WALTHERS™
P.O. Box 3039
Milwaukee, WI 53201-3039
(414) 527-0770
http://www.walthers.com

ISBN 0-941952-58-4

Printed in the USA

WELCOME TO WALTHERS 2000 HO SCALE MODEL RAILROAD REFERENCE BOOK

The local depot used to be the best place in town to get all the latest news. Passenger trains brought daily papers from big cities, as well as mail and magazines. And the arrivals and departures of visitors or local residents was often newsworthy.

Inside the depot, the dots and dashes of Morse code kept the railroad running. But in many villages, the railroad also handled private telegrams. When really big news was breaking, such as an election or sporting event, it would sometimes be transmitted live over the telegraph. Folks would crowd into the depot and anxiously listen as the station agent read off each incoming message.

Technology has replaced the depot as our main source of information for major news. But keeping up to date on all that's happening in our hobby also requires new and better resources. Since our first HO Catalog in 1937, Walthers has been committed to providing you with the most accurate model railroad information available.

Each year, we completely update the Reference Book with the latest new products, more pictures, more information and current prices. It remains a unique resource, listing thousands of products and providing new modeling techniques.

Many ideas can be found in the all-new "Magic of Model Railroading" photos. You'll find a spectacular shot at the beginning of each section of the book, plus a showcase of additional photos in their very own "Magic" section. Contributed by modelers from around the world, each photo spotlights the builder's creative methods and uses of materials.

For additional ideas or just plain fun, be sure to read the "Information Station" articles appearing in each section. We've created a new collection of fun facts, modeling ideas and how-to articles with practical ideas you can use.

And, you can update your Book every day through our Web site at www.walthers.com. You can check on any item in this and other Reference Books to see if it's in stock, or when we expect delivery if it isn't. We've recently added a special Product Locator™ feature to help you find Dealers who may still have hard-to-find items in stock too. You can read the latest new product announcements and find additional information, photos and more on the thousands of products in this book.

Your comments, questions and suggestions are a vital part of the information we receive every day, which help us to better meet your needs. Whether by phone, fax, e-mail or letter, your ideas are always welcome.

Happy modeling!

Phil Walthers

Phil Walthers

What's New In 2000

This is just a sampling of the new products you'll find throughout Walthers 2000 HO Scale Reference Book.

O scale model shown.

3D Railroad Concept & Design™

See the Books, Video & Railroadiana Section Page 903

The new version 2.01 for Windows contains these requested new features: The "Track Wizard" for quickly creating complex track pieces, the "Terrain Tool" for easily mapping custom terrain, a precision track-cutting tool, more track libraries, new 3D objects, more textures, grades and elevation across multiple track pieces.

AEM-7/ALP-44 Electric Locomotives

Atlas introduces its first-ever electric locomotive. Exciting features of each engine include operating pantographs, marker lights and headlights, a full-cab interior with painted crew members and dual flywheels. Available in undecorated versions and a variety of popular roadnames.

Turf, Ballast and Snow Shakers

See the Scenery Section Pages 352, 353 and 356

Big projects requiring a lot of scenic detail will benefit from these shakers. Each shaker can hold 32oz of scenic material. Choose from easy-to-apply styles such as ballast, snow or turf to create the perfect look for your layout.

WALTHERS™

Oscar & Piker Passenger Cars

See the Passenger Cars Section Pages 210 & 211

Introduce luxury passenger service to your layout with these exclusive private rail cars. Each style features separate wire grab irons, styrene bodies, working diaphragms, one-piece plastic interiors, body-mounted working knuckle couplers and a smooth rolling truck.

Auto Dealership Figures

See the Figures Section Page 625

From a devoted sales staff to customers eager to get behind the wheel of a new car, these figures are the perfect complement to your automotive dealership. They'll look perfect when placed in the Uptown Motors building (#933, 3077, sold separately).

Track Bed Sheets

See the Track & Accessories Section Page 284

This state-of-the-art roadbed is constructed from sound-deadening material, so your layout will run more quietly. Each sheet measures 5 x 24"; six sheets come in each package. The flexible roadbed is easy-to-use – just tack or glue to your layout.

KALMBACH PUBLISHING CO.

F Units: The Diesels That Did It

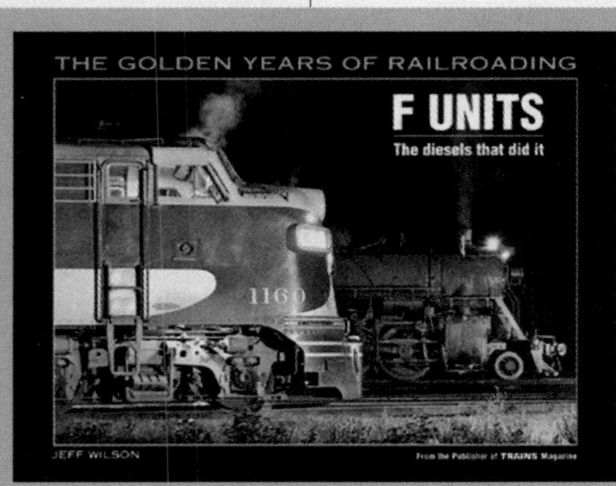

See the Books, Video & Railroadiana Section Page 923

Learn how this revolutionary diesel locomotive became such a primary freight hauler that it drove steam engines out of operation. Text details prototype histories, while photos and illustrations show original units and prototypes.

What's New In 2000

This is just a sampling of the new products you'll find throughout Walthers 2000 HO Scale Reference Book.

International Hobby Corp.

Diesel Alco C-628 Powered Locomotives

See the Locomotives Section Page 62

Introduced in 1963, these high-horsepower units were designed as dual service machines, equally at home with heavy freight or passenger trains. The long hood area directly behind the cab provided additional space for the installation of a steam generator, used to provide heat to passenger cars. Most buyers opted for the freight-only version, which remained in production until January of 1968. These accurately detailed and painted locomotives feature an operating headlight and horn-hook couplers. A variety of vintage roadnames are available to meet the motive power needs of your HO Scale railroad, or add color to your collection.

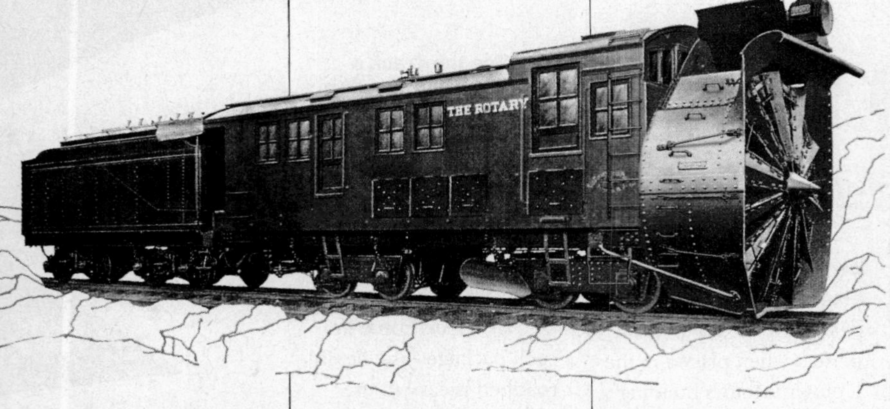

WALTHERS™

Alco Leslie Snow Plow

See the Freight Section Page 123

Problems with snow on the tracks are a thing of the past! These Leslie snow plows are based on early 20th-century prototypes. Fully assembled models include a drive motor and a tender with working knuckle coupler.

KALMBACH PUBLISHING CO.

Maintaining and Repairing Your Scale Model Trains

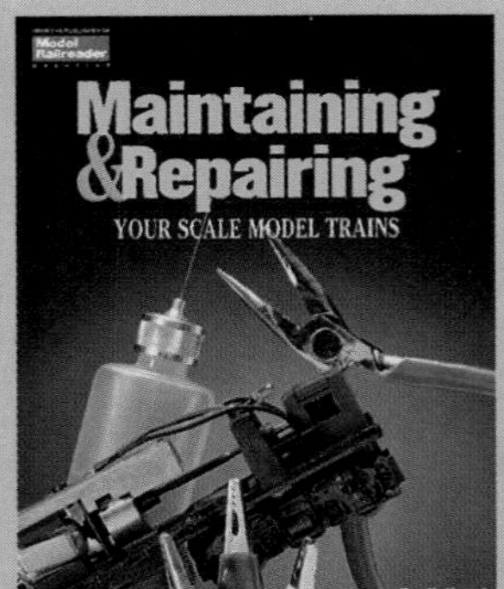

See the Books, Video & Railroadiana Section Page 922

Read about money-saving techniques on repairing your model trains. Learn the basic repair skills needed to fix your locomotives, rolling stock and layouts.

FALLER

Wild Mouse Working Rolling Coaster

See the Circus Section Page 363

Walthers Exclusive

The daredevil in you is sure to love this roller coaster. Four cars, powered by a 12-16V drive motor, sail along a thrilling track punctuated by sharp turns and gravity-defying drops from the track's highest points. Kit includes a ticket booth, working lights and detailed plastic parts.

Coal River Passenger & Freight Depots

See the Structures Section Page 482

Two buildings in one kit loaded with over 40 white metal castings, enough detail parts to create an entire scene on your layout.

What's New In 2000

This is just a sampling of the new products you'll find throughout Walthers 2000 HO Scale Reference Book.

Train-Teasers™

See the Books, Video & Railroadiana Section
Page 903

The all-new Train-Teasers series of games will bring hours of fun and relaxation to train enthusiasts everywhere. These challenging games have a special touch of nostalgia to add to the enjoyment.

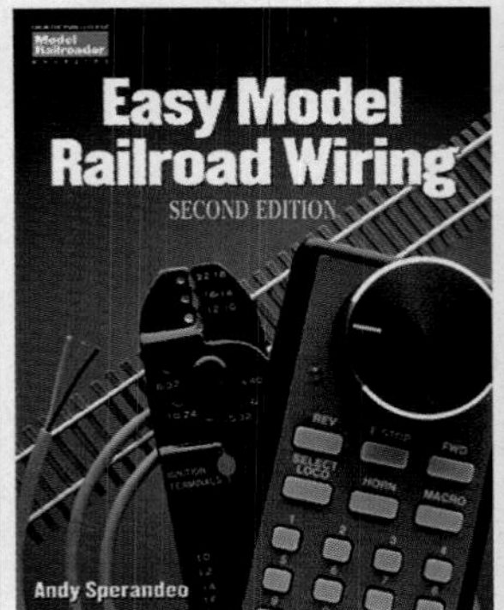

Easy Model Railroad Wiring

See the Books, Video & Railroadiana Section
Page 922

Increase the operating possibilites of your train set or layout with this comprehensive new book as your guide. Written especially for beginners in a clear, easy to read style, it explains the basic terms and provides simple hands-on projects to learn the techniques every modeler needs to know to wire a two-rail, DC-powered, permanent layout. Plenty of large, clear illustrations, along with many color and black and white photos accompany the text in this 160-page softcover book.

ORIGINAL Preiser

Military Figures

See the Figures Section
Page 625

Populate your airfield with this package of twelve figures, including standing pilots and members of a ground crew. The perfect accompaniment to World War Two flying machines like the C-47 and the P-51D (#933-1150 and #933-1170, each sold separately).

Sunlit Vistas
THE LOOK OF SUNLIGHT IN YOUR WORLD

Trees

See the Scenery Section
Page 336

Whatever the season, whatever the setting, these trees are certain to add just the right touch of color and authenticity to your layout. Choose from various types of trees in kits or assembled styles.

New Deluxe Backwoods Locomotive or Car Shop

See the Structures Section Page 378

- *Parts for Loco or Car Shop in Both Deluxe and Standard Kits
- *Deluxe Kit includes Add-On Resin Details
- *Interior Cut Lines for Easy Customizing
- * Fits Any Era
- *Plastic Parts Molded in Color

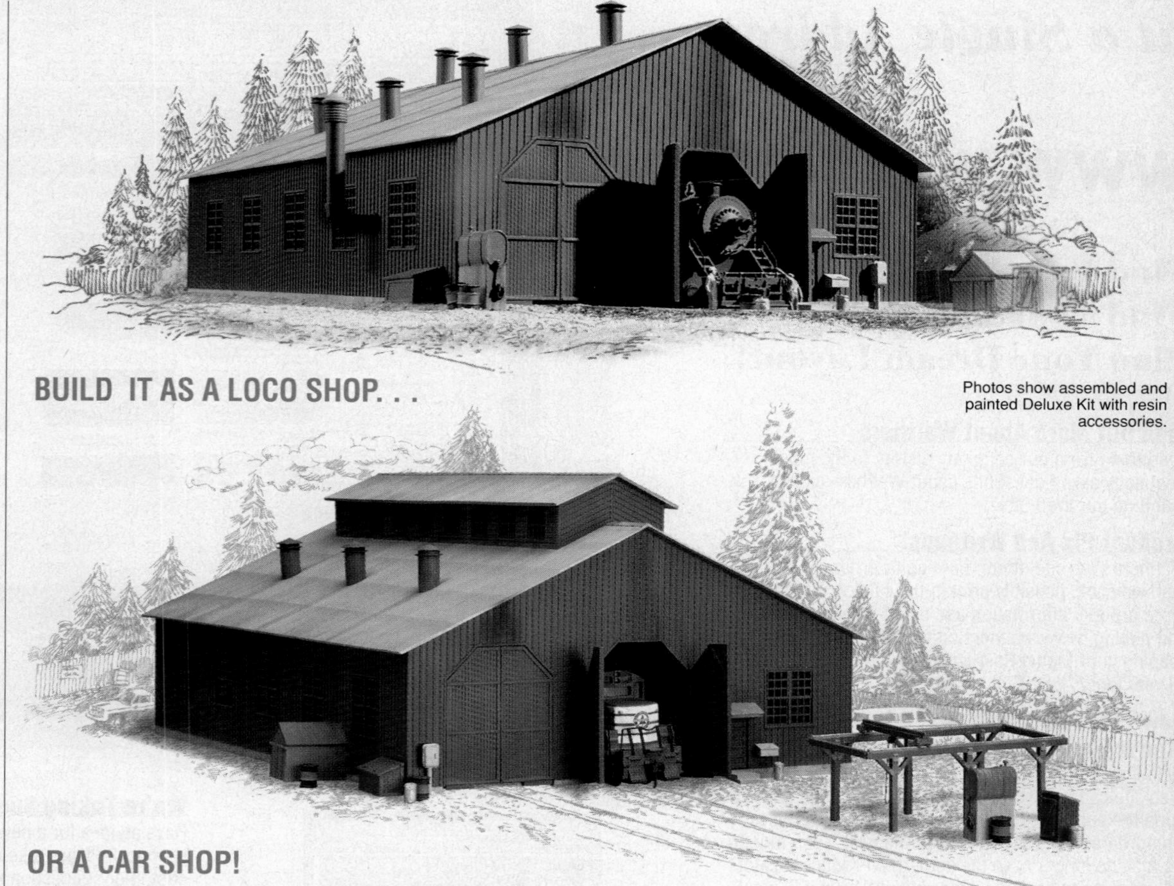

BUILD IT AS A LOCO SHOP. . .

Photos show assembled and painted Deluxe Kit with resin accessories.

OR A CAR SHOP!

BUSCH

1997 Chevrolet S-10 Blazers

See the Vehicles Section Page 653

Walthers Exclusive

Give a touch of class and driving elegance to roadways, auto dealerships and assembly plants with these Chevy Blazers. These special versions of the popular 1997 sports utility vehicles are painted in shades of red and black.

SCALE SHOPS

HO, HOn3 SIGNALS

Choose from a variety of signals to best illuminate the railways of your HO/HOn3 layout. Choose from two assembled styles: a two-aspect dwarf signal (#649-5202) or a three-aspect low profile signal (#649-5206) with LEDs and resistors.

You can also choose these models in basic brass castings (dwarf signal #649-5200; low-profile signal #649-5204) or in ready-to-assemble kits (dwarf signal #649-5201; low-profile signal #649-5205).

Get Everything You Need at a Single Address:

www.walthers.com

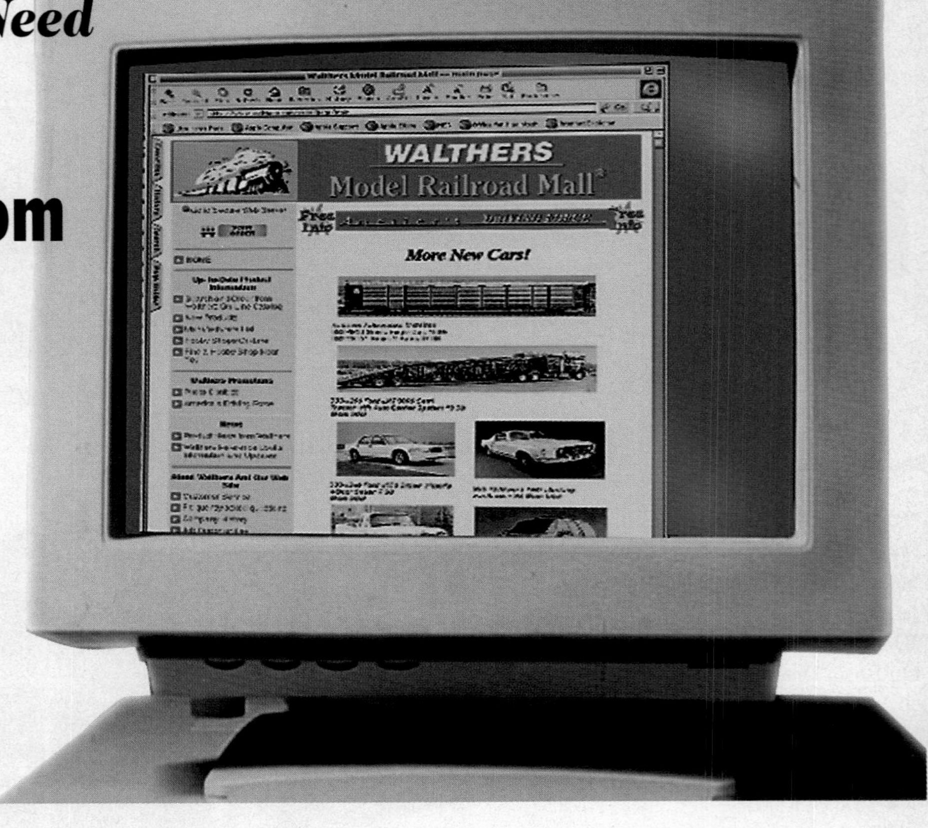

Find Your Trains!
Find Your Tools!
Plan Your Dream Layout!

Find Out More About Walthers
Everything from our company history to the most frequently asked questions about Walthers can be found on our Web Site.

Product Pix And Writeups!
Walthers Web site offers more color product photos than we could possibly print in the catalog. Along with more product information and up-to-date availability and pricing, www.walthers.com is a great tool for keeping your Model Railroad Reference Books current all year long!

New Product Locator™ Service— Find It Even If It's Already Sold Out!
Even if an item is out of stock or discontinued, our Web site can help you find it. Our search page draws upon the purchase history of selected dealers to see who ordered the item from us in the past. Even though we may no longer have the item, this Product Locator™ will lead you to dealers who might still have it in stock. Our research shows that when using this new feature, one in four dealers are likely to still have the item in stock.

Walthers Model Railroad Mall®
The Walthers Model Railroad Mall® is an online gathering of Walthers dealers from which you can order through our Web site. Select dealers have storefronts on the Mall; all you have to do is choose which dealer you want to order from. Your shopping cart order goes directly to the dealer you specify. We have a secure Web server available for your protection!

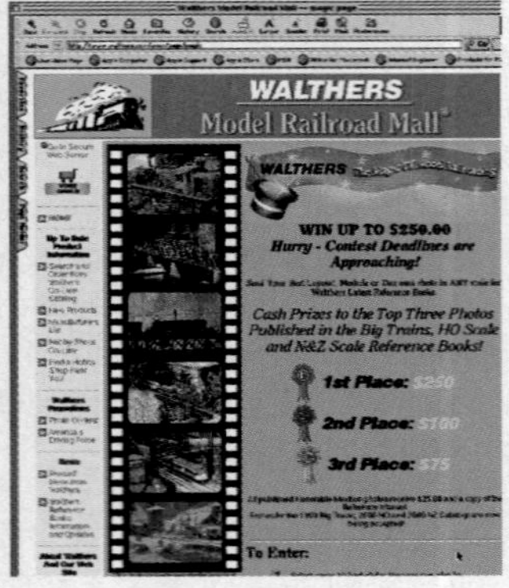

Contests
Get all the info about the annual Walthers Magic of Model Railroading photo contest. Prize-winning photos are published each year in the Magic of Model Railroading section of our Reference Books. Check out the entry rules, deadlines and some of the fantastic photos on our site.

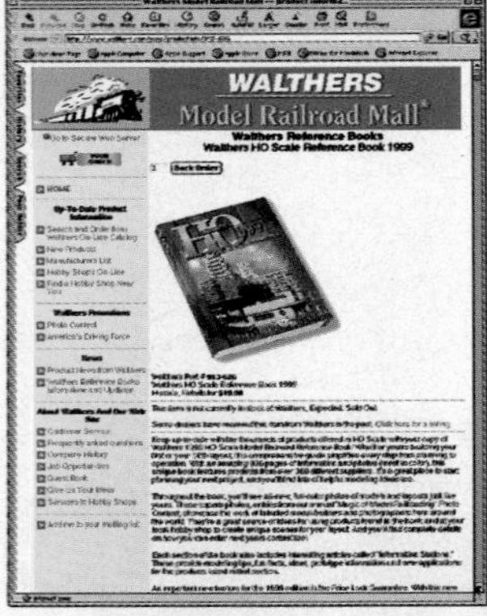

Keep Your Model Railroad Reference Book Current
The Walthers site is the best way to update the information in your Model Railroad Reference Books. With the click of your mouse you can keep track of constantly changing availability and pricing. You'll also be in the know about new products introduced between Reference Books. With all the new information on the site each day, you'll want to keep this page bookmarked and check it often!

Hobby Shop Locator
Find the top Walthers dealers from around the world with our Dealer Locator. Use this service to find a nearby store or to find stores along your travel and vacation routes!

Who Makes What?
Our Manufacturer List is a great way to learn a little about your favorite manufacturers. Selected manufacturer listings tell about the history of the vendor and the products they produce.

We're Taking Suggestions
Have an idea for a new product you would like us to produce? Please take a few minutes to fill out our customer suggestion form. It'll be mailed directly to our marketing department. We read 'em all, so your suggestions and ideas for new products really count! Have a problem with a product? Contact our customer service department with a click of your mouse.

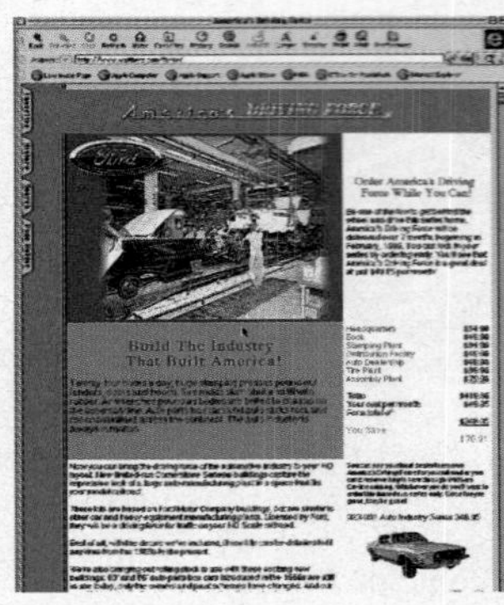

Get The Latest Scoop!
Get the most current information on what's hot and what's new. Our site is updated daily, so you'll always know what's in stock. Just try our search page — it covers every item we have on hand and more. Check availability on our Web site along with your Reference Book when putting together your shopping list before visiting your favorite hobby shop! You might just find some products you didn't know existed!

walthers.com is Your Greatest Resource for Finding the Products you Need on the Internet!

WM. K. WALTHERS, INC:

FROM ONE MILLENNIUM TO THE NEXT

For all intent and purposes, Wm. K. Walthers, Inc. was founded in 1932, in Milwaukee, Wisconsin. But the idea truly began 33 years earlier when seven-year-old Bill Walthers received his first taste of the hobby for Christmas, a windup toy train. He continued in the hobby, growing as it did. Eventually, he had an attic layout composed primarily of his own scratchbuilt creations. It was then that he realized his dream: Bill Walthers sought to make his hobby into a business. He succeeded far beyond any of the dreams he had.

An advertisement was placed in the May, 1932 issue of *Modelmaker Magazine*, and Wm. K. Walthers, Inc. was born. The first sale was made a few days later, marking the beginning of nearly $500.00 in sales for the year.

Five years later, after starting out merely with a few designs of electrical controls that turned toy railroads into working model systems, the company had to move to a larger building to accommodate all the in-house work that was now being done. At this time Walthers was producing everything from milled wood parts to metal castings to decals. The hobby was growing. So was Walthers.

By the time 1958 rolled along, Bill Walthers was ready to retire. Having decided he wanted to spend more time with the hobby he helped make popular all over the globe, he handed the reins over to his son Bruce, who had been a part of the company since 1946. Bruce Walthers possessed the same passion and business sense that his father had. It was under his guidance that Wm. K. Walthers, Inc. became a full-line distributor of other manufacturers' products while continuing to expand the Walthers lines. He was also responsible for Walthers becoming an international company with the advent of the Walthers Importing Division.

IMPROVE YOUR TOY RAILROAD

Why not make your toy railroad into a *Model System?* Send 15 cents in stamps for 24 page catalog on signal and control equipment, rails, ties and track; real automatic switches; reversing mechanisms, automatic couplers and uncouplers, supplies, parts, drawings, etc. Also SIGNAL AND CONTROL MANUAL — 250 pages and drawings — $3.00.

W. K. WALTHERS

1566 W. Pierce Street *Milwaukee, Wis.*

Thirty-eight years of service were under Bruce's belt when he retired in 1984. His son Phil became the 3rd generation of the Walthers family to head the company. Under his tenure, in 1985, Walthers introduced Code 83 Track making it possible for many modelers to build realistic track for the first time. The accessories soon followed. 1990 saw the introduction of the Cornerstone Series® kits. In 1994, Trainline Deluxe Train Sets and Locomotives debuted, giving the beginning modeler a train set that had many features of interest to serious modelers, for a reasonable price. It's with Phil Walthers at the helm that Wm. K. Walthers, Inc. sails into the New Millennium.

A lot has happened since the doors opened 68 years ago. Wm. K. Walthers, Inc. has survived a World War and its labor shortages, more than one recession, competitive forces to the hobby that threatened to take spare time away from the prospective hobbyist (such as television and other popular hobbies like slot cars), several "deaths" of the hobby (as well as the subsequent "rebirths") and, finally, the introduction and explosion of computers. Walthers has met these obstacles head-on and has strived to keep moving forward, succeeding more often than not.

When the industry bowed to the needs and wants of the modelers and cut the O Scale in half to create the more manageable HO Scale, Walthers was there. When cast metal and brass cars gave way to mass produced plastic ones, Walthers was there. And now, when the hobby seems to be shifting from a hands-on building hobby to a collectors hobby, Walthers is there. This was realized in the early 1990s when the Cornerstone Series® and Trainline® products came out. Ready-to-run models were being asked for and Walthers delivered, saving the modeler vast amounts of time. This allows people to enjoy the hobby even if they do not possess a lot of that great commodity called "spare time." Walthers has not changed its general

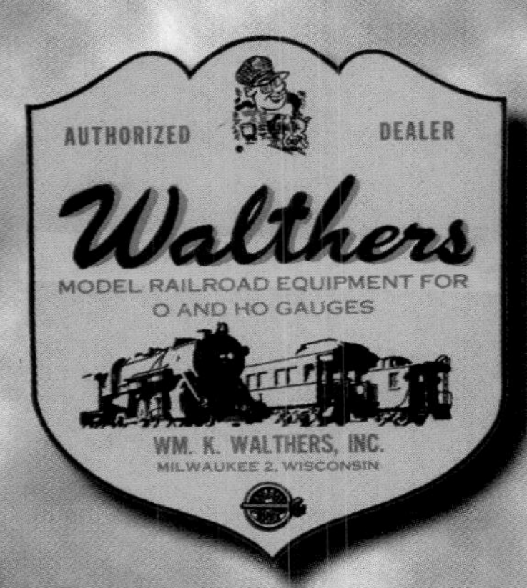

Clockwise From Far Left: In 1937 Walthers occupied part of this warehouse. Our first advertisement appeared in the May, 1932 issue of *Modelmaker Magazine*. One of the first Walthers logos. Cover of Phil Walthers first HO catalog. The first Cornerstone Series® structure, Don's Shoe Store. Code 83 track in its present packaging. The current building at 5601 W. Florist Ave., Milwaukee, WI.

philosophy with every shift in the train modeling industry, though. They have recognized that the hobby sometimes leans in different and new directions. And while they have taken the time to explore these avenues, Walthers has also made the effort to remain loyal to the methods and ideas that have been at the heart of the hobby for many years. This has allowed Wm. K. Walthers, Inc. to cater to all model railroaders of all kinds.

With the start of the 21st Century, the age of computers is being fully realized by businesses all over the world, and Walthers is no exception. The Internet has opened the widest of possibilities; the world can now shop at Walthers. The newly redesigned Web site, entitled "Walthers Model Railroad Mall®," can be found on the World Wide Web at www.walthers.com. This site is updated DAILY, allowing access to all the information any modeler would need. It offers a search engine that encompasses over 80,000 items (the very same items found in the Reference Books); a Product Locator™ that gives users the ability to find items that Walthers does not currently have in-stock; a new products page that lists the latest items offered by the manufacturers carried in the Reference Books; a list of manufacturers and information about them; information about hobby shops on-line and where to find hobby shops across the US; information on current Walthers promotions (such as the Magic Photo Contest); product news about Walthers most recent in-house creations; Reference Book information and updates; a suggestion box to help Walthers keep the pulse of the modern modeler; a Walthers mailing list; and information on Wm. K. Walthers, Inc. itself. Virtually everything anyone needs to know within the model railroading hobby can be found here. Providing the most recent and fastest information available is just another way in which Walthers attempts to make model railroading easier and more enjoyable.

The popular use of the Internet and Web sites like Walthers has drastically changed the model railroad industry. Products can now be ordered on-line through your local hobby store. Chat rooms dedicated to model railroading give modelers a venue in which they can exchange ideas and methods with other enthusiasts half a world away. One cannot forget the thousands of Web sites offered by clubs, modelers, official associations and prototype railroads. A wealth of knowledge is out there and it can all be easily accessed via a computer in your own living room. For more detailed information on what Walthers Web site has to offer, check out page 8.

Another way Walthers has embraced the New Millennium and its technology is with the "Weekly Wire." To better serve the model railroader, Walthers sends out a weekly 8-10 page newsletter to participating hobby shops detailing ALL the newest items in EVERY scale. This enables the consumer to remain informed about newly released products and lets dealers know what the future will bring as far as the modeling world is concerned. Being up-to-date and well informed makes it that much easier to keep the shelves filled with the latest items that modelers want and need for their layouts.

Wm. K. Walthers, Inc. would like to thank all the modelers and hobby shops around the world who have kept Model Railroading alive and growing. Thank you.

If Bill Walthers could see how far his dream has come and what his company has accomplished, he would be a proud man.

FREQUENTLY ASKED QUESTIONS

WHAT DOES WALTHERS DO?

We're a manufacturer of freight cars, locomotives, Trainline® Models, Cornerstone Series® buildings and other kits, some of which are made for us.

We're also a wholesaler, distributing products from over 300 manufacturers to hobby shops worldwide.

And we're an importer, bringing you products from around the world.

Combined as one operation, we're the world's largest distributor of model railroad products, offering over 80,000 items so you and your dealer have the best possible selection.

DOES WALTHERS HAVE A WORLD WIDE WEB SITE?

Yes, the Model Railroad Mall™ at **www.walthers.com**. The Model Railroad Mall™ is the quickest and easiest way to contact Walthers directly. The Railroad Mall offers an abundance of information about products, vendors, the latest Walthers publications, On-Line ordering from local hobby shops, model railroad industry services and much more.

HOW DOES THIS REFERENCE BOOK HELP ME AND MY DEALER?

This is a comprehensive listing of merchandise that's available or will be delivered shortly.

Each manufacturer has reviewed and updated their listing. Based on this, we list items we believe will be available during the life of this book. Many things are beyond our control, so all items are offered subject to availability at the time of shipment.

I'M BUILDING MY FIRST RAILROAD - WILL THIS REFERENCE BOOK HELP ME?

You bet! Whether starting out with a new Trainline® Deluxe Train Set, or older equipment, you'll want cars, buildings, track, industries, electrical supplies, scenery materials or another locomotive. This book shows what's available, and provides ideas and information to get you started.

HOW DO I PURCHASE ITEMS SHOWN IN THIS REFERENCE BOOK?

Walthers is a wholesaler and sells only to approved hobby shops who are committed to helping you enjoy the hobby and supplying products from this book. Please support your local shop by purchasing materials and supplies there. Your dealer can order any item listed in this Book at any time.

If your dealer has Walthers EXPRES™ III, he or she can find out almost instantly if we have the product you want in stock and the current price. We can usually ship it the next day.

HOW DO I FIND A HOBBY SHOP IN MY AREA?

Simply send Walthers a SASE and we will send you a list of dealers in your area. Please send to:

Walthers—DEALER LIST
5601 W. Florist Ave.
P.O. Box 3039
Milwaukee, WI 53201-3039

The Model Railroad Mall™ at **www.walthers.com** also has a link to a current list of more than 1,000 hobby shops across the U.S.

WHAT IF MY DEALER DOESN'T HAVE THE ITEM I WANT?

There are more products than your dealer can possibly have in stock. If you don't find what you want, ask to place a special order. You or your dealer can check our Web site to find out if the item is available. Special orders can be placed at any time. Some dealers have policies, so ask first.

THE ITEM IS OUT OF STOCK - WHAT DOES THAT MEAN?

We try to stock these products at all times, but some manufacturers' products run out and are temporarily unavailable. Ask your dealer to place it on backorder. This is important, since we don't do this automatically! Backorders are shipped as soon as we have the merchandise from the supplier.

I RECEIVED THE ITEM, BUT I'M NOT HAPPY - WHO CAN HELP?

We try to describe each item in this Reference Book accurately. If it's not what you expected, your dealer can return it. If the kit is too difficult, it can be returned. But, do this BEFORE starting construction. We cannot accept returns of items that have been worked on.

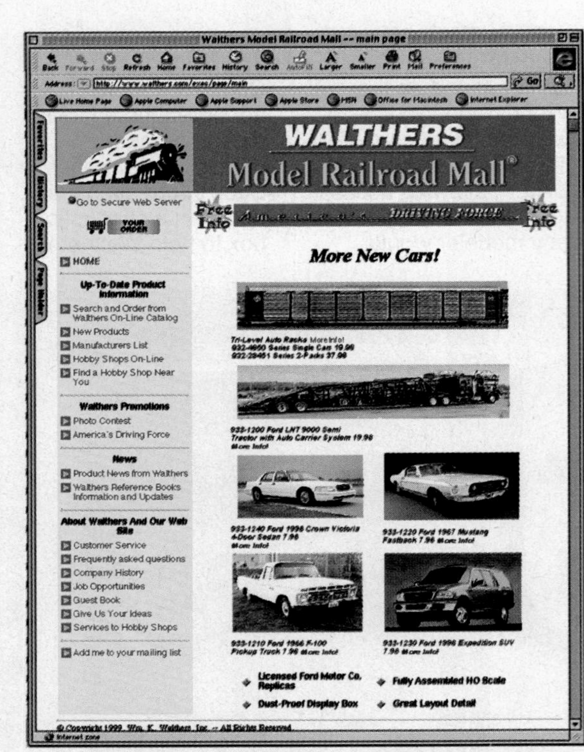

Use the power of the Internet to step into the warehouse. Visit us at www.walthers.com

I STILL DON'T HAVE MY ORDER - WHY NOT?

Most manufacturers make every effort to ship products to us on schedule, but many are small businesses with limited resources. They may rely on outside suppliers for parts, packaging, use of a molding machine, etc., which they can't always get. This means items may be temporarily out of stock, or in extreme cases, may never go into production.

Some manufacturers use "batch production," making just enough product to satisfy current demand. Orders are then allowed to accumulate to a specific level before another batch is made. With slow-moving items, there can be long delays (sometimes several years) until enough orders are received. Items that we know will be out of stock are printed in blue.

There are things that no one can control. Weather delays, shortages of materials, delays at customs, fires—all of these and other unforeseen problems can change the situation in a hurry.

WHY ARE SOME LISTINGS PRINTED IN BLUE INK?

This is our way of letting you know we haven't received these products for quite some time, and they may not be in stock. They haven't been discontinued, but you may not be able to get them right away. We expect delivery sometime this year and suggest you backorder them with your dealer.

ARE SOME PRODUCTS PRINTED IN BLUE FROM LAST YEAR MISSING?

Yes, some items printed in blue in the 1999 Reference Book have not arrived. If the supplier didn't tell us when they're coming, we have not listed them.

WHY ARE SOME MODELS CALLED "CRAFT TRAIN" KITS?

To identify the difficulty and skills needed to build a model, we use these descriptions:

Ready-to-Run = Fully assembled model, ready to use.

Easy-To-Build = A simple kit, molded in colors, or painted and lettered, that can be assembled quickly with basic hobby tools.

Craft Train Kits = Designed for experienced modelers, parts may have to be made from wood, metal or plastic and assembled using templates and drawings. Most include small detail parts in plastic or metal. All parts are unpainted.

HOW CAN I KEEP THIS REFERENCE BOOK UPDATED?

The fastest way to find out the latest information on what's new and in stock at Walthers is to visit the Model Railroad Mall™ at **www.walthers.com**. You'll find new product and new arrival information updated daily. Or, if you don't have on-line access, ask your dealer about the latest edition of Walthers Weekly Wire. These resources tell you what new items are in stock and ready for delivery, and what new items are expected in the future.

WHO SHOULD I CONTACT WITH A QUESTION ABOUT A PRODUCT?

We do our best to describe each item in this Reference Book thoroughly and accurately, but sometimes a question still remains. We are happy to answer all questions sent to us with a SASE or on-line.

Another on-line source of information is the news group rec.models.railroad. This news group contains a wealth of information and puts you in touch with other modelers from around the world!

For questions about techniques or materials, see your dealer. There are many "how-to" books and videos available that may have the answers you need. Your dealer probably knows several experienced modelers who visit the shop and can answer your questions.

There may also be a club in your area where you can visit their layout. You can ask questions, watch trains and see how things are done.

A membership in the National Model Railroad Association (NMRA) will put you in touch with thousands of modelers worldwide. A monthly magazine, "The Bulletin," provides listings of clubs, special interest groups and helpful articles.

(An application for membership is printed in this manual; please see the index listing under NMRA for the page.)

If you are looking for information on an actual car, locomotive or rail line, consider joining a railroad historical society. These addresses are listed in some hobby magazines. Members are dedicated to studying and preserving the history and equipment of their favorite lines. Most issue a newsletter or magazine and can answer in-depth questions.

WALTHERS REFERENCE BOOK POLICY/ WARRANTY INFORMATION

WALTHERS REFERENCE BOOK POLICY

We realize there are more products listed in this book than the average hobby shop can stock at one time. Therefore, we try to describe every item as accurately as possible so you can special order them with confidence. However, if the item is not as you expected, your dealer can return it to us. If it is clearly our mistake, we will pay return transportation; otherwise your dealer must pay the return transportation, plus restock fees.

PRICES

All prices are subject to change without notice. All items are invoiced at the prices in effect at the time of shipment.

IMPORTANT

There are certain things beyond our control, therefore: 1) All items offered are subject to availability at the time of shipment. 2) We reserve the right to correct errors, change prices and modify designs without notice and without obligation to previous purchasers. If you do not like the change or correction, the item may be returned by your dealer.

ABOUT WARRANTIES

As a prospective buyer of materials offered in this book, you benefit from three separate warranties:

1) The warranty offered by the manufacturer

2) The warranty we extend to our dealers

3) The warranty offered by the dealer to you, the purchaser

Some warranties are better than others; we suggest you ask before you buy.

WALTHERS LIMITED WARRANTY

We will replace any part of a Walthers kit that's defective at the time of purchase or was lost or damaged during assembly. We reserve the right to ask you to send the damaged or defective part back to us; however, DO NOT send it back until we ask for it, as we will not be responsible for this shipping cost. If the part was defective, we'll pay the transportation costs to send you a new one. If you are asking for a replacement because the part was lost or damaged during assembly, please include $5.00 service fee payment (in US funds), payable to Wm. K. Walthers, Inc. This warranty applies to the original purchaser only, with a time limit of 90 days.

We reserve the right to request proof of purchase. To save time, write to us directly regarding replacement or repair and DO NOT RETURN THE MERCHANDISE UNLESS REQUESTED. Since our designs are subject to change, we reserve the right to make reasonable substitution if the item requested is no longer available. Remember, Walthers warranties apply ONLY to merchandise purchased through authorized retail establishments.

OTHER MANUFACTURERS' WARRANTIES

Manufacturers establish their own policies. Detailed information may be included with the product, or may be obtained by contacting the company. Most require that parts be returned to them with proof of purchase. Under Federal regulations, this is defined as a limited warranty. Your rights on warranty repairs vary depending on which state you live in. If you have problems with another manufacturer's warranty, we'll try to help, but again, DON'T SEND MERCHANDISE UNLESS WE ASK FOR IT.

DEALER WARRANTIES AND POLICIES

Dealers set their own policies for returns, refunds, credits or exchanges. Ask before you buy as some are unable or unwilling to return merchandise. We can't accept responsibility or issue refunds for merchandise sent to us without authorization.

KITS VS ASSEMBLY

Unless stated otherwise, the merchandise offered is in kit form, for assembly by you. If you feel that you are unable to put it together, this is a reason for return under our policy, but please do this BEFORE starting construction. We normally will not accept the return of items which have been worked on or are otherwise in unsellable condition. Please note that we do not have an assembly service.

PUT "SAFETY FIRST" ON YOUR RAILROAD

Working on a real railroad can be dangerous. The "Safety First" message on equipment reminds employees to work carefully, think about what they're doing and follow proper procedures.

"Safety First" is a good message for model railroaders too. Properly used, hobby products provide hours of enjoyment. But you must understand and appreciate the tools and materials. That's especially important if younger members of the family are going to help.

The items in this Reference Book are NOT toys, and should only be used by children with adult supervision. You can set a good example by working carefully and taking the time to read and follow directions.

The use of hazardous substances in hobby products is declining, but you can be exposed to TOXIC, MECHANICAL (including heat) and ELECTRICAL hazards. The following is a partial list of things to be aware of:

TOXIC CHEMICALS: ALWAYS READ AND FOLLOW THE INSTRUCTIONS ON THE CAN, BOTTLE OR OTHER PACKAGING.

If you use the material indoors, adequate ventilation is required. Work in a large room, open doors and windows and use an exhaust fan to circulate the air, especially AFTER you finish. The use of a respirator, eye protection and protective gloves is a must, AND NO SMOKING! Empty containers should also be handled carefully and disposed of properly. Following are some specific chemical hazards:

METHYL ALCOHOL

Extremely poisonous when ingested or absorbed through the skin. Causes severe nervous system toxicity and can cause blindness. Used as a solvent in some shellac and varnishes, and in some paint strippers.

TEFLON

Harmful near fire or flame-including smoking materials. Heated Teflon produces fumes that can cause congestion of the lungs.

1,1,1 TRICHLOROETHANE

A substitute for carbon tetra-chloride that is much safer but still very toxic. Can cause fatal heart disturbances.

TRICHLOROETHYLENE

Can cause severe central nervous system depression and lung damage.

PETROLEUM HYDROCARBONS

(Petroleum distillates) are found in some paint and thinners. May produce coma, depression or convulsions, as well as pulmonary irritation. Use with adequate ventilation, wear an approved respirator and gloves. Avoid breathing mists or vapors. If swallowed, do not induce vomiting.

TOLUOL

(Toulene) is used in some paints and plastic glues. Depresses the nervous system and may damage bone marrow.

XYLENE

Produces the same side effects as Toluol, found in some lubricants, cleaning fluids, dull coating sprays, plastic glue, matte finish sprays, paints and solvents.

MODEL LOCOMOTIVE SMOKE

Usually consists of volatile oils that can be harmful or fatal if swallowed.

EPOXY CEMENTS

The hardener is extremely irritating to the skin and should be washed off immediately.

INSTANT GLUES - (ACC, CA OR CYANOACRYLATES)

These instant-drying glues bond skin, or objects to the skin, so that surgery may be needed to remove them. Fumes from some of these glues and their accelerators are eye irritants.

ACETONE (INCLUDING ISOPROPYL AND ISOBUTYL ACETATES)

As little as 50 grams can be fatal. Produces skin and mucous membrane irritation and depression of the central nervous system. Contained in some cements and debonding agents for instant glues. Use with adequate ventilation.

GASOLINE - DO NOT USE UNDER ANY CIRCUMSTANCE!

Gasoline is highly flammable and potentially explosive - one cup can lift a ton of weight 1000 feet instantly. Use a non-flammable cleaning agent instead.

CARBON TETRA-CHLORIDE - DO NOT USE UNDER ANY CIRCUMSTANCE!

Ingesting 1/10 to 1/6 of an ounce is fatal. It injures all cells of the body, especially the kidneys.

SOLDERING FLUX

Often contains hydrochloric acid and sometimes oxalic acid, which irritates mucous membranes and the skin on contact or inhalation.

LEAD

For many years, lead and various lead-based alloys were used in metal castings and paints. Today, lead has been removed from hobby paints; however, some lead castings are still in use. Always dispose of lead filings carefully. Wash your hands thoroughly when done and NO SMOKING.

MECHANICAL AND HEAT HAZARDS

Pay attention to castings, punched metal parts, wire forms, strips, shapes and plastic parts that can have very sharp edges.

Tools should be handled with extreme care and inspected for any signs of wear or damage. Read and follow proper procedures for use and always wear eye protection. Never wear loose clothing or jewelry, and tie back long hair that could get caught in machinery.

Using power tools for cutting, sanding or grinding will transfer heat to the object you are working on. Some power tools require regular oiling, and air vents should always be kept clear to prevent overheating the motor.

Soldering irons, torches or hot knives can create heat and fire hazards. These items can cause severe burns, and soldering fumes can be harmful.

ELECTRICAL HAZARDS

As little as 10 milliamps at a high voltage can paralyze you. Only 50 milliamps are needed to produce cardiac arrest, and a normal household fuse is 15 amps - almost 300 times more than needed to stop your heart!

MAKE SURE YOUR POWER TOOLS AND OTHER ELECTRICAL ACCESSORIES ARE PROPERLY GROUNDED SO THAT STRAY CURRENT IS DRAWN AWAY FROM YOU!

Three-prong adapters are useless unless the pigtail is connected to ground. An inexpensive but almost fool-proof appliance is a "Ground Fault Circuit Interrupter." These devices shut off the power after sensing a current leak as small as 5 milliamps.

Electrical cords should be checked frequently. At the first sign of wear or damage, repair or replace them immediately. When working on or around electrical items, make sure they're unplugged and the power is shut off before starting. If repairs are needed on an item that uses house current, it should be done ONLY by qualified personnel.

FLAMMABLE ITEMS

Use and store paint, thinner, glue or ANY item marked "FLAMMABLE" with care. Fumes and vapors are heavier than air and collect near the floor. Air currents can move them from room to room, where they could be ignited by a pilot light or electrical spark.

NEVER STORE NOR USE THESE ITEMS NEAR A WATER HEATER, FURNACE, ELECTRIC MOTOR OR OTHER SOURCE OF FLAME OR SPARK IGNITION!

Always make sure the can or bottle is tightly closed to prevent fumes from escaping. These potentially dangerous liquids should only be stored in their original marked container! Most are harmful or fatal if swallowed, so keep them out of the reach of children.

SAFETY IS HABIT FORMING

By paying attention, reading instructions and using common sense, you can safely use a variety of materials. Model railroading is fun, and by making safety a habit, you can keep it that way!

Adapted from an April 1976 feature in Model Railroader written by Dr. W.T. Watkins Jr., M.D.

AAR
The Association of American Railroads (Formerly the American Railroad Association, ARA). This trade group establishes standards for equipment and safety.

ACC
Alphacyanoacrylate, also called CA. Instant-bonding, "super" glues. See Safety First for more information.

ABS Plastic
A modeling plastic that's harder than styrene.

Airbrush
Small spray gun for use with hobby paints and stains, powered by compressed air.

B

Backdrop
Painted or photographic scene on the wall behind the layout. Creates illusion of great distance.

Back Saw
A fine-toothed saw with a reinforcing strap on the back of the blade, also called a razor saw.

Ballast
Crushed rock or stone, used by railroads to hold ties in place and improve drainage.

Balsa
Very lightweight wood used for modeling, easily cut.

Basswood (American Linden)
A lightweight, close-grained wood that's harder than balsa. (May show signs of fuzzing when painted or stained.)

Block
A section of track electrically isolated from adjoining sections. Used for multi-train operation, signal systems or to prevent short circuits.

Board and Batten Siding
Vertical wooden planking with small wooden strips (battens) nailed over the seams between each plank.

Bolster
Part of a railroad car body that runs across the underbody and connects the trucks' pivot points to the body. Sometimes used to describe all the cross members, including the ends of a car's underframe. On a truck, the transverse part between the sideframes.

Branch
A portion of a railroad line that diverges off from the main line to serve a town or industry, or connect with another railroad.

Bristol Board
Heavy-duty paper board with a soft surface, sold in thickness based on weight.

Bumper
A device placed at the end of a track siding to prevent cars or locos from running off and derailing.

Butt Joint
A wood joint where one end of a board is glued (butted) directly to the end of another board.

Caboose
The last car of a freight train, used as an office and living quarters by the crew.

Caliper
A precision measuring tool, fitted with adjustable jaws and a measuring scale, for determining very small dimensions.

Cardstock
Generic name for all laminated paper sheet material.

Casting
The process of making copies of an original item using a mold and a free-flowing material such as metal, plaster or resin. Finished pieces are called castings.

Catenary
Overhead wires that supply current for electric locomotives.

Corner Board
Trim on the outside corner of a wood frame building. Siding fits tight against corner boards.

Cornice
Horizontal molding or trim which crowns or finishes a wall.

Coursed Rubble
A type of masonry wall made from random sized stones in crude rows (courses) with smaller stones used to fill gaps. Often used for older building foundations.

Craft Train Kits
Kits designed for the experienced modeler, with unpainted wood, metal or plastic parts. Assembly usually requires use of drawings or templates.

Cribbing
A framework of wood, concrete or metal beams filled with stones or earth to act as a retaining wall.

Crossing
A special kind of track where two lines cross each other. (Sometimes used to describe a grade crossing, where a road crosses the tracks.)

Crossover
A pair of switches that allow trains to cross from one set of tracks to another on a double-track line.

Cut
Construction term for the area removed from a hill or mountain to permit construction of level roadbed. Also refers to a small group of cars coupled together.

D

DPDT - Double Pole, Double Throw
Type of electrical switch used to reverse the flow of current. Some types have an "off" position midway through the throw, and these "center-off" switches are frequently used for wiring layouts to allow for two train and two throttle operation.

Dental Plaster
A hard casting plaster used for molding.

Diecast
Casting process where molten metal or other liquid is forced into a mold.

Diorama
A small scene with great detail. Used as a setting for photographs or model display.

Double-Hung Window
Window with two sliding sashes that move vertically next to each other.

Draft Gear
On a model, the box where the coupler is spring mounted.

Dry Brushing
A weathering technique, where an almost "dry brush" is used to highlight details on the model with paint.

E

Easy-To-Build Kits
Kits featuring simple construction with few parts. Most are prepainted or molded in color and can be assembled in a short time using only basic tools.

Elevation
1) A kind of engineering drawing showing only one side of a structure. 2) The vertical distance above an established level or grade.

Epoxy
A two-part adhesive consisting of a resin and hardener, which cures rather than dries. Good for gluing nonporous materials such as plastic and metal.

Escutcheon Pins
Small pins or nails used with ornamental fasteners, originally used with keyhole plates.

F

Fascia
Board nailed vertically to the end of roof rafters, sometimes used to support gutters.

Fiddle Yard
Hidden tracks where a modeler can couple or uncouple cars, usually lifting them by hand.

Fill
A construction term used to describe an area where dirt or rock has been dumped so a level roadbed can be constructed.

Flange
The inner edge of a railroad wheel that guides it down the rails. The flange extends around the inner edge of the wheel.

Flash
Thin sections of material that have oozed out from a mold, but remain attached to the casting.

Frog
The point where the track rails cross at a switch or rail/rail crossing.

Gap
A space between rails to electrically isolate some portion of the track. Used to prevent short circuits, or to allow multiple train operation on the same track.

Gauge
The spacing between the inside of the rail heads. Standard gauge for North American railroads is 4' 8-1/2". Narrow gauge is anything smaller than standard, with 2' and 3' being the most common. Sometimes used to describe the size of models, such as HO Gauge. (See Scale.)

Grab Iron (Grab)
Steel hand rails on the sides, roofs or ends of equipment.

Grade
The angle of rise or fall of the tracks so they follow the contour of the land.

Grain
The direction and stratification of fibers in wood and cardboard, or some kinds of stone.

Ground Foam
Synthetic foam rubber, ground into various sizes and dyed to match vegetation.

Gypsum
A common calcium sulfate used to make plaster of Paris.

H

Head-End Cars
Express Reefers, Baggage Cars or Railway Post Offices, coupled at the front or head end of a passenger train.

Helper
A locomotive used to help a train over a steep grade, usually by pushing at the rear.

Herald
A Railroad's logo.

Hostler
A person who moves and services locomotives at a terminal.

Hotbox
An overheated wheel bearing on a car or a locomotive. Caused by lack of lubrication.

Hydrocal®
A trade name of US Gypsum Corporation for a very hard, dense plaster. Much stronger than patching plaster or plaster of Paris.

I

Interchange
The movement of cars between railroads, also the track where cars are left for pickup by another railroad.

Interlocking
A system of mechanical and/or electrical controls allowing only one train to move through a junction of two or more tracks.

Intermodal
"Between Modes." Refers to the movement of containers by ship, train and truck, or the specialized rail cars which carry containers and trailers.

Interurban
A type of shortline railroad, usually equipped with electrically powered cars, to provide passenger and freight service between two or more cities. The self-propelled cars, (also called interurbans) drew electrical power from overhead lines or a third rail.

J-K

Journal
The load-bearing end of an axle which rides in the support bearing.

Keystone
A wedge-shaped piece at the top of an arch which holds the other pieces in place.

Kingpin
The pivot point of a wheel set (truck), it connects to the bolster. In modeling, a plastic pin used to attach the truck to the bolster.

Kitbash
To combine parts from two or more different models into an entirely new design. Sometimes called cross-kitting, customizing or converting.

L

LCL
"Less-than-Carload-Lot." Small freight shipments that don't require an entire car.

Lap Joint
A wood joint made by cutting two boards to 1/2 of their thickness and joining them.

Lintel
Structural element across the top of a window, made of stone or concrete when those materials are used in construction. Hidden on modern buildings by a siding cover.

M

Main Line
The primary route where traffic on a railroad is heaviest.

Maintenance-Of-Way (MOW)
Usually refers to the equipment used by work crews to maintain the tracks, buildings and other railroad property.

Modules
Small, portable sections of layouts that can be joined to form a larger model railroad.

Mortise and Tenon Joint
Wood joint made by cutting a hole in one board, and cutting the other to fit into the hole.

Motor Tool
A hand-held power tool with exchangeable collets, used for cutting, sanding, polishing, etc.

Muntin
Framing to hold window panes, also called a glazing bar.

N-P

NMRA
National Model Railroad Association.

Narrow Gauge
Any trackage with rails spaced closer than 4' 8-1/2" (Standard Gauge)

Nut-Bolt-Washer Casting (NBW)
A plastic or metal piece representing the visible portion of a threaded rod with washer and locking nut in place.

Parting Line
Point where two halves of a mold join, also a visible ridge on casting made in such a mold.

Peddler Freight
A small freight train, switching towns and industries along a specific route, also called a wayfreight.

Piggyback
Term to describe moving highway trailers aboard flat cars, sometimes called Trailer-On-Flat-Car (TOFC). See Intermodal.

Pike
Short for turnpike, used to describe an entire model railroad.

Pilaster
An architectural feature describing a low-relief pier or column which is not a supporting member of the structure. May have a base, wall or capital as part of the wall itself.

Points
The portions of a switch that move to change a track route from the main line to the siding. The point where the rails actually cross is called a frog.

Prototype
The actual car, locomotive, structure or other object on which a model is based.

Pullman
A type of diner, sleeper or parlor car operated by the Pullman Company in passenger service. Sometimes used to describe any sleeping car.

R

R-T-R
Ready-To-Run, a model which requires no assembly.

Rail Joiner
A piece of folded metal used to connect two sections of model track and provide a complete electrical circuit between the rails.

Razor Saw
A type of modeler's saw with very fine teeth and a ribbed reinforcement on top. (Resembles an old-fashioned razor.)

Reefer
Slang for any type of refrigerated car used to haul perishables.

Resin
A type of liquid material used for castings, which dries to a hard plastic substance.

Right-Of-Way
The railroad track and adjacent property.

S

Scale
The size of a model, expressed as a mathematical ratio. An HO model is 1/87 Scale.

Scale Lumber
Small pieces of wood cut to scale proportions of commercial building materials, such as 2 x 4"s, etc.

Scratchbuilding
Construction of a model from scratch, using plastic, wood or paper.

Scribe
To cut or mark. Scribed material (often used to simulate siding) has lines cut into its surface.

Selective Compression
A modeling technique where a model is made smaller than its actual dimensions in order to fit on a layout. (Often used with structures.)

Sill
Horizontal piece directly below a window, angled downward for drainage.

Solder
A mixture of metal which melts at different temperatures. Used for electrical work as well as joining brass and other metals.

SPDT
Single Pole, Double Throw. A type of electrical switch

Spot
A switching maneuver to move a car to a desired location (spot).

Strathmore
Commercial name for high-grade card stock with a hard surface, often used for structure construction. Supplied in thicknesses based on plies.

Styrene
A common modeling plastic used in injection molding, also available in sheets and strips for scratchbuilding.

Superelevation
Banking tracks on a curve so trains can maintain a higher speed.

Switch
On a railroad, a type of track that allows trains to change routes. Modelers use this term to indicate electrical switches. See Turnouts.

Switch Machine
An electrical device, operated by remote control, that moves the points of a track switch from one route to the other.

T

Talgo Truck
A type of model railroad truck with a coupler mounted on it. Often used on toy train equipment so cars can negotiate tighter curves, but prone to derailments when a long train is pushed or backed.

Tangent
Straight sections of track.

Tank Engine
A small steam engine that carries fuel and water in tanks on the side of the boiler instead of in a tender.

Tender
Car behind larger steam engines that carries fuel and water.

Throat
Point in a yard where the mainline diverges into multiple tracks for storage and switching.

Traction
A term used to describe all prototype locomotives and self-propelled cars (i.e., trolleys and interurbans) that operated by electrical power.

Transistor Throttle
An electric speed control used in place of wire-bound rheostat. Provides better slow speed and starting control.

Transition Curve
Also called an Easement. Length of track on a layout where a curve joins a tangent with gradually diminishing radius. Eases the sudden shift from straight to curved track to help prevent derailments, especially of longer equipment.

Trolley
A self-propelled, electrically powered car that ran on city streets. (Interurbans were generally bigger cars and ran between cities.) Also the device used to collect current from the overhead lines.

Truck
The sprung frame and wheels under each end of a car or locomotive.

Turnout
Modeler's term describing a track switch, where two tracks join.

Turntable
Rotating steel or wooden bridge for turning locomotives.

U-Z

Vestibule
Enclosed area at the end of a passenger car where riders board, and also pass between cars.

Wayfreight
See Peddler Freight

Weathering
Process of painting, staining or coloring, showing the affects of aging and exposure to the elements on a model.

White Glue
A polymer suspension in water, sold under various brand names such as Elmer's®, Ambroid®, etc. Some can be sanded, others peel when sanded.

Wye
A track where routes curve to the left and right of a single straight track. Also describes the triangular trackage sometimes used for reversing trains.

This glossary combines material from Model Railroad Structures from A to Z by Carstens Publications Inc., and The HO Model Railroading Handbook by Robert Schleicher, published by Chilton Book Company. Reprinted with permission.

YOU'VE GOT QUESTIONS? WE'VE GOT ANSWERS!

With our 2000 edition of the Walthers Reference Book, we've tried to make sure that each manufacturer's listing has as much information as possible to make your decisions on what to buy a little easier. As a result, there may be some terms and abbreviations you may not be familiar with. To make sure you are "up-to-speed," below are a series of roadname abbreviations and special codes you might find on a page. Use these lists as guides to better understanding all the information within the Walthers Reference Book.

US & CANADIAN ROADNAME ABBREVIATION KEY

Amtrak (AMTK on Maintenance/some freight equipment)
ATSF Santa Fe (Actual = Atchinson, Topeka & Santa Fe)
B&O Baltimore & Ohio
BN Burlington Northern
BNSF Burlington Northern **Santa Fe** (1996 Merger)
C&O Chesapeake & Ohio
CB&Q Chicago, Burlington & Quincy
CN Canadian National
CNJ Central Railroad of New Jersey/Jersey Central
CNW Chicago & North Western
CP Canadian Pacific
CR Conrail
CSX CSX Transportation
D&H Delaware & Hudson
DRGW Rio Grande (Actual = Denver & Rio Grande Western)
EL (Also E-L in some cases) Erie Lackawanna
GN Great Northern
IC Illinois Central
L&N Louisville & Nashville
LV Lehigh Valley
MILW Milwaukee Road (Actual = Chicago, Milwaukee, St. Paul & Pacific)
MKT Katy (Actual = Missouri, Kansas, Texas)
MON Monon (Actual = Chicago, Indianapolis & Louisville-)
MP Missouri Pacific
MOW Maintenance-Of-Way
N&W Norfolk & Western
NH New Haven (Actual = New York, New Haven & Hartford)
NKP Nickel Plate Road (Actual = New York, Chicago & St. Louis)
NP Northern Pacific
NS Norfolk Southern
NYC New York Central
PFE Pacific Fruit Express
PRR Pennsylvania
RDG Reading
ROCK Rock Island (Actual = Chicago, Rock Island & Pacific)
SOO Soo Line (Actual = Minneapolis, St. Paul & Saulte St. Marie)
SOU Southern Railway
SP Southern Pacific
UP Union Pacific
WC Wisconsin Central Limited
WM Western Maryland

EUROPEAN ERAS

To identify equipment and color/lettering schemes from specific time periods, most European manufacturers use the following eras:

ERA I: 1870-1920
ERA II: 1920-1945
ERA III: 1945-1970
ERA IV: 1968-1985
ERA V: 1985-Present

EUROPEAN ROADNAMES & ABBREVIATIONS

GERMANY

1) REGIONAL RAILWAYS BEFORE 1920
KPEV Royal Prussian State Railways
KBAY Bavarian State Railways
KWStE Royal Württemburg State Railways
K.Sächs. Sts. E. B. Royal Saxonian State Railways

2) GOVERNMENT RAILWAYS
DRG = German State Railways 1920-1945
DB = German Federal Railways 1945-1985
DB-AG = German Railway Union 1985-Present

EAST GERMANY

DR = East German State Railways 1945-1985

AUSTRIA

BBÖ Federal Railways of Austria-Through 1956
ÖBB Austrian Federal Railways 1956-Present

BELGIUM

SNCB National Railways of Belgium

CZECH REPUBLIC

CD

DENMARK

DSB Danish State Railways

FRANCE

SNCF French National Railway Company

HUNGARY

MAV

ITALY

FS Italian State Railways

LUXEMBOURG

CFL

HOLLAND/NETHERLANDS

NS Netherlands State Railways

NORWAY

NSB Norwegian State Railways

POLAND

PKP State Railway of Poland

SLOVENIA

SZ

SLOVAKIA

ZSR

SPAIN

RENFE

SWEDEN

SJ Swedish State Railways

SWITZERLAND

Numerous regional lines operated as Swiss Federal Railways. Modern engines are marked SBB CFF FFS, but you may see them individually as:

SBB
BLS Bern-Lötschberg-Simplon
CFF
FFS
BT
GBS
S.T.B.
S.O.B South East Railway
(Sud Ost Bahn)

SYMBOLS

NEW - Identifies a brand new item, appearing for the first time in this book.

NEW
SUPPLIER

NEW SUPPLIER - Identifies an all-new line of products, making their first appearance in this book.

BLUE LINE ITEMS -
When an item is listed in blue, it's because the manufacturer has not been able to deliver them regularly. The item was out of stock when the catalog was printed and delivery was not known. All "blue line" items CAN still be placed on backorder. Ask your dealer or check our Web site at www.walthers.com for current delivery information.

Limited Quantity Available
When products appear under this heading, it means we are running out of the item/s and are unable to order more. The item/s may have been discontinued by the manufacturer, or is produced on an irregular schedule and will not be available again for quite some time.

PACKAGE QUANTITY - (pkg#) - Indicates the number of items included in the package. Some items used in pairs (trucks, diaphragms) are listed as 1 Pair, 2 Pair etc.

RETIRED MODEL - Indicates a Walthers product which has been taken out of production. Supplies are limited to the remaining inventory at your dealer or in our warehouse. A future production run may be scheduled.

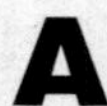

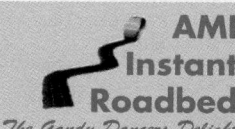

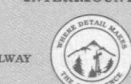

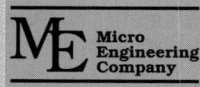

P

LOCOMOTIVES

Photo by Ken Patterson, courtesy of Bachmann

Bigger, heavier, faster. Those are the watchwords along the railroad these days. It isn't just freight and passenger cars that are growing. These innovative car designs demand a new kind of steam loco.

Now each railroad has its likes and dislikes. Every single superintendent of motive power knows exactly what his railroad needs when it comes to locomotive design. But these new 4-8-2 "Mountains," well, they're changing things.

Sure, the railroads were skeptical at first, especially when the United States Railroad Administration insisted on using a standardized plan. But over time, the railroads came to admit this 4-8-2 was pretty good. So good in fact, that some are copying the design for their own new locos!

Now the debate seems to be whether it's a better passenger or freight engine. They've got what it takes to roll the varnish at speed. A bigger boiler and towering 69" drivers provide almost twice the pulling power of the aging Atlantics. Even the newer Pacifics are hard-pressed to keep up. Others swear the combination of size and power makes them the best fast freight engines their road has ever owned. Some roads are using them in both assignments.

Whether your favorite loco is an early 4-4-0 steamer or the latest Dash 9 wide cab diesel, you'll find the motive power (including the new Bachmann Spectrum® 4-8-2 shown above) your railroad needs on the following pages.

WALTHERS™

TRAINLINE®
by WALTHERS

With Trainline® locomotives, you can count on years of reliable service for your railroad. These detailed models are ready to run, with prepainted plastic bodies, diecast metal frames, powerful motor, 8-wheel electrical pick-up and drive, plus a working headlight.

EMD F40PH LOCOMOTIVES

EA 49.98

Move passengers in style with the F40PH on the head-end. Introduced in the 1980s and still going strong today, you'll find them in Amtrak and regional commuter service. Models are ready-to-run with diecast metal frame, dual flywheel drive, directional headlight and optional pilot plow.

931-301

931-306

931-308

931-304

931-307

931-303

Preproduction Model Shown
931-313

931-301 Amtrak Phase III #300
931-302 Amtrak Phase III #303
931-303 Chicago METRA
931-304 Boston MBTA
931-308 Via Rail Canada
931-309 Amtrak Phase II #259
931-311 Amtrak Phase III #339
931-310 Amtrak Phase II #272
931-313 GO Transit
931-314 Metro Link
931-315 Tri-Rail
931-316 VIA - Canadian Flag Scheme #6450 ***NEW***
931-317 Florida Fun Train #374 ***NEW - LIMITED RUN***
931-318 New Jersey Transit #4125 ***NEW***
931-300 Undecorated

Limited Quantity Available
931-306 San Francisco Caltrain
931-307 San Diego Coaster

Daily New Arrival Updates! Visit Walthers Web site at

www.walthers.com

WALTHERS™

TRAINLINE®
by WALTHERS

931-172

931-173

931-176

931-177

931-179

931-191
Preproduction Model Shown

Roadnumber Shown Not Available

931-190
Preproduction Model Shown

931-187
Preproduction Model Shown

931-188
Preproduction Model Shown

GE DASH 8-40B LOCOMOTIVE

EA 59.98

These modern locos pack 4000 horsepower into a single unit and serve primarily in high speed intermodal service. Due to their speed capabilities, a passenger version was also built for Amtrak. (These engines are ideal for use with Walthers intermodal equipment, plus Superliner II, Amfleet and Horizon Fleet passenger cars).

This detailed engine has all the features you look for in a quality locomotive: dual flywheels, five-pole can motor with skew-wound armature, reversing headlight, superbly detailed trucks with separate brake gear and shock absorber struts, and a heavy die-cast frame for superior performance.

AMTRAK-WIDE

931-166 #510
931-185 Phase II #506

ATSF

931-168 #553 Wide Cab (red, silver)
931-175 #7410 Standard Cab (blue, yellow)

Limited Quantity Available

931-176 #7435 Standard Cab (blue, yellow)

LMX LEASING-STANDARD CAB

Limited Quantity Available

931-169 #8554

CSX-STANDARD CAB

931-170 #5930

NS-STANDARD CAB

931-171 #3554 (black & white)

UP

931-172 #9503-Wide Cab
931-189 #5637-Standard Cab (Ex-SP, yellow w/small UP herald)

Limited Quantity Available

931-190 #5646-Standard Cab (Ex-SP, yellow w/small UP herald)

SUSQUEHANNA-STANDARD CAB

931-173 #4002

Limited Quantity Available

931-174 #4006

SSW-STANDARD CAB

Limited Quantity Available

931-177 #8041
931-178 #8072

SP-STANDARD CAB

Limited Quantity Available

931-179 #8000
931-180 #8003

BNSF "WARBONNET" WIDE CAB

931-181 #517 (red, silver)
931-187 #557 (red, silver w/small lettering)

Limited Quantity Available

931-182 #533 (red, silver)

BNSF "PUMPKIN" STANDARD CAB

931-183 #8615 (green, orange)
931-188 #8630 (green, orange)

Limited Quantity Available

931-184 #8623 (green, orange)

CONRAIL

931-167 CR #5068 Wide Cab
931-191 #5072 Standard Cab w/ Labor Management Project Nose Art

UNDECORATED

931-150 Standard Cab
931-151 Wide Cab

TRAINLINE®
by WALTHERS

EMD GP9M DIESELS

EA 32.98

The Electro-Motive Division (EMD) of General Motors was the last major builder to enter the road switcher market, introducing the GP7 (GP for General Purpose) in 1949. In 1954, the more powerful GP9 was unveiled with a 1750 horsepower prime-mover. This became the most successful of the early geeps, with sales of more than 3,800 locos in the U.S. and Canada. As the GP9s were bumped from major freight and passenger trains by newer locos, they began new careers as switchers. Many roads rebuilt them with a low nose to improve forward visibility and they continue to serve in switching, wayfreight and transfer assignments today.

This HO Scale model will be a real workhorse on your model railroad. Fully assembled and ready for service, they come prepainted in a variety of schemes.

931-101 BN #1709 w/White Front
931-102 UP
931-103 ATSF (Freight)
931-104 CN
931-105 CSX
931-106 CR
931-107 SP
931-108 NS
931-109 PRR
931-110 CNW
931-111 MILW
931-113 ATSF (Superfleet®)
931-114 CP
931-115 Guilford (B&M)
931-116 SOO
931-117 SOU
931-118 WC
931-119 Montana Rail Link
931-120 BNSF "Pumpkin" (orange, green)
931-121 IC
931-122 Florida East Coast
931-123 Amtrak
931-124 C&O/Chessie #6073 (blue, yellow, orange)
931-125 DRGW (black, orange)
932-126 Alaska Railroad #1809 (blue, yellow) ***NEW*** Features correct Alco Type B trucks.

932-127 US Army #4616 (red, yellow) ***NEW***
931-100 Undecorated

Limited Quantity available

931-112 Ashley, Drew & Northern

931-101
931-102
931-104
931-105
931-106
931-107

931-103
931-108
931-109
931-110
931-111
931-113
931-114

TRAINLINE®
by WALTHERS

931-115

931-116

931-117

931-118

931-119

931-120

931-121

931-122

931-123

*Preproduction Model Shown
931-124

*Preproduction Model Shown
931-125

931-126

931-127
Different Unit Number Shown

Get Daily Info, Photos and News at

www.walthers.com

TRAINLINE®
by WALTHERS

ALCO FA-1/FB-1 DIESEL LOCOMOTIVES

Alco's answer to EMD's Fs, running side-by-side with first generation diesels and the last of steam. Colorful period paint and lettering, different numbers and matching B-units for roads which had them, make these powered models a must for vintage rosters. All locos feature cast metal frame, all-wheel drive and electrical pickup, powerful motor with flywheel, working headlight (FA only) and body-mounted couplers.

ALCO FA-1 LOCOMOTIVES EA 29.98

GREAT NORTHERN
931-201 #310A
931-202 #310C

UNION PACIFIC
931-203 #1500A
931-204 #1503A

PENNSYLVANIA
931-205 #9600
931-206 #9602

SANTA FE
931-207 #202A
931-208 #205A

SOUTHERN
931-209 #2853A

Limited Quantity Available
931-210 #2858A

NEW YORK CENTRAL
931-211 #1000A
931-212 #1043A

ERIE
931-213 #729A

Limited Quantity Available
931-214 #725A

READING
931-215 #300
931-216 #305

SPOKANE, PORTLAND & SEATTLE
931-217 #859
931-218 #867

WABASH
931-219 #1200A
931-220 #1202A

ROCK ISLAND
931-221 #147

Limited Quantity Available
931-222 #158

NEW HAVEN
931-223 #0400
931-224 #0419

ERIE LACKAWANNA
(maroon, yellow, gray)
931-225 #7254
931-226 #7344

LEHIGH VALLEY
(Cornell Red)
931-227 #538
931-228 #542

SOO LINE
(maroon, Dulux Gold)

931-229 #207A
931-230 #210B
931-200 Undecorated

ALCO FB-1 LOCOMOTIVES EA 29.98

931-261 GN #310B
931-262 UP #1524B
931-263 PRR #9601
931-264 ATSF #202B
931-266 NYC #2304B
931-267 Erie #732B
931-268 RDG #302
931-269 Wabash #1203B
931-270 ROCK #151B
931-271 NH #0464
931-272 Spokane, Portland & Seattle #205
931-273 EL #7263
931-274 LV #531
931-260 Undecorated

Limited Quantity Available
931-265 SOU #2853B

931-203/262

931-205/263

931-207/264

931-209/265

931-211/266

931-213/267

931-215/268

931-201/261

TRAINLINE® by WALTHERS

931-220/269

931-221/270

931-224/271

931-218/272

Preproduction Model Shown
931-225/273

Preproduction Model Shown
931-227/274

TRAINLINE®
by WALTHERS

US Army 931-701

Alaska Railroad 931-700

LOCO & CABOOSE SETS

EA 39.98

Enjoy the color and variety of your favorite railroads any time you run trains! With these combination loco and caboose packs, you can collect a whole series of equipment from great American railroads that will make any operating session more fun.

Each set comes with a powerful GP9M diesel, packed with features including a diecast metal frame, five-pole, skew wound armature motor with flywheel, working headlight and much more.

To complete your train, a wide-vision caboose, painted in the same colors as the engine, is also included. And, these models have DIFFERENT NUMBERS from individual Trainline® GP9M locos and cabooses so you can easily expand your fleet in a matter of minutes. Both loco and caboose are fully assembled and ready for work on your railroad.

931-700 Alaska Railroad (blue & yellow) ***NEW***
Loco features correct Alco Type B trucks.

931-701 US Army (red, yellow) ***NEW***
931-702 BN (white front scheme) ***NEW***
931-703 UP (yellow, gray & red) ***NEW***
931-704 CSX (blue & gray) ***NEW***
931-705 NS (black & white) ***NEW***
931-706 Wisconsin Central (maroon & yellow) ***NEW***
931-707 BNSF (orange & green) ***NEW***
931-708 ATSF (red & silver "Warbonnet" w/red caboose) ***NEW***
931-709 DRGW (black & orange) ***NEW***

*Preproduction Model Shown
931-352

*Preproduction Model Shown
931-353

EMD GP15-1 DIESELS

EA 49.98

EMD introduced the GP15-1 in 1975 as a replacement for aging GP7s and GP9s still being used for switching, transfer and wayfreight service. Buyers had to provide a trade-in unit for the traction motors, trucks and main generators. Outwardly, GP15-1s looked like 35 Series engines, with a long hood, road-style cab and short nose. The most distinguishing feature was the single 48" fan and "tunnel motor" air intake for the radiators. Later versions included the GP15-1AC, equipped with an alternator instead of a generator, and the GP15T, which added a turbocharger to the AC model. Nearly 370 of the three styles were built for US railroads between 1976 and 1983, and most are still going strong.

The models are detailed to match their prototype with the correct style of Inertial or Louvered air intakes.

Each includes full handrails, directional lighting, all-wheel drive and electrical pick-up, five-pole motor with dual flywheels and a heavy cast frame. Models are equipped with knuckle type couplers; optional horn-hook couplers are also provided.

931-351 BN (green, black, white)
931-352 CNW (yellow, green)
931-353 UP (yellow, gray, red)
931-354 MP (blue, white)
931-355 Chessie (orange, yellow, blue)
931-356 CR (blue, white)
931-357 SLSF (red/orange, white)
931-358 BNSF #1478 ***NEW***
931-359 CSX #1511 (blue & gray) ***NEW***
931-350 Undecorated-Louvered Air Filter
931-399 Undecorated-Inertial Air Filter

SECOND SERIES ENGINE NUMBERS

Same great schemes, but with another factory-printed engine number to expand your fleet in minutes.

931-361 BN #1397 ***NEW***
931-362 CNW #4413 ***NEW***
931-363 UP #1649 ***NEW***
931-364 MP #1695 ***NEW***
931-365 Chessie System #1508 ***NEW***
931-366 CR #1645 ***NEW***
931-367 SLSF #105 ***NEW***
931-368 BNSF #1485 ***NEW***
931-369 CSX #1523 (blue & gray) ***NEW***

NO UNIT NUMBER

Customize your roster in minutes with these models. Locos are painted and lettered in the same schemes, but with NO unit numbers so you can model any engine in the fleet. Simply add the number you choose with your favorite decals, sold separately.

931-371 BN ***NEW***
931-372 CNW ***NEW***
931-373 UP ***NEW***
931-374 MP ***NEW***
931-375 Chessie System ***NEW***
931-376 CR ***NEW***
931-377 SLSF ***NEW***
931-378 BNSF ***NEW***
931-379 CSX ***NEW***

WALTHERS™

MODERNIZE MASS TRANSIT SERVICE ON YOUR LAYOUT

Operate modern intercity passenger service with Walthers Rapid Transit Cars. Based on equipment of the Bay Area Rapid Transit (BART) system in San Francisco and the METRO system in Washington, D.C.

Easy-to-build kits feature an injection molded styrene body. All cars are prepainted silver, with decals provided for logos and numbers. (METRO cars have prepainted metallic brown trim and include decals for the red, white and blue stripe.) Kits include separately molded underbody details, diaphragms and tinted window "glass." BART cars have separately molded grab irons. Powered models are driven by an under-floor mounted, self-contained power truck.

BAY AREA RAPID TRANSIT

BART CARS

Serves Oakland, San Francisco, and nearby suburbs.

932-6030 A Unit Powered **49.98**
932-6031 A Unit Dummy **19.98**
932-6032 B Unit Dummy **19.98**

WASHINGTON D.C. METRO

METRO CARS

Serving the District of Columbia and suburbs in Maryland and Virginia.

932-6035 Powered **49.98**
932-6036 Dummy **19.98**

932-1367

EMD SW-1 DIESELS

EA 79.98

From the late 30s to the present day, the SW-1 has a proven track record as one of the most successful switchers ever built. Their small size makes them ideal for all types of heavy industries that require a reliable, in-plant loco to keep rail cars moving.

Both front and rear trucks are powered and a heavy diecast frame (model weighs 11 ounces) insures plenty of pulling power. A skew-wound, five-pole, can motor with dual flywheels and all-wheel electrical pick-up insure smooth operations at any speed. Each is painted and lettered, with a basic cab interior, window "glass," working headlight and a complete set of add-on handrails. (For easy superdetailing, starter points are molded on the body to drill mounting holes for wire grab irons, sold separately.)

932-1367 Erie #360 (black, yellow)
932-1368 B&O #8401 (blue, yellow)
932-1369 SP #1010 (black & orange "Tiger Stripes")
932-1370 SOU #2007 (black, gold)
932-1371 GN #77 (orange, green, yellow)
932-1372 PRR #9137 (Brunswick Green, red & white herald)
932-1373 CNJ #1012 (green, yellow, with Liberty herald)
932-1350 Undecorated

932-6035

932-6030

TRAINS Athearn IN MINIATURE

C44-9W 140-4936

C44-9W

All models are ready to run (hood units require installation of handrails which are included) with prepainted and lettered styrene bodies and metal underframes. All wheels are powered and engines feature flywheel drives where noted. All locos include horn-hook couplers.

POWERED EA 59.50

140-4901 GE Demonstrator #8601
140-4902 ATSF #601
140-4906 SP #8125
140-4910 UP #9703
140-4914 CNW #8651
140-4918 CSX #9003
140-4922 CN #2514
140-4926 BCR #4641
140-4932 NS #8890
140-4936 BNSF #968 **59.50**
140-4940 BNSF (Warbonnet) #701
140-4900 Undecorated, High Boards
140-4930 Undecorated, Low Boards
140-4931 ATSF Cab Undecorated

DUMMY EA 35.75

140-4951 GE Demonstrator # 8601
140-4952 ATSF #601
140-4956 SP #8125
140-4960 UP #9703
140-4964 CNW #8651
140-4968 CSX #9003
140-4972 CN #2514
140-4976 BCR
140-4982 NS #1
140-4986 BN #968
140-4990 BNSF (Warbonnet) #701
140-4950 Undecorated, High Boards
140-4980 Undecorated, Low Boards
140-4981 ATSF Cab Undecorated

EMD F7

One of the all-time great locos, the F7 was an upgrade of earlier F unit models. Packing 1500 horsepower, they were built in A (with control cab) and B (cabless booster) unit configurations, so they could be MUed. Many were fitted with water tanks and steam generators for use in passenger service. Nearly 2,400 were purchased for use in the US, Canada and Mexico, and some remained in service until the 1980s.

F7A "SUPER" W/FLYWHEELS-POWERED EA 33.50

140-3201 ATSF Passenger (Warbonnet, yellow, silver)
140-3203 ATSF Freight (blue, yellow)
140-3205 PRR Passenger (maroon, yellow)
140-3207 PRR Freight (green, yellow)
140-3209 SP (red, gray)
140-3211 BN (Cascade Green, black, white)
140-3213 UP (gray, yellow)
140-3215 DRGW (black yellow, silver)
140-3217 MILW (gray, yellow)
140-3219 B&O (blue, black, gray)
140-3221 NH (red, white, black)
140-3225 CN (green, yellow, black)
140-3227 C&O (blue, yellow)
140-3229 NP (green, yellow, red)
140-3231 CNW (green, yellow)
140-3233 Amtrak
140-3235 SP Daylight (red, orange)
140-3237 CP (red, white black)
140-3241 SP "Black Widow"
140-3243 CSX
140-3245 CR
140-3247 CN "Zebra"
140-3249 Western Pacific (orange & silver)
140-3271 Amtrak Phase III
140-3273 NP Freight
140-3223 Undecorated, 2 Headlights
140-3239 Undecorated, 1 Headlight

EMD F7A ATSF 140-3101

F7A STANDARD-POWERED EA 29.50

140-3101 ATSF Passenger (Warbonnet, yellow, silver)
140-3103 ATSF Freight (blue, yellow)
140-3105 PRR Passenger (maroon, yellow)
140-3107 PRR Freight (green, yellow)
140-3109 SP (red, gray)
140-3111 BN (Cascade Green, black, white)
140-3113 UP (gray, yellow)
140-3115 DRGW (black, yellow, silver)
140-3117 MILW (gray, yellow)
140-3119 B&O (blue black, gray)
140-3121 NH
140-3125 CN (green, yellow, black)
140-3127 C&O (blue, yellow)
140-3129 NP (green, yellow, red)
140-3131 CNW (green, yellow)
140-3133 Amtrak
140-3135 SP Daylight (red, orange)
140-3137 CP Rail
140-3141 SP "Black Widow"
140-3143 CSX
140-3145 Cr
140-3147 CN "Zebra"
140-3149 Western Pacific (orange, silver)

140-3171 Amtrak Phase III
140-3173 NP Freight
140-3123 Undecorated, Double Headlight
140-3139 Undecorated, Single Headlight

F7A DUMMY EA 17.75

140-3001 ATSF Passenger (silver, red)
140-3003 ATSF Freight (blue, yellow)
140-3005 PRR Passenger (maroon, yellow)
140-3007 PRR Freight (green, yellow)
140-3009 SP (red, gray)
140-3011 BN (green)
140-3013 UP (yellow)
140-3015 DRGW (aluminum, yellow w/black stripes)
140-3017 MILW (gray)
140-3019 B&O (blue, black, gray)
140-3021 NH (black, orange, white)
140-3025 CN (green, yellow, black)
140-3027 C&O (blue, gold silver)
140-3029 NP (green, yellow)
140-3031 CNW (green, yellow)
140-3033 Amtrak (silver w/black roof)
140-3035 SP Daylight (red, orange)
140-3037 CP (red, white, black)
140-3041 SP "Black Widow"
140-3043 CSX
140-3045 Cr
140-3047 CN "Zebra"
140-3049 Western Pacific (orange, silver)
140-3071 Amtrak Phase III
140-3073 NP Freight
140-3023 Undecorated, 2 headlights (black)
140-3039 Undecorated

F7B WITH FLYWHEELS-POWERED EA 33.50

140-3202 ATSF Passenger (Warbonnet, yellow, silver)
140-3204 ATSF Freight (blue w/yellow stripe)
140-3206 PRR Passenger (Tuscan w/yellow stripes)
140-3208 PRR Freight (olive w/yellow stripes)
140-3210 SP (gray, red)
140-3212 BN (green & white w/black roof)
140-3214 UP (yellow w/gray roof & red stripes)
140-3216 DRGW (aluminum, yellow w/black stripes)
140-3218 MILW
140-3220 B&O (black, blue, gray w/gold stripes)
140-3222 NH (black, orange, white)
140-3226 CN (green, yellow & black)
140-3228 C&O (blue, yellow)
140-3230 NP (green, yellow w/red stripes)
140-3232 CNW (green, yellow)
140-3234 Amtrak (silver w/black roof)
140-3236 SP Daylight (red, orange)
140-3238 CP Rail (red w/silver stripe)
140-3242 SP "Black Widow"
140-3244 CSX
140-3248 CN "Zebra"
140-3250 Western Pacific (orange, silver)
140-3272 Amtrak Phase III
140-3274 NP Freight
140-3224 Undecorated

WALTHERS™

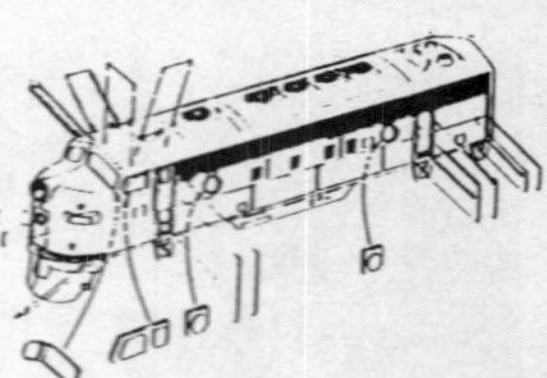

F UNIT SUPERDETAILING KIT

933-822 51 Pieces **4.98**
Dress up F7 and F9 A and B units with this superdetailing kit. Designed especially for Athearn Fs, the kit contains enough parts for one A and one B Unit, including clear plastic windshield, windows and port holes, pre-formed wire grab irons and two clear plastic headlight lenses. Complete instructions and placement diagram included.

F7B DUMMY EA 17.75

140-3002 ATSF Passenger (silver, red)
140-3004 ATSF Freight (blue, yellow)
140-3006 PRR Passenger (maroon, yellow)
140-3008 PRR Freight (green, yellow)
140-3010 SP (red, gray)
140-3012 BN (green)
140-3014 UP (yellow)
140-3016 DRGW (gold, silver)
140-3018 MILW
140-3020 B&O (blue, black, gray)
140-3022 NH (black, orange, white)
140-3026 CN (green, yellow, black)
140-3028 C&O (blue, gold, silver)
140-3030 NP (green, yellow)
140-3032 CNW (green, yellow)
140-3034 Amtrak (silver w/black roof)
140-3036 SP Daylight (black, red, orange)
140-3038 CP (red, white, black)
140-3042 SP "Black Widow"
140-3044 CSX
140-3048 CN "Zebra"
140-3049 Western Pacific (orange & silver)
140-3050 Western Pacific (orange, silver) NW
140-3072 Amtrak Phase III
140-3074 NP Freight
140-3024 Undecorated (black)

EMD GP38-2

WITH FLYWHEELS-POWERED EA 41.50

140-4601 BN (green, black)
140-4602 CR (Big Sky Blue)
140-4603 IC Gulf (gray, orange, red)
140-4604 Seaboard System (gray)
140-4605 MP (blue, white)
140-4606 MILW (black, orange)
140-4607 NS (black)
140-4608 ATSF (blue, yellow)
140-4609 SOO (white, red, black)
140-4610 SP (gray, red)
140-4611 UP (gray, yellow)
140-4613 BN (Cascade Green, white)
140-4614 CP (cascade green, white)
140-4615 CSX
140-4616 CP (2 Flags)
140-4617 CSX
140-4618 SP (speed lettering)
140-4619 BNSF (orange, green)
140-4620 ATSF "Kodachrome" 1983 Merger
140-4640 Boston & Maine (blue w/white lettering) ***NEW***
140-4641 CP (Beaver Herald, red w/white lettering) ***NEW***
140-4642 Frisco (red w/white stripe) ***NEW***
140-4643 Penn Central (black w/white lettering) ***NEW***
140-4600 Undecorated, Dynamic (black)
140-4612 Undecorated, Nondynamic (black)

DUMMY EA 24.75

140-4651 BN (green, black)
1404652 CR (Big Sky Blue)
140-4653 IC Gulf (gray, orange, red)
140-4654 Seaboard System (gray)
140-4655 MP (blue, white)
140-4656 MILW (black, orange)
140-4657 NS (black)
140-4658 ATSF (blue, yellow)
140-4659 SOO (white, red, black)
140-4660 SP (gray, red)
140-4661 UP (gray, yellow)
140-4663 BN (white face)
140-4664 CP (2 Flags)
140-4665 CSX
140-4666 CP System "Dual Flags" Scheme (red, white)
140-4667 CSX (blue, gray)
140-4668 SP (speed lettering)
140-4669 BNSF (orange, green)
140-4662 Undecorated Nondynamic (black)
140-4670 ATSF "Kodachrome" 1983 Merger
140-4690 Boston & Maine (blue w/white lettering) ***NEW***
140-4691 CP (Beaver Herald, red w/white lettering) ***NEW***
140-4692 Frisco (red w/white stripe) ***NEW***
140-4693 Penn Central (black w/white lettering) ***NEW***
140-4650 Undecorated, Dynamic (black)

EMD GP9 GN 140-3157

EMD GP35 CR 140-4210

EMD GP9

Beginning with Alco's RS-2 in the late 1940s and EMD's GP7 and GP9 a few years later, "road switchers" became the most common type of diesel. Also called "hood units," they featured outside walkways and improved visibility for crews doing switching.

WITH FLYWHEELS-POWERED EA 34.50

140-3152 B&O (blue, black, gray)
140-3153 SP (red, gray)
140-3154 UP (yellow, gray)
140-3155 CB&Q
140-3156 ATSF Freight (blue, yellow)
140-3157 GN (orange, green)
140-3159 MILW (black, orange)
140-3160 CR (blue)
140-3161 CN (red, black, white)
140-3162 SP "Black Widow"
140-3163 CN "Zebra"
140-3151 Undecorated (black)

DUMMY EA 20.75

140-3052 B&O (blue, black, gray)
140-3053 SP (red, gray)
140-3054 UP (yellow, gray)
140-3055 CB&Q (red, white, gray)
140-3056 ATSF Freight (blue, yellow)
140-3057 GN (orange, green)
140-3059 MILW (black, orange)
140-3060 CR (blue)
140-3061 CN (black, red, white)
140-3062 SP "Black Widow"
140-3063 CN "Zebra"
140-3051 Undecorated (black)

EMD GP38-2 BN 140-4601

EMD GP38-2 Boston & Maine 140-4640

EMD GP38-2 CP 140-4641

EMD GP38-2 Frisco 140-4642

EMD GP38-2 Penn Central 140-4643

EMD GP35

WITH FLYWHEELS-POWERED EA 34.50

140-4201 Atlantic Coast Line (black, yellow)
140-4202 B&O (blue, yellow)
140-4203 CB&Q (red, white, gray)
140-4204 IC (black, white)
140-4205 ATSF Freight (blue, yellow)
140-4206 SP (red, gray)
140-4207 EL (gray, maroon, yellow)
140-4208 Chessie System (orange, yellow, blue)
140-4209 SOO (red, white)
140-4210 CR
140-4211 CN "Zebra"
140-4200 Undecorated (black)

DUMMY EA 20.75

140-4221 Atlantic Coast Line (black, yellow)
140-4222 B&O (blue, yellow)
140-4223 CB&Q (red, white, gray)
140-4224 IC (black, white)
140-4225 ATSF Freight (blue, yellow)
140-4226 SP (red, gray)
140-4227 EL (gray, maroon, yellow)
140-4228 Chessie System (orange, yellow, blue)
140-4229 SOO (red, white)
140-4230 CR
140-4231 CN "Zebra"
140-4220 Undecorated (black)

EMD GP40-2

POWERED EA 41.50

140-4702 BN (green, white)
140-4703 CR (blue, white)
140-4704 CSX Transportation (blue, gray)
140-4705 DRGW (black, orange)
140-4706 Seaboard System (red, yellow, gray)
140-4707 SP (red, gray, white)

140-4708 SP Speed Lettering (red, gray, white)
140-4709 BN (Cascade Green, white)
140-4710 CSX
140-4711 CR "Q" Logo
140-4712 B&O
140-4713 C&O
140-4714 WM

140-4715 UP (Former SP Loco Repaint) ***NEW***
140-4716 SSW (black w/red ends, white lettering) ***NEW***
140-4717 Detroit, Toledo & Ironton (orange) ***NEW***
140-4718 Florida East Coast (blue w/white lettering) ***NEW***
140-4719 Western Pacific (Perlman Green) ***NEW***
140-4700 Undecorated w/Dynamics (black)
140-4701 Undecorated

DUMMY EA 24.75

140-4722 BN (green, white)
140-4723 CR (blue, white)
140-4724 CSX Transportation (blue, gray)
140-4725 DRGW (black, orange)
140-4726 Seaboard System (red, yellow, gray)
140-4727 SP (red, gray, white)
140-4728 SP Speed Lettering
140-4729 BN (Cascade Green, white)
140-4730 CSX
140-4731 CR "Q" Logo
140-4732 B&O
140-4733 C&O
140-4734 WM
140-4735 UP (Former SP Loco Repaint) ***NEW***
140-4736 SSW (black w/red ends, white lettering) ***NEW***
140-4737 Detroit, Toledo & Ironton (orange) ***NEW***
140-4738 Florida East Coast (blue w/white lettering) ***NEW***
140-4739 Western Pacific (Perlman Green) ***NEW***
140-4720 Undecorated w/Dynamics (black)
140-4721 Undecorated

EMD GP40-2 Florida East Coast 140-4718

EMD GP50

WITH FLYWHEELS-POWERED EA 41.50

140-4628 CNW (yellow, green)
140-4629 MP (dark blue)
140-4630 NS (black)
140-4631 ATSF (yellow, blue)

140-4632 UP (gray, yellow)
140-4633 BN (Cascade Green, black)
140-4634 BN (Cascade Green, white)
140-4635 ATSF "Kodachrome" 1983 Merger
140-4626 Undecorated, w/Dynamics (black)
140-4627 Undecorated, Less Dynamics (black)

DUMMY EA 24.75

140-4678 CNW (yellow, green)
140-4679 MP (dark blue)
140-4680 NS (black)
140-4681 ATSF (yellow, blue)
140-4682 UP (gray, yellow)
140-4683 BN (Cascade Green, black)
140-4684 BN (Cascade Green, white)
140-4685 ATSF "Kodachrome" 1983 Merger
140-4676 Undecorated, With Dynamics (black)
140-4677 Undecorated, Less Dynamics (black)

GP50 Phase II ATSF 140-4581

EMD GP40-2 SSW 140-4716

EMD GP60 UP (Former SP Loco Repaint 140-4767

GP50 PHASE II

POWERED EA 41.50

140-4581 ATSF #3841
140-4584 BN #3142

140-4585 GP50 Phase II BN #3125
140-4580 Undecorated

DUMMY EA 24.75

140-4591 ATSF #3841
140-4594 BN #3142
140-4590 Undecorated

EMD GP60

EMD's newest 4-axle power, these 3800 horsepower units are working all types of freight service. This model captures all the details, from the free-flow blower duct to the angular dynamic brake housing.

WITH FLYWHEELS-POWERED EA 41.50

140-4752 NS #7102 (black, white)
140-4754 NS "Operation Lifesaver" #7140 (black, white)
140-4756 SP Speed Lettering #9715 (gray, red)
140-4758 ATSF #4020 (blue, yellow)
140-4759 ATSF #4039 (blue, yellow)
140-4760 SSW #9651 (gray, red)

140-4762 DRGW #3154 (black, orange)
140-4763 DRGW #3156 (black, orange)
140-4764 EMD Demonstrator #5 (blue, white)
140-4766 NS-SOU 100th Anniversary (green)
140-4767 UP (Former SP Loco Repaint) ***NEW***
140-4750 Undecorated w/Brake Lever
140-4751 Undecorated w/Brake Wheel

DUMMY EA 24.75

140-4772 NS #7102 (black, white)
140-4774 NS "Operation Lifesaver" #7140 (black, white)
140-4776 SP Speed Lettering #9715 (gray, red)
140-4778 ATSF #4020 (blue, yellow)
140-4780 SSW #9651 (gray, red)
140-4782 DRGW #3154 (black, orange)
140-4784 EMD Demonstrator #5 (blue, white)
140-4786 NS-SOU 100th Anniversary (green)
140-4787 UP (Former SP Loco Repaint) ***NEW***
140-4770 Undecorated w/Brake Lever
140-4771 Undecorated w/Brake Wheel

AMD-103

The AMD-103, also known as a Genesis, is the latest passenger diesel from Amtrak. The P40, a 4000 horsepower unit arrived in 1991, and was followed by the 4250 horsepower P42 in 1996. Each powered model features a distinctive, highly detailed paint scheme and includes detail parts such as air horns, exhaust stack, etched fan grill, headlight and classification light lenses, radio antenna, steps, plastic air tanks, battery boxes, pilots, front snowplow and more.

POWERED EA 56.50

P40
140-3643 Amtrak #1
140-3644 Amtrak #2
140-3645 Amtrak #838
140-3646 Amtrak No #
140-3650 Metro North #1
140-3651 Metro North #2
140-3652 Metro North No #
140-3656 Amtrak Intercity #1 *NEW*
140-3657 Amtrak Intercity #2 *NEW*
140-3640 Amtrak Undecorated

P42
140-3647 Amtrak #1
140-3648 Amtrak #2
140-3649 Amtrak No #
140-3653 Amtrak NE Corridor #1
140-3654 Amtrak NE Corridor #2
140-3655 Amtrak NE Corridor No #
140-3658 Amtrak Intercity #1 *NEW*
140-3659 Amtrak Intercity #2 *NEW*
140-3641 Amtrak Undecorated

P40/P42
140-3660 Amtrak Intercity No # *NEW*

DUMMY EA 33.75 (UNLESS NOTED)

P40
140-3673 Amtrak #1
140-3674 Amtrak #2
140-3675 Amtrak #838
140-3676 Amtrak No #
140-3680 Metro North #1
140-3681 Metro North #2
140-3682 Metro North No #
140-3686 Intercity #1 *NEW*
140-3687 Intercity #2 *NEW*
140-3670 Amtrak Undecorated

P42
140-3677 Amtrak #1
140-3678 Amtrak #2
140-3679 Amtrak No #
140-3683 Amtrak NE Corridor #1
140-3684 Amtrak NE Corridor #2
140-3685 Amtrak NE Corridor No #
140-3688 Intercity #1 *NEW*
140-3689 Intercity #2 *NEW*
140-3671 Amtrak Undecorated

P40/P42
140-3690 Intercity No # *NEW*

EMD SD9

WITH FLYWHEELS-POWERED EA 36.50

140-3801 ATSF (yellow, blue)
140-3802 BN (green, black, white)
140-3803 MILW (orange black)
140-3804 PRR (black, yellow)
140-3805 SP (gray, red)
140-3806 UP (yellow, gray)
140-3807 SP "Black Widow"
140-3800 Undecorated (black)

AMD-103 P40 140-3643

EMD SD40-2 140-4431

DUMMY EA 21.75

140-3821 ATSF (blue, yellow)
140-3822 BN (green, black white)
140-3823 MILW (orange, black)
140-3824 PRR (black, yellow)
140-3825 SP (gray, red)
140-3826 UP (yellow, gray)
140-3827 SP "Black Widow"
140-3820 Undecorated (black)

EMD SD40T-2 "TUNNEL MOTOR"

POWERED EA 44.50

140-4501 SP (gray, red)
140-4502 SSW (gray, red, white)
140-4503 DRGW (black, orange)
140-4505 SP Speed Lettering This is the standard design with medium length nose and front "porch."
140-4506 SP Speed Lettering This version includes the extra headlights and the long "nose."
140-4507 UP #4555
140-4508 SP Short-Nose Early Logo
140-4509 SP Short Nose "Kodachrome" 1983 Merger
140-4510 SP Snoot "Kodachrome" 1983 Merger
140-4511 UP Snoot w/Long Nose (Former SP Loco Repaint) *NEW*
140-4500 Undecorated, SP Details (black)
140-4504 Undecorated, DRGW Details (black)

EMD SD40T-2 "Tunnel Motor" UP 140-4511

EMD SD40T-2 "Tunnel Motor" SP 140-4501

DUMMY EA 26.75

140-4551 SP (gray, red)
140-4552 SSW (gray, red, white)
140-4553 DRGW (black, orange)
140-4555 SP Speed Lettering This is the standard design with the medium length nose and front "porch."
140-4556 SP Speed Lettering This version includes the extra headlights and the long "nose."
140-4557 UP #4555
140-4558 SP Short-Nose Early Logo
140-4559 SP Short Nose "Kodachrome" 1983 Merger
140-4560 SP Snoot "Kodachrome" 1983 Merger
140-4561 UP Snoot w/Long Nose (Former SP Loco Repaint) *NEW*
140-4550 Undecorated, SP Details (black)
140-4554 Undecorated, DRGW Details (black)

EMD SD40-2

WITH TWIN FLYWHEELS POWERED EA 44.50

140-4401 ATSF (blue, yellow)
140-4402 B&O, Chessie (blue, orange, yellow)
140-4403 BN (green, black)
140-4404 CR (blue)
140-4405 L&N, Family Lines System (gray, yellow, red)
140-4406 N&W (black, white)
140-4407 SOO (white, red, black)
140-4408 UP (yellow, gray, red)
140-4410 ROCK (orange, white, yellow)
140-4411 MP (blue, white)
140-4412 CP (orange)
140-4413 SP/ATSF (black, red, yellow)
140-4414 BN (Cascade Green, white)
140-4415 IC
140-4416 CP, 2 Flags
140-4417 SOO (red)
140-4418 Montana Rail Link
140-4419 L&N (yellow)
140-4420 MKT (green)
140-4421 CN-North America
140-4422 CN "Zebra"
140-4423 Grand Trunk Western (blue/red)
140-4424 Kansas City Southern (white)
140-4425 MILW
140-4426 NS "Thoroughbred"
140-4427 CNW

140-4428 CNW "Operation Lifesaver"
140-4429 CSX
140-4430 Frisco
140-4431 CR "Q" Logo
140-4432 BNSF (green, orange)
140-4400 Undecorated (black)
140-4409 Undecorated, Non-Dynamic (black)

DUMMY EA 26.75

140-4451 ATSF (blue, yellow)
140-4452 B&O, Chessie (blue, orange, yellow)
140-4453 BN (green, black)
140-4454 CR (blue)
140-4455 L&N, Family Lines System (gray, yellow, red)
140-4456 NW (black, white)
140-4457 SOO (white, red, black)
140-4458 UP (yellow, gray, red)
140-4460 ROCK (orange, white, yellow)
140-4461 MP (blue, white)
140-4462 CP (orange)
140-4463 SP/ATSF (black, red, yellow)
140-4464 BN (Cascade Green, white)
140-4465 IC
140-4466 CP, 2 Flags
140-4467 SOO (red)
140-4468 Montana Rail Link
140-4469 L&N (yellow)
140-4470 MKT (green)
140-4471 CN-North America
140-4472 CN "Zebra"
140-4473 Grand Trunk Western (blue, red)
140-4474 Kansas City Southern (white)
140-4475 MILW
140-4476 NS "Thoroughbred"
140-4477 CNW
140-4478 CNW "Operation Lifesaver"
140-4479 CSX
140-4480 Frisco
140-4481 CR "Q" Logo
140-4482 BNSF (green, orange)
140-4450 Undecorated (black)
140-4459 Undecorated, Non-Dynamic (black)

EMD FP45

WITH FLYWHEELS-POWERED EA 36.50

140-3621 ATSF (silver, red)
140-3622 MILW (yellow, gray)
140-3623 B&O (blue, yellow)
140-3624 Amtrak (black, silver, red)
140-3625 ATSF Passenger Early
140-3620 Undecorated (black)

DUMMY EA 21.75

140-3631 ATSF (silver, red)
140-3632 MILW (yellow, gray)
140-3633 B&O (blue, yellow)
140-3634 Amtrak (black, silver, red)
140-3635 ATSF Passenger Early
140-3630 Undecorated (black)

EMD SDP40

WITH FLYWHEELS-POWERED EA 36.50

140-4101 B&O (blue, yellow)
140-4102 CNW (green, yellow)
140-4103 NH (black, orange, white)
140-4104 NYC (black, white)
140-4105 ATSF Freight (blue, yellow)
140-4106 SP (gray, red)
140-4107 ATSF Passenger (Warbonnet, yellow silver)
140-4108 GN (blue)
140-4100 Undecorated (black)

DUMMY EA 21.75

140-4121 B&O (blue, yellow)

140-4122 CNW (green, yellow)
140-4123 NH
140-4124 NYC (black, white)
140-4125 ATSF Freight (blue, yellow)
140-4126 SP (gray, red)
140-4127 ATSF Passenger (Warbonnet, yellow, silver)
140-4128 GN (blue)
140-4120 Undecorated (black)

EMD SW7 "COW"

WITH FLYWHEELS-POWERED EA 32.50

140-4002 BN (green, black)
140-4003 IC (black, white)
140-4004 SOU (black, white)
140-4005 ATSF Freight (blue, yellow)
140-4006 SP (red, gray)
140-4007 UP (gray, yellow)
140-4008 PRR (black, yellow)
140-4009 B&O (blue, white)
140-4010 CR (blue)
140-4011 CP (red)
140-4012 CN (red, black, white)
140-4013 Amtrak (silver, black)
140-4001 Undecorated (black)

DUMMY EA 19.75

140-4052 BN (green, black)
140-4053 IC (black, white)
140-4054 SOU (black, white)
140-4055 ATSF Freight (blue, yellow)
140-4056 SP (red, gray)
140-4057 UP (gray, yellow)
140-4058 PRR (black, yellow)
140-4059 B&O (blue, white)
140-4060 CR (blue)
140-4061 CP (red)
140-4062 CN (red, black, white)
140-4063 Amtrak (silver, black)
140-4051 Undecorated

EMD SW7 "CALF"

WITH FLYWHEELS-POWERED EA 32.50

140-4027 BN (green, black)
140-4028 IC (black)
140-4029 SOU (black, white)
140-4030 ATSF Freight (blue, yellow)
140-4031 SP (red, gray)
140-4032 UP (gray, yellow)
140-4033 PRR (black, yellow)
140-4034 B&O (blue, white)
140-4035 CR (blue)
140-4036 CP (red)
140-4037 CN (black, red)
140-4026 Undecorated (black)

DUMMY EA 19.75

140-4077 BN (green, black)
140-4078 IC (black)
140-4079 SOU (black, white)
140-4080 ATSF Freight (blue, yellow)
140-4081 SP (red, gray)
140-4082 UP (gray, yellow)
140-4083 PRR (black, yellow)
140-4084 B&O (blue, white)
140-4085 CR (blue)
140-4086 CP (red)
140-4087 CN (black, red)
140-4076 Undecorated (black)

EMD SD45

WITH FLYWHEELS-POWERED EA 36.50

140-4161 Seaboard Air Line (red, black, yellow)
140-4162 SP (gray, red)
140-4163 UP (gray, yellow)
140-4164 CB&Q (gray, red, white)
140-4165 ATSF Freight (blue, yellow)
140-4166 PRR (black, yellow)
140-4167 GM Demo (blue, white)
140-4168 CR (blue, white)
140-4169 SP
140-4170 BN
140-4171 DRGW (Large Rio Grande)
140-4172 DRGW (Small Rio Grande)
140-4173 ATSF Freight Warbonnet
140-4174 WC
140-4175 SP "Kodachrome" 1983 Merger
140-4176 ATSF "Kodachrome" 1983 Merger
140-4160 Undecorated (black)

DUMMY EA 21.75

140-4181 Seaboard Air Line (red, black, yellow)
140-4182 SP
140-4183 UP (gray, yellow)
140-4184 CB&Q (gray, red, white)
140-4185 ATSF Freight (blue, yellow)
140-4186 PRR (black, yellow)
140-4187 GM Demo (blue, white)
140-4188 CR
140-4189 SP
140-4190 BN
140-4191 DRGW (Large Rio Grande)
140-4192 DRGW (Small Rio Grande)
140-4193 ATSF Freight Warbonnet
140-4194 WC
140-4195 SP "Kodachrome" 1983 Merger
140-4196 ATSF "Kodachrome" 1983 Merger
140-4180 Undecorated (black)

See What's Available at

www.walthers.com

EMD SW7 "Cow" 140-4013

EMD SW1500 NASA 140-3942

EMD SW7 "Cow & Calf" 140-4010

EMD SD45 CR 140-4168

EMD SW1500 140-3902

EMD SW1000

The SW1000 is a stock version with AAR type A trucks.

WITH FLYWHEELS-POWERED EA 36.50

140-3931 BN (green)
140-3932 DRGW (black)
140-3930 Undecorated (black)

DUMMY EA 21.75

140-3951 BN (green)
140-3952 DRGW (black)
140-3950 Undecorated (black)

EMD SW1500

The SW1500 is available in two versions: stock with Flexicoil trucks, or with AAR type A trucks to match a specific prototype.

WITH FLYWHEELS-POWERED EA 36.50

140-3902 BN (green)
140-3903 CR (blue)
140-3904 NS (black)
140-3905 Seaboard System (gray)
140-3906 SP (gray)
140-3907 CSX Transportation (blue, gray)
140-3908 Family Lines (gray)
140-3909 ROCK (light blue)
140-3933 UP (yellow, gray w/red stripe)
140-3934 CN (black, red, white, yellow)
140-3935 Western Pacific (green, orange)
140-3936 CR-Quality Logo
140-3937 CSX New Image
140-3938 Frisco (orange, white)
140-3939 SP Speed Lettering
140-3940 SP "Kodachrome" 1983 Merger
140-3941 UP "We Will Deliver"
140-3942 NASA
140-3943 BNSF (green & orange)
140-3900 Undecorated (black)
140-3901 Undecorated, SP Details (black)

DUMMY EA 21.75

140-3922 BN (green)
140-3923 CR (blue)
140-3924 NS (black)
140-3925 Seaboard System (gray)
140-3926 SP (gray)
140-3927 CSX Transportation (blue, gray)
140-3928 Family Lines (gray)
140-3929 Rock (light blue)
140-3953 UP (yellow, gray w/red stripe)
140-3954 CN (black, red white, yellow)
140-3955 Western Pacific (green, orange)
140-3956 CR-Quality Logo
140-3957 CSX New Image
140-3958 Frisco (orange, white)
140-3959 SP Speed Lettering
140-3960 SP "Kodachrome" 1983 Merger
140-3961 UP "We Will Deliver"
140-3962 NASA
140-3963 BNSF (green, orange)
140-3920 Undecorated (black)
140-3921 Undecorated, SP Details (black)

FM TRAIN MASTER

POWERED EA 36.50 (UNLESS NOTED)

140-4302 MILW (orange, black)
140-4303 CNW (green, yellow)
140-4304 N&W (dark blue)
140-4305 PRR (black)
140-4306 ATSF (blue, yellow)
140-4307 SP (gray, red)
140-4308 SP "Black Widow" **35.50**
140-4309 Virginian (yellow, black)
140-4310 N&W (black)
140-4300 Undecorated
140-4301 Undecorated, SP Details

DUMMY EA 21.75 (UNLESS NOTED)

140-4322 MILW (orange, black)
140-4323 CNW (green, yellow)
140-4324 N&W (dark blue)
140-4325 PRR (black)
140-4326 ATSF (blue, yellow)
140-4327 SP (gray, red)
140-4328 SP "Black Widow" **17.75**
140-4329 Virginian (yellow, black)
140-4330 N&W (black)
140-4321 Undecorated, SP Details
140-4320 Undecorated

GE U SERIES

Nicknamed "U boats," GE U Series locomotives were built from the late 1960s to the mid-1970s for heavy freight service. Models ending in "B" have four axles. Those ending in "C" have six.

GE U28B

WITH FLYWHEELS-POWERED EA 34.50

140-3401 BN (green, black)
140-3402 N&W (blue)
140-3403 Western Pacific (silver, orange, gold)
140-3400 Undecorated (black)

DUMMY EA 20.75

140-3411 BN (green, black)
140-3412 N&W (blue)
140-3413 Western Pacific (silver, orange, gold)
140-3410 Undecorated (black)

GE U28C

WITH FLYWHEELS-POWERED EA 36.50

140-3421 SP (red, gray)
140-3422 UP (gray, yellow)
140-3423 Penn Central (black, white)
140-3420 Undecorated (black)

DUMMY EA 21.75

140-3431 SP (red, gray)
140-3432 UP (gray, yellow)
140-3433 Penn Central (black, white)
140-3430 Undecorated (black)

GE U30C 140-3464

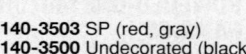

FM Train Master 140-4323

GE U28C 140-3422

Alco PA1 140-3307

GE U30C

WITH FLYWHEELS-POWERED EA 36.50

140-3461 C&O (blue, yellow)
140-3462 MILW
140-3463 PRR (black, yellow)
140-3464 BN
140-3465 L&N
140-3466 MP
140-3467 NS
140-3468 SP
140-3469 UP
140-3460 Undecorated (black)

DUMMY EA 21.75

140-3471 C&O (blue, yellow)
140-3472 MILW (orange, black)
140-3473 PRR (black, yellow)
140-3474 BN
140-3475 L&N
140-3476 MP
140-3477 NS
140-3478 SP
140-3479 UP
140-3470 Undecorated (black)

GE U30B

WITH FLYWHEELS-POWERED EA 34.50

140-3441 CB&Q (gray, red, white)
140-3442 IC (white, orange)
140-3443 ATSF Freight (yellow, blue)
140-3444 Chessie System (orange, yellow, blue)
140-3440 Undecorated (black)

DUMMY EA 20.75

140-3451 CB&Q (gray, red, white)
140-3452 IC (white, orange)
140-3453 ATSF Freight (yellow, blue)
140-3454 Chessie System (orange, yellow, blue)
140-3450 Undecorated (black)

GE U33B

WITH FLYWHEELS-POWERED EA 34.50

140-3481 ROCK (red)
140-3482 NYC (black)
140-3483 Seaboard Coast Line (black)
140-3480 Undecorated

DUMMY EA 20.75

140-3491 ROCK (red)
140-3492 NYC (black)
140-3493 Seaboard Coast Line (black)
140-3490 Undecorated

GE U33C

WITH FLYWHEELS-POWERED EA 36.50

140-3501 ATSF Freight (blue, yellow)
140-3502 GN (blue, gray, white)
140-3503 SP (red, gray)
140-3500 Undecorated (black)

DUMMY EA 21.75

140-3511 ATSF Freight (blue, yellow)
140-3512 GN (blue, gray, white)
140-3513 SP (red, gray)
140-3510 Undecorated (black)

EMD F45

WITH FLYWHEELS-POWERED EA 36.50

140-3601 ATSF Freight (blue, yellow)
140-3602 GN (gray, blue, white)
140-3603 BN (green, black, white)
140-3604 WC
140-3605 ATSF "Kodachrome" 1983 Merger
140-3600 Undecorated

DUMMY EA 21.75

140-3611 ATSF Freight (blue, yellow)
140-3612 GN (gray, blue white)
140-3613 BN (green, black, white)
140-3614 WC
140-3615 ATSF "Kodachrome" 1983 Merger
140-3610 Undecorated

ALCO PA-1

WITH FLYWHEELS-POWERED EA 44.50

140-3302 B&O (blue, black, gray)
140-3303 NYC (white, gray)
140-3304 PRR (maroon, yellow)
140-3305 ATSF (Warbonnet Red, yellow, silver)
140-3306 SP Daylight (red, orange)
140-3307 UP (yellow, gray)
140-3308 D&H (yellow, blue, silver)
140-3309 EL (gray, yellow, maroon)
140-3310 NKP
140-3301 Undecorated (black)

DUMMY EA 26.75

140-3322 B&O (blue, black, gray)
140-3323 NYC (white, gray)
140-3324 PRR (maroon, yellow)
140-3325 ATSF (Warbonnet Red, yellow, silver)
140-3326 SP "Daylight" (red, orange)
140-3327 UP
140-3328 D&H (yellow, blue, silver)
140-3329 EL (gray, yellow, maroon)
140-3330 NKP (blue, white)
140-3321 Undecorated (black)

BALDWIN S12

WITH FLYWHEELS-POWERED EA 32.50

140-3701 ATSF (blue, yellow)
140-3702 B&O
140-3703 EL
140-3704 GN (orange, green)
140-3705 MILW (orange, black)
140-3706 NYC (black, white)
140-3707 PRR (black, yellow)
140-3708 SP (red, gray)
140-3700 Undecorated (black)

DUMMY EA 19.75

140-3721 ATSF (blue, yellow)
140-3722 B&O (blue, yellow)
140-3723 EL (gray, brown, gold)
140-3724 GN (orange, green)
140-3725 MILW (orange, black)
140-3726 NYC (black, white)
140-3727 PRR (black, yellow)
140-3728 SP (red, gray)
140-3720 Undecorated (black)

ALCO PB-1

WITH FLYWHEELS-POWERED EA 44.50

140-3342 B&O (blue, black, gray)
140-3343 NYC (white, gray)
140-3344 PRR (maroon, yellow)
140-3345 ATSF (Warbonnet Red, yellow, silver)
140-3346 SP "Daylight" (red, orange)
140-3347 UP (yellow, gray)
140-3348 D&H (yellow, blue, silver)
140-3349 EL (gray, yellow, maroon)
140-3350 NKP (blue white)
140-3341 Undecorated (black)

DUMMY EA 26.75

140-3362 B&O (blue, black, gray)
140-3363 NYC (white, gray)
140-3364 PRR (maroon, yellow)
140-3365 ATSF (Warbonnet Red, yellow, silver)
140-3366 SP "Daylight" (red, orange)
140-3367 UP
140-3368 D&H (yellow, blue, silver)
140-3369 EL (gray, yellow, maroon)
140-3370 NKP (blue, white)
140-3361 Undecorated (black)

Diesel AC4400 CP #1 140-4363

EMD DD40 UP #70 140-4285

Diesel AC4400 CSX #4 140-4346

EMD DD40

POWERED-ONE MOTOR EA 42.50

140-4241 B&O
140-4242 CB&Q
140-4243 EMD Demonstrator
140-4244 PRR
140-4245 UP #70
140-4246 SP #9503
140-4247 SP #9504
140-4248 SP #9505
140-4249 UP #77
140-4250 UP #78
140-4240 Undecorated

POWERED-TWO MOTORS EA 52.50

140-4281 B&O
140-4282 CB&Q
140-4283 EMD Demonstrator
140-4284 PRR
140-4285 UP #70
140-4286 SP #9503
140-4287 SP #9504
140-4288 SP #9505
140-4289 UP #77
140-4290 UP #78
140-4280 Undecorated

DUMMY EA 25.75

140-4261 B&O
140-4262 CB&Q
140-4263 EMD Demonstrator
140-4264 PRR
140-4265 UP #70
140-4266 SP #9503
140-4267 SP #9504
140-4268 SP #9505
140-4269 UP #77
140-4270 UP #78
140-4260 Undecorated

DIESEL AC4400

GE's AC4400 was the first locomotive with an AC (alternating current) traction motor to be widely accepted by railroads. The AC4400 distinguishes itself from its predecessor, the C44-9W, most noticeably because of the large box located behind the cab on the left side that houses the air cooled AC inverters.

POWERED EA 59.50

140-4342 GE Demonstrator #2000
140-4343 CP Rail #9503
140-4346 CSX #4
140-4349 CNW #8804
140-4352 SP #3144
140-4355 UP #6839
140-4358 UP "Operation Lifesaver"
140-4362 GECX (Used By UP)
140-4363 CP #1 (Bright Red w/Beaver Herald) ***NEW***
140-4364 CP #2 (Bright Red w/Beaver Herald) ***NEW***
140-4365 CP No # (Bright Red w/Beaver Herald) ***NEW***
140-4340 Undecorated Hi Board Cab
140-4341 Undecorated Low Board Cab

DUMMY 35.75 (UNLESS NOTED)

140-4372 GE Demonstrator #2000
140-4373 CP Rail #9503
140-4376 CSX #4
140-4379 CNW #8804
140-4382 SP #144
140-4385 UP#6839
140-4388 UP "Operation Lifesaver"
140-4392 GECX (Used By UP)
140-4393 CP #1 (Bright Red w/Beaver Herald) ***NEW***
140-4394 CP #2 (Bright Red w/Beaver Herald) ***NEW***
140-4395 CP No # (Bright Red w/Beaver Herald) ***NEW***
140-4370 Undecorated Hi Board Cab
140-4371 Undecorated Low Board Cab
140-43910 GE Demo Version Undecorated Body **16.75** (Gullwing Cab, 3 Dynamic, Phase I Rear Grills)

140-43900 GE Demo Version Undecorated Body **16.75** (2 Dynamic Low Board Cab)

PRICE GUIDE

140-99998 1996 Athearn Price Guide **1.50**

Information STATION

Small Steam Power

Most small steam locos led very long lives, as they could be used at virtually any place on a railroad. Those same characteristics make them ideal for model railroads as well. Here are some typical engines:

0-4-0
Very short wheelbase. Built with tenders or boiler-mounted water tanks and a small fuel bunker. Used as a shop, inner-city and industrial switcher.

4-4-0 "American"
(Also "8-Wheeler" or "American Standard")

Dual purpose for passenger and freight work. Used from about 1836 on, some rebuilt examples ran into the early 1950s.

0-6-0
Built with and without tenders. One of the most common switchers, many lasted until the end of steam.

2-6-0 "Mogul"
A light, dual-purpose engine primarily used in freight service, but sometimes used for passenger service. Many ended their days on short lines and branches.

4-6-0 "Ten Wheeler"
Dual purpose engines, originally built for passenger service and later used for both passenger and freight work.

2-6-2 "Prairie"
Originally built for fast freight service, but also used as a passenger engine when larger drivers were specified.

0-8-0
The biggest switchers built, used for heavy yard and industrial service.

GENESIS premium line ready-to-run HO locomotives feature true-to-prototype body detail that includes full cab interior, true-to-prototype lettering, acetal plastic handrails and separate grab irons. Each locomotive features a new power chassis and drive system, and features constant/directional lighting, chemically blackened solid nickel-silver wheels, all wheel pickup and isolated can motor and motor mounts ready to accept your DCC circuit board.

EMD F UNITS

EA 114.98 (UNLESS NOTED)

F7A
141-1000 ATSF Passenger (red, silver "Warbonnet") ***NEW***
141-1001 PRR (Brunswick Green) ***NEW***
141-1002 DRGW (4 Stripe) ***NEW***

F7B
141-1500 ATSF Passenger (red, silver "Warbonnet") ***NEW***
141-1501 PRR (Brunswick Green) ***NEW***
141-1502 DRGW (4 Stripe) ***NEW***

F3A
141-2000 NYC ***NEW***
141-2001 SP "Black Widow" (black, red, silver, orange, white) ***NEW***
141-2002 ATSF Freight (blue, yellow) ***NEW***

F3B
141-2500 NYC ***NEW***
141-2501 SP "Black Widow" (black, red, silver, orange, white) ***NEW***
141-2502 ATSF Freight (blue, yellow) ***NEW***
141-2505 ATSF Freight (blue, yellow) **TBA** ***NEW***

F9A
141-3000 MILW (orange, black) ***NEW***

F9B
141-3200 MILW (orange, black) ***NEW***

EMD SD70

SD70 EA TBA

141-6110 IC #1
141-6111 IC #2
141-6112 IC No #
141-6113 NS #1
141-6114 NS #2
141-6115 NS No #
141-6143 CR #1
141-6144 CR #2
141-6145 CR No #

SD70I EA 114.98

141-6131 CN #1
141-6132 CN #2
141-6133 CN No #
141-6020 Undecorated ***NEW***

SD70M

141-6116 EMD Demo #7000 **TBA**
141-6117 EMD Demo #7001 **TBA**
141-6118 EMD Demo #7002 **TBA**
141-6119 Lease #1 (burgundy) **114.98**
141-6120 Lease #2 (burgundy) **114.98**
141-6121 Lease No # (burgundy) **114.98**
141-6122 Lease #1 (burgundy, silver, gray) **114.98**
141-6123 Lease #2 (burgundy, silver, gray) **114.98**
141-6124 Lease No # (burgundy, silver, gray) **114.98**
141-6125 SP #1 **114.98**
141-6126 SP #2 **114.98**
141-6127 SP No # **114.98**
141-6128 New York, Susquehanna & Western #4050 **TBA**
141-6129 New York, Susquehanna & Western #4052 **TBA**
141-6130 New York, Susquehanna & Western #4054 **TBA**
141-6030 Undecorated (SP version) **114.98**

SD75I

141-6140 CN #1 **TBA**
141-6141 CN #2 **TBA**
141-6142 CN No # **TBA**
141-6146 BNSF #1 (red & silver "Warbonnet") **114.98** ***NEW***
141-6147 BNSF #2 (red & silver "Warbonnet") **114.98** ***NEW***
141-6148 BNSF No # (red & silver "Warbonnet") **114.98** ***NEW***
141-6021 Undecorated **114.98** ***NEW***

SD75M

141-6134 BNSF #1 **TBA**
141-6135 BNSF #2 **TBA**
141-6136 BNSF No # **TBA**
141-6137 ATSF #1 **114.98**
141-6138 ATSF #2 **114.98**
141-6139 ATSF No # **114.98**
141-6033 Undecorated (ATSF/BNSF version) **114.98** ***NEW***
141-6031 Undecorated (Lease/New York, Susquehanna & Western version) **114.98** ***NEW***

See What's Available at

www.walthers.com

141-6146

EMD F7A 141-1000 & EMD F7B 141-1500

USRA 2-8-2 141-9002

USRA 2-8-2 141-9004

USRA 2-8-2 LIGHT

EA 139.98

From its introduction in 1918 until the end of the steam-era, the USRA Light 2-8-2 "Mikado" proved to be one of the most popular American designs. Used primarily for heavy freight service, over 1200 were eventually built and served some 50 different railroads.

The legendary loco lives again in these new HO Scale models from the Genesis Series by Athearn. An ultra-quiet Samhongsa drive provides smooth performance and comes DCC ready for easy conversion. Each model features nickel silver plated wheels, working valvegear, blackened handrails and directional lighting. The highly detailed boiler and tender body are molded plastic, so customizing with detail parts (sold separately) to match your favorite lines is fast and easy.

141-9002 B&O #4531 ***NEW***
141-9003 PRR #9627 ***NEW***
141-9004 MP #1318 ***NEW***
141-9005 NYC #5155 ***NEW***
141-9006 NKP #586 ***NEW***
141-9007 Frisco #4030 ***NEW***
141-9008 UP #2297 ***NEW***
141-9000 Undecorated w/Road Pilot ***NEW***
141-9001 Undecorated w/Foot Board Pilot ***NEW***

Atlas engines feature prepainted and lettered plastic bodies with flywheels and can motors for smooth operation at all speeds. Heavy cast-metal frames and all-wheel drive provide excellent tractive effort and pulling power.

Alco S-2 Different Roadname Shown

GE C30-7 150-8632

GE C30-7 150-8630

Alco RS-3 Classic Locomotive 150-8460

DIESEL LOCOMOTIVES

GE C30-7 EA 94.95

Features fine quality, highly detailed moldings, two-turned brass flywheels, blackened metal wheels, Kadee® compatible coupler pockets, printed number boards and directional lighting. Cabs feature two or four windows as correct with prototype. Formed wire grab irons are provided for the modeler to attach. DCC ready.

150-8602 ATSF #8015, Adirondack Trucks
150-8603 ATSF #8033, Adirondack Trucks
150-8604 ATSF #8076, Adirondack Trucks
150-8605 BN #5028, GSC Trucks
150-8606 BN #5112, GSC Trucks
150-8607 BN #5509, GSC Trucks
150-8608 CR #6600, GSC Trucks
150-8609 CR #6601, GSC Trucks
150-8610 CR #6609, GSC Trucks
150-8613 CSX #7057, GSC Trucks
150-8614 N&W #8010 (maroon), Adirondack Trucks
150-8615 N&W #8025 (black), Adirondack Trucks
150-8616 N&W #8072 (black), Adirondack Trucks
150-8617 UP #2501, GSC Trucks
150-8618 UP #2515, GSC Trucks
150-8619 UP #2530, GSC Trucks
150-8620 BN "Whiteface" #5004
150-8621 BN "Whiteface" #5019
150-8622 BN "Whiteface" #5114
150-8623 Family Lines #7030
150-8624 Family Lines #7033
150-8625 Family Lines #7037
150-8626 NS #8006
150-8627 NS #8020
150-8628 NS #8028
150-8630 ATSF Merger #8078
150-8631 ATSF Merger #8141
150-8632 UP #2416
150-8633 UP #2423
150-8634 UP #2432

GEU33C/36C EA 89.95

Handle heavy freight assignments with these U33C/36C locomotives. Built from the late 1960s to the mid-1970s, many of the U36C's are still in service today. These ready-to-run models are designed to accept command control with minimum modification, and conform to new NMRA standards. Other features include 5-pole skew-armature motor, two turned brass flywheels, blackened metal wheels and directional lighting. A 22" radius is recommended for these engines.

150-8545 Guilford (D&H) #651 (dark gray & orange)
150-8553 Seaboard System (gray) #7301
150-8554 Seaboard System (gray) #7304

Limited Quantity Available
150-8506 BN #5761
150-8511 CR #6889
150-8521 IC #5059
150-8527 SP #8641
150-8531 GN #2544
150-8532 PC #6540
150-8533 PC #6545
150-8534 PC #6549
150-8543 EL/NJ DOT #3371

ALCO S-2 EA 84.95

150-8705 CNW #1035
150-8706 CNW #1093
150-8707 Grand Trunk Western #8099
150-8708 Grand Trunk Western #8107
150-8711 WP #552
150-8712 WP #553

ALCO RS-3 CLASSIC LOCO EA 94.95

150-8451 CN #1807 (green, gold)
150-8452 CN #1812 (green, gold)
150-8453 CN No # (green, gold)
150-8454 Central of Georgia #108 (gray, blue)
150-8455 Central of Georgia #109 (gray, blue)
150-8456 Central of Georgia No # (gray, blue)
150-8457 Erie #918 (black, yellow)
150-8458 Erie #925 (black, yellow)
150-8459 Erie No # (black, yellow)
150-8460 ROCK #479 (red, black "Route of the Rockets")
150-8461 ROCK #495 (red, black "Route of the Rockets")
150-8462 ROCK No # (red, black "Route of the Rockets")
150-8463 Rutland #205 (green, yellow)
150-8464 Rutland #208 (green, yellow)
150-8465 Rutland No # (green, yellow)
150-8450 Undecorated

ALCO RSD-4/5 CLASSIC LOCO

150-8491 CNJ #1604 (green, yellow stripes)
150-8492 CNJ #1607 (green, yellow stripes)
150-8493 CNJ No # (green, yellow stripes)
150-8494 Utah #300 (gray, red stripes, yellow lettering)
150-8495 Utah #301 (gray, red stripes, yellow lettering)
150-8496 Utah No # (gray, red stripes, yellow lettering)
150-8490 Undecorated

U23B W/AAR TRUCKS EA 99.95

Limited Quantity Available
150-8653 ATSF #6305
150-8655 CR #2735

SHELL ASSEMBLIES

Bodies are molded in gray plastic and are complete with window "glass," add-on details and full sets of handrails, which are molded in black engineering plastic.

DECORATED

150-850226 U33C/36C SP **15.00**

UNDECORATED

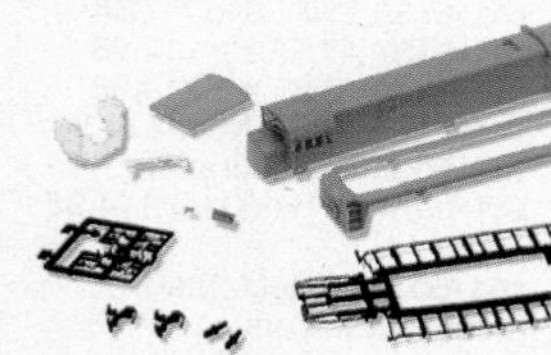

150-803210 C424/C425 **12.50**
150-805210 C424 Phase II **12.50**
150-805225 C424 Phase I **12.75**
150-850225 U33C/36 **15.00**
150-860225 C30-7 (4 Window Cab) **16.35**
150-860226 C30-7 (2 Window Cab) **16.35**

LOCOMOTIVE MAINTENANCE

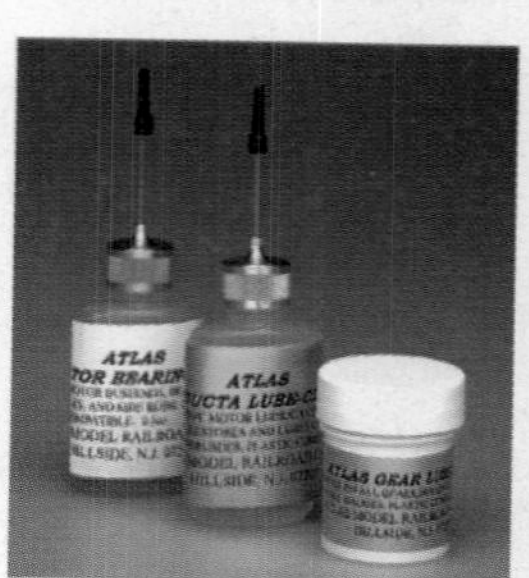

150-193 Loco & Track Maintenance 3-Pack **16.50**
Contains one each of above.

HO Scale locomotives are ready to run and feature prepainted and lettered plastic bodies, operating headlights and horn-hook couplers. Engines feature an all-metal chassis with additional weight, worm gear and flywheel drive, five-pole motor and a new idler gear box.

STEAM LOCOMOTIVES

Vanderbilt Tender w/Smoke 160-50701

Short Haul Tender 160-50440

Slope Tender w/Smoke 160-50614

USRA 0-6-0 EA 56.00

VANDERBILT TENDER W/SMOKE
160-50701 UP Greyhound

SHORT HAUL TENDER
160-50440 Smokey Mountain Express

SLOPE TENDER W/SMOKE
160-50602 ATSF
160-50614 PRR

2-6-2 PRAIRIE W/SMOKE EA 74.00

160-51501 UP
160-51520 NYC

4-8-4 W/SMOKE EA 112.00

With plenty of power for freight or passenger trains, the 4-8-4 was one of the most popular dual-service engines in North America.

160-11301 SP Daylight, GS-4 #4449
160-11302 SP Daylight #4446
160-11305 NYC, Niagara
160-11306 NYC Niagara #5016
160-11315 N&W, Class J
160-11316 Class J N&W
160-11322 SP #4446
160-11323 SP #4454

2-6-2 Prairie w/ Smoke 160-51501

4-8-4 w/Smoke 160-11301

American 4-4-0 & Tender 160-51101

AMERICAN 4-4-0 & TENDER EA 74.00

160-51101 UP #119
160-51124 Central Pacific "Jupiter"

DIESEL LOCOMOTIVES

Feature five-pole, skew-wound motors, dual flywheels, helical cut gears, metal chassis and eight-wheel drive.

GP 50

160-61241 NS **26.00**

SPECTRUM® EMD GP40

160-63502 ATSF (red, silver) **26.00**

SMOKE FLUID

160-99993 2-1/4 fl. oz. **3.00**

Superdetail your motive power with these easy-to-assemble, injection-molded plastic diaphragms. Kits include complete instructions.

GP 50 160-61241

EMD GP40 160-63502

4-8-4 w/Smoke 160-11305

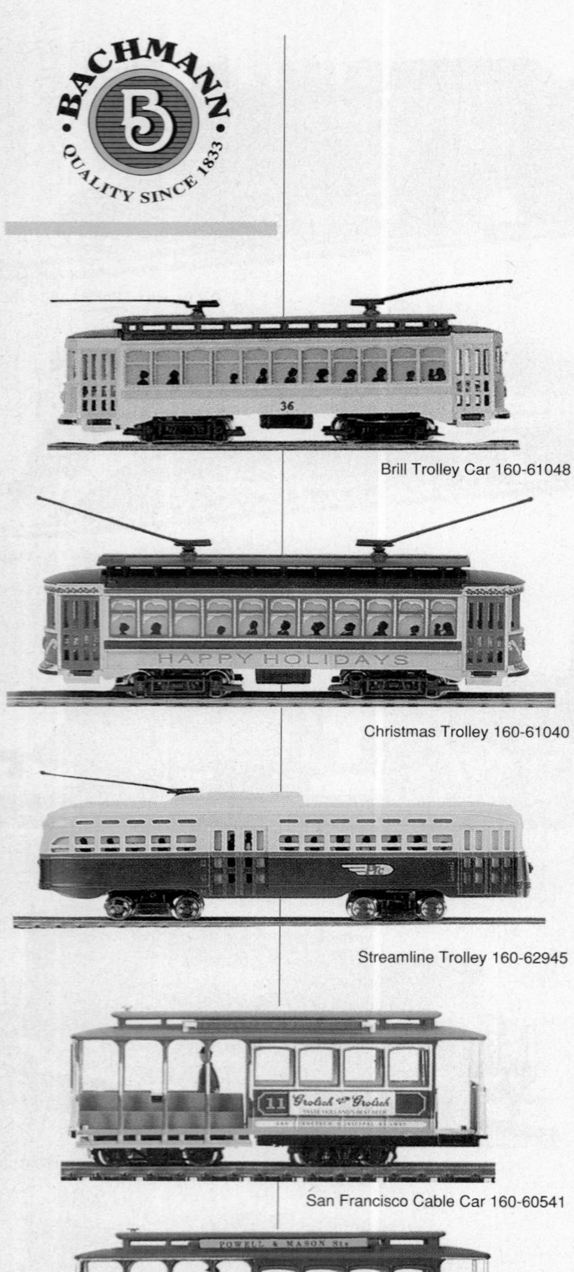

Brill Trolley Car 160-61048

Christmas Trolley 160-61040

Streamline Trolley 160-62945

San Francisco Cable Car 160-60541

San Francisco Cable Car 160-60542

TROLLEYS

These models are ready to run and feature prepainted and lettered plastic bodies, operating headlights and horn-hook couplers (unless noted).

BRILL TROLLEY CAR EA 28.00

160-61047 Mainstreet
160-61048 36 Yellow

CHRISTMAS TROLLEY

160-61040 31.00

STREAMLINE TROLLEY

160-62945 Philadelphia Transportation Company (dark green, tan) **33.00**

SAN FRANCISCO CABLE CAR EA 45.00

160-60541 Powell & Hyde
160-60542 Powell & Mason

INTERMOUNTAIN RAILWAY COMPANY

These highly detailed kits allow the modeler to select an F unit and customize it for a specific railroad. All units listed here are in kit form.

85-44002

EMD F SERIES

A UNITS F7A - PHASE I

85-44001 NYC (Lightning Stripe) **74.95** ***NEW***
85-44002 SP "Black Widow" **74.95** ***NEW***
85-44003 UP **74.95** ***NEW***
85-44004 CNW **TBA** ***NEW***
85-44005 ATSF **TBA** ***NEW***
85-44006 PRR **TBA** ***NEW***
85-44007 CB&Q **TBA** ***NEW***
85-44008 B&O **TBA** ***NEW***
85-44009 GN **TBA** ***NEW***
85-44097 Undecorated **49.95** ***NEW***

A UNITS EA TBA

85-44091 F2 Undecorated
85-44092 F3 (Phase I) Undecorated
85-44093 F3 (Phase II) Undecorated
85-44094 F3 (Phase III) Undecorated
85-44095 F3 (Phase IV) Undecorated
85-44096 F5 Undecorated
85-44098 F7 (Phase II) Undecorated
85-44099 F9 Undecorated

B UNITS F7B

85-44501 NYC (Lightning Stripe) **74.95** ***NEW***
85-44502 SP "Black Widow" **74.95** ***NEW***
85-44503 UP **TBA** ***NEW***
85-44504 CNW **TBA** ***NEW***
85-44505 ATSF **TBA** ***NEW***
85-44506 PRR **TBA** ***NEW***
85-44507 CB&Q **TBA** ***NEW***
85-44508 B&O **TBA** ***NEW***
85-44509 GN **TBA** ***NEW***
85-44597 Undecorated **44.95** ***NEW***

American Limited

Superdetail your motive power with these easy-to-assemble, injection-molded plastic diaphragms. Kits include complete instructions.

DIAPHRAGMS

FOR STEWART HOBBIES F-UNITS

147-9900

Designed for use with Stewart Hobbies F Units and Kadee® #450 close couplers. Includes diaphragms and an alignment spacer .

147-9900 Gray, 1 Pair **4.95**
147-9903 Gray, 3 Pair **12.95**
147-9910 Black, 1 Pair **4.95**
147-9913 Black, 3 Pair **12.95**

STEWART FT'S AB SET EA 4.95

147-9700/9710

Includes new diaphragm for connection of A B set.

147-9700 Gray
147-9710 Black

FOR ATHEARN F-UNITS

147-9800/9803

Complete with diaphragms and close coupling draft gear boxes. Draft gear boxes fit Kadee #5 couplers.

147-9800 1 Pair **4.95**
One pair of diaphragms and draft gear boxes for two A units or one B unit.

147-6100 2 Pair **2.75**
Draft gear box for A-B-A set (4 locomotive ends).

147-9803 3 Pair **13.95**
Diaphragms and draft gear for A-B-B-A sets (six locomotive ends).

147-9810 Black **4.95**
147-9813 Black, 3 Pair **13.50**

Clear Case

Protect your investment in your favorite models with Clear Case display cases. These handmade cases are constructed of rich-grain solid oak or walnut, with a mitered edge to ensure a dust-free enclosure and felt pad feet to protect your furniture. The cover is crystal clear optical grade acrylic. The result is a display case that makes your model look like a museum masterpiece.

Note: Clear Case displays can be ordered in other sizes that are more appropriate for G, O, N and Z Scale models. See your Walthers dealer for more information.

Sports Display Case 248-1615

Model Car Case 248-12533

Multi-Shelf Display Case 248-18223

Train Display Case 248-87133

SPORTS DISPLAY CASES

Show off your sports memorabilia in these handcrafted Medium Oak display cases. Though not all shown here, Clear Case offers a variety of sports display cases, sized appropriately for holding everything from baseballs to basketballs. See your Walthers dealer for more information.

248-1615 Football Case **68.56**
248-1620 Football Helmet Case **102.99**

MODEL CAR CASES

Though not all listed here, Clear Case displays to protect your scale model automobiles are available in 12 different sizes; contact your Walthers dealer for more information.

6" LONG x 2-3/4" WIDE x 2-1/2" HIGH

248-1230 Light Oak **25.56**
248-12303 Medium Oak **25.56**
248-12301 Dark Oak **25.56**
248-12302 Black Walnut **26.67**

10" LONG x 3-3/4" WIDE x 5-1/2" HIGH

248-1245 Light Oak **48.78**
248-12453 Medium Oak **48.78**
248-12451 Dark Oak **48.78**
248-12452 Black Walnut **42.00**

13" LONG x 5" WIDE x 4" HIGH

248-1253 Light Oak **48.78**
248-12533 Medium Oak **48.78**
248-12531 Dark Oak **48.78**
248-12532 Black Walnut **51.78**

Daily New Product Announcements! Visit Walthers Web site at

www.walthers.com

TRAIN DISPLAY CASES

Interior dimensions of covers are 2-3/4" wide by 3-1/4" high. Dimension shown with part number is interior length.

LIGHT OAK

248-8710 10-5/8" **34.00**
248-8713 13" **41.56**
248-8716 16-1/2" **48.89**
248-8722 22" **60.56**

MEDIUM OAK

248-87103 10-5/8" **34.00**
248-87133 13" **41.56**
248-87163 16-1/2" **48.89**
248-87223 22" **60.56**

DARK OAK

248-87101 10-5/8" **34.00**
248-87131 13" **41.56**
248-87161 16-1/2" **48.89**
248-87221 22" **60.56**

BLACK WALNUT

248-87102 10-5/8" **35.78**
248-87132 13" **44.67**
248-87162 16-1/2" **52.12**
248-87222 22" **63.67**

MULTI-SHELF DISPLAY CASES

These beautiful wall-mounted cases are ideal for displaying HO Scale trains and 1:43 Scale model cars. Each case is 27-1/2" tall and 5" deep; there are 8 shelves per case. Dimension shown with part number is case width.

LIGHT OAK

248-1822 24-1/2" **226.67**
248-1836 38-1/2" **339.12**

MEDIUM OAK

248-18223 24-1/2" **226.67**
248-18363 38-1/2" **339.12**

DARK OAK

248-18221 24-1/2" **226.67**
248-18361 38-1/2" **339.12**

DISPLAY CASE RISERS

Use these solid wood risers to adapt HO Scale Clear Cases for displaying N and Z Scale models.

LIGHT OAK

248-10 For #8710 **5.34**
248-13 For #8713 **6.56**
248-16 For #8716 **7.78**
248-22 For #8722 **10.23**

MEDIUM OAK

248-103 For #87103 **5.34**
248-133 For #87133 **6.56**
248-163 For #87163 **7.78**
248-223 For #87223 **10.23**

DARK OAK

248-101 For #87101 **5.34**
248-131 For #87131 **6.56**
248-161 For #87161 **7.78**
248-221 For #87221 **10.23**

BLACK WALNUT

248-102 For #87102 **7.78**
248-132 For #87132 **8.67**
248-162 For #87162 **9.45**
248-222 For #87222 **12.67**

ANTI-STATIC CLEANER

248-500 Spray Cleaner 4oz **6.65**
Spray cleaner for plastic and acrylics: the perfect way to keep your Clear Case display covers crystal clear and sparkling like new. Polishes, repels dust and resists fingerprints.

BRAWA

IMPORTED FROM GERMANY BY WALTHERS

Engines include add-on details and three styles of couplers. AC locos are designed for use with Marklin equipment.

2-8-4T Class 65 186-610

Class 132 186-300

E242 Era IV 186-204

GERMAN STATE RAILWAYS (DRG)

0-6-0T CLASS T3

Between 1891 and 1913, over 100 of these switchers were built. Some also saw branchline service. Most remained in use until the late 30s, when all but three were sold to private industries. Model includes complete cab interior with positionable doors.

186-600 DC **419.99**
186-601 AC **499.99**

CLASS 95 AS-DELIVERED ERA II

A superbly detailed replica of these mighty engines, as they appeared at delivery in 1927-28. In addition to specific period details and painting, a reprint of the original engineer's operating manual is included.

186-211 DC **629.99** ***NEW***
186-241 AC **699.99** ***NEW***

EAST GERMAN STATE RAILWAYS (DR)

STEAM

CLASS 65 2-8-4T ERA IV

Introduced in 1954, some 88 engines of this class were eventually constructed. Fast starters, they were often used on commuter runs and were finally retired in 1975. Includes complete cab interior with crew. A Seuthe smoke generator, sold separately, can be added.

186-610 DC **529.99** ***NEW***
186-611 AC **599.99** ***NEW***

DIESELS

CLASS 132 "RUSSIAN ORIGINAL"

Over 700 of these engines were purchased by the East German rail authority from the Soviet Union between 1973 and 1983. Model is correctly detailed for a unit of the mid 1970s.

186-300 DC **249.99** ***NEW***
186-301 AC **309.99** ***NEW***

KOF SWITCHERS

186-473 KöF I AC (black) **339.99**
186-497 KöF II AC (black) **337.49**

KOF "SHARKMOUTH"

This ferocious little loco is based on a prototype painted by trainees at the Limburg shops. The colorful graphics remained when the engine was later converted to an industrial unit. Limited-run scheme.

186-459 DC **299.99**
186-460 AC **379.99**
186-461 AC w/Marklin Digital Decoder **459.99**

CLASS V 100

186-418 Rebuilt Industrial (green, white) DC **269.99**
186-448 Rebuilt Industrial (green, white) AC **339.99**
186-419 Meter Gauge-12mm (red, white) DC **379.99**
186-420 Meter Gauge-9mm (red, white) DC **379.99**
186-421 865 Series Engine (white, green) DC **269.99**
186-451 865 Series Engine (white green) AC **339.99**

186-422 Wine Red-Late 1960s DC **269.99**
186-452 Wine Red-Late 1960s AC **339.99**

CLASS 110

Latest version of the prototype V100 series. Models feature dual flywheels and both trucks are powered. Open radiator fans and positionable drop steps for more realism.

186-423 DC (red) **279.99**
186-453 AC (red) **339.99**

CLASS 102

Introduced in 1968, these powerful switchers can still be found in service.

186-552 DC **279.99**
186-557 AC **369.99**

CLASS 232

186-410 DC **239.99**

CLASS 312

186-556 AC w/Marklin Digital Decoder (yellow) **449.99**

ELECTRICS

E42

186-202 DC (green) **309.99**
186-232 AC (green) **379.99**

E242 ERA IV

Converted to push-pull engines for urban rapid transit lines in the 1970s

186-204 DC **319.99** ***NEW***
186-234 AC **389.99** ***NEW***

E95

186-210 DC (DB red, white) **549.99**
186-240 AC (DB red, white) **629.99**

GERMAN FEDERAL RAILWAYS (DB & DB-AG)

DIESELS

KO I CLASS 322

186-470 DC (red) **259.99**
186-472 AC (red) **339.99**

KOF II CLASS 323

186-484 DC (red) **259.99**

BATTERY-POWERED SWITCHER

Limited Quantity Available
186-482 DC (red) **227.49**

INDUSTRIAL SWITCHERS

186-468 DC **269.99**
186-469 AC **369.99**

CLASS 216

Over 200 were built between 1964 and 1968, serving in both freight and passenger service.

186-380 DC **299.99**
186-381 AC **379.99**

CLASS 219

Introduced in 1977, these six-axle units replaced steam on many East German lines. They were nicknamed "submarines" because of the six porthole windows on the sides. Two separate prime movers and hydraulic transmissions were originally used, and rebuilt units are still in service.

186-405 DC **219.99**
186-435 AC **289.99**

BRAWA

CLASS 216 - NEW CARGO SCHEME ERA V
Designed in 1956 and still in service today.

186-384 DC **299.99** ***NEW***
186-385 AC **369.99** ***NEW***

CLASS 219 - NEW CARGO SCHEME ERA V
Built in Romania and later rebuilt, some are now in DB-AG Service in the new Cargo colors.

186-406 DC **219.99** ***NEW***
186-436 AC **279.99** ***NEW***

CLASS 232 - NEW CARGO SCHEME ERA V
These are former DR Class 132 Russian-built locos now in service with the DB-AG.

186-414 DC **229.99** ***NEW***
186-444 AC **299.99** ***NEW***

CLASS 298 SWITCHER ERA V
Introduced to replace steam switchers in East Germany, 82 of these hardy diesels have been rebuilt for switching and freight service on the DB-AG.

186-417 DC **289.99** ***NEW***
186-447 AC **349.99** ***NEW***

CLASS 312 - NEW CARGO SCHEME ERA V
These former East German locos date from the late 1950s, but remain in service across the DB-AG.

186-551 DC **289.99** ***NEW***
186-553 AC **369.99** ***NEW***

CLASS 643 "TALENT" PUSH-PULL RAILCAR SET ERA V
A Brawa Exclusive! Similar in appearance to the new ICE 3 trains, these multi-unit sets are scheduled to enter DB-AG service on suburban lines in late 1999.

186-710 DC **359.95** ***NEW***
186-711 AC **419.99** ***NEW***

ELECTRICS

E69 SWITCHER ERA V
Built in 1913, Class 69 #06 served regularly until 1953 and is now being restored.

186-220 DC **379.99** ***NEW***
186-221 AC **459.99** ***NEW***

CLASS E42
Introduced by the DR in 1963 for freight service, 292 were built through 1976. Some were repainted in DB red with a white "bib" following reunification and remain in use.

186-203 DC (DB red, white) **299.99**
186-233 AC (DB red, white) **379.99**

HELLA ERA IV LIMITED-RUN
Painted and lettered as #1378-88.

186-580 DC **289.99** ***NEW***
186-581 AC **369.99** ***NEW***
186-582 AC w/DCC Decoder **419.99** ***NEW***

SWISS RAILWAYS

ELECTRICS

SBB SWITCHER CLASS TE III
Introduced between 1941 and 1949, these tiny electrics handled switching at medium sized stations. Some were also built for private lines and the Swiss Post Office. Both axles of the model are powered by a hidden motor.

186-560 DC **339.99**
186-565 AC **419.99**

NEW SBB RED SCHEME ERA V
186-5611 DC **359.99** ***NEW***
186-566 AC **439.99** ***NEW***

SWISS PRIVATE RAILWAYS

ELECTRICS

FORMER E42-REBUILT AE 477 EA TBA
Purchased used from the DB-AG, these former Class E42 electrics are used by the Mittel Thurgau Bahn (MThB) and the Südostbahn (South East Railway). All were extensively rebuilt with numerous modifications for service in Switzerland. Many now carry colorful advertising schemes.

186-2051 Südostbahn Kantonalbank DC
186-2055 Biberbau DC
186-2351 MThB Kantonalbank AC
186-2355 Südostbahn Biberbau AC

SOB "HELVETIA PATRIA" ERA V

186-205 DC **389.99** ***NEW***
186-235 AC **449.99** ***NEW***

Class 298 Diesel Switcher Era V 186-417

Hella Era IV 186-580

USEDOMER BADERBAHN GMBH
This German shortline transports passengers on the Baltic Island of Usedom. Models duplicate the current (Era V) "hog carrier" railbuses. Includes one powered Class 772 Power Unit #201-0 and one unpowered Class 972 Trailer #201-8.

186-532 DC **349.99** ***NEW***
186-538 AC **429.99** ***NEW***

MAINTENANCE EQUIPMENT

KLV 60 CATENARY CAR

186-522 DC **479.99**
186-527 AC **399.99**

KLV 60 TOWER INSPECTION CAR
186-520 DC **289.99**

186-526 AC **459.99**

KLV 53 WORK CAR W/CRANE

186-500 DC **299.99**
186-510 AC **389.99**
186-512 AC w/Digital **479.99**

KLA GONDOLA

186-501 DC **75.99**
For use with #186-500, sold separately.

KLV 96 PROPANE CARRIER
Includes one powered cab, one unpowered cab and one center unit.

186-505 DC **569.99**
186-515 AC **649.99**

REPLACEMENT MOTOR
Limited Quantity Available
186-9703 **45.99**
Fits work train cars.

EMD E7A DIESELS-AC POWERED

186-890 UP **349.99**
186-891 Florida East Coast **369.99**

These HO Scale, ready-to-run locomotives are offered in several paint schemes and most feature two different unit numbers. Each loco has a detailed plastic body, can motor, flywheels and truck assemblies geared for low speeds, unless noted.

We have worked closely with this manufacturer to provide accurate delivery information at the time this catalog was published. Items listed in blue ink may not be available at all times. Current delivery information, along with a list of in-stock products for this line, can be found on our Web site at www.walthers.com.

4-6-4 Hudson 223-1200

4-8-8-4 Big Boy 223-1201

MP15 223-155401

STEAM LOCOMOTIVES

Nonoperating, unpowered plastic kits.

4-6-4 HUDSON

223-1200 NYC **18.98**
223-1202 Chessie **14.98**

4-8-8-4 BIG BOY

223-1201 UP 19.98

DIESEL LOCOMOTIVES

EMD MP15 EA 64.98

This model features a 5-pole skewed armature motor, cab interior with painted engineer and fireman figures, cab lighting, factory-mounted handrails and upgraded printing.

223-155101 BN #1000 (green, black, white face)
223-155102 BN #1003 (green, black, white face)
223-155201 SP Speed Lettering #2695 (gray, red)
223-155202 SP Speed Lettering #2698 (gray, red)
223-155301 UP #1004 (gray, yellow, red)
223-155302 UP #1007 (gray, yellow, red)
223-155401 Chessie #5311 (blue, yellow, orange)
223-155402 Chessie #5316 (blue, yellow, orange)
223-155501 ATSF #912 (blue, yellow)
223-155502 ATSF #924 (blue, yellow)
223-155601 CR "Quality" #9627 (blue)
223-155602 CR "Quality" #9630 (blue)
223-155701 NS #2380 (black, white)
223-155702 NS #2384 (black, white)
223-155801 WC #1559 (maroon & yellow)
223-155901 MP #1356 (yellow & gray)
223-156001 ATSF #1212 (Warbonnet Scheme)
223-156101 CB&Q #580 (black and red)
223-156201 MP # 1379
223-156202 MP
223-156301 IC # 1356
223-156302 IC # 1364
223-156401 Amtrak # 531
223-156402 Amtrak # 536
223-156501 SP # 2690
223-156502 SP # 2700
223-155000 Undecorated

Keystone Locomotive Works

These HO Scale craft train kits are unpainted metal, and include trucks.

Shay Locomotive 395-105

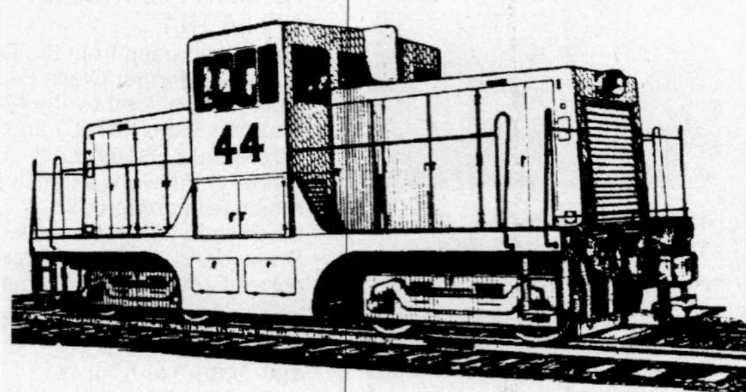

GE 44-Ton Diesel 395-108

Cab Interior 395-3304

STEAM LOCOMOTIVES

SHAY EA 49.95

Based on engine No. 31 of the Kelly Island Lime & Transport Co., this model includes an optional oil bunker and wood burning or shotgun stacks. The unpowered model can be made operational with a North West Shortline Shay powering kit, available separately. Model is less couplers.

395-105 20-Ton Class A, HO
395-1053 20-Ton Class A, HOn3

DIESEL LOCOMOTIVES

GE 44-TON

395-108 Powered Loco **89.95**
This loco includes an assembled chassis with North West Shortline gears and a Sagami motor. Electrical pickup is through all eight nickel-silver wheels. The model can be built as a Phase III or Phase IV loco. Includes brass-etched hoods, cast-metal cab, pilots and details. The kit accepts Kadee® couplers and can be adapted for constant lighting.

CAB INTERIORS

EA 9.98

Add a realistic touch to your next model with these interior kits. Adaptable to powered or dummy units, kits feature plastic and metal parts, with complete instructions.

395-3301 F Unit
395-3302 EMD SW & NW Switchers
Fits Athearn SW7 as well as other diesels.
395-3304 EMD 1st Generation GP/SD
Fits the following models: GP7 9, 18, 20, and SD7, 9, 18, and 24.
395-3305 EMD 2nd Generation GP/SD
Fits the following models: 40-2, 38-2, 35, 40 and 50. Can also be modified to fit Bachmann GP30.

395-3309 E Unit

ERTL®

TOY TRAINS

Delight your little ones with the popular Thomas the Tank Engine line of toys. A popular TV show and family favorite for several years, Thomas and his friends offer hours of entertainment for boys and girls of all ages. Each well-built toy is constructed of diecast metal and plastic, and is colorfully decorated and painted. Collect them all!

Gordon 264-1091

ENGINES EA 7.29

264-1091 Gordon

264-1183 Edward

264-1191 Henry

264-1192 James

264-4019 Duke

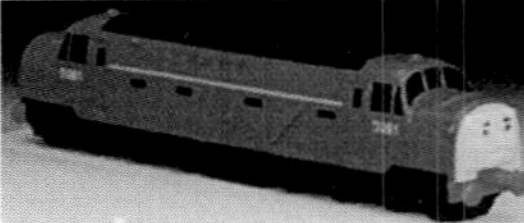
264-4100 Diesel Engine
264-4102 Skarloey

264-4113 Lord Harry

264-4538 Wilbert

264-4539 Sixteen

ENGINES EA 5.76

264-1022 Percy

264-1237 Thomas

264-4003 Mavis
264-4103 Sir Handle
264-4104 Rheneas
264-4391 Peter Sam

264-4508 Rusty Engine

MISCELLANEOUS EA 5.76

264-1012 Toby the Tram
264-1293 Harietta the Coach

264-1705 Troublesome Trucks

264-1707 Harold the Helicopter

264-4001 Tar & Milk Wagon

264-4023 Trevor the Tractor

264-4040 Sir Topham Hatt & Engineer

264-4057 Breakdown Truck

264-4107 Old Coaches

264-4370 Toad Wagon

Henry's Forest Log Car 264-4491

Scrap Trevor 264-4372

264-4371 Sodor Mail Coaches
264-4389 Express Coaches

MISCELLANEOUS EA 7.29

264-4029 D Fusit *NEW*
264-4372 Scrap Trevor
264-4490 Sodor Soft Side Truck *NEW*
264-4491 Henry's Forest Log Car **7.29**
264-4569 Bluebell *NEW*

264-4795 Canal Boat *NEW*

264-4796 Crane *NEW*

264-4822 Sodor Mail Van *NEW*

264-4975 S.C. Ruffey Truck **7.29**

264-4976 Bulstrode the Barge **7.29**

PLAYSETS

264-1019 Branch Line Playset **34.49**

264-1033 Roundhouse Playset **49.99** *NEW*

264-1395 Stationhouse Playset **41.99** *NEW*

ASSORTMENTS

264-4018 Donald & Douglas **173.39**
264-4039 Deluxe Set **77.76** *NEW*

MISCELLANEOUS TOYS

264-4075 Carrying Case **18.69** *NEW*

HIGHLINERS

F UNIT BODY SHELL KITS

Body shell kits can build any version of the F2, F3, F5, F7 or F9 diesel. They are for use with powered or unpowered Athearn F7 chassis, or Stewart Hobbies/Kato F Unit drives.

B Unit kits include molded plastic detail parts: four versions of the dynamic brake hatch, tall and short roof fans, five sets of side panel inserts, steam generator parts, two styles of sand filler hatches, flush-mounted porthole "glass", photo-etched stainless steel fan grills, door handles, lift rings and other detail parts.

A Unit kits include all the details found in the B Unit kits plus true-to-scale headlights, three styles of number boards, two styles of pilots, two styles of cab doors, three nose doors (with and without lights), two styles of lights, horns, five types of side porthole arrangement inserts, "winterization hatch" and coupler door cover, photo-etched stainless steel windshield wipers, windshield and porthole "gaskets", cab side-window "wind wings", cab door "kick plates," pilot corner steps and winterization hatch screen.

328-1001 A Unit **47.95**
328-1002 B Unit **35.95**

Stainless Steel F7 & F9 "Farr-Air" Grill
328-10017 thru 328-10029

Decorated F-Unit Shown

WIRE SCREENING

These "see through," photo-etched preblackened .003" thick stainless-steel screens simulate the "chicken wire" applied over air intakes on prototype F3s.

328-10010 A Unit **12.95**
328-10020 B Unit **12.95**

STAINLESS STEEL "FARR" AIR GRILL

328-10017 A Unit F7 pkg(2) **16.95**
328-10019 A Unit F9 pkg(2) **16.95**
328-10027 B Unit F7 pkg(2) **18.95**
328-10029 B Unit F9 pkg(2) **18.95**

FAN & DETAIL PARTS SETS

Includes five 36" low fans, four 34" talls fans, one 48" fan, 8 sand filler hatches, 4 exhaust stacks, steam generator vents etc.

Used for E/F units, GP7, GP9, GP18, GP20 and SD units.

328-2001 #1 **14.95** ***NEW***
328-2002 #2 Photo-Etched Fan Grills and Detail Parts **5.95** ***NEW***

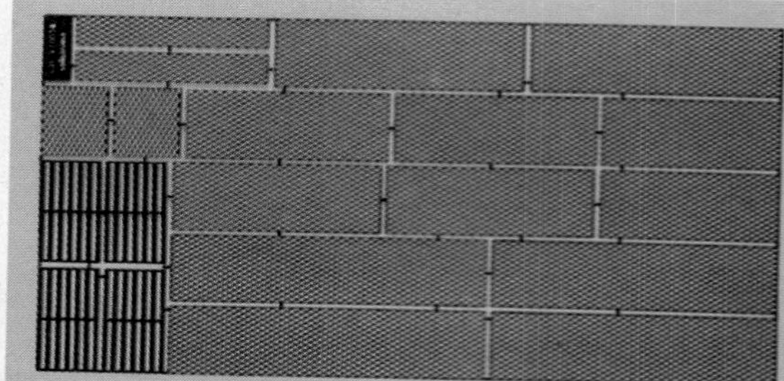

Wire Screening

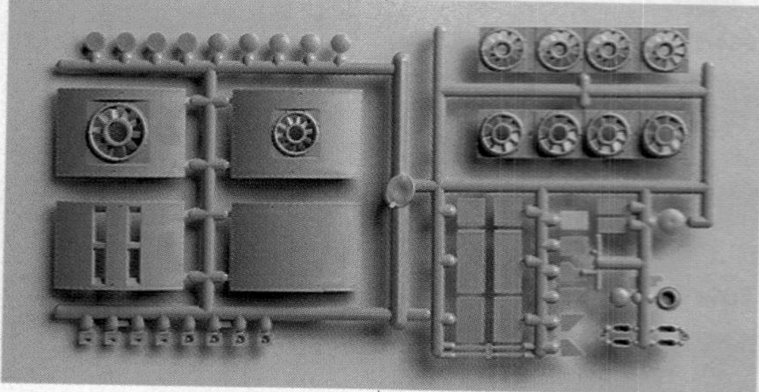

328-2001

328-2002

Photos by Steve Crise

These HO Scale locos feature prepainted and lettered plastic shells and diecast chassis. All models are ready to run with operating headlights and include horn-hook couplers and RP25 wheels.

Old Time Shifter 490-6779

2-6-0 Locomotive 490-6720

Casey Jones 10-Wheeler 490-6587

EMD F3A
Different Roadname Shown

STEAM LOCOMOTIVES

OLD TIME SHIFTER W/TENDER EA 37.98 (UNLESS NOTED)

490-6779 Dickens Railroad **39.98**
490-6780 ATSF
490-6781 PRR
490-6782 SOU
490-6783 CP
490-6784 DRGW

2-6-0 W/TENDER EA 35.00

490-6720 ATSF
490-6721 PRR
490-6722 GN
490-6723 SOU

CASEY JONES 10-WHEELER EA 79.99

490-6580 IC
490-6581 SP
490-6582 DRGW
490-6584 ATSF
490-6585 CN
490-6586 CP
490-6587 PRR

0-4-0 EA 25.00

490-6500 ATSF
490-6501 PRR
490-6502 CN
490-6503 Number Only
490-6504 SOU
490-6505 B&O

0-4-0 W/TENDER EA 35.00

490-6635

490-6632 CN
490-6633 CP
490-6634 ATSF
490-6635 PRR
490-6636 SOU

2-8-0 CONSOLIDATION EA 79.99

490-6550 SP
490-6551 PRR
490-6552 GN
490-6554 CP
490-6555 CN
490-6556 ATSF
490-6557 B&O
490-6558 Grand Canyon
490-6559 N&W
490-6560 NP
490-6561 MA & PA
490-6562 DRGW

Limited Quantity Available
490-6563 Erie

0-8-0 EA 79.98

490-6662 ATSF
490-6663 PRR
490-6664 Southern
490-6665 SP
490-6666 DRGW

DIESEL LOCOMOTIVES

ALCO DUAL DRIVE

RS-2 EA 39.98

490-6842

490-6841 CN (black)
490-6842 CP
490-6843 ATSF
490-6844 BN
490-6845 CR
490-6846 SOU

RS-11 EA 36.00

Different Roadname Shown

490-6692 ATSF (black, yellow)
490-6699 BN

C-430 EA 39.98

490-6775

490-6770 CN (red, black, white)
490-6771 CP
490-6773 CR
490-6774 BN (green, black)
490-6775 MKT (green)

Limited Quantity Available
490-6772 ATSF

ALCO 1000 POWERED

490-6834 BN **36.00**

EMD DUAL DRIVE

F3A

Eight-wheel pick-up with metal chassis. Painted in ATSF scheme.

490-6730 ATSF Powered **36.00**
490-6731 ATSF Dummy **15.50**

F2A EA 33.00

490-6801

490-6800 ATSF
490-6801 PRR
490-6802 Chessie
490-6803 UP
490-6804 SP
490-6805 BN
490-6806 Amtrak
490-6807 CR
490-6808 SOU
490-6809 CN
490-6810 CP
490-6812 SP "Daylight"
490-6813 United States Army

EMD F3A DUMMY

490-6730 ATSF Powered (silver & red) **36.00**
490-6731 ATSF Dummy (silver & red) **15.50**

BALDWIN "SHARK NOSE" COLLECTOR SERIES

A-UNIT EA 82.50

490-724 NYC
490-740 ATSF

A UNIT DUMMY EA 19.78

490-730 ATSF
490-731 PRR
490-733 CN
490-729 Undecorated

B UNIT DUMMY EA 17.58

490-750 ATSF
490-753 CN
490-754 NYC

EMD GP9 EA 39.98

490-6750 ATSF
490-6751 SOU
490-6752 CR
490-6754 CN
490-6755 BN

For Daily Product Updates Point Your Browser to

www.walthers.com

ALCO COLLECTOR SERIES

FA2

490-823 CP **82.50**
490-850840 ATSF **92.50**

FB2 EA 82.50

490-840 ATSF
490-842 PRR
490-844 UP
490-845 BN

FA2 DUMMY EA 19.78

490-850 ATSF
490-852 CP

FB2 DUMMY EA 18.68

490-860 ATSF
490-861 PRR
490-863 UP
490-864 BN
490-859 Undecorated

LOCO DUMMIES EA 11.00

490-66024 CP
490-66074 ATSF
490-66124 F9 CP
490-66134 F9 CN
490-66974 RS1 Chessie
490-77104 RI
490-98014 F9 Firefighter

PORTER HUSTLER EA 24.95

Directional lighting.

490-6705 ATSF
490-6706 BN
490-6707 SOU
490-6708 SP
490-6709 PRR
490-6710 Chessie
490-6711 Amtrak
490-6712 CN

DDT PLYMOUTH INDUSTRIAL DIESEL EA 25.00

490-6669 BN
490-6670 ATSF
490-6673 CN

490-6674 CP
490-6676 Amtrak
490-6678 Chessie
490-6679 CR

EMD SW1

Limited Quantity Available
490-6826 BN **38.00**

HO Scale locomotives are ready-to-run with plastic and diecast bodies that are prepainted and lettered. Steam locos feature working valve gear. All locos have working headlights and Magic Mate couplers.

0-4-0 Switcher 348-8004

0-4-0 Old Timer 348-8006

4-8-2 Mountain 348-925

2-8-2 Mikado 348-9805

2-6-0 Mogul w/Oil Tender 348-512

STEAM LOCOMOTIVES

0-4-0 SWITCHER

348-8004 UP (black) **14.98**

0-4-0 OLD TIMER

348-8006 ATSF (red & black) **14.98**

2-8-2 Mikado 348-9815

2-6-0 Mogul w/Coal Tender 348-531

PREMIER SERIES STEAM LOCOMOTIVES

These authentically reproduced models feature additional body details, extra pick-ups in the tenders and metal handrails.

4-8-2 MOUNTAIN EA 139.98 (UNLESS NOTED)

These locos were some of the biggest in service on many roads. With plenty of power, they handled both heavy freight and passenger trains. Ideal for either service on your layout, these new versions are equipped with a larger can motor for improved performance. To match prototype practice, most models now feature the correct deck-mounted airpumps and headlight centered on the smokebox door. For more realism, each engine also includes the correct style of tender used by the prototype. There's an all-new rectangular type, matching the style used by most roads, that's highly detailed and features a working back-up light. Roads that used Vanderbilt tenders include that style.

SQUARE TENDER

348-901 B&O
348-910 Florida East Coast **99.98**
348-916 LV
348-918 Mopac **119.98**
348-919 NdeM (National of Mexico) **99.98**
348-922 NYC
348-925 N&W
348-926 PRR
348-929 DRGW **119.98**
348-931 Seaboard **119.98**
348-932 SOU
348-933 SOO **119.98**
348-938 UP
348-939 Wabash **99.98**
348-940 WP **99.98**
348-937 Undecorated

VANDERBILT TENDER

348-905 C&O (High Pumps & Low Headlight)
348-909 CN
348-912 Grand Trunk Western **95.98**
348-913 GN
348-920 Nashville, Chattanooga & St. Louis **99.98**
348-934 SP

2-8-2 MIKADO EA 99.98 (UNLESS NOTED)

Features retooled drivers for smoother operation, can motor with flywheel, metal hand rails mounted on boiler, real brass bell, metal coupler lift bar on tender body, reversing headlight on tender and additional weight in cab and smokebox.

348-9800 ATSF
348-9801 SOU
348-9802 SP
348-9803 C&O **79.98**
348-9804 C&O Chessie
348-9805 GN
348-9806 PRR
348-9807 Atlantic Coast Line
348-9808 Louisville & Nashville
348-9809 CN
348-9810 CNW
348-9811 UP
348-9813 WM
348-9814 RDG
348-9815 SP
348-9816 NYC
348-9817 NKP **79.98**
348-9818 Frisco
348-9819 MILW **79.98**
348-9820 Erie
348-9821 B&O
348-9822 NH
348-9823 Lackawanna **79.98**
348-9824 Burlington
348-9825 CP
348-9826 LV **79.98**
348-9827 DRGW
348-9828 NP **79.98**
348-9829 Texas & Pacific **79.98**
348-9830 NdeM (Mexico) **79.98**
348-9831 Maine Central **79.98**
348-9812 Undecorated

2-6-0 MOGUL EA 89.98 (UNLESS NOTED)

WITH OIL TENDER

348-510 ATSF
348-511 PRR
348-512 SP
348-513 SOU (green)
348-514 Central Vermont **59.98**
348-515 B&O
348-516 CNW
348-517 Green Bay & Western **59.98**
348-518 NYC
348-519 Central of Georgia **59.98**
348-520 NH
348-521 Texas & Pacific **59.98**
348-522 IC **59.98**
348-523 CN **59.98**
348-526 Boston & Maine
348-527 New York, Ontario & Western
348-524 Undecorated

WITH COAL TENDER

348-528 ATSF
348-529 PRR **59.98**
348-530 SP
348-531 SOU
348-532 Central Vermont **59.98**
348-533 B&O
348-534 CNW
348-535 Green Bay & Western
348-536 NYC
348-537 Central of Georgia **59.98**
348-538 NH **59.98**
348-539 Texas & Pacific
348-540 IC
348-541 CN
348-543 Boston & Maine
348-544 RDG
348-545 C&O **59.98**
348-546 L&N **59.98**
348-547 Richmond, Fredricksburg & Potomac **59.98**
348-548 LV **59.98**
348-549 Florida East Coast **59.98**
348-550 GN
348-551 NP **59.98**
348-552 CNJ **59.98**
348-553 Atlantic Coast Line **59.98**
348-554 MP **59.98**
348-555 Kansas City Southern **59.98**
348-556 WM **59.98**
348-557 UP
348-558 D&H **59.98**
348-542 Undecorated

International Hobby Corp.

4-6-2 PACIFIC EA 99.98 (UNLESS NOTED)

Includes can motor with flywheel, metal hand rails mounted on boiler, retooled drivers for smoother operation, real brass bell, metal coupler lift bar on tender body, reversing headlight on tender and additional weight in cab and smokebox. New Pacifics are equipped with Magic Mate couplers, compatible with horn-hook and knuckle type couplers.

348-9888 Florida East Coast **79.98**
348-9889 N&W **79.98**
348-9890 Pere Marquette **79.98**
348-9891 Atlantic Coast Line (FDR Special) **79.98**
348-9892 ROCK **79.98**
348-9893 LV **79.98**
348-9894 DRGW
348-9895 Boston & Maine **79.98**
348-9896 B&O (Royal Blue)
348-9897 NP **79.98**
348-9898 Texas & Pacific **79.98**
348-9899 Toronto, Hamilton & Buffalo
348-9900 Atlantic Coast Line **79.98**
348-9901 ATSF
348-9902 B&O President Washington
348-9903 B&O President Fillmore **79.98**
348-9904 Burlington
348-9905 Chicago & Alton **79.98**
348-9906 CNW
348-9907 C&O
348-9908 C&O Chessie
348-9909 CN
348-9910 CP
348-9911 Erie **79.98**
348-9912 Frisco
348-9913 GN
348-9914 L&N **79.98**
348-9915 Delaware, Lackawanna & Western **79.98**
348-9916 MILW
348-9917 MILW Chippewa **79.98**
348-9918 NH
348-9919 NKP **79.98**
348-9920 NYC
348-9921 PRR
348-9922 RDG
348-9923 SOU **79.98**
348-9924 Southern Crescent
348-9925 SP
348-9926 SP
348-9928 UP
348-9929 WM **79.98**
348-9930 CNJ
348-9931 B&O
348-9932 B&O President Lincoln
348-9933 B&O President Polk
348-9934 B&O President Jefferson **79.98**
348-9927 Undecorated

2-8-0 CONSOLIDATION EA 89.98 (UNLESS NOTED)

348-9500 ATSF
348-9501 Atlantic Coast Line **59.98**
348-9502 B&O
348-9503 Bessmer & Lake Erie **59.98**
348-9504 Boston & Maine
348-9505 CN
348-9506 CP **59.98**
348-9507 Central Vermont **59.98**
348-9508 Chesapeake & Ohio **59.98**
348-9509 CB&Q
348-9510 CNW
348-9511 D&H
348-9512 Delaware, Lackawanna & Western **59.98**
348-9513 DRGW
348-9514 Erie
348-9515 San Francisco **69.98**
348-9516 GN
348-9517 IC **69.98**
348-9518 Kansas City Southern **69.98**
348-9519 Lehigh & New England **69.98**
348-9520 LV **69.98**
348-9521 L&N **59.98**
348-9522 Maine Central **59.98**
348-9523 Milwaukee **59.98**
348-9524 MKT
348-9525 MOPAC **69.98**
348-9526 MON **69.98**
348-9527 NH **69.98**
348-9528 NYC **59.98**
348-9529 New York, Ontario & Western **69.98**
348-9530 NKP
348-9531 N&W
348-9532 NP **69.98**
348-9533 Pennsylvania Lines
348-9534 Philadelphia & RDG **55.98**
348-9535 ROCK **55.98**
348-9536 Seaboard **55.98**
348-9537 Southern **59.98**
348-9538 SP **69.98**
348-9539 UP
348-9540 Wabash **59.98**
348-9541 WM **59.98**
348-9542 Western Pacific **49.98**
348-9543 Duluth, Missabe & Iron Range
348-9544 Lake Superior & Ishpeming **49.98**
348-9545 Buffalo Creek & Gauley **49.98**
348-9546 Grand Trunk Western **49.98**
348-9547 Lehigh & Hudson River **49.98**
348-9548 Florida East Coast **49.98**
348-9549 Spokane, Portland & Seattle **49.98**
348-9551 Virginian **49.98**
348-9552 Long Island
348-9553 Duluth, Winnipeg & Pacific
348-9554 Chicago Great Western
348-9555 Wheeling & Lake Erie
348-9556 SOO **59.98**
348-9557 Bangor & Aroostook **59.98**
348-9558 Chicago & Illinois Midland **49.98**
348-9559 NdeM (National of Mexico) **49.98**
348-9560 Susquehanna & New York **49.98**
348-9561 Meridian & Bigbee **49.98**
348-9562 Pere Marquette **49.98**
348-9550 Undecorated **59.98**

SEMI-STREAMLINED PACIFICS EA 99.98 (UNLESS NOTED)

Add a touch of class to your layout with these spectacular models featuring Mabuchi motors with precision flywheels, metal handrails and lift bars, and directional lighting.

348-9850 ATSF (Valley Flyer) #1369 **79.98**
348-9851 B&O (The Royal Blue) #5304
348-9852 D&H (Loree) 3607 **79.98**
348-9853 LV (Asa Packer) #2022
348-9854 LV (John Wilkes) #2101 **79.98**
348-9855 NYC (The Mercury) #6515 **79.98**
348-9856 Boston & Maine #3710 **79.98**
348-9857 Lackawanna #1124 **79.98**
348-9858 St. Louis-San Francisco **79.98**
348-9859 WAB (Blue Bird) **79.98**
348-9860 PRR #5399
348-9861 RDG #210 **79.98**
348-9862 SP (Sunbeam) #4365
348-9863 UP #2906
348-9864 Milwaukee (Hiawatha) #6160 **79.98**
348-9865 CNW (Route of the 400) **79.98**
348-9866 Southern (Tennessean) **79.98**
348-9867 CP
348-9868 SOU **79.98**

4-4-0 AMERICAN EA 79.98 (UNLESS NOTED)

This classic design was invented in the United States, where the addition of the four-wheel lead truck helped steer the engine over rough track. Many of these older engines were eventually sold to shortlines and industrial roads, where they served for many years after being "retired." These historic models come fully assembled and are equipped with Magic Mate Couplers, which can be used with horn-hook or knuckle type couplers.

348-13800 ATSF
348-13801 PRR
348-13802 SP
348-13803 SOU
348-13804 B&O
348-13805 CNW
348-13806 NYC **59.98**
348-13807 Central of Georgia
348-13808 RDG
348-13809 IC **59.98**
348-13810 Central Vermont
348-13811 Green Bay & Western **59.98**
348-13812 NH
348-13813 CN
348-13815 Boston & Maine
348-13816 New York, Ontario & Western
348-13817 L&N
348-13818 GN
348-13819 LV
348-13820 Delaware, Lackawanna & Western
348-13821 UP
348-13822 Virginia & Truckee
348-13814 Undecorated

4-6-2 Pacific 348-9922

2-8-0 Consolidation 348-9516

2-8-0 Consolidation 348-9541

Semi-Streamlined Pacific 348-9851

Semi-Streamlined Pacific 348-9862

4-4-0 American 348-13822

2-6-0 "Camelback" - "Mother Hubbard" 348-23252

Alco C-628 Powered 348-23250

Alco C-628 Powered 348-23252

Alco C-628 Powered 348-23264

SD35 348-13713

2-6-0 "CAMELBACK" - "MOTHER HUBBARD" EA 89.98 (UNLESS NOTED)

In 1877, John E. Wooten invented a new style of engine firebox designed to burn anthracite coal. To accommodate the design's extra width at the rear, the engine cab was moved forward to the middle of the boiler. Some folks thought this resembled a camel's hump, hence the name "camelbacks." Others thought it looked like the hood worn by Old Mother Hubbard in the popular nursery rhyme and referred to them as "Mother Hubbards." Finely detailed and ready for service on your railroad, each comes equipped with Magic Mate couplers, which can be used with horn-hook or knuckle type couplers.

348-20307 New York, Ontario & Western *NEW*
348-23150 Atlantic City Railroad **79.98**
348-23151 Atlantic Coast Line **69.98**
348-23152 ATSF **69.98**
348-23153 B&O
348-23154 Boston & Maine
348-23155 CN **69.98**
348-23156 CP **69.98**
348-23157 CNJ
348-23158 C&O
348-23159 Chicago, Milwaukee, St. Paul & Pacific **69.98**
348-23161 D&H
348-23162 DRGW
348-23163 Lackawanna **69.98**
348-23164 Erie
348-23166 GN **69.88**
348-23169 Lehigh Coal & Navigation **69.88**
348-23170 LV
348-23172 L&N
348-23174 NYC & Hudson River **69.98**
348-23175 New York & New England **69.98**
348-23176 N&W
348-23177 Pennsylvania Lines

348-23178 RDG **69.98**
348-23180 SOU **69.98**
348-23181 SP
348-23182 UP **69.98**
348-23202 Undecorated

DIESEL LOCOMOTIVES

ALCO C-628 POWERED EA 29.98

348-23250 ATSF #1814 (blue & yellow) *NEW*
348-23251 CP #4503 (Tuscan, gray, black & gold) *NEW*
348-23252 D&H (blue, gray & yellow) *NEW*
348-23253 L&N #1413 *NEW*
348-23254 L&N #1405 *NEW*
348-23255 LV #628 (Cornell Red) *NEW*
348-23256 LV #629 (Cornell Red) *NEW*
348-23257 LV #630 Snowbird *NEW*
348-23258 LV #631 Snowbird *NEW*
348-23259 MON #404 (black & gold) *NEW*
348-23260 PRR #6311 (black) *NEW*
348-23261 PRR #6310 (black) *NEW*
348-23262 SP #3125 *NEW*
348-23263 SP #4850 *NEW*
348-23264 UP #3222 (yellow & red) *NEW*

EMD E8 A-UNIT SET EA 49.98 (UNLESS NOTED)

Designed for passenger service, the first E8s were delivered in 1949. In later years, they served in commuter and freight service. Sets include two A-units; one powered with working headlight and one dummy.

348-1929 IC (dark brown & orange)
348-1930 Chicago & Alton (red & maroon) **39.98**
348-1931 PRR (Tuscan Red) **39.98**
348-1933 SP Daylight (orange & red) **39.98**
348-1940 MILW (yellow & gray) **39.98**
348-1942 New Jersey Transit (black & silver)
348-1944 Richmond, Fredricksburg & Potomac (dark blue & gray)
348-1949 C&O (blue, yellow & gray)
348-1950 BN (green & white) **39.98**
348-1951 MILW (maroon & orange)
348-1953 PRR (green)
348-1954 VIA (yellow & blue w/yellow lettering) **39.98**
348-1958 N&W (maroon & gold)
348-1960 Wabash (blue & silver)
348-1965 RDG (black & green w/yellow stripe)
348-1968 PRR **39.98**
348-1971 CP Rail **39.98**
348-1972 Lackawanna
348-1966 Undecorated

EMD SD40 DIESEL

348-350 ATSF (black & gold) **15.98**

SD35 EA 59.98 (UNLESS NOTED)

348-13700 CR
348-13702 Atlantic Coast Line
348-13703 B&O **39.98**
348-13704 CP
348-13705 CSX
348-13706 Central RR of NJ
348-13707 Family Lines System L&N **29.98**
348-13708 Gulf Mobile & Ohio
348-13709 L&N **29.98**
348-13710 N&W **29.98**
348-13711 PRR **29.98**
348-13712 Seaboard System
348-13713 SP **39.98**
348-13714 UP **39.98**
348-13715 WM
348-13716 CN

CENTER CAB DIESEL EA 12.98 (UNLESS NOTED)

348-500 General Electric (black, orange & silver)

348-501 UP

348-502 ATSF

348-505 MILW (black & orange) **9.98**
348-506 PRR

International Hobby Corp.

These HO Scale models are ready to run.

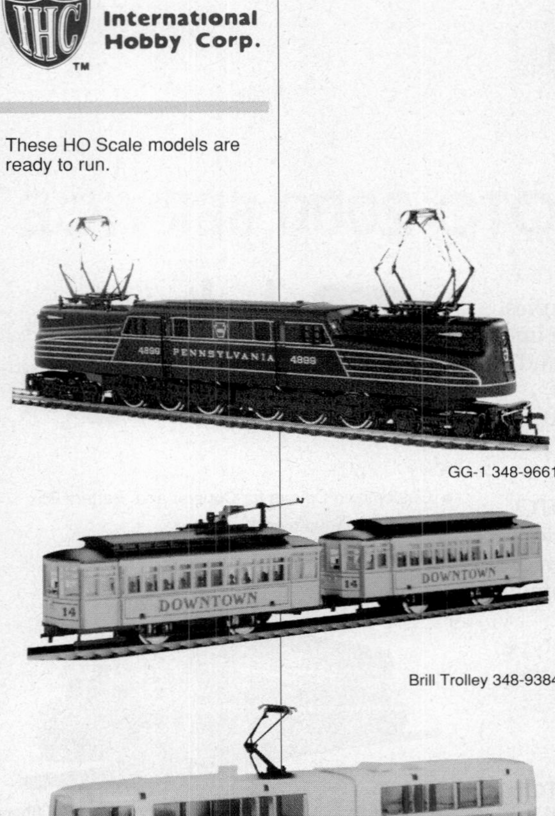
GG-1 348-9661

Brill Trolley 348-9384

Boeing LRV 348-9386

ELECTRICS

GG-1 EA 79.98

A new upgraded version of Pennsy's popular electric locomotive.

348-9650 PRR Tuscan, #4828
348-9651 PRR Brunswick Green, #4828
348-9652 PRR Silver, #4880
348-9653 PRR "Black Jack", #4935
348-9654 PRR Single Stripe Tuscan, #4907
348-9655 PRR Single Stripe Brunswick Green, #4907
348-9656 PRR 5 Stripe Tuscan, #4856
348-9657 PRR 5 Stripe Brunswick Green, #4856
348-9658 PRR 5 Stripe "Futura", #4824
348-9659 CR (blue)
348-9660 Amtrak (black)
348-9661 PRR Pre-Loewy, #4899
348-9662 Amtrak Bloody Nose
348-9663 NJ Transit
348-9664 Amtrak "Savings Bond"
348-9665 PRR, JFK Funeral
348-9666 Spirit of '76 (white)
348-9667 Spirit of '76 (red, white & blue)
348-9668 PRR, Dark Green Stripe, #4829
348-9669 PRR Washington, D.C. Crash, #4876
348-9670 Milwaukee Premier
348-9671 NH Premier
348-9672 VGN Premier
348-9673 GN Premier
348-9674 NYC Lightning Premier

BRILL TROLLEY EA 34.98

These four-wheel cars were common on big city streetcar lines. Set features a powered unit pulling a trailer.

348-9381 PTC
348-9382 Connecticut Company
348-9383 United Transit Lines
348-9384 Downtown
348-9380 Your Town

BOEING LRV EA 59.98

This model is based on the Light Rail Vehicle built by Boeing. The model is powered, with a prepainted and lettered plastic body.

348-9385 Boston
348-9386 San Francisco

KATO PRECISION RAILROAD MODELS

NW2 Phase 1 381-371008

NW2 Phase 1 381-371009

NW2 Phase 1 381-371010

NW2 Phase 1 381-371011

NW2 PHASE 1

First introduced by EMD in 1939, the dependable NW2 was utilized by numerous North American railroads. The safety striped paint scheme of two of the most well-known roads — Santa Fe and Southern Pacific — is accurately reproduced with precision detail.

ATSF "ZEBRA STRIPE" (BLACK & WHITE) EA 109.98

381-371008 #2405
381-371009 #2406

SP "TIGER STRIPE" (BLACK & ORANGE) EA 109.98

381-371010 #1313
381-371011 #1319

Grandt Line

These HO Scale kits contain injection-molded, black plastic parts and nonmagnetic wheelsets. They will accept Kadee® couplers. Powered kits include Mabuchi Motor and Grandt Line gears with 80:1 reduction.

GE 25-TON INDUSTRIAL LOCOS

EA 39.95

300-7090

Small switchers like these are owned and operated by many types of heavy industries including steel mills, cement plants, grain elevators and more. This powered model accepts Kadee® No. 714 (narrow gauge) or No. 711 (standard gauge) couplers.

300-7091 HO
300-7090 HOn3

23-TON BOX CAB DIESEL LOCOS

300-7088

Early box cab diesels were found in many large cities, where smoke from steam locos and tight clearances created problems. In later years, they were often sold to on-line industries for use as plant switchers.

POWERED EA 39.95

300-7089 Standard Gauge
300-7088 Narrow Gauge

UNPOWERED EA 19.25

300-5127 Standard Gauge
300-5114 Narrow Gauge

THE GLORIOUS HISTORY OF PROTO 2000 SERVICE

Beginning in 1989, Life Like introduced the PROTO 2000 series. Soon after, the series became a line of models that hobbyists, collectors and merchants celebrated. Ten years and thousands of models later, the PROTO 2000 series is still producing models with the same level of quality.

Attention to quality makes the PROTO 2000 line a must-have for avid collectors. Models feature exceptional recreation of the prototype, with each model becoming increasingly detailed until there is near-perfect accuracy between prototype and model. Paint schemes exhibit to-the-letter perfection, while laser-quality printing and decoration increase the model's superior detailing.

Superior craftsmanship of the PROTO 2000 line can also be evidenced in the detail parts of each model. The state-of-the-art motor ensures flawless track performance: it's a five-pole skew-wound balanced armature model. Each piece also features exceptional tractive force and pulling power. Detail parts like all-wheel drive and electrical pick-up, dual brass flywheels and sintered oil-free bearing also bear the PROTO 2000 markings of superior workmanship.

Innovative design is essential to the growth and development of the PROTO 2000 line. As the hobby continues to grow, as well as the interests of modelers, the line continues to evolve its design to keep up with the changing direction of the industry. Developments to the PROTO 2000 line have included working magnetic knuckle couplers and readying engines for Digital Command Control operation.

The toll-free consumer hotline reflects how the happiness of each customer is most important to the PROTO 2000 series. This communication allows modelers to register comments and questions directly to the manufacturer. This interaction allows designers to determine what is a success and where changes are needed. Models also feature a lifetime limited warranty and free replacement parts to guarantee modelers that their model is always at its best.

BL2

- Cast Safety Railing & Stanchions
- See-Through Grating on Pilots & Fan Grills
- Correct Number of Bolts on Roof Hatches

FA2/FB2

- Motor-Driven Exhaust Fans
- Functional Rear Door
- Working Side Louvers
- Dual Operating Headlights
- Working Diaphragms

GP18

- Accurate MU Connections
- Operating Drop Step & Cab Door
- Includes Dynamic Brakes (when appropriate)

E7A/B

- Interior Bracing Visible Through Sidescreens
- Sideframes with Floating Journal Covers
- See-Through Steps
- Standard & Extended Range Fuel & Water Tanks

SW9/1200

- Customized Covers for Coupler and Battery Box
- Sand Line Hoses on Trucks
- All-Weather Windows

SD7 Shown

SD7/SD9

- See-Through Sill Steps
- DCC Plugs
- Fan Grills with Blades
- RP25 Flanges

E8/9

- Photo-Etched Grills
- Operating Mars Light
- See-Through Screening on Winterization Hatch
- Realistic Cab Interior with Crew

See the Freight Cars section of this Reference Manual to see what the PROTO 2000 line has to offer you in Cabooses and Freight Cars!

PROTO 1000 LOCOMOTIVES: OUTSTANDING QUALITY AT AFFORDABLE PRICES!

- Micro-Molded Details
- Magnetic Knuckle Couplers
- Prototypically Correct Paint Schemes
- Laser-Quality Lettering
- Blackened Metal Wheels

With top-of-the-line production quality at a price that allows enthusiasts to collect all variations on the line, the PROTO 1000 series is a fantastic value for any serious modeler! These prototypically accurate locomotives feature some of the qualities that made the PROTO 2000 series such a sensation. Features include blackened metal wheels, PROTO 2000 magnetic knuckle couplers, micro-molded details, laser-quality printing and paint schemes to match the appropriate prototype.

433-8157

433-8170

433-8160

433-8172

433-8166

433-8174

F3A EA 50.00

Features include constant and directional lighting, five-pole skew-wound armature motor with low-amp draw and dual brass flywheels.

The screw-in universal couplers are mounted to each frame. The diecast chassis has eight-wheel drive and eight-wheel electrical pick-up.

433-8157 ATSF #2000 (blue, yellow freight scheme) ***NEW***
433-8158 ATSF #201C (blue, yellow freight scheme) ***NEW***
433-8160 CNW #4064 (green, black, yellow freight scheme) ***NEW***
433-8163 CNW #4056 (green, black, yellow freight scheme) ***NEW***
433-8170 LV #510 (Cornell Red, black stripes) ***NEW***
433-8171 LV #514 (Cornell Red, black stripes) ***NEW***
433-8172 PRR #9502 (Brunswick Green freight scheme) ***NEW***
433-8173 PRR #9508 (Brunswick Green freight scheme) ***NEW***
433-8174 UP #1401 (Armour Yellow) ***NEW***
433-8175 UP #1403 (Armour Yellow) ***NEW***

EMD F40PH 433-8241

EMD F7A 433-8684

Low Nose 433-8288

STEAM LOCOMOTIVES

Classic steam locomotives from the "Golden Era" of railroading. Ideal for light service and switching.

OLD TIME TEA KETTLE

433-8300 B&O (black, maroon) **27.50**

0-4-0 SWITCHER W/TENDER EA 33.00

433-8344 PRR (black)
433-8394 UP (black)

0-4-0 DOCKSIDE EA 27.50

433-8301 B&O (black)
433-8302 ATSF (black)

DIESEL LOCOMOTIVES

EMD F40PH

433-8241 Amtrak **36.00**

EMD F7A EA 36.00

433-8684 Amtrak (black, silver & blue)
433-8689 ATSF (silver & red)

EMD GP38-2 EA 36.00

LOW NOSE

433-8288 Chessie System (blue, orange & yellow)
433-8294 ATSF

HIGH NOSE

433-8067 ATSF
433-8068 BN
433-8073 N&W
433-8074 CR
433-8075 UP

MAINTENANCE KIT

ALL-PURPOSE LOCO MAINTENANCE KIT

433-8629 13.25
This kit includes track cleaner, track brite, oil gun, grease gun and electrical tester.

ON-TRAK MODEL PRODUCTS

HO Scale, cast-metal craft train kits.

SHAY CONVERSION BOILER

786-5019 13.40
Cast-alloy boiler will backdate the Roundhouse Shay prior to 1915. Boiler is straight version with a fluted steam and sand dome with removable hatch and cast number boards.

LOCO KITS UNPOWERED

786-5203 Mack Switcher **18.95**
With conventional draft gear; less couplers.

786-5206 Mack Switcher **18.95**
With link-and-pin type draft gear; less couplers.

786-5205 Westminster Kerosene **17.95**
HO/HOn3.

JORDAN HIGHWAY MINIATURES

15-TON MACK SWITCHER LOCOMOTIVE

360-302 9.95 ***NEW***
Kit is based on the Mack gas-electric switch locomotive that was in use from 1930 to 1980. Unpowered model molded of styrene plastic.

CUSTOM FINISHING

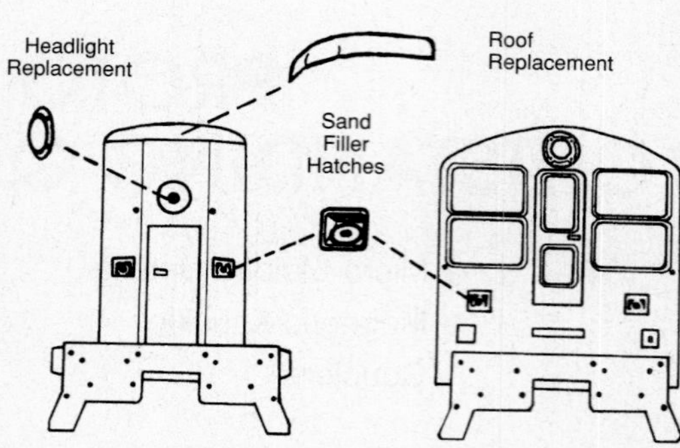

H12-44 CONVERSION KIT FOR WALTHERS LOCO

247-264 Fairbanks-Morse H12-44 Conversion Kit **11.95**
In September of 1952, F-M changed the styling of the H12-44. The cab overhang was removed, the sloped nose was changed slightly, the headlight was lowered and new sand fillers were installed. Production of this body style continued through February of 1953.

This set features a cast brass nose piece to match the roof contour, a replacement front headlight (which accepts a 1.5V mini-bulb and M.V. Products lens #516-159, both available separately) and sloped sand filler hatches for the nose and rear of the cab. An illustrated instruction sheet covers basic body modifications and the installation of new parts on the Walthers loco.

KADEE®

LOCO DRIVER CLEANER

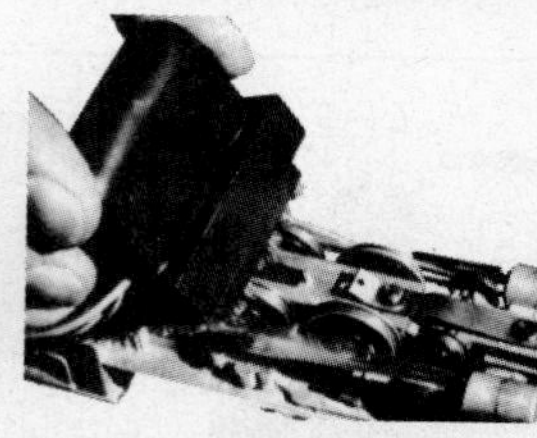

380-236 Speedi-Driver Cleaner Brush **9.95**
Cleans corrosion from loco driver treads to improve electrical conductivity. No special wiring is needed to operate.

NOCH

IMPORTED FROM GERMANY BY WALTHERS

TUNNEL CATENARY SETS

528-51260 Large **33.99**
Designed for use in tunnels and other hidden areas, this catenary features a sturdier design to add extra support to your catenary system. Includes seven masts and 56° of wire.

Roadname Abbreviation Key

ATSF Santa Fe
B&O Baltimore & Ohio
BN Burlington Northern
BNSF Burlington Northern Santa Fe (1996 Merger)
C&O Chesapeake & Ohio
CN Canadian National
CNJ Central Railroad of New Jersey
CNW Chicago & North Western
CP Canadian Pacific
CR Conrail
CSX CSX
D&H Delaware & Hudson
DRGW Rio Grande
EL Erie Lackawanna
GN Great Northern
IC Illinois Central
L&N Louisville & Nashville
LV Lehigh Valley
MILW Milwaukee Road
MKT Katy (Missouri, Kansas, Texas)
MON Monon
MOPAC Missouri Pacific
MOW Maintenance Of Way
N&W Norfolk & Western
NH New Haven
NKP Nickel Plate Road
NP Northern Pacific
NS Norfolk Southern
NYC New York Central
PFE Pacific Fruit Express
PRR Pennsylvania
RDG Reading
ROCK Rock Island
SOO Soo Line
SOU Southern Railway
SP Southern Pacific
UP Union Pacific
WC Wisconsin Central
WM Western Maryland

MANTUA

MANTUA COLLECTIBLES

These are real working locomotives, each with a certificate of authenticity that certifies it as a genuine Mantua, and each collectible is issued a unique serial number, keyed in to the order in which it was manufactured. Between runs, there's a solid wood base with track and a brass nameplate to display your locomotive. In operation or on display, these models will be the showpiece of your collection. Each model is produced in limited quantities.

B&O "President Adams" 455-3007

B&O "President Washington" 455-3002

PRR "Lindbergh Special" 455-3008

Southern Crescent 455-3001

UP "Grey Goose" 455-3004

THE NYC HUDSON

455-3006 195.00
This beautiful limited-edition locomotive celebrates the heyday of passenger travel. The 1927 debut of the NYC Hudson steam locomotive introduced a new level of first-class travel. Passengers could enjoy many of the amenities of the time, from prime roast beef to decadent Russian caviar. This diecast locomotive measures 12-3/8" long and features over 100 handcrafted details, including boxpok drivers, Baker valve gear and "Art Deco" style lettering.

PRR "LINDBERGH SPECIAL"

455-3008 195.00
The Lindbergh Special earned the name when it delivered a newsreel, developed in a converted baggage car, from Washington D.C. to New York City, and had it playing at Broadway theaters an hour before any other news agency even made it to New York. The film was of a celebration of Lindbergh's non-stop solo flight across the Atlantic, held in Washington D.C. When it wasn't racing films across the system, it was assigned to various passenger trains. Extra detailing includes brass coal shovel, Pennsy marker lights, cut levers, air compressors, brass railings and bell, brass dummy knuckle couplers and more.

SOUTHERN CRESCENT

455-3001 195.00
Named to honor the Crescent City of New Orleans, the Southern's "Crescent Limited" was a deluxe all-Pullman train, regarded as one of the most beautiful of all time. They were pulled by class Ps-4, 4-6-2 Heavy Pacifics. Sporting gold crescents on the cylinders and cab sides, a light graphite smoke box and a Virginia Green boiler and cab, highlighted with gold trim, each had 73" drivers with 47,500lbs of tractive force, and displayed many innovations, such as a long-distance tender with 6-wheel commonwealth trucks carrying 14,000 gallons of water and 16 tons of coal. The Crescent Limited scale model from Mantua compliments its life-size counterpart virtually detail for detail.

B&O "PRESIDENT ADAMS"

455-3007 195.00
The "President Adams" was the second of 20 class P7 Pacifics named for past American Presidents by the B&O. Wearing an olive and gold leaf livery, these locomotives were frequently seen pulling the "Cincinnatian." The President Adams served with distinction through the Depression years and was retired in 1957. From the headlight and gleaming brass bell, clear to the end of the tender with its rear backup light (lit when the model is in reverse), this engine is truly a masterpiece to be collected and treasured. The President Adams has over 100 handcrafted, precision parts, including full working valve gear, just like the 1927 original.

B&O "PRESIDENT WASHINGTON"

455-3002 195.00
Pride of the Baltimore & Ohio "President" class Pacifics handled some of the line's finest passenger trains. Finished in authentic green, gray and black paint, delicate gold and red pinstrips have been printed onthe cab, cylinders and tender. Sharp gold lettering includes "President Washington" on the cab, the B&O name and the engine number on the tender. Features over 100 handcrafted and precision parts, including working valve gear and numerous brass details.

UP "GREY GOOSE"

455-3004 195.00
Built by Baldwin Locomotive Works, this engine was delivered to the Union Pacific in 1920. The "Grey Goose" was the heaviest Pacific on the line, weighing in at over 230 tons. Its tender could carry 12,000 gallons of water and 20 tons of coal. The die-cast model measures 12-3/8" long and features a distinctive two-tone gray scheme with white lettering.

STEAM LOCOMOTIVES

Steam locomotives are powered and have prepainted and lettered diecast and plastic bodies. All have operating headlights, back-up lights and smoke units (unless noted), moving metal bells, wire handrails and horn-hook couplers.

4-6-0 Rogers 455-346097

2-6-0 Mogul 455-313003

4-4-0 American 455-369044

2-8-0 Camelback 455-397021

4-4-0 American 455-394061

0-4-0 Shifter 455-375020

4-6-2 Heavy Pacific 455-349021

4-6-2 Heavy Pacific 455-349036

2-6-0 MOGUL

455-313003 UP **169.99**
Less smoke unit.

2-8-0 CAMELBACK POWERED W/TENDER

455-397021 RDG **195.99**

0-4-0 SHIFTER POWERED

455-375020 PRR **109.99** *NEW*

4-6-2 HEAVY PACIFIC EA 234.99

455-349021 RDG *NEW*
455-349036 WM
455-349080 CP
455-349520 PRR

4-6-0 ROGERS EA 174.99

455-346097 Denver, South Park & Pacific
455-377565 Clinchfield
This is the coal-burning version of the "Ten Wheeler" as built by Roger Locomotive Works. It served in main line freight and passenger service. Features include metal handrails, a three-piece brass bell and turned brass domes.

4-4-0 AMERICAN EA 184.99

455-369044 W&ARR "General"
On April 12, 1862 at Big Shanty, Georgia, the Western & Atlantic RR engine called the "General" was stolen by a group of volunteers from Company H, 33rd Ohio Infantry Division. Their mission was to destroy the main line between Atlanta and the central front of Chattanooga. Less smoke units and back-up lights.

455-394061 GN

2-8-2 HEAVY MIKADO W/TENDER & SMOKE EA 249.99

The Mikado was the dependable workhorse of virtually every Class-1 railroad. These handmade beauties feature diecast metal boilers, full working valve gear, metal handrails and a three-piece brass bell.

455-348004 NP
455-348023 C&O
455-348025 RDG *NEW*
455-386040 SOU

4-4-2 ATLANTIC

455-336561 GN **179.99**
Less smoke unit.

4-6-2 LIGHT PACIFIC

455-340098 Erie w/Vanderbilt Tender **234.99** *NEW*
455-340511 SP **259.99**

MANTUA
Fine Craftsmanship Since 1926

4-6-0 Rogers 455-377565

2-8-2 Heavy Mikado 455-348004

4-4-2 Atlantic 455-336561

4-6-2 Light Pacific 455-340098

4-6-2 Light Pacific 455-340511

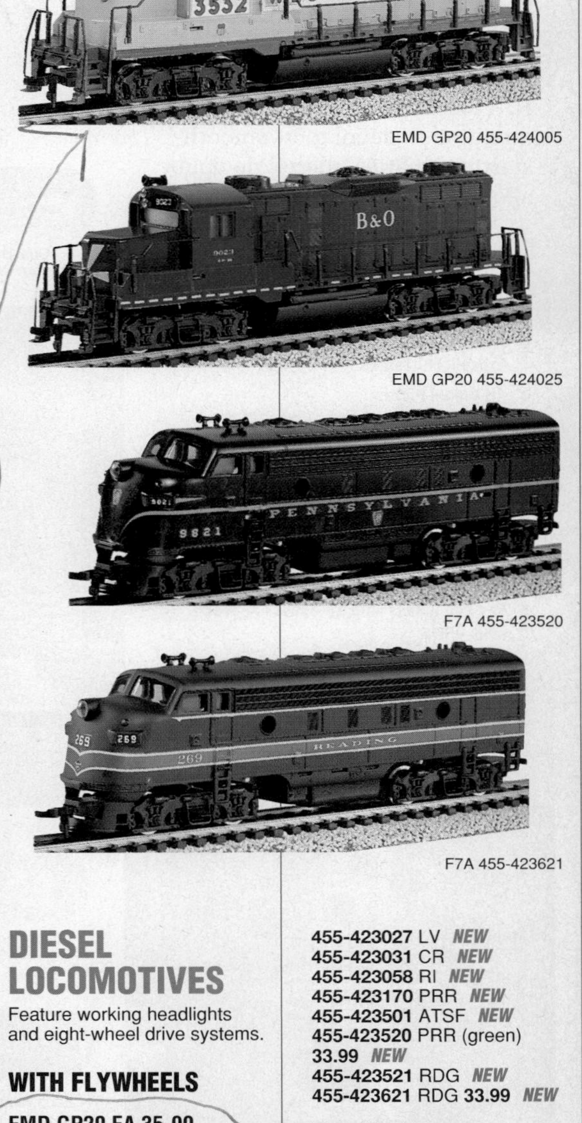

EMD GP20 455-424005

EMD GP20 455-424025

F7A 455-423520

F7A 455-423621

DIESEL LOCOMOTIVES

Feature working headlights and eight-wheel drive systems.

WITH FLYWHEELS

EMD GP20 EA 35.99 (UNLESS NOTED)
455-424005 WP **37.99** ***NEW***

455-424020 PRR
Less smoke unit.

455-424025 B&O **37.99** ***NEW***
455-424063 BN ***NEW***
455-424521 RDG w/New Number
455-424522 NYC ***NEW***
455-424530 EL ***NEW***
455-424583 CR Quality ***NEW***

F7A EA 30.99 (UNLESS NOTED)
455-423003 UP ***NEW***
455-423011 SP **37.99** ***NEW***
455-423022 NYC **37.99** ***NEW***
455-423027 LV ***NEW***
455-423031 CR ***NEW***
455-423058 RI ***NEW***
455-423170 PRR ***NEW***
455-423501 ATSF ***NEW***
455-423520 PRR (green) **33.99** ***NEW***
455-423521 RDG ***NEW***
455-423621 RDG **33.99** ***NEW***

F7B EA 14.99
455-412001 ATSF Dummy ***NEW***
455-412022 NYC ***NEW***
455-412031 CR ***NEW***

455-412520 PRR (green) ***NEW***

455-412521 RDG ***NEW***

Everything you ever wanted in a locomotive is available in MRC's new F7A locomotive. From its fantastic attention to detail to its smooth-starting abilities, there's no doubt about the excellence of this engine.

Introducing MRC's NEW F7A Platinum Series Locomotive

Everything About It Is For Real!

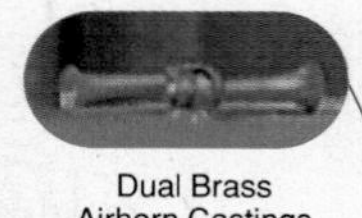

Dual Brass Airhorn Castings

Blackened Wheels

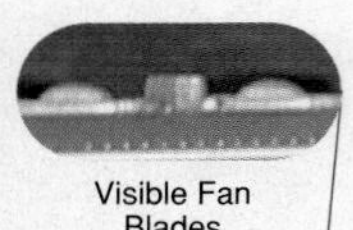

Visible Fan Blades

Stainless-Steel Side Grille

- Five-Pole Skewed Armature Motor with Exceptional Torque
- All-Wheel Pickup
- Two Massive, Balanced Flywheels
- Extremely Low Starting Characteristics
- Metal Hand Grips
- Stainless-Steel Side Grille
- Dual Brass Horns
- Fully Detailed Cab with Engineer
- Fan Has Blades with Air Spaces Between Each Blade
- All Locomotives Feature Metal Parts
- Blackened Wheels
- Available with Factory-Installed Decoder
- Each Roadname Available in Two Different Roadnumbers

Metal Hand Grips

Each Roadname Available In Two Different Roadnumbers

F7A Locomotives

500-32100 ATSF #300
500-32101 ATSF #260
500-32104 NYC #1830
500-32105 NYC #1650
500-32108 SP #6262
500-32109 SP #6264
500-32112 BN #758
500-32113 BN #759
500-32116 Undecorated

Special Introductory Price: $69*

Decoder-Equipped

500-33100 ATSF #300
500-33101 ATSF #260
500-33104 NYC #1830
500-33105 NYC #1650
500-33108 SP #6262
500-33109 SP #6264
500-33112 BN #758
500-33113 BN #759
500-33116 Undecorated

Special Introductory Price $94**

** Prices increase to $99 begining January 1, 2000*
*** Prices increase to $125 beginning January 1, 2000*

OTHER MRC ENGINES W/DECODER

ALCO FA-1 EA 79.98

500-2100 UP
500-2110 ATSF
500-2120 PRR
500-2130 NYC

EMD F40PH

500-2220 Amtrak **89.98**

EMD GP9M EA 79.98

500-2230 UP
500-2231 CSX
500-2232 BN
500-2233 CR

GE DASH 8 EA 99.98

500-2240 BNSF
500-2241 CSX

MRC 50TH ANNIVERSARY ENGINE

500-50 Limited Run C44-9W **79.98**
Specially painted GE features the MRC logo and an attractive red, black and white scheme. Each engine is numbered to insure its status as a collector's item.

RAIL POWER PRODUCTS

LOCOMOTIVE SHELLS

These body shells can be mounted on Rail Power frames (listed in the Super Detailing Parts section), or Overland Models chassis and will fit Athearn frames and drive trains with minor modification. Kits are unpowered and less trucks, chassis (unless noted), handrails and couplers. Chassis are diecast metal. Pictured models are shown assembled, painted, detailed and lettered.

B23-7 Shell 60-504

SD90 Mac w/Chassis 60-547

SD7/9 Dynamic Shell w/Chassis 60-523

GP60 Shell w/Chassis 60-529

KITS EA 15.00 (UNLESS NOTED)

60-500 C32-8
60-501 C30-7
60-502 SD60
60-504 B23-7
60-505 CF-7 Round Cab
60-507 CF-7 Angle Cab
60-509 Dash 8-40B
60-511 SD45
60-512 GP35 Dynamic
60-513 GP35 Nondynamic
60-514 Dash 8-40CW
60-516 Dash 8-40CW ATSF "Gull Wing" Cab
60-518 SD60M, 2-Window
60-520 SD60M, 3-Window
60-522 SD7/9 Dynamic
60-524 SD7/9 Nondynamic
60-526 SD45-2
60-528 GP60
60-530 GP60M.
60-532 GP60B
60-534 Dash 9-44CW
60-536 Dash 9-44CW ATSF Cab
60-538 SD40 Dynamic
60-539 SD40 Nondynamic
60-542 SD38 Dynamic
60-543 SD38 Nondynamic
60-546 SD90 Mac **16.00**
60-548 SD90 Mac w/H Kit **18.00**
60-550 GP40X *NEW*

KITS & CHASSIS EA 25.00 (UNLESS NOTED)

60-503 SD60
60-506 CF-7 Round Cab
60-508 CF-7 Angle Cab
60-510 Dash 8-40B
60-515 Dash 8-40CW
60-517 Dash 8-40CW ATSF "Gull Wing" Cab
60-519 SD60M, 2-Window
60-521 SD60M, 3-WIndow
60-523 SD7/9 Dynamic
60-525 SD7/9 Nondynamic
60-527 SD45-2
60-529 GP60
60-531 GP60M
60-533 GP60B
60-535 Dash 9-44CW
60-537 Dash 9-44CW ATSF Cab
60-540 SD40 Dynamic
60-541 SD40 Nondynamic
60-544 SD38 Dynamic
60-545 SD38 Nondynamic
60-547 SD90 Mac
60-549 SD90 Mac w/H Kit **27.00**
60-551 GP40X *NEW*
60-5115 SD45 **23.00**

TOMAR INDUSTRIES

Drumheads were used for many years on the last car of interurbans, making it easy for passengers to find their train in a terminal. The lighted sign was also useful for advertising, especially after dark. These kits are complete with cast and machined drum housing, 1.5V micro-miniature lamp, full color sign, light diffuser, diodes, hookup wire and complete instructions.

TRACTION DRUMHEADS

EA 10.95

CHICAGO SOUTH SHORE & SOUTH BEND

81-1540 Herald

CINCINNATI & LAKE ERIE

1535  1536

81-1535 Fleeting Sun
81-1536 Valley Queen

ILLINOIS TERMINAL RAILROAD

81-1525 Company

ILLINOIS TRACTION SYSTEM

1510 1511

81-1510 The Owl
81-1511 St. Louis/Peoria Limited

LEHIGH VALLEY TRANSIT

LIBERTY BELL ROUTE

1550

81-1550 Liberty Bell Route
81-1551 Liberty Bell Limited

THE MILWAUKEE ELECTRIC RAILWAY & LIGHT COMPANY

81-1530 Land O'Lakes Limited

NORTH SHORE LINE

1515 1516 1517

81-1515 Gold Coast Limited
81-1516 The Eastern Limited
81-1517 Prairie State Special

SACRAMENTO NORTHERN

1500 1501 1502

81-1500 Comet
81-1501 Meteor
81-1502 Sacramento Valley Limited

SACRAMENTO SHORT LINE

1505 1506

81-1505 The Comet
81-1506 The Meteor

YE OLDE HUFF-N-PUFF

CLIMAX LOCOMOTIVE

792-1050 25.00
This unpowered, undecorated dummy locomotive kit consists of wood sides, floor and roof plus plastic and metal detail parts. The HO scale kit is less trucks and couplers.

4-6-6-4 Challenger w/Tender
UP #3967 635-1591

2-8-8-2 Mallet B&O EL5 #7165
635-5400

4-8-4 UP Northern #844
Gray Excursion 635-1587

4-6-2 Heavy Pacific Crescent Limited
635-5401 (Rolling Stock Not Included)

4-6-2 Heavy Pacific B&O 635-5403

4-6-2 Heavy Pacific B&O 635-5404

4-6-2 Heavy Pacific CNJ 635-5405

STEAM LOCOMOTIVES

UNION PACIFIC 4-8-8-4 BIG BOYS W/TENDER EA 299.99

The new Big Boys have a powerful five-pole Japanese motor that provides the tractive power needed for realistic in-scale acceleration, speed and pulling power. The chassis and truck carriages are metal for better balance, a lower center of gravity and extra strength. Reduced diameter flanges on trucks and drivers conform to NMRA RP25, allowing operation on Code 70, 83 or 100 track. Now that the motor is concealed in the boiler, you'll find a fully detailed engineer's cab, firebox and controls.

635-5439 #4008 (black) ***NEW***
635-5440 #4010
635-5441 #4011 (silver & black) ***NEW***

DIGITAL VERSIONS EA 329.99

635-54398 UP #4008
635-54408 UP #4010
635-54418 UP #4011

4-6-6-4 CHALLENGERS W/TENDER EA 289.99

These are the locomotives everyone has been waiting for. Driven by powerful five-pole Japanese motors, now located in the boiler. Fully detailed cab interiors and cast metal chassis.

635-1591 UP #3967 (black & silver)
635-1592 UP #3979 (Two-Tone gray)
635-1596 UP Excursion Locomotive #3985 (black & Graphite)
635-1597 Clinchfield #670 (black)
635-1598 DRGW #3800 (black & silver)
635-1599 D&H #1519 (black)

2-8-8-2 MALLETS EA 279.99

635-1593 N&W Y6b #2174
635-5400 B&O EL5 #7165

UP NORTHERNS EA 249.99 (UNLESS NOTED)

635-1587 #844 (gray excursion) **229.99**
635-5427 #835 (gray)
635-5428 #844 (black & silver)
635-5429 #844 (Graphite)

4-6-2 HEAVY PACIFICS EA 199.99

Heavy Pacifics feature powerful five-pole motors and metal chassis. All have RP25 wheels and run on code 70, 83 and 100 track.

635-5401 Crescent Limited
635-5402 MILW
635-5403 B&O (green)
635-5404 B&O (blue)
635-5405 CNJ
635-5406 Chicago & Alton
635-5407 ATSF #3423

UP FEF 3 #844 635-5429
Passenger Cars Sold Separately

RIVAROSSI

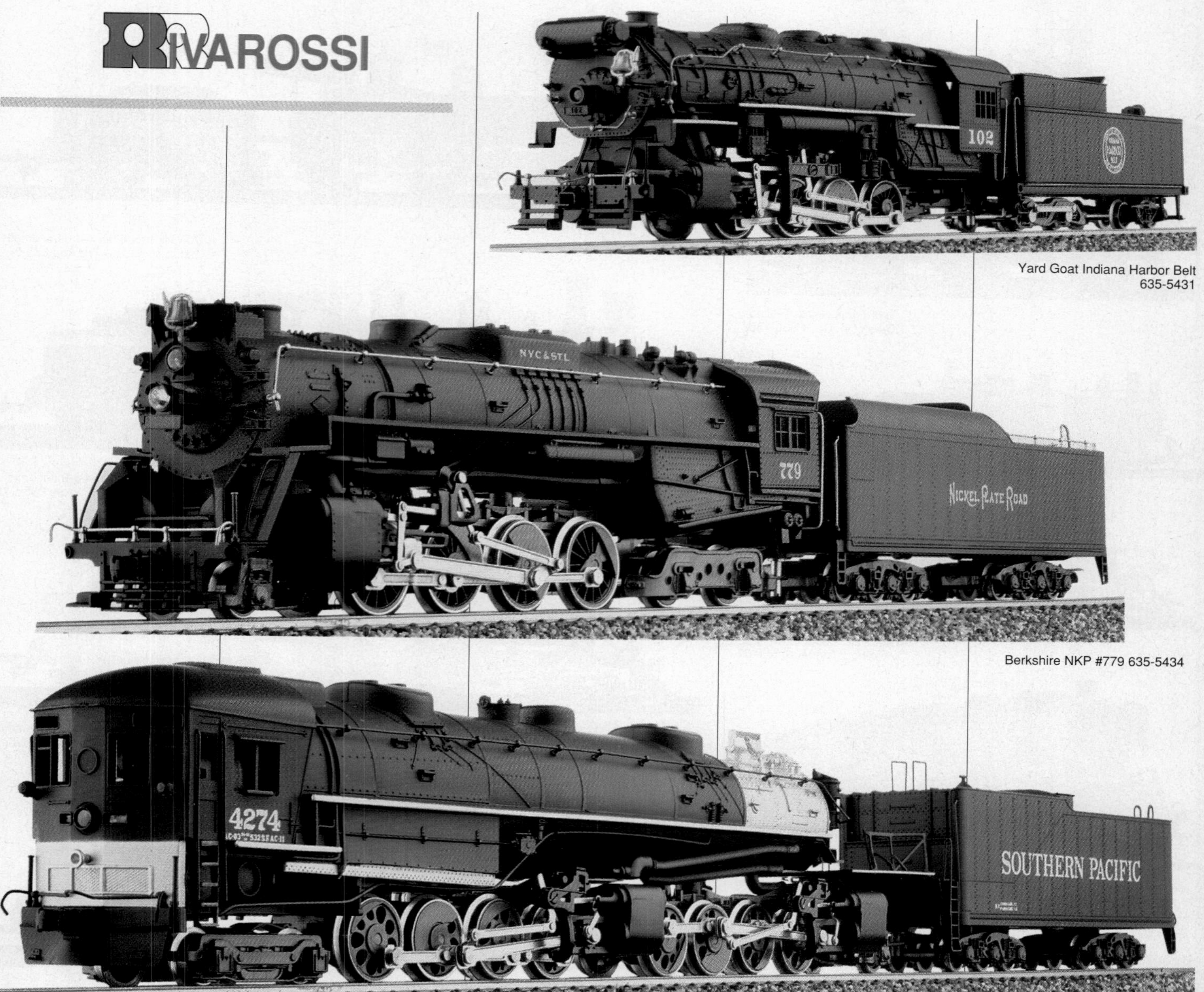

Yard Goat Indiana Harbor Belt 635-5431

Berkshire NKP #779 635-5434

Cab Forward SP #4274 635-5424

4-8-8-2 CAB FORWARD LOCOMOTIVES EA 289.99

When SP tried conventional mallet type locos in the tunnels and snow sheds on the busy Sierra Nevada line, the build-up of blinding smoke was so thick that boiler fires were sometimes extinguished and engine crews asphyxiated. To remedy these short-comings, the cab was put up front in 1911, creating the locomotive which would become Southern Pacific's trademark—the Cab-Forward.

Each model locomotive and tender is complete with the same number of nuts, bolts and rivets as its prototype. Handrails are made of steel wire, individually threaded through each stanchion. Working rods are nickel-plated and walkways are etched to look like the real thing.

635-5424 SP #4274
635-5426 SP #4294
635-5430 SP #4247 ***NEW***

BERKSHIRES EA 229.99

In 1924 Lima's William E. Woodard designed a loco that could pull long trains at sustained high speeds. Demonstrator No. 1, class A-1, became the first 2-8-4. It had 28 x 30" cylinders, 63" drivers and a boiler pressure of 240 pounds. Its grate was an unheard-of 100 square feet. The frame ended behind the rear drivers, with the trailing truck transmitting pulling forces and supporting the rear of the firebox. In addition, the trailing truck was equipped with a booster.

The engine was an immediate success and railroads ordered "Berkshires" by the dozens. Before production ended in 1949, 611 were built.

Rivarossi's Berkshires feature smooth wormgear transmissions. Powerful five-pole Japanese motors with flywheel in the boiler and metal chassis for stability. All Berkshires have RP25 wheels and will run on code 70, 83 or 100 track.

635-5434 NKP #779
635-5435 Richmond, Fredricksburg & Potomac #574
635-5436 Pere Marquette #1222
635-5437 American Railroads **229.99** ***NEW***
635-5438 NKP w/Double Tender **269.99** ***NEW***

YARD GOATS EA 199.99

Indiana Harbor Belt's Yard Goat was the most powerful of all 0-8-0 switchers. It had a Franklin Booster on the front truck of the tender, adding another 13,800 pounds of tractive force for a grand total of 89,500 pounds. It was the heaviest 0-8-0 at 294,00 pounds without tender. In addition, it was equipped with an Elesco feadwater heater.

The 0-8-0 Yard Goats feature powerful Rivarossi motors with wormgear transmission and new metal chassis for improved stability. Yard Goats have RP25 wheels and run on code 70, 83 or 100 track.

635-5431 Indiana Harbor Belt
635-5432 ATSF
635-5433 MP

RIVAROSSI

Two Truck Heisler Salmon Creek Co. No. 4 635-1568

Three Truck Heisler Ohio Match Co. No. 1 635-1569

Mikado 2-8-2 Locomotive SOU w/Short Tender 635-5409

Mikado 2-8-2 Locomotive GN w/Vanderbilt Tender
Roadname Shown Not Available

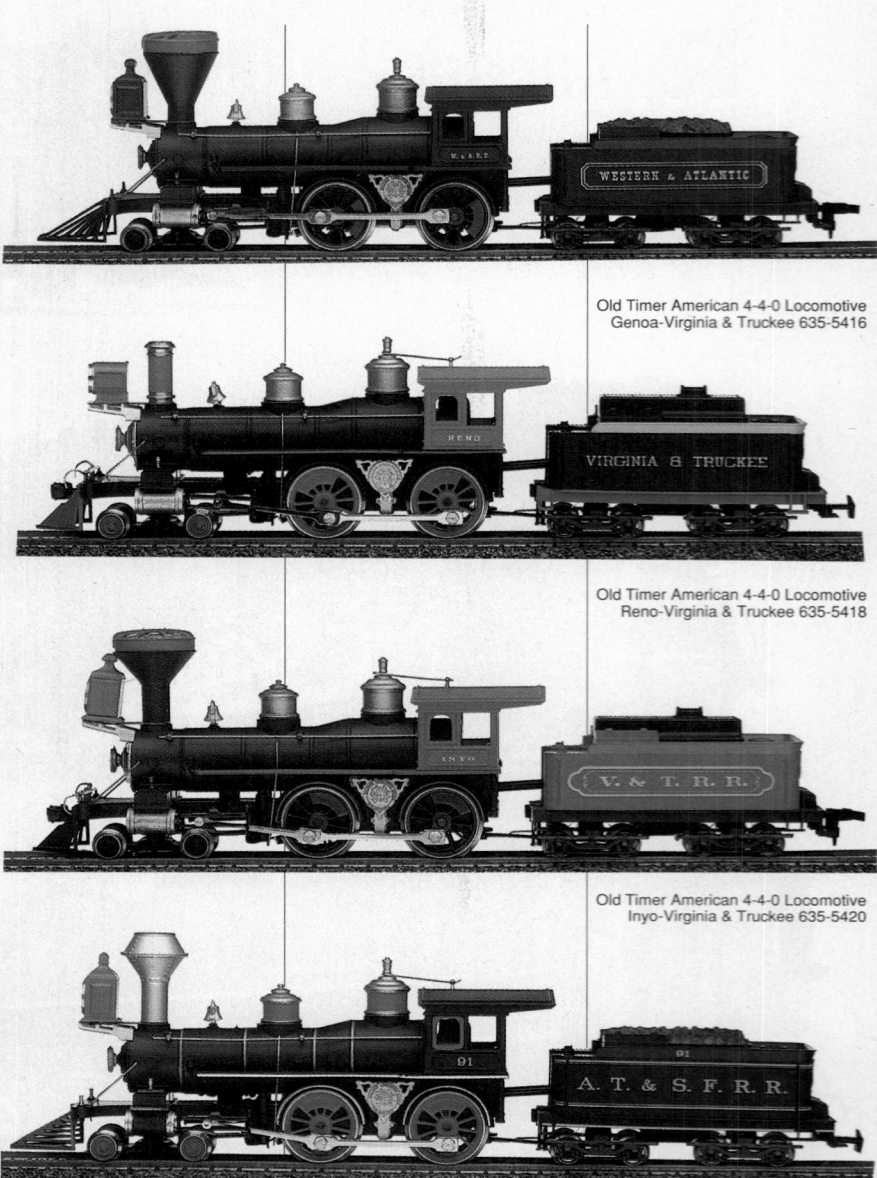

Old Timer American 4-4-0 Locomotive Genoa-Virginia & Truckee 635-5416

Old Timer American 4-4-0 Locomotive Reno-Virginia & Truckee 635-5418

Old Timer American 4-4-0 Locomotive Inyo-Virginia & Truckee 635-5420

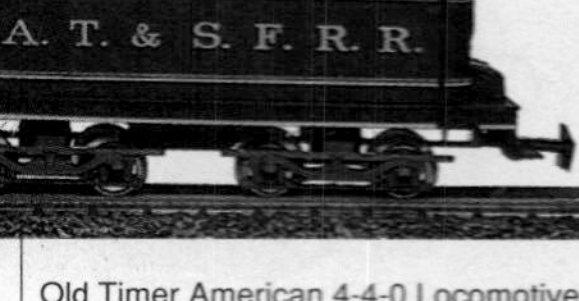

Old Timer American 4-4-0 Locomotive American-ATSF 635-5422

HEISLER LOCOMOTIVES

With steep grades, sharp curves, snow and swampland to conquer, the logging industry needed a locomotive that would stand up to nature's rough elements. Charles Heisler solved this problem with the Heisler Locomotive.

Both model versions are exact mechanical reproductions of the prototypes.

Nickel-plated piston rods connect to a center geared transmission that powers flexible coupled drive shafts, which turn bevel gears housed within the axles. Drive-wheel trucks float, allowing your loco to operate on the roughest track. Can motors married to worm-gear power trains will pull the heaviest logging and mining loads you can create.

TWO TRUCK HEISLERS EA 219.99

635-1228 West Side Lumber Co.
635-1568 Salmon Creek Co. No. 4

THREE TRUCK HEISLERS EA 239.99

635-1532 Green Brier & Elk River
635-1569 Ohio Match Co. No. 1

LOGGING BUGGIES

635-2349 19.00
Each buggy is 4" long and 1-7/8" high

MIKADO 2-8-2 LOCOMOTIVES EA 199.99

Feature powerful five-pole motors and metal chassis. All have RP25 wheels and run on code 70, 83 and 100 track.

635-5408 Erie Railroad w/Short Tender
635-5409 SOU w/Short Tender
635-5410 GN w/Short Tender
635-5411 GN w/Vanderbilt Tender *NEW*
635-5454 Undecorated w/Vanderbilt Tender *NEW*

HUDSON 4-6-4 LOCOMOTIVES

STANDARD EA 209.99

635-5446 NYC #5405 *NEW*
635-5447 NYC #5442 *NEW*
635-5449 Boston & Albany #604 *NEW*
635-5452 C&O #303 *NEW*

STREAMLINED EA 239.99

635-5445 Empire State Express *NEW*
635-5448 NYC #5453 *NEW*
635-5444 NYC #5445 *NEW*
635-5450 MILW "Hiawatha" *NEW*
635-5451 #3460 "Blue Goose" *NEW*

OLD TIMER AMERICAN 4-4-0 LOCOMOTIVES EA 99.99

Improved versions feature motor in tender and cab interior details, plus sharp paint and lettering. Can be run on Code 70, 83 or 100 track.

635-5416 Genoa-Virginia & Truckee
635-5417 Genoa-Western & Atlantic
635-5418 Reno-Virginia & Truckee
635-5419 Reno-Kansas, St. Louis & Chicago
635-5420 Inyo-Virginia & Truckee
635-5421 Inyo-Kansas, St. Louis & Chicago
635-5422 American-ATSF
635-5423 American-UP

These models feature plastic bodies and diecast frames, trucks, motor with flywheels and drive train. F units include couplers; the following units are kits and less couplers. F units and other models as noted include motors.

Baldwin AS-16
691-4170

EMD FT AB Set
691-5030

Century 628
691-6211

BALDWIN

BALDWIN AS-16 (ATHEARN DRIVE) EA 45.00 (UNLESS NOTED)

691-4170 SOO (black)
691-4180 MKT (orange)
691-4000 Undecorated, Powered (gray)
691-4050 Undecorated, Dummy **23.00**

ALCO

RS-3 (ATHEARN DRIVE)

All models undecorated.

PHASE I

Features punched louvers in side doors.

691-1000 Powered **39.95**
691-1050 Dummy **21.95**

PHASE II

Features horizontal box filters in side doors.

691-2000 Powered (gray) **39.95**
691-2050 Dummy (gray) **21.95**

PHASE III

Features vertical box filters in side doors.

691-3000 Powered (gray) **39.95**
691-3050 Dummy (gray) **21.95**

CENTURY 628 POWERED EA 135.00

691-6210 PRR
691-6211 LV (Snowbird Scheme) ***NEW***
691-6212 Penn Central ***NEW***
691-6213 Alco Demonstrator 628-1 ***NEW***
691-6214 Alco Demonstrator 628-2 ***NEW***
691-6215 L&N ***NEW***
691-6220 SP
691-6200 Undecorated Single Sand Filler
691-6201 Undecorated Double Sand Filler

GENERAL ELECTRIC

U25B (ATHEARN DRIVE) EA 54.99

Different Roadname Shown

691-7120 C&O
691-7140 NYC
691-7000 Undecorated
691-7001 Phase III Undecorated ***NEW***
691-7002 Phase IV Undecorated ***NEW***

EMD

FT AB SET EA 185.00

691-5018 DRGW
691-5019 DRGW (5 Port Holes in B Unit)
691-5020 LV (Cornell Red)
691-5021 SOU
691-5022 GN
691-5023 GN (Light Side Panel)
691-5027 SSW Black Widow
691-5028 Atlantic Coast Line (purple)
691-5029 ATSF Passenger
691-5030 Boston & Maine
691-5031 CB&Q
691-5032 WP
691-5033 Erie
691-5034 Baltimore & Ohio

Limited Quantity Available
691-5024 RDG (black, green & yellow)
691-5025 NP

FTA SINGLE LIGHT EA 130.00 (UNLESS NOTED)

691-5014 NYC
691-5000 Undecorated
691-5001 Undecorated w/Large Side Panels **99.98**

FTA DOUBLE LIGHT EA 130.00

691-5002 Undecorated
691-5003 Undecorated w/Large Side Panels

FTB DUMMY EA 55.00

691-5015 NYC
691-5004 Undecorated
691-5005 Undecorated, 5 Port Holes

POWER CHASSIS

691-5198 F3A/F7A/F9A **95.00** ***NEW***
691-5199 F3B/F7B/F9B **95.00** ***NEW***
691-5999 FTB **85.00**

F UNITS A/B SETS

F3 EA 150.00

PHASE I POWERED

Includes chicken wire, three porthole A units and high fans.

691-5100 Undecorated Single Headlight ***NEW***
691-5101 Undecorated Double Headlight ***NEW***

PHASE III

Includes chicken wire, horizontal louvers and low fans.

691-5400 Undecorated Single Headlight ***NEW***
691-5401 Undecorated Double Hedalight ***NEW***

F7 EA 150.00

PHASE I EARLY

691-5610 PRR Single Headlight ***NEW***
691-5611 CN (Wet Noodle) CN (Wet Noodle) ***NEW***
691-5612 SP (Black Widow) Double Headlight ***NEW***
691-5613 Amtrak Double Headlight ***NEW***
691-5600 Undecorated Single Headlight ***NEW***
691-5601 Undecorated Double Headlight ***NEW***

PHASE II

48" dynamic fan, low fans and vertical grill and louvers.

691-5810 Penn Central Single Headlight ***NEW***
691-5811 C&O Double Headlight ***NEW***

F9 EA 150.00

48" dynamic fan, extra louvers, low fans and vertical grill and louvers.

691-5900 Undecorated Single Headlight ***NEW***
691-5901 Undecorated Double Headlight ***NEW***

Information
STATION

PICKING THE PROPER MOTIVE POWER-PART II DIESELS

By the late 1940s, railroads were buying new diesels as fast as they could. While steam engines were often built for very specific jobs, diesels could be ordered with options, such as different gearing for higher or lower speeds, or steam heating for passenger service. It wasn't uncommon for diesels to handle both freight and passenger traffic. If you model a specific railroad or time period, your choice will be a little easier. Here are some basic guidelines for using diesels on your line.

Smaller engines were built especially for switching chores and these were often the first diesels a railroad purchased. Examples include early Box Cabs from various industrial builders, the EMD SW and NW series, the GE 44- and 70-Tonner, Alco's S series and Baldwin's V and later DS models. These engines had small fuel tanks and were intended for use only in yards or industrial areas.

IMPORTED FROM AUSTRIA BY WALTHERS

These engines feature authentically painted and lettered plastic bodies with diecast frames, metal gears and European-style couplers. Many have operating, reversing headlights and include multiple locomotive numbers. All Roco engines operate on 2-rail DC (unless otherwise indicated). Engines with pantographs can also be powered from overhead wire. Many models are also available equipped for 3-rail AC operation.

EUROPEAN RAILROAD ERAS

Roco categorizes each of its models into eras to assist hobbyists and collectors specializing in specific time periods. Five eras are used to classify equipment from the 1830s to the present:

ERA I

Equipment used by provincial and private railways between 1835 and 1920.

ERA II

Locomotives and rolling stock from 1920 through 1945, following the formation of the large national state railways (DRG, BBO, SBB, etc.).

ERA III

Engines, freight and passenger equipment representing the time period between 1945 and 1970.

ERA IV

Locomotives and rolling stock having computer-readable UIC lettering, in service since approximately 1968 through 1985.

ERA V

Equipment covering the modern era of 1985 to the present.

ROYAL WUERTTEMBERG STATE RAILWAYS

CLASS C

625-43259 150th Anniversary Edition **274.99**

SAXONIAN STATE RAILWAY

CLASS XIII H 2-10-0

625-43328 Era I **239.99**

PRUSSIAN RAILWAY ADMINISTRATION (P. ST. E.V.)

CLASS T14-1 2-8-2T

625-63260 "8976 Berlin" **TBA** *NEW*
Rebuilt from class 14 locos for heavy freight service on short runs and on some passenger assignments. Finished in deep green and black, model includes gas lanterns, additional gas containers, cover for coal bunker and a modified pipe arrangement. Ideal for use with the new Prussian Railway cars (625-45410, 45411, 45412, 45413, sold separately) in the Passenger Car section.

ROYAL PRUSSIAN STATE RAILWAYS

CLASS S10 4-6-0

625-43312 #1112 (Era III black w/red striping) **259.99**

GERMAN STATE RAILWAY (DRG 1920-1945)

CLASS 01 4-6-2

625-43316 Era II **289.99**

CLASS G10 0-10-0

625-43221 Era I **274.99**

CLASS 57 0-10-0

625-43222 Era II **234.99**

E18.18 ELECTRIC W/FRONT APRON

625-43758 E18.18 **209.99**

CLASS E 16 ELECTRIC

625-63620 Era II (green) **TBA** *NEW*
Features new motor with heavy flywheels and low center of gravity. New superstructure has the correct lower roof found on engines #01 to 17 in this era. Model a complete train with the new Fast Train Coaches in the Passenger Cars section.

CLASS E17 ELECTRIC

625-43719 DC Powered (gray) Era II **239.99**
625-43856 AC Powered (gray) Era II **289.99**

CLASS 91 ELECTRIC

625-43737 Era II (green) **199.99**

CLASS 17 4-6-0

625-43314 With Two Domes (Era II, black) **199.99**

CLASS 444 2-10-0

625-43352 Era II (gray) **259.99**

PANORAMA MOTOR COACH

625-43598 EIT 1998 Panorama **249.99**

GERMAN FEDERAL RAILWAYS (DB 1945-1985)

CLASS 041 2-8-2

625-43366 #293-2 w/Rebuilt Boiler & Tender (black, red) **TBA** *NEW*

CLASS V100 DIESEL

625-63417 Switcher #1224 (red, gray/black) Era III **154.99** *NEW*

CLASS 332 DIESEL

625-43829 Light Switcher #015-7 Era IV (red) **TBA** *NEW*

CLASS 140 ELECTRIC

625-43387 #542-2 (Ocean Blue, Beige) Era IV **159.99** *NEW*

CLASS E 94 ELECTRIC

625-43714 #036 (green) **229.99** *NEW*

CLASS E 60 ELECTRIC

625-43817 Switcher Era III **TBA** *NEW*

CLASS 111 ELECTRIC

625-63640 (Ocean Blue, Beige) Era IV **TBA** *NEW*
Prototypes entered fast freight service in the early 1970s.. Models are completely revised with new drive and numerous add-on details.

CLASS 012 STEAM LOCOMOTIVE

625-43340 Era IV **359.99**
625-43874 AC, 3-Rail **389.99**

CLASS 41 2-8-2T

625-43245 Era III **269.99**

CLASS 58 2-10-0

625-43204 Era IV-V, Museum Edition-Ulmer Railway Friends **264.99**

CLASS 44 2-10-0 EA 259.99

625-43260 Oil Tender Era III
625-43351 Coal Tender Era III

CLASS 01 4-6-2

625-43359 Era III **259.99**

CLASS 93 2-8-2T

625-43320 DC Powered Era III **239.99**
625-43875 AC Powered Era IV **289.99**

CLASS E17 ELECTRIC

Prototype Photo

625-43717 Era III **229.99**
625-43876 Era III, AC 3-Rail **279.99**

CLASS E 10 "CREASE" ELECTRIC

625-43791 DC Powered (blue) Era III **199.99**
625-43843 AC Powered (blue) Era III **249.99**

CLASS E18 ELECTRIC

625-43660 Museum Edition (gray) **249.99**
625-43981 Museum Edition, AC 3-Rail (gray) **299.99**

625-43729 Era III (blue, double silver stripe) **209.99**
625-43886 Era III, AC 3-Rail (blue, double silver stripe) **269.99**

CLASS 103 ELECTRIC W/SHORT CAB

625-43839 DC Powered Era IV **229.99**
625-43849 AC Powered Era IV **289.99**

CLASS 50 2-10-0

625-43306 Cabin Tender (Era III black, red) **299.99**

CLASS 23 2-6-2

625-63223 Era IV **229.99**

CLASS 01 4-6-2

625-43341 Era III w/Coal Tender **339.99**

CLASS 80 0-6-0T

625-43371 Era III **129.99**

E71 ELECTRIC

625-43816 Era III (green) **199.99**

CLASS 112 ELECTRIC

625-43792 Era IV TEE Scheme (Cream & maroon) **209.99**

GERMAN FEDERAL RAILWAYS

V 160 003 "LOLLO"

625-43840 Era V Museum Edition **219.99**

6-AXLE TRAMWAY CAR "REISSDORF KOLSCH"

625-43186 Era V **189.99**

CLASS E41 ELECTRIC

625-43956 Era III, AC 3-Rail (blue) **219.99**
625-43957 Era III, AC 3-Rail (green) **219.99**

Limited Quantity Available
625-43636 Era III (blue) **169.99**
625-43637 Era III (green) **169.99**

CLASS E94 ELECTRIC

625-43712 Museum Edition (green) **239.99**

CLASS 110 ELECTRIC

625-43790 Era IV, w/apron, newly designed surperstructure "Flatiron Crease" **219.99**

625-43889 AC, 3-Rail **269.99**
625-43990 Era IV, AC 3-Rail (blue) **239.99**

CLASS 111 ELECTRIC

625-43413 Era IV-V (blue, beige) **149.99**

CLASS 140 ELECTRIC

Limited Quantity Available
625-43388 Era IV (gray) **209.99**
625-43991 Era IV, AC 3-Rail (gray) **259.99**

CLASS 141 ELECTRIC

625-43638 Era IV (blue) **179.99**

Limited Quantity Available
625-43888 Era IV, AC 3-Rail (blue) **219.99**

CLASS 150 ELECTRIC

625-43585 Era IV (green) **199.99**

Limited Quantity Available
625-43924 Era IV, AC 3-Rail (green) **249.99**

CLASS 181 ELECTRIC

625-43692 Era IV, "Lorraine" (beige, blue) **209.99**
625-43984 Era IV, "Lorraine," AC 3-Rail (beige, blue) **259.99**

625-43693 Era IV, "Scar" (beige, blue) **209.99**
625-43890 Era IV, "Scar," AC 3-Rail (beige, blue) **259.99**
625-43690 Era IV (blue) **199.99**

Limited Quantity Available
625-43985 Era IV, AC 3-Rail (blue) **259.99**

CLASS V200 DIESEL

625-43522 Era III (red, gray) **159.99**
625-43928 Era III, AC 3-Rail (red, gray) **209.99**

CLASS 211 DIESEL

Limited Quantity Available
625-43989 Era IV, AC 3-Rail (blue) **179.99**

V 290 DIESEL

625-824 Era IV-V, Bundeswehr Lettering **134.99**
625-63422 Era V (blue) **TBA**

CLASS 215 DIESEL

625-43417 Era IV (red, gray) **119.99**

CLASS 260

625-43830 Era IV, DB **149.99**

CLASS 333 DIESEL

625-43477 Era III-IV (red) **99.99**

KOF 331/332/333 DIESEL

625-63410 Red, White Scheme Era III **99.99**

GERMAN STATE RAILWAY (DR - FORMER EAST GERMAN LINES 1945- 1985)

CLASS 58 2-10-0

625-43202 With Tender Era III (black, red) **219.99** ***NEW***

CLASS 57 0-10-0

625-43346 Era III **239.99**

CLASS 44 2-10-0

625-43351 Era III **259.99**

CLASS 93 2-8-2T

625-43321 Era III **239.99**

CLASS 50 2-10-0

625-43360 With Tender Era III (black, red) **TBA** ***NEW***
Based on prototypes rebuilt from 1958 to 1963, with new boiler, feedwater heater and firebox.

CLASS 35-10 2-6-2

625-63231 With Tender Era IV (black, red) **TBA** ***NEW***

CLASS 142 DIESEL

625-63430 Era IV (red) **164.99** ***NEW***

CLASS 01 4-6-2

625-43317 Era II **249.99**

CLASS 80 0-6-0T

625-43372 Era III **129.99**

CLASS E 18 MUSEUM ELECTRIC

625-43815 209.99
Restored to the original dark green, red, and gray scheme and now used for occasional fan trips.

UNITED GERMAN RAILWAYS DB-AG

CLASS 364 DIESEL

625-63421 Switcher #796-3 (Traffic Red "DB Cargo") Era V **TBA** ***NEW***

INTERCITY CAB CAR

625-44937 Era V (Traffic Red) **54.99** ***NEW***
For push-pull commuter trains, matches coaches #625-45068, 45254 and Cab Car #45262, all sold separately, listed in Passenger Cars.

CLASS 101 ELECTRIC

625-43740 Era V **199.99**
625-43741 DC Powered (Traffic Red) Era V **189.99**
625-43858 AC Powered (Traffic Red) Era V **229.99**
625-43880 AC, 3-Rail **245.99**
625-63720 #130-3 "Metropolitan" (two-tone gray) **TBA** ***NEW***

CLASS 112 ELECTRIC

625-43681 Era V (red) **199.99**

625-43684 Era V (red) **199.99**
625-43979 Era V, AC 3-Rail (red) **239.99**
625-43993 Era V, AC 3-Rail (red) **259.99**

CLASS 140 ELECTRIC

625-43382 Era V (red) **149.99**

CLASS 143 ELECTRIC

625-43683 Era V, "S-Bahn" (white, orange, yellow) **189.99**
625-43680 Era V (maroon) **199.99**
625-43978 Era V, AC 3-Rail (maroon) **239.99**
625-63559 Era V (red) **199.99**

Limited Quantity Available
625-43992 Era V, "S-Bahn," AC 3-Rail (white, orange, yellow) **259.99**

CLASS 145 ELECTRIC

625-63560 Era V (red) **209.99**

CLASS 151 ELECTRIC
625-43380 Era V (red) **179.99**

CLASS 181 ELECTRIC

625-43695 Era V, (oriental red) **209.99**
625-43891 Era V, AC 3-Rail (oriental red) **259.99**

CLASS 211 DIESEL

625-63416 Era V (red) **149.99**

CLASS 232
Limited Quantity Available
625-43705 Era V, (oriental red) **159.99**

CLASS 232 DIESEL

625-63689 Era V "DB-Cargo" (red) **169.99**

CLASS 361 DIESEL
Limited Quantity Available
625-43960 Era V, AC 3-Rail (red) **219.99**

CAB CAR 1/100 SCALE
Limited Quantity Available
625-44935 Interegio (blue, white scheme) Era V **54.99**

ICE 2
625-43071 Set w/Driving Trailer 1/100 Scale Era V **239.99**

CLASS ET 420 3-UNIT COMMUTER TRAIN
625-63007 DB-AG (red) **339.99**
625-63008 DB-AG Munich Airport (blue) **359.99**

AUSTRIAN FEDERAL RAILWAYS

CLASS 310 2-6-4
625-43330 #23 - Museum Edition **TBA** ***NEW***
Authentic model of the engine owned by the Vienna Technical Museum, currently undergoing a complete overhaul for fantrip service. Limited to 8,000 models worldwide, comes with special packaging and an accompanying book.

CLASS 1014 ELECTRIC

625-43820 DC Powered (Modern red, white) **249.99**
625-43860 AC Powered (Modern red, white) **299.99**
625-63610 Multi-Nation Service w/4 Pantographs (red, white, gray) **TBA** ***NEW***
Based on prototypes equipped with multiple pantographs for service in Hungary and other routes.

CLASS 1044 ELECTRIC
625-63580 Era V (Traffic Red) **189.99**

625-63582 "Kids Art Loco" #282-0 Era V **279.99** ***NEW***
Special paint scheme features winners from a children's coloring contest and has been in service since November, 1998. Limited-Run, features over 100 impressions and different schemes on each side.

CLASS RH 1016 ELECTRIC
625-63680 "Taurus" (red, black, white lettering) Era V **TBA** ***NEW***

CLASS 50 2-10-0
Limited Quantity Available
625-43289 Era III-IV **299.99**

CLASS 110 ELECTRIC "CROCODILE"
625-43378 Museum Edition (green) **299.99**
Based on preserved engine #102, includes book on the prototypes.

CLASS 310 2-6-4
625-43330 Era V **TBA**
Limited-edition of 7000 models world-wide. Based on restored prototype at the Vienna Technical Museum.

CLASS 1020.010-3 ELECTRIC

625-43738 Era IV-V **219.99**

CLASS 1045 ELECTRIC
625-43700 Era IV-V (orange) **169.99**
625-43819 Era III (green) **TBA**

CLASS 1044.240-8 ELECTRIC

624-43724 Era IV-V **179.99**
624-43998 AC, 3-Rail **249.99**

CLASS 1044.006-3 ELECTRIC
625-43720 Era IV (orange) **179.99**

CLASS 1044.77 ELECTRIC
Limited Quantity Available
625-43971 Era IV, AC 3-Rail (orange) **219.99**

625-43760 Era IV-V (orange, white, gray) **242.99**

625-43766 Era IV Solid Orange/Red Scheme **219.99**

CLASS 1110 ELECTRIC

625-43767 Era V (Traffic Red) **239.99**

CLASS 1141 ELECTRIC
Limited Quantity Available
625-43962 Era III-IV, AC 3-Rail (green) **259.99**
625-63576 With Computer Unit Numbers (Blood Orange) **TBA** ***NEW***

CLASS 2045 DIESEL
625-43702 Era IV-V (orange) **159.99**

SWISS FEDERAL RAILWAYS

CLASS C 5/6 2-10-0
625-63320 With Oil Tender Era V **TBA** ***NEW***
Matches Diner #625-44877 and coaches 44878 and #44880, all sold separately, listed in Passenger Cars.

CLASS AE 8/14 DOUBLE
625-63771 #11852 Era III (green) **429.99** ***NEW***

CLASS AE 8/8 DOUBLE ELECTRIC LOCO
625-63880 Era IV (brown) **TBA** ***NEW***

CLASS BE4/6 II ELECTRIC

625-43507 Era II-III (green) **219.99**

CLASS CE6/8 II ELECTRIC

625-43538 Era III (green) **289.99**
625-43940 Era III, AC 3-Rail (green) **349.99**

CLASS AE 4/6 ELECTRIC
625-63530 Era IV **249.99**

BERN-LOTSCHBERG-SEMPION CLASS AE 6/8 ELECTRIC
These handsome collector's editions come in a wood presentation box.

625-43711 Era V (brown) DC Powered **319.99**
625-43855 Era V (brown) AC Powered **369.99**

CLASS 460 ELECTRIC

625-43655 Era V (red) **219.99**
625-43970 Era V, AC 3-Rail (red) **269.99**

CLASS AE6/6 ELECTRIC
625-43986 Era IV-V, AC 3-Rail (green) **259.99**
Limited Quantity Available
625-43698 Era IV (red, gray, white stripe) DC Powered **219.99**
625-43938 Era V, AC 3-Rail (red) **179.99**

CLASS RE460 ELECTRIC
These modern locos sport a variety of colorful advertising schemes.

625-63513 TSR, Era V **229.99**
625-63514 Western Union, Era V **229.99**
625-63515 RSI, Era V **219.99**
Limited Quantity Available
625-43652 AGFA (gray, white, orange) **249.99**

CHINA
625-63507 Kowloon Canton Railway Corporation-KCRC Locomotive 2000, Era V **229.99**

ITALIAN STATE RAILWAYS

CLASS E 636 ELECTRIC
625-63628 #041 Era IV/V (brown) **TBA** ***NEW***

CLASS D345 DIESEL
625-63450 With New Front Windows Era V (green, brown) **TBA** ***NEW***

CLASS 880 STEAM 2-6-0
625-43277 Era III-IV **209.99**

CLASS 214 DIESEL
625-43728 Era IV (green) **119.99**

E645 ELECTRIC
625-63627 Articulated, Era V (brown) **229.99**

FRENCH NATIONAL RAILWAYS

CLASS BB63000 DIESEL

625-63437 Arsenz-Lackierung, Era V **159.99**

CLASS 22387 ELECTRIC
625-43780 "Corail Plus" Scheme, Era V **219.99**

Class ET 420 3-Unit Commuter Train
625-63007

CLASS BB 25155 ELECTRIC

625-43566 Era IV **219.99**

CLASS BB5282 ELECTRIC

625-43564 Era IV (gray, orange, white) **199.99**

CLASS BB63000 DIESEL-ELECTRIC

625-43575 Era IV-V **149.99**

CLASS BB 16007 ELECTRIC

625-43568 Era IV (gray/green scheme) **199.99**

RGP MOTOR TRAIN

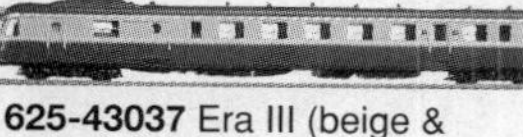

625-43037 Era III (beige & green) **329.99**

NETHERLANDS STATE RAILWAYS

CLASS 1700 ELECTRIC

625-43679 Era IV-V (gray, yellow) **199.99**

BELGIAN NATIONAL RAILWAYS

CLASS 25 4-10-0

625-43268 #021 With Modified Headlights Era III (green, black) **TBA** ***NEW***

CLASS 20 ELECTRIC

625-43670 Era IV-V (blue-green, yellow) **209.99**

625-43974 Era IV-V, AC 3-Rail (blue-green, yellow) **259.99**

NORWEGIAN STATE RAILWAYS

CLASS EL16 ELECTRIC

Limited Quantity Available
625-43668 Era IV (red) **209.99**
625-43973 Era IV, AC 3-Rail (red) **259.99**
625-43933 Era IV-V, AC 3-Rail (red, black) **269.99**

CLASS EL 18 ELECTRIC

625-63503 Era V DC Powered (red) **229.99**
625-69503 Era V AC Powered (red) **269.99**

SWEDISH STATE RAILWAYS

CLASS RC6 ELECTRIC

625-63570 Era V (blue, red, gray) **209.99**

MODERN STREETCARS

625-43182 6-Axle "Gotha-Versicherung" Rhine Rail Corporation Streetcar **159.99**

625-43183 8-Axle "Persil" Cologne Public Transport Services Streetcar **169.99**

Modern Streetcar 625-43182

FINNISH STATE RAILWAYS

CLASS RE465

625-43656 Era IV (blue) **229.99**
625-43953 Era IV, AC 3-Rail (blue) **279.99**

CLASS AE 6/8

625-43710 Era IV-V (brown) **279.99**

LOCOMOTIVE DETAIL SET

625-40014 4.99
Superdetail your Roco locomotives with this detail set, complete with hoses, couplers and more.

DIGITAL SYSTEM

The Digital system combines the fun of model railroading with computer technology. Digital is an easy-to-operate system that allows independent control of multiple locomotives. A computer chip, programmed with a special identifying number (called an address), is mounted in each loco and responds to the commands from the "mouse," which features controls for loco speed and direction, lights on/off, emergency stops and loco address programming. Up to eight digitally equipped locos can be controlled independently within a power circuit.

LOCOMOTIVE MOUSE

625-10750 99.99
Controls all functions of digital locomotives: speed and direction, selection of locomotives, illumination on/off, emergency stop and programming of locomotive addresses.

DIGITAL BUS CONNECTOR

625-10755 12.99

RAILWAY BREAKDOWN CRANE

Digitally controlled crane with real operating functions makes it possible to turn cab boom left or right up to 90°, and raise and lower crane boom and hook.

625-46800 DC Powered **269.99**
625-46900 AC Powered **319.99**

DIGITAL CENTRE

625-10751 164.99
Small digital centre for independent multiple train control up to eight digital locomotives.

DISPLAY CASE

625-40025 6.99
9-1/2 x 3 x 3"
23.8 x 7.5 x 7.5cm
Show off your favorite Roco engine or rolling stock in this handsome display. A great way to protect against dust and prevent others from handling your models.

MODELTRONICS
LIGHTING ACCESSORIES FOR MODEL LOCOS

Ready-to-run locomotives with special sound system and constant brightness lighting. System is entirely contained in the locomotives, does not require a special power supply and can be used on any conventionally wired layout. Sound is produced by electronics and a speaker that create the whine and clatter of various diesel types, it is adjustable and changes as the engine accelerates and decelerates.

LOCOMOTIVES WITH SOUND

510-8341

POWERED LOCOMOTIVES PKG(2) EA 169.95

510-8321 GP35 Atlantic Coast Line
510-8322 GP35 B&O
510-8323 GP35 Burlington
510-8324 GP35 IC
510-8325 GP35 ATSF Freight
510-8326 GP35 SP
510-8327 GP35 EL
510-8328 GP35 Chessie
510-8331 GP9 B&O
510-8332 GP9 Burlington
510-8333 GP9 ATSF Freight
510-8334 GP9 SP
510-8335 GP9 UP
510-8336 GP9 GN
510-8337 GP9 MILW
510-8341 EMD F7A & B ATSF Passenger
510-8342 EMD F7A & B ATSF Freight
510-8343 EMD F7A & B SP
510-8344 EMD F7A & B BN
510-8345 EMD F7A & B UP
510-8346 EMD F7A & B B&O
510-8347 EMD F7A & B Amtrak

DUMMY LOCOMOTIVES EA 149.95

510-8421 GP35 Atlantic Coast Line
510-8422 GP35 B&O
510-8423 GP35 Burlington
510-8424 GP35 IC
510-8425 GP35 ATSF Freight
510-8426 GP35 SP
510-8427 GP35 EL
510-8428 GP35 Chessie
510-8431 GP9 B&O
510-8432 GP9 CBO
510-8433 GP9 ATSF Freight
510-8434 GP9 SP
510-8435 GP9 UP
510-8436 GP9 GN
510-8437 GP9 MILW
510-8441 EMD F7B ATSF Passenger
510-8442 EMD F7B ATSF Freight
510-8443 EMD F7B SP
510-8444 EMD F7B BN
510-8445 EMD F7B UP
510-8446 EMD F7B B&O
510-8447 EMD F7B Amtrak

DIVISION OF BACHMANN
These HO Scale locomotives feature many separate detail parts, working headlights and authentic paint schemes. Each is ready to run and produced as a limited-run model.

2-8-0 Consolidation w/Smoke 160-11414

GE Dash 8-40CW 160-86026

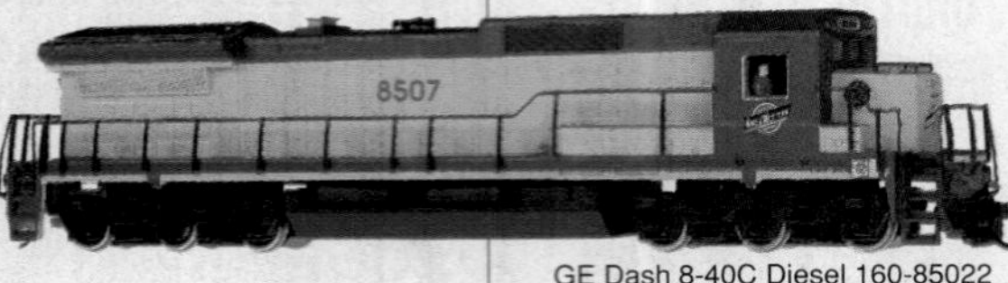

GE Dash 8-40C Diesel 160-85022

EMC Gas Electric Doodlebug 160-81403

4-8-2 USRA 160-81602

F40PH Diesel 160-87014

STEAM LOCOMOTIVES

2-8-0 CONSOLIDATION W/SMOKE EA 135.00

160-11411 UP #721
160-11412 B&O #2784
160-11413 SOU #722
160-11414 WM #763 (Fireball)
160-11415 ATSF *NEW*
160-11416 Boston & Maine *NEW*
160-11418 ROCK *NEW*
160-11419 NKP *NEW*
160-11420 NYC *NEW*
160-11421 Western Pacific *NEW*
160-11422 Clinchfield *NEW*
160-11410 Undecorated

K4 4-6-2 PACIFIC POWERED EA 114.00

160-84013 PRR #3750 w/Tender Post War w/Modern Pilot
160-84014 PRR #1361 w/Tender Post War w/Modern Pilot

4-8-2 USRA LIGHT MOUNTAIN EA 170.00

160-81602 Southern *NEW*
160-81603 UP *NEW*
160-81604 Nashville, Chattanooga & St. Louis *NEW*
160-81605 NH *NEW*
160-81606 MOPAC *NEW*
160-81607 SP *NEW*
160-81601 Painted, Unlettered *NEW*

DIESEL LOCOMOTIVES

GE DASH 8-40CW EA 72.00 (UNLESS NOTED)

160-86025 UP #9375
160-86026 ATSF #804
160-86027 BNSF #814
160-86028 CR #6059
160-86029 CR Quality #6108
160-86030 LMS #728
160-86031 CSX #7654
160-86032 CNW #8612
160-86001 Undecorated

Limited Quantity Available
160-86014 UP #9449 **59.95**
160-86015 UP #9381 **59.95**
160-86016 CSX #7658 **59.95**
160-86022 CNW #8606 **59.95**
160-86023 CNW #8618 **59.95**
160-86024 CNW #8611 **59.95**

EMD DD40AX EA 114.00

160-81303 UP #6922
160-81305 UP #6900
160-81306 UP #6926

160-81307 UP #6941
160-81301 Undecorated

FM H16-44 BABY TRAINMASTER EA 62.00

160-81220 ATSF (Zebra Stripe) #3015
160-81221 B&O (Cobalt Blue) #927
160-81222 PRR #8810
160-81223 CP #8551
160-81224 B&O (Enchantment Blue) #9744
160-81225 N&W #146
160-81226 Virginian #33
160-81227 Southern #2149
160-81228 NH #1605
160-81201 Undecorated

EMD GP30 EA 62.00

160-82013 B&O (Capitol Dome) #6954

160-82018 CP #8200
160-82020 PRR #2206
160-82021 PRR #2215
160-82022 RDG #5515
160-82023 RDG #5518
160-82024 UP #733
160-82026 GN #3008
160-82027 GN #3011
160-82028 NKP #904

Limited Quantity Available
160-82849 Undecorated

GE DASH 8-40C EA 72.00

160-85008 NS #8665
160-85009 CR #6034
160-85010 CSX #7564
160-85011 UP
160-85022 CNW #8507
160-85001 Undecorated

EMD F40 PH EA 70.00

160-87009 New Jersey Transit *NEW*
160-87012 Phase II #209 Amtrak
160-87013 Phase III #231 Amtrak
160-87014 VIA #6406 Canada **59.95**
160-87001 Undecorated

EMD SD45 EA 72.00

160-11614 EL #3614
160-11615 NP #3605
160-11616 GN #408
160-11617 RDG #7603 "Bee Line"
160-11630 PRR #6119
160-11631 BN #6470
160-11632 CR #6148
160-11633 SP "Bloody Nose" #8941
160-11634 UP #14
160-11635 ATSF #5410 Blue & Yellow Warbonnet
160-11601 Undecorated

GE 44-TON SWITCHER EA 52.00

160-80010 GN #50
160-80025 Maine Central #15
160-80026 ATSF Zebra Stripe #464
160-80028 Southern #1951
160-80029 DRGW #40
160-80030 SP #1903
160-80031 PRR #9325
160-80032 Boston & Maine "Minuteman" #115

160-80033 NH #0815
160-80312 B&O #20
160-80617 WM #75
160-80001 Undecorated

GE 70-TON SWITCHER EA 52.00

160-81110 South Pacific (black and orange) #5104

160-81111 Bethlehem Steel #44
160-81009 Painted, Unlettered
160-81101 Undecorated

EMD GP35 EA 62.00

160-11502 UP #749

160-11504 ATSF #2894
160-11506 CR #2271
160-11508 GN #3018
160-11510 PRR #2262
160-11512 CP
160-11514 CSX #4404
160-11501 Undecorated

GAS ELECTRIC

EMC GAS DOODLEBUG EA 72.00

The Doodlebug has been around almost as long as railroading itself, but you better hurry and pick one up today before they're all gone.

160-81403 ATSF (Mustache)
160-81404 B&O
160-81405 UP
160-81406 PRR (Post War)
160-81407 GN
160-81408 ROCK
160-81409 Boston & Maine
160-81410 ATSF War Bonnet
160-81411 CB&Q
160-81412 NYC "Safety Stripe"
160-81401 Undecorated
160-81402 Undecorated Pullman Green

Spectrum® 2-8-0 Consolidation

Named 1998 Product Of The Year Award by the readers of Model Railroader

Our thanks goes to the readers of *Model Railroader* and discerning modelers everywhere who helped make the Spectrum® 2-8-0 Consolidation "1998 Product Of The Year." We are truly honored! In celebration of this achievement, we're adding seven new roadnames to the 2-8-0 lineup this fall. Now you'll have even more ways to enjoy this outstanding locomotive.

From our large scale Shay and HO 2-8-0 (winners of 1997 and 1998 Product of the Year, respectively), to our On30 line and large scale Climax, the recognition of our efforts has inspired us to even greater heights of excellence. We urge you to look for additional product introductions coming your way this fall: our HO Scale Cityscenes® building kits, On30 freight cars and HO USRA 4-8-2 Light Mountain.

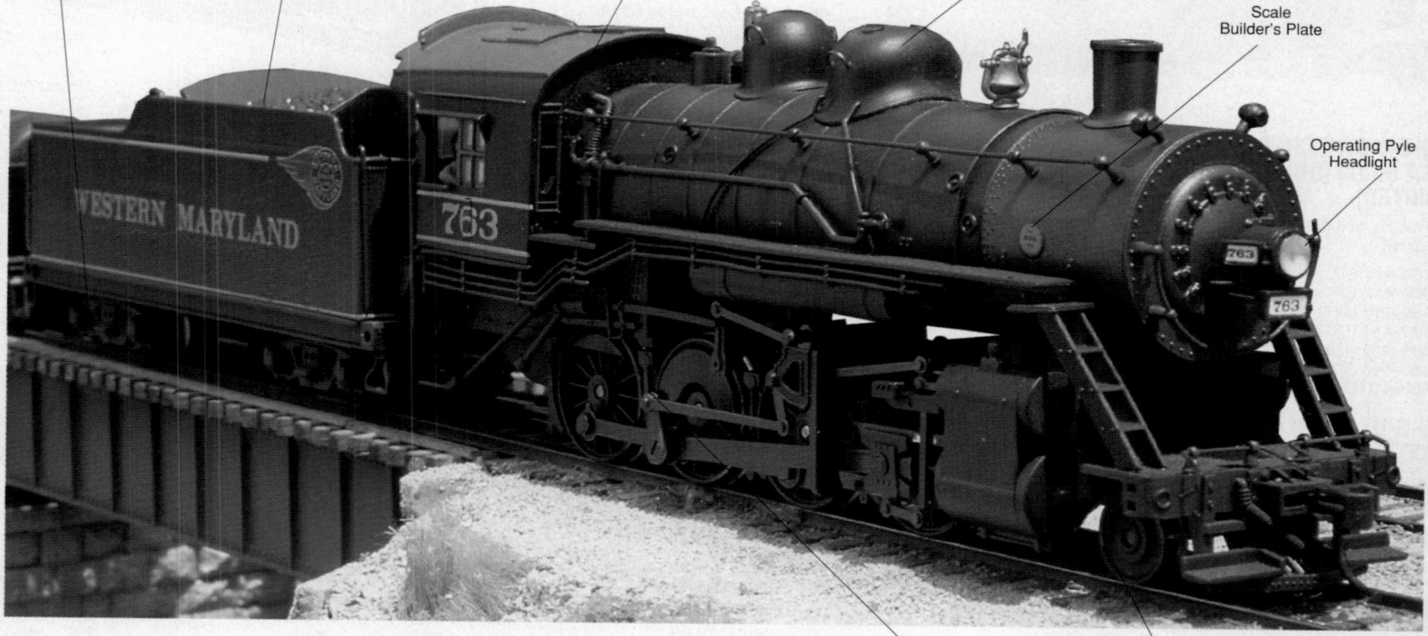

Detailed Andrews Leaf Spring Trucks

Wood-Grained Coal Boards

Superdetailed Injectors

Separate Cab, Domes and Stack for Easier Kitbashing

Scale Builder's Plate

Operating Pyle Headlight

Power Reverse Linkage

Sprung Lead Truck

Additional Locomotive Features

- HO Scale Spectrum Model
- DCC Interface Plug
- Belt Drive for See-Through Clearance Between Boiler and Diecast Frame
- Completely Hidden Drive Train
- Precision, Sealed Can Motor
- Metal Motor Bearings
- Precision-Balanced Brass Flywheel Drive
- Electrical Pickup on All Locomotive Drivers (and Tender Wheels)
- Quiet, Strong Performance Without Traction Tires
- Detailed Leaf Springs Over Drivers
- Sprung Axles on Second and Fourth Drivers for Best Pickup and Tracking Performances
- Accurate Paint Schemes
- Superb Detailing to Match Prototype

Additional Tender Features

- Short Coupled to Locomotive for Excellent Performance on 18" Radius Track
- Detailed Underframe with I-Beam "X" Bracing
- Separately Molded Brake Rigging
- Needlepoint Bearings
- All-Wheel Positive and Negative Pickup
- Sophisticated Electronic Circuitry
- Miniature Power Plugs with Polarized Nickel-Silver Contacts

Roadnames Available Ea 135.00

160-11411 UP
160-11412 Baltimore & Ohio
160-11413 Southern (green)
160-11414 WM Fireball
160-11415 ATSF
160-11416 B&M
160-11418 ROCK
160-11419 NKP
160-11420 NYC
160-11421 WP
160-11422 Clinchfield
160-11410 Unlettered (black)

You Can Expect the Best from Bachmann!

These HO Scale craft train locomotive kits feature diecast zinc boilers and underframes, molded plastic cabs, tenders or bodies and illustrated instructions.

STEAM LOCOMOTIVES

0-6-0 Switcher 480-411

2-8-0 Old Timer 480-481

0-6-0 SWITCHER EA 65.00 (UNLESS NOTED)

This kit includes slope back tender.

480-411 SP
480-412 UP
480-413 NYC
480-414 PRR
480-415 CNW
480-416 CB&Q
480-410 Undecorated **59.95**

0-6-0T SADDLE TANKER KIT EA 45.00 (UNLESS NOTED)

480-421 SP (NM&SP)
480-422 ATSF
480-425 UP
480-426 Weyerhaeuser
480-420 Undecorated **35.00**

2-8-0 CONSOLIDATION EA 95.00 (UNLESS NOTED)

480-461 SP w/Vanderbilt Tender
480-462 Pennsy, Undecorated **85.00**
480-463 PRR w/Coal Tender
480-465 GN, Harriman Boiler w/Oil Tender
480-466 CB&Q, Harriman Boiler w/Oil Tender
480-467 Nickel Plate, Harriman Boiler w/Oil Tender
480-468 NYC, Harriman
480-469 Western Pacific, Harriman
480-470 UP, Harriman
480-471 CNW, Harriman
480-460 Undecorated, Harriman Boiler w/Vanderbilt Tender **85.00**

2-6-2 HARRIMAN STYLE PRAIRIE KIT

Kits feature Harriman type boilers and Vanderbilt tenders.

480-443 SP **82.50**
480-442 Undecorated **75.00**
480-444 Harriman UP **82.50**

2-8-0 OLD TIMER

480-481 SP **99.98**
480-482 ATSF **69.98**
480-483 PRR **69.98**
480-484 UP **69.98**
480-485 DRGW **69.98**
480-486 Maryland & Pennsylvania **69.98**
480-480 Undecorated **59.98**

2-6-0 OLD TIMER EA 80.00 (UNLESS NOTED)

WITH 63" DRIVERS

480-491 B&O
480-492 NYC
480-493 SP
480-494 ATSF
480-495 IC
480-496 Colorado & Southern
480-490 Undecorated **70.00**

WITH 51" DRIVERS

480-511 DRGW El Durando **80.00**
480-512 Mogul V&T Comstock **80.00**
480-510 Undecorated **70.00**

Shay Locomotive 480-370

SHAY LOCOMOTIVES

Kits are powered with a 12V in-line motor, which is included. Frame and boiler insert are diecast metal, while the cab and tender are molded plastic. Models are offered for the 2- and 3-Truck versions in both standard and narrow (HOn3) gauges.

CLASS B 2-TRUCK STANDARD GAUGE

480-361 DRGW **79.98**
480-362 Westside Lumber **79.98**
480-360 Undecorated **69.98**

CLASS B 2-TRUCK HOn3

480-381 DRGW **79.98**
480-380 Undecorated **69.98**

CLASS C 3-TRUCK STANDARD GAUGE EA 89.98 (UNLESS NOTED)

480-371 Sierra Railroad
480-372 UP
480-373 Little River Lumber
480-374 Ely Thomas Lumber Co. ***NEW***
480-375 Pickering Lumber Co. ***NEW***
480-370 Undecorated **79.98**

CLASS C 3-TRUCK HOn3

480-391 DRGW **89.98**
480-390 Undecorated **79.98**

4-4-2 SANTA FE STYLE ATLANTIC

480-431 ATSF **95.00**
480-430 Undecorated **89.98**

4-4-2 ATLANTIC KIT

Kits feature a Harriman Boiler with Vanderbilt Tender.

480-429 SP **79.98**
480-434 UP **79.98**
480-428 Undecorated **69.98**

2-6-2 SANTA FE STYLE PRAIRIE

480-441 ATSF **95.00**
480-440 Undecorated **89.98**

2-6-2 "PENNSY STYLE" LOCO

480-451 PRR w/Coal Tender **95.00**
480-450 Undecorated **85.00**

4-4-2 "PENNSY STYLE" LOCO

480-436 PRR w/Coal Tender **85.00**
480-435 Undecorated **75.00**

4-6-0 "PENNSY STYLE" LOCO

480-453 PRR w/Coal Tender **82.50**
480-452 Undecorated **75.00**

2-6-0 Old Timer 480-510

2-6-2 Prairie 480-440

2-6-2 "Pennsy Style" 480-451

4-4-2 "Pennsy Style" 480-436

4-6-0 TEN WHEELER KIT

480-454 CP, Harriman Boiler w/Coal Tender **85.00**
480-456 SP, Harriman Type Boiler & Vanderbilt Tender **85.00**
480-457 UP, Harriman **85.00**
480-455 Undecorated, Harriman Boiler w/Vanderbilt Tender **75.00**

3-IN-1 HOn3 STATIC STEAM

480-1550 3-in-1 HOn3 Static Steam Articulated Kit **23.50**
This unpowered kit features one molded plastic saddle tanker body, plastic detail parts, metal "outside frame" chassis with two sets of steam cylinders, counter weights and main rods. Unassembled drivers consist of brass rims, steel axles, molded centers, plus screws. Includes instructions to kitbash one of the following: 2-4-4-0T, 0-8-0T (logging type), or 0-8-0T (plantation type).

2-8-0 CONSOLIDATION, HOn3

480-472 Outside Frame, Undecorated **80.00**
480-473 Inside Frame, Undecorated **80.00**
480-474 Outside Frame, DRGW **90.00**
480-477 Inside Frame, DRGW **90.00**

DIESEL LOCOMOTIVES

Alco RS3 480-2385

Box Cab Diesel Track Cleaner Kit 480-2796

CLIMAX 2-TRUCK CLASS "B" KIT EA 29.98 (UNLESS NOTED)

"Old Timer" logging complex 2-truck locos are prepainted and lettered.

480-2772 White Pass & Yukon Lumber Co.
480-2773 Moose Jaws Saskachewan Lumber

480-2774 DRGW
480-2770 Undecorated **26.50**
480-2771 Undecorated (brown)

ALCO RS-3 READY-TO-RUN EA 75.00 (UNLESS NOTED)

Features new power mechanism and detailed body, which is painted and lettered in appropriate colors. Includes add-on details and wire handrails.

480-2371 RDG
480-2372 DRGW
480-2373 ROCK
480-2374 CR
480-2375 Gulf, Mobile & Ohio
480-2376 National Railways of Mexico
480-2377 Green Bay & Western
480-2378 MP
480-2381 WM (black, yellow)
480-2382 ATSF (black, white)
480-2383 NYC (black, white, red)
480-2384 CN (black, white)
480-2385 SP (black, red)
480-2386 UP (yellow, gray)
480-2387 CNW (yellow, green)
480-2388 PRR (green, yellow)
480-2389 BN (cascade green, black, white)
480-2390 Rutland
480-2391 NH
480-2392 Frisco
480-2393 MKT
480-2394 Spokane, Portland & Seattle
480-2395 LV
480-2396 Boston & Maine
480-2397 Vermont Railway
480-2398 Amtrak
480-2399 N&W
480-2380 Undecorated **72.50**

BOX CAB DIESEL KIT EA 29.98 (UNLESS NOTED)

This kit features molded plastic body and zinc underframe.

480-2811 Decorated
480-2812 Maintenance of Way
480-2813 Ingersoll-Rand
480-2814 Ford
480-2815 UP
480-2816 Erie
480-2810 Undecorated **26.50**

BOX CAB DIESEL TRACK CLEANER KIT

This track cleaning diesel works without fluid! The model is equipped with a 12 volt in-line motor and all-metal flywheel, plus spring-loaded track cleaning plungers with flat sanding discs that ride on rail tops and clean track.

480-2806 Decorated **35.00**
480-2807 MOW **35.00**
480-2805 Undecorated **29.98**
480-2796 Undecorated, Unpowered **12.50**
480-2799 Accessory Kit **2.98**
This kit includes track cleaning assemblies to convert the standard Roundhouse box cab diesel to a track cleaner. Complete kit with instructions.

480-2835 Replacement Discs pkg(12) **1.00**

TENDERS

TENDER EA 15.00

Kits feature black plastic bodies with diecast zamac underframes. Tenders are undecorated and include trucks.

480-400 Slope Back (Switcher)
480-401 Oil (ATSF Type)
480-402 Coal (PRR Type)
480-403 Vanderbilt
This kit is convertible to either coal or oil.

480-404 "Old Timer" Coal

480-405 DRGW HOn3

DETAILING SET

LOCO DETAILING SET

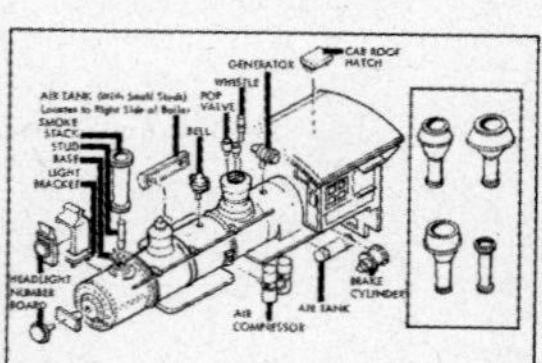

This set includes molded plastic detail parts; less cab and boiler.

480-2980 Baldwin Detailing Set pkg(26 pieces) **3.50**
480-2981 Shay Detailing Pack **6.50**

VOLLMER

IMPORTED FROM GERMANY BY WALTHERS

Complete HO Scale catenary system is designed to provide overhead power or can be used for nonoperating catenary with standard track power. Based on German Railways prototypes, equipment can be adapted for any model railroad.

All wiring is made from chrome-nickel steel for improved conductivity. Masts are molded in break-resistant plastic to prevent short-circuits. Each is approximately 3-7/8" tall (97mm) and provides a wire height of about 3" (76mm).

CATENARY

Catenary Wire 770-1315

Catenary Wire 770-1339

MASTS

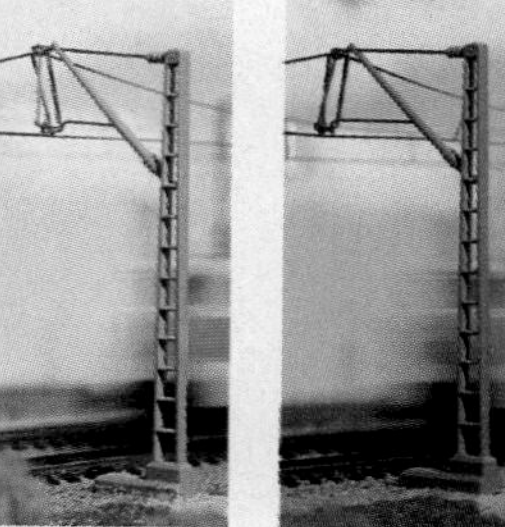

770-1300 770-1301

770-1300 Mast w/Short Arm pkg(10) **43.99**
770-1301 Mast w/Long Arm pkg(10) **43.99**

770-1304 770-1308

770-1304 Terminal/Feeder pkg(5) **39.99**
770-1308 Tower Mast pkg(10) **64.99**
770-1311 Registration For Tower Mast pkg(10) **19.99**
For use with #1300 and #1301.

770-1314 Mast Bracket pkg(10) **22.99**

Limited Quantity Available
770-4021 Mast Base **.99**

WIRE

770-1310 Cross Span w/Accessories 310mm Long **12.99**
770-1315 Bridging Section pkg(5) **17.99**
Used between two bridges.

770-1316 Bridging Section pkg(5) **13.99**
770-1320 Insulating Unit 1" pkg(5) **19.99**

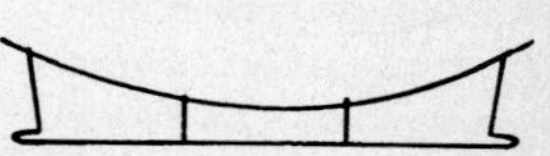

770-1331 3.9" pkg(10) **27.99**
For radii under 10" 280 mm.

770-1335 5.5" Long 140mm pkg(10) **28.99**
For radii over 10" 280 mm.

770-1339 1.95 x 7.4" 190mm pkg(10) **31.99**
For radii over 17.5" 437 mm.

770-1343 Contact Wire 15.8" pkg(10) **38.99**
770-1345 For Loco Shed #5750 pkg(2) **8.99**
770-1347 For Loco Shed #5752 pkg(2) **10.99**
770-1349 For Loco Shed #5760 pkg(2) **10.99**
770-1351 For Bridge #2506 pkg(2) **10.99**

SET

770-1390 Overhead Set **149.99**
This set includes 9 #1300, 10 #1301, 1 #1304, 18 #1335 and 2 contact wires 15.6" long.

Information STATION

The Whyte Numbering System

2-6-0? 0-4-0? 2-8-2? What do all these numbers mean when looking at a steam locomotive? This series of numbers is part of a classification method called the Whyte System, a United States standard reference for steam power.

The Whyte System came into being at the dawn of the 20th century. A gentleman named F.M. Whyte created a system of classifying steam locomotives by counting the wheels on both sides of the locomotive, but not counting the tender wheels or trucks. Using the number scheme 2-4-6T as an example, the 2 indicates there are two small wheels on the pilot truck (at the front of the locomotive). The 4 indicates the four drivers in the middle. The 6 designates the six wheels at the rear on the trailing truck. If the steam locomotive is a tank engine (a steam loco without a tender), the Whyte system adds a T to the final number.

The Whyte system helped decipher each railroad's unique practices of identifying engines by a class, series numbers or a specific nickname. For example, Soo Line 4-8-4s were actually the O-20 class, but were also known as the 5000s, (since they were numbered 5000-5004) or simply as "Northerns." (Many of these nicknames were universally used and understood, so that calling an engine a "Northern" referred to a 4-8-4 on almost every railroad.)

TRAIN SETS

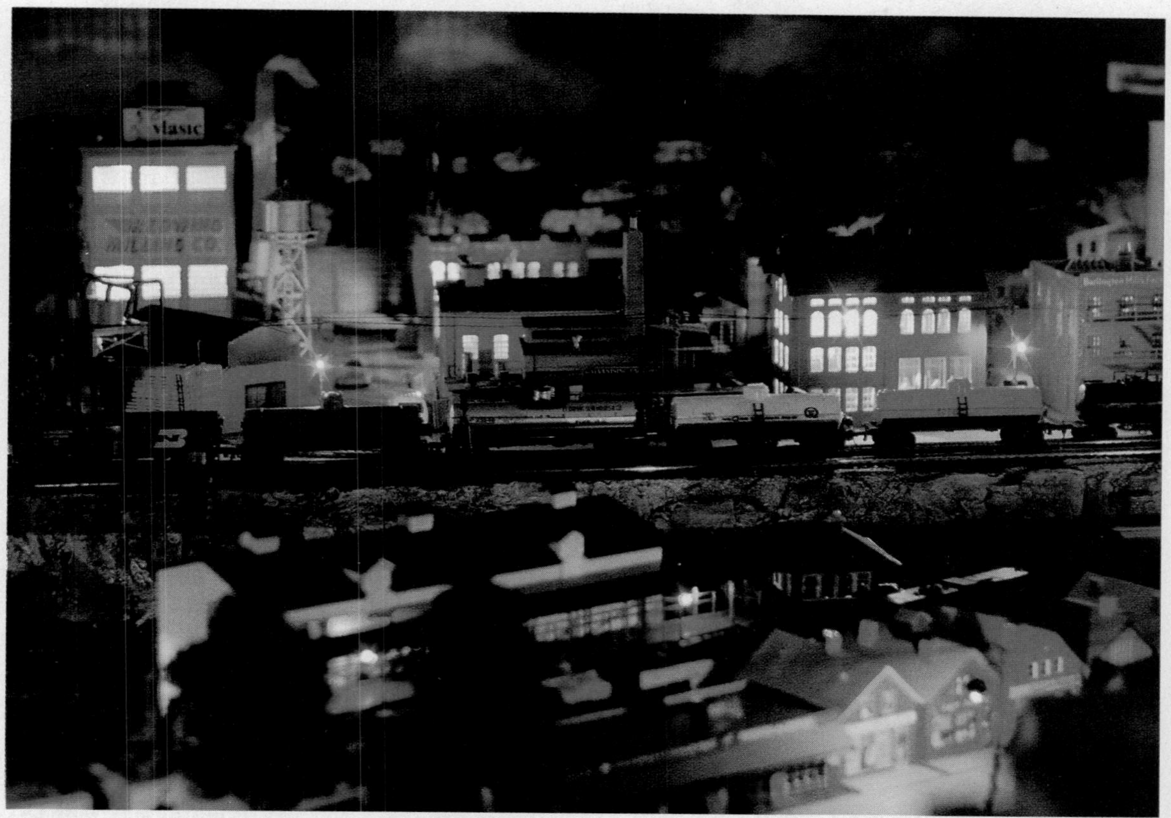

Models and Photo by Jim Lipnos

The last rays of sunset glow from the western sky. While the day may be over for some, for others it is just beginning. And for the railroad, the workday is never really over. City lights gleam as second shift employees keep the machinery running. Headlights and signals burn brightly along the railroad, keeping freight and commuters on the move.

Brakes squeal as a wayfreight eases off the main and into the maze of industrial yard trackage. The head and rear brakeman have plenty of work tonight. With lanterns gleaming, waybills are checked, switches thrown, cars spotted, loaded cars picked up and made into new trains.

All it takes is a little imagination to turn a basic set into a working railroad. Jim Lipnos' layout in Cleveland, Ohio, reflects his long-time love for the hobby. He admits his layout has never truly been completed, but it now occupies an impressive 400 square feet of the family room! This busy night scene shows just a few of the 250-plus buildings along the right-of-way.

TRAINLINE®
by WALTHERS

TRAINLINE® DELUXE SETS

Enjoy years of model railroading fun when you start out with the very best, Walthers Trainline® Deluxe. Each set features a powerful GP9M diesel loco with working headlight and many other features. Freight cars are ready-to-run, with a 40' plug door box car, a 40' steel reefer, a 40' hopper, a tank car and a bay window caboose that's painted and lettered to match the engine, included in each set. A solid state MRC™ 1300 power pack is provided for smooth, dependable operation.

Best of all, you choose the track system that's right for you; sets are available with Atlas® Code 100 or Bachmann EZ-Track® to meet the needs of any modeler. All sets include a 36 x 45" oval, and can easily be expanded with additional products from your local hobby dealer. (You'll find complete listings for both lines in the Track Section of this book.)

Daily New Arrival Updates! Visit Walthers Web site at **www.walthers.com**

SETS WITH ATLAS® TRACK EA 106.98

Traditional sectional track system features Code 100 nickel silver rail for improved electrical conductivity and engine performance.

931-20 UP
931-22 CSX
931-23 NS
931-24 ATSF
931-25 CR
931-26 Wisconsin Central
931-30 CP
931-31 BNSF (orange, green w/red caboose) *NEW*

SETS WITH BACHMANN EZ-TRACK® EA 116.98

Designed for fast and easy set-up, each section is fully assembled with a unique plastic roadbed. Special clips lock sections together, and replace rail joiners with built-in electrical contacts for perfect assembly every time. Can be set-up on a rug or any other suitable surface in minutes.

931-70 UP
931-72 CSX
931-73 NS
931-74 ATSF
931-75 CR
931-76 Wisconsin Central
931-80 CP
931-81 BNSF (orange, green w/red caboose) *NEW*

- **Solid state MRC™ Railpower 1300 power pack. Simple two-wire hook-up to track. Master on-off switch means no more plugging and unplugging. AC terminals for accessories such as switch machines and lights.**

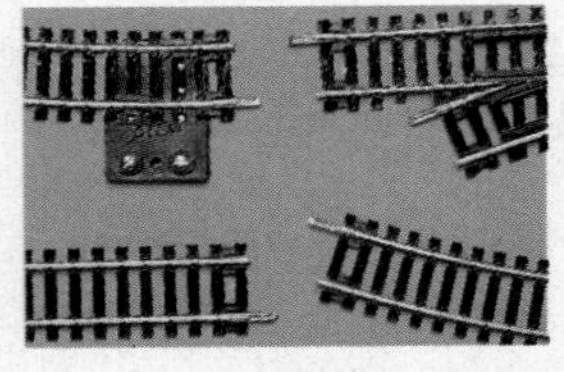

- **Sets come with your choice of Atlas or Bachmann track systems.**

- **Features a rugged GP9M Locomotive for hauling heavy loads.**
- **Highly detailed, ready-to-run freight cars include: a 40' Plug Door Box Car, a 40' Steel Reefer, a 40' Hopper, a Tank Car, and a Bay Window Caboose.**
- **A Big 36 x 54" oval of Atlas® Nickel Silver, or Bachmann E-Z Track® that can be expanded as your interest in the hobby grows.**
- **Easy to operate MRC™ 1300 Power Pack.**
- **A Lifetime Limited Warranty.**
- **Derailment-reducing couplers to keep your train on track.**

TRAINLINE® SUPER-POWER HO TRAIN SET

TRAINLINE® SUPER POWER SETS

Step up to big time railroading when you take the throttle of the Trainline® Super Power Set. A great start for any new modeler, each complete HO Scale set includes a solid state MRC™ 1300 power pack to insure smooth, steady operation and outstanding performance from your engine. Pulling the train is the highly detailed GE Dash 8-40B, based on diesels now in service with many major railroads. You also get six freight cars: Stand-Alone Double-Stack Car with two removable containers, Flat Car with removable trailer, 50' Airslide® Covered Hopper, Bethgon Coal Hopper, Box Car and Cushioned Steel Coil Car with removable hoods. For the finishing touch, there's a colorful bay window caboose, painted to match the engine. And, the set also comes with a Cornerstone Series® United Trucking Terminal structure kit. This easy-to-build model features plastic parts molded in color, complete instructions and colorful decals.

Best of all, you choose the track system that's right for you; sets are available with Atlas® Code 100 or Bachmann EZ-Track® to meet the needs of any modeler. All sets include a 36 x 45" oval, and can easily be expanded with additional products from your local hobby dealer. (You'll find complete listings for both lines in the Track Section of this book.)

SETS WITH ATLAS® TRACK EA 159.98

Traditional sectional track system features Code 100 nickel silver rail for improved electrical conductivity and engine performance.

931-10 ATSF (Super Fleet Colors)
931-11 Union Pacific
931-12 Conrail
931-13 Norfolk Southern
931-14 CSX
931-15 BNSF

SETS WITH BACHMANN EZ-TRACK® EA 169.98

Designed for fast and easy set-up, each section is fully assembled with a unique plastic roadbed. Special clips lock sections together, and replace rail joiners with built-in electrical contacts for perfect assembly every time. Can be set-up on a rug or any other suitable surface in minutes.

931-90 ATSF
931-91 Union Pacific
931-92 Conrail
931-93 Norfolk Southern
931-94 CSX
931-95 BNSF

• **Solid state MRC™ Railpower 1300 power pack. Features advanced circuitry for superior performance at slow speeds. Simple two-wire hook-up to track. Master on-off switch means no more plugging and unplugging. Built-in circuit protector. AC terminals for accessories such as switch machines and lights.**

• **Powerful Dash 8-40B locomotive featuring can motor, dual flywheels and reversing headlights. Pulled more than 30 cars on our test track.**

• **Walthers Cornerstone Series® United Trucking Terminal. Easy to build, detailed structure kit has plastic parts molded in colors.**

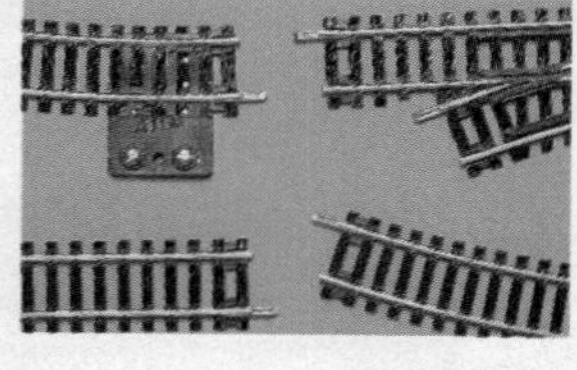

• **Sets come with your choice of Atlas or Bachmann track systems.**

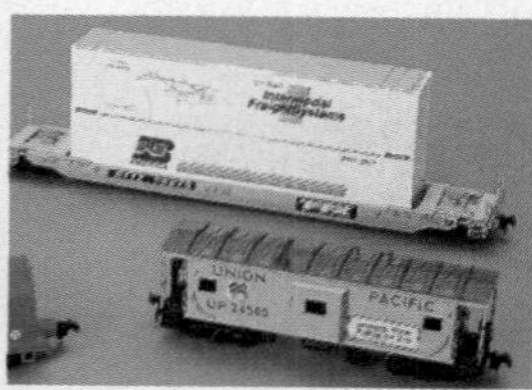

• **Six ready-to-run freight cars and Bay Window Caboose.**

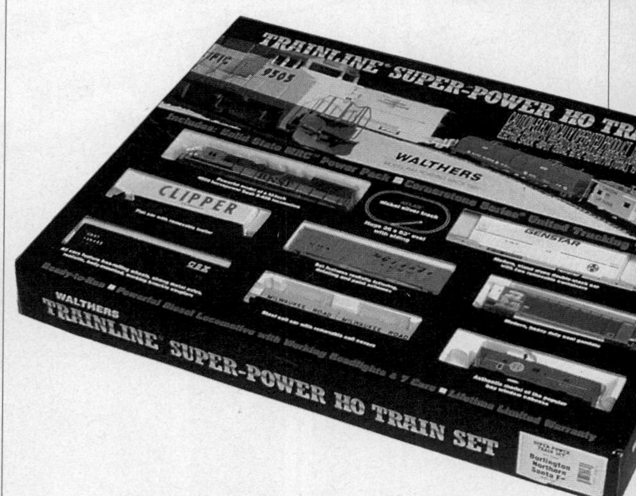

- **A Powerful Dash 8-40B Locomotive.**
- **Seven ready-to-run freight cars including: a 55' Cushion Coil Car with removable covers, a modern Stand Alone Double-Stack Well Car with 2 removable containers, a 40' Plug Door Box Car, 39' Airslide® Covered Hopper, a Flatcar with removable Trailer, a Bethgon Coalporter™ Gondola, and a Bay Window Caboose.**
- **Easy to operate MRC™ 1300 Power Pack.**
- **A Cornerstone Series® United Trucking Terminal.**
- **Derailment-reducing couplers to keep your train on track.**
- **A Lifetime Limited Warranty.**

TRAINLINE®
by WALTHERS

AMTRAK LUXURY LINER

931-42 Revised Amtrak Luxury Liner Train Set **159.98**
All the color and excitement of contemporary passenger trains comes rumbling down the rails aboard the revised Amtrak Luxury Liner! This HO Scale set features colorful, modern equipment and is perfect for beginners or experienced modelers.

Leading the way is the Trainline® Dash 8-40B diesel, painted in the same red, white, blue and silver scheme used on the real engines. Passengers will enjoy a spectacular view of the scenery from the three bi-level Superliner II cars. There's a Coach and a Diner, plus, this revised set now includes a Sightseer Lounge car! All three cars are painted in the current Phase IV scheme and come fully assembled, with working knuckle couplers.

To start service right away, the set includes a 44 x 71" 110 x 177.5cm oval of Atlas® nickel silver track with big 22" 55cm radius curves. An MRC 1300 power pack is also included to insure smooth and steady operation. The set can be expanded at any time with additional track (See the complete line of Atlas track and accessories in the Track section.), cars (See Walthers listing in the Passenger Cars Section.) and other accessories, available separately. All items included in the set are covered by a lifetime limited warranty.

Best of all, you get this complete set - a $185.88 value if purchased separately - for only $159.98!

New Sightseer Lounge

Amtrak Luxury Liner Train Set

TRAINLINE®

by WALTHERS

READY-TO-RUN LOCOMOTIVES

Every railroad needs plenty of motive power, like the Trainline® EMD GP9M, GE Dash 8-40B, Alco FAs, and new GP15-1.

These models will be the workhorses of your model railroad, with great features like heavy die-cast metal frames for superior performance, powerful can motors with flywheels, eight-wheel electrical pick-up and drive, and working headlights.

See the Locomotives section for a complete listing of roadnames and roadnumbers for these engines.

EASY SNAP-TOGETHER ACCESSORIES

These great-looking kits are a snap to build! Each features snap-together construction, and plastic parts molded in colors, so no painting is needed.

WHISTLE STOP STATION

931-800 Whistle Stop Station **9.98**
It's "All Aboard" at the Whistle Stop Station, where passengers and freight are ready for boarding. Includes crates and stickers with station names.

SAWMILL

Preproduction models shown assembled; colors and some details may vary.

931-801 Sawmill with Accessories **24.98**
You can almost smell the sawdust coming from the Trainline® Sawmill! This deluxe kit includes a Working Dump Car, Logs, Lumber Carrier and Sawdust Burner. For added fun, the dump car empties its load of logs with the pull of a lever!

See the complete listing in the Locomotives Section of this Catalog

F40PH

931-305

GE DASH 8-40B EA 59.98

931-173

EMD GP9M AND CABOOSE SETS EA 39.98

931-701

ALCO FA1 AND FB1 29.98

931-203/931-262

GP15-1

931-352

TRAINLINE®

by WALTHERS

READY-TO-RUN FREIGHT CARS

Flat cars, tank cars, logging cars, box cars - you can move all kinds of freight down the line aboard Trainline® freight cars. Finished in authentic paint schemes, these detailed models are ready to run, with free-rolling wheels, strong metal axles and body-mounted couplers.

40' X-29 Box Car 931-621

40' Plug Door Box Car-Track Cleaning Car 931-751

40' Tank Car 931-612

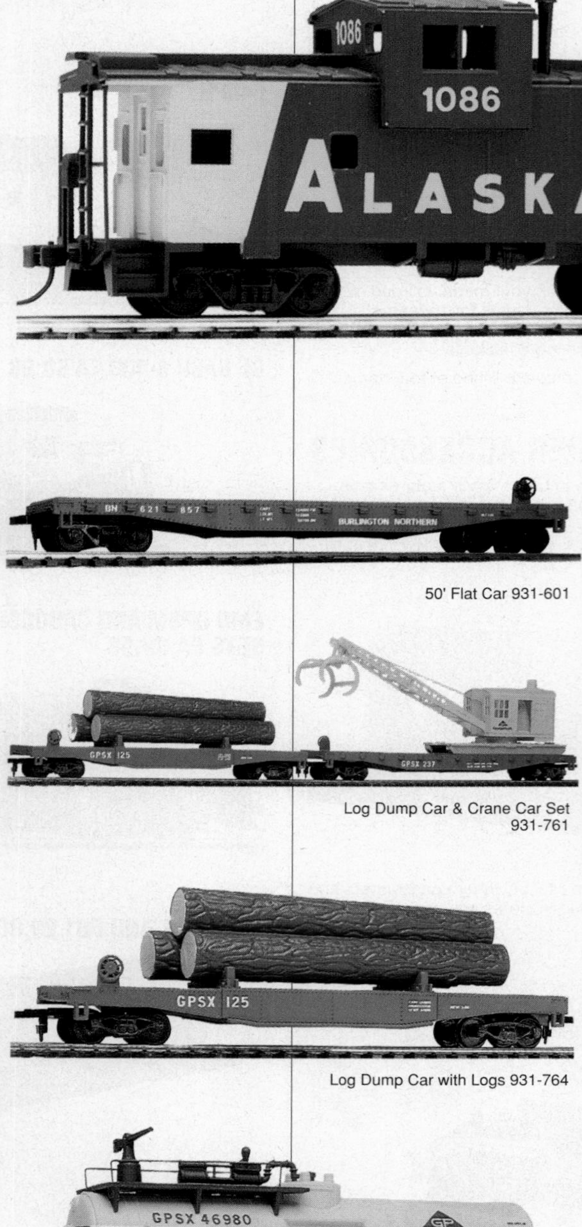

Wide Vision Caboose 931-526

50' Flat Car 931-601

Log Dump Car & Crane Car Set 931-761

Log Dump Car with Logs 931-764

Firefighting Car 931-767

40' X-29 BOX CAR EA 5.98

931-621 Pennsylvania
931-622 Reading
931-623 Nickel Plate Road

40' PLUG DOOR BOX CAR-TRACK CLEANING CAR EA 15.98

Just couple this car into your train and start cleaning! Cleans tracks for better performance while you run your trains. Soft-abrasive pad mounted under car wipes away grime without scratching rail surfaces.

931-751 Union Pacific
931-752 CSX

40' TANK CAR EA 5.98

931-611 Sinclair
931-612 Gulf
931-613 Standard
931-614 Conoco

50' FLAT CAR EA 4.98

931-601 Burlington Northern
931-602 Conrail
931-603 Union Pacific
931-604 Norfolk Southern

LOGGING CARS

931-761 Log Dump Car & Crane Car Set **11.98**
Crane car features movable cab, boom and grapple. Log dump car will dump included logs when used with Trainline® Sawmill #931-801.

931-764 Log Dump Car with Logs **6.98**
Same car as in set listed above, but with different road number.

931-767 Firefighting Car **6.98**
Complete with pump details and movable water cannon!

WIDE VISION CABOOSE EA 6.98

Keep a safe eye on your train from the cupola of one of these cabooses. Models are painted to match roadnames in Trainline® train sets and on Trainline® locos.

931-501 Burlington Northern
931-502 Union Pacific
931-503 Santa Fe
931-504 Canadian National
931-505 CSX
931-506 Conrail
931-508 Norfolk Southern
931-509 Pennsylvania
931-510 CNW
931-514 CP
931-516 SOO
931-517 Southern
931-518 Wisconsin Central
931-520 BNSF
931-521 Illinois Central
931-523 Amtrak
931-524 Chessie System
931-525 DRGW
931-526 Alaska RR ***NEW***
931-527 US Army ***NEW***

Limited Quantity Available
931-511 Milwaukee Road
931-512 Ashley, Drew & Northern
931-515 Guilford (B&M)
931-519 Montana Rail Link

Ready-to-run train sets are decorated in authentic colors.

FREIGHT SETS

Sets include locomotive, three freight cars, caboose, Bachmann E-Z Track® and Athearn Trainpak (Power Pack).

THUNDER RAILS FREIGHT TRAIN SETS EA 119.50

These complete starter sets are a great way to introduce the fun of model railroading to kids of any age. Each is complete with a powered diesel loco with working headlight, three freight cars, matching caboose, power pack and nickel silver E-Z Track® from Bachmann.

140-1034 With BNSF GP38-2
140-1036 CP w/Beaver Logo
NEW

Limited Quantity Available
140-1031 With SOU GP59

YARD MASTER FREIGHT TRAIN SET EA 119.50

Hours of family fun are packed into these brand-new sets! Each is complete with a powered SW1500 loco with a working headlight, three freight cars, matching caboose, power pack and nickel silver E-Z Track® from Bachmann.

140-1044 With BNSF SW1500
140-1045 With NASA SW1500
NEW

Limited Quantity Available
140-1042 With CSX SW1500 (yellow, blue and gray)
140-1043 With UP SW1500 (yellow & gray)

HERITAGE SERIES FREIGHT TRAIN SETS EA 119.50

One of the most famous American diesels, the F7A, leads these colorful sets. Ready for years of modeling fun, each includes a powered loco with working headlight, three freight cars, matching caboose, power pack and nickel silver E-Z Track® from Bachmann.

140-1051 With ATSF F7A (warbonnet red & silver)
140-1057 With SOU F7A

Limited Quantity Available
140-1052 With UP F7A (yellow and gray)

1999 CHRISTMAS TRAIN SET

140-1099 129.50 ***NEW***
Featuring exclusive packaging and graphics created by railroad artist Ernie Towler, this is the first Christmas train set produced by Athearn. Set includes an F7A loco, three freight cars, a caboose, Athearn TrainPak power supply, 14 pieces of Bachmann Nickel-Silver E-Z Track® and high quality knuckle couplers. Only 2000 of this limited edition set are being made.

PASSENGER SETS

Set includes locomotive, three passenger cars, Bachmann E-Z Track®, and AthearnTrainpak (Power Pack).

EXPEDITION SERIES PASSENGER SET EA 119.50

Now ready for boarding on track one, these sets bring back happy memories for anyone who ever traveled by train, or dreams of those glory days. On the head end is the classic F7A with working headlight. A trio of matching passenger cars make up the consist. Each set is complete with power pack and nickel silver E-Z Track® from Bachmann.

140-1060 With Amtrak F7A (Phase III red, white & blue)
140-1061 With ATSF F7A (warbonnet red & silver)

Limited Quantity Available
140-1062 With UP F7A (yellow and gray)

COMPLETE STARTER SETS EA 149.95

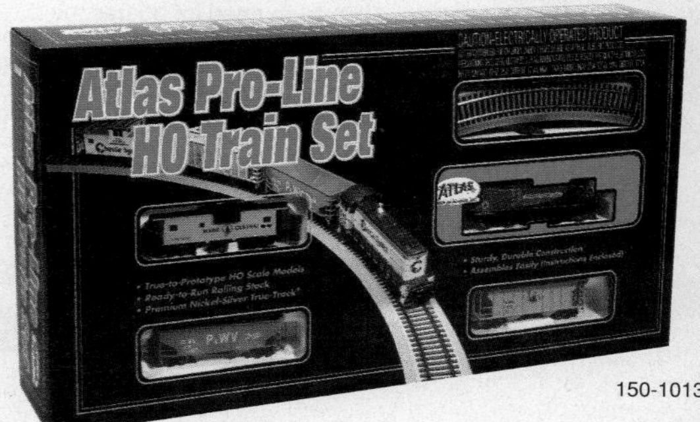

150-1013

These train sets, available in four popular roadnames, offer everything you need to get started in HO Scale model railroading. Each set includes an Alco S-2 or S-4 locomotive, two freight cars, a caboose, True-Track with roadbed, one structure kit, terminal joiners and a Custom Power 1700 power pack.

150-1010 Santa Fe, S-2
150-1011 Burlington, S-2
150-1012 Chessie, S-4
150-1013 Maine Central, S-4

Roadname Abbreviation Key

ATSF Santa Fe
B&O Baltimore & Ohio
BN Burlington Northern
BNSF Burlington Northern Santa Fe (1996 Merger)
C&O Chesapeake & Ohio
CB&Q Chicago Burlington & Quincy
CN Canadian National
CNJ Central Railroad of New Jersey
CNW Chicago & North Western
CP Canadian Pacific
CR Conrail
CSX CSX
D&H Delaware & Hudson
DRGW Rio Grande
EL Erie Lackawanna
GN Great Northern
IC Illinois Central
L&N Louisville & Nashville
LV Lehigh Valley
MILW Milwaukee Road
MKT Katy (Missouri, Kansas, Texas)
MON Monon
MP Missouri Pacific
MOW Maintenance Of Way
N&W Norfolk & Western
NH New Haven
NKP Nickel Plate Road
NP Northern Pacific
NS Norfolk Southern
NYC New York Central
PFE Pacific Fruit Express
PRR Pennsylvania
RDG Reading
ROCK Rock Island
SOO Soo Line
SOU Southern Railway
SSW St. Louis Southwestern (Cotton Belt)
SP Southern Pacific
UP Union Pacific
WC Wisconsin Central
WM Western Maryland

TRAIN SETS

These sets include E-Z Track®, the snap-fit track system that can be set up almost anywhere. There's no need for boards, nails, screws or tools. E-Z Track combines track and roadbed together into one track section, so you can get your trains up and running in minutes. Track sections are designed with a special snap-fit locking feature that holds the pieces securely together, for smooth and trouble-free operation.

The Monopoly Train 160-1201

OLD TYME VILLAGE FREIGHT

160-604 133.00
4-4-0 steam loco with tender and operating headlight, water tank car, box car, wood gondola, flat car, bobber caboose, 47 x 38" oval of E-Z Track, power pack and instructions.

OLD TYME VILLAGE EXPRESS

160-605 133.00
4-4-0 steam loco with tender and operating headlight, old-time combine, two old-time coach cars, 47 x 38" oval of E-Z Track, power pack and instructions.

WHITE CHRISTMAS® EXPRESS

160-609 134.00
Features E-Z Track snap-fit track and roadbed system, and E-Z plug-in wiring. The train is headed by a USRA 0-6-0 steam locomotive and tender with operating headlight. Locomotives and festively decorated freight cars all feature magnetically operated E-Z Mate® knuckle couplers operated by an under-track magnet with brakeman figure. This set is powered by a UL-listed power pack and includes an illustrated instruction manual.

OVERLAND LIMITED

160-614 200.00
Union Pacific 4-8-4 steam loco with tender and operating smoke and headlight, 3-dome tank car, grain car, flat car with logs, center-flow hopper, open quad offset hopper, two plug door box cars, wood stock car, wide vision caboose, 65 x 38" oval of E-Z Track, power pack and instructions.

GOLDEN SPIKE® SET

160-615 129.00
Features E-Z Track snap-fit track and roadbed system, and E-Z plug-in wiring. The train is hauled by a EMD GP40 diesel locomotive with operating headlight. Freight cars include an open quad hopper, plug door box car, single dome tank car, stock car and off-center caboose. Accessories include signal bridge, suburban station, 48 figures, 36 telephone poles, 48 street signs, UL-listed power pack and illustrated instruction manual. Runs on a 65 x 38" oval.

Old Tyme Village Freight 160-604

Old Tyme Village Express 160-605

RAIL KING

160-616 105.00
Lay claim to your kingdom with the Rail King Set! The Rail King features E-Z Track snap-fit track and roadbed system, and E-Z plug-in wiring, so setting up the 47 x 38" oval and 20" siding is easy. A powerful EMD GP40 diesel locomotive with operating headlight leads the train. Freight cars include an open quad hopper, mechanical reefer and off-center caboose. Extras include signal bridge, 36 figures, 24 telephone poles, 48 railroad and street signs. The set is powered by a UL-listed power pack and illustrated instruction manual.

CASEY JONES®

Limited Quantity Available
160-617 140.00
Features E-Z Track snap-fit track and roadbed system, and E-Z plug-in wiring, so setting up the 56 x 38" oval and 20" siding is a breeze! The locomotive is a 0-6-0 steam locomotive and tender with operating headlight and smoke. Freight cars include a plug door box car, single dome tank car, open quad hopper and an off-center caboose. Accessories include suburban station, signal bridge, 48 figures, 36 telephone poles, 48 railroad and street signs, a UL-listed power pack and illustrated instruction manual.

THE CHALLENGER

Limited Quantity Available
160-621 53.00
Set features a diesel locomotive with eight-wheel pickup and operating headlight, two freight cars, caboose, 38 x 38" circle of E-Z Track, plug-in wiring and power pack.

CANNONBALL EXPRESS® W/MOTORIZED HAND CAR

160-625 121.00
F9 Diesel locomotive with Lustra Chrome finish, powered hand car, gondola, open quad hopper, plug door box car, steel off-center caboose, 65 x 38" oval of E-Z Track®, two switches, phone poles, figures, street signs and power pack.

CHATTANOOGA CHOO CHOO™

160-626 145.00 ***NEW***
Set is led by a 0-6-0 steam locomotive and tender with operating headlight and smoke. Freight cars to follow include a plug door box car, open quad hopper, single-dome tank car and an off-center caboose. Train set runs on a 47 x 38" oval of track. Accessories include suburban station, signal bridge, 48 figures, 36 telephone poles, 48 railroad and street signs and a power pack. Instructional VHS video included.

SILVER STREAK

160-627 110.00 ***NEW***
Pulled by an EMD GP40 diesel locomotive with Lustra Chrome finish and operating headlight, this train set includes a gondola, single-dome tank car, open quad hopper, wood stock car, reefer and an off-center caboose. A 56 x 38" oval of track is included. Accessories include a 14-piece pier set, signal bridge, 12 crossing signals and gates, 48 figures, 36 telephone poles, 48 railroad and street signs and a power pack. Assembly instructions are provided on a VHS video cassette.

THE MONOPOLY TRAIN

160-1201 200.00 ***NEW***
This collector series train set is inspired by the classic Parker Brothers board game. Includes 0-6-0 steam locomotive and tender with operating headlight and smoke, four box cars and an off-center caboose. Set runs on a 47 x 47" E-Z Track oval. Accessories include 24 street signs with Monopoly property names, a 53 x 53" vinyl mat recreating the appearance of the Monopoly board game, a snap-fit jail/police station building, power pack and assembly video.

THE GALAXY

Limited Quantity Available
160-610 65.00
F9 diesel loco with Lustra Chrome finish and operating headlight, open quad hopper, plug door box car, steel off-center caboose, 47 x 38" oval of E-Z Track, 24 figures, 12 telephone poles, 24 railroad and street signs, power pack and instructions.

SILVER SERIES® TRAIN SETS

Premium quality sets featuring an oval of nickel-silver E-Z Track, a Spectrum® Series locomotive with operating headlight, upgraded rolling stock (with detailed underframes, brass nonmagnetic axles and body-mounted couplers) and a Spectrum power pack.

MOUNTAINEER EA 118.00

Sets feature GP35 loco and three freight cars.

160-1101 ATSF
160-1116 CR
160-1117 PRR
160-1118 CSX

TRAIL BLAZER EA 129.00

Sets feature B23-7 loco and four freight cars.

160-1102 CR
160-1106 UP
160-1107 Chessie
160-1108 ATSF

PIONEER EA 146.00

Sets feature F7A loco, unpowered F7B loco and four freight cars.

160-1103 UP
160-1111 PRR
160-1112 GN
160-1113 SP Black Widow

PATRIOT

160-1104 163.00
Spectrum F40PH loco, three lighted Amfleet passenger cars and oval of nickel-silver E-Z Track.

THE FRONTIERSMAN EA 217.00

Sets feature a Baldwin 2-8-0 locomotive with tender and operating headlight, open quad hopper, plug door box car and extended vision caboose. Assembly instructions are explained on a VHS videotape included with each set.

160-1121 UP
160-1122 WM
160-1123 Southern

THE EXPLORER EA 258.00

Sets feature a Baldwin 2-8-0 locomotive with tender and operating headlight and three passenger cars with interior lighting (combine, coach and observation car). Assembly instructions are explained on a VHS videotape included with each set.

160-1126 UP
160-1127 B&O

The Frontiersman Train Set
160-1121

The Explorer Train Set
160-1126

Mountaineer Train Set
160-1101

Trail Blazer Train Set
160-1102

Pioneer Train Set
160-1103

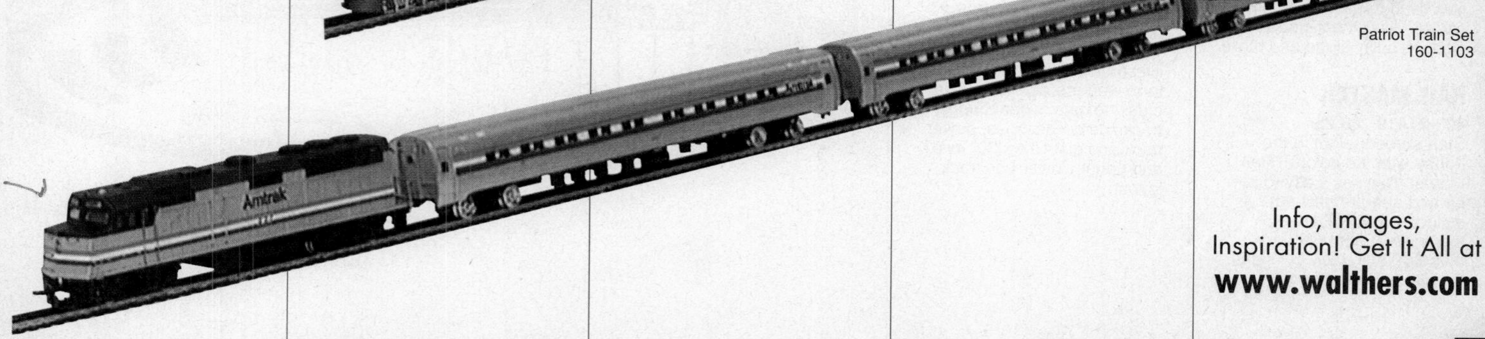

Patriot Train Set
160-1103

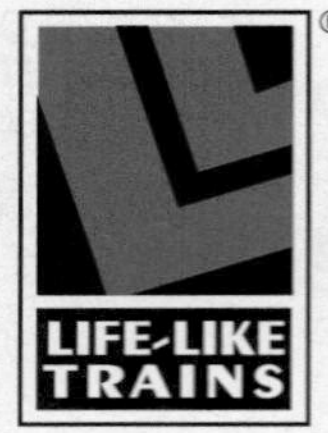

TRAIN SETS W/POWER-LOC™ TRACK

These sets include Life-Like's Power-Loc track, the unique side-locking track system that clicks together instantly and locks track securely in place. There's no need for rail joiners, so set-up is quick and easy. Solid roadbed base offers durability and support on any surface (even carpet), eliminating the need for boards, nails, screws or tools. Sets also include a UL-listed power pack with forward and reverse, and a terminal rerailer. All sets (excluding sets with Power-Loc track) feature the Trac-Loc™ system, which keeps track connected for superior running.

Freightline USA Train Set 433-8644

IRON HORSE

433-8603 95.00
You'll know you're in the steam age when the mighty 0-4-0 steam locomotive rumbles down the track on the Iron Horse train set. The set includes: 0-4-0 steam locomotive and tender, 4 freight cars, 47 x 38" oval track, 10-piece bridge and pier set, 62 signs, 12 utility poles and more.

FREIGHTLINE USA

433-8644 193.75
Freightline USA is loaded with action! This top-of-the-line train set has it all: GP38-2 diesel locomotive, 6 freight cars, 49 x 76" double loop track, 2 manual switches, 18-piece bridge and pier set, coal tipple, gravel dump station, operating dual crossing gate, 3 shanty kits, 3 vehicles, 6 figures, 3 trees, tunnel, signal bridge, 24 authentic street signs, 6 utility signs and more.

RAIL MASTER

433-21419 66.25
Start someone out in the hobby with the colorful Rail Master train set. Easy to set up and operate, this set includes: F40PH diesel locomotive, 3 freight cars, 47 x 38" oval track, 62 signs, 6 utility poles and more.

RAIL BLASTER

433-8965 100.00 ***NEW***
Includes lo-nose GP38-2 diesel locomotive with working headlight, 5 railroad cars with matching 8-wheel caboose, 74 x 38" track oval with terminal rerailer, UL-approved power pack, snap-together station, 4 cars, 3 trucks, 12 utility poles, gravel dump station, 110 different signs, plug-in terminal wires, extra couplers and illustrated instructions.

POWER CHARGER

433-21429 132.50
Includes high-nose GP38-2 diesel locomotive, 6 freight cars, 18-piece bridge and pier set, livestock pen with cows, pigs, farm workers, operating dual crossing gate, signal bridge, trackside accessories, power pack and giant 74 x 38" over and under Power-Loc track layout.

Rail Blaster Train Set 433-8965

Iron Horse Train Set 433-8603

Rail Master Train Set 433-21419

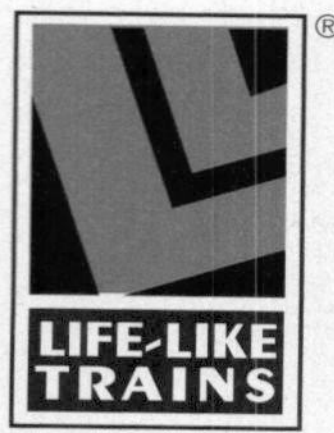

BRANCH LINE

433-21401 56.50
Set includes an F7 diesel loco with working headlight, 3 railroad cars with a matching 8-wheel caboose, 38" track circle and terminal/rerailer, UL-listed power pack, plug-in terminal wires and extra couplers.

FREIGHT CHARGER

433-21416 76.25
Includes an F7 diesel loco with working headlight, 4 railroad cars with a matching 8-wheel caboose, a 47 x 38" oval track with Power-Loc track and terminal rerailer, UL-listed power pack, log dump station with logs, 6 figures, 67 authentic railroad and street signs, 12 utility poles, plug-in terminal wires and extra couplers.

BLAZING RAILS

433-21420 86.25
Includes GP38-2 diesel locomotive, 5 freight cars, bridge and pier set, 86 authentic railroad, street and road signs, 6 utility poles, 47 x 38" oval of Power-Loc track and power pack.

DOUBLE TRAIN EXPRESS

433-21430 225.00
The ultimate adventure in model railroad, the Double Train Express features two complete trains and separated elevated figure-8 and circular tracks. Layout can reach up to 90 x 46". Set includes grass mat, earth and lake materials, trees, decorated tunnel, lichen shrubs, an operating dual-crossing gate with arms, building kits, vehicles, authentic signs and assembly glue.

DIESEL BLASTER

433-21506 105.00
Includes powered and unpowered GP38-2 diesel locomotive, 5 freight cars, 10-piece bridge and pier set, shanty buildings, livestock pen, livestock, farmers, autos and trucks, trees, signal bridge, 12 utility poles, power pack, mammoth 72 x 36" oval of Power-Loc track and 91 railroad, street and road signs.

Latest New Product News Daily! Visit Walthers Web site at
www.walthers.com

Double Train Express Train Set 433-21430

Branch Line Train Set 433-21401

Blazing Rails Train Set 433-21420

Freight Charger Train Set 433-21416

Diesel Blaster Train Set 433-21506

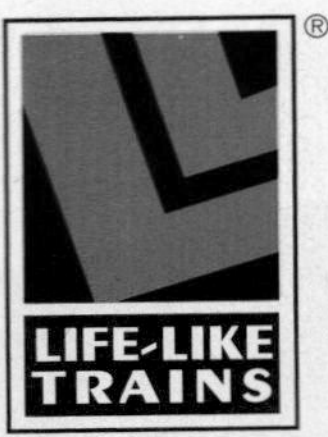

TRAIN SETS W/ CONVENTIONAL TRACK

Start your model railroading fun right away with these complete HO Scale train sets. Each includes a ready-to-run loco with working headlight and freight cars, all equipped with universal couplers. Sets are complete with track and accessories, plus a UL-listed power pack with forward and reverse, and a terminal rerailer. All sets (excluding sets with Power-Loc track) feature the Trac-Loc™ system, which keeps track connected for superior running.

Diesel Master Train Set 433-8740

Thundering Rails Train Set 433-8766

Rail Master Train Set 433-8916

Golden Flyer Train Set 433-8803

UP DIESEL MASTER

433-8740 100.00
Complete with F40PH diesel locomotive, 4 freight cars, caboose, 35-piece bridge and trestle set, 6 autos, 67 signs, 12 utility poles and a 48 x 49" double oval over and under track and power pack.

ATSF THUNDERING RAILS

433-8766 87.00
Includes GP38-2 diesel locomotive, 5 freight cars, 8-wheel caboose, operating blinking bridge, 17-piece trestle set, signal bridge with trackside accessories, 67 signs, 6 utility poles, 24 authentic Burma Shave signs, hook-up wires, extra couplers and rail joiners, illustrated instructions and a 45 x 45" track layout and power pack.

GOLDEN FLYER

433-8803 54.00
Features F40PH diesel loco, 3 freight cars and 8-wheel caboose, track circle with Power-Loc fasteners and terminal rerailer, UL-listed power pack, plug-in terminal wires and extra couplers.

RAIL MASTER

433-8916 61.00
Includes F40PH diesel locomotive, 3 freight cars, 62 railroad and street signs, 6 utility poles, 36" circle track w/Trac-LocTM fasteners and power pack.

PROTO 1000 SERIES TRAIN SETS

Featured elements of the PROTO 1000 series include trucks with needle point axles, PROTO 2000 magnetic knuckle couplers, blackened metal wheels, micro-molded details, laser-quality printing and paint schemes to accurately represent the designated paint scheme.

GREAT AMERICAN RAILWAY TRAIN SETS EA 160.00

With easy assembly and quick set-up time, the Great American Railway is a perfect starter set. Contents of train set include: PROTO 1000 F3A locomotive with working headlight and matching caboose, three freight cars, snap-together freight and passenger station kit, 56 x 38" nickel-silver Power-Loc track oval, a listed power pack, hook-up wires and illustrated instructions.

433-23901 ATSF ***NEW***
433-23902 PRR ***NEW***
433-23903 CNW ***NEW***

PRR Great American Railway Train Set 433-23902

ATSF Great American Railway Train Set - Engine Style Only Shown 433-23901

CNW Great American Railway Train Set - Engine Style Only Shown 433-23903

Mogul Train Set 348-308

GGI Milleniun Express Train Set 348-312

PREMIER SERIES MOGUL TRAIN SETS EA 99.98

Sets include a 2-6-0 steam engine and tender, five freight cars, an oval of track and a deluxe UL-listed power pack with automatic resetting circuit breaker.

348-308 PRR ***NEW***
348-311 SP ***NEW***
348-313 SOU ***NEW***

GG-1 MILLENIUM EXPRESS TRAIN SETS EA 99.98

Set is pulled by a premier GG-1 locomotive with a powerful twin-can motor, independent flywheels, diode directional lighting, working pantographs and twelve-wheel drive. Includes four collector's edition freight cars, an oval of track and a UL-listed power pack.

348-309 PRR (green stripe) ***NEW***
348-312 PRR (red stripe) ***NEW***

Information STATION

Is My Old Train Set Worth Money?

Many factors determine values of toy trains. Guide books help you identify toys and determine current market prices. Typically, collectors look at the following:

Condition: The most desirable items were never played with nor removed from their original box. These rare items command the best prices.

Packaging: Overall condition of the box substantially impacts value and an excellent original can double the value of a used toy.

Age: A true antique is 100 years old or more. Since toys were once a luxury made in small numbers, older items are most desirable.

Scarcity: If fewer were made, they are more collectable. One-off engineering models, or factory errors with the wrong color or lettering are good examples. Some items produced only for sets and not sold separately qualify too. Sets produced with unique colors and packaging fit this group.

Desirability: If a set is eagerly sought by collectors, it will drive up prices and lower the supply.

Survival Rate: Recent sets were produced in huge numbers and survived their owner's childhood . They are readily available so prices stay low. But when few originals exist, survivors are highly desirable.

Here's a great way to add life to your train set! Just imagine having a complete layout like this with houses, roads, vehicles and businesses up and running in just one evening! Best of all, you don't have to be an advanced model railroader to build this model railroad empire. Anybody can do it!

Complete Your Own Model Railroad Empire In Just One Evening!

The IHC One Evening Model Railroad Empire is just as its name says: a one-evening project! No special tools or skills are required-- all you need to do is plunk the pieces down on your train board! Great for you, your kids, spouse, nieces, nephews, grandchildren and friends.

Preassembled structures, vehicles and accessories make assembling this layout a breeze! Ardent model railroaders will also appreciate the usefulness of these items on their pikes!

The One Evening Model Railroad Empire is a fun, affordable family activity! Placing trains, vehicles, roads and buildings on the layout will get your creative juices flowing.

Everybody will love designing their own ideal village! Get everyone involved and set up your model railroad empire with these layout ready products.

It's easy!

All you need to get started is a 4' x 8' x 1/2" piece of plywood and an HO train set of your choice! Attach the track to the board and start adding your scenery! Choose from these easy-to-use scenic details shown in the photo and listed here. They're ready to go right on the board! Check out these low prices!

Look for more additions to your One Evening Model Railroad Empire soon. Coming soon: trees, shrubs and cars, all layout-ready and at affordable prices!

Stock#	Description	Retail
348-1	Tower Crane w/Platform	6.98
348-2	Cement Plant w/Platform	9.98
348-3	Harvester	2.98
348-4	Farm Accessory Set	4.98
348-5	Greenhouse	3.98
348-7	Farm House	4.98
348-8	8 Straight & 2 Corner Pavements	2.98
348-9	Large Equipment Shed	4.98
348-10	5 Straight & 1 Curved Road Sections	2.98
348-11	1940's Style Bus	2.98
348-12	Heavy Duty Tow Truck	2.98
348-130	Large Open Bed Truck (cab over engine)	2.98
348-140	Front End Loader (w/blade)	2.98
348-150	Front End Loader (w/bucket)	2.98
348-160	Ready Mix Concrete Truck	2.98
348-170	Delivery Truck (cab over engine)	2.98
348-180	Livestock Transporter	2.98
348-190	Oil Tanker w/40' Oil Tank	3.98
348-200	Flatbed Truck w/Tank Container	3.98
348-210	40' Tractor Trailer	3.98
348-222	Village Green Accessories	3.98
348-223	Mobile Office Site	1.98
348-225	Farm Silo	2.98
348-226	Road Roller	2.98
348-227	Open Truck w/Boom Crane	2.98
348-228	Corn Crops (3 3 x 1.5')	4.98

Ready-to-run electric train sets include lighted locomotives, steel track, power packs with hook-up wire and instructions. Locomotives feature all-wheel drive.

LI'L DONKEY

490-1024 61.00
Lighted loco, 2 freight cars, caboose, dual lights and 36" circle of track.

SANTA 6

490-1031 85.00
Loco, 3 Christmas cars, 45 x 36" oval of track and 6 Santa figures.

NORTHERN STAR

490-1045 91.00
Diesel loco, 4 freight cars, 45 x 36" oval of track and 2 track overhead signal bridge.

DICKENS RAILROAD CO.

490-1077 127.00
Old-time loco and tender, two passenger cars, four lighted buildings and 54 x 36" oval of track.

490-1075 Buildings Set 1 **47.98**
490-1078 Train Set (Less Buildings) **77.98**

TUXEDO JUNCTION

490-1046 101.00
Diesel loco, 3 freight cars, caboose, dual automatic crossing gate with watchman's house and 45 x 36" oval of track.

DOUBLE DIESEL

490-1061 124.00
Powered and dummy diesel locos, 4 freight cars, caboose, bridge and trestle set, 40 piece building set, 22 telephone poles and signs, figures, tunnel and 54 x 36" oval of track.

MIDNIGHT EXPRESS

490-1065 91.00
Lighted 0-4-0 steam loco, 3 freight cars, caboose and 36" circle of track.

PENNZOIL TRAIN SETS EA 120.00

490-1300 Z-7 Diesel Express
Diesel loco, 4 cars, 7-piece signal bridge and 45 x 36" oval of track.

490-1301 Old Timer
Steam loco & tender, 3 cars, cargo dock and 45 x 36" oval of track.

SMOKIN' JOE

490-1073 96.00
Includes lighted loco with tender, old-time bridge, 4 freight cars, caboose and 45 x 36" oval of track.

THE WORLD'S FASTEST TRAINS

490-1084 101.00
Powered loco, 1 unpowered loco, 2 passenger cars and 45 x 36" oval of track.

THE CHRISTMAS TRAIN

490-1093 107.00
Loco, 4 Christmas freight cars, and 45 x 36" oval of track and blinking bridge.

PRESIDENTIAL SPECIAL EA 194.00

Steam loco, 2 passenger coaches, observation and 45 x 36" oval of track.

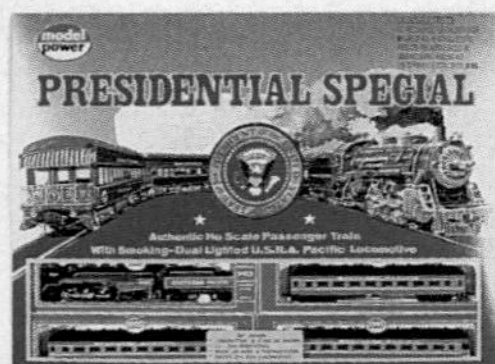

490-1008 PRR
490-1009 SP
490-1011 B&O
490-1012 ATSF
490-1013 CP
490-1014 CN
490-1015 CP
490-1016 CNR

BLUE EAGLE

490-1049 81.00
Diesel loco, 3 cars and circle of track.

ATLANTIC PACIFIC - OLD TIMER EA 118.00

Fat Boy steam loco, 3 wooden passenger cars, station building, telephone poles, signs and 45 x 36" oval of track.

490-1252 ATSF
490-1253 PRR
490-1254 SOU
490-1255 CP
490-1256 DRGW

ATLANTIC PACIFIC - STREAMLINE EA 137.00

FA2 diesel loco, 3 streamline passenger cars, station building, 7-piece signal bridge, telephone poles, signs and 45 x 36" oval of track.

490-1262 Amtrak
490-1263 PRR
490-1264 SP
490-1265 CN
490-1266 CP
490-1267 ATSF

ATLANTIC PACIFIC - HARRIMAN EA 177.00

Steam loco, 3 Harriman passenger cars with interiors, station building, 7-piece signal bridge, telephone poles, sign, and 45 x 36" oval of track.

490-1280 SP
490-1281 SOU
490-1282 ATSF
490-1283 CN
490-1284 CP
490-1285 PRR
490-1287 DRGW

DOUBLE EAGLE

490-1055 124.00
Diesel loco, 4 freight cars, caboose, 54 x 36" oval of track with two switches, snap-together plastic station, telephone poles and signs.

SILVER STAR

490-1063 81.00
Diesel loco, 2 freight cars, caboose, 40-piece pop-out building set, telephone poles, signs and circle of track.

THE CHAMP

490-1025 61.00
Switcher, 2 freight cars, caboose and 36' circle of track.

GOLDEN SPIKE OLD TIMER

490-1052 110.00
Steam loco & tender, 5 freight cars, 144 unpainted figures, 24 signs, power pack, roadbed and E-Z Track.

ROLLING THUNDER

490-1062 118.00
Lighted steam loco & tender, 4 freight cars, 72 figures, 12 x 18" tunnel, bridge & trestle set, 40-piece building set, 22 painted signs & telephone poles, 54 x 36" track oval and deluxe power pack.

MISSILE FORCE

490-1068 134.00
GP9 diesel loco, flat car w/tank, tank buster car, railway gun, exploding car, caboose, 3 missiles w/launcher, 144 figures and oval of track.

PRIDE OF THE LINE

490-1035 66.00
Diesel loco, 2 freight cars, caboose and 36" circle of track.

Mantua train sets are ready-to-run and decorated in authentic colors. Engines feature operating headlights.

Toy Express Train Set 455-972414

War Bonnet Special 455-9018

Conrail "Tru-Blu" Quality 455-9019

Union Pacific "Steam with Safety" 455-9020

WAR BONNET SPECIAL

455-9018 59.95 ***NEW***
Set is led by a F-7A ATSF diesel locomotive with eight-wheel drive and flywheel, GD-500 can motor, operating headlight, eight-wheel electrical pickup, diecast frame and horn-hook-style couplers.

Includes IC 41' reefer, Westinghouse flat car with crates, Boston & Maine 41' steel box car, Du Pont 35' single-dome tank car and ATSF 36' caboose.

CONRAIL "TRU-BLU" QUALITY

455-9019 64.95 ***NEW***
Train set features a GP20 Conrail "Quality" diesel engine with eight-wheel drive and flywheel, GD-500 can motor, operating headlight, eight-wheel electrical pickup, diecast frame and horn-hook-style couplers. Along for the ride are a Dubuque 41' reefer, N&W 41' hopper, ART 40' wood side reefer, Baby Ruth 35' single-dome tank car and CR 36' caboose.

UNION PACIFIC "STEAM WITH SAFETY"

455-9020 174.95 ***NEW***
A 2-6-0 UP locomotive gets this set headed down the rails. The steam locomotive features a can motor, working headlight, diecast metal frame with brass bearings, three-piece brass bell and horn-hook-style couplers The locomotive pulls two 41' steel box car (DRGW and LINDE schemes), Hood Milk 41' steel reefer, Hercules 35' single-dome tank car and UP Safety Slogan 36' caboose.

TOY EXPRESS TRAIN SET

455-972414 99.00 ***NEW***
Christmas will burst with excitement when collectors get their hands on this Toy Express train set. Set includes a GP20 eight-wheel drive diesel locomotive, 41' steel box car, 36' single dome tank car, 41' steel reefer, heavy flat car with crates, 36" wheel caboose, a UL-listed power pack and 14 pieces of track (with rerailer) to make a 36 x 45" oval.

Hot New Products Announced Daily! Visit Walthers Web site at **www.walthers.com**

IMPORTED FROM AUSTRIA BY WALTHERS

These models are authentically painted and lettered with plastic bodies and die-cast metal frames, metal gears and European-style couplers. Many have operating, reversing headlights and interior lighting. Models with pantographs may be powered from overhead catenary or track. All models operate on 2-rail D.C. (unless otherwise indicated).

GERMAN STATE RAILWAY (COMPANY)

CLASS BR601 "MAX LIEBERMANN" MULTIPLE-UNIT TRAIN

Limited Quantity Available

625-43905 3-Unit Supplement Set, Era V, AC 3-Rail (red, cream) **129.99**

GERMAN FEDERAL RAILWAYS

CLASS ET85/ES85 MULTIPLE-UNIT TRAIN

With powered car, trailer car and center coach.

625-43065 3-Unit Set, Era III (maroon) **279.99**

Limited Quantity Available

625-43893 3-Unit Set, Era III, AC 3-Rail (maroon) **339.99**

ICE 2 MULTIPLE-UNIT TRAIN

625-43071 DC Power 1:100 Scale w/Driving Trailer DB-AG Scheme **239.99**
625-43877 AC Power, 3 Rail **299.99**
Extensively new design. 1:100 scale. Era V (white body, red striping).

CLASS ET 420 MULTIPLE-UNIT TRAIN

625-43006 3-Unit Set, Era V (white, orange) **359.99**

CLASS ET491 "GLASS TRAIN"

Limited Quantity Available

625-43930 Era IV, AC 3-Rail (powder blue, gray) **279.99**

WORK TRAIN SET

Limited Quantity Available

625-41084 Era IV **179.99**
Includes class 333 diesel, kitchen-lounge car, shower car, sleeper, foreman's car and a section of ROCO-LINE track to display the set.

CLASS VT98/VS98 "CHIEMGAU RAILWAY" DIESEL RAILCAR

Limited Quantity Available

625-43040 Powered & Trailer Car, Era V (sky blue, light green, gray) **199.99**

CLASS VT98/VS98 DIESEL RAILCAR

Limited Quantity Available

625-43945 Powered & Trailer Car, Era III, AC 3-Rail (red) **169.99**

CLASS 798/998 DIESEL RAILCAR

Limited Quantity Available

625-43046 Center Car, Era IV-V (red) **64.99**
625-43969 Center Car, Era IV-V, AC 3-Rail (red) **69.99**

CLASS VT11 "TEE" MULTIPLE-UNIT TRAIN

625-43903 3 Car Set, Era III, AC 3-Rail (red, cream) **159.99**
Two coaches and dining car.

Limited Quantity Available

625-43949 Powered & Trailer Car, Era V, AC 3-Rail (sky blue, light green, gray) **319.99**

CLASS VT601 "INTERCITY" MULTIPLE-UNIT TRAIN

Limited Quantity Available

625-43904 4-Unit Set, Era IV, AC 3-Rail (red, cream) **149.99**

AUSTRIAN FEDERAL RAILWAYS

MARIAZELL "JAFFA" PASSENGER COACHES HOe EA 39.99

625-34000 Era IV, Type AB 1st/2nd Class
625-34001 Era IV, Type B 2nd Class
625-34002 Era IV, Type BD 2nd Class Combine

MARIAZELL "ORIGINAL" PASSENGER COACHES HOe EA 35.99

625-34003 Era III-IV, Type AB 1st/2nd Class
625-34004 Era III-IV, Type B 2nd Class
625-34005 Era III-IV, Type BD 2nd Class Combine

CLASS 5081 DIESEL RAILCAR

625-43051 Powered & Trailer Car, Era IV (blue, silver) **199.99**
625-43052 Center Car, Era IV (blue, silver) **69.99**

625-43947 Powered & Trailer Car, Era III-IV, AC 3-Rail (blue, silver) **249.99**
625-43948 Center Car, Era III-IV, AC 3-Rail (blue, silver) **64.99**

Limited Quantity Available

625-43020 Powered & Trailer Car, Era III-IV (blue, silver) **149.99**

CLASS 4010 "TRANSALPIN" MULTIPLE-UNIT TRAIN

625-43894 3-Unit Set, Era III-IV, AC 3-Rail (blue, white) **499.99**
Powered lead car, dining car and trailer.

625-43895 3-Unit Coach Supplement Set, Era III-IV, AC 3-Rail (blue, white) **249.99**

Limited Quantity Available

625-43054 3-Unit Coach Supplement Set, Era III-IV (blue, white) **239.99**

3-UNIT TRAIN

625-43061 DC Power **449.99**
With power unit, driving trailer and buffet car. Era IV, (red, white)

625-43898 AC Power **499.99**
With power unit, driving trailer and buffet car. Era IV, (red, white) 3 Rail.

EUROPEAN TRAMWAYS

625-43189 8-Axle, Undecorated (white) **132.99**

STARTER SETS

These sets come complete with Roco Line track, which features Code 83 nickel-silver rail with plastic ties mounted on a premolded roadbed section.

DIGITAL TRAIN SETS

625-41101 Freight Set **469.99**
Features diesel loco, three freight cars, track with turnout, power pack, Digital central control unit and mouse.

625-41200 ICE II Passenger Set **489.99**
Includes two powered ICE II cars, a first-class center car, track with turnout, power pack, Digital central control unit and mouse.

NARROW GAUGE INDUSTRIAL RAILROADS

Roco offers a complete selection of ready-to-run industrial narrow gauge rolling stock and locomotives. HOe narrow gauge track and turnouts (with a gauge of 9 mm) are also available. Track products use correctly scaled and spaced HO ties.

DIESEL INDUSTRIAL SET

625-31004 Diesel Set **129.99**
This kit includes a diesel locomotive (No. 33205), two wood gondolas (No. 34503), two timber cars (No. 34502), two dump cars (No. 34500), a shed building kit and an oval of Roco HOe narrow gauge track.

"SCHWARZ" DIESEL INDUSTRIAL SET-UNPOWERED

625-1599 Schwarz Set **89.99**
Includes industrial diesel locomotive (unpowered), Unimog U1300L, wood trailer, 3 cement cars, 3 gondolas and oval of Roco HOe narrow gauge track.

LOCOMOTIVES

625-33201 Steam (black, green) **74.99**

625-33205 Diesel (dark green) **64.99**

MINE CARS

625-34500 Dump Car pkg(6) **39.99**
625-34501 Cement Car pkg(6) **39.99**
625-34502 Timber Car pkg(6) **39.99**
625-34503 Wood Gondola pkg(6) **39.99**
625-34504 Bulkhead Flat Car pkg(6) **39.99**
625-34505 Coal Car pkg(4) **39.99**
625-34506 Mine Car pkg(4) **39.99**
625-34507 Flat Car pkg(6) **39.99**

625-34511 Disconnect Logging Trucks w/Wood Logs 1 Pair **33.99**
625-34512 Betriebsausflug Railway Cars w/Figures pkg(3) **29.99**

NARROW GAUGE TRACK

Roco HOe narrow gauge track products are exactly to prototype in type, size and spacing of ties. The track "gauge" is 9 mm (N Scale), but it is HO "scale."

625-32200 28" Flexible Track (730 mm) **4.99**
Dealers MUST order in multiples of 24.

625-32201 28" Flexible Track, Temporary Ties (730 mm) **4.99**
Dealers MUST order in multiples of 24.

625-32202 5-3/8" Straight (134 mm) pkg(12) **22.99**

625-32203 2" Straight (48 mm) pkg(12) **22.99**

625-32204 30° Curved pkg(12) **22.99**

625-32205 15° Curved pkg(12) **22.99**

FILL-IN TIES PKG(24)

625-32211 Temporary Track **8.99**

Model classic passenger service of the past and present with this matching locomotive and passenger cars. Locomotive is ready to run with powerful three-pole motor and worm gear drive insure smooth operation, and a working headlight is standard equipment. Cars are finished in authentic colors and each is fully assembled, ready for service.

AMERICAN ORIENT EXPRESS TRAIN

635-824 American Orient Express **299.99**
Limited-Run Set
Now, you can be one of the select few to own a limited edition American Orient Express train set. Produced with the authorization of TCS Expeditions, the operator of the American Orient Express, Rivarossi's eight-piece set is an authentic replica of the train that carries passengers in comfort and luxury.

The HO Scale American Orient Express is driven by a powered E8 diesel, and a matching dummy A unit is also included. Metal wheels conform to RP25 standards, so your train can be used on code 70, 83 or 100 track.

Six smoothside cars, most complete with interior details, make up the consist. You'll get three roomettes, a baggage car, diner and observation car. The blue and gold colors duplicate the prototype paint scheme. Exterior details are faithfully reproduced–including the distinct American Orient Express crest.

To ensure its value as a true collectible, Rivarossi has limited production of the American Orient Express to just 3,000 sets world-wide. We guarantee a fabulous train set to run now, and a rare collectible to be treasured for a lifetime.

Information STATION

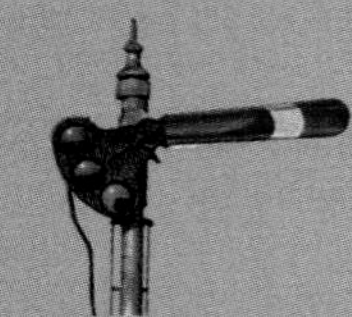

Beginner's Books & Videos

The wrapping paper is off, the box is open and you're starting to set up your new train set. Once you're ready to make the transition from basic set to model railroad, there are plenty of how-to materials available.

Krause Publications offers The HO Model Railroading Handbook (213-8346) which provides all kinds of information and lots of helpful photos throughout its 240 pages.

Kalmbach Books HO Railroad From Set To Scenery begins with helpful hits on how to select the starter train set that is best for your needs. The 96-page book then goes on to discuss a variety of other interesting topics, including track laying, benchwork construction and instruction for further expanding your layout. The ABC's of Model Railroading (400-12036) and The Practical Guide to HO Model Railroading (400-12075) answer frequently asked questions from new modelers.

Green Frog Productions offers step-by-step ideas and inspiration on video with Building a Model Railroad - The Apple Valley Branch. This set of 10 tapes (302-70000, also available individually as 302-70001 - 70010) covers all aspects of layout construction from initial planning to operation.

One lonely box car. By itself, it doesn't seem like much. Day in and day out, it has rumbled obediently along behind far more exciting motive power. Kids just watch it pass, saving their excited waves for the crew in the caboose. It has sat patiently through long days on side tracks and spurs, waiting to be loaded or unloaded. In every kind of weather, it has gone about its assigned jobs, never complaining.

But couple it with two, three , four others - as many as the engines can pull and they become a force to deal with. They are a mile-long steel conveyor, moving everything you can imagine across country, safe from the weather and other potential harm. You simply can't run a railroad without them. And if that was you down there rolling out loaded 55 gallon drums, one at a time by hand, you wouldn't think that one car was so small either!

All across the nation, the same scene is being played out on team tracks, factory sidings and loading docks. Soon those empty cars will be reloaded and rolling together to a new destination. Martin Pollizotto of East Islip, New York, built this small industrial scene.

Models and Photo by Martin Pollizotto

WALTHERS™

Walthers HO Scale kits feature detailed styrene parts and are designed for easy construction with basic hobby tools. Each car is prepainted and lettered in an authentic scheme that includes end reporting marks. All kits are complete with instructions, weights, trucks with nonmagnetic brass axles and horn-hook couplers.

AMERICA'S DRIVING FORCE SERIES FREIGHT CARS

America's DRIVING FORCE

PULLMAN-STANDARD 86' 4-DOOR HI-CUBE BOX CARS

Designed to move lightweight sheet metal parts economically, these big cars are a fixture of modern auto production. Introduced in the mid 60s by Pullman-Standard, the cars feature large double-doors for easy access by forklifts. Parts are carried in special baskets to simplify loading or unloading. Assigned to pool service, they can be spotted moving in priority parts trains on many railroads.

Based on the common four-door design originally built for Ford and Chrysler plants, the models feature the correct ribbed ends and the unique sidesills with visible interior posts found on the prototypes. Models are fully assembled with working knuckle couplers. To match your timeframe, cars are prepainted in 1960s or 1990s schemes. Choose from single cars or 2-Packs, each with a different number to expand your fleet in seconds.

SINGLE CARS EA 18.98

932-3501 PRR (1960s scheme) ***NEW***
932-3502 Detroit, Toledo & Ironton (1960s scheme) ***NEW***
932-3503 NYC (1960s scheme) ***NEW***
932-3504 C&O (1960s scheme) ***NEW***
932-3505 ATSF (1960s scheme) ***NEW***
932-3506 WP (1960s scheme) ***NEW***
932-3507 CR (1990s scheme) ***NEW***
932-3508 CNW (1990s scheme) ***NEW***
932-3509 Golden West (1990s scheme) ***NEW***
932-3510 NS (1990s scheme) ***NEW***
932-3511 CP (1990s scheme) ***NEW***
932-3512 CSX (1990s scheme ***NEW***
932-3513 MILW (1960s scheme) ***NEW***
932-3514 GTW (1970s scheme) ***NEW***
932-3515 NS (gray 1990s scheme) ***NEW***
932-3516 Detroit, Toledo & Ironton (1960s scheme) ***NEW***
932-3500 Undecorated ***NEW***

2-PACKS EA 35.98

932-23501 PRR (1960s scheme) ***NEW***
932-23502 Detroit, Toledo & Ironton (1960s ***NEW***
932-23503 NYC (1960s scheme) ***NEW***
932-23504 C&O (1960s scheme) ***NEW***
932-23505 ATSF (1960s scheme) ***NEW***
932-23506 WP (1960s scheme) ***NEW***
932-23507 CR (1990s scheme) ***NEW***
932-23508 CNW (1990s scheme) ***NEW***
932-23519 Golden West (1990s scheme) ***NEW***
932-23510 NS (1990s scheme) ***NEW***
932-23511 CP (1990s scheme) ***NEW***
932-23512 CSX (1990s scheme) ***NEW***
932-23513 MILW (1960s scheme) ***NEW***
932-23514 GTW (1970s scheme) ***NEW***
932-23515 NS (gray 1990s scheme) ***NEW***
932-23516 Detroit, Toledo & Ironton (1960s scheme) ***NEW***

86' 8-DOOR HI-CUBE BOX CARS

SINGLE CARS EA 18.98

932-3531 B&O (1960s scheme) ***NEW***
932-3532 MILW (1960s scheme) ***NEW***
932-3533 NYC (1960s scheme) ***NEW***
932-3534 MP/UP (1990s scheme) ***NEW***
932-3535 Grand Trunk (1990s scheme) ***NEW***
932-3536 CR (1990s scheme) ***NEW***
932-3530 Undecorated ***NEW***

2-PACKS EA 35.98

932-23531 B&O (1960s scheme) ***NEW***
932-23532 MILW (1960s scheme) ***NEW***
932-23533 NYC (1960s scheme) ***NEW***
932-23534 MP/UP (1990s scheme) ***NEW***
932-23535 Grand Trunk (1990s scheme) ***NEW***
932-23536 CR (1990s scheme) ***NEW***

Pullman-Standard 86' Hi-Cube Box Car 933-3502

86' 8-Door Hi-Cube Box Car 933-3533

Pullman-Standard 60' Single Door Auto Parts Box Car 933-3551

PULLMAN-STANDARD 60' SINGLE DOOR AUTO PARTS BOX CARS

Faced with increasing numbers of parts and expensive shipping systems, automakers approached freight car builders in the early 1960s about creating a universal box car for heavy parts. The basic design evolved into a smooth-side, interior post car, where load restraints could be mounted.

Heavier castings such as brake drums, engine blocks, transmissions and so on are carried in special baskets, designed for easy unloading/loading with forklifts. The large single door provides easy access to the interior. These cars can still be seen moving in priority trains to and from America's auto assembly plants.

The models come fully assembled and are offered in 1960s or 1990s paint schemes. Working knuckle couplers are also provided.

SINGLE CARS EA 15.98

932-3551 ATSF (1960s scheme) ***NEW***
932-3552 B&O (1960s scheme) ***NEW***
932-3553 DRGW (1960s scheme) ***NEW***
932-3554 UP (1960s scheme) ***NEW***
932-3555 NS (1990s scheme) ***NEW***
932-3556 CNW (1990s scheme) ***NEW***
932-3557 BN (1990s scheme) ***NEW***
932-3558 CSX (1990s scheme) ***NEW***
932-3559 MILW (1960s scheme) ***NEW***
932-3560 BNSF (1990s scheme) ***NEW***
932-3561 SOU (1970s scheme) ***NEW***
932-3562 CN (1990s "Noodle" Herald scheme) ***NEW***
932-3550 Undecorated ***NEW***

2-PACKS EA 29.98

932-23551 ATSF (1960s scheme) ***NEW***
932-23552 B&O (1960s scheme) ***NEW***
932-23553 DRGW (1960s scheme) ***NEW***
932-23554 UP (1960s scheme) ***NEW***
932-23555 NS (1990s scheme) ***NEW***
932-23556 CNW (1990s scheme) ***NEW***
932-23557 BN (1990s scheme) ***NEW***
932-23558 CSX (1990s scheme) ***NEW***
932-23559 MILW (1960s scheme) ***NEW***
932-23560 BNSF (1990s scheme) ***NEW***
932-23561 SOU (1970s scheme) ***NEW***
932-23562 CN (1990s "Noodle" Herald scheme) ***NEW***

WALTHERS™

PULLMAN-STANDARD 60' DOUBLE-DOOR AUTO PARTS BOX CAR

A common variation of the Pullman-Standard 60' auto parts box cars was the installation of two eight foot wide doors. This large opening allowed plenty of clearance to move in or out with a forklift. Like the single door car, they were used to carry heavy components such as engine blocks, axles, transmissions or brake drums in special baskets. You'll still find them in this specialized service across America today.

The models are fully assembled with working knuckle couplers and come prepainted in 1960s (old) or 1990s (new) paint schemes. Modeling several cars is a snap with the matching 2-Pack sets (932-23581 series sold separately), which feature two different car numbers.

SINGLE CARS EA 15.98

932-3581 CB&Q (1960s scheme) *NEW*
932-3582 NYC (1960s scheme) *NEW*
932-3583 UP (1960s scheme) *NEW*
932-3584 CNW (1960s scheme) *NEW*
932-3585 CR (1990s scheme) *NEW*
932-3586 Grand Trunk Western (1990s scheme) *NEW*
932-3587 BN (1990s scheme) *NEW*
932-3588 ATSF (1990s scheme) *NEW*
932-3580 Undecorated *NEW*

2-PACKS EA 29.98

932-23581 CB&Q (1960s scheme) *NEW*
932-23582 NYC (1960s scheme) *NEW*
932-23583 UP (1960s scheme) *NEW*
932-23584 CNW (1960s scheme) *NEW*
932-23585 CR (1990s scheme) *NEW*
932-23586 Grand Trunk Western (1990s scheme) *NEW*
932-23587 BN (1990s scheme) *NEW*
932-23588 ATSF (1990s scheme) *NEW*

89' TRI-LEVEL ENCLOSED AUTO CARRIERS

Over half of all new autos make their first long trip by train, riding in enclosed tri-level auto rack cars. Since autos are smaller and shorter than trucks or vans, the third deck increases carrying capacity; usually 15 mid-size or 18 compact cars make up a full load. As some of the longest and tallest equipment in operation, tunnels, bridges or other obstructions can present routing problems that require detours. To avoid this, a modified tri-level design was introduced in the mid 1970s. The 89' flat car that carries the rack is a special low-level car, easily identified by the side-sill cut outs that provide left and right side clearance for the trucks. In place of the usual 33" wheels, these cars ride on smaller 28" wheels to further reduce overall height. In service with most major roads, they can be found in the staging areas of every auto assembly plant, as well as reloading with import cars for their return trip.

Fully assembled and ready for service, these models come in a variety of colorful, modern schemes and are complete with working knuckle couplers. They're perfect for use with the Distribution Facility (933-3076) or to model bridge traffic moving across your layout.

SINGLE CARS EA 19.98

932-4851 ATSF *NEW*
932-4852 UP *NEW*
932-4853 CNW *NEW*
932-4854 BN *NEW*
932-4855 CSX *NEW*
932-4856 BNSF *NEW*
932-4857 CR *NEW*
932-4858 NS *NEW*
932-4859 TTX (New Scheme w/TTX Rack) *NEW*
932-4860 UP ("We Will Deliver") *NEW*
932-4861 GTW *NEW*
932-4862 SP (Speed Lettering) *NEW*
932-4850 Undecorated *NEW*

2-PACKS EA 37.98

932-24851 ATSF *NEW*
932-24852 UP *NEW*
932-24853 CNW *NEW*
932-24854 BN *NEW*
932-24855 CSX *NEW*
932-24856 BNSF *NEW*
932-24857 CR *NEW*
932-24858 NS *NEW*
932-24859 TTX (New Scheme w/TTX Rack) *NEW*
932-24860 UP ("We Will Deliver") *NEW*
932-24861 GTW *NEW*
932-24862 SP (Speed Lettering) *NEW*

Pullman-Standard 60' Double-Door Auto Parts Box Car 933-3585

89' Tri-Level Enclosed Auto Carriers 933-4851

Thrall 89' Bi-Level Enclosed Auto Carier Kit 933-4804

THRALL 89' BI-LEVEL ENCLOSED AUTO CARRIER KITS EA 14.98

With the increased popularity of trucks, vans and sport utility vehicles, bi-level enclosed auto carriers now play a more important role in moving new vehicles to customers. Although outwardly similar to tri-level rail cars, only two decks are used because trucks are taller, longer and heavier than automobiles (10 trucks is typically a full load).

Walthers kits produce a great-looking model with a minimum of effort. The one-piece body (the flat car portion of the model, end doors and superstructure are molded as a single unit, similar to a box car kit) comes prepainted and lettered in the correct color. Separate side panel sections are prepainted and lettered to match the prototypes, along with a separate roof that's painted aluminum.

The cars are the proper 89' length and include a special swinging (radial) coupler mounting to improve operation on curves. (Minimum track radius is 22"; however, 24" or larger is recommended for best performance.)

932-4801 DRGW (orange, yellow)
932-4803 CR (Tuscan Red, yellow)
932-4804 GTW (blue with blue panels)
932-4806 CNW (yellow)
932-4808 UP (Armour Yellow)
932-4809 CSX Transportation (yellow, New TTX color)
932-4810 BN (Cascade Green)
932-4813 ATSF (red)
932-4814 UP (yellow)
932-4815 NS (Tuscan Red)
932-4816 C&O-Chessie (yellow)
932-4817 CNW (Bright Yellow)
932-4818 SP (speed lettering)
932-4800 Undecorated

LIMITED-RUN CARS EA 19.98

Special paint and lettering schemes make these colorful collectibles that will dress up your distribution facility or auto trains.

932-4802 CP *NEW*
932-4805 MKT *NEW*
932-4807 SP *NEW*
932-4811 MILW *NEW*
932-4812 ATSF *NEW*

WALTHERS™

AN INTRODUCTION TO INTERMODAL

Some historians trace the start of intermodal service to 1872, when William Coup loaded circus wagons on flat cars to move his show. In 1884, the Long Island Rail Road hauled loaded farm wagons to market in New York City. By the early 1920s, the New York Central was using small containers for some freight shipments. In 1926, the North Shore line began hauling tiny highway trailers on special flat cars between Milwaukee and Chicago. On July 7, 1936, the Chicago Great Western began what many consider the first true intermodal service, hauling another company's trailers on specially modified flat cars.

In the 1950s, every large railroad began handling trailers on flat cars.

In the 1960s, standardized containers, 89' flat cars and 40' trailers appeared.

In the 1970s and 1980s new fuel-saving car designs, articulated cars, double-stacks, domestic service containers, tank containers and larger trailers were introduced.

FLAT CARS

F89F 89' "CHANNEL-SIDE" FLAT CAR EA 11.98

Introduced in the 1960s, these cars are easily identified by their steel channel sides. As trailer sizes increased, these cars were rebuilt into various "new" types. Our kit can be built in three versions: Standard, Twin 45 or Triple 28 using the hitches and other parts included.

These cars use the same proven underframe found on our Enclosed Auto Carriers, so they can be operated on small layouts with tight radius curves. Each kit also has a nearly full-length weight to improve performance.

932-4951 TTX - Standard (Elephant-style loading)
932-4952 TTX - "Twin 45"
932-4953 TTX - "Triple 28"
932-4954 UP
932-4955 SP
932-4956 ATSF
932-4950 Undecorated

GSC "COMMONWEALTH" 53' 6" FLAT CAR EA 9.98

This kit is the correct length and includes early and late piggyback hitches, plus parts for bulkhead and standard versions. They're perfect for use on any layout from the 1950s to the present. See the Vehicles and Freight Cars sections for loads to use with these cars.

932-3751 PRR (oxide red)

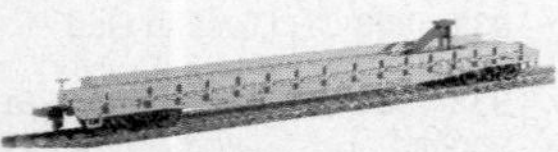

932-3752 UP (Armor Yellow)
932-3753 DRGW (black)
932-3754 ATSF (red)
932-3755 Soo Line (white)
932-3756 BN (Cascade Green)
932-3758 GN
932-3760 Conrail
932-3761 SP
932-3762 CNW/CGW
932-3763 IC
932-3765 ROCK
932-3766 N&W
932-3767 SOU
932-3768 Wabash
932-3769 Seaboard Coast Line
932-3750 Undecorated

Limited Quantity Available
932-3757 NP
932-3759 CB&Q
932-3764 MP

GSC Flat Car 932-3768

GSC Flat Car - Bulkhead Version 932-3755

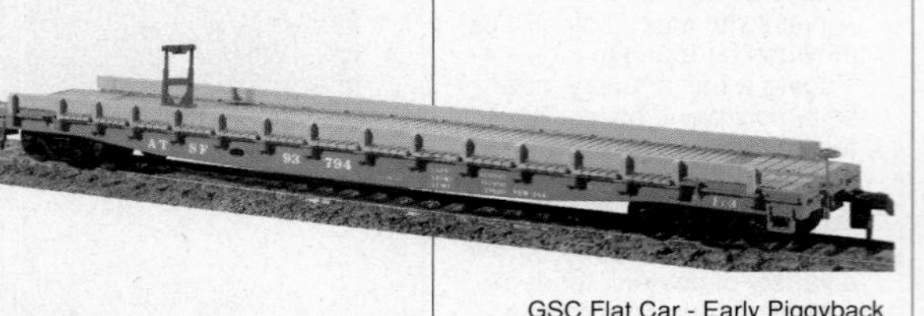

GSC Flat Car - Early Piggyback Version 932-3754

ROCK 932-3765
Preproduction Model Shown

GN 932-3769
Preproduction Model Shown

F89F 89' "Channel Side" Flat Car 932-4951

AMERICAN MODEL BUILDERS

WOOD FLAT CAR DECK

Designed especially for use with Walthers GSC "Commonwealth" Flat Car, these realistic planking kits are laser-cut from 1/32" plywood.

152-234 Wood Flat Car Deck **3.25**

152-233 With Laser-Etched Bolt Holes **7.95**

WOOD BULKHEAD PLANKING

152-260 Bulkhead Planking **7.95**
152-261 Bulkhead Planking w/Wood Flat Car Deck **14.95**

FLAT CAR LOADS EA 10.95

Neat detail for any era car, loads are laser-cut from wood or acrylic and fit together easily. Includes laser-cut bracing to hold load in place.

152-287 Wood Crate/Box Load-Plywood w/Wood Bracing

152-288 Crankshaft-Acrylic w/Wood Bracing

152-289 Stacked Lumber-All Wood

WALTHERS™

69' All-Purpose Husky-Stacks®

Stand Alone Well Cars

WELL CARS

69' ALL-PURPOSE HUSKY-STACKS® EA 14.98

Ready-to-run cars feature authentic paint schemes, diecast body, unique car numbers and a see-through floor just like the prototype.

932-4301 TTX
932-4302 BN
932-4303 NS Southwind
932-4304 CRLE
932-34301 TTX #1 3-Pack **44.98**
932-34302 TTX #2 3-Pack **44.98**
932-34303 BN 3-Pack **44.98**
932-4300 Undecorated

STAND-ALONE WELL CARS

Stand-alone well cars entered service in the early 1990s as larger and heavier containers came into use. With a truck at each end, they have a larger carrying capacity and are easier to maintain than articulated cars. Some owners run them with drawbars as three, four or five "unit cars."

932-3901 TTX, Single Unit (new TTX yellow) **9.98**
932-3902 TTX, Three-Pack (new TTX yellow) **27.98**
932-3903 TTX Original "TT" Logo, Four-Pack (new TTX yellow) **36.98**
932-3904 CN, Single Unit (blue) **9.98**
932-3900 Undecorated, Single Unit **9.98**

Limited Quantity Available
932-3905 CN, Five-Unit Car (blue) **44.98**
Prototype consists of five stand-alone cars, connected by drawbars.

SPINE CARS

FIVE-UNIT ALL-PURPOSE SPINE CAR EA 39.98

Hitch Detail

This model features a prepainted and lettered die-cast metal body for improved performance.

Add-on brake gear, hitches, container pedestals and other plastic details are included.

Limited Quantitiy Available On All Items
932-3932 BN (green)
932-3933 ATSF (red)
932-3934 UP (yellow)
932-3935 Conrail (blue)
932-3930 Undecorated

FRONT RUNNER®

These models feature a metal frame and body mounted working knuckle couplers for smooth operation. (Front Runner is a registered trademark of TTX Corporation.)

INDIVIDUAL CARS EA 10.98

932-3981 TTX (old)
932-3982 TTX (new)
932-3980 Undecorated

FOUR RUNNERS

Lightweight Four Runners were some of the first intermodal cars built to handle 45' trailers. The 4-platform models feature metal frames, appropriate drawbars and body-mounted, working knuckle couplers for smooth operation.

FOUR-PACKS EA 39.98

932-3991 TTX (Old Scheme)
932-3992 TTX (New Scheme)
932-3990 Undecorated

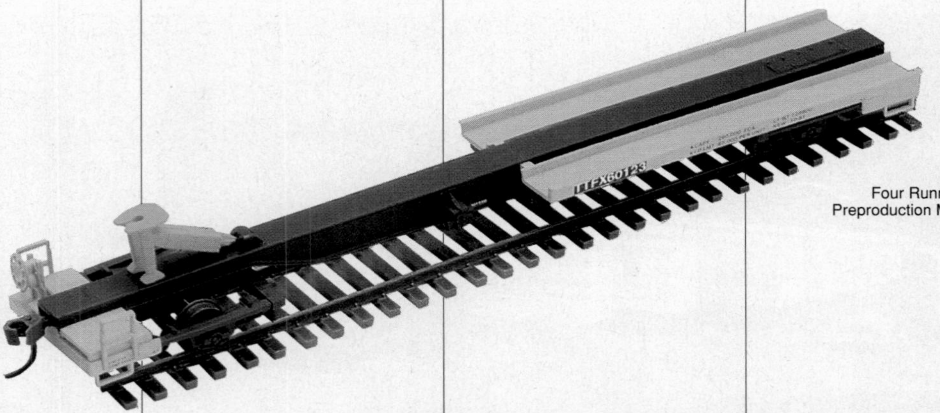

Four Runner 932-3991
Preproduction Model Shown

WALTHERS™

EXTENDIBLE CONTAINER CHASSIS

933-3110 pkg(2) **8.98**
When containers arrive for delivery, they're usually reloaded on extendible chassis. Kit can be adjusted from 40 to 48' scale feet, and looks great behind the semi tractors you'll find in Vehicles.

48' STOUGHTON SEMI TRAILERS EA 4.98

Some of the most common trailers on the road or the rails are the 48' Stoughton Semi Trailers. These easy-to-build kits come decorated in a variety of popular roadnames, which are seen on intermodal trains throughout the US.

933-1901 XTRA Intermodal (white)
933-1904 JB Hunt (white)
933-1905 TransAmerica (white)
933-1906 Schneider (white)
933-1907 Strick Lease (white)
933-1908 Tip Lease (white)
933-1909 Schneider (orange)
933-1910 BN America
933-1913 IC
933-1915 England
933-1917 CRST
933-1918 Navajo
933-1919 BNSF *NEW*
933-1920 ATSF *NEW*
933-1921 CSX Intermodal *NEW*
933-1922 Ryder *NEW*
933-1923 Terminal *NEW*
933-1924 Anderson *NEW*
933-1925 Werner *NEW*
933-1926 Crete *NEW*
933-1900 Undecorated

Limited Quantity Available
933-1911 Swift
933-1914 Dart
933-1916 KLLM

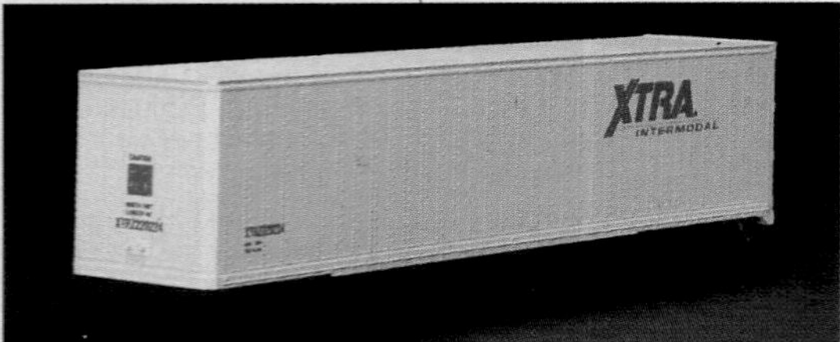

48' Stoughton Semi Trailer 933-1901

48' Stoughton Semi Trailer 933-1905

48' Stoughton Semi Trailer 933-1904

48' Stoughton Semi Trailer 933-1906

48' Stoughton Semi Trailer 933-1907

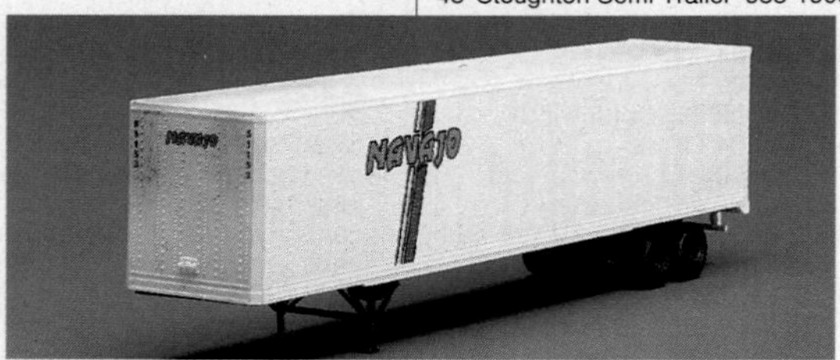

48' Stoughton Semi Trailer 933-1918

WALTHERS™

Walthers HO Scale kits feature detailed styrene parts and are designed for easy construction with basic hobby tools. Each car is prepainted and lettered in an authentic scheme that includes end reporting marks. All kits are complete with instructions, weights, trucks with nonmagnetic brass axles and horn-hook couplers.

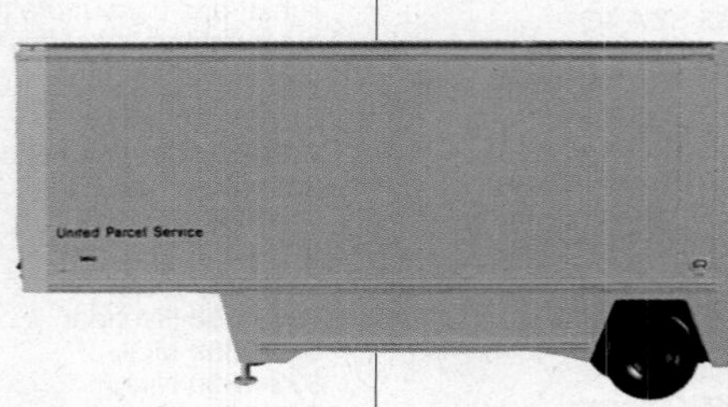

26' Parcel Trailer 933-1581

TRAILERS

26' PARCEL TRAILERS

933-1581 Parcel Van w/Decals **3.98**
933-1580 Undecorated **3.98**

45' STOUGHTON® 45/102 TRAILER EA 4.98

933-1401 SP (Golden Pig)
933-1403 CSX
933-1404 XTRA
933-1407 UP
933-1408 Transamerica Leasing
933-1409 Redon
933-1410 Minnesota, Duluth & Western
933-1411 KCS
933-1412 ATSF

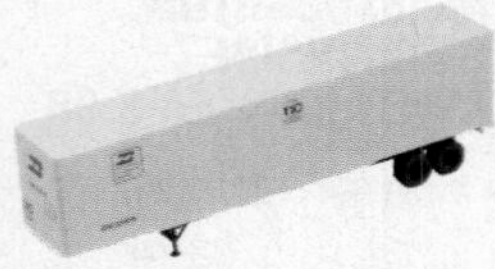

932-1413 BN
932-1414 Florida East Coast
932-1415 CP America
932-1416 Tote
932-1417 Toledo, Peoria & Western
932-1418 Iowa Interstate
932-1419 DRGW
932-1420 WP
933-1400 Undecorated

Limited Quantity Available

933-1402 Vermont Railway
933-1405 IC
933-1406 NS

32' VAN TRAILER EA 3.49

933-1601 Erie (aluminum)
933-1602 PRR (tuscan red)
933-1611 NiKP(dark blue)
933-1616 Pacific Intermountain Express (white)
933-1617 Roadway (aluminum)
933-1620 Glendenning (maroon)

933-1623 SLSF (yellow)
933-1600 Undecorated

40' TRAILER EA 3.98

933-1655 Railway Express Agency (dark green)
933-1658 UP (aluminum)
933-1660 US Mail (white)
933-1663 ATSF (aluminum)
933-1668 A&P (aluminum)
933-1671 CNW
933-1673 UP "We Can Handle It"
933-1674 IC (New scheme)
933-1650 Undecorated

Limited Quantity Available

933-1666 Time DC (white)
933-1670 Seaboard
933-1672 Strick
933-1675 SOU

40' Trailer 933-1663

40' Trailer 933-1668

40' Trailer 933-1673

40' Trailer 933-1674

Front Runner 932-3981
45' Stoughton Trailer 933-1401

Roadname Abbreviation Key

ATSF Santa Fe
B&O Baltimore & Ohio
BN Burlington Northern
BNSF Burlington Northern Santa Fe (1996 Merger)
C&O Chesapeake & Ohio
CB&Q Chicago Burlington & Quincy
CN Canadian National
CNJ Central Railroad of New Jersey
CNW Chicago & North Western
CP Canadian Pacific
CR Conrail
CSX CSX
D&H Delaware & Hudson
DRGW Rio Grande
EL Erie Lackawanna
GN Great Northern
IC Illinois Central
L&N Louisville & Nashville
LV Lehigh Valley
MILW Milwaukee Road
MKT Katy (Missouri, Kansas, Texas)
MON Monon
MP Missouri Pacific
MOW Maintenance Of Way
N&W Norfolk & Western
NH New Haven
NKP Nickel Plate Road
NP Northern Pacific
NS Norfolk Southern
NYC New York Central
PFE Pacific Fruit Express
PRR Pennsylvania
RDG Reading
ROCK Rock Island
SOO Soo Line
SOU Southern Railway
SSW St. Louis Southwestern (Cotton Belt)
SP Southern Pacific
UP Union Pacific
WC Wisconsin Central
WM Western Maryland

WALTHERS™

MI-Jack Crane 933-3122

Kalmar Container Crane 933-3109

CONTAINER CRANES

MI-JACK TRANSLIFT INTERMODAL CRANE

933-3122 MI-Jack Crane **21.98**
The Translift Crane is used to lift trailers or containers. It's wide enough to straddle the intermodal car and two rows of trailers or containers parked side by side, making short work of loading or unloading.

Many parts on the model are adjustable to simulate a working crane. Magnets are included to hold containers securely without gluing. Decals and complete instructions are included.

KALMAR CONTAINER CRANE

933-3109 Kalmar Container Crane **19.98**
These mobile cranes are used for side loading or unloading and are especially well suited to smaller terminals. Model is molded in safety yellow and includes decals and instructions.

CONTAINERS

Walthers containers, available in the four most common prototype lengths of 20, 28, 40 and 48', are great loads for any modern intermodal car and a must for realistic terminal scenes. Each package includes one prepainted and assembled container.

20' RIBBED-SIDE CONTAINER EA 2.98

933-1754

933-1751 Maersk
933-1752 K-Line
933-1753 Hanjin
933-1754 Evergreen
933-1755 Genstar
933-1756 OOCL
933-1757 Mitsui OSK
933-1758 Triton
933-1759 Nedlloyd
933-1760 GELCO
933-1761 CP Ships
933-1762 CAST
933-1763 American President Lines (APL)
933-1764 Flexi-Van
933-1765 NOL
933-1766 NYK
933-1767 Hamburg Sud
933-1768 Xtra International
933-1769 UASC
933-1750 Undecorated

20' TANK CONTAINER EA 3.98

933-1953

933-1951 ATSF
933-1952 UP
933-1953 SEACO
933-1954 TransAmerica
933-1955 K&W Alaska
933-1956 Matlack
933-1957 Tiphook
933-1958 Trans Ocean
933-1959 Agmark
933-1960 Northbrook
933-1961 Bond
933-1962 Vanhool
933-1963 Hoyer
933-1964 Stolt
933-1965 Cronos
933-1966 Miller
933-1950 Undecorated

28' CONTAINER EA 2.98 (UNLESS NOTED)

933-1553

933-1551 American Freightways
933-1552 BN America
933-1553 Parcel Trailer w/Decals
933-1569 Assembled Parcel Trailer and Chassis w/Decals **6.98**
933-1570 Chassis Kit w/Decals
933-1550 Undecorated

40' HIGH CUBE CONTAINER EA 2.98

933-1701

933-1701 Maersk
933-1702 APL
933-1703 Evergreen
933-1704 K-Line
933-1705 Hapag-Lloyd
933-1706 Matson
933-1707 ITEL
933-1708 CAST
933-1709 CP Ship
933-1710 OOCL
933-1711 Hyundai
933-1712 Hanjin
933-1713 TransAmerica
933-1714 Genstar
933-1715 XTRA
933-1716 Tropical
933-1717 P&O
933-1718 Nedlloyd
933-1719 Yang Ming Line
933-1720 Columbus Line
933-1721 Crowley
933-1700 Undecorated

40' REEFER CONTAINER EA 3.49

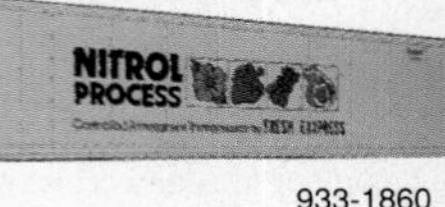

933-1860

Equipped with a "picture frame" refrigeration unit that draws power from a separate generator, these containers are lighter and carry more than other containers of this type.

933-1851 K- Line
933-1852 Sea-Land
933-1853 TransAmerica
933-1854 Evergreen
933-1855 Maersk
933-1856 APL
933-1857 Dole
933-1858 Hyundai
933-1859 MOL
933-1860 Nitrol
933-1861 NYK
933-1862 P&O
933-1863 Cosco
933-1864 Trans Ocean
933-1850 Undecorated

48' STOUGHTON RIBSIDE EXTERIOR POST CONTAINER EA 3.98

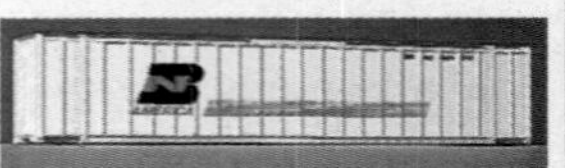
933-1818

933-1805 Norfolk Southern
933-1816 EMP
933-1817 Santa Fe
933-1818 BN America
933-1819 J.B. Hunt®
933-1820 APL
933-1821 NACS
933-1822 Carolina
933-1823 Union Pacific
933-1849 Undecorated

48' STOUGHTON SMOOTHSIDE CONTAINER EA 3.98

933-1807

933-1801 CP/US Service
933-1802 CN Laser
933-1803 BN America
933-1804 Conrail Mercury
933-1806 APL
933-1807 Conquest
933-1808 Genstar
933-1809 CSX/SL
933-1810 XTRA
933-1811 ATSF
933-1812 SP
933-1813 UP/Genstar
933-1814 ITEL
933-1815 J.B. Hunt®
933-1824 BCL
933-1825 CWT
933-1800 Undecorated

WALTHERS™

Walthers HO Scale kits feature detailed styrene parts and are designed for easy construction with basic hobby tools. Each car is prepainted and lettered in an authentic scheme that includes end reporting marks. All kits are complete with instructions, weights, trucks with nonmagnetic brass axles and horn-hook couplers.

GONDOLAS

Gondolas carry a wide range of heavy and unusual loads.

All-steel construction has long been standard, because of the rough service and constant exposure to the elements. As a result, these cars survive many years of revenue service despite their beat-up appearance.

READY-TO-RUN BETHGON COALPORTER™ GONDOLA SIX-PACKS EA 59.98 (UNLESS NOTED)

The BethGon Coalporter™ can be seen on railroads across the country, with more than 10,000 cars in service. The BethGon features all-aluminum construction and a unique trough-style bottom for added carrying capacity. Because there are no discharge chutes on the bottom of the car, these cars are unloaded strictly by rotary dump.

With these new models, you'll be able to model a unit train in minutes. The six-packs come ready to run, and each car features a different number. The cars are sharply detailed, with the authentic trough bottom and a hidden weight for better operation.

READY-TO-RUN BETHGON COALPORTER™ GONDOLAS

6-PACKS EA 59.98

FIRST NUMBER SERIES

932-5301 BN
932-5302 CSXT
932-5303 UP
932-5304 NS
932-5319 BNSF (green)
932-5330 CN New
932-5331 BNSF (Mineral Red) ***NEW***
932-5332 CSXT (silver) ***NEW***

Limited Quantity Available

932-5305 Wisconsin Electric WPEX
932-5308 Somerset

SECOND NUMBER SERIES

932-5309 Detroit Edison DEEX
932-5311 BN
932-5312 CSXT
932-5313 UP
932-5314 NS
932-5317 BNSF-Early Merger Scheme (black, white)
932-5318 CSX
932-5327 BNSF-Later Merger Scheme (aluminum, green)

SINGLE CAR

932-5300 Undecorated Kit **9.98**

BETHGON COAL LOADS

These one-piece castings are designed especially for the Bethgons and feature realistic color and texture. Drop-in mounting.

933-1038 Two-Pack **6.98**
933-1039 Six-Pack **12.98**

53' THRALL GONDOLA EA 10.98

In the late 1960s, a 53' gondola with corrugated side panels was introduced by Thrall. The corrugation made the side panels stronger and more resistant to dents and damage. A smooth-side version, designed for service where side panel strength is not as critical, is also used by numerous railroads.

Limited Quantity Available

932-5901 UP, Corrugated Sides
932-5903 SP, Smooth Sides
932-5949 Undecorated, Corrugated Sides

65' MILL GONDOLA EA 9.98

Getting finished steel or scrap metal to the customer is a job for railroads, and when the load is large or odd-shaped 65' Mill Gondolas are frequently called into action. Walthers kit contains parts to build three versions: Standard, with fixed, short ends for hauling beams and other loads; Drop End, with short, folding ends for handling long items that exceed the length of the car; and Bulkhead, with higher fixed ends to accomodate lighter loads like pipe.

Bethgon Gondola 932-5301

Bethgon Gondola 932-5302

Bethgon Gondola 932-5306

53' Thrall Gondola 932-5901

Limited Quantity Available

932-3251 BN
932-3253 DRGW
932-3255 CNW
932-3250 Undecorated
932-3254 MILW
932-3256 Elgin, Joliet & Eastern

WALTHERS™

55' Cushion Coil Car 932-3870

55' Cushion Coil Car 932-3857

55' Cushion Coil Car w/Round Hood 932-3882

Steel Coil Loads

COIL CARS

55' CUSHION COIL CAR EA 11.98

Among the unusual loads moved by railroads are large steel coils used to make automobile bodies, appliances and other products. Because of their size (6 to 10' in diameter) and weight, coils are more easily shipped by rail than by truck.

Classified as both gondolas and flat cars, coil cars feature a "V" shaped cradle in place of the usual floor. Adjustable retainers hold the coils in place and a cushion underframe helps prevent end-to-end load shifting. Removable hoods protect the coils from the weather.

932-3857 CNW (green, yellow)
932-3864 MILW (black, yellow)
932-3867 GTW (blue)
932-3870 CSX Transportation (yellow, black)
932-3873 NS (black)
932-3850 Undecorated

55' CUSHION COIL CARS W/ROUND HOODS EA 11.98

932-3881 CSXT
932-3882 Conrail
932-3883 NS
932-3884 ATSF
932-3885 BN
932-3886 CNW
932-3887 BNSF
932-3888 Indiana Harbor Belt (HARBOR Scheme)
932-3889 IC
932-3890 UP
932-3899 Undecorated

STEEL COIL LOADS

933-1499 Steel Coil Loads pkg(12) **4.98**

Load your Walthers or other steel service cars with this kit! Injection-molded parts capture the look of the huge coils but are easy to build. Parts for 12 coils in two sizes are included.

State Tool & Die Co.

HOT METAL CAR

661-720 Pollock 75-Ton Kling Hot Metal Car w/Trucks & Couplers **17.95**

SPACER CAR

661-740 With Trucks & Couplers **11.95**

COIL CAR HOODS

Add variety to steel service cars or detail your mill scene with these round and corrugated coil car hoods. Matching the styles commonly seen on prototype equipment, these parts are designed for use with Walthers Coil Cars (3850 series), Roundhouse gondolas (1680 series) or Life-Like D.E. Gondolas.

Basic kits include a pair of unpainted hoods. For big projects, sets of six hoods are available. All kits include add-on stacking braces and instructions.

ROUND - REVISED

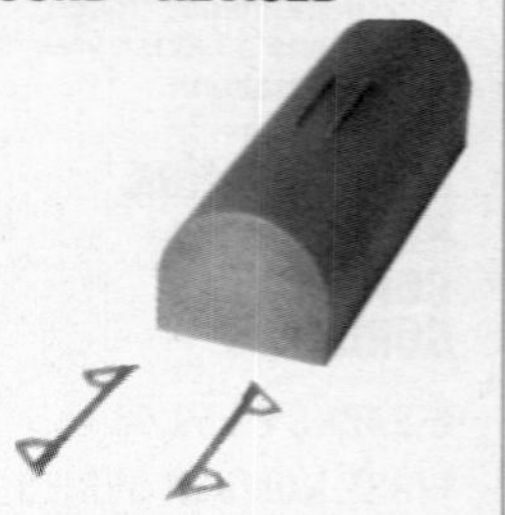

661-1012 Set of 2 **3.79**
661-1016 Set of 6 **9.95**

CORRUGATED

661-2012 Set of 2 **4.25**
661-2016 Set of 6 **11.95**

DRAWBARS

661-600 Multi-Purpose Drawbars pkg(10) **3.00** *NEW*

WALTHERS™

"THE WORKS"

These steel-service cars are ready to meet the vigorous demands of a blistering day at "The Works."

SLAG CAR

Kit features separate ladle, simulated dump mechanism, plus trucks and horn-hook couplers.

932-3140 Slag Car **15.98**
932-3141 Slag Car 3-Pack **44.98**

HOT METAL CAR

Easy to build, highly detailed cars feature a positionable ladle, six-wheel trucks, drive housing and horn-hook couplers.

932-3130 Hot Metal Car **16.98**
932-3131 Hot Metal Car 3-Pack **49.98**

COKE CAR

932-3091 Coke Car 3-Pack **24.98**
These cars are Converted from older 36' two-bay hoppers and feature side and end extensions.

ORE CARS

Based on "Minnesota" cars that served the Missabe range. At home in the mills or mines, many are still used today. Highly accurate kits feature diecast underframes. One pair of working knuckle couplers (or optional horn-hooks) are included for the end cars, with dummy couplers for all intermediate cars.

FOUR PACKS EA 21.98

932-4401 UP
932-4402 GN
932-4403 CNW
932-4404 Duluth, Missabe & Iron Range
932-4406 Bessemer & Lake Erie
932-4407 SOO
932-4408 Data Only (oxide)
932-4449 Wisconsin Southern *NEW*
932-4400 Undecorated

Limited Quantity Available
932-4405 NP

12-PACKS - FIRST SERIES

932-4459 CN 59.98

ORE CAR 12-PACKS - SECOND SERIES EA 59.98

Same roadnames, but with 12 new numbers to model a longer train in minutes. One pair of working knuckle couplers (or optional horn-hooks) are included for the end cars, with dummy couplers for all intermediate cars.

932-4459 CN #1
932-4461 UP
932-4462 GN
932-4463 CNW
932-4464 Duluth, Missabe & Iron Range
932-4465 NP
932-4466 Bessemer & Lake Erie
932-4467 SOO

TACONITE PELLET CARS

Expand mining or steel mill operations in minutes with these models! Older ore jennies were rebuilt with short side and end extensions to increase carrying capacity and some roads combined four cars into one, by connecting the intermediate cars with drawbars.

Sporting authentic paint and extensions, these models fill an important gap in HO freight car fleets. They come in 4- and 12-packs, each with different car numbers.

One pair of working knuckle couplers (optional horn-hooks are also provided) are included for the end cars. Intermediate cars can be connected with dummy couplers OR drawbars (both included) to match your favorite prototypes.

FOUR-PACKS EA 21.98

932-4501 Bessemer & Lake Erie
932-4502 BN
932-4503 CN
932-4504 Duluth, Missabe & Iron Range
932-4505 GN
932-4506 Lake Superior & Ishpeming
932-4508 Data Only
932-4500 Undecorated

12-PACKS EA 59.98

932-4551 Bessemer & Lake Erie
932-4552 BN
932-4553 CN
932-4554 Duluth, Missabe & Iron Range
932-4555 GN
932-4556 Lake Superior & Ishpeming
932-4550 Undecorated

TACONITE PELLET CAR BN 932-4552

Ore Car CN 932-4459

Ore Car UP 932-4461

Ore Car GN 932-4462

Ore Car CNW 932-4463

Ore Car NP 932-4465

Ore Car SOO 932-4467

Taconite Pellet Car 932-4504

Taconite Pellet Car Data Only 932-4508

Taconite Pellet Car 932-4551

Taconite Pellet Car 932-4553

Taconite Pellet Car GN 932-4555

Taconite Pellet Car 932-4556

WALTHERS™

Thrall 56' All-Door Box Car
932-7008

50' Single-Sheathed
Double-Door Box Car 932-5853

Fruit Growers Express RBL
Insulated Box Car 932-4753

BOX CARS

50' SINGLE-SHEATHED DOUBLE-DOOR BOX CAR EA 9.98

Cars of this style appeared around 1929-1930 on several Western railroads, where they were used to handle automobiles, furniture and lumber products. Their double-wide doors simplified loading these cargoes, which did not fit well in smaller cars. To handle larger vehicles, some roads added a door at one end, and when spotted at a ramp, the cargo could be driven on or off in a matter of minutes. Like most cars of this period, steel and wood parts were used in construction. Many remained in service into the 1960s.

This model features a detailed plastic body, and both standard and automobile door ends to match prototype practice.

Limited Quantity Available
932-5851 GN
932-5852 UP
932-5853 NP
932-5855 SP
932-5856 ATSF
932-5850 Undecorated

CRYOGENIC REFRIGERATED BOX CAR EA 11.98

First built in 1992, these cars use carbon dioxide vapor and "snow" to keep their loads frozen in transit. They're now hard at work hauling frozen juice, meat, potatoes, poultry and more.

Limited Quantity Available

Roadname Shown Unavailable

932-5451 Arcticar/GATX Demonstrator (white)
932-5454 Carnation (white)
932-5455 Cryo-Trans (white)
932-5456 Universal Frozen Foods (white)

All roadnames shown are registered trademarks, used with permission of the trademark owner/s.

FRUIT GROWERS EXPRESS RBL INSULATED BOX CAR EA 9.98

Palletized shipments of perishables led to the introduction of this class in the early 1960s. The interior is fitted with restraints, which hold the loads securely and protect them against damage caused by slack action. To speed loading times, 10'6" plug doors are used, providing easier access for forklifts. These cars also carry electronic items, furniture, paper and machinery.

932-4753 UP (yellow)
932-4755 Conrail (yellow)
932-4757 CNW
932-4758 CP Rail
932-4759 N&W
932-4760 ROCK
932-4761 WP
932-4762 BC Rail
932-4763 EL (blue, white lettering)
932-4764 CSXT (dark blue, yellow lettering)
932-4765 CP (yellow scheme, black lettering)
932-4766 CN (Box Car Red, white lettering)
932-4750 Undecorated

THRALL 56' ALL-DOOR BOX CARS

Lumber has always been difficult to ship by rail. Box cars were used to provide protection, but were hard to load and unload. Flat cars eliminated those problems, but loads had to be tarped to protect them.

In 1967, Thrall took the best of both ideas and created the All-Door Box Car. Equipped with four large doors, this provided a 25' wide opening for easy handling, but loads remained completely enclosed in transit.

Our ready-to-run cars are packed with detail and painted for a variety of private owners. Plus, three different numbers are available for each scheme. Free-rolling trucks and working knuckle couplers are included.

SINGLE CARS EA 15.98
932-7001 Weyerhaeuser *NEW*
932-7002 US Plywood *NEW*
932-7003 Boise Cascade *NEW*
932-7004 St. Regis Paper *NEW*
932-7005 Idaho Forest Industries *NEW*
932-7006 Masonite Corporation *NEW*
932-7007 Canfor *NEW*
932-7008 Georgia-Pacific *NEW*
932-7000 Undecorated *NEW*

TWO-PACKS WITH DIFFERENT NUMBERS EA 29.98
932-27001 Weyerhaeuser *NEW*
932-27002 US Plywood *NEW*
932-27003 Boise Cascade *NEW*
932-27004 St. Regis Paper *NEW*
932-27005 Idaho Forest Industries *NEW*
932-27006 Masonite Corporation *NEW*
932-27007 Canfor *NEW*
932-27008 Georgia-Pacific *NEW*

Hot New Products Announced Daily! Visit Walthers Web site at

www.walthers.com

Roadname Abbreviation Key

ATSF Santa Fe
B&O Baltimore & Ohio
BN Burlington Northern
BNSF Burlington Northern Santa Fe (1996 Merger)
C&O Chesapeake & Ohio
CB&Q Chicago Burlington & Quincy
CN Canadian National
CNJ Central Railroad of New Jersey
CNW Chicago & North Western
CP Canadian Pacific
CR Conrail
CSX CSX
D&H Delaware & Hudson
DRGW Rio Grande
EL Erie Lackawanna
GN Great Northern
IC Illinois Central
L&N Louisville & Nashville
LV Lehigh Valley
MILW Milwaukee Road
MKT Katy (Missouri, Kansas, Texas)
MON Monon
MP Missouri Pacific
MOW Maintenance Of Way
N&W Norfolk & Western
NH New Haven
NKP Nickel Plate Road
NP Northern Pacific
NS Norfolk Southern
NYC New York Central
PFE Pacific Fruit Express
PRR Pennsylvania
RDG Reading
ROCK Rock Island
SOO Soo Line
SOU Southern Railway
SSW St. Louis Southwestern (Cotton Belt)
SP Southern Pacific
UP Union Pacific
WC Wisconsin Central
WM Western Maryland

WALTHERS™

Walthers HO Scale kits feature detailed styrene parts and are designed for easy construction with basic hobby tools. Each car is prepainted and lettered in an authentic scheme that includes end reporting marks. All kits are complete with instructions, weights, trucks with nonmagnetic brass axles and horn-hook couplers.

50' NORTH AMERICAN PLUG DOOR EXTERIOR POST INSULATED BOX CAR EA 12.98

Introduced in 1964, these insulated box cars were leased to a number of railroads and private industries. In service, they carried loads which required a constant temperature, but didn't need to be refrigerated in transit. This included foodstuffs like cereal, beer, canned goods and chocolate, as well as a variety of lubricants and chemicals. Using the same basic body, three variations were built, which differed in inside length, types and thickness of insulation and load restraints. Just over 1300 roamed the rails and a few remain in use today.

These ready-to-run cars feature a detailed body, colorful paint and working knuckle couplers. Perfect for modeling bridge traffic or serving on-line users and producers, they'll brighten any freight from the 60s to the 90s.

932-3601 CNW
932-3602 DRGW
932-3603 Green Bay & Western
932-3604 Nestle (TCNX)
932-3605 WP
932-3606 Quaker Oats (QOCX)
932-3607 D&H
932-3608 Johnson Wax (JWAX)
932-3600 Undecorated.

NORTH AMERICAN 50' RBL INSULATED SMOOTHSIDE BOX CARS

North American began building its own 50' insulated box cars in 1963. They featured smoothside steel construction, underframe cushioning and a large, tight-fitting Superior plug door. This made them well suited to handle food and chemicals.

In all, 750 were built before production ended in 1965. Of those still in service, most are now privately owned.

Our fully assembled cars feature a detailed body, authentic paint, free-rolling trucks and working knuckle couplers. Plus, single and two-pack cars have different numbers.

SINGLE CARS EA 12.98

932-3451 CNW *NEW*
932-3452 DRGW *NEW*
932-3453 SP *NEW*
932-3454 NYC *NEW*
932-3455 Burlington Refrigerator Express *NEW*
932-3456 Western Pacific *NEW*
932-3457 Magcobar *NEW*
932-3458 Sterling Salt *NEW*
932-3450 Undecorated *NEW*

TWO-PACKS WITH DIFFERENT NUMBERS EA 24.98

932-23451 CNW *NEW*
932-23452 DRGW *NEW*
932-23453 SP *NEW*
932-23454 NYC *NEW*
932-23455 Burlington Refrigerator Express *NEW*
932-23456 Western Pacific *NEW*
932-23457 Magcobar *NEW*
932-23458 Sterling Salt *NEW*

North American 50' Plug Door Exterior Post Insulated Box Car 932-3603
Preproduction Model Shown

North American 50' RBL Insulated Smoothside Box Car 932-3456

WALTHERS™

REEFERS

The introduction of refrigerated cars in the 1880s made it possible to ship perishables for long distances. Early reefers had all-wood bodies for maximum insulation and loads were cooled by melting ice. These cars could only travel about 250 to 400 miles before they would need re-icing.

Reefers were among the last cars rebuilt with steel parts, as wood offered the best insulation. As a result, cars often had a steel roof and Dreadnaught ends, but retained their wood sides. Many cars of this style remained in service through the 1950s.

Ice-cooled, steel cars appeared in the early 1940s and some were upgraded in the 50s with plug doors. They remained in use until the 1970s.

40' GENERAL AMERICAN MEAT REEFERS EA 10.98

932-2551 Swift
932-2552 American Refrigerator Transit Co.

932-2553 Armour (PCX & TRAX)

932-2554 Dubuque Packing Co. (GACX)
932-2555 Wilson Car Lines
932-2556 URTX/Milwaukee Road
932-2557 Raskin Packing Co.
932-2560 American Beef Packers
932-2561 Iowa Beef Packers
932-2562 Rock Island
932-2599 Undecorated-Notched Sills
932-2550 Undecorated

Limited Quantity Available
932-2558 Royal Packing Co.
932-2559 Mid-States Packers Inc.

40' General American Meat Reefer
932-2557

40' General American Meat Reefer
932-2558

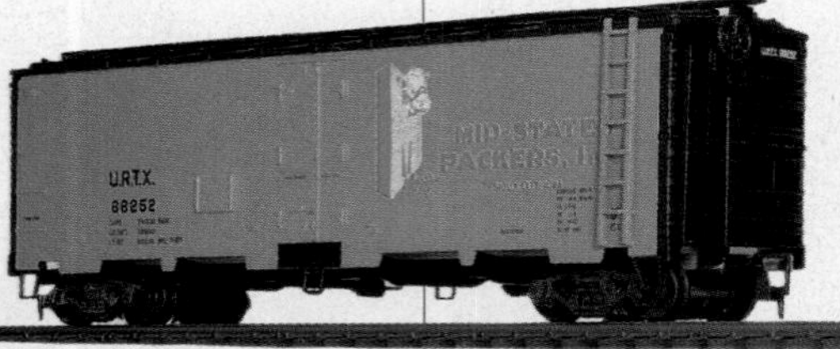

40' General American Meat Reefer
932-2559

932-2560

40' General American Meat Reefer
932-2561

40' General American Meat Reefer
932-2562

40' Reefer Six-Pack
932-950

40' Reefer Six-Pack
932-952

40' Reefer Six-Pack
932-953

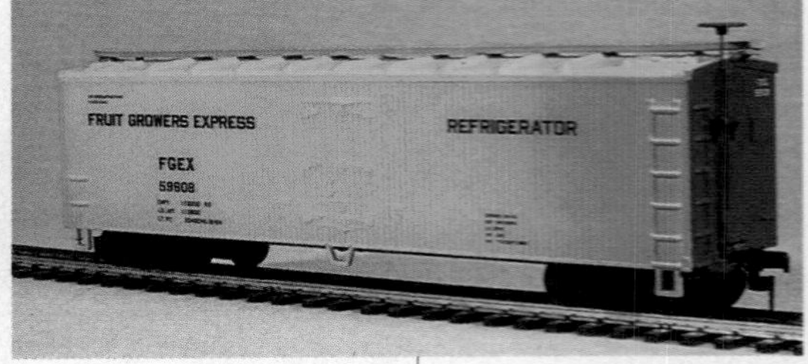

40' Reefer Six-Pack
932-954

40' REEFER SIX-PACKS EA 59.98

Six classic reefer roadnames, available only in these sets. Each car features a different number. Great for ice service or perishable loading.

932-950 BREX-CB&Q (All Steel)
932-951 St. Louis Refrigerator Car Co. (SLRX–All Steel)
932-952 Western Fruit Express–GN (Wood Sides & Ends)
932-953 Merchant's Despatch Transportation–NYC (All Steel)
932-954 Fruit Growers Express (Wood Sides & Ends)
932-955 NWX–CNW (Wood Sides & Ends)
932-956 Pacific Fruit Express *NEW*
932-957 West India Fruit *NEW*
932-958 Canadian Pacific *NEW*

WALTHERS™

Walthers HO Scale kits feature detailed styrene parts and are designed for easy construction with basic hobby tools. Each car is prepainted and lettered in an authentic scheme that includes end reporting marks. All kits are complete with instructions, weights, trucks with nonmagnetic brass axles and horn-hook couplers.

COVERED HOPPERS

Since their introduction in the late 19th century, the covered hopper has become increasingly important. Protecting cargo from dirt, insects, moisture and other contaminants, they're ideal for shipping powdered or granular materials in bulk.

The cars were first built in large numbers in the 1920s, primarily for cement service, and were fairly common by the 1940s, when the first Airslide® hopper appeared.

In the 1950s, larger capacity cars like the PS2 were introduced. During this period, covered hoppers began replacing box cars for many types of loads. Today, they are the most widely used car type on the nation's rails and whether railroad owned or leased from a private firm, they often sport colorful paint jobs.

PULLMAN-STANDARD PS2 CENTER DISCHARGE HOPPER EA 9.98

With their assembly line manufacturing, Pullman-Standard was able to modify its PS2 hopper to meet the needs of many customers. In the 1960s, a new version was introduced for the grain industry with a trough-style roof hatch for faster loading and the proven center discharge for fast unloading. Immensely popular, the cars were purchased by dozens of railroads and private firms, and many are still going strong.

This kit features a superbly detailed body, separate roofwalk, brake gear and hatches, plus a variety of authentic paint schemes.

932-5701 UP (gray)
932-5702 BN (Cascade green)
932-5703 CNW (new yellow)
932-5709 ATSF
932-5713 SOO
932-5718 Wisconsin Central
932-5720 LV
932-5700 Undecorated

Limited Quantity Available

932-5707 CB&Q
932-5710 DRGW
932-5711 Corn Products
932-5715 Chessie
932-5719 Far-Mar Co-Op

Pullman-Standard PS2 Center Discharge Hopper 932-5702

Pullman-Standard PS2 Center Discharge Hopper 932-5703

Pullman-Standard PS2 Center Discharge Hopper Roadname Shown Not Available

Pullman-Standard PS2 Center Discharge Hopper 932-5720

932-5708

WALTHERS™

50' Airslide Covered Hopper
932-3665

AIRSLIDE® COVERED HOPPERS

Developed in the late 1940s for cement service, the Airslide® Covered Hopper began to appear in large numbers after 1954. These air-tight cars kept loads clean and dry, while a special fabric liner simplified unloading. Thousands are still in use today, hauling food products, chemicals and other powdered materials.

Each easy-to-build kit has a one-piece body, with numerous add-on details like loading hatches with separate securing clamps, a see-through roofwalk, brake gear and more.

"Airslide" is a registered trademark of the General American Transportation Corporation.

50' AIRSLIDE® COVERED HOPPERS WITH NEW NUMBERS EA 9.98

In the early 1960s, demand for larger cars capable of carrying heavier loads led to the development of a 100 ton capacity, 50' Airslide® hopper.

932-3659 ADM® Milling
932-3665 Burlington Northern
932-3667 Wonder Bread
932-3668 Chicago and North Western
932-3678 Norfolk Southern
932-3679 GATX Modern
932-3650 Undecorated

Limited Quantity Available
932-3680 CSXT

FREIGHT CAR ACCESSORIES

933-1030

Simulate end-of-car cushioning devices on modern freight cars with this kit. The longer draft gear increases the distance between cars for more realism.

The Walthers Cushion Car Coupler Pocket Kit is molded in rust-colored styrene that's easily painted. Assembly drawings and detailed instructions make this modeling project easy and fun. Parts to modify four cars are included. Horn hook or knuckle couplers work well with this kit.

CUSHION CAR COUPLERS

933-1030 Cushion Car Coupler Pocket Kit pkg (4 pair) **3.98**

HORN-HOOK COUPLERS

933-995 X2F Horn-Hook Couplers pkg(12) **1.98**
Standard replacement fits all Walthers kits. Molded in Delrin® plastic.

ATHEARN COUPLER POCKET CONVERSION KIT

933-997 2 Pair **3.98**
Converts Athearn 85' Hi-Cube box cars and 85' flat cars from a truck-mounted coupler bar system to a body-mounted swinging coupler bar system as used on Walthers Enclosed Auto Carrier. Kit includes parts to convert 2 cars.

50' Airslide Covered Hopper
932-3667

WALTHERS™

Walthers HO Scale kits feature detailed styrene parts and are designed for easy construction with basic hobby tools. Each car is prepainted and lettered in an authentic scheme that includes end reporting marks. All kits are complete with instructions, weights, trucks with nonmagnetic brass axles and horn-hook couplers.

Ballast Hopper 932-4201

HOPPERS

Open-top hoppers transport a wide variety of bulk materials including coal, sand, ore, gravel and even sugar beets which do not require protection from the weather.

49' 100-TON QUAD HOPPER EA 9.98

As new clean air standards were mandated in the 1970s, coal-fired power plants around the country found themselves in need of clean-burning, low sulfur coal. The vast deposits in the western US met this criteria and demand skyrocketed. New rail lines were built to serve the coal field and orders for 100-ton cars poured in.

932-4901 BN (black)
932-4902 UP (black)
932-4903 DRGW (black)
932-4906 CSX Transportation (black)

932-4908 UP
932-4900 Undecorated (black)

Limited Quantity Available
932-4907 CB&Q
932-4909 CHTT
932-4910 GN

100 TON QUAD HOPPER 6-PACKS EA 54.98

932-49411 MP *NEW*
932-49421 Clinchfield *NEW*
932-49431 NS (silver) *NEW*

SPECIAL LIMITED RE-RUN FIRST NUMBER SERIES 6-PACKS AVAILABLE ONLY WHILE SUPPLIES LAST EA 54.98

932-49311 BN
932-49321 UP
932-49331 DRGW
932-49351 NS
932-49361 CSX

COAL LOAD

933-1037 2-Pack **6.98**
One-piece resin castings, ready to install in your cars.

BALLAST HOPPER EA 9.98

Railroads always maintain a fleet of these cars for moving ballast.

Limited Quantity Available
932-4201 UP
932-4202 CSX
932-4207 NS
932-4212 CP
932-4200 Undecorated
932-4203 ATSF
932-4204 Conrail
932-4205 MOW
932-4206 BN
932-4208 CNW
932-4209 SP
932-4210 DRGW
932-4211 Amtrak

3-PACKS EA 29.98

Limited Quantity Available
932-34201 UP
932-34203 ATSF
932-34204 CR
932-34205 MOW
932-34206 BN
932-34207 NS
932-34208 CNW
932-34210 DRGW
932-34211 Amtrak
932-34212 CP
932-34213 MILW
932-34214 CN
932-34215 SOO
932-34216 SP

PRE-SIZE MODEL SPECIALTIES

FREIGHT LOAD

483-455 Ballast **5.60**
For Walthers 4200 Series Ballast Hoppers.

SCRAP LOADS EA 6.00

483-453 For Walthers 53' Thrall Gondola
483-454 For MDC Roundhouse 1680 Series 50' Mill Gondola

WALTHERS™

Walthers HO Scale kits feature detailed styrene parts and are designed for easy construction with basic hobby tools. Each car is prepainted and lettered in an authentic scheme that includes end reporting marks. All kits are complete with instructions, weights, trucks with nonmagnetic brass axles and horn-hook couplers.

37' Cement Service Covered Hopper
932-5406

37' CEMENT SERVICE COVERED HOPPERS EA 9.98

In the early 1980s, Greenville Steel Car Company introduced a new hopper for powdered materials. Cement proved to be too heavy for the car, so a slightly smaller version was created for cement service. This smaller car was also sold as a general purpose covered hopper, and can be found carrying plastic pellets, roofing granules, flour, grain and more.

This kit has a one-piece body with end ladders molded in place, separate hatches, a thin profile roofwalk and other add-on details.

932-5401 UP (gray)
932-5402 BN (gray)
932-5403 CSX Transportation (gray)
932-5404 CNW (yellow)
932-5405 Wisconsin Central (gray)
932-5406 ATSF (Mineral Red)
932-5407 Maryland Midland
932-5408 Winchester & Western
932-5409 N&W
932-5410 Blue Circle Cement
932-5411 Dakota, Minnesota & Eastern
932-5400 Undecorated

STOCK CARS

Moving livestock from range to market was once an important part of the traffic on virtually every railroad.

Livestock were shipped from virtually every town. Small stock pens were built alongside the team track to handle one or two cars. Loaded cars would be routed as quickly as possible to a classification yard. From there, dedicated stock trains raced their cargo to the packing plants.

By the 1930s, increased truck competition, changing packing plant operations and the development of better refrigerated rail cars contributed to a steady decline in livestock shipments. By 1970, most US roads were out of the business altogether. Some rail shipments of livestock continued on the UP as well as the CP and CN into the late 1980s.

40' STOCK CARS EA 9.98

End Detail

Roll livestock to market in these improved cars, now featuring separate letter boards. Stock cars are an essential part of the traffic on any layout set before 1960. Since the basic design remained in service for decades, these cars are also right at home behind your favorite steam or first generation diesel power.

These models feature authentic slatted sides, and are available with braced wood or dreadnaught ends.

Limited Quantity Available
932-2750 Undecorated - Dreadnaught Ends
932-3400 Undecorated - Braced Wood Ends

MAINTENANCE-OF-WAY EQUIPMENT

Keeping structures, bridges and track in good repair is the responsibility of the Maintenance-of-Way (MOW) department. These jobs require a variety of specialized equipment, much of which is rebuilt from "retired" freight cars. To keep costs down, virtually any kind of car is used. As a result, you may still see old wood freight cars or 40' box cars on modern railroads.

Since these cars often no longer meet certain safety requirements, they can not be interchanged with another railroad. To identify their new role, they are repainted in a special color scheme and lettered as MOW equipment. With different cars to choose from, Walthers has MOW equipment that will be right at home on your railroad, no matter what era you model!

SHEEPSCOT SCALE PRODUCTS

Pile Driver Conversion
668-75005

PILE DRIVER

668-1340 Large Brownhoist **135.00** ***NEW***
Pile driver on rail chassis can either be made operational or folded for travel. Car mounted.

PILE DRIVER CONVERSION

668-75005 Industrial Brownhoist Type **25.00**
Convert any Walthers 25-Ton Crane (sold separately) into a pile driver with this kit. Prototypes are used in bridge construction and repair, driving pilings down to firm ground that will support the structure. Kit includes photo-etched booms, with detail castings including pulley, head sheaves and steam hammer. Cables, decals and window "glass" are also provided. Recommended for builders with some experience. Complete instructions also include notes on soldering and working with brass.

WALTHERS™

Walthers HO Scale kits feature detailed styrene parts and are designed for easy construction with basic hobby tools. Each car is prepainted and lettered in an authentic scheme that includes end reporting marks. All kits are complete with instructions, weights, trucks with nonmagnetic brass axles and horn-hook couplers.

Jordan Spreader 932-5359

Roadname Shown Not Available

Russell Snow Plow 932-5762

25 TON CRANE EA 9.98

Used by railroads, these versatile cranes are also operated by all types of private industries.

932-5612 Electric Company
932-5610 Vulcan Steel
932-5611 Brownhoist
932-5500 Undecorated

JORDAN SPREADER EA 24.98

The Jordan Spreader can be found cleaning up after rock slides and spreading ballast, but cutting drainage ditches is where it is found most often. Jordans plow snow to the side of the right-of-way after the Russell Plow has cleared the line.

This model features detailed styrene parts and authentic paint schemes.

932-5351 UP
932-5352 ATSF
932-5354 SP
932-5355 GN
932-5356 PRR
932-5357 CR
932-5358 BN
932-5359 CNW
932-5360 CSX
932-5361 CP
932-5362 NS

DIFCO DUMP CAR EA 14.98

These cars are the railroad equivalent of a dump truck. Designed to carry up to 100 tons of load, they are fitted with large pneumatic cylinders and side doors, and can dump to the left or right of the tracks. They can also be used in revenue service to carry sand, gravel, cinders, coal and other loose bulk material.

Kits are easy to build, and can be positioned in a dump mode, with moveable cylinders and side doors.

932-5951 UP
932-5954 Conrail
932-5955 BN
932-5957 CNW
932-5958 SP
932-5962 CN
932-5963 Amtrak

RUSSELL SNOW PLOW EA 14.98

This style of push-type plow is owned by dozens of railroads. The "Russells" are either painted in standard maintenance colors, or a bright scheme to contrast with the snow for added safety.

The model features basic cab interior, separate underbody details, including a flanger, positionable wings and many other details.

932-5751 MOW
932-5752 UP
932-5755 PRR
932-5759 Boston &Maine
932-5762 Wisconsin Central
932-5750 Undecorated

Limited Quantity Available

932-5753 GN
932-5754 BN
932-5756 ATSF
932-5757 CNW
932-5758 CR
932-5760 MILW

25 Ton Crane 932-5610

WALTHERS™

AMERICAN LOCOMOTIVE CRANE

By the 1950s, the days of steam-powered wrecking cranes were numbered. Railroads began replacing the "big hook" with smaller, more versatile diesel-powered cranes. These self-propelled units eliminated the need for a separate loco and crew, making them more cost effective. Since they could pull a few loaded cars at low speeds, they proved ideal for track and bridge repairs, where you'll often find them today. Many private industries, such as steel mills, scrap yards and others that require a crane, found these units an ideal choice. They can function as a crane or a switcher, doing two jobs for less money.

These kits offer you the same versatility of the real thing! Choose from a powered model, complete with hidden motor and gear drive, capable of pulling a few cars. Or, for a static display, there's a dummy version. Both kits come in subassemblies, requiring only final assembly and rigging for the finishing touch.

POWERED EA 54.95

932-5071 MOW
932-5072 UP
932-5073 ATSF
932-5074 SP
932-5075 GN
932-5076 CSX
932-5077 BN
932-5078 NS
932-5079 PRR
932-5080 Amtrak
932-5081 CR
932-5082 WC
932-5083 MILW *NEW*
932-5084 CNW *NEW*
932-5085 B&O *NEW*
932-5086 C&O *NEW*
932-5070 Undecorated

DUMMY EA 29.98

932-5051 MOW
932-5052 UP
932-5053 ATSF
932-5054 SP
932-5055 GN
932-5056 CSX
932-5057 BN
932-5058 NS
932-5059 PRR
932-5060 Amtrak
932-5061 CR
932-5062 WC
932-5063 MILW *NEW*
932-5064 CNW *NEW*
932-5065 B&O *NEW*
932-5066 C&O *NEW*
932-5050 Undecorated

932-5082
Preproduction Model Shown

WORK TRAIN SETS

Keep your railroad running smoothly with these maintenance-of-way sets. Two different sets are offered, each with six different styles of cars. Both sets are available decorated in the same roadnames with matching paint schemes, so you can create a complete work train.

WORK TRAIN SET #1 EA 49.98

Limited Quantity Available
Include two Bunk Cars, one Kitchen Car, one Engineering Car, one assembled, 40' Tank Car and one 40' Single-Sheathed Box Car.

932-911 Maintenance of Way (gray)
932-912 ATSF (silver)
932-913 UP (green)
932-914 BN (mineral red)
932-915 CSX (orange)

WORK TRAIN SET #2 EA 49.98

Limited Quantity Available
Include one 25-Ton Crane, one Crane Tender, one 50' Flat Car, one 50' Gondola, one 40' Steel Box Car and one Combination Box Car/Caboose.

932-932 ATSF (silver)
932-933 UP (green)
932-931 Maintenance of Way (gray)
932-934 BN (Mineral Red)

Work Train Set #1

Work Train Set #2

WALTHERS™

Blacksmith Car 932-5587

INDIVIDUAL WORK CARS

WORK FLAT CAR
EA 8.98

Limited Quantity Available

An all-purpose 40' flat car. Includes details to build with a load of supplies, or as a rail & tie car.

932-5562 SP
932-5564 ATSF
932-5565 PRR
932-5568 UP
932-5569 GN
932-5560 Undecorated

BLACKSMITH CAR
EA 8.98

Limited Quantity Available

Complete with covered forge, tools and blacksmith figure.

932-5582 Central Pacific
932-5585 PRR (early scheme)
932-5580 Undecorated

42' CRANE TENDER

932-5510 Undecorated **8.98**

ALCO/LESLIE ROTARY SNOW PLOW WITH TENDER

EA 49.98

Howling winds, heavy snowfall and bitter cold mean trouble along the line! As trains slow and drifts pile up beyond the capacity of the push plows, the call goes out for the Rotary Snow Plow!

Since their commercial introduction in the late 1880s, these amazing machines have kept the rails open when nothing else would. On the business end, a huge, spinning wheel cuts drifts down to size, then feeds the snow into scoops. Centrifugal force hurls snow hundreds of feet away from the line, keeping trains moving safely.

From mountain passes to open prairies, wherever winter winds howl, generations of railroaders came to rely on these rugged machines. Now, your HO line can take on winter and win with your own WORKING rotary plow!

Our model is a faithful replica of steam-era prototypes built by Alco under the Leslie patents between 1900 and 1940. Roads large and small rostered plows of this style - where snow was a real headache, area railroads usually owned several! Many led long lives and were later rebuilt for use with diesel power.

Fully assembled and ready for duty, our new model includes a drive motor to spin the wheel*. Move your power pack throttle and the wheel spins faster or slower! Just couple your favorite motive power behind the detailed Tender (also included) with its working knuckle coupler, and you're ready to take on winter's worst.

*Of course, it just looks strong enough to plow real snow - please don't try using it like the prototype!

932-1951 ATSF *NEW*
932-1952 DRGW *NEW*
932-1953 CNW *NEW*
932-1954 SP *NEW*
932-1955 UP *NEW*
932-1956 Alaska Railroad *NEW*
932-1957 Colorado & Southern (Burlington) *NEW*
932-1958 NYC *NEW*
932-1959 MILW *NEW*
932-1960 Western Pacific *NEW*
932-1961 GN *NEW*
932-1962 NP *NEW*
932-1950 Undecorated *NEW*

Work Flat Car 932-5564

Rotary Snow Plow Prototype Shown

International Bay Window Caboose 932-4365

CABOOSES

INTERNATIONAL BAY WINDOW CABOOSE
EA 14.98

For nearly forty years, the International Bay Window Caboose was a familiar sight behind freight trains. Serving as office, lookout, restaurant and hotel to crews on the road, no other piece of rolling stock may be as much a part of railroading as this caboose.

This authentic model features separate railings and wire grab irons, all-new trucks, a full underbody and roof details. The bay windows are also separate parts, and each kit includes the correct window for its prototype.

932-4355 CNW
932-4360 MILW
932-4363 ATSF
932-4364 CR
932-4365 NYC
932-4366 NP
932-4367 WC
932-4369 NS
932-4350 Undecorated

Limited Quantity Available

932-4351 UP
932-4352 SP
932-4353 Chessie System
932-4354 BN
932-4357 N&W
932-4359 WP
932-4361 EL
932-4362 SSW (Cotton Belt)
932-4368 GN
932-4370 MP
932-4371 KCS
932-4372 L&N/Family Lines
932-4373 SLSF
932-4374 ROCK (blue)

WALTHERS™

TREES & TRAINS FREIGHT CARS

73' CENTERBEAM FLAT CARS EA 12.98

The models come fully assembled and feature the correct "opera window" or standard centerbeam to match the prototype car.

932-4101 British Columbia Railway (opera)
932-4102 UP (standard)
932-4103 TTX (standard)
932-4104 CSX (opera)
932-4105 BN (standard)
932-4106 Plum Creek (standard)
932-4107 Hampton Lumber (standard)
932-4108 Cascade Warehouse (opera)
932-4109 Tobacco Valley Lumber (opera, light blue)
932-4110 NS (standard, Box Car Red)
932-4112 CN (standard, Mineral Red)
932-4113 CP (standard, Action Red)
932-4114 Atlanta & St Andrews Bay (opera, yellow)
932-4116 Wisconsin Central (standard)
932-4117 UP (opera)
932-4118 BC Rail (opera)
932-4100 Undecorated - Standard
932-4149 Undecorated - Opera

Limited Quantity Available
932-4111 Columbia & Cowlitz (standard, dark blue)
932-4115 Tri-Con Forest Products (opera, red)

THREE-PACKS EA 35.98

932-34101 British Columbia Railway (opera)
932-34102 UP (standard)
932-34104 CSX (opera)
932-34106 Plum Creek (standard)
932-34107 Hampton Lumber (standard)
932-34108 Cascade Warehouse (opera)
932-34109 Tobacco Valley Lumber (light blue)
932-34110 NS (Standard, Box Car Red)
932-34111 Columbia & Cowlitz (Box Car Red)
932-34112 CN (Mineral Red)
932-34113 CP (Action Red)
932-34114 Atlanta & St Andrews Bay (yellow)
932-34115 Tri-Con Forest Products (red)

Limited Quantity Available
932-34105 BN (standard)

73' CENTERBEAM FLAT CAR LOADS EA 5.98

Add wrapped lumber loads to your Bulkhead Flats with these kits. Assembles in minutes, with no cutting or gluing. Each features a one-piece plastic load (one for each side of the car) that's prepainted and lettered. Just snap them on and send them down the line!

933-1101 Georgia-Pacific
933-1102 Slocan Group
933-1103 Louisiana Pacific
933-1104 Plum Creek
933-1105 Pope & Talbot
933-1106 High Cascade Lumber
933-1107 Mountain Lumber
933-1109 Crown Pacific
933-1110 West Frazer
933-1111 Northwood
933-1112 Weyerhaeuser Lumber
933-1113 Finlay Premium
933-1114 Tolko
933-1115 Potlach *NEW*
933-1116 Williamette Industries *NEW*
933-1117 Tree Source *NEW*
933-1100 Undecorated

Limited Quantity Available
933-1108 Buse

45' LOGGING FLAT CAR W/LOGS EA 12.98

Designed to haul logs safely on common-carrier railroads.

932-4001 MILW
932-4002 BN
932-4003 Chehalis Western
932-4004 Georgia-Pacific
932-4005 UP
932-4006 Southern Pacific
932-4000 Undecorated

THREE PACKS EA 35.98

932-34001 MILW
932-34002 BN
932-34003 Chehalis Western
932-34004 Georgia-Pacific
932-34005 UP
932-34006 SP

LOG LOAD

933-1031 For Walthers 45' Logging Flats pkg(30) **9.98**
One-piece resin castings. Use as car loads, fresh-cut trees at the cutting site or floating logs in a mill pond.

63' PULPWOOD CARS EA 10.98

Many lumber companies also grow and harvest pulpwood for the paper industry. Cut into short lengths, the pulpwood logs are shipped on special cars equipped with side and end bracing to prevent shifting in transit.

932-3151 CN
932-3152 CP
932-3153 Wisconsin Central
932-3154 Georgia Pacific
932-3155 TTX
932-3156 SOU
932-3150 Undecorated

63' Pulpwood Car 932-3152

THREE-PACKS EA 29.98

932-33151 CN
932-33152 CP
932-33153 Wisconsin Central
932-33154 Georgia Pacific
932-33155 TTX
932-33156 SOU

PULPWOOD LOADS

Resin Pulpwood Car load fits one Walthers Pulpwood Car. Pulpwood Truck load is designed to fit the trailer included with the Pulpwood Truck (933-4014).

933-1033 Pulpwood Car Load pkg(7) **9.98**
933-1036 Pulpwood Truck Load **6.98**

WOODCHIP CARS EA 10.98

Although they're one of the lightest loads, they require one of the biggest cars! Wood chips are big business for saw mills and lumber operations. Once burned as scrap or fuel on-site, these by-products of the lumber industry are used to make paper.

932-4051 GN
932-4052 BN
932-4053 NP
932-4054 UP

932-4055 MILW
932-4056 Chattahoochee Industrial Railroad
932-4057 CN
932-4058 Seaboard Coast Line
932-4059 NS
932-4060 WP

932-4061 CSX
932-4050 Undecorated

THREE-PACK EA 29.98

932-34051 GN
932-34052 BN
932-34053 NP
932-34054 UP
932-34055 MILW
932-34056 Chattahoochee Industrial Railroad
932-34057 CN

Lumber Car 932-4103

Center Beam Flat w/ Opera Window 932-4115

Woodchip Car 932-4058
Preproduction Model Shown

Center Beam Load 933-1101

45' Logging Flat Car w/Logs 932-34002

WOODCHIP LOADS

One-piece castings with realistic look (not molded in color) are designed for drop-in mounting on Walthers Woodchip Hoppers and Truck.

933-1034 Woodchip Car Load 2-Pack **6.98**

Limited Quantity Available
933-1035 Woodchip Truck Load **2.98**

TRAINLINE®

by WALTHERS

READY-TO-RUN FREIGHT CARS

Flat cars, tank cars, logging cars, box cars - you can move all kinds of freight down the line aboard Trainline® freight cars. Finished in authentic paint schemes, these detailed models are ready to run, with free-rolling wheels, strong metal axles and body-mounted couplers.

40' X-29 Box Car 931-621

40' Plug Door Box Car-Track Cleaning Car 931-751

40' X-29 BOX CAR EA 5.98

931-621 Pennsylvania
931-622 Reading
931-623 Nickel Plate Road

40' PLUG DOOR BOX CAR-TRACK CLEANING CAR EA 15.98

Just couple this car into your train and start cleaning! Cleans tracks for better performance while you run your trains. Soft-abrasive pad mounted under car wipes away grime without scratching rail surfaces.

931-751 Union Pacific
931-752 CSX

40' TANK CAR EA 5.98

931-611 Sinclair
931-612 Gulf
931-613 Standard
931-614 Conoco

50' FLAT CAR EA 4.98

931-601 Burlington Northern
931-602 Conrail
931-603 Union Pacific
931-604 Norfolk Southern

Wide Vision Caboose 931-524
Preproduction Model Shown

Log Dump Car & Crane Car Set 931-761

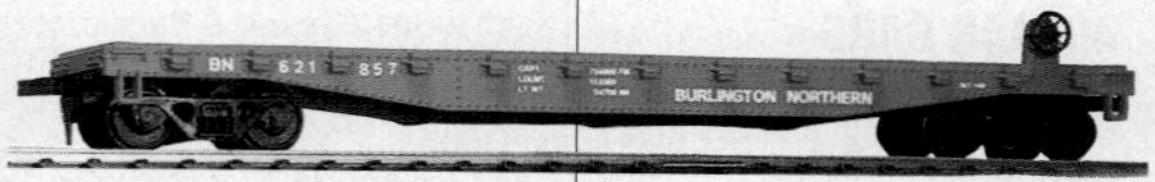

50' Flat Car 931-601

40' Tank Car 931-612

Log Dump Car with Logs 931-764

Firefighting Car 931-767

LOGGING CARS

931-761 Log Dump Car & Crane Car Set **11.98**
Crane car features movable cab, boom and grapple. Log dump car will dump included logs when used with Trainline® Sawmill #931-801.

931-764 Log Dump Car with Logs **6.98**
Same car as in set listed above, but with different road number.

931-767 Firefighting Car **6.98**
Complete with pump details and movable water cannon!

WIDE VISION CABOOSE EA 6.98

Keep a safe eye on your train from the cupola of one of these cabooses.

931-501 Burlington Northern
931-502 Union Pacific
931-503 Santa Fe
931-504 Canadian National
931-505 CSX
931-506 Conrail
931-508 Norfolk Southern
931-509 Pennsylvania
931-510 CNW
931-514 CP
931-516 SOO
931-517 Southern
931-518 Wisconsin Central
931-520 BNSF
931-521 Illinois Central
931-523 Amtrak
931-524 Chessie System
931-525 DRGW
931-526 Alaska Railroad ***NEW***
931-527 US Army ***NEW***

Limited Quantity Available
931-511 Milwaukee Road
931-512 Ashley, Drew & Northern
931-515 Guilford (B&M)
931-519 Montana Rail Link
931-522 Florida East Coast

These easy-to-build HO Scale plastic car kits feature a one-piece body with details molded in place. Decorated models feature authentic paint and lettering schemes with end reporting marks. In addition, the trucks feature nonmagnetic axles, and the coupler pockets accept Kadee® No. 5 couplers. Another special detail of these Accurail kits is that they have exceptionally free-rolling wheels.

One look and you'd swear these cars were really made of wood! Actually, the kits have a one-piece styrene body with superb wood grain detail, along with a detailed underframe, doors and other parts. Typical of cars built by many roads during the steam-era, the models are prepainted and lettered in a wide selection of period schemes.

BOX CARS

40' WOOD OUTSIDE BRACED CARS EA 9.98

WITH WOOD DOOR & ENDS

Limited Quantity Available

112-4007 N&W (Box Car Red)

WITH WOOD DOOR & STEEL ENDS EA 9.98

Limited Quantity Available

112-4202 D&H (Lt. Freight Car Red)
112-4212 Clinchfield (oxide)
112-4215 N&W (Lt. Freight Car Red)

WITH STEEL DOOR & ENDS EA 9.98

Limited Quantity Available

112-4404 MP (oxide)
112-4406 Duluth, Missabe & Iron Range
112-4408 Wabash (Mineral Red)
112-4498 Data Only (Lt. Freight Car Red)
112-4499 Data Only (oxide)
112-4400 Undecorated (black)

MOW EA 9.98

Limited Quantity Available

112-4280 Gray
112-4281 Silver
112-4283 Dark Green
112-4284 Yellow

40' STEEL DOUBLE DOOR CARS EA 8.98

Limited Quantity Available

112-3008 NYC (Mineral Red)
112-3014 SP (Mineral Red)
112-3021 NP (Mineral Red)
112-3023 WM (Mineral Red)
112-3098 Data Only (Mineral Red)
112-3099 Data Only (oxide)
112-3000 Undecorated (black)

40' PS-1 STEEL CARS EA 9.98

112-3401 ATSF (Scarlet)
112-3402 Akron, Canton & Youngstown (yellow)
112-3403 Illinois Central Gulf (orange)
112-3404 RDG (green)
112-3405 ROCK (blue)
112-3406 Seaboard Coast Line (silver)
112-3407 Illinois Terminal (yellow)
112-3408 Elgin, Joliet & Eastern (green)
112-3409 L&N (blue)
112-3410 LV (white)
112-3411 Penn Central (Jade Green)
112-3412 UP (oxide)
112-3413 CN (dark)
112-3414 Lackawanna
112-3415 N&W (black)
112-3416 Wabash
112-3417 MP (blue-gray)
112-3418 Maine Central (yellow)
112-3419 WP
112-3420 Toledo, Peoria & Western
112-3421 PRR (oxide)
112-3422 Atlanta & West Point
112-3423 SOO
112-3424 Central of Georgia
112-3496 Data Only (Bright Red)
112-3498 Data Only (Mineral Red)
112-3499 Data Only (Oxide Red)
112-3400 Undecorated

40' AAR CARS

PLUG DOOR EA 9.95

Cars feature high ladders and roofwalks.

112-3101 ATSF (Mineral Red w/orange door)
112-3102 PRR (Mineral Red)
112-3103 Fruit Growers Express (yellow)
112-3104 SOO (white)
112-3105 CP (silver)
112-3106 SLSF (Mineral Red)
112-3107 Detroit, Toledo & Ironton (yellow)
112-3108 CN (oxide)
112-3199 Data Only (oxide)
112-3100 Undecorated

STEEL EA 8.98

Limited Quantity Available

112-3209 SP (Mineral Red)
112-3217 B&O (oxide)
112-3219 BN (BN Green)
112-3223 IC (Lt. Freight Car Red)

STEEL MOW EA 8.98

Limited Quantity Available

112-3281 Silver
112-3282 Orange
112-3283 Dark Green
112-3284 Yellow

50' STEEL CARS-RIVETED SIDES EA 8.98

SINGLE DOOR

112-5001 ATSF (Mineral Red)
112-5002 IC (orange)
112-5003 C&O (black)
112-5004 NYC (Jade Green)
112-5005 UP (oxide)
112-5006 PRR (oxide)
112-5007 B&O (oxide)
112-5008 CB&Q (oxide)
112-5009 NP (oxide)
112-5010 Lackawanna (Mineral Red)
112-5011 ROCK (oxide)
112-5012 SP (Mineral Red)
112-5098 Data Only (Mineral Red)
112-5099 Data Only (oxide)
112-5000 Undecorated

DOUBLE-DOOR

112-5201 ATSF (red)
112-5202 B&O (oxide)
112-5203 BN (green)
112-5204 PRR (oxide)
112-5205 DRGW (Mineral Red)
112-5206 SP (Mineral Red)
112-5207 CB&Q (bright red)
112-5208 MKT (yellow)
112-5209 NYC (Jade Green)
112-5210 UP (oxide)
112-5211 Erie (oxide)
112-5212 Texas & Pacific (Mineral Red)
112-5298 Data Only (Mineral Red)
112-5299 Data Only (oxide)
112-5200 Undecorated

50' AAR PLUG DOOR CARS EA 9.98

RIVETED

Cars feature high ladders and roofwalks.

112-5101 ATSF (Mineral Red w/orange door)
112-5102 CN (Mineral Red)
112-5103 C&O (dark blue)
112-5104 BN (green)
112-5105 SP (oxide)
112-5106 NKP (Mineral Red)
112-5198 Data Only (Mineral Red)
112-5199 Data Only (oxide)
112-5100 Undecorated

WELDED

Cars feature low ladders and no roofwalks.

112-5801 ATSF (bright red)
112-5802 BN (Mineral Red)
112-5803 EL (oxide)
112-5804 CN (Mineral Red)
112-5805 LV (white)
112-5806 MP (oxide)
112-5898 Data Only (Mineral Red)
112-5899 Data Only (oxide)
112-5800 Undecorated

50' COMBO-DOOR RIVETED CARS EA 8.98

Cars feature high ladders and roofwalks.

112-5301 ATSF (Mineral Red)
112-5302 Akron, Canton & Youngstown (yellow)
112-5303 CN (dark gray)
112-5304 DRGW (oxide)
112-5305 NKP
112-5306 IC (orange)
112-5307 MILW (Mineral Red)
112-5308 GN (bright red)
112-5309 Atlantic Coast Line (black)
112-5310 NS-Old (gray)
112-5311 EL (oxide)
112-5398 Data Only (Mineral Red)
112-5399 Data Only (oxide)
112-5300 Undecorated

40' PS-1 Steel Box Car
112-3401

50' Steel Double Door Box Car
112-5204

50' EXTERIOR POST EA 8.98

112-5610

112-5601 ATSF
112-5602 BN
112-5603 SOU
112-5604 CSX
112-5605 SOO
112-5606 GN
112-5607 Frisco
112-5608 SP
112-5609 ROCK
112-5610 CNW
112-5611 CP Rail
112-5612 Rail Box
112-5613 NS
112-5614 CN
112-5615 N&W
112-5616 Grand Trunk Western
112-5698 Data Only
112-5600 Undecorated

50' AAR CARS EA 8.98

SLIDING DOORS

Cars feature low ladders and no roofwalks.

112-5701 ATSF (bright red)
112-5702 MILW (Mineral Red)
112-5703 WM (oxide)
112-5704 SSW (Mineral Red)
112-5705 MKT
112-5706 Chessie System (blue)
112-5798 Data Only (Mineral Red)
112-5799 Data Only (oxide)
112-5700 Undecorated

DOUBLE-DOOR

Cars feature low ladders and no roofwalks.

112-5901 ATSF (Mineral Red)
112-5902 Grand Trunk Western (blue)
112-5903 Minneapolis, Northfield & Southern (white)
112-5904 ROCK (blue)
112-5905 N&W (Mineral Red)
112-5906 MKT (green)
112-5998 Data Only (Mineral Red)
112-5999 Data Only (oxide)
112-5900 Undecorated

ACCURAIL®

HOPPERS

55-TON USRA HOPPERS

EA 8.98

112-2501 ATSF (oxide)
112-2502 N&W (black)
112-2503 Lackawanna (black)

112-2504 NYC (oxide)
112-2505 B&O (black)
112-2506 PRR (oxide)
112-2507 SLSF (oxide)
112-2508 C&O (black)
112-2509 RDG (black)
112-2510 MP
112-2511 CN (oxide)
112-2512 CB&Q
112-2513 Peabody Coal Co.
112-2514 SP (Mineral Red)
112-2515 Wabash (black)
112-2516 NKP (black)
112-2517 Berwind Coal Co. (black)
112-2518 IC (black)
112-2519 Pittsburgh & West Virginia (black)
112-2520 Virginian (black)
112-2521 Akron, Canton & Youngstown (black)
112-2522 Interstate Railroad (black)
112-2523 Grand Trunk Western
112-2524 Minneapolis & St. Louis
112-2525 NH
112-2526 Montour
112-2527 LV
112-2528 Rutland (black)
112-2529 Bessemer & Lake Erie (black)
112-2530 WM (oxide)
112-2531 L&N (black)
112-2598 Data Only (black)
112-2599 Data Only (oxide)
112-2500 Undecorated

6-PACK EA 49.98

Includes six cars painted in the same scheme, with different numbers.

112-2601 ATSF
112-2602 N&W
112-2603 Lackawanna
112-2604 NYC
112-2605 B&O
112-2606 PRR
112-2608 C&O
112-2609 RDG
112-2612 CB&Q
112-2614 SP (Mineral Red)
112-2616 NKP (black)

47' ACF 3-BAY CENTER FLOW HOPPERS

EA 9.98

These cars carry 4600 cubic feet and were "Plate B" cars used on a large number of railroads.

112-2001 Data Only (dark gray)
112-2002 ATSF (brown)
112-2003 NYC (light gray)
112-2005 UP (gray)

112-2006 CNW (green)
112-2007 MILW (gray)
112-2008 SP (gray)
112-2009 Illinois Central Gulf (gray)
112-2010 GN (Glacier Green)
112-2011 WP (light gray)
112-2012 MP (gray)
112-2013 CR (brown)
112-2014 Grand Trunk Western (blue)
112-2015 BN (BN Green)
112-2016 PRR (gray)
112-2017 CB&Q (gray)
112-2018 SOO (white)
112-2019 ROCK (blue)
112-2020 N&W (dark gray)
112-2021 SSW (light gray)
112-2022 B&O (dark gray)
112-2023 CSX (tan)
112-2024 Chicago & Eastern Illinois (light gray)
112-2025 SOU (light gray)
112-2026 L&N (blue)
112-2027 Seaboard (tan)
112-2028 Detroit, Toledo & Ironton (light gray)
112-2029 EL (light gray)
112-2030 CP Rail (gray)
112-2031 NP (gray)
112-2032 Golden West Service (blue)
112-2033 FMC Chemicals (gray)
112-2034 DRGW (orange)
112-2035 Kansas City Southern (Mineral Red)
112-2036 Chessie (yellow)
112-2037 ADM® (blue)
112-2038 NS (gray)
112-2039 RDG (gray)
112-2040 C&O (gray)
112-2041 Duluth, Missabe & Iron Range (gray)
112-2042 Ashely, Drew & Northern
112-2043 Montana Rail Link
112-2044 Penn Central
112-2045 Englhard
112-2046 CN (Undercoat Gray)
112-2047 ATSF (Mineral Red w/"Q Quality" Logo)
112-2048 BNSF (green)
112-2049 BNSF (Mineral Red)
112-2050 UP/CNW (light gray)
112-2051 ACF (light gray with blue stripe)
112-2052 Family Lines (tan)
112-2053 Kansas City Southern (oxide)
112-2054 ROCK (gray)
112-2055 IC (modern, dark gray)
112-2056 CR (gray)
112-2057 GN (blue)
112-2000 Undecorated (black)

SIX-PACK SETS EA 59.98

Includes six cars painted in the same scheme, with different numbers.

112-12023 CSX (tan)
112-12030 CP Rail/SOO
112-12048 BNSF

REEFERS

40' WOODEN REEFERS

EA 9.98 (UNLESS NOTED)

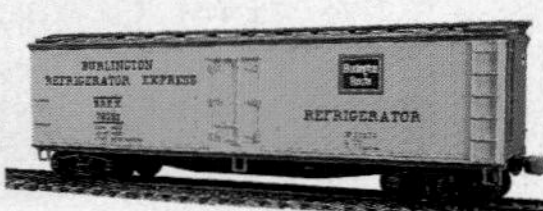

112-4801 Burlington Refrigerator Express
112-4802 Fruit Growers Express
112-4803 Western Fruit Express
112-4804 MILW
112-4805 Green Bay & Western
112-4806 West India Fruit & Steamship Co.
112-4807 CN
112-4808 ATSF
112-4809 NP
112-4810 NYC
112-4811 NKP
112-4812 SP/UP
112-4813 Erie
112-4814 ATSF-Map- "Grand Canyon" (Engine Black)
112-4815 ATSF-Map- "Scout" (black, orange)
112-4816 ATSF-Map- "Super Chief" (black, orange)
112-4817 ATSF-Map- "Chief" (black, orange)
112-4818 ATSF-Map- "El Capitan" (black, orange)
112-4819 CNW (red, gray)
112-4820 Swift (silver)
112-4821 National Car Co. (Mineral Red, Railbox Yellow)
112-4822 CP (Mineral Red)
112-4823 WP (red, orange)
112-4824 New York Dispatch (Mineral Red, ATSF Orange)
112-4825 BN (Railbox Yellow)
112-4852 Merchants Dispatch-NYC (Mineral Red, Reefer White) **12.98**
112-4895 Data Only (Yellow, Brown)
112-4851 American Refrigerator Transit Co. **12.98**
112-4800 Undecorated

THREE-PACKS EA 29.98

112-4901 Burlington
112-4902 Fruit Growers Express
112-4903 Western Fruit Growers
112-4908 ATSF
112-4909 NP
112-4910 NYC
112-4912 SP/UP
112-4914 Western Fruit Express

FLAT CARS

89' TOFC FLAT CARS

EA 9.98

112-8901 TTX #156478 (brown)
112-8902 TTAX #973552 (brown)
112-8903 TTCX #975131 (brown)
112-8904 TTWX #981575 (Trailer Train)
112-8905 KTTX #157134 (Trailer Train)
112-8906 RTTX #156237 (Trailer Train)
112-8907 TTWX #971283 (TTX Corp)
112-8908 KTTX #158917 (TTX Corp)
112-8909 RTTX #975501 (TTX Corp)

89' TOFC Flat Car 112-9105

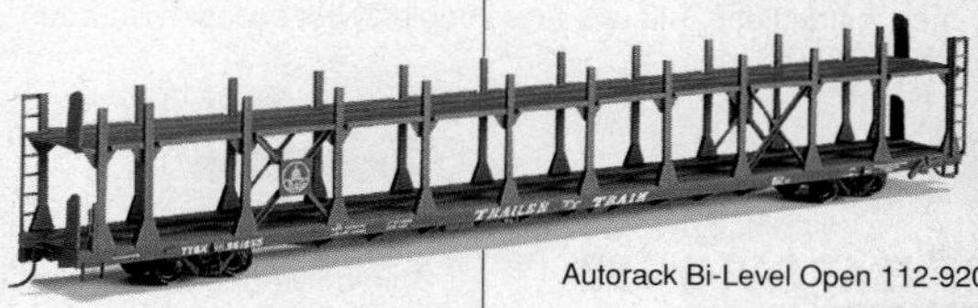

Autorack Bi-Level Open 112-9203

Autorack Tri-Level Open 112-9314

112-8910 TTWX #991595 (Lemon Yellow)
112-8911 ATSF (white)
112-8912 SOU (brown)
112-8913 UP (yellow)
112-8914 MP (brown)
112-8915 CP Rail (Action Red)
112-8916 SP (Mineral Red)
112-8900 Undecorated

WITH TWO 45' TRAILERS EA 19.98

112-9104 TTWX #981575 (TT Yellow)
112-9105 KTTX #157134 (TT Yellow)
112-9106 RTTX #156237 (TT Yellow)
112-9107 TTWX #971283 (Lt. Yellow)
112-9108 KTTX #158917 (Lt. Yellow)
112-9109 RTTX #975501 (Lt. Yellow)
112-9110 TTWX #991595 (Lt. Yellow)
112-9111 ATSF (white)
112-9112 SOU (oxide)
112-9113 UP (yellow)
112-9114 MP (Lt. Freight Car Red)
112-9115 CP Rail (red)
112-9116 SP (Mineral Red)
112-9100 Undecorated

TRAILERS

45' HIGHWAY TRAILERS EA 5.98 (UNLESS NOTED)

Plastic trailers are prepainted and lettered.

112-9904

112-9901 Preferred 45 (white, gray, red)
112-9902 ATSF (white, blue)
112-9903 CR (white, blue)
112-9904 BN (green, white)
112-9905 CN (silver, orange, black)
112-9906 SP (silver, black, yellow) **7.98**
112-9907 TransAmerica (white, red, blue)
112-9908 Kankakee, Beaverville & Southern (green, white)
112-9909 SOU (silver, green)
112-9900 Undecorated

AUTORACKS

EA 14.98

BI-LEVEL OPEN

112-9201 ATSF *NEW*
112-9202 UP *NEW*
112-9203 B&O *NEW*
112-9204 PRR *NEW*
112-9205 NYC *NEW*
112-9206 CN *NEW*
112-9207 N&W *NEW*
112-9208 Wabash *NEW*
112-9209 CP Rail *NEW*
112-9210 Boston & Maine *NEW*
112-9211 C&O *NEW*
112-9212 Gulf, Mobile & Ohio *NEW*
112-9213 EL *NEW*
112-9214 L&N *NEW*
112-9215 Southern *NEW*
112-9216 WM *NEW*
112-9217 ROCK *NEW*
112-9218 SSW *NEW*
112-9219 Burlington *NEW*
112-9200 Undecorated TTX *NEW*

TRI-LEVEL OPEN

112-9301 ATSF *NEW*
112-9302 UP *NEW*
112-9303 B&O *NEW*
112-9304 PRR *NEW*
112-9305 NYC *NEW*
112-9306 CN *NEW*
112-9307 N&W *NEW*
112-9308 Wabash *NEW*
112-9309 CP Rail *NEW*
112-9310 Boston & Maine *NEW*
112-9311 C&O *NEW*
112-9312 Gulf, Mobile & Ohio *NEW*
112-9313 EL *NEW*
112-9314 L&N *NEW*
112-9315 Southern *NEW*
112-9316 WM *NEW*
112-9317 ROCK *NEW*
112-9318 SSW *NEW*
112-9319 Burlington *NEW*
112-9300 Undecorated TTX *NEW*

These easy-to-build HO Scale kits are based on contemporary intermodal equipment used by many roads. They include unpainted injection-molded plastic parts, trucks, weights and step-by-step instructions. Kits are less couplers, but accept horn-hook or Kadee® styles.

FLAT CARS

85' FLAT CAR W/END WEIGHT

116-13202 Undecorated **11.75**
Commonly used for intermodal service, this flat car kit includes an undecorated Athearn body with trucks. The custom end and center sill weights improve performance of car by lowering car height and center of gravity. End weights simplify installing body-mounted couplers and come with springs to simulate cushioning effect.

DOUBLE STACK CONTAINER CARS

40' & 45' THRALL

These five-unit cars are used by American President Lines/APC and Trailer Train/TTX. The 40 and 45' units can carry two 20' or one 40 or 45' container on the bottom, and a 40, 45, 48 or 53' container on the top (depending on the kit). The cars are packaged as either two end units, two center units, or a five-unit set (prototypical). The end and center unit kits can be combined to build shorter cars for small layouts.

116-26100 40' End Units, Undecorated pkg(2) **20.95**
116-26102 40' Mid Units, Undecorated pkg(2) **19.95**
116-26103 40' 5-Unit Set, Undecorated **46.95**
116-26104 45' Mid Units, Undecorated pkg(2) **20.95**
116-26105 40'/45' 5-Unit Set, Undecorated **47.95**
This kit includes two 40' end units and three 45' mid units.

116-26900 Thrall Extra-Detail Kit **8.80**

GUNDERSON

TWIN-STACK

These five-unit cars are used by Trailer Train, ATSF, SP, BN, CR, SOO, Sea Land (NYSW & CSX) and others. Units can carry two 20' or one 40' container on the bottom, and a 40, 45 or 48' container on top. The cars are packaged as either two end units, two center units, or a five-unit set (prototypical). The end and center unit kits can be combined to build shorter cars for small layouts.

116-27100 40' End Units, Undecorated pkg(2) **22.95**
116-27102 40' Mid Units, Undecorated pkg(2) **21.95**
116-27103 5-Unit Set, Undecorated **49.95**
116-27900 Twin Stack Extra-Detail Kit **5.80**
One package will detail five cars.

HUSKY-STACK™

116-27200 Undecorated **8.95**
This single-unit, 48' well car is used by Trailer Train/TTX, BN, Greenbrier Leasing, Coe Rail and others. The car can carry either two 20' or one 40, 45 or 48' container on the bottom, and a 40, 45, 48 or 53' container on top.

Thrall Double-Stack 116-26103 w/APL/APC Decals 116-26700; 40' Ribbed 116-25100, 45' Ribbed Containers 116-25200 w/APL 40' and 45' Decals 116-25800.

Gunderson "Twin Stack" 116-27200 w/BN Decals 116-27805; 48' Smooth Containers 116-25300 w/48' BN American Decal 116-25804 & 48' BN American Special Decal 116-25814.

Gunderson "Twin Stack" 116-27103 w/TTX Decals 116-27700; 48' Smooth Container 116-25300 w/APC 48' Decal 116-25805.

CONTAINERS

20 & 40' CORRUGATED PKG(2) EA 5.95 (UNLESS NOTED)

Used by NYK, Mitsui, OSK, YS Line, OOCL, Triton, Hyundai, Matson, IEA, Evergreen, CGM, Transamerica, Maersk and others. Each kit features the "beveled" style of corrugation, 2-logo panel or all corrugated sides, smooth or corrugated doors, see-through forklift pockets, corrugated roofs and one-piece body with separate floor, stacking pins, vents and door bars. Undecorated containers are molded in gray styrene. Painted containers are ready for decals, which are available separately.

45' Ribbed Container 116-25200 w/Maersk Decal 116-25803; 20' Containers 116-25520 & 116-25530 w/Maersk & NOL Decal 116-25819, 116-25803

116-25500 20' Undecorated 2-Logo Panel Sides/Smooth Doors
116-25510 20' Undecorated 2-Logo Panel Sides/Corrugated Doors
116-25520 20' Undecorated Corrugated Sides/Smooth Doors
116-25530 20' Undecorated Corrugated Sides/Corrugated Doors
116-25610 40' Undecorated, Smooth Doors, All Corrugated Sides **TBA**
116-25700 20' Flat Rack **TBA**

40' Ribbed 116-25100 & 45' Ribbed Containers 116-25200 w/APL 40'/45' Decals 116-25800.

Gunderson "Twin Stack" 116-27103 w/Sealand Decals 116-27705; 45' Ribbed Container 116-25200 w/Maersk Decal 116-25803; 20' Containers 116-25520 & 116-25530 w/Maersk & NOL Decal 116-25819, 116-25803

48 & 53' SMOOTH SIDE PKG(2) EA 11.50 (UNLESS NOTED)

Used by APL/APC, CSX/CSL, ITEL, XTRA, BN, CN, SP, CR, ATSF, Canadian Pacific, Genstar, Con-Way and others. Based on a Monon prototype, these are the most common domestic containers in use today. Each kit features a one-piece body with separate roof and stacking pins. The undecorated containers are molded in white styrene. Decorated containers are ready to run.

116-25301 48' ATSF
116-25303 48' APL
116-25300 48' Undecorated **7.50**
116-25400 53' Undecorated **7.50**

40 & 45' RIBBED SIDE

Used by APL, Maersk, Sea Land and others, these containers are seen around the world. These kits feature a one-piece body with separate floor and stacking pins. Undecorated containers are molded in silver styrene. Painted containers are ready for decals, which are available separately.

116-25101 40' Painted (silver) pkg(2) **7.95**
116-25201 45' Painted (silver) pkg(2) **7.95**
116-25100 40' Undecorated pkg(2) **7.50**
116-25200 45' Undecorated pkg(2) **7.50**

Racing containers east and west, double stack cars are the backbone of the railroad's intermodal fleets. The modular design of A-Line models allows you to build longer or shorter cars to fit your operation. Add-on details, containers, and decals are available separately.

53' Smooth 116-25400 & 48' Smooth Containers 116-25300 w/53' APC Decals 116-25806 & 48' APC Decals 116-25805.

DECALS

EA 4.50

CONTAINER

Each set includes detailed lettering diagram of container.

116-25800 APL 40'/45'
116-25801 Maersk 20'/40' (original)
116-25802 Sea Land 40'
116-25803 Maersk 40'/45'
116-25804 BN America 48'
116-25805 APC 48'
116-25806 APC 53'
116-25807 ITEL/BN/ITEL 48'
116-25808 ATSF 45'/48'/53'
116-25809 CSX/CSL 48'
116-25810 XTRA 48'
116-25811 SP 48'
116-25812 CN Intermodal 48'
116-25813 CP Intermodal 48'
116-25814 BN America Special 48'
116-25815 CR Mercury 48'
116-25816 CR Mercury 53'
116-25817 Con-Quest 48'
116-25819 NOL 20'/40'

LOCOMOTIVE

116-25900 Maersk GP60M **4.50**

THRALL CAR

Each set includes complete decals for one 5-unit set and detailed lettering diagram.

116-26700 APL/APC (blue or red car)
116-26701 Trailer Train (yellow car)

TWIN-STACK CAR

Each set includes complete decals for one 5-unit set and detailed lettering diagram.

116-27700 TTX/SP (yellow car)
116-27701 TTX/ATSF (yellow car)
116-27702 TTX/BN (yellow car)
116-27703 SP (red car)
116-27704 ATSF (red car)
116-27705 Sea Land (red car)
116-27706 BN (cascade green car)
116-27707 SOO Line (red car)
116-27708 CR (Box Car Red)

HUSKY-STACK™

Each set includes detailed lettering diagram and color photo of car.

116-27800 TTX
Enough to do four single cars.

116-27805 BN
Enough to do two single and one three-stack units.

116-27806 GBRX/BN
116-27807 CRLE/GBRX

TRAINS
Athearn
IN MINIATURE

These easy-to-build HO scale kits are prepainted and lettered, molded in styrene, and weighted. They can be assembled with a screwdriver, and come complete with horn-hook couplers and Delrin® trucks.

86' Hi Cube 4-Door Box Car 140-2940

BOX CARS

86' HI CUBE 4-DOOR BOX CAR EA 11.00

140-1969 NYC
140-1970 PRR
140-1971 L&N
140-1972 SOU
140-1973 Penn Central
140-1975 ATSF
140-1976 UP
140-1977 CB&Q
140-1978 Detroit, Toledo & Ironton
140-1979 Wabash
140-1980 N&W
140-1981 NS
140-1982 CR
140-1983 MP
140-1984 Western Pacific (yellow)
140-1999 Western Pacific (white)
140-1974 Undecorated
140-2940 BN (green)
140-2941 CN (Box Car Red)
140-2942 CNW (Box Car Red)
140-2943 CNW (yellow)
140-2944 DRGW (Box Car Red)
140-2945 Detroit, Toledo & Ironton (red)
140-2946 EL
140-2947 Frisco (yellow)
140-2948 ROCK (Box Car Red)
140-2949 MKT (red)

140-2950 MILW (yellow)
140-2951 UP "We Can Handle It" (yellow)
140-2952 ATSF "Q" (Oxide Red)
140-2953 CP (Action Red)
140-2954 C&O
140-2955 CSX
140-2956 SSW
140-2957 DRGW (orange)
140-2958 Golden West Service
140-2959 NS (Thoroughbred Gray)

40' STEAM ERA BOX CAR EA 5.75

140-5001 Atlantic Coast Line (Box Car Red)
140-5002 CB&Q (Box Car Red)
140-5003 CNW (Box Car Red)
140-5004 Seaboard Air Line (Box Car Red)
140-5005 CP (Box Car Red)
140-5006 Gulf Mobile & Ohio (Box Car Red)
140-5007 GN (Box Car Red)
140-5008 Delaware, Lackawanna & Western (Box Car Red)
140-5009 NH (Box Car Red)
140-5010 NP (Box Car Red)
140-5011 SP (Box Car Red)
140-5012 UP (Box Car Red)
140-5013 ATSF "El Capitain" (Box Car Red)
140-5014 ATSF "Grand Canyon" (Box Car Red)
140-5015 ATSF "Scout" (Box Car Red)
140-5016 ATSF "Chief" (Box Car Red)
140-5017 ATSF "Super Chief" (Box Car Red)
140-5018 ATSF "San Francisco Chief" (Box Car Red)

40' WOODEN BOX CAR EA 5.75

140-5231 ATSF
140-5232 Erie
140-5233 GN
140-5234 SOU
140-5235 SP
140-5236 Western Pacific
140-5230 Undecorated

86' HI CUBE 8-DOOR BOX CAR EA 11.00

140-1986 SP
140-1987 B&O
140-1988 Grand Trunk Western
140-1989 MP
140-1990 NYC
140-1991 PRR
140-1992 CR
140-1993 IC
140-1994 N&W
140-1995 Chessie
140-1996 Maxi-Cube
140-1997 Detroit, Toledo & Ironton
140-1998 ATSF
140-2970 CNW (yellow)
140-2971 ROCK (Box Car Red)
140-2972 Route Rock (Light Blue)
140-1985 Undecorated
140-2973 CN (blue)
140-2974 CSX (blue)
140-2975 B&O (yellow doors)
140-2976 DRGW (dark brown)
140-2977 Penn Central

40' HI CUBE PLUG DOOR EA 7.00

140-1961 CB&Q
140-1962 IC
140-1963 MILW
140-1964 DRGW
140-1965 ATSF
140-1966 UP
140-1967 NP
140-1968 BN
140-1960 Undecorated

40' HI CUBE OUTSIDE BRACED BOX CAR EA 7.00

140-1951 B&O
140-1952 SSW
140-1953 GN
140-1954 Penn Central
140-1955 Seaboard Coast Line
140-1956 SP
140-1957 BN
140-1958 Great Western Sugar
140-1959 CR
140-1950 Undecorated

WALTHERS™

ATHEARN COUPLER POCKET CONVERSION KIT

933-997 2 Pair **3.98**
This kit converts Athearn 86' Hi-Cube box cars and 86' flat cars from a truck-mounted coupler bar system to a body-mounted swinging coupler bar system, as used on Walthers Enclosed Auto Carriers. Kit includes parts to convert 2 cars.

40' Single Door Box Car 140-1204

86' Hi Cube 8-Door Box Car 140-2970

40' SINGLE DOOR BOX CAR EA 5.75

140-1201 Gulf, Mobile & Ohio (Caboose Red)
140-1204 GN (Big Sky Blue)
140-1205 SP (Box Car Red)
140-1206 Penn Central (PC Green)
140-1207 IC (Box Car Red)
140-1209 CN (Box Car Red)
140-1210 N&W (Tuscan Red)
140-1211 Grand Trunk Western (Box Car Red)
140-1212 Akron, Canton & Youngstown (yellow)
140-1213 Ontario Northland (Dark Green)
140-1214 Vermont Railway (Dark Green)
140-1221 ATSF "Shock Control" (Caboose Red)
140-1223 GN (turquoise)
140-1224 BN (green)
140-1225 CP Rail (red w/"Pac-Man" logo)
140-1226 DRGW (white/"Cookie Box" logo)
140-1227 EL (gray w/red logo)
140-1228 SP "Overnight" (black)
140-1229 SP "Overnight" (silver)
140-1230 Western Pacific
140-1200 Undecorated (black)

50' PLUG DOOR BOX CAR EA 6.50

140-1322 IC
140-1323 Western Pacific (Tuscan Red)
140-1324 MKT (red)
140-1325 ATSF
140-1326 ROCK (Tuscan Red)
140-1327 Penn Central
140-1328 CP
140-1330 MILW (orange, black)
140-1332 Pearl Brewery
140-1335 SOO
140-1361 Green Bay & Western (yellow)
140-1362 American Refrigerator Transport
140-1329 Undecorated (black)

50' OUTSIDE BRACED PLUG DOOR BOX CAR EA 6.50

140-1337 B&O
140-1339 GN
140-1342 UP
140-1343 LV
140-1344 ATSF
140-1345 SOU
140-1346 Kansas City Southern
140-1336 Undecorated

AUTO LOADER EA 8.75

140-1481 ATSF (early, black w/silver lettering)
140-1482 B&O (early, black w/white lettering)
140-1483 NYC (early, black w/white lettering)
140-1484 PRR (early, Box Car Red w/white lettering)
140-1485 UP (early, Box Car Red w/white lettering)
140-1486 ATSF (late, yellow TTX floor, red sides, white lettering)
140-1487 BN (yellow TTX floor, green sides, white lettering)
140-1488 BNSF (yellow TTX floor, green sides, white lettering)
140-1489 CN (black floor, red sides, white lettering)
140-1490 CR (yellow TTX floor, Box Car Red sides, white "Q" logo)
140-1491 CSX (yellow TTX floor, gray sides, yellow logo)
140-1492 Grand Truck Western (yellow TTX floor, blue sides, white lettering)
140-1493 NS (yellow TTX floor, black sides, white lettering)
140-1494 UP (yellow UP floor, yellow sides, red/white/blue herald)
140-1480 Undecorated

TRAINS
Athearn
IN MINIATURE

50' DOUBLE-DOOR RAILBOX BOX CAR EA 6.75

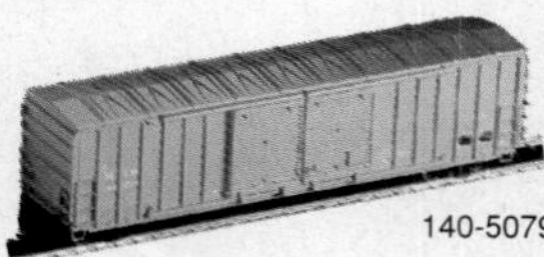
140-5079

140-5071 Union Railroad of Oregon
140-5072 Arcata
140-5073 Prineville
140-5074 SP
140-5075 BN
140-5076 Yreka
140-5077 Western Pacific
140-5078 McCloud
140-5079 MILW
140-5080 Longview, Portland & Northern
140-5081 Galveston
140-5082 Camino, Placerville & Lake Tahoe
140-5083 SSW
140-5070 Undecorated

50' OUTSIDE BRACED BOX CAR EA 6.75

140-5521 Railbox
140-5522 Railbox (1996 Version)
140-5524 BN
140-5525 CN
140-5526 CR

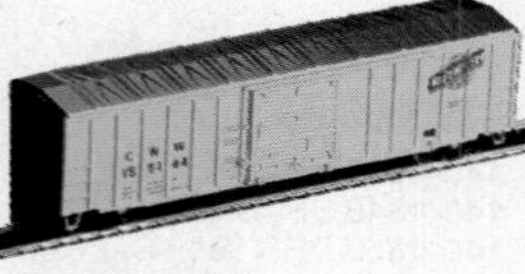

140-5527 CNW
140-5528 Chessie
140-5529 CSX
140-5530 Family Lines
140-5531 Florida East Coast
140-5532 Frisco
140-5537 MP (w/UP shield)
140-5538 Montana Rail Link

140-5541 Richmond, Fredericksburg & Potomac
140-5542 ROCK (Route Rock)
140-5543 ATSF
140-5545 WC
140-5520 Undecorated

40' GRAIN LOADING BOX CAR EA 5.75

140-2091 CB&Q
140-2092 GN
140-2093 NP
140-2094 ATSF
140-2095 SOO
140-2096 UP (yellow door)

140-2097 UP w/Damage Free Loader
140-2098 UP (silver, yellow)
140-2090 Undecorated

50' STEEL SINGLE DOOR BOX CAR EA 5.75

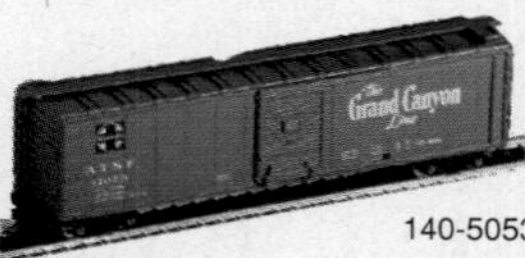
140-5053

140-5051 ATSF "Super Chief"
140-5052 ATSF "El Capitan"
140-5053 ATSF "Grand Canyon"
140-5054 ATSF "Chief"
140-5055 ATSF "Santa Fe Chief"
140-5056 ATSF "Texas Chief"
140-5057 NYC
140-5058 NP (Box Car Red)
140-5059 PRR
140-5060 SOU (Box Car Red)
140-5061 SP (Box Car Red)
140-5062 UP
140-5050 Undecorated (black)

50' PLUG DOOR RIB SIDE BOX CAR (MODERN BILLBOARD) EA 6.50

140-5281 Rohm-Haas
140-5282 Johnson Wax
140-5283 Borg Warner
140-5284 Nestles

50' DOUBLE-DOOR AUTO CAR BOX CAR-STEAM ERA EA 5.75

140-5040

140-5031 Kansas City Southern
140-5032 SSW (Box Car Red)
140-5033 MKT
140-5034 ATSF
140-5035 SP
140-5036 UP (Box Car Red)
140-5037 ROCK (Box Car Red)
140-5038 PRR (Box Car Red)
140-5039 DRGW (Box Car Red)
140-5040 CB&Q
140-5041 Seaboard Air Line
140-5042 Pere Marquette

50' DOUBLE-DOOR AUTO CAR EA 5.75

140-1305 Seaboard Coast Line (Box Car Red)
140-1306 Chicago & Eastern Illinois
140-1307 Detroit & Toledo Shoreline
140-1308 N&S (light gray)
140-1310 CB&Q (red)
140-1311 GN (red)
140-1315 SP Hydro-Cushion (Box Car Red)
140-1316 NYC (Penn Central green)
140-1317 ATSF (red)
140-1319 UP (reefer yellow)
140-1309 Undecorated (black)

50' PLUG DOOR SMOOTHSIDE BOX CAR

INSULATED-BILLBOARD

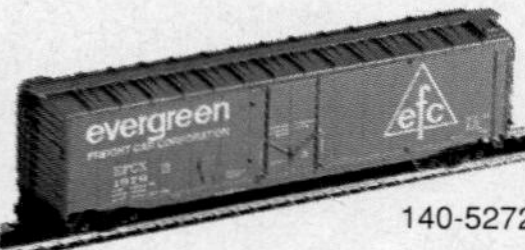
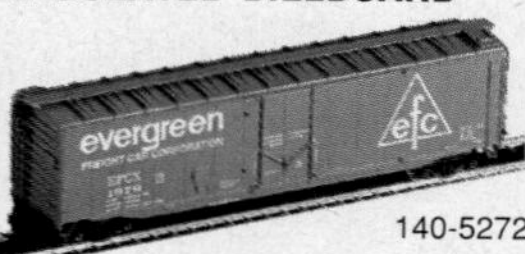
140-5272

140-5271 Hamms Beer
140-5272 Evergreen
140-5273 Evans
140-5274 Dresser
140-5275 Abbott Lab
140-5276 Volclay
140-5277 Evans (EELX)
140-5278 Richmond, Fredericksburg & Potomac

MODEL RAILROADER ANNIVERSARY CARS

To complete your train, a Standard Heavyweight Observation Car (140-5633) is also available and can be found in the Passenger Car section.

140-5631 40' Wood Side Box Car **7.25**

140-5632 86' Hi-Cube 4-Door Box Car **13.25**

HOPPERS

55' ACF CENTERFLOW COVERED HOPPER EA 7.25

140-1901 ACF Demonstrator
140-1902 Dow Chemical
140-1903 DuPont (red)
140-1904 Enjay (white)
140-1905 Grace
140-1906 DRGW
140-1907 Gulf Oil (light gray-green)
140-1908 NYC (Jade Green)

40' Quad Hopper 140-1759

54' PS 3-Bay Covered Hopper 140-5311

140-1909 Co-op Fertilizers (white)
140-1910 Shell Plastics
140-1911 SP
140-1912 UP
140-1913 Diamond Plastic (light gray-green)
140-1914 United Carbon (black)
140-1915 ATSF (mineral brown)
140-1916 Tenneco
140-1917 Borg-Warner
140-1918 SSW (light gray-green)
140-1919 Firestone (light gray-green)
140-1920 Chevron (light gray-green)
140-1921 Union Carbide (light gray-green)
140-1922 Stauffer Chemical (light gray-green)
140-1923 CB&Q (light gray-green)
140-1924 Sinclair-Koppers (light gray-green)
140-1925 ACFX
140-1926 ADMX
140-1927 BN
140-1928 CSX
140-1929 Golden West Service
140-1931 GN (Glacier Green)
140-1933 HERCULES
140-1940 WC
140-1941 BNSF (BN Green)
140-1942 BNSF (Oxide Red)
140-1900 Undecorated (black)

34' TWIN COMPOSITE HOPPER EA 5.75

140-5421 ATSF (Box Car Red)
140-5422 CB&Q (Box Car Red)
140-5423 LV (Box Car Red)
140-5424 SOU (Box Car Red)
140-5425 SP (Box Car Red)
140-5426 UP (Tuscan Red)
140-5420 Undecorated (black)

34' OFFSET-SIDE TWIN HOPPER EA 5.75

140-5401 ATSF (Box Car Red)
140-5402 CP (Box Car Red)
140-5403 EL (black)
140-5404 Frisco (Box Car Red)
140-5405 GN (Tuscan Red)
140-5406 MILW (Box Car Red)
140-5400 Undecorated (black)
140-5407 Undecorated, Flat End (black)

34' TWIN RIBBED-SIDE HOPPER EA 4.75

140-5444

140-5441 B&O (black)
140-5442 D&H (Box Car Red)
140-5443 NYC (Box Car Red)
140-5444 N&W (black)
140-5445 PRR (Tuscan red)
140-5446 Virginian (black)
140-5440 Undecorated, Peaked End (black)
140-5447 Undecorated, Flat End (black)

40' QUAD HOPPER EA 5.75

140-1750 LV (Box Car Red)
140-1751 Elgin, Joliet & Eastern (black)
140-1752 Boston & Maine (light blue)
140-1753 B&O (black)
140-1754 CB&Q (red)
140-1756 Peabody (yellow)
140-1757 WM (gray)
140-1758 ATSF (Box Car Red)
140-1759 IC (black)
140-1760 Seaboard Coast Line (Box Car Red)
140-1749 Undecorated (black)

54' PS 3-BAY COVERED HOPPER EA 7.25

140-5301 ATSF (Box Car Red)
140-5302 CB&Q (dark gray-green)
140-5303 Cargill (yellow)
140-5304 CO-OP
140-5305 MKT
140-5306 MILW (Reefer Yellow)
140-5307 NP
140-5308 Pillsbury (light gray-green)
140-5309 DRGW (light green)
140-5310 ROCK
140-5311 SOO
140-5312 UP
140-5314 BNSF (BN Green)
140-5315 BNSF (Oxide Red)
140-5300 Undecorated (black)

40' Single-Dome Tank Car 140-1572

40' Three Dome Tank Car 140-1500

40' Chemical Tank Car 140-1553

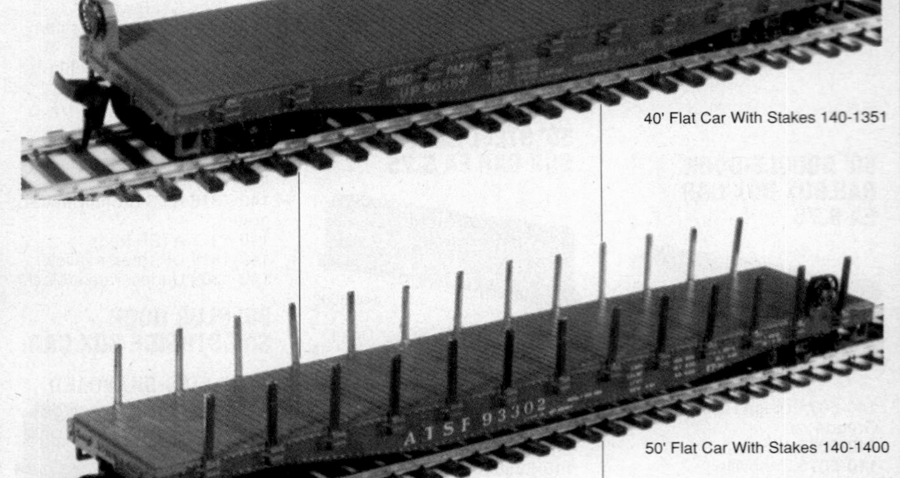

40' Flat Car With Stakes 140-1351

50' Flat Car With Stakes 140-1400

34' AAR HOPPER EA 29.50

140-5570 ATSF
140-5572 B&O
140-5573 CNJ
140-5574 CP
140-5575 C&O
140-5577 CNW (Omaha)
140-5579 Erie
140-5581 IC
140-5584 MP
140-5585 NKP
140-5586 NYC/Pittsburgh & Lake Erie
140-5587 NP
140-5588 RDG
140-5589 SOU
140-5590 Texas & Pacific
140-5591 Gulf, Mobile & Ohio

COVERED HOPPER 12-PACK

140-2906 BNSF **87.00** ***NEW***
Set includes six ACF Centerflow Hoppers (3 Oxide Red, 3 green) and six Pullman-Standard cars (three Oxide Red, three green). Each car in the set has its own number, end reporting marks and the sharp lettering of the BNSF. HO Scale models are easy to build and are complete with trucks and couplers.

TANK CARS

40' SINGLE-DOME TANK CAR EA 5.75

140-1571 Conoco (silver)
140-1572 Phillips Petroleum (black)
140-1574 ATSF (black)
140-1575 SP (yellow)
140-1577 B&O (black)
140-1578 SP (silver)
140-1579 Firestone (light green, black)
140-1570 Undecorated (black)

40' THREE DOME TANK CAR EA 5.75

140-1500 Shell (yellow)
140-1501 Texaco (silver)
140-1504 Union Oil (dark blue)
140-1506 Koppers (black)
140-1507 Ethyl Corporation (light gray-green)
140-1499 Undecorated (black)

40' CHEMICAL TANK CAR EA 5.75

140-1550 Gulf Oil (orange)
140-1551 Michigan Alky
140-1552 Dow Chemical (blue)
140-1553 DuPont (silver)
140-1557 Hooker (orange)
140-1558 Staley (gray)
140-1549 Undecorated (black)

PICKLE CAR EA 7.75

140-1475 Heinz w/Tanks
140-1476 Heinz w/Closed Sides

62' TANK CAR EA 6.75

140-1522 CB&Q
140-1524 General Dynamics
140-1526 UP
140-1527 North American Car Corporation
140-1528 San Angelo Tank Car (yellow)
140-1529 ACF Industries
140-1530 Conslidated Gas
140-1520 Undecorated (black)

85' PIGGYBACK FLAT CARS EA 8.00

140-2001 Trailer Train ***NEW***
140-2002 PFE ***NEW***
140-2003 North American Car ***NEW***
140-2004 GN ***NEW***
140-2005 ATSF ***NEW***
140-2006 SP ***NEW***
140-2000 Undecorated ***NEW***

85' ALL PURPOSE FLAT CAR EA 8.00

140-2016 Trailer Train ***NEW***
140-2017 C&O ***NEW***
140-2018 SSW ***NEW***
140-2019 PFE ***NEW***
140-2020 SP ***NEW***
140-2021 UP ***NEW***
140-2022 BNSF (Oxide Red) ***NEW***
140-2023 CP (Action Red) ***NEW***
140-2024 DRGW ***NEW***
140-2025 Florida East Coast (Box Car Red) ***NEW***
140-2026 MP ***NEW***
140-2027 New Orleans Public Belt ***NEW***
140-2028 ROCK ***NEW***
140-2029 ATSF (white) ***NEW***
140-2080 ATSF (orange) ***NEW***
140-2081 SOU (brown) ***NEW***
140-2082 Trailer Train (yellow) ***NEW***
140-2083 TTX (yellow) ***NEW***
140-2084 Terminal Alabama State Docks (yellow) ***NEW***
140-2085 Western Pacific (black) ***NEW***
140-2086 Western Pacific (yellow, Trailer Train repaint) ***NEW***
140-2000 Undecorated Piggyback ***NEW***
140-2015 Undecorated All-Purpose ***NEW***

FLAT CARS

40' FLAT CAR WITH STAKES EA 5.75

140-1347 DRGW
140-1348 SP (Box Car Red)
140-1350 PRR (Box Car Red)
140-1351 UP (Box Car Red)
140-1352 NYC
140-1356 SOU
140-1357 C&O
140-1358 ROCK
140-1359 L&N
140-1377 BN (green)
140-1378 UP (yellow)
140-1379 ATSF (red)
140-1380 IC Gulf (orange)
140-1381 CP (red)
140-1382 CR (maroon)
140-1349 Undecorated (black)

50' FLAT CAR WITH STAKES EA 5.75

140-1391 N&W
140-1392 B&O
140-1393 PRR
140-1394 Wabash
140-1395 SOU
140-1396 GN
140-1397 UP
140-1398 SP
140-1400 ATSF
140-1401 MILW (Box Car Red)
140-1399 Undecorated (black)

Gunderson Maxi-III 5-Unit Container Well Car 140-5912

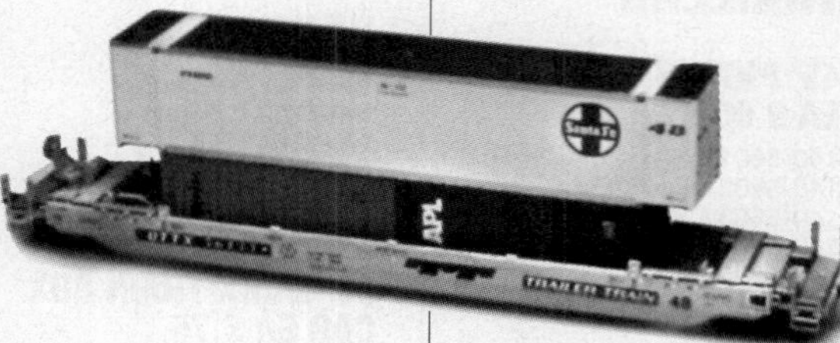

GWF 10 Husky Stack Car 140-5870

50' FLAT CAR WITH TWO 20' TRAILERS EA 10.00

140-1402 RDG Flat w/International Forwarding Trailers
140-1403 Wabash
140-1404 PRR Flat w/Cooper-Garrett Trailers
140-1405 ATSF
140-1406 B&O Flat w/B&O TOFCEE Trailers
140-1408 SP w/ACME Trailers
140-1409 ATSF w/National Trailers
140-1410 SP w/SP Trailers
140-1411 Undecorated

20' TRAILERS PKG (4) EA 12.00

140-1425 SP
140-1426 B&O
140-1427 Wabash
140-1428 Garrett
140-1429 International Forwarding
140-1431 ACME
140-1430 National
140-1432 ATSF
140-1424 Undecorated

50' HEAVY DUTY FLATCAR EA 10.00

140-1295 Department of Defense
140-1296 ATSF
140-1297 Trailer Train
140-1298 TTX
140-1300 Westinghouse
140-1301 CNW
140-1302 Erie
140-1303 PRR
140-1304 UP
140-1299 Undecorated

40' FLAT CAR WITH BOAT EA 7.75

140-1353 Gulf, Mobile & Ohio
140-1354 Seaboard Air Line

40' FLAT CAR WITH PLANE

140-1355 NKP **7.75**

40' FLAT LOAD PKG(4) EA 12.00

140-1375 Boat
140-1376 Plane

40' PULPWOOD CAR EA 5.75

140-1450 SP
140-1452 CB&Q
140-1453 L&N
140-1449 Undecorated

WELL CARS

GWF10 HUSKY STACK CAR EA 8.50 (UNLESS NOTED)

140-5870 ARZC #100015
140-5871 ARZC #100018
140-5875 CSX #61515
140-5876 CSX #61518
140-5880 SP Speed Lettering #513901
140-5881 SP Speed Lettering #513905
140-5901 Trailer Train (yellow)
140-5902 TTX (yellow)
140-5903 Greenbrier Leasing Corporation (red)
140-5904 BN (red)
140-5905 Coe Rail (red)
140-5906 BN pkg(3) **21.50**
140-5900 Undecorated

GUNDERSON MAXI-III 5-UNIT CONTAINER WELL CAR EA 39.50

140-5911 Trailer Train (yellow)
140-5912 TTX (yellow)
140-5913 APC (yellow)
140-5914 Greenbrier APC (red)
140-5915 BN (yellow)
140-5916 BN (red)
140-5917 CSX Transportation (blue)
140-5918 ATSF (red)
140-5919 SP (Ely red)
140-5920 SP (light red)
140-5921 Centrex
140-5922 SP Original
140-5923 APLX #4820
140-5924 APLX #4825
140-5925 BNSF
140-5930 BN #65069 (red)
140-5931 BN #65023 (red)
140-5910 Undecorated

REEFERS

40' ICE BUNKER REEFER-STEEL SIDE EA 5.75

140-1601 PFE (Reefer Orange)
140-1602 Carnation
140-1603 Blatz (Reefer Yellow)
140-1604 CN
140-1605 ATSF, Chief (Reefer Orange)
140-1609 Railway Express Agency
140-1610 CB&Q
140-1615 Bangor & Aroostock (orange)
140-1599 Undecorated (black)

ICE BUNKER REEFER-STEAM ERA EA 5.75

140-5019 ATSF "El Capitan" (Reefer Orange)
140-5020 ATSF "Grand Canyon" (Reefer Orange)
140-5021 ATSF "Scout"
140-5022 ATSF "Chief" (Reefer Orange)
140-5023 ATSF "Super Chief" (Reefer Orange)
140-5024 ATSF "Texas Chief" (Reefer Orange)
140-5025 Merchants
140-5026 IC (yellow)
140-5027 Burlington Refrigerator Express (yellow)
140-5028 NP (Reefer Orange)
140-5029 American Refrigerator Transit
140-5030 PFE (Reefer Orange)

50' Plug-Door Outside Braced Reefer 140-1633

57' Mechanical Reefer 140-5473

50' Reefer smoothside140-1623

50' EXPRESS REEFER EA 6.50

140-5331 ATSF
140-5332 GN
140-5333 MILW
140-5334 PRR
140-5335 PFE
140-5336 Railway Express Agency
140-5341 Hood
140-5342 Western Dairy
140-5343 Sheffield
140-5344 Standard Fruit
140-5345 GACX
140-5346 Abbott
140-5330 Undecorated

50' PLUG-DOOR OUTSIDE BRACED REEFER EA 6.50

140-1632 CB&Q (yellow)
140-1633 Fruit Growers Express (yellow)
140-1634 GN
140-1636 PFE
140-1637 ATSF
140-1631 Undecorated (black)

50' REEFER-SMOOTHSIDE EA 6.50

140-1619 CP
140-1620 MILW
140-1622 CNJ
140-1623 Burlington Refrigerator Express (BN Green)
140-1625 Libby Famous Foods
140-1627 Pacific Fruit Express
140-1628 NP
140-1629 Safeway
140-1630 ATSF "Ship & Travel"
140-1624 Undecorated

57' MECHANICAL REEFER EA 7.25

140-5461 American Refrigerator Transit (red)
140-5462 ATSF (Reefer Orange)
140-5463 Bangor & Aroostock (Reefer Orange)
140-5464 Burlington Refrigerator Express - Burlington Route (Reefer Yellow)
140-5465 UP Fruit Express - BN
140-5466 Western Fruit Express
140-5467 Pacific Fruit Express - UP
140-5468 BN (white)
140-5469 Fruit Growers Express
140-5470 Golden West Service
140-5471 NP
140-5472 WC
140-5473 BNSF (green)

140-5474 BNSF (Oxide Red)
140-5460 Undecorated (black)

20' Container Chassis 140-5763
(Tractor not included)

50' Gondola 140-1643

50' Gondola w/Frozen Food Lockers
140-1676

40' ICE BUNKER REEFER-WOOD EA 5.75

140-5201 Baby Ruth (red)
140-5202 Canada Dry
140-5203 Coors Beer
140-5204 Crisco

140-5205 Kraft
140-5207 Morrell (Reefer Orange)
140-5208 Old Dutch
140-5209 Oscar Mayer
140-5210 Pluto Water
140-5211 Schlitz (Reefer Yellow)
140-5212 Swift (Reefer Orange)
140-5213 SOO (Reefer Orange)
140-5214 PFE/Western Pacific
140-5215 CNW
140-5216 Western Fruit Express-GN (Reefer Yellow)
140-5217 Burlington Refrigerator Express
140-5218 Fruit Growers Express
140-5200 Undecorated (black)

GONDOLAS

50' GONDOLA EA 5.75

140-1643 GN (green)
140-1644 UP (Box Car Red)
140-1645 EL (black)
140-1646 SOO (white)
140-1648 CB&Q (red)
140-1649 DRGW (orange)
140-1650 BN (green)
140-1651 ROCK
140-1652 CP Rail (red)
140-1654 BNSF (black)
140-1655 BNSF (Oxide Red)
140-1647 Undecorated (black)

50' COVERED GONDOLA EA 7.25

140-1660 SOU
140-1661 CB&Q
140-1664 Chicago & Eastern Illinois
140-1665 SP
140-1659 Undecorated

50' GONDOLA W/CANISTERS EA 7.75

140-1653 Erie

50' GONDOLA W/FROZEN FOOD LOCKERS EA 7.25

140-1676 N&W

STOCK CARS

40' STOCK CAR EA 5.75

140-1771 GN
140-1772 ROCK
140-1773 Texas & Pacific
140-1776 ATSF
140-1777 DRGW
140-1779 UP
140-1774 Undecorated

CONTAINERS

20' CORRUGATED-SQUARE PKG(4) EA 10.00

140-2031 Triton
140-2032 Kline
140-2033 Flexivan
140-2034 Itel
140-2030 Undecorated

20' CORRUGATED-BEVELED PKG(4) EA 10.00

140-2051 Tiphook
140-2052 Matson
140-2053 Genstar
140-2054 Seaco
140-2056 APL
140-2050 Undecorated

20' SMOOTH SIDE PKG(4) EA 10.00

140-2041 President
140-2042 YS Line
140-2043 Japan Line
140-2044 Contrans
140-2045 Matson
140-2040 Undecorated

20' RIBBED SIDE PKG(4) EA 10.00

140-2061 Matson
140-2062 Showa
140-2063 Seatrain
140-2064 Compass
140-2060 Undecorated

20' CONTAINER CHASSIS EA 37.50

140-5761 APL (black)
140-5762 Evergreen (green)
140-5763 Flexi-Van (black)
140-5764 Hyundai
140-5765 K-Line (red)
140-5766 Maersk (light blue)
140-5767 OOCL (yellow)
140-5760 Undecorated

40' CONTAINERS PKG(2) EA 9.00

140-5741 Matson
140-5742 Genstar
140-5743 Hanjin
140-5744 APC-APL
140-5745 Itel-Maersk
140-5746 Tiphook-Triton
140-5747 Evergreen
140-5748 NYK
140-5749 Zim
140-5740 Undecorated

48' CONTAINERS PKG(2) EA 10.00

140-5701 APL
140-5702 APC
140-5703 CSX-CSL
140-5704 NYK
140-5705 SP
140-5706 ATSF
140-5707 BN
140-5708 TransAmerica
140-5709 Itel
140-5710 BNSF
140-5700 Undecorated

40' SMOOTH SIDE CONTAINER PKG(6) EA 27.00

140-5721 APL
140-5722 Japan
140-5723 K-Line
140-5724 KS Line
140-5725 Matson
140-5726 Mitsui
140-5727 NYK
140-5728 Sealand
140-5729 States
140-5730 YM Line
140-5720 Undecorated

TRAILERS

45' PIGGYBACK PKG(2) EA 9.00

140-5601 BN
140-5602 CR
140-5603 CSX
140-5604 NS
140-5605 DRGW
140-5606 ATSF
140-5607 SP
140-5608 Owner
140-5600 Undecorated

PARTS

140-14240 25' Body Undecorated **2.00**
140-14251 25' Underframe pkg(2) **1.50**
140-14252 25' Stand pkg(3) **1.50**
140-14253 25' Van Wheel Assembly **1.50**
140-14257 Dual Trailer Mount for 50' Flat Car pkg(4) **1.50**
140-51513 40' Dual Wheel Assembly **2.00**
140-51515 40' Refrigeration Unit pkg(3) **1.50**
140-51516 40' Fuel Tank pkg(3) **1.50**
140-51521 40' Trailer Hardware Set **2.00**

40' TRAILER PKG(2) EA 8.00

140-5153 IC
140-5154 NW
140-5155 Penn Central
140-5156 DRGW
140-5157 ATSF
140-5158 Seaboard Coast Line
140-5159 SOU
140-5160 SP
140-5161 L&N
140-5162 C&O
140-5163 NP
140-5165 SSW
140-5167 MILW
140-5168 ROCK
140-5169 PFE
140-5170 ATSF
140-5171 Seaboard Coast Line
140-5172 SeaLand
140-5173 UP
140-5174 Western Pacific
140-5175 Owner Operated
140-5151 Undecorated

MOW EQUIPMENT

WORK TRAIN RPO TOOL CAR EA 10.50

140-1150 ATSF
140-1151 B&O
140-1152 BN
140-1153 CP Rail
140-1154 CSX
140-1155 MOW
140-1156 PRR
140-1157 UP

40' WORK TRAIN BOX CAR EA 5.75

140-1100 ATSF
140-1101 B&O
140-1102 BN
140-1103 CP Rail
140-1104 CSX
140-1105 MOW
140-1106 PRR
140-1107 UP

50' WORK TRAIN BOX CAR EA 5.75

140-1110 ATSF
140-1111 B&O
140-1112 BN
140-1113 CP Rail
140-1114 CSX
140-1115 MOW
140-1116 PRR
140-1117 UP

50' WORK TRAIN GONDOLA EA 5.75

140-1120 ATSF
140-1121 B&O
140-1122 BN
140-1123 CP Rail
140-1124 CSX
140-1125 MOW
140-1126 PRR
140-1127 UP

SINGLE DOME TANK CAR WORK TRAIN EA 5.75

140-1130 ATSF
140-1131 B&O
140-1132 BN
140-1133 CP Rail
140-1134 CSX
140-1135 MOW
140-1136 PRR
140-1137 UP

BAGGAGE TOOL CAR WORK TRAIN EA 10.50

140-1140 ATSF
140-1141 B&O
140-1142 BN
140-1143 CP Rail
140-1144 CSX
140-1145 MOW
140-1146 PRR
140-1147 UP

Impack Piggyback Intermediate 140-5561

Rotary Snow Plow 140-1198

40' WORK CABOOSE EA 6.75

140-1275 Boston & Maine
140-1276 PRR
140-1278 Wabash
140-1279 B&O
140-1280 ATSF
140-1281 MOW

40' WORK CABOOSE CRANE TENDER EA 6.75

140-1277 BN
140-1282 CP Rail
140-1283 CSX
140-1284 UP
140-1274 Undecorated

200 TON CRANE EA 14.00

140-1700 UP
140-1701 PRR
140-1702 ATSF
140-1703 Boston & Maine
140-1704 B&O
140-1705 BN
140-1706 CP Rail
140-1707 CSX
140-1708 MOW
140-1709 Wabash
140-1699 Undecorated

ROTARY SNOW PLOW EA 12.50

140-1195 CN
140-1196 GN
140-1198 UP
140-1197 NYC
140-1194 Undecorated

IMPACK CARS

IMPACK PIGGYBACK END PKG(2) EA 10.00

140-5551 BN
140-5552 SSW
140-5553 Itel
140-5554 ATSF
140-5555 SP
140-5556 Trailer Train
140-5550 Undecorated

IMPACK PIGGYBACK INTERMEDIATE PKG(3) EA 15.00

140-5561 BN
140-5562 SSW
140-5563 Itel
140-5564 ATSF
140-5565 SP
140-5566 Trailer Train
140-5560 Undecorated

CABOOSES

34' CUPOLA CABOOSE EA 6.75

140-1250 ATSF
140-1251 SP (Box Car Red)
140-1252 UP (yellow)
140-1253 PRR
140-1254 CB&Q
140-1255 B&O (Caboose Red)
140-1256 MILW
140-1258 DRGW (yellow)
140-1259 NH
140-1260 GN
140-1262 CN
140-1265 C&O
140-1266 NP
140-1267 CNW (Tuscan Red)
140-1268 NYC (Box Car Red)
140-1269 ATSF (Caboose Red)
140-1249 Undecorated (black)

34' Cupola Caboose 140-1262

Bay Window Caboose 140-1179

BAY WINDOW CABOOSE EA 6.75

140-1165 BN
140-1166 Chessie System
140-1167 SSW
140-1168 D&H
140-1170 Kansas City Southern
140-1171 L&N
140-1172 EL
140-1173 Florida East Coast
140-1174 MILW
140-1175 MP
140-1176 NKP
140-1177 N&W
140-1178 ROCK (white)
140-1179 SOU
140-1180 UP
140-1181 Western Pacific
140-1286 ATSF
140-1287 B&O
140-1288 CB&Q
140-1289 CNW
140-1290 NH
140-1291 NYC
140-1292 PRR
140-1293 SP
140-1294 CSX
140-1285 Undecorated

29' WIDE VISION CABOOSE EA 6.75

140-5361 BN
140-5362 C&O
140-5363 SSW

140-5364 IC
140-5365 Penn Central
140-5366 ROCK (Caboose Red)

140-5367 ATSF
140-5368 UP
140-5369 Chessie System (yellow)

140-5370 SOO

140-5371 CR
140-5372 CN
140-5373 CP
140-5375 Frisco
140-5378 MILW
140-5379 Montana Rail Link
140-5380 MKT
140-5381 MP
140-5382 Seaboard Coast Line
140-5384 CR "Q" Logo
140-5360 Undecorated (black)

Roadname Abbreviation Key

ATSF Santa Fe
B&O Baltimore & Ohio
BN Burlington Northern
BNSF Burlington Northern Santa Fe (1996 Merger)
C&O Chesapeake & Ohio
CB&Q Chicago Burlington & Quincy
CN Canadian National
CNJ Central Railroad of New Jersey
CNW Chicago & North Western
CP Canadian Pacific
CR Conrail
CSX CSX
D&H Delaware & Hudson
DRGW Rio Grande
EL Erie Lackawanna
GN Great Northern
IC Illinois Central
L&N Louisville & Nashville
LV Lehigh Valley
MILW Milwaukee Road
MKT Katy (Missouri, Kansas, Texas)
MON Monon
MP Missouri Pacific
MOW Maintenance Of Way
N&W Norfolk & Western
NH New Haven
NKP Nickel Plate Road
NP Northern Pacific
NS Norfolk Southern
NYC New York Central
PFE Pacific Fruit Express
PRR Pennsylvania
RDG Reading
ROCK Rock Island
SOO Soo Line
SOU Southern Railway
SSW St. Louis Southwestern (Cotton Belt)
SP Southern Pacific
UP Union Pacific
WC Wisconsin Central
WM Western Maryland

3-Bay Cylindrical Hopper
150-19345

6-Bay Cylindrical Hopper
150-19584

2-Bay Offset Side Open Hopper
w/Flat Ends 150-1852

53' Evans Double Plug-Door Box Car
150-17563

PS2 2-Bay Covered Hopper
150-18253

ACF 3-Bay Cylindrical Hopper
150-19422

ACF 3-Bay Cylindrical Hopper
150-19411

BOX CARS

53' EVANS DOUBLE PLUG-DOOR BOX CAR EA 14.95

Make sure all your freight arrives safely with a fleet of 53' Evans Double Plug-Door Box Cars. Each car features 70-ton roller-bearing trucks, blackened metal wheels, a two-piece underframe, separate brake cylinder, air reservoir and end platforms.

150-17514 BN ***NEW***
150-17524 Ralston Purina ***NEW***
150-17534 UP ***NEW***
150-17544 CNW ***NEW***
150-17554 Boston & Maine ***NEW***
150-17564 British Columbia Rail ***NEW***
150-17574 Evans Products ***NEW***
150-17581 Minneapolis, Northfield & Southern
150-17582 Minneapolis, Northfield & Southern
150-17591 Northwest Hardwood
150-17592 Northwest Hardwood
150-17601 Tropicana

HOPPERS

PS2 2-BAY COVERED HOPPER EA 12.95

Expand your hopper fleet with the ever popular PS2 2-Bay Covered Hopper. Perfect for carrying sand, powdered cement and similar products. Each car features free-rolling, blackened metal wheels, detailed brake gear and body mounted coupler pockets.

150-18022 BN ***NEW***
150-18072 UP ***NEW***
150-18081 D&H
150-18092 CNW ***NEW***
150-18101 SP #4129
150-18111 DRGW
150-18122 B&O ***NEW***
150-18131 ATSF
150-18141 NH
150-18151 LV #50794
150-18161 N&W
150-18171 Clinchfield
150-18181 Maine Central
150-18191 GN
150-18201 Western Pacific
150-18211 MILW
150-18242 Lehigh & New England ***NEW***
150-18253 Minneapolis & St. Louis ***NEW***
150-18263 ROCK ***NEW***
150-1800 Undecorated

Limited Quantity Available
150-18031 Chessie (WM) #5825
150-18041 CR #879821
150-18061 SOU #900171

2-BAY OFFSET SIDE OPEN HOPPER WITH FLAT ENDS EA 11.95 (UNLESS NOTED)

All new freight cars include blackened metal wheels, detailed brake gear, body mounted couplers and improved coupler pockets with screw-attached covers.

150-1851 B&O
150-1852 Frisco
150-1853 Pittsburgh & Lake Erie
150-1854 SOU
150-1855 ATSF
150-1856 CNJ
150-1857 D&H
150-1858 Lehigh & New England
150-1859 NP
150-1860 RDG
150-1861 MP
150-1863 CNW
150-1864 Erie
150-1865 C&O
150-18624 Boston & Maine ***NEW***
150-18681 Chicago & Eastern Illinois #1 **12.95**
150-18682 Chicago & Eastern Illinois #2 **12.95**
150-18683 Chicago & Eastern Illinois #3 **12.95**
150-18694 Lehigh & New England **12.95** ***NEW***
150-18704 RDG **12.95** ***NEW***
150-1850 Undecorated

ACF 3-BAY CYLINDRICAL HOPPER EA 17.95 (UNLESS NOTED)

Each Atlas 3-bay Cylindrical Hopper features blackened metal wheels, free rolling 100-ton roller bearing trucks, detailed brake gear, body mounted couplers and improved coupler pockets with screw attached covers.

150-19315 B&O ***NEW***
150-19325 BN ***NEW***
150-19335 CR ***NEW***
150-19345 EL ***NEW***
150-19355 PRR ***NEW***
150-19364 MKT
150-19374 NYC
150-19384 SP
150-19394 Sterling Salt
150-19404 Toledo, Peoria & Western
150-19411 French's
150-19412 French's
150-19413 French's
150-19422 Wayne Feed's
150-19423 Wayne Feed's
150-1930 Undecorated

6-BAY CYLINDRICAL HOPPER EA 15.95 (UNLESS NOTED)

Carry more grain with this 3960 cu. ft. cylindrical hopper car, produced between 1962 and 1964. It contains five inlet roof hatches and six outlet bays, and features 100-ton roller bearing trucks, blackened metal wheels and detailed brake gear.

150-19515 BN ***NEW***
150-19525 C&O ***NEW***
150-19535 GN ***NEW***
150-19545 Illinois Terminal
150-19555 Seaboard Air Line
150-19565 BN **17.95** ***NEW***
150-19574 MP **17.95**
150-19584 N&W **17.95**
150-19594 Wabash **17.95**
150-19611 C&O
150-19612 C&O
150-19613 C&O
150-19621 GN (aluminum)
150-19622 GN (aluminum)
150-19623 GN (aluminum)
150-1950 Undecorated

2-BAY OFFSET SIDE OPEN HOPPER WITH OVAL ENDS EA 12.95

Back by popular demand! Atlas Oval End Open Hoppers come equipped with blackened metal wheels, free-rolling 50-ton friction bearing trucks, detailed brake gear, and for the first time ever these cars come factory-equipped with body mounted Accumate® couplers! (For those of you who prefer the horn-hook couplers, those will be included in the box for your convenience.)

150-18915 C&O #1
150-18916 C&O #2 *NEW*
150-18925 Clinchfield #1
150-18926 Clinchfield #2 *NEW*
150-18935 NKP #1
150-18936 NKP #2 *NEW*
150-1894 C&O "For Progress"
150-1895 Montour
150-1890 Undecorated *NEW*

FLAT CARS

PULPWOOD FLAT CARS EA 17.95 (UNLESS NOTED)

150-16021 Atlantic Coast Line #1
150-16022 Atlantic Coast Line #2
150-16023 Atlantic Coast Line #3 *NEW*
150-16031 C&O #1
150-16032 C&O #2
150-16033 C&O #3 *NEW*
150-16041 D&H #1 (red)
150-16042 D&H #2 (red)
150-16043 D&H #3 (red) *NEW*
150-16051 Gulf, Mobile & Ohio #1 (yellow)
150-16052 Gulf, Mobile & Ohio #2 (yellow)
150-16053 Gulf, Mobile & Ohio #3 (yellow) *NEW*
150-16061 ATSF #1
150-16062 ATSF #2
150-16063 ATSF #3 *NEW*
150-16071 WM #1
150-16072 WM #2
150-16073 WM #3 *NEW*
150-1600 Undecorated Open Ends **12.95**
150-1601 Undecorated Closed Ends **12.95**

FLAT CAR LOAD

GIRDERS

150-790 Girder Load pkg(4) **2.45**
Molded in black styrene plastic.

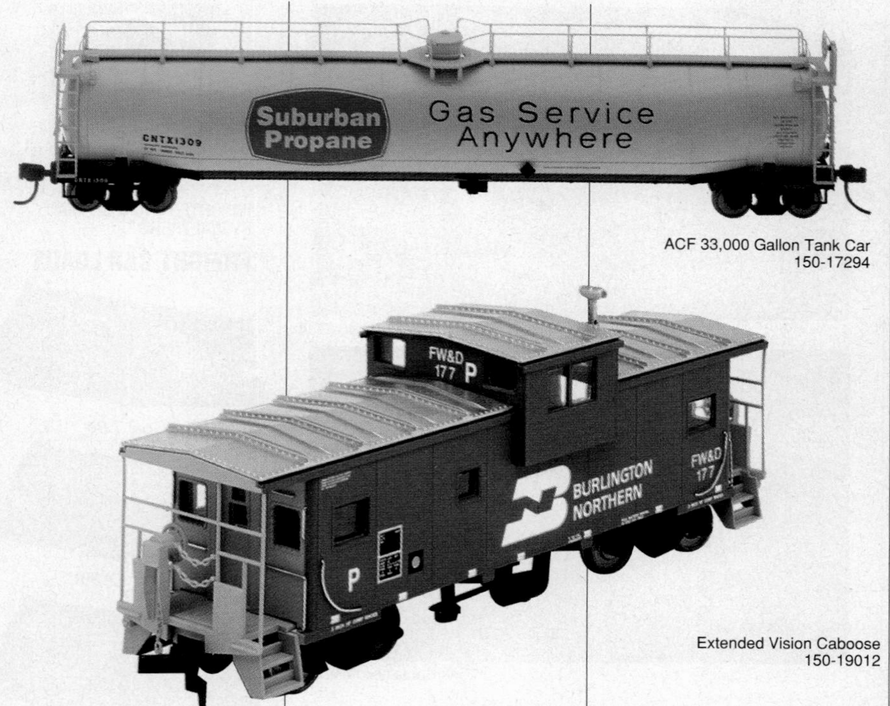

ACF 33,000 Gallon Tank Car 150-17294

Extended Vision Caboose 150-19012

TANK CARS

KAOLIN TANK CAR EA 16.95

Popular on layouts and prototype railroads alike, the HO Kaolin Tank Car was the first Atlas freight car ever made! Representing the 14,000 gallon non-pressure tank cars used to haul Kaolin clay slurry and other liquids, each tank car features new brake details, safety bars molded in place, screw attaching coupler covers and highly accurate printing and paint schemes.

150-17071 Omya
150-17072 Omya
150-17081 Thiele (gray)
150-17082 Thiele (gray)
150-17091 DuPont TiPure
150-17092 DuPont TiPure
150-17101 Freeport Kaolin
150-17102 Freeport Kaolin

Limited Quantity Available

150-17044 Thiele, 4th Car
150-17054 ECC, 4th Car
150-17055 ECC, 5th Car

ACF 33,000 GALLON TANK CAR EA 18.95 (UNLESS NOTED)

The popular ACF 33,000 Gallon Tank Car is used to carry liquefied petroleum gas and anhydrous ammonia. Each tank car features blackened metal wheels, 100-ton roller bearing trucks and improved coupler pockets with screw-attached covers. Details include end ladders arched over the sides, air reservoir, walkway and end platforms.

150-17214 ACFX #17433 *NEW*
150-17224 Royster
150-17234 Shell
150-17244 Shippers Car Line
150-17254 Technical Propellants
150-17264 United Petroleum
150-17274 Bottled Gas of Virginia **20.95**
150-17284 Pyrofax **20.95**
150-17294 Suburban Propane #1312 **20.95** *NEW*
150-17304 Union Texas Petroleum #933019 **20.95** *NEW*
150-17311 CNTX
150-17312 CNTX
150-17313 CNTX
150-17321 Cumberland Corp.
150-17322 Cumberland Corp.
150-17323 Cumberland Corp.
150-17331 Virginian Petroleum Corp.
150-17333 Virginian Petroleum Corp.
150-17342 Cal Gas
116-1720 Undecorated

CABOOSES

EXTENDED VISION CABOOSE

Immortalized in story and song, the caboose has slowly become a railroading icon. Features of the Atlas' Extended Vision Caboose include detailed air reservoir, brake cylinder and triple valve, blackened metal wheels, free-rolling Barber Bettendorf roller-bearing caboose trucks, complete window glazing and pre-formed wire grab-irons.

150-1902 Cotton Belt **15.95**
150-1907 C&O **15.95**
150-1908 CB&Q **15.95**
150-1909 Maine Central **15.95**
150-1910 RDG **15.95**
150-1911 DRGW **15.95**
150-1912 SOO **15.95**
150-1913 BN "Freedom" **22.95**
150-1914 Family Lines **16.95**
150-1915 Grand Trunk Western **16.95**
150-1916 MILW **16.95**
150-1917 MKT **16.95**
150-19012 BN **16.95** *NEW*
150-19031 CR **16.95**
150-19041 D&H **15.95**
150-19181 NP **16.95**
150-19191 C&O **21.95**
150-19202 Duluth, Missabe & Iron Range **27.95**
150-19212 GN **20.95** *NEW*
150-19241 Montana Rail Link **19.95**
150-19251 Richmond, Fredricksburg & Potomac **22.95**
150-1900 Undecorated **16.95**

Information STATION

Freight Car Slang

Band Wagon - a railroad pay car
Big Hook - wrecking crane
Black Snake - solid train of loaded coal cars
Box Car Tourist - hobo
Can - tank car
Car Catcher - rear brakeman
Catwalk - plank walk on top of boxcars
Checker - a company spy, checking loss of materials or receipts of a conductor
Chippies - narrow gauge cars
Consist - contents or equipment of a train
Cornered - when a car, not in the clear on a siding, is struck by a train or engine
Cornfield Meet - head on collision or one narrowly averted
Cow Cage - stock car
Cradle - gondola or other open top car
Crummy - caboose
Donegan - old car, with wheels removed, used as residence or office
Doodlebug - motorcar used by section men
Drag - heavy train of "dead" freight; any slow freight train
Fish Wagon - gas-electric car or other motorcar with an air horn
Flat - flat car
Foreign Car - car running over any railroad other than its own
Glory - string of empty cars; also to be killed accidently, as in "gone to glory"
Gon - gondola
Grab Iron - steel bar attached to cars and engines as a hand hold
Graveyard - siding occupied by obsolete and unused engines and cars; scrap pile

American Limited

TANK CONTAINERS

One of the latest intermodal innovations, 20' tank containers have quickly caught on with railroads and shippers because of their durability and size. Available in framed and unframed versions, these tanks are molded in color, easy to assemble and are compatible with the Athearn 86' intermodal flat car, Walthers All-Purpose Spine Car and all well cars, where they are often placed on the lower level. Kits also include full-color Microscale® decals.

20' TANK CONTAINER TRAILERS EA 9.95 (UNLESS NOTED)

Precise replicas of the 40' drop center trailers used to move 20' tank containers, as well as 20' box containers that are too heavy for a standard chassis. Easy-to-build kits feature rubber tires, photo-etched fenders and custom Microscale decals with optional lettering and numbers. Compatible with all 20' tank and box container models.

147-7710 UP (yellow)
Includes UP decals, with trailer parts molded in yellow.

147-7720 Blue
Used by UP, ATSF and Chemical Leaman, parts are molded in blue.

147-7800 BNSF **12.95**
Chassis with BNSF markings. Blue chassis with blue/white tank.

147-7810 UP **12.95**
Union Pacific chassis in yellow with UP Bulktainer tank container.

UNFRAMED TANK CONTAINERS EA 5.95

Also called "beam" tanks, the prototype is designed for the US domestic market.

147-7510 UP Bulktainer®
Latest version with "New American Tank Truck" graphics. White tank with blue framework. Six-color decals.

"Bulktainer" is a registered trademark of the Union Pacific Railroad Company.

Tank Container 147-7710

Tank Container 147-7800

147-7520 Alaska West Express
Alaska West has pioneered containerized liquid transport from the midwest to Alaska's oil fields and industrial areas. White tank with blue framework.

FRAMED TANK CONTAINERS EA 5.95 (UNLESS NOTED)

These tanks are a European prototype commonly seen in the US and around the world.

147-7610 Stolt
Silver tank with black frame and bright red, yellow and black logo.

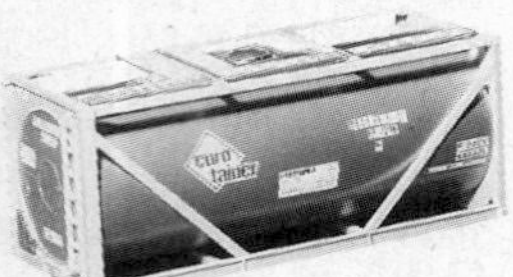

147-7620 Eurotainer
Silver tank with light blue frame.

147-7630 TransAmerica Leasing
Silver tank with dark blue frame and red pyramid logo.

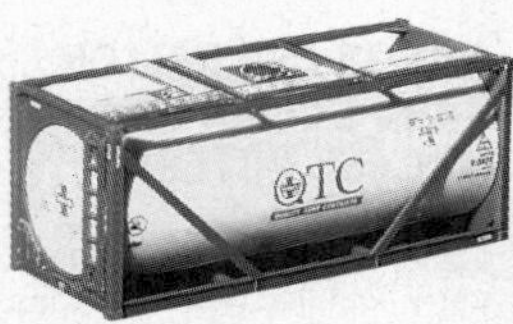

147-7640 ATSF QTC
White tank with dark blue frame and lettering.

147-7600 Undecorated **5.49**

TANK CONTAINER DECAL SETS

For use with undecorated tank container #147-7600 or Walthers 20' Tank Container. Sets include decals for two tanks.

147-6210 Stolt pkg(2) **3.00**
147-6220 Eurotainer pkg(2) **3.00**
147-6200 Placards & Chemical Stencils **2.50**

IMPORTED FROM GERMANY BY WALTHERS

FREIGHT CAR LOADS

189-7600 Coal **7.99**

189-7601 Sand **7.99**

189-7602 Sugar Beets **7.99**

189-7603 Scrap Metal Load **7.99**

189-7604 Tires **10.99**

189-7605 Pressed Automobile **11.99**

189-7606 Truck Cabs **17.99**

189-7607 Two Bundles of Wood **11.99**

189-7608 Four Wire Cable Rolls **11.99**

189-7609 Steel Fabric
96 x 29 x 5mm **11.99**

189-7610 Ore **7.99**

189-7611 Dirt/Top Soil **8.99**

189-7612 Stacked Pulpwood **12.99**

189-7613 Loose Pulpwood **11.99**

189-7614 Scrap Lumber **8.99**

189-7615 Two Truck Chassis w/Cabs **15.99** *NEW*
Measures 3-13/16 x 1"
9.5 x 2.5cm.

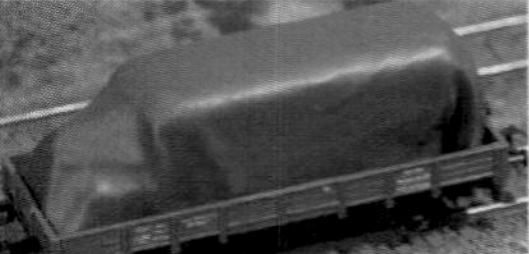

189-7616 Covered Tour Bus **7.99** *NEW*
Measures 3-27/32 x 1-13/64"
9.6 x 3cm

189-7617 Covered Machinery Load **7.99** *NEW*
Measures 3-27/32 x 1-13/64"
9.6 x 3cm

Model accurate freight trains of the 1940s, 50s and 60s with this line of easy-to-build, HO Scale kits. These colorful models capture the details found on their prototypes and come prepainted and lettered in period schemes. Cars listed will be carried in stock; additional styles and/or roadnames can be special ordered.

REEFERS

ATSF STEEL REBUILT ICE COOLED REEFERS EA 13.88

5' swing doors and 3" recessed eaves.

VERSION A

193-7002 "Grand Canyon"/ Ship & Travel Class Rr19
193-7003 Big Circle Herald-1959
193-7005 "El Capitan"/Ship & Travel Class Rr23
193-7020 "El Capitan"/Curved Line Map Class Rr27
193-7035 Big Circle Herald Class Rr28
193-7037 "Super Chief"/ Straight Line Map Class Rr32

VERSION B

4/4 dreadnaught ends.

193-7104 "El Capitan"/Straight Line Map Class Rr34
193-7110 "El Capitan"/Ship & Travel Class Rr33
193-7112 Big Circle Herald Class Rr33

BOX CARS

AAR 40' BOX CARS EA 8.95

Models feature 10 panel side, flat roof and 4-4 ends, unless noted.

6' DOORS

193-10101 Wabash "Flag"
193-10102 UP
193-10103 Spokane, Portland & Seattle In-line Initials
193-10104 Spokane, Portland & Seattle Angled Initials
193-10106 NH Block Herald
193-10107 NH Script Herald
193-10110 NP Arched Lettering
193-10111 NP "Mainstreet"

193-10112 NP Large Round Herald
193-10113 Illinois Terminal (Early)
193-10114 CNW (Early)
193-10115 IC "Mainline of Mid-America"
193-10116 MON "Hoosier" in Script
193-10117 N&W 1944 Railroad Roman
193-10118 N&W 1954 Railroad Roman
193-10119 N&W Half Moon Herald
193-10100 Undecorated

7' DOORS

193-10201 B&O "Timesaver" (Vermillion)
193-10202 B&O "Sentinel" (Vermillion)
193-10204 B&O M-55H Round Herald
193-10208 WP 1940s
193-10209 WP 1950s
193-10210 WP 1960s
193-10211 NKP

8' DOORS

193-10301 SOU Round Herald "Serves the South"
193-10302 PRR X-43c w/Round Keystone (Tuscan)
193-10303 RDG Early Scheme
193-10304 Erie Small Diamond Herald

STAGGERED DOUBLE-DOORS

193-10401 ATSF "Scout"/ Straight Line Map
193-10402 ATSF "El Capitan"/ Straight Line Map
193-10403 ATSF "Chief"/ Straight Line Map
193-10404 ATSF "Super Chief"/ Straight Line Map
193-10405 ATSF "Grand Canyon"/Straight Line Map
193-10406 WAB w/Flag Herald
193-10407 UP "Streamliners"
193-10408 NYC Oxide Red Oval
193-10409 B&O M-59 Automobile Service, Round Herald
193-10410 DRGW Automobile Service (Box Car Red)
193-10414 Seaboard Air Line "Route of Courteous Service"
193-10415 Seaboard Air Line "Route of the Silver Meteor"

6' DOORS, 12 PANEL

193-10501 ATSF "Scout"/ Straight Line Map
193-10502 ATSF "El Capitan"/ Straight Line Map
193-10503 ATSF "Chief"/ Straight Line Map
193-10504 ATSF "Super Chief"/Straight Line Map
193-10505 ATSF "Grand Canyon"/Straight Line Map
193-10506 DRGW (Box Car Red)

6' DOORS, 4/3/1 ENDS

193-10901 MP "Route of the Eagles"
193-10902 CB&Q (Chinese Red) "Zephyr"/Everywhere West

STAGGERED 14' DOUBLE-DOORS, 4/3/1 ENDS

193-11201 MP "Route of the Eagles"
193-11202 CB&Q (Chinese Red) "Zephyr"/Everywhere West
193-11203 B&O "Timesaver" (Vermillion)
193-11204 B&O "Sentinel" (Vermillion)

ATSF 6' DOORS, 12 PANEL, DIAGONAL ROOF

193-12501 "Chief" Bx53
193-12502 "El Capitan" Bx60
193-12503 "Super Chief" Bx62
193-12504 "Grand Canyon" Bx63

SOO 6' DOORS, 4/3/1 ENDS

193-13105 "$" Herald
193-13106 Billboard Large Letters

14' DOUBLE-DOORS, 4/3/1 ENDS, DIAGONAL ROOF

193-13401 BN (Cascade Green)

6' DOORS, 4/3/1 ENDS, 12 PANEL DIAGONAL ROOF

193-13501 GN Large Goat Herald (Tuscan Red)

8' DOORS, TAPER ENDS, DIAGONAL ROOF

193-14301 Seaboard Air Line, "STB Loader"
193-14302 RDG Small "Savings Bonds"

4/3/1 ENDS, 6' DOORS, 12 PANEL

193-11302 SP Early Ball Herald
193-11303 SP Late Ball Herald

ANGLE ROOF

193-12103 CN "Serves All Canada"
6' Door.

193-13602 Buffalo Creek Flour Co.
4/3/1 End, 7' Door, 12 Panel.

GN EXPERIMENTAL SCHEMES EA 8.95

14' DOUBLE-DOORS, TAPER ENDS, DIAGONAL PANEL ROOF

193-14401 #6 Gray #3345
193-14402 #7 Box Car Red #3384
193-14403 #8 Dark Green #3336
193-14404 #9 Vermillion Red #3249
193-14405 #10 Box Car Red #3486

6' DOORS, TAPER ENDS, 12 PANEL DIAGONAL ROOF

193-14501 #1 Orange #19038
193-14502 #2 Oxide Red #18588

CENTRAL VALLEY

STOCK CAR

210-1001 Undecorated **10.95**
After the round-up, ship your livestock to market in this detailed car. Based on a Northern Pacific prototype, it's typical of stock cars used by many Western roads from the 1930s into the early 1970s.

Champ decal HC-112 provides the correct lettering for the Northern Pacific car this model is based on. This easy-to-build HO Scale kit features highly detailed plastic parts with separate details and a detailed underframe. Less trucks and couplers.

LASER CUT WOOD CABOOSES

This HO Scale car features "outboard" style cupola roofwalks, and grab iron holes designed to accept Detail Associates parts. Cabooses feature tabbed and slotted construction, peel and stick windows and doors, and custom Laser-Scribed siding. Includes Athearn floor and frame, AMB cast white metal marker lights, needle beams and queen posts.

152-850 Katy #751-795 Series Wood Caboose **32.95**

152-851 NKP **33.95**

152-852 IC (Side Door) **34.95**

152-853 C-30-1 SP Caboose **34.95**
Add the finishing touch to your Southern Pacific freights with this detailed replica of the C-30-1 series caboose of the 1920s. Features a carefully engineered cupola that can be built with full glazing or with the windows blanked out with wood.

152-854 Seaboard Air Line **34.95** ***NEW***
Features window awnings, screens for doors and windows and an Athearn floor and frame with provisions for modification.

These ready-to-run cars are prepainted and lettered, and include trucks and horn-hook couplers.

50' Steel Reefer 160-17901

BOX CARS

50' PLUG-DOOR EA 10.00

160-18001 UP
160-18006 CR
160-18009 Chessie
160-18010 RDG
160-18017 MILW
160-18025 Frisco
160-18028 EL
160-18030 Triangle Pacific

REEFERS

50' STEEL EA 10.00

160-17901 UP
160-17902 ATSF
160-17913 CN
160-17927 LV
160-17947 Tropicana
160-17948 PFE

HOPPERS

56' CENTERFLOW EA 10.00

160-17508 ROCK
160-17513 CN
160-17527 LV
160-17534 Shell
160-17544 Enjay
160-17545 Corning

40' QUAD EA 10.00

160-17604 Southern
160-17613 CN
160-17618 CSX
160-17626 D&H
160-17635 Morris & Knudson
160-17642 N&W
160-17643 Napierville Junction
160-17646 Minneapolis & St. Louis

GONDOLAS

40' EA 10.00

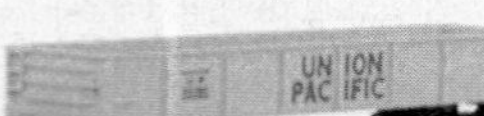

160-17201 UP
160-17204 Southern
160-17209 Chessie
160-17216 Burlington

FLAT CARS

52' DEPRESSED CENTER

160-18347 With Missile Load **16.00**
160-18348 With Transformer Load **13.00**
160-18349 Empty-Car Only **12.00**

89' Tri-Level Transporter 160-46002

51' UP Floodlight Car Only 160-46311

250-Ton Crane & 51' Boom Car 160-46213

TANK CARS

40' 3-DOME EA 10.00

HO deluxe freight cars with metal wheels and EZ-Mate™ magnetic couplers.

160-17134 Shell
160-17136 Pennsalt
160-17137 Quaker State
160-17138 Exxon
160-17140 Phillips 66

40' SINGLE DOME EA 10.00

160-17834 Shell
160-17836 Pennsalt

160-17837 Quaker State
160-17838 Exxon
160-17840 Phillips 66

CABOOSES

36' WIDE VISION EA 10.00

160-17701 UP
160-17702 ATSF
160-17703 BN
160-17709 Chessie
160-17711 GN
160-17718 CSX
160-17728 EL
160-17742 N&W

OPERATING CARS

250-TON CRANE & 51' FLOODLIGHT CARS

160-46101 UP (yellow) **28.00**
160-46103 EL (black, Box Car red) **28.00**
160-46105 Amtrak (orange) **28.00**
160-46311 UP Floodlight Car Only (yellow, silver) **18.00**
160-46313 EL Floodlight Car Only **18.00**
160-46315 Amtrak Floodlight Car Only (orange) **18.00**

250-TON CRANE & 51' BOOM CARS EA 26.00

160-46111 UP (yellow)
160-46115 Amtrak (orange)
160-46213 EL (black, box car red)

MISCELLANEOUS

89' TRI-LEVEL TRANSPORTERS EA 22.00

Transporter includes 15 autos.

160-46002 ATSF (Caboose Red, white)
160-46032 Penn Central (green, white)

GANDY DANCER HAND CAR

160-46202 Powered (yellow, red, green) **28.00**

BACHMANN SILVER SERIES®

HO deluxe freight cars with metal wheels and EZ-Mate™ magnetic couplers.

BOX CARS EA 10.00

40'

160-17010 RDG/Bee Line
160-17033 Lancaster & Chester
160-17034 Alton & Southern
160-17036 Green Bay & Western
160-17038 Bangor & Aroostock
160-17039 DRGW "Cookie Box"

HI CUBE

160-18201 UP
160-18216 CB&Q
160-18220 DRGW
160-18239 NYC

40' STOCK CARS EA 10.00 (UNLESS NOTED)

160-18501 UP
160-18502 ATSF
160-18511 GN
160-18541 CNW

160-18549 Humane Livestock Car **12.00**

45' TRIPLE BAY 100-TON HOPPERS 6-PACK EA 93.00

160-18703 BN
160-18706 CR
160-18707 SP
160-18710 RDG
160-18714 PRR
160-18737 WM
160-18739 DRGW
160-18742 N&W

ORE CARS EA 9.00

160-18601 UP
160-18641 CNW
160-18642 N&W
160-18643 Duluth, Missabe & Iron Range

34' Box Car 160-72324

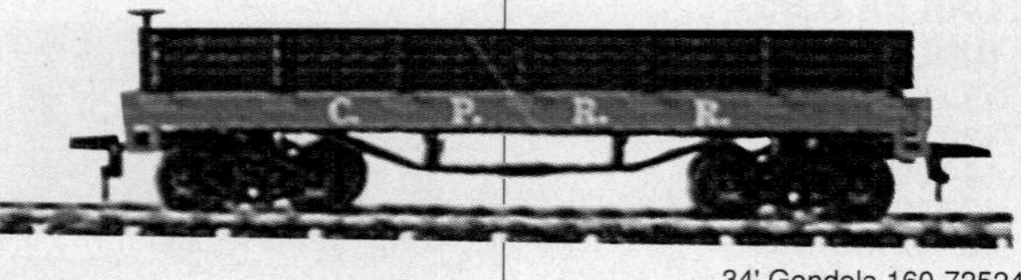

34' Gondola 160-72524

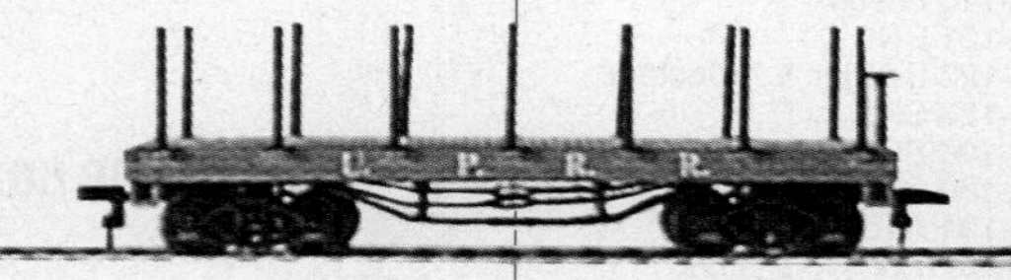

34' Flat Car w/Stakes 160-72424

34' Water Tank Car 160-72601

OLD TIMERS

"Old Timers" are scaled authentically from prototypes in use on western railroads during the mid-1800s.

34' BOX CARS EA 9.00

160-72301 UP (caboose red, black)
160-72324 Central Pacific (green, yellow)

34' GONDOLAS EA 9.00

160-72501 UP (black, caboose red)
160-72524 Central Pacific (black, caboose red)

34' FLAT CARS W/STAKES EA 9.00

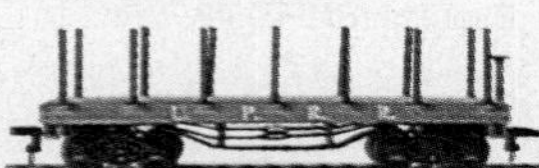

160-72424 Central Pacific (caboose red)
160-72401 UP (gray)

34' WATER TANK CARS EA 9.00

160-72601 UP (caboose red, black)

160-72624 Central Pacific (caboose red, gray)

21' 4-WHEEL CABOOSES EA 9.00

160-72701 UP (yellow)

160-72724 Central Pacific (caboose red, black)

50' Insulated Smooth Side Plug-Door Box Car 235-806

50' Double Plug-Door Box Car 235-505

BOX CARS

These easy-to-build HO Scale kits feature one-piece plastic bodies with separate ladders and brake gear. They also include a nonoperating detailed cushion underframe and Delrin® trucks.

50' INSULATED SINGLE PLUG-DOOR BOX CAR EA 9.95 (UNLESS NOTED)

235-701 Fruit Growers Express-SOU (yellow)
235-702 Fruit Growers Express-BN (Cascade Green)
235-703 Fruit Growers Express-L&N (yellow)
235-704 Fruit Growers Express-CR (yellow)
235-705 Fruit Growers Express-RBNX (yellow)
235-706 Fruit Growers Express-N&W (yellow)
235-707 PC (green)
235-708 SP-Food Loading Only (tuscan)
235-709 N&W Modern (black)
235-710 Green Bay & Western (yellow)
235-711 Fruit Growers Express-Solid Gold (yellow)
235-712 EL (blue)
235-700 Undecorated **7.95**

50' INSULATED SMOOTH SIDE SINGLE PLUG-DOOR BOX CAR EA 9.95 (UNLESS NOTED)

235-801 ATSF
235-802 SOO (white w/red door)
235-803 Boston & Maine (light blue)
235-804 ROCK (blue)
235-805 N&W (tuscan)
235-806 Providence & Worcester
235-800 Undecorated **7.95**

52' DOUBLE PLUG-DOOR BOX CAR EA 9.95 (UNLESS NOTED)

235-501 Bend Mill Works
235-502 CNW **7.95**
235-505 UP
235-506 Weyerhauser
235-507 Cascade
235-508 Georgia-Pacific
235-513 Ralston-Purina
235-514 Boston & Maine
235-515 Florida East Coast
235-516 WC
235-517 Thomasville
235-518 Virginia Central (green w/silver roof) ***NEW***
235-519 L&N/Seaboard Coast Line (black w/silver roof) ***NEW***
235-500 Undecorated **7.95**

C M SHOPS, INC.

These easy-to build HO Scale plastic car kits are prepainted and lettered, and include weights, trucks and horn-hook couplers.

BOX CARS

40' Box Car 12-103

50' Plug Door Box Car 12-145

50' Single Door Box Car 12-133

50' Double Door Box Car 12-120

40' BOX CAR EA 8.95

12-101 EL
12-102 D&H
12-103 N&W
12-104 ATSF
12-106 IC
12-111 CN
12-161 LV (green)
12-188 Erie
12-190 NYC
12-191 UP
12-192 SOU, "Green Light"
12-193 Frisco, "Ship It"
12-194 Lackawanna, "Phoebe Snow"
12-195 Cotton Belt, "Blue Streak"
12-208 Buffalo Creek
12-209 GN
12-211 LV (white)
12-216 B&O
12-217 Indiana Harbor Belt
12-254 Grand Trunk Western "Maple Leaf"
12-289 NH #1 *NEW*
12-2891 NH #2 *NEW*

50' PLUG DOOR BOX CAR EA 9.95

12-105 Chessie/B&O
12-113 Providence & Worcester
12-114 The Rock
12-125 MILW
12-134 Boston & Maine
12-143 ATSF
12-144 Western Pacific
12-145 Chicago Great Western
12-147 Chessie System/C&O
12-159 EL
12-162 Napierville Junction
12-163 CNW "Employee Owned"
12-166 NH
12-168 MOPAC
12-170 SP
12-177 C&O
12-181 Maine Central
12-182 Texas & Pacific
12-196 NP
12-203 CP
12-224 CR
12-225 CN
12-269 Chicago & Illinois Midland
12-2791 LV #2 *NEW*

50' OUTSIDE-BRACED PLUG DOOR BOX CAR EA 9.95

12-157 Pittsburgh & Lake Erie
12-158 EL
12-279 LV 1st # (green)
12-280 CR
12-2801 CR 2nd #

50' SINGLE DOOR BOX CAR EA 9.95 (UNLESS NOTED)

12-107 RDG
12-108 CNW
12-109 Vermont
12-110 Family Lines (L&N)
12-112 MOPAC
12-115 Grand Trunk Western
12-116 Frisco
12-121 BN
12-122 Bangor & Aroostook
12-123 SP
12-126 SOU
12-130 Chessie System/WM
12-131 ATSF
12-132 PC
12-133 CR
12-135 Ashley, Drew & Northern
12-136 Gulf, Mobile & Ohio
12-137 IC Gulf
12-146 Seaboard Air Line
12-151 Atlantic Coast Line
12-152 Nacionales de Mexico
12-153 WM
12-155 Seaboard Coast Line
12-156 IC
12-164 N&W
12-165 Lackawanna
12-167 Maine Central
12-169 UP
12-172 Louisiana Midland
12-173 Clinchfield
12-175 SOO
12-176 L&N
12-178 MILW
12-179 Wabash
12-180 ROCK
12-218 Gulf, Mobile & Ohio "Cushioned"
12-246 Seaboard Coast/Line Family Lines **9.50**
12-2261 D&H "I Love New York" 2nd Edition **11.95**
12-2262 D&H "I Love New York" 3rd Edition **11.95**

50' RAILBOX-TYPE BOX CAR EA 9.95

12-212 Bangor & Aroostook
12-213 N&W
12-214 CNW "Employee Owned"
12-276 The Rock (blue)
12-277 CN
12-278 CR
12-283 Railbox "Next Load, Any Road" (yellow w/black door)
12-285 Richmond, Fredericksburg & Potomac #1 *NEW*
12-2761 The Rock 2nd #
12-2771 CN 2nd #
12-2781 CR
12-2831 Railbox "Next Load, Any Road" 2nd #(yellow w/black door)
12-2851 Richmond, Fredericksburg & Potomac #2 *NEW*

57' Mechanical Reefer 12-227

54' Pullman Standard Ribside Covered Hopper 12-220

50' DOUBLE DOOR BOX CAR EA 9.95

12-120 Erie
12-183 Texas & Pacific
12-197 UP
12-198 CN
12-215 NYC
12-288 LV "Processed Food Loading Only" #1 (Tuscan w/white & black print) *NEW*
12-292 DRGW #1 (Tuscan w/white print) *NEW*
12-1541 Spokane, Portland & Seattle #1 *NEW*
12-1542 Spokane, Portland & Seattle #2 *NEW*
12-2881 LV "Processed Food Loading Only" #2 (Tuscan w/white & black print) *NEW*
12-2921 DRGW #2 (Tuscan w/white print) *NEW*

REEFERS

57' MECHANICAL REEFER EA 10.95

12-141 EL
12-227 Pacific Fruit Express
12-274 BN (white)
12-275 FGE/Real Cold (tan)
12-286 Western Fruit Express (BNFE) #1 *NEW*
12-2741 BN (white w/large lettering)
12-2751 FGE Real Gold (tan w/blue logos)
12-2861 Western Fruit Express (BNFE) #2 *NEW*

HOPPERS

54' PULLMAN STANDARD RIBSIDE COVERED HOPPER EA 10.95

12-124 D&H
12-187 CR
12-199 CNW "Employee Owned"
12-200 CNW "Employee Owned" (yellow)
12-201 Chessie System/B&O
12-202 MKT
12-220 BN
12-221 SOO
12-222 Transportation Corporation of America
12-223 UP "Sugar"
12-230 N&W
12-231 Frito-Lay
12-232 UP
12-233 NYC
12-234 EL
12-235 SOU
12-236 IC
12-237 IC Gulf
12-238 DRGW
12-239 GN (blue)
12-253 PC
12-255 BN (1991)
12-262 CNW "Employee Owned" (gray)
12-264 The Rock
12-2511 SBD (new #)
12-2522 Family Lines (new #)

C M SHOPS, INC.

55' ACF Centerflo Covered Hopper 12-268

50' Gondola 12-184

50' Covered Gondola 12-118

62' Tank Car 12-174

Wide Vision Caboose 12-258

Bay Window Caboose 12-263

55' ACF CENTERFLOW COVERED HOPPER EA 10.95 (UNLESS NOTED)

12-127 Arco Polymers
12-128 Hercules
12-186 CR
12-189 SOO
12-204 EL
12-205 El Rexene
12-206 Chessie System/B&O
12-207 CNW "Employee Owned" (yellow)
12-219 BN
12-228 Chessie System pkg(3) **29.95**
12-229 Robintech
12-240 NYC
12-241 B&O
12-242 C&O
12-243 PRR
12-244 GN (gray)
12-245 Cotton Belt
12-247 Grand Trunk Western
12-248 N&W
12-249 L&N
12-250 Grand Trunk Western (blue)
12-265 The Rock
12-266 UP (white)
12-267 E.C.C. International
12-268 BN (1991)
12-270 GN (Jade Green)
12-271 GN (Big Sky Blue)
12-272 Engelhard (white)
12-290 WP #1 ***NEW***
12-291 WP "Feather" #1 ***NEW***
12-2281 Chessie - Includes 1 Each B&O, C&O and WM pkg(3) **29.95**
12-2701 GN "Grain Loading" (Jade Green)
12-2711 GN (Big Sky Blue)
12-2721 Engelhard 2nd # (white w/blue & black graphics)
12-2901 WP #2 ***NEW***
12-2911 WP "Feather" #2 ***NEW***

GONDOLAS

50' GONDOLA EA 8.95

12-129 PRR
12-139 RDG
12-148 Pittsburgh & Lake Erie
12-149 Detroit, Toledo & Ironton
12-150 IC
12-160 B&O/Chessie
12-171 Rutland
12-184 CR
12-210 D&H
12-281 CN
12-2811 CN ***NEW***

50' COVERED GONDOLA EA 9.95

These covered gondolas are an economical car for both model and prototype railroads. With their covers in place, the cars are used to carry steel coils which are protected from the weather. If business is slow, the covers can be removed and the car used as a standard gondola. This model comes prepainted and requires only minor assembly.

12-117 NKP
12-118 B&O
12-119 C&O
12-138 CNW
12-140 NH
12-185 Bessemer & Lake Erie
12-287 EL #1(black w/white print) ***NEW***
12-2871 EL #2 (black w/white print) ***NEW***

TANK CARS

62' TANK CAR

12-174 Publicker **9.95**

CABOOSES

WIDE VISION CABOOSE EA 10.95

12-256 CR
12-257 DRGW
12-258 D&H
12-259 Spokane, Portland & Seattle
12-260 Seaboard Air Line
12-261 CN

BAY WINDOW CABOOSE EA 10.95

12-263 BN
12-273 The Rock (blue)
12-284 CR "Operation Lifesaver"
12-2731 The Rock (Light Blue)

HOPPER LOADS

These hopper and gondola loads are cast plastic. They will also fit AHM, Tyco and Bachmann cars with some modification.

COAL PKG(2) 3.75 (UNLESS NOTED)

12-3101 Athearn Twin Hopper, Single "Hump" Contour **2.95**
12-3102 Athearn Twin Hopper, Double "Hump" Contour **2.95**
12-3103 Stewart Fishbelly Hopper **2.95**
12-3104 Athearn Quad Hopper
12-3108 Roundhouse Triple Hopper
12-3110 Roundhouse Thrall Gondola
12-3112 McKean Triple Hopper
12-3114 Roundhouse Bathtub
12-3116 Walthers/TMI Twin Hopper or Gondola
12-3118 MDC Ortner Hopper
12-3121 Stewart AAR 14-Panel Hopper
12-3123 Stewart H39 12-Panel Hopper
12-3124 Stewart Offset-Side 9-Panel Hopper
12-3125 Bowser H21 Hopper

GRAVEL PKG(2) 3.75 (UNLESS NOTED)

12-3106 Athearn Twin Hopper **2.95**
12-3107 Athearn Quad Hopper
12-3109 Roundhouse Triple Hopper
12-3119 Walthers/TMI Twin Hopper

ORE

12-3105 MDC 21' Ore Car pkg(2) **2.95**
12-3115 MDC Modern 26' Gondola pkg(2) **3.75**

SAND

12-3113 Athearn 50' Gondola pkg(2) **3.75**

WOOD CHIP

12-3117 Walthers/TMI 36' Hopper pkg(2) **3.75**

These HO Scale easy-to-build kits are prepainted and lettered and include trucks and horn-hook couplers.

We have worked closely with this manufacturer to provide accurate delivery information at the time this catalog was published. Items listed in blue ink may not be available at all times. Current delivery information, along with a list of in-stock products for this line, can be found on our Web site at www.walthers.com.

40' Airslide Covered Hopper
223-9701

Greenville 12 Panel Hopper
223-9315

BOX CARS

60' GREENVILLE SINGLE DOOR BOX CAR

223-9630 Undecorated 9.98

OLD-TIME BOX EA 9.98

223-520101 DRGW
223-520102 PRR
223-520103 Atlantic Coast Line
223-520104 Chicago & Illinois Midland
223-520105 UP
223-520106 MOW (gray)
223-520107 N&S (Tuscan)
223-520108 ATSF (Tuscan)
223-520109 Seaboard
223-520110 SP (Tuscan)
223-520109 Seaboard
223-520111 Nashville, Chattanooga & St. Louis (Tuscan)
223-520112 Florida East Coast (Tuscan)
223-520100 Undecorated

40' PS-1 BOX EA 6.98

These kits include separate weights and feature working Pullman Standard panel doors. The underframe has been modified and will accept body-mounted horn-hook or Kadee No. 5 couplers.

223-9402 SP
223-9404 CR 5.98
223-9410 Grand Trunk Western (Tuscan)
223-9412 MKT (Tuscan)
223-9414 Green Bay & Western
223-9418 Western Pacific (Tuscan, orange)
223-9419 Pittsburgh & West Virginia (black)
223-9423 IC (orange)
223-9429 ATSF #2
223-9430 ATSF #3
223-9431 NYC (red)
223-9432 NYC (green, black)
223-9433 PRR (Not Shaded)
223-9434 PRR (Shaded)
223-9400 Undecorated

40' PS-1 INSULATED BOX EA 5.98

223-9451 CB&Q
223-9452 UP
223-9460 BN
223-9461 DRGW
223-9463 Hormel
223-9464 Thermal Ice (silver)
223-9466 American Refrigerator (Tuscan, yellow)
223-9468 CN (Tuscan)
223-9469 SP (REA green)
223-9450 Undecorated

60' GREENVILLE DOUBLE PLUG DOOR BOX EA 9.98

223-9602 CR (Box Car Red)
223-9603 UP (Oxide Red)
223-9604 SP
223-9605 Chessie
223-9606 BN
223-9607 Data (red)
223-9610 NYC
223-9611 Western Pacific (Box Car Red)
223-9613 SOU System
223-9615 Illinois Central Gulf
223-9617 MP (Box Car Red)
223-9618 Data (Oxide Red)
223-9619 Data (Box Car Red)
223-9600 Undecorated

50' DOUBLE-DOOR AUTO BOX

223-1000988 Christmas 1998 Twelve Days of Christmas Series "A Partridge In A Pear Tree" 10.98 *NEW*

HOPPERS

40' AIRSLIDE COVERED HOPPER-ORIGINAL EA 9.49

223-9701 ATSF (dark gray)
223-9702 PRR (original, gray)
223-9703 SP (gray w/small black "Southern Pacific" lettering)
223-9704 SP (gray w/large red "Southern Pacific" lettering)
233-9006 Firestone (black, red)
223-9708 Bond Baking (gray)
223-9713 CB&Q
223-9714 NKP
223-9715 CR (Oxide Red)
223-9716 UP
223-9717 UP 1970s
223-9718 UP 1990s
223-9719 WM
223-9700 Undecorated

40' AIRSLIDE COVERED HOPPER-MODERN EA 9.49

223-9751 ATSF #2 (dark gray)
223-9752 PRR (modern)
223-9753 N&W
223-9765 CR #2
223-9750 Undecorated

40' AIRSLIDE COVERED HOPPER ASSORTMENT PKG(12) EA 113.88

223-175 CR

GREENVILLE 12 PANEL HOPPER EA 6.98

223-9300 Data (black)
223-9301 Data (red)
223-9302 Chessie
223-9303 CR
223-9304 SOU
223-9305 SP
223-9306 BN
223-9307 DRGW
223-9308 ATSF
223-9309 UP
223-9310 N&W
223-9311 CNW
223-9312 C&O
223-9313 Frisco (Box Car Red)
223-9314 IC
223-9315 PRR
223-9316 Seaboard Coast Line
223-9317 Chattahoochee Industrial
223-9318 SOO
223-9319 Western Pacific
223-9321 IC #2
223-9322 DRGW
223-9323 Penn Central
223-9324 CR Quality
223-9332 ATSF
223-9320 Undecorated

GREENVILLE 15 PANEL HOPPER EA 6.98 (UNLESS NOTED)

223-9350 Data (black)
223-9351 Data (red)
223-9352 B&O
223-9353 Detroit, Toledo & Ironton
223-9354 WM
223-9355 ATSF
223-9356 L&N
223-9357 N&W
223-9359 L&N Dixie
223-9360 EL
223-9361 D&H
223-9362 NP 5.98
223-9363 CB&Q 5.98
223-9364 NYC
223-9365 ATSF "Quality" 5.98
223-9358 Undecorated (black)

40' PS-2 COVERED HOPPER EA 9.98 (UNLESS NOTED)

These kits will accept body-mounted couplers. Some kits include add-on lettering panels that mount over the ribs and simulate the sheet metal plates used on the prototypes.

223-9501 UP
223-9504 CR
223-9509 MOW (gray)
223-9511 Wabash
223-9512 B&O
223-9519 Elgin, Joliet & Eastern (gray)
223-9523 Jack Frost Cane Sugar (blue, white) 8.98
223-9524 Great Western Malt (gray, green) 8.98
223-9525 BakeLite Plastics (red, white) 8.98
223-9530 Warps Plastic (yellow) 8.98
223-9534 Sutton Co-Op (blue) 8.98

GONDOLAS

54' MILL EA 6.98

223-9001 CNW (Chinese Red)
223-9002 UP
223-9003 PRR
223-9004 SP (Box Car Red)
223-9005 ATSF
223-9006 Wabash (black)
223-9007 CR
223-9008 CSX Transportation
223-9010 SP (Modern)
223-9011 BN
223-9012 DRGW
223-9013 Pittsburgh & Lake Erie
223-9014 C&O
223-9015 L&N
223-9016 MP
223-9017 N&W (black)
223-9019 SSW (Box Car Red)
223-9021 UP (Modern)
223-9022 SOU System
223-9023 MILW
223-9025 Data (black)
223-9026 Data (red)
223-9000 Undecorated

54' MILL W/LOAD EA 8.49 (UNLESS NOTED)

223-9029 WC 7.98
223-9030 Florida East Coast
223-9031 CNJ (Olive Green)
223-9032 CR
223-9033 UP 7.98
223-9034 WC 7.98
223-9035 NS

WITH MOUNTED MOW CRANE EA 21.98

223-9121 MOW (gray)
223-9122 MOW (yellow)
223-9123 MOW (black)
223-9120 Undecorated

REEFERS

57' EA 9.49

223-9805 Golden West
223-9806 BN Temp-Lok

223-9807 SOO
223-9808 CR

COIL CARS

54' EA 10.98

223-9054 CR (Box Car Red)
223-9055 PRR
223-9056 NYC (black)
223-9057 Detroit, Toledo & Ironton
223-9061 CNW
223-9062 UP
223-9063 N&W
223-9064 CR Quality
223-9050 Round Undecorated
223-9059 Angled Undecorated

FLAT CARS

54' PULPWOOD EA 7.98 (UNLESS NOTED)

Each kit includes a one-piece removable pulpwood load.

223-9201 ATSF (red) 10.98

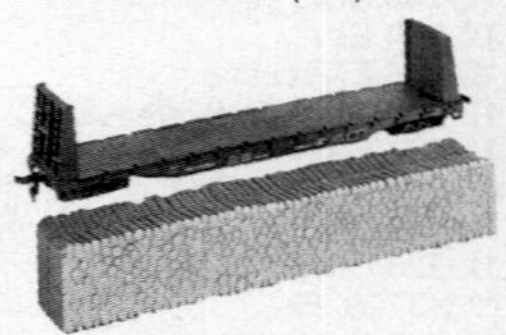

223-9202 TTX 10.98
223-9203 SOO (white)
223-9204 BN (Cascade Green) 8.98
223-9205 SOU 9.20
223-9206 Ontario Northland (blue) 8.98
223-9207 GN
223-9208 N&W (black)
223-9209 CNW
223-9200 Undecorated 10.98

54' W/TRAILER EA 10.98 (UNLESS NOTED)

223-9173 Illinois Central Gulf (black, silver)
223-9182 NP #2
223-9183 N&W #2
223-9184 Western Pacific #2
223-9185 B&O #1
223-9277 DRGW (black, gray)
223-9281 IC
223-9282 N&W
223-9283 Royal American Shows
223-9285 With Royal American Rib Trailer
223-9286 With Royal American 28' Trailer
223-9150 Undecorated 9.98

54' W/CABLE LOAD EA 6.98 (UNLESS NOTED)

223-9251 SP (Box Car Red)

223-9252 Trailer Train **5.98**
223-9253 BN
223-9254 Illinois Central Gulf (orange) **5.98**
223-9255 N&W **5.98**
223-9256 UP **5.98**
223-9257 ATSF (red)
223-9258 DRGW (orange)
223-9259 CR (Box Car Red)
223-9260 CSX Transportation **5.98**
223-9261 SOU
223-9262 Family Lines
223-9250 Undecorated

54' W/40' CONTAINER ON CHASSIS EA 10.98

223-9177 CP/CP Ships (box car red, green)
223-9178 CR/Spanish Line (Box Car Red, blue)
223-9180 Chessie/American President Lines (black, silver)
223-9181 SOO Hanjin (white, light blue)

WITH MOUNTED MOW CRANE EA 21.98

223-9101 MOW (gray)
223-9102 MOW (yellow)
223-9103 MOW (black)
223-9100 Undecorated

INTERMODAL

125-TON 5-UNIT CONTAINER WELL CAR EA 59.98

223-195401 ATSF #1
223-195402 ATSF #2
223-195403 ATSF #3
223-195501 BN #1
223-195502 BN #2
223-195503 BN #3
223-195601 CSX #1
223-195602 CSX #2
223-195603 CSX #3

125-TON GUNDERSON FLAT CAR W/LOADS EA 18.98

223-198101 Trialer Train w/48' "ATS" Trailer #1
223-198102 Trailer Train w/48' "ATS" Trailer #2
223-198201 BN w/2 28' BN Trailers #1
223-198202 BN w/2 28' BN Trailers #2
223-198301 ATSF w/JB Hunt Trailer #1
223-198302 ATSF w/JB Hunt Trailer #2
223-198401 Sealand w/48' "Sealand" Container #1
223-198402 Sealand w/48' "Sealand" Container #2
223-198501 SP w/2 28' Overnite Trans. Trailers #1
223-198502 SP w/2 28' Overnite Trans. Trailers #2
223-198601 CSX w/48' North American Trailer #1
223-198602 CSX w/48' North American Trailer #2
223-198000 Undecorated

CONTAINERS

40' RIBBED SIDE PKG(3) EA 9.98

223-8304 Cast Container Line
223-8300 Undecorated

40' SMOOTH SIDE PKG(3) EA 9.98

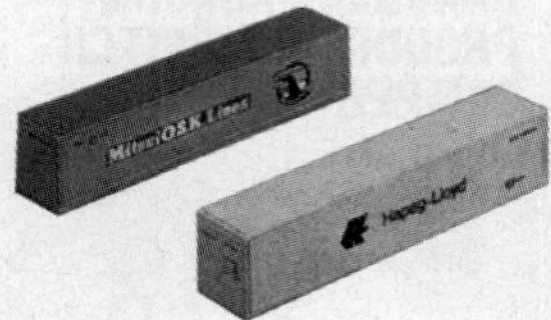

223-8401 OOCL
223-8403 Showa Container Line
223-8400 Undecorated

45' RIBBED SIDE

223-8350 45' Smooth Side **9.98**
223-8450 45' Ribbed Side **11.98**

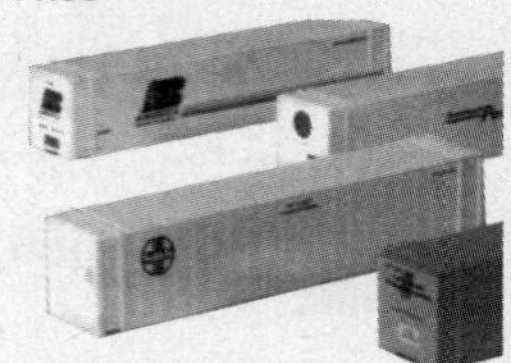

223-8351 CP Intermodal Freight Systems pkg(2) **9.98**
223-8352 SP (new 1992 logo) pkg(2) **9.98**
223-8355 Model Railroader 60th Anniversary (White) **6.98**

40' OLDIES TRAILER PKG(2) EA 11.98

223-8139 NP
223-8140 N&W
223-8141 Western Pacific

30' BULK CONTAINER EA 7.98

223-8331 UP ***NEW***
223-8332 Sealand ***NEW***

48' CONTAINER

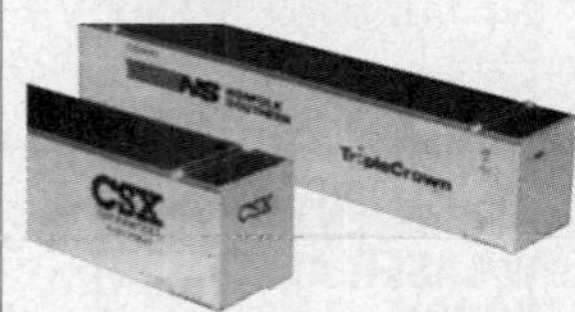

223-8552 XTRA **4.29**
223-8553 CN Intermodal **4.29**
223-8554 BN America **5.98**
223-8555 Itel **5.98**
223-8557 SP **5.98**
223-8559 NS Triple Crown **5.98**
223-8560 J.B. Hunt **5.98**
233-8561 Schneider National **4.29**
233-8562 NYK **4.29**
223-8550 Undecorated **4.29**

TRAILERS

40' PKG(3) EA 10.98 (UNLESS NOTED)

223-8103 Consolidated Rail pkg(3) **9.98**
223-8104 TransAmerica pkg(3) **9.98**
223-8107 UP
223-8108 Budd of California
223-8109 Illinois Central Gulf pkg(3) **9.98**
223-8111 Boston & Maine
223-8114 N&W
223-8115 DRGW

45' SEMI TRAILERS PKG(2) EA 11.98

223-8201 Nitrol
223-8202 Crab Orchard & Egyptian Railway
223-8203 Texas-Mexican Railway
223-8204 Cornucopia Transport
223-8205 CP Rail Intermodal
223-8206 Seaboard System
223-8208 UP w/Flag
223-8209 Lynden Transport w/Alaska Map
223-8210 Illinois Central Gulf
223-8211 BN "Expediter" Logo
223-8213 Co-Op
223-8214 BN
223-8200 Undecorated

Limited Quantity Available
223-8212 Preferred Pool Trailer

45' UNDECORATED SEMI TRAILERS EA 9.98

223-8200 Ribbed Side

223-8250 45' Ribbed Side

48' EA 5.98

223-8502 TransAmerica
223-8503 CP
223-8505 J.B. Hunt
223-8506 Schneider National
223-8507 JB Hunt "Quantum"
223-8508 XTRA Intermodal
223-8500 Undecorated

These easy-to-build HO Scale kits feature highly detailed plastic parts, separate ladders and grab irons. Underbody details, trucks and step-by-step instructions are also included. Coupler pockets accept horn-hook or Kadee® couplers.

HOPPERS

ACF 2970 2-BAY COVERED HOPPER

The ACF 2970 covered hopper was built by American Car & Foundry from 1966 to 1970. Approximately 1555 of this Phase 2 car were built and used by at least 17 different railroads for hauling concentrated loads such as sand, cement and potash.

This kit includes three types of hatches and two types of hopper outlets to match prototype equipment. Other details include separate brake components, wire grab irons, stirrup steps and wire coupler lift bars.

229-245

229-243 ACFX (gray) **17.50**
229-245 NP (gray) **17.50**
229-248 CB&Q (gray) **18.50**
229-250 EL (gray) **17.50**
229-258 CNW (yellow) **18.50**
229-240 Undecorated **15.50**

GONDOLAS

May be built with drop doors open or closed.

40' GENERAL SERVICE GONDOLA EA 18.95

229-200 Composite Sides, Undecorated
229-220 Steel Sides, Undecorated

40' GENERAL SERVICE SUGAR BEET GONDOLA EA 21.95

Originally built as standard general service drop-bottom gondolas, these SP sugar beet gondolas had side extensions added in the mid-1950s to increase hauling capacity. These cars are still in use today hauling the same load, usually under private sugar company ownership. Detailed kits include side panel extensions to match the prototype wood or plywood conversions.

229-201 Wood Extensions, Undecorated

229-202 Plywood Extensions, Undecorated

SUGAR BEET LOAD

229-7301 For Sugar Beet Gondola **TBA**

WELL CARS

GUNDERSON ALL-PURPOSE WELL CAR

229-261 Undecorated **TBA**
Introduced in 1993, the Gunderson single-unit well car features a totally revised car design allowing it to carry either double stack containers or trailers of various lengths. This kit features a one-piece body, with separate walkways, trailer hitches, brake components, stirrup steps, stanchions, wire grab irons, air hoses and coupler lift bars.

Custom Finishing

These HO Scale kits feature detailed brass and white-metal parts, and include rotating, insulated wheels. All kits include decals.

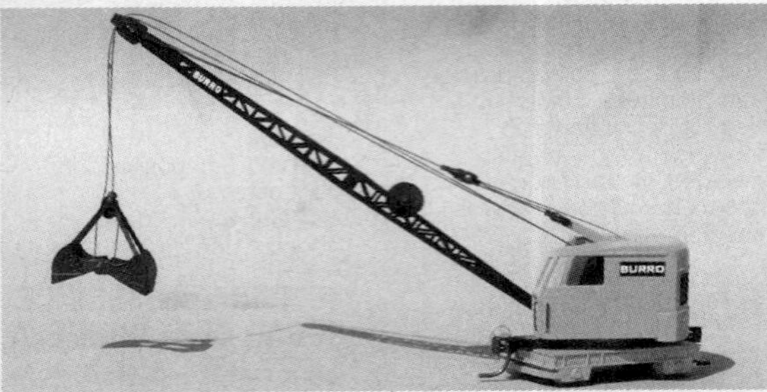

Burro Crane 247-7000

Pyke Ballast Regulator 247-7011

Tamper Track Alignment Machine 247-7014

TRACK MAINTENANCE EQUIPMENT

BURRO CRANE

247-7000 Model 40, 12-1/2 Ton **49.95**

247-7008 Model 50, 20 Ton **64.95**
247-7057 Model 30 **51.95** ***NEW***
This 7-1/2-ton crane can rotate or be secured by a pivot system. Over 55 detail parts, including a brass boom, windshield wipers, window glazing and a 39" magnet. Couplers not included.

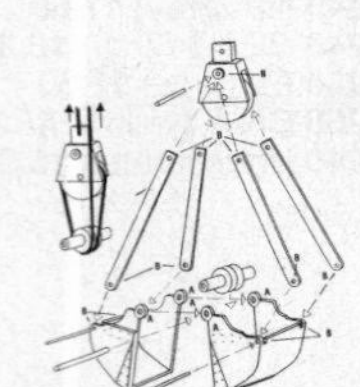

247-7282 Clamshell Bucket **16.95**
This 1/2 cubic yard bucket includes brass castings and can be assembled to operate.

247-70001 Crane Boom Only **10.95**
247-7808 Model 50 Extra Decals **4.95**

247-7283 Crane Accessories **6.95**
This set of brass castings includes a 39" nonoperating magnet, hoistblock, hook and railtongs.

247-7800 Extra Decals **4.95**

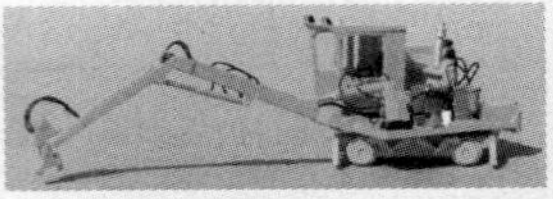

FAIRMONT TIE HANDLER

247-7001 27.95
The kit can be assembled so the cab rotates.

247-7801 Extra Decals **4.95**

FAIRMONT PRECISION RAIL SPOT GRINDER

247-7002 39.95
247-7802 Extra Fairmont Decals **4.95**

PERMAQUIP/FAIRMONT WELDERS VEHICLE

247-7003 27.95
Side shutter panels operate and may be left open to show interior detail (available separately).

247-7284 Permaquip Welders Vehicle Interior **3.95**
The details in this kit include a welder console, V6-style engine and hoist winches

247-7803 Extra Decals **4.95**

NORDBERG/NORDCO SPIKE PULLER

247-7005 Super Claws LS w/Figures **22.95**
247-7805 Extra Decals **4.95**

PYKE BALLAST REGULATOR

247-7011 Model M **74.95**
247-7811 Extra Decals **4.95**

PERMAQUIP/FAIRMONT PERMACLIPPER

This machine is used to remove and replace "Pandrol" rail clips quickly and efficiently.

247-7004 27.95
247-7804 Extra Decals **4.95**

NORDBERG/NORDCO RAIL SPIKER

247-7006 Hydra-Hammer **26.95**
247-7806 Extra Decals **4.95**

SWINGMASTER SPEED SWING

247-7007 Model 181 **29.95**
247-7285 Swingmaster Loader Bucket **2.95**
247-7807 Extra Decals **4.95**

PANDROL-JACKSON PRODUCTION/SWITCH TAMPER

247-7021 Model 6700 **79.95**
247-7821 Extra Decals **4.95**

PYKE UTILITY CRANE

247-7010 1 Ton **36.95**
247-7810 Extra Decals **4.95**

PYKE SNOW CLEARING MACHINE

247-7017 Model M **79.95**
247-7817 Extra Decals **4.95**

TAMPER SWITCH TAMPING MACHINE W/LASER ALIGNMENT BUGGY

247-7012 Model STM-XLC **54.95**
247-7812 Extra Decals **4.95**

TAMPER TRACK ALIGNMENT MACHINE W/LASER ALIGNMENT BUGGY

247-7014 Model MK III **47.95**
247-7814 Extra Decals **4.95**

PYKE ON-TRACK BRUSH CUTTER

247-7013 65.95
247-7813 Extra Decals **4.95**

NORDBERG/NORDCO ANCHOR APPLICATOR

247-7018 27.95
247-7818 Extra Decals **4.95**

NORDBERG/NORDCO SCARFIER/TIE INSERTER

247-7019 Model C OMSI **32.95**
247-7819 Extra Decals **4.95**

PANDROL-JACKSON ULTRASONIC RAIL FLAW DETECTION VEHICLE

247-7023 34.95
247-7823 Extra Decals **4.95**

NORDCO RIDE ON ADZER

247-7035 27.95
Operating lever to raise and lower cutter head onto ties. More than thirty parts. Includes decals and operator figure.

FAIRMONT HEAVY-DUTY GANG CAR

247-7020 With Trailer **19.95**
247-7220 Extra Trailer for Gang Car **6.95**

Custom Finishing

TRACKMOBILE MOBILE RAILCAR MOVING VEHICLE

247-7025 Model 4500 **42.95**
247-7825 Extra Decals **4.95**

PYKE BRIDGE TIMBER INSERTER

Features positionable parts with telescoping brass cylinders. Cab can be built to rotate. Kit features over 60 parts cast in lead-free pewter.

247-7028 39.95
247-7828 Extra Decals **4.95**

18 TON STEEL-DECKED EQUIPMENT TRAILER W/PINTEL HOOK

247-7048 19.95
247-7248 Operating Pintel Hooks pkg(3) **4.95**

KERSHAW SELF-PROPELLED CRIBBER

247-7037 17.95

FAIRMONT SPEEDER

247-7038 23.95
Kit makes two vehicles.

PYKE TIE CRANE W/BASKET GRAPPLE

Cab rotates and grapple swivels. Boom, dipper stick and basket grapple are all movable.

247-7039 42.95
247-7839 Decals **4.95**

KERSHAW KLEARWAY 10-10 RIGHT OF WAY VEGETATION CONTROL MACHINE

Cutterhead raises and lowers via brass telescopic tubing hydraulic cylinders.

247-7045 29.95
247-7845 Decals **4.95**

KERSHAW BALLAST REGULATOR

One of the most versatile machines in railroading, the Kershaw Model 26 Ballast Regulator can be found on the maintenance roster of every Class 1 US and Canadian railroad. On the prototype, these machines spread and shape the ballast between and alongside the rails, preparing it for the tampers. This kit has many parts that are positionable. The side wing plows can be raised and lowered by cable and drum like the prototype. The front transfer plow blade swings, and can be raised and lowered, as can the sweeping machinery at the rear. The model includes a full cab interior, plus decals, window glazing and etched brass windshield wipers. The kit features over 100 metal parts and includes complete assembly instructions.

247-7027 Model 26 **61.95**
247-7127 Window Glazing **3.95**
247-7327 Windshield Wipers **5.95**
247-7827 Extra Decals **4.95**

FAIRMONT A4 SERIES E MOTOR CAR

247-7056 26.95 *NEW*
This double kit features over 30 detail parts, including windshield wipers and window glazing.

KERSHAW MOBILE WRECKING CRANE

Make quick work of heavy repairs anywhere along your railroad with this Kershaw truck crane, based on the RCH 100, now in service with many roads. The all-metal kit is packed with details, including an optional front frame extension with a winch. With careful assembly, virtually all of the hydraulic system parts can be raised and lowered, while the crane can be rotated and the boom extended. This kit also introduces all-new steerable front tandem axles, which can be positioned at various angles for more realism. Both cabs feature full interiors, plus new laser-printed window "glass" and photo-etched windshield wipers. Authentic Kershaw decals are included to complete this impressive model.

247-7030 RCH 100 **81.95**
247-7330 Window Glazing **3.95**
247-7130 Windshield Wipers **5.95**
247-7830 Extra Decals **4.95**

KERSHAW RCT 130 MOBILE WRECKING CRANE KIT

247-7049 81.95 *NEW*
The stabilizers of this 130-ton wrecking crane are positionable. Over 150 detail parts, including windshield wipers and window glazing. Cabs feature full interior detail.

TAMPER MODEL CSC BALLAST COMPACTOR KIT

247-7053 41.95 *NEW*
Side-shoulder compact assemblies can be raised and lowered. Over 60 detail parts, piece includes cab interior detail, window glazing and windshield wipers.

FAIRMONT TAMPER

247-7031 Mark IV Production Tamper w/Laser Alignment Buggy Kit **95.95**
247-7831 Extra Mark IV Decals **4.95**

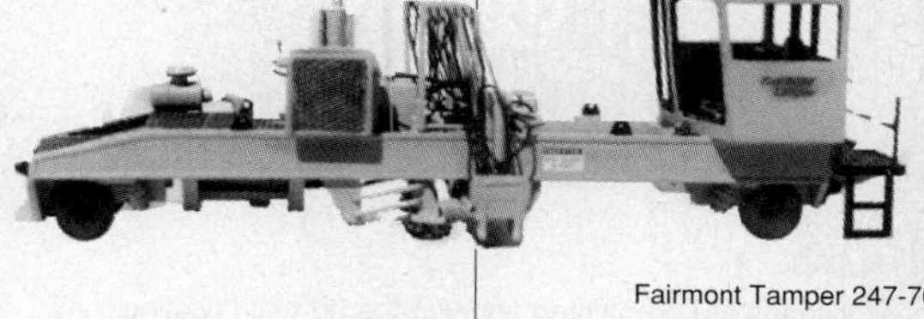

Fairmont Tamper 247-7034

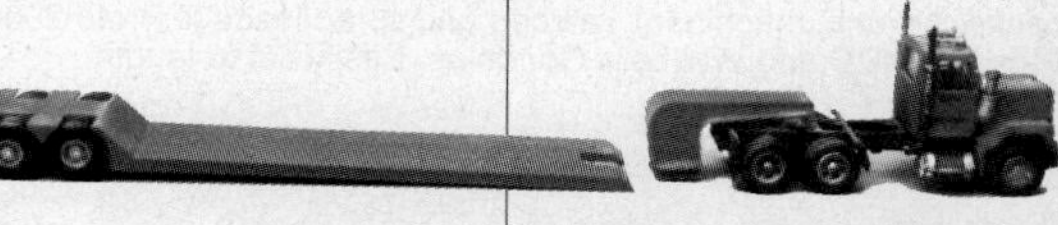

Equipment Transport Flatbed Trailer 247-7047

247-7034 Model TR-10 Tie Exchanger **58.95**
247-7834 Extra Model TR-10 Decals **4.95**

50' EQUIPMENT TRANSPORT FLATBED TRAILER

247-7047 23.95
Heavy duty detachable gooseneck. Fits Herpa/Con-Cor & other tractors (not included).

KERSHAW KLIPPER

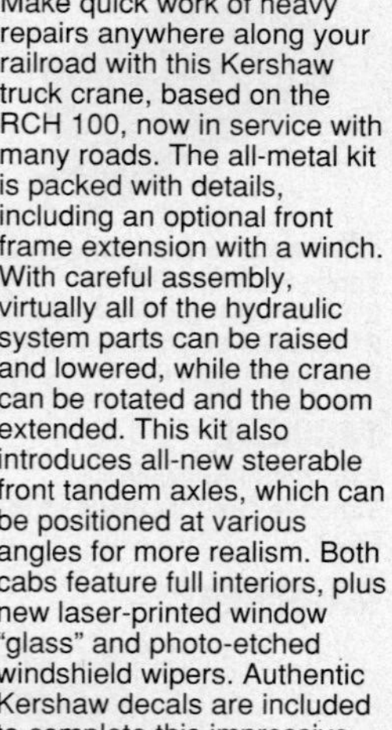

247-7046 55 High-Reach Vegetation Control Machine **49.95**
Keep your line free from brush and debris with this all-metal kit. Features include: front debris blade that raises and lowers, stabilizer arms with swivel pads that raise and lower, a boom that swivels and elevates to 60' from ground level and a cutter head that swivels and rotates on boom. The body also articulates to negotiate any rough terrain that it might encounter. Includes 70+ parts, decals and laser-printed "glass" windows.

LOG STAKE CAR

62' 9"

247-318 National Steel Car Company **19.95**
This log car is easily assembled and features an all pewter make-up. Kit includes all castings, preformed grabs, predrilled end platforms for truck installation (brass screws included) and illustrated instructions. Less trucks, couplers and decals.

ACCESSORIES

COMPRESSOR

247-7024 160 psi, w/Hy-Rail Wheels **11.95**

HY-RAIL GUIDE WHEELS

247-7009 For Light-Duty Vehicles **2.95**

FLAT CAR LOADING RAMP

247-7016 For Track Maintenance Equipment **9.95**

SIX SEATED FIGURES

247-7036 pkg(6) **3.95**
Hard hat operators for maintenance equipment. Three each of two different positions.

Chooch ENTERPRISES INC.®

LOADS

Realistic loads are prepainted and weathered resin castings. All coal loads come in nine different piles packed randomly in two packs. All junk, machinery, railroad and scrap loads fit Proto 2000, Athearn, MDC and Walthers Gondolas. Easily cut to length.

Ore for Walthers Car 214-7212

Taconite for Walthers Car 214-7213

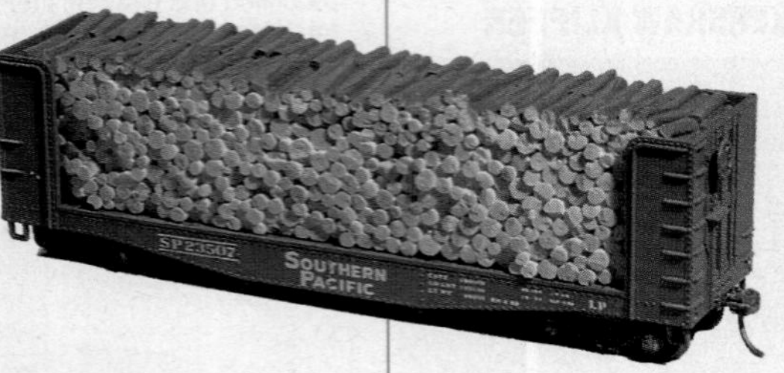

Pulpwood for Athearn Car 214-7214

Bundled Lumber for 40' Flat Car 214-7217

Bundled Lumber for 50' Flat Car 214-7218

Bundled Lumber for 50' Box Car 214-7219

ORE

214-7088 For Roundhouse 26' Taper-Side Ore Car 2-1/2 x 1-1/4" pkg(4) **7.99**
214-7212 For Walthers Ore Car pkg(4) **5.99**

TACONITE

214-7213 For Walthers Taconite/Ore Car pkg(4) **5.99** *NEW*

MACHINERY

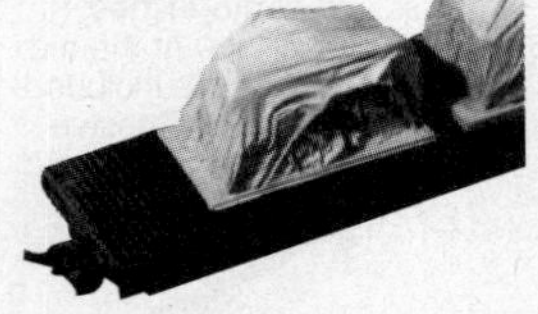

214-7087 Covered for Flat Car (1 x 1-3/4") pkg(6) **7.99**
214-7220 Wrapped pkg(6) **9.99** *NEW*

JUNK & SCRAP LOADS EA 5.99 (UNLESS NOTED)

The following loads fit into the following gondolas: Proto 2000, Athearn, Roundhouse and Walthers cars.

214-7224 Junk for Gondolas *NEW*
214-7222 Baled Scrap for Gondolas **4.99** *NEW*
214-7223 Random Baled Scrap for Gondolas **4.99** *NEW*
214-7225 Scrap for Gondolas *NEW*
214-7226 Railroad Scrap for Gondolas *NEW*
214-7227 Automobile Scrap for Gondolas *NEW*
214-7228 Machinery Scrap for Gondolas *NEW*

Limited Quantity Available

214-7053 Scrap for Athearn 50' Gondola (6-3/4 x 1-1/4") pkg(2)
214-7069 Scrap for Roundhouse 50' Mill Gondola (7-1/4 x 1-1/4") pkg(2)

PULPWOOD EA 5.99

214-7214 For Athearn Car *NEW*
214-7215 For 40' Flat Car *NEW*
214-7216 For 40' Gondola *NEW*

Limited Quantity Available

214-7058 For Athearn Cars (5-1/2 x 1-1/4") pkg(2)

Wrapped Machinery 214-7220

Random Scrap Baled for Gondolas 214-7223

Baled Scrap for Gondolas 214-7222

BUNDLED LUMBER EA 7.99

214-7086 For Flat Car (1-1/8 x 2-1/4") pkg(4)
214-7217 For 40' Flat Car *NEW*
214-7218 For 50' Flat Car *NEW*
214-7219 For 50' Box Car *NEW*

COAL PKG(2) EA 5.99

214-7056 For Athearn 40' Quad Hopper (5-3/4 x 1-1/4")
214-7057 For Athearn 34' Offset-Side Twin Hopper (4-1/2 x 1-1/4")
214-7063 For Roundhouse 40' 3-Bay Rib-Side Hopper (5-1/2 x 1-1/4")

214-7089 For Accurail 55-Ton USRA Hopper

214-7090 For Atlas 50-Ton 2-Bay Offset Side Hopper

214-7202 For Stewart Offset 70-Ton Triple Hopper
214-7203 For Walthers Bethgon Coalporter

214-7204 For Walthers 100-Ton Quad Hopper

BALLAST

214-7211 For Walthers 41' Ballast Car pkg(2) **5.99**

COILED WIRE

214-7221 For Gondola **4.99** *NEW*

RAZOR SAW FOR CUTTING LOADS

214-7400 **9.99** *NEW*

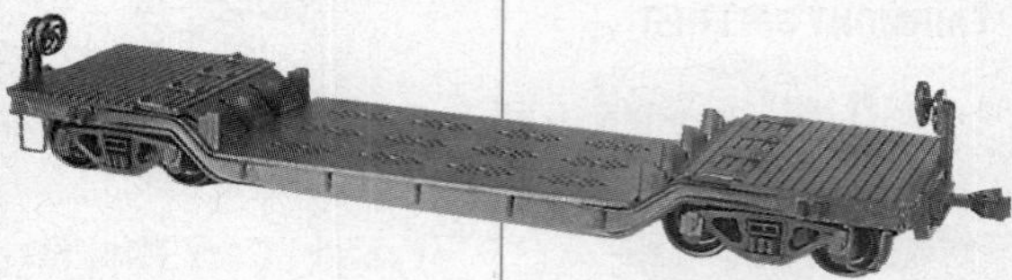
90-Ton Depressed Center Flat Car 117-4800

These undecorated HO Scale kits feature highly detailed plastic parts and include trucks. Couplers are not included, but Kadee® couplers can be easily installed.

90-TON DEPRESSED CENTER FLAT CAR

117-4800 Commonwealth Depressed Center Flat Car **10.00**
Generally, the cast steel bodies of these cars were sent to the railroads, where final assembly was completed. This accounts for the many variations in trucks, decking and brake equipment used on these cars by different roads.

70-TON ACF COVERED HOPPER EA 8.95

117-2000

Developed in 1938 as a standardized design for handling bulk cement. The first cars built had ten roof hatches for loading, while later versions had eight loading hatches. These kits feature parts to model three different side variations built by ACF, along with two different discharge hatches.

117-2000 8-Hatch
117-2001 8-Hatch - Wide Spacing
117-2002 Round Hatch

70-TON ACF/M-K BALLAST HOPPER

117-2200 MOW **8.95**
In the late 1960s, laws were passed to remove cars over 30 years old from railroad interchange. To comply with the laws, many older 70-ton covered hoppers were converted to ballast service with the installation of special control flow doors developed by the Morrison-Knudsen Company.

70-TON ENTERPRISE COVERED HOPPER EA 8.95

117-2020

Developed by the Enterprise Railway Equipment Company to compete with the ACF 70-ton covered hopper.

117-2020 NYC Version
117-2021 CN Version

40' SINGLE-BAY AIRSLIDE® COVERED HOPPER

117-2600 2600 Cu. Ft. **8.95**
Includes parts to model early or late version.

65' MILL GONDOLA EA 7.95

117-3010

The 65' mill gondola first appeared in the 1930s. The two most common were Pennsy's G-26 and the AAR 70-ton design.

117-3000 PRR G-26
117-3010 AAR 70-Ton

CABOOSE

117-4000 Northeast Standard **20.00**
This kit includes parts to build over 50 variations of the basic northeast standard caboose.

FALLER

IMPORTED FROM GERMANY BY WALTHERS
Loads are finished in realistic colors and ready to install.

FREIGHT LOADS

272-1550 Timber Load **9.99**
4 x 1-1/4 x 1-3/8"
98 x 30 x 35mm

272-1551 Coal Load **8.99**
4 x 1-1/4 x 7/8"
100 x 30 x 20mm

272-1552 Scrap Load **8.99**
4 x 1-1/4 x 1/2"
100 x 30 x 14mm

272-1553 Timber Load **8.99**
3-3/8 x 1 x 1" 85 x 27 x 23mm

272-1554 Steel Fabric Load **11.99**
2-3/4 x 1 x 5/8"
69 x 24 x 15mm

272-1555 Sugar Beet Load **9.99**
4 x 1-1/4 x 7/8"
100 x 30 x 20mm

272-1556 Waste Glass Load **8.99**
4 x 1-1/4 x 1/2"
100 x 30 x 16mm

272-1557 Waste Wood Load **8.99**
4 x 1-1/4 x 1/2"
100 x 30 x 16mm

272-1558 Slab Boards **12.99**
Bundles 2 x 1-3/4 x 1-1/4"
49 x 43 x 30mm

272-1559 Pipes **12.99**
4-1/4 x 1 -1/4 x 1"
111 x 29 x 26mm

272-1560 Cable Drum **14.99**
3 x 1 x 1" 80 x 23 x 24, 3mm

272-1561 Wood Pieces 10g **17.99**

272-1562 Waste Glass 10g **10.99**

272-1563 Timber 10g **13.99**

272-1564 Steel Plates 14g **13.99**

272-1565 Apples .35oz 10g **9.99**

272-1566 Wooden Mine Pilings .35oz 10g **12.99**

272-1567 Wooden Planks .35oz 10g **16.99**

These HO and HOn3 craft train kits include various combinations of wood, plastic, cast-metal and cardstock parts. Special note: The Wheel Works line of freight cars has been acquired by Durango Press.

GONDOLAS

All gondolas are HOn3 scale with DRGW roadname.

HIGH-SIDE GONDOLA

254-112 16.95

PIPE GONDOLA

254-114 16.95

FLAT CARS

WESTSIDE LUMBER CO. EA 16.95

Car bodies are one-piece metal castings, so no extra weight is needed. All add-on details are also cast metal. Trucks included.

254-50 HOn3
254-53 Aged Deck HOn3
Includes a weathered deck with rotten boards.

IDLER FLAT CAR

254-116 DRGW HOn3 **15.95**

INTERMODAL EQUIPMENT

Now in use on some major railroads, the RoadRailer® can be operated as a truck trailer or rail car using the retractable running gear. A special coupler is used so that RoadRailers are run as unit trains. Kits include unpainted plastic and metal parts.

ROADRAILER®

254-101 16.95
Kit is designed to run on rails, but can be modified for highway use with some scratchbuilding.

ADAPTERRAILER®

254-102 19.95
This unit is used as an idler between the loco and other RoadRailer units. It has a standard coupler at the front, and the special RoadRailer coupler at the rear.

Rotary Snow Plow 254-31

Roadrailer® 254-101

Adapterrailer® 254-102

CABOOSE

WESTSIDE LUMBER CO.

254-55 HOn3 **19.95**
All-plastic kit with trucks.

MAINTENANCE OF WAY

ROTARY SNOW PLOW KITS EA 89.95

Meet winter head-on with this rugged rotary plow. The kit is based on Rotary OM, which was built by Cooke and delivered to the Rio Grande narrow gauge in 1889. The same design was also used by many standard-gauge roads.

254-30 HOn3
Includes decals for Rio Grande Rotary OM.

254-31 HO
Includes decals for SP, UP, CP, GN and SOO.

DRAG FLANGERS

254-51 Rio Grande Southern Drag Flanger #01 HOn3 **34.95**
Came to the RGS new in 1890 from the Denver & Rio Grande shops.

254-126 Rio Grande Southern Decals **1.00**
Set includes numbers and data for use with #254-51 as shown above, printed in white.

HAND CARS

254- 12

Taken directly from Rio Grande plans, this kit consists of detail metal castings, brass wire and scale lumber.

254-12 HO **8.95**
254-22 HOn3 **10.95**
254-14 Hand Car Wheels pkg(4) **1.95**
These wheels are for use with kits #254-12 and 254-22.

TRACK MAINTENANCE EQUIPMENT

TRACK EQUIPMENT SET

254-100 36.95
This set includes one each of kits #37, 97, 98 & 99.

FAIRMONT SPEEDER

254-37 6.95

FAIRMONT SPIKE PULLER

254-97 6.95
The prototype of this unit is used to pull spikes from bad ties.

FAIRMONT TIE SHEAR

254-98 14.95
The prototype of this machine cuts bad ties in half, for faster removal.

KERSHAW TIE CRANE

254-99 13.95
This small crane is used to lift new ties and put them in place.

LOG CAR

DRGW/NEW MEXICO LUMBER CO.

254-58 13.95
This car was used by the New Mexico Lumber Co. and other lumber companies along the Rio Grande line.

MINE CAR

254-43 18" Gauge **3.25**

Information STATION

Freight Cars That Fit

Selecting the "right" freight cars for your fleet can be a tough choice. Railroads purchase cars to serve the needs of on-line customers who either produce or consume materials, and the same approach can be used on your own line.

Certain industries dominate areas of the country, so you're likely to see a lot of the cars they require. For example, in the corn belt, lots of covered hoppers are needed to move grain. In the east and west, coal hoppers or modern gondolas handle much of the traffic.

Industries that require many different raw materials in bulk are good choices for your layout, as they require a variety of cars. A paper maker needs chemicals delivered in tank cars, pulp wood which comes in on special flat cars or gondolas, wood chips that arrive in giant purpose-built open hopper cars and empty box cars to ship the finished product. A steel works needs coal, coke, taconite, limestone and ore, which may arrive in hoppers. Finished steel will be delivered to customers in specialized cars such as coil steel cars, or flat cars and gondolas.

Grandt Line

Narrow gauge styrene craftsman car kits. Underbody details, brake gear, wire parts, dummy couplers, trucks and decals (where appropriate) are included. All kits are HOn3 unless noted.

NARROW GAUGE CARS

30' WOOD BOX CAR
300-5226 C&S/RGS **19.95**

30' REEFER
300-5231 C&S/RGS **19.95**

STEEL UNDERFRAME STOCK CAR
300-5253 C&S/RGS **19.95**
Over 60 parts; Murphy roof and positionable door.

30' GONDOLAS
300-5188 Drop Bottom DRGW **29.95**
Includes over 200 parts.

300-5214 Steel Underframe C&S **19.95**

30' FLAT CAR
300-5186 DRGW **16.45**

30' CABOOSE

300-5235 C&S **19.95**

30' WHEEL & TIE CAR
300-5187 DRGW **20.95**

DUMP CAR PKG(2) EA 7.50
Easy-to-build Koppel 3-1/2 yard, 4-wheel gable bottom dump car from the "Baby Railroad," a two-foot Borax mine road in Death Valley, California. All-plastic construction with silver-colored Delrin wheels and brass axles.

300-5147 HOn30" pkg(2)
300-5148 HOn3 pkg(2)

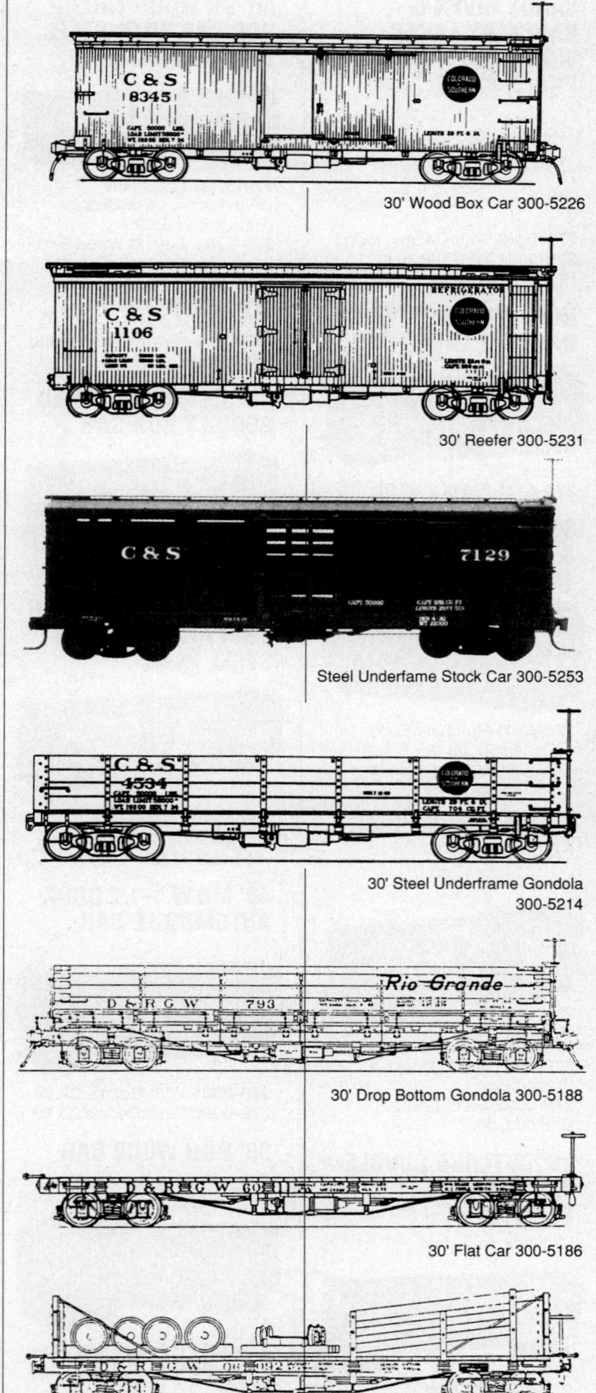

30' Wood Box Car 300-5226

30' Reefer 300-5231

Steel Underfame Stock Car 300-5253

30' Steel Underframe Gondola 300-5214

30' Drop Bottom Gondola 300-5188

30' Flat Car 300-5186

30' Wheel & Tie Car 300-5187

Dump Car 300-5147

JV MODELS

LUMBER LOAD

345-2010 pkg(3) **19.98**
This easy-to-build HO Scale kit includes wooden loads for three 40-60' flat or gondola cars, plus braces and stake posts. Loads are designed to be removable for more operating possibilities.3

HI-TECH DETAILS

BOX CAR

PULLMAN STANDARD 40' HI-CUBE BOX CAR

331-7000 Undecorated **13.95**
NEW
A highly detailed, injection-molded styrene kit. This type of car was most commonly used by the CB&Q, DRGW, MILW, IC, NP, and BN railroads.

Roadname Abbreviation Key

ATSF Santa Fe
B&O Baltimore & Ohio
BN Burlington Northern
BNSF Burlington Northern Santa Fe (1996 Merger)
C&O Chesapeake & Ohio
CB&Q Chicago Burlington & Quincy
CN Canadian National
CNJ Central Railroad of New Jersey
CNW Chicago & North Western
CP Canadian Pacific
CR Conrail
CSX CSX
D&H Delaware & Hudson
DRGW Rio Grande
EL Erie Lackawanna
GN Great Northern
IC Illinois Central
L&N Louisville & Nashville
LV Lehigh Valley
MILW Milwaukee Road
MKT Katy (Missouri, Kansas, Texas)
MON Monon
MP Missouri Pacific
MOW Maintenance Of Way
N&W Norfolk & Western
NH New Haven
NKP Nickel Plate Road
NP Northern Pacific
NS Norfolk Southern
NYC New York Central
PFE Pacific Fruit Express
PRR Pennsylvania
RDG Reading
ROCK Rock Island
SOO Soo Line
SOU Southern Railway
SSW St. Louis Southwestern (Cotton Belt)
SP Southern Pacific
UP Union Pacific
WC Wisconsin Central
WM Western Maryland

FUNARO & CAMERLENGO

These kits consist of thin flexible styro-urethane castings, stripwood, Tichy brake parts, preformed wire grab irons and instructions. Cars do not include couplers or trucks. Kits include decals where noted.

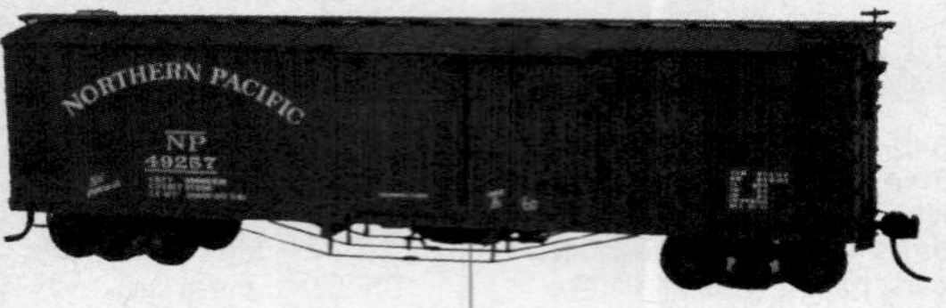
NP 40' Box Car 279-1007

40' B&M XM-1 Single-Sheathed Wood Car 279-6000

BOX CARS

NP 40' BOX CARS EA 27.99

Built by the company shops in Brainerd, Minnesota, these wooden box cars were used to avoid the USRA allocations. The cars were based on an earlier, but shorter design, and were fitted with both a steel centersill and trussrods to provide additional strength. The second series was six inches taller, but featured many of the same characteristics, such as the B end lumber door and radial roof of the first group. Some lasted into the 1950s.

279-1007 1916 Version-8' Interior Height
279-1008 1918 Version-8' 6" Interior Height

40' B&M XM-1 SINGLE-SHEATHED WOOD CAR EA 27.99

Each kit includes decals and Tichy trucks.

279-6000 Flat Pullman Roof
279-6001 Rib Outside Carline Roof

CAIRO & KANAWHA WOOD CAR EA PKG(2) 29.99

279-1003 Less Decals, HOn3
279-1004 Less Decals, HOn2-1/2

36' NP WOOD CAR

279-1006 Fishbelly Side Sill, w/Decals (Retooled) **27.99**

36' SOU WOOD CAR

279-3130 Hutchins Ends, Less Decals **26.99**
279-3132 Hutchins Ends, w/Decals **27.99**

36' DOUBLE-SHEATHED CAR

WITH STRAP-BRACED ENDS

279-6290 NYC/P&LE, w/Decals (Retooled) **27.99**

WITH REVERSE DREADNAUGHT ENDS

279-6340 Boston & Albany w/Decals **27.99**

SANDY RIVER & RANGELEY LAKES WOOD CAR PKG(2) 32.99

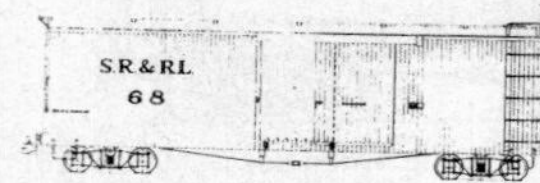

279-5040 With Decals, HOn3
279-5041 With Decals, HOn2-1/2

HOn30 SANDY RIVER & RANGLEY LAKES CAR

279-6191 Set of 2 **32.99**

36' NEW YORK, ONTARIO & WESTERN WOOD TRUSS-ROD CAR

279-3201 Hutchins Ends, w/Decals **27.99**
279-3200 Hutchins Ends, Less Decals **26.99**

36' NH REBUILT CAR EA 27.99

Kits include decals.

279-5090 Steel Doors & Ends
279-5091 Wood Doors & Braced Ends
279-5092 Steel Doors & Braced Ends

36' RUTLAND DOUBLE-SHEATHED CAR EA 27.99

Kits include decals.

279-6230 Rutland
279-6240 Boston & Albany

40' ARA DELAWARE, LACKAWANNA & WESTERN

279-6321 With Steel Ends & Replacement Panel Roof, 45000-45999 Series **27.99** *NEW*

40' GN WOOD TRUSS-ROD CAR WITH STEEL CENTER SILL

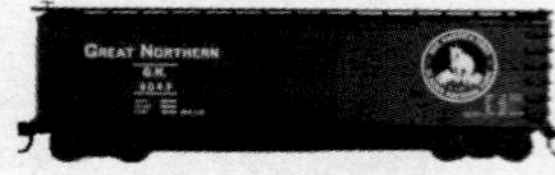

279-3700 Truss-Rod Underframe, Less Decals (Retooled) **26.99**
279-3701 Braced Wood End w/Lumber Doors, w/Decals (Retooled) **27.99**
279-3702 Hopper Doors w/Decals **27.99**
279-3703 Murphy Corrugated Steel Ends **27.99**

40' SINGLE-SHEATHED REBUILT BOX CAR

279-6270 IC, w/Decals **27.99**

40' DOUBLE-SHEATHED 1924 ARA CAR WITH STEEL ENDS

279-6320 Delaware, Lackawanna & Western, w/Decals **27.99**

40' MILW 1-1/2 DOOR AUTOMOBILE CAR

279-3301 With Decals **27.99**
279-3300 Less Decals **26.99**

36' D&H WOOD CAR

The following kits include decals.

279-3404 Burnett Ends **27.99**
279-3405 Rebuilt Z-Bar Ends **27.99**
279-3406 Reverse Hutchins Ends **27.99**
279-3409 Sand Service **27.99**

The following kits do not include decals.

279-3400 Burnett Ends **26.99**
279-3401 Rebuilt Z-Bar Ends **26.99**
279-3402 Reverse Hutchins Ends **26.99**
279-3408 Sand Service **26.99**

40' USRA DOUBLE-SHEATHED CARS EA 27.99

Kits include decals.

279-3052 Wabash
279-3053 Delaware, Lackawanna & Western
279-3054 CB&Q
279-3055 ATSF
279-3056 NYC
279-3057 Atlantic Coast Line
279-3058 CNW

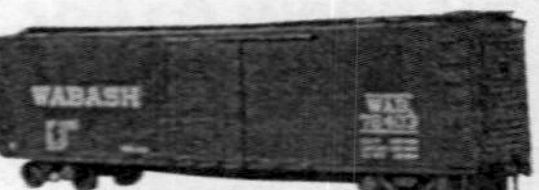

279-3059 MP/Missouri Illinois, w/Decals **27.99**
279-3050 Less Decals **26.99**

36' ULSTER & DELAWARE WOOD CAR

279-5120 Fishbelly Center Sill, w/Decals **27.99**

SINGLE-SHEATHED AUTO CAR WITH CAST STEEL UNDERFRAME

279-6250 Kansas City Southern w/Decals **27.99**

40' WABASH SINGLE-SHEATHED WOOD AUTO CAR-RADIAL ROOF

The following kits include decals.

279-3504 Wood Doors & Murphy Ends **27.99**
279-3505 Steel Doors & End Loading Door **27.99**

279-3506 Steel Doors & 3/3/3 Dreadnaught Ends **27.99**

The following kits do not include decals.

279-3500 Wood Doors & Murphy Ends **26.99**
279-3501 Steel Doors & End Loading Door **26.99**
279-3502 Steel Doors & 3/3/3 Dreadnaught Ends **26.99**

1890s WOOD CAR

279-3800 Less Decals **23.99**

EAST BROAD TOP STEEL CAR

279-1005 Less Decals, HOn3 **23.99**

34' NEW YORK, ONTARIO & WESTERN CAR EA 27.99

279-5110 As-Built, w/Decals
279-5111 Upgraded, w/Decals

40' ALL-WOOD CAR

279-3060 Steel Underframe, Less Decals **26.99**

FUNARO & CAMERLENGO

40' USRA SHORT STEEL REBUILT CAR EA 27.99

Kits include decals.

279-6160 Frisco Fast Freight, Multicolor
279-6161 Frisco
279-6162 Atlantic Coast Line

279-6163 Charleston & Western Carolina

40' USRA TALL STEEL REBUILT CAR-VIKING ROOF EA 27.99

Kits include decals.

279-6170 CNW/Chicago, Minneapolis, St. Paul & Omaha
279-6171 Chicago, Minneapolis, St. Paul & Omaha "Route of the 400s"
279-6172 Rock Island

1938 40' "PS-0" PULLMAN WELDED CAR EA 27.99

Kits include decals.

279-6350 Bessemer & Lake Erie, 6-Panel Superior Door-9 Rib Ends

279-6351 UP/Chicago Great Western, 6-Uneven Panel Superior Door-9 Rib Ends
279-6352 Pere Marquette/NKP/Wheeling & Lake Erie, 7-Panel Superior Door-10 Rib End

STATE OF MAINE INSULATED PLUG DOOR STEEL CAR EA 27.99

Kits include decals.

279-6390 NH/Bangor & Aroostook
279-6391 Modernized "McGuiness" Era Decals

FLORIDA EAST COAST VENTILATED CAR EA 27.99

USRA W/DECALS
279-6400 As-Built
279-6401 Modernized with Facia Boards & Enlarged Doors

1924 ERA W/DECALS.
279-6410 Original
279-6411 FEC/Savannah & Atlanta, Rebuilt to Insulated Box Car

ARA BANGOR & AROOSTOOK SINGLE SHEATHED CARS EA 27.99

279-6550 1927 w/Reverse Hutchins Ends *NEW*
279-6551 1927 w/Flat Steel Ends *NEW*
279-6552 1950s Rebuild w/Youngstown Steel Doors & Flat Ends *NEW*

CP CAR

279-6440 27.99
Includes Hutchins Radial roof, 4/5 Dreadnaught ends and Youngstown door. Decals for CP and "Spans the World" schemes.

43' BOX TRAILER

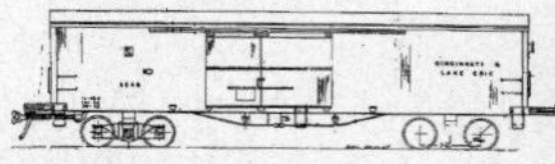

279-4400 Cincinnati & Lake Erie **26.99**

50' A50-6 SINGLE SHEATHED AUTO CAR

279-6560 SP w/Decals **29.99** *NEW*

REEFERS

MILK REEFERS

50' GPEX WOOD CAR-WIDE DOOR EA 29.99 (UNLESS NOTED)

Kits include decals, unless noted.

279-1062 Borden's

279-1063 United Farmers, Billboard
279-1064 H.P. Hood & Sons
279-1065 Sheffield Farms
279-1066 United Farmers, Roman Lettering
279-1060 Less Decals **28.99**

50' D&H WOOD CAR

279-2001 With Decals **29.99**
279-2000 Less Decals **28.99**

50' GPEX WOOD EXPRESS CAR

279-1070 Less Decals **28.99**

NEW YORK, ONTARIO & WESTERN

279-1091 With Decals **29.99**
279-1090 Less Decals **28.99**

40' GREENVILLE STEEL CAR EA 29.99 (UNLESS NOTED)

Upgraded kits feature more detail, plus Viking roofs. Kits include decals, unless noted.

279-5020 Boston & Maine

279-5021 Erie
279-5022 Less Decals **28.99**

40' GPEX STEEL CAR EA 34.99 (UNLESS NOTED)

Kits include decals, unless noted.

279-1032

279-1031 H.P. Hood & Sons (Retooled)
279-1032 Borden's, Roman Lettering (Retooled)
279-1034 Milky Way (Retooled)
279-1030 Less Decals (Retooled) **33.99**

40' GPEX STEEL CAR-ROUND FLOOR EA 34.99 (UNLESS NOTED)

Kits include decals, unless noted.

279-3022

279-3021 H.P. Hood & Sons, Roman Lettering (Retooled)
279-3022 Borden's, Roman Lettering (Retooled)
279-3023 Milky Way (Retooled)
279-3024 Baker's Chocolate (Retooled)
279-3020 Less Decals (Retooled) **33.99**

50' GPEX STEEL CAR-ROUND FLOOR EA 39.99 (UNLESS NOTED)

Kits include decals, unless noted.

279-1081 H.P. Hood & Sons (Retooled)

279-1082 Borden's, Roman Lettering
279-1080 Less Decals **38.99**

40' GPEX Wood Milk Reefer 279-1042

40' GPEX Wood Milk Reefer Narrow Door 279-1053

Single Sheathed Cars 279-6551

40' GPEX CAR EA 29.99 (UNLESS NOTED)

Kits include decals.

279-1041 Sheffield Farms (Retooled)
279-1042 Borden's (Retooled)
279-1044 Abbot's Milk (Retooled)
279-1045 Hood's (Retooled)
279-1046 Sheffield Farms (Retooled)
279-1047 Nestle's (Retooled)
279-1048 Borden's (gold sign) (Retooled)
279-4200 Renken's
279-1040 Less Decals (Retooled) **28.99**

50' GPEX CAR-NARROW DOOR EA 29.99 (UNLESS NOTED)

Kits include decals, unless noted.

279-1052 Borden's, Roman Lettering
279-1053 Eversweet Orange Juice
279-1054 Baker's Chocolate
279-1055 H.P. Hood & Sons
279-1050 Less Decals **28.99**

40' B&M WOOD CAR

279-2061 With Decals **29.99**
279-2060 Less Decals **28.99**

50' B&M WOOD CAR

279-3011 With Decals **29.99**
279-3010 Less Decals **28.99**

ALL-PURPOSE REEFERS

36' CN 8-HATCH EA 27.99

Kits include decals.

279-5130 Dreadnaught Ends

279-5131 Improved Dreadnaught Ends
279-5132 Plug Door
279-5133 Hinged Door, NSC Ends
279-5134 Plug Door, Dreadnaught Ends

37' WOOD MEAT CAR EA 27.99 (UNLESS NOTED)

Kits include decals, unless noted.

279-3607

279-3602 Wilson & Co., 1920-1949
279-3603 Wilson & Co., 1940-1960
279-3605 Kahn's
279-3606 Patrick Cudahy
279-3607 Oscar Mayer
279-3608 American Refrigerator Transit
279-3609 Hormel
279-3600 Less Decals **26.99**

40' RDG OUTSIDE-BRACED WOOD CAR

279-1015 With Decals **27.99**
279-10151 Less Decals **26.99**

FUNARO & CAMERLENGO

50' NYC/RUTLAND WOOD W/TRUSS ROD UNDERFRAME

MILK-WIDE LETTERBOARD EA 29.99 (UNLESS NOTED)
Kits include decals, unless noted.

279-3031 Rutland
279-3032 NYC
279-3030 Less Decals **28.99**

NARROW LETTERBOARD EA 29.99 (UNLESS NOTED)
Kits include decals, unless noted.

279-3041 Rutland
279-3042 NYC
279-3040 Undecorated **28.99**

MILK-NARROW LETTERBOARD & STEEL UNDERFRAME EA 29.99 (UNLESS NOTED)
Kits include decals, unless noted.

279-2021 Rutland

279-2022 NYC, San Serif Lettering
279-2020 Less Decals **28.99**

WIDE LETTERBOARD & STEEL UNDERFRAME EA 29.99 (UNLESS NOTED)
Kits include decals, unless noted.

279-2011 Rutland
279-2012 NYC, San Serif Lettering
279-2010 Less Decals **28.99**

ARMOUR MEAT EA 27.99

Kits include decals.

279-6300 Armour Refrigerator Line, Modernized, Truss-Rod Underframe

279-6301 Armour Refrigerator Line & Supplementary Heralds, Modernized

CP 8-HATCH EA 27.99

279-6470 Dreadnaught Ends, Hinged Door w/Decals
279-6471 Dreadnaught Ends, Plug Door w/Decals
279-6472 NSC-2 Ends, Plug Door w/Decals

HOPPERS

EAST BROAD TOP STEEL

279-5102 With Decals, HOn3 **24.99**

D&H COMPOSITE

THREE-BAY

279-3112 With Decals **27.99**
279-3110 Less Decals **26.99**

FOUR-BAY
279-3122 With Decals **27.99**
279-3120 Less Decals **26.99**

RDG CHANNEL-SIDE STEEL EA 27.99 (UNLESS NOTED)

279-1019 Plain Ends, w/Decals
279-10191 Plain Ends, Less Decals **26.99**
279-1020 Pressed Metal Ends, w/Decals
279-10201 Pressed Metal Ends, Less Decals **26.99**

SOU 1918 WOOD SEALY EA 27.99

279-6180 K-Brakes w/Decals
279-6181 AB Brakes, Modernized, w/Decals

RUTLAND BOTTOM DUMO COAL CAR EA 27.99

Kits include decals.

279-6220 As-Built

279-6221 Modernized
279-6222 Modernized & Weathered

CARBON BLACK EA 27.99

Kits include decals.

279-6310 SHPX
279-6311 Cabot's w/Steel Roofwalk (1940s-1950s)

279-6312 Cabot's Spheron Billboard

COVERED

279-6370 National Plate Glass, w/Decals **27.99**

CN SLAB SIDE EA 27.99

279-6450 Series 113170-113269 w/Metal Hatches, Red & White Decals
279-6451 Series 113270-113394, w/Stamped Metal Hatches, Red Decals

34' 4" COAL & ORE CAR

279-6460 GN **27.99**

PRR G39 & G39A ORE JENNIES

279-6430 Set of 2 **32.99**

34' PRR H30A RIVETED COVERED EA 27.99 (UNLESS NOTED)

279-30010 With Decals, White Steam-Era Lettering
279-30040 With Decals, Black Steam-Era Lettering
279-30001 Less Decals **26.99**

52' PRR H32 COVERED EA 27.99 (UNLESS NOTED)

279-2091 With Decals, White Steam-Era Lettering
279-2092 With Decals, Black Modern Lettering
279-2094 With Decals, Black Steam-Era Lettering
279-2090 Less Decals **26.99**

40' HORIZONTAL RIB

279-5050 Erie/New York, Susquehanna & Western **27.99**
Kit includes decals for both roadnames.

D&H COMPOSITE TWIN

279-3083 As-Built, w/Decals **27.99**
279-3081 As-Built, Less Decals **26.99**
279-3092 Modernized, w/Decals **27.99**
279-3090 Modernized, Less Decals **26.99**
279-3102 Modernized-Peaked Ends, w/Decals **27.99**
279-3100 Modernized-Peak Ends, Less Decals **26.99**

34' PRR H30A Riveted Covered Hopper 279-30010

40' Horizontal Rib Hopper 279-5050

D&H Composite Twin Hopper 279-3083

KCS 45' Hopper/Gondola 279-6510

38' GSH Steel Gon 279-6531

34' NEW YORK, ONTARIO & WESTERN WOOD

279-2081 With Decals **27.99**
279-2080 Less Decals **26.99**

GONDOLAS

40' ATLANTIC COAST LINE LOW-SIDE STEEL GON

279-5080 With Decals **27.99**

40' MP STEEL GON EA 27.99

279-6140 With Decals (Retooled)
279-6141 Panel-Side With Decals (Retooled)

PRR 38' STEEL GON 2-PACKS EA 32.99

Includes two cars and decals.

279-6530 GS *NEW*
279-6531 GSH *NEW*

KCS 45' HOPPER/GONDOLA

279-6510 With Decals **27.99**
This unusual combination car served coal fields in Kansas, Missouri and Arkansas, but could have been intended as dual-purpose equipment. Built in the company shops at Pittsburgh, Kansas, some of the unique cars lasted in maintenance service until the 1980s. Kit consists of five major resin castings, with full interior detail. Ladders and a set of Tichy AB brake gear are also included.

40' B&O COMPOSITE GON

279-1021 With Decals **27.99**
279-1022 Less Decals **26.99**

FUNARO & CAMERLENGO

PRR "GR" COMPOSITE GON-DROP ENDS PKG(2) 32.99

Upgraded kits feature all-new patterns with more detail, plus decals.

279-5000 PRR
279-5001 Long Island
279-5002 Less Decals

50' VIRGINIAN "BATTLESHIP" GON

279-2071 With Decals **27.99**
279-2070 Less Decals **26.99**

41' 6" WAR EMERGENCY GON EA 27.99 (UNLESS NOTED)

Kits include decals.

279-6260 Wabash, Original Wood Version
279-6261 Atlantic Coast Line, Original Wood Version
279-6262 Atlantic Coast Line, Rebuilt Steel Version
279-6263 Texas & New Orleans w/Dreadnaught Ends **25.00**
279-6264 Texas & New Orleans w/Improved Dreadnaught Ends

MAINE CENTRAL LOW SIDE STEEL GON

279-6330 With Decals pkg(2) **32.99**

RUTLAND 36' 4100 SERIES STEEL UNDERFRAME WOOD GON

279-6480 With Decals **27.99**

52' 6" STEEL WAR EMERGENCY COMPOSITE GON EA 27.99

279-6421 ATSF

279-6422 N&W
279-6423 PRR
279-6424 NYC

53' 6" WOOD WAR EMERGENCY COMPOSITE GON EA 27.99

Kits include decals.

279-6150 Rock Island
279-6151 ATSF
279-6152 N&W

279-6153 PRR
279-6154 NYC

D&H COMPOSITE GONS

36' W/TRUSS RODS

279-4601 With Decals **27.99**
279-4600 Less Decals **26.99**

33' CARS

279-4621 3' Height, w/Decals **27.99**
279-4620 3' Height, Less Decals **26.99**
279-4631 3' 8" Height, w/Decals **27.99**
279-4630 3' 8" Height, Less Decals **26.99**
279-4641 4' 6" Height-Extended Sides, w/Decals **27.99**
279-4640 4' 6" Height-Extended Sides, Less Decals **26.99**

CP

279-6280 CP "Big Otis," w/Decals **27.99**

FLAT CARS

EAST BROAD TOP CAR

Kits include decals.

279-5100 No. 103-124, HOn3 pkg(2) **29.99**
279-5101 No. 73, HOn3 **19.99**

RUTLAND 36' 2300/2600 SERIES CARS

279-6490 With Marble Load & Decals **27.99**
279-6491 With Decals pkg(2) **32.99**
279-6492 With Banded, Sawed Marble Load & Decals **27.99**

HOn30 SANDY RIVER & RANGLEY LAKES CAR

279-6211 Set of Two **29.99**

PRR CLASS FM FLAT CARS

279-6500 pkg(2) **29.99**

MILK TANK CARS

"BUTTERDISH" TANK CAR EA 32.99 (UNLESS NOTED)

Kits include decals, unless noted.

279-1010 Borden's, White Roman Lettering
279-1011 Borden's, Yellow Roman Lettering
279-1012 Borden's, Black Roman Lettering
279-1013 Borden's Chemical Division
279-1009 Less Decals **31.99**

TWIN TANK CAR EA 32.99 (UNLESS NOTED)

Kits include decals.

279-5060 Borden's Tanks, Fishbelly Side
279-5061 Bell Tanks, Fishbelly Side
279-5062 Borden's Tanks, Fishbelly Center

279-5063 Bell Tanks, Fishbelly Center
279-5064 Tank Only, Borden's pkg(2) **14.99**
279-5065 Tank Only, Bell pkg(2) **14.99**

CABOOSES

Caboose kits do not include decals, unless noted.

WOOD EA 24.99

279-501 Long Island Class N52A, Original w/Decals (Retooled)
279-502 Long Island Class N52A, Rebuilt w/Decals (Retooled)
279-504 Long Island/New York, Ontario & Western Class N52B

STEEL EA 24.99

279-503 Long Island Class N22A One Piece Body w/Decals
279-505 Long Island Class N22B Bay Window

PRR "GR" Composite Gon-Drop Ends 279-5000

D&H Composite Gon 279-4631

4' 6" Height-Extended Sides 279-4641

"Butterdish" Tank Car 279-1012

Steel Long Island Class Caboose 279-503

Caboose NH Class NE 279-508

SOU WOOD EA 24.99

Kits include decals.

279-506 Single-Light Windows (Retooled) **24.99**
279-507 4-Light Windows (Retooled) **24.99**

CABOOSES EA 24.99

Kits include decals.

279-508 NH Class NE
279-509 IC Outside Braced
279-510 Ulster & Delaware USRA Design
279-511 Rutland 4-Window #11-14

NARROW-GAUGE WOOD EA 24.99

279-1001 DRGW Short HOn3 w/Decals
279-1002 DRGW Short HOn2-1/2 w/Decals
279-5030 Sandy River & Rangeley Lakes #551 HOn3 w/Decals
279-5031 Sandy River & Rangeley Lakes #551 HOn2-1/2 w/Decals
279-6201 HOn30 Sandy River & Rangley Lakes Short Caboose

GLOOR CRAFT MODELS

These HO Scale craft train kits feature precut basswood parts, color-coded stripwood, metal castings, decals (unless undecorated), step-by-step instructions and full-size drawings. Trucks and couplers are not included.

We have worked closely with this manufacturer to provide accurate availability information at the time this catalog was published. Items listed in blue ink may not be available at all times. Please see you dealer for current delivery information.

BOX CARS

HOn3 BOX CAR

288-3501 East Broad Top, No. 170 **18.95**

70' LUMBER BOX CAR

288-3003 "Hello Dolly" **26.95**

50' 1-1/2 DOOR GRAIN LOADING BOX CAR

288-3002 CB&Q **23.95**

40' XML BOX CAR

288-3001 DRGW **21.95**

50' DOUBLE-DOOR AUTO BOX CAR

288-3005 ATSF, Fe-27 "The Chief" **23.95**

60' INSULATED BOX CAR

288-3000 CB&Q **25.95**

50' XL "CANSTOCK" BOX CAR

288-3012 B&O **25.95**

HOPPERS

3-BAY HOPPER

288-3503 East Broad Top, HOn3 **17.95**

34' 50-TON 2-BAY HOPPER

288-3400 NKP **20.95**

32' H-31 2-BAY HOPPER

288-3403 PRR **20.95**

34' COVERED 2-BAY HOPPER EA 20.95

288-3401 70-Ton, Undecorated
288-3402 100-Ton, Undecorated

2-BAY HOPPER

288-3502 East Broad Top, HOn3 **17.95**

AUTO RACKS

89' BI-LEVEL AUTO RACK

288-3200 Trailer Train **22.95**

89' TRI-LEVEL AUTO RACK

288-3201 Trailer Train **25.95**

MAINTENANCE OF WAY

Maintenance-of-way cars are often old coaches or freight cars which have been specially rebuilt for their new use.

FLANGER WITH PLOW

288-3600 Undecorated **18.95**

FLAT CARS

50' CONVERTED FLAT CAR WITH 45' TRAILER

288-3208 Undecorated **25.95**

GONDOLAS

HON3 GONDOLA

288-3504 East Broad Top, No. 346 **12.95**

3-Bay Hopper 288-3503

Wood Caboose 288-3116

Wood Caboose 288-3101

CABOOSES

WOOD CABOOSE EA 24.95 (UNLESS NOTED)

288-3100 PRR Class N6A
288-3101 PRR Class N6B
288-3102 NKP
288-3103 32' NW
288-3104 PRR Class ND Caboose, 33" Wheels
288-3105 UP, CA-1
288-3106 30' C&O
288-3110 Pittsburgh & Lake Erie, Standard
288-3111 NYC, 19000 Series
288-3114 30' Delaware & Hudson
288-3115 32' Erie
288-3116 35' CN
288-3500 East Broad Top, No. 27/28 HOn3 **18.95**
288-3506 32' DRGW, HOn3 **19.95**

REEFERS

37' WOOD REEFER

288-3020 Olympia Beer **22.95**

50' WOOD REEFER

288-3009 ATSF, Rr-37 "The Chief" **19.95**

PAYROLL CAR

288-3601 55' Long **22.95**

HEICO MODELL

FREIGHT CAR LOADS

Transform empty cars into detailed models in seconds! Fully assembled, one-piece loads are complete with real wood bracing and are ideal for use with various flat cars and gondolas. Simply set in place for loads-in/empties out operation, or glue down for permanent detail. Can be used to model finished products stacked for loading or unloading alongside industries too. Short loads may be kitbashed for use with trucks. Dimension shown is overall length.

NEW SUPPLIER

Banded Steel Pipe 335-870051

Large Air Compressor 335-870835

Large Printing Press Wrapped in Plastic 335-870872

Heat Exchanger 335-870873

335-870011 Construction Steel Matting 5-13/64" 13cm **13.99** ***NEW***

335-870021 Flat Steel Plates 5-13/64" 13cm **14.99** ***NEW***

335-870022 Large Steel Plates 8-13/32" 21cm **17.99** ***NEW***

335-870041 Short Steel Pipe 5-5/8" 14cm **11.99** ***NEW***

335-870042 Long Steel Pipe 7-13/32" 18.5cm **13.99** ***NEW***
335-870051 Banded Steel Pipe 5-13/32" 13.5cm **11.99** ***NEW***

335-870101 Short H-Beams 3-5/8" 9cm **18.99** ***NEW***

335-870102 Long H-Beams 5-5/8" 14cm **19.99** ***NEW***

335-870112 Long Steel Square Section 5-5/8" 14cm **19.99** ***NEW***

335-870141 Steel Slabs 4" 10cm **18.99** ***NEW***

335-870301 Concrete Slabs 4" 10cm **11.99** ***NEW***

335-870311 Concrete Water/Sewer Pipe 3-13/32" 8.5cm **14.99** ***NEW***

335-870331 Prefab Concrete Underpass Sections 5-13/64" 13cm **10.99** ***NEW***

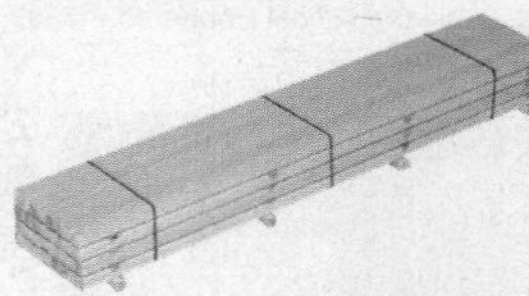

335-870412 Large Square Wooden Beams 5-5/8" 14cm **12.99** ***NEW***

335-870431 Cut Board Lumber 3-5/8" 9cm **13.99** ***NEW***

335-870435 Plywood Sheets 5-5/8" 14cm **16.99** ***NEW***

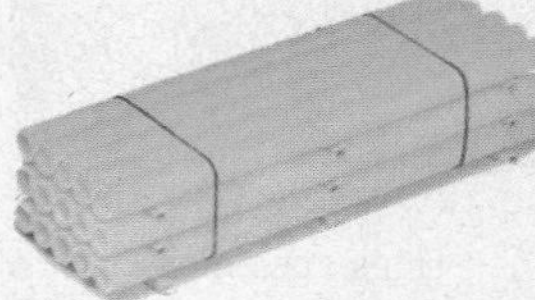

335-870501 Short Plastic Pipes (yellow) 3-5/8" 9cm **13.99** ***NEW***

335-870502 Long Plastic Pipes (yellow) 8" 20cm **14.99** ***NEW***

335-870611 Marble Slabs 4" 10cm **10.99** ***NEW***

335-870805 Steam-Powered Road Roller Era III 2-13/16" 7cm **17.99** ***NEW***

335-870831 Large Boiler 3-13/16" 9.5cm **14.99** ***NEW***
335-870835 Large Air Compressor 5-13/32" 13.5cm **16.99** ***NEW***

335-870841 Wooden Cable Reels 3-5/8" 9cm pkg(3) **14.99** ***NEW***

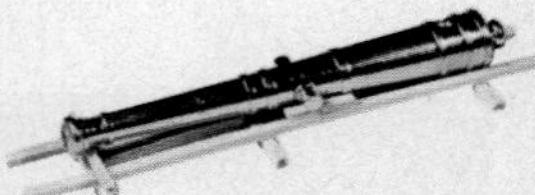

335-870851 Cannon Barrel Era II 3-5/8" 9cm **16.99** ***NEW***

335-870852 Large Equipment Tires 3-5/8" 9cm **15.99** ***NEW***

335-870854 Clay Buckets-Stacked & Wrapped in Plastic 3-13/32" 8.5cm **10.99** ***NEW***

335-870855 Newsprint Paper Rolls 5-13/32" 13.5cm **14.99** ***NEW***
335-870872 Large Printing Press Wrapped in Plastic 3-13/64" 8cm **16.99** ***NEW***
335-870873 Heat Exchanger 3-13/64" 8cm **16.99** ***NEW***

335-870931 Crated Machinery 4" 10cm **11.99** ***NEW***

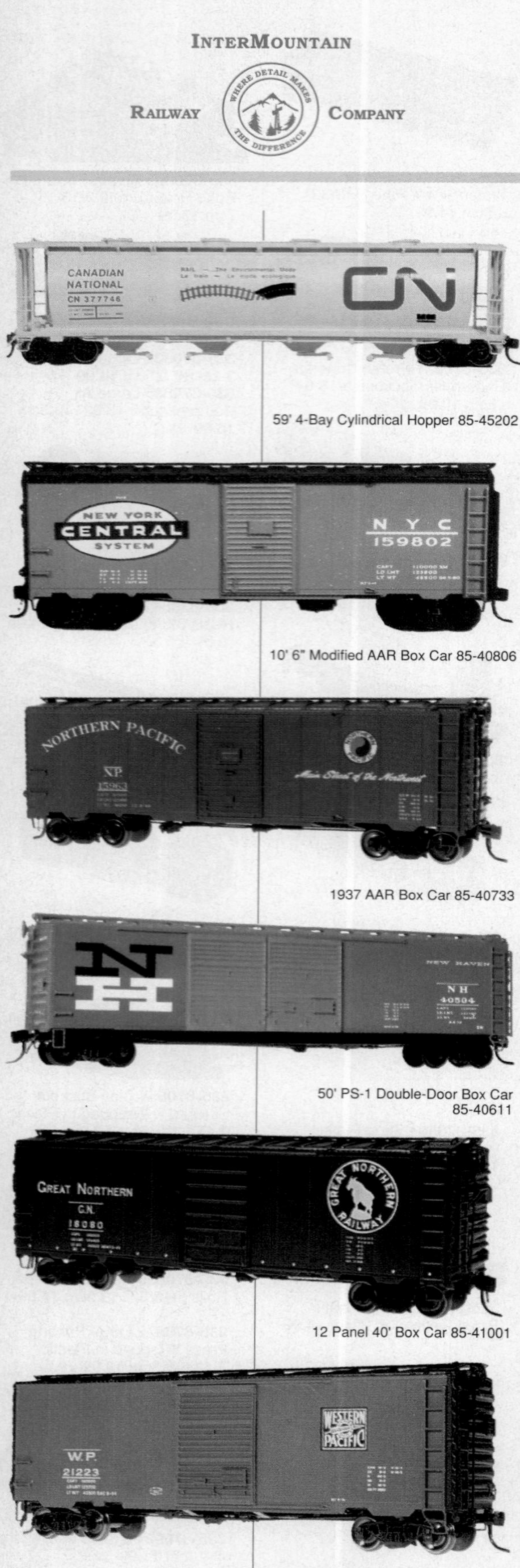

59' 4-Bay Cylindrical Hopper 85-45202

10' 6" Modified AAR Box Car 85-40806

1937 AAR Box Car 85-40733

50' PS-1 Double-Door Box Car 85-40611

12 Panel 40' Box Car 85-41001

40' PS-1 with 7' Door 85-40471

ASSEMBLED MODELS

Ready-to-run with trucks and brass wheelsets, weights and couplers.

BOX CARS

40' PS-1 W/6' DOOR

85-45401 NYC **22.95**
85-45402 CNW **22.95**
85-45464 Ann Arbor (Large Flag) **24.95**

40' PS-1 W/8' DOOR

85-45451 Western Pacific **22.95**

50' PS-1 SINGLE DOOR

85-45910 Atlanta & West Point **22.95**
85-45913 Gulf, Mobile & Ohio **24.95**

REEFERS

R-40-23 REEFER EA 24.95

85-45501 PFE
85-45525 Dubuque

HOPPERS

59' 4-BAY CYLINDRICAL W/TROUGH HATCHES EA 24.95

85-45101 Red Canada CNWX
85-45102 Red Canada CPWX
85-45121 SKNX
85-45122 SKPX

59' 4-BAY CYLINDRICAL W/ROUND HATCHES

85-45202 CN "Environmental Mode" **22.95**

PULLMAN STANDARD CENTER DISCHARGE 4750 EA 22.95

85-45301 CNW
85-45307 CSX

UNASSEMBLED MODELS

These easy-to-build styrene kits have numerous add-on parts. Each is complete with trucks and step-by-step instructions, but does not include weights or couplers. Coupler pockets will accept InterMountain Couplers and other brands of magnetic couplers. Some car styles are also available as built-up assembled models.

BOX CARS

10' 6" MODIFIED AAR EA 13.95 (UNLESS NOTED)

85-40801 NP

85-40802 CB&Q

85-40803 ATSF
85-40804 ROCK
85-40805 NYC
85-40806 NYC
85-40807 SOU w/6' Door ***NEW***
85-40808 CNW
85-40812 MP **14.95** ***NEW***
85-40813 IC **14.95** ***NEW***
85-40814 SOU (billboard paint scheme) **14.95** ***NEW***
85-40815 UP **14.95** ***NEW***
85-40816 SOO **14.95** ***NEW***
85-40898 Undecorated (Box Car Red) **10.95**
85-40899 Undecorated (gray) **10.95**

40' PS-1 W/6' DOOR EA 13.95

85-40401 NYC
85-40406 Burlington Route
85-40407 CP

1937 AAR 40' EA 13.95 (UNLESS NOTED)

85-40701 NYC
85-40702 UP
85-40706 C&O
85-40707 Western Pacific
85-40733 NP
85-40708 CNW **14.95** ***NEW***
85-40716 B&O **14.95** ***NEW***
85-40717 EL **14.95** ***NEW***
85-40718 Gulf, Mobile & Ohio **14.95** ***NEW***
85-40719 Minneapolis & St. Louis **14.95** ***NEW***
85-40720 Western Pacific (yellow) **14.95** ***NEW***
85-40734 ROCK **14.95** ***NEW***
85-40798 Undecorated (Box Car Red) **10.95**
85-40799 Undecorated (Gray) **10.95**

40' PS-1 W/7' DOOR EA 14.95 (UNLESS NOTED)

85-40471 Western Pacific ***NEW***
85-40473 Boston & Maine ***NEW***
85-40474 Erie ***NEW***
85-40475 Maine Central ***NEW***
85-40494 Undecorated (Box Car Red) **11.50** ***NEW***
85-40495 Undecorated (Gray) **11.50** ***NEW***

40' PS-1 W/8' DOOR EA 13.95 (UNLESS NOTED)

85-40452 Erie
85-40453 GN
85-40457 NW
85-40458 Virginian
85-40461 UP
85-40464 Ann Arbor
85-40496 Undecorated (red) **10.95**
85-40497 Undecorated (gray) **10.95**
85-40498 Undecorated (red) **10.95**
85-40499 Undecorated (gray) **10.95**

50' PS-1 SINGLE-DOOR EA 14.95 (UNLESS NOTED)

85-40901 Chicago, Rock Island & Pacific
85-40902 SOU
85-40908 ATSF
85-40909 Frisco
85-40910 Atlanta & West Point
85-40911 MP ***NEW***
85-40912 Maine Central ***NEW***
85-40913 Gulf, Mobile & Ohio ***NEW***
85-40914 Boston & Maine ***NEW***
85-40915 L&N ***NEW***
85-40998 Undecorated (red) **11.50**
85-40999 Undecorated (gray) **11.50**

50' PS-1 DOUBLE-DOOR EA 14.95 (UNLESS NOTED)

85-40601 UP
85-40602 NW
85-40604 SSW
85-40605 IC
85-40606 C&O
85-40607 SP
85-40608 Western Pacific
85-40609 Erie
85-40610 DRGW
85-40611 NH
85-40612 DRGW ***NEW***
85-40613 MKT ***NEW***
85-40614 Chicago & Eastern Illinois ***NEW***
85-40698 Undecorated (red) **11.50**
85-40699 Undecorated (gray) **11.50**

12 PANEL 40' EA 14.95 (UNLESS NOTED)

85-41001 GN (Mineral Red)

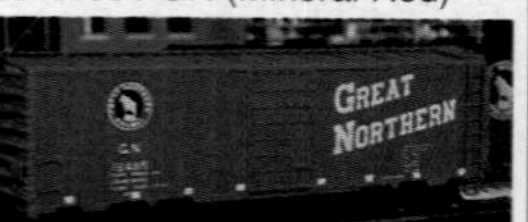

85-41002 GN (Vermilion Red, Slant Serif)
85-41003 GN (Big Sky Blue)
85-41004 GN (Glacier Green)
85-41005 GN (Vermilion Red, Empire Builder)
85-41006 Spokane, Portland & Seattle
85-41009 GN (Glacier Green, large goat herald)
85-41010 GN Express
85-41011 GN (Glacier Green, Empire Builder) ***NEW***
85-41012 GN Express (orange/green) **16.95** ***NEW***
85-41013 SP (4-3 Improved Dreadnaught End) **15.95** ***NEW***
85-41014 Texas & New Orleans **15.95** ***NEW***
85-41098 Undecorated (Box Car Red) **11.50**
85-41099 Undecorated (gray) **11.50**

REEFERS

ATSF EA 16.95 (UNLESS NOTED)

85-41101 "Super Chief"

85-41102 "El Capitan"
85-41103 Grand Canyon RR-32 Curved Line Map
85-41104 Scout RR-27 Curved Line Map ***NEW***
85-41105 "The Chief" RR-23
85-41106 "The Chief" RR-27 Curved Line Map
85-41107 "El Capitan" RR-23 Ship & Travel
85-41112 "El Capitan"
85-41113 "Super Chief" RR-28 Straight Line Map
85-41114 "Grand Canyon" Straight Line Map
85-41115 Scout RR-32
85-41116 The Chief West RR-32 Straight Line Map ***NEW***
85-41198 Undecorated (painted) **15.95**
85-41199 Undecorated **15.95**

InterMountain Railway Company

Where Detail Makes The Difference

R-40-23 EA 15.95 (UNLESS NOTED)

85-40501 PFE (double herald)
85-40506 Swift
85-40509 PFE Overland Herald ***NEW***
85-40510 Armour
85-40511 Hormel
85-40512 PFE Express Reefer
85-40514 MILW
85-40515 Rath Packing Co
85-40516 PFE/Western Pacific
85-40517 Libby's
85-40518 Northern Refrigerator Company/IC (Green Diamond)
85-40519 Wilson
85-40520 Oscar Meyer
85-40522 Needham Packing Co. (yellow)
85-40523 Needham Packing Co. (blue)
85-40524 Morrell
85-40525 Dubuque
85-40526 Patrick Cudahy
85-40527 Swift Premium
85-40528 Supreme Beef
85-40529 MDT/NYC
85-40530 Iowa Beef Packers
85-40531 West India Fruit and Steamship Co.
85-40532 PFE
85-40533 National Packing
85-40599 Undecorated **11.50**

HOPPERS

59' 4-BAY CYLINDRICAL W/TROUGH HATCHES EA 15.95 (UNLESS NOTED)

Introduced in 1972, these cylindrical hoppers are commonly known as "Canadian grain cars." Almost 20,000 were built for grain service throughout Canada and the cars are frequent visitors to the US.

85-40101 Canadian Wheat Board CNWX
85-40102 Canadian Wheat Board CPWX
85-40103 Alberta Heritage ALNX
85-40104 Alberta Heritage ALPX
85-40111 ATSF
85-40116 Canadian Wheat Board
85-40117 Alberta "Heritage Fund" CN (APLX), "Take a Break" Scheme
85-40118 Alberta "Heritage Fund" CP Rail (APLX), "Take a Break" Scheme
85-40119 CPWX **17.95**
85-40120 CPWX**17.95**
85-40199 Undecorated **11.50**

59' 4-BAY CYLINDRICAL W/ROUND HATCHES EA 15.95 (UNLESS NOTED)

85-40201 Potash
85-40204 GN
85-40205 CN "Wet Noodle"
85-40208 CP Rail (Multi-Mark)
85-40212 CP (Script)
85-40214 Canpotex Ltd.
85-40216 CB&Q ***NEW***
85-40299 Undecorated **11.50**

PULLMAN STANDARD 4750 CUBIC FT. RIB SIDE 3-BAY COVERED EA 14.95 (UNLESS NOTED)

Introduced in the early 1970s by Pullman-Standard, 30 railroads and some 120 private firms have purchased these cars. Several builders have also constructed similar three-bay hoppers with a 4,750 cubic-foot capacity.

85-40304 SOO
85-40314 GoldKist
85-40316 Monfort
85-40318 Lincoln
85-40320 CNW (yellow)
85-40321 Penn Central
85-40323 SOU
85-40324 Grand Trunk Western
85-40325 NW
85-40326 UP
85-40327 GATX
85-40328 Canada Malting
85-40329 Corn Sweetener
85-40331 Terra Chemicals ***NEW***
85-40332 Ann Arbor ***NEW***
85-40334 BN ***NEW***
85-40335 MILW ***NEW***
85-40336 Frito Lay Inc. ***NEW***
85-40399 Undecorated **10.95**

FLAT CARS

60' W/LASER CUT WOOD DECK EA 17.95 (UNLESS NOTED)

85-41401 Trailer Train
85-41402 BN
85-41403 ATSF "Super Shock Control"
85-41404 UP
85-41405 TTX (Mineral Red)
85-41406 MP ***NEW***
85-41407 Kansas City Southern ***NEW***
85-41408 GN ***NEW***
85-41409 BNSF ***NEW***
85-41410 IC ***NEW***
85-41411 Elgin, Joilet & Eastern ***NEW***
85-41499 Undecorated **13.95** ***NEW***

TANK CARS

10,000 GALLON ACF TYPE 27 EA 15.95 (UNLESS NOTED)

85-41201 Shippers Car Line
85-41202 USQX-US Government War Department
85-41203 Gulf
85-41204 US Army
85-41205 Frontenac
85-41207 GATX
85-41208 Belcher Oil Co.
85-41209 Union Tank Car
85-41210 Pan Am Oils
85-41211 Canadian General Transit Inc.
85-41212 SP ***NEW***
85-41213 Semet-Solvay Co. ***NEW***
85-41214 Hartol Products ***NEW***
85-41299 Undecorated **11.50**

ACF 27 RIVETED 8000 GALLON EA 15.95 (UNLESS NOTED)

85-41301 Robeson
85-41302 Shell Chem
85-41303 Spencer Kellogg
85-41304 Shippers Car Line
85-41305 Canton Tank Car Co.
85-41306 Harbor Tank Line
85-41307 Hercules Powder Co
85-41308 Bell Oil & Gas Co.
85-41309 Wolf's Head Oil
85-41310 Navy Gas & Supply Co.
85-41311 A.E. Staley MFG. Co. (silver, black)
85-41312 A.E. Staley MFG. Co (black)
85-41313 Globe Oil & Refining Co. ***NEW***
85-41316 Mobilgas ***NEW***
85-41318 John Grace Co. ***NEW***
85-41319 King Taste Products ***NEW***
85-41321 Stauffer Chemical ***NEW***
85-41399 Undecorated **11.50**

R-40-23 Reefer 85-40528

R-40-23 Reefer 85-40529

Center Discharge Hopper 85-40329

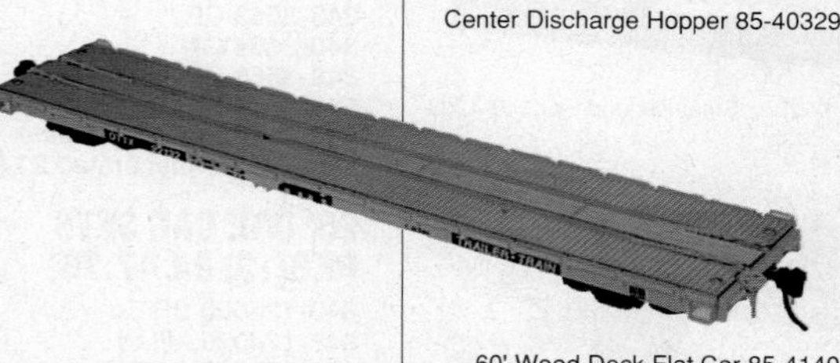

60' Wood Deck Flat Car 85-41401

Rib Side 3-Bay Hopper 85-40332

10,000 Gallon ACF Type 27 Tank Car 85-41203

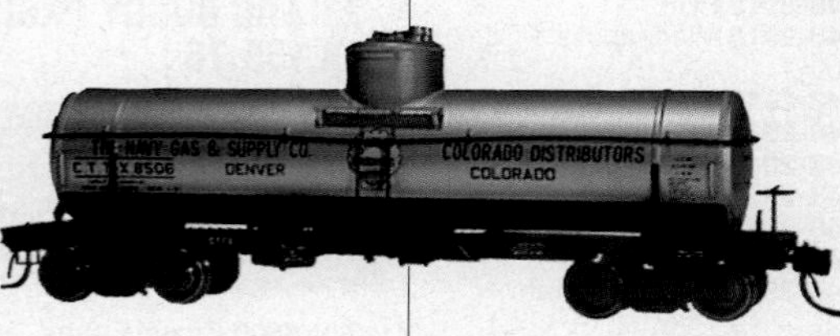

ACF 27 Riveted 8000 Gallon Tank Car 85-41309

Information STATION

Mail Crane

About one hundred thirty years ago a man by the name of George B. Armstrong came up with the of the standard mail crane and hook. His creation made it possible for trains to pick up bags of mail while running at normal speeds.

The hook, or catcher, was attached to railroad mail cars and the crane, or holder, was planted into the ground along the railroad tracks near a station. A bag of mail would hang from the crane. As the train would pass the mail crane, the clerk would swing the catcher out so that it would hook the mail bag. At the same time he would kick out the bag of mail that was to be delivered to that particular town.

Though the trains themselves changed through time, the design of the mail catcher stayed relatively the same. In fact, the mail hook specifications from 1979 are nearly identical to the specifications of 1940. The mail crane, though having numerous designs, remained with the same basic principles and measurements.

These ready-to-run cars are prepainted and lettered in a variety of roadnames and include Talgo trucks with horn-hook couplers.

Track Cleaning Car 348-4356

Steam Sound Car 348-4303

Heavy Duty Snow Plow 348-2903

MAINTENANCE-OF-WAY

TRACK CLEANING CAR EA 17.98

It's a caboose AND a track cleaning car all in one. The perfect way to clean your track whenever you run a train.

348-4355 UP
348-4356 ATSF (Caboose Red)
348-4357 PRR (Tuscan)
348-4358 CNW (yellow)
348-4359 B&O (gold)
348-4368 NYC (aqua)
348-4369 SOU
348-4370 CP

TRACK CLEANING CAR REPLACEMENT PADS

348-4398 pkg(6) **3.98**

STEAM SOUND CAR EA 22.98

These cars include a sound unit (hidden in a crate) that produces authentic steam sounds. Requires a 9V battery, available separately.

348-4300 UP (gold, brown)
348-4301 ATSF (brown)
348-4302 PRR (black, brown)
348-4303 Burlington
348-4304 NYC
348-4305 SP (brown)

HEAVY DUTY SNOW PLOW EA 7.98

348-2902 MILW
348-2903 GN
348-2904 NYC
348-2905 Alaska
348-2906 Boston & Maine
348-2907 UP
348-2908 ATSF
348-2909 CN
348-2910 DRGW
348-2911 Grand Trunk
348-2912 CP
348-2913 Lehigh & New England
348-2914 Wabash
348-2915 PRR
348-2916 Minneapolis & St. Louis
348-2917 CNW
348-2918 SOO
348-2919 LV
348-2920 CB&Q
348-2921 RDG
348-2922 SP
348-2923 Maine Central

Wreck Crane & Boom Tender 348-3557

WRECK CRANE & BOOM TENDER EA 29.98 (UNLESS NOTED)

Modeled after a 200-ton Bucyrus-style diesel wreck crane, or "Big Hook." Features pivoting cab, a boom that can be raised or lowered and a center hook that can be reeled in or out.

348-3554 PRR
348-3555 ATSF
348-3556 UP
348-3557 CNW
348-3558 NYC
348-3559 Amtrak
348-3560 RDG
348-3561 Seaboard
348-3562 CSX
348-3563 CP
348-3564 GN
348-3565 CR
348-3566 SOU
348-3567 Boston & Maine
348-3550 Undecorated **21.98**

25' ORE CAR SETS PKG(12) EA 47.76

348-134000 SP
348-134025 MILW
348-134050 SOO
348-134075 Duluth, Missabe & Iron Range
348-134100 UP
348-134125 Bessemer & Lake Erie
348-134150 CNW
348-134175 CR
348-134200 Lake Superior & Ishpeming
348-134225 Penn Central

348-134250 GN
348-134275 CN

23' LOG BUGGY PKG(12) EA 155.76

348-4800 Brown Frame
348-4820 Red Frame
348-4840 Green Frame
348-4860 Black Frame
348-4880 Olive Frame
348-4900 Gray Frame
348-4920 Assorted Colors

OLD TIME MAINTENANCE-OF-WAY

All cars are easy-to-build kits.

30' BOX CAR EA 9.98

348-8127 B&O
348-8128 PRR
348-8129 Denver, South Park & Pacific
348-8130 SP
348-8131 Virginia & Truckee
348-8132 Lake Shore & Michigan Southern
348-8133 DRGW
348-8134 ATSF
348-8135 Central Pacific
348-8136 MOW
348-8137 US Military Railroad
348-8138 CP
348-8139 Philadelphia & RDG
348-8140 NH
348-8141 IC
348-8142 Western & Atlantic
348-8143 Orange & Alexandria
348-8144 UP
348-8145 LV
348-8146 Denver, Lackawanna & Western
348-8147 D&H
348-8148 Wabash
348-8149 Central Vermont
348-8150 CNJ

30' BUNK CAR EA 10.98

348-8161 B&O
348-8162 PRR
348-8163 Denver, South Park & Pacific
348-8164 SP
348-8165 Virginia & Truckee
348-8166 Lake Shore & Michigan Southern
348-8167 DRGW
348-8168 ATSF
348-8169 Central Pacific
348-8170 MOW
348-8171 US Military Railroad
348-8172 CP
348-8173 Philadelphia & RDG
348-8174 NH
348-8175 IC
348-8176 Western & Atlantic
348-8177 Orange & Alexandria

348-8178 UP
348-8179 LV
348-8180 Denver, Lackawanna & Western
348-8181 D&H
348-8182 Wabash
348-8183 Central Vermont
348-8184 CNJ

30' GONDOLA EA 10.98

348-8195 B&O
348-8196 PRR
348-8197 Denver, South Park & Pacific
348-8198 SP
348-8199 Virginia & Truckee
348-8200 Lake Shore & Michigan Southern
348-8201 DRGW
348-8202 ATSF
348-8203 Central Pacific
348-8204 MOW
348-8205 US Military Railroad
348-8206 CP
348-8207 Philadelphia & RDG
348-8208 NH
348-8209 IC
348-8210 Western & Atlantic
348-8211 Orange & Alexandria
348-8212 UP
348-8213 LV
348-8214 Denver, Lackawanna & Western
348-8215 D&H
348-8216 Wabash
348-8217 Central Vermont
348-8218 CNJ

WOODEN TANK CAR EA 11.98

348-8264

348-8263 B&O
348-8264 PRR
348-8265 Denver, South Park & Pacific
348-8266 SP
348-8267 Virginia & Truckee
348-8268 Lake Shore & Michigan Southern
348-8269 DRGW
348-8270 ATSF
348-8271 Central Pacific
348-8272 MOW
348-8273 US Military Railroad
348-8274 CP
348-8275 Philadelphia & RDG
348-8276 NH
348-8277 IC
348-8278 Western & Atlantic
348-8279 Orange & Alexandria
348-8280 UP
348-8281 LV
348-8282 Denver, Lackawanna & Western
348-8283 D&H
348-8284 Wabash
348-8285 Central Vermont
348-8286 CNJ

International Hobby Corp.

30' BLACKSMITH CAR EA 12.98

348-8229 B&O
348-8230 PRR
348-8231 Denver, South Park & Pacific
348-8232 SP
348-8233 Virginia & Truckee
348-8234 Lake Shore & Michigan Southern
348-8235 DRGW
348-8236 ATSF
348-8237 Central Pacific
348-8238 MOW
348-8239 US Military Railroad
348-8240 CP
348-8241 Philadelphia & RDG
348-8242 NH
348-8243 IC
348-8244 Western & Atlantic
348-8245 Orange & Alexandria
348-8246 UP
348-8247 LV
348-8248 Denver, Lackawanna & Western
348-8249 D&H
348-8250 Wabash
348-8251 Central Vermont
348-8252 CNJ

DERRICK CAR EA 12.98

348-8297 B&O
348-8298 PRR
348-8299 Denver, South Park & Pacific
348-8300 SP
348-8301 Virginia & Truckee
348-8302 Lake Shore & Michigan Southern
348-8303 DRGW
348-8304 ATSF
348-8305 Central Pacific
348-8306 MOW
348-8307 US Military Railroad
348-8308 CP
348-8309 Philadelphia & RDG
348-8310 NH
348-8311 IC
348-8312 Western & Atlantic
348-8313 Orange & Alexandria
348-8314 UP
348-8315 LV
348-8316 Denver, Lackawanna & Western
348-8317 D&H
348-8318 Wabash
348-8319 Central Vermont
348-8320 CNJ

RAIL & TIE CAR EA 9.98

348-8331 B&O
348-8332 PRR
348-8333 Denver, South Park & Pacific
348-8334 SP
348-8335 Virginia & Truckee
348-8336 Lake Shore & Michigan Southern
348-8337 DRGW
348-8338 ATSF
348-8339 Central Pacific
348-8340 MOW
348-8341 US Military Railroad
348-8342 CP
348-8343 Philadelphia & RDG
348-8344 NH
348-8345 IC
348-8346 Western & Atlantic
348-8347 Orange & Alexandria
348-8348 UP
348-8349 LV
348-8350 Denver, Lackawanna & Western
348-8351 D&H
348-8352 Wabash
348-8353 Central Vermont
348-8354 CNJ

FLAT CAR EA 9.98

348-8371 B&O
348-8372 PRR
348-8373 Denver, South Pacific
348-8734 SP
348-8375 Virginia Truckee
348-8376 Lake Shore & Michigan Southern
348-8377 DRGW
348-8378 ATSF
348-8379 Central Pacific
348-8380 MOW
348-8381 US Military Railroad
348-8382 CP
348-8383 Philadelphia & RDG
348-8384 NH
348-8385 IC
348-8386 Western & Atlantic
348-8387 Orange & Alexandria
348-8388 UP
348-8389 LV
348-8390 Denver, Lackawanna & Western
348-8391 D&H
348-8392 Wabash
348-8393 Central Vermont
348-8394 CNJ

Flat Car 348-8378

50' Single Plug Door Box Car 348-35080

ASSEMBLED BARNHART LOG LOADERS EA 19.98

Load log cars with fresh-cut timber easily with the Barnhart Log Loader. Developed by the Marion Steam Shovel Company in the 1880s, the Barnhart loaders operated directly on log cars, allowing them to move down the length of trains. The crew would advance the Barnhart along the train, using the Barnhart's winch, until it reached the last car, where it was often left. Comes fully assembled and crafted in metal and plastic. Perfect accessory for skeleton log cars 348-4800, etc.

348-36000 Alamagordo Lumber Company
348-36001 Conasauga River Lumber Company
348-36002 Cherry River Boom & Lumber Company
348-36003 United States Lumber Company
348-36004 Goodyear Lumber Company
348-36005 Emporium Forestry Company
348-36006 Barnhart's Lumber Company
348-36007 Diamond Lumber Company

348-36008 Woodside Lumber Company
348-36009 Unlettered (brown)

CABOOSE

348-3254 Woodside Lumber **3.98**

ASSEMBLED FREIGHT CAR ASSORTMENTS

OLD TIME FREIGHT EA 47.76

Create an authentic freight train from the early days of railroading with these sets. Perfect for use behind those handsome 4-4-0s, the assortments include various combinations of these six kits: 34' Drovers Caboose, Cattle Car, Ventilated Box Car, Flat Car and 29' Tank Car. The majority of cars in each set are decorated for the roadname listed, with additional cars from other roads.

348-11930 ATSF w/Overland Oil Tank, UP Cattle Car
348-11931 B&O w/Sun Oil Tank
348-11932 CP w/Milwaukee Tank, UP Cattle Car
348-11933 DRGW w/Virginia & Truckee Cattle Car
348-11934 Denver, South Park & Pacific w/Virginia & Truckee Tank
348-11935 Maryland & Pennsylvania w/Drane Oil & Conoco Tank
348-11936 NH w/U.S. Military Railroad Tank, PRR Ventilated Box & W&A Flat
348-11937 PRR w/Sun Oil Tank, NH Ventilated Box Car
348-11938 UP w/Central Pacific Tank
348-11939 US Military Railroad w/Western & Atlantic Cattle Car
348-11940 Virginia & Truckee w/Denver, South Park & Pacific Ventilated Box Car
348-11941 Western & Atlantic w/U.S. Military Railroad Ventilated Box Car

50' SINGLE DOME TANK CAR

348-1509 GATX Tank Train **2.98**

40' SINGLE DOME TANKERS ASSORMENTS EA 35.76

348-35000 (2 each of Dupont, Sacony, Celanese, Shamrock, Goodyear and Gulf)
348-35030 (2 each of Shell, RDG, Union Carbide, Diamond Alkali, Hooker and Ethyl Corp)
348-35040 (2 each of Amstar, Corn Products, NJ Zinc, National Lead, Hudson Bay & BASF)

50' SINGLE PLUG DOOR BOX CAR ASSORMENTS EA 35.76

348-35050 #1 (2 each of RDG Lines, Florida East Coast, LV, CR, CP & CNJ)
348-35080 #2 (2 each of Railway Express Agency, CNW, MILW, GN Cushion Ride, GN & NKP)

62' HI-CUBE DOUBLE DOOR BOX CAR ASSORMENTS EA 35.76

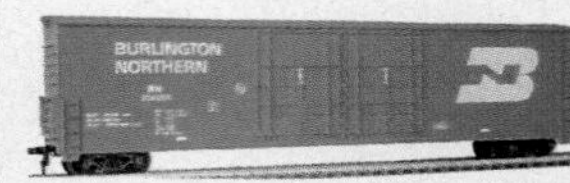

348-35150 #1 (2 each of UP, ATSF, NYC, Detroit, Toledo & Ironton, BN & Ann Arbor)
348-35170 #2 (2 each of UP, Detroit, Toledo & Ironton, MILW, Wabash, Frisco & NS)

56' ACF COVERED HOPPER

348-35200 56' ACF Center Flow Hopper Assortment (2 each of DRGW, C&O, CNW, CB&Q, CR & PC) **35.76**

54' 3-BAY COVERED HOPPER ASSORTMENTS EA 35.76

348-35250 #1 (2 each of D&H, Seaboard Coast Line, Central Soya, BN, Cargill Salt and Ann Arbor)
348-35270 #2 (2 each of PC, Miles, ADM, Norchem, CON AGRA & LV)
348-35280 #3 (2 each of CHEMPLEX, Welch Grain, UP, FMC, Detroit, Toledo & Ironton and FGDA)

38' EXTENDED VISION CABOOSE ASSORTMENTS EA 35.76

348-35300 #1 (2 each of Montana Rail Link, SBD, CNW, Deroit, Toledo & Ironton, TH&B & UP)
348-35330 #2 (2 each of BN, CR, D&H, Gulf, Mobile & Ohio, MOPAC & CP Rail)
348-35340 #3 (2 each of C&O, Richmond, Fredricksbugh & Potomic, Maine Central, ATSF, WM & SP)

40' HOPPER

348-132650 Assortment **35.76**

42' HOPPER

348-35110 42' 4-Bay Open Hopper Assortment (2 each of Pennsy Power & Light, Ontario Northland, D&H, Frisco, CRR & LEF&C) **35.76**

FREIGHT CAR ASSORTMENTS PKG(12) 35.76 (UNLESS NOTED)

348-1650

348-1500 Single Dome Tank Car
348-1550 50' Reefer, Assorted Roadnames
348-1600 50' Box Car
348-1650 50' Box Cars, Assorted Roadname
348-1700 40' Double Door Box Car
348-1750 40' Reefer
348-1800 50' Stock Car
348-1850 50' Gondola
348-1900 50' Hopper
348-2550 40' Stock Car
348-2600 36' Extended Vision Caboose **43.49**
348-2800 Undecorated **34.67**

International Hobby Corp.

OLD TIME ASSEMBLED CARS

30' BOX (TOOL) CAR EA 17.98

348-58127 B&O
348-58128 PRR
348-58129 Denver, South Park & Pacific
348-58130 SP
348-58131 Virginia & Truckee
348-58132 Lake Shore & Michigan Southern
348-58133 DRGW
348-58134 ATSF
348-58135 Central Pacific Railroad
348-58136 MOW
348-58137 US Military Railroad
348-58138 Central Pacific
348-58139 Philadelphia & RDG
348-58140 NH
348-58141 IC
348-58142 Western & Atlantic
348-58143 Orange & Alexandria
348-58144 UP
348-58145 LV
348-58146 Delaware, Lackawanna & Western
348-58147 D&H
348-58148 Wabash
348-58149 Central Vermont
348-58150 CNJ

30' BUNK CAR EA 16.98

348-58161 B&O
348-58162 PRR
348-58163 Denver, South Park & Pacific
348-58164 SP
348-58165 Virginia & Truckee
348-58166 Lake Shore & Michigan Southern
348-58167 DRGW
348-58168 ATSF
348-58169 Central Pacific Railroad
348-58170 MOW
348-58171 US Military Railroad
348-58172 CP
348-58173 Philadelphia & RDG
348-58174 NH
348-58175 IC
348-58176 Western & Atlantic
348-58177 Orange & Alexandria
348-58178 UP
348-58179 LV
348-58180 Delaware, Lackawanna & Western
348-58181 D&H
348-58182 WAB
348-58183 CV
348-58184 CNJ

GONDOLA EA 16.98

348-58195 B&O
348-58196 PRR
348-58197 Denver, South Park & Pacific
348-58198 SP
348-58199 Virginia & Truckee
348-58200 Lake Shore & Michigan Southern
348-58201 DRGW
348-58202 ATSF
348-58203 Central Pacific Railroad
348-58204 MOW
348-58205 US Military Railroad
348-58206 CP
348-58207 Philadelphia & RDG
348-58208 NH
348-58209 IC
348-58210 Western & Atlantic
348-58211 Orange & Alexandria
348-58212 UP
348-58213 LV
348-58214 Delaware, Lackawanna & Western
348-58215 D&H
348-58216 Wabash
348-58217 Central Vermont
348-58218 CNJ

BLACKSMITH CAR EA 24.98

348-58229 C&O
348-58230 PRR
348-58231 Denver, South Park & Pacific
348-58232 SP
348-58233 Virginia & Truckee
348-58234 Lake Shore & Michigan Southern
348-58235 DRGW
348-58236 ATSF
348-58237 Central Pacific Railroad
348-58238 MOW
348-58239 US Military Railroad
348-58240 CP
348-58241 Philadelphia & RDG
348-58242 NH
348-58243 IC
348-58244 Western & Atlantic
348-58245 Orange & Alexandria
348-58246 UP
348-58247 LV
348-58248 Delaware, Lackawanna & Western
348-58249 D&H
348-58250 Wabash
348-58251 Central Vermont
348-58252 CNJ

30' Box Car 348-58127

WOODEN TANK CAR EA 17.98

348-58263 B&O
348-58264 PRR
348-58265 Denver, South Park & Pacific
348-58266 SP
348-58267 Virginia & Truckee
348-58268 Lake Shore & Michigan Southern
348-58269 DRGW
348-58270 ATSF
348-58271 Central Pacific Railroad
348-58272 MOW
348-58273 US Military Railroad
348-58274 CP **348-58275** Philadelphia & RDG
348-58276 NH
348-58277 IC
348-58278 Western & Atlantic
348-58279 Orange & Alexandria
348-58280 UP
348-58281 LV
348-58282 Delaware, Lackawanna & Western
348-58283 D&H
348-58284 Wabash
348-58285 Central Vermont
348-58286 CNJ

Derrick Car 348-58298

Gondola 348-58195

DERRICK CAR EA 19.98

348-58297 B&O
348-58298 PRR
348-58299 Denver, South Park & Pacific
348-58300 SP
348-58301 Virginia & Truckee
348-58302 Lake Shore & Michigan Southern
348-58303 DRGW
348-58304 ATSF
348-58305 Central Pacific Railroad
348-58306 MOW
348-58307 US Military Railroad
348-58308 CP
348-58309 Philadelphia & RDG
348-58310 NH
348-58311 IC
348-58312 Western & Atlantic
348-58313 Orange & Alexandria
348-58314 UP
348-58315 LV
348-58316 Delaware, Lackawanna & Western
348-58317 D&H
348-58318 Wabash
348-58319 Central Vermont
348-58320 CNJ

RAIL & TIE CAR EA 15.98

348-58353 CV
348-58331 B&O

348-58332 PRR
348-58333 Denver, South Park & Pacific
348-58334 SP
348-58335 Virginia & Truckee
348-58336 Lake Shore & Michigan Southern
348-58337 DRGW
348-58338 ATSF
348-58339 Central Pacific Railroad
348-58340 MOW
348-58341 US Military Railroad
348-58342 CP
348-58343 Philadelphia & RDG
348-58344 NH
348-58345 IC
348-58346 Western & Atlantic
348-58347 Orange & Alexandria
348-58348 UP
348-58349 LV
348-58350 Delaware, Lackawanna & Western
348-58351 D&H
348-58352 Wabash
348-58354 CNJ

FLAT CAR EA 10.98

348-58371 B&O
348-58372 PRR
348-58373 Denver, South Park & Pacific
348-58374 SP
348-58375 Virginia & Truckee
348-58376 Lake Shore & Michigan Southern
348-58377 DRGW
348-58378 ATSF
348-58379 CPRR
348-58380 MOW
348-58381 US Military Railroad
348-58382 CP
348-58383 Philadelphia & RDG
348-58384 NH
348-58385 IC
348-58386 Western & Atlantic
348-58387 Orange & Alexandria
348-58388 UP
348-58389 LV
348-58390 Delaware, Lackawanna & Western
348-58391 D&H
348-58392 Wabash
348-58393 Central Vermont
348-58394 CNJ

Jaeger

Easy-to-build load kits include coated paper, wood blocks, banding material, spacers and instructions.

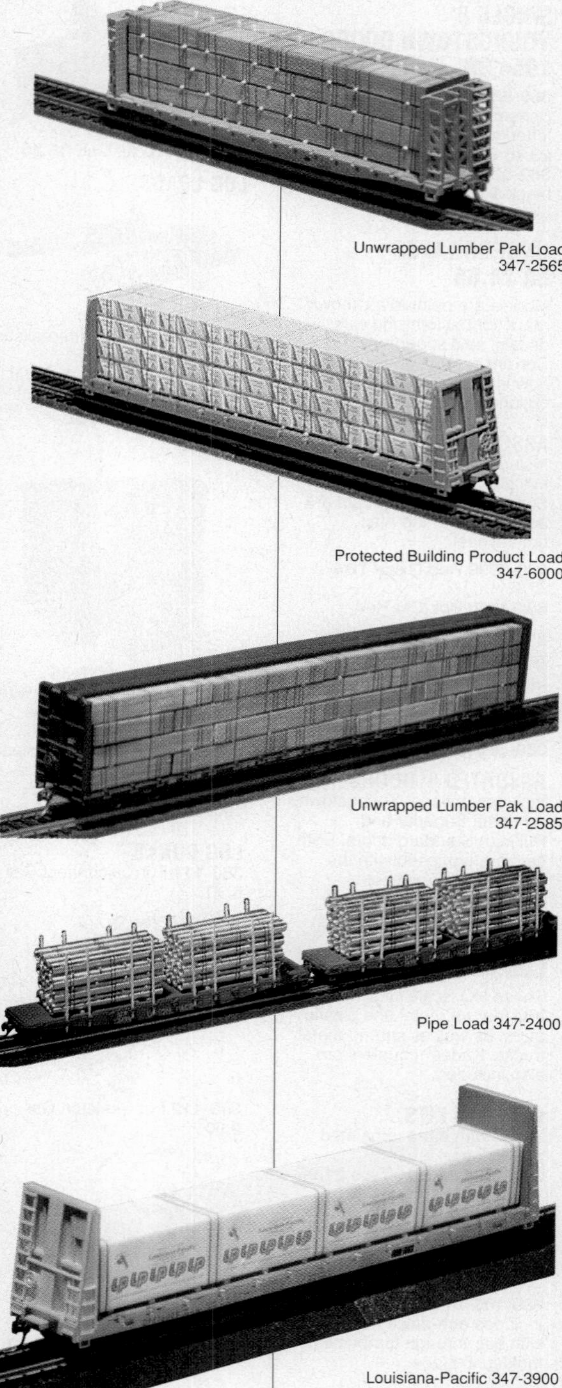

Unwrapped Lumber Pak Load 347-2565

Protected Building Product Load 347-6000

Unwrapped Lumber Pak Load 347-2585

Pipe Load 347-2400

Louisiana-Pacific 347-3900

LOADS

PROTECTED BUILDING PRODUCT LOAD EA 8.95

Assembled, fits Roundhouse 60' bulkhead flats.

347-3100 Evans Products
347-3200 Gold Bond Products
347-3300 Johns-Manville Building Products
347-3350 Ligmun
347-3400 Masonite
347-3500 Plum Creek Timber Co.
347-3600 US Gypsum
347-3700 Centex
347-3800 Georgia-Pacific
347-3850 Georgia-Pacific (blue)
347-3900 Louisiana-Pacific
347-3950 Louisiana-Pacific (Particle Board)
347-3000 Undecorated (black)

PIPE LOAD

Builds two complete loads, fits most 40 or 50' flats or gons.

347-2400 Corrugated **16.95**
347-2900 Aluminum **12.95**

UNWRAPPED LUMBER PAK LOAD EA 14.95

Contains material for two loads each.

347-2555 For Athearn 50' Flat Car
347-2565 For Walthers GSC Bulkhead Flat Car
347-2575 For MDC 60' Bulkhead Flat Car
347-2585 For E&C Shops 63' Centerbeam Flat Car
347-2595 For Walthers 73' Centerbeam Flat Car

60' FLAT CAR LUMBER LOAD EA 12.95

Fits standard or bulkhead car.

347-4000 ATCO Lumber Ltd.
347-4100 Canfor
347-4200 Carrier Western Lumber
347-4300 Champion Lumber
347-4400 Crown Zellerbach
347-4500 Evans Products
347-4600 Grande Prairie
347-4700 Hines
347-4800 Northwood
347-4900 Pope & Talbot
347-5000 Publishers Forest Products
347-5100 Roseburg
347-5200 Simpson Timber
347-5300 Washington Idaho Forest Products
347-5400 Weyerhaeuser Building Products
347-5500 Clearwater Forest Industries
347-5600 Great West Timber
347-5700 Hanel Lumber Company
347-5800 Sierra Pacific
347-5900 Slocan
347-6000 Weyerhaeuser Lumber/Kamloops

40'/50' FLAT CAR LUMBER LOAD EA 6.95

Fits standard or bulkhead car.

347-100 Boise Cascade
347-200 Bulkley Valley
347-250 Canfor
347-300 Edward Hines
347-400 Georgia-Pacific
347-450 Georgia-Pacific (blue)
347-500 Pack River
347-600 Weyerhaeuser Shed-Pak
347-650 ATCO Lumber Ltd
347-700 Babine
347-750 Croman Corp.
347-800 Idapine Mills
347-900 Louisiana-Pacific
347-1000 Modoc
347-1100 St. Regis
347-1150 Tricon Timber, Inc.
347-1200 West Fraser
347-1300 Bennett Lumber
347-1400 Collins Pine Co.
347-1450 Crown Pacific
347-1500 High Cascade
347-1600 International Paper-IP Building Materials
347-1700 Keystone
347-1800 Potlatch
347-1900 Weldwood

CABLE LOAD

347-2800 6.95
12 assembled reels, fits 50' gondolas.

WALTHERS GSC FLAT CAR LUMBER LOAD EA 10.95

347-6800 ATCO Lumber Ltd.
347-6805 Bennett Lumber
347-6810 Boise Cascade
347-6815 Champion Lumber
347-6820 Georgia-Pacific
347-6825 Grande Prairie
347-6830 High Cascade
347-6835 Idaho Timber
347-6840 Idapine Mills
347-6845 International Paper

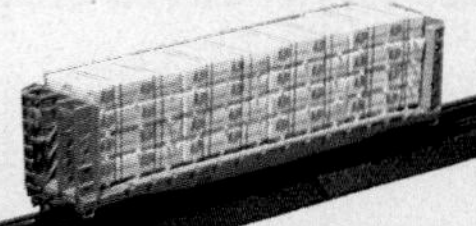

347-6850 Louisiana-Pacific
347-6855 MacMillian Bloedel
347-6860 Northwood
347-6865 Plum Creek Timber
347-6870 Publishers Forest Products
347-6875 Ranger
347-6880 Rustad Brothers
347-6885 St. Regis
347-6890 Weldwood
347-6895 Weyerhaeuser

CENTERBEAM LUMBER LOAD EA 11.95

347-7000 Boise Cascade
347-7100 MacMillian Bloedel
347-7200 Quandra Wood Products
347-7300 Rustad Brothers
347-7400 Snow Mountain Pine Co.
347-7500 Weyerhaeuser
347-7600 Jacobson Brothers
347-7650 Jacobson Brothers (red, green)
347-7700 Millar Western
347-7800 Plum Creek Timber
347-7900 Ranger
347-8000 Georgia-Pacific
347-8100 Idaho Timber
347-8200 Potlatch
347-8300 Simpson

LUMBER-PAK FOR WALTHERS 73' CENTERBEAM CARS EA 15.95

347-6900 Boise Cascade

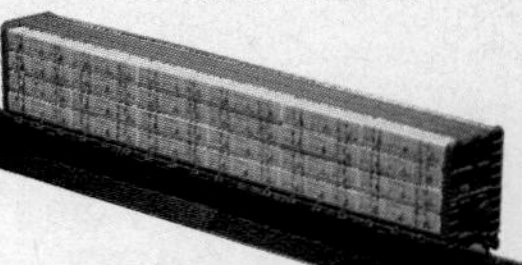

347-6910 Clearwater/Idapine
347-6920 Hampton Lumber
347-6930 Lignum
347-6940 Manfor Ltd.
347-6950 Moose River Lumber Co.
347-6960 Weyerhaeuser
347-6970 Norwegian Termite
347-6980 Simpson Timber

GONDOLA RAIL LOAD

347-2700 39' Rail **7.95**
Fits any 40' or longer car.

INGOT LOAD

347-2600 Aluminum **6.95**
Two loads for 50' gondolas or 60' bulkhead flats.

UTILITY POLE LOAD

Two complete loads for gondolas or bulkhead flats.

347-2300 Natural **6.95**
347-2350 Dark Brown **8.95**

TIMBER LOAD EA 15.95

Four assembled, stained and banded bundles for Athearn 40 or 50' flat cars.

347-2500 No Markings
347-2525 Georgia-Pacific
347-2550 Publishers Forest Products

SIGNODE GRAIN DOORS

347-2000 Red Lettering pkg(24) **1.00**
347-2050 Grain Tainer, Green Lettering pkg(24) **1.00**

FREIGHT CAR PLACARDS

Assorted placards for gondolas, box and flat cars.

347-2100 Set 1 pkg(400) **1.00**
347-2150 Set 2 **2.00**
Includes modern Home Shop For Repairs on green paper.

DETAILING KITS

347-2200 Freight Dock pkg(47) **6.95**
Pallets, barrels, cable reels, drums, crates, bottle cases and sacks.

347-2275 Lumber Yard (100 Pieces) **9.95**

PULLMAN-STANDARD PS-1 40' BOX CARS

Single 6' Youngstown Doors 1950-54 380-4041

Single 8' Youngstown Doors 380-5206

One of the most popular designs, over 100,000 were built between 1947 and 1963 to serve 78 railroads! Welded steel construction kept most rolling into the 1980s. Each car is a faithful replica of the prototype and comes fully assembled, ready for service. Smooth rolling, self-centering trucks and Kadee® Magne-Matic® metal couplers are standard on all models. For improved operation, cars are the NMRA recommended weight and have a low center of gravity. Finely detailed handrails, ladders, stirrups, grab irons, see-through roofwalk, prototypical brakewheel and full underbody details are all included. Models feature specific doors and brake gear to match their prototypes and come fully painted and lettered in authentic schemes.

SINGLE 6' YOUNGSTOWN DOORS 1950-54

380-4002 Akron, Canton & Youngstown #750 **24.65**
380-4004 D&H #19114 **28.95**
380-4005 Chicago Great Western #5200 **27.95**
380-4006 CP #269142 **27.95**

380-4007 NYC #170699 **27.95** April, 1960 Repaint.

380-4008 CRIP #22172 As Built December, 1951 Centennial Scheme **29.95** Decorated with "100 Years of Progress 1852-1952" herald and "Route of the ROCKETS" slogans.

380-4010 D&H #18570 **27.95** ***NEW***
380-4013 Monon #843 **28.95**
380-4014 Monon #741 **27.95** ***NEW***

380-4015 ATSF #31440 ("Super Chief") **29.95**
380-4018 ATSF #31698 ("Grand Canyon") **29.95** ***NEW***
380-4019 LaSalle & Bureau County #170685 **28.95**
380-4022 Chicago Great Western #5106 **28.95** ***NEW***
380-4025 Maryland & Pennsylvania #3165 **27.95** ***NEW***
380-4041 Akron, Canton & Youngstown #772 **27.95** ***NEW***
380-4042 D&H #19114 **29.45**
380-4043 Fort Dodge, Des Moines & Southern #12300 (Box Car Red) **28.95** ***NEW***
380-4044 CP #268885 International of Maine Division (Oxide Red) **27.95** ***NEW***

SINGLE 6' 5 PANEL YOUNGSTOWN DOORS 1950-54

380-4021 Minneapolis, Northfield & Southern #1035 **28.95**

380-4023 CP #268899 **28.45** ***NEW***
380-4024 New York, Susquehanna & Western #418 (Light Tuscan) **29.95**

SINGLE 6' 7 PANEL YOUNGSTOWN DOORS 1950-54

380-4016 Green Bay & Western #799 **29.95**
380-4020 CRI&P #21110 **29.95** ***NEW***
380-4026 Lake Superior & Ispheming #2266 **28.95** ***NEW***
380-4027 Lake Superior & Ispheming #2236 **28.95** ***NEW***
380-4028 Lake Superior & Ispheming #2241 **28.95** ***NEW***
380-4029 Chicago & Eastern Illinois #65596 **27.95** ***NEW***

380-4030 Chicago & Eastern Illinois #65593 **27.95** ***NEW***
380-4031 Chicago & Eastern Illinois #65599 **27.95** ***NEW***
380-4032 NYC #169000 **28.95** ***NEW***
380-4033 NYC #169004 **28.95** ***NEW***
380-4034 NYC #169016 **28.95** ***NEW***

SINGLE 8' YOUNGSTOWN DOORS 1950-54

380-5001 N&W #44324 **27.95**

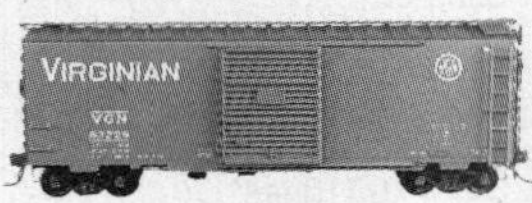

380-5002 Virginian #63226 **28.95**
380-5003 Lake Superior & Ispheming #2413 **28.95**
380-5004 N&W #44025 **27.95**

SINGLE 8' PS DOORS 1954 ON

380-5201 Texas Mexican #8956 (1965 Scheme-Box Car Red) **27.95** ***NEW***
380-5202 CRI&P #5809 (1959 Scheme-Box Car Red) **28.45** ***NEW***

380-5204 CNJ #23527 (1957 Scheme-Box Car Red) **29.45** ***NEW***
380-5205 CNW #24739 (1958 Scheme-Oxide Red) **28.45** ***NEW***
380-5207 MP #39075 (1959 Scheme-Box Car Red, black ends) **27.45** ***NEW***
380-5208 Wabash #7609 (1959 Scheme-Oxide Red, black ends, roof) **29.95** ***NEW***

SINGLE 8' YOUNGSTOWN DOORS 1954 ON

380-5203 UP #126176 (1964 Scheme-Oxide Red, yellow lettering, black roof & ends) **29.45** ***NEW***
380-5206 SLSF #18299 (1954 black & white scheme) **29.45** ***NEW***

UNDECORATED EA 24.65

Models are painted as shown, ready for customizing with decals, sold separately. Current production models now include three styles of optional doors unless noted.

ASSORTED 6' DOORS

Includes optional Youngstown, five panel and seven panel Superior doors. Both cars are equipped with the Ajax brakewheel.

380-3999 Red Oxide **TBA** ***NEW***
380-4000 Box Car Red

8' CAMEL-YOUNGSTOWN DOORS ONLY

Both cars are equipped with the Ajax brakewheel.

380-4999 Red Oxide ***NEW***
380-5000 Box Car Red

ASSORTED 8' DOORS

Includes optional Youngstown, six panel Superior and Pullman Standard doors. Both cars are equipped with the Universal brakewheel.

380-5199 Red Oxide
380-5200 Box Car Red ***NEW***

LOGGING EQUIPMENT

These HO Scale Craft Train Kits feature metal and plastic parts, as well as sprung metal trucks. Kadee® couplers are also included.

FLAT CAR KITS

Metal, with three unpainted plastic logs.
380-102 Skeleton Type **21.95**

380-103 Truss Type **27.95** Includes one-piece truss rods with see-through turnbuckles molded in place,

DISCONNECT LOGGING TRUCKS

Arch bar style trucks with couplers and footboards. Prototypes served loggers for over 80 years.

380-101 With Unpainted Log Load **17.55**

380-107 Trucks Only **15.35**

LOG LOADS

380-110 pkg(4) **3.60** One-piece plastic with realistic ends and bark detail. Unpainted.

LOGGING CABOOSE

380-104 Kit (red) **16.45** Move timber trains safely with this caboose, typical of the home-made equipment on many logging lines. One-piece plastic body with removable roof. Includes Magne-Matic® couplers.

LOG BUNKS

380-111 For Disconnect Car **5.30**

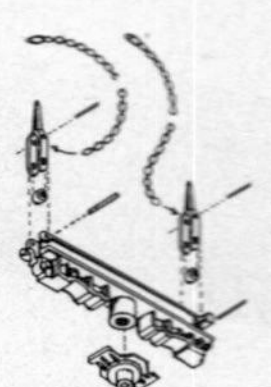

380-112 For Skeleton Car **9.90**

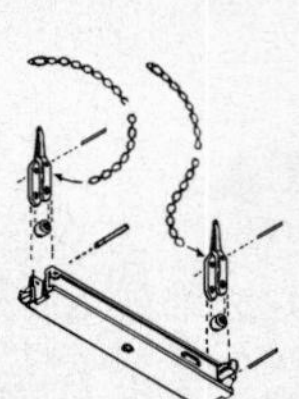

380-113 For Truss Car **8.80**

Keystone Locomotive Works

All items are HO Scale craft train kits. Many of the models are based on equipment used by the Grasse River Railroad in New York, but can be easily adapted to equipment used on other lines. The Grasse River was located in northeastern New York in the Adirondack Mountains and ran from Cranberry Lake to Conifer, New York.

Barnhart Log Loader 395-104

LUMBER CARS

BARNHART LOG LOADER

395-104 39.95
Barnhart log loaders were widely used by logging railways from coast to coast. Since they could be transported anywhere along the railway, they provided the logging companies flexibility in loading schedules. This kit is designed for use with Keystone, Alexander and Model Engineering Works log buggies. It includes a cast body with interior and exterior wood planking, interior details with boiler and steam engine, corrugated metal roof and a brass chain for the drive mechanism. The kit also features a boom and cable.

LOG BUGGIE

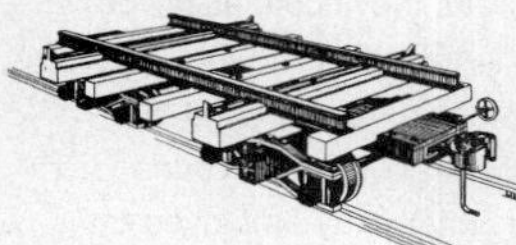

395-100 pkg(2) **11.95**
This kit is modeled after a Grasse River prototype, which carried hardwood logs from 14 to 21" in diameter. The average train size was 20 to 22 of these cars. Loading was accomplished by a Barnhart log loader which ran along the top of the car on rails and was left on the last car. The kit includes a cast-metal body, Code 100 rails for loader to run on, brass chain, cast brake cylinders and brake wheel. Trucks, couplers and logs are not included. Kit accepts horn-hook, Kadee®, or other similiar couplers.

SKELETON LOG CAR

395-103 pkg(2) **11.95**
Varying in length from 20' to 50', skeleton log cars were used on both standard- and narrow-gauge logging lines throughout the United States. This model is a replica of a typical 29' log car, which is short enough for small layouts. The kit includes pressure-cast body, separate cheese block castings and brake parts. Trucks and couplers are not included. Kit accepts Kadee® #380-714 couplers or other manufacturer's similiar couplers.

LOGGING CABOOSE

395-106 18.95
Rebuilt and repainted repeatedly during its lifetime, caboose No. 71 of the Grasse River Railroad measured under 20' long. This kit features a cast-metal frame, positionable cupola, ends, windows, steps and details. The sides, floor, and roof pieces are all wood. Trucks are also included.

CLIMAX LOG CAR

395-107 pkg(2) **11.95**
The rugged, simple design of the Climax log car made it one of the most versatile and popular logging cars of its time. This kit includes a wood center beam that can be cut to the desired car length (26 to 42'). Other details include all-in-one cast metal ends with bunk and cheese blocks, bunk straps, NBW details, wire brake staffs and bunk release rings. This kit does not include logs, trucks or couplers. The car is designed to use Model Die Casting arch-bar trucks or the trucks of your choice.

LOGGING TRUCKS

395-30 Grasse River Logging pkg(2) **3.95**
This kit builds one pair of Grasse River Logging trucks for the Grasse River log buggie. Includes cast-metal bolsters and sideframes, plus RP25 wheels.

CABOOSE INTERIOR

WIDE VISION

395-3501 12.98
This interior kit represents standard equipment in a modern-day caboose and fits Athearn, Bachmann and AHM wide-vision cabooses without modification. Features over 25 cast-metal and plastic parts, including seats, lockers, a desk, water cooler, heater, fuel tank, fire extinguisher, telephone and more.

DISPLAY CASE

357-1847 Display Case **169.95**
Great for displaying HO Scale equipment, this case features a solid oak frame and shelves, white plastic back and plastic sliding doors. Mounting hardware and self-sticking door handles also included. Outside dimensions: 18 x 47".

AC&F 70-Ton Open-Side Covered Hoppers

AC&F 70-TON COVERED HOPPER 3-PACK EA 45.00

OPEN SIDE

An open space between the two bays is the only thing distinguishing these easy-to-assemble kits from the Closed Side units. All units are crisply printed and precisely detailed. Kits include ASF "Ride Control" trucks.

381-380201 Boston & Maine 5502, 5511 & 5516 (gray) *NEW*
381-380202 GE Lamps 313, 317 & 318 (black) *NEW*
381-380203 GN 71233, 71247 & 71283 (gray) *NEW*
381-380204 MON 4331, 4376 & 4382 (gray) *NEW*
381-380205 Wabash 30000, 30001 & 30004 (black) *NEW*
381-380206 WM 5102, 5124 & 5187 (gray) *NEW*

CLOSED SIDE

Limited Quantity Available

381-380107 EL
381-380108 MILW
381-380109 NKP
381-380111 Seaboard Air Line
381-380112 SP

FREIGHT CAR SET

Limited Quantity Available

381-1808 Wamu 80000 **48.60**

kibri

IMPORTED FROM GERMANY BY WALTHERS

Railroad Telescoping Crane 405-16000

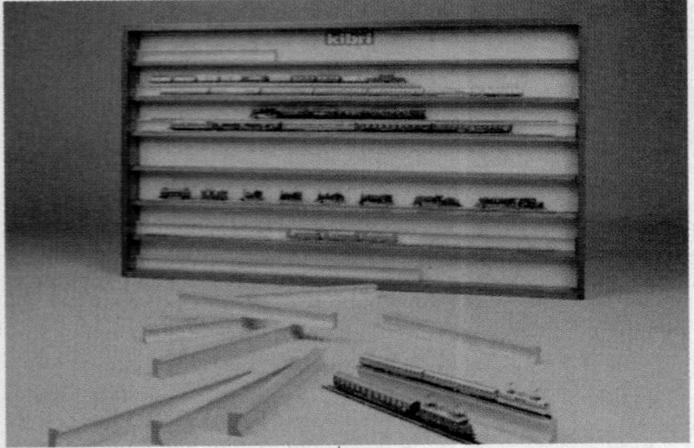

Display Case 405-12000

WORK TRAIN EQUIPMENT

405-16000 Railroad Telescoping Crane **99.99** ***NEW***
This versatile crane is a must-have for the modern maintenance fleet. Based on a prototype built by Gottwald, cranes like this are entering service on many of Europe's railroads, but it's modern lines and rugged good looks are typical of equipment used on American lines too. In service, it can be found repairing and building track, bridges, buildings and tunnels.

The easy-to-build kit features parts molded in several realistic colors. Construction is fast and easy with numbered parts and exploded view instructions.

DISPLAY CASES

High-quality hardwood display cases. (Dimensions shown are approximate.)

405-12000 5 Shelves, Natural Finish (14 x 14.8 x 1.8") **45.99**
405-12002 5 Shelves, Natural Finish (28 x 14.8 x 1.8") **84.99**

405-12005 7 Shelves, Dark Finish (32 x 24") **109.99**
Molded plastic shelf insert.

405-12006 9 Shelves, Natural Finish (32 x 24") **109.99**
Molded plastic shelf insert.

405-12010 7 Shelves, Glass Doors, Dark Finish (41.6 x 24.4 x 2.8") **279.99**
405-12012 3 Shelves, Glass Doors, Dark Finish (83.2 x 11 x 2.8") **329.99**
405-12018 3 Shelves, Glass Doors, Dark Finish (41.6 x 11 x 2.8") **169.99**

Limited Quantity Available

405-12020 For Marklin Gauge 1 Crocodile Loco & Other Large Scale Locos, Dark Finish (31.6 x 8.2 x 11.2") **189.99**
Wood base with acrylic top & side panels framed in wood.

405-12048 For Kibri Telescoping Cranes, Natural Finish (41.6 x 25.6 x 3.6") **169.99**

405-12056 Five Shelves, Glass Doors (28-3/8 x 24-3/8 x 4-5/8" Shelves are 4" Deep) **169.99**
Wood base with acrylic top and side panels framed in wood.

NOCH

IMPORTED FROM GERMANY BY WALTHERS

FREIGHT CAR LOADS EA 7.99 (UNLESS NOTED)

3.9 x 1.1" (10 x 2.8cm)

528-52610

528-52600 Coal
528-52610 Iron Scrap
528-52620 Railway Scrap
528-52630 Machinery Scrap
528-52640 Steel Girder Scrap
528-52650 Scrap Glass-Green
528-52660 Wood Chips
528-52670 Apples
528-52675 Potatoes
528-52680 Covered Machinery pkg(2)
Each measures 1.8 x 1.04 x 1.04" 4.5 x 2.6 x 2.6cm

528-52690 Stacked Lumber pkg(2) **10.99**
Each measures 2.2 x 1.16 x .8" 5.5 x 2.9 x 2cm.

ON-TRAK MODEL PRODUCTS

WEED SPRAYER

786-5014 With Arch Bar Trucks **15.20**
Kit features white metal and wood detail parts.

Information STATION

Where Have All The Cabooses Gone?

For over a century, the caboose was a common sight on the tail end of virtually every freight train that made its way down the line. You could always count on a friendly wave from the crew. And the cheery glow of the lights and markers helped give the mighty iron horse a human quality. Over time, the caboose became firmly connected to American literature, music and folk lore.

By the 1980s, time and technology were catching up to the caboose. Since they could not carry any freight, they made no money for their owners. Coupled at the back of the train, they could easily be damaged by the force of slack running in and out, which could also cause injury to any employee on board. Cabooses required frequent, regular maintenance and many were fast-approaching the end of their useful service lives. Faced with the prospect of purchasing expensive replacement cars, railroads turned to a new technology.

These ready-to-run models are finished in authentic colors and feature trucks and horn-hook couplers.

PROTO 1000 BOX CARS

Features include PROTO 2000 magnetic knuckle coiplers, blackened metal wheels, PROTO 2000 trucks with needle point axles and micro-molded details.

60' THRALL DOOR BOX CARS EA 12.00

433-23936 LUNX #4323 ***NEW***
433-23937 LUNX #4329 ***NEW***
433-23938 TCAX #30030 ***NEW***
433-23939 TCAX #30032 ***NEW***
433-23940 LUNX #4315 ***NEW***
433-23941 TCAX #30033 ***NEW***

50' HIGH ROOF BOX CAR EA 12.00

433-23942 PC #229046 ***NEW***
433-23943 PC #229258 ***NEW***
433-23944 PC #229408 ***NEW***
433-23945 WP #4052 ***NEW***
433-23946 WP #4057 ***NEW***
433-23947 WP #4060 ***NEW***

HOPPERS

PROTO 1000 100-TON HOPPERS EA 12.00

Features include PROTO 2000 magnetic knuckle couplers, blackened metal wheels, PROTO 2000 trucks with needle point axles and micro-molded details.

433-23930 SP #480182 ***NEW***
433-23931 SP #481136 ***NEW***
433-23932 SP #481147 ***NEW***

433-23933 B&O #82541 ***NEW***
433-23934 B&O #82967 ***NEW***
433-23935 B&O #83746 ***NEW***

AUTO CARRIER

50' BI-LEVEL AUTO CARRIER

433-8089 ATSF/Trailer Train w/6 Cars (red, yellow) **15.25**

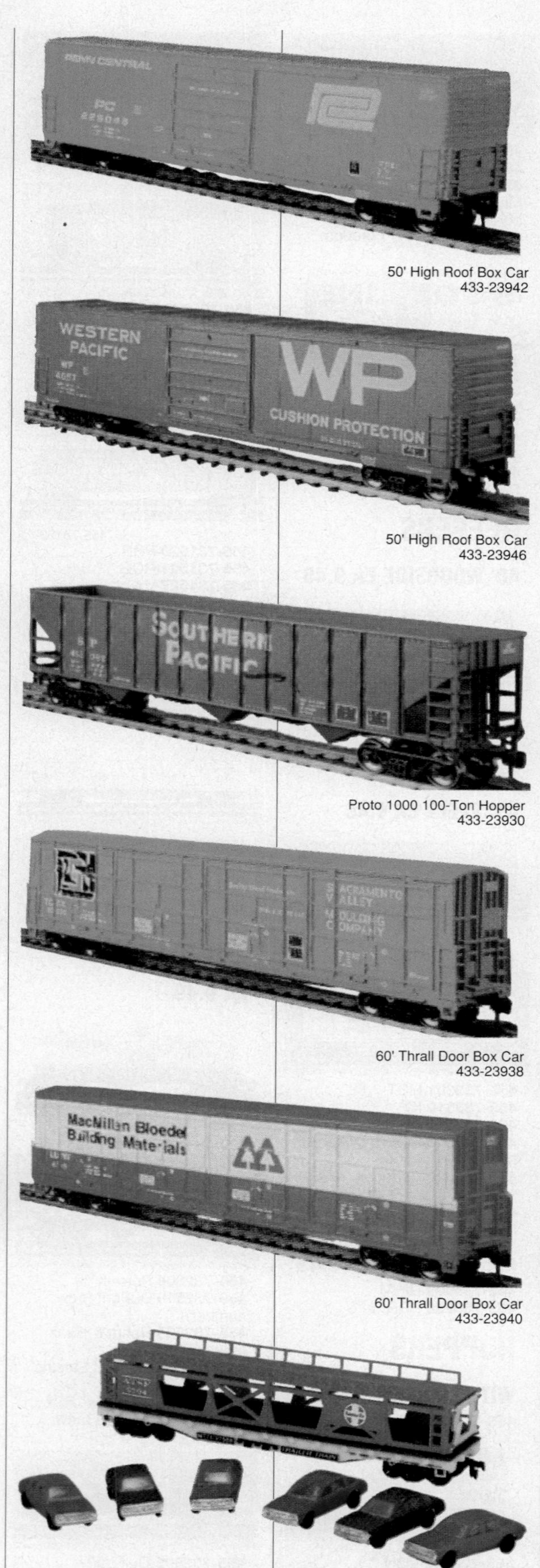

50' High Roof Box Car
433-23942

50' High Roof Box Car
433-23946

Proto 1000 100-Ton Hopper
433-23930

60' Thrall Door Box Car
433-23938

60' Thrall Door Box Car
433-23940

Auto Carrier 433-8089

PLASTRUCT

HOT METAL CARS

570-1040 Undecorated pkg(2) **20.95**
Perfect for hauling hot metal from blast furnaces to converters, these Pollock 12-wheel cars are a must for any layout serving the steel industry. Includes plastic parts to build two cars, based on Dean Freytag's article in the November 1994 issue of Railroad Model Craftsman. A reprint of the article is provided for instructions. Kits are less trucks, hardware and couplers; some model building experience is helpful in constructing this scratch model Kit.

Easy-to-build kits feature detailed plastic parts, plus authentic decals, less trucks and couplers.

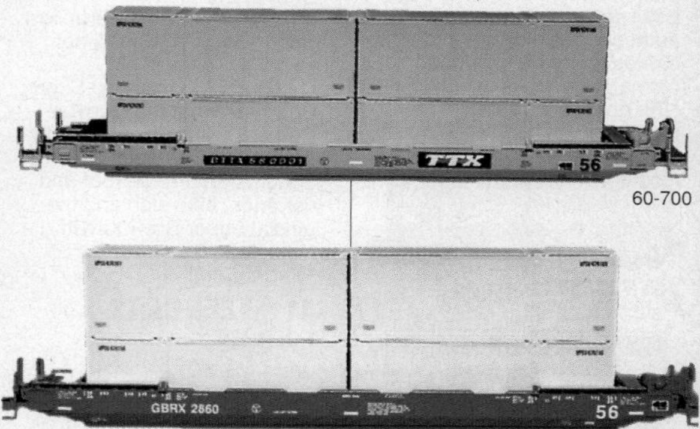

60-700

60-701

56' GUNDERSON HUSKY 2+2

TTX
60-700 With 2 #802 Containers **16.00**
60-702 Well Car Only **9.00**
NEW

GREENBRIER
60-701 With 2 #802 Containers **16.00**
60-703 Well Car Only **9.00**
NEW

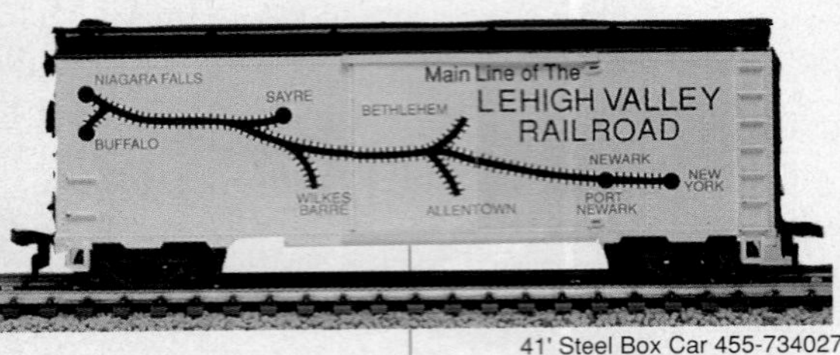

41' Steel Box Car 455-734027

41' Steel Box Car 455-734586

BOX CARS

NFL CARS EA 19.75

Add all the teams in the league to your Super Bowl® Express train set. Each car is made with the same care and attention to detail as the Super Bowl set, and is painted in authentic team colors and carries the team logo and helmet, as well as the Official NFL and Conference markings.

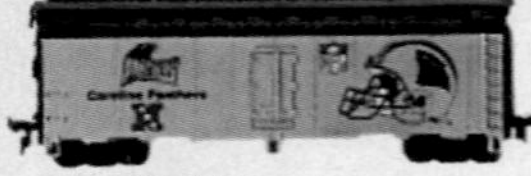

455-733830 Carolina Panthers

455-733834 St. Louis Rams

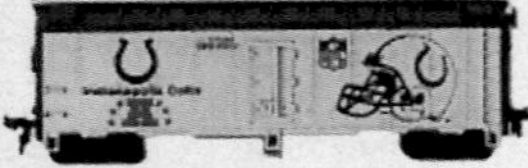

455-733836 Indianapolis Colts

455-733837 New England Patriots

455-733932 Dallas Cowboys Super Bowl XXX Winner

Limited Quantity Available

455-733831 Baltimore Ravens
455-733832 Philadelphia Eagles
455-733835 Arizona Cardinals
455-733838 Oakland Raiders

455-733904 Buffalo Bills
455-733933 Green Bay Packers

455-733934 Super Bowl XXXII Denver Broncos
455-733935 Denver Broncos Super Bowl XXXIII Winner *NEW*
Celebrate the fantastic Super Bowl victory of the Denver Broncos with this collectable freight car. The paint scheme features an orange roof and car ends, blue side and the official Super Bowl XXXIII insignia

41' STEEL CARS EA 9.49

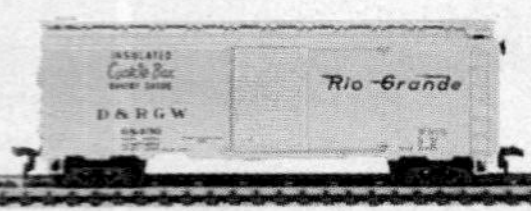

455-734008 DRGW
455-734027 LV Billboard *NEW*
455-734177 NYC Pacemaker
455-734231 Railbox

455-734251 B&O Time Saver (New #) *NEW*

455-734302 Seaboard *NEW*

455-734520 PRR *NEW*
455-734530 B&M
455-734549 PRR Merchandising Service (new number)
455-734586 RDG Freedom *NEW*

455-734590 SOO *NEW*
455-734601 Linde

1860 CARS EA 9.49

455-721011 SP
455-721020 PRR
455-721303 Maryland & Pennsylvania *NEW*

REEFERS

40' WOODSIDE EA 9.49

455-739179 Union Refrigerator
455-739180 GN Western Fruit Express
455-739181 North Western
455-739182 ART

41' STEEL EA 9.49

455-733020 PRR

455-733301 MDT *NEW*
455-733510 IC
455-733515 NP
455-733543 Hood's Milk (new number)
455-733590 Dubuque *NEW*

STOCK CARS

40' WOOD CAR EA 9.49

455-735003 UP
455-735250 PRR *NEW*

HOPPERS

WITH LOAD EA 9.49

455-729041 N&W *NEW*

455-729042 VGN
455-729202 PP&L #140 *NEW*
455-729203 PP&L #147 *NEW*

455-729204 PP&L #130 *NEW*
455-729205 PP&L #133 *NEW*

455-729620 PRR *NEW*
455-729621 RDG (orange) *NEW*

GONDOLAS

43' W/LOAD EA 9.49

455-731527

455-731020 PRR
455-731521 RDG
455-731527 LV

FLAT CARS

WITH CRATES EA 9.49

455-727523 C&O
455-727570 US Navy

455-727607 Westinghouse

WITH STAKES

455-727520 PRR **9.49** *NEW*

TANK CARS

EA 9.49

455-732148 Baby Ruth

455-732304 Pure *NEW*
455-732516 DuPont (new number)
455-732535 Rohm & Haas (new number)
455-732570 General Electric *NEW*
455-732580 Hercules *NEW*
455-732584 Sunoco (new number)

455-732593 Gulf *NEW*

455-732594 Mobil *NEW*

CABOOSES

COMBINE EA 9.49

455-725006 Central Pacific (red)
455-725008 DRGW
455-725025 B&O (Caboose Red)
455-725085 Rock & Peoria (Tuscan)

36' EA 9.49

455-726025

455-726002 ATSF
455-726008 DRGW
455-726012 Frisco (red)
455-726022 NYC (Jade Green)
455-726025 B&O
455-726027 LV *NEW*
455-726030 EL
455-726087 Chicago & Illinois Midland (dark green)
455-726088 Midland Valley (brown)
455-726174 Radio Dispatch (bright red)

455-726503 UP *NEW*
455-726561 GN *NEW*
455-726572 CR (new number) *NEW*

455-726620 PRR *NEW*
455-726621 RDG (new number, red) *NEW*

1860 HORSE CAR

455-722003 UP **9.49**

Get Daily Info, Photos and News at

www.walthers.com

These HO Scale ready-to-run cars are prepainted and lettered. An asterisk (*) after a car name indicates that the model is a "Heavy Weight" series car, which features a heavier body for improved performance, metal springs for coupler return and coupler height pockets.

40' Box Car 490-7973

36' 2-Bay Covered Hopper 490-8084

36' 2-Bay Open Hopper 490-8067

BOX CARS

40' EA 5.98 (UNLESS NOTED)

WITH SLIDING DOORS

490-7970 B&O Sentinel* (silver, blue)
490-7971 GN* (green w/orange stripe)
490-7972 Central of Georgia* (purple, silver)
490-7973 Timken* (yellow, silver)
490-7974 SP* (brown)
490-7976 Operation Lifesaver*
490-7977 PRR "Don't Stand Me Still"
490-7978 Gortons* **6.98**
490-7991 Operation Lifesaver Anniversary **6.98**
490-7992 Willy Wonka **6.98**
NEW

HEAVYWEIGHT CANADIAN

490-7950 Algoma Central*
490-7951 BC Rail*
490-7952 CP*
490-7953 CN*
490-7954 GTW*
490-7955 Ontario Northland*
490-7956 Pacific Great Eastern*
490-7957 Toronto, Hamilton & Buffalo*
490-7958 CN Manitoba*
490-7960 Unlettered (white)*

SLIDING-DOOR STEEL EA 4.98

490-8001 CR

490-8002 Baby Ruth (red)
490-8003 Maine Central (bright orange)
490-8004 CN
490-8005 CP Rail
490-8006 Domino
490-8007 Nabisco
490-8008 Napa Filters
490-80052 Champion Plugs

50' EA 6.98

Different Roadname Shown

490-8043 CP
490-8044 General Electric

PLUG-DOOR/SLIDING-DOOR COMBO

490-9031 Western Pacific (silver w/orange feather)
490-9034 IC Gulf (orange)
490-9037 Frisco (yellow)

REEFERS

50' THERMO-KING

490-9057 Olympia Beer (white) **6.98**

40' STEEL W/ICE HATCHES EA 11.98 (UNLESS NOTED)

490-8255 A. Y. Cleopatra

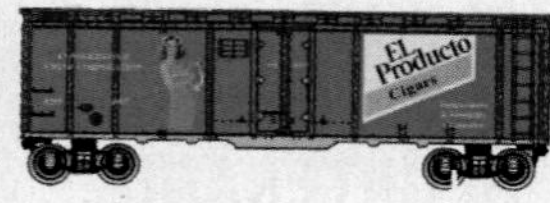

490-8256 El Producto
490-8257 Dutch Masters
490-8258 Muriel
490-8265 Muriel & Antonio Y Cleopatra **23.96**
490-8266 Dutch Masters & El Producto **23.96**

STOCK CARS

40' CATTLE CARS EA 5.98

490-6916 DRGW

490-8013 MKT (yellow)

HOPPERS

36' 2-BAY EA 4.98

COVERED

490-8080 N&W* (gray)
490-8081 Portland Cement* (gray)
490-8082 Ontario Northland* (blue)
490-8083 Jack Frost Cane Sugar* (gray, blue)
490-8084 Granite Rock* (orange)

OPEN

490-8060 L&N-Dixie Line* (gray)
490-8061 WM* (red)
490-8062 Frisco* (white)
490-8063 PRR* (Tuscan)
490-8064 SP* (red)
490-8065 CN
490-8066 C&O
490-8067 NYC

40' 4-BAY EA 4.98

490-6931 DRGW (orange)
490-6932 Illinois Central Gulf (orange)
490-6933 Peabody

490-8050 ATSF (red)
490-8051 PC (green)

40' Depressed Center Flat Car w/Searchlight 490-8220

40' Depressed Center Flat Car w/2 Cables & Figures 490-8221

54' Flat Car w/40' Trailer 490-8350

51' CYLINDRICAL COVERED GRAIN EA 10.98

490-9501 Canada (brown)
490-9502 Canada (silver)
490-9509 Wheat Board
490-9510 Heritage
490-9513 Canada (red)
490-9514 Saskatchewan

490-9515 Alberta (blue)
490-9516 Winnipeg
490-9517 CP

GONDOLAS

40' EA 4.98

490-8501 SP* (brown)
490-8502 PRR* (tuscan)

490-8503 SOU* (silver)
490-8504 CN* (tuscan)
490-8506 Soo* (white)
490-8507 Recycled Steel* (white)
490-8508 Recycled Steel* (black)
490-8509 CSX-B&O

FLAT CARS

40' DEPRESSED CENTER

WITH SEARCHLIGHT

490-8220 Safety* (red) **9.98**
All-metal car features dual electrical pickup, constant lighting and two handpainted figures.

WITH 2 CABLES & FIGURES EA 7.98

490-8221 ATSF*
490-8222 PRR*
490-8223 CN*
490-8224 Jet Copter Red

40' W/LOGS

490-8210 Burlington* (red) **6.98**

40' W/TWIN REMOVABLE TANKS EA 7.98

490-8160 Cities Service*

490-8161 Gulf* (blue w/white tanks)
490-8162 Sonoma Wine*
490-8163 Water Car*

54' W/40' TRAILER EA 12.98

490-8350 ATSF w/Union 76 Trailer
490-8351 PRR
490-8352 CR
490-8353 SP
490-8354 CP
490-8355 SOU w/US Mail Trailer
490-8356 CNW w/Fedex Trailer
490-8357 Schenker
490-8358 Union 76
490-8359 Phillips 66
490-8360 Conoco
490-8361 Marathon
490-8362 ATSF Unlettered
490-8363 TTX
490-8364 ATSF w/Sunkist
490-8365 Mason Dixon

50' W/TRAILER

490-6913 ATSF w/ATSF Trailer-Old **7.98**

WITH 50' TRACTOR & 32' TRAILER EA 14.98

490-6950 ATSF
490-6951 PRR
490-6952 US Mail
490-6953 US Army

WITH GRADER LOAD EA 13.98

490-6970 ATSF
490-6971 PRR
490-6972 Southern
490-9159 US Army

50' W/2 CONTAINERS EA 9.98

490-8303 ATSF
490-8304 PRR
490-8305 Trailer Train
490-8306 Southern
490-8307 DRGW
490-8308 Maine Casket Co.

40' W/GUARD RAILS EA 6.98

490-8230 ATSF *NEW**
490-8231 PRR *NEW**
490-8232 CP *NEW**
490-8233 SOU *NEW**

50' HEAVWYEIGHT

490-6962 With Red Copter * **13.98**

TANK CARS

50' HEATED EA 6.98

490-9083 Shell
490-9084 Tank Train (black)
490-9086 Hudson's Bay

40' EA 5.98

490-6920 Texaco (silver)
490-6921 DuPont (yellow, olive green)

490-8032 Cities Service Oils (green)
490-8033 Michigan Alkali Co. (white)
490-8034 Hooker
490-8035 Celeanese
490-8103 Shell

Limited Quantity Available
490-6923 Hooker (black)

CHEMICAL TANK CAR EA 5.98 (UNLESS NOTED)

490-8125

490-8101 Tank Train*
490-8102 Kodak*
490-8104 Hudson's Bay Oil & Gas* (yellow)
490-8105 Exxon*
490-8106 Texaco*
490-8108 Sunkist
490-8110 Champion Oil **6.98**
490-8111 Dominion Sugar Co. Ltd. **6.98**
490-8112 Imperial Oil Ltd. **6.98**
490-8119 Ashland Oil
490-8120 Union 76
490-8122 Phillips 66
490-8123 Conoco *NEW*
490-8124 Marathon
490-8125 SP
490-8126 MCP Corn

Limited Quantity Available
490-8107 Baker's Chocolate

CABOOSES

EXTENDED VISION

490-9113 36' Assortment pkg(12) 71.76 *NEW*
490-9165 Army (Olive Drab) **6.98**

36' BAY-WINDOW EA 5.98

490-8240 Safety*
490-8241 ATSF
490-8242 CR*
490-8243 PRR*
490-8244 SOU*
490-8245 BN*

490-8246 CN*
490-8247 SP*
490-8248 CP Rail

38'

Limited Quantity Available
490-9125 Safety (red) **5.98**

40' WORK EA 6.98

WITH TANK

490-8181 Amtrak*
490-8182 Weed Control*
490-8180 Undecorated* (white)

WITH CRANE EA 6.98

490-8191 ATSF*
490-8192 PRR
490-8193 DRGW
490-8194 C&O

WITH TOOL BOXES

490-8200 Safety First* (red, silver) **6.98**

32' WOOD EA 6.98

Wooden cabooses were used well into the 1950s by many railroads, so this handsome model is right at home behind your favorite steam or early diesel power.

490-9141 PRR
490-9142 B&O
490-9143 ATSF
490-9144 SP
490-9145 Southern
490-9146 DRGW
490-9147 CP
490-9148 CN
490-9149 Transfer

MAINTENANCE OF WAY

RAILROAD CRANE W/METAL WHEELS EA 24.95

490-9175 ATSF
490-9176 PRR
490-9177 AMTRAK
490-9178 Southern
490-9179 CN

CONTAINERS

WITH OPENING DOOR

490-7850 #1 pkg(4) **11.98**
490-7851 #2 pkg(4) **10.98**
490-7852 #3 pkg(4) **10.98**

TRAILERS

40' REEFER PKG(2) EA 10.98

490-7602 USDA Meat
490-7603 Union Ice
490-7600 Undecorated (black)
490-7601 Undecorated (white)

40' TANK PKG(2) EA 11.98

490-7622 Water
490-7623 General Cesspool
490-7620 Undecorated (white)
490-7621 Undecorated (black)

40' RACING PKG(2) EA 11.98

490-7642 Racing Dynamics
490-7643 Bekins
490-7640 Undecorated (black)
490-7641 Undecorated (white)

40' HEAVYWEIGHT W/OPERATING DOORS PKG(2) EA 11.98

490-6860 ATSF
490-6861 PRR
490-6862 UP
490-6863 Boston & Maine
490-6864 N&W
490-6865 NYC
490-6867 CP

Flat Car w/50' Tractor & 32' Trailer 490-6951

Flat Car w/Grader Load 490-6972

50' Heated Tank Car 490-9084

40' Work Caboose w/Crane 490-8191

32' Wood Caboose 490-9143

ORE CARS

TWO-PACKS EA 13.98

490-865 UP (silver) *NEW*
490-866 GN (green) *NEW*
490-867 CNW *NEW*
490-868 PRR *NEW*
490-869 Bessemer & Lake Erie *NEW*
490-870 CN (brown) *NEW*
490-871 ATSF *NEW*
490-872 Minnesota Smelting (orange) *NEW*

CHRISTMAS CARS

490-9700 4-Car Set **29.98**
Special Christmas set includes a Season's Greetings caboose, Millie's Egg Nog tank car, Christmas Tree box car and Mother's Apple Cider flat car with two tanks.

490-9701 4-Car Set **29.98**
Includes Season's Greetings box car, Holiday Express hopper, flat car with sleigh and Santa, and a white and gold caboose.

MILITARY ACTION CARS

U.S. ARMY FLAT CARS W/ROCO-MP MINI TANKS

OLIVE GREEEN EA 14.98
490-8450 Long Tom Gun Load
490-8452 With 2 Howitzers

490-8453 Sherman Tank Load *NEW*
490-8455 With Patton Tank
490-8459 With 2 Fords
490-8460 With Chaparrel AFV 15.98
490-8463 With Jeep & Trailer
490-8468 With Troop Carrier 15.98
490-8470 With Hummer & 20' Container
490-8472 With Desert Copter *NEW*

DESERT SAND EA 15.98
490-8461 With Half Track & Sherman Tank
490-8464 With 20' Fuel Container & Bradley APC
490-8458 With 2 Dodge 4x4 Trucks

CAMOUFLAGE EA 17.98
490-8451 Long Tom Gun Load
490-8454 With Half Track & Sherman Tank
490-8456 With 20' Container & Patton Tank
490-8457 With 2 Dodge 4x4 Trucks
490-8462 With Jeep & Trailer
490-8465 With 20' Fuel Container & Bradley AFV
490-8467 With Troop Carrier
490-8469 With Hummer & 20' Container

U.S. ARMY RAILROAD CARS

490-9159 With Grader **13.98**

490-9160 With M-47 Tank **13.98**
490-9180 With Launch & MS/S **14.98**

U.S. AIR FORCE

Models are decorated in U.S. Air Force colors of blue and white.

490-91611 Searchlight Command Center Car **12.98**

490-91621 Tank Buster Hidden Gun Car **12.98**

490-91641 Launcher w/Planes and Missiles **14.98**

490-91661 Tank Car **12.98**

MISCELLANEOUS

490-6953 Flat Car w/50' Tractor & Trailer **14.98**
490-9162 Hidden "Q Gun Car" **13.98**

490-9163 Big Thunder Railway Gun **14.98**

490-9164 Exploding Car When missile hits car, car "explodes" **14.98**
490-9165 Extended Vision Caboose **6.98**

TOMAR INDUSTRIES

PICK-UP SHOES PKG(4) EA 3.95

Shoes mount on the trucks of passenger cars, cabooses or locomotives. Kits include detailed installation drawings.

81-804 For Passenger Cars & Cabooses
81-805 For Locomotives

These undecorated HOn3 kits are made of laser-cut wood, injection-molded plastic and metal parts, unless otherwise noted. Detailed assembly instructions and drawings are provided. All kits are less trucks and couplers.

BOX CARS

D&RG 1878 STANDARD BOX CAR

464-417 18.95

COLORADO CENTRAL 24' BOX CAR

464-403 14.95

DENVER, SOUTH PARK & PACIFIC 27' WOOD BOX CAR

464-413 14.95

RGS 24' BOX CAR

464-419 18.95

REEFERS

DENVER, SOUTH PARK & PACIFIC 27' WOOD REEFER

The Tiffany Summer & Winter Car was one of the first cars built especially for refrigeration and the design was used for both standard- and narrow-gauge transit of perishables.

464-405 Undecorated **15.95**
464-406 With Decals **17.95** *NEW*

Skeleton Log Car 464-415

26' Flat/Gondola 464-407

18-Ton Ore Car 464-401

Covered Ore Car 464-411

FLAT CARS

RUSSEL WHEEL & FOUNDRY SKELETON LOG CARS

464-415 16.95
Used with minor variations on a number of Northwestern logging railroads including Mich-Cal Lumber Co., Carter Brothers Lumber and Feather River Lumber. Includes enough material and details for 2 cars.

DENVER, SOUTH PARK & PACIFIC 26' FLAT/GONDOLA

464-407 14.95
These kits include parts for any one of the following cars: flat car, lime car, two types of lumber cars, log car or coal loader. It can also be shortened to make a Colorado Central 23 or 24' gondola.

WEST SIDE STANDARD FLAT CAR - HON3

464-421 13.95 ***NEW***
Over 300 of these 24' flat car prototypes were constructed and used regularly in logging operations until the longer skeleton cars arrived in the 1940s. They were often rebuilt many times due to the rough treatment they received while in service.

ORE CARS

SILVER PLUME & MONTEZUMA 18-TON ORE CAR

464-401 16.95
These kits feature injection-molded plastic bodies and frame parts.

COLORADO CENTRAL COVERED ORE CAR

464-411 14.95
This unusual car was built in the Colorado Central shops from a flat car or gondola. The car may have been used to haul black powder or other commodities.

EXCURSION CARS

COLORADO CENTRAL EXCURSION CAR

464-409 14.95
The Colorado Central Railroad and its Georgetown Loop were famous tourist attractions known the world over. To supplement its regular passenger service and to provide a better scenic view of the mountains, the CC rebuilt six of its 26' flat cars into excursion cars.

RED CABOOSE

All freight car kits packaged after September 1, 1998, come with weights and Accumate® couplers except tank cars, which come with Accumate® couplers only.

BOX CARS

1937 AAR Single-Door Box Car 629-8037

40' Double Door-Door Box Car 629-8504

1937 AAR SINGLE-DOOR EA 14.95 (UNLESS NOTED)

629-8003 C&O
629-8004 Atlantic Coast Line with "W" Corner Post
629-8006 Indiana Harbor Belt with "W" Corner Post
629-8008 CN
629-8009 CP
629-8011 MON
629-8012 Florida East Coast
629-8013 DRGW
629-8014 ROCK
629-8015 NKP
629-8017 ATSF "Chief" w/Map
629-8018 ATSF "Texas Chief"
629-8019 ATSF "San Francisco Chief"
629-8020 L&N
629-8021 LV
629-8022 Maine Central
629-8023 Boston & Maine
629-8024 Minneapolis & St. Louis "The Peoria Gateway"
629-8025 Minneapolis & St. Louis
629-8027 Frisco
629-8028 NH
629-8031 IC
629-8032 Seaboard
629-8033 Seaboard "Silver Star"
629-8034 Seaboard "Silver Meteor"
629-8035 SOU
629-8036 SP Overnight (black)
629-8037 SP Overnight (silver)
629-8039 Texas & Pacific
629-8042 Virginian
629-8043 Western Pacific
629-8044 UP
629-8045 Pacific Great Eastern
629-8046 Norfolk Southern Railway (old)
629-8047 Illinois Terminal
629-8048 Lake Superior & Ishpeming
629-8049 Gulf, Mobile & Ohio
629-8050 SP "Express"
629-8051 SP/Texas & New Orleans
629-8052 C&O "For Progress"
629-8053 Pittsburgh & Lake Erie
629-8054 NYC
629-8055 Pittsburgh & Lake Erie "Steel Centers"
629-8056 Spokane, Portland & Seattle
629-8057 MKT
629-8058 Maine Central
629-8059 Wheeling & Lake Erie
629-8060 ATSF (MOW)
629-8061 Chicago Great Western
629-8062 Texas & New Orleans
629-8063 Clinchfield
629-8067 Wabash
629-80051 CB&Q
629-80052 Fort Worth & Denver
629-80053 Colorado & Southern
629-80102 Lackawanna "Phoebe Snow"
629-80161 D&H Large Herald
629-80261 NYC
629-80262 Pittsburgh & Lake Erie (red)
629-80263 Pittsburgh & Lake Erie (green)
629-80381 SP
629-80382 SP Initials
629-80411 UP
629-80412 Oregon Washington Railroad & Navigation Co.
629-80413 Oregon Short Line
629-8001 Undecorated Square Corner **11.75**
629-8002 Undecorated "W" Corner **11.75**

ATSF WITH MAP

629-80301 "El Capitan"
629-80302 "Scout"
629-80303 "Super Chief"
629-80304 "Grand Canyon"

UP

629-80401 "Serves All the West"
629-80402 Oregon Washington Railroad & Navigation Co.
629-80403 Oregon Short Line

X-29 Box Car 629-7024

CNW

629-80071 "Overland Route"-Omaha
629-80072 "Railway" Herald
629-80073 "Route of the 400 Fleet"

NP

629-80291 3' Herald
629-80292 4' Herald With "Mainstreet"
629-80293 4' NP Railway Herald With "Mainstreet"
629-80294 NP "Main St"

40' DOUBLE DOOR EA 14.95 (UNLESS NOTED)

629-8503 ATSF (MOW)
629-8504 Atlantic Coast Line
629-8505 CB&Q
629-8507 CNW
629-8508 MKT
629-8513 DRGW
629-8529 NP
629-8531 IC
629-8532 Seaboard
629-8535 SOU
629-8538 SP
629-8540 UP
629-8541 UP (yellow lettering)
629-8543 Western Pacific
629-8567 Wabash
629-85211 LV
629-85261 NYC **15.95**
629-8500 Undecorated "W" Corner **12.75**
629-8501 Undecorated Square Corner **12.75**

X-29

SINGLE CARS EA 15.95 (UNLESS NOTED)

629-7010 PRR "Circle Keystone" (steel plate ends)
629-7012 N&W
629-7014 Lehigh & New England
629-7016 Wheeling & Lake Erie
629-7018 C&O
629-7020 Boston & Maine
629-7022 EL
629-7024 PRR "Shadow Keystone"
629-7026 PRR "Merchandise Service" **16.95**
629-7028 PRR "Railway Express"
629-7030 PRR "Buy War Bonds"
629-7032 NKP
629-7034 Seaboard
629-7036 Maine Central
629-7038 Detroit, Toledo & Ironton
629-7040 Erie
629-7044 CNJ
629-7042 B&O
629-7046 RDG
629-7048 Chicago Great Western
629-7050 NYC
629-7052 Georgia Northern
629-7054 US Army Munitions
629-7056 High Point, Thomasville & Denton
629-7058 West India Fruit Express & Steamship
629-7060 Pere Marquette
629-7000 Undecorated '28 Body w/Steel Plate Ends
629-7002 Undecorated '24 Body w/Steel Plate Ends
629-7003 Undecorated AAR Body w/Steel Plate Ends

6-PACKS EA 95.70

629-7013 N&W
629-7015 Lehigh & New England
629-7017 Wheeling & Lake Erie
629-7019 C&O
629-7021 Boston & Maine
629-7023 EL
629-7033 NKP
629-7035 Seaboard
629-7037 Maine Central
629-7039 Detroit, Toledo & Ironton
629-7041 Erie
629-7045 CNJ
629-7047 RDG
629-7049 Chicago Great Western
629-7053 Georgia Northern
629-7055 US Army Munitions
629-7057 High Point, Thomasville & Denton
629-7059 West India Fruit Express & Steamship
629-7061 Pere Marquette

12-PACKS EA 191.40 (UNLESS NOTED)

629-7011 PRR "Circle Keystone" (steel plate ends)
629-7025 PRR "Shadow Keystone"
629-7027 PRR "Merchandise Service" **203.40**
629-7029 PRR "Railway Express"
629-7043 B&O
629-7051 NYC

ACF 4-3-1 10' 6" EA 14.95 (UNLESS NOTED)

All cars come in 6 road numbers unless otherwise noted.

RIVETED SIDES 6' DOOR

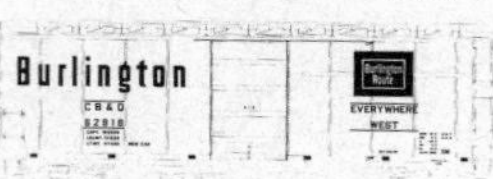

629-8601 CB&Q (Chinese Red) *NEW*
629-8602 Colorado & Southern "Way of the Zephyrs" (Box Car Red) *NEW*
629-8603 SOO (billboard) *NEW*
629-8604 Texas & Pacific (Box Car Red) *NEW*
629-8600 Undecorated **12.95** *NEW*

RIVETED SIDES 8' DOOR

629-8703 MP *NEW*
629-8704 Erie *NEW*
629-8705 B&O *NEW*
629-8706 Kansas City Southern *NEW*
629-8707 New Jersey, Indiana & Illinois (Wabash) *NEW*
629-8708 Texas & Pacific *NEW*
629-8709 Wabash *NEW*
629-8700 Undecorated **12.95** *NEW*

WELDED SIDES 8' DOOR

629-8901 Maine Central (Pine Green) *NEW*
629-8902 RDG (Box Car Red) *NEW*
629-8903 Western Pacific *NEW*
629-8904 Louisville & Nashville (blue) *NEW*
629-8905 Chicago & Eastern Illinois *NEW*
629-8906 Rock Island *NEW*
629-8900 Undecorated **12.95** *NEW*

REEFERS

WOOD REEFERS

SINGLE CARS EA 15.95 (UNLESS NOTED)

629-4421 Bangor & Aroostook (Reefer Orange)
629-4429 NP "Yellowstone Park"
629-4431 NP Herald
629-4433 Lackawanna
629-4435 NP "Northern Pacific" (yellow)
629-4437 Fruit Growers Express
629-4440 Merchants Despatch Transit
629-4442 Northern Refrigerator Line
629-4444 Boston & Maine
629-4446 Pacific Great Eastern (silver)
629-4448 Western Fruit Express w/GN Herald
629-4450 American Refrigerator Transport (shield)
629-4451 American Refrigerator Transport (MP/Wabash)
629-4461 Burlington Refrigerator Express
629-4462 Fort Worth & Denver
629-4463 Colorado & Southern

6-PACKS EA 95.70

629-4422 Bangor & Aroostook
629-4434 Lackawanna
629-4445 Boston & Maine
629-4447 Pacific Great Eastern (silver)

RED CABOOSE

12-PACKS EA 191.40
629-4430 NP "Yellowstone Park"
629-4432 NP Herald
629-4436 NP "Northern Pacific" (yellow)
629-4438 Fruit Growers Express
629-4441 Merchants Despatch Transit
629-4443 Northern Refrigerator Line
629-4449 Western Fruit Express w/GN Herald
629-4460 Burlington Refrigerator Express /FWD/CS

PACIFIC FRUIT EXPRESS/UNION PACIFIC R-30-12 WOOD REEFERS
629-4001 SP/UP "Overland" **15.95**
629-4013 SP/UP "Overland" 12-Pack **191.40**
629-4000 Undecorated **12.95**

PACIFIC FRUIT EXPRESS/WESTERN PACIFIC R-30-12 WOOD REEFERS
Reconditioned cars with wooden ice platforms and hatches, Equipco brake gear, ladders, K type brakes and Bettendorf trucks.

629-4221 Western Pacific/PFE w/Grab Irons **15.95**
629-4223 Western Pacific/PFE w/Grab Irons 12-Pack **191.40**

R-30-12-9 ICE SERVICE WOOD REEFERS
629-4114 SP/UP (orange) **15.95**
629-4115 SP/UP (orange) 6-Pack **95.70**
629-4214 Western Pacific (silver) **15.95**
629-4215 Western Pacific (silver) 6-Pack **95.70**

R-30-12-9 "RECONDITIONED" WOOD REEFERS
Reconditioned cars with wooden or steel ice hatches, Equipco brake gear, ladders, K type brakes or AB Brakes and Bettendorf trucks.

629-4151 SP/UP **15.95**
629-4153 SP/UP 12-Pack **191.40**
629-4231 Western Pacific/PFE **15.95**
629-4233 Western Pacific/PFE 12-Pack **191.40**
629-4120 SP/UP PFE (Script) **16.95**
629-4121 SP/UP PFE **15.95**
629-4122 SP/UP PFE **16.95**
629-4123 SP/UP PFE 12-Pack of 4121 **191.40**
629-4154 SP/UP PFE **15.95**
629-4155 SP/UP PFE 6-Pack **89.70**
629-4150 Undecorated (steel hatch) **12.95**
629-4250 Undecorated (wood hatch) **12.95**

WINE COMPANY R-30 REEFERS
629-4301 Roma Wine **16.95**
629-4302 Ambrose Wine **15.95**
629-4303 Bearcreek Vineyard Association **16.95**
629-4304 Fruit Industries **15.95**
629-4300 Undecorated **12.75**

37' MATHER MEAT REEFERS EA 15.95 (UNLESS NOTED)
629-1001 Mather (MRRX)
629-1002 Mather (MUNX)
629-1003 Armour
629-1004 Rath
629-1005 Morrell
629-1006 Cudahy
629-1007 Hygrade
629-1008 Swift
629-1009 Wilson
629-1010 Oscar Mayer
629-1011 Dubuque Packing Co.
629-1012 Rasking Packing Co., Inc.
629-1013 Sioux City Dressed Beef, Inc.
629-1014 Minnesota, Iowa, Dakotas
629-1015 Swift (silver)
629-1016 Iowa Beef Packers
629-1000 Undecorated **12.95**

R-30-12 Wood Reefer 629-4221

37' Mather Meat Reefer 629-1004

42' Flat Car 629-2219

GONDOLAS

DROP BOTTOM GONDOLAS EA TBA

WITH STEEL SIDES
629-50011 SP w/Black & White Herald ***NEW***
629-50021 UP ***NEW***
629-50031 Boston & Maine ***NEW***
629-50041 NP ***NEW***
629-50051 IC ***NEW***
629-50061 Western Pacific ***NEW***
629-50071 DRGW ***NEW***
629-50081 Maine Central ***NEW***
629-50091 SP w/White Herald ***NEW***
629-50101 GN ***NEW***
629-50111 CN ***NEW***
629-50121 CP ***NEW***
629-50001 Undecorated ***NEW***

WITH COMPOSITE SIDES
629-5101 SP w/Black & White Herald ***NEW***
629-5102 Western Pacific ***NEW***
629-5103 UP ***NEW***
629-5104 SP w/White Herald ***NEW***
629-5100 Undecorated ***NEW***

WITH COMPOSITE SIDES & SUGAR BEET EXTENSIONS
629-5177 SP w/Black & White Herald (board) ***NEW***
629-5178 SP w/White Herald (plywood) ***NEW***
629-5179 Western Pacific ***NEW***
629-5175 Undecorated w/Board Extensions ***NEW***
629-5176 Undecorated w/Plywood Extensions ***NEW***

10,000 Gallon Tank Car 629-3018

FLAT CARS

42' FLAT CARS EA 9.50 (UNLESS NOTED)
629-2203 NYC (black)
629-2204 SP (red)
629-2205 CNW (red)
629-2206 UP (red)
629-2207 C&O (black)
629-2208 ROCK (red)
629-2209 GN (red)
629-2210 Frisco (red)
629-2211 Northwestern Pacific (red)
629-2212 NP (black)
629-2213 DRGW (black)
629-2214 B&O (black)
629-2215 ATSF (brown)
629-2216 CP (black)
629-2217 Western Pacific (red)
629-2218 CN (red)
629-2219 B&M (black)
629-2220 SOO (red)
629-2221 NKP (red)
629-2222 MILW (red)
629-2223 SOU (red)
629-2224 NYC (red)
629-2225 CB&Q (red)
629-2226 PRR (red)
629-2227 Erie
629-2229 IC
629-2230 Gulf, Mobile & Ohio
629-2231 Wabash
629-2233 L&N
629-2234 NH
629-2235 LV
629-2237 Virgina &Truckee
629-2240 Dept. of Defense
629-2241 Railway Express Agency
629-2242 Atlantic Coast Line
629-2243 Texas & Pacific
629-2244 Grand Trunk Western
629-2245 Pere Marquette
629-2246 Seaboard
629-2247 Texas & New Orleans
629-2248 Duluth, South Shore & Atlantic
629-2249 EL
629-2250 Pacific Great Eastern
629-2251 MP
629-2252 Michigan Central
629-2253 SSW
629-2254 Wheeling & Lake Erie
629-2255 N&W
629-2256 MON
629-2257 Akron, Canton & Youngstown
629-2258 Central of Georgia
629-2259 Minneapolis & St. Louis
629-2260 Denver & Salt Lake
629-2261 El Paso & South Western
629-2262 Toledo, Peoria & Western
629-2263 Spokane International
629-2265 US Army
629-2201 Undecorated (black) **8.50**
629-2202 Undecorated (red) **8.50**

TANK CARS
Hauling all types of petroleum and chemical products, tank cars of this type first appeared in the late 40s. Built by the thousands in the 50s and 60s, some are still in diesel fuel or maintenance service today. Available in both HO and O Scale versions, the models look great behind steam and diesel power. Each kit features detailed plastic parts and comes prepainted and lettered.

10,000 GALLON TANK CARS 15.95 (UNLESS NOTED)
629-3001 Union Tank Car Line
629-3002 Shipper's Car Line
629-3003 Dupont
629-3004 Texaco
629-3005 Conoco
629-3006 Shell Oil
629-3007 Standard Oil
629-3008 Dow Chemical
629-3009 Gulf Oil
629-3010 Sunoco
629-3011 City Service
629-3012 Phillips 66
629-3013 Union 76
629-3014 Mobil
629-3015 Sinclair
629-3016 Deep Rock
629-3017 General American
629-3018 Flying A Oil
629-3019 Richfield
629-3020 Carter Petrol
629-3021 Roma Wine
629-3022 Fruit Industries Limited Wine
629-3023 Ambrose Wines
629-3024 Conoco
629-3025 Magnolia
629-3026 Skelgas
629-3027 Anchor
629-3028 Arrow
629-3029 Humble
629-3030 Warren
629-3031 Dow 2nd Number
629-3032 US Army
629-3033 Koppers
629-3034 Pure
629-3035 Shamrock
629-3036 SP
629-3037 PRR
629-3038 ATSF
629-3039 NYC
629-3040 Data Only Black
629-3041 Data Only Silver
629-3042 Bakelite
629-3043 Frisco
629-3044 Atlantic Coast Line
629-3000 Undecorated **13.95**

These detailed HO Scale models are fully assembled and painted in authentic colors.

Snow Plow w/Working Headlight 635-2290

Big Boy Set 1 635-6991

Big Boy Set 2 635-6992

Old Timer Set 635-6990

28' Logging Buggy 635-2349

LOGGING BUGGY

635-2349 Logging Buggy **19.00**
Car is complete with wooden logs tied down by real chain. Each buggy is 4 x 1-7/8".

SNOW PLOW

SNOW PLOW W/WORKING HEADLIGHT

635-2290 UP **21.99**
Headlight is battery operated, battery not included.

FREIGHT CAR SETS

BIG BOY SET 1

635-6991 49.99
Includes the following: CN reefer, Santa Fe stock car, Soo Line hopper, Union Pacific gondola, "Miller" MHLX box car and Norfolk & Western caboose.

BIG BOY SET 2

635-6992 49.99
Includes the following: New Haven box car, Missouri & St. Louis hopper, Fruit Growers Express reefer, MKT stock car, Boston & Maine gondola and Union Pacific caboose.

OLD TIMER SIX CAR FREIGHT SET

635-6990 74.99
Includes the following: Southern Pacific box car, ATSF gondola with coal, Virginia & Truckee flat car, gondola, tank car and caboose.

IMPORTED FROM AUSTRIA BY WALTHERS

Roco models are prepainted and lettered in authentic period schemes. Each car is fully assembled and ready-to-run with NEM style couplers (unless noted).

BOX CARS

625-46654 DR w/Warning Markings Era III (Box Car Red) **23.99** ***NEW***
625-46655 DRG w/Smooth Roof & Ends Era II (Box Car Red) **21.99** ***NEW***
625-46742 DB Era III (Box Car Red) **22.99** ***NEW***

625-46743 DR, "Motorräder aus Zschopau" Era IV (Box Car Red) **29.99** ***NEW***
625-46829 DR Contractor's Supply Car Era III (gray) **19.99** ***NEW***
625-46833 FS Era IV/V (oxide, gray roof) **23.99** ***NEW***
625-46839 DB Era IV (Box Car Red) **TBA** ***NEW***
625-46843 DB Era III (Box Car Red) **22.99** ***NEW***
625-46845 DBS Dresden Era IV (Box Car Red) **21.99** ***NEW***
625-47270 DB 2-Axle Car w/Chalk Markings Era IV (Box Car Red) **16.99** ***NEW***

G10 CLASS EA 16.99 (UNLESS NOTED)

625-46820 DB 1945-68 **17.99**
625-46822 DRG-Unbraced Ends (brown)
625-46825 KBAY (green)

33' BARREL ROOF OUTSIDE BRACED CAR

625-46014 DB, Steel (Box Car Red) **9.99**

35' OUTSIDE BRACED WOOD CAR

625-46105 DB (Box Car Red) **22.99**

35' CAR GMS-54 EA 24.99

625-46256 DB, With Brakeman's Platform (Box Car Red)
625-46259 DB, Converted Crew Car

46' BOX CAR

625-46210 DB, Taes 891 (Box Car Red) **24.99**
Roof moves sideways.

RIV EUROP TYPE

1950s European freight car pool markings.
625-46823 OBB **16.99**
625-46835 NS Ventilated **22.99**
625-46836 DB **19.99**

34' BARREL ROOF OUTSIDE BRACED WOOD CAR

625-46016 DB (Box Car Red) **9.99**

35' BARREL ROOF OUTSIDE BRACED STEEL CAR

625-46408 DB, Class 254 **24.99**

Limited Quantity Available
625-46052 DB Lowenbrau **14.99**

30' WOOD CARS

625-46001 DB (Box Car Red) **9.99**

59' BOX CAR

Limited Quantity Available
625-46222 Bromberg (Box Car Red) **29.99**

39' VENTILATED CARS

625-46457 SNCF, GS **27.99**
625-46830 DB Gs Class **19.99**

625-46831 SBB K4 Class **22.99**

46' ALL DOOR CAR

625-46456 SJ Class Hbi KKS (blue, silver) **25.99**

MOVABLE SIDEWALL VANS

625-46509 Hbbillns FS **28.99**
625-46511 DR Type Hbbillns **29.99**
625-46641 Tbis SBB **27.99**

Limited Quantity Available
625-46593 Jelmoli/SBB **24.99**

SMOOTH SIDEWALL VAN

625-46597 Hbis "Chocolate Frey" SBB **25.99**

625-46636 DB/Fewa Era III (white, oxide ends) **31.99** ***NEW***
625-46639 SJ/SKF Steel Hellefors Era IV (white, blue) **TBA** ***NEW***
625-46647 DB **26.99**
625-46648 SBB Zuckermuhle Rupperswil A.G. **31.99**
625-46814 British Railways/Transfesa Era V (blue, silver) **29.99** ***NEW***

625-46920 Czech Republic-CD **26.99**
625-46921 DB-AG DB-Cargo (red) **26.99**

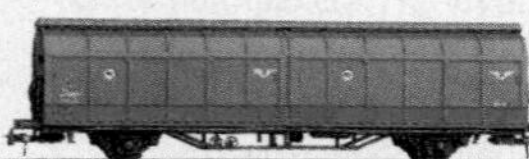

625-46922 SJ (blue, red) **26.99**
625-46923 ÖBB "Rail Cargo Austria" **29.99**
625-46926 Hungary-MAV (silver) **25.99**
625-46927 Finnish Railways (VR) Era V (Steel Gray) **34.99** ***NEW***
625-46928 SJ Nordwaggon (gray, silver, blue) Era V **34.99** ***NEW***
625-46932 DSB Era V (gray, white) **34.99** ***NEW***
625-46936 DB/ATA Era IV (white, oxide ends) **34.99** ***NEW***
625-47130 DB/Danzas Cargowaggon Era V (blue, silver, orange) **TBA** ***NEW***

DOUBLE BOX CAR

625-46121 DB, "Leig" Unit Gllm(e)hs 52 **44.99**

FERRYBOAT BOX CAR

625-46324 DB, "Tiphook" **29.99**

NARROW GAUGE CAR

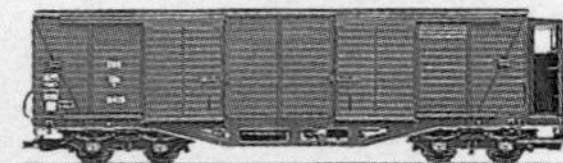

625-34526 OBB, GGm **28.99**

MARIAZELL CARS

625-34520 Type OOm Gondola, Era III-IV **25.99**
625-34521 Type SSm Flat Car, Era III-IV **25.99**
625-34522 Type GGm Box Car, Era III-IV **28.99**

Hungary-MAV (silver) 625-46926

G10 Class 625-46825

Smooth Sidewall Van 625-46923

REEFERS

625-44143 DB/"Diebels Bier" Car & Truck Set (white) **TBA** ***NEW***
Includes matching insulated box car and Opel Blitz beer delivery truck, in white with colorful Diebels Bier graphics and lettering.

625-46881 DB/Interfrigo ICF Banana Carrier (yellow, gray, green) **29.99** ***NEW***

625-46880 DB-AG/Interfrigo Banana Car WAI 28 B **29.99**

48' CLOSED RIB REEFER

625-46403 DB "Transthermos" **25.99**

REFRIGERATOR VAN

625-46235 DB Class T38 **19.99**
625-46556 Interfrigo/Spar **29.99**

Limited Quantity Available
625-46555 FS, Interfrigo **27.99**

STOCK CARS

STOCK CAR

625-46035 35' DB, For Sheep (tuscan) **9.99**

HOPPERS

625-44150 Kirow Liepzeg Ballast Cars Era V (oxide) pkg(2) **79.99** ***NEW***

625-46389 Grain Car Tppps SBB **29.99**

SIDE DUMP HOPPERS

23' EA 23.99

625-46128 DB "Talbot" (Box Car Red)
625-46130 DRG, "Stuttgart" (Box Car Red)

IMPORTED FROM AUSTRIA BY WALTHERS

32'
625-46132 DB "Talbot" (Box Car Red) **28.99**
625-46248 NS-BL (blue) **31.99**
625-46432 SNCF (Box Car Red) **31.99**

625-46679 DB-AG **29.99**

Limited Quantity Available
625-46433 DR **32.99**

GRAVEL WAGON

625-44128 DB Class 266 pkg(2) **79.99**

SWIVEL ROOF CARS

625-46725 DB-AG DB Cargo (red) **29.99**
625-46731 DR "Getreide" (brown) **27.99**
625-48082 Czech Republic-CD Class TDS **29.99**

BALLAST HOPPER

625-44138 DB/Rurkohle-AG Self-Unloading Car Set Era IV/V pkg(3) **94.99** ***NEW***

625-46728 DSB Ballast Class Fccs (brown) **26.99**

GARBAGE DUMP CAR

Limited Quantity Available
625-46345 "Vam Compost" (green) **31.99**

40' 8 WHEEL HOPPER EA 29.99

625-46239 DB oot 42 (Box Car Red)
625-46242 DRG (Box Car Red)

49' 12 WHEEL HOPPER EA 36.99 (UNLESS NOTED)

625-46250 DB/Peine & Salzgitter (Box Car Red)

625-46251 DB (Box Car Red)
625-46919 DB-AG DB-Cargo Class Faals (red) **33.99**

COVERED HOPPERS

625-46432 SNCF (Box Car Red) **31.99**
625-46852 BLS-Herald Cement Carrier Era V (gray) **TBA** ***NEW***
625-46951 Slovenian Railways (SV) Swivel-Roof Car (oxide) **29.99** ***NEW***

625-46958 DB Swivel-Roof Car Era IV (oxide) **29.99** ***NEW***
625-47169 DB/BO-SCH-KI Five-Compartment Era IV/V **34.99** ***NEW***
625-47320 DR Coal Dust Hopper Era III **TBA** ***NEW***

WOOD HOPPER

625-34510 Industrial Railway pkg(2) **25.99**

GONDOLAS

625-46614 DR w/20' Container **17.99**
625-46617 Hi-side, DB Omm 55 **13.99**
625-46892 Hungarian Railways (MAV) Era V (red) **14.99** ***NEW***
625-46894 BLS w/Real Wood Load Era IV (oxide) **TBA** ***NEW***
625-46948 SNCB RIV EUROP Era III (Box Car Red) **8.99** ***NEW***

625-46952 DB Era V (oxide) **12.99** ***NEW***
625-47201 DB-AG Era V (oxide) **TBA** ***NEW***
625-47203 DR Era IV (oxide) **TBA** ***NEW***

Limited Quantity Available
625-16071 DB Type Tamns 893 **36.99**

27' GONDOLAS EA 9.99

625-46011 DB, Low Side
625-46043 DB, High Side

30' GONDOLA

625-46039 DB (Box Car Red) **9.99**

31' GONDOLA

625-46280 DRG w/Brakeman's Cabin (Box Car Red) **18.99**
625-46612 Open DSB Riv Europ w/Ramp **12.99**
625-46696 Open Container, DR Om 21 (brown) **8.99**
625-46890 Open SBB E (brown) **12.99**
625-46949 Open CFL Riv Europ **8.99**
625-46950 Open OBB w/Ramp (brown) **12.99**

33' GONDOLA

625-46010 DB (Box Car Red) **9.99**

FLAT CARS

625-839 DRG 2-Axle w/2 VW Kubelwagens (gray) Era II **39.99** ***NEW***

625-841 DB German Army Heavy-Duty Flat w/Gepard Tank Era IV/V **59.99** ***NEW***
Modern Gepard tank in camouflage paint. Models come in special presentation box.

625-1910 With Helicopter **34.99**
625-46116 DB, w/2 Containers **25.99**
625-46492 DB Rail Carrier With Rail **39.99**

625-46486 Royal Saxonian Railways Class R10 w/Log Load (brown) **29.99**
625-46528 DB Carrier Flat w/3 Sudzucker Containers **41.99**

625-46538 DB Carrier Wagon w/5 "Haus zu Haus" Containers DB **39.99**
625-46570 "P&O" w/40' Container **54.99**
625-46572 "Barilla" **54.99**

625-46580 SNFC w/40' Container "CNC" **49.99**
625-46584 DB-AG "DB-Cargo" **49.99**
625-46588 SNCB Well Flat w/Hyundai Trailer **49.99**
625-46912 DB Carrier Flat w/SBB Container **24.99**

625-47001 DB-AG Standard w/2 Schenker 20' Reefer Containers **49.99**

625-47002 DB-AG Standard w/3-Axle Slide-Tarpaulin "Burger King" Trailer **45.99**
625-47003 ÖBB "Rail Cargo Austria" w/2 Containers **49.99**
625-47045 DR w/Side Stakes, Guard's Cabin & Load Era III (Box Car Red) **TBA** ***NEW***
625-47193 K.Bay.St.B w/Stakes & Log Load (black) Era I **TBA** ***NEW***
625-47195 DB Heavy-Duty Car w/Side Stakes & Pipe Load Era IV (black) **TBA** ***NEW***

HEAVY DUTY CAR

625-46385 DR **22.99**

35' DEPRESSED CENTER WELL CAR

625-46380 DB (Box Car Red, black) **22.99**

40' CAR

625-46576 DB w/"Arcus Logistic" **49.99**

49' CUSHION CAR

625-46110 DB (black) **19.99**

STAKED CARS

625-1907 With 2 Mercedes Tractors **49.99**

35'
625-46031 DB **9.99**
625-46482 DB w/Brakeman's Platform **26.99**

45'
625-46313 OBB **23.99**
625-46315 SNCF **23.99**
625-46481 DB, Class R10 w/Brakeman's Cabin (Box Car Red) **26.99**
625-46490 DB, "Cologne," Class SS15 **39.99**

Limited Quantity Available
625-46322 SNCF w/20' Container **28.99**

TARPAULIN COVERED CARS

625-46661 NS Cargo Era V (red) **34.99** ***NEW***
625-46780 DB w/3 Containers "Cho Yang" **44.99**
625-46914 DB "On Rail" Era V **TBA** ***NEW***

625-46916 SNCF S58 Class **31.99**
625-46917 SNCB "B-Cargo" Scheme **32.99**

625-46941 ÖBB Steel Stahlwaggon Era V (blue) **34.99** ***NEW***
625-1905 With Tractors **49.99**

Limited Quantity Available
625-46560 SNCB, w/2 20' Containers **49.99**
625-46563 OBB Double Flat Car, w/4 20' Containers **79.99**

54' CARS W/CONTAINER EA 49.99 (UNLESS NOTED)

625-46377 SNCF w/Regular Flatbed (gray, white, green)

Limited Quantity Available
625-46371 SBB/Jacky Maeder **44.99**
625-46372 OBB/LKW Augustin **44.99**
625-46374 SNCF/Guyon (gray, bright blue)
625-46379 OBB w/2 Flatbeds

CONTAINERS FOR FLAT CARS

Limited Quantity Available
625-40060 Containers (red, gray) pkg (2) **10.99**

STEEL TRANSPORTS

625-44125 CFL Set **139.99**
Includes large 2-truck flat with a pair of 4-wheel idler cars; used to safely move oversize loads

625-46553 DB Coil Transporter w/4 Coils **33.99**
625-46779 RENFE Coil Transporter w/3 Coils **33.99**

625-46778 SNCB Coil Transporter w/Removable Coils Era IV (oxide) **29.99** ***NEW***

INTERMODAL EQUIPMENT

625-47014 DSB w/2 Ceres/Strongale Export Breweries Containers Era V (brown) **49.99** ***NEW***

625-47098 SNCF w/2 Intercontainer ICF Containers Era V (Box Car Red) **34.99** ***NEW***
625-47100 DB Six-Axle Articulated Car w/Containers Era IV **TBA** ***NEW***
Suitable for small radii; containers can be removed.

IMPORTED FROM AUSTRIA BY WALTHERS

STANDARD WELL FLATS

625-46574 RENFE w/2 20' Containers Era V (blue) **49.99** *NEW*
625-47008 SNCB w/Arthur Pierre & Maersk Containers Era V (orange) **TBA** *NEW*
625-47013 DB w/2 Skandi Containers Era IV (oxide) **49.99** *NEW*
625-47016 SBB w/2 Removable Containers Era V (gray) **49.99** *NEW*
625-47017 DB-AG w/Kitekat Reefer 3-Axle Trailer Era V (red) **TBA** *NEW*

COWL CARS

625-46776 SJ Shimmns (blue) **23.99**
625-46918 DB-AG DB-Cargo (red) Class Sahmms 900 **24.99**

625-47191 SBB/Tiphook Rail Era V (blue, black) **24.99** *NEW*

39' CARS

625-46284 DB, Telescoping (Box Car Red) **25.99**
625-46292 FS, Telescoping (Box Car Red, gray) **25.99**
625-46294 SNCB, Shis **25.99**

Limited Quantity Available
625-44076 39' Flat Standard DB 2-Cars **49.99**
625-46517 DR Cowl Flat, Shims 708 **25.99**

49' TELESCOPING CAR

625-46286 DB (Box Car Red) **26.99**

TANK CARS

625-46076 DB, Bogies Tank Car of VTG **29.99**
625-46329 Brandt/VTG **22.99**
625-46666 SBB, Tank Wagon "Motorex" **29.99**
625-46668 SBB, Tank Wagon, VTG Leased to AGIP **32.99**

625-46702 DB, Tank Car "KVG" **26.99**
625-46706 DB/Wacker Chemie Era III (blue, black) **TBA** *NEW*
625-46716 DB, Chlorine Tank Car of VTG, **35.99**
625-46783 Slovenian Railways-SZ Petrol (silver) **33.99**
625-46785 ÖBB/ÖMV Propane Gas w/Shield Era V (white, orange stripe) **39.99** *NEW*
625-46786 DR/Waggon Union Propane Gas w/Shield Era IV (white, orange stripe) **39.99** *NEW*
625-46787 DB/Westfallen AG Propane Gas Era IV (white, orange stripe) **39.99** *NEW*
625-46788 Hungarian Railways (MAV) MOL Propane Gas Era V (white, orange stripe) **TBA** *NEW*
625-46797 DB/Swiss Etra Propane Gas w/Shield Era V (white, orange stripe) **39.99** *NEW*
625-46798 Slovakian Railways-ZSR Pressurized Slovnaft Gas **39.98**
625-46978 SNCB/KVG-Esso Switzerland Era V (black) **34.99** *NEW*
625-47063 DB/Lowenbrau Era IV (blue-green) **TBA** *NEW*
625-47067 CFL/Gulf Oil Era IV (silver, black w/orange & blue logo) **29.99** *NEW*
625-47068 ÖBB/Castrol Era V (green ends, white body) **34.99** *NEW*
625-47072 DB/Texaco Era IV/V (blue-green w/logo) **34.99** *NEW*
625-47080 SBB/VTG/Kemira Era V (white, orange stripe) **24.99** *NEW*
625-47081 DB/VTG Era III (white, orange stripe) **24.99** *NEW*

625-47091 DR Drinking Water Service Era IV (gray, black) **21.99** *NEW*

29' CARS

625-46662 SBB Rexwal (gray) **29.99**
625-46675 ÖBB OMV **29.99**
625-46708 DB-AG Minol **21.99**
625-46710 CFL Shell **19.99**
625-47078 DR (silver) **19.99**

29' CAR (220HL)

625-46143 DB/VTG **21.99**

47' CARS

625-46072 DB/EVA, 220hl (black, white, orange) **34.99**

625-46188 DB/VTG, 400hl (gray) **26.99**

625-46712 OBB Schwechat 2000 **39.99**

TANK CAR SETS

625-44113 SBB, Tank Wagon Set "Esso Chemical" "Esso Lubeoil" **64.99**

Limited Quantity Available
625-14108 DB Assorted **89.99**
625-16118 DB, Tank Wagon "Esso" **28.99**
625-44073 DB 88OHL Tank 3-Car Set **99.99**
625-46616 Agip/DB **34.99**
625-48040 AS Praha **12.99**

SILO WAGONS

625-46473 DB, UCS 909 **34.99**
625-46474 VTG Type Kds 56 **29.99**

625-46477 DB, Silo Car-"Dykerhoff" **39.99**

625-46715 CEVA OBB **32.99**

625-46860 NS (gray) **29.99**
625-46862 DSB Phoenix **31.99**
625-46864 SJ Cementa **29.99**

Limited Quantity Available
625-44035 DB Kds 56 Silo Car Set **74.98**
625-44073 DB 88OHL Tank 3-Car Set **99.99**

Crane & Jib Car 625-46331

CABOOSES/VANS

625-46960 SBB Class Db "Sputnik" Era IV (green) **TBA** *NEW*

MOW EQUIPMENT

625-1926 DSB Hy-Rail Unimog (Unpowered) Era V (yellow) **19.99** *NEW*
625-47170 Swivel Stanchion Flat for Truck Transport Era V (blue) **TBA** *NEW*

35' MOW BOX CAR

623-34525 OBB HOe **28.99**

CRANE & JIB CAR

625-46331 DB **44.99**

MISCELLANEOUS CARS

TRACK CLEANING CAR

Clean track is essential to your layout, but out-of-scale hands can't reach everywhere. Roco Track Cleaning Cars go where the track goes. Rails are cleaned quickly and easily in hard-to-reach spots, in tunnels, beneath catenary and next to delicate scenery. Just couple a Roco track cleaner into your train and start cleaning! As the car is pulled, the soft-abrasive pad wipes away grime without scratching rail surfaces.

625-46400 Roco **29.99**
625-40019 Replacement Wiper **9.99**
For use with #46400.

AUTO TRANSPORTER

625-46467 DB-AG "DB-Autozug" DDm (blue) **46.99**

625-46468 DB-AG DDm915 (red) **46.99**
625-46630 DB Modern (With 10 Cars) **79.99**
625-46634 SBB Articulated Goth Transports (blue) **79.99**

Limited Quantity Available
625-1900 DB w/Vehicles (Forest Green) **89.99**
625-46460 DB (Forest Green) **49.99**
625-46462 OBB (red) **49.99**
625-46465 DB, Class DDm 915 (green) **49.99**

39' COIL CAR

625-46304 SNCB (Box Car Red) **25.99**
With 5 sheet metal coils.

WOOD WRECK CAR

625-46212 DB, 75' (yellow) **31.99**

COLLECTOR CAR SETS

BERLIN BLOCKADE SET

625-43145 DR Class 50 2-10-0 w/4 Freight Cars **TBA** *NEW*
Commemorates the early days of the post-war German Railways, when Berlin was divided into four occupation zones. Railroads transported US and British troops into the western zones, along with many daily essentials. Set includes powered 2-10-0 steamer with US and English flags on smokebox front, two DR box cars, an empty high-side DR gondola and a high-side DR gondola with brakeman's cabin and a load of coal.

These easy-to-build HO Scale kits feature one-piece plastic bodies, prepainted and lettered for a variety of railroads. Trucks, couplers and weights are included.

BOX CARS

36' BILLBOARD BOX CAR EA 6.98

480-3022

480-3021 Standard Wagon (Box Car Red)
480-3022 Lindsay Brothers (green)
480-3023 Ball Glass Jar Company (Box Car Red)
480-3024 NK Fairbanks (Box Car Red)
480-3025 Hercules Powder Company (gray)
480-3026 Racine Wagon
480-3020 Undecorated

36' OLD TIME BOX EA 6.98

480-3281 SP
480-3282 PRR
480-3283 Virginia & Truckee
480-3284 NH
480-3285 DRGW
480-3286 CNW
480-3287 Kansas City, Mexico & Orient (Large Orient)
480-3288 Atlanta & West Point
480-3289 B&O
480-3290 Maryland & Pennsylvania
480-3291 Salt Lake Route (brown)
480-3292 Nevada Copper Belt (brown)
480-3293 Colorado Midland
480-3294 CP
480-3295 Oregon Short Line
480-3296 New York Central & Hudson River *NEW*
480-3297 PRR - Empire Line *NEW*
480-3298 C&O **7.98** *NEW*
480-3280 Undecorated

40' AAR BOX CAR EA 6.25 (UNLESS NOTED)

480-1041 BN (BN Cascade Green)
480-1042 PRR (Box Car Red)
480-1043 NKP
480-1044 UP (Box Car Red)
480-1047 GN (silver)
480-1048 DRGW (white)
480-1049 CN (Tuscan)
480-1050 SP "Overnight" (black)
480-1051 ATSF - Map Side
480-1053 B&O (dark blue)
480-1054 NP
480-1056 CP (Tuscan)
480-1057 Spokane, Portland & Seattle
480-1062 CP Rail (red) **7.25**
480-1063 Ontario Northland (blue)
480-1064 British Columbia Railway (Olive Green)
480-1066 CN (Box Car Red)
480-1067 NYC **7.25**
480-1068 B&O (Box Car Red)
480-1069 Western Pacific (Tuscan)
480-1070 C&O "For Progress" (Box Car Red)
480-1071 SP "Overnight" (silver)
480-1072 C&O/REA (green)
480-1073 SOO (Tuscan)
480-1074 Frisco (Tuscan)
480-1075 Western Pacific w/Feather (orange)
480-1076 Erie (Mineral Red)
480-1077 ATSF (Mineral Red)
480-1078 WM, Speed Lettering (Tuscan)
480-1079 WM (Tuscan)
480-2041 NYC "Early Bird" (Mineral Red)
480-2042 Pittsburgh & Lake Erie (Mineral Red)
480-2043 Pittsburgh & Lake Erie (Jade Green)
480-2044 Peoria & Eastern (Mineral Red)
480-2045 MKT
480-2046 NYC Pacemaker (red, gray) **8.00**
480-2047 NYC Pacemaker (brown, white lettering)
480-1040 Undecorated

40' HORIZONTAL RIB BOX CAR EA 6.25 (UNLESS NOTED)

480-1025

These kits include operating doors.

480-1021 MILW Olympian (Tuscan)
480-1022 MILW Hiawatha (Tuscan)
480-1023 Chicago, Milwaukee, St. Paul & Pacific Olympian (Tuscan)
480-1024 Chicago, Milwaukee, St. Paul & Pacific Hiawatha (Tuscan)
480-1025 Western Pacific (orange)
480-1026 MILW **7.50**
480-1020 Undecorated

40' MODERN BOX CAR EA 6.25 (UNLESS NOTED)

480-1106

480-1101 SP (Box Car Red)
480-1102 SOO (Box Car Red)
480-1103 BN (BN Cascade Green)
480-1104 CP (Tuscan)
480-1105 SOU (Box Car Red) **6.98**
480-1106 ATSF (Box Car Red)
480-1107 EL (Tuscan)
480-1108 CB&Q
480-1109 Frisco
480-1110 Pickens
480-1111 Grand Trunk Western
480-1112 Gulf, Mobile & Ohio
480-1113 MKT
480-1114 CNW
480-1115 RDG
480-1116 Green Bay & Western
480-1117 Minneapolis, Northfield & Southern
480-1118 Western Pacific
480-1100 Undecorated

40' ROUND TOP BOX CAR EA 6.25

These kits include operating doors.

480-1081 PRR (Tuscan)
480-1082 Bessemer & Lake Erie (Tuscan)
480-1083 N&W (Tuscan)
480-1084 Seaboard Air Line (Tuscan)
480-1085 B&O (Tuscan)
480-1086 ATSF
480-1087 NP (brown)
480-1088 B&O (REA Blue)
480-1089 B&O (REA Green)
480-1080 Undecorated

40' TRUSS SIDE BOX CAR EA 6.25

480-1034

480-1027 Frisco
480-1028 CNW
480-1029 C&O
480-1031 ATSF (Tuscan)
480-1032 Seaboard (Tuscan)
480-1033 CB&Q (Tuscan)
480-1034 SP (Tuscan)
480-1035 NKP (Box Car Red)
480-1036 Erie (Box Car Red)
480-1037 Boston & Maine
480-1038 Akron, Canton & Youngstown
480-1039 Chicago & Eastern
480-1030 Undecorated

50' BOX CAR EA 6.25 (UNLESS NOTED)

480-1190 CB&Q **7.50**
480-1191 Green Bay & Western (green) **7.50**
480-1192 Penn Central (green) **7.50**
480-1199 CR (Box Car Red)
480-1201 DRGW
480-1202 IC (orange)
480-1203 CN (Box Car Red)
480-1207 Seaboard Coast Line
480-1209 Wabash (red)
480-1210 PRR/REA (Olive)
480-1211 UP (Box Car Red)
480-1212 GN (orange, green)
480-1215 SOU (brown)
480-1216 SP (red, gray)
480-1219 UP/Map **9.98**
480-1220 Western Pacific (orange) **7.25**
480-1221 Western Pacific (Mineral Red) **7.25**
480-1222 ATSF Modern (Box Car Red)
480-1223 EL (Box Car Red)
480-1200 Undecorated

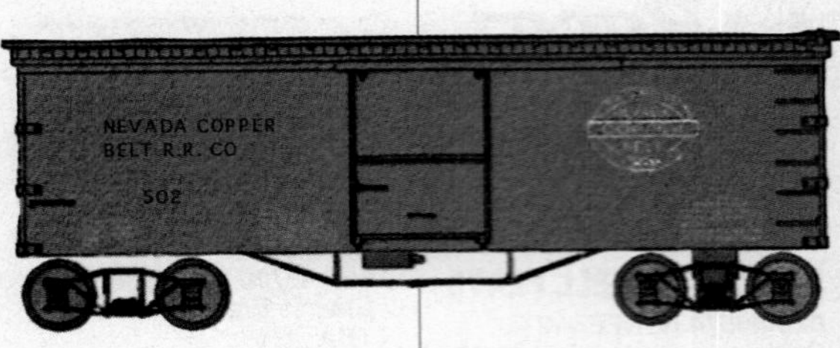

36' Old Time Box Car 480-3292

40' AAR Box Car 480-2046

40' Round Top Box Car 480-1087

50' Flat Top Hi Cube 480-1767

50' Ribbed Side Flat Top Hi Cube 480-1823

50' FLAT TOP HI CUBE EA 7.25 (UNLESS NOTED)

These kits have single plug doors.

480-1761 UP (Tuscan) **8.50**
480-1762 EL (blue)
480-1763 Seaboard Coast Line (black)
480-1764 BN (Cascade Green)
480-1765 ATSF (black, red)
480-1766 SP (Box Car Red)
480-1767 Golden West Service **8.00**
480-1768 SP (Speed Lettering)
480-1769 C&O
480-1760 Undecorated

50' RIBBED SIDE FLAT TOP HI CUBE EA 7.25

These kits have single plug doors.

480-1821 ATSF (red, black)
480-1822 CR (Tuscan)
480-1823 BN
480-1824 SP (Box Car Red)

480-1825 Ontario Northland (dark blue)
480-1826 C&O (black)
480-1827 SOO (white, red door)
480-1828 Frisco (beige)
480-1820 Undecorated

50' FLAT TOP (WAFFLE SIDE) EA 7.25

480-1801 Seaboard Coast Line (Box Car Red)
480-1802 L&N
480-1803 D&H (Reefer Yellow)
480-1804 SP (Box Car Red)
480-1805 BN (Cascade Green)
480-1806 Chessie (Royal Blue)
480-1807 UP/Rock Island (blue)
480-1808 Frisco (beige)
480-1809 L&N - Family Lines
480-1800 Undecorated

50' FLAT TOP HI CUBE EA 7.25 (UNLESS NOTED)

These kits have double plug doors.

480-1781 UP **8.00**
480-1782 SP (Box Car Red)
480-1783 ATSF (black, red)
480-1784 CR (Tuscan)
480-1785 N&W (black)
480-1786 Western Pacific (Tuscan)
480-1787 UP Automated (silver, yellow) **9.98**
480-1780 Undecorated

50' FMC 1-1/2 DOOR BOX EA 7.25 (UNLESS NOTED)

These kits include combination door-sliders and plug door.

480-1931 Railbox (yellow) **9.98**
480-1932 Seaboard Coast Line (Box Car Red)
480-1933 MP (Box Car Red)
480-1934 Minnesota, Dakota & Western (white, green door)
480-1935 BN (Cascade Green)
480-1936 BCR (light green) **8.00**
480-1937 UP (Tuscan)
480-1938 ABOX (Railbox) **9.98**
480-1944 Railbox (CN) (yellow) **9.98**
480-1930 Undecorated

50' FMC SINGLE DOOR BOX EA 7.25 (UNLESS NOTED)

This is a ribbed side box car.

480-1951 Grand Trunk Western
480-1952 Maine Central
480-1953 Warwick Railway (Dark Green)
480-1954 Ashley, Drew & Northern (green)
480-1955 Providence & Worcester (red)
480-1956 Lake Erie, Franklin & Clarion (yellow)
480-1958 Sabine River (red)
480-1959 Savannah State Docks (blue) **8.50**
480-1960 Marinette, Tomahawk & Western (green)
480-1961 Meridian & Bigbee (blue)
480-1962 Bath & Hammondsport (Tuscan)
480-1963 Port Huron & Detroit (blue)
480-1964 Seaboard System (black)
480-1965 Seaboard System (red)
480-1966 CSX/C&O (blue)
480-1967 NS
480-1972 RBOX (Railbox)
480-1973 Railbox (yellow) **9.98**
480-1974 Railbox - SOU (yellow) **9.98**
480-1975 Railbox **9.98**
480-1976 Railbox - BN (yellow) **9.98**
480-1977 Railbox - ATSF (yellow) **9.98**
480-1978 Railbox - Seaboard (yellow) **9.98**
480-1979 Railbox - Richmond, Fredricksburg & Potomac (yellow) **9.98**
480-1950 Undecorated

50' FMC DOUBLE DOOR BOX EA 7.25 (UNLESS NOTED)

480-1981 Western Pacific (Mineral Red)
480-1982 Amador Central (Sky Blue)
480-1983 CNW (Box Car Red)
480-1984 MILW (blue)
480-1985 SSW(Box Car Red)
480-1986 SP (Box Car Red)
480-1987 Seattle & North Coast (Dark Green) **8.00**
480-1988 Longview Piedmont & Northern (orange)
480-1989 McCloud River (white)
480-1993 BCR (green) **8.00**
480-1994 BN (Cascade Green)
480-1995 C&O - Chessie (blue)
480-1996 UP **8.00**
480-1980 Undecorated

50' Flat Top Hi Cube 480-1783

50' FMC 1-1/2 Door Box 490-1935

50' FMC Single Door Box Car 480-1967

50' FMC Double Door Box Car 480-1983

50' FMC DOUBLE DOOR OFFSET EA 7.25 (UNLESS NOTED)

480-3643

480-3641 UP **9.50**
480-3642 East St. Louis Junction (yellow)
480-3643 Columbia & Cowlitz (blue)
480-3644 Pend Oreille Valley (blue)
480-3645 Oregon, Pacific & Eastern (blue)
480-3646 Galveston Wharves (orange)
480-3647 Yreka Western (blue)
480-3640 Undecorated

50' FMC PLUG DOOR BOX EA 7.25 (UNLESS NOTED)

480-3621 ATSF (red)
480-3622 Grand Trunk Western
480-3623 BN (Cascade Green)
480-3624 MILW (Tuscan)
480-3625 Minnesota, Dakota & Western (green, white)
480-3626 CP (green)
480-3627 SOO (black lettering) **9.50**
480-3628 SOO (red lettering) **9.50**
480-3629 DRGW **9.50**
480-3630 BNSF ***NEW***
480-3620 Undecorated

50' PLUG DOOR BOX EA 6.25 (UNLESS NOTED)

480-1238

480-1230 PRR **7.50**
480-1231 N&W **7.50**
480-1232 SP **7.50**
480-1233 UP **7.50**
480-1234 Frisco **7.50**
480-1235 CNW **7.50**
480-1236 NKP (yellow) **7.50**
480-1237 SSW (orange) **7.50**
480-1238 Texas & Pacific (yellow) **7.50**
480-1251 BN (BN Cascade Green)
480-1255 UP
480-1256 UP - Map Side (silver, yellow, black letters) **9.98**
480-1257 UP (silver, yellow, red letters) **9.98**
480-1258 EL
480-1261 Railway Express Agency
480-1262 ROCK Modern (blue)
480-1263 CP (green, new styling lettering) **8.50**
480-1264 CP (Insulated) **8.50**
480-1265 BCR
480-1266 Pacific Great Eastern
480-1267 Frisco (blue)
480-1268 Frisco (Tuscan)
480-1269 UP "Automated" Map (yellow) **9.98**
480-1271 Western Pacific (Mineral Red) **7.50**
480-1272 Tidewater South (Mineral Red) **7.50**
480-1273 ATSF, Modern (Mineral Red) **6.98**
480-1250 Undecorated

50' PULLMAN STANDARD EA 6.25

480-1901 Frisco (Tuscan)
480-1902 MILW (Box Car Red)
480-1903 L&N (Box Car Red)
480-1904 SOU (Tuscan)
480-1905 CNW (Box Car Red)
480-1906 Boston & Maine (blue)
480-1907 CNW/Rock Island (white)
480-1908 South Branch Valley (yellow)
480-1909 Texas-Mexican Railway
480-1910 Ann Arbor Railway System (orange)
480-1911 New Orleans Public (orange)
480-1912 St. Mary's Railroad (white)
480-1913 Lamoille Valley (yellow)
480-1914 Alabama State Docks (yellow)
480-1915 CSX Transportation/Seaboard System (blue)
480-1900 Undecorated

50' SINGLE SHEATHED CARS EA 9.98

STEEL SINGLE DOOR

480-2101 Texas & Pacific
480-2103 MILW
480-2104 GN
480-2105 IC
480-2107 Ashley, Drew & Northern
480-2100 Undecorated

DOUBLE WOOD DOORS

480-2112 SP
480-2113 NP
480-2117 UP
480-2118 IC
480-2110 Undecorated

DOUBLE STEEL DOORS

480-2161 Texas & Pacific
480-2162 MP
480-2163 SP
480-2164 NP
480-2165 GN
480-2166 UP
480-2160 Undecorated

WOOD AUTO DOOR END

480-2121 GN
480-2122 MP
480-2123 Chicago, Rock Island & Pacific
480-2120 Undecorated

STEEL AUTO DOOR END

480-2131 Texas & Pacific
480-2132 GN
480-2133 ATSF
480-2134 SP
480-2130 Undecorated

STEEL DOUBLE DOOR AUTO END

480-2141 Western Pacific
480-2142 CB&Q
480-2140 Undecorated

STEEL DOUBLE DOOR LUMBER END

480-2151 Western Pacific
480-2152 CB&Q
480-2150 Undecorated

REEFERS

36' BILLBOARD REEFER EA 8.25

Different Roadname Shown

480-3130 Columbia Soup (red)

36' REEFERS EA 8.50 (UNLESS NOTED)

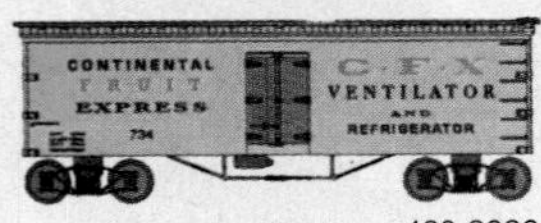

480-3086

480-3071 Snickers
480-3072 Asco Milk
480-3073 Land O' Lakes
480-3074 Hormel
480-3075 Parrot Potatoes
480-3076 Carnation Milk
480-3077 Old Heidelberg/Blatz
480-3078 Budweiser (green)
480-3079 Miller High Life
480-3080 San Antonio & Aransas Pass - SP Mission Route
480-3081 SP Sunset
480-3082 Hershey's Chocolate (chocolate brown w/silver roof & ends)

480-3083 PFE (orange with black roof & ends) **6.98**
480-3084 Denver, Texas & Fort Worth
480-3085 DRGW **6.98**
480-3086 Continental Fruit Express (yellow)
480-3087 Tivoli Beer (green)
480-3088 Yakima Apples (Northern Refrigerator) **6.98** ***NEW***

480-3090 Old Dutch Cleanser (Cudahy) **8.98** ***NEW***
480-3092 CP **6.98** ***NEW***
480-3093 Heinz Chow Chow **8.98** ***NEW***
480-3094 Chicago, St. Paul, Minneapolis & Omaha **7.98** ***NEW***
480-3070 Undecorated **6.98**

36' "STEEL UNDERFRAME" MEAT REEFER

480-3182 Cudahy (yellow) **8.25**
480-3180 Undecorated **5.50**

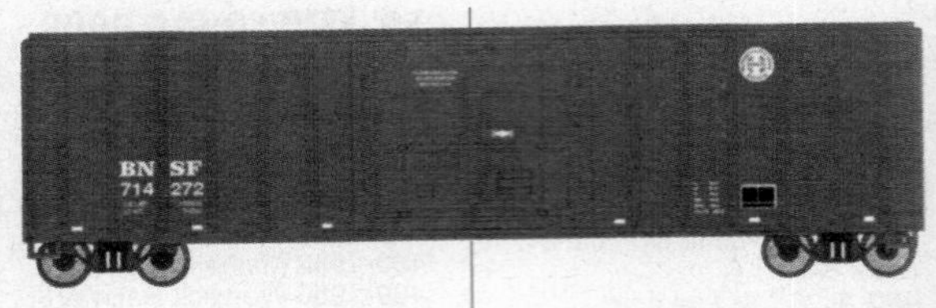

50' FMC Plug Door Box Car 480-3630

50' Plug Door 480-1231

50' Pullman Standard 480-1915

50' Single-Sheathed Box Car 480-2165

36' Reefer 480-3090

36' "STEEL UNDERFRAME" WOOD SIDE MEAT REEFER NEW TOOLING EA 8.98

480-3191 Evansville Packing Co.

480-3192 Oppenheimer Casing Co.

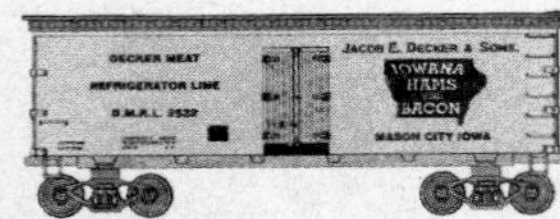

480-3193 Decker Meat

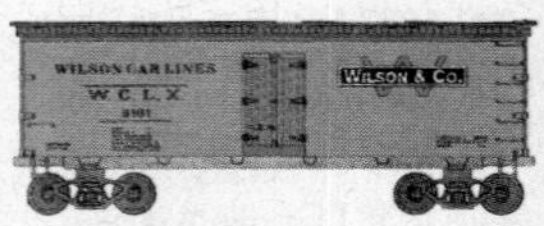

480-3194 Wilson Car Lines

480-3195 Swift Refrigerator Line (red)
480-3196 Swift Refrigerator Line (yellow)
480-3190 Undecorated

36' REFRIGERATOR EA 5.98 (UNLESS NOTED)

480-3161 PRR (Reefer Yellow)
480-3167 Erie (Reefer Yellow)
480-3160 Undecorated **5.50**

50' EXPRESS REEFER EA 8.98

480-3605 PRR
480-3607 Dairyman's League (white, blue & red)
480-3608 Central Vermont (silver)
480-3610 Railway Express Agency (green)
480-3611 Borden's Milk (Pullman Green, yellow)
380-3612 Chateau Martin Wines (burgundy)
480-3600 Undecorated

GONDOLAS

40' GONDOLA EA 6.25 (UNLESS NOTED)

480-1342 ATSF (Tuscan)
480-1343 SP (Tuscan)
480-1344 UP
480-1345 PRR (Tuscan)
480-1346 NYC (black)
480-1347 GN
480-1350 BN
480-1353 CP (Tuscan)
480-1354 CN (black)
480-1356 BCR (Olive) **7.50**
480-1359 Erie (black)
480-1340 Undecorated

40' OVAL- END GONDOLA EA 6.25

480-1331 C&O (black)
480-1330 Undecorated

50' MILL GONDOLA EA 6.25 (UNLESS NOTED)

480-1681 Railgon (black, yellow) **8.50**
480-1682 Elgin, Joilet & Eastern (black)
480-1683 Illinois Terminal (yellow)
480-1684 SOO (Box Car Red)
480-1685 MP (Box Car Red)
480-1686 MILW
480-1687 CNW (black)
480-1688 Kansas City Southern
480-1689 Philadelphia, Bethlehem & New England (orange)
480-1690 Maine Central (green)
480-1691 Boston & Maine (orange)
480-1692 D&H (black)
480-1693 N&W (blue)
480-1694 Frisco (Box Car Red)
480-1696 C&O - Chessie
480-1698 B&O Railgon (black, yellow) **8.50**
480-1699 C&O (Railgon Repaint) ***NEW***
480-1680 Undecorated

50' THRALL HIGH SIDE GONDOLA EA 7.50 (UNLESS NOTED)

480-1641 Commonwealth Edison
480-1642 Wisconsin Electric (ochre, black)
480-1643 UP (black, yellow)
480-1644 DRGW - Coal Liner (black, orange)
480-1645 BN (black)
480-1646 NP
480-1647 Peabody Coal
480-1648 Northern Indiana Public Service Company
480-1649 Detroit Edison
480-1650 CP (orange) **8.50**
480-1651 Greenlease
480-1652 ATSF (black, yellow) **8.50**
480-1640 Undecorated

50' BATHTUB GONDOLA EA 6.25

480-1661 C&O - Chessie (yellow, black)
480-1662 UP (yellow, black)
480-1665 BN (black)
480-1666 DRGW (orange, black)
480-1660 Undecorated

HOPPERS

34' 2-BAY COVERED HOPPER EA 8.25

480-1431 PRR
480-1432 UP (gray)
480-1434 Jack Frost Sugar
480-1435 SP
480-1436 MILW (gray)
480-1437 Haliburton (red, white)
480-1438 US Borax
480-1439 Boston & Maine
480-1440 Boraxo
480-1441 GN (Big Sky Blue)
480-1442 Penn Central
480-1443 BN (Cascade Green)
480-1444 ROCK (blue)
480-1445 CR (Box Car Red)
480-1446 C&O (black)
480-1447 SOO (Tuscan)
480-1448 EL (gray)
480-1464 ATSF
480-1465 NKP (black)
480-1466 Wabash (black)
480-1467 Ann Arbor (gray)
480-1468 LV
480-1469 WM
480-1630 CNW
480-1631 WM/C&O
480-1632 Detroit, Toledo & Ironton
480-1633 SSW
480-1634 NH
480-1635 CSX
480-1636 Rutland
480-1637 CNJ
480-1638 B&O - Chessie
480-1639 Minneapolis & St. Louis
480-2060 GN
480-2061 Western Pacific
480-2062 RDG
480-1430 Undecorated

38' SAND AND GRAVEL HOPPER EA 6.25 (UNLESS NOTED)

480-1476

480-1471 CN
480-1472 ATSF
480-1473 SP
480-1474 B&O
480-1475 C&O
480-1476 MOW (dark gray) **9.98**
480-1470 Undecorated

40' 3-BAY OFFSET SIDE HOPPER EA 6.25 (UNLESS NOTED)

480-1621

480-1611 Erie (black)
480-1612 IC (black)
480-1613 NKP (black)
480-1614 CP (Box Car Red) **7.25**
480-1615 NYC (black)
480-1616 MP (black)
480-1617 CN (Box Car Red)
480-1618 Bessemer & Lake Erie (brown)
480-1619 B&O (black)
480-1620 SOO (Mineral Red)
480-1621 CB&Q (red)
480-1622 C&O - Progress
480-1610 Undecorated

40' OFFSET BALLAST HOPPER EA 6.25

480-1584

480-1581 UP "Be Specific" (Mineral Red)
480-1582 UP "Streamliner" (Mineral Red)
480-1583 UP - Large Lettering (Mineral Red)
480-1584 DRGW (black)
480-1585 SOU (black)
480-1586 SOU (red)
480-1580 Undecorated

40' 3-BAY RIB SIDE HOPPER EA 6.25 (UNLESS NOTED)

480-1546

480-1486 WM (black)
480-1488 PRR (Tuscan)
480-1489 Virginian (black)
480-1490 N&W (black)
480-1492 CR
480-1493 DRGW (black)
480-1494 UP (Tuscan)
480-1495 C&O (black)
480-1496 B&O (black)
480-1498 BN (black)
480-1499 C&O Progress
480-1531 EL (black, yellow)
480-1532 Seaboard (black)
480-1533 MKT (red)
480-1535 CSX/C&O (black)
480-1537 SOU (Mineral Red)
480-1538 PRR (black)
480-1539 CNW
480-1540 CSX/C&O-Revised Scheme (black)
480-1541 CB&Q (black)
480-1542 NS (black)
480-1543 NYC (black)
480-1544 B&O **6.75**
480-1545 WM
480-1546 Minneapolis & St. Louis (red w/white lettering)
480-1547 RDG (black w/white lettering)
480-1485 Undecorated

50' Express Reefer 480-3610

40' Gondola 480-1343

50' Mill Gondola 480-1684

50' Thrall High Side Gondola 480-1652

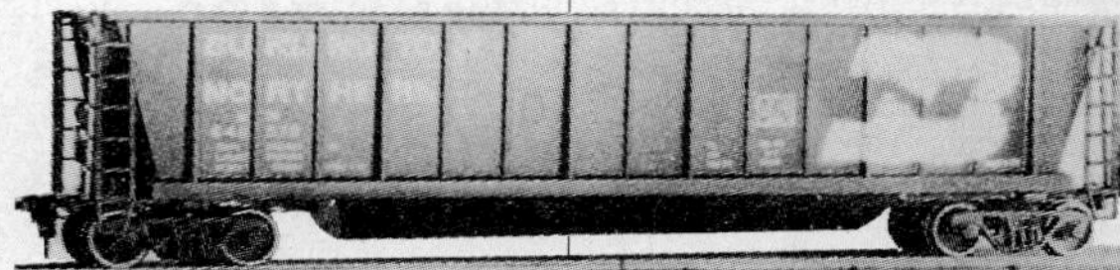

50' Bathtub Gondola 480-1665

40' 2-Bay Covered Hopper 480-1441

48' RIB BALLAST HOPPER EA 6.25

480-1563

480-1561 UP MOW (green)
480-1562 Pittsburgh & Lake Erie (black)
480-1563 NYC (black)
480-1564 DRGW
480-1565 GN
480-1566 PRR
480-1567 CR
480-1568 Western Pacific
480-1569 N&W
480-1570 ATSF
480-1560 Undecorated

50' 5-BAY RAPID DISCHARGE HOPPER EA 6.25

480-1721 ATSF (Box Car Red)
480-1723 US Steel - Cumberland Mine (light blue)
480-1724 Black Mesa & Lake Powell (dark blue)
480-1725 UP
480-1726 Colorado Springs (black)
480-1727 C&O (black)
480-1728 SOU (Box Car Red)
480-1729 Missouri Public Service
480-1730 National Steel
480-1732 Colorado & Wyoming
480-1733 Itel
480-1735 Seaboard Coast Line (black)
480-1736 N&W (black)
480-1758 SOU (silver)
480-1759 SOU/Ortner
480-1720 Undecorated

50' FMC 3-BAY COVERED HOPPER EA 8.98

When the grain rush starts, you'll see plenty of these distinctive covered hoppers in every train. Introduced in the early 1980s, these 100-ton capacity cars are being used by many railroads and private companies. The large carrying capacity (4,750 cubic feet) makes them an ideal choice for grain and many other loads.

The highly detailed body has the unique horizontal stiffening ridge that makes both the prototype and the model stand out from other hoppers. The low-profile roofwalk is nicely detailed, adding to the overall realism of the finished car. Prepainted and lettered for a variety of roadnames, this easy-to-build kit is a great addition to your modern layout.

480-3521 BN (Cascade Green, white)
480-3522 DRGW (The Action Road)
480-3523 CNW (green)
480-3524 CNW (yellow)
480-3525 Western Pacific (gray)
480-3526 Percival Grain
480-3527 Mid Iowa (medium blue, white)
480-3528 Val-Hi Supply (Cascade Green, white)
480-3529 Arthur Farms (yellow, black)
480-3530 Klemme Co-op (pink, black)
480-3531 Farnhamville, Iowa (pink, black)
480-3532 NAHX (gray w/red FMC logo)
480-3533 Cook Industries (gray, blue logo)
480-3534 XTRA (gray, red logo)
480-3535 Procor (gray, blue logo)
480-3537 BNSF
480-3536 Seaboard Coast Line
480-3520 Undecorated

STOCK CARS

36' OLD TIME STOCK CAR EA 7.50

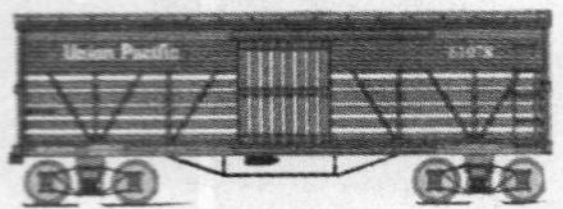

480-3276

480-3261 DRGW (black)
480-3262 CNW
480-3263 GN (Box Car Red)
480-3264 PRR (Box Car Red)
480-3265 ATSF (Box Car Red)
480-3266 NYC (black)
480-3267 Clinchfield
480-3268 Colorado Midland (black)
480-3269 Colorado & Southern
480-3270 NP
480-3271 MP
480-3272 B&O
480-3273 Kansas City, Mexico & Orient
480-3274 B&O
480-3275 Atlanta & West Point
480-3276 UP
480-3260 Undecorated

TANK CARS

26' OLD TIME TANK CAR EA 8.50

480-3373

480-3361 PRR (black)
480-3362 ATSF (black)
480-3363 SP (black)
480-3364 Sun Oil (black)
480-3365 UP (black)
480-3366 Union Tank Line (black)
480-3367 Conoco (black)
480-3368 Zerolene (silver)
480-3369 Standard Oil (black)
480-3370 Gramps (black)
480-3371 Battle Mountain Liquid Gold (burgundy)
480-3372 RPM Motor Oil (silver)
480-3373 Central Tank Lines
480-3374 German-American Tank Lines (black w/white lettering)
480-3360 Undecorated

30' MODERN TANK CAR EA 8.50 (UNLESS NOTED)

480-3307

480-3301 GATX (black)
480-3302 Hooker
480-3303 UTLX (black)
480-3304 GATX (white)
480-3305 Freeport (white) 9.50 *NEW*
480-3306 Cargill (black) *NEW*
480-3307 Emery *NEW*
480-3300 Undecorated

50' TANK CAR EA 9.75 (UNLESS NOTED)

480-1372 ATSF
480-1373 General American Transportation (black)
480-1374 SP
480-1375 Sunoco
480-1376 BN
480-1377 Cargill
480-3251 ADM Corn Sweetener (white) **10.50**
480-1370 Undecorated

50' TANK TRAIN EA 9.98

480-1391 Tank Train (black)
480-1392 Quaker State
480-1390 Undecorated

OLD TIME WOOD CABOOSES

30' 3-WINDOW STANDARD EA 8.98

480-3441 DRGW (Caboose Red)
480-3442 NP (Caboose Red)
480-3443 PRR
480-3444 Wabash (Caboose Red)
480-3445 SP (Caboose Red)
480-3447 CN (orange)
480-3448 GN (Caboose Red)
480-3449 UP
480-3450 CNW
480-3451 NYC
480-3452 Western Pacific
480-3453 Maryland & Pennsylvania
480-3440 Undecorated

30' SMALL SIDE DOOR EA 8.98

480-3401 UP (Box Car Red)
480-3402 Atlantic Coast Line
480-3403 CB&Q (Box Car Red)
480-3404 LV
480-3405 Atlanta & West Point
480-3400 Undecorated

50' 5-Bay Rapid Discharge Hopper 480-1723

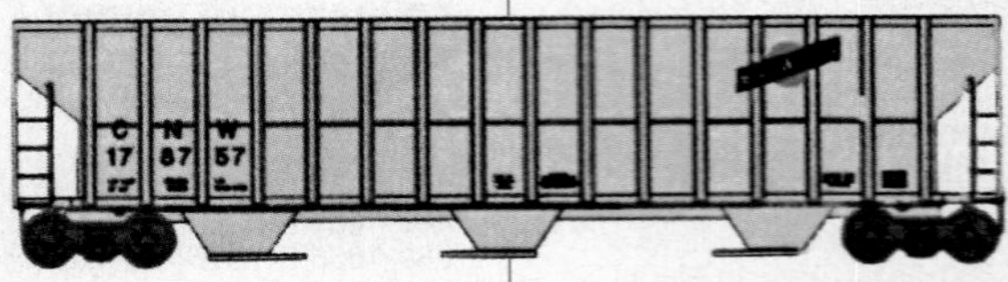

50' FMC 3-Bay Covered Hopper 480-3524

50' Tank Train 480-1391

50' Tank Car 480-3251

30' 3-Window Standard 480-3442

30' Small Side Door 480-3401

30' OUTSIDE BRACED EA 8.98

480-3463

480-3461 MKT (Reefer Yellow)
480-3462 ROCK (Box Car Red)
480-3463 Western Pacific (silver, orange)
480-3464 N&W (Tuscan)
480-3460 Undecorated

30' BLIND END SIDE DOOR EA 8.98

480-3421 ATSF (Tuscan)
480-3422 Erie (Box Car Red)
480-3423 IC (Box Car Red)
480-3424 NYC & Hudson
480-3425 Kansas City, Mexico & Orient
480-3420 Undecorated

30' OPEN END SIDE DOOR EA 8.98

480-3431 B&O (Caboose Red)
480-3432 Colorado Midland (Caboose Red)
480-3433 SSW
480-3434 SP (Caboose Red)
480-3435 Virginia & Truckee Transfer Style, No Cupola (yellow)
480-3430 Undecorated

MODERN STEEL CABOOSES

26' 2-WINDOW EA 8.98

480-3471 PRR (Caboose Red)
480-3472 Amtrak (gold, blue)
480-3473 BN (BN Cascade Green)
480-3475 B&O (Caboose Red)
480-3476 Duluth, Missabe & Iron Range
480-3478 ROCK (light blue)
480-3479 CR (blue)
480-3511 C&O (red)
480-3512 Clinchfield "Family Lines"
480-3470 Undecorated

26' 4-WINDOW EA 8.98

480-3481 SP (Box Car Red)
480-3483 GN
480-3484 GN (Big Sky Blue)
480-3485 UP (Reefer Yellow)
480-3486 ATSF (Caboose Red)
480-3487 SP "Overland" (silver)
480-3488 EL
480-3480 Undecorated

30' 3-WINDOW EA 8.98

480-3492 Ontario Northland (yellow, blue)
480-3493 Grand Trunk Western (black, orange)
480-3494 Frisco
480-3495 CB&Q (silver)
480-3496 DRGW
480-3497 ATSF
480-3491 Undecorated

ORE CARS

22' TAPER-SIDE ORE CAR EA 5.25

480-1405 DRGW (black)
480-1406 CP (Tuscan)
480-1407 CN (Tuscan)
480-1408 C&O (black)
480-1409 PRR (Tuscan)
480-1410 GN (Tuscan)
480-1411 SOO (Tuscan)
480-1412 CNW (Tuscan)
480-1413 Lake Superior & Ishpeming (Tuscan)
480-1414 SP (Tuscan)
480-1415 BN (BN Cascade Green)
480-1401 Undecorated

22' RECTANGULAR-SIDE ORE CAR EA 5.25

480-1322 Bessemer & Lake Erie (brown)
480-1323 Duluth, Missabe & Iron Range (brown)
480-1324 DRGW (silver)
480-1417 CN (silver)
480-1418 Ontario Northland (Ontario Northland Blue)
480-1419 ROCK
480-1420 GN
480-1421 Duluth, Missabe & Iron Range (Tuscan)
480-1422 CN (Tuscan)
480-1423 Chicago, Terre Haute & South Eastern (MILW) (Tuscan)
480-1424 UP (Tuscan)
480-1425 GN (Big Sky blue)
480-1426 Penn Central (green)
480-1427 B&O (Tuscan)
480-1428 ATSF (Tuscan)
480-1429 UP (silver)
480-1402 Undecorated

26' TIGHT-BOTTOM "HI SIDE" ORE CAR EA 7.25

480-1701

480-1702 SP
480-1703 PRR
480-1701 Undecorated

26' LOW SIDE ORE CAR EA 7.25

480-1715

480-1712 SP
480-1713 UP
480-1714 CP
480-1715 PRR
480-1716 CR
480-1711 Undecorated

FLAT CARS

30' FLAT CAR EA 5.25

480-1451 MOW
480-1453 MILW (black)
480-1454 PRR (Box Car Red)
480-1455 SP (Box Car Red)
480-1456 UP (Box Car Red)
480-1457 ATSF (Box Car Red)
480-1458 B&O (black)
480-1459 CN (Box Car Red)
480-1460 NYC (black)
480-1450 Undecorated

30' Open End Side Door 480-3435

26' 2-Window 480-3473

26' 4-Window 480-3484

22' Taper Side Ore Car 480-1405

22' Rectangular-Side Ore Car 480-1324

30' Flat Car 480-1460

60' BULKHEAD FLAT CAR EA 7.98

480-1299 Columbia & Cowlitz
480-1301 Trailer Train (yellow)
480-1302 BN (BN Cascade Green)
480-1303 CP (red)
480-1306 SSW (red)
480-1307 MILW (yellow)
480-1308 SOO (white)
480-1310 UP (yellow)
480-1311 ATSF (red)
480-1312 Western Pacific (black)
480-1314 BCR (Olive)
480-1315 SP (Box Car Red)
480-1316 MP (Box Car Red)
480-1317 Kansas City Southern (Box Car Red)
480-1318 Oregon, Pacific & Eastern (orange)
480-1319 Longview, Portland & Northern (orange)
480-1320 Trailer Train
480-1321 UP (Brown Body)
480-1300 Undecorated

60' FLAT CAR EA 6.25

480-1281 Trailer Train (yellow)
480-1282 SOO (white)
480-1283 SP (red)
480-1284 ATSF (red)
480-1285 MP (red)
480-1286 UP (yellow)
480-1287 SOU (red)
480-1288 Frisco (yellow)
480-1291 TTX (Modern)
480-1280 Undecorated

3-IN-1 CAR KITS

3-in-1 Kits represent the use of more than one kit which can be combined with "partner" kits, to establish an overall theme. Not all 3-in-1 Kits contain 3 individual kits. Kit-bashing and the purchase of some details from other manufacturers is necessary. Rolling stock kits come undecorated, with trucks and couplers.

480-1500 26' Log Car Set pkg(3) **11.98**
This kit includes three 26' metal log car kits and detailing parts, less logs.

480-1501 21' Wood Chip Car Set pkg(3) **15.00**
This kit includes three one car kits and gondola sides, less load.

480-1502 MOW Car Set pkg(3) **15.00**
This kit includes three 26' shorty flat car kits with gondola sides, less load.

480-1503 MOW Passenger Car Set pkg(3) **15.00**
This kit includes three 30' wood style molded work cars, MOW Supply, MOW Bunk, MOW Repair, less details.

480-1515 Rotary Snowplow & Tender pkg(2) **15.00**
480-1516 Jordan Spreader & Snow Crab pkg(3) **15.00**
This kit also includes one flanger car.

Rotary Snowplow & Tender 480-1515

Fire Fighting Train Set 480-1507

Austin City Street Scene 480-1514

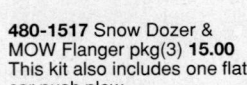

60' Bulkhead Flat Car 480-1321

60' Flat Car 480-1285

480-1517 Snow Dozer & MOW Flanger pkg(3) **15.00**
This kit also includes one flat car push plow.

480-1518 Galloping Goose Diesel Conversion Dummy **15.00**
This kit includes one each: box car, diesel body and details, and 4 wheel lead truck, less diesel truck.

480-1555 Rip Track - Car Body Assortment **5.98**

BATTLE MOUNTAIN THEME KITS

Battle Mountain represents America's silver mining boom, from the 1870s to 1930s. Battle Mountain was located on the Central Pacific (later Southern Pacific) line between Elko and Reno, Nevada, and was also the northern terminus of the narrow gauge Nevada Central Railroad which supplied the silver town of Austin.

480-1507 Fire Fighting Train Set pkg(2) **15.00**
This kit includes a water tank car, chemical tank car and a tower car.

480-1509 Log Car & Building Set pkg(2) **15.00**
This kit includes three 36' log cars and one building.

480-1510 Climax Mine Loco (Dummy) **15.00**
This kit featurs molded body, detailing parts, HO and HOn3 trucks, 30' flat car body, less boiler and metal underframe.

480-1514 Austin City Street Scene **15.00**
This kit is a molded two story stone building, 8-1/2 x 4-1/4".

SHANTY TOWN THEME KITS

When steam was king, the railroads needed plenty of men, and they needed places to live. Wherever the steam loco stopped for water you could find a small telegraph station, coal or oil loading facility and a section gang's living quarters.

480-1504 Yard Office pkg(2) **15.00**
This kit includes two 36' wood style box car kits and a molded single story brick freight station, less details. The station measures 8-1/2 x 5 x 2".

480-1505 Section Gang House pkg(2) **15.00**
This kit includes one each 36' Overton coach, 36' reefer car kit and a molded single story stone building which measures 4-1/2 x 6 x 2".

480-1506 Telegraph Office & Service Facility pkg(2) **15.00**
This kit includes one each 26' tank car, 30' Shorty flat car kit and a molded single story brick telegraph office, less figures and details. The building measures 8-1/2 x 6 x 3-1/4".

HANDCAR

These kits are molded plastic.

480-2976 Handcar Kit (black) pkg(2) **3.50**

JIMMIES

480-1508 Steel Ore Jimmies **15.00**

These easy-to-build HO Scale plastic models feature one-piece, prepainted and lettered bodies. Kits include trucks and weights, and coupler pockets accept Kadee® couplers.

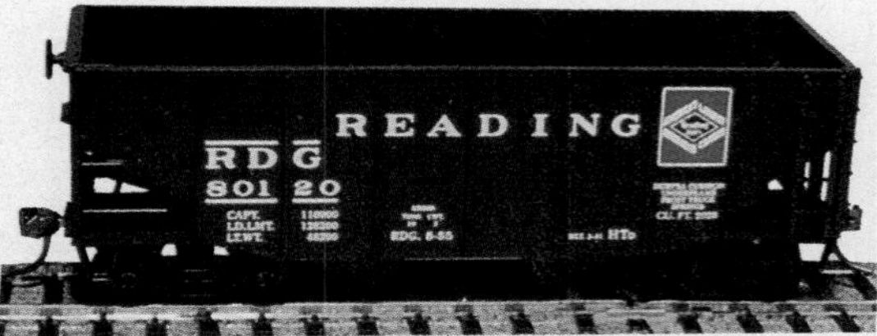

2-Bay 55-Ton Fishbelly Hopper 691-10145

70-Ton NYC/AAR 14-Panel Triple Hopper 691-10004

H39 12-Panel Triple Hopper 691-10225

Triple Offset Hopper 691-10320

U Channel 2-Bay Hopper 691-10403

BOX CARS

50' GENERAL AMERICAN RBL PLUG DOOR

691-11000 Undecorated **TBA** *NEW*

HOPPERS

55-TON FISHBELLY

2-BAY

691-10145 RDG Anthracite pkg(6) **59.88**
691-10146 Cambria & Indiana pkg(3) **29.94**

EA 9.98

691-10120 D&H #5895 (black)
691-10122 WM #10939 (Oxide Red)
691-10123 WM #10942 (Oxide Red)
691-10133 Jersey Central (CRP) #67069
691-10134 Jersey Central (CRP) #67179
691-10135 Jersey Central (CRP) #67194
691-10137 RDG (Speed) #66731
691-10138 RDG (Speed) #66739
691-10101 Data Only (black)
691-10100 Undecorated (black)

PEAKED ENDS EA 9.98

691-10181 Atlantic Coast Line #81758 (black)

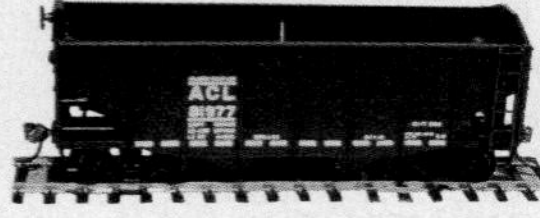

691-10182 Atlantic Coast Line #81977 (black)
691-10174 Undecorated (black)

70-TON

NYC/AAR 14-PANEL TRIPLE EA 9.98

691-10001 NYC #905035 (black)
691-10002 DRGW #17341 (black)
691-10003 WM #80293 (Oxide Red)
691-10004 ATSF #80000 (Box Car Red)
691-10018 D&H #9000 (black)
691-10019 D&H #9014 (black)
691-10020 D&H #9028 (black)
691-10021 GN #70528 (black)
691-10022 GN #70549 (black)
691-10023 GN #70558 (black)
691-10024 Seaboard #40215 (Box Car Red)
691-10025 Seaboard #40322 (Box Car Red)
691-10026 Seaboard #40496 (Box Car Red)
691-10027 CR #421008 (Box Car Red)
691-10028 CR #421135 (Box Car Red)
691-10029 CR #421679 (Box Car Red)
691-10030 Chicago & Eastern Illinois #99074
691-10031 Chicago & Eastern Illinois #99088
691-10032 Chicago & Eastern Illinois #99095
691-10033 Detroit, Toledo & Ironton #1826
691-10034 Detroit, Toledo & Ironton #1835
691-10035 Detroit, Toledo & Ironton #1839
691-10036 Penn Central #459730
691-10037 Penn Central #459734
691-10038 Penn Central #459755
691-10039 Seaboard Coast Line #163145
691-10040 Seaboard Coast Line #163159
691-10041 Seaboard Coast Line #163188
691-10042 Pittsburgh & Shawmut #12000
691-10043 Pittsburgh & Shawmut #12003
691-10044 Pittsburgh & Shawmut #12005
691-10045 Montour
691-10053 Boston & Albany #910224
691-10000 Undecorated (black)

H39 12-PANEL TRIPLE EA 9.98

691-10208 DRGW #17735 (black)
691-10209 DRGW #17749 (black)
691-10210 DRGW #17896 (black)
691-10211 EL #33460 (black)
691-10212 EL #33482 (black)
691-10213 EL #33508 (black)
691-10214 Pittsburgh & Lake Erie #62329 (black)
691-10215 Pittsburgh & Lake Erie # 62411 (black)
691-10216 Pittsburgh & Lake Erie #64031 (black)
691-10217 WM #72081 (Oxide Red)
691-10218 WM #72120 (Oxide Red)
691-10219 WM #72247 (Oxide Red)
691-10220 CR #431431 (Box Car Red)
691-10221 CR #435048 (Box Car Red)
691-10222 CR #443699 (Box Car Red)
691-10223 PRR #671632 (black)
691-10224 PRR #671669 (black)
691-10225 PRR #671729 (black)
691-10228 MILW #371080 (Box Car Red)
691-10229 MILW #371122 (Box Car Red)
691-10230 MILW #371202 (Box Car Red)
691-10231 L&N #182125
691-10232 L&N #182133
691-10233 L&N #182156
691-10234 SOU #74745 (Box Car Red)
691-10235 SOU #74751 (Box Car Red)
691-10237 CN #111137 (oxide red)
691-10238 CN #111302 (oxide red)
691-10239 CN #111486 (oxide red)
691-10242 CSX #141222
691-10243 CSX #141234
691-10207 Data Only (black)
691-10370 Undecorated
691-10371 Data Only
691-10200 Undecorated (black)

H39 12-PANEL TRIPLE-PEAKED ENDS EA 9.98

691-10276 PRR #274001 (black)
691-10277 C&O #151949 (black)
691-10278 C&O #151975 (black)

691-10279 C&O #151998 (black)
691-10280 N&W #59000 (black)
691-10275 Undecorated (black)

TRIPLE OFFSET EA 9.98

691-10301 Data Only
691-10300 Undecorated

TRIPLE-OFFSET SIX-PACKS EA 59.88 (UNLESS NOTED)

691-10304 Seaboard As Delivered Scheme
Includes #38378, 38403, 38467, 38522, 38621 and 38645.

691-10306 SP As Delivered-T&NO
Includes #4252, 4267, 4339, 4345, 4414 and 4440.

691-10309 NYC
691-10314 MOPAC
691-10316 ROCK
691-10318 B&O
691-10319 ATSF
691-10320 CB&Q
691-10321 CN
691-10322 Atlantic Coast Line
691-10323 Bangor & Aroostook
691-10324 Kansas City Southern
691-10326 Illinois Terminal (2 Schemes) **65.88** *NEW*
691-10327 Family Lines **65.88** *NEW*
691-10328 Toronto, Hamilton & Buffalo **65.88** *NEW*

Limited Quantity Available
691-10317 Chicago Great Western/Minneapolis & St. Louis

3-BAY OFFSET PKG(3) EA 32.95

691-10332 Minneapolis & St. Louis *NEW*
691-10334 Chicago Great Western *NEW*

3-BAY OFFSET PKG(6) EA 65.88

691-10329 Boston & Maine *NEW*
691-10330 NKP *NEW*
691-10331 Detroit, Toledo & Ironton *NEW*
691-10333 Pittsburgh & Lake Erie *NEW*
691-10335 CP (Script Lettering) *NEW*

13-PANEL EA 9.98

691-10371 Data Only *NEW*
691-10370 Undecorated *NEW*

13-PANEL SIX-PACKS EA 59.95

691-10372 PRR (traditional)
691-10373 PRR (simplified scheme)

14-PANEL SIX-PACKS EA 59.88

691-10054 Chessie (4 WM, 2 C&O)
691-10055 Florida East Coast (black)

U CHANNEL 2-BAY

EA 10.98

691-10401 Data Only
691-10400 Undecorated

PKG(3) EA 32.94

691-10406 Pittsburgh & West Virginia
691-10408 Toronto, Hamilton & Buffalo *NEW*

PKG(6) EA 65.88

691-10404 WM
691-10405 WM w/Circle Herald
691-10407 Boston & Maine *NEW*

TICHY TRAIN GROUP

These easy-to-build HO Scale kits feature unpainted plastic parts, underbody details, separate ladders and grab irons (unless noted). Coupler pockets accept horn-hook or Kadee® couplers.

BOX CARS

40' USRA WOOD BOX CAR

Built under the mandate of the United States Railway Administration, these single-sheathed box cars were built for more than 20 railroads starting in 1918. Some were in nonrevenue service as late as 1965.

293-4026 Single Car **14.50**
293-6026 6-Pack **75.00**

DECAL SETS EA 2.50

293-9026 LIRR (white) *NEW*
293-9126 D&H (white) *NEW*

40' USRA WOOD BOX CAR REBUILT W/RIBBED STEEL SIDES

The Georgia and several other railroads chose to upgrade their USRA single-sheathed box cars with steel plates welded to the bracing. Kits include AB brake gear. Decals feature lettering for the Georgia Railroad.

293-4032 Single Car **14.50**

293-40324 Single Car, w/Decals **16.50**
293-6032 6-Pack **75.00**
293-60324 6-Pack, w/Decals **87.00**

GEORGIA DECAL SETS EA 2.50

293-9032 Black *NEW*
293-9132 White *NEW*

40' USRA WOOD BOX CAR REBUILT W/STEEL SIDES UPGRADE

These cars were rebuilt during the late 1930s and early 1940s from USRA single-sheathed box cars. Kits feature both ribbed and nonribbed extended ends, plus AB-type brake gear. Decals include lettering for NYC, Pittsburgh & Lake Erie and Pittsburgh, McKeesport & Youghiogheny cars.

293-4028 Single Car **14.50**
293-40284 Single Car, w/Decals **16.50**
293-6028 6-Pack **75.00**
293-60284 6-Pack, w/Decals **87.00**

X-29

293-1021 PRR **10.50**
293-1020 Undecorated **9.50**

MK-26

293-1031 B&O **10.50**
293-1030 Undecorated **9.50**

DECAL SETS EA 2.50

293-9028 Pittsburgh & Lake Erie, Pittsburgh, McKeesport & Youghiogheny (white) *NEW*
293-9128 PRR & Detroit, Toledo & Ironton (white) *NEW*

REEFERS

40' PFE WOOD REEFER

Kit is based on class R-40 PFE wood reefers as operated by the SP/UP and WP railroads. Includes parts to build class R-40-4, R-30-9 or WP-style car. By substituting grab irons (available separately), class R-30-13 and R-40-2 reefers can also be built.

293-4024 Single Car **14.50**
293-6024 6-Pack **75.00**

40' PFE Wood Reefer 293-4024

HOPPERS

USRA 36' 2-BAY

293-4027 Single Car **14.50**
293-6027 6-Pack **75.00**
293-9029 Decal Set **2.50**
Includes lettering for C&O, D&H, Wabash and NH.

DECAL SETS EA 2.50

293-9027 LIRR (white) *NEW*
293-9029 NH, D&H, C&O, Wabash (white) *NEW*
Also works on 36' 2-bay hopper with rebuilt panel side (#293-4029).

36' 2-BAY REBUILT PANEL SIDE

When USRA hoppers came due for rebuilding in the 1930s and 1940s, many roads elected to replace the flat sides with panel sides, resulting in a capacity increase of 80 cubic feet. Kits include AB brakes. Decals include lettering for C&O, D&H, Wabash and NH.

293-4029 Single Car **14.50**

293-40294 Single Car, w/Decals **16.50**
293-6029 6-Pack **75.00**
293-60294 6-Pack, w/Decals **87.00**

USRA D&H CEMENT CONVERSION

293-4030 Single Car **14.50**
293-40304 Single Car, w/Decals **16.50**
293-6030 6-Pack **75.00**
293-60304 6-Pack, w/Decals **87.00**

USRA D&H Cement Conversion Hopper 293-4030

DECAL SETS EA 2.50

293-9030 D&H (black) *NEW*
293-9130 D&H (white) *NEW*
293-9230 B&O (white) *NEW*

PANEL HOPPER-ANDERSONS CO. GRAIN CONVERSION W/DECALS

This model represents a series of 114 cars acquired by The Andersons Company in 1961 and used in grain transport. The kit includes a cast-resin top and custom decals for The Andersons Co.

293-4031 Single Car **18.50**
293-6031 6-Pack **96.00**
293-9031 Decal Set (black) **2.50** *NEW*

Panel Hopper 293-4031

GONDOLAS

USRA COMPOSITE GONDOLA

293-4033 Single Car **14.50**
293-6033 6-Pack **75.00**

FLAT CARS

40' FLAT CAR

50-TON STEEL

This flat car was built by American Car & Foundry in 1926. The kit features a molded deck, straight side sills, detailed underframe and complete brake rigging.

293-4021 Single Car **8.95**
293-6021 6-Pack **45.98**

WHEEL

These cars were converted by the MILW and other lines to transport wheelsets for company use. Kit includes 40 wheelsets.

293-4023 Single Car **14.50**
293-6023 Wheel Car 6-Pack **75.00**
293-3010 Extra Wheelset pkg(96) **9.50**
Nonoperating wheelsets for use with kit #4023.

53' GSC COMMONWEALTH FLAT CAR EA 9.00 (UNLESS NOTED)

These prepainted and decorated kits include trucks and couplers.

293-1001 PRR
293-1002 Wabash

293-1003 SOO
293-1004 UP
293-1000 Undecorated **8.00**

FLAT CAR LOAD

293-3056 Pipe Load pkg(2 Loads) **9.50**
Pictured above with 53' GSC Commonwealth Flat Car, sold separately.

TANK CARS

36' USRA TANK CAR

The 36' USRA 10,000-gallon tank car was used from the 1920s through the 1960s to haul crude oil and other products.

54" DOME

293-4020 Single Car **14.50**
293-6020 6-Pack **75.00**

60" DOME

293-4025 Single Car **14.50**
293-6025 6-Pack **75.00**

TICHY TRAIN GROUP

120-Ton Brownhoist Crane 293-4010

40' Boom Car 293-4022

22' Wood Ore Car 293-4012

MAINTENANCE OF WAY

120-TON BROWNHOIST CRANE

293-4010 Undecorated **28.50**
Ready to go on a moment's notice, the 120-ton crane was an important piece of maintenance equipment for any railroad. This kit is based on a Brownhoist prototype, many of which lasted well into the diesel-era. The detailed model has over 200 parts and features a working boom plus heavy-duty trucks. Complete instructions are included.

40' BOOM CAR

This kit features a toolbox underframe, deck cabin and many accessories to customize the design.

293-4022 Single Car **14.50**
293-6022 6-Pack **74.98**

ORE CARS

22' WOOD ORE CAR

The heavy-duty "Great Lakes" ore car captures the look of Eastern and Western mining equipment.

293-4012 2-Car Set **14.50**
293-6012 12-Car Set **75.00**

HANDCARS

293-4011 Handcars/Trailers pkg(12) **9.50**
This kit contains six handcars with optional side benches and six trailers.

RIBBONRAIL

TRACK CLEANING CARS EA 34.95

Cars are equipped with rubber blocks impregnated with fine grain abrasive that clean the rails as the cars roll around the track. Ready-to-run models feature solid brass bodies and trucks. Couplers are included with car No. 7.

170-6 For Standard 2-Rail Track
170-7 For Marklin Track

RIX PRODUCTS

INGOT BUGGIES & MOLDS

628-601 pkg(3) **9.95**

INGOT MOLDS W/STOOLS

628-602 pkg(2) **2.49**

WHITEGROUND MODEL WORKS

These HOn3 Scale plaster loads are for Hallmark, Quality Craft and Car Shop hoppers.

We have worked closely with this manufacturer to provide accurate delivery information at the time this catalog was published. Items listed in blue ink may not be available at all times. Current delivery information, along with a list of in-stock products for this line, can be found on our Web site at www.walthers.com.

HOPPER LOADS PKG(6) EA 9.95

771-5012 Ganister Rock
771-5013 Mine Run Coal
771-5014 Processed Coal

DECAL

771-5002 EBT Hopper (white) **2.00**

TAURUS PRODUCTS/ TROUT CREEK ENGINEERING

These kits feature scale lumber and plastic and metal detail parts. They do not include trucks or couplers. Custom Microscale decals are included with all kits except ore cars.

Tank Car HO Scale 707-2881

Tank Car HOn3 Scale 707-3882

40' WOOD SHEATHED REEFERS EA 19.00

707-2871 PFE
Pacific Fruit Express was a jointly owned corporation of the Union Pacific and the Southern Pacific Railroads. In 1926, it purchased over 4000 of these R-30-13 class wood sheathed reefers. Many lasted well into the 1950s and a few into the 60s. The car features a UP herald on one side and SP herald on the other.

707-8272 ROCK
Two hundred fifty of these cars were purchased in 1942 by the Rock Island and numbered 67750 to 67999. They served for more than 30 years on the line.

TANK CARS EA 38.00

HO SCALE

707-2880 Conoco
707-2881 Standard Oil ***NEW***
707-2882 Zerolene Oil ***NEW***
707-2883 RPM oil ***NEW***

HOn3 SCALE

707-2880 Conoco
707-2881 Standard Oil ***NEW***
707-2882 Zerolene Oil ***NEW***
707-2883 RPM Oil ***NEW***

STOCK CAR

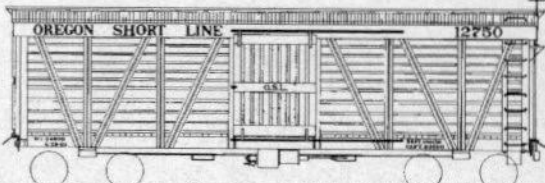

707-2870 Oregon Short Line **20.00**
These stock cars were built for the Oregon Short Line in 1903. The Oregon Short Line was ultimately absorbed into the Union Pacific system.

20' WOOD ORE CAR

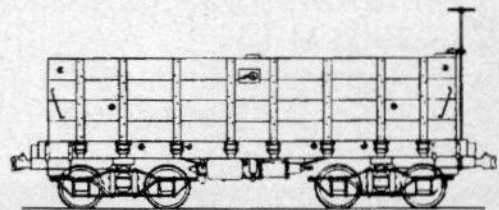

707-3860 Undecorated pkg(2) **21.00**
This car is typical of small wooden ore cars used by narrow- and standard-gauge railroads around the country.

Westerfield specializes in cars from 1895 to 1930, the "golden age" of railroading. HO Scale craft train kits feature unpainted, ultra-thin, impact-resistant, urethane castings with add-on detail parts. Prototypical custom decals are included in the decorated kits. Models include weights, but are less trucks and couplers. Note: Walthers carries the most popular kits in the extensive Westerfield line. Other kits not listed can be special ordered from Walthers. For a complete listing of what's in stock, see our Web site at www.walthers.com

BOX CARS

Fowler 40' w/5' Door Box Car 783-1501

40' Automobile Car 783-2001

783-1151 50' A-50-4 Automobile Car UP **29.00**
783-1352 36' Modernized XL Maryland & Pennsylvania **27.00**
783-4751 ATSF BX-12 w/Raised Roof **28.00**

B&O M-15 CLASS EA 27.00

783-5001 M-15B Original 1916 w/Reverse Murphy Ends
783-5002 M-15E As-Built 1923 w/Reverse Murphy End
783-5003 M-15D As-Built 1922 w/USRA Alternate End
783-5004 M-15C As-Built 1921 w/Reverse Murphy Ends
783-5006 M-15F w/Indestructible Ends *NEW*
783-5051 C-8 Express Car *NEW*

783-5052 M-15H 1937 Rebuild w/Indestructible Ends *NEW*
783-5053 M-15J w/Indestructible Ends *NEW*
783-5054 C-8A Express Car *NEW*
783-5055 M-15B Maryland & Pennsylvania *NEW*

40' USRA/NYC MODIFIED DESIGN STEEL CAR EA 27.00

783-2901 NYC
783-2902 Boston & Albany

783-2903 Cleveland, Cincinnati, Chicago & St. Louis
783-2904 Michigan Central
783-2905 Cincinnati Northern
783-2906 Peoria & Eastern

TEXAS & PACIFIC REBUILT 40' AUTOMOBILE CARS EA 28.00

783-2001 40' Double-Sheathed, Double-Door
783-2051 Double Sheathed, Single Door 1935-50
783-2052 Steel, Single Door 1935-70s

40' Double Sheathed Box Car 783-7001

CANADIAN PACIFIC FOWLER 40' W/5' DOOR EA 27.00

783-1501 Phase IIIA/B As-Built w/2-Brace End
783-1502 Phase II As-Delivered w/ 4-Brace End
783-1551 Phase II/IIIA/B Rebuild w/Poling Pockets
783-1552 Phase IIIC Rebuild w/Poling Flanges

36' FOWLER MODERNIZED CAR W/6' DOOR

738-4352 Erie/Susquehanna
738-4354 Grand Trunk Western
738-4355 Nashville, Chattanooga & St. Louis
738-4357 CN (Built 1912) 1930s-60s Rebuild w/3-Brace End
738-4358 CN (Built 1913) 1930s-60s Rebuild w/Steel Roof
738-4359 CN (Built 1913) 1930s-60s Rebuild w/3-Brace End
738-4360 CN (Built 1918) 1930s-60s Rebuild w/Steel Roof

40' FOWLER CLONE SINGLE SHEATHED CARS EA 27.00

738-6453 DRGW Modernized 1935-48
738-6456 Minneapolis & St. Louis Modernized 1934-49
738-6463 DRGW Modernized w/AB Brakes 1948-65

40' UP HARRIMAN B-50-6 DOUBLE SHEATHED BOX CARS EA 27.00

783-7353 Modernized w/Corrugated 5-5-5 Murphy Ends 1939-1950s Lettering *NEW*
783-7354 Modernized w/Dreadnaught Ends 1939-1950s Lettering *NEW*
783-7355 Modernized w/Corrugated 5-5-5 Murphy Ends 1924-1936 Lettering *NEW*
783-7356 Modernized w/Dreadnaught Ends 1924-1936 Lettering *NEW*

40' DOUBLE SHEATHED VENTILATED USRA CLONE EA 28.00

783-7001 Atlantic Coast Line/Atlantic Coast Despatch 1921-29 Yellow Scheme
783-7002 Atlantic Coast Despatch 1929-40s w/Roman Lettering
783-7003 Atlantic Coast Line/Atlantic Coast Despatch 1940s-50s w/Gothic Lettering
783-7004 Atlantic Coast Line 1950s-60s
783-7005 Atlantic Coast Line/Atlantic Coast Despatch Late 1930s-40s w/Roman Lettering
783-7006 Atlantic Coast Line/Atlantic Coast Despatch Rebuilt 1940s-50s w/Gothic Lettering

ATSF 36' COMPOSITE BX SERIES EA 27.00

783-7801 Class Bx.O Pre-Safety Appliances 1905-1910+
783-7811 Class Bx.O w/Safety Appliances Teens-1920s
783-7851 Class Bx-O/5 Rebuild w/Murphy Ends 1925-Mid 40s
783-7852 Class Bx-O/14 Rebuild w/Dreadnaught Ends 1931-40s
783-7861 Class Bx-O5 w/Murphy Ends-1930s Rebuild w/New Roof & Bottom Door Rollers
783-7862 Class Bx.O/14 w/Dreadnaught Ends 1930s Rebuild w/new Roof, Bottom Door Rollers
783-7863 Class Bx-O 1930s Rebuild w/Double Sheathed Ends, New Roof, Bottom Door Rollers

1916 DESIGN AUTO CARS EA 27.00

783-7901 NYC As-Built 1916 w/Tight A End *NEW*
783-7902 Michigan Central As-Built 1916 w/Tight A End *NEW*
783-7903 Michigan Central-End Door First Series As-Built 1916 *NEW*
783-7951 NYC Rebuild 1937-50s Box Car *NEW*
783-7952 Michigan Central Rebuild 1937-50s *NEW*

783-7953 Canada Southern 1941-mid 60s *NEW*

REEFERS

UNION REFRIGERATOR TRANSIT CO. 42' CARS

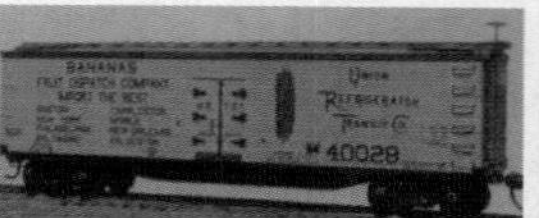

783-2601 Bananas **28.00**
783-2602 MILW 1920s-30s **28.00**
783-2600 Undecorated **26.00**

AMERICAN CAR & FOUNDRY 40' TYPE 1

783-6001 Union Refrigerator Transit Co./Bananas 1911-20 **28.00**
783-6002 GN/Western Fruit Express 1920-30 **27.00**

783-6003 American Refrigerator Transit Co. 1911-1920s **28.00**

34' HEINZ INSULATED BOX CARS

783-3951 Large "57" Lettering - Modernized Car **27.00**

PFE R-50-1 CLASS

783-8301 PFE **29.00** ***NEW***

STOCK CARS

HARRIMAN STANDARD 40'

S-40-4 CLASS SINGLE CENTERSILL-ORIGINAL 1912-14 EA 29.00

783-5201 SP & Subsidiaries
783-5202 UP & Subsidiaries

783-5203 North Western Pacific/Pacific Electric/SP of Mexico

S-40-4 CLASS MODERNIZED EA 29.00

783-5251 SP/Texas & New Orleans 1930-60+

783-5252 UP/Oregon Short Line 1940s-50s

S-40-5 CLASS MODERNIZED EA 29.00

783-5351 SP/North Western Pacific/Texas & New Orleans 1930s-60s
783-5352 UP 1940s-1970

S-40-8 CLASS EA 29.00

783-5401 Modernized S40-8/9/10 1923-40s SP **29.00**
783-5402 Original S-40-8 1924-40s SP/Arizona Eastern/San Diego & Arizona

783-5403 Modernized S-40-8 Single Deck 1924-50s Western Pacific
783-5451 Modernized S40-8/9/10 1930s-70 SP
783-5453 S-40-8 1930s-60s Western Pacific Double Deck

ATSF SK SERIES CARS EA 29.00

783-7601 Class Sk-2 w/Original Side Door 1942-74
783-7602 Class Sk-3 w/Radial Roof & New Doors 1940s-74

MILW 36' CARS EA 29.00

783-8201 Single Deck ***NEW***
783-8202 Solid Bottom ***NEW***
783-8203 Double Deck ***NEW***

HOPPERS

USRA 70 TON 39' 3-BAY

783-2151 C&O w/Flat Radial Ends
783-2152 C&O w/Dreadnaught Radial Ends
783-2153 NYC w/Center Saw Tooth
783-2154 Pittsburgh & Lake Erie/Pittsburgh McKeesport & Youghiogheny w/Center Saw Tooth

GLA 2-BAY HOPPERS EA 26.00

783-5751 PRR 1911-40
783-5752 Berwind Coal 1911-40 (BWCX/BWCMCO)
783-5753 Berwind/New River & Pocahontas 1930s-40s
783-5754 B&O (Ex-Jamison Coal) 1917-30

STANDARD STEEL CAR CO. 2-BAY HOPPER

783-7402 CNJ 1900s-Teens **26.00**
783-7403 Lackawanna Class B4 1900s-Teens **28.00**
783-7405 Erie 1905-20 **28.00**

783-7407 Jamison Coal & Coke Co. 1904-17 **26.00**
783-7408 LV 1900s-20s **26.00**
783-7409 Susquehanna 1900s-Teens **26.00**
783-7410 PRR Class GLB (& All Subsidiaries) 1900s-20s **28.00**
783-7411 Philadelphia & Reading/Reading 1900s-Teens **26.00**
783-7457 B&O Class N-14 1917-30 **26.00**
783-7460 PRR Class GLB w/Safety Appliances 1910-Late 20s **26.00**
783-7463 PRR Class GLE Covered Hopper Rebuild 1931-60s **30.00**

31' VANDERBILT HOPPER EA 26.00

783-8401 West Virginia Coal-Original ***NEW***
783-8451 WM-Modern ***NEW***

GONDOLAS

783-1251 46' PRR G22 Original **26.00**

783-2501 40' Composite MILW **26.00**

46' "LONG GONDOLA" 1933-65 27.00

783-7101 Canadian National Railway - No Side Stakes **27.00**

783-7111 Canadian National Railway w/Side Stakes **28.00**
783-7110 Undecorated w/Side Stakes **27.00**

34' Heinz Insulated Box Car 783-3951

"Coffin" Pickle Tank Cars 783-2202

Drover's Service Car 783-8001

46' USRA STEEL GONDOLA EA 27.00

783-8101 B&O Class O-27 ***NEW***
783-8102 NYC/Pittsburgh McKeesport & Youghiogheny ***NEW***
783-8103 PRR Class G-25 ***NEW***
783-8104 Reading Class GMK ***NEW***
783-8105 Wheeling & Lake Erie ***NEW***

TANK CARS

"COFFIN" PICKLE TANK CARS EA 27.00

783-2201 Claussen
783-2202 Heinz

OTHER CARS

22' STEEL ORE CARS

AS-BUILT CIRCA 1900

783-3401 GN pkg(2) **31.00**
783-3402 Algoma Central/Lake Champlain & Moriah pkg(2) **31.00**
783-3400 Undecorated pkg(2) **29.00**

MODERNIZED CIRCA 1914 PKG(2)

783-3451 GN **31.00**
783-3452 Sierra Railroad/Yosemite Valley **31.00**
783-3450 Undecorated **29.00**

DROVER'S SERVICE CAR

783-8001 UP/Los Angeles & Salt Lake Class B-50-4 1926-57 **27.00**

GLA 2-Bay Hoppers 783-5751

RAIL LINE

30' Box Car 620-130

30' Idler Flat Car 620-131

30' Stock Car 620-132

NARROW GAUGE CARS

These HOn3 kits are based on Rio Grande prototypes. They feature injection-molded styrene bodies, detailed underframes, separate grab wires and other details. They also include dummy couplers, but do not come with trucks or decals.

30' BOX CAR

620-130 Rio Grande **14.95**
Haul in supplies to the high country aboard this authentic 30' box car, a replica of the Rio Grande's rebuilt 3000 series cars. Sliding side doors are great for showing off interior details.

30' IDLER FLAT CAR

620-131 Rio Grande **11.95**
These 6700 series flat cars were converted from 5500 series stock cars in 1955 for pipe train service.

30' STOCK CAR

620-132 Rio Grande **14.95**
Based on 5500 series cars as rebuilt after 1940. The kit features sliding doors, positionable end door and molded details.

These HO Scale craft train kits feature unpainted metal castings.

203 220 204 205

216 216, 217 210 209

220

FLAT CARS

683-230 Heavy Duty Flat Car **12.95** ***NEW***

FLAT CAR LOADS

(Cars shown in photos not included.)

683-203 Air-Cooled Transformer **7.95**
683-204 Turbine Gear & Blocking **7.95**
683-205 Diesel Generator **7.95**
683-209 Ship Propellers pkg(4) **7.95**
This package includes two 4-blade and two 3-blade propellers.

683-210 Steel Coils pkg(6) **7.95**

683-216 Refinery Pressure Tank **9.95**

683-217 Extra Sections for Tank No. 216 pkg(4) **6.95**
683-220 High-Voltage Cells pkg(3) **7.95**

683-225 Steel Mill Ingots pkg(6) **6.95**

CLAMSHELL BUCKET

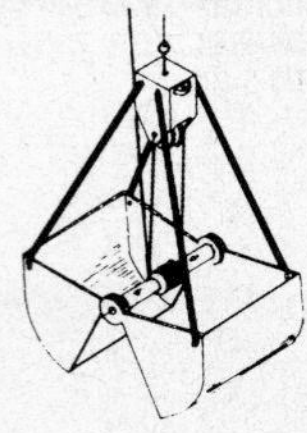

683-201 Clamshell Bucket Kit **11.95**
This operating bucket is for use with any HO crane. The all-metal kit includes complete assembly instructions.

20' FLATBED CONTAINER KIT

Includes a set of Virnex Alphabet and number decals. 2-5/8 x 1-1/16 x 1-11/16" high.

683-206 Smooth End pkg(2) **7.95**
683-207 Smooth End pkg(2) w/StripCoil **9.95**
683-208 Smooth End w/Machinery Load pkg(2) **9.95**
683-226 Ribbed End pkg(2) **7.95**
683-227 Ribbed End w/Steel Coil Load pkg(2) **9.95**
683-228 Ribbed End w/Machinery Load pkg(2) **9.95**

Models and Photo by Steve Sencaj

Someone once said that everything old is new again, and that certainly applies to railroading.

When the first rails were laid and the trains began running over the small shortline, it opened up the outside world to the local residents. As its success grew, new owners came calling, intent on making it part of their ever-expanding railroad empire. And when the red ink finally overflowed the ledgers, it was sold and began a return to its roots as a regional shortline.

The old-timers will tell you it isn't like it used to be. Gone now are the steam-powered Limiteds that roared through town. Gone are the bright streamliners. Gone are the work-a-day black diesels that pulled the wayfreights.

Despite all the changes, much is the same. The tracks are still here. On-line customers feel rail service is essential to their business. So with new owners and used equipment, another chapter in the history of the line begins.

Bright as the future they represent, the Erie Western equipment is spotless on this beautiful fall day. A second-hand Alco RS-3 drags a cut of covered hoppers down the mainline. The recently harvested cornfields along the tracks indicate plenty of work is waiting at the elevator!

Capturing the color of the prototype, Steve Sencaj of Highland, Indiana, repainted and decaled this Kato RS-3 and Athearn hopper. A pair of Walthers grain bins are alongside the tracks. A variety of natural materials were used to create the different kinds of foliage and groundcover.

WALTHERS™

BLANK DECAL PAPER

Create custom decals for any kind of models with these blank sheets. Same high-quality paper used in Walthers decals, ready to use. Choose from larger 8-1/2 x 11" sheets, ideal for making decals on a computer printer or photocopier, or the standard 9 x 6" sheets.

934-706821 8-1/2 x 11" Sheet pkg(4) **7.98**
934-706820 9 x 6" Sheet pkg(4) **3.98**

DECALS

ALL SETS $3.98

From the classic paint schemes of the steam-era to the flashy colors of today, creating custom equipment is easy with Walthers decals. Based on period photos and original railroad lettering diagrams, each set includes heralds, data and other lettering for one complete car or loco. Sets for most equipment include lettering diagrams with painting information. Color shown indicates primary color of lettering.

ALASKA RAILROAD

934-119001 Combination Freight–Steam-Era–white
934-119100 50' Box–Steam-Era–white
934-119750 GP35–yellow
934-119800 Streamline Passenger–yellow

ALGOMA CENTRAL

934-23010 Combination Freight–Modern–white
934-23320 52' Gondolas #601-875–white
934-23750 GP7 #150 series–yellow

ANN ARBOR

934-3100 40' Box #1200-1399 –white
934-3402 Covered Hopper #500-599–black

ATLANTIC COAST LINE

934-25060 Caboose #1352–white
934-25081 Caboose #0600 "Thanks" slogans–black
934-25110 40' Box–Steam-Era–white
934-25150 40' Box–Round Herald–white
934-25200 50' Box–"Thanks" slogans–yellow
934-25210 50' Box #35100-99–yellow
934-25401 53' Covered Hopper #50000–black
934-25760 GP7 #100-253–purple & silver
934-25771 ALCO C628 #2000-5–silver
934-25780 GP35 #907–white
934-25910 EMD #384 Diesel Freight–silver

BALTIMORE & OHIO

934-26060 Caboose–Steam-Era–white
934-26070 Caboose C1897 "Serving 13 Great States"–yellow
934-26110 40' Box "Timesaver"–white
934-26120 40' Box "Sentinel"–white
934-26150 40' Box–Steam–white
934-26331 40' Box–black herald–white
934-26470 40' Box "Fast Freight"–blue
934-26480 40' Box "Timesaver"–orange
934-26610 Passenger–1947 Scheme–yellow
934-26710 Steam Loco–yellow
934-26720 Steam Loco–white
934-26740 Steam Loco #12 William Mason–gold
934-26770 GPs–New Style–yellow
934-26810 Passenger Cars "Capital Limited"–gold
934-26870 Piggyback Reefer–"Tofcee"–blue
934-26871 Piggyback–New Herald–blue
934-26890 RDC–blue
934-26921 E7 Passenger Diesel–New yellow

BANGOR & AROOSTOOK

934-28060 Caboose #900 w/Large Shield Herald–white
934-28110 40' Box Car–"Maine Products"-red, white & blue
934-28130 40' Box–red, white & blue Herald
934-28160 40' Box Small Herald–white
934-28440 40' Box Cars–#2000-2299
934-28480 40' Box #5100-99–black
934-28760 GP7 #550-60–yellow
934-28920 EMD Diesel Passenger–blue

BERWIND WHITE COAL CO.

Limited Quantity Available
934-219020 Combination Freight–Modern–Black
934-219750 Diesel Loco–white

BESSEMER & LAKE ERIE

934-121060 Caboose #7061–white
934-121110 40' Box–white
934-121750 GP Diesel–white
934-121900 EMD Diesel Freight–white

BOSTON & MAINE

934-29060 Caboose #C-100 large "BM" Herald–white
934-29600 Passenger–Steam-Era–gold
934-29750 Diesel Switcher–Minuteman Herald–white
934-29760 GP7 #1555-77–yellow
934-29770 GP9 Black Cab, "BM" Herald–white
934-29890 RDC #6100–black

BRITISH COLUMBIA RAILWAY

934-284770 GP/SD Loco white

BURLINGTON NORTHERN

934-219010 Combination Freight–Modern–white

CANADIAN NATIONAL

934-30100 40' Box Maple Leaf Herald–white
934-30480 Reefer Pre-1960 Maple Leaf Herald–red
934-30600 Passenger Pre-1960s–gold
934-30700 Steam Loco–gold
934-30710 Steam Loco–white
934-30760 Diesel Switchers #8500-8625–black
934-30780 GP9–green-yellow
934-30930 EMD Diesel Passenger–1960's–white

CANADIAN PACIFIC

934-31300 Open/Covered Hopper–black
934-31331 35' Covered Hopper–white Script Lettering
934-31700 Steam Loco Beaver
934-31790 Multimark Logo for GP, SD, F & E Units–white
934-31800 Steam Passenger Letterboard

Ann Arbor Covered Hopper
934-3402

Atlantic Coast Line Caboose
934-25081

Baltimore & Ohio "Wm. Mason"
4-4-0 Steam Loco 934-26740

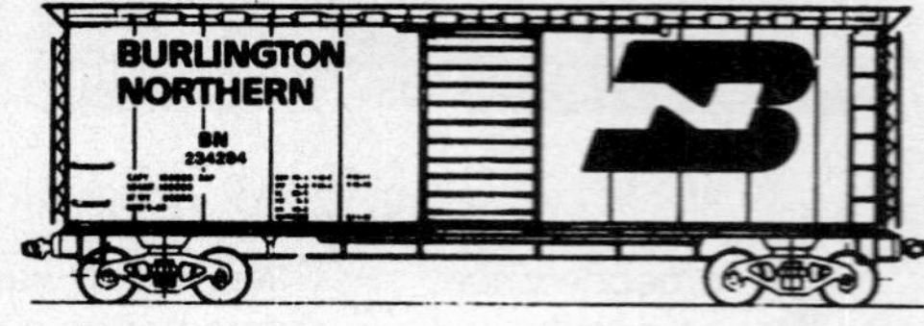

Burlington Northern
Combination Freight Set 934-219010

Canadian Pacific Diesels
w/Multimark Herald 934-31790

CENTRAL OF GEORGIA

934-32060 Caboose "Right Way"–white
934-32110 50' Box "Right Way"–white
934-32140 50' Box DF–white
934-32480 50' Box -1955–black
934-32600 Passenger Steam-Era–gold
934-32760 ALCO Loco Series #130–gold
934-32770 EMD Yard Switchers–white
934-32810 1947 Passenger Car–gold
934-32900 Diesel/Freight/ Passenger–gold

See What's Available at
www.walthers.com

CENTRAL VERMONT

934-34110 40' Box "Wet Noodle"–white
934-34700 Steam Loco–gold

CENTRAL RAILROAD OF NEW JERSEY

934-33060 Caboose–Steam #91538–white
934-33070 Caboose–Modern #91320–yellow
934-33150 40' Box Steam-Era–white
934-33600 Passenger–Steam-Era–gold
934-33610 Passenger–Steam-Era–yellow
934-33700 Steam Loco–Dulux
934-33750 Diesel Switcher–Dulux
934-33770 SD7–New Heralds–yellow
934-33810 Passenger–"Blue Comet"–gold
934-33890 RDC–black

WALTHERS™

ALL SETS $3.98

CHESAPEAKE & OHIO

934-35001 Combination Freight–Steam-Era–white
934-35060 Caboose #634–Steam-Era–white
934-35110 40' Box USRA Single Sheathed
934-35260 86' Hi-Cube Box–yellow
934-35620 Passenger–Steam-Era–blue
934-35700 Steam Loco–gold
934-35720 Streamline Steam Loco–white
934-35750 GP7 #5049 Older Lettering–yellow
934-35770 GP30 #3000–Yellow Nose
934-35900 EMD Freight–Original yellow

CHESSIE SYSTEM

934-282080 Caboose–blue

CHICAGO & ALTON

934-7100 40' Box #53039–white
934-7700 Steam Loco–gold

CHICAGO & EASTERN ILLINOIS

934-36760 GP7–White Nose Stripe

CHICAGO & ILLINOIS MIDLAND

934-37120 40' Box–No Herald–white
934-37760 GP9 & Other Diesels–white

CHICAGO & NORTH WESTERN

934-38050 "Flag Caboose"–black
934-38090 Caboose "Employee Owned"–green
934-38110 40' Box "Overland"–white
934-38130 50' Box–Large CNW–white
934-38170 40' Box–white "Route of the 400"-white
934-38200 40' Box–Omaha Road "Route of the 400"–green
934-38403 40' Airslide® Hopper–black
934-38600 Passenger–Steam-Era–gold
934-38750 FM Locos "Route of the 400"–green
934-38760 Diesel Switchers–white
934-38770 Early GP & Road Loco–green & yellow
934-38780 SD40-2 "Falcon Service"–green
934-38840 Streamline Passenger–black
934-38880 Piggyback–Original–yellow, green
934-38900 Diesel Freight EMD Units–Early–yellow

CHICAGO, BURLINGTON & QUINCY

934-40110 40' Box–Large Herald–white
934-40440 Reefer "Route of the Zephyrs"–black
934-40451 50' Reefer–Yellow Stripes–white
934-40700 Steam Loco–gold
934-40810 Streamline Passenger–"California Zephyr" –black
934-40910 EMD Diesel Freight #9900 Series–black

CHICAGO GREAT WESTERN

934-41060 Caboose #140–Modern Herald–white
934-41150 Box "Insulated DF" Modern Herald–white
934-41200 50' Box "Insulated DF"–yellow

CLINCHFIELD

934-39001 Combination Freight–Steam-Era–white
934-39100 40' Box–white
934-39110 50' Box "Cushion Car"–white
934-39751 EMD Switchers, Pre-1970–yellow

COLORADO MIDLAND

934-141120 Narrow Gauge Box–white

CONRAIL

934-325060 Caboose–white
934-325100 Box "Wheel On Rail"–white
934-325110 Box (Early) Ex-PC–white
934-325760 Diesel Hood Units–May, 1976–white

CSX

934-329900 Diesel Scheme September, 1986–blue

DELAWARE & HUDSON

934-46060 Caboose–Steam-Era–white
934-46110 40' Box–Old Herald–white
934-46120 40' Box–New Herald–white
934-46700 Steam Loco–Dulux

DELAWARE, LACKAWANNA & WESTERN

934-48060 Caboose–white
934-48110 40' Box "Phoebe Snow"–white
934-48320 52' Gondola Billboard Scheme–white
934-48331 40' Hopper Billboard Scheme–white
934-48600 Passenger–Steam-Era–gold
934-48700 Steam Loco–Dulux
934-48750 Diesel Switcher–yellow

DETROIT & MACKINAC

934-16210 Covered Hopper #6100-49–black

DETROIT, TOLEDO & IRONTON

934-17001 Combination Freight–Steam-Era–white
934-17700 Steam Loco–silver

DULUTH, MISSABE & IRON RANGE

934-19090 Caboose C200–Modern–maroon
934-19340 20' Ore Car–white
934-19600 Passenger–Steam-Era–gold

DULUTH, SOUTH SHORE & ATLANTIC

934-18200 50' "Merchandise Service" Box #18090-99–red
934-18340 Ore Car #80002-82049–white

EDAVILLE RAILROAD

934-161100 Box Ocean Spray–white

ELGIN, JOLIET & EASTERN

934-20760 GPs & Yard Switchers–yellow

ERIE / ERIE-LACKAWANNA

934-49001 Combination Freight–Steam-Era–white
934-49010 E-L Combination Freight–white
934-49060 Caboose–white
934-49600 Passenger Steam-Era–gold
934-49700 Steam Loco–Dulux
934-49750 Diesel Switcher–yellow
934-49760 Alco Road Switcher–yellow
934-49800 "Erie Limited" Streamline Passenger Car–yellow
934-49880 Piggyback Trailer–Early-black, yellow
934-49900 Diesel Freight–yellow
934-49920 Alco Diesel Freight/Passenger–yellow

FLORIDA EAST COAST

Limited Quantity Available

934-50600 Passenger–Steam-Era–gold

GRAND TRUNK WESTERN

934-51001 Combination Freight–Steam-Era–white
934-51770 GP9–Large "GT" Herald–white

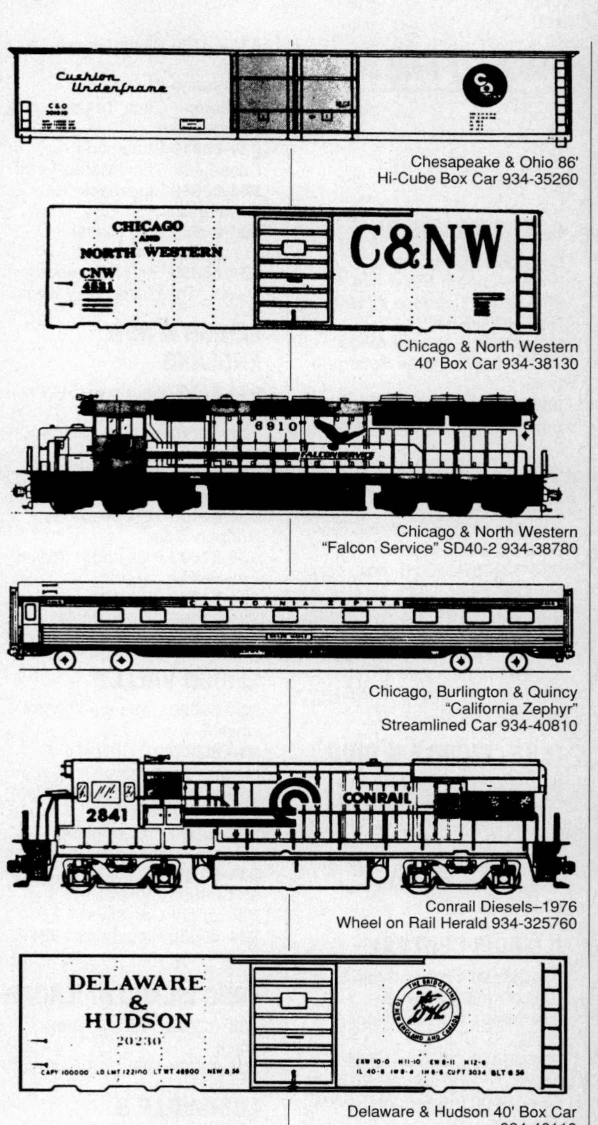

Chesapeake & Ohio 86' Hi-Cube Box Car 934-35260

Chicago & North Western 40' Box Car 934-38130

Chicago & North Western "Falcon Service" SD40-2 934-38780

Chicago, Burlington & Quincy "California Zephyr" Streamlined Car 934-40810

Conrail Diesels–1976 Wheel on Rail Herald 934-325760

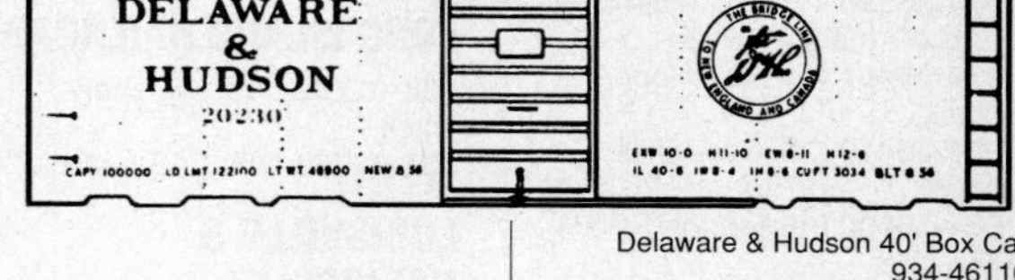

Delaware & Hudson 40' Box Car 934-46110

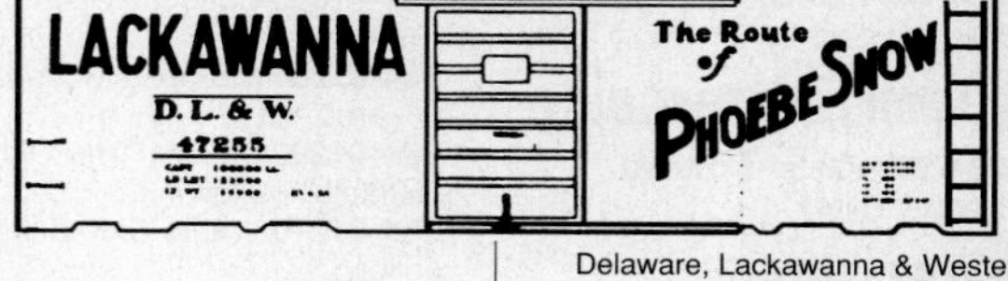

Delaware, Lackawanna & Western 40' Box Car 934-48110

Grand Trunk Western GP Diesels 934-51770

WALTHERS™

ALL SETS $3.98

GREAT NORTHERN

934-52001 Combination Freight–Steam-Era–white
934-52061 Caboose #X600 New Herald–white
934-52062 Caboose–Wide Vision–Big Sky Blue Scheme–white
934-52070 Caboose #X270 Big Sky Blue Scheme–white
934-52130 40' Box "Rocky" Logo & Herald–white
934-52131 50' Box "Cushion Ride"–white
934-52140 Box Cars–Big Sky Blue Scheme–white
934-52403 41' Covered Hopper–Flour–black
934-52700 Steam Loco–white
934-52710 Steam Loco–silver
934-52770 Diesels–Big Sky Blue Scheme–white
934-52880 Piggyback 1954–orange

GULF, MOBILE & OHIO

934-55060 Caboose–white
934-55110 40' Box Steam-Era–white
934-55600 Passenger–Steam-Era–gold
934-55900 Diesel Freight–Early, yellow

ILLINOIS CENTRAL

934-56150 40' Box "Main Line of Mid-America"–white
934-56401 Covered Hopper–black
934-56410 Coil Car–white, black
934-56600 Passenger–Steam-Era–gold
934-56700 Steam Loco–white
934-56910 Diesel Passenger–Early–brown

ILLINOIS CENTRAL GULF

934-228400 54' Covered Hopper–black

INTERSTATE

934-104330 Coal Hopper–white

KATY MISSOURI-KANSAS-TEXAS

934-68060 Caboose–Steam-Era–black
934-68070 Caboose #30 New Herald–yellow
934-68080 Caboose #801–black
934-68300 Center Flow Hopper–white
934-68600 Passenger–Steam-Era–gold
934-68750 Diesel Switcher–white
934-68800 Streamline Passenger Cars "Texas Special"–red
934-68810 Streamline Passenger Cars "Meteor"–red
934-68880 Piggyback "Katy"–Early–black
934-68900 Alco Diesel Freight/Passenger–red
934-68920 EMD Passenger Diesel "Texas Special"–silver

LEHIGH & NEW ENGLAND

934-67060 Caboose–Steam-Era–white
934-67110 40' Box Billboard Scheme–white
934-67150 40' Box Steam-Era–white
934-67400 32' Covered Hopper–black
934-67600 Passenger Steam-Era–yellow
934-67700 Steam Loco–white
934-67900 Alco #700 Series–black

LEHIGH VALLEY

934-60060 Caboose #95604–white
934-60400 31' Covered Hopper–black
934-60600 Passenger–Steam-Era–Dulux
934-60610 Passenger–Modern–yellow
934-60700 Steam Loco–silver
934-60800 Streamline Passenger Car–silver
934-60880 Piggyback 1954–white

LONG ISLAND RAILROAD

934-62762 Alco Switcher–black
934-62780 Alco C420–black

LOUISVILLE & NASHVILLE

934-61060 Caboose Steam-Era–white
934-61080 Caboose Modern w/Large "L&N"–red
934-61200 50' Box "The Old Reliable"–yellow
934-61270 Waffle-Side Box–yellow
934-61600 Passenger–Steam-Era–gold
934-61610 Passenger–Modern–yellow
934-61700 Steam Loco–gold
934-61770 GP7, 9, 18, 30–yellow
934-61771 U25B–No Name–yellow
934-61820 Streamline Passenger Car–black

MAINE CENTRAL

934-63001 Combination Freight–Steam-Era–white
934-63200 40' Box–Pine Tree–yellow
934-63223 40' Box–Green Door–green
934-63580 33' Tank–yellow
934-63600 Passenger–Steam-Era–gold
934-63710 Steam Loco–New Script–yellow
934-63770 GP7 Name Panel–yellow

MILWAUKEE ROAD

934-43111 50' Box–yellow stripe–maroon
934-43140 40' Box–Large Name–white
934-43170 50' Reefer–Aluminum Roof–white
934-43331 40' Hopper–Large Name–white
934-43401 46' Covered Hopper–black
934-43402 PS2 Yellow Covered Hopper–black
934-43470 URTX 40' Plug Door Reefer
934-43610 Passenger-Steam-Era–gold
934-43620 Passenger-UP Style–red
934-43700 Steam Loco–white
934-43760 FM Diesel–gold
934-43761 Orange & Black Hood Diesels–black
934-43762 SD40-2 Bicentennial red, white & blue scheme
934-43820 "Olympian Hiawatha" Streamline Passenger Cars–silver
934-43830 "Twin Cities Hiawatha" Streamline Passenger Cars–red
934-43880 Piggyback "Flexivan"–red

MINNEAPOLIS & ST. LOUIS

934-65110 40' Box "Peoria Gateway"–white
934-65770 GP7–New Herald–white
934-65930 Diesel Passenger–red

MISSOURI PACIFIC

934-69150 40' Box "Route of the Eagles"–white
934-69400 40' Covered Hopper–Flour–black
934-69480 40' Box "Merchandise Service"–black
934-69600 Passenger–Steam-Era–gold
934-69770 GP30 w/Eagle Herald–white
934-69920 EMD Passenger–Eagle Nose Herald–silver
934-69940 EMD Passenger–New Herald–white

Illinois Central Covered Hopper 934-56401

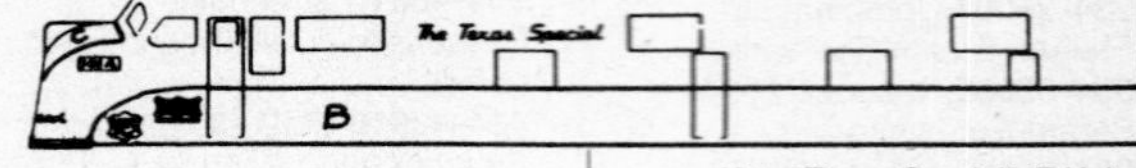

Katy "Texas Special" E Units 934-68920

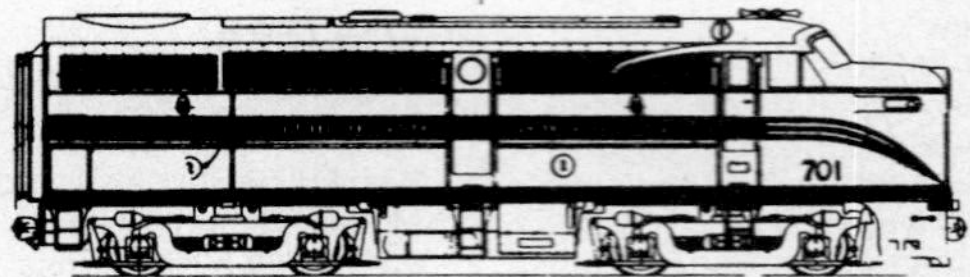

Lehigh & New England Alco Diesels 934-67900

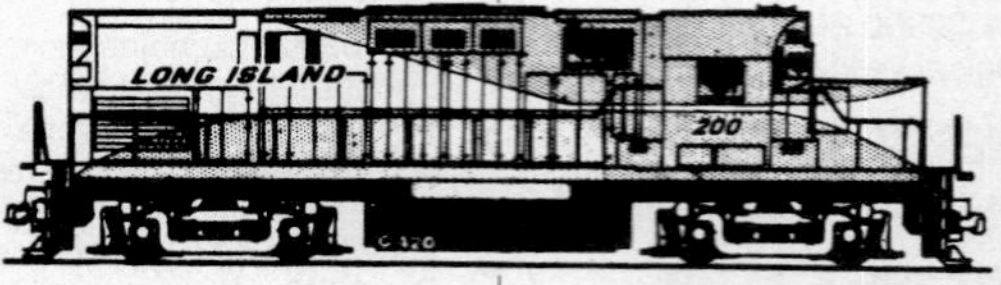

Long Island Railroad Alco Diesel Locos 934-62780

Milwaukee Road Bicentennial SD40-2 934-43762

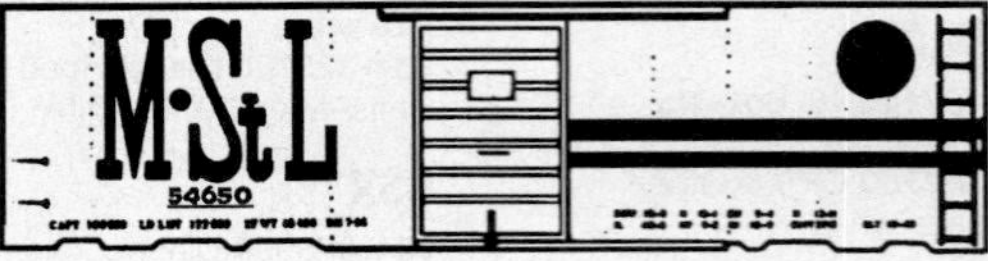

Minneapolis & St. Louis 40' Box Car 934-65110

MONON

934-42010 Combination Freight–Modern–white
934-42060 Caboose "Monon"–white
934-42110 40' Box #1-500 "Monon"–white
934-42120 40' Box w/Large "Hoosier Line"–white
934-42130 40' Box New Herald–white
934-42331 33' Hopper Large "MONON"–white
934-42630 Passenger Steam-Era–gold
934-42760 Alco C628–black, gold
934-42920 Diesel Passenger–white

NASHVILLE, CHATTANOOGA & ST. LOUIS

934-70060 Caboose "Dixieland" Slogan–white
934-70100 40' Box–Wide Yellow Stripe, white
934-70700 Steam Loco–yellow
934-70750 Diesel Switcher–yellow

NATIONAL OF MEXICO

934-64210 FCM 40' Box Large "M"–white
934-64230 40' Box–black

NEW HAVEN

934-73050 Caboose #C418 Steam-Era–white
934-73060 Caboose #678 Large "NH"–white
934-73080 Caboose #C581 "Trailiner"–black
934-73110 40' Box w/black and white "NH" Herald
934-73130 40' Reefer red, white & blue, "State of Maine"
934-73600 Passenger–Steam-Era–gold
934-73650 Express Reefer–gold

WALTHERS™

ALL SETS $3.98

Limited Quantity Available

934-73700 Steam Loco, Retired 1952–silver
934-73752 Alco C424 "NH"–white
934-73760 Alco #500–black
934-73810 Streamline Passenger–black

Limited Quantity Available

934-73880 Piggyback "Trailiner"–orange, black
934-73930 Electric Locos 1908 Paint Scheme "NH"–white

NEW YORK CENTRAL

934-71001 Combination Freight–Steam-Era–white
934-71060 Caboose–Steam-Era–white
934-71061 Caboose–No Herald–white
934-71070 Caboose–Jade Green–white
934-71120 40' Box "Early Bird"–white
934-71130 50' Jade Green Box–white
934-71140 60' Box "Cushion Underframe"–white
934-71160 40' Box "Pacemaker"–white
934-71600 Passenger–Steam-Era–gold
934-71640 Passenger–Steam-Era–black
934-71700 Steam Loco–Standard–white
934-71730 Streamlined Steam Loco–silver
934-71760 Jade Green Diesels–white
934-71820 Streamlined Passenger Cars "20th Century Limited"–1938 Scheme–white
934-71840 Streamlined Passenger Cars Passenger Pool–yellow
934-71880 Piggyback Trailer "Flexivan"–black
934-71901 Diesel Freight 1961 Style–white
934-71920 EMD Diesel Passenger–white
934-71930 Alco #4100 Series Diesels–white

NEW YORK, ONTARIO & WESTERN

934-140001 Combination Freight–Steam-Era–white

NICKEL PLATE

934-72001 Combination Freight–Steam-Era–white
934-72060 Caboose "High Speed Service"–white, black
934-72110 40' Box "DF"–white
934-72120 40' Insulated Box–white
934-72321 Gondola–white
934-72440 MDT Reefer–black
934-72700 Steam Loco–yellow
934-72750 Diesel Switcher–white
934-72800 Streamline Passenger–blue
934-72880 Piggyback 1954 Style–blue

NORFOLK & WESTERN

934-74060 Caboose–Steam-Era–white
934-74061 Caboose–New Style Round Herald–white
934-74130 Box Plug Door & Standard 1971 NW Scheme–white
934-74600 Passenger Steam-Era–gold
934-74710 Steam Loco–Dulux
934-74750 GP7 #710-812–gold

NORFOLK SOUTHERN–MODERN

934-327900 Diesel–white

NORFOLK SOUTHERN–ORIGINAL

934-108001 Combination Freight–Steam-Era–white
934-108200 50' Box #1200/1300 Series–black

NORTHERN PACIFIC

934-75321 60' Wood Chip Car–white
934-75371 40' Stock "Pig Palace"–white
934-75760 GP9 #200-375 & GP18 Diesels–Dulux
934-75900 EMD Diesel Freight–yellow

NORTHWESTERN PACIFIC

934-138100 Box Billboard Name–white

PENN CENTRAL

934-205020 Combination Freight–Modern–black
934-205060 Caboose–white
934-205150 Box Cars–white
934-205310 Coil Cars–white
934-205750 Diesel Locos–white

PENNSYLVANIA

934-77001 Combination Freight–Steam-Era–white
934-77060 Caboose Keystone Herald–white
934-77100 40' Box Steam-Era–white
934-77110 60' Box "Merchandise Service"–silver, red
934-77130 50' Box "No Damage," Special Herald–white
934-77140 40' Box New Herald, 14" Reporting Marks–white
934-77170 50' Box "Cushioned Car"–white
934-77331 Open Hopper, Old–white
934-77600 Passenger Car Steam-Era–gold
934-77610 Passenger Car Modern–Dulux
934-77700 Steam Loco–gold
934-77710 Steam Loco–Dulux
934-77730 Streamline Steam Loco–gold
934-77750 Diesel Switchers & Geeps–gold
934-77760 EMD Yard Switcher–Dulux
934-77800 Streamlined Cars "Broadway"–gold
934-77810 Streamlined Cars "Trail Blazer"–gold
934-77860 Streamlined "Congressional Limited"–gold
934-77880 Piggyback 1954 Style–yellow
934-77881 Piggyback w/Round Herald–yellow
934-77900 EMD #9200 Series Single Stripe–gold
934-77910 EMD Freight Diesel 5 Stripe–Dulux
934-77925 Alco Passenger Diesel–Dulux
934-77940 GG1 5-Stripe 1934–gold

PERE MARQUETTE

934-78060 Caboose–white
934-78920 Diesel Passenger–yellow, blue

PIEDMONT & NORTHERN

934-167750 Alco Road Switcher–yellow

PITTSBURGH & SHAWMUT

934-146001 Combination Freight–Steam-Era–white
934-146750 Diesel Switcher–black

PITTSBURGH & WEST VIRGINIA

934-79100 40' Box #1200–white

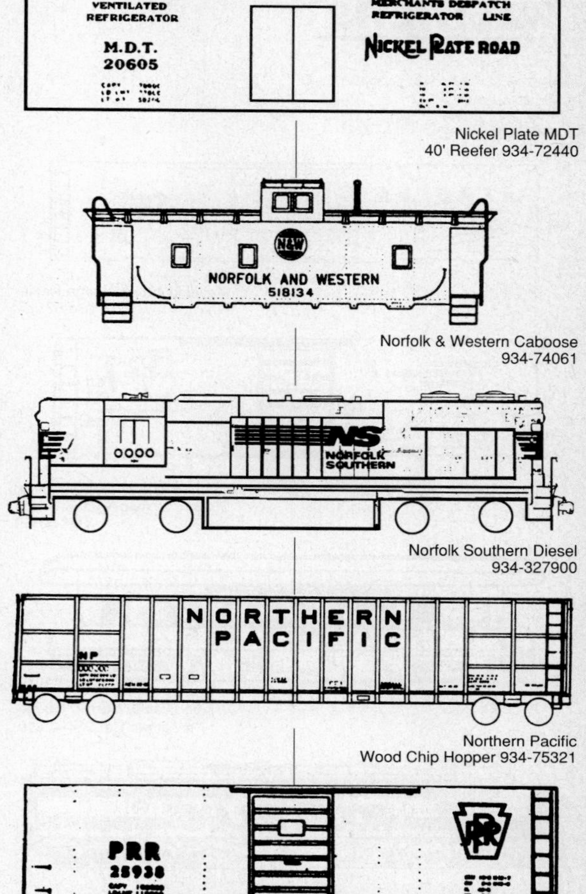

Nickel Plate MDT 40' Reefer 934-72440

Norfolk & Western Caboose 934-74061

Norfolk Southern Diesel 934-327900

Northern Pacific Wood Chip Hopper 934-75321

Pennsylvania 40' Box New Herald 934-77140

Pennsylvania Alco Passenger Diesel 934-77925

PORT HURON & DETROIT

934-81110 40' Box Billboard–white

PORTLAND TERMINAL RAILROAD

934-160100 40' Box–white

PULLMAN

934-80610 Passenger Roman/Gothic–gold

RAILWAY EXPRESS AGENCY

934-124440 43' Reefer Green Bands–black
934-124650 Express Reefer–gold
934-124660 46' Express Reefer–New–white

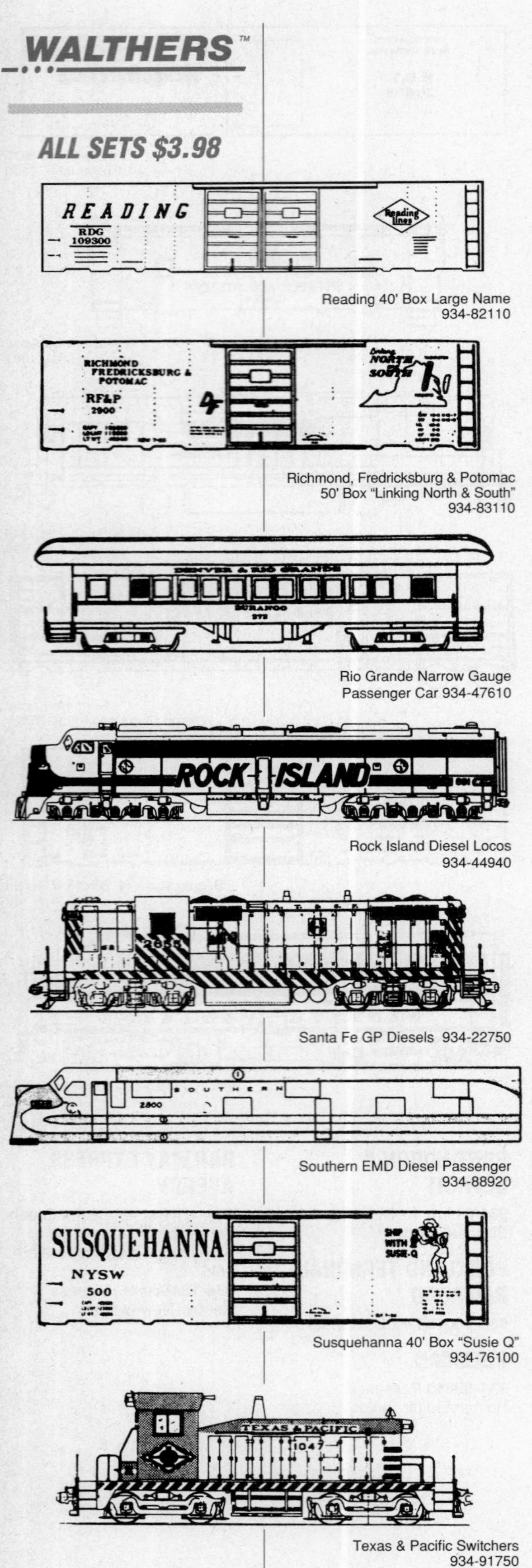

Reading 40' Box Large Name 934-82110

Richmond, Fredricksburg & Potomac 50' Box "Linking North & South" 934-83110

Rio Grande Narrow Gauge Passenger Car 934-47610

Rock Island Diesel Locos 934-44940

Santa Fe GP Diesels 934-22750

Southern EMD Diesel Passenger 934-88920

Susquehanna 40' Box "Susie Q" 934-76100

Texas & Pacific Switchers 934-91750

READING

934-82001 Combination Freight–Steam-Era–white
934-82060 Caboose #920680–white
934-82070 Caboose #9230–yellow
934-82100 40' Box Old Letters–white
934-82110 40' Box Large Name–white
934-82200 50' Box w/Name on Yellow Panel–yellow
934-82600 Passenger–Steam-Era–gold
934-82610 Passenger–Modern–yellow
934-82700 Steam Loco–gold
934-82770 GP30 #5513 Series–black
934-82880 Piggyback Trailer–blue

RICHMOND, FREDRICKSBURG & POTOMAC

934-83060 Caboose Steam-Era–white
934-83110 50' Box "Linking North & South"–white
934-83920 Old Diesel Passenger #1101–black

RIO GRANDE

934-47110 40' Box Steam-Era–white
934-47130 30' Box Narrow Gauge–white
934-47470 40' Box–black
934-47610 Passenger–Narrow Gauge–gold
934-47700 Steam Loco–white
934-47750 Diesel Switcher–yellow

ROCK ISLAND

934-44080 Caboose–black
934-44100 40' Box "Ship Rocket Freight"– white
934-44150 Box Steam–white
934-44210 Box "The Rock"–black
934-44331 40' Hopper–Billboard Scheme–white
934-44400 Center Flow Hopper–black
934-44470 GARX 50' Reefer–black
934-44600 Passenger Steam-Era–gold
934-44820 Streamline Passenger–black
934-44920 EMD Passenger "Rocket"–black
934-44940 Diesel Freight–1969 Scheme–white
934-44950 EMD Freight "The Rock"–black

ROSCOE, SNYDER & PACIFIC

934-177200 40' Box–black

RUTLAND

934-100001 Combination Freight–Steam-Era–white
934-100060 Caboose–white
934-100070 Caboose–yellow
934-100200 40' Box "Green Mountain Gateway"–green
934-100600 Passenger Steam-Era–gold
934-100750 Diesel Switcher Yellow Stripe–yellow

SANTA FE

934-22001 Combination Freight–Steam-Era–white
934-22151 86' Box–Auto Parts –white
934-22280 40' Box #16700-899–yellow
934-22600 Passenger–Steam-Era–gold
934-22710 Steam Loco–white
934-22750 GP7, FM etc.–silver
934-22910 EMD Freight Diesels–1960's–yellow
934-22920 ALCO & EMD Passenger Diesels–black

Limited Quantity Available
934-22180 50' Box #16950-98 –white

SEABOARD AIR LINE

934-86060 Caboose #5602–Steam-Era–white
934-86160 40' Box Large "Seaboard"–white
934-86200 50' Box "Cushion Underframe"–white
934-86210 50' Box "Seaboard"–yellow
934-86600 Passenger–Steam-Era–black
934-86800 Streamlined "Silver Meteor"–black
934-86900 EMD Diesel Freight #4000–yellow
934-86920 EMD Diesel Passenger Old–black

SEABOARD COASTLINE

Limited Quantity Available
934-206400 SCL Covered Hopper
934-206080 Caboose–black

SOO LINE

934-66001 Combination Freight–Steam-Era–white
934-66060 Caboose through 1962–white
934-66070 Wide Vision Caboose–Modern–black
934-66402 49' Covered Hopper "Custom Equipped"–black
934-66600 Passenger–Steam-Era–gold
934-66700 Steam Loco–white
934-66900 EMD Freight–Early –gold

Get Your Daily Dose of Product News at
www.walthers.com

SOUTHERN

934-88001 Combination Freight–Steam-Era–white
934-88060 Caboose–Steam-Era–white
934-88070 Caboose #X3064–Modern–yellow
934-88110 40' Box "DF"–white
934-88140 50' Box "Super Cushion Service"–white
934-88150 40' Box Old Letters–white
934-88490 Work Car/MOW–black
934-88600 Passenger–Steam-Era–gold
934-88610 Passenger–Modern–yellow
934-88640 Passenger–Steam-Era–black
934-88700 Steam Loco–white
934-88750 Diesel Switcher–white
934-88770 EMD Diesel Switcher–yellow
934-88810 Streamlined Passenger Cars "Crescent Limited"–gold
934-88880 Piggyback "Containerized"–black
934-88900 EMD Diesel Freight–yellow
934-88920 EMD Diesel Passenger–gold

SOUTHERN PACIFIC

934-89080 Caboose #501–black, red
934-89100 40' Box–white
934-89140 86' Hi-Cube Box–white
934-89700 Steam Loco–white
934-89880 Piggyback–black

SPOKANE, PORTLAND & SEATTLE

934-122120 40' Box 1960's–white

ST. LOUIS–SAN FRANCISCO–"FRISCO"

934-84110 40' Box "Frisco Fast Freight"–white
934-84402 50' Covered Hopper "Ship IT" slogan–black
934-84620 Passenger Steam-Era–red

SUSQUEHANNA

934-76100 40' Box "Susie Q"–yellow
934-76750 Diesel Switchers 1945–silver

TENNESSEE, ALABAMA & GEORGIA

934-169100 50' Box–yellow

TENNESSEE CENTRAL

934-94001 Combination Freight–Steam-Era–white
934-94100 40' Box–white
934-94600 Passenger Heavyweight–yellow

WALTHERS™

ALL SETS $3.98

TERMINAL RAILROAD ASSOCIATION OF ST. LOUIS

934-117750 Diesel Switcher–white

TEXAS & PACIFIC

934-91001 Combination Freight–Steam-Era–white
934-91060 Caboose #7234–white
934-91100 40' Box–Steam-Era Diamond Herald–white
934-91380 Tank Diesel Oil–yellow
934-91480 40' Reefer "DF"–black
934-91600 Passenger Heavyweight–gold
934-91710 Steam Loco–white
934-91750 Diesel Switcher Diamond Herald–orange
934-91751 Diesel Switcher Diamond Herald–black

TOLEDO, PEORIA & WESTERN

934-90530 40' Hopper "Links East & West"–yellow

TRANSPORT LEASING CORP.

934-163200 50' Box Spruce Falls Power & Paper–yellow

UNION PACIFIC

934-93080 Caboose–red
934-93200 40' Box "Streamliner"–yellow
934-93401 40' Covered Hopper–black
934-93590 Auto Rack–yellow
934-93600 Passenger–Steam-Era–gold
934-93640 Passenger–1952 Style–red
934-93700 Steam Loco–white
934-93761 GP30–Red Stripes
934-93780 GP "We Can Handle It"–red, black
934-93910 EMD Freight Double Wing–red
934-93920 Diesel Passenger "Cities"–red
934-93930 Gas Turbine–red
934-93940 E6 Diesel "Cities/ Overland"–multicolor

UNITED STATES ARMED FORCES

934-131100 Box Transportation Corps–white
934-131110 Box Army/Navy–white
934-131380 Tank Car Transportation Corps–white
934-131610 Army Hospital Car–white
934-131620 Troop Train–gold

VIRGINIA & TRUCKEE

934-123080 Caboose–red
934-123100 Box–white
934-123600 Passenger–gold
934-123700 Steam Loco–gold

VIRGINIAN

934-95001 Combination, Freight–Steam-Era–white
934-95060 Caboose–white
934-95110 40' Box New Herald–white
934-95750 GP & FM Trainmaster–yellow

WABASH

934-96060 Caboose #2773–white
934-96110 40' Box "Heart of America"–white
934-96501 41' Covered Hopper "Cannonball Freight"–blue
934-96760 GP7–yellow
934-96770 GP30–yellow
934-96910 EMD Freight–yellow

WESTERN MARYLAND

934-97001 Combination Freight–Steam-Era–white
934-97060 Caboose #1600–white
934-97110 40' Box Pre-1953–white
934-97770 GP9 Yellow Stripes–yellow
934-97880 Piggyback–black
934-97900 Alco Diesel Freight–Dulux

WESTERN PACIFIC

934-98120 40' Box "Shock Protected"–black
934-98220 50' Reefer–"DF"/Feather–yellow
934-98600 Passenger–Steam-Era–gold

PRIVATE OWNERS

PRIVATE OWNER COVERED HOPPERS

934-1205 HWCX 29' Haliburton Oil Well Cement–black
934-1441 NAHX 41' Centerflow–International Minerals–green

PRIVATE OWNER/GACX AIRSLIDE® HOPPERS

934-1416 29' Brach's–white, blue
934-1417 29' Nebraska Consolidated Mills–black, red

PRIVATE OWNER–OPEN-TOP HOPPER

934-1380 Peabody Coal Co.–black

PRIVATE OWNER REEFERS

934-1104 URTC A&P Tea Co.–black
934-1110 URTC Carnation–black, red
934-1111 Carnation Wheat–black, red, green
934-1137 GARE Hoods Dairy–yellow, red
934-1151 Snickers/Mars–black
934-1177 Phenix Cheese–black
934-1183 URTC Schlitz–w/Globes–red, black
934-1201 URTX Heidelberg–black
934-1204 URTX Bordens Milk–old
934-1214 Milky Way (Mars)–white
934-1288 SLRX–Budweiser–white
934-1292 Heinz 57 w/Pickle Herald–multicolor
934-1397 NADX Safeway Foods–black
934-1502 URTC Van Camps–ed, black, white
934-1503 PFE

PRIVATE OWNER TANK CARS

934-1117 CONX Conoco Billboard Scheme–white
934-1122 DRX Deep-Rock Billboard Scheme–yellow
934-1150 MPCX Magnolia Oil–black
934-1154 SOVX Mobilgas–Flying Horse–red, black
934-1155 SEOX Mobilgas–silver
934-1184 SCCX Shell Oil–yellow
934-1190 TCX Texaco Billboard Scheme–black
934-1233 GATX Hooker Chemical–Steam-Era–yellow
934-1268 GATX Anheuser-Busch Corn Syrup–black
934-1274 SCCX Shell Oil–black
934-1300 GATX Celanese–red
934-1333 GATX Klarer Lard–red, black
934-1342 NATX North American–silver
934-1351 POTX Pure Oil–blue
934-1365 NATX Rohm/Haas–yellow

Limited Quantity Available

934-1387 SPX Solvay–black
934-1395 CCBX Union Carbide–green, white
934-1396 UCPX Ucon Fluorocarbons (Union Carbide)–black
934-1404 WRNX Gulf Oil–white
934-1408 GATX DuPont Budium–black, red

Union Pacific Gas Turbine 934-93930

Wabash 40' Box "Heart of America" 934-96110

Brach's Candy Single Bay Airslide® Hopper 934-1416

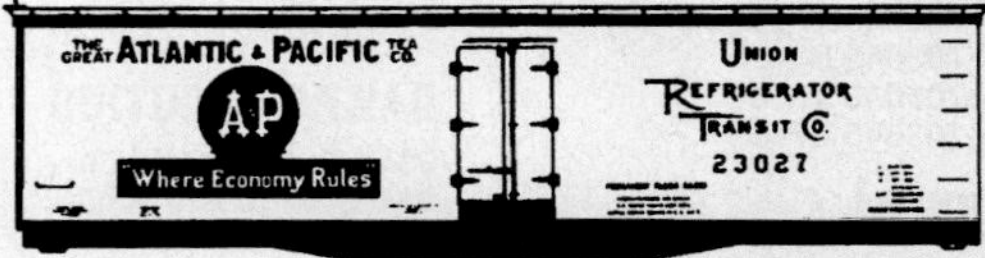

Atlantic & Pacific Tea Co. 40' Wood Reefer 934-1104

Blatz "Old Heidelberg Brew" 40' Wood Reefer 934-1201

DRX Deep-Rock Billboard Scheme 934-1122

WALTHERS™

ALL SETS $3.98

TRAILER TRAIN
934-1500 Various Flat Cars–black, white

STRIPES

1/64" STRIPES
934-703011 White
934-703012 Black
934-703013 Yellow
934-703016 Gold

1/32" STRIPES
934-703021 White
934-703023 Yellow
934-703024 Red
934-703025 Silver
934-703026 Gold

1/16" STRIPES
934-703041 White
934-703042 Black
934-703043 Yellow
934-703045 Silver

BARNUM
934-809110 #10 White
934-809410 #10 Red

BLOCK W/SHADOW
934-812108 #8 White
934-812408 #8 Red

COMBINATION STRIPES

SMALL WIDTH (1/64–1/16")
934-704501 White
934-704503 Yellow
934-704504 Red
934-704505 Silver
934-704506 Gold

LARGE WIDTH (3/64–1/8")
934-704561 White
934-704562 Black
934-704563 Yellow
934-704564 Red

CURVED DIESEL STRIPES (1/64–1/8")
934-704633 Yellow

EXTENDED GOTHIC ROUND #8
934-802108 White
934-802208 Black

EXTENDED ROMAN OVAL
934-845308 #8 Yellow

Limited Quantity Available
934-845310 #10 Yellow
934-845312 #12 Yellow
934-845410 #10 Red
934-845412 #12 Red
934-845610 #10 Silver

EXTENDED ROMAN SQUARE
934-846508 #8 Gold

MISCELLANEOUS STRIPES
934-703061 3/32" white
934-703101 1/4" white

SAFETY STRIPES
934-701471 White
934-701472 Black
934-701473 Yellow

STRIPES

Limited Quantity Available
934-703014 1/64" Red
934-703069 3/32" Orange

LETTERING

RAILROAD EXTENDED GOTHIC SQUARE
934-808108 #8 White
934-808110 #10 White
934-808116 #16 White
934-808208 #8 Black
934-808210 #10 Black

RAILROAD GOTHIC
934-806108 #8 White
934-806110 #10 White
934-806112 #12 White
934-806116 #16 White
934-806120 #20 White
934-806208 #8 Black
934-806210 #10 Black
934-806212 #12 Black
934-806216 #16 Black
934-806220 #20 Black
934-806310 #10 Yellow
934-806320 #20 Yellow
934-806408 #8 Red
934-806608 #8 Silver

Limited Quantity Available
934-806610 #10 Silver
934-806616 #16 Silver
934-806620 #20 Silver

RAILROAD ROMAN
934-804108 #8 White
934-804110 #10 White
934-804112 #12 White
934-804116 #16 White
934-804120 #20 White
934-804208 #8 Black
934-804210 #10 Black
934-804212 #12 Black
934-804308 #8 Yellow
934-804312 #12 Yellow
934-804408 #8 Red
934-804508 #8 Gold
934-804608 #8 Silver

CONDENSED
934-807108 #8 White
934-807216 #16 Black
934-807308 #8 Yellow
934-807508 # 8 Gold

Limited Quantity Available
934-807310 #10 Yellow
934-807312 #12 Yellow

CIRCUS ALPHABET
934-706932 Black
934-706934 Red
934-706935 Silver
934-706936 Gold

CIRCUS LETTERING
934-701630 Ringling Wagons–white
934-1489 Ringling Brothers, Barnum & Bailey® Circus Advance Car–multicolored
934-2008 Pullman Passenger Names–gold

Limited Quantity Available
934-701640 Ringling Passenger Cars–red
934-701670 Ringling Passenger Cars- gold
934-706760 Ringling Passenger Cars–red
934-701660 Ringling Stock Cars–white

ENGINE LETTERING
934-702090 Diesel Numberboards–black, white
934-701440 Steam Loco Panels–red, green, gold
934-706830 Diesel Loco Data–red, white

FREIGHT CAR LETTERING
934-706900 FRA Lubrication Plates

GRAFFITTI & SCRIBBLES
934-701070 White
934-701080 Black

DATA

COMBINATION FREIGHT

1920-60
934-706061 White
934-706062 Black

DATA 1920-60
Limited Quantity Available
934-706068 Blue

POST 1960
934-706371 White
934-706372 Black
934-706373 Yellow

AIRSLIDE® HOPPER
934-705601 White
934-705602 Black

ACF/PULLMAN HOPPER
934-705611 White
934-705612 Black

MODERN

CABOOSE
934-700861 White

BOX CAR
934-706351 White
934-706352 Black

STEAM-ERA DATA

BOX CAR
934-700101 White
934-700102 Black

WORK CAR
934-700391 White

TANK CAR DATA
934-706631 White

OLD TIME FREIGHT DATA
934-706191 White
934-706192 Black

PASSENGER CAR DATA
934-700601 White

NUMBER JUNGLES

ALTERNATIVE GOTHIC
934-706361 White

GOTHIC FUTURA
934-2510 White
934-2511 Black

RAILROAD ROMAN
934-2540 White
934-2543 Yellow

EXTENDED
934-2560 White
934-2562 Gold

PASSENGER CAR LETTERING
934-702060 Passenger Car Scrolls–gold

TRACTION EQUIPMENT
934-1457 Chicago, Aurora & Elgin–gold
934-1464 Sacramento Northern–Passenger–gold

CHICAGO, NORTH SHORE & MILWAUKEE
934-702170 Greenliner–gold
934-702190 Silverliner–silver

CHICAGO, SOUTH SHORE & SOUTH BEND
934-702210 Passenger–gold
934-702220 New–red

PACIFIC ELECTRIC
934-702640 #1100 Series–silver

PHILADELPHIA TRANSIT
934-702920 Red

VENETIAN BLINDS

Each decal set includes approximately 64" of Venetian blinds, ready to install on windows.

934-701180 Silver
934-701190 Gold

PRISM WINDOWS
934-701310 Silver

WAGON SCROLLS
934-701780 Silver
934-701790 Gold
934-706850 Circus Data

See Signals & Detection & Signs for signs, graffitti, fire engine names, stars.

Information STATION

WHAT IS A DECAL?

Ever wonder what a decal is made of, or how it works? The first use of preprinted transfers, known as "decalcomania," was in the 19th century. Designed to replace expensive and time consuming handpainting needed to decorate ceramic and glass products, they were very similar to modern decals. Decals for model railroads appeared in the 1930s as undecorated kits became available. Today's decals are still made in much the same way.

The process starts by taking photos and measurements from actual cars or locos, or obtaining company painting and lettering diagrams. From this material, the colors, sizes and styles of lettering are determined. These are also used to make the lettering diagrams, showing where each item will be used, that come with most sets. Most railroad equipment also carries a stylized logo, known as a "herald," which requires additional artwork. At one time this all had to be drawn by hand or typeset. Today, much of the work can be done using computers.

Decals are printed using the silk-screen process. Finished artwork is made into films which are used to make the screens.

Decals require special paper. The visible portion, usually a light blue, is called the backing paper. Next, a thin coating of water-soluble adhesive is applied. After it dries, a clear topcoat is applied, which forms a continuous film surface. Finally, all of the lettering is silk-screened on the clear surface.

Each color that makes up a decal requires a separate run through the silk-screening process, the sheets must be in perfect registration each time. Each color requires a separate set of screens for the images being printed.

Once dry, the sheets are cut to size, packaged and shipped, ready for your next custom painting project.

MICROSCALE®

DECAL ACCESSORIES

460-50 Microscale System Pack **19.80**
Complete starter kit with one bottle each: Micro Set, Micro Sol, Micro Coat Flat, Satin and Gloss finishes, Micro Mask, Kristal Kleer, Micro Metal Foil Adhesive, Micro Weld Cement, Micro Liquitape and Micro Liquid Decal Film.

ADHESIVES 1OZ (30ML) EA 2.00

460-114 Kristal Kleer
Perfect for attaching window glass, aircraft canopies, headlights and other clear parts to models. Dries completely clear, or tint with food coloring to make light lenses, stained glass or other special applications. Can be used to model window glass by applying in a thin layer to window openings. Cleans up with water; waterproof when dry.

460-115 Micro Liquitape
Make any part removable with this special formula. Holds parts firmly, but gentle finger pressure will loosen them. Works over and over. Great for test fitting parts, or for showing off "hidden" features, such as interior detail.

460-116 Micro Metal Foil Adhesive
Give models the look of real aluminum with this adhesive. Works with thin metallic foils, (including common aluminum foil) to simulate stainless steel, chrome plating, or natural metal finishes.

DECAL SETTING SOLUTION 1OZ (30ML) EA 2.00

Setting solutions soften decal film, allowing it to stretch over details for the best appearance. Prevents air bubbles and results in an invisible carrier film, reducing silvering. Formulated especially for Micro Scale decals, can be used with most other brands.

460-104 Micro Set
Brush over area where decal is to be applied. Special wetting agents cut oils in new paint and strengthen adhesive on decal.

460-105 Micro Sol
A stronger formula, for use on larger details or stubborn areas. Just brush on and let it work, actually makes decal part of the paint.

CLEAR FINISH EA 2.00

Water clear, nonyellowing, acrylic resins adhere strongly to paint and plastics and hide decal film. Can be applied with a brush, or airbrushed (40 pounds pressure), cleans-up with water.

460-103 Micro Coat Flat
Dead-flat for dirty, weathered or camouflaged look.

460-106 Micro Coat Satin
Semi-gloss, for a less shiny or slightly dirty look.

460-108 Micro Coat Gloss
Provides a smooth surface for decaling and produces a high-gloss, "wet look" when dry.

LIQUID DECAL FILM 1OZ (30ML) EA 2.00

460-117 Micro Liquid Decal Film
Create your own decals or save old ones. To make your own, brush film on a flat clean surface, allow to dry and draw or paint on your image. When brushed over an old decal, film seals and provides a new surface.

MASKING LIQUID 1OZ (30ML) EA 2.00

460-110 Micro Mask
Works like masking tape in a bottle! Just brush on surface and allow to dry. Can be cut with sharp hobby knife to create special effects. For use with solvent based paints. (Micro Mask is water soluble.)

DECAL CATALOG

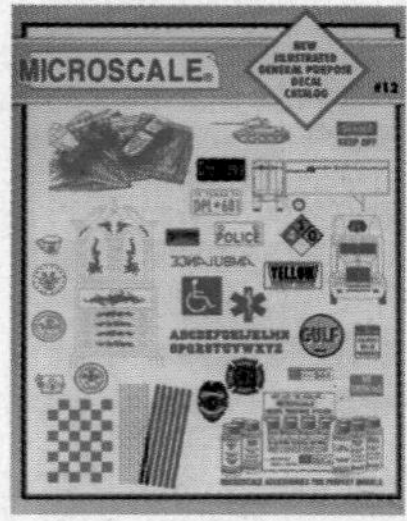

460-300 General Purpose **4.00**
Sets for larger models, including alphabets, signs, Pinewood Derby Cars, military equipment, dollhouses and more.

ACCESSORY DECAL SETS

TRIM FILM EA 1.50

Solid sheets of a single color for all kinds of special effects, backgrounds, or custom art.

460-1 White
460-2 Black
460-3 Metallic Gold
460-4 Metallic Silver
460-5 Red
460-6 Yellow
460-7 Dark Blue
460-8 Dulux Gold
460-9 Dark Green
460-10 SP "Daylight" Orange
460-11 Guilford Gray
460-12 UP/Amtrak Blue
460-13 Brown
460-14 Bright Blue
460-15 Gray Green
460-16 B&M Gray
460-17 Emerald Green
460-18 Maroon
460-19 Light Blue
460-20 DRGW Orange
460-21 NYC Gray
460-22 Royal Blue
460-23 CR Blue
460-24 Box Car Red
460-25 Caboose Red
460-26 Pullman Green
460-27 Stainless Steel
460-38 Flat Black *NEW*
460-39 Dark Dulux Gold *NEW*
460-100 Clear

PARALLEL STRIPES EA 1.50

A handy way to insure straight lines, create special schemes or shadow effects. Each sheet includes several stripes of the same width and color as shown.

BLACK
460-212 1/2"
460-214 1/4"
460-218 1/8"
460-2116 1/16"
460-2132 1/32"
460-2164 1/64"

GOLD
460-312 1/2"
460-314 1/4"
460-318 1/8"
460-3116 1/16"
460-3132 1/32"
460-3164 1/64"

SILVER
460-412 1/2"
460-414 1/4"
460-418 1/8"
460-4132 1/32"
460-4164 1/64"

RED
460-512 1/2"
460-514 1/4"
460-518 1/8"
460-5116 1/16" *NEW*
460-5132 1/32"
460-5164 1/64"

YELLOW
460-612 1/2"
460-614 1/4"
460-618 1/8"
460-6116 1/16"
460-6132 1/32"
460-6164 1/64"

WHITE
460-1112 1/2"
460-1114 1/4"
460-1116 1/16"
460-1118 1/8"
460-1132 1/32"
460-1164 1/64"

DARK BLUE
460-712 1/2"
460-714 1/4"
460-718 1/8"
460-7116 1/16"
460-7132 1/32"
460-7164 1/64"

DULUX GOLD
460-812 1/2"
460-814 1/4"
460-818 1/8"
460-8116 1/16"
460-8132 1/32"
460-8164 1/64"

HO SCALE WIDTH STRIPES EA 4.00

1 & 2" WIDE
460-8712401 White
460-8712402 Black
460-8712403 Gold
460-8712404 Silver
460-8712405 Red
460-8712406 Yellow
460-8712407 Blue
460-8712408 Dulux Gold
460-8712409 Dark Green
460-8712402 SP Gray

3" & 4-3/4" WIDE
460-8711001 White
460-8711002 Black
460-8711003 Gold
460-8711004 Silver
460-8711005 Red (Fits UP Diesels)
460-8711006 Yellow
460-8711007 Dark Blue
460-8711008 Dulux
460-8711009 Dark Green

4 & 6" WIDE
460-8721401 White
460-8721402 Black
460-8721403 Gold
460-8721404 Silver
460-8721405 Red
460-8721406 Yellow
460-8721408 Dulux Gold
460-8721409 Green

BARRICADE STRIPES EA 4.00

6" WIDE
460-8722601 White
460-8722602 Black
460-8722603 Gold
460-8722604 Silver
460-8722606 Yellow
460-8722607 Blue
460-8722608 Dulux Gold
460-8722609 Green

45° ANGLE
460-8724901 White
460-8724902 Black
460-8724904 Silver
460-8724905 Red
460-8724906 Yellow
460-8724907 Dark Blue
460-8724908 Dulux Gold
460-8724909 Green

8" WIDE
460-8728301 White
460-8728302 Black
460-8728304 Silver
460-8728305 Red
460-8728309 Dark Green

12" WIDE
460-8726601 White
460-8726604 Silver
460-8726606 Yellow

ALPHABET & NUMBER SETS EA 4.00

ART DECO-CONDENSED
460-87338 Black

EXTRA BOLD MODERN GOTHIC
460-87334 4" 6" 12" (black)

RAILROAD ROMAN
460-876901 White
460-876902 Black
460-876903 Gold
460-876904 Silver
460-876905 Red
460-876906 Yellow
460-876907 Dark Blue
460-876908 Dulux Gold
460-876909 Green

RAILROAD GOTHIC
460-877001 White
460-877002 Black
460-877003 Gold
460-877004 Silver
460-877005 Red
460-877006 Yellow
460-877007 Blue
460-877008 Dulux Gold
460-877009 Green

MICROSCALE®

EXTENDED ROMAN-PASSENGER CARS
460-878001 White
460-878002 Black
460-878003 Gold
460-878004 Silver
460-878005 Red
460-878006 Yellow
460-878007 Blue
460-878008 Dulux Gold
460-878009 Green

CONDENSED GOTHIC
460-879301 White
460-879302 Black
460-879303 Gold
460-879304 Silver
460-879305 Red
460-879306 Yellow
460-879307 Blue
460-879308 Dulux Gold
460-879309 Green

CONDENSED ROMAN
460-879401 White
460-879402 Black
460-879403 Gold
460-879404 Silver
460-879405 Red
460-879406 Yellow
460-879407 Blue
460-879408 Dulux Gold
460-879409 Green

EUROSTYLE
460-87294 Black

NEON
460-87245 Neon Lettering-Black Background

STENCIL
460-87326 Standard Roman Stencil Letters & Numbers (black)

OLD WEST
460-8711101 White
460-8711102 Black
460-8711103 Gold
460-8711104 Silver
460-8711105 Red
460-8711106 Yellow
460-8711107 Blue
460-8711108 Dulux Gold
460-8711109 Green

BLOCK GOTHIC
460-8712301 White
460-8712302 Black
460-8712303 Gold
460-8712304 Silver
460-8712305 Red
460-8712306 Yellow
460-8712307 Blue
460-8712308 Dulux Gold
460-8712309 Dark Green

EXTENDED ROMAN-SOUTHERN PACIFIC STYLE 6 & 15"
460-8720201 White
460-8720202 Black
460-8720203 Gold
460-8720204 Silver
460-8720205 Red
460-8720206 Yellow
460-8720207 Blue
460-8720208 Dulux Gold
460-8720209 Green

3, 9 & 12"
460-8720301 White
460-8720302 Black
460-8720303 Gold
460-8720304 Silver
460-8720305 Red
460-8720306 Yellow
460-8720307 Blue
460-8720308 Dulux Gold
460-8720309 Green

EXTENDED GOTHIC-NEW HAVEN STYLE
460-8721001 White
460-8721002 Black
460-8721003 Gold
460-8721004 Silver
460-8721005 Yellow
460-8721007 Blue
460-8721008 Dulux Gold
460-8721009 Green

QUENTIN
460-8724001 White
460-8724002 Black
460-8724003 Gold
460-8724004 Silver
460-8724005 Red
460-8724006 Yellow
460-8724007 Blue
460-8724008 Dulux Gold
460-8724009 Green

1920S STYLE ULTRA-MODERN
460-87329 4, 6 & 12" Black

UP STYLE LETTERING WITH NO OUTLINE
460-8763201 White
460-8763202 Black
460-8763203 Gold
460-8763204 Silver
460-8763205 Red
460-8763206 Yellow

WITH BLACK OUTLINE
460-8763301 White
460-8763303 Gold
460-8763304 Silver
460-8763305 Red
460-8763306 Yellow

DATA SETS EA 4.00 (UNLESS NOTED)

FREIGHT CARS
Capacity, weight limit, load limit, builder's plates ACI Lube Plates, Plate C markings and more, ideal for use with custom decals.

460-4035 Center Beam Bulkhead Flat Car Data **2.00**
460-4126 Consolidated Lube Plates 1985+ **2.00**
460-4236 Data for 33,000 Gallon Propane Tank Cars 1965+ **2.00** ***NEW***
460-4281 Automatic Car Identification ACI "Kartrack" Computer ID Plates 1967-77 **2.00** ***NEW***
460-87286 Miscellaneous Box Car Door Markings
460-87260 For Large Capacity Cars
460-87235 Tank Cars-White; GATX, UTLX, SHPX & More
460-87236 Tank Cars-Yellow; GATX, UTLX, SHPX & More
460-871016 6000-8000 Gallon Tank Cars 1910-50 ***NEW***

ROMAN LETTERING
460-8701 Black
460-87462 Red & Yellow

GOTHIC LETTERING
460-8702 Black
460-87260 200 Ton Cars
460-87460 Red & Yellow
460-87463 100 Ton Cars, w/Black & Yellow Wheel Inspection Dots
460-87193 Black & White w/Black & Yellow Wheel Inspection Dots
460-871936 Black & Yellow w/Black & Yellow Wheel Inspection Dots

DIESELS
460-8748 Data & Builders Plates (black & white)
460-87134 Data & Builders Plates #2 Red & Yellow
460-87205 Numberboards-Assorted (Clear Letters on Black Background)
460-87527 GE & EMD Late 1980s Data & Builders Plates
460-87793 E & F Unit Data & Number Boards 1944+
460-87794 FT Units Data & Number Boards 1939+ (yellow & red)
460-87925 GE Dash-9 & AC-4400 Data 1995+

RAILROAD SETS EA 4.00 (UNLESS NOTED)

Create models from your favorite eras and railroads. Sets are printed in authentic colors, with heralds, stripes, data and other markings. Each includes a lettering diagram with prototype paint colors. Dates indicate when a scheme was introduced, or in use. Sets priced at $2.00 include special lettering for a single car or loco.

ALASKA RAILROAD
460-4094 50' High Cube Box Cars 1993+ **2.00**
460-87256 General Freight
460-87279 Cabooses
460-87280 Diesels 1960-70
460-87480 Diesels (Hood & Alco Units) 1980s

AMERICAN CAR & FOUNDRY ACFX
460-4045 50' Tank Car Data (black & white) **2.00**
460-4213 10,000 Gallon Tank Car, The Barrett Co., 1910-50 **2.00**
460-4123 Pressure Aide Covered Hoppers 1994+ **2.00**
460-4236 Tank Car Data 1965+ **2.00**
460-87986 10,000 Gallon Tank Cars; WP, CNW, CB&Q, SLSF, Texas Co. 1910-50
460-871016 Tank Cars 6,000 & 8,000 Gallon 1910-1950

ALCO AMERICAN LOCOMOTIVE CO.
460-4019 PA Diesels for Original Freedom Train 1947 **2.00**
460-87681 Century Demonstrators; C-415, C-636 & C-430

ALGOMA CENTRAL RAILWAY
460-4187 FP9 Diesels 1995+ **2.00**

AMTRAK
460-4155 Material Handling Cars 1986+ **2.00**
460-4170 "Vermonter" Baggage Cars 1995+ **2.00**
460-4231 "Adirondack" Cars 1996+ **2.00**
460-8799 Cars Phase I (white lettering)
460-87100 E, F & F40 Diesels Phase I 1970
460-87191 Diesels Phase I Red & Blue Stripes
460-87362 SDP40F & F40PH Diesels-Phase III
460-87423 E8, F40PH & SDP40F Phase II 1970-80
460-87424 F40PH Phase III 1980+
460-87425 Superliners Phase II 1970-80
460-87426 Heritage Fleet Cars Phase III 1980
460-87427 Superliner Phase II Scotchlite Striping (Use with 87425)
460-87428 Heritage Fleet Phase III Striping (Use with 87426)
460-87518 Superliners Phase III
460-87519 Superliner Stripes Phase III (Use with 87518)
460-87525 Amfleet Cars Phase III Paint
460-87526 Amfleet Cars Stripes Phase III (Use with 87525)
460-87675 Dash 8-32BWH Phase IV 1991+
460-87867 Superliners Phase IV 1994+
460-87868 Superliner Stripes Phase IV 1994+
460-87869 Superliner Names Phase IV 1994+
460-87949 Hi-Level Cars Phase III 1980+
460-87950 Hi-Level Car Stripes Phase III 1980+
460-87971 Amfleet Cars, Phase IV 1996+
460-871022 P42 "Northeast Direct" Diesels 1997+ ***NEW***
460-871022 Diesels P-42 1997+
460-871036 Station Signs 1971+

DIESEL ANTI-GLARE PANELS
460-87431 Green & Gray (UP Diesels)
460-87440 Black & Light Blue
460-87449 Light Blue & Maroon
460-87451 Red & Orange

ATLANTIC COAST LINE
460-87768 Diesels (yellow & black) 1957-66
460-87773 E & F Units (purple & silver) 1939-57
460-87774 Switchers & GP7 (purple & silver) 1940-57
460-87907 ACL-Subsidiaries Late Switchers & GP7 1950-57
460-87908 Diesel Stripes (purple & silver) 1949-57
460-87940 Freight Cars, New Gothic Lettering 1956-67
460-87976 Cabooses 1930-67

BALTIMORE & OHIO
460-4053 GP30 Sunburst Scheme **2.00**
460-8752 Cab Diesels; FB-2, F7, Alco FA-1, F3
460-8783 Medium Steam Locos
460-87396 EA, E6, 7, 8 & 9 Diesels (blue & gray)
460-87401 EMD & GE Diesels 1970
460-87486 2-Bay Covered Hoppers Class N-42 & N-43
460-87797 Passenger Cars 1949-70
460-87798 Passenger Car Stripes 1949-70
460-87799 Passenger Car Names 1949-70

BANGOR & AROOSTOOK
460-4133 Diesels (Solid Blue) 1960-70 **2.00**
460-4191 Hood Units, Iron Roads Scheme, 1996+ **2.00**
460- 87626 F Units 1947 & 1991 Restoration
460-87863 Passenger Cars; 1945-70
460-87980 Diesels (blue & gray) 1952-63
460-871015 BAR & NH "State of Maine" 40 & 50' Box Cars 1938-65

BRITISH COLUMBIA RAILWAY-BC RAIL
460-87726 Late 1980s Diesels
460-87783 Two-Tone Green Diesels 1972+
460-87931 Wide Vision Caboose; Pacific Great Eastern, British Columbia Railway, BC Rail 1986+

BURLINGTON NORTHERN SANTA FE - BNSF
460-4148 SD70MAC #9647 1995+ **2.00**
460-4178 Aluminum Coalporter Gondolas 1996+ **2.00**
460-4183 SD60M #9297 (orange & green) 1996+ **2.00**
460-4254 "Patches" for Renumbered Diesels (yellow & green), use with #871035 and standard BN or ATSF sets. **2.00**
460-4258 48' Trailers or Containers 1997+ ***NEW***
460-87943 SD75M Diesels-Super Fleet Colors 1996+
460-87944 SD70MAC Diesels-BN Executive Colors 1996+
460-87967 GP60M Diesels (red & silver) 1996+
460-87968 Dash 9-44CW Diesels (orange & green) 1996+

MICROSCALE®

460-87979 GE Dash-8 Diesels (red & silver) 1996+
460-871008 Dash 9-44CAW Diesels (red & silver) 1997+
460-871009 Dash 9-44CW Diesels (red & silver) w/BNSF Nose Logo 1997+
460-871023 Orange & Green Repainted Diesels 1996+
460-871024 Orange & Green New Heritage Scheme Dash 9-44CW 1997+

460-871035 Renumbered Diesels (Use with Standard BN or ATSF Sets ႞.)
460-871037 Centerflow Covered Hoppers 1996+ ***NEW***
460-871038 3-Unit All Purpose Double Stack Cars 1997+ ***NEW***
460-871044 SD70MAC "Premium Heritage" Hood Unit Diesels w/"Cigar-Band" Nose Herald ***NEW***
460-871050 Heritage II/Premium Heritage Scheme Stripes Only (871024 or 871044 for lettering, sold separately) **2.00** ***NEW***

BOSTON & MAINE
460-4208 E7 Diesels As-Delivered 1945-48 **2.00**
460-4241 Milk Cars **2.00**
460-871014 Passenger Cars 1900-60
460-87176 Cab Unit Diesels 1960-70
460-87863 Passenger Cars; 1945-70
460-87885 FT Diesels Original Scheme 1943-50
460-87909 E & F Unit Diesels (maroon & gold) 1948-60
460-87919 GP7 (maroon & gold) 1950-60
460-87934 Late Blue Scheme 1978-85
460-87970 RS-2 & -3 Diesels (maroon & gold) 1950-60
460-87984 Switchers (black) 1940-60

BURLINGTON - CHICAGO, BURLINGTON & QUINCY
460-4026 25' & 35' Piggyback Trailers & Tractors 1949 **2.00**
460-4186 50' Mather Stock Cars 1963-70 **2.00**
460-4265 3-Bay Open Hoppers 1960+ **2.00** ***NEW***
Chinese Red scheme with "Route of the Zephyrs" and "Everywhere West" slogans, plus rebuilt hoppers painted black.
460-8715 Later Freight Diesels (red, white, gray)
460-8790 FT, F3, F7 & F9 Diesels
460-8798 Passenger Diesels E5, E7, E8
460-87108 California Zephyr Passenger Cars 1950-70
460-87412 XM-32 40' Steel Box Cars
460-87481 50' & 60' Outside Braced Plug Door Insulated Box Cars
460-87485 50' & 60' Insulated Box Cars #2
460-87535 Refrigerator Cars
460-87572 Refrigerator Cars #2
460-87581 E-5 Diesels
460-87609 Switchers-Early
460-87610 Switcher Stripes-Early
460-87659 Modern Style Switcher Lettering
460-87734 40' Wood Box Cars 1915-70
460-87752 Passenger Cars; Heavyweight & Streamlined 1940-70
460-87830 Covered Hoppers (gray) 1958-70
460-87836 24' & 40' Trailers w/Tractors 1950s-70s

BURLINGTON NORTHERN
460-4106 BN/Western Fruit Express 57' Mechanical Reefers 1993+ **2.00**
460-4055 Natural Gas Loco & Cryogenic Tender 199 **2.00**
460-4069 Freedom Caboose-(red, white & blue) **2.00**
460-4072 BN/EMD SD60MAC Demonstrator **2.00**
460-4085 Commuter E Units 1975-92 **2.00**
460-4097 Thrall Double Stack Cars (Use with #87688) **2.00**
460-4119 31,000 Gallon 59' Fuel Tank Cars 1994+ **2.00**
460-4135 "Hustle Muscle" SD45 #6430 1973-85 **2.00**
460-4157 BN/Trinity Industries 67' Composite Box Car 1995+ **2.00**
460-4256 GP38M #1524 "Operation Lifesaver" Diesel **2.00** ***NEW***
460-8725 Diesels (green & black)
460-87190 Early BN, Late CB&Q Diesels (green, black, white lettering)
460-87251 General Freight
460-87252 General Freight #2
460-87364 GP30/35 Diesels
460-87458 45' Trailers (green or white schemes)
460-87459 Bicentennial Units SD40-2, SDP40, U30C
460-87484 SD40, GP50 & SD60 "Tiger Stripe Nose" 1985
460-87492 Fuel Tenders & Locomotive Data
460-87549 Diesels w/White Front 1989
460-87559 BN America 48' Containers 1989
460-87569 45' Trailers #2
460-87576 57' Mechanical Reefers, Cryogenic & Temp-Loc Cars
460-87621 Desert Storm SD60M 1991
460-87631 20th Anniversary GP38
460-87649 Hoppers, Box Cars 1990 Scheme w/Herald
460-87669 Husky Stack Stand-Alone & 3-Unit Cars 1991 to Present
460-87674 48' Containers; BN America Special Schemes
460-87695 Executive F Units
460-87760 SD60M 1990+
460-87716 Diesel Data 1980s+
460-87723 BN America 48' Container #2, 48' Chassis & Terminal Tractor 1990+
460-87711 Auto Rack
460-87779 Business Train & E Unit 1989+
460-87780 Business Train Stripes 1989+
460-87803 SD70MAC 1994+
460-87826 Gunderson Maxi III Double-Stack Car 1990+
460-87842 Cabooses 1970+

CANADIAN NATIONAL
460-4086 Manitoba 40' Box Cars 1985+ **2.00**
460-4121 Gondolas 1980+ **2.00**
460-4227 Modern Cabooses, Noodle Scheme 1970+ **2.00**
460-4228 Centerflow Covered Hoppers 1995+ **2.00**
460-4246 Passenger Service Steam Locos 1938-60 **2.00**
460-87234 General Freight & Cabooses 1970-80
460-87374 F Unit Diesels 1940-50
460-87567 Hood Unit Diesels 1990+
460-87568 Hood Unit Diesel Stripes 1990+
460-87641 Diesel Switchers 1990+
460-87664 CN Intermodal 48' Containers, Trailers & Tractors 1991
460-87707 4-Bay Cylindrical Covered Hoppers
460-87720 Autoracks
460-87746 CN "North America" Diesels 1992+
460-87804 CN Laser 48' Refrigerated Containers 1993+
460-87829 5-Unit Drawbar Connected Double-Stack Cars (blue or orange) 1990+
460-87849 48' Trailers & Tractors 1970+
460-87939 Diesels 1995+
460-87947 Freight Diesels (green & yellow) 1953-60
460-87948 GP7/9 & RS-10/18 (green & yellow) 1953-60
460-87957 H16-44, H24-66 & RS-3 Diesels (green & yellow) 1953-60
460-871019 Steam Locos 1931-60
460-871033 Wood Cabooses 1920-61

CANADIAN PACIFIC
460-8787 Cab Unit Diesels
460-8792 Hood Unit Diesels
460-871052 "Golden Beaver" Modern Hood Unit Diesels ***NEW***

CENTRAL OF NEW JERSEY
460-87231 Hood Unit Diesels 1950-65
460-87232 Hood Unit Diesels 1965-70 (red & white)

CENTRAL OF GEORGIA
460-87382 Freight & Passenger Diesels F3A, E7A & E8A 1950-60
460-87604 Hood Unit Diesels RS-3, GP9 & SD9 1950s
460-4062 Switchers 1952-69 **2.00**

CENTRAL VERMONT
460-87846 Diesels & Cabooses 1989 (blue & orange)
460-87990 Diesels (green & yellow) 1956-60
460-1020 Steam Loco 1931-60
460-871031 Wood Cabooses 1920-61
460-871039 Black & Orange Diesels 1963-77 ***NEW***
460-871040 Green & Yellow Diesels 1977-95 ***NEW***

CHESAPEAKE & OHIO
460-4245 Piggyback Flat Cars 1959-70 **2.00**
460-8747 C&O/Pere Marquette Cab Diesels & Caboose
460-8776 Medium Steam Locos (yellow)
460-8795 C&O/Pere Marquette Berkshire Steam Locos
460-871042 C&O or Pere Marquette E7A Cab Unit Diesels 1948-1955 ***NEW***
460-871045 Open Top Coal Hoppers w/Roman Lettering 1935-56+ ***NEW***
460-87401 EMD & GE Hood Unit Diesels 1970
460-87875 Diesel Road Units & Switchers 1950-60
460-87881 Hood & Cab Unit Diesels 1957-1965

CHESSIE SYSTEM

460-4257 Chessie/EMD 50th Anniversary Diesel
460-87400 EMD & GE Diesels 1970-80
460-87790 Chessie/WM Safety Cabooses
460-87952 Chessie/C&O Safety Cabooses 1976-89

CHICAGO & EASTERN ILLINOIS
460-87375 Passenger & Freight Cab Unit Diesels 1940-50
460-87376 E4A Passenger Diesels (orange & blue) 1940-50
460-4074 E & F Unit Diesels (Dark Blue) 1959-72 **2.00**

CHICAGO & ILLINOIS MIDLAND
460-87595 Diesels 1950s+
460-87596 Diesel Stripes 1950s+

CHICAGO & NORTH WESTERN
460-4006 Dash 9-44CW Diesels 1993+ **2.00**
460-4047 Wyoming Centennial C40-8 Diesel **2.00**
460-4054 C40-8 Diesel-Safety & Reliability Logos 1991 **2.00**
460-4229 40' Box Cars-No Slogans 1944-62 **2.00**
460-4230 40' Box Cars-Yellow Lettering 1963-69 **2.00**
460-4113 Aluminum Rapid Discharge Coal Hoppers 1994+ **2.00**
460-4166 Early RS-1 Diesels "Route of the Streamliner", "400", & "Challenger" Slogans 1944-55 **2.00**
460-8751 Cab Diesels; E6 through E8 1950-60
460-8789 Steam Locos 1930-50
460-87290 Employee Owned & Falcon Service Slogan SD40-2 Diesels 1970-80
460-87370 GP50 #5050-5099 1980
460-87541 Late 1980s GE & EMD Diesels
460-87560 F Unit Diesels 1949-75 (Use #87561 for Stripes)
460-87561 E & F Unit Striping (Use with #8751 or #87560) 1950s
460-87562 Modern Coal Hoppers & Gondolas
460-87735 Fowler 40' Wood Box Cars 1914-59
460-87781 Operation Life Saver Diesels 1990+
460-87845 Freight Cars w/Large Block CNW Letters 1992+
460-87859 Passenger Cars 1940+
460-87928 GE AC4400CW & Dash-9 Diesels w/Operation Lifesaver Logos 1995+
460-87962 Early Hood Unit Diesels & Switchers 1948-60

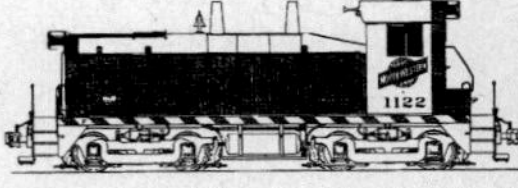

460-87963 Early Hood Unit Diesel & Switcher Stripes 1948-60

CHICAGO GREAT WESTERN
460-4011 EMD or Baldwin Diesel Switchers 1950 **2.00**
460-87593 F & GP Unit Diesels
460-87594 F & GP Unit Diesel Stripes

CLINCHFIELD
460-87913 Diesels 1948-77
460-87966 40' & 50' Box Cars 1947-70

CONRAIL
460-4049 Desert Storm SD50 Diesel #6707 1991 **2.00**
460-4065 57' Mechanical Reefer 1989
460-4066 Executive E Unit Diesel or Passenger Car 1980-92 **2.00**
460-4070 US Olympic Cycling GP40-2 Diesel 1992 **2.00**
460-4222 C32-8 Ballast Express Diesels 1997+ **2.00**
460-4223 Operation Lifesaver Diesels 1997+ **2.00**

460-4255 Keep It Moving With Conrail B23-7 Diesel #1980 **2.00**
460-4271 Engine Numbers Only for SD70/80MAC Diesels **2.00** ***NEW***
460-87157 Hood Unit Diesels 1970-80
460-87161 Rolling Stock 1970-80
460-87614 GE Painted Diesels & Labor-Management Project Nose Art 1976-92
460-87627 EMD & Conrail Painted Diesels 1970-Present
460-87628 Diesel Data & Stripes
460-87684 Mercury 48' Containers 1992
460-87685 Mercury 48' Trailer & 53' Container
460-87740 Quality SD60M, GP10, SW1200 Diesels 1992+
460-87742 50' Coil Steel Cars
460-87856 Hoppers w/Quality Logos (gray) 1985+
460-87862 Quality 50', 60 '& 86' Box Cars; 52' Gondola 1992+

MICROSCALE®

ALL SETS $4.00 (UNLESS NOTED)

460-87899 Quality Coal Hoppers 1992+
460-87987 Quality Diesels Repainted by Conrail 1995+
460-87994 SD80MAC Diesels 1996+
460-871034 United Way/Savings Bonds Diesels
460-871046 Assorted 50' Box Cars *NEW*
Includes PRR and NYC reporting marks to show cars going to CSX or NS.

460-871051 SD70MAC Hood Unit Diesels (blue, white matches SD80MACS) *NEW*

COTTON BELT-ST. LOUIS SOUTH WESTERN
460-8711 Diesels (gray) w/Roman Lettering 1960-70
460-87201 Black Widow E, F, GP9, SD9 & Trainmaster Diesels 1950-60
460-87219 General Freight 1970
460-87447 Diesels Red Wings Scheme 1980
460-87472 4- & 8-Pack Intermodal Flat Cars
460-87835 Bicentennial Locos & Caboose 1975-80
460-87992 FT Diesels As-Delivered (light blue & yellow) 1944-55

CP RAIL-CP RAIL SYSTEM
460-4115 Smokey Bear 50th Anniversary SD40-2 Diesel 1994+ **2.00**
460-4137 3-Bay Center Flow Covered Hoppers 1994+ **2.00**
460-4142 SD40-2 Diesels in UP Colors 1995+ **2.00**
460-87221 General Freight 1970-80
460-87671 48' Containers & Tractors 1991
460-87706 Cylindrical Covered Hoppers
460-87721 Autoracks
460-87733 Diesels 1969+
460-87737 Diesel Multimarks Mid 1970s to Date
460-87738 Diesel 8" Stripes Mid 1970s to Date
460-87753 Double-Stack Cars 1992+
460-87754 Dual Flag Scheme Diesels 1993+
460-87844 Bathtub Gondolas 1985
460-87974 Dual Flag Scheme AC-4400CW Diesels 1995+

CSX
460-4075 Bay Window Cabooses 1991+ **2.00**
460-4082 Presidential Tour 8-40CW Diesels 1992+ **2.00**
460-4141 Maintenance of Way Locos & Cabooses 1995+ **2.00**
460-4145 Rebuilt Coal Hoppers (gray) 1995+ **2.00**
460-4162 CSX Diesel Data 1990+ **2.00**
460-4184 Fuel Tenders 1995+ **2.00**
460-4200 Aluminum Coal Porter Gondolas 1995+ **2.00**
460-4212 Center Flow Hoppers, Grain Express 1996+ **2.00**
460-4248 Switchers 1990+ **2.00**
460-87497 CSX & CSX Transportation Diesels 1986
460-87504 CSX Transportation Box Cars, Open & Covered Hoppers & Gondola 1986
460-87536 Diesels-After 9/4/87 with Operation Red Block Logos
460-87575 Diesels (blue gray & yellow) 1990
460-87640 CSX & CSL Intermodal 48' Containers & Chassis
460-87682 Cabooses Operation Life Saver & Red Block
460-87697 CSX Transportation Auto Racks
460-87988 Freight Car Data 1985+
460-87915 GE Wide Cab Dash 8/9 & AC Units 1990+

DELAWARE & HUDSON
460-4010 Baldwin Shark Diesels-Blue Warbonnet on Silver
460-4061 Alco PA Diesels 1960-80
460-8731 Diesels & Cabooses (blue & yellow lettering & shield) 1970
460-87582 Hood Unit Diesels 1978-85 (blue & yellow)
460-87587 Hood Unit Diesels (blue & gray) 1970s through 1980

DELAWARE, LACKAWANNA & WESTERN
460-87812 Diesels 1939-1960
460-87813 Freight F Unit Diesel Stripes 1945-60
460-87821 Stripes for Passenger Service E, F & Trainmaster Diesels 1945-60

DETROIT, TOLEDO & IRONTON
460-4041 70 Ton, 14 Panel Triple Bay Hopper **2.00**
460-4268 50' Outside-Post "Railbox" Box Car 1973+ **2.00** *NEW*

DULUTH, MISSABE & IRON RANGE - MISSABE ROAD
460-87854 Cabooses 1945-90
460-87131 Hood Unit Diesels 1950-80
460-87357 SD9 Diesels

DULUTH, SOUTH SHORE & ATLANTIC
460-4112 50' Double Door Box Car 1957-65 **2.00**

DULUTH, WINNIPEG & PACIFIC RAILWAY
460-4093 Diesels 1970-93 **2.00**
460-87991 Diesels (CN Green & yellow) 1956-60
460-871020 Steam Locos 1931-1960
460-871031 Wood Cabooses 1920-61

ELGIN, JOLIET & EASTERN
460-87642 Diesels
460-87715 Freight Cars 1980+

EMD
460-4020 Test Car 1970 **2.00**
460-4056 Builders Plates-US & Canadian **2.00**
460-4068 SD7, SW8 & TR-6 Demo Units 1950-58 **2.00**
460-4073 SD70MAC Demo (Big MAC) 1992 **2.00**
460-4078 SD40-3MPR Demo Unit 1992+ **2.00**
460-4130 Round Number Board Numbers 1950+ **2.00**
460-4131 Square Number Board Numbers 1960+ **2.00**
460-4161 70 Series Data 1990+ **2.00**
460-4221 SD80/90MAC Data 1996+ **2.00**
460-4232 SD90MAC Demo Unit 1997+ **2.00**
460-871003 GP7 & BL-1 Demo Units 1949-53
460-87141 E, F & SD45 Demo Units 1950-70
460-87524 Demo Units GP59, GP60 & SD60 1987
460-87602 Lease Fleet Diesels 1987
460-87603 SW1001, SW1500 & MP15AC Demo Switchers
460-87613 FT #103 Demonstrator A & B Units
460-87858 GP20, GP30, DD30 Demo Units & Test Car 1959-63
460-87904 Number Boards 1985+
460-87927 Lease Fleet Diesels (Wine Red) 1994+

ERIE
460-8791 Steam Locos 1930-50
460-87360 F Unit Diesels 1940-60
460-87876 Road Units & Switchers 1945-1960

ERIE LACKAWANNA
460-8716 Diesels (maroon & yellow lettering) 1960-70
460-87573 Stripes for E, F & PA 1960-75

EVERGREEN
460-87877 Containers, 20' & 40' & 40' Refrigerated, 1980+

FAMILY LINES
460-87397 EMD & GE Diesels 1970s
460-87399 F Units & Switchers 1970
Grand Trunk Western
460-87991 RS-1, RS-11 & GP9 Diesels (CN Green & yellow) 1956-60
460-871020 Steam Locos 1931-1960

FLORIDA EAST COAST
4460-4100 Ortner Hopper Cars 1988+ **2.00**
4460-4244 Ortner Hopper Cars 1996+ **2.00**
460-87140 Diesels 1960-80
460-87142 Early Hood Unit Diesels 1950-80
460-87556 Hood Unit Diesels 1980s
460-87767 E & F Unit Diesels 1939-60

FRISCO-ST. LOUIS SAN FRANCISCO
460-8785 Cab Unit Diesels & Cabooses 1960-70
460-87115 Diesels 1970-80
460-87137 Modern 50 to 86' Box Cars (yellow) 1970
460-87149 40-50' Box Cars (black & white) "Ship It On The Frisco!" 1970-80
460-87455 EMD E Unit Diesels 1950-60
460-87711 Auto Racks

FRUIT GROWERS EXPRESS
460-4022 "Real Cold" 57' Mechanical Reefers 1986 **2.00**
460-87238 Mechanical Reefers; "For Greater Efficiency," N&W Herald
460-87450 50' Insulated Box Cars & 57' Mechanical Reefers "Solid Cold/Gold" & "The Chiller" Slogans

GATX-GENERAL AMERICAN
460-4005 Tank Trainer Tank Car 1993+ **2.00**
460-4058 Capital Corp. Ex UP SD40-2 Diesels 1991 **2.00**
460-4076 63' & 66' Liquid Petroleum Gas Tank Cars 1990 **2.00**
460-87413 Tank Train 50' Tank Cars (black w/white lettering) 1980
460-87625 Tank Train Tank Cars 1980s
460-87736 50' Tank Cars 1970
460-87770 Covered Hoppers; 50' Airslide®, 4-Bay ACF 1970+
460-4146 Lamb Weston Cryogenic Box Cars, Arcticar, 1995+
460-87557 GATX Leasing Hood Unit Diesels 1989

GENERAL ELECTRIC
460-4056 Builders Plates-US & Canadian **2.00**
460-4125 U-25B Demo Units 1962
460-4129 Number Boards 1960+ **2.00**
460-4189 AC-6000CW Demo Unit 1996+ **2.00**
460-4237 GECX AC4400-CW Diesels 1997+ **2.00**
460-87532 GE Leasing GECX B40-8 Diesels 1987
460-87904 Number Boards 1985+
460-87607 Dash 8 Demo Units 1988-1991
460-87834 Dash 9 & AC4400CW Demo Units 1994+

GEORGIA GROUPS RAILROADS
460-4193 Passenger Cars 1940-1970 **2.00**
460-87889 Georgia Railroad, Atlantic & West Point, Western Railroad of Alabama Diesels 1948-76

GOLDEN WEST SERVICE
460-87658 Freight Cars 1990
460-87693 62' Bulkhead Flat, Ballast Hopper, 89' Flat Car 60' Woodchip Car 1992
460-87694 57' Mechanical & 60' Cryogenic Reefers 1992

GOVERNMENT OF CANADA GRAIN HOPPERS
460-87714 Saskatchewan 4-Bay Cylindrical
460-87717 4-Bay Cylindrical 1973+
460-87718 Wheat Board 4-Bay Cylindrical
460-87724 4-Bay Cylindrical 1982+ (Bright Red)
460-87729 Aluminum 4-Bay Cylindrical
460-87710 "Take an Alberta Break" 4-Bay Cylindrical
460-87725 Original Heritage Fund Alberta 4-Bay Cylindrical 1976+

GPEX
460-871030 Leased Milk Cars 1920-70 *NEW*

GRAND TRUNK
460-87990 Diesels (green & yellow) 1956-60
460-87991 Diesels (CN Green & yellow) 1956-60

GRAND TRUNK RAILWAY
460-871020 Steam Locos 1931-1960
460-871031 Wood Cabooses 1920-61

GRAND TRUNK WESTERN
460-4015 EMD & Alco Diesel Switchers 1950 **2.00**
460-4246 Passenger Service Steam Locos 1938-60 **2.00**
460-87103 Cab & Hood Unit Diesels 1950-60
460-87366 F3 Diesels 1940-50
460-87650 Late Diesels (large GT Herald)
460-871020 Steam Locos 1931-1960
460-871032 Wood Cabooses 1920-61

GREAT NORTHERN
460-4014 Passenger-Script Lettering for E7 Diesels 1950 **2.00**
460-4060 RDC-3 1956-70 **2.00**
460-8745 Cab Unit Diesels (orange & green w/yellow lettering) 1950-70
460-8786 Switchers 1940-60
460-87153 "Empire Builder" Passenger Cars 1950-60
460-87154 Passenger Car Gold & Silver Stripes 1950-60
460-87185 40' Single Door Box Car 1950-60
460-87268 40' & 50' Box Cars & 3-Bay Hoppers 1940-60
460-87269 Refrigerator Cars-Western Fruit Express 1960-70
460-87284 Hood & Cab Unit Diesels (Big Sky Blue) 1970
460-87285 SD45-"Hustle Muscle," RCU Cars & Cabooses (Big Sky Blue) 1970
460-87372 "Empire Builder" Passenger Cars Owned by Pullman 1920-50
460-87571 40' Express Box Cars 1945-55
460-87757 Cabooses (red) 1922-70
460-87808 RS-1 Diesels 1944-60
460-87815 Hood Unit Diesels (orange & green) 1950-70
460-87926 40' Glacier Green Box Cars 1961-1967
460-87996 50' Glacier Green Box Cars 1961-1967

MICROSCALE®

ALL SETS $4.00 (UNLESS NOTED)

GUILFORD
460-87457 EMD & GE Diesels 1980
460-87951 Guilford System & Springfield Terminal Diesels 1995+

GULF, MOBILE & OHIO
460-8743 Hood & Cab Unit Diesels 1960-70
460-87365 GP30 & GP35 Diesels 1960-70
460-87895 GM&O/MDT Late Steel Ice Reefers 1960-73

ILLINOIS CENTRAL
460-4002 EMD Switchers-Black w/Green Diamond Herald **2.00**
460-4029 45' Trailer 1987 **2.00**
460-4144 Executive E Units 1995+ **2.00**
460-4210 Operation Lifesaver Diesels 1993+ **2.00**
460-8727 Diesels (white & orange) & Cabooses (black & orange) 1970
460-87348 E7 & E8 Diesels 1960-70
460-87528 Diesels Black w/White Lettering & "Deathstar" Herald 1988
460-87655 Diesel & Passenger Car Stripes 1980+
460-87895 IC/MDT Late Steel Ice Reefers 1960-73

ILLINOIS CENTRAL GULF
460-8742 Hood Unit Diesels & Cabooses (orange & white) 1970
460-87402 Modern Hood Unit & Diesel Switchers (gray & orange) 1980

ILLINOIS TERMINAL
460-87651 Diesels
460-87652 Diesel Stripes

INDIANA HARBOR BELT
460-87782 Locomotives 1950+

INTERMODAL EQUIPMENT
460-4043 Dole 40' Refrigerated Container & Chassis **2.00**
460-4063 Monon Corporation 48' Display Container **2.00**
460-4095 APC Thrall Double-Stack Cars (Use w/#87788) 1986+ **2.00**
460-4096 APL Thrall Double-Stack Cars (Use w/#87788) 1986+ **2.00**
460-4117 International Container Data, 20', 40' & 45' 1980+ **2.00**
460-4204 28' Trailer Data 1980+ **2.00**
460-4262 Redon 48' Box Containers **2.00** ***NEW***
460-4263 EMP 48' Box Containers **2.00** ***NEW***
460-87298 40' Containers & Vans; PCL & KS Lines, Transamerica, IW Leasing
460-87299 20' & 40' Containers; Mitsui OSK., Showa, Evergreen & Lykers
460-87300 20' Containers; ITS, Hansetanier, Con Trans & Evergreen Line
460-87310 American President Lines, Barber Blue Sea & NOL Containers
460-87311 40' & 20' Containers; Japan Line, Sea Land & American President Lines
460-87312 20' Johnson Line & 20' & 40' YM Line Containers
460-87443 20' & 40' Containers; Matson, HKIL, Genstar, ICCU & CTI
460-87477 K&W 3-Unit Articulated & BN 5- & 10-Unit Versa-Deck Intermodal Cars
460-87478 Itel Rail 4- & 10-Pack Impack & Intermodal Flat Cars
460-87487 American President Lines 40' & 45' Containers & Chassis
460-87634 Containers; 48' Itel, BN-Itel, Interdom, 45' Rail-Bridge
460-87647 XTRA 48' Containers, ATSF & CSX Versions
460-87657 SP 48' Container & Itel 40' Reefer Container 1990
460-87704 Conway Intermodal Conquest 48' Containers
460-87719 Genstar Containers 20, 40 & 48'
460-87731 Sea Land Containers; 40' Reefer, 40' Smoothside & 45' Corrugated
460-87741 Greenbrier Intermodal Husky-Stack Cars 1990+
460-87743 Genstar Containers Leased to Railroads 1992+
460-87748 Neptune Orient Lines (NOL) 20' & 40'
460-87756 20' & 40' Containers CP Ships, Canada Maritime 1980+
460-87766 NYK Containers 20' 40' & 48' 1970+
460-87778 Maersk Gunderson Maxi-I Double Stack Cars 1989+
460-87838 Gunderson Twin Stack 5-Unit Articulated Double Stack Cars 1986+
460-87852 Trailer & Domestic Container Data 1965+
460-87784 K-Line Containers, 20',40' & 45' 1970+
460-87805 Mitsui OSK Lines (MOL) 20' 40' & 45' Containers 1980+

IOWA INTERSTATE
460-87551 Diesel Hood Units & Switchers 1988
460-87742 50' Coil Steel Cars

KANSAS CITY SOUTHERN
460-4238 Executive Train Locos & Cars 1995+ **2.00**
460-87138 E & F Unit Diesels 1950-60
460-87139 Passenger Cars 1950-60
460-87146 Modern EMD Diesels
460-87148 Switchers 1950-60
460-87430 SD40-2 & GP7 Diesels 1950-80
460-87550 Diesels (gray) 1989
460-87656 Freight Cars 1970s
460-87942 Diesels with Cab Side Logo (gray) 1995+

LEASE FLEET DIESELS
460-4038 VMV Enterprises Leasing (gray) **2.00**
460-4059 Preferred Lease Management (PLM) SD40 **2.00**
460-4154 LMS (Lease Management Services) 8-40CW 1994+ **2.00**
460-87520 GE Leasing LMX B39-8 1988
460-87524 Oakway Leasing SD60 1987
460-87537 VMV Rebuilt Diesels "Paducahbilt" GP35/36
460-87601 Capital Corporation (GATX) Diesels 1990
460-87629 Morrison-Knudsen MPI 1990 to Present
460-87865 Morrison Knudsen 1994+

LEHIGH & NEW ENGLAND
460-87882 Diesels 1948-1961

LEHIGH VALLEY
460-4098 Pre-War Switchers 1937-45 **2.00**
460-4143 Bicentennial Caboose 1975-80 **2.00**
460-4197 Passenger Cars 1939-72 **2.00**
460-4218 Wide Yellow Band Scheme Diesels 1971-74 **2.00**
460-87775 Diesels (Cornell Red & black stripe) 1940-60
460-87776 Diesel Stripes (Cornell Red & black) 1940-60
460-87855 Late Cornell Red GP38, GP38-2, U-23B Diesels 1970-76
460-87861 Late Cornell Red Diesel Switchers, GP9, C-420, 1970-76
460-87880 Alco C-420 & C-628 Diesels As-Delivered 1964-76
460-87922 Cabooses 1932-80
460-87995 Diesels (Tuscan Red w/White Flag) 1966-72

LOGGING LINES
460-8708 Locos; LK&L, Coos Bay, Long Bell, Pickering Lumber etc. (white)

LONG ISLAND RAILROAD
460-87759 Diesels & Passenger Cars 1980+

LOUISVILLE & NASHVILLE
460-4105 Cabooses 1963-80 **2.00**
460-8761 E & F Unit Diesels (tan & orange stripes) 1950-60
460-87639 Alco FA-2 & RS-3 Diesels 1950s
460-87817 Diesels (gray & yellow) 1963-70
460-87823 Diesels (gray & yellow) 1970-80
460-87824 Diesel Stripes (gray & yellow) 1963-70
460-87888 RS-3, GP7/9 Diesels (black & yellow) 1950-1963
460-87917 Diesels, (solid blue or black) 1958-62

MAINE CENTRAL
460-4181 EMD Switchers, Solid Green 1975-82
460-4209 E7 Diesels, As-Delivered 1945-48
460-87863 Passenger Cars 1945-70
460-87903 Cabooses 1955-75
460-87910 E & F Unit Diesels (maroon & gold or green & gold) 1948-66
460-87920 MEC/Portland Terminal GP7 (maroon & gold or green & gold)
460-87935 Diesels (Harvest Gold) 1974-85
460-87958 Diesels (green) 1960-70
460-87985 MEC/ Portland Terminal Switchers (black) 1950-60
460-871028 40' & 50' Steel Box Cars 1954-70

MAINTENANCE-OF-WAY
460-871012 Gothic Lettering 1950+
460-871013 Roman Lettering 1950+

MEXICAN RAILWAYS
460-4081 FNM Diesels National Railways of Mexico 1991+ **2.00**
460-87538 National Railways of Mexico Diesels 1987
460-87175 Nacionales De Mexico Hood Unit Diesels 1960-80

MILWAUKEE ROAD
460-4031 50' Steel Coil Car 1988 **2.00**
460-8753 E & F Unit Diesels 1953-60
460-87389 E9A & B Diesels 1960-70 (UP Style Lettering)
460-87441 Diesels New Hiawatha Scheme 1980
460-87514 50' Box Cars 1970s
460-87789 Diesels (orange & black) 1960-87
460-871004 1939 Hiawatha Passenger Cars 1939-46

MINING COMPANIES
460-87145 Oliver Mining Hood Unit Diesels 1960-70
460-87147 Erie Mining Hood & Cab Unit Diesels 1960-70
460-87209 Kaiser Steel Eagle Mountain Mine

MINNEAPOLIS & ST. LOUIS
460-87953 Diesels (red & white) 1956-60
460-871018 F Unit Diesels 1945-56

MINNEAPOLIS, NORTHFIELD & SOUTHERN
460-4179 Diesels 1950-90

MISSOURI PACIFIC
460-4091 Cabooses 1979-90 **2.00**
460-4272 2-Bay Centerflow Covered Hoppers **2.00** ***NEW*** Includes additional lettering for Texas & Pacific and Chicago & Eastern Illinois cars.
460-8774 Hood Unit Diesels (dark blue w/Eagle) 1960-70
460-87113 EMD & GE Diesels w/Buzzsaw & Eagle Heralds 1970-80
460-87183 Cabooses w/Buzzsaw Heralds 1960-70
460-87192 Steam Locos 1930-50
460-87388 EMD E7 & E8 Diesels 1950-60
460-87442 Diesels UP North Little Rock Lettering 1980
460-87493 MP & C&EI Pullman-Standard 3-Bay Covered Hoppers 1980

MISSOURI-KANSAS-TEXAS KATY
460-87180 Diesel Numbers & Letters (green & yellow) 1970-80
460-87181 Diesel Stripes (green & yellow) 1970-80
460-87277 Diesel Numbers & Letters (red & white) 1950-80
460-87278 Diesel Heralds & Stripes (red & white) 1950-80
460-87446 Freight Cars 1970-80
460-87479 General Freight; 50' Box Car, 2-Bay Covered Hopper, 50' Flat Car 1960-70

MONON-CHICAGO, INDIANAPOLIS & LOUISVILLE
460-87358 Early F3 Passenger Diesels 1940-60
460-87359 F3 Freight Diesels 1940-60

MONONGAHELA
460-87586 GP7, GP38, B23-8 & Super 7 Diesels 1970-90

MONTANA RAIL LINK
460-87544 Diesels 1988
460-87600 ACF Center Flow & Pullman-Standard Hopper, plus 52' Gondola 1987
460-87605 50' Box Cars 1988+
460-87606 Cabooses & Freight Cars #2 1988
460-87606 Diesels 1988
460-87887 Montana Centennial, F45 & Operation Lifesaver Diesels 1989+
460-87954 Diesels w/ New Image Lions Head Logo 1996+
460-87964 2- & 3-Bay Covered Hoppers, 62' Bulkhead Flat Cars
460-871027 I&M Rail Link Diesels 1997+ ***NEW***

NARROW GAUGE LINES
COLORADO & SOUTHERN
460-87158 Steam Locos 1920-40
460-87159 Cabooses & Freight Cars 1920-40
DRGW
460-8760 Steam Locos & Cabooses
460-8773 Freight Cars
460-87156 Work Cars
RIO GRANDE SOUTHERN
460-8759 Locos & Cabooses
460-87170 Passenger Cars
460-87171 Galloping Goose
460-87179 Cabooses, Freight & MOW Cars

MICROSCALE®

ALL SETS $4.00 (UNLESS NOTED)

NASHVILLE, CHATTANOOGA & ST. LOUIS
460-87901 Diesels 1949-1963

NEW HAVEN-NEW YORK, NEW HAVEN & HARTFORD
460-8768 Diesels; McGinnis & Alpert Schemes 1954-68
460-87207 Passenger Cars 1950-60
460-87666 EF-4 Electrics
460-87864 Steam Locos 1900-55
460-87884 Passenger Cars, Head End & 8200, 8500, 8600 Series Cars
460-87937 Cab Diesels 1954-68
460-871000 Cab Diesels (green & orange) 1947-55
460-871001 Hood Unit Diesels (green & orange) 1947-55
460-871015 40 & 50' Box Cars 1938-65
460-871060 Early Green & Yellow Diesel Lettering Only (use #871061 for stripes, sold separately) 1941-54 *NEW*
460-871061 Stripes Only-Green & Yellow Diesels & Electrics (use #871060 for lettering, sold separately) *NEW*

NEW YORK CENTRAL
460-4004 Diesel Switchers Alco, Baldwin & EMD 1950 **2.00**
460-4186 50' Mather Stock Cars 1963-70 **2.00**
460-8749 Cab Unit Diesels Red Herald, Gray Stripes 1950-60
460-8758 40 & 50' Jade Green Box Cars 1960-68
460-8778 Steam Locos-Medium 1930-50
460-8788 Single Stripe Cab Unit Diesels 1960
460-87618 Lightning Stripes for Hood Unit Diesels 1950s
460-87890 Merchants Despatch Early Ice Reefers 1930-73
460-87895 Merchants Despatch Late Steel Ice Reefers 1960-73
460-87912 NYC/Boston & Albany Early Passenger Cars 1900-39
460-87932 General Service Passenger Cars 1939-68
460-87933 General Service Passenger & Head End Cars 1939-68

NICKEL PLATE-NEW YORK, CHICAGO & ST. LOUIS
460-4186 50' Mather Stock Cars 1963-70 **2.00**
460-4243 Cabooses "High Speed Service" 1930-62 **2.00**
460-8741 Hood & Cab Unit Diesels 1950-60
460-87189 40 & 50' Box Cars 1950-60

NORFOLK & WESTERN
460-4017 Passenger Service GP9 Diesels 1950 **2.00**
460-8722 Hood Unit Diesels (blue or black) 1950-70
460-87106 Steam Locos 1930-80
460-87391 Streamline Passenger Cars 1950-80
460-87482 Cabooses (red, white) 1940-80
460-87554 Hood Unit Diesels & Switchers 1982
460-87728 Auto Racks 1980+

NORFOLK SOUTHERN
460-4007 Coil Steel Cars (Protect II) 1993+ **2.00**
460-4057 Operation Life Saver GP60 Diesel 1991 **2.00**
460-4147 Southern Railway 100th Anniversary GP59 Diesel #4610 1994+ **2.00**
460-4206 Triple Crown Service 53' Plate Wall Road Railers 1995+ **2.00**
460-4270 48' Semi Trailer w/NS Herald **2.00** *NEW*
460-87435 Thoroughbred for GE & EMD Diesels 1984
460-87574 50 & 60' Box Cars & 100 Ton Hopper 1988
460-87591 Covered Hoppers, Coil Steel Car 1988+
460-87597 Triple Crown Services Road Railers
460-87705 Autoracks 189+
460-87713 48' Outside Post Containers
460-87945 GE Dash-8/9 Diesels 1984+

NORFOLK SOUTHERN RAILWAY CO.
460-87135 Diesels 1950-70

NORTHERN PACIFIC
460-4109 40' Plug & Single Door Box Cars Staggered NP 1958-70
460-4235 40' Double-Sheathed Box Cars 1918-68 **2.00**
460-87118 Steam Locos 1920-50
460-87132 EMD & GE Hood Unit Diesels (yellow & black) w/Gothic Lettering 1960-70
460-87133 NP Hood Unit Diesels (& GE-44 Tonner) Roman Lettering 1950-70
460-87143 Diesel Switchers 1950-70
460-87184 Cabooses Early Pre Merger 1960-70
460-87208 Passenger Cars (Two-Tone Green) 1950-70
460-8737 40, 50 & 60' Box Cars, Large Billboard, NP & Monad 1958-70
460-8746 Freight Cab Unit Diesels 1950-70
460-87488 40' Ice Cooled Reefers 1930-60
460-87530 Passenger F Unit Diesels 1950s
460-87555 NP 40, 50, & 57' Mechanical Reefers 1970-80
460-87584 Stripes for Freight F Unit Diesels 1950
460-87777 Gondola Tank, Hopper, Flat & Bulkhead Flat 1940-70
460-87786 Passenger Cars Original Two-Tone Green 1946-54
460-87787 Stripes for Two-Tone Green Passenger Cars 1946-54
460-87837 Covered Hoppers Pullman-Standard 3-Bay, ACF 2-& 3-Bay 1964-70
460-87843 40 & 50' Box Cars w/Arch Lettering 1942-70
460-871011 MOW Equipment 1920-69 *NEW*

NEW YORK, SUSQUEHANNA & WESTERN
460-4195 SD70M Diesels 1996+

NEW YORK, ONTARIO & WESTERN
460-8744 FT Diesels & Cabooses to 1957

PACIFIC ELECTRIC
460-87563 Trolleys 1911-47
460-87564 Car Stripes 1911-47
460-87589 Freight Motors 1903-65
460-87590 Electric & Diesel Locos 1903-65

PACIFIC FRUIT EXPRESS
460-4021 Ice Reefer with Overland Herald
460-4240 Early Ice Reefers 1920-42 **2.00**
460-8717 Mechanical Reefers 40, 50, & 57' 1960-70
460-87250 40, 50 & 57' Reefers 1960-80
460-87414 40' Ice Reefers, w/Color Heralds 1946-52
460-87501 40' Reefers 1949-60

PENN CENTRAL
460-8784 Cab & Hood Unit Diesels

PENNSYLVANIA
460-8721 Hood Unit Diesels (Tuscan Red & Dulux Gold or white) 1960-70
460-8739 5-Stripe E, F, PA, PB Diesels & GG1 Electrics 1950-60
460-8766 Steam Locos
460-8767 Single Stripe E & F Unit Diesels 1960-70
460-87108 California Zephyr Passenger Cars 1950-70
460-87677 5-Stripe Gold Leaf Scheme Locos 1939-52
460-87810 Single Stripe E Unit Diesels 1953-68
460-87891 Tuscan Red Passenger Cars 1947-68
460-87892 Stripes for Tuscan Red Passenger Cars 1947-68
460-87893 Tuscan Red Lightweight Car Names 1949-68
460-87894 Tuscan Red Heavyweight Car Names 1945-68

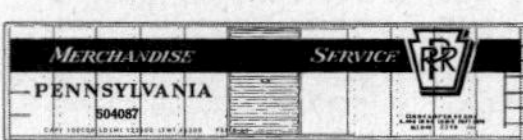

460-87972 40' Merchandise Service Box Cars 1947-57

PERE MARQUETTE
460-8747 Cab Diesels & Caboose
460-8795 Berkshire Steam Locos
460-871042 C&O or Pere Marquette E7A Cab Unit Diesels 1948-1955 *NEW*

PITTSBURGH & LAKE ERIE
460-87702 Covered Hoppers 1960+

PLACARDS & GRAFFITTI
460-87228 Graffiti & Placards
460-87243 Graffiti #2
460-87840 Hazardous Material Placards US & Canada 1984+
460-87975 Transition Era Placards 1945-70

PRIVATE OWNER CARS
460-4023 ADM® Uni-Temp 50' Tank Car 1986 **2.00**
460-4032 ADM® UELX 50' Tank Car **2.00**
460-4033 ADM® UTLX Tank Car-Corn Sweeteners **2.00**
460-4034 ADMX 50' Tank Car-Corn Sweeteners **2.00**
460-4036 ACF 4-Bay Center Flow Hopper-POLYSAR Resins **2.00**
460-4052 Dupont Training Tank Car w/Classroom (Refrigerator Car) **2.00**
460-4064 Tropicana 60' Insulated Box Car **2.00**
460-4103 Holly Sugar Rapid Discharge Beet Hoppers 1990+ **2.00**
460-4107 Americold Cryogenic Box Car 1993+ **2.00**
460-4118 Occidental Chemical 41' Tank Cars 1994+ **2.00**
460-4123 Minnesota Corn Processors Covered Hoppers, ACF Pressure Aid, Trinity Power Flow **2.00**
460-4124 Minnesota Corn Processors 40 & 50' Tank Cars 1994+ **2.00**
460-4165 Northern Indiana Public Service (NORX) Aluminum Coalporter Gondolas 1992+ **2.00**
460-4198 Kansas City Power & Light Coal Porter Gondolas 1984+ **2.00**
460-4264 Richmond Tank Car Co. 65' Propane Gas Tank Car **2.00** *NEW*
460-4267 Kodak/Eastman Chemical ACF 4-Bay Centerflow Covered Hopper 1960s Scheme **2.00** *NEW*
460-4269 Georgia-Pacific Thrall All-Door Box Cars **2.00** *NEW*
460-4275 AGP Grain Trinity 3-Bay Covered Hopper **2.00** *NEW*
460-4276 ConAgra Pullman-Standard 4750 3-Bay Covered Hopper 1973+ **2.00** *NEW*
460-4277 Southdown Cement Co. 2-Bay Covered Hopper 1998+ **2.00** *NEW*
460-87689 ADM Tank Cars; Carbon Dioxide, Alcohol, Corn Syrup
460-87244 Kerr McGee Covered Hoppers
460-87615 Staley Tank Cars Mid 1970s to 1991
460-87645 Cargill Tank Cars; Corn Syrup, Vegetable Oils, Molasses. 1970-91
460-87660 ACF Covered Hoppers; Private Owners (gray & aluminum) 1939-70
460-87661 ACF Covered Hoppers Private Owners (black) 1939-70s
460-87739 North American Chemical Covered & Open 1992+
460-87727 Corn Products; 40' Tank Car, 4-Bay ACF Hopper
460-87809 Canadian Pot Ash Cylindrical & ACF Hoppers 1979+
460-87900 ADM Covered Hoppers, ACF 3- & 4-Bay Trinity Power Flow 1980+

PULLMAN
460-87371 Early Passenger Cars 1920-50

RICHMOND, FREDRICKSBURG & POTOMAC
460-87608 Hood Unit Diesels 1989
460-87474 Hood Unit Diesels 1970-80+

RAILBOX
460-4173 Repainted 50' Box Cars 1992+ **2.00**
460-87160 50' Outside Braced Single Door Box Cars
460-87316 50' Plug & Single Door Box Car, Rail Gon 52' Gondola 1970-80

RAILWAY EXPRESS AGENCY
460-871010 50' Express Reefers 1929-67

READING
460-4138 2-Bay Open Hoppers 1944-76 **2.00**
460-87125 FT, F3, F7, FP7 & FA-1 Diesels 1950-60
460-87686 Diesels 1962-73
460-87691 RS-3, GP9 & SD40-2 Diesels (green)
460-87708 Diesel "Barricade Stripes" 1947-73
460-87883 Cabooses 1924-76

RIO GRANDE-DENVER, & RIO GRANDE WESTERN
(Narrow gauge equipment sets are listed under Narrow Gauge Lines.)
460-4083 GP60 Diesels 1991+ **2.00**
460-8728 Diesels-Large & Small Lettering 1960-80
460-8740 1 & 4 Stripe Cab Unit Diesels 1950-60
460-8756 Cab Unit Diesels (black & yellow) 1950s
460-8782 50' Single & Double Door Box Cars 1954-72
460-8796 Early Hood Unit Diesels (black & yellow)
460-87108 California Zephyr Passenger Cars 1950-70
460-87199 Cabooses (orange) 1970-80
460-87200 Cabooses (black, orange & silver) 1940-60
460-87271 Stripes for EMD Hood Unit Diesels 1960-80
460-87542 Standard Gauge Steam Locos 1930s
460-87577 Ski Train and Business Cars 1986
460-87816 12-Panel 4-Bay Hoppers 1970+
460-871047 Pullman PS2CD 4427 Covered Hoppers *NEW* Fits Walthers or Life-Like cars.
460-871058 Striping for Passenger Cars or Diesels (Use w/#8740, sold separately) *NEW*

ROCK-ROCK ISLAND-CHICAGO, ROCK ISLAND & PACIFIC
460-4104 "Golden State" Sleeping Cars 1947-60 **2.00**
460-8718 Hood & Cab Unit Diesels 1960-70
460-8719 Freight Cars-Block Lettering 1960-70

MICROSCALE®

ALL SETS $4.00 (UNLESS NOTED)

460-8720 Freight Cars-Speed Lettering 1960-70
460-87229 ROCK General Freight (Route ROCK) 1970
460-87230 ROCK Hood Unit Diesels 1970
460-87361 Early F Unit Diesels 1940-60
460-87956 E & F Unit Diesels Rocket Scheme 1943-60

460-87989 GP7 & RS-3 Diesels Rocket Scheme 1950-60
460-87259 Last "Fallen Flag" Freight Cars w/CNW, SP & SSW Reporting Marks
460-871041 GP7/9 Diesels THE ROCK w/Names 1975-80 ***NEW***

RUTLAND

460-4001 Diesels 1956-64 **2.00**
460-4251 Diesels 1956-64 (yellow lettering & stripes) **2.00** ***NEW***

SANTA FE-ATCHISON, TOPEKA & SANTA FE

460-4003 EMD Diesel Yard Switchers 1960-80 **2.00**
460-4012 Stainless Steel RDC Cars 1950 **2.00**
460-4025 50' Steel Coil Car "Super Shock Control" 1988 **2.00**
460-4037 25' Piggyback Van & Tractor-1950-60s **2.00**
460-4128 Woodchip Car 1985+ **2.00**
460-4174 Hi-Level Passenger Cars (El Capitan) 1956-70 **2.00**
460-4190 Streamlined General Service Passenger Cars 1939-70 **2.00**
460-8709 Box Cars & Reefers w/Super Shock Control, Ship & Travel Slogans 1960-70
460-8712 Freight Diesels (blue & yellow) 1950-70
460-8729 Freight Diesels blue & yellow Warbonnet 1972
460-8730 Freight Cars w/Large Round Herald, black & white Lettering 1972
460-8764 Steam Locos-Silver Lettering 1930-50
460-8772 Passenger Warbonnet E3, E6, PA & PB-1 Diesels 1940-60
460-8777 Freight Service Cab Unit Diesels 1940-70
460-8779 Maintenance-of-Way Cars 1940-80
460-876401 Steam Locos-White Lettering 1930-50
460-87101 Warbonnet Passenger Diesels 1950-70
460-87112 Express Box Cars 50' (Straight Line Map, yellow lettering) 1950-60
460-87114 "Super Chief" Passenger Cars 1946-72
460-87121 Cabooses 1940-80
460-87127 "Scout" Passenger Cars 1950-60
460-87128 Company Service Tank Cars 1950-80
460-87136 40' Reefers (Straight Line Map black Lettering) 1940-50
460-87168 Gas Electrics 1920-50
460-87188 Red & Silver Warbonnet U28C/G & U30C/G 1960-70
460-87215 50' Map Box Cars Super Chief & El Capitan (Box Car Red) 1950-60
460-87216 50' Map Box Cars Chief, Scout & Grand Canyon 1950-60
460-8724701 Zebra Stripes-White
460-8724704 Zebra Stripes-Silver
460-87248 Zebra Stripes for Hood Unit Diesels (silver) 1950-60
460-87255 Mechanical Reefers 1960-80
460-87263 50' Double-Door Box Cars Mid 1960s
460-87264 Insulated 50' Plug Door Cars 1960-80
460-87267 Food & Auto Parts Box Cars w/black & white Heralds 1960-70
460-87288 Covered Hoppers for MDC & E&B Kits 1950-80
460-87291 40' Trailers; Blue & Red Logo, Piggyback Logo 1960-70
460-87363 Steam Loco Tender Data 1920-50
460-87369 SD40-2 "Snoot" Diesels 1980
460-87383 Heavyweight Passenger Cars 1920-50
460-87384 Pullman Heavyweight Cars Assigned to ATSF
460-87390 Two-Tone Gray Passenger Car Stripes 1940+
460-87444 4-Bay Cylindrical & 3-Bay Covered Hoppers 1970
460-87470 10-Pack Fuel Foiler 1970-80
460-87483 Bicentennial SD45-2 Diesel 1976
460-87498 40' Box Cars w/Straight Line Map "Grand Canyon", "Scout", "El Capitan", "Super Chief" & "Chief" 1940-47
460-87505 40 & 50' Box Cars "El Capitan", "Chief" & "Super Chief 1947-59
460-87506 40 & 50' Damage Free Box Cars "Texas Chief", "Chief", Ship & Travel ATSF All the Way & Grand Canyon Line (white)1947-59
460-87509 40' Ice Reefers Ship & Travel Slogan 1940
460-87510 50' Mechanical Reefers Ship & Travel Slogan 1950
460-87516 40' Box Cars w/Curved Line Map 1940
460-87517 40' Ice Reefers w/Curved Line Map 1930-40
460-87548 Alco Hood Unit Diesels 1960
460-87558 Freight Cars w/24" Logo 1988
460-87585 GP60M Superfleet® Diesels (red & silver) 1990
460-87599 FP45 in Original & Superfleet® Schemes 1970-90
460-87619 Hood Unit Diesels w/EMD Style Lettering & 12 x 20" US Flags 1990
460-87637 Superfleet® GE Dash 8 (1991-92) & 9 (1994) Diesels
460-87638 45, 48 & 53' Containers & Chassis 1990+
460-87662 "Valley Flyer" Steam Locos 1938-1940s
460-87663 "Valley Flyer" Steam Loco Stripes 1938-40s
460-87676 GP60B Superfleet® Diesels 1991+
460-87688 Auto Racks 1980s
460-87699 F Unit "Cat Whiskers" Scheme 1940-52
460-87772 Thrall 5-Unit Articulated Double-Stack Cars 1989+
460-87791 "Quality" Covered Hoppers 1990+
460-87800 "Quality" Box Cars 1990+
460-87831 DL-109 & Erie-Built F-M Diesels 1941-63
460-87832 Two-Tone Gray Sleeping Cars 1940-65
460-87906 SD75M Diesels 1995+
460-87914 Late Cabooses, Ce-1 to Ce-13 1979+
460-87936 Roadrailers (Autorailer) 1985+
460-87961 Streamlined General Service Sleepers 1939-70
460-871043 Head End Horse Express, Mail & Railway Express Agency Cars 1924-71 ***NEW***
460-871067 Extra Numbers for Diesels (use w/#8729, 87369, 87619 all sold separately) ***NEW***

SFSP PROPOSED MERGER

(Merger denied July, 1986 by the ICC.)
460-4273 SFSP Cabooses 1986+ **2.00** ***NEW***
460-87469 Premerger Experimental Scheme w/Large SP or SF Lettering 1985
460-87475 Merger Warbonnet Yellow Outlines for ATSF Blue/Yellow Diesels
460-87476 Merger Warbonnet Red Outlines for SFSP Red/Yellow Diesels
460-87496 Premerger Diesels (red, yellow "Kodachromes") w/Large SP or SF 1986

SEABOARD AIR LINE

460-4013 Passenger EMD E7 Diesels 1950 **2.00**
460-87104 F3A, FA-1 & FT A&B Diesels 1950-60
460-87151 Cabooses 1950-60
460-87152 Switchers 1950-60
460-87439 EMD E Unit Diesels 1950-60
460-87565 Switchers & Diesel Freight Units 1950s
460-87566 Freight Diesel Stripes 1950s
460-87965 40 & 50' Box Cars 1950-65
460-871007 Covered Hoppers 1947-63

SEABOARD COAST LINE

460-8706 Freight Cars 1960-70
460-87896 Diesels 1967-72

SEABOARD SYSTEM

460-87398 EMD & GE Diesels 1980

SOO LINE

460-4215 85 & 89' Flat Cars 1961-90 **2.00**
460-87116 Diesels (yellow & Maroon) 1950-60
460-87117 Diesels (red, white) 1970-80
460-87119 Diesel Switchers (black, Dulux Gold) 1950-60
460-87553 Diesels (Action Red) 1989
460-87998 Early Piggyback Trailers 24, 35 & 40' 1955-63
460-87999 40' Piggyback Trailers 1963-80

SHORTLINES

460-4008 Gateway Western Operation Lifesaver & Gateway Eastern Diesels 1993+ **2.00**
460-4018 McCloud River SD38 Diesels **2.00**
460-4030 Chicago Central & Pacific Diesels 1985 **2.00**
460-4046 Eureka Southern GP38 Diesels **2.00**
460-4050 East Erie Commercial Railroad GE70 & 85-Ton Switchers **2.00**
460-4067 Providence & Worcester Diesel Locos 1982-92 **2.00**
460-4090 Midsouth GP7, 9 & 18 w/Operation Life Saver 1988+ **2.00**
460-4092 Twin Cities & Western Diesels 1989+ **2.00**
460-4099 Arizona & California Husky-Stack Cars 1993+ **2.00**
460-4108 Blue Mountain Railroad Diesels 1993+ **2.00**
460-4110 Spokane International RS-1 Diesels, UP Colors 1962-67 **2.00**
460-4114 South Shore GP38-2 Diesels 1989+ **2.00**
460-4116 Red River Valley & Western Diesels
460-4127 Indiana Southern Railroad Diesels 1990+ **2.00**
460-4132 Cape Breton & Central Nova Scotia Railway Diesels 1993+ **2.00**
460-4134 Birmingham Southern Diesels 1980+ **2.00**
460-4139 Virginia Railway Express Diesels 1990+ **2.00**
460-4140 New England Central Diesels 1995+ **2.00**
460-4153 Central Oregon & Pacific Diesels 1995+ **2.00**
460-4156 TransKentucky Transportation Railroad Inc. (TTI) Diesels 1985+ **2.00**
460-4158 Finger Lakes Railway Diesels 1995+ **2.00**
460-4164 Blue Mountain & Reading Diesels & Passenger Cars 1987+ **2.00**
460-4167 Reading Blue Mountain & Northern Locomotives 1991+ **2.00**
460-4175 Arkansas Midland Railroad Diesels 1992+ **2.00**
460-4176 Bay Colony Railroad Diesels 1994+ **2.00**
460-4177 Cape Cod Railroad Diesels & Passenger Cars 1993+ **2.00**

460-4182 Masscentral Diesels 1990+ **2.00**
460-4185 Reading & Northern Diesels 1992+ **2.00**
460-4188 Northwestern Pacific Diesels, Black Widow 1996+ **2.00**
460-4205 Great Western Railway Diesels 1990+ **2.00**
460-4207 Connecticut Central Hood Unit Diesels 1996+ **2.00**
460-4216 Canadian American Railroad Diesels 1996+ **2.00**
460-4217 St. Lawrence & Hudson Diesels 1996+ **2.00**
460-4220 Vermont Railway Hood Unit Diesels 1975+ **2.00**
460-4225 Clarendon & Pittsford Hood Unit Diesels 1985+ **2.00**
460-4233 Hudson Bay Railway Diesels 1997 **2.00**
460-4249 Vermont Northern Diesels 1996+ **2.00**
460-4250 Quebec Southern Diesels 1996+ **2.00**
460-4252 Green Mountain Diesels 1965-88 **2.00**
460-4253 Green Mountain Diesels 1988-98 **2.00**
460-4261 Allegheny Railroad Diesels (red lettering) 1990+ **2.00** ***NEW***
460-87545 Middletown & Unionville, Middletown & New Jersey, Locos & Rolling Stock
460-87570 Washington Central Diesels & Caboose 1987
460-87583 Paducah & Louisville Diesels (gray) & Switchers (green & black)
460-87588 Paducah & Louisville Diesels & Caboose (green & black)
460-87592 The Indiana Railroad CF-7, GP9 & Other Diesels 1988+
460-87598 Kyle SW8, GP9, GP40 & GP20 Diesels
460-87696 Gateway Western & Chicago Missouri & Western Diesels 1987
460-87701 St. Louis Area Short Lines 1954+
460-87755 Georgia Northeastern Diesels & Caboose 1988+
460-87785 Belt Railway of Chicago Diesels 1950+
460-87801 California Short Lines; 70 Ton Locos. Modesto & Empire Traction, Ventura County
460-87820 Dakota, Minnesota & Eastern Diesels 1990+
460-87825 Arizona & California/California Northern Diesels 1992+
460-87827 Willamette & Pacific Diesels 1993+
460-87860 Lake Superior & Ishpeming Diesels 1950+
460-87886 Arkansas & Missouri Diesels 1989+
460-87955 Genesee & Wyoming Group Diesels, Buffalo & Pittsburgh, Rochester & Southern
460-87960 Virginia Railway Express Passenger Cars, 1990+

MICROSCALE®

ALL SETS $4.00 (UNLESS NOTED)

SOUTHERN PACIFIC

460-4001 GP9 Passenger Diesels Black Widow 1950-70 **2.00**
460-4024 50' Steel Coil Car "Hydra-Cushion" 1975 **2.00**
460-4027 25' Piggyback Trailers & Tractors 1950 **2.00**
460-4044 12,500 Gal. Tank Cars 1950 **2.00**
460-4101 Woodchip Cars Steel Sides 1975+ **2.00**
460-4136 Trailer Flat Car Service Cabooses 1954-65 **2.00**
460-4160 50' Speed Lettering Box Cars 1995+ **2.00**
460-8703 General Freight w/Hydra-Cushion & C, LD, DF, CP Logos 1950-70
460-8711 Diesels (gray) w/Roman Lettering 1960-70
460-8733 Steam Locos-"Daylight", "Sunbeam" & "San Joaquin" 1940-50
460-8734 Passenger Cars "Daylight", "Sun Beam" & "San Joaquin" SP Lines 1940-60
460-8750 "Daylight" Diesels; PA, PB, E7, E8A & B & FP7 1950-60
460-8765 Medium Steam Locos 1920-50
460-8771 Tiger Stripe Switchers 1950-60
460-8775 Heavy Steam Locos 1940-50
460-87105 Light Steam Locos 1930-50
460-87107 General Service Passenger Cars gray lettering) 1960-80
460-87122 Passenger Cars "Golden State" 1950-60
460-87126 "City"/"Overland" Post-War Passenger Cars (red lettering) 1950-60
460-87155 Maintenance-of-Way Equipment 1940-80
460-87177 Cab & Hood Unit Diesels (gray, red) 1960-80
460-87178 Letterboard Striping for "Sunset Limited" Passenger Cars 1960-80
460-87186 Diesels Experimental "Daylight" 1970
460-87194 Ore Cars 1960-80
460-87201 Black Widow E, F, GP9, SD9 & Trainmaster Diesels 1950-60
460-87204 "Sunset Limited" Passenger Cars 1950-60
460-87227 Cabooses 1940-80
460-87239 Covered Hoppers
460-87258 Loading Symbols 1970-80
460-87262 "Daylight" Passenger Car Stripes
460-87270 70 Ton 2-Bay Covered Hoppers 1960-80
460-87390 Two-Tone Gray Passenger Car Stripes 1940+
460-87407 SPFE 50 & 57' Outside Braced Mechanical Reefers 1980
460-87408 White SPFE 57' Outside Braced Mechanical Reefers
460-87409 Orange SPFE 57' Outside Braced Mechanical Reefers
460-87447 Diesels Red Wings Scheme (use with #87612) 1980
460-87464 SD40 Diesel & 45' Trailers in Olympic Schemes 1980s
460-87472 4-Pack Intermodal Flat Cars 1980
460-87529 57' Mechanical Reefers w/8 Different Colored Heralds 1960
460-87611 Police Cabooses & Passenger Cars 1985
460-87612 Diesel Road Names & Numbers (red, use with #87447) 1989
460-87617 Red Wings for Atlas, Athearn, Con-Cor & Rail Power Model Diesels 1950s
460-87620 Speed Lettering Merger Scheme-Rebuilt GP40s 1991
460-87646 GP60 Diesels w/Speed Lettering 1991+
460-87835 Bicentennial Diesels & Caboose 1975-80
460-87745 Gunderson Maxi III Double Stack Cars 1990+
460-87761 "Daylight", "Lark", "Golden State", "Overland", "Sunset Limited" Insignia for Passenger Cars 1937-70
460-87857 Speed Lettering for SD70, Dash 9-44CW & Switchers 1994
460-87911 Single Sheathed Wood Box Cars Classes B-50-13, B-50-14, 1923-62
460-87923 "Overnight" Service Box Cars 1946-59
460-87973 AC-4400CW Diesels 1995+
460-871055 "Shasta Daylight" & "Coast Daylight" Passenger Cars 1947-58 ***NEW***
460-871057 "Shasta Daylight" E7A/B Cab Unit Diesels ***NEW***
460-8724103 Heavyweight Passenger Car-Metallic Gold Lettering 1920-50
460-8724108 Heavyweight Passenger Car-Dulux Gold Lettering 1920-50

SOUTHERN RAILWAY

460-4084 Bay Window Cabooses 1960-90 **2.00**
460-4196 Coil Steel Car 1974-85 **2.00**
460-8713 Freight Cars; Serves The South, Big John 1960-70
460-8714 Freight Cars; Green Light, White Lettering, DF Logos 1960-70
460-8732 Hood Unit Diesels, Southern, Interstate, Savannah & Atlanta, Central of Georgia 1950-70
460-8762 Diesel Cab Units (gold & white stripes) 1950-80
460-87539 Diesels-Dulux Gold Lettering 1971
460-87540 Diesels-Dulux Gold Stripes 1971
460-87878 Early Hood Unit Diesels & Switchers, (green) 1940-60
460-87879 Early Cab Units (green) 1940-60

SPOKANE, PORTLAND & SEATTLE

460-4016 EMD or Alco Cab Unit Diesels 1950 **2.00**
460-87102 E, F & FA Diesels 1950-70
460-87195 Hood Unit Diesels (yellow & green) 1960-70
460-87196 Diesel Switchers (black) 1950-60
460-871026 40 & 50' Steel Box Cars 1946-68

SUSQUEHANNA-NEW YORK, SUSQUEHANNA & WESTERN

460-87531 Diesels 1988

TEXAS & PACIFIC

460-4088 Diesel Switchers (orange & black) 1950-62 **2.00**
460-87452 Cab Unit Diesels
460-87764 Early Hood Unit Diesels 1950-62

TOLEDO, PEORIA & WESTERN

460-87129 Hood Unit Diesels 1950-70
460-87648 Diesels 1991

TRAILER TRAIN-TTX

460-4040 62 & 74' Thrall or Gunderson Centerbeam Bulkhead Flats 1977-90 **2.00**
460-87471 Impack, Front Runner & 4 Runner Intermodal Cars 1980
460-87552 50, 60, 68, 85 & 89' Flat Cars (Box Car Red)
460-87578 50, 60, 68 & 85' Flat Cars (yellow) 1970+
460-87579 89' & Long Runner Flat Cars (yellow)
460-87670 Trailer Train/TTX Husky Stack Container Cars 1991+
460-87722 TTX Thrall Stand-Alone & 3-Unit Container Double-Stack Cars
460-87732 TTX Thrall 4-Unit Double-Stack Cars (Drawbar Connected) 1991+
460-87747 TTX Long Runner Flat Cars (Two 89' Cars) 1990+
460-87750 Thrall 4-Unit Drawbar Connected Double-Stack Cars 1990+
460-87788 Trailer Train/TTX Thrall 5-Unit Articulated Double-Stack Car 1989+
460-87792 TTX Gunderson Maxi III 5-Unit Articulated Double-Stack Cars 1992+
460-87822 Trailer Train/TTX 48 & 53' All-Purpose Spine Cars 1990+
460-87839 TTX Twin Stack 5-Unit Articulated Double-Stack Cars 1993+

TRONA RAILWAY

460-87209 Baldwin Cab Unit Diesels 1970-80
460-87758 SD45-2 Diesels 1992+

UNION PACIFIC

460-4009 Diesel Yard Switchers Overland Route Shield 1950 **2.00**
460-4028 Operation Red Block Diesels 1988 **2.00**
460-4039 UP/GE 1000th Dash 8 #9400 1990 **2.00**
460-4048 Desert Victory Camouflage SD40-2 Diesel 1991 **2.00**
460-4071 Diesel Safety Plaques & B Unit Lettering (Use with #87523) 1990 **2.00**
460-4077 57' Mechanical Reefers Late 1980s **2.00**
460-4079 12,500 Gal Tank Cars As-Built 1937-55 **2.00**
460-4080 12,500 Gal Tank Cars 1955+ **2.00**
460-4120 SD40-2 Diesel #3301, North Little Rock "Pulling for Safety" 1994+ **2.00**
460-4180 Center Flow Hoppers "We Will Deliver" 1996+ **2.00**
460-8707 Freight Cars; Automated Railway, Map & Shield 1960-70
460-8710 40 & 50' Box Cars, 1950-70
460-8735 Diesels & Turbine (gray & yellow) 1960-80
460-8736 Freight Diesels w/Centennial Curved Wings 1960-80
460-8763 Steam Locos-White, Yellow or Silver Lettering 1930-80
460-8797 Cabooses w/Billboard Safety Slogans 1970
460-87109 Passenger E & F Unit Diesels 1950-80
460-87169 Hood Unit Diesels w/Modern, Large Lettering & Numbers 1979+
460-87222 Bathtub Gondola 1970-80
460-87223 Cabooses CA11 1970-80
460-87242 UP Fruit Express 57' Mechanical Reefer.1970-80
460-87254 Maintenance-Of-Way Equipment 1960-70
460-87257 Caboose Safety Slogans & Class Numbers 1970-80
460-87265 100 Ton Grain Hoppers 1960-80
460-87354 Hood Unit Diesels 1970-80
460-87373 Diesel Switchers 1980
460-87390 Two-Tone Gray Passenger Car Stripes 1940+
460-87392 Two-Tone Gray Passenger Cars 1950
460-87453 SD40 Diesels w/"Energy" Slogans
460-87465 UP 50' Single Plug Door Box Cars "We Can Handle It"
460-87466 50, 60 & 86' Box Cars w/Plug Door 1980
460-87467 50' Plug & Sliding Door Box Cars 1980
460-87468 50 & 86' Plug & Sliding Door Box Cars 1970-80
460-87489 40 & 50' Box Cars 1939-50
460-87490 30, 40 & 45' Trailers & Tractors 1980
460-87494 40 & 50' Box Cars 1952-59
460-87499 Box Cars w/"Road of the Streamliners" & "Serves the West" 1926-39
460-87512 Stock Cars Class 5-40-10, 11& 12
460-87522 Diesels w/North Little Rock Style Lettering 1987
460-87523 High Tech Diesels; Dash 8-40C & SD60M 1987
460-87580 #80 or #8080 Coal Turbine Loco
460-87616 Passenger Cars 1947-89 (Stripes in #871105)
460-87622 Early E Unit Diesels "City of San Francisco" 1950s
460-87623 Stripes for Early E Unit & "City" Cars 1950s
460-87624 Early E Units "City of Los Angeles" 1950-60
460-87630 Sleepers & Business Cars-1947-89
460-87635 Names for Lightweight Passenger Cars 1947-71
460-87636 Heavyweight & Special Passenger Cars 1947-91
460-87653 E Unit Diesels w/"Overland Route" 1950s
460-87679 Auto Racks 1990
460-87683 40' Express Box Cars 1960+
460-87833 Two-Tone Gray Passenger Car Names 1942-53
460-87841 Early Piggyback Trailers 24, 36 & 40' w/Tractors 1947-60
460-87847 60' Beer Cars, 1977+
460-87850 Covered Hoppers 1976+
460-87851 United Way Campaign SD40-2 Diesel 1994
460-87905 Early Cabooses CA-1 to -9 (red or yellow) 1941-77

460-87977 Diesels "We Will Deliver" 1996+
460-87978 Natural Gas Powered Switchers & Tenders 1992+
460-87997 SD90MAC Diesels 1996+
460-871053 1996 Olympic Torch Relay SD40-2 Diesel ***NEW***
460-871054 1996 Olympic Torch Relay Passenger Cars ***NEW***
460-871056 Business/Excursion Passenger Cars 1996+ ***NEW***

US ARMY

460-4278 Diesels 1990+ **2.00** ***NEW***

UTAH RAILWAY

460-87182 Hood Unit Diesels (gray & Maroon) 1960-70
460-87668 Morrison-Knudsen Rebuilt SD40 Diesels 1992

VIA RAIL CANADA

460-87667 Diesels 1979-92
460-87672 Passenger Cars 1990+
460-87673 Passenger Car Stripes 1990+
460-87678 Passenger Car Names 1990+

VIRGINIAN RAILWAY

460-87120 Steam Locos 1920-50

MICROSCALE®

ALL SETS $4.00 (UNLESS NOTED)

WABASH
460-87643 Diesels (blue and gray) 1949-64
460-87644 Diesel Stripes 1949-64
460-87698 Road Diesels & Switchers 1960-64

WASHINGTON STATE DEPT. OF TRANSPORTATION "GRAIN TRAIN"
460-4259 Pullman-Standard/Trinity Covered Hoppers 1996+ **2.00** ***NEW***
460-4260 ACF Centerflow Covered Hoppers 1996+ **2.00** ***NEW***

WESTERN MARYLAND
460-87130 Hood Unit Diesels 1950-70
460-87700 Cabooses 1936-80
460-87916 40, 50 & 60' Box Car Speed Lettering 1953-70
460-871005 Hood & Cab Unit Diesels "Fireball" Scheme 1947-54

WESTERN PACIFIC
460-4266 50' Single Sheathed Automobile Service Box Cars-Original White Lettering **2.00** ***NEW***
460-4274 Bicentennial GP40 Diesel **2.00** ***NEW***
460-8726 Silver & Orange Hood & Cab Unit Diesels (Sacramento Northern) 1950-70
460-87108 California Zephyr Passenger Cars 1950-70
460-87187 Green Diesels (Sacramento Northern, Tidewater Southern) 1970
460-87211 Diesel Switchers 1950-80
460-87212 Standard (1960-70) & Bay Window (1950-80) Cabooses
460-87220 General Freight (white lettering) 1970-80
460-87253 Freight Cars 1960-70
460-87272 Freight Cars-New Image 1980
460-87274 Hood Unit Diesels (Sacramento Northern)-New Image 1970-80
470-87433 40' Box Cars 1950-60
460-87438 40 & 50' Box Cars 1950-60
460-87445 Merger Cabooses (UP red lettering) 1980
460-87448 GP40 Diesels (UP scheme) & Cabooses 1985
460-87491 40' Wood Reefers 1920-40
460-87802 FT Diesels 1940-65
460-87818 60' Box Car, 62' Bulkhead Flat, 89' Auto Rack 1970
460-87871 60' Beer Cars, 1969+

WHEELING & LAKE ERIE
460-87981 Diesels 1991+

WISCONSIN & CALUMET
460-87654 Diesels & Passenger Cars 1980+
460-87655 Diesel & Passenger Car Stripes (Also for IC cars) 1980+

WISCONSIN & SOUTHERN
460-87762 Diesel Switchers & Road Units 1985+
460-87763 Diesel Stripes 1985+

WISCONSIN CENTRAL
460-4102 Model Railroader 60th Anniversary 50' Box Car 1993 **2.00**
460-87533 GP38-2, GP35 & SD45 Diesels 1988+
460-87534 Diesel Stripes-30" Wide (yellow) 1988+
460-87543 Diesel Switchers 1988+
460-87546 Box Cars 1989+
460-87547 Hoppers & Gondolas 1989
460-87712 GP40 Diesels 1991 New Paint Scheme
460-87921 F45 Diesels 1995+

MULTIPLE FREIGHT CAR SETS EA 4.00 (UNLESS NOTED)
Sets include lettering for various individual cars

AIRSLIDE® HOPPERS
40' CARS
460-87434 Wabash, L&N, B&O, CB&Q, Minneapolis & St. Louis
460-87417 UP, NP, GN
460-87419 Atlantic Coast Line, SOU, SP, Chicago Great Western
460-87749 Domino Sugar, Bay State Milling, Golden Loaf Flour
50' CARS
460-87511 CB&Q, GN, NP
460-87515 BN, CNW, DRGW
460-87503 ATSF, SP & SSW
460-87507 UP, WP, MP

ASSORTED CARS
460-87261 SP, NKP ATSF & LV
460-87322 Hoppers UP, SSW, N-F-O, Gondola-Bessemer & Lake Erie
460-87324 55' ACF 4-Bay Hoppers; ADM & Rock Island, 50' Outside Braced Box Car Helena Southwestern
460-87342 FMC Hopper; ICG 50' Single Door Box Car, WCTR 50' Double-Door Box Car
460-87356 52' Gondola Chessie, ATSF, UP & DRGW, 50' Chessie Flat Car
460-87394 ACF Hopper; Hercules, 50' Box Cars; Marinette, Tomahawk & Western, ICG & MD&W
460-87395 54' ACF Hoppers; Southern, Chemplex, 52' Gondola D&H
460-87406 UP 40' Ballast Car, 3-Bay Hoppers; Lincoln Grain, Boone Valley Co-Op, Detroit & Mackinac Box Car
460-87742 50' Coil Steel Cars; Iowa Interstate, Conrail, CNW, Little Rock & Western 1969+

AUTO RACKS
460-87687 SP, SSW, DRGW
460-87692 MILW, Soo Line, CNW
460-87709 CR & Waterloo (WLO)

BOX CARS
460-8738 SSW 50' Double-Door, PRR, L&N, CPR, D&H 40' Single Door
460-8754 UP, Pacifio, Buffalo Creek, Linde
460-8755 B&O, Chessie, SP&S, MP, S&A, DRGW
460-8781 50' MEC, Evergreen, MA&PA, N&W, DRGW, GTW, WP, B&O
460-87217 50' Outside Braced Rahway Valley, St. Lawrence, Western Erie
460-87218 50' Outside Braced ROCK, Sabine River & Northern, Hutchinson Northern
460-87224 50' Outside Braced FEC, Mississippi Export, Providence & Worchester, Bath & Hammondsport
460-87225 50' Outside Braced Double Door Yreka Western, Sierra, Simpson Timber, City of Prineville
460-87303 Family Lines, Sandersville, V&S
460-87304 50' Single Door Hutchinson Northern, MCSA & MILW
460-87305 50' Ashley Drew & Northern, MP, SP
460-87306 GN, GTW & WAB
460-87307 50' N&W, Georgia-Pacific & Seaboard
460-87309 E&N, CNJ, St. Marys
460-87313 40' Monon, CP & EL
460-87315 50' WAB, SBD, GTW, DT&I
460-87317 40 & 50' MN&S, P&LE
460-87318 40' Union Carbide/Linde (green Logo)
460-87319 50' NdeM, Lake Erie Franklin & Clarindon, MA&PA
460-87320 50' South Shore, Amador Central, Roscoe, Snyder & Pacific
460-87321 50' UP & Providence & Worchester
460-87323 40 & 50' ATSF, Boise Cascade, DRGW
460-87328 50' ATSF, SP&S, Oregon & Pacific Eastern
460-87330 50' Peninsula Terminal, Middletown & New Jersey, New Hope & Ivy.
460-87333 50' Hi-Cube ATSF 50' Outside Braced, Double-Door Oregon & Northwestern
460-87335 50' Outside Braced P&LE, Virginia Central, 40' CN
460-87336 50' Louisiana Midland, GB&W, Manufacturers Railway Service
460-87349 50' Oregon, California & Eastern & Longview, Portland & Northern
460-87353 50' Plug & Double-Door N&W, Willamette, Bessemer & Lake Erie
460-87377 50' Outside Braced Vermont Northern & The Bay Line
460-87378 50' Ralston Purina & Ontario Northland
460-87379 50' Outside Braced B&M, RDG

460-87381 50' Outside Brace D&H, Union Railroad of Oregon, Angelina & Neches River
460-87404 50' NP "Freedom" & WP w/Large Feather
460-87405 50' All-Door & Double Door Louisiana-Pacific, Ashley, Drew & Northern, Sacramento Valley & Tillamook Bay
460-87411 40' DRGW, ICG & Pickins Railroad
460-87415 50' All Door Anderson-Tully, 50' Double-Door Pend Oreille Valley
460-87416 50' Outside Braced Lancaster & Chester, TOE, BAR

62' BULKHEAD CENTERBEAM FLAT CARS
460-87339 Trailer Train, CP Rail, CR
460-87340 BN, UP & CLC
460-87436 CB&Q, WP
460-87437 UP, MILW

75' BULKHEAD CENTERBEAM FLAT CARS
460-871025 Set #1: Cascade Warehouse, Hampton Lumber Sales, Desticon Transportation, Tricon Forest Products, Tobacco Valley 1987+ ***NEW***
460-871029 Set #2 BN, UP, British Columbia Rail, BC Rail 1987+ ***NEW***
460-4247 Data Only 1987+ **2.00** ***NEW***

COVERED HOPPERS
460-8723 54' Center Flow Ethyl, El Rexene, Hercules,Chemplex
460-8724 Pullman-Standard Commodity Traders, Trona, Equity, Cargill, Cosden
460-8757 LD, RF&P, Welch Grain, TP&W
460-87301 ACF 55' 4-Bay Arco, Gulf, Amoco
460-87302 Pullman Standard Open & Covered; SLSF, Amoco & Scoular
460-87314 ACF 54' Centerflow CB&Q, Stauffer & Continental
460-87325 50, 54 & 60' City Service Co., CITCO & Camden & Highland
460-87331 54 & 55' ADM, Norchem, Augora Co-op
460-87351 54' 3-Bay RI, Cylindrical; Pillsbury
460-87352 55' ACF 5-Bay North American & American Hochest Plastics
460-87355 54' Pullman & ACF 4-Bay Dupont, Carlon
460-87410 55' ACF 4-Bay Centerflow Rexall, WR Grace & Plaskon
460-87429 55' ACF 4-Bay Centerflow Englehard, Amoco & Shell
460-87432 50' 100 Ton American Chemical, Sinclair, Koppers, Reynolds Metals
460-87690 Wonder Bread, NAAS Foods, Englehard
460-87730 ACF 4-Bay Centerflow Amaizo, Goodyear, Penford
460-87744 ACF 2- & 3-Bay Centerflow Saskatchewan Minerals, Genesse & Wyoming, Dupont 1966+
460-87765 COOP Pullman-Standard 17 Panel & 4-Bay Cylindrical 1973+

REEFERS
460-87144 RDG, Dubuque, Miller, Armour, Evans
460-87150 Hormel, Boise Cascade & GN
460-87167 Billboard-Wescott & Winks, Land O' Lakes, White Rock
460-87172 Billboard-Red Top, Wilson Milk, Jelke Good Luck Margarine
460-87173 Billboard-Black Hawk, Southern Star, Hygrade, Rath's
460-87174 Billboard-Jersey Gold, "W" Brand, Midwest Hennery
460-87418 57' Mechanical SOO, BAR & 50' MEC
460-87680 60' Insulated Beer Cars, SP, ATSF &BN
460-87871 60' Beer Cars, MP, MKT, WP 1969+

TWO-& 3-BAY OPEN HOPPERS
460-87368 Virginian, NYC & Cleveland, Cincinnati, Chicago & St. Louis
460-87380 RDG, LV; 3-Bay Shawmut, Pittsburgh & Lake Erie

GONDOLAS
460-87327 65' Erie & 50' Soo & N&W
460-87332 50' Chessie, B&O, BN, CR & ATSF
460-87337 52' Chicago West Pullman & Southern, SOU, GB&W, PC

TANK CARS
460-87350 50' Van Gas & Olin Chemicals
460-87796 Seneca, Amstar, CPC International 1970+
460-87828 42' SCM Chemicals, Engelhard, Thiele 1975+
460-87502 50' Corn Products, Trusweet, Amaizo & Hubinger

SIGNS EA 4.00 (UNLESS NOTED)

AMERICAN FLAGS EA 2.00
460-4201 48 Star 1912-59
460-4202 50 Star 1960+

FARM COMMUNITY
460-87163 Small Towns
460-87166 Rural Towns 1800-1920
460-87795 #1 Grain Elevators, Feed Stores 1960+
460-87811 #2 Grain Elevators, Feed Stores 1960+

CANADIAN GRAIN ELEVATORS
460-87866 Alberta 1980+
460-87870 Saskatchewan 1985+
460-87898 Manitoba 1980+

MICROSCALE®

GAS STATIONS
460-87853 Detail Signs 1945+
460-87874 Texaco & Flying A 1949-60
460-87902 Gulf 1936-63
460-87938 Mobil 1940-66
460-87959 Esso 1946-65
460-87969 Sinclair 1935-60
460-87993 Shell 1935-60
460-871002 Ashland & Pepper 1924-60
460-871017 Atlantic Refining Co. 1935-60 *NEW*

CITY BUILDING SIGNS
460-87275 Streets & Buildings
460-87848 Set #1 1960+
460-87982 Diners #1 1950+
460-87983 Diners #2 1950+
460-871049 Commercial Buildings/Stores Late 1950s - Mid 1960s *NEW*

PACKING HOUSE/COLD STORAGE
460-87771 Sunkist Packing House 1955+
460-87806 #1 1970+
460-87807 #2 1970+

WESTERN TOWN SIGNS
460-87162 Cowtowns
460-87164 Town Signs

20TH CENTURY SIGNS
460-87197 1900-1930
460-87198 Mid Century

1930S & 40S SIGNS
460-87287 1930s Window Signs
460-87420 Commercial Signs
460-87421 Commercial Signs
460-87422 Commercial Signs

RAILROAD SIGNS
460-87206 Right-Of-Way Crossing, Warnings etc. (black)

INDUSTRIAL SIGNS
460-87165 Town & City Industry Signs
460-87273 Set #1
460-87289 Set #2
460-87924 Industrial Safety and Warning Signs 1985+

PROPANE TERMINAL & VEHICLES
460-87941 Superior & Suburban Propane 1985+

TRUCK & VEHICLE SETS EA 4.00 (UNLESS NOTED)

DELIVERY VANS
460-87385 Svenhard, Jags Diesel, Peninsula Creamery, Langendorf
460-87387 Mothers Cookies, Earth Grains & Kilpatrick's Bread

TRUCKING COMPANIES
460-4042 J.B. Hunt-ATSF Quantum 48' Trailer **2.00**
460-4051 J.B. Hunt 48' Trailers & Tractor **2.00**
460-4087 Sunkist 40' Trailer & Tractor 1970+ **2.00**
460-4159 Yellow Freight System Tractors & Trailers 1975+
460-4163 Trans Western Express Tractors, 48' Trailers & Containers 1990+
460-4169 Overnite Transportation Co. 28 & 45' Trailers & Tractors 1990+ **2.00**
460-4171 Martrac 42, 45 & 48' Refrigerated Trailers 1985+ **2.00**
460-4172 XTRA Lease 45' Trailers 1990+ **2.00**
460-4192 England 48' Trailers & Tractor 1990+ **2.00**
460-4194 ABF 28' Trailers & Tractor 1970+ **2.00**
460-4199 Nations Way 28' Trailers & Tractors 1990+ **2.00**
460-4203 Viking Freight System Inc. 28' Trailers & Tractors, Old 1990+ **2.00**
460-4211 Old Dominion Freight Line 28' Trailers & Tractors 1994 + **2.00**
460-4214 Watkins Motor Lines Inc., 28' Trailers & Tractors 1990 + **2.00**
460-4219 Bullocks Express 28' Trailers & Tractors 1994+ **2.00**
460-4224 GI Trucking Co. 28' Trailers & Tractors 1980+ **2.00**
460-4226 American Freightways 28' Trailers & Tractors 1990+ **2.00**
460-4234 Interstate Distributing Co.Tractor/Trailer 1990+ **2.00**
460-4239 Gordon Trucking Inc. Tractor/Trailer 1990+ **2.00**
460-4242 Preston 151 Line Tractor/Trailer 1990+ **2.00**
460-87386 20 & 40' Vans & Cabs; Viking Freight, McLean, Nashville & Ashland
460-87500 Pacific Motor Trucking 40' Trailers, SP & Union Ice Tractor (1985) & Trailers (1982 & 1985)
460-87769 J.B. Hunt 48 & 53' Containers & Chassis 1993+
460-87814 Schneider National 48 & 53' Trailers/Tractors 1980+
460-87872 May Trucking 28 & 53' Trailers 1989+
460-87873 Tractor Striping and May Trucking Tractors 1989+

SEMI TRAILERS
460-8704 40' Navajo, CF, PIE, DOX, TC, Republic
460-8705 40' SCL, REA, DRGW, WM, Monon, EL, PC, L&N, MP
460-87233 Preferred Pool Coop, Shippers, ATSF, XTRA, RI
460-87237 40' Bekins, Frisco, ICG, Brillion &Forest Junction
460-87246 20 & 40' Trailers & Tractors ICX, Consolidated, FW Leeway, Digby's
460-87276 40' IC, Family Lines, CNW
460-87282 40 & 45' N&W & Matson Lines
460-87292 40' Crab, Orchard & Egyptian, Texas Mexican, BN
460-87293 40' ATSF, B&M & Erie Western
460-87295 40' Container & Trailers; Clinchfield, K-Line, B&O
460-87296 20, 40, & 45' Trailers; N&W, WP, & NP
460-87297 40' CR, FGE, PFE, SOU
460-87308 40' Chief, Chessie, NYC & SOU
460-87341 40' ATSF, Western Express & Gelco Rail Services
460-87343 40' Brea Corp, UP & Transamerica
460-87344 40' IMEX, Nevada Northern, Fresh Approach, Intermodal Systems Inc.
460-87345 40' International Nu-Way Shippers, Cornucopia, 40' Container Nitrol Process
460-87346 40' Agricultural Express of America, MSA Lamda & MP
460-87347 40' Columbus & Greenville, Metro Shippers & Clipper Express
460-87393 Tractors & 40' Vans; UP, Wilson Trucking, Mason & Dixon, Carolina
460-87403 40' KLM, Superior Fast Freight, SP Golden Pig Service
460-87454 45' Trailers; Preferred Pool & Milwaukee Road
460-87456 45' DRGW, WP
460-87461 45' Vermont, SOU, 40' Trailers; Crafton, UP, C&U
460-87495 40' Rail Services, Interstate, SP & SSW
460-87508 45' CSX, Seaboard System, US Mail & XTRA
460-87513 40 & 45' Trailers & Tractors; Pennzoil & Valvoline
460-87521 40 & 45' Trailers & Tractors; Quaker State & Castrol
460-87665 45' Minnesota, Dakota & Western, Kankakee, Beaverville & Southern, Chicago Central
460-87703 Transamerica Trailers #2 45 & 48'
460-87819 48' ; Ida Cal, Bulldog, Knight Trans, XTRA, Intermodal+ 45' 1990+
460-87897 45 & 48' Toledo, Peoria & Western, Iowa Interstate, KCS, Terminal Consolidated 1992+

VEHICLE MARKINGS
460-4122 Red & White Trailer Safety Striping 1993+
460-4149 Vehicle License Plates 1975-1985 **2.00**
460-4150 Emergency Vehicle Markings, Police, Fire, Ambulance 1970+ **2.00**
460-4168 Commercial Vehicle License Plates 1970-1995 **2.00**
460-87281 Custom Truck Tractor Schemes - Owner/Operators

RAIL POWER PRODUCTS

HUSKY STACK 2+2 56' WELL CAR DECAL SETS EA 1.50
60-1700 TTX *NEW*
60-1701 GBRX "Greenbrier Lease" *NEW*

TRAILER DECALS SETS EA 1.50 (UNLESS NOTED)

28'
60-1805 ABF *NEW*
60-1806 CF *NEW*
60-1808 Roadway *NEW*
60-1811 "New" CF *NEW*
60-1824 Roadway Express *NEW*
60-1825 Viking *NEW*
60-1827 "New" Yellow **2.00** *NEW*
60-1828 "New" Roadway *NEW*

28/48'
60-1807 NW *NEW*
60-1809 Overnight *NEW*
60-1810 Carolina *NEW*
60-1812 Transcon *NEW*
60-1813 Preston *NEW*
60-1814 Leeway *NEW*
60-1822 Yellow *NEW*

48'
60-1850 Roadway **2.25** *NEW*

Information STATION

MODEL QUICK CAR REPAINTS WITH DECALS

Watch a freight train pass and you might see a "used car!" When cars are sold to new owners, old reporting marks, data and special instructions are painted over. Only areas where new lettering is applied are repainted. These temporary paint jobs are common following mergers and sometimes last for years. This is easy to do on decorated models. Mask the areas to be relettered and weather. Now, reverse your masking, leaving the clean areas exposed. Paint over the existing lettering with a lighter or darker color. Don't worry if the factory lettering bleeds through or the masking isn't straight, this is a down and dirty job in prototype paint shops! Apply a gloss coat and add the new decals. Seal with gloss.

Prototype roads often repaint cars tagged by vandals the same way. Start with an undecorated car and paint in the finish color. Mask, weather and gloss coat. Now add some of the lettering, such as a herald that was too high to paint over. Seal with gloss, then mask off unlettered areas and weather. Add remaining lettering and seal with gloss. The patches of fresh paint and lettering will contrast nicely with the "original" paint.

Models and Photo by Gary Hoover

PASSENGER CARS

"Ladies and gentlemen . . . Ocean View Bay is our next stop, Ocean View Bay."

Excitement ripples through the passengers as they arrive on time. Local residents will tell you that summer would never be the same without the tourist trains. Since the late 1880s when this line was built, people have been riding the trains to Ocean View Bay to enjoy sun, sand and surf. Wasn't long before there was a streetcar line and an amusement park. And every weekend there were crowds of people everywhere.

A lot has changed, but people still flock to the beaches on weekends. Nowadays, you'll ride in on Amtrak and take a cab to your hotel. But the fun of travel by train hasn't changed one tiny bit.

While crowds are heaviest in summer, many a snow belt resident skips town in December or January for two weeks in the warm California weather. And getting here is a snap with Amtrak's nation-wide connections.

Weekdays find a smaller crowd on the platform, but that will change in a few minutes as the F40s drift to a smooth stop.

Looking back from the seawall, this view of Gary Hoover's layout in Florissant, Missouri, records the arrival of the repowered and detailed Life-Like locos alongside the Walthers station.

Milwaukee Road Piker 933-25

Milwaukee Road Oscar 933-15

FOR THE ULTIMATE MILLENNIUM PARTY BOOK A TRIP ON THE OSCAR AND PIKER!

In an elegant age when traveling by train was the only way to go, every railroad owner could boast of a private car. No expense was spared to build these rolling palaces. Only the very best materials and craftsmanship would do. Handsome interior furniture was custom made. Formal dinners were prepared by trained chefs. Uniformed waiters served each course on fine china and cut-crystal, emblazoned with the railroad's herald and colors.

In service, these cars had no rivals - except perhaps for the private cars of other railroad owners! Politicians were wined and dined on memorable sight-seeing trips. Deals were made with important industrialists that owned the massive factories bordering the tracks. And in summer, the owner's family would vacation to their multi-room "cottage," complete with its own private rail siding.

As owner of your very own railroad, you deserve to travel in the lap of luxury too. And instead of just a simple private car, imagine rubbing shoulders with the likes of the Vanderbilts or Harrimans as your own private train rolls into the station!

After many years and with major improvements, the classic "Oscar" and "Piker" are ready to roll once more! Now every HO Scale railroad owner with big dreams and a small budget can afford the luxury of his or her very own private rail cars.

The "Piker" offers guests the ultimate in Pullman service and comfort. As a two-section sleeper-solarium-diner, it's actually a complete train in just one tiny car! Big windows and traditional styling give it a charm all its own.

Its partner is "Oscar," a nice, short name for a nice, short Observation Car. It features a dramatically different body than the Piker, with paired windows and traditional "brass" railed observation platform at the back.

The Oscar interior, complete with galley, observation area and commodes, comes ready for figures. It's shown here with the figures from 590-10021 and the new Transition-Era Passenger Train Crew, #590-10452.

Milwaukee Road Oscar, Ready-To-Run 933-15

Santa Fe Oscar, Ready-To-Run 933-16

WALTHERS™

Measuring just 21 scale feet long each, tight curves pose no problems to Oscar or Piker! Riding on a single six-wheel truck with plenty of pivot room, they can handle radii that would make a streetcar cry!

With tongue planted firmly in cheek, we've brought back the Oscar and Piker and we've updated them to modern standards for today's busy railroad president.

These collectible replicas feature:

- **Ready-To-Run**
- **Detailed, injection molded styrene bodies**
- **Separate wire grab irons**
- **Crisp, detailed lettering**
- **Realistic satin paint finish**
- **Working diaphragms**
- **One-piece plastic interiors**
- **Body mounted working knuckle couplers**
- **Smooth rolling truck with realistic sideframe**

And best of all - Piker and Oscar now come fully assembled, ready for same-day service on your railroad!

Just what can you do with the Oscar and Piker? These cars are the ultimate party cars. Company brass, elected officials and shippers can all be treated to your road's hospitality.

Couple up Oscar and Piker behind your favorite motive power, hang the markers, put your feet up and tour your line in real style. A better car was never built for "short" lines! Or put 'em to work in mixed train service. Run them as a contractor's, civil engineer's or foreman's office with the work trains. In an emergency, they can double as a caboose or a telegraph office on wheels. **Run some money-making railfan excursions across the line.** How about a military train for the general or visiting dignitary? Or invite state and local politicians to celebrate April 15th with a "Busted Budget Limited."

The Piker interior features a section, solarium and a galley complete with pots on the stove. Shown here with the figures from #590-14095 and the new Transition-Era Passenger Train Crew, #590-10452.

OSCAR & PIKER, READY-TO-RUN SETS
EA 39.98

Includes one each Observation ("Oscar") and Solarium-Diner-Pullman ("Piker") in matching paint and lettering.

932-31 UP ***NEW***
932-32 SP ***NEW***
932-33 PRR ***NEW***
932-34 Amtrak ***NEW***
932-35 MILW ***NEW***
932-36 ATSF ***NEW***
932-37 Pullman ***NEW***

"OSCAR" INDIVIDUAL CARS, READY-TO-RUN
EA 21.98

A unique Observation car in a class by itself.

932-11 UP ***NEW***
932-12 SP ***NEW***
932-13 PRR ***NEW***
932-14 Amtrak ***NEW***
932-15 MILW ***NEW***
932-16 ATSF ***NEW***
932-17 Pullman ***NEW***
932-10 Undecorated ***NEW***

"PIKER" - INDIVIDUAL CARS, READY-TO-RUN
EA 21.98

The ultimate two-section Pullman sleeper-solarium-diner.

932-21 UP ***NEW***
932-22 SP ***NEW***
932-23 PRR ***NEW***
932-24 Amtrak ***NEW***
932-25 MILW ***NEW***
932-26 ATST ***NEW***
932-27 Pullman ***NEW***
932-20 Undecorated ***NEW***

Pennsylvania Oscar, Ready-To-Run 933-13

Union Pacific Piker, Ready-To-Run 933-21

Southern Pacific Piker, Ready-To-Run 933-22

Pullman Piker, Ready-To-Run 933-27

Amtrak Piker, Ready-To-Run 933-24

Tack the Oscar and Piker onto the rear of your Amtrak trains as private varnish.

WALTHERS™

Features of Walthers detailed passenger car models:

- **Ready to Run**
- **Authentic Paint Schemes**
- **Decals for Car Markings and Numbers**
- **Correct Trucks**
- **Tinted Window "Glass"**
- **Complete Underbody**
- **Swinging Coupler Pockets**

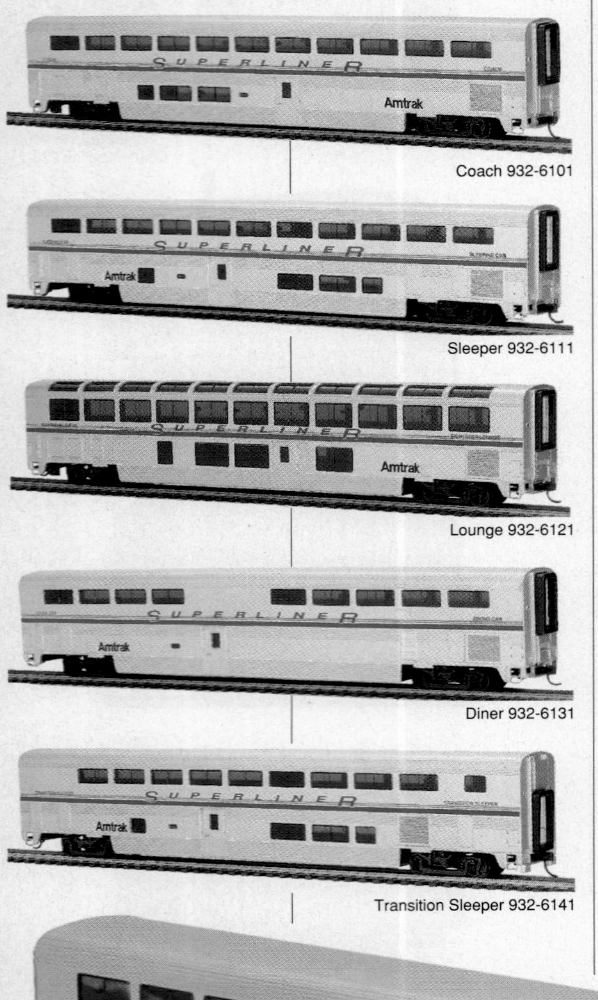

Coach 932-6101

Sleeper 932-6111

Lounge 932-6121

Diner 932-6131

Transition Sleeper 932-6141

Superliner I Coach Baggage Car
932-6151

Amtrak Material
Handling Car 932-6021

SUPERLINER II CARS

Add Amtrak's long-distance trains to your layout. The ready-to-run cars ride on authentic, smooth-rolling GSC trucks with metal wheels, and include working knuckle couplers, as well as sprung diaphragms. To model several cars, a sheet of decals is included with car numbers, handicapped entrance signs and other lettering. For more realism, separate wire grab irons are included, and the cars are molded with starter points to make drilling easy. Complete instructions and a decal lettering diagram are included too. (Walthers Amtrak F40PH diesels are available separately in the Locomotives section.)

AMTRAK EA 24.98

932-6101 Coach
932-6111 Sleeper
932-6121 Lounge
932-6131 Diner
932-6141 Transition Sleeper

UNDECORATED EA 24.98

932-6100 Coach
932-6110 Sleeper
932-6120 Lounge
932-6130 Diner
932-6140 Transition Sleeper

PASSENGER TRAIN FIGURES

See the complete Figures section in this Book for passengers and travelers to complete your station scenes or detail car interiors.

590-10452 Transition-Era Passenger Train Crew pkg(6) **12.99**
Now revised with correct figures, this set provides a complete crew for any size passenger train of the 1940s to the 1960s. A seated engineer and hard-working fireman are included, along with a uniformed conductor, trainman, porter and waiter/steward to see to each passenger's every need.

590-1010054 Amtrak Crew pkg(6) **14.98**
Provide first class service at any stop along your line. Wearing authentic Amtrak colors, the figures are a perfect accessory to detail a station platform and look great alongside any Walthers Amtrak equipment. Each figure is molded in a realistic pose and hand-painted in authentic colors. The set include six different figures, ready to add action to your scenes.

SUPERLINER I COACH-BAGGAGE CARS

EA 24.98

Delivered with the original Superliners, this car was designed for short-haul trains. The upper level seats 78. Standard entrance doors and rest rooms were installed on the lower level, but there were no seats. This open area, accessible through a large side door, is used to store baggage. The models are ready-to-run with movable diaphragms, working knuckle couplers and correct trucks with metal wheelsets.

932-6151 Amtrak Phase III Paint (Tri-Stripe)
932-6152 Amtrak Phase IV Paint (Current)
932-6154 Coach Smoker Phase IV
932-6150 Undecorated

AMTRAK MATERIAL HANDLING CARS - 1500 SERIES

Material Handling Cars (MHCs) are common on many long-distance Amtrak runs. They can be found at the head or rear of the train to handle mail, express packages and baggage. Our model is based on the MHC II 1500 Series cars. The model includes separate ladders, GSC trucks and the correct diagonal panel roof. Working knuckle type couplers are also standard.

TWO-PACKS EA 39.98

932-26021 Amtrak Phase III (Tri-Stripe)
932-26022 Amtrak Phase III with US Mail Emblem

SINGLE CARS EA 19.98

932-6021 Amtrak Phase III (Tri-Stripe)
932-6022 Amtrak Phase III with US Mail Emblem
932-6020 Undecorated

WALTHERS™

HORIZON FLEET CARS

These versatile cars are now in service with Amtrak and several regional commuter operations.

AMTRAK CARS EA 19.98

Cars ride on detailed models of the GSI roller bearing truck, and are finished in the correct Phase III scheme.

932-6051 Coach
932-6061 Food Service

COMMUTER SERVICE CARS EA 19.98

All cars feature improved inside bearing trucks.

CONNECTICUT DOT

Silver, red window band, black lettering, state seal in blue and white.

932-6075 Coach
932-6085 Cab Car

NEW JERSEY (DOT)

Early color scheme.

932-6076 Coach
932-6086 Cab Car

NEW JERSEY (NJ TRANSIT)

Silver car, black window band, orange, red and blue hash marks with NJ Transit logos.

932-6072 Coach
932-6082 Cab Car

PHILADELPHIA (SEPTA)

Silver with red and blue stripes, plus "S" logo.

932-6071 Coach
932-6081 Cab Car

BOSTON (MBTA)

Silver, purple window band, yellow pinstripes, "T" logo.

932-6073 Coach
932-6083 Cab Car

NEW YORK (NY METRO MTA)

Silver, blue window band, black lettering, "M" logo.

932-6074 Coach

932-6084 Cab Car

UNDECORATED

932-6050 Coach, Amtrak Style
932-6060 Food Service
932-6070 Commuter Coach
932-6080 Cab Car

AMFLEET I CARS

EA 19.98

Introduced in the mid 1970s, these cars have been the backbone of the Amtrak fleet. Models are offered in the four paint schemes (called phases) used on coach and food service cars. Models feature improved inside bearing trucks with electrical pickup.

PHASE I

As-built scheme: wide red and blue stripes, separated by narrow white stripes, plus headless arrow logos.

932-6002 Coach

932-6012 Food Service

PHASE II

Wide red and blue stripes, and white pinstripes.

932-6001 Coach
932-6011 Food Service

PHASE III

Equal red, white and blue stripes, Amtrak logo in black on white background.

932-6003 Coach
932-6013 Food Service

PHASE IV

932-6004 Coach
932-6014 Food Service

PHASE IV "NORTHEAST DIRECT" SCHEME

932-6005 Coach ***NEW***
932-6015 Food Service ***NEW***

LIGHTING KIT

933-717 Standard Car Lighting Kit **6.98**
Add working lights to any car. Includes two 16v bulbs, sockets and wiring diagram. Insulated sockets can be glued directly to any roof. Tubular bulbs clear most interior details and are milk white for uniform lighting. Wired as directed, bulbs last for hundreds of hours.

To use track power for lighting, your car must be equipped with metal wheels on metal axles, insulated on one side. One car with pickups can light an entire train using feeder wires. Kit uses two 16v bulbs (942-352) for best results on track voltages ranging from 10v to 24v AC or DC.

Horizon Fleet Coach 932-6051

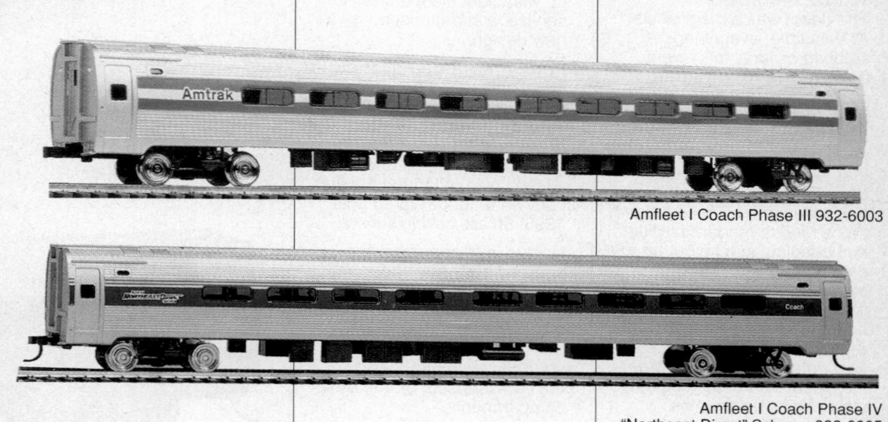

Amfleet I Coach Phase III 932-6003

Amfleet I Coach Phase IV "Northeast Direct" Scheme 932-6005

Horizon Fleet Food Service Car 932-6061

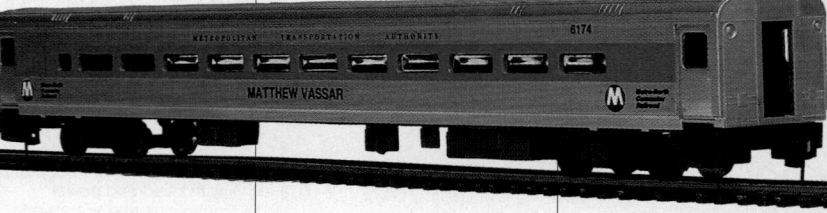

Horizon Fleet Commuter Coach 932-6074

Amfleet Food Service Car - Phase II 932-6011

DIAPHRAGMS

PKG(2) EA 2.98

933-429 Folded Bellows
With vinyl striker plate, use on heavyweight cars.

933-977 Black Rubber
One-piece molding, use on streamlined cars.

WALTHERS™

AMTRAK STATION

933-3038 19.98 SPECIAL VALUE PRICING

The depot was a magical place. At train time, everything stopped as local folks went down to watch the varnish come in. The old depot may be gone, but the magic is still there! Today, shiny Amtrak streamliners glide by, and in many areas, daily commuter trains make up much of the trackside action. These modern trains require modern facilities and bringing your layout up-to-date is easy with this kit. It's based on a design first used in the late 1970s, which was adapted for use in several Amtrak served communities. This detailed model captures the clean lines of the original in a size that's right for the contemporary layout. Full-color Amtrak station signs add the finishing touch.

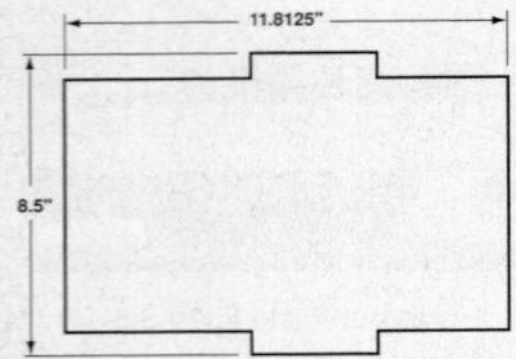

VIEWLINER SLEEPER

EA 24.98

As Amfleet I Coaches and Food Service Cars entered service in the mid 1970s, Amtrak found the body was not suitable for conversion to a sleeping car. As time caught up with older sleepers still in service, a search began for a new design.

In 1987, Morrison-Knudsen unveiled a new sleeper, called a "Viewliner." Designed to meet the clearance restrictions of the eastern US, the cars had a unique shape and style all their own. Although the first cars were not delivered until 1996, 50 are now in service.

Unique in appearance, the squared body has upper and lower rows of windows for a large, roomy feel inside and out. Passengers can choose from two deluxe bedrooms, a specially equipped room for the handicapped, or one of 12 compartments.

Now, HO passengers can spend the night in style aboard this detailed model. All the lines of the prototype are here, from the angular, fluted sides to the triangular shock supports mounted above the trucks. Both rows of tinted windows, authentic Amtrak paint and lettering, separate wire grabs and stirrups, everything down to the electrical conduit on the roof is included. A great addition to your Amtrak trains, the model comes fully assembled with free-rolling trucks and working knuckle couplers.

932-6091 Amtrak Phase IV *NEW*
932-6090 Undecorated *NEW*

60' Express Box Car 932-26041

Viewliner Sleeper 932-6091

60' EXPRESS BOX CARS

Amtrak handles more bulk mail and packages than ever and many of today's trains now include these specialized freight haulers in the consist. Purpose-built for the job starting in 1996, the cars are fitted with high-speed brakes and other Amtrak equipment. While they can carry more than Material Handling Cars (MHCs), they are not equipped with head-end power couplings and are always hauled at the rear of the train.

Modernize your Amtrak Superliner II, Amfleet and Horizon Fleet long-distance trains in minutes with these models. Each comes fully assembled and includes separately applied door latch bars, ladders and door release wheels. Working knuckle couplers and metal wheelsets are standard equipment.

Expanding your fleet is easy, with two prototype paint schemes to choose from, each with three different cars numbers. (Two in each 2-Pack and a third on Single Cars.)

2-PACKS EA 34.98

Each car in the set has its own roadnumber.

932-26041 Amtrak Phase IV *NEW*
932-26042 Amtrak Silver Scheme *NEW*

SINGLE CARS EA 17.98

932-6041 Amtrak Phase IV *NEW*
932-6042 Amtrak Silver Scheme *NEW*
932-6040 Undecorated *NEW*

Amtrak Station 932-3038

PASSENGER CAR KITS

These kits include laser-cut and laser-etched acrylic car sides, Eastern Car Works Car Core Kit and laser-cut interior partition kits. Cast white metal seating is available separately. Cars feature pre-drilled grab iron holes, stirrup steps as one piece with car side, flush mount gasketed windows and pre-masked sides for easy painting.

UNION PACIFIC

152-1011 1504 Club/Lounge/ Barber Shop "Hollywood" **TBA** ***NEW***

SOUTHERN PACIFIC

152-1101 79' 44 Seat Coach Lot 6593 **59.95** ***NEW***

CHICAGO & NORTH WESTERN EA 46.95

152-1203

152-1201 PS Plan W-53194, 155 Seat Gallery Cab
152-1203 PS Plan W-53194, 161 Seat Gallery Commuter Coach

MILWAUKEE ROAD

152-1302 PS Plan 4135, 8 Duplex 6 RMT, 4 DB **44.95**

SANTA FE EA TBA

152-1500 PS "Valley" Series Sleeper (6-6-4) Pool Service
152-1502 64' 3750-3799 Baggage Car
152-1503 74' 3800-3939 Baggage Car ***NEW***

ILLINOIS CENTRAL

152-1600 PS "B" Series Sleeper **TBA**

PULLMAN POOL CARS

152-2000 Cascade Series 10-5 Plan 4072B **TBA**

PASSENGER CAR SIDES

Laser-cut, acrylic sides, pre-masked for ease of painting. For use with Eastern Car Works Car Core Kit (sold separately).

UNION PACIFIC SIDES EA 22.95

152-1000 5631 Series Baggage Car
152-1001 5816 Series RPO
152-1002 4000 Series Lunch Counter Diner
152-1003 5007 Series Lunch Counter/Cafe/Lounge
152-1004 5488 Series Chair Car
152-1005 "Ocean" Series Sleeper
152-1006 "Placid" Series Sleeper, 11 Bed
152-1007 "National" Series Sleeper, 6-6-4
152-1008 4800 Series Dining Car
152-1009 5900 Series Postal/Mail Storage ***NEW***
152-1010 6000 Series Baggage/Dormitory

NORFOLK & WESTERN EA 22.95

152-1400 #502 Crew Coach
152-1401 PM Class Coach
152-1402 D-1 Diner

PENNSYLVANIA EA 22.95

152-1700 Harbor Series Sleeper/Lounge
152-1701 PS Plan 4129, 10-6 Rapid Series

PASSENGER CAR DETAIL PARTS

152-900 Grab Iron Bending & Drilling Template **5.95**
152-905 Cast Metal Passenger Car Seats **9.95** Includes 12 left and 12 right.

152-910 Full Width Diaphragms **11.95** ***NEW***
152-915 Caboose Grab Iron Bending Template **4.95**
152-920 Window Shades - Metallic (2 Coaches) **5.95** ***NEW***

American Limited

DIAPHRAGMS

Operating passenger car diaphragms are accurate models of specific prototypes. Easy-to-build kits feature injection molded plastic parts, in black or gray plastic. Sprung to hold together on curves down to 24" radius, no minimum radius limitation. Will not interfere with operation of most couplers. All kits include complete instructions.

STREAMLINE CARS-GRAY

Can be modified to look like Pullman or Budd diaphragms. Fit on Athearn Streamliners.

147-9000 1 Pair **4.45**
147-9006 6 Pair **20.95**

STREAMLINE CARS-BLACK

147-9010 1 Pair **4.45**
147-9016 6 Pair **20.95**

HEAVYWEIGHT CARS-ATHEARN-BLACK

147-9100 1 Pair **4.45**
147-9106 12 Pair **20.95**

HEAVYWEIGHT CARS-RIVAROSSI & OTHERS

147-9200 1 Pair **4.45**
147-9206 12 Pair **20.95**

BACHMANN SPECTRUM CARS-BLACK

Complete set includes car end doors. Unit is designed for use with Kadee® #23 couplers.

147-9300 1 Pair **4.45**
147-9306 6 Pair **20.95**

CON-COR SUPERLINERS-GRAY

Improve the operation and appearance of your Superliner fleet. Simplifies installation of knuckle-type couplers (sold separately) and provides prototypical close-coupling between cars. Kits include diaphragms molded in gray plastic, coupler and truck adapter in black plastic, plus mounting screws.

147-9400 1 Pair **4.75**
147-9406 3 Pair **23.95**

FULL WIDTH DIAPHRAGMS

The flexibility of these styrene diaphragms is achieved via a two-piece telescoping arrangement that allows operation on curves down to 34 inches. Kit features step and handrail details, springs and mounting frames. Can fit Rivarossi and Athearn, in addition to others.

147-9500 Single Car **5.25** ***NEW***
147-9504 Four-Car Set **18.95** ***NEW***

F UNIT DIESEL DIAPHRAGMS

Make your classic A and B passenger (or freight) units look as good as the cars they pull with prototypical close-coupling and detailed diaphragms between units. Parts are molded in gray or black to match prototype practice.

STEWART F3/F7 A&B UNITS

SINGLE (1 PAIR) EA 4.75

Parts for two A or one B unit. Includes spacers and works with close-coupling adapter.

147-9900 Gray
147-9910 Black

SET OF 6 (3 PAIR) EA 12.95

Three complete sets for A-B-B-A or other combinations.

147-9903 Gray
147-9913 Black

FT A&B UNITS EA 4.95

Make your earliest F units look their best with these parts. Uses the loco's scale (short) drawbar and includes three complete diaphragm assemblies, enough for one A and one B unit.
147-9700 Gray
147-9710 Black

ATHEARN F7 A&B UNITS

Close-coupling draft gear boxes and diaphragms make those classic lash-ups look more realistic. Draft gear boxes accept Kadee® #5 couplers (sold separately) and sets the units at 32" between diaphragm mounts, less than half the distance of the Standard Athearn coupling.

SINGLE (1 PAIR) EA 4.95

Enough parts to do two A or one B unit.
147-9800 Gray
147-9810 Black

SET OF 6 (3 PAIR) EA 13.95

Enough parts to do an A-B-B-A set, or other combinations.
147-9803 Gray
147-9813 Black

TRAINS **Athearn** IN MINIATURE

Easy-to-build kits feature prepainted and lettered plastic bodies. Length is ideal for small layouts and sharper radius curves. Kits are complete with horn-hook couplers and Delrin® trucks with metal and plastic wheels.

DELIVERY PROBLEMS: All items are not produced on a regular schedule and may not be available for several months. Items not listed in this catalog are temporarily out of stock. Watch Walthers Publications for the latest delivery information.

72' Streamline Diner 140-1792

72' Streamline RPO 140-1808

72' Streamline RPO 140-2132

72' STREAMLINE CARS

PENNSYLVANIA EA 10.50

(maroon, gold lettering, black roof)

140-1782 Baggage
140-1792 Diner
140-1802 Railway Post Office
140-1812 Coach
140-1822 Vista Dome
140-1832 Observation

CHICAGO, BURLINGTON & QUINCY EA 10.50

(silver, black)

140-1783 Baggage
140-1793 Diner
140-1803 Railway Post Office
140-1813 Coach
140-1823 Vista Dome
140-1833 Observation

NEW HAVEN EA 10.50

(silver, red window band, black lettering)

140-1784 Baggage
140-1794 Diner
140-1804 Railway Post Office
140-1814 Coach
140-1824 Vista Dome
140-1834 Observation

UNION PACIFIC EA 10.50

140-2110 Baggage
140-2120 Diner
140-2130 Railway Post Office
140-2140 Coach
140-2150 Vista Dome
140-2160 Observation

CALIFORNIA ZEPHYR EA 10.50

140-2111 Baggage
140-2121 Diner
140-2131 Railway Post Office
140-2141 Coach
140-2151 Vista Dome
140-2161 Observation

AMTRAK PHASE I EA 10.50

(silver with red, white and blue stripes, headless arrow logos)

140-1789 Baggage
140-1799 Diner
140-1809 Railway Post Office
140-1819 Coach
140-1829 Vista Dome
140-1839 Observation

72' Streamline Observation 140-1831

72' Streamline Vista Dome 140-2152

72' Streamline Baggage 140-1789

AMTRAK PHASE III

(silver with red, white and blue stripe, black lettering)

140-2112 Baggage *NEW*
140-2122 Diner *NEW*
140-2132 RPO *NEW*
140-2142 Coach *NEW*
140-2152 Dome *NEW*
140-2162 Observation *NEW*

BALTIMORE & OHIO EA 10.50

(silver, blue window band, black lettering)

140-1785 Baggage
140-1795 Diner
140-1805 Railway Post Office
140-1815 Coach
140-1825 Vista Dome
140-1835 Observation

SANTA FE EA 10.50

(silver, black)

140-1781 Baggage
140-1791 Diner
140-1801 Railway Post Office
140-1811 Coach
140-1821 Vista Dome
140-1831 Observation

NORTHERN PACIFIC EA 10.50

(dark green, red and yellow stripes, yellow and black lettering)

140-1786 Baggage
140-1796 Diner
140-1806 Railway Post Office
140-1816 Coach
140-1826 Vista Dome
140-1836 Observation

NEW YORK CENTRAL EA 10.50

(silver, black lettering)

140-1787 Baggage
140-1797 Diner
140-1807 Railway Post Office
140-1817 Coach
140-1827 Vista Dome
140-1837 Observation

SOUTHERN PACIFIC "DAYLIGHT" EA 10.50

(orange, red, black roof, silver stripes and lettering)

140-1788 Baggage
140-1798 Diner
140-1808 Railway Post Office
140-1818 Coach
140-1828 Vista Dome
140-1838 Observation

UNDECORATED EA 10.50

140-1780 Baggage
140-1790 Diner
140-1800 Railway Post Office
140-1810 Coach
140-1820 Vista Dome
140-1830 Observation

MODEL RAILROADER ANNIVERSARY CARS

140-5633 Standard Heavyweight Observation Car **13.25** *NEW*
To complete your train, a 40' Wood Side Box Car (140-5631), and a 86' Hi-Cube 4-Door Box Car (140-5632) are also available and can be found in the Freight section.

70' STANDARD CARS

70' Standard Observation 140-1871

67' Standard RPO 140-1843

70' Standard Baggage 140-1885

70' Standard Observation 140-1860

BALTIMORE & OHIO EA 10.50

140-1845 67' Railway Post Office
140-1855 Standard Coach
140-1859 Arch Roof Coach
140-1865 Pullman
140-1875 Observation
140-1885 Baggage
140-1895 Diner

NEW YORK CENTRAL EA 10.50

140-1842 67' Railway Post Office
140-1852 Standard Coach
140-1857 Arch Roof Coach
140-1862 Pullman
140-1872 Observation
140-1882 Baggage
140-1892 Diner

UNDECORATED EA 10.50

140-1840 67' Railway Post Office
140-1850 Standard Coach
140-1854 Arch Roof Coach
140-1860 Pullman
140-1870 Observation
140-1880 Baggage
140-1890 Diner

SANTA FE EA 10.50

140-1841 67' Railway Post Office
140-1851 Arch Roof Coach
140-1856 Standard Coach
140-1861 Pullman
140-1871 Observation
140-1881 Baggage
140-1891 Diner

SOUTHERN PACIFIC EA 10.50

140-1843 67' Railway Post Office
140-1853 Standard Coach
140-1858 Arch Roof Coach
140-1863 Pullman
140-1873 Observation
140-1883 Baggage
140-1893 Diner

LIGHTING KITS

140-90200 For Streamline (4-wheel truck) **2.00**
140-90201 For Standard (6-wheel truck) **2.00**

Ready-to-run passenger cars feature molded plastic bodies, which are prepainted and lettered. Complete with trucks and horn-hook couplers.

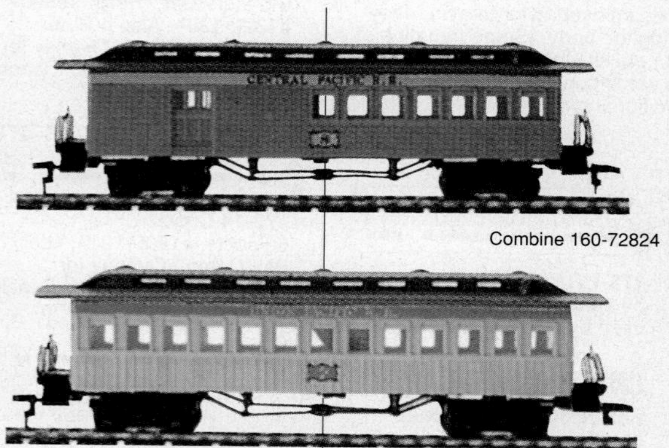
Combine 160-72824

Coach 160-72901

Full Dome Car 160-71705

Amfleet Coach 160-72205

OLD TIMERS

Prototypes are 47' cars used on Western Railroads, circa 1860.

CENTRAL PACIFIC EA 10.00

160-72824 Combine
160-72924 Coach

UNION PACIFIC EA 10.00

160-72801 Combine
160-72901 Coach

STREAMLINERS

Modern 85' cars are ready to run, and finished in Phase I Scheme–silver with red, white and blue stripes. Scheme features headless arrow logos.

AMTRAK

160-71705 Full Dome Car **20.00**
160-72205 Amfleet Coach, Lighted **25.00**

Information STATION

Headend Cars

A headend car is defined by the American Association of Railroads as a car "classified as Class B and Class M." A clearer explanation is that a headend car is a design built to handle express freight, or cargo considered to be of a larger value. Examples of express freight carried on freight cars include currency, perishable food items and business contracts. Most were designed for use with passenger equipment and were fitted with high-speed trucks, plus steam and signal communication lines.

There are a variety of cars classified by the AAR as Class B headend cars. Baggage express cars could be used as passenger cars but mostly carried express material. Horse-express cars transported expensive livestock ranging from race horses to cattle. There were also a number of cars designed to transport liquids, from milk cars to express refrigerator cars to container flat cars.

Class M cars are also known as postals, a style of headend car that carried United States Mail. Postal cars were designed for picking up and sorting mail en route to their destination. Baggage and mail cars were divided into two sections by bulkheads; one section for mail, the other for baggage. Postal service cars are best described as a gutted version of the postal cars. These were designed to carry bulk mail rather than individually sorted letters.

BRASS CAR SIDES

Photo-etched brass sides and kits for streamlined passenger cars. Window openings and grab iron holes are etched through, with additional etched details on the surface. These craft train kits can be used with either Basic (173-101) or Deluxe (173-102) Body Kits. Some kits, as noted, are designed as an overlay for use on ready-to-run plastic cars, without shortening the body. (Some trimming of plastic around windows is required.) All kits include instructions and are undecorated. Because the same construction plans were often used by several railroads, additional roadnames are listed where appropriate.

BRASS SIDES

CANADIAN NATIONAL EA 28.75

Later used by VIA.

173-34 Pullman
6-4-6 sleeper, "Green" series, #1162-1181. Overlay for IHC/Rivarossi 1930 85' Coach or Sleeper.

173-38 Pullman
8-4-4 sleeper, "Eastport" series #1110-1161. Overlay for IHC/Rivarossi 1930 85' Coach or Sleeper.

173-39 CCF Coach
#5437-5654. Later used by VIA.

CHESAPEAKE & OHIO COACHES EA 28.75

Pullman-Standard Plan 7600, 52 seats. Use Evergreen 4525 & 4527 siding for as-built fluting. Also built for DRGW and NKP, later used on D&H, SAL, CNW, SP, and Amtrak. Overlay for IHC/Rivarossi 1930 85' Coach or Sleeper.

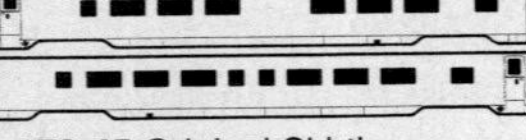

173-45 Original Skirting

173-46 Partial Skirting

CHICAGO & NORTH WESTERN EA 28.75

173-6 Pullman - North Western Limited
16-3-1 Sleeper, "Northern" series. Overlay for IHC/Rivarossi 1930 85' Coach or Sleeper.

173-1 Coach - "400"
56 seat, #3431-3476. Also used by GN, NP and CB&Q.

CNW BI-LEVEL CARS

Boxed kits include etched brass sides, cast brass ends, etched grilles and vents, basswood roof, copper clad fiberglass floor, green window glazing, cab end details (if used) and instructions. Later used by RTA and METRA, also purchased by CRIP.

173-47 Coach **66.75**
#49-150, 201-329, 700-709, 6400, 600, used in Chicago area commuter service and on some "400" fleet trains. Also used on Amtrak.

173-48 Cab Car **71.75**
#151-200, 251-264, used in Chicago area push-pull commuter service, has operator's control cab at one end.

GREAT NORTHERN EMPIRE BUILDER EA 28.75 (UNLESS NOTED)

173-10 Coffee Shop
#1240-1245 "Ranch" series. Also built for CB&Q. Overlay for IHC/Rivarossi 1930 85' Coach or Sleeper.

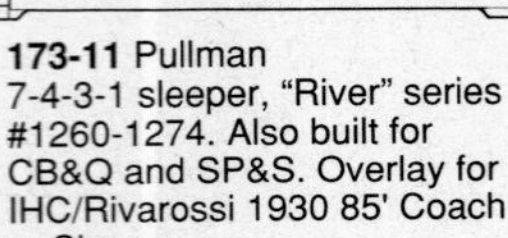

173-11 Pullman
7-4-3-1 sleeper, "River" series #1260-1274. Also built for CB&Q and SP&S. Overlay for IHC/Rivarossi 1930 85' Coach or Sleeper.

173-12 Coach
48 seats, #1215-1231. Also built for CB&Q and SP&S. Overlay for IHC/Rivarossi 1930 85' Coach or Sleeper.

173-13 Pullman
6-5-2 sleeper, "Pass" series #1370-1384. Also built for CB&Q and SP&S. Overlay for IHC/Rivarossi 1930 85' Coach or Sleeper.

173-14 Coach
60 seats, #1209-1214, later BN "Como." Overlay for IHC/Rivarossi 1930 85' Coach or Sleeper.

173-15 Diner
"Lake" series #1250-1255. Also built for CB&Q. Overlay for IHC/Rivarossi 1930 85' Coach or Sleeper.

173-18 Baggage/Dorm
#1200-1205. Overlay for IHC/Rivarossi 1930 85' Coach or Sleeper.

173-20 Coach
Budd dome #1320-1331. Also built for CB&Q, NP, SP&S and GN. Overlay for Con-Cor Dome car

173-25 Pullman - Western Star
16-4 sleeper, "Glacier" series #1181-1188. Overlay for IHC/Rivarossi 1930 85' Coach or Sleeper.

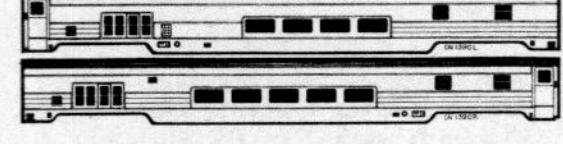

173-27 Dome Lounge
#1390-95 "View" series Great Dome lounge. Overlay for Bachmann full dome coach.

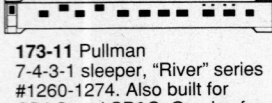

173-43 Baggage/Dorm **33.75**
Baggage and mail doors are separate etched parts. GN #37-44, also built for UP and CNW. Overlay for IHC/Rivarossi 1930 85' Coach or Sleeper.

ILLINOIS CENTRAL EA 28.75

Overlay for IHC/Rivarossi 1930 85' Coach or Sleeper.

173-41 Pullman
10-6 sleeper, "C" series. Pullman-Standard plan 4167. Also built for B&O as #7040-49.

173-44 Streamlined Coach
56 seats, #2614-40. Used on City of New Orleans, Daylight, Land O' Corn, Green Diamond and in pool service.

LOUISVILLE & NASHVILLE

173-35 Pullman **28.75**
6-6-4 sleeper, "Pine" series. Also built for C&EI and NC&StL. Overlay for IHC/Rivarossi 1930 85' Coach or Sleeper.

MILWAUKEE ROAD EA 28.75

173-2 Coach - 1948 Hiawatha
52 seats, #480-497, 535-551 and 600-661.

173-3 Parlor- 1948 Hiawatha
"Valley" series #190-197.

173-7 Pullman - Pioneer Limited
16-4 Sleeper "Raymond" series, #27-30.

173-8 Pullman - Pioneer Limited
8-6-4 Sleeper "River" series, #19-26.

NORTHERN PACIFIC EA 28.75 (UNLESS NOTED)

173-4 Coach - North Coast Limited
56 seats, #588-597, CB&Q #598-99, SP&S #300.

173-5 Pullman - North Coast Limited
8-6-3-1, #350-363. Also built for SP&S #366, CB&Q #480-482. Overlay for IHC/Rivarossi 1930 85' Coach or Sleeper.

173-19 Lounge - North Coast Limited
#494-499 "Traveler's Rest." Also built for CB&Q. Overlay for IHC/Rivarossi 1930 85' Coach or Sleeper.

173-20 Budd Dome Coach - North Coast Limited
#550-559. Also built for CB&Q and SP&S. Overlay for Con-Cor Budd Dome Coach.

173-24 Pullman/Budd Dome - North Coast Limited
4-4-4 sleeper, #304-314. Also built for CB&Q and SP&S. Overlay for Con-Cor Budd dome coach.

173-29 Budd Diner - North Coast Limited
#459-463. Also built for CB&Q. Overlay for Con-Cor Budd 10-6 Sleeper.

173-30 Coach - Mainstreeter
56 seats, #500-517. Also built for SP&S. Overlay for IHC/Rivarossi 1930 85' Coach or Sleeper.

173-50 Mail-Dorm - North Coast Limited **30.75** ***NEW***
Includes two separate brass two-window mail door, and full skirting. Overlay for Rivarossi coach or sleeper body.

PENNSYLVANIA EA 28.75

Overlay for IHC/Rivarossi 1930 85' Coach or Sleeper.

173-32 Coach "Jeffersonian"
P-85BR type, 44 seats. Matches Altoona-built #4100-4169, and ACF-built #4068-4091.

173-33 Pullman
10-6 sleeper, Plan 4140. PRR "Rapids," N&W "County," RF&P "King" and L&N "River" series.

BRASS CAR SIDES

PULLMAN EA 28.75

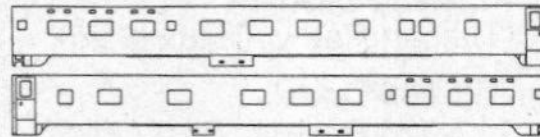

173-9 "American" Series
Plan #4099, 6-6-4 sleeper, used on UP, SP, CNW, ATSF, Erie, MP, IC and CRIP.

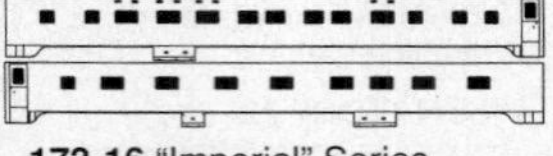

173-16 "Imperial" Series
Plan #4069, 4-4-2 sleeper, used on NYC, PRR, UP, SP, CNW, CRIP, IC and CN.

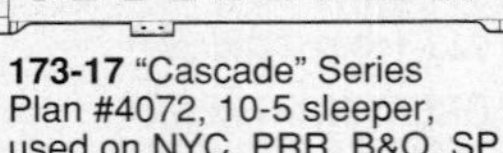

173-17 "Cascade" Series
Plan #4072, 10-5 sleeper, used on NYC, PRR, B&O, SP, ATSF and CP

173-21 "County" Series
Plan #4071, 13 bedroom sleeper, used on PRR, NYC and SP.

173-23 "City" Series
Plan #4068, 18 Roomette sleeper, used on PRR, NYC, NKP, CN, NdeM and IC.

173-28 14-4 Sleeper
Plan #4153, used on B&O, KCS, MP and T&P. Overlay for IHC/Rivarossi 1930 85' Coach or Sleeper.

173-37 "Bay " Series
Plan #4122, 22 Roomette sleeper, used on NYC, CN, IC and SP. Overlay for IHC/Rivarossi 1930 85' Coach or Sleeper.

SOUTHERN PACIFIC

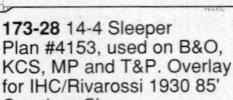

173-49 Bi-Level Gallery Coach **62.75**
Boxed kit includes etched brass sides, stainless steel doors, cast brass ends, etched grilles and vents, basswood roof, copper clad fiberglass floor, green window glazing, MDC trucks and instructions.

173-51 Sleeper **28.75** *NEW*
Works on Northern Pacific. P-S 10-6 Sleeper Plan 4140C for Cascade pool and other trains. End skirts only.

UNION PACIFIC EA 28.75

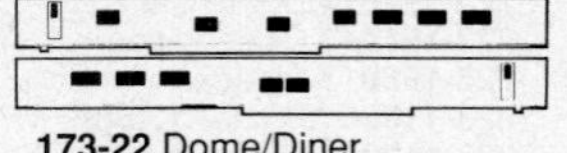

173-22 Dome/Diner
#8000-8009. Later used by Auto-Train. Overlay for IHC/Rivarossi Vista Dome coach.

173-26 Mid-Train Dome Lounge
#9000-9014, later used on Auto Train. Overlay for IHC/Rivarossi Vista Dome Coach. See 173-36 for illustration.

173-31 Coach
48 seat chair cars, #5331-5365, used on Challenger & Cities trains. Overlay for IHC/Rivarossi 1930 85' Coach or Sleeper.

173-36 Dome Observation Lounge
#9000-14, tail end version. Overlay for IHC/Rivarossi Vista Dome Coach.

173-40 Chair Car
44 seat Chair Car, #5450-87. Also built for CNW as #3477-82. Later used by SP, GTW, GN and Amtrak. Overlay for IHC/Rivarossi 1930 85' Coach or Sleeper.

BODY KITS

Use with all non-dome brass side sets. Some cutting required for shorter cars. Instructions included. Less trucks and couplers.

173-101 Basic Kit **10.75**
American Pewter metal ends, scale-width milled basswood roof, floor, and centersill for one car.

173-102 Deluxe Kit **18.75**
Includes lost-wax brass ends, heavy copper-clad fiberglass (pc board) floor, milled basswood roof for one car.

BRAWA

ROYAL WUERTTEMBERG STATE RAILROAD

TWO-AXLE PASSENGER CARS EA 59.99

Brawa unveils its first HO Scale passenger car models, with these detailed replicas of 4th Class Coaches built for the Royal Württemberg State Railroad (K.W.St.E). Introduced early in the 20th century, many of these interesting cars survive in museums and some are still in operation on tourist lines.

Each model comes fully assembled and painted, with many fine details that make them ideal for operation or display.

186-2150 4th Class Coach *NEW*
When Fourth Class service was added in 1907, a new style of coach was required. By 1914, 395 of these purpose-built cars were in operation, becoming a mainstay of passenger service in Württemberg.

186-2151 3rd Class Coach
Though outwardly similar to Fourth Class cars, these coaches were built for 2nd class service from 1904-07. The smaller double windows were replaced with large single windows.

186-2152 4th Class Coach
When delivered in 1899-1900, these cars were considered highly advanced. The nearly 9' (8m) long wheelbase and spacious interiors were major design improvements. Movable platform railings allowed them to be used as Hospital Cars during World War One.

DETAIL ASSOCIATES

HI-LEVEL CARS

Recreate the first hi-level passenger cars, a design so advanced, they're still in use today. Built by Budd for the Santa Fe, these pioneer cars were originally used on the "El Capitan." Easy-to-build kits are available in both coach and step-up coach styles. For the final touch, detail kits are available separately.

Prototype Photo

UNDECORATED COACHES - SUPER KITS EA 32.95

Unpainted kits include separate grab irons, head-end power receptacles, coupler lift bars and air hoses.

229-601 Hi-Level
229-611 Step-Up

PASSENGER CAR DETAIL KITS

229-901 Con-Cor Superliner Car **10.50**
229-902 Con-Cor Material Handling Car **8.50**
229-903 Walthers Horizon Cars **9.50**
229-904 Train Station Products Budd Hi-Level Car **9.50**

JAY BEE

INTERIOR LIGHTING KITS

Kits fit most popular brands of passenger cars and come fully assembled, ready to install. No soldering is required.

369-150 Rivarossi 1920 Series **23.85**
369-151 Rivarossi 1930/40 Series **20.85**
369-154 Con-Cor Budd **15.30**
369-155 Con-Cor Superliner **15.50**
369-156 Con-Cor 72' Budd **14.85**
369-159 Athearn **14.85**
369-1501 Rivarossi 72' 1920 Baggage Car **23.60**
369-1511 Rivarossi 72' 1930 Series **19.30**

GRANDT LINE

INTERIOR DETAILS

Parts are injection-molded styrene plastic.

CAR STOVE W/STACK

300-5008 DRGW Passenger **1.85**

COACH SEATS W/WOOD ENDS

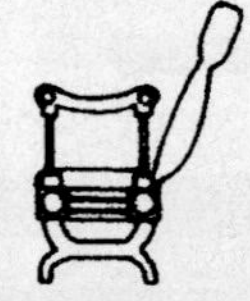

300-5048 Narrow Gauge pkg(12) **3.10**
300-5049 Standard Gauge pkg(12) **3.40**

See PARTS Section for Grandt Line detail parts.

Roadname Abbreviation Key

ATSF Santa Fe
B&O Baltimore & Ohio
BN Burlington Northern
BNSF Burlington Northern Santa Fe (1996 Merger)
C&O Chesapeake & Ohio
CN Canadian National
CNJ Central Railroad of New Jersey
CNW Chicago & North Western
CP Canadian Pacific
CR Conrail
CSX CSX
D&H Delaware & Hudson
DRGW Rio Grande
EL Erie Lackawanna
GN Great Northern
IC Illinois Central
L&N Louisville & Nashville
LV Lehigh Valley
MILW Milwaukee Road
MKT Katy (Missouri, Kansas, Texas)
MON Monon
MOPAC Missouri Pacific
MOW Maintenance Of Way
N&W Norfolk & Western
NH New Haven
NKP Nickel Plate Road
NP Northern Pacific
NS Norfolk Southern
NYC New York Central
PFE Pacific Fruit Express
PRR Pennsylvania
RDG Reading
ROCK Rock Island
SOO Soo Line
SOU Southern Railway
SP Southern Pacific
UP Union Pacific
WC Wisconsin Central
WM Western Maryland

Easy-to-build kits feature prepainted and lettered plastic bodies. Complete with horn-hook couplers and trucks with brass wheels. Most streamlined cars are available in 72' (ideal for smaller layouts or tight radius curves) and full-length, 85' versions.

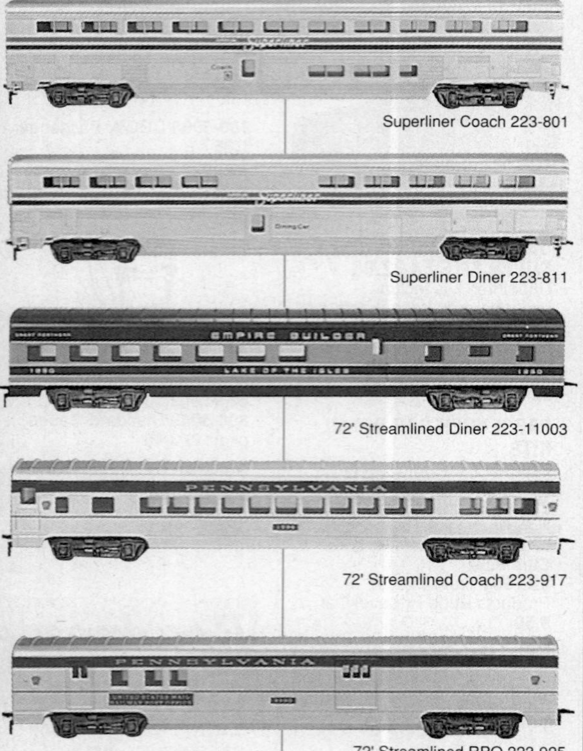

Superliner Coach 223-801

Superliner Diner 223-811

72' Streamlined Diner 223-11003

72' Streamlined Coach 223-917

72' Streamlined RPO 223-925

19TH CENTURY CARS

AMERICAN VINTAGE SETS PKG(4) EA 44.98

A complete train in a single set: two coaches, a full baggage car and a combine, in matching paint and lettering. Authentic 1880s styling.

223-3000101 PRR (Tuscan, gold, black roof)
223-3000102 UP (yellow, red, gray roof)
223-3000103 DRGW (yellow, silver)
223-3000104 MOW (gray, black)
223-3000105 ATSF (Pullman Green, gold, black roof)
223-3000106 N&W (Tuscan Red, gold, black roof)
223-3000107 SP (Pullman Green, gold, black roof)

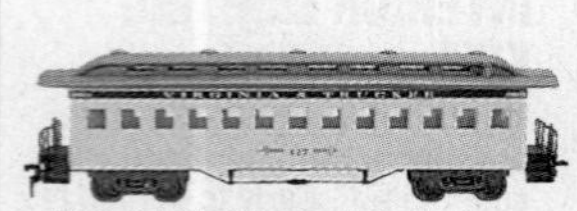

223-3000108 Virginia & Truckee
223-3000109 Central Pacific (red, black)

223-3000110 B&O (blue, gray)
223-3000111 NYC (two-tone gray)
223-3000112 SOU - "Southern Crescent" (two-tone green, gold)
223-3000100 Undecorated

SUPERLINER

AMTRAK SUPERLINERS EA 16.98 (UNLESS NOTED)

Double-deck, 85' cars, introduced in late 70s for long-distance runs. Available in Phase II, Phase III and latest Phase IV schemes.

PHASE II
223-801 Coach
223-811 Diner
223-821 Coach/Baggage
223-831 Sleeper
223-841 Lounge/Cafe

PHASE III
223-802 Coach
223-812 Diner
223-822 Coach/Baggage
223-832 Sleeper
223-842 Lounge/Cafe

PHASE IV
223-803 Coach
223-813 Diner
223-823 Coach/Baggage
223-833 Sleeper
223-843 Lounge/Cafe

UNDECORATED
223-800 Coach **14.98**
223-810 Diner **14.98**
223-820 Coach/Baggage
223-830 Sleeping Car
223-840 Lounge/Cafe **14.98**

72' STREAMLINED CARS EA 14.98
(Phase II scheme)

223-906 Coach
223-926 Railway Post Office
223-946 Dome
223-966 Observation Car
223-986 Sleeper
223-11006 Diner
223-11026 Baggage

AMTRAK 60' MATERIAL HANDLING CARS

Special box cars carry mail, express packages and baggage on most Amtrak runs. Trains have up to three cars, coupled between the loco and first passenger car.

INDIVIDUAL CARS
223-871 Single Car **13.98**
223-872 Railway Express Agency **13.98**
223-873 With Post Office Logo **13.98**
223-874 Phase IV **14.98**
223-870 Undecorated **12.98**

3-PACKS
Cars in 3-packs feature different numbers.

223-90603 Set #1 **41.94**
223-90604 Railway Express Agency **41.94**
223-90605 Set #2 **41.94**
223-90606 Amtrak Phase III, Set #1 **44.98**
223-87003 Undecorated **35.94**

72' PASSENGER

EA 14.98 (UNLESS NOTED)

BURLINGTON NORTHERN EXECUTIVE
223-190013 Coach
223-192013 Railway Post Office
223-194013 Dome Car
223-196013 Observation
223-198013 Sleeper
223-1100013 Diner **13.98**
223-1102013 Baggage
223-92031 4-Pack (Coach, RPO, Dome, Observation) **59.89**

NEW HAVEN
(red, orange)

223-190014 Coach
223-192014 Railway Post Office
223-194014 Dome Car
223-196014 Observation
223-198014 Sleeper
223-1100014 Diner
223-1102014 Baggage
223-92032 4-Pack (Coach, RPO, Dome, Observation) **59.89**

LOUISVILLE & NASHVILLE
223-190017 Coach
223-192017 Railway Post Office
223-194017 Dome Car
223-196017 Observation
223-198017 Sleeper
223-1100017 Diner
223-1102017 Baggage
223-92034 4-Pack (Coach, RPO, Dome, Observation) **59.89**

MISSOURI PACIFIC
223-190018 Coach
223-192018 Railway Post Office
223-194018 Dome Car
223-196018 Observation
223-198018 Sleeper
223-1100018 Diner
223-1102018 Baggage
223-92035 4-Pack (Coach, RPO, Dome, Observation) **59.89**

NORTHERN PACIFIC
223-190019 Coach
223-192019 Railway Post Office
223-194019 Dome Car
223-196019 Observation
223-198019 Sleeper
223-1100019 Diner
223-1102019 Baggage
223-92036 4-Pack (Coach, RPO, Dome, Observation) **59.89**

BALTIMORE & OHIO
223-10003 Diner
223-10203 Baggage **13.98**
223-19003 Coach **13.98**
223-19203 Railway Post Office
223-19403 Vista Dome
223-19603 Observation **13.98**
223-19803 Sleeper

UNION PACIFIC
(yellow, gray)

223-901 Coach
223-921 Railway Post Office
223-941 Dome
223-961 Observation Car
223-981 Sleeper
223-11001 Diner
223-11021 Baggage

PENNSYLVANIA
(Tuscan Red w/Dulux Gold)

223-905 Coach
223-925 Railway Post Office
223-945 Dome
223-965 Observation Car
223-985 Sleeper
223-11005 Diner
223-11025 Baggage
223-11045 60' Material Handling Car

"SENATOR" 72'
(silver, Tuscan letterboards, Dulux lettering)

223-917 Coach
223-937 Railway Post Office
223-957 Dome
223-977 Observation Car
223-997 Sleeper
223-11017 Diner
223-11037 Baggage

GREAT NORTHERN "EMPIRE BUILDER"
(orange, green, yellow)

223-903 Coach **17.98**
223-923 Railway Post Office **17.98**
223-943 Dome **17.98**
223-983 Sleeper **14.98**
223-963 Observation Car **17.98**
223-11003 Diner **17.98**
223-11023 Baggage **17.98**

SOUTHERN RAILWAY "CRESCENT LIMITED"
(Two-Tone Green, Dulux lettering, black roof)

223-904 Coach
223-924 Railway Post Office
223-944 Dome
223-964 Observation Car
223-984 Sleeper
223-11004 Diner
223-11024 Baggage

NORFOLK & WESTERN
(Tuscan with gold stripes)

223-907 Coach
223-927 Railway Post Office
223-947 Dome
223-967 Observation Car
223-987 Sleeper
223-11007 Diner
223-11027 Baggage

ROYAL AMERICAN SHOWS CARNIVAL
(5-color scheme)

223-908 Coach
223-928 Railway Post Office
223-948 Dome
223-968 Observation Car
223-988 Sleeper
223-11008 Diner
223-11028 Baggage

MILWAUKEE ROAD
(yellow, gray)

223-909 Coach
223-929 Railway Post Office
223-949 Dome
223-969 Observation Car
223-989 Sleeper
223-11009 Diner
223-11029 Baggage

ATSF

"VALLEY FLYER"
(silver, with red, black, yellow trim)

223-910 Coach
223-930 Railway Post Office
223-950 Dome
223-970 Observation Car
223-990 Sleeper
223-11010 Diner
223-11030 Baggage

"SCOUT" 72' STREAMLINED CARS
223-10004 Diner **13.98**
223-10204 Baggage **13.98**
223-19004 Coach **13.98**
223-19204 Railway Post Office **13.98**
223-19404 Vista Dome
223-19604 Observation
223-19804 Sleeper **13.98**

CHICAGO & NORTH WESTERN
(yellow, green)

223-916 Coach
223-936 Railway Post Office
223-956 Dome
223-976 Observation Car
223-996 Sleeper
223-11016 Diner
223-11036 Baggage

NICKEL PLATE ROAD
223-10002 Diner
223-10202 Baggage
223-19002 Coach **13.98**
223-19202 Railway Post Office
223-19402 Vista Dome **13.98**
223-19602 Observation **13.98**
223-19802 Sleeper **13.98**

SOUTHERN PACIFIC

GOLDEN STATE
(red, silver)

223-918 Coach
223-938 Railway Post Office
223-958 Dome
223-978 Observation Car
223-998 Sleeper
223-11018 Diner
223-11038 Baggage

"DAYLIGHT"
(orange, red)

223-902 Coach
223-922 Railway Post Office
223-942 Dome
223-962 Observation Car
223-982 Sleeper
223-11002 Diner
223-11022 Baggage

SP GOLDEN STATE
223-190020 Coach
223-192020 Railway Post Office
223-194020 Dome Car
223-196020 Observation
223-198020 Sleeper
223-1100020 Diner
223-1102020 Baggage
223-92037 4-Pack (Coach, RPO, Dome, Observation) **59.89**

"LARK"
(gray, white)

223-914 Coach
223-934 Railway Post Office
223-954 Dome
223-974 Observation Car
223-994 Sleeper
223-11014 Diner
223-11034 Baggage

CHESAPEAKE & OHIO
(silver)

223-919 Coach
223-939 Railway Post Office
223-959 Dome
223-979 Observation Car
223-999 Sleeper
223-11039 Baggage
223-11019 Diner

CANADIAN NATIONAL
223-190011 Coach
223-192011 Railway Post Office
223-194011 Dome **13.98**
223-196011 Observation
223-198011 Sleeper
223-1100011 Diner **13.98**
223-1102011 Baggage

ERIE
223-19008 Coach
223-19208 Railway Post Office
223-19808 Sleeper
223-110008 Diner
223-110208 Baggage

LACKAWANNA
(gray, yellow and maroon scheme)

223-19007 Coach **13.98**
223-19207 Railway Post Office
223-19407 Dome Car **13.98**
223-19607 Observation **13.98**
223-19807 Sleeper **13.98**
223-110007 Diner **13.98**
223-110207 Baggage Car **13.98**

ERIE-LACKAWANNA
(gray, yellow and maroon scheme)

223-190010 Coach **13.98**
223-192010 Railway Post Office
223-194010 Dome Car
223-196010 Observation
223-198010 Sleeper
223-1100010 Diner **13.98**
223-1102010 Baggage Car **13.98**

RIO GRANDE "SKI TRAIN"
(orange, silver)

223-10001 Diner **13.98**
223-10201 Baggage
223-19001 Coach **13.98**
223-19201 Railway Post Office **13.98**
223-19401 Dome **13.98**
223-19601 Observation Car **13.98**
223-19801 Sleeper **13.98**

VIA
(blue, yellow stripes)

223-912 Coach
223-932 Railway Post Office
223-952 Dome
223-972 Observation Car
223-992 Sleeper
223-11012 Diner
223-11032 Baggage

DELAWARE & HUDSON
223-190012 Coach
223-192012 Railway Post Office
223-194012 Dome **13.98**
223-196012 Observation
223-198012 Sleeper
223-1100012 Diner **13.98**
223-1102012 Baggage **13.98**

NORFOLK SOUTHERN
(maroon, gold)

223-911 Coach
223-931 Railway Post Office
223-951 Dome
223-971 Observation Car
223-991 Sleeper
223-11011 Diner
223-11031 Baggage

NEW YORK CENTRAL
(two-tone gray)

223-913 Coach
223-933 Railway Post Office
223-953 Dome
223-973 Observation Car
223-993 Sleeper
223-11013 Diner
223-11033 Baggage

20TH CENTURY SCHEME
223-190016 Coach
223-192016 Railway Post Office
223-194016 Dome Car
223-196016 Observation
223-198016 Sleeper
223-1100016 Diner
223-1102016 Baggage
223-92033 4-Pack (Coach, RPO, Dome, Observation) **59.89**

OVERLAND MAIL
223-915 Coach
223-935 Railway Post Office
223-955 Dome
223-975 Observation Car
223-995 Sleeper
223-11015 Diner
223-11035 Baggage

72' Streamlined Dome 223-950

72' Streamlined Dome Observation 223-970

72' Streamlined Dome 223-958

72' Streamlined Sleeper 223-982

72' Streamlined Coach 223-919

72' Streamlined Baggage 223-11031

72' Strea mlined Sleeper 223-993

KANSAS CITY SOUTHERN
223-19005 Coach **13.98**
223-19205 Railway Post Office **13.98**
223-19405 Dome **13.98**
223-19605 Observation **13.98**
223-19805 Sleeper **13.98**
223-110005 Diner **13.98**
223-110205 Baggage **13.98**

ILLINOIS CENTRAL
(brown, orange scheme)

223-19006 Coach **13.98**
223-19206 Railway Post Office
223-19406 Dome Car
223-19606 Observation
223-19806 Sleeper
223-110006 Diner **13.98**
223-110206 Baggage Car

WABASH
223-190022 Coach ***NEW***
223-192022 Railway Post Office ***NEW***
223-194022 Dome ***NEW***
223-196022 Observation ***NEW***
223-198022 Sleeper ***NEW***
223-1100022 Diner ***NEW***
223-1102022 Baggage ***NEW***
223-92038 4-Pack (Coach, Dome, RPO & Observation) **59.89** ***NEW***

UNDECORATED
223-900 Coach
223-920 Railway Post Office
223-940 Dome
223-960 Observation Car
223-980 Sleeper
223-11000 Diner
223-11020 Baggage

85' CORRUGATED PASSENGER

EA 16.98 (UNLESS NOTED)

NEW HAVEN
(silver, red)

223-70103 Coach
223-71103 Dome
223-72103 Diner
223-73103 Observation
223-74103 72' Baggage
223-75103 Slumbercoach
223-77103 Dome Observation
223-78103 Budd Dome
223-79103 10-6 Sleeper

FRISCO-TEXAS SPECIAL
(red, silver)

223-70104 Coach
223-71104 Dome
223-72104 Diner
223-73104 Observation
223-74104 72' Baggage
223-75104 Slumbercoach
223-77104 Dome Observation
223-78104 Budd Dome
223-79104 10-6 Sleepe

CHESAPEAKE & OHIO
(silver, blue, yellow)

223-70105 Coach
223-71105 Dome
223-72105 Diner
223-73105 Observation
223-74105 72' Baggage
223-75105 Slumbercoach
223-77105 Dome Observation
223-78105 Budd Dome
223-79105 10-6 Sleeper

COLORADO EAGLE
(red, orange)

223-70106 Coach
223-71106 Dome
223-72106 Dine
223-73106 Observation
223-74106 72' Baggage
223-75106 Slumbercoach
223-77106 Dome Observation
223-78106 Budd Dome
223-79106 10-6 Sleeper

"SP DAYLIGHT"
(red, orange)

223-70107 Coach
223-71107 Dome
223-72107 Diner
223-73107 Observation
223-74107 72' Baggage
223-75107 Slumbercoach
223-77107 Dome Observation
223-78107 Budd Dome
223-79107 10-6 Sleeper

85' Streamlined Baggage 223-743

85' Streamlined Slumbercoach 223-753

85' Streamlined 10-6 Pullman 223-793

ROCK ISLAND GOLDEN ROCKET
(silver, red)

223-70108 Coach
223-71108 Dome
223-72108 Diner
223-73108 Observation
223-74108 72' Baggage
223-75108 Slumbercoach
223-77108 Dome Observation
223-78108 Budd Dome
223-79108 10-6 Sleeper

PENNSYLVANIA "SENATOR"
223-708 Coach
223-718 Dome
223-728 Diner
223-738 Observation
223-748 Baggage
223-758 Slumbercoach
223-778 Dome-Observation
223-788 Budd-Dome
223-798 10-6 Sleeper

AMTRAK
223-7105 Coach
223-7205 Dome
223-7305 Diner
223-7405 Observation
223-7505 Baggage
223-7605 Budd Slumbercoach
223-7805 85' Budd Dome
223-7905 Budd Dome

CANADIAN PACIFIC
223-70109 Coach *NEW*
223-71109 Dome *NEW*
223-72109 Diner *NEW*
223-73109 Observation *NEW*
223-74109 Baggage *NEW*
223-75109 Slumber Coach *NEW*
223-77109 Dome/Observation *NEW*
223-78109 Budd Dome *NEW*
223-79109 10-6 Sleeper *NEW*

CANADIAN PACIFIC W/"BEAVER" LOGO
223-709 Coach
223-719 Dome
223-729 Diner
223-739 Observation Car
223-749 Baggage (70')
223-759 Sleeper
223-779 Dome-Observation
223-789 Budd-Dome
223-799 10-6 Sleeper

ATLANTIC COAST LINE
(with purple letterboards)

223-70101 Coach
223-71101 Dome
223-72101 Diner
223-73101 Observation
223-74101 Baggage (70')
223-75101 Sleeper
223-77101 Dome-Observation
223-78101 Budd-Dome
223-79101 10-6 Sleeper

EA 14.98

SOUTHERN
(black, silver)

223-17106 Coach
223-17206 Dome
223-17306 Diner
223-17506 Baggage
223-17606 Sleeper
223-17906 Budd Dome
223-17406 Observation
223-17806 Dome Observation
223-18006 10-6 Pullman

PENNSYLVANIA
223-703 Coach
223-713 Dome
223-723 Diner
223-733 Observation
223-743 Baggage
223-753 Budd Slumbercoach
223-783 Budd Dome
223-793 10-6 Pullman

NEW YORK CENTRAL
223-705 Coach
223-715 Dome
223-725 Diner
223-735 Observation
223-745 Baggage
223-755 Sleeper
223-775 Dome-Observation
223-785 Budd Dome
223-795 10-6 Pullman

CALIFORNIA ZEPHYR
223-706 Coach
223-716 Dome
223-726 Diner
223-736 Observation
223-746 70' Baggage
223-756 Budd Slumbercoach
223-776 Dome-Observation
223-786 Budd Dome
223-796 10-6 Pullman

CHICAGO, BURLINGTON & QUINCY
(silver)

223-70102 Coach
223-71102 Dome
223-72102 Diner
223-73102 Observation
223-74102 Baggage
223-75102 Sleeper
223-77102 Dome-Observation
223-78102 Budd-Dome
223-79102 10-6 Sleeper

ATSF
223-702 Coach
223-712 Dome
223-722 Diner
223-732 Observation
223-742 Baggage
223-752 Budd Slumbercoach
223-772 Dome-Observation
223-782 Budd Dome
223-792 10-6 Pullman

UNDECORATED
223-701 Coach
223-711 Dome
223-721 Diner
223-731 Observation
223-741 Baggage (70')
223-751 Budd Slumbercoach
223-771 Dome-Observation
223-781 Budd Dome
223-791 10-6 Pullman Sleeper

PASSENGER CAR PARTS

223-73 Standard Roof pkg(2) **6.95**
223-74 Passenger Car Truck Pin pkg(8) **1.25**

BUDD STYLE CAR ROOFS PKG(2)

223-70 Regular **7.98**
223-72 Dome **6.95**

MANTUA

Ready-to-run models are pre-painted plastic, and include trucks and horn-hook couplers.

OLD TIME CARS EA 9.49

PRR 1860 ERA

455-717520 Coach *NEW*

455-718520 Combine *NEW*

1890 ERA COMBINES

455-720008 Denver, South Park & Pacific (yellow)
455-720097 DRGW

Roadname Abbreviation Key

ATSF Santa Fe
B&O Baltimore & Ohio
BN Burlington Northern
BNSF Burlington Northern Santa Fe (1996 Merger)
C&O Chesapeake & Ohio
CN Canadian National
CNJ Central Railroad of New Jersey
CNW Chicago & North Western
CP Canadian Pacific
CR Conrail
CSX CSX
D&H Delaware & Hudson
DRGW Rio Grande
EL Erie Lackawanna
GN Great Northern
IC Illinois Central
L&N Louisville & Nashville
LV Lehigh Valley
MILW Milwaukee Road
MKT Katy (Missouri, Kansas, Texas)
MON Monon
MOPAC Missouri Pacific
MOW Maintenance Of Way
N&W Norfolk & Western
NH New Haven
NKP Nickel Plate Road
NP Northern Pacific
NS Norfolk Southern
NYC New York Central
PFE Pacific Fruit Express
PRR Pennsylvania
RDG Reading
ROCK Rock Island
SOO Soo Line
SOU Southern Railway
SP Southern Pacific
UP Union Pacific
WC Wisconsin Central
WM Western Maryland

Easy-to-build kits feature molded plastic parts and are undecorated. Cars are compatible with Kadee® draft gear (not included) and feature trucks with RP25, 36" Delrin wheel sets. Less couplers.

Coach 117-1030

Baggage/Lounge 117-1311

Osgood Bradley Coach 117-1300

P-70 SERIES 80' STANDARD HEAVYWEIGHTS

UNDECORATED 6-WHEEL TRUCKS EA 24.95 (UNLESS NOTED)

117-1001 78' PB-70 Combine
117-1010 B-60 Baggage Car **35.00**
117-1020 M-70b Railway Post Office **35.00**
117-1030 Coach
117-1100 Z-74 Business/ Observation w/Clerestory Roof
117-1120 P-70 FBR Arch Roof Coach
117-1123 P-70 FBR Clerestory Roof Coach

UNDECORATED 4-WHEEL PRR STYLE TRUCKS, EA 24.95

117-1122 P-70 FBR Arch Roof Coach
117-1125 P-70 FBR Clerestory Roof Coach
117-1141 P-70 FAR Low Arch Roof Coach

UNDECORATED 4-WHEEL TRUCKS , EA 24.95

117-1031 Coach
117-1101 Z-74 Business/ Observation w/Clerestory Roof - CommonwealthTrucks
117-1121 P-70 FBR Arch Roof Coach
117-1124 P-70 FBR Clerestory Roof Coach - Commonwealth Trucks

CAR CORE KITS

Kits include roof and floor to complete American Model Builders Limited car side conversions, sold separately.

117-1029 70' Head End Car Core Kit **15.00** *NEW*
117-1200 Basic Core **10.00**
117-1299 Pullman Standard Core **10.00**
117-1319 NH 85' Car Core Kit **20.00** *NEW*
117-1399 Budd **15.00**

PULLMAN-STANDARD LIGHTWEIGHTS

UNDECORATED STAINLESS STEEL, EA 19.95

117-1300 Osgood Bradley 84-Seat Commuter Coach
117-1310 Commuter Coach
117-1311 Baggage/Lounge
117-1330 4-4-2 Sleeper
117-1331 6-6-4 Sleeper

85' PULLMAN-STANDARD STREAMLINED

UNDECORATED EA 14.95

117-1201 RPO - Baggage
117-1202 Coach
117-1203 Diner
117-1204 Dormitory - Lounge
117-1205 6-6-4 Sleeper
117-1206 4-4-2 Sleeper
117-1207 Observation
117-1208 7-4-3-1 Sleeper

HEAVYWEIGHTS

Plastic bodies are prepainted and lettered in period schemes. Details include working lights, separate metal grab irons, rubber diaphragms and full underbody with brake gear. Cars come with weights, trucks and swing coupler pockets with E-Z Mate™ knuckle couplers.

BALTIMORE & OHIO EA 34.00

160-89044 Diner "Molly Pitcher"
160-89047 Pullman "Loch Ness"
160-89341 Combine #1445
160-89342 Coach #5481
160-89343 Coach #5483
160-89345 Coach #5490
160-89346 Observation Car #901

GREAT NORTHERN EA 34.00

160-89034 Diner "Minnesota"
160-89037 Pullman "Buccaneer"
160-89331 Combine #575
160-89332 Coach #963
160-89333 Coach #965
160-89335 Coach #956
160-89336 Observation Car #810

MISSOURI PACIFIC EA 34.00

160-89511 Combine *NEW*
160-89512 Coach *NEW*
160-89513 Coach *NEW*
160-89514 Diner *NEW*
160-89515 Coach *NEW*
160-89516 Observation Car *NEW*
160-89517 Pullman *NEW*

NASHVILLE, CHATTANOOGA & ST. LOUIS EA 34.00

160-89431 Combine *NEW*
160-89432 Coach *NEW*
160-89433 Coach *NEW*
160-89434 Diner *NEW*
160-89435 Coach *NEW*
160-89436 Observation Car *NEW*
160-89437 Pullman *NEW*

NEW HAVEN EA 34.00

160-89201 Combine *NEW*
160-89202 Coach *NEW*
160-89203 Coach *NEW*
160-89204 Diner *NEW*
160-89205 Coach *NEW*
160-89206 Observation Car *NEW*
160-89207 Pullman *NEW*

NEW YORK CENTRAL EA 34.00

160-89106 Observation Car "Detroit"
160-89401 Combine #305
160-89402 Coach #411
160-89403 Coach #810
160-89404 Diner #637
160-89405 Coach #965

NORFOLK & WESTERN EA 34.00

160-89411 Combine #1518
160-89412 Coach #1633
160-89413 Coach #1642
160-89414 Diner #1012
160-89415 Coach #1647
160-89416 Observation Car #102

PENNSYLVANIA EA 34.00

PULLMAN
160-89117 "Edgar Allan Poe" **34.00**

POST-WAR SCHEME
160-89241 Combine #9920
160-89242 Coach #4533
160-89243 Coach #3748
160-89244 Diner #8018
160-89245 Coach #3816
160-89246 Observation #130

PRE-WAR SCHEME
160-89301 Combine #5109
160-89302 Coach #1703
160-89303 Coach #3323
160-89304 Diner #4491
160-89305 Coach #1704
160-89306 Observation Car #1705

SANTA FE EA 34.00

160-89147 Pullman "Echo Lake"
160-89311 Combine #1525
160-89312 Coach #828
160-89313 Coach #837
160-89314 Diner #1416
160-89315 Coach #892
160-89316 Observation Car #407

SOUTHERN EA 34.00

160-89441 Combine *NEW*
160-89442 Coach *NEW*
160-89443 Coach *NEW*
160-89444 Diner *NEW*
160-89445 Coach *NEW*
160-89446 Observation Car *NEW*
160-89447 Pullman *NEW*

SOUTHERN PACIFIC EA 34.00

160-89421 Combine #3051
160-89422 Coach #1013
160-89423 Coach #1015
160-89424 Diner #10202
160-89425 Coach #1997
160-89426 Observation Car #2903

UNION PACIFIC EA 34.00

160-89027 Pullman "Lake Crystal"
160-89321 Combine #2513
160-89322 Coach #1084
160-89323 Coach #1111
160-89324 Diner #4050
160-89325 Coach #1125
160-89326 Observation Car #1503

International Hobby Corp.

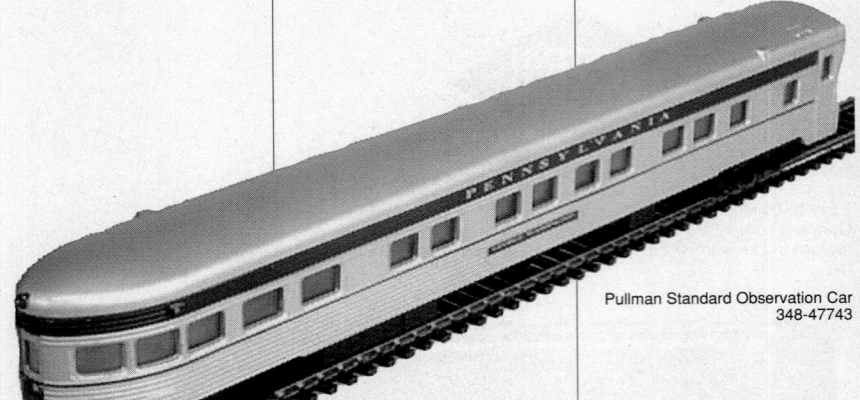

PULLMAN STANDARD CARS

CORRUGATED SIDES EA 14.98

ATLANTIC COAST LINE
348-47750 Baggage
348-47751 Coach
348-47752 Diner
348-47753 Observation
348-47755 RPO
348-47756 Sleeper
348-147754 Combine
348-147757 Vista Dome
348-50000 8-Car Set **119.84**

ALGOMA CENTRAL
348-47760 Baggage
348-47762 Coach
348-47763 Diner
348-47765 RPO
348-47766 Sleeper
348-147761 Coach
348-147764 Combine
348-147767 Vista Dome
348-50001 8-Car Set **119.84**

AMTRAK
348-47770 Baggage
348-47773 Observation
348-47777 Vista Dome
348-147771 Coach
348-147772 Diner
348-147774 Combine
348-147775 RPO
348-147776 Sleeper
348-50002 8-Car Set **119.84**

ATCHINSON, TOPEKA & SANTA FE
348-47781 Coach
348-47782 Diner
348-47783 Observation
348-47784 Combine
348-47786 Sleeper
348-47787 Vista Dome
348-147780 Baggage
348-147785 RPO
348-50003 8-Car Set **119.84**

BOSTON & MAINE
348-47790 Baggage
348-47791 Coach
348-47792 Diner
348-47793 Observation
348-47794 Combine
348-47795 RPO
348-147796 Sleeper
348-147797 Vista Dome
348-50004 8-Car Set **119.84**

BALTIMORE & OHIO
348-47800 Baggage
348-47801 Coach
348-47802 Diner
348-47803 Observation
348-47804 Combine
348-47805 RPO
348-47806 Sleeper
348-47807 Vista Dome
348-50005 8-Car Set **119.84**

CALIFORNIA ZEPHYR
348-47830 Baggage
348-47831 Coach
348-47832 Diner
348-47833 Observation
348-47834 Combine
348-47835 RPO
348-47836 Sleeper
348-47837 Vista Dome
348-50007 8-Car Set **119.84**

CANADIAN PACIFIC
348-47850 Baggage
348-47851 Coach
348-47852 Diner
348-47853 Observation
348-47854 Combine
348-47855 RPO
348-47856 Sleeper
348-47857 Vista Dome
348-50009 8-Car Set **119.84**

CHESAPEAKE & OHIO
348-47820 Baggage
348-47821 Coach
348-47822 Diner
348-47823 Observation
348-47824 Combine
348-47825 RPO
348-47826 Sleeper
348-47827 Vista Dome
348-50006 8-Car Set **119.84**

CHICAGO, BURLINGTON & QUINCY
348-47810 Baggage
348-47811 Coach
348-47812 Diner
348-47813 Observation
348-47814 Combine
348-47815 RPO
348-47816 Sleeper
348-47817 Vista Dome
348-50008 8-Car Set **119.84**

FLORIDA EAST COAST
348-47860 Baggage
348-47861 Coach
348-47862 Diner
348-47863 Observation
348-47864 Combine
348-47865 RPO
348-47866 Sleeper
348-47867 Vista Dome
348-50010 8-Car Set **119.84**

FRISCO
348-47870 Baggage
348-47871 Coach
348-47872 Diner
348-47873 Observation
348-47874 Combine
348-47875 RPO
348-47876 Sleeper
348-47877 Vista Dome
348-50011 8-Car Set **119.84**

Pullman Standard Observation Car
348-47743

LOUISVILLE & NASHVILLE
348-47880 Baggage
348-47881 Coach
348-47882 Diner
348-47883 Observation
348-47884 Combine
348-47885 RPO
348-47886 Sleeper
348-47887 Vista Dome
348-50012 8-Car Set **119.84**

NEW YORK CENTRAL
348-47890 Baggage
348-47891 Coach
348-47892 Diner
348-47893 Observation
348-47894 Combine
348-47895 RPO
348-47896 Sleeper
348-47897 Vista Dome
348-50013 8-Car Set **119.84**

PENN CENTRAL
348-50014 8-Car Set **119.84**

PENNSYLVANIA
348-47900 Baggage
348-47901 Coach
348-47902 Diner
348-47903 Observation
348-47904 Combine
348-47905 RPO
348-47906 Sleeper
348-47907 Vista Dome
348-50015 8-Car Set **119.84**

PENNSYLVANIA "THE FLEET OF MODERNISM"
348-47730 Baggage
348-47731 Coach
348-47732 Diner
348-47733 Observation
348-47734 Combine
348-47735 RPO
348-47736 Sleeper
348-47737 Vista Dome
348-50016 8-Car Set **119.84**

PENNSYLVANIA "THE CONGRESSIONAL"
348-47740 Baggage
348-47741 Coach
348-47742 Diner
348-47743 Observation
348-47744 Combine
348-47745 RPO
348-47746 Sleeper
348-47747 Vista Dome
348-50017 8-Car Set **119.84**

READING
348-47910 Baggage
348-47911 Coach
348-47912 Diner
348-47913 Observation
348-47914 Combine
348-47915 RPO
348-47916 Sleeper
348-47917 Vista Dome
348-50018 8-Car Set **119.84**

ROCK ISLAND
348-47920 Baggage
348-47921 Coach
348-47922 Diner
348-47923 Observation
348-47924 Combine
348-47925 RPO
348-47926 Sleeper
348-47927 Vista Dome
348-50019 8-Car Set **119.84**

SEABOARD
348-47930 Baggage
348-47931 Coach
348-47932 Diner
348-47933 Observation
348-47934 Combine
348-47935 RPO
348-47936 Sleeper
348-47937 Vista Dome
348-50020 8-Car Set **119.84**

SOUTHERN RAILWAY
348-47940 Baggage
348-47941 Coach
348-47942 Diner
348-47943 Observation
348-47944 Combine
348-47945 RPO
348-47946 Sleeper
348-47947 Vista Dome
348-50021 8-Car Set **119.84**

SOUTHERN PACIFIC
348-47950 Baggage
348-47951 Coach
348-47952 Diner
348-47953 Observation
348-47954 Combine
348-47955 RPO
348-47956 Sleeper
348-47957 Vista Dome
348-50022 8-Car Set **119.84**

TEXAS SPECIAL
348-47720 Baggage
348-47721 Coach
348-47722 Diner
348-47723 Observation
348-47724 Combine
348-47725 RPO
348-47726 Sleeper
348-47727 Vista Dome
348-50023 8-Car Set **119.84**

UNION PACIFIC
348-47960 Baggage
348-47961 Coach
348-47962 Diner
348-47963 Observation
348-47964 Combine
348-47965 RPO
348-47966 Sleeper
348-47967 Vista Dome
348-50024 8-Car Set **119.84**

WABASH
348-47970 Baggage
348-47971 Coach
348-47972 Diner
348-47973 Observation
348-47974 Combine
348-47975 RPO
348-47976 Sleeper
348-47977 Vista Dome
348-50024 8-Car Set **119.84**

SMOOTH SIDES EA 14.98

AMTRAK
348-48000 Baggage
348-48001 Coach
348-48002 Diner
348-48003 Observation
348-48004 Combine
348-48005 RPO
348-48006 Sleeper
348-48007 Vista Dome
348-50400 8-Car Set **119.84**

ATCHINSON, TOPEKA & SANTA FE
348-48010 Baggage
348-48011 Coach
348-48012 Diner
348-48013 Observation
348-48014 Combine
348-48015 RPO
348-48016 Sleeper
348-48017 Vista Dome
348-50401 8-Car Set **119.84**

BALTIMORE & OHIO
348-48020 Baggage
348-48021 Coach
348-48022 Diner
348-48023 Observation
348-48024 Combine
348-48025 RPO
348-48026 Sleeper
348-48027 Vista Dome
348-50402 8-Car Set **119.84**

BURLINGTON NORTHERN
348-48030 Baggage
348-48031 Coach
348-48032 Diner
348-48033 Observation
348-48034 Combine
348-48035 RPO
348-48036 Sleeper
348-48037 Vista Dome
348-50403 8-Car Set **119.84**

CANADIAN NATIONAL
348-48050 Baggage
348-48051 Coach
348-48052 Diner
348-48053 Observation
348-48054 Combine
348-48055 RPO
348-48056 Sleeper
348-48057 Vista Dome
348-50406 8-Car Set **119.84**

CHESAPEAKE & OHIO STEAM SPECIAL
348-48350 Baggage
348-48351 Coach
348-48352 Diner
348-48353 Observation
348-48354 Combine
348-48355 RPO
348-48356 Sleeper
348-48357 Vista Dome
348-50405 8-Car Set **119.84**

CHICAGO & NORTH WESTERN
348-48040 Baggage
348-48041 Coach
348-48042 Diner
348-48043 Observation
348-48044 Combine
348-48045 RPO
348-48046 Sleeper
348-48047 Vista Dome
348-50404 8-Car Set **119.84**

DELAWARE, LACKAWANNA & WESTERN
348-48140 Baggage
348-48141 Coach
348-48142 Diner
348-48143 Observation
348-48144 Combine
348-48145 RPO
348-48146 Sleeper
348-48147 Vista Dome
348-50417 8-Car Set **119.84**

DENVER & RIO GRANDE WESTERN
348-48060 Baggage
348-48061 Coach
348-48062 Diner
348-48063 Observation
348-48064 Combine
348-48065 RPO
348-48066 Sleeper
348-48067 Vista Dome
348-50407 8-Car Set **119.84**

ERIE LACKAWANNA
348-48300 Baggage
348-48301 Coach
348-48302 Diner
348-48303 Observation
348-48304 Combine
348-48305 RPO
348-48306 Sleeper
348-48307 Vista Dome
348-50409 8-Car Set **119.84**

ERIE
348-48070 Baggage
348-48071 Coach
348-48072 Diner
348-48073 Observation
348-48074 Combine
348-48075 RPO
348-48076 Sleeper
348-48077 Vista Dome
348-50408 8-Car Set **119.84**

GOLDEN STATE
348-50412 8-Car Set **119.84**

GULF, MOBILE & OHIO
348-48080 Baggage
348-48081 Coach
348-48082 Diner
348-48083 Observation
348-48084 Combine
348-48085 RPO
348-48086 Sleeper
348-48087 Vista Dome
348-50410 8-Car Set **119.84**

GREAT NORTHERN
348-48090 Baggage
348-48091 Coach
348-48092 Diner
348-48093 Observation
348-48094 Combine
348-48095 RPO
348-48096 Sleeper
348-48097 Vista Dome
348-50411 8-Car Set **119.84**

ILLINOIS CENTRAL
348-48110 Baggage
348-48111 Coach
348-48112 Diner
348-48113 Observation
348-48114 Combine
348-48115 RPO
348-48116 Sleeper
348-48117 Vista Dome
348-50413 8-Car Set **119.84**

ILLINOIS CENTRAL "CITY OF MIAMI"
348-48330 Baggage
348-48331 Coach
348-48332 Diner
348-48333 Observation
348-48334 Combine
348-48335 RPO
348-48336 Sleeper
348-48337 Vista Dome
348-50414 8-Car Set **119.84**

KANSAS CITY SOUTHERN
348-48120 Baggage
348-48121 Coach
348-48122 Diner
348-48123 Observation
348-48124 Combine
348-48125 RPO
348-48126 Sleeper
348-48127 Vista Dome
348-50415 8-Car Set **119.84**

LEHIGH VALLEY
348-48150 Baggage
348-48151 Coach
348-48152 Diner
348-48153 Observation
348-48154 Combine
348-48155 RPO
348-48156 Sleeper
348-48157 Vista Dome
348-50418 8-Car Set **119.84**

LOUISVILLE & NASHVILLE
348-48130 Baggage
348-48131 Coach
348-48132 Diner
348-48133 Observation
348-48134 Combine
348-48135 RPO
348-48136 Sleeper
348-48137 Vista Dome
348-50416 8-Car Set **119.84**

MOPAC
348-48160 Baggage
348-48161 Coach
348-48162 Diner
348-48163 Observation
348-48164 Combine
348-48165 RPO
348-48166 Sleeper
348-48167 Vista Dome
348-50419 8-Car Set **119.84**

NEW JERSEY TRANSIT
348-48180 Baggage
348-48181 Coach
348-48182 Diner
348-48183 Observation
348-48184 Combine
348-48185 RPO
348-48186 Sleeper
348-48187 Vista Dome
348-50421 8-Car Set **119.84**

NEW YORK CENTRAL
348-48200 Baggage
348-48201 Coach
348-48202 Diner
348-48203 Observation
348-48204 Combine
348-48205 RPO
348-48206 Sleeper
348-48207 Vista Dome
348-50423 8-Car Set **119.84**

NEW YORK CENTRAL "MERCURY"
348-48290 Baggage
348-48291 Coach
348-48292 Diner
348-48293 Observation
348-48294 Combine
348-48295 RPO
348-48296 Sleeper
348-48297 Vista Dome
348-50424 8-Car Set **119.84**

NORFOLK & WESTERN
348-48170 Baggage
348-48171 Coach
348-48172 Diner
348-48173 Observation
348-48174 Combine
348-48175 RPO
348-48176 Sleeper
348-48177 Vista Dome
348-50420 8-Car Set **119.84**

NORTHERN PACIFIC
348-48190 Baggage
348-48191 Coach
348-48192 Diner
348-48193 Observation
348-48194 Combine
348-48195 RPO
348-48196 Sleeper
348-48197 Vista Dome
348-50422 8-Car Set **119.84**

PENNSYLVANIA
348-48210 Baggage
348-48211 Coach
348-48212 Diner
348-48213 Observation
348-48214 Combine
348-48215 RPO
348-48216 Sleeper
348-48217 Vista Dome
348-50425 8-Car Set **119.84**

PENNSYLVANIA "EASTWIND"
348-48320 Baggage
348-48321 Coach
348-48322 Diner
348-48323 Observation
348-48324 Combine
348-48325 RPO
348-48326 Sleeper
348-48327 Vista Dome
348-50427 8-Car Set **119.84**

PENNSYLVANIA "THE FLEET OF MODERNISM"
348-48310 Baggage
348-48311 Coach
348-48312 Diner
348-48313 Observation
348-48314 Combine
348-48315 RPO
348-48316 Sleeper
348-48317 Vista Dome
348-50426 8-Car Set **119.84**

READING
348-48220 Baggage
348-48221 Coach
348-48222 Diner
348-48223 Observation
348-48224 Combine
348-48225 RPO
348-48226 Sleeper
348-48227 Vista Dome
348-50428 8-Car Set **119.84**

RICHMOND, FREDERICKSBURG & POTOMAC
348-48230 Baggage
348-48231 Coach
348-48232 Diner
348-48233 Observation
348-48234 Combine
348-48235 RPO
348-48236 Sleeper
348-48237 Vista Dome
348-50429 8-Car Set **119.84**

ROCK ISLAND
348-48240 Baggage
348-48241 Coach
348-48242 Diner
348-48243 Observation
348-48244 Combine
348-48245 RPO
348-48246 Sleeper
348-48247 Vista Dome
348-50430 8-Car Set **119.84**

SEABOARD COAST LINE
348-48360 Baggage
348-48361 Coach
348-48362 Diner
348-48363 Observation
348-48364 Combine
348-48365 RPO
348-48366 Sleeper
348-48367 Vista Dome
348-50431 8-Car Set **119.84**

SOUTHERN PACIFIC
348-48250 Baggage
348-48251 Coach
348-48252 Diner
348-48253 Observation
348-48254 Combine
348-48255 RPO
348-48256 Sleeper
348-48257 Vista Dome
348-50432 8-Car Set **119.84**

SOUTHERN PACIFIC GOLD
348-48100 Baggage
348-48101 Coach
348-48102 Diner
348-48103 Observation
348-48104 Combine
348-48105 RPO
348-48106 Sleeper
348-48107 Vista Dome

SPOKANE PORTLAND & SEATTLE
348-48340 Baggage
348-48341 Coach
348-48342 Diner
348-48343 Observation
348-48344 Combine
348-48345 RPO
348-48346 Sleeper
348-48347 Vista Dome

UNION PACIFIC
348-48270 Baggage
348-48271 Coach
348-48272 Diner
348-48273 Observation
348-48274 Combine
348-48275 RPO
348-48276 Sleeper
348-48277 Vista Dome
348-50435 8-Car Set **119.84**

VIA
348-48280 Baggage
348-48281 Coach
348-48282 Diner
348-48283 Observation
348-48284 Combine
348-48285 RPO
348-48286 Sleeper
348-48287 Vista Dome
348-50436 8-Car Set **119.84**

UNDECORATED
348-48260 Baggage
348-48261 Coach
348-48262 Diner
348-48263 Observation
348-48264 Combine
348-48265 RPO
348-48266 Sleeper
348-48267 Vista Dome
348-50434 8-Car Set **119.84**

INTERIORS EA TBA

348-20150 Baggage *NEW*
348-20151 Coach *NEW*
348-20152 Diner *NEW*
348-20153 Observation *NEW*
348-20154 Combine *NEW*
348-20155 RPO *NEW*
348-20156 Sleeper *NEW*
348-20157 Vista Dome *NEW*

FUNARO & CAMERLENGO

Craft Train Kits consist of thin flexible styro-urethane castings with details molded in place, stripwood, wire and instructions. Cars are less trucks and couplers.

LONG ISLAND RAILROAD EA 29.99

279-103

279-102 MU "World's Fair" Coach
279-103 Double Deck Coach
279-5010 "Ping-Pong" Coach
279-5011 "Ping-Pong" Combine
279-6380 1950-Current Coach
Includes decals for white lettering and red numbers.

ERIE EA 29.99

279-201 Stillwell Coach
279-202 Stillwell Combine

NEW YORK, ONTARIO & WESTERN EA 29.99

279-301 Coach
279-302 Combine
279-303 Baggage
279-304 Railway Post Office
279-306 Osgood Bradley Coach
279-309 Observation Car
Also used on Southern Pacific and St. Louis Southwestern

CAR SETS PKG(2) EA 58.99

279-3001 Coach & Combine
Includes one each #301 and #302.

279-3002 Baggage & RPO
Includes one each #303 and #304.

NEW YORK CENTRAL EA 29.99

279-5070 Standard Coach, Less Decals
279-5071 Steel Coach
Includes decals for Rutland.

DELAWARE, LACKAWANNA & WESTERN

279-401 Boonton Coach **29.99**

CENTRAL OF NEW JERSEY

279-701 Clerestory Roof Coach **29.99**

READING

279-601 Arch Roof Coach **29.99**

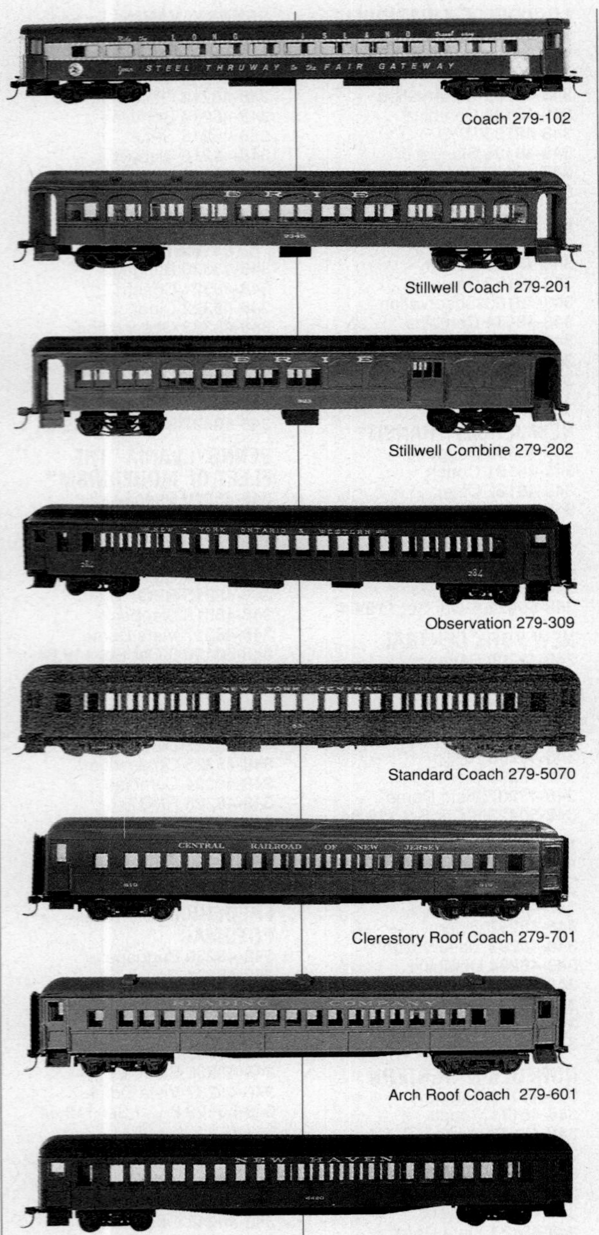
Coach 279-102
Stillwell Coach 279-201
Stillwell Combine 279-202
Observation 279-309
Standard Coach 279-5070
Clerestory Roof Coach 279-701
Arch Roof Coach 279-601
Osgood Bradley Coach 279-308

NEW HAVEN EA 29.99

279-308 Osgood Bradley Coach
279-801 70' Baggage Car w/Turtle Back Roof & Decals *NEW*
This car models the prototypes numbered 5570-5589.

279-802 70' Messenger Car w/Turtle Back Roof & Decals *NEW*
This car models the prototypes numbered 5570-5589.

279-803 70' Baggage Car w/Clerestory Roof & Decals *NEW*
This car models the prototypes numbered 5500-5569.

279-804 70' Messenger Car w/Clerestory Roof & Decals *NEW*
This car models the prototypes numbered 5500-5569.

MARYLAND & PENNSYLVANIA EA 29.99 (UNLESS NOTED)

279-4001 Wooden Coach
279-4002 Wooden Railway Post Office
279-4003 Wooden Baggage
279-4004 Complete Train pkg(3) **80.99**

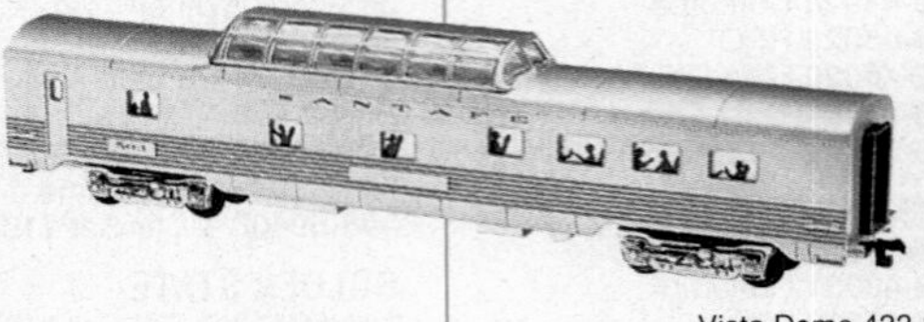
Vista Dome 433-8052

Full Dome 433-8059

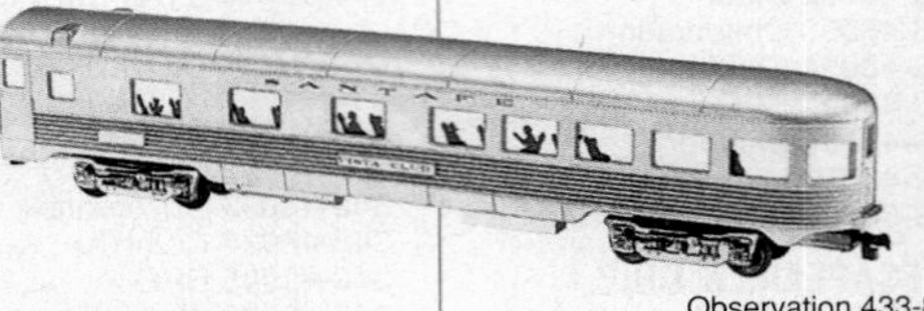
Observation 433-8080

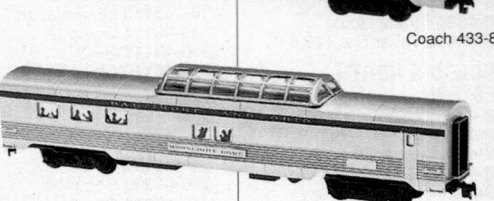

Coach 433-8085

Diner 433-8093

Ready-to-run cars are made of colored plastic, and include trucks plus horn-hook couplers.

60' STREAMLINED CARS W/LIGHTS

AMTRAK EA 15.00

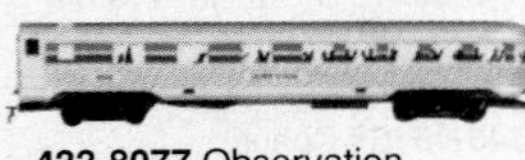

433-8077 Observation
433-8078 Full Dome
433-8079 Coach
433-8090 Diner
433-8091 Vista Dome

ATSF EA 15.00

433-8052 Vista Dome *NEW*
433-8056 Diner *NEW*
433-8057 Coach *NEW*
433-8059 Full Dome *NEW*
433-8080 Observation *NEW*

B&O EA 15.00

433-8083 Observation *NEW*
433-8084 Full Dome *NEW*
433-8085 Coach *NEW*
433-8093 Diner *NEW*
433-8094 Vista Dome *NEW*

CAR ASSORTMENTS PKG(12) EA 180.00

Includes three each of Coach and Vista Dome, and two each of Observation, Full Dome and Diner.

433-8051 ATSF *NEW*
433-8076 Amtrak
433-8082 B&O *NEW*

Ready-to-run cars feature plastic bodies and come prepainted and lettered.

PASSENGER CARS

AMTRAK

BUDD CARS EA 14.98

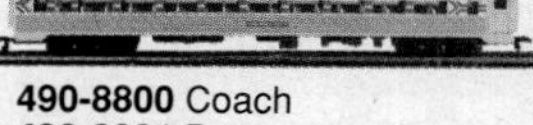

490-8800 Coach
490-8801 Baggage
490-8802 Dining
490-8803 Observation
490-8804 Sleeper

BALTIMORE & OHIO

67' HARRIMAN CARS W/ INTERIOR (BLUE) EA 14.98
490-9903 Coach
490-9913 Observation Car

CANADIAN NATIONAL EA 14.98

67' HARRIMAN CARS W/INTERIOR (GREEN)
490-9906 Coach (gray, black)
490-9908 Coach
490-9916 Observation Car (modern gray, black)
490-9918 Observation Car

BUDD CARS
490-8840 Coach
490-8841 Baggage
490-8842 Dining
490-8843 Observation
490-8844 Sleeper

CANADIAN PACIFIC

40' OLD-TIME WOOD CARS EA 12.98
490-5508 Coach
490-5518 Baggage

67' HARRIMAN CARS W/INTERIOR (SILVER, RED) EA 14.98

490-9915

490-9905 Coach
490-9907 Coach (older Maroon scheme)
490-9915 Observation Car
490-9917 Observation Car (older Maroon scheme)

BUDD CARS EA 14.98
490-8850 Coach
490-8851 Baggage
490-8852 Dining
490-8853 Observation
490-8854 Sleeper

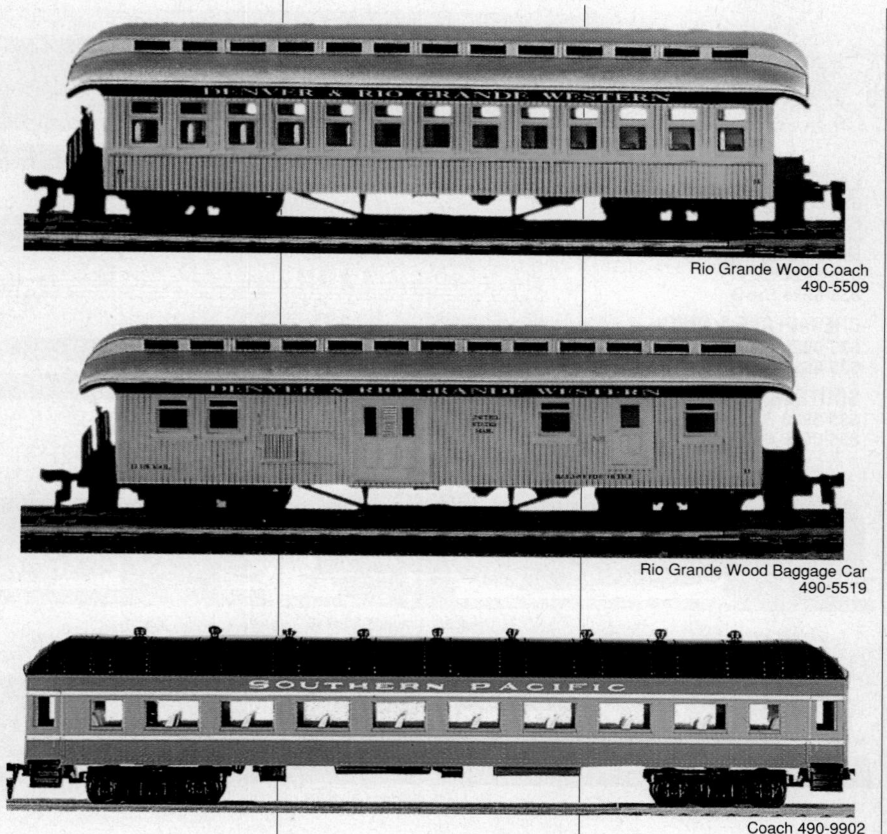

Rio Grande Wood Coach
490-5509

Rio Grande Wood Baggage Car
490-5519

Coach 490-9902

DICKENS RAILROAD EA 12.98

Cars are painted and lettered to match equipment in Christmas Village Sets.

490-5504 48' Old-Time Wooden Deluxe Coach
490-5514 48' Old-Time Wooden Baggage

ERIE LACKAWANNA

67' HARRIMAN CARS W/INTERIOR EA 14.98
490-9910 Coach
490-9920 Observation Car

PENNSYLVANIA EA 14.98 (UNLESS NOTED)

40' OLD-TIME WOOD CARS EA 12.98
490-5506 Coach
490-5516 Baggage

67' HARRIMAN CARS W/INTERIOR
490-9909 Coach
490-9919 Observation Car

"THE CONGRESSIONAL"
490-8870 Coach #1569
490-8871 Coach "Henry Knox"
490-8875 Diner #1154
490-8877 Observation Car #7128

"THE SENATOR"
490-8880 Coach #1576
490-8881 Coach "Betsy Ross"
490-8885 Diner #1156
490-8887 Observation Car #7126

RIO GRANDE

40' OLD-TIME WOOD CARS EA 11.98
490-5509 Coach
490-5519 Baggage

SANTA FE

40' OLD-TIME WOOD CARS EA 12.98
490-5505 Coach
490-5515 Baggage

67' HARRIMAN CARS W/INTERIOR (SILVER) EA 14.98
490-9904 Coach
490-9914 Observation

BUDD CARS EA 14.98
490-8860 Coach
490-8861 Baggage
490-8862 Dining
490-8863 Observation
490-8864 Sleeper

SOUTHERN

40' OLD-TIME WOOD CARS EA 12.98
490-5507 Coach
490-5517 Baggage

67' HARRIMAN CARS W/INTERIOR (GREEN) EA 14.98
490-9902 Coach
490-9912 Observation Car

SOUTHERN PACIFIC EA 14.98

67' HARRIMAN CARS W/INTERIOR (RED, ORANGE)

490-9901 Coach
490-9911 Observation Car

BUDD CARS
490-8820 Coach
490-8821 Baggage

490-8822 Dining
490-8823 Observation
490-8824 Sleeper

UNDECORATED

67' HARRIMAN CARS W/INTERIOR EA 14.98
490-9899 Coach
490-9900 Observation Car

Information STATION

Fish Travel By Train

Railroads have long been used to transport a variety of special, oversize and heavy loads, many of which require special cars. But one of the strangest loads to move by train has to be live fish!

Special fish tank cars were moved on fast passenger trains throughout the United States from 1881 to 1947. Operated by the Department of Commerce, they were used to transport fingerlings and fish eggs for stocking in awaiting streams, rivers and lakes throughout the country. (Some of the major aquariums and marine institutes also operated their own cars, which were used to move exotic and saltwater fish over long distances.)

In the early stages, normal baggage cars were loaded with milk cans housing the fry. They required constant attention while traveling, and frequent use of hand-pumped aerators to put oxygen back into the water.

In later years, all-new cars were designed and built specifically for the task of carrying the fish to their destination. These were equipped with large storage tanks to speed transfer of fish to and from the car. Air pumps and filtration equipment were developed which could be operated from the train's electrical and steam systems.

OLD-TIMER FOUR-CAR SETS

EA 74.99

Each includes a fully assembled Baggage car, Combine, Coach and Barnum Advertising Car.

635-6900 Virginia & Truckee
635-6901 ATSF
635-6986 Kansas, St. Louis & Chicago

1920S ERA HEAVYWEIGHT SETS

PKG(4) EA 99.99

All models come fully assembled, with RP25 metal wheels, full interiors and superb paint and lettering schemes. Each roadname is offered only in two sets of four cars, painted in the same scheme (sorry, cars are not available separately). "A" Sets include one each: Baggage Express, Combine, Pullman and Diner. "B" Sets include one each RPO/Baggage, Coach, Duplex Sleeper and an Observation.

"CRESCENT LIMITED"
635-6902 Set A
635-6903 Set B

MILWAUKEE ROAD
635-6904 Set A
635-6905 Set B

BALTIMORE & OHIO
GREEN
635-6906 Set A
635-6907 Set B
ROYAL BLUE
635-6908 Set A
635-6909 Set B

CENTRAL RAILROAD OF NEW JERSEY
635-6910 Set A
635-6911 Set B

CHICAGO & ALTON
635-6912 Set A
635-6913 Set B

SANTA FE
635-6914 Set A
635-6915 Set B

PENNSYLVANIA
635-6916 Set A
635-6917 Set B

CANADIAN NATIONAL
635-6918 Set A
635-6919 Set B

DENVER & RIO GRANDE
635-6920 Set A
635-6921 Set B

UNION PACIFIC
635-6922 Set A
635-6923 Set B

LACKAWANNA
635-6930 Set A
635-6931 Set B

NEW YORK CENTRAL
635-6924 Set A
635-6925 Set B

CHESAPEAKE & OHIO
635-6926 Set A
635-6927 Set B

SOUTHERN PACIFIC
635-6928 Set A
635-6929 Set B

Chicago & Alton 635-6912

Denver & Rio Grande 635-6920

Crescent Limited 635-6902

Pennsylvania 635-6916

Milwaukee Road 635-6904

Union Pacific 635-6922

Baltimore & Ohio 635-6906

New York Central 635-6924

Baltimore & Ohio 635-6908

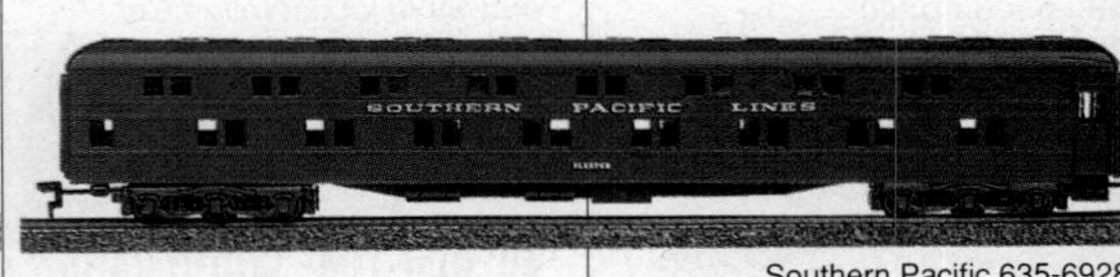

Chesapeake & Ohio 635-6926

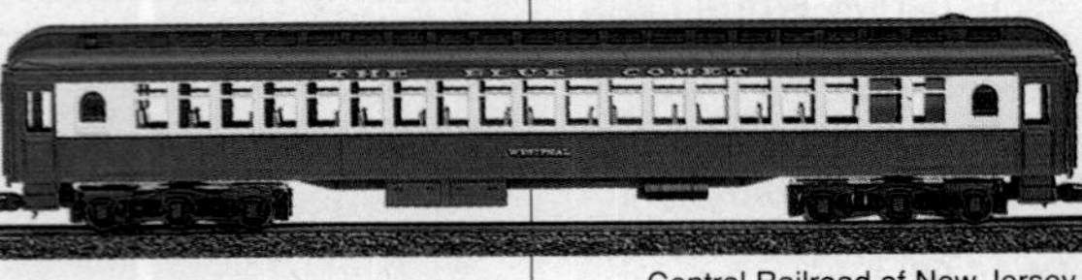

Central Railroad of New Jersey 635-6910

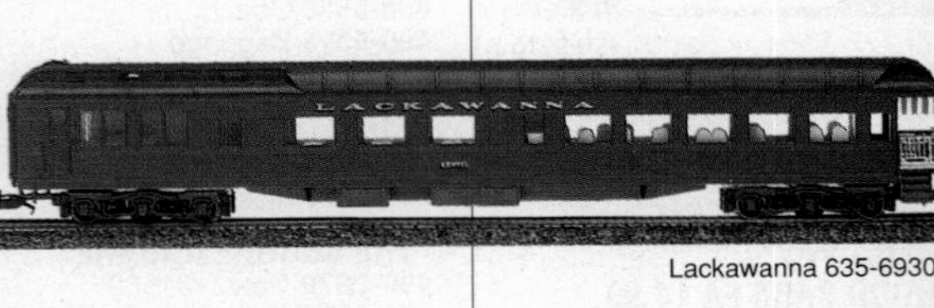

Southern Pacific 635-6928

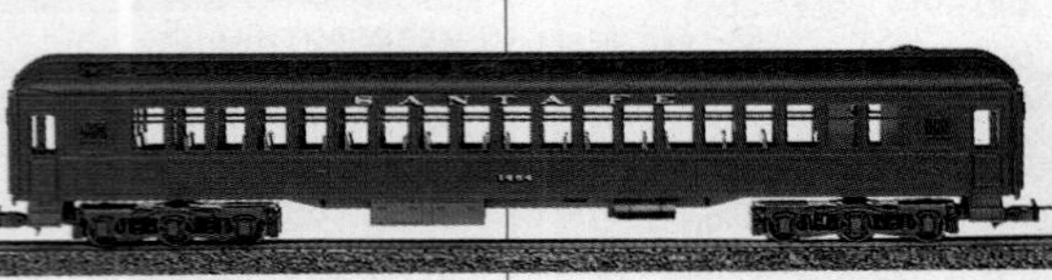

Santa Fe 635-6914

Lackawanna 635-6930

Old Timer Four-Car Set 635-6901

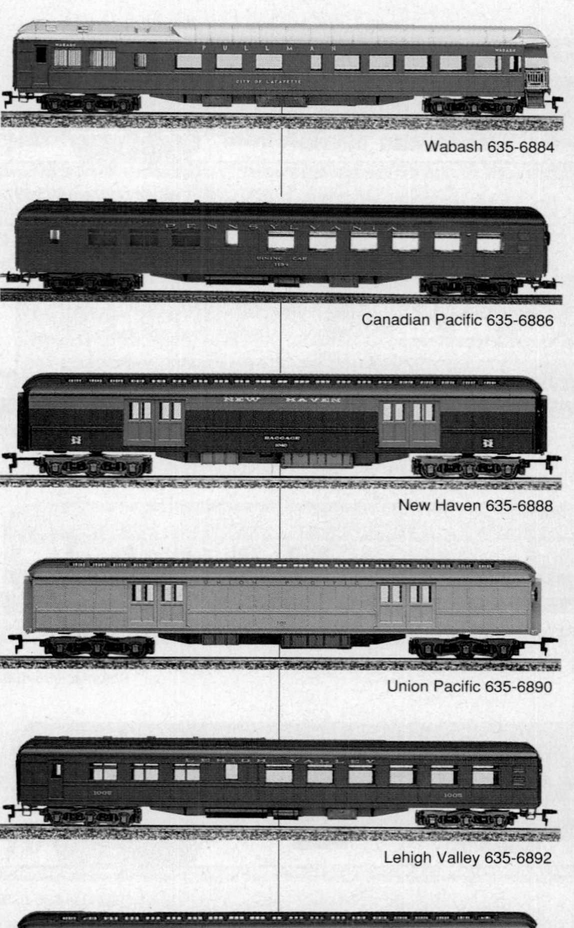

Wabash 635-6884

Canadian Pacific 635-6886

New Haven 635-6888

Union Pacific 635-6890

Lehigh Valley 635-6892

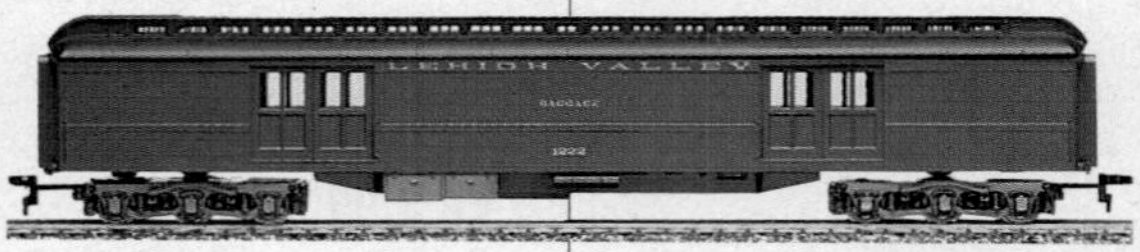

Lehigh Valley 635-6898

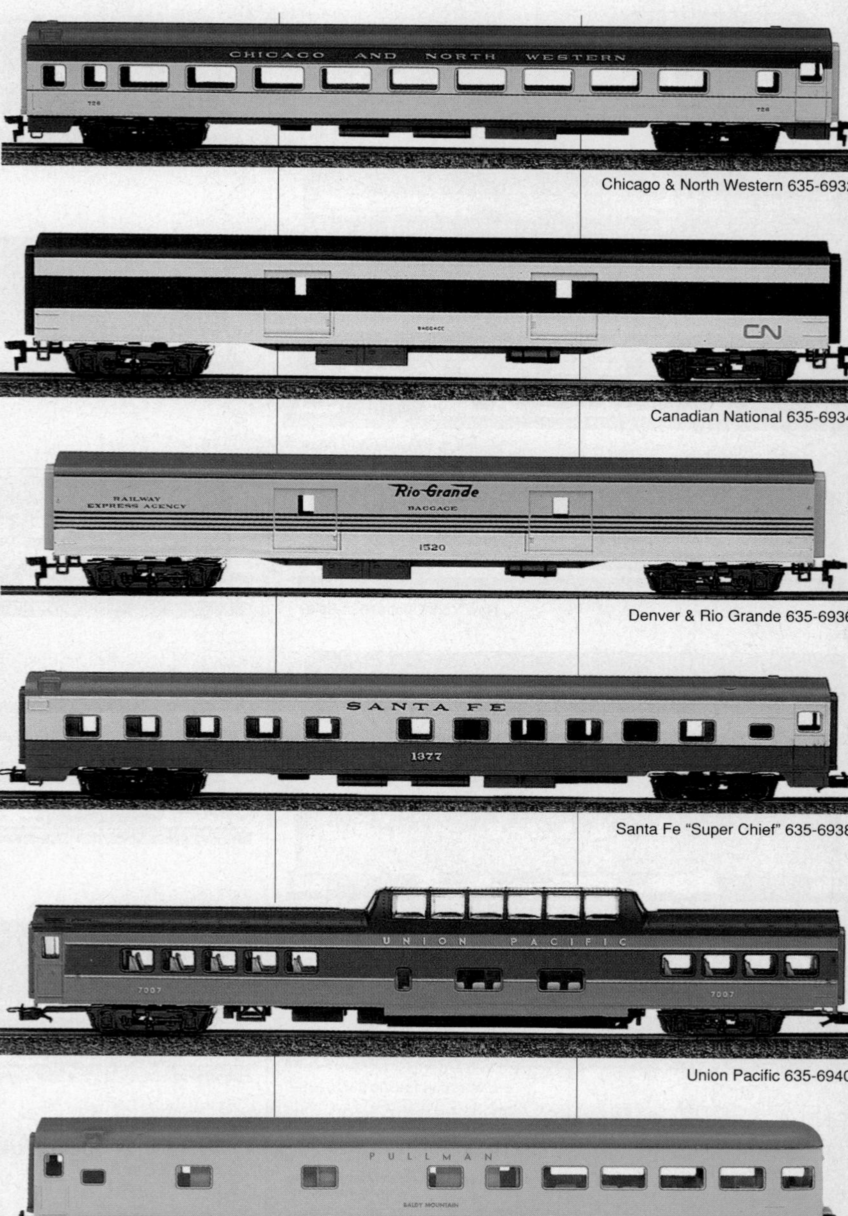

Chicago & North Western 635-6932

Canadian National 635-6934

Denver & Rio Grande 635-6936

Santa Fe "Super Chief" 635-6938

Union Pacific 635-6940

UP Excursion Sets 635-6962

WABASH
635-6884 Set A
635-6885 Set B

CANADIAN PACIFIC
635-6886 Set A
635-6887 Set B

NEW HAVEN
635-6888 Set A
635-6889 Set B

UNION PACIFIC
635-6890 Set A
635-6891 Set B

LEHIGH VALLEY

PULLMAN GREEN
635-6892 Set A
635-6893 Set B

BROWN
635-6898 Set A
635-6899 Set B

DELAWARE & HUDSON
635-6894 Set A
635-6895 Set B

MISSOURI PACIFIC
635-6896 Set A
635-6897 Set B

1930S ERA STREAMLINED CARS

PKG(4) EA 99.99

Ushering a new age in travel by train, these deluxe streamliners were the pride of the roads who ran them. All models come fully assembled, with RP25 metal wheels, full interiors and superb paint and lettering schemes. Each roadname is offered only in two sets of four cars, painted in the same scheme (sorry, cars are not available separately).

"A" Sets include one each: Baggage, Coach, Diner and Vista Dome. "B" Sets include one each RPO, Roomette, Duplex Sleeper and Tail Car (Observation).

CHICAGO & NORTH WESTERN
635-6932 Set A
635-6933 Set B

CANADIAN NATIONAL
635-6934 Set A
635-6935 Set B

DENVER & RIO GRANDE
635-6936 Set A
635-6937 Set B

SANTA FE "SUPER CHIEF"
635-6938 Set A
635-6939 Set B

UNION PACIFIC

GRAY
635-6940 Set A
635-6941 Set B

EXCURSION SETS
635-6962 Set A
635-6963 Set B

YELLOW
635-6964 Set A
635-6965 Set B

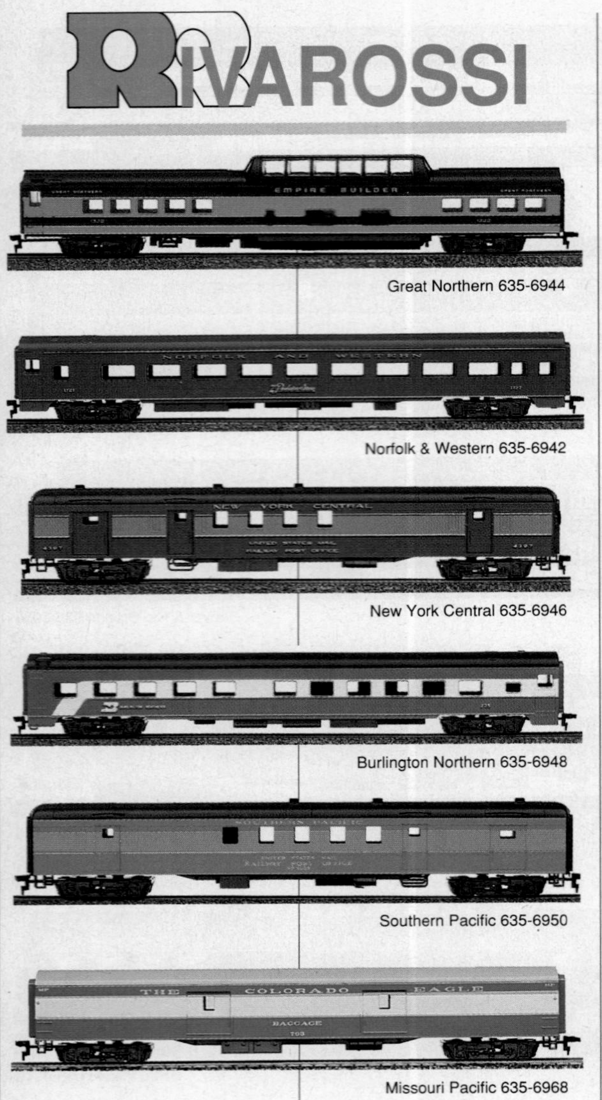

Great Northern 635-6944

Norfolk & Western 635-6942

New York Central 635-6946

Burlington Northern 635-6948

Southern Pacific 635-6950

Missouri Pacific 635-6968

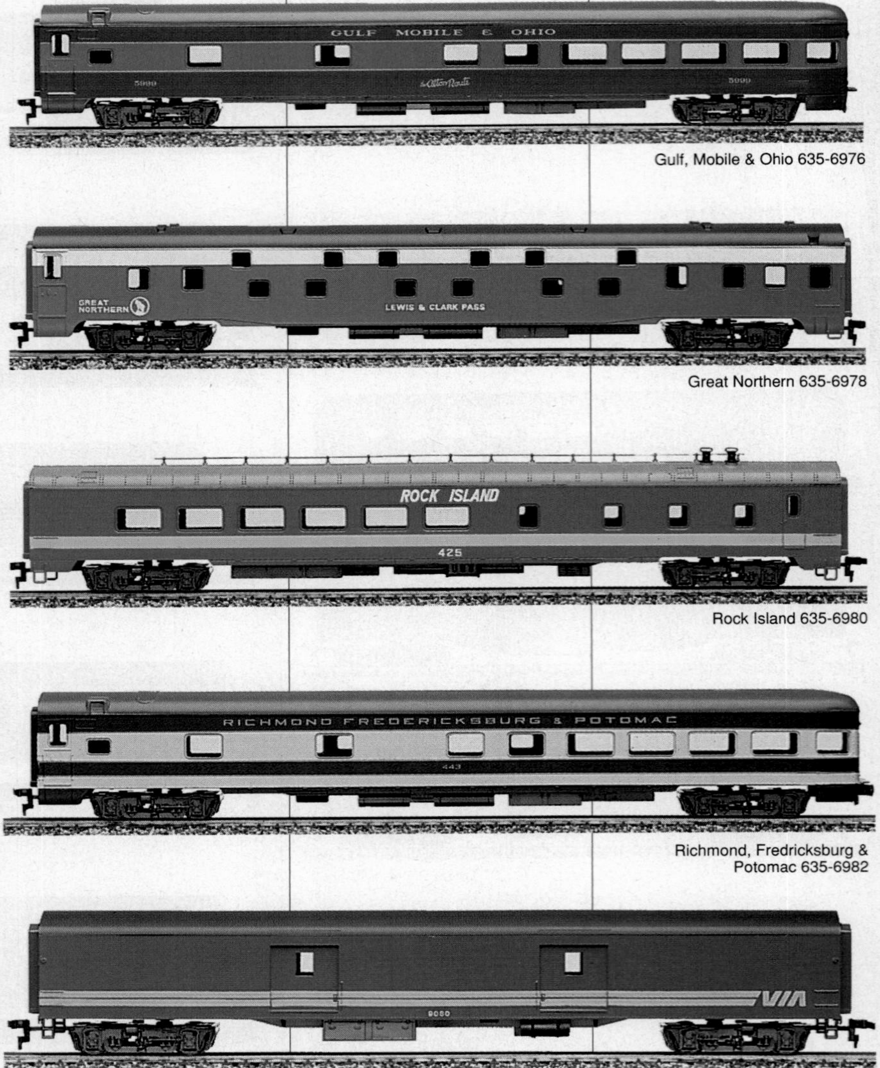

Gulf, Mobile & Ohio 635-6976

Great Northern 635-6978

Rock Island 635-6980

Richmond, Fredricksburg & Potomac 635-6982

Via Rail 635-6984

GREAT NORTHERN
635-6944 Set A
635-6945 Set B

NORFOLK & WESTERN
635-6942 Set A
635-6943 Set B

NEW YORK CENTRAL
635-6946 Set A
635-6947 Set B

BURLINGTON NORTHERN
635-6948 Set A
635-6949 Set B

SOUTHERN PACIFIC
635-6950 Set A
635-6951 Set B

ILLINOIS CENTRAL

635-6952 Set A
635-6953 Set B

LACKAWANNA
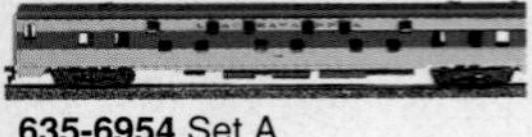

635-6954 Set A
635-6955 Set B

AMTRAK
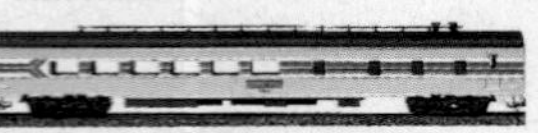

635-6956 Set A
635-6957 Set B

PENNSYLVANIA

635-6958 Set A
635-6959 Set B

BALTIMORE & OHIO

635-6960 Set A
635-6961 Set B

MILWAUKEE ROAD
635-6966 Set A
635-6967 Set B

MISSOURI PACIFIC
635-6968 Set A
635-6969 Set B

NORTHERN PACIFIC
635-6970 Set A
635-6971 Set B

KANSAS CITY SOUTHERN
635-6972 Set A
635-6973 Set B

SOUTHERN PACIFIC
635-6974 Set A
635-6975 Set B

GULF, MOBILE & OHIO
635-6976 Set A
635-6977 Set B

GREAT NORTHERN
635-6978 Set A
635-6979 Set B

ROCK ISLAND
635-6980 Set A
635-6981 Set B

RICHMOND, FREDERICKSBURG & POTOMAC
635-6982 Set A
635-6983 Set B

VIA RAIL
635-6984 Set A
635-6985 Set B

UNDECORATED MODELS

EA 19.99

These unpainted and unlettered models are ideal for custom painting, or as starting points for kitbashed models. Cars are sold individually.

1920s HEAVYWEIGHT CARS
635-6596 Full Baggage Car
635-6597 Baggage-Post Office
635-6598 Combine
635-6599 Coach
635-6600 Diner
635-6601 Pullman
635-6602 Sleeper
635-6603 Observation

1930s STREAMLINE CARS
635-6604 Baggage Car
635-6605 Railway Post Office
635-6606 Coach
635-6607 Roomette
635-6608 Dome Car
635-6609 Sleeper
635-6610 Diner
635-6611 Tail Car (Observation)

INTERIORS

EA 3.99

One-piece, molded plastic interiors to detail your Rivarossi models in minutes. Complete with all the seats, walls and other items you'd find inside the prototype. Simply remove the car roof and drop in place. Easily painted and superdetailed to create a miniature masterpiece for your railroad!

1920s HEAVYWEIGHTS
635-90050 Coach
635-83162 Pullman
635-83172 Observation
635-85822 Diner
635-83152 Combine

1930s STREAMLINERS
635-90090 Railway Post Office
635-96460 Lower Vista Dome
635-96480 Upper Vista Dome
635-90510 Tail Car (Observation)
635-90520 Roomette
635-201400 Coach
635-209770 Diner

Add international flavor to your passenger traffic with these authentic models. Representing cars from over a dozen different nations and many time periods, each is ready-to-run with exact paint and lettering. Superbly detailed, cars include full-underbody, interiors, diaphragms, European NEM couplers and blackened brass wheels. Most are made to exact scale length, and several are offered in 1/100 scale (as noted), for smaller layouts. Easy to install Interior lighting kits are offered separately for most cars. Additional information about these models, accessories and prototype history can be found in the Roco Catalog (#625-80196).

PRUSSIAN STATE RAILWAY ADMINISTRATION (P.ST.E.V.)

German regional railway 1835-1920.

STEAM-ERA CARS EA 44.99

Models are finished in the green paint scheme from Era I. A matching Class T14 2-8-2T (sold separately), is listed in the Locomotives section.

625-45410 1st/2nd Class Compartment Coach ***NEW***

625-45411 3rd Class Compartment Coach ***NEW***

625-45412 4th Class Compartment Coach ***NEW***

625-45413 Railway Post Office ***NEW***

GERMAN STATE RAILWAYS (DRG)

Deutsche Reichsbahn Gesellschaft (DRG) 1920-1945.

"LONG BAVARIAN BRANCHLINE COACH"

625-44227 Postwar 4-Wheel **16.99**

FULL-LENGTH COACHES EA 49.99

625-44855 3rd Class Coach

625-44862 2nd/3rd Class Coach
These cars can be combined to model a typical passenger train of the period. The correct electric class E17 electric loco (#43719 DC or 43856 AC) in gray, is available separately.

SIX-WHEEL BRANCHLINE COACH

Limited Quantity Available
625-44863 2nd/3rd Class Coach **44.99**
Matches set #43048.

FAST TRAIN COACHES EA TBA

Cars look great behind matching Class E 16 (available separately) electric, listed in the Locomotives section.

625-45443 1st Class Coach Era II (green) ***NEW***
625-45444 1st/2nd Class Coach Era II (green) ***NEW***
625-45445 3rd Class Coach Era II (green) ***NEW***
625-45446 3rd Class Coach/Sleeper -MITROPA Era II (red, yellow) ***NEW***
625-45447 Baggage Coach Era II (green) ***NEW***
625-45448 Railway Post Office Era II (green) ***NEW***

GERMAN STATE RAILWAYS (DR)

Deutsche Reichsbahn (DR) former East German lines from 1945 on.

INTEREGIO CARS

Used on inter-regional express trains.

625-44542 Wurttemburg Baggage Car **54.99**

TYPE 36 EXPRESS

625-45344 1st Class Coach (green) **44.99**

625-45346 Baggage (green) **44.99**

625-45347 Express Baggage (green) **42.99**

RAILBUS

625-13001 VT2 Railbus Set **269.99**
Includes one powered car and one nonpowered trailer.

STANDARD BRANCHLINE COACHES EA 36.99

Limited Quantity Available
625-14207 2nd Class Coach (former Bi31 - Riveted)
625-14210 2nd Class Coach (former BCi34 - Welded)
625-14213 2nd Class Coach (former Ci-31a - Riveted)

RECONDITIONED COACHES EA 39.99 (UNLESS NOTED)

Limited Quantity Available
625-14367 Restaurant Car ("Mitropa" Sand color)
625-14371 2nd Class Coach w/Baggage Compartment (green)

FAST TRAIN COACHES

Limited Quantity Available
625-44028 2nd Class Coach **44.99**
Matches cars in set 44027

"ITALIAN" COACH

Limited Quantity Available
625-44678 2nd Class Coach **59.99**

BI-LEVEL CARS

Limited Quantity Available

625-14382 Two-Unit Bi-Level with Center Trailer **64.99**

THREE-AXLE CARS

625-44860 3rd Class Coach **49.99**

625-44583 2nd Class Compartment Coach **44.99** w/Brakeman's Cabin **44.99**
625-44584 2nd Class Compartment Coach **44.99**
625-44585 2nd Class Compartment Coach **44.99**
625-44586 Twin-Unit 2nd Class Compartment Coach **64.99**

"THUNDERBOX" CARS EA 29.99

Representing downgraded cars still in service during Era IV.

625-44996 2nd Class Coach Era IV (green w/silver roof) ***NEW***
625-44997 2nd Class Coach Era IV(green w/silver roof) ***NEW***
625-44998 2nd Class Coach Era IV (green w/silver roof) ***NEW***
625-44999 Baggage Car Era IV (green w/silver roof) ***NEW***

GERMAN FEDERAL RAILWAYS

Deutsche Bundesbahn (DB) from 1949 on.

RAILBUS

Limited Quantity Available
625-43019 Railbus Trailer VB 98 **64.99**

"TEN" POOL SLEEPER

625-44841 German Federal Railways (DB) **59.99**
"Trans Euro Nacht" (TEN) car pool, with "European Ends." Blue and white paint.

"THUNDERBOX COACHES" EA 26.99 (UNLESS NOTED)

625-44201 2nd Class Coach
625-44211 1st/2nd Class Coach
625-44212 1st Class Coach
625-44222 Standard Baggage **28.99**

REBUILT 44' COACHES EA 26.99

625-44252 2nd Class Coach
625-44253 1st/2nd Class Coach

625-44254 2nd Class Coach w/Baggage Compartment

"STANDARD BRANCHLINE COACHES"

625-44255 40' Mail Car **26.99**
Lettered for the German Federal Postal Service.

Limited Quantity Available
625-14322 Baggage Car **39.99**
625-44223 2nd Class Coach **16.99**

THREE-AXLE COACHES EA 49.99

625-44858 2nd Class Coach
625-44865 1st/2nd Class Coach

FAST TRAIN COACHES

United States Transportation Corps.

625-838 Limited-Run US Army Railway Diner Era III (green, yellow, silver-gray roof) **49.99** ***NEW***

1960S ERA PAINT & LETTERING EA 44.99 (UNLESS NOTED)
625-44543 Baggage (green) **49.99**
625-44546 70' 2nd Class Coach
625-44547 67' 1st/2nd Class Coach
625-44548 70' 1st Class Coach
625-44549 70' Baggage Car
625-44591 Restaurant (green) **52.99**
625-44592 Provisional Baggage Car (green) **41.99**

Limited Quantity Available
625-14008 Coach Set pkg(4) **169.99**
Includes four 2nd Class coaches with different car numbers, paint and lettering of the 1970s.

EXPRESS CARS EA 52.99

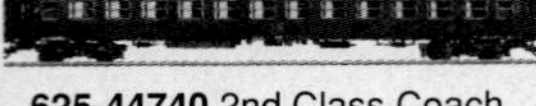

625-44740 2nd Class Coach (green)
625-44741 Express Coach
625-44742 Express Coach

1970s/80s CARS EA 59.99
Blue and cream paint with dark gray roof from Era IV. A matching Class 111 electric loco (625-63640) is available separately, and listed in the Locomotives section of this reference book.

625-44746 2nd Class Coach *NEW*

625-44747 1st Class Coach *NEW*
625-44748 1st/2nd Class Coach *NEW*
625-44749 2nd Class Coach w/Baggage Compartment *NEW*
625-44750 Baggage Car *NEW*

REBUILT CARS EA 33.99

625-45242 2nd Class Coach
625-45243 1st/2nd Class Coach

625-45244 2nd Class/ Baggage

REBUILT "BOGIES" COACHES EA 34.99
Rebuilt during the 1950s with new trucks.

625-44363 64' 2nd Coach
625-44367 64' 1st/2nd Class Coach
625-44370 64' 2nd Class Coach/ Baggage

"PIKE" COACHES EA 35.99

625-44439 67' 2nd Class Express Coach
625-44444 67' 1st Class Express Coach

625-44449 65' Baggage Car
625-44450 67' 1st /2nd Class Express Coach
625-44452 67' 2nd Class Express Sleeper
Painted red and lettered for the German Sleeping and Dining Car Company (DSG)

625-44454 70' Express Mail Car

EXPRESS CARS

1960S CARS EA 59.99
Green scheme, larger 26.4 (about 87') length.

625-44752 2nd Class Coach
625-44753 1st Class Coach (blue)
625-44754 1st/2nd Class Coach
625-44755 2nd Class Coach/ Baggage
625-44756 Baggage

1960S SCHEMES EA 59.99

625-44902 Half Dining Car (maroon, green)

625-44903 2nd Class Coach (green)

DINING CARS

625-44761 Half Dining Car **79.99**
Red and blue "Cockatoo" scheme, with roof-top pantograph, used to power kitchen equipment on prototype.

625-44762 Half Dining Car (red, cream) **64.99**

1970S CARS EA 59.99
Blue & cream paint.

625-44748 1st/2nd Class Coach

"POP" LIVERY CARS EA 59.99
625-44918 2nd Class Coach (blue, white)

Limited Quantity Available
625-44920 2nd Class Coach (blue, Flint Gray)
625-44921 2nd Class Coach (green, Flint Gray)

GERMAN DINING & SLEEPING CAR COMPANY (DSG)
625-44928 Sleeping Car Finished in red w/DSG markings **44.99**

625-45069 Sleeper Era III (Maroon, gold lettering, silver-gray roof) **59.99** *NEW*

SCALE LENGTH CENTER-ENTRY CARS
Models are finished in Ocean Blue and Beige scheme from Era IV.

625-44686 2nd Class Coach **54.99** *NEW*
625-44687 1st/2nd Class Coach **54.99** *NEW*
625-44688 2nd Class Coach w/Baggage Area & Control Cab **69.99** *NEW*
With reversing headlights and red marker lights for push-pull train service.

1/100 CENTER ENTRY CARS EA 34.99
Finished in 1960s green scheme.

625-44932 2nd Class Coach w/Baggage Compartment

Limited Quantity Available
625-44930 2nd Class Coach
625-44931 1st/2nd Class Coach

1/100 SCALE - CORRUGATED METAL ROOFS EA 38.99
Limited Quantity Available
625-44413 1st/2nd Class Coach
625-44414 2nd Class Coach

SPECIAL SCHEMES

625-829 British Army Parlor Car **64.99**
Operated as part of the Berlin Military Train during the cold war. Special paint and lettering includes Royal Corps of Transport and full-color English flags.

625-44900 75' Coach "Touropa" (blue) **54.99**
625-44907 Hummel Tours Couchette Coach **52.99**

625-45300 Touropa Couchette Coach w/Fairing Era III (blue, silver-gray roof) **TBA** *NEW*
625-44137 Tour Group Set-1/100 Scale Era IV pkg(3) **TBA** *NEW*
Includes a Touropa Couchette Coach (blue, silver), and two slightly different styles of Couchette Coaches (one in green and one in blue) with special Scharnow Travel Agency markings.

Limited Quantity Available
625-823 US Army Transport Corps Sleeper **59.99**

1/100 SCALE EA 34.99 (UNLESS NOTED)
Blue and cream, same great detail in a smaller length.

625-44380 2nd Class Coach (green)
625-44381 1st Class Coach (blue)
625-44382 Baggage

Limited Quantity Available
625-44383 2nd Class Couchette Coach **36.99**

75' "SILVERFISH" PUSH-PULL TRAIN

NEW REGIONAL PAINT SCHEME
Limited Quantity Available
625-44247 1st/2nd Class Coach **44.99**

"EUROFIMA"
(Red & cream 1970s colors)

Limited Quantity Available
625-44751 Half Dining Car **79.99**
Equipped with roof-mounted pantograph, to power on-board kitchen.

BI-LEVEL COACHES

Limited Quantity Available
625-14014 Three Car Set **219.99**
Set includes two 2nd Class Coaches and one 1st/2nd Class Coach.

INDIVIDUAL CARS EA 74.99
Cars match equipment in set #14014, but feature different numbers.

Limited Quantity Available
625-14429 2nd Class Coach
625-14431 1st/2nd Class Coach

TOURIST UNION INTERNATIONAL CHARTER CARS EA 49.99
Red, brown and cream paint and are operated by the DB. Cars are 1/100 scale.

625-44228 Party Coach
625-44229 Compartment Coach

CENTER ENTRY CARS
625-44681 1st/2nd Class Coach (green) **39.99**

Limited Quantity Available
625-44683 2nd Class Coach (blue & cream) **59.99**
625-44684 1st/2nd Class Coach (blue & cream) **59.99**
625-44685 2nd Class Coach/ Baggage (blue & cream) **74.99**

SUBURBAN SERVICE (S-BAHN) CARS
Limited Quantity Available
625-44674 75' 1st/2nd Class Coach (orange, white) **49.99**
625-44675 75' 2nd Class Coach (orange, white) **49.99**
625-44676 75' 1st Class Cab Car (orange, white) **79.99**

TRANS EUROPE EXPRESS (TEE)
625-43011 VT115 Four Part Basic Set Era III (red, cream) **329.99** *NEW*
Revised edition now includes digital interface. Set includes powered and dummy cab control cars, Compartment Coach and Bar Coach.

625-43014 Three Car Supplement Set Era III (red, cream) **149.99** *NEW*
Matches cars in set #43011 and includes an Open Plan Coach, Dining Coach and Compartment Coach

COACHES
These models are based on cars in service during 1969-1974, when TEE trains were widely used in western Europe. All finished in the correct red and cream. A matching class 103 electric locomotive (#43839 DC or #43849 AC) is available separately.

FULL-LENGTH

Limited Quantity Available
625-44117 IC Coach Set DB 1969-1974 pkg(3) **169.99**
Includes two First Class coaches and a Restaurant car, equipped with a pantograph to provide power to the kitchen.

1/100 SETS EA 109.99

625-44120 Diner & Two First Class Coaches
625-44121 Bar-Lounge, Half-Restaurant & 1st Class Coach Matches set 44120.

INTERCITY EQUIPMENT

Introduced in 1986, these red, pink and white cars can be seen on "Intercity" routes.

1/100 SCALE

Limited Quantity Available
625-44784 75' Diner **59.99**

FULL-LENGTH CARS

625-44785 2nd Class Coach **59.99**

"INTEREGIO" EQUIPMENT

INTEREGIO COACHES

625-45050 1st Class Coach Aim (Two-Tone Blue) **54.99**
625-45051 2nd Class Coach Bim (Two-Tone Blue) **54.99**
625-45052 "Bistro Cafe" **59.99**

1/100 SCALE EA 34.99

625-45080 1st Class Coach
625-45081 2nd Class Coach
625-45082 Coach "Bistro Cafe"

TRAVEL AGENCY SETS EA 179.99

Each limited-run set includes a trio of coaches with special lettering for travel agency charters.

Limited Quantity Available
625-44098 Set #1 pkg(3)
625-44099 Set #2 pkg(3)

ICE COACH EA 29.99

625-44896 2nd Class Coach

625-44897 1st Class Coach (For #43070)

UNITED GERMAN RAILWAYS (DB-AG)

Former DB and DR lines.

"HALBERSTADT" EXPRESS COACHES EA 64.99

Finished in cream and Linden Green, with Fawn-Brown roof.

Limited Quantity Available
625-14418 2nd Class Couchette Coach
625-14421 2nd Class Coach w/Baggage Compartment

1/100 COMMUTER CARS

625-44940 2nd Class Commuter Coach **39.99**
625-44941 Commuter Coach **39.99**
625-44942 Cab Coach **49.99**

1/100 IC CARS EA 34.99

625-45086 1st Class Coach

625-45087 2nd Class Coach

INTERCITY (IC) COACHES EA 59.99 (UNLESS NOTED)

WHITE & RED W/STRIPE

625-45255 Half-Restaurant Car **64.99**
625-45256 1st Class Coach
625-45257 2nd Class Coach
625-45260 IC Cab Coach **89.99**
Matches others cars in series, includes reversing white (forward) and red (reverse) headlights.

WHITE & RED

625-45267 1st Class IC Coach
625-45268 Coach
625-45269 1st Class Half-Restaurant **79.99**
625-45270 2nd Class Coach
625-45271 2nd Class Coach

625-45068 Sleeper Era V (Traffic Red) DB Auto Train (Auto Zug) Scheme **59.99** ***NEW***
625-45254 1st Class Coach Era V (Orient Red) **59.99** ***NEW***
625-45262 2nd Class Cab Control Car Era V (Traffic Red) **89.99** ***NEW***
Represents the latest prototype with no front flap, additional MU socket and separately mounted boarding steps.

BI-LEVEL COACHES

SECOND SERIES

(Red & white, matches engine #625-63559, sold separately. See Lighting Sets for additional accessories.)

625-45280 2nd Class Bi-Level Coach **89.99**
625-45281 1st Class Bi-Level Coach **89.99**
625-45282 Cab Coach **119.99**

ORIGINAL SERIES

(Turquoise & white, see Lighting Sets for additional Accessories)

625-45285 1st/2nd Class Bi-Level Coach **89.99**

625-45286 2nd Class Bi-Level Coach **89.99**
625-45287 2nd Class Cab Coach **119.99**

MASS TRANSIT EQUIPMENT

625-45297 Coach **54.99**
625-45298 2nd Class Coach **54.99**
625-45299 Cab Coach **79.99**

INTEREGIO

625-45261 2nd Class Cab Coach **89.99**
Matches others cars in series, includes reversing white (forward) and red (reverse) headlights.

ROYAL WUERTTEMBERG STATE RAILWAYS (K.W.ST.E)

German regional railway, 1845-1920.

625-44545 3rd Class Coach **59.99**
Matches equipment in set #44096.

625-44096 Express Coach Set pkg(5) **309.99**
A tribute to the 150th anniversary of this famed regional line, includes four coaches (two in brown and two in green) plus a baggage car. A matching locomotive, #625-43259 is available separately.

Limited Quantity Available
625-44540 Limited-Run Baggage Car Type Gep **59.99**

AUSTRIAN FEDERAL RAILWAYS

Federal Railways of Austria (BBO) until 1956, now Austrian Federal Railways (OBB).

"EUROFIMA" EXPRESS EQUIPMENT

Purchased for international traffic beginning in 1977, cars were delivered in "Blood Orange." In 1990, this was changed to a darker "Traffic Red" and gray scheme. Cars in the older scheme are still in service.

FULL-LENGTH EA 49.99 (UNLESS NOTED)

625-44645 1st/2nd Class Coach (red, gray)
625-44668 2nd Class Coach (red, gray)
625-44647 Dining Car (red, gray) **54.99**
625-44648 2nd Class Coach/Baggage (red, gray) **54.99**

625-44665 1st Class Coach (red, gray)
625-44666 2nd Class Coach (red, gray)

625-45020 2nd Class Coach (orange) **59.99**
625-45021 1st Class Coach (orange) **59.99**

625-45023 2nd Class/ Baggage Car (orange) **59.99**
625-45024 Domestic Service Restaurant Car (orange) **59.99**

625-45075 Trans Euro Nacht (TEN) Pool Sleeper (blue) **59.99**

1/100 SCALE EA 35.99

"Traffic Red" and gray.
625-44318 1st Class Coach-New Graphics
625-44319 2nd Class Coach - New Graphics

MARIAZELLERBAHN NARROW GAUGE (HOE) EA 39.99

625-34007 2nd Class Coach
625-34008 2nd Class Coach/Baggage
Latest brown, white and red scheme of the famous narrow gauge line.

SCHLIEREN CARS EA 49.99

Shorter cars, used on domestic Austrian trains and some international runs.

625-45124 1st Class Coach (red & cream)
625-45125 2nd Class Coach (red & cream)
625-45126 1st/2nd Class Coach/Baggage (red & cream)
625-44488 2nd Class Coach

MULTIPLE-UNIT TRAIN COACHES EA 79.99

Used on the new 4010 trains, these cars match the equipment in sets #43061 (DC power) and #43898 (AC power, cars require new wheelsets, sold separately).

625-43058 1st/2nd Class Coach
625-43059 2nd Class Coach
625-43060 2nd Class Open Interior Coach

PUSH-PULL TRAIN

(Red & silver, matches engine #625-43820, sold separately.)

625-45013 2nd Class Cab Coach **TBA**

625-45015 Middle Unit 2nd Class Coach **59.99**

SWISS FEDERAL RAILWAYS

Includes SBB, CFF and FFS.

BERN-LOTSCHBERG-SIMPLON (BLS) CARS

625-44868 3rd Class Coach (green) **51.99**
625-44893 EW-IV 1st Class IC Coach **56.99**
625-44894 EW-IV 2nd Class IC Coach **56.99**

625-44476 EW-II Baggage Car Era IV/V (blue, white) **49.99** ***NEW***

RIC COACHES

MODERN FULL-LENGTH CARS

625-44891 EW-IV "Children of the SBB" Coach **99.99**
625-44892 2nd Class EW IV Cab Coach **TBA**

625-45088 Baggage Car Type D EW II **49.99**
625-45073 Sleeper Era V (blue) **64.99** *NEW*
Matches rebuilt prototypes, with new window arrangement, modified roof and side fairings.

625-45189 EW-II Baggage/Bicycle Car Era V (green, white) **44.99** *NEW*

EW-IV SERIES CARS

625-44887 Saloon Coach Era V (green, white) **64.99** *NEW*
625-44891 "Children of the SBB" Coach **99.99**
625-44892 Cab Control Car/2nd Class Coach Era V (red, green, white) **TBA** *NEW*
625-44963 Commuter Dining Car Era V (red, white) **89.99** *NEW*
625-44964 1st Class Express Commuter Coach Era V (green, white) **54.99** *NEW*
625-44965 2nd Class Commuter Coach Era V **59.99** *NEW*

150TH ANNIVERSARY EQUIPMENT

Celebrate 150 years of railroad service in Switzerland with these limited edition models.

625-63010 Three Coaches w/Class C 5/6 2-10-0 Loco Era V **TBA** *NEW*
This handsome collector's set is based on the "Historical Train 1930" of restored fantrip equipment. Powering the train is a superb replica of 2-10-0 #2978, one of only four surviving engines of this type. The consist includes a 1st/2nd Class Coach, 2nd Class Coach and 3rd Class Coach (all in green), which match the prototypes. (Three matching cars, #625-44877, #625-44878 and #625-44880, are available separately.)

HISTORIC TRAIN 1930 CARS

Matching cars for set #625-63010 (sold separately) in the current, Era V, green scheme.

625-44877 Dining Car **69.99** *NEW*
625-44878 2nd Class Steel Coach **54.99** *NEW*
625-44880 1st Class Steel Coach w/Barrel Roof **54.99** *NEW*

STANDARD CARS

Purchased in the early 1960s for domestic service.

ORIGINAL GREEN

625-44438 Swiss Federal Postal Administration Mail Car **39.99**

LIGHTWEIGHT "SEETAL" COACHES EA 49.99

625-44730 1st/2nd Class
625-44731 2nd Class

EUROCITY CARS

(Two-tone gray)

COACHES EA 54.99

625-44770 2nd Class Express
625-44771 1st Class Express

PANORAMIC VIEW CARS

Unique cars have large arched windows extending into the roof, providing a panoramic view of the scenery.

625-44769 1st Class Coach Only **99.99**
Can be lighted with set #625-40312 , sold separately.

ITALIAN STATE RAILWAYS (FS)

"CENTO-PORTE " COACHES EA 59.99

Ordered in 1929 and still in use by the late 70s.

625-44691 2nd Class (gray)
625-44775 1st/2nd Class (gray)

EUROFIMA COACHES EA 54.99

625-45218 1st Class-Current Turquoise & Gray Scheme
625-45219 2nd Class-Current Turquoise & Gray Scheme

625-45220 1st Class-Old Two-Tone Gray Scheme
625-45221 2nd Class Old Two-Tone Gray Scheme

NETHERLANDS STATE RAILWAYS

"BLOKKENDOOS" CAR

625-44988 Passenger Coach Era III **TBA** *NEW*
Matches cars in set 43744, which is out of production.

SPANISH STATE RAILWAYS

1/100 SCALE CARS EA 24.99

Limited Quantity Available
625-44462 Baggage

FRENCH NATIONAL RAILWAYS (SNCF)

"CORAIL" COACHES

Each full-length model measures 87 scale feet long.

625-45111 2nd Class Type Vu/B11U **69.99**
625-45113 2nd Class Coach **69.99**
625-45207 Couchette Coach **44.99**
Coach Class
625-45381 1st Class Express VU Era IV-V (gray, white, orange) **69.99** *NEW*

BRUHAT COACH

Limited Quantity Available
625-44273 2nd Class **44.99**

UIC INTERNATIONAL SERVICE COACH EA 49.99

625-45200 1st Class Coach (green & gray) w/"Spaghetti Logo"
625-45201 Coach (green & gray) w/"Spaghetti Logo"

625-45202 2nd Class Coach (green & gray) w/"Spaghetti Logo"
625-45131 1st Class Coach Era IV (gray) **TBA** *NEW*
625-44631 2nd Class Coach Era IV (gray) **TBA** *NEW*

Sleeper Era V 625-45073

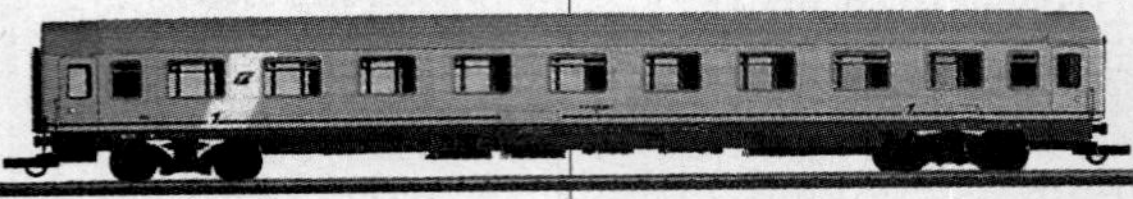

1st Class 625-45218

2nd Class B9 Coach 625-45290

625-45207 2nd Class Couchette **44.99**

Limited Quantity Available

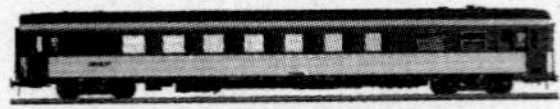

625-45206 Coach VRU in "Corail" (Two-Tone gray & orange) Colors **44.99**

UIC DESIGN COACHES

625-44607 1st/2nd Class Coach (green, cream) **46.99**

Limited Quantity Available
625-44612 1st Class Express Coach "Capitole" **45.99**
Additional coach for sets 44080-and 44087.

LUXEMBOURG NATIONAL RAILWAYS

HISTORIC WURTTEMBURG COACH

Limited Quantity Available
625-44529 2nd /3rd Class (green) **44.99**

SWEDISH STATE RAILWAYS

INTEREGIO CARS EA 54.99

(Blue w/red stripe, matches engine #625-63570, sold separately.)

625-45290 2nd Class B9 Coach

625-45292 2nd Class ABP Coach

THROUGH TRAIN STREAMLINE COACHES EA 54.99

625-44725 1st Class
625-44726 2nd Class
Fluted-side cars are finished in gray, blue and black with white lettering.

CZECHOSLOVAKIAN STATE RAILWAYS (CSD)

Limited Quantity Available
625-14355 Long-Distance Sleeping Car (blue, white) **64.99**

INTERIOR LIGHTING KITS

Sets contain all parts needed, require only minor assembly for installation. For best results, wheels and track should be clean. Specific information on sets to fit each car is provided in the Roco catalog, #625-80196.

625-40300 8-Wheel Short Coaches **12.99**
625-40302 Modern Coaches **12.99**
625-40303 4-Wheel Coaches **10.99**
625-40305 Commuter Baggage **13.99**
625-40306 Commuter Coach **13.99**
625-40307 Prussian Car **13.99**
625-40308 Modern Long Coach **13.99**
625-40310 WURTT Coaches **13.99**
625-40311 FS Coaches **13.99**
625-40312 For Swiss Panoramic View Car #44769 **23.99**
625-40314 Light Set For IR/IC Coaches **22.99**
625-40315 Bi-Level Coach **34.99**
625-40316 Bi-Level Driving Trailer **TBA**

Create authentic steam-era passenger trains with these easy-to-build kits. Five different styles, (30' Overton, 50' Pullman, 50' Overland with Clerestory Roof, 86' Pullman Palace and 60' Harriman) represent cars built from the 1870's to the 1920's. Each is prepainted and lettered. Kits include underbody details, trucks and horn-hook couplers.

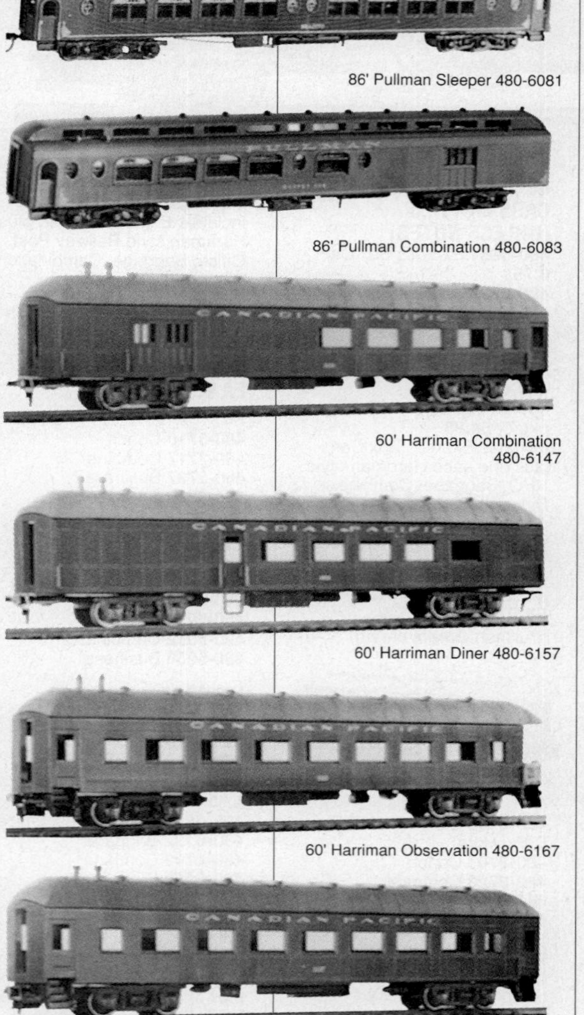

86' Pullman Sleeper 480-6081

86' Pullman Combination 480-6083

60' Harriman Combination 480-6147

60' Harriman Diner 480-6157

60' Harriman Observation 480-6167

60' Harriman Coach 480-6177

UNDECORATED

34' OVERTON CARS EA 9.98
480-3700 Coach
480-3720 Combine
480-3730 Business
480-3740 Baggage
480-3760 Drovers Caboose

50' PULLMAN CARS EA 9.98
480-5001 Coach
480-5021 Baggage
480-5035 Combine
480-5045 Business

50' Overland SleeperCombination 480-5256

50' Pullman Business 480-5071

50' OVERLAND CARS W/CLERESTORY ROOF EA 10.98 (UNLESS NOTED)
480-5200 Mail
480-5210 Baggage
480-5230 Business
480-5250 Sleeper
480-2999 50' Roof Only **3.00**

60' HARRIMAN STYLE CARS EA 10.25
480-5970 Diner
480-5980 Railway Post Office
480-5990 Combination
480-6000 Observation
480-6010 Coach
480-6020 Baggage

86' PULLMAN PALACE CARS EA 10.25
480-6081 Sleeper
480-6082 Observation
480-6083 Combination
480-6084 Diner

BALTIMORE & OHIO

30' OVERTON CARS EA 9.98
(blue, cream)

480-3709 Coach
480-3716 Combine
480-3729 Business
480-3749 Baggage

50' PULLMAN CARS EA 9.98
(blue, cream)

480-5009 Coach
480-5020 Baggage
480-5065 Combination
480-5071 Business

CANADIAN NATIONAL

60' HARRIMAN-STYLE CARS EA 10.25 (UNLESS NOTED)
(light gray, black)

480-6116 Express Reefer **8.98**
480-6126 Railway Post Office
480-6136 Baggage
480-6146 Combination
480-6156 Diner
480-6166 Observation
480-6176 Coach
480-6106 Complete Train pkg(6) **54.98**
Includes Express Reefer, plus Harriman-style Railway Post Office, Baggage, Combination, Diner and Observation.

CANADIAN PACIFIC

60' HARRIMAN-STYLE CARS EA 10.25 (UNLESS NOTED)
(maroon, black)

480-6117 Express Reefer **8.98**
480-6127 Railway Post Office
480-6137 Baggage
480-6147 Combination
480-6157 Diner
480-6167 Observation
480-6177 Coach
480-6107 Complete Train pkg(6) **54.98**
Includes Express Reefer, plus Harriman-style Railway Post Office, Baggage, Combination, Diner and Observation.

CENTRAL PACIFIC

34' OVERTON CARS EA 9.98
(Pullman Green, cream)

480-3705 Coach
480-3725 Combine
480-3735 Business
480-3745 Baggage

CHESAPEAKE & OHIO

50' OVERLAND CARS EA 10.98

480-5215

480-5205 Mail Car ***NEW***
480-5215 Baggage ***NEW***
480-5235 Business ***NEW***
480-5255 Sleeper ***NEW***

CHICAGO, BURLINGTON & QUINCY

34' OVERTON CARS EA 9.98
480-3712 Coach
480-3719 Combine
480-3739 Business
480-3752 Baggage

50' OVERLAND CARS EA 10.98
(Chinese Red and cream, red roof, black and white lettering)

480-5203 Mail
480-5213 Baggage
480-5233 Business
480-5253 Sleeper

CHICAGO & NORTH WESTERN

50' OVERLAND CARS EA 10.98
480-5206 Mail Car ***NEW***
480-5216 Baggage ***NEW***
480-5236 Business ***NEW***
480-5256 Sleeper ***NEW***

COLORADO & SOUTHERN

34' OVERTON EA 9.98
(Pullman Green with black roof and yellow lettering)

480-3754 Coach
480-3772 Business-Observation
480-3782 Baggage
480-3794 Combine

ROUNDHOUSE Products

50' Pullman Coach 480-5006

DENVER & RIO GRANDE WESTERN

34' OVERTON CARS EA 9.98
(cream, red)

480-3702 Coach
480-3732 Business
480-3742 Baggage
480-3722 Combine

50' OVERLAND CARS EA 10.98
480-5201 Mail
480-5211 Baggage
480-5231 Business
480-5251 Sleeper

DENVER & RIO GRANDE WESTERN - "SILVERTON"

34' OVERTON CARS EA 9.98
(black, yellow)

480-3767

480-3707 Coach
480-3714 Combine
480-3727 Business
480-3747 Baggage
480-3767 Drovers Caboose

ILLINOIS CENTRAL

34' OVERTON EA 9.98
(Dark Green with black roof and yellow lettering)

480-3773

480-3755 Coach
480-3773 Business-Observation
480-3783 Baggage
480-3797 Combine

MARYLAND & PENNSYLVANIA

34' OVERTON CARS EA 9.98
480-3711 Coach
480-3718 Combine
480-3738 Business
480-3751 Baggage

NEW YORK CENTRAL

50' OVERLAND CARS EA 10.98
(Pullman Green, gray roof, yellow lettering.)

480-5204 Mail
480-5214 Baggage
480-5234 Business
480-5254 Sleeper

60' HARRIMAN-STYLE CARS EA 10.25 (UNLESS NOTED)
480-6115 Express Reefer **8.98**
480-6125 Railway Post Office
480-6135 Baggage
480-6145 Combine
480-6155 Diner
480-6165 Observation
480-6175 Coach
480-6105 Complete Train pkg(6) **54.98**
Includes Express Reefer, plus one each Harriman-style RPO, Baggage, Combine, Diner and Observation.

NORTHERN PACIFIC

34' OVERTON CARS EA 9.98
(green, silver)

480-3704 Coach
480-3724 Combine
480-3734 Business
480-3744 Baggage

PENNSYLVANIA

34' OVERTON CARS EA 9.98
(maroon, cream)

480-3736

480-3706 Coach
480-3726 Combine
480-3736 Business
480-3746 Baggage

50' PULLMAN CARS EA 9.98
(maroon)

480-5006 Coach
480-5026 Baggage
480-5061 Combination
480-5067 Business

60' HARRIMAN-STYLE CARS EA 10.25 (UNLESS NOTED)
(Tuscan, black)

480-6113 Express Reefer **7.25**
480-6123 Railway Post Office

50' Overland Business 480-5231

50' Pullman Baggage 480-5027

480-6133 Baggage
480-6143 Combination
480-6153 Diner
480-6163 Observation
480-6173 Coach
480-6103 Complete Train pkg(6) **54.98**
Includes Express Reefer, plus Harriman-style Railway Post Office, Baggage, Combination, Diner and Observation.

SANTA FE

34' OVERTON CARS EA 9.98
480-3753 Coach
480-3793 Combine
480-3771 Business
480-3779 Baggage

50' OVERLAND CARS EA 10.98
(Dark Green, black roof, yellow lettering)

480-5202 Mail
480-5212 Baggage
480-5232 Business
480-5252 Sleeper

SIERRA RAILROAD

34' OVERTON CARS EA 9.98
(Pullman Green, cream)

480-3708 Coach
480-3715 Combine
480-3728 Business
480-3748 Baggage

SOUTHERN PACIFIC

34' OVERTON CARS EA 9.98
(yellow/maroon letterboard with black roof, gold and red lettering)

480-3798

480-3756 Coach
480-3774 Business-Observation
480-3784 Baggage
480-3798 Combine

60' HARRIMAN-STYLE CARS EA 10.25 (UNLESS NOTED)
480-5961 Express Box Car **6.75**
480-6121 Railway Post Office
480-6131 Baggage
480-6141 Combine
480-6151 Diner
480-6161 Observation
480-6171 Coach
480-6101 Complete Train pkg(6) **54.98**
Includes Express Box Car, plus one each Harriman-style RPO, Baggage, Combine, Diner and Observation.

UNION PACIFIC

34' OVERTON CARS EA 9.98
(Pullman Green, cream)

480-3723

480-3108 Old Timer UP Photo Car (white)
480-3703 Coach
480-3723 Combine
480-3733 Business
480-3743 Baggage

50' PULLMAN CARS EA 9.98
(Union-Central Pacific, Pullman Green)

480-5002 Coach
480-5022 Baggage
480-5060 Combination
480-5066 Business

60' HARRIMAN-STYLE CARS EA 10.25 (UNLESS NOTED)
(yellow, brown)

480-6114 Express Reefer **8.98**
480-6124 Railway Post Office
480-6134 Baggage
480-6144 Combination
480-6154 Diner
480-6164 Observation
480-6174 Coach
480-6104 Complete Train pkg(6) **54.98**
Includes Express Reefer, plus Harriman style Railway Post Office, Baggage, Combination, Diner and Observation.

VIRGINIA & TRUCKEE

30' OVERTON CARS EA 9.98
(green, yellow)

480-3710 Coach
480-3717 Combine
480-3737 Business
480-3750 Baggage

50' PULLMAN CARS EA 9.98
(green, yellow)

480-5007 Coach
480-5027 Baggage
480-5062 Combination
480-5068 Business

WESTERN PACIFIC

60' HARRIMAN-STYLE CARS EA 10.25
480-5962 Express Box Car **6.75**
480-6122 Railway Post Office
480-6132 Baggage
480-6142 Combine
480-6152 Diner
480-6162 Observation
480-6172 Coach
480-6102 Complete Train pkg(6) **54.98**
Includes Express Box Car, plus one each Harriman-style RPO, Baggage, Combine, Diner and Observation.

WHITE PASS & YUKON

34' OVERTON CARS EA 9.98
480-3713 Coach
480-3770 Business
480-3778 Baggage
480-3792 Combine

TOMAR INDUSTRIES

Drumhead kits include illustrated instructions, cast and machined housing, 1.5V micro-miniature lamp, full-color sign, light diffuser and constant lighting components (4 diodes, ballast lamp and hookup wire) which operate from track power. (Cars may require modification to provide electrical pick-up.) Kits can also be battery powered using #81-812, sold separately. Double kits contain parts for one car with two tailsigns and are $17.45 each.

LIGHTED DRUMHEAD KITS

EA 10.95 (UNLESS NOTED)

TYPICAL APPLICATIONS

Rectangular housing mounted on streamlined observation car.

Round drumhead mounted on heavy-weight observation platform railings. (Some may use rectangular housing).

HW -- Used on Heavyweight Trains (Older style heavy steel or wood cars)

LW -- Used on Lightweight Trains (New style lightweight streamlined cars)

HOUSING STYLES & SHAPES

Pennsy Keystone
Square
Round
Used on observation car railings, tailgates and streamlined cars.

Rectangular & Vertical (Horizontal mounting) Used on all types of tail end cars.

ALASKA

81-89 Herald (LW round)
81-91 Herald NG (HW round)

ALGOMA CENTRAL

81-90 Algoma Central (HW round)

AMTRAK

LW rect.
81-129 Amtrak
81-770 Pere Marquette
81-771 Panama Ltd
81-772 Carolinian
81-773 Lake Shore Ltd
81-774 Abraham Lincoln

ATCHISON, TOPEKA & SANTA FE

81-95 Chief (yellow) (LW round)
81-96 Ranger (LW round)
81-97 Tulsan (LW Round)
81-98 El Capitan (yellow) (LW round)
81-99 San Diegan (blue) (LW round)
81-100 California Ltd (HW round)
81-101 Chief (LW or HW round)
81-102 El Capitan (LW round)
81-103 X-Fare Deluxe (HW round)
81-104 Grand Canyon (HW round)
81-105 Ranger (HW round)
81-106 San Diegan (LW round)
81-107 Super Chief (LW round)
81-108 Conquistador (LW round)
81-109 Kansas City Chief (LW round)
81-110 San Francisco Chief (LW round)
81-111 Texas Chief (LW round)
81-112 Chicagoan (LW round)
81-113 Kansas Cityan (LW round)

81-114 Golden Gate (LW round)
81-115 Grand Canyon (LW round)
81-116 Super Chief/El Capitan (LW round)
81-117 Super Chief (purple) (LW round)
81-118 California Ltd, Scout (HW round)
81-119 Scout (1937) (HW round)
81-600 Oil Flyer (LW round)
81-601 El Pasoan (LW round)
81-602 Scout (LW round)
81-603 Herald (LW round)
81-604 Herald (HW square)
81-605 Chicago-KC-Flyer (HW round)
81-606 Texas Chief, Dallas (HW round)
81-607 Texas Chief, FW-H-G (HW round)
81-608 Valley Flyer (LW round)
81-609 Navajo (HW round)

ATLANTIC COAST LINE

81-120 Florida Special (HW round)
81-121 The Champion (LW rect)
81-122 Florida Special (HW rect)
81-123 Gulf Coast Ltd (HW round)
81-124 Herald (round)

BALTIMORE & OHIO

81-130 Capitol Ltd (HW round)
81-131 Capitol Ltd (LW rect)
81-132 Cincinnatian (LW rect)
81-133 Columbian (HW round)
81-134 National Ltd (HW round)
81-135 Royal Blue (LW Round)
81-136 Shenandoah (LW round)
81-137 Capitol Ltd, 1929 (HW round)
81-138 National Ltd, 1929 (HW round)
81-139 Royal Blue (white) (LW rect)
81-720 Royal Blue (blue) (LW square)
81-721 National Ltd (LW rect)
81-722 Columbian (LW square)
81-723 Great Lakes (HW round)
81-724 Cincinnatian (HW round)
81-725 Diplomat (HW round)
81-726 Royal Blue (HW round)
81-727 Baltimore Special (HW Round)
81-728 Ambassador (HW round)
81-729 Chicago, Washington, New York & Capital Ltd. (Double Kit) (HW round) **17.45**

BOSTON & MAINE

81-140 Alouette (HW round)
81-141 Minuteman (HW rect)
81-142 Flying Yankee (HW rect)
81-143 Alouette (HW rect)
81-220 Bar Harbor Express (LW rect)

CANADIAN NATIONAL

81-150 CNR w/Maple Leaf (HW square)
81-151 Herald (HW square)
81-152 Herald (LW rect)
81-153 The Continental (LW rect)

81-154 Ocean Ltd (HW square)

CANADIAN PACIFIC

81-160 Alouette (HW round)
81-161 Herald (HW square)
81-162 Shield w/Beaver (HW rect)
81-163 Plain Shield w/Beaver (HW rect)
81-164 Canadian (1968) (LW square)
81-165 Dominion (LW square)

81-166 Canadian (1955) (LW rect)
81-167 Alouette (HW rect)
81-168 The Mountaineer (HW round)
81-169 Empress (HW round)
81-920 Expo Ltd (LW rect)
81-921 Trans-Canada Ltd (HW rect)
81-922 Canadian Shield (HW rect)
81-923 Le Quebec (LW rect)

CENTRAL NEW JERSEY

81-260 Blue Comet (HW round)
81-440 Herald (HW rect)

CHESAPEAKE & OHIO

81-170 C&O for Progress (HW round)
81-171 C&O Lines (HW square)
81-172 Flying Virginian (HW square)
81-173 George Washington (HW round)
81-174 George Washington Portrait (HW round)
81-175 The Sportsman (HW square)
81-176 Chessie (LW rect)

CHICAGO & ALTON

81-93 Alton Ltd (HW round)

CHICAGO, BURLINGTON & QUINCY

81-177 Pioneer Zephyr (LW rect)

81-178 Kansas City Zephyr (Double Kit) (LW rect) **17.45**
81-179 Burlington & Denver Zephyr (Double Kit) (LW rect) **17.45**
81-180 Advance Texas Zephyr (HW rect)
81-181 Buffalo Bill (HW rect)
81-182 Burlington Route (HW rect)
81-183 California Zephyr (LW rect)
81-184 Colorado Ltd (HW rect)
81-185 Texas Zephyr (LW rect)
81-635 Sam Houston Zephyr (LW rect)
81-636 Texas Zephyr w/Star (LW rect)
81-637 Twin City Zephyr 1938 (LW rect)
81-638 Twin City Zephyr 1937 (LW Square)

CHICAGO & EASTERN ILLINOIS

81-186 Cardinal (HW round)
81-187 Dixieland (HW round)
81-500 Dixie Flagler (LW rect)
81-501 Dixie Mail (HW round)
81-502 Dixie Flyer (HW round)
81-503 Dixie Ltd (HW round)
81-504 Dixie Express (HW round)
81-505 Silent Knight (HW round)
81-506 Zipper (HW round)
81-507 Cardinal (HW round)

CHICAGO GREAT WESTERN

81-189 Corn Belt Route (HW round)

CHICAGO, INDIANAPOLIS & LOUISVILLE (MONON)

81-410 The Hoosier Line (HW round)

81-411 Monon Special (HW round)
81-412 The Hoosier (LW round)
81-413 The Tippecanoe (LW round)
81-414 Thoroughbred (HW round)
81-415 Herald (HW round)
81-416 Red Devil (HW round)

CHICAGO & NORTH WESTERN

81-190 "400" (HW round)
81-191 "400" (LW rect)
81-192 Columbine (HW round)
81-193 Overland Ltd (HW round)
81-194 Viking (HW round)
81-195 San Fran Overland Ltd (HW round)
81-196 "49er" (LW rect)
81-197 Herald (HW round)
81-198 NW Ltd (HW round)
81-199 Flambeau (HW round)
81-790 The Namekagon (Double Kit) (LW rect) **17.45**
81-791 The 400 & Herald (Double Kit) (HW round) **17.45**
81-792 Northwestern & Herald Double Kit (HW square) **17.45**

CHICAGO, ROCK ISLAND & PACIFIC

81-450 Twin Star Rocket (LW rect)
81-451 Corn Belt Rocket (LW rect)
81-452 Oklahoma Rocket (LW rect)
81-453 Golden State (LW rect)

81-454 Golden State (HW round)
81-455 Apache (HW round)
81-456 Rocky Mountain Ltd (HW round)
81-457 Choctaw Rocket (LW rect)
81-458 Golden Rocket (LW rect)
81-459 Arizona Ltd (LW rect)
81-730 The Rocket (LW round)
81-731 Texas Rocket (LW rect)
81-732 Rocket (LW round)
81-733 Quad City Rocket (LW round)
81-734 RI, Route of the Rocket (LW round)
81-735 Zephyr Rocket (LW rect)
81-736 Rocky Mountain Rocket (LW rect)
81-737 Golden State (LW square)
81-738 Rocky Mountain Limited (HW rect)

TOMAR INDUSTRIES

CMSTP&P (MILW)
81-200 Olympian (HW round)
81-201 Pioneer Ltd (HW round)
81-202 Sioux (HW round)
81-203 Southwest Ltd (HW round)
81-204 Columbian w/MILW (HW round)

81-205 Olympian w/MILW (HW round)
81-206 Olympian Hiawatha (HW round)
81-207 Pacific Express w/MILW (HW round)
81-208 Varsity w/MILW (HW round)
81-209 Arrow w/MILW (HW round)
81-570 Pioneer Ltd w/MILW (HW round)
81-571 Marquette w/MILW (HW round)
81-572 Chippewa w/MILW (HW round)
81-573 Omaha Chicago Limited (LW round)
81-574 Hiawatha (LW round)
81-575 Arrow (HW square)

COLORADO MIDLAND
81-210 Pikes Peak Route (HW round)

COTTON BELT
81-700 Lone Star Trains (HW rect)

DELAWARE & HUDSON
81-220 Bar Harbor Express (LW rect)
81-221 Champlain (LW rect)
81-222 D&H Shield (HW round)
81-223 Laurentian (LW rect)

81-224 Montreal Ltd (LW rect)
81-225 Plain Shield (HW round)
81-226 Adirondack (LW round)

DELAWARE, LACKAWANNA & WESTERN
81-227 Phoebe Snow, Double Kit (LW rect) 17.45

81-228 Phoebe Snow (HW round)
81-229 Lackawanna Limited (HW rect)
81-473 Sussex County Express (HW round)
81-474 Lackawanna Ltd (HW round)

DENVER & RIO GRANDE WESTERN
(Narrow Gauge & Standard Gauge)
81-230 California Zephyr (LW rect)
81-231 Panoramic (HW round)
81-232 Prospector (LW round)
81-233 San Juan (NG round)
81-234 Scenic Lines (HW round)
81-235 Scenic Ltd (HW round)
81-236 Shavano (NG round)
81-237 The Royal Gorge (LW round)

DULUTH, MISSABE & IRON RANGE
81-215 Herald (HW round)

EAST BROAD TOP
81-149 Herald, Narrow Gauge (rectangular)

ERIE
81-240 Erie Ltd (HW rect)
81-241 Herald (HW square)
81-242 Pacific Express (HW square)
81-243 Atlantic Express (HW square)
81-244 The Midlander (HW square)
81-568 Erie Limited (HW square)
81-569 Herald (HW round)

FLORIDA EAST COAST
81-550 Florida East Coast Ltd (HW round)
81-551 Miamian (HW round)
81-552 Herald (HW round)

GRAND TRUNK WESTERN
81-480 International (HW rect)
81-481 Maple Leaf (HW square)
81-482 La Salle (HW square)
81-483 Inter-City Ltd (HW square)

GREAT NORTHERN
81-250 Cascadian (HW rect)
81-251 Empire Builder, Goat (HW square)
81-252 Empire Builder, Neon (LW square)
81-253 Herald (HW round)
81-254 Oriental Ltd, Red Dot (HW rect)
81-255 Oriental Ltd, Goat (HW rect)
81-256 Western Star (LW square)
81-262 Badger (LW rect)
81-263 Gopher (LW rect)
81-264 Badger/Gopher Double Kit (LW rect) 17.45
81-490 Oriental Limited, Double Kit (HW rect) 17.45
81-491 Empire Builder (HW square)
81-492 International Ltd (HW rect)
81-493 International Ltd (LW square)
81-494 Herald (HW square)
81-495 The Red River Neon (LW square)

GREEN BAY & WESTERN
81-685 Green Bay Route (HW round)

GULF, MOBILE & NORTHERN
81-760 The Rebel (LW rect)
81-761 Road of Service (HW round)

GULF, MOBILE & OHIO
81-257 Abe Lincoln (LW square)

81-258 Alton Ltd (HW round)
81-259 Ann Rutledge (LW rect)
81-540 Abraham Lincoln (LW square)
81-541 Gulf Coast Rebel (LW round)
81-542 St Tammany Special (HW round)
81-543 Rebel (LW square)

ILLINOIS CENTRAL
81-245 Panama Ltd (HW rect)
81-246 City of New Orleans (LW rect)
81-247 Seminole (HW square)
81-248 Daylight (LW square)
81-249 Night Diamond (HW square)
81-900 Green Diamond (HW square)
81-901 Herald (LW rect)
81-902 Panama Ltd (LW rect)
81-903 Daylight (LW rect)
81-904 City of Miami (LW rect)
81-905 Panama Limited (LW square)
81-906 Herald (HW round)

KANSAS CITY SOUTHERN
81-405 Flying Crow (HW round)
81-406 Southern Belle (LW rect)
81-407 Herald (LW square)

LAKE ERIE, FRANKLIN & CLARION
81-559 Herald (rect)

LEHIGH & NEW ENGLAND
81-265 Herald (HW round)

LEHIGH VALLEY
81-460 Black Herald (HW rect)
81-461 Black Diamond, Double Kit (HW rect) 17.45
81-462 Black Diamond (HW round)

LONG ISLAND
81-750 Sunrise Special (HW keys)
81-751 Sundowner (HW rect)
81-752 Cannonball (HW square)

LOUISIANA & ARKANSAS
81-408 Southern Belle-Portrait (LW rect)
81-716 Hustler (HW rect)
81-717 Shreveporter (HW rect)

LOUISVILLE & NASHVILLE
81-261 Pan-American (HW round)
81-640 Humming Bird (LW rect)
81-641 Herald (HW round)

MICHIGAN CENTRAL
81-449 Niagara Falls Deluxe (HW square)

MISSOURI-KANSAS-TEXAS

81-530 Texas Special, Double Kit (HW rect) 17.45
81-531 Texas Special (red) (LW rect)
81-532 Texas Special (white) (LW rect)
81-533 Katy Flyer (HW square)
81-534 Herald (HW rect)

MISSOURI & KANSAS
81-715 Herald (HW round)

MISSOURI PACIFIC

81-273 Sunshine Special (HW rect)
81-274 Texas Eagle (LW rect)
81-275 Herald (HW round)
81-276 The Star (HW round)
81-277 The Texan (HW round)
81-660 The Orleanan (HW round)
81-661 Hot Springs Special (HW rect)
81-662 Delta Eagle (LW rect)
81-663 The Westerner (LW rect)
81-664 Kay See Flyer (LW rect)
81-665 Sunshine Special (HW round)
81-667 Royal Gorge (HW square)
81-668 Royal Gorge (HW round)
81-669 Texan (LW rect)

NdeM
81-995 (LW square)

NEW YORK, NEW HAVEN & HARTFORD
81-270 Yankee Clippers (HW rect)
81-271 Merchants Ltd (LW rect)
81-272 Herald (square)

NEW YORK CENTRAL
81-278 Pacemaker (HW rect)
81-279 James Whitcomb Riley (LW rect)
81-280 20th Century Ltd (HW rect)
81-281 20th Century Scroll (HW rect)

81-282 20th Century Ltd (LW rect)
81-283 Empire State Express (HW rect)
81-284 New England States (LW rect)
81-285 Pacemaker (LW rect)
81-286 Twilight Ltd (LW rect)
81-287 Wolverine (HW rect)
81-288 Commodore Vanderbilt (HW rect)
81-289 Advance 20th Century (HW rect)
81-520 Knickerbocker (HW rect)
81-521 The Michigan (HW rect)
81-522 Cleveland Flyer (HW round)
81-523 New England States (LW rect)
81-524 Ohio State Ltd (LW rect)
81-525 Mercury (LW rect)
81-526 Laurentian (LW rect)
81-527 NYC System (LW rect)
81-528 NYC System (black) (HW rect)
81-529 South Western Ltd (LW rect)
81-670 James Whitcomb Riley (LW rect)
81-671 Commodore Vanderbilt (LW rect)
81-672 Detroiter (HW rect)
81-673 Southwestern Ltd (HW rect)
81-674 Lake Shore Ltd (HW rect)
81-675 Empire State Express (HW round)
81-676 Motor Queen (HW square)

NICKEL PLATE

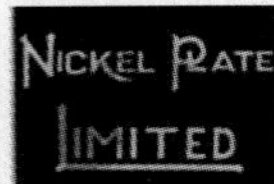

81-296 Nickel Plate Ltd (HW rect)
81-298 Herald (HW square)
81-299 Herald (HW rect)

NORFOLK & WESTERN
81-290 Cavalier (LW rect)
81-291 Herald (HW round)
81-292 Herald (HW rect)
81-293 Pocahontas (LW rect)
81-294 Powhatan Arrow (LW rect)
81-295 Banner Blue (LW rect)

NORTHERN PACIFIC
81-300 North Coast Ltd (LW rect)
81-301 North Coast Ltd (HW round)
81-302 Herald (HW round)
81-303 Puget Sound Ltd (HW round)
81-304 Yellowstone Comet (HW round)
81-305 Yellowstone Park (HW round)

NORTHWESTERN PACIFIC
81-780 Herald (HW round)
81-781 Redwood Empire Route (HW round)

ONTARIO NORTHLAND
81-269 Shield (LW rect)

TOMAR INDUSTRIES

PENNSYLVANIA

81-310 Broadway Ltd (HW keys)
81-311 Broadway Ltd (LW keys)
81-312 Cincinnati Ltd (HW keys)
81-313 General (HW keys)
81-314 Golden Arrow (HW keys)
81-315 Jeffersonian (LW keys)
81-316 Liberty Ltd (LW keys)
81-317 Manhattan Ltd (HW keys)
81-318 Pennsylvania Ltd (HW keys)
81-319 Rainbow (HW keys)
81-320 Senator (LW keys)
81-321 South Wind (LW keys)
81-322 Spirit of St Louis (HW keys)
81-323 Congressional (LW keys)
81-324 Trail Blazer (LW keys)

81-325 Statesman (HW keys)
81-326 Representative (HW keys)
81-580 Pittsburger (HW keys)
81-581 Congressional (HW keys)

PENNSYLVANIA

81-582 President (HW keys)
81-583 Liberty Ltd Chicago (HW keys)
81-584 Red Bird (LW keys)
81-585 Spirit of St Louis (HW keys)
81-586 Detroit Arrow (HW keys)
81-587 Pennsylvania Special (HW keys)
81-588 Herald (LW keys)
81-589 The Red Arrow (HW keys)
81-590 The Steeler (HW keys)
81-591 The Clevelander (HW keys)
81-592 The Southland (HW keys)
81-593 Buckeye Ltd (HW keys)
81-594 The Senator (HW keys)
81-595 Gotham Ltd (HW keys)
81-596 The Metropolitan (HW keys)
81-597 The St Louisan (HW keys)
81-598 The American (HW keys)
81-599 St Louis Express (HW keys)
81-945 Herald (round)
81-946 Trail Blazer (LW keys)

PERE MARQUETTE

81-327 Resort Special (HW round)
81-445 Pere Marquette (Double Kit) (LW round) **17.45**

READING

81-560 Herald (LW rect)
81-561 Iron Horse Ramble (HW round)

RICHMOND, FREDERICKSBURG & POTOMAC

81-475 Old Dominion (HW round)

RUTLAND

81-710 Mount Royal (HW rect)

ST LOUIS -- SAN FRANCISCO

HW round.

81-328 Firefly
81-329 Meteor
81-510 5000 Mile Service
81-511 Will Rogers
81-512 Lead Belt Special

SAN DIEGO & ARIZONA

81-94 San Diego Short Line -- Herald (HW round)

SEABOARD AIR LINE

81-362 Silver Meteor (LW square)
81-363 Orange Blossom (LW square)
81-364 Herald (HW round)
81-365 Silver Comet (LW square)

SEABOARD COAST LINE

81-690 Herald (LW round)

SIERRA

81-748 Preserving Yesterday for Tomorrow (HW round)
81-749 Herald (HW round)

SOO LINE

81-420 Twin City - Seattle (HW round)
81-421 Soo-Spokane-Portland (Train Deluxe) (HW round)
81-422 Herald (HW rect)
81-423 The Mountaineer (HW round)

SOUTHERN

81-350 Crescent Ltd (LW rect)
81-351 Crescent (LW rect)
81-352 Queen Crescent Ltd (HW round)
81-353 Herald (HW round)
81-354 Carolina Special (HW rect)
81-355 Royal Palm (HW round)
81-356 Southerner (LW rect)
81-357 Tennessean (Double Kit) (LW rect) **17.45**
81-358 Royal Palm (HW rect)
81-359 Memphis Special (HW rect)
81-910 Crescent-Sunset Ltd (HW round)

SOUTHERN PACIFIC

81-330 Cascade (HW round)
81-331 Daylight Ltd (HW round)
81-332 Daylight (LW rect)
81-333 Daylight (HW round)
81-334 Del Monte (HW round)
81-335 Golden State (HW round)
81-430 Golden State (LW rect)
81-336 Lark (LW rect)
81-337 Oregonian (HW round)
81-338 Overland Ltd (HW round)
81-339 Owl (Photo) (HW round)
81-340 San Joaquin (LW rect)
81-935 Sunbeam (LW square)
81-341 Shasta (HW round)
81-342 Sunbeam (LW rect)
81-343 Sunset Ltd (HW round)
81-344 San Fran Overland Ltd (HW round)
81-345 West Coast (HW round)
81-346 Sunset Ltd (LW rect)
81-347 Sunbeam (HW round)
81-348 Pacific Ltd (HW round)
81-349 "49er" (LW rect)
81-431 Herald (LW round)
81-432 Owl (HW round)
81-433 Apache (HW round)
81-434 Argonaut (HW round)
81-435 Imperial (HW round)
81-436 Crescent/Sunset (HW round)
81-437 Golden State (LW square)
81-438 Klamath (HW round)
81-439 Sun-Tan Special (HW round)
81-930 St Louis Express (HW round)
81-931 Golden Coast Ltd (HW round)
81-932 Cascade (LW rect)
81-933 Lark (LW round)
81-934 Shasta Ltd. (HW round)

SPOKANE, PORTLAND & SEATTLE

81-360 Columbia River Express (HW rect)
81-361 Empire Builder (HW square)
81-680 Herald (HW rect)

TEXAS & PACIFIC

81-297 Herald (LW rect)

TEXAS STATE

81-709 Herald (LW round)

UNION PACIFIC

81-370 Cheyenne (LW square)
81-371 City Of Los Angeles (LW square)
81-372 City Of San Francisco (LW round)
81-373 City of Los Angeles (LW round)
81-374 Columbine (HW round)
81-375 Denver Ltd (HW round)
81-376 Los Angeles Ltd (HW round)
81-377 LA Ltd, Flower (HW round)
81-378 Overland Ltd (HW round)
81-379 Portland Rose (HW round)
81-380 SF Overland Ltd (HW round)
81-381 "49er" (LW rect)
81-382 City of Denver (HW square)
81-383 City of Denver (LW round)
81-384 City of Las Vegas (LW round)
81-385 Old Timer (LW round)
81-386 Pony Express (HW round)
81-387 Challenger (HW round)
81-388 Streamline Challenger (LW round)
81-389 Streamline (LW round)
81-620 City of Portland (LW round)
81-621 Adios (LW round)
81-622 City of St Louis (LW round)
81-623 Herald (LW round)
81-624 Continental Ltd (HW round)
81-625 City of San Francisco (LW square)

VIA

81-470 Herald (LW rect)

VIRGINIA & TRUCKEE

81-214 Herald (round)

WABASH

81-390 Wabash Cannonball (HW round)
81-391 Bluebird (LW rect)
81-392 Banner Blue (HW round)
81-393 City of St Louis (LW rect)
81-394 City of Kansas City (LW rect)
81-395 Banner Ltd (HW round)
81-396 Kansas City-Omaha-Des Moines Limited (HW round)
81-397 The Midnight (HW round)
81-398 Detroit-St Louis Ltd (HW round)
81-399 Kansas City-Pacific Coast Ltd (LW round)
81-650 Banner Blue (LW rect)
81-651 Detroit-St Louis Ltd (LW round)
81-652 Midnight (LW round)
81-653 City of St Louis (LW round)
81-654 Blue Bird-Cannon Ball (LW square)

WESTERN MARYLAND

81-479 Fast Freight Lines (HW round)

WESTERN PACIFIC

81-400 California Zephyr (LW rect)
81-401 Scenic Ltd (HW round)

WHITE PASS & YUKON

81-92 Herald (HW round)

MISCELLANEOUS

81-990 Clown (round)
81-991 Freedom Train (LW square)
81-992 Santa Claus (round)
81-993 Hot Dog Special (round)
81-994 Chessie Steam Special (square)
81-996 Circus Parade Ltd (round)

ACCESSORIES

BATTERY POWER HOOK-UP KIT

81-812 2.95
Use wherever 1.5V is needed. Ideal for drumheads, markers etc. Fits inside most HO or larger cars. Includes AA battery holder (less battery), micro-switch and wire.

PICK-UP SHOES

Preformed metal shoes for better electrical pick-up.

081-801 Constant Intensity Light **2.95**
Includes 14V ballast lamp, four diodes and hook-up wire. Powers up to four 1.5V lamps from track power.

081-816 Ballast Bulb pkg(2) **1.39**
Replacement for #801.

081-802 Micro Miniature Slide Switch pkg(2) **2.50**
Very small SPDT switch.

81-804 Passenger Car pkg(4) **3.95**
81-805 Loco pkg(4) **3.95**
#804, 805 include drawings, instructions, wire and screws.
81-814 Bulk Passenger & Caboose pkg(8) **2.95**
81-815 Bulk Locomotive Only pkg(8) **2.95**
#814, 815 are bulk packs with shoes only. Less hardware and instructions.

END-OF-TRAIN DEVICE EA 11.95

Choose from red or amber lens to match prototype practice. Fully assembled and painted, includes metal casting with permanent lens, 1.5V lamp, electronic flasher unit, AA battery holder (less battery) and instructions.

81-806 Amber
81-822 Red
081-819 1.5V Lamps pkg(2) **4.95**
Replacement bulbs for #806 or #822.

AXIALIGHT GREEN

81-820 1.5V pkg(2) **3.50**
Very small size, ideal for limited space.

ADLAKE MARKER LIGHTS EA 12.45

The finishing touch for any observation car or caboose! Available in two authentic color combinations to match prototype practice.

Includes two brass markers with lenses installed, 1.5V lamp and instructions.

081-807 Green & Red.
081-809 Yellow & Red
081-818 Adlake Replacement Lamps pkg(2) **7.45**
1.5V bulbs for #807 or #809, also fits all drumheads.

081-813 Red Tail Light Kit **2.95**
Includes 1.5V red lamp and instructions.

CATALOG

For a free copy of the latest catalog, please write Tomar at: 9520 E. Napier Ave. Benton Harbor, MI 49022

All products made in the USA.

Diner 732-830

BUDD HI-LEVEL PASSENGER CARS

Introduced on Santa Fe's "El Capitan" in 1954, these streamlined, hi-level cars were later acquired by Amtrak. Easy-to-build kits feature plastic bodies and are available undecorated, prepainted and unlettered in silver (correct for ATSF or Amtrak schemes) or as ATSF cars, painted silver with black lettering. Models are also offered with blackened brass wheelsets as noted.

STEP-UP COACH

These cars were used between conventional equipment and hi-level cars.

732-801 Undecorated Body **10.95**
732-810 Less Couplers & Wheels **25.95**
732-811 Painted Silver w/Blackened Wheels **29.95**
732-812 ATSF w/Blackened Wheels **32.95**
732-814 Amtrak Remodeled Coach-Dorm (Phase III) **35.95**
732-818 Unpainted Remodeled Coach-Dorm **29.95**
732-434 Amtrak Hi-Level Coach/Dorm Window Inserts **4.95**
Converts Train Station Products/Detail Associates High-Level, Step-Up Coach to a modern Amtrak Hi-Level Coach-Dorm.

COACH

732-820 Less Couplers & Wheels **25.95**
732-821 Silver w/Blackened Wheels **29.95**
732-822 ATSF w/Blackened Wheels **32.95**
732-802 Undecorated Body **10.95**

DINER

732-830 Less Couplers & Wheels **25.95**
732-831 Painted Silver w/Blackened Wheels **32.95**
732-832 ATSF w/Blackened Wheels **35.95**
732-803 Undecorated Body **10.95**

MATERIAL HANDLING CAR PARTS

CONVERSION KIT

732-440 MHC II **10.95**
Modernizes the Con-Cor Material Handling Car from the MHC I to the current MHC II (1500 series) cars now in Amtrak service. Includes side ladders, door locking wheels and the correct GSI trucks. All parts are also sold separately.

INDIVIDUAL PARTS

732-441 Locking Wheels pkg(2) **2.95**
Now in use on MHC I (1400 series) and newer MHC II (1500 series) cars.

732-442 Side Ladders pkg(4) **2.95**
Current style, now in use on most MHC I and MHC II cars.

732-443 Ladder & Wheel Set **4.95**
Complete set of four ladders and two locking wheels, as used on MHC I and MHC II type cars.

Step-Up Coach 732-812
Coach 732-822

Amtrak Coach Dorm 732-814-Painted, 732-818-Unpainted

MHC II Conversion Kit 732-440

DIAPHRAGMS

Unpainted plastic parts, unless noted.

AMFLEET STYLE

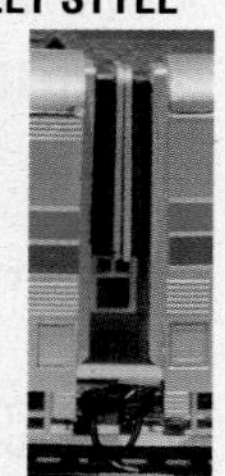

For Amfleet, Superliner I and II, Horizon, High-Level, Metroliner/Cab Control cars and some Heritage Fleet cars. Fits Train Station Products, Detail Associates, Con-Cor, Bachmann, Walthers and others.

732-400 1 Pair **2.95**
732-401 3 Pair **7.95**

HI-LEVEL STYLE

A unique design, used on the Budd Hi-Level cars which operated on Santa Fe's "El Capitan," and were later acquired by Amtrak. Includes support bars and leaf springs.

732-407 1 Pair **2.95**
732-452 Working 1 Pair **TBA**
NEW

UP STYLE

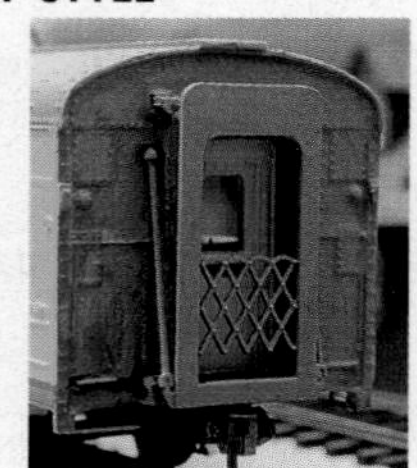

For Con-Cor, AHM, Rivarossi, Athearn, brass and other models. Easily modified to make other styles. This diaphragm was installed on most of Union Pacific's modern passenger fleet and remained in use when the cars entered Amtrak service. Includes end gates, support bars and leaf springs.

732-403 1 Pair **2.95**
732-404 3 Pair **7.95**
732-453 Working 1 Pair **TBA**
NEW

TUBULAR STYLE

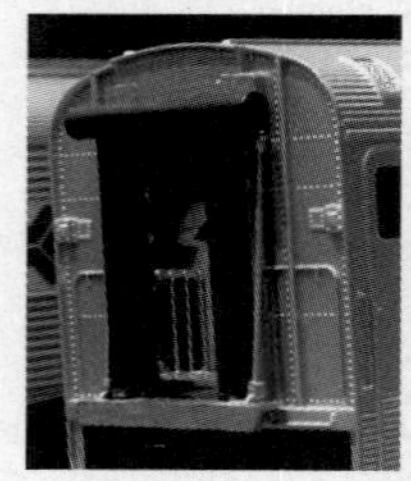

732-405 1 Pair **3.95**
For Con-Cor, AHM, Rivarossi, Athearn, brass and other models. This style of diaphragm is still in use on most privately owned cars and was found on many Amtrak Heritage Fleet cars.

STANDARD MODERN STYLE

Many railroads used this style of diaphragm, or a very similar style, on modern, streamlined cars. Subsequently, they could be found on much of Amtrak's Heritage Fleet. Includes support bars and leaf springs.

732-406 1 Pair **2.95**
732-451 Working 1 Pair **TBA**
NEW

COUPLERS & TRUCKS

From the roundhouse to the board room, everyone wants to know what happened over on the SP this morning. Detours across the Lost Creek usually come later in the year, when the fruit and vegetable harvest clogs the SP main with dozens of extra reefer drags.

Rumor has it that a coupler knuckle let go on a fast freight somewhere up in the Sierras. No one was hurt, but the line is blocked. More detour trains are coming - and coming fast!

All the stops have been pulled out to keep Espee's pride and joy, the famed "Daylight", rolling. Still off schedule and running like her tail is on fire, the "most beautiful train in the world" makes a rare appearance on the Lost Creek line. And what a show it is! An unearthly roar of prime movers at full throttle, screaming air horns and a blast of air as the train flies by. They're nudging past the speed limit now, and you can imagine what will happen when they hit the edge of town!

Ken Estes of Lakewood, California, is the owner/operator of the Lost Creek Railroad, a shortline set in the California foothills. This is one of two modules Ken built and photographed outdoors, which he hopes will one day be part of a complete layout.

Models and Photo by Ken Estes

WALTHERS™

Couplers, coupler pockets and trucks for use with Walthers and other freight and passenger cars.

COUPLERS

CUSHION CAR COUPLER POCKET

933-1030 Coupler Pocket Kit pkg(8) **3.98**
Freight cars coupled at speeds over five miles per hour can hit with enough force to severely damage loads. End-of-car cushioning devices are used on freight cars that carry automobiles, glass, canned goods, paper and other fragile loads.

Easy to install, this kit simulates end-of-car cushioning devices used on box cars, auto racks, cabooses and other types of cars. The longer draft gear increases the distance between cars for a more realistic appearance. Parts to modify four cars and complete instructions are included. Horn-hook or Kadee® #5 couplers work well with this kit.

DUMMY COUPLERS

933-1045 12 Pair **2.98**

HORN-HOOK COUPLERS

933-995 pkg(12) **1.98**
Replacement coupler fits all Walthers freight and passenger cars. Molded in Delrin® plastic.

PASSENGER CAR TRUCKS

RIGID PLASTIC W/METAL WHEELS

Trucks are molded in black Delrin® plastic, with one-piece rigid sideframes. Nonmagnetic brass axles. RP25 wheels.

933-996 GSC 1 Pair **5.98**

SUPERLINER CARS

933-1046 Air Sprung Type 1 pair 5.98
Original style used on Superliner cars, prototypes were fitted with a large airbag in place of springs.

FREIGHT TRUCKS

Suitable for all types of freight equipment. Trucks are assembled, unless noted.

RIGID PLASTIC W/PLASTIC WHEELS 1 PAIR EA 1.98

Molded in black Delrin® plastic with one-piece, rigid sideframes, nonmagnetic brass axles with Delrin RP25 wheels.

933-1010 Arch Bar

933-1011 "T" Section

933-1012 Bettendorf

933-1013 Roller Bearing

RIGID PLASTIC W/METAL WHEELS 1 PAIR EA 2.98

Black Delrin® plastic, with one-piece rigid sideframe, nonmagnetic brass axles and RP25 blackened brass wheels.

933-1007 Roller Bearing

933-1008 Bettendorf

933-1009 "T" Section

933-1018 Arch Bar 1 Pair

SPRUNG PLASTIC W/PLASTIC WHEELS EA 2.98

Easy-to-assemble with black Delrin® sideframes, bolsters and wheels. Sprung and equalized. Nonmagnetic brass axles.

933-1001 Bettendorf 1 Pair

933-1002 Diamond Arch Bar 1 Pair

933-1003 "T" Section Bettendorf 1 Pair

933-1004 Andrews 1 Pair

933-1005 Roller Bearing 1 Pair

WHEELSETS

With nonmagnetic brass axles.

BRASS WHEELS

933-383 36" pkg(4) **2.98**
933-870 33" pkg(4) **2.79**

BLACK PLASTIC WHEELS

933-1006 33" pkg(12) **2.98**

AMERICAN LIMITED MODELS

COUPLING KIT

147-6100 Close Coupling Adaptor Kit **2.50**
For Athearn F7A/B diaphragms and draft gear box.

ACCURAIL®

TRUCKS

1 PAIR EA 2.98

Trucks feature acetal plastic sideframes and wheelsets.

112-100 Bettendorf

112-102 Roller Bearing

WHEELSETS

112-101 33" Acetal Plastic pkg(12) **2.98**

COUPLERS

ACCUMATE COUPLERS

Easy-to-use coupler works well manually or magnetically, and can be dropped into the coupler box of most cars. With no tiny springs or small metal stampings to lose, it's great for beginners. Draftless knuckle profile allows operation of long, heavy trains without the effects of "coupler rideup."

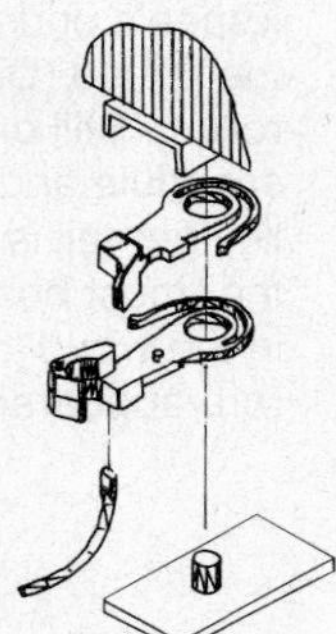

112-1011 2 Pair **1.59**
112-1012 12 Pair **8.98**
112-1013 Medium Shank 2 Pair **1.98**
112-1014 Long Shank 2 Pair **1.98**
112-1020 Scale Knuckle & Draft Gear Box 2 Pair **2.98**

COUPLER TOOLS

112-1001 Accumate Switchman **1.99**
Hand-held uncoupler works anywhere on your layout; simply insert between Accumate couplers and turn.

112-1010 Height Gauge **2.49**
Make sure your Accumate couplers are positioned correctly.

ALEXANDER SCALE MODELS

We have worked closely with this manufacturer to provide accurate delivery information at the time this catalog was published. Items listed in blue ink may not be available at all times. Current delivery information, along with a list of in-stock products for this line, can be found on our Web site at www.walthers.com.

COUPLERS

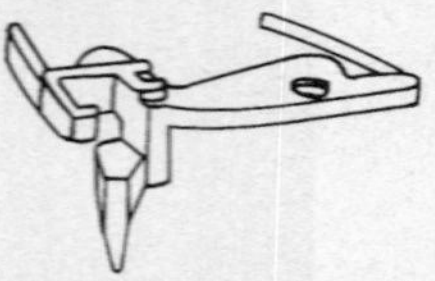

120-6001 Plastic 1 Pair .60
HO scale universal, automatic couplers accurately designed to NMRA standards. Easily installed on almost all cars.

ATLAS

FREIGHT CAR TRUCKS 1 PAIR EA 3.95

Trucks feature Delrin® sideframes and metal wheelsets.

150-180000 70-Ton Roller-Bearing

150-185000 50-Ton Bettendorf Friction-Bearing

150-190000 Barber-Bettendorf Roller-Bearing Caboose

150-195000 100-Ton Roller-Bearing

HO Scale couplers and trucks for use with Athearn and other compatible equipment. Trucks come assembled and ready-to run. See the Super Detailing Parts section for more Athearn truck-related items, such as gear parts, drive assemblies and more. Parts are available only for current production items.

COUPLERS

EA 2.00

140-90601 Regular Horn-Hook Style pkg(6)
140-90602 Snap-On Coupler Cover Plates, Metal pkg(12)
140-90606 Snap-On Coupler Cover Plates, Plastic pkg(12)

LOCOMOTIVE TRUCKS

The following Athearn trucks have drive or partial drive mechanisms (or mountings) attached. With some cutting and refabricating of bolsters, these trucks can be used for other manufacturers' products. Sideframes are either Delrin® or metal. Power trucks have metal wheels while dummies have Delrin wheels.

H24-66 LOCOS

140-43016 Front Power **6.50**
140-43017 Rear Power **6.50**
140-43018 Front Dummy **4.50**
140-43019 Rear Dummy **4.50**

PA1/PB1

140-33233 Front Dummy PA1 **5.00**
140-33234 Rear Dummy PA1/PB1 **5.00**
140-33236 Front Power PB1 **6.50**
140-33237 Front Dummy PB1 **5.00**

U28B, U30B & U33B LOCOS

140-34021 Front Power **5.00**
140-34022 Rear Power **5.00**
140-34023 Front & Rear Dummy 1 Pair **4.00**

U28C, U30C & U33C LOCOS

140-34213 Rear Power **6.50**
140-34215 Rear Dummy **3.15**

SW-1500 LOCO

140-39021 Front Power **5.50**
140-39022 Rear Power **5.50**
140-39023 Dummy **4.50**

FOR SW-7/1000

140-41022 Front/Rear Dummy **3.00**

F7/GP LOCOS EA 5.50

140-42010 Front Power
140-42020 Rear Power

GP50/38-2 LOCOS

140-46010 Front Power **5.50**
140-46020 Rear Power **5.50**
140-90460 Dummy **3.00**
140-90470 Dummy **3.00**

SD9 LOCO

140-38019 Front Power **6.50**
140-38020 Rear Power **6.50**
140-38021 Front Dummy **5.00**
140-38022 Rear Dummy **5.00**

SD40-2 LOCO

140-44011 Front Power **6.50**
140-44012 Rear Power **6.50**
140-44021 Front Dummy **5.00**
140-44022 Rear Dummy **5.00**

SD40/45 F-FP LOCOS

140-40024 Front Power **6.50**
140-40025 Rear Power **6.50**
140-40034 Front/Rear Dummy **3.50**

RDC

140-90454 Front Power **3.00**
140-90457 Rear Power **3.00**
140-90455 Dummy **3.00**
140-90565 Large Insulators for #90457 pkg(6) **1.80**
140-90566 Small Insulators for #90457 pkg(6) **1.80**

DD40

140-42030 Front Power **7.00**
140-42031 Rear Power **7.00**
140-42034 Rear Dummy **5.00**

SIDEFRAMES

140-42009 Blomberg "B" Set pkg(4) **4.50**
140-45036 For SD40-2 Set **4.00**
140-46036 Blomberg "M" Set **4.00**

TRUCKS

BLOMBERG TRUCKS

Molded plastic trucks have sideframes with arch contour, individual brake cylinders with brake levers and separate outside swing hangers (less worm housing).

140-42011 F7 Power Truck Set **11.00**
140-46011 Blomberg Power Set **11.00**
140-90469 Dummy "M" 1 Pair **6.00**

FREIGHT TRUCKS EA 2.00

Trucks have RP-25 Delrin wheels.

140-90396 28' Impack 1 Pair
140-90397 Caboose Roller Bearing 1 Pair
140-90398 Timken Roller Bearing, Working 1 Pair
140-90399 Hyatt Roller Bearing 1 Pair
140-90400 Bettendorf 1 Pair
140-90401 Hyatt 36" Bearing 1 Pair
140-90407 6-Wheel Buckeye 1 Pair

PASSENGER TRUCKS

Trucks have RP-25 metal wheels.

140-90379 Pick-Up Wiper 4-Wheel pkg(6) **1.80**
140-90380 Pick-Up Wiper 6-Wheel pkg(6) **1.80**
140-90410 4-Wheel Black pkg(2) **3.00**
140-90411 Streamline Talgo 1 Pair **3.00**
140-90412 Streamline Observation 1 Pair **3.00**
140-90413 6-Wheel Talgo 1 Pair **3.00**
140-90414 4-Wheel Observation (black) 1 Pair **3.00**

SNOWPLOW TRUCKS

140-90409 Rear **2.00**

WHEEL ASSEMBLIES

140-40019 40" Drive Wheels pkg(12) **13.80**
140-40023 Geared Drive Wheels pkg(12) **10.80**
140-45034 40" Wheelsets w/Bearings pkg(4) **2.00**
140-45035 Plastic Locomotive Wheel Bearing **2.00**
140-90501 33" Plastic pkg(8) **2.50**
140-90502 36" Plastic Wheelset pkg(8) **2.50**
140-90503 33" Brass pkg(8) **2.50**
140-90504 36" Metal Wheelsets pkg(8) **2.50**
140-90505 42" Plastic Wheelsets pkg(8) **2.50**
140-90506 42" Metal Wheelsets pkg(2) **1.50**
140-90508 36" Metal Wheelsets pkg(2) **1.50**
140-90510 28" Impack pkg(8) **2.00**

BACHMANN

E-Z MATE™ COUPLERS 1 PAIR EA 1.00

E-Z Mate™ knuckle couplers have springs molded as an integral part of the knuckle coupler. They operate with a standard metal "glad hand" and under-track magnet. Completely compatible with all magnetically operated knuckle couplers currently on the market.

OVER SHANK

160-78001 Long
160-78002 Medium
160-78003 Short

CENTER SHANK

160-78004 Long

160-78005 Medium
160-78006 Short

UNDER SHANK

160-78007 Long
160-78008 Medium
160-78009 Short

ECONOMY PACK

160-78105 Center Shank (25 Pair) **21.00**
160-78999 Magnet w/Brakeman Figure **2.00**

E-Z MATE MARK II

Center-shank medium couplers feature metal coil springs.

160-78025 12 Pair **16.00**
160-78125 25 Pair **26.00**

CENTRAL VALLEY

"UN-DEE" UNCOUPLER

210-3001 9.95
Place the "UN-DEE" between cars and depress the plunger. Two miniature magnets move toward the couplers from each side, attracting the steel trip pins on the couplers and opening the knuckles. Eliminates need to modify trackwork or install Kadee magnets in track.

Information STATION

Changing Couplers-Standard Installations

As your layout grows or you desire more realistic models, you'll probably want to change coupler styles.

Virtually all models use a standard draft gear which easily accepts most brands of couplers. Before starting, purchase a coupler standards gauge to help set the correct height for top performance. Some lines also offer specialized couplers for specific cars or locos with unique mountings.

If you are working with an unassembled model, simply add the springs and couplers as the last step.

On assembled models, remove the trucks. The draft gear has a separate cover which may clip, screw or press-fit in place. Inside, a mounting pin centers the coupler and serves as pivot point on corners. Install springs or other parts, add the knuckle and replace the cover. Check your installation with the gauge to be sure the knuckles align at the proper height.

Some styles include a steel trip wire which looks like an air hose, but works with magnetic uncouplers. This may need to be adjusted with a small pliers for best performance.

Ready-to-run trucks with brass axles and Delrin® sideframes.

We have worked closely with this manufacturer to provide accurate delivery information at the time this catalog was published. Items listed in blue ink may not be available at all times. Current delivery information, along with a list of in-stock products for this line, can be found on our Web site at www.walthers.com.

TRUCKS

BARBER "S-2" ROLLER BEARING

223-99200 33" Delrin Wheels **1.49**
223-99220 33" Brass Wheels **2.89**
223-99221 36" Brass Wheels **2.89**

FREIGHT

223-99222 Roller Bearing Trucks w/Celcon RP-25 36" 1 Pair **TBA**
223-99250 Bettendorf Trucks, Celcon 33" Wheelsets 1 Pair **TBA**
223-99251 Bettendorf Trucks, Brass RP-25 33" Wheelsets 1 Pair **TBA**

STREAMLINED PASSENGER FOR 72' PASSENGER CARS (CELCON SIDEFRAMES)

223-970219 With Silver Sideframes, Metal RP-25 Wheelsets 1 Pair **6.98**
223-97022 With Black Sideframes, Metal RP-25 Wheelsets 1 Pair **6.98**

STREAMLINED PASSENGER FOR 85' & SUPERLINER PASSENGER CARS (CELCON SIDEFRAMES)

223-970019 With Silver Sides, Metal RP-25 Wheelsets 1 Pair **6.98**
223-97002 With Black Sides, Metal RP-25 Wheelsets 1 Pair **6.98**
223-970119 With Silver Sides & Plastic RP-25 Wheelsets 1 Pair **3.98**
223-97012 With Black Sideframes & Plastic RP-25 Wheelsets 1 Pair **3.98**

WHEELSETS

8-PIECE PACKS

223-99201 RP-25 33" Celcon **2.49**
223-99202 RP-25 33" Brass **7.98**
223-99203 PR-25 36" Brass **7.98**
223-99204 RP-25 36" Celcon **2.49**

PLASTIC RP-25 1 PAIR

223-970139 Silver Sideframes **3.98**
223-97032 Black Sideframes **TBA**

CAL-SCALE

HO Scale couplers and truck kits are cast in brass.

DUMMY COUPLERS

292

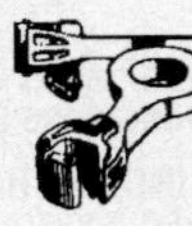
302

190-292 Standard 1 Pair **3.10**
190-302 Standard "E" 1 Pair **3.00**

BRASS WHEELS PKG(4) EA 4.20

190-467 30" 1/16 diameter
190-468 36" Needle Point
190-469 33" Needle Point
190-470 30" Needle Point
190-471 36" Flush
190-472 33" Flush
190-473 30" Flush

NON-MAGNETIC NICKEL PLATED WHEELSETS EA 4.20

190-453 33"
190-454 36"

TRUCKS

LOCOMOTIVE TRUCKS

190-2000 USRA **16.75**
Includes opening journal lids.

TENDER TRUCKS EA 20.95

190-310 Andrews 1 Pair

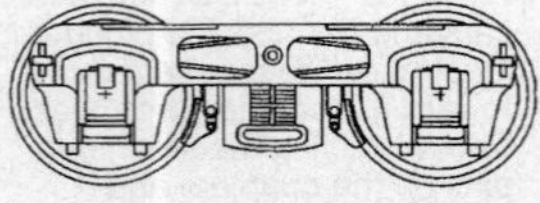

190-311 4-Wheel USRA 1 Pair

Custom Finishing

Easy-to-build modern freight and passenger car trucks feature brass parts, springs and NorthWest Short Line wheelsets.

TRUCK KITS

PASSENGER CARS

247-185 GSC 41N/41ND, Less Details 1 Pair **32.95**

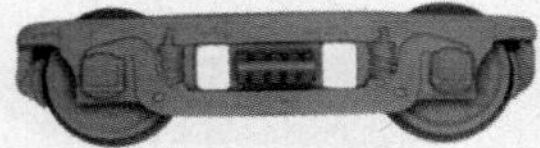

247-244 Standard Motor Car 1 Pair **13.95**
White metal, wheels unsprung.

41-BNO W/NWSL WHEELS 1 PAIR EA 21.95

247-309 Friction Bearings

247-310 Roller Bearings

ROLLERBEARING 1 PAIR EA 26.95

247-177 70 Ton, 33" Wheels

247-218 100 Ton, 36" Wheels

TRUCK ACCESSORIES

GSC 41N/41ND TRUCK DETAILS

Each package contains enough parts for one pair of trucks.

247-186 12 x 10 Brake Cylinders w/Stack Adjusters pkg(4) **10.95**

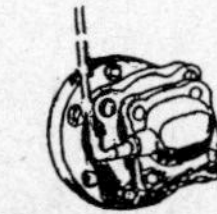

247-217 Decelostat Caps pkg(4) **3.95**

SHOCKS/SNUBBERS PKG(4) EA 4.95

187

188

247-187 Monroe
247-188 Houde

BEARING CAPS PKG(8) EA 5.95

189

190

247-189 Hyatt
247-190 Timken, Round

191

216

247-191 Timken
247-216 SKF, Oil Filled Type

TRUCK SPRINGS PKG(12) EA 2.95

247-132 .150" Long, .092" Diameter

247-180 .130" Long, .060" Diameter
247-227 .250" Long, .164" Diameter

ERNST MANUFACTURING

GEARING KITS

Self-lubricating gearing kits for Athearn locomotive trucks. Kits produce more realistic control and smoother operation, with lower low speeds, twice the power and brighter headlights. Keeps motor running cooler, increasing motor life. Triple reduction.

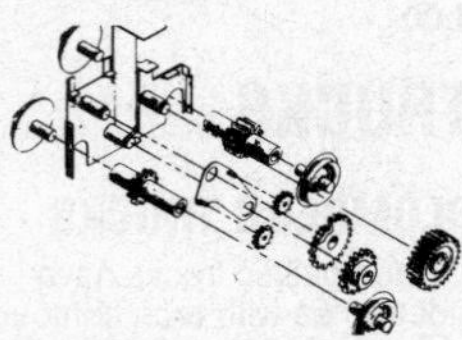

259-44 Gearing Kit MKII for 4-Axle Trucks **7.98**
F7 A & B, GP9, GP35, U28B, S12, SW1500 Cow and SW1500 Calf.

259-6 Super Gearing Kit for 6-Axle Trucks **7.98**
EMD SD9, F45, SDP40, SD45, U28C, U33C, Trainmaster, Alco PA1 and PB1 (Alco requires modeling skill).

259-66 Gearing Kit for SD40-2 **7.98**
Converts 12:1 ratio of the stock SD40-2 to a 32:1 gear ratio. Greater pulling power, slower speed and less current draw.

259-2 Gearing Kit for Hustler **11.98**
Provides a 36:1 gear ratio with two 1/2" flywheels. Includes two flywheels, brass worms and gearboxes with all gears necessary.

259-3 Gearing Kit for RDC **11.98**
Provides a 12:1 gear ratio with a large flywheel for smoother operation. Includes a gearbox, geared axle pieces, worm gears, 1" flywheel and added components.

GLOOR-CRAFT MODELS

Ready-to-run trucks feature metal sideframes and fully equalized, black Delrin® wheels with RP-25 contours.

We have worked closely with this manufacturer to provide accurate delivery information at the time this catalog was published. Items listed in blue ink may not be available at all times. Current delivery information, along with a list of in-stock products for this line, can be found on our Web site at www.walthers.com.

FREIGHT TRUCKS 1 PAIR EA 4.25

288-801 Bettendorf w/33" Wheels
288-803 Roller Bearing w/36" Wheels

288-805 Bettendorf w/36" Wheels

288-804 Arch Bar w/33" Wheels

288-800 Roller Bearing w/33" Wheels

288-802 Andrews w/33" Wheels

WHEELSETS PKG(4) 2.25

288-807 33"
288-808 36"

Easy-to-build kits with plastic parts. Kits come without wheels, but wheelsets are available separately.

TRUCKS

PASSENGER TRUCKS EA 5.00

117-9001 Pennsylvania 2D-P5 4-Wheel pkg(2)
117-9002 Commonwealth 4-Wheel Leaf Spring pkg(2)
117-9003 Pullman Standard 4-Wheel Lightweight pkg(2)
117-9004 Commonwealth 4-Wheel Swing Motion pkg(2)
117-9005 Pullman Standard
117-9006 Taylor
117-9007 Pullman-Standard 41-BNO
117-9008 Pullman-Standard Low Profile
117-9009 4-Wheel General Steel Casting Double Equalized
117-9021 Pennsylvania 3D-P1, 3D-P7 6-Wheel pkg(2)
117-9022 Pennsylvania 3D5P2 6-Wheel
117-9023 Pullman-Standard 61-NO

FREIGHT TRUCKS EA 3.00

117-9051 Barber-Bettendorf Caboose
117-9052 Taylor 70-Ton Caboose/Freight
117-9053 Bettendorf Friction Bearing
117-9054 Barber S-2
117-9055 Birdsboro/Andrews Caboose/Freight
116-9056 Bett RB Conversion
117-9057 Pyle-National B-1
117-9058 Buckeye Roller Bearing 125-Ton
117-9059 C-1 Friction Bearing
117-9060 C-1 Roller Bearing
117-9061 2 Level Dalman
117-9062 C-1 National Super
117-9063 Commonwealth High Capacity
117-9064 70 Ton Bettendorf 5' Wheel Base, Roller Bearing
117-9065 High Capacity 2-Lever Dalma 5' Wheel Base, Roller Bearing
117-9066 50-Ton Andrews Trucks
117-9067 55-Ton Andrews
117-9068 Vulcan

SIX WHEEL FREIGHT TRUCKS EA 4.00

117-9081 Commonwealth Integral Pedestal
117-9082 Buckeye Friction Bearing
117-9083 Buckeye Roller Bearing

EXPRESS TRUCKS EA 5.00

117-9040 Commonwealth, 8' Wheel Base

117-9041 ACF Mechanical Ventilation Fans, 6' Wheel Base
117-9042 Commonwealth Box
117-9043 Allied Full Cushion

WHEELSETS

PASSENGER

117-9000 36" pkg(6) **2.00**

FREIGHT

117-9050 33" pkg(4) **1.50**
117-9080 33" pkg(6) **2.00**

Grandt Line

Couplers are injection-molded plastic, except where noted. Trucks are ready-to-run and molded in Delrin. Wheelsets are metal unless noted.

COUPLERS

DRGW COUPLER POCKETS PKG(4) EA 2.05 (UNLESS NOTED)

300-5006 For Box Car

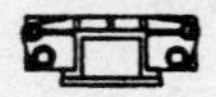

300-5044 For 30' Refrigerator

300-5047 For Drop Bottom Gondola

300-5086 For High Side Gondola 2 Sets **1.85**
Includes end details.

DUMMY COUPLERS

300-5003 Plastic pkg(10) **2.05**
300-86003 Brass pkg(2) **5.65**

TRUCKS

BETTENDORF

300-5120 54" Wheelbase, Brown 1 Pair **4.95**
Used by Colorado & Southern, Rio Grande Southern and White Pass & Yukon.

ANDREWS HON3 1 PAIR EA 4.95

DRGW style for 5900 stock car, 150 reefer and 6400 flat. 4'-8" wheelbase.

300-5144 Brown
300-5145 Black

ARCHBAR

300-5159 Brown 1 Pair **4.95**
DRGW style, 4'-8" wheelbase.

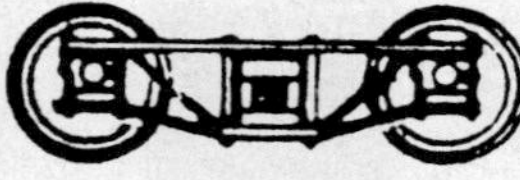

300-5257 SR&RL/NWSL Wheels **6.50**
300-5146 HOn3z, 1 Pair **4.95**
SR&RL style, 4' wheelbase with silver Delrin wheels.

FREIGHT CAR 1 PAIR EA 4.95

DRGW style, 3'-7" wheelbase.

300-5110 Brown
300-5111 Black

WHEELSETS

20" WHEELSETS PKG(4) EA 2.40

With brass axles and silver Delrin wheels.

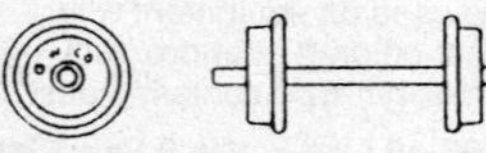

300-5141 HOn3
300-5142 HOn3

26" WHEELSETS

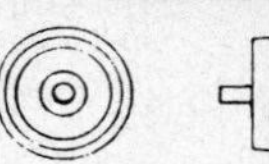
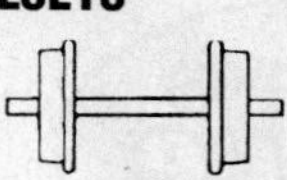

300-5132 HOn3, Nonmagnetic pkg(4) **3.50**

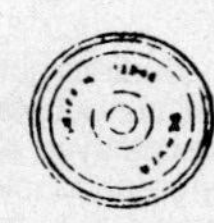

300-5055 Griffin-Denver, Nonoperating Plastic pkg(16) **3.40**

WHEELSETS FOR 23-TON BOX CAB & 25-TON SWITCHER EA 12.95

Includes one plain and one geared axle.

300-7092 HOn3
300-7093 HO

INTERMOUNTAIN RAILWAY

TRUCKS

85-40001 100-Ton Barber S-2 **1.75**

TRUCKS W/BRASS WHEELSETS 1 PAIR EA 3.95

85-40060 Barber S-2

85-40061 ASF 50-Ton

COUPLERS

LESS DRAFT GEAR

85-40005 Black, 2 Pair **1.99**
85-40006 Black, 10 Pair **9.25**
85-40007 Black, 25 Pair **21.25**
85-40025 Rust, 2 Pair **1.99**
85-40026 Rust, 10 Pair **9.25**
85-40027 Rust, 25 Pair **21.25**

WITH DRAFT GEAR

85-40015 Black, 2 Pair **2.29**
85-40016 Black, 10 Pair **10.50**
85-40017 Black, 25 Pair **24.50**
85-40035 Rust, 2 Pair **2.29**
85-40036 Rust,10 Pair **10.50**
85-40037 Rust, 25 Pair **24.50**

ALL BRASS INSULATED WHEELSETS 12 PACKS (UNLESS NOTED)

85-40050 33" Wheels **7.95**
85-40051 36" Wheels **7.95**
85-40052 33" Semi-Scale **7.95** *NEW*
85-40053 28" Semi-Scale **7.95**
85-40054 36" Semi-Scale **7.95** *NEW*
85-40055 33" Wheels, Pack of 100 **58.00**
85-40056 36" Wheels, Pack of 100 **58.00**
85-40059 36" Ball Bearing, Pack of 6 **19.95** *NEW*

International Hobby Corp.

COUPLERS

348-19001 Magic Mate 2 Pair **3.50**

TRUCKS

PASSENGER TRUCKS

TALGO

348-220020 6-Wheel 1920 Heavyweight Passenger Car w/Long Shank Coupler pkg(2) **9.58**
Couplers are mounted on trucks and feature plastic wheels.

COMMONWEALTH 4-WHEEL

For use on IHC/Rivarossi passenger cars and other equipment. One side of the nickel-silver wheels is insulated to allow for interior lighting.

348-4240 Black 1 Pair **20.98**
348-4241 Silver 1 Pair **20.98**
348-4242 IHC/Rivarossi Adapters **3.98**

6-WHEEL EA 24.98

348-4256 Friction/Black
348-4257 Friction/Silver
348-4258 Roller/Black
348-4259 Roller/Silver

WHEELSETS

31" RP25 WHEELSETS

Nickel-silver plated brass wheelsets are insulated on one side and are nonmagnetic.

348-4254 pkg(12) **13.98**
348-4255 pkg(36) **38.98**

Kadee® Magne-Matic® delayed-action couplers automatically uncouple when stopped over a magnetic uncoupler (see illustrations below). Kadee® makes both delayed action and nondelayed action uncouplers to fit different coupling and uncoupling requirements.

See the Coupler Conversion List on the following pages for aid in adapting and installing Kadee® couplers.

THE MAGNE-MATIC® COUPLING AND UNCOUPLING SYSTEM

1. Stopped over a Magnetic upcoupler allowing slack to occur between the couplers. Knuckles have opened.

2. Withdraw slightly to disengage couplers. Magnetic force of the uncoupler draws couplers apart, uncoupling them.

3. Enter over uncoupler again, couplers are in delayed position allowing pushing of car(s) without causing re-coupling.

4. Withdraw, leaving uncoupled car(s) on desired track. Couplers automatically return to normal coupling position.

Kadee® and Magne-matic® are Registered Trademarks.

CATALOG

380-84 1998 Whole-Line Catalog **3.95** *NEW*
A complete list of couplers and accessories for all scales. Packed with black and white photos and illustrations, plus helpful information, coupler conversion charts and more. Softcover, 52 pages.

COUPLERS

Couplers are part of the "Delayed Action Series" using delayed magnetic uncoupling. Two pairs of couplers per package.

#5 UNIVERSAL COUPLERS

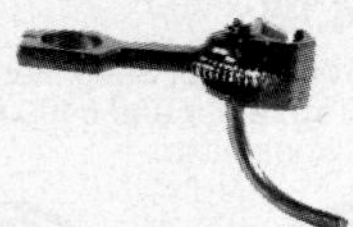

The most popular Kadee® coupler. Fits virtually any HO equipment. Metal coupler with insulated plastic gear box and cover, bronze centering spring plate. #9 coupler is identical to #5, except for smaller draft gear center hole, for truck mounting situations.

380-3 Fully Assembled 2 Pair **5.25**
380-5 Kit 2 Pair **2.95**
380-9 Truck Mounting 2 Pair **3.30**

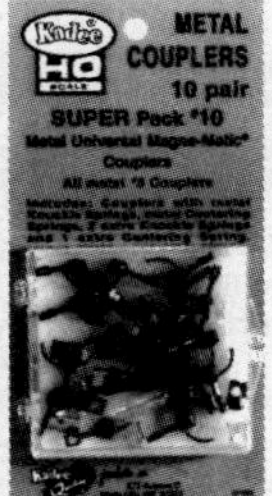

380-10 Less Draft Gear, 10 Pair **11.95**
380-11 Less Draft Gear, 20 Pair **21.95**

#4 COUPLERS

380-4 4 Standard 2 Pair **2.95**
All-metal coupler. Especially for mounting on wooden floored car kits and trains that require additional drawbar slack action. With #204 Adapter Plate, can be used on equipment with cast-on draft gear box with small pin-type centering post.

380-15 Low Profile 2 Pair **3.30**
Metal coupler with plastic insulating draft gear box. Includes centering springs with spacer dowels. For use with Kadee® log cars and other cars or locos that require a lower profile draft gear box.

20 SERIES COUPLERS 2 PAIR EA 3.75

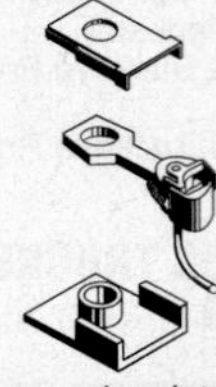

Multipurpose insulated couplers designed for locomotive pilot mounting and unusual mounting situations on Talgo-style trucks. With Talgo-mounting adaptors and #5 draft gear boxes for body mounting.

380-21 Long Underset Shank (25/64")
For low mounting platforms and locomotive pilots.

380-22 Medium Overset Shank (9/32")
For high mounting platforms and tight clearances.

380-23 Short Centerset Shank (1/4")
For standard height mounting platforms with tight clearances.

380-24 Short Underset Shank (1/4")
For low mounting platforms with tight clearances.

380-25 Short Overset Shank (1/4")
For low mounting platforms with tight clearances.

380-26 Long Centerset Shank (25/64")
For extended locomotive pilots and cars that are difficult to convert.

380-27 Medium Underset Shank (9/32")
For low mounting platforms with tight clearances.

380-28 Medium Centerset Shank (19/64")
For standard height mounting platforms.

380-29 Long Overset Shank (25/64")
For high mounting platforms and locomotive pilots.

30 SERIES COUPLERS 2 PAIR EA 3.30

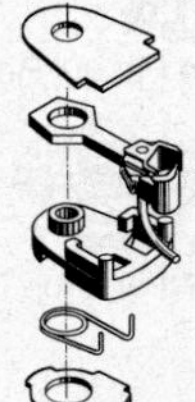

Body mounting couplers with small, versatile draft gear box. Ideal for mounting on locomotives with space limitations and varying mounting heights.

380-31 Long Underset Shank (25/64")
For low mounting platforms and locomotive pilots.

380-32 Medium Overset Shank (9/32")
For high mounting platforms and tight clearances.

380-33 Short Centerset Shank (1/4")
For standard height mounting platforms with tight clearances.

380-34 Short Underset Shank (1/4")
For low mounting platforms with tight clearances.

380-35 Short Overset Shank (1/4")
For low mounting platforms with tight clearances.

380-36 Long Centerset Shank (25/64")
For extended locomotive pilots and cars that are difficult to convert.

380-37 Medium Underset Shank (9/32")
For low mounting platforms with tight clearances.

380-38 Medium Centerset Shank (19/64")
For standard height mounting platforms.

380-39 Long Overset Shank (25/64")
For high mounting platforms and locomotive pilots.

40 SERIES COUPLERS 2 PAIR EA 2.95

Interchangeable with #5, 20 and 30 Series couplers.

380-41 Long (25/64") Underset Shank
380-42 Medium (9/32") Overset Shank *NEW*
380-43 Short (1/4") Centerset Shank *NEW*
380-44 Short (1/4") Underset Shank *NEW*
380-45 Short (1/4") Overset Shank *NEW*
380-46 Long (25/64") Centerset Shank
380-47 Medium (9/32") Underset Shank *NEW*
380-49 Long (25/64") Overset Shank *NEW*

NEM (362) EUROPEAN STYLE COUPLERS 2 PAIR 3.95

380-17 Very Short 7.11mm (.280")

380-18 Short 8.63mm (.340")
380-19 Medium Long 10.76mm (.400")
380-20 Long 11.68mm (.460")

OLD-TIME COUPLERS 2 PAIR 2.95

3/4 size couplers for old-time locos and cars.

380-711 HO
380-714 HOn3

COUPLERS FOR LOCOMOTIVE PILOTS 2 PAIR EA 3.30

Designed to fit unusual mountings of many loco pilots and cars with limited space. Plastic draft gear box insulates couplers. From the center of the screw hole to the rear of draft gear is 5/32", shortest of all draft gears.

380-6 13/32" Long Shank
380-7 1/4" Long Shank
380-8 5/16" Long Shank
380-16 1/4" Long Shank
Combines #6 coupler with shorter #7 draft gear box. For certain traction applications and European equipment with buffers.

COUPLER SAMPLE KIT

Find out which couplers are right for your cars and locomotives with this sample set of HO couplers. Includes couplers #4-9, 21-29, 31-39 & 711. Also includes Magne-Matic® Uncouplers #308 & 321.

380-13 Sampler Kit **23.95**
380-91 20-Series Sample Kit **8.45**
Includes one coupler each of numbers 21-29.

380-92 30 Series Sample Kit **7.45**
Includes one coupler each of numbers 31-39.

For Daily Product Information Click
www.walthers.com

COUPLER CONVERSION KITS

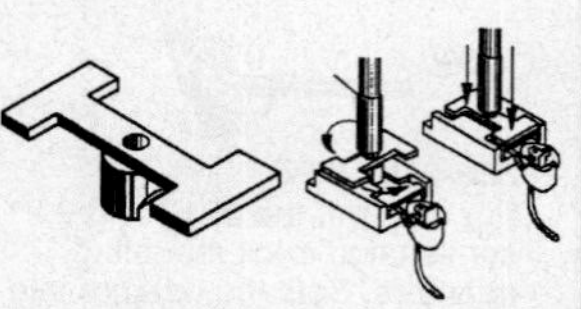

380-212 Talgo Truck Adaptors pkg(24) **2.95**

380-450 Stewart F Units (1 Pair) **4.95**
Special bracket converts Stewart F units to 30 Series couplers.

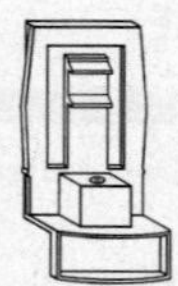

380-452 Spectrum® F7 A & B Units (1 Pair) **5.95**
Contains parts to convert F7 A & B units to prototypical 5' spacing, or 3' spacing between units.

380-453 Life Like Proto 2000 E8/9 1 Set **11.95**

380-454 Swing Bracket Adaptor Kit 1 Set **6.95**
380-455 Life-Like® Proto 2000™ E7 or PA 1 Set **8.95** ***NEW***
Close-coupling conversion fits E7 A and B units, or Alco PA and PB.

PASSENGER TRUCK CONVERSION BOLSTERS W/COUPLERS EA 3.30

Each package contains two conversion bolsters and one Pair of #5 couplers.

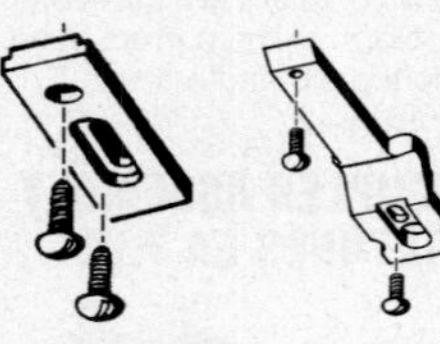
505 506

380-505 For International Hobby 6-Wheel Passenger Trucks
Adjusts to different car lengths.

380-506 For Central Valley 4-Wheel Passenger Trucks

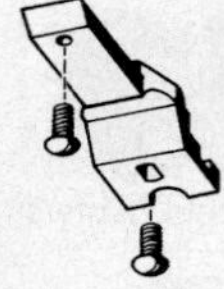
507

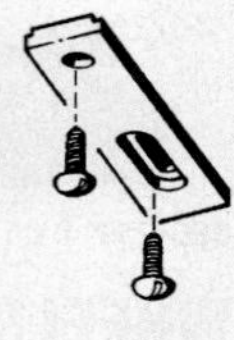
508

380-507 For Central Valley 6-Wheel Passenger Trucks
380-508 For International Hobby 4-Wheel Passenger Trucks
Adjusts to different carlengths.

COUPLER DRAFT GEAR BOXES & SHIMS

232

Draft gear boxes with covers only.

380-211 Draft Gear Shims pkg(40) **1.60**
For #4-9 couplers. Includes 20 each of .010" and .015" thick draft gear shims.
380-213 Boxes & Sleeves for 20 Series pkg(24) **2.95** ***NEW***
380-228 For #4 Couplers, Metal 10 Pair **2.50**
380-232 For #5 Couplers, Plastic 10 Pair **2.50**
380-233 For 30 Series Couplers 10 Pair **3.50**
380-234 Boxes w/Lids for #23, 24, 25, 43, 44 & 45 Couplers 10 Pair **2.50** ***NEW***

MINIMUM SPACE ADAPTER PLATE

380-204 pkg(20) **2.65**
Use with #4 coupler where space is limited. Takes place of #4 draft gear box and cover plate. Use same spacer dowel and centering spring.

UNCOUPLERS

MAGNE-MATIC® UNCOUPLERS

For use with Kadee® couplers.

380-308 Under Track **3.90**
Extra strong magnet can be completely concealed under ties and ballasted over. For use from HOn3 to O Scale.

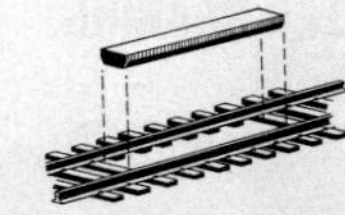

380-312 Nondelayed pkg(2) **4.65**
Automatically uncouples cars when couplers are stopped over magnet. You can then pull away, leaving the cars.

DELAYED

When couplers are stopped over uncoupler, knuckles open and move off center to "delayed" position (see Magne-Matic® system diagram at beginning of listing). You can then push uncoupled cars to any location, beyond the uncoupler, without recoupling.
380-321 pkg(2) **4.45**
380-709 HOn3 pkg(2) **4.65**

MAGNE-ELECTRIC UNCOUPLERS

Delayed action uncouplers effectively eliminate false uncoupling sometimes experienced with permanent magnetic uncouplers. Push button switch (not included) activates magnet. Ideal for secondary and siding tracks. Mounts through the track. Requires 16V AC power supply.

380-307 HO **8.50**
380-708 HOn3 **8.90**

SPRINGS

CENTERING SPRINGS

380-620 For #17-20 Couplers pkg(20) **2.00**

380-623 For #4 & #205 Height Gauge Couplers, w/Spacer Dowels pkg(12) **.98**

380-634 For #5 & #20 Series Couplers pkg(12) **2.40**

380-635 For #6, 7, 8 & 16 Couplers pkg(12) **.98**
380-636 For #711 & 714 Couplers pkg(12) **1.10**

KNUCKLE SPRINGS

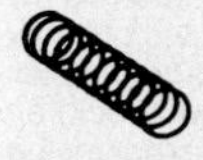

380-622 pkg(12) **.98**
For all HO couplers except #711 and 714.

TORSION SPRINGS

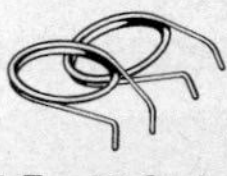

380-621 For 30 Series Gear Boxes pkg(12) **1.60**

TRUCK SPRINGS

380-624 HOn3 pkg(12) **.98**

380-637 HO pkg(18) **1.95**
380-638 HO pkg(18) **1.95**
For #513 roller bearing trucks.

SCREWS

COUPLER MOUNTING SCREWS PKG(24) EA 3.95

Metal roundhead screws; 0-48 size.

380-400 1/8" Long
380-401 3/16" Long
380-402 1/4" Long
380-403 3/8" Long

PLASTIC SCREWS

380-256 2-56 x 1/2" Long pkg(12) **1.65**
Insulated phillips head screws. Uses include mounting couplers, draft gear boxes and trucks. Can be easily trimmed to appropriate length.

TRUCKS

Kadee® offers two styles of trucks, Talgo style (with couplers and coupler pockets mounted on truck) and standard style (does not include couplers and coupler pockets). All trucks feature blackened nonmagnetic metal sideframes and wheels with Delrin axles. Cannot be used for car lighting unless wipers are used on wheels.

BETTENDORF TRUCKS

380-500 Standard 1 Pair **5.75**
With 33" smooth back wheels.

380-502 Talgo 1 Pair **8.00**
With 33" smooth back wheels and ready-to-mount couplers.

380-511 T-Section, Standard 1 Pair **5.75**
With 33" ribbed back wheels.

380-512 T-Section, Talgo 1 Pair **8.00**
With 33" ribbed back wheels and ready-to-mount couplers.

ARCH BAR TRUCKS

380-501 Standard 1 Pair **5.75**
With 33" ribbed back wheels.

380-503 Talgo 1 Pair **8.00**
With 33" ribbed back wheels and ready-to-mount couplers.

ANDREWS TRUCKS

380-509 Standard 1 Pair **5.75**
With 33" ribbed back wheels.

380-510 Talgo 1 Pair **8.00**
With 33" ribbed back wheels and ready-to-mount couplers.

ROLLER BEARING TRUCKS

380-513 Standard 1 Pair **7.25**
With 36" smooth back wheels.

BARBER S-2 70-TON ROLLER BEARING TRUCKS

380-518 Standard 1 Pair **6.75**
33" smooth back wheels.

VULCAN DOUBLE-TRUSS TRUCKS

380-515 Standard 1 Pair **5.75**
With 33" ribbed back wheels.

380-516 Talgo 1 Pair **8.00**
With 33" ribbed back wheels and ready-to-mount couplers.

ASF 50-TON RIDE CONTROL TRUCKS

380-504 Standard 1 Pair **5.75**
33" smooth back wheels.

PRR CLASS 2DF8 50-TON TRUCKS

380-517 Standard 1 Pair **5.75**
33" smooth back wheels.

LOGGING TRUCKS

380-107 Disconnect Logging Trucks 1 Pair **15.35**
Two trucks to make a disconnect logging car. Ribbed back wheels. Includes two Pairs of couplers.

HON3 TRUCKS 1 PAIR EA 7.95

Kits include body and truck bolsters, sideframes, spring planks, wheelsets with ribbed back wheels, truck bushings and springs.

380-716 3' 7" Wheel Centers

380-717 4' 6" Wheel Centers

WHEELSETS

FREIGHT & PASSENGER CAR WHEELSETS

RP-25 contour, tapered axles and founding data on wheels.

380-520

380-521

380-520 33" Freight Car, Smooth Back Wheels 12 Pair **7.20**
380-521 36" Passenger Car, Ribbed Back Wheels 12 Pair **9.00**

380-522 36" Passenger Car, Smooth Back Wheels 12 Pair **9.00**

380-523

380-524

380-523 33" Freight Car, Ribbed Back Wheels 12 Pair **7.20**
380-524 28" Freight Car, Smooth Back Wheels 12 Pair **7.20**
For modern freight cars such as TOFC, auto carriers.

WASHERS

FIBER WASHERS PKG(48) EA 2.30

Truck spacer washers for adjusting car height or coupler height.

380-208 .015" Thick
380-209 .010 Thick

TOOLS

COUPLER HEIGHT GAUGES

Height gauges gauge coupler height, trip pin height, trackage and correct height of permanent magnet uncouplers.

380-205 HO **3.90**
380-704 HOn3 **5.95**

ADAPTER INSERTION PIC

380-230 2.25
For use with the #212 and 20 series talgo truck mounting adaptors. Sets the adaptor into the Talgo mount holding the spring and coupler.

THE GRIPPER

380-238 The Four-Prong Gripper **4.75**
Use to pick up and position small, hard to hold items.

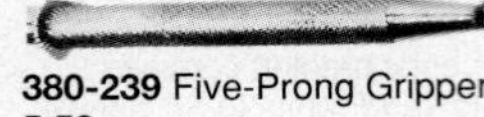

380-239 Five-Prong Gripper **5.50**

PIN VISE

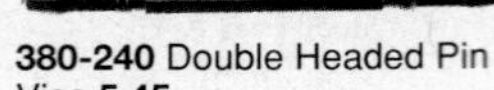

380-240 Double Headed Pin Vise **5.45**

SPRING PIC

380-235 Spring Pic **1.80**
Crowned tip grips miniature springs used in couplers and trucks, making them easier to handle.

TWEEZERS

380-1020 Coupler Tweezers **3.50**

TRIP PIN PLIERS

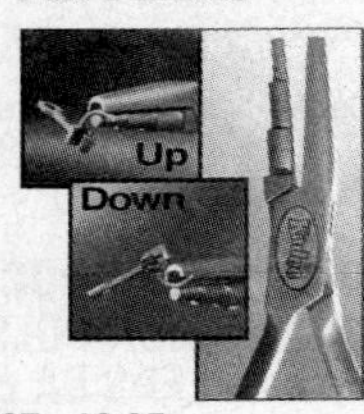

380-237 10.95
Special pliers for adjusting the height of coupler trip pins. Jaws of pliers are curved, to conform to the correct bend in the trip pin and prevent kinking.

COUPLER ASSEMBLY FIXTURES EA 7.95

Fixtures holds coupler parts in place for easier assembly.

380-701 For #4, 5 & 9 Couplers
380-702 For #711 & 714 Couplers
380-703 For #6, 7 & 8 Couplers

UNCOUPLER GLUING JIG

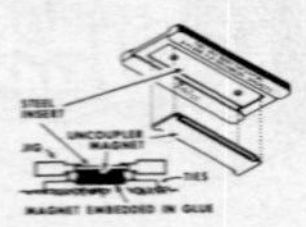

380-334 2.55
For installing #312 & 321 magnetic uncouplers in track.

TAP & DRILL SETS EA 5.05

380-246 2-56 Tap, #43 & 50 Drills
For 2-56 screw mounting most HO couplers and trucks.

380-780 0-80 Tap, #52 & 55 Drills
For 0-80 and 0-48 screws used in the side lugs of the #5 draft gear box, #4, #9, #711 and #714.

380-247 1-72 Tap, #48 & 53 Drills
For miscellaneous applications.

HON3 TRUCK ASSEMBLY FIXTURE

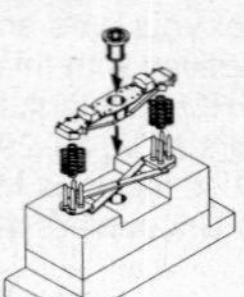

380-715 3.95
Fixture holds truck parts in place for easier assembly.

LUBRICANT

GREAS-EM LUBRICANT

380-231 1/4oz Tube **1.95**
Fine, dry lubricant for friction-free coupler performance. Add to the assembled coupler box; will not become gummy. Can also be used as a general-purpose lubricant around the layout.

HO SCALE COUPLER CONVERSION LIST

ACCURAIL
All Rolling Stock 5

AHM (RIVAROSSI)
STEAM
0-4-0 Dockside (Early model) .34 Pilot, 31 Rear
0-4-0 Dockside (Late model) .34 Pilot, 34 Rear
0-4-0 Switcher w/Tender 37
0-8-0 Switcher .38 Pilot, 5 Tender
2-4-0 Bowker (Tender only) . . .34
2-8-4 Berkshire 34 Pilot, 26 Tender
2-10-2 Santa Fe Class, ...38
2-8-8-2 USRA Mallet 5
4-4-0 Genoa or Reno (Tender only) .34
4-6-0 Casey Jones (Tender only) .37
4-6-2 Heavy Pacific 5
4-6-4 J3a Hudson Pilot 28
Tender 5
4-6-6-4 Challenger .33 Pilot, 27 Tender
4-8-8-2 Cab Forward (Early model) ...34
4-8-8-2 Cab Forward(Late model) .Pilot 33, Tender 27
4-8-8-4 Big Boy .33 Pilot, 27 Tender
Heisler (2 & 3 truck)BM 32 TM 21
DIESEL
Alco RS-2 5
EMD BL-2 5
EMD E-8/9 .....27 Pilot, 24 Rear
EMD GP-18 21
Fairbanks Morse 'C' Liner .31 Pilot, 37 Rear
GE U25C 38
GG1 37
Krauss/Maffi ....5 or 28
Plymouth MDT Switcher 27
Whitcomb Switcher 38
ROLLING STOCK
All Freight Cars-Talgo trucks .37 TM
Caboose (Plastic) ....5 or 38
Box, Reefer, Stock Cars .5 or 38
Hoppers, 4 Bay ....5 or 38
Hoppers, 50' Covered ....5 or 38
Gondolas ....5 or 38
Tank Car ....5 or 38
Old Time Freight Cars 5
Old Time 4-Wheel Pass. Truck .508
4-Wheel Pass. Trucks 508
6-Wheel Pass. Trucks 505

NOTE:
1. See "Rivarossi" for post 1993 models.
2. Most late model RTR European Locos and Rolling Stock come equipped with "NEM" style couplers. Kadee® offers HO-Scale NEM-362 Couplers in four different lengths .17, 18, 19 & 20

A-LINE (Proto Power West)
All Rolling Stock 5

ALCO (BRASS)
All Imports 5

AMBROID
All Rolling Stock Kits 5

AMERICAN BEAUTY
All Rolling Stock 5

AMERICAN FLYER (GILBERT)
All Rolling Stock .....27 in 5box

AMERICAN MODEL BUILDERS
All Passenger Car Kits 5

AMERICAN TRAIN & TRACK
DIESEL
Alco 415 ....5 TM
Plymouth MDT Switcher 27
ROLLING STOCK
All Freight Cars (Generic) . .37 TM
Box Car & Reefers ....5 BM
Flat Car, 3 Container ......5 BM
Coach, Old Time 27

ARISTO-CRAFT
STEAM
All Steam Locomotives (Generic)5
0-4-0 Switcher 5
0-4-4 Mason 5
0-6-0 Tank Switcher 5
0-8-0 Ashland Switcher 5
2-4-2 Columbia 5
2-6-0 Thomas Rogers (Tender only) 5
2-8-0 Consolidation 5
2-8-2 Mikado 5
4-2-2 Baldwin 5
4-4-2 Atlantic 5
4-6-0 Ten Wheeler 5
4-8-2 Mountain 5

ATHEARN
STEAM
0-4-2T "Little Monster" 5
0-6-0 Switcher with Tender 5
4-6-2 Pacific 5
DIESEL
Alco PA-1 & PB-7 .....27 or 37
AMD 103 P40 and P42 27
Baldwin S-12 27
Budd RDC ...37 Metal Body, 21 Plastic Body
EMD DD40X 38
EMD F7A & B (Rubberband drive) 31
EMD F7A & B (Gear drive) 37
EMD F45 38
EMD FP45 38
EMD GP9 38
EMD GP30 38
EMD GP35 32
EMD GP38-2 37
EMD GP40-2 38
EMD GP50 38
EMD GP50 Phase II 38
EMD GP60 38
EMD SD9 38
EMD SD35 37
EMD SDP40 37
EMD SD40-2 37
EMD SD40T-2 37
EMD SD45 37
EMD SW7 5
EMD SW7, Calf 5
EMD SW1000 (Late) 38 (Early) 37
EMD SW1500 .(Late) 38 (Early) 5
FM H 24-66 (Trainmaster) 37
GE Dash 9-44CW ......27 or 28
GE U28B 37
GE U28C 38
GE U30B 37
GE U30C 38
GE U33C 38
GE U33B 37
GE AC 4400 28
Hustler 5

ATHEARN CONT'D
ROLLING STOCK
All Freight Cars (Generic) .4, 5, 20-Series
Freight Cars-Generic (Metal/wood) 4
Freight Cars-Generic (Plastic) . .5
Box Car 40' ....5+Shims
Box Car 40' (High cube) .5+Shims
Box Car 50' Double Door 5+Shims
Box Car 50' Plug Door . .5+Shims
Box Car 50' Rail Box . . .5+Shims
Box Car 50' Single Door .5+Shims
Box Car 56' All Door . . .5+Shims
Box Car 86' Hi-Cube 27
Caboose ATSF Type 27
Caboose Bay Window 27
Caboose Extended Vision 27
Container Well Car 27
Flat Car 40' 5
Flat Car 50' ....5+Shims
Flat Car 50' Bulkhead 5
Flat Car 50' Piggy Back 5
Flat Car 86' 27
Gondola 50' 5
Hopper 34' ....5+Shim
Hopper 40' Quad 5
Hopper Covered PS-3 5
Hopper Covered ACF Center Flow .5+Shim
Husky Stack Gunderson GWF-10 .27
Impack End Car or Unit 22
Pickle Car 5
Reefer 40' Ice Wood Sides 5
Reefer 40' Ice Metal Sides 5
Reefer 50' Express .....5+Shim
Reefer 50' Mechanical 5
Reefer 50' Plug Door ....5+Shim
Reefer 57' Mechanical 5
Stock Car 27
Tank Car, 40' 5
Tank Car, 40' Chemical 5
Tank Car, 40' Three Dome 5
Tank Car, 62' 27
TOFC, 86' 27
Rotary Snow Plow 5
200 Ton Crane (Metal & Plastic) 5
Work Caboose on Flat 27
Passenger Car Heavyweight .5 TM
Passenger Car Streamlined .5 TM or 26 TM
Passenger Car Streamlined Observation ......22 TM

ATLAS
DIESEL
Alco B-425 & 426 Century 5
Alco C-424 Phase I and II 5
Alco C-425 5
Alco RS-1 5
Alco RS-3 5
Alco RS-11 5
Alco RSD-4/5 38
Alco RSD-12 5
Alco S-1 28
Alco S-2 27
Alco S-3 28
Alco S-4 27
EMD F3 37
EMD F7 37
EMD FP7 Austria 34
EMD FP7 Japan - Kato 38
EMD GP7 38
EMD GP38 37
EMD GP40 37
EMD SD9 38
EMD SD24 37
EMD SD35 37
GE C 30-7 ....33 or 454 Kit
U23B 5
GE U33/36C ....38 or 454 Kit
ROLLING STOCK
Box Car 50' Double Plug Door . .5

ATLAS CONT'D
Box Car 50' Evans Double Plg Dr5
Caboose, Extended Vision 27
Hopper, 2-Bay Offset 5
Hopper, 2-Bay Offset-Oval Ends .5
Hopper, 3- Bay Cylindrical 5
Hopper, 6-Bay Cylindrical 5
Hopper, Covered PS-2 . . .5+Shim
Tank Car, ACF (Kaoline) 5

AUTHENTICAST
All Rolling Stock 5

BACHMANN
STEAM
0-6-0 USRA Switcher 5
2-6-2 Prairie ....5 ?
2-8-0 Consolidation 5
2-8-2 Mikado ....5 ?
2-10-4 Texas ....5 ?
4-4-0 American (Tender only) .33
4-8-4 GS4 (Tender only) 37
DIESEL
EMD F9 37
EMD F45 37
EMD GP18 28
EMD GP40 37
EMD GP50 37
EMD SD40-2 27
GE E60-CP Electric (Amtrak) . .38
GE U36-B 37
Plymouth 35 Ton Switcher 37
ROLLING STOCK
All Freight Cars (Generic) .37 TM or 5 BM
Box Car, 56' All Door 38
All Cabooses 37
Flat Car ....37 TM or 5 BM
Flat Car Depr. Cent.37 TM or 5 BM
Gondola ....37 TM or 5 BM
Hopper Quad ....37 TM or 5 BM
Hopper 55' Grain Car .37 TM or 5 BM
Ore Car 27' ......37 TM or 5 BM
Reefer 51' Steel ..37 TM or 5 BM
Stock Car ....37 TM or 5 BM
Tank Car ....37 TM or 5 BM
Vinegar Car .....37 TM or 5 BM
Tri-Level 89' Auto Car .37 TM or 5 BM
Box Car, Old Time 37 TM or 5 BM
Caboose, Old Time ....5 BM
Flat Car, Old Time .37 TM or 5 BM
Gondola, Old Time 37 TM or 5 BM
Water Tank Car . . .37 TM or 5 BM
Crane Car (Lifting) ....27 ?
Search Light /Boom Car ...37 TM
Budd 85' Coach ....38 TM or 454
Passenger Cars 85' ....37 or 454

BACHMANN SILVER SERIES
ROLLING STOCK
Freight Cars 5

BACHMANN PLUS
STEAM
4-8-4 GS-4 (Tender only) 37
4-8-4 N&W J (Tender only) 37
4-8-4 Niagara (Tender only) . . .37
4-8-4 Northern (Tender only) . .37
DIESEL
EMD F7 A & B 452
EMD GP35 27
EMD SD45 38
GE B23-7 5
GE B30-7 33

BACHMANN SPECTRUM
STEAM
4-6-2 K4 Pacific 4 Pilot, 37 Tender
2-8-0 Consolidation 36 Pilot, 38 Tender
DIESEL
EMC Gas Elec Doodlebug .Rear 5 or 38
For Small Radius Track 454 w/31
EMD DD40AX 38
EMD FH40PH 27
EMD GP30 37
EMD SD45 33
FM H16-44 34
GE 44-Tonner 33
GE 70-Tonner 21
GE Dash 8-40C 37, (31 Front w/Plow)
GE Dash 8-40CW Wide Cab 37, (31 Front w/Plow)
ROLLING STOCK
Observation Car Front 27, Rear 27+5 box
Passenger Cars (non obs.) . . .27
When running Bachmann Spectrum Passenger Cars on tight radius track use ....454+36
1998 Production Passenger cars 5

BALBOA/TRAINMASTERS
See Manufacturers Instructions .5

BRANCHLINE
Passenger Cars (Con-Cor) . . .508
Other Rolling Stock 5

BEAVER CREEK MODELS (BRASS)
See Manufacturers Instructions .5

BOWSER
STEAM
2-8-0 Consolidation 5
2-8-2 Mikado 5
2-10-0 Decapod 5
4-4-2 Atlantic 5
4-6-2 Pacific 5
4-8-2 Mountain ....5 ?
4-6-6-4 Challenger ....36 Pilot, 5 Tender
Tenders (Penn Line) 5
T-7 Type Tender 5
DIESEL
FM H-16 -44 Diesel (Bowser Box) 28 (In a Kadee Box) 5
ROLLING STOCK
RoadRailer® 53' 5
Hopper, 45' 3-Bay 100 Ton 5
Hopper,4-Bay H-21 5
Box Car, 50' x32 Rnd Roof Dbl Dr5

BRASS CAR SIDES
See Manufacturers Instructions .5

BRAWA See LIFE-LIKE
NOTE: Most late model RTR European Locos and Rolling Stock come equipped with "NEM" style couplers. Kadee® also offers HO-Scale NEM-362 Couplers in four different lengths .17, 18, 19 & 20

CANADIAN RAILWAY MODEL
All Freight Cars 5

CASCADE MODELS
Wood Chip Car 5

KEY: BM = Mounting, CM = Clip Mounting, SM = Screw Mounting, TM = Truck Mounting, ?5 Or ? = Not Verified/Converted by Kadee®

HO SCALE COUPLER CONVERSION LIST

C&BT
AAR 40' Box Car .... .27

C&M SHOPS
All Rolling Stock 5

CENTRAL VALLEY
All Freight Cars .... .4 or 5
Passenger Cars4 Wheel Truck 506
.... .6 Wheel Truck 507

CHALLENGER IMPORTS (Brass)
All Rolling Stock 5
36' Stock Car .... .38
Freight Cars 5

CON-COR
STEAM
4-6-4 Hudson . .28 Pilot, 5 Tender
4-8-8-4 Big Boy33 Pilot, 27 Tender
DIESEL
BUDD RDC (Plastic Body) 21
EMD E7A & B . .Pilot 31, Rear 33
EMD GP38 .... .37
EMD GP40 .... .37
EMD MP15 .... .22
EMD SD24 .... .37
EMD SD35 .... .37
EMD SD40 .... .38
EMD SW7 .... .37
ROLLING STOCK
All Freight Car Kits (Wood) 4 or 5
Box Cars 60' Greenville ...... .27
Box Cars (Empire Builder Series)5
Box Car PS-1 .... .27
Flat Car 54' 5
Mill Gondola 54" 5
Hopper Greenville .... .27 ?
Covered Hopper Airslide . . . .27 ?
Covered Hopper PS-2 .... .38
1890 Oldie Passenger Car ..... .33
Gunderson 5 Unit Twin Stack . . .5
Amtrak Mail Car (60' PD Box Car)5
Amtrak Phase III Car. . .508 & 22
Streamlined Passenger Car
.... .5 BM, 37 TM
Amtrak Superliner . . .27 in 5 box
New Passenger Cars
.... .4 Wheel Trucks 508
.... .6 Wheel Trucks 505
72' Passenger Cars w/4 Wheel
Trucks .... .505

COOPER & OSHTEMO
All Rolling Stock 5

COX
DIESEL
Hustler .... .28
ROLLING STOCK
Freight Cars 5
Caboose Extended Vision
.... .21 TM or 32 BM

CROWN (Brass)
See Manufacturers Instructions .5

CUSTOM RAIL
89' TOFC 5

DETAIL ASSOCIATES
Covered Hopper ACF 2970 5
Gondola 40' GS 5

DETAILS WEST
Box Car, Comb. Door 50' 5
Box Car, Plug Door 50' 5

DIAMOND SCALE MODELS
Wood Chip Car 5

E&B VALLEY
Mill Gondola 65' 5
Covered Hopper .... .22

EASTERN CAR WORKS
Caboose 5
Gondola 65' Mill 5
Hoppers 5
All Heavywt. Passenger Cars ....
.... .5 BM, 21 TM
All Streamlined Passenger Cars 22

E&C SHOPS
ROLLING STOCK
Wood Chip Car 5
Coal Porter Hopper 5
Box Car 50' ACF Double Door . .5
Box Car 52'ACF Modern 5

ENGLISH MODEL TRAINS
DIESEL
ALCO FA-1 .... .38

ERM
Insulated Box (Beer) 62'Car . . .26

ERTL
All Rolling Stock 5

EURO-MODELS IMPORTERS LTD.
DIESEL
EMD FP7 .... .34
Baldwin Shark .... .34
Track Cleaning Car (Roco) ......
.... .37 BM, 21 TM

FLEISHMAN (Germany)
DIESEL
O-C-O Switcher (German) 37
ROLLING STOCK
Non-"NEM" .... .39
Most Fleischmann cars and locomotives that do not have "NEM" coupler pockets will use the #39 coupler mounted on the original pin or screw hole.
NOTE: Most late model RTR European Locos and Rolling Stock come equipped with "NEM" style couplers. Kadee® also offers HO-Scale NEM-362 Couplers in four different lengths
.... .17, 18, 19, & 20

FRATESCHI (E.R. MODELS)
DIESEL
FA-1 (Brazil) .... .37

FRONT RANGE
DIESEL
EMD GP9 5
ROLLING STOCK
Box Car 50' SD 5
TOFC Articulated A & B ends . .27

FUNARO AND CAMERLENGO
All Rolling Stock 5

GEM MODELS (Brass)
See Manufacturers Instructions .5

A.C.GILBERT (American Flyer)
Freight Cars .... .27 in 5 box

GLOBE MODELS
DIESEL
EMD F7 A & B 5
ROLLING STOCK
Freight Cars 5

GLOOR CRAFT MODELS
All Rolling Stock 5

GOULD CO.
ROLLING STOCK
120-Ton Wrecking Crane ..... .22
Boom Car 5
Flat Car 5
Tank Car 5
Wood Ore Car 5

GRANDT LINE HOn3
All HOn3 Rolling Stock ...... .714

HALLMARK (Brass)
See Manufacturers Instructions . .
.... .27 or 28

HERKIMER
All Passenger Cars 7

HOBBYTOWN
DIESEL
ALCO 1600 HP RS/RSD 6
EMD GP9 and GP30 (Athearn) . .8
Chassis GP20 (TYCO) 8
Chassis SDP40, SD45 6
Chassis GE U-28C 6

IHC (Mehano)
STEAM
0-4-0 Dockside .... .27
0-4-0 Switcher 34 Pilot, 34 Tender
2-6-0 Mogul (Mehano)
.... .38 Pilot, 27 Tender
2-6-0 Mogul ..... .38 Pilot, 38 or
.... .28 TM Tender
2-6-0 Camelback Mother Hubbard
.... .Pilot 26
.... .Tender Talgo Type 28
2-8-0 Consolidation ....
.... .39 Pilot, 5 Tender
2-8-2 Mikado .38 Pilot, 27 Tender
4-4-0 American29 Pilot, 28 Tender
4-6-2 Pacific (Mehano) ....
.... .38 Pilot, 27 Tender
4-6-2 Pacific (IHC) ....
.... .31 Pilot, 5 Tender
4-8-2 Mountain 36 Pilot, 5 Tender
DIESEL
EMD E8/9 A and B Units ....
.... .26 Pilot, 27 Rear
EMD SD35 .... .23
EMD SD40 .... .22
GG-1 Electric . . . .New 27 Old 37
MDT Switcher .... .31
SETS
Thunder Bolt Set (Mehano) .....
.... .SD40 Loco 22
.... .Cars 28
ROLLING STOCK
Crane Car and Boom Tender ....
.... .28 TM or 22 BM
Log Car (Buggy) 5
Freight Cars . . . .27 TM or 28 TM
(New) Old Time Freight Cars . . .5
Heavyweight PassCars 6 wheel trucks .... .505
Streamlined Pass Cars 4 wheel trucks .... .508
Passenger Car Truck, 6 Wheel
Die Cast Metal (After Market) .505

IMWX
Box Cars 5

INTERMOUNTAIN
All Freight Cars 5

J-C MODELS
All Passenger Cars Kits 5

KASINER
All Passenger Cars Kits 5

KATO (Japan)
DIESEL
EMD GP35 5
EMD GP35 Phase 1a 5
EMD NW2 ... . .27 in 5 Box
SD40 5
SD45 .... .33
GE C44-9C (Dash 9) ..... .38 or 5
FREIGHT CARS
ACF 70 TON Covered Hopper . . .5

KAZAN (Japan)
45' Whale Belly Tank Car ......
With Kadee #500 Trucks ..... .38

KEN KIDDER (Brass)
STEAM
Generic for most equipment . . .5
0-4-0 Tank 8

KEY (Brass)
See Manufacturers Instructions .5

KEYSTONE LOCOMOTIVE
Log Buggy 5
Climax Log Car (HOn3) ..... .711
(HO) 5

LA BELLE
All Rolling Stock Kits 5

LACONIA
All Rolling Stock Kits 5

LAMBERT ASSOCIATES
See Manufacturers Instructions .5

LBF COMPANY
ROLLING STOCK
8200 Cu. ft Woodchip Car 5
Other Rolling stock 5

LIFE-LIKE®
STEAM
0-4-0 Old Time Tea Kettle 28
0-4-0 Tank (Dockside) .... .27
0-4-0 Switcher .... .27
DIESEL
EMD F7A .... .Pilot 37,
.... .Rear 35 or 27 TM
EMD F7B .... .35 or 27 TM
EMD F40PH .... .28TM
EMD GP38-2 ....
...... .New 33 BM, Old 28 TM
ROLLING STOCK
Generic Freight Cars ..... .27 TM
Box Cars 40' .... .27 TM
Box Cars 50' Thrall ...... .27 TM
Gondola 40' .... .27 TM
Hopper 2 Bay .... .27 TM
Covered Hopper .... .27 TM
Reefer 40' .... .28 TM
Stock Car 40' .... .28 TM
Tank Car 40' .... .28 TM
Lighted Caboose .... .28 TM
Searchlight Car .... .28 TM

LIFE-LIKE CONT'D
Crane Car .... .28 TM
Track Cleaning Car .... .27 TM
Passenger Cars .... .28 TM
Observation (Back End) 26 TM
Body Mounted For all above Life-Like cars 5

LIFE-LIKE® PROTO 1000™ SERIES
DIESEL
EMD F3A .... .23
ROLLING STOCK
Freight Cars 5

LIFE-LIKE® PROTO 2000™ SERIES
DIESEL
Alco FA-2 .... .36 or 26 Front,
.... .38 or 28 Rear
Alco FB-2 .... .38 or 28
Alco PA/PB 26 Pilot, 23 Ends, For
Close Coupling .... .455
EMD BL2 Diesel .... .32 or 22
EMD E6 A&B 23, For Close
Coupling .... .455
EMD E8/9 A .... .33 or 453
EMD E7 A&B 26 Pilot 23 Ends,
For Close-Coupling .... .455
EMD E8/9A .... .33 or 453
EMD GP9 5
EMD GP18 .... .38 or 28
EMD SD7 .... .33 or 23 CM
EMD SD9 .... .33
EMD SW 9/1200 5
ROLLING STOCK
Box Car, 50' DD Auto . . . .5 or 33
Caboose .... .38
Other Freight Car Kits 5
Factory Assembled Cars (RTR) .5

LIMA
STEAM
2-8-2 Mikado .... .37 Tender
DIESEL
Alco C-420 .... .38

LINDBERG
DIESEL
EMD SW600 5
ROLLING STOCK
Freight Cars (Plastic) 5

LIONEL
STEAM
4-8-4 GS-4 (Tender only) 37
DIESEL
EMD F7 A & B . . . .7 Pilot, 8 Rear
EMD GP9 ....?
Lionel Rolling Stock ....?

LMB MODELS (BRASS)
See Manufacturers Instructions .5

L&W
All Rolling Stock Kits 5

MAINLINE
All Rolling Stock Kits 5

KEY: BM = Mounting, CM = Clip Mounting, SM = Screw Mounting, TM = Truck Mounting, ?5 Or ? = Not Verified/Converted by Kadee®

HO SCALE COUPLER CONVERSION LIST

MANTUA
STEAM
0-4-0 Booster 37
0-4-0 Camelback 37
0-4-0 Switcher 37
0-6-0 Tank Switcher 37
0-6-0 Little Six Switcher 37
0-8-0 USRA Switcher . . . .
. . . . .27 Pilot, 37 Tender
2-6-0 Mogul 37
2-6-2 Prairie 37
2-8-0 Consolidation 37
2-8-2 Mikado (Camelback) 37
2-8-2 Mikado (Old- Pwr. in Tender)
5
2-8-2 Mikado 38
2-8-4 Berkshire 37
2-6-6-2 Mallet . .22 Pilot, 28 Rear
4-4-0 American31 Pilot, 37 Tender
4-4-2 Atlantic (Camelback) . . .28
4-6-0 Ten Wheeler (Rogers) . . . .
. . . . .31 Pilot, 37 Tender
4-6-2 Pacific .39 Pilot, 37 Tender
4-6-4 Hudson .31 Pilot, 38 Tender
DIESEL
EMD F7A & B . . . . .28 TM
EMD GP20 . . . . .28 TM
ROLLING STOCK
Box Car (Plastic Chassis) 38
Caboose 4 Wheel Bobber 38
Flat Car 38
Gondola 38
Hopper 2-Bay 38
Covered Hopper 38
Reefer 40' 38
Wood Stock Car 38
Tank Car 38
Water Car (Old Time) 27
Streamlined Pass. Car (Metal) . . .28
Passenger Cars, Old Time 1860 . .27

MARKLIN
Most Marklin Cars and locomotives that have Non-NEM coupler pockets can easily be adapted to use Kadee couplers (mostly 30 series). Contact Kadee with the type of car or locomotive and the Marklin product number.
***NOTE:* Most late model RTR European Locos and Rolling Stock come equipped with "NEM" style couplers. Kadee also offers HO-Scale NEM-362 Couplers in four different lengths . . . . .17, 18, 19, & 20**

MCKEAN
ROLLING STOCK
All Rolling Stock Kits 29
Box Cars PS-1, 40' 29
Flat Car Center Beam, 60' 29

MDC MODEL DIE CASTING CO. (ROUNDHOUSE)
STEAM
0-6-0 Yard Hog (Metal) 4
0-6-0 Switcher (Old) . . . .
. . . . .26 Pilot, 4 Tender
0-6-0 Switcher (New) . . . .
. . . . .26 Pilot, 28 Tender
2-6-0 Mogul (Old) . . . .
. . . . .26 Pilot, 4 Tender
2-6-0 Mogul (New) . . . .
. . . . .26 Pilot, 28 Tender
2-6-2 Prairie (Old) . . . .
. . . . .26 Pilot, 4 Tender
2-6-2 Prairie (New) . . . .
. . . . .26 Pilot, 28 Tender
2-8-0 Consolidation (Old) . . . . .
. . . . .26 Pilot, 4 Tender

MDC CONT'D
2-8-0 Consolidation (New) . . . . .
. . . . .26 Pilot, 28 Tender
4-4-2 Atlantic (Old) . . . .
. . . . .26 Pilot, 4 Tender
4-4-2 Atlantic (New) . . . .
. . . . .26 Pilot, 28 Tender
4-6-0 Ten Wheeler (Old) . . . .
. . . . .26 Pilot, 4 Tender
4-6-0 Ten Wheeler (New) . . . . . .
. . . . .26 Pilot, 28 Tender
Climax 5
Shay .27
DIESEL
Alco RS-3 5
Box Cab Diesel 5
Track Cleaner 5
ROLLING STOCK
All Rolling Stock 5
Hopper, Sand (Metal) .4 with 204
Ore Car (Older Metal) 37
Tank Cars Old Time 26' 28
Harriman Passenger Cars 5

MEHANO (See IHC)

MICRO-ENGINEERING
ROLLING STOCK
All HOn3 Rolling Stock 714
Adapte-Railer 5

MODEL POWER
STEAM
0-4-0 27
2-8-0 Consolidation . . . . .26 Pilot
. . . . .5 Tender
4-6-0 Casey Jones . . . . . .26 Pilot
. . . . .5 Tender
4-6-2 Pacific . . . . .38 Pilot
. . . . .27 Tender
DIESEL
ALCO C-430 28
ALCO C-628 25
ALCO FA-2 & FB-2 . . . . .Front 37
. . . . .Rear 27
ALCO RS-11 . . . . .33 BM, 29 TM
Baldwin Shark Nose A & B . . . . .
. . . . .Front 37, Rear 27
EMD E7 . . . . . .Front 36, Rear 38
EMD E8/9 . . . . .Front 36, Rear 38
Porter Hustler 28
ROLLING STOCK
All Freight Cars (Generic) . . . .
. . . . .5 BM, 28 TM
Streamlined Pass. Cars (Tri-Ang)37
Streamlined Passenger Cars 27 TM
***NOTE:* Most late model RTR European Locos and Rolling Stock come equipped with "NEM" style couplers. Kadee® also offers HO-Scale NEM-362 Couplers in four different lengths**
. . . . .17, 18, 19, & 20

MODEL EXPO (RIVAROSSI)
All Rolling Stock see Rivarossi

MTS IMPORTS (Brass)
See Manufacturers Instructions .5

NEW ENGLAND RAIL SERVICE
All Rolling Stock 5

NICKLE PLATE PRODUCTS
See Manufacturers Instructions .5

NORTHEASTERN
All Rolling Stock 5

NORTHWEST SHORTLINE
All HO Rolling Stock 5
All HOn3 Rolling Stock 714

OVERLAND MODELS (BRASS)
See Manufacturers Instructions .5

PECOS RIVER BRASS
See Manufacturers Instructions .5

PENN LINE
Midget Whitcomb Switcher . . .38
See Bowser for Steam Locomotives

PFM (Brass)
See Manufacturers Instructions
. . . . .HO 5
HOn3 714

PMI (LIMA)
STEAM
0-4-0 Switcher . . . . .27 ?
2-8-2 Mikado .38 Pilot, 27 Tender
DIESEL
ALCO C 420 . . . . .27 TM
EMD FP45 . . . . .27 with 5 Lid
ROLLING STOCK
All Freight Cars 38
Caboose 5
All Passenger Cars . . . . . . .27 TM

PRECISION SCALE CO.
All Products in HO 5
All Products in HOn3 714

PROTO POWER WEST
Thrall Container Car 5

QUALITY CRAFT MODELS
All Rolling Stock 5

RAIL POWER PRODUCTS
DIESEL
EMD SD60M (SD75M) 27
GE DASH 8-40B 27
ROLLING STOCK
Gunderson Well Car 5
See Manufacturers Instructions for other Kadee coupler recommendations.

RAILWORKS (Brass)
See Manufacturers Instructions .5

RED CABOOSE
All Rolling Stock 5

REVELL
STEAM
0-4-0 Switcher 33
0-6-0T Switcher 33
DIESEL
EMD SW7 . . . . .36 Front, 37 Rear
ROLLING STOCK
All Freight Cars 5

RIVAROSSI (Post 1993)
STEAM
0-8-0 Switcher . . . .
. . . . .38 Pilot, 38 Tender BM
2-8-4 Berkshire34 Pilot, 26 Tender
2-8-8-0 and 2-8-8-2 Mallet 33 Pilot
Vanderbilt Tender 38
Standard Tender 27BM
4-4-0 Amer, Inyo, Reno, Genoa . .
. . . . .38 Tender
4-6-2 Pacific . . . .
. . . .33 Pilot, Tender 5 BM 31 TM
4-6-4 Hudson . .28 Pilot, 5 Tender

RIVAROSSI CONT'D
4-8-4 UP Northern . . . .
. . . . .33 Pilot, 27 Tender
4-6-6-4 Challenger . . . .
. . . . .33 Pilot, 27 Tender
4-8-8-2 Cab Forward . . . .
. . . . .33 Pilot, 27 Tender
4-8-8-4 Big Boy 33 Pilot, 27 Tender
Heisler Two and Three Truck . . . .
. . . . .32 BM 21 TM
DIESEL
ALCO C-420 5
EMD E8/9 . . . . .27 Pilot, 24 Rear
ROLLING STOCK
Log Car Buggy 33
Hvywt. Passenger Car, 6 Wheel505
Streamlined Pass. Car, 4 Wheel508

ROCO
LOCOMOTIVES and ROLLING STOCK
200-Ton Crane 31
All Passenger Cars (NEM-362) 18
***NOTE:* Most late model RTR European Locos and Rolling Stock come equipped with "NEM" style couplers. Kadee® also offers HO-Scale NEM-362 Couplers in four different lengths** 17, 18, 19, & 20

ROLLER BEARING MODELS
All Rolling Stock 5

ROUNDHOUSE (MDC)
See MDC-Model Die Casting Co.

RSO (Mehano)
DIESEL
RSD-12 26

SILVER STREAK
All Rolling Stock 5

SPECTRUM (See Bachmann)

S. SOHO AND CO. (Brass)
See Manufacturers Instructions .5

STEWART HOBBIES
DIESEL
ALCO RS-3 5
Baldwin AS-16 22
EMD FT A & B (Pilot and Rear of B)
. 5
(Between A & B) 35
EMD F3 A & B 450
EMD F7 A & B 450
GE U25B 5
ROLLING STOCK
Rolling Stock 5

SUNSET MODELS (Brass)
See Manufacturers Instructions .5

SUNSHINE MODELS
All Rolling Stock 5

SYLVAN
All Rolling Stock (w/Kadee #500 Trucks) 5

TENSHODO (Brass)
See Manufacturers Instructions .5

TICHY TRAIN GROUP
Box Car 28
Flat Car 5
Hopper 2-Bay U.S.R.A 5
Reefer 40' Wood 5

TIGER VALLEY
All Diesels 5

TRAIN-MASTER
All Rolling Stock 5

TRAIN MINIATURES
DIESEL
Alco FA-1 . . . . .6 Pilot, 8 Rear
Alco FB-1 8

TRAIN STATION PRODUCTS
Hi- Level Passenger Car 5

TRU-SCALE
All Rolling Stock 5

TYCO
STEAM
0-4-0 Booster . .37 Pilot, 5 Tender
0-6-0 Little Six . . . .
. . . . .37 Pilot, 5 Tender
0-6-0 Big Six 37
0-8-0 Chattanooga . . . .
. . . . .5 Pilot, 27 TM Tender
2-6-2 Prairie 37
2-8-2 Mikado 38
4-4-0 General (Tender only) 5
4-6-2 Pacific .39 Pilot, 37 Tender
DIESEL
ALCO C-430 . . . . .27 TM
EMD F9 A & B.. 33 BM and 33 TM
EMD GP20 9
GG-1 Electric . . . . .26 TM
Plymouth Switcher 5
ROLLING STOCK
All Freight Cars (Generic) . . .9 Old
. . . . .27 or 28 New
Box Car 40' . . . . .9 Old, 28 New
Box Car 50' Plug Door 27
Caboose . . . . .9 Old, 27 New
Flat Car . . . . .9 Old, 28 New
Gondola . . . . .9 Old, 28 New
Hopper 2-Bay . . . . .9 Old, 28 New
Covered Hopper 54' 27
Reefer 40' . . . . .9 Old, 28 New
Reefer 60' Plug Door 27
Stock Car . . . . .9 Old, 28 New
Tank Car . . . . .9 Old, 28 New
Tank Car 60' 3-Dome 27
All Old Time Freight Cars 9
Streamlined Passenger Cars . . .5
Old Time Passenger Cars 9

ULRICH
All Rolling Stock, Metal 4
All Rolling Stock, Wood 5

U.S. HOBBIES, INC. (Brass)
See Manufacturers Instructions .5

VAN HOBBIES MODELS
Canadian Models sold by PFM . .5

VARNEY
STEAM
0-4-0 Dockside 5
2-8-0 Consolidation (Old Lady) .5
4-6-0 Ten Wheeler (Casey Jones)5
4-6-2 Pacific 5
DIESEL
EMD F7 A and B 5
EMD SW1 (NW-1) 5
ROLLING STOCK
All Freight Cars (Metal) 4
All Freight Cars (Plastic) 5
Ore Car 37

KEY: BM = Mounting, CM = Clip Mounting, SM = Screw Mounting, TM = Truck Mounting, ?5 Or ? = Not Verified/Converted by Kadee®

WALTHERS

ROLLING STOCK
Box Car 40' Wood 5
Box Car 40' Steel 5
Box Car 40' PS-1 5
Box Car 50' DD 5
Box Car 50' Waffle Side 5
Coil Car 55' 5
All Flat Cars 42' 5
All Flat Cars 53' 6" 5
Flat Car Depressed Center, 4 Truck 5
Flat Cars 75' Piggy Back 5
Flat Cars 89' Channel-Side 5
All Purpose Spline Cars 5
Well Car-Stand Alone 5
Well Cars-5 Unit Articulated 5
Auto Carrier 89' 5
Gondola 40' 5
Gondola 53' Thrall 5
All Hoppers 36' 5
All Hoppers 49' 5
Covered Hoppers 37' Cement ..5
Covered Hoppers 39' Airslide ...5
Covered Hoppers 50' Airslide ...5
Covered Hoppers 84' Airslide ...5
Covered Hoppers PD 5
Covered Hoppers PS-2 5
Reefers 40' Wood 5
Reefers 40' Steel 5
Reefers 40' Plug Door 5
Reefers Cryogenic 5
Reefers RBL Insulated 5
Stock Car 40' 5
Tank Car 10,000 Gallon 5
Tank Car 40' UTLX 5
Tank Car 30' Funnel-Flow® 5
Tank Car 40' Funnel-Flow® 5
Tank Car 54' Funnel-Flow® 5
Tank Car 65' LPG 5
Tank Car 65' Ammonia 5
M.O.W. 25 Ton Crane 5
M.O.W. Scale Test Car 5
M.O.W. Russell Snow Plow 5
All M.O.W. Work Cars 5
All M.O.W. Work Train Sets 5
M.O.W. Difco Dump Car (Metal Chassis) 28
Hot Metal Car 5
Slag Car 5
Jordan Spreader .Front 36, Rear 5
Amfleet Passenger Car 5
Horizon Commuter Pass. Car ....5 or 454w/36
Superliner Passenger Cars 26
On small radius curves use 454 with 38
DIESEL
EMD SW-1 Switcher 5
FM H10/12-44 5

WALTHERS TRAINLINE

DIESEL
Alco FA-1 and FB-1 5
EMD F40PH 28
EMD GP9M 28
GE Dash 8-40B 5

WALTHERS TRAINLINE SETS

DIESEL
EMD GP9M 28
ROLLING STOCK
Box Car 29
Caboose, Extended Vision 27
Flat Car 28
Gondola 28
Tank Car 22

WESTERFIELD

All Rolling Stock Kits 5

WESTSIDE MODEL CO. (Brass)

See Manufacturers Instructions .5

YANKEE CLIPPER MODELS

All Rolling Stock Kits 5

YE OLDE HUFF-N-PUFF

ROLLING STOCK
All HO Rolling Stock Kits 5
All HOn3 Rolling Stock Kits 714

ALL HOn3 MANUFACTURERS

You may choose "Old Time" 3/4 size Kadee® #711, Or HOn3 Kadee® #714 Couplers

Note: Please use Kadee® HOn3 Coupler Height Gauge #704 to assure proper Trip Pin clearance and correct coupler height.

Please see adjacent General Notes and Helpful Hints.

ILLUSTRATIONS

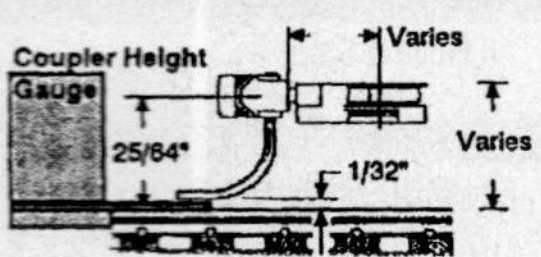

Critical HO Scale Coupler dimensions

Kadee's® 20 and 30 series couplers are specifically designed to accommodate widely varying coupler mounting conditions on equipment from various U.S. manufactures and importers.

Try these first; They offer numerous adaptation possibilities in couplers, draft gear box orientation, and height and length.

Should you still require more adjustment, cutting away or shimming the mounting platform may be necessary..

Floor

Floor

TYPICAL METHOD TO ADJUST COUPLER DRAFT GEAR BOX HEIGHT.

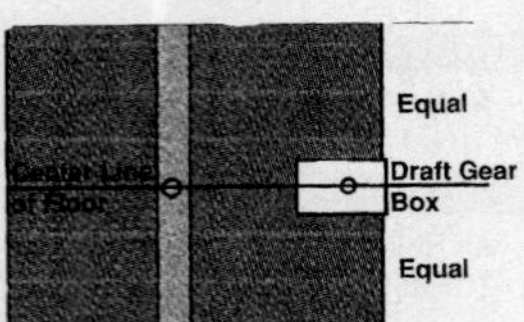

PLACEMENT OF DRAFT GEAR BOX AND COUPLER EXACTLY ON CENTERLINE OF EQUIPMENT IS VERY IMPORTANT TO ASSURE PROPER KADEE® COUPLER OPERATION.

Designers and Producers of Kadee®

GENERAL NOTES & HELPFUL HINTS

1. Most craftsman style kits requiring built up construction from wood, plastic, brass or a combination of these materials, are easily fitted with the **#5 Kadee® Draft Gear Box and Coupler.** Height adjustments can usually be made by removing car body material under the Draft Gear Box, or by addition of shims. Kadee® **#211 Shims** are ideal for this purpose.

2. Many "HO Brass" imports are already "set up" to accommodate a #5 Draft Gear Box and Coupler with drilled and tapped holes (usually metric) for mounting. You may still need to adjust for height and/or refit by "trial and error" to find the best Kadee® Coupler for a given condition, on a particular model. **The #13 Sample Kit** is ideal for this purpose.

3. Special conditions such as pilot/cow catcher/front end coupler mounting on steam or diesel locomotives may require a longer coupler shank to "clear" front obstructions. Different coupler mounting heights on the front and rear of locomotives are also common, and need to be taken into consideration when choosing the correct Kadee® Coupler and Draft Gear Box combination.

4. Some adaptations of Kadee® Couplers may require modifications to the frame, body, and/or truck or other components to allow for proper mounting height, location and free operation of the coupler. In some cases this may require advanced skills in model building.

5. **The 20 and 30 Series of Kadee® Couplers were specifically created to provide the model railroader with numerous choices in coupler mounting.** The 20 and 30 Series gives you choices in height and length by providing Underset, Centerset, and Overset Coupler Shanks, plus Top or Bottom Draft Gear Box positioning, with four different coupler lengths. This should provide the modeler with a coupler to fit almost any condition and minimize the time-consuming "cut and fit" process.

6. To assure uniform and consistent performance of Kadee® Couplers, the mounting height and coupler trip pin clearance are critical. Please use our **#205 Height Gauge and #237 Coupler Trip Pin Pliers** to help you establish and maintain the correct dimensions.

WHAT IS DELAYED-ACTION UNCOUPLING?

Spotting a car (removing a car from the train, usually placing it at a siding or spur track) is an easy procedure with Kadee® Magne-Matic® couplers. When stopped over the uncoupler, the couplers are in the "open" position. When pushed back together again, they are in the "delayed" position. In this position, the coupler lips (the flat area of the couplers) are pressed into the center of the opposite coupler. Consequently, the knuckles can't couple together. It is now possible to push back the car to be spotted to any location on any track beyond the uncoupler without recoupling. Once stopped, the train leaves the car in position. When pulling away, the couplers return to the normal "couple" position, ready to pick-up.

All Kadee® Magne-Matic® couplers will operate in the delayed-action mode. However, Kadee® makes both delayed-action and nondelayed action uncouplers, as well as the Magne-electrics which will operate either way. The difference between the delayed and nondelayed uncouplers is the width of the magnet and the corresponding amount of off-center draw the magnet has on the trip pins. The nondelayed action uncoupler has sufficient width to cause the couplers to uncouple, but not enough to draw the couplers wide enough to put them in the delayed position. Once pushed off the uncoupler, the couplers will return to the "coupled" position, preventing the cars from being spotted without another uncoupler.

All wheelsets are brass with black nickel plating (unless noted) and are RP25 contour, .110" tread.

METAL WHEELSETS & AXLES

369-10620 36" Wheels pkg(12) 20K Ohm **19.90**
369-10639 36" Wheels pkg(12) 39K Ohm **19.90**
369-10820 33" Wheels pkg(12) 20K Ohm **18.90**
369-10839 33" Wheels pkg(12) 39K Ohm **18.90**

FOR ATHEARN EMD SD60

369-10242 42" Solid Nickel 1/2 Axle **13.50**

ATHEARN DIESEL

369-100 36" Wheels w/1/2 Axle pkg(12) **7.50**
369-101 42" Wheels w/1/2 Axle pkg(8) **5.60**
369-102 40" Solid Nickel Silver Wheels w/1/2 Axle pkg(8) **8.95**
For use in newer Athearn diesels with molded plastic sideframes. Includes parts to convert one four-axle loco.

POINTED END AXLES

369-98 38" pkg(12) **12.70**
369-106 36" pkg(12) **11.95**
369-107 28" pkg(8) **7.25**
369-108 33" pkg(12) **11.75**
369-109 40" pkg(4) **4.10**
369-988 33" & 38" pkg(12) **12.10**
Includes four 33" and eight 38" pointed end axles for Walthers Double Stack cars.

SHOULDER END AXLES PKG(4) EA 4.90

369-1012 42"
369-1062 36"
369-1072 28"
369-1082 33"
369-1092 40"

BLUNT END AXLES PKG(4) EA 4.90

369-1011 42"
369-1061 36"
369-1081 33"
369-1091 40"

AXLES & MOLDED PLASTIC WHEELS

369-105 Nonmagnetic Axles pkg(24) **3.25**
For Athearn and Roundhouse freight cars with 33" molded wheels.

METAL WHEEL REPLACEMENTS PKG(6) EA 5.95

369-1094 40" Wheelset For Athearn Dummy
369-1095 42" Wheelset For Athearn Dummy

COUPLER MOUNT PADS

Improve the handling of long HO Scale passenger cars by replacing the Talgo couplers with these body-mounted coupler mounting pads. Use to mount Kadee® type couplers to Athearn, Bachmann, Con-Cor, Rivarossi and Roundhouse cars. When used with the proper size wheels, these pads provide correct coupler heights. Each mounting pad is adjustable, so cars can be spaced close together or apart when coupled. Parts to convert three cars are included in each pack.

RIVAROSSI EA 2.90

369-110 1920 Baggage Cars
369-111 1920 Cars Except Baggage
369-112 1930 Cars
369-117 1940 Cars

ATHEARN EA 2.90

369-113 Streamline
369-114 Heavyweight

CON-COR EA 2.90

369-115 Budd 72 & 85' Cars
369-116 Superliners

BACHMANN

369-118 Spectrum Cars **3.25**

DETAIL ASSOCIATES

369-120 ATSF "El Capitan" **3.25**

RAIL POWER

SD90-MAC & ATHEARN SD-40-2

369-10245 45" Solid Nickel 1/2 Axle **13.50**

KEYSTONE LOCOMOTIVE WORKS

All-metal craft train kits, unless noted.

FREIGHT TRUCKS

395-30 Grasse River Logging 1 Pair **3.95**
This kit builds one pair of Grasse River Logging trucks for the Grasse River log buggie. Includes cast-metal bolsters and sideframes, plus RP25 wheels.

PASSENGER TRUCKS

395-9 Pennsylvania 6-Wheel 1 Pair **10.95**
Pre-assembled with NorthWest Short Line nickel-silver wheelsets.

KATO

TRUCKS

ASF RIDE CONTROL TRUCK

381-31601 A-3 pkg(2) **4.98**
Based on American Steel Foundries A-3 freight car truck. Fully assembled, molded in black plastic with metal wheels.

BARBER S-2 TRUCK

381-31602 70-Ton Roller Bearing pkg(2) **5.98**
Features a wheel bearing cap that spins as truck is rolling, simultaneously maintaining the vehicle's smooth rolling ability.

COUPLER

381-7602 Knuckle Coupler 10 Pair **5.00**
Prototypical in size and shape, the coupler is the same semi-automatic version featured on the Kato Covered Hopper Cars. Compatible with most other brands of couplers.

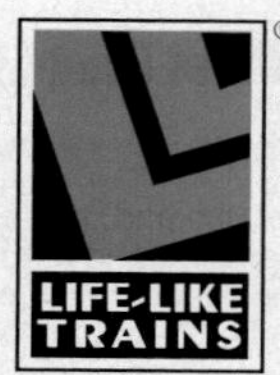

Molded plastic trucks and couplers.

COUPLERS

433-1433 Horn-Hook pkg(4) **3.75**

PROTO 2000 COUPLERS

433-21095 1 Pair **1.50**
433-21096 10 Pair **11.00**

TRUCKS

433-1435 Bettendorf 1 Pair **3.75**
Ready-to-run, with couplers.

PROTO 2000 TRUCKS PKG(2) EA 3.95

50-TON SPRING PLANKLESS W/33" WHEELSETS

433-21251 Ribbed Back
433-21253 Flat Back

NATIONAL B-1 W/33" WHEELSETS

433-21254 Ribbed Back
433-21255 Flat Back

BARBER S-2 100-TON

433-21256 With 36" Wheelsets pkg(2)

WHEELSETS

PROTO 2000 WHEELSETS PKG(12) EA 7.00

433-21257 36"
433-21258 33" Flat Back
433-21259 33" Ribbed Back

McHenry Couplers™

COUPLERS

STANDARD

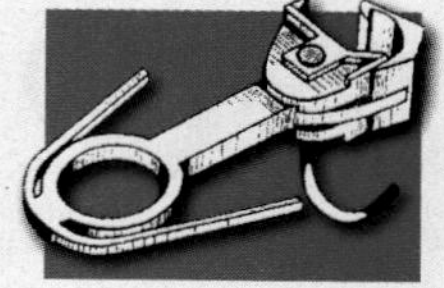

443-1 1 Pair **.99**
443-5 With Draft Boxes 2 Pair **2.19**
443-112 6 Pair **5.79**
443-150 25 Pair **19.95**
443-500 250 Pair **195.00**

KNUCKLE SPRING STYLE

443-51 1 Pair **1.19**
443-512 6 Pair **5.99**
443-550 25 Pair **22.99**

FOR IHC/RIVAROSSI PASSENGER CARS 1 PAIR EA 3.69

Simply clips in place on the standard mounting, requires no adapter kit for installation.

443-2 Fits 4-Wheel Trucks
443-3 Fits 6-Wheel Trucks

FOR RIVAROSSI LOCOS & FREIGHT CARS

443-6 2 Pair **3.69** *NEW*

SPECIALTY COUPLERS 2 PAIR EA 1.98

443-10 Short Shank, Lowered Head
443-11 Standard Shank, Lowered Head

443-12 Long Shank, Lowered Head
443-13 Short Shank, Centered Head
443-14 Long Shank, Centered Head

443-15 Short Shank, Raised Head
443-16 Standard Shank, Raised Head
443-17 Long Shank, Raised Head

UNCOUPLER

443-4 Magnetic Uncoupler **1.98**

MODEL POWER

HO Scale plastic couplers and trucks.

COUPLERS EA 2.29

490-96002 Standard Cars
490-97002 Heavyweight Cars

TRUCKS

490-94002 RP25 **2.29**
490-95002 Standard **2.29**
490-6512 Metal Wheels for Freight Cars **TBA**

KEIL-LINE MODELS

HO Scale craft train kits.

FREIGHT TRUCKS EA 6.59

Kits contain three pair of all-metal sprung trucks, less wheelsets. For use with Kadee® wheelsets.

382-8721 Bettendorf
382-8722 Timken

NEW ENGLAND HOBBY SUPPLY

THE COUPLER SELECTOR

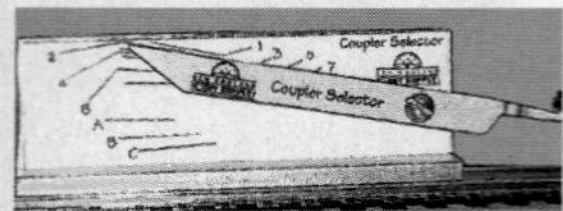

522-5 11.98
Convert your equipment to knuckle couplers quickly and easily. Easy-to-read gauge provides instant height and depth requirements for all locos and cars, including those equipped with talgo and body mounted couplers. Works with Kadee®, Bachmann®, Intermountain and McHenry Coupler® styles. Selector chart included.

OLD PULLMAN

TRUCKS

Assembled trucks with needle-point nonmagnetic axles and sprung Delrin sideframes and bolsters. "Black Label" trucks have precision-made NMRA RP-25 black nickel-plated brass wheelsets. "Red Label" trucks feature Walthers RP-25 plastic wheels.

TIMKEN ROLLER BEARING
1955 to present, 1 pair each.

536-40021 Black Label 33" Wheels **5.75**
536-40091 Red Label 33" Wheels **2.75**
536-40031 Black Label 36" Wheels **5.75**

BETTENDORF
50-ton AAR, 1940/1950 era, 33" wheels, 1 pair each.

536-40001 Black Label **5.75**
536-40081 Red Label **2.75**

ANDREWS
1930-1939 era, 33" wheels, 1 pair each.

536-40011 Black Label **5.75**
536-40061 Red Label **2.75**

ON-TRAK MODEL PRODUCTS

White metal castings with Delrin wheels.

TRUCKS 1 PAIR EA 5.50 (UNLESS NOTED)

786-5301 PSC Arch Bar

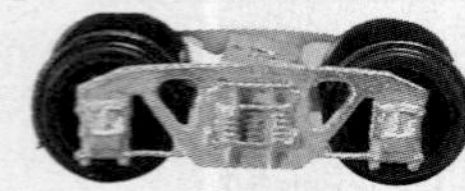

786-5302 PRR 70-Ton

786-5303 Swing Motion
5' wheel base.

786-5304 Arch Bar
5' wheel base.

786-5305 Grasse River Arch Bar **5.95**

NorthWest Short Line

Power trucks and drive units are assembled and ready to run. Wheelsets are all-metal and can be used with Athearn and other HO and HOn3 Scale equipment.

A NorthWest Short Line catalog (#53-1, 7.00) is available for more detailed information on these products.

DRIVE UNITS

FLEA II

53-2076 Auxiliary Gearbox **7.50**
15:1 ratio, less geared wheelset.

POWER TRUCK UPGRADE

53-3286 GSB/Kumata Worm Kit **4.25**
Worm replacement kit for GSB/Kumata vertical motor style power truck mechanism. Provides a steel worm plus spacer to adapt the worm to the original brass wormgear. Truck disassembly not required.

SIDEFRAMES

BRILL SIDEFRAMES

53-4325 Brill 77EI pkg(4) **4.50**
As used on Brill master units and other streetcars. 5'-6" wheelbase, forged brass.

WHEELSETS

Nonmagnetic wheelsets with nickel-plated brass wheels (insulated on one side only for electrical pick-up) and 3/32" diameter axles. In general, 110 size tread is used in HO Scale, 88 in HOn3.

FLEA II GEARED WHEELSETS EA 4.95 (UNLESS NOTED)

Geared wheelsets have a shoulder style axle, except for #053-20196, which is flush. 1/16" journal on shouldered style. Wheelsets fit Flea II #53-2056, #53-2066 or Auxiliary Gearbox #53-2076.

53-20056 26"/110 Wheels
53-20016 33"/110 Wheels
53-20026 36"/110 Wheels
53-20036 40"/110 Wheels
53-20046 42"/110 Wheels
53-20086 26"/88 Wheels, HO
53-20186 26"/88 Wheels, HOn3
53-20196 26"/88 Wheels, Flush Axle
53-20096 33"/88 Wheels
53-20106 36"/88 Wheels
53-20236 3/32" Shaft (Axle) w/Gear **3.50**

BLUNT AXLE WHEELSETS PKG(6) EA 8.95

53-71434 36"/110 Wheels
53-71094 40"/110 Wheels
53-71394 40"/110 Wheels, Athearn Half Axle
53-71414 40"/110 Wheels, Athearn Inside Frame
53-71104 42"/110 Wheels
53-71404 42"/110 Wheels, Athearn Half Axle
53-71424 42"/110 Wheels, Athearn Inside Frame
53-72394 40"/88 Wheels, Athearn Half Axle
53-72414 40"/88 Wheels, Athearn Inside Frame

FLUSH AXLE WHEELSETS

53-71234 26"/110 Wheels pkg(4) **5.95**
53-71244 26"/110 Wheels pkg(4) **5.95**
For PCC cars.

53-71254 28"/110 Wheels pkg(4) **5.95**
53-1166 36"/110 Wheels, Geared pkg(4) **19.95**
For Keystone 44-Tonner.

53-1106 36"/110 Wheels, 2 Geared pkg(6) **12.95**
For AHM/Rivarossi E8/9.

53-71294 40"/110 Wheels pkg(6) **8.95**
53-71304 42"/110 Wheels pkg(6) **8.95**
53-73224 24"/88 Wheels pkg(4) **5.95**
53-73234 26"/88 Wheels pkg(4) **5.95**
53-72244 26"/88 Wheels pkg(4) **5.95**
For PCC cars.

53-72254 28"/88 Wheels pkg(4) **6.95**

POINTED AXLE WHEELSETS

53-71154 28"/110 Wheels pkg(4) **5.95**
53-71164 30"/110 Wheels pkg(4) **5.95**
53-71174 33"/110 Wheels pkg(4) **5.95**
53-1176 33"/110 Wheels, Geared pkg(4) **14.95**
For Keystone 44-Tonner.

53-71184 36"/110 Wheels pkg(6) **8.95**
53-1156 36"/110 Wheels, Geared pkg(4) **10.00**
For Keystone 44-Tonner.

53-71364 38"/110 Wheels pkg(4) **5.95**
53-71194 40"/110 Wheels pkg(6) **8.95**
53-71204 42"/110 Wheels pkg(6) **8.95**
53-73124 24"/88 Wheels pkg(4) **3.95**
53-73134 26"/88 Wheels pkg(4) **5.95**
53-72154 28"/88 Wheels, HO pkg(4) **5.95**
53-73154 28"/88 Wheels, HOn3 pkg(4) **5.95**
53-73164 30"/88 Wheels pkg(4) **5.95**
53-72174 33"/88 Wheels pkg(4) **5.95**
53-72184 36"/88 Wheels pkg(6) **8.95**
53-72364 38"/88 Wheels pkg(4) **5.95**

FOR LIFE-LIKE PROTO 2000 E8 UNITS PKG(12) EA 9.95

Half axle with needle point, available in two tread sizes.

53-71454 36"/110
53-72454 36"/88

POINTED AXLE WHEELSETS-WEATHERED

53-171154 28"/110 Wheels pkg(4) **5.95**
53-171174 33"/110 Wheels pkg(4) **5.95**
53-171184 36"/110 Wheels pkg(4) **8.95**
53-171364 38"/110 Wheels pkg(4) **5.95**
53-172364 38"/88 Wheels pkg(4) **3.95**

SHOULDERED AXLE WHEELSETS

1/16" journal.

53-71034 26"/110 Wheels pkg(4) **5.95**
53-71054 28"/110 Wheels pkg(4) **5.95**
53-71064 30"/110 Wheels pkg(4) **5.95**
53-71074 33"/110 Wheels pkg(4) **5.95**
53-71084 36"/110 Wheels pkg(6) **8.95**
53-71314 40"/110 Wheels pkg(6) **8.95**
53-71324 42"/110 Wheels pkg(6) **8.95**
53-73024 24"/88 Wheels pkg(4) **5.95**
53-73034 26"/88 Wheels pkg(4) **5.95**
53-72054 28"/88 Wheels pkg(4) **5.95**
53-72074 33"/88 Wheels pkg(4) **5.95**
53-72084 36"/88 Wheels pkg(6) **8.95**

NICKEL PLATED NON-MAGNETIC ATHEARN™ WHEELSETS EA 8.95

53-71444 45"/110 Inside Frame pkg(6)
53-71424 42"/88 Inside Frame pkg(6)
53-72444 45"/88 Needle Point
53-72424 42"/88 Needle Point

RED CABOOSE

FREIGHT CAR WEIGHTS

629-5006 pkg(4) **2.95**

FREIGHT TRUCKS

629-5004 T Section, Black **2.75**
629-5005 T Section, Black pkg(12) **33.00**
629-5007 Andrews **2.75**
629-5008 Andrews pkg(12) **33.00**
629-5009 PRR 2DF8, Black **2.75**
629-5010 PRR 2DF8, Black pkg(12) **33.00**
629-5011 T Section Bettendorf Truck Less Wheels 1 Pair, Black **2.00**
629-5012 Andrews Less Wheels, Black **2.00**
629-5013 PRR 2DF8 Less Wheels, Black **2.00**

RAIL LINE

Couplers are molded in black nylon.

COUPLERS

620-101 Magnetic w/Draft Gear pkg(4) **2.50**

620-107 Regular NMRA Style Less Draft Gear pkg(4) **1.20**
620-106 Regular NMRA Style w/Draft Gear pkg(4) **2.00**

620-116 HOn3 "Sharon" pkg(6) **1.00**
Nonoperating, long shank.

UNCOUPLERS

620-102 Magnet for No. 101 pkg(2) **3.00**

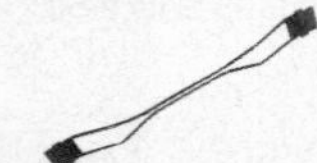

620-112 Uncoupling Ramp, Stationary pkg(2) **1.20**
One-piece, black nylon uncoupling ramp assures positive, automatic switching. Installs anywhere on layout.

IMPORTED FROM AUSTRIA
BY WALTHERS
Couplers are injection-molded plastic.

DELAYED CLOSE COUPLERS

Delayed close couplers are specially designed so that the ends of locomotives and cars separate around curves so that the buffers align correctly. While running on straight track the separation between coaches reduces itself realistically. Couplers conform to European Model Railway standards (NEM 362), and can be used with Roco and other equipment.

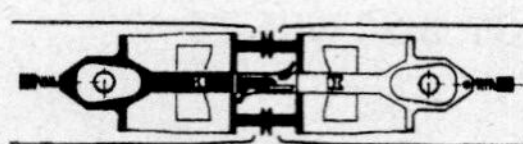

An underside view of two close-coupled cars, after removal of the trucks. On straight track, the buffers are close together, as on the prototype.

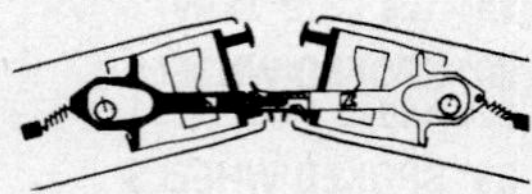

As soon as the cars enter a curve, the coupler shafts push the cars apart. When the cars return to a straight section of track, they are pulled together again as the coupler shafts follow the gull-winged grooves in the car floors.

625-40243

625-40244

625-40243 Loop-Type Coupler **2.49**
625-40244 For Fleischmann Freight Cars **2.99**

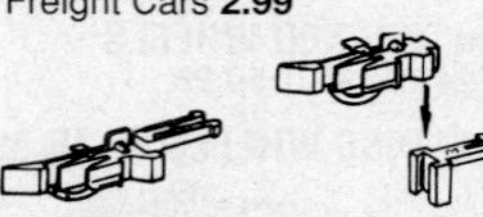

625-40270 625-40287

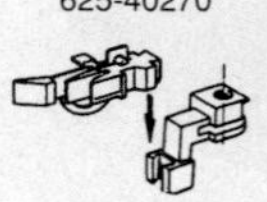

625-40280

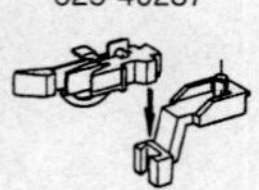

625-40281

625-40270 Standard Close Coupler pkg(4) **3.99**
625-40271 Standard Close Coupler pkg(50) **26.99**
625-40280 For Fleischmann Cars 1 Pair **3.99**
625-40281 For Fleischmann Cars 1 Pair **3.99**

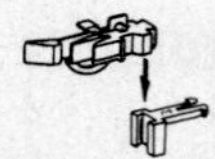

625-40286 For Ade Cars **3.99**
625-40287 Standard Close Coupler-Adjustable Height 1 Pair **3.99**
Height can be adjusted up or down for correct alignment between couplers.

Limited Quantity Available

625-40201 For Cars #46106-46107 **1.99**
625-40202 For Cars #46176-46180 **1.99**
625-40203 For Cars #44360-44461 **1.99**
625-40220 Close Coupler pkg(4) **2.49**
Without delayed uncoupling ability
625-40233 For Cars #46250-46251 **2.49**
625-40273 Close Couplers 1 Pair **2.99**
625-40276 Close Couplers 1 Pair **2.99**
625-40277 Close Couplers 1 Pair **2.99**
625-40279 Close Couplers 1 Pair **2.99**
625-40282 Close Couplers 1 Pair **2.99**
625-40330 Close Couplers 1 Pair **2.99**

625-40335 For Cars #46227-46229 1 Pair **2.99**
625-40337 Close Couplers 1 Pair **2.99**

RETROFIT COUPLER MECHANISMS

Retrofit mechanisms to convert older-style cars with delayed close-couplers.

625-40341 2-Axle Cars **5.99**
For cars up to 5-5/8" (140mm) long; with two #40287 couplers.

625-40343 2-Axle Cars pkg(12) **19.99**
Same as #40341, but without #40287 couplers.

625-40344 2-Axle Cars pkg(12) **19.99**
For cars over 5-5/8" (140mm) long.

UNIVERSAL COUPLERS

625-40350 Standard pkg(12) **9.99**
625-40351 Adjustable pkg(12) **10.99**

UNCOUPLER

625-40292 Undertrack Mount Uncoupler **13.99**
Universal undertrack mount uncoupler. Can be fitted to all 2-rail DC track.

TRACTION TIRES

625-85602 For Large Steam Locos pkg(10) **3.99**
Fits wheels having a tire groove diameter of approximately 9/16" (14-15mm).

WHEELSETS

NEM

European standard wheelsets.

625-40189 19/64" (7.5mm) Dia., One Side Insulated 1 Pair **3.99**
625-40194 23/64" (9mm) Dia., One Side Insulated 1 Pair **3.99**
625-40192 7/16" (11mm) Dia., Split Axles 1 Pair **4.99**
625-40198 7/16" (11mm) Dia., One Side Insulated 1 Pair **3.99**

RP-25

American standard wheelsets.

625-40266 23/64" (9 mm) Dia., One Side Insulated 1 Pair **4.99**
625-40268 23/64" (9mm) Dia., Split Axles 1 Pair **6.99**
625-40195 23/64" (9mm) Dia., 3-Rail AC 1 Pair **3.99**
625-40187 23/64" (9mm) Dia. 1 Pair **6.99**
With built-in resistor for track occupancy indication (for vehicles without interior lighting).
625-40264 7/16" (11mm) Dia., One Side Insulated 1 Pair **4.99**
625-40267 7/16" (11mm) Dia., Split Axles 1 Pair **6.99**
625-40196 7/16" (11mm) Dia., 3-Rail AC 1 Pair **3.99**
625-40186 7/16" (11mm) Dia. 1 Pair **6.99**
With built-in resistor for track occupancy indication (for vehicles without interior lighting).

Information STATION

Talgo Conversions

Train set equipment often comes with a combination truck and draft gear box. These "Talgo trucks" allow operation on narrow curves, but transmit force to the truck, which can cause derailments.

Most are easily modified with basic tools to allow installation of other types of couplers. You'll need separate draft gear boxes, often included with the couplers. A razor saw or cutting pliers to remove the draft gear. And a small screwdriver if your trucks are attached with screws. Use a ruler to locate the center of the car floor for the new draft gear. You can glue the draft gear in place, but screws provide a more secure, adjustable mount. With screws, a pin vise, drill bit and tap for cutting threads are required. Use a coupler height gauge for correct alignment.

Remove the trucks. Cut off the molded-on draft gear. Locate the center of the car floor. Assemble the couplers as directed. Using the draft gear box as a guide, mark the mounting point on the car center. Don't glue it down; you may need to make adjustments. Hold it in place with double-side tape. Add the trucks, check your height gauge and make any adjustments. Secure the draft gear box and your car should be ready for operation.

HO and HOn3 couplers and trucks for freight and passenger cars, locomotives and tenders.

COUPLERS

DUMMY COUPLERS

Molded in precolored plastic.

480-2972 HO pkg(12) **1.50**
480-2973 HOn3 pkg(12) **1.50**
480-2974 NMRA pkg(12) **1.80**

LONG COUPLER ARM/BOLSTER

480-2930 Long Throw Talgo Coupler Arm/Bolster 3 Sets **2.00**

TRUCKS

Trucks feature one-piece molded Delrin® frames, RP25 wheels and steel needle-point axles. Trucks are assembled, unless noted.

FREIGHT TRUCKS

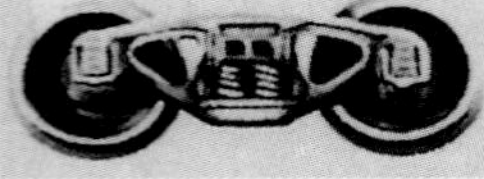

480-2903

480-2902

480-2925

480-2918

480-2923 Bettendorf, Plastic Wheels 1 Pair **2.00**
480-2903 Bettendorf, Metal Wheels 1 Pair **3.75**
480-2922 Arch Bar, Plastic Wheels 1 Pair **2.00**
480-2902 Arch Bar, Metal Wheels 1 Pair **3.75**
480-2917 HOn3 Arch Bar, Plastic Wheels 1 Pair **3.50**
480-2928 HOn3 Arch Bar, Metal Wheels 1 Pair **3.75**
480-2925 Express Roller Bearing, Plastic Wheels 1 Pair **2.00**
480-2918 Modern Roller Bearing, Plastic Wheels 1 Pair **2.00**
480-2919 Heavy Duty Roller Bearing, Plastic Wheels **2.00**

LOCOMOTIVE TRUCK KITS

480-2860 4-Wheel Lead **2.75**
480-2861 2-Wheel Lead **2.00**
480-2862 Pennsylvania 2-Wheel Trailing **3.50**
480-2863 Santa Fe 2-Wheel Trailing **3.50**
480-2864 Modern 2-Wheel Trailing **2.00**
480-2865 Old Time 2-Wheel Lead **2.00**
480-2866 HOn3 2-Wheel Lead **3.50**

TENDER TRUCKS

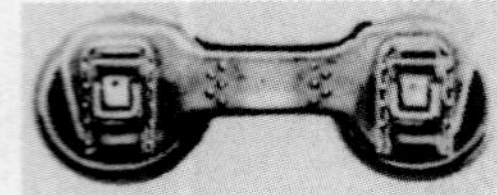

480-2924

480-2925

480-2904 Fox, Metal Wheels 1 Pair **3.75**
480-2924 Fox, Plastic Wheels 1 Pair **2.00**
480-2925 Express Roller Bearing, Plastic Wheels **2.00**

PASSENGER TRUCKS

480-2933

480-2934

480-2936

Passenger trucks feature plastic wheels.

480-2929 HOn3 4-Wheel 1 Pair **3.75**
480-2931 6-Wheel Pullman 1 Pair **2.50**
480-2933 Pennsylvania Roller Bearing 1 Pair **2.50**
480-2934 Challenger 1 Pair **2.50**
480-2935 Commonwealth 1 Pair **2.50**
480-2936 Wood Beam Passenger 1 Pair **2.50**
480-2937 Pullman 4-Wheel Talgo 1 Pair **2.50**

RIX PRODUCTS

UNCOUPLING TOOL

628-14 Rix Sticker **2.99**
When inserted between two cars with Kadee® couplers, the tool will cause the couplers to open immediately.

STEWART PRODUCTS

Vinyl traction tires increase pulling power and give a smoother ride with less bounce. (These tires can only be used on wheels that had traction tires on them originally. Wheels must be grooved to accept tires.)

SUPER TRACTION TIRE ASSORTMENTS EA 5.95

683-505 Diesel Tires pkg(20)
683-510 Small Steam pkg(18)
Fits AHM GG-1, 0-8-0 Switcher, 2-8-8-2 Mallet and others.

683-511 Medium Steam pkg(18)
Fits AHM Mikado, Berkshire, Bowser, Challenger, Reno and others.

683-512 Large Steam pkg(18)
Fits AHM Hudson, Heavy Pacific and others.

683-513 Steam Assortment pkg(18)
Includes six each of Nos. 510, 511 and 512.

683-515 Steam Tender Tires pkg(20)
Fits TYCO "Chattanooga" and 0-8-0 Tender Drives.

TRACTION TIRE TOOL

683-504 9.95
For easy application and replacement of diesel traction tires. Includes ten tires.

Tenshodo

Power trucks can be adapted to fit any self-propelled equipment, such as locomotives, doodlebugs, traction and streetcars. Sideframes are not included, but parts are included for mounting. Measurement next to each part number indicates wheelbase scale size.

POWER TRUCKS

GT-1 SERIES

Diecast metal body with sealed ball bearings on each end of the motor shaft for smooth running. Prewired electrical pick-ups. Attached connections for interior lighting. Self-lubricating gears.

36" DISC WHEELS

724-126 7-1/2' **71.99**

36" SPOKED WHEELS

724-12619 7-1/2' **78.99**

39" SPOKED WHEELS EA 78.99

724-13119 9'
724-128519 8'

WB SERIES

Plastic body with pick-up shoes. Metal tabs on both sides at the top of the body for interior lighting. Self-lubricating gears.

34" SPOKED WHEELS

724-3519 10' **50.99**

36" DISC WHEELS EA 45.99

724-245 7'
724-262 7-1/2'
724-287 8'
724-31 9'
724-35 10'

36" SPOKED WHEELS EA 50.99

724-24519 7'
724-26219 7-1/2'
724-28719 8'

39" SPOKED WHEELS

724-3119 9' **35.99**
724-3529 10' **50.99**

39" DISC WHEELS

724-31194 9' **50.99**

48" WHEELS

724-3514 10' **45.99**

TICHY TRAIN GROUP

FREIGHT TRUCKS

Heavy-duty trucks have a 5-1/2' wheel base and include wheelsets. Arch bar trucks are molded in paintable styrene with nylon bearings. All other trucks are molded black Delrin and self-lubricating.

ARCH BAR KITS

293-3002 1 Pair **2.95**
293-3022 100 Ton, 1 Pair **2.95**
293-3035 10 Pair **14.50**

ANDREWS

293-3012 Kit 1 Pair **2.95**
293-3016 Kit 10 Pair **15.50**
293-3026 Assembled 1 Pair **2.95**
293-3027 Assembled 10 Pair **15.50**

BETTENDORF

293-3008 Kit 1 Pair **2.95**
293-3014 Kit 10 Pair **14.50**
293-3024 Assembled 1 Pair **2.95**
293-3025 Assembled 10 Pair **14.50**
293-3049 Leaf/Coil 1 Pair **2.95**
293-3050 Leaf/Coil 10 Pair **15.50**
293-3051 Caboose, Leaf Springs 1 Pair **2.95**
293-3052 Caboose, Leaf Springs 10 Pair **15.50**

ROLLER BEARING ASSEMBLED

293-3009 1 Pair **2.95**
293-3036 10 Pair **14.50**

WHEELSETS

These are the same wheelsets included in Tichy Wheelcar kit #4023. Great for detailing yard and engine terminal scenes, the 33" wheelsets are nonoperating and molded in rust-colored styrene. Wheels and axles are molded separately. Axles have square ends and bearing seats.

293-3004 8 Sets **1.50**
293-3010 96 Sets **9.50**

These detailed plastic parts can be combined with other manufacturers' products to create customized or superdetailed cars and locomotives. Basic instructions for assembly and installation are included.

SIDEFRAMES

EA 8.95

All kits include one set of sideframes.

732-24 Athearn AAR Switcher w/Roller Bearings
Fits switcher trucks.

732-114 FM C-Liner pkg(4)
Fits Athearn "B" 2-axle power trucks.

732-119 Alco Blunt Switcher
Fits Athearn "B" 2-axle power trucks.

GE

732-77 GSC Dash 7
Fits Athearn "C" 3-axle power trucks.

732-78 GSC Dash 8
Fits Athearn "C" 3-axle power trucks.

732-79 GSC Dash 8
Fits Bachmann Dash 8-40C power trucks.

732-83 AD Dash 7
Fits Athearn "C" 3-axle power trucks.

732-84 AD Dash 8
Fits Athearn "C" 3-axle power trucks.

732-85 AD Dash 8
Fits Bachmann Dash 8-40C power trucks.

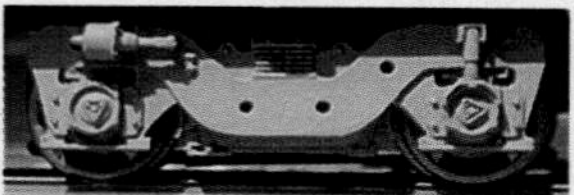

732-112 F-B2 Phase I (Floating Bolster 2-Axle) *NEW*
Fits Athearn "B" 2-axle power trucks.

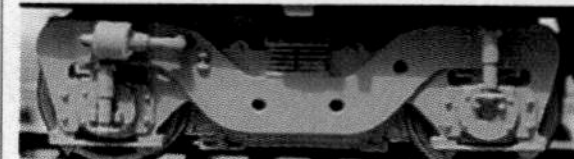

732-121 F-B2 Phase II (Floating Bolster 2-Axle)
Fits Athearn "B" 2-axle power trucks.

EMD

732-90 Blomberg "M" Phase 2
Fits Athearn "B" 2-axle power trucks.

732-98 Flex-i-Coil "C" Type w/Low Mounted Brake Cylinders
Fits Bachmann 3-axle (6 wheel) SD45 power truck .

732-99 SD45 Flex-i-Coil "C" Type w/Low Mounted Brake Cylinders
Fits Athearn "C" 3-axle power trucks.

732-120 SW Flex-i-Coil "B" Type Switcher
Fits Athearn switcher power trucks.

732-137 SD60 HTC w/Roller Bearing Journals
Fits Athearn 3-axle Dash 2 power trucks.

732-142 HTCR Radial
Fits Athearn "C" 3-axle power trucks.

732-145 HTCR II Radial
Fits Athearn 3-axle Dash 2 power trucks.

PASSENGER TRUCKS

SUPERLINER I 1 PAIR EA 8.95 (UNLESS NOTED)

Accepts Con-Cor, Kadee® or Jay-Bee 36" wheelsets.

732-410 Con-Cor
Coupler pocket accepts most couplers.

732-413 Walthers
Modifies Superliner II Cars to resemble the earlier Superliner I. Also fits Walthers coach/baggage.

SUPERLINER II 1 PAIR EA 8.98

Accepts Con-Cor, Jay-Bee and Kadee 36" wheelsets.

732-422 Con-Cor
Coupler pockets accept Intermountain, McHenry or Kadee #5 couplers.

732-423 Walthers

MODERN SIX-WHEEL PASSENGER CARS WITHOUT WHEELSETS EA 9.95

Accepts Con-Cor, Jay-Bee and Kadee 36" wheelsets. Coupler pockets accept Intermountain, McHenry or Kadee #5 couplers.

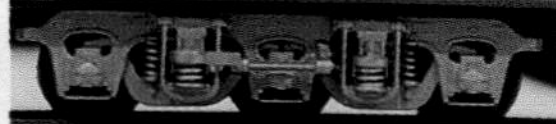

732-424 UP
732-425 UP (silver) **10.95**
NEW

732-426 ATSF

OUTSIDE SWING HANGER

Used by Amtrak, UP, ATSF and others. Fits Rivarossi, Con-Cor, Athearn, AHM and other cars. Accepts Kadee, Con-Cor and Jay-Bee 36" wheelsets. Coupler pocket accepts Intermountain or Kadee® No. 5 couplers.

732-414 1 Pair **8.95**
732-415 With Blackend 36" Brass Wheelsets 1 Pair **15.95**
Fits Train Station Products, Detail Associates, Rivarossi, Con-Cor, Athearn, AHM and other passenger cars. Pockets also accept McHenry couplers.

732-417 Silver Painted **10.95**

GSI ROLLER BEARING

For Amtrak Horizon Passenger Cars. Fits Walthers and other passenger cars.

732-420 1 Pair **8.95**

TRUCK PARTS

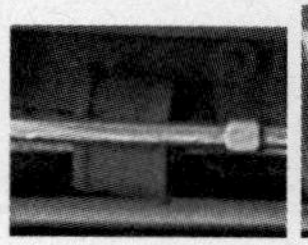
732-100

732-122

732-100 Low Mounted Brake Cylinders w/Brake Shoes pkg(8) **3.95**
732-122 Truck Exposed Roller Bearing Journals pkg(8) **3.95**
732-130 Engine Truck Brake Cylinders pkg(8) **2.95**

732-132 Vertical Struts/Shock Absorbers for EMD HTC & Other Trucks pkg(8) **3.95**
732-409 Truck Bolster w/Coupler Boxes pkg(4) **5.95** *NEW*
732-416 Bolster Anchors & Timkin Wheel Journal Covers **3.95** *NEW*

MOUNTING SCREWS

732-402 pkg(12) **4.95**
For attaching passenger car trucks to Con-Cor, AHM or Rivarossi passenger cars. Nonmagnetic, stainless steel screws.

GE F-B2 JOURNAL COVERS W/STRUTS EA 3.95

732-123 Phase II
732-136 Phase I

See What's Available at **www.walthers.com**

WESTERN RAIL PRODUCTS

UNCOUPLERS

Magnetic uncouplers require cars equipped with couplers activated by a magnetic field.

757-201 Magnetic Uncoupler **1.95**
Uncouples cars automatically when they are stopped above magnetic uncoupler. You can then pull away, leaving cars behind. Mounts under track (not included) and can be hidden when covered with ballast.

757-202 Delayed Magnetic Uncoupler **2.95**
When cars are spotted over delayed magnetic uncoupler, coupler knuckles will open and move slightly off center to the delayed position, allowing you to push cars down the track without recoupling. Mounts under track (not included) and can be hidden when covered with ballast.

WHITEGROUND MODEL WORKS

VULCAN FREIGHT TRUCK KIT

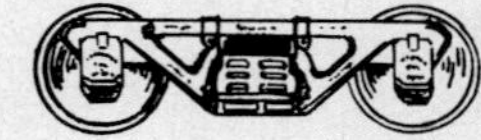

771-5001 East Broad Top, HOn3, 1 Pair **5.00**
Delrin sideframes and wheels with brass axles.

Scale
WALTHERS
HO
2000
MODEL RAILROAD
REFERENCE BOOK

And you thought spring cleaning was a big deal at your house! Out here, it has to be done on a much larger scale. Each section of the line needs to be inspected. Broken ties have to come out and be replaced. Dirty ballast needs to be removed, cleaned and tamped down. Rails need to be aligned and spiked firmly in place. Joints need tightening. Low spots must be filled. Culverts need cleaning, ditches must be profiled. And it all has to be done while dozens of trains rumble past.

Careful scheduling allows the dispatchers to set up maintenance windows, periods where traffic can be kept to a minimum. During those lulls, the work crews own the railroad. From late morning to late afternoon, only the most important trains are allowed to pass, and then only at greatly reduced speed.

Major rebuilding programs continue in and around "CP" on the West Shore Model Railroad Club line in Kingston, New York, where Patrick Cassidy captured the action. A custom-painted Athearn GP38-2 eases several more tons of fresh ballast ahead, while work continues on the new turnout.

Photo by Patrick Cassidy

Models by the West Shore Model Railroad Club

WALTHERS™

MADE EXCLUSIVELY BY SHINOHARA FOR WALTHERS

Get the look of hand-laid track without the work using Walthers Code 83 track system. Rolling stock and accessories look more like the real thing because the Code 83 rail is correctly proportioned for HO Scale. The system is perfect for building a complete layout, or can be combined with an existing Code 100 layout to create realistic branchlines, yards and sidings.

CODE 83 TRACK

Walthers Code 83 track system sets a new standard for realism and performance.

A COMPLETE TRACK SYSTEM

- Everything needed to build an entire layout!
- Choose from flex track, several sizes of turnouts, crossings, double slips, bulk rail and rail joiners.

REALISTIC DETAIL

- Code 83 simulates 132 pound mainline rail used by many railroads.
- Prototypical "all-rail" frogs and rail made of nickel silver for best conductivity.
- Correctly proportioned for HO Scale - gives your equipment a more massive, realistic appearance.
- Thin profile ties are molded in dark brown with fine woodgrain detail.

EASY TO INSTALL

- Track comes fully assembled and ready to install.
- Can be combined with Code 100 or Code 70 track for realistic variety of rail sizes on the same layout.
- Turnouts are route selective, with power controlled by turnout setting.

FLEX TRACK

948-815 39" Section **6.98**
Dealers MUST order in multiples of 10.

TURNOUTS

948-891 #5 Left Hand 14.98
A. Total Length: 10-3/8" (263.5mm)
B. Points to Frog: 5-21/32" (143.7mm)
C. Frog Angle: 11° 26´

948-892 #5 Right Hand 14.98
A. Total Length: 10-3/8" (263.5mm)
B. Points to Frog: 5-21/32" (143.7mm)
C. Frog Angle: 11° 26´

948-803 #6 Left Hand 14.98
A. Total Length: 11-5/16" (287.3mm)
B. Points to Frog: 6-9/16" (166.7mm)
C. Frog Angle: 9° 32´

948-804 #6 Right Hand 14.98
A. Total Length: 11-5/16" (287.3mm)
B. Points to Frog: 6-9/16" (166.7mm)
C. Frog Angle: 9° 32´

948-805 #8 Left Hand 16.98
A. Total Length: 13-7/8" (352.4mm)
B. Points to Frog: 8-1/32" (204mm)
C. Frog Angle: 7° 9´

948-806 #8 Right Hand 16.98
A. Total Length: 13-7/8" (352.4mm)
B. Points to Frog: 8-1/32" (204mm)
C. Frog Angle: 7° 9´

WYE TURNOUTS

948-890 #2-1/2 (Matches #5 Turnouts) 14.98
A. Total Length: 7-3/16" (182.6mm)
B. Points to Frog: 3-19/32" (91.3mm)
C. Frog Angle: 22° 54´

948-893 #3 (Matches #6 Turnouts) 14.98
A. Total Length: 7-7/8" (200mm)
B. Points to Frog: 3-3/4" (95.2mm)
C. Frog Angle: 19° 5´

948-807 #4 (Matches #8 Turnouts) 14.98
A. Total Length: 9-23/32" (247.8mm)
B. Points to Frog: 4-5/16" (134.9mm)
C. Frog Angle: 14° 15´

CURVED TURNOUTS

948-827 #6-1/2 Right Hand 26.98
A. Total Length: 12-25/32" (324.6mm)
R1. Inside Radius: 20" (508mm)
R2. Outside Radius: 24" (609.6mm)

948-826 #6-1/2 Left Hand 26.98
A. Total Length: 12-25/32" (324.6mm)
R1. Inside Radius: 20" (508mm)
R2. Outside Radius: 24" (609.6mm)

948-894 #7 Left Hand 27.98
A. Total Length: 14-31/32" (380.2mm)
R1. Inside Radius: 24" (609.6mm)
R2. Outside Radius: 28" (711.2mm)

948-895 #7 Right Hand 27.98
A. Total Length: 14-31/32" (380.2mm)
R1. Inside Radius: 24" (609.6mm)
R2. Outside Radius: 28" (711.2mm)

948-888 #7-1/2 Left Hand 28.98
A. Total Length: 17-7/32" (437.4mm)
R1. Inside Radius: 28" (711.2mm)
R2. Outside Radius: 32" (812.8mm)

948-889 #7-1/2 Right Hand 28.98
A. Total Length: 17-7/32" (437.4mm)
R1. Inside Radius: 28" (711.2mm)
R2. Outside Radius: 32" (812.8mm)

948-828 #8 Left Hand 29.98
A. Total Length: 19" (482.6mm)
R1. Inside Radius: 32" (812.8mm)
R2. Outside Radius: 36" (914.4mm)

948-829 #8 Right Hand 29.98
A. Total Length: 19" (482.6mm)
R1. Inside Radius: 32" (812.8mm)
R2. Outside Radius: 36" (914.4mm)

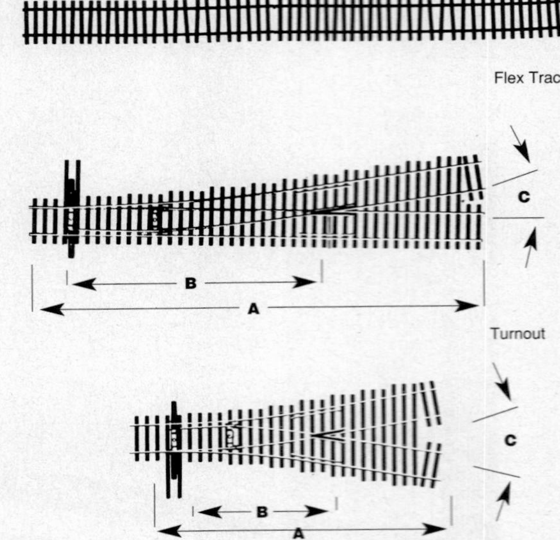

Flex Track

Turnout

Wye Turnout

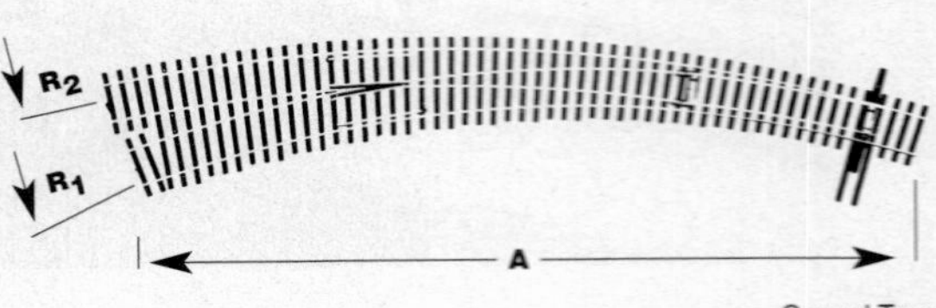

Curved Turnout

WALTHERS™

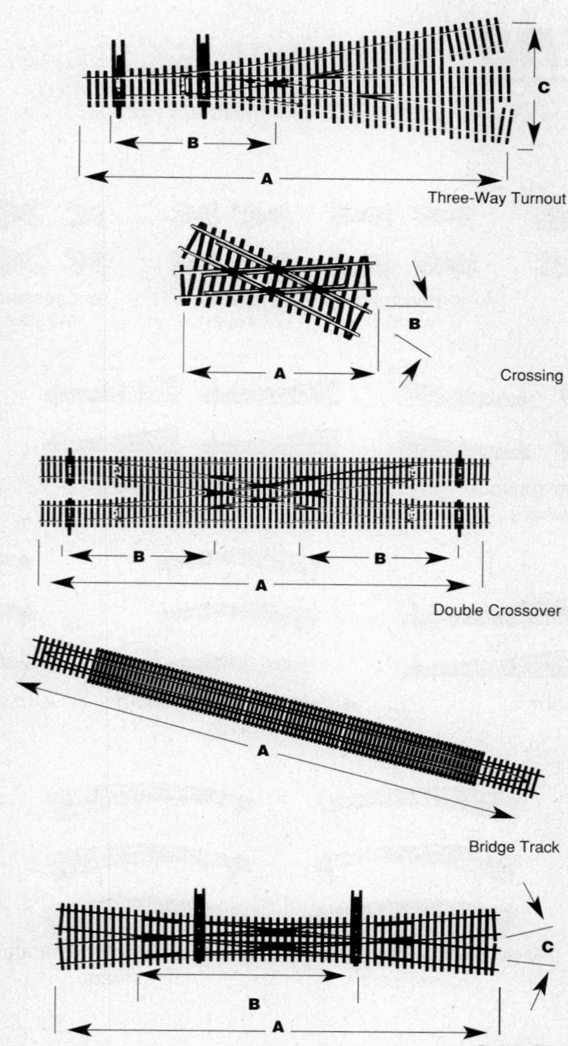

Three-Way Turnout

Crossing

Double Crossover

Bridge Track

Double Slip

3-WAY TURNOUT

948-808 #6 29.98
A. Total Length: 13-3/8" (339.7mm)
B. Points to Frog: 5-1/8" (130.2mm)
C. Width: 3-23/32" (94.4mm)

CROSSINGS

948-830 30° 15.98
A. Total Length: 6-11/32" (161.5mm)
B. Angle: 30°

948-831 45° 15.98
A. Total Length: 5-9/16" (141.9mm)
B. Angle: 45°

948-832 60° 15.98
A. Total Length: 4-13/16" (123mm)
B. Angle: 60°

948-833 90° 15.98
A. Total Length: 3-7/32" (82mm)
B. Angle: 90°

DOUBLE CROSSOVER

948-812 #6 49.98
A. Total Length: 19-5/32" (486.6mm)
B. Points to Frog: 6-19/32" (167.5mm)
Frog Angle: 9° 30´

BRIDGE TRACK

Designed especially for the Cornerstone Series® Double-Track Truss Bridge, this single track section features detailed bridge ties and inside guard rails with Code 70 rail. Two bridge tracks required for each bridge. Can also be used with most HO bridges.

948-899 Truss Bridge Track **14.98**
A. Total Length: 19-11/16" (500mm)

DOUBLE SLIPS

948-814 #6 49.98
A. Total Length: 15-7/16" (392.1mm)
B. Points to Frog: 7" (177.8mm)
C. Frog Angle: 9° 30´

948-896 #8 54.98
A. Total Length: 20-1/4" (515mm)
B. Points to Frog: 7-7/8" (200mm)
C. Frog Angle: 7° 9´

Transition Track

TRANSITION TRACK

Using these transition tracks, you can combine other rail sizes with Walthers Code 83 system to create realistic mainlines, yards and sidings. Each 6-inch track section has a small section of Code 83, combined with Code 100 or 70 track, to provide a smooth transition between rail sizes.

948-897 Code 83 to Code 100 **5.98**
948-898 Code 83 to Code 70 **5.98**

RAIL JOINERS

948-841 Code 83 pkg(50) **6.98**

RAIL SPIKES

For Code 83 and Code 70 track.

948-360 .024 x 3/8" pkg(500*) **6.98**
*Package is sold by weight, number shown is approximate.

BULK RAIL

948-870 Code 83, 150' 45m pkg(50) **100.00**
Includes 50 rail sections, each 3' long.

BRIGHT BOY TRACK CLEANER

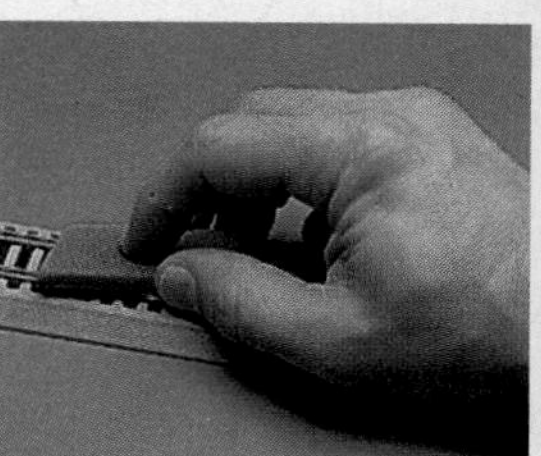

949-521 Bright Boy (2 x 1 x 1/4" **4.98**
Easy-to-use Bright Boy track cleaning block keeps rails and wheels clean and bright. Just run Bright Boy over rails for clean track with better conductivity.

WALTHERS™ CODE 83 TRACK PLANNING TEMPLATE SCALE 3/4"=1'

Use these illustrations to plan your HO layout with Walthers Code 83 track system.

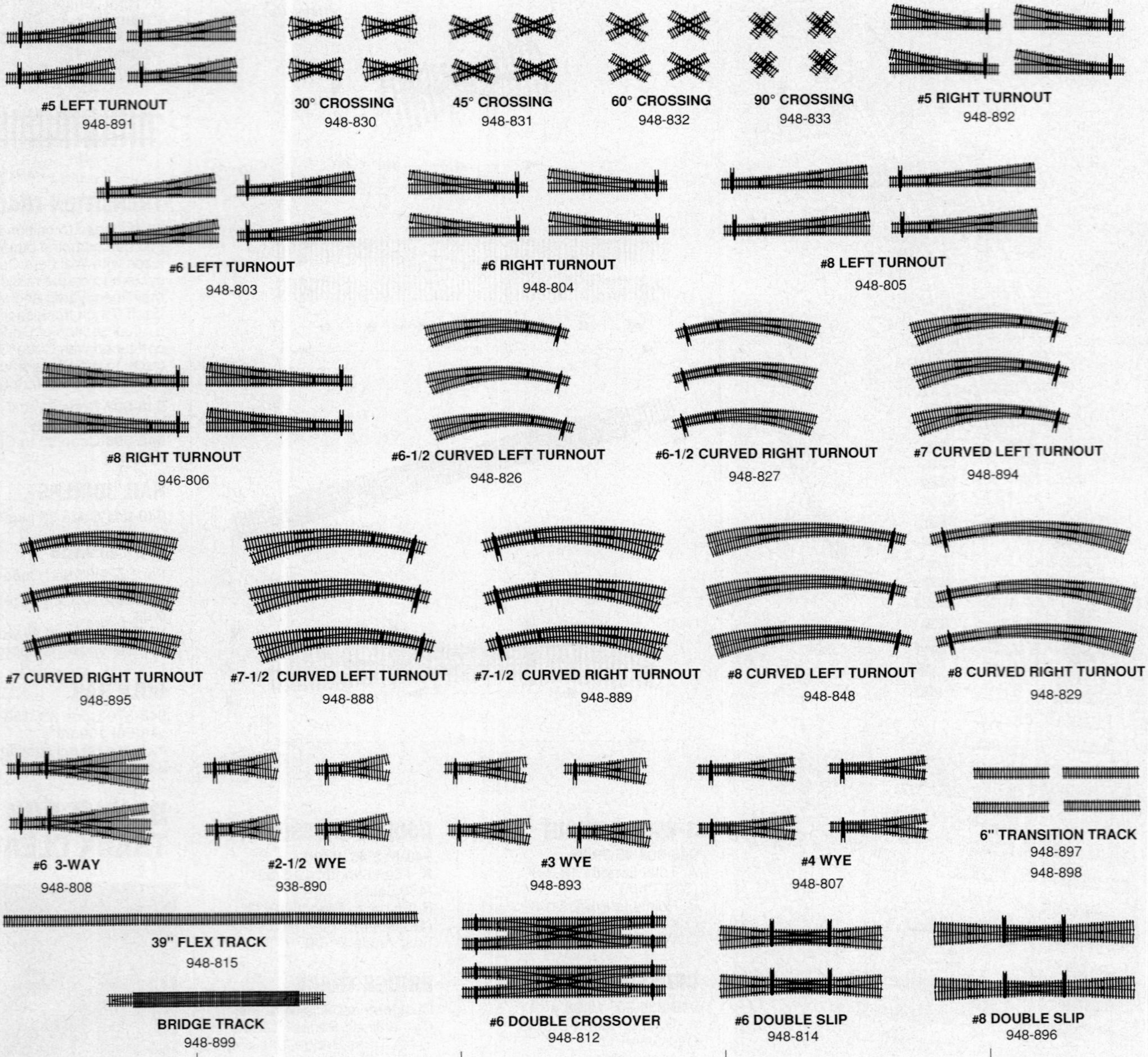

#5 LEFT TURNOUT
948-891

30° CROSSING
948-830

45° CROSSING
948-831

60° CROSSING
948-832

90° CROSSING
948-833

#5 RIGHT TURNOUT
948-892

#6 LEFT TURNOUT
948-803

#6 RIGHT TURNOUT
948-804

#8 LEFT TURNOUT
948-805

#8 RIGHT TURNOUT
946-806

#6-1/2 CURVED LEFT TURNOUT
948-826

#6-1/2 CURVED RIGHT TURNOUT
948-827

#7 CURVED LEFT TURNOUT
948-894

#7 CURVED RIGHT TURNOUT
948-895

#7-1/2 CURVED LEFT TURNOUT
948-888

#7-1/2 CURVED RIGHT TURNOUT
948-889

#8 CURVED LEFT TURNOUT
948-848

#8 CURVED RIGHT TURNOUT
948-829

#6 3-WAY
948-808

#2-1/2 WYE
938-890

#3 WYE
948-893

#4 WYE
948-807

6" TRANSITION TRACK
948-897
948-898

39" FLEX TRACK
948-815

BRIDGE TRACK
948-899

#6 DOUBLE CROSSOVER
948-812

#6 DOUBLE SLIP
948-814

#8 DOUBLE SLIP
948-896

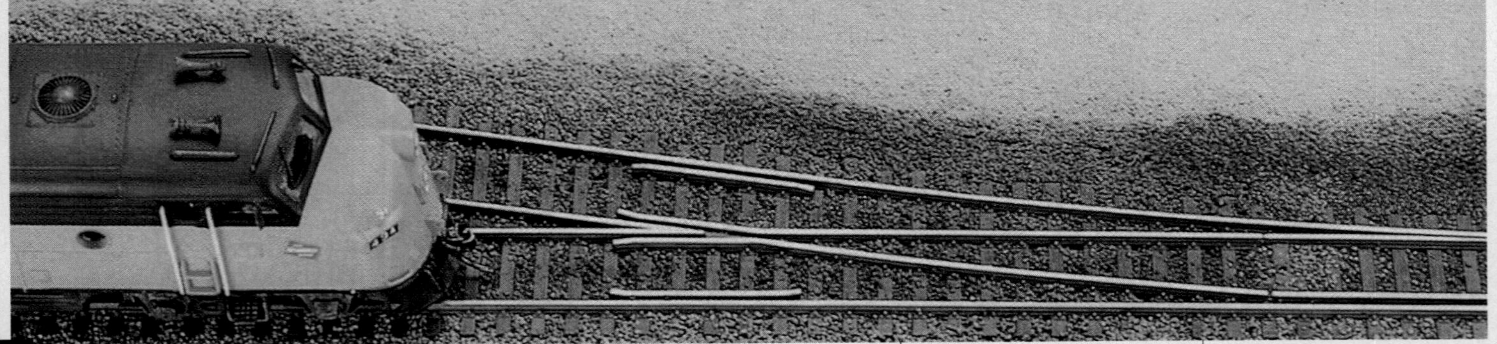

YOU'RE ON THE RIGHT TRACK ...WITH ATLAS®!

Atlas Model Railroad Company has three different HO track lines to suit the needs of all model railroaders. On the following two pages you will find a complete listing of all Atlas track available; below is some information that may help you determine which track is best for your layout.

True-Track® - Contains code 83 track that can be removed from roadbed.

ATLAS HO TRUE-TRACK® BROWN TIES/NICKEL SILVER RAIL/GRAY ROADBED

Atlas' True-Track line features versatile roadbed track with a realistic look. Each piece of True-Track contains fine-scale code 83 track snapped into a gray graveled roadbed. True-Track is perfect for beginning modelers because it snaps together quickly and easily. As modelers advance, the code 83 track can be taken out of the roadbed and used separately, making it a great long-term investment.

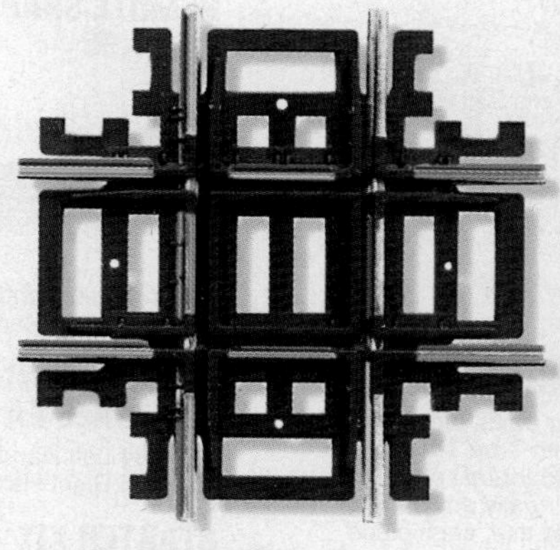

Code 83 90° Crossing

ATLAS HO CODE 83 TRACK - BROWN TIES/NICKEL SILVER RAIL

Atlas code 83 is known as fine-scale track because its rail has a lower profile and its ties are finer than code 100 track. It has a very prototypical look due to its thinner, brown ties. With the same high quality and durability as Atlas' popular code 100 line, code 83 is quickly becoming a favorite. The line includes Atlas' famous Super-Flex® Track, Snap-Track, Snap-Switches and numbered Turnouts.

Code 83 9" Straight Track

Code 100 30° Rail Crossing

Code 100 18" Radius Track

ATLAS HO CODE 100 TRACK - BLACK TIES/NICKEL SILVER RAIL

Atlas' line of code 100 track was started almost 50 years ago, and it is well-known for its high quality and durability. Made with black injection-molded plastic ties and nickel silver rail, it is sturdy, reliable and looks great on any layout. The code 100 line is very extensive, and includes Super-Flex® Track, Snap-Track, Snap-Switches, Custom-Line Turnouts and accessories.

TRUE-TRACK®

Get your trains running right away with True-Track®, designed for fast and easy set-up on virtually any surface. Ready to use, each piece features Code 83 nickel silver rail on realistic brown ties, plus roadbed molded in gray and detailed to look like real ballast. Just connect the sections together, wire to your power pack and your railroad is up and running!

Best of all, True-Track is adaptable to your changing needs. It can be nailed down for use on a permanent layout. Or remove and paint the roadbed sections for added realism. The sections can also be removed from the roadbed and used with cork roadbed, ballast and other Atlas Code 83 track products to build a traditional layout.

STRAIGHT SECTIONS

150-450 9" pkg(4) **4.95**
150-452 3" pkg(4) **3.35**
150-453 1-1/2" pkg(4) **3.35**
150-454 2" pkg(4) **3.35**
150-476 90° Crossing **8.35**

CURVE SECTIONS EA 4.95

150-460 18" Radius Curve pkg(4)
150-463 22" Radius Curve pkg(4)

TRACK ACCESSORIES

150-465 Terminal Joiners pkg(2) **1.75**
150-470 Track Bumper pkg(2) **1.95**

MANUAL SNAP-SWITCH EA 10.95

150-478 Left Hand
150-479 Right Hand

MANUAL SWITCH MACHINES EA 2.75

150-586 Left Hand
150-587 Right Hand

REMOTE SNAP-SWITCH EA 14.95

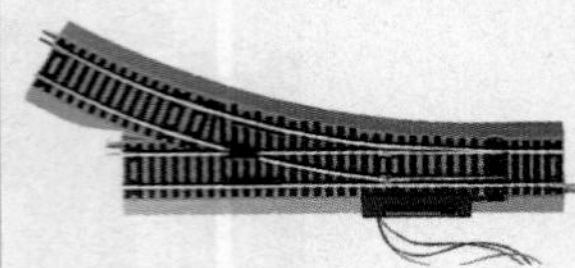

150-480 Left Hand
150-481 Right Hand

REMOTE SWITCH MACHINES EA 6.95

150-584 Left Hand
150-585 Right Hand

STARTER KIT

150-488 True-Track Starter Set **42.95**
Includes 18 sections of track, plus two manual switches and terminal rail joiners, enough track for a 38 x 56" layout.

CODE 100 TRACK

Code 100 comes with black ties and nickel silver rail. For all skill levels, it can be used to build any one of the 36 HO layouts featured in the four Atlas layout instruction books that appear in the Books section of this catalog.

HO SCALE SNAP-TRACK® STARTER SET

150-88 Nickel Silver Rail, Black Ties **29.95**

36" SUPER-FLEX TRACK®

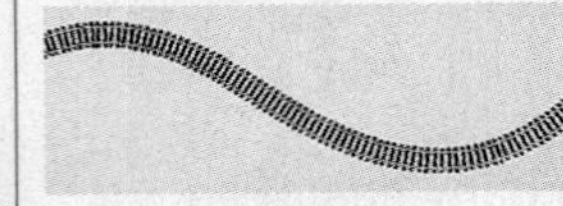

NICKEL SILVER RAIL

150-168 Black Ties **2.95**
150-178 Black Ties pkg(5) **15.95**

STRAIGHT SNAP-TRACK®

NICKEL SILVER RAIL

150-821 9", Black Ties pkg(6) **4.30**
150-822 6", Black Ties pkg(4) **2.35**
150-823 3", Black Ties pkg(4) **2.35**
150-825 1-1/2", Black Ties pkg(4) **2.35**

CURVED SNAP-TRACK®

NICKEL SILVER RAIL

150-831 15" Radius, Black Ties pkg(6) **4.30**
150-90831 15" Radius, Brown Ties pkg(6) **4.30**
150-832 1/2 - 15" Radius, Black Ties pkg(4) **2.35**
150-90832 1/2 - 15" Radius, Brown Ties pkg(4) **2.35**

150-833 18" Radius, Black Ties pkg(6) **4.30**
150-90833 18" Radius, Brown Ties pkg(6) **4.30**
150-834 1/2 - 18" Radius, Black Ties pkg(4) **2.35**
150-90834 1/2 - 18" Radius, Brown Ties pkg(4) **2.35**
150-835 1/3 - 18" Radius, Black Ties pkg(4) **2.35**
150-90835 1/3 - 18" Radius, Brown Ties pkg(4) **2.35**
150-836 22" Radius, Black Ties pkg(6) **4.30**
150-90836 22" Radius, Brown Ties pkg(6) **4.30**

SNAP-TRACK® ASSORTMENT

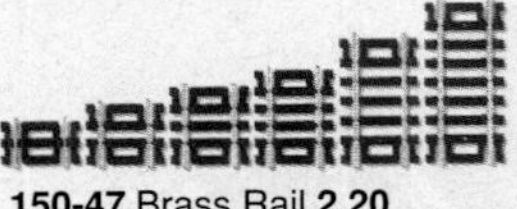

150-47 Brass Rail **2.20**
150-847 Nickel Silver Rail, Black Ties **2.95**
150-90847 Nickel Silver Rail, Brown Ties **2.95**

BULK SNAP-TRACK®

NICKEL SILVER RAIL-BLACK TIES EA .68

150-150 9" Straight Track
150-151 15" Radius
150-152 18" Radius
150-153 22" Radius

RAIL

150-102 Nickel Silver **31.90**
Each bundle includes 99' of bulk rail.

SNAP CROSSINGS

150-839 30°, Nickel Silver Rail, Black Ties **5.95**

SNAP-TRACK® TERMINAL SECTIONS

NICKEL SILVER RAIL EA 2.95

150-840 9" Straight, Black Ties

150-845 18" Radius Curved, Black Ties

SNAP-SWITCHES®

REMOTE CONTROL-NICKEL SILVER RAIL EA 12.95

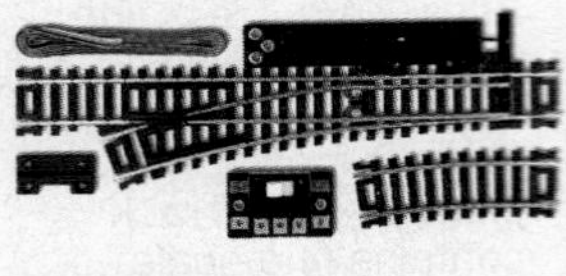

150-850 Left Hand, Black Ties
150-851 Right Hand, Black Ties

MANUAL-NICKEL SILVER RAIL EA 8.35

150-860 Left Hand, Black Ties

150-861 Right Hand, Black Ties

RAIL JOINERS

150-55 Plastic Insulating pkg(24) **1.10**

150-170 Nickel Silver pkg(48) **1.85**

SWITCH MACHINES

REMOTE CONTROL EA 6.50

150-52 Left Hand, Black Ties
150-53 Right Hand, Black Ties
150-65 Under Table-Right or Left

MANUAL EA 1.95

150-62 Left Hand, Black Ties
150-63 Right Hand, Black Ties

For Daily Product Information Click
www.walthers.com

BUMPER

150-843 Nickel Silver Rail, Black Ties pkg(2) **2.35**

RERAILER

150-155 Nickel Silver w/Black Ties pkg **1.35**
150-844 Nickel Silver Rail, Black Ties pkg(3) **4.75**

DEAD-END UNCOUPLER

150-849 Nickel Silver Rail **2.95**

TERMINAL JOINERS

150-842 Nickel Silver 1 Pair **1.95**

CUSTOM-LINE® CROSSINGS

NICKEL SILVER RAIL EA 5.95 (UNLESS NOTED)

150-171 19° - 6", Black Ties
150-172 25° - 4-1/2", Black Ties
150-173 30° - 4", Black Ties
150-174 45° - 3", Black Ties

150-175 60° - 3", Black Ties
150-176 90° - 6", Black Ties
150-177 12-1/2° - 9", Black Ties **6.50**

CUSTOM-LINE® MARK 3 TURNOUTS

NICKEL SILVER RAIL EA 9.75

150-280 Wye, Black Ties

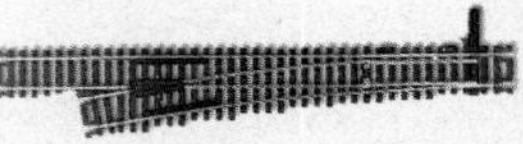

150-281 #4 Left, Black Ties
150-282 #4 Right, Black Ties
150-283 #6 Left, Black Ties
150-284 #6 Right, Black Ties

CODE 83 TRACK

Code 83 track features brown ties and nickel silver rail. Perfect for modelers of all skill levels looking for high quality prototypical-looking track. Can be used to build any twelve layouts in the Atlas book "Beginner's Guide to Ho Model Railroading."

Track features nickel-silver rail and brown ties (unless noted).

150-511 15" Radius Curve **.68**
150-513 22" Radius Curve **.68**
150-521 6" Straight Section pkg(4) **2.35**
150-522 3" Straight Section pkg(4) **2.35**
150-524 Straight Track Assortment **2.95**
150-525 2" Straight Section pkg(4) **2.35**

SWITCH MACHINES

For use with Code 83 Snap-Switches, #540-#543.

REMOTE EA 6.95
150-584 Left Hand
150-585 Right Hand

MANUAL EA 2.75
150-586 Left Hand
150-587 Right Hand

HO SCALE SNAP-TRACK® STARTER SET

150-588 Starter Set **29.95**

36" SUPER-FLEX® TRACK

150-500 Brown Ties **3.50**

SNAP-TRACK®

150-510 9" Straight Track **.68**
150-512 18" Radius **.68**
150-520 9" Straight pkg(6) **4.30**
150-523 1-1/2" Straight Section pkg(4) **2.35**
150-530 15" Radius pkg(6) **4.30**
150-531 1/2 - 15" Radius pkg(4) **2.35**
150-532 18" Radius pkg(6) **4.30**
150-533 1/2 - 18" Radius pkg(4) **2.35**
150-534 1/3 - 18" Radius pkg(4) **2.35**
150-535 22" Radius pkg(6) **4.30**

CROSSINGS EA 5.95 (UNLESS NOTED)

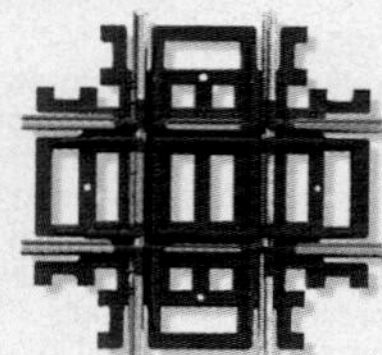

Each crossing includes brown ties and nickel silver rail.

150-571 12-1/2° **6.50** ***NEW***
150-572 19° ***NEW***
150-573 25° ***NEW***
150-574 30° ***NEW***
150-575 45° **6.95** ***NEW***
150-576 60° ***NEW***
150-577 90° ***NEW***

CODE 83 TURNOUTS EA 11.50

150-505 #6 Left Hand
150-506 #6 Right Hand

RAIL JOINERS

150-551 Transition (Code 83 to 100), Nickel Silver pkg(12) **1.95**
150-552 Plastic Insulating pkg(24) **1.10**

TERMINAL JOINERS

150-553 Nickel Silver (1 Pair) **2.15**

SNAP-SWITCHES®

150-540 Left Hand, Remote (18" Radius) **12.95**
150-541 Right Hand, Remote (18" Radius) **12.95**
150-542 Left Hand, Manual **8.35**
150-543 Right Hand, Manual **8.35**

CUSTOM-LINE® TURNOUTS

150-560 Wye **TBA**
150-561 #4 Left Hand **10.95**
150-562 #4 Right Hand **10.95**
150-563 #6 Left Hand **TBA**
150-564 #6 Right Hand **TBA**

ELECTRICAL CONTROLS

SNAP RELAY

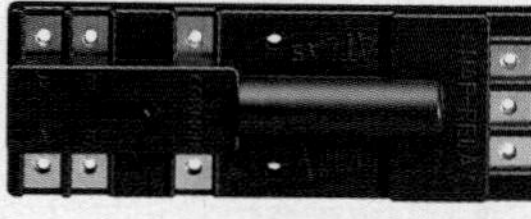

150-200 7.95
Feeds control panel lamps and allows selective power control (i.e. frogs and signals).

CONNECTOR

150-205 6.25
Three SPST on-off switches in parallel. Use to control power to sidings, accessories, etc. Can be coupled together in any number.

TWIN

150-210 6.25
Two DPDT switches in parallel. Useful for reversing section and turntable control on single-cab layouts, etc.

SWITCH CONTROL BOX

150-56 2.95

SELECTOR

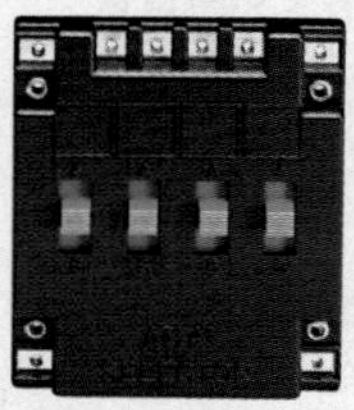

150-215 6.25
Four single-pole, double-throw switches provide two-cab operation for four blocks. May be coupled together in any number for control of additional blocks without interswitch wiring. Can be used as area selectors for four-cab operation. Can be used with No. 220.

CONTROLLER

150-220 6.50
Simple way to wire and control reversing loops, wyes and turntables. Has reversing switches for two mainline cabs plus a switch, selectable for either cab, for directional control on reversing loops, etc. Can be used with No. 215.

WIRE & ACCESSORIES

20 GAUGE HOOK-UP WIRE EA 5.45

Each role includes 50' of stranded, copper wire.

150-315 Black
150-316 Red
150-317 Green
150-318 Yellow
150-319 Light Blue

SPADE CONNECTORS

150-201 #3 Spade Connectors pkg(24) **3.25**

REDESIGNED TURNTABLE

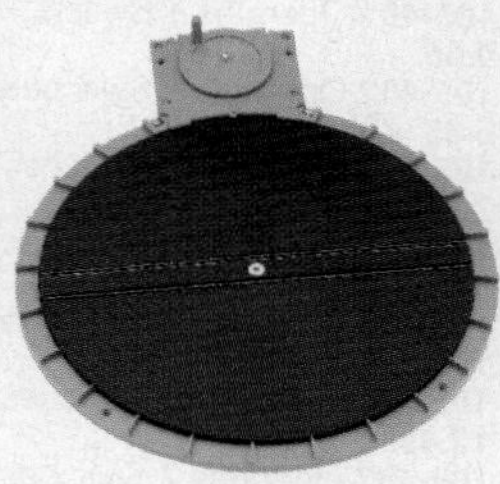

150-305 19.95
Fully assembled, 9" diameter turntable has the ability to stop at 21 positions, 15° apart. Geneva movement locks table in exact position every time. Simulated wood brown turntable deck and concrete pit ring. Surface mount; no cutting necessary. Manual crank operation; can be easily motorized for remote control operation with the #304 Turntable Drive Unit.

150-304 Turntable Drive Unit **19.95**

ACCESSORIES

MODELER'S SUPER SAW

150-400 Super Saw **2.50**

TRACK NAILS

150-2540 Track Nails (2 oz) **2.95**
No. 19, 1/2" long, round head, black oxidized steel.

TRACK PLANNING TEMPLATE SET

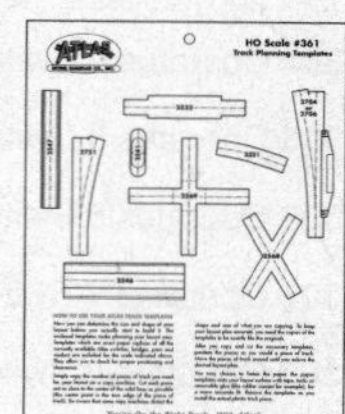

150-361 3.95
Exact paper replicas of all currently available Atlas track. Just cut out and position, like pieces of track, into the desired layout shape.

ATLAS CD-ROM LIBRARY

150-371 19.95
Includes entire contents of each Atlas HO and N gauge layout instruction book, plus the Parts Catalogue, Wiring Book and product catalog. You can access every one of Atlas' 54 layout plans, exploded loco diagrams and more than 300 pages of text. Requires a PC with system 486SX or better, Windows 3.1 or '95, 4MB RAM, 5MB free disk space and a mouse.

ATLAS RIGHT TRACK® SOFTWARE

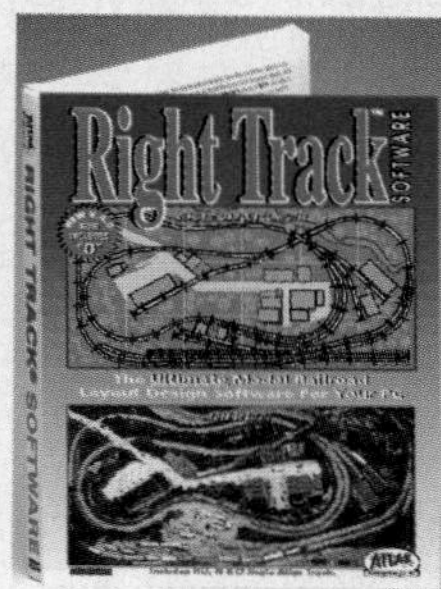

150-370 Version 4.0 **34.95**
Users can draw in the size and shape of their layout table; place and connect track; add elevations, helices, parallel tracks, transition curves, roadbed and more.

Features new Atlas O libraries; updated graphical user interface; the ability to create crossovers and ladders and to search and replace elements; gradients can now be calculated; several undo steps (adjustable); color can be added to elements according to layer number or height; easier zoom function; autosave function and more.

System requirements: PC with Windows 95, 98 or NT; Pentium I, 66Mhz; 16MB RAM; 10MB free disk space.

CONTROLLERS

LIGHTED SWITCH CONTROLLERS

Will operate all switches and switch motors including Lionel, Atlas and others. Light remains on after corresponding button is pressed. Instructions, red and green light bulbs, mounting screws and self-stick number sheet are included.

Each #498 and #444 comes with a contact plate. Each #894 and #888 is equipped with electro-mechanical switching circuitry controls and switches red and green light automatically. No need for contact plates or relays; unit is completely self-contained. Bulbs use the AC current from the power supply.

SURFACE MOUNT

105-444 Standard **8.95**
105-888 Electro-Mechanical **14.95**

INSERT MOUNT

105-498 7.95
105-894 13.95
105-4994 GE Bulb 12-18V (red) pkg(2) **.70**
105-4995 GE Bulb 12-18V (blue) pkg(2) **.70**

PUSH-BUTTON UNITS

105-439 Double **2.50**
Can be installed in any position. Dealers MUST order multiples of 12.

PANELS

FRAME-MOUNTED

With polished aluminum mounting frame.

105-401 Operates 1 Switch **4.65**
105-402 Operates 2 Switches **6.35**
105-403 Operates 3 Switches **7.95**
105-404 Operates 4 Switches **9.65**
105-405 Operates 5 Switches **10.65**
105-406 Operates 6 Switches **12.45**
105-407 Operates 7 Switches **13.95**
105-408 Operates 8 Switches **15.95**

105-916 Operates 16 Switches **29.95**

TERMINAL

105-416 Less Switches **7.95**

105-516 With Switches **9.65**

FLUSH-MOUNTED

EXCLUSIVE FEATURE: All Acme switch controllers are equipped with crimp or solder terminals.

105-301 Operates 1 Switch **3.95**
105-302 Operates 2 Switches **5.25**
105-303 Operates 3 Switches **6.75**
105-304 Operates 4 Switches **8.45**
105-305 Operates 5 Switches **9.65**
105-306 Operates 6 Switches **11.25**
105-307 Operates 7 Switches **12.85**
105-308 Operates 8 Switches **14.45**

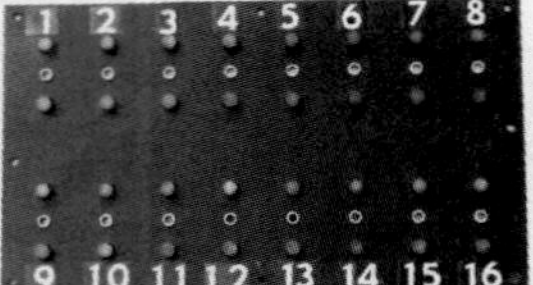

105-816 Operates 16 Switches **26.55**

TURNOUT CONTROL SYSTEM ACCESSORIES

Easy-to-install turnout control system is ideal for any size layout. All accessories install with basic tools (screwdriver, drill, pliers). Simple mechanical design with rugged Delrin® plastic parts insures years of trouble-free operation. Controls include illustrated, step-by-step instructions and can be used with scales from Z to O.

QUICK KNOBS

362-40 pkg(6) **1.95**
Delrin® plastic control knobs for use with music wire push rods; just heat wire and press on. Knobs are 3/8" diameter and 1/2" long.

QUICK SWITCH

362-1000 6.95
Remote turnout control with no wiring. Control lever has built-in indication and provides positive point contact.

QUICK GUIDE

362-1060 3.95
Simple push-rod system for Micro-Engineering and Peco turnouts only. Includes guide assembly, wire and knob. Accepts Hot Frog for power routing.

QUICK SWITCH WITH HOT FROG

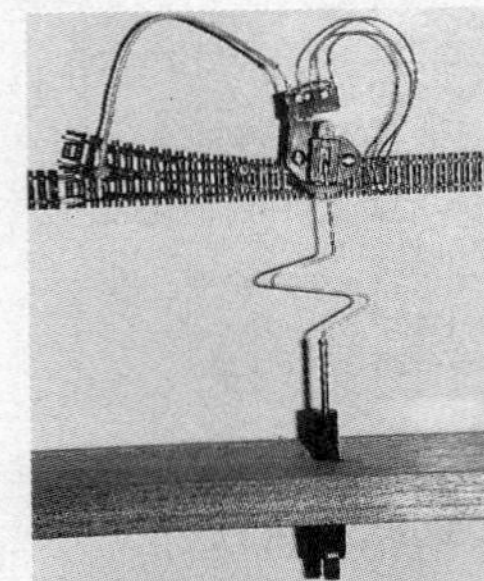

362-2000 8.95
Includes a SPDT micro-switch for power routing. Great for passing sidings, yard tracks - anywhere power needs to be shut-off to one set of tracks. Also provides power for two-color signals at turnout. Control lever has built in indication and provides positive point contact.

HOT FROG

362-2050 pkg(2) **4.25**
SPDT micro switch, as found in No. 2000.

QUICK TURN

362-4000 pkg(2) **3.95**
Special mounted bell crank, use with control wires wherever a 90° turn is needed.

FREIGHT BRAKE

362-3000 7.95
Holds cars on grades; includes parts to convert to HO horn-hook or N Scale Rapido uncoupler. Control lever has built in indication.

Information STATION

Turntables

Among the problems facing early railroad builders was turning engines for the return trip. Steam locos were designed to operate with the pilot forward. If space allowed, a wye could be built, but this required three turnouts and a connecting track. This took a lot of space, making it impractical in many places.

The answer was the turntable. In its basic form, a turntable is a bridge supported on a center pivot point, with small wheeled supports on the outside edges. To align with the tracks and allow 360° of movement, a circular pit was dug. The pivot was mounted in the center and rails laid around the edge to guide the support wheels.

HO Scale track and accessories.

E-Z TRACK®

Building a new railroad is a snap with E-Z Track. Each section combines track and roadbed into a single unit, with snap-fit assembly and plug-in wiring to provide instant railroad fun. A hidden locking feature holds sections securely together until you're ready to take them apart. Easy to set up on any surface, including floors and rugs, no special tools, nails or boards are needed. A great system for Christmas time, displays or permanent layouts. 12 sections of curved 18" radius track make a full circle; 16 sections of curved 22" radius track make a full circle.

NICKEL-SILVER TRACK W/GRAY ROADBED

44501 44502

160-44501 18" Radius Curved pkg(4) **9.00**
160-44502 18" Radius Terminal/Rerailer **6.00**
160-44503 22" Radius Curved pkg(4) **10.00**

44504 44507

160-44504 33.25" Radius, 18° Curve pkg(5) **15.00** *NEW*
160-44507 35.50" Radius, 18° Curve pkg(5) **15.00** *NEW*

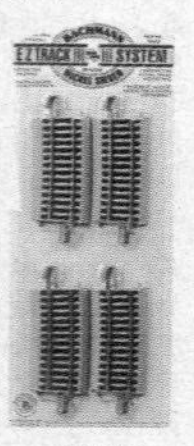

44508

160-44508 33.25" Radius, 6° Curve pkg(4) **9.00** *NEW*
160-44509 33.25" Radius, 12° Curve pkg(4) **11.00** *NEW*

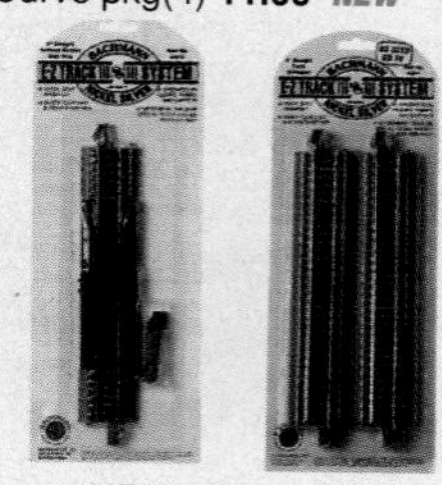

44510 44511

160-44510 9" Straight Terminal/Rerailer **6.00**
160-44511 9" Straight pkg(4) **9.00**
160-44512 3" Straight pkg(4) **6.00**

44513 44514 44528

160-44513 2.25" Straight pkg(4) **6.00** *NEW*
160-44514 4.50" Straight pkg(4) **7.00** *NEW*
160-44528 9" Straight Rerailer pkg(2) **6.00** *NEW*

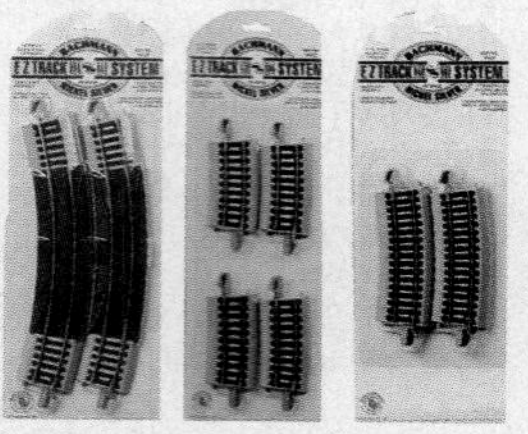

44529 44530 44531

160-44529 18" Radius Curved Rerailer pkg(2) **6.00** *NEW*
160-44530 1/2 18" Radius Curve pkg(4) **6.00** *NEW*
160-44531 1/2 18" Radius Curve pkg(4) **7.00** *NEW*

44540 44541

160-44540 30° Crossing **7.00**
160-44541 90° Crossing **11.00** *NEW*

44561 44562

160-44561 Remote Left Hand Switch **17.00**
160-44562 Remote Right Hand Switch **17.00**
160-44565 #5 Left Hand Remote Switch **TBA** *NEW*
160-44566 #5 Right Hand Remote Switch **TBA** *NEW*
160-44569 #5 Wye Switch **TBA** *NEW*
160-44591 Hayes Bumpers pkg(2) **7.50**
160-44594 Layout Expander **64.00**

STEEL TRACK W/BLACK ROADBED

160-44401 18" Radius Curved pkg(4) **6.00**
160-44402 18" Radius Terminal/Rerailer **5.00**
160-44403 22" Radius Curved pkg(4) **7.00**
160-44410 9" Straight Terminal/Rerailer **5.00**
160-44411 9" Straight pkg(4) **6.00**
160-44412 3" Straight pkg(4) **4.00**
160-44428 9" Straight Rerailer pkg(2) **5.00** *NEW*
160-44429 18" Radius Curved Rerailer pkg(2) **5.00** *NEW*
160-44440 30° Crossing **5.00**
160-44441 90° Crossing **9.00** *NEW*
160-44461 Remote Left Hand Switch **12.00**
160-44462 Remote Right Hand Switch **12.00**
160-44488 Switch Assortment **264.00**
160-44489 Assorted pkg(72) **396.00**
160-44491 Hayes Bumpers pkg(2) **6.50**
160-44494 Layout Expander **38.00**

BULK TRACK- CASE OF 50

NICKEL SILVER
160-44580 18" Radius Curved **85.00**
160-44581 9" Straight **85.00**
160-44583 22" Radius Curve **95.00** *NEW*

STEEL
160-44480 18" Steel Radius Curved **57.00**
160-44481 9" Straight **57.00**
160-44483 22" Steel Radius Curved **65.00** *NEW*

TRACK ACCESSORIES

GATE

160-44579 Deluxe Crossing Gate **25.00**

TRACK CLEANER

160-99991 8oz **4.00**

MANUAL

160-99979 E-Z Track Manual #1 **4.00**

CABOOSE INDUSTRIES

OPERATING GROUND THROWS

Strong, self-lubricating, black Delrin ground throws with external cam for strength and maximum throw. Molded on a pin for direct mounting. All 100 series (Rigid) stands require modelers to fabricate a spring connecting link between the stand and the turnout. All 200 series stands have internal springs so they can be connected directly to the turnout throwbar.

.135" TRAVEL

97-105 Rigid **2.73**
97-206 Sprung **2.90**

.190" TRAVEL

97-101 Rigid **2.63**
97-202 Sprung **2.80**
97-5202 Sprung 5-Pack **13.25** *NEW*

.280" TRAVEL

97-107 Rigid **2.83**
97-208 Sprung **3.00**

.190" TRAVEL W/TARGETS

97-109 Rigid **3.68**
97-210 Sprung **3.85**

.165" TRAVEL W/SELECTABLE END FITTINGS

Operating ground throws including five different connectors: flat blade for Roco, small diameter pin for Micro Engineering, .083" hole for Peco, 90° slender shaft for Atlas, and large pin for most other turnouts. Also includes shim plate to raise the stand to height if needed.

97-117 Rigid **2.73**
97-218 Spring **2.90**
97-5218 Sprung 5-Pack **13.75** *NEW*

.165" TRAVEL W/SPDT CONTACTS

With parts to assemble one low current SPDT contact set.

97-119 Rigid **4.34**
97-220 Sprung **4.60**

HIGH LEVEL SWITCH STANDS

These operating models are typical of switch stands used by many railroads. Working parts are Delrin, but kit also includes six targets, nonworking lantern and a square diamond made of ABS plastic. Manual targets can be adapted to operate from an electric switch machine (sold separately) below the benchwork, .190" travel. Kits now include a shim to raise the stand to tie level, along with five different fittings for use with most turnouts, including Atlas®, Roco, Peco, Micro Engineering and Shinohara.

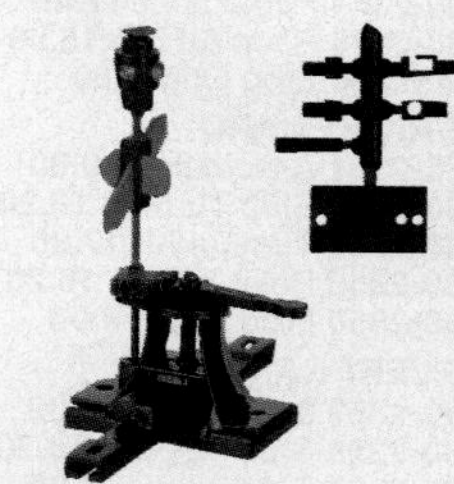

97-103 Rigid **5.15**
97-204 Sprung **5.50**

CREATIVE MODEL ASSOCIATES

TRACK STOP

363-1005 pkg(2) **5.95**
HO Scale replica of the most widely used track bumper, made by the Hayes Manufacturing Corporation from 1926 to the present. Includes bolt reinforcing plate details for outside of rails; great for sidings.

BK Enterprises
QUALITY TRACK PRODUCTS

Build your own custom trackwork with these turnouts and crossings. Recommended for the advance modeler, each features accurately gauged nickel-silver rails, without ties (ties are available separately). Turnouts are offered assembled and ready for spiking, or as a kit which requires bending the outside rail and gauging the track. Frogs and point and frog sets are also available. **PLEASE NOTE:** All kits are made to order and are not available for immediate delivery. A backorder is required for all track items.

CODE 40

HO TURNOUTS

180-2840 #4, Frog Only **10.20**
180-2850 #5, Frog Only **10.40**
180-2860 #6, Frog Only **10.60**

CODE 55

HO TURNOUTS

#4 RIGHT HAND
180-2341 Assembled **18.60**
180-2347 Stub Turnout **17.80**
180-2343 Turnout Kit **17.40**
180-2345 Point & Frog **15.80**
180-2340 Frog Only **9.80**

#4 LEFT HAND
180-2342 Assembled **18.60**
180-2348 Stub Turnout **17.80**
180-2344 Turnout Kit **17.40**
180-2346 Point & Frog **15.80**
180-2340 Frog Only **9.80**

#5 RIGHT HAND
180-2351 Assembled **19.00**
180-2357 Stub Turnout **18.20**
180-2353 Turnout Kit **17.80**
180-2355 Point & Frog **16.20**
180-2350 Frog Only **10.00**

#5 LEFT HAND
180-2352 Assembled **19.00**
180-2358 Stub Turnout **18.20**
180-2354 Turnout Kit **17.80**
180-2356 Point & Frog **16.20**
180-2350 Frog Only **10.00**

#6 RIGHT HAND
180-2361 Assembled **19.40**
180-2367 Stub Turnout **18.60**
180-2363 Turnout Kit **18.20**
180-2365 Point & Frog **16.60**
180-2360 Frog Only **10.20**

#6 LEFT HAND
180-2362 Assembled **19.40**
180-2368 Stub Turnout **18.60**
180-2364 Turnout Kit **18.20**
180-2366 Point & Frog **16.60**
180-2360 Frog Only **10.20**

#2-1/2 WYE
180-2391 Assembled **18.60**
180-2397 Stub Turnout **17.80**
180-2393 Turnout Kit **17.40**
180-2395 Point & Frog **15.80**
180-2390 Frog Only **9.80**

#4 WYE
180-2392 Assembled **18.60**
180-2398 Stub Turnout **17.80**
180-2394 Turnout Kit **17.40**
180-2396 Point & Frog **15.80**

HOn3 TURNOUTS

#4 RIGHT HAND
180-941 Assembled **18.80**
180-947 Stub Turnout **18.00**
180-943 Turnout Kit **17.60**
180-945 Point & Frog **16.00**
180-940 Frog Only **9.40**

#4 LEFT HAND
180-942 Assembled **18.80**
180-948 Stub Turnout **18.00**
180-944 Turnout Kit **17.60**
180-946 Point & Frog **16.00**
180-940 Frog Only **9.40**

#5 LEFT HAND
180-951 Assembled **19.20**
180-957 Stub Turnout **18.40**
180-953 Turnout Kit **18.00**
180-955 Point & Frog **16.40**
180-950 Frog Only **9.60**

#5 LEFT HAND
180-952 Assembled **19.20**
180-958 Stub Turnout **18.40**
180-954 Turnout Kit **18.00**
180-956 Point & Frog **16.40**
180-950 Frog Only **9.60**

#6 RIGHT HAND
180-961 Assembled **19.60**
180-967 Stub Turnout **18.80**
180-963 Turnout Kit **18.40**
180-965 Point & Frog **16.80**
180-960 Frog Only **9.80**

#6 LEFT HAND
180-962 Assembled **19.60**
180-968 Stub Turnout **18.80**
180-964 Turnout Kit **18.40**
180-966 Point & Frog **16.80**
180-960 Frog Only **9.80**

#2-1/2 WYE
180-991 Assembled **18.80**
180-997 Stub Turnout **18.00**
180-993 Turnout Kit **17.60**
180-995 Point & Frog **16.00**
180-990 Frog Only **9.40**

#4 WYE
180-992 Assembled **18.80**
180-998 Stub Turnout **18.00**
180-994 Turnout Kit **17.60**
180-996 Point & Frog **16.00**
180-980 Frog Only **10.00**

HOn30 TURNOUTS

#4 RIGHT HAND
180-2941 Assembled **18.80**
180-2947 Stub Turnout **18.00**
180-2943 Turnout Kit **17.60**
180-2945 Point & Frog **16.00**

#4 LEFT HAND
180-2942 Assembled **18.80**
180-2948 Stub Turnout **18.00**
180-2944 Turnout Kit **17.60**
180-2946 Point & Frog **16.00**

#5 RIGHT HAND
180-2951 Assembled **19.20**
180-2957 Stub Turnout **18.40**
180-2953 Turnout Kit **18.00**
180-2955 Point & Frog **16.40**

#5 LEFT HAND
180-2952 Assembled **19.20**
180-2958 Stub Turnout **18.40**
180-2954 Turnout Kit **18.00**
180-2956 Point & Frog **16.40**

#6 RIGHT HAND
180-2961 Assembled **19.60**
180-2967 Stub Turnout **18.80**
180-2963 Turnout Kit **18.40**
180-2965 Point & Frog **16.80**

#6 LEFT HAND
180-2962 Assembled **19.60**
180-2968 Stub Turnout **18.80**
180-2964 Turnout Kit **18.40**
180-2966 Point & Frog **16.80**

#2-1/2 WYE
180-2991 Assembled **18.80**
180-2997 Stub Turnout **18.00**
180-2993 Turnout Kit **17.60**
180-2995 Point & Frog **16.00**

#4 WYE
180-2992 Assembled **18.80**
180-2998 Stub Turnout **18.00**
180-2994 Turnout Kit **17.60**
180-2996 Point & Frog **16.00**

HOn3 CURVED TURNOUTS

#4 CURVED
180-9241 Right Hand **28.00**
180-9242 Left Hand **28.00**

#5 CURVED
180-9251 Right Hand **29.00**
180-9252 Left Hand **29.00**

#6 CURVED
180-9261 Right Hand **30.00**
180-9262 Left Hand **30.00**

HOn3 CROSSINGS

180-931 90° **37.00**
180-932 70° **37.00**
180-933 45° **37.00**
180-934 30° **37.00**
180-935 28° **39.00**

CODE 70

HO TURNOUTS

#4 RIGHT HAND
180-741 Assembled **17.40**
180-747 Stub Turnout **16.60**
180-743 Turnout Kit **16.20**
180-745 Point & Frog **14.60**
180-740 Frog Only **8.80**

#4 LEFT HAND
180-742 Assembled **17.40**
180-748 Stub Turnout **16.60**
180-744 Turnout Kit **16.20**
180-746 Point & Frog **14.60**
180-740 Frog Only **8.80**

#5 RIGHT HAND
180-751 Assembled **17.80**
180-757 Stub Turnout **17.00**
180-753 Turnout Kit **16.60**
180-755 Point & Frog **15.00**
180-750 Frog Only **9.00**

#5 LEFT HAND
180-752 Assembled **17.80**
180-758 Stub Turnout **17.00**
180-754 Turnout Kit **16.60**
180-756 Point & Frog **15.00**
180-750 Frog Only **9.00**

#6 RIGHT HAND
180-761 Assembled **18.20**
180-767 Stub Turnout **17.40**
180-763 Turnout Kit **17.00**
180-765 Point & Frog **15.40**
180-760 Frog Only **9.20**

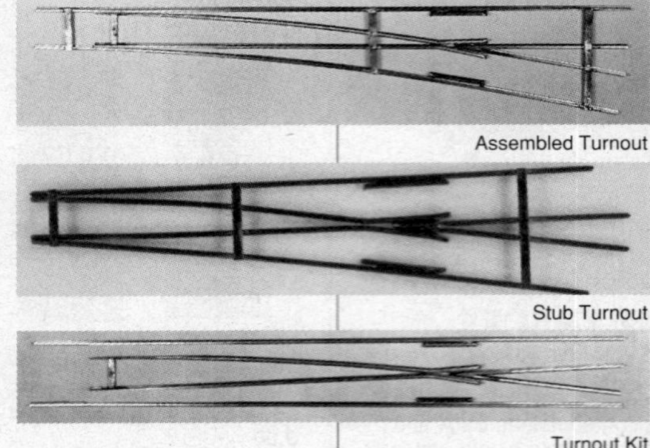
Assembled Turnout
Stub Turnout
Turnout Kit
Point & Frog

#6 LEFT HAND
180-762 Assembled **18.20**
180-768 Stub Turnout **17.40**
180-764 Turnout Kit **17.00**
180-766 Point & Frog **15.40**
180-760 Frog Only **9.20**

#8 RIGHT HAND
180-781 Assembled **19.00**
180-787 Stub Turnout **18.20**
180-783 Turnout Kit **17.80**
180-785 Point & Frog **16.20**
180-780 Frog Only **9.40**

#8 LEFT HAND
180-782 Assembled **19.00**
180-788 Stub Turnout **18.20**
180-784 Turnout Kit **17.80**
180-786 Point & Frog **16.20**
180-780 Frog Only **9.40**

#2-1/2 WYE
180-791 Assembled **17.40**
180-797 Stub Turnout **16.60**
180-793 Turnout Kit **16.20**

Frog Only

180-795 Point & Frog **14.60**
180-790 Frog Only **8.80**

#4 WYE
180-792 Assembled **17.40**
180-798 Stub Turnout **16.60**
180-794 Turnout Kit **16.20**
180-796 Point & Frog **14.60**

HO CURVED TURNOUTS

#4 CURVED
180-7241 Right Hand **22.00**
180-7242 Left Hand **22.00**

#5 CURVED
180-7251 Right Hand **23.00**
180-7252 Left Hand **23.00**

#6 CURVED
180-7261 Right Hand **24.00**
180-7262 Left Hand **24.00**

#7 CURVED
180-7271 Right Hand **25.00**
180-7272 Left Hand **25.00**

#8 CURVED
180-7281 Right Hand **26.00**
180-7282 Left Hand **26.00**

HO 3-WAY TURNOUTS EA 46.00

180-729 Blade
180-730 Stub

HO/HOn3 DUAL GUAGE TURNOUTS EA 51.00

180-7211 Right Hand, Narrow on Right
180-7212 Right Hand, Narrow on Left
180-7221 Left Hand, Narrow on Right
180-7222 Left Hand, Narrow on Left

HO CROSSINGS

180-737 14° **34.00**
180-736 19° **34.00**
180-735 28° **33.00**
180-734 30° **32.00**
180-733 45° **32.00**
180-732 60° **32.00**
180-738 70° **32.00**
180-731 90° **32.00**

HOn3 TURNOUTS

#4 RIGHT HAND
180-841 Assembled **17.00**
180-847 Stub Turnout **16.20**
180-843 Turnout Kit **15.80**
180-845 Point & Frog **14.20**
180-840 Frog Only **8.80**

#4 LEFT HAND
180-842 Assembled **17.00**
180-848 Stub Turnout **16.20**
180-844 Turnout Kit **15.80**
180-846 Point & Frog **14.20**
180-840 Frog Only **8.80**

#5 RIGHT HAND
180-851 Assembled **17.40**
180-857 Stub Turnout **16.60**
180-853 Turnout Kit **16.20**
180-855 Point & Frog **14.60**
180-850 Frog Only **9.00**

#5 LEFT HAND
180-852 Assembled **17.40**
180-858 Stub Turnout **16.60**
180-854 Turnout Kit **16.20**
180-856 Point & Frog **14.60**
180-850 Frog Only **9.00**

#6 RIGHT HAND
180-861 Assembled **17.80**
180-867 Stub Turnout **17.00**
180-863 Turnout Kit **16.60**
180-865 Point & Frog **15.00**
180-860 Frog Only **9.20**

BK Enterprises
QUALITY TRACK PRODUCTS

#6 LEFT HAND
180-862 Assembled 17.80
180-868 Stub Turnout 17.00
180-864 Turnout Kit 16.60
180-866 Point & Frog 15.00
180-860 Frog Only 9.20

#8 RIGHT HAND
180-880 Frog Only 9.20

#8 LEFT HAND
180-880 Frog Only 9.20

#2-1/2 WYE
180-891 Assembled 17.00
180-897 Stub Turnout 16.20
180-893 Turnout Kit 15.80
180-895 Point & Frog 14.20
180-890 Frog Only 8.80

#4 WYE
180-892 Assembled 17.00
180-898 Stub Turnout 16.20
180-894 Turnout Kit 15.80
180-896 Point & Frog 14.20

HOn3 CURVED TURNOUTS

#4 CURVED
180-8241 Right 26.00
180-8242 Left 26.00

#5 CURVED
180-8251 Right Hand 27.00
180-8252 Left Hand 27.00

#6 CURVED
180-8261 Right Hand 28.00
180-8262 Left Hand 28.00

HOn3 3-WAY TURNOUTS

180-830 Stub 48.00

HOn3 CROSSINGS EA 34.00 (UNLESS NOTED)

180-831 90°
180-832 70°
180-833 45°
180-834 30°
180-835 28° 36.00

HOn3 TRANSITION TRACK EA 16.00

180-8201 Right to Left
180-8202 Left to Right

CODE 83

HO TURNOUTS

#4 RIGHT HAND
180-241 Assembled 17.60
180-247 Stub Turnout 16.80
180-243 Turnout Kit 16.40
180-245 Point & Frog 14.80
180-240 Frog Only 9.00

#4 LEFT HAND
180-242 Assembled 18.00
180-248 Stub Turnout 16.80
180-244 Turnout Kit 16.40
180-246 Point & Frog 14.80
180-240 Frog Only 9.00

#5 RIGHT HAND
180-251 Assembled 18.00
180-257 Stub Turnout 17.20
180-253 Turnout Kit 16.80
180-255 Point & Frog 15.20
180-250 Frog Only 9.20

#5 LEFT HAND
180-252 Assembled 18.00
180-258 Stub Turnout 17.20
180-254 Turnout Kit 16.80
180-256 Point & Frog 15.20
180-250 Frog Only 9.20

#6 RIGHT HAND
180-261 Assembled 18.40
180-267 Stub Turnout 17.00
180-263 Turnout Kit 17.20
180-265 Point & Frog 15.60
180-260 Frog Only 9.40

#6 LEFT HAND
180-262 Assembled 18.40
180-268 Stub Turnout 17.60
180-264 Turnout Kit 17.20
180-266 Point & Frog 15.60
180-260 Frog Only 9.40

#7 RIGHT HAND
180-271 Assembled 18.80
180-273 Turnout Kit 17.60
180-275 Points & Frog 16.00
180-277 Stub Turnout 18.00

#7 LEFT HAND
180-272 Assembled 18.80
180-274 Turnout Kit 17.60
180-276 Points & Frog 16.00
180-278 Stub Turnout 18.00

#8 RIGHT HAND
180-281 Assembled 19.20
180-287 Stub Turnout 18.40
180-283 Turnout Kit 18.00
180-285 Point & Frog 16.40
180-280 Frog Only 9.80

#8 LEFT HAND
180-282 Assembled 19.20
180-288 Stub Turnout 18.40
180-284 Turnout Kit 18.00
180-286 Point & Frog 16.40
180-290 Frog Only 8.80

#10 RIGHT HAND
180-211 Assembled 20.40
180-213 Turnout Kit 19.20
180-215 Points & Frog 17.60
180-217 Stub Turnout 19.60

#10 LEFT HAND
180-212 Assembled 20.40
180-214 Turnout Kit 19.20
180-216 Points & Frog 17.60
180-218 Stub Turnout 19.60

#2-1/2 WYE
180-291 Assembled 17.60
180-297 Stub Turnout 16.80
180-293 Turnout Kit 16.40
180-295 Point & Frog 14.80
180-290 Frog Only 8.80

#4 WYE
180-292 Assembled 17.60
180-298 Stub Turnout 16.80
180-294 Turnout Kit 16.40
180-296 Point & Frog 14.80

HO CURVED TURNOUTS

#4 CURVED
180-2241 Right Hand 23.00
180-2242 Left Hand 23.00

#5 CURVED
180-2251 Right Hand 24.00
180-2252 Left Hand 24.00

#6 CURVED
180-2261 Right Hand 25.00
180-2262 Left Hand 25.00

#7 CURVED
180-2271 Right Hand 26.00
180-2272 Left Hand 26.00

#8 CURVED
180-2281 Right Hand 27.00
180-2282 Left Hand 27.00

HO 3-WAY TURNOUTS

180-229 Blade 48.00
180-230 Stub 48.00

HO/HOn3 DUAL GAUGE TURNOUTS

180-2211 Right Hand, Narrow on Right 52.00
180-2212 Right Hand, Narrow on Left 52.00
180-2221 Left Hand, Narrow on Right 52.00
180-2222 Left Hand, Narrow on Left 52.00

HO CROSSINGS

180-237 14° 34.00
180-236 19° 34.00
180-235 28° 33.00
180-234 30° 32.00
180-233 45° 32.00
180-232 60° 32.00
180-231 90° 32.00

HO DOUBLE SLIP CROSSINGS

180-238 #4 Frog 40.00
180-239 #6 Frog 42.00

CODE 100

HO TURNOUTS

#4 RIGHT HAND
180-141 Assembled 18.00
180-147 Stub Turnout 17.20
180-143 Turnout Kit 16.80
180-145 Point & Frog 15.20
180-140 Frog Only 9.00

#4 LEFT HAND
180-142 Assembled 18.00
180-148 Stub Turnout 17.20
180-144 Turnout Kit 16.80
180-146 Point & Frog 15.20
180-140 Frog Only 9.00

#5 RIGHT HAND
180-151 Assembled 18.40
180-157 Stub Turnout 17.60
180-153 Turnout Kit 17.20
180-155 Point & Frog 15.60
180-150 Frog Only 9.20

#5 LEFT HAND
180-152 Assembled 18.40
180-158 Stub Turnout 17.60
180-154 Turnout Kit 17.20
180-156 Point & Frog 15.60
180-150 Frog Only 9.20

#6 RIGHT HAND
180-161 Assembled 18.80
180-167 Stub Turnout 18.00
180-163 Turnout Kit 17.60
180-165 Point & Frog 16.00
180-160 Frog Only 9.40

#6 LEFT HAND
180-162 Assembled 18.80
180-168 Stub Turnout 18.00
180-164 Turnout Kit 17.60
180-166 Point & Frog 16.00
180-160 Frog Only 9.40

#7 RIGHT HAND
180-171 Assembled 19.20
180-177 Stub Turnout 18.40
180-173 Turnout Kit 18.00
180-175 Point & Frog 16.40
180-170 Frog Only 9.60

#7 LEFT HAND
180-172 Assembled 19.20
180-178 Stub Turnout 18.40
180-174 Turnout Kit 18.00
180-176 Point & Frog 16.40
180-170 Frog Only 9.60

#8 RIGHT HAND
180-181 Assembled 19.60
180-187 Stub Turnout 18.80
180-183 Turnout Kit 18.40
180-185 Point & Frog 16.80
180-180 Frog Only 9.80

#8 LEFT HAND
180-182 Assembled 19.60
180-188 Stub Turnout 18.80
180-184 Turnout Kit 18.40
180-186 Point & Frog 16.80
180-180 Frog Only 9.80

#8-1/2 RIGHT HAND
180-1811 Turnout 19.80
180-1831 Right Hand Turnout Kit 18.60
180-1851 Right Hand Point & Frog 17.00
180-1871 Right Hand Stub Turnout 19.00

#8-1/2 LEFT HAND
180-1821 Left Hand Turnout 19.80
180-1841 Left Hand Turnout Kit 18.60
180-1861 Left Hand Point & Frog 17.00
180-1881 Left Hand Stub Turnout 19.00

#10 RIGHT HAND
180-111 Assembled 20.80
180-117 Stub Turnout 20.00
180-113 Turnout Kit 19.60
180-115 Point & Frog 18.00
180-110 Frog Only 10.20

#10 LEFT HAND
180-112 Assembled 20.80
180-118 Stub Turnout 20.00
180-114 Turnout Kit 19.60
180-116 Point & Frog 18.00
180-110 Frog Only 10.20

#12 RIGHT HAND
180-1111 Right Hand Turnout 21.60
180-1131 Right Hand Turnout Kit 20.40
180-1151 Right Hand Point & Frog 18.80
180-1171 Right Hand Stub Turnout 20.80

#12 LEFT HAND
180-1121 Left Hand Turnout 21.60
180-1141 Left Hand Turnout Kit 20.40
180-1161 Left Hand Point & Frog 18.80
180-1181 Left Hand Stub Turnout 20.80

#16 RIGHT HAND
180-101 Assembled 23.20
180-103 Turnout Kit 22.00
180-105 Points & Frog 20.40
180-107 Stub Turnout 22.40

#16 LEFT HAND
180-102 Assembled 23.20
180-104 Turnout Kit 22.00
180-106 Points & Frog 20.40
180-108 Stub Turnout 22.40

#2-1/2 WYE
180-191 Assembled 18.00
180-197 Stub Turnout 17.20
180-193 Turnout Kit 16.80
180-195 Point & Frog 15.20
180-190 Frog Only 9.00

#4 WYE
180-192 Assembled 18.00
180-198 Stub Turnout 17.20
180-194 Turnout Kit 16.80
180-196 Point & Frog 15.20

HO CURVED TURNOUTS

#4 CURVED
180-1241 Right Hand 24.00
180-1242 Left Hand 24.00

#5 CURVED
180-1251 Right Hand 25.00
180-1252 Left Hand 25.00

#6 CURVED
180-1261 Right Hand 26.00
180-1262 Left Hand 26.00

#7 CURVED
180-1271 Right Hand 27.00
180-1272 Left Hand 27.00

#8 CURVED
180-1281 Right Hand 28.00
180-1282 Left Hand 28.00

HO 3-WAY TURNOUTS

180-129 Blade 48.00
180-130 Stub 48.00

HO CROSSINGS

180-137 14° 34.00
180-136 19° 34.00
180-135 28° 33.00
180-134 30° 32.00
180-133 45° 32.00
180-132 60° 32.00
180-131 90° 32.00

HO DOUBLE SLIP CROSSINGS

180-138 #4 Frog 40.00
180-139 #6 Frog 42.00

TRANSITION RAIL

Use to connect two different rail sizes.

180-31 Code 40 to 55 pkg(2) 6.60
180-32 Code 55 to 70 pkg(2) 6.60
180-33 Code 70 to 83 pkg(2) 6.80
180-34 Code 83 to 100 pkg(2) 6.80

TIES

Prestained basswood ties

HO PROFILE

REGULAR
180-11 Gray pkg(1200) 12.00
180-13 Brown pkg(1200) 12.00
180-15 Black pkg(1200) 12.00
180-17 Plain pkg(1200) 11.00

TURNOUT
180-12 Gray pkg(700) 12.00
180-14 Brown pkg(700) 12.00
180-16 Black pkg(700) 12.00
180-18 Plain pkg(700) 11.00

HOn3 PROFILE

REGULAR
180-25 Gray pkg(1200) 12.00
180-19 Brown pkg(1200) 12.00
180-21 Black pkg(1200) 12.00
180-23 Plain pkg(1200) 11.00

TURNOUT
180-26 Gray pkg(700) 12.00
180-20 Brown pkg(700) 12.00
180-22 Black pkg(700) 12.00
180-24 Plain pkg(700) 11.00

CAR WEIGHTS

180-37 1/2 Ounce pkg(8) 5.60
180-38 1 Ounce pkg(8) 8.80

AMI INSTANT ROADBED

INSTANT ROADBED

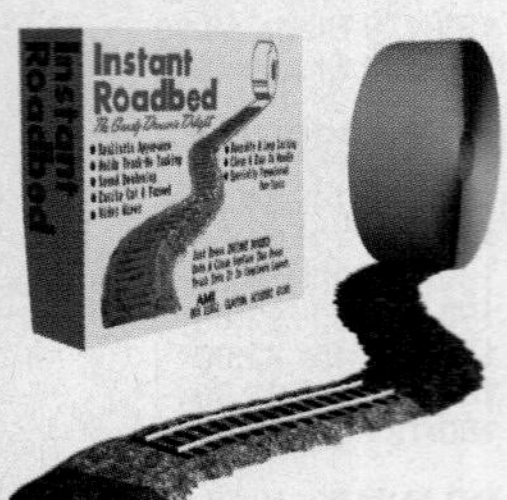

Just press realistic appearing Instant Roadbed onto a clean surface, then press track into it to complete layout. Made of uncured butyl rubber. Easily cut and formed. Sound deadening, self-adhesive, nontoxic. Can be used with any scale 2" x 1/8" x 30' rolls.

Also makes it easy to model very realistic asphalt, concrete, bricks and other material for sidewalks, cobblestone streets, highways and more.

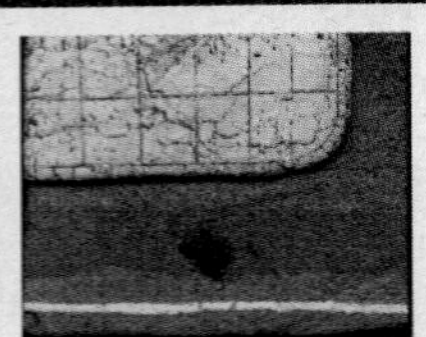

128-30 Black **15.95**
128-130 Gray **17.95**
128-25 Black **13.95**
1 x 1/8 x 30' roll.

Dealer: MUST order dealer pack of 8 rolls.

INSTA BASE

128-18 Insta Base pkg(10) **3.95**
Same material as Instant Roadbed, but in sheets measuring 18 x 8-3/4 x 1/8".

BUSCH

IMPORTED FROM GERMANY BY WALTHERS
Track ballast tape and cork roadbed for HO and HOn3 track.

TRACK BALLAST TAPE

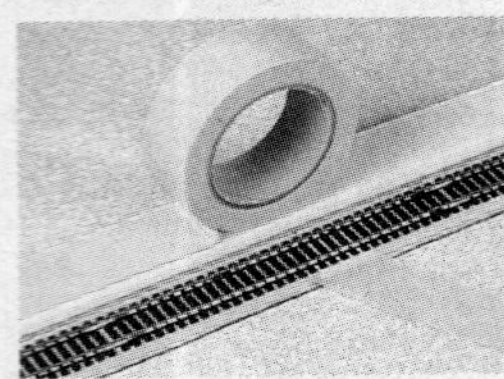

189-7119 Ballast Tape **10.99**
10' 3.3m long, 1-5/8" 41mm wide.

CORK ROADBED

3/16" 5mm thick.

189-7501 8' 3" 2.5m Long, 45° Beveled Edge **14.99**
189-7502 Cork Sheet 12 x 8" 300 x 200mm **8.99**

CAMPBELL SCALE MODELS

HO Scale track ties and accessories.

PROFILE TIES EA 12.00

200-796 Standard pkg(1000)
200-797 Turnout & Crossover pkg(250)
200-798 Bridge pkg(500)
200-799 Narrow Gauge pkg(1000)

TRACK TEST LIGHT

200-550 6.00
When set on track, test light shines if power is on. Works with any gauge. In green, red or amber.

Circuitron

THE TORTOISE™ SWITCH MACHINE

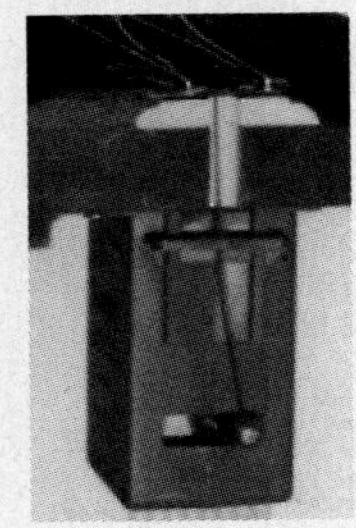

- Easy-to-mount slow-motion switch machine features:
- Prototypical slow-motion action - 3 seconds to complete throw
- Low current drain
- Precision-engineered gear drive mechanism
- Simple mounting with linkage included - no additional brackets or linkage necessary
- Convenient auxilliary contacts- two sets SPDT provided
- Easy wiring - 2 wire connection possible

800-6000 The Tortoise **15.95**

TORTOISE VALUE PACKS

(Dealers Note: items are not labeled for individual sale.)

800-6006 Pack of 6 **92.95**
800-6012 Pack of 12 **179.95**

REMOTE TORTOISE™ MOUNT

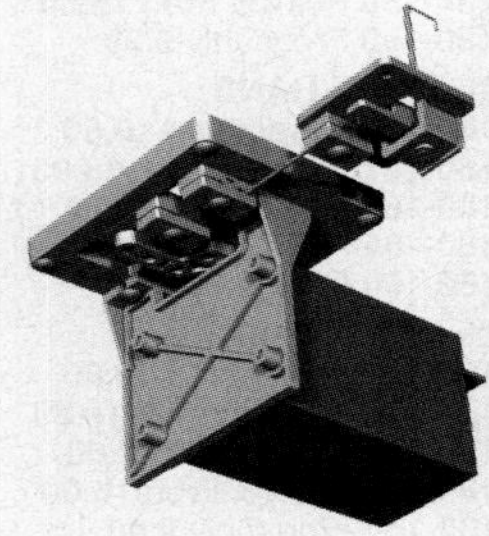

800-6100 8.95 ***NEW***
Mounting bracket and special linkage allow you to mount the Tortoise™ above or below the benchwork and up to 18" from the turnout. Suitable for all scales and brands of turnouts.

AC ADAPTER

800-7212 11.95
110 volt AC wall plug adapter outputs filtered 12 volts DC at 500 ma, sufficient to power up to 30 Tortoise™ Switch Machines.

CTT. INC.

Designing and planning your next layout will be easy with CTT track-planning templates and layout design sheets. All items are calibrated to a 1" = 12" scale.

TEMPLATE

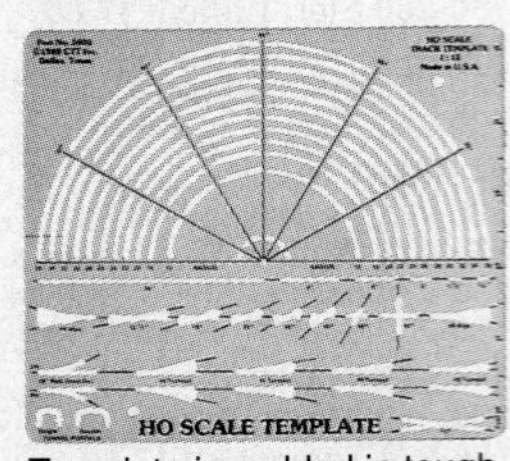

Template is molded in tough, see-through plastic with outlines for HO Scale curves, crossings, turnouts and other track.

233-5000 Template Only **10.95**
233-5003 Template & Layout Design Paper **14.50**

LAYOUT DESIGN PAPER

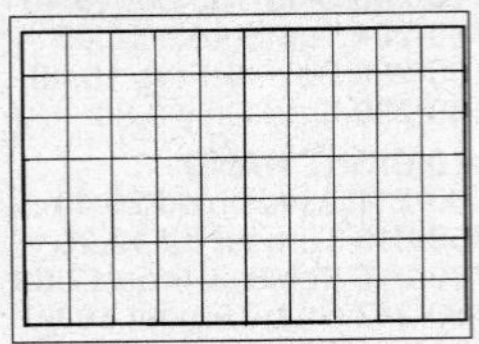

Design sheets feature a 1" square grid pattern, printed in light gray. Available for 7 x 10', 9 x 16', or 16 x 23' rooms. (Sheets can be overlapped for larger areas.)

233-4000 Paper Kit **4.25**
233-4001 7 x 10' **.35**
233-4002 9 x 16' **.90**
233-4003 16 x 23' **2.35**

SCALE RULER EA 3.25

12" clear plastic. Includes scale feet, inches, full-size inch, millimeter, decimal and metric conversion table.

233-9022 1:22.5 (G) Scale
233-9024 1:24 Scale
233-9025 1:25 Scale
233-9032 1:32 Scale
233-9035 1:35 Scale
233-9048 1:48 Scale
233-9064 1:64 Scale
233-9072 1:72 Scale
233-9087 1:87 (HO) Scale
233-9160 1:160 (N) Scale

EVERGREEN HILL DESIGNS

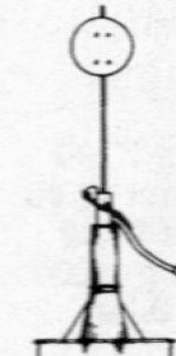

SWITCH STAND

261-620 Sierra Switch Stand **2.25**
Nonoperating, cast white-metal HO Scale kit.

EARL R. ESHLEMAN

TURNOUT LINKS EA 2.45 (UNLESS NOTED)

Designed for under-the-table operation of turnouts with choke rod or switch machine. Works with any scale or gauge.

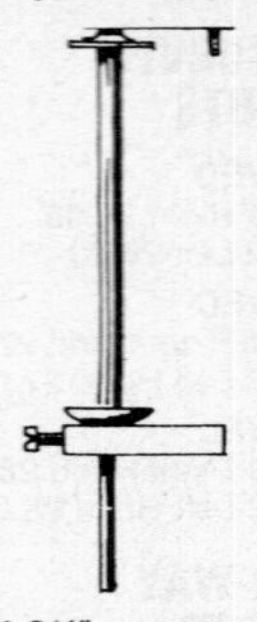

257-1 3/4"
257-2 1-3/8"
257-3 1-7/8"
257-4 1-7/8" w/Spring **2.50**

DRILLING JIG

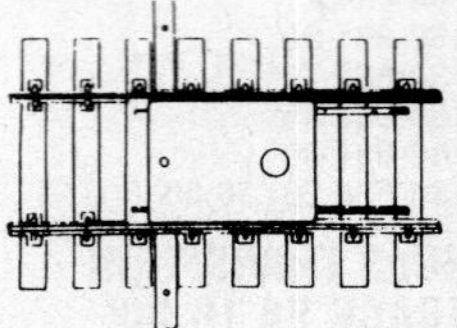

257-10 1.45

HO ROADBED

One-piece cork roadbed turnout sections provide a smooth transition between turnouts and track. Each section is 5mm thick with beveled edges. Color and profile match other popular brands of roadbed. Works with all HO Scale track.

#4/#6 TURNOUTS EA 4.45

357-1500 Right Hand pkg(2)

357-1501 Left Hand pkg(2)

#8 TURNOUTS EA 5.25

357-1502 Right Hand pkg(2)
357-1503 Left Hand pkg(2)

CROSSINGS & WYE

357-1504 12.5° Crossing **3.45**

357-1505 25/30° Crossing **3.25**

357-1506 Wye **3.35**

MULTI-TRACK YARD PADS

357-1518 6 x 18" **3.95**
Dealers MUST Buy Packs of 12.

HOm & TT ROADBED

18" SINGLE TRACK

357-1400 pkg(5) **5.95**
357-14001 pkg(24) **22.95**

TURNOUTS PKG(2) EA 3.25

357-1401 Right Hand

357-1402 Left Hand

CURVED TURNOUTS EA 2.25

357-1403 Right Hand
357-1404 Left Hand

357-1405 15° Crossing **2.25**

FALLER

IMPORTED FROM GERMANY BY WALTHERS

HO Scale roadbed and accessories.

CORK ROADBED

272-765 pkg(6) **16.99**
Flexible, sloped sections. Dimensions: 50cm (20-11/16") long, 5mm (3/16") high. Total 12 sections: 118" long.

TRACK BUFFER

Limited Quantity Available

272-15900 With Contact **1.99**

GRANDT LINE

HO Scale track items.

SWITCH STAND

300-5061 Kit **1.85**
Model of a heavy cast-iron switch stand. Kit features styrene parts with jewels.

RAIL CLIPS

300-5155 Dummy pkg(55) **2.05**

KADEE®

HO Scale switches, track gauges and accessories.

"QUICKIE" PANEL SWITCHES PKG(3) 3.45

Single pole, single throw, momentary push button switches for uncouplers, turnout motors, etc. 16V AC or DC, 1 amp.

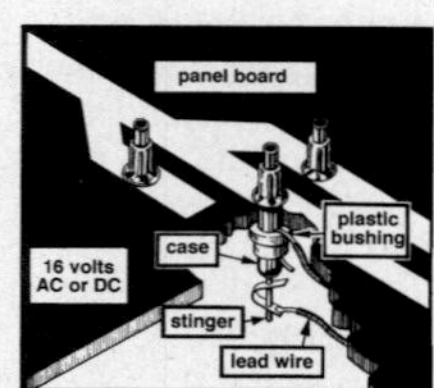

380-160 Amber
380-161 Green
380-162 Red

TRACK GAUGES EA 2.15

"Flip-over" multi-purpose gauge.

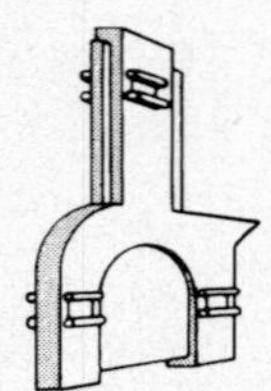

380-341 Code 70 & 100
380-342 Code 55, 66 & 70 HOn3

TRACK SPIKES FOR KADEE® RAIL SPIKER PKG(4000) EA 6.15

These spikes can only be used with the Kadee® Rail Spiker.

380-372 Code 70 & 83
380-392 Code 100

N.J. International

TRACK ACCESSORIES

SWITCH MACHINES & ACCESSORIES

525-6000 Twin Coil Switch Machine **14.99**
525-6001 Extra Contacts **4.79**
525-6002 Extra Throw Springs pkg(2) **1.59**
525-6003 Under Table Mounting Kit pkg(2) **4.99**
525-6004 Wiring Connector **4.99**

SWITCH STANDS EA 7.95

All brass-jeweled, operating.

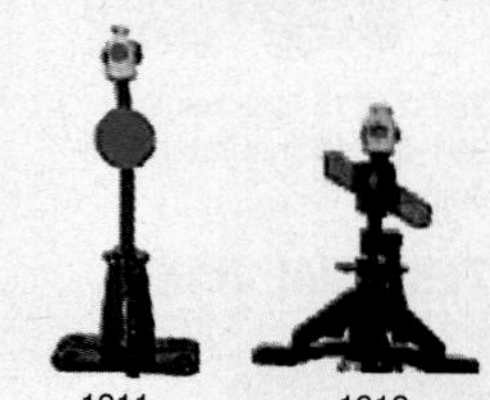

525-1911 Star
525-1912 Branch Line

525-1913 Main Line
525-1914 Low Ramapo
525-1915 High Ramapo

SWITCH INDICATORS

All brass with LEDs.

525-13000 Silver (pair) **16.95**
525-13010 Black (pair) **16.95**

SWITCH INDICATOR DRESS-UP KIT

All brass.

525-1305 Silver **6.99**
525-1306 Black **6.99**

KAPPLER MILL & LUMBER CO.

These HO and HOn3 Scale ties are made of unstained sugar pine. Dimensions are in prototype inches.

REGULAR TIES

HOn3 PKG(1000) EA 10.95

385-51 5 x 7" x 6'
385-52 5 x 7" x 6' 6"

HO PKG(1000) EA 11.95

385-53 7 x 9" x 8'
385-54 7 x 9" x 8' 6"

SWITCH TIES

385-59 5 x 7" x 12', HOn3 pkg(500) **10.95**
385-60 7 x 9" x 16', HO pkg(500) **11.95**

KONTOUR SWITCH TIES

385-84 4 x 7" x 12', HOn3 pkg(500) **10.95**
385-85 4 x 9" x 16', HO pkg(500) **11.95**

BRIDGE & TRESTLE TIES

385-69 8 x 8" x 10', HO/HOn3 pkg(500) **11.95**

KONTOUR CROSS TIES

Kontour cross ties are about 1/2 the thickness of regular scale ties in order to use less ballast.

HOn3 PKG(1000) EA 10.95

385-72 4 x 7" x 6'
385-73 4 x 7" x 6' 6"

HO PKG(1000) EA 11.95

385-74 4 x 9" x 8'
385-75 4 x 9" x 8' 6"

UNITRACK SYSTEM

With Kato's HO Scale Unitrack Modular Roadbed Track System you can have an operating layout in minutes. Whether you're a beginner or expert, Unitrack offers hours of enjoyment and trouble-free operation. Suitable for all types of layouts, whether temporary or permanent.

This modular track system features an integrally molded roadbed for realistic appearance. Uni-Joiners (included) lock the track sections together for easy assembly and solid electrical connections.

NOW WITH NICKEL-SILVER CODE 83 RAIL

STRAIGHT TRACK

Dealers MUST order in multiples of 4.

381-2120 4-1/2" **2.50**

381-2130 6-7/8" **2.63**

381-2150 9-3/4" **2.75**

FEEDER TRACK

381-2151 9-3/4" **5.00**

BUMPER

381-2170 pkg(2) **10.00**

CURVED TRACK

Dealers MUST order in multiples of 4. Four packages makes a full circle; listed dimension indicates radius. 22.5°

381-2210 21-5/8" **2.75**
381-2220 24" **3.00**
381-2240 28-3/4" **3.25**
381-2250 31-1/8" **3.50**

ELECTRIC TURNOUTS

Each turnout includes a switch machine that is prewired and installed inside the roadbed.

#4 POWER ROUTING TURNOUTS EA 44.00

381-2850 Left Hand
381-2851 Right Hand

#6 EA 53.00

Can have live or insulated frogs.

381-2860 Left Hand
381-2861 Right Hand

UNI-JOINERS PKG(20) EA 5.25

381-24815 Uni-Joiners
381-24816 Insulated Uni-Joiners

TERMINAL JOINER

381-24818 4.25
Feeds power anywhere on a layout without the need for an additional track section.

ADAPTER CORD

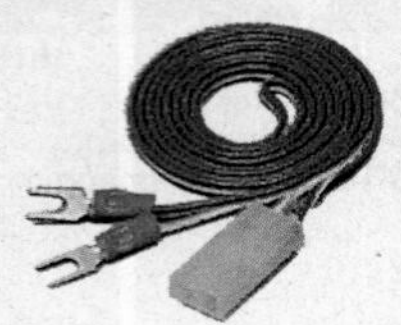

381-24843 3.25
For use between power pack and feeder track or accessories.

TURNOUT CONTROL SWITCH

381-24840 7.75
Use to operate turnout electrically.

DC CONVERTER

381-24842 6.50
Connect to your power pack's AC 16/17V accessory output. Only one converter is required to connect as many turnout control switches as your layout requires.

EXTENSION CORDS

All cords 35".

381-24841 Turnout **3.25**
381-24825 DC **3.25**
381-24826 AC **3.25**

381-24827 3-Way **5.25**
Can be used to power multiple feeder tracks or operate multiple turnouts with single turnout control switch #381-24840.

RERAILER

381-2502 With Uni-Joiner Removal Tool **3.60**

SWITCHES

381-24830 Connector (green) **3.25**
381-24831 Selector (red) **3.75**
381-24832 Reverse (blue) **4.00**

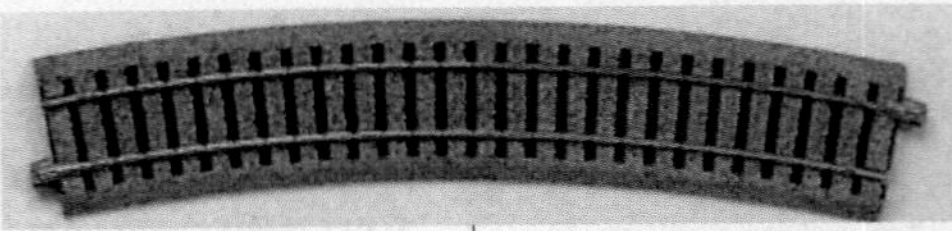

Curved Track 21-5/8" 381-2210

Curved Track 24" 381-2220

Curved Track 28-3/4" 381-2240

Curved Track 31-1/8" 381-2250

Left Hand #4 Power Routing Electric Turnout 381-2850

Right Hand #4 Power Routing Electric Turnout 381-2851

Left Hand #6 Electric Turnout 381-2860

Right Hand #6 Electric Turnout 381-2861

HO Scale cork roadbed and sheet.

CORK ROADBED

These lightweight pieces of cork roadbed are easy to use by any modeler: materials can be easily shaped and easily cut. Constructed with consistent thickness, each section is beveled for a realistic look. Features excellent sound absorption.

3' SECTIONS

472-3013 1.20
Dealers MUST order multiples of 25.

472-3015 pkg(5) **8.25**

#4/6 TURNOUTS

Install roadbed under turnouts in seconds with these precut easy-to-use cork sections. Simply position and nail in place. One-piece design eliminates difficult alignment of diverging route and cutting. Beveled edges, height and color match other cork roadbed and sheets. Can be used with most US standard turnouts.

472-3022 Right Hand pkg(2) **4.75**
3/16 x 2-15/16 x 8-5/8"

472-3023 Left Hand pkg(2) **4.75**
3/16 x 2-15/16 x 8-5/8"

472-3024 Wye **3.95**
3/16 x 3-1/8 x 8-23/32"

CORKSHEET PACK

472-3014 3.30
Sheet stock can be used on switches, sidings, yards and loading areas. Each sheet is 5mm x 5 x 36". Dealers MUST order multiples of 9.

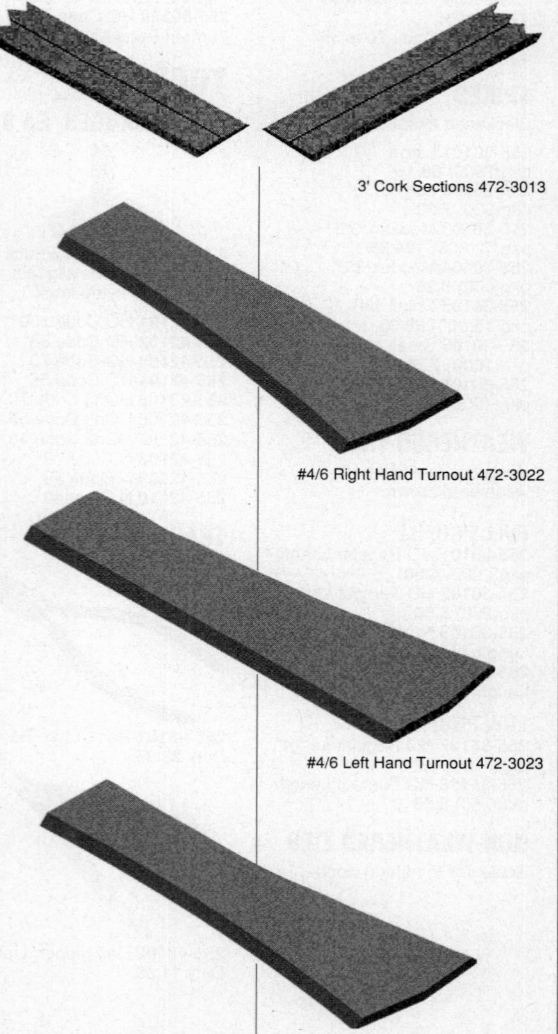

3' Cork Sections 472-3013

#4/6 Right Hand Turnout 472-3022

#4/6 Left Hand Turnout 472-3023

#4/6 Wye Turnout 472-3024

HO Scale nickel-silver track, cork roadbed and accessories.

TRACK

SUPER FLEX FLEXIBLE TRACK

490-105 Code 100, 36" **2.70**

CURVED TRACK

490-3344 Code 100, 18" pkg(4) **1.98**
2 packages make a complete circle

AUTOMATIC TURNOUTS

Turnouts include electric switch machine and black plastic ties.

#6
490-170 Left Hand **39.98**
490-171 Right Hand **39.98**
490-198 3-Way **74.98**
490-189 Double Slip **79.98**

18/22" CURVED EA 39.98

490-180 Left Hand
490-181 Right Hand

REMOTE EA 9.98

490-5044 Left Switch
490-5144 Right Switch

TERMINAL TRACK EA 2.25

490-40 Straight
490-4544 Curved, Code 100, 9"

TRACK ACCESSORIES

SHUTTLE UNIT

490-1 Reversing **79.98**

SWITCH CONTROL

490-3 Nickel Silver **2.25**

RERAILER

490-108 Curved Track **1.98**

TRACK LOCKS

490-6538 1.98

CORK ROADBED

SINGLE TRACK 36"

490-4311 pkg(25) **28.75**
490-4315 pkg(5) **7.75**

SWITCH BLOCK 9"

490-4316 pkg(2) **4.35**
490-4317 pkg(20) **39.60**

TRACK NAILS EA 2.49

490-220 Long
490-245 Short

RAIL JOINERS

490-125 Nickel Silver pkg(24) **1.50**

TRACK BUMPER-LIGHTED

490-8744 Code 100, Nickel Silver pkg(2) **2.98**

TRACK TEST LIGHT

490-16628 6.98

CLEANING BLOCK

490-250 2.49
Contains pumice stone.

Peerless Industries Inc.

Offers easy-to-install electronic controls for directional reversing, delayed reversing and intermediate stops. Designed for use with HO Scale track, the units come completely assembled with color-coded wires and easy-to-follow instructions. Operates from any 12V DC power supply.

AUTOMATIC REVERSING UNIT

564-525 HO Scale **65.95**
Automatically reverses train direction without the need for track switches, optical sensors, special lights or other devices. Unit is less track. Can be used for:

- automatic single or multitrack point-to-point operation.
- a wall or bookcase mini-layout or display track for your favorite locomotive
- a test or break-in track

AUTOMATIC TRAIN STOPS EA 69.95

564-550 Control
For use with Peerless #525, 535, 542 & 545. Provides automatic delayed stops at the end points of your reversing section. Delay is adjustable from 1 to 30 seconds. Takes only a few minutes to install.

564-555 Intermediate
Train will make automatic stops at intermediate points such as a station, water tower, etc. Train will stop-delay-start automatically. Delay time is adjustable from 1 to 30 seconds. For use with #525, 535, 545 or 542. Can operate from AC power supply.

NORTHEASTERN SCALE MODELS INC.

ROADBED

Give your railroad a solid surface using these precut sections of wooden roadbed.

Each section is laser-cut for accuracy and features male and female ends to insure precise self-alignment. The surface of each section is smoothly milled, ready for your favorite brand of track.

STRAIGHT

521-80001 12" pkg(2) **2.70**
521-80002 16" pkg(2) **3.70**
521-80003 24" pkg(2) **4.70**

CURVED

521-80004 18" Radius pkg(2) **4.90**
521-80005 22" Radius pkg(2) **5.20**
521-80006 26" Radius pkg(2) **6.00**
521-80007 28" Radius pkg(2) **6.30**
521-80008 30" Radius pkg(2) **5.10**
521-80009 32" Radius pkg(2) **5.40**
521-80010 34" Radius pkg(2) **5.70**
521-80011 36" Radius pkg(2) **6.00**

CONNECTORS

521-80012 Assorted pkg(6) **2.00**

TURNOUTS

#4 EA 4.00

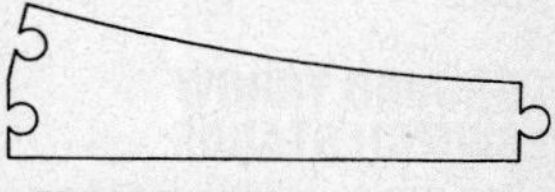

521-80016 Left
521-80017 Right

#5 EA 4.50

521-80018 Left
521-80019 Right

#6 EA 4.80

521-80020 Left
521-80021 Right

#8 EA 5.00

521-80022 Left
521-80023 Right

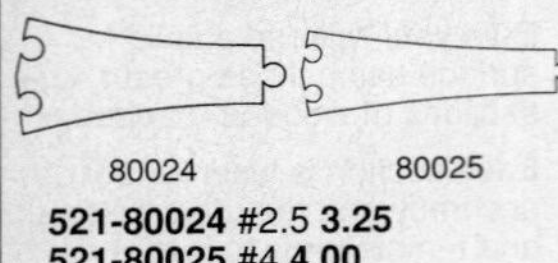

WYE TURNOUTS

521-80024 #2.5 **3.25**
521-80025 #4 **4.00**

521-80026 Three-Way **6.00**

CROSSINGS EA 4.00

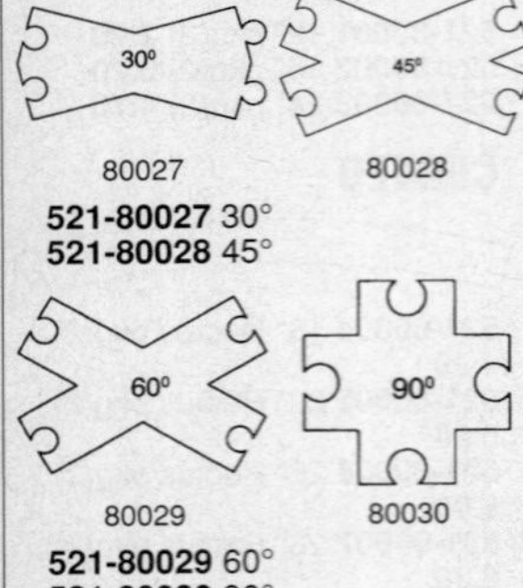

521-80027 30°
521-80028 45°

521-80029 60°
521-80030 90°

OLD PULLMAN

SPIKES 5/16" LONG

536-195 pkg(1000) **5.95**
536-196 pkg(2500) **13.95**
536-197 pkg(5000) **26.95**

ON-TRAK MODEL PRODUCTS

HO Scale cast-metal detail parts.

GROUND THROW SWITCH STANDS

786-818 Switch Stand Only pkg(2) **1.60**
786-819 With Lamp pkg(2) **2.45**
786-820 With Lamp & Jewels pkg(2) **3.95**

HO and HOn3 Flex-Trak with nickel-silver rail.

FLEX-TRAK™

Flex-Trak features scale size ties, tie plates and spikes, irregular tie spacing, natural brown tie color and nickel-silver rail. 3' lengths.

HO STANDARD GAUGE NON-WEATHERED FLEX-TRAK

255-10102 Code 100 pkg(6) **27.25**
255-10104 Code 83 pkg(6) **25.75**
255-10106 Code 70 pkg(6) **25.75**
255-10108 Code 55 pkg(6) **25.75**

HO STANDARD GAUGE WEATHERED FLEX-TRAK

255-12102 Code 100 pkg(6) **28.30**
255-12104 Code 83 pkg(6) **26.80**
255-12106 Code 70 pkg(6) **26.80**
255-12108 Code 55 pkg(6) **26.80**

HOn3 NARROW GAUGE NON-WEATHERED FLEX-TRAK

255-10114 Code 70 pkg(6) **25.75**
255-10116 Code 55 pkg(6) **24.10**
255-10118 Code 40 pkg(6) **24.10**

HOn3 NARROW GAUGE WEATHERED FLEX-TRAK

255-12114 Code 70 pkg(6) **26.80**
255-12116 Code 55 pkg(6) **25.15**
255-12118 Code 40 pkg(6) **25.15**

HO-HOn3 DUAL GAUGE NON-WEATHERED FLEX-TRAK

255-10110 Code 70 pkg(6) **31.45**
255-10112 Code 55 pkg(6) **30.40**

HO-HOn3 DUAL GAUGE WEATHERED FLEX-TRAK

255-12110 Code 70 pkg(6) **33.10**
255-12112 Code 55 pkg(6) **31.45**

BRIDGE FLEX-TRAK

Flex-Trak with bridge tie dimensions, ties are wider with closer spacing. The HO track includes guard rails, guard timbers and 4 barrel platforms with barrels.

255-11101 HO Code 83 pkg(1) **8.50** ***NEW***
36" length.

255-11103 HO Code 70 pkg(1) **8.50** ***NEW***
36" length.

255-11102 HOn3 Code 55 pkg(2) **5.20**
7" length.

FLEX-TRAK TURNOUTS EA 16.95

255-14705 HO Code 83, No.6 Left Hand
255-14706 HO Code 83, No.6 Right Hand
255-14805 HO Code 70, No.6 Left Hand
255-14806 HO Code 70, No.6 Right Hand

NICKEL SILVER RAIL

WEATHERED

Preblackened nickel-silver rail sections. 3' lengths.

255-16040 Code 40 pkg(33) **32.95**
255-16055 Code 55 pkg(33) **32.95**
255-16070 Code 70 pkg(33) **37.75**
255-16083 Code 83 pkg(33) **40.90**
255-16100 Code 100 pkg(33) **47.20**

NON-WEATHERED

3' lengths.

255-17040 Code 40 pkg(33) **30.40**
255-17055 Code 55 pkg(33) **30.40**
255-17070 Code 70 pkg(33) **35.15**
255-17083 Code 83 pkg(33) **37.95**
255-17100 Code 100 pkg(33) **43.95**

ACCESSORIES

RAIL JOINERS-METAL

Low profile, nickel silver, slip-on type joiners.

255-26055 Code 55 pkg(50) **6.25**
255-26070 Code 70 pkg(50) **6.25**
255-26083 Code 83 pkg(50) **6.25**
255-26100 Code 100 pkg(48) **4.70**
255-26148 Code 148 pkg(50) **6.25**

RAIL JOINERS-PLASTIC INSULATED EA 2.95

255-26084 Code 83 Pkg(12)
255-26071 Code 70 Pkg(12)
255-26056 Code 55 Pkg(12)

TRANSITION RAIL JOINERS PLASTIC INSULATED EA 2.95

255-26001 Code 100 to 83 4 Pair ***NEW***
255-26002 Code 100 to 70 4 Pair ***NEW***
255-26003 Code 83 to 70 4 Pair ***NEW***
255-26004 Code 80 to 55 4 Pair ***NEW***
255-26005 Code 70 to 55 4 Pair ***NEW***

SPIKES

Blackened metal.

255-30101 Large, 1/2" pkg(7500) **88.15**
255-30102 Large, 1/2" pkg(500) **7.30**
255-30103 Medium, 3/8" pkg(12,000) **104.95**
255-30104 Medium 3/8" pkg(800) **8.35**
255-30105 Small 1/4" pkg(15,000) **86.00**
255-30106 Small 1/4" pkg(1000) **7.30**
255-30108 Micro, 3/16" pkg(1000) **7.30**

WEATHERED TIES

Scale ties, stained and weathered brown.

FULL PROFILE

255-36101 HO Regular Length pkg(1000) **8.90**
255-36102 HO Turnout Length pkg(250) **5.50**
255-36103 HOn3 Regular Length pkg(1000) **7.60**
255-36104 HOn3 Turnout Length pkg(250) **4.95**

LOW PROFILE

255-36107 HO Regular Length pkg(1000) **8.90**
255-36108 HO Turnout Length pkg(250) **5.50**

NON-WEATHERED TIES

Scale ties in natural wood.

FULL PROFILE

255-37101 HO Regular Length pkg(100) **7.80**
255-37102 HO Turnout Length pkg(250) **4.70**
255-37103 HOn3 Regular Length pkg(1000) **6.55**
255-37104 HOn3 Turnout Length pkg(250) **4.45**

LOW PROFILE

255-37107 HO Regular Length pkg(1000) **7.80**
255-37108 HO Turnout Length pkg(250) **4.70**

RAIL WEATHERING SOLUTION

255-49103 3oz **6.25**
Same solution used to weather Flex-Trak™ and Rail.

TURNOUT PARTS

255-80301 Switchstand, non-operating pkg(2) **1.95**
255-80316 HO Code 83 Turnout Parts Kit #6 **6.95**
255-80320 HO Code 70 Turnout Parts Kit #6 **6.95**

TOOLS

TRACK GAUGES EA 3.75

3-point, diecast metal track gauge keeps rails aligned when hand-laying track.

255-42101 HO Code 100
255-42102 HO Code 83
255-42103 HO Code 70
255-42104 HO Code 55
255-42105 HOn3 Code 70
255-42106 HOn3 Code 55
255-42107 HOn3 Code 40
255-42108 N Code 70
255-42109 N Code 55
255-42110 N Code 40

TRACK TOOLS

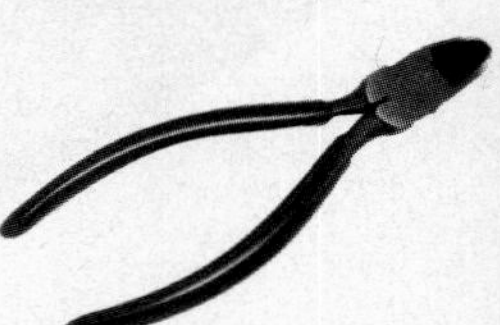

255-48101 Rail Cutter, Heavy Duty **23.95**

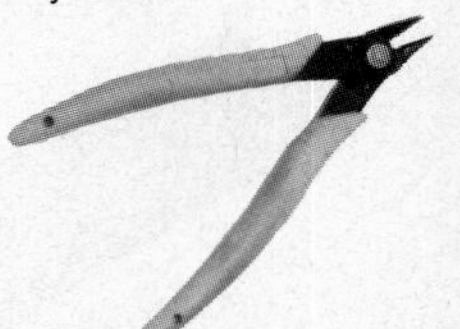

255-48102 Rail Nipper, Light Duty **11.95**

Track tools for use with HO and HOn3 track.

TRACK TOOLS

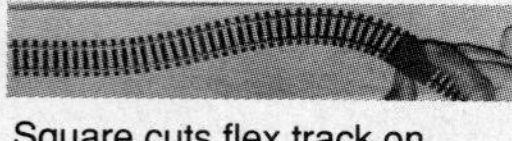

Square cuts flex track on straight-aways and curves without tie separation; helps locate misaligned rail joints and straightens used flex track in seconds.

479-5001 HO **2.96**
479-5003 HO & HOn3 **2.96**

479-5002 Parallel, HO & HOn3 **2.96**
Allows uniform spacing maintenance on straight-aways and curves while laying parallel tracks with HO or HOn3 track.

SOLDER TOOLS EA 2.96

Tool holds rail alignment for soldering rail joint.

479-5005 HO
479-5006 HOn3

RADIUS TOOL

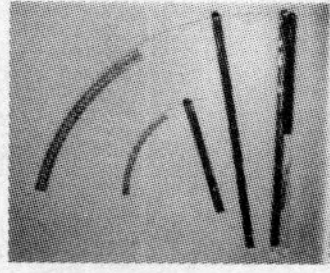

479-5007 7.67
Set contains two units–short unit will swing a radius from 7 to 11", long unit 11 to 23".

FLEX TRACK ALIGNMENT TOOLS EA 4.26

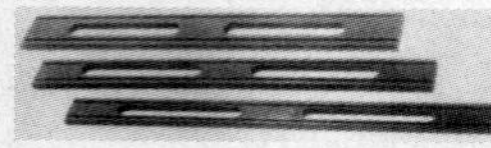

8" section will keep rail straight during construction of hand-laid mainlines, sidings and yard tracks.

479-5016 HO
479-5017 HOn3

TRACK TOOL SETS

Sets contain track tool, parallel tool, soldering tool and ballast spreader.

479-5012 HO **16.81**
479-5013 HOn3 **16.81**
479-5014 Assortment **302.58**
Contains 6 track tool sets each of N-HO-HOn3.

479-5019 Deluxe HO **29.74**
Includes one each of 5001, 5002, 5005, 5007, 5016 and 5008 (Ballast Spreader located in Scenery).

POWER-LOC™ TRACK

This side-locking track system and solid roadbed base offer durability and support on any surface, even carpet, eliminating the need for boards, nails, screws and other tools. Maximum strength without frustrating rail joiners. So simple, beginners can set up an entire layout in five minutes or less.

433-21302 9" Straight pkg(4) **4.50**
433-21303 18" Curved pkg(4) **4.50**
433-21304 Curved Terminal Rerailer **4.50**
433-21317 3" Straight Track pkg(2) **3.75**
433-21318 22" Curved Track pkg(4) **6.25**

REMOTE CONTROL SWITCH EA 10.25

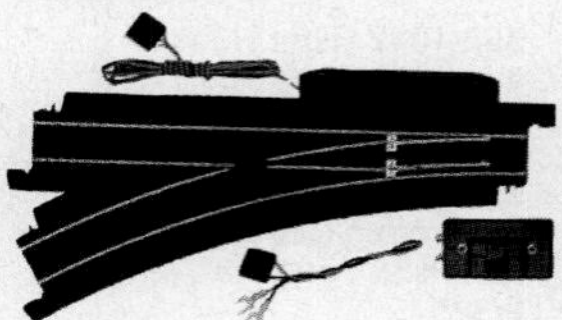

433-21305 Right Hand
433-21306 Left Hand

MISCELLANEOUS TRACK

433-21308 Illuminated Bumper pkg(2) **5.25**

433-21309 Track Expander **28.00**
Turns an oval into a double oval. Includes 2 pieces of 9" straight track, 2 pieces of 18" curved track, one left and right hand switch, and hook-up wires.

433-21314 Power Link Adapter Track **2.75**
Allows modeler to connect Power-Loc to existing layouts and all standard rail joiner track.

NICKEL-SILVER POWER-LOC

433-21332 9" Straight pkg(4) **8.00**
433-21347 3" Straight pkg(2) **5.25**
433-21333 18" Radius pkg(4) **8.00**
433-21348 22" Radius pkg(4) **10.25**

TURNOUTS EA 15.00

433-21335 Right Hand
433-21336 Left Hand

TERMINAL/RERAILER

433-21334 18" Radius **8.00**

POWER LINK ADAPTOR

433-21344 3.75

433-21338 Illuminated Bumpers pkg(2) **5.00** *NEW*

CODE 100 TRACK

Code 100 track and accessories. Track features steel rails, unless noted.

FLEX TRACK

433-8616 3' pkg(5) **10.75**

TERMINAL/RERAILER

433-8622 Curved **3.00**

ROADBED

433-8627 Cork pkg(5) **9.25**

STRAIGHT TRACK

433-8609 9" pkg(4) **2.25**

CURVED TRACK

433-8602 18" Radius pkg(4) **2.25**
2 packages make a full circle.

NAILS/SCREWS/SPIKES EA 3.75

1405 1404 1407

433-1405 1/2" Track Nails pkg(20 grams)
433-1404 1/2" Track Screws pkg(24)
433-1407 HO Spikes pkg(20 grams)

433-1434 3/4" Track Nails for Cork pkg(20 grams)

BUMPER

433-8628 Lighted pkg(2) **3.50**

RAIL JOINERS

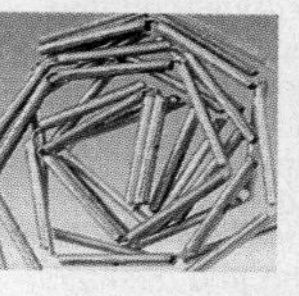

433-1412 Steel pkg(24) **3.75**

TRACK EXPANDER SETS

433-8617 Double Oval **24.25**
Turns an oval into a double oval.

433-8618 Figure 8 **13.50**
Turns a circle of track into a giant figure 8.

TURNOUTS, REMOTE CONTROL EA 9.75

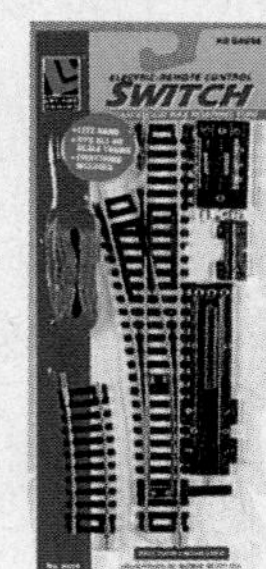

433-8610 Right Hand
433-8611 Left Hand

PECO

IMPORTED FROM GREAT BRITAIN BY WALTHERS
Peco track features nickel-silver rail for excellent conductivity. Setrack is a sectional track system ideal for beginners. Streamline is a more advanced, flexible track system. Insulfrog turnouts feature an insulated, plastic frog for easier wiring. Electrofrog turnouts provide continuous electrical current across the frog to help prevent stalling and hesitation. Turnouts are route selective.

SETRACK

CURVED TRACK

552-409 No. 3 Radius, Double Curve **86.99**
552-408 No. 3 Radius, Standard Curve **99.99**

TURNOUTS

Radius: 17-1/4" (438mm)

Length: 6-5/8" (168mm)

Angle: 22-1/2°

552-1240 Right Hand, Insulfrog **12.99**
552-1241 Left Hand, Insulfrog **12.99**

CURVED DOUBLE RADIUS TURNOUTS

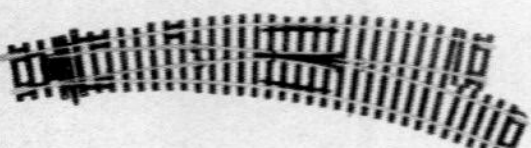

552-244 Code 100, Right Hand **20.99** *NEW*
552-245 Code 100, Left Hand **20.99** *NEW*

STREAMLINE TRACK

FLEX TRACK

Each piece measures 36" long and features nickel-silver rail.

Available only in boxes of 25.

552-1162 Code 100, Concrete Ties **104.99**
Simulates modern concrete ties being tested on some railroads.

552-1163 Code 75, Wooden Ties **109.99**

552-11603 Code 100, Wooden Ties **103.99**

CROSSINGS

552-1049 Short, Insulfrog, Code 100 **12.99**
Approximate length: 5" (127mm), Angle: 24°.

552-529 Short, Insulfrog, Code 75 **15.99**

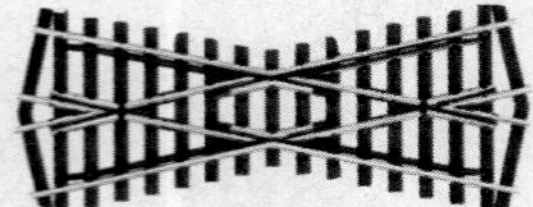

552-193 Short, Electrofrog, Code 75 **TBA** *NEW*

552-1050 Long, Insulfrog, Code 100 **14.99**
Approximate length: 10" (250mm) Angle: 12°

552-1194 Long, Insulfrog, Code 75 **14.99**

3-WAY TURNOUTS

Nominal Radius: 914mm (36")
Angle: 12°, Length: 220mm (8-21/32")

552-1055 Medium Radius, Insulfrog, Code 100 **36.99**
552-1907 Medium Radius Electrofrog, Code 100 **37.99**

SINGLE SLIP

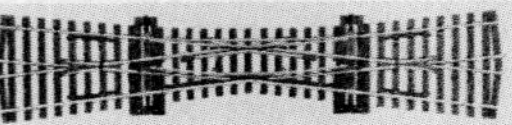

552-80 Code 100 Insulfrog-New Design **43.99**

552-1180 Insulfrog, Code 75 **50.99**

DOUBLE SLIP

552-90 Code 100 Insulfrog-New Design **47.99**

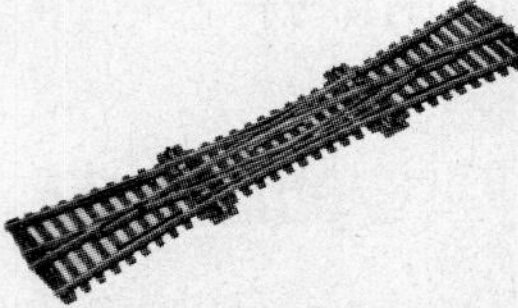

552-1046 Code 100, Insulfrog **47.99**
Matches Long Crossing No. 1050. Angle: 12°, Length: 250mm (9-13/16").

552-190 Code 75, Insulfrog **54.99**

WYE TURNOUTS

Nominal Radius: 610mm (24"), Angle: 24° Length: 148 mm (5-13/16").

552-1053 Small Radius, Insulfrog, Code 100 **13.99**

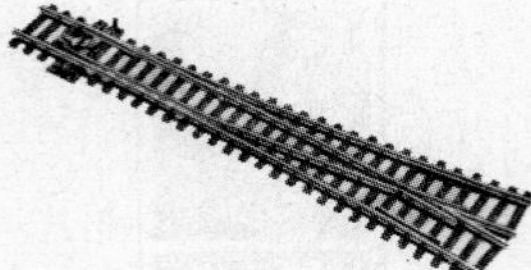

552-1054 Large Radius, Insulfrog, Code 100 **15.99**
552-1197 Small Radius, Electrofrog, Code 75 **15.99**
552-1198 Large Radius, Electrofrog, Code 75 **17.99**
552-1397 Nominal Radius 30", angle 8°, length 5", Code 80 Electrofrog **13.99**
552-1901 Small Radius, Electrofrog, Code 100 **14.99**
552-1902 Large Radius, Electrofrog, Code 100 **16.99**

CURVED DOUBLE RADIUS TURNOUTS

Nominal Radius Outside: 1524mm (60"), Inside: 762mm (30"), Length: 256mm (10-5/32").

552-917 Right Hand, Electrofrog, Code 75 **18.99**
552-918 Left Hand, Electrofrog, Code 75 **18.99**

552-1042 Right Hand, Insulfrog, Code 100 **17.99**
552-1043 Left Hand, Insulfrog, Code 100 **17.99**
552-1386 Right Hand **15.99** Electrofrog Code 80, nominal radius 36", angle 8°, length 6-9/32".
552-1387 Left Hand **15.99** Electrofrog Code 80, Nominal radius 36", angle 8°, length 6-9/32".
552-1910 Right Hand, Electrofrog, Code 100 **17.99**
552-1911 Left Hand, Electrofrog, Code 100 **17.99**

SMALL RADIUS TURNOUTS

Nominal Radius: 610mm (24"), Angle: 12°, Length: 185mm (7-9/32").

552-1047 Right Hand, Insulfrog, Code 100 **13.99**

552-1048 Left Hand, Insulfrog, Code 100 **13.99**
552-1903 Right Hand, Electrofrog, Code 100 **13.99**
552-1904 Left Hand, Electrofrog, Code 100 **13.99**
552-1916 Right Hand, Electrofrog, Code 75 **15.99**
552-1917 Left Hand, Electrofrog, Code 75 **15.99**

MEDIUM RADIUS TURNOUTS

Nominal Radius: 914mm (36"), Angle: 12°, Length: 219mm (8-5/8").

552-1051 Right Hand, Insulfrog, Code 100 **14.99**

552-1052 Left Hand, Insulfrog, Code 100 **14.99**
552-1905 Right Hand, Electrofrog, Code 100 **15.99**
552-1906 Left Hand, Electrofrog, Code 100 **15.99**
552-1912 Right Hand, Electrofrog, Code 75 **16.99**
552-1913 Left Hand, Electrofrog, Code 75 **16.99**

LARGE RADIUS TURNOUTS

Nominal Radius: 1524mm (60"), Angle: 12°, Length: 258mm (10-5/32").

552-1044 Right Hand, Insulfrog, Code 100 **16.99**
552-1045 Left Hand, Insulfrog, Code 100 **16.99**
552-1908 Right Hand, Electrofrog, Code 100 **17.99**
552-1909 Left Hand, Electrofrog, Code 100 **17.99**
552-1914 Right Hand, Electrofrog, Code 75 **18.99**
552-1915 Left Hand, Electrofrog, Code 75 **18.99**

STREAMLINE NARROW GAUGE TRACK

METRE GAUGE TRACK

Used throughout Switzerland. Metre gauge can also be found in parts of Europe, Asia and South America. In HO, it scales out to 3' 6"(HOn3-1/2) which is used in many parts of the world. Modelers working in OO can use this trackage for OOn3, matching the 3' gauge lines used in Ireland and on the Isle of Man. The selection includes flex track, turnouts and other accessories, which are fully assembled with simulated wood ties and Code 75 nickel silver rail.

FLEX TRACK

Dealer MUST order in multiples of 25.

552-1400 **5.80**

PECO

CROSSINGS
552-1493 Short Crossing 20° Angle w/Electrofrog **13.99**

MEDIUM RADIUS TURNOUTS
552-1495 Right Hand w/Electrofrog **18.99**
552-1496 Left Hand w/Electrofrog **18.99**

CURVED TURNOUTS

552-1486 Right Hand **TBA**

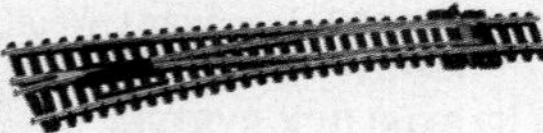

552-1487 Left Hand **TBA**

ACCESSORIES
552-1440 Buffer Stop Rail Type pkg(6) **11.99**
552-1455 Turntable **56.99**
Builds your choice of an open pit or an enclosed version for areas where snow can be a problem.

HO (HOn2-1/2) NARROW GAUGE FLEX TRACK
Features Code 80 nickel-silver rail and randomly spaced wooden ties.

Dealers MUST order in multiples of 25.

552-500 36" **4.95**

HOE (HOn2-1/2) NARROW GAUGE TURNOUTS
Features Code 80 nickel-silver rail and randomly spaced wooden ties.

552-492 Left Hand, 12" Radius, Electrofrog **12.99**
552-491 Right Hand, 12" Radius, Electrofrog **12.99**
552-497 Wye, 18" Radius, Electrofrog **12.99**

ACCESSORIES

LOCO LIFTER

552-43 SL-43 Loco-Lift & Storage 305mm (12") **17.99**

Pickup, move and store your locos without touching them! Perfect way to handle your favorite motive power and equipment without damaging details or paint jobs. Can be used anywhere along your layout. Simply place on tracks and rails in the lifter are electrified so the whole train can run through. Stacking beams at both ends allow the units to be used for storage between operating sessions.

BULK RAIL
Simulate the wide variety of rail sizes found on mainlines and sidings with these packs of bulk rail. Rail is made of nickel silver for realistic appearance and improved electrical conductivity.

552-4000 Code 60 **8.99**
552-4002 Code 75 **9.99**
552-4003 Code 80 **9.99**
552-4004 Code 100 **11.99**
552-4008 Code 250 **57.99**

RAIL JOINERS
Dealers MUST order in multiples of 12.

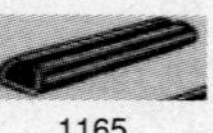

1165 1164

552-1165 Code 75, Nickel Silver **2.85**
552-1164 Code 75, Nylon-Insulated **2.85**
552-10 Code 100, Nickel Silver **2.65**
552-11 Code 100, Nylon-Insulated **2.65**

THIRD RAIL CONDUCTOR MOUNTS
552-4009 Code 60 Rail pkg(100) **5.99**

SWITCH MACHINE

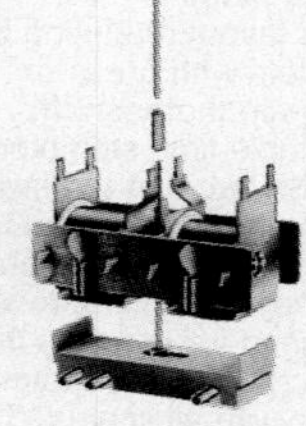

Unit installs directly beneath the turnout and makes positive contact without linkage or other complex connections. Just cut a hole in your benchwork deep enough to clear the motor and install. An extension pin is included to mount the motor beneath the benchwork. Can be adapted to other brands of turnouts with extension pin (included) and motor adapter, available separately.

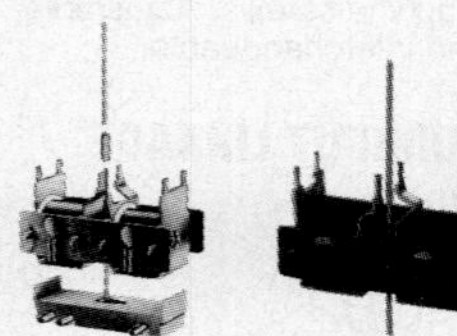

552-3010 552-105

552-3010 Switch Machine **7.99**
552-105 Switch Machine w/Extended Pin **7.99**
552-1023 Switch Machine For Digital Applications **8.99**
Designed to consume less power than standard (3010) Switch Machine.

MOTOR ADAPTER

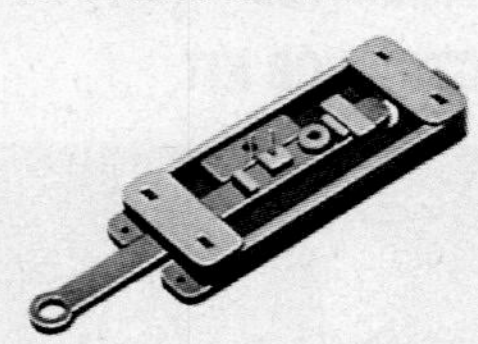

552-3003 Motor Adapter **2.99**
Allows mounting of the switch machine on the benchwork, alongside of the turnout. Can be adapted for use with various makes of turnouts.

ACCESSORY SWITCH

552-3013 Switch **3.99**
Can be used with switch machine to control turnout polarity, operate signals or other trackside devices.

MICRO SWITCH

552-15 9.99

MOUNTING PLATE

552-9 5.99
For 3010, 105, 1023.

PASSING CONTACT SWITCH EA 7.99

Lever type switch for turnout control. Can be mounted on a panel or inside #552-28, sold separately.

552-26 Black
552-30 White
552-31 Yellow
552-32 Red

552-22 On/Off Switch Light Blue **7.99** ***NEW***
552-23 On/On Green **7.99** ***NEW***
552-24 Switch Joining Bar **3.99** ***NEW***

MOUNTING PLATE
552-29 For Contact Switches **7.99**

CONSOLE

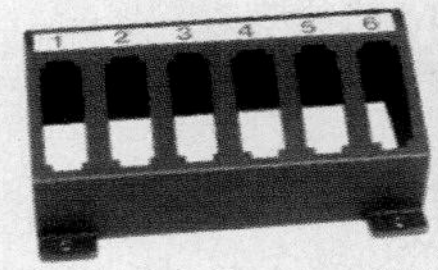

552-28 Switch Console **7.99**
Create a neat-looking control panel in minutes. Plastic unit holds up to six Passing Contact Switches, #552-22, 23, 26 and 32, switches sold separately. Small size can easily be hidden behind scenery or inside some structures if mounting space is limited.

SUBWAY STAIRCASE KIT

552-7 7.99

PECO CATALOG

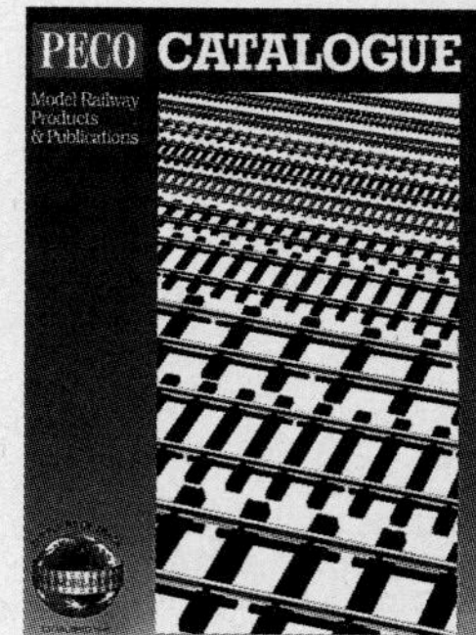

552-1995 8.99
Features the complete line of Peco products, including track, locomotives and rolling stock, structures, scenery and more.

TRACK ACCESSORIES

HO Scale switch machines and accessories.

SWITCH MACHINES

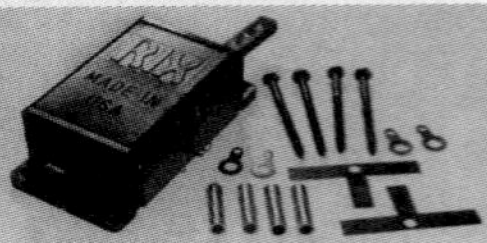

628-4 T-C **6.99**
Controls turnouts from above or below the layout. Includes two SPDT add-on sets of contacts and needed hardware. Operates on 6-32V.

628-15 Economy **6.25**
Same as #628-4 less contacts and mounting screws.

PUSH BUTTONS

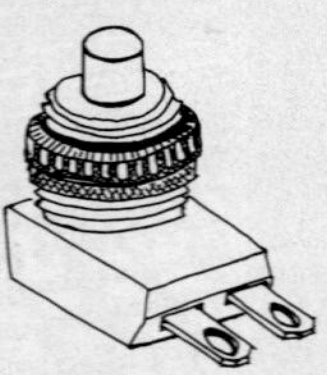

628-16 Momentary Contact pkg(4) **3.99**
Buttons are complete with mounting nut and soldering terminals. For controlling switch machines. 3 amps, 125V.

RAIL-IT

628-2 2.49
Set on track and roll cars down ramp; automatically places wheels on track. Works with code 70, 83 and 100 track.

SWITCH STAND KIT

628-13 Shorty Type, 2' **2.99**
Works directly off throw bar from any type turnout. 90° rotation. Includes switch ties, throw bar, target, linkage and housing.

MOUNTING BRACKETS

628-1 Rix-Rax Mounting Bracket **2.99**
Under layout bracket, completely adjustable. Includes nuts, bolts, screws and throw rod. For use with most twin coil switch machines.

628-5 Rix-Rax Flat Mounting Bracket Kit **2.99**
Under layout mounting bracket works with most any switch machine for flat mounting.

DIODE MATRIX BOARD

Diode matrix board makes it possible to control several switch machines at once so that an extra route can be aligned with the push of a button. Will work with most twin coil switch machines and motor drives, including Hanscraft and Tortoise. Use 1 amp diodes with motor drives and 3 amp diodes with twin coil switch machines.

628-50 9.95
628-52 1K Resistors pkg(12) **1.20**
628-51 1 Amp Diodes pkg(14) **2.99**
628-53 3 Amp Diodes pkg(14) **3.99**

RIX-RAX II

628-21 2.99
Under layout mounting bracket complete with press-on linkage to motor shaft, adjustable limit stop blocks to limit the force on the switch points, mounting holes for most brands of adjustable limit switches and all hardware. Designed for use with the Hanscraft Display Motor. Works with all scales.

RIX ADJUSTO PAD

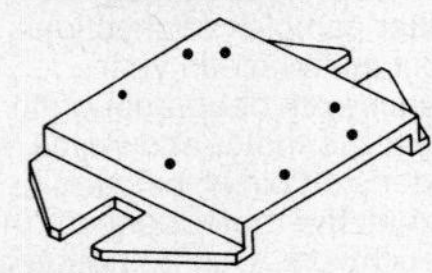

628-7 2.25
For mounting switch machine above or below layout. Includes wood and switch machine screws. Adjustable and interchangeable.

TURNOUT LINKAGE

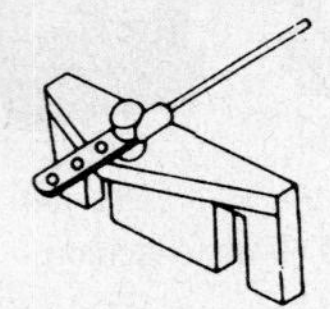

628-6 Pivoting Turnout Linkage **2.25**
For controlling turnout from underneath layout.

TURNOUT CONTROL

628-60 Cable Turnout Control System **11.95**

CTC KNOB KIT

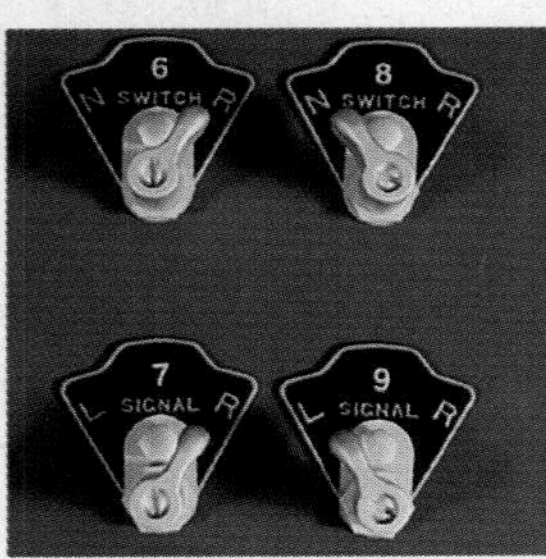

628-61 6.95

RIVAROSSI

STRAIGHT TRACK

635-3140 12-1/4" Long pkg(12) **22.68**
635-3141 6-1/8" Long pkg(12) **15.48**
635-3142 6.4" Long pkg(12) **15.48**
635-3143 Flexible Track Sections pkg(24) **119.76**

CURVED TRACK SECTIONS

One package of, or 12 individual pieces of #3210 will make a complete circle. One package of, or 12 individual pieces of #3330 will make a complete circle. Three packages of, or 36 individual pieces of #3331 will make a complete circle.

635-3210 23-1/2" Radius 30° Curve pkg(12) **22.68**
635-3330 25-1/2" Radius 30° Curve pkg(12) **22.68**
635-3331 6.4" Long Curve pkg(12) **15.48**

TURNOUTS

MANUAL TURNOUTS PKG(2) EA 29.98

635-3340 Right Hand
635-3342 Left Hand

LARGE MANUAL TURNOUTS PKG(2) EA 43.98

635-3352 Right Hand
635-3354 Left Hand

ELECTRIC TURNOUTS PKG(2) EA 69.98

635-3341 Right Hand
635-3343 Left Hand

LARGE ELECTRIC TURNOUTS PKG(2) EA 69.98

635-3353 Right Hand
635-3355 Left Hand

CROSSOVERS

QUADRUPLE CROSSOVER

635-3346 Manual pkg(2) **99.96**
635-3347 Electric pkg(2) **159.98**

DOUBLE CROSSOVER

635-3348 Double Parallel Style pkg(2) **89.98**

SINGLE CROSSED SECTION PKG(2) EA 29.98

635-3349 Right Hand
635-3350 Left Hand

CROSSING

635-3356 Track Crossing pkg(2) **21.98**

ACCESSORIES

POWER FEED CLIPS

635-4610 Hook-Up Wires w/Clips **2.99**

BUMPER

635-4611 Track Bumper pkg(6) **8.94**

PLANNING TEMPLATE

635-4612 Transparent Layout Planing Template **11.99**

FLEXIBLOCK SYSTEM

635-4614 Parallel Track Alignment Tool **19.99**

SWITCHMACHINES

BELOW SURFACE MOUNTED

635-4613 29.99

SURFACE MOUNTED PKG(2) EA 35.98

635-4616 Right Hand
635-4617 Left Hand

RAIL JOINERS

635-4615 Insulating Joiners pkg(24) **2.49**
635-4618 Metal Joiners pkg(24) **2.99**

HO Scale Upson board roadbed, track alignment gauges and ground throws.

ROADBED

Precut Upson board pieces feature beveled edges. Easy to spike into; sound-deadening.

FLEX TRACK SECTION

170-9020 24" pkg(4) **7.00**

STRAIGHT SECTIONS

170-9010 24" pkg(4) **4.95**
170-9030 Double Track, 24" pkg(4) **9.25**

TURNOUT SECTIONS

#4 PKG(4) EA 8.50
170-9041 Right Hand
170-9042 Left Hand

#6 PKG(4) EA 9.25
170-9061 Right Hand
170-9062 Left Hand

#8 PKG(4) 9.95
170-9081 Right Hand
170-9082 Left Hand

CURVED SECTIONS

8 pieces form a complete circle.

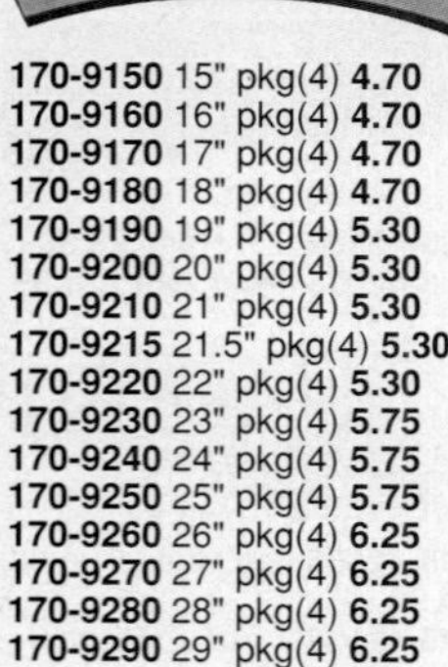

170-9150 15" pkg(4) **4.70**
170-9160 16" pkg(4) **4.70**
170-9170 17" pkg(4) **4.70**
170-9180 18" pkg(4) **4.70**
170-9190 19" pkg(4) **5.30**
170-9200 20" pkg(4) **5.30**
170-9210 21" pkg(4) **5.30**
170-9215 21.5" pkg(4) **5.30**
170-9220 22" pkg(4) **5.30**
170-9230 23" pkg(4) **5.75**
170-9240 24" pkg(4) **5.75**
170-9250 25" pkg(4) **5.75**
170-9260 26" pkg(4) **6.25**
170-9270 27" pkg(4) **6.25**
170-9280 28" pkg(4) **6.25**
170-9290 29" pkg(4) **6.25**

12 pieces form a complete circle.

170-9300 30" pkg(4) **5.50**
170-9310 31" pkg(4) **5.50**
170-9320 32" pkg(4) **5.50**
170-9330 33" pkg(4) **5.50**
170-9340 34" pkg(4) **6.25**
170-9350 35" pkg(4) **6.25**
170-9360 36" pkg(4) **6.25**
170-9370 37" pkg(4) **6.25**
170-9380 38" pkg(4) **6.25**
170-9390 39" pkg(4) **6.25**
170-9400 40" pkg(4) **7.00**
170-9410 41" pkg(4) **7.00**
170-9420 42" pkg(4) **7.00**
170-9430 43" pkg(4) **7.00**
170-9440 44" pkg(4) **7.00**
170-9450 45" pkg(4) **7.75**
170-9460 46" pkg(4) **7.75**
170-9470 47" pkg(4) **7.75**
170-9480 48" pkg(4) **7.75**

TRACK ALIGNMENT GAUGES

Slide between rails to correctly gauge rails. Helps in laying, spiking and joining rail. Precision machined to NMRA standards.

RADIUS GAUGES EA 3.80

HO

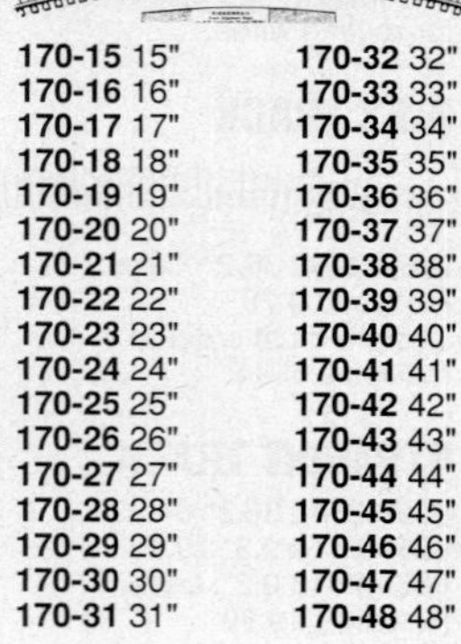

170-15 15"	**170-32** 32"
170-16 16"	**170-33** 33"
170-17 17"	**170-34** 34"
170-18 18"	**170-35** 35"
170-19 19"	**170-36** 36"
170-20 20"	**170-37** 37"
170-21 21"	**170-38** 38"
170-22 22"	**170-39** 39"
170-23 23"	**170-40** 40"
170-24 24"	**170-41** 41"
170-25 25"	**170-42** 42"
170-26 26"	**170-43** 43"
170-27 27"	**170-44** 44"
170-28 28"	**170-45** 45"
170-29 29"	**170-46** 46"
170-30 30"	**170-47** 47"
170-31 31"	**170-48** 48"

HON3

170-315 15"	**170-332** 32"
170-316 16"	**170-333** 33"
170-317 17"	**170-334** 34"
170-318 18"	**170-335** 35"
170-319 19"	**170-336** 36"
170-320 20"	**170-337** 37"
170-321 21"	**170-338** 38"
170-322 22"	**170-339** 39"
170-323 23"	**170-340** 40"
170-324 24"	**170-341** 41"
170-325 25"	**170-342** 42"
170-326 26"	**170-343** 43"
170-327 27"	**170-344** 44"
170-328 28"	**170-345** 45"
170-329 29"	**170-346** 46"
170-330 30"	**170-347** 47"
170-331 31"	**170-348** 48"

STRAIGHT GAUGES

5" EA 3.80
170-5 HO
170-305 HOn3

10" EA 4.00
170-10 HO
170-310 HOn3

MICRO MATIC TRACK GAUGE

170-8 9.95
Use to check for correct spacing between rails. Helps to eliminate derailments.

GROUND THROWS

170-9 Manual pkg(2) **5.00**
Assembled, all-metal construction. Includes linkage and universal mounting for either side. Operating 3/8" maximum throw.

SELLEY FINISHING TOUCHES

Assembled HO Scale details are unpainted metal castings.

BUMPER

675-89 End of Line **2.50**

HAYES WHEEL STOPS

675-677 pkg(6) **2.00**

SCALE SHOPS

HO Scale switch machines and accessories.

SWITCH MACHINES

Slow motion, motorized, threaded-shaft type switch machines. Each includes one pair of contacts and switch linkage. Available fully assembled and in kit form.

649-1040 Assembled **13.98**
649-1030 Kit **7.98**
Easy-to-build kit assembles in six steps. Includes cut-out contacts, diodes and complete assembly, wiring and installation instructions.

649-1006 Kit pkg(6) **44.98**
649-1012 Kit pkg(12) **74.98**

SWITCH MACHINE CONTACTS

649-4080 pkg(2) **.98**
649-4082 pkg(12) **4.98**
649-4085 pkg(50) **16.98**

Information STATION

What Is Narrow Gauge?

Exactly what is narrow gauge? Some of the more advanced model railroaders may scoff at such a question, but those of you that are just getting started in the hobby may not know.

Gauge is the measurement of how far apart the rails are from each other. It is the distance between the rail heads. Standard gauge, which is what is used for the most part nowadays, is four feet eight and a half inches. Narrow gauge encompasses anything that is less than the standard measurement. When this occurs, both the track and the entire railroad take on the name of narrow gauge. In the modeling world it is designated by listing scale, then a small "n" followed by the gauge. HOn3 would stand for three foot narrow gauge in the HO scale.

The most common narrow gauge in the U.S. was three feet, although some two foot was used around the Maine area for a while. But by the mid to late 19th century most railroads in the U.S. were standard gauge. However, the Denver and Rio Grande Western railroad used three foot narrow gauge up until the 1980's. In Europe, meter was the most popular narrow gauge used making the rails roughly 39 inches apart from each other.

ROCO CODE 100 TRACK

FLEX TRACK

Two types of flex-track are available: very flexible for tight curves and semi-rigid for straight tracks or slight curves. Dealers must order in multiples of 24.

625-42200 Very Flexible 38.5" (970mm) **3.96**
625-42201 Semi Rigid 36" (914.4mm) **3.54**
625-42262 Tie Sections pkg(24) **8.99**
Molded plastic ties for filling in flex track. Simplifies connecting flex track to itself and to other track sections.

STRAIGHT TRACK

625-42202 9" (228.6mm) pkg(12) **16.99**
625-42203 8" (204mm) pkg(12) **16.99**
625-42204 3.3" (85mm) pkg(24) **31.99**
625-42206 2.2" (57mm) pkg(12) **15.99**
625-42207 2" (51mm) pkg(12) **15.99**
625-42208 1.1" (29mm) pkg(24) **31.99**
625-42209 1" (26.5mm) pkg(24) **31.99**
625-42210 1" (26.5mm) pkg(24) **31.99**
625-42211 .9" (24.5mm) pkg(24) **31.99**
625-42212 25/32" pkg(24) **31.99**
625-42213 .2" (6mm) pkg(24) **31.99**

UNCOUPLING TRACK

625-42261 4.5" (1143mm) for Close Coupling **19.99**

CURVED TRACK

10" RADIUS - 1/6 CIRCLE

625-42221 60° pkg(12) **16.99**

14" RADIUS - 1/12 CIRCLE

625-42222 30° pkg(12) **16.99**
625-42232 12° 10' pkg(12) **15.99**
625-42242 7° 30' pkg(12) **15.99**

17" RADIUS - 1/12 CIRCLE

625-42223 30° pkg(12) **16.99**
625-42233 12° 10' pkg(24) **31.99**
625-42243 7° 30' pkg(12) **15.99**

19" RADIUS - 1/12 CIRCLE

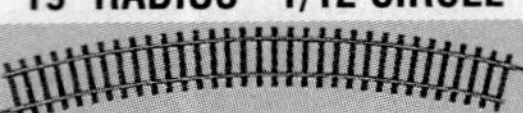

625-42224 30° pkg(12) **18.99**
625-42234 7° 30' pkg(12) **15.99**

21" RADIUS - 1/12 CIRCLE

625-42225 30° pkg(12) **18.99**
625-42235 7° 30' pkg(12) **15.99**

CURVED TERMINAL TRACK

Limited Quantity Available
625-42252 30°, 14" Radius pkg(12) **34.99**

TURNOUTS

Electro-magnetically operated standard turnouts are actuated by motors which have disconnect circuits to avoid burn-out of coil. All switches may be operated manually. Available in under layout mounting, remote control and manual.

Because European standards don't match those of the United States, turnouts approximate U.S. number shown.

3-WAY TURNOUT

Straight track 9" (226mm), radius of diverging track 28" (700mm), turn off angle 12° 50'.

625-42318 Unpolarized **59.99**

DOUBLE SLIP

625-42320 Remote **59.99**

Length of tracks 9" (228.6mm) crossing angle 12° 50'.

CROSSINGS

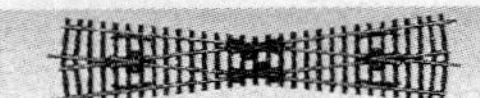

625-42270 13° **13.99**
625-42271 90° **13.99**

SWITCH MACHINES

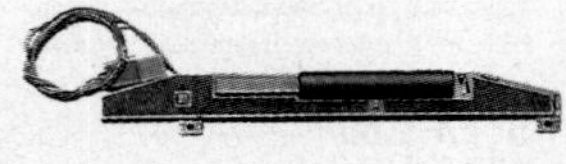

625-10010 Left **18.99**
Twin coil drive and power-disconnect after actuation, single-pole.

625-10011 Right **18.99**
Twin coil drive and power-disconnect after actuation, single-pole.

625-10014 Underfloor Operation Conversion Kit **6.99**
Left hand, fits turnout motor No. 10008 and 10010.

625-10016 Underfloor Operation Conversion Kit **6.99**
Right hand, fits turnout motor No. 10009 and 10011.

POLARIZING SET

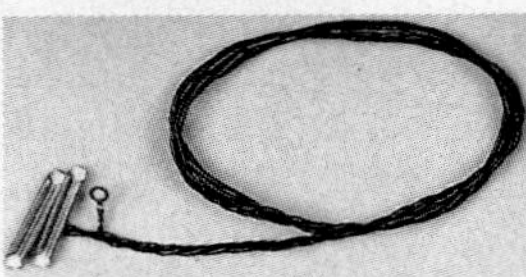

625-40289 Polarizing Set **3.99**

TRACK BUMPER

625-42267 Bumper Kit **4.99**

TRACK NAILS

625-10000 1/2" Track Nails pkg(400) **4.99**

RAIL JOINERS EA 3.99

625-42263 Nickel Silver Noninsulated pkg(30)
625-42264 Insulated pkg(24)
625-42265 Noninsulated
With connecting cable set.

DIGITAL TRACK

625-42517 Digital Terminal Track, Single **7.99**

ROCO LINE CODE 83 TRACK

Fully assembled track with Code 83 nickel-silver rail, realistic plastic ties and a unique two-piece roadbed system. The top piece duplicates the ballasted right-of-way, with realistic size and colored "stones" (molded in light gray, but easily painted to match your favorite prototype), plus a sloping edge. Underneath is the plastic core which locks with other sections to provide a rigid track assembly that's strong enough to use for temporary operations. The space underneath can also be used for routing wires.

FLEX TRACK

625-42400 36.2", Less Roadbed **4.79**
Dealers must order In multiples of 24.

STRAIGHT TRACK

625-42506 36.8" **64.99**
625-42510 9.2" **19.99**
625-42410 9.2", Less Roadbed **19.99**
625-42511 4.7" Diagonal Straight **17.99**
625-42411 4.7" Diagonal Straight, Less Roadbed **18.99**
625-42512 4.5" **17.99**
625-42412 4.5", Less Roadbed **18.99**
625-42513 2.5" **16.99**
625-42413 2.5", Less Roadbed **8.99**
625-42518 4.5" w/FDR Contact Relay **18.99**
625-42519 4.5" w/Uncoupler **22.99**
625-42520 Terminal Track **7.99**
With wire leads for easy hook up to power pack.

CURVED TRACK

625-42522 14.1" Radius x 30° **19.99**
625-42422 14.1" Radius x 30°, Less Roadbed **9.99**
625-42523 16.5" Radius x 30° **21.99**
625-42423 16.5" Radius x 30°, Less Roadbed **19.99**
625-42524 18.9" Radius x 30° **24.99**
625-42424 18.9" Radius x 30°, Less Roadbed **22.99**
625-42525 21.4" Radius x 30° **26.99**
625-42425 21.4" Radius x 30°, Less Roadbed **23.99**
625-42426 24" Radius x 15° **12.99**
625-42526 24" Radius x 30° **26.99**
625-42527 32.5" Radius x 15° **27.99**
625-42528 35" Radius x 15° **27.99**
Reverse curve for #4 turnouts.
625-42530 77.2" Radius x 5° **22.99**
625-42430 77.2" Radius x 5°, Less Roadbed **11.99**
Two pieces form a reverse curve for #6 turnouts.

CROSSINGS

625-42591 Cross 13.6" x 10° w/Roadbed **64.99**
625-42597 Cross 9.1" x 15° w/Roadbed **34.99**
625-42598 Double Cross-Over **24.99**
625-42609 Rerailer Set **4.99**

TURNOUTS

Manually controlled turnouts with preformed roadbed sections. Can be fitted with motor No. 42620 for remote control.

#4 TURNOUTS

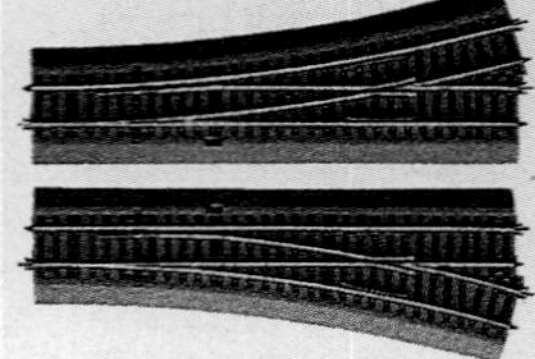

625-42532 Left Hand **28.99**
625-42533 Right Hand **28.99**

625-42556 Left Hand Curved **34.99**
625-42538 Turnout, Manual Left 15° **21.99**
625-42539 Turnout, Manual Right 15° **21.99**
625-42558 Curved Turnout Manual Left **29.99**
625-42559 Curved Turnout Manual Right **29.99**
625-42464 Left Hand Curved, Less Roadbed **25.99**
14" inside radius, 16-1/2" outside radius
625-42557 Right Hand Curved **34.99**
625-42465 Right Hand Curved, Less Roadbed **25.99**

#6 TURNOUTS

625-42580 Left Hand **44.99**
13.6" length x 10°.
625-42581 Right Hand **44.99**
13.6" Length x 10°.

625-42570 Left Hand, Curved **44.99**
625-42470 Left Hand Curved, Less Roadbed **35.99**
625-42571 Right Hand, Curved **44.99**
625-42471 Right Hand, Curved Less Roadbed **34.99**

#8 TURNOUTS

625-42568 Left Hand, Curved **64.99**
32.5" inside radius, 35" outside radius.
625-42569 Right Hand Curved **64.99**

3-WAY TURNOUT

625-42543 15° **54.99**

SINGLE SLIP

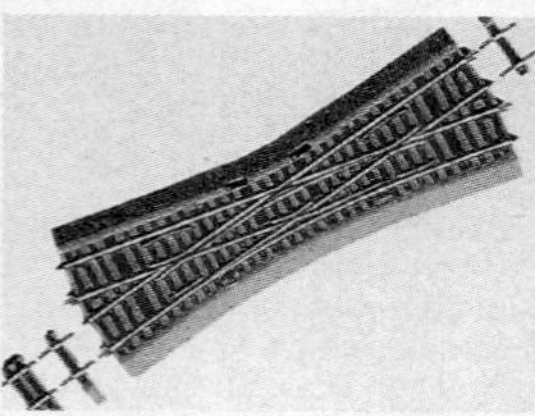

625-42546 15° **54.99**

DOUBLE SLIP

625-42549 10° **74.99**
625-42594 15° **79.99**

TIE STRIPS EA 3.99

Use to fill gap at the end of flex track sections, or when cutting rail.

42600

42601

625-42600 Wooden Ties pkg(12)
625-42601 Concrete Ties pkg(12)

REED RELAY

625-42605 Reed Relay **8.99**
Wooden tie with built-in reed switch, for activating electrical accessories.

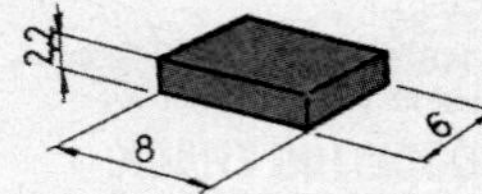

625-42256 Magnet for No. 42605 **9.99**

TRACK BUMPER

625-42608 Track Bumper **4.99**

SWITCH LAMPS

625-40293 **11.99**
Based on lamps used by the German Federal Railways. Lanterns indicate if turnout is open or closed. Fits motor No. 10030.

SWITCH MACHINES

625-42620 Roadbed Switch Machine **21.99**
Low profile switch machine for mounting under Roco-Line roadbed sections. Prewired, easy to install, machine features end of stroke power disconnect.

625-40295 Left Hand Turnout **22.99**
625-40296 Right Hand Turnout **22.99**
Fits all Roco turnouts and mounts on switch, above the benchwork. Prewired, easy to install, machine features end of stroke power disconnect.

625-10030 Universal Underfloor Motor **28.99**
Designed for mounting under benchwork, fits all Roco-Line and can be adapted to other track systems. Prewired, easy to install, machine features end of stroke disconnect.

MANUAL CONTROLS

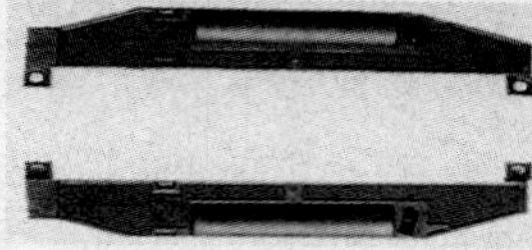

625-40297 Left Hand Turnout **5.99**
625-40298 Right Hand Turnout **5.99**
Manual controls fit all Roco turnouts and make it easier to open or close switch. Ideal for fiddle yards or other trackage where remote control is not needed.

TURNTABLE

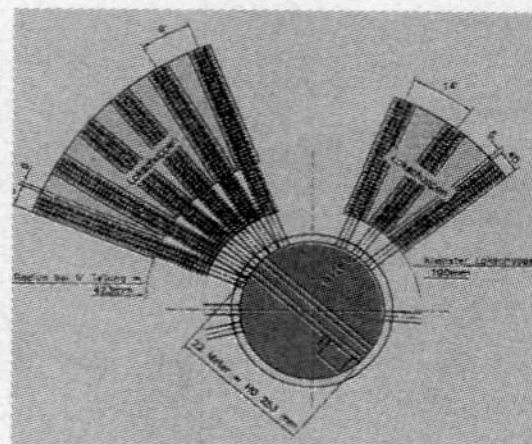

625-42615 **389.99**
Turntable with 22 meters (72 feet) prototype diameter and electric operation, track separation variable.
625-42616 Track Connections for Turntable pkg(2) **13.99**

RAIL JOINERS

42610

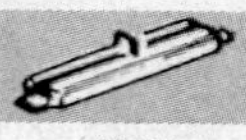
42611

625-42612

625-42610 Standard Steel pkg(24) **2.99**
625-42611 Insulated pkg(24) **2.99**
625-42612 Code 83 to 100 Conversion Rail Joiners pkg(12) **4.99**
Use for transition from track with Code 83 to Code 100 rail. Ideal for use where sidings join mainline.
625-42613 Joiner w/Wire Leads **4.99**
Preassembled rail joiners with wire leads.

ROADBED

625-42650 Roadbed Filler Piece 14.2" pkg(12) **13.99**
Sloped side pieces for Roco Line roadbed sections.

625-42651 Roadbed End Piece pkg(6) **6.99**
Realistic, rounded piece fits on end of roadbed section. Ideal for use on sidings or display tracks.

625-42652 Ballast Gravel, Loose **4.99**
Matches size and color of molded roadbed sections.
625-42653 Ballast Sheet (345 x 93mm) **15.99**

FLEXIBLE ROADBED EA 13.99

For use with flex track section.
625-42660 For No. 42400 w/Wooden Ties
625-42661 For No. 42401 w/Concrete Ties

WHEEL STOPS

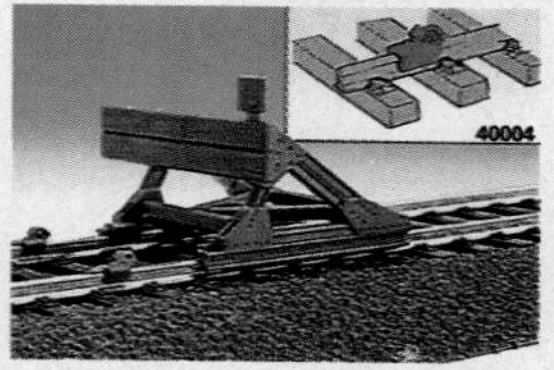

625-40004 Wheel Stops pkg(12) **4.99**

TRACK NAILS

625-10001 pkg(500) **5.99**
Correct length for mounting Roco Line track and roadbed to benchwork.

TRACK SETS

Expand the basic oval of Roco Line track included with starter train sets. A variety of track pieces that add more operating possibilities, such as turnouts, curves and more are included.

625-42011 Passing Siding Expansion Set **74.99**
Add a passing siding to your mainline and automatic uncoupling with this set. Includes one No. 4 right hand turnout, one No. 4 right hand curved turnout, a manually operated uncoupler and one 4.5" straight section.

625-42012 Double Track Expansion Set **139.99**
Build a double track mainline and add an extra siding with this set. Includes 10 straight sections, one 4.5" straight section, one track bumper, 10 curve sections, one No. 4 right hand turnout, one No. 4 left hand turnout, one No. 4 left hand curved turnout and replacement roadbed wedges.

625-42010 Industrial Siding Expansion Set **64.99**
Add an industrial siding and lengthen the basic oval with this set. Includes one No. 4 left hand turnout, 13 straight sections and one track bumper.

625-42013 Crossover Extension Set **119.99**
Add a crossover in station or yard area and convert single track spur to double track. Includes one 10" straight section, one 4.5" straight section, one track bumper, one #4 left hand turnout and one #4 right hand turnout.

SEQUOIA SCALE MODELS

We have worked closely with this manufacturer to provide accurate delivery information at the time this catalog was published. Items listed in blue ink may not be available at all times. Current delivery information, along with a list of in-stock products for this line, can be found on our Web site at www.walthers.com.

Nonoperating HO Scale switch stands feature metal or plastic castings.

SWITCH STANDS PKG(2) EA 3.25

135-2041 DRGW No. 4
135-2042 DRGW No. 6

135-2045 Low Ramapo, Red/Green Jewels
135-2046 Low Ramapo, Red/Amber Jewels

Division of Builders In Scale

SWITCHMASTER SWITCH MACHINE

Slow motion switch machine completes throw in 4 seconds. Mounting hardware and linkage included. Current to switch machine is on constantly, so panel lights and track signals can be wired to the same current running the switch machine. Eliminates contacts with complicated wiring. Durable motor. Operates on 12V DC. Can be used in all scales.

169-1001 Single **16.00**
169-1006 Six-Pack **92.00**
169-1025 25-Pack **366.00**
169-1002 Switch Machine Kit **21.00**
Includes switch machine, linkage and mounting hardware, DPDT toggle switch (#169-1106), a pair of dual color LEDs (#169-1103) and two LED mounting rings.

SWITCH MACHINE ACCESSORIES

169-1003 M-1 Switchmaster Motor Only (w/resistor) **14.50**
For animation or other layout purposes. 4 RPM motor with resistor for 12V DC power supplies.

169-1101 Power Routing Contact **3.29**
For switching power to points or blocks.

169-1102 Panel Lighting Kit **1.89**
Two pairs of LEDs (red and green), resistors and instructions.

169-1103 Bi-Color LED Panel Lighting Kit **2.98**
One pair LEDs (red and green), resistors and instructions.

169-1104 Signal Kit **.79**
Converts power from switch machine #169-1001 for use with signals.

169-1105 LED Mounting Ring pkg(6) **1.29**
Mounting rings for use with LEDs #169-1102 and 169-1103.

TOGGLE SWITCHES

DPDT toggle switch with red handle.

169-1106 Single **3.59**
169-1107 Two-Pack **6.59**
169-1110 Push Button Switch **6.98**
Offers constant contact, DPDT control of signals. Red button.

HANDLE COVERS PKG(6) EA 1.49

169-1108 Black
169-1109 White

PUSH BUTTON CAPS PKG(2) EA 2.79

169-1111 Black
169-1112 White

REPLACEMENT HARDWARE EA 1.50

169-1113 Mounting *NEW*
Four mounting sleeves and four mounting screws required when moving SwitchMasters.

169-1114 Linkage *NEW*
Three crank wires and three crank wire tubes required when moving SwitchMasters.

SHINOHARA

Build busy mainlines, sidings and yards all along your layout with this line of ready to use track and accessories. Available in two popular sizes, Code 100 simulates heavy (155+ pounds) mainline trackage, while Code 70 can be used for medium rail (100 pounds) found on branchlines and sidings. The two can be combined for a more realistic variety of rail sizes, or used with other brands of track. All items come fully assembled, ready to install with nickel silver rail and dark brown plastic ties, unless noted.

CODE 100

#4 TURNOUT EA 17.95

948-101 Left Hand
948-102 Right Hand

#6 TURNOUT EA 17.95

948-103 Left Hand
948-104 Right Hand

#8 TURNOUT EA 19.50

Measures 12-3/4", frog angle 7° 9'.

948-105 Left Hand
948-106 Right Hand

WYE TURNOUTS

948-107 #4 **19.00**
Measures 9-5/8", frog angle 14° 15'.
948-118 #6 **19.50**

THREE-WAY TURNOUT

948-108 #6 **38.00**
Measures 12-1/16".

CROSSOVERS

948-109 #6 Single Left Hand **34.35**
Measures 9-3/8", frog angle 9° 30'.

948-110 #6 Single Right Hand **34.35**
Measures 9-3/8", frog angle 9° 30'.

948-111 #4 Double **57.25**
Measures 14-15/32", frog angle 14°.

948-112 #6 Double **57.25**
Measures 19-1/8", frog angle 9° 30'.

DOUBLE SLIP SWITCHES

948-113 #4 **48.35**
Measures 9-3/4", frog angle 15°.
948-114 #6 **53.00**
Measures 12-1/8" frog angle 9° 30'.

FLEX-TRACK

948-115 Flex-Track **88.95**
948-116 Single Guard Rail **95.00**
20" (50cm) long.
948-117 Double Guard Rail **155.00**
39" (1m) long.
948-119 Flex-Track for Branch Line **87.95**

CURVED TURNOUTS

#6 EA 27.25

Measures 12-31/32".

948-126 Left Hand
948-127 Right Hand

#8 EA 31.75

Measures 16-11/16".

948-128 Left Hand
948-129 Right Hand

TURNOUT ACCESSORIES

948-173 Throw Bar pkg(12) **1.25**
948-178 Linkage **8.40**
948-180 Operating Ground Throw, Left Hand **6.98**
948-181 Operating Ground Throw, Right Hand **6.98**

CROSSINGS EA 18.25 (UNLESS NOTED)

948-130 30°
948-131 45°
Measures 4-17/32".

948-132 60°
Measures 4-15/32".

948-133 90°
Measures 3-3/32".

948-134 9-1/2° Left Hand **24.95**
948-135 9-1/2° Right Hand **24.95**

STRAIGHT TRACK

948-144 2" Terminal Section **3.35**
948-145 9" Straight Track pkg(10) **34.00**
948-146 9" Terminal Section **4.50**

CURVED TRACK PKG(12)

948-147 16" Radius **34.95**
948-148 18" Radius **34.95**
948-149 20" Radius **34.95**
948-150 22" Radius 30° **34.95**
948-151 24" Radius 30° **45.00**
948-152 26" Radius 30° **45.00**
948-153 28" Radius 30° **60.00**
948-154 30" Radius 30° **64.40**
948-155 32" Radius 30° **64.40**
948-156 34" Radius 30° **64.40**
948-157 36" Radius 30° **64.40**

TRACK W/CONCRETE TIES

Some roads have experimented with concrete ties in place of wood. Track sections feature plastic ties molded in concrete gray, with prototypical mountings.

948-185 Flex-Track 1m Long **9.98**
948-191 #5 Turnout Left Hand **17.95**
948-192 #5 Turnout Right Hand **17.95**

CODE 100 TRACK ACCESSORIES

948-141 Rail Joiners-Nickel Silver pkg(50) **8.40**
948-160 Spikes .35 oz (10g) pkg **5.80**
948-170 Bulk Rail 99' **50.00**

SPACER TIES PKG(24) EA 2.75

Use to fill in "empty" spaces between track sections.

948-175 Brown (Wood)
948-179 Cement

UNCOUPLER

948-172 Uncoupling Base **1.50**

TRACK CLEANER

948-177 Rail Cleaner **2.98**

CODE 70

#4 TURNOUT EA 17.25

948-301 Left Hand
948-302 Right Hand

#6 TURNOUT EA 17.25

Measures 10-7/8", frog angle 9° 30'.

948-303 Left Hand
948-304 Right Hand

#8 TURNOUT EA 18.85

Measures 14-13/32", frog angle 7° 9'.

948-305 Left Hand
948-306 Right Hand

SPECIAL TURNOUTS

948-307 #4 Wye **17.25**
948-308 #6 Three-Way **38.00**

DOUBLE CROSSOVERS

948-312 #4 **54.75**
948-314 #6 **46.00**

FLEX TRACK

948-315 Flex-Track pkg(10) **82.95**
948-317 Double Guard Rails **155.00**
39" (1m) long.

#6 CURVED TURNOUTS EA 31.65

948-326 Left Hand
948-327 Right Hand

CURVABLE TURNOUTS EA 31.65

948-371 Left Hand
948-372 Right Hand

CROSSINGS EA 18.25

948-330 30°
Measures 5-13/32".

948-331 45°
Measures 4-23/32".

948-332 60°
Measures 4-3/32".

948-333 90°
Measures 4-3/32".

CODE 70 TRACK ACCESSORIES

948-370 Bulk Rail 99' **50.00**
948-375 Space Tie pkg(24) **2.75**
948-341 Rail Joiner-Nickel Silver pkg(50) **8.40**
948-342 Insulated Rail Joiners pkg(12) **2.75**

HON3

#4 TURNOUT EA 15.40

948-401 Left Hand
948-402 Right Hand

#6 TURNOUT EA 15.40

948-403 Left Hand
948-404 Right Hand

FLEX TRACK

948-415 HOn3 pkg(10) **82.95**
948-465 Dual Gauge pkg(10) **119.95**

CROSSINGS EA 16.90

948-430 30°
948-431 45°
948-432 60°
948-433 90°

DUAL GAUGE #6 TURNOUTS EA 39.95

948-450 Left Hand-1
Narrow gauge on left.

948-451 Left Hand-2
Narrow gauge on right.

948-452 Right Hand-1
Narrow gauge on right.

948-453 Right Hand-2
Narrow gauge on left.

TRANSITION TRACK EA 12.00

948-470 Narrow Gauge-Left
948-471 Narrow Gauge-Right

TOMAR INDUSTRIES

HAYES WHEEL STOP

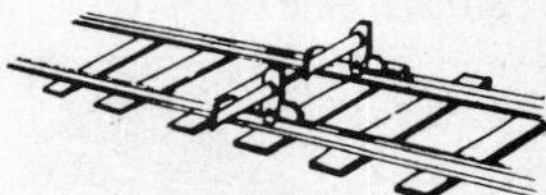

81-803 Type SF pkg(4) **1.50**
Cast white-metal "stops" protect your spur ends. They won't come off when bumped by a car. Used on heavy or lightweight service.

BUMPING POSTS

81-808 Hayes **3.45**
Assembled post mounted on track with insulated rail joiners.

81-80870 For Code 70 Track **3.95**
81-80883 For Code 83 Track **3.95**

Tru-Scale Models offers four interchangeable HO track systems: Plain Roadbed, Self-Gauging Roadbed, Milled Roadbed and Ready-Track. Each is made from kiln-dried basswood, which will not change shape or size and easily accepts spikes. Roadbed is easy to install and helps muffle track noise.

SELF-GAUGING ROADBED

Self-gauging roadbed features milled ties and tie plates.

STRAIGHT

730-1201 1' Straight **1.80**
Dealers MUST order in multiples of 5.

TURNOUT

730-1950 Wye Switch **5.50**
730-1951 #4 Right **4.83**
730-1952 #4 Left **4.83**
730-1953 #6 Right **5.16**
730-1954 #6 Left **5.16**
730-1955 #8 Right **5.66**
730-1956 #8 Left **5.66**
Dealers MUST order in multiples of 6.

CROSSOVER

730-1975 No. 8 Right **5.00**
Dealers MUST order in multiples of 8.

Limited Quantity Available

730-1477 #4 Scissors, Kit **58.00**

PLAIN ROADBED

Designed to be a sub-base and embankment for flex-track or for laying individual ties and rail.

STRAIGHT

730-1301 1' **1.50**
Dealers MUST order in multiples of 6.

730-1302 2' **2.80**
Dealers MUST order in multiples of 10.

730-1303 3' **3.80**
Dealers MUST order in multiples of 18.

730-1304 2' Super-Flex **3.40**
730-1305 Bulk Pack (Random Lengths-20') **25.00**

CIRCLE

730-1316 16" Radius **2.60**
730-1318 18" Radius **2.80**
730-1320 20" Radius **3.00**
730-1322 22" Radius **3.20**
730-1324 24" Radius **3.40**
730-1326 26" Radius **3.60**
730-1328 28" Radius **3.80**
Dealers MUST order in multiples of 8.

730-1330 30" Radius **3.00**
730-1332 32" Radius **3.20**
730-1334 34" Radius **3.40**
730-1336 36" Radius **3.60**
730-1338 38" Radius **3.80**
730-1340 40" Radius **4.00**
730-1342 42" Radius **4.20**
730-1344 44" Radius **4.40**
730-1346 46" Radius **4.60**
730-1348 48" Radius **4.80**
Dealers MUST order in multiples of 12.

730-1306 16 to 26" Radius Assortment **19.60**
730-1307 26 to 36" Radius Assortment **21.80**
730-1308 36 to 48" Radius Assortment **26.00**

TURNOUT

730-1350 Wye Switch **4.80**
730-1351 #4 Right **4.40**
730-1352 #4 Left **4.40**
Dealers MUST order in multiples of 6.

730-1353 #6 Right **4.60**
730-1354 #6 Left **4.60**
730-1355 #8 Right **5.00**
730-1356 #8 Left **5.00**
730-1375 #8 Crossover **4.20**
Dealers MUST order in multiples of 6.

HOn3 ROADBED

STRAIGHT

730-1601 1' **1.38**
Dealers MUST order in multiples of 8.

730-1602 2' **2.50**
730-1604 2' Super-Flex **4.13**
Dealers MUST order in multiples of 8.

730-1603 3' **3.50**
Dealers MUST order in multiples of 8.

730-1605 Bulk Pack **20.00**

CIRCLE

730-1612 12" Radius **1.55**
730-1614 14" Radius **2.60**
730-1616 16" Radius **2.80**
730-1618 18" Radius **3.00**
730-1620 20" Radius **3.20**
730-1622 22" Radius **3.40**
730-1624 24" Radius **3.60**
730-1626 26" Radius **3.80**
730-1628 28" Radius **4.00**
Dealers MUST order in multiples of 8.

730-1630 30" Radius **2.80**
Dealers MUST order in multiples of 12.

730-1606 16 to 26" Radius Assortment **19.00**
730-1607 26 to 36" Radius Assortment **21.00**

TURNOUT

730-1650 Wye Switch **5.00**
730-1651 #4 Right **4.50**
730-1652 #4 Left **4.50**
730-1653 #6 Right **4.80**
730-1654 #6 Left **4.80**
730-1675 #8 Crossover **4.33**
Dealers MUST order in multiples of 6.

MILLED ROADBED

Roadbed with milled ties, for use with Code 70 or 83 rail.

STRAIGHT

730-1901 1' **1.73**
Dealers MUST order in multiples of 6.

730-1902 2' **3.00**
730-1903 3' **4.40**
Dealers MUST order in multiples of 16.

730-1904 2' Super-Flex **4.75**
Dealers MUST order in multiples of 8.

730-1905 Bulk Pack **1.50**
Dealers MUST order in multiples of 16.

CIRCLE

730-1916 16" Radius **3.20**
730-1918 18" Radius **3.40**
730-1920 20" Radius **3.60**
730-1922 22" Radius **3.80**
730-1924 24" Radius **4.00**
730-1926 26" Radius **4.20**
730-1928 28" Radius **4.40**
Dealers MUST order in multiples of 8.

730-1930 30" Radius **3.60**
730-1932 32" Radius **3.80**
730-1934 34" Radius **4.00**
730-1936 36" Radius **4.20**
730-1938 38" Radius **4.40**
730-1940 40" Radius **4.60**
730-1942 42" Radius **4.80**
730-1944 44" Radius **5.00**
730-1946 46" Radius **5.20**
730-1948 48" Radius **5.40**
Dealers MUST order in multiples of 12.

730-1906 16 to 26" Radius Assortment **22.00**
730-1907 26 to 36" Radius Assortment **24.00**
730-1908 38 to 48" Radius Assortment **29.80**

READY TRACK

Ready-Track comes ready for installation, with Code 100 nickel-silver rail spiked on an accurately milled sub-base with tie plates and ties. The ties are stained and the base is ballasted.

STRAIGHT

730-1101 1' **4.40**
Dealers MUST order in multiples of 4.

730-1102 2' **7.40**
730-1103 3' **10.40**
Dealers MUST order in multiples of 12.

730-1104 2' Super-Flex **9.00**
Dealers MUST order in multiples of 6.

730-1112 Modular Track **17.00**
Consists of one 41" straight Ready-Track and two 9" Ready-Track connectors.

730-1115 Modular Track **17.00**
Consists of one 41" straight Ready-Track, and two 9" Atlas straight track connectors.

730-1180 Rerailer (7" long) **19.00**

CIRCLE

Eight packages of, or 8 individual pieces of, the following items will make a complete circle.

730-1118 18" Radius **5.20**
730-1120 20" Radius **5.60**
730-1122 22" Radius **6.00**
730-1124 24" Radius **6.60**
730-1126 26" Radius **7.20**
730-1128 28" Radius **7.80**
Dealers MUST order in multiples of 8.

Twelve packages of, or 12 individual pieces of each of the following items will make a complete circle.

730-1130 30" Radius **5.60**
730-1132 32" Radius **6.20**
730-1134 34" Radius **6.80**
730-1136 36" Radius **7.40**
730-1138 38" Radius **8.00**
730-1140 40" Radius **8.60**
730-1142 42" Radius **9.20**
730-1144 44" Radius **9.80**
730-1146 46" Radius **10.40**
730-1148 48" Radius **11.00**
Dealers MUST order in multiples of 12.

TURNOUT-ASSEMBLED

730-1150 Wye Switch **35.00**
730-1151 #4 Right Hand **31.00**
730-1152 #4 Left Hand **31.00**
730-1153 #6 Single Right **33.00**
730-1154 #6 Single Left **33.00**
730-1155 #8 Single Right **35.00**
730-1156 #8 Single Left **35.00**

TURNOUT-KIT

730-1450 Wye Switch **15.00**
730-1451 #4 Single Right **15.00**
730-1452 #4 Single Left **15.00**
730-1453 #6 Single Right **16.20**
730-1454 #6 Single Left **16.20**
730-1455 #8 Single Right **17.40**
730-1456 #8 Single Left **17.40**
730-1457 #4 Double Right **60.00**
730-1458 #4 Double Left **60.00**

CROSSING

730-1190 14° **39.00**
730-1191 19° **39.00**
730-1192 28° **37.00**
730-1193 45° **37.00**
730-1194 60° **36.00**
730-1195 90° **36.00**

CROSSOVER

Less motors.

730-1171 #4 Single Right **47.00**
730-1172 #4 Single Left **47.00**
730-1173 #6 Single Right **47.00**
730-1174 #6 Single Left **49.00**
730-1175 #8 Single Right **51.00**
730-1176 #8 Single Left **51.00**

ACCESSORIES

TEST CAR

Clear plastic car allows you to see problems with laying of track, switches and crossovers. Fully sprung trucks let you "feel" the conditions of the rail by keeping fingers on the car.

730-1420 Track Laying Test Car, HO **16.00**
730-1421 Track Laying Test Car, HOn3 **14.00**

TEST TRACK

730-1440 Test Track **35.00**

CAST FROG

730-1412 Wye pkg(2) **6.00**
730-1413 #4 pkg(2) **6.00**
730-1414 #6 pkg(2) **6.00**
730-1415 #8 pkg(2) **6.00**

RAIL JOINERS

730-1446 Code 100, Nickel Silver pkg(50) **5.00**

BUMPERS

730-2001 Tie **13.00**
730-2002 Rail **14.00**

UNCOUPLER TRACK

730-2008 With Kadee® Ramp **14.00**

RERAILER

730-1480 Rerailer Kit **11.00**

GRADE CROSSING

730-2010 Crossing **13.00**

BRIDGE STOCK

730-1416 6" **9.00**
730-1417 12" **11.60**
730-1418 18" **15.00**

TRACK-BED

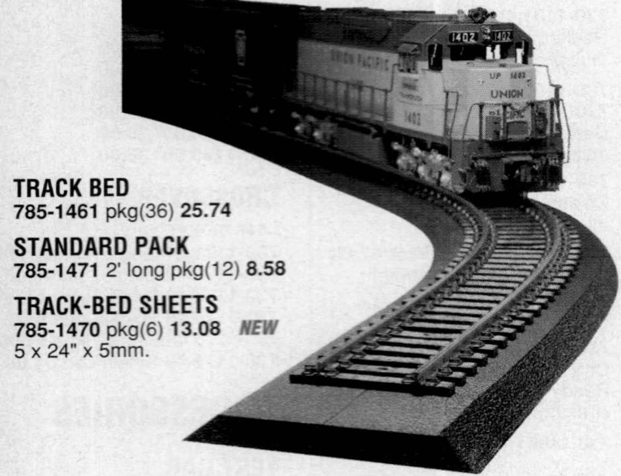

TRACK BED
785-1461 pkg(36) **25.74**

STANDARD PACK
785-1471 2' long pkg(12) **8.58**

TRACK-BED SHEETS
785-1470 pkg(6) **13.08** ***NEW***
5 x 24" x 5mm.

NEW HO Scale Roadbed

Conforms To Applicable NMRA Standards

- **Quieter Operation** (Sound Deadening Material)
- **Smoother Operation** (Cushions Vibrations)
- **Easier to Use** (Tack or Glue Down, Flexible, No Soaking, Compatible with Cork, Won't Dry Out or Crumble)
- **Better Value** (Higher Quality...Lower Cost)

SIGNALS

Old timers remember when the chatter of the telegraph key was sweet music. Some learned to "sling lightning" as kids, taught by their fathers or grandfathers who worked for the road. Others remember the excitement of being in the depot and hearing those mysterious dots and dashes flit through the air. A series of clicks and the agent would rise, set the semaphore, then return to type out the message coming across the wires.

In those days, telegraphy was essential, for train orders sent to stations along the line kept things moving safely. In small towns, the telegraph was the only link to a far-away world. Telegrams were only part of it. Locals would drift in to listen in as sporting events or election results were sent live. And the agent who understood the code was looked on as a local hero.

Telephones and centralized traffic control are replacing the Morse Code. Here and there, a few towers are still open, at least until new relays are in place. Colored lights keep today's heavier, faster and longer trains rolling safely.

Passing freights still shake the windows of this tower, but how much longer, no one can say. So amidst the blazing fall colors, we're in time to watch local #2706 take the siding as a long Chessie coal drag snakes by. And if you listen very, very closely, you may hear the sounds of the past.

Models and Photo by Fred Lagno

WALTHERS™

OLD TIME STREET LAMPS

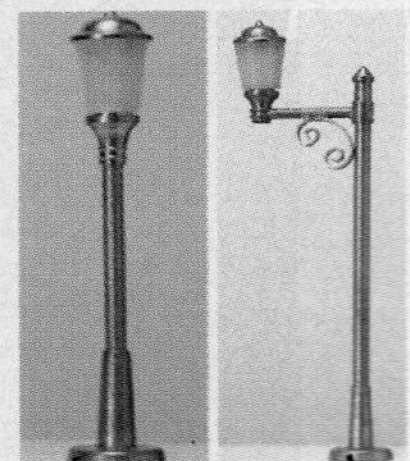
933-939 933-1022

933-1023

Operating lamps can be used in scenes from the 1920s to the present for lighting streets, boulevards or station platforms. Lamps are fully assembled, unpainted brass with plastic globes.

933-939 2-1/4" Tall (12v bulb) pkg(2) **6.98**
933-1022 Single Arm, 3-1/2" Tall (18v bulb) **6.98**
933-1023 Double Arm, 3-1/2" Tall (18v bulb) **8.98**

ROADSIDE BILLBOARDS

These easy-to-assemble kits include three billboards with nonilluminated light fixtures and 12 full-color signs. Plastic parts are molded in color, and instructions are included with tips for adding signs to existing scenery.

933-3103 Steam-/Diesel-Era Signs **8.98**

933-3106 Food Signs **8.98**

933-3107 Automotive Signs **8.98**
933-3133 Plain Billboards pkg(2) **4.98**

DECAL SIGNS

GRAFFITI EA 3.98

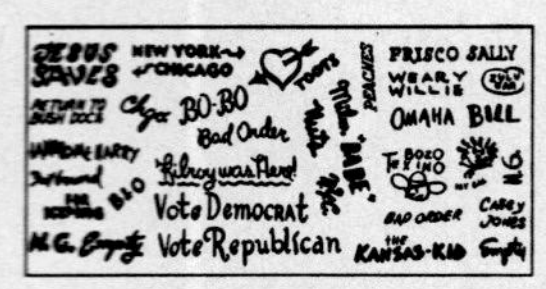

Give your layout extra realism with these graffiti decals, great for rolling stock, structures, bridges or rock formations.

934-701070 White
934-701080 Black

FIRE ENGINE NAMES

ENGINE LADDER RESCUE / ENGINE LADDER COMBINATION / ENGINE SALVAGE HIGH PRESSURE

934-1495 3.98
Detail your fire trucks with these engine name decals, printed in gold.

STARS

934-706870 3.98
A collection of red, white and blue star decals. Each set includes two sets of each color.

A.W. ENTERPRISES

DRESS-UP KITS EA 2.95

Bring new life to boring downtown shops! Full-color sheets contain appropriate interior scenes and numerous signs for exterior as well.

699-16005 Dime Store & Offices
699-16006 Hardware Store
699-16017 Florist's Shop
699-16018 Drug Store

IMPORTED FROM GERMANY BY WALTHERS

Pre-wired plastic signals are assembled and ready to install.

SIGNALS

189-5802 189-5803 189-5804

189-5802 Blocksignal 2 LEDs **13.99**
189-5803 Hauptsignal 4 LEDs **17.99**
189-5804 Vorsingal 4 LEDs **17.99**

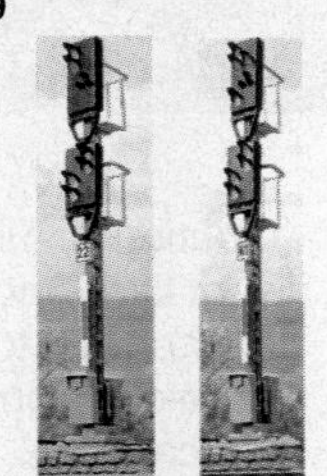
189-5805 189-5806

189-5805 Block/Vorsignal 6 LEDs **31.99**
189-5806 Haupt/Vorsignal 8 LEDs **35.99**

189-5821 189-5822 189-5823

189-5821 Block Signal, 2 LEDs **18.99**
189-5822 Main Signal, 3 LEDs **19.99**
189-5823 Block/Warning Signal, 4 LEDs **24.99**

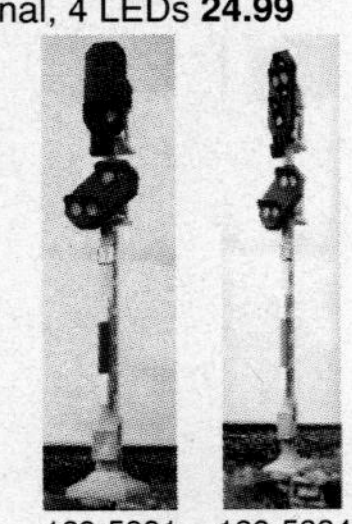
189-5831 189-5834

189-5831 Block/Warning Signal, 6 LEDs **35.99**
189-5834 Departure/Warning Signal, 10 LEDs **44.99**

CROSSING SIGNALS

Signals include control units.

189-5300 Modern Crossing Gates w/Electronic Drive **60.99** *NEW*

189-5968 Belgian Railways Crossing Flashers **TBA** *NEW*

189-5903 Crossing Blinkers **22.99**
189-5913 4-Pack with Signs **36.99**

189-5934 Crossing Blinkers **29.99**
Set includes 2 crossing signals and control unit.

189-5966 Swiss Style pkg(2) **34.99**

Limited Quantity Available
189-5910 2-Pack **21.99**

TRAFFIC SIGNALS

Signals include control units.

189-5902 189-5916

189-5902 pkg(2) **49.99**
189-5916 Pedestrian Crossing Set pkg(2) **36.99**

CONSTRUCTION BARRICADES

189-5905 Barricades pkg(2) **31.99**
With control unit.

189-5907 Construction Zone Set pkg(7) **38.99**
Includes seven stanchion barricades (four with blinking lights) and control unit.

189-5917 Construction Zone Set pkg(15) **65.99**
Includes 15 stanchion barricades (eight with blinking lights), three signs and control unit.

189-6022 Guardrail & Speed Limit Set **5.99**

189-6048 Road Construction Set **14.99**

CONSTRUCTION TRAILERS

189-5904 Construction Trailer w/Lights **32.99**
With control unit.

189-5912 Road Construction Warning Trailer **29.99**
Trailer features blinking lights. With control unit.

TRANSMITTER TOWER

189-5965 41.99
Features three red LEDs at the top of the tower that blink in sequence. 14-3/4" (370mm) tall.

SIGNAL KITS

189-5490 Compact Light Signal Kit **13.99** *NEW*
Includes base, masts, LEDs and resistors to construct a pair of signals.

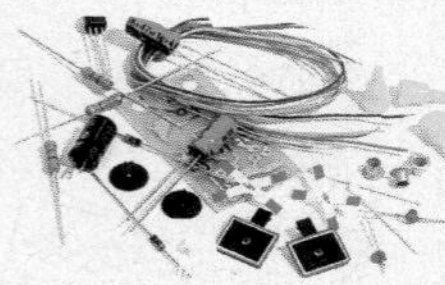

189-5491 Modern Crossing Flasher Kit **10.99** *NEW*
Parts to construct a pair of contemporary German crossing flashers with red LEDs, signs, resistors, assembled circuit board and wiring.

189-5492 Highway Construction Barricades w/Flasher **19.99** *NEW*
Kit includes parts for seven barricades, plus LEDs and flasher circuit to equip four barricades with flashing yellow lights.

DRY TRANSFER DECALS

Decal sets include rub-on pen.

189-6024 German Federal Railways (DB) Logos **3.99**

189-6035 Graffiti Detail Set **7.99**

ADVERTISEMENTS

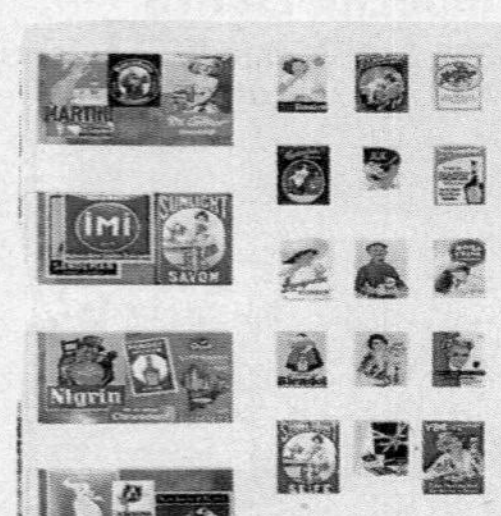

189-6002 Sign Set **5.99**

FENCES & GATES

189-6018 120cm+ **4.99**

Precolored plastic signals, lights and signs.

SIGNALS

160-42101 Block Signals pkg(4) **5.00**

160-42200 Crossing Signals & Gates (6 each) pkg(12) **6.00**

SIGNAL BRIDGE

160-45134 6.00

GRADE CROSSING

160-42208 Nonoperating **6.00**

SIGNS

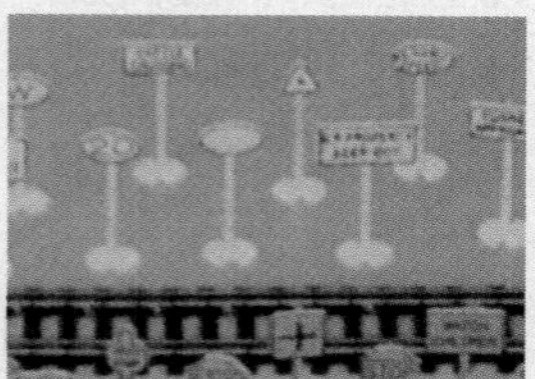

160-42204 Rail & Street Signs pkg(24) **6.00**

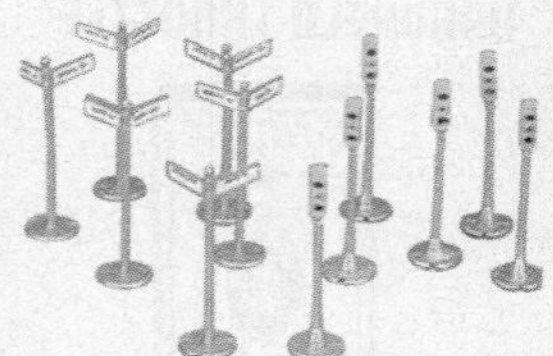

160-42207 Traffic Lights & Signs pkg(12) **6.00**

TELEPHONE POLES

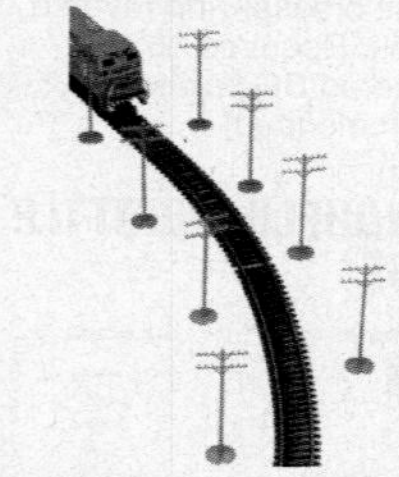

160-42102 pkg(12) **6.00**

ATLAS

TELEPHONE POLES

150-775 Telephone Poles pkg(12) **3.25**
Styrene parts, molded in appropriate colors.

CAMPBELL SCALE MODELS

STREET LAMPS

200-928 pkg(3) **3.00**
Nonoperating plastic lamp kit with clear plastic "glass."

CREATIVE MODEL ASSOCIATES

CROSSING SIGNS EA 4.95

363-1008 Warning pkg(20)
Yellow with black lettering.

363-1009 Crossbucks pkg(20)
White with black lettering.

363-1021 Canadian *NEW*
White with black lettering.

363-1022 Diamond pkg(10)
363-1023 Early Warning pkg(10)

MILE POST MARKERS

363-1011 Printed 1 to 50 pkg(50) **7.95**

WHISTLE POST SIGNS PKG(32) EA 4.95

363-1026 Early *NEW*
363-1027 Modern *NEW*

CRESCENT STATION

SIGNS

513-550 2.95
Over 425 different signs printed on sturdy cardstock in full color, black and white and brown and white.

LICENSE PLATES

513-602 6.50
Over 100 pair of license plates representing 47 US states and 10 Canadian provinces, in full color. Best applied with a light adhesive, such as Microscale LiquiTape.

COUNTRY TRAINS

Signs are printed in appropriate colors on glossy, coated cardstock. Two sheets included with each set.

ROAD SIGNS EA 1.50

203-1 Street Corner, Road Signs & Construction (110 signs)

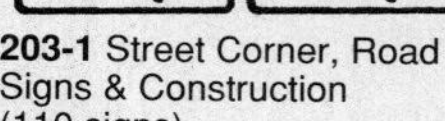

203-2 Highway Signs (56 signs)

203-3 Speed Limit, Railroad Crossing, Stop & Warning (72 signs)

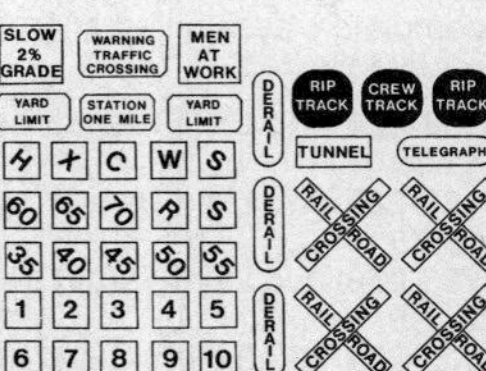

203-4 Railroad Track & Crossbucks (86 signs)

ROAD DECALS EA 2.98

203-5 Railroad Stop pkg(28)
203-6 Railroad Pedestrian pkg(18)

BL HOBBY PRODUCTS

All signals and controls include detailed installation instructions.

SIGNALS

FIBER OPTIC SIGNALS

Fiber optics transmit light from base-mounted bulbs to show the proper indications. Plastic and metal construction. Fully assembled, wired and ready to install.

183-222 183-231

183-221 Two Light Standard **11.95**
183-222 Two Light Dwarf **10.95**
183-223 Two Light Target **11.95**
183-231 Three Light Standard **12.95**
183-232 Three Light Dwarf **10.95**
183-233 Three Light Target **12.75**

LED SIGNALS

Light-emitting diode signals completely assembled and ready to install.

183-224 Two Light Standard **11.35**
183-225 Two Light Dwarf **10.75**
183-226 Two Light Target **11.95**
183-234 Three Light Standard **12.25**
183-235 Three Light Dwarf **11.95**
183-236 Three Light Target **14.95**

PANEL TRAIN CONTROL

Train control system is built into panels for direct mounting onto a control board. Each panel is 9" wide by 2, 4, 6 or 8" high. Units can be used together or integrated with your present train control system. Units will operate all scales from O to Z. Panels feature brushed metal finish with black lettering. Color-coded wires for installation.

THROTTLE

183-450 2 Amp **84.50**
Transistor speed control with full 2 amps of power. Features circuit breaker, overload indicator, power and reverse switches and direction indicator light.

RHEOSTAT THROTTLE

183-451 2 Amp **95.50**
Same as #183-450, but with rheostat speed control.

SWITCHER TRANSISTOR THROTTLE

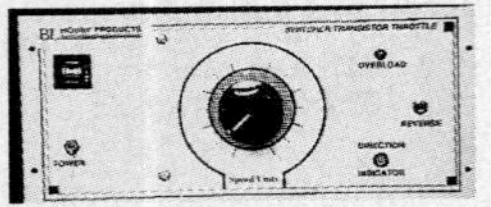

183-452 75.00
Slow switching speed control with 1 amp of power. Features circuit breaker, overload indicator, power and reverse switches and direction indicator light.

DC POWER SUPPLY

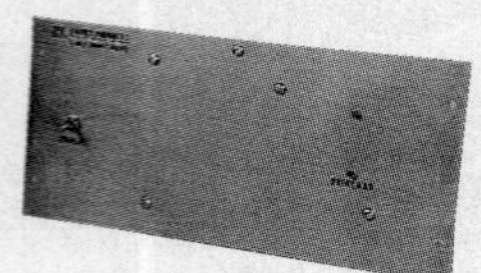

183-460 63.75
Use for auto block control or any DC accessories. 16V filtered power at 2 amps. Features circuit breaker and overload indicator.

AC POWER SUPPLY

183-462 55.00
12V of 2 amp power. With circuit breaker, overload indicator light and power on indicator light.

HANDHELD THROTTLE

183-458 54.95
Exceptional slow speed control. Includes 10 foot cable with plug and socket. With circuit breaker and reverse switch. Requires 16V unfiltered DC power (#183-461 recommended).

HANDHELD THROTTLE BASE

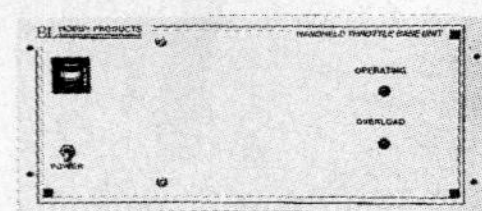

183-461 59.95
Designed specially for the handheld throttle, but can serve as DC power supply (can power four handheld throttles at once). Full 2 amp 16V unfiltered DC power. With circuit breaker, overload indicator, power switch and power on indicator.

SOCKET FOR HANDHELD THROTTLE

183-463 6.00
Allows for additional plug-ins for handheld throttles.

TRAIN DETECTION SYSTEM

Create block occupancy indicator or complete block control systems with these light-activated detection units. Compatible with most command control systems, rolling stock requires no modification. Units activate when light is blocked by a train, and long trains activate all occupied blocks.

Each block is controlled by a "Regular" unit that runs two-color signals (sold separately) so trains stop on red, proceed on green. A "Closing" unit must be installed at the end of a series of occupancy or automatic blocks. (Continuous loop layouts require only Regular units.) New design eliminates "opening" block and panel mountings, but is compatible with older train control products. Requires separate 12V DC power supply, which will operate multiple units.

BLOCK OCCUPANCY "REGULAR" UNIT

183-441 29.95
Occupancy indication only, use #183-442 as "Closing" unit in last block. Includes yellow LED for panel, mounting hardware and color-coded wiring.

AUTOMATIC BLOCK "REGULAR" UNIT

183-444 43.00
For full block control, works with any two-color signal (sold separately). Includes yellow LED for panel, push-button for manual control, color-coded wiring and instructions.

BLOCK "CLOSING" UNIT

183-442 27.95
Use as last unit in series of occupancy or automatic block units, unless running continuous loop. Includes mounting hardware and instructions.

ACCESSORIES

SWITCH A ROO

Builds and stores up to 25V to operate a switch machine. Quick recovery allows another switch machine to be activated within two seconds.

183-300 31.50
183-468 Panel Switch-A-Roo **36.00**
Same as #300, but mounted on a 9 x 4" panel.

WIRING HARNESS

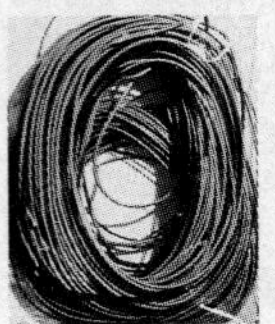

183-473 16.75
25' of color coded wire. Simplifies installation of train detection systems.

BLANK PANELS

For use on control board. Easily drilled for toggle switches for accessories.

183-470 2 x 9" **3.50**
183-471 4 x 9" **7.00**
183-472 6 x 9" **10.50**

TRAIN REVERSE KIT

183-466 34.00
Can be installed on any length of track to allow the train to automatically reverse itself. Just turn on the throttle and the train will run continuously.

DEPOTS BY JOHN

TRACKSIDE SIGNS

Signs feature easy-to-apply self-adhesive backing.

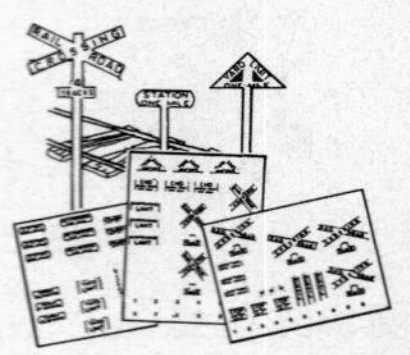

87-101/102/103

87-101 MILW Trackside **2.00**
87-102 MILW Mainline Set **2.00**
87-103 MILW Yard Set **2.00**
87-104 MILW Red Chevrons, Targets & Heralds **2.25**
87-105 MILW Red Chevrons, Heralds & Targets **2.25**
87-107 MILW Freight House & No Clearance (O, S, HO, N Scales) **2.00**
87-108 MILW Yellow Speed & Restriction **2.25**

HELJAN

Plastic models molded in realistic colors.

TELEPHONE POLES

322-512 Telephone Poles pkg(10) **4.98**

MODERN LIGHTS

322-513 Modern Street Lights Nonworking pkg(12) **3.98**

BRAWA

Brawa signals are made of brass (except as noted) and come fully assembled. The line features models of signals used by the German Federal Railways (DB) and include decals, where appropriate, to identify the signal type. The Brawa Signal Manual (#186-29) provides detailed information on wiring and operation of a model signal system. Signals equipped with bulbs or LEDs can be wired to AC or DC transformers with a maximum output of 10 to 16V. For longer bulb life, 10 to 12V is recommended. Brawa relays #186-2760 or 2761 are designed for switching these signals and feature matching color-coded wiring.

SIGNALS

SEMAPHORE SIGNALS

Semaphore signals were a common sight during the steam-era and are still in widespread service today in Europe. The moving signal arm adds realistic action to a layout, while providing a visual indication of the route setting. Signals are approximately 4" high.

186-8530 186-8930 186-8538

186-8530 Home Signal, 1-Arm w/Slow Memory Drive (2 position) **59.99**
186-8930 Home Signal, 1-Arm (2 position) **47.99**
186-8538 Home Signal, 2-Arm w/Slow Memory Drive (3 position) **69.99**

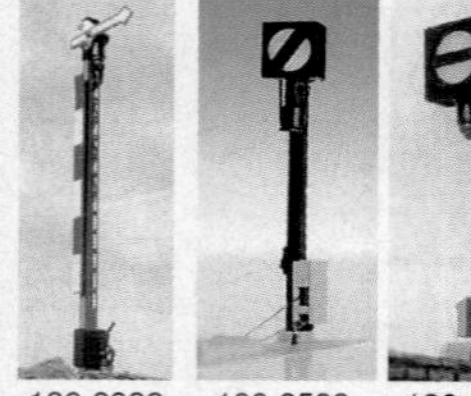

186-8932 186-8533 186-8933

186-8932 Bavarian Stop Signal **47.99**
186-8533 Track Stop Signal w/Slow Memory Drive **59.99**
186-8933 Track Stop Signal **45.99**

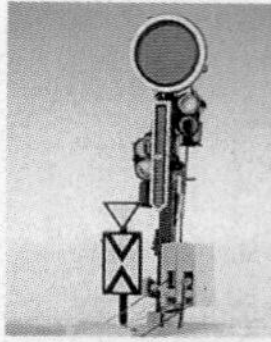

186-8536 186-8534

186-8536 Repeater Signal w/Slow Memory Drive, 3 Aspect (Vr 0/1/2) **79.99**
Movable arm, disk and aspects.

186-8534 Repeater Signal w/Slow Memory Drive, 2 Aspect (Vr 0/1) **69.99**
Movable disk and aspects.

186-8535 Repeater Signal w/Slow Memory Drive, 2 Aspect (Vr 0/2) **69.99**
Fixed disk, movable arm and one aspect.

COLOR LIGHT SIGNALS

Most European State and private railways have begun replacing semaphores with color-light signals which display a variety of aspects. The signals have a built-in resistor for use with any AC or DC 14-16V power supply. Signals are approximately 3-1/2" high, unless noted.

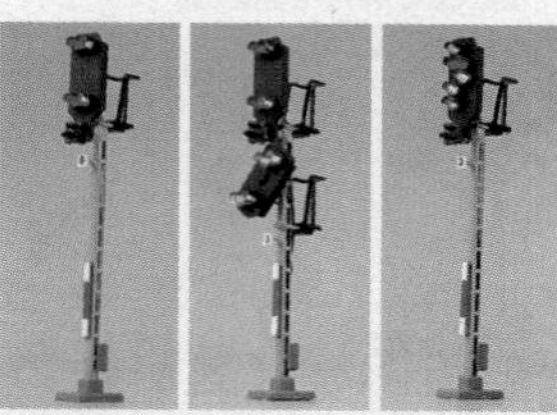

186-8801 186-8802 186-8803

186-8801 Home Signal **29.99**
186-8802 Home & Distant Signal **49.99**
186-8803 Starter Signal w/Track Block Signal **39.99**

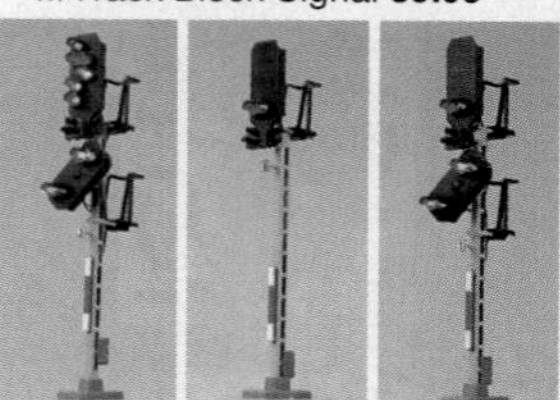

186-8804 186-8805 186-8806

186-8804 Starter Signal w/Distant & Track Block Signal **59.99**
186-8805 Automatic Block Signal **25.99**
186-8806 Automatic Block & Distant Signal **47.99**

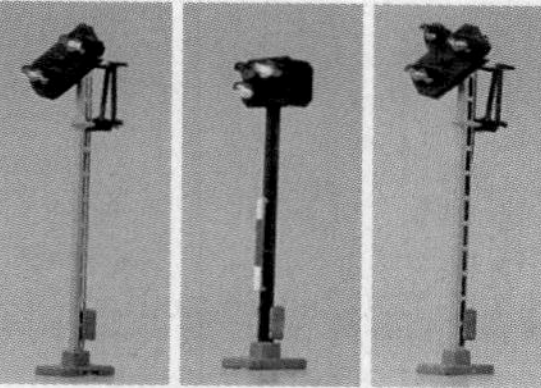

186-8808 186-8809 186-8817

186-8808 Distant Signal **29.99**
186-8809 Trackside Stop Signal **29.99**
Approximately 2-1/2" high.

Limited Quantity Available
186-8817 Distant Signal w/Marker Light **37.49**

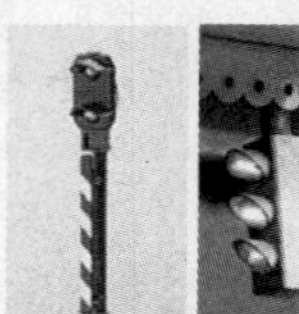

186-8811 186-8810

186-8811 Flashing Warning Signal **18.99**
Approximately 2" high.

Limited Quantity Available
186-8810 Brake Test Signal **17.49**
Installed at stations, signal indicates if train brakes are working properly. Approximately .8" high (22 mm).

LED COLOR LIGHT SIGNALS

Signals feature LEDs (Light-Emitting Diodes) and have a built-in resistor for use with any AC or DC 14-16V power supply. The low current draw (15mA from 14V supply) allows use of Brawa LED signals with transistor or integrated circuits. To install Brawa LED signals on benchwork, drill a 23/64" 9mm hole and simply press into place. Signals are approximately 3-1/2" high, unless noted.

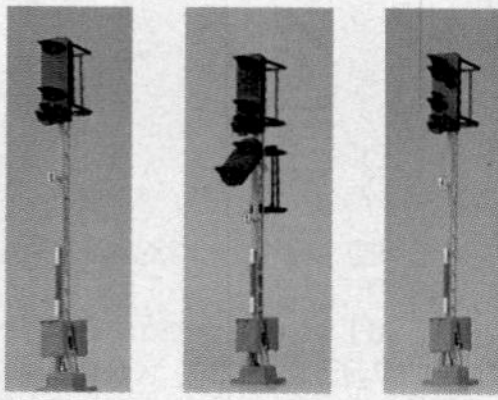

186-8831 186-8832 186-8833

186-8831 Home Signal, 4 LEDs **49.99**
186-8832 Home & Distant Signal, 8 LEDs **79.99**
186-8833 Starter Signal, 6 LEDs **59.99**

186-8834 186-8835 186-8836

186-8834 Starter Signal w/Distant & Track Block Signal, 10 LEDs **89.99**
186-8835 Block Signal, 2 LEDs **44.99**
Prototype automatic block signals are located at the start of each track block and are operated by passing trains.

186-8836 Block & Distant Signal, 6 LEDs **79.99**

186-8837

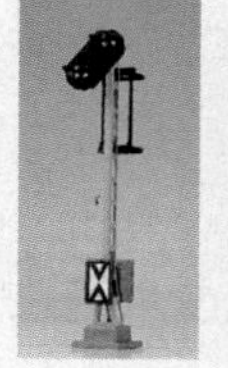

186-8838 186-8839

186-8837 Trackside Stop Signal-Dwarf, 4 LEDs **47.99**
Head: 4.8 x 7.2 x 1.8mm.

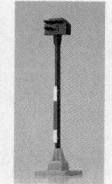

186-8838 Distant Signal, 4 LEDs **49.99**
Distant signals give train crews advance warning of the next signal aspect.

186-8839 Trackside Stop Signal, 4 LEDs **49.99**
Head: 4.8 x 7.2 x 1.8mm.

SIGNAL BRIDGES & SIGNALS

Brawa signal bridges and cantilever masts do not include cages or signals. Individual signals include cages, which can be glued on the bridge.

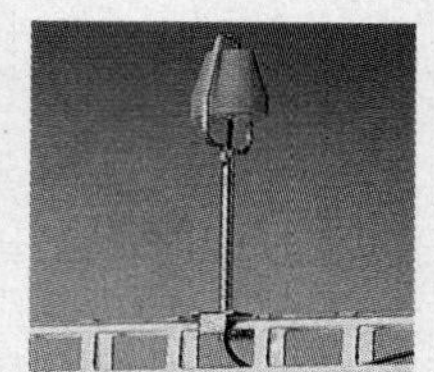

186-5531 Catenary Light, Swiss Style **11.99**

186-8620 Cantilever Signal Mast **11.99**
Less signals; approximately 4-1/4 x 3".

186-8621 Signal Bridge **16.99**
Less signals; approximately 5 x 7".

186-8822 186-8825 186-8845

186-8822 Home Signal **25.99**
With cage and head, 4 bulbs.

186-8825 Distant Signal **25.99**
With cage and head, 4 bulbs.

186-8845 Home Signal **36.99**
With cage and 4 LEDs.

186-8846 186-8847 186-8848

186-8846 Starting Signal **45.99**
With cage and 6 LEDs.

186-8847 Block Signal **34.99**
With cage and 2 LEDs.

186-8848 Distant Signal **39.99**
With cage and 4 LEDs.

CROSSING SIGNALS

Crossing signals are made of brass (except where noted) and feature red LEDs. Can be operated automatically with relay #186-2760 and track contacts.

186-6128/6131 186-6130/6129

186-6128 Crossing Signal w/Flashing Light (plastic) **9.99**
Approximately 1-1/2" (42mm) high.

186-6131 Crossing Signal Set pkg(4) **49.99**
Includes four of #6128 crossing signals with alternating electronic flashing unit.

186-6130 Crossing Signal w/Guard Ring **14.99**
Approximately 1-1/4" (35mm) high.

186-6129 Crossing Signal Set pkg(4) **69.99**
Includes four of #6130 crossing signals with alternating electronic flasher unit.

BRAWA

CROSSING GATE SET

186-1194 Crossing Gate Set **279.99**
Set features two gates with slow memory drive for realistic gate action. Also includes four brass crossing signs, two street lights (#186-5496), road section, warning loudspeaker (#186-2650), crossing shanty, electronic control unit (#186-2765) for gates with outputs for bell and flasher unit (#186-6129), two magnets (#186-3543), four switches (#186-3530), two resistors (#186-6154) and a bell (#186-1141).

TELEPHONE POLES

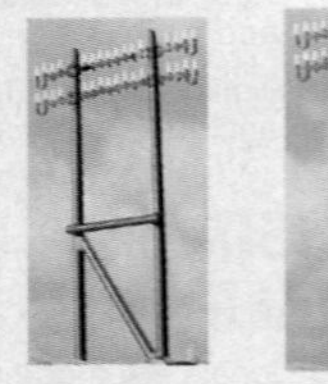

186-2668 186-2669

186-2668 Twin Poles pkg(3) **25.99**
Approximately 3-1/4" high.

186-2669 With Supports pkg(3) **18.99**
Approximately 3-1/4" high.

186-2670 186-5277

186-2670 With Base Supports pkg(3) **16.99**
Approximately 3" high.

Limited Quantity Available
186-5277 With Light **12.99**

HIGH TENSION TOWERS

Suitable for use in HO or N Scale, towers are made of metal. Approximate height 4" 100mm.

186-2658 High Tension Tower **18.99**
186-2659 High Tension Tower Set pkg(4) **79.99**
Set of four #186-2658 high tension towers with wires, warning globes and tension springs.

LIGHTS

Lights are made of brass (with plastic parts where appropriate), fully assembled and ready to install. Lamps can be powered from an AC or DC transformer with a maximum output of 16V.

STATION LIGHTS

186-5040 186-5050 186-5175

186-5040 St. Paul Streetlight **14.99**
186-5050 Station Light, 4-1/2" **9.99**
186-5175 Waiblingen, 2-1/2" High **15.99**

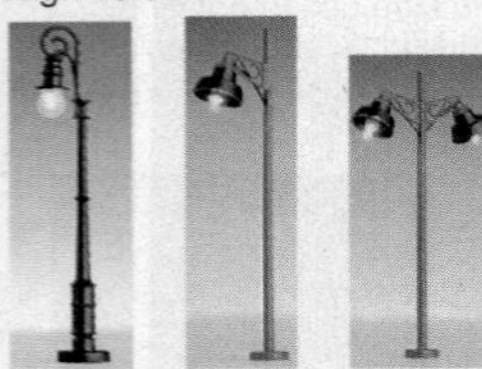

186-5176 186-5271 186-5272

186-5176 Stettin Station-Berlin, 3" High **16.99**
186-5271 One Arm w/Wooden Mast, 3" High **10.99**
186-5272 Two Arm w/Wooden Mast, 3" High **16.99**

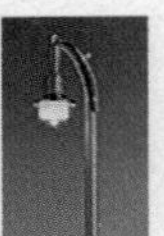
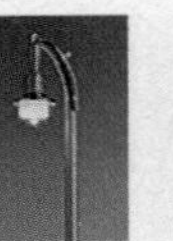

186-5273 186-5276 186-5451

186-5273 Tall Goose Neck, 4" High **11.99**
186-5275 With Wood Mast, 3-1/4" High **9.99**
186-5276 With Wood Mast-Birkenau, 5-1/2" High **10.99**
186-5451 Tall Station Light, 5" High **10.99**

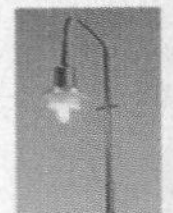
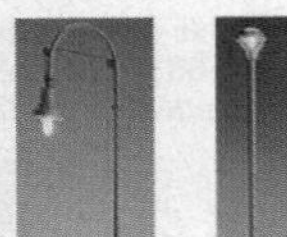

186-5453 186-5454 186-5458

186-5453 Station Forecourt, 3" High **10.99**
186-5454 Depot Light, 4" High **16.99**
186-5458 With Wood Mast, 6-1/2" High **10.99**

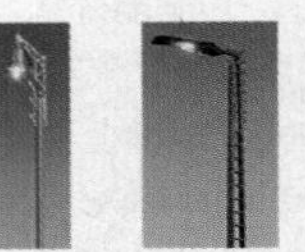

186-5459 186-5518 186-5525

186-5459 With Wood Mast, 6-1/2" High **12.99**
186-5518 With Lattice Mast, 5" High **13.99**
186-5525 Depot Light-Munich, 3-1/2" High **14.99**

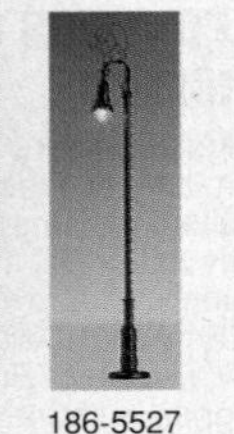

186-5472 186-5527

186-5472 Station Light **9.99**
186-5527 Depot Light-Frankfurt, 3-1/2" High **11.99**

PLATFORM LIGHTS

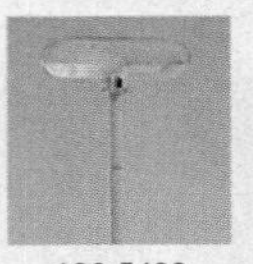
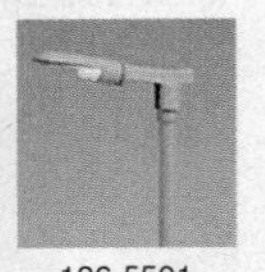

186-5499 186-5501

186-5499 Modern, 2-3/4" High **10.99**
186-5501 Single Arm, 2-3/4" High **10.99**

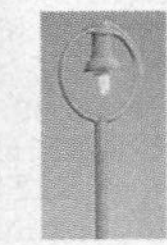

186-5502 186-5504

186-5502 Double Arm, 2-3/4" High **16.99**
186-5504 Ring Post, 3-1/2" High **10.99**

CATENARY TOWER LIGHTS

Lights fit Vollmer, Marklin and Sommerfeld towers.

186-5532 186-5533

Limited Quantity Available
186-5532 Single Add-on Light **8.99**
186-5533 Twin Add-on Light **14.49**

186-5534 186-5535

186-5534 Single Add-on Light **8.99**
186-5535 Twin Add-on Light **13.99**

UNDER-ROOF MOUNTED LIGHTS

186-5320 186-5536 186-5537

186-5320 Under Roof Mount, 1" Long **8.99**
186-5536 Under Roof Mount **7.99**
186-5537 Under Roof Mount, 3/4" Long **8.99**

WALL-MOUNTED LIGHTS

186-5352 186-5353 186-5356

186-5352 Wall Light **9.99**
186-5353 Wall Light **9.99**
186-5356 Baden-Baden **11.49**

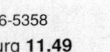

186-5357 186-5358

186-5357 Nuremburg **11.49**
186-5358 Wall Light **8.99**

LATTICE MAST LIGHTS

186-5450 186-5460

186-5450 Single Arm, 5" High **10.99**
186-5460 Double Arm , 5" High **13.99**

186-5470 186-5471 186-5505

186-5470 Ring Post, 5" High **10.99**
186-5471 Yard Light 5-11/32" High **12.99**
186-5505 Narrow Rectangular Mast, 6" High **13.99**

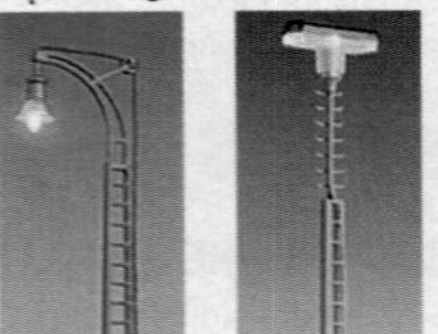

186-5506 186-5507

186-5506 Flat Design, 6" High **13.99**
186-5507 Flat Light, 5" High **13.99**

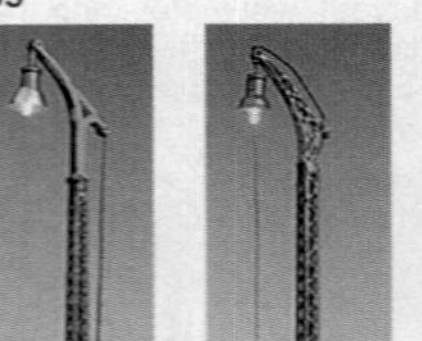

186-5509 186-5519

186-5509 Narrow Rectangular Mast, 6" High **13.99**
186-5519 Single Arm, 6" High **16.99**

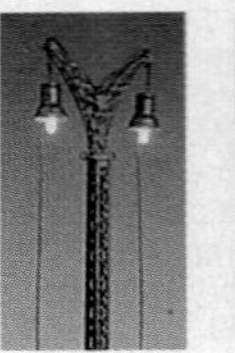
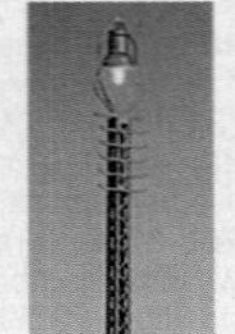

186-5520 186-5522

186-5520 Two Arm, 6" High **25.99**
186-5522 Ring Post, 5-1/2" High **16.99**

BRAWA

PARK LIGHTS

186-5001 186-5090

186-5001 Park Light, 2-1/2" High **8.99**
186-5090 Park Light, 2-1/2" High **9.49**

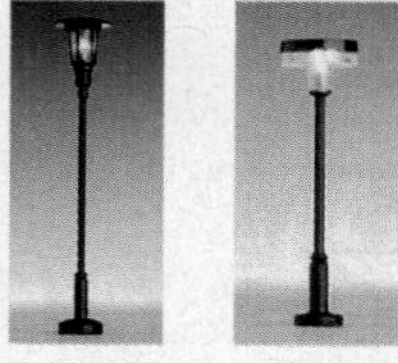
186-5100 186-5230

186-5100 Park Light, 2-1/2" High **8.99**
186-5230 Park Light, 2" High **8.99**

HISTORIC PARK LIGHTS

186-5220 186-5222

186-5220 Three Arm, 3-1/2" High **27.99**
186-5222 Double Arm, 3-1/2" High **23.99**

186-5223 186-5224

186-5223 Triple Arm, 3-1/2" High **31.99**
186-5224 Six Arm-Baden Baden, 3" High **78.99**

186-5225 186-5226

186-5225 Single Arm, 3-1/2" High **17.99**
186-5226 Double Arm, 3-1/2" High **23.99**

186-5171 Five Arm, 3-1/2" High **39.99**

186-5092 186-5093 186-5253

186-5092 Oldtime Park Light, 1-1/2" High **9.99**
186-5093 Park/Street Light, 1-3/8" High **9.99**
186-5253 Park/Street Light-Round, 1-21/32" High **9.99**

STREET LIGHTS

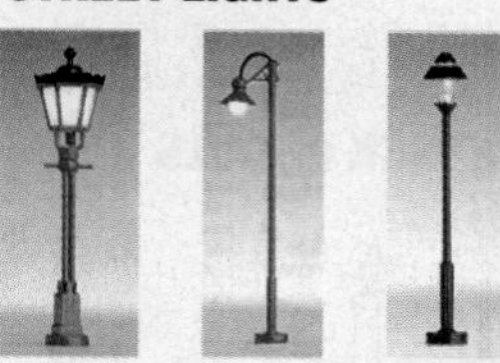
186-5000 186-5005 186-5007

186-5000 Old Street Lamp, 2-1/2" High **12.99**
186-5005 Urbach, 2" High **9.99**
186-5007 Bad Homburg, 1-3/4" High **9.99**

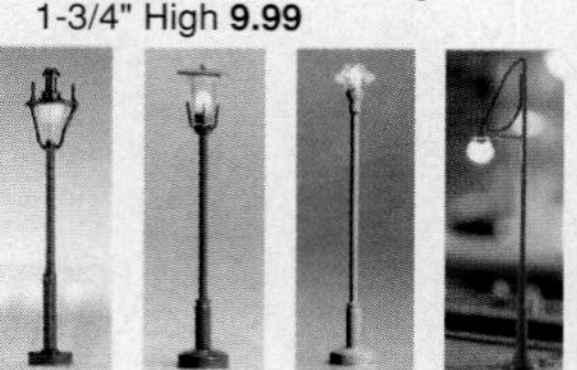
186-5008 186-5101 186-5013 186-5041

186-5008 Lunen-Rye Market, 1-3/4" High **9.99**
186-5101 Stuttgart Rosenstein Park Lamp **10.99** ***NEW***
186-5013 Wernigrode Street Light **9.99** ***NEW***
186-5041 Berlin City Streetlight **10.00** ***NEW***

186-5172 186-5173 186-5204

186-5172 Nuremberg, 2" High **14.99**
186-5173 Nuremberg, 2-1/2" High **34.99**
186-5204 Cologne Boulevard Light, 6-1/4" High **25.99**

186-5205 186-5210 186-5240

186-5205 Munich Boulevard Light, 4-3/4" High **14.99**
186-5210 Street Light, 2-1/2" High **8.99**
186-5240 Street Light, 2-1/2" High **8.99**

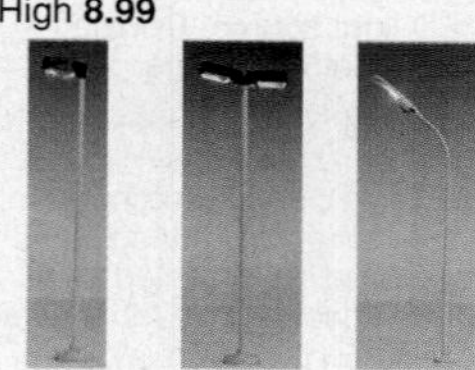
186-5280 186-5515 186-5020

186-5280 Rectangular Head, 4-1/2" High **9.99**
186-5515 Twin Rectangular Head, 4-1/2" High **15.99**
186-5020 Curved Mast-Single Arm, 4" High **8.99**

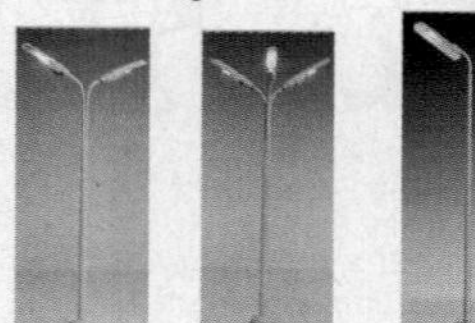
186-5400 186-5410 186-5452

186-5400 Curved Mast-Double Arm, 4-1/2" High **15.99**
186-5410 Curved Mast-Triple Arm, 5" High **22.99**
186-5452 Single Arm, 4-1/2" High **10.99**

186-5510 186-5514 186-5512

186-5510 Curved Mast-Single Arm, 5" High (yellow light) **8.99**
186-5514 Curved Mast-Double Arm, 5" High (yellow light) **13.99**
186-5512 Curved Mast-Single Arm, 4" High **8.99**

186-5513 186-5179 186-5456

186-5513 Curved Mast-Double Arm, 4" High **13.99**
Limited Quantity Available
186-5179 Cologne Street Light, 6-1/4" High **23.49**
186-5456 Octagon Ring Post City Light, 3" High **12.49**

HISTORIC STREET LIGHTS

These models are based on actual lamps from various German cities, that are being restored to their original appearance.

186-5174 186-5177

186-5174 Berlin-Charlottenburg, 4-1/2" High **19.99**
Limited Quantity Available
186-5177 Cologne Rhine Bank, 3" High **17.99**

MODERN STREET LIGHTS

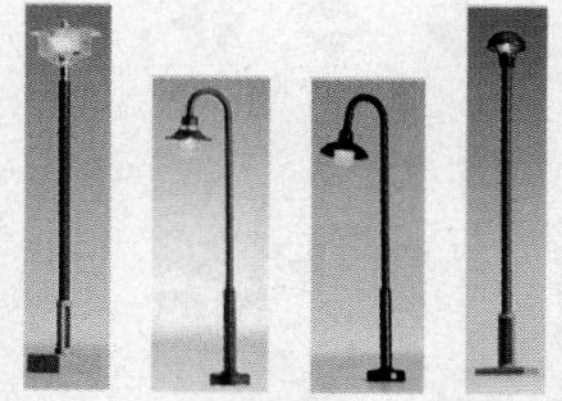
186-5014 186-5015 186-5016 186-5019

186-5014 Street Light, 2-1/8" High **9.99**
186-5015 Neuss, 1-3/4" High **9.99**
186-5016 Munich, 2" High **9.99**
186-5018 Harz, 3-1/2" High **9.99**
186-5019 Modern, 3-15/16" High **9.99**

GAS LIGHTS

186-5010 186-5180 186-5190

186-5010 Gas Light, 2" High **12.99**
186-5180 Gas Light, 2-1/2" High **9.99**
186-5190 Gas Light, 2" High **9.99**

186-5200 186-5201 186-5202 186-5203

186-5200 Old Gas Light, 2" High **9.99**
186-5201 Gas Light-Baden Baden, 2" High **14.99**
186-5202 Gas Light-Hamburg, 2" High **9.99**
186-5203 Gas Light-Stuttgart, 4" High **19.99**

FLOODLIGHTS

Floodlights pivot horizontally and vertically.

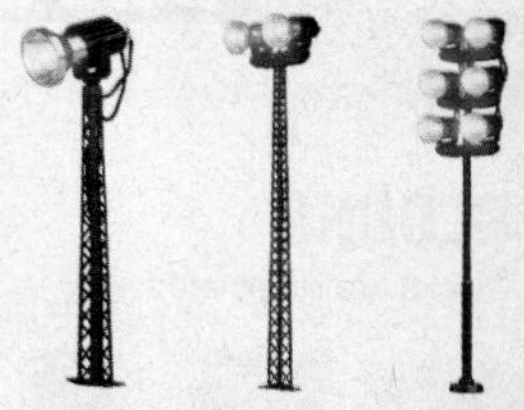
186-5581 186-5582 186-5583

186-5581 Single Light, 3-1/4" High **15.99**
186-5582 Double Light, 5-1/2" HIgh **28.99**
186-5583 Six Light, 6" High **57.99**

186-5370

186-3278

186-5370 Spotlight **12.99**
Approximate dimensions: .7 x .6 x .5"; pivots vertically.
186-3278 Spare Bulb pkg(2) **8.99**

RELAYS

WITH TWO CONTACTS

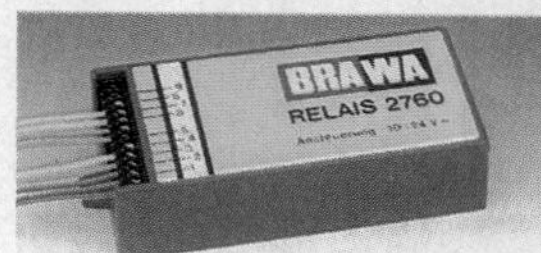

186-2760 47.99
Precision relay for reliable switching of signals, electromagnetic and motor drives. Two separate inputs. Power supply 10 to 24V AC. Switching current max. 60 mA. Contact load approximately 3A per contact. Voltage up to 24V AC or DC. Operated by momentary contact, track contact or reed contact.

WITH THREE CONTACTS

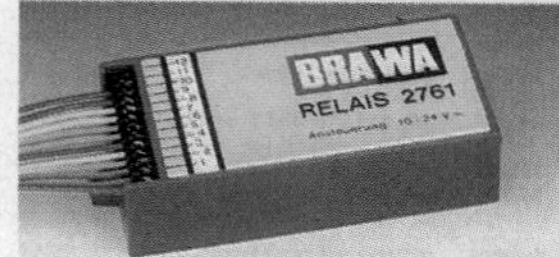

186-2761 62.99
Same as #186-2760, but with a third contact.

BRAWA

CLOCKS

Clocks are illuminated.

186-5361 186-5761 186-5340

186-5361 Historic Wall Clock-Baden-Baden **15.99**
With adjustable hands.

186-5761 Kiosk with Clock, 1-1/2" High **24.99**
With adjustable hands.

186-5340 Station/Yard Clock, 3" High **15.99**
With adjustable hands.

186-5294 186-5362 186-5366

186-5294 Clock w/DB/S Bahn Signs, 2-1/8" High **17.99**

186-5362 Baden-Baden Clock w/3 Faces, 2-1/2" High **35.99**
With adjustable hands.

186-5366 Berlin Stettin Station Clock, 3-1/4" High **29.99**
With adjustable hands.

186-5260 186-5261 186-5290

186-5260 Platform Clock, 2" High **8.99**

186-5261 Wall Clock **8.99**
Horizontal or vertical mounting. Frame diameter approximately 1/2".

186-5290 Platform Clock w/Train Direction Signs, 2" High **24.99**

186-5265 186-5368 186-5495

186-5265 Station Platform Clock **10.99** ***NEW***

186-5368 With Lattice Mast & Platform, 4-1/2" High **21.99**

186-5495 Platform Light w/Clock, 2-3/4" High **15.99**

SIGNS

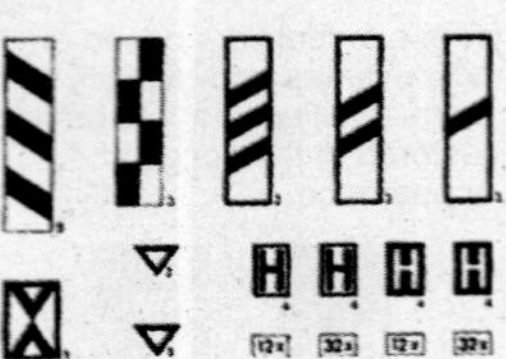

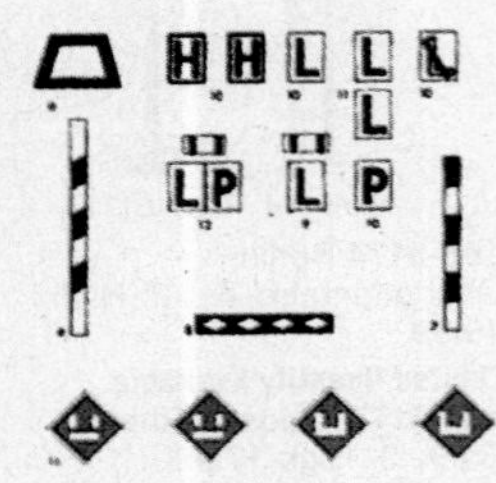

186-8618

186-5295

186-8618 Advance Warning Signs **11.99**
Set includes all types of trackside signs used by the DB. Posts are molded in black plastic; signs are printed in full color with self-adhesive backing.

Limited Quantity Available
Indicates where reserved seat or through cars will stop at station platforms. Illuminated, installs under platform roof. Includes decals "A" to "E"; approx. 1/2 x 1/2".

186-5295 U-Bahn Sign **7.49**
Illuminated, hanging mount.

Signal kits include an assortment of number and ID plates, plus fiber optics. Can be fully illuminated using a LED light source. Detailed white-metal castings.

We have worked closely with this manufacturer to provide accurate delivery information at the time this catalog was published. Items listed in blue ink may not be available at all times. Current delivery information, along with a list of in-stock products for this line, can be found on our Web site at www.walthers.com.

SEARCHLIGHT SIGNALS

215-130 215-1301

215-130 Dwarf Type SA; w/Safety Light **2.75**

215-1301 Dwarf Type SA, w/Sighting Alignment **2.75**

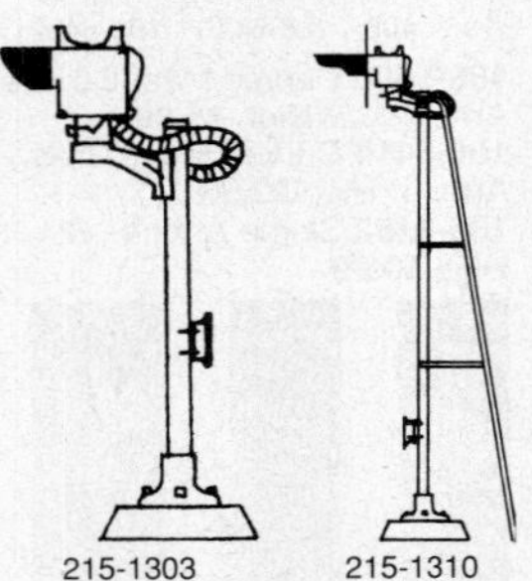

215-1303 215-1310

215-1303 Siding Signal, Low **5.00**

215-1310 With Footrest & Ladder **7.25**

WIG-WAG SIGNALS

215-115 215-116

215-115 Short **2.75**

215-116 Tall **3.25**

FIBER OPTICS

215-10 .010 Diameter, 12' **1.50**

215-20 .020 Diameter, 12' **1.75**

215-30 .030 Diameter, 12' **2.50**

215-40 .040 Diameter, 6' **2.50**

215-50 .050 Diameter, 6' **2.75**

215-60 .060 Diameter, 6' **4.00**

JACKETED FIBER OPTIC BUNDLES

215-87 .087 x 4' (16 Fibers of .010 Dia.) **5.50**

215-117 .117 x 4' (32 Fibers of .010 Dia.) **5.75**

215-140 .140 x 3' (19 Fibers of .020 Dia.) **4.50**

SIGNAL FINIALS PKG(6) EA 1.50

215-1361 Pointed, For Side Mount Signal Head

215-1362 Round, For Side Mount Signal Head

215-1363 Teardrop, For Side Mount Signal Head

215-1364 Dome, For Front Mount Signal Head

TRACK DETAILS

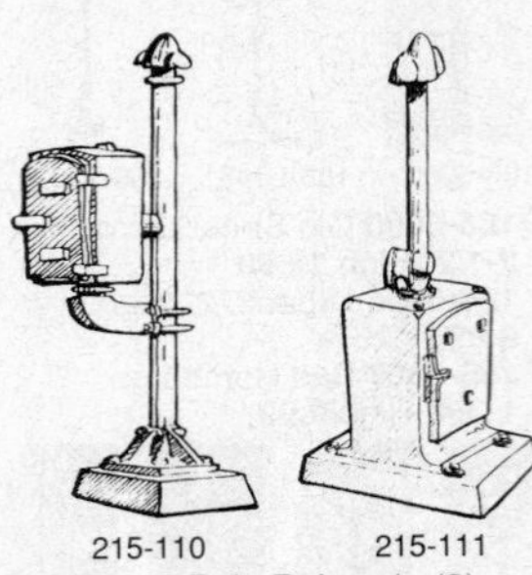

215-110 215-111

215-110 Pole Relay pkg(3) **1.95**

215-111 Ground Relay Box & Mast pkg(3) **2.50**

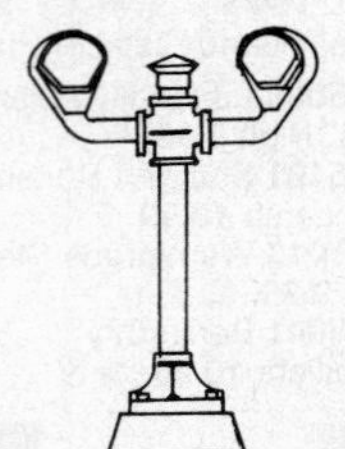

215-112 Block Indicator pkg(4) **1.95**

215-113 Trackside Battery Box pkg(6) **1.95**

SWITCH MOTOR

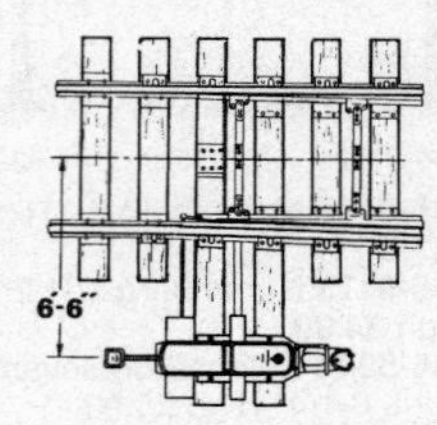

215-135 Switch Motor pkg(2) **2.75**
For installation in signal kits.

Information STATION

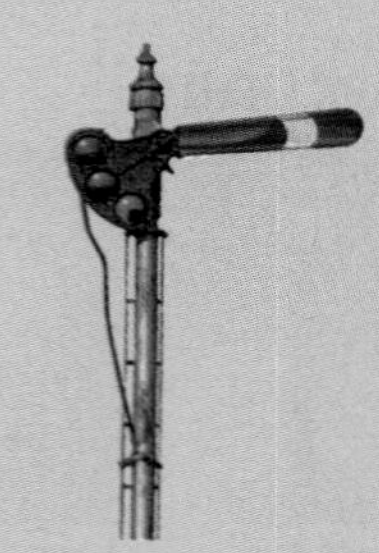

Custom Signs

It doesn't take much to figure out that every model railroader's layout is different and every model railroader is trying to achieve something unique with that layout. Personalizing a diorama is half the fun of building it. For those who chose to set their layouts in the past, here's an idea. Create billboards and signs from old magazine adds. Sure you can buy packaged signs, but they are mass produced, insuring that countless of others will have the same signs in their layout as you. By making your own signs from old magazines you'll be able to get exactly what you want for your layout and also have a one of a kind set-up.

The magazines are easy enough to find. They can often be found at rummage sales or used book stores and prices will vary. Once the magazines are obtained, flip through them looking for the right sized ads that you will be able to use as billboards or signs. Cut out the selected ad, paste it where you want to, weather and seal it and you have just created a custom sign that fits perfectly into the time frame of your layout.

Circuitron products are constructed on printed circuit boards and are designed to snap into a section of Circuitron's PCMT (Printed Circuit Mounting Track). Solid state integrated circuit technology. Connections to any Circuitron printed circuit board can be made using solderless connectors or by soldering the leads directly to the terminals on the board. Complete instructions are included.

We have worked closely with this manufacturer to provide accurate delivery information at the time this catalog was published. Items listed in blue ink may not be available at all times. Current delivery information, along with a list of in-stock products for this line, can be found on our Web site at www.walthers.com.

PRINTED CIRCUIT MOUNTING TRACK (PCMT)

800-9506 PCMT, 6" **4.95**
Plastic assembly provides simple, snap-in mounting of all Circuitron printed circuit boards. Prepunched with mounting holes; can be mounted using screws, adhesive, or double-backed tape. After PCMT is mounted, circuit boards simply snap into the track and can easily be removed for service.

BLOCK OCCUPANCY DETECTION UNITS

Tiny Opto-Sensors detect train movement. Sensors mount between the rails and activate circuitry when shaded by a passing train. Independent of track power, rolling stock requires no modifications. Sensors fit between HO Scale ties and may be ballasted over in most cases. Circuitry is extremely sensitive and will operate properly under very low levels of room light.

BD-1 OPTICAL DETECTORS

Positive indication whenever a section of a layout is occupied by rolling stock. Contains all circuitry to power two-color block signals at each end of the protected block. Will give proper indications if a train leaves a block by backing out. No modifications to rolling stock needed. Completely bi-directional. No additional driver boards or relays are needed. 250 ma. output can power lamp or LED-type signals. Requires 6-20V DC input. Independent of track power. Compatible with radio or carrier control systems.

800-5501 BD-1 Optical Detector **29.95**
800-5521 BD-1HD Optical Detector **32.95**
Same as #800-5501, but with 500 ma. output.

BD-2 CURRENT SENSING DETECTION UNIT

Detects current drawn by a locomotive or lighted piece of rolling stock. Unpowered equipment can be detected by using metal wheelsets with resistors connected across the insulator. Will directly drive 2-color lamp or LED-type block signals. 250 ma. output (500 ma. for BD-2HD). Circuit boards are designed for easy daisy chain wiring of multiple blocks and will snap into a section of Printed Circuit Mounting Track. Requires 10-18V DC. Works in any scale and with most track power, systems including most forms of carrier control.

800-5502 BD-2, 3 amp Capacity **18.95**
800-5522 BD-2HD, 6 amp Capacity **22.95**

ROLLING STOCK DETECTION UNIT

DT-4 ROLLING STOCK DETECTOR

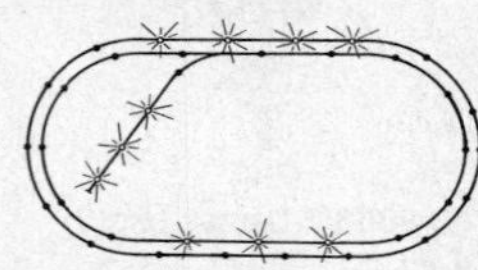

800-5204 34.95
Ideal for spotting a hidden train or piece of rolling stock. Four independent detection units combined onto one circuit board, can be used separately or together to control external devices. Supplied with four Opto-Sensors that mount between rails to detect movement. When train covers a sensor, the unit activates any connected DC accessory, such as an indicator light on a control panel. Independent sensitivity controls are provided for adjusting each Opto-Sensor to lighting conditions. Constructed on a 3 x 3" printed circuit board. Requires 10-18V DC. Independent of track power. Compatible with radio or carrier control systems.

GRADE CROSSING DETECTION UNITS

Specifically designed for use at grade crossings, using Opto-Sensors to detect the train. Output controls flashers, gates, bells, etc. Note: DT-1, DT-2 and DT-3 Detection Units require an Alternating Flasher Unit (FL-2 or FL-3) to operate flashing lamps.

DT-1 DETECTION UNIT

800-5201 29.95
Detects train when an Opto-Sensor is covered. Senses track polarity and activates only the Opto-Sensors for the direction of travel. Always turns off after the last piece of rolling stock clears the crossing. Includes four Opto-Sensors. Note: DT-1 cannot detect a short train or loco if it falls between Opto-Sensors. Use in any scale with DC track power. 2 x 3" printed circuit board. 10-18V AC or DC input.

DT-2 DETECTION UNIT

800-5202 DT-2 Logic Grade Crossing Detection Unit **42.95**
Full logic system duplicates prototype grade crossing action. Does not require sensor to stay covered to activate. Integrated memory keeps output "on" until last car clears the crossing. Activates whenever a train approaches from either direction. If train stops short then backs away, unit will detect that and turn output "off." Independent of train length - will detect a short train even if it falls between Opto-Sensors. Includes four Opto-Sensors. 3 x 4" printed circuit board. 10-18V AC or DC input.

DT-3 SINGLE-DIRECTION DETECTION UNIT

800-5203 21.95
Single-direction unit for crossings where bi-directional detection is unnecessary, such as a mainline with trains traveling in only one direction. Operates with any length train. Completely independent of track power. Use in any scale. Requires 10-18V AC or DC input.

DF-1 DETECTOR WITH FLASHER

800-5250 34.95
Single-direction grade crossing detector with alternating flasher on one circuit board. Operates with any length train. Independent of track power. Use in any scale. Can power two 250 ma loads (5 grain-of-wheat lamps or 10 LEDs per side). 10-18V AC or DC input.

DRIVERS

SD-1 SIGNAL DRIVER

800-5510 12.95
Logic and output drivers to control any 3 lamp, 3 color block signal. Will power LED or lamp-type signals. LED-type requires common positive (anode) connection of all LEDs. Detection circuits (such as BD-1) are needed for a minimum of 3 blocks to display all three aspects. 10-18V DC input.

SD-2 3-POSITION SEMAPHORE DRIVER

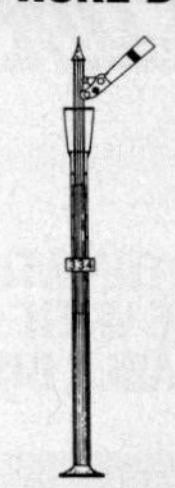

800-5520 19.95
Use with the Tortoise Switch Machine and an upper or lower quadrant semaphore-style signal. Includes all the logic circuitry to drive the signal to all three positions. Works with BD-1 or BD-2 Block Occupancy Detectors. A minimum of two blocks must have detectors installed for the SD-2 to indicate all three positions. Requires 10-18V DC power.

SD-3 SIGNAL DRIVER

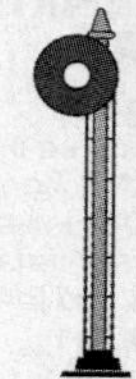

800-5530 15.95
Drives any single target tri-color LED-type signal to red, green and amber aspects. Will not drive lamp signals. Amber hue fully adjustable. May be controlled by 3 position switch or automatically by detection circuits such as BD-1 (minimum of 3 blocks required). 10-18V AC or DC.

TRAIN CONTROL CIRCUITS

AR-1 AUTOMATIC REVERSING CIRCUIT

800-5400 39.95
Changes direction when the Opto-Sensor is covered. Use for test track, window display, mine train or automatic reverse loop operation. Pushbuttons can be connected for manual reversing. Requires 12V DC power source. Constructed on 2 x 3" printed circuit board.

AR-1CC REVERSE LOOP CONTROLLER

800-5400 39.95
Same as AR-1, but with four Opto-Sensors for automatic reverse loop switching on command control layout. Trains must be shorter than loop for proper operation.

AR-2 AUTOMATIC REVERSE WITH ADJUSTABLE DISPLAY

800-5401 49.95
Same as AR-1, but with adjustable delay to hold train at sensor before reversing. Adjustable delay from 1 second to over 1 minute. Can be connected to pushbutton or DT-4 to permit stops and delays without reversing. Requires 12-18V AC or DC power supply. Constructed on 3 x 3" printed circuit board.

AS-1 AUTOMATIC SLOWDOWN

800-5601 16.95
Slows train speed in a section of track. Bi-directional; use with AC or DC power. Output is continuously variable between 1/4 and 3/4 of the input voltage.

TD-1 TIME DELAY CIRCUIT

800-5602 24.95
Use with Detection Units for adjustable delay with self-contained relay on the output. Great for automatic stop at a station or siding. Time delay adjustable from 0 to over 1 minute. Requires 12V DC power supply.

SOUND

BELL RINGER CIRCUITS

Connects to Detection Unit to simulate crossing bell. Rate and volume are adjustable.

BR-1 includes separate 2-1/2" bell. BR-2 includes circuit board, but no bell (use any dual-coil electromagnetic doorbell). Designed for under layout mounting. Use with 10-18V AC or DC.
800-5700 BR-1 with Bell **42.95**
800-5702 BR-2 less Bell **26.95**

ALTERNATING FLASHERS

Use to flash signals, emergency vehicle lights, signs and more.

FL-2 ALTERNATING FLASHER

Flashes LEDs or lamps. Connects to Detection Units. Maintains constant flash rate. 1.5 x 3" printed circuit board. Requires 10-18V AC or DC input. 250 ma. output.

800-5102 FL-2 **16.95**
800-5122 FL-2HD **18.95**
Same as FL-2, but with 500 ma. load capability per side. Adaptable for all scales.

FL-3 ALTERNATING FLASHER

800-5103 29.95
Heavy-duty, with three control terminals and three outputs. Independent flashing at up to three locations. Outputs can control 250 ma. Can flash LEDs or lamps. 3 x 3" printed circuit board. 10-18V AC or DC input.

CROSSING SIGNALS

CROSSBUCKS

Highly detailed, low-current LEDs for pure color and long life. Available assembled and painted, or as a kit (requires soldering and painting). Use with FL-2 or FL-3.

800-8001 Assembled pkg(2) **24.95**
800-8011 Kit pkg(2) **14.95**

CROSSING GATES

Scale size with slow motion drive for prototypical action. Available assembled and painted (requires mounting and adjustment) or in kits. Use with crossbucks above. Requires 12V DC power supply.
800-8005 Assembled pkg(2) **44.95**
800-8015 Kit pkg(2) **29.95**

COMBINATION SIGNALS

Modern highway type with single gate and crossbuck on post. Assembled and painted (requires mounting and adjustment) with front (2-Lamp) or front and rear facing (4-Lamp) signals.

800-8006 2-Lamps pkg(2) **74.95**
800-8007 4-Lamps pkg(2) **94.95**

GATE DRIVER CIRCUIT

800-5550 14.95
Use with detection circuits and alternating flashers to automate 8000 series gates. Adjustable speed and flasher hold-on for realistic operation. 10-18V DC input.

HIDDEN ACCESSORY SWITCHES

On-Off reed switches for strobe flashers, marker lights or other electrical accessories. Operated by holding a magnet near the loco or car. Nothing to detract from the look of the model. Kits contain a subminiature reed switch and a tiny bias magnet. RS-1 requires adjustment before mounting. RS-2 requires no adjustment.
800-9101 RS-1 Kit **4.95**
800-9102 RS-2 Kit **6.95**
800-9100 Magnet **1.50**
800-9103 Subminiature Slide Switch pkg(2) **2.95**

TURNOUT CONTROL CIRCUITS

SNAPPER SWITCH MACHINE POWER SUPPLY

800-5303 29.95
Solid state, provides positive power to dual-coil switch machines. Protects from burnout due to stuck pushbuttons, short circuits, etc. Operates off accessory terminals of power pack or transformer up to 25V. 24V input can activate 5 to 10 coils simultaneously if connected to same control. Instant recycle time. Includes a section of Printed Circuit Mounting Track (PCMT).

3 AMP DIODE

800-9350 pkg(2) **1.50**
Heavy-duty, silicon rectifiers with 50V rating, axial leads and surge rating of 300 amps. Use in turnout control diode matrix with Snapper Power Supply or wire across a gap in the track to stop a train automatically.

TC-1 AUTOMATIC TURNOUT CONTROL

800-5605 27.95
Activates dual-coil switch machine when used with DT-4. Momentary pulse when detection unit is activated, protects from burnout. Can be used to control both directions. Requires 10-18V AC or DC input. The higher the voltage input, the greater the output power. Recycle time on each side is 1-2 seconds.

TC-2 TURNOUT DIRECTION ALTERNATOR

800-5606 29.95
Automatically alternates turnout direction when used with DT-4. Sends momentary pulse to one coil of the switch machine, throwing the turnout in one direction. Next activation throws it in the other direction. Allows train to travel alternate routes automatically. Requires 10-18V AC or DC input.

TC-3 AUTOMATIC TORTOISE CONTROL

800-5615 17.95
Automatically activates Tortoise switch machine when used with Detection Unit. Two drive inputs control direction. Only momentary inputs are required; can be used for pushbutton or matrix control. Requires 12-18V DC.

TC-4 TORTOISE DIRECTION ALTERNATOR

800-5616 18.95
Similar to #800-5606, but output is designed to drive the Tortoise switch machine. Requires 12-18V DC.

PB-1 POWER BOOSTER

800-5603 11.95
Connects directly to the output of any Detection Unit to raise load capacity to 1 amp DC. Can only be used for DC circuits. Up to 50 Power Boosters can be controlled by one Detection Unit. Requires 10-18V AC or DC input.

ER-1 EXTERNAL RELAY

800-5604 SPDT **13.95**
Single pole, double throw, 6 amp relay mounted on a circuit board, with driver circuitry to be directly connected to the output of any Detection Unit. Provides high current, bi-directional contacts for train control. Ideal for use with Block Occupancy Detectors to power blocks for automatic train control. Requires 12V DC power supply.

ER-2 EXTERNAL RELAY

800-5624 DPDT **19.95**
Double pole, double throw version of ER-1 with 2 amp rating.

POWER SUPPLIES

Most Circuitron accessories operate off AC or DC , but perform best with a DC supply. These units convert power from AC to DC, for improved operation and include a section of PCMT.

PS-1 CONVERTER

800-5301 Filtered AC to DC Converter **14.95**
Highly filtered AC to DC converter. Maximum load capacity 1 amp, maximum input voltage 22V AC. Output is not regulated; voltage will vary depending upon input voltage and output load. (Requires transformer or power pack for AC input.)

PS-2 CONVERTER

800-5302 Filtered & Regulated AC to DC Converter **24.95**

PS-2A CONVERTER & REGULATOR

800-5305 26.95
Self-contained AC to DC converter with adjustable output between 1.25 and 12V DC. Maximum continuous current output in excess of one amp. Ideal for powering any low current DC accessories, including 1.5V micro-lamps. AC or unfiltered DC input should be about 5-6V higher for maximum current output. Input voltage up to 22V, but may result in reduced current available a the output, particularly at lower voltage settings.

INTERFACE CIRCUITS

Circuit boards change polarity so different electronic products can be used together.

800-5271 LT-1 Positive Logic Translator **8.95**
800-5272 LT-2 Negative Logic Translator **8.95**

ACCESSORIES

IN-LINE FUSE HOLDER

800-9601 In-line Fuse Holder **2.00**
Accepts any standard length, 1/4" diameter fuse. With wire leads.

DIODES

800-9350 3 amp pkg(2) **1.50**
800-9351 1 amp pkg(6) **1.50**
800-9352 6 amp pkg(2) **2.95**
800-935012 3 amp pkg(12) **6.95**
800-935212 6 amp pkg(12) **12.95**

OPTO-SENSORS

For use with all Circuitron Detection Circuits. .185" diameter.

800-9201 Single **3.95**
800-9202 Two-Pack **7.50**
800-9206 Six-Pack **19.95**

DETAILS WEST

SWITCH STANDS

253-914 235-915

253-914 Style 1 pkg(2) **2.95**
253-915 Style 2 pkg(2) **2.95**

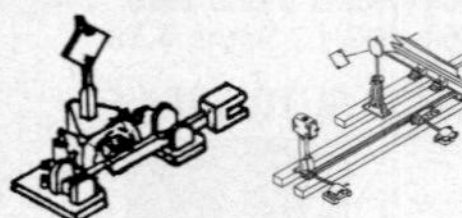

253-916 235-917

235-916 Ground Throw Switch 2 Sets **2.75**
235-917 With Interlock **3.75**

STREET LIGHT

464-732 Undecorated **1.00**
Nonoperating, cast-metal lamp post.

POSTERS EA 1.95

Each set includes 17 to 20 original color posters.

464-906 Set #1

464-908 Set #2

464-910 Set #3

464-912 Set #4

STREET SIGNS

464-914 OSHA/Street Signs (2 sets) **1.00**

BILLBOARDS

Billboards for Franz Falk Brewery. Prototype dimensions.

464-916 22' 6" x 14' 6" **1.00**
464-918 42' 6" x 27' **2.95**

WARNING SIGNS

464-930 "Keep out," "Danger," "Slow," etc. **1.00**

DECAL SET

464-1115 Frank's New Deal Garage **5.95**
Color decal set.

FALLER

IMPORTED FROM GERMANY BY WALTHERS

Assembled plastic models molded in realistic colors.

TRAFFIC SIGNS

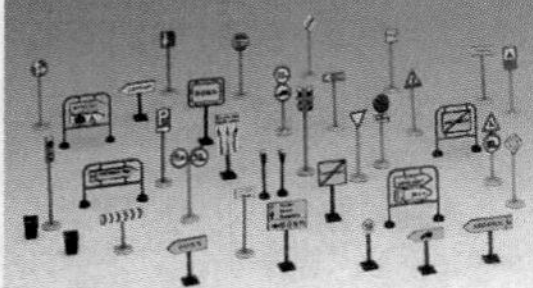

272-578 17.99
City signs, direction signs, traffic signs and lights, parking meters and waste baskets.

272-594 German Traffic Signs 1948-1977 **11.99**
272-595 European Traffic Signs 1977-1985 **11.99**

DRY TRANSFER LETTERING EA 6.99

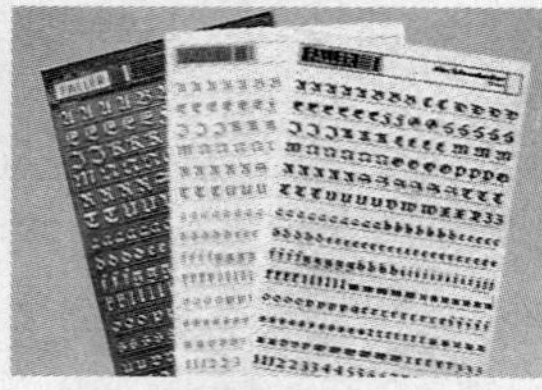

Each set includes a sheet of white, gold and black letters.

272-692 .2" (5mm) High Letters
272-693 .14" (3.5mm) High Letters

International Hobby Corp.

Easy-to-build precolored plastic models.

SIGNALS

CROSSBUCK SIGNALS

348-5202 Operating pkg(2) **39.98**
Includes flashing red LEDs, realistic bell sound, optical sensors and hook-up wires.

348-4550 Nonoperating pkg(2) **2.98**

CROSSING GATES/ CROSS BUCKS

348-422300 pkg(12) **1.98**

SIGNS & TRAFFIC LIGHTS

348-422307 pkg(12) **1.98**

BLINKING BEACON LIGHTS EA 6.98

Blinking unit with LED.

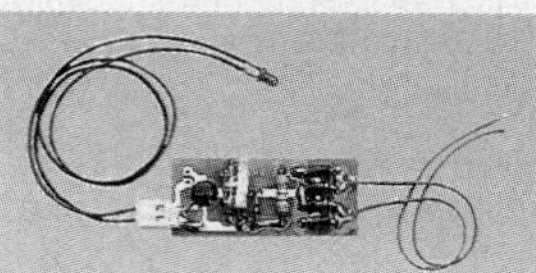

348-5200 Red
348-5201 Yellow

SIGNAL BRIDGES EA 9.98

Designed to fit a four-track layout but can be easily modified to fit fewer tracks. Target faces for the appropriate railroad are included. Extra piping is included to hide wiring when installing LEDs (not included).

348-5011 PRR
348-5012 B&O
348-5013 N&W
348-5014 UP/DRGW
348-5015 Universal/All Other Signal Faces

TARGET FACES PKG(2) EA .98

All target faces accept 2mm LEDs (not included).

348-4421 348-4422

348-4421 2 Aspect
348-4422 3 Aspect

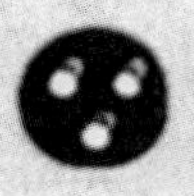

348-4423 348-4424

348-4423 3 Aspect Triangular
348-4424 3 Aspect Sunbonnet

348-4425 348-4426 348-4427

348-4425 PRR
348-4426 B&O
348-4427 N&W

DETAIL SETS

348-4551 Railroad Details **2.98**
Includes block signal (less target face), trackside instrument case, line side call box, relay cabinet and end-of-track bumper.

JL INNOVATIVE DESIGN

These full-color posters and signs add color and life to layouts of any era. Printed on two 4 x 5-1/2" heavy paper sheets. Application and weathering instructions included.

POSTERS & SIGNS

CONSUMER PRODUCTS EA 2.89 (UNLESS NOTED)

361-182 1940s & 1950s Household (41 signs)

361-185 1940s-1960s Alcohol/Tobacco/Chewing Gum (40 signs)

361-197 1930s-1960s Vintage Soft Drink (72 signs)

361-282 1940s & 1950s Consumer Products (42 signs)

361-285 1890s-1920s Turn of the Century pkg(40)

361-297 1930s- 1950s Soft Drink Series II

361-322 1930s-1950s Country Store **3.49**

361-682 Consumer Signs/Posters 1940s-50s

FEED & SEED EA 2.89

361-183 1940s & 1950s Farm Implement (54 signs)
361-383 1950s-Present Grain Elevator
361-483 1950s-Present Grain Elevator II

TRANSPORTATION EA 2.89 (UNLESS NOTED)

361-204 1900s-1960s Vintage Motorcycle & Auto (63 signs)

361-283 1940s & 1950s Planes/Trains/Industrial (55 signs)

361-304 Motorcylces 1920s Up **3.49** ***NEW***

361-404 Auto 1940s-1950s **3.49** ***NEW***

GAS STATIONS

361-184 1940s & 1950s Gas Station & Oil (41 signs) **2.89**

361-284 1940s-1960s (55 signs) **2.89**

361-384 Series III **2.89**
Signs are printed on heavy paper and measure approximately 3-1/8" wide and 1-5/8" high.

1930S-1950S EA 3.49

361-484 Texaco ***NEW***

361-485 Mobil ***NEW***

361-486 Sinclair ***NEW***

361-487 Phillips ***NEW***

ROAD SIGNS EA 2.89

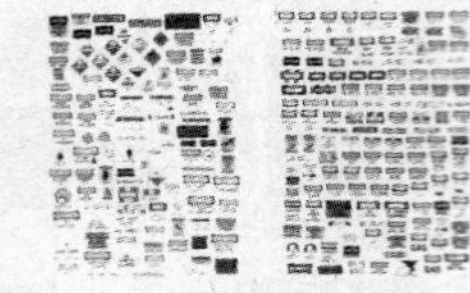

361-196 Danger/Warning (250 signs)

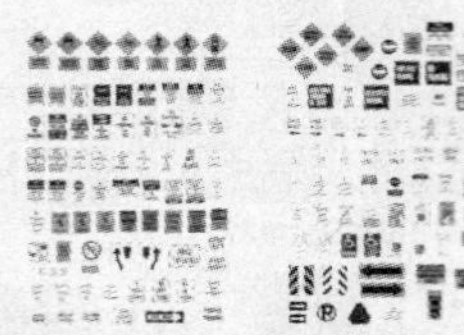

361-202 Uncommon Street & Parking (150 signs)

SALOON/TAVERN SIGNS EA 3.49

361-332 Series 1 1900-1920

361-333 Series 2 1930-1950

BILLBOARD SIGNS

TRANSPORTATION

1940S & 1950S AUTOMOBILE

361-172 6 Signs **2.89**
361-173 12 Signs **4.59**

1960S AUTOMOBILE

361-174 361-175

361-174 5 Signs **2.89**
361-175 10 Signs **4.59**

1940S RAILROAD THEME

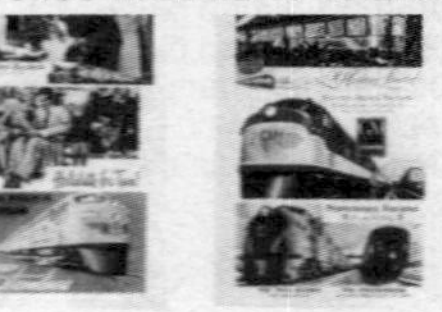

361-186 6 Signs **2.89**
361-187 12 Signs **4.59**

1940S AUTOMOBILE

361-188 6 Signs **2.89**
361-189 12 Signs **4.59**

1950S AUTO & TRANSPORTATION

361-192

361-193

361-192 6 Signs **2.89**
361-193 12 Signs **4.59**

1970S AUTOMOBILE

361-272 6 Signs **2.89**

JL INNOVATIVE DESIGN

361-273 12 Signs **4.89**

1960S AUTOMOBILE

361-274 6 Signs **2.89**

361-275 12 Signs **4.89**

CONSUMER PRODUCTS

1930S-1960S VINTAGE SOFT DRINK

361-198 6 Signs **2.89**
361-199 12 Signs **4.59**

1930S-1960S VINTAGE TOBACCO

361-212 6 Signs **2.89**
361-213 12 Signs **4.59**

RC COLA SIGNS

361-298 6 Signs **3.49**
361-299 12 Signs **5.49**

BILLBOARDS

TELEPHONE POLE

361-176 Two Billboards **7.49**
Kit includes Northeastern basswood, full-color auto billboard signs, four nonilluminated lamps per billboard, chain-link fencing and illustrated instructions.

SIDEWALK LATTICE

361-277 6.79
Kit includes Northeastern basswood for 4 signs, 4 full color billboard signs and molded plastic lattice.

FENCE BASE

361-276 pkg(2) **7.49**
Billboards feature movie stars promoting RC Cola.

CUSTOM 2-RAIL FENCING

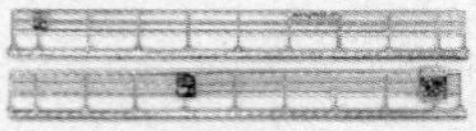

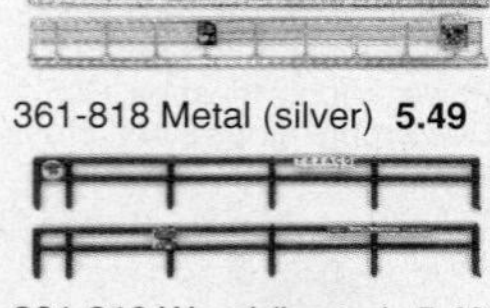

361-818 Metal (silver) **5.49**

361-819 Wood (brown) **5.49**

MISCELLANEOUS

TRAIN ORDER SIGNALS

361-252 Nonoperating **3.49**

CATALOG

361-5 Catalog #5 **3.50**

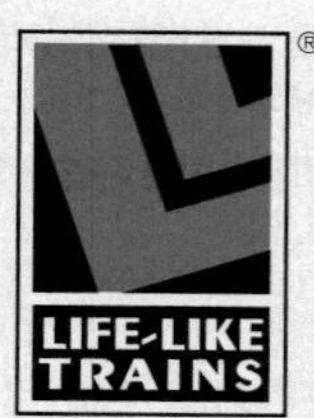

Assembled signals and accessories feature prepainted plastic parts.

SIGNALS

Operating signals include switches and wire.

RAILROAD SIGNALS

433-1180 Nonoperating pkg(8) **8.75**

CROSSING SIGNAL

433-1207 Operating **8.25**

SEMAPHORE

433-1261 Operating **11.00**

2-LIGHT TARGET

433-1262 Red/Green, Operating **11.00**

SIGNAL BRIDGE

433-8215 Nonoperating **7.00**
Includes five trackside signals and a power transformer.

LIGHT-UPS

Detailed, lighted accessories molded in appropriately colored plastic.

LIGHT POLES

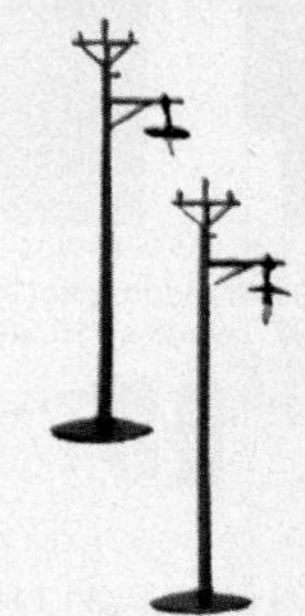

433-1206 pkg(3) **8.25**

LIGHTS

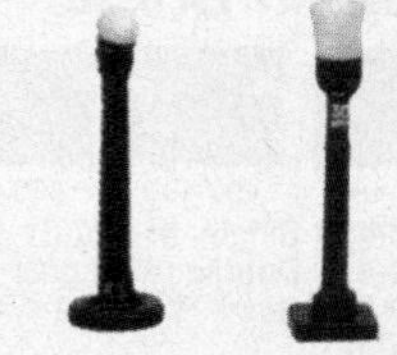

433-1208 433-1505

433-1208 Street pkg(3) **8.25**
433-1505 Gas pkg(3) **8.25**
433-1506 Highway pkg(3) **8.25**

SPOTLIGHTS

433-1209 pkg(2) **8.25**
Lights swivel up and down and turn 360°.

LIGHT-UP ASSORTMENT

433-1240 198.00 ***NEW***
Includes three each: 1201, 1206-1209 and 1504-1506.

EXPRESSWAY LIGHTS

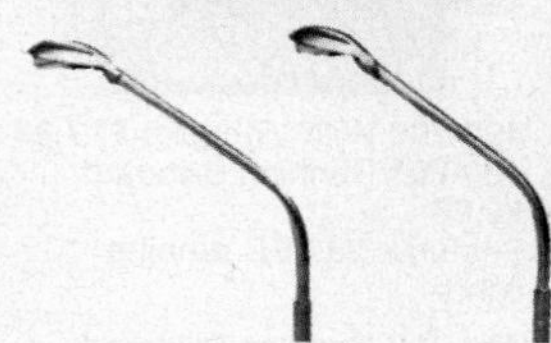

433-1504 pkg(2) **8.25**

ACCESSORIES

Appropriately colored, molded plastic accessories.

CITY SIDEWALKS

433-1121 8.75
Includes telephone poles, fire hydrants, trash cans, vending machines and telephone booth.

TELEPHONE POLES

433-1114 pkg(12) **8.75**

SIGNS

433-1115 Railroad pkg(19)
433-1116 Street & Highway pkg(24)

OPERATING ACCESSORIES

9" brass straight track included.

SWITCHMAN

433-8203 With Lighted Building **19.50**
Switchman emerges automatically from lighted shack as train nears, goes inside after last car passes.

CROSSING GATE

433-8209 12.50
Gate lowers automatically as train nears, raises after last car crosses.

POWER-LOC™ OPERATING ACCESSORIES

For use with Power-Loc track.

DUAL CROSSING GATE

433-21313 18.75
Safety gates lower to warn oncoming traffic as train approaches and remain down until the last car passes.

SWITCHMAN

433-21315 19.50
As train approaches grade crossing, switchman emerges from the lighted shack; goes back inside after the last car passes.

Assembled signals and lights are operating, handcrafted brass, unless noted.

SIGNALS

BLOCK EA 10.98 (UNLESS NOTED)

490-1451 pkg(6) **5.98**
Molded gray plastic. Three green and three red signal lights and two relay cabinets. Nonoperating.

490-1675

490-1680

490-1675 2 Indication
490-1676 2 Indication w/Relay
490-1677 3 Indication
490-1678 3 Indication w/ Relay
490-1679 3 Indication
490-1680 3 Indication
490-1682 2 Color w/Relay

MISCELLANEOUS

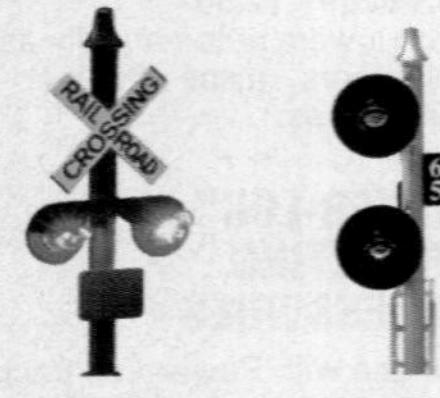

490-1681 490-1684

490-1681 Crossing Signal pkg(2) **13.98**
490-1684 North American Signal **11.98**

LIGHTS

SUBURBAN PKG(3) EA 6.98

490-593 Clear, 1-1/2"
490-594 Frosted, 1-1/2"

BOULEVARD PKG(3) EA 6.98

490-499

490-500

490-595

490-499 Square, Clear, 2"
490-500 Round, Clear, 2"
490-595 Round, Frosted, 2" Station Lamp

GLOBE POST LAMP

490-498 2" pkg(3) **6.98**

TRAFFIC

Lights include 4-way slide switch and red, green and amber bulbs. Painted and prewired.

490-596

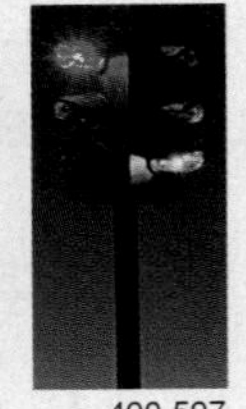
490-597

490-596 Standard pkg(2) **11.98**
490-597 Two-Way **10.98**

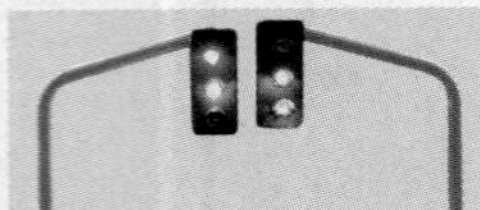

490-599 Left & Right **14.98**
490-5961 Standard **9.98**
490-5991 Left **9.98**
490-5992 Right **9.98**

HIGHWAY EA 6.98

490-495

490-496

490-497

490-495 Single, 4" pkg(3)
490-496 Double, 4" pkg(2)
490-497 Small Single, 2-1/4" pkg(3)

GAS PKG(3) EA 6.98

490-493 Clear, 1-1/2"
490-494 Frosted, 1-1/2"

CLOCK

490-598 Lighted, 2-Sided pkg(2) **8.98**

SIGNS

BILLBOARDS

490-700 With Light pkg(2) **7.98**
490-701 Running Billboard **29.98**
Features 28 LED running lights.

490-703 Running Billboard w/Base **29.98**
Features 28 LED running lights.

GAS STATION SIGNS PKG(2) EA 6.98

Illuminated, brass parts.

490-704 Shell
490-705 Exxon
490-706 Gulf

ROAD & RAIL SIGNS

490-1454 pkg(24) **5.98**

MOVIE POSTERS PKG(8) EA 6.98

490-702 1924-1940 Era
490-7021 1940-1960 Era

TELEPHONE POLES

490-1452 pkg(12) **5.98**

"N"-WAY PRODUCTS

Operating signals, lighting kits and accessories.

We have worked closely with this manufacturer to provide accurate delivery information at the time this catalog was published. Items listed in blue ink may not be available at all times. Current delivery information, along with a list of in-stock products for this line, can be found on our Web site at www.walthers.com.

SIGNALS

CROSSING SIGNALS

Typical of many railroad standard crossing signals. Can be operated manually, mechanically or automatically by Train Detection Kit #535-400. The Flasher is powered by two 9V batteries or Power Supply Kit #535-425 and will operate up to six signals at one time.

535-151 With Flasher pkg(2) **22.95**
535-152 Signals Only pkg(2) **16.95**
535-155 Two Directions pkg(2) **28.95**
Same as #535-151, except each signal has two crossbucks and lights that flash in both directions.

BOULEVARD CROSSING

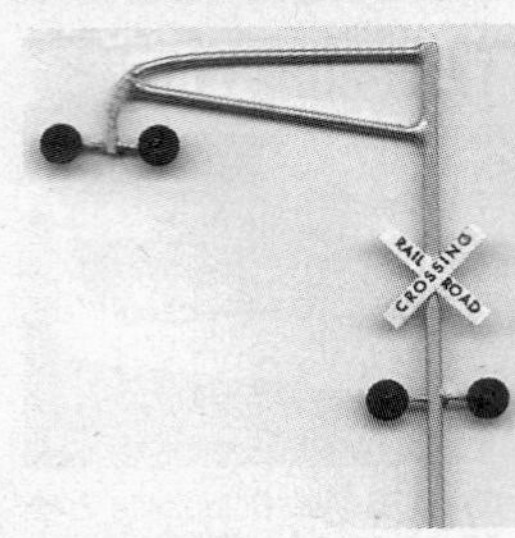

535-251 pkg(2) **28.95**
Stylized overhead "flashing" signal. Because of the number of lights on the signals, additional flashing crossing signals should not be used with this unit's flasher. The flasher is powered by two 9V batteries or Power Supply Kit #535-425.

RAILROAD CROSSING BELL

535-191 22.95
3" bell provides a loud, clear tone to be used with warning signals. Kit requires assembly of 110V components (included). Bell will operate in conjunction with Train Detection Kit #535-400.

TRAIN DETECTION KIT

535-400 14.95
Kit will operate N-Way and other signals in N or HO. It will make two complete detection units that will activate signals at two locations. Magnets are used to activate reed switches you mount in the tracks. Kit requires soldering. Magnets, reed switches and wiring instructions included. Automatic block control requires extensive technical knowledge and a number of Train Detection Kits.

SEARCHLIGHT SIGNALS

These signals are used to indicate location and condition of manual or automatic blocks. Power supply must be 12V DC. Dropping resistors, brass ladder stock included.

535-351 Green-Red pkg(2) **14.95**
535-352 Red-Red pkg(2) **9.95**
535-353 Red pkg(2) **8.95**

535-354 Green-Yellow-Red pkg(2) **16.95**
Each color is separately controlled.

GAS STREET LIGHTS

535-851 Gas Street Lights pkg(5) 22.95
Turn of the century style, with a yellow LED light to give the realistic glow of a gas lamp.

FLICKERING FLAMES KIT

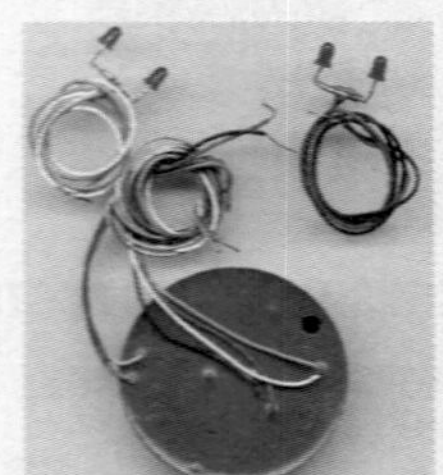

535-901 19.95
Can be used to simulate fires in buildings, sheds and homes. This hearth lighting unit is a solid state device made to flash two sets of dual LEDs to simulate the flames. Requires 12V transformer.

KEYSTONE LOCOMOTIVE WORKS

BLOCK SIGNAL

395-13 Old-Time Banjo Block Signal pkg(2) **7.95**
Kit contains metal pressure castings, brass rod and wire. Nonoperating.

KIBRI

IMPORTED FROM GERMANY BY WALTHERS

LIGHTS

Operating lights are constructed of appropriately colored plastic and include bulb and wiring.

405-5830 Platform Light Fixture (less pole) **19.99**

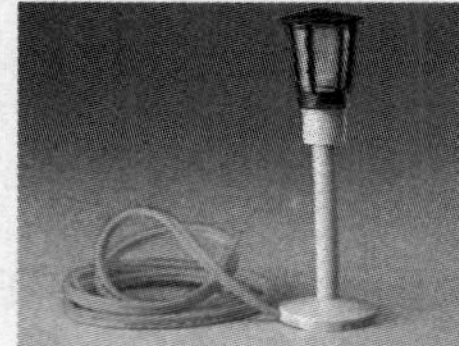

Limited Quantity Available
405-5660 Boulevard Lamp, 2-1/8" High **13.99**

NOCH

IMPORTED FROM WEST GERMANY BY WALTHERS

Molded in realistically colored plastic.

SIGNS

528-10860 Sign & Clock Assortment pkg(4) **6.99**
528-11290 Advertising Sign & Kiosk **9.99**
528-60511 Crash Barriers **8.99**
528-60521 Assorted Traffic Signs **13.99**

PREISER

SIGNS

Sign kits include styrene masts and adhesive signs.

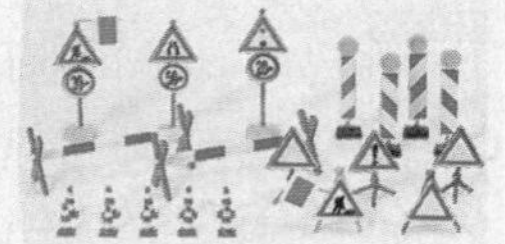

590-17176 Traffic & Construction Signs **18.99**

590-17211 1900s Era Signs for Buildings **19.99**

590-18203 Sign Assortment pkg(40) **11.99**

POLA

IMPORTED FROM GERMANY BY WALTHERS

STREET LIGHT & TELEPHONE POLE SETS

Operating street lights feature plastic construction. Sets include two street lights and six telephone poles. 14-19V.

578-70 Residential Street Lights **11.99**

578-71 Girder-Style Street Lights **11.99**

PIKESTUFF

CROSSBUCKS

541-1017 pkg(4) **2.99**
Set includes plastic molded parts, decals and assembly instructions.

Hot New Products Announced Daily! Visit Walthers Web site at **www.walthers.com**

Plastruct

Nonoperating lights are molded in styrene plastic, unless noted.

STREET LIGHTS

570-94802 1920s Era pkg(4) **4.00**

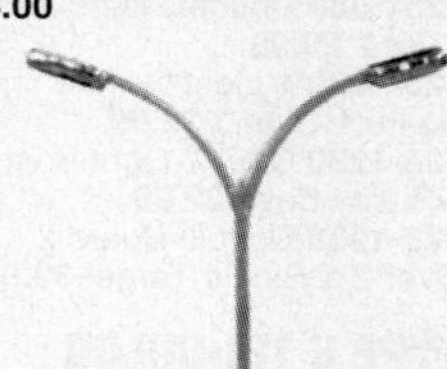

570-94808 1980s Era pkg(4) **3.75**

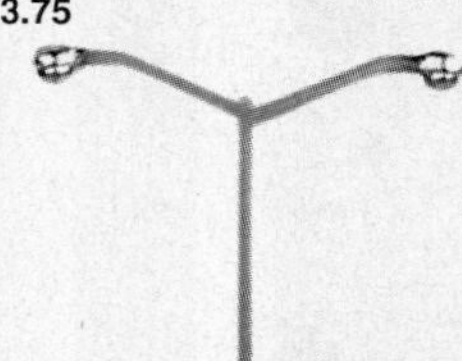

570-94812 1960s Era pkg(4) **3.75**

570-94816 1980s Era (metal) pkg(2) **8.00**

94821 94826

570-94821 4 Globe Walkway pkg(5) **14.00**
570-94826 3 Globe Walkway pkg(5) **14.00**

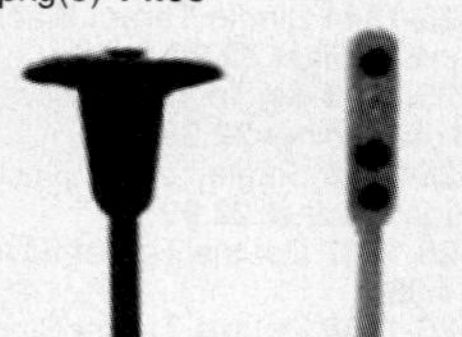

94829 94842

570-94829 Halogen Walkway pkg(5) **10.95**
570-94842 Traffic Signal pkg(5) **4.50**

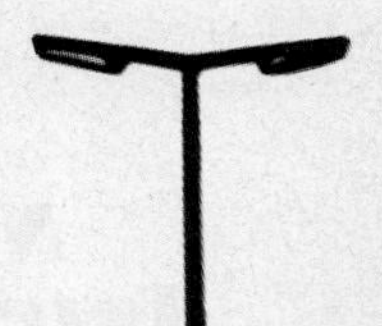

570-94831 1990s Era pkg(5) **10.95**

570-94836 1990s Era pkg(5) **10.95**

570-94852 Wood Phone Poles pkg(10) **6.25**

SIGNS

570-96052 Oil Company Decal Set pkg(2) **1.75**
Full-color logos and warning signs are a great detail for storage tanks, fences and structures. Each sheet features nine decals.

BILLBOARDS

570-1013 Billboards pkg(4) **10.95**
Scratch model kit contains enough materials to construct four modern, steel billboards, including posters.

N.J. International

SIGNALS & SIGNAL SYSTEMS

All brass construction, assembled, painted and lighted.

SEMAPHORES

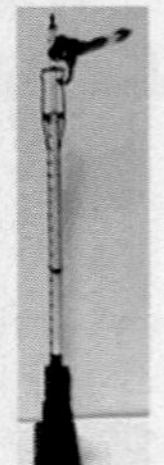

525-1000 3-Light Upper Quadrant **37.99**
525-1010 2-Light Lower Quadrant **29.99**

POSITION LIGHTS

525-1040 PRR 8-Light **39.99**
525-10411 PRR 8-Light Absolute Stop **39.99**
525-1210 B&O Color Position **29.99**

TYPE D COLOR LIGHTS

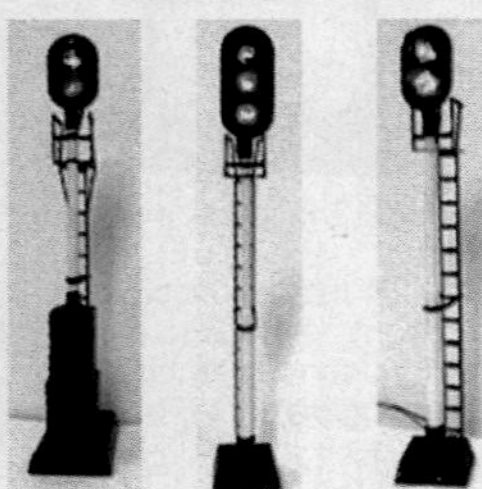

525-1020 525-1031 525-1081

525-1020 2-Light w/Relay Base **19.99**
525-1023 3-Light w/Relay Base **19.99**
525-1031 3-Light Board (black) **17.99**
525-1032 3-Light Board (silver) **17.99**
525-1033 Double Board 3 Over 3 **31.99**
525-1038 Double Board 3 Over 2 **29.99**
525-1081 2-Light Board (black) **16.99**
525-1082 2-Light Board (silver) **16.99**
525-1088 Double Board 2 Over 2 **29.99**
525-1089 1-Light Double Board 1 Over 1 **29.99**
525-1230 C&O 1-Light Board w/Relay Base **22.99**
525-1233 Double Board 2 Over 2 & Single Target **39.99**

TYPE G TRI-COLOR

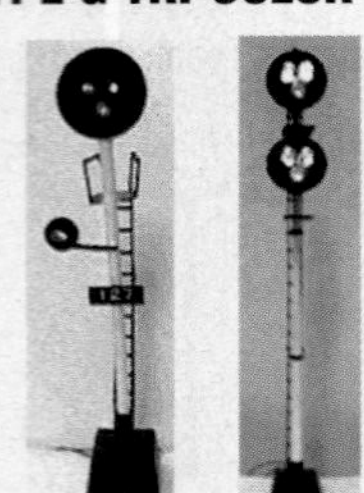

525-1050 525-1060

525-1050 3-Light Hooded Target **19.99**
525-1060 Double Target 3 Over 3 Light **29.99**

SA TYPE TARGET

Signals exact scale. All brass with bi-color LEDs.

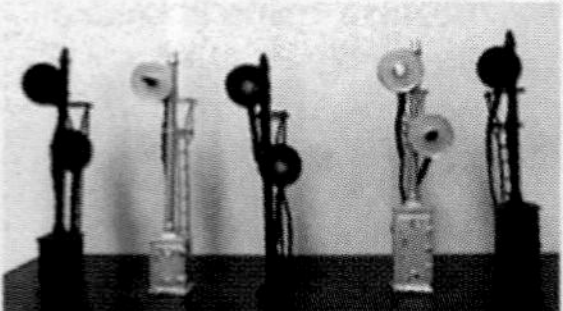

525-1341 Single Target Silver **19.99**
525-1342 Single Target Black **19.99**
525-1343 Single Target Silver Low Cabinet **22.99**
525-1344 Single Target Black Low Cabinet **22.99**
525-1345 Single Target Silver High Cabinet **22.99**
525-1346 Single Target Black High Cabinet **22.99**
525-1347 Double Target Silver **24.99**
525-1348 Double Target Black **24.99**
525-1349 Double Target Silver Low Cabinet **26.99**
525-1350 Double Target Black Low Cabinet **26.99**
525-1351 Double Target Silver High Cabinet **26.99**
525-1352 Double Target Black High Cabinet **26.99**

OTHER SA TARGET LIGHTS

525-1070 Double Single Target w/Relay Base **19.99**
525-1270 N&W 2-Light Target **19.99**
525-1280 Triple Target 3-Light **35.99**

SA SEARCHLIGHT

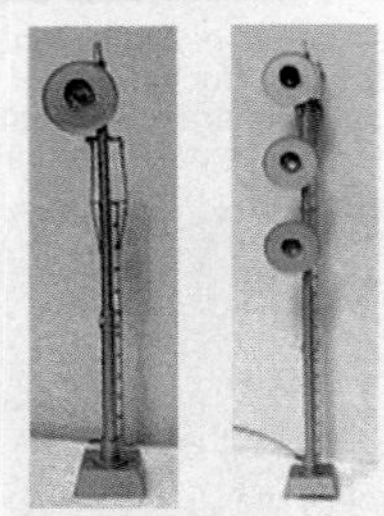

525-1200 525-1220

525-1200 1-Light Target w/Relay Base & Red/Green LEDs **26.99**
525-1220 Triple Single Target **19.99**

GROUND TYPE DWARF

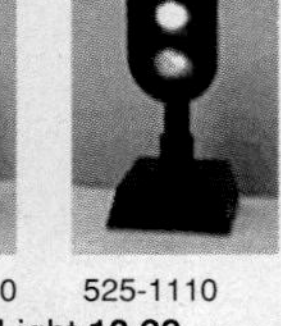

525-1100 525-1110

525-1100 2-Light **10.99**
525-1110 3-Light **11.99**
525-1130 3-Light Position LH **11.99**
525-1140 3-Light Position RH **11.99**

GROUND DWARF SIGNALS 14.99 PAIR

Exact scale, all brass, painted, with LEDs.

525-1290 Silver w/Red LED
525-1291 Black w/Red LED
525-1292 Silver w/Green LED
525-1293 Black w/Green LED
525-1294 Silver w/Amber LED
525-1295 Black w/Amber LED

TRAIN ORDER

525-1150 3-Light **24.99**

SIGNAL SYSTEMS

Realistic prototype operation, bi-directional indication, block occupancy indication to control panel, reverse loop operation, no track gaps required.

TWO LIGHT SYSTEM

525-8300 Signal Module w/Sensor **33.99**

THREE LIGHT SYSTEM

525-8330 Signal Module w/Sensor **48.99**

EXTRA ACTIVATING SENSORS

525-8301 CDS Sensor **3.79**
525-8306 CDS Sensor pkg(6) **19.99**

SIGNAL ACCESSORIES - BRASS

525-1337 Relay Cabinet-Silver Low pkg(2) **6.99**
525-1338 Relay Cabinet-Black Low pkg(2) **6.99**
525-1339 Relay Cabinet-Silver High pkg(2) **6.99**
525-1340 Relay Cabinet-Black High pkg(2) **6.99**
525-1800 Line Shed pkg(2) **6.99**
525-1820 Relay Box pkg(2) **4.99**
525-1886 Ladder w/Loop Top pkg(2) **4.99**
525-1887 Ladder Straight pkg(2) **4.99**
525-4410 Signal Mounting Stems pkg(4) **2.99**
525-4440 Track Clips pkg(2) **1.99**

SIGNAL DISC HEADS-BRASS

525-4100 Semaphore 3-Light **7.99**
525-4101 Semaphore 2-Light **6.99**
525-4103 3-Light Board **2.39**
525-4104 PRR 8-Light **4.99**
525-4106 3-Light Target **2.59**
525-4107 Small Single Target **2.09**
525-4108 2-Light Board **2.29**
525-4122 Single Target **2.19**
525-4130 N&W 2-Light **2.29**

SIGNAL BRIDGE KITS

Injection molded plastic.

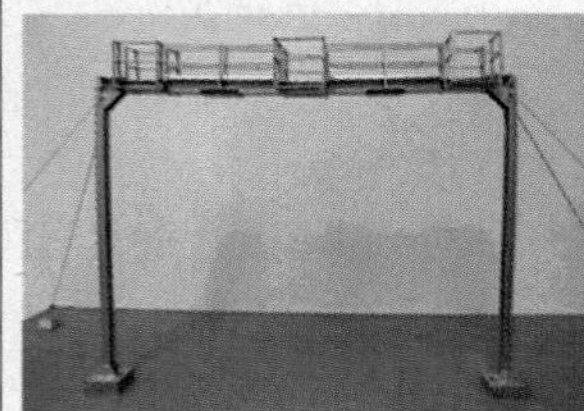

525-4006 I-Beam 2 Track **13.95**

CANTILEVER SIGNAL BRIDGES

525-4001 1 Track Silver **12.95**
525-4002 1 Track Black **12.95**
525-4003 2 Track Silver **13.95**
525-4004 2 Track Black **13.95**

SIGNAL MASTS

Brass, for mounting on all signal bridges.

525-13020 2 Targets Kit **15.99**
525-13030 2 Targets Black **21.99**
525-13040 2 Targets Silver **21.99**

CROSSINGS & CROSSING SYSTEMS

Signals are all brass, painted and lettered. All gates swing freely but are not motorized

CROSSING GATES 27.95 (PAIR)

525-1171

525-1170 "A" Arm Red & White
525-1171 "A" Arm Black & White
525-1172 Bar Arm Red & White
525-1173 Bar Arm Black & White

CROSSBUCKS W/GATE & LEDS 39.95 (PAIR)

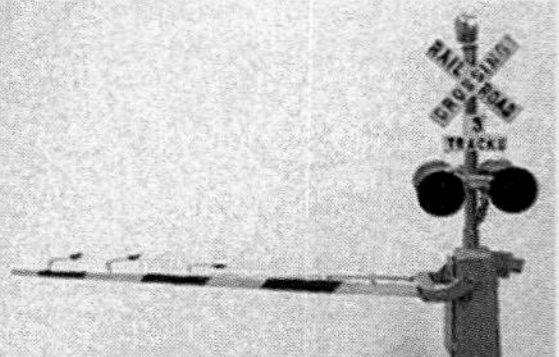

525-11600 "A" Arm Red & White
525-11610 "A" Arm Black & White
525-1162 Bar Arm Red & White
525-1163 Bar Arm Black & White

N.J. International

WIG WAG CROSSINGS

525-1180 525-1181

525-1180 Wig Wag pkg(2) **24.95**
525-1181 UP Type Wig Wag pkg(2) **29.95**

CROSSBUCK W/BULBS & LENSES

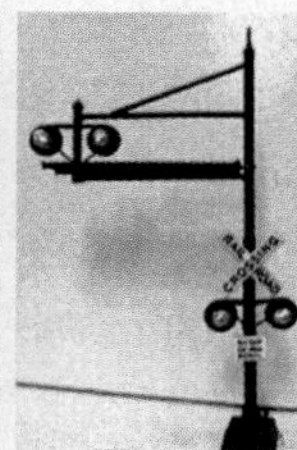

525-1090 525-1190

525-1090 Crossbuck **15.99**
525-1190 Over the Road **37.99**

CROSSING FLASHERS

525-8020 Flasher Module **19.99**
525-8021 Sound Module **29.99**
525-8022 Flasher/Sound Module **37.99**
525-8109 Flasher & HO Crossbuck **34.99**

STREET LIGHTS

525-5002 525-5003

525-5002 Dome Type pkg(2) **17.95**
525-5003 Boulevard Light Single Arm **10.99**

525-5004 525-5005

525-5004 Boulevard Light Double Arm **14.99**
525-5005 Street Light **8.99**

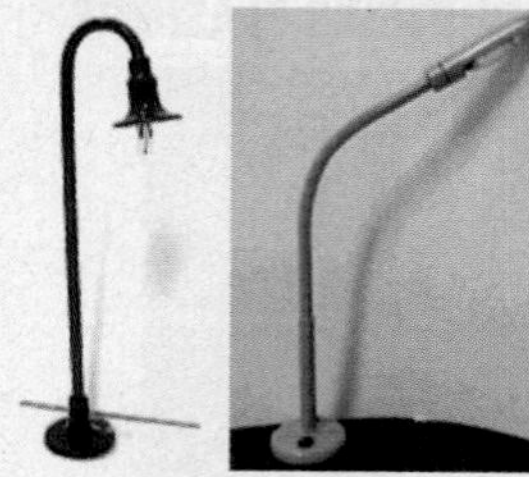

525-5006 525-5009

525-5006 Hook Neck Street Lamp pkg(2) **19.99**
525-5009 Boulevard Lamp **8.99**

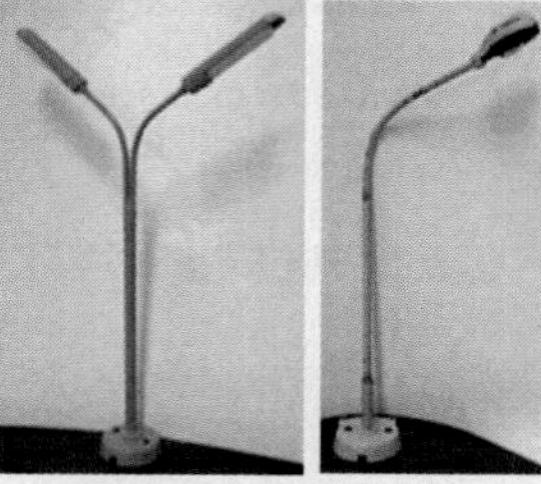

525-5010 525-5012

525-5010 Boulevard Lamp Double Arm **13.99**
525-5012 Large Boulevard Lamp **8.99**

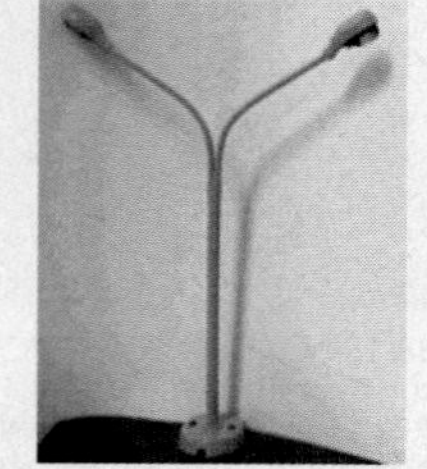

525-5013 Street Lamp Double Arm **12.99**

SIGNS

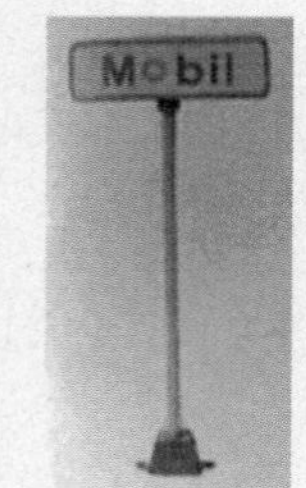

525-1979 7.99
525-1240 Round Railroad Warning pkg(2) **6.99**
525-1250 Illuminated Stop Sign **9.99**
525-1260 Railroad Crossing Sign pkg(2) **6.99**

TRAFFIC LIGHT

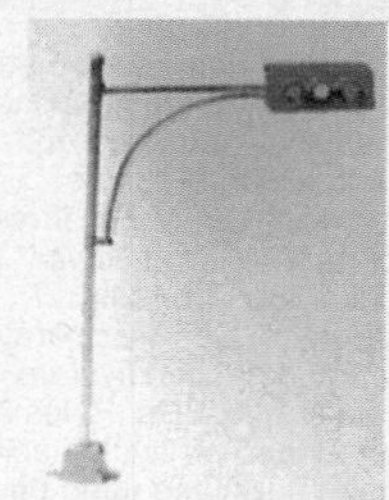

525-1978 14.99

TOWER LIGHTS

METAL

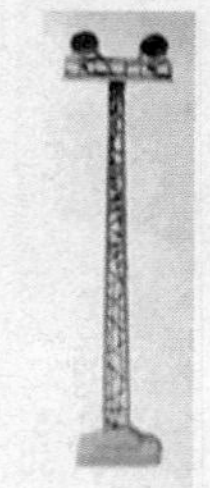

525-1972 525-1973

525-1972 Twin Searchlight **15.99**
525-1973 Quad Searchlight **19.99**

PLASTIC

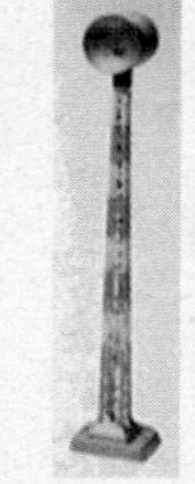
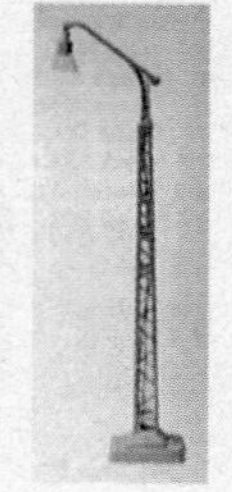

525-1974 525-1975

525-1974 Micro Wave Tower **12.99**
525-1975 Yard Tower **13.99**

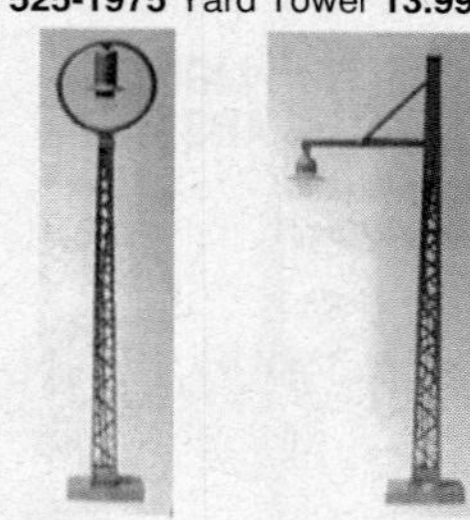

525-1976 525-1977

525-1976 Loop Yard Light **10.99**
525-1977 Yard Light **10.99**

NEW ENGLAND HOBBY SUPPLY

STREET LIGHTS

These working models will brighten any street scene. Used throughout the steam- and diesel-eras, they're authentic replicas of lights found all over the US. Perfect for any size town, station platform, residential, commercial or industrial district streets. Kits consist of unpainted pewter castings and brass poles (in some kits) which are easily assembled with epoxy or CA adhesives. Each is complete with clear 12V bulb/s and instructions.

GASLIGHT

522-80011 Single Lamp **8.98**
522-80014 Set of Four **29.98**

STATION PLATFORM LIGHT

Adjustable to 3" tall.

522-80021 Single Lamp **7.98**
522-80024 Set of Four **24.98**

BISHOP'S CROOK

Adjustable to 6", used world wide from the early 1900s to the present.

522-80031 Single Lamp **7.98**
522-80034 Set of Four **24.98**

UNIVERSAL SINGLE BOULEVARD LAMPS

Adjustable to 4" tall, includes clear plastic globe.

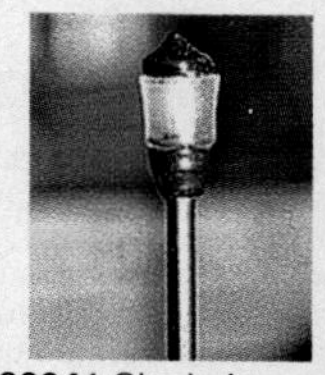

522-80041 Single Lamp **6.98**
522-80044 Set of Four **19.98**

UNIVERSAL DOUBLE BOULEVARD LAMPS

Adjustable to 4" tall, includes clear plastic globes.

522-80051 Single Lamp **9.98**
522-80054 Set of Four **32.98**

BRACKET ARM STREETLIGHT

Typically seen along industrial streets. Includes pewter pole with groove to hide wire leads.

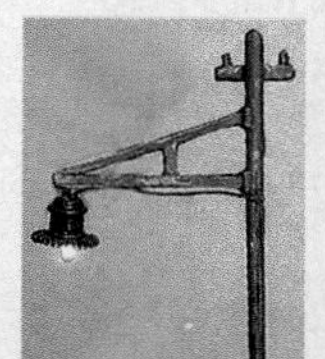

522-80101 Single Lamp **8.98**
522-80104 Set of Four **29.98**

SPAN-HUNG

Includes two pewter poles adjustable to 5" high, typically seen at city and some rural intersections.

522-80111 Single Lamp **9.98**
522-80114 Set of Four **32.98**

Flexible system of signal heads, LEDs and accessories can be used to create a variety of working signals. All parts are molded in black styrene and can be illuminated using LEDs or fiber optics.

SIGNALS

Each kit builds a complete signal with target, mast, ladder, base and finale. Small LEDs and resistors also included.

125 127 130

538-125 Single **9.95**
538-127 2 Target Single **15.95**
538-128 3 Color Single **34.95**
538-130 Triple Target Single **17.95**

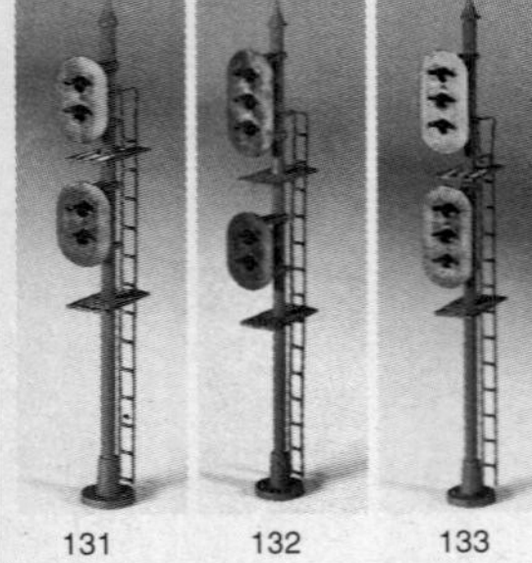

131 132 133

538-131 2 Over 2 **14.95**
538-132 3 Over 2 **15.95**
538-133 3 Over 3 **16.95**

134 114 115

538-134 3 Over 3, Circular **16.95**
538-114 Two Light **7.95**
538-115 Three Light **8.95**

116 117

538-116 Three Light, Circular **8.95**
538-117 PRR Intermediate **16.95**
538-118 PRR Absolute **16.95**
538-120 UP/DRGW Hooded **8.95**

121

538-121 UP/DRGW Hooded Targets Only pkg(3) **5.95**

DWARF SIGNALS

Signals change to colors shown when polarity is reversed. Great for use as turnout indicators.

SINGLE LITE PKG(2) EA 8.95

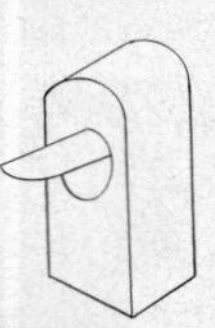

538-122 Red/Green
538-135 Red/Yellow

DOUBLE LITE PKG(2) EA 7.50

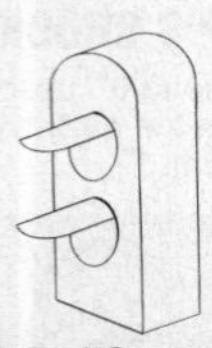

538-123 Red/Green
538-136 Red/Yellow

DWARF TURNOUT INDICATORS

538-140 pkg(10) **27.95** ***NEW***
Single two-color (red/green) LED with three leads.

ASSEMBLED BLOCK SIGNALS

Ready for service anywhere along your line, these signals come fully assembled and complete with bi-color (red/green) LEDs. For three-color aspects, add Driver Circuit #538-303 (sold separately). Can be operated with any detection system designed for LEDs. Poles are finished in silver, with black targets, like those used on most prototype roads.

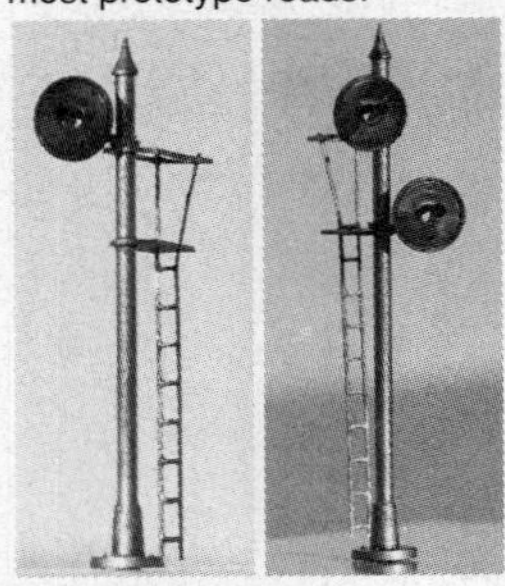

401 402

538-401 Single Target **21.95**
538-402 Double Target **31.50**

"SEARCHLIGHT" SIGNAL LIGHT TARGETS

Each set includes three heads with brackets and finales. Based on prototype introduced in 1920s and still in use on many railroads.

103

538-102 Single pkg(3) **3.95**
538-103 Double pkg(3) **4.50**
538-104 Triple pkg(3) **4.50**

"POSITION LIGHT" SIGNAL HEADS

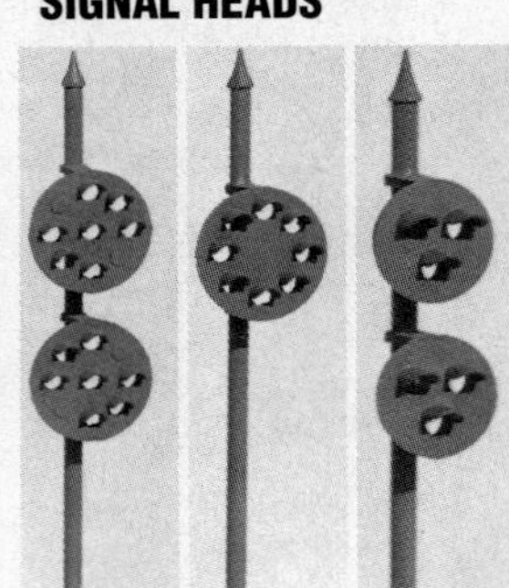

105 106 107

Commonly used by eastern railroads, these signals were introduced in 1915 and use lights in various positions to prevent misreading signals. Each includes accessories.

538-105 PRR/N&W pkg(6) **7.95**
538-106 B&O pkg(3) **5.95**
538-107 NYC/ROCK pkg(3) **4.50**

SAMPLER SET

538-108 7.95
Includes one of each type of signal head, with bases, walkway grating, brackets and more.

SIGNAL HOOK-UP WIRE

538-304 28 Gauge **2.95**

CROSSING FLASHERS

538-113 pkg(2) **15.95**
Easy-to-build with targets, crossbucks, base, mast, red LEDs and decals.

CANTILEVERED SIGNAL BRIDGES

538-101 C&O **14.95**
Prototype at Peach Creek, West Virginia. Can be installed on single or double track and includes wire handrails and assembly instructions.

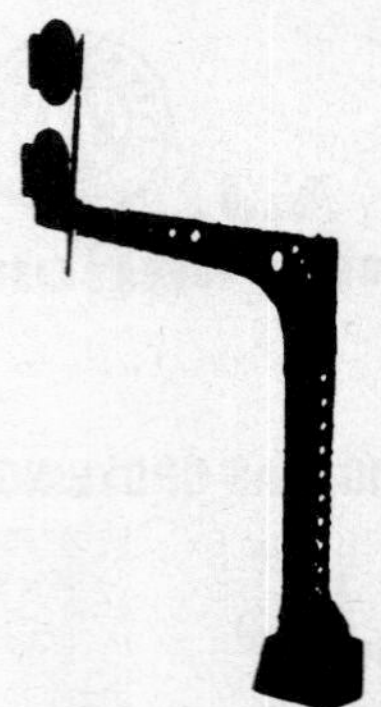

538-99 UP/DRGW **21.95**
Includes hooded UP targets, LEDs and resistors.

538-129 Single Searchlight Bridge Unit **12.95**
Two complete targets with LEDs for mounting on signal bridge.

LEDS EA 3.50

Correct sizes for press fit into signal heads.

.088" SQUARE PKG(3)

538-109 Green
538-110 Red
538-111 Yellow

1/8" 3MM PKG(6)

538-137 Red
538-138 Green
538-139 Yellow

BI-COLOR

538-126 Red/Green pkg(2) **4.95**
Changes color when polarity is reversed, measures 1/8" 3mm.

LED DRIVER CIRCUIT

538-303 3-Color **27.95**
Circuit used in #538-128. Converts any 2-color LED signal to 3-color with a simple wiring change. Circuit will operate on an input voltage range of 9 to 15 volts DC.

DIODE LOGIC BOARD

538-124 4.95
This device is required to operate Pennsylvania style signals #538-117 and 118. The unit activates the center lamp and is designed to be used between a detection system and the signal. Assembled with logic circuit and resistor to drive the signal.

RAILROAD TELEPHONE POLES EA 3.99

Two-piece plastic poles molded in realistic brown color. Any number of crossarms can be added to the poles. Notches are provided in the poles for easy assembly of the crossarms.

628-32 628-34

628-30 30' & 40' Poles pkg(36)
628-31 Crossarms Only pkg(72)
628-32 2 Arm Poles pkg(18)
628-34 4 Arm Poles pkg(12)
628-35 Clear Crossarms pkg(36)
628-40 40' Poles Only pkg(36)

ROCO

IMPORTED FROM AUSTRIA BY WALTHERS

SIGNALS

Operating, assembled signals feature precolored plastic parts.

625-40020 625-40021

625-40020 2 Color **14.99**
625-40021 3 Color, SNCF Style **18.99**

S&S HOBBY PRODUCTS

ROAD SIGN KITS

Kits include etched brass signs, steel posts and color decals.

643-303 Street Sign Set pkg(10) **7.99**
Includes two each: Fallout Shelter, No U Turn, No Passing, Truck Route and Stop Ahead.

643-302 Interstate Sign Set pkg(10) **7.99**
Includes two each: Train Station, Bus Stop, Yield, Do Not Enter and Interstate (with decals to select your own interstate numbers).

643-300 Stop Sign Set pkg(12) **8.99**
Includes four Stop signs, two Railroad Crossing signs, two Pedestrian Crossing signs, plus one 25, 35, 45 and 55 MPH speed limit sign.

643-301 Route Sign Set pkg(10) **6.99**
Includes two each: Slippery When Wet, Soft Shoulder, No Parking, Do Not Stop on Tracks and Route (with decals to select your own route numbers).

643-304 Smokey Sign Set pkg(8) **8.99**
Includes two each: Smokey Bear, Deer Crossing, National Forest and Falling Rock.

SCALE STRUCTURES LIMITED

BILLBOARDS PKG(2) EA 15.95

Kits include wood and metal parts, plus assorted 4-color signs.

650-1108 1920s

650-1155 #2

SELLEY FINISHING TOUCHES

BURMA SHAVE SIGNS EA 3.30

Sets include cast-metal sign posts and self-adhesive Burma Shave signs printed in red and white.

1941-1949
HO

REMEMBER THIS	WHISTLE BECAUSE
IF YOU'D BE	THEY'RE SCARED
SPARED TRAINS DON'T	Burma-Shave

675-6282

675-6281 1930s Era
675-6282 1940s Era
675-6283 1950s Era

SRE
Sunrise Enterprises

SIGNALS

TARGET SIGNALS W/BI-COLOR LED

695-111000 With Twin Relay Single SP/ATSF Style **29.95**
695-111001 Diverging Single w/Single Relay Box - Assembled **26.95**
695-111050 With Twin Relay Dual SP/ATSF Style **32.95**

695-111002 Single on 20' Pole **29.95** *NEW*

695-111051 695-111052

695-111051 Dual Target, Signal Relay Box **32.95** *NEW*
695-111052 Dual Target on 20' Pole **32.95** *NEW*

SINGLE TARGET BI-COLOR SIGNALS EA 26.95

695-112002 695-112001

695-112001 Single Relay Box *NEW*
695-112002 Double Relay Box *NEW*

DWARF POT SIGNALS EA 20.95

695-112005 Single Head w/Electrical Box *NEW*
695-142005 GS Single Target 20'

CLUSTER ASSEMBLIES EA 3.95

695-13122 SP, Assembled, Life-Like GP9/20 *NEW*
695-13123 SP, No Gyralights, Blank Plates & Brackets *NEW*

SEMAPHORE

695-11850 Single Blade **TBA** *NEW*

ELECTRICAL BOXES

695-14124 Twin Relay **5.95** *NEW*
695-14125 Single Relay **3.95** *NEW*

TRAIN ORDER BOARD

695-11550 TBA *NEW*

TRU-SCALE MODELS

SIGNALS

Assembled signals wired with electrical binding posts for use with any signal control system. Red and green 12-16 volt pea bulbs are installed.

730-1409 Dwarf Signal **11.00**

730-1410 Two-Color Signal **14.00**

WHITEGROUND MODEL WORKS

POSTERS

771-5017 2.25

POWER LINES

683-113 45' Hi-Tension Tower Kit **7.95**
(2pcs) 1-1/2 x 1-1/2 x 6-1/2".

RURAL UTILITY POLES PKG(12) EA 9.95

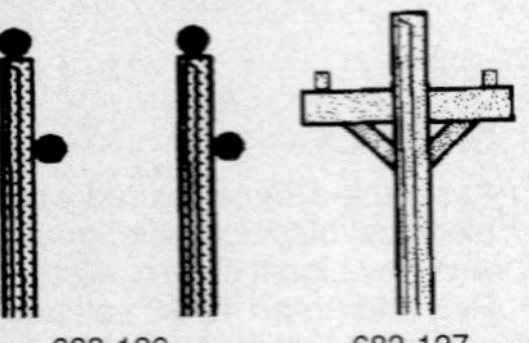

683-126 683-127

683-126 4-1/2"
683-127 With Brackets 4-1/2"

OVERHEAD SIGNAL WIRE KITS EA 8.95

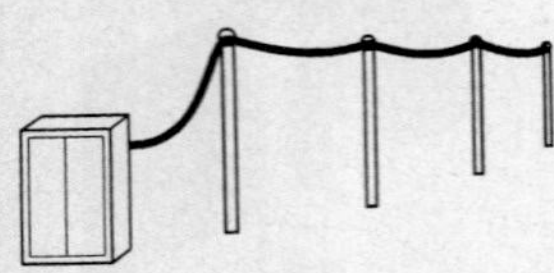

683-121 Includes 12 Metal Poles
683-122 Includes 12 Concrete Post
683-123 Includes 8 Utility Poles

SIGN KITS EA 3.95

NO TRESPASSING SIGNS

683-850 Railroad pkg(4)

WHISTLEPOSTS

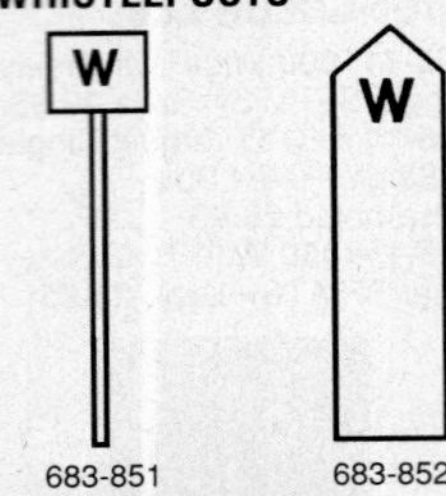

683-851 683-852

683-851 Metal pkg(6)
683-852 Concrete pkg(6)

MILEPOSTS

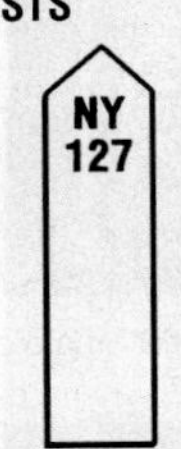

683-854 Concrete, Pointed Top pkg(4)

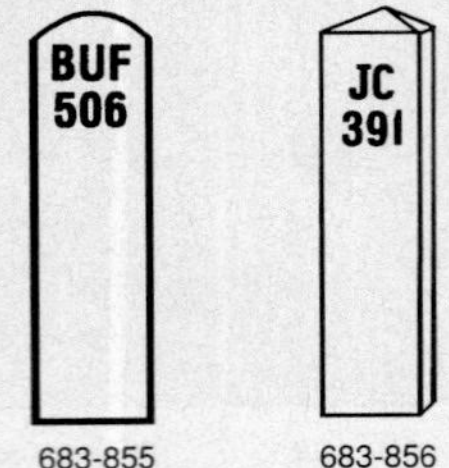

683-855 683-856

683-855 Concrete, Rounded Top pkg(4)
683-856 Concrete, 3-Sided pkg(4)

RR SPEED LIMIT SIGNS

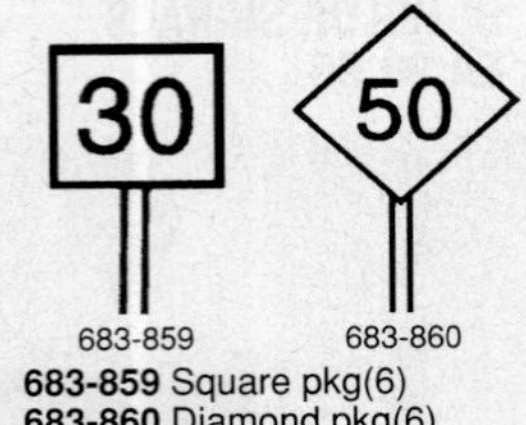

683-859 683-860

683-859 Square pkg(6)
683-860 Diamond pkg(6)

FLAG WITH FLAGPOLE EA 5.95

Perfect addition to stations, company buildings, yard offices and facility entrances. Includes 3 aluminum flagpoles, draw ropes, concrete base and finely detailed paper flags.

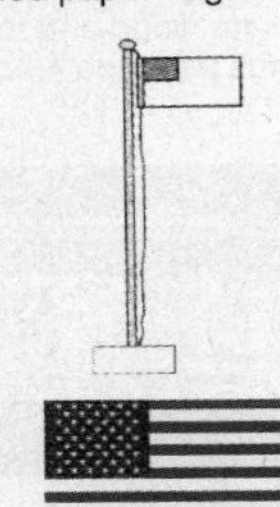

683-950 USA
683-951 Canada

683-952 UP
683-953 NS
683-954 CR
683-955 CP/SOO
683-956 CN/Grand Trunk Western

683-957 WC

683-958 Amtrak
683-959 Florida East Coast
683-960 BNSF
683-961 CSX
683-962 IC
683-963 Kansas City Southern

Prebuilt and tested electronics for train control, signal operation and lighting.

AUTOMATIC REVERSING CIRCUIT

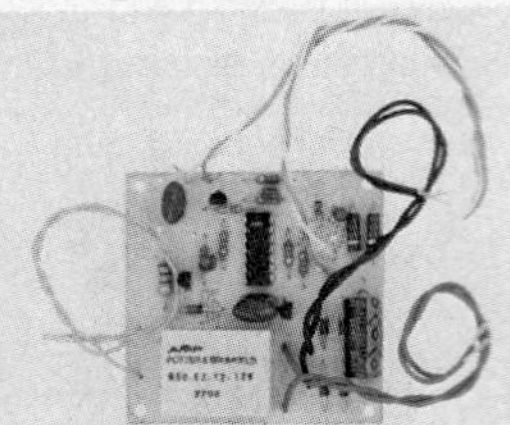

723-601 39.95
Automatically reverses locomotive on any predetermined length of track. Track reversing length can be adjusted by the placement of the magnetic sensors. No need to replace existing trackage. Works with any type of rail power.

AUTOMATIC TURNOUT CONTROL

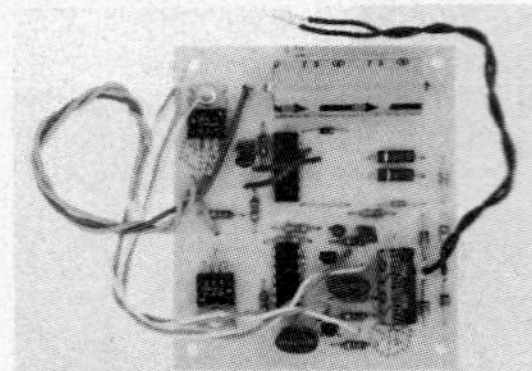

723-602 36.95
Alternates the route your locomotives travels and throws up to two turnouts simultaneously. Can be used with #723-601 to permit reverse operation on alternate sidings and automatic reverse loops.

SWITCHES

723-406 Reed Switch & Magnet pkg(2) **6.95**
Provides momentary switch that is activated by magnets placed on bottom of train. Use to operate various track detection systems, controls and signals. Includes two subminiature reed switches with magnets.

723-407 Pushbutton pkg(4) **6.95**
SPST - normally open, momentary, mounts in 5/16" hole.

GRADE CROSSING FLASHER

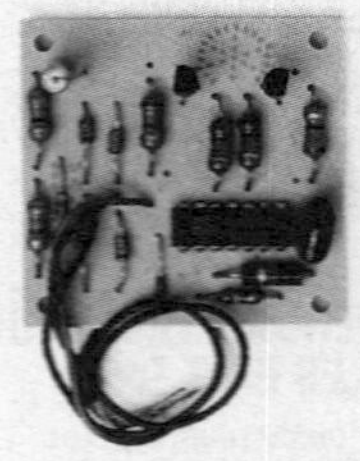

723-501 Signal Flasher **17.95**
For use with #723-505 bulb or #723-510 LED crossing signals. Will run several sets of crossing signals with the proper switching set up. 6 to 16V AC or DC.

CROSSING ACTIVATOR

723-502 22.95
Connects to Flasher #723-501 for realistic operation. Crossing signals turn on as train approaches crossing and remain flashing until train has passed. Placement of sensors on track allows operation in either direction. Includes printed circuit, magnets and magnet sensors.

CROSSING SIGNALS

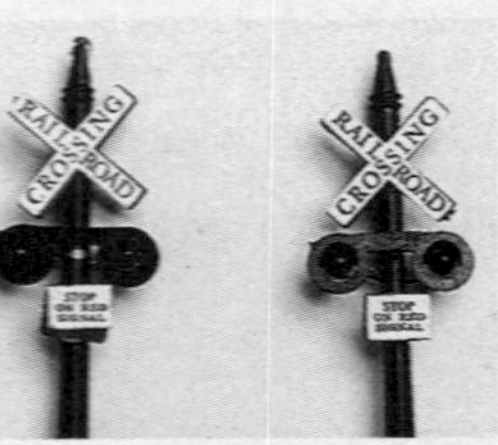

723-505 Bulb pkg(2) **9.95**
723-510 LED pkg(2) **8.95**
Use with Flasher #723-501 for true signal action. Available in LED or bulb models. Can be used with included base or hole mounted. 2-1/4" high.

CROSSING CONTROL W/BELL

723-515 32.95
Turns crossing signals and electronic bell on and off automatically as train enters and leaves crossing area. Unit is bi-directional and comes complete with track detector, crossing flasher, electronic bell and speaker. This unit for use with LED crossing signals only (#723-510 crossing signals suggested).

TRAIN TRONICS

CHASE LIGHT

723-201 Sign Border Chase Light Kit **34.95**
Realistic marquee with chasing lights, just like those on movie theaters, car dealerships, restaurants and taverns. Tiny tips of light, via fiber optics, chase around the sign to provide light action. The kit comes complete with sign material, prebuilt circuit board and enough fiber optics to build a 36 light sign. Uses 12-16V DC power supply (not included). Completed sign operates either in a chasing mode or alternating mode; change from one to the other with the push of a button. To expand the kit to 72 lights, use #723-401 fiber optic kit.

PROGRESSIVE LIGHT KIT

723-205 39.95
Up to nine lights turn on in sequence, one at a time. When all bulbs are illuminated they turn off and repeat the sequence. Use it as a sign to identify factories, banks, motels, restaurants and many other structures. Kit is complete with all prebuilt electronics, plastic sign front, stick-on letters and all parts necessary to assemble sign.

FIBER OPTICS

Use in dwarf signals, streetlights, railroad block signals and more.

723-401 20 mil (25') **7.95**
723-413 30 mil (25') **7.95**
723-414 40 mil (25') **11.95**

TOMAR INDUSTRIES

Assembled signals are painted and wired with bulbs or LEDs and feature brass construction. Complete instructions included.

SIGNALS

SWITCH STAND

81-851 81-848

81-851 13.25
Finished in black with red and green lenses, red and white target blades. Illuminated with 1.5V bulb, rotates 360°.

81-848 90° Operator **6.25**
Assembled, links switch machine to switch stand. Indexes to 90°.

DWARF SIGNALS

Feature black finish.

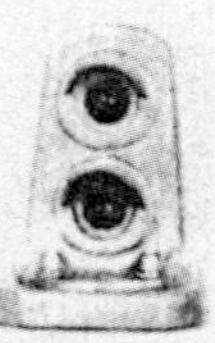

81-847 Two Light **8.45**
Yellow over red.

81-852 Two Light **8.45**
Green over red.

81-850 Three Light **9.95**
Red, yellow and green LEDs.

SEARCHLIGHT SIGNALS

3 colors from one LED.

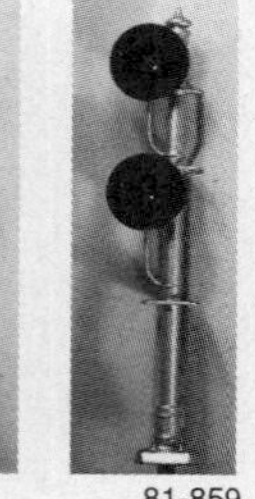

81-858 81-859

81-858 Single Head **24.75**
81-859 Double Head **33.00**

SEMAPHORE SIGNALS

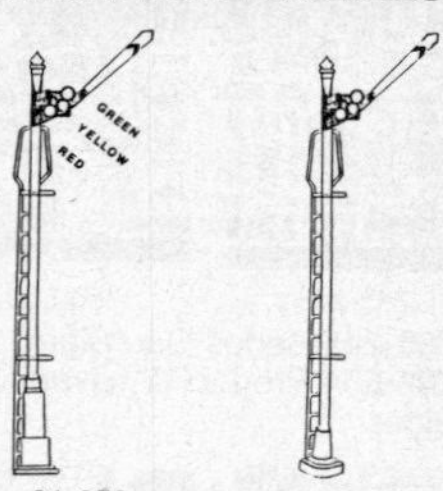

81-853 81-854

81-853 3-Position Semaphore **21.95**
1.5V bulb.

81-854 3-Position Semaphore **23.95**
With relay box for base, 1.5V bulb.

81-849 Operating Mechanism for Semaphore #81-853 & 854 **24.95**
Allows three-position stop of semaphore arm. Uses Switchman motor for slow motion operation. Includes instructions and mounting screws.

81-860 Lower Quadrant Semaphore w/Relay Base **23.95** ***NEW***
Brass hand-constructed signal is assembled and painted.

VERTICAL SIGNALS

81-843 Train Order **36.95**
NEW
Brass hand-constructed signal is assembled and painted.

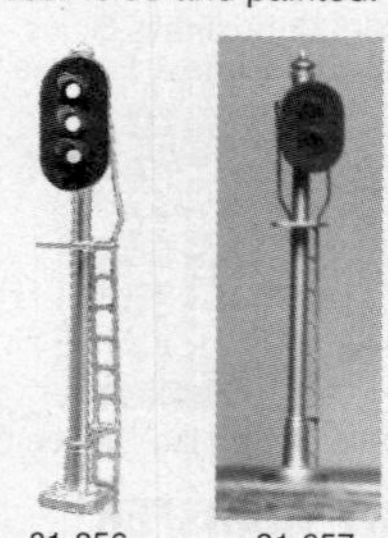

81-856 81-857

81-856 Three Light w/LEDs **18.45**
81-857 Two Light **16.75**

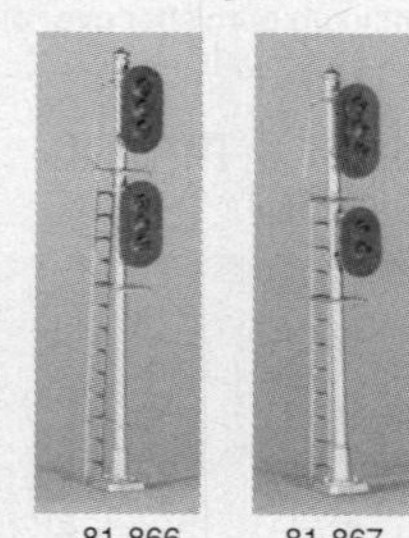

81-866 81-867

81-866 Two Head 3 Light **36.75**
81-867 Two Head **33.50**

FLASHER UNIT

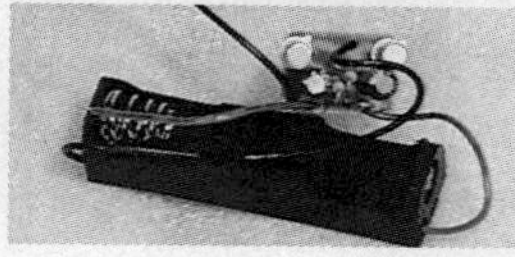

81-823 9.95

SIGNAL RESISTORS KIT EA .19

Signal resistors for Tomar signals using LEDs. Resistors limit the current to the LEDs, allowing usage of higher supply voltage than the LED rating.

81-864390 Green
81-864560 Yellow
81-8641500 Red

CROSSING SIGNAL

81-862 Without Gate pkg(2) **46.95**
Features operating LEDs.

RAILROAD CROSSBUCKS

Completely assembled, painted and decaled solid Beryllium signs.

81-868 81-869

81-868 pkg(2) **10.45**
81-869 With Track Numbers pkg(2) **11.45**

SIGNAL LADDER

81-899 12" **4.95**

TARGET SIGNALS

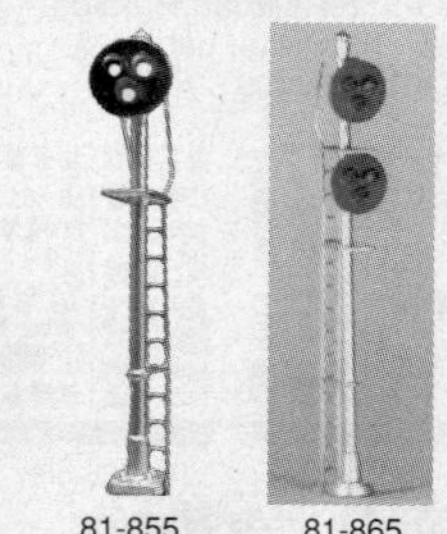

81-855 81-865

81-855 With LEDs **18.45**
81-865 Two Head **36.75**

Information STATION

Trackside Signs

While we usually think of illuminated signals or semaphores, many of the "signals" by the tracks are really just signs. Small and easily overlooked, they add a lot of realism to the most basic scene.

Whistle posts at every grade crossing signal the engineer to sound the whistle. Most are just a large letter W on a white or yellow background, mounted on a post. Speed limit signs indicate a maximum safe speed. Some display one number for all trains, others show two. When two numbers appear, the top regulates passenger trains, the lower freights.

Other signs indicate yard limits, junctions, fouling points (the point where cars on a siding block the mainline) or the capacity of a siding. In cold areas, signs at crossings and bridges alert plow operators to raise or lower flangers. Some sidings are protected by a Derail, (which causes cars to jump the tracks before they can reach the mainline and do more damage) which is marked with a sign.

A number of manufacturers offer ready-made signs that will work along your railroad, or you can create your own with decals and a bit of styrene or wood.

Lost-wax brass castings.

JEWELS PKG(12) EA 1.50

Without backing.

755-56 Clear
755-57 Red
755-58 Green
755-59 Yellow

LANTERNS

755-86 Switch Stand Kit **3.00**
Includes one lantern casting and four jewels (two red and two green).

755-95 Illuminated **7.95**
1.5V kit. Adaptable to various colors and scales.

MARKER LIGHTS

755-64 1 Pair **12.45**
1.2V kit with lights installed. Includes assorted transparent colored jewels.

SWITCH STAND

755-89 Nonilluminated Kit **5.95**

DRY TRANSFER SIGNS EA 4.98

Full-color dry transfers can be applied to a smooth or textured surface such as wood, metal or plastic by positioning the sign in the desired area, rubbing gently on the back and peeling away the carrier sheet. One 4 x 5" sheet per package.

785-551 785-552

785-551 Tavern, Gas Station & Commercial Signs
785-552 Assorted Business Signs

785-553 785-555

785-553 Depot, REA & Advertising Signs
785-555 Road, Product, & Burma Shave Signs

785-556 785-557

785-556 Assorted Logos & Advertising Signs
785-557 Data/Warning Labels & Commercial Signs

785-558 785-560

785-558 Railroad Heralds
785-560 Crate, Labels & Warning Signs

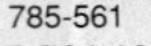

785-561  785-563

785-561 1960s Signs & Posters
785-563 1940s Signs & Posters

785-245 785-554

785-245 Series One Signs
785-554 Product & Advertising Signs

785-559 785-562

785-559 Business Signs
785-562 1950s Signs & Posters

MINI-SERIES DRY TRANSFER SIGNS EA 4.98

These N Scale transfers can be used as small signs for HO Scale.

785-570 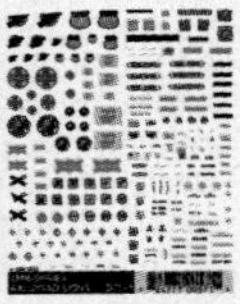 785-571

785-570 Product Logos
785-571 Railroad Signs

785-572 785-573

785-572 Business Signs
785-573 Signs & Posters

785-574 Service Station Signs

DRY TRANSFER BURNISHER

785-600 3.49
For applying dry transfers. Gently rub burnisher over dry transfer to apply.

STREET & TRAFFIC LIGHT SET

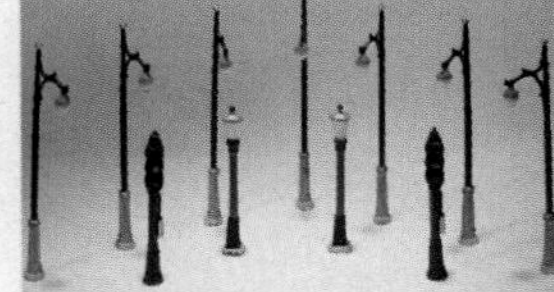

785-248 6.49
Detailed white metal castings. Set includes two traffic lights, seven tall single arm lights and two short street lights.

Adding scenery to your layout can transform your simple train set into a realistic model railroad.

Scenery gives you a chance to build an entire setting for your train.

Today's landscaping and terrain products let you add a variety of features, regardless of the time period or geographical area you are modeling.

With modern scenery systems, you can build rolling terrain features with easy to find materials like plaster cloth and rolled up newspaper.

You can even add highly detailed realistic rock faces by using simple rubber molds and lightweight plaster products.

Vegetation of almost any kind is easily modeled using ground covers of various densities and colors. Just sprinkle these products over the desired area until you achieve the color and consistency that meets your taste.

Realistic trees can be added to a layout by either buying them ready-made or in kits that you assemble yourself.

Today, modelers are not limited by scenery products that are too brightly colored or crudely detailed. They can model a scene that looks like the real thing.

The scene above shows DPM's Coal River Passenger and Freight Depot enhanced by a variety of Woodland Scenics scenery products. The trees were made using Realistic Tree Kits. The white stone bluff was modeled with a variety of Woodland Scenics Rock Molds. Bushes around the track and platform were made with Woodland Scenics Clump-Foliage and Medium Ground Cover. The track is detailed with Woodland Scenics Gray Blend Ballast.

Model and Photo by Woodland Scenics

INSTANT HORIZONS™

Take your layout beyond the basement with panoramic mountains, deserts, big cities and more, in full-color. Instant Horizons and Instant Buildings are a complete background system, expanding your perception of distance, adding miles of scenery to your layout. Perfect for every era, they can be mixed and matched to show an ever changing landscape. Easily added to layouts that are "finished" or under construction, complete instructions are included in each set.

BACKGROUND SCENES

INSTANT HORIZONS™ SCENES EA 7.98

24 x 36"

The Docks
949-713

Mountain to Desert
949-703

Drywash Desert
949-705

Saguaro Desert
949-706

Desert to Country
949-707

DESERT

With little vegetation and distant foothills, these scenes capture the look of the southwestern US.

For variety, several transition scenes are designed especially for use with these views.

949-705 Drywash Desert
949-706 Saguaro Desert

TRANSITION SCENES

These special views smooth the transition between different kinds of scenery, creating a more natural and realistic change.

949-703 Mountain to Desert
949-704 Desert to Mountain
949-707 Desert to Country
949-708 Country to Desert
949-714 Country to Eastern Foothills
949-716 Country to City
949-717 City to Country

MOUNTAIN SCENES

From foothills to snow capped peaks, put your layout in a mountain setting with any of these scenes.

949-701 Sierra Boomtown (Gold Rush)
949-702 Tall Timber
949-715 Eastern Foothills

RURAL SCENES

Fewer details and plenty of sky add miles of scenery and a wide, open look to any layout.

949-709 Prairie/Grain Elevator
949-710 Whistle Stop

CITY SCENES

Busy industrial and commercial scenes are perfect for rail yards, terminals and big city skylines.

949-711 Freight Yards
949-712 Hotel/Business
949-713 The Docks

Instant Horizons™

MANUFACTURED BY WM. K. WALTHERS, INC.

Scenes can be arranged side by side for a panoramic background. All Instant Horizons are drawn so they can easily be combined for a realistic transition between different kinds of scenery.

Tall Timber
949-702

Sierra Boomtown
Gold Rush 949-701

Prairie/Grain Elevator
949-709

Whistle Stop
949-710

Country to Desert
949-708

Desert to Mountain
949-704

INSTANT HORIZONS™

MANUFACTURED BY WM. K. WALTHERS, INC.

Eastern Foothills
949-715

City to Country
949-717

Country to City
949-716

Country to
Eastern Foothills
949-714

Hotel/Business
949-712

Freight Yards
949-711

Instant Buildings©

MANUFACTURED BY WM. K. WALTHERS, INC.

INSTANT BUILDINGS

EA 5.98

Put more scenery in less space combining Instant Buildings with Instant Horizons. These printed buildings fit between actual structures and scenes, smoothing the transition from foreground to backdrop. Where space is limited, or to hide seams, glue Instant Buildings on the scene. For a 3-D effect, arrange Instant Buildings in tiers and elevate structures at the rear to add depth. Or, mount the buildings on a sheet of styrofoam and cut out small angles and openings using a hot wire cutter. For a quick change photo backdrop, or more layout variety, assemble Instant Buildings but don't glue them in place. The scene can be changed over and over again. Easy to use, they can be mixed and matched to create a unique backdrop for your layout or module. Each includes complete instructions. (Some sets include additional details, not illustrated.)

949-723 Old West Frontier
A collection of wooden and brick businesses, right out of the old west. Use with: 949-701 Sierra Boomtown, 949-702 Tall Timber, 949-703 Mountain to Desert, 949-705 Dry Wash Desert, 949-706 Saguaro Desert, 949-707 Desert to Country.

949-722 Back Street Structures
Rear views of older brick structures, just like you see beside the tracks in most big cities. Use with: 949-711 Freight Yards, 949-712 Hotel/Business, 949-713 The Docks.

949-724 Industrial District
Large industrial structures, with a variety of interesting roof-top vents, smokestacks and more. Use with: 949-711 Freight Yards, 949-712 Hotel/Business, 949-713 The Docks 949-723.

949-725 Main Street Stores
Brick storefronts, suitable for scenes from the 1890s to the present. Use with: 949-709 Prairie/Grain Elevator, 949-710 Whistle Stop, 949-711 Freight Yards, 949-712 Hotel/Business.

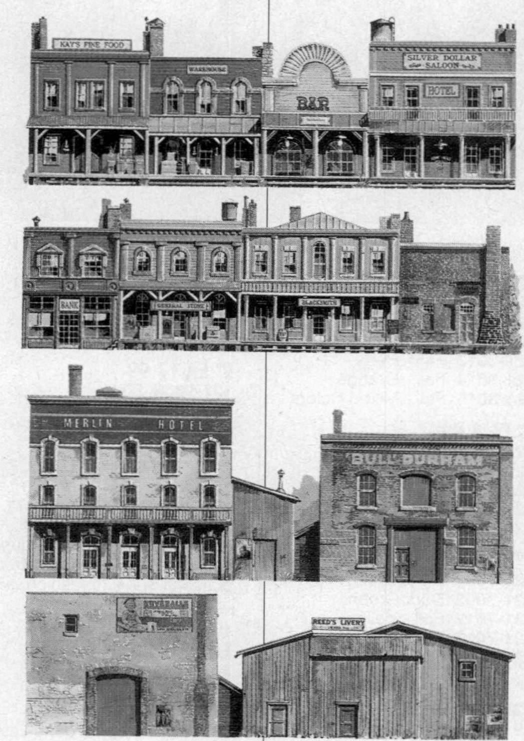

Old West Frontier Buildings 949-723

Back Street Structure Buildings 949-722

Industrial District Buildings 949-724

Main Street Store Buildings 949-725

Accurate Dimensionals
SCALE LANDSCAPING

Give your forests, city parks and residential areas a new level of detail with these scenic accessories. Adding these trees, bushes and ground cover to your layout will add interest and attention.

TREES

Suitable for use in virtually any scale, these trees are constructed to stand up to the rigors of handling not only during installation, but throughout the life of your layout.

Each tree is entirely hand-crafted using natural plant material. Plant material is systemically preserved to insure that branches and foliage remain soft, resilient and will not shed. Bark and foliage colors are carefully selected to insure realistic, natural colors.

Branches and bark are handpainted to show such details as aspen/birch gall marks and rough-textured bark of deciduous varieties.

ASPEN/BIRCH

1" PKG(4) EA 15.99
121-1003 Yellow
121-1004 Red
121-1005 Orange
121-1006 Mixed Colors
121-1007 Green

1.5" PKG(3) EA 14.99
121-1503 Yellow
121-1504 Red
121-1505 Orange
121-1506 Mixed Colors
121-1507 Green

3" PKG(3) EA 21.99
121-3003 Yellow
121-3004 Red
121-3005 Orange
121-3006 Mixed Colors
121-3007 Green

5" PKG(2) EA 16.99
121-5003 Yellow
121-5004 Red
121-5005 Orange
121-5006 Mixed Colors
121-5007 Green

7" EA 16.99
121-7003 Yellow
121-7004 Red
121-7005 Orange
121-7007 Green

9" EA 17.99
121-9003 Yellow
121-9004 Red
121-9005 Orange
121-9007 Green

CONIFERS

1" PKG(4) EA 17.99
121-1010 Green
121-1011 Blue

1.5" PKG(3) EA 16.99
121-1510 Green
121-1511 Blue

3" PKG(2) EA 16.99
121-3010 Green
121-3011 Blue

5" PKG(2) EA 18.99
121-5010 Green
121-5011 Blue

7" EA 18.99
121-7010 Green
121-7011 Blue

9" EA 19.99
121-9010 Green
121-9011 Blue

SNOW-COVERED CONIFERS

1" PKG(4) EA 19.99
121-1019 Green w/Snow
121-1020 Blue w/Snow

1.5" PKG(3) EA 18.99
121-1519 Green w/Snow
121-1520 Blue w/Snow

3" PKG(2) EA 18.99
121-3019 Green w/Snow
121-3020 Blue w/Snow

5" PKG(2) EA 20.99
121-5019 Green w/Snow
121-5020 Blue w/Snow

7" EA 20.99
121-7019 Green w/Snow
121-7020 Blue w/Snow

9" EA 21.99
121-9019 Green w/Snow
121-9020 Blue w/Snow

DECIDUOUS TREES

1" PKG(4) EA 15.99
121-1001 Light Green
121-1002 Dark Green
121-1012 Fall - Yellow
121-1013 Fall - Red
121-1014 Fall - Orange
121-1015 Fall - Mixed Colors

1.5" PKG(3) EA 15.99
121-1501 Light Green
121-1502 Dark Green
121-1512 Fall - Yellow
121-1513 Fall - Red
121-1514 Fall - Orange
121-1515 Fall - Mixed Colors

3" PKG(2) EA 14.99
121-3001 Light Green
121-3002 Dark Green
121-3012 Fall - Yellow
121-3013 Fall - Red
121-3014 Fall - Orange
121-3015 Fall - Mixed Colors

5" EA 8.99
121-5001 Light Green
121-5002 Dark Green
121-5012 Fall - Yellow
121-5013 Fall - Red
121-5014 Fall - Orange

7" EA 16.99
121-7001 Light Green
121-7002 Dark Green
121-7012 Fall - Yellow
121-7013 Fall - Red
121-7014 Fall - Orange

9" EA 17.99
121-9001 Light Green
121-9002 Dark Green
121-9012 Fall - Yellow
121-9013 Fall - Red
121-9014 Fall - Orange

FRUIT TREES

1" PKG(4) EA 15.99
121-1008 Pink
121-1009 Lavender
121-1016 White

1.5" PKG(3) EA 15.99
121-1508 Pink
121-1509 Lavender
121-1516 White

3" PKG(2) EA 14.99
121-3008 Pink
121-3009 Lavender
121-3016 White

5" EA 8.99
121-5008 Pink
121-5009 Lavender
121-5016 White

7" EA 16.99
121-7008 Pink
121-7009 Lavender
121-7016 White

9" EA 17.99
121-9008 Pink
121-9009 Lavender
121-9016 White

GROUND COVER

Add dimension, variety and color to any forest floor or lamdscape with these ground cover materials. Choose from plants or snow to fashion the appropriate look.

LOOSE PLANT MATERIAL .5OZ EA 2.49

121-11 Conifer Ground Litter
121-12 Flower & Shrub Material-Mixed Colors

SNOW 4OZ PKG EA 2.49

121-13 Shimmering Snow
121-14 Slushy Snow

BUSHES

.5" PKG(4) EA 14.99
121-205001 Light Green
121-205002 Dark Green
121-205008 Pink
121-205009 Lavender
121-205012 Yellow
121-205013 Red
121-205014 Orange

1" PKG(4) EA 15.99
121-10001 Light Green
121-10002 Dark Green
121-10008 Pink
121-10009 Lavender
121-10012 Yellow
121-10013 Red
121-10014 Orange

1.5" PKG(3) EA 14.99
121-15001 Light Green
121-15002 Dark Green
121-15008 Pink
121-15009 Lavender
121-15012 Yellow
121-15013 Red
121-15014 Orange

2.5" PKG(2) EA 14.99
121-25001 Light Green
121-25002 Dark Green
121-25008 Pink
121-25009 Lavender
121-25012 Yellow
121-25013 Red
121-25014 Orange

3.5" EA 8.99
121-35001 Light Green
121-35002 Dark Green
121-35008 Pink
121-35009 Lavender
121-35012 Yellow
121-35013 Red
121-35014 Orange

TREE KITS

EA 15.99

Now you can make these beautiful, high-quality trees yourself. Kits contain all of the unique materials needed for constructing these trees. Enough materials for approximately 50 to 60 - 1.5" or 5 to 6 - 9" trees. Clear Step-by-step instructions.

121-101 Light Green Deciduous
121-102 Dark Green Deciduous
121-103 Aspen/Birch - Yellow
121-104 Aspen/Birch - Red
121-105 Aspen/Birch - Orange
121-107 Aspen/Birch - Green
121-108 Pink Fruit
121-109 Lavender Fruit
121-112 Fall Deciduous - Yellow
121-113 Fall Deciduous - Red
121-114 Fall Deciduous - Orange

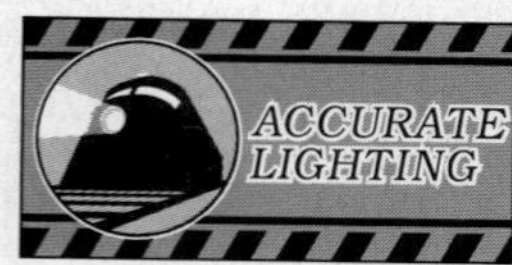

MINI SCENES EA 29.95

Each mini-scene is fully assembled with handpainted figures and scenery, plus a flickering fire, powered by an FM radio headset jack (less radio).

144-90000 Bums in Paradise
Two hobos swap stories.

144-90001 Bum Up a Tree
Bum meets hungry bear and heads for the trees.

144-90002 Prospector Camp
Prospector and donkey settle in for the night.

144-90003 Beach Bum
Bum by the fire ring, watching jogger hurry past.

144-90004 Bayou Bum
Hungry crocodile joins bum for dinner.

144-90005 Bummed Hunter
Hunter sits by the fire as deer strolls past.
144-90006 Buffalo Chase
144-90007 Moose Hunt
144-90008 Turkey Shoot

CAMPFIRE SIMULATION KITS

144-90010 Flame Magic I **12.98**
Add a flickering fire to a fireplace, cook-out or other scene. Unit is powered by an FM radio headset jack (radio not included)

144-90011 Flame Magic II **21.98**
Simulates a flickering fire using power from your power pack.

TREES

144-40 Deciduous Trees 1-1/2" pkg(4) **14.95**

ACTIVA PRODUCTS, INC.

MOLDING MATERIAL

A clean, instant papier mache for sculpting scenery, etc.

142-225 Art Plaster 5lb **7.19**

142-230 Rigid Wrap **4.19**

142-250 142-350

142-250 Instamold 12oz **7.99**
142-350 Permastone™ 28oz **4.99**

CELLUCLAY

142-100 142-200

142-100 Brown 1lb **4.99**
142-105 Brown 5lb**19.29**
142-200 White 1lb **5.49**
142-205 White 5lb **21.99**

LANDSCAPING KIT

142-177 38.59

GROUND COVER

SCENIC SAND 1LB EA 1.99

142-4581 Red
142-4582 Dark Brown
142-4583 White
142-4584 Black
142-4585 Light Blue
142-4586 Dark Blue
142-4587 Light Green
142-4588 Dark Green
142-4589 Yellow
142-4590 Orange
142-4591 Rust
142-4592 Lilac
142-4594 Purple
142-4595 Light Brown
142-4596 Turquoise

AMACO®

MOLDING MATERIAL

INSTANT PAPIER MACHE

Dry powder mixes with water, ready to use in 15 to 20 minutes. Material is nontoxic. Dries white, can be painted with any type of paint when dry.

126-41810 1lb **5.49**
126-41811 5lbs **21.65**

Get Daily Info, Photos and News at

www.walthers.com

SCULPTAMOLD

126-41821 3lbs **5.39**
126-41822 25lbs **36.75**
126-41823 50lbs **68.25**

CASTING COMPOUND

126-52761 5lbs **8.99**

CREA-STONE

126-53301 5lbs **17.99**
Dry powder mixes with water to make castings or moldings. Can be sculpted and carved for long periods if kept moist.

RUBBER LATEX

126-89915 16oz **11.95**
Use to make your own custom molds for casting scenery, small parts and other hobby or craft items.

MIX-A-MOLD

Nontoxic material for creating molds using 3-D objects. Picks up every detail of original. Powder mixes with water and molds are ready in two minutes.

126-75541 8oz **9.59**
126-75542 2-1/2lbs **32.00**

WIREFORM®

Perfect for sculpting and model making, modelers can easily create any three-dimensional shapes simply by manipulating these wire sheets. Each folded sheet measures 16 x 20".

EXPANDABLE WIREMESH MINI-PACKS

Ideal for any detailed projects you may find on your layout.

125-50004 Contour Aluminum 1/16" Pattern **5.50** *NEW*
125-50005 Sparkle Aluminum 1/8" Pattern **4.75** *NEW*
125-50006 Diamond Aluminum 1/4" Pattern **4.75** *NEW*
125-50007 Impression Copper 1/8" Pattern **7.75** *NEW*
125-50008 CopperForm Copper 1/4" Pattern **7.75** *NEW*

WOVEN WIREMESH

125-50023 Modeler's Aluminum **12.95** *NEW*
The woven wires create a structural grid, assuming different textures when shaped. Includes two sheets of 16 x 20" wiremesh.

ALLOY FORMS

FENCES

119-2009 Chain Link Fence Kit 30" **19.95**
Builds 200 scale feet of fence. Includes posts, corner posts, left and right gate posts, plus two 8' swinging gates. Parts are brass castings for added strength, with aluminum fencing material and simulated barbed wire.

119-2013 Corrugated Iron Fence Kit w/Working Gates 30" **12.95**
Builds 200 scale feet of fence.

A.I.M. Products are cast in high-density plaster to give maximum strength and stain absorption. This process is exclusive with A.I.M. Products.

WALLS

Overall height 3-5/8", overall width 5-5/8", overall thickness 3/4".

110-106 Cut Stone pkg(2) **7.95**

110-107 Fieldstone pkg(2) **7.95**

110-108 Random Stone pkg(2) **7.95**
110-114 Poured Concrete pkg(2) **7.95**

110-122 Wood Outside Braced pkg(2) **7.95**

110-127 Concrete Board – Formed pkg(4) **6.95**
1-3/4 x 4" (4.3 x 10cm)

110-139 Log pkg(2) **8.95**
5 x 7" (12.5 x 17.5cm)

110-140 Fractured Rock – Large **8.95**
6 x 12" (15 x 30cm)

110-141 Log Cribbed – Large **8.95**
6 x 12" (15 x 30cm)

110-702 Staggered Wall-Split Stone pkg(2) **7.95**
110-706 Interlocking Wall-Split Wall pkg(2) **7.95**

PRE-FINISHED WALLS PKG(2) EA 9.95

Stained in authentic color, these models are ready to add to your trackside scenery.

SPLIT STONE

110-802 Staggered Wall
110-806 Interlocking Wall

RETAINING WALLS

110-506 Cut Stone
110-514 Poured Concrete

ABUTMENT WINGS

Height: high end 3-1/2", low end 2'; width 5-5/8", thickness 3/4".

PKG(2) EA 7.95

110-102 Cut Stone
110-103 Fieldstone

110-105 Random Stone

110-115 Poured Concrete
110-123 Wood Outside Braced
110-126 Poured Concrete Board – Formed

PRE-FINISHED EA 9.95

110-502 Cut Stone
110-515 Poured Concrete

TUNNEL PORTALS

PRE-FINISHED

SINGLE TRACK EA 8.95 (UNLESS NOTED)

110-510 Cut Stone
110-516 Concrete-Grooved Face
110-517 Concrete-Plain Face
110-533 Lough
110-810 Split Stone **9.95**

DOUBLE TRACK EA 9.95

110-511 Cut Stone
110-534 B&O
110-634 Weathered

UNFINISHED

110-710 Split Stone **7.95**

3/4" THICK PORTALS

SINGLE TRACK EA 6.95

Overall height 5-1/4", overall width 6-1/4".

110-109 Blasted Rock

110-110 Cut Stone
110-112 Random Stone

110-116 Groove Face

110-117 Plain Face
110-119 Concrete Lined

110-120 Blasted Rock, HOn3

110-121 Wood Outside Braced
110-128 Poured Concrete Board – Formed
110-130 Eroded Limestone
110-131 Granite Gingerbread

DOUBLE TRACK EA 7.95

Overall height 5-5/8", overall width at base 7-1/2".

110-113 Random Stone
110-111 Cut Stone
110-129 Poured Concrete Board – Formed
110-132 Granite Face
110-134 Concrete

110-133 Modern Concrete

BRIDGE ABUTMENTS

Overall height 5-3/4", width at base 4", overall thickness 3/4". Numbers 110-124 and 125 are designed to fit Micro-Engineering structures #255, 501-504, 507 and 508.

110-100 Cut Stone pkg(2) **7.95**

110-101 Fieldstone pkg(2) **7.95**
110-104 Random Stone pkg(2) **7.95**

110-118 Concrete pkg(2) **7.95**

110-124 Poured Concrete Board – Formed pkg(2) **7.95**
110-125 Pier w/Cutwater **13.95**
110-135 Pier **10.95**
110-136 Cutwater Only pkg(2) **7.50**
110-137 Pylon Bent Footing pkg(4) **6.95**
110-138 Double pkg(2) **10.95**
110-501 Cut Stone Pre-Finished pkg(2) **9.95**
110-518 Poured Concrete Pre-Finished pkg(2) **9.95**

SPLIT STONE

38' TALL PIER

110-735 Standard **11.95**
110-835 Pre-Finished **13.95**

CUTWATER

110-736 Standard pkg(2) **8.50**
110-836 Pre-Finished pkg(2) **10.50**

TURNTABLE PIT

110-757 66' Diameter **79.95**

ROCKS

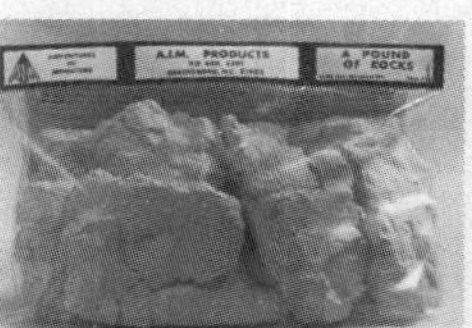

110-500 1lb **5.95**
Assorted rock castings sold by the pound, about 9 castings per package.

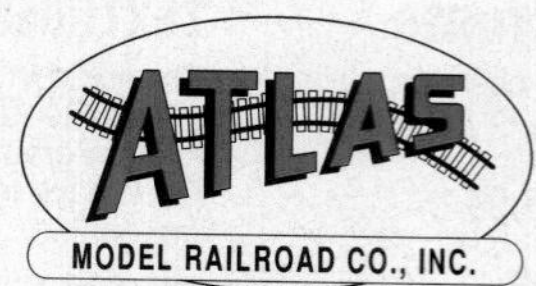

FENCES EA 3.25

Parts are molded of styrene in appropriate colors. Figures sold separately.

150-776 Picket Fence & Gate-White 6' **3.25**

150-777 Rustic Fence & Gate-Brown 6' **3.25**

AM MODELS

ROCKS

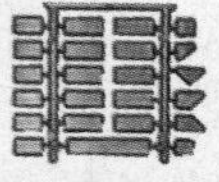

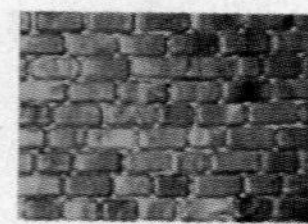

129-502 1.98
Molded in various shapes and colors, enough to cover 10 square inches.

FENCES

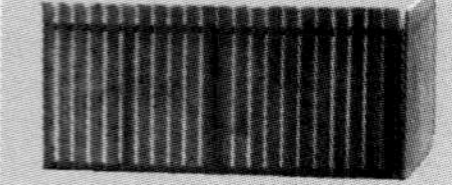

129-503 pkg(4) **1.98**
Includes four sections, each 8 scale feet long.

A-WEST

WEATHERING EA 5.98

158-1 158-2 158-4

Comes in 4oz bottles.

158-1 Weather-It
Gives unpainted wood a gray, aged look. Not a paint or stain. Use for old paint effects and realistic plaster "concrete" too.

158-2 Blacken-It
Works on most metals; not a paint. Conducts electricity, can be soldered.

158-4 Patina-It
Produces shades of blue/green on copper, brass and bronze. Not a paint. Also for Corrode-It technique on white metal, producing a pewter-gray/black patina.

FENCES

169-592 Ornate Wrought Iron **12.98**
100 scale feet of fencing.

169-604 Chain Link **6.98**
Includes 150 scale feet of chain link material, cast metal posts, corner posts, gates and gate posts.

169-5608 UP Snow Fence Kit pkg(2) **3.98**
Includes parts to build a pair of Union Pacific-style snow fences used to reduce blowing and drifting along the right-of-way. Each fence 16 scale feet long.

GROUND COVER

169-252 Snow 8oz **3.29**
Create a permanent snow scene with marble dust. Sprinkle over plaster that has been brushed with water and matte medium.

SEAWEED

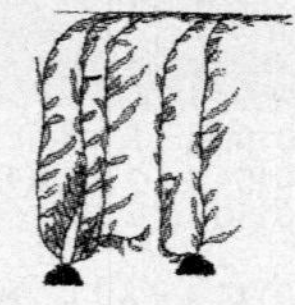

169-258 Seaweed/Kelp **6.98**
Create unique scenery for beaches, piers or underwater areas with this material. Translucent green strands with long blades can be suspended in resin to model plants in the water, or piled up along the shore as wrack.

WEATHERING

STAIN

169-106 Silverwood Stain 4oz **5.98**
Produce a dark, aged look on wood, plaster and other porous materials with this stain. Material is alcohol based and includes an applicator.

CHALKS

169-107 Weathering Chalk Set **12.98**
Add lots of neat weathering effects to your models with this set of eight chalks. Includes Terra Cotta, Red-Brown, Brown, Rust, Black, Light Gray, Medium Gray and Dark Gray chalks, plus an applicator brush.

Campbell Scale Models

TREES

200-100 Pine Tree Kit pkg(5) **25.00**
Enough material for five trees. Suitable for N, HO, S and O Scales.

TUNNEL PORTAL

200-351 Timber **17.00**
11-1/2" x 5"
Can be used as O Scale mine portal.

GROUND COVER

200-793 Decomposed Granite Ballast **5.00**
7oz per package.

200-795 Coal **5.00**
For tenders, gondolas and hopper loads.

MISCELLANEOUS

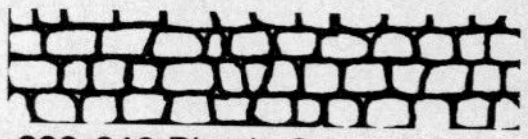

200-810 Plastic Stone **8.00**
5-3/8 x 17-1/4"
Clear plastic. Model random stone foundations, retaining walls, etc.

200-930 200-931

200-930 Park Bench pkg(4) **3.50**

200-931 48-Star Flag & Pole **3.25**

CENTRAL VALLEY

FENCE ASSORTMENTS EA 5.49

210-1601 Fence & Railing
Includes picket fence with gate, post and board fence with gate, board fence with gate (great for wooden sidewalk), plus welded pipe handrails and stair rails. Molded in black styrene.

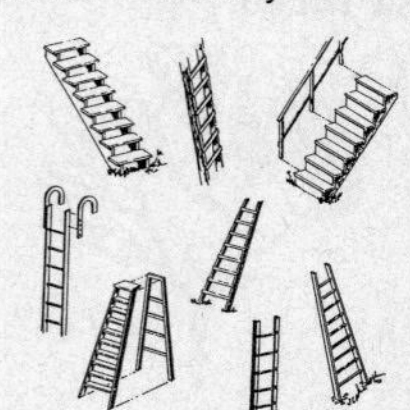

210-1602 Ladders, Stairs & Railing
Open and closed riser staircases, wood and steel ladder stock, wooden ladders with round and slat rungs, two 10' step ladders, four pairs of steel ladder loop tops, freight car ladder and wooden stair railings. Ideal for detailing kit or scratchbuilt structures. Molded in black plastic.

A•M•S•I
SCALE MODEL SUPPLIES

TREES

BIG TREE KIT

137-50 22.50
Tree is approximately 18" high with a 12" spread. Kit includes green cloth wire, putty powder, green covering material, ground foam and instruction book.

BIG TREE PUTTY POWDER

137-26 3.99
8oz package, mix with water to form a putty and sculpt realistic tree bark over your wire forms.

BIG TREE WIRE KIT

137-30 8.25
#24 green cloth wire for making tree armatures. Cover with Putty Powder or plaster.

TREE STRUCTURE KIT

Flat metal forms, painted brown.

OAK TREES

137-102 Large **3.99**
5-1/2 x 4-1/4" 44 HO feet tall.

137-105 Medium **3.99**
4 x 5"

137-90618 Small pkg(6) **11.98**
4 x 2-1/2", includes foliage material.

ROUND HEAD OAKS PKG(6) EA 3.99

137-134 Large
2 x 1-1/4", 12 HO feet tall.
137-135 Small
1-1/4 x 1", 9 HO feet tall.

MONTEREY PINES EA 3.99 (UNLESS NOTED)

137-103 Large
7-1/2 x 3-1/2", 56 HO feet tall.

137-109 Medium
5-1/2 x 2-1/2", 44 HO feet tall.

137-117 Small pkg(3)
3 x 1-1/2", 22 HO feet tall.

137-120 Small pkg(3)
3 x 1", 20 HO feet tall.

137-129 Small pkg(5)
1-1/2 x 1", 9 HO feet tall.

137-90620 Small pkg(8) **9.98**
3 x 1-1/2", 20 HO feet tall. Includes foliage.

REDWOODS

137-104 Large **3.99**
137-90604 Large pkg(6) **14.98**
7-1/2 x 1-3/4", 56 HO feet tall. Includes foliage.

137-90610 Medium pkg(6) **10.98**
5-1/2 x 1-5/8", 40 HO feet tall. Includes foliage.

137-110 Medium pkg(2) **3.99**
5 x 1-1/2" 44 HO feet tall.

137-125 Small pkg(2) **3.99**
3-1/2 x 1-1/4", 22 HO feet tall.

ROUND HEAD TREES EA 3.99

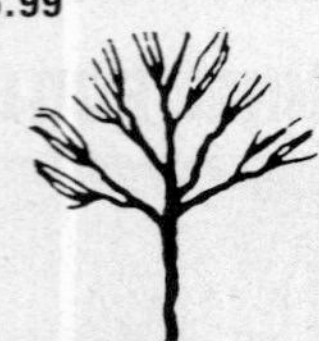

137-106 Large
4-1/2 x 4", 40 HO feet tall.

137-118 Medium pkg(2)
3-1/4 x 2-1/2", 24 HO feet tall.

137-119 Small pkg(3)
2-3/4 x 2-1/2", 18 HO feet tall.

137-132 Small pkg(5)
1-1/2 x 1", 14 HO feet tall.

BIRCH/EUCALYPTUS TREES

137-90612 Large pkg(4) **9.98**
5", 36 HO feet tall. Includes foliage.

137-112 Medium pkg(2) **3.99**
4-1/2 x 1-1/2", 33 HO feet tall.

137-124 Small pkg(3) **3.99**
3 x 1", 17 HO feet tall.

ELM TREES

137-107 Small pkg(2) **3.99**
3-1/2 x 3", 25 HO feet tall.

137-116 Medium - Round Head **3.99**
4-1/2 x 2-1/2", 36 HO feet tall.

137-90616 Large pkg(6) **14.98**
5 x 2-1/2", 36 HO feet tall. Includes foliage.

TREE COVER MATERIAL

137-1 Green - Steel Wool **3.49**
137-2 Green **3.99**
6 x 9" pad, nonmagnetic, flexible mesh material.

137-3 Brown **3.99**
6 x 9" pad, nonmagnetic, flexible mesh material.

HEDGE MATERIAL

Black nylon foam pad of various thicknesses can be cut in any shape and covered with foam to look like trimmed hedges or bushes.

137-100 5 x 5 x 1/4" pkg(2) **3.99**
137-200 5 x 5 x 1/2" **3.99**
137-350 5 x 5 x 1" **4.49**

FINISHED HEDGES

Ready to use, natural variegated exterior.

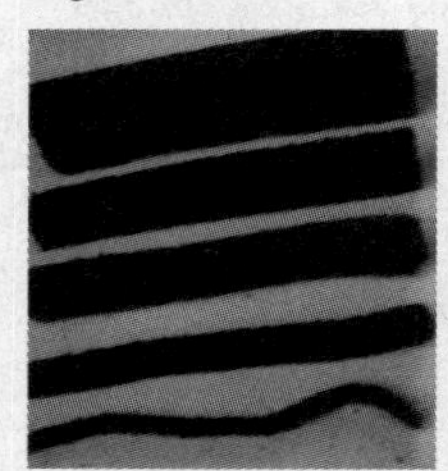

137-80100 1 x 2" pkg(2) **13.49**
137-80101 1 x 1" pkg(4) **13.49**
137-80110 1/2 x 1" pkg(4) **11.99**
137-80111 1/2 x 1/2" pkg(4) **11.99**
137-80120 1/4 x 1/2" pkg(4) **10.99**
137-80121 1/4 x 1/4" pkg(4) **10.99**

WISTERIA VINE KIT

137-90670 17.99

SOLID STRUCTURES

One-piece metal castings, painted gray.

CONIFERS EA 3.99

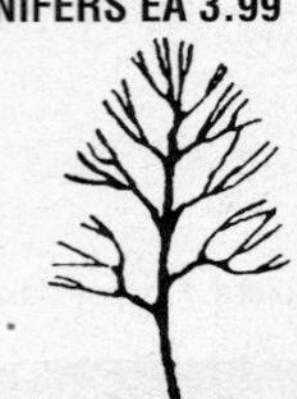

137-140 Small pkg(10)
1/2 x 1/8", 4 HO feet tall.

137-141 Medium pkg(8)
3/4 x 3/16", 6 HO feet tall.

137-142 Large pkg(8)
1-1/8 x 1/4", 8 HO feet tall.

137-143 Large pkg(6)
1-3/8 x 3/8", 10 HO feet tall.

137-144 Large pkg(4)
1-5/8 x 1/2", 12 HO feet tall.

MONTEREY PINE

137-145 pkg(6) **3.99**
1 x 3/8", 7 HO feet tall.

ROUND HEAD TREES EA 3.99

137-146 Small pkg(8)
5/8 x 3/16", 4 HO feet tall.

137-147 Medium pkg(6)
3/4 x 5/16", 6 HO feet tall.

137-148 Large pkg(5)
1 x 1/2", 9 HO feet tall.

GROUND COVER

FLOWER FOAM PACKS EA 8.49

137-800 Spring Color Pack
1/2oz each of white, canary, bluebell and coral.

137-820 Fall Color Pack
1/2oz each of red, gold, orange and plum.

137-830 Summer Color Pack
1/2oz each of fuchsia, delphinium, rose and violet.

FLOWER COLORS - GROUND FOAM EA 2.49

1/2oz of ground foam in each package.

137-10801 White
137-10802 Canary
137-10803 Bluebell
137-10804 Salmon Pink
137-10805 Pink Raspberry
137-10810 Fuchsia
137-10811 Delphinium
137-10812 Violet
137-10813 Calico Rose
137-10821 Maple Red
137-10822 Fall Orange
137-10823 Aspen Gold
137-10824 Plum
137-10825 Cherry Red
137-10826 Purple
137-10827 Wisteria
137-10828 Baby Pink

TEXTURES EA 3.99

Premixed in combinations of green. Ready to apply as foliage, grass or ground cover. Each pack includes 1oz of material.

137-205 Medium Dark Tree Texture
137-309 Coarse Grade Ground Cover, Dark Conifer
137-1109 Lawn
137-1206 Light Tree
137-1207 Medium Tree
137-1208 Dark Tree

FLEX-TURF EA 7.99

Ground foam texture on cloth backing material. 12 x 24".

137-1010 Turf Green
137-1020 Gravel Gray
137-1030 Topsoil Brown
137-1040 Hillside Tan

TERRAIN BRUSH EA 7.99

Topographical relief material for landscape models. 12 x 12".

137-2010 Sage Brush
137-2020 High Mountain Brush
137-2030 Riverbank Brush
137-2040 Hill Country Brush

SNOW

137-900 3.99
Non-metallic powder you can sift on your layout. Economical 1/2lb package.

GROUND FOAM

Soft foam material in three grades: fine (for grass and flowers, ideal for small scales), medium (for large scale ground cover or foliage) and coarse (for small shrubs or tree plantings). All are offered in regular one ounce or economy five ounce packages.

FINE - REGULAR EA 3.99

1oz packages.

137-401 Spring Green
137-411 Yellow Green
137-421 Ochre Green
137-431 Olive Green
137-441 Grass Green
137-451 Conifer Green
137-461 Dirt Brown
137-471 Gray Green
137-481 Black Forest
137-491 Straw
137-501 Plum
137-511 Aspen Gold
137-521 Fall Orange
137-531 Maple Red
137-541 Leaf Green
137-551 Spruce Green
137-561 Eucalyptus
137-571 Dust
137-581 Top Soil
137-591 Gravel Gray
137-601 Coal Black
137-611 Apple Green
137-631 Pumpkin
137-641 Orange
137-651 Hunter Green
137-661 Milk Chocolate
137-10621 Jungle Green

A*M*S*I SCALE MODEL SUPPLIES

MEDIUM - REGULAR
EA 3.99
1oz packages.

137-402 Spring Green
137-412 Yellow Green
137-422 Ochre Green
137-432 Olive Green
137-442 Grass Green
137-452 Conifer Green
137-462 Dirt Brown
137-472 Gray Green
137-482 Black Forest
137-492 Straw
137-502 Plum
137-512 Aspen Gold
137-522 Fall Orange
137-532 Maple Red
137-542 Leaf Green
137-552 Spruce Green
137-562 Eucalyptus
137-572 Dust
137-582 Top Soil
137-592 Gravel Gray
137-602 Coal Black
137-612 Apple Green
137-632 Pumpkin
137-642 Orange
137-652 Hunter Green
137-662 Milk Chocolate
137-10622 Jungle Green

COARSE - REGULAR
EA 3.99
1oz packages.

137-403 Spring Green
137-413 Yellow Green
137-423 Ochre Green
137-433 Olive Green
137-443 Grass Green
137-453 Conifer Green
137-463 Dirt Brown
137-473 Gray Green
137-483 Black Forest
137-493 Straw
137-503 Plum
137-513 Aspen Gold
137-523 Fall Orange
137-533 Maple Red
137-543 Leaf Green
137-553 Spruce Green
137-563 Eucalyptus
137-573 Dust
137-583 Top Soil
137-593 Gravel Gray
137-603 Coal Black
137-613 Apple Green
137-633 Pumpkin
137-643 Orange
137-653 Hunter Green
137-663 Milk Chocolate
137-10623 Jungle Green

FINE - ECONOMY EA 16.00
5oz packages.

137-4015 Spring Green
137-4115 Yellow Green
137-4215 Ochre Green
137-4315 Olive Green
137-4415 Grass Green
137-4515 Conifer Green
137-4615 Dirt Brown
137-4715 Gray Green
137-4815 Black Forest
137-4915 Straw
137-5015 Plum
137-5115 Aspen Gold
137-5215 Fall Orange
137-5315 Maple Red
137-5415 Leaf Green
137-5515 Spruce Green
137-5615 Eucalyptus
137-5715 Dust
137-5815 Top Soil
137-5915 Gravel Gray
137-6015 Coal Black
137-6115 Apple Green
137-6215 Jungle Green
137-6315 Pumpkin
137-6415 Orange
137-6515 Hunter Green
137-6615 Milk Chocolate

MEDIUM - ECONOMY
EA 16.00
5oz packages.

137-4025 Spring Green
137-4125 Yellow Green
137-4225 Ochre Green
137-4325 Olive Green
137-4425 Grass Green
137-4525 Conifer Green
137-4625 Dirt Brown
137-4725 Gray Green
137-4825 Black Forest
137-4925 Straw
137-5025 Plum
137-5125 Aspen Gold
137-5225 Fall Orange
137-5325 Maple Red
137-5425 Leaf Green
137-5525 Spruce Green
137-5625 Eucalyptus
137-5725 Dust
137-5825 Top Soil
137-5925 Gravel Gray
137-6025 Coal Black
137-6125 Apple Green
137-6225 Jungle Green
137-6325 Pumpkin
137-6425 Orange
137-6525 Hunter Green
137-6625 Milk Chocolate

COARSE - ECONOMY
EA 16.00
5oz packages.

137-4035 Spring Green
137-4135 Yellow Green
137-4235 Ochre Green
137-4335 Olive Green
137-4435 Grass Green
137-4535 Conifer Green
137-4635 Dirt Brown
137-4735 Gray Green
137-4835 Black Forest
137-4935 Straw
137-5035 Plum
137-5135 Aspen Gold
137-5235 Fall Orange
137-5335 Maple Red
137-5435 Leaf Green
137-5535 Spruce Green
137-5635 Eucalyptus
137-5735 Dust
137-5835 Top Soil
137-5935 Gravel Gray
137-6035 Coal Black
137-6135 Apple Green
137-6235 Jungle Green
137-6335 Pumpkin
137-6435 Orange
137-6535 Hunter Green
137-6635 Milk Chocolate

MISCELLANEOUS

FLEX MAT
137-1002 42.35
48 x 54 x 1/2"
Black, open cell foam mat.

POLYURETHANE FOAM BOARD
Rigid polyurethane foam, can be carved and sanded. Use for building bases, terrain, layouts and dioramas.

137-20202 Foam Poly-Rigid **3.99**
12 x 24 x 1/2".

137-20204 6.99
12 x 24 x 1" thick.

LANDSCAPING TECHNIQUES
137-20006 5.98
Six-page booklet explains basic landscaping techniques and ideas for using all AMSI landscaping and building materials. For railroaders and general landscaping.

VIDEO
137-20000 29.98
Video Master Miniaturists - Landscaping Primer. 90 minutes.

PARK BENCHES
137-90500 Kit **10.49**
137-90501 Ornate **15.49**
137-90502 1/2" **9.99**
137-90503 Ornate 1/2" **11.99**
137-90504 1/4" **9.99**

CM SHOPS, INC.

TUNNEL PORTALS
Full-size modern-style portals designed to clear today's larger rolling stock, such as double-stack and auto rack cars. Molded in concrete colored plastic, which is easily painted or weathered.

ARCHED OPENING
12-2001 Single Track **6.75**
12-2002 Double Track **7.75**

SQUARE OPENING
12-2011 Single Track **6.75**
12-2012 Double Track **7.75**

ETI ENVIRONMENTAL TECHNOLOGY, INC.

MOLDING MATERIALS

POLYMER COATINGS
Simply mix, measure and pour these decoupage resins to create realistic water in any scale. These materials do not produce the odors and heat associated with polyester and are nonflammable. Transparent dyes can be added to produce different "colors" of water. Dries to a hard, high gloss finish. Set includes decoupage resin and hardener, plus complete instructions.

207-27 Ultra-Glo 8oz **8.00**
207-35 Ultra-Glo 16oz **13.29**

ENVIROTEX LITE

Now available in several sizes for modeling large or small bodies of water. Pour-on plastic material dries to a hard, clear finish.

207-2007 4oz **5.45**
207-2008 8oz **8.00**
207-2016 16oz **13.29**
207-2032 1qt **21.79**
207-2064 1/2gal **37.75**
207-2128 1gal **66.00**

MIXING CUPS

207-1013 Mixing Cup Set **4.65**
Includes 6 disposable mixing cups, stirring paddles and 3 craft brushes. Use with decoupage or casting resins.

LIQUID LATEX

207-779 Mold Builder 16oz **8.40**
Liquid latex rubber for mold making.

CASTING RESIN
Water-clear, less catalyst. Shelf-life of approximately nine months, can be extended if stored at cool temperatures.

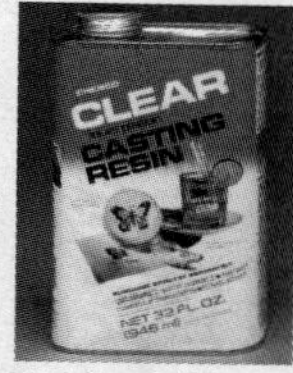

207-175 16oz **9.20**
207-183 32oz **15.49**
207-191 1gal **43.29**

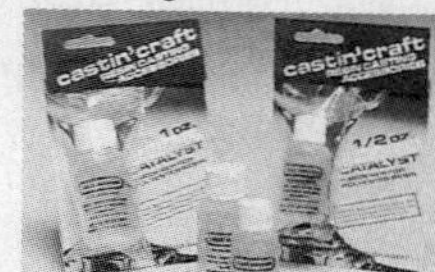

207-46388 Catalyst 1/2oz **2.65**
Needed to cure (harden) resin, for use with #s 175, 183 and 191.

TRANSPARENT DYE 1/2OZ EA 3.25

Add for see-through color in resin.

207-46418 Pearl
207-46434 Blue
207-46469 Green
207-46493 Amber

IMPORTED FROM GERMANY BY WALTHERS

TREES

APPLE TREES

189-6628 1-13/16" 45mm pkg(2) **4.99**

189-6648 3" 75mm pkg(2) **4.99**
189-6658 4-13/32" 110mm pkg(2) **7.99**

BEECHES

189-6739 3-5/8" 90mm pkg(2) **6.99**
189-6749 4-5/8" 115mm pkg(2) **7.99**
189-6759 6" 150mm pkg(2) **11.99**
189-6769 7-3/16" 180mm **11.99**
189-6779 8-13/32" 210mm **11.99**

BIRCHES

189-6736 3-5/8" 90mm pkg(2) **6.99**
189-6746 4-5/8" 115mm pkg(2) **7.99**
189-6756 6" 15mm pkg(2) **11.99**
189-6766 7-3/16" 180mm **11.99**
189-6776 8-13/32" 210mm **11.99**

BLOOMING TREES

189-6643 3" 75mm pkg(2) **6.99**
189-6653 4-13/32" 110mm pkg(2) **7.99**
189-6252 Small 2-13/16" 7cm Tall pkg(2) **2.99** *NEW*
189-6253 Medium 3-5/8" 9cm Tall pkg(2) **2.99** *NEW*
189-6254 Large 4-3/16" 10.5cm Tall pkg(2) **3.99** *NEW*

CHESTNUT EA 11.99

189-6761 7-3/16" 180mm
189-6771 8-13/32" 210mm

DECIDUOUS TREE ASSORTMENT

189-6484 Spring Trees pkg(16) **14.99** *NEW*
Includes a variety of trees from 2-13/16" 7cm to 5" 12.5cm tall.

189-6487 pkg(25) **21.99**

DECIDUOUS/PINE ASSORTMENT

189-6490 pkg(35) **19.99**

FOREST TREES

189-6489 Mixed Assortment pkg(24) **23.99**

FRUIT TREES

189-6647 3" 75mm pkg(2) **6.99**
189-6657 4-13/32" 110mm pkg(2) **7.99**

PINE TREE ASSORTMENTS

189-6470 pkg(15) **9.99**
Includes three each: 2-1/2, 3, and 3-1/2" (60, 75, 90mm) and two: 2, 4-1/2 and 5-1/2" (50, 110, 135mm).

189-6471 pkg(30) **18.99**
Includes six each: 2-1/2, 3 and 3-1/2" (60, 75, 90mm) and four each: 2, 4-1/2 and 5-1/2" (50, 110, 135mm).

189-6472 pkg(60) **35.99**
Includes 12 each: 2-1/2, 3 and 3-1/2" (60, 75, 90mm) and eight each: 2, 4-1/2 and 5-1/2" (50, 110, 135mm).

189-6497 pkg(50) **19.99**
189-6498 pkg(20) **7.99**
Trees range in height from about 1-1/2 - 3-1/2" 40-90mm.

189-6499 pkg(100) **31.99**
Trees range in height from about 2-1/2 - 4-1/2" 60-110mm

189-6412 Serbian Pines 3-13/32-5-5/8" 8.5-14cm Tall pkg(20) **17.99** *NEW*

189-6466 Snow Covered Pines 2-3/8-5-3/8" 6-13.5cm Tall pkg(6) **17.99** *NEW*

PINE TREES W/ROOTS

189-6475 pkg(10) **7.99**
Includes two each: 2-1/2, 3-1/2 and 4-1/2" (60, 90, 110mm) three 3" (75mm) and one 5-1/2" (135mm).

189-6476 pkg(20) **14.99**
Includes four each: 2-1/2, 3-1/2 and 4-1/2" (60, 90, 110mm), six 3" (75mm) and two 5-1/2" (135mm).

189-6477 pkg(40) **28.99**
Includes eight 2-1/2, 3-1/2 and 4-1/2" (60, 90, 110mm), twelve 3" (75 mm) and four 5-1/2" (135mm)

189-6577 pkg(40) **19.99**
1-3/16 to 2-3/16" 30-60mm

POPLARS

189-6229 Poplars pkg(10) **11.99** *NEW*
Includes six 4-13/16" 12cm and four 3-13/16" 9.5cm tall trees.

189-6733 3-5/8" 90mm pkg(2) **6.99**
189-6743 4-5/8" 115mm pkg(2) **7.99**
189-6753 6" 150mm pkg(2) **11.99**

WEEPING WILLOWS

189-6650 4-13/16" 120mm pkg(2) **11.99**

SNOW

189-7171 Snow Powder 500g **6.99**

WALL CARDS

EA 1.99

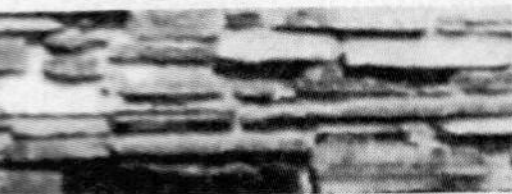

189-7421 Layered Stone

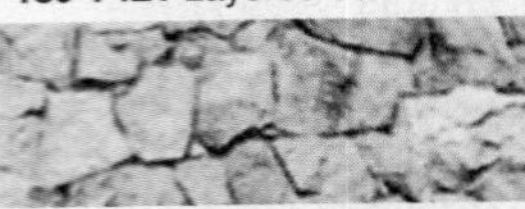

189-7422 Natural Stone

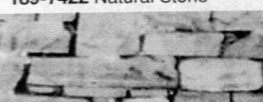

189-7423 Sandstone

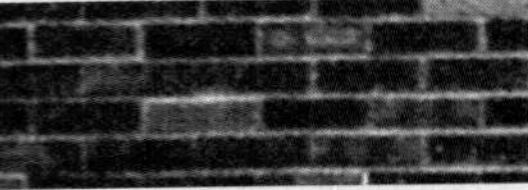

189-7424 Dark Brick

189-7425 Red Brick

WATER

189-7180 Foil/Paper **7.99**
18 x 14" 45 x 35cm

189-7426 Sheet **1.99**

GROUND COVER

GRASS FLOCKING EA 2.99

189-7110 Dark Green

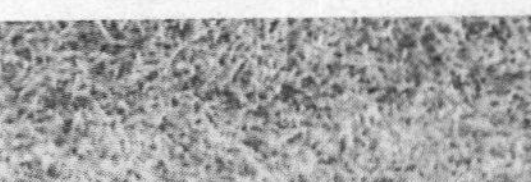

189-7111 Spring Green

PLOWED FIELD

189-7182 pkg(2) **4.99**
19 x 11" 48 x 28cm

GRASS MATS EA 5.99

Limited Quantity Available

189-7187 Moor Landscape

LARGE GRASS MATS

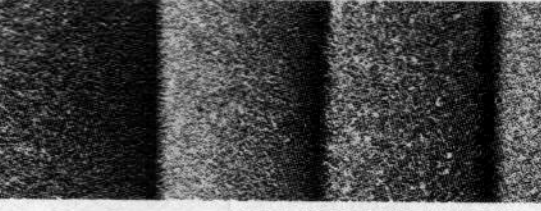

189-7220/7221/7231

189-7220 Dark Green **11.99**
40 x 32"

189-7221 Spring **11.99**
40 x 32"

189-7231 Spring **21.99**
79 x 32"

MICRO FLOCKING EA 2.99

189-7321 Spring Green

189-7323 Dark Green

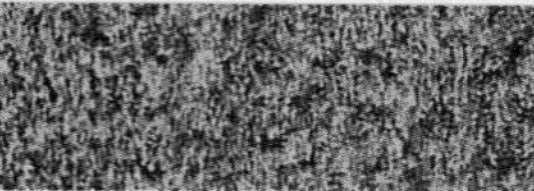

189-7327 Light Green
189-7322 Medium Green

FLOCKING EA 2.99

189-7331 Spring Green
189-7332 Medium Green
189-7333 Dark Green
189-7337 Light Green

FOAM SCATTER MATERIAL

Ground foam in a variety of colors and textures, suitable for trees, weeds, grass and other plants.

FINE EA 4.99

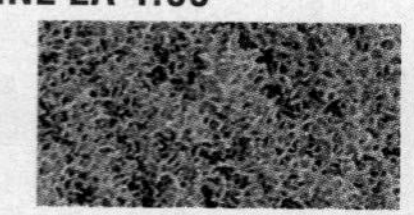

189-7311 Spring Green ***NEW***

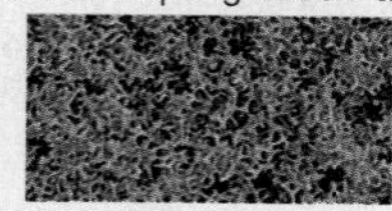

189-7312 Medium Green ***NEW***

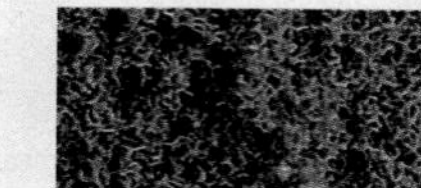

189-7313 Dark Green ***NEW***

189-7314 White ***NEW***

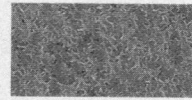

189-7315 Red ***NEW***

COARSE EA 3.99

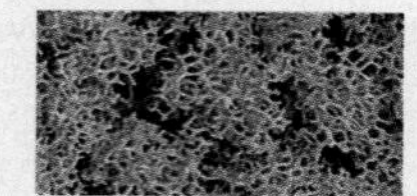

189-7317 Spring Green ***NEW***

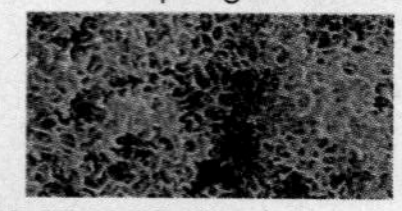

189-7318 Medium Green ***NEW***

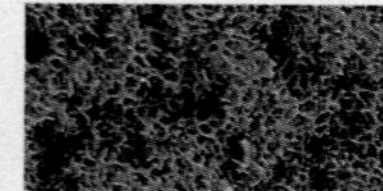

189-7319 Dark Green ***NEW***

WILD GRASS MATS

Longer material is ideal for modeling fields, pastures, meadows and more.

SMALL EA 8.99

Each measures: 20 x 16"
50 x 40cm

189-7210 Dark Green ***NEW***
189-7211 Spring Green ***NEW***
189-7214 Corn Field ***NEW***

LARGE EA 23.99

Each measures: 32 x 32"
80 x 80cm

189-7215 Dark Green ***NEW***
189-7216 Spring Green ***NEW***
189-7219 Corn Field ***NEW***

ROADWAY

FLEXIBLE ROADWAY

189-7098 Street Curve 120mm **6.99**

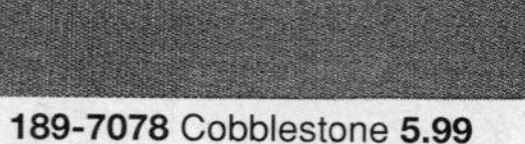

189-7078 Cobblestone **5.99**
189-7082 Bicycle Path **6.99**
14.5mm (5/8") wide, printed in gray/red with bicycle symbol.

189-7084 Flexible Field Path **4.99**
23mm (1") wide.

189-7085 Asphalt **7.99**
189-7086 Asphalt - Wide **9.99**
22" x 6'1"

189-7090 Asphalt Tape - Double-Faced **12.99**
189-7093 Country Asphalt **5.99**

SIDEWALK SHEET

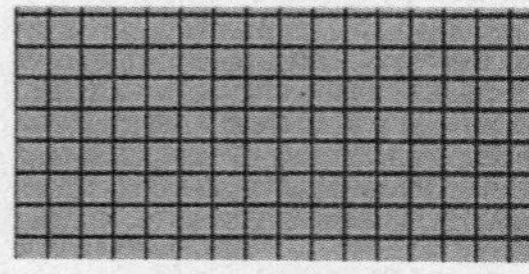

189-7094 pkg(6) **3.99**
8-1/2 x 6" 21 x 15cm

PARKING LOT

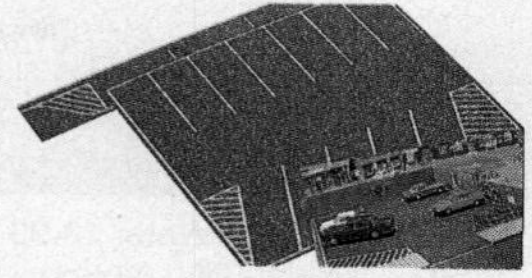

189-7076 **3.99**
8 x 6-1/2" 20 x 16cm

ROAD CONSTRUCTION SET

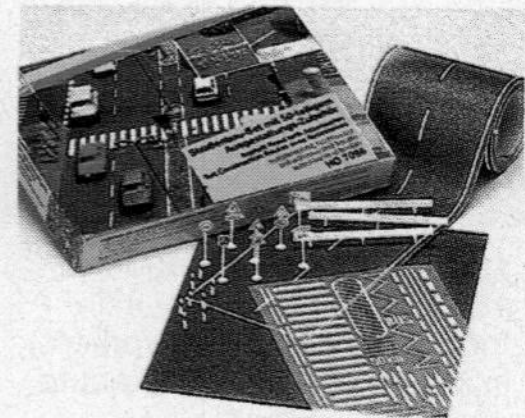

189-7096 **15.99**
Includes roadway, signs and markings.

MORTAR EA 7.99

Self-adhesive putty can be used to create all kinds of scenic formations. Mix one part mortar with one part water, knead into a pasty dough and apply. Stays workable for up to four hours, dries completely in two days. Package includes 17-1/2oz (500 grams).

189-7590 Rocks (Gray)

189-7591 Soil (Tan)

WALLS

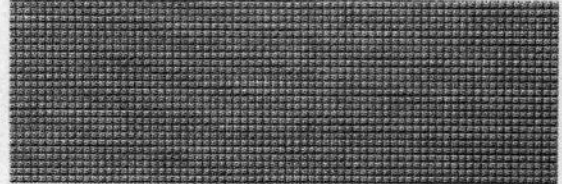

189-7401 Tile Gray **4.99**

189-7402 Even Brick Brown **4.99**

189-7403 Natural Stone **4.99**

PLASTIC SHEETS PKG(2) EA 1.99

189-7035 Interlocked Stone
189-7036 Hex Stone
189-7037 Random Stone
189-7038 Cut Stone
189-7039 Wood Planking

TUNNEL PORTALS

"ICE" TUNNEL PORTALS

Modern designs are based on portals used on the German Railways Inter City Express (ICE) line.

189-7020 Single Track **6.99**

189-7021 Double Track **7.99**

TUNNEL PORTALS W/WINGS

189-7022 Single Track **9.99**
189-7023 Double Track **9.99**

LEFT HAND TUNNEL PORTALS

LESS LINER

189-7024 pkg(2) **2.99**

WITH LINER

189-7026 pkg(2) **3.99**

DOUBLE-TRACK TUNNEL PORTAL

189-7027 pkg(2) **3.99**

SCENIC DETAILS

189-5408 Summer Night Party Set **23.99**
Features a garland with 12 colored lights, two wooden masts, four benches and two tables.

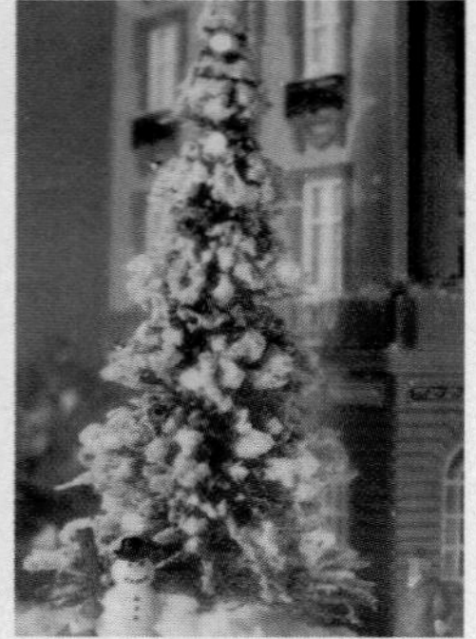

189-5409 Christmas Tree w/7 Yellow Lights **22.99**

189-5450 Construction Zone pkg(4) **29.99**
Contains 4 stantions (2 blinking) and control unit.

189-6465 Winter Set **15.99**
Includes 10 white trees, snowman, aviary and snow-powder.

189-6045 Construction Scene **13.99**
189-6044 Coal Mining Scene **14.99**

COMPLETE MINI-SCENES

These collectible miniatures look great on your layout or on display. Fully assembled with figures and scenery material, most also include a vehicle and accessories. For safe, dust-free display, each comes in a clear plastic box with base.

189-5631 Complete Radar Trap Set **33.99**

189-6046 Gliding Field **26.99**
Turn a vacant field into an airfield! Set includes two gliders, a VW "Beetle" tow car with winch, plus a mobile control tower van with special markings, fire extinguisher and wind speed indicator, a wind sock and runway foil.

189-7620 Live to Work **15.99**
Two workmen load a Goliath truck. Includes small shed and freight.

189-7621 Thirst is the Worst **15.99**
Soldiers stash a case of beer. Includes tent, VW "Beetle" figures and tree.

189-7622 Joe the Sprayer **13.99**
Graffiti "artist" tags a wooden fence. Includes van, painter and decorated wooden fence.

189-7623 Oh Happy Day **14.99**
Bride and groom about to depart in Mercedes convertible, decorated with flowers and tin cans.

189-7624 Circus Breakdown **15.99**
Who needs a tow truck when you've got a baby elephant! Mercedes panel truck sports colorful Krone Circus scheme. Includes ringmaster and elephant.

189-7625 Billposter at Work **13.99**
Worker puts the finishing touches on a new sign. Includes van and ladder

189-7626 Underground Telephone Repair Crew **13.99**
Includes worker, traffic barricades, small tent, van and large cable reel.

189-7627 Flensburg Speed Trap **14.99**
Police field radar unit with two figures and vehicle.

189-7628 On the Water **13.99**
Boater "accidentally" meets sunbather. Includes figures, raft, tree, signs and simulated water base.

189-7629 Fender Bender **15.99**
Includes two rescue workers, injured motorist, dented auto and bent lamp pole.

189-7630 Cutting Firewood **10.99**
Two men trimming a fresh-cut tree. Includes figures, stump, tree and stacks of firewood.

189-7631 Hunter's Dilemma **13.99**
A day in the woods, and no deer to be found – unless you know where to look! Includes hunter, dog, trees, rock, deer and monument.

189-7632 The Place We Walk **15.99**

189-7633 Free Culture (Freie Knips Kultur) **15.99**

189-7634 Much Cackling About Nothing **15.99**

189-7635 Merry Christmas **17.99**

189-7636 Dinosaur Escape **15.99**

189-7637 Graffiti Artist at Work **17.99**

189-7638 Santa Driving Convertible **17.99**

189-7639 Merry Christmas-1999 **19.99** ***NEW***
Santa hitches reindeer to a Goli 3-Wheeler. Includes figures, snowman, fence, pine tree and specially lettered vehicle.

189-7660 Big Ones are Biting **10.99** ***NEW***
Two fishermen, small pier, small bush and circling sharks!

189-7661 Backyard Dilemma **12.99** ***NEW***
Includes two neighbors, bird feeder, flowering bush, fence and scarecrow.

189-7662 Danger-Glass! **12.99** ***NEW***
Two workers lifting a large pane of glass and a fast-moving bike rider spell trouble.

189-7663 Blind Justice **14.99** ***NEW***
Traffic cop writes ticket while thief makes off with bike. Includes sign, figures and vehicles.

189-7664 Tire Changer **14.99** ***NEW***
Includes figure, tools and automobile.

189-7665 Telephone Repair Crew **11.99** ***NEW***
Two workers, barricades and more.

189-7666 Street Repair Crew **9.99** ***NEW***
Two workers, warning signs and tools.

189-7667 Railroad Signal Maintainers **14.99** ***NEW***
Two workers and assorted accessories.

189-7680 Picnic on the Green **14.99** ***NEW***
Two figures, automobile and more.

189-7668 The Slow Apprentice **14.99** ***NEW***
New mechanic learns the tricks of the trade. Includes auto, lift, welding tanks and figures.

189-7669 Rest in Peace **16.99** ***NEW***
Graveside scene includes Priest, Undertaker, 1931 Ford Hearse, casket and more.

189-7671 Garden Party **9.99** ***NEW***
Three figures with picnic table.

189-7670 Occupied Outhouse **11.99** ***NEW***
Includes two figures, tree, outhouse and fence.

189-7672 Asphalt Swallows **13.99** ***NEW***
Two figures, nonworking street light and automobile.

189-7673 Teenager's Hang-Out **15.99** ***NEW***
Three figures, two vehicles, nonworking streetlight and bench.

189-7674 The Fast Traveling Salesman **10.99** ***NEW***
Open gate, angry dog! Includes figures, fence, sign and more

189-7675 The Blind Date **9.99** ***NEW***
Includes two figures, clock and fence.

189-7681 Any Landing You Can Walk Away From. . . **14.99** ***NEW***
Includes glider in tree, two figures, fence.

BACHMANN

FENCES

160-42100 pkg(24) **5.00**

PARK ITEMS

160-42209 City Park Accessories **6.00**

BRAWA

IMPORTED FROM GERMANY BY WALTHERS

VIADUCT

186-2880 16.99
"Berlin Stadbahn" railroad arches w/shops. Plastic kit is molded in appropriate colors. With 2 arch sections; approximately 3 x 8-1/2". Arches are about 4-1/4" long.

WALLS

Additional wall sections for use with 186-2880.

ARCH W/RECESS

186-2881 Arcade Wall pkg(2) **14.99**

ARCH W/ENCLOSED WINDOWS

186-2882 Arcade Wall pkg(2) **14.99**

ARCHED RETAINING WALLS PKG(2) EA 4.99

6 x 4"

186-2860 Gray - 6 Arches
186-2865 Gray - 4 Arches

186-2866 Brick Red- 4 Arches

CS DESIGN, INC.

ROADWAYS

155-7001 Scale Crete™ 32oz **13.95**
Ready-to-use latex for modeling concrete with authentic color and texture. Apply with putty knife. Covers 6 square feet at 1/16" thickness.

CUSTOM RAILWAY SUPPLY

Limited Quantity Available On All Items

WROUGHT IRON FENCES EA 3.95

Made of photo-etched metal to capture prototype detail and thickness. Use around homes, cemeteries or other models.

212-1065 Gate Only

212-1066 Gate & Panel

DEPOTS BY JOHN

BRICK TUNNEL PORTAL

87-130 6.95

Chooch Enterprises Inc.®

TUNNEL PORTALS

SINGLE TRACK EA 6.25

214-8320 Concrete

214-8321 Cascade

214-8322 High Cube Concrete

214-8340 Cut Stone

214-8360 Random Stone

DOUBLE TRACK EA 6.49

214-8330 Concrete

214-8350 Cut Stone

214-8370 Random Stone

BRIDGE ABUTMENTS

SINGLE TRACK EA 6.49

Fits Central Valley Rigid Truss Bridge (#210-1902)

214-8440 Cut Stone
214-8460 Cut Stone Tapered

DOUBLE TRACK

214-8450 Cut Stone **6.99**

BRIDGE PIERS

214-8430 Cut Stone **6.99**
For Central Valley Bridge.
214-8431 Cut Stone Rectangular **6.99**
For Central Valley Bridge.

WALLS

STEPPED WALLS EA 6.99

214-8400 Cut Stone
6.6 x 3.75"

214-8420 Concrete
6.75 x 3.75"

INTERLOCKING RETAINING EA 6.99 (UNLESS NOTED)

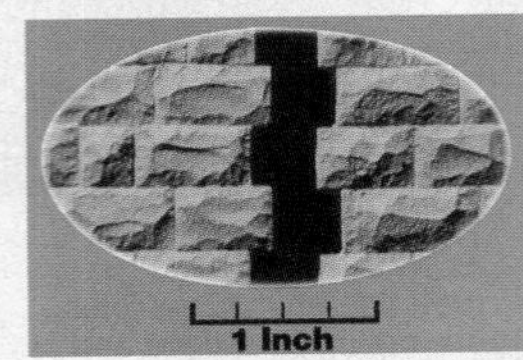

Diagram reflects size of interlocking retaining walls.

RANDOM STONE

214-8300 Small

214-8302 Medium

214-8304 Large

CUT STONE

214-8310 Small

214-8312 Medium

214-8314 Large
214-8315 Extra Large **17.99**
NEW
10 x 7.25"

Bridge Pier 214-8430

Bridge Pier 214-8431

Stepped Wall 214-8400

Stepped Wall 214-8420

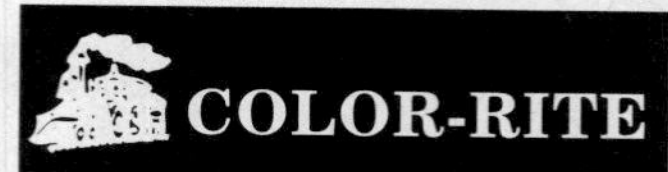

ROCK MOLDS

ROCK MOLDS EA 3.69

Made of soft vinyl for the "Wet Method" of applying rock castings. Each mold allows unlimited variations, using finger and thumb pressure. Almost indestructible, will not lose detail with use. Unconditional, free, lifetime replacement guarantee by Color Rite.

211-801 8 Mold Set **27.95**
Includes one each #802 - 809.

211-802 3-1/2 x 3-1/2"

211-803 6 x 2-1/2"

211-804 4 x 4-1/4"

211-805 8 x 3-1/2"

211-806 4-1/4 x 2-1/2"

211-807 4-3/4 x 3-1/2"

211-808 6-1/2 x 4-1/4"

211-809 5 x 3-1/2"

ROCK MOLD SET

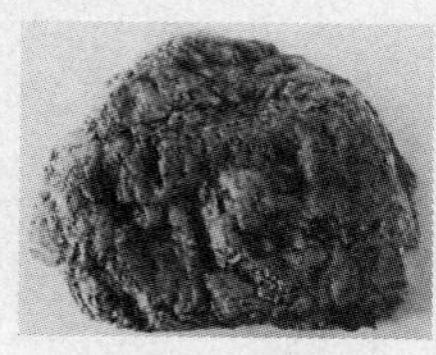

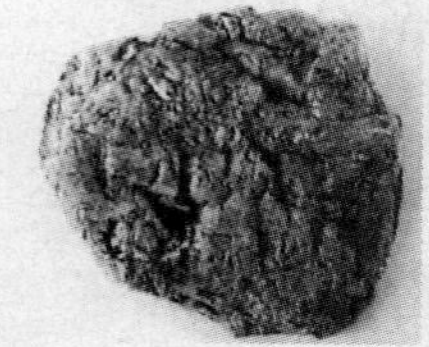

211-810 5 Mold Set (Large) **27.95**
Bigger molds cover large area in less time. Molds are 6 x 6-1/2" to 6-1/2 x 8" in area and 1/2" deep.

Lake & River Kit 211-702

Waterfall Kit 211-701

WATER

LAKE & RIVER KIT

211-702 9.95
Realistic water without the danger and smell of flammable resins. Contains wax base and high gloss finish that won't affect wax. Covers about 300 square inches.

WATERFALL KIT

211-701 4.95
62' high by 26' wide (HO Scale).
Easy way to model realistic waterfalls. Heat-sensitive plastic is easily cut, and can be shaped using hot water. Material is semi-transparent; spray paint the back to model water of any color.

COLORING

COLOR PIGMENTS 3OZ EA 3.95 (UNLESS NOTED)

According to "Scenery for Model Railroads" (Kalmbach #400-12008), Pure Paint Pigments are the only coloring recommended for mixing with plaster for "zip-texturing" or hardshell scenicking.

211-301 Chrome Green **4.95**
211-302 Chrome Yellow **4.95**
211-303 Burnt Sienna
211-304 Raw Sienna
211-305 Burnt Umber
211-306 Raw Umber

ROCK & EARTH STAINS 4OZ EA 2.50 (UNLESS NOTED)

Highly concentrated will not fade like water colors. Acrylic base stains for recreating Nature's coloring on exposed rock.

211-402 Yellow Ochre
211-403 Burnt Sienna
211-404 Raw Sienna
211-405 Burnt Umber
211-406 Raw Umber
211-407 Lamp Black
211-408 Ultra-Marine Blue
211-401 Assortment **14.95**
One each #402-408.

DETAIL ASSOCIATES

Create a unique backdrop for your layout, module or diorama with Rail Scenes. Printed modules can be joined in any order, creating a unique scene. Each measures 8-1/2 x 22" (21.25 x 55cm).

BACKGROUND SCENES

229-7501

229-7502

229-7503

229-7504

229-7505

229-7506

229-7507

229-7508

229-7509

229-7510

229-7511

229-7512

RAIL SCENES EA 6.98

229-7501 City
229-7502 Downtown
229-7503 Industrial District
229-7504 Lumber Yard
229-7505 Estuary
229-7506 Tank Farm
229-7507 Oil Fields
229-7508 Farm Town
229-7509 Land
229-7510 Woods
229-7511 Forest
229-7512 Mountains

INSTRUCTION MANUAL

229-7550 4.98
38-page illustrated booklet contains instructions for creating backdrops, shows possible combinations and suggestions for details.
11 x 8-1/2"

Information STATION

Scenery Source Materials

Real railroads were built through the existing scenery. But if they had had a choice, they might have made things a lot easier! For modelers, scenery construction is a fast and easy part of creating a complete layout. You don't have to be an artist, and you can work at your own pace over areas large or small. There's a huge range of materials available to recreate everything from snow-capped mountains, to lush forests to barren deserts.

To help you understand what materials are available and how they can be used, here are just a few of the innovative and interesting books and videos you can select:

Kalmbach has several books dedicated to improving the scenery on a layout. HO Railroad from Set to Scenery (400-12144) offers advice for beginners, including plenty of hands-on scenery construction tips. 303 Tips For Detailing Model Railroad Scenery and Structures (400-12153) offers practical and effective advice for improving the realism of the buildings and scenery on your model railroad. The Pennsy Middle Division in HO Scale (400-12170) shows how to use many of today's scenery materials to capture the look of a real railroad.

Model Railroading with John Allen (400-12177) examines the philosophy, techniques and ideas of this legendary modeler who was a pioneer in the creation of realistic layouts.

FALLER

Creating realistic scenery is fast and fun with the complete Faller line. No matter what kind of terrain you're creating, you'll find trees, groundcover and many other easy to use materials that produce realistic miniature scenes.

TREES

DECIDUOUS

272-1412 Small 2-1/2" pkg(4) **5.99**

272-1410 Large 5-1/4" pkg(3) **6.99**
272-1413 Small 2-1/2" pkg(4) **5.99**
272-1416 Medium 4-1/4" pkg(4) **6.99**

272-1488 Small 2-3/8" pkg(6) **6.99**

272-1452 Beech 8" 20cm Tall **10.99** ***NEW***

272-1453 Large, 5-1/2" pkg(2) **7.99**

272-1470 Trees 5" 13 cm pkg(14) **21.99**
272-1471 Small 1-3/16 - 2-3/8" pkg(15) **18.99**

272-1473 Mixed Woodland Trees Height 2 to 3-5/8" 5-9cm pkg(15) **18.99**

FRUIT EA 6.99 (UNLESS NOTED)

272-1400 Large 4-1/2" w/o Fruit pkg(3)
272-1401 Medium 3-1/4" w/o Fruit pkg(3)
272-1402 Small 2-1/2" w/o Fruit pkg(4)
272-1403 Apple 3-1/4 - 4" pkg(3)
272-1406 Cherry pkg(3)
272-1407 Small 2-1/3" w/Fruit pkg(4)
272-1408 Medium 4-1/4" Rowan w/Fruit pkg(3)
272-1414 Small 1-3/16 - 2-3/8" pkg(5)

272-1417 Green Foliage w/Fruit pkg(5)
272-1418 Red & Green Foliage w/Fruit pkg(5)
Trees are about 1-1/8 to 1-1/2" tall (3-4 cm).
272-1419 Wall Fruit-Small 1-3/16 - 1-5/8" pkg(5)
272-1445 Fruit Trees pkg(4) **7.99**

272-1472 Assorted Height 2-3/8 to 4-3/8" 5-9cm pkg(15) **21.99**

272-1484 Lime 6-13/32" 16cm Tall **8.99** ***NEW***

ELM

272-1458 Large 7-3/16" **10.99**

OAK

272-1450 Large Oak 6-5/8" **7.99**
272-1483 Small Oaks 4-1/4" pkg(2) **12.99**

WEEPING WILLOW

272-1424 Medium 3-7/8" pkg(2) **7.99**

BIRCH EA 6.99 (UNLESS NOTED)

272-1423 3-1/2" pkg(4)
272-1422 Medium 4-1/4" pkg(4)
272-1456 Assorted 4-1/2" pkg(3) **5.99**

272-1420 Medium 5-1/8" pkg(3)
272-1457 6-3/4" **7.99**
272-1415 1-3/4" Mini pkg(5) **5.99**
272-1486 Small 2-3/16" pkg(5)

BEECH

272-1454 7" 18 cm pkg(2) **6.99**

POPLAR EA 6.99 (UNLESS NOTED)

272-1421 6" 15cm pkg(4) **10.99**

272-1425 Large 5-1/4" pkg(3)
272-1426 White 5-1/2" pkg(4) **7.99**
272-1460 Black, Medium pkg(4)

272-1487 Small 2-1/2" pkg(5)

FLOWERING

272-1475 Forsythia -Yellow Flowers pkg(6) **6.99**

CHESTNUT

272-1463 Large 6-3/4" **7.99**

TREE ASSORTMENTS

272-1491 Deciduous 4" 10cm Tall pkg(15) **18.99** ***NEW***

272-1492 Mixed Deciduous & Coniferous 4 to 5-5/8" 10 to 14cm Tall pkg(15) **21.99** ***NEW***

272-1493 Silver Firs 2 to 4-13/16" 5 to 12cm Tall pkg(40) **33.99** ***NEW***

EVERGREENS

BLUE SPRUCE

272-1432 Blue Spruce pkg(3) **6.99**
One medium 4-1/2" and two large 5-1/2"

TAMARACK (LARGE) EA 6.99

272-1437 Assorted 4-1/2" pkg(3)
272-1438 Small 3-1/2" pkg(4)

PINE EA 6.99 (UNLESS NOTED)

272-1433 Large Fir 4-1/2" pkg(3)
272-1435 Tall Spruce 6-1/2" pkg(8)
272-1436 Medium 4" pkg(3)
272-1434 Small Fir 2" pkg(5)
272-1431 Medium Fir 3-3/4" pkg(4)
272-1430 Large Fir 5-1/2" pkg(3)
272-1441 Nordic Pine 5 1/4" pkg(3)

FALLER

272-1462 Nordic, 3" 8 cm pkg(4)
272-1482 Fir 7" pkg(8) **10.99**

272-1485 Pines 2-3/8" pkg(5)

COLORADO SPRUCE

272-1439 5 ea: 3-1/2, 4-3/4 & 6" pkg(15) **12.99**
272-1480 pkg(6) **6.99**

HEDGES

EA 5.99 (UNLESS NOTED)

272-1446 Large 6-1/2" pkg(2)

272-1449 Small 19" pkg(2)

272-1447 Small 4" pkg(3)

PINE ASSORTMENTS

272-1318 4 ea: 1-1/4 & 5-1/2" kit pkg(8) **13.99**

272-1440 10 ea: 1-1/4, 2 & 2-3/4" pkg(30) **13.99**

272-1461 Silver Firs Height 2 to 3-5/8" 5-9cm pkg(15) **27.99** ***NEW***

272-1464 Fir, Assorted pkg(50) Sizes ranging from 4 to 6" **22.99**

272-1465 Fir, Assorted pkg(25) Sizes ranging from 4-3/4 to 6-1/2" **17.99**

272-1448 Medium 19" pkg(2)
272-1466 Flowering, White pkg(2)
5-1/2 x 1/2" 14 x 1.4 cm
272-1467 Flowering Hedge pkg(2)
272-1469 Flowering Hedge pkg(3)
272-1489 Long - pkg(3) **8.99**
20 x 1" 50 x 1 x 2.7 cm

BUSHES (SHRUBS) EA 6.99 (UNLESS NOTED)

272-1474 Assortment pkg(12) **11.99**
272-1476 Red Flowers pkg(6)
272-1478 Blooming 1-1/2" pkg(6)
272-1479 Green 1-1/2" pkg(6)
272-1442 Hazel Bushes pkg(10)
Stick-in mounting.

272-1443 Large Bushes pkg(3) **5.99**
272-1444 Small Bushes pkg(3) **5.99**

VINES

272-1490 Vineyard w/Poles pkg(36) **13.99**
Complete vineyard with foliage and poles, each about 1-1/4" 3 cm tall.

GROUND COVER

GROUND COVER MATERIAL EA 2.99 (UNLESS NOTED)

272-701 Black **1.99**
272-712 Spring Green
272-713 Forest Green
272-714 Flowery Meadow

FLOCK EA 2.99

FINE .88OZ
272-756 Spring Green
272-757 Dark Green

MEDIUM .53OZ
272-758 Spring Green
272-759 Dark Green

COARSE .53OZ
272-760 Spring Green, Coarse
272-761 Dark Green, Coarse
272-762 Multicolor, Coarse

SCATTER MATERIAL

1oz packages.

272-702 Spring Green **1.99**
272-703 Forest Green **1.99**
272-707 Yellow **1.99**
272-710 Meadow Green **1.99**
272-725 Grass Fiber **4.99**
272-726 Grass, Dark Green **4.99**

272-716 Marsh Reeds pkg(20) **7.99**

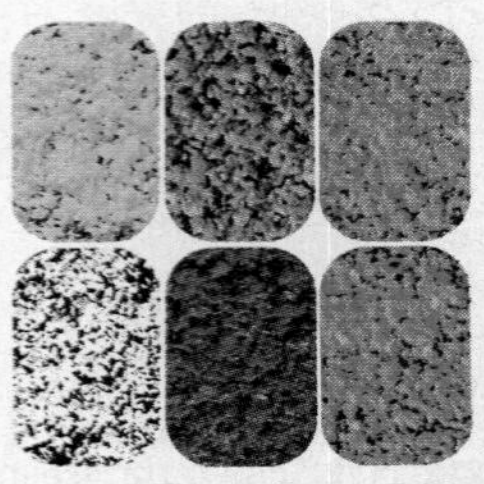

272-717 Flower Decor **7.99**
272-718 Green Foam **8.99**
272-727 Dark Brown **4.99**
272-708 Light Blue **1.99**
272-709 Flower Red **1.99**

LICHEN

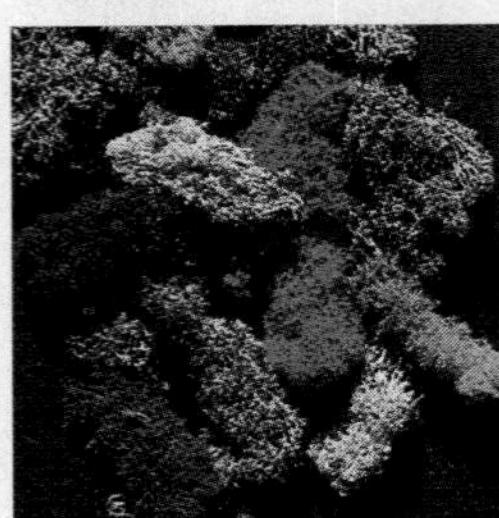

272-730 5 Assorted Colors 2.8oz **7.99**

SAND 1-1/2LB EA 12.99
272-749 Earth Brown
272-750 Soil Brown

FALLER

SCENERY MATERIAL ASSORTMENTS

Contains 10 colors of scatter material: 3 shades of green, 2 shades of brown, and one of each: gray, red, black, blue and yellow.

272-700 Large Material Assortment **11.99**
Contains: 6 shades of scatter material, 2 shades of fibers (brown & green), green lichen and green flocks.

272-698 Small Material Assortment **9.99**

272-735 Winter Scene Making Set **39.99**
Set includes enough material to completely cover an area about 39-1/ 4 x 39-1/4" (100 x 100cm) or three to four houses and some trees. Comes complete with detailed instructions, six trees, spatula and large and small Icicles.

CASTING MATERIAL

Colored compound for landscape formations, rock castings etc.One each: brown, gray and ochre.

272-502 Hydrozell Powder Assortment 3/4oz **6.99**
272-503 Hydrozell Powder 4-1/2oz **5.99**
Uncolored.

272-657 Hydrozell Powder 8-3/4oz **10.99**
Gray, 240 gram package.

GROUND MATS

LIGHT GREEN

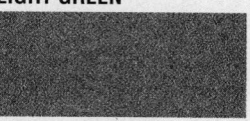

272-766 Small **9.99**
40 x 30" 100 x 75cm

272-767 Medium **19.99**
40 x 60" 100 x 150cm

272-769 Large **31.99**
40 x 100" 100 x 250cm

MEADOW GREEN

272-781 Small **9.99**
40 x 30" 100 x 75cm

272-782 Medium **19.99**
40 x 60" 100 x 150cm

272-783 Large **31.99**
40 x 100" 100 x 250cm

DARK GREEN

272-770 Small **9.99**
40 x 30" 100 x 75cm

272-771 Medium **19.99**
40 x 60" 100 x 150cm

272-773 Large **31.99**
40 x 100" 100 x 250cm

FLOWERING MEADOW

272-774 Small **9.99**
40 x 30" 100 x 75cm

272-775 Medium **19.99**
40 x 60" 100 x 150cm

272-777 Large **31.99**
40 x 100" 100 x 250cm

272-784 Wild Flowers **7.99**
NEW
40 x 30" 100 x 75cm

BALLAST EA 7.99

40 x 30" 100 x 75cm

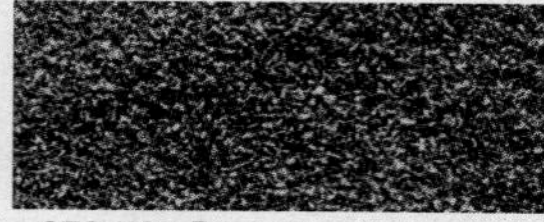

272-785 Dark Brown New

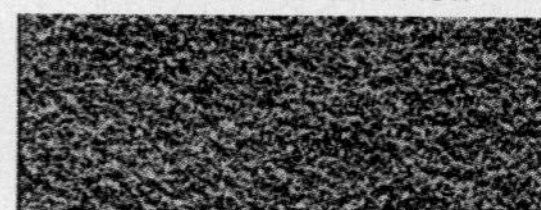

272-786 Light Brown Ballast
NEW

GRASS WITH SHAKER APPLICATOR EA 8.99

Makes neat, easy work of applying grass. Includes shaker, ready for use.

272-752 Light Green w/Shaker 7oz
272-753 Dark Green w/Shaker 7oz
272-754 Meadow Flowers w/Shaker 7oz
272-755 Ground Cover-Brown 6oz w/o Shaker

GRASS SHAKER REFILLS 3-1/2OZ EA 7.99

272-736 Light Green
272-737 Dark Green

SOIL 1OZ EA 1.99

272-704 Plowed Field
272-705 Sand Brown

COAL

272-723 2.99

ROCKS EA 2.99 (UNLESS NOTED)

272-741 Natural Gray 8-3/4oz (250g)

272-742 Dark Brown (Soil) 8-3/4oz (250g)

272-745 Quarry Stones - Gray Granite 8-3/4oz (250g)
272-722 Gravel, Stone Gray
272-740 Slate, Natural 8.9oz
272-743 Slate, Gray 8.9oz
272-744 Quartz 8.9oz
272-747 Beach Pebble, Beige 8.9oz

Limited Quantity Available
272-715 Assorted Rocks 2.1oz **7.99**
Made of foam material for easy shaping and installation.

ROCK WALLS EA 13.99

Realistic texture and hand-painted to enhance detail, each section is made of polyurethane foam, and is easily cut to fit your layout

272-793 Gneiss

272-794 Stratified Rock

272-795 Red Sandstone

BALLAST

272-706 Gray 1.58oz **1.99**
272-720 Gravel Brown 1.6oz **2.99**
272-721 Brown/Gray **2.99**
272-731 Dark Brown 10.5oz **5.99**
272-732 Light Brown 10.5oz **5.99**
272-751 Track (Brown) 24oz **12.99**
272-778 Gray Mat **8.99**
Use for yards, parking lots etc. Measures 40 x 30" 100 x 75cm.

BUILDING MATERIALS

EA 1.30 (UNLESS NOTED)

Embossed panels are preprinted in appropriate colors. Panels measure: 9-7/8 x 4-7/8" 25 x 12.5 cm. Dealers MUST order in multiples of 10.

272-608 Red Brick

272-601 Cobblestone

272-604 Cut Stone-Brown

272-605 Cut Stone-Yellow

272-606 Cut Stone-Gray

272-610 Natural Stone

272-614 Cut Stone-Brown

272-615 Cut Stone-Yellow

272-616 Cut Stone-Gray

272-613 Cut Stone-Red

272-600 Sidewalk

272-607 Glazed Brick

272-617 Cut Stone-Basalt

272-618 Cut Stone-Slate

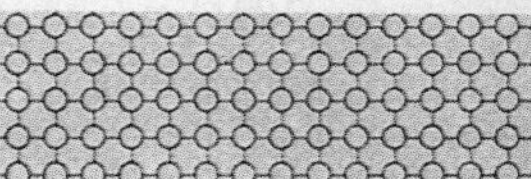

272-619 Ornamental Pavement

272-620 Cut Stone-Limestone

FALLER

MINI-SCENES

272-575 Barbecue Site 3 x 2" 7.8 x 5.4cm **19.99**
Includes wooden hut with benches, tables and stools, open and stone fireplaces and pile of firewood. A smoke generator can be fitted into the stone fireplace to bring the scene to life.

WATER

272-791 Lake Construction Kit 21-1/4 x 10-1/4" 53 x 26cm **9.99**
Includes rippled plastic sheet for realistic wave surface, which can be painted or use the blue paper (included) for coloring. Easily cut and shaped.

BACKGROUND SCENES

Each scene is a full color photo, printed on several paper panels.

272-511 Black Forest-Baar Extension **29.99**
Set of four panels can be used to enlarge #514 (sold separately) to the right or left as desired. 155-3/16 x 26" 388 x 65cm total length. Panels can also be used alone.

272-512 "Neuschwanstein" **21.99**
2 sections, totaling 10' - 8" x 40" 320 x 100cm

272-513 "Karwendelgebirge" **21.99**
2 sections, totaling 10' - 8" x 40" 320 x 100cm

272-514 Schwarzwald-Baar **29.99**
4 sections totaling 12'-9" x 26" 388 x 65cm

272-515 "Lowenstein" **22.99**
3 sections totaling 9'-8" x 17-3/4" 290 x 45cm

272-516 "Oberstdorf" **22.99**
3 sections totaling 9'-8" x 17-3/4" 290 x 45cm

272-517 Oberstdorf Expander Scene **22.99**
Three part expander scene use with #516 to increase over-all length to about 6 yards (5.8 meters).

Black Forest-Baar Extension Scene 272-511

"Neuschwanstein" Scene 272-512

"Karwendelgebirge" Scene 272-513

Schwarzwald-Baar Scene 272-514

"Lowenstein" Scene 272-515

Oberdorf Scene 272-516

Oberdorf Expander Scene 272-517

TUNNEL PORTALS

Tunnel portal kits are pre-colored plastic and include numbered instructions.

SINGLE TRACK

272-558 Low Clearance - Steam Era **5.99**
2-3/4" 7.2cm clearance

272-557 Loreley Tunnel pkg(2) **29.99**
5-3/4 x 3-1/2" (14 x 8.5cm) North and South portal
6-3/4 x 6" (17 x 15cm) Ornate castle design, includes North portal.

272-559 High Clearance - Steam Era **7.99**
Optional cap for 3-31/2" or 4" 9 or 9.8cm clearance.

272-561 Low Clearance for Steam Era pkg(2) **4.49**
2-3/4" 7.2cm clearance

272-563 High Clearance for Catenary pkg(2) **4.99**
3-3/4" 8.5cm clearance

DOUBLE TRACK

272-564 Kyllburg **14.99**
4" (10cm) Clearance
This ornate entry is based on an actual portal in use at Kyllburg. It can be used with steam or electric locos.

272-565 Steam & Catenary Operation pkg(2) **5.99**
4" 10cm clearance

272-566 Portal Set pkg(2) **10.99**
4" 10cm clearance

Matching portals will add realism to every tunnel along your line. Enough clearance for overhead catenary, and perfect for use with steam or diesel power too.

TUNNEL ACCESSORIES

272-540 Assorted Structural Sections **8.99**

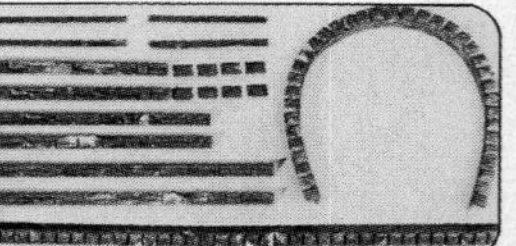

272-550 Facing Strips **9.99**
272-424 Interior Wall Card **34.99**

FALLER

WATER PUMP

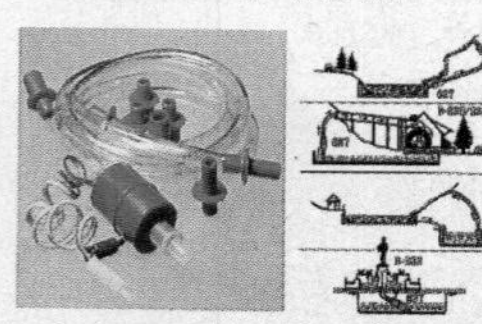

272-627 Water Pump & Accessories **27.99**
Pump real water anywhere on your layout. Includes 12-16V AC electric pump, 36" 90 cm PVC hose and two connecting pieces, plus detailed instructions.

PLASTER CLOTH

A neat and easy way to create hills and other landscapes. Special cloth is pretreated with plaster. Dip in water and apply. Rolls include 80" of cloth.

272-663 4" Wide **5.99**
272-664 8" Wide **8.99**

LANDSCAPE PAPER

272-666 Gray Crepe Paper **7.99** *NEW*
Use to model a variety of surfaces, such as lightly eroded rocks, roadways, stream beds and many other applications. Sheet measures 60 x 30" 150 x 75cm.

WIRE MESH

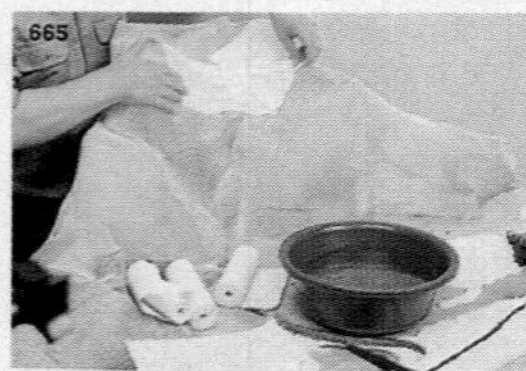

272-665 Aluminum Screening **17.99**
Flexible and easily formed as a base for mountains, hills and other scenic formations. Measures 40 x 32" 100 x 80cm.

BOOKS

272-840 Scenic Modeling Made Easy **10.99**
English text, introduction to scenic modeling using Faller materials. Covers initial planning, tools and materials, getting started, mountain building, rock design, water, assembling structures, backgrounds, laying track, ballasting, bridges and viaducts, winter landscaping, dioramas and electrical tips. Over 120 color illustrations, soft cover, 35 pages, 8-1/4 x 11-1/2".

FENCES

272-518 Iron Fence w/Concrete Posts **11.99**
12 wire sections each 8" 20cm and 80 concrete posts.

272-520 Metal Industrial Fencing **12.99**
272-521 Ornate Garden Fence pkg(18) **12.99**
A neat touch for any older home.

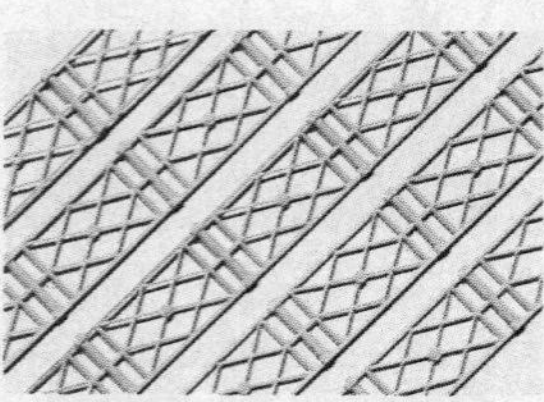

272-522 Railing Fence 7" pkg(8) **12.99**

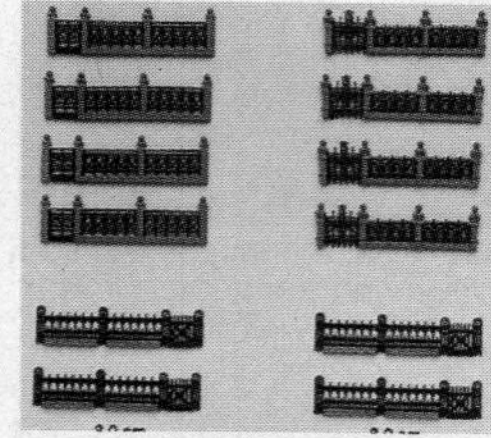

272-523 Wrought Iron 3 - 3-1/4" pkg(24) **12.99**
Includes fine mesh, concrete posts, corner posts, entry and moveable, wide sliding door. 41" 105cm total length.

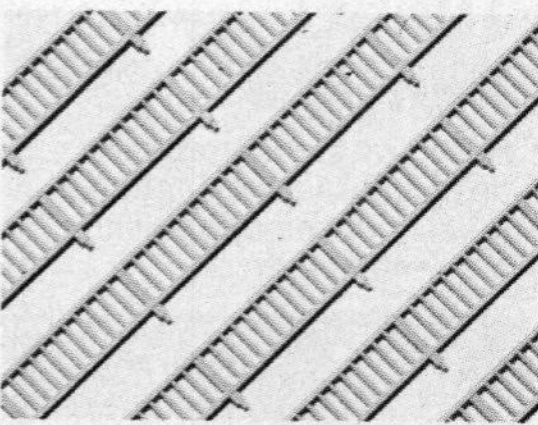

272-524 Fencing 57-1/2" pkg(8) **9.99**

272-525 Garden & Field 142" **10.99**

272-526 Assorted Fences 7" pkg(10) **10.99**

272-527 Black Metal 7" pkg(10) **10.99**
Assorted fences and matching gates.

272-528 Rough Wooden Picket Fence w/Gate 31-3/4" pkg(6) **7.99**

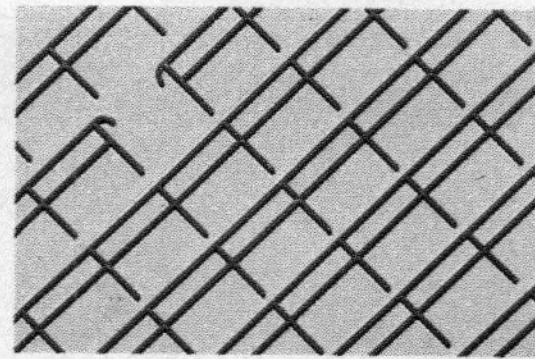

272-529 Iron Hand Railing pkg(6) 3' **9.99**

GLUE

Colofix glues are tinted and dry to the color listed. Ideal for use with various shades of ground cover, grass and ballast.

272-660 Colofix-Brown 9.2oz **7.99**

272-661 Colofix-Green 9.2oz **7.99**

272-662 Colofix-Gray 7.5oz **5.99**
Packaged in a special applicator for use with track.

272-501 Colofix Wood Compound-White **6.99**
White wood cement, dries clear and is perfect for applying scenery material.

PAINT

Water-based acrylic paint can be thinned with water.

272-796 Granite Rock Paint 3.5oz 118ml **9.99**
Adds realistic coloring to rock surfaces.

272-797 Sand Ground Paint 3.5oz 118ml **9.99**
Perfect for country roads, beaches or other sandy areas.

272-507 Roadway Paint 7.5oz 250ml **7.99**
Realistic asphalt color for highways, parking lots, driveways or other paved surfaces.

FILLER MATERIAL

272-654 Terrain Filler Putty 17.5oz 500g **7.99**
Dark gray powder mixes with water for easy-to-use putty. Make rocks and other terrain, or spread smooth to model roads.

272-500 Filler **7.99**
Build all kinds of realistic roads and terrain with this material. Filler is self-adhesive and easy to use. Ideal for constructing your own road surfaces for the Faller car system.

272-655 Terrain Filler-Brown 17.5oz 500g **7.99**
Realistic brown color is perfect for rock and landscape formations. Material is self-adhesive and designed for ease of use.

272-658 Putty Compound-Green 8.4oz 240g **10.99**
This green material is perfect for landscaping yards, parks, fields or meadows that will be covered with grass (sold separately). Helps hide spots where grass may be brushed off.

ROADWAY

Self-adhesive rub on transfers.

FLEXIBLE

272-591 Roadway Markings **9.99**

272-650 2-Lane Flexible - w/Markings 3 x 3" **6.99**
272-651 2-Lane Flexible - Less Markings 3 x 3" **4.99**
272-652 Roman Stone 2 x 3" **5.99**
272-1677 Junction Branch Off **22.99**

PARKING SPAVE MARKINGS EA 6.99

4 x 2-1/2

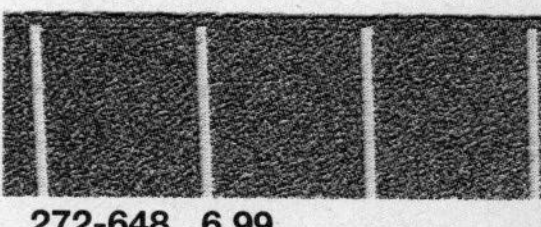

272-648 **6.99**

272-649 **6.99**

FALLER

COBBLESTONE PAVEMENT

Self-adhesive material with realistic color.

272-646 Square **9.99**
Measures 19-3/16 x 9-5/8" 48 x 24cm.

272-647 Arch **6.99**
Measures 4 x 2-13/16" 10 x 7cm.

MISCELLANEOUS

272-573 Picnic Accessories **13.99**
Includes two tables, benches, stools, fountain and wood pile to finish any park scene.

272-576 Playground Equipment **13.99**
Complete with slide, swings, merry-go-round, sandbox, jungle gym, pipes and more. Great for school or park scene.

272-955 Telegraph Poles pkg(10) **8.99**

INDUSTRIAL HERITAGE SCALE MODELS

We have worked closely with this manufacturer to provide accurate delivery information at the time this catalog was published. Items listed in blue ink may not be available at all times. Current delivery information, along with a list of in-stock products for this line, can be found on our Web site at www.walthers.com.

TREES

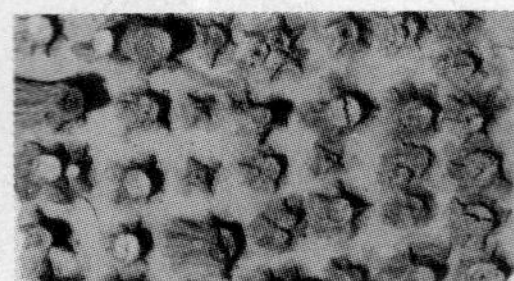

356-1201 Stumps pkg(36) **6.75**
Resin castings, easily stained to represent a variety of stumps.

356-1202 Western Stumps **7.75**
Similar to #1201, but larger diameter, many have spring platform notches.

356-1203 Fallen Logs **7.75**
A set of 10 resin logs of various sizes cast from hand carved masters reflecting various levels of the rot and decay found on logs lying on the forest floor.

WALLS

356-1120 Tie Cribbing Wall pkg(4) **7.75**
Four interlocking pieces, each 3/4 x 5-1/2"

356-1121 Rail Reinforced Tie Wall pkg(4) **7.75**
Four interlocking pieces, each 3/4 x 5-1/2", of stacked ties supported by lengths of rail driven into the ground.

356-1122 Precast Concrete Cribbing Wall pkg(2) **7.75**
Two interlocking pieces, each 1-1/4 x 6". Will interlock end to end, or stack vertically to match common prototype construction.

356-1212 Rectangular **9.75**
Will interlock with itself or Sloping Walls (#356-1213) to represent large, cut stone masonry common in the eastern US. 3-1/4 x 9-1/2"

356-1213 Sloping pkg(2) **9.75**
Will interlock together or with rectangular wall #356-1212.

356-1214 Interlocking Stone pkg(3) **7.75**
Each measures 1 x 5-3/4", will interlock with #1212 and 1213.

TUNNEL PORTALS

Based on standard B&O designs. Cast polyurethane resin, requires only painting and weathering.

356-1101 Wide Stone Portal 5-1/2 x 10" **7.75**
Use for early steam-era double track, or as a rebuilt single track tunnel, with clearance for modern equipment.

356-1102 Double Track Brick Portal **7.75**

356-1104 Single Track Stone Portal **6.50**

CULVERTS

356-1105 16' Stone Arch pkg(2) **10.50**
Includes stone wing walls

356-1106 Steel Pipe w/Concrete Head Wall pkg(2) **6.50**
1 pair each 12" and 24" diameter pipes.

356-1107 Wood Box Culvert **6.50**
Used for crossing small streams with a span of 7 ft., 7 ft. height.

356-1108 Small Culverts 2 Pair **6.50**
Two pairs of culverts, 1 wood and 1 concrete, designed to be inserted into cork roadbed for layouts with no sub-roadbed.

WATER

356-1210 Falling Water **7.75**
3-1/2 x 6" Clear resin casting is easily cut to represent a large waterfall or light cascade from drain pipe.

TREES

TREE ASSORTMENTS EA 19.99

Assortments include Shade, Birch, Cedar, Oak, Ash, Maple, Evergreen, Juniper, Fir, Forest Pine and Hedgerows. Each assortment includes trees in various heights (as noted) which can be used in any scale. Trees are fully assembled, with plastic trunks and realistic foam foliage.

338-301 Small Trees 1-1/2 - 3-1/2" pkg(40)

338-302 Small Trees 2 - 3-1/2" pkg(40)

338-303 Medium Trees 2-1/2 - 4" pkg(30)

338-304 Medium Trees 3-5" pkg(24)

338-305 Medium Trees 2-1/2 - 5" pkg(12)

338-306 Small Pines 2 - 3-1/2" pkg(30)

338-307 Large Pines 4-7" pkg(12)

338-308 Large Trees 4-7" pkg(12)

338-309 Small Pines 1-1/2 - 3" pkg(100)

An entire forest in a single set! Great for use by themselves, or combine with larger trees to model a variety of scenes. Pines are fully assembled, ready for use on your layout.

LICHEN

5OZ EA 7.99
338-401 Light Green
338-402 Dark Green
338-403 Assorted Colors

FEATHER LITE
Scenic Railroad™

All units are manufactured in a lightweight low-density foam. This enables the modeler to make any useful changes to suit the requirement of the layout. All units represent American Railroading precisely. Designs by Doug Goodsell.

We have worked closely with this manufacturer to provide accurate delivery information at the time this catalog was published. Items listed in blue ink may not be available at all times. Current delivery information, along with a list of in-stock products for this line, can be found on our Web site at www.walthers.com.

BOOK

311-100 Small Spaces **10.00**
Step-by-step guide shows how to build a small, lightweight layout using Feather Lite materials.

BRIDGES

311-42602 Double - 5 x 14" 12.5 x 35cm **12.00**

BRIDGE ABUTMENTS & PIERS

CAJON CREEK

311-43020 Single Track - Cut Stone Bridge Abutment w/Insert 3 x 5" 7.5 x 12.5cm **10.00**

311-44010 Pier 3-1/2 x 3" 8.7 x 7.5cm **8.00**

DARBY CREEK

311-43000 Single Track Concrete Abutment w/Adjuster 3-1/2 x 2-7/8" **10.00**
311-43002 Double Track Concrete Abutment w/Adjustable Insert 5-3/4 x 3-1/2" **12.00**

311-43010 Single Track Concrete Pier 3 x 3-3/4" 7.5 x 8.1cm **8.00**
311-43012 Double Track Concrete Pier 6 x 4" **10.00**

311-43013 Pier Extender 3 x 3-1/4" 7.5 x 8.1cm **5.00**

311-43030 Single Track Cut Stone Bridge Pier w/Debris Deflector 3 x 3-1/2" **8.00**
311-43040 Single Track Concrete Foundation 4 x 1-1/2" **5.00**

ROCK CASTINGS

SMALL EA 7.00

7 x 9" 17.5 x 22.5cm

311-102 Midway Rock (Granite)
311-103 Standing Bear (Limestone)

311-104 Colorado Shale

311-106 Liberty Rock (Basalt)

LARGE

311-123 Pennsylvania Shale 9 x 13" 22.5 x 32.5cm **12.00**

311-124 Ultimate Shale 9 x 25" 22.5 x 62.5cm **40.00**
311-125 Marsh Rock (Fine Detail Granite) 3-12 x 12" 8.8 x 30cm **10.00**
311-126 The Castles (Fine Detail Granite) 6 x 12" 15 x 30cm **10.00**
311-127 Savaged Rock (Layered Granite) 5 x 12" 12.5 x 30cm **10.00**
311-128 Pitsburg Cut Layered Sandstone 4-1/2 x 15" **10.00**
311-129 Pittsburg Cut Layered Limestone 3 x 12" 7.5 x 30cm **10.00**

ROCK MOLD KIT

311-140 Make-A-Mold Kit **40.00**
Includes four quart rock castings, one pint of Mold Compound, two ounces of Mold Release and complete instructions.

TUNNELS

311-1003 "Plop Down" Deadman's Corner 15 x 19 x 5" **25.00**
311-1004 "Plop Down" Mountain Tunnel Deadman's Corner 19 x 19 x 19" **45.00**

TUNNEL PORTALS

SINGLE TRACK

311-41530 Single Blasted Rock 8 x 9-1/4" 20 x 23.1cm **6.00**

311-41590 Single Cut Stone 2-1/2 x 3-1/4" Inside **7.00**

311-41630 Single Cut Stone Dated - Double Stacked Option 2-1/2 x 3-3/4" Inside **7.00**

311-41650 Single Concrete 2-3/8 x 3-1/2" Inside **6.00**
311-41654 Single Concrete (Dated) Double Stacked Option 2-1/2 x 3-3/4" Inside **7.00**
311-41690 Single Random Stone (Dated) Double Stacked Option 2-1/2 x 3-3/4" Inside **7.00**

DOUBLE TRACK EA 8.00 (UNLESS NOTED)

311-42540 Double Blasted Rock 8 x 10" 20 x 25cm

311-42600 Double Cut Stone 4-1/2 x 3-1/4" Inside
311-42660 Double Concrete 4-1/2 x 3-1/2" Inside
311-42640 Double Cut Stone (Dated) Double Stacked Option 4-1/2 x 3-3/4" Inside
311-42664 Double Concrete (Dated) Double Stacked Option 4-1/2 x 3-3/4" Inside **6.00**
311-42700 Double Random Stone - Double Stacked Option 4-1/2 x 3-3/4" Inside

PORTAL WING ABUTMENTS EA 6.00

311-4190 Cut Stone (use w/41590 & 42600) 4 x 4-1/2 10 x 11.2cm

311-4194 Cut Stone (use w/41630 & 42640) 4 x 4" 10 x 10cm
311-4200 Concrete (use w/41650 & 42660) 4 x 5" 10 x 11.2cm

311-4204 Concrete (use w/41654 & 42664) 4 x 4-1/2" 10 x 11.2cm
311-4210 Random Stone (use w/41690 & 42700) 4 x 4-1/2" 10 x 11.2cm

PORTAL SEAM SEALERS

311-4152 Seam Sealer 1 x 5" 1.8 x 11.2cm pkg(6) **7.00**
For use with #415 or 42600 (sold separately).
311-4182 Seam Sealer 1 x 5" (use w/418) pkg(3) **6.00**

RETAINING WALLS

EA 12.00 (UNLESS NOTED)

311-4151 Square Cut Sandstone Small Stones 3-3/4 x 12"

311-4130 Toltec **13.00**
311-4131 Square Cut Sandstone (Rough) 5 x 12"

311-4150 Square Cut Sandstone (Neat) Dove Tails 5 x 12"
311-4170 Dry Stacked Field Stone 5 x 12"
311-4180 Dry Stacked Colonial Sandstone 5 x 12"

HELJAN

SCENIC ACCESSORIES EA 3.98

322-501 Park Benches pkg(15)
322-502 Barrels, Cases & Ladders pkg(28)
322-503 Telephone Booth pkg(3)
322-520 Assorted Fences 72-3/4" 181.8cm pkg(12)
322-521 Railings 58" 145cm pkg(10)
322-522 Stairway pkg(4)

HOBBY HELPERS

WEATHERING

CHALK-EZ 1OZ EA 1.08
Add the grit and grime of the real world to your models. Authentic colors of artist chalk can be used straight, or blended to match all kinds of weathering. Easily removed with water so you can start over. Cakes come in plastic storage boxes.

99-103 Light Brown
99-104 Gray
99-106 White
99-107 Black
99-108 Rust
99-109 Yellow
99-110 Blue
99-111 Red
99-112 Green
99-113 Orange
99-114 Light Blue
99-115 Red-Orange
99-116 Yellow-Green
99-117 Turquoise
99-118 Amber/Light Rust
99-119 Yellow-Orange
99-120 Dark Green

CHALK-EZ SETS

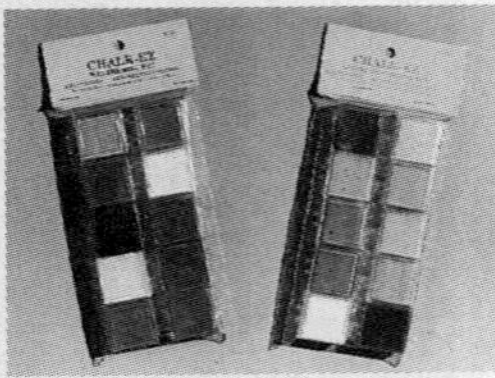

99-301 Master Set **13.67**
Set of ten: brown, light brown, black, white, gray, red, yellow, rust, blue and green.

99-101 Railroad Equipment pkg(10) **6.99**
Set of ten: orange, red-orange, light rust, yellow-orange, turquoise, light blue, dark green, white and black.

99-102 Buildings & Scenery pkg(10) **6.99**

HIGHBALL PRODUCTS

GROUND COVER

HO SCALE 5LBS EA 24.95
330-2205 Limestone
330-2215 Light Gray
330-2225 Dark Gray
330-2235 Black
330-2245 Cinder
330-2255 Brown
330-2265 Light Gray/Dark Gray Blend

COAL EA 6.95

330-130 Stoker 1-3" 14oz
330-131 Egg 2-5" 14oz
330-132 Lump-over 6" 14oz
330-134 Dust 5oz

SCENIC ROCK 1LB EA 6.95
330-150 Sand-White
330-151 Stone
330-153 Iron Ore
330-154 Sand-Brown

BALLAST

N SCALE 1LB EA 4.99
330-120 Limestone
330-121 Light Gray
330-122 Dark Gray
330-123 Black
330-124 Cinder
330-125 Brown

HO SCALE 1LB EA 4.99
Genuine limestone.

330-220 Limestone
330-221 Light Gray
330-222 Dark Gray
330-223 Black
330-224 Cinder
330-225 Brown
330-226 Light Gray/Dark Gray Blend

GRASS 3OZ EA 6.95
Regular and electrostatic, can be used in Noch grass applicator #528-5018.

330-160 Green - Regular - Static
330-161 Light Green - Regular - Static
330-162 Green - Fine
330-163 Light Green - Fine
330-164 Moss Green - Regular - Static

EARTH 3OZ EA 6.95

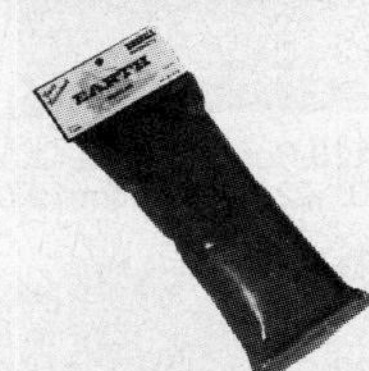

330-172 Dark Brown - Regular
330-170 Light Brown - Regular
330-171 Light Brown - Fine
330-173 Dark Brown - Fine
330-174 Top Soil
330-175 Red

MISCELLANEOUS
330-400 Sawdust Pack 4oz **17.95**
Six assorted packs of sawdust.

330-510 Dirt 12oz **6.95**
Real dirt, specially processed for model scenery.

330-520 Gravel 1lb **6.95**
Creating realistic scenery is fast and fun with the complete

GRS MICRO-LITING

MINI-SCENES

296-2000 Hobo Camp w/Working Fire **39.95**
A pair of hobos camp for the night, cooking stew over a small fire. Complete kit with detailed base casting, two painted soft metal tote-stick, FM-1 Micro-Flamemaker lamp kit, plus complete instructions for wiring, installation and painting.

INTERNATIONAL HOBBY CORP.

ACCESSORIES

348-4 Farm Accessory Set **4.98**

348-222 Village Green Accessories **3.98**

ROADS & PAVEMENT EA 2.98

348-8 Pavements (8 Straight, 2 Corner)

348-10 Road Section (5 Straight, 1 Curved)

MINI-HIGHWAYS

Division of Leisuretime Products

ROADWAYS EA 5.79 (UNLESS NOTED)
Thin precut material with realistic black/brown color and authentic markings. Will lie flat without adhesive, but can be glued for permanent scenery.

406-201 Straight Passing Zone 9'
406-203 Curved Roadway 6'
406-205 RR Crossing & Intersection 2 Each
406-209 Airport Runways pkg(12) **6.79** ***NEW***

KEIL-LINE MODELS

We have worked closely with this manufacturer to provide accurate delivery information at the time this catalog was published. Items listed in blue ink may not be available at all times. Current delivery information, along with a list of in-stock products for this line, can be found on our Web site at www.walthers.com

CACTUS

SAGUARO CACTUS
Cactus are white metal castings.

382-8774 Small pkg(5) **4.99**
382-8775 Medium pkg(2) 4.99
382-8776 Large pkg(2) 5.99
382-8777 Medium-Tall pkg(2) 4.99

CACTUS ASSORTMENT
382-8780 pkg(10) 11.99

LABELLE INDUSTRIES

We have worked closely with this manufacturer to provide accurate delivery information at the time this catalog was published. Items listed in blue ink may not be available at all times. Current delivery information, along with a list of in-stock products for this line, can be found on our Web site at www.walthers.com

LICHEN

1-1/2 OZ PACKAGES EA 1.99
430-5002 Dark Green
430-5004 Fall Red
430-5005 Fall Yellow
430-5006 Mixed Colors
430-5007 Sunset Orange

4 OZ PACKAGES EA 4.99
430-5101 Light Green
430-5102 Dark Green
430-5103 Gray
430-5104 Fall Red
430-5105 Fall Yellow
430-5107 Sunset Orange

kibri

TREES

Trees are assembled, ready to install.

PINES EA 11.99

405-6290 Set of Four
405-6292 Assorted Pines pkg(7)

ASSEMBLED LEAFED TREES

405-6281 Assortment 3-13/64 to 6-13/32" 8-16cm Tall pkg(4) **11.99** ***NEW***

405-6287 Single Large Tree 8-13/16" 22cm Tall **15.99** ***NEW***

BALLAST

7-1/2OZ PKG EA 2.99

405-5891 405-5893

405-5891 White
405-5893 Brown

405-5894 405-5895

405-5894 Black
405-5895 Natural Cork

GROUND COVER

FLOCKING MATERIAL

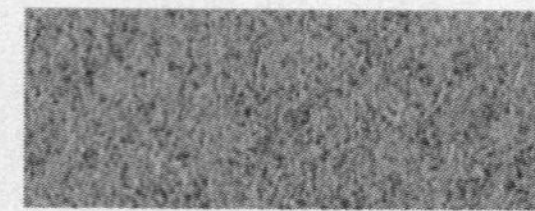

405-5990 Mixed pkg (1/2 oz) **2.99**

LICHEN

1OZ PKG EA 3.99

405-5971 Light Green
405-5972 Medium Green
405-5973 Medium Gray
405-5976 Mixture

2OZ PKG EA 6.99

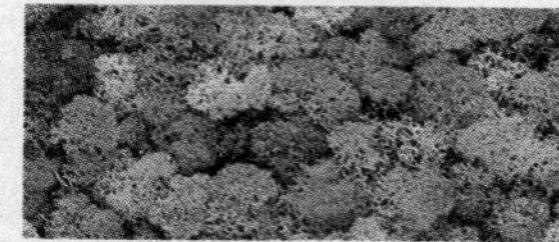

405-5977 Large Green
405-5978 Large Mixed

BUILDING MATERIALS

Stone, brick and concrete sheets are molded in appropriately colored plastic. Each sheet is 8 x 4-3/4".

STONE EA 4.99

405-4119 405-4145

405-4119 Cut Stone (beige)
405-4145 Smooth Cut Stone (beige)

405-4121 Natural (gray)

BRICK EA 4.99

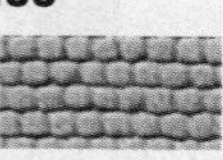

405-4122 405-4124

405-4122 (red)
405-4147 (brown)

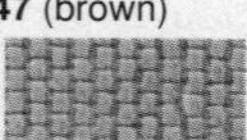

405-4124 Cobblestone
405-4125 Cobblestone with Grooves for Track

ROOF SECTIONS EA 4.99

Roof sections are molded in appropriately colored plastic. Each sheet is 8 x 4-3/4".

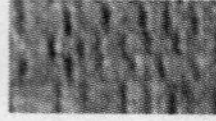

405-4140 405-4141

405-4140 Flat Tile (red)
405-4141 Shingle (gray)

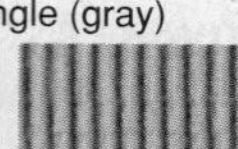

405-4142 405-4143

405-4142 Round Tile (red)
405-4143 Corrugated Metal (light gray)

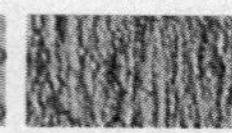

405-4144 405-4139

405-4144 Slate Tile
405-4116 Tile (brown)
405-4139 Thatched (tan)

CONCRETE EA 4.99

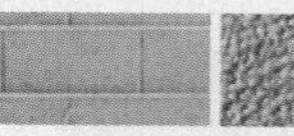

405-4148 405-4128

405-4148 Concrete 20 x 21cm
405-4128 Concrete Slab 5 x 8"

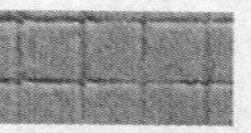

405-4123 Concrete (light gray)

FLOWERS

405-8106 Assorted Flowers & Window Boxes pkg(57) **6.99**

WALLS

WALL SECTIONS EA 4.99

Plastic sheets measure 4 x 7-3/4".

405-4120 405-4118

405-4120 Random Cut Stone
405-4118 Cut Stone

AVALANCHE WALL SECTION

405-4110 5.99
8" length HO.

WATER

405-4126 4.99
Sheet measures 5 x 8".

ROCKS

405-4112 pkg(10) **22.99**
Gray molded plastic.

TUNNEL PORTALS

SINGLE TRACK

405-4101 2-3/4" pkg(2) **7.99**
405-4102 8-7/8" **6.99**
405-4103 2-3/4" w/Tunnel Tube **8.99**
405-4105 8-7/8" w/Tunnel Tube **9.99**

DOUBLE TRACK

405-4104 4-1/8" **6.99**

ROADWAY

405-8102 City Street Assortment **18.99**

FENCES

405-9353 Picket w/Gate **11.99**
Total length 33".

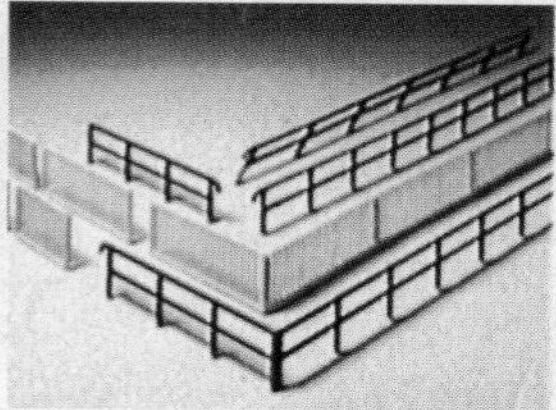

405-9356 Fence **11.99**
405-8008 Cattle **10.99**
With water trough & accessories.

NEW LONDON INDUSTRIES

BACKGROUND SCENE STENCILS EA 9.98

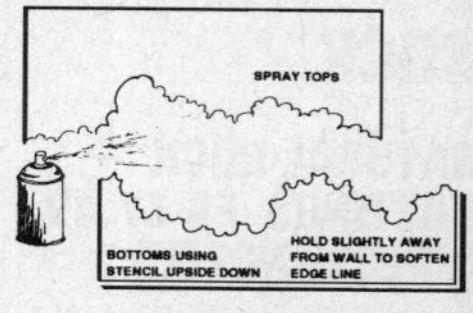

Create a unique background scene. Stencils are cut from heavy cardstock and can be used over and over. May be used for various scales. Includes instructions.

519-1 The Clouds pkg(4)
519-2 The Mountains pkg(4)
519-3 The City pkg(4)
519-4 The Details pkg(2)
Two fine-cut cloud stencils, ideal for adding extra detail to #519-1 and for smaller scales near the horizon.

519-8 The Hills pkg(4)

SCENERY VIDEO

519-6 "The Sky's the Limit" **19.98**
Explains and demonstrates the techniques of making a background scene using stencils.

MLR MFG. CO.

CACTUS

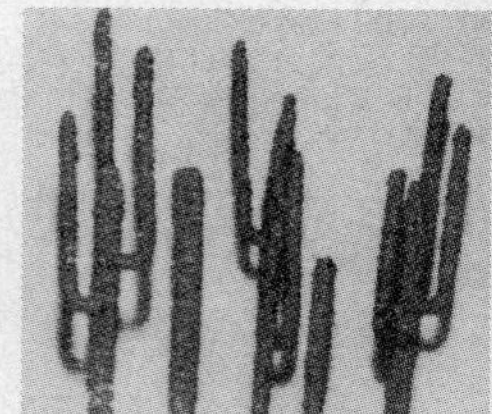

479-5301 pkg(5) **5.95**
Painted resin.

BALLAST SPREADER EA 8.93

Easy to use. Adjustable for heavy or light flow.

479-5008 HO Scale
479-5010 HOn3

Mountains in Minutes™
I.S.L.E. LABORATORIES

Build custom scenery for your layout, diorama or module with these accessories.

ROCK

NATURAL ROCK CASTINGS EA 17.49 (UNLESS NOTED)

Foam duplicates of actual rocks. Use as masters to produce duplicate castings with Mountains in Minutes Polyfoam, or cut and fit into your layout. Each casting comes with instructions and painting tips. Rock castings are 12 x 12" 30.5 x 30.5cm.

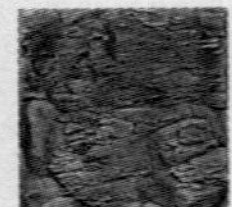
473-801

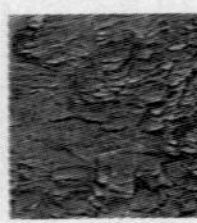
473-802

473-801 Agawa Canyon Wall
473-802 Kitanning Slope

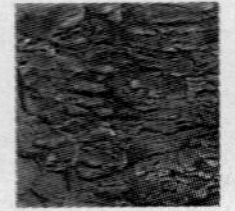
473-803

473-804

473-803 Royal Gorge
473-804 Colorado Red Rock

473-501

473-502

473-501 Flexrock Rock Canyon Wall **15.98**
473-502 Flexrock Rock Embankment Wall **15.98**
473-503 Flexrock Rock Gorge **15.98**

MULTI-SCALE EMBANKMENT

473-820 17.49
15 x 6-1/2" 38 x 16cm.
Easily cut with serrated knife or modeling knife. Paint with enamels, oils or water base acrylics. (Lacquer base paints may cause cracking).

MULTI-SCALE MOUNTAIN - LARGE

473-880 79.98

MULTI-SCALE MOUNTAIN - MEDIUM

473-860 44.98
Approximate size:
10 x 18 x 20"
254 x 470 x 508mm.
Premolded rigid foam mountain in variable color and detail of natural rock. Templates provided for easy carving of optional size tunnel openings.

MULTI-SCALE MOUNTAIN - SMALL

473-855 18.98

MOLDING MATERIAL

CRAFT CAST SET

473-900 23.49
Includes 1 pint each Polyfoam "A" and "B." Expands up to 30 times amount of original material. Forms rigid foam that can be stained, carved, sanded or molded.

MODEL LANDSCAPE KIT

473-701 43.98
Make your own foam castings and rubber molds. Perfect for use in the field, using real rocks as masters. Includes 1 pint each of "A" and "B" Polyfoam, latex mold compound and mold release.

POLYFOAM 2 QUART REFILLS EA 19.98

473-702 Part "A"
473-703 Part "B"

LATEX MOLD COMPOUND

473-704 Quart bottle **16.98**
473-705 Pint bottle **8.98**

MOLD RELEASE COMPOUND

473-706 2oz bottle **2.49**

WALLS

CUT STONE WALL W/STAIRCASE

473-821 6.98
10 x 3-1/2".

LOG CRIBBING

473-822 6.98
Used for reinforcing, embankments or holding steep banks. 8" long x 3-1/2" high.

CUT STONE WALL

473-824 8.98
11-1/2 x 7".

WATER

LAKE STREAM & FALLS KIT

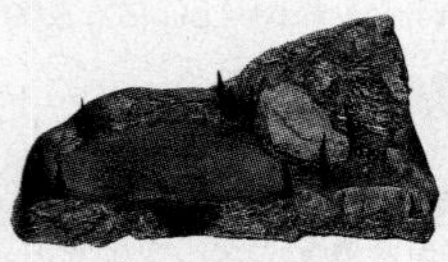

473-890 94.98
Approximately 28 x 20 x 8"
71 x 50 x 20cm.
Operating unit features long-lasting water pump that sends water over the falls and down stream into the lake. Includes water tinting and spruce trees. Use with all scales.

WATERFALL PLANTER

473-895 279.98
28 x 36 x 29" 71 x 91 x 73cm.
Molded from authentic rock formations and hand-painted in six realistic colors. Made of urethane foam, the planter can be used indoors or out. The basin holds up to three gallons of water, circulated with a UL listed submersible pump, which has an adjustable flow rate.

CULVERTS

473-204 pkg(2) **6.98**
Approx. 4-1/8 x 7/87 x 3/4"
105 x 22 x 19mm.
Molded in rigid plastic foam.

TUNNEL PORTALS

Tunnel Portals molded in rigid plastic foam, with a two-tone, golden brown and burnt umber finish. The "Brick Portal" is surrounded by a mixture of boulders and stratified rock. The rough hewn "Cut Stone Portal" is set back into a sheer rock wall. The "Wolfe's Cove Portal" is a scale model of a Canadian Pacific portal of concrete with wooden snow doors, also surrounded with stratified rock. The "Hoosac Tunnel Portal' will allow for double track.

473-101 Brick 6-1/4 x 7-1/4" **6.98**

473-102 Cut Stone 6 x 7-1/4" **6.98**

473-103 Wolfe's Cove 6 x 7-3/4" **6.98**

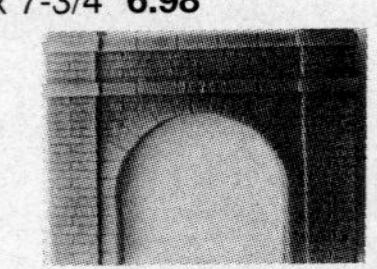

473-104 West Face - Hoosac Tunnel 6 x 7" **6.98**

BOX STYLE TUNNEL PORTAL

473-105 4-3/4 x 5-1/4" **7.98**

DUAL SCALE TUNNEL PORTAL

473-201 6-3/4 x 7-3/4" **6.98**
Use for double track portal in N Scale, single track in HO.

MODEL POWER

TREES

490-1425 5-1/2" 14cm pkg(15) **15.98**

GROUND COVER

490-172 Grass Mat 54 x 99" **19.98**
490-1430 Green Lichen 12oz **4.98**
490-1431 Grass & Mixed Colors 12oz **4.98**

TUNNELS

Flocked, decorated plastic tunnels from Germany.

490-373 Straight Tunnel **14.99**
NEW
10 x 7.6 x 7.2"

490-1324 Curved Corner **23.99**
Brown styrene, with flocking and lichen ground cover.
13.6 x 10.8 x 6.4"

FENCES EA 5.98

490-548 Iron 54"
490-547 White Picket 54"

MINI SCENES

490-5710 Park Scenes Hand-painted. 1/2" to 1" high pkg(6) **10.98**
490-5712 Winter Scenes 3/4" tall pkg(6) **5.98**

PIKESTUFF

CULVERTS

541-2 Concrete 2 x 1" 5 x 2.5cm pkg(2) **1.50**
Molded gray plastic, use as a bridge type culvert or at the base of a hill emptying into a creek, river or drainage ditch

SCALE STRUCTURES LIMITED

FARM YARD DETAILS

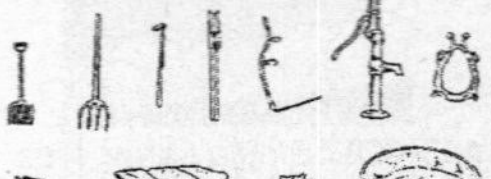

650-7269 9.95

SMALLTOWN U.S.A.

SIDEWALKS

699-7000 pkg(6) **3.95**
Finish your city scene with these plastic sidewalk sections. Each piece measures 10 scale feet by 40 scale feet long.

TREES

Trees are assembled self-standing, appropriately colored. Sizes are approximate.

433-1951 433-1952 433-1950

AUTUMN & SPRING PKG(4) EA 7.50

433-1903 Autumn 3"
433-1922 Autumn 4"
433-1926 Spring 4"

BLUE SPRUCE

433-1952 5-1/2" pkg(2) **7.50**

DECIDUOUS

433-1924 White Birch 4" pkg(4) **7.50**
433-1925 Poplar 4" pkg(4) **7.50**
433-1950 Redwood 5-1/2" pkg(2) **7.50**
433-1971 Oak 6-1/2" pkg(2) **13.00**

EVERGREENS

433-1941 Small - 2" pkg(4) **7.50**
433-1907 3" pkg(4) **7.50**
433-1923 4" pkg(4) **7.50**
433-1972 6-1/2" pkg(2) **13.00**

3" FRUIT PKG(4) EA 7.50

433-1908 Apple
433-1909 Orange

SHADE TREES EA 7.50

433-1940 2" pkg(4)
433-1902 3" pkg(4)
433-1921 4" pkg(4)
433-1951 5-1/2" pkg(2)

SUMMER SHADE PKG(4) EA 7.50

433-1910 Small
433-1927 Large

WINTER

Flocked to simulate snow on branches.

433-1901 Small 3" pkg(4) **7.50**
433-1970 Big 8-1/2" pkg(2) **13.00**

433-1910 433-1912 433-1913 433-1914

433-1924 433-1923 433-1925 433-1921

433-1907 433-1909 433-1903 433-1908 433-1901

SCENEMASTER TREES (W/BENDABLE ARMATURES)

Give outdoor scenes a burst of realism and beauty with SceneMaster trees. Each tree is individually handcrafted and finely detailed through realistic forms, colors and sizes. Each tree features bendable armatures, giving modelers a wide variety of shaping options.

ELM

433-1912 Small pkg(6) **9.00**
433-1931 Medium pkg(4) **9.50**
433-1955 Large pkg(4) **10.00**

MAPLE

433-1913 Small pkg(6) **9.00**
433-1932 Medium pkg(4) **9.50**
433-1956 Large pkg(3) **10.00**

OAK

433-1914 Small pkg(6) **9.00**
433-1933 Medium pkg(4) **9.50**
433-1957 Large pkg(3) **10.00**

GROUND COVER

LICHEN

2OZ EA 7.50
433-1060 Mixed
433-1061 Green

3OZ EA 10.00
433-1062 Mixed Colors Bulk
433-1063 Green Bulk

BALLAST

433-1104 Ballast/Gray 15oz **4.00**
433-1105 Coal 15oz **4.00**
433-1106 Gravel 15oz **4.00**
433-1109 Earth 7oz **4.50**
433-1111 Economy Earth **6.25**

GRASS MATS

Quick and easy to use, mats can be modified or removed when landscaping progresses and are completely reusable. Paper backing for easy cutting. Each features realistic textures with bright, pure colors. All flocking is nonmagnetic. Dealers MUST order in multiples of 12.

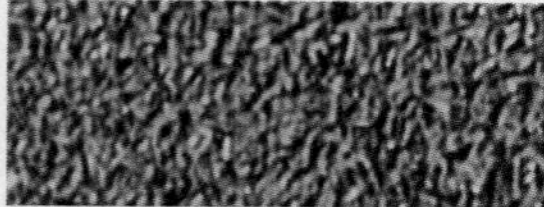

433-1151 50 x 33" **5.25**
433-1156 50 x 99" **10.75**
433-1152 Meadow Mat 50 x 33" **5.25**

433-1155 Scenemaster Velour-Soft Mat **17.00** ***NEW***

Constructed of non-shredding, highly durable velour-like texture. Measures 50 x 99".

GRASS

433-1107 7oz **4.50**
433-1108 Economy 1lb. **6.25**
Big one-pound package covers a large area.

TUNNELS

Tunnels are lightweight durable LiFoam® and are finished in realistic colors.

433-1304 Straight **5.00**

433-1305 Large Straight **10.00**

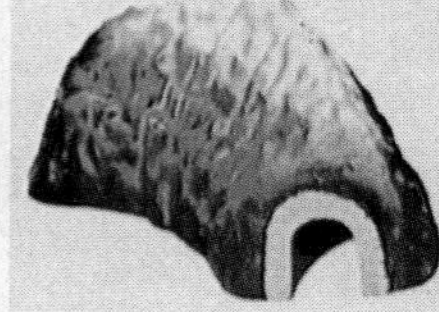

433-1306 Curved **11.00**

ACCESSORIES

MOUNTAIN PAPER

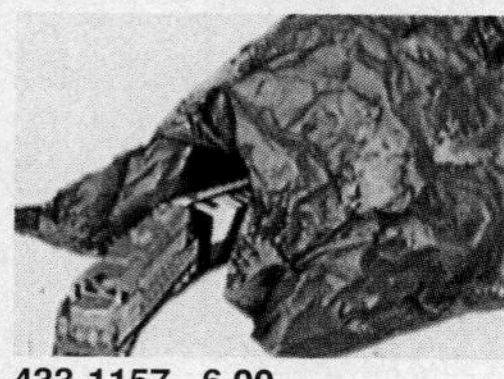

433-1157 6.00
Ready-to-use mountain paper can be used to create mountains, tunnels and scenes. Just wet, shape and install as desired. The paper is finished in a realistic color and is reusable. Measures 24 x 72".

LANDSCAPING CEMENT

433-1403 6.00
Clean, nontoxic, non-flammable adhesive. Dries hard and clean on almost any surface. Resealable 1 pint can.

POLA

IMPORTED FROM GERMANY BY WALTHERS

FENCES EA 9.99

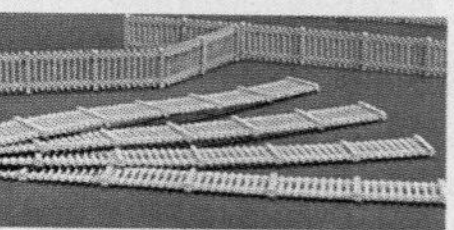

578-455 Cement 4'11"

578-456 Iron 5' 10-3/4"

FURNITURE

578-459 Sun Shades & Benches **9.99**
Assortment of patio umbrellas, benches, tables and stools.

PREISER

ROADWAY

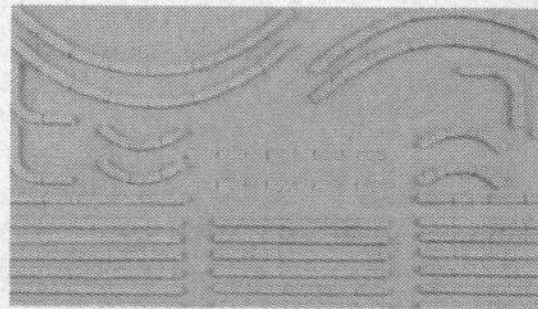

590-18200 Curb Set 38 Pieces **8.99**

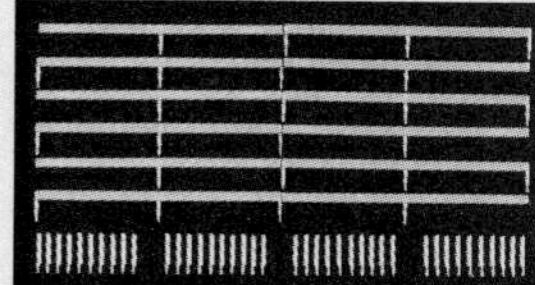

590-18202 Guardrail Set 40 Pieces **8.99**

TREES

590-18600 Palm Trees pkg(4) **14.99**
Easy-to-assemble, appropriately colored plastic.

Sunlit Vistas™
THE LOOK OF SUNLIGHT IN YOUR WORLD

TREE KITS

DECIDUOUS EA 12.98

TALL TREES
252-6001 Small 2 - 3-1/2" (Green Mix) pkg(48) *NEW*
252-6002 Medium 4 - 5-1/2" (Green Mix) pkg(24) *NEW*
252-6003 Large 6 - 7-1/2" (Green Mix) pkg(16) *NEW*
252-6020 Fall Mix 2 - 7-1/2" (Fall Colors) pkg(22) *NEW*

BROAD TREES
252-6101 Small 2 - 3-1/2" (Green Mix) pkg(32) *NEW*
252-6102 Medium 4 - 5-1/2" (Green Mix) pkg(16) *NEW*
252-6103 Large 6 - 7-1/2" (Green Mix) pkg(8) *NEW*
252-6120 Fall Mix 2 - 7-1/2" (Fall Colors) pkg(14) *NEW*

ASPENS
252-6030 Fall Yellow 2 - 7-1/2" pkg(22) *NEW*

CONIFERS EA 12.98

252-6211 Small 2 - 3-1/2" (Conifer Green) pkg(48) *NEW*
252-6212 Medium 4 - 5-1/2" (Conifer Green) pkg(24) *NEW*
252-6213 Large 6 - 7-1/2" (Conifer Green) pkg(16) *NEW*

ASSEMBLED-READY TO PLANT TREES

DECIDUOUS EA 7.98

TALL TREES-GREEN MIX COLORS
252-6601 Large *NEW*
252-6602 Medium *NEW*
252-6603 Small *NEW*

TALL TREES-FALL MIX COLORS
252-6604 Large *NEW*
252-6605 Medium *NEW*
252-6606 Small *NEW*

BROAD TREES-GREEN MIX COLORS
252-6611 Large *NEW*
252-6612 Medium *NEW*
252-6613 Small *NEW*

BROAD TREES-FALL MIX COLORS
252-6614 Large *NEW*
252-6615 Medium *NEW*
252-6616 Small *NEW*

CONIFERS EA 7.98

252-6621 Large *NEW*
252-6622 Medium *NEW*
252-6623 Small *NEW*

MIXED TREES EA 19.98

252-6631 Summer Color Mix *NEW*
252-6641 Fall Color Mix *NEW*
252-6651 Conifers *NEW*
252-6661 Aspens (Fall Yellow) *NEW*

GROUND COVER

Polyurethane foam in four sizes and several natural colors can be used to model grass, weeds, fallen leaves, soil and more.

FINE EA 2.59

252-1101 Light Green *NEW*
252-1102 Medium Green *NEW*
252-1103 Dark Green *NEW*
252-1104 Burnt Green *NEW*
252-1105 Conifer Green *NEW*
252-1106 Aspen Yellow *NEW*
252-1107 Autumn Red *NEW*
252-1108 Autumn Yellow *NEW*
252-1109 Light Brown *NEW*
252-1110 Dark Brown *NEW*
252-1112 Dark Soil *NEW*
252-1113 Light Soil *NEW*
252-1115 Earth Blend *NEW*
252-1116 Light Green Blend *NEW*
252-1117 Dark Green Blend *NEW*

MEDIUM EA 2.59

252-1201 Light Green *NEW*
252-1202 Medium Green *NEW*
252-1203 Dark Green *NEW*
252-1204 Burnt Green *NEW*
252-1205 Conifer Green *NEW*
252-1212 Dark Soil *NEW*
252-1213 Light Soil *NEW*
252-1216 Light Green Blend *NEW*
252-1217 Dark Green Blend *NEW*

COARSE EA 2.59

252-1301 Light Green *NEW*
252-1302 Medium Green *NEW*
252-1303 Dark Green *NEW*
252-1304 Burnt Green *NEW*
252-1305 Conifer Green *NEW*
252-1306 Aspen Yellow *NEW*
252-1307 Autumn Red *NEW*
252-1308 Autumn Yellow *NEW*
252-1309 Light Brown *NEW*
252-1310 Dark Brown *NEW*
252-1311 Sagebrush *NEW*
252-1314 Bramble Bush *NEW*
252-1316 Light Green Blend *NEW*
252-1317 Dark Green Blend *NEW*

BRAMBLE EA 2.59

252-1411 Sagebrush *NEW*
252-1414 Bramble Bush *NEW*

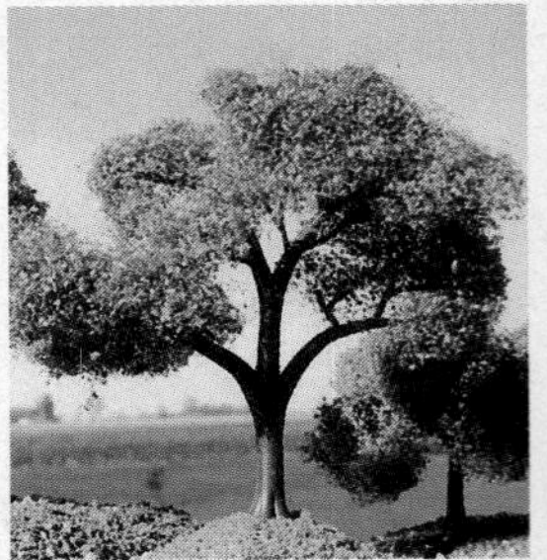

ROCO

IMPORTED FROM AUSTRIA BY WALTHERS

BALLAST

625-42652 1.4oz Gravel, Loose **4.99**

Matches size and color of molded roadbed sections.

BALLAST FILLER PLATE

625-42653 13-1/2 x 3-3/4" 34.5 x 9.3cm **15.99**

SUPERIOR HOBBY PRODUCTS

MOLDING MATERIAL

STAIN EA 1.80

Water-based, nontoxic stain for rock castings. Mix directly with plaster or water to make "paint" for coloring rocks, structures etc.

This line of unique scenery products takes your layout to a new level of realism. Perfect for new construction or refurbishing your existing layout, items are designed to produce realistic results without special tools or skills.

Limited Quantities Available
697-501 White
697-503 Blue
697-509 Red
697-510 Orange
697-517 Aqua Blue
697-519 Cloud White
697-522 Clay Red
697-524 Burnt Orange

TRU-SCALE

STACKED TIES

Detail for yard scenes, near buildings, along the right-of-way or as loads on work cars.

730-2005 Treated (Stained) 1-1/4 x 1-1/4 x 3/4" pkg(2) **12.00**

730-2006 Untreated (Natural Wood) 1-1/4 x 1-1/4 x 3/4" pkg(2) **11.00**

SCALE SCENICS

DIVISION OF CIRCUITRON

ROADWAY

Scale sized, ultra-thin vinyl tape segments are properly spaced on a clear flexible carrier, making roadway striping quick and easy. Flexes easily to follow curves. Permanent acrylic adhesive adheres to most surfaces. Each includes 20' of stripping.

"BROKEN" STRIPES EA 4.95

652-2500 Yellow
652-2501 White

SOLID STRIPES EA 2.95 (UNLESS NOTED)

652-2520 Yellow
652-2521 White
652-2532 Double Yellow **3.95**

SAFETY PYLONS

652-3506 Safety Pylons pkg(24) **2.95**
Bright orange plastic, great detail for construction scenes.

SCALE WORKS MODELS

MORTAR EA 4.00

For all brick and stone mortar, or as a scenery base. Can be applied to any material. Clean up with warm water. 2oz bottle.

644-10 Weathered White
644-20 Concrete Gray
644-30 Light Gray
644-40 Light Sand
644-50 Red
644-60 Tar Black
644-70 Turf Green
644-80 Earth Brown

SUGAR PINE MODELS

FENCES

Easy-to-build kits include pre-cut wood and templates for fast construction.

685-1108 Plank Style **6.00**
16" long.

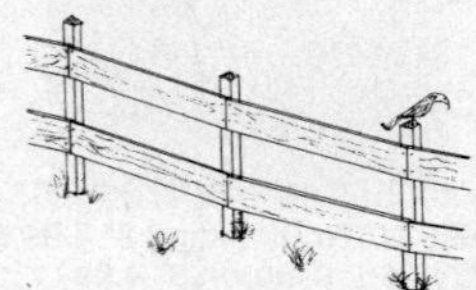

685-1109 Cattle Style **5.00**
16" long.

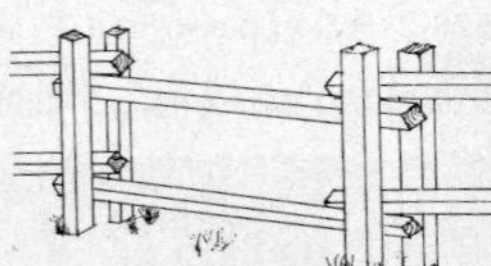

685-1110 Rustic Style **5.00**
35" long.

S&S HOBBY PRODUCTS

ROADWAY

643-305 E-Z Streets Kit **9.99**
Add paved roads to every part of your layout with this easy to use kit. Printed on waterproof styrene, kit includes six 12" straight sections (two with railroad crossing lines), curves and an intersection with crosswalk lines.

ROAD SIGNS EA 4.49

643-1

643-2

MPH 25

643-3

643-1 Etched Brass Stop Ahead Stencil
643-2 Etched Brass R/R Crossing Stencil
643-3 Etched Brass 25 MPH Street Stencil

SUN RAY SCENICS

Limited Quantity Available On All Items

Produce realistic scenery for almost any region with this line of easy to use materials. From trees to rock molds, to turf and other ground cover, the various materials can be combined to model a wide range of terrain.

TREES

Trees are bendable, nontoxic pewter, so you may modify them to suit any situation.

TREE KITS EA 9.49

FIR TREES
687-1090 pkg(3)

LARGE POPLAR
687-1050 Summer pkg(5)

LICHEN

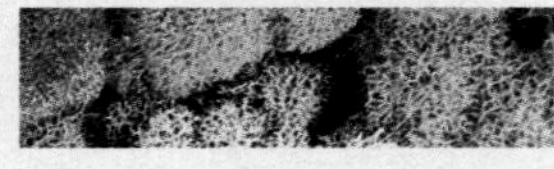

Lichen is thick and soft and works well for shrubs, trees, bushes, hedges, etc.

1OZ PACKAGES EA 2.98

687-7020 Light Green
687-7030 Leaf Green
687-7040 Mixed Green

2-1/2OZ PACKAGES EA 5.49

687-7120 Light Green
687-7130 Leaf Green
687-7160 Autumn Red
687-7170 Autumn Yellow

BALLAST

Light Gray

Medium Gray

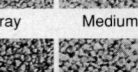

Dark Gray

Light Brown

Medium Brown

Dark Brown

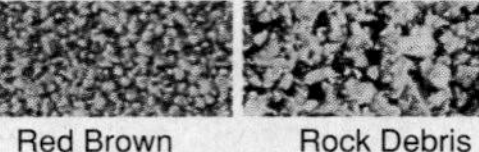
Red Brown

Rock Debris

Will not fade, nonmagnetic, no powder particles, very light-weight. Available in 7 or 17oz packages.

COARSE 7OZ EA 2.49

687-3004 Light Gray
687-3014 Medium Gray
687-3024 Dark Gray
687-3034 Light Brown
687-3044 Medium Brown
687-3054 Dark Brown
687-3064 Red Brown

17OZ

687-4064 Red Brown **5.49**

WHITEGROUND MODEL WORKS

We have worked closely with this manufacturer to provide accurate delivery information at the time this catalog was published. Items listed in blue ink may not be available at all times. Current delivery information, along with a list of in-stock products for this line, can be found on our Web site at www.walthers.com.

LOGS

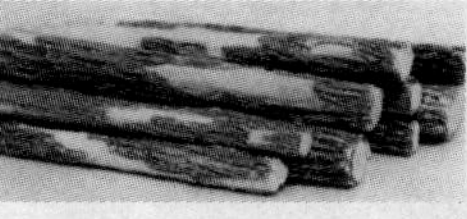

All logs are molded plaster.

771-5004 Logs On Land 5 x 4" pkg(12) **9.95**
771-5005 Floating Logs 6-1/2 x 4-1/2" pkg(12) **8.00**
771-5018 Sugarpine/Redwood Logs pkg(6) **11.95**

TAR PAPER

EA 2.00

Paper measures 6 x 9".

771-50031 Black
771-50032 Red
771-50033 Green
771-50034 Blue
771-50035 Brown

TUNNEL PORTALS

771-5010 Portal **8.95**

771-5015 Rocky Ridge HOn3 5-1/2 x 2-3/4" **8.95**

771-5016 Sideling Wall HOn3 **10.95**

BRIDGE PIER

771-5011 **8.95**

50" for single track

TREES

ACACIA

528-21660 Multi-Trunk 15cm 6" **11.99**

DECIDUOUS

ASH
528-21650 Mountain Ash ("Bird Berry") 4-5/8" **5.99**

528-21790 7-1/2" **11.99**

528-21710 Nut 5-1/2" **7.99**

528-25570 8cm 3-1/8" **7.99**

BEECH EA 7.99 (UNLESS NOTED)

528-25750 4-3/4" pkg(2) **8.99**
528-21690 5-3/16"
528-21720 5"

528-21730 5-1/2"

BIRCH

528-22340 3.9" **2.99**
528-21640 4" **5.99**

BLOSSOM

528-25580 Blossom Tree 8cm 3-1/8" **5.99**

528-21770 Weeping Willow 4-1/2" **7.99**

CHESTNUT

528-21800 , 7-3/4" **12.99**

ELM

528-25560 pkg(2) **10.99**

FRUIT

528-21570 Blooming 3" **4.99**
528-21550 Green 3" **4.99**
528-21580 Cherry 3" **4.99**
528-21600 Pear - Green 4-1/2" **5.99**
528-21560 Apple w/Fruit 3" **4.99**
528-22170 Blossoming 3" **2.99**

528-25540 Apple pkg(3) 2-3/4" **7.99**

528-22270 Pear - Green 4" **2.99**

528-25790 Plum, 3-1/4" pkg(2) **7.99**

LIME

528-21780 Lime Tree 7-1/4" **11.99**

Assorted Fruit 528-25510

OAK

528-22730 Green 5.9" **5.99**
528-21760 6-1/4" **11.99**

POPLAR

528-21680 4-3/4" **5.99**

SUPER TREES

These deluxe models are fully assembled, with a highly detailed plastic form and realistic colors of foliage. Can be used for very large HO trees, or with larger scales.

528-21870 Kandelaber Fir 17cm (7") **31.99**

BLACK PINE

528-21914 14cm (5-1/2") **18.99**
528-21916 18cm (7 1/4") **21.99**
528-21918 25cm (10") **24.99**

PALM

528-21970 15cm (6") **24.99**
528-21980 19cm (7-1/2") **27.99**

CONIFERS

528-21830 Light Green 10-3/16" **34.99**

FIR

528-21880 528-21890

528-21880 6-3/4" **24.99**
528-21890 8-3/4" **29.99**
528-25930 Blue Fir pkg(3) **7.99**

PINES

528-25960 Withered 5" pkg(3) **15.99**
528-22580 Weathered 9" **9.99**

SPRUCE

528-22540 4.3" **4.99**
528-22550 5-1/2" **4.99**
528-21930 6" **24.99**
528-21940 8" **29.99**
528-21950 9-5/8" **34.99**

TREE ASSORTMENTS

528-23350 Natural Tree 2-13/32-3-13/32" (light green) pkg(2) **6.99** *NEW*

528-23355 Natural Tree 2-13/32-3-13/32" (dark green) pkg(2) **6.99** *NEW*

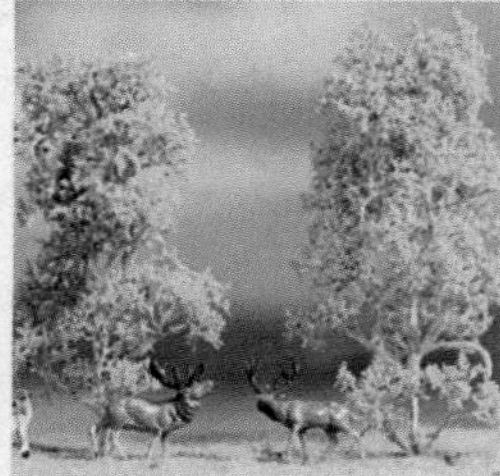

528-23360 Natural Tree 4-4-5/8" (light green) pkg(2) **8.99** *NEW*

528-23365 Natural Tree 4-4-5/8" (dark green) pkg(2) **8.99** *NEW*

528-23370 Natural Tree 5-5/8-6-13/32" (light green) pkg(2) **11.99** *NEW*

Pine Assortment 528-25640

Assorted Spruce 528-25600

528-23375 Natural Tree 5-5/8-6-13/32" (dark green) pkg(2) **11.99** *NEW*

528-23390 Natural Tree 6-13/16-8" (medium green) **7.99** *NEW*

528-26300 Deciduous pkg(25) **21.99** *NEW*

528-26310 Mixed Forest 3-5/8-6" pkg(25) **20.99** *NEW*
528-26320 Model Fir 4-6" pkg(25) **19.99** *NEW*

528-26330 Fir 8-15cm pkg(50) **20.99** *NEW*

528-23800 Large (Natural Tree Form) pkg(5) **31.99**
528-23820 Medium (Natural Tree Form) pkg(5) **16.99**

528-24240 Fir 2.3" pkg(10) **12.99**

528-24250 Fir 3.5" pkg(10) **17.99**
528-24260 Fir 5.1" pkg(10) **22.99**
528-24270 Fir 7" pkg(10) **30.99**
528-25510 Assorted Fruit pkg(5) **12.99**
528-25530 Vines pkg(24) **9.99**
528-25600 Spruce - Assorted pkg(5) **7.99**
528-25630 Fir 2-3" pkg(5) **7.99**
528-25640 Pine Assortment pkg(5) **9.99**

528-25760 Birch, Pine & Willow 3-5" **10.99**
528-75010 Bulk Trees 3-5/8" pkg(140) **189.99**
528-75030 Bulk Trees 2-13/16" pkg(300) **199.99**
528-75220 Bulk Deciduous & Pine Assortment pkg(135) **279.99**
528-75250 Bulk Deciduous & Pine Assortment pkg(75) **129.99**

BUSHES & VINES

528-22080 Flowering Bushes 1.6" pkg(2) **2.99**
528-22090 Bushes pkg(2) **2.99**
528-22120 Vines pkg(12) **2.99**
528-22050 Red/White pkg(2) **5.99**

HEDGES

528-22060 Privet Hedge 20" pkg(2) **7.99**

528-22070 Privet & Barberry **7.99**
528-21530 Blooming Bushes 1-3/4" pkg(2) **5.99**

GROUND COVER

GRASS MATS EA 10.99 (UNLESS NOTED)

Ready-to-use mats are available in many colors and textures to simulate natural ground cover. Grass mats are made with static grass, so that the blades are standing. Mats are 24 x 48" unless noted.

528-1 Spring 40 x 78" **28.99**
528-110 Spring 29 x 40"
528-120 Autumn 29 x 40"

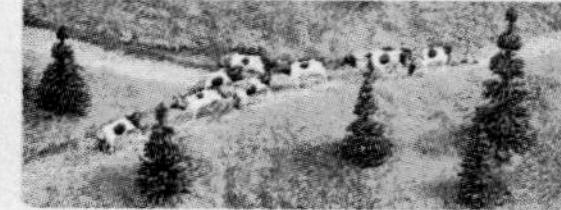

528-240 Meadow

528-280 Autumn Meadow
528-8330 Flowering **2.99**

SNOW

528-8750 Powdered Snow 8-3/4oz **7.99**

STATIC GRASS APPLICATORS

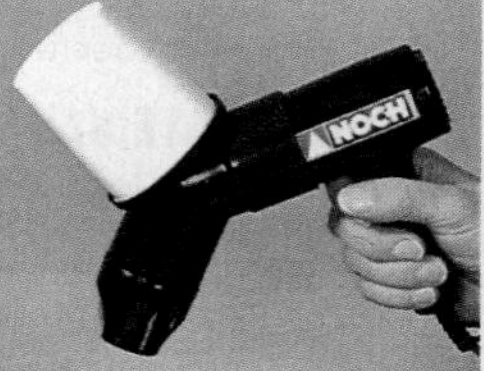

528-50180

528-8100

528-50180 Turbostat Grass Applier **139.99**
Electrostatically charges grass fibers, to produce more realistic, standing grass. Use with 12-16V transformer (not included).

528-8100 Dispenser Bottle **4.99**
Hand-held bottle with sprinkler opening, allows for precise application in small area. Can be used with various materials.

528-61130 Cement for Grass 7-1/2oz (250ml) **8.99**

STATIC GRASS

528-230 Dark Green Meadow **10.99**

3/8OZ EA 2.99
528-8300 Spring Green
528-8310 Light Green
528-8320 Dark Green
528-8340 Brown

3-1/2OZ EA 9.99

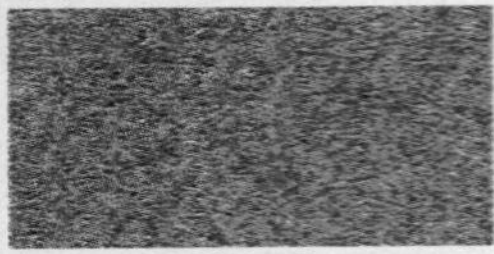

528-50190 Light Green
528-50200 Dark Green
528-50210 Spring Green

TERRAIN MAT SURFACER
528-60920 7.99

FLOCK 3/4OZ EA 3.99

528-6550 528-6570

528-6500 Light Brown
528-6520 Medium Brown
528-6550 Light Green
528-6560 Dark Green
528-6570 Medium Green

SCATTER MATERIAL
528-8350 Forest 3/4oz. **3.99**
Combination of materials, ideal for blending with grass mats and other scenery.

LEAVES 3/4OZ EA 4.99

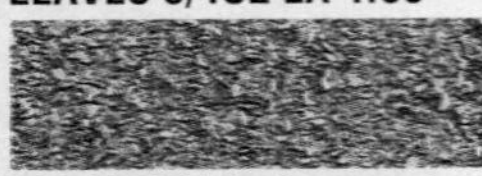

528-8010 Light Green

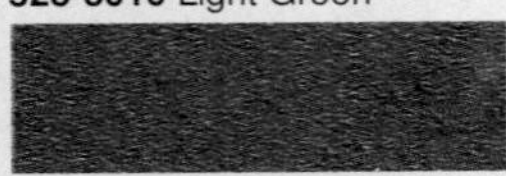

528-8020 Medium Green

528-8040 Yellow
528-8050 Fir Needles

FOLIAGE 3/4OZ EA 9.99
528-6300 Light Green
528-6310 Medium Green
528-6320 Dark Green
528-6350 Spring Green/Yellow
528-6430 Forest

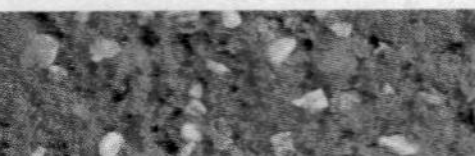

528-6440 Mountain Meadow

528-6450 Moorland
Use to make realistic trees or bushes. Tear into small pieces, glue in place.

1OZ SHAKER-TOP CONTAINER EA 4.99

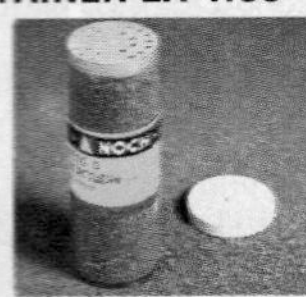

528-8210 Light Green
528-8200 Flower Meadow
528-8220 Dark Green
528-8240 Brown
528-8250 Alp
528-8260 Gray
528-8270 Forest Ground

LICHEN

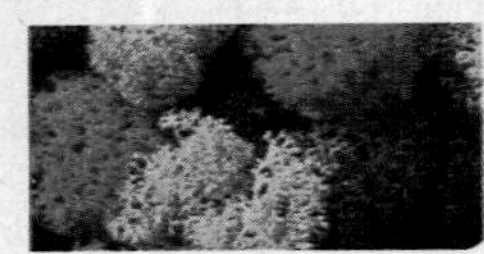

528-8630

SINGLE PACKS 1OZ EA 3.99
528-8610 Assorted Green
528-8630 Autumn Assorted Double
528-8600 Stone Gray

DOUBLE PACKS 2-3/4OZ EA 6.99
528-8621 Light & Dark Green
528-8620 Autumn

1.4OZ PACKS EA 1.99
528-8400 Flower Red
528-8410 Light Green
528-8420 Dark Green
528-8440 Brown
528-8450 Mountain Grass
528-8460 Gray
528-8470 Forest

6.3OZ PACKS EA 5.99
Each color comes in a reclosable plastic bag for easy storage.

528-8401 Summer Flowers
528-8411 Alpine Meadow (Light Green)
528-8421 Dark Green
528-8441 Brown
528-8461 Gray

WATER

SEA MATS

528-60860 Wild Water Set **10.99**
Includes 1-3/4oz multi-colored pebbles and 1.6 fl oz bottle each: blue paint and transparent blue gloss.

528-60850 16-1/2 x 10-3/4" **7.49**
528-60851 30 x 20" **19.99**

ROADWAYS
528-48570 Paved Square 8 x 3-7/8" pkg(2) **8.99**
528-58300 Subway Crossing 5 1/2 x 4 1/2" 14 x 11cm **11.99**

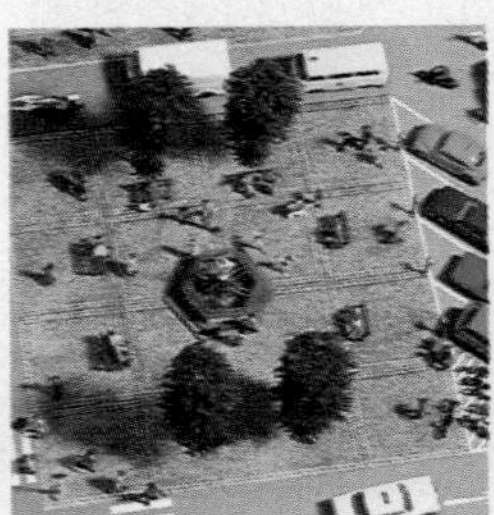

528-60460 Paved Courtyard Cobblestone 8 x 3-7/8" 20.5 x 10cm pkg(2) **7.99**

528-60470 Highway 40" 1m pkg(2) **9.99**
528-60540 Transfers Street Markings 8 x 4" 20.5 x 10cm **8.99**

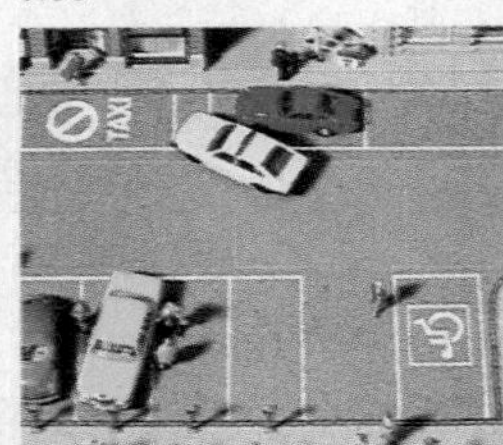

528-60550 Parking Lot, Gray pkg(2) **8.99**
Adhesive backed with printed parking spaces. Includes 4 plastic parking meters. 4 x 8" 10 x 20.3cm

528-60600 Country Road pkg(2) **9.99**

FLEXIBLE

528-60410 Road, Black 39 x 1" **7.99**

528-60430 Roadway, Cobblestone 40" 1m **7.99**

528-60440 Roadway, Old-Town 80" 2m **7.99**

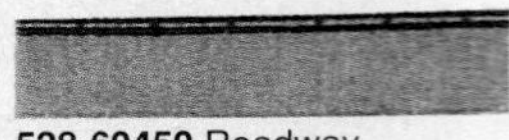

528-60450 Roadway, Pavement 40" (1/2" wide) **7.99**

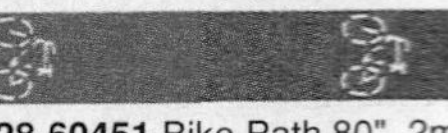

528-60451 Bike Path 80" 2m **7.99**
528-60480 Roadway, Country 40" (1/2" wide) **5.99**

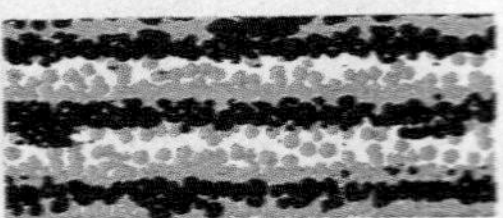

528-60481 Gravel Road **6.99**

528-60490 Highway, Gray 40" pkg(2) **11.99**
528-60530 Roadway Paving Station 8 x 4" 20 x 10cm pkg(2) **8.99**

528-60570 Sheet Paved 8 x 3.9" 20.5 x 10cm **8.99**
528-60610 Roadway, Country **10.99**

528-60620 Roadway, Pavement **6.99**

528-60630 Roadway, Garden 40" 1m **5.99**

FENCES

EA 6.99
528-60640 Iron Railings
528-60650 Pasture Fence
528-60660 Garden Fence

WALLS
Standard walls measure 9-13/32 x 4-5/8" 23.5 x 11.5cm (unless noted); large walls 28-13/32 x 4-5/8" 71 x 11.5cm.

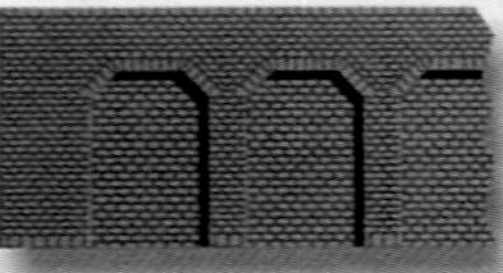

528-57888 Arcade (Gray Brick) **12.99** ***NEW***
20 x 5" 50 x 12.5cm

528-57898 Arcade (Beige Brick) **12.99** ***NEW***
20 x 5" 50 x 12.5cm

528-58324 Gray **9.99** ***NEW***
528-58325 Large Gray **34.99** ***NEW***

528-58327 Retaining **9.99** ***NEW***
528-58328 Large Retaining **34.99** ***NEW***

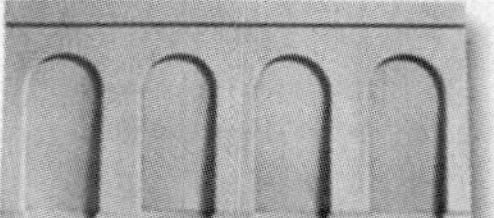

528-58330 Arcade **9.99** ***NEW***
528-58331 Large Arcade **34.99** ***NEW***

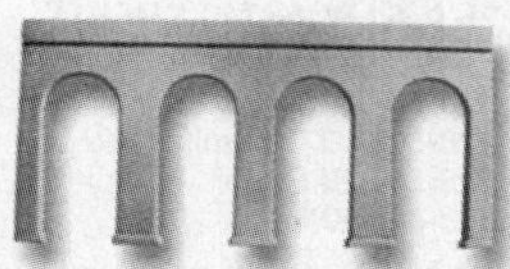

528-58333 Arcade Open **9.99** *NEW*
528-58334 Large Arcade Open **34.99** *NEW*

STYRO-FLEX WALLS

528-57811 Square Stone, Beige 10-1/2 x 5-1/2" 24 x 14cm **2.99**
528-57831 Brick, Red 10-1/2 x 5-1/2" 24 x 14cm **2.99**
528-57871 Stone, Red 10-1/2 x 5-1/2" 24 x 14cm **2.99**
528-57980 Styro-Flex Wall Set #1 **219.99**
Includes 22 each of 57871, 57891, 57881, and 57831 10 1/2 x 5 1/2" 24 x 14cm.

528-57990 Styro-Flex Wall Set #2 **221.99**
Includes 22 each of 57801, 57841, 57851, and 57811 10-1/2" x 5-1/2" 24 x 14cm.

HARD FOAM WALLS

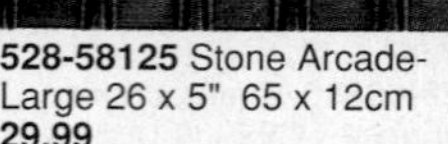

528-58115 Retaining Stone 26 x 5" 65 x 12cm **29.99**

528-58125 Stone Arcade-Large 26 x 5" 65 x 12cm **29.99**
528-58320 Ashlar Facing Wall **10.99**

PLASTIC WALL SHEETS

528-58430 Sandstone Arcade Wall **9.99**
9-5/8 x 5" 25 x 12.5cm

528-58440 Sandstone Retaining Wall **9.99**
9-5/8 x 5" 25 x 12.5cm

528-58160 Stone 9-1/2 x 5-1/4" **9.99**

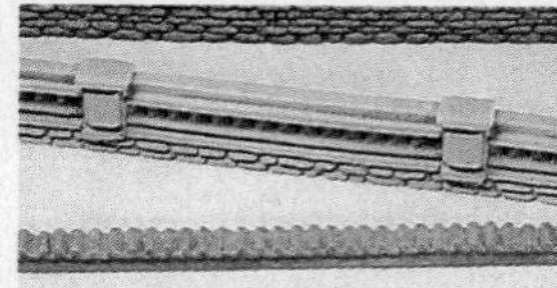

528-58190 Ledge 14-3/8" 36.5cm **13.99**

528-58180 Brick 9-1/2 x 5-1/4" 24 x 13cm **9.99**
Made of hard foam, easily cut to fit with hobby saw.

528-58240 Brick Arcades 14-3/8 x 4-1/4" 36.5 x 10.5cm **12.99**

528-58090 Rock Arcade Wall 14 x 5" 35 x 13cm **23.99**

528-58150 Retaining Wall w/Rock **18.99**

528-58110 Wall w/Pillars 10 x 4-3/4" **9.99**

528-58120 Wall w/Arches 10 x 4-3/4" **9.99**

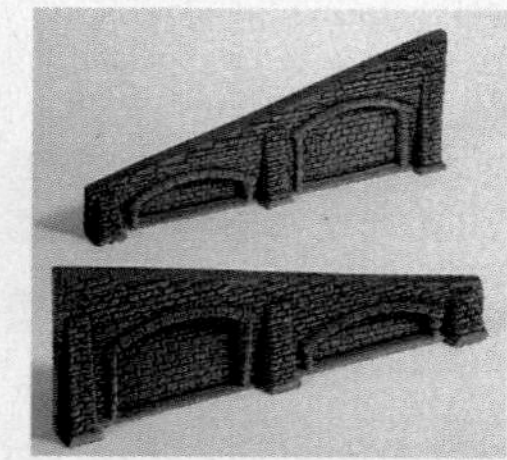

528-58132 Arcades - Rising 10-1/2 x 4" 26 x 10cm pkg(2) **13.99**

528-58170 Stone Arcade 9-1/2 x 5-1/8" 24 x 13cm **9.99**
528-58560 Sandstone 6-3/4 x 3-1/2" 17 x 9cm **6.99**
528-58580 Rock Plate Stratified 6-3/4 x 3-1/2" 17 x 9cm **7.49**

528-58220 Brick Wall 9-1/2 x 5-1/4" 24 x 13cm **9.99**

528-58250 Quarry Stone Wall 9-1/2 x 5-1/4" 24 x 13cm **9.99**

528-58260 Quarry Stone Arcade Wall 10-3/4 x 5-1/4" 27 x 13cm **12.99**

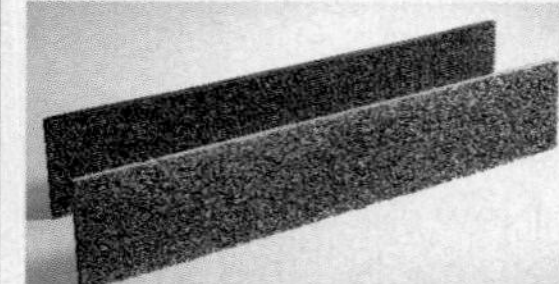

528-58200 Natural Stone Wall 26 x 5" 65 x 13cm **29.99**

528-58590 Rock Plate Limestone 6-3/4 x 3-1/2" 17 x 9cm **7.49**
528-58100 Stone 9-1/2 x 5" 23.7 x 12.5cm **9.99**
528-58210 Quarry Stone 6.5 x 12.5" **29.99**
528-58490 Structured Limestone Wall **19.99**

ROCK ARCADE

528-58090 23.99

TUNNELS

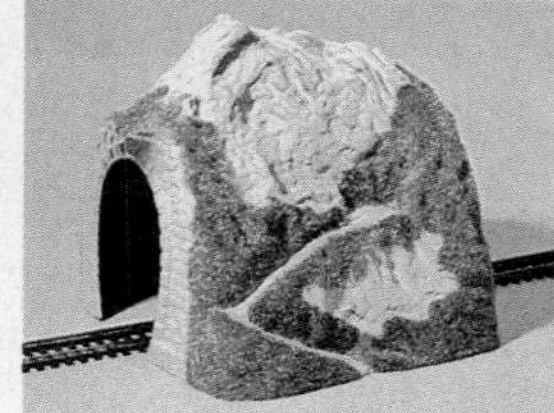

528-2120 Single Track **9.99**
7 x 6-1/2 x 6-3/4" 18 x 16.5 x 17cm

528-2200 With Creek **20.99**
13-3/8 x 6-3/4 x 6-3/8" 34 x 17 x 16cm

528-5080 With Pond **29.99**
17-3/4 x 17-1/2 x 6-3/4" 45 x 44 x 17cm

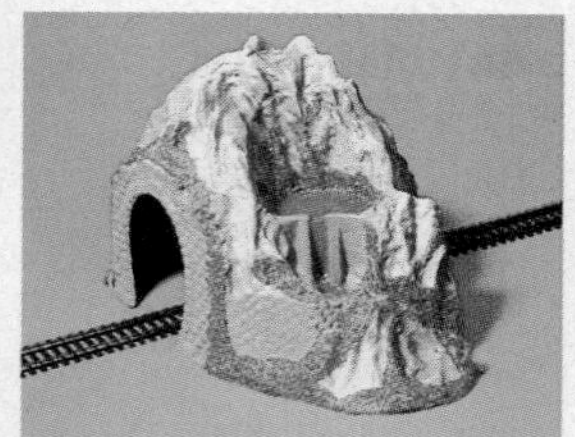

528-2110 Straight & Curved 7 x 9-1/2" 7" high 18 x 24cm 18cm high **13.99**

528-5180 Curved Tunnel - Single Track **29.99**
17-1/8 x 12-1/2 x 9-1/8" 43 x 31 x 23cm

528-48670 Single Track, Straight **16.99**
12-1/2 x 7 x 5-1/2" 31 x 18 x 14cm

528-48730 Single Track, Curved **24.99**
14-3/4 x 13 x 6-1/2" 37 x 33 x 16cm

528-2220 25.99
13-5/8 x 10-7/16 x 7-5/8" 34 x 26 x 19cm

528-2430 29.99
12 x 11-1/4 x 6-13/16" 30 x 28 x 17cm

528-5170 Curved **34.99**
15-1/4 x 12-13/16 x 12" 38 x 32 x 30cm

TUNNEL PORTALS

Tunnel portals are made of hard foam material with realistic colors and textures.

528-58290 Street Portal 5-1/2 x 4-1/2" 14 x 11cm **11.99**

SINGLE TRACK

528-58400 Sandstone 5.8 x 4.8" 14.5 x 12cm **10.99**

528-60010 Cut Stone - Gray pkg(2) **3.99**

528-58270 Quarry Stone Arcade Tunnel pkg(4) **23.99**
528-48790 TT Scale **12.99**
528-58010 Portal 4 x 4.7" **9.99**

528-57884 Gray Brick 24 x 14cm **6.99** *NEW*

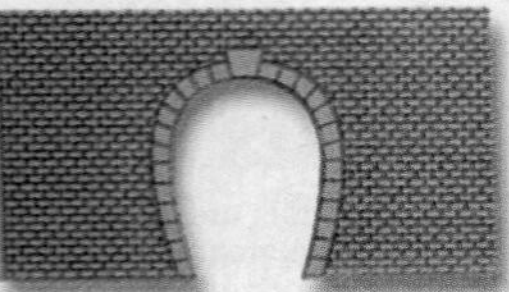

528-57894 Beige Brick 24 x 14cm **6.99** *NEW*

528-58320 Gray 11 x 11.5cm **10.99** *NEW*

DOUBLE TRACK

528-57885 Gray Brick 24 x 14cm **6.99** *NEW*

528-57895 Beige Brick 24 x 14cm **6.99** *NEW*
528-58020 Rough Cut Stone Brown 4 x 4.7" **11.99**

528-58040 Modern Inter City Express (ICE) **16.99**
Partly scenicked with grass.

528-58310 Tunnel Portal 10-1/2 x 7-1/2" 26 x 18.5cm **12.99**

528-58322 Gray 18 x 11.5cm **12.99** *NEW*

528-58410 Sandstone 5.8 x 4.8" 14.5 x 12cm **12.99**

528-60020 Cut Stone - Tan pkg(2) **5.99**
Suitable for use with overhead catenary.

528-48800 TT Scale **12.99**

ROCK

NATURAL STONE 17-1/2OZ EA 5.99

Limited Quantity Available
528-9240 Fine, White Limestone **5.99**
528-9320 Coarse, Pink
528-9170 Sand - Natural

BALLAST, FINE 17OZ EA 5.99

528-9350 Brown
528-9360 Gray

PLASTIC ROCK WALLS EA 3.99

These flat mountain sides can be cut to fit with a scissors and are easily glued in place. Each flat section is made of realistically colored plastic. 10-5/8 x 5-1/8" 27 x 13cm

528-60780 Slate

528-60790 Granite

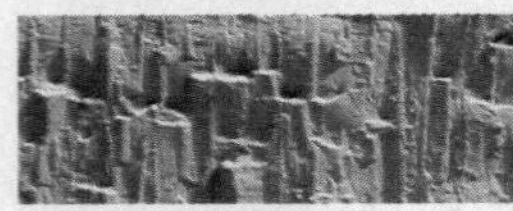

528-60800 Multi-Colored Sandstone

FOAM ROCK FORMATIONS

Highly detailed, hard foam castings can be used as a single piece, or easily cut with a saw to fit your layout. Foam material is molded in realistic colors, and is easily painted to match existing scenery, or model different types of rock. Models are less figures, vehicles, trees and other details.

528-5930 Three Peaks **37.99**
11-3/4 x 7" 30 x 18cm

528-58470 Granite Panel **19.99**
13 x 6-3/4" 32 x 17cm
Use randomly with other scenery, or join several to form a continuous wall.

528-5900 Quarry **36.99**
12-3/4 x 6-3/4 x 4-3/4" 32 x 17 x 12cm

528-60820 Wendelstein Rock Wall pkg(2) **19.99**
528-58460 Elbsandstein **19.99**
13 x 7-1/8" 32 x 18cm

528-58480 Schichtgestein **19.99**
13-1/2 x 8-3/4" 34 x 22cm
Rocky plate with partial grass.

528-60810 Rock Moldings **18.99**
One-piece molding provides several rocks, just cut out and install. Use them to model outcroppings, or joined to form a wall.

CORK ROCK SECTIONS

528-8810 Small 2-3/4oz 80g **6.99**
528-8820 Large 6-1/oz 180g **13.99**
Chunks of cork, ideal for stratified rock formations.

STONE SHEETS

9 X 6" PLASTIC SHEETS EA 1.99

528-57510  528-57520

528-57510 Granite
528-57520 Dolomite

528-57530  528-57550

528-57530 Basalt
528-57550 Brick

528-57560 528-57570

528-57560 Square Stone
528-57570 Sandstone

26 X 6" PLASTIC SHEETS EA 4.99

528-57700 Granite
528-57710 Dolomite
528-57720 Basalt
528-57730 Brick

STONE WALLS EA 12.99

One-piece foam castings, can be cut to fit your scenery. Each section measures 9-5/8 x 5-3/64" 24 x 13cm

528-58560 Sandstone
528-58570 Granite
528-58580 Layered Stone

BUILDING SHEETS

528-65050 Street w/Houses & Shops (6 Buildings) **9.99**
528-65450 Dwelling Houses (6 Buildings) **9.99**
528-65980 Building Sheets Assortment **239.99**

MINI SCENES

Put life in your layout with this assortment of figures and accessories. Each item is prepainted, ready to install.

528-605 Castle Ruin **26.99**
528-11700 Campers & Tents **17.99**
528-60580 Tennis Court w/Fence **14.99**
528-64820 Snackbar **6.99**
528-64830 Fruit Stand **6.99**

Elbsandstein 528-58460

Campers & Tents 528-11700

ACCESSORIES

528-11690 City Scooter Trip **14.99**
Includes 2 scooters, 3 figures, and 1 bench.

528-11841 Country Market **17.99**
Includes market stand, 2 figures and animal.

528-11940 Funeral **20.99**
Includes mortuary van and 3 figures.
528-11340 Graves pkg(5) **11.99**
528-11580 Playground Equipment **14.99**

528-11650 Table Tennis Scene **17.99**

Graves 528-11340

Playground Equipment 528-11580

528-10970 Wild Water Scene w/Bridge **6.99**

528-10900 528-10910

528-10900 Well **6.99**
528-10910 Outdoor Privy **6.99**

528-11360 Wood Cutters Scene **11.99**

528-10870 Patio Umbrella Set **6.99**

528-10920 528-10930

528-10920 Roofed Shrine **6.99**
528-10930 Feeding Hut w/Hay **6.99**

528-10940 Hunter's Lookout w/Ladder **6.99**
528-10950 Footbridge without Figure **6.99**
528-11370 Country Yard Set **11.99**
528-11680 Memorial Cross **14.99**
528-10960 Footbridge w/Figures & Accessories **6.99**

2000 CATALOG

528-71990 **7.99** ***NEW***
Full-color listing of all HO, N&Z and G Scale items. 147 pages.

Tunnel portals and accessories are odorless urethane castings in a natural "smoky gray" color, which can be used as-is or painted.

TUNNEL PORTALS

SINGLE TRACK

483-113 Concrete **7.50**
4-3/4 x 4-3/4" 11.5 x 11.5cm
483-101 Timber **7.50**
4-1/4 x 4" 11 x 10.5cm
483-103 Random Stone **7.50**
4-3/4 x 5" 11.5 x 13cm
483-105 Cut Stone **7.50**
4-3/4 x 5" 11.5 x 12.5cm

483-117 Rough Square **8.00** ***NEW***
483-118 Rough Round **8.00** ***NEW***
483-119 Smooth Square **8.00** ***NEW***
483-120 Smooth Round **8.00** ***NEW***

DOUBLE TRACK EA 8.00

483-104 Random Stone
4-3/4 x 7" 11.5 x 17.5cm
483-102 Timber
4-3/4 x 7" 11.5 x 17.5cm
483-106 Cut Stone
4-3/4 x 7" 11.5 x 17.5cm
483-114 Concrete
4-3/4 x 6" 11.5 x 15.5cm

AUTO PORTALS EA 6.00

483-180 Modern Concrete
483-181 Old Concrete
483-182 Random Stone

WALLS

TUNNEL ABUTMENTS PKG(2) EA 10.00

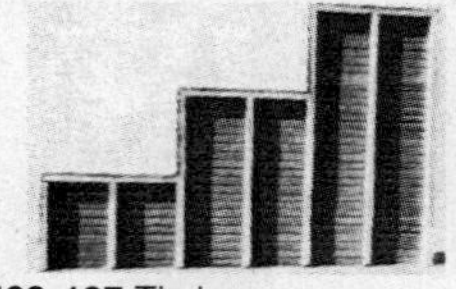

483-107 Timber
6-3/4 x 4-1/2" 17 x 11.5cm
483-108 Random Stone
483-109 Cut Stone
5-3/4 x 4-3/4" 14.5 x 11.5cm
483-115 Concrete ***NEW***

RETAINING WALLS EA 6.00

483-110 Timber
6-1/4 x 3-1/2" 15.5 x 8.5cm
483-111 Random Stone
6-1/4 x 3-1/2" 15.5 x 8.5cm
483-112 Cut Stone
6 x 3-1/2" 15 x 8.5cm
483-116 Concrete ***NEW***

SINGLE DECK BRIDGE ABUTMENTS EA 8.00 (UNLESS NOTED)

483-140 4' Timber w/Rock Base pkg(2) **9.00**
483-141 15' Timber

483-142 30' Random Stone
483-143 30' Cut Stone
483-144 30' Old Concrete
483-145 30' Smooth Concrete

SINGLE DECK BRIDGE PIERS

EA 11.00

483-130 33' Random Stone
483-131 33' Cut Stone
483-132 30' Old Concrete
483-133 35' Smooth Concrete

CULVERTS

PKG(2) EA 6.50 (UNLESS NOTED)

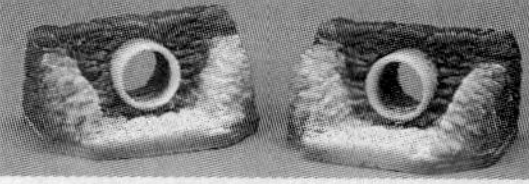

483-122 Random Stone, 48"
483-150 Random Stone Double Pipe, 48"

483-123 Cut Stone, 8' Arch

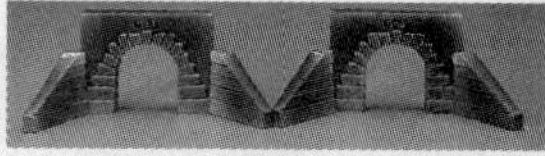

483-124 Concrete, 8' Arch
483-125 Concrete, 36" Double Pipe

483-127 20' Single Bridge **9.00**

CULVERT WALLS

483-126 Concrete, 2 - 6' Rectangular pkg(2) **6.50**
483-128 20' Double Bridge **11.00**

FIELDS

483-701 Plowed **7.00**
483-702 Disced **7.00**

SCRAP PILE

483-703 15.00

TREES

Fully assembled, ready for planting.

ARMATURES

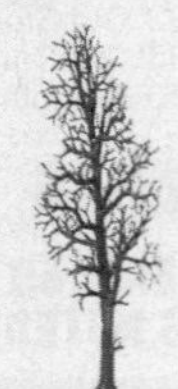

Bare plastic forms are ideal for winter scenes or detailing with foliage, sold separately.

570-94031 1-1/4" pkg(5) **5.95**
570-94032 2" pkg(5) **6.95**
570-94033 3" pkg(5) **7.95**
570-94034 4" pkg(4) **7.95**
570-94035 6" pkg(2) **6.95**
570-94036 8" pkg(2) **6.95**

POPLAR

Fully assembled, with twisted wire form and mixed green foliage.

570-94021 1/4" pkg(5) **7.50**
570-94022 1/2" pkg(5) **7.95**
570-94023 1-1/2" pkg(5) **8.50**
570-94024 1-7/8" pkg(5) **9.50**
570-94025 2-5/8" pkg(5) **10.95**
570-94026 3-1/2" pkg(4) **12.95**
570-94027 4-3/4" pkg(3) **13.95**
570-94028 6-3/4" pkg(2) **14.95**

SYCAMORE

Fully assembled with etched brass form, painted brown and flocked.

570-94101 1/4" pkg(5) **8.00**
570-94102 1/2" pkg(5) **12.50**
570-94103 3/4" pkg(5) **15.00**
570-94104 1" pkg(4) **17.50**
570-94105 1-3/8" pkg(4) **20.00**
570-94106 1-7/8" pkg(3) **20.00**
570-94107 2-1/4" pkg(2) **17.50**
570-94108 2-7/8" **12.50**
570-94109 3-1/4" **15.00**
570-94110 3-7/8" **18.00**
570-94111 4-7/8" **24.00**

ELM

Each pack includes a mix of up to 5 different shades of green foliage.

570-94001 1/4" pkg(5) **6.50**
570-94002 1/2" pkg(5) **7.25**
570-94003 7/8" pkg(5) **8.00**
570-94004 1-1/8" pkg(5) **8.75**
570-94005 1-1/4" pkg(5) **9.50**
570-94006 1-1/2" pkg(5) **10.25**
570-94007 1-7/8" pkg(5) **11.00**
570-94008 2 1/4" pkg(4) **11.25**
570-94009 2-3/4" pkg(4) **11.75**
570-94010 3-1/2" pkg(3) **12.50**
570-94011 4-3/4" pkg(3) **13.50**
570-94012 6-1/4" pkg(2) **15.00**
570-94013 7" pkg(2) **17.50**

FIR

Each pack includes a mix of dark and medium green shades.

570-94041 1/2" pkg(5) **7.50**
570-94042 3/4" pkg(5) **8.50**
570-94043 1-1/4" pkg(5) **9.50**
570-94044 2" pkg(5) **10.50**
570-94045 2-7/16" pkg(5) **11.50**
570-94046 3-3/4" pkg(4) **12.50**
570-94047 4-7/8" pkg(3) **13.50**
570-94048 6-3/4" pkg(2) **14.50**

PALM

Easily bent for natural, curved appearance.

570-94061 1-1/4" pkg(5) **7.50**
570-94062 1-1/2" pkg(5) **8.50**
570-94063 1-5/8" pkg(2) **10.95**
570-94064 2-3/8" pkg(2) **12.95**
570-94065 3-7/8" pkg(2) **14.95**
570-94068 5" pkg(2) **7.95**
570-94066 6" **16.95**
570-94067 9-1/2" **18.95**

ECONO PALM TREES

570-94261 1-1/2" pkg(5) **10.95**
570-94262 2" pkg(4) **10.95**
570-94263 3-1/2" pkg(3) **10.95**
570-94264 5" pkg(2) **10.95**
570-94265 7" pkg(2) **10.95**
570-94266 12" **7.95**

TREE TRUNKS

Adds realistic detail and stability to plastic trees, or use alone to model stumps. Simply press wire trunk of tree into place. Molded in brown styrene.

570-94091 Fits Small Tree pkg(5) **2.25**
570-94092 Fits Medium Tree pkg(5) **2.25**
570-94093 Fits Large Fir/Poplar pkg(3) **1.75**

CACTUS

SAGUARO

570-94051 3/4" pkg(5) **8.50**
570-94052 1" pkg(5) **10.00**

570-94053 1-3/16" pkg(4) **11.00**
570-94054 2" pkg(2) **11.00**
570-94254 4" pkg(3) **7.25**
NEW

PRICKLY PEAR

570-94071 1/2" pkg(18) **3.25**
570-94072 3/4" pkg(20) **4.25**
570-94073 1-3/8" pkg(16) **5.50**

GROUND COVER

GRAVEL

570-94501

570-94502

8oz EA 1.95

570-94501 Extra Fine Mixed
570-94502 Fine Mixed
570-94503 Super Fine Mixed

10oz EA 3.95 (UNLESS NOTED)

570-94512 Super Fine Beige **4.95**
570-94513 Super Fine Gray **4.95**
570-94514 Fine Beige
570-94515 Fine Gray
570-94516 Fine Brown
570-94517 Fine Red
570-94518 Fine Black
570-94519 Fine White
570-94520 Fine Dark Brown

BALLAST

570-94505 Super Fine Black 8oz **1.95**

GROUND FOAM EA 4.95

Use to model grass, weeds, foliage and more.

Spring Green

Grass Green

Conifer Green

Olive Green

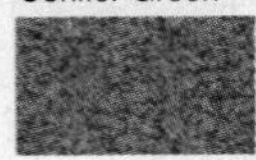
Gold Straw

Dark Earth

FINE

Each package contains 1oz of ground foam.

570-94401 Spring Green
570-94402 Grass Green
570-94403 Conifer Green
570-94404 Olive Green
570-94405 Gold Straw
570-94406 Dark Earth

MEDIUM

Each package contains 20g of ground foam.

570-94411 Spring Green
570-94412 Grass Green
570-94413 Conifer Green
570-94414 Olive Green
570-94415 Gold Straw
570-94416 Dark Earth

COARSE

Each package contains 20g of ground foam.

570-94421 Spring Green
570-94422 Grass Green
570-94423 Conifer Green
570-94424 Olive Green
570-94425 Gold Straw
570-94426 Dark Earth

BUILDING SHEETS

ROCK & STONE SHEETS PKG(2) EA 8.25

7 x 12" patterned sheets are vacuum-formed styrene, .020 thick.

570-91560

570-91561

570-91560 O Coursed Stone
570-91561 HO Coursed Stone

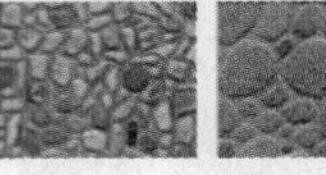
570-91581 570-91582

570-91581 HO Random Stone
570-91582 HO Polished Stone

570-91584

570-91590

570-91584 N Polished Stone
570-91590 HO Dressed Stone

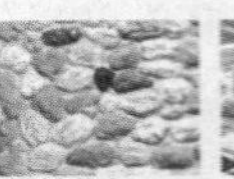
570-91559

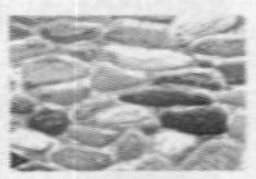
570-91563

570-91559 Stone Wall
570-91563 HO Field Stone

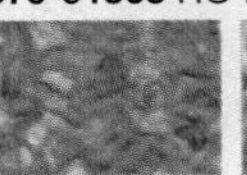
570-91570

570-91571

570-91570 HO Rock Embankment
570-91571 O Rock Embankment

570-91690

570-91690 Parkway Sidewalks
Neat detail for city streets, complete pieces feature grass parkway with realistic concrete curb and 30" of straight sidewalk. Also includes two corners and two driveways.

CRATERS

570-91695 Moon/Bomb Craters pkg(2) **8.25**
An easy way to create realistic landscapes for science fiction or military dioramas.

WATER

7 x 12" plastic sheets with patterned surfaces.

CALM/SHALLOW EA 7.50

570-91801 Blue
570-91811 Clear

AGITATED/SHALLOW EA 8.50

570-91802 Blue
570-91812 Clear

CHOPPY/DEEP EA 9.50

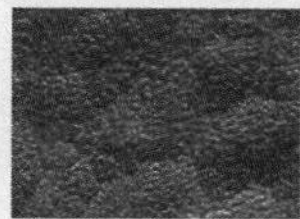

570-91803 Blue
570-91813 Clear

STORMY/DEEP EA 6.50

570-91804 Blue
570-91814 Clear

CELLULAR FOAM

A Lichen type ground foam for modeling tree foliage and brush. Won't dry out.

MEDIUM EA 5.95

Each package contains 20 grams of ground foam.

570-94450 Green Mix
570-94451 Spring Green
570-94452 Grass Green
570-94453 Evergreen
570-94454 Sugar Maple Mix
570-94455 Autumn Mix
570-94456 Leaf Green
570-94457 Bright Green
570-94458 Mint Green

FINE EA 5.95

Each package contains 20 grams of ground foam.

570-94460 Green Mix
570-94461 Spring Green
570-94462 Grass Green
570-94463 Evergreen
570-94465 Autumn Mix
570-94466 Leaf Green
570-94467 Bright Green
570-94468 Mint Green Green
570-94469 Autumn Gold
570-94470 Autumn Red

MIXED EA 5.95

Each package contains 50 grams of ground foam.

570-94441 Light Green Mix
570-94442 Medium Green Mix
570-94443 Dark Green Mix
570-94445 Dark Cedar Mix
570-94446 Lush Green Mix

ROADS

Ideal for modeling all types of paved surfaces. Choose from printed paper or Flex Mat with finely ground aggregate surface.

ASPHALT

570-94535

570-94531

570-94535 Paper
11-3/4" x 26-3/4" **4.00**
570-94531 Flex Mat
12 x 24" **18.95**
570-94551 Roadway Kit
21.95

CONCRETE

570-94536

570-94532

570-94536 Paper
11-3/4" x 26-3/4" **4.00**
570-94532 Flex Matt
12 x 24" **18.95**
570-94552 Roadway Kit
21.95

FENCES

CHAIN LINK

570-90451 Mesh & Rod
48" **7.95**
Includes two strips of precut fencing, which measure 1-1/8" tall by 24" long, plus five, 15" lengths of plastic rod for posts.

4-BAR HORIZONTAL

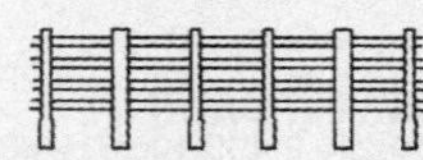

570-90453 Plastic 20" **6.95**

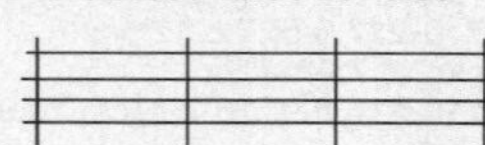

570-90454 Brass 9-1/2" **11.95**

PICKET

570-90456 Plastic 20" **6.95**

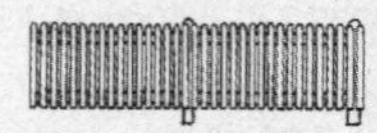

570-90460 Plastic 20" **6.95**

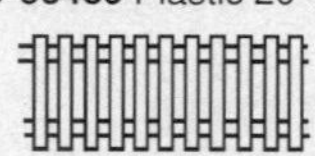

570-90464 Plastic 28" **5.95**
570-90466 Plastic 20" **5.95**

VISTA SCENIC HOBBY PRODUCTS

STARTER KITS

767-2010 Scenery **18.99**
This basic scenery kit lets you begin creating beautiful scenery. Includes 500 grams of brown ballast, 60 grams of mixed lichen, 500 grams of gray ballast, 60 grams of forest floor mixture and 75 grams of scenic grass.

767-2110 Roadway **26.99**
NEW
Includes one each: 30" two-lane passing, 14" curve, 30" one-lane passing and 30" unmarked.

ROADWAY

Create realistic paved highways, streets, parking lots and more. Made from foam material, with self-adhesive backing that sticks to most surfaces. Sections are 30" long except curves, which are 14."

YELLOW MARKINGS EA 6.99

GRAY ROAD

767-800 Two Passing Lanes
767-801 One Passing Lane
767-802 No Passing Zone
767-803 Curve
767-804 RR Crossing
767-805 Unmarked

BLACK ROAD

767-810 Two Passing Lanes
767-811 One Passing Lane
767-812 No Passing Zone
767-813 Curve
767-814 RR Crossing
767-815 Unmarked

WHITE MARKINGS EA 6.99

GRAY ROAD

767-820 Two Passing Lanes
767-821 One Passing Lane
767-822 No Passing Zone
767-823 Curve
767-824 RR Crossing

BLACK ROAD

767-830 Two Passing Lanes
767-831 One Passing Lane
767-832 No Passing Zone
767-833 Curve
767-834 RR Crossing

GROUND COVER

LICHEN

Add the smell of a real forest to your layout with pine scented lichen! Great for modeling trees, bushes or shrubs in any scale.

2.1OZ EA 4.99

767-500 Light Green
767-501 Dark Green
767-502 Mixed Colors
767-503 Autumn
767-505 Gray
767-506 June Green
767-507 Forest Green
767-508 Fall Browns

1OZ EA 2.99

767-550 Light Green ***NEW***
767-551 Dark Green ***NEW***
767-552 Mixed ***NEW***
767-553 Autumn ***NEW***
767-555 Gray ***NEW***
767-556 June Greens ***NEW***
767-557 Forest Greens ***NEW***
767-558 Fall Browns ***NEW***

Limited Quantity Available

8.8OZ EA 16.95

767-571 Dark Green
767-572 Mixed Colors
767-573 Autumn
767-574 June Green
767-575 Gray
767-578 Fall Browns

STATIC GRASS 1OZ EA 3.99

Rayon fibers, a few thousandths of an inch thick, produce a surface with a velvet smooth texture. Suitable for HO, N, and Z Scale scenery. One ounce (30 grams) per package.

767-360 Light Green
767-361 Dark Green
767-362 Brown
767-363 Yellow ***NEW***

BLENDED STATIC GRASS 1OZ EA 3.99

Blended colors to produce different effects.

767-370 Sea Blue
767-371 Desert Sand

DYED SAWDUST EA 3.29

Medium grade sawdust dyed to simulate grass, ground cover and earth. Use in any scale. For custom applications, mix two or more colors, or sift for finer texture. Covers approximately 400 square inches (2500 sq. cm) with 2.6 ounces (75 grams) per package.

767-300 Light Green
767-301 Medium Green
767-302 Dark Green
767-303 Grass w/Flowers
767-304 Brown Earth Mix
767-308 Light Brown

GROUND FOAM 1/2OZ EA 3.99

Simulate trees, shrubs or ground with this medium ground foam. Perfect for any kid's project.

767-400 Light Green ***NEW***
767-402 Dark Green ***NEW***
767-404 Burnt Orange ***NEW***
767-405 Brown ***NEW***
767-407 Yellow ***NEW***
767-409 Cherry Black ***NEW***

SCENIC ROCK & LICHEN

767-1060 75g **5.99** ***NEW***
An easy way to add landscape definition to your layout. This unique product mixes lightweight rock formations with lichen shrubbery.

TREE KITS

LICHEN

The base, trunk and branches of these detailed trees are constructed from plastic and topped with lichen.

2-3"
767-706 3-Pack **4.99** ***NEW***
767-708 10-Pack **14.99** ***NEW***

3-4"
767-707 3-Pack **4.99** ***NEW***
767-709 10-Pack **14.99** ***NEW***

EVERGREEN 3-PACKS

767-720 2-3" **6.99** ***NEW***
767-721 4-5" **9.99** ***NEW***
767-722 6-7" **12.99** ***NEW***
767-723 8-9" **14.99** ***NEW***

FOREST FLOOR

767-1050 2.1oz **3.99** ***NEW***
Simulate natural products found on any forest floor. Mixture includes lichen, pine needles and other products.

FIELD/PRAIRIE GRASS

767-1070 Natural **TBA** ***NEW***

VISTA SCENIC HOBBY PRODUCTS

TUNNELS

Molded from polystyrene plastic, these tunnels and painted with up to five different colors and flocked with static grass.

767-1100 Stoney Point **16.99** ***NEW***
9.5 x 9.75 x 6".

767-1101 Twin Peaks **19.99** ***NEW***
9.5 x 15 x 7".

767-1102 Avalanche **19.99** ***NEW***
9.5 x 15 x 7.5".

767-1103 Burkes Falls **16.99** ***NEW***
9.25 x 9.75 x 6".

ROCK CUTS

767-1110 Ramma Ridge **16.99** ***NEW***
6.75 x 14.75 x 5.25".

767-1111 Orrs Ridge **14.99** ***NEW***
6.75 x 12.75 x 4".

767-1112 Eagles Pass **26.99** ***NEW***

LAKE

767-1150 Crystal Lake **15.99**
Lake is constructed from black polystyrene plastic. Each is vacuum formed, die cut and hand-painted to create an individual look.

ACCESSORIES

767-921 Farm Windmill **3.49**
767-980 Farm Fences **3.49**
767-981 Footbridges pkg(2) **3.49**
767-982 Road Signs - Unmarked pkg(12) **3.49**
767-991 Road & Track Side Sign Sets **2.99** ***NEW***

Timberline Scenery Co., LLC

NEW SUPPLIER

Create a realistic forest in any scale with these detailed tree replicas. Each is hand-built one at a time, to insure the highest quality and that no two are ever identical. Pine trees (conifers) are available with real wood trunks for dioramas or foreground, or with wire forms for backgrounds and scenes requiring many trees. All leafed (deciduous) trees feature real wood trunks.

TREES

CONIFERS W/WIRE FORM TRUNKS

NORTHWOODS GREEN

710-101 1/2-2" 1.25-5cm pkg(6) **6.98** ***NEW***
710-102 2-4" 5-10cm pkg(3) **6.98** ***NEW***
710-103 4-6" 10-15cm pkg(2) **6.98** ***NEW***
710-104 6-9" 15-22.5cm **7.98** ***NEW***
710-105 9-11" 22.5-27.5cm **8.98** ***NEW***

DEEP WOODS GREEN

710-106 1/2-2" 1.25-5cm pkg(6) **6.98** ***NEW***
710-107 2-4" 5-10cm pkg(3) **6.98** ***NEW***
710-108 4-6" 10-15cm pkg(2) **6.98** ***NEW***
710-109 6-9" 15-22.5cm **7.98** ***NEW***
710-110 9-11" 22.5-27.5cm **8.98** ***NEW***

LODGE POLE GREEN

710-111 1/2-2" 1.25-5cm pkg(6) **6.98** ***NEW***
710-112 2-4" 5-10cm pkg(3) **6.98** ***NEW***
710-113 4-6" 10-15cm pkg(2) **6.98** ***NEW***
710-114 6-9" 15-22.5cm **7.98** ***NEW***
710-115 9-11" 22.5-27.5cm **8.98** ***NEW***

DEADWOOD BROWN

710-116 1/2-2" 1.25-5cm pkg(6) **6.98** ***NEW***
710-117 2-4" 5-10cm pkg(3) **6.98** ***NEW***
710-118 4-6" 10-15cm pkg(2) **6.98** ***NEW***
710-119 6-9" 15-22.5cm **7.98** ***NEW***
710-120 9-11" 22.5-27.5cm **8.98** ***NEW***

ASSORTMENT

710-190 Alpine Forest 1/2-6" 1.25-10cm pkg(20) **29.95** ***NEW***

PINE TREES W/REAL WOOD TRUNKS

NORTHWOODS GREEN

710-1102 2-4" 5-10cm pkg(3) **7.98** ***NEW***
710-1103 4-6" 10-15cm pkg(2) **7.98** ***NEW***
710-1104 6-9" 15-22.5cm **9.98** ***NEW***
710-1105 9-11" 22.5-27.5cm **10.98** ***NEW***

DEEP WOODS GREEN

710-1107 2-4" 5-10cm pkg(3) **7.98** ***NEW***
710-1108 4-6" 10-15cm pkg(2) **7.98** ***NEW***
710-1109 6-9" 15-22.5cm **9.98** ***NEW***
710-1110 9-11" 22.5-27.5cm **10.98** ***NEW***

LODGE POLE GREEN

710-1112 2-4" 5-10cm pkg(3) **7.98** ***NEW***
710-1113 4-6" 10-15cm pkg(2) **7.98** ***NEW***
710-1114 6-9" 15-22.5cm **9.98** ***NEW***
710-1115 9-11" 22.5-27.5cm **10.98** ***NEW***

DEADWOOD BROWN

710-1117 2-4" 5-10cm pkg(3) **7.98** ***NEW***
710-1118 4-6" 10-15cm pkg(2) **7.98** ***NEW***
710-1119 6-9" 15-22.5cm **9.98** ***NEW***
710-1120 9-11" 22.5-27.5cm **10.98** ***NEW***

ASSORTMENT

710-1190 1/2-6"1.25-10cm pkg(11) **29.95** ***NEW***

DECIDUOUS W/REAL WOOD TRUNKS

SUMMER LEAVES

710-201 2-4" 5-10cm pkg(3) **7.98** ***NEW***
710-202 3-5" 7.5-12.5cm pkg(2) **7.98** ***NEW***
710-203 6-9" 15-22.5cm **10.98** ***NEW***

SPRING GREEN

710-204 2-4" 5-10cm pkg(3) **7.98** ***NEW***
710-205 3-5" 7.5-12.5cm pkg(2) **7.98** ***NEW***
710-206 6-9" 15-22.5cm **10.98** ***NEW***

LATE AUTUMN

710-207 2-4" 5-10cm pkg(3) **7.98** ***NEW***
710-208 3-5" 7.5-12.5cm pkg(2) **7.98** ***NEW***
710-209 6-9" 15-22.5cm **10.98** ***NEW***

FALL SPLENDOR

710-210 2-4" 5-10cm pkg(3) **7.98** ***NEW***
710-211 3-5" 7.5-12.5cm pkg(2) **7.98** ***NEW***
710-212 6-9" 15-22.5cm **10.98** ***NEW***

AUTUMN GOLD

710-213 2-4" 5-10cm pkg(3) **7.98** ***NEW***
710-214 3-5" 7.5-12.5cm pkg(2) **7.98** ***NEW***
710-215 6-9" 15-22.5cm **10.98** ***NEW***

Deep Woods Green

Tree Assortment

Pine Trees w/Real Wood Trunks

HARVEST DAWN

710-216 2-4" 5-10cm pkg(3) **7.98** ***NEW***
710-217 3-5" 7.5-12.5cm pkg(2) **7.98** ***NEW***
710-218 6-9" 15-22.5cm **10.98** ***NEW***

OCTOBER ORANGE

710-219 2-4" 5-10cm pkg(3) **7.98** ***NEW***
710-220 3-5" 7.5-12.5cm pkg(2) **7.98** ***NEW***
710-221 6-9" 15-22.5cm **10.98** ***NEW***

INDIAN SUMMER

710-222 2-4" 5-10cm pkg(3) **7.98** ***NEW***
710-223 3-5" 7.5-12.5cm pkg(2) **7.98** ***NEW***
710-224 6-9" 15-22.5cm **10.98** ***NEW***

FRUIT TREES

LEMON

710-225 2-4" 5-10cm pkg(3) **7.98** ***NEW***
710-226 3-5" 7.5-12.5cm pkg(2) **7.98** ***NEW***
710-227 6-9" 15-22.5cm **10.98** ***NEW***

ORANGE

710-228 2-4" 5-10cm pkg(3) **7.98** ***NEW***
710-229 3-5" 7.5-12.5cm pkg(2) **7.98** ***NEW***
710-230 6-9" 15-22.5cm **10.98** ***NEW***

APPLE

710-231 2-4" 5-10cm pkg(3) **7.98** ***NEW***
710-232 3-5" 7.5-12.5cm pkg(2) **7.98** ***NEW***
710-233 6-9" 15-22.5cm **10.98** ***NEW***

ASSORTMENTS PKG(11) EA 29.95

Trees measure 3-5" 7.5-12.5cm in each assortment.

710-290 Summer Grove ***NEW***
710-291 Autumn Grove ***NEW***

VOLLMER

Create unique scenes along your railroad with this assortment of materials and supplies.

Foothills & Mountain Scene 770-6110

"Alpenvorland" 770-6111

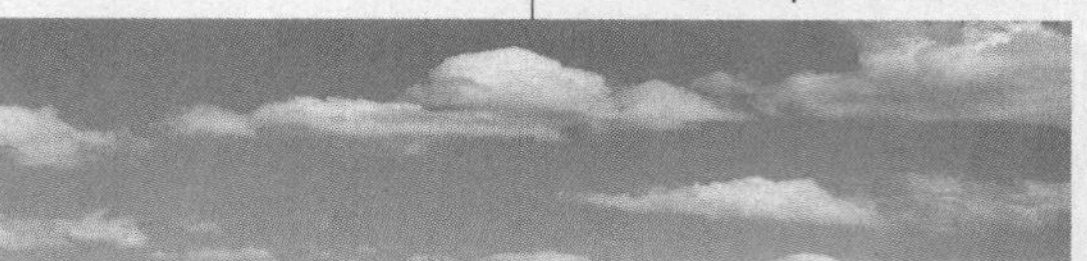

Background Clouds 770-6112

"Sauerland" 770-6113

ROADWAY

COBBLESTONE STREET EA 15.99

Both are printed on adhesive paper.

770-6023 6 x 39" Strip
770-6024 3 x 78" Strip

FOIL

770-6020 6.99
Road 39 x 3"

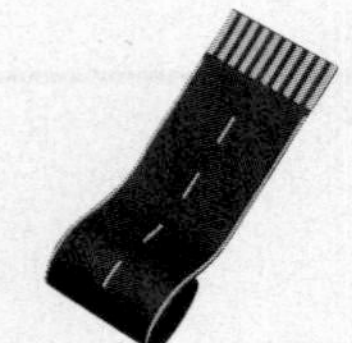

770-6021 7.99
Street 39 x 3"

770-6022 7.99
Cobblestone 39 x 3"

BACKGROUND SCENES

Full-color photographic backgrounds, printed on heavy paper.

770-6105 Clouds 112 x 32" 280 x 80cm **27.99**

770-6110 Foothills & Mountain Scene **28.99**
(2 sections) 112 x 20" 280 x 50cm

770-6111 "Alpenvorland" 10 x 2' 300 x 60cm **31.99**

770-6112 Background Clouds **25.99**
108 x 20" 270 x 50cm

770-6113 "Sauerland" 10 x 2' 300 x 60cm **31.99**

GROUND COVER

770-5224 Coal **5.99**
770-5240 Gravel **5.99**

BUILDING MATERIALS

ROOFING PKG(5) EA 26.99

Each plastic sheet measures 4-1/2 x 8-1/2"

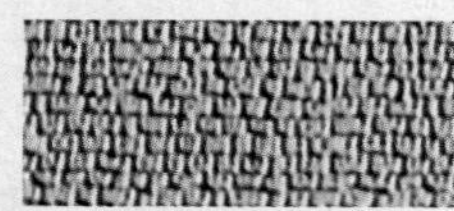

770-6025 Wood Shingles

770-6026 Red Tile

770-6027 Corrugated Iron

770-6028 Brick

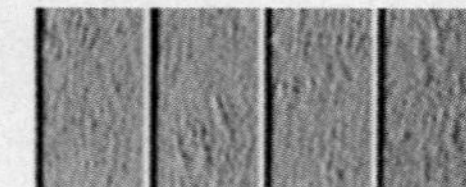

770-6029 Tar Paper

770-6030 Slate

770-6031 Stone Wall

770-6032 Tile

STONE PATTERN EMBOSSED PAPER PKG(10) EA 16.99

Embossed paper can be used as pavement or building materials. Less adhesive. Each sheet measures 10 x 5" 25 x 12.5cm.

770-6041 Cobblestone

770-6042 Red Brick

770-6043 Brown Stone

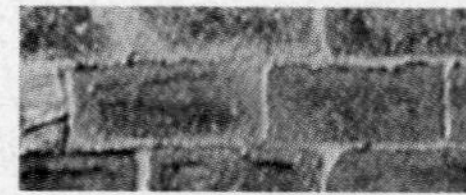

770-6045 Gray Sandstone

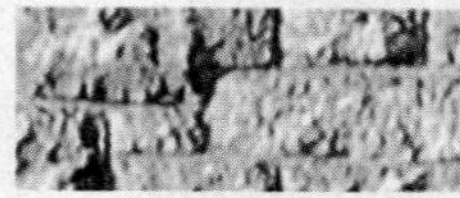

770-6046 Marble

770-6047 Red Sandstone

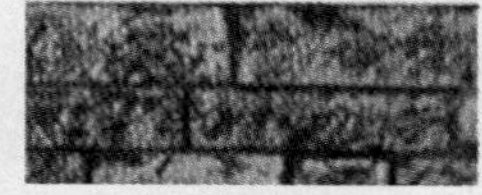

770-6048 Granite

WALLS PKG(10) EA 16.99

10 x 5" 25 x 12-1/2cm.

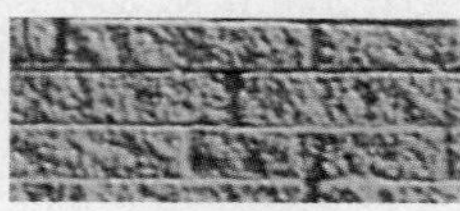

770-6039 Gneiss

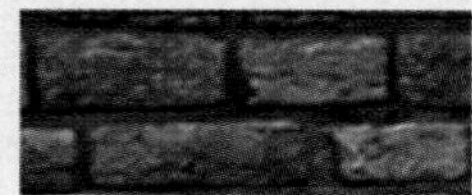

770-6040 Granite

WALL SECTIONS

Molded of appropriately colored plastic.

770-4508 Retaining Wall pkg(5) **29.99**
36 x 41-1/2" 90 x 104cm

770-6028 Red Brick pkg(5) **26.99**
4-1/2 x 8-1/2"
11.25 x 21.25cm

770-6031 Rough Stone pkg(5) **26.99**
36 x 41-1/2" 90 x 104cm

FENCE

770-5009 Chain Link **14.99**
With six frames, each 6" 150mm long, 1.1 yard (1m) wire mesh and 2 gates.

770-5011 Fence **7.99**

770-5012 Meadow **7.99**

770-5013 Garden **7.99**

770-5014 Factory **7.99**
770-5133 Ornate **9.99**
Approximately 39" 97.5cm long

TUNNEL PORTALS

770-2501 Single Track pkg(2) **6.99**
Cut stone, maximum clearance, 3-1/2" 9cm.

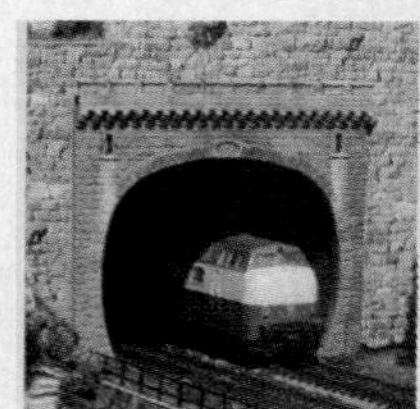

770-2502 Double Track pkg(2) **7.99**

770-2503 Double Track pkg(2) **7.99**
Cut stone, maximum clearance, 3-3/4" 9.5cm

MISCELLANEOUS

770-5136 Turnout Scenic Accessories **10.90**

SUBTERRAIN FOAM PRODUCTS

The Revolutionary Layout System for beginners or experienced modelers.

- **No Expensive Power Tools**
- **No Dusty Mess**
- **No Complicated Calculations**

CREATE THE IDEAL BASE FOR REALISTIC SCENERY IN JUST FIVE EASY STEPS................YOU CAN DO IT!

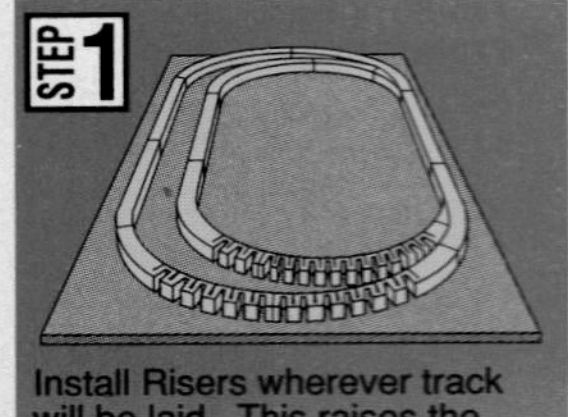

Install Risers wherever track will be laid. This raises the track level to the height of the Risers, causing surrounding areas to be lower. You can quickly and easily make creeks and other low-lying areas without cutting into the layout base.

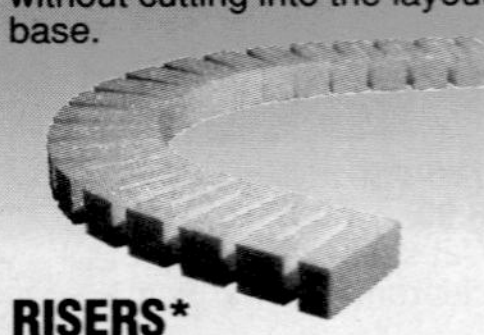

RISERS*

785-1406 1/2" pkg(4) **3.98**
785-1407 1" pkg(4) **5.98**
785-1408 2" pkg(4) **7.98**
785-1409 4" pkg(2) **7.98**

Use at least 2" Risers to elevate track, 4" Risers give maximum elevation for steep relief. 1/2" & 1" Risers are generally used with Incline Starters to create varying grades. Each piece is 2-1/2" wide x 24" long.

Use flexible Inclines to easily change track elevations on curves or straights. The SubTerrain System's precut Inclines (with 2% or 4% grade) remove the guesswork and complicated calculations.

INCLINE SETS*

785-1410 2% (Set) **12.98**
785-1411 4% (Set) **7.98**

4% Set elevates your track 4" in 8'.
2% Set elevates your track 4" in 16'.
Stack the precut Inclines on top of Risers for quick & easy elevation changes. Each piece is 2-1/2" wide x 24" long.

INCLINE STARTERS*

785-1412 2% pkg(8) **3.98**
785-1413 4% pkg(4) **3.98**
Can be used alone or with sets to start your track on an incline. 4% Starter includes 4 identical pieces each 24" long that raise the elevation 1".

2% Starter includes 8 identical pieces each 24" long that raise the elevation 1/2". Each piece is 2-1/2" wide x 24" long.

*Patent Pending

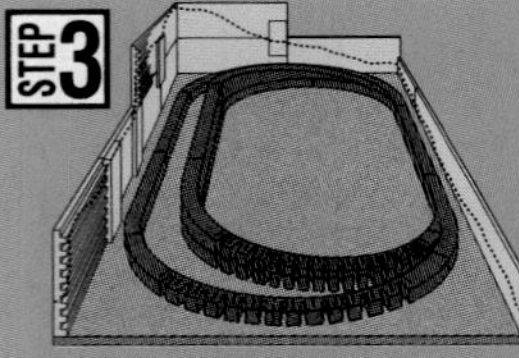

Install interlocking Profile Boards with matching Connectors to make a sturdy layout perimeter that can easily be cut with the Hot Wire Foam Cutter or a hobby knife to conform to any profile desired.

PROFILE BOARDS

785-1419 (2 Connectors and 2 Boards) **6.98**
Profile Boards are used around the perimeter of your layout to define the contours. Their special interlocking design allows them to be stacked and locked together. Each board is 8" high & 24" long.

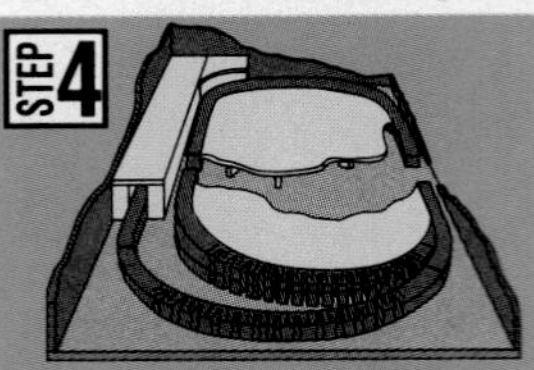

Cut Foam Sheets to enclose tunnels, create interior terrain profiles and form level, elevated areas for buildings and towns.

FOAM SHEETS

785-1422 1/4" **2.98**
785-1423 1/2" **2.98**
785-1424 1" **3.49**
785-1425 2" **6.98**
785-1426 3" **9.98**
785-1427 4" **12.98**
Use Foam Sheets to create elevated flat areas for towns, tunnels and contour supports. The 1/4 & 1/2" can be bent to a tight radius. Each piece 12 x 24".

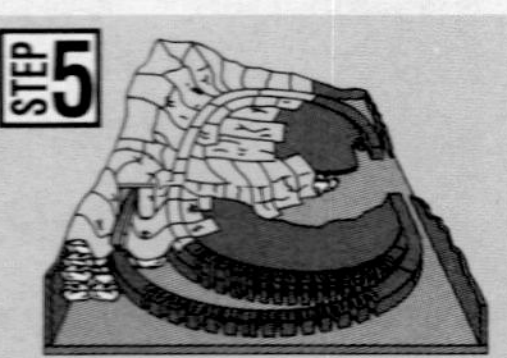

Form terrain with newspaper wads and cover with Plaster Cloth that has been dipped in water. The Plaster Cloth will dry to a hard shell without adding any plaster. Install the Track-Bed.

PLASTER CLOTH

785-1203 6.98
A simple, convenient, and lightweight way to create a durable terrain shell or base. Just wad newspaper and stack to form the desired shape. Dip Plaster Cloth in water. Lay over newspaper wads. Plaster Cloth will dry to a hard shell without adding any plaster. 8" wide x 15' long. (10 sq. ft.)

SUBTERRAIN LEARNING AIDS

HOW TO VIDEO

785-1401 24.98
Approx. 60 minutes. A step-by-step video that shows you how to build a model railroad layout with the revolutionary SubTerrain Layout System.

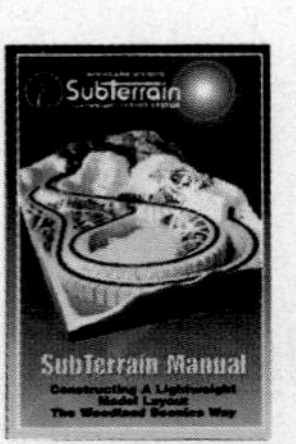

HOW TO MANUAL

785-1402 4.98
An illustrated how-to manual that teaches you how to create the ideal base for scenery and landscaping in five easy steps. 101 pages with 43 illustrations and 160 photos.

ACCESSORIES

All of these accessories are available to help you successfully build your SubTerrain Layout.

FOAM PENCILS
785-1431 3.98
Foam Pencils have special lead that allows you to draw on foam without causing any damage. The colors will not bleed through paint or other coverings. Each package contains 2 red and 2 black pencils.

FLEX PASTE
785-1205 16oz **11.98**
A specially formulated, non-cracking modeling paste. Use for a filler, surfacer or primer on styrofoam.

2" FOAM NAILS
785-1432 pkg(75) **4.98**
Use Foam Nails to temporarily pin track, foam or other products to your layout.

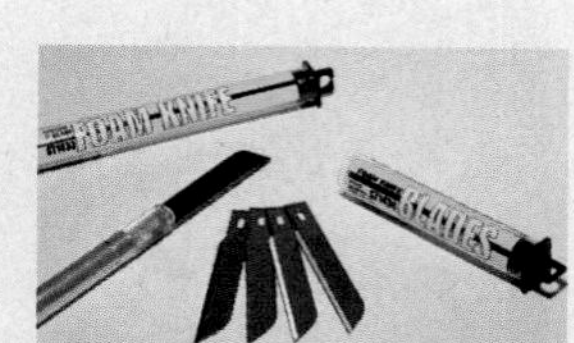

FOAM KNIFE
785-1433 5.98
The Foam Knife comes with a 2" replaceable blade that is ideal for cutting thick pieces of foam.

FOAM KNIFE BLADES
785-1434 pkg(4) **4.98**

FOAM TACK GLUE
785-1444 12oz **9.98**
This specially formulated glue is high tack and effective on most materials. Use as a contact cement whenever bonding two large surfaces.

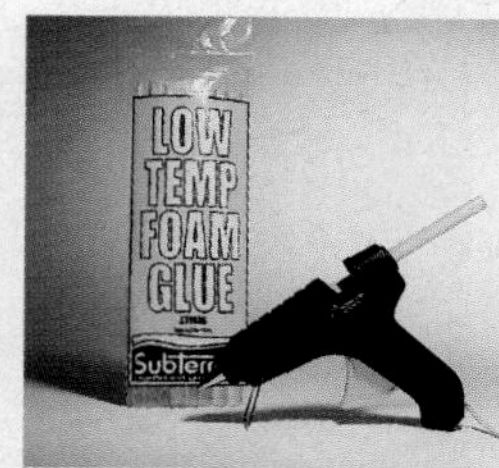

LOW TEMP FOAM GLUE GUN
785-1445 16.98
The Glue Gun with the Low Temp Glue Sticks operates at a temperature that will not damage foam and bonds instantly.

LOW TEMP FOAM GLUE STICKS
785-1446 pkg(10) **3.98**
10" Sticks.

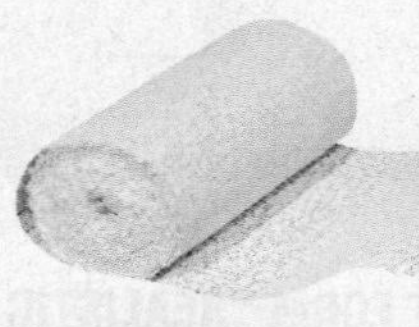

PLASTER CLOTH
785-1203 6.98
A simple, convenient, and lightweight way to create a durable terrain shell or base. Just wad newspaper and stack to form the desired shape. Dip Plaster Cloth in water, lay over newspaper and allow to dry. A quick, no mess scenery base. Includes 8" wide x 15' long (10 sq. ft.) roll.

FOAM PUTTY
785-1447 16oz **7.98**
A non-shrinking, lightweight filling material that has same characteristics as foam. Fill cracks and gaps then sand.

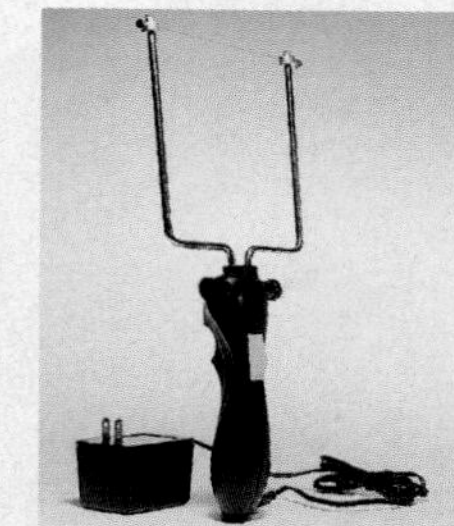

HOT WIRE FOAM CUTTER
785-1435 29.98
The Hot Wire Foam Cutter has adjustable collars allowing for clean, accurate cuts in foam. Woodland Scenics recommends using this tool only with SubTerrain white foam, which has no toxic fumes. Use only special nichrome replacement wire, listed below.

4' HOT WIRE REPLACEMENT WIRE
785-1436 1.98
Special Nichrome wire retains an even temperature required to cut Woodland Scenics foam products. Use only with Hot Wire Foam Cutter #1435, sold separately.

FOAM CUTTER BOW & GUIDE
785-1437 7.49
This Bow Attachment adds versatility to the Hot Wire Cutter. Attach the guide to make precise angle cuts (handle not included).

COMPLETE ROAD SYSTEM

Making roads, parking lots or any asphalt or concrete surface has never been easier with the Woodland Scenics Road System. Use directly on any clean hard surface.

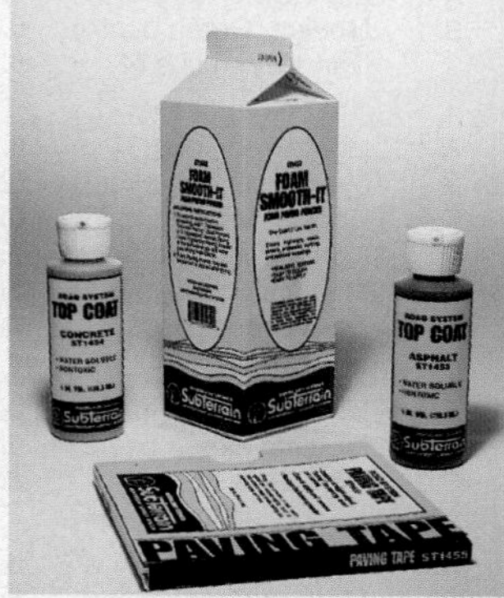

PAVING TAPE
785-1455 1/4" x 30' **5.98**
An adhesive backed foam tape that is used to outline streets, roads and sidewalks, fill with Smooth-It, sold separately. A spreader is included.

SMOOTH-IT
785-1452 1qt **3.98**
Mix with water and apply directly to any hard surface. Smooth-It is a plaster material that is used to smooth rough spots, create streets, roads and parking lots.

TOP COAT EA 3.98
785-1453 Asphalt 4oz
785-1454 Concrete 4oz
Two realistic Top Coat colors are available: Asphalt and Concrete. Use full strength or thin with water.

STEP 1
Draw road and apply Paving Tape.

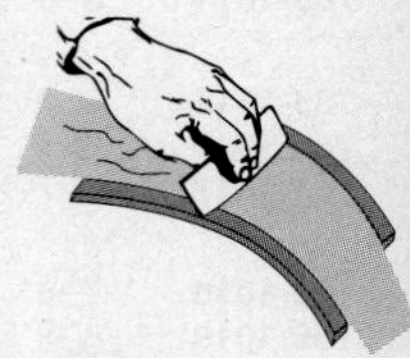

STEP 2
Fill and spread Smooth-It.

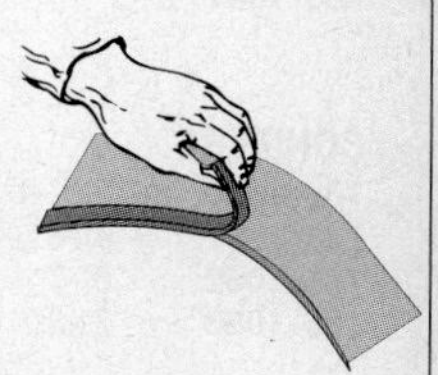

STEP 3
Remove Paving Tape.

TRACK-BED

HO SCALE ROADBED & TRACK-BED SHEETS

- **Quieter Operation** (Sound Deadening Material)
- **Smoother Operation** (Cushions Vibrations)
- **Easier to Use** (Tack or Glue Down, Flexible, No Soaking, Compatible with Cork, Won't Dry Out or Crumble)
- **Better Value** (Higher Quality...Lower Cost)

TRACK-BED
785-1461 2' pkg(36) **25.74**

TRACK-BED SHEETS
785-1470 5 x 24" x 5mm pkg(6) **13.08** *NEW*

STANDARD PACK
785-1471 2' pkg(12) **8.58**

TREES

REALISTIC TREES...READY MADE & KITS

Ready Made "Realistic Trees" are ready to use right out of the box. Or make your own with Realistic Tree Kits. Both styles include bendable plastic armatures which will not break. Realistic Trees lend instant authenticity to a layout or diorama. Natural colors and realistic texture duplicate nature and blend with other Woodland Scenics landscaping products.

READY MADE "REALISTIC TREES"

There are 25 different packages of trees for variety. Each tree is hand crafted; individually shaped and uniquely foliated. No two trees are exactly the same.

GREEN DECIDUOUS

785-1001	.75"-1.25"	B	Medium Green pkg(8)	**5.98**
785-1002	1.25"-2"	B	Medium Green pkg(5)	**5.98**
785-1003	2"-3"	A	Light Green pkg(4)	**6.49**
785-1004	2"-3"	B	Medium Green pkg(4)	**6.49**
785-1005	2"-3"	C	Dark Green pkg (4)	**6.49**
785-1006	3"-4"	A	Light Green pkg(3)	**6.98**
785-1007	3"-4"	B	Medium Green pkg(3)	**6.98**
785-1008	3"-4"	C	Dark Green pkg(3)	**6.98**
785-1009	4"-5"	A	Light Green pkg(3)	**7.49**
785-1010	4"-5"	B	Medium Green pkg(3)	**7.49**
785-1011	4"-5"	C	Dark Green pkg(3)	**7.49**
785-1012	5"-6"	A	Light Green pkg(2)	**6.98**
785-1013	5"-6"	B	Medium Green pkg(2)	**6.98**
785-1014	5"-6"	C	Dark Green pkg(2)	**6.98**
785-1015	6"-7"	A	Light Green pkg(2)	**8.49**
785-1016	6"-7"	B	Medium Green pkg(2)	**8.49**
785-1017	6"-7"	C	Dark Green pkg(2)	**8.49**
785-1018	7"-8"	B	Medium Green pkg(2)	**10.49**
785-1019	8"-9"	B	Medium Green pkg(2)	**12.49**

FALL DECIDUOUS

785-1040	1.25"-3"	E	Fall Mix pkg(9)	**11.49**
785-1041	3"-5"	E	Fall Mix pkg(6)	**13.49**

CONIFERS

785-1060	2.5"-4"	D	Conifer Green pkg(5)	**6.98**
785-1061	4"-6"	D	Conifer Green pkg(4)	**6.98**
785-1062	6"-7"	D	Conifer Green pkg(3)	**7.49**
785-1063	7"-8"	D	Conifer Green pkg(3)	**9.49**

KIT FORM "REALISTIC TREES" EA 13.98

Six selections of tree kits in deciduous or conifer styles ranging in size from 3/4" to 8" give you the opportunity to make easy and truly unique trees for your layout. Create the armature shape you want then add as much or as little foliage as desired. Easy for beginners.

GREEN DECIDUOUS

785-1101	.75"-3"	ABC	Mixed Green pkg(36)
785-1102	3"-5"	ABC	Mixed Green pkg(14)
785-1103	5"-7"	ABC	Mixed Green pkg(7)

CONIFERS

785-1104	2.5"-4"	D	Conifer Green pkg(42)
785-1105	4"-6"	D	Conifer Green pkg(24)
785-1106	6"-8"	D	Conifer Green pkg(16)

READY MADE VALUE PACKS EA 22.98

Nine different Value Packs contain deciduous or pine trees ranging in size from 3/4" to 8". Quantities vary according to size. Mixed green conifer or fall colors.

GREEN DECIDUOUS

785-1070	.75"- 2"	ABC	Mixed Green pkg(38)
785-1071	2"- 3"	ABC	Mixed Green pkg(23)
785-1072	3"- 5"	ABC	Mixed Green pkg(14)

FALL DECIDUOUS

785-1075	.75"-2"	E	Fall Colors pkg(38)
785-1076	2"- 3"	E	Fall Colors pkg(24)
785-1077	3"- 5"	E	Fall Colors pkg(16)

CONIFERS

785-1080	2.5"-4"	D	Conifer Green pkg(33)
785-1081	4"-6"	D	Conifer Green pkg(24)
785-1082	6"-8"	D	Conifer Green pkg(12)

CLUMP-FOLIAGE EA 10.98

Clump-Foliage is a patented foliage product available in 3qt. bags in six realistic colors. Use for ground cover, bushes, shrubs, and tree foliage. Previously available in Realistic Tree Kits only.

785-181	F	Burnt Grass	3qt
785-182	A	Light Green	3qt
785-183	B	Medium Green	3qt
785-184	C	Dark Green	3qt
785-185	D	Conifer Green	3qt
785-186	E	Fall Mix	3qt

A

B

C

D

E

F

ADHESIVE

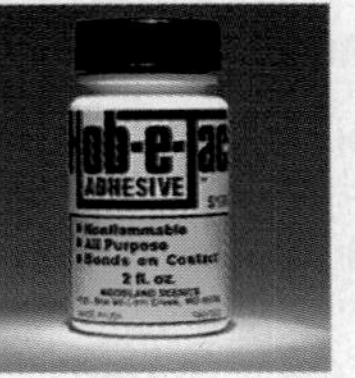

HOB-E-TAC
785-195 2oz. **4.79**
All purpose, nonflammable, aggressive high tack adhesive. For making trees and for attaching Clump-Foliage, Field Grass and Foliage Clusters. Can also be used as a contact adhesive.

TREES

With Woodland Scenics Kits, no two trees need ever look alike because you design each tree! You bend the branches and shape the tree. You position the foliage. Try using different colors of foliage with varied placement for realism and variety.

THREE BASIC STEPS

Bend and twist the soft metal armature to a realistic shape. Stretch out the foliage until thin and lacy. Apply foliage to tree and glue as desired.

SMALL TREE KITS

Each tree kit contains two to five bendable metal trunk castings with bark texture; pre-colored, nonmetallic foliage material; and easy to follow instructions. These are highly detailed, extremely versatile trees, designed to lend realism and variety to any layout.

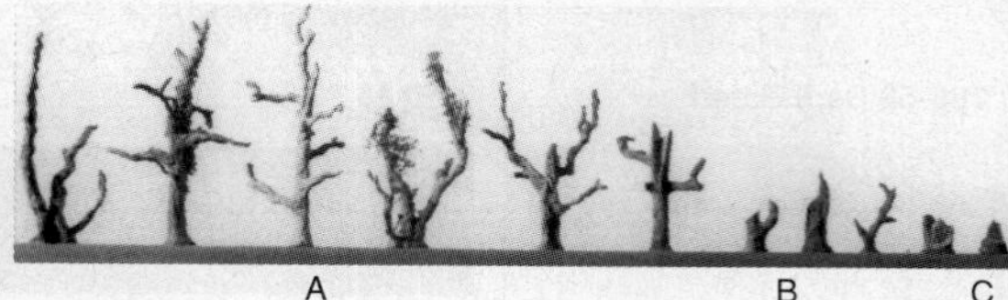

A **785-22** Dead Trees pkg(5) **5.49**
B **785-31** Cut Stumps pkg(14) **2.49**
C **785-32** Broken Stumps pkg(14) **2.49**

785-11 Forked Trunk 2-1/4" pkg(4) **5.49**

785-13 Straight Trunk 2-1/2" pkg(5) **5.49**

785-18 Double Fork 3-1/2" pkg(2) **5.49**

785-21 Gnarled 4-1/2" pkg(2) **5.49**

785-12 Ornamental 2-1/2" pkg(5) **5.49**

785-14 Softwood Pine 3-1/4" pkg(5) **5.49**
785-20 Columnar Pine 4-1/2" pkg(4) **5.49**

785-19 Shade Tree 4" pkg(2) **5.49**

785-17 Shag Bark 3-1/2" pkg(3) **5.49**

LARGE TREE KITS

The soft white metal tree kits provide realism for the special scenes in your layout.

785-23 Pine Trees approx. 6-9" tall pkg(5) **9.98**

785-25 Hardwood Trees approx. 5-1/2 to 6-1/2" tall pkg(3) **9.98**

785-27 Pine Forest approx. 2-4" tall pkg(24) **10.98**

785-24 9.98
Hedge Row Scene 24-30 inches long. Contains: 18 trees, 6 bushes, 3 colors foliage, 2 colors turf.

785-26 Big Old Trees approx. 7 to 7-1/2" tall pkg(2) **9.98**

785-28 Hardwood Forest approx. 2-4" tall pkg(24) **10.98**

COMPLETE LANDSCAPE KIT

785-926 19.98
Contains: 18 trunks (2-4" tall), 3 packs foliage, 7 stumps, 2 packs green blend turf, 3 packs accent turf.

785-47 Fruit (Orange and Red) **2.59**

785-48 Flowers (4 Colors) **2.59**

TURF

32OZ TURF SHAKER *NEW*

Turf is a ground foam material for modeling grass, dead grass, and various types of plant life. Easy to apply. A variety of colors and sizes allow you to create combinations and textures for any season in any scale.

BLENDED TURF BAG EA 5.59
32OZ SHAKER EA 7.98 *NEW*

785-49 Green Blend 45 cu. in.
785-1349 Green Blend 32oz Shaker *NEW*

785-50 Earth Blend 45 cu. in.
785-1350 Earth Blend 32oz Shaker *NEW*

FINE TURF BAG EA 2.79
32OZ SHAKER EA 7.98 *NEW*

785-41 Soil 18 cu. in.
785-1341 Soil 32oz Shaker *NEW*

785-42 Earth 18 cu. in.
785-1342 Earth 32oz Shaker *NEW*

785-43 Yellow Grass 18 cu. in.
785-1343 Yellow Grass 32oz Shaker *NEW*

785-44 Burnt Grass 18 cu. in
785-1344 Burnt Grass 32oz Shaker *NEW*

785-45 Green Grass 18 cu. in.
785-1345 Green Grass 32oz Shaker *NEW*

785-46 Weeds 18 cu. in.
785-1346 Weeds 32oz Shaker *NEW*

COARSE TURF BAG EA 2.79
32OZ SHAKER EA 7.98 *NEW*

785-60 Earth 18 cu. in.

785-61 Yellow Grass 18 cu. in.
785-1361 Yellow Grass 32oz Shaker *NEW*

785-62 Burnt Grass 18 cu. in.
785-1362 Burnt Grass 32oz Shaker *NEW*

785-63 Light Green 18 cu. in.
785-1363 Light Green 32oz Shaker *NEW*

785-64 Medium Green 18 cu. in.
785-1364 Medium Green 32oz Shaker *NEW*

785-65 Dark Green 18 cu. in.
785-1365 Dark Green 32oz Shaker *NEW*

785-1353 Yellow Fall 32oz Shaker *NEW*

785-1354 Orange Fall 32oz Shaker *NEW*

785-1355 Red Fall 32oz Shaker *NEW*

785-1356 Rust Fall 32oz Shaker *NEW*

785-1366 Conifer Green 32oz Shaker *NEW*

FOLIAGE EA 2.98

Foliage can be used for trees, vines, weeds, bushes, or any other low growth. Simply stretch foliage material to desired density and apply. Each 60 sq. in.

785-51 Light Green

785-52 Medium Green

785-53 Dark Green

785-54 Conifer Green

785-55 Early Fall

785-56 Late Fall

FOLIAGE CLUSTERS EA 5.98

A specially produced ground foam cluster for bushes, undergrowth and foliage. Use as is or break into smaller clusters. Each 45 cu. in.

785-57 Light Green

785-58 Medium Green

785-59 Dark Green

EXTRA COARSE TURF EA 2.79

18 cu. in per pack

785-34 Yellow Grass

785-35 Burnt Grass

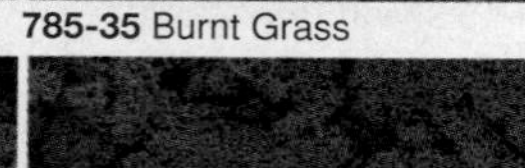

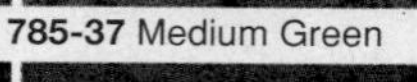

785-36 Light Green

785-37 Medium Green

785-38 Dark Green

785-39 Conifer Green

POLY FIBER

785-178 Green **2.29**
A synthetic fiber intended for use with ground foam to create undergrowth, vines, and economical trees.

COAL

785-92 Mine Run Coal 6oz vol. Unsorted **2.49**
785-93 Lump Coal 6oz vol. Chunks 4" or greater in diameter **2.49**

BOOKS

THE SCENERY MANUAL

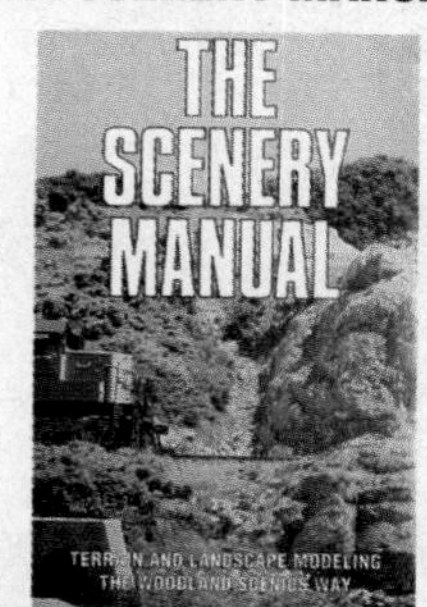

785-1207 9.98
An illustrated start-to-finish guide to terrain construction and landscaping. It is full of basics for beginners and secrets of skilled scenery modelers.

FOLIAGE

CLUMP-FOLIAGE EA 10.98

Clump-Foliage is a patented foliage product available in 3qt bags in six realistic colors. Use as ground cover, bushes, shrubs, and tree foliage. Previously available in Realistic Tree Kits only.

785-181 Burnt Grass

785-182 Light Green

785-183 Medium Green

785-184 Dark Green

785-185 Conifer Green

785-186 Fall Mix

LICHEN EA 4.98 (UNLESS NOTED)

This natural product blends in a limitless variety of colors and textures when combined with Woodland Scenics turf and Foliage lines. Two package sizes and several colors offer variety and economy.

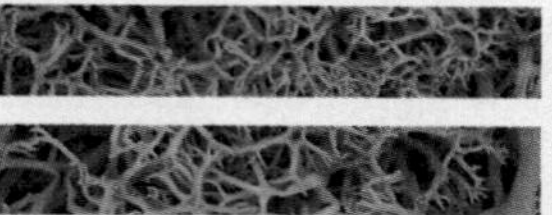

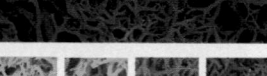

785-161 Spring Green 1-1/2qts

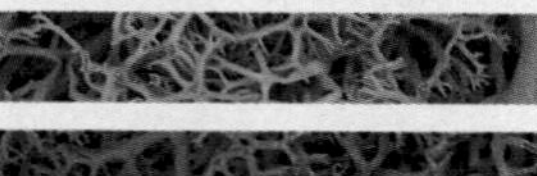

785-162 Light Green 1-1/2qts

785-163 Medium Green 1-1/2qts

785-164 Dark Green 1-1/2qts

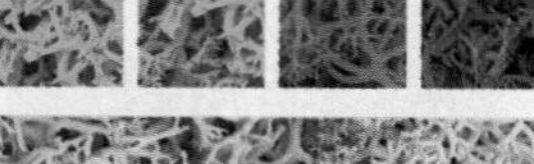

785-165 Autumn Mix 1-1/2qts

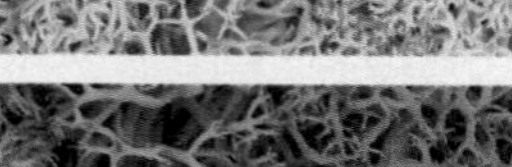

785-166 Natural 1-1/2qts

785-167 Light Green Mix 3qts **9.98**

785-168 Dark Green Mix 3qts **9.98**

FIELD GRASS EA 2.79

An extremely fine natural hair product that models tall grass, field grass and weeds. Easy to follow instructions. Four realistic colors. Net 8gr.

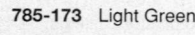

785-171 Natural Straw

785-172 Harvest Gold

785-173 Light Green

785-174 Medium Green

SNOW *NEW*

WOODLAND SCENICS SOFT FLAKE SNOW EA 7.98

785-140 This realistic, easy-to-use snow is available in a 32oz shaker with a sifter top. Perfect for adding either light dustings or heavy drifts.

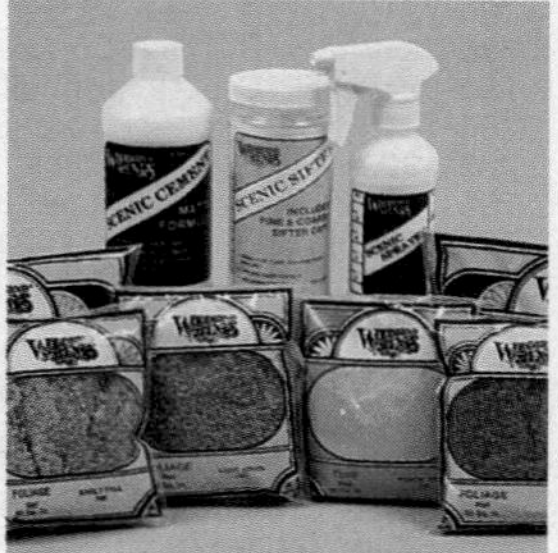

ACCESSORIES

785-191 Scenic Cement **5.49**
Ready to use matte medium. Nontoxic, dries clear, flat 16oz.

785-192 Scenic Sprayer **3.29**
Safe, durable plastic 8oz bottle. Adjustable nozzle.

785-193 Scenic Sifter **2.98**
Includes two interchangeable snap-on shaker caps for sprinkling turf, dirt, ballast, etc.

HOW TO VIDEO 24.98

785-1401

Approx. 60 minutes. A step-by-step video that shows you how to build a model railroad layout with the revolutionary SubTerrain Layout System.

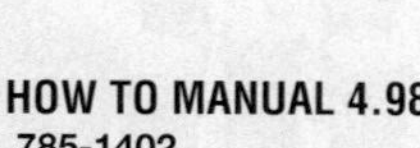

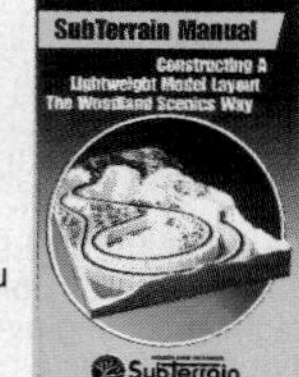

HOW TO MANUAL 4.98

785-1402

An illustrated how-to manual that teaches you how to create the ideal base for scenery and landscaping in five easy steps. 101 pages with 43 illustrations and 160 photos.

TUNNEL LINER

785-1250 3.49
You can cast realistic rock walls and ceilings for single or double track tunnel.

THE CLINIC VIDEO

785-990 24.95
Learn by watching the professionals demonstrate landscaping and terrain modeling techniques at a recent National Model Railroad Convention. In this video, you'll see just how easy it is. 1 hour and 15 min. length.

HOB-E-TAC ADHESIVE

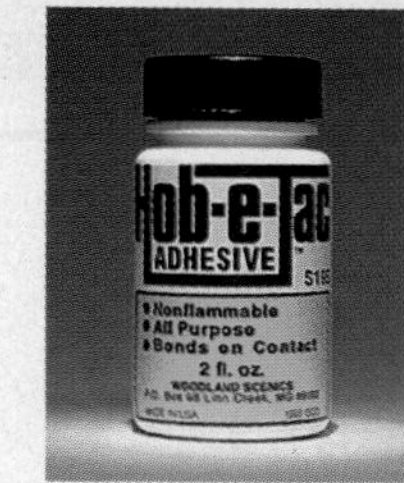

785-195 4.79
All purpose, nonflammable, aggressive high tack adhesive. Perfect for attaching Clump-Foliage, Field Grass and Foliage Clusters. Can also be used as a contact adhesive. 2 fl. oz.

BUYERS GUIDE

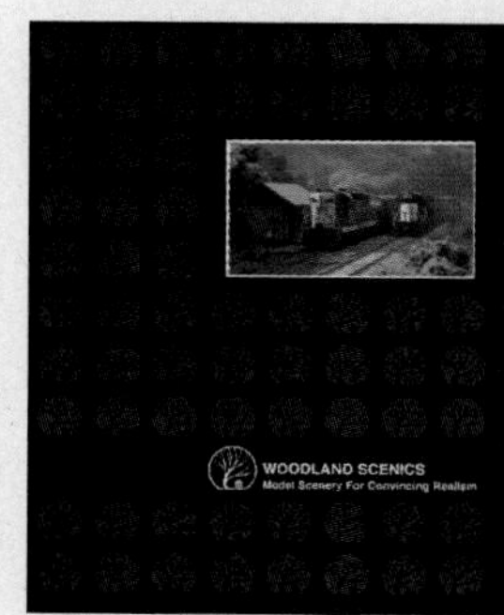

785-100 1.50
Full color, 28 page complete guide to Woodland Scenics products.

THE COMPLETE TERRAIN SYSTEM

Woodland Scenics Terrain products are a complete system for beginners and craftsmen alike. The Terrain System has all the products needed to make earth contour models that reflect any type of terrain. The system includes Lightweight Hydrocal, Mold-A-Scene, Plaster Cloth, E-Z Water, Flex Paste, Latex Rubber, Tunnel Portals, Retaining Walls, Culverts, Talus, Tunnel Liner Form, Earth Color Liquid Pigments, Scenic Sprayer, Rock Molds and The Scenery Manual. Each product has easy to follow instructions

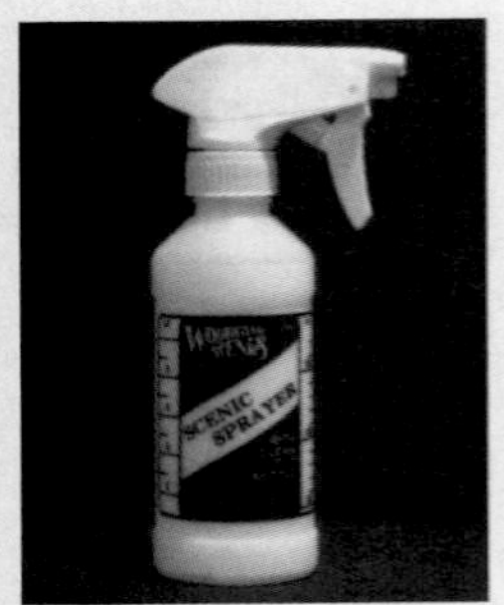

SCENIC SPRAYER

785-192 8oz **3.29**
The Scenic Sprayer comes with a long siphon tube and spray head that fits the Scenic Cement bottle. Nozzle is adjustable from a very fine mist to a steady stream. May be used to spray water, diluted Earth Color Liquid Pigment and Scenic Cement.

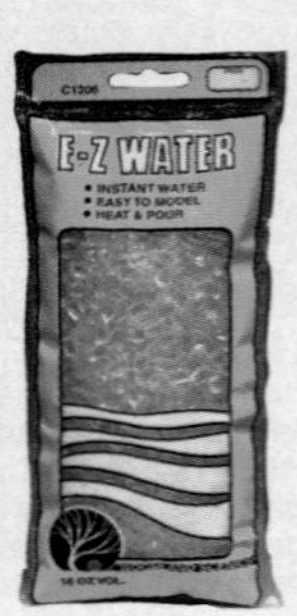

E-Z WATER

785-1206 16oz **8.49**
This heat activated water modeling material has been developed for the special needs of the scenery modeler. Melt on stove and pour.

THE CLINIC VIDEO

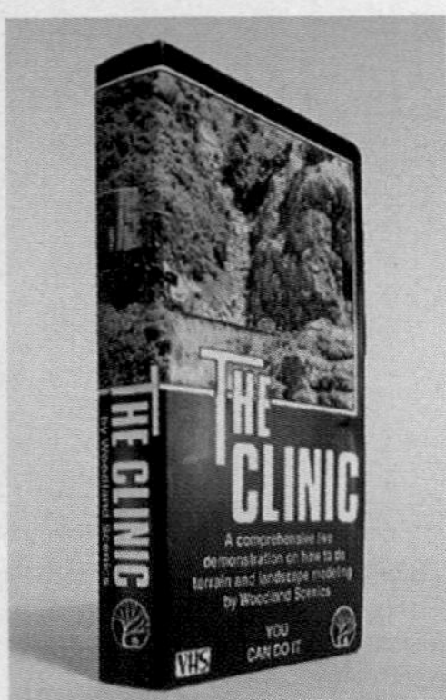

785-990 24.98
Learn by watching the professionals demonstrate landscaping and terrain modeling techniques at a recent National Model Railroad Convention. In this video, you'll see just how easy it is. 1 hour and 15 min. length.

FLEX PASTE

785-1205 16oz **11.98**
Use this as a flexible, non-cracking coating over Styrofoam or as a road base for concrete or asphalt modeling.

PIGMENTS EA 3.98 (UNLESS NOTED)

EARTH COLOR LIQUID PIGMENTS

Use the eight different colors of Earth Color Liquid Pigment to color rocks, terrain, and plaster castings. They are water soluble and can be diluted and blended in limitless combinations. Extremely concentrated for economical use. 4oz each. (Photo shows plaster rock castings, sold separately, stained with color.)

785-1216	A	White
785-1217	B	Concrete
785-1218	C	Stone Gray
785-1219	D	Slate Gray
785-1220	E	Black
785-1221	F	Raw Umber
785-1222	G	Burnt Umber
785-1223	H	Yellow Ocher

UNDERCOAT PIGMENTS

Formulated for use under Green Blend and Earth Blend Turf (785-49 and 785-50) to provide a base color. These two colors of Liquid Pigment can also be used for rocks and plaster castings. Extremely concentrated. 8oz each. (Photo shows plaster rock castings, sold separately, stained with color.)

785-1228	I	Green Undercoat **5.49**
785-1229	J	Earth Undercoat **5.49**

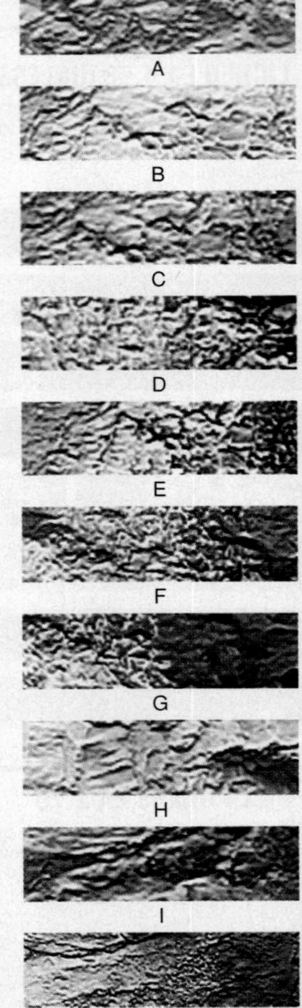

EARTH COLOR KIT

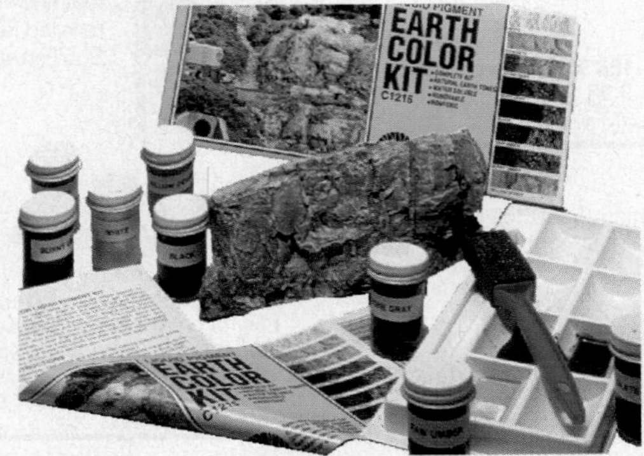

785-1215 Earth Color Kit **14.98**
A simple system for staining rocks, terrain, and plaster castings such as portals. Beginners get quality results. The Earth Color Kits include instructions, applicator, palette, and eight 1oz bottles each of Earth Color Liquid Pigment (White, Concrete, Stone Gray, Slate Gray, Raw Umber, Burnt Umber, Yellow Ocher).

PLASTER

PLASTER CLOTH

785-1203 6.98
A simple, convenient, and lightweight way to create a durable terrain shell or base. Just wad newspaper and stack to form the desired shape. Dip Plaster Cloth in water, lay over newspaper and allow to dry. A quick, no mess scenery base. Includes approx. 10 square feet of cloth.

LIGHTWEIGHT HYDROCAL*

785-1201 1/2gal **7.49**
A specially formulated new Lightweight Hydrocal for terrain model builders. Lightweight Hydrocal is nearly half the weight of Hydrocal, goes almost twice as far, and is the tough, quick setting product.

*Hydrocal is a product of U.S. Gypsum

LATEX RUBBER

785-1204 16oz **9.98**
Make your own rock molds with this ready to use Latex Rubber. It is formulated to reproduce fine detail and to be durable.

MOLD-A-SCENE PLASTER

785-1202 1/2gal **7.49**
Mold-A-Scene is a plaster material that can be shaped without a mold like modeling clay. Its longer setting time allows a scenery modeler to add terrain contours to new or existing scenery.

FLEX PASTE

785-1205 16oz **11.98**
Use this as a flexible, non-cracking coating over Styrofoam or as a road base for concrete or asphalt modeling.

ROCK MOLDS

Highly detailed, flexible, and durable rock molds. Use to cast small boulders, rock outcroppings, top rock for fields and creeks, or make entire rock faces by combining castings produced with these molds.

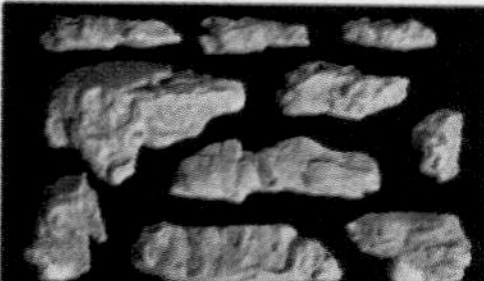
785-1230 Outcroppings **5.98**

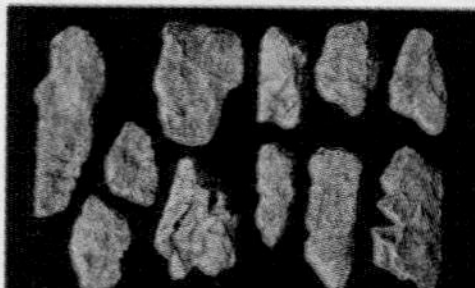
785-1231 Surface Rocks **5.98**

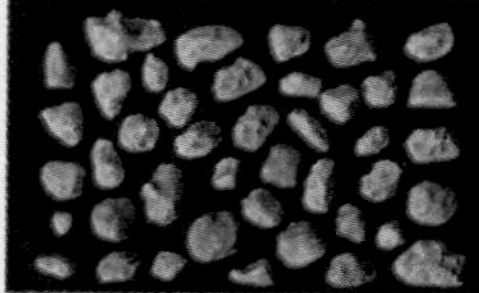
785-1232 Boulders **5.98**

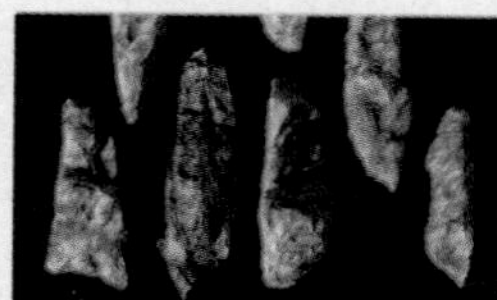
785-1233 Embankments **5.98**

785-1234 Random Rock **5.98**

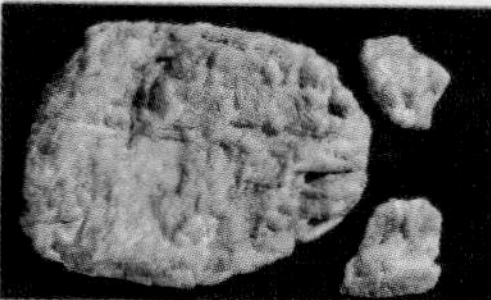
785-1235 Laced Face Rock **5.98**

785-1236 Classic Rock **5.98**

785-1237 Wind Rock **5.98**

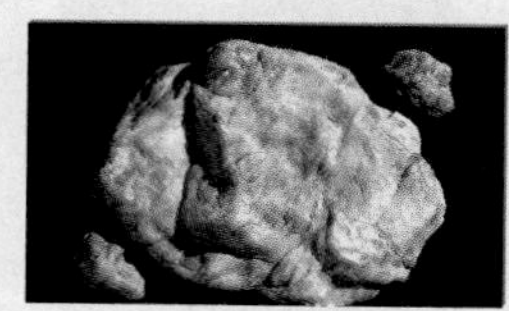
785-1238 Weathered Rock **5.98**

785-1239 Strata Stone **5.98**

785-1240 Rock Mass **5.98**

785-1241 Layered Rock **5.98**

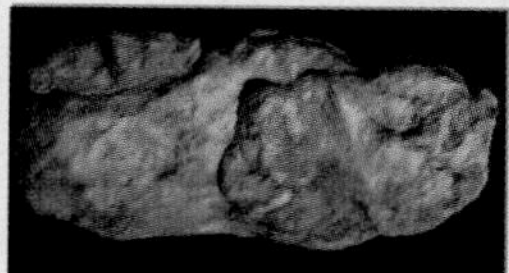
785-1242 Washed Rock **6.98**

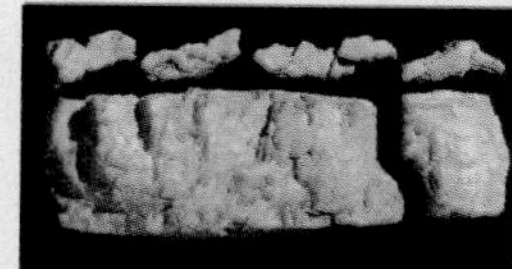
785-1243 Base Rock **6.98**

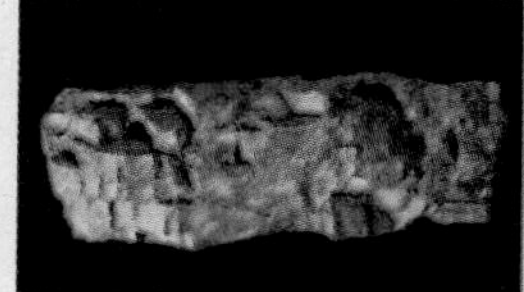
785-1244 Facet Rock **6.98**

PORTALS AND RETAINING WALLS

EA 6.98 (UNLESS NOTED)

Tunnel Portals and Retaining Walls are high density Hydrocal castings that are easy to stain with Earth Color Liquid Pigments and are available in concrete, cut stone, random stone and timber styles. Retaining Walls come in three sections per package. Each section can be used alone or installed adjacent to another in an endless chain fashion. They can be cut to varying heights to accommodate the adjoining terrain.

785-1252 Concrete - Single

785-1253 Cut Stone - Single

785-1254 Timber - Single

785-1255 Random Stone - Single

785-1256 Concrete-Double **7.49**

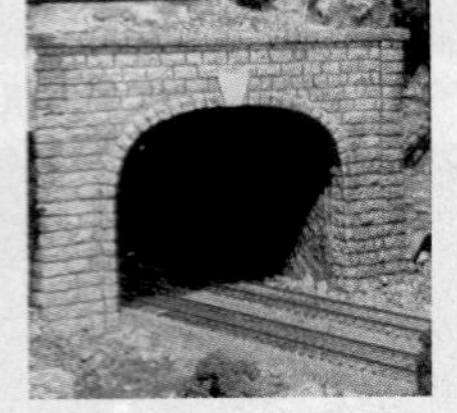

785-1257 Cut Stone - Double **7.49**

785-1258 Concrete pkg(3)

785-1259 Cut Stone pkg(3)

785-1260 Timber pkg(3)

785-1261 Random Stone pkg(3)

CULVERTS

PKG(2) EA 6.49

Culverts are also high density Hydrocal castings. There are two culverts per package.

785-1262 Concrete

785-1263 Masonry Arch

785-1264 Random Stone)

785-1265 Timber

TALUS EA 2.69

Natural rock debris usually occurs near rock faces and outcroppings, near culverts and portals and in creeks and ditches. For super detailing add talus to models in appropriate areas with white glue. Intermix grades, blend shades, and even stain your own to match rock castings with Woodland Scenics Earth Colors. 12oz bags.

FOUR COLORS / **FOUR GRADES**

Buff / Fine

Brown / Medium

Gray / Coarse

Natural / Extra Coarse

COLOR	FINE	MED.	COARSE	EXTRA COARSE
Buff	**785-1270**	**785-1271**	**785-1272**	**785-1273**
Brown	**785-1274**	**785-1275**	**785-1276**	**785-1277**
Gray	**785-1278**	**785-1279**	**785-1280**	**785-1281**
Natural	**785-1282**	**785-1283**	**785-1284**	**785-1285**

BALLAST EA 2.69 (UNLESS NOTED)

NEW 32OZ BALLAST SHAKER EA 7.98

Woodland Scenics standard bag of ballast contains 12 ounces (volume) and only weighs 7oz, but is equivalent to approximately 20oz (weight) of stone ballast.

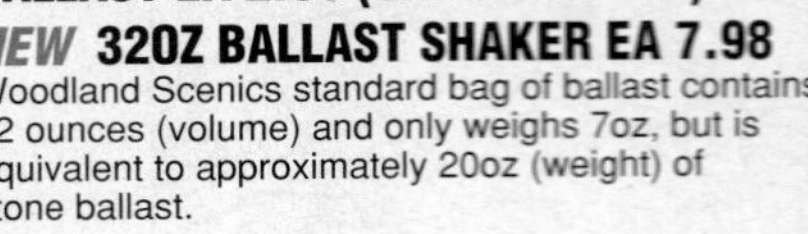

A B C D

E F G H

COLOR	FINE	MED.	COARSE
A **Iron Ore**	**785-70**	**785-77**	**785-84**
B **Dk. Brown**	**785-71**	**785-78**	**785-85**
C **Brown**	**785-72**	**785-79**	**785-86**
NEW 32oz	**785-1372**	**785-1379**	**785-1386**
D **Buff**	**785-73**	**785-80**	**785-87**
NEW 32oz	**785-1373**	**785-1380**	**785-1387**
E **Lt. Gray**	**785-74**	**785-81**	**785-88**
NEW 32oz	**785-1374**	**785-1381**	**785-1388**
F **Gray**	**785-75**	**785-82**	**785-89**
NEW 32oz	**785-1375**	**785-1382**	**785-1389**
G **Cinders**	**785-76**	**785-83**	**785-90**
NEW 32oz	**785-1376**	**785-1383**	**785-1390**
H **785-94** Blended Med. Gray 24 oz. vol			**5.49**
NEW 32oz	**785-1393**	**785-1394**	**785-1395**
785-91 Dry Ballast Cement			**2.99**

SCALE REFERENCE CHART: BALLAST

SCALE	FINE	MED.	COARSE
Z	2.2"-7.3"	7.3"-11"	11"-18.3"
N	1.6"-5.3"	5.3"-8"	8"-13.3"
HO	9"-2.9"	2.9"-4.3"	4.4"-7.2"
S	.6"-2.1"	2.1"-3.2"	3.2"-5.3"
O	.5"-1.6"	1.6"-2.4"	2.4"-3.9"
1	.3"-1"	1.1"-1.6"	1.6"-2.6"
G	.24"-.8"	.8"-1.2"	1.2"-1.9"

MINI-SCENES

EA 9.98 (UNLESS NOTED)

These kits contain everything required to build Mini-Scenes, including pewter castings, landscape materials and instructions. (Less paint and glue). Mini-Scene kits can be finished in pewter or painted as realistic miniatures. They can be built into an HO layout, complete HO scenes, for display or added to your layout.

785-101 Abandoned Log Cabin

785-102 Moonshine Still

785-103 The Windmill

785-104 The Hunter

785-105 The Sign Painter

785-106 The Tack Shed

785-107 Tommy's Treehouse

785-108 Outhouse Mischief

785-109 Ernie's Fruit Stand

785-110 Saturday Night Bath

785-111 Floyd's Barber Shop

785-112 Tractor Pit Stop

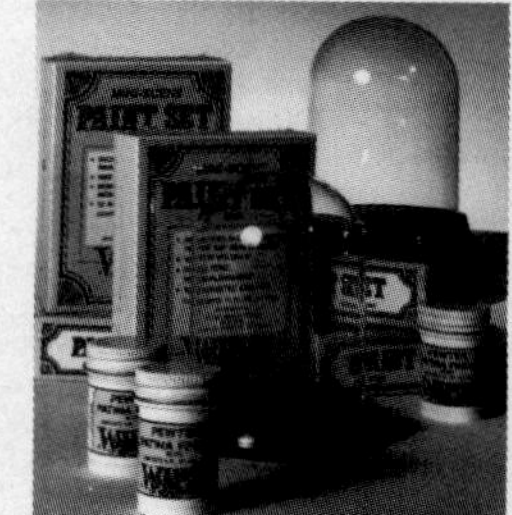

785-125 Paint Set **4.49**
785-126 Pewter Patina Finish **1.98**
785-127 Display Dome **6.98**

LEARNING AIDS... YOU CAN DO IT

THE SCENERY KIT 785-927

Whether beginner or expert, with The Scenery Kit modelers learn scenery techniques that dramatically improve their skills...in just hours! A 10 x 18" diorama displays your favorite rolling stock or engine when finished.

You Will Learn To:
Make Trees, Create Mountains, Build Rolling Terrain, Stain Rocks Realistically, Plant Grass, Weeds & Bushes, Install Track & Ballast.

- **Includes a piece of HO track, but N scale can be substituted**
- **All scenery materials included...even paint and hardboard base (Everything!).**
- **785-927 If purchased separately $61.00. Suggested retail only $39.98**

THE SCENERY MANUAL

785-1207 9.98
An illustrated start-to-finish guide to terrain construction and landscaping. It is full of basics for beginners and secrets of skilled scenery modelers.

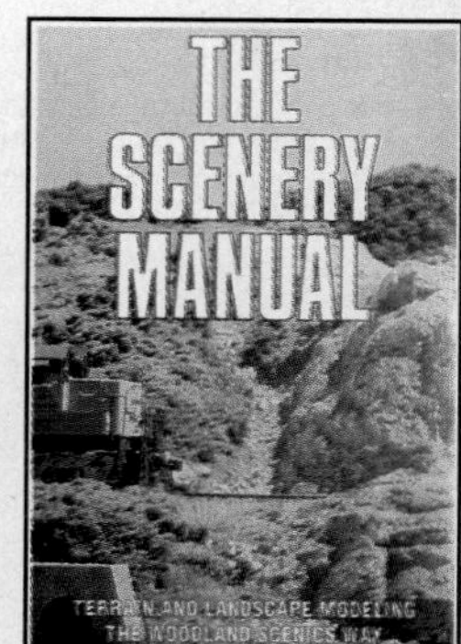

VIDEO

THE CLINIC

785-990 24.95
Learn by watching the professionals demonstrate landscaping and terrain modeling techniques. In this video, you'll see just how easy it is. 1 hour and 15 min. length.

WOODLAND SCENICS

TURN YOUR TRAIN SET INTO A MODEL RAILROAD!

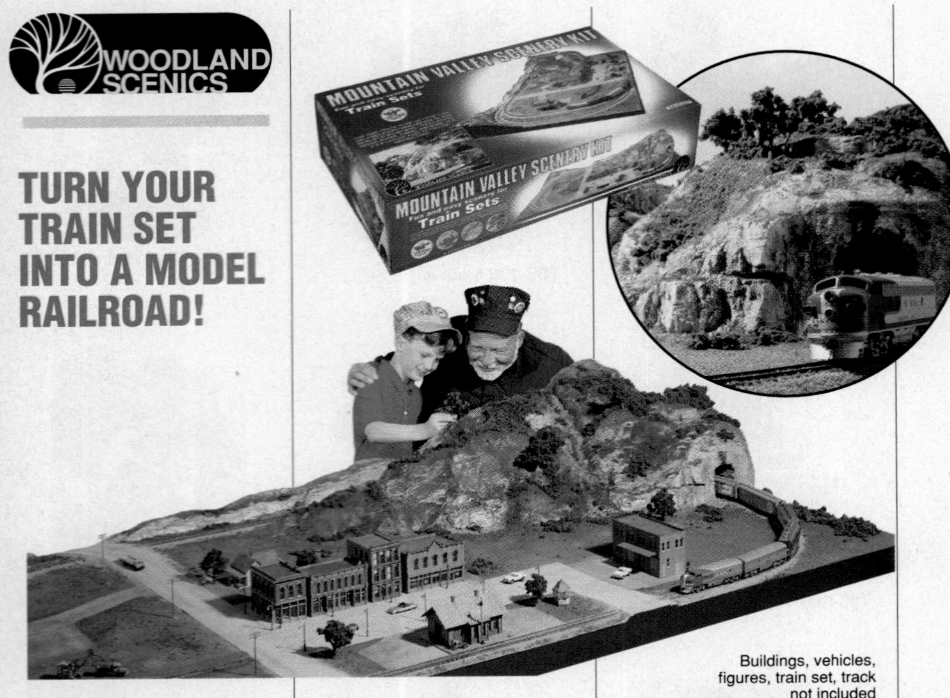

Buildings, vehicles, figures, train set, track not included

The Mountain Valley Scenery Kit from Woodland Scenics is for beginners who want scenery for train sets, model railroaders just beginning scenery, or experienced modelers looking for a bargin. It includes everything neede to add trees, grass, weeds, rocks, mountains, tunnel, ballast and more to a 4' x 8', layout. Use our HO scale track plan or yours. Step-by-step instructions make this kit fun and easy!

785-928 $104 value if items purchased separately, only **$69.98**

ATTACH TERRAIN SUPPORT

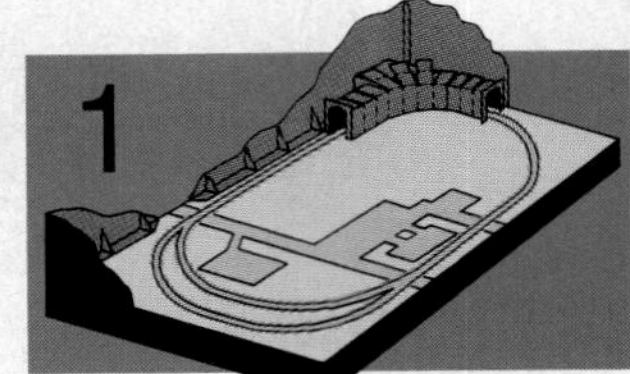

BUILD MOUNTAIN SHAPES

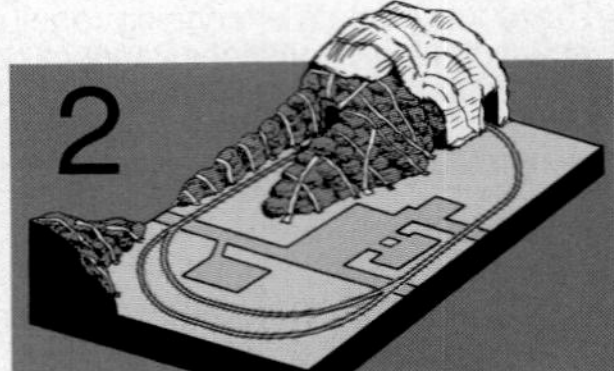

MAKE AND PLACE ROCK CASTINGS

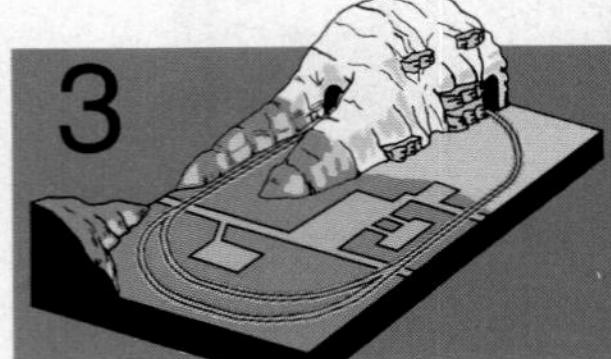

ADD GROUND COVER AND TREES

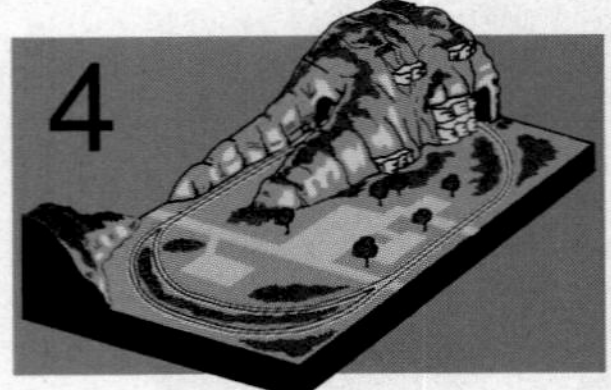

COMPLETE SCENE KITS

EA. 24.98

Nearly any model railroad can be improved with the addition of one or more of the Complete Scene Kits. The kits contain highly detailed castings plus all other materials needed to build one of the three scenes pictured (except paint and glue). all are HO scale and can be assembled in several different ways to fit the available space.

785-130 Smiley's Tow Service (7 x 9")
Includes: Basswood building & fence, seven trees (with two colors of foliage), four different colors of grass & soil, three colors of foliage for bushes & weeds, and over 60 white metal castings including tires, concrete blocks, fuel tanks, oil rums, firewood, mail box, man and several other assorted pieces including junk pile.

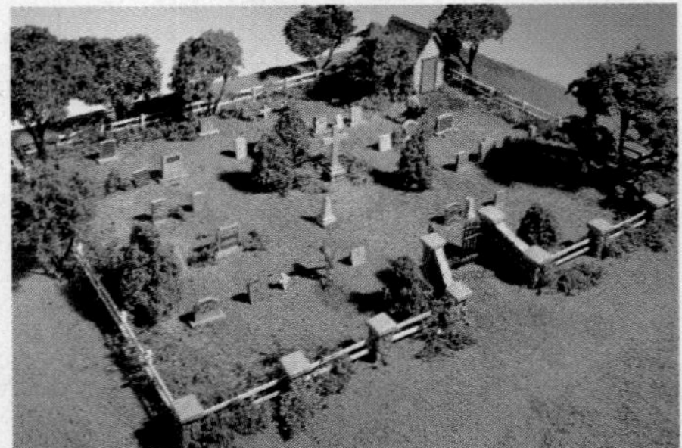

785-131 Maple Leaf Cemetery (8 x 11")
Includes: Basswood tool shed & fence rail, eight trees (with two colors of foliage), four colors of grass & soil, two colors of foliage for bushes & weeds, and over 40 white metal castings including stone fence posts & walls, gates, two men, a central monument & 28 tombstones with names.

785-132 Memorial Park (8 x 14")
Includes: Shelter House, basswood fence, nine trees (with two colors of foliage), Four colors of grass & soil, two colors of foliage for bushes 7 weeds, & over 40 white metal castings including bar-b-q ovens, tire swing, teeter-totter, picnic tables, people, trash cans & park swing.

"Hold your horses... the elephants are coming!" You can feel the electric thrill shoot through the crowd as the uniformed rider approaches and shouts a warning. Just as the posters promised, here's a real-live "Parade of Ponderous Pachyderms" swaying down main street! And it really is a good idea to hold on to your horses. The exotic aroma of such strange creatures will send the calmest old plug running for cover!

Once, the highlight of every summer was the arrival of the circus train. Weeks before, brilliant color posters blazed across every wall and fence, urging you to wait for the coming show. On the big day, folks would arrive well before dawn to stake their claim on the best spots to watch the train unload. For many, the spectacle of colorful cars, rumbling wagons, roaring animals and the orchestrated movements of the train crew was every bit as exciting as the performance under the big top.

Today's circuses move by truck, but once each summer, the glory days of the rail shows live again. On a magical morning in July, a train of restored flat and stock cars ease out of the Circus World Museum grounds at Baraboo enroute to Milwaukee. This colorful caravan attracts thousands of on-lookers along its route and to the unloading area.

Back in 1989, Walthers unveiled an HO Scale replica of the Great Circus Train as it appeared in the late 1960s. Though long out of production, the James Strates Elephant Car shown here may still be the most colorful HO car ever produced - nine different colors were applied, a process which required 23 steps to decorate each model!

If you were one of the lucky subscribers who purchased this limited-run set back then, you know how much fun circus modeling can be. If you're just getting started, you'll find a colorful collection of cars, wagons, animals and accessories to build a big show on the following pages.

ACCURATE LIGHTING

CIRCUS BANNERS

"Step right up! Step right up! Come and see the world's most amazing freaks at the circus sideshow. If that isn't enough to totally amaze you, let the sight of revolting reptiles put a chill down your spine!" Printed in color on 100% polyester, #971 includes the bearded lady, fire eater, tallest man, contortionist and more while #972 includes all sorts of amazing reptiles.

144-971 Sideshow Banner 23.95

144-972 Reptile Banner **12.95**

ALLOY FORMS

CIRCUS TENT VAN

119-7077 Mack Circus Tent Van **22.95**
1930s Mack (CJ) universal tractor with dual axle, canvas circus van and spoke wheels. Kit consists of unpainted white-metal parts. Also includes styrene, brass and rubber details.

CIRCUS CRAFT

Craftsman kits consist of precut wood, unpainted plastic wheels and hardware.

CIRCUS CARS

ELEPHANT CARS EA 7.25

220-161 72' Slatted Sides
220-162 Solid Sides

HORSE CARS

220-163 72' Horse Car **7.25**

FLAT CARS EA 4.25

220-164 72' Mt. Vernon
220-165 72' Warren

220-161 72' Slatted Sides

220-163 72' Horse Car

220-164 72' Mt. Vernon

WAGONS

COMMISSARY WAGON

220-16 4.00

SIDE SHOW CANVAS WAGON

220-17 4.00

GOLIATH WAGON

220-18 4.00

QUARTER POLE WAGON

220-19 With Poles **4.75**

DINING DEPARTMENT WAGON

220-15 4.00

BARNES DOG WAGON

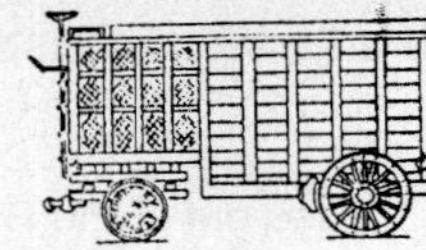

220-23 4.00

STAKE DRIVER

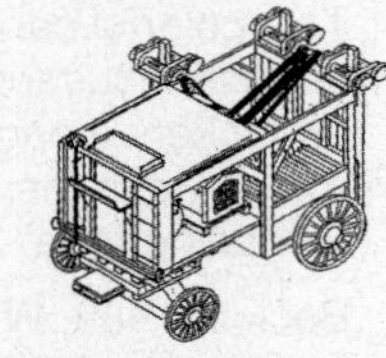

220-28 4.75

HOT DOG WAGON

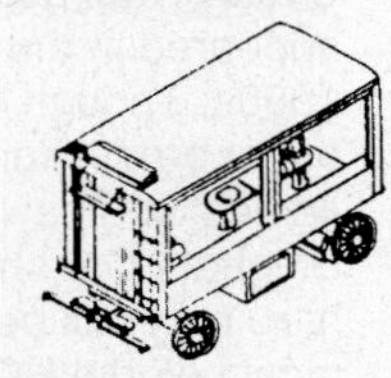

220-24 4.00

GIRAFFE COMPANION WAGON

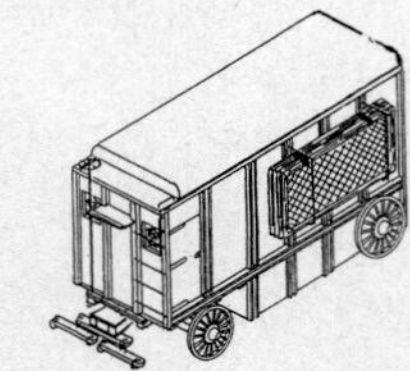

220-26 4.50

GIRAFFE WAGON

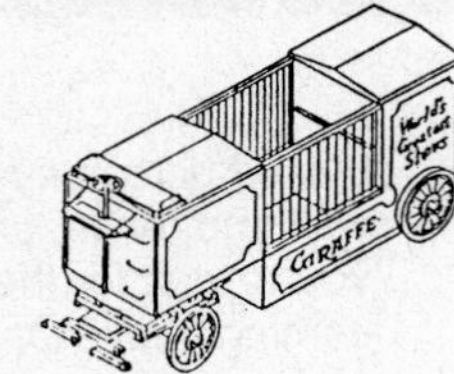

220-20 4.50

LION CAGE WAGON

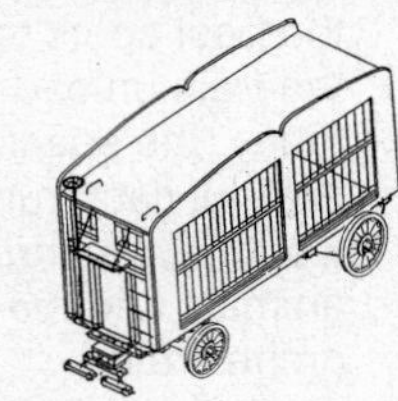

220-25 4.50

COOKHOUSE WATER/ EQUIPMENT WAGON

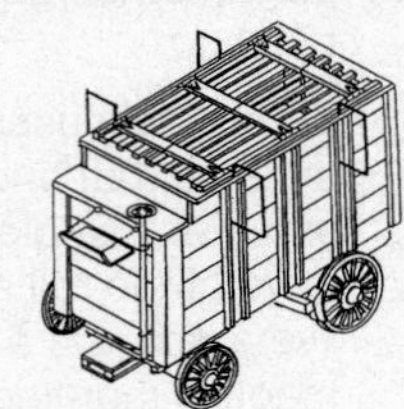

220-27 4.25

FOLDING SEAT WAGON EA 4.00

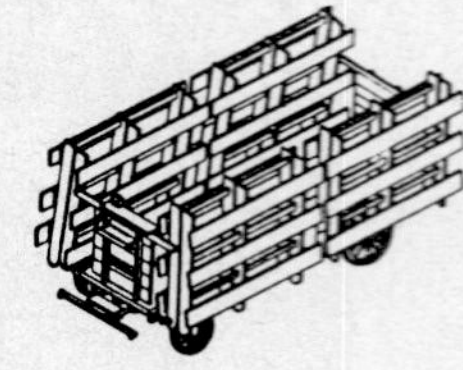

220-1 20'
220-2 30'

FIGURES

Plastic figures molded in realistic poses.

PAINTED EA 3.25

220-1021 Men pkg(6)
220-1022 Women pkg(6)

UNPAINTED

220-1020 Men/Women, Seated pkg(24) **2.50**
220-1025 Men/Women, Seated pkg(102) **7.95**

WHEELS

WAGON PKG(2) .50

220-220 220-221

1/8" Scale. Can be used with HO Scale. Two each of 36" and 48".
220-220 Sunburst
220-221 Baggage

TRUCK

220-226 Truck pkg(12) **1.50**

CIRCUS WHEEL OVERLAYS

220-303 1.50
Before the days of sunburst wheels, painted inserts were placed between the spokes. These overlays simulate those early inserts, and are printed on high-gloss paper in red, yellow and blue. 12 Sets of overlays per package.

BOOKS

CIRCUS TRAINS, TRUCKS & MODELS

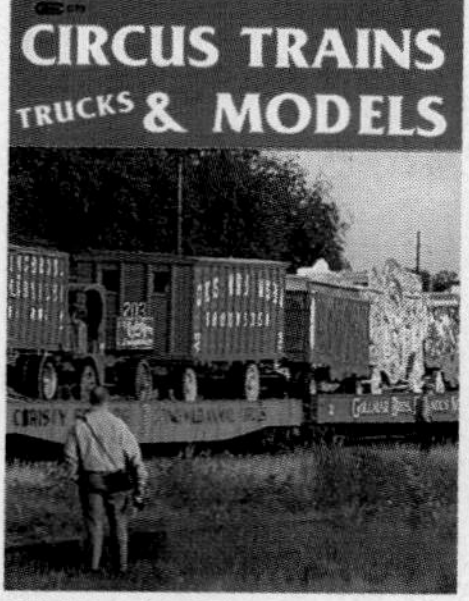

205-70 12.95
Discover the fun of modeling a railroad or truck circus with this historic and informative book. Period black-and-white and color photos of prototype equipment and operations, plus an up-to-date listing of available circus kits. New chapters examine some of today's typical truck shows, along with special trains, like the American Freedom Train, which were similar to the operations of circus trains. 52 pages, softcover.

THE CIRCUS MOVES BY RAIL

A giant collection of rare photos, posters, illustrations and documents covering the railroad circus from its infancy to today. Features in-depth details on circus operations by rail, the evolution of circus car designs, train consists and more. By noted circus historians Tom Parkinson and Chappie Fox. 400 pages.

205-83 Softcover **39.95**
205-85 Hardcover **54.95**

GEM CITY AMUSEMENTS

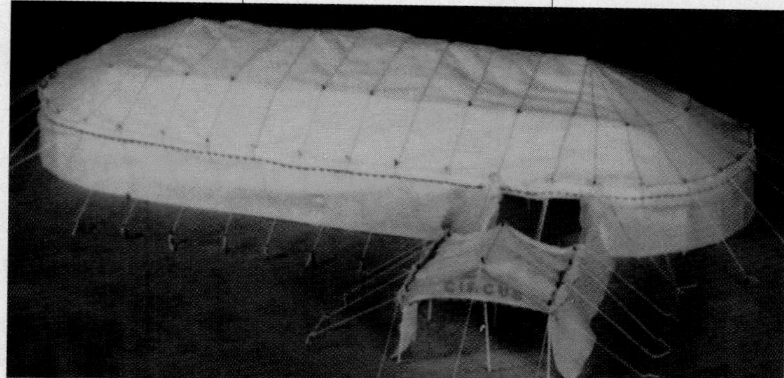

Big Top & Entrance Marquee
294-8902

TENTS

Kits are made of fabric and come complete with precut poles, braided "rope" and brass eyelets. Instructions with diagrams and placement templates are also included.

FULL CIRCUS SET

294-8901 179.95
Includes a Big Top, Entrance Marquee, Menagerie and Side Show tents. To help set things up, a video tape of instructions is included.

BIG TOP & ENTRANCE MARQUEE

294-8902 99.95
For building a smaller circus scene or diorama.

ACCESSORY TENTS

294-8903 99.95
Four accessory tents with hip and gable roofs. These tents can be used for the cookhouse, horse tents, dining tent, dressing table or other tents.

GIANT BIG TOP TENT

294-9704 179.95
The tent needed for a real-size circus model. Room for a three-ring circus with plenty of space for acts and seating. Requires set-up space of 20 x 38".

BUSCH

CARNIVAL LIGHTING

For use on carnival booths, rides and more. Each light strip measures 2-3/8 x 1/8" (60 x 3mm), and includes six LEDs. Control unit (14-16V AC or DC) also included.

189-5932 Blinking **28.99**
189-5933 Constant **33.99**

CON-COR

Assembled, ready-to-run plastic models decorated in authentic colors.

COLONEL BARNUM TRAILERS PKG(2) 10.98

223-8144 28'
223-8146 40'
223-8147 45'
223-8148 48'

ROYAL AMERICAN SHOWS TRAILERS PKG(2) 10.98 (UNLESS NOTED)

223-8133 Ribbed Side
223-8134 Smooth Side
223-8135 40' Trailer "World's Largest Midway"
223-8136 40' Trailer
223-8137 Elliptical Tank Trailers **11.98**

Information STATION

Circus Wagons

Arena Wagon-carried the barred sections of the wild animal arena

Canvas Wagon-carried huge bundles of canvas needed for the various tops

Light Plant-carried engines and generators used to supply the circus with electricity

Plank Wagon-carried the boards, or planks, for the general admission seating

Sanitary Wagon-contained clean, modern restrooms

Spool Wagon-an improvement of the canvas wagon, had a motorized spool on which the big top canvas could be wound

Stake Driver-wagon that carried a gasoline powered machine that mechanically pounded up to three stakes at once

Steam Calliope-a parade wagon with a boiler that provided steam to a manifold, which was released through a tuned pipe via valves operated by a keyboard

Tableau Wagon-solid sided parade wagon decorated with paintings, carvings and sometimes corner statues

Unafon Wagon-a small tableau wagon that carried an unafon on its roof, a unafon is a keyboard instrument which uses hammers to hit tone bars much like a xylophone

Water Wagon-a large wooden tank, generally filled from a fire hydrant or stream, both performers and stock received their water from here

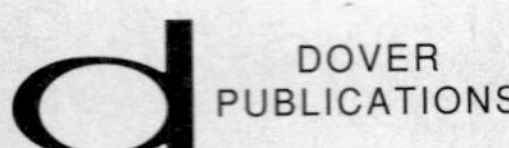

BOOKS

POSTER BOOKS

AMERICAN CIRCUS POSTERS IN FULL COLOR

241-23693 11.95
Features reproductions of original posters from 1890 through 1940, highlights unusual acts, wild animals, performers and more. Softcover, 48 pages, 10-1/4 x 14-1/4".

CUT & ASSEMBLE BOOKS

High-quality, full-color paper cut-out books. Printed one side only on heavy cardstock. Easy-to-follow, step-by-step instructions. 9-1/4 x 12-1/4".

241-24861 Cut & Assemble a Circus Parade **7.95**
Includes horses, wild animals, circus wagons, clowns and a Roman chariot.

241-24992 Cut & Assemble an Old-Fashioned Carousel **7.95**
More than a foot in diameter, with bright red and white canopy, colorful banners and exotic animals, including a camel, pig, zebra, lion, ostrich and horses.

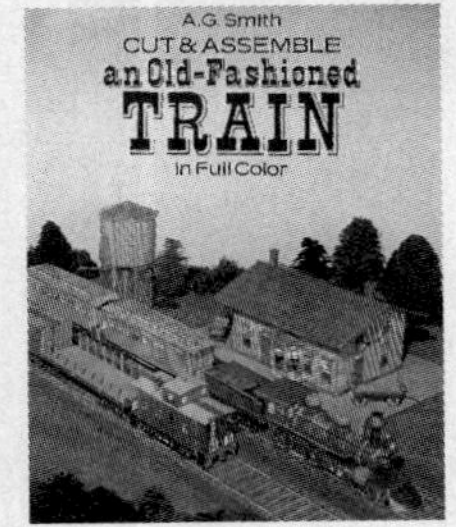

241-25324 Cut & Assemble an Old-Fashioned Train **6.95**
Also includes small town station, water tower and baggage carts. Finished train measures over 44" long.

JORDAN HIGHWAY MINIATURES

VEHICLES EA 6.95

Models are molded of colored polystyrene and require only minimum painting.

WATER TRUCK

360-232 Mack Water Truck
Includes decals for red or white version.

CALLIOPE TRUCK

360-233 Air Calliope Truck

POPCORN WAGON

360-235 1913 Popcorn Wagon w/Horses

FALLER

IMPORTED FROM GERMANY BY WALTHERS
These plastic kits are easy to build and molded in authentic colors. Many include signs and self-adhesive decals to decorate the model. Complete, illustrated instructions are also included.

Break Dancer Roundabout 272-440

Octopus Roundabout 272-441

Music Express Roundabout 272-437

RIDES

BREAK DANCER ROUNDABOUT

272-440 65.99
After a dizzying ride on this roundabout, riders won't be in any shape for break dancing! 16 colorful gondolas spin on four rotary tables. Complete with motor, ticket booths and full-color background scene and signs. 10 x 9-5/8" 25 x 24cm.

OCTOPUS ROUNDABOUT

272-441 46.99
The Octopus features arms that move up and down as the body rotates. With ticket booth and motor. 8.5 x 6" 21.3 x 15 cm.

MUSIC EXPRESS ROUNDABOUT

272-437 79.99
Jump in and hang on as the Music Express whirls your car around at super speed! Includes 20 colored cars, chrome-plated parts, 12-16V AC motor and lighting.

FALLER

Wildwater Log Ride "Pirate's Island"
272-430

Wild Mouse Working Roller Coaster
272-432

WILDWATER LOG RIDE "PIRATE'S ISLAND"

272-430 Wildwater Log Ride (motorized) **199.99**
Add the excitement of a real WORKING water ride to your layout! You've seen log rides like "Pirate's Island" in amusement parks and maybe even gotten soaked on them after splashing down the steep, whitewater drops. Now you can recreate that same fun with "Pirate's Island" Wildwater Log Ride.

The log boats race along the course on real water, powered by two water pumps that keep the water jetting along. Two motor lifts carry the logs up the hills where they soon shoot down the steep inclines. Includes everything you need to recreate a thrilling water ride. Motors and pumps each require 12-16V AC.
21-3/16 x 17 x 8.3"
20.8 x 53 x 43 x 21cm

WILD MOUSE WORKING ROLLER COASTER

272-432 159.99 *NEW*
Enjoy all the thrills of the real ride in this detailed, working model! A drive motor (requires 12-16V AC) pulls the four cars up to the top of the ramp. From there, gravity takes over, speeding the cars down and around the track and back to the station. Kit is complete with ticket booth, colorful graphics, detailed plastic parts, four cars, working lights, drive motor and complete instructions. Preiser figures shown not included; see the complete listing in the Figures section.
22-13/32 x 9-3/32 x 10-13/16"
56 x 22.7 x 27cm

Jungle Train Working Carousel Ride
272-433

JUNGLE TRAIN WORKING CAROUSEL RIDE

272-433 79.99 *NEW*
Take a journey of discovery along these winding jungle trails, where thrills and chills await at every twist and turn! The 20 gondolas included on this WORKING ride spin forward and backward, thanks to a hidden drive motor included with the kit (requires 12-16V AC power supply). Complete colorful signs and instructions. Preiser figures shown not included; see the complete listing in the Figures section.
8-21/64 x 7-31/32 x 3-3/4"
20.8 x 19.9 x 9.3cm

FLIPPER ROUNDABOUT

272-439 73.99
Twelve colorful gondolas spin around at breathtaking speed, with the rotating table rising and falling at the same time. Complete with motor, background scene and ticket booth. Can be illuminated with Lighting Kit #272-671.
10-3/8 x 9" 26 x 22.5cm.

CHAIROPLANE

272-315 64.99
Put a swirl of color in your midway with the Chair-O-Plane! The operating model features 12 seats and brightly colored roof panels, motor and lighting for night scenes.
8 x 8" 20 x 20cm.

SWINGBOATS

272-318 49.99
Includes motor to move boats back and forth. Special feature on motor makes red lamps flash on and off (requires Lighting Kit #272-671).
7-3/8 x 4" 18.4 x 9.8cm.

BUMPER CARS

272-328 84.99
Be sure to buckle up at the bumper cars - and watch out for the crazy drivers! A motorized driving mechanism moves six cars around the running surface, while three nonoperating cars stay parked on the side. 8 x 7-3/8"
20 x 18.5cm

RAINBOW ROUNDABOUT

272-436 99.99
Touch the sky in the Rainbow Roundabout. This exciting ride is not for the faint of heart, as riders test their courage while spinning through the air. The operating model includes motor (629) with 12-16V AC, lighting and panorama decoration. 9.6 x 7.3 x 10.3"
24.5 x 18.5 x 26cm

FALLER

Ghost Train 272-460

Big Dipper Roller Coaster 272-451

Ferris Wheel 272-312

Indiago 272-438

GHOST TRAIN

272-460 99.99
LIMITED AVAILABILITY
Get ready for the ride of a lifetime on the Ghost Train. Sixteen cars move individually around the track of this three-story model, as mechanically-controlled monster figures like serpents, dragons and a huge Cyclops move back and forth, testing riders' courage.

The model is powered by two motors for smooth operation, (requires 12-16V AC) and includes lights and a sound unit that produces ghost sounds. A ticket booth and numbered certificate are also included.
14-5/8 x 9-1/4" 36.5 x 23cm.

BIG DIPPER ROLLER COASTER

272-451 159.99
Fully functional roller coaster has a 12-16V DC or AC motor that pulls cars up to the top of the run where their own momentum carries them around the track with the help of ball bearings. Astonishingly similar to the real thing!
28-5/8 x 17-1/8 x 16-3/8"
71.5 x 43 x x 41cm.

FERRIS WHEEL

This is a must for every county fair, carnival or amusement park scene! This kit includes over 275 parts, molded in 10 different colors. Unpowered Ferris Wheel can be powered with Electric Motor #272-629 and lighted with #272-635. Wheel measures
9 x 7-1/2 x 22-3/8"
22.5 x 18.7 x 56cm.

272-312 Unpowered Ferris Wheel **74.99**
272-635 Lighting Set For Ferris Wheel **37.99**
272-636 Replacement Bulbs **14.99**
272-629 Electric Motor **22.99**
272-628 High Power Motor **26.99** ***NEW***
Reversible, 4/15 RPM, Produces 35% more power than #629.

INDIAGO

272-438 129.99
Indiana Jones is your guide on the Indiago, the lastest ride from Faller. Adventure awaits as a large gondola spins between two support arms that move back and forth. Kit includes two motors, electronic controls, background scenery and lighting.
11 x 9-1/4 x 7-5/8"
27.5 x 23 x 19cm

FALLER

Scrambler "Insider" 272-434

Top In Dodgem Car Ride 272-435

Tent 272-329

Food Booths 272-455

SCRAMBLER "INSIDER"

272-434 109.99
For the risk-taker in all of us comes this working carnival ride. Twenty double-occupancy gondolas actually swing and somersault, drawing power from a 12-16V AC motor that's included with the kit.
Ticket Booth:
1-1/4 x 1-1/4 x 1-1/2"
3.2 x 3.2 x 3.7cm
Ride Only: 10 x 9-5/8 x 5-3/4"
25 x 24 x 14.3cm

TOP IN DODGEM CAR RIDE

272-435 119.99
An exact replica of the Mack original. Twelve dodgem cars bump about, thanks to a hidden magnet drive powered by a 12-16V AC motor. The ride features detailed decoration and eye-catching colors. A raised platform and ticket booth provide additional detail.
15-5/8 x 7-13/16 x 4-13/16"
39 x 19.5 x 12cm

CONCESSION STANDS & TENTS

TENT

272-329 63.99
Large-size tent with hand-sewn "canvas" cover, benches, bar, kitchen and stage for the band.
14 x 11 x 3"
35 x 27.5 x 7.5cm

Pizza & Popcorn Stands 272-324

Candy & Crepes Stands 272-453

Midway Booths 272-320

Midway Food & Game Stands 272-464

Flipper Vehicle Set 272-467

FOOD BOOTHS

272-455 pkg(2) **19.99**
Liven up any midway with this set. One features fruit drinks and the other is an Asian food stand.

PIZZA & POPCORN STANDS

272-324 pkg(2) **19.99**
3-3/4 x 2-3/8" 9.4 x 6.1cm
2-3/4 x 1-5/8" 7 x 4.1cm

CANDY & CREPES STANDS

272-453 pkg(2) **16.99**
1-7/8 x 1-7/8" 4.5 x 4.5cm.

MIDWAY BOOTHS

272-320 pkg(2) **16.99**
Can be illuminated with Lighting Set #272-314.
3-7/8 x 1-1/4" 9.6 x 3.2cm

FLIPPER VEHICLE SET

272-467 47.99
Transport the Flipper ride (272-439) with this vehicle set.

MIDWAY FOOD & GAME STANDS

272-464 Set of Two **19.99** *NEW*
Make any model midway more fun with these colorful stands. Show-off your throwing arm at the Power Ball tossing game! Then celebrate with everybody's favorite meal on a bun at the delightful Hot Dog stand. Kits are complete with printed signs. Preiser figures shown not included; see the complete listing in the Figures section.
Mr. Hot Dog:
2-1/2 x 1-5/8 x 2-3/8"
6.4 x 4 x 5.9cm
Power Ball Toss:
2-11/16 x 1-3/4 x 3-27/32"
6.7 x 4.3 x 9.6cm

STAND ACCESSORIES

272-448 12.99
Trash cans, tables and table umbrellas to detail concession stands.

BENCHES & TABLES

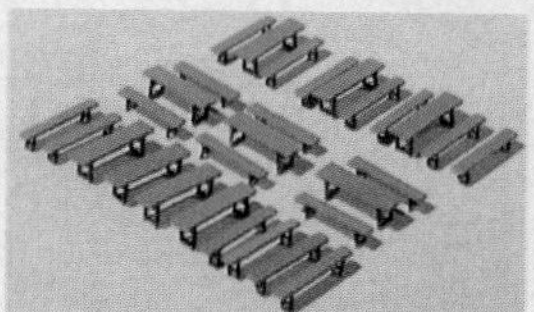

272-449 pkg(72) **15.99**

VEHICLES

INDIAGO VEHICLE SET

Looks great parked next to the Indiago ride (#272-438).
272-468 45.99
272-469 Fairground Vehicle Set **29.99**

Limited Quantity Available
272-1026 Break Dancer Truck **24.99**
272-1032 2-Axle Trailer **19.99**
272-1036 3-Axle Trailer **17.99**
272-1038 Trailer w/Container **18.99**

FAIRGROUND VEHICLE SET

272-469 29.99
Includes truck with covered flatbed and mobile Showman's Trailer.

SHOWMAN'S TRAILER

Limited Quantity Available
272-1030 Trailer (creme) **28.99**
Includes a covered verandah and cardboard curtain inserts. With extendible, slide-out wall panels to increase the size of the trailer.

FALLER

Game Booths 272-452

Showman's Booth 272-456

Fairground Booths 272-457

Sport Show Booth 272-458

GAME BOOTHS

272-452 25.99
10-1/8 x 2-1/4" 25.3 x 5.5cm.

SHOWMAN'S BOOTH

272-456 22.99
Witness the world's most amazing spectacles at the Showman's booth. Includes cash box and front decoration. 8 x 4 x 4.1" 20 x 10 x 10.5cm

FAIRGROUND BOOTHS

272-457 pkg(2) **13.99**
Try your luck at one of these games and maybe you'll win a prize for your sweetheart! Your layout just won't be complete without the familiar site of these gaming booths, common at fairs and carnivals across the land. 2.5 x 2 x 2.2" 6.5 x 4 x 5.5cm

SPORT SHOW BOOTH

272-458 22.99
In this corner, with lots of flash and color, we have the Sports Show Booth! A great addition to any carnival. 8 x 4 x 4.1" 20 x 10 x 10.5cm.

Funfair Stands 272-462

Magic Vision 272-459

Shark Show 272-443

FUNFAIR STANDS

272-462 pkg(2) **19.99**
Two colorful booths to delight young and old along your model midway! Grab a bite to eat at the "Maize Man," a unique corn-cob design that makes a great food stand (especially for sweet corn sales at county or state fair scenes). Then test your skills and take home a prize with a game or two at the colorful "Throw The Hat" booth. Hat Toss:
2-1/2 x 1-1/2 x 2"
6.4 x 3.9 x 5cm
Maize Man:
2-1/2 x 1-1/2 x 3-5/8"
6.3 x 3.9 x 9.1cm

SHOWS

MAGIC VISION

272-459 22.99
A universe of sorcery, imagination and fantasy await those who venture into this magic show. Eye-catching artistry draws the eye of every passerby. A showman's booth with ticket office is also provided. 7-7/8 x 3-13/16 x 4" 19.6 x 9.5 x 10cm

SHARK SHOW

272-443 27.99
Step right up and see the greatest mobile sea show on earth. With stairway, ticket booth, colorful show signs and sharks.
7-3/8 x 4-1/2" 18.5 x 11.4cm.

Information STATION

History of the Circus

The word "circus" comes to us from Roman Empire times when horse and chariot races, gladiatorial combats and barbaric athletic contests were known as Circensian games. These games took place in a round or oval structure with tiers of spectator seats enclosing the area. The so-called "modern circus" has its origins in the late 18th century equestrian feats performed in a horse ring.

Now it encompasses a tent show that features wild and trained animals, freaks, acrobats and clowns. Its heyday is considered to have been in the years of 1880-1920. After a large decline in the 50s and 60s, the circus revived somewhat in the early 1980s.

P.T. Barnum is probably the most well known name associated with the circus. He opened his American Museum in 1842 and instantly became famous for his advertising and exhibits of freaks. In 1871 he opened his famous circus called The Greatest Show on Earth and ten years he later merged with his largest competitor to form the Barnum & Bailey circus.

Country Carnival 348-5310

Country Circus 348-5311

BACKGROUNDS

Full-color backgrounds for circuses, carnivals or country fairs. Backgrounds measure 36 x 24".

COUNTRY CARNIVAL

348-5310 .98
With rides, gazebo, concession stands, hot air balloon and more.

COUNTRY CIRCUS

348-5311 .98
With circus tent, elephants, hot air balloon and more.

FIGURES

Fully painted plastic figures.

CLOWN FIGURES EA 2.98

348-8851 Assorted Clowns

348-8853 Hobo Clowns

CIRCUS TRAIN SET

CORKEY'S SPECIAL

348-401 18.98
Featuring 8-wheel drive locomotive, Corkey's caboose, Tiger box car, a Carousel box car, a Ferris Wheel box car, clown figures and a carnival background.

RIDES

Customize your midway with these easy-to-build plastic kits. Models are molded in colors and include full-color printed signs. Each can be built as a working model, using motorizing kit #5115 or #5190, sold separately.

FERRIS WHEEL

348-5110 15.98

CAROUSEL

348-5111 17.98
Approximately 9" in diameter with two rows of horses and chair cars. When fitted with a motorizing kit (available separately), the horses will move up and down!

SKY WHEEL DOUBLE FERRIS WHEEL

348-5112 17.98
When motorized, the two smaller wheels turn as they rotate around the larger axis. Stands about 12" tall.

SWINGER

348-5113 14.98
Hanging seats spin out and up, the faster the ride turns.

FALLING STAR

348-5117 19.98
Platform rises, falls and turns just like the real thing.

SEA DRAGON

348-5118 19.98
Colorful ship sweeps back and forth.

OCTOPUS

348-5124 14.98
With eight spinning arms.

THUNDER BOLT

348-5119 19.98
Cars rise up as they swing around the central column.

SPIDER

348-5125 14.98
Six spinning arms, each with twin cars.

BREAK DANCER

348-5131 19.98

MEGA DANCER

348-5132 19.98

TORNADO

348-5133 19.98

MOTORIZING KITS

348-5115 For Rides **4.98**
348-5190 Deluxe, For Rides **7.98**
348-5198 Battery Box w/Switch & Wiring Harness **2.98**
348-5188 Gearhead Motor **39.98**

CONCESSIONS & GAME BOOTHS

WEIGHT GUESSING & BASEBALL BULL'S EYE

348-5123 12.98

CONCESSION BOOTHS

348-5121 #1 4.98
Shooting Gallery, Dart and Balloon Game and Birthday Game.

348-5122 #2 4.98
King Kong Hoop Toss, Barney's Basketball Game and Spinning Wheel Game.

348-5129 #3 12.98
Kentucky Derby, Ring a Bottle and Frog Pond.

348-5130 #4 12.98
Big Mouth Pig, Squirt Gun and Milk Can Toss.

CARNIVAL RAIL/TICKET OFFICE

348-4407 1.98

SNACK SHACKS EA 2.98

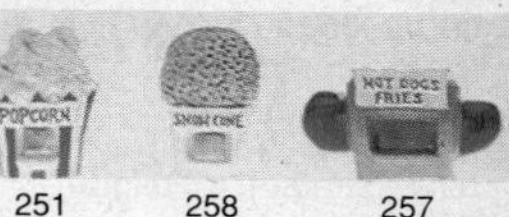

251 258 257

259 252 253

348-251 Popcorn *NEW*
348-252 Lemonade *NEW*
348-253 Ice Cream *NEW*
348-257 Hot Dog *NEW*
348-258 Snow Cone
348-259 Cotton Candy *NEW*

ORIGINAL Preiser

IMPORTED FROM GERMANY BY WALTHERS

Decorated plastic models are assembled, unless noted.

Baggage Wagon 590-21016

Toilet Wagon 590-21025

Krone Equipment Wagon 590-21026

WAGONS

590-20005 Wagon Set (undecorated), Kit pkg(3) **32.99**
590-20006 Equipment Wagon Set (undecorated), Kit pkg(4) **32.99**
590-20007 Animal Wagon Set (undecorated), Kit pkg(3) **32.99**
590-20008 Wagon Set (undecorated), Kit pkg(3) **32.99**
590-21016 Baggage Wagon **17.99**

590-21017 Krone Baggage Wagon w/Windows **17.99**

590-21018 Animal Wagon-Closed **17.99**

590-21019 Animal Wagon-Open **17.99**

590-21020 Krone Equipment Wagon **17.99**

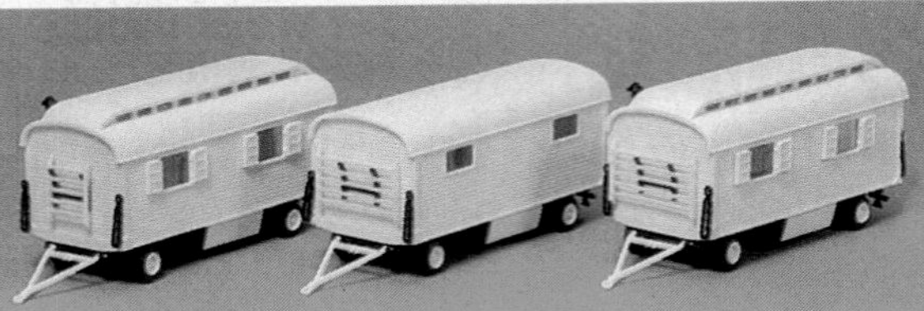
Wagon Set 590-20005

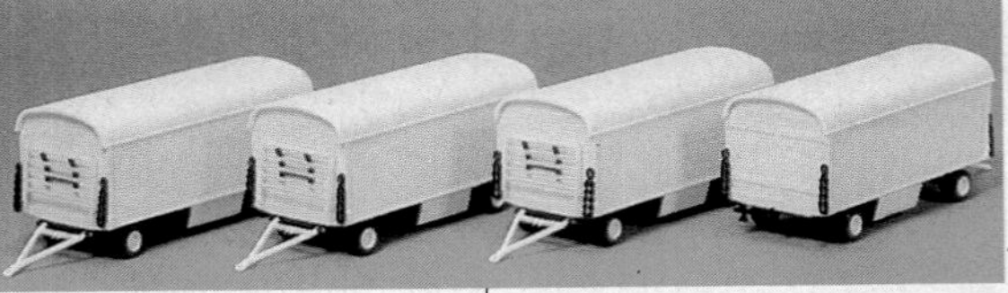
Equipment Wagon Set 590-20006

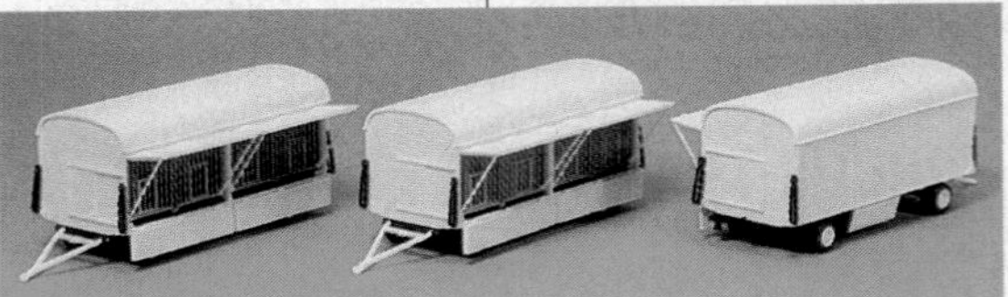
Animal Wagon Set 590-20007

Wagon Set 590-20008

590-21021 Krone Equipment Caravan **17.99**
590-21023 Krone Equipment Wagon **17.99**
590-21025 Toilet Wagon **17.99**

590-21026 Krone Equipment Wagon **17.99**

Limited Quantity Available

590-21030 Krone Electronic Wagon **23.99**
590-21031 Krone Cashier's Wagon **27.99**
590-22100 Barnes Wagon **13.99**
590-22102 Hagenbeck-Wallace 2 Arch Cage Wagon **19.99**

590-22105 Jaeger Baggage Wagon Less Horses **18.99**

590-22106 Jaeger Mirror Bandwagon Less Horses **30.99**

590-22107 Jaeger 2 Arch Cage Wagon Less Horses **24.99**

590-22150 Barnes Wagon w/Driver & Horses **19.99**
590-22155 Jaeger Baggage Wagon w/2 Horses **27.99**

590-22156 Jaeger Mirror Bandwagon w/2 Horses **38.99**

590-22157 Jaeger 2 Arch Cage Wagon w/2 Horses **33.99**

590-22158 Jaeger 3 Arch Cage Wagon w/2 Horses **33.99**

TRAILERS

EA 14.99

Detail your circus or carnival scene with these colorful concession trailers. Models are assembled and ready for service!

590-24702 Snack Trailer

590-24703 Candy Trailer

590-24704 Lucky Dip Trailer

ORIGINAL Preiser

VEHICLES

590-24679 Hanomag R55 (white), Kit pkg(2) **19.99**

Limited Quantity Available
590-24680 Mercedes 710 w/Baggage Wagon **31.99**

FIGURES

590-10109 Concession Workers & Customers pkg(6) **12.99**
590-20254 Magician, Clowns, Acrobats pkg(8) **25.99**

590-20257 Girl w/Monkeys **12.99**

590-20258 Clowns **25.99**
590-20259 Seated Circus Band **18.99**

590-20260 Sea Lions w/Tamer **11.99**

590-20261 Circus Workers **15.99**

590-20262 Circus Workers **15.99**

590-20263 Circus Workers **15.99**

Hanomag R55 590-24679

Mercedes 710 w/Baggage Wagon 590-24680

590-20264 Circus Workers w/Driver **15.99**

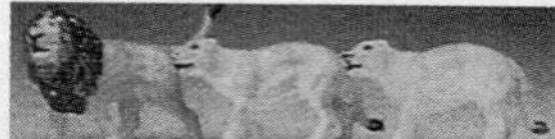

590-20379 Lions pkg(3) **10.99**

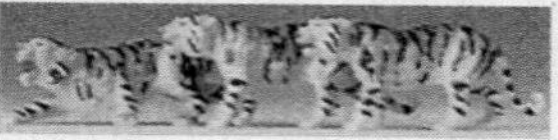

590-20380 Tigers pkg(3) **10.99**
590-20381 Performing Lions pkg(3) **10.99**

590-20382 Horses pkg(6) **18.99**
590-20383 Camels pkg(6) **14.99**

590-20384 Polar Bears pkg(4) **11.99**
590-20388 Monkeys **10.99**

590-20389 Llamas pkg(3) **10.99**
590-20391 Buffaloes pkg(4) **14.99**

590-20392 Kangaroos pkg(3) **10.99**

590-20394 Reindeer pkg(6) **15.99**

590-20397 Camels pkg(3) **12.99**

590-24652 For Merry-Go-Round #590-24650 pkg(6) **11.99**
590-24656 Weight Lifter, Sword Swallower, Stilt Walker **25.99**
590-24659 Selling Balloons **18.99**

590-24660 For Swings #590-24658 pkg(6) **11.99**
590-24661 Ice Cream Stands **23.99**

590-24662 For Shooting Gallery #590-24694 **12.99**

590-24663 Circus Goers **13.99**

590-24664 For Chairoplane **11.99**

Magician, Clowns, Acrobats 590-20254

Seated Circus Band 590-20259

Performing Lions 590-20381

Camels 590-20383

Monkeys 590-20388

Buffaloes 590-20391

Weight Lifter, Sword Swallower, Stilt Walker 590-24656

Selling Balloons 590-24659

Ice Cream Stands 590-24661

ORIGINAL Preiser

CIRCUS DECALS

590-21049 Krone **15.99**

Limited Quantity Available

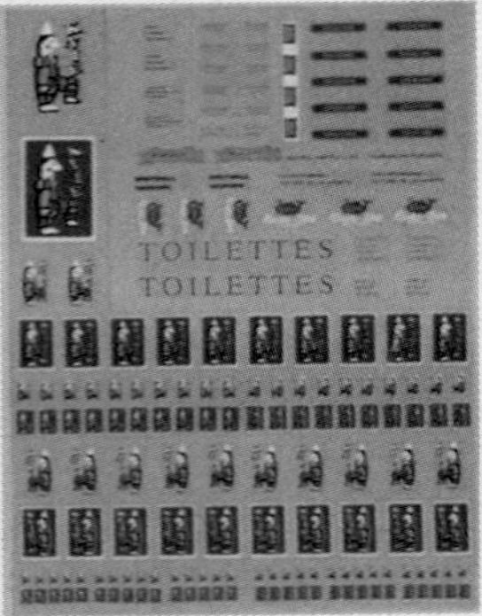

590-20078 Knie **15.49**

GAME BOOTHS

590-24692 Toy Game **37.99**
590-24693 China Game **37.99**
590-24701 Variety Show w/Figures **37.99**

CONCESSION STANDS

590-24690 Ginger Bread Stand **37.99**

590-24691 Hot Dog Stand **37.99**

Variety Show w/Figures 590-24701

Toy Game 590-24692

China Game 590-24693

590-24694 Shooting Gallery **37.99**
590-24695 Market Stall **37.99**
590-24696 Market Stall **37.99**

590-24697 Pottery Market Booth **37.99**

590-24700 Hammer Game **19.99**
590-24705 Dance Floor w/Figures **18.99**

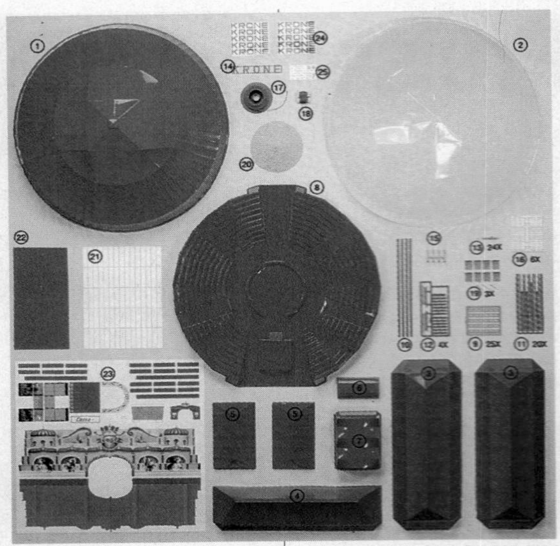

Circus Tent Set 590-21045

Accessories for Krone Circus Tent 590-21048

CIRCUS TENT & ACCESSORIES

CIRCUS TENT SET

590-21045 Circus Tent Set **189.99**
A complete set of circus tents in one kit! Features 19-1/4" (480 mm) diameter big top that's 6-3/8" (160 mm) high, plus a transparent insert to protect interior of big top from dust when cutting open for display. Also includes a horse tent (15-1/4 x 6 x 3" 380 x 150 x 75 mm), open animal tent (14-3/4 x 4-3/8 x 3" 370 x 110 x 75 mm), entrance and restaurant tents, baseplate with preformed benches and 18-3/8" (460 mm) diameter ring, tent poles, entrance stairways, signs, tent rigging and more. Tents are preformed plastic.

ACCESSORIES FOR KRONE CIRCUS TENT

590-21048 25.99
Includes seats, lights, poles, posters, hand trucks, wheelbarrows, pitchforks, shovels and more.

Roco

IMPORTED FROM AUSTRIA
BY WALTHERS

CIRCUS SETS

KRONE CIRCUS BOX CAR SET

Limited Quantity Available
625-44009 Krone Circus Box Car Set **149.99**
Includes three ventilated box cars and one elephant car, a model of the original "Zirkus Krone" elephant car.

CIRCUS FLAT CAR SET I

625-44130 Circus Flat Car Set #1 **249.99**
The "Williams" Circus Set includes 4 stake wagons with Preiser Circus Vehicles (1945-1970) not available separately.

VOLLMER

Roundabout Ride 770-3622

Swingboat Ride 770-3620

Ghost Train 770-3627

RIDES & ACCESSORIES

Build a midway in miniature with these thrilling rides and accessories. Each kit is easy to build and molded in realistic colors, so no painting is needed.

ROUNDABOUT RIDE

770-3622 42.99
You can build this colorful roundabout as a static model, or add motor #4200 (available separately) for a working ride!
7-3/8 x 6-3/8 x 4-1/2"
18.5 x 16 x 11.2cm.

SWINGBOAT RIDE

770-3620 42.99
Ahoy mates, this swingboat ride will be a popular attraction on any midway! The kit can be built for display, or powered with motor #4200 (available separately) to animate your scene.
7-1/4 x 4-5/8 x 5-1/4"
18 x 11.6 x 13.2cm.

GHOST TRAIN

770-3627 48.99
Add thrills and chills to your model midway with this haunted house ride! For added excitement, there's a special electronic sound unit that produces eerie noises.
7-3/4 x 4-1/2 x 3-7/8"
20 x 11.5 x 10cm.

Tent 770-3623

Game Booths 770-3625

Fair Assortment 770-3626

TENT

770-3623 28.99
Take a break from a day at the fair under the cool shade of this colorful tent. Add some appropriate figures and details to turn it into a dining tent, exhibit hall or beer garden.
7-1/4 x 4-3/4 x 3-3/8"
18 x 12 x 8.5cm.

GAME BOOTHS

770-3625 pkg(2) **18.99**
You're a winner every time with these games of luck and skill! The kit includes parts to build a toy lottery and a plant lottery. Full color panels make these eyecatching models for any miniature midway.

FAIR ASSORTMENT

770-3626 125.99
Get your midway started with this set of four kits, perfect for a carnival, county fair or amusement park. Try your luck at either of the two game booths in kit #3625. Then it's on to a thrilling ride aboard the Swingboats, #3620 or the Roundabout, #3622. Finally, relax out of the sun under tent #3623, all included in this set.

WALTHERS
Scale
HO
2000
MODEL RAILROAD
REFERENCE BOOK

There's an old poem that begins "I must go down to the sea again. . . ." And such is the daily chore of trains on the Knowlton & Northerly, which make their way to and from the harbors along the line.

Where space is limited by the many inlets and bays, bigger customers must remain well inland. There, connections to the Maine Central make it easy to receive supplies from the rest of the US and Canada. This also simplifies transferring freight to and from the 30" narrow gauge K&N. Local ship-owners have come to appreciate the arrangement too, for their orders can be consolidated into a single car and delivered right alongside their vessels.

Shipyards shuttered by the depression are re-opening along the line. The fishing fleets are refitting as business picks up. These days, the air shakes with the sounds of steam locos, cranes and winches as freight and supplies are transferred from shore to ship and back. And there's a different sound in the air now days, for the K&N recently took delivery of one of those new-fangled oil-electric locos.

As the biggest employer in Marcus Hook, this busy ships chandler has supplied generations of mariners with everything from anchors to portholes. The company's big headquarters and warehouse building began life as a pair of International Hobby Corp. buildings. Sam Parker of Media, Pennsylvania, did the kitbashing. Custom decal signs, made by friend Jim Hart on his computer, completed the project.

Models and Photo by Sam Parker

Finally... Classic Building Kits with Maximum Detail AND Easy Assembly, Designed Especially for Today's Busy Model Railroader

Here's What Advanced Modelers Are Saying About Gold Ribbon Series™ Snap Together Building Kits

GARY HOOVER
Florissant, Missouri

"The package arrived on Thursday afternoon and by 10:00 I was installing the structure on the layout for the photos! This was truly a fun, no stress, one evening project."

Gary's Missouri, Kansas & Quincy layout has been featured in many model railroad magazines and images taken on his pike have graced the pages of the Walthers Model Railroad Reference Books for years.

Gary photographed Aunt Lucy's House in Oak Grove, Illinois on his MK&Q. To highlight the cast-in detail of the kit, Gary used some weathering chalks. The roof and porch were drybrushed with Floquil Polly Scale light grays which brought out the rich shingle and plank detailing.

Gary Hoover had Aunt Lucy's House built and placed in this scene on his MK&Q in just one evening.

JOHN NEHRICH
Project Coordinator
Rensselaer Railroad Heritage Center

"With their new Gold Ribbon Series™... Walthers is extending the range down to the beginner as yet unskilled, or the serious operator who'd rather run trains than build. These new kits basically snap together— if you can handle opening the box you can get the kit together— yet produce a structure almost any modeler would welcome on his or her layout."

The Rensselaer Railroad Heritage Center at the Rensselaer Polytechnic Institute is the home of the legendary New England, Berkshire & Western, a 1950s-era pike set in New England. Members of this organization have demonstrated their attention to detail and excellent modeling skills throughout the years in various model railroad publications.

Spearheading many projects on the NEB&W is John Nehrich. John sings the praises of the Gold Ribbon Series® as bringing the detail of advanced modeling to the beginner.

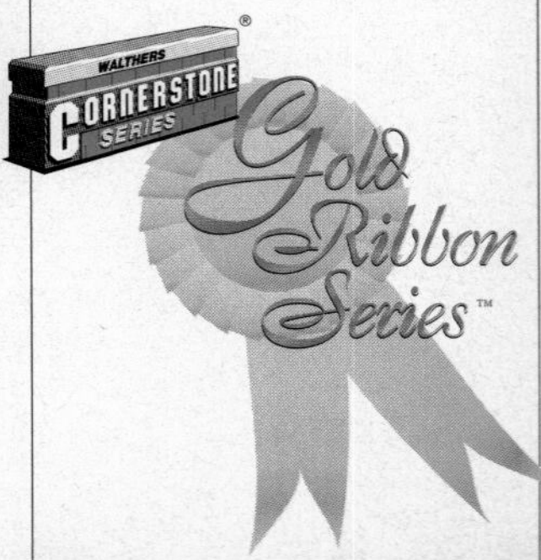

AUNT LUCY'S HOUSE

933-3601 29.98 ***NEW***
4 x 5-3/4" 10 x 14.3cm and stands 5-1/8" 12.8cm tall.

Remember those summer nights when it was just too hot to sleep? You'd open the windows wide. Sometimes, you'd sit on the floor and look up at the stars. Or just lie there and listen. The old porch swing would creak back and forth a little. And sometimes, if you could stay awake long enough, you'd hear lonesome whistles. Gradually, you'd drift off, wondering where those trains were going and hoping someday you'd be on board.

Whether you grew up on a busy city block or a quiet farm, here's a new kit that brings back memories of home. It's the kind of house we all wish we could have grown up in, a comfortable two-story design perfect for city or country and packed with details.

Check out the turned "wood" railings and eave trim. Or the elegance of those shingled gables, a reminder of an era when builders took extra pride in their work. The inviting front porch is a natural for superdetailing with figures and other accessories, sold separately. This timeless classic also includes a sheet of printed interior details, including curtains, to dress-up your finished model to fit in almost any era.

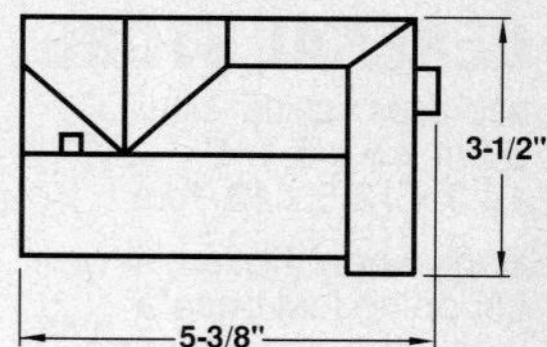

Victorian Styling and Detail, Snap-Together Construction

It was an age of elegance. Clothes, carriages, buildings -- especially buildings -- had a distinctive style and lavish ornaments. Many still survive, lovingly restored to their former glory.

Capture the elegance of those long-ago days with the all-new Gold Ribbon Series™ buildings from Walthers Cornerstone Series®. This collection of HO Scale kits is designed for simple snap-together assembly with a minimum of gluing. The finished models are perfect for layouts, dioramas or Christmas Villages.

Major parts snap together and you just glue on a few small details for the finishing touch. Main walls and trim are molded as one assembly, but in two different colors, so no painting is required. Windows feature true-to-scale mullions and frames molded in color over clear glazing for more realism. Decals and interior detail sheets are included as appropriate, along with complete instructions.

Packed with details, you'll be proud to display the finished buildings in any setting.

All parts feature alignment tabs for easy, snap-together assembly.

Two color molding allows detail, depth and contrast without painting.

Snap in windows with molded mullions and glass eliminate the spread of glue onto window panes.

SMITH'S GENERAL STORE

933-3604 29.98 ***NEW***
5-3/4 x 5 x 5-1/2"
14.3 x 12.5 x 13.7cm

Back when the family went shopping just once a week, the general store was among your first stops. You gave your list to the owner who filled your order with personal service, from shelves brimming with all sorts of fancy goods and household supplies. Big barrels of flour, crackers and dill pickles stood guard by the old wooden counter. The huge coffee grinder dominated the other end of the room, and the place smelled so wonderful whenever someone bought a pound or two. A big coal stove stood in the center, with folks crowded around to gossip, play checkers and warm-up in colder weather. The big brass cash register was always shiny and its bells could be heard above the loudest conversations. Kids spent long minutes at the penny candy jars, agonizing over their final choice of licorice sticks or peppermint drops.

Now, the old General Store can once again be a thriving business in the nearest town or rural crossroads. It's a must for steam-era scenes, and a few can still be found here and there, often serving other purposes. This elegant model is complete with the ornate bay window, which mounts on a tall "false front" wall, so typical of Victorian commercial buildings. Add your personal touch with the printed interior detail sheets, as well as colorful decal signs, and you'll be open for business in no time!

Smith's General Store features a second story bay window and a one-piece stairwell with open treads.

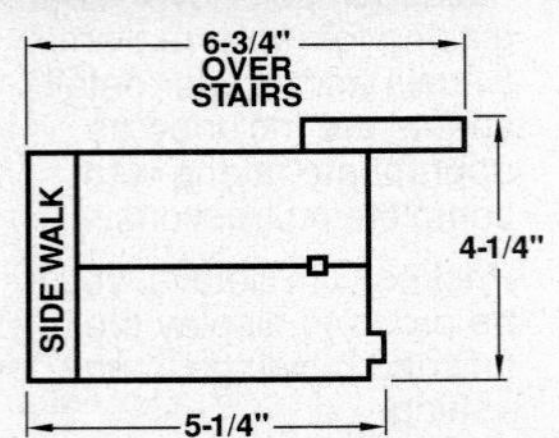

Easy-To-Build Premium HO Scale Structure Kit

WILLOW GLEN BRIDGE

933-3602 24.98 *NEW*
8-1/2 x 3-1/2 x 3-1/2"
21.2 x 8.7 x 8.7cm at the roofline.

We always knew we were home when we crossed the old bridge at Willow Glen. In summer, we'd play inside its dusty shadows, or carve our initials in some hidden spot so no would know we had done it! If Dad was working the south 40, he'd drive our Belgian horses, Boss and Beauty, over to the shady side and let them drink. The clatter of their hooves and the creak of wagon wheels would thunder around us, making it sound like they were moving much faster than they really ever did.

Time was, you could travel from Maine to Mexico and cross many a covered bridge just like this. Most were simple designs, and before chemical preservatives, the roof and sides protected the all-important beams from rot. Now some folks insist they were designed and painted to look like barns on purpose. The idea was that a horse or cow would walk right into one and not be scared by the rushing water below.

Give any rural road a unique charm when you add this model to your HO Scale layout. Typical of covered bridges from coast-to-coast, its detailed beams and boards look like real wood. Of course, they're molded in color so painting is an option and the major parts just snap together. Realistic stone abutments are provided so it's easy to add to a new section of your layout, or blend with existing scenery. And, we've included colorful decal signs from different eras for the finishing touch.

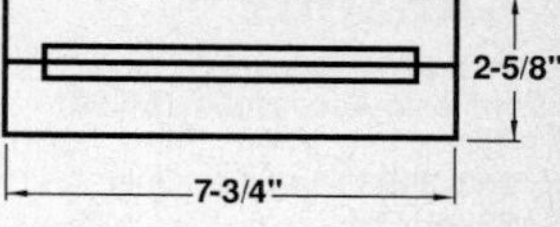

RIVER ROAD MERCANTILE

933-3600 29.98 *NEW*
5-3/4 x 5 x 5-1/2"
14.3 x 12.5 x 13.7cm.

When great grandpa was a boy, a trip to town was a real chore. A rough ride over miles of dusty dirt roads meant you only went once a week. And only when the weather was dry. But in between, you counted on the local Mercantile.

Conveniently located nearby, the Mercantile offered a little something for everyone. There were shelves full of hardware and horse tack to keep the farm running. The lady of the house could swap butter and eggs for flour, sugar or other staples. Kids found a special treat in the penny candy jars. Retired folks could count on daily checker games and pleasant conversation to pass the time. As the hub of activity in rural areas, many served as the local post office and town hall too.

Whether in its bustling prime or bypassed and neglected, River Road Mercantile is an important addition to the rural area of your HO Scale layout. It can be the most important building in a tiny village, or stand by itself at a country crossroads. Add horses and wagons, or gas pumps and pick-ups (sold separately) to blend with your favorite era.

Designed for easy construction, the main walls are detailed to look like real wood and are molded as separate parts in two colors. You can build it as-is without painting, or easily repaint in your favorite scheme. For the final touch of detail, printed interior scenes and a set of colorful decal signs* are included.

*Photo shows preproduction model with decal signs from Micro Scale set #460-87165 and 87166, both available separately.

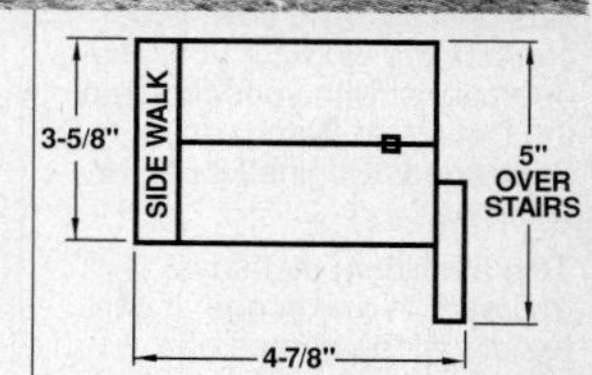

WALTHERS
CORNERSTONE SERIES
NEW DELUXE BACKWOODS SHOP KIT WITH RESIN ACCESSORIES
BUILD IT AS A LOCO SHOP. . .

BACKWOODS LOCOMOTIVE OR CARSHOP

933-3701 Deluxe Version w/Resin Accessories **54.98** *NEW*
933-3083 Structure Only **39.98** *NEW*

***PARTS FOR LOCO OR CAR SHOP IN DELUXE AND STANDARD KITS**

***DELUXE KIT INCLUDES RESIN DETAILS**

***INTERIOR CUT LINES FOR EASY CUSTOMIZING**

*** FITS ANY ERA**

***PLASTIC PARTS MOLDED IN COLOR**

When 4-4-0s worked this line, this building was the busiest place on the branch. Every morning, locos were wheeled out, polished and oiled before starting the day's work. Once the shop floor was clear, wooden freight or passenger cars were led in by the switcher. Sometimes a loco would be there needing some attention. Then, the carpenter and blacksmith took over, the ringing of their tools drifting out through the big wooden doors.

Down through the years, the old shop has tasted coal smoke and diesel soot. It's still standing, still doing the jobs it was built for. And now, you can put it to work for your HO operations, with your choice of the Deluxe or Standard Backwoods Engine House or Carshop.

This a building that says "railroad" in any scene. It can handle all the chores of a branch, shortline or industrial road. Picture it with steam or diesel power, wood or steel cars ... they'll all look great spotted here.

Its detailed board and batten siding fits any era and the building is easily customized. Scribed interior cut lines simplify adding a through track or a third door. Plus, the roof can be built with stacks for locos, or a clerestory skylight for car repairs. Parts for both versions are included.

The Deluxe kit comes with a complete set of resin castings to bring your building to life; overhead crane, forge smoke stack, two small sheds, three ash cans, three 55 gallon drums, an awning for the office door, a bin, waybill/mail box, phone/electrical box and a fuel oil tank are all there! Or, do it yourself and start out with the basic building.

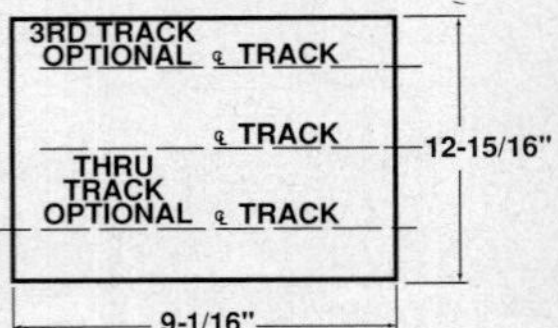

For Daily Product Information Click

www.walthers.com

ENGINE HOUSE/CARSHOP DETAIL KIT

933-3512 19.98 *NEW*

THE DELUXE KIT COMES WITH A COMPLETE SET OF RESIN ACCESSORIES, WHICH ARE ALSO SOLD SEPARATELY IN ITEM #933-3512.

Dress-up and detail any shop scene with this set of accessories, identical to those included with the Deluxe Backwoods Engine or Carshop. The finely detailed resin castings are ready to paint and easy to add to your structures. Set includes; overhead crane, forge smoke stack, two small sheds, three ash cans, three 55 gallon drums, an awning for the office door, a bin, waybill/mail box, phone/electrical box and a fuel oil tank.

MIRANDA'S BANANAS

933-3080 39.98 ***NEW***

Flags flying and cranes at the ready, a cargo ship makes port. Railroad tugs muscle carfloats of empty reefers alongside and the race is on! Fresh bananas, lemons, oranges - all have to be moved and moved quickly! Soon, these strings of reefers will be racing the clock with their cargoes, heading for the fruit brokers in the big city markets across the country.

Keeping America fed and healthy is a big job, one which the railroads have handled for decades. Near the freight yards in virtually every big city, fruit brokers supply supermarkets and other commercial buyers with fruit and vegetables from all over the world. Reefers and insulated box cars handle the traffic and refrigerated containers can also be found on the job.

If your railroad needs more business, you'll find plenty of fast-paced operations at Miranda's Bananas! Switch crews will always have work here as freight cars arrive and are unloaded quickly. It's perfect for simulating loads in-empties out traffic on any line.

This unique structure can be a brand-new building on a transition-era layout, or an older structure in a modern scene. It fits any industrial area and is a natural with the Cornerstone Series® Waterfront buildings.

An angled corner allows the building to be placed between closely spaced sidings or on an odd-shaped lot. Separate rail and truck docks with canopies, rooftop machinery house, and colorful decal signs are all included.

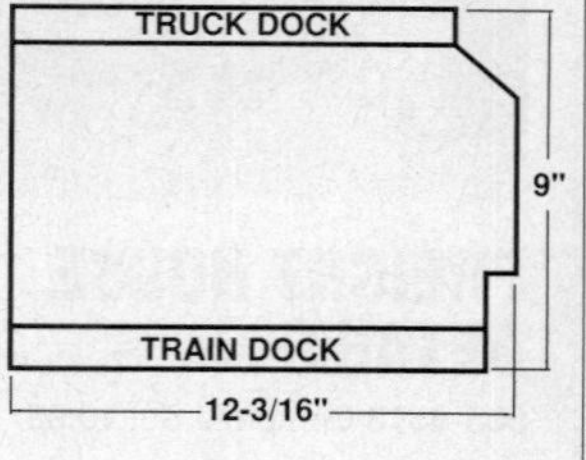

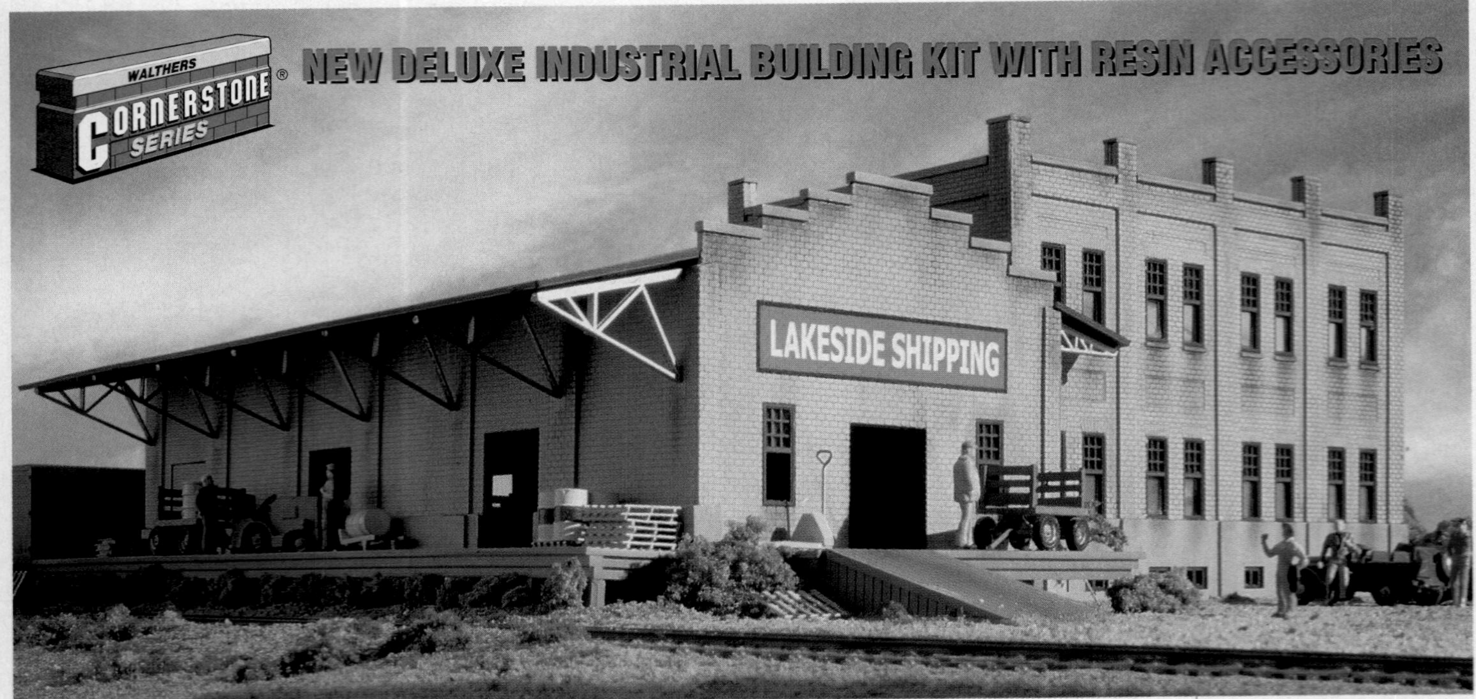

LAKESIDE SHIPPING

933-3702 Deluxe Version w/Resin Accessories **49.98** *NEW*
933-3084 Structure Only **32.98** *NEW*

Time is money they say, not just for big business, but for small ones too. Keeping the freight moving is a tough job. It takes planning and timing to make sure loads arrive on schedule and empties are ready when new loads need to move. And that's where the freight forwarders come in.

Coordinating shipments to and from local customers, these busy facilities consolidate smaller loads into big ones. They contract with the railroads and truckers to keep them moving on time and under budget.

And they make a great addition to your layout! Boxes, barrels, pallets, sacks, crates, packing cases - no two freight shipments are ever alike from this busy operation. Up front is a handsome brick office to monitor the paperwork. At the rear is the transfer building, where loads are exchanged from train to truck. When completed, the shape of the finished building is ideal for a small space or odd shaped area.

Great for late steam- and diesel-eras, this beautiful building comes in two versions. Choose the Deluxe kit with a pair of tow motors, five freight wagons, two pallet jacks, two platform scales and three hand trucks, molded in resin. Just paint and install to complete the scene. Or, start with the basic kit to create your own small industry or other business. Both kits come with colorful sign decals and complete instructions.

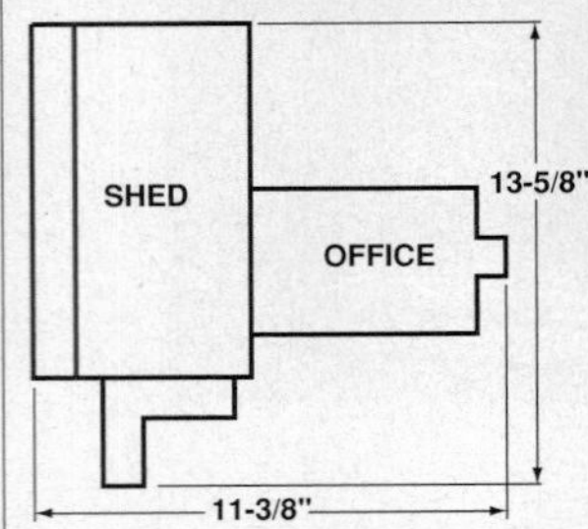

FREIGHT HOUSE DETAILS

933-3513 Complete Set **19.98** *NEW*

Transform any freight handling facility with this set of highly detailed resin castings. The set comes with a pair of tow motors, five freight wagons, two pallet jacks, two platform scales and three hand trucks. Add your personal touch with paint and install them on any loading dock to add life to the scene.

50' NORTH AMERICAN SMOOTHSIDE BOX CARS

SINGLE CARS EA 12.98:
932-3451 CNW, 932-3452 DRGW, 932-3453 SP, 932-3454 NYC, 932-3455 Burlington Refrigerator Express, 932-3456 Western Pacific, 932-3457 Magcobar, 932-3458 Sterling Salt, 932-3450 Undecorated

TWO-PACKS WITH DIFFERENT ROAD NUMBERS EA 24.98
932-23451 CNW, 932-23452 DRGW, 932-23453 SP, 932-23454 NYC, 932-23455 Burlington Refrigerator Express, 932-23456 Western Pacific, 932-23457 Magcobar, 932-23458 Sterling Salt

MILLS BROS. LUMBER

933-3082 49.98 ***NEW***
From the Pacific Northwest, from Canada, from the southern states, colorful freight cars arrive daily with loads of lumber. The fragrant smell of fresh-cut wood is everywhere as crews begin unloading. At the office, contractors and builders take delivery of lumber and other materials. Trucks groan out onto the street, working through the gears as they move loads to area building projects.

As the local lumber yard evolved into a building materials center, the operation grew larger in scope and size. Lumber is only part of the business these days. Most carry anything and everything, from insulating materials to plumbing fixtures to electrical supplies. Some also fabricate major components, such as roof trusses, decks and other structural sub-assemblies. And the business still depends on the local railroad to bring in the raw materials in bulk.

With Mills Bros. Lumber, building more action into your operations is a snap! Add a siding and expand your freight car fleet with Walthers Thrall All-Door Box Cars and Bulkhead or Centerbeam Flats (See the complete listing in the Freight Cars section of this Book.) to serve this busy complex.

The kit includes six separate structures; a large shed, two small sheds, an outdoor canopy, an open shed/garage and a corrugated office building. You can arrange them to fit your layout space and create a perfect business for any trackside town. All parts are molded in realistic colors and complete instructions make construction fast and fun. Plus, colorful sign decals are included for the finishing touch.

Corrugated Office Building

Outdoor Canopy

Open Shed/Garage

Small Shed (two in kit)

Large Shed

SMALL SHED 6-13/16 x 2-13/16"
OPEN CANOPY BASE 5-11/16 x 2-13/16"
OPEN SHED/ GARAGE 5-13/16 x 3-5/8"
LARGE SHED WITH DOCK 5-3/4 x 8"
SMALL SHED 6-13/16 x 2-13/16"
OFFICE 3-13/16 x 2-13/16"

THRALL 56' ALL-DOOR BOX CARS

Single Cars Ea 15.98
932-7001 Weyerhaeuser
932-7002 US Plywood
932-7003 Boise Cascade
932-7004 St. Regis Paper
932-7005 Idaho Forest Industries
932-7006 Masonite Corp.
932-7007 Canfor
932-7008 Georgia-Pacific
932-7000 Undecorated

Two-Packs With Different Road Numbers Ea 29.98
932-27001 Weyerhaeuser
932-27002 US Plywood
932-27003 Boise Cascade
932-27004 St. Regis Paper
932-27005 Idaho Forest Industries
932-27006 Masonite Corp.
932-27007 Canfor
932-27008 Georgia-Pacific

AIRCRAFT

P51-D "MUSTANG"

933-1170 pkg(2) **19.98** *NEW*
"Left waist gunner to crew... little friends at four o' clock low!"

To World War Two bomber crews, those were some of the sweetest words ever heard. "Little friends" were escort fighters, protecting the vulnerable bomber formations as they headed to and from the target.

Among the first fighters that could go round-trip with its bigger brothers was the legendary P-51 "Mustang."

Designed and built for the British in 1940, the P-51 was North American Aviation's first fighter. Its Allison engine

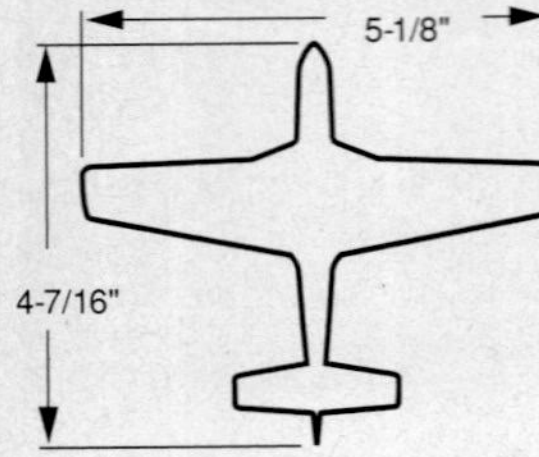

proved unsuitable at high-altitudes, but the aircraft was ideal for photo and ground attack missions. By mid 1941, the US Army Air Corps. ordered its first samples.

Lessons learned in combat were quickly incorporated on the production line. In 1942, the Rolls Royce "Merlin" engine was coupled with a new supercharger and a four-blade propeller, dramatically improving performance and range. Designated P51-B/C, the Allies finally had a fighter that could escort bombers to and from the target and take on any opposition.

Later improvements created the P51-D. Its streamlined "bubble" canopy required changes in the fuselage that gave the D a unique appearance. Six .50 caliber, wing-mounted machine guns provided more punch, while stronger pylons allowed bombs or rockets to be carried. Just over 9600 were built and by 1945, most US fighter squadrons flew P51-Ds.

Outdated by jets, Mustangs were quickly transferred to the reserves. Some were briefly recalled to service during the Korean War. And some soldiered on in Latin America and Israel through the late 50s. Others were rebuilt as air racers or preserved as museum pieces, where a few remain in flying condition.

Now, take the controls and add this legendary fighter to your stable of aircraft. All-new tooling captures every line of these sleek planes, from the huge four blade prop to the distinct tail.

Parts for two complete aircraft are included in this first-ever HO Scale kit to get your squadron airborne. And since no fighter of this era is complete without colorful nose art, each kit includes full-color decal markings for four different planes! Based on period photos and research, build your choice of "Betty Lee III", "Louisiana Heat Wave", "Missouri Armada" or "Scat IV."

Then, park your completed P51s on the flight line with our C-47 (933-1150). Add Roco Minitanks, Trident Miniatures or other HO Scale military vehicles and you'll have the makings of a great diorama. The small size is perfect for wargaming, and makes the finished models much easier to display than larger scale replicas.

625-444

625-225

625-646

590-1010056

YOUR FLIGHTLINE COMES ALIVE WITH THESE ACCESSORIES

625-225 Dodge 4x4 w/Closed Cab **4.99**
625-444 Willys Jeep w/Trailer **9.99**
625-646 GMC Truck w/US Star logo **14.99** *NEW*
590-1010056 US Army Air Force Flight & Ground Figures pkg(12) **14.98** *NEW*

CENTENNIAL MILLS - BUILDING BACK

933-3160 21.98 *NEW*
10-3/16 Wide x 1-15/16 Deep x 8-7/16" Tall 25.4 x 4.8 x 21cm

VARIETY PRINTING CO. LTD. BUILDING FRONT

933-3161 21.98 *NEW*
12-1/4 Wide x 1-3/4 Deep x 6-11/16" Tall 30.6 x 4.3 x 16.7cm

ADD NEW DIMENSION TO YOUR BACKGROUND SCENES

Finally! There's a quick, affordable way to add scenery anywhere space is limited - without the added time and trouble of kitbashing!

Background Building Walls let you use that last little bit of space to create a realistic background for any industrial area. These kits can be used on the edge of your benchwork, along a shelf or modular layout and in dioramas. Once installed, they provide a smooth, realistic transition between 3-D foreground scenes and printed or painted backgrounds. (Check out the complete listing of Instant Horizons™ printed backgrounds in the Scenery Section for more ideas on creating a backdrop for your layout.)

Based on popular Cornerstone Series® structures, you can build them stock or easily customize them. Each has scribed cut lines molded on the inside so you can cut new angles or reduce the width to fit your pike. Each building also comes with a variety of add-on details, a partial roof and colorful sign decals.

NEW ADD-ON DETAILS GIVE HO SCALE BUILDINGS A NEW LOOK!

Turn ho-hum kits into realistic replicas with this new series of structural details and smaller structures! Perfect as add-ons for other kits, superdetails or the finishing touch to kitbashed and scratchbuilt buildings. Easy-to-build kits feature plastic parts molded in colors, or detailed resin castings you can paint yourself. Complete instructions are included with every kit to show you how to assemble and install your new details.

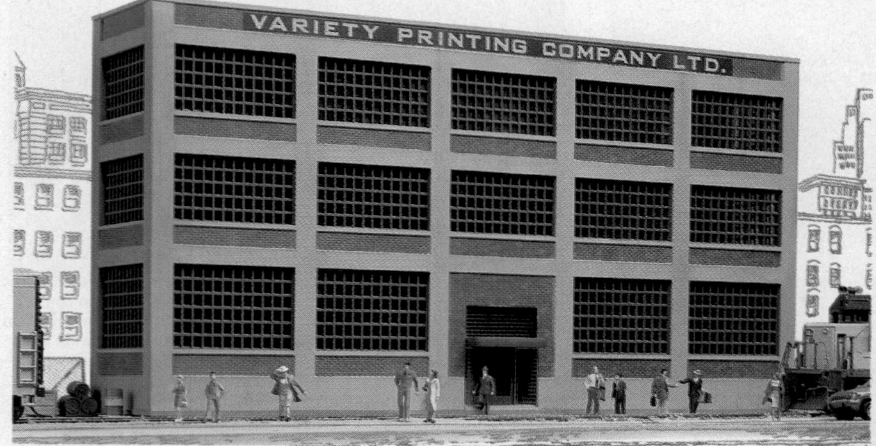

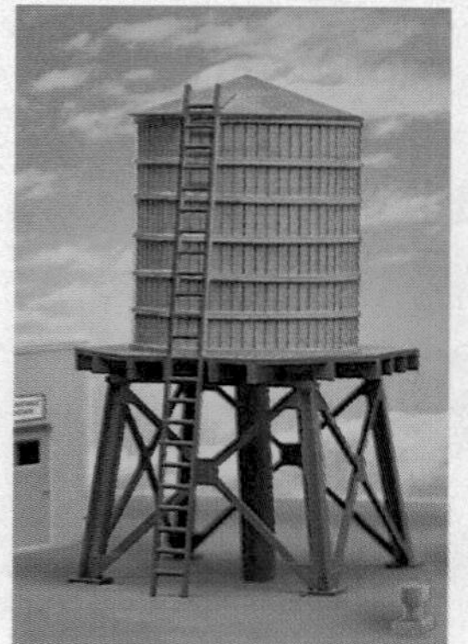

WOOD WATER TANKS

933-3507 pkg(3) 9.98 *NEW*
As much a part of a city skyline as clouds! Look at any big city scene and you'll see tanks perched on the roofs of all kinds of buildings. From downtown offices, stores and apartments, to grimy industries, here's a detail that's perfect for every tall building on your layout.

Detailed plastic parts look like real wood and are molded in colors. A separate roof and supports are also included. Each kit comes with parts for three complete tanks.

TRACK BUMPERS

933-3511 pkg(16) 9.98 *NEW*
Keep freight cars and sidings safe in your industrial areas. Typical of the track bumpers installed in every factory district, these easy-to build kits feature plastic parts molded in realistic color. Simply snap into place when complete.

BRICK SMOKESTACK

933-3509 9.98 *NEW*
When coal was the life-blood of American industry, smokestacks were a symbol of power and progress. Rising majestically into the city skyline, many carried their company's name in fancy brickwork or as a painted sign. Today, many of these old stacks still stand as an unused monument to a by-gone industrial age.

A great detail for any big industry, several can be combined in the same scene. By themselves, they can stand alongside heating plants, hospitals, small powerhouses, creameries, - any vintage industry that burns coal for power. Or, replace the stacks that come with other kits to create a custom building for your layout.

COOLING TOWER

933-3504 9.98 *NEW*
Evaporative coolers are some of the biggest air conditioners in use. In addition to cooling air, they also filter it to remove dust and other particulates and lower the humidity. As a result, they are vital to many modern manufacturing operations. Installed as both stand-alone and roof-top units, they can be found in service at factory and office buildings. This kit features highly detailed resin castings.

AIR FILTRATION BUILDING AND DUCTWORK

933-3503 29.98 ***NEW***
To meet today's air quality standards, many manufacturing processes now require air to be cleaned before it's released back into the atmosphere. This type of machinery is commonly seen on all kinds of factories, especially around areas where dust and dirt or solvents and chemicals may be released. The air filtration systems work like huge vacuum cleaners to trap these materials and remove them. This resin model adds a modern touch to any big factory and includes a variety of ductwork, simulated filtration machinery and three large exhaust stacks

WALL-MOUNT DUST COLLECTORS

933-3510 9.98 ***NEW***
Modernize older industries for your contemporary railroad with this neat accessory. Today's clean air laws require that dust, solvents and particulate matter be trapped before it can be blown out of the factory. You'll see these big collectors hard at work on the sides of food processing plants, mills, woodworking plants, furniture factories, chemical plants, textile mills, industrial painting operations and businesses that handle or cut paper. Highly detailed, unpainted plastic castings make it easy to model the complex piping and other details found on the real thing.

ROOF DETAILING KIT-ASSORTED VENTS

933-3158 pkg(62) **11.98** ***NEW***
Detail the most visible area of your HO Scale buildings - the roof! This highly realistic set is a great value, with parts for 62 vents in 10 different styles. A surprising variety of vents are found on industrial buildings, so you can install several styles as desired. You'll also find smaller vents on commercial buildings, such as restaurants. With some careful cutting and fitting, many can be adjusted to fit peaked roofs, or simulate wall-mounted units.

INDUSTRIAL SUBSTATION

933-3506 20.98 ***NEW***
Modern offices and industries are almost exclusively powered by electricity. These high-demand customers often have their own on-site substations and transformers, which reduce high voltage supplied from overhead lines and re-route power within the complex. This HO Scale kit is complete with three transformers, a distribution rack with detailed insulators and fencing to secure the area. The major parts are detailed resin castings, and the finished model will look great alongside any large industrial building.

GUARD STATION

933-3505 29.98 ***NEW***
Most large industries protect their property with guarded entrances. This model builds into a typical facility, which is perfect for an auto assembly plant or distribution facility, steel works, paper mill and more. The kit is complete with a Guard Station which features detailed resin parts, and plastic parts to simulate the modern motorized access gates now used at many facilities.

With some additional decal signs and details (sold separately), the basic building lends itself to easy conversion projects, such as a roadside drive-in, used car lot or other small business.

ROOF AIR CONDITIONING KIT

933-3157 11.98 ***NEW***
Make any building a cool model with these detailed roof-top air conditioners. Since the 1930s, units like these have been installed on commercial, industrial and public buildings. In addition to cooling air, they also control humidity and remove dust and other materials, which makes them essential to modern manufacturing plants. The finished models are an easy way to detail and modernize any structure with a flat roof. And you can combine kits to detail larger buildings, which usually require several to provide adequate cooling for the entire structure, or to serve specific areas inside. Each kit consists of detailed plastic parts simulating a variety of equipment.

Ford logo used by license from Ford Motor Company

America's DRIVING FORCE

WALTHERS CORNERSTONE® SERIES

HEADQUARTERS BUILDING

933-3074 54.98 ***NEW***

13-1/2 x 6-1/2 x 7-1/4"
33.7 x 16.2 x 18.1cm

As small industries became successful companies, most needed purpose-built office space. Though dwarfed by ever-larger manufacturing or assembly plants designed to do one or two jobs, no other building on the property typically did as much work under one roof. Here, an army of bookkeepers, stenographers, secretaries, mail clerks, accountants, telephone operators, janitors, typists and others were needed to handle the volume of work.

Constructed alongside a busy street or other highly visible location, the office projected power, strength and confidence. They were often constructed of stone or brick and included a variety of dignified trim elements. This also required they be remodeled fairly often, to keep them looking modern and up-to-date.

Based on a prototype built by the Ford Motor Company at Dearborn, Michigan, in the 1920s, this building once served as the headquarters of the Detroit, Toledo & Ironton railroad. On your layout, virtually any large industrial complex, such as a steel mill, brewery, or manufacturing plant needs a building like this located on the property. With its shape, size and numerous windows, it's typical of many public buildings as well. With appropriate details and figures available separately, it could be used to model a school, city hall, hospital, courthouse or other government offices as well.

Photos and base diorama by Ken Patterson

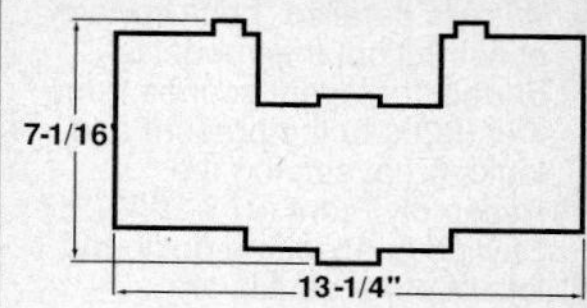

Ford logo used by license from Ford Motor Company

STAMPING PLANT

933-3075 64.98 *NEW*

15-3/4 x 8 x 7-3/4"
39.3 x 20 x 19.3cm (Height Over Vents)

Every new car or truck begins as sheet steel, which will be transformed into nearly 300 stamped metal parts to build an average car. This is done by massive stamping machines, which may use large steel sheets called blanks, or steel from continuous coils. The machines hammer the metal into shape over special forms called dies, which produce everything from doors to trunk decks, down to small brackets and reinforcing pieces.

With its detailed "brick curtain" construction, this model is perfect for layout scenes from the 1920s to the present and looks great serving the Assembly Plant (933-3079). Skylights, a loading dock and lots of other details are included. Plants of this type are an integral part of appliance manufacturing too, turning out steel shapes for refrigerators, freezers, washers, dryers, hot water heaters and other durable goods.

932-3882

933-1499

EXPAND OPERATIONS WITH THESE CARS

Producing parts on tight "just in time" schedules requires a steady flow of rail cars. Steel arrives in Cushion Coil Cars (932-3850 series with square hoods or 932-3881 series with round hoods) which can be loaded with Steel Coils (933-1499) for more realism. Scrap goes back to the mills in 65' Mill Gondolas (932-3250 series). Finished parts head for auto assembly plants in 86' Hi-Cube Box Cars with four (Individual Cars 932-3500 series, 2-Packs 932-23501 Series) or eight doors (Individual Cars 932-3530 series, 2-Packs 932-23531 Series) to speed loading and unloading.

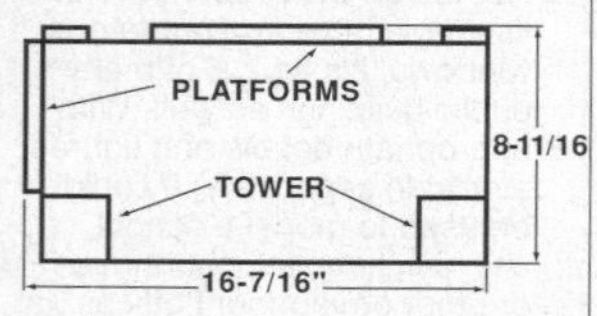

Photos and base diorama by Ken Patterson

America's DRIVING FORCE

WALTHERS CORNERSTONE® SERIES

UPTOWN MOTORS AUTO DEALERSHIP

933-3077 49.98 ***NEW***

9 x 12-1/4 x 3-3/4" 22.5 x 30.6 x 9.3cm (Height Over Vents)

Brand new or slightly used, you'll find outstanding deals at this modern auto dealership. Perfect for city or suburban street scenes, this model is typical of older dealerships which have been remodeled to keep pace with the latest trends. Out front is the showroom with its huge glass windows, perfect for displaying the latest from the factory. Directly behind is a two-story brick office area, which leads out to the garage and service center. Lots of rooftop vents, air conditioners and more complete the basic building. And, colorful decal signs to build your choice of a 1960s or 1990s dealership are included so the finished model fits perfectly in your favorite era.

Photos and base diorama by Ken Patterson

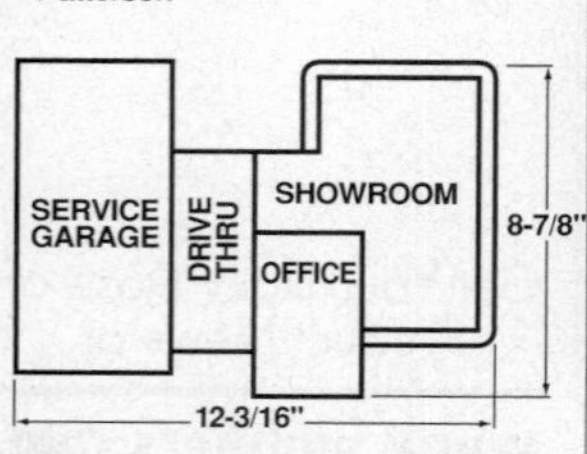

CARS AND TRUCKS SET THE SCENE

To detail the scene, check out the selection of Walthers assembled plastic vehicles. For modern scenes, load your parking lots with the 1998 Ford Crown Victoria Four-Door Sedan (933-1240), or the Expedition SUV m(933-1230). Or turn back the clock with the 1967 Mustang Fastback 2-Door (933-1220) or the 1966 F-100 Pickup (933-1210). Add shoppers and a sales staff from the Auto Dealership Figure Set (590-1010119) and you're ready to open for business.

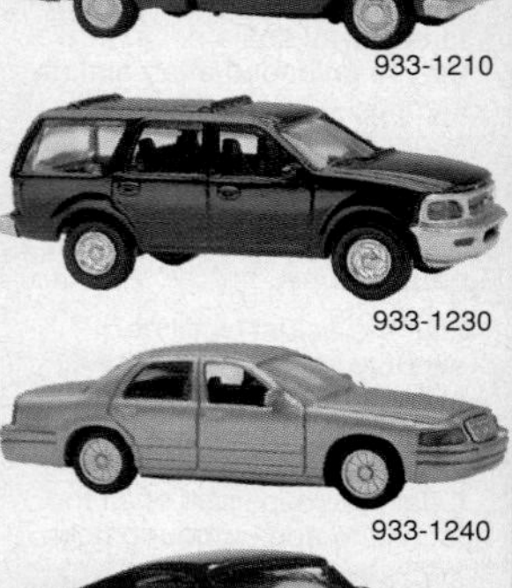

933-1210

933-1230

933-1240

933-1220

Ford logo used by license from Ford Motor Company

DISTRIBUTION FACILITY

933-3076 49.98 ***NEW***

Office: 4 x 3 x 1-5/8" 10 x 7.5 x 4.2cm; 1-5/16 x 1 x 1-1/8" 4 x 2.5 x 2.8cm

Your new car or truck took its first long trip by train, and was loaded at a facility much like this. Once assembly and inspection are complete, vehicles are driven to these large lots for staging. Here, they'll be ramped aboard waiting auto racks for the trip to far-away dealers. On arrival, they're unloaded at an almost identical facility, which may serve one or two large markets. For the final trip to the showroom, cars or trucks are reloaded aboard special carrier semis.

Like the actual facilities, security is important. The kit includes easy-to-assemble Chain Link Fencing, a Guard Shack, a corrugated metal Office to keep track of all the incoming and outbound new vehicles, two Unloading Ramps, two Auto Carrier Trailers and a set of colorful sign decals.

Photos and base diorama by Ken Patterson

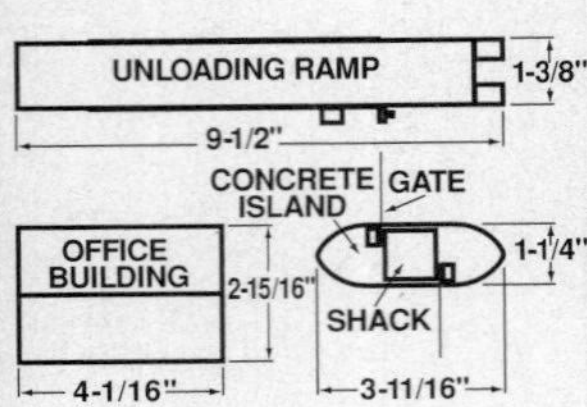

932-3551

932-3585

933-1200

933-1250

MAKE THIS FACILITY COME TO LIFE

For modern scenes, autos can arrive aboard the Enclosed Tri-Level Auto Racks (932-4850 series single cars, 932-24851 series 2-Packs) and trucks can come in on the Enclosed Bi-Level Auto Racks (932-4800 series single cars), all sold separately. New cars can then be loaded aboard the Auto Carrier Semi (933-1200), with a detailed Ford LNT 9000 tractor pulling an Auto Carrier Trailer.

And be sure to check out Walthers assembled auto and trucks to detail your scene, priced to move at just $7.98 each:

1998 Ford Crown Victoria Four-Door Police Car (933-1250),

1998 Ford Expedition SUV (933-1230)

1967 Ford Mustang Fastback 2-Door (933-1220)

1966 Ford F-100 Pickup (933-1210)

America's DRIVING FORCE

TIRE PLANT

933-3078 69.98 ***NEW***

13-1/4 x 16 x 12"
33.1 x 40 x 30cm (Height Over Smoke Stacks)

Since the 1900s, pneumatic tires have smoothed the ride for generations of drivers. Auto makers are among the biggest single buyers of new tires, but Tire Plants also make tires for bicycles, airplanes, construction equipment and farm machinery as well. Making tires requires an amazing variety of raw materials: the average radial tire requires 30 different types of natural rubber, 8 types of synthetic rubber, 8 different types of carbon black, 1 pound of steel belts, 1 pound of polyester and nylon, 1 pound of steel bead wire and 3 pounds of 40 different chemicals! And virtually all of it arrives at the plant by rail.

As a stand-alone industry supporting your Auto Assembly Plant (932-3079 sold separately), this big factory will provide plenty of traffic for any railroad. Built in the "brick curtain" style which first appeared in the 1920s, buildings like this are still going strong today. The finished model is a 3-story brick structure, complete with two smoke stacks, a roof-top water tank, an enclosed rail car loading dock, truck dock, and a huge storage silo for carbon black. Separate doors and windows are standard, while complete instructions and colorful signs round out this impressive industry.

Photos and base diorama by Ken Patterson

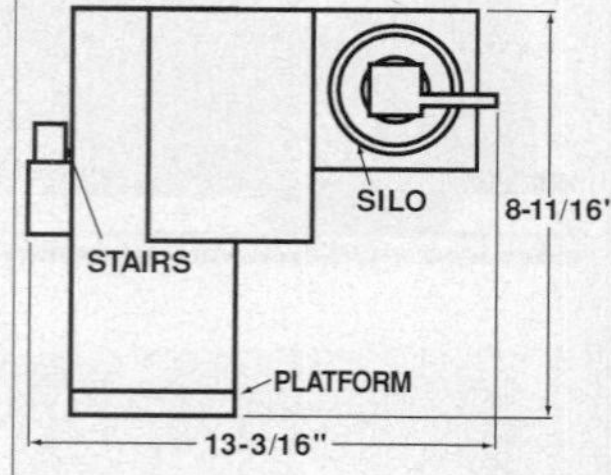

America's DRIVING FORCE

Ford logo used by license from Ford Motor Company

WALTHERS CORNERSTONE SERIES®

AUTO ASSEMBLY PLANT

933-3079 79.98 ***NEW***

23-3/16 x 12 x 4-3/4" 58 x 30 x 11.8cm

From tiny screws to solid steel frames, here's where the 30,000+ parts of your new car or truck are brought together as one. Most of those parts are made by other suppliers, then shipped here by rail. Shipping is carefully timed and closely watched, as the parts must arrive on the day they're needed. Finally, your new vehicle begins its trip down a moving assembly line. Body panels are welded, cleaned and painted. Frames are connected to drivetrains and exhaust systems. From radiator to radio, workers on the line add another component at each station. Finally, a gleaming new car or truck is completed. After inspection, it's moved to the Distribution Facility (933-3076, sold separately) for another train trip.

Some of the biggest buildings on the property, Assembly Plants are the heart of any automaker's operations. This model builds into a detailed replica, sized to fit most layouts. It features a modern brick front office, while the plant itself is made of corrugated metal on a concrete foundation. Big overhead doors on the back wall can be built open to handle box cars. Lots of windows, roof-top vents and many other details are included, along with 1960s and 1990s vintage signs.

Photos and base diorama by Ken Patterson

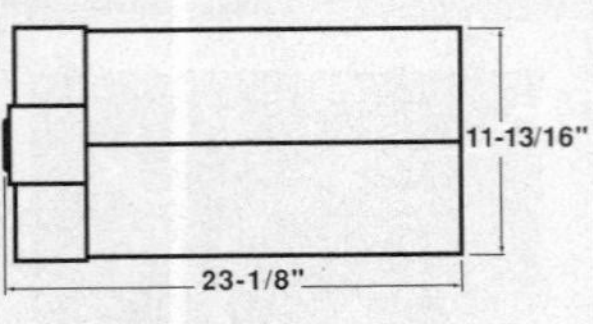

FREIGHT CARS TO SERVE YOUR PLANT

Sheet metal, seats and other lightweight parts can be delivered to your new plant in Walthers 86' Hi-Cube Box Cars with four (Individual Cars 932-3500 series, 2-Packs 932-23501 Series) or eight doors (Individual Cars 932-3530 series, 2-Packs 932-23531 Series) to speed loading and unloading. Heavy components like engines, axles, transmissions and wheels arrive in Pullman-Standard 60' Single Door (Individual Cars 932-3550 series, 2-Packs 932-23551 Series) or Double-Door Auto Parts Box Cars (Individual Cars 932-3580 series, 2-Packs 932-23581 Series).

932-3551

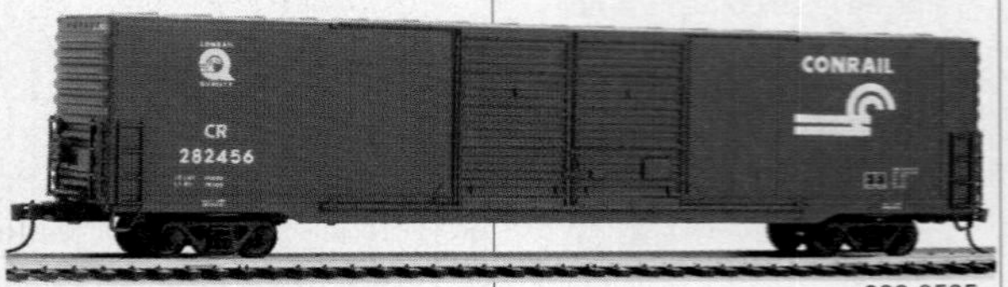

932-3585

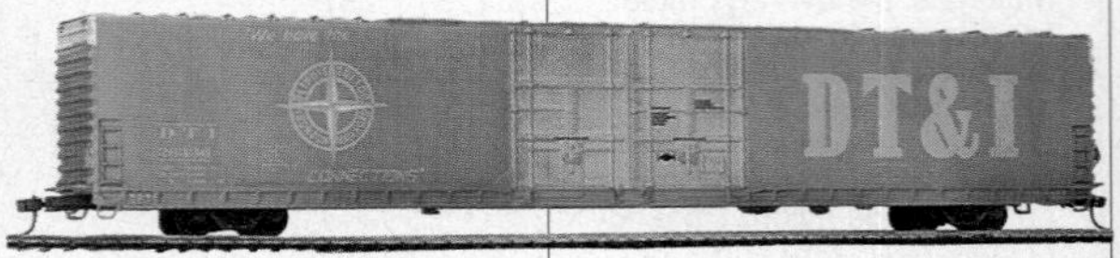

932-3502

932-3533

For Up-To-Date Information and News Bookmark Walthers Web site at

www.walthers.com

PIER & TRAVELING CRANE

933-3067 74.98
Pier: 12-5/8 x 5-3/4 x 1-1/2"
31.5 x 14.3 x 3.7cm
Crane: 4 x 4 x 9-1/8"
10 x 10 x 22.8cm

Essential to any waterfront scene, the Pier & Traveling Crane is sure to be a focal point of activity on your layout. Here, ships unload and take on cargo with the aid of a traveling crane which traverses the length of the pier. A siding on the pier allows switchers to spot freight cars next to the ship for convenient loading. The rails are embedded into the surface so that trucks, forklifts and other vehicles can also use the pier. The basic HO Scale kit includes plain and grooved pier sections. The grooved sections are molded to accept Code 83 or Code 100 rail (sold separately) so you can run a spur right out on the dock. With its modular design, the Pier can be lengthened with the Pier Add-On Kit (933-3154, sold separately), which includes two matching sections.

Plastic rails are molded onto the deck for the unpowered crane. Complete instructions and decals round out this model.

Photos and base dioramas by Ken Patterson

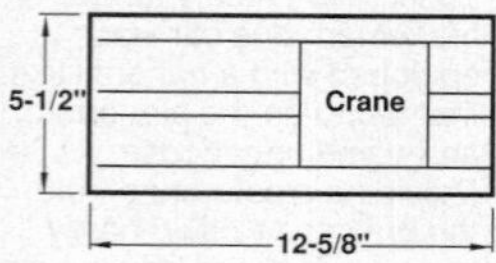

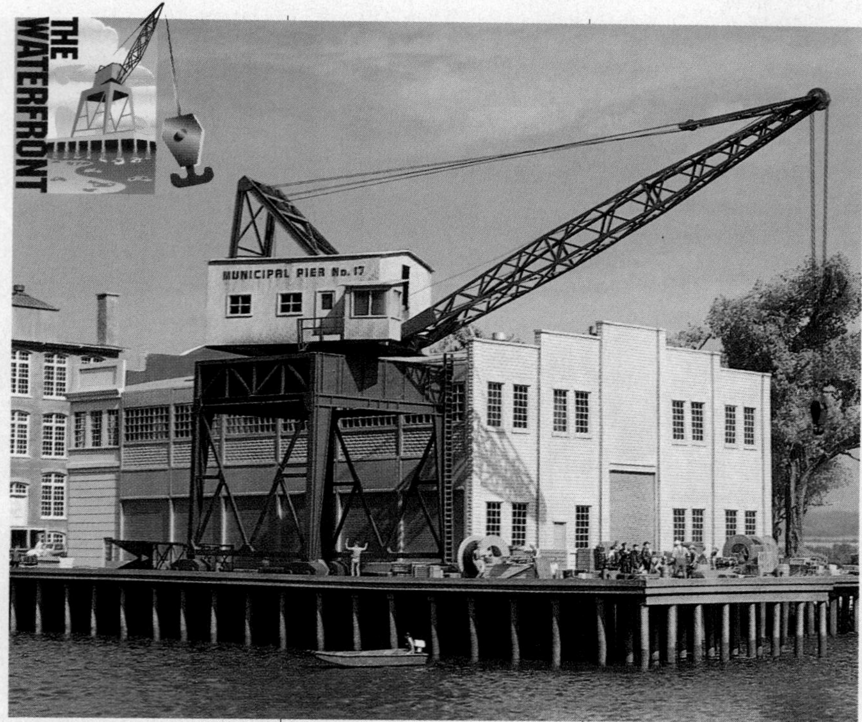

ADD-ON PIER

This kit is no longer in production and supplies are limited to stock on hand. A future producton run may be scheduled if there is enough demand. Please see your dealer or check out our Web site at www.walthers.com for current availability.

933-3154 Two Additional Sections **19.98**
Build a longer pier with this set of parts that match parts from #3067, sold separately.

CARFLOAT APRON

933-3068 39.98
(Height Above Water)
8-1/2 x 8-1/2 x 8-5/8"
21.2 x 21.2 x 21.5cm

To move freight cars between land and carfloats, railroads and some private industries constructed Carfloat Aprons. These structures consist of a moving apron (similar to a bridge) that can be locked with the float. This keeps the tracks aligned during switching and allows the float and the apron to move up and down with the tides. Counterweights and lifting machinery are housed in the towers at the end of the apron.

This detailed HO Scale model is an ideal way to add waterfront traffic to your operations. Built on the water's edge, they require little space, but add plenty of interchange traffic. Often found serving large yards as well as industrial areas, they can be among the busiest spots on a railroad. The model features a positionable apron, detailed hoisting towers (unpowered), as well as supporting piers. The three-track apron matches the track pattern on Walthers Railroad Carfloat (933-3152), sold separately.

Photos and base dioramas by Ken Patterson

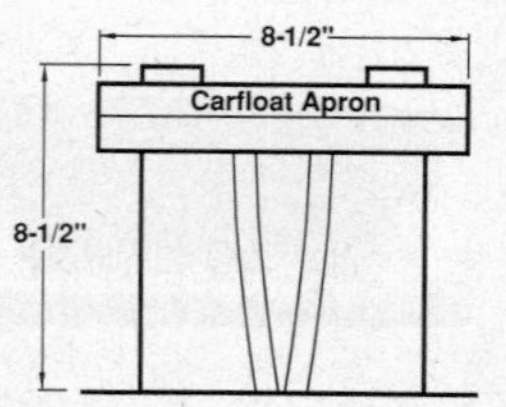

RAILROAD TUG BOAT

933-3153 59.98
13 x 3-1/2 x 3-7/8"
32 x 8.7 x 9.6cm

Once a common sight on big city harbors, the Railroad Tug was a specialized version of the familiar tug boat. In order to improve visibility over freight cars on the deck of a carfloat, Railroad Tugs were built with a taller pilot house. Starting in the 1930s, many railroads began modernizing their fleets with diesel-electric tugs. Not only did they use similar technology to the then-new diesel locos, many were painted in the same colorful schemes. These newer tugs remained in service for years, with a few serving new owners yet today.

Ready to handle chores in any busy HO harbor, Walthers Railroad Tug Boat builds into a detailed replica of the later diesel-electric designs. It features the tall pilot house, along with various roof details, towing bitts, masts and a host of other details. Complete instructions simplify construction and decals are also included. The kit builds into a waterline model with no lower hull detail, so it's easy to add to your new or existing scenery. For more realism, you can add the Tug Boat Crew which includes six hand-painted figures (590-1010052, sold separately). Your completed model is perfect for use with the Railroad Carfloat (933-3152, sold separately), or any of the other facilities in the Waterfront series.

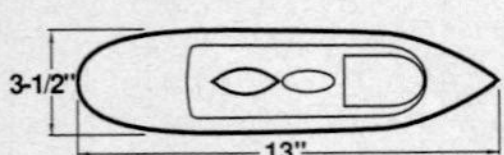

RAILROAD CARFLOAT

933-3152 39.98
39 x 5-1/2 x 1"
97 x 13.7 x 2.5cm

Where bridges were too expensive or impossible to build, railroads turned to carfloats. These big barges feature a flat deck with up to three sets of tracks, allowing for quick movement of virtually any rail car over water.

These "floating rail yards" were especially common in big city harbors and on many inland rivers, in many cases providing the only rail connection to the main line. Since they were unpowered, they required the services of a railroad tug to move them from point to point. The basic design was used for decades, so many steam-era veterans lasted until the end of operations on most lines.

This HO Scale model builds into a detailed replica of a carfloat and is equally at home in the steam- or diesel era. For added-realism, it's designed as a waterline model with no lower hull. When finished, the carfloat appears to be floating in the water, making it much easier to add to new or existing scenery. Three plastic tracks are included (a common prototype practice) which matches the Carfloat Apron (933-3068, sold separately). To model a float underway, add Walthers Railroad Tug (933-3153), which is available separately.

Railroad Carfloat
5-1/2"
36"

IDLER CAR SET

933-968 pkg(3) **21.98**
Due to their great weight, waterfront switchers were seldom allowed on the apron or carfloat tracks. During switching operations, this required the use of additional cars, placed between the engine and the cars coming on or off the float. In the days before two-way radios, all of the signals to come ahead, stop or back-up had to be passed by hand or lantern. This made good visibility essential for safe operation. As a result, older flat cars with no obstructions on their decks were used for this job and were known as idler cars.

To increase safety for the brakeman, one car was equipped with a handrail like that found on the platform of an engine or caboose. Providing a safe hand-hold, the brakeman could easily climb aboard and ride the car. This set includes a trio of "retired" 40' flat cars equipped for service as idler cars. Two are standard HO Scale models, while the third includes a handrail and end steps. Perfect for steam- or diesel-era operations, the cars are prepainted and easy to assemble.

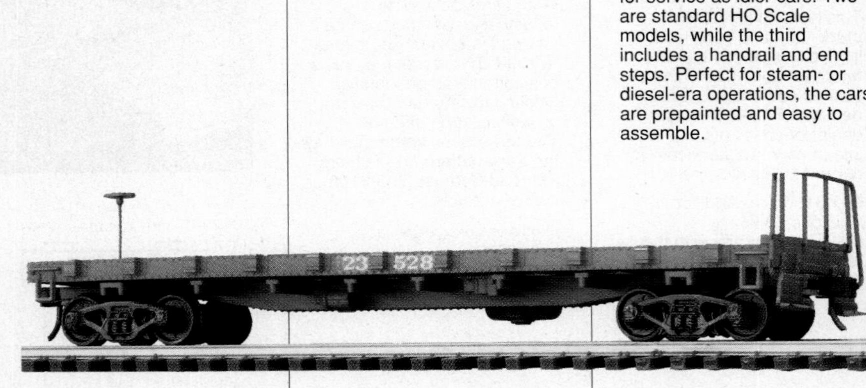

PIER TERMINAL

933-3066 59.98
12 x 16 x 7-1/4"
30 x 40 x 18.1cm

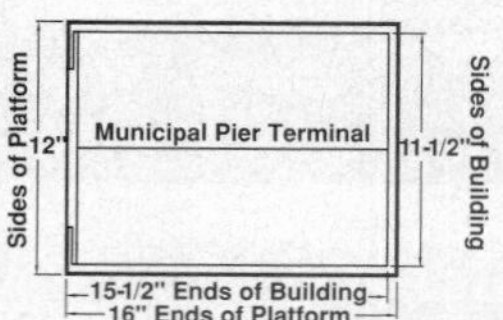

Municipal Pier Terminals are found at cargo piers throughout North America. These distinctive buildings are usually flanked by piers with railroad spurs and cranes which traverse their length. Traveling cranes unload cargo from ships onto the pier and stevedores wheel it inside through the large roll-up doors that run the length of the building. Inside the Municipal Pier Terminal, dockworkers transfer cargo to freight cars and trucks.

On your layout the HO Scale Municipal Pier Terminal makes a great destination for box cars, reefers and other cars. Many ports have several similar pier terminals on adjacent piers, so adding more than one Municipal Pier Terminal to your waterfront district is easy by just changing the decals. With its detailed facade and rows of doors, the Municipal Pier Terminal is also a prime candidate for kitbashing or enlarging. This kit comes molded in realistic colors and includes colorful decals.

Photos and base dioramas by Ken Patterson

FRONT STREET WAREHOUSE

933-3069 49.98
6-3/4 x 15-3/8 x 10"
16.8 x 38.4 x 25cm

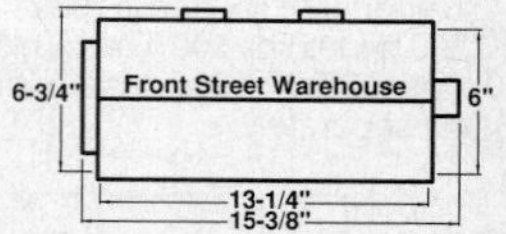

Among the first industries constructed alongside water-front areas were warehouses. These buildings made it possible to store cargo coming ashore from ships until enough wagons, freight cars or trucks could be made available. They could also hold outbound freight until a ship arrived. Brick rapidly became the building material of choice in the 1800s, to provide a sturdy, fire-resistant building. Large windows let in plenty of natural light, and skylights were also added to the roof. Many of these older buildings are still standing, some still serving as industrial structures, others converted into up-scale condominiums or apartments. From the days of sail to the present day, this handsome building makes a fine addition to any sea, lake or river port city. The HO Scale model comes molded in a variety of colors, and the parts are highly detailed to capture the look of brick-by-brick construction.

TRI-STATE POWER ATHORITY

933-3055 39.98
13-7/8 x 10 x 13"
34.5 x 4 x 32.5cm

Today, America demands a steady supply of electrical power, and much of it comes from up-to-date facilities like this. Here, a steady stream of unit trains bring in clean-burning coal to feed the turbines that drive the generators. You'll also find a variety of air and water treatment equipment to reduce harmful emissions into the environment. Outside, clean, simple lines using colored steel panels produce a building that blends easily into the surrounding landscape.

The contemporary lines of this imposing steel structure will look great in any modern skyline. A tall smokestack and a variety of roof-top details add lots of interesting angles. Capturing the look of the real thing in a size that fits most layouts, your finished model will create lots of new operations for your railroad. It's perfect for use with the Rotary Dumper (933-3145), Substation (933-3025) and High Voltage Transmission Towers (933-3121) along with Walthers BethGon Coalporter™ six-packs (932-5300 series) or 100 Ton Quad Hoppers (933-4900 series), all sold separately.

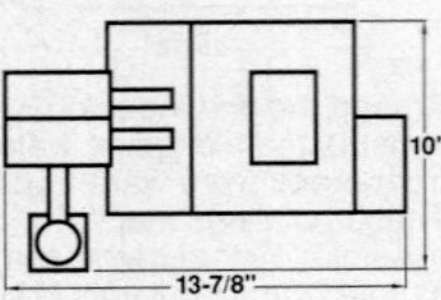

13" Tall
Smoke Stack: Base 2-1/4 x 2-1/4"
5.6 x5.6cm
18" Tall 45cm

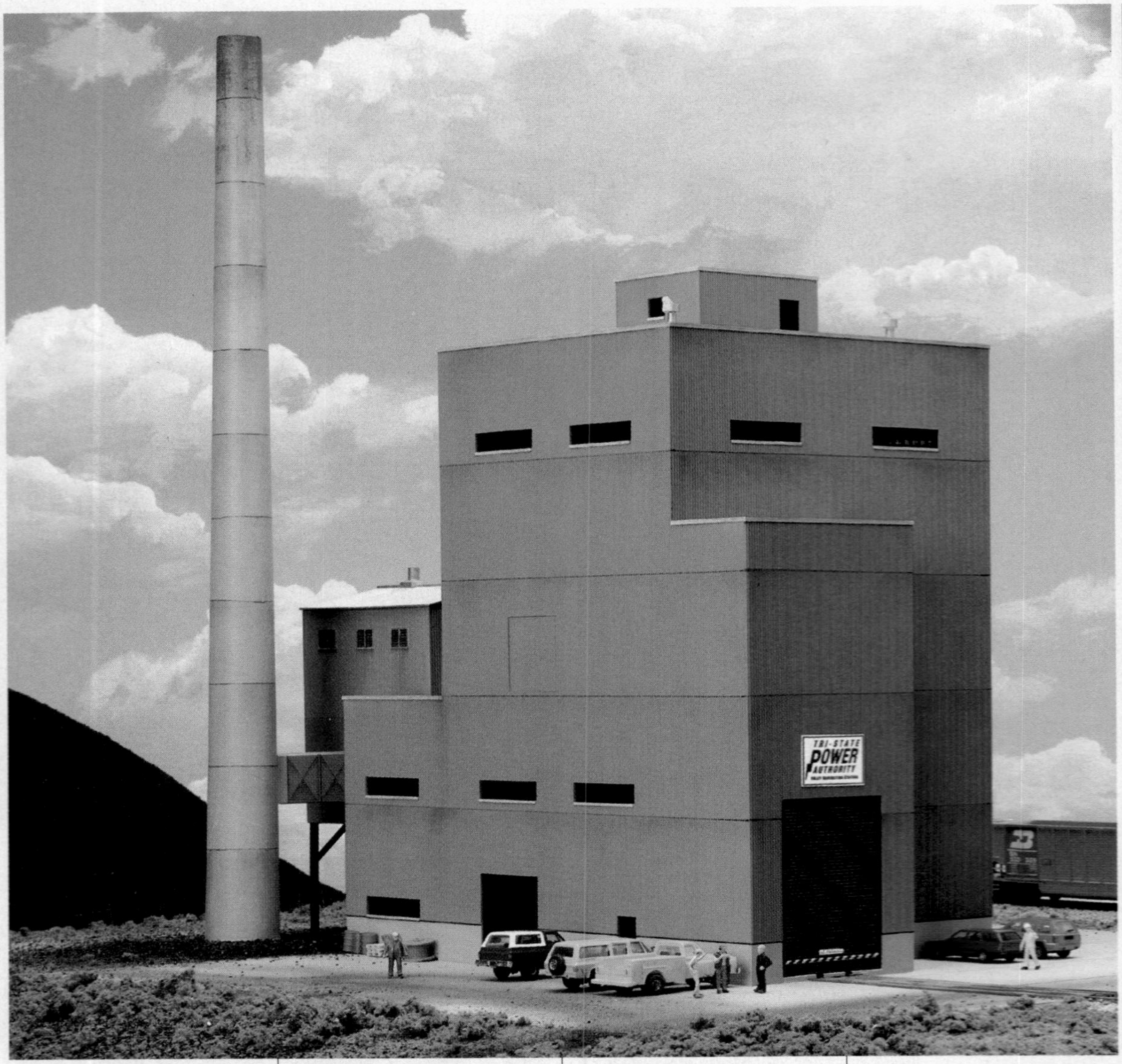

DOUGLAS DC-3/C-47

EA 24.98

933-1150 US Army Air Force (W.W.II)
933-1151 US Air Force
933-1160 North Central
933-1161 Delta
933-1162 Eastern Airlines
933-1163 Pacific Southwest Airlines
933-1164 Ozark
933-1165 North West Airlines
933-1166 Canadian Pacific

Finally, an aircraft kit compatible with Roco Minitanks and Trident military vehicles! Complete your HO Scale military diorama with our new DC-3/C-47.

The DC-3, and its military counterpart the C-47, revolutionized both commercial and military air transport. Sleek DC3s first took to the air in the mid-1930s. Reliable and cheap to operate, they helped to make commercial aviation profitable. With thousands constructed and flown worldwide, the DC-3 was the best-known airliner in the world.

During World War Two, the DC-3 was rebuilt as a cargo carrier for the Army and Navy. Large double-wide cargo/personnel doors were added and the military version was redesignated the C-47. C-47s were flown by virtually every Allied country. While C-47s were used mainly during W.W. II, some flew in the Korean War and a few even made it into Vietnam.

In the commercial world, versatile DC-3s hauled passengers and freight for most major airlines. They were also used on charters and for special services like survey work and hauling recreational skydivers. Today, over 60 years after the first ones took to the air, many DC-3s, and a few former military C-47s, can still be found in specialized service. In some remote corners of the globe, many still haul passengers.

This display-quality HO Scale aircraft kit can be built two ways, as a civilian DC-3 or as a military C-47. Both versions of the kit include correct fuselage sections to make commercial DC-3s with small side-entry doors or military C-47s with double-wide cargo/personnel doors. Models also include separate engines, propellers, wheels and authentic decals.

Best of all, now you can bring together all of your Roco Minitanks, Trident and other HO Scale military vehicles and figures into a single scene featuring the DC-3/C-47.And don't forget, on a model railroad this aircraft flew in both the steam- and diesel-eras!

AL'S VICTORY SERVICE STATION

933-3072 21.98
4 x 6 x 2-1/16"
10 x 15 x 5.8cm

Not too long ago, stations like Al's could be found at every busy city intersection and along most major highways. Premium was 25 cents a gallon, maps were free, restrooms were clean. There was a mechanic on duty who could fix anything. And Al always wore a spotless uniform when he came out to pump your gas, check the oil and wash the windows.

Introduced in the late 1930s, "box" style stations like this sprang up from coast to coast and remained a standard well into the 1950s. Combining the office, restrooms and service bays into one structure, they provided a uniform, neat appearance that attracted motorists. Lots of windows made them bright and cheerful, as did the enameled steel walls decorated in company colors. Although newer stations have taken their place, many survive today as independent garages, body shops, retail stores and offices. A few have even been converted into private homes!

Authentic styling looks great on any vintage or modern street scene. Optional pumps are included to match your era, along with colorful decal signs for the finishing touch. Just add vehicles, figures and interior details, available separately, to create a busy scene anywhere along your layout.

Preproduction model shown, color may vary.

SERVICE TRUCK

189-48291 16.98

Roadside service is just a phone call away! Vintage Chevy pick-up sports colorful graphics, airhorns, nonworking amber light, tool box and towing winch. Fully assembled.

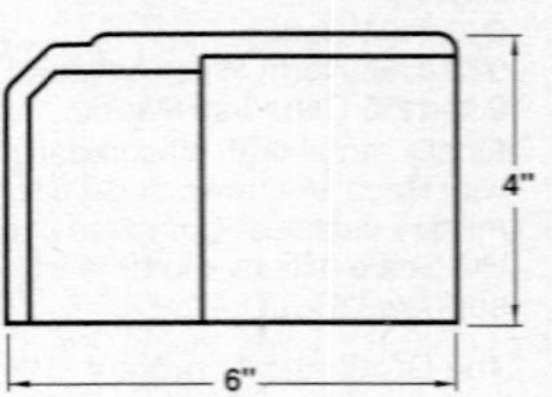

STATION DETAILING KITS EA 20.98

Turn your new station into a real showplace with these resin parts, which can backdate or modernize your scene. Each includes 17 highly detailed, unpainted castings for a soda machine, ice machine, rolling tool chest, two wooden benches, a counter with cash register, automobile lift, two mechanic's creepers, two oil can display racks, three trash cans, a free-standing air pump, a canopy to mount over the pumps and a portable engine hosit. The soda machine, canopy and oil display racks differ in each kit, so they are correct for the time period.

933-3501 Vintage 30s-60s Accessories
933-3502 Modern 70s-90s Accessories

TRESTLE W/STEEL DECK GIRDER BRIDGE

933-3147 29.98

KIT INCLUDES TWO COMPLETE TRESTLE/GIRDER BRIDGE SECTIONS

Each single-track trestle with deck girder bridge measures: 15-1/2" long with 3-1/2" deck girder bridge section, 3" wide at the bottom of the tallest girder, 4" tall.

Perhaps the most common trestle/bridge combination in North America, the Trestle with Deck Girder Bridge is a must for every steam- or diesel-era layout. Trestles consist of a series of piers, called bents, which support the track. Wood trestles were built through the 1940s and are still common on branches and secondary lines across the continent. Where piers could not be erected, such as in a flowing stream, a highway, or across another railroad, a deck girder bridge would be installed between two bents as part of the structure.

This versatile kit can be built two ways: with or without the girder bridge. With two complete trestle/girder bridges per kit, you can combine parts to open up lots of detailing options along your right-of-way. By combining both trestles you can construct a structure spanning gaps up to 31" long. Place the pair side by side for a double track mainline. And don't forget, you can also shorten the height of the bents by simply cutting them shorter from the bottom--perfect for crossing marshes and swamps just above the water level.

Place the two structures next to each other for double track

Both trestles combined yield a 31" span

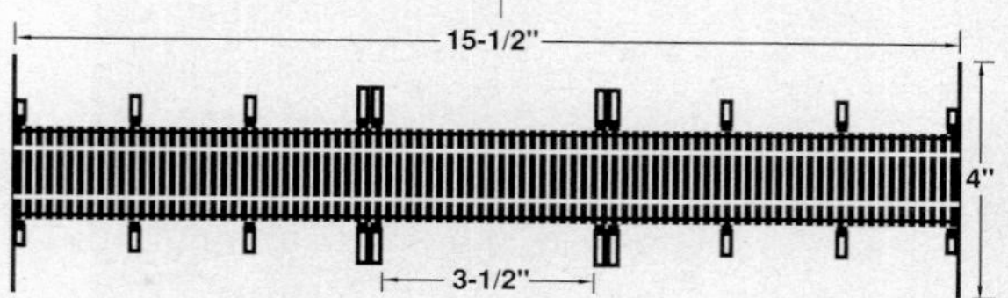

4" Tall
(Dimensions for each of the sections)

Perfect for use in any era, the detailed plastic parts simulate the all-wood construction of the prototypes. The optional deck girder bridge gives you added flexibility, whether installed with existing scenery, or in planning new construction. Complete instructions make construction quick and easy.

MILWAUKEE BEER & ALE

933-3024 69.98
12-3/8 x 10 x 12"
30.9 x 4 x 30cm

Skoal! Prost! Salut! No matter how you say it, this handsome brewery building will be the toast of your railroad. Many started as small, local suppliers, eventually growing into huge operations, thanks to the railroads. In every era, these facilities require an amazing variety of freight cars. Box cars and hoppers bring in grains and malt, as well as empty barrels, bottles, bottle caps or cans. Hoppers haul in coal and one or two may depart with loads of broken glass. Gondolas haul scrap aluminum. Tank cars arrive with natural gas, or corn syrup, while others carry beer in bulk. Insulated box cars and reefers bring in hops, then haul the finished products to market.

Milwaukee Beer & Ale will add plenty of operation to your present railroad, and if space is limited, it can be the main industry of a small switching layout. Its ornate trim, brick construction and various sizes and shapes of windows and doors (all molded separately) make it look right in any era. It's perfect as the main building in a vintage scene, or as an older part of a modern complex.

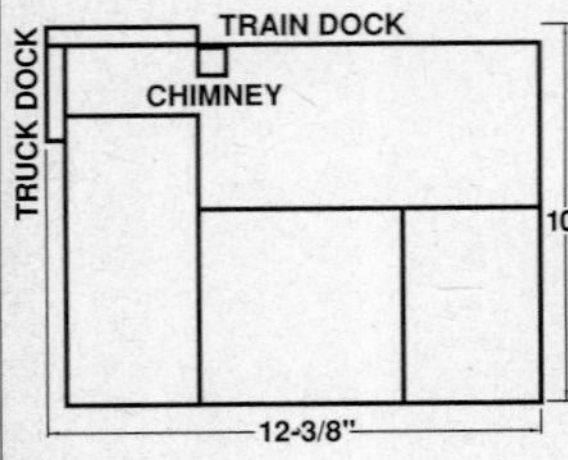

12" Tall

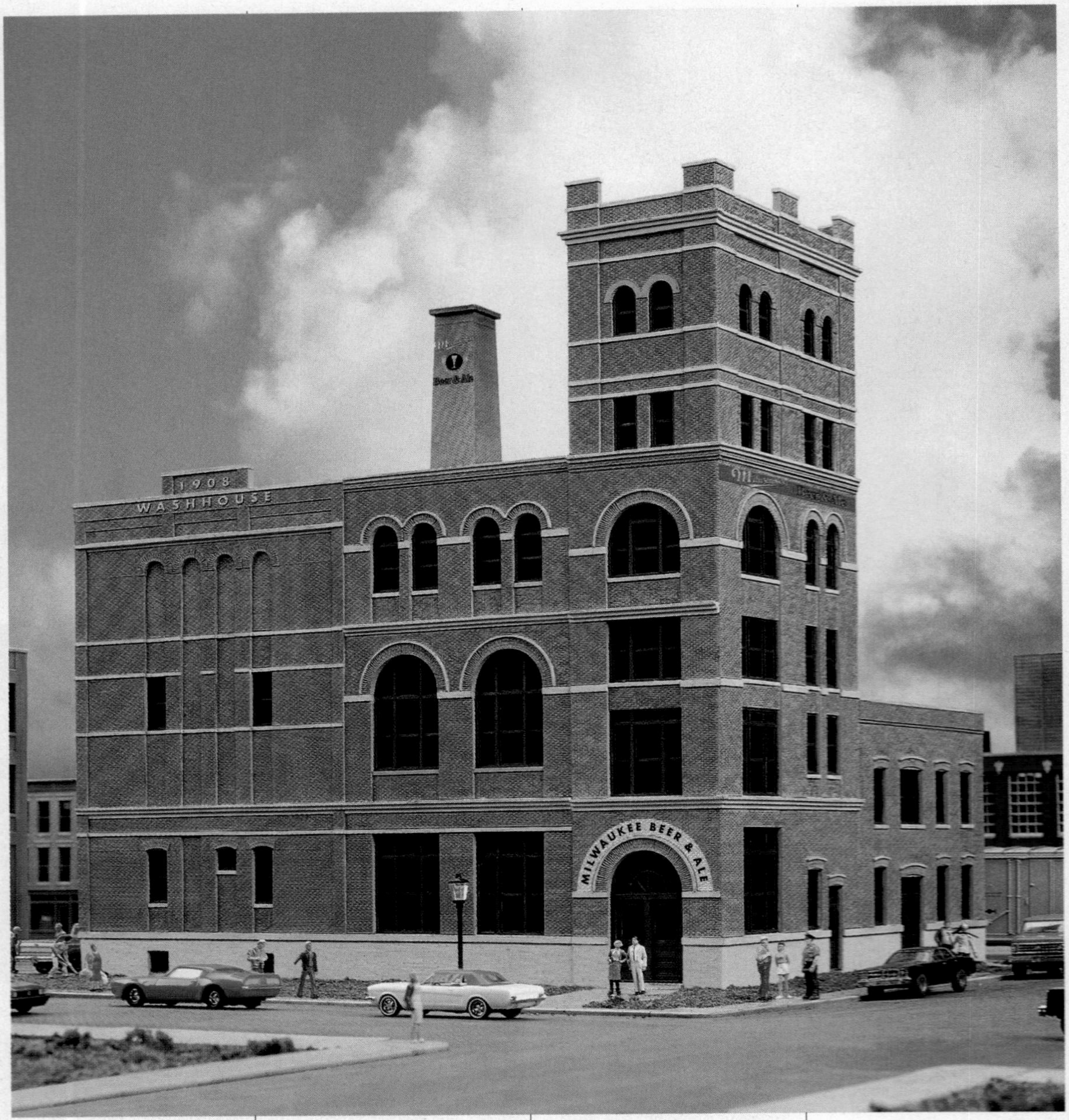

MIDSTATE MARBLE PRODUCTS

933-3073 39.98
Main Building: 10 x 5-1/2 x 4-1/2" 25 x 13.7 x 11.2cm

For thousands of years, humans have shaped stone into a variety of building materials. For many decades, much of it has come from operations like this. The stone is quarried from nearby deposits then hauled to cutting operations for sizing. Inside, huge powered saws, water-cooled to reduce dust and friction, cut blocks to the required size. Large blocks may serve as a base for monuments and small blocks as tombstones. Slabs are used as floors or exterior treatments. The surface is then polished and the finished piece ready to ship. And given the size and weight, this is definitely a job for the railroads! Flat cars or gondolas are used to ease loading and unloading of the valuable and heavy cargo.

A neat addition to the industries along any railroad, this kit includes a detailed main building, with lots of big windows that invite adding a customized interior of your own design. To handle those heavy loads coming in from the quarry, the kit comes with an overhead crane, complete with craneway supports, bridge and operator's cab. A positionable derrick and machine house are also included to hoist really big blocks on or off waiting rail cars.

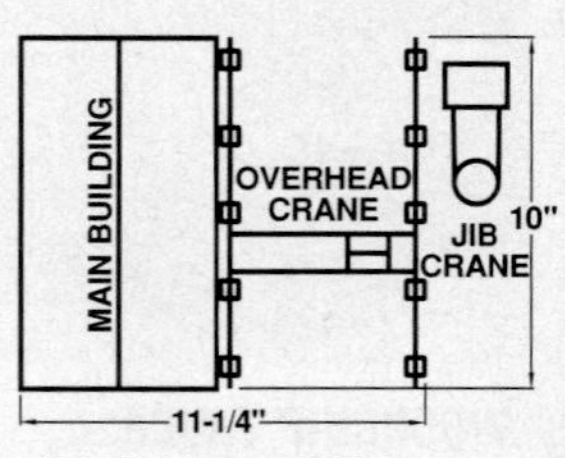

Main Building: 4-1/2" Tall

MOUNTAIN LUMBER COMPANY SAW MILL

933-3058 69.98
A fine scent of wood smoke hangs in the damp morning air. Over at the mill, they're raising steam for another busy day on the job. Any minute now, you'll hear the log conveyor rattle into action. Soon after, the shrill wine of the cutting blades will split the forest. A few minutes later, rough-cut lumber will emerge at the far end of the building, where it will be stacked and allowed to air dry. Through the day, several trains will arrive with new logs to keep the mill running smoothly.

Whether set in the days when Shays and Heislers ruled the forests, or served by contemporary diesels, this complete kit can be the centerpiece of any logging operation. Everything you'll need to start work is included, from the Log Conveyor to the Burner. The Saw Mill Building is enclosed with board and batten siding and covered by a corrugated metal roof. This style is typical of permanent operations or those that ran in areas where the weather could turn cold. At the back is a canopied area, where timbers are sorted. To keep the machinery running at capacity, there's a nicely detailed Powerhouse with twin smokestacks. And for the final touch, you get a Sawdust Burner, used to get rid of the waste products from the mill. Operations can be expanded with the Planning Mill (933-3059) or modernized with the Saw Mill Outbuildings (933-3144), both sold separately.

From any angle, the Mountain Lumber Co. Saw Mill puts realistic detail into your logging layout. Here's a rear-view showing the Slash Burner, sorting area of the Main Building and Powerhouse, which are all included in the basic kit. Easily adapted to any era, just add appropriate details, figures and scenery materials you'll find in this catalog to finish the scene.

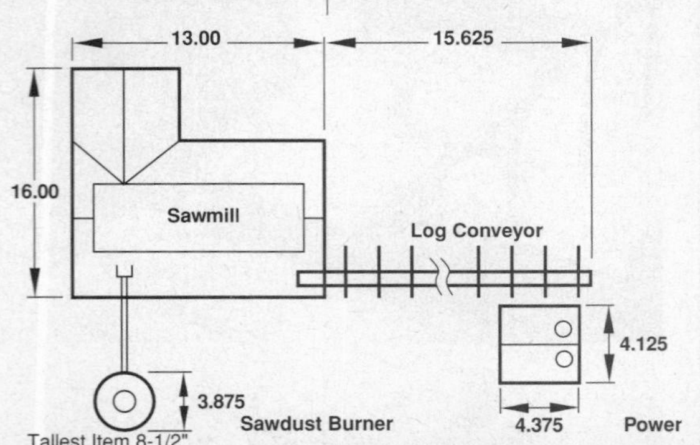

WOODCHIP TRUCK

933-4013 19.98
Woodchips are a valuable by-product, sold to paper mills to make wood pulp. Since the chips are light, a huge quantity can be shipped in specialized trailers like these. Detailed cab and trailer are molded in resin. See the Walthers listing in the Vehicles Section for more models!

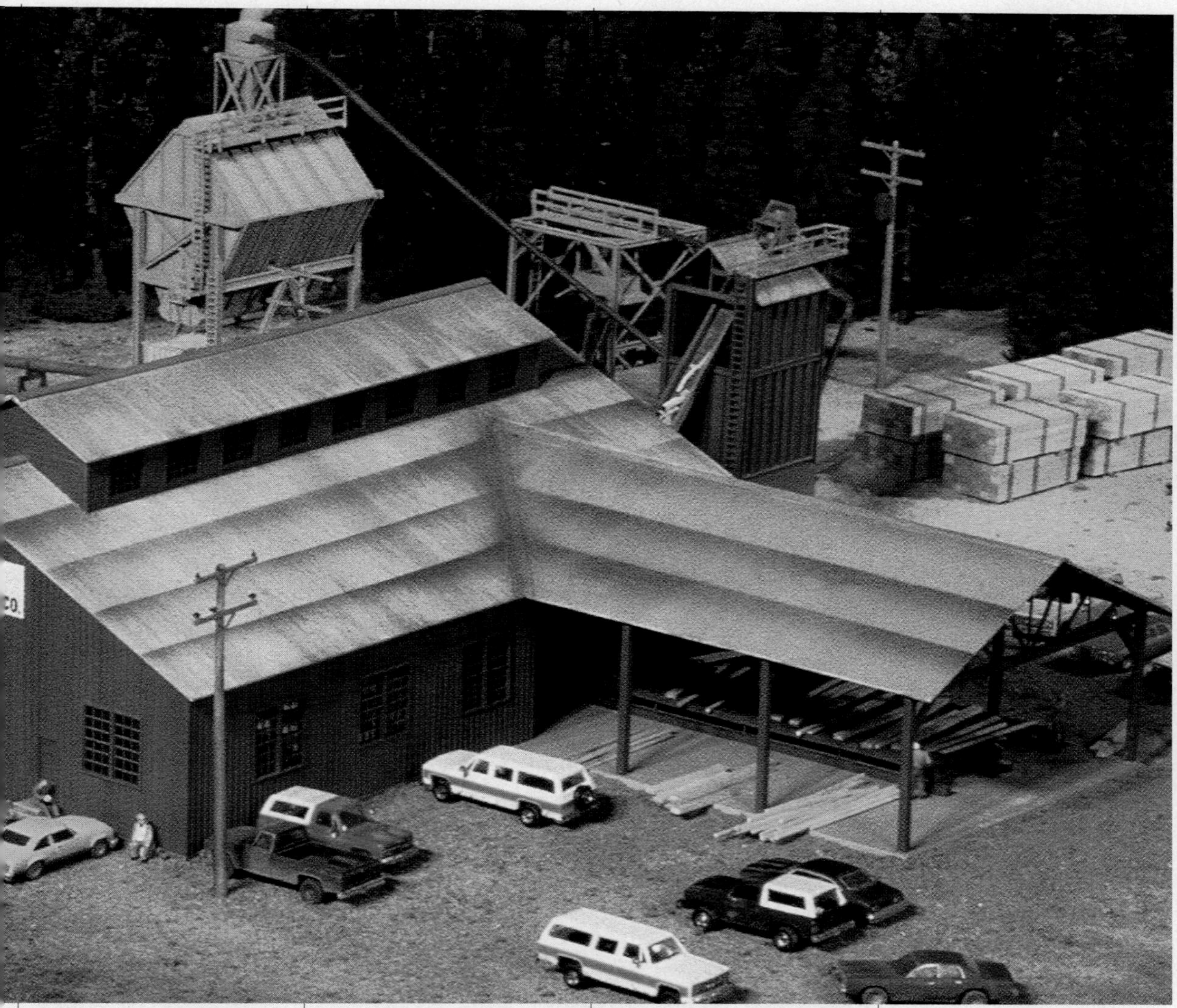

SAW MILL OUTBUILDINGS

933-3144 39.98

Things have changed down at the saw mill over the years. We're getting more timber from every log we cut thanks to the debarker. The scrap and sawdust we once burned is now ground into wood chips and sold to nearby paper mills as wood pulp. Most of it ships from here in special rail cars or trucks. Sure it changed the way we did things, but it's good for the environment, and for our bottom line!

Meet the needs of today's logging operations by adding this set of structures to the Mountain Lumber Co. Saw Mill (933-3058, sold separately). The kit consists of four complete buildings, typical of the equipment installed at contemporary mills. The Log Debarker is the first stop for logs heading into the mill. Inside, the bark is ground away, producing more useful timber and less waste. Much of the scrap lumber that once went directly to the boilerhouse or sawdust burner is also being saved. A quick pass through the Wood Chipper reduces these scraps to chips about 1/2" square and an 1/8" thick. The light-weight chips are blown through pipes into the Chip Loaders. The kit includes both a Rail Car Loader, with its special equipment for loading wood chip gondolas, and a Truck Loader, with a gravity fed storage bin and blower details.

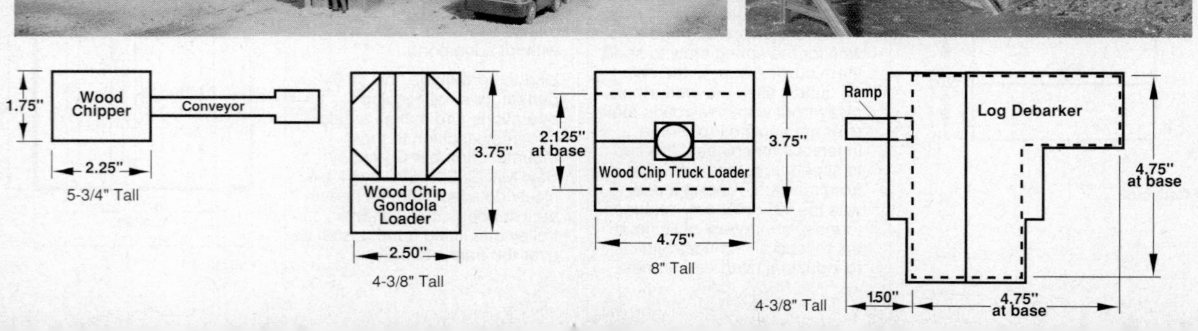

PLANING MILL

RETIRED MODEL

This kit is no longer in production and supplies are limited to stock on hand. A future producton run may be scheduled if there is enough demand. Please see your dealer or check out our Web site at www.walthers.com for current availability.

933-3059 49.98

The steady roar of machinery fills the air, already heavy with the smell of fresh-cut trees. Inside this busy part of the mill operations, rough-cut timber is being run through planers, emerging as standard sized lumber. Once this process is completed, the material is moved outside for additional drying, or readied for shipment by train or truck. Making everything from tiny shims to 2 x 4" studs to big wooden beams, the Planing Mill remains an integral part of the forest products industry. You'll find them working right alongside the saw mills, as free-standing industries or as part of other operations, such as furniture or building materials manufacturers that need a steady supply of dimensioned lumber.

This impressive model is a great addition to your logging operations. Suitable for any era, it includes a two-story Main Building with simulated board & batten construction, a modern Saw Dust Collector with blower and storage bin, plus an outdoor drying and loading area for the finished products. The completed model can be used by itself anywhere along your line. You can also combine it with the Mountain Lumber Co. Saw Mill (933-3058) for an on-site operation, or build it as part of a larger industrial complex alongside the Hardwood Furniture Company (933-3044).

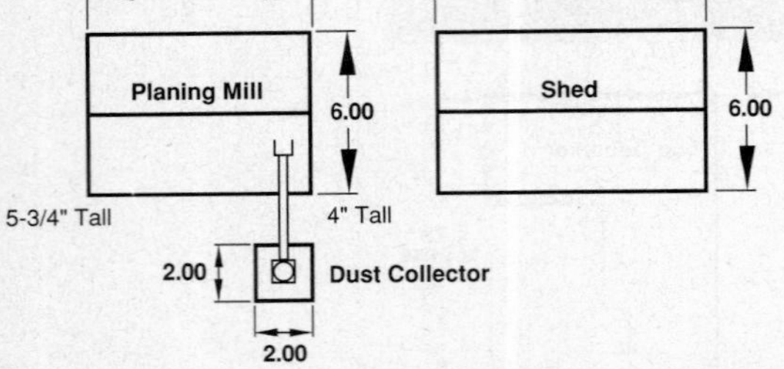

8.00
Planing Mill
6.00
5-3/4" Tall
4" Tall
2.00
Dust Collector
2.00

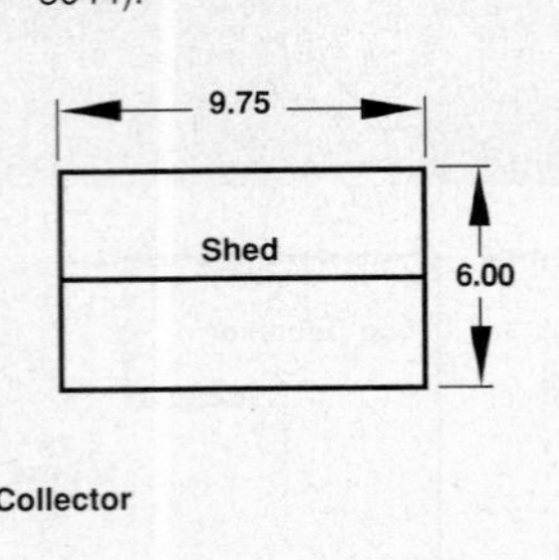

LOG UNLOADER

933-3146 19.98

Moving logs from cutting site to saw mill was once a difficult task. The work had to be done in winter, when trails froze enough so fresh-cut logs could be dragged to the nearest river. There, they were dumped in to wait for the spring thaw to send them downstream to the mill. As cutting sites moved further away from water, railroads took over the hauling job. Some ingenious machines appeared to speed up removal of logs from rail cars. Among these was the log unloader, designed to make short work of lifting an entire load all at once. Similar to industrial overhead cranes, these machines feature a moving trolley mechanism, but use giant arms to lift their loads. Log unloaders could be found at all sizes of operations, but were well suited to small mills where space was limited. They could also be constructed in virtually any location, so it was possible to build a saw mill without a log pond.

Like the prototype, this kit is perfect for small logging operations and makes a quick and easy addition to the Mountain Lumber Company Saw Mill (933-3058). The kit is nicely detailed, with the heavy-duty supports, positionable trolley and lifting arms. Install it over the tracks to service Walthers Log Flats (932-4000 Series Series) and the Logging Truck (933-4012) to add action and interest to your logging line.

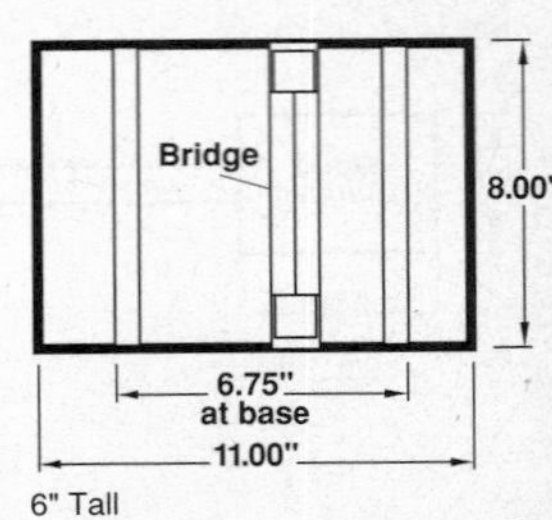

WALTHERS CORNERSTONE SERIES®

WALTON & SONS LUMBER COMPANY

933-3057 39.98
Among the most common trackside businesses are local lumber yards. A vital part of small towns, they can also be found in the heart of the biggest cities. Here, dimensioned lumber, hardware and building materials of every kind still arrives in box cars. Workers unload, sort and stack the lumber under cover to protect it from moisture. In damp or cold areas, these storage buildings are sometimes constructed over the tracks with a large opening at each end. Others are left open on one side to ease handling and removal of long heavy products. Up front is the office, usually a small structure where the coffee is always hot and you can get good advice for finishing your project.

Today, the small lumber yard is often part of a national chain of building suppliers, but much of the product is still shipped by train.

A great trackside business, lumber yards like this are still found in the every town. They are often owned and operated by the local grain elevator or oil dealer as a source of year 'round income. A perfect destination for wayfreights of every era, this model builds into a typical operation that fits almost any available space. The storage buildings are designed so you can construct one large, covered structure, or two free-standing, open sided buildings. And of course the main office is here too. Lots of colorful sign decals brighten up the place and illustrated, step-by-step instructions make construction easy.

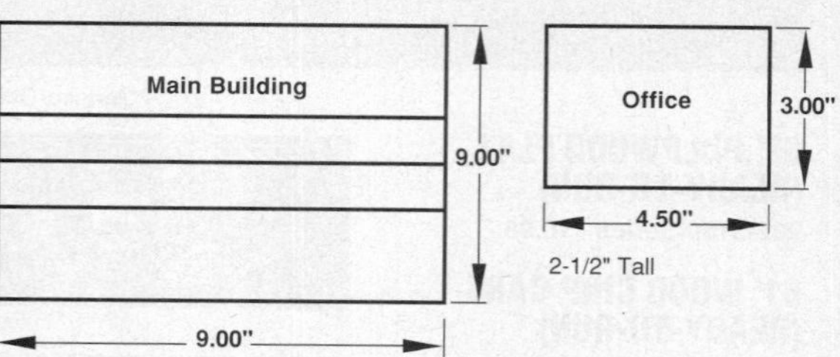

73' Center Beam Flat Car

45' Log Flat Car

Logging Truck

73' CENTER BEAM FLAT CAR (READY-TO-RUN)

932-4100 Series 12.98
Carry finished lumber from mill to market with these cars. Models feature the correct "opera window" or standard centerbeam to match their prototypes.

45' LOG FLAT CAR W/LOGS (READY-TO-RUN)

932-4000 Series 12.98
Transport timber safely across your line. Modern design features sturdy braces and a load of logs. Authentic roadnames are available with four different numbers.

LOGGING TRUCK

933-4012 19.98
Get logs from the cutting site to the trackside loading point with this rig. Resin kit assembles just like styrene and features an open cab.

LOG LOADER

This kit is no longer in production and supplies are limited to stock on hand. A future producton run may be scheduled if there is enough demand. Please see your dealer or check out our Web site at www.walthers.com for current availability.

933-3148 29.98
This modern machine makes quick work of loading trailers at the cutting site. Easy-to-build plastic kit is molded in colors.

SUPERIOR PAPER

RETIRED MODEL

This kit is no longer in production and supplies are limited to stock on hand. A future producton run may b scheduled if there is enoufh demand. Please see your dealer or check out our Web site at www.walthers.com for current availability.

933-3060 99.98
675 pounds. That's how much paper the average American will use this year. And most of it comes from facilities just like this. Starting with pulp logs and wood chips, wood fibers are gradually modified and formed into thousands of useful paper products. The process starts in the "kraft" (German for "strength") mill, where a chemical bath removes the natural glue that holds wood fibers together. The fibers are washed, whitened and mashed into fine pulp before they enter the paper making machinery next door. The watery mixture is then pressed into huge sheets, treated, dried and rolled, ready for use. These modern facilities are some of the most rail-intensive industries in operation, requiring specialized Wood Chip and Pulpwood cars for raw materials, armies of tank cars to bring in chemicals and slurries, plus box cars to haul finished products to market.

This kit is complete with the Kraft Mill, a modern steel structure with tall smokestacks and more. The Main Building is packed with details, including pulp vats, loading docks and more. Detailed instructions are provided for the entire complex, along with colorful industrial sign decals. Sized right to look right on any railroad, this modern industry is perfect for use with other kits from the Trees & Trains Series.

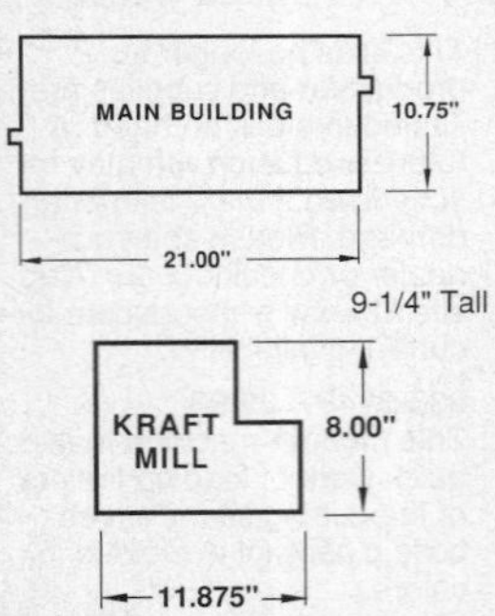

9-1/4" Tall

17" Tall

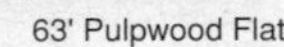

63' Pulpwood Flat

61' Woodchip Car

Pulpwood Truck

63' PULPWOOD FLAT (READY-TO-RUN)

932-3150 Series 10.98

61' WOOD CHIP CARS (READY-TO-RUN)

932-4050 Series 10.98

PULPWOOD TRUCK

933-4014 19.98

PAPER MILL CREW

590-1010051 pkg(10) 19.99

ROTARY DUMPER

933-3145 39.98

Time is money at today's industries. That's why many operations, like unloading rail cars, are now mechanized. Many processes require tons of materials which can only be delivered in sufficient quantity by train. To move the cars through as quickly as possible, Rotary Dumpers make short work of emptying hoppers and purpose-built gondolas. As the name implies, these massive machines actually clamp the car in place, then rotate 180°. As the car tilts, gravity takes over, spilling the load into a dump pit below. The mechanism returns to the upright position and the process begins again. Meanwhile, the coal, wood chips, stone or other materials are moved by conveyors and stockpiled where they're needed. You'll find these machines in use at paper plants handling huge quantities of wood chips, at power plants unloading unit coal trains and at steel works, unloading limestone, coal and other commodities.

With highly detailed plastic parts, this unique model is sure to be an eye-catching addition to any heavy industry. Detailed parts simulate the massive steel construction and include positionable turning machinery. (Mechanically minded builders will find this kit makes a great starting point for an animated model!) A safety fence, decal signs and other details are included. Perfect for use alongside the Cornerstone Series® Superior Paper Mill, the Coke Ovens from "The Works" or the Northern Light & Power Powerhouse, featured elsewhere in this section.

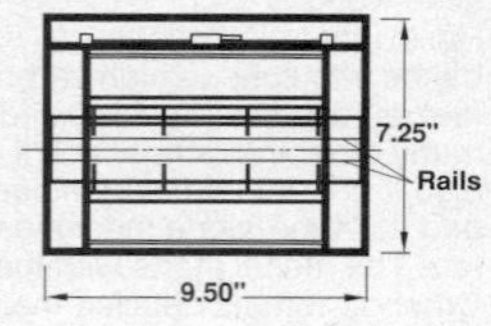

2-3/4" Deep 3" Tall

ROLLING MILL

933-3052 49.98
16-1/4 x 10 x 10"
41.2 x 25 x 25 cm
Glowing with an inner fire of 2200°F, a fresh ingot thunders onto the tables and into the rollers. Inside massive mill buildings, ingots are transformed into the beams, pipes, tubes, sheets and hundreds of other shapes that are the raw materials of other industries. This big building is ideal for housing specialized mill operations, but its steel construction and size make it a natural for any modern industry. With a modular design, plus optional cut-out end doors and walls, you can easily customize the building. The baseplate includes simulated rails so you can roll cars inside. The big roof invites plenty of detail, so we've included both a full-length monitor-type as well as individual round vents, used on the prototypes to release the tremendous heat that builds up inside.

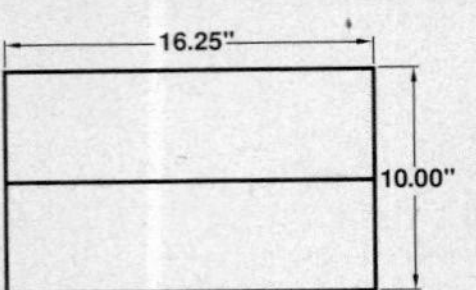

STEEL MILL DAY CREW

590-1010067 pkg(10) 19.99
This set includes a variety of hand-painted figures in realistic poses, dressed in safety gear and ready to go to work.

LOADING CREW

590-1010066 pkg(6) 13.99
Dressed in protective gear and ready for a long day on the job, these hand-painted figures put life into any part of your new Rolling Mill scene.

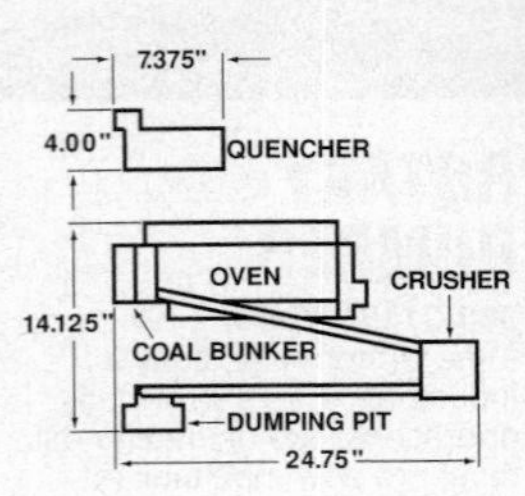

COKE OVENS & QUENCHER

This kit is no longer in production and supplies are limited to stock on hand. A future producton run may be scheduled if there is enough demand. Please see your dealer or check out our Web site at www.walthers.com for current availability.

933-3053 99.98
Area for all Buildings: 28 x 19 x 14"
70 x 47.5 x 35 cm
A waterfall of fire flashes orange against the night sky, silhouetting clouds of steam. Running nonstop to feed the blast furnaces, Coke Ovens are an essential part of most steel works.
Here, unit trains of coal are baked into coke, a high carbon fuel used in steel making and many other industries. You'll also find coke ovens at mines, and as stand-alone industries too! The model starts with the Crusher, with its detailed metal siding, rugged I-beam supports, safety cage ladders and other details, including a simulated dump pit to receive loads of coal. The Storage Bunker also features steel construction and an enclosed conveyor. The heart of the operation is the battery of coke ovens, with detailed doors, walkways, large concrete smokestack, governor house and many other parts. For the final step, car loads of coke can be run through the Quench Tower with its many authentic details.

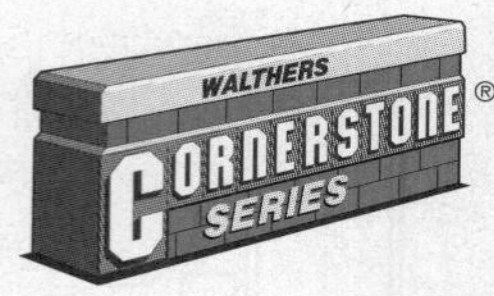

BLAST FURNACE WITH CAST HOUSE

This kit is no longer in production and supplies are limited to stock on hand. A future producton run may be scheduled if there is enough demand. Please see your dealer or check out our Web site at www.walthers.com for current availability.

933-3054 129.98
28 x 14 x 21-1/2"
70 x 35 x 53.8 cm

Say the word "steel" to even the most casual observer and they picture these towering giants. Looming hundreds of feet into the skyline, their maze of pipes and equipment stands in stark contrast to the lines of newer buildings. Running nonstop, no other part of The Works generates as much rail traffic. Hoppers bring up load after load of iron ore or taconite, coke and limestone. Hot metal cars carry the molten steel to the converters, while slag cars take their loads to the dump. At last, here's a model that captures the power of the prototype and still fits the average layout. This complete kit includes the furnace, stoves, dust collectors and cleaning system, piping, cast house, hearth, skip hoist, high line supports -- over 300 parts in all. Yet, it's designed for easy construction and includes complete instructions.

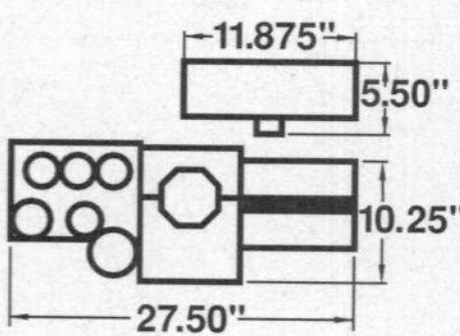

BLAST FURNACE CREW

590-1010064 pkg(6) **13.99**

Dressed in protective gear known as "silvers," that allows them to work in the incredible heat of the cast house.

ELECTRIC FURNACE

RETIRED MODEL

This kit is no longer in production and supplies are limited to stock on hand. A future producton run may be scheduled if there is enough demand. Please see your dealer or check out our Web site at www.walthers.com for current availability.

933-3056 69.98
12-5/8 x 11-3/4 x 12"
31.5 x 29.4 x 30 cm

The cost-effective electric furnace is the backbone of a modernized steel works. They're also the heart of mini-mills, built in various parts of the US, that create new steel from scrap. As impressive as the real thing, our kit includes the furnace with electrodes and other interior details. Craneways accommodate the Heavy-Duty Overhead Crane (933-3150, sold separately) and spreader bars and monstrous "J" hooks are included to convert the crane for steel service. With its modular construction and optional cut-out end doors, it's a snap to create a custom building.

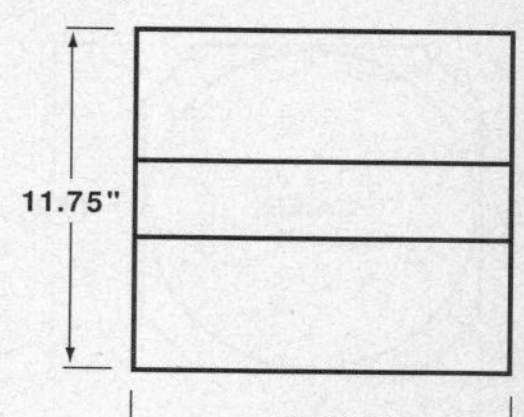

ELECTRIC FURNACE CREW

590-1010065 pkg(6) **13.99**

STEEL WATER TANK

933-3043 24.98
Perfect for serving your biggest and best steam power, this kit offers all the versatility of the prototype. It requires a small amount of layout space and comes with two standpipes which you can install wherever you want. Detailed parts are molded in color, while complete instructions make construction fast and fun. For the finishing touch, decal signs are provided.

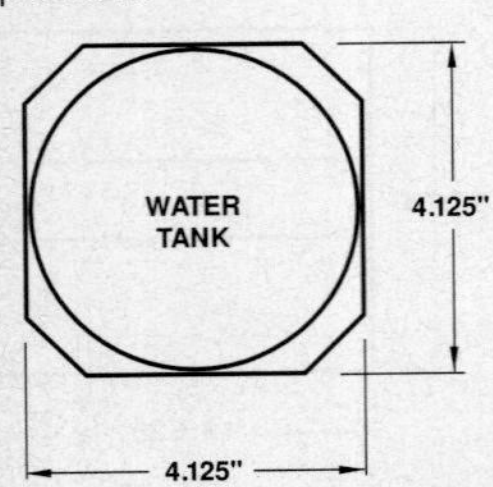

7" Tall

CONCRETE COALING TOWER

933-3042 39.98
Whether alive with action or quiet and abandoned, this model can be the focal point of your engine service facilities. It's complete with covered pit, machinery house, lifting equipment and chutes to serve two tracks. As the prototypes go, this model represents a medium sized tower, making it ideal for layouts large or small. The plastic parts feature realistic concrete and steel detailing and are molded in realistic colors. A complete set of instructions and decal signs round out the kit.

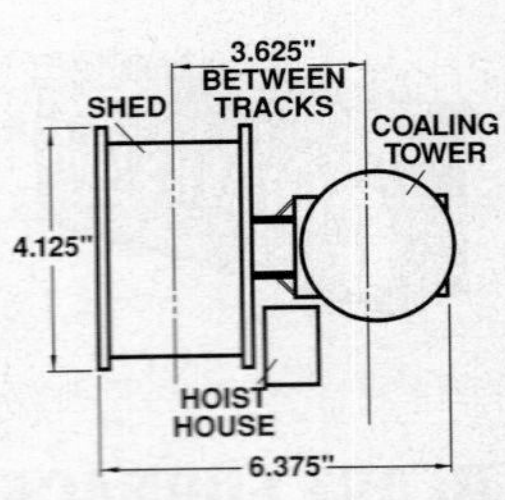

11" Tall

INTERLOCKING TOWER

933-3071 19.98
A great starting point for a trackside scene, this model is complete with an outside stairway, as well as simulated rods for the control system. It has the look and feel of prototypes built by roads large and small. You can easily use several along your line, giving your operations the "family" styling so common to railroad buildings. Plastic parts are molded in color and detailed to simulate the look of wood construction. A set of decal signs and complete instructions are also provided.

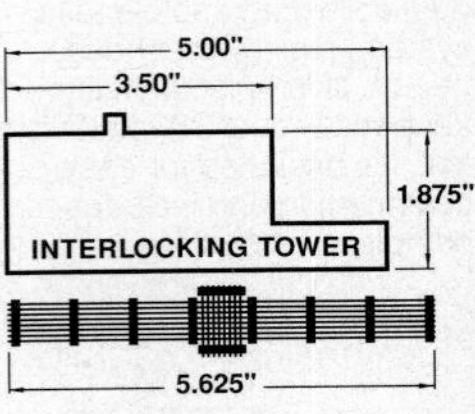

4" Tall

AMTRAK STATION

933-3038 19.98
SPECIAL VALUE PRICING
The depot was a magical place. At train time, everything stopped as local folks went down to watch the varnish come in. The old depot may be gone, but the magic is still there! Today, shiny Amtrak streamliners glide by, and in many areas, daily commuter trains make up much of the trackside action. These modern trains require modern facilities and bringing your layout up-to-date is easy with this kit. It's based on a design first used in the late 1970s, which was adapted for use in several Amtrak served communities. This detailed model captures the clean lines of the original in a size that's right for the contemporary layout. Full-color Amtrak station signs add the finishing touch.

GLACIER GRAVEL CO.

933-3062 39.98
9-3/8 x 11 x 10-1/4"
23.4 x 27.5 x 25.6cm
Sand and gravel for new roads, sewers, subdivisions and parking lots. Ballast for new railroad right-of-ways. Rip-rap to hold back raging waters. Limestone and dolomite for the steel mills. Reclaimed slag for construction materials.

Those are just some of many crushed stone products moved quickly and economically from quarry to customer by train. This detailed building is typical of the trackside crushers where the final product is loaded into hoppers and trucks. The kit features a detailed main building with concrete and steel construction. Separate conveyors allow more flexibility for various layout installations and there's also a loader grating for more realistic detail.

CONVEYORS

933-3149 pkg(3) 8.98
Extend the reach of your new rock crusher! These parts match the conveyors included in #933-3062, so you can customize your installation to fit your layout. Shown in large photo.

CLARKESVILLE DEPOT

933-3063 24.98
9-3/4 x 3-1/4 x 3-1/4"
24.7 x 8.2 x 8.2cm
One of the most important buildings in a small town was the depot. As the first building visitors saw, it was a source of great pride to local residents. Inside, it served as a freight storage room and office for the agent, who did everything from wash windows to deliver telegrams. This charming structure is the perfect choice for every town on your line. All the classic features are here, from the bay window to the platform. And for more variety, the eaves can be built one of two ways, plus two styles of eave brackets are included.

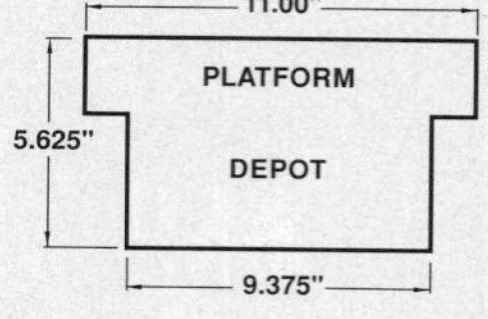

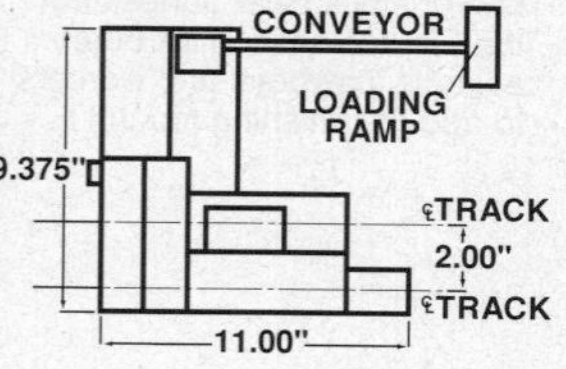

Amtrak Station 932-3038

CHAMPION PACKING COMPANY

933-3048 39.98
Measures 40.9 x 17.8 x 13.2cm
Based on a prototype at Waterloo, Iowa, it's perfect for adding action and operation to your railroad. The multi-story building has an elevated cattle chute, attached office, power plant, roof-top details, colorful decals – everything you need, including four dressed beef for the loading dock.

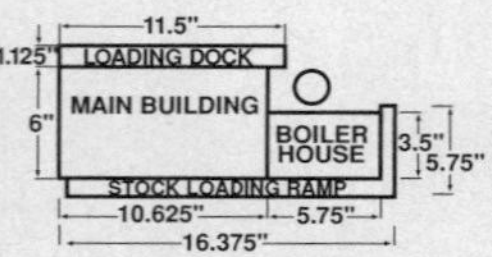

5-5/16" Tall

BEEF CATTLE SET

933-3143 pkg(16) **4.98**
Each set features 16 Hereford cattle in realistic poses, that look great in your new stock pen or stock cars. (Check out the Figures section for other animals, cowboys and workers to add the finishing touch!)

STOCKYARD

933-3047 24.98
Measures 9 x 7"
22.5 x 17.5 cm.

With its modular design, this kit builds everything from the small town loading pen to the big city stockyard. Includes detailed parts for two pens with loading chutes, which align with 40' stock cars, plus a lean-to for shelter or feeding.

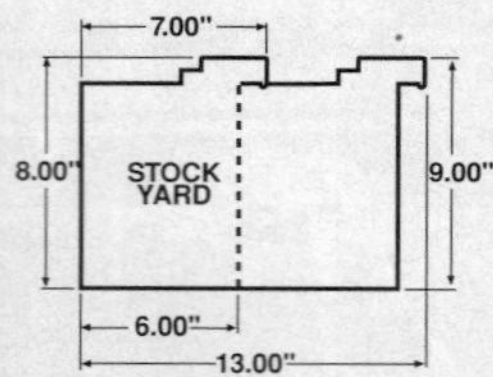

ICE HOUSE AND ICING PLATFORM

933-3049 30.98
Measures 4-3/4 x 11-/14 x 5-1/2" 12 x 28,5 x 14cm

This complete kit includes a detailed Ice House, based on a prototype at Antigo, Wisconsin, plus a modular Icing Platform, from a Pacific Fruit Express design. Lots of add-on details, including an optional platform roof (used in warm areas to shade ice and slow melting), roof vents and 24 ice blocks are included.

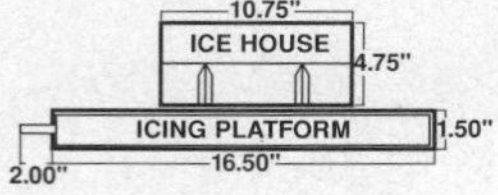

5-1/2" Tall

REEFER SIX-PACKS 59.98

These colorful sets are a great way to boost reefer traffic on your line and increase operations around your new Ice House & Platform. Each set includes six ready-to-run cars painted in the same schemes, each with its own number.

932-950 BREX-Chicago, Burlington & Quincy (All Steel)
932-951 St. Louis Refrigerator Car Co-SLRX (All Steel)
932-952 Western Fruit Express-Great Northern (Wood Sides & Ends)
932-953 Merchant's Despatch Transportation-New York Central (All-Steel)
932-954 Fruit Growers Express (Wood Sides & Ends)
932-955 NWX-CNW (Wood Sides & Ends)

ROUNDHOUSE

933-3041 39.98
Adding one to your engine terminal is a snap with this American style kit. All of the prototype details are there, including the traditional two-level roof, with separate clerestory windows and smokejacks, plus 23 large windows for natural lighting. It holds engines up to 13" long, typical of the power found on most lines. Stalls are spaced on 10° angle, requiring less approach trackage. With its modular design, the basic 3-stall kit can be enlarged up to a full-circle, to meet the needs of your railroad. To finish the scene, install the 90' Motorized Turntable to serve your new Roundhouse.

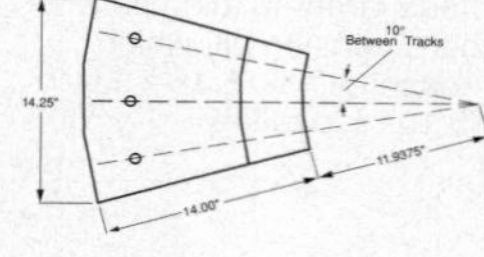

90' MOTORIZED TURNTABLE

933-3135 49.98
Pit diameter: 13-3/16" 33 cm, Bridge holds locos up to 12-3/8" 30.9 cm.

In the steam-era, every loco had to be turned for its next run. Today, diesels are still turned for safe operation, or to facilitate repairs. Found at engine terminals of every size and some shops, the turntable remains an essential part of today's railroading.

Adding a working turntable to your engine terminal or shop has never been easier. Carefully designed to fit most layouts, this model has a one-piece pit for drop-in mounting. A low-speed motor and worm gear drive insure smooth and realistic operation. And complete hook-up instructions cover wiring, adding track and more. The detailed bridge includes the operator's cab, handrails and a traditional arch (used to supply electrical power to the drive motors on the prototypes). When completed, it's ideal for use with the Three-Stall Roundhouse, 933-3041.

WORK TRAIN CARS 49.98

You'll often find work cars stored near the roundhouse. Modeling them is easy with these new sets in six new paint and lettering schemes. Each has different equipment, but painted in matching schemes.

SET #1 INCLUDES:

Two Bunk Cars, One Kitchen Car, One Engineering Car, One 40' Tank Car, One 40' Single . Sheathed Box Car

932-911 Maintenance-Of-Way (gray)
932-912 Santa Fe (silver)
932-913 Union Pacific (green)
932-914 Burlington Northern (Mineral Red)

SET 2 INCLUDES:

One 25 Ton Crane, One Crane Tender, One 50' Flat Car, One 50' Gondola, One 40' Steel Box Car and One Combination Box Car/ Caboose

932-932 Santa Fe (silver)
932-933 Union Pacific (green)

2-STALL ENGINE HOUSE & ACCESSORIES

933-3007 28.98
This authentic brick engine house is modeled after facilities constructed in the steam era and still used today. Inside, inspections and light repairs are completed on all types of locos and cars. This kit is detailed with moveable doors, oil drums, separate windows and a pillar crane. Parts are included to extend one track through the building. Engines or cars up to 11-5/8" long can be stored inside.

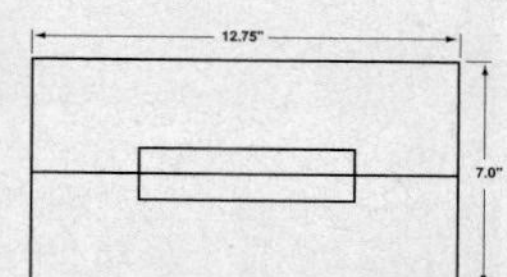

BACKSHOP & ACCESSORIES

933-3039 36.98
11-5/8 x 8-13/16 x 8-3/4"
29 x 22 x 21.8cm

Here, in grimy buildings that stretched for acres, every need of the iron horse was taken care of. From new wheels to a complete rebuilding, they had the tools and the know-how to keep 'em running.

Now, a Backshop can be an essential part of your railroad with this new kit. Big enough to look right, small enough to fit your steam- or diesel-era layout, this HO Scale Backshop is packed with features. Detailed brick work, 28 separate windows, interior trusses, roll-up doors, inspection pit openings in the floor, everything right down to the decal signs, it's all here.

The kit builds into a three-stall Backshop (great for modeling a running repair shop where light repairs were done) and its modular design makes it easy to create a bigger building by combining kits.

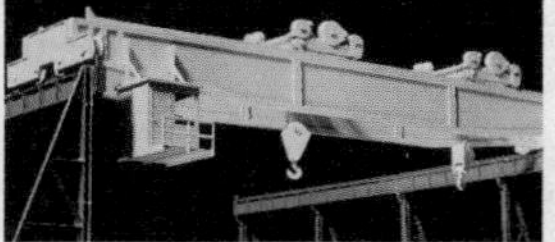

HEAVY DUTY CRANE

933-3150 12.98
11 x 2-3/8 x 2-5/16"
27.3 x 5.7 x 6.5cm

The steel cables are pulled tight. The foreman signals his approval. The winches start turning. And nearly half a million pounds of locomotive rise toward the roof of the backshop.

These heavy duty cranes, with a lifting capacity of 250 tons, are essential to the work of every engine shop. And this kit is the finishing touch for the interior of your Backshop (933-3039). All of the features of the real thing, the heavy steel construction, the motor and winch mechanisms, the operator's cab, the big lifting hooks, even the decal signs are included in this easy-to-build kit.

With a little scratchbuilding, you can install this Heavy Duty Crane in other industries, like a steel mill, ship builder, or anywhere heavy lifting is done on your layout.

TRANSFER TABLE & ACCESSORIES

RETIRED MODEL

This kit is no longer in production and supplies are limited to stock on hand. A future producton run may be scheduled if there is enough demand. Please see your dealer or check out our Web site at www.walthers.com for current availability.

933-3131 49.98
A cold, biting wind is blowing out of the north. Normally, the big shop walls offer some protection, but not today. The little electric heater won't cut it, so you blow on your hands and start the electric motors. The table shudders, sending sharp vibrations right through the bottom of your boots. Ease off a little, the drive is stiff and cold. If the switch crew shows up with those crippled cars soon, you might be able to get inside for a quick cup of coffee.

Before now, adding a Transfer Table to your HO Shops meant long hours of scratchbuilding and electrical work. But this kit changes that! Everything you need is inside: electric motor, drive, detailed table, operators' cab, detailed pit walls, and a modular baseplate so you can build a longer pit to serve your car or loco shops. Pit measures 11-15/16 x 11-15/10" Lip to Lip.

TRANSFER TABLE EXTENSION PIT

This kit is no longer in production and supplies are limited to stock on hand. A future producton run may b scheduled if there is enoufh demand. Please see your dealer or check out our Web site at www.walthers.com for current availability.

933-3132 19.98
For a bigger shop complex, your Transfer Table can be made larger in minutes with this extension pit, which measures 11-15/16 x 11-15/10" Lip to Lip.

CAR SHOP & ACCESORIES

933-3040 36.98
11-5/8 x 8-13/16 x 7-5/8"
29 x 22 x 19cm.

Without the Car Shop, a railroad just doesn't run. Until now, adding one to your HO railroad meant lots of work. But this new kit changes that.

Big enough to look right, small enough to fit steam- or diesel-era layouts, this HO Scale Car Shop is packed with features. Detailed brick work, authentic saw-tooth style roof with skylights, separate windows, roll-up doors, openings in the floor for rail, everything right down to the decal signs, is included. A basic kit builds a three-stall shop. But the design is modular, so you can build one as big as you need, by combining kits.

ALLIED RAIL REBUILDERS & ACCESSORIES

933-3016 27.98
Measures 10 x 10 x 6"
25 x 25 x 15cm.

Performing everything from painting to complete rebuilds, Allied Rail Rebuilders captures the realism in a size that works on most layouts. Lots of details are included, such as an EMD 567 prime mover, separate roof vents, interior trusses, doors and windows. It can also be used for other types of heavy industry.

OVERHEAD TRAVELING CRANE & ACCESSORIES

933-3102 12.98
Overhead traveling cranes are used where heavy materials are moved. This kit represents a crane with a capacity of 25 tons, used at industries, scrapyards, steel mills and railroad shops. The bridge and covered motor housing can be positioned.

An operator's cab with "glass," hoist hooks and a nonworking electromagnet are included.

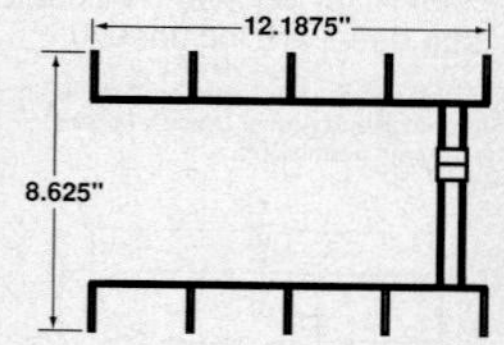

EMD 567 PRIME MOVER

933-3119 3.98
From 1938 to 1966, the 567 was used in all types of EMD locos, from switchers to high-speed passenger power. Many are being rebuilt and still going strong today. This styrene kit is easy to build, and makes a great detail out on the shop floor or as a flat car load.

FARMERS COOPERATIVE RURAL GRAIN ELEVATOR

933-3036 27.98
Measures 8-7/8 x 7-1/4 x 10" 22 x 18.1 x 4cm.
Shed Measures 7 x 4-1/2" 17.5 x 11.2cm.

The rural elevator was more than just a trackside industry. It was the center of many rural communities. And in some places it WAS the community. Handling grain from local farms and selling it to distant markets, these older buildings are still active today.

With its colorful signs and period styling, this HO Scale elevator is perfect for your layout and your favorite era, from the 1880s to present day. The kit includes the main elevator, plus a storage building and a scalehouse, all with realistic "wood" walls. Separate doors and windows add to the realism, along with colorful decals for several grain companies.

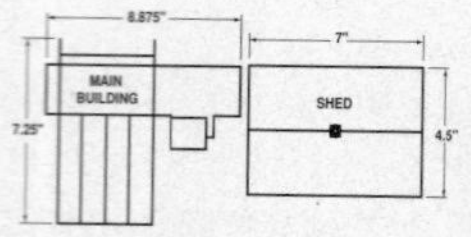

ADM® GRAIN ELEVATOR & ACCESSORIES

933-3022 32.98
Measures 13-1/2 x 9-1/2 x 13-1/2" 33.7 x 23.7 x 33.7cm

This detailed kit includes an elevator, eight storage silos, dust bins, head house and sheds for rail and trucks. Full-color ADM logos and billboard sign decal are included.

"ADM" and the ADM logo are registered trademarks of Archer Daniels Midland, used with permission.

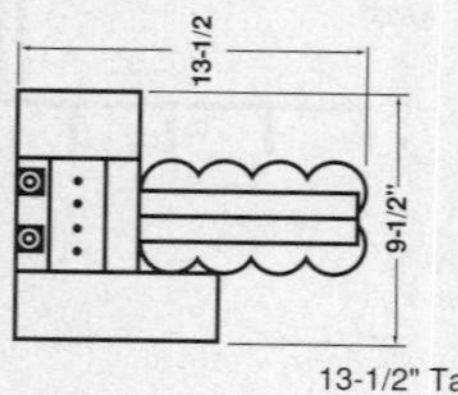

13-1/2" Tall

PROPANE TANKS

933-3129 pkg(2) **10.98**
A great detail alongside your line, many elevators sell propane or offer grain drying services to their customers, and install their own propane tanks to insure a ready supply of fuel.

Similar tanks are used to store anhydrous ammonia, used as a fertilizer. This kit includes two complete tanks with propane decals. Decals for anhydrous are sold separately in set 933-3112.

GRAIN HANDLING EQUIPMENT

Drying and storing grain are important functions of a grain elevator complex. With these kits, you can model the complete operation!

GRAIN BIN
933-3123 14.98

GRAIN CONVEYOR
933-3124 14.98

GRAIN DRYER
933-3128 9.98

RED WING FLOUR MILL

933-3026 29.98
8 x 11 x 10-3/8"
20 x 27.5 x 26.5cm

Flour mills have changed dramatically since the water-powered mills of the 1800s. Today's mills produce enormous quantities of flour and other milled grains. This modern concrete mill features truck and rail loading facilities, blowers, vents, separate doors and windows, and full-color decal signs.

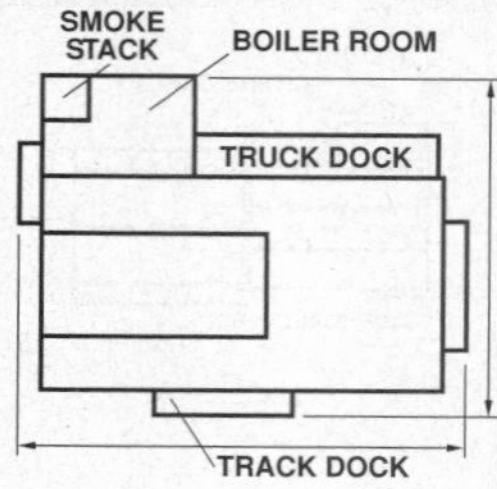

COAL FLOOD LOADER

933-3051 29.98
4 x 6 x 11"
10 x 15 x 27.5cm.

Coal is the life-blood of 1990s railroading. Unit trains feed the hungry boilers of power plants and industries. To keep those trains moving, the Coal Floodloader has become one of the most important buildings at any modern mine.

Your mining operations can be updated in a few hours with this kit. It captures all the detail of the real thing, in a space that fits most layouts. Detailed hillside conveyor, metal siding, stairways, I-beams and more are included.

BETHGON®/COAL PORTER® COAL LOADS

One-piece casting, realistic color and texture, drop-in mounting.

933-1038 2-Pack **6.98**
933-1039 6-Pack **12.98**

VULCAN MANUFACTURING COMPANY

933-3045 30.98
Main Building: 9 x 9-3/8 x 8"
22.8 x 23.8 x 20.3cm

When steel became a common building material early in the 20th century, the trackside steel fabricator or ironworks was born. These plants turn raw steel shapes into precut parts for new structures. Others specialize in producing components like fencing, fire escapes, stairways and windows. Rail service is a must for bringing in raw materials and hauling out finished pieces and scrap.

Here's the perfect starting point for a larger operation, or use it right out of the box to model a small fabricator. The kit includes the main building, smokestack, plus a separate stairway, windows and doors. Lifting and carrying steel is no problem, as a canopy and trusses are included to model the overhead crane. (These parts are designed for use with the bridge in The Overhead Traveling Crane kit #933-3102, available separately.)

932-5901

Limited Quantity Available

53' THRALL GONDOLAS 10.98 EA

The most versatile cars on any railroad. Models have smooth or corrugated sides, like their prototypes. Great for moving steel shapes or scrap at Vulcan Manufacturing, or serving any industry that uses gons.

932-5901 UP–Corrugated Sides
932-5903 SP–Smooth Sides
932-5949 Undecorated–Corrugated Sides

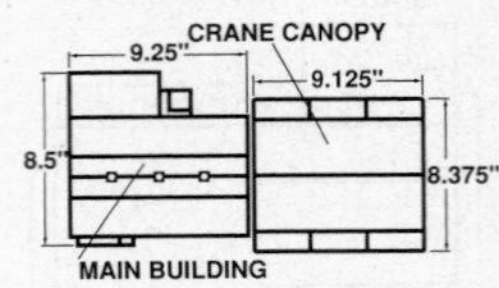

NEW RIVER MINING COMPANY & ACCESSORIES

933-3017 36.98
Main Building:
12-1/2 x 9 x 9-3/8"
31.2 x 22.5 x 23.2cm

Loading unit trains is a big job that requires heavy facilities like this. The prototype was built in the early 1950s and is typical of loading facilities found in all parts of the country. A conveyor brings coal from the mine to the tipple, where it's crushed and screened. The finished model fits most layouts and comes with building, truck loading facility, enclosed conveyors, plus separate windows and doors.

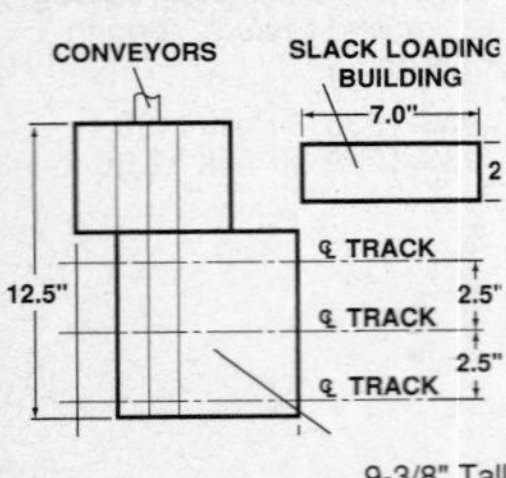

NORTHERN LIGHT & POWER POWERHOUSE & ACCESSORIES

933-3021 32.98
Measures: 12-3/4 x 6-1/2 x 7"
31.8 x 16.2 x 17.5cm

Generate new revenue for your steam- or diesel-era railroad with Northern Light & Power. This detailed model is similar to power stations operated by utility companies, private industries and institutions, as well as streetcar or interurban lines. The easy-to-build kit features a brick main building, large smokestack, coal dump pit, separate doors, roof and windows, clear window "glass" and complete instructions. Decal signs and a special billboard are also included.

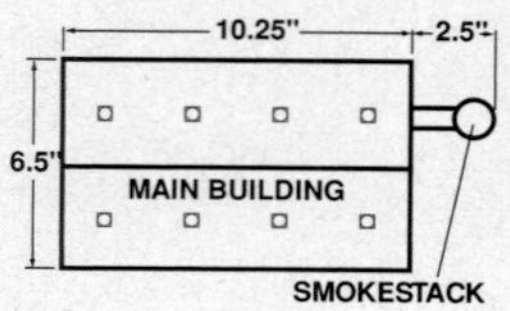

7" Tall

NORTHERN LIGHT & POWER INTERIOR

933-3130 9.98
Superdetail your powerhouse with this interior kit, complete with boiler walls, generators and turbines. (Also shown: Overhead Traveling Crane, 933-3102, sold separately.)

CHAIN-LINK FENCE

933-3125 9.98
Kit comes with styrene parts for poles, gates and other details, plus a separate piece of chain-link material.

HIGH-VOLTAGE TRANSMISSION TOWERS

933-3121 14.98
These tall towers will add realism to your railroad's skyline. The set includes four easy-to-build towers with molded-on eyelets for stringing "wire."

NORTHERN LIGHT & POWER SUBSTATION & ACCESSORIES

933-3025 24.98
Baseplate measures:
8.5 x 12.5" 21.2 x 31.2 cm.

This model's a must for an authentic electrical operation. Installations like the Northern Light & Power Substation are used to lower the current of high voltage before routing it to residential and commercial customers. This kit includes all the details of the prototype, from the transformers and steel framework to the chain-link fencing around the facility. Warning signs and billboard decal for the Basic Billboards are included.

TRANSFORMER

933-3126 9.98
High-tonnage equipment like this transformer is just the ticket for a flat car load, or a detail around the Northern Light & Power plant or substation.

ELECTRIC UTILITY POLE SET

933-3101 9.98
This electric pole set includes 24 easy-to-assemble power poles, transformers, insulators, nonilluminated street lights and realistic "wire."

MEDUSA CEMENT COMPANY & ACCESSORIES

933-3019 32.98
Measures: 9 x 7 x 11"
22.5 x 17.5 x 27.5cm

Cement distribution plants are vital to the construction industry, providing the bulk cement used to make concrete. This kit makes a great addition to an industrial district, with eight tall storage silos, conveyor tower and rail car unloading shed. Other details include separate roll-up doors for truck loading, plus separate roof-top piping, railing and dust collectors. (To create a larger structure, use the Cornerstone Series Add-On Silos (933-3023).)

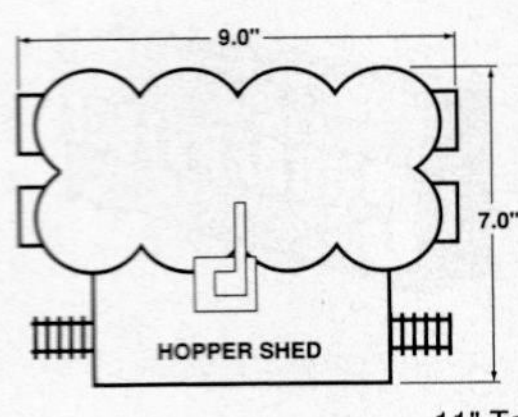

O.L. KING & SONS COAL YARD & ACCESSORIES

933-3015 21.98
The kit comes complete with a brick office, fencing, shed, elevated trestle and decals.

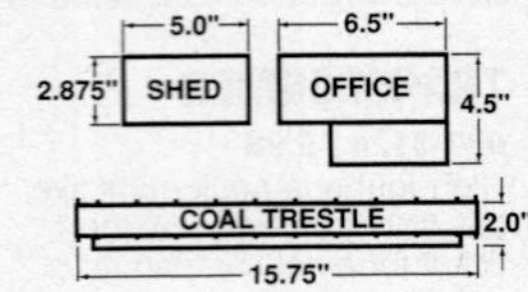

SUNRISE FEED MILL

933-3061 24.98
4 x 15-1/8 x 7-3/4"
10 x 37.8 x 19.3cm
Back when America moved by horses instead of horsepower, the local feed mill was an important trackside business in towns of every size. Here, all types of grains were ground for animal feed, then bagged for easier handling and storage. They're still going strong in areas where livestock and dairy production requires a constant supply of feed. Others serve suburban customers with pet foods, bird food, lawn and garden supplies and more. This detailed model is complete with authentic "wooden" drop siding, a large dust collector for the roof, rail and truck/wagon unloading docks and colorful decals.

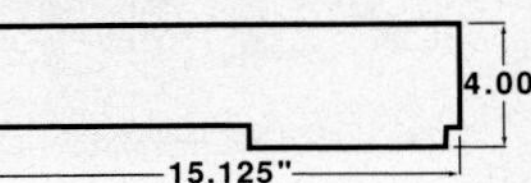

HARDWOOD FURNITURE COMPANY

933-3044 39.98
Measures: 11-7/8 x 10-5/8 x 8-7/8" 23.5 x 29.5 x 22.5cm
The box car doors slide open. Ramps clang into place from the loading dock. Strong backs bend to their task as the first crates are carried out of the warehouse and on to the car.

Tucked into the cramped quarters of the industrial district, the Hardwood Furniture Company is the kind of industry that every layout needs. Big enough to look right, small enough to fit. And packed with realism.

Check out the authentic architectural trim molded on each wall, or the over 50 separate windows! There's a covered loading dock for box cars, and roll-up doors for trucks. Up on the roof, a water tank, elevator house and chimney are included to detail this important area. Complete instructions and colorful signs round out the kit. Plus, modelers who desire a larger building will find it's easy to expand with some minor kitbashing.

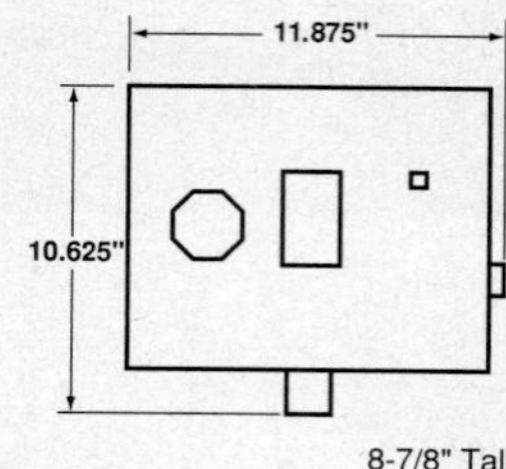

GOLDEN VALLEY CANNING COMPANY & ACCESSORIES

933-3018 26.98
Railroads play a big part in putting food on the tables of Americans each and every day. Canned and frozen foods move in bulk from regional operations like the Golden Valley Canning Company to cities around the country, where they are transported to local stores for sale. Canneries can be found in small towns and large cities, producing everything from fruits and vegetables to meats, jellies and sauces. This kit comes with everything needed to create an authentic steam- or diesel-era cannery, including a main canning building, boiler house, smokestack, steam pipes, roof-top water tank and separate windows and doors.

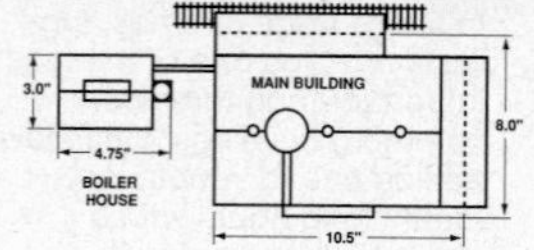

PALLETS

590-17104 11.99
Stack boxes of canned and frozen goods produced by your cannery on these sturdy pallets. This set includes 60 pallets, molded in a realistic wood color. From Preiser.

WATER STREET FREIGHT TERMINAL & ACCESSORIES

933-3009 26.98
Freight terminals were essential to railroads, handling less-than-carload lot (lcl) shipments. Loads arrived in box cars or reefers and were transferred to trucks for local delivery. Each railroad serving a community had its own terminal, usually near the main passenger station or classification yard. This detailed structure features a large office building, freight house with loading docks to service freight cars and trucks, plus an assortment of crates, barrels and pallets.

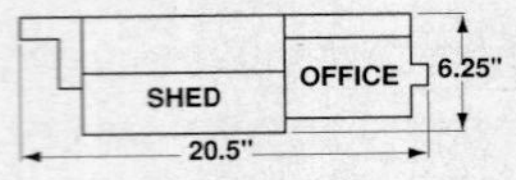

4-3/4" Tall

FREIGHT LOAD SET WITH FORKLIFT

405-9458 9.99
Load up on details for your freight house with this kit, which includes pallet jacks, a forklift, oil drums, pallets, boxes and carts. From Kibri.

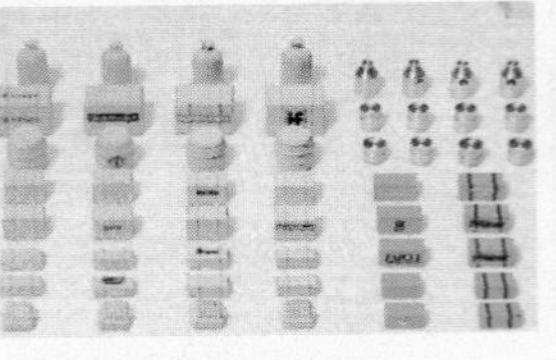

CARGO SET

590-17100 11.99
Keep your freight terminal full with this assortment of boxes, barrels, sacks, milk cans, labels and more. From Preiser.

OIL DRUM/FIGURE SET

933-3100 10.98

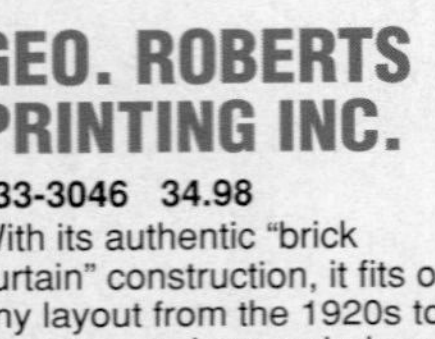

GEO. ROBERTS PRINTING INC.

933-3046 34.98
With its authentic "brick curtain" construction, it fits on any layout from the 1920s to the present. Large windows, a hallmark of this architectural style, provide plenty of natural illumination and made this type of building a popular choice for all types of industries. To save space in the cramped industrial district, a covered loading dock is built into the rear of the building and will add plenty of operation to your railroading. For the finishing touch, authentic "extras" like the roof-top water tank, 3-story fire escape and colorful decal signs are included.

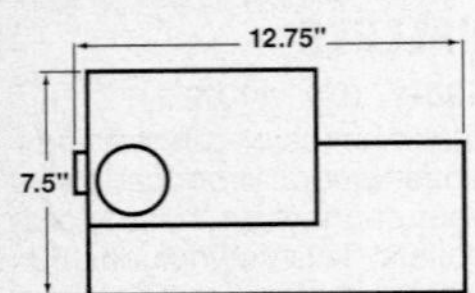

9" Tall

BAILEY SAVINGS & LOAN

933-3031 24.98
In towns large or small, the bank remains one of the most important (and the most common) buildings. Until now, adding one to your layout meant long hours with a difficult kit, or weeks of scratchbuilding.

Bailey Savings and Loan features authentic Beaux Arts (Fine Arts) styling which used ornamental columns, arches and cut stone to project an image of power and strength. (Many libraries and city halls were constructed in this style as well.) Ideal for any business district from the 1900s to the present day, buildings like this were common downtown, and in the suburbs.

This kit features highly detailed plastic walls which look just like cut stone and a the front includes the columns. Bank and library decals are also included.

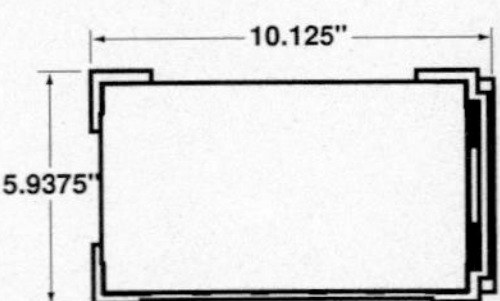

NORTH ISLAND REFINERY & ACCESSORIES

933-3013 36.98
Railroads are vital to refinery operations, from the switchers that move cars to the mainline freights that hustle finished products to market. The North Island Refinery is carefully designed to capture the realism of the prototype, in a size that works on most layouts. The superdetailed kit includes a main fractioning tower, furnace, piping group and heat exchangers, vacuum pipe still and decal warning signs.

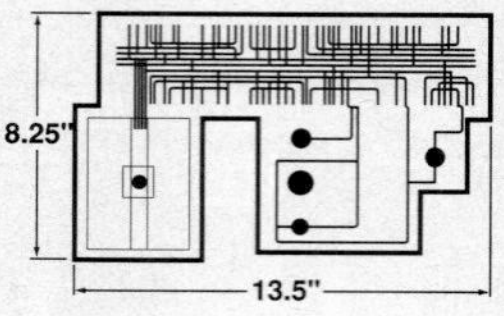

INTERSTATE FUEL & OIL & ACCESSORIES

933-3006 25.98
Bulk oil distributors have been important for every railroad. At home in cities and towns, dealerships like this distribute fuel oil, gasoline and other products locally. This kit includes horizontal and vertical storage tanks, above-ground piping, pump house with header stand to unload tank cars, truck loading rack and corrugated metal office. Like the prototypes, the various pieces can be arranged to fit available space. A gas pump, oil drums and other details are also provided.

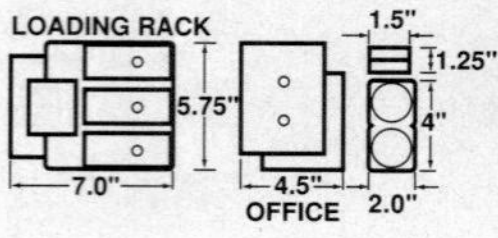

REFINERY PIPING KIT

933-3114 9.98
Includes overhead supports, angles and other fixtures. Modular design allows for many possible configurations to fit your refinery complex.

OIL TANK DECALS

933-3117 4.98
Ten full-color oil company logos, for use with oil storage tanks #3115 and #3120.

OIL LOADING PLATFORM

933-3104 11.98
This detailed kit simulates a typical tank car loading platform which serves two tracks. Complete with piping, nozzles, platforms and stairway, safety sign decals, nonworking light fixtures and more. Illustration shows two kits combined to build a longer platform.

OIL STORAGE TANKS

Used to store oil and other petroleum products, these tanks are a common sight at oil refineries and terminals. Kits include one-piece styrene tank bodies, spiral access ladders, safety railing, outlet valves and decal warning signs.

575,000 GALLON HORIZONTAL OIL STORAGE TANK

933-3120 19.98
(7-1/2" diameter by 4" tall)

500,000 GALLON VERTICAL OIL STORAGE TANK

933-3115 19.98
(6" diameter by 6-1/4" tall)

LPG STORAGE TANK DECAL SETS EA 4.98

933-3112 Anhydrous Ammonia
933-3111 LPG Gas
Additional lettering to customize Propane Tanks #933-3129.

PIPING KIT

933-3105 5.98
Here's an easy way to model supply lines used to bring oil and other materials to and from the platforms. The kit includes a variety of angles, elbows, tees, straight pipes, valves and more.

WELCOME TO MAIN STREET USA

Every town has a Main Street USA. And everyone has memories of the Main Street in his or her hometown. It might be the ice cream parlor where you had your first triple scoop cone, or the dime store you rode your bike to on Saturdays for baseball cards. Now you can recapture the excitement and nostalgia of Main Street on your layout with the "Main Street USA" collection from the Cornerstone Series.

Each kit is easy to build, with styrene parts molded in colors, including a roof and numerous details. All of the architectural features such as trim, windows and doors, are molded in place to speed construction. Each kit also includes full-color decals with a wide range of business names so you can build a custom structure, or model several versions of the same kit.

NEIGHBORHOOD FOOD MART

933-3033 12.98
This double store-front can be home to one large or two small businesses. The kit fits city or small town scenes and includes various sheds and a base plate.

Dimensions: 5 x 8-1/4 x 4" 12.5 x 20.6 x 10cm

GEMINI BUILDING

933-3001 11.98
It's a modeling twin bill - two duplicate storefronts make up the marvelous Gemini Building. Complete with chimney, the kit will look great in any steam- or diesel-era city scene.

Dimensions: 4-1/4 x 3-5/8 x 3-3/8" 10.6 x 9 x 8.2cm

UNITED TRUCKING TRANSFER TERMINAL

933-3005 11.98
Fill up those small spaces with this attractive freight terminal. The kit has roll-up doors molded into the sidewalls to serve box cars or trucks.

Dimensions: 2-5/8 x 6 x 3-3/8" 6.5 x 15 x 8.2cm

BILL'S GLASS SHOP

933-3002 11.98
This three-story brick building has plenty of space for a growing HO Scale business. The upper floors can be rented out for additional offices or apartments.

Dimensions: 3 x 4 x 4-3/8" 7.5 x 10 x 16.7cm

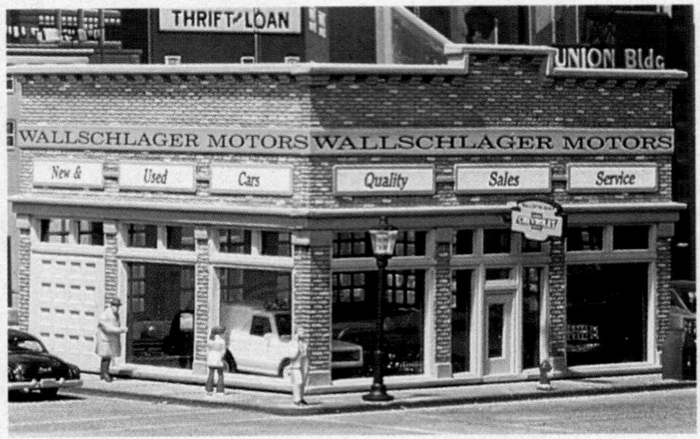

WALLSCHLAGER MOTORS

933-3004 11.98
You can almost hear the salesman hawking those new cars down at Wallschlager Motors. You'll love the large windows of this building, which are great for showing off interior details.

Dimensions: 5-1/4 x 5 x 3-1/2" 13.1 x 12.5 x 8.7cm

ADAM'S RIBS RESTAURANT

933-3034 11.98
From the turn of the century to the present, buildings like this have been an integral part of many neighborhoods. The kit is ideal for any busy street corner and includes a distinctive corner tower/entry way.

Dimensions: 5-1/2 x 3 x 6" 13.7 x 7.5 x 15cm

STREET SYSTEMS

Modeling realistic streets has always been a tough job, requiring messy plaster, or endless cutting and fitting of styrene pieces. Until now. Walthers street system makes quick and easy work of modeling everything from busy downtowns, to tree-lined residential areas, to narrow alleyways in the grimy industrial district

The secret is the detailed plastic parts, that install just like sectional track. Glue the sections together. Add sidewalks, curbs and other details. Weather for more realism (if desired) and install on your layout. 3139 and 3138 include approximately 25" (63cm) of roadway. Parts for one complete intersection, sidewalks, curbs, driveway and alley entrances, plus complete instructions are included.

WESTERN AVENUE FIRE STATION

933-3037 14.98
A superdetailer's delight! This kit is similar to stations throughout the country that were built in the early 1900s and later upgraded for use with modern equipment. Includes a special set of fire station decals.

Dimensions: 4-1/4 x 6-3/4 x 5-3/4"
10.6 x 16.8 x 14.3cm

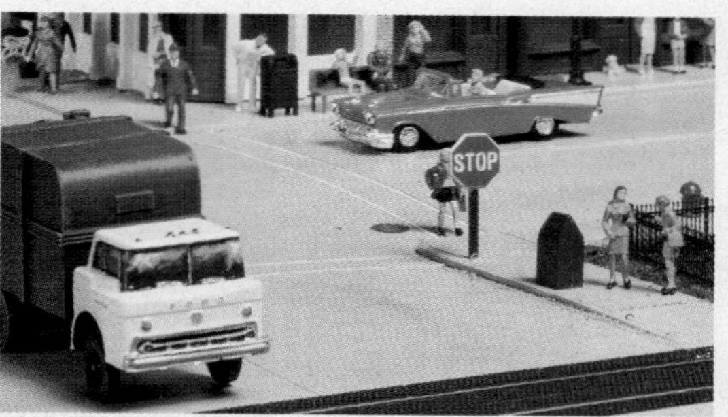

CONCRETE STREETS

933-3138 11.98
For a modern steam-era highway, or a modern stretch of road handling today's traffic. Plastic parts have realistic texture and center crown for ultimate realism.

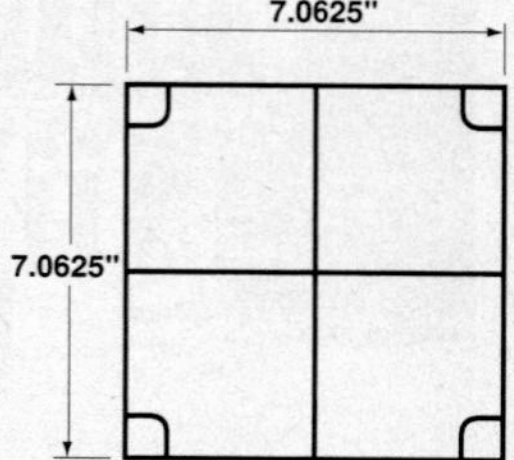

BRICK STREETS

933-3139 11.98
An authentic detail for steam-era street scenes of any kind, or the older parts of a modern city. Each piece captures the look of brick-by-brick construction to model authentic streets on your steam- or diesel-era layout.

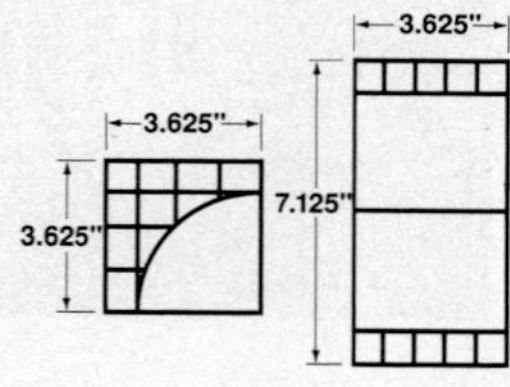

WHITE TOWER RESTAURANT

933-3030 14.98
Can we take your order for this classic hamburger stand? The original White Tower Restaurants were built in the 1930s, springing up from Boston to Los Angeles.

Dimensions: 4-5/8 x 3 x 2-7/8" 11.5 x 7.5 x 7cm

GRADE CROSSING

933-3137 4.98
Local motorists will thank you for installing these kits at every grade crossing. The detailed parts replicate the rubber mat style of crossing, now in use on railroads large and small. A neat detail for modern street scenes, ideal for use with Code 83 track.

STREET TRACK INSERT SET

933-3140 11.98
In the narrow confines of most industrial areas, railroads were often forced to lay tracks in the city streets. Adding this authentic detail to your HO Scale operations is a snap with this new kit. Sized to fit Code 83 track, the kit includes straight sections, plus pieces for 15, 18 and 22" radius curves, and parts to fit #4 and 18" radius turnouts. Simulated concrete detail matches Walthers Street System kits 933-3138 (Concrete) or 933-3139 (Brick), both sold separately.

STRAIGHT STREET SECTIONS EA 9.98

Expand the basic street kits with these add-on sets of straight pieces. Each pack includes 8 sections of straight streets only, plus 1 set of curbs.

933-3155 Concrete
933-3156 Brick

MAINSTREET USA

MERCHANT'S ROW SERIES

Model a bustling business district in a big city, suburb or small town while you save valuable layout space, time and money. These affordably priced kits feature front and rear walls which look like several different buildings standing side-by-side, but are actually one-piece parts. They're ideal for steam- or diesel-era scenes. Architectural details are molded in place to speed assembly. Add your personal touch with paint from your dealer, then complete construction with the variety of decal signs in each kit. (For the finishing touch, check out Walthers Street System, also listed in this section.)

MERCHANT'S ROW I

933-3028 29.98
11 x 5 x 4"
27.5 x 12.5 x 10cm

Five different stores in one complete structure.

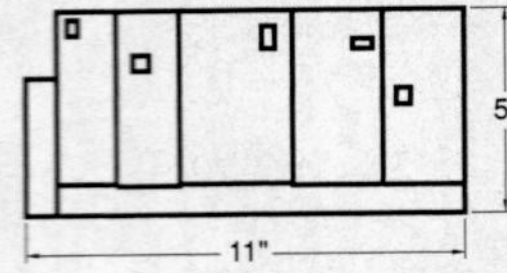

4" Tall

MERCHANT'S ROW II

933-3029 29.98
10 x 5"
4 x 12.5cm

Three storefronts, highlighted by an elaborate corner building with turret.

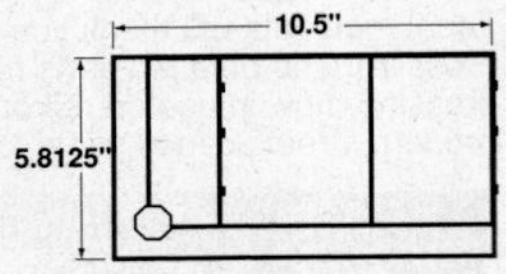

MERCHANT'S ROW III

933-3064 19.98
6-1/4 x 7-3/4 x 4-3/4"
15.9 x 19.7 x 12cm

Based on a real building in eastern Ohio, with three small businesses under one roof.

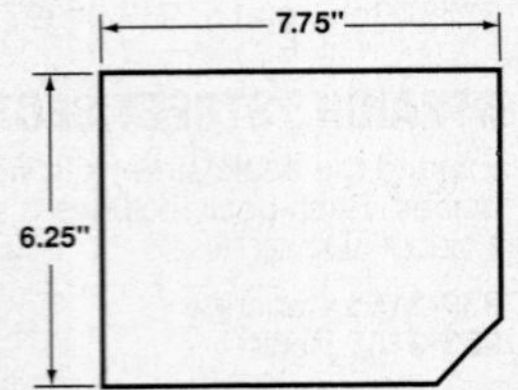

4-3/4" Tall

INTERSTATE FUEL & OIL GAS STATION

933-3035 11.98
Deliver fuel from Interstate Fuel & Oil to this gas station, bearing the same name as the Cornerstone Series® bulk oil distributor. The model comes with a covered service island with pumps, highway sign, service bays and air pump.

Dimensions: 9-1/4 x 7-3/4 x 1-3/4" 23.1 x 19.3 x 4.3cm

DON'S SHOE STORE

933-3000 11.98
Here's a building with a lot of sole! Graceful curved windows and a recessed doorway make Don's Shoe Store a favorite for downtown districts.

Dimensions: 2-1/2 x 3-1/2 x 3-3/8" 6.2 x 8.7 x 8.2cm

TRAINLINE®

by WALTHERS

EASY SNAP-TOGETHER ACCESSORIES

These great-looking kits are a snap to build! Each features snap-together construction, and plastic parts molded in colors, so no painting is needed.

WHISTLE STOP STATION

931-800 9.98

It's "All Aboard" at the Whistle Stop Station, where passengers and freight are ready for boarding. Includes crates and stickers with station names.

Preproduction models shown assembled; colors and some details may vary.

SAWMILL W/ACCESSORIES

931-801 24.98

You can almost smell the sawdust coming from the Trainline® Sawmill! This deluxe kit includes a Working Dump Car, Logs, Lumber Carrier and Sawdust Burner. For added fun, the dump car empties its load of logs with the pull of a lever!

DOUBLE-TRACK TRUSS BRIDGE & ACCESSORIES

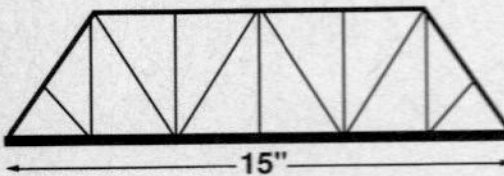

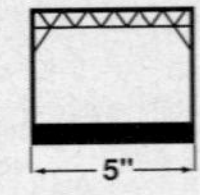

933-3012 21.98
The truss-type bridge is among the most common railroad styles. Early designs date to the 1820s, when wood was standard. As trains became heavier, cast-iron and wood were used. The development of the Bessemer process made steel bridges possible. This kit is typical of steel bridges found throughout North America. Trusses, chords and bridge shoes, plus safety sign and graffiti decals are included.

WING WALLS

439-560 4.49
For realistic detail, you can add these Wing Walls, which simulate the retaining walls used with abutments on many bridges. The kit includes two one-piece resin wings, each measuring 3-3/8" high and 3-3/4" wide at the base.

BRIDGE ABUTMENT

439-558 6.98
This abutment makes bridge installation a snap. Matching the width of the bridge, the one-piece casting is 3-3/8" high, allowing enough clearance for trains to be run underneath. One kit is required to do each end of the bridge.

BRIDGE PIER

439-559 11.98
To create a longer bridge, additional bridge kits can be combined to produce a longer span, which can be supported with this Bridge Pier. The one-piece casting has a height of 3-3/8" (matching the height of the Bridge Abutment and Wings), a base width of 5-3/8" and a thickness of approximately 1-1/8" at the base. (Not pictured).

BRIDGE TRACK

948-899 14.98
Roll trains across your new truss bridge with the Code 83 Bridge Track. Designed especially for this bridge, the single track section features nickel-silver rails, bridge ties and inside guard rails with Code 70 rail. Length: 19-11/16". (#933-3012 requires two sections for double track.)

MOTORIZED BASCULE BRIDGE

933-3070 79.98
You can always count on plenty of action wherever railway meets waterway. Some of the most impressive structures on any railroad are its bridges. Especially lift bridges that gracefully rise out of the way. These engineering marvels support tremendous weight, but allow safe passage of trains and water traffic. For railroads, lift bridges are the preferred design, as they can be built with less machinery and no center pivot point in the water below.
Now, you can add that same level of intense action to your operations, with this working Bascule Bridge. This single-track design is used by many railroads and the model is sure to be a highlight along your line. Big enough to look right, small enough to fit most layouts, it's equally at home supporting big steam power or modern double-stacks.

The kit is complete with detailed plastic parts that capture all of the rivets and cross-sections of the steel work. On the business end, a huge "concrete" counterweight simulates the massive assembly that lifts the prototype. Rounding out the details are the Bridge Tender's shanty high in the beams, and a trackside Interlocking Tower to keep things moving safely. Hidden inside is the reliable low-speed motor that raises and lowers your bridge just like the real thing.

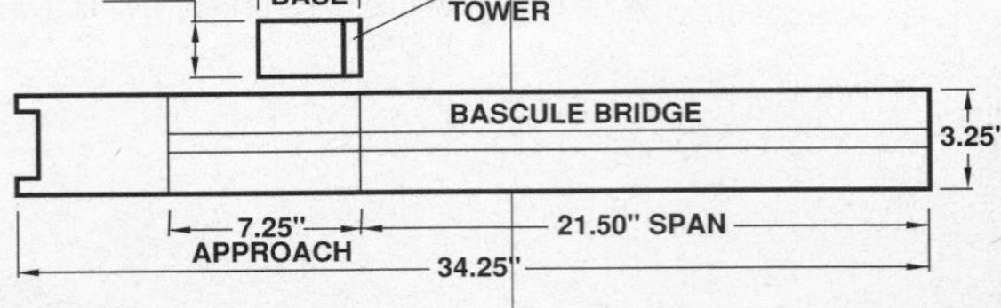

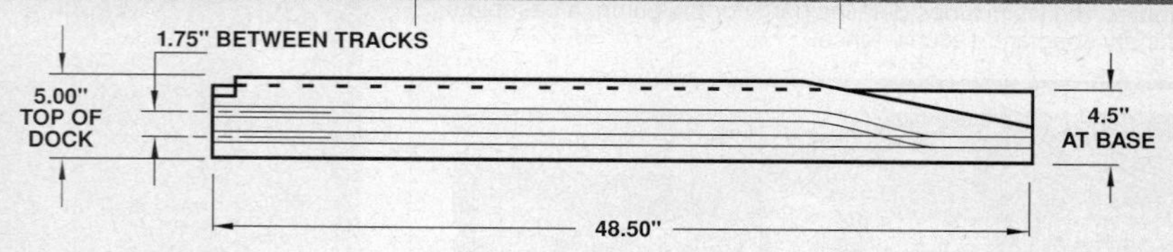

WINNER OF THE MODEL RAILROADER READER'S CHOICE AWARD-1997

ORE DOCK

933-3065 79.95

Getting iron ore from the mines to the furnaces has always been a huge job. As the furnaces grew, so too did their appetites, requiring loading facilities that were up to the task. Many steel companies and railroads erected these big loading docks at Great Lakes ports to keep the iron ore (and later taconite) moving down to the steel centers. Often stretching for hundreds of feet, these engineering masterpieces were first made of wood and later of concrete and steel. Through a series of pockets lining the sides, iron ore could be loaded by gravity into the waiting holds of the big ore boats.

Still in use today, ore docks are home to some of the most fascinating railroading in the world. And, with this superb kit, it's easy to make it part of your model railroad as well.

Carefully engineered to look right without being overwhelming, the basic kit builds into a two-track, single-sided dock. But, the modular design offers complete flexibility without the need for cutting and kitbashing. Just combine kits as desired to make a wider, longer, customized dock to fit your space.

Ideal for installation along a wall or as a scenic view block, the model features loads of detailed parts, along with elevated approaches, all molded in color. The chutes are positionable and can be built up or down. Complete instructions and decal signs are also included.

FALLER

IMPORTED FROM GERMANY BY WALTHERS

These easy-to-build kits consist of prototypically colored plastic parts, printed signs and details where applicable, with fully illustrated, step-by-step instructions.

WALKING BEAM OIL PUMP

272-994 24.99 *BACK IN PRODUCTION*
7-1/8 x 3-13/16 x 4-1/2" 17.8 x 9.5 x 11.3cm

A WALTHERS US EXCLUSIVE

These unique pumps can be seen wherever oil is moving underground. Also called "horse head pumps" because the slow up and down motion resembles a walking horse, this model is a must for any railroad that runs where petroleum is produced. The basic kit builds into a detailed static model, but you can add the slow speed electric motor (272-629, sold separately), to turn this into a working model that moves just like a real one. Easily Americanized in minutes, the kit includes detailed parts for the pump, a baseplate, machinery shed and security fence.

"BONN" PASSENGER STATION

272-113 109.95
27-1/2 x 6-1/4" 70 x 16cm
This classic station is typical of those found in large cities around the world and is based on the prototype at Bonn, Germany. To complete the scene, add several Passenger Station Canopy kits (272-180), patterned after the actual Bonn train shed.

"FRIEDRICHSHOHE" PASSENGER STATION W/COVERED PLATFORM & BUILT-ON FREIGHT DEPOT

272-110 52.99
16 x 6" 40.7 x 15.6cm
This depot is typical of structures built to serve larger towns. The building features a passenger waiting room, a freight station and living quarters for the agent.

"PICKPOCKET" JAIL - LIMITED-RUN FOR 1999-2000

272-999 179.99 *NEW*
12 x 10 x 7-13/16" 30 x 25 x 19.5cm
Maintain law and order along your railroad with this impressive model. And if you're looking for something out of the ordinary to expand operations, this is it! (Many of these facilities have their have own powerplants, so add a powerhouse and a siding to deliver car loads of coal inside.)

The perfect starting point for a busy mini-scene, it's sized to fit layouts or modules without overwhelming other buildings. You'll get the five-story prison building, a high wall with an entrance gate and two wall-mounted guard towers. For more fun, a special electronics package activates a loud warning horn and lights on the towers if the barbed wire is touched!

Special custom-painted figure sets are included to model guards and prisoners. A second set of prisoners walks in a circle in the exercise yard, driven by a hidden motor. Additional prisoners and basketball equipment are provided to model a game of hoops.

Each kit includes a special numbered certificate to indicate its limited-edition status.

BIESTCHTAL BRIDGE

272-535 74.99
43-13/16 x 3-13/16 x 8-13/16" 109.5 x 9.5 x 22cm
This impressive steel span, an authentic replica of the Biestchtal bridge, is perfect for carrying your line across a river or other natural obstacle. Prototype is located on the south side of the Lotschberg tunnel. Use with any type of track.

NEUSTADT "WEINSTRASSE" STATION

272-111 149.99
31-11/16 x 11 x 10-3/4" 79.2 x 27.5 x 26.8cm
Built at the turn-of-the-century this impressive station is still serving the city of Neustadt. This special edition model for 1997 includes a variety of interior details, opening doors, decorative trim and many other features. Its many windows make it a natural for lighting (sold separately). For more "special effects," the clock tower can be fitted with the real Quartz Clock (272-639, sold separately). The model is designed to be built in stages for ease of construction, then assembled into one large structure.

FALLER

IMPORTED FROM GERMANY BY WALTHERS

SERVICE AREA SET – SPECIAL VALUE PACKAGE

Limited Quantity Available
272-70 56.99
A great value for the modeler looking to set up a complete locomotive servicing area. This set combines six popular kits in a single, specially priced package. The kits included are: Back Shop (#272-159); Water Tower (#272-143); Overhead Crane (#272-164); Small Coaling Station (#272-131); Inspection Pit (#272-136); and Water Spout (#272-137). Each easy-to-assemble kit consists of appropriately colored plastic parts.

GATE KEEPER'S LODGE

272-169 29.99
4-3/4 x 6 x 4-3/8"
12 x 15 x 11cm
In the days of steam, these small homes were built for crossing watchmen. An upstairs apartment provided living quarters, with a workshop and storage on the ground floor.

3-STALL ROUNDHOUSE - LONG

272-177 71.99
16 x 13-1/2 x 5"
40 x 34 x 12.5cm
Store big power in style in this building, which can be used with kits 175 or 176 (sold separately) to create a bigger facility. Holds locos up to 9-3/16" 23cm.

KONIGSBACH STATION

272-109 99.99
24-3/16 x 8-13/16 x 8-13/16" 60.5 x 22 x 22cm
This timeless design will look great in a busy suburb or city. It's turn-of-the-century styling fits perfectly in the steam-era, or add appropriate details to model an older structure in a modern setting.

LUTZEN STATION

272-103 41.99 ***NEW***
16-11/64 x 5-3/8 x 6" 40.4 x 13.4 x 15cm
Any town would consider itself lucky to have this handsome depot! Its ornate half-timber construction and elaborate construction are typical of buildings used on branchlines and some narrow gauge routes. Includes a small freight house too.

GROCER'S SHOP & HOUSE

272-278 27.99 ***NEW***
8 x 6 x 4-9/32" 20 x 15 x 10.7cm
This handsome building combines a two-story home and an attached store that looks great in any modern business area.

"MITTELSTADT" PASSENGER STATION

272-115 69.99
17-1/2 x 6-1/4" 44.6 x 16cm
This nicely sized passenger depot is ideal for the larger town or city. It can easily be adapted to a layout or module. Just add a Faller platform and other accessories for a superdetailed scene!

TWO STALL ENGINE SHED

272-165 44.99
14-1/4 x 7-7/8 x 5-1/4" 35.5 x 19.5 x 13cm
Make sure your motive power is well cared for between runs with this handsome shed. Engines up to 10-13/16" (27cm) long can be stored in either stall. Detailed plastic parts simulate wood and stone construction. Ideal for a shortline or industrial road.

ALPINE INN "ZUM ALMDUDLER"

272-273 31.99
7-3/8 x 4-3/8 x 4" 18.5 x 11 x 9.8cm
Provide a bit of ethnic flavor on your layout with this stylish guest house. Ideal for use as a bed and breakfast or a fancy restaurant, the kit includes typical construction details found on Swiss structures in the Alps, and features a Village Pub on the ground floor.

QUARTZ REAL TIME CLOCK

272-639 54.99
Diameter: 7-13/32" 18.5cm
An actual, battery-powered clock that fits many Faller models and can be adapted to other kits. Features gothic numerals and ornate brass hands.

DUMPSTERS

272-354 pkg(8) **9.99** ***NEW***
A great detail for your modern factories, restaurants, railroad shops - any building that throws things away or recycles! Set of eight assorted dumpsters, ideal for a variety of materials. Fits most model dumpster trucks (sold separately).

FALLER

IMPORTED FROM GERMANY
BY WALTHERS

LOADING CRANE

272-129 11.99
1 x 3-1/4" 2.6 x 8.3cm
Nonworking model.

STORAGE SHED W/LOADING CRANE

272-152 22.99
Handle oversize shipments of parts and freight in any industrial complex with this warehouse. The trackside platform is covered and has plenty of space to speed loading and unloading. For larger and heavy items, there's a small gantry crane supported by "steel" beams.

PASSENGER STATION CANOPY, BONN

272-180 39.99
11-7/8 x 7" 30.2 x 17.8cm

PLATFORM LIGHTING FOR #180

272-183 14.99

GARDEN CHAIRS W/TABLES

272-571 pkg(45) **6.99**
Set includes 36 chairs and nine tables, perfect for detailing picnic areas, beer gardens or restaurants.

OVERHEAD SIGNAL TOWER NEUSTADT

272-124 44.99
11-3/32 x 6-3/4 x 8-3/8" 28 x 16.8 x 21cm
Keep trains moving safely along your mainline with this stylish signal tower. The kit includes interior details for the tower and provides clearance of 3-3/16" (80cm) without tracks installed. Model is based on a prototype at Neustadt/Weinstrasse.

FREIGHT HOUSE

272-153 44.99 ***NEW***
12 x 7-13/64 x 5-5/8" 30 x 18 x 14cm
This old building will look great at trackside in almost any era. Build it as new structure during the days of steam. Or weather and detail it to look run down and unused in the modern era. Features loading ramps on each side, with positionable side doors, plus various roof details.

SNACK BAR "ZUR MUHLE"

272-210 29.99
7 x 4-5/8 x 2-3/8"
17.5 x 11.5 x 6cm
Take a quick break anytime at the Mill Snackbar. Waterwheel can be powered with motor 272-629 (sold separately).

"LENGMOOS" PASSENGER STATION

272-100 49.99
12 x 6-7/8" 30.6 x 17.5cm
Bring rail service to a small town on your layout with this station! The Alpine style station includes a covered platform and freight shed.

Limited Quantity Available

SERVICE STATION (BOSCH)

272-349 59.99
6-1/2 x 4" 16 x 10cm,
4-1/2 x 2-3/4" 11 x 6.8cm
Car not running right? Maybe it's time for a tune-up. Servicing any make or model is easy with this complete kit, that includes a main office, workshop & garage with various details. Less figures and vehicles.

BREITENBACH STATION

272-94 24.99
7-13/32 x 3-13/64 x 2-5/8" 18.5 x 8 x 6.5cm
Provide first class service to any small town with this combination depot handling freight and passengers.

ARCADE

272-567 pkg(4) **13.99**
Each 7-3/64" 17.6cm Long x 2-5/32" 5.4cm Tall
Elevate your right-of-way with this set of detailed arcade walls. Each features realistic brick detail, suitable for any era.

COVERED FOOTBRIDGE

272-198 24.99
Overall: 11 x 7-13/16 x 5-3/16" 27.3 x 19.5 x 13.8cm
Clearance: 3-3/4" 9.3 cm
Cross tracks or busy streets safely with this bridge. Two-level open stairways lead to an enclosed walkway that can span up to four tracks. Plenty of room underneath for steam-era models or modern double-stacks, bi-level cars or electrified equipment.

ONE FAMILY HOUSE W/HALF-TIMBER FRAMING

272-257 20.99
4-5/8 x 3-13/16 x 4-5/8"
11.5 x 9.5 x 11.5cm
The perfect starter home for the new family, or a great retirement cottage for grandma and grandpa. This small home fits city or country settings and features authentic half-timber framing for added realism.

FREIGHT DEPOT

272-154 24.99
8-1/4 x 3-7/16" 21 x 8.8cm

FALLER

IMPORTED FROM GERMANY BY WALTHERS

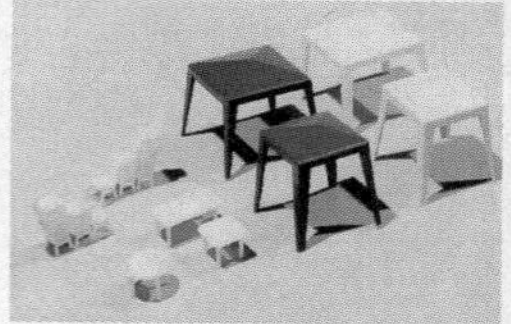

PARTY TENTS & FURNITURE

272-358 5.99 ***NEW***
Set of four outdoor tents, plus tables and chairs. Perfect for detailing any outdoor get-together.

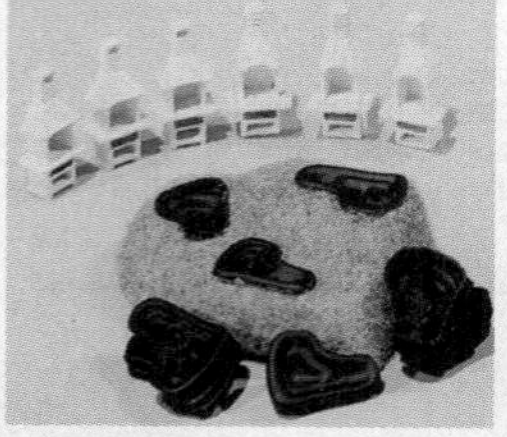

GARDEN GRILLS & PONDS

272-359 6.99 ***NEW***
A modern touch for today's backyards. Includes six barbecue grills and seven plastic pond forms.

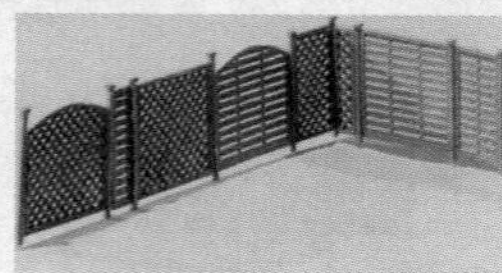

GARDEN FENCES

272-361 6.99 ***NEW***
Add privacy to your model yards with this set, featuring 62 sections of assorted styles of modern fencing.

PLANT STONES

272-362 pkg(80) **4.99** ***NEW***
A neat detail for any sloping area. Perfect for hillside plantings in the suburbs, or alongside a busy freeway.

STEINHEIM HALF-TIMBERED HOUSE

272-410 54.99
8-3/8 x 4-3/8 x 8-5/8" 21 x 11 x 21.5cm
Old-World craftsmanship and attention to detail make this majestic structure a must for any village. Ground-level archways, covered staircase, flowering window boxes and a centered steeple add character and color.

GARDEN CENTER

272-357 49.99 ***NEW***
11-13/64 x 7-13/32 x 7-13/64" 28 x 18.5 x 9.5cm
Model communities look their best all season long because of this modern business. Great for any modern street scene. Includes large showroom with interior, plus a variety of garden furniture, barbecue grills, ponds, fencing, planting stones and other details, all protected by an outdoor fence. (Matching accessories to expand your inventory are included in #272-358, 359, 361 and 362, all sold separately)

CHAPEL W/WAYSIDE CROSSES

272-235 19.99
2-5/8 x 2-3/16 x 4"
6.5 x 5.5 x 10cm
Nestled high on a mountainside, this charming Swiss Chapel will add a nice touch of detail to any layout. The kit includes wayside crosses, typically found alongside the path leading to the Chapel.

CORNER SHOP "BALDREICH"

272-341 26.99
6-3/16 x 6-3/16 x 4-3/16"
15.5 x 15.5 x 10.5cm
The staff at Baldreich's Corner Market are always glad to have you stop by. Whether it's for a few groceries or the evening paper, corner stores like this are a neat addition to any neighborhood. The two-story building features a first floor store, while the upper floor can be used as offices or apartments. The kit includes lots of details and has been designed for easy construction, making it a good choice for new modelers.

OLD WOODEN BRIDGE

272-539 21.99
Clearance: 2" 5cm
This old fashioned highway bridge will look great in steam-era scenes. It could easily be used in a modern park or museum too. Complete with two stone abutments to support the finished model.

BLACK FOREST FARMYARD W/ACCESSORIES

272-366 54.99
10-13/16 x 9-5/8 x 6-1/4" 27 x 24 x 15.6cm
These classic farmhouses can be found scattered throughout the Black Forest region. Combining the home, barn and milk house into one large structure, they have remained virtually the same for decades. The kit captures all of the charming detail of the real thing, and includes a variety of accessories for the finishing touch.

ROOFED PLATFORM

272-190 13.99
7-1/8 x 2-7/8" 18 x 7.2cm

OPERATIONS BUILDING

272-973 31.99
6-1/8 x 5-7/8" 15.5 x 14.8cm

IMPORTED FROM GERMANY
BY WALTHERS

STONE ARCH BRIDGE

272-555 16.99
15-1/8 x 1 x 3-5/16"
18 x 6.5 x 8.4cm

RURAL STATION "GUGLINGEN"

272-107 46.99
12-1/16 x 5-1/4"
30.8 x 13.5cm

WORLD'S LARGEST CUCKOO CLOCK

272-389 79.99
4-5/16 x 3-3/4" 11 x 9.5cm
Germany's Black Forest is the home of the famed Cuckoo Clocks, as well as the prototype of this unique model! The actual building was constructed between 1979 and 1981 by Joseph Dubold, in the style of a traditional home which houses the world's largest cuckoo clock. The working model is complete with battery-powered clock mechanism, which includes the cuckoo and its familiar song. There is also an electric motor to drive the waterwheel.

COUNTRY STATION

272-92 17.99
8 x 4-1/8" 20.3 x 10.4cm

KRAMER MACHINING CO.

272-970 37.99
11-3/16 x 6-5/8 x 4" 28 x 16.5 x 10cm

Doing all kinds of contract and specialty work, small machine shops like this are a neat addition to your older industrial areas. Located in a vintage building with brick and half-timber construction, there's a large end door and loading platform to handle shipments by truck. A great steam- or diesel-era industry.

OLD BRICK WORKS

272-952 66.99
9-13/16 x 8-13/16 x 13-5/8" 24.5 x 22 x 34cm

Whether it's building materials, paving blocks, new linings for blast furnaces or any other kind of brick products, this old style factory will generate lots of interesting traffic for your railroad. The central building doubles as the kiln and includes the tall smokestack. A modular design allows you to arrange the buildings as needed to fit your layout space.

HOUSE "KRISTALL"

272-306 22.99
6-5/8 x 5-11/16 x 3-13/16"
16.6 x 14.2 x 9.5cm
Start your new subdivision in style with this handsome house. This two-family home is perfect for city scenes and includes terraces on each side for the residents.

TWO-FAMILY HOUSE W/GARAGE

272-260 25.99
6-7/16 x 6-3/16 x 6"
16 x 15.5 x 15cm
With plenty of space for everyone, this two-family home is perfect for an extended family or a duplex in a subdivision. Realistic stucco walls and other details add to the realistic look of the finished model. There's also a one-car garage to finish the scene.

S-BAHN RAILWAY BRIDGE

272-551 44.99
Overall: 14.4 x 5.6 x 4" 36 x 14 x 10cm
Clearance: 2-13/16" 7cm
From the late 1800s to the present day, elevated railroads have been a vital part of big city transit systems. Based on German S-Bahn prototypes, this timeless iron design is easily adapted to American layouts of the steam- or diesel-era. Wide enough for two tracks. Add the Station (272-119), or Arcades (272-#568 and 272-569), each sold separately, to detail your right-of-way.

S-BAHN RAILWAY STATION

272-119 59.99
28-13/16 x 8 x 8" 72 x 20 x 19.8cm
Passengers will appreciate these handsome stations at every stop on your transit line. Platform buildings and an underground passage that can be reached by stairway add to the realistic detail. Bridge parts and columns are identical to the S-Bahn Railway Bridge (#272-551, sold separately).

FALLER

IMPORTED FROM GERMANY
BY WALTHERS

HOUSE "CHIEMGA"

272-274 29.99
5-3/16 x 4-3/8 x 3-15/16"
13 x 11 x 9.8cm
This charming Alpine home will look great in your miniature mountain range. Authentic timber construction and numerous details produce a highly realistic model.

GLASS TRAIN SHED W/ACCESSORIES

272-188 24.99
19-1/4 x 2-1/8" 48.8 x 5.3cm

BEET LOADER W/ACCESSORIES

272-128 16.99
7-1/8 x 2-1/2" 18 x 6.5cm
Ship beets by rail with this machine, used to load gondolas. Includes a load of beets for added detail.

TWO-FAMILY HOUSE & GARAGE

272-261 29.99
6-7/16 x 6-3/16 x 6"
16.5 x 15.5 x 15cm
Growing family? Need extra income? Then this duplex will be just the ticket for your city residential area. One family can occupy the entire building, or rent out half. Detailed half-timber construction provides a stylish look, and there's a one-car garage for the owner.

HOUSE "ENZIAN"

272-275 27.99
5-13/16 x 5-1/2 x 3-5/8"
14.5 x 13.8 x 9cm
This typical Alpine home adds a nice touch to a meadow or mountain scene. It features the traditional balcony and many other details.

"TALHEIM" RURAL STATION

272-105 34.99
9-7/16 x 4-1/2" 23.9 x 11.5cm

NEWSPAPER & WAFFLE STAND

272-211 pkg(2) **14.99**
Newstand: 3-1/4 x 2"
8.5 x 5cm
Waffle Stand: 2-3/4 x 1-1/2"
6.8 x 3.8
Great detail for parks, city streets, fair scenes and more.

Limited Quantity Available

TWO-STALL ENGINE HOUSE

272-156 51.99
15-3/4 x 6-3/4 x 5-1/8"
40 x 17.2 x 13cm
For use as electric or diesel engine shed. Motor not included for mechanical door operation.

SANDING FACILITY

272-146 23.99
6 x 2-1/8" 15.5 x 5.5cm
1-1/2 x 1-1/2" 3.7 x 3.7cm
Includes sanding tower, sand house and bag of sand.

INDUSTRIAL CHIMNEY

272-949 7.99
10" 25cm Tall, Diameter 1-21/64" 3.3cm
A must-have detail for steam-era industries, many of these ornate brick stacks are still standing. Add your personal touch with decal lettering and weathering to create a neat detail for any factory, railroad shop, powerhouse or other big industry.

SUMMER HOUSES

272-208 pkg(3) **13.99**
1-7/16 x 1-7/16 x 1-9/32"
3.6 x 3.6 x 3.2cm
2-11/64 x 1-31/32 x 1-9/32"
5.4 x 4.9 x 3.2cm
2-13/32 x 2-1/8 x 1-9/32"
6 x 5.3 x 3.2cm
These tiny timber homes are great for tourist cabins, roadside motels, backyard playhouses and hundreds of other uses around your layout.

DIESEL FUEL FACILITY

272-157 32.99
8-7/8 x 4-7/8" 22.5 x 12.4cm

BACK SHOP

272-159 42.99
10-3/8 x 6" 26.6 x 15cm
This shop building is perfect for heavy repairs to locos or cars. The brick structure features one stall, large smokestack and lots of details. For a bigger repair shop, just combine a few kits!

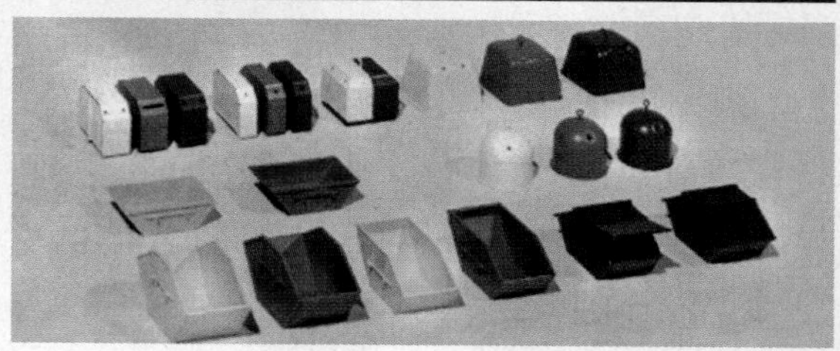

RECYCLING CENTER

272-351 Bins & Dumpsters pkg(21) **17.99**
Virtually every modern industry, apartment complex and many other businesses will have these big bins out back. You could also group them together at the city garage for a contemporary recycling center scene.

PARK HOTEL

272-934 59.99 ***NEW***
10-13/32 x 9-5/8 x 9-13/32" 26 x 24 x 23.5cm
In the heart of a busy city or as a quaint country resort, this attractive building can be a focal point in any scene. The covered entry is perfect for detailing and a variety of parts are included to personalize the model.

FALLER

IMPORTED FROM GERMANY BY WALTHERS

"ALLMANNSDORF" TOWN HALL

272-427 52.99
7 x 6-3/8 x 9-3/16"
17.5 x 16 23cm
Housing important local offices and providing meeting rooms for the council and local organizations, no town or village should be without a City Hall building. This charming kit is based on a prototype at Allmannsdorf, which is still standing. For additional realism, the kit can be fitted with the Working Clock (#272-639), sold separately.

DEPARTMENT STORE

272-920 46.99
6-13/16 x 5-1/4 x 6-7/16"
17 x 13 x 16cm
You'll find everything you need in this busy downtown building. With its late 19th century styling, it can be used in various time periods and matches the City Hall #901, sold separately.

SMALL SIGNAL BOX

272-123 24.99
5-3/8 x 1-7/8 x 4-7/16"
13.6 x 4.7 x 11.3cm
A small signal tower which can be installed between tracks.

OLD-TOWN TOWER HOUSE

272-402 25.99 ***NEW***
4 x 2-3/32 x 8-5/8"
10 x 5.2 x 21.5cm
Use this unique building by itself or to add a different look to your walled city. Matches parts in kits 401, 403 and 404, all sold separately.

OLD-TOWN PEEL TOWERS

272-403 25.99 ***NEW***
1-5/8 x 1-5/8 x 5"
4 x 4 x 12.5cm
5-13/32 x 2 x 5"
6 x 5 x 12.5cm
Use these towers to add corners to your walled city. Includes one each 45° and 90° towers, which can be used with kits 401, 402, and 404, all sold separately.

OLD-TOWN WALLS

272-404 18.99 ***NEW***
6-1/8 x 2-13/16 x 5"
15.3 x 7 x 12.5
Highly detailed wall sections, for use with kits 401, 402, and 403, all sold separately.

OLD-TOWN WALL SET

272-401 109.99 ***NEW***
Re-create a medieval city for an amusement park, diorama, adventure/war game or European city scene. Basic kit includes old town wall with attached half-timber house, wall with stairway, wall with battlements, two peel towers and the city gate with an attached house (both with entrances). This starter set can be expanded and customized with kits #272-402, 403 and 404, all sold separately.

TRANSFORMER STATION

272-954 17.99
2-5/8 x 2-3/8 x 4-3/8"
6.5 x 6 x 11cm
Provide a safe and scenic housing for electrical transformers along your layout with this neat building. A great detail for steam-era scenes, a few can still be found in some rural areas in Germany. For more realism, this building can serve telegraph lines using the Telegraph Poles Set (#272-955), sold separately.

GUTERMANN KNITTING MILL

272-979 89.99 ***NEW***
15-13/64 x 7-3/4 x 12-13/16" 38 x 19.3 x 32cm
This charming building can be home to virtually any small factory. With its lavish 19th century styling, it fits perfectly in steam-era scenes. The kit includes a loading ramp, a tall smokestack and a variety of period details.

GANTRY CRANE

272-162 42.99
13-3/8 x 2-1/4" 34 x 5.8cm
Give heavy loads a lift with this big Gantry Crane! The kit can be built with a hook, a clamshell bucket or logging hooks. The crane cab can be rotated 360 degrees; use motor 272-629 (available separately) for remote control, or operate manually.

STATION SCHWARZBURG

272-116 89.99
19 x 7" 47.6 x 17.5cm
This city station is highly detailed and includes numerous accessories.

FALLER

IMPORTED FROM GERMANY BY WALTHERS

GAS STATION W/CAR WASH

272-296 27.99
Car Wash: 4 x 3-13/16 x 1-5/8" 10 x 9.5 x 4.9cm
Office: 3-3/8 x 2-5/8 x 1-1/2" 8.5 x 6.5 x 3.9cm
Pump Island: 3-3/8 x 1-13/16 x 2" 8.4 x 4.5 x 5cm
Turn a vacant layout lot into a thriving business with this modern fueling facility. Great for the business district or any busy highway, the kit includes three separate buildings, which can easily be arranged to fit available space. A set of signs is also included.

GATEKEEPER'S HOUSE

272-132 13.99
3-7/8 x 2-15/16" 9.8 x 7.5cm

HEATING & POWER PLANT

272-982 45.99
9 x 8-1/4" 23 x 21cm
Power small cities on your layout with this Heating and Power Plant! Always ready for coal shipments from your HO Scale railroad, the kit includes a brick boiler house and power station. For added realism, the smokestack can be fitted with Seuthe Steam generator #667-7 (listed in the Sound & Smoke section of this catalog).

TRACKSIDE ACCESSORIES

272-142 19.99
Includes four propane tanks for switch heaters, shanty, switch box and plank walkways.

TRACK SCALE & LOADING CLEARANCE GAUGE

272-134 13.99
3-1/4 x 3" 8.5 x 8cm
1 x 1/2" 2.4 x 1cm

PLATFORM ACCESSORIES

272-182 17.99
Kit includes newsstand, hut, lamps, signs, benches, fountains, clocks, fences and many other parts.

ENGINE DRIVER'S CABIN

272-133 13.99
1-1/4 x 1-1/8" 3.2 x 2cm

COALING STATION

272-148 74.99
13 -3/8 x 10-3/4" 34 x 27.4cm
Perfect for loading coal, ore, gravel or stone, this detailed coaling tower can easily be adapted to mining operations. The kit is complete with a large gantry crane, equipped with a clamshell bucket.

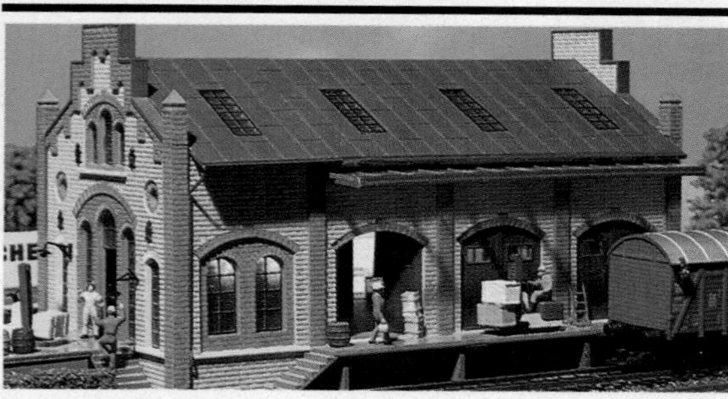

FREIGHT HOUSE

272-150 42.99
9-3/4 x 5-5/8" 24.8 x 14.4cm
Freight houses could be found in every large yard to handle small freight shipments. Combine several of these kits and build a larger, unique structure for your layout

BLACK FOREST HOUSE

272-367 35.99
6-5/8 x 4-13/32 x 4-1/2" 16.5 x 11 x 11.3cm

This diminutive country home is representative of the Black Forest. Its design is perfect for any forest, hillside or meadow. A great addition to the Black Forest Farmyard #272-366, sold separately.

DIESEL OIL FACILITY

272-145 13.99
4-1/8 x 1-3/8" 10.5 x 3.5cm

SMALL SHED

272-151 16.99
4-3/4 x 3" 12 x 6.7cm

INSPECTION PITS

272-136 pkg(2) **25.99**
13-1/2 x 5-3/4" 34.4 x 14.7cm
Rails are molded on baseplate.

FREIGHT LOAD

272-588 8.99
Assorted barrels, crates and other details, less building and figures.

OVERHEAD CRANE

272-164 17.99
5-3/8 x 1-1/4" 13.7 x 3cm

FALLER

IMPORTED FROM GERMANY BY WALTHERS

MITTLESTADT SIGNAL TOWER

272-120 19.99
3-3/16 x 2-1/2" 8.4 x 6.4cm

DOUBLE SILO

272-167 24.99
3 x 6" 7.8 x 14.8cm

GLASS COVERED PLATFORM

272-187 17.99
19-1/4 x 2-1/8" 48.8 x 5.3cm

WAYSIDE STATION

272-91 11.99
4-7/8 x 3-3/16" 12.4 x 8.1cm

FREIGHT STATION

272-155 20.99
7-9/16 x 4-1/4"
19.2 x 10.8cm

BLACK FOREST SAWMILL

272-230 With Motor **67.99**
272-227 Less Motor **43.99**
9-1/16 x 6-1/4" 23 x 16cm
You can almost smell the fresh sawdust around this busy mill. The rustic structure can easily be adapted to many time periods. For extra realism, an electric motor is included in kit 272-230 to power the saw and water wheel.

OVERHEAD SIGNAL TOWER

272-125 34.99
7 x 6-5/8" 18 x 17cm

OLD GRIST MILL

272-368 54.99
8 x 4-1/4 x 5-1/8" 20 x 10.7 x 12.8cm
This old-fashioned grain mill is based on a prototype still in use in the Black Forest. A motorized water wheel drives cams on the exterior that power the machinery inside. The kit also includes simulated rope, sound effects and optional landscaping for building the structure on a hillside.

RURAL FIRE STATION

272-268 21.99
5-1/8 x 4" 13 x 10cm
This small fire house will be the pride of your volunteer department! The building features two operating apparatus bays and a rooftop hose drying tower, roof siren and scaffolding. Suitable for use with TT Scale.

LUMBER ASSORTMENT

272-589 8.99

FALLER

IMPORTED FROM GERMANY BY WALTHERS

WATER TOWER

272-144 18.99
3-7/16 x 3-7/16" 8.7 x 8.7cm

CINDER REMOVAL FACILITY

272-149 45.99
13-1/2 x 5-3/4" 34.4 x 14.7cm
Includes a hoist, two swivel water cranes, two slag hoppers, base plate with slag pit, slag wagon and slag wheel barrow.

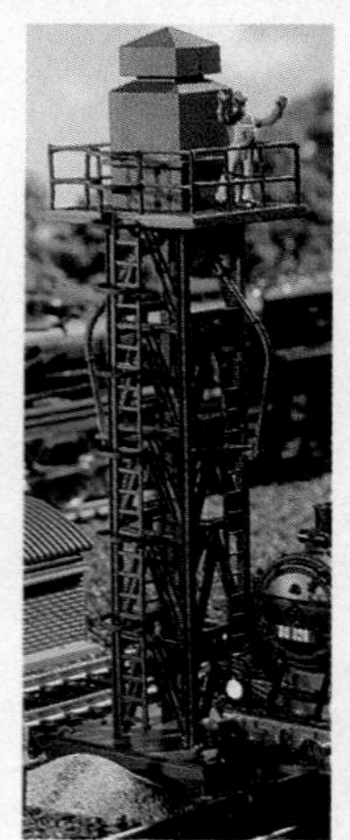

SANDING TOWER

272-138 13.99
1-3/8 x 1-3/8" 3.7 x 3.7cm
Includes hopper and ramp.

TELEVISION TOWER RESTAURANT

272-969 Rotating Cafe, Beacon & Motor **99.99**
8-13/16 x 7-3/16 x 36"
22 x 18 x 90cm
Transform your big city skyline with this working model! From top to bottom, this superb building is packed with realistic detail. There's a ground-floor restaurant, open observation decks, a rotating restaurant and a detailed antennae array at the very top. The kit is complete with a motor drive for the restaurant, as well as flashing red lamp to warn aircraft away from the tower. The finished model stands an impressive 36" tall, making it an ideal way to draw attention to any part of your layout.

PASSENGER STATION PLATFORM

272-191 pkg(2) **29.99**
11-7/8 x 1-7/8" 30.2 x 4.8cm

"DUDERSTADT" ENGINEHOUSE

272-160 59.99
12-1/4 x 7-1/4" 31 x 18.5cm
This three-stall engine house is perfect for shortlines, or as part of a larger engine terminal. Locos up to 11" can be stored inside. The working doors can be opened or closed by hand.

WOODEN HUT

272-947 13.99
4 -3/8 x 2-7/8" 11.1 x 7.2cm

2-STALL ENGINEHOUSE

272-161 41.99
8-1/4 x 6-1/8" 21 x 15.7cm

CROSSING W/WARNING LIGHTS

272-630 29.99

SWIVEL WATER SPOUT

272-137 pkg(2) **12.99**
3 x 9/16" 7.8 x 1.5cm
Includes external heater device and two gully covers.

VILLA

272-364 44.99
7 x 5-3/4" 17.5 x 14.5cm

THREE TRACKSIDE SHANTIES

272-140 13.99

TWO-FAMILY HOUSE

272-262 26.99
House: 6-5/16 x 6 x 6-1/8" 15.8 x 15 x 15.3
Garage: 2-5/8 x 1-5.8 x 1-7/16" 6.6 x 4 x 3.6cm
This two-family unit radiates warmth with cozy features and simple design. A ground-level fenced courtyard, a second-story terrace and an attached one-car garage make this multi-level a great new home in any neighborhood.

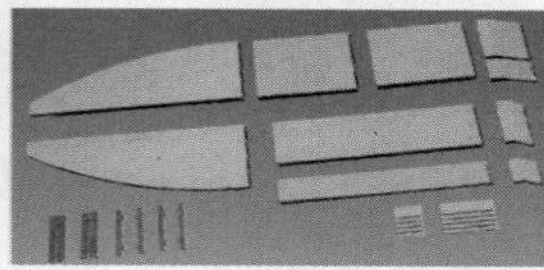

ASSORTED LEVEL PLATFORMS

272-184 17.99

ALPINE BLACKSMITH

272-332 35.99
7-1/4 x 4-1/2" 18.5 x 11.5cm

FALLER

IMPORTED FROM GERMANY BY WALTHERS

WATER TOWER

272-143 24.99
radius: 3-7/8" 10cm
height: 9-1/2" 24.2cm

LOG BARN

272-294 11.99
4-3/16 x 2-1/4" 10.6 x 5.7cm

TIMBER YARD

272-288 13.99
5-1/8 x 3-1/2" 13 x 9cm

BREWERY

272-960 39.99
6-15/16 x 6-1/2"
17.6 x 16.5cm

WATERMILL

272-225 With Pump **54.99**
272-226 Less Pump **29.99**
9-1/2 x 5-1/8" 24 x 13cm
Nearly every small village once had a mill. Powered by a stream, the waterwheel turned the millstone to grind grain into flour. This charming kit (#225) includes an electronic pump to circulate real water which turns the wheel! (Also available less pump).

HUNTER'S LODGE "FALKENECK"

272-385 49.99
7-3/8 x 5-1/4" 18.8 x 13.4cm
Includes wooden draw-bridge and walkway.

SWIMMING POND W/ACCESSORIES

272-375 36.99 ***NEW***
Add a neat detail to any resort area, small town or farm with this unique model. It features a water-tight, one-piece pond that can be filled with water. To set the scene, a small boathouse, row boats in several colors and surfboards are all included.

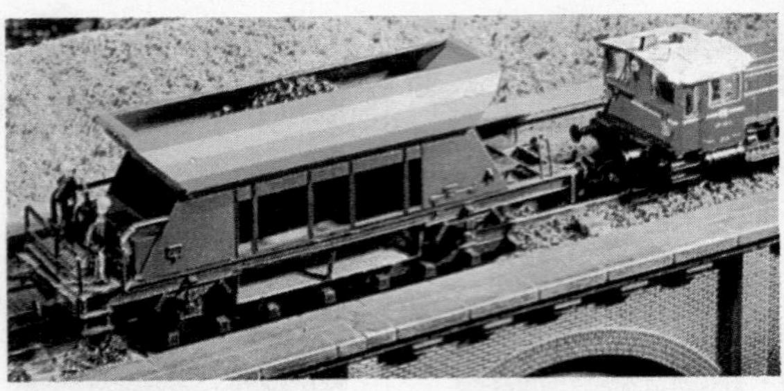

COAL FREIGHT CAR

272-941 20.99
Carry coal to any customer with this car, which matches the equipment included with the Hildegard Mine (#272-940, sold separately).

COAL CHIPS

272-724 2.99
These specially-designed chips look like real coal but can be used without the mess. For use with the Hildegard Coal Mine (#272-940, sold separately).

COMPRESSOR HOUSING & ACCESSORIES

272-139 29.99
3-5/8 x 2-1/8" 9.4 x 5.6cm
3 x 3-5/8" 7.6 x 9.3cm
This small facility is used to clean the flues and fireboxes of steam locos. A shed with compressor, sand blasting frame and fire cleaning tools with rack are included.

HUNTER'S LOOKOUT

272-290 12.99
1-9/16 x 1-3/16" 4 x 3cm

NORDEX WIND GENERATOR

272-381 27.99
2 x 2 x 13-3/16" 5 x 5 x 33cm
Make your layout environmentally friendly with this powered generator. Based on a prototype installed in the Black Forest in 1996, it's typical of modern units seen around the world. Includes 12-16V AC motor and three-blade propeller.

FALLER

IMPORTED FROM GERMANY BY WALTHERS

"ALSFELD" TOWN HALL

272-936 39.99
4-3/8 x 4-1/16" 11.1 x 10.3cm
Includes four turrets, arcades and many details.

GRAIN STORE W/ACCESSORIES

272-333 15.99
3-1/2 x 3-1/8" 9 x 8cm

GUTACH VALLEY FARMHOUSE

272-289 33.99
5-3/4 x 4-15/16"
14.6 x 12.6cm

LOG CABIN

272-299 10.99
3-1/4 x 30" 8.2 x 7.6cm

FOREST LOG CABIN

272-293 11.99
3-7/16 x 2" 8.7 x 5.1cm

LOWER-SAXON FARMHOUSE

272-371 36.99
4-1/4 x 7" 11 x 17.5cm

FARM BUILDING W/DETAILS

272-276 35.99
6-3/8 x 3-7/8" 16.2 x 9.8cm
3-3/4 x 2-1/16" 9.6 x 5.3cm
5-3/8 x 3-7/8" 13.7 x 9.8cm

HOUSE UNDER CONSTRUCTION

272-303 19.99
4-11/16 x 3-1/2" 12 x 9cm

TIMBERED HOUSE W/GARAGE

272-215 16.99
4-7/8 x 2-13/16" 12.6 x 6.2cm

DETACHED HOUSE

272-214 16.99
3-1/2 x 2-13/16" 9.1 x 7.2cm

SMALL COALING STATION

272-147 21.99
8-1/8 x 3-1/8" 20.7 x 8cm

UNTERBRUNN STATION

272-106 29.99
10-1/2 x 5-5/16 x 43/8"
26.3 x 13.4 x 11cm
Designed for easy construction, this country station features traditional half-timber construction, with an attached wooden freight house.

TOWN HALL

272-930 31.99
5-5/16 x 4-1/16"
13.5 x 10.3cm
This ornate town hall is loaded with architectural features!

L-SHAPED MOE TREFF TOWN HOUSE

272-428 42.99
5-5/8 x 5-5/8 x 6-13/32" 14 x 14 x 16cm
The business district will be booming with this multi-storied commercial complex, complete with an arcade. A ground-floor boutique and half-timbered second floor accent the building's design. The L-shaped scheme matches models #272-411 through 427, each sold separately.

L-SHAPED UHL HAIRDRESSING SALON TOWN HOUSE

272-429 39.99
5-5/8 x 5-5/8 x 6-13/32" 14 x 14 x 16cm
Give your layout a new look with this L-shaped town house. An arcade, ground-level boutique and hairdressing salon rent space in this two-story structure. Its design matches models #272-411 through 427, each sold separately.

ROOFED PLATFORM W/ACCESSORIES

272-192 13.99
17-3/4 x 1-7/8" 45 x 4.8cm

FALLER

IMPORTED FROM GERMANY
BY WALTHERS

TWO TOWN HOUSES W/SHOP

272-418 37.99
4-3/4 x 5-7/8" 12 x 14.9cm

MULTI-STORY HOUSE W/ANTIQUE SHOP

272-422 34.99
3-3/4 x 6-1/2" 9.7 x 16.5cm

HOUSE "FLAIR"

272-392 36.99
7 x 6 x 3-3/4"
17.8 x 15.3 x 9.5cm
This handsome home is sure to be a focal point of any HO subdivision. It's complete with a winter garden, patio, upper balcony and a carport.

ONE-FAMILY HOUSE

272-221 12.99
3-3/4 x 3-1/2" 9.3 x 8.5cm
Easy-to-build kit with decorative parts.

VILLAGE INN

272-269 23.99
5-5/8 x 5-5/8" 14.5 x 14.5cm
This charming inn is the perfect place to hold a wedding reception or other celebration. The building is complete with an outdoor bandstand plus tables and chairs.

GUGLINGEN CENTENNIAL SET

272-118 pkg(4) **84.99**
Passenger Shelter: 5-1/8 x 2-1/4 x 2-3/8" 12.8 x 5.6 x 6cm
Station 12-5/16 x 5-3/8 x 5-11/16" 30.8 x 13.5 x 14.2cm
Engine Shed: 10-7/8 x 5 x 3-13/16" 27.2 x 12.7 x 9.5cm
Crane: 5-3/16 x 2 x 3-13/16" 13 x 5.4 x 9.5cm
Celebrating a century of service to the people of Guglingen, this set includes the restored station building with attached passenger shelters, gantry crane and single-stall engine house.

GOETHE STREET TOWNHOUSES

272-915 109.99 ***NEW***
28-13/16 x 5 x 9-13/16" 72 x 12.5 x 24.5cm
Turn a plain city street into a detailed residential district with this handsome set of homes. The kit includes parts for four complete buildings, dating from about 1929. Build them right from the box for steam-era layouts, or weather and customize them to fit a modern setting.

FARM

272-370 69.99
8-3/4 x 13-1/4" 22.5 x 34cm
Includes 1/2-timber farmhouse, shed for sheep, barn, pigsty with fence, dog house and dung cart.

STATION "THALBACH"

272-1212 37.99
Finish your small town in minutes with this fully assembled station building. Model is complete with freight shed and loading dock.

ONE-FAMILY HOUSE

272-254 16.99
4-3/16 x 4 x 4-13/32" 10.5 x 10 x 11cm
Economical in its structure, this simple single family home creates a cozy feeling in every neighborhood.

3 TERRACED HOUSES

272-399 35.99
6-3/16 x 5-13/16 x 3" 15.5 x 14.5 x 7.5cm
A great touch for a modern housing development. Each has a unique character so they can be used together as an apartment or condominium, or as separate buildings.

TOWN HOUSE W/SHOPS

272-421 31.99
3-3/4 x 6-1/2" 9.7 16.5cm
Entrance to hair salon and pub, both of which are located on the ground floor of this building.

BEIGE PLASTER HOUSE

272-1205 15.99
3-5/8 x 3-3/8" 9.3 x 8.6cm
(Assembled)

1-1/2 STORY HOUSE

272-205 12.99
5-3/16 x 3-1/4" 13.2 x 8.3cm

FALLER

IMPORTED FROM GERMANY
BY WALTHERS

HOUSE W/DORMER

272-200 11.99
3-17/32 x 3-1/8" 9 x 8cm

COTTAGES

272-590 pkg(4) **19.99**

HALF-TIMBERED CHALET

272-277 15.99
4-1/2 x 3-3/8" 11.5 x 8.7cm

STUCCO TIMBERED HOUSE

272-1207 15.99
3-5/8 x 3-3/8" 9.3 x 8.6cm

WHITE PLASTER HOUSE W/TILE ROOF

272-1209 15.99
3-5/8 x 3-3/8" 9.3 x 8.6cm
(Assembled)

BASIC VILLAGE SET

272-255 63.99
Here's everything you need to build a small village in one complete set! Including three Cape Cod homes and a small church, the set also features an assortment of fir trees and a playground which is detailed with teeter-totters, a swing set and more.

L-SHAPED BUNGALOW

272-398 17.99
6-3/16 x 5-13/16 x 3" 15.5 x 14.5 x 7.5cm
This Weber house is unique in its L-shaped layout. A covered terrace accents the home second level, while an enclosed patio marks the entryway.

HOUSE W/BALCONY

272-209 13.99
4 x 3-3/4" 10.1 x 9.5cm

HOUSE UNDER CONSTRUCTION

272-246 11.99
2-15/16 x 2-3/4" 7.5 x 7.1cm

CHALET W/PORCH

272-204 11.99
3-15/16 x 3-1/4" 10 x 8.3cm

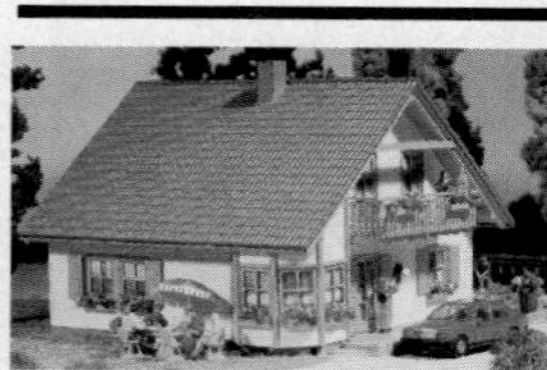

SINGLE FAMILY HOME ROMANTIC

272-301 22.99
5 x 5" 12.7 x 12.6cm

CONSTRUCTION SITE BARRICADE SET

272-682 59.99
Prepare your crews and ready your equipment – construction season is underway. Eight countdown markers and eight traffic cones divert traffic and protect workers. In addition, four of each are equipped with flashing lights. One barricade comes equipped with three flashing lights as well. European traffic signs are also provided.

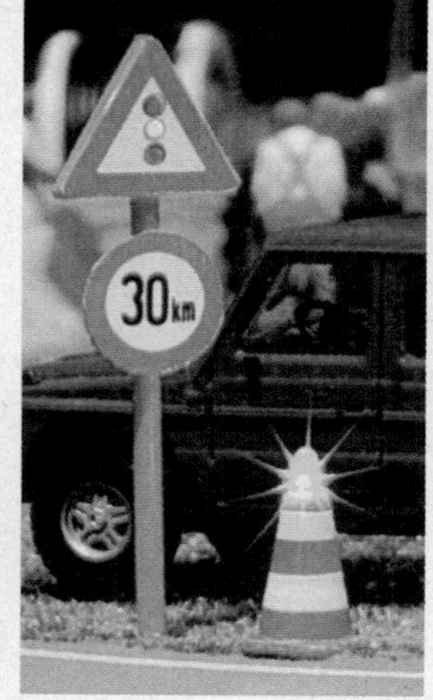

BUILDING SITE SECURITY SET

272-683 32.99
Set yourself up with the basics for construction season. The building site security set contains one barricade, eight traffic cones and eight countdown markers. The kit is ready for connection to #682, sold separately.

SCAFFOLDING W/ACCESSORIES

272-352 13.99
Decrepit buildings are a thing of the past. This scaffolding kit makes renovation and restoration easy! Two complete sets of scaffolding provide lots of construction possibilities. Additional supplies include protective nets, worker's sheds and contractor's advertising signs.

FALLER

IMPORTED FROM GERMANY BY WALTHERS

SMALL MOUNTAIN CHALET

272-297 14.99
4-11/16 x 3-7/8" 11.9 x 9.9cm

COVERED PLATFORM

272-189 17.99
11-1/2 x 2-1/4" 29.5 x 5.3cm

Covered platform, suitable for use with all track.

ENGINE SHED

272-168 34.99
10-7/8 x 5 x 3-13/16"
27.2 x 12.7 x 9.5cm

Doors open and close automatically as engines roll in or out. Features detailed brick and half-timber construction, holds locos up to 9-3/16" 23cm.

ROUNDHOUSE W/WATER SUPPLY

272-175 79.99
13-1/2 x 2" 34 x 5cm

Based on an actual structure, the separate office building also houses a water tank. Doors automatically open and close as engines arrive and depart. Will hold engines up to 8-3/4" (22cm) long. Can be used with Roco Turntable (#625-42615, sold separately.) A larger structure can be built with add-on stalls in kit #272-176.

WIESENTAL STATION W/PLATFORM

272-93 35.99
14-3/4 x 5-1/2" 37 x 14cm

Small town station with attached freight house, includes benches and other details.

272-377

272-376

"THE CAT" WINDMILL W/MOTOR

272-377 69.99
11-1/4 x 5-1/8 x 13-1/8" 28.5 x 13 x 33cm

Built in 1646 and still in operation as a museum. Prototype located in Zaandamn, The Netherlands. Includes 12-16V AC motor to move the sails at realistic slow speeds.

SMALL WINDMILL W/MOTOR

272-376 54.99
4-1/2 x 4-1/2 x 10-1/4" 11.5 x 11.5 x 26cm

Typical of mills found throughout the Netherlands. Includes 12-16V AC motor to move the sails at realistic slow speeds.

DISTRICT COURT

272-420 67.99
This ornate building makes a fitting monument to the cultural heritage of your model city. It includes a number of details and accessories to complement its design.

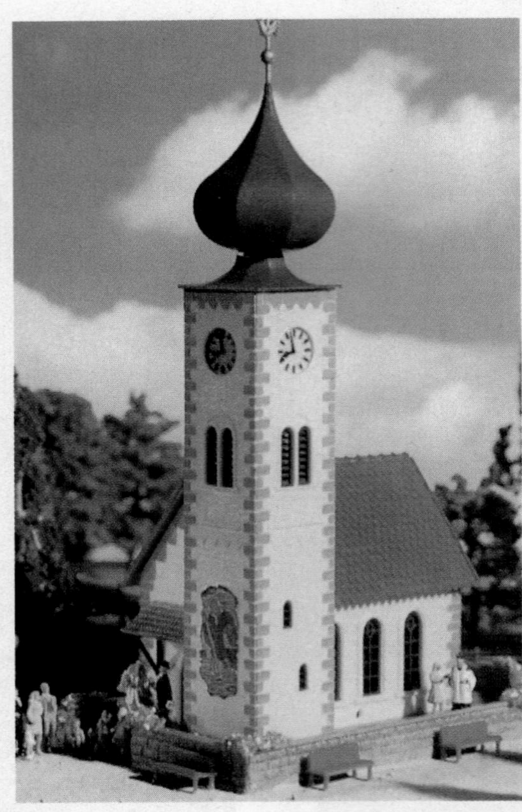

CHURCH

272-238 25.99
5-13/16 x 3-1/2" 14.8 x 8.8cm

CITY HALL W/FIRE STATION

272-901 84.99
10-3/8 x 9-1/2" 26.3 x 24.2cm

This beautiful structure combines the City Hall and Fire Station into a single building. Three apparatus bays are provided to showcase your fire equipment. A large hose drying tower rounds out the structure.

FALLER

IMPORTED FROM GERMANY
BY WALTHERS

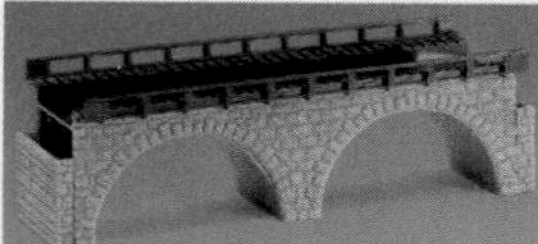

STRAIGHT STONE VIADUCT

272-545 12.99
7-1/16" 18cm

CURVED STONE VIADUCT

272-546 12.99
30", approximate 14" radius

SMALL FOOT BRIDGES

272-537 pkg(2) **13.99**
8-5/8 x 7/8" 22 x 2,2cm
10 x 2-1/8" 25.6 x 5.5cm

CONCRETE BRIDGE PIERS

272-538 pkg(18) **16.99**
for #'s 534, 536 and 541

TRACKBED, CURVED

272-552 8.99
R42, 4cm

HIGH PIERS FOR #543

272-544 pkg(6) **9.99**

BRIDGES & ACCESSORIES FOR MARKLIN C TRACK

UP & OVER BRIDGE SET EA 54.99

272-470 Outside Circle-Large Radius *NEW*

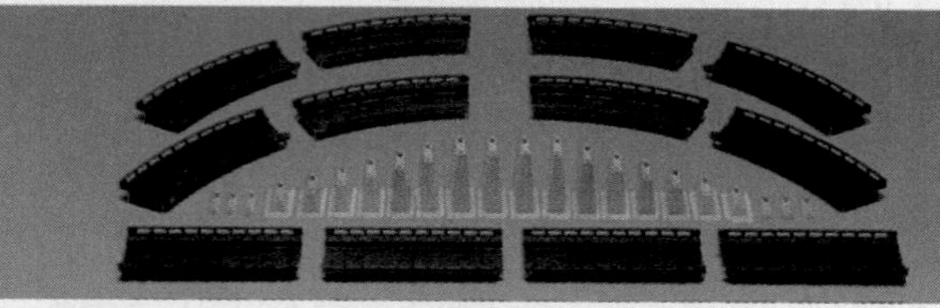

272-471 Inside Circle-Smaller 17-1/2" 43.7cm Radius *NEW*
Smaller radius allows you to build another bridge inside of #470, sold separately

BRIDGE PIERS PKG(6) EA 9.99

For use with #470, 474 and 475, all sold separately.

272-472

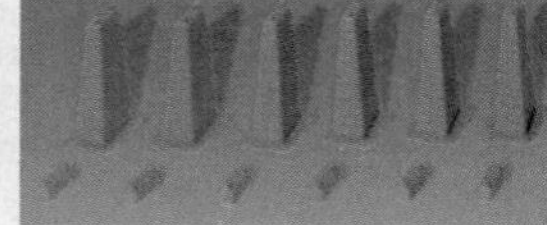

272-4736

272-472 Graduated *NEW*
From 5/8 to 3" 1.5 to 7.5cm tall.
272-473 Tall *NEW*
Each stands 3" 7.5cm tall, and includes a 21/64" 0.8cm cap which locks into Bridge Track Beds, sold separately.

BRIDGE TRACK BED EA 7.99

Matching parts that can be used to customize #470/471.

272-474

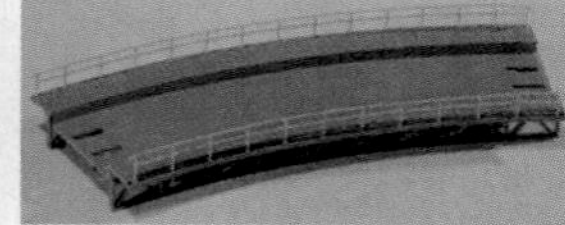

272-475

272-474 Straight 7-1/2" 18.9cm Tall *NEW*
272-475 Curved 14-13/32" 36cm Radius *NEW*
272-476 Curved 17-1/2" 43.7cm Radius *NEW*

VIADUCT TOP SECTION EA 14.99

Sections stand 2-5/8" 6.5cm tall.

272-477 Straight 7-1/2" 18.9cm Long *NEW*

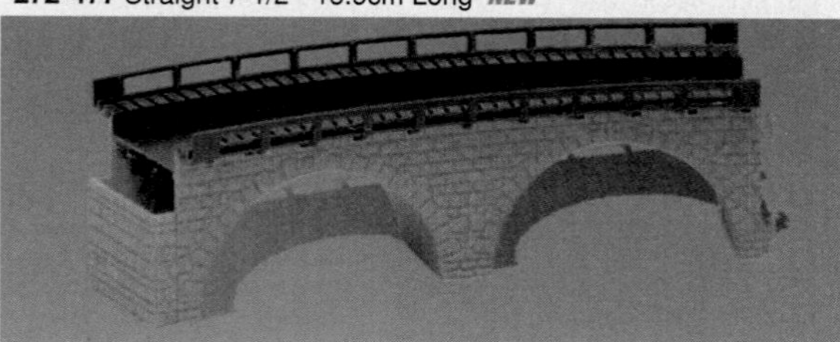

272-478 Curved 14-13/32" 36cm Radius *NEW*

CUT STONE VIADUCT PIERS

Use with #477 and 478, both sold separately.

272-479

272-480

272-479 Tall 7-13/64" 18cm pkg(3) **16.99** *NEW*
272-480 Short 2-13/32" 6cm pkg(6) **15.99** *NEW*

HOTEL SONNE

272-927 36.99
4-1/16 x 4-1/16" 10.4 x 10.4cm

Dress up any corner of your downtown with this superb model! The four story building is designed especially for a corner location and can be used with other Faller buildings to create a complete city scene!

MITTELSTADT APARTMENTS

272-926 pkg(2) **44.99**
5-5/8 x 3-1/8" 14.5 x 8cm

FALLER

IMPORTED FROM GERMANY BY WALTHERS

GUEST HOUSE "ROSEL"

272-286 18.99
3-15/16 x 3-3/8" 10 x 8.7cm

TOWNHOUSE SCHWABENTOR

272-424 34.99
6 x 3-9/16" 15 x 9cm
A neat part of an old city scene, with large and small arches.

BLUMENFELD DEPOT

272-97 29.99
9-1/4 x 5-1/4" 24 x 13.5cm

AUTO SERVICE/FACTORY

272-946 19.99
6-1/4 x 3-5/8" 15.8 x 9.6cm

TOWN ACCESSORIES

272-585 16.99

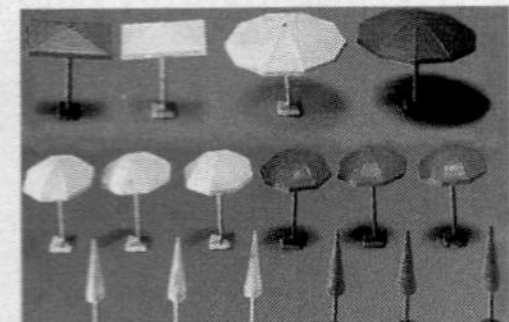

PARASOLS

272-572 pkg(16) **6.99**
Various sizes of garden umbrellas, perfect for detailing summertime backyards, beaches or restaurant scenes.

SINGLE FAMILY HOUSE

272-251 16.99
4-13/64 x 4 x 4-13/32"
10.5 x 10 x 11cm
Modernize your suburbs with this small home.

GARAGES

272-586 pkg(2) **12.99**

Limited Quantity Available

GEAR FACTORY

272-953 45.99
16-3/16 x 4-7/8"
17.4 x 12.4cm
This busy factory includes a storage shed (4-11/16 x 2-3/4") and other details.

SMALL COALING STATION

272-131 20.99
8-1/4 x 3-1/8" 21 x 8cm
This small facility is perfect for a branch or shortline railroad. Includes positionable crane with bucket and coal storage bins

"ROMERBERG" ROWHOUSES

272-911 pkg(6) **109.99**
14 x 3-1/8" 35.5 x 8cm
This detailed kit is based on an actual street in Frankfurt, Germany. These ornate buildings date back to the 15th century and were restored in 1983. The kit is complete with six different structures. Special plastic sheets to simulate half-timber construction are included, so the finished buildings can be used in various time periods. Includes six structures from #912, #913, and #914.

BUILDING SHELL W/SCAFFOLDING

272-309 19.99
5-1/8 x 4" 13 x 10cm

"KIRCHBACH" STATION

272-104 34.99
10-3/8 x 4" 26.5 x 10.3cm

SINGLE FAMILY HOME "ERLENSEE"

272-300 23.99
6 x 5-3/8" 15 x 13.6cm
This attractive single-family home is nicely detailed, with wooden shutters, a roofed terrace and a separate one-car garage.

CAR WASH

272-343 46.99
8-13/16 x 3 x 2-13/64" 20.2 x 7.7 x 5.5cm
6-5/32 x 2-1/2 x 2-5/8" 15.4 x 6.4 x 6.5cm
3/4 x 1/2 x 27/32" 2 x 1 x 2.1cm
Clean up with this richly detailed, motorized car wash. For drivers in a hurry, the automated washrack moves backward and forward while brushes spin overhead and along the sides. Do-it-yourself stalls and an open-air bay for trucks and other big vehicles, all with complete details, are also included. A 12-16V AC motor runs the automated parts, and lots of accessories and advertising signs are also included.

SASBACH WINE PRESS

272-353 12.99
2 x 1-7/8 x 2" 5.2 x 4.7 x 5.0cm
Wine making was an essential activity in many villages. The grape press often became the town square, where friends and family gathered to share stories and news. Kit comes with wine-harvesting accessories such as grape vats and a wine cask.

FALLER

IMPORTED FROM GERMANY BY WALTHERS

FARMERS COOPERATIVE

272-959 69.99
14-3/4 x 5-1/8" 37.2 x 13cm
This rural co-op keeps farmers supplied with fertilizer, feed and more. Excellent detail, with sliding door, loading docks for road and rail service and many add-on parts.

PHARMACY W/ MULTI-STORY HOUSE

272-417 32.99
4-1/2 x 3-3/4" 11.6 x 9.6cm

NEWSSTANDS

272-135 pkg(2) **13.99**
Round: 2-3/4 x 1-9/16"
7 x 4cm
Square: 1-15/16 x 1-15/16"
5 x 5cm

VILLAGE CHURCH

272-241 54.99
9-5/16 x 5" 24 x 12.9cm
This medium sized church is perfect for smaller towns and cities. The kit features a single bell tower which can be built with a spire or "onion" dome.

VILLAGE CHURCH

272-240 23.99
4-3/4 x 4" 12 x 10.2cm
Nestled in a small village, this tiny church puts big detail in a small space. The building has a single bell tower, with a traditional steeple. Can be equipped with bell 272-638 (sold separately) for realistic chime sounds. Suitable for use with TT Scale.

V-A-G AUTO DEALERSHIP

272-348 79.99
Showroom: 13 x 9" 32.5 x 22.3cm
Service Center: 6-1/4 x 4" 15.8 x 9.6cm
Pump Island: 4-3/4 x 2-1/2" 12 x 6.3cm
Everything for the new car buyer under one roof! Set includes a showroom, service center and covered gas pump island. A special Volkswagen from Wiking is also included.

CORNER DRUG STORE

272-929 36.99
4-1/16 x 4-1/16" 10.4 x 10.4cm

POST OFFICE W/ACCESSORIES

272-356 42.99
6-3/4 x 6-3/8" 2-1/4 x 1"
17.2 x 17.4cm 5.7 x 2.7cm

URBAN DWELLING HOUSE

272-425 21.99
3 x 3-1/8" 7.5 x 8cm
Includes eaves, timber framing and dormers.

FALLER

IMPORTED FROM GERMANY BY WALTHERS

MINI MARKET

272-342 36.99
7-3/4 x 7-3/4" 19.8 x 19.8cm
Don't forget to pick up a few groceries on the way home! Shopping will be easy in this modern mini-mart which features a complete interior with shelves, merchandise and cash registers. For added realism, the sign on the roof can be made to rotate with motor #629 and the building can be illuminated with lighting set #671, both sold separately.

CITY GATE "ST. MARTIN'S"

272-922 46.99
4-3/8 x 3" 11.2 x 7.8cm

OLD TIME FACTORY

272-980 72.99
20-1/8 x 6-7/8" 51.2 x 17.3cm
From steam-era to the diesel age, this old factory building can be used in many time periods. The three buildings can be built as individual structures or combined into one large building. A covered loading ramp and large smokestack (which can be fitted with a smoke generator) are included.

6 HIGH-VOLTAGE MASTS

272-956 pkg(6) **19.99**
Each Tower: 8-27/32" 22.1cm Tall
Carrying current from generator to customers, these tall high-tension lines make a great detail in city or country scenes. Includes roll of nonconductive line to simulate the wires.

MERCEDES-BENZ DEALERSHIP

272-344 64.99
9-1/4 x 7-1/2" 6 x 3-3/4"
23.7 x 19.7cm 15.5 x 9.5cm
Modern 2-story dealership with showroom and parts store located on ground level. Office, information rooms and living area on upper floor. Can be illuminated with bulbs (272-671), rotating turntables in showroom and roof emblem can be motorized with Faller motor 272-629. (272-671 and 272-629, sold separately).

GAS STATION W/SERVICE BAY

272-345 29.99
6-1/4 x 3-5/8" 15.8 x 9.6cm

HALF-TIMBERED HOUSE W/SHOP

272-938 29.99
4-3/8 x 3-3/4" 11 x 9.5cm

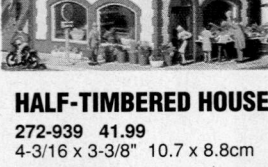

HALF-TIMBERED HOUSE

272-939 41.99
4-3/16 x 3-3/8" 10.7 x 8.8cm

LARGE MOUNTAIN CHALET

272-287 17.99
5 x 3-3/4" 12.7 x 9.3cm

HOUSE

272-280 22.99
4-5/8 x 4-1/2" 11.7 x 11.5cm
Includes stork's nest.

"KRONE" INN W/BEER GARDEN

272-415 29.99
4-1/2 x 5" 11.6 x 13cm

FALLER

IMPORTED FROM GERMANY BY WALTHERS

HAY SHEDS

272-334 pkg(2) **16.99**
3 x 2-1/2" 7.5 x 6.5cm

SINGLE FAMILY HOME "WIESENTAL"

272-305 24.99
6 x 5-3/8" 15 x 13.6cm

"BRILLIANT" HOUSE

272-395 17.99
5-13/16 x 5 x 3"
14.5 x 12.7 x 7.7cm
This model home is based on an actual design made by the Weberhaus firm. It combines contemporary features with older styling to produce a neat addition to any suburb.

"THE SUN" TRAVEL AGENCY

272-928 31.99
3-5/8 x 3-3/8" 9.2 x 8.6cm
Connects with Structure kits #927 and #929 to create a city street.

SMALL VILLAGE CHURCH

272-236 17.99
4-3/4 x 2-3/4" 12 x 5.5cm

ENGEL & GREIF ROWHOUSES

272-912 44.99
3-5/8 x 2-3/4" 9.2 x 7cm

HOTEL ROMANTIC

272-937 49.99
5-1/2 x 5-1/8" 14 x 13cm

SCHILLERSTRASSE CITY BLOCK

272-925 109.99
15-1/4 x 4-1/4" 38.9 x 11cm
Build a better business district with this complete kit! The set combines two large corner buildings with two adjoining structures for the middle of the block. The modular construction makes it possible to arrange the buildings in different combinations to fit available space. A variety of finishing details, including ground foam "flowers" are included to complete a realistic scene.

GROBER & KLEINER ROWHOUSES

272-914 44.99
4-13/16 x 3-1/8" 2.3 x 8cm

4-FACE CLOCK TOWER W/NEWSSTAND

272-583 19.99
2 x 2" 5.2 x 5.2cm
Prototype is from pre-war Frankfurt.

MINEHEAD W/WINCH HOUSE

272-945 49.99
10-1/4 x 6-7/8" 26 x 17.5cm
Powering underground conveyors, the winch house is an essential part of any mining operation. The kit is complete with a minehead building and can be used with the mine kits available from various manufacturers. For extra realism, the winch can be powered with an electric motor (272-629), available separately).

GARDEN CENTER

272-253 36.99
Includes house, 3 greenhouses, 2 hot beds, straw mats and accessories.

SMALL GREENHOUSE

272-213 19.99
3-5/8 x 1-7/8" 9.2 x 4.7cm
2-3/4 x 1-5/8" 7.1 x 4.2cm

IMPORTED FROM GERMANY BY WALTHERS

WILDER & DACHSBERG ROWHOUSES

272-913 44.99
5-3/8 x 2-3/4" 13.8 x 7.1cm

COVERED PLATFORM

272-181 20.99
13 x 3-1/2" 33.8 x 9.2cm
Platform with passenger exit. Suitable for all track.

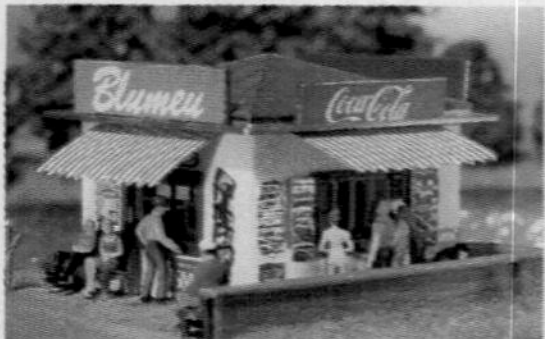

SMALL FOOD STAND

272-212 12.99
3-1/8 x 3" 8 x 7.7cm

STRAIGHT BRIDGE SECTION

272-553 8.99
7" 18cm Long

CURVED BRIDGE SECTION

272-554 8.99
7" 18cm
30°, approximate 14" radius

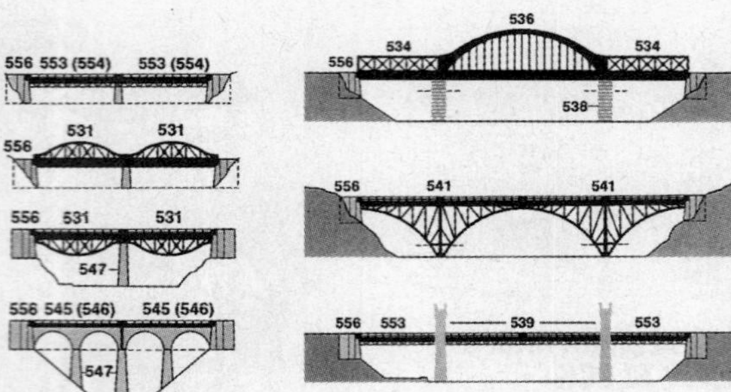

Bridges add an extra dimension of reality, depth and perspective that is difficult to capture in a small area. Faller offers a wide range of bridges and ramps to suit all kinds of terrain. These drawings are a sampling of the many combinations attainable with Faller bridges and piers.

ARCH BRIDGE

272-536 22.99
14-1/4 x 2-1/2 x 4-3/4" 36 x 6.5 x 11.9cm
This detailed bridge looks super on any mainline! It can easily be used with other Faller bridges to cross wide rivers or valleys.

ROADWAY BRIDGE

272-532 21.99
14-1/8" 36cm long

RAILWAY BRIDGE, DOUBLE TRACK

272-542 29.99
15-1/4 x 6" 40 x 15.5cm
Clearance Height
3-1/4" 8.3cm

THREE-STALL ROUNDHOUSE

272-176 54.99
13-1/2 x 16" 34 x 40cm
Matching structure for #175, can also be used by itself. Will hold engines up to 8-3/4" (22cm) long.

DECK ARCH BRIDGE

272-541 19.99
14-1/4 x 2-1/2 x 4-3/4" 36 x 6.5 x 11.9cm
This modern steel bridge is typical of railroad designs used around the world. Detailed steel work and girders highlight this single track bridge.

4-TRACK CONCRETE FOOT BRIDGE

272-179 20.99
13-1/8" 33 x 19.5cm
This modern pedestrian bridge will be a great addition to a yard or industrial area. The basic kit will cross four tracks and additional kits can be combined to build a longer bridge.

UP & OVER BRIDGE SET

272-543 49.99
Includes straight and curved track beds and piers.

CIRCLE SET FOR #543

272-548 54.99

STONE ARCH BRIDGE

272-533 34.99
14 x 1-3/4" 36 x 4.4cm
Several bridges can be built and interconnected with each other.

FALLER

IMPORTED FROM GERMANY
BY WALTHERS

BRICK/TIMBERED HOUSE

272-1208 15.99
3-5/8 x 3-3/8" 9.3 x 8.6cm
(Assembled)

MOUNTAIN CHAPEL

272-243 11.99
2-3/4 x 2-3/4" 7.1 x 7.1cm

HOUSE W/WINE SHOP

272-413 27.99
3-1/2 x 2-15/16" 9.1 x 7.5cm

2 FLATS W/LOWER SHOPS

272-414 41.99
3-5/16 x 2-1/2" 8.4 x 6.4cm
3-1/2 x 3" 9.1 x 7.5cm

CORNER HOUSE W/TOY SHOP

272-411 24.99
3-1/4 x 2-1/2" 8.4 x 6.4cm

CHAPEL

272-234 11.99
2 x 2-3/8" 5 x 6cm

"FAMILIA" HOUSE

272-397 17.99
5 x 5 x 3-1/2"
12.7 x 12.6 x 8.8cm

A handsome smaller home, based on a real design from Hansa-Haus. Like the prototype, the model is complete with a balcony, terrace and more.

STONE BRIDGE ABUTMENT SET

272-556 17.99
For #'s 553, 554, 531, 534 and 536

VIADUCT PIERS

272-549 pkg(6) **13.99**
1-7/8" long
for #'s 545 and 546

HEXENLOCH MILL

272-388 64.99
9-3/4 x 4-3/4" 24.7 x 11.9cm
This working model includes an electric motor that turns the waterwheels in opposite directions, like the prototype.

TRESTLE SET

272-530 24.99
Includes approach ramp for all track types.

VIADUCT PIERS

272-547 pkg(3) **15.99**

ARCH BRIDGE

272-531 15.99
7" 18cm

GIRDER BRIDGE

272-534 13.99
7 x 4-3/4" 18 x 11.9cm

OLD CASTLE "LICHTENSTEIN"

272-245 31.99
5-1/2 x 2-15/16" 13.3 x 7.5cm
This imposing castle is specially designed for use as a backdrop building. The finished model is slightly smaller than HO Scale, so it will not overwhelm surrounding scenery.

GAS PUMPS W/SERVICE BAY

272-346 12.99
4-7/8 x 2-1/2" 12.4 x 6.3cm

FALLER

IMPORTED FROM GERMANY BY WALTHERS

2-TRACK STEEL FOOT BRIDGE

272-178 17.99
9-1/8 x 7" 23.3 x 17.8cm

GRADE CROSSING W/GATES

272-174 59.99
8-5/8 x 10" 22 x 25.5cm

BLUMENFELD WAYSIDE STATION

272-97 29.99
9-1/2 x 5-1/4" 24 x 13.5cm
Suitable for use with TT Scale.

FREIGHT WAREHOUSE "DISCHINGER"

272-983 46.99
14-3/4 x 7-1/4 x 5"
37.2 x 18.5 x 12.9cm
Start a modern industrial park on your layout with this contemporary building that's based on an actual structure. Modular construction makes it easy to build a custom structure to fit your available space.

BP GAS STATION

272-347 22.99
7-11/16 x 3-5/8 x 2-3/32"
19.2 x 9 x 5.5cm
This 1950s vintage station projected a clean, modern image to motorists. The large windows showcase the office details, while, pumps and signs are provided for the canopy.

CITY OPTICAL SHOP W/HOUSE

272-426 23.99
3 x 3-1/8" 7.5 x 8cm
Combines a ground floor optical center with upstairs apartment, that features half-timber framing.

CURVED GRADE CROSSING W/GATES (DUMMY)

272-173 17.99
5-7/8 x 5-11/16" 15 x 14.5cm

BOATHOUSE & BOAT

272-284 10.99
3-5/8 x 2-23/32" 9.2 x 6.9cm

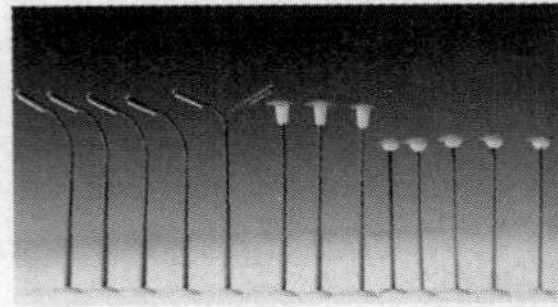

NONWORKING STREET LAMP SET

272-625 pkg(56) **10.99** ***NEW***
Decorate your downtown, station platform, city park or subdivision with these detailed plastic lamps. Set includes six different styles and a total of 56 lamps in all. (Plastic parts, cannot be converted to working models.)

Limited Quantity Available

SWIMMING POOL

272-383 82.99
15-1/2 x 10-3/4 x 2-5/8" 39 x 27 x 6cm
Last one in is a rotten egg - just fill the pool with water and the swimmers begin moving! Includes magnets,12-16V AC motor, locker room, 9 swimmers, outdoor furniture, playground equipment and diving board.

Limited Quantity Available

RESCUE STATION W/VEHICLES

272-990 119.99
14-1/2 x 6-3/4" 36.5 x 17cm
Limited edition kit captures the charm of an older building, and is ideal for a small town. Turn-of-the-century styling combines with four attached bays for the emergency vehicles. The model includes a working clock (battery powered) for the tower, three rescue/fire service vehicles from Wiking and Brekina, an electronic fire siren with speaker (operates from 12-16V AC or DC), interior lighting and a special numbered certificate of authenticity.

1-1/2 STORY HALF-TIMBERED HOUSE

272-218 22.99
5-1/4 x 4-7/8" 13.3 x 12.3cm

CURVED GRADE CROSSING W/GATES

272-172 17.99
7-1/2 x 6-5/16" 19 x 16cm

CHALET

272-249 13.99
3-3/4 x 3-3/8" 9.6 x 8.6cm

ORNAMENTAL FOUNTAIN

272-232 13.99
4-1/2 x 4-5/16" 11.5 x 11cm

FALLER

IMPORTED FROM GERMANY BY WALTHERS

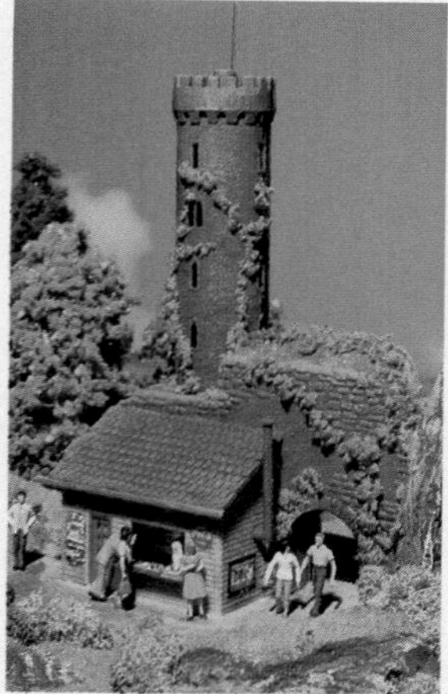

OBSERVATION TOWER

272-291 14.99
4-1/2 x 2-1/2" 11.5 x 6.5cm

CASTLE TOWER RUINS

272-285 17.99
5-11/16 x 3-1/8" 14.5 x 8cm

HOLLAND WINDMILL W/MOTOR

272-231 54.99
8-1/16 x 6-1/2"
20.5 x 16.5cm
Includes 12-16 volt motor.

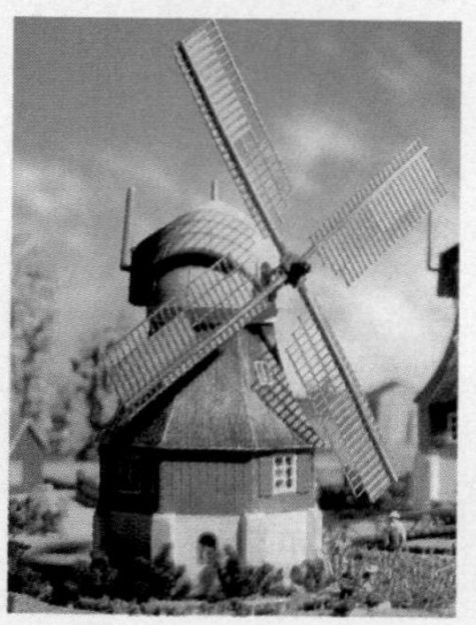

WINDMILL W/MOTOR

272-233 49.99
4 x 3-1/2" 9.8 x 8.8cm
Powered model includes 12-16V AC motor to turn the blades.

FOUNTAIN W/FIGURE

272-581 9.99
1-5/8 x 1-5/8" 4.3 x 4.3cm
Non-operating.

ALPINE HOUSE

272-335 29.99
6-3/8 x 5-3/8 x 3-5/8"
16 x 13.5 x 9cm

Built to withstand Alpine snows and summers, this rugged home is an ideal choice for the mountains of your layout. Model is based on a structure preserved at the Bavarian Forest Museum, and will look great with kits #330-334, sold separately.

OIL TANK W/GASOLINE PUMPS & HOSES

272-948 13.99
3-3/4 x 1-11/16" 9.6 x 4.3cm

VINE GROWING ESTATE TAVERN

272-372 75.99
13-7/32 x 12-13/32 x 4-13/16" 33 x 31 x 12cm
Here's a terrific roadside attraction in the rural part of your layout. This big building includes a tavern and a winery. Plenty of accessories are provided for detailing, including a large wine press, tables and benches, vats, wine casks, buckets and more. It can also model a typical European farmstead.

CEMENT WORKS

272-950 35.99
8-1/8 x 3" 20.7 x 9cm
This detailed cement plant makes a great trackside industry! Similar plants are found by themselves, or as part of a large gravel pit. The plant mixes and loads cement into waiting trucks. The building is complete with storage silos, a loading elevator, walkways and an attached office.

MINI GOLF COURSE W/TICKET BOOTH

272-384 44.99
20 x 13-13/16 x 2-13/32" 50 x 34.5 x 6cm
A great place to take the family for an afternoon of fun! This complete set includes an 18 hole miniature golf course with the some tricky obstacles, the snackbar (water wheel can be powered with Motor #272-629, sold separately) and an eating area with tables, umbrellas, chairs and other accessories.

FALLER

IMPORTED FROM GERMANY
BY WALTHERS

HALF-TIMBERED HOUSE W/DORMERS

272-219 22.99
4-3/4 x 3-1/2" 12 x 9cm
Includes three dormers and dark "wood" timbers.

HALF-TIMBERED HOUSE

272-222 12.99
3-3/4 x 3-1/2" 9.3 x 8.5cm
Easy-to-build kit with dark half timbers

2 BICYCLE STANDS & 16 BIKES

272-584 17.99
2-1/4 x 1-1/8" 5.9 x 2.7cm
2 x 5/8" 5.1 x 1.7cm

ADVENTURE PLAYGROUND

272-577 13.99
Superdetail a park with this assortment of equipment, including a wooden train, tower, teeter-totter, sandbox, benches and more.

PAVILION

272-355 32.99
8-5/8 x 6-1/8" 22 x 15.8cm

SMALL GRADE CROSSING W/GATES

272-170 13.99
5-1/8 x 4-3/4" 13 x 12cm

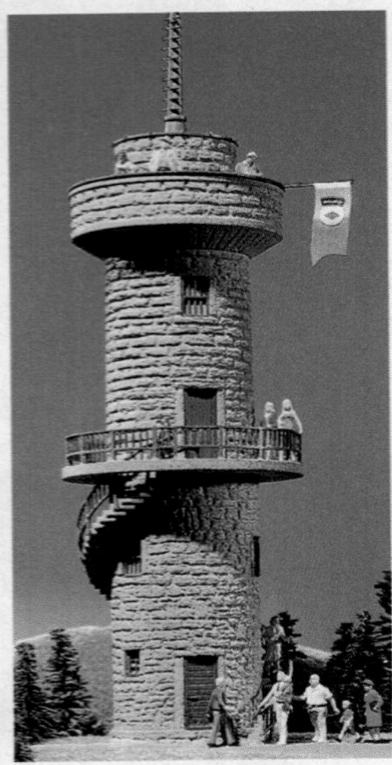

OBSERVATION TOWER "BREND"

272-386 24.99
2 x 11" 5.2 x 28cm
A narrow, two-story observation tower of natural stone, with an outside stairway on the lower area and an observation platform above.

PLATFORM EXTENSION

272-185 15.99
Extensions for use with station platform #272-181, sold separately.

HALF-TIMBERED HOUSE

272-252 21.99
4-13/32 x 3-13/32 x 4-1/4"
11 x 8.5 x 10.7cm
This small home makes a charming country cottage, or use it in a big city blue collar neighborhood.

DWELLING HOUSE

272-279 37.99
7-5/8 x 5 x 5-13/64"
19 x 12.5 x 13cm
Built from a variety of natural materials at the turn-of-the-century, this ornate house is based on a prototype located in the Black Forest.

"TURKIS" HOUSE

272-396 17.99
8-13/64 x 5-11/64 x 3-13/32"
20.5 x 12.9 x 8.5cm
A great building for the suburban homeowner, this model home (prototype built by Weberhaus) comes with a two-car garage with roof-top deck, covered entry and many other fine details.

MOUNTAIN CHAPEL

272-242 13.99
3-13/16 x 2-5/8 x 4-3/16"
9.5 x 6.5 x 10.5cm
A perfect addition to any scenic mountain path or forest area. Model features realistic timber walls and a belfry.

GANTRY CRANE

272-127 14.99
Crane: 5-3/16 x 2 x 3-13/16"
13 x 5.4 x 9.5cm

Heavy timber construction adds to the realistic look of this model.

BUS STOP SHELTERS

272-587 Set of Two **13.99**
2-3/8 x 1-5/16 x 1-1/2"
6 x 3.3 x 3.8cm
2-13/16 x 1 x 1-7/16"
7 x 2.5 x 3.6cm
Local citizens will appreciate having several of these shelters along bus or light rail lines in your city scene. Simulating wooden construction, they look great in any setting and provide a neat detail for busy streets. The kit includes parts for two complete buildings.

American Limited

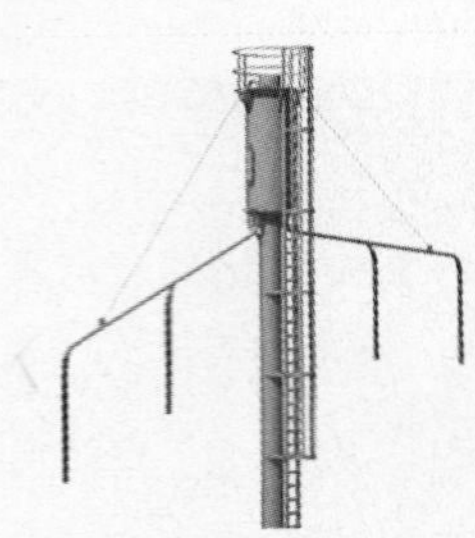

DIESEL SANDING TOWER

147-5100 12.95
Upgrade your engine terminal with this authentic replica, typical of towers used throughout the US and Canada. Model features moveable arms and operating counterweights, and can be built with one or two arms to service any size terminal. Easy-to-build kit features plastic parts, a photo-etched safety cage ladder and handrail, plus step-by-step instructions.

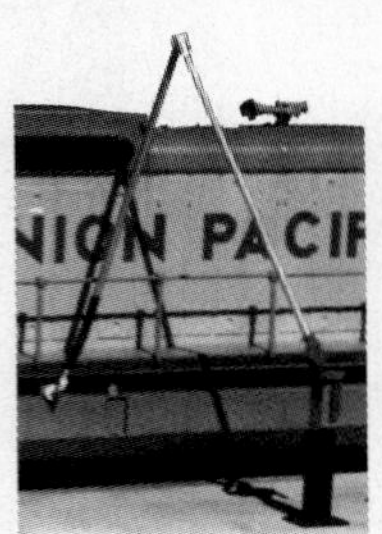

SYNDER FUEL CRANE

147-5200 2 Kits **5.95**
Movable styrene kit can be set to "fuel" diesel locos.

CHASSIS STACKERS

147-5300 pkg(2) **9.95**
Holds 18 van container chassis each. Used in many intermodal terminals.

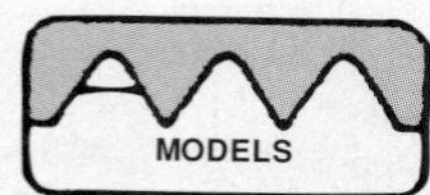

These smaller buildings add realism to any railroad. Each is designed for easy construction with injection molded parts.

FREIGHT PLATFORM
129-107 2.98
2-1/4 x 5-1/2" 5.6 x 13.9cm

TOWER
129-105 3.50
1 x 1-1/2" 2.5 x 4cm

SHANTY
129-102 2.98
1 x 1" 1.5 x 2cm
Prototype located in Hudsonville, Michigan, next to the C&O tracks.

FREIGHT STATION
129-104 3.50
1-1/2 x 2-1/16" 4 x 5.2cm

SHORT TRESTLE BRIDGE
129-302 3.50
2-1/4 x 1-1/4" 5.7 x 3.2cm

SIMPLE BEAM BRIDGE
129-301 1.98
4" x 1-9/16" 10 x 4cm, 4" tall

LONG TRESTLE BRIDGE
129-303 4.50
6' x 1-5/8" road bed.

LONG FREIGHT STATION
129-110 5.98

WORKSHED
129-106 5.98
1-1/2 x 4-3/4" 4 x 12cm

HAMELTON FREIGHT STATION
129-111 9.98

WILLIAMSBURG YARD OFFICE
129-103 3.50
1-1/2 x 2-1/16" 4 x 5.2cm

TRACKSIDE SHANTY
129-101 1.50
5/8 x 3/4" 1.5 x 2cm

SMALL SHANTY
129-112 With Windows **2.00**
5/8 x 3/4" 1.6 x 1.9cm

SMALL SHANTY
129-113 Without Windows **1.50**
5/8 x 3/4" 1.6 x 1.9cm

BUNKHOUSE
129-109 3.50
2-1/4 x 5-1/2" 5.6 x 13.9cm

FREIGHT STATION
129-108 5.98
2-1/2 x 2-1/4" 6.2 x 5.6cm

GARAGE
129-114 3.95
2-1/2 x 2-1/4" 6.2 x 5.6cm
Clapboard siding, includes doors and windows.

STORAGE SHED
129-115 3.50
2-1/2 x 2-1/4" 6.2 x 5.6cm
Clapboard siding, includes large sliding door, no windows.

A.W. ENTERPRISES

BUILDING WINDOW DRESS-UP KITS EA 2.95
Bring new life to dull downtown buildings. Full-color sheets contain appropriate interior scenes and numerous signs for the exterior as well. Designed to fit Smalltown USA buildings, adaptable to others.

157-16001 Mike's Market
157-16002 Tony's Gym
157-16003 Jessica's Salon
157-16004 Madlene's Deli
157-16005 Dime Store & Offices

157-16006 Hardware Store -
157-16009 Roy's Fix-It Shop
157-16011 John's Place
157-16010 Sally's Antiques
NEW
157-16012 Helen's Country Kitchen
157-16013 Family Shoe Store
NEW
157-16014 Old Indian Tobacco Shop
157-16016 Florist's Shop
157-16017 Drug Store
157-16025 Freytag's Furnaces

Information STATION

AMERICANIZING FOREIGN STRUCTURES
Before starting your next big building project, take a closer look at many of the structures available from over-seas manufacturers.

While many architectural details reflect a European sensibility or distinctly non-American appearance, it may be easier than you think to modify them for use on your layout. And, depending on the ethnic make-up of a city, you may see some of these same architectural elements copied or simplified when similar buildings were constructed in the US. For example, a successful brewer of German heritage may have constructed a warehouse that looked like a castle. The challenge is to integrate such models with the rest of your layout so the building "belongs" with the structures surrounding them.

One important thing to note, the entire structure may not be European. As you know, most structures come in kits and are not fully assembled. There may be distinct elements with a European design, but the rest of the building may have a universal appearance. It may be as easy as not using some parts during construction, or replacing them with new parts that look more like those found on American structures.

Look at the basic design, break the building down into its simplest elements and replace those pieces that don't fit. It's that simple!

ALPINE DIVISION
Scale Models

These HO craft train kits feature cardstock or metal construction (as noted). Mat board is printed or embossed to simulate brick, concrete block, board and batten, clapboard or stucco. These kits also include stripwood for bracing and trim. Corrugated Metal buildings require soldering skills. Kits include signs and detail parts. Interiors and lighting are included with some models.

WYOMING COAL MINE-METAL
700-24 32.00
5 x 10" 12.8 x 25.5cm

MODERN STATION
700-503 8.75
4-1/2 x 7" 11.5 x 8cm

3-TRACK CAR BARN-METAL
700-20 25.50
17 x 16" 18 x 40.5cm

DR. WHYTE'S HOUSE W/GARAGE
700-577 20.25
5-1/2 x 5-1/4" 14 x 13.4cm

MAIN STREET STATION
700-73 27.75
10 x 12" 25.5 x 30.5cm

STANDARD STATION
700-504 12.00
4 x 6" 10 x 15.3cm

2-STALL ENGINE HOUSE-METAL
700-9 21.50
5 x 14" 12.8 x 35.5cm

THE BROWN BUNGALOW WITH GARAGE
700-576 17.50
5-3/8 x 4" 13.7 x 10cm

WAREHOUSE-METAL
700-7 19.50
4-1/2 x 12" 11.5 x 30.5cm

UNION ICE COMPANY
700-566 28.25
Building: 6-3/4 x 8" 17.2 x 20.5cm
Platform: 1-1/2 x 16" 4 x 40.5cm

OLD TOWN LODGINGS
700-572 17.75
3-1/4 x 4" 8.3 x 10cm
4 x 4-7/8" 10 x 12.5cm

WELLS FARGO STATION
700-86 9.25
3-1/2 x 5" 9 x 12.8cm

1886 FREIGHT STATION EA 15.75
5-1/4 x 6" 13.5 x 15.3cm
700-5111 Orange
700-5112 Gray
700-5113 Red

WOOD BILLBOARD W/4 SP "DAYLIGHT" SIGNS

700-89 7.98

STATION DETAIL KIT
700-602 6.95

Get Daily Info, Photos and News at
www.walthers.com

BEKINS STORAGE WAREHOUSE
700-88 32.50
Mat, 5-3/4 x 15" 14.2 x 38cm

LUMBER YARD, COMPLETE
700-563 39.25
8-1/2 x 16" 21.5 x 40.5cm area

DIESEL HOUSE W/INTERIOR
700-522 27.75
6-1/2 x 16-1/2" 16.5 x 42cm

1887 PASSENGER DEPOT EA 22.95
5-1/2 x 8" 14 x 20.5cm
700-5021 Orange
700-5022 Gray
700-5023 Red

1870 WATER TANK EA 7.50
2 x 3-3/8" 5 x 8.5cm
700-5361 Orange
700-5362 Gray
700-5363 Red

COMBINATION TOWN DEPOT EA 36.50
6 x 12-1/2" 15.3 x 32cm
700-7001 Orange
700-7002 Gray
700-7003 Red

CENTRAL MFG. CO. FACTORY
700-541 15.95
4-1/2 x 10" 11.5 x 12.8cm

SUNKIST CITRUS EXCHANGE
700-83 15.75
4-1/2 x 6-1/2" 11.5 x 16.5cm
"Stucco" mat board.

ALPINE DIVISION
Scale Models

MAIL POUCH TOBACCO BARN
700-87 8.50
Mat, 4-1/2 x 5" 11.5 x 12.8cm

YARD TOWER, MODERN
700-80 17.50
2 x 2" 5 x 5cm

GRAIN ELEVATOR-METAL
700-12 23.50
5 x 5" 12.8 x 12.8cm

SUGAR ELEVATOR
700-26 32.00 ***NEW***

700-22

700-23

AMERICAN CHEMICAL & POTASH CO. & ANNEX-METAL
700-22 Plant **34.00**
6 x 14" 15 x 35cm

700-23 Annex **39.00**
6 x 14" 15 x 35cm

OLD TOWN HOMES
700-574 pkg(3) **21.95**
3-3/4 x 1-3/4" 9.5 x 4.5cm
3-1/2 x 5" 9 x 12.8cm
3-1/2 x 5" 9 x 12.8cm

OLD TOWN BUILDINGS
700-571 pkg(3) **28.25**
2-1/4 x 4" 5.7 x 10cm
5-3/4 x 5" 14.7 x 12.8cm
4-1/4 x 5-1/2" 10.8 x 14cm

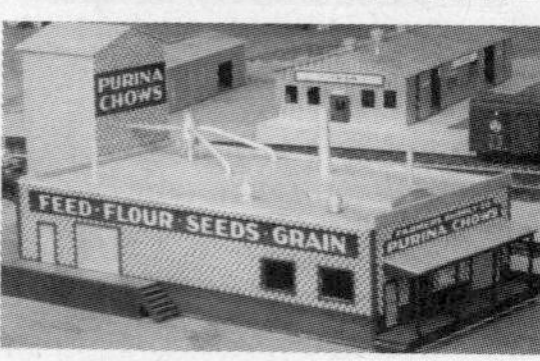

PURINA CHOWS FEED MILL
700-82 22.95
Mat, 5 x 9" 12.8 x 23cm

SWIFT MEAT PACKING PLANT
700-85 22.95
4 x 8" 10 x 20.5cm

ELECTRONICS PLANT
700-74 16.75
5-1/4 x 11" 13.5 x 28cm

MINING COMPANY MILL-METAL
700-18 12.00
4 x 6" 10 x 15.3cm

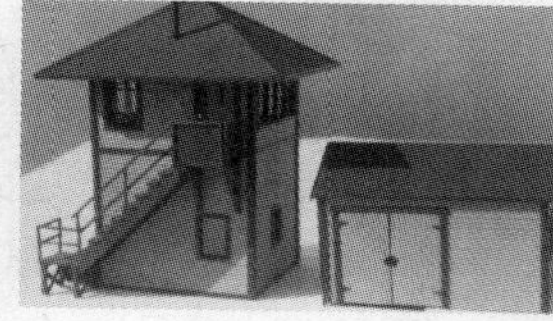

INTERLOCKING TOWER & SHED
700-61 12.75
2 x 2" 5 x 5cm

GRAND JUNCTION BOX WORKS
700-81 13.95
5 x 10" 12.8 x 25.5cm
Board and batt embossed mat board.

CURIO SHOP
700-575 17.50
3-1/4" 8.3 x 10cm

INDUSTRIAL OFFICE BUILDING - METAL
700-16 10.75
3 x 6" 7.5 x 15.3cm

PACIFIC FOUNDRY-METAL
700-19 15.50
5 x 8" 12.8 x 20.5cm

RED LAKE HILLSIDE MINE-METAL
700-6 13.85
5 x 7" 12.8 x 17.8cm
For hillside construction.

FURNITURE FACTORY-METAL
700-1 19.50
4-1/2 x 12" 11.5 x 30.5cm

OLD TOWN BUSINESS BLOCK
700-573 22.95
3-7/8 x 2-1/2" 9.8 x 6.5cm
3-7/8 x 3-5/8" 9.8 x 9.2cm

ED'S MARKET
700-76 22.00
5-1/2 x 6" 14 x 15.6cm
With interior and lights.

RAIL-TRUCK TERMINAL
700-542 15.95
5 x 9" 12.8 x 23cm

MODERN STORES
700-552 pkg(2) **7.50**
Each: 3-1/2 x 5" 9 x 12.8cm

ALPINE DIVISION
Scale Models

BLACK BART MINE & SHAFT-METAL
700-5 11.95
3 x 7" 7.5 x 18cm

TRIANGLE CAFE
700-75 27.75
4 x 5-1/2" 10 x 14cm
With interior and lights.

BUCKHORN MINE ORE PLANT-METAL
700-4 25.95
6 x 16" 15.3 x 40.5cm

3-STALL ROUNDHOUSE-METAL
700-8 31.50
12 x 12" 30.5 x 30.5cm

EXTRA STALL FOR ROUNDHOUSE-METAL
700-8241 8.50

3 EXTRA STALLS FOR ROUNDHOUSE-METAL
700-8243 20.25

YOUR HOBBY SHOP
700-71 17.50
5-1/2 x 6" 14 x 15.3cm

ILLUMINATED SIGN FOR HOBBY SHOP
700-7112 3.95

MODERN INDUSTRY
700-543 15.95
5 x 11-1/4" 12.8 x 28.5cm

POWER SUB-STATION
700-66 23.25
4-1/4 x 8-1/4" 10.8 x 21cm

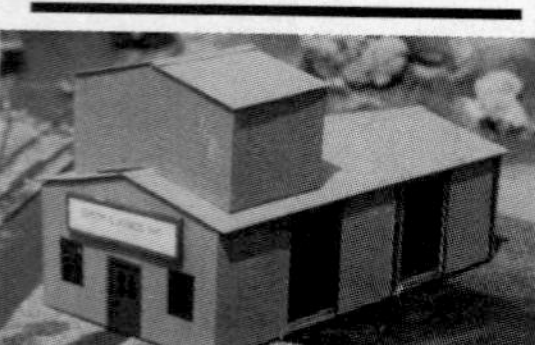

MINING HOIST HOUSE-METAL
700-17 12.00
3 x 5" 7.5 x 12.8cm

NORTHSIDE TOOL & DIE COMPANY
700-25 13.95
6 x 7" 15.3 x 18cm

LUMBER RACK & OFFICE
700-561 15.95

LUMBER COMPANY STORE & SHED
700-562 17.75

LUMBER COMPANY OFFICE ONLY
700-564 5.75

SCALE LUMBER PACKAGE
700-565 5.75

700-21

700-214

BRICK CAR BARN
700-21 2-Track **28.00**
700-214 4-Track **34.00**

CMA
Creative Model Associates

Add the finishing touch to your layout with these easy-to-build plastic kits. Each is finely detailed and comes with complete instructions.

MAIL CRANE
363-1001 5.95
Terrific detail for every station on your steam-era line. Includes one-piece arm with mail pouch molded in place.

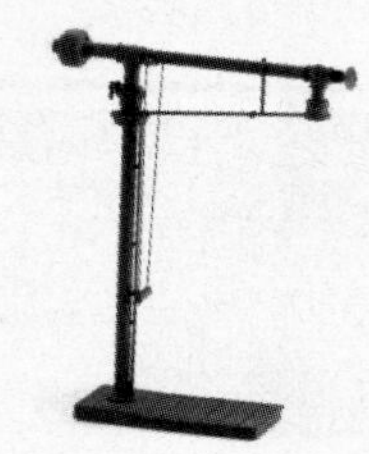

OIL COLUMN
363-1002 6.95
Refuel oil-burning steamers at this detailed column.

TELLTALE
363-1004 4.95
For safe operation near overhead obstacles.

OUTHOUSES
363-1025 pkg(3) **5.95** ***NEW***

ICING PLATFORM
Platforms were constructed about every 250 miles to fill ice in refrigerator cars. Model is based on a PFE design, used in many locations.

363-1014 18" (45cm) **29.50**
363-1015 36" (90cm) **49.50**

MILK STATION W/CANS
363-1007 9.95
Farmers brought their milk and cream to platforms like this for shipment to dairies. Usually spaced about a mile apart, they were often built near a small town station or rural road crossing. The covered shelter helped keep full cans cool during hot weather. Includes 27 cans, additional cans are available in #363-1006, sold separately.

CRESCENT STATION

PHONE BOOTH KIT
513-566 pkg(3) **3.95**
3/8 x 3/8" 1 x 1cm

Unique construction method uses adhesive-backed film, which is wrapped around an acrylic cube. Includes cardstock details and enough parts to build three booths.

GAS STATION
513-553 29.95
4-1/4 x 4-7/8"
Craft train kit features die-cut walls, plastic doors and windows and corrugated aluminum sheathing. Cast metal gas pumps, oil bunker, signs, a phone booth and other details are included. For the finishing touch, there's a plastic 1935 Ford from Williams Brothers, that looks great parked out front.

CITYSCENES™

The Cityscenes™ line of Spectrum® building kits offers a dramatic skyline for your diesel- or steam-era railroad. All structures are richly detailed and accurately modeled for amazing realism. Kits require glue for assembly, and previous model building experience is recommended for best results.

DEPARTMENT STORE

160-88006 60.00
For a sophisticated shopping experience at the end of the 1800s, you had to make your way to one of the new department stores. With their multiple floors of merchandise showrooms, the department store was a dream-come-true for product selection and convenience.

THE METROPOLITAN BUILDING

160-88003 80.00
With its Art Deco details, this skyscraper would typically contain luxury apartments on the upper floors, offices in the middle and retail shops on the ground floor. The building is appropriate for middle-of-the-block use.

TRADE TOWER

160-88007 90.00
Reminiscent of the Empire State Building, this magnificent skyscraper's top floors are configured to comply with the "setback laws" passed in many cities to ensure that sunlight reached the sidewalks and streets below. This building is designed for use as a corner property.

BUS STATION

160-88005 40.00
Sweeping lines and bold Art Deco styling make this downtown bus station a standout.

AMBASSADOR HOTEL

160-88002 80.00
With a ballroom and colonnade on the upper floor, guest rooms in the middle and a lobby and restaurant on the first floor, this hotel is typical of those built in any medium- to large-size city from 1910-1940. "U"-shape configuration was a practical consideration to provide the maximum amount of windows and natural light to the hotel's guests.

VARIETY STORE

160-88004 50.00
Modeled from period photographs, this building represents the ubiquitous five-and-dime stores that found their way into most cities and towns during the first half of the 1900s.

For Daily Product Information Click

www.walthers.com

SAVINGS AND LOAN CO.

160-88008 40.00
By reducing the masonry mass needed to support the building's upper floors, a cast iron facade permitted the installation of large street-side windows. The result was more light and timeless architecture.

These kits are more challenging, and are designed for builders with some experience. Parts are molded in color and complete instructions are included. Assembly requires glue for plastic, sold separately.

LOCO MAINTENANCE BUILDING
160-15115 31.00

CAR REPAIR SHOP
160-15124 31.00
Keep your freight car fleet in top shape with regular repairs in this facility.

SUBURBAN STATION
160-45173 8.00
1-7/8 x 5-1/2" 14 x 4.8cm

STORAGE BUILDING W/STEAM WHISTLE SOUND
160-46209 26.00

RANCH STYLE HOUSE
160-45154 7.00
2-1/4 x 5-1/2" 5.7 x 14cm

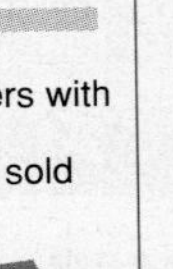

PLATFORM
160-45194 9.00
2-1/8 x 7" 5.5 x 18cm

WATER TANK
160-45153 7.00
3-1/4" 8.2cm diameter

SWITCH TOWER
160-45132 6.00
1-5/8" 4.2cm square

SUPER MARKET
160-45141 6.00
2-1/8 x 4-5/8" 5.5 x 11.8cm

DRIVE-IN HAMBURGER STAND
160-45434 12.00

HARDWARE STORE
160-45143 6.00
2-1/8 x 4-5/8" 5.5 x 11.8cm

OIL TANK
4-3/4" 12.1cm diameter

WITH DIESEL HORN
160-46208 26.00

WITH BLINKING LIGHT
160-46212 18.00
4-3/4" 12.1cm diameter

COALING STATION
160-45211 10.00
3-3/8 x 3" 8.6 x 7.6cm

PASSENGER STATION W/LIGHT
160-46217 24.00
5-3/8 x 9-3/8" 13.7 x 23.8cm
Preassembled.

FREIGHTHOUSE W/LIGHT
160-46216 24.00
5-1/2 x 9-1/2" 14 x 24.1cm
Preassembled.

FARM BUILDING W/ANIMALS
160-45152 7.00

HOUSE UNDER CONSTRUCTION
160-45191 9.00
2-7/8 x 5-1/4" 7.3 x 13cm

FREIGHTHOUSE
160-45171 8.00
2-3/8 x 4-3/4" 12.1 x 6cm

CONTEMPORARY HOUSE
160-45432 12.00
2-7/8 x 8-3/4" 7.3 x 22.3cm

BARN
160-45151 7.00
2-1/2 x 3-1/2" 6.4 x 9cm

CATHEDRAL
160-45192 9.00

POLICE STATION
160-45145 6.00

SPLIT LEVEL HOUSE
160-45213 10.00
2-7/8 x 6-1/8" 7.3 x 15.5cm

MOTEL W/SWIMMING POOL
160-45214 10.00
4-1/8 x 12-3/4" 10.5 x 32.4cm

CAPE COD STYLE HOUSE
160-45131 6.00
1-7/8 x 3" 4.8 x 7.5cm

PEDESTRIAN FOOT BRIDGE
160-45172 8.00

TOY & HOBBY SHOP
160-45431 12.00
3-3/8 x 5-7/8" 8.6 x 15cm

These easy-to-build structures feature plastic parts molded in colors. and snap-together

SCHOOL HOUSE

160-45133 6.00
6 x 7-1/8" 15.3 x 4.8cm

5 & 10 STORE

160-45142 6.00
2-1/8 x 4-5/8" 5.5 x 11.8cm

POST OFFICE

160-45144 6.00
2-1/8 x 4-5/8 5.5 x 11.8cm

GAS STATION

160-45174 10.00

EMIL'S DRY GOODS

160-45535 17.00

RURAL STATION

160-45521 12.00

BUD'S CONVENIENCE STORE

160-45522 12.00

TWO-STORY HOUSE

160-45523 12.00

MAIN STREET APOTHECARY

160-45536 17.00

LIBRARY

160-45524 12.00

THEATER

160-45525 12.00

JOE'S PIZZA & VIDEO STORE

160-45526 pkg(2) **12.00**

SILVER SERIES™ BUILDINGS

A great addition to Silver Series train sets, these easy-to-build kits are perfect for any layout. Models feature parts molded in color and simple snap and lock "E-Z Build" Plasticville USA® construction.

GEORGIAN MANSION

160-45531 17.00

VINTAGE AUTO REPAIR

160-45532 17.00

1930s SCHOOL HOUSE

160-45533 17.00

PINK LADY BOUTIQUE

160-45534 17.00

BH MODELS

These easy-to-build kits add realistic detail to industrial and railroad scenes. Tank kits consist of individual 1/4 round sections, which are "stacked" to simulate plate steel construction. All kits are molded in color and include instructions.

Limited Quantity Available on All Items

24' DIAMETER BLACK WATER TANKS EA 19.50

42' tall.

159-322 30° Peaked Top
159-326 15° Peaked Top

KIRBY WAGON WORKS

159-502 19.95
Board and batten siding, plus a galvanized tin roof

SOMEPLACE ELSE CIRCA 1880

159-503 19.95
Board and batten siding, plus a galvanized tin roof. Door and window openings are cut out, frames are separate for easy painting if desired.

COUNTRY CROSSING

159-504 26.95
5 x 5" 12.5 x 12.5cm
Board and batten siding, plus a galvanized tin roof.

HITCHIN' POST

159-505 34.95
5 x 10" 12.5 x 25cm
Board and batten siding, plus a galvanized tin roof.
30° peaked top,

BUILDING W/TANK, CYCLONE & VENTS

159-5001 50.00
70 x 80'
Use for any small industry.

Designed for easy construction, Laser-Kit® kits feature styrene and wood parts which have been cut to exact size and shape using a computer-controlled laser. Models are highly detailed and assemble much like plastic kits. Most include peel & stick roofing and press-fit windows and doors.

CATALOG

152-99999 HO Catalog **2.00**

TWO STORY SECTION HOUSE

152-128 39.95
3-3/4 x 4-1/2 x 3"
9.7 x 11.5 x 7.5cm

When section gangs were assigned to each part of the railroad, many lines built company houses for workers and their families. This two-story design is based on a Missouri Pacific prototype that looks great on any railroad. The model features authentic clapboard siding, plus small front and rear covered porches.

PENNSYLVANIA TOOL HOUSE

152-131 17.95
3 x 2-1/4 x 2"
7.5 x 5.6 x 5cm

INTERLOCKING TOWER N&W "FOREST"

152-132 44.95
2-1/4 x 1-3/4 x 4"
12.5 x 6.2 x 10.6cm

PACIFIC ELECTRIC PASSENGER SHELTER

152-137 pkg(2) **12.95**
Figures not included

1-1/2 STORY HOUSE WITH PORCH - 139 MAPLE STREET

152-139 29.95
3-1/2 x 3 x 2-1/2"
8.7 x 7.5 x 6.2cm
In the city or out on the farm, this little house will be a real showpiece along your railroad. It includes a delicate front porch made of laser-cut parts, plus a fully screened back porch for those hot summer nights. Clapboard siding and rolled roofing add to the realism of the finished model.

FARMER'S GRAIN & STOCK CO

152-115 49.95
9 x 5 x 7"
Not just another grain elevator... this kit includes an attached, elevated loading dock with ramps, office and machinery shed and scale. 100% laser-cut from clapboard siding with tin style roof featuring peel and stick backing for easy application.

BURLINGTON ROUTE DEPOT

152-144 64.95

TWO STORY FARM HOUSE W/FRONT PORCH

152-140 42.95
Perfect for the big HO family, this home looks great in the country (especially alongside the Country Barn #119, or Feeder Barn #71, both sold separately) or in an older part of town. Features laser-cut clapboard siding, an attached rear "kitchen," plus a detailed front porch with laser-cut steps and trim. The roof is covered with self-adhesive, tin-style material and a cast metal chimney adds the final touch.

WINDSOR HOTEL

152-143 54.95
2-1/2 x 6-1/2 x 4-1/2"
6.2 x 16.2 x 11.2cm

FARBER STATION

152-111 89.95
This delightful structure is based on a plan used by the Chicago & Alton Railroad in the late 1800s, which has been preserved and is still standing today. The kit is perfect for any small town and features upstairs living quarters for the agent and his family, along with many period details.

RAILROAD SUPPLY BUILDING

152-118 25.95
4-7/8 x 2-5/8" 12.1 x 6.5cm
Built by the Chicago & Alton, at Roodhouse, Illinois, later used by Illinois Central Gulf. Supplies for track and signal crews were stored here. Buildings of this type were also found in terminals, housing car and loco supplies.

A.C. BROWN MANUFACTURING COMPANY

152-715 99.95 ***NEW***
12 x 6-1/4 x 5-1/4"
A wonderful factory for your HO Scale layout. 100% laser-cut wood with pre-cut window and door openings; layered peel and stick window and door assembly; covered loading dock; outside staircase; and a roof with laser-cut watertank, skylights, access hatch with door, smokejacks and chimneys.

SOUTHERN PACIFIC COMBINATION TYPE 23 DEPOT W/DOCK

152-150 99.95 ***NEW***
Features 100% laser-cut wood with layered, peel and stick windows, doors and shingles, tabbed and notched wall and roof pieces, laser-cut wood loading dock with laser-scribed decking and correct Southern Pacific style, cast white metal chimneys.

NINE MILE HOUSE & TAVERN

152-145 59.95
4 x 5 x 4-1/2"
10 x 12.5 x 11.2cm

Designed from an old St. Louis tavern located exactly nine miles from the St. Louis City/County line, this building is still standing, although there have been some changes over the years. It is now called the Train Wreck Saloon, features a rear beer garden, complete with an old wood caboose, and is a popular "hot spot." This kit is 100% laser-cut wood with layered, peel and stick window and door assembly, "tin" style roof, corner doors and windows and two AMB cast white metal chimneys. Includes full color signage and front sign board.

WEST END EXCHANGE

152-146 38.95
3-1/2 x 7 x 2"
8.7 x 17.5 x 5cm

Designed from photos of the Massachusetts Transit Authority waiting room at Arlington Heights, MA, this kit could be a local bus depot, post office, barber shop, mercantile or whatever your imagination dictates. Features 100% laser-cut clapboard siding with layered, peel and stick windows and door assembly, covered front waiting area, rear loading area, flat roof with peel and stick tarpaper strips and an extra-tall AMB cast white metal chimney with wire stays. Comes complete with full color signage.

SANTA FE DEPOT #3 - GOLD SERIES

152-801 69.95
8-3/4 x 4-1/8 x 3-1/4"
21.8 x 10.3 x 9.3cm
As part of your layout or diorama, this stunning depot takes kit building to a new level. A faithful replica of the Santa Fe design, it's complete with the road's unique bay window, clapboard siding above the belt rail and drop siding below. Laser-cut, diamond shaped shingles , a complete set of detailed doors, windows, eave brackets, even the Santa Fe style chimney are included!

RAILROAD ROOMING HOUSE

152-713 52.95
11-1/2 x 2 x 3"
28.7 x 5 x 7.5cm

LONG BELL LUMBER CO. SKID SHACKS

152-710 pkg(3) **24.95**
2-1/2 x 1-3/4 x 1-1/2"
6.2 x 4.3 x 3.7cm
Built to house loggers, these "mobile homes" were built on large skids so they could be dragged to a new cutting area. Build them without the skids and you've got a great set of miner's cabins, an early tourist camp, or seasonal homes for farm workers. Includes parts for three shacks, plus cast metal smokejacks.

FREIGHT HOUSE

152-701 29.95
Laser-cut kit.

FEEDER BARN

152-711 26.95
7 x 4-3/4 x 3-1/2"
17.5 x 11.8 x 8.7cm
The perfect addition to your farm operations, this barn is ideal for housing cows, sheep, hogs, horses or other animals. The model features laser-cut siding, plus peel and stick material for the tin roof

SPRINGFIELD DEPOT

152-138 39.95
A great small town depot, this one-story design features laser-cut eave brackets and traditional bay window.

MRS. WILLIAMS HOUSE

152-126 39.95
6 x 3-3/4"
15 x 9.3cm
This structure makes a great home in any setting from the 1920s to the present. The frame bungalow includes covered front and rear porches, outside cellar doors, laser-cut lattice work under the front porch and self-adhesive, laser-cut roofing.

OLD MAN DAN'S HOUSE

152-151 39.95 *NEW*
4 x 4 x 2-1/4"
A great little town or country house with covered front porch and delicate, laser-cut trim. The siding comes scribed and the house can be built with or without the laser-cut peel and stick shingle strips. Includes AMB cast white metal chimney.

ATLANTIC COAST LINE DEPOT

152-130 64.95
13 x 5 x 3-1/2"
32.5 x 12.5 x 8.7cm
This classic depot is a must-have for the ACL fan and will look great on any layout set in the south. It includes the unique bay window and dormer, wrap-around freight dock and chimneys found on actual ACL depots of this style.

ELEVATED WAREHOUSE

152-706 26.95
Small storage buildings like this are common on farms, in small towns and along busy sidings. Kit includes loading dock and ladder, plus cast metal chimney and piers.

SPRINGFIELD CAFE

152-136 26.95
Includes covered front porch, rear shed and live-over second floor.

SANTA FE ONE STORY DEPOT

152-707 39.95
8-3/4 x 3-1/4 x 2-3/4"
21.8 x 9.3 x 6.8cm
Whether a new building in the days of steam, or worn and weather-beaten in the present, this handsome depot makes a great addition to your railroad. Based on a Santa Fe design, it includes the road's traditional bay window, ornate eave brackets and loads of additional features.

SANTA FE TWO STORY DEPOT

152-142 86.95
The model includes accurate ATSF style windows and doors, along with the correct diamond-shaped shingles for the roof. A neat bay window and laser-cut eave brackets are just some of the fine details included.

ELLINGTON'S MERCANTILE

152-135 39.95
Perfect for any town, any time. 100% laser-cut scribed siding with two story front and covered front porch with peel and stick front decking. A special feature is the newly designed, recessed entryway with large display windows which were typical on this type of store.

NEW FREEDOM, PENNSYLVANIA DEPOT

152-141 72.95 *NEW*
13 x 5 x 3-3/4"
This Pennsy prototype features board and batten siding; layered, peel and stick windows and doors; beautifully designed three window bay; and a raised passenger loading platform. The perfect addition to any layout.

SOUTHERN PACIFIC DEPOT

152-134 124.95
Station Building Alone:
11 x 3-1/2 x 4-1/2"
27.5 x 8.7 x 11.2cm
Loading Dock Adds:
5" 12.5cm to Length,
1" 2.5cm to width.
Designed from the original railroad drawings, this depot was built by the SP on both narrow and standard gauge lines, and many are still standing today. Features two-story bay window, laser-cut shingles and a loading dock.

NORTHERN PACIFIC DEPOT

152-149 74.95 *NEW*
10-1/2 x 3 x 3-1/2"
Designed from plans for a Class A Depot built between 1889 and 1900, this kit can also be built to represent Class B or C depots with a bit of modification. 100% laser-cut wood with clapboard and scribed siding and pre-cut door and window openings. Windows feature layered construction with peel and stick backing and a precise fit. Roofing is peel and stick tabbed shingle strips and two AMB cast white metal chimneys are included.

COUNTRY GRAIN ELEVATOR

152-110 39.95
4-1/4 x 6-3/4 x 10"
10.8 x 17 x 25.2cm
These prairie skyscrapers still dot rural landscapes. The model features laser-cut Evergreen styrene walls, with Grandt Line windows and a plastic spout for loading box cars. A great structure for steam- or diesel-era lines.

TRANSFER BUILDING

152-704 87.95
11-3/4 x 8-3/4 x 5-1/2"
29.3 x 21.8 x 13.7cm
Locate your newest trackside industry inside this roomy building. Perfect for any kind of manufacturing or storage, the kit includes 350 laser-cut parts.

LINEMAN'S TOOL HOUSE

152-116 17.95
3-7/8 x 1-1/4"
9.8 x 3.1cm
A must-have detail for the right-of-way. Includes motor car set-off. Doors can be positioned open or closed. Combine with Handcar House #114 (sold separately) for a great mini-scene.

ILLINOIS CENTRAL TYPE B DEPOT

152-124 24.95
3 x 4-1/4"
7.5 x 10.6cm
Built for very small towns and remote areas to provide the agent with a modest office and freight house.

COUNTRY BARN

152-119 69.95
7-1/2 x 5-1/2"
18.8 x 13.8cm
The perfect shelter for any livestock or dairy farm.

ENGINE/WAREHOUSE

152-708 45.95
9 x 5 x 4" 22.5 x 12.5 x 10cm
The perfect shop to store and service the lone engine of a shortline, or an engine shed for the local switcher in a bigger community. The kit is based on an Illinois Terminal structure and features board and batten siding, plus an extra-long cast metal chimney.

SANTA FE TWO-STORY DEPOT

152-125 Original **47.95**
5 x 2-1/2 x 3-3/4"
12.5 x 6.2 x 9.4cm
Based on the Engel, New Mexico, depot, built to ATSF #1 Standard Two-Story design. Almost identical structures were built throughout Colorado, New Mexico and western Kansas from the 1880s on. Includes ATSF style shingles and paint mixing formulas to match various schemes.

BIG FOUR FREIGHT HOUSE

152-152 49.95 *NEW*
Structure: 7 x 3 x 3-1/2"
Dock: 9-1/4 x 1-1/4"
A New York Central design, used on the CCC&St.L Railroad, a subsidiary of the NYC. Includes laser-cut scribed siding with cast white metal piers, a flared hip roof and windows and doors with layered peel and stick assembly. Also included is an extra-long freight dock.

INTERLOCKING TOWER

152-702 29.95
2-1/4 x 1-3/4 x 4"
5.6 x 4.3 x 10cm
Found at yards, junctions and other busy spots along the right-of-way, this tower makes a neat addition to your line. Features laser-cut basswood and veneer plywood, along with an impressive stairway and a traditional hip roof.

HILLVIEW VOLUNTEER FIRE COMPANY

152-147 42.95 *NEW*
2-3/4 x 3-3/4 x 4-3/4"
Designed from a photo of an old fire house in Hillview, IL, but appropriate for anywhere in the country. This two story fire house is just large enough to house the town pumper truck on the lower level, with an office and storage above. Features unusual Queen Anne style windows which assemble in layers with peel and stick backing, double doors which can be modeled open or closed, an outside stairway and hexagonal peel and stick shingle strips.

WETHERSFIELD NEW HAVEN DEPOT

152-148 54.95 *NEW*
6-1/4 x 3-1/2 x 3-1/2"
Originally constructed as a freight depot, this building was put into service for passenger use when the original depot burned. Very similar in design to other New Haven depots, this one is 100% laser-cut wood with tabbed and notched wall and roof pieces, pre-cut window and door openings and peel and stick layered windows and doors. Includes a freight dock and comes complete with the typical NYC signs in full color.

YARD OFFICE

152-709 24.50
2-1/2 x 1-3/4 x 3"
10 x 4.3 x 7.5cm
Keep yard operations moving smoothly from this handsome little building. The Boston & Maine prototype looks great in a small yard, but can also serve as a hotel, boarding house or store across the tracks.

GREAT NORTHERN DEPOT

152-133 59.95
8-1/4 x 4-1/8 x 3-1/4"
20.6 x 10.3 x 9.3cm
Local residents will be mighty proud to have this depot in their town. Based on a Great Northern prototype, it has all the features that make it a perfect choice for any layout. Detailed laser-cut parts include the bay window and a ladder.

UNION PACIFIC STANDARD 24 X 64' DEPOT

152-127 59.95
10 x 3-1/2 x 2-1/3"
8.4 x 17.1cm
Used all along the UP, ideal for small towns on your road too. Includes laser-cut brackets and roof trusses.

LAKE JUNCTION STATION

152-120 32.95
2-1/4 x 2" 5.6 x 5cm
Built by Missouri Pacific at Lake Junction, Missouri, a suburb of Webster Grove. Can be used as a small yard office.

HITZEMAN FEED MILL

152-117 41.95
9 x 5-1/2 x 5.75"
22.5 x 13.8 x 14.4cm
Found in small towns throughout the US, this trackside industry looks great next to the Country Grain Elevator #110 (sold separately).

DILL'S MARKET

152-122 19.95
4-1/4 x 3"
10.6 x 7.5cm
Corner grocery, gas station - just about any small business can use this building, based on an actual structure.

SONNY'S SHACK

152-705 19.95
4-1/2 x 2-1/2 x 1-3/4"
11.2 x 6.2 x 4.3cm
A great building down by the tracks, out on the farm or alongside the road. Kit includes laser-cut tar paper (so no painting is needed) plus "Laser-Cracked" window glass. Build it like new or ready for the wreckers!

TOOL & HAND CAR HOUSE

152-114 14.00
Paint it to match, and this small structure will look great alongside any station or junction tower. Based on a Missouri Pacific prototype, it's similar to designs used on just about every US railroad. The kit includes set off tracks to park a hand car or motor car (sold separately).

CORYDON GENERAL STORE/POST OFFICE

152-123 36.95
A classic that fits many areas and time periods. Build it for any country crossroads on your layout.

SILEX ELEVATOR

152-121 44.95
4.5 x 5.5 x 7.75"
11.2 x 13.8 x 19.4cm
Prototype in Silex, Missouri. A great elevator for any grain growing region of your railroad.

MINER'S CABIN

152-703 14.00
2-3/4 x 1-3/4 x 1-3/4"
6.8 x 4.3 x 4.3cm
This small structure can be used almost anywhere. It makes a great cabin up in the woods, but it can also serve as a crossing shanty, industrial guard house, company house or other general purpose building.

ONE-STORY SECTION HOUSE

152-129 22.95
Many railroads built small, wooden homes for workers. Single-story home is based on a Rio Grande design and also makes a dandy cabin, gas station or small store.

AMERICAN CLASSIC NARROW GAUGE SERIES

Specific prototype kits for the narrow gauge railroads from east to west.

DOLORES DEPOT

152-803 TBA *NEW*
Prototype was on the Rio Grande Southern Railroad.

CUMBRES STATION

152-112 45.95
5-1/4 x 3-1/4 x 2-7/8"
This famous New Mexico depot was located atop Cumbres Pass, NM, along the route of the DRGW's San Juan narrow gauge extension. The kit is carefully scaled after the original depot, yet it's versatile enough for most railroads in any era. Includes laser-cut roof brackets, doors and windows.

STRONG DEPOT

152-804 TBA *NEW*
Prototype is located on the Sandy River and Rangely Lakes Railroad.

LASERKIT® XPRESS

Priced under 15.95 so you can put multiples of these products on your layout, these kits are designed to be simple enough for the first time modeler to complete assembly in under two hours.

BILLBOARD W/COLOR SIGNAGE

152-795 TBA *NEW*

ONE CAR GARAGE

152-796 10.95 *NEW*

GAS STATION

152-797 15.95 *NEW*

COMPANY HOUSE

152-798 10.95 *NEW*

SMALL FALSE FRONT STORE

152-799 10.95 *NEW*

These craft train kits include detailed plaster walls, with beveled corners for easier assembly. Doors and windows are cast in place, and stripwood is provided for window sashes.

SALIDA MACHINE SHOP

231-3 22.50
3-1/4 x 3-1/4"
9 x 9cm

SALIDA COAL COMPANY

231-1 29.95
3-3/4 x 8-3/4"
9.5 x 22cm
Includes dry transfer sign.

SALIDA COAL BINS

231-2 16.50
2-1/2 x 10-1/2" 6 x 26.5cm
Wood kit with plastic details.

231-6 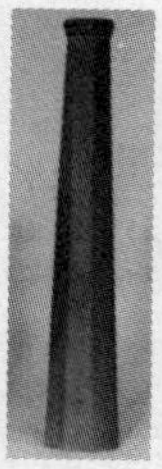 231-7

70' SQUARE BRICK CHIMNEY

231-6 9.95

70' OCTAGONAL BRICK CHIMNEY

231-7 9.95
1-1/2 x 9-5/8"
3.8 x 24.4cm
Smokestacks are one-piece plaster castings with realistic brick detail.

BLACKSMITH SHOP

231-14 19.95
4 x 4" 10 x 10cm
Wooden building. Includes plastic windows and preweathered wood.

MENARD WOOL & MOHAIR

231-8 34.95
3-1/2 x 7-1/2" 9 x 18.5cm
Includes plastic windows.
Prototype in Menard, Texas.

ALAMOSA OIL SERVICE

231-9 29.95
4-1/2 x 5" 12 x 13cm
Includes plastic windows.
Prototype in Alamosa, Colorado.

DYNAMITE IGLOOS

231-4 pkg(3) **14.95**
2-1/2 x 1-3/4" 6.4 x 4.5cm
One-piece Hydrocal® castings.

TAPERED, 9' DIAMETER WATER TANK W/TOWER

231-24 22.95
1-3/8 x 3-7/8" 3.5 x 10cm
Includes rod banding. Water tanks can be built with tower, or free-standing as a roof-top detail. Kits feature preweathered wood parts.

STRAIGHT 6' DIAMETER WATER TANK W/TOWER

231-25 20.95
1-1/4 x 4-5/8" 3 x 11.5cm
Includes hoop banding.

LIGHTED MINE TUNNEL W/MIRROR

231-20 TBA *NEW*

Start a construction boom on your layout with the Atlas line of trackside structures and accessories! Based on authentic American prototypes, the kits are molded in realistically colored styrene. The kits also include easy-to-follow instructions, decals and printed window glazing where appropriate

ROADSIDE RESTAURANT ↑OK

150-760 9.45
5-5/8 x 8-3/4" 14.3 x 21.9cm

LUMBER YARD & OFFICE

150-750 8.95
3-3/4 x 8-1/2" 9.5 x 21.3cm
Mill lumber sold separately (150-791).

SCALE LUMBER

150-791 3.25
Easy-to-build kit features stacks of lumber, molded in realistic color of plastic.

TRACKSIDE SHANTY

150-702 5.60
2-1/4 x 3-1/8" 5.7 x 8cm

PASSENGER STATION ←OK

150-706 9.45
4-1/8 x 9"
10.3 x 22.5cm
Includes 1 station platform.

PIER SET

150-80 11.80
Includes 46 stone masonry piers, graduated in height, 1 pier girder; snap-in shims.

WATER TOWER

150-703 7.20
3-1/8 x 3-1/4" 7.8 x 8.2cm

REFRESHMENT STAND

150-715 5.45
3-3/8 x 4-1/4" 8.4 x 10.7cm

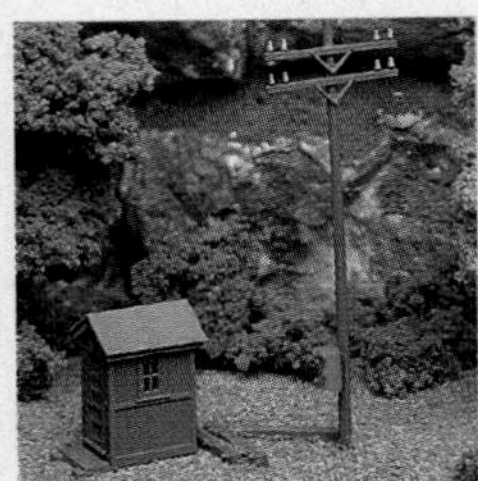

TELEPHONE SHANTY & POLE

150-705 3.85
1-1/2 x 3" 3.8 x 7.5cm

SIGNAL TOWER

150-704 7.20
2-5/8 x 3-1/8" 6.5 x 14cm

STATION PLATFORM

150-707 pkg(2) **4.40**
2-1/8 x 6-1/2" 5.4 x 16.3cm

ELEVATED GATE TOWER

150-701 5.60
1-1/4 x 2" 3.1 x 5cm

TURNTABLE

150-305 19.95
Fully assembled, 9" diameter turntable has the ability to stop at 21 positions, 15° apart. Geneva movement locks table in exact position every time. Simulated wood brown turntable deck and concrete pit ring. Surface mount; no cutting necessary. Manual crank operation; can be easily motorized for remote control operation with the #304 Turntable Drive Unit.

PIER GIRDER

150-82 pkg(4) **2.35**

65' DECK TRUSS BRIDGE

150-884 Nickel Silver Rail **4.75**
9"
23cm

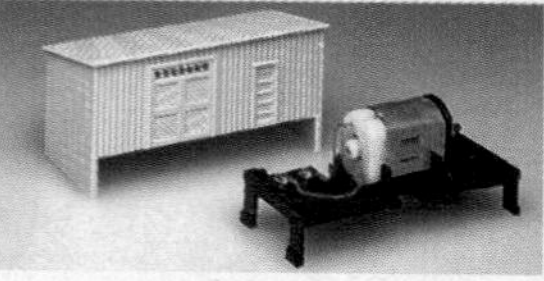

NEW & IMPROVED TURNTABLE MOTOR DRIVE UNIT

150-304 19.95
Belt-driven for quiet operation.

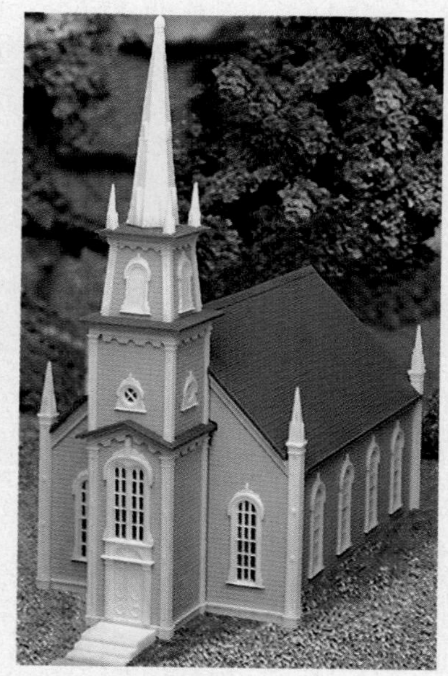

19TH CENTURY CHURCH

150-708 21.95
9-1/2 x 4-3/4 x 10-3/4"
23.8 x 11.9 x 26.9cm
A charming addition to any community, based on an actual structure. Molded in blue and white ABS plastic, no painting is needed. Requires ABS cement for assembly (sold separately).

BRIDGE PIER

150-81 pkg(4) **3.00**
3"
7.5cm

65' PONY TRUSS BRIDGE

150-886 Nickel Silver Rail **11.95**
9"
23cm

65' WARREN TRUSS BRIDGE

150-883 Nickel Silver Rail **4.75**
9"
23cm

130' CURVED CORD BRIDGE

150-887 Nickel Silver Rail **19.50**
18"
45.7cm

65' THRU PLATE GIRDER BRIDGE

150-885 Nickel Silver Rail **4.75**
9 x 2-5/8"
23 x 6.5cm
Comes assembled.

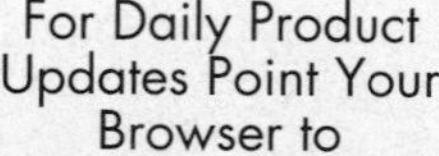

TRANSMITTER TOWER

189-5965 41.99
14-3/4" 37cm

Modernize communications on your layout with this modern radio tower. To protect aircraft, there are three LEDs at the top of the tower which flash in sequence. Model is fully assembled, ready to install.

PEDESTRIAN STONE BRIDGE

189-6041 13.99

TIMBER SHOP

189-6047 14.99

These craft train kits include diecut siding, Grandt Line plastic doors and windows, scale lumber and cast metal detail parts.

JOHNSON MOTOR SERVICE

216-8701 22.95
4-1/8 x 2" 10.5 x 5cm

1940-50S GAS PUMPS

216-187 pkg(2) **3.95**
13/16" 2.1cm tall

BUTLER BINS®

216-8704 pkg(2) **15.95**
2-1/8" 5.4cm diameter

VICTORIAN COTTAGE

216-8703 32.95
4 x 3-1/8" 10 x 8cm

HOUSE

216-8702 31.95
3-1/2 x 5" 9 x 12.7cm
Turn-of-the-century design.

BRAWA

These detailed sturctures feature metal, plastic and wood parts, and require only minor assembly or instillation. Powered models require a 14-16V DC power supply, or can be converted for AC power using Bridge Rectifier #2185, sold separately.

CABLEWAYS

These working models look great on mountain ranges. Each is complete with drive cable, mechanism and cars. Systems can be expanded with additional cable and pylons, as well as other accessories listed with the various sets. The speed can be controlled with Brawa controllers 6149 or 6150 (sold separately). Structures to house the cable mechanisms are also available separately.

KANZELWANDBAHN CABLEWAY SET

186-6280 165.99
Complete with both valley and summit cable mechanisms, 6 cars, a center pylon that's about 7-1/2" 190mm tall and drive cables.

EXTRA CABIN WITH FIGURE

186-6281 11.99

CENTER PYLON

186-6283 24.99
Matches pylon in set #6280, to support a longer cableway. About 7-1/2", 190mm tall

STATION BUILDINGS

186-6290 pkg(2) **35.99**
House your summit and valley cable mechanisms inside these structure kits. Parts for two complete buildings are provided. Summit station measures about 5 x 7-1/2" 165 x 125mm while the Valley station is approximately 4-1/2 x 6" 155 x 125mm.

SPARE DRIVE CABLE

186-6292 6.99
Approximately 11 yards of cable, for use with #6280, 6210, 6270 and 6560.

TOWER BOTTOM

186-6231 11.99

TOWER MIDDLE

186-6232 5.99

TOWER TOP

186-6233 9.99

DRIVE SUPPORT CABLES (35.5'/10M)

186-6241 9.99

CABLES WITH MOTOR FOR SUMMIT MECHANISM

186-6253 68.99

CHAIR LIFT SET

186-6270 152.99
Give HO skiers a quick ride to the top of the slopes with this fun accessory. Includes summit and valley mechanisms, support mast, 6 chairs and drive cable.

CHAIR LIFT STATION BUILDINGS

186-6271 pkg(2) **22.99**
Summit 3 x 3", 70 x 77mm
Valley 4 x 4", 95 x 100mm Buildings for Chair Lift.

SUPPORT MAST FOR #6270

186-6272 14.99

EXTRA CHAIR WITH FIGURE

186-6273 10.99

NEBELHORNBAHN CABLEWAY SET

186-6200 165.99
Includes valley and summit cable mechanisms, 2 cars, a center pylon that's about 11" (280 mm) tall and drive cables.

STATION BUILDINGS

186-6201 pkg(2) **39.99**
Parts for two complete buildings. Summit station measures about 6-1/2 x 5" 165 x 125mm and the Valley station is approximately 6-1/4 x 5" 155 x 125mm

TITLIS CABLEWAY

186-6330 328.99
One of Switzerland's newest attractions, recreated as a working model in HO Scale! Offering breathtaking views of the Alps, the prototype is located in Engelberg and climbs nearly 10,000 feet on its 45 minute trip. During the journey, the cabin rotates, offering an ever-changing view of the area. This superb replica will be a hit in any scene. The set comes with a cabin, which has a rotating floor like the real one, plus summit and valley mechanisms, drive motors and a speed control.

REPLACEMENT MOTORS

186-9712 28.99
For cableways made before August,1992.

186-9713 19.99
For cableways made after September, 1992.

BRAWA

MINERAL CABLEWAY SET

186-6210 139.99
Neat detail for mine or quarry operations. Includes cable mechanisms, 3" 77mm tall center pylon, six dump skips and drive cable. Expand with accessories listed below.

BUILDINGS FOR #6210

186-6211 pkg(2) **28.99**
Includes summit 3 x 5", 70 x 130mm and valley 6 x 5", 150 x 130mm station buildings.

CENTER PYLON

186-6212 14.99

EXTRA DUMP SKIP

186-6213 8.99

SUMMIT MECHANISM WITH MOTOR

186-6214 58.99

PLATFORM EDGES

186-2869 8.99
Includes four straight sections (8-5/16", 208mm long), four ramps (3", 78mm long) and two transition sections (2", 52mm long). Use Brawa building material sheets for platform surface (sold separately in Scratchbuilding Supplies.)

FUNICULAR RAILWAY SET

Based on a prototype in Stuttgart, Germany. Set includes 2 passenger cars, 4 straight tracks with rollers, one passing track, drive motor with automatic stop and drive cable. Approximately 48" 120cm long when assembled.

SET WITH RED CARS

186-6310 227.99

STATION BUILDINGS

186-6311 pkg(2) **42.99**
Kits for summit 3-1/4 x 9", 82 x 255mm and valley 5 x 7-1/2", 127 x 185mm station buildings.

STRAIGHT TRACK SECTION (4")

186-6312 pkg(2) **9.99**

REEL OF DRIVE CABLE

186-6320 6.99
13', use with #6309 or 6310.

TRANSFER TABLE

186-1180 318.99
Complete unit includes controller, base and transfer table.
Railroad shops use transfer tables to move equipment between repair bays. This requires less room than switches or a turntable.

This model will add action to your layout. Locos or cars up to 11-1/2" long(290mm) can fit on the bridge, and up to 11 service tracks (with one approach track) can be installed. When complete, the unit measures just 14-3/4 x 17 x 1/2" 372 x 427 x 15mm.

REPLACEMENT MOTOR

186-1184 67.99
Same motor as used in #1180, ideal for repair or custom projects.

CONTAINER TERMINAL

Animate your intermodal terminal with this WORKING model! Overhead crane lifts and lowers containers onto freight cars, using two motors for lifting and movement on the rack-rail.

CONTROL UNIT FOR CRANE

186-1156 51.99
Control up and down and back and forth movement of container crane (#1161 and 1170 required) with this fully-assembled unit.

CONTAINER TERMINAL SET

186-1162 329.99
Complete set includes: Baseplate (#1170), Overhead Crane (#1161), Control Unit (#1156) and four 20' containers (#1163).

LOADING PLATFORM

186-1170 119.99
16 x 8 x 1" 40 x 20.3 x 2.5cm
Plastic baseplate, identical to plate in #1162.

CONTAINER CRANE

186-1161 161.99
Imagine the fun of two working cranes in your intermodal terminal! Fully functional model has a motor to control the lifting mechanism and another for back and forth movement. Use with the Baseplate (#1170) and Control unit #1156, sold separately.

CONTAINER SET

186-1163 pkg(4) **17.99**
Use these 20' smoothside containers to detail your terminal scene. Includes two each ACL (Tuscan and white) and Seatrain (gray, blue) containers, which are fully assembled, ready to use.

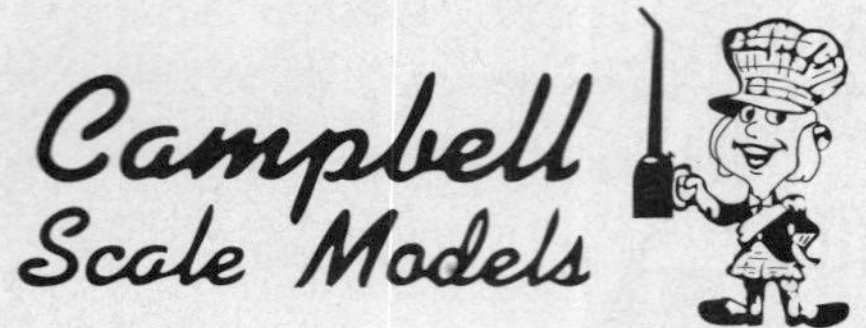

These craft train kits feature precision-cut wood, "profile shingles," molded plastic windows and doors, vents, signs, corrugated aluminum siding, etc., as needed. Each kit includes templates and complete instructions.

SKULL VALLEY STATION
200-367 50.50
3-7/8 x 10-1/4" 9.52 x 26.3cm

SHED UNDER CONSTRUCTION & DOUBLE HANDCAR HOUSE
200-368 30.00
Shed: 2-1/2 x 5-1/4" 6.3 x 13.3cm
House: 3-1/8 x 3-7/8" 7.9 x 9.8cm

SUPPLY SHED & SINGLE HANDCAR HOUSE
200-370 31.00
Shed: 2-1/2 x 5-1/4" 6.3 x 13.3cm
House: 2 x 3-7/8" 5 x 10.1cm

LARGE FREIGHT STATION
200-447 61.50
5-3/4 x 10-5/8" 14.6 x 27cm
SP Coast Railroad prototype.

Latest New Product News Daily! Visit Walthers Web site at **www.walthers.com**

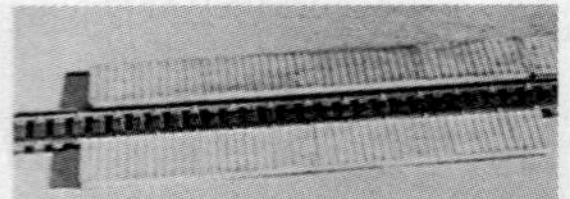

PASSENGER PLATFORM
200-786 pkg(3) **10.00**
1-3/32 x 6-7/8" 2.8 x 17.7cm

KIOWA JUNCTION STATION
200-423 50.50
2-7/8 x 7-1/2" 7.3 x 19.2cm
Prototype in Junction, Kansas.

GRAN'MA'S HOUSE
200-387 62.50
House: 5 x 5-1/4"
12.7 x 13.3cm
Garage: 2-1/2 x 1-3/4"
6.3 x 4.5cm

BRANCH LINE WATER TANK & TOOL HOUSE
200-372 31.00
Tank: 2 x 3-1/2" 5 x 9cm
Tool House: 1.5 x 3.8cm square

FREIGHT PLATFORM PLUS RAMPS
200-785 pkg(2) **12.50**
1-3/8 x 6-7/8" 2.8 x 17.7cm

WINDY GULCH ENGINE HOUSE
200-389 60.25
3 x 12" 7.6 x 30.4cm

200-382 200-381

BARN
200-382 39.25
4-1/8 x 6-3/4" 10.4 x 17.1cm

FARM HOUSE
200-381 32.00
3-1/2 x 4-1/2" 8.8 x 10.7cm

POST OFFICE
200-446 30.00
2-1/2 x 5-7/8" 6.5 x 15cm

MONTGOMERY FEED & SEED
200-419 65.50
3-1/4 x 9" 8.3 x 22.8cm

FREIGHT STORAGE SHED
200-427 32.00
3-5/8 x 4-5/8" 9.3 x 11.9cm

WAYSIDE FREIGHT STATION
200-361 36.00
2-7/8 x 6-5/8" 7.62 x 16.8cm

SQUARE WATER TOWER
200-421 30.00
3 x 3-1/4" 7.5 x 8.5cm

FREIGHT HOUSE & PASSENGER STATION
200-442 31.00
3-1/16 x 3-3/8" 7.8 x 6.8cm

PASSENGER SHELTER
200-362 30.50
2 x 9-7/8" 4.5 x 24.8cm

POPO-AGIE CANNING CO.
200-452 75.50
4-3/4 x 14-3/8" 12 x 36.5cm

BRECKENRIDGE FIRE HOUSE
200-441 57.00
5 x 6-1/4" 13 x 16cm
Prototype in Breckenridge, Colorado, until 1941

QUICK'S COAL
200-386 65.50
Yard: 3 x 8" 7.6 x 20.3cm
Office: 2 x 3-1/2" 5 x 8.9cm

The "Norm's Landing" complex, pictured above, consists of the following three kits: #'s 392, 396 and 397.

FISHING PIER
200-392 52.00
Pier: 7-1/2x 10" 19 x 25.4cm
Ramp: 2-1/2 x 10" 6.3 x 25.4cm
Float: 4 x 7-1/8" 10.1 x 18cm

ICE HOUSE & CAFE
200-397 48.25
Ice House: 2-1/2 x 4-1/4" 6.3 x 10.8cm
Cafe: 3-1/2 square 8.9cm square

BOAT SHOP
200-396 52.00
3-1/2 x 6-1/4" 8.9 x 15.8cm

SHERRY'S SCARLET SLIPPER SALOON
200-378 53.00
Saloon: 4-1/4" 10.8cm square
Frame: 2-1/8 x 4" 5.3 x 10.1cm

DOCTOR'S OFFICE
200-398 52.00
3-5/8 x 5" 9.5 x 12.7cm

IRON FOUNDRY
200-444 47.00
4-3/8 x 9-5/8" 11.1 x 24.5cm

ABANDONED HOUSE
200-393 37.00
4 x 4-1/2" 10.1 x 10.8cm

1875 FIRE HOUSE
200-355 32.00
2-3/4 x 3-5/8" 7 x 9.2cm

Trackside Details #2 Trackside Details #1

KIOWA TRACKSIDE DETAILS #1
200-426 32.00

KIOWA TRACKSIDE DETAILS #2
200-425 30.50
3-9/16 x 6" 9 x 15.2cm

200-230

200-231

PORTABLE BUNKHOUSE "A" & "B"
200-230 8.50
1-1/4 x 3" 3.2 x 7.7cm
200-231 9.50
1-1/4 x 3" 3.2 x 7.7cm
These kits are designed to introduce modelers to Craft Train Kit construction. The buildings feature simple design and fewer parts, making them ideal for beginners. Kits include precut wood with plastic castings for the windows and details. Complete step-by-step instructions make construction fast and easy.

THE PAINT FACTORY
200-457 52.00
6-1/2 x 11-1/8" 16.5 x 28.2cm

SEEBOLD & SONS MANUFACTURING COMPANY
200-377 44.00

STOCKPENS W/DOUBLE CHUTES
200-437 30.00
10-1/2 x 1" 26.7 x 27.9cm

CATTLE LOADING PENS
200-781 15.00
7-7/8 x 5-3/4" 20.3 x 14.6cm

DEWITT'S DEPOSITORY
200-412 52.50
3 x 7" 7.6 x 17.7cm

KIOWA TOWER
200-424 42.00
2-5/16 x 6-1/8" 13.5 x 15.5cm

SAND HOUSE
200-358 41.50
3 x 8" 7.6 x 20.3cm

TILT-UP BUILDING #1
200-451 44.00

SHERIFF'S OFFICE
200-364 31.50
3-1/2 x 5" 8.9 x 12.7cm

CORRUGATED WAREHOUSE
200-373 32.00
3 x 5-3/4"
7.6 x 14.6cm

RICHMOND BARREL MANUFACTURING COMPANY
200-422 50.50
3-1/4 x 6-5/8" 8.3 x 16.8cm

COMMUNITY CHURCH
200-359 53.00
3-1/4 x 7-5/8" 8.3 x 19.3cm
With "stained" glass windows.

WATER TANK
200-356 45.00
4" square 10.1cm square

NORTHERN WATER TANK
200-376 45.00
4" square 10.1cm square

CARSTENS' FLOP HOUSE
200-413 75.00
3-3/4 x 6" 9.5 x 15.2cm

SAEZ SASH & DOOR MILL HOUSE & LOFT
200-416 65.50
5-5/8 x 10" 14.3 x 25.4cm

GRAIN ELEVATOR
200-384 53.00
3-1/2 x 10-1/2" 8.9 x 26.6cm

KOHLER DISTRIBUTING CO.
200-459 49.00
13-1/2 x 8-3/4" 34.4 x 22.3cm

TALC PLANT
200-399 75.00
7-3/8 x 12-3/4" 18.6 x 32.4cm

BARNETT PLASTIC CO.
200-458 50.25
11" square 26.6cm square

LCL FREIGHT STATION
200-353 30.00
3-1/2 x 7" 8.7 x 17.5cm
Plus ramp.

COALING STATION
200-357 53.75
5 x 6" 12.7 x 15.2cm

TIMBER OIL DERRICK
200-354 40.50
3-3/4 x 9" 9.5 x 22.8cm

FREDERICK J. HAMILTON DINGHYS
200-394 60.00
3-3/4 x 8-3/4" 9.5 x 22.1cm
Includes two rowboats.

SANTANGELO FRUIT CO.
200-420 65.00
4-7/8 x 9-1/2" 12.4 x 23.5cm

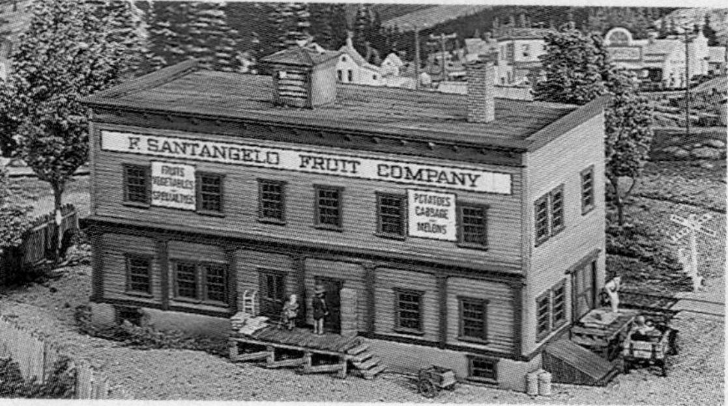

PRODUCE HOUSE
200-379 54.25
4 x 16"
10.1 x 40.6cm

AYRES CHAIR FACTORY
200-391 63.00
6-3/4 x 7-1/4" 17.1 x 18.4cm

CORDAGE WORKS
200-455 48.00
5-3/8 x 6-3/8" 13.6 x 16.1cm

GRAIN STORAGE BIN
200-449 42.50
3-5/8 x 7-1/2" 9.2 x 18.5cm

SCHROCK'S MEAT CO.
200-411 75.25
3-11/16 x 11-1/16" 9.8 x 28.1cm

FARM CO-OP CREAMERY
200-418 58.00
9-1/2 x 5-5/8" 24.2 x 14.3cm

SAEZ SASH & DOOR MACHINE SHOP, SHED & HOPPER
200-417 72.00
6 x 12" 15.6 x 27.9cm

GRIST MILL
200-374 44.00
3-1/4 x 4-1/2" 8.3 x 10.8cm

For Daily Product
Information Click
www.walthers.com

THE BLACKSMITH SHOP
200-461 31.00
3 x 5-1/8" 7.7 x 13cm

DONNA'S DINER
200-432 36.50
4-3/16 x 1-3/8" 10.7 x 3.5cm

TOWERS FLOWERS
200-460 75.00
3-1/2 x 10" 9 x 25.5cm

CITY TRANSFER
200-454 44.00
13-3/4 x 6-1/2" 35 x 16.5cm

MATTHEW'S MERCANTILE
200-371 45.75
3 x 3-1/2" 7.6 x 8.9cm

BRET'S BREWERY
200-385 61.00
5-1/2 x 10-1/2" 13.9 x 26.6cm

KEE LING LAUNDRY & CIGAR STORE
200-365 44.25
Cigar Store: 2-11/16 x 3-3/16" 7 x 8.3cm
Shelter: 2 x 9-7/8" 5 x 25.4cm

TEN STAMP MILL
200-428 45.50
7-7/8 x 7-1/4" 20 x 18.5cm

CAMPBELL SUPPLY COMPANY
200-363 45.50
4 x 10" 10.1 x 25.4cm

TRAVELING CRANE
200-404 31.00
1-5/8 x 6-1/8" 4 x 15.6cm

CABINET MAKERS SHOP
200-443 45.50
5 x 7-3/8" 12.7 x 18.7cm

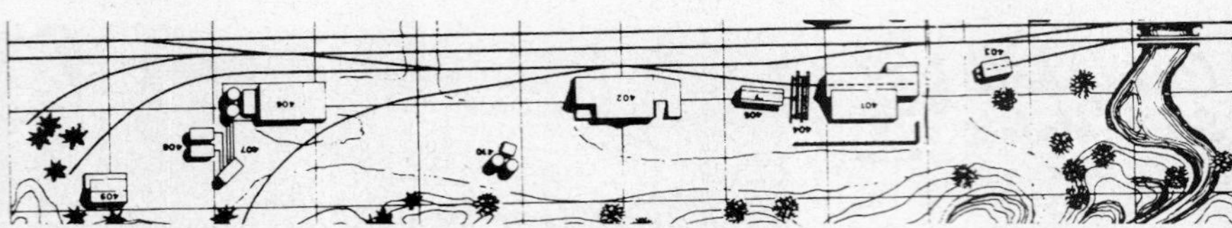

QUINCY MODULE

The Quincy Railroad is a three-mile line owned by the di Giorgio Fruit Company. Located in California's Feather River country, it connects the agricultural community of Quincy with the Western Pacific at Quincy Junction. The map portrays the layout of the Quincy Railroad at Quincy.

J. BRICE PRODUCE WAREHOUSE
200-435 49.50
7-1/2 x 4-3/8" 19 x 11.2cm

WATER TOWER
200-453 31.25
1-5/8" square
4.2cm square

PUMP HOUSE
200-360
29.25
2-3/4 x 3-1/4"
6.9 x 7.6cm

W. T. STEPHENSON DRUG COMPANY & BARBER SHOP
200-366 44.25
Drug Co.: 3-1/2 x 3-3/16" 8.9 x 17.8cm
Barber: 2-3/8 x 3" 5.8 x 8.9cm

OIL WAREHOUSE & OFFICE
200-406 45.00
4-1/8 x 8-1/4" 10.5 x 21cm

QUINCY STATION
200-402 67.00
5-1/8 x 12" 13.1 x 30.6cm

KING'S CANNERY
200-439 74.50
6-3/4 x 12-1/2" 17.2 x 31.8cm
Santa Fe prototype from Irvine, California.

M E NELSON LIVESTOCK COMPANY
200-400 48.25
7-1/2 x 14" 19 x 35.5cm

SUSANNAH'S FROCKS
200-375 45.75
3-1/4 x 4" 8.3 x 10.1cm

GUNSMITH SHOP
200-456 36.50
3-1/4 x 5-5/8" 8.2 x 14.4cm

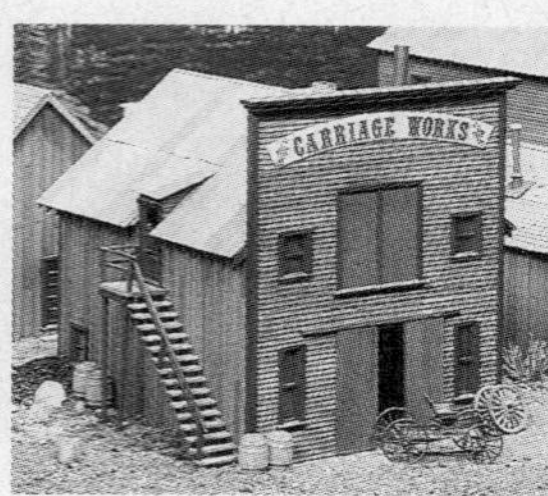

CARRIAGE WORKS
200-430 45.75
3-3/4 x 4-3/4" 9.6 x 12.1cm

RED MOUNTAIN MINE
200-429 62.25

SILVER SPUR MINE
200-388 58.50
Shaft House: 4-1/2 x 6-1/2" 10.8 x 16.5cm
Tunnel & Tipple: 1-3/4 x 3-3/4" 4.5 x 9.5cm

IDAHO SPRINGS MINE
200-433 35.25
Main Structure: 3 x 3-3/8" 7.7 x 8.6cm
Trestle: 12-1/2" 31.8cm

ASSAY OFFICE/ CLOTHING STORE
200-431 34.25
3-3/4 x 4-7/8" 9.6 x 12.5cm

COLUMBIA GAZETTE OFFICE
200-380 32.25
4 x 5" 10.1 x 12.7cm

TOBACCO SHOP
200-434 32.50
2-3/4 x 3-7/8" 7 x 9.9cm

WATER TREATMENT PLANT
200-440 36.00
5 x 6-1/2" 12.7 x 16.5

ENGINE HOUSE
200-401 65.25
6-3/4 x 11" 17.2 x 28cm

IOWA SCHOOL HOUSE
200-369 45.00
2-3/4 x 4-1/2" 7 x 10.8cm

24' HORIZONTAL TANKS
200-408 pkg(2) 25.00
Each: 3-3/4 x 1-5/8" 9.5 x 4cm

GROCERY WAREHOUSE
200-436 43.50
7-3/8 x 4-1/4" 18.7 x 10.8cm

18' HORIZONTAL TANKS
200-407 pkg(2) 25.00
Each: 3-3/4 x 1-5/8" 9.5 x 4cm

LOADING TANKS
200-410 29.00
4-1/8 x 2-1/8" 10.5 x 5.5cm
Vertical tanks with small loading rack.

PICKEN'S PLACE
200-395 36.25
4 x 4-1/2" 10.1 x 10.8cm
1-5/8 x 1-5/8" 4.2 x 4.2cm

MARJORIE'S MILLINERY
200-390 36.25
3-1/8 x 2-7/8" 7.9 x 7.3cm

FUEL OIL DOCK
200-405 45.00
Each: 3 x 1-5/8" 7.5 x 4cm

ORE BIN
200-438 37.00
3-7/8 x 3" 9.9 x 7.7cm

SUMMER BANDSTAND
200-383 36.50
3-1/2 x 3-1/2" 8.8 x 8.8cm

OIL COMPOUND HOUSE (INCLUDING DOCK)
200-409 33.50
4 x 5-1/2" 10.2 x 14cm

PLASTIC WINDMILL
200-1604 5.00

BRIDGES W/HIGHWAY ACCESSORIES
Plastic kit
200-1605 Concrete **6.50**
200-1606 Stone **6.50**

MINE HEAD FRAME
200-352 32.50
3-3/4 x 11-1/2" 9.5 x 29.2cm

WHARF
200-307 52.00
22-3/8 x 5-1/4"
56.6 x 13.3cm

AUXILIARY SHEDS & SIGNS
200-403 31.25
Shed: 2 x 3" 5.1 x 7.7cm
Ice house: 1-3/4" square
4.5cm square

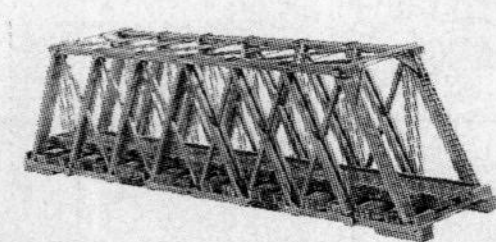

HOWE TRUSS BRIDGE
200-305 45.00
14-1/2 x 3-1/8" 36.8 x 7.6cm

144-216' TALL TIMBER TRESTLE
200-751 44.00
20 x 29" 50.8 x 73.6cm

70' THRU TIMBER BRIDGE
200-762 40.00
14 x 3-3/4" 35.5 x 9.5cm

70' CURVED TRESTLE
200-303 30.00
15-1/4 x 1-3/8" 38.7 x 3.5cm

110' TALL CURVED TRESTLE
200-304 39.25
15-1/4 x 1-3/8" 38.7 x 3.5cm

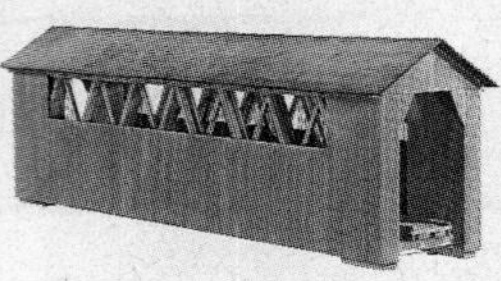

COVERED BRIDGE
200-306 49.50
14-5/8 x 3-1/4" 37.2 x 8.2cm

50' DECK TIMBER BRIDGE
200-761 37.50
14" 35.5cm

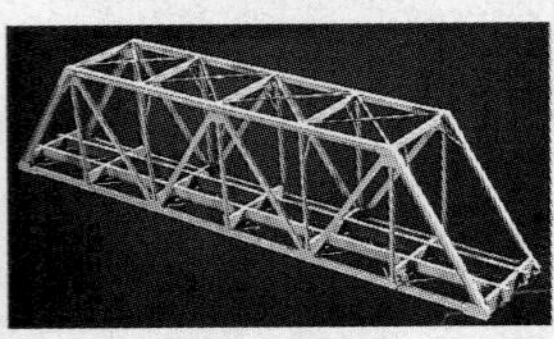

125' SINGLE TRACK TRUSS BRIDGE (LESS TIES)
200-763 35.00
17-1/4 x 3" 40.2 x 7.6cm

125' DOUBLE TRACK TRUSS BRIDGE
200-764 39.50
16-7/8 x 3-3/8" 35.8 x 8.5cm

50' OPEN DECK PILE TRESTLE
200-302 20.50
6-7/8 x 3" 17.3 x 7.6cm

50' BALLASTED DECK PILE TRESTLE (LESS TIES)
200-301 20.50
6-7/8 x 3" 17.3 x 7.6cm

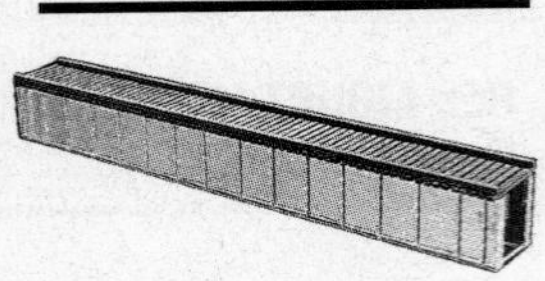

70' DECK PLATE GIRDER BRIDGE
200-765 28.50
9-5/8 x 1-3/8" 24.4 x 3.5cm

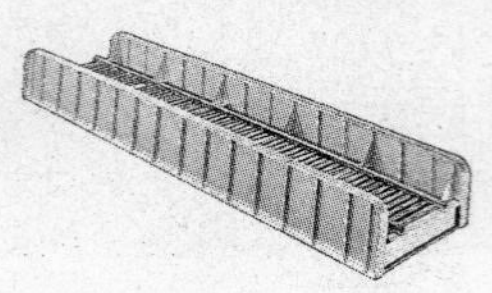

70' THRU PLATE GIRDER BRIDGE
200-766 29.75
9-5/8 x 2-1/2" 24.4 x 5.2cm

For Up-To-Date Information and News Bookmark Walthers Web site at **www.walthers.com**

CENTRAL VALLEY

PLATE GIRDER BRIDGES
72', one-piece floor and bridge tie sections.

210-1903 Single Track **13.50**
Each 5-7/8" (14.8cm) long.

210-1904 Double Track **19.95**
Each 3-1/4" (8.2cm) long.

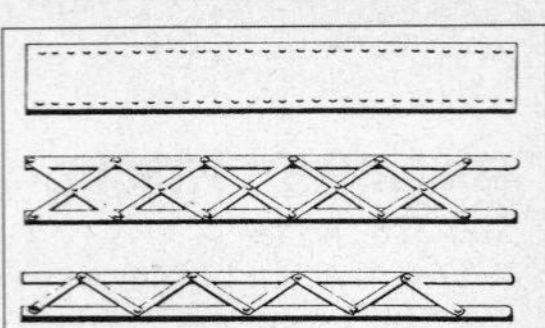

BOX GIRDER SECTIONS
210-19025 5-7/8" pkg(30) **10.95**

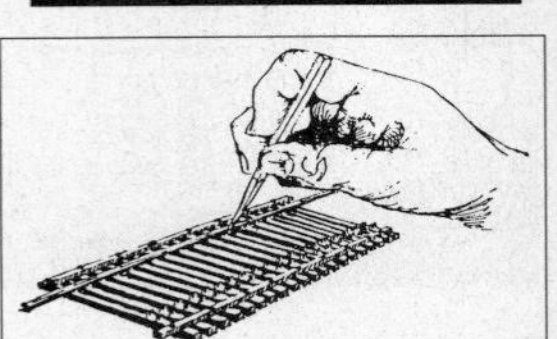

BRIDGE TIE SECTIONS
210-190210 3-1/4" pkg(10) **10.95**

150' RIGID TRUSS BRIDGE
210-1902 36.95
20-5/8" 52.5cm

Single-track bridge features a removable upper truss, premolded bridge ties and extra long girder components. (Ties accept code 70 or 83 rail, easily modified for code 100 rail.)

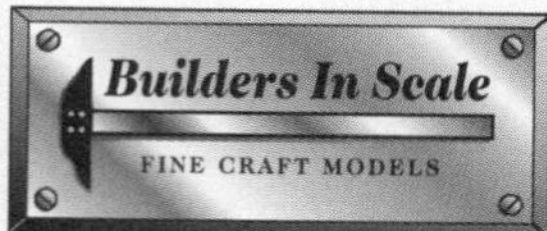

These highly detailed craft train kits feature wood construction with metal details and architectural plans.

Evening Express kits are easy to assemble and feature wood and metal parts. When completed, they make dandy mini-scenes. Each includes easy to follow instructions with weathering tips.

GETZ GAS WAREHOUSE

169-611 34.89
4-1/2 x 4" 11.2 x 10cm

A small trackside bottled gas dealer, with both rail and truck docks. Laser-cut walls, over 25 metal detail parts and color signs.

GINGERBREAD LACE HOUSE

169-614 59.98
4-1/2 x 4" 11.2 x 9.4cm

A classic home loaded with gingerbread trim, plus porch and windows. Etched brass parts, laser-cut wood and over 30 metal castings included.

CHAMPION MILL

169-11 TBA
11 x 5" 27.5 x 12.5cm

A four-story water fed mill, with cast mill chase and stonework foundation, laser-cut wood, color signs and cast metal details.

SCALE HOUSE

169-610 24.98
3-1/2 x 3-1/2" 9 x 9cm (w/truck pad)

3-1/2 x 9" 9 x 23cm (w/rail pad)

Includes a 10 x 10' building, detailed casting of the scale mechanism, "concrete" foundation and separate scale platforms for rail or truck. Rail car scale comes with nonoperating ground throws. Over 25 detail castings are included. Laser-cut wood.

FISHERMAN'S SHANTY

169-613 34.98
3 x 3" 7.5 x 7.5cm

A two-level structure built on pilings for use along the coast. Laser-cut wood and over 20 metal detail castings, including a boat, floating dock and other nautical items.

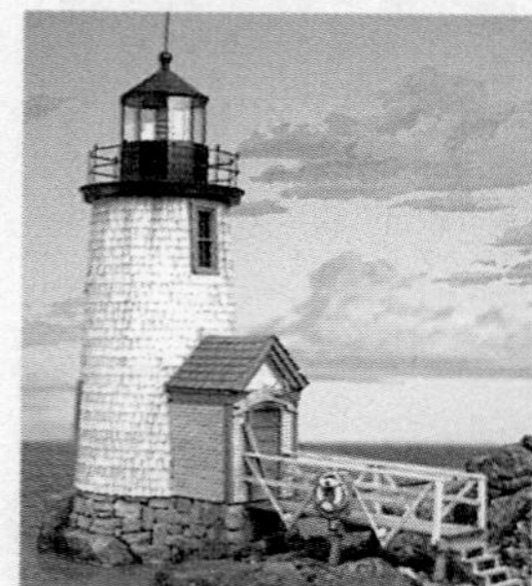

THE LIGHTHOUSE

169-612 49.98
2 x 5 x 5-1/2"
5 x 12.5 x 13.8cm

A shingled structure with cast stone foundation. Includes laser-cut parts, etched brass parts, special white metal castings and other details.

TRACKSIDE SHED

169-601 17.98
2 x 4" 5 x 10cm

Includes aluminum ribbed seam roofing and siding material, over 20 metal detail castings and handcar track.

HOUSE

169-606 "630 Elm Street" **49.98**
4 x 8" 10 x 20cm

Precast brick walls, laser-cut wood, stone foundation and period details (coal door, fireplace ash door, clapboard gables, venetian blinds). Separate garage and over 60 cast metal details (flower boxes, dog house, old bathtub, clothesline poles, swing set) are all included.

PUMP & BOILER HOUSE

169-602 24.98
3-1/2 x 3" 8.8 x 7.5cm

Includes cast plaster stonework foundation and over 25 detail castings. Laser-cut wood.

FLYBINYTE CONSTRUCTION COMPANY

169-603 18.98
4 x 4" 10 x 10cm

Small job site trailer and three-man housing cabin on skids. Prototype 1930s. Laser-cut wood.

Information STATION

EARLY STATIONS

By the 1880s, railroad stations were unique structures. New depots were custom designed by architects to project a positive image of the railroad and the town it served. Based on these ideas, three principal styles were constructed.

The simplest were called flag-stops, because trains would only stop when a signal flag was displayed. These included covered platforms or shelters and tiny waiting/room office buildings. Most were only a few square feet in size and had a small platform trackside.

In towns where more passengers and packages were handled, a combination station was used. These larger buildings combined the freight handling and passenger waiting rooms into one structure. A ticket/telegraph/business office was included for the agent. Low platforms for passengers and taller freight platforms for wagons were used.

Bigger towns and cities had separate freight and passenger stations to allow space for each operation. Stations retained the office and platforms, but had separate waiting rooms for ladies and gentlemen. Some even boasted indoor restrooms - a very modern touch at the time. A separate baggage room was sometimes provided to store luggage until trains arrived. Most of the designs were flexible to build larger or smaller variations.

DIVISION OF TAURUS PRODUCTS
Wood kits feature template construction, Kappler and Northeastern lumber, roofing material, plastic and metal cast details.

MT. PRINCETON STATION
225-31121 24.00
2-3/4 x 4" 7 x 10.2cm
DSP&P Railroad.

COLUMBIA MINER'S CABIN
225-38918 23.00
2 x 3-3/4" 5.1 x 9.5cm
Columbia, CA.

THE RUINS
225-38927 32.00 ***NEW***
Mostly urethane.

RED LIGHT DISTRICT
225-38910 pkg(5) **22.00**
2-1/2 x 11" 6.5 x 28cm total length.

GENOA SALOON
225-38920 30.00 ***NEW***

LAWS STATION
225-31415 42.00 ***NEW***
Carson & Colorado Railroad.

NATIONAL SALOON
225-38919 26.00 ***NEW***

OPHIR STATION
225-31156 48.00 ***NEW***
Rio Grande Southern Railroad.

ILIUM STATION
225-31155 Ilium Station **48.00** ***NEW***
Rio Grande Southern.

SP SPARKS DEPOT
225-31905 31.00
5 x 6-1/2"
12.5 x 6.5cm
Sparks, NV.

UNION BRASS FOUNDRY
225-38928 28.00 ***NEW***
All urethane.

LEADVILLE HOUSE
225-38104 41.00
4 x 6"
10 x 15cm
Leadville, CO, circa 1900.

QUEEN ANNE COTTAGE
225-38903 37.00
3-3/4 x 5"
9.5 x 12.5cm
Arcadia, CA, circa 1890.

GOLD HILL HOUSE
225-38430 29.00
4-1/2 x 5"
11.5 x 12.5cm
Gold Hill, Nevada, circa 1881.

WINTERS MANSION
225-38908 41.00
5-1/2 x 7"
14 x 18cm

FORKS CREEK STATION
225-31141 31.00
2-3/4 x 5-1/2"
7 x 14cm
Colorado Central Railroad.

GENERAL STORE
225-38904 26.00
3-3/4 x 5"
9.5 x 12.5cm
Sutter Creek, CA, circa 1897.

GRAND CENTRAL GOLD MINE W/POWDER HOUSE
225-38916 31.00
Mine: 5-3/8 x 3-5/8"
13.6 x 9.2cm.
Powder house: 1-1/2 x 1-3/16"
3.8 x 3.0cm

NEVADA FIRE STATION
225-38912 29.00
3 x 6-1/2"
7.6 x 16.5cm
Nevada City, CA, circa 1861.

FRATERNITY HALL
225-38902 24.00
3-1/2 x 5-1/2"
9 x 14cm
Elkhorn, MT, circa 1890.

VIRGINIA CITY ORE BIN
225-38431 23.00
3-3/8 x 1-11/16"
8.5 x 4.2cm
Prototype in Virginia City, Nevada.

MASONIC LODGE
225-38906 24.00
3-3/4 x 8"
9.5 x 20.5cm
Los Angeles, CA, circa 1858.

ATSF MAINLINE STATION #4
225-31904 56.00 ***NEW***

SP ENGINE HOUSE
225-32401 29.00
2-3/4 x 8-1/2"
7 x 21.5cm
Prototype built in 1883 for the Carson & Colorado. Will accept most HOn3 locos.

BODIE CHURCH
225-38914 31.00
4 x 6-1/8" 10.1 x 15.5cm
Bodie, CA.

SILVER PLUME STORE
225-38140 23.00
2-1/4 x 4-1/2"
5.5 x 11.5cm
Silver Plume, CO, circa 1883.

WORK'S HARDWARE
225-38151 47.00
4-1/2 x 7"
10.4 x 17.8cm
Telluride, CO, circa 1890.

BRIDGEPORT HOUSE
225-38915 38.00
5 x 4" 12.5 x 10cm
Bridgeport, CA.

See What's Available at
www.walthers.com

WELLS FARGO & CO. OFFICE
225-38905 22.00
3 x 6-1/2" 7.5 x 16.5cm
Prototype built in Columbia, CA, in 1857 to handle express service, still stands today.

BANK BUILDING
225-38913 22.00
3-1/2 x 4-1/2" 9 x 11.5cm
Circa 1900.

MINE HOUSE
225-38907 35.00
5 x 6-1/2" 12.7 x 16.5cm
Mojave, CA, circa 1890.

MONTEZUMA POST OFFICE
225-38917 31.00

LUCKY MINE
225-38909 26.00
Virginia City, NV.

These Craft Train kits feature wood parts, with metal details and complete instructions.

We have worked closely with this manufacturer to provide accurate delivery information at the time this catalog was published. Items listed in blue ink may not be available at all times. Current delivery information, along with a list of in-stock products for this line, can be found on our Web site at www.walthers.com.

ASH DRUGS
261-203 42.95
4 x 6-1/2" 10.2 x 16.5cm
Includes business with interior, plus home, garage and doghouse.

30s GAS STATION
261-206 35.95
3 x 4" 7.5 x 10.2cm
In the steam-era, service stations like this could be found along many state and county highways. This detailed kit comes with two gravity-feed gas pumps, plus tires, tools and welding equipment for making repairs.

RAVINE TRESTLE
261-514 23.95
3-1/8 x 11-1/8" 8 x 28.3cm

GULLY TRESTLE
261-504 21.95
3-1/8 x 11-1/8" 8 x 28.3cm

BACKMASTER'S TRUCK & RADIATOR SUPPLY
261-209 42.95

BRANCHLINE WATER TANK
261-513 24.95

CITY CLASSICS

Photos by John Polyak.

These easy-to-build kits capture the look of various styles of architecture and are ideal for steam-or diesel-era layouts. Kits feature injection molded, plastic parts, styrene roof material, clear window glazing and easy-to-follow instructions. Kits 101, 102, 105, and 106 do not include signs shown. Most are available from Main Street Graphics shown elsewhere in this book.

ROUTE 22 DINER

195-110 17.98
6-1/2 x 4"
16.5 x 10cm
The easy-to-build plastic kit includes the "stainless steel" diner, a concrete block kitchen addition, a free-standing sign and easy to follow instructions.

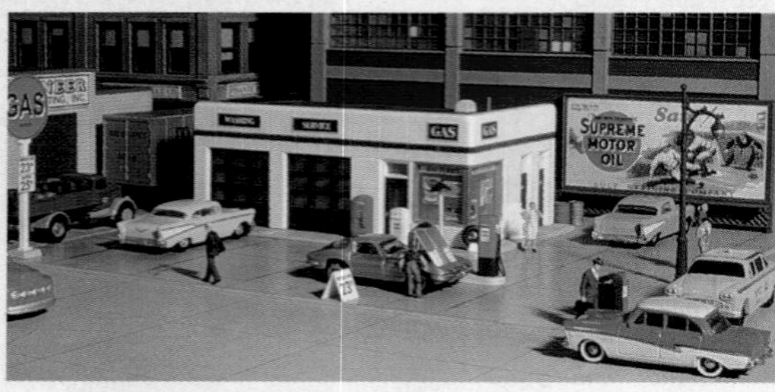

1930S CRAFTON AVENUE SERVICE STATION

195-108 17.98
5 x 3"
25.4 x 12.7cm
Includes the station building, gas island with nonworking lamp, two different pump styles, two different sign posts and heads, soda and ice machines, oil and tire displays plus printed signs for a number of different oil companies.

SMALLMAN STREET WAREHOUSE

195-103 18.98
8-1/2 x 6"
21.6 x 15.2cm
Ideal for just about any era being modeled. Add extra stories with #104 Two Story Add-On Kit.

CARSON STREET RAIL/TRUCK TERMINAL

195-107 10.98
8-1/2 x 6"
21.6 x 15.2cm
A small building that's perfect for a variety of small industries.

FORBES AVENUE THEATER

195-111 TBA *NEW*

GRANT STREET IRON FRONT BUILDING

195-101 15.98
5-1/4 x 3-1/2"
13.4 x 8.9cm
Accurately captures the look of an ornate cast iron facade that was common during the late 1800s.

PENN AVENUE TILE FRONT BUILDING

195-102 15.98
5-1/4 x 3-1/2"
13.4 x 8.9cm
This unique style of architecture using tera cotta blocks will stand out among dark masonry buildings and brighten up your towns at the same time!

2-STORY ADD-ON FOR #103

195-104 10.98

CARNEGIE STREET MANUFACTURING BUILDING

195-109 16.98
10 x 5"
25.4 x 12.7cm
A common small industrial building that may be built a variety of ways using the extra parts.

EAST OHIO STREET BUILDING

195-106 15.98
5-1/4 x 3-1/2"
13.4 x 8.9cm
A classic structure that may be found in just about every city and town! Features a modular front that makes it easy to combine additional kits to get larger buildings.

BAUM BOULEVARD ART DECO BUILDING

195-105 15.98
5-1/4 x 3-1/2"
13.4 x 8.9cm
This seldom modeled art deco style building will really stand out on your layout! The unique modular front makes kitbashing easier than ever.

Items #201-207 can be used with the basic Smallman Street Warehouse (#103) to build a larger or customized structure.

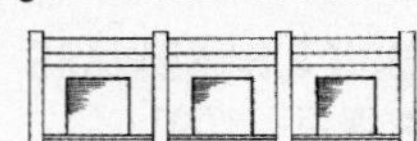

LONG LOWER WALLS W/DOORS

195-201 pkg(2) **3.50**

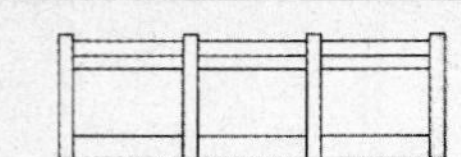

LONG LOWER WALLS LESS DOORS

195-202 pkg(2) **3.50**

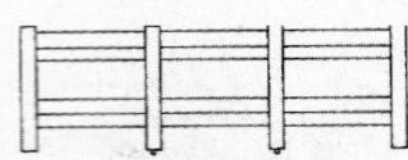

LONG UPPER WALLS W/WINDOWS

195-203 pkg(2) **3.50**

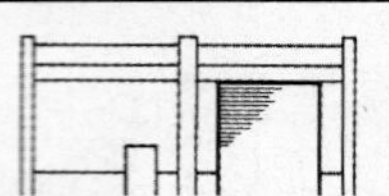

SHORT LOWER WALLS W/DOORS

195-204 pkg(2) **3.50**

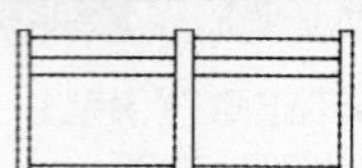

SHORT LOWER WALLS LESS DOORS

195-205 pkg(2) **3.50**

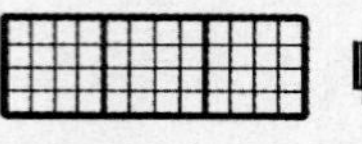

FACTORY WINDOWS & ROOF VENTS

195-207 3.50
Set includes 10 windows and two roof vents.

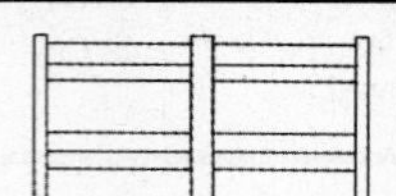

SHORT UPPER WALLS W/WINDOWS

195-206 pkg(2) **3.50**

See What's Available at
www.walthers.com

DEPOTS BY JOHN

D-3 DEPOT
87-131 15.95

MILW SPEEDER SHED
87-106 9.95
Used to store track speeders, tools and supplies. Includes information on four different paint schemes used from the 1920s to the 1980s.

COUNTRY DEPOT
87-110 43.95
Any small town along your railroad would be proud to have this depot at trackside. The kit has lots of traditional details, including the operator's bay window, detailed roof eaves, brick chimney and a tiny waybill box. Perfect for use in any era or region.

2-HOLE OUTHOUSE
87-132 3.99

FAIRBANKS-MORSE SCALEHOUSE
87-114 8.95
Six-sided building is a one-piece casting, typical of similar buildings used by many railroads.

GARAGE/TRACKSIDE MOW BUILDING
87-122 9.95
Keep the family sedan shiny and neat when you store it in this handsome one-car garage. Hundreds of thousands of these buildings were constructed from 1920 to around 1940 and many are still in use today. A common sight in the older residential areas, they were also built by some railroads to house track inspection cars or as tool sheds.

TRACKSIDE UTILITY BUILDINGS
87-113 pkg(3) 18.95
Includes outside braced wood/coal shed, elevated fuel oil tank and small tool shed. Great detail near a depot or section gang house.

MANNED CROSSING GATE TOWER
87-115 19.95
Used to control crossing gates in busy areas, prototype stood in Wauwatosa, Wisconsin. Includes phone box and walk-in maintenance shed.

PHONE BOOTHS PKG(3) EA 7.95
87-116 NKP
87-117 IC
87-118 MILW
87-119 ATSF

STORAGE SHED
222-9065 33.98
8-1/2 x 5-1/8"
21.2 x 13cm

Ready to serve rural customers along your line, this big building serves as center stage for your grain elevator. It features truck and rail car loading docks, and matches kits 9066 and 9067 (sold separately).

SHED
222-9033 5.98

SANDHOUSE & FUEL FACILITY

222-9029 14.98

OIL TANK FARM-SHELL
222-9069 22.98
5-1/2 x 3-1/2 x 5-1/4"
13.7 x 8.7 x 13.1cm
A great way to store plenty of petroleum products. Neat detail for a refinery, local oil dealer, industry or railroad refueling area.

YARDMASTER'S OFFICE
222-9032 5.98

SUMMER STOCK THEATER
222-9035 14.98

GRAIN ELEVATOR
222-9066 28.98
3-1/2 x 4-3/4 x 8-5/8"
8.5 x 12 x 21.5cm

The business end of the elevator is housed in this structure. The kit includes vents, pipes, loading spout and many other details.

BUTANE GAS DIST. CENTER
222-1704 15.50

ELECTRIC SUB-STATION
222-9060 12.98

WAREHOUSE TRANSFER
222-9058 15.98

MA'S PLACE
222-9051 12.98

HARDWARE STORE
222-9053 15.98

AUNT MILLIE'S HOUSE
222-9050 12.98

GRAIN SILOS

222-9067 24.98
2-1/2 x 6-1/2 x 6"
6 x 16 x 15cm

A fast and easy way to load or unload grain, this kit includes steel braces, vents, pipes, bins, blower and other realistic details.

RURAL SCHOOLHOUSE STRUCTURE & VEHICLE SET

222-90361 School House w/Unified School District #2 Bus **14.98**
This structure kit comes with a a fully assembled vehicle.

STOCKYARDS

222-9052 16.98

MOXHAM SOAP WORKS

222-1714 13.98

YARD CRANE

222-9041 9.98

STONEY CREEK BRIDGE

222-9031 3.25

WEEKLY HERALD PRINT SHOP

222-9038 14.98

WEEKLY HERALD PRINT SHOP STRUCTURE AND VEHICLE SET

222-90381 Weekly Herald w/Helping Hands Temporary Labor Bus **14.98**
This structure kit comes with a fully assembled vehicle.

WELDING SHOP

222-9059 12.98

SMALL TOWN STATION

222-9001 14.98

GRAVEL RAMP WITH OPERATING HOPPER

222-6100 19.98
Shipping rock, sand, gravel or other bulk materials, this working loading ramp and hopper car make a great team on any HO layout. The kit includes graduated ramps and an open pit dump site. The bridge over the pit has riggers that actuate the dump mechanism on the car, allowing it to dump its load. The set includes one operating car, but more are available separately.

INDIVIDUAL OPERATING HOPPERS 8.98

Designed for use with #6100, cars feature working dump doors.

222-6101 ATSF (Tuscan, white)
222-6102 PRR (Tuscan, white)
222-6103 UP (Oxide Red, white)
222-6104 SP (Tuscan, white)
222-6105 BN (green, white)
222-6106 CR (Tuscan, white)
222-6107 Undecorated

CAMBRIA IRON WORKS

222-9054 29.98

CAMBRIA BOILER HOUSE

222-9055 12.98

CAMBRIA STORAGE TANKS

222-9056 11.98

CAMBRIA ACCESSORY PACK

222-9057 9.98

CAMBRIA FUEL DEPOT

222-9061 17.98

CAMBRIA FUEL TANKS

222-9062 16.98

CAMBRIA FUEL RACK

222-9063 16.98

CAMBRIA FUEL RACK STRUCTURE & VEHICLE SET

222-90631 Fuel Rack w/LaBelle Oil Tank Truck **16.98**
This structure kit comes with a fully assembled vehicle.

CAMBRIA TIRE REPAIR SHOP

222-9064 15.98

STAR GLASS FACTORY COMPLEX

Star Glass Factory Complex (Each Item Sold Separately)

Turning out practical items like window panes, jars and bottles, or art glass such as vases and ashtrays, there's plenty of work for any railroad around the Star Glass Company. By combining the four kits from the series (each sold separately), you can customize the operation to fit your plans. The big Main Building (222-9070) is three stories tall and forms the heart of the plant. With lots of heat required, the Five-Story Chimney (222-9071) is a great addition, and will look good with many other buildings too. For more action around the loading area, you can add the Crane and Accessory Package (222-9072), that can also be used with other kits.

222-9070 Main Building w/Dump Truck **48.98**

Building: 8-13/16 x 5 x 5-7/8"
22.5 x 13 x 15cm
Base: 16-1/2 x 8-3/8"
42 x 21cm
Includes a specially painted semi with dump trailer, lettered for Star Glass Recycling.

222-9071 Five Story Chimney **16.98**
2 x 2 x 10"
5 x 5 x 26cm

222-9072 Crane & Accessories **24.98**
Crane: 5 x 3 x 11-1/2"
12 x 9 x 7cm
Base: 16-1/2 x 4"
42 x 1cm

222-9073 Fencing **16.98**
6' 1.8m overall length.
Ornate iron and brick fence is ideal for fencing in a park, cemetery, mansion or industry. Fencing can be arranged in many different ways to fit your space.

SUPERIOR BAKERY

222-9037 14.98

RURAL SCHOOLHOUSE

222-9036 14.98

Great West Models, Inc.

Easy-to-build plastic kits. Create-A-Scene details shown in some photos are sold separately. Industrial buildings are based on modern concrete "tip-up" style buildings.

GOLDEN FOODS

24-505 44.95 *NEW*
21-1/2 x 11-1/2 x 4-1/8"
This structure is made to have two service sidings along with two truck docks and is ideal for shelf or modular layouts.

FERGUS DISTRIBUTING

24-504 35.95 *NEW*
14-3/4 x 11-1/2 x 4-1/8"
Similar to #24-505 except smaller.

ELLIS MANUFACTURING

24-503 34.95 *NEW*
14-3/4 x 12-3/4 x 4-1/8"

ALL AMERICAN TRACTOR & TRAILER

24-502 26.95 *NEW*
11-1/2 x 9-1/4 x 4-1/2"
A great structure to use as a backdrop for your tractor & trailer collection. Can also be used as intermodal maintenance facility.

ALLIED CHEMICAL

24-501 26.95 *NEW*
10-1/2 x 10-1/2 x 4-1/8"

ANGLED ACME DIST.

24-500 24.95
11-12 x 7-1/8 x 4-1/8"

MITCHELL'S MACHINE SERVICE

24-102 19.95
8 x 6 x 4-1/8"

STAN'S FABRICATING

24-101 17.95
7 x 5 x 4-1/8"
A slightly smaller version of #102.

ACME DISTRIBUTING

24-103 23.95
9-1/8 x 7-1/8 x 4-1/8"
A slightly larger version of #102.

1 STORY OFFICE/WAREHOUSE

24-110 19.95
11-3/8 x 6 x 2-1/2"

RITEWAY ENGINEERING

24-108 16.95
5-7/8 x 7 x 2-1/2"

WINSLOW CONST CO.

24-109 17.95
7 x 9-1/4 x 2-1/2"

STAR MANUFACTURING

24-104 29.95
14-3/4 x 7-1/8 x 4-1/8"

MATRIX COMPONENTS

24-105 32.95
16 x 9-1/4 x 4-1/8"

ST PLASTICS

24-106 24.95
10-1/4 x 9-1/4 x 4-1/8"
Same as #105, but without one-story office area.

ENGINE/CAR SHOP

24-107 24.95
9-1/4 x 11-1/2 x 4-1/8"

ROADSIDE COTTAGES

24-1050 20.95
Includes add-on details, makes a great steam- or early diesel-era motel too!

All house and garage kits feature numerous choices of door and window locations to suit your particular layout.

HOUSE KITS EA 7.95

Kits are complete with chimney, 1 door and 3 windows.

24-1060 Hip Roof
24-1070 Gable Roof

GARAGE KITS

24-1010 Single Door, 2-Car w/Gable Roof **7.95**
24-1020 Double-Door, 2-Car w/Gable Roof **7.95**
24-1030 Single Door, 2-Car w/Hip Roof **7.95**
24-1040 Single Door, 1 Car w/Gable Roof pkg(2) **9.95**

GAS STATION & REPAIR GARAGE

24-1100 25.95
Includes add-on details.

GAS STATION ONLY

24-1090 19.95

GARAGE ONLY

24-1080 7.95

CREATE-A-SCENE

24-301 House Details **5.98**

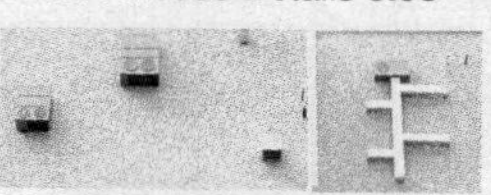

24-302 Roof Details **12.98**
Small air conditioning unit, assorted ductwork, large evaporation cooler and assorted vents.

24-303 Roof Details **12.98**
Medium air conditioning unit, large evaporantive cooler, J vent, assorted vents and two small evaporation coolers.

24-304 Roof Details **15.98**
Large air conditioning unit, small air conditioning unit, assorted ductwork, "J" vent and assorted vents.

24-305 Warehouse Details **13.98**
Dumpster, large gas meter, fire plug, parking and dock bumpers, building protector posts and industrial electric meter.

24-306 Assorted Warehouse Details **6.98**
24-310 Assorted Roof Details **13.98** *NEW*
Assorted duct work, small air conditioning unit, one large and one small domed vents, and five assorted vents.

24-311 Assorted Roof Details **12.98** *NEW*
One small evaporative cooler and 13 large and small assorted vents.

24-312 Assorted Roof Details **12.98** *NEW*
Two small evaporative coolers, nine assorted vents and one large and one small roof or wall exhaust blowers.

FENCE

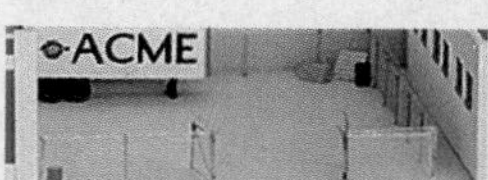

24-309 150' Metal Chainlink Fencing **15.98**

ASSORTED INDUSTRIAL SIGNS EA 3.95

Each colored sheet has assorted warning, parking, and company signs.

24-400
24-401 *NEW*
24-402 *NEW*

Roof Toppers

Make your buildings stand out with these arched and flat tar-paper styrene roofs. Add Create-A-Scene evaporative coolers and vents to RoofToppers and really detail a roof.

ROOF TOPPERS EA 4.95

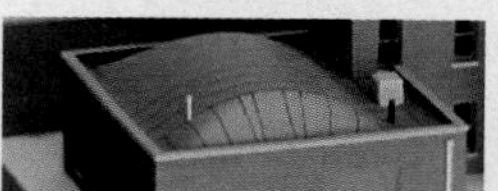

24-901 For City Classics #107 (sold separately) *NEW*
24-902 For City Classics #109 (sold separately) *NEW*
24-903 For Design Preservation Models #112 (sold separately) *NEW*
24-904 Universal for Flat Roofs *NEW*

100 SERIES KITS

#100 Series plastic kits include authentically detailed walls plus roof, clear window material, and complete instructions. Architectural details are molded in place for easy assembly in minutes. Use any plastic model cement or solvent. Figures, vehicles, decals not included.

LAUBE'S LINEN MILL

243-106 10.98
6-3/4 x 3-1/4"
17.2 x 8.4cm

FREIGHT DEPOT

243-107 10.98
5-3/4 x 4-3/4"
14.5 x 12cm

CUTTING'S SCISSOR CO.

243-103 10.98
7-1/4 x 3" 18.5 x 7.7cm

CARR'S PARTS

243-116 10.98
4-3/4 x 3-3/4" 12 x 9.5cm

SKIP'S CHICKEN AND RIBS

243-105 9.98
2-3/4 x 4" 7 x 10.2cm

B. MOORE CATALOG SHOWROOM

243-104 10.98
4-3/4 x 5" 13 x 12.9cm

CAROL'S CORNER CAFE

243-113 10.98
4-1/4 x 2-3/4" 11 x 7cm

KELLY'S SALOON

243-101 9.98
2-3/4 x 4" 7 x 10.2cm

DPM GOLD KITS

Gold Kits are plastic kits with numerous white metal casting details and dry transfer decals included.

COAL RIVER PASSENGER & FREIGHT DEPOTS

243-405 39.98 ***NEW***
15-1/2 x 6-3/8" 39.5 x 16.1cm
The depot set comes with a hydrocal passenger platform with wood plank details and a realistic-looking "concrete" freight dock. Both models feature the molded-in architectural details that add an extra touch of realism. More than 40 white metal castings transform these depots into an entire scene! (People and vehicles not included.)

EMERY LANE

243-404 34.98
8-53/64 x 5-1/2" 22.4 x 13.9cm
Two different DPM Victorian houses come to life with over 90 white metal castings. Includes motorcycle, dog with dog house, mail box, street light, lawn mower, wash lady, picket fence, chimneys, clothesline with clothes. (People not included.)

ENTERTAINMENT DISTRICT

243-403 39.98
8-53/64 x 5-1/2" 22.4 x 13.9cm
Two different DPM buildings come to life with over 80 white metal castings. Includes 16 full color movie and burlesque posters, billboard, 2 marquees, canopy, theatre and bar sign, "Premiering Tonight" search light, street lights, dry transfer decals and more. (Cars and people not included.)

DRYWELL INKS

243-401 37.98
13-3/4 x 9-1/2" 34.9 x 17.7cm
Comes with storage tank, loading dock, awnings, barrels, ladders, stairs, handrail, sign, lights, electric junction box, dry transfer decals and over 30 highly detailed white metal castings. (Truck, cars and people not included.)

WHITEWATER BREWING CO.

243-402 44.98
6 x 9-1/2" 15.2 x 24.1cm
This DPM Gold Series Kit comes with dry transfer decals, smokestack, loading dock and over 50 white metal castings including aluminum and wooden beer kegs, full and empty crates, louvered wall fan and more. (Truck, cars and people not included.)

DPM URBAN DETAIL

JC NICKELS
243-117 10.98
6-3/4 x 4"
17 x 10.2cm

SEYMOUR BLOCK
243-121 11.98
7 x 3"
18 x 10.2cm

FRONT STREET BUILDING
243-120 10.98
5-3/4 x 4"
14.7 x 10.2cm

M.T. ARMS HOTEL
243-119 18.98
7-3/4 x 2-3/4" 20 x 7cm

1ST NATIONAL BANK
243-118 10.98
3 x 4-1/2" 7.7 x 11.5cm

TOWNHOUSE #3
243-111 9.98
2-1/2 x 4-1/4" 6.4 x 11cm

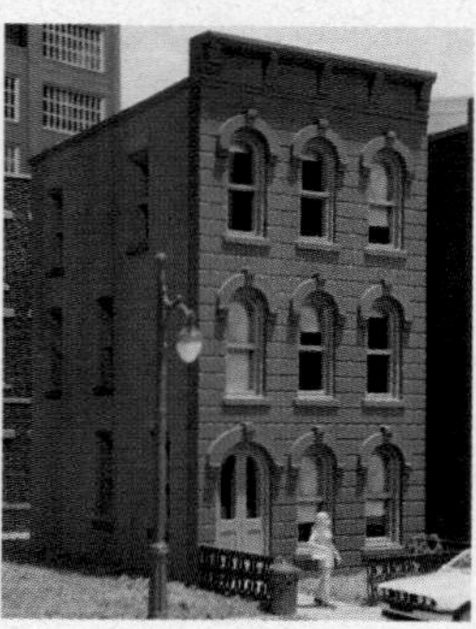

TOWNHOUSE #2
243-110 9.98
2-1/2 x 4-1/4" 6.4 x 11cm

TOWNHOUSE #1
243-109 9.98
2-1/2 x 4-1/4" 6.4 x 11cm

THE OTHER CORNER CAFE
243-115 10.98
4-3/4 x 3"
12 x 7.7cm

TOWNHOUSE FLATS 3 FRONTS
243-114 9.98
2-1/2 x 4-7/8" each
6.4 x 12.2cm

CITY CAB CO.
243-112 10.98
6-1/4 x 5-3/4"
16 x 14.5cm

GOODFELLOWS HALL
243-108 10.98
6-1/4 x 4-3/4" 16 x 12cm

ROBERTS DRY GOODS
243-102 9.98
4-1/2 x 3-3/4" 11.5 x 9.5cm

POWERHOUSE
243-356 29.98
11-1/4 x 5-3/4" 30 x 14.9cm
An industrial structure with dramatic 3-story windows.

TERA SURPLUS WINDOW WAREHOUSE
243-355 29.98
8-3/4 x 11-1/2" 22.2 x 29.5cm
An industrial/warehouse structure with a high profile.

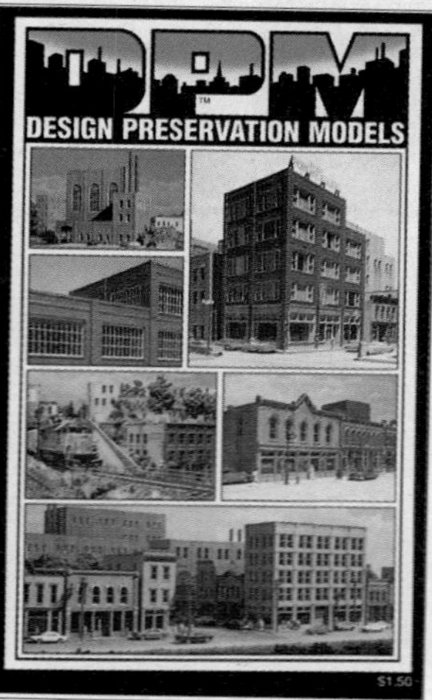

STRUCTURE CATALOG
243-13 1.50
A complete listing of all HO (plus N and O Scale) kits, shown in full-color.

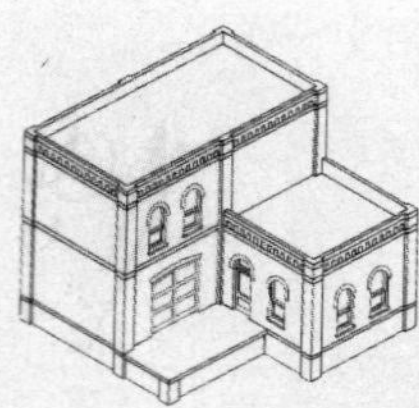

THREE-IN-ONE KIT
243-351 19.98
Complete either of two buildings up to 8-1/2 x 6" (21.9 x 15.4cm) or a 23" (59cm) long 3-D "flat".

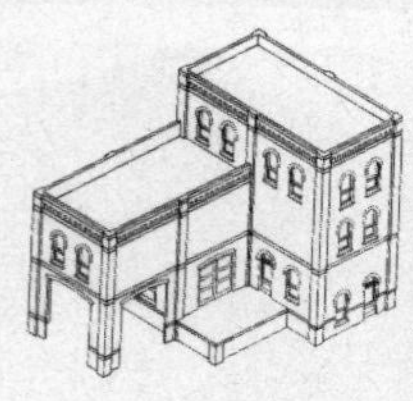

FOUR-IN-ONE KIT
243-352 26.98
Complete any of three buildings up to 7-1/2 x 8-1/2" (19 x 21.9cm) or a 17" (41.9cm) long 3-D "flat".

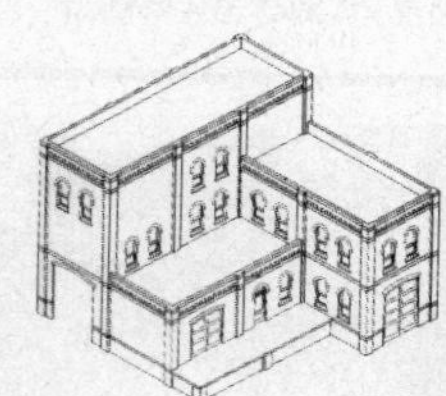

FOUR-IN-ONE KIT
243-353 29.98
Complete any of three buildings up to 11-1/2 x 8-1/2" (29 x 21.9cm) or a 20" (50.5cm) long 3-D "flat".

FEDUPS FREIGHT CO.
243-354 29.98
19-3/4 x 8-3/4" 50 x 22.2cm
A shipping and receiving center with an action-oriented focal point.

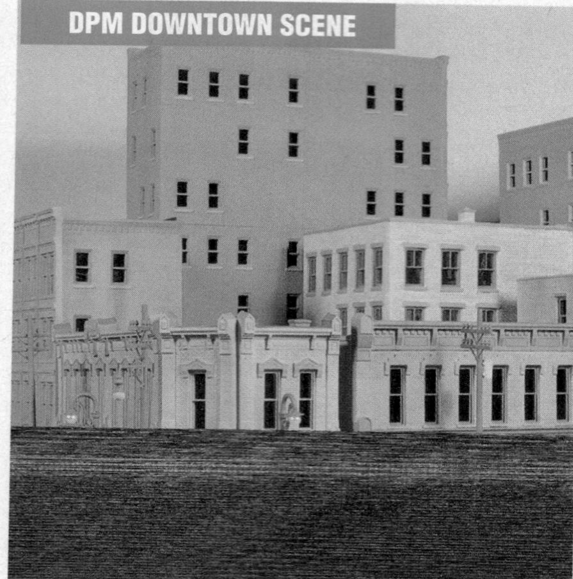

Authentic detail and architecture are portrayed in this DPM downtown scene.

200 SERIES KITS

#200 Series kits make painting optional because the walls are one color, doors and windows another. These plastic kits include detailed walls and separate window and doors. Roof, clear window material, and complete instructions are also included. Use plastic model cement or solvent. Figures, vehicles, decals not included.

PAM'S PET SHOP
243-202 9.98
2-1/8 x 3" 5.4 x 7.7cm

WALKER BUILDING
243-204 10.98
3 x 4-1/2" 7.7 x 11.5cm

SCHULTZ'S GARAGE
243-201 9.98
3 x 4-3/4" 7.7 x 12.2cm

C. SMITH PACKING HOUSE
243-203 10.98
4-3/4 x 5-3/8" 12.2 x 14.8cm

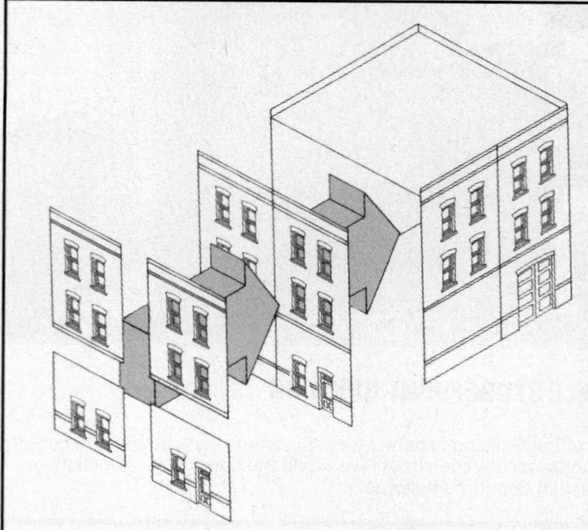

MODULAR BUILDING SYSTEM

UNLIMITED BUILDING OPTIONS

Interchangeable plastic wall sections make it possible to create buildings of any size, shape, and height. Build a variety of styles - whatever you want or need.

- One story building - use street or dock level wall sections and cornice.
- Two story building - use street or dock level wall sections, top with one story wall sections and cornice.
- Three story building - use street or dock level wall sections, top with two story wall sections and cornice.
- More stories - add additional wall sections to create as many stories as desired.

Packages include 4 identical wall sections with pilasters, plus doors, windows, and clear window material where needed. All sections are the same width (2-3/4" 7cm) and color. Cornice packages include 8 sections of Cornice with Cornice pilasters, Dock Riser Wall packages include 8 Dock Riser Wall sections with dock pilasters. Powerhouse Window packages include 2 two-story windows and 4 walls. Packages are 3.49 - 4.49 each. Designer Bulk Packs are an economical way to purchase modular wall sections for your own designs (see facing page).

DOCK LEVEL WALL SECTIONS

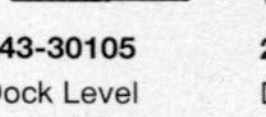

243-30105
Dock Level Arched Entry

243-30103
Dock Level Arched Window

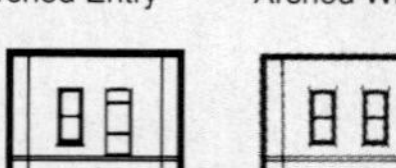

243-30136
Dock Level Rectangular Entry

243-30133
Dock Level Rectangular Window

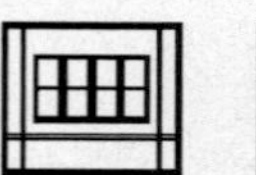

243-30143
Dock Level Victorian Window

243-30163
Dock Level 20th Century Window

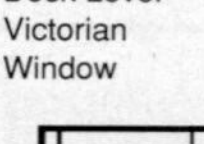

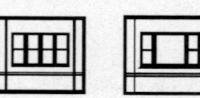

243-30172
Dock Level Steel Sash Entry

243-30173
Dock Level Steel Sash Window

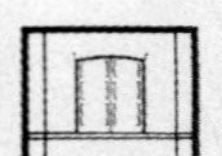

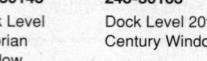

243-30106
Dock Level Freight Door

243-30135
Dock Level Overhead Door

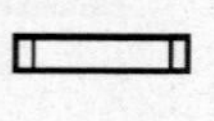

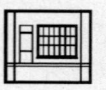

243-30115
Dock Riser Wall (8 per package)

243-30104
Street/Dock Level Blank Wall

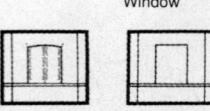

STREET LEVEL WALL SECTIONS

243-30101
Street Level Arched Entry

243-30131
Street Level Rectangular Entry

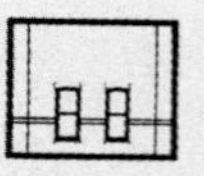

243-30134
Street Level Rectangular Window

243-30141
Street Level Victorian Entry

243-30142
Street Level Victorian Window

243-30161
Street Level 20th Century Entry

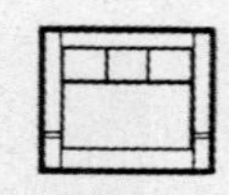

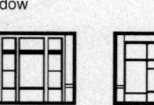

243-30162
Street Level 20th Century Window

243-30171
Street Level Steel Sash Entry

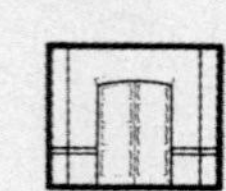

243-30102
Street Level Freight Door

243-30132
Street Level Overhead Door

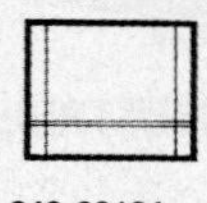

243-30107
Street Level Open Arch

243-30104
Street/Dock Level Blank Wall

TWO STORY WALL SECTIONS

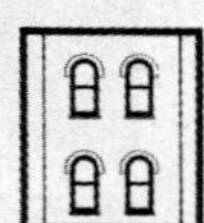

243-30108
Two Story Arched 4 Window

243-30109
Two Story Arched 2 Window (HIGH)

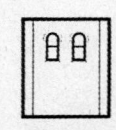

243-30110
Two Story Arched 2 Window (LOW)

243-30138
Two Story Rectangular 4 Window

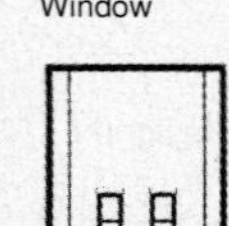

243-30139
Two Story Rectangular 2 Window (HIGH)

243-30137
Two Story Rectangular 2 Window (LOW)

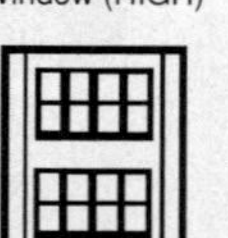

243-30144
Two Story Victorian Window

243-30164
Two Story 20th Century Window

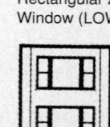

243-30174
Two Story Steel Sash Window

243-30111
Two Story Blank Wall

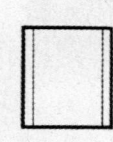

ONE STORY WALL SECTIONS

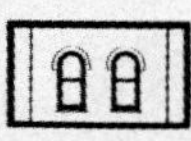

243-30112
One Story Arched Window

243-30130
One Story Rectangular Window

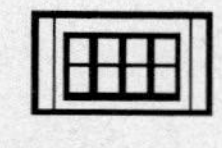

243-30147
One Story Victorian Window

243-30167
One Story 20th Century Window

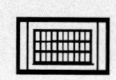

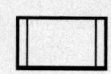

243-30175
One Story Steel Sash Window

243-30113
One Story Blank Wall

CORNICE

243-30117
Cornice - Plain

243-30114
Cornice - Fancy

POWERHOUSE WINDOW

243-30118
Powerhouse Window (2 per package)

See What's Available at
www.walthers.com

ROOF & TRIM KIT

243-30190 3.49
For modular buildings, this plastic kit includes styrene roof material, brick detailed parapet wall trim and styrene supports for "inside" corners. Assorted roof vents and hatches suitable for all buildings are also included. All add fine detail and realism to building tops.

PLANNING PACKET

243-30191 .98
Pre-plan buildings with paper mock-ups. The HO scale Planning Packet contains full size drawings of wall sections. To use, make photo copies of wall sections, cut out the wall sections you want and arrange into walls. Tape walls on cardboard, cut out cardboard and tape together to form a 3-dimensional paper mock-up. Modify mock-up until it is satisfactory, then purchase the required wall sections to construct your building.

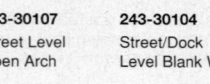

"HO" SCALE MODULAR LEARNING KIT

243-360 5.98
Learn the techniques for building with DPM's Modular System components. Complete instructions and planning packet show you how to do it. The result is this 5-3/4 x 3" (14.8 x 7.7cm) building with a variety of uses on your HO layout. Kit includes decals, roof and clear window material. Use any plastic model cement or solvent. Figures and vehicles not included.

DESIGNER BULK PACKS

Designer Bulk Packs each feature one of the five different architectural styles represented in the modular system. Each pack contains plans for three specific buildings and all plastic modular parts needed to finish any one of the three. Styrene roof material, clear window material, complete instructions, building plans, and painting and weathering tips are included. Use plastic model cement or solvent. Note: Designer Bulk Packs provide approximately 40% in savings over buying modular parts in separate packages. Figures, vehicles, decals not included.

ARCHED WINDOW INDUSTRIAL BUILDING

243-361 29.98
Arched Window Industrial Buildings embody classic architectural features. Designed for factory, warehouse or institutional usage, they endure in every skyline.

RECTANGULAR WINDOW INDUSTRIAL BUILDING

243-362 29.98
Rectangular Window Industrial Buildings premiered in the late 1800s. Popular as factories, warehouses, and institutional buildings, they maintain their profiles in cities and towns today.

VICTORIAN STYLE STOREFRONT BUILDING

243-363 29.98
Victorian Style Storefront Buildings characterize the ornate style of the 19th century. Retail stores commonly occupy the street level while the upper floors function as offices, showrooms, and department stores.

20TH CENTURY STOREFRONT BUILDING

243-364 29.98
20th Century Storefront Buildings enhance the marketplace with dignified style. The upper floors accommodate offices, showrooms, and financial institutions, while large display windows at street level attract customers to the retail activity within.

STEEL SASH INDUSTRIAL BUILDING

243-365 29.98
Steel Sash Industrial Buildings gained popularity early in the 20th Century. Larger windows provide energy conserving light to the workplace while multiple panes of glass supported by steel framework create an open feeling.

Model a variety of authentic railroad structures with these craft train kits, which are complete with scale lumber, plastic and/or metal castings, signs and instructions.

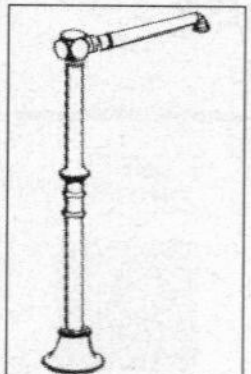

WATER COLUMN

254-27 2.95

FLEMING MAIL CATCHER

254-70 5.95
1/4 x 7/8"
.7 x 2.3cm

JIB CRANE

254-68 10.95
2-3/4 x 3/4"
7 x 2cm

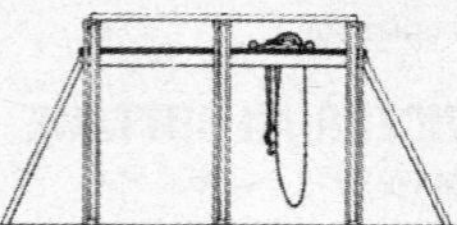

TRAVELLING CRANE

254-73 13.95
4-1/2 x 3-5/8" 11.5 x 9.2cm

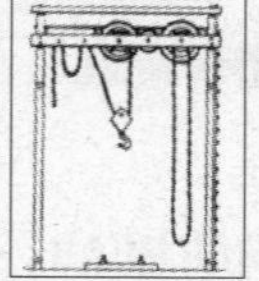

OVERHEAD CRANE

254-72 8.95
2-3/4 x 3"
7 x 7.7cm

D&RG ORE LOADING RAMP

254-125 19.95
Based on a Rio Grande prototype located on Marshall Pass, this HO Scale kit features precut wood parts.

Q&TL WATER TANK

254-28 13.95

RGS TROUT LAKE WATER TANK

254-119 49.95
3-3/4" diameter
9.5cm

WATER TANKS EA 49.95

4-1/4 x 4-1/2" 11 x 11.5cm

254-59 DRGW, HOn3
254-67 Standard, HO

EXTRA SPOUT KIT

254-66 3.95
1-1/2 x 5/8" 4 x 1.7cm

For use with kits #67 or 59.

GOOSE/GANDER OUTHOUSES

254-120 10.95
Two outhouses and Trout Lake station signs.

GRAVITY STAMP

254-35 11.95
1-5/8 x 1"
4.2 x 2.5cm

PALMS STATION

254-19 54.95
4 x 6" 16.16 x 15.24cm
This charming depot will provide excellent service to a small town. The prototype was built in 1887, and the model includes over 70 detail parts to capture the look of the original. Includes detailed step-by-step instructions and drawings.

CLEANOUT RACK

254-39 5.95
3/4 x 1/16"
2 x .2cm

COAL LOADER

254-41 16.95
5-1/8 x 1-5/8" 9.5 x 4.2cm

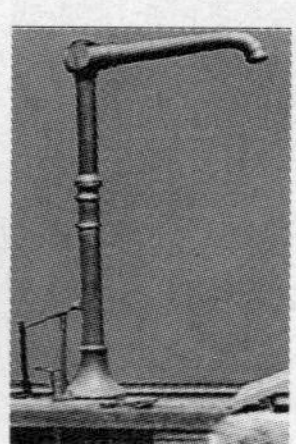

WATER CRANE

254-17 8.95
7/8 x 1-5/8"
2.3 x 4.2cm

COLUMBINE CAFE

254-118 49.95
Includes curtains, cast metal tables and chairs. Choice of three dry transfer names for cafe.

HANDCAR SHED KITS EA 24.95

Both sheds include handcar kits. 2 x 3" 5 x 7.7cm

254-29 HOn3
254-32 HO

ASHPIT

254-40 21.95
3-3/4 x 2-5/8"
9.5 x 6.7cm

THE NEWSPAPER OFFICE

254-56 18.95
3-5/8 x 3-1/2" 9.2 x 9cm
Easy to assemble. Includes die-cut walls, white metal detail parts, plastic windows and doors.

Daily New Arrival Updates! Visit Walthers Web site at
www.walthers.com

Information STATION

Railroad Slang

Gandy Dancer - track worker: May have originated from the Gandy Tool Company, or an Irish jig known as a "gandy" which resembled their rhythmic work.
Gay Cat - tramp held in contempt by fellow vagrants because he is willing to work if a job comes along
Hobo - Folks who sneak rides on or in freight cars (not the same as a bum or a tramp).
Hogger - An engineer
Lizard Scorcher - dining car chef
Music Master - paymaster
Ringmaster - yardmaster
Sandhog - laborer who works in a caisson tunneling under a river, boring either a railroad tunnel, subway or highway tunnel.
Scab - nonunion worker
Seat Hog - passenger who monopolizes more than one seat in a car or a station waiting room while others have to stand.
Star Gazer - brakeman who fails to see signals.
Stude Tallow - student fireman.
Tallow Pot - fireman, from the days when beef tallow was used as a lubricant.

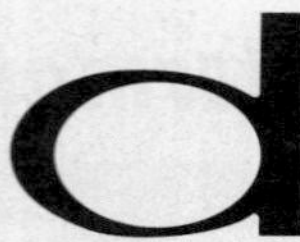

DOVER PUBLICATIONS

These easy-to-build kits are full-color buildings printed on cardstock. Each includes illustrated instructions.

1920S MAIN STREET

241-24473 6.95
9 buildings.

VICTORIAN HOUSES

241-23849 7.95
4 buildings.

EARLY NEW ENGLAND VILLAGE

241-23536 6.95
12 buildings.

WESTERN FRONTIER TOWN

241-23736 6.95
10 buildings.

SUBURBAN HOUSES OF THE 1920S

241-27714 6.95
4 buildings.

EARLY AMERICAN SEAPORT

241-24754 7.95
11 buildings.

HOUSE OF SEVEN GABLES

241-26150 4.95

OLD TIME FARM

241-24589 6.95
9 buildings.

GREENFIELD VILLAGE

241-25635 7.95

For Daily Product Information Click
www.walthers.com

CAERNAVON CASTLE IN WALES

241-24663 6.95

VICTORIAN SEASIDE RESORT

241-25097 6.95
9 buildings.

241-25198

241-25368

OLD ENGLISH VILLAGE

241-25198 6.95
12 buildings.

ROBIE HOUSE

241-25368 6.95
Designed by Frank Lloyd Wright.

241-26017

241-26279

SOUTHERN PLANTATION

241-26017 6.95

LINCOLN'S SPRINGFIELD HOME

241-26279 4.95

241-26337

241-26547

OLD IRISH VILLAGE

241-26337 6.95
6 buildings.

OLD BETHPAGE VILLAGE

241-26547 5.95
6 early American buildings.

241-26899  241-26910

PAUL REVERE HOUSE

241-26899 4.95

OLD STURBRIDGE VILLAGE MEETINGHOUSE

241-26910 4.95

241-29082  241-29276

VICTORIAN SHINGLE-STYLE HOUSE

241-29082 4.95

VICTORIAN "PAINTED LADY"

241-29276 5.95

241-27125

241-27311

COLONIAL HOUSES

241-27125 6.95
5 buildings.

VICTORIAN COTTAGE

241-27311 4.95

241-27473

241-28045

19TH CENTURY MILL TOWN

241-27473 6.95

VICTORIAN RAILROAD STATION

241-28045 5.95

VICTORIAN GOTHIC HOUSE

241-28770 4.95
9 x 9 x 8" 22.5 x 22.5 x 20cm
With their arched windows, high roofs and lavish ornamental carvings, homes of this type were very popular in the northeastern US during the mid-19th century. Model is based on the historic Delamater House built in 1844, preserved today at Rhinebeck, New York.

DYNA-MODEL PRODUCTS COMPANY

These craft train kits feature milled, die cut basswood, fully formed plastic shingle roofing and cast metal windows and doors. Details shown in illustrations are included, unless noted. Some kits can be constructed with removable roof and/or side. Most are available with either painted or unpainted accessories.

SLAUGHTER HOUSE

8 x 6"
20.5 x 15.3cm

260-307 Unpainted Accessories **25.95**
260-3071 Painted Accessories **49.95**

HOLDING PENS W/PAINTED CATTLE

260-4001 31.95

HOLDING PENS W/PAINTED CATTLE, PIGS/SHEEP

260-4002 31.95
9-3/4 x 4-3/4"
25 x 12cm

SMALL PASSENGER STATION

260-1 22.95
6 x 2-3/4"
15.5 x 7cm
Less people and benches.

NEWSSTAND

260-3161 Painted Accessories
9.95

VEGETABLE STAND

260-5001 Painted Accessories
9.95 ***NEW***

MAC DOUGAL'S FARM HOUSE

4-3/4 x 3-1/8"
12 x 8cm

260-313 Unpainted Accessories **22.95**
260-3131 Painted Accessories **39.95**

COUNTRY CHURCH

260-317 Unpainted Accessories **23.95**
260-3171 Painted Accessories **37.95**

SMALL FREIGHTHOUSE

260-100 22.95

BUTCHER SHOP

4-5/8 x 2-5/8"
11.8 x 6.7cm

260-301 Unpainted Accessories **22.95**
260-3011 Painted Accessories **43.95**

MRS. O'MALLEY'S PLACE

3-3/4 x 2-1/2"
9.5 x 6.5cm

260-312 Unpainted Accessories **21.95**
260-3121 Painted Accessories **37.95**

SHANTY

260-306 22.95
4 x 3-3/8"
10 x 8.5cm

LIVERY STABLE

4 x 7"
10 x 18cm

260-311 Unpainted Accessories **29.95**
260-3111 Painted Accessories **47.95**

SMALL BARN

4-1/2 x 4-3/8"
11.5 x 11.2cm

260-309 Unpainted Accessories **18.95**
260-3091 Painted Accessories **29.95**

PASSENGER STATION W/TOWER

260-2 22.95
6 x 3-5/8"
15.5 x 9.3cm
Less people and benches.

GROCERY STORE

5-1/2 x 3-3/16"
14 x 8.1cm

260-308 Unpainted Accessories **23.95**
260-3081 Painted Accessories **42.95**

MABEL'S BOARDING HOUSE FOR RAILROAD MEN

5-3/16 x 5-3/16"
13.5 x 13.5cm

260-314 Unpainted Accessories **24.95**
260-3141 Painted Accessories **43.95**

GRIST MILL & FEED STORE

6-1/2 x 4-3/4"
16.5 x 12cm

260-304 Unpainted Accessories **22.95**
260-3041 Painted Accessories **43.95**

CORRAL W/PAINTED HORSES

260-4011 26.95
3-1/2 x 5-1/2"
9 x 14cm

PLUMBING SUPPLY

6 x 5"
15.5 x 12.8cm

260-305 Unpainted Accessories **23.95**
260-305 Painted Accessories **43.95**
Less pickup truck.

LARGE FREIGHT HOUSE

4 x 8-1/2"
10 x 21.5cm

260-101 Unpainted Accessories **23.95**
260-1011 Painted Accessories **42.95**

DYNA-MODEL PRODUCTS COMPANY

OUTDOOR PRIVY

260-3151 Painted Accessories **9.95**
7/8 x 7/8"
2.2 x 2.2cm

BARBER SHOP & POOL ROOM

2-7/8 x 4-3/16"
7.3 x 10.7cm

260-303 Unpainted Accessories **22.95**
260-3031 Painted Accessories **43.95**

TWO SMALL HOUSES

3-5/8 x 3-3/4"
9.3 x 9.5cm

260-310 Unpainted Accessories **22.95**
260-3101 Painted Accessories **39.95**

BLACKSMITH SHOP

3-1/2 x 3-1/2"
9 x 9cm

260-302 Unpainted Accessories **21.95**
260-3021 Painted Accessories **42.95**
Less team of horses.

CATALOG

260-99 1.00

GLOOR CRAFT MODELS

These HO, craft train kits feature basswood, precut parts, color coded stripwood, metal castings, step-by-step instructions and full size drawings.

We have worked closely with this manufacturer to provide accurate delivery information at the time this catalog was published. Items listed in blue ink may not be available at all times. Current delivery information, along with a list of in-stock products for this line, can be found on our Web site at www.walthers.com.

HAYDENTON COVERED DEPOT

288-4002 38.95
11-1/2 x 5" 29.3 x 12.7cm

BRYAN'S FARM SUPPLY

288-4008 30.95
6 x 7" 15.3 x 17.8cm

SINGLE STALL ENGINE HOUSE

288-4005 38.95
15-1/2 x 6-1/2" 39.4 x 16.5cm

FREIGHT HOUSE

288-4007 20.95
9 x 3-1/2" 23 x 9cm

MARLINTON STATION

288-4021 50.95

SMALL FREIGHT HOUSE

288-4012 18.95
2-3/4 x 4" 7 x 10cm

LINESIDE SECTION HOUSE

288-4013 16.95
2-1/4 x 2-3/4" 5.7 x 7cm

YARDMASTER'S OFFICE

288-4010 11.95
4 x 2-1/2" 10.2 x 6.4cm

WATCHMAN'S SHANTY

288-4014 18.95
2-1/8 x 3-1/8" 5 x 8cm

TOOL & SUPPLY SHED

288-4015 26.95
3-3/8 x 7" 8.6 x 17.8cm

INTERLOCKING TOWER

288-4004 32.95
2 x 3-1/4" 5 x 8.3cm
Prototype in Mt. Union, Pennsylvania.

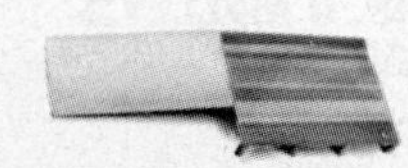

LOADING PLATFORM

288-4022 14.95
2-7/8 x 7" 7.3 x 17.8cm

CHUCK'S HARDWARE

288-4031 23.95
4-1/2 x 5-1/2" 11.5 x 14cm

OLD STYLE HOUSE

288-4006 27.95
7-1/2 x 5" 19 x 12.7cm

CASH & CARRY LUMBER CO.

288-4023 54.95
Space varies with arrangement.

MIDWESTERN GRAIN ELEVATOR

288-4009 58.95
5 x 16" 12.8 x 47cm

STOVER'S MOTORS

288-4025 23.95
5-3/4 x 5-3/4" 14.6 x 14.6cm

SUNSET FIREWORKS INC.

288-4026 22.95
10-1/2 x 7" 26.8 x 17.8cm

LUMBER STORAGE RACK

288-4024 20.95
2-1/2 x 7" 6.6 x 17.8cm

ROGER'S PLUMBING & HEATING

288-4016 31.95
6 x 7" 15.3 x 17.8cm
Clapboard siding and metal roof. Includes lean-to shanty plus a 2-color sign.

DIESEL SERVICE FACILITY

288-4035 32.95
12 x 10-1/4" 35 x 26cm

COALING TOWER

288-4001 43.95
5 x 7" 12.7 x 18cm

STORE & WAREHOUSE

288-4003 37.95

FUNARO & CAMERLENGO

Craft Train Kits feature thin, flexible styro-urethane castings with architectural details cast in place, stripwood and wire.

SEARS CATALOG HOME
279-1 49.99
4-1/4 x 4-1/4" 10.7 x 10.7cm

ART DECO CORNER BUILDING
279-9 42.99
6-1/4 x 3-1/2" 16 x 9cm

ART DECO CENTER BLOCK
279-11 36.99
6-1/16 x 2-1/4" 15.5 x 5.7cm

ART DECO FRONT BUILDING
279-10 42.99
6-1/4 x 4-1/2" 16 x 11.5cm

D&H COMPANY HOUSE
279-14 29.99
2-5/8 x 4-3/4" 6.7 x 12.2cm
As-built.

D&H COMPANY HOUSE
279-15 29.99
2-5/8 x 4-3/4" 6.7 x 12.2cm
Modernized.

RUSHLAND STATION W/ASPHALT ROOF
279-4 26.99
2-1/4 x 4-1/2" 5.5 x 11.5cm

RUSHLAND STATION W/SLATE ROOF
279-8 26.99
2-1/4 x 4-1/2" 5.5 x 11.5cm

GULF SUMMIT COTTAGE
279-2 15.99
2-1/4 x 2" 5.7 x 5cm

COMPANY HOUSE
279-6 15.99
3-3/4 x 3-5/8" 9.5 x 9.2cm

COMPANY PRESIDENT'S HOME
279-5 26.99
5 x 4-5/16" 12.7 x 11cm

ISLAND CREEK STORE
279-7 49.99
6 x 6" 15.3 x 15.3cm

OLD TIME GAS STATION
279-3 15.99
1-1/2 x 1-1/2" 3.8 x 3.8cm

ART DECO STORE
279-12 9.99
2-1/4 x 2-1/4" 5.7 x 5.7cm

INDUSTRIAL HERITAGE SCALE MODELS

We have worked closely with this manufacturer to provide accurate delivery information at the time this catalog was published. Items listed in blue ink may not be available at all times. Current delivery information, along with a list of in-stock products for this line, can be found on our Web site at www.walthers.com.

TRUCK DUMP TIPPLE
356-101 80.00
5-1/2 x 13-3/4"
14 x 34.3cm
For sand, gravel, ore and coal. Uses two tracks.

RETAIL COAL DEALER
356-201 70.00
7-5/8 x 6-3/16"
19.2 x 15.8cm
Based on the Sexton Lumber Co. in Nichols, New York.

MICHIGAN ARROW MOBILE HOME
356-1152 15.75

1950s MOBILE HOME
356-1150 15.75
Molded in clear resin, less details and figures.

1970s MOBILE HOME
356-1151 16.75
Newer prototype, molded in clear resin.

Grandt Line

Easy-to-build kits feature finely detailed parts made of injection-molded styrene.

MIDWEST PETROLEUM DISTRIBUTORS

300-5907 TBA
Features a main warehouse, pump house, full loading dock and three oil tanks.

REESE STREET ROWHOUSES

300-5903 pkg(3) **24.95**
Total Area: 10 x 5" 26.2 x 12.5cm
Based on actual row houses built in Silverton, Colorado. These small homes are perfect for any area. Includes parts for three complete buildings. Windows and doors are separate parts. Four different eave trims are included. Extra details include three outhouses, interior floors and three lengths of boardwalk.

CORRUGATED IRON WAREHOUSE KIT

300-5908 24.95 ***NEW***
4-3/4 x 6-1/4" 11.9 x 15.7cm
Based on a prototype facility located in Placerville, California, the design of this structure is common to industrial sites from the 1920s to today. Building features two sliding warehouse doors and an office that opens out onto the loading platforms. The risers can be left off so structures can sit directly on the ground. Windows and doors and molded separately.

THE SILVERTON ORE CHUTE

300-5904 19.95
2 x 3" 5 x 7.6cm
Located on the south side of the tracks at Silverton, Colorado, this Ore Chute makes an interesting addition to any HO Scale line. Built sometime in the late 1930s or early 40s, the prototype was served by trucks and used to load box cars with high-grade ore, which required more protection in transit. The complete kit is molded in styrene with a high level of detail. Designed for easy construction, the ore chutes and cribing can be configured to fit your available space. The model includes a complete set of optional stairs and railings which can be arranged as needed to add character to the finished model, or left off to match the appearance of the actual structure.

STANDARD SECTION TOOL HOUSE

300-5905 5.95
One of the most common buildings along any right-of-way are small toolsheds. Generations of maintenance and track crews used these handy buildings to store all kinds of tools and supplies, as well as track inspection cars. This kit represents a pre-fabricated steel design, used system-wide on the Rio Grande starting around 1940. (The prototype is at Pando, Colorado.) Still in use today, its styling is typical of similar buildings used on many roads. The kit features detailed plastic parts and the large doors can be built in the open or closed position.

EAST TERRIBLE MILL & MINING CO.

300-5901 27.95
7-1/2 x 7-1/8" 19 x 18cm
This 10-stamp mill complex is typical of many built in the 1890s. Features separate doors and windows.

NO PROBLEM JOE'S

300-5906 24.95
This structure is based on the still-standing home of "No Problem Joe," a local fix-it man in Aspen, Colorado. Ski-lift operators in Aspen often called on Joe to correct seasonal problems that threatened business operation. Joe was always able to rectify the crisis, swearing there was "no problem."
Model is constructed of styrene components and can be built on a 7 x 3.6" footprint. Kit contains a main house with front porch, coal shed and outhouse.

WENTAMUCK MINE

300-5902 24.95
Total Area: 4-1/2 x 9" 11.2 x 22.5cm
Typical of small "new venture" mines that appeared in Colorado and Nevada around 1910.

SECOND CLASS SALOON

300-5900 16.95
4-3/4 x 3-1/8" 12 x 8cm
Includes Thin Film® decals, five-color signs printed on cardstock, barrels and more.

Add a variety of small commercial and industrial buildings to your layout with these kits. Walls are Hydrocal® plaster castings, which capture fine details. Separate Grandt Line windows and wood parts are also provided.

BOB'S LIQUOR
308-138 99.95

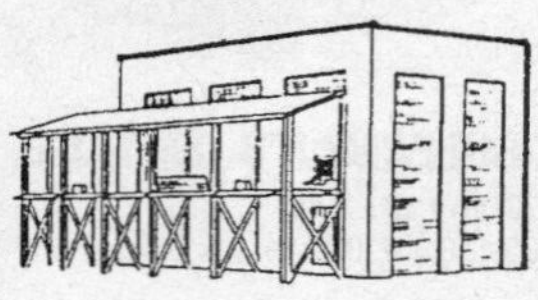

S. KAULMAN ICE PLANT
308-135 29.95
6-1/2 x 11-1/2" 16.5 x 29.2cm

CLIFF'S AUTO WORKS
308-145 39.95
5-1/4 x 6-1/2" 13.3 x 16.5cm

LYON BANK
308-108 24.95
5 x 6-1/2" 12.7 x 16.5cm

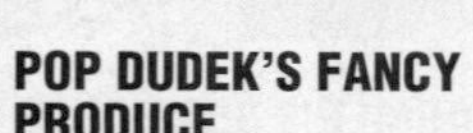

POP DUDEK'S FANCY PRODUCE
308-144 16.95

BAKER'S POOL HALL
308-128 10.95
2-1/4 x 5" 5.7 x 12.7cm

EDWARD'S PLACE
308-101 6.95
3-1/2 x 2" 8.9 x 5.1cm

ED SMITH CABINETMAKER
308-139 29.95
5 x 9-1/2" 12.7 x 24.1cm

PAQUETTE HARDWARE
308-116 10.95
2-1/4 x 4-1/2" 5.7 x 11.4cm

D'ORSEY GAS STATION W/PIT, 1930S
308-126 19.95
2-7/8 x 4-3/4" 7.3 x 12.1cm

GREASE PIT FOR GAS STATION, 1930s
308-127 5.95
1-1/4 x 4-3/4" 3.2 x 12.1cm

CULBERTSON'S FUEL & SOLVENT
308-129 12.95
4 x 5-1/2" 10.2 x 14cm

BURRUS LIVERY
308-130 10.95
3-1/2 x 5-1/4" 8.9 x 13.3cm

ORR'S BROKEN BUTT CAFE
308-131 9.95
2-1/8 x 3-1/2" 5.4 x 8.9cm

LORD'S HOTEL
308-151 49.95
4-3/4 x 3-3/4" 12 x 9.5cm

DULAND'S REPAIR SHED
308-124 5.95
3-1/4 x 2-1/4" 8.3 x 5.7cm

PAYNES CLOCK WORKS
308-102 8.95
2-1/2 x 2" 6.4 x 5.1cm

FAIRY'S MACHINE SHOP
308-169 35.95
12-1/4 x 6-1/4" 31.1 x 15.9cm

TINNER'S WHEAT CO.
308-148 29.95
3 x 4 x 8" tall
7.6 x 10.1 x 20.3cm

REDIGER'S STORAGE
308-109 8.95
1-7/8 x 4" 4.8 x 10.2cm

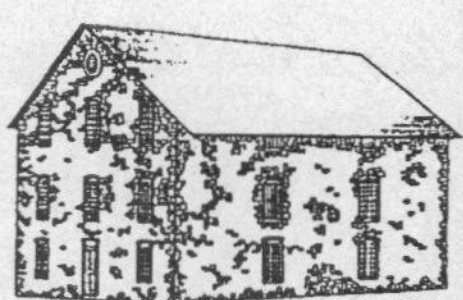

LYLE LARD & LUBRICANTS
308-142 25.95
4-1/2 x 4-7/8" 11.2 x 12cm

J. LOTT WELDING & BLACKSMITH
308-106 9.95
4-1/4 x 2-3/4" 10.8 x 6.9cm

MOTTE'S MINING SUPPLY
308-112 7.95
3 x 2" 7.6 x 5.1cm

ERTNER'S FEED & GRAIN
308-105 14.95
6-1/4 x 4-1/4" 15.9 x 10.8cm

WISBY'S GROCERY
308-122 9.95
3 x 2-1/2" 7.6 x 6.4cm

WALLY'S HOT DOG HAVEN
308-161 8.95
2-3/8 x 2-1/2" 6 x 6.4cm

KYLE'S KOFFEE SHOPPE
308-162 8.95
2-1/2 x 2-1/2" 6.4 x 6.4cm

ROBBIE'S BURGER ROOST
308-163 8.95
5-11/16 x 2-9/16"
14.4 x 6.5cm

ROUTE 66 EATERIES
308-164 (set of 3) 24.95
Includes one each #161-163.

SLICK'S PLUMBING
308-147 19.95
2-1/4 x 4-1/4" 5.7 x 10.8cm

CLARK'S FUR & HIDE CO.
308-149 19.95
8-1/2 x 3-3/8" 21.6 x 8.6cm

WU TANG LAUNDRY & DRUGS
308-104 9.95
3 x 2-3/8" 7.6 x 6cm

COPELAND LEATHER & BOOT COMPANY
308-140 39.95
7 x 7" 17.8 x 17.8cm

H. SMITH WAGON WORKS
308-143 19.95
3-7/8 x 4" 9.8 x 10.2cm

TATER HILL SCHOOL
308-141 54.95
5-7/16 x 8-3/4" 13.8 x 22.2cm

CLAIRMONT TEXAS JAIL
308-110 11.95
4-1/4 x 3-1/4" 10.8 x 8.3cm

GANDY'S WIRE & FENCE
308-150 19.95
3-7/8 x 5" 9.8 x 12.7cm

JACK'S SADDLE SHOP
308-170 14.95

BRENT'S POWDER & SHOT
308-171 19.95

GREER'S BUTCHER SHOP
308-172 14.95

THREE LITTLE JOHNS
308-113 pkg(3) 7.95

MIGRANT WORKERS' ROOMS
308-103 8.95
2-1/4 x 4-1/2" 5.7 x 11.4cm

CROMWELL'S CABIN
308-114 8.95
2-1/8 x 3-1/4" 5.4 x 8.3cm

CLEAR GRIT MINE
308-167 99.95

FANNY RAWLIN'S MINE
308-157 59.95
7 x 12" 17.8 x 30.5cm

SIMMON'S POWER PLANT
308-154 39.95

MCCARTNEY BROTHERS MILL ENGINE HOUSE
308-125 24.95
6-3/8 x 11" 16.2 x 27.9cm

SCHACHT'S SHACK (DOG HOUSE)
308-115 10.95

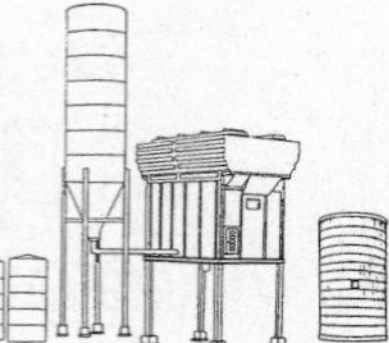

CEMENT PLANT COMPLEX
308-152 49.95

MINER'S HALF DUGOUT
308-156 8.98
2-1/2 x 3" 6.4 x 7.6cm

BUEERMAN'S COTTAGE
308-118 8.95
2-5/8 x 2-3/8" 6.7 x 6cm

SHOTGUN HOUSE
308-111 9.95
4-1/2 x 1-3/4" 11.4 x 4.4cm

GRIMES MILL COMPLEX
308-146 109.95
14 x 10" 35.6 x 25.4cm

FARMER'S SOD HOUSE
308-160 8.95

JOHN HALL FEED & SILAGE
308-136 29.95
3-1/2 x 4-3/4" 8.9 x 12.1cm

REEDS CRIB & CARRIAGE
308-137 59.95
7 x 16-1/2" 17.8 x 41.9cm

WELCH'S DAIRY & FEED MILL
308-168 39.95

BURKHOLTZ'S TEN STAMP MILL
308-132 29.95
3-3/4 x 9" 9.5 x 22.9cm

BRAKEMAN'S SHACK
308-153 10.95
1-1/2 x 3-5/8" 3.8 x 9.2cm

SANTA FE STATION
308-155 54.95

HOWARD FARM BARN
308-121 10.95
4 x 5" 10.2 x 12.7cm

MARTIN'S POLE BARN
308-123 7.95
2-3/4 x 2" 6.9 x 5.1cm

PRICHETT MOUNTAIN TATTLER
308-117 9.95
2 x 3-1/2" 5.1 x 8.9cm

Mountains in Minutes™
I.S.L.E. LABORATORIES

The "Old Hometown Series" are unpainted, precast, rigid foam plastic building fronts. Printed windows and signs are included.

MULTI SCALE ARCH BRIDGE
473-826 12.98
1-3/4 x 11-7/8"
4.5 x 30cm
For HO or N Scales.

TAYLOR'S GARAGE
473-407 15.98
12-1/4 x 5"
31.2 x 12.7cm

BANK BUILDING
473-402 10.98
4 x 2-1/2"
10 x 6.5cm

WAREHOUSE
473-404 15.98
7-1/4 x 2-1/8"
18.5 x 5.5cm

FACTORY
473-408 15.98
12 x 5"
30.5 x 12.7cm

GENERAL STORE
473-401 10.98
7-1/2 x 1-3/8"
19 x 3.5cm

ROCK BREWERY
473-406 15.98
14-1/4 x 4-1/2"
36.3 x 11.5cm

GRAIN ELEVATOR
473-405 14.98
11 x 1-3/4"
28 x 4.5cm

MEMORIAL HALL
473-403 10.98
7 x 2"
18 x 5cm

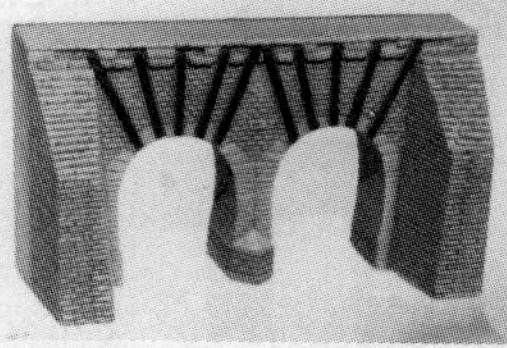

CROSS-OVER BRIDGE TUNNEL
473-828 16.98
11 x 4-1/4"
27.9 x 10.7cm

MULTI SCALE VIADUCT
473-827 24.98
8 x 21"
20 x 44cm
Use with HO, O or N Scales.

BRIDGE ABUTMENTS
473-825 pkg(2) **8.98**
3-1/2 x 8-3/4"
9 x 22.5cm

These easy-to-build kits consist of prototypically precolored plastic parts and complete instructions. Kits are European prototypes. With minor modifications most can easily be Americanized.

FARM HOUSE

322-138 10.98
2-3/16 x 1-5/8 x 1-58"
5.5 x 4 x 4cm

BRITISH PEDESTRIAN OVERPASS

322-715 8.98
9-1/4 x 5-1/4 x 4-3/4"
23 x 13 x 12cm

AMERICAN WEEKEND COTTAGE

322-217 7.98
7-1/16 x 3-15/16" 18 x 10cm

BAR & BEAUTY SALON W/APARTMENTS

322-465 13.98
4 x 2-1/2" 10 x 6.5cm

SMALL RETAIL STORE

322-462 7.98
2-3/8 x 2-3/16 x 4-1/8"
6 x 5.5 x 10.5cm

BRITISH YARD TOWER

322-711 9.98
6-13/16 x 2-5/8 x 4-7/16"
17 x 6.5 x 11cm

COUNTRY CHURCH

322-713 12.50
7-5/8 x 3-5/8 x 4-13/16"
19 x 9 x 12.5cm

BRITISH WAYSIDE

322-714 9.98
24 x 3-1/2 x 2-1/2"
60 x 9 x 6.5cm

RANCH HOUSE

322-1774 6.98
4 x 3-1/2" 10 x 9cm

TERRACE HOUSES

322-1706 pkg(2) **12.98**
8-3/8 x 7-5/8 x 4-7/16"
21 x 19 x 11cm

BLACKSMITH SHOP

322-210 7.25
5-1/8 x 2-3/4" 13 x 7cm

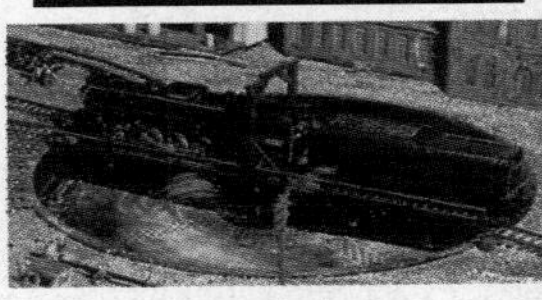

MANUAL TURNTABLE

322-804 29.98
Turntables date from the earliest days of railroading and are used to turn locomotives so they face the right way to pull a train. Kit is typical of a steam-era turntable but many are used to turn diesels today.

WALTHERS TURNTABLE DRIVE

942-472 29.98
Motorize your Walthers N Scale (933-3203) or Heljan HO Scale Turntable (322-804) with this easy conversion kit. Includes one RPM 12V DC motor, motor support bracket, mounting hardware and instructions. Complete unit mounts out of sight below the turntable pit.

ROAD BRIDGE OVERPASS

322-102 6.98
9-1/2 x 2-3/8 x 3-3/4"
5 x 10cm

3-STALL ROUNDHOUSE

322-802 39.98
15-5/8 x 16 x 4-3/4" 39 x 40 x 12cm
During the steam era, the roundhouse was an essential part of every engine terminal and many are still in use today. This kit is typical of structures found on large or small lines and includes parts for three stalls. For a larger facility, an add-on kit (#322-803) is available.

3-STALL ADD-ON (FOR ROUNDHOUSE #322-802)

322-803 36.98
Includes three extra stalls and a rear extension to hold locomotives up to 19-1/4" in length.

STREET HOUSES

322-155 pkg(2) **10.25**
3-3/8 x 2" 8.5 x 5cm

MODERN FREIGHT WAREHOUSE

322-145 22.98
15 x 9-13/16" 38 x 25cm

HANS CHRISTIAN ANDERSEN HOUSE

322-220 7.98
4-5/16 x 4" 11 x 10cm

2-STORY ALPINE HOUSE W/BALCONY

322-1791 14.50
5-1/2 x 4-5/16" 14 x 11cm

RAILROAD STATION

322-1752 22.98
15-3/4 x 6-5/8" 40 x 17cm

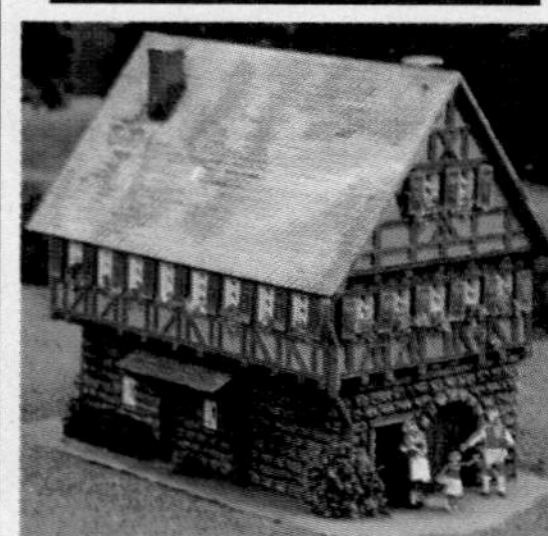

HOUSE AGAINST CITY WALL

322-1797 16.98
4-1/2 x 3-3/8" 11.5 x 8.5cm

SMALL FREIGHT STATION

322-1760 7.98
4 x 2-3/4" 10 x 7cm

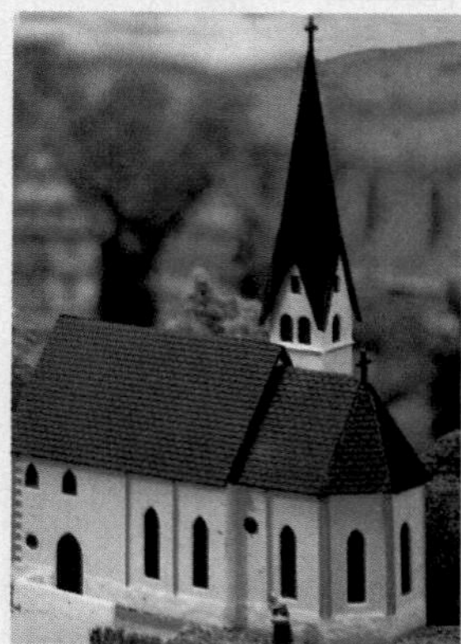

CHURCH

322-1785 12.98
6-1/2 x 4-3/4" 16.5 x 12cm

MODERN YARD TOWER

322-1754 6.75
4-7/8 x 2-1/2" 9 x 6.5cm

HALF-TIMBERED HOUSE

322-203 6.75
5-5/8 x 3 x 2-5/8"
14 x 7.5 x 6.5cm

LARGE PASSENGER STATION

322-151 29.98
16 x 6-13/16 x 4-13/16"
40 x 17 x 12cm

BREWERY COMPLEX

322-690 44.99
When immigrants came to America, they brought many old traditions and skills, including the art of brewing beer. Many a town could boast of its local brewery, and railroads were vital to the success of the business.

This superb kit includes four structures, which you can arrange to fit your layout, and create a custom brewery complex. There's the large malt house with separate tower, the bottling plant and a cooling tower. Plus, there's a brick smokestack, separate windows and doors and more. Be sure to see the Freight Car section for colorful billboard reefers and other cars to serve your industry.

RANCH HOUSE W/ATTACHED GARAGE

322-218 10.98
10-5/8 x 6-5/16" 27 x 16cm

STONE BRIDGE PIER (2-IN-1 KIT)

322-1765 4.99
3-13/64 1-13/64 x 3-13/64"
8 x 3 x 8cm

2-STORY BRICK STATION

322-153 21.98
9-7/8 x 5-7/8" 25 x 15cm

BREWERY MALT HOUSE

322-807 56.98
26 x 7-3/5 x 22" 65 x 19 x 55cm

TIMBER TRESTLE

322-174 19.98
Larger trestle used for main or branch line operations. Molded in dark brown plastic. Its modular design can be used to arrange the various pieces to fit your scenery.

KINDERGARTEN
322-1707 10.98
7-3/16 x 5-3/16 x 1-13/16"
18 x 13 x 4.5cm

DIESEL SERVICE FACILITY
322-1711 14.98
12-13/16 x 2 x 3-5/8"
32 x 5 x 9cm

YARD TOWER 1910 ERA
322-1751 6.75
3-1/2 x 2-1/2 x 4-3/4"
12.5 x 5 x 9.5cm

OVERTRACK SWITCH TOWER
322-1757 12.98
6-3/8 x 4 x 5-3/16"
16 x 10 x 13cm

TUNNEL PORTALS
322-1759 6.98
19-5/8 x 1-7/16 x 5-3/8"
49 x 3 x 13.5cm

OLD WINDMILL
322-201 9.00
4" 10cm square

SPANISH STYLE STATION
322-152 19.98
9 x 7-5/8 x 3-5/8"
22.5 x 19 x 9cm

SMALL BRICK STATION
322-130 11.25
7-5/8 x 3 x 4-13/64"
19 x 7.7 x 10.5cm

LONG PASSENGER PLATFORM
322-1753 11.25
18-3/4 x 2-3/4" 47.5 x 7cm

DANISH CITY HALL
322-221 15.25
5-1/8 x 4-5/16" 13 x 11cm

ROADSIDE INN
322-206 12.50
7-1/8 x 4-1/8 x 3-1/2"
18 x 10.5 x 9cm

DAIRY PLANT
322-207 14.50
7-1/8 x 4-3/4 x 6-1/4"
18 x 12 x 16cm

GENERAL STORE
322-208 14.98
6-3/4 x 4-3/4 x 3-3/8"
17 x 12 x 8.5cm

SMALL TRACT HOUSE
322-216 6.75
4-1/8 x 3-1/2 x 2"
10.5 x 9 x 5cm

CITY HALL
322-1788 13.75
4-7/8 x 4-3/4" 12.5 x 12cm

WAYSIDE STATION
322-156 16.98
8-13/64 x 2-13/16 x 2-5/8"
20.5 x 7 x 6.5cm

COUNTRY INN
322-1789 13.75
6-13/32 x 5-13/16 x 4"
16 x 14.5 x 10cm

COUNTRY STATION
322-1712 16.98
9-5/8 x 3-13/16 x 4-13/32"
24 x 9.5 x 11cm

SHOPPING CENTER W/5 STORES
322-1775 15.98
6-3/4 x 5-7/8" 17 x 15cm

BRICK STATION - 1910 ERA
322-1750 19.50
13 x 4-3/4" 32.5 x 11cm

FREIGHT & PASSENGER STATION
322-1756 29.98
19-13/16 x 7-5/8 x 6"
49.5 x 19 x 15cm

SUBURBAN PASSENGER STATION
322-1755 16.98
10-5/8 x 4-3/8" 27 x 11.2cm

SUMMER HOMES
322-351 pkg(2) **5.75**
1-9/16 x 2-3/4 x 1-3/8"
4 x 7 x 3.5cm
1-9/16 x 2-15/16 x 1-9/16"
4 x 7.5 x 4cm

DRUG STORE
322-461 9.98
2-3/4 x 2-3/8 x 5-1/2"
7 x 6 x 14cm

COALING STATION
322-1767 15.98
7-3/16 x 4 x 3-5/8"
18 x 10 x 9cm

WOOD RAILROAD HOTEL - 1900 ERA
322-820 19.98
5-1/16 x 5-5/16" 13 x 13.5cm

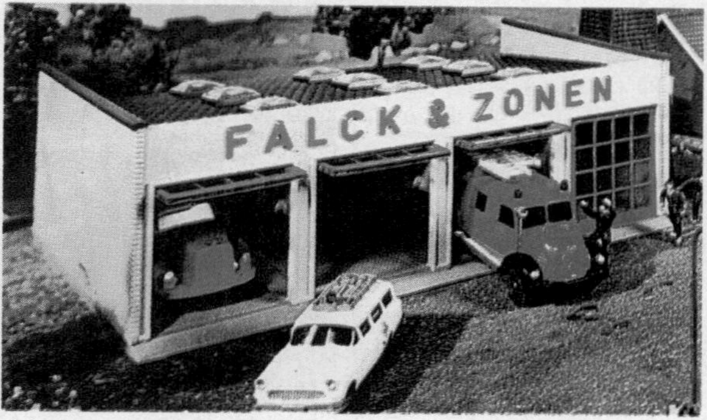

MODERN FIRE STATION
322-1778 11.50
7-1/2 x 4-5/16" 19 x 11cm

STATION
322-157 16.98
19 x 6-5/8 x 3-13/16" 47.5 x 16.5 x 9.5cm

WEEKEND COTTAGE (2-IN-1 KIT)
322-350 7.25
2-1/4 x 3-1/8" 5.8 x 8cm
2-1/4 x 2-7/8" 5.8 x 6.8cm

OLD SUBURBAN HOUSE
322-1773 7.98
4 x 3-5/8 x 2-3/8" 10 x 9 x 6cm

COURTHOUSE
322-906 39.98
15-3/4 x 11-3/8 x 10-13/32" 40 x 29 x 26cm

MODERN 2-STORY HOUSE
322-1794 13.98
6-1/8" 15.5cm square

THE OLD INN
322-1777 8.98
7 x 4-5/8 x 3-3/8"
17.5 x 11.5 x 8.5cm

TRACT HOUSE
322-1772 7.95
4 x 3-3/8 x 2" 10 x 8.5 x 5cm

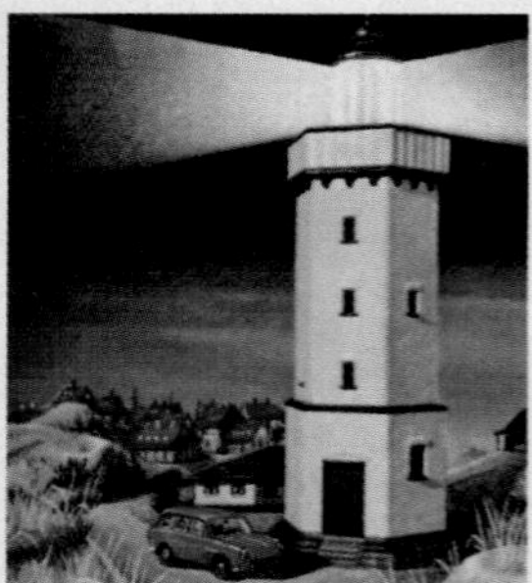

LIGHTHOUSE
322-355 10.25
3 x 3 x 7-1/2" 7.5 x 7.5 x 19cm
(Non-operating light)

APPLIANCE WAREHOUSE
322-1780 11.25
8-3/16 x 4-3/8 x 3-3/16"
20.5 x 11 x 8cm

HOUSE W/GARDEN
322-1781 8.98
5-13/16 x 3-3/8 x 2-5/8"
14.5 x 8.5 x 6.5cm

MODERN HOUSE W/GARAGE
322-1783 8.98
9 x 4-13/16 x 7-5/8"
22.5 x 12 x 19cm

SWIMMING POOL
322-1704 15.98
8-4/5 x 6 x 2-1/5"
22 x 15 x 5-1/2cm

WINDMILL
322-1795 15.25
7-1/2 x 5-1/2 x 10"
19 x 13.5 x 25cm

CHALET
322-1786 9.98
4 x 3-5/8 x 2-5/8"
10 x 9 x 6.5cm

HOTEL CHALET
322-1787 9.25
5-5/8 x 4-3/8 x 2-3/8"
14 x 11 x 6cm

COTTAGE
322-1792 9.00
8-5/8 x 3-3/16 x 1-5/8"
21.5 x 8 x 4cm

FARM HOUSE
322-1790 13.00
7-1/16 x 4-7/8" 18 x 12-1/2cm

SMALL BRICK HOUSE
322-211 6.98
3-5/8 x 4 x 3-13/64"
9 x 10 x 8cm

DOWNTOWN HOUSE
322-1798 16.50
4-5/8 x 3-5/8 x 4-5/8"
11.5 x 9 x 11.5cm

SWITCH TOWER
322-2075 15.98
7-3/8 x 3-3/8 x 4-3/16"
18.6 x 8.5 x 10.5cm

SWEDISH CHURCH
322-136 12.25
9-7/8 x 3" 18 x 12cm

SELF-SERVICE STORE
322-1702 11.49
5-13/16 x 8 x 2-5/8"
14.5 x 20 x 6.5cm

WATERMILL
322-1771 7.25
4-1/2 x 3-5/16" 11.5 x 8.5cm

PEDESTRIAN OVERPASS
322-1736 7.98
9-1/2 x 2-1/2" 24 x 6.5cm

G.W.R. STATION
322-712 21.98
14-4/5 x 4-4/5 x 2-4/5" 37 x 12 x 7cm

MODERN PASSENGER STATION
322-120 23.50
19-1/5 x 5-1/5 x 4" 48 x 13 x 10cm

SWEDISH FARM BUILDINGS
322-137 18.98
10-4/5 x 6 x 3-1/5" 27 x 15 x 8cm

AMERICAN FARM HOUSE
322-301 8.98
4-1/8 x 3" 10.5 x 7.5cm

CONTAINER TERMINAL
322-1716 21.98
8 x 10 x 7-5/8"
20 x 25 x 19cm

WATER TOWER
322-1735 11.98
4 x 4 x 8-13/16"
10 x 10 x 22cm

VILLAGE CHURCH
322-202 9.98
6-1/5 x 3-3/5 x 5-1/5"
15-1/2 x 9 x 13cm

WOODEN WATER TANK CANADIAN
322-1001 11.50
4 x 4 x 6-1/5"
10 x 10 x 15-1/2cm

TRACT HOUSE W/TERRACE
322-213 12.98
4 x 3-1/2" 18 x 12cm

CUSTOMS HOUSE
322-2019 24.98
11-1/2 x 9-13/64 x 4-13/32" 28.7 x 23 x 11cm

FIRE STATION
322-1703 15.98
12-4/5 x 6-1/5 5-3/5" 32 x 15-1/2 x 14cm

COUNTRY HOME
322-139 12.25
5-1/5 x 4-1/5 x 4"
13 x 10-1/2 x 10cm

AUTO UNLOADING RAMP
322-1717 11.98
12 x 4 x 4-3/5"
30 x 10 x 11-1/2cm

BRICK ENGINE HOUSE 2-STALL
322-842 33.98
15-3/5 x 9-3/5 x 5-3/5"
39 x 24 x 14cm

MODERN GAS STATION
322-1776 9.50
6 x 4 x 2-13/64"
15 x 10 x 5.5cm

FREIGHT LOADING ACCESSORIES
322-1733 4.98

2-STORY HOUSE W/BALCONY
322-1779 11.50
6 x 4-4/5 x 3-3/5"
15 x 12 x 8-1/2cm

MODERN HOUSE W/CARPORT
322-1793 13.98
7-3/5 x 7-1/5 x 3-1/5"
19 x 18 x 8cm

These easy-to-build kits feature pre-colored molded plastic parts, with base and concrete sidewalks, trim details and clear plastic windows (unless noted).

KAVANAUGH
348-1001 14.98

QUEEN ANN
348-1002 14.98

STEINER
348-1003 14.98

PAINTED LADY
348-1004 14.98

VICTORIAN
348-1005 14.98

VICTORIAN ASSORTMENT
348-10091 pkg(5) 54.98

HUNTINGTON
348-1007 14.98

STEVENSON
348-1009 14.98

BALDWIN
348-10011 14.98

VANDERBILT
348-1008 14.98

PULLMAN
348-10010 14.98

COLONIAL HOUSE ASSORTMENT
348-10089 pkg(5) 39.98

SECOND HAND ROSE
348-10014 12.98

RITA'S ANTIQUES
348-10016 12.98
Includes roof-top shed.

GRANT CARY'S APOTHECARY
348-10018 12.98

THE SOUTH STREET SMOKE SHOP
348-10015 12.98
Includes wooden Indian.

O'WEEDS GREENERY
348-10017 12.98
Includes window displays.

STORE FRONT HOUSE ASSORTMENT
348-10090 pkg(5) 54.98

TOWER CRANE W/PLATFORM
348-1 6.98

CEMENT PLANT W/PLATFORM
348-2 9.98

GREENHOUSE
348-5 3.98

FARMHOUSE
348-7 4.98

LARGE EQUIPMENT SHED
348-9 4.98

MOBILE OFFICE SITE
348-223 1.98

FARM SILO
348-225 2.98

SAW MILL
348-3630 19.98 *NEW*

RANCH HOUSE
348-4944 12.98 *NEW*

COLONIAL HOUSE
348-4945 12.98 *NEW*

HEAVY DUTY PIER
348-5501 15.98 *NEW*

LARGE TRANSFER PIER
348-5505 17.98 *NEW*

EXPANSION PACKS EA 4.98
348-5513 Wide Pier *NEW*
348-5514 Narrow Pier *NEW*
348-5515 Track Pier *NEW*

348-7002 348-7001

PACKING HOUSE
348-7001 9.98

CANNERY
348-7002 9.98

TRUCK TERMINAL
348-47758 14.98

SCHOOL HOUSE
348-47775 14.98

RICO STATION
348-807 22.98

AUNT MILLIE'S HOUSE
348-47776 14.98

MA'S PLACE
348-47779 9.98

PICKLE FACTORY
348-47780 9.98

MAINLINE STATION
348-3502 14.98

FREIGHT STATION
348-3510 11.98

GENERAL STORE & BILLIARDS PARLOR
348-3508 14.98

SERVICE STATION
348-3509 9.98

RAILROAD YARD BUILDINGS
348-3501 14.98

LUMBER MILL
348-709 19.98

FACTORY W/LOADING SILO
348-3503 14.98

VILLAGE IN A BAG
348-1100 6.98

STORE & AUTO REPAIR
348-3504 14.98

LUIGI'S RESTAURANT
348-810 12.98

COUNTY COURT HOUSE
348-805 22.98

TEXACO STATION
348-4108 7.98

WINDMILL PUMPING STATION
348-706 22.98

WATER BRIDGE
348-5006 6.98

ICE CREAM PARLOR & BOARDING HOUSE
348-3507 14.98

FAST PHOTO
348-10044 3.98

DINO'S PIZZA
348-10046 3.98

CHARISMA DRESS SHOP
348-10045 3.98

PARLOR CARDS & UNUSUAL GIFTS
348-10047 3.98

HEALTH AIDS SHOPPING CENTER ASSORTMENT
348-10048 3.49348-100100 pkg(5) 19.98
Includes 1 each: 10044, 10045, 10046, 10047 & 10048.

FREIGHT STATION W/LOADING PLATFORM
348-3505 10.98

POLYBAG KITS

ABERCROMBIE MANSION
348-19 7.98

REAGAN MANSION
348-20 7.98

MORGAN MANSION
348-21 7.98

CARRINGTON MANSION
348-22 7.98

MELLON MANSION
348-23 7.98

5-PACK BROWNSTONE KITS
348-10083 pkg(5) 49.98
Fill up an entire city block on your layout with this series of Brownstone Buildings!

Uniquely designed to create rows of realistic structures, the three-story brick and stone mansions are super detailed with bay windows, front stairs with railings, simulated plaster trim, concrete sidewalks and window "glass".

BARN W/SILO
348-812 14.98

650-TON COAL BUNKER
348-5000 39.98

1ST NATIONAL BANK
348-10025 9.98

For Daily Product Updates Point Your Browser to
www.walthers.com

OLD TIME GAS STATION
348-712 21.98

LEGAL & PROFESSIONAL OFFICE
348-10026 9.98

COLONIAL CHURCH
348-804 20.98

CONCRETE MIXING PLANT
348-5007 18.98

HERALD STAR NEWSPAPER
348-806 19.98

SNAP-EAZE SERIES

"SNAP-EAZE" kits feature snap-together construction. No glue required.

COUNTRY CHURCH
348-4105 7.98

SWITCH TOWER
348-4102 5.98

COUNTRY BARN
348-4100 7.98

SCHOOL HOUSE
348-4104 7.98

RURAL FREIGHT/ PASSENGER STATION
348-4101 7.98

LOCOMOTIVE MAINTENANCE BUILDING
348-4103 7.98

AMERICAN FARM HOUSE
348-4107 7.98

SOCIETY HILL TOWNHOUSE
348-809 12.98

2 SUBURBAN HOUSES
348-4106 7.98

SAND TOWER
348-5005 7.98

MASTERPIECE SERIES

Easy-to-build kits, construction time varies with kit size.

3 HOUSES UNDER CONSTRUCTION
348-711 7.98

INTERLOCKING TOWER
348-602 9.98

OPEN TOP WATER TOWER
348-3512 7.98
Great for railroad or ranch.

OPERATING GRAVEL LOADER
348-4110 3.98

TWO STALL ENGINE HOUSE
348-3500 14.98

SMALL AIRPORT TERMINAL
348-2080 10.98
Complete with control tower and restaurant.

HANGER W/2 PLANES
348-2081 10.98
All-metal building holds three aircraft safely inside. Includes windsock, equipment locker and two single-engine airplanes.

PLANE & GLIDER SET
348-2086 pkg(4) 3.98
Things will be taking off with two twin-engine planes, a single-engine sail plane and a glider.

SINGLE-ENGINE AIRPLANES
348-2084 pkg(6) 7.98
Great replicas of the Piper 140, Super Cub and Cessna 150. Includes two of each airplane.

SAND & FUELING DEPOT
348-3506 13.98

POWER PLANT
348-2018 3.98

HIGH TENSION MASTS
348-2014 pkg(5) 3.98

TRANSFORMER PLANT
348-2015 3.98

TIMBER YARD W/SAWMILL
348-2059 5.98

INTERMODAL CRANE W/2 CONTAINERS
348-4310 19.98
Great for small terminals, easily kitbashed for shorter bridge. Includes two 20' containers.

MIX & MATCH BUILDING SETS EA 2.98
348-3610 Sousa House
348-3611 Barnum House
348-3612 Hill House
348-3613 Mason House

CENTER STREET SERIES

Center Street Series buildings look great on any main street. Most come with interiors and lighting. Parts are molded in colors with lots of detail.

HOWARD JOHNSON'S RESTAURANT

348-47754 14.98
An authentic replica of the famous roadside stop.

BARBER SHOP & CHINESE LAUNDRY

348-47771 13.98
A great business complete with chairs, counters and cash register.

GENERAL STORE & FINANCE CENTER

348-47798 12.98
You'll find everything you're shopping for here and you can get a loan to buy it upstairs! Lots of tools, handtrucks, wheelbarrows and sacks are included for superdetailing.

MACHINE SHOP

348-47764 14.98
A perfect small industry, use as part of a larger complex or by itself.

CROSSOVER SIGNAL BRIDGE

348-47767 9.98
Keep trains moving safely. Bridge also has pedestrian walkway for those busy mainlines in urban areas.

DRUG STORE & CAMERA SHOP

348-47772 13.98
Two stores in one, with booth-style seats, camera on tripod, movie projector and counters.

ARLEE STATION

348-47761 10.98
A typical small town or suburban station, combining passenger and freight operations. Complete with bay window and attached platform.

FURNITURE STORE

348-47774 10.98
A full inventory of lamps, chairs, tables, a bedroom set, grandfather clock and more.

JOE'S FRUIT STORE & DENTIST OFFICE

348-47797 12.98
Detailing is a snap as this kit includes 24 crates of produce.

SIGNAL TOWER

348-47768 8.98
Perfect for any junction makes a neat yard tower too!

WATER TOWER

348-47769 9.98
A must for steam-era operations. Wooden tank with spout and other details.

LOEW'S MOVIE THEATRE

348-47799 13.98
Will our hero be dashed to bits on the jagged rocks below? You'll have to add this kit to your downtown to find out. An ornate old-time structure, complete with a big three-sided marquee, a ticket booth and a fire escape - everything you need but the popcorn.

FREIGHT STATION

348-47785 14.98
A great rail-served building that can be used by just about any industry as a warehouse. The first floor has a covered loading dock, and the upper floor can be used as an office.

HONEST SAM'S USED CAR LOT

348-47796 12.98
Honest Sam won't steer you wrong! Just look at those shiny cars out front, included for the showroom or the lot.

JL INNOVATIVE DESIGN

This line of craft train kits features precut Northeastern siding and Kappler stripwood, with illustrated instructions.

MCLEOD SUPER SERVICE

361-311 32.95
Better check your gauge–you won't want to pass up this super gas station. Over the years, McLeod has added a covered garage and some of those fancy new electric pumps on the island. Stations like this are still standing in many areas (often remodeled as other businesses), making this a natural for any busy HO highway. The model comes with over 60 different signs, a fence-base billboard, Grandt Line windows and doors, pumps and complete instructions.

DUNN PROCESSING

361-151 44.95
9 x 9" 22.5 x 22.5cm

HUBERMILL WAREHOUSE

361-121 34.95
9-1/4 x 3" 23 x 7.5cm

WOODY'S

361-211 34.95
5-1/2 x 3" 12.5 x 7.5cm

BAGWELL JUNCTION TOWER

361-291 29.95
2-3/8 x 1-7/8 x 3-3/8"
5.7 x 4.5 x 8.4cm
Protect a busy interlocking yard or junction along your railroad with this handsome tower. Typical of designs used by most US railroads, the finished model fits steam- or diesel-era scenes. The kit features precut siding, laser-cut shingles, separate doors, windows, steps and railings. To detail the area around the tower, you also get a separate storage shed, nonoperating train order signal, seven relay/phone boxes, train order hoop stand, battery cellar and extra rail fencing.

JL INC. BOATWORKS

361-101 36.95
9 x 5" 22.5 x 12.5cm

LABOSKY'S MOTORCYCLE REPAIR

361-141 29.95
5-3/4 x 4-1/2" 14.3 x 11.2cm

VAL'S HAMBURGERS

361-131 24.95
5 x 3" 12.5 x 7.5cm

MCDOUGALL TELEGRAPH OFFICE

361-271 18.95
3-1/4 x 2-7/8" 8.1 x 7.2cm

AVON ST. ELEVATED CROSSING TOWER

361-241 19.95
A Milwaukee Road prototype, it can also be used as switch tower. Includes pre-bent rail support truss, precut Northeastern siding, Grandt Line windows and doors, Central Valley steps and railings and Campbell shingles.

BROOKSIDE ICE HOUSE

361-191 29.95
5-3/8 x 9" 13.6 x 22.5cm

ICE BLOCKS

361-205 pkg(25) **2.50**

PICKARD MOTORS

361-171 39.95
11-1/2 x 8-1/2"
28.8 x 21.3cm

SAW PIT STORE

361-321 32.95
Wander along the back roads and you'll probably pass by an old filling station like this. A common sight from the 1920s to the 1950s, a few lasted into the 1970s. The kit is based on an actual building and comes loaded with details. Northeastern basswood walls, Grandt Line doors and windows, over 20 cast metal accessories, a complete set of parts to build the Socony Vacuum shield sign, and a pair of custom-painted JL barrels are all included. You'll also get a set of Country Store Posters/Signs (185 different styles) plus illustrated instructions with multi-view, detailed drawings.

FRYXELL FEED & SEED

361-181 32.95
4-1/2 x 4-1/4" 11.2 x 10.7cm

EASTSIDE OIL CO.

361-221 29.95

MCSORELEY'S OLD ALE HOUSE

361-331 44.95
A uniquely designed tavern, McSoreley's Old Ale House is a perfect building for the main street running through any small- or medium-size city layout. Kit includes 40 cast metal details and plastic accessory parts, custom-designed full color signs, precut basswood siding, Grandt Line injection-molded windows and doors, detailed roof and a rear add-on section.

MCGREGOR DEPOT

361-251 49.95
8 x 4" 20 x 10cm
Based on Soo Line Second Class design with upstairs living quarters. Prototype was modified with operator's window at corner, to protect Northern Pacific/Soo crossing at McGregor, Minnesota. Includes precut Northeastern siding, over 30 Grandt Line windows and doors, baggage cart, 20 metal details, Campbell shingles, Rix pole, plus separate tool shed and nonoperating train order signal board.

JL INNOVATIVE DESIGN

WABASHA ENGINE HOUSE

361-281 38.95
7-5/8 x 6" 19.1 x 15cm

VIC'S AUTO ALIGNMENT

361-161 23.95
7-3/4 x 3-3/4" 19.4 x 9.4cm

EAST JUNCTION SECTION HOUSE

361-261 19.95
5-3/8 x 2-7/8" 13.4 x 7.2cm

COMPANY STORE

395-125 21.95
4-1/4 x 7-1/4" 10.8 x 18.5cm

TRACKSIDE JAMBOREE

361-231 pkg(2) **24.95**
Large Building: 3-3/4 x 1-1/2" 9.5 x 3.7cm
Small Building: 2-5/8 x 1-3/4" 6.4 x 3.2cm
Section crews will be ready for any job with this structure set. Over 20 Grandt Line windows, doors and accessories, including standard gauge Fairmont pushcar. Woodland Scenics pallets and junk are included, along with JL's own crimped metal and tarpaper roofing.

Figures and Vehicles Not Included

BROWNIES NORTHSIDE SERVICE

361-341 36.95 ***NEW***
This classically designed filling station first began popping up in the 1930s, but its look was still being used into the 1960s. Kit features precut basswood walls and Grandt Line windows and doors. Gravity-feed and electric pumps allow modelers to help determine the service station's appropriate era. In addition, 217 gas station signs allow you to decide if your station is affiliated with Shell, Texaco and Flying A.

Keystone Locomotive Works

Build distinctive business and commercial establishments with these Craft Train kits. Models feature wood construction, with injection molded styrene and cast metal details.

DANBY SAW MILL

395-111 29.95
7 x 7" 18 x 18cm
Includes logs and other details.

FLATWHEEL HOTEL & SALOON

395-126 34.95
5-1/2 x 8-1/2" 14 x 21.8cm
False front, sloped roof, porch on three sides.

PASSENGER SHELTER

395-117 17.95
Now features laser-cut wood for the distinctive "V" shaped roof sections. Rafter and stringer positions are cut into roof sections to speed construction. Kit builds a 130' platform. Includes cast columns, scrolls and light shades, pre-cut stringers and wire for drain pipes.

KINDLING WOOD FACTORY

395-124 48.95
3 x 3" 7.6 x 7.6cm
7 x 4" 18 x 10.3cm
Double kit, with Sawing Building connected to Drying Building.

LOGGING ENGINE SHOP

395-133 34.95
6 x 9-1/2" 15.3 x 23.6cm

Create detailed scenes for any railroad with this line of easy-to-build kits. Models feature laser-cut wood for easy construction, plus cast metal and plastic details. Each includes complete instructions and a color photo of the finished model.

HANDCAR/TOOL SHED

482-1001 12.99
Every section gang had a small trackside building like this in the days of steam. Kit is complete with tie stack, outhouse, power pole and track tool set.

MOTORCAR/BLACKSMITH SHED

482-1002 12.99

FISHING SHACK/DOCK

482-1005 12.99
Looks great along any waterway and comes with wooden dock and shack, two cast metal boats, buckets, lamps and more.

DOUBLE HANDCAR SHED

482-1003 12.99

YARDMASTER'S OFFICE

482-1004 12.99
Action never stops around this tiny office. Complete with cast metal window cooler, outhouse and track tool set.

BILLBOARD KITS

482-1006 pkg(2) **12.99**
Typical of signs from the 1920s to the 1960s. Includes six full-color signs and 110 nut-bolt-washer castings.

ROADSIDE DINER

482-1007 19.99

RAIL AUTO FERRY "JUBILEE"

482-1008 19.99

WOOD FREIGHT DEPOT

482-1009 19.99

WOOD OUTHOUSE KIT

482-6009 2.69
Great period detail for stations, homes and farms. Laser-cut wood parts insure easy construction, right down to the door.

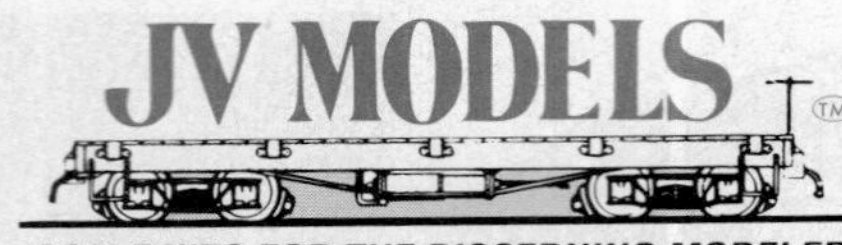

These Craft Train kits feature Northeastern Scale Lumber, metal and/or Grandt Line plastic castings, full size templates and detailed instructions.

GABLED ROOF DAIRY BARN
345-2001 27.98
5-1/4 x 10-1/2" 13.3 x 26.5cm
Build 72 or 84' long barn. Includes strip shingles.

CURVED WOOD TRESTLE
345-2016 39.98
These wooden trestle kits are typical of designs used by many roads. Kits are complete with longer bridge ties for the deck. Instructions include diagrams and color photos. Straight trestle (#2014) can be built up to 18" long. The Curved Trestle (#2016) can be built up to 36" long and can be constructed in any radius or an S curve. Additional kits can be combined to build longer versions

BURNT RIVER MINING CO.
345-2019 32.98
Scale 23 x 15'
Includes ore shoots and ore bins, can be made to operate.

WOOD TIMBER TRESTLE
345-2014 29.98

ROADSIDE FRUIT STAND & BAIT SHOP
345-2004 11.98
2 x 2-3/4" 4.5 x 6.4cm
Includes cast metal produce.

SMALL BOAT LANDING
345-2003 14.98
2-3/4 x 7-1/4" 7 x 18.2cm
With corrugated aluminum roofing and cast metal boat.

BRANCHLINE WOOD WATER TOWER
345-2012 22.98
Scale 22 x 42'
60,000 gallon capacity.
Includes spout.

PONTYPOOL FARM SUPPLY
345-2023 29.98
Scale 57 x 24'
Craftsman style kit builds elevator, storage sheds, store, office scalehouse and two loading docks. Includes color photo, scenery ideas and directions to build as a new or old building.

40-TON COALING TOWER
345-2029 26.98
Scale 16 x 16 x 65'
Scribed siding, timbers, ladder stock and Grandt Line parts are included in this kit. Detailed plans include unloading pit. Can be modified for narrow gauge.

WARD'S SALVAGE
345-2022 34.98
Scale 50 x 60'
Includes office, garage, equipment shed, fences, benches, instructions and color photo of finished model.

AUSTINBURG LUMBER YARD
345-2031 42.98
Scale 64 x 92'
Includes two story office with covered attached rail siding, storage, lumber and tool sheds, fence and color photo.

MAINLINE WOOD WATER TOWER
345-2013 25.98
Scale 28 x 56'
124,000 gallon capacity.
Includes spout.

SAND TOWER & DRYING HOUSE
345-2008 29.98
5-3/8 x 6-1/8" 13.5 x 15.3cm
Upgrade your engine service facilities with this double-track tower, based on a Northern Pacific prototype. Includes sand to finish the scene.

MOTOR CAR HOUSE
345-2006 pkg(2) **16.98**
2 x 4-1/8" 4.5 x 9.5cm
Northern Pacific prototypes, kits include parts for two structures. Figures not included.

ALDEN FARMS STOCKYARD
345-2028 32.98
Scale 80 x 120'
Parts for pens, pole barn, office, platforms, ramps, water tanks and more. Includes templates, scenery ideas and color photo of finished model.

LUCAS SAWMILL
345-2021 39.98
Scale 50 x 95'
Based on the historic Haliburton Sawmills, this Craftsman-style kit has board-by-board construction over timber framing. Includes mill, log deck, machine shop, racks, benches, lumber and more. Quality pine and basswood, full instructions with templates, scenery details and color photo.

FOREST RANGER TOWER
345-2002 22.98
3 x 3" 7.5 x 7.5cm
Includes strip shingles and cast metal stairs.

BUNKHOUSES OR LINE STORAGE SHED
345-2011 pkg(2) **19.98**
Scale 10 x 20'

SECTION TOOL HOUSE
345-2005 pkg(2) **16.98**
2 x 4-1/8" 4.5 x 9.5cm
Double kit, figures not included.

FARM SILO
345-2000 TBA
Scale 18 x 44'
Board on board construction.

WATSON'S SIDING
345-2020 35.98
Scale 40 x 30'
Derelict village includes general store, freight station, blacksmith's shop, sheds and fences.

Get Daily Info, Photos and News at

BOYD LOGGING CAMP
345-2018 42.98
Scale 50 x 85'
Craft train kit builds Rail Shed, Company Store, Dining Hall, Water Tower, Kitchen and 3 Bunkhouses. Includes lumber, scenery details and easy-to-follow instructions.

HALIBURTON ENGINE HOUSE
345-2024 32.98
Scale 23 x 79'
Engine and shop crews will appreciate working inside this single stall engine house. The prototype was built in 1878 for the Victoria Railway. Diagrams, scenery details and color photo are provided (Utility Shed not included).

36' BOXCAR UTILITY SHED
345-2026 pkg(2) **26.98**

VICTORIA STATION
345-2025 30.98
Scale 23 x 56'
Grandt Line detail parts. Figures not included.

N.J. INTERNATIONAL

PLASTIC KITS

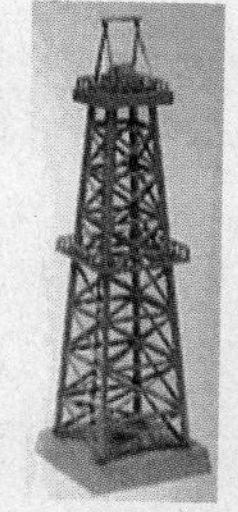
525-1970

525-1971

525-1970 Oil Derrick **8.99**
525-1971 Water Tower **8.99**

MAINTENANCE PLATFORM KITS
With etched see-through stainless steel walkways and stair treads.

525-4020 68' Platform pkg(2) **19.95**
525-4021 102' Platform pkg(2) **25.95**
525-4022 136' Platform pkg(2) **29.95**
525-4023 68' Handrail Kit **3.99**
525-4024 68' Walkway **9.99**

OTHER PLASTIC KITS
525-6179 Short Bridge Kit **3.99**
525-6183 Outhouse Kit pkg(2) **3.29**
525-6184 Oil Tank & Stand **3.99**
525-6185 Gantry Crane **3.29**
525-6186 Signal Cabinets pkg(2) **3.99**
525-6187 Tool Shed Kit **3.99**
525-6190 Hand Car pkg(2) **3.99**
525-6196 Play Yard Set **3.29**

kibri

IMPORTED FROM GERMANY BY WALTHERS

These easy-to-build, plastic kits are based on a wide range of European buildings, many of which are easily converted for American layouts. Parts are molded in realistic colors and are numbered to match the instructions, for fast and easy assembly.

VILLAGE OF SOLIS SET

405-8037 pkg(5) **119.99** *NEW*
A complete community in one kit! Includes one each Ernen House (#8031), Gletsch House (#8033), Barn with Hayloft (#8035) Solis Station (#9513) and Alpine Farm Accessories (#8111).

"SCHAWABIA" HOUSE SET WITH CITY GATE

405-8477 109.98 *NEW*
Add a touch of history to your old-world city scene with this set of four complete kits. Historic homes feature modern businesses, while retaining their as-built appearance. Includes Ice Cream Parlor (#8469), Folklore Museum (#8473), Retirement Home (#8471) and City Gate Tower (#8075).

ERNEN 2-STORY HOUSE

405-8031 25.99 *NEW*
4-13/32 x 3-13/32 x 3-13/16"
11 x 8.5 x 9.5cm
Typical Swiss mountain home made of heavy timbers with traditional stone base. Lots of details, including piles of firewood, colorful shutters and more, add life to the finished model.

GLETSCH HOUSE

405-8033 25.99 *NEW*
4-13/32 x 3-13/32 x 3-13/16"
11 x 8.5 x 9.5cm
This Swiss mountain home is packed with details, including a rear storage shed, balcony with awning and more.

CONTAINER CRANE

405-8530 69.99 *NEW*
12-13/16 x 7 x 6-13/16" 32 x 17.5 x 17cm
Make quick work of moving containers in your terminal scenes with this detailed model. Includes operator's cab, positionable lifting mechanism and more. Great starting point for kitbashing an ore bridge or bulk material unloader for your waterfront too!

DOCKSIDE ACCESSORIES

405-8528 23.99 *NEW*
Transform your waterfront in seconds with this set of plastic parts. Includes both modern steel pilings and old-time piled stones to protect your docks and quays. Also includes a small jib crane, life rings, a small pleasure boat and trailer.

BARN W/HAYLOFT

405-8035 23.99 *NEW*
2-5/8 x 2-13/64 x 3-5/8"
6.5 x 5.5 x 9cm
This Swiss barn is loaded with rural charm and character. Detailed plastic parts look like rough timbers and many details are included to complete the scene.

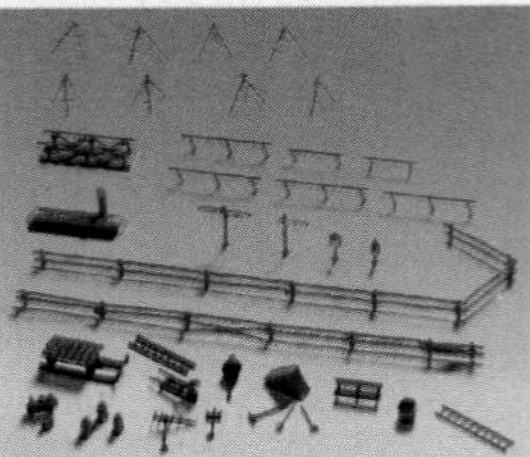

ALPINE FARM ACCESSORIES

405-8111 19.99 *NEW*
Set the scene on any rural part of your layout with this set. Includes rustic split rail fences, watering trough, small foot bridge, handrails, milk cans, tools, sled for winter chores, rural road signs, bell, roof-top details and more.

ICE CREAM PARLOR

405-8469 29.99 *NEW*
4-13/32 x 3-5/8 x 5"
11 x 9 x 12.5cm
A sweet addition to your downtown area. Traditional half-timber and stucco, with ornate shutters make this building standout on any street.

UNGUARDED RURAL GRADE CROSSING

405-8113 17.99 *NEW*
Length: 2-13/16" 7cm
Width: 4-3/16 10.5cm
Ideal for use in many eras, this grade crossing is perfect for country roads or private rail crossings. Each plastic piece looks like old timber and installs in minutes. Can be used for single or double track crossings.

CITY GATE TOWER

405-8475 27.99 *NEW*
3-5/8 x 2-13/32 x 8-13/32"
9 x 6 x 21cm
Re-live the days of old with this handsome section of the city wall to guard your community. Detailed to look as though it's built of stone and timber.

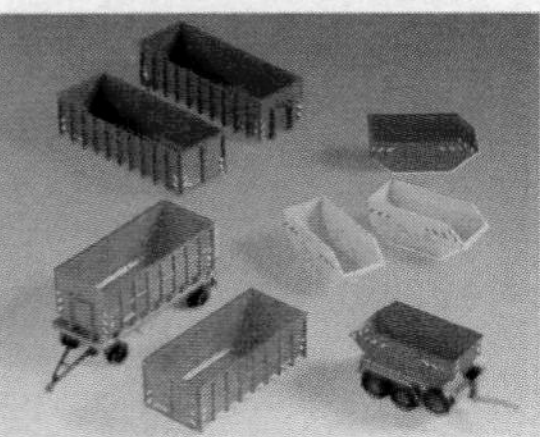

REFUSE/RECYCLING CONTAINER SET

405-8109 19.99 *NEW*
Every modern industry can use these important details. You'll see them alongside virtually every manufacturing plant collecting scrap metals and paper for recycling, along with trash. Set includes a variety of styles, along with two trailers for moving from site to site.

kibri

IMPORTED FROM GERMANY BY WALTHERS

WORKER'S RETIREMENT HOME

405-8471 31.99 ***NEW***
4 x 3-13/64 x 5-5/8"
10 x 8 x 14cm
Make your golden years the best when you rent a room at this handsome facility. Stucco walls, add-on downspouts, colorful shutters and lots of windows add to the charming appearance.

INDUSTRIAL ACCESSORIES

405-8103 19.99 ***NEW***
Give tired factories a face-lift with this set of accessories. Loads of piping, tanks and other details to convert basic kits into detailed models.

LIFTING EQUIPMENT SET W/CRANE

405-8101 19.99 ***NEW***
Give any industrial scene a lift with this set of accessories. Includes a small winch-type crane for the finishing touch.

SOLIS STATION

405-9513 35.99 ***NEW***
13-13/32 x 5-5/8 x 4-5/8" 33.5 x 14 x 11.5cm
This two-story station is perfect for a small town. Living quarters for the agent and family are on the second floor, while the lower half includes the waiting room and a freight storage room. Timber construction and lots of add-on details make the finished model a real eye-catcher.

WLZ FARM SUPPLY ELEVATOR/WAREHOUSE

405-9408 64.99 ***NEW***
14 x 5-5/8 x 10" 35 x 14 x 25cm
Transform any rural siding into a busy spot with this big farm supply building. It includes a tall grain elevator, offices and a warehouse for all types of agricultural needs.

FOLKLORE MUSEUM

405-8473 27.99 ***NEW***
4-13/32 2-13/16 x 4-13/64"
11 x 7 x 10.5cm
Explore the past of your community inside this historic building. Superbly detailed for use in any downtown.

WORKING CITY/STATION CLOCKS & SIGNS

405-8121 pkg(4) **23.99** ***NEW***
7/8 x 21/64 x 1-31/64"
2.2 x .8 x 3.7cm
Animate your station platforms, bus stops, subway stations and more with these modern accessories. Includes plastic signs and self-adhesive lettering. Real-time digital clock is easily set and battery powered for long service.

MODERN FACTORY BUILDING

405-9793 35.99 ***NEW***
10-13/32 x 5 x 3" 26 x 12.5 x 7.5cm
Add appropriate details and signs and this handsome building can be home to any modern business. Looks great in any industrial park and features a variety of parts molded in colors.

FREIGHT SHED W/LOADING CRANE

405-9410 21.99 ***NEW***
10-3/16 x 4 x 3-3/16" 25.5 x10 x 8cm
Handle small freight shipments for your railroad, or use this great building as small factory or warehouse. Modern design includes overhead canopies, positionable loading dock doors, lots of details and a small winch type crane for moving heavy loads.

LOADING DOCK ACCESSORY SET

405-8105 19.99 ***NEW***
Go from dull to detailed in minutes with this accessory set. Includes various crates, barrels, pallets and sacks, plus a small forklift, pallet jacks and a small winch type crane. Also includes a loading gauge to make sure cars can move safely across your railroad. Perfect for any freight station or industry.

STATION LIGHTING ASSORTMENT-NONWORKING

405-8107 19.99 ***NEW***
Add an important detail to city streets and station platforms with this set of nonworking lights. Includes a variety of modern and vintage designs on poles and for mounting directly on buildings.

BUILDING SITE ACCESSORIES

405-8123 15.99 ***NEW***
Keep the crew working down at the job site with this assortment of machinery and accessories. A great detail for almost any kind of building project, the set includes a small air compressor trailer, cement mixer, table saw, portable toilet and more.

kibri

IMPORTED FROM GERMANY
BY WALTHERS

LENZERHEIDE VILLAGE SET

405-8071 149.99
Build a brand-new community with this complete set that includes one each of 8067, 8068, 8069 and the Litziruti Station #9497.

LENZHERHEIDE CHALET

405-8067 34.99
7-3/16 x 5-13/16 x 3-3/8"
18 x 14.5 x 8.5cm
Traditional wood and stucco construction, updated for today's lifestyles. Great home for a city suburb or rural retreat.

VALBELLA LAND HOUSE

405-8068 34.99
7-3/16 x 5-13/16 x 3-3/8"
18 x 14.5 x 8.5cm
Built-in fireplace, balcony and patio-this handsome home has it all!

DAVOS RURAL VILLAGE SET

405-8066 99.99
Model a brand new suburb with this set that includes #8061, 8063, 8065 and the Monstein Station, #9503

LENZERHORN HOTEL W/TAVERN

405-8069 44.99
3-3/16 x 5-5/8 x 4-13/16"
8 x 14 x 12cm
Enjoy a night in the finest hotel in town! This beautiful building is complete with guest rooms on two floors. After checking in, enjoy a relaxing evening in the outdoor beer garden.

LITZIRUTI STATION

405-9497 33.99
6-13/32 x 5-13/16 x 5-5/8"
16 x 14.5 x 14cm
Combining the best of the old and the new, this attractive station features much of its original wood and stucco construction, with a few modern touches.

SURSVELA HOUSE

405-8065 29.99
4-3/8 x 5-1/8 x 3-13/16"
11 x 12.9 x 9.5cm
Spend time indoors or out when you buy this home, complete with wood deck and upstairs balconies.

CASANNA HOUSE

405-8063 29.99
5-13/16 x 5-5/8 x 3-13/16"
14.5 x 14 x 9.5cm
Neat blend of old and new, stucco walls and timber balconies look great in any residential area.

PARSENN HOUSE

405-8061 29.99
3-13/16 x 5 x 3-13/16"
9.5 x 12.5 x 9.5cm
Big detail for small city lots. Two-story home features an upstairs balconies, lots of extra details too!

MONSTEIN STATION

405-9503 26.99
14-5/8 x 6 x 43/8"
36.5 x 15 x 11cm
With its modern lines and timber construction, this station looks great in an outlying city or suburb. Lots of accessories to complete the scene are included.

SPREEWALD VILLAGE SET

405-8215 104.99
A complete community in one kit! Includes 1 each of #8209, 8211, 8213 and 8270 (Small Boat Assortment).

SPREEWALDECK CAFE

405-8213 26.99
6-13/16 x 4 x 4"
17 x 10 x 10cm
This appealing inn will attract dinner guests from all over. Half-timber construction and outdoor accommodations make it a great starting point for a detailed scene.

FURSTENBERG STATION

405-9501 49.99
16-13/16 x 6 x 5-5/8" 42 x 15 x 14cm
This ornate station combines wood, brick and tile construction to produce a typical turn-of-the-century design.

CEMENT PLANT

405-9822 Office, Storage Building & 3 Trucks **109.99**
405-9820 Storage Building Only **64.99**
7-3/16 x 5-3/16 x 11" 18 x 13 x 27.5cm
Lay a new siding and you'll have everything you need to add new industry to your layout. Complete set #9822 includes a small office and shop with fuel pumps, large cement plant with dump pit, lifting machinery and storage tanks, plus a trio of trucks, including a dump truck with dump trailer, powdered cement tanker semi and a mixer to haul cement to the job site.

MUNLENWUG HOUSE

405-8209 19.99
5 x 4 x 4" 12.5 x 10 x 10cm
Perfect as a summer cottage, makes a neat addition to any residential area.

LANDGRABEN HOUSE

405-8211 19.99
4 x 4 x 3-13/16"
10 x 10 x 9.5cm
A handsome home in a rural scene or older suburb of a big city.

BURG-SPREEWALD STATION

405-9509 36.99
10 x 6-3/8 x 8"
25 x 16 x 20cm
This small-town station is perfect for rural scenes. Includes ornate waiting area and decorative turret.

BURG-SPREEWALD FREIGHT SHED

405-9459 22.99
6 x 4-3/16 x 2-5/8"
15 x 10.5 x 6.5cm
Handle small freight shipments to and from any town. A great warehouse or storage building for a heavy industrial complex too.

kibri

IMPORTED FROM GERMANY BY WALTHERS

Special Value Price Shown In Red

HOUSE "STADTPLATZ"

405-8085 31.99
5-3/8 x 6-1/2 x 6-3/8"
13.5 x 16.2 x 16cm
For the downtown decor, a bakery and delicatessen. Eat and relax as you enjoy the view of the city square.

HOUSE "KURPARK"

405-8086 33.99
5-3/8 x 6-1/2 x 6-1/16"
13.5 x 16.2 x 15.4cm
One last shopping stop at this neighborhood store before you return to the guest house for a well-deserved rest.

PLATFORM "LANDWIED"

405-9546 33.99
40-5/8 x 2-3/16 x 2-3/8"
101.5 x 5.5 x 6cm

SULSBERG PLATFORM

405-9556 29.99
40-5/8 x 1-1/2 x 2-3/8"
101.5 x 3.8 x 6cm
Protect passengers in any weather. Modern design with large glass shelter and loads of details to finish any contemporary station scene.

HOFHEIM PLATFORM

405-9558 22.99
26-5/8 x 1-1/2 x 2-3/8"
66.5 x 3.8 x 6cm
Modern design is perfect for city commuters or a modern Amtrak stop. Includes glass shelter, nonworking lamps, signs and other details.

HOUSE "AUGUSTINERPLATZ"

405-8088 29.99
5-3/8 x 6-1/2 x 5"
13.5 x 16.2 x 12.5cm
Handle with care inside the glass and porcelain shop as you browse while waiting for your friend to arrive home next door.

MUNGSTENNER BRIDGE

405-9670 56.99
27 x 2-3/5 x 7-1/5"
67.5 x 6.5 x 18cm
Authentic model of Germany's tallest railroad bridge, typical of designs used in many countries. Detailed plastic parts capture the look of the steel prototype.

DETTINGEN STATION

405-9507 39.99
13-5/8 x 4-13/16 x 6"
34 x 12 x 15cm
This station is perfect for serving smaller towns out on the line. Upstairs living quarters, passenger waiting room and a freight house are combined into a single building.

STATION DETAIL SET

405-8108 19.99
Modernize your station scene in minutes with these easy-to-build details. Includes modern covered waiting shelter (great for a bus stop too), bike rack, sign boards, posters, benches, luggage, baggage cart and four nonworking lamp posts.

HOUSE "RATHAUS"

405-8087 31.99
5-3/8 x 6-1/2 x 5-5/16"
13.5 x 16.2 x 14.5cm
After attending the latest important meeting at the town hall, stop on the way home and pick up a nice bouquet for someone special at the flower shop.

PLATFORM "KARLSFELD"

405-9548 23.99
15 x 2-3/16 x 2-5/8"
37.5 x 5.5 x 6.5cm
As the mid-day sun hangs in the sky, a few pedestrians wait patiently as the next train arrives.

SKY SCRAPER

405-8218 ~~71.99~~ **34.99**
8 x 7-1/4 x 13-1/2"
20 x 18 x 32.8cm
A modern look. Add this to your city scene and "modernize" it. From the shops at ground level to the penthouse atop, this building stands out.

HOUSE SET "GORLITZER"

405-8309 154.99
Includes 1 each of #8301, 8303, 8305, 8307 and City Street Assortment (#405-8102). Your whole downtown scene will be greatly enhanced when you use this set to bring the town square area to life.

HOUSE SET "TOLZ"

405-8089 Includes 1 Each of #8085, 8086, 8087 & 8088 **114.99**
Add to all of your downtown or village setting with this set of detailed and colorful buildings.

CORNER CITY HOME BONN

405-8280 47.99
5-1/4 x 5-1/4 x 7-1/16"

CITY HOME W/BAY WINDOW BONN

405-8282 36.99
3-7/8 x 5-1/4 x 6-5/8"

CITY HOME W/LAWN BONN

405-8284 36.99
3-1/8 x 5-1/4 x 7-1/16" 8 x 13.5 x 18cm

CITY HOUSE W/BALCONY

405-8286 36.99
3-1/2 x 5-1/4" 9 x 13.5cm

kibri

IMPORTED FROM GERMANY BY WALTHERS

HOUSE "WALLGRABEN"

405-8303 36.99
5-3/8 x 4-13/16 x 7-3/4"
13.5 x 12 x 19.4cm
This beautiful house and neighborhood scene is an elegant addition to any downtown scene.

MODERN TOWN BUILDING

405-8219 54.99
9-1/4 x 4-5/8 x 10-1/4"
23 x 11.5 x 25.5cm
In this modern town building, tenants enjoy the view from their balconies as the people below window-shop the stores for deals.

TOWN MUSEUM

405-8301 42.99
5-3/8 x 4-13/16 x 10"
13.5 x 12 x 25cm
What better place to visit downtown than the museum. Lots of interesting and rare items will be found inside, as well as hours of fun.

BACKYARD ASSORTMENT SET

405-8313 33.99
A large assortment of items for use in the back-yards of your buildings. Includes light poles, crates, sheds and more!

POTSDAMER HOUSE ASSORTMENT

405-8349 159.99
Includes 1 each of #8341, 8343, 8347 and City Street Assortment (405-8102). This assortment enhances your downtown scene by giving it a small town, friendly feel.

HOUSE "BALLHAUSPLATZ"

405-8305 54.99
5-3/8 x 4-13/16 x 7-9/16"
13.5 x 12 x 18.9cm
Sitting right next to the Cocktail Bar, this house makes a comfortable and welcome retreat for the weary home-owner after a long day of work.

SIGNAL BOX

405-9481 19.99
Overlooking the track below, this signal tower makes sure that the train keeps running smoothly and efficiently.

HOUSE "GLOCKENGIEBERPLATZ"

405-8307 42.99
5-3/8 x 6-3/4 x 6-3/8 x 1-5/16"
13.5 x 16.8 x 16 x 3.3cm
Add some class to your downtown scene with this magnificent house. Tastefully decorated with trim, flowers and balconies, this one certainly impresses passers-by.

TOWN HOUSE W/FACTORY ANNEX

405-8311 46.99
5-1/4 x 7 x 7-7/16"
13 x 17.5 x 18.5cm
Another beautiful town house next to an annexed factory to place in your downtown diorama.

SWISS VILLAGE GRECASALCAS

405-8010 129.99
Set includes one each of #s 8012, 8014, 8016, 8018, 8020 and 8022.

SWISS ALPINE HOUSE "PALUE"

405-8012 25.99
6-5/8 x 4-3/4 x 3"
17 x 12 x 7.5cm

SWISS ALPINE HOUSE "FEXTAL"

405-8014 25.99
6-1/8 x 5-7/8 x 3-1/2"
15.5 x 15 x 9cm

SWISS ALPINE HOUSE "STEINBOCK"

405-8016 25.99
6-1/4 x 5-7/8 x 3-3/4"
16 x 15 9.5cm

SWISS ALPINE HOUSE "SILS"

405-8018 25.99
6-1/4 x 5-1/8 x 4"
16 x 13 x 10cm

SWISS ALPINE CHAPEL

405-8020 28.99
6-5/8 x 4-3/4 x 7-1/8"
17 x 12 x 18cm

SWISS ALPINE STABLE W/ACCESSORIES

405-8022 25.99
5-7/8 x 4-1/4 x 3-1/8"
15 x 11 x 8cm

kibri

IMPORTED FROM GERMANY BY WALTHERS

Special Value Price Shown In Red

CORNER HOUSE "SACHSENPLATZ"

405-8345 35.99
5-3/8 x 6-3/4 x 6-3/8 x 1-5/16"
13.5 x 16.8 x 16 x 3.3cm
With an ornate gate as the entryway, a colorful paint scheme and stylish construction, this corner house has that lived in look and "welcome home" feel to it.

CHEMIST SHOP

405-8341 33.99
5-3/8 x 4-13/16 x 6-1/4"
13.5 x 12 x 15.5cm
Have your prescription filled at this neighborhood pharmacy while you wait.

STREET CAFE

405-8347 33.99
5-3/8 x 3-3/4 x 6-5/8"
13.5 x 9.4 x 16.5cm
Stop in for something to eat or drink as you enjoy the day and watch the people walk by at this colorful cafe.

CORNER HOUSE "SCHILLERPLATZ"

405-8343 35.99
5-3/8 x 6-3/4 x 6-3/8 x 1-5/16"
13.5 x 16.8 x 16 x 3.3cm
The classic construction and fixtures make this attractive house something that looks very nice on any corner.

"URACH" TOWN HALL

405-8464 46.99
5-13/16 x 4-3/16 x 8"
14.5 x 10.5 x 20cm
Keep track of not only what's happening in town affairs, but also of the time with this beautiful town hall building, featuring two clocks and some wonderful woodwork on the exterior.

FOUNTAIN WITH ACCESSORIES

405-8467 19.99
A perfect centerpiece for your town. Imagine sitting by this cool fountain on a hot day and enjoying a cold drink as you watch the people walk by.

URACHER HOUSE ASSORTMENT

405-8468 Includes 1 each of #8464, 8465, 8466 & 8467
119.99
Make your town area look lived in with this assortment of houses and buildings. Not to mention the fountain in the center.

FREIGHT HOUSE W/LOADING DOCK

405-9462 ~~51.49~~ **31.99**
18-1/2 x 5-1/2" 47 x 14cm

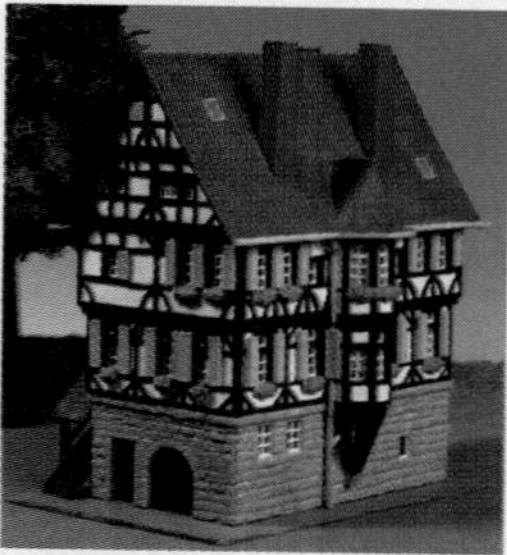

HALF TIMBERED HOUSE

405-8465 33.99
4-5/8 x 3-7/16 x 5-1/4"
11.5 x 8.5 x 13cm
Featuring both stone and timber, this half timbered house has a rear stairway, shuttered windows and two sturdy chimneys on the roof. There's no place like home.

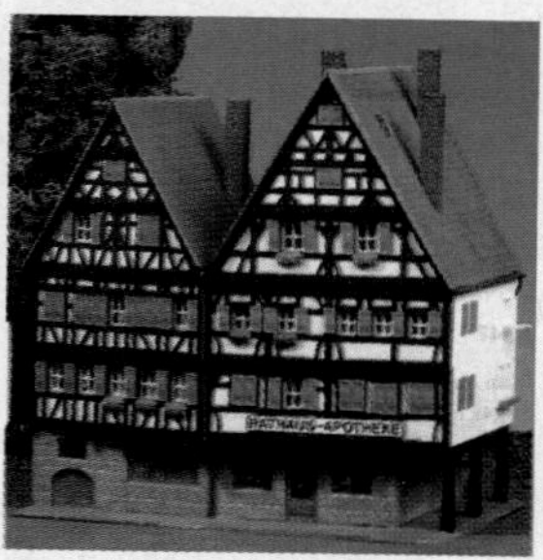

TWIN TIMBERED HOUSES

405-8466 37.99
5-3/8 x 3-13/16 x 5-5/8"
13.5 x 9.5 x 14cm
These twin timbered houses sit side by side here, artfully decorated with shutters and flowers, featuring slanted roofs and detailed chimneys.

MARBACH SIGNAL TOWER

405-9477 23.99
4-13/16 x 2-3/16 x 4-3/8"
12 x 5.5 x 11cm
This detailed interlocking tower will keep trains moving safely. Great for steam- or diesel-era layouts.

Limited Quantity Available

STATION SET ALPENLAND

405-9531 99.99
Includes #'s 8040, 8044, 8058 and 9533.

Limited Quantity Available

RAILWAY STATION SHOP

405-9493 33.99
5-1/2 x 3-1/2" 14 x 9cm

OLD BRICK STATION

405-9494 25.99
7-1/2 x 4-1/4" 19.5 x 11cm

STATION "KOTTENFORST"

405-9500 49.99
12 x 8" 30 x 20cm

STATION "CALW"

405-9518 69.99
21-5/8 x 6-1/4" 55 x 16cm

kibri

IMPORTED FROM GERMANY BY WALTHERS

Special Value Price Shown In Red

Limited Quantity Available

"ALTES LAND" STATION SET

405-8245 129.99
Creating an entire country town is easy with this set of rustic buildings. Set includes four timber and brick houses (one each of kits #405-8241, 8242, 8243 and 8244), and the "Konigsmoor" Station (#405-9515).

OCTAGONAL WINDMILL

405-8246 57.99
5-1/2 x 4-1/2" 14 x 11.5cm
Can be powered with Motor #8248, sold separately.

SURAVA STATION

405-9519 42.99
13-1/4 x 5-1/2" 33.5 x 14cm
Based on a Swiss prototype, this depot combines the waiting room, freight house, and living quarters for the agent into one structure. Lots of extra details, including flower boxes, benches and more are provided to complete your station scene.

LANGENTHAL STATION

405-9504 39.99
17-1/8 x 5-1/2" 43 x 14cm

STATION SET "REICHELSHEIM"

405-8186 69.99
Consists of #'s 8180, 8182, 8184 and 9492.

KONIGSMOOR STATION

405-9515 33.99
9-3/4 x 6-1/8" 25 x 15.5cm

PAINT SHOP

405-9402 38.99
7-1/16 x 6-1/2" 18 x 16.5cm
Neat addition to any industry.

PLATFORM ALTBACH

405-9544 33.99
2 x 2-3/8" 5 x 6cm
47-5/8 x 2-1/8" 121.5 x 5.5cm

FELDAFING STATION

405-9530 ~~69.99~~ 34.99
25.2 x 7.5 x 6.7" 64 x 19 x 17cm
Built in the 1860s, this impressive station is still in use today! The model is highly detailed and can be used in various time periods.

SIGNAL TOWER "BEISLINGEN/STEIGE"

405-9478 29.99
5-3/4 x 3-1/2" 14.5 x 9cm
Control yard operations from this modern building! The structure features an attached office and interior details for the tower.

STATION "BLAUSEE"

405-9508 39.99
13-1/2 x 4-3/4" 34 x 12cm

STATION PLATFORM

405-9550 29.99
47-5/8 x 1-1/2" 121.5 x 3.8cm

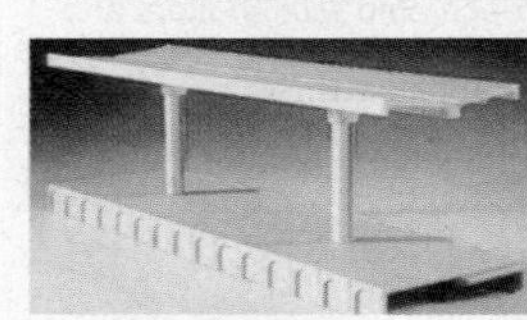

PLATFORM EXTENSION FOR #9544

405-9538 10.99
7.2" 18cm

PLATFORM EXTENSION FOR #9554

405-9539 10.99
7.2" 18cm

PLATFORM EXTENSION & DETAILS FOR #'S 9542, 9544 & 9554

405-9540 10.99
7.2" 18cm

PLATFORM EXTENSION FOR #9550

405-9551 9.99
7.2" 18cm

STEAM LOCO SAND FACILITY

405-9418 28.99
5-1/2 x 2-3/4" 14 x 7cm
2-3/4 x 3-3/8" 7 x 8.5cm

COAL MERCHANT'S YARD WITH ACCESSORIES

405-9442 49.99
10-5/8 x 6" 27 x 15cm

COALING STATION W/CRANE

405-9420 54.99
15-1/2 x 5-1/2" 39.5 x 14cm

DIESEL OIL STATION

405-9430 14.99
4-3/4 x 3-7/8" 12 x 10cm

WATER COLUMN

405-9422 pkg(2) **23.99**
3-3/8 x 7/8" 8.5 x 2cm

kibri

IMPORTED FROM GERMANY BY WALTHERS

3-TRACK DIESEL SHED

405-9450 54.99
13-3/8 x 4-7/8" 34 x 17.5cm

REISCHELSHEIM STATION

405-9492 33.99
9-1/2 x 5-1/2" 24 x 14cm
This two-story station is typical of small town depots and includes an attached freight shed.

BRICK STATION "ESCHBRONN"

405-9502 49.99
13-3/8 x 5-1/8" 34 x 13cm

ALTKIRCHEN STATION

405-9532 54.99
15-1/2 x 8" 39 x 20cm

COALING STORAGE

405-9434 28.99
9-1/2 x 3-7/8" 24 x 6cm

SIGNAL BOX OTTBERGEN

405-9474 28.99
8-1/2 x 2-1/4" 22 x 6cm

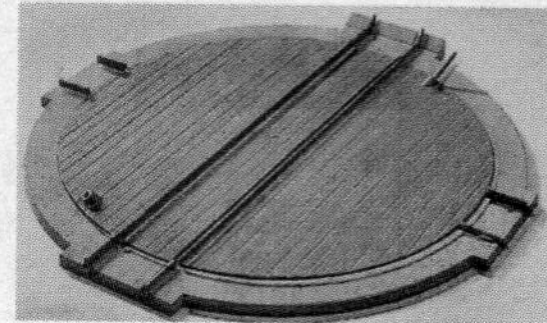

TURNTABLE

405-4130 7.99
4-3/4 x 4-3/4" 12 x 12cm

LOCOMOTIVE REPAIR SHED

405-9438 42.99
10-1/4 x 5-7/8" 26 x 15cm

SHED-SCHENKER

405-9468 29.99

SINGLE STALL ENGINE HOUSE

405-9436 31.99
7-7/8 x 4-3/4" 20 x 12cm
This single stall engine house is a perfect shelter for a branch line loco or local switcher. Many are used today to store maintenance equipment.

BONN STATION

405-9524 With 2 Train Sheds **188.99**
Station: 19-3/8 x 10" 99 x 25.5cm
Sheds: 33-1/2 x 17-1/4" 86 x 44cm
Based on the Bonn Station in Germany, this realistically detailed model is ideal for use on American or European layouts. The kit also includes two simulated "glass" train sheds to protect your passengers and trains during inclement weather.

TRAIN SHED BONN, GERMANY

405-9522 47.99
17 x 8-5/8" 43 x 22cm
Train sheds were an important part of stations in large cities. This kit is based on the prototype at Bonn, Germany, and is ideal for use with the Bonn Station kit (#405-9524) or other large stations.

SCRAPYARD

405-9400 36.99
16 x 4-3/4" 40 x 12cm
Includes mobile crane with claws and dump truck.

COLBE SIGNAL TOWER

405-9488 29.99
6-1/2 x 2-3/4" 16.5 x 7cm

RAILROAD SIGNAL TOWER

405-9472 45.99
11 x 3-7/8" 28 x 10cm

COALING DISTRIBUTION CENTER

405-9406 36.99
For customer convenience, you can buy coal in bulk or bags here. This modern facility includes a dump truck, loading crane, scale house, bins, pallets and machinery.

GANTRY CRANE

405-9602 33.99
5-1/8 x 2" 13 x 5cm
This heavy crane is perfect for industrial areas served by road or rail. Prototypes move large or bulky loads from trucks to freight cars.

FREIGHT HOUSE "ESCHBRONN"

405-9466 22.99
7-5/16 x 4-3/4" 18.5 x 12cm

TOWN HALL

405-8416 44.99
6 x 5" 15.5 x 13cm

GARAGE

405-8136 31.99
12-5/8 x 4-3/8" 32 x 11cm

kibri

IMPORTED FROM GERMANY
BY WALTHERS

Special Value Pricing Shown In Red

RAILWAY POST OFFICE
405-8199 31.99
5-1/8 x 4-3/4" 13 x 12cm

MUNDERKINGEN POST OFFICE
405-8198 44.99
9-1/4 x 4-5/8 x 6-1/4"
23.5 x 11 x 16cm

CITY GATE TOWER "CHATENOIS"
405-8470 28.99
3-1/2 x 2-3/8" 9 x 6cm

ALPINE SET W/STATION
405-8078 pkg(3) **85.99**
A complete village in a single kit! Includes #8075, 8076 and 9497.

FIREHOUSE "GOLDBACH"
405-8032 33.99
5-1/4 x 4-5/8" 13 x 11.5cm

TIE BUMPER
405-9470 6.99
2-1/8 x 1-3/4" 5.5 x 4.5cm

TRANSFORMER STATION
405-8131 16.99
1-3/4 x 1-9/16" 4.5 x 4cm

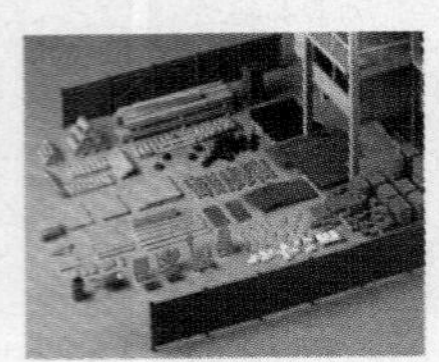

SKYSCRAPER SITE ACCESSORIES
405-8226 42.99

ALPINE SET W/STATION
405-8078 pkg(3) **85.99**
A complete village in a single kit! Includes #8075, 8076 and 9497.

ROUNDHOUSE ENGINE SHED
405-9452 ~~51.49~~ **31.99**
9-3/8 x 15-1/4" 24 x 39cm
This 3-stall brick roundhouse holds steam or diesel locos up to 9-1/2" (24cm) long. Engines up to 8" can be turned on the manual turntable.

SINGLE STALL ADD-ON SHED
405-9454 12.99
3-1/2 x 6-1/8" 9 15.5cm

MANUAL TURNTABLE
405-9456 12.99
8 x 8" 20.5 x 20.5cm

BOILER HOUSE
405-9784 ~~24.99~~ **14.99**
7-1/8 x 5-7/8" 18 x 15cm
Boiler houses generated steam and electricity for railroad shops and industrial complexes. The kit includes the smokestack.

CITY HALL W/FOUNTAIN
405-8418 57.99
Beautiful half-timber and stone construction highlight this ornate structure, and a fountain is included to complete the scene.

INDUSTRIAL FENCES W/GATE
405-9792 19.99
49-1/4" 124cm

SAWMILL W/INTERIOR
405-9960 76.99
23-5/8 x 6-3/4" 60 x 17cm

THW VEHICLE DEPOT KITZINGEN
405-8134 76.99
Used by the German Rescue Service as a garage for heavy equipment, this building makes a great office for a small construction firm, trucking company or other business with a fleet of vehicles.

CITY HALL "LEER"
405-8380 76.99
11-3/4 x 9 x 13-3/4"
30 x 22.5 x 35cm

WAREHOUSE ANNEX
405-9790 33.99
8-7-16 x 4-3/8" 21.5 x 11cm

WAREHOUSE
405-9404 36.99
10-13/32 x 5-13/16 x 4-13/32"
26 x 14.5 x 11cm

kibri

IMPORTED FROM GERMANY BY WALTHERS

Special Value Pricing Shown In Red

WIESENTAL FARMHOUSE

405-8152 21.99
4 x 3-5/8 x 4-13/32"
10 x 9 x 11cm
Sturdy stucco construction and a gambrel, tile roof make this a house to be proud of! Comes with a TV aerial and a small backyard storage shed.

CEMENT SILO

405-10000 pkg(2) **8.99**
1-1/8 x 1-1/8" 3 x 3cm

SINGLE FAMILY HOUSE

405-8180 15.99
5-1/2 x 4-3/4 x 4"
14 x 12 x 10cm

WATERMILL MOISBURGER

405-8240 49.99
Water power runs the machinery at this country mill. Excellent detail highlights the thatched roof and brick and stone walls. The wheel is powered by an electric motor, included with the kit. The motor is also sold separately for your own projects.

MOTOR FOR #8240

405-8248 31.99

STONE HOUSE

405-8080 18.99
4-3/8 x 3-3/4 x 3-1/2"
11 x 9.5 x 9cm

OUTDOOR CHAPEL W/ACCESSORIES

405-9780 22.99
2-3/8 x 2-3/8 x 3-7/8"
6 x 6 x 10cm

SIX CONTAINERS/ MOBILE OFFICES

405-11970 pkg(6) **19.99**
2-3/4 x 1-1/8" 6.9 x 2.8cm

SKYSCRAPER UNDER CONSTRUCTION

405-8224 69.99
8 x 7-1/4" 20 x 18cm
Perfect for a city under construction, this kit comes complete with fencing, cement mixer, piles of construction material and other details. For added realism, superdetail the scene with a construction crane (#405-10202), or Kibri construction equipment listed in the Vehicles section.

MINIATURE "KUEHTZAGL" CHAPEL

405-9781 10.99
2 x 1-5/8" 5 x 4cm

MODERN APARTMENT BUILDING

405-8222 ~~39.99~~ **24.99**
9 x 4-1/2 x 5-1/2" 23 x 11.5 x 14cm
These attractive apartments add a city look to any scene. The first floor features small shops, so the structure can be used in a business district or suburb.

kibri

IMPORTED FROM GERMANY BY WALTHERS

Special Value Pricing Shown In Red

VILLAGE CHURCH "SERTIG"

405-8006 25.99
5-1/8 x 4-3/8 x 6-1/2"
13 x 11 x 15cm

CHAPEL "ELLMAU"

405-9764 24.99
4-1/2 x 4-3/8 x 6-3/4"
11.5 x 11 x 17cm

VILLAGE CHURCH

405-9772 39.99
8-7/8 x 5-3/4 x 11"
22 x 14.5 x 28cm

COMPLETE FACTORY COMPLEX

405-9798 ~~166.49~~ **89.99**
Everything you need in one kit includes on each #9784, 9786, 9788, 9790 and two of #9792

FACTORY ANNEX BUILDING

405-9786 ~~42.99~~ **26.99**
13 x 6-5/8" 28 x 17cm

CONSTRUCTION CRANE

405-10202 49.99
These tall cranes can be found on construction sights around the world. To fit your building needs, the height can be adjusted from 10 to 22".

RAILROAD WORKER'S HOUSE & OUTBUILDING

405-8194 36.99
5-1/8 x 2-3/8" 13 x 6cm
7 x 5-1/2" 17.6 x 14cm

BREWERY GUEST HOUSE

405-8197 39.99
9 x 7" 22.5 x 17.5cm

BREWERY

405-9799 ~~65.39~~ **39.99**
13 x 8" 33 x 20cm

FACTORY BUILDING

405-9786 42.99
11-5/8 x 10-3/16" 27 x 25cm
This factory includes blower housing, palets, oil drums and more.

kibri

IMPORTED FROM GERMANY BY WALTHERS

Special Value Pricing Shown In Red

STUCCO HOUSE WITH GAS STATION

405-8202 29.99
6 x 4.4" 15 x 11cm

STUCCO HOUSE W/MANSARD ROOF

405-8160 19.99
4.8 x 4.4" 12 x 11cm

"LANGNAU" HOUSE

405-8026 33.99
5-3/4 x 5-1/8" 14 x 13cm

SINGLE FAMILY HOUSE

405-8062 14.99
4-1/8x 3-3/4" 10.5 x 9.5cm

COUNTRY HOUSE W/TIMBERING

405-8184 15.99
5-1/2 x 4-3/4 x 4"
14 x 12 x 10cm

HOUSE W/GARAGE

405-8084 24.99
5-3/4 x 4-3/4 x 3"
14.5 x 12 x 7.5cm

CHALET "SEEBLICK"

405-8001 18.99
3-3/8 x 3-1/8 x 2"
8.5 x 8 x 5cm

STUCCO HOUSE WITH GABLE

405-8164 22.99
4.8 x 4.4" 12 x 11cm

CHALET "EDELWEISS"

405-8002 19.99
4-3/8 x 3-3/8 x 2-3/4"
11 x 8.5 x 7cm

STUCCO HOUSE W/WINDOWS

405-8166 22.99
4.8 x 4.4" 12 x 11cm

BOTTROP HOUSE (2 BUILDINGS)

405-8190 25.99
6-1/2 x 5-1/8 x 4-1/2"
6.5 x 13 x 11.5cm
4-1/4 x 2-5/8 x 2-1/2"
11 x 6 x 6.5cm

BOTTROP HOUSE W/WORKSHOP

405-8192 25.99
6-1/2 x 5-1/8 x 4-1/2"
6.5 x 13 x 11.5cm
4-1/4 x 2-5/8 x 2-1/2"
11 x 6 x 6.5cm

SINGLE FAMILY HOUSE

405-8156 21.99
4-13/64" x 3-5/8 x 4"
10.5 x 9 x 10cm
A neat addition to a city street or subdivision.

ROMAN CATHOLIC CHURCH

405-9760 ~~85.49~~ **49.99**
12-1/4 x 7-1/2 x 14-1/8" 31 x 19 x 36cm
Roman style brick church can be equipped with Bell Tape & Speaker Set #405-9762.

BELL TAPE & SPEAKER SET

405-9762 31.99
Cassette tape of actual church bells and assembled speaker.

WAREHOUSE BUILDING

405-9782 ~~29.99~~ **19.99**
9-1/2 x 5" 24 x 12.5cm
This small kit can be used to store raw materials or to house a small manufacturing plant. The large roll-up door can accommodate freight cars or trucks.

Limited Quantity Available

STATION "OBERWALD"

405-8046 24.99
4-1/4 x 3-1/4" 11 x 8.5cm

Limited Quantity Available

STATION W/RURAL HOUSES

405-8158 85.99
Set-up a suburb with this set that includes #8152, 8154, 8156 and 9499.

kibri

IMPORTED FROM GERMANY BY WALTHERS

Limited Quantity Available

HOUSE "FURKA"

405-8048 24.99
4-1/4 x 3-1/4" 11 x 8.5cm

HOUSE "BICHLBERG"

405-8058 29.99
5-1/2 x 4-1/4" 14 x 11cm

GUEST HOUSE THREE BEARS

405-8056 57.99
7-1/2 x 5-7/8" 19 x 15cm

COUNTRY HOUSE

405-8182 15.99
5-1/2 x 4-3/4 x 4"
14 x 12 x 10cm
Here's a home that's ideal for the growing HO family! The structure features two floors and will fit into a modest sized lot in any HO city.

INN W/BEER GARDEN

405-8174 39.99
5-13/16 x 5-13/64 x 5-13/64"
14.5 x 13 x 13cm
Enjoy a hearty meal and good conversation every time you dine at this stylish inn. During warm weather, patrons can be found enjoying the tables, chairs and umbrellas provided for the outdoor beer garden.

THE WHITE HORSE INN

405-8434 29.99
3-7/8 x 3-7/8" 10 x 10cm

Limited Quantity Available

TIMBER & BRICK, BORSTEL

405-8243 29.99
5-1/8 x 3-5/8" 13 x 9.5cm

Limited Quantity Available

TIMBER & BRICK, NIEDERELBE

405-8244 29.99
6-7/8 x 3-7/8" 17.5 x 10cm

Limited Quantity Available

TIMBER & BRICK, JORK

405-8242 24.99
3-7/8 x 3-5/8" 10 x 9cm

HALF TIMBER HOUSE/TILE ROOF

405-8124 22.99
3-7/8 x 3-1/2" 10 x 9cm

HALF TIMBER HOUSE W/HIP ROOF

405-8126 29.99
3-7/8 x 3-1/2" 10 x 9cm

FAMILY HOUSE "BERGWALD"

405-8176 25.99
6-5/8 X 5-13/64 X 4-5/8"
16.5 x 13 x 11.5
Sturdy brick construction and lots of vintage details make this the perfect house, or converted apartment, for an older neighborhood in any city.

CHALET "BRIENZ"

405-8040 25.99
4-3/4 x 3-1/2 x 2-3/4"
12 x 9 x 7cm

AUMENAO CHURCH

405-9774 47.99
9-1/2 x 6-3/4" 24 x 17cm
This stylish church fits big city or small town locations. The kit features rough stone construction, tall steeple and covered entryway.

405-8440 405-8442 405-8444 405-8446

HALF TIMBER MARKET

405-8440 42.99
3-3/4 x 3-3/4" 9.5 x 9.5cm

HALF TIMBER GUEST HOUSE

405-8442 42.99
4 x 3-3/4" 10 x 9.5cm

HALF TIMBER W/2 SHOPS

405-8444 42.99
2-3/4 x 3-1/2" 7 x 9cm
1-3/4 x 3-3/4" 4.5 x 9.5cm

HALF TIMBER W/SHOPS

405-8446 39.99
4-5/8 x 3-3/4" 4.5 x 9.5cm

HALF TIMBERED HOUSES

405-8448 139.99
Includes #'s 8440, 8442, 8444 and 8446

LARGE & SMALL HAY BARNS

405-8007 15.99
2-3/4 x 2-5/8 x 1-5/8"
7 x 6.5 x 4cm
2-1/8 x 2 x 1-3/8"
5.5 x 5 x 3.5cm

CHALET "SIGRISWIL"

405-8042 28.99
5-3/8 x 3-7/8 x 3-1/2"
13.5 x 10 x 9cm

kibri

IMPORTED FROM GERMANY BY WALTHERS

FARM "SIMMENTAL"

405-8050 44.99
7-7/8 x 5-1/2 x 3-1/2"
20 x 14 x 9cm

ALPENHOF CHALET

405-8077 33.99
6-13/16 x 6-13/32 x 4-13/16"
17 x 16 x 12cm
With a few extra details, you can convert this three-story building into a hotel or apartment complex.

COMPLETE VILLAGE, 6 BUILDINGS

405-8009 pkg(6) **83.99**
Set includes one each of #'s 8001, 8002, 8004, 8006, 8007 and 8008.

ALPINE STORE & INN

405-8003 22.99
4-3/4 x 3-3/8 x 3-1/2"
12 x 8.5 x 9cm

DIORAMA "BRAUEREI" — SMALL

405-9796 169.99
11-1/8 x 12" 28 x 30cm

CHALET "SONNENHALDE"

405-8004 24.99
4-3/4 x 4-3/4 x 3-3/8"
12 x 12 x 8.5cm

FARM IN TYROL

405-8052 36.99
6-3/4 x 5-1/8 x 4-1/4"
17 x 13 x 11cm

FARMHOUSE FROM EMMENTAL

405-8054 59.99
7-1/4 x 11-3/8" 18.5 x 29cm

STARTING RAMP

405-9654 7.99
12 x 2-3/4 x 3/4"
30 x 7 x 1.8cm

BRIDGE, DECK TRUSS

405-9698 36.99

STARTING RAMP R14

405-9660 7.99
13.7"

VIADUCT CURVED KIT

405-9664 46.99

MARKET PLACE TERRACE HOUSE

405-8296 44.99
6-1/2 x 6-3/4"
16 x 16.8cm

HALF TIMBER HOUSE, TECKLENBERG

405-8130 29.99
5-1/8 x 4-1/2" 13 x 11.5cm

HALF TIMBER HOUSE "MUNSTERLAND"

405-8128 28.99
5.5 x 3-3/8" 14 x 10cm
This charming home is perfect for country settings or city suburbs. It features detailed plastic parts to simulate the traditional half-timber and stucco construction.

MIDDLE BRIDGE PIER

405-9690 10.99
3-1/8" 8cm high

STONE VIADUCT

405-9644 24.99
16-1/2" radius x 45°

STEEL BRIDGE, CURVED 14" RADIUS

405-9682 22.99
11 x 2-3/4 x 1-1/8"
28.2 x 7 x 3cm

FOOTBRIDGE

405-9612 29.99
9 x 7-7/8 x 4-3/4"
23 x 20 x 12cm

STEEL BRIDGE, STRAIGHT

405-9680 19.99
10-5/8 x 2-3/4 x 1-1/8"
27 x 7 x 3cm

SINGLE SECTION FLEXIBLE BRIDGE

405-9620 9.99
7-1/4" 18.5cm

STRAIGHT STONE ARCH BRIDGE

405-9640 22.99
13-3/4 x 3-1/4" 34 x 8cm

STONE VIADUCT

405-9642 19.99
14" radius x 45°

PAVING FOR DOCKSIDE CRANE

405-4127 4.99
7-7/8 x 4-3/4" 20 x 12cm

kibri

IMPORTED FROM GERMANY BY WALTHERS

Special Value Pricing Shown In Red

DRAWBRIDGE POTSHAUSEN
405-8256 36.99
7-3/4 x 3-1/2" 19.5 x 9cm

STONE ARCH VIADUCT
405-9650 25.99
12-3/4 x 2-1/2" 33.6 x 7cm

HEIMSBACH CHEESE DAIRY
405-8024 33.99
7-1/4 x 4-7/8" 18 x 12cm
With its old-world styling, this small cheese plant also makes an attractive retail store! Add some tourists and cars out front for a super mini-scene.

Limited Quantity Available

SCHOOL HOUSE W/THATCH ROOF
405-8238 39.99
5-7/8 x 5-3/8" 15 x 13.5cm

STORE HOUSE GRAINARY W/LOFT
405-8028 25.99
4-1/4 x 4-1/4 x 4-3/8"
10.5 x 10.5 x 11cm
Detail a farm scene with this ornate and truly different building! This detailed kit simulates the detailed wood construction of a Swiss prototype.

Limited Quantity Available

BARN AND HAYLOFT
405-8049 26.99
2-1/4 x 1-3/4" 6.5 x 7cm
2-1/4 x 1-3/4" 6.5 x 9cm

FOOT BRIDGE
405-9606 13.99
5-3/4 x 2-1/2" 14.6 x 6.5cm

FLEXIBLE BRIDGE
405-9610 54.99
58.2" 148cm

ARCHED RETAINING WALL
405-9648 19.99
12" 30cm

CORNER TERRACE HOUSE SET
405-8292 ~~142.99~~ 69.99
Set of three kits, #8294, 8296 and 8298 to model a complete city scene.

STONE MULTI-ARCH VIADUCT
405-9652 25.99

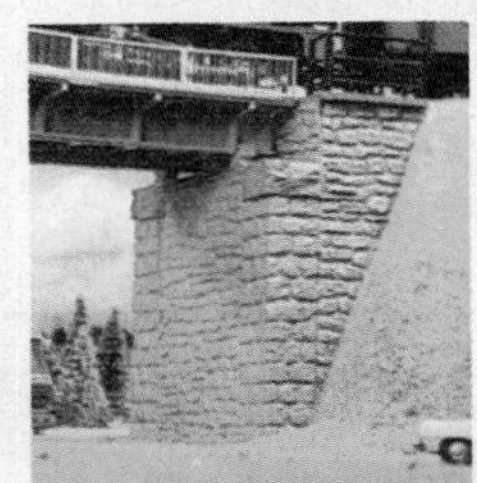

BRIDGE END PIERS
405-9691 pkg(2) 24.99
4" 10cm high

GIRDER BRIDGE
405-9694 29.99
10-3/4 x 3-1/8 x 3"
27.5 x 7.5cm

TRUSS BRIDGE 15" LONG
405-9630 35.99
15 x 2.6" 38.5 x 6.5cm

HALF-TIMBERED HOUSE W/GATE
405-8452 38.99
5-3/8 x 5-1/4 x 6-1/4"
14 x 13.5 x 16cm

HALF-TIMBERED HOUSE W/RECESS
405-8454 38.99
6 x 4 x 8" 15 x 10 x 20cm

HALF-TIMBERED HOUSE W/MARKET
405-8456 36.99
4-1/8 x 3-1/8 x 6-3/8"
10.5 x 8 x 16.5cm

STATUE W/FOUNTAIN
405-8458 9.99
2-1/4 x 2-1/4 x 2-3/4"
6 x 6 x 7cm

HALF-TIMBERED CORNER HOUSE
405-8460 39.99
6 x 5-1/4 x 6-1/4"
15 x 13.5 x 16cm

"ODENWALD" HALF-TIMBERED SET
405-8462 139.99
Includes all of the above #'s.

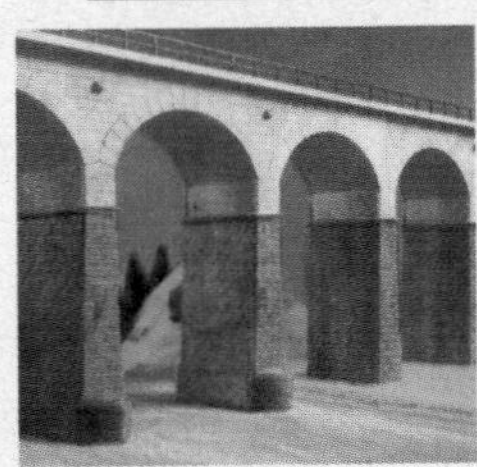

STONE VIADUCT PIERS
405-9646 pkg(4) 16.99
4" 10cm high

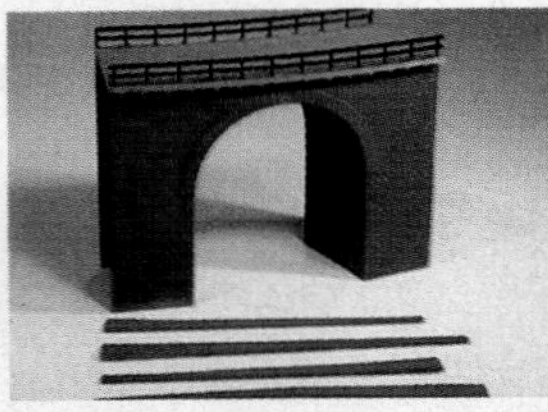

VIADUCT CURVED R14
405-9662 7.99

kibri

IMPORTED FROM GERMANY
BY WALTHERS

VIADUCT STRAIGHT

405-9656 7.99

CONCRETE BRIDGE

405-9668 24.99
13-1/2 x 2-3/4 x 5-1/8"
33.8 x 5.9 x 12.3cm

BAMBERG FIREHOUSE

405-8172 33.99
4-1/8 x 4-1/8 x 6-3/4"
11 x 11 x 17cm

GATEKEEPER'S COTTAGE

405-9485 23.99
Cottage: 5-13/64 x 4-13/32 x 3-13/32" 13 x 11 x 8.5cm
Stable: 4-13/16 x 2-13/32 x 2-13/32" 12 x 6 x 6cm
Protecting a busy rural crossing, homes like this were often built for railway employees and their families. This kit has many "extras" including a livestock stable.

BOUTIQUE TERRACE HOUSE W/TOWER

405-8298 52.99
7-3/4 x 6-3/4" 19.2 x 16.7cm

STATION BUILDING

405-9491 33.99

COUNTRY SIGNAL TOWER

405-9486 25.99

FARM HOUSE W/BARN

405-8146 25.99
6 x 4-3/4" 15 x 12cm

HALF-TIMBERED RURAL FARM HOUSE

405-8138 16.99
4 x 3-1/2" 10.5 x 9cm

CASTLE "FALKENSTEIN"

405-9010 99.99
18-7/8 x 11 x 13" 48 x 28 x 33cm
Built in the 13th century, this castle was restored in 1905 and remains a favorite with tourists. The model is nicely detailed, with rough stone and timber construction.

CONCRETE BRIDGE-CURVED

405-9666 29.99
25-1/2 x 2-3/4 x 5-1/8"
64 x 7 x 13cm

HALF-TIMBERED FARM HOUSE

405-8142 21.99
4 x 3-1/2" 10 x 9cm

RURAL TOWN HALL

405-8144 29.99
4-1/2 x 4-1/4" 11.5 x 11cm

ALPENBLICK GUEST HOUSE

405-8070 33.99
7-1/2 x 6-1/2" 19 x 16.5cm

FORESTER'S LODGE

405-8072 33.99
6 x 4-1/2" 15 x 11.5cm

BLACK FOREST FARM HOUSE

405-8074 42.99
8 x 6" 20.5 x 15cm

kibri

IMPORTED FROM GERMANY
BY WALTHERS

Limited Quantity Available

RURAL MARKET SET

405-8150 pkg(3) **85.99**
Includes #8130, 8144, 8146, 8456 and accessories.

RURAL HOUSE W/FRONT GARDEN

405-8140 19.99
4-3/4 x 4-1/2" 12 x 11cm

FAMILY HOUSE

405-8154 21.99
4 x 3-5/8 x 4" 10 x 9 x 10cm
Living in this handsome home will always be a pleasure. It's complete shutters, window boxes and a TV aerial.

COWS BEING SHIPPED BY TRAIN

405-8059 25.99
6-13/16 x 3-13/64" 17 x 8cm
Modernize your rural livestock shipping with this kit, complete with loading ramp, fence, cows, stock truck and figures.

"DETMOLD" PLATFORM

405-9554 39.99

EMMENTAL SET

405-9489 119.99
Set includes one each of #9490, 8024, 8026, 8028 and 8008.

BARN W/EQUIPMENT

405-8055 42.99
5-5/8 x 4-13/64 x 3-5/8"
14 x 10.5 x 9cm
Keep your equipment clean and serviceable by storing it inside this machine shed. Includes forage wagon, roll-over plow, mower, box wagon and other accessories, which can be used with the Kibri Mercedes Tractor (sold separately), listed in Vehicles.

BARN ONLY

405-8057 16.99
5-5/8 x 4-13/64 x 3-5/8"
14 x 10.5 x 9cm
Machine shed, less trailers and equipment.

DUISBURG WATER TOWER

405-9457 61.99
4-13-16 x 4-13/16 x 13-13/16"
12 x 12 x 34.5cm
Keep thirsty steamers ready for the road at all times with this tank in your terminal. Can also be used as a city or industrial tower too.

KARWENDEL CHALET

405-8076 25.99
4-13/16 x 4 x 3-13/64"
12 x 10 x 8cm
This attractive two-story home is loaded with details and features stucco construction.

HOUSE W/BOUTIQUE & GARAGE

405-8075 27.99
6-13/32 x 6 x 4"
16 x 15 x 10cm
Run any business from the house with this kit. Two-story home has ground floor shop with large windows, and an attached one-car garage.

TERRACE HOUSE W/TOWER

405-8294 59.99
11 x 9-1/2" 27.6 x 23.5cm

DIORAMA "BRAUEREI" — LARGE

405-9794 274.99
33-1/8 x 16" 83 x 40cm

LARGE TRUSS BRIDGE

405-9696 49.99
17-3/4 x 3-1/8 x 4-1/2" 45 x 8 x 11.5cm
This big bridge is typical of railroad bridges found around the world. Lattice girder work, plenty of rivets and heavy I beams give the finished model a realistic appearance.

FISCHBACH STATION

405-9499 25.99
8 x 6 x 3-13/16"
20 x 15 x 9.5cm
This busy suburban station is a great way to serve an outlying suburb. Model features detailed "wood" walls, with an outdoor snack bar, complete with table, chairs and umbrellas.

Limited Quantity Available

STATION SET

405-8179 pkg(3) **85.99**
Create an upscale older neighborhood for your layout with this set, which includes #8176, 8178 and 9501.

HOUSE "AM PAPPELWEG"

405-8178 23.99
5-13/64 x 4-13/32 x 5-13/64"
13 x 11 x 13cm
This stately home could easily be "Americanized" with a shingle roof. It has many details, like the large bay window, attic windows and column entryway that you'll find on homes in your town.

Make industrial or railroad scenes more realistic with these easy-to-build kits, which can be used in many eras. Water towers feature injection-molded parts, other structures feature urethane castings.

66' ELLIPSOIDAL WATER TANK KIT
411-126 16.95

74' 1900s VINTAGE WATER TANK KIT
411-127 16.95

H.L. BROWN 5¢ & 10¢ STORE
411-808 14.95

70' 1960s VINTAGE WATER TANK KIT
411-125 14.95

THREE-STALL ROUNDHOUSE
411-104 59.95
15-1/2 x 8-1/2" Front 16-1/2" Back 5"

American-style Roundhouse includes 20 windows, 3 smokestacks and detailed doors for each stall. A larger building can be constructed using the add-on stall in kit #411-105.

ADD-ON STALL FOR ROUNDHOUSE
411-105 16.95
Additional stall for #411-104.

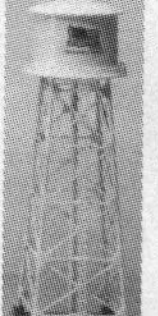

1930S ERA WATER TANK
411-128 16.95

ACME NUTS & BOLTS
411-802 29.95

BAYVIEW MIDDLE SCHOOL
411-803 19.95

CAMBRIDGE FURNITURE
411-805 17.95

INTERSTATE TRANSPORTATION
411-801 17.95

BAYVIEW OFFICE CENTER
411-806 14.95

JACK'S HARDWARE
411-807 7.95

A.C. POWER COMPANY
411-809 9.95

S.M.I. TOOL CO.
411-804 14.95

ALPHA PRINTING CO.
411-810 7.95

These easy-to-build kits feature pre-colored plastic parts.

SAND FACILITY
625-40105 17.99
Facilities like this provide clean, dry sand for steam and diesel locos. Includes tower, sand house and bin.

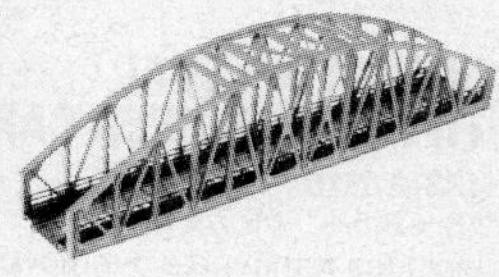

CURVED GIRDER BRIDGE
625-40081 27.99
Length 18" 45.7cm

BRIDGE PIERS SET
625-40082 pkg(2) 11.99
1-1/2 x 5" 3.8 x 12.7cm
3-3/4" high 9.5cm high

STRAIGHT GIRDER BRIDGE
625-40080 13.99
Length 9" 23cm

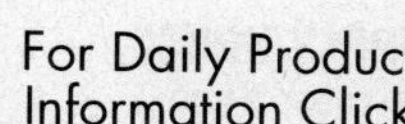

These craft train kits are molded plastic, undecorated and some require modification and components from other manufacturers.

VICTORIA SHOP & BARN KIT
480-1513 15.00

VICTORIA CABLE POWER HOUSE & PASSENGER CAR KITS
480-1512 15.00
5 x 2-1/2 x 4"
12.7 x 6.4 x 10.2cm
With two old timer style passenger car kits.

VICTORIA STATION RESTAURANT
480-1511 15.00
8 x 8 x 2" 20.4 x 20 x 5cm
With metal box car and modern caboose.

These easy-to-build, structures feature plastic parts molded in colors and hand-painted details.

FREIGHT STATION KIT

433-1353 18.50
12-1/2 x 5-3/4" 31.4 x 14.5cm

PASSENGER STATION

433-1352 9.50

TRAIN STATION

433-1347 7.50
2 x 11-5/8" 5.1 x 29.5cm

MAINLINE STATION

433-1342 24.00
12-3/8 x 4-7/8" 31.4 x 12.4cm

COALING TOWER

433-1377 24.00

OPERATING COAL TIPPLE W/HOPPER CAR

433-21310 19.50
18 x 2-5/8" 45.7 x 6.7cm
Includes removable overflow tray, ramps and coal.

OPERATING LOGGING MILL

433-8201 33.50
12 x 7-3/4" 30.5 x 19.7cm
Includes dump car, logs and log pond.

OPERATING GRAVEL UNLOADER W/DUMP CAR

433-8204 15.25
6-5/8 x 5-1/2" 16.8 x 14cm
Includes gravel.

SUPPLY HOUSE

433-1398 24.00

ACE SUPER MARKET

433-1330 12.25
5-1/2 x 9-3/8 x 3-1/2" 13.7 x 23.7 x 8.7cm
Part of the urban landscape for decades, convenience stores like this can be found in virtually any town. Detailed model is complete with ads for the windows, a full interior with shelves, cash registers and an ice machine, plus phone booth and a loading door in the rear.

NATIONAL OIL CO.

433-1331 12.25
5-1/2 x 4-1/2 x 2-3/4" 13.7 x 11.2 x 6.8cm
These retired railroad tank cars are still doing their duty for their new owner. Converted storage tanks like these can be found at lots of industries, railroad shops, or alongside bulk oil dealers. Kit includes two storage tanks which can be positioned together or used separately, a pump house, barrels, tools and wood stacks.

DOWNTOWN BUSINESS CENTER

433-1373 12.25
6-1/4 x 8-3/8 x 4-1/2" 2.5 x 20.9 x 11.2cm
Revitalize your downtown with this new building. The first floor is home to an Italian restaurant, a phone communications company and a barber shop, while the upstairs is leased to a bowling alley. Realistic signs, a chimney and a roof-mounted air conditioner are all included.

ENGINE HOUSE KIT

433-1354 18.50
7-1/4 x 3" 18.4 x 7cm

TRACKSIDE SHANTIES

433-1348 7.50
Includes one of each: Line Shack (2 x 2-1/4" 5.1 x 5.9cm), Switchman's Shanty (1-5/8 x 2-1/8" 4 x 5.5cm) and Whistle Stop (2 x 2-1/4" 5.1 x 5.9cm).

WESTERN HOMESTEAD

433-1338 13.50
7-3/4 x 5-1/2" 19.7 x 14cm

GENERAL STORE

433-1351 7.50
6 x 4-7/8" 15.2 x 12.4cm

BELVEDERE DOWNTOWN HOTEL

433-1339 13.50
5-1/2 x 2-1/2" 14 x 64cm

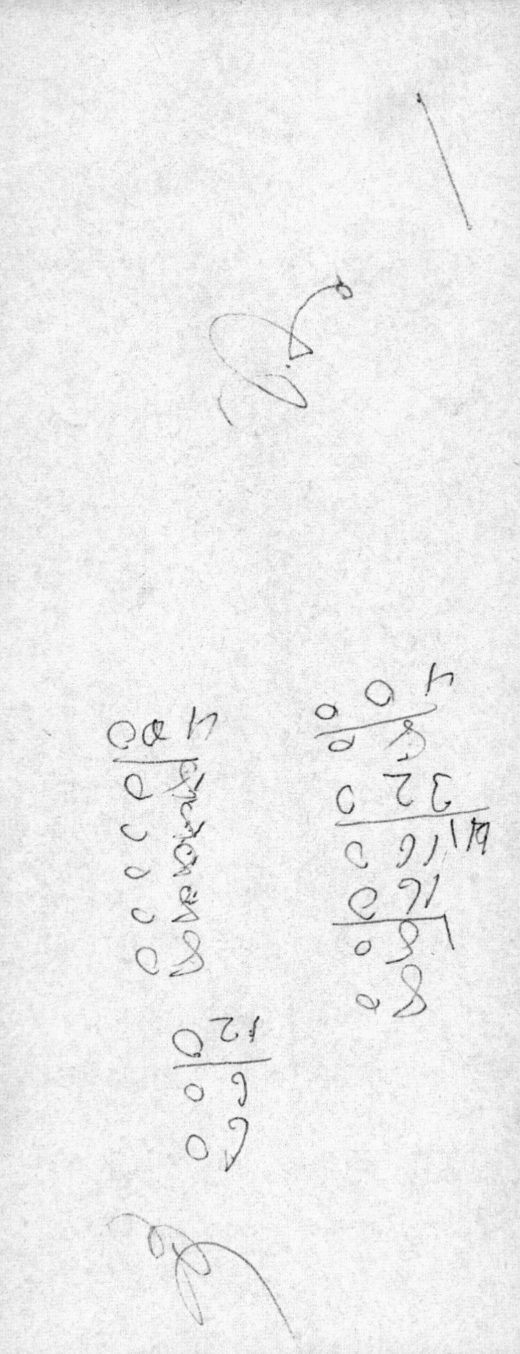

Hobbyland Inc.

41[illegible] [illegible] Blvd.

Fort Wayne In [illegible]

[illegible]

Date: [illegible]/2000

Time: [illegible] AM

Clerk: [illegible]

Station: [illegible]

Transaction: [illegible]

Transaction Type: Sale

[illegible] 32

[illegible] [illegible] $29.99

[illegible] COMPATIBLE [illegible]

[illegible] [illegible] [illegible]

Subtotal: [illegible]

Sales Tax: [illegible]

Total Due: [illegible]

Cash: [illegible]

Cash: [illegible]

Change: [illegible]

Thank You!

TOWN CHURCH
433-1350 7.50
5 x 6" 12.8 x 15.3cm

WOODLAWN POLICE STATION
433-1382 12.25
6-1/4 x 8-3/8" 15.9 x 21.3cm

STOCK PEN
433-1378 11.50
5-7/8 x 5-7/8" 14.9 x 14.9cm

HOUSE LIGHTING KIT
433-1200 3.75
All day, the lights burn brightly in stores and industries. At dusk, they come on in the houses at the edge of town. Over at the roundhouse, the lights burn night and day to keep the railroad running. Working lights will add drama and action to your entire layout, and this economical kit makes it easy to install lighting in almost any building. It's completely assembled, with screw-type bulb, socket with hook-up wires and a plastic mounting base, which can be nailed to your layout surface, or glued inside your buildings.

FLASHING LIGHT STORAGE TANK
433-8205 12.50
2-7/8" 7.3cm square
With blinking light and graffiti decals.

LIGHTED YARD TOWER
433-8208 12.50
2-7/8" 7.3cm square
Includes working light.

KENTUCKY FRIED CHICKEN® DRIVE-IN
433-1394 12.25
8-3/8 x 4-1/4" 21.3 x 10.8cm

ARCH SPAN BRIDGE
433-8213 18.00
18-5/8 x 5-1/4" 46.6 x 13.1cm

BRIDGE & TRESTLE SET
433-8210 9.75

HAMPDEN FIRE ENGINE HOUSE #46
433-1390 12.25
6-1/4 x 8-3/8" 15.9 x 21.3cm

MT VERNON MANUFACTURING CO
433-1337 13.50
8-14 x 5-1/2" 21 x 14cm
Modular design allows for easy kitbashing.

TRACKSIDE BUILDINGS
433-1392 pkg(12) **90.00**
Includes 3 each of Train Station, General Store, Trackside Shanties and Town Church

OPERATING ACCESSORIES, ASSORTMENT
433-8731 551.75
Includes two each of #8201 Operating Log Mill, #8203 Switchman with Lighted Building and #8205 Flashing Light Storage Tank; three each of #21310 Coal Tipple with Hopper Car and #8204 Gravel Unloader; six each of #8089 Bi-Level Auto Carrier with six cars and #8208 Lighted Yard Tower; and 12 each of #8209 Crossing Gate.

COUNTRYSIDE BUSINESS ASSORTMENT
433-1388 pkg(12) **147.00**
Four each #1330 Ace Super Market, #1331 National Oil Co. and #1394 Kentucky Fried Chicken.

OLD TOWN BUILDINGS
433-1395 pkg(12) **162.00**
Includes 4 each Mt. Vernon Manufacturing, Western Homestead and Belvedere Downtown Hotel.

HOMETOWN BUILDING ASSORTMENT
433-1393 pkg(12) **147.00**
Includes 4 each of #1382 Woodlawn Police Station, #1390 Hampden Fire Station and #1373 Downtown Business Center.

POWER-LOC™ OPERATING ACCESSORIES
Make any model railroad more fun with these working structures! Models are designed for Power-Loc™ track-and-roadbed system, but are compatible with standard track.

433-8234

433-21310

BRIDGE/PIER SET
433-8234 10.00

OPERATING COAL TIPPLE
433-21310 19.50
Send coal to customers with the pull of a lever! Includes hopper, scale coal and a handy pick-up tray to catch spills.

433-21311

433-21312

GRAVEL UNLOADER
433-21311 15.25
Keep construction materials moving on your line with this set! A detailed plastic building hides the mechanical dump, which you control with a lever. Complete with operating dump car and simulated gravel load, plus gravel storage bin.

LOG DUMP STATION
433-21312 15.25
Car loads of lumber arrive and drop logs for the mill at this busy siding. Includes a small building, lever dump, working log dump car, logs and storage bin.

Limited Quantity Available

MOORE & COMPANY WAREHOUSE
433-1372 60.00
18 x 5-3/4 x 7"
Proto 2000's latest warehouse is actually three distinct units: a tower, a loading dock and a main building. Features multicolored molding, sharp printing, and fine detailing on the walls, doors and foundation.

Main Street Graphics

WM. K. WALTHERS EXCLUSIVE VENDOR

These Retail Store Window kits replace the plastic windows in Cornerstone Series®, City Classics and Design Preservation Models buildings. Sets include large windows and colorful signs (most for two different shops) for the first floor, with curtains, window shades or business lettering for upstairs windows. Each set is preprinted on thin acetate. Easily adapted to most eras, as well as scratchbuilt or kitbashed buildings.

FOR WALTHERS CORNERSTONE SERIES® BUILDINGS

398-1001 Gemini Building **4.25**
Flower shop, shoe repair or train/hobby shop.

398-2028 Merchants Row I **7.50**
S & L, real estate, beauty parlor and restaurant.
398-2029 Merchant's Row II **7.50**
398-2030 Merchants Row III Windows **TBA**
398-2034 Adam's Ribs Restaurant **4.25**

398-2033 Neighborhood Food Market **4.25**
Deli and pastry shops.

398-2032 Crown Paint & Hardware **6.25**
Mitchell's Army and Navy

398-1002 Bill's Glass **4.25**
Travel agent or bookstore.

STREET STRIPES TBA

398-3100 Yellow
398-3101 White

CITY CLASSICS EA 6.75

Each kit contains enough signs to fill-up four stories of windows.

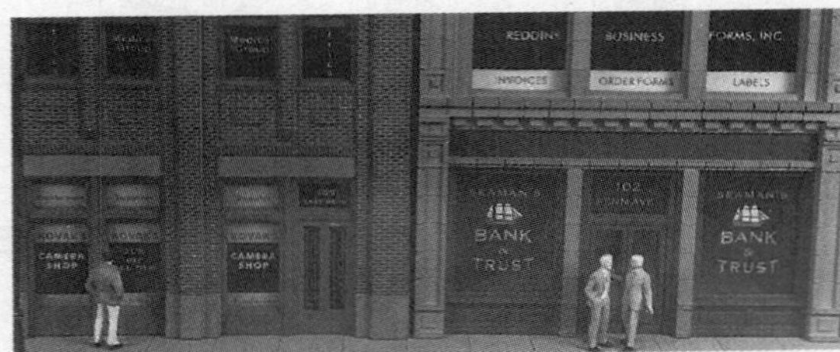

398-2335 102 Penn Ave. Tile-Front Building
398-2337 105 Baum Boulevard Art Deco Building
398-2336 101 Grant St. Iron Front Building

398-2338 East Ohio Street Building

FOR DESIGN PRESERVATION MODELS BUILDINGS

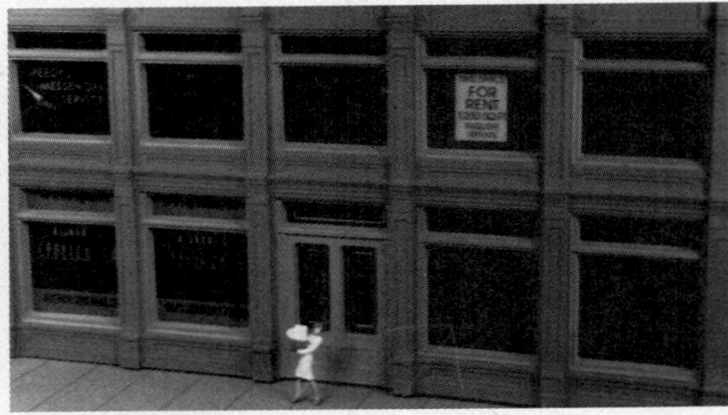

398-1117 J.C. Nickels **4.95**
Appliance and variety store, assorted services on upper floor.

398-1101 Kelly's Saloon **3.95**
Pool hall or barber shop.

398-1102 Robert's Dry Goods **4.50**
Tobacco or pawn shop.

398-1120 Front Street Building **4.50**
Accountant, laundry or tailor.

398-1104 B. Moore Catalog Showroom **4.95**
City cab or flooring store.

398-1105 Skip's Chicken & Ribs **3.95**
Hardware or seafood shop.

398-1108 Goodfellows Hall **4.50**
Drug store and ice cream parlor.

398-1113 Carol's Corner Cafe **4.50**
Coffee shop or produce market

398-1115 The Other Corner Cafe **4.50**
Meat market or newsstand/ fountain.

398-1116 Carr's Parts **4.50**
Harley cycle shop or plumbing & heating.

398-1119 M.T. Arms Hotel **6.50**
Window curtains, cafe or jewelry store.

398-1121 Seymour Block **4.95**
Bar, bakery or dry cleaners.

398-1122 Modular Venetian Blinds **4.50**
Includes 16 small for any factory, office or home, 14 medium and 7 large for DPM™ modular windows.

398-1123 Modular Curtains **4.50**
Includes 20 single windows in 4 colors, 4 double wide (side curtains & valence, 2 each in 2 colors).

398-1124 Modular Shades **3.95**
Includes 14 medium in 2 colors, 4 large in 2 colors.

BRIDGE & TRESTLE KITS

Skill Level 1 kits are designed for first-time builders (a few parts need cutting and fitting) and can be assembled with basic hobby tools. Skill Level 2 kits are for builders with some experience shaping, cutting or fitting parts and include assembly jigs to simplify some steps. All kits feature micro-cut basswood parts, many of which are precut and/or shaped. A variety of details are included. Each kit comes with a multi-page, step-by-step instruction manual with tips for installing the finished model on your layout, as well as customizing ideas.

SILVER CREEK TIMBER BRIDGE

SKILL 1 LEVEL

472-3050 19.95
10-3/8 x 2-9/16 x 2"
26.3 x 6.5 x 5.1cm
Cross obstacles by installing this bridge on your railroad. Skill Level 1 kit includes pre-cut wooden channels, beveled angle posts and a special construction jig so you can build with confidence. Can be used with all popular brands of track, including various track and roadbed systems.

FOX RIVER THRU-TRUSS BRIDGE

SKILL 2 LEVEL

472-3054 49.99
11-7/8 x 2-5/32 x 3-1/2"
29.7 x 5.4 x 8.8cm
Used primarily to span rivers, this Skill Level 2 kit allows modelers to construct their own thru-truss bridge. The pre-painted construction jig and guide blocks allow for accurate assembly. Kit include pre-cut, beveled wood parts, injection-molded nut-bolt-washer castings, music wire for tension rods, styrene for tension plates, drill bit, styrene U-channel stock and plan sheets.

CANYON CITY TRESTLE

SKILL 2 LEVEL

472-3051 44.95
14 x 6 x 3-3/8"
35.5 x 15.2 x 8.6cm
Create an accurate, authentic wooden trestle for any stretch of your layout. Versatile design can build straight, curved or S-curved structure. Includes vacuum-formed jig for trestle assembly. An injection-molded trestle buddy is provided so you can accurately locate the bents on your layout, taking the guesswork out of installation. Includes precut, beveled parts for 6" 15.2cm tall bents, scale lumber for all girts and diagonals, plus material for stringers. Instructions also cover building a longer or double-track model.

BOULDER CREEK DECK BRIDGE

SKILL 2 LEVEL

472-3052 39.95
9-7/16 x 2-5/32 x 2-7/32"
24 x 5.5 x 5.6cm
Skill Level 2 kit is easily installed with trestles or abutments (sold separately). Prototypes were frequently installed in the middle of a trestle to cross rivers, creeks or streams. Complete with material for stringers, a corner jig for accurately mitered corners, and a jig to assemble end panels. Music wire is provided for tension rods, along with the correct size drill bit for installation. Plastic nut-bolt-washer castings are included for the finishing touch. Instruction manual includes tips for building a shorter or narrow gauge version.

EAGLE PASS TRUSS BRIDGE

SKILL 2 LEVEL

472-3053 39.95
11-7/8 x 2-5/32 x 3-1/2"
30.1 x 5.4 x 8.9cm
Authentic truss bridge has lots of layout applications. Easily used as a display for a favorite car or loco too. Can be built with zero clearance for use on floor or plywood surface and used with all popular brands of flex or sectional track, including Bachmann EZ-Track™, Atlas True-Track® or Life-Like Power-Loc™. Skill Level 2 kit includes pre-beveled top chords and end angle braces, plus precut floor beams, bottom beams, vertical posts, stringer stock and more. Music wire and a matching diameter drill bit are included to build tension rods. Plastic nut-bolt-washer castings and strip styrene for iron plates are also included.

CONSTRUCTION ACCESSORIES

TRESTLE BUDDY

472-3049 14.95
Keep your trestle in perfect alignment from assembly through final installation with this ingenious flexible roadbed system. The Trestle Buddy is a chain of flexible joints that keep the bents properly spaced, and the top caps aligned in a plane to simplify installing sectional or flex track. It also holds the completed trestle securely while you install it on your layout. Once in place, remove the Buddy and add stringers, or leave in place and ballast it to model a decked trestle. Ideal for straight trackage. The complete flexibility allows easy construction of large, small or "S" curve trestles. One kit installs up to 6 bents of any height over a distance of 11 to 14" 27.9 to 35.5cm, and several can be combined to build longer structures. Each kit is complete with 8 plastic joints, nuts and bolts to secure track, rubber bands to temporarily hold bents in place, plus an illustrated assembly/use manual.

This line of craft train kits feature laser-cut Northeastern Lumber, Scale Works and Grandt Line details, color-coded stripwood and complete assembly instructions with templates.

2-IN-1 DERRICK/HOIST HOUSE

644-1 29.95

QUARRY STONE CUTTING BUILDING

644-2 98.95
Office: 2-3/8 x 1-3/4"
6 x 4.4cm
Main Building : 6-1/8 x 15-1/8"
15.6 x 38.4cm
Boiler House: 2 x 4-1/4"
5.1 x 10.8cm

Typical of New England quarrying buildings, this kit includes a cast polyurethane smokestack. Foundation pieces, plus other details included.

CHICKERING'S GRIST & FEED MILL

644-9 82.95
Kit includes laser-cut mill and waterwheel; cast foundation pieces and sluiceway materials.

YARD OFFICE

644-100 16.59
2-3/8 x 1-3/4" 6 x 4.4cm

YARD BUILDING

644-6 11.95

Information STATION

EARLY STATIONS

By the 1880s, railroad stations were unique structures. New depots were custom designed by architects to project a positive image of the railroad and the town it served. Based on these ideas, three principal styles were constructed.

The simplest were called flag-stops, because trains would only stop when a signal flag was displayed. These included covered platforms or shelters and tiny waiting room/office buildings. Most were only a few square feet in size and had a small platform trackside.

In towns where more passengers and packages were handled, a combination station was used. These larger buildings combined the freight handling and passenger waiting rooms into one structure. A ticket/telegraph/business office was included for the agent. Low platforms for passengers and taller freight platforms for wagons were used.

Bigger towns and cities had separate freight and passenger stations to allow space for each operation. Stations retained the office and platforms, but had separate waiting rooms for ladies and gentlemen. Some even boasted indoor restrooms - a very modern touch at the time. A separate baggage room was sometimes provided to store luggage until trains arrived. Most of the designs were flexible to build larger or smaller variations.

Capture the look of these classic American buildings for your layout with this series of easy-to-build kits. Models consist of very fine photo-etched brass and stainless steel parts that assemble in layers, producing detailed 3-D structures. Each comes complete with step-by-step, easy to follow instructions. Figures, vehicles and other details shown in photos are not included.

THE PARKWAY DINER

502-871001 69.95 ***NEW***
6-5/16" x 4-13/32" 15.7cm x 11cm
A great detail for busy streets from the 40s to the present. Made of real stainless steel with art deco style, just like the prototypes!

CITY SCOOP

502-871002 58.95 ***NEW***
3-5/8 x 3-3/4" 9.3cm x 9cm
The perfect place to spend those hot summer nights, hanging out with the classic car club or your buddies from school. Photo-etched stainless steel construction provides super realism. Colorful sign decals are included for the finishing touch.

GULF GAS STATION

502-879300 89.95 ***NEW***
6-1/8" x 3-5/8" 9cm x 15.2cm
Turn any empty corner into a superdetailed scene with this art deco style station. Licensed, HO Scale replica of the original Gulf design, reproduced in photo-etched brass. Complete with authentic decals and painting tips.

These craft train kits include laser-cut components which are accurate up to .001". Kits also include one or all of the following: white metal castings, brass castings, color signs, figures, scenery items, rust powder, electronics, lighting and more. All models include full assembly instructions.

HYDE PULP MILL

464-95 379.95
Expanded and modified over the years, this detailed industry converts scrap lumber and wood from the McCabe Logging operations into wood pulp for the paper industry. Lots of interesting construction elements and details.

MCCABE SAWDUST SHED

464-220 TBA
Kit includes laser-cut shed, foundation and many details, including a very nicely detailed blower and pipe system, with realistic hollow-top piping.

MCCABE POWER HOUSE

464-225 TBA
Many prototype operations used this type of set-up to run their mills and provide power for other buildings. Lots of piping is included to connect it to the sawmill or the Sawdust Shed, both sold separately.

MCCABE PUMP HOUSE

464-230 TBA
This kit houses a small, WORKING pump that's based on an interesting prototype, along with lots of other details.

MCCABE LOG DUMP

464-235 TBA
Make sure there's plenty of timber ready for cutting with these log dumps along your line. This kit includes a storage shed, trestle structure, dump structure and a crane. Many additional details are also provided.

LOGGING WAGONS

464-504 Assembled **39.95**
A delightful addition to your logging operations, this limited-edition (only 200 were made) model comes fully assembled from brass parts. Use it in a vintage setting or as a restored wagon outside the offices of a modern logging operation.

FLAGSTOP AT SLAPOUT

464-1400 22.95
Typical small town depot, can be used almost anywhere.

LOGGING BUNKHOUSES

464-1425 24.95
Lumberjacks will appreciate clean, comfortable quarters like these models, similar to a style used by the actual Westside Lumber Company. Kit includes parts for three structures and all wood items are laser-cut to speed construction. Roofs are removable so it's easy to add your own interiors.

JUNIOR'S SHINER

464-1405 24.95
This early mobile home fits any layout from the 1930's to the present. Great detail on the "wrong side of the tracks," a home for a hired hand on a farm or anywhere you can imagine. Includes laser-cut parts, venetian blinds, scale door handle, detail castings, scale screen wire, color awning and color instructions with an exploded view diagram.

CLEATORS GAS STATION

464-1410 24.95
First appearing in the 1920s, filling stations of this type were in service for many years. Kit includes pumps, island, color signs and other details. Can be superdetailed with Gas Station Detail Kit #774, listed in the Parts section.

PRITCHARD'S BARN

464-1420 29.95
The right size building for any scene, this small structure makes a great outbuilding down on the farm, or it could be any kind of industrial shop. A removable roof allows you to show off the full interior framing detail, and any interior details you might want to add. Scale door handles are also included. Color instructions with an exploded view diagram are also included.

SLADE'S ASSAY OFFICE

464-1430 24.95
A great office for any business, this small structure also makes a dandy little house. Kit includes four pewter wall castings and many small details. Laser-cut rafter tails, plus roof and porch parts are included. Full-color instructions provide additional detailing tips.

WILLET'S SUPPLY COMPANY

464-1435 32.95
Carrying just about anything and everything, this thriving business can be used in any city or town scene. Loads of details are included. Less figures.

BABE'S DINER

464-1440 34.95
A must for any layout from the 1930s to the 1950s, these eateries are coming back in many cities! Authentic Art Deco styling and full-color signs make this an eye-catcher along any HO highway.

MCCABE BACKWOODS ENGINE HOUSE

464-1450 39.95
Just the right size for a Shay, Heisler or Climax logging loco, this one-stall engine house has a removable roof so interior detailing can be added. A stencil is provided for the company name on the roof.

BUCK'S DYNAMITE BUILDING

464-1455 31.95
Highly detailed stone, brick and cement walls highlight this small explosives storage shed, which features laser-cut and metal parts. A great addition to any mine or construction scene.

KEE'S CHINESE LAUNDRY

464-1465 21.95
3-1/2 x 2-3/4" 8.7 x 6.8cm

The local laundry was an essential service in many western and boom towns. Here, miners, loggers, railroaders and residents alike could have their clothes cleaned good as new. The small building fits on any size layout and is right at home from the 1800s to the 1950s. The kit features laser-cut wood parts, brass door knobs, full-color signs and instructions. Can be combined with the Red Eye Saloon (464-1460) to create a unique building.

CLEGG'S CABIN

464-1470 12.95
Whether home to a miner or a fisherman's weekend get-away retreat, this small cabin will look great nestled in your scenery. Laser-cut walls feature realistic nail hole detail, also made with the laser. Laser-cut shingles, a brass doorknob and full-color instructions are all included.

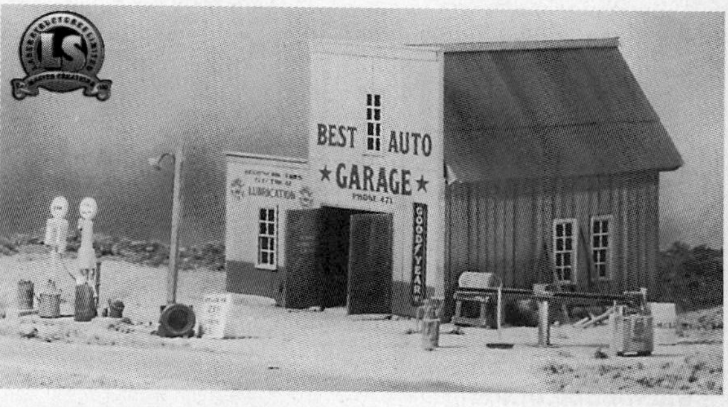

BEST AUTO GARAGE

464-1415 49.95
This charming kit is complete with pumps, island, color signs and many other exterior details.

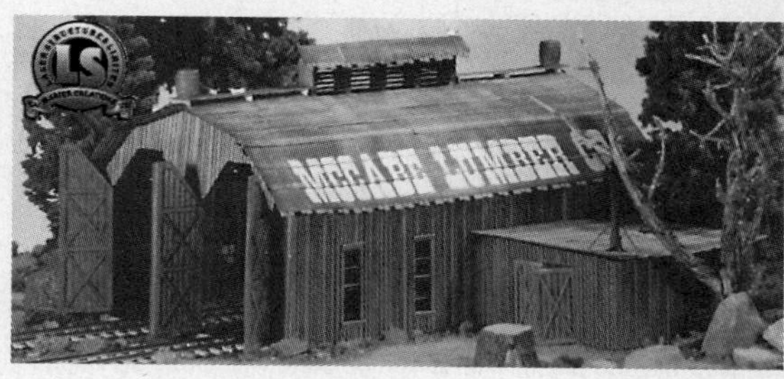

COYOTE DRAW ENGINE HOUSE

464-1445 49.95
When the McCabe Lumber Company outgrew their single stall shed (464-1450), they built this new two-stall building. Your shortline operations will be right at home in this detailed model which holds locos up to the size of a Westside 3-truck Shay. The building has laser-cut parts for a board-by-board look with far less work. Also includes full interior framing, scale brass door handles, photo-etched hinges, positionable windows and a side shop area. The building can be constructed with a removable roof if desired. Color instructions with an exploded view diagram are provided, along with an interactive MCinfodisk catalog, with additional views of the model.

RED EYE SALOON

464-1460 19.95
3-1/2 x 1-5/8" 8.7 x 6.8cm
Saloons like these could be found on many western main streets from the 1800s to the 1950s. The kit is complete with laser-cut wood parts, brass door knobs, full-color signs and complete instructions. Small size fits any layout, and the model is designed so it can be kitbashed with Kee's Chinese Laundry (464-1465) to create a unique building.

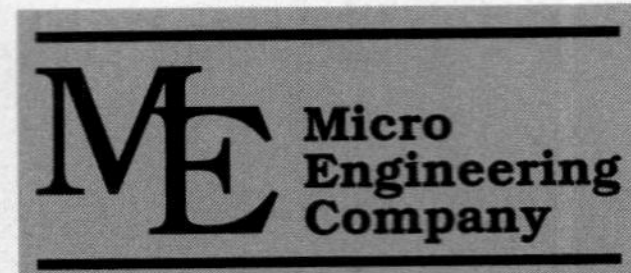

OLD TIME BUILDINGS
False front buildings include plastic windows and doors and white metal details.

MODERN BUILDINGS
Injection molded styrene kits feature precolored parts. Choice of various door and window locations. Includes steps, sidewalks, pallets and ventilators.

CITY VIADUCTS
Includes HO Code 83 Bridge Flex-Trak™. Details include girder lateral bracing, girder X-bracing, lattice bracing, cross lacing, bridge shoes and extensive rivet detail.

TALL STEEL VIADUCTS
Includes HO Code 83 Bridge Flex-Trak™. Details include girder X-bracing, bent X-bracing, tower bracing, rivet plates, bridge shoes and extensive cross-lacing and rivet detail.

DECK GIRDER BRIDGES
Includes Bridge Flex-Trak™. Details include lateral bracing, X-bracing, bridge shoes and extensive rivet detail.

THRU GIRDER BRIDGES
Injection-molded plastic kits come complete with Code 83 Bridge Flex-Trak™ and a "concrete" trough or troughs which allow the bridge to be built with either an open or ballasted deck.

HO CITY VIADUCT 90' SINGLE TRACK
255-75509 18.85

HO CITY VIADUCT 90' DOUBLE TRACK
255-75510 29.95

HO CITY VIADUCT 150' SINGLE TRACK
255-75511 29.95

HO CITY VIADUCT 150' DOUBLE TRACK
255-75512 46.15

CITY VIADUCT TOWER
255-80168 5.25
3-1/2" high.

HO COMBINATION BRIDGE, 110' THREE SPAN
255-75530 26.35
15-1/8 x 3-3/4"
Includes two 30' deck girder bridges and one 50' thru girder bridge.

150' HO TALL STEEL VIADUCT
255-75514 35.20

150' HOn3 TALL STEEL VIADUCT
255-75516 35.20

HO COMBINATION BRIDGE, 160' FOUR SPAN
255-75532 31.85
22 x 3-3/4"
Includes two 30' deck girder bridges and two 50' thru girder bridges.

DECK GIRDER BRIDGES, OPEN DECK

255-75501 HO 50' **7.30**
7 x 1-3/8" 18 x 3.5cm

255-75502 HO 30' **6.55**
4-1/8 x 1-3/8" 10.5 x 3.5cm

255-75503 HOn3 50' **7.30**
7 x 1-3/8" 18 x 3.5cm

255-75504 HOn3 30' **6.55**
4-1/8 x 1-3/8" 10.5 x 3.5cm

DECK GIRDER BRIDGES, BALLASTED DECK

255-75507 HO 50' **7.30**
7 x 1-13/16" 18 x 4.5cm
Less track and ballast.

255-75508 HO 30' **6.55**
4-1/8 x 1-13/16" 10.5 x 4.5cm
Less track and ballast.

TALL STEEL VIADUCT TOWER
255-80169 7.95
10" high.

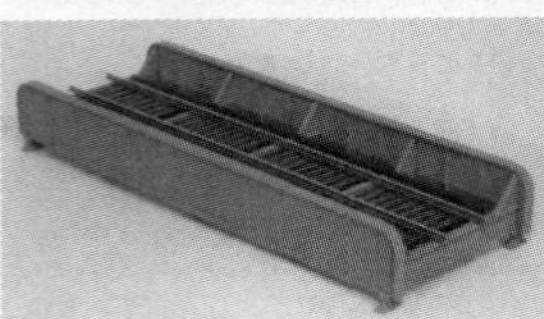

HO THRU GIRDER BRIDGE 50' SINGLE TRACK
255-75520 9.95

HO THRU GIRDER BRIDGE 50' DOUBLE TRACK
255-75521 15.70

HO THRU GIRDER BRIDGE 100' SINGLE TRACK
255-75522 17.80
Includes center support legs.

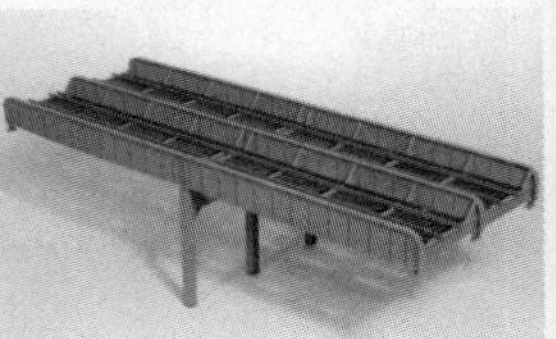

HO THRU GIRDER BRIDGE 100' DOUBLE TRACK
255-75523 28.90
Includes center support legs.

BRIDGE SUPPORT
255-80175 7.30
3-3/8 x 9-1/2" 8.4 x 24cm

OUTHOUSE
255-80172 2.50

TRANS WORLD TRUCK TERMINAL
255-55005 15.70
4-1/4 x 13-1/2" 10.8 x 34.2cm

PETROFF PLUMBING SUPPLY
255-55006 15.70
8-3/8 x 9-1/2" 21.1 x 24cm

GROGER'S GROCERY
255-70604 11.50
5 x 5" 12.8 x 12.8cm
Includes signs, awning, shed and clutter parts

MURPHY MANUFACTURING
255-55004 13.60
4-1/4 x 9-1/2" 10.8 x 24cm

All structures are molded in appropriately colored plastic.

MOUNTAIN CHAPEL
528-64800 6.99

MOUNTAIN LODGE
528-64810 6.99

LOOKOUT POST/ACCESS
528-64900 6.99

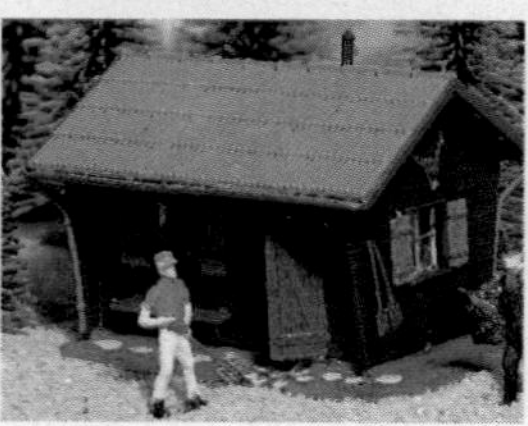

FOREST CABIN
528-64840 6.99

WEEKEND HOUSE
528-64850 6.99

FRUIT STAND
528-64830 6.99

SNACKBAR
528-64820 6.99

1.5' BRIDGE PIER
528-21410 pkg(5) **8.99**
1/4" .5cm
Can be used with #21400 to build a higher pier.

9' BRIDGE PIER
528-21400 pkg(5) **13.99**
1-1/4" 3cm high
Realistic detail for any Noch bridge.

DOUBLE BRIDGE PIERS
528-21420 14.99
3-3/4" 9.4cm high

STRAIGHT STEEL BRIDGE
528-21340 9.99
7 x 2-1/4" 17.8 x 5.7cm

CURVED STEEL BRIDGE
528-21350 9.99
7 x 2-1/4" 17.8 x 5.7cm

SMALL FOOT BRIDGES
528-11050 pkg(4) **8.99**

LAGGIES BRIDGE KITS

PYLON SUSPENSION BRIDGE
528-53506 92.99
14-1/2" 36cm
Modern suspension bridge with single support piling.

STRAIGHT BRIDGE SECTION
528-53508 19.99
7" 18cm
Straight section to lengthen #53506.

CURVED BRIDGE SECTION
528-53509 19.99
7" 18cm
Curved section for approaches to #53506.

GIRDER BRIDGE
528-21310 24.99
14 x 1-3/4" high 36 x 4.5cm

THRU TRUSS BRIDGE
528-21320 24.99
14 x 2-1/4" 35.6 x 5.7cm

TRUSS BRIDGE
528-21330 13.99
7 x 2-1/4" 17.8 x 5.7cm

These HO, easy-to-build kits include pre-colored plastic parts and step-by-step instructions. 500 series are built-up structures.

KITS

FERTILIZER BUNKER W/FERTILIZER
490-313 16.99 *NEW*

OFFICES & OFFICE ACCESSORIES
490-314 16.99 *NEW*

OLD COAL MINE
490-316 34.98 *NEW*

CONVEYOR W/INDUSTRIAL ACCESSORIES
490-320 14.98 *NEW*

MOVABLE CRANE
490-315 16.99 *NEW*

HOFFA CEMENT FACTORY
490-297 22.99 *NEW*
490-670 Built Up 34.98 *NEW*

HOFFA STORAGE SILOS & OFFICES
490-298 22.99 *NEW*

HOFFA SAND BUNKER
490-299 18.99 *NEW*
490-671 Built Up 18.99 *NEW*

LOADING BRIDGE
490-300 22.99 *NEW*
490-646 Built Up 34.99 *NEW*

UNLOADING CRANE
490-303 18.49 *NEW*

GRADING TOWER
490-301 22.99 *NEW*
490-647 Built Up 34.99 *NEW*

SILO & TRANSPORTER
490-302 18.99 *NEW*

OFFICES & SHED
490-304 14.99 *NEW*
490-650 Built Up 21.99 *NEW*

IRS ON FIRE
490-470 39.98

2-STORY RAILROAD STATION
490-480 19.98
9-1/2 x 5" 24 x 12.5cm

LUMBER YARD
490-407 17.98
4 x 6" 10 x 15cm

INDUSTRIAL BUILDING
490-458 18.98

BLUE COAL DEPOT
490-453 19.98
4 x 6-1/2" 10.2 x 16.5cm

TWO STATION PLATFORMS
490-478 pkg(2) 18.98
each: 2 x 14" 5.5 x 36cm

CHESTER STATION
490-454 17.98
4 x 7-3/4" 11 x 9.7cm

SILVERADO STATION
490-605 18.98
4-1/4 x 6-1/2" 11 x 16cm

REDWOOD STATION
490-564 Built Up 21.98

SMALL FREIGHT STATION
490-404 13.98
6-3/4 x 3-3/4" 17 x 7cm

PORT CHESTER STATION
490-542 18.98
5-3/8 x 12-3/8" 13.7 x 31.6cm

WHISTLE STOP STATION
490-444 12.98
490-562 Built Up 15.98

RAIL CRANE
490-424 14.98
3 x 9-1/2" 7.7 x 24cm

WATER TANK W/SHED
490-428 pkg(2) **15.98**
490-561 Built Up **17.98**
tank: 3-1/2 x 4" 9 x 10.4cm
shed: 1-3/4 x 2" 4.5 x 5.4cm

COALING STATION
490-410 19.98
490-560 Built Up **25.98**
6 x 6" 15.3 x 15.3cm

RAILROAD SIGNAL BRIDGE
490-419 5.98
4 x 5-1/2" 10.2 x 14cm

GLOBE NEWS & PRINTING
490-477 17.98
490-578 Built Up **21.98**
6-3/4 x 9-1/4" 17 x 23.5cm
Hand-weathered.

Hot New Products Announced Daily! Visit Walthers Web site at

www.walthers.com

HEINZ PICKLE FACTORY
490-465 19.50
5-1/2 x 12" 14 x 30.5cm

OVER & UNDER PIER SET
490-99 5.98

TRACKSIDE MAINTENANCE
490-408 pkg(3) **13.98**
Storage Shed: 1-3/4 x 2"
4.5 x 5.1cm

Transformer Box: 1-1/4 x 2"
4.5 x 5.1cm

Shed w/Extension: 3 x 8"
7.6 x 20.3cm

ROOMING HOUSE
490-426 16.98
6-1/4 x 6-1/2" 16 x 16.5cm

LITTLE RED SCHOOL HOUSE
490-604 16.98
3-1/2 x 5-1/2" 8.9 x 14cm

BUILDING UNDER DEMOLITION
490-469 18.98
4-1/2 x 8-1/2" 11.5 x 21cm

BARN
490-601 15.98
490-567 Built Up **19.98**
4-5/16 x 5-1/2" 11 x 14cm

URBAN RENEWAL PROJECT
490-420 19.98
490-579 Built Up **21.98**
4-1/2 x 9-1/4" 11.4 x 23.5cm

FIRE HOUSE W/2 ENGINES
490-409 17.98
4-1/2 x 5-1/4" 11.5 x 13.5cm

HAUNTED HOUSE
490-486 17.98
490-586 Built Up **19.98**
7-1/2 x 9" 19 x 23cm

INTERLOCKING TOWER
490-481 14.98

MODERN HOUSE
490-606 15.98
5 x 3-1/4" 12.7 x 8.2cm

DELTA FRATERNITY HOUSE
490-456 18.98
3-1/2 x 7" 9 x 17.5cm

FARM HOUSE
490-433 16.98
3 x 7" 7.7 x 17.7cm

SULLIVAN HOUSE
490-488 17.98
490-588 Built Up **19.98**
7-1/2 x 9" 19 x 23cm

BLINKING BRIDGE
490-111 6.98

HIGH TRESTLE BRIDGE
490-112 10.98

TRUSS BRIDGE
490-102 5.98

BELLA'S FARM HOUSE
490-490 17.98
7-1/2 x 9" 19 x 23cm

JORDAN'S HOUSE
490-590 Built Up **19.98**

MOVING IN HOUSE
490-484 17.98
7-1/2 x 9" 19 x 23cm

MR. & MRS DIGGER'S HOUSE
490-489 17.98
7-1/2 x 9" 19 x 23cm

SIMPSON'S HOUSE
490-589 Built Up 19.98

BURNED TOWNHOUSE
490-466 16.98
2-3/4 x 6" 7 x 15cm

THE GRABITSKI HOUSE
490-485 17.98
7-1/2 x 9" 19 x 23cm

MR. ROGERS' HOUSE
490-585 Built-Up 18.98
4 x 4-1/2" 10.2 x 11.4cm

GRANDMA'S HOUSE
490-487 17.98
490-587 Built Up 19.98
7-1/2 x 9" 19 x 23cm

2 TWIN CAPE COD HOUSES
490-479 pkg(2) 17.98
3-3/4 x 5" 9.5 x 12.5cm

GIRDER BRIDGES EA 5.98
Models are fully assembled with realistic, brown painted ties, colorful railroad logos and two figures.
490-120 ATSF
490-121 PRR

DECK BRIDGE
490-103 5.98
Fully assembled with brown painted ties and two figures.

ROBERT SHAW WINE & CHEESE
490-543 12.98
3-3/8 x 7-3/8" 8.6 x 18.9cm

LUIGI'S LA TROTTERIA
490-544 12.98
3-3/8 x 7-3/8" 8.6 x 18.9cm

CATHY'S FLOWER SHOP
490-545 12.98
3-3/8 x 7-3/8" 8.6 x 18.9cm

SPOTLESS DRY CLEANERS
490-546 12.98
3-3/8 x 7-3/8" 8.6 x 18.9cm

HOUSE W/GARAGE
490-425 15.98
4 x 6-3/4" 10 x 14.5cm

MARRYIN' SAM'S CHAPEL
490-457 18.98
3-1/2 x 7" 8.8 x 17.8cm

2 STORY POLICE STATION
490-447 20.00
5-3/4 x 11-1/4" 14.6 x 28.5cm

BUILDING ON FIRE
490-449 18.98
490-569 Built Up 24.98
2-3/4 x 6" 7 x 15.2cm

MERCEDES CAR AGENCY
490-429 19.98
5-1/4 x 8-1/2" 13.3 x 21.6cm

RILEYS BUILDING RENOVATION
490-468 16.98
2-3/4 x 6" 7 x 15cm

ANNIE'S ANTIQUES
490-464 18.98
3-1/2 x 6" 9 x 15.2cm

WESTERN UNION OFFICE
490-452 17.98
4-1/2 x 6-1/2" 11.5 x 16.5cm

JAN'S ICE CREAM PARLOR
490-475 18.98
7 x 4-1/4" 18 x 11cm
Hand-weathered.

REAL ESTATE OFFICE
490-442 14.98
3-7/8 x 4-1/2" 10 x 12cm

INTERSTATE FREIGHT
490-411 16.98
490-574 Built Up 18.98
3-1/2 x 7" 8.4 x 18cm

GEORGE'S GROCERY
490-463 18.98
3-1/2 x 6" 9 x 15.2cm

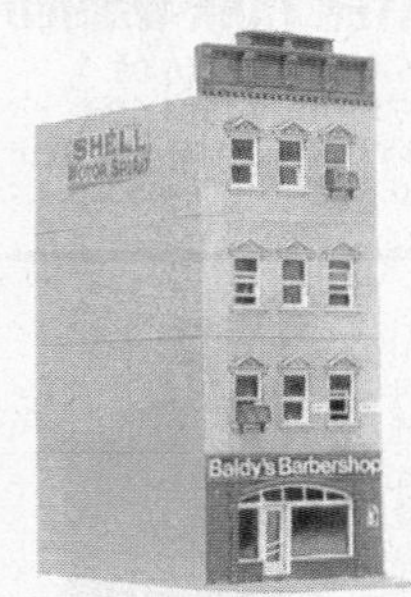

BALDY'S BARBER SHOP
490-472 18.98
2-3/4 x 6" 7 x 15.2cm

JIMMY'S BARBER SHOP
490-462 18.98
3-1/2 x 6" 9 x 15.2cm

PURE WATER SUPPLY CO.
490-415 18.98
490-563 Built Up 20.98

ACE HARDWARE
490-461 18.98
490-577 Built Up 20.98
3-1/2 x 7" 9 x 17.7cm

BUILDING INTERIOR & LIGHTING KIT
490-602 10.98
Includes 3 interior lights with wire, sockets and bulbs, plus assorted furniture.

SNEED'S FEEDS & TOOLS
490-474 18.98
3-1/2 x 6" 9 x 15.2cm

NATURAL GAS SUPPLY CO.
490-417 16.98

BUILDERS DEPOT
490-418 16.98

NICK'S PICKLES
490-471 18.98
3-1/2 x 6" 9 x 15.2cm

UNITED MILLS FACTORY
490-455 18.98
3-1/2 x 7" 9 x 17.8cm

CITY POWER STATION NO. 15
490-416 15.98

MICKY'S FRUIT STAND
490-476 18.98
5 x 5" 12.5 x 12.5cm
Hand-weathered.

THRU-WAY TRUCKSTOP
490-607 17.98
6 x 6-3/4" 15.2 x 17.1cm

AVERILL GOLD REFINING CO.
490-423 15.98
7-1/2 x 4-1/2" 19 x 11.5cm

DURKIN PICKLE FACTORY
490-573 Built Up 20.98

TRESTLE BRIDGE 15PC SET
490-79 4.98

BILLY'S AUTO BODY
490-414 16.98
490-575 Built Up 19.98
5 x 6" 12.5 x 15.4cm

BOB'S HOT DOG STAND
490-441 13.98
490-573 Built Up 15.98
2-1/2 x 4-1/4" 6.5 x 10.8cm

CITIBANK
490-445 19.98
3-5/8 x 8-1/4" 9.2 x 21cm

POWER STATION
490-443 12.98
490-580 Built Up 18.98

SHELL SERVICE CENTER
490-549 19.98
Keep your car or truck on the road in this modern service station.

DUAL LOCO SHED
490-541 19.98

GRAIN SILOS
490-307 19.98
490-653 Built Up 34.98

BANKED PIER SET W/GIRDER BRIDGE
490-113 10.98

TWIN OIL TANKS
490-308 15.98
490-654 Built Up 24.98

TANK FILLING STATION
490-309 15.98
490-655 Built Up 27.98

BREWERY
490-451 19.98

GRAIN DEPOT
490-305 22.98
490-651 Built Up 34.98

GRAIN ELEVATOR
490-306 22.98
490-652 Built Up 34.98

3500 GALLON TANKS
490-1455 pkg(4) 9.98

STATION & FREIGHT SHED
490-427 19.98
490-570 Built Up 25.98

HUNTER'S LOG CABIN
490-434 8.98
490-640 Built Up 12.98

OLD STORAGE SHED
490-435 8.98
490-641 Built Up 12.98

LUMBER SHED
490-436 11.98
490-642 Built Up 13.98

3 TRACKSIDE BUILDINGS
490-437 11.98
490-643 Built Up 14.98

RANGER LOOKOUT W/TREES
490-438 8.98
490-644 Built Up 11.98

FISHERMAN'S CABIN
490-439 8.98
490-645 Built Up 12.98

TRACKSIDE YARD TOWER
490-551 8.98
490-627 Built Up 11.98

INDUSTRIAL WATER TOWER
490-552 8.98
490-628 Built-Up 10.98

LOCO MAINTENANCE BUILDING
490-553 18.98
490-629 Built-Up 24.98

DELUXE BARN KIT
490-482 17.98
490-592 Built Up 23.98

OIL FACILITY OFFICE
490-310 14.98 *NEW*
490-656 Built Up 18.98

TWIN HIGH OIL TANKS
490-311 19.98
490-657 Built Up 34.98

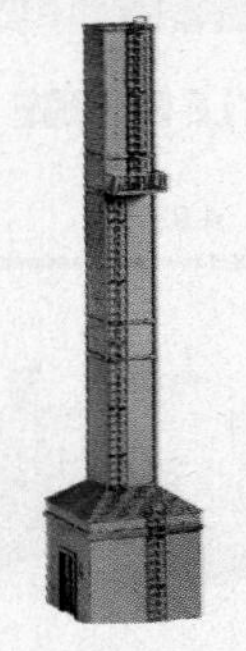

FACTORY SMOKE STACK
490-312 12.98

EMBASSY
490-540 18.98

STEAM LOCOMOTIVE SUPPLY DEPOT
490-617 19.98
490-572 Built Up 23.98

KITS W/FIGURES

RAILROAD PLATFORMS
490-612 pkg(4) 15.98
1 x 6-1/2" 2.5 x 16.5cm

WEST END SHOPPING CENTER
490-615 17.98
Four small shops in one building.

2-STORY HOUSE
490-609 18.98
3-3/8 x 4-3/8" 8.6 x 11.1cm

CHURCH
490-613 17.98
490-582 Built Up 19.98
7-1/2 x 9" 19 x 22.9cm

TWIN LOCO SHED
490-611 19.98
10 x 6-13/16" 25.7 x 17.4cm

ADMINISTRATION OFFICE & FACTORY COMPLEX
490-610 22.98
Office: 3-1/8 x 7-13/16"
7.9 x 19.9cm
Factory: 3-13/16"
7.9 x 20cm

DELUXE GAS TANKS EA 19.98
490-618 Shell
490-619 Gulf

LENNY'S CLAM BOX
490-608 17.98
5-1/2 x 6-13/16" 14 x 17.4cm

AMERICAN MACHINE & FOUNDRY
490-614 17.98

STATION PLATFORM
490-616 15.98
490-583 Built Up 19.98

ASSEMBLED & LIGHTED BUILDINGS W/2 FIGURES

SINATRA'S HOUSE
490-584 18.98
2-5/8 x 5-1/2" 6.7 x 14cm

WATER TOWER
490-630 10.98

SEARCH TOWER
490-631 10.98

DELUXE SHELL TANK LTD
490-565 25.98
6-1/2 x 6-1/2" 16.2 x 16.2cm

DURANGO STATION PLATFORM
490-566 19.98
4-1/4 x 6-3/4" 10.6 x 16.8cm

HOUSE ON FIRE
490-568 19.98

GULF GAS TANK
490-571 25.98

ARMY MOTOR POOL
490-667 24.98

ARMY MUNITION DEPOT W/2 MINITANKS
490-668 24.98

NORTHEASTERN SCALE MODELS INC.

These small trackside structures are easy to assemble laser-cut kits that feature multiple use buildings that can be placed in nearly any small area on your layout. Kits do not include detailing parts.

MOTOR CAR SHED
521-40004 7.95 *NEW*

PASSENGER SHELTER
521-40001 6.95 *NEW*

STORAGE SHED
521-40002 8.95 *NEW*

WATCH BOX
521-40005 pkg(2) 5.95 *NEW*

WATCH TOWER
521-40006 7.95 *NEW*

FREIGHT DEPOT
521-40003 19.95 *NEW*

EARL SMALLSHAW'S TENEMENT ROW
521-20108 pkg(3) 119.95 *NEW*

SEQUOIA SCALE MODELS

These craft train kits include stripwood and/or diecut scribed wood, and metal castings.

BRANCH LINE PASSENGER STATION
135-4005 5.95
1-1/2 x 2" 4 x 5cm

SANDY RIVER GALLOWS TURNTABLE
135-4007 15.95
Based on a turntable used on Maine's famous Sandy River & Rangely Lakes, this detailed kit is a perfect choice for your shortline engine facilities.

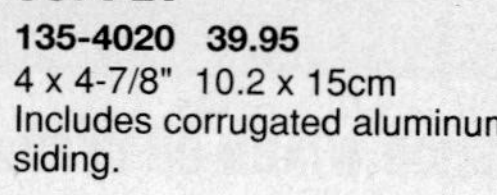

RON'S ELECTRICAL SUPPLY
135-4020 39.95
4 x 4-7/8" 10.2 x 15cm
Includes corrugated aluminum siding.

These craft train kits feature molded plastic parts with separate doors and windows. All wall sections are molded without window or door openings, enabling you to add them where you want. Easily kitbashed or combined with more kits to build a larger structure.

MILTON A. CORPORATION
541-104 29.95
4-1/8 x 8-1/4" 10.3 x 20.6cm
9-3/4 x 11 x 7" 24.3 x 27.5 x 17.5cm
Add interest to any industrial park with the character and versatility of this kit. Includes a rail car-height door for inside unloading, with freight doors for outside truck and railroad service. Versatile design uses parts from other kits, and can be arranged to fit just about any space.

SHOP W/ADD-ON OFFICE

541-15 18.95
70 x 80 scale feet

FIRE STATION
541-19 Blue **9.95**
541-191 Green **9.95**
541-192 Red **9.95**
7 x 5-1/2" 17.5 x 12.5cm
This modern building will be the pride of your small town volunteers. Features three apparatus bays and comes in your choice of red, green or blue.

MODERN 2-STORY OFFICE BUILDING
541-5002 8.45

THE WAREHOUSE

541-4 11.95
4-1/8 x 8-1/4" 10.8 x 21cm

YARD OFFICE
541-16 6.95
Includes material to build one of three heights; 12', 18', 22 x 40' scale feet.

AUTO REPAIR SHOP
541-9 14.95
3-1/2 x 8-1/4" 9 x 21cm

DIAMOND TOOL & ENGINEERING CO.
541-18 10.95
5-1/2 x 8-1/4" 14 x 21cm

TRI-STAR INDUSTRIES
541-20 Blue **12.95**
541-201 Green **12.95**
9-5/8 x 8-1/4" 24.5 x 21cm

RETAIL/WAREHOUSE CENTER
541-7 16.95
4-1/4 x 8-1/4" 10.8 x 21cm
Includes outdoor sign and decals for a variety of stores.

DISTRIBUTION CENTER
541-10 11.95
9-5/8 x 5-1/2" 24.5 x 14cm

ADD-ON WALL SECTION FOR MOST KITS
541-14 3.25
20 scale feet long.

ADD-ON OFFICE SHOWROOM
541-11 5.99

MACHINE TOOL CENTER

541-101 15.95
Includes one each: Smalltown, USA Hardware Kit, USA Sidewalks Kit, Three Size Yard Office and Loading Docks.

RAIL/TRUCK TRANSFER FACILITY

541-100 17.98

MOTOR FREIGHT TERMINAL

541-5001 9.95
4-3/16 x 11-1/8"
10.5 x 28cm

MULTI-PURPOSE STEEL BUILDING

541-5005 9.25

MODERN 1 OR 2 STALL ENGINE HOUSE

541-8 14.95
5-1/2 x 11" 14 x 28cm

CONTRACTORS BUILDING

541-5006 9.95

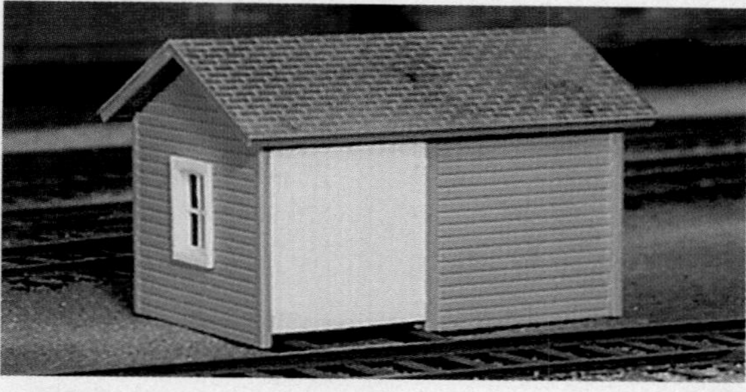

WOOD HANDCAR SHED

541-6 3.50
1-5/8 x 1-1/4" 4.2 x 3.2cm

PIPING & MECHANICAL CONTRACTORS

541-103 16.95

CONTRACTORS BUILDING

541-5006 9.95

SMALL YARD OFFICE

541-5 3.95
1-5/8 x 1-1/4" 4.2 x 3.2cm

MODERN SMALL ENGINE HOUSE

541-5000 8.25
4-3/16 x 8-5/16" 10.5 x 21cm

U&K PLASTICS

541-102 17.95
Includes a factory that's 70' wide 60' deep, plus an attached two-story office that measures 50' wide by 40' deep. All wall sections are molded in "Monsoon Green" so no painting is needed. Also includes concrete parking barriers, for the employee lot.

LOADING DOCKS & RAMP

541-17 3.99
Includes ramp and four modular docks, each scale 40' long, 10' wide and 5'3" tall.

EXTENSION KITS (ADD-ON WALL SECTIONS)

541-141 Green 3.25
541-142 Red 3.25
Make virtually any of the modern metal buildings larger. Includes two wall sections molded in color, plus white roof and other details.

YARD OFFICE KIT

541-162 6.95

ATKINSON ENGINE FACILITY

541-5007 17.95

OREGON RAIL SUPPLY

MENOMONEE FALLS DEPOT

538-501 44.95
16 x 5" 40.6 x 12.7cm
Easy-to-build plastic kit, molded in color.

Plastruct

These craft train kits feature a variety of plastic shapes and parts and are complete with construction plans.

PETRO/CHEMICAL REFINERY

570-1008 79.95
20 x 24" 51 x 70cm
Keep petroleum or chemical products moving on your layout with this superb kit! Includes all of the piping, angles, valves, tanks and other details to model a storage and rail car loading facility. Flexible design allows you to put the various components where you want them. Complete instructions and blueprints are included.

STEEL MILL FAKEFRONT

570-1030 44.95
22 x 3 x 12" 56 x 7.5 x 30cm
Fill background voids and add an impressive structure at the same time. Design versatility allows use in several types of industrial settings as well as the switching of building positions. Designed for HO Scale, but with slight modifications, may also be used in N, S and possibly O. Complete instructions and blueprints are included.

WELDED STEEL WATER TANK

570-1009 23.95
3-1/2" diameter 9cm diameter
100,000 gallon, used during the last days of steam.

TWIN LAMP POSTS

570-1012 pkg(4) **6.95**
6-1/4" high, nonoperating.

OIL STORAGE TANK

570-1015 14.95
2-1/4 x 3-1/4" 5.7 x 8.3cm
For expanding your refinery, tank farm or bulk oil distribution center.

TWIN LP GAS STORAGE TANKS

570-1019 pkg(2) **17.95**
1-1/2" 3.81cm diameter, 10" 25.4cm long

UTILITY WATER TOWER

570-1016 16.95
2 x 2 x 15"
5.08 x 5.08 x 38.1cm.
A must for all modern industries. Adjustable height.

PROPANE STORAGE TANK

570-1017 10.95
1-1/2 x 5" 3.81 x 12.7cm
Can be used at refineries, large industries or propane distributors.

SIDE BY SIDE VERTICAL TANKS

570-1018 24.95
3" 7.62cm tall,
1-1/2" 3.81cm diameter.
Use as chemical tanks or silos.

2" OIL TANK

570-94876 pkg(2) **3.25**
45/64" 1.27cm tall,
2" 5.08cm diameter.

ELECTRICAL TOWERS & OIL WELL

570-1005 21.95
Contains enough material to build either one Oil Well Derrick or one each of the Transmission Towers.

SAND TOWER

570-1011 10.95
1 x 6-3/4" 2.5 x 17.2cm
Includes material for concrete slabs, walkways, etc.

SILOS & GRAIN ELEVATORS

570-1025 47.95
Tanks: 3 x 7" 7.6 x 17.7cm

Office: 3-1/8 x 2-1/8"
7.9 x 5.4cm

Elevator: 3/4 x 1 x 15"
1.9 x 2.54 x 38.1cm
An important industry on every railroad. Typical of smaller facilities, includes three silos, headhouse, and small office building.

CONE ROOF ELEVATED WATER TANK

570-1028 21.95
Probably the most common style of water tower found in industrial settings.

3-1/2" TOWER

570-94893 5.00

5-1/2" TOWER

570-94892 5.50

8" TOWER

570-94891 6.25

SPHERICAL STORAGE TANK

570-1026 20.95
3 x 3-1/2" 7.6 x 8.9cm

EXTERNAL FLOATING ROOF TANK

570-1027 32.95
5 x 4" 12.7 x 10.1cm

TWIN BULK OIL STORAGE TANKS

570-1014 16.95
2-1/4 x 5-1/4" 5.7 x 13.3cm

WATER TANKS

570-94884 1/4" O.D. .6cm pkg(8) **2.50**
570-94883 1/2" O.D. .2cm pkg(4) **2.75**
570-94882 1" O.D. 2.5cm pkg(2) **3.50**
570-94881 1-3/4" O.D. 4.5cm **3.50**

OLD TIME MOVING BRIDGE

570-1007 24.95
24" long, 13-1/2" wide over piers 70cm long 34.5cm wide. Opens horizontally using a central pivoting system.

TRUSS BRIDGE

570-1002 20.95

SIMPLE SPAN BRIDGE

570-1001 15.95
15-1/8" 38.4cm
Includes parts for concrete overpass and simple beam bridge.

GAS PUMP

570-94872 pkg(3) **3.95**

SERVICE PLATFORMS

570-1010 pkg(2) **13.95**
3-1/2 x 1" 9 x 2.5cm

P&M BRIDGES & BENTS

Cross obstacles along your right-of-way in no time with these wood kits and fully assembled models. The finished items are typical of railroad bridges or trestles found on almost every line and can be used in any time period.

TRUSS BRIDGES - ASSEMBLED

12"
551-400 Single Track **46.98**
551-401 Double Track **56.98**

18"

551-402 Single Track **59.98**

551-403 Double Track **69.98**

24"
551-404 Single Track **79.98**
551-405 Double Track **89.98**

SINGLE TRACK BENTS

551-300 21' High pkg(2) **5.98**
551-301 41' High pkg(2) **6.98**
551-302 62' High pkg(2) **7.98**
551-303 82' High pkg(2) **8.98**
551-304 102' High pkg(2) **10.98**
551-305 122' High pkg(2) **12.98**

SINGLE TRACK TRESTLE KITS

551-340 Low 21' High **23.98**

551-341 Standard 21' to 41' High **25.98**
551-342 High 21' to 62' High **26.98**

DOUBLE TRACK BENTS

551-320 21' High **6.49**
551-321 41' High **7.49**
551-322 62' High **8.49**
551-323 82' High **9.49**
551-324 102' High **11.49**

DOUBLE TRACK TRESTLE KITS

551-360 Low 21' High **25.98**
551-361 Standard 21' to 41' High **27.98**
551-362 High 21' to 62' High **28.98**

12" THRU TRUSS BRIDGES

551-406 Single Kit **38.98**
551-407 Double Kit **48.98**

TURNTABLE BRIDGE

551-408 "A" Frame Turntable Bridge Kit **14.98**

12" LONG EXTENSION KITS FOR ADDING BENTS

551-420 Single Track **8..98**
551-421 Double Track **10.49**

Information STATION

Tunnel Tidbits

At 901 feet long, the Staple Bend Tunnel, east of Johnstown, Pennsylvania, on the Allegheny Portage Railroad, was the first American railroad tunnel. The tunnel itself became open for use on October 7, 1834. It cost the J. & E. Applton company $37,500 to complete the tunnel. It is twenty feet wide, nineteen feet high and is lined with cut stone for 150 feet at each end.

Tunnels were in existence long before they were introduced on the American continent, however. An underground line at Newcastle upon Tyne, England, produced the first railway tunnel. This tunnel was first built in 1770. However, railroad passengers had to wait until 1830 to ride passenger service through a man-made tunnel. The Tyler Hill Tunnel first opened for crossing on May 4, 1830 for transit along the Canterbury & Whistle Railway.

Not long after above-ground tunnels were in place, underwater tunnels began to surface below the depths of the world's greatest bodies of water. The Thames Tunnel was first opened to pedestrian traffic in March of 1843, and is now a part of the London Transport system

These HO, easy-to-build plastic kits have European prototypes — most can be Americanized with minor modifications. Parts are injection molded, appropriately colored plastic. Instructions included.

TOWN HOUSE ROW

578-115 129.99
28.8 x 5 x 9.8" 11.5 x 12.5 x 24.5cm
Any street will stand out with this row of town houses. The set consists of four- and three-story models and can be combined with #116-118, each sold separately. Easily Americanized into a complete block of city apartments with ornate fronts. Or install them with their brick back walls facing the tracks as big city tenements.

TOWN HOUSE

578-116 39.99
7.2 x 5 x 9.8"
18 x 12.5 x 24.5cm
This commanding four-story town house boasts a gable roof and a portal on the entry level. Fancy front with red brick rear makes this a great kit for a trackside apartment in a city scene.

TOWN HOUSE

578-117 37.99
7.2 x 5 x 7.2"
18 x 12.5 x 18cm
Lower-level shops and a small rear building give this traditional three-story town house extra personality. Change a few details to expand your urban American city scenes.

TOWN HOUSE

578-118 44.99
7.2 x 5 x 9.4"
18 x 12.5 x 23.5cm
A rear building, shops and attention to detail lend historical appeal to this four-story town house. Easily Americanized for any era.

TOWN HOUSE

578-119 44.99
7.2 x 5 x 7.6"
18 x 12.5 x 19cm
Turn your neighborhood into the talk of the town with this fashionable three-story residence. This classic structure features roof apartments as an architectural bonus. Great for big city American apartments in any era.

FIRE HOUSE

578-155 19.99
4.72 x 2.88 x 5.6"
11.8 x 7.2 x 14cm
This simple one-stall structure features a hose-drying tower and moving doors. Great for a very small village or rural town.

VILLAGE SET

578-134 59.99
A complete community in one kit, perfect for a first layout or seasonal display. Basic village includes three detached houses and a church with steeple.

SIGNAL TOWER

578-514 29.99 ***NEW***
4-5/8 x 3-1/4 x 5" 11.6 x 8.1 x 12.3cm
The upper part of the tower features half-timbered construction, while the structure itself is brickwork design.

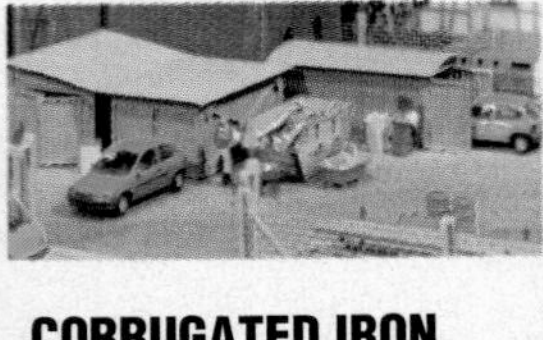

CORRUGATED IRON GARAGES

575-158 pkg(3) **12.99**
2.44 x 1.52 x 1.24"
6.1 x 3.8 x 3.1cm
Excellent industrial sheds, equipment storage for railroad crews or big city garages. Three complete kits, each with a different roof for variety.

POST OFFICE

578-146 39.99
8-5/16 x 8-5/8 x 5-1/2"
21 x 22 x 14cm
This small-town post office features traditional half-timber construction and realistic brick work. The package check-in around the back is included, along with a storage shed. Parts are preweathered.

OLD COAL MINE

578-708 39.99
16-1/8 x 14-5/8 x 7-1/2"
40.3 x 36.5 x 18.7cm

WALDBRUNN STATION

578-1000 21.99
9-5/8 x 5" 24 x 12.5cm
Includes a covered platform, which can be enlarged with platform kit #1005.

NARROW GAUGE BRIDGES

578-807 pkg(2) **22.99**
4-1/2 x 2 x 2-1/8 & 12-13/64 x 2 x 3-1/8"
11.5 x 5 x 55 & 31 x 5 x 8cm
Designed for narrow gauge, these bridges can also be built to accommodate a wider gauge as well.

PASSENGER PLATFORM

578-1005 19.99
14-1/4 x 2-1/4" 36 x 5.6cm

SUSCH PASSENGER STATION

578-740 39.99
13-1/8 x 5-3/4" 33.5 x 15cm

HAUNTED HOUSE

578-198 69.99
8 x 8-5/8" 20 x 21.7cm
We dare you to spend the night working on this scary old house! A neat addition to your layout, all of the parts are heavily weathered, windows are broken and boarded up, and the chimney has collapsed. To send shivers up your spine, there's a spooky red light that flashes in the belfry.

BORDER POST

578-818 33.99

HOFHEIM FREIGHT SHED

578-2012 9.99

ST. NIKLAUS STATION

578-650 33.99
12-3/8 x 5" 31 x 12.7cm
This old-time station will be right at home on steam-era pikes! The model is complete with an attached waiting room and an outhouse. Swiss prototype, ideal for narrow gauge.

NIEDLINGEN STATION

578-551 19.99
9-3/4 x 4-3/4" 24.5 x 12cm
This stucco city station features a clock tower and a covered platform.

HOFHEIM COVERED PLATFORM

578-2011 9.99

Limited Quantity Available

STATION EBELSBACH

578-604 14.99
8-1/4 x 4-3/4" 22 x 12cm

Limited Quantity Available

STATION SET

578-2052 pkg(5) **59.99**
Includes: station, warehouse with crane, switch tower, keeper's cottage, platform and cement.

"NEUFELD" STATION

578-663 41.99
13-3/4 x 5-3/4" 35 x 14.5cm
Framed with two small natural stone annexes, this station is similar to many structures built during the steam-era and still in use today. Other details include movable windows and doors, a hip roof and pre-weathered parts.

THREE TOWNHOUSES

578-133 34.99
8-13/64 x 4-5/16 x 5-1/2"
21 x 11 x 14cm
Typical of suburban areas in many European countries, this building can be part of an old-world neighborhood on a US layout. Two of the townhouses feature first-floor shops. Weathered parts speed construction time.

BACKYARD CAR REPAIR

578-199 29.99
6-13/16 x 9-5/16 x 3-51/6"
17.2 x 23.6 x 8.3cm
Years ago, neighborhood garages like this could be found in many large cities. An old-fashioned gas pump is mounted on the front sidewalk for quick service, and the large garage doors are movable.

TWO-STALL ENGINE HOUSE

578-1020 34.99
13 x 6-7/8" 32.3 x 17.2cm
Engine houses like this could be found on branch and mainline railroads. The kit has movable doors and holds locos or cars up to 11-5/8".

TRAM STOP

578-676 22.99
17-5/16 x 2" 44 x 5.1cm

SIGNAL TOWER (BRICK)

578-512 14.99
4-5/16 x 2-3/4" 11 x 7cm

SWISS VILLAGE

578-571 pkg(4) **44.99**
5-1/8 x 3-1/2 x 7"
13 x 9 x 18cm
A complete set of four buildings: two homes, a barn and church, that capture the look of a typical Swiss village.

COALING TOWER

578-704 19.99
6-1/4 x 6" 16 x 15cm
Includes coal buckets, machinery house and coal chute.

SAND HOUSE-LOADER

578-702 14.99
9-1/4 x 4" 23.5 x 10cm
Kit includes a drying house, timber bunker with one-piece sand pile and a tower.

COAL LOADER

578-561 14.99
7-1/4 x 2" 18 x 5.5cm
Kit includes traveling crane, loading bucket and water crane.

BAYWA COAL DEPOT

578-847 38.99
8-5/16 x 5-1/8" 21 x 13cm

ROUNDHOUSE "FREILASSING"

578-670 139.99
Shed is divided into five stalls, each holding a loco up to 32cm in length; each stand is at a 75˚ angle. Doors are operated by special mechanism: engines driving in close the doors, engines driving out open them automatically.

COAL STOCK YARD

578-671 56.99
10-3/16 x 6-11/16" 26 x 17cm
There's a lot of work to be done at the coal stock yard. This is the place where the engines are fed. Coal is delivered at the top level and then shoveled down to keep the wheels in motion.

RAILROAD ADMINISTRATION BUILDING

578-677 45.99
13-13/32 x 4-5/16 x 7-11/16" 34 x 11 x 19.5cm
Keep every part of your railroad running smoothly when you house your corporate offices in this building. Ideal for a factory office, too.

STORAGE DEPOT RAIFFEISEN

578-662 44.99
6-1/2 x 4-1/2" 16.5 x 11cm
Complete with freight details and a specially painted and lettered truck, this small storage depot will be right at home on steam- or diesel-era layouts!

WAALDRECHT SIGNAL TOWER

578-553 9.99
3-3/4 x 2-3/4" 9.5 x 7cm

BAYWA GRAIN ELEVATOR

578-844 49.99
9-1/2 x 7-3/4" 24 x 19.5cm

OLD SMITHY

578-569 12.99
5-1/2 x 4-5/16" 14 x 11cm
This village smithy is housed in an old barn and comes complete with anvil, grind stone, forge and other accessories. Just add some animals and figures to finish the scene!

Limited Quantity Available

HOUSE "JUGENDSTIL"

578-178 37.99
5-1/4 x 4" 13.6 x 10cm

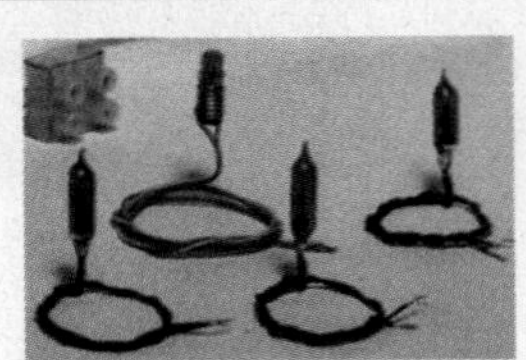

RED FLASHING LIGHTS

578-87 pkg(2) **6.99**
Blinking lights to simulate crackling flames. Combine with smoke generator #84 (sold separately) to model a large fire.

Limited Quantity Available

REPLACEMENT BULBS

578-88 pkg(10) **9.99**
Clear screw-type bulbs, for all Pola lighting units.

ATTIC APARTMENT

578-750 35.99
5-5/8 x 3-5/8" 14.2 x 9cm
Enjoy sea-side living in this elegant old warehouse, renovated as a fashionable apartment. Prototype in Holland.

KINDERGARTEN

578-400 119.99
9-13/16 x 9-3/8" 25 x 24cm
This set comes complete with tables, stools, shelves, matching bus, six children, a mommy and a teacher.

SMALL COUNTRY CHAPEL

578-2017 6.99

"BAYWA" STORAGE DEPOT

578-843 49.99
9 x 7" 23 x 18.5cm
To handle freight shipments in and out of your small town, use this storage depot! Authentically detailed with half-timbered construction and a broken stone base, the pre-weathered depot features a roof with overhang, loading ramps and a fence with opening gate.

APARTMENT BUILDING UNDER DEMOLITION

578-166 42.99
9-7/16 x 5" 24 x 12.5cm

CHURCH

578-1030 23.99
8-1/8 x 4-3/8"

CUSTOMS HOUSE

578-197 34.99
A 1920s style structure, ideal for the office of any industry or government agency.

SERVICE STATION

578-131 54.99
A 1950s vintage filling station, with built-on sales and parts center. Includes custom Brekina service truck.

CHRIST'S JEWELERS

578-112 54.99
8-1/3 x 7-1/2" 21 x19cm
This handsome 3-story, corner townhouse has recently been renovated and now has a plastered facade. The ground floor is complete with marble accents and interior lighting. Also included are glass showcases with displays of jewelry; mirrors and pictures on the wall, flower arrangements, etc. Parts are pre-weathered.

TRAM TERMINAL "DRESDEN"

578-675 99.99
14-1/3 x 12" 36 x 30.4cm
Here's the perfect home for your city streetcars! Front doors open and close, and the modular design makes it easy to build a larger or smaller facility. The four-track shed will hold eight-axle articulated cars with a maximum length of 14" (35cm).

HOSPITAL

578-192 59.99
11-1/2 x 11" 29.5 x 28.5cm
This hospital will give your layout a healthy dose of detail! Based on a turn-of-the-century building converted into a hospital, the structure is detailed with sandstone walls, an entrance drive for ambulances, canopied porch, opening doors and windows, a parking lot and more.

MEDIEVAL WATCH TOWER

578-130 44.99
A remaining section of the old city walls, with gate for cars and pedestrian walkway. Can be illuminated with spotlight, sold separately.

DEVELOPMENT HOUSES EA 29.99

Each measures: 6-1/4 x 5 x 5-3/64" 15.6 x 12.5 x 12.6cm
578-142 Clinker Brick *NEW*
With bricked-up base.

578-143 Render Finish *NEW*
With side entrance and dormer windows.

MUNICIPAL GARAGE

578-180 42.99
6-7/8 x 9-3/8" 17 x 23.5cm
Keep your fleet on the road with this handsome HO Scale garage! The doors can be left open to display vehicles parked inside. To start your scene, a truck is included!

CORNER TOWNHOUSE

578-184 46.99
8-1/2 x 6" 21.2 x 15cm

APARTMENT BUILDING W/THEATER

578-167 42.99
5-1/4 x 6-5/8" 13.5 x 17cm

TOWNHOUSE W/CITY BUILDINGS

578-190 54.99
5-5/8 x 5" 14.5 x 12.7cm

BURNING IRS OFFICE

578-160 64.99
7-3/4 x 5-5/16" 19.5 x 13.3cm

HOUSES UNDER CONSTRUCTION

578-566 pkg(2) **11.99**
Each: 3-1/2 x 3" 8.7 x 7.4cm
A pair of brick houses, with scaffolding, rafters and other details.

BUTCHER SHOP W/APARTMENTS

578-168 42.99
5-3/4 x 4-7/8" 14.5 x 12.7cm

1930S GAS STATION

578-159 17.99
7-7/8 x 4-7/8" 20 x 12.7cm

FARM HOUSE

578-509 8.99

BOILER HOUSE

578-541 11.99
7-1/2 x 4-3/4" 18.8 x 11.8cm
Detail for any industrial scene.

BOEKELO SIGNAL TOWER

578-560 9.99
5-1/8 x 2-3/8" 13 x 5.8cm

PARADISE BAR

578-191 59.99
7-5/16 x 4-7/8" 18.3 x 12.5cm

CROSSING KEEPER'S HOUSE W/GATES

578-558 15.99
Gates: 3-3/4 x 1-5/8" 9.5 x 4cm
House: 4 x 3-5/8" 10 x 9cm

PLUMBING SHOP & APARTMENTS

578-164 44.99
5-1/4 x 6-5/8" 13.5 x 17cm

FLASHING LIGHTS FOR #193

578-82 45.99
Illuminates gambling machines, must be put in before #193 is assembled. 14-17V AC/DC.

RAILWAY/ROADWAY BRIDGE

578-621 34.99
13 x 8-5/8" 33.5 x 22.5cm

CORNER PUB UNDER REPAIR

578-177 46.99
8-3/8 x 7-5/8" 21 x 19cm

CROSSING KEEPER'S HOUSE

578-519 7.99
3-3/4 x 2-5/8" 9.5 x 6.7cm

AUTO GARAGE W/APARTMENTS

578-165 44.99
5-1/4 x 6-5/8" 13.5 x 17cm

FACTORY HALL

578-841 16.99
4-1/2 x 3-7/8" 11.5 x 10cm

"BAYWA" AGRICULTURAL MACHINERY WORKSHOP

578-846 39.99
4-1/3 x 4-1/3" 11 x 11cm
Includes bike stands, scrap, diesel fuel tank and fencing!

WUPPERTAL SIGNAL TOWER

578-562 29.99
3 x 2-1/2" 7.5 x 6.1cm
Prototype served in Wuppertal-Elberfeld area.

RAILWAY STATION SET

578-664 74.99
7-1/8 x 4-1/2" 18.5 x 11.5cm
Includes Oberndorf station, roofed platform, signal tower and gated level crossing with gatekeeper's ledge.

LAUERTAL DAM

578-619 49.99
15 x 8.5" 38.2 x 21.5cm

CORNER TOWN HOUSES

Structure is accented by stucco work and dormer windows. Features a shop on the ground floor of the town house.

578-120 4-Story **44.99** *NEW*
4-5/8 x 3-27/32 x 8-13/16" 11.6 x 9.6 x 22cm
578-121 3-Story **39.99** *NEW*
4-5/8 x 3-27/32 x 7-13/64" 11.6 x 9.6 x 18cm

CORNER HOUSE

578-174 46.99
8-1/4 x 6-1/4" 21 x 15.6cm
This city apartment building provides housing on three detailed floors. The main entrance is at the back. Opening doors, interior lights and weathered parts make this model more realistic.

STORAGE TANKS

578-842 pkg(2) **14.99**
3-3/4 x 2" 9.5 x 5.5cm

BAYWA OFFICE

578-849 31.99
7-3/4 x 7-1/4" 19.5 x 18.5cm
The stone construction of this two-story building provides realistic detail for any location. Kit is complete with flagpoles and flags.

FREIGHT STATION W/RAMP

578-839 54.99
23-13/64 x 6-3/4 x 4-3/4"
59 x 17 x 12cm
Typical of small-town freight stations, this model includes an easily "Americanized" main building, with an open freight platform to serve the team track. Includes lots of freight for the finishing touch.

CHIMNEY

578-855 19.99
2-1/2 x 1-3/4" 6.5 x 4.5cm
12-3/4" 32cm high

ROTH ROOF TILE FACTORY

578-616 79.99
5 x 3-3/4" 12.4 x 9.5cm
Still making clay roof tiles the old-fashioned way, this intricate factory still stands. Lots of extra details, shovels, stacks of tiles, sacks and more are included, along with a special Brekina truck featuring Roth decals.

FREIGHT DEPOT

578-542 9.99

GALVANIZING WORKS

578-840 49.99
9-3/8 x 6-5/8" 24 x 17cm
This factory building will be a boom to your industrial district! The brick building with tall smokestack is detailed with a loading dock, ventilation ducts, air conditioning units, crates, barrels, pallets and lamps. To complete the scene, add Factory Hall #841 and Storage Tanks #842 (shown at left).

INDUSTRIAL FENCE

578-850 19.99
Increase safety and security around any factory complex with this attractive wrought iron fencing. Includes vehicle and pedestrian gates.

POWER STATION

578-617 54.99
7.3 x 4.5" 18.5 x 12.5cm

TRANSFORMER STATION

578-618 49.99
12.2 x 3.5" 31 x 9cm.

SCHONBRUN PLATFORM

578-860 39.99
19-5/8 x 4-3/4 x 2-1/2"
50 x 12 x 6.5cm
Passengers can board trains safely from this handsome steam-era platform, which is designed for use with station #627. Includes benches and a small sales stand. Can be expanded with add-on Platform #861, sold separately.

PLATFORM ADD-ON

578-861 26.99
9-13/16 x 4-3/4 x 2-1/2"
25 x 12 x 6.5cm
Use with #860 to build a longer platform. Includes covered platform without stairs and open platform section, plus several accessories.

UNEMPLOYMENT OFFICE

578-826 119.99
7-3/4 x 5-1/4" 19.6 x 13.2cm
The limited-run model includes a special set of Preiser figures, a Brekina VW bus, interior details and lighting, movable door and a powered roof-top sign. For the finishing touch, all of the exterior walls are pre-weathered.

BAYWA BUILDING MATERIALS STORE

578-845 39.99
9-3/8 x 8" 24 x 20.5cm

TOWN GAS CYLINDER

578-854 54.99
6-1/2 x 7-3/4" 16.3 x 17cm

BAYWA FUEL DEPOT

578-848 24.99
8-3/8 x 6-1/4" 21.6 x 16cm
Receiving oil by rail, this small industry is a great addition to your layout. The kit includes the stone office, three large storage tanks and a pair of gas pumps. (Less figures and vehicle.)

SCHWEINFURT GAS CO. COAL PROCESSOR

578-851 39.99
Used to make coke from coal, this kit includes a baking oven and a cooling tower, where gases are captured for other products.

BICYCLE SHOP

578-157 29.99
7-1/8 x 4-5/16 x 5-3/4"
18 x 11 x 14.5cm
The store comes completely furnished with shelves, bikes, counter and more. The kit also features movable windows and doors.

ROTHHAUSEN STATION
578-660 19.99
6-1/2 x 4-5/16" 16.6 x 11.2cm
The depot was an important part of every small town, and this model is a great addition to a layout scene. Weathered walls and working doors make this a very realistic model.

FARM HOUSE
578-819 39.99
11-1/8 x 7-1/4" 28 x 19cm
Complete with house, barn and machine shed, plus fence, feed sacks, wheelbarrow and shovel.

RURAL DUPLEX
578-539 29.99
7 x 4-3/4" 17.7 x 11.8cm
Realistic brick walls and wooden windows. Opening doors, interior lighting and fencing material are included.

BUS DEPOT
578-678 52.99
10-1/2 x 8-3/8" 26.2 x 21.5cm
Many older buildings have been converted for new uses, like this former streetcar barn that's now a garage for the bus fleet.

ROADSIDE BUSINESS
578-538 7.99
8-1/4 x 3" 11 x 7.4cm
Open your own small business with this detailed building. A great structure for a news stand, snack bar, neighborhood grocery - whatever your busy layout needs!

SCHWEINFURT GAS CO. ADMINISTRATION BUILDING
578-853 26.99
9-1/4 x 5-1/4" 24 x 14cm
A great central office for an industry or railroad, the kit includes interior lights and various add-on details.

SCHWEINFURT GAS WORKS
578-401 119.99
12 x 6-1/4" 30 x 16.5cm
Relying on the railroad for raw materials, this model puts action into any layout setting. For more realism, parts are weathered by hand to capture the grime and grit of the real thing. Working doors, interior lights, a special Brekina truck and trailer and figures are all included. There's also a decal, designed especially for Smokestack #855 (sold separately) to finish the scene.

SCHWEINFURT GAS CO. SEPARATOR
578-852 18.99
6-1/8 x 4-1/2" 15.5 x 11.6cm
Kit is complete with tower, bunker and vehicle.

BUILDING UNDER DEMOLITION
578-162 39.99
8-1/2 x 4-1/2" 21.5 x 11.5cm
There are plenty of extra details included, like the old sinks and radiators, a bath tub and torn wallpaper, plus a site office trailer. The model has been weathered by hand and captures the grimy look of an actual structure!

SIGNAL TOWER
578-672 39.99
8 x 2-5/8" 20 x 6cm
Move trains through a yard or busy junction with this facility. Can be built on a hillside or as a free-standing building. The second floor interior is highly detailed.

ZWEINITZ STATION
578-804 16.99
8-3/4 x 4-3/4" 22 x 12cm
This Austrian prototype building is well suited to narrow gauge operations.

COUNTRY TOWNHOUSE
578-1040 9.99
5 x 3-3/4" 12.5 x 9.5

SMALL STORAGE SHED
578-802 12.99
6-1/2 x 3-1/4" 17.5 x 8.4cm
This small structure makes a great freight station for a village, or a storage building for a trackside industry.

LAKEVIEW CAFE
578-559 9.99
7-1/4 x 4-1/8" 18.5 x 10.5cm

WAALDRECHT PLATFORM
578-552 9.99
11-1/4 2-1/8" 278.5 x 5.5cm

TOWN MILLING SECTION
578-2059 pkg(3) **39.99**
Houses: 4-3/4 x 4-1/2"
11.8 x 11.4cm
Windmill: 5 x 3-1/4 x 7-1/8"
12.5 x 8.5 x 18cm
Typical of buildings found in northern Holland, this attractive trio includes two houses and a large windmill.

GAS COMPANY - SULFUR SEPARATOR
578-856 54.99
7-1/4 x 4" 18.5 x 10cm
This building houses the cleaning machinery and storage tanks for useful by-products, including sulfuric acid. Realistically weathered walls are a highlight and three gas cleaning tanks are included.

GAS COMPANY GAS WASHER
578-857 44.99
4-1/4 x 4-1/4" 11 x 11cm
Kit features weathered walls and a large gantry crane to handle the movement of chemicals used in the cleaning process into the building.

FREILASSING RAILROAD CAR SHOP
578-674 119.99
7 x 28" 17.5 x 70cm
This kit has a modular design, so several can be joined to create a customized building that's just right for your railroad. Parts are weathered and the large doors can be opened or closed. Smokejacks, sky lights and other details are also included.

Limited Quantity Available

CROSSING KEEPER'S SHANTY
578-707 16.99
6-3/4 x 4-3/4" 17 x 12cm
Found in rural areas, includes covered entry way.

MAIN DISPATCHER'S BUILDING
578-679 52.99
13 x 6-11/16 x 5-1/2"
33 x 17 x 14cm
A neat yard office, this kit consists of the front offices and a one-stall car shed with movable doors. Lots of "extra" details are all included to set the scene.

CORNER HOUSE DISTILLERY
578-145 34.99
8-5/16 x 6-1/8 x 5-1/8"
21 x 15.5 x 13cm
This corner building houses both the pub and distillery, and features weathered parts and working doors.

ST. MARTIN STATION
578-780 31.99
17-5/16 x 5-1/2 x 6"
44 x 14 x 15cm
This station is based on a prototype that serves the historic Furka-Oberalp Line in Switzerland. The attached freight house features movable doors.

FREIGHT STATION
578-838 68.99
18-1/2 x 6-5/16 x 7-13/16"
47 x 16 x 20cm
This big city freight station will generate lots of traffic for road and rail. Includes large front offices and a large freight area with platforms and movable doors on both sides. Lots of freight is included for detailing. Works well with station #839, sold separately.

These HO Scale, craft train kits consist of die cast, stamped and formed metal parts and vinyl tubing, as noted. Complete instructions included.

DIESEL OIL STORAGE TANK CENTER & PUMP HOUSE
683-107 14.95
1-1/4 x 4" 3.2 x 10.2cm

WATCHMAN'S SHANTY
683-108 8.95
1-1/4 x 1-1/2" 3.2 x 3.8cm
Includes figure and super details.

TRACKSIDE SHANTY W/STOVE
683-116 6.95
1 x 1" 2.54 x 2.54cm

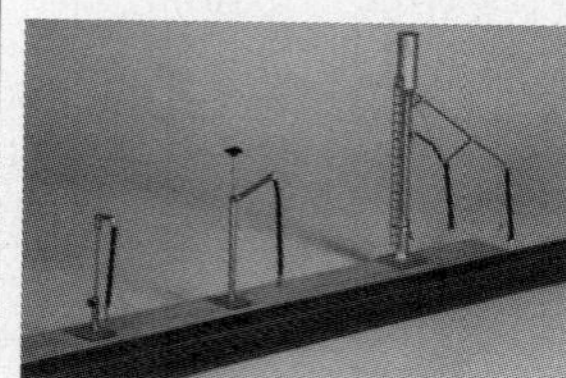

WATER COLUMN
683-101 7.95
1/2 x 3/4" 1.3 x 2cm

FUEL COLUMN
683-100 7.95
1/2 x 1-1/2" 1.3 x 3.8cm

SAND TOWER
683-102 12.95
3/4 x 3-1/2" 2 x 9cm

SAND, FUEL & WATER COLUMN
683-103 21.95
3/4 x 5/8" 1.9 x 1.6cm

2 BRUSH CAR WASHER
683-104 12.95
1 x 1/2" 2.5 x 3.9cm

4 BRUSH CAR WASHER
683-105 17.95
1 x 2-1/2" 2.5 x 6.4cm

6 BRUSH CAR WASHER
683-106 22.95
1 x 3-1/2" 2.5 x 9cm
Swing arms are movable.

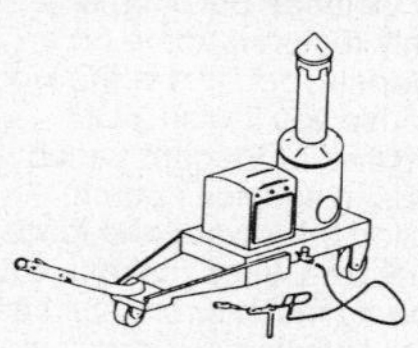

PORTABLE STEAM CLEANER
683-212 6.95
1 x 1/4" 2.54 x .6cm

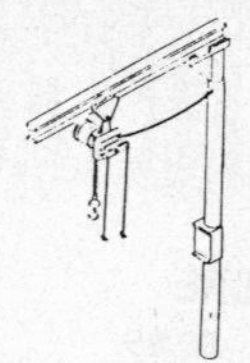

I BEAM CRANE HOIST
683-214 7.95
3-1/2 x 2-1/2" 8.9 x 6.3cm

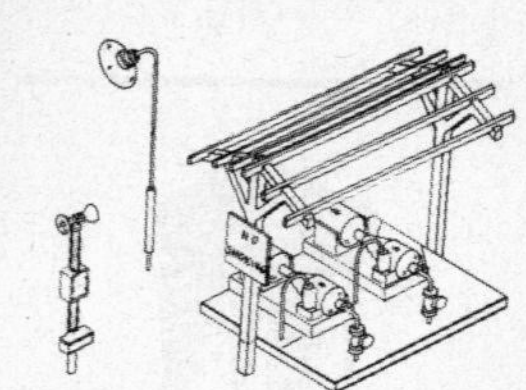

OIL PUMP & SHELTER
683-215 9.95
1 x 1-3/8" 2.5 x 3.5cm

DIESEL OIL STORAGE TANK
683-218 9.95
7/8 x 2-1/2" 2.2 x 6.3cm

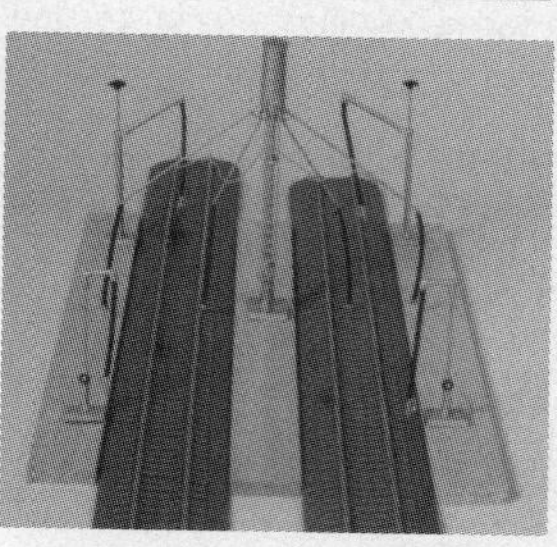

DOUBLE TRACK DIESEL SAND TOWER, FUEL & WATER COLUMNS
683-115 31.95
3/4 x 5/8 x 4-7/8"
1.9 x 1.6 x 12.3cm

DOUBLE TRACK DIESEL SAND TOWER KIT
683-114 14.95
4-7/8" 12.3cm tall

CREW SHELTER
683-117 6.95
1 x 1-3/8" 2.54 x 3.4cm

TWO-STORY YARD TOWER
683-118 9.95
1 x 1-3/8" 2.54 x 3.4cm

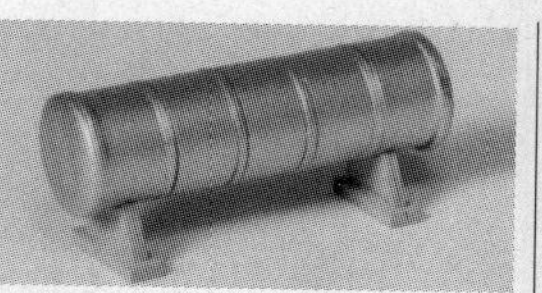

REFINERY TYPE PRESSURE TANK
683-216 8.95
7/8 x 2-1/2" 2.2 x 6.3cm

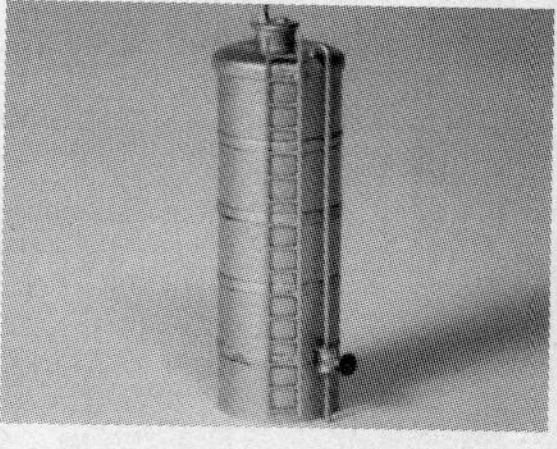

VERTICAL OIL STORAGE TANK
683-219 9.95
7/8 x 2-1/2" 2.2 x 6.3cm

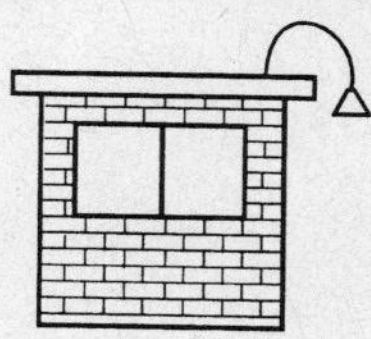

WATER PUMPING STATION
683-119 7.95
1-1/4 x 1-3/4 x 2"
3.1 x 4.3 x 5cm
An important part of engine terminals, this small structure houses the pumps and machinery that supply water for locos, car washers, fire sprinklers and more.

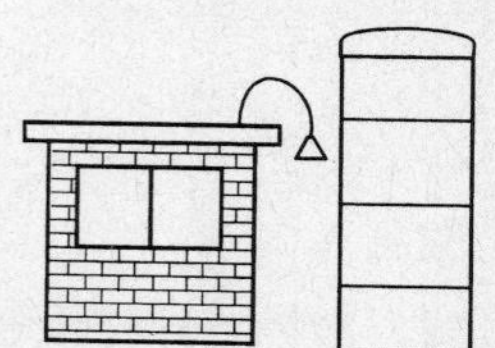

WATER PUMPING STATION W/TANK
683-120 12.95
This kit includes the Pump House (#119) plus a large storage tank, suitable for water treatment chemicals or clean water.

The charm and attention to detail of yesteryear can be part of your layout, with this line of kits. Each structure consists of wood and cast metal parts, numerous add-on details and complete instructions. Instant Kit 1400/1500 series buildings are constructed of resin castings and include various add-on details and full-color printed signs.

PLEASE NOTE: The entire line of SS Ltd. furniture, detail parts and other items, which are listed in their catalog, #650-9997, are available by special order through your dealer.

TOADSUCK CANNING COMPANY
650-1157 169.95
Fresh as the catch of the day, this local cannery really adds "flavor" to your entire layout. This dockside industry is a natural for a busy rail siding, bringing in tin cans, paper labels and parts for the machinery. Empty cars can be reloaded with canned goods for distant markets. Lots of neat wood, resin and metal parts provide hours of construction fun.

VICTORIAN STATION W/INTERIOR
650-1115 139.95

GOTHIC CROSSING SHANTY
650-1153 12.95
Metal kit.

DOROTHY'S HOME
650-1125 79.95
Whether modeled as a brand new Victorian building, or a freshly restored home on a modern layout, this is the kind of house you'll wish YOU could live in! Elegant period details, a spacious porch, detailed brick work and loads of metal castings make this home as much fun to build as it is to show off on your layout.

THE STORE
650-1118 89.95
In the days before mail-order catalogs, folks relied on the local mercantile for almost everything. This wonderful kit recaptures that simpler time, with its detailed trim, large windows and various other details.

TELEPHONE SHACK
650-1107 6.95

HOMETOWN GAZEBO
650-1154 29.95
A perfect place for summer band concerts, this kit makes a neat detail for any city park scene.

RIO GRANDE CAR REPAIR BARN
650-1158 87.95
Prototype at Durango, Colorado, kit is based on the building as it appeared circa 1938.

PURINA GRAIN LOADER
650-1441 24.95

V & T JIB CRANE
650-9126 31.95

COUNTRY CORN CRIB
650-1156 22.95

1929 GAS STATION
650-1101 29.95

AUTOMOBILE JUNK YARD
650-8016 16.95

BROKEN BACK MINE
650-8075 19.95

FLUE RACK & FIRE STAND
650-1109 15.95

NEW YORK BROWNSTONE
650-1103 34.95

SAN FRANCISCO APARTMENT
650-1104 34.95

CHICAGO TOWNHOUSE
650-1105 34.95

CORNER DRUG STORE
650-1111 69.95

TOOL HOUSE & PILLAR CRANE
650-1106 28.95

TIMBER GANTRY
650-1146 59.95

OIL TANKS
650-1112 34.95

SAN FRANCISCO OFFICE BUILDING
650-1113 49.95

SAN FRANCISCO OFFICE BUILDING - WALLS ONLY
650-1150 pkg(2) 4.95

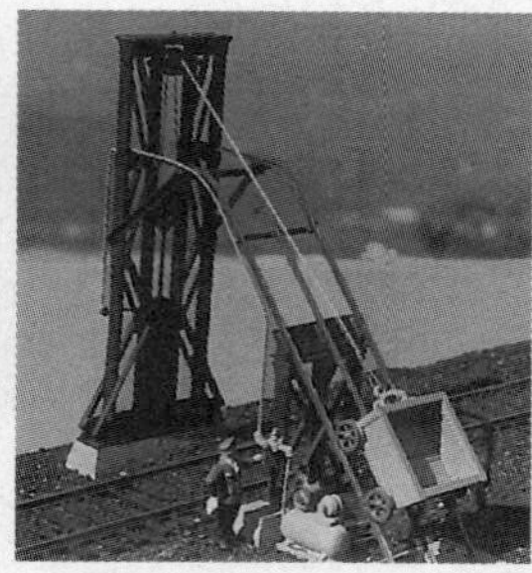

ROBERTSON CINDER CONVEYOR
650-1110 26.95

PILLAR CRANE & PLATFORM
650-1120 16.95

T.W. SNOW COALING TOWER
650-1116 69.95

TWIN WATER TANKS
650-1145 43.95

JENNINGS LUMBER CO.
650-1117 219.95
The only thing this kit needs is the smell of fresh-cut sawdust! A miniature masterpiece, the model is packed with detail inside and out. The exterior includes a variety of roof vents, cyclone dust collector with wooden storage tank and water barrels for fire protection. Inside, there's a complete set of belt-driven machinery and furniture for the offices.

STERLING, COLORADO, ROUNDHOUSE
650-1121 154.95
Tired iron horses rest in style inside this ornate roundhouse. The numerous large windows make this a natural for interior detailing. It's based on an actual structure in Sterling, Colorado, and can be made larger with the add-on stall in kit #650-1122.

EXTRA STALL FOR ROUNDHOUSE
650-1122 34.95
Same fine detail as kit #650-1121, several can be added to the roundhouse to build a custom structure. Use to enlarge the Sterling, Colorado, Roundhouse kit #1121, sold separately.

BOILER HOUSE
650-1102 69.95

COUNTRY STORE W/INTERIOR
650-1114 TBA

OIL LOADING FACILITY
650-1123 27.95

BOARD & BATTEN CROSSING SHANTY
650-1151 12.95

FREIGHT TRANSFER PLATFORM
650-1148 13.95

1880 UNION HOTEL
650-1149 59.95

110'-130' TURNTABLE
650-1124 69.95

70'-90' TURNTABLE
650-1126 59.95

DINKY CREEK BRIDGE
650-1127 47.95

DECK BRIDGE
650-1144 29.95

VICTORIAN CROSSING SHANTY
650-1152
12.95
Metal kit.

GRIZZLY FLATS DEPOT
650-1147 38.95

SUPER KITS

Each kit includes detail castings.

650-1001 Baker Street Super Kits **199.95**
Includes 1 each of kit #1101,1103,1104,1105, and 1108.

650-1002 The Tank Farm Super Kit **149.95**
Includes 1 of kit #1120, 2 of kit #1123 and 9124 and 3 of kit #1112.

650-1003 English Service Facility Super Kit **199.95**
Includes 1 of kit #1109, 1110, 1116 and 1151 and 3 of kit #7232.

INSTANT KIT SERIES

This series of kits (1400/1500) feature cast resin walls, add-on details, printed signs and complete instructions.

COUNTRY STORE
650-1402 TBA

MACHINERY SALES BUILDING
650-1403 TBA

CONCRETE LOADING DOCK
650-1405 9.95

FEED & GRAIN SUPPLY
650-1406 TBA

GENERAL STORE
650-1407 TBA

HILLSIDE OIL FACILITY
650-1412 19.95

RUSTON SHANTIES
650-1451 16.95

MCHUGH'S HARDWARE STORE
650-1453 24.95

CONCRETE LOADING DOCK & RAMP
650-1446 12.95

TRIANGLE CORNER DRUG STORE
650-1414 TBA

DIXIE'S DINER
650-1415 19.95

HALLOWAY'S PLUMBING SUPPLY
650-1410 19.95

1930S SERVICE STATION
650-1411 TBA

STEEL WATER TANK
650-1424 19.95

For Daily Product Information Click

www.walthers.com

WOOD BRANCHLINE WATER TANK
650-1443 19.95

MAPLE VALLEY COAL & ICE
650-1416 16.95

TRACK GANG BAGGAGE HOUSE
650-1421 16.95

J.E. WORK'S GRAVEL YARD
650-1449 21.95

REGGIE'S VEGGIE MARKET
650-1437 21.95

WOOD LOADING DOCK & RAMP
650-1447 12.95

THE POWERHOUSE
650-1519 89.95
With covered siding.

QUINCY STREET
650-1539 59.99

WISCHER'S WASHER COMPANY
650-1523 49.95

OIL STORAGE TANK FACILITY
650-1455 19.95

WESTON'S WAREHOUSE
650-1442 TBA

THE COUNTRY GARAGE
650-1418 21.95

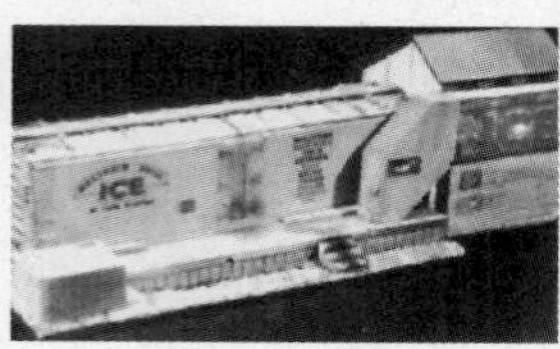

MELTNICK'S ICE STATION
650-1423 21.95

COLUMBIA DEPOT
650-1404 31.95

TRACKSIDE SHANTIES
650-1422 pkg(3) 19.95

BELOW GROUND STORAGE TANK FACILITY
650-1417 19.95

FOUNTAIN BREWERY
650-1510 69.95

WANGLIE'S DEPARTMENT STORE
650-1521 TBA

TICKNER'S WATCHWORKS
650-1524 39.95

RICK'S PLACE
650-1525 24.95

VFWD PUMPING STATION
650-1527 TBA

BURLINGTON STREET
650-1534 47.95

WISE SUPPLY COMPANY
650-1529 TBA

1940s GAS STATION
650-1531 48.95

MUNICIPAL BUILDING
650-1530 59.95

VICTORIA FALLS TRANSFER CO.
650-1533 TBA

ART DECO MOVIE THEATER
650-1536 49.95

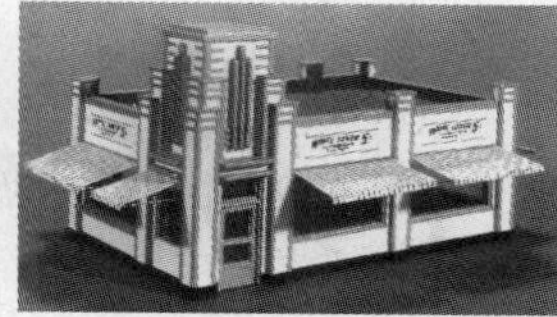

WHITE TOWER RESTAURANT
650-1540 29.95

SMILEY'S PLACE
650-1537 21.95

MINERS UNION HALL
650-1502 29.99

BIRTHPLACE OF MODEL RAILROADING
650-1543 34.95

DES PLAINES AVENUE
650-1545 34.99

EDISON STREET POWERHOUSE
650-1550 TBA

MENASHA WOODEN WARE COMPANY
650-1551 TBA

BRACH'S CANDY COMPANY
650-1556 69.95

SCALE STRUCTURES LTD. CATALOG
650-9997 4.00
A complete listing of all structures, parts, interior details, scale machinery and many other items.

SHEEPSCOT SCALE PRODUCTS

This line of craft train kits takes structure modeling to a new level of detail. Kits include Northeastern lumber and siding, Grandt Line windows, doors and other details (as appropriate), Evergreen styrene, metal castings from Model Masterpieces and Alloy Forms, as well as the firm's own roofing material (simulating asphalt shingles), photo-etched brass and cast-metal detail parts. Board-by-board construction is made easier through the use of solid wood formers, which keep parts aligned. Scale drawings and extensive instructions are provided with every model.

CAT'S HEAD PIER

668-1250 140.00
Loading rail cars and trucks, this model is sure to be the star of your harbor. The heart of the operation is the detailed machinery house, complete with triangular mast and clamshell bucket. The house sits on a detailed trestle that's 17" long and 8" tall, and features an elevated track running inside. A surge hopper (used on the prototype to load rail cars) and storage bins for different sizes of coal are also included. Detailed instructions feature several templates to simplify building the trestle and the board-by-board construction of the machinery house. The model can be carefully configured to fit in a fairly small space.

COAL TOWER-150 TON

668-1040 85.00
4 x 11 x 13" 10 x 27.5 x 32.5cm
Wooden towers were found in most terminals and along the main line where locos needed refueling. The kit includes a tool house, a brass chute, brass chain, laser-cut stair stringers, wooden formers, cutting block with special jigs and 22 pages of instructions and drawings.

ACADIA GRANITE WORKS

668-1200 225.00
Large granite blocks from quarries like this model are some of the heaviest loads moved by rail. Kit includes garage, storeroom, office and toolroom, detailed traveling bridge crane, three brass trailers and signs.

LIME COMPANY

668-1070 215.00
Lime plants like this can still be found shipping their product by rail. This kit depicts a company that also supplies livestock feed, and it can fit any time frame from 1900 to the present. Scale lumber, signs, castings and details are all included, along with truck bodies for dumps, bulk feed, flatbeds and spreaders.

BEANFIELD SIDING

668-1170 160.00
Industrial action abounds on every side of this complete packing house and icing platform. The kit includes a unique ice house, a milk shed and a big diesel storage tank. There's also an office, privy and a truck scale.

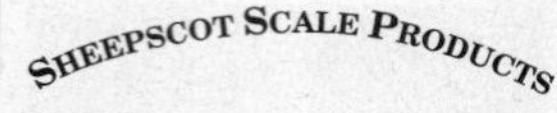

FREIGHT BUILDING W/PLATFORM

668-1010 35.00
12 x 5" 30 x 12.5cm
(with platform)

Model is based on a Maine Central design from 1892 and includes a tar and gravel roof.

NEW ENGLAND STATION

668-1020 38.00
19 x 6" 47.5 x 15cm
(with platform)

Includes hip roof, bay window, semaphore train order signal and passenger platform.

SIGNAL TOWER-20 LEVER

668-1030 35.00
2 x 3 x 4-3/4" 5 x 7.5 x 11.8cm

Keep a busy interlocking or junction working safely and smoothly with this terrific tower. Based on a Maine Central design from 1912, kit also includes a crossing shanty and a ball signal.

PHILIPS BEACH STATION

668-1050 48.00
This ornate station is the perfect choice for a seaside community. It's complete with ornate gingerbread trim, eave brackets and clock tower.

HOCKING BROS. HOISTING CO.

668-1063 40.00
This big derrick is complete with block and tackle, machinery house, gears and more.

50,000-GALLON WATER TOWER

668-1080 35.00
A perfect companion to the Coaling Tower, or by the station in a "tank town," this typical railroad design features a variety of fine details and real wood construction.

100-TON PEDESTAL-MOUNT WATERFRONT CRANE

668-1233 85.00
12-24 x 4 x 16"
30-60 x 10 x 40cm

Move cargo on or off any vessel, or detail an industrial scene with this big crane. Rigs of this type have moved coal, containers, steel, stone, pulpwood and other big, heavy loads from the early 1900s to the present. The kit comes with a brass A-frame gantry, a photo-etched brass 100' boom with a 35' jib, optional hooks or clamshell for loading duties, numerous metal detail parts, a simulated concrete mounting pad, linen thread and brass wire for rigging and complete assembly instructions.

RED HERRING PACKING CO.

668-1270 215.00
Dockside canneries are big industries and this model captures everything but the smell! Five structures make up the complex: Office & Bait Shop, Fish Tanks, Packing House, Shipping Room and a large Water Tank. This kit also includes a unique system to build the granite pier walls. There are numerous details, including a crane for unloading fishing boats, large fuel tank, door frames, wind mill, doors, louvers, flag, weather vane and much more!

HAWK'S NEST LODGE

668-1240 210.00
An ideal weekend get-away, fishing lodge resort or hotel, there's a covered platform at trackside to welcome visitors.

STARTERS MILKHOUSE

668-1290 30.00
2-1/2 x 3" 6.2 x 7.5cm
Versatile design can be customized with your choice of wall configuration, corner boards, foundation, roof overhang, cornice details or a loading platform. The kit is designed for easy construction with laser-cut Northeastern clapboard siding, Grandt Line windows and a door, plus a wood former for the platform. Comprehensive instructions are written for the first-time builder, with drawings and 24 photos to make construction a snap.

ROAD BED SUPPLY SAND & GRAVEL DIORAMAS EA TBA

668-1381 Screening Plant *NEW*
668-1382 Trestle & Crusher Building *NEW*
668-1383 Two-Track Hopper & Charging Conveyor *NEW*

TRAVELING/GANTRY CRANE

668-1232 140.00
Make quick work of loading or unloading with this detailed model, typical of cranes used for containers and other material handling. Includes 100-ton crane with brass boom, riding on a 20' high traveling gantry.

PHOTO-ETCHED BRASS MODELS

Made from solid sheets that are just 0.012" thick, easily soldered or assembled with adhesive of your choice.

RADIO/HIGH TENSION TOWER

668-75008 10.00
These modern towers can be seen in rural and urban areas. Includes two cast insulators, measures 52' tall and 20' wide at base. Leave the top in place and build a 62' tall radio tower. Includes microwave dish and open grid antenna.

PUMP HOUSE

668-75010 15.00
This unique design eliminates stone joints by bending the walls from the front. Two choices for the brick ends are included, and the bricks are exactly to scale. Separate doors, windows, frames and sashes simplify painting. Measures 12 x 17 scale feet.

WINDMILL

668-75011 15.00
A common sight on farms before rural electricity, the windmill was used to pump water. Some railroads used them to keep water tanks filled at trackside. This brass kit can be assembled with adhesive or soldered.

Recreate many of the structures seen along US railroads with these easy-to-build plastic kits. Detailed styrene parts are molded in realistic colors.

MODERN HIGHWAY OVERPASSES

These overpass kits feature details to match newer construction. Each overpass section is a scale 50' long and 25' wide. Modular design and interlocking parts make it easy to build longer overpasses.

628-111 50' **5.99**
628-112 50' w/Pier **9.95**
628-113 150' w/4 Piers **29.95**
Kit includes 3 overpass kits and 4 piers.

VINTAGE HIGHWAY OVERPASSES

These vintage highway overpass kits model concrete bridges built in the 1930s and 1940s, which are still used today. All parts are molded in realistic concrete color. Each overpass section is a scale 50' long and 25' wide. Modular design and interlocking parts make it easy to build longer overpasses.

628-101 50' **5.99**
628-102 50' w/Pier **9.95**
628-103 150' w/4 Piers **29.95**
Kit includes 3 overpass kits and 4 piers.

VINTAGE HIGHWAY PIER

628-100 3.99

1930S OVERPASS RAILINGS

628-104 pkg(4) **3.99**

BEAMS

628-105 pkg(10) **3.99**

ROADWAY

628-106 pkg(4) **3.99**

MODERN RAILINGS

628-114 pkg(4) **3.99**

MODERN MEDIAN DIVIDER

628-115 pkg(4) **3.99**
Individual parts match those used in the overpass kits.

ONE STORY HOUSE W/SIDE PORCH

628-203 9.95
3-1/2 x 3-7/8" 9 x 9.9cm

ONE STORY HOUSE W/FRONT PORCH

628-202 9.95
3 x 4-3/8" 7.7 x 11.2cm
Each house kit features white weatherboard walls, red brick foundations, brown asphalt roofing and clear windows.

PORCH KIT

628-204 4.99
1/2 x 1" 1.3 x 2.5cm
Includes brick porch, steps, doors, porch floor, gable and porch roof.

ONE STORY HOUSE

628-201 8.95
3 x 3-7/8" 7.7 x 9.9cm

GRAIN BINS 30° PEAKED TOP

Typical of steel bins found on farms and at elevators to store all types of grains. Each section consists of six bands, which are stacked to various heights. Kits include parts to build the height shown. Also includes door, vents, dryer, chutes and grain head. All parts are molded in realistic galvanized color.

628-304 33' Tall **10.99**

628-305 44' Tall **13.99**

GALVANIZED COLOR GRAIN BIN ROOFS EA 2.99

628-356 15° Pitch
628-357 30° Pitch

GRAIN BIN DETAIL PARTS

628-358 2.99
Includes door, vents, dryer, chutes and grain head. Use with any grain bin kit.

GRAIN BIN EXTENSION

628-354 3.99
Three complete bin sections, add up to 30' to #304 or #305.

RURAL WOODEN OVERPASS

628-200 10.98
Great detail for rural right-of-way, typical of crossings built for farm roads.

GRAIN ELEVATOR

628-407 14.99
Detailed replica of the pipes and machinery used to move grain from bins, great for use with #304 or #305. Includes ladders with safety cages, platforms, chutes and tubes. Can be built in scale 10' increments, up to 90' tall.

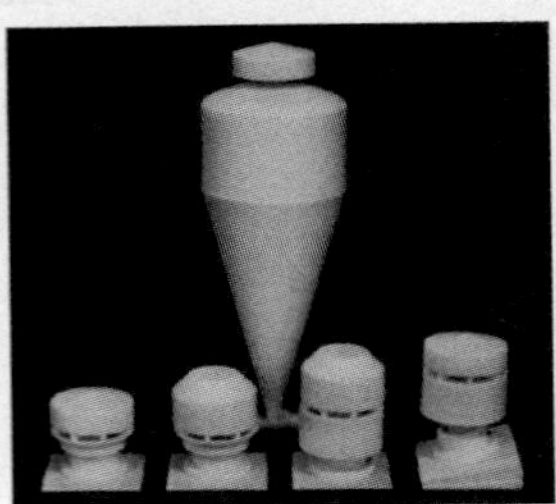

CYCLONES & VENTS

628-611 9.95
This set includes the large cyclone type dust collectors that are mounted on the roofs and walls of many manufacturing plants, along with the vents found in kit #610.

QUONSET HUT

628-410 9.99
Built by the thousands during WWII, these pre-fab metal buildings found all sorts of post-war uses. Kit includes one complete building. Measures a scale 24 x 26 x 12' and features pre-cut door and window openings.

WATER/OIL TANK FLAT TOP

628-500 29' 6.99

628-501 43' 9.99

628-502 60' 12.99

WATER/OIL TANK PEAK TOP

628-503 29' 6.99

628-504 43' 9.99

628-505 60' 12.99

WATER/OIL TANK LADDER KIT

628-506 1.99

OLD HENDERSON WAREHOUSE

628-250 29.95
A lot of history has passed through this old warehouse and it's still in daily operation. Looks great on layouts from the mid 1800s to the present day. Features board and batten siding, large windows, freight doors and many other details.

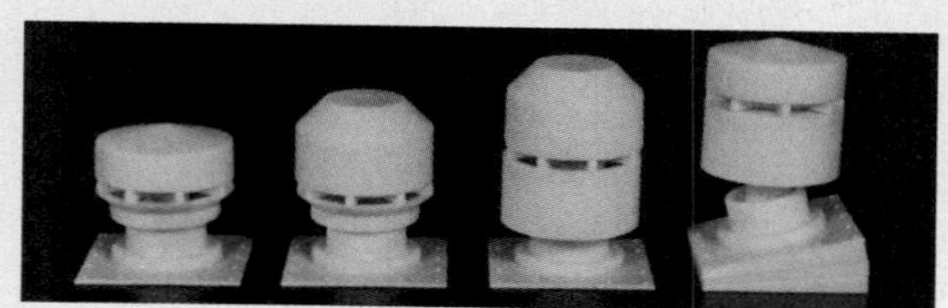

ROOF VENTS

628-610 5.95
Realistic detail for the most-seen part of model industrial buildings - the roof! Includes separate bases, spacers and vent bodies to make eight vents (four of one and four of another, in five possible combinations).

BIG BLUE STORAGE SILO

628-510 9.99
A great storage system for farm or industry, measures a scale 24' diameter by 49" tall (at eave).

ELEVATED TANK

628-520 7.99

STONE CULVERTS EA 6.95

628-651 Small Cut

628-652 Large Cut

BOARD & BATTEN EA 9.95

628-251 Building #1

628-252 Building #2

Craft train kits feature die cut wood walls, plastic, etched brass or metal details and templates.

"ROLL AWAY" CATTLE LOADING RAMP

707-38921 19.00
5-7/8 x 1" 15 x 2.5cm
Prototype was in Yorba Linda, California. Features "working" roll away ramp and code 40 rail.

DALEY BROS. PIPE & SUPPLY CO

707-38922 29.00
3-1/2 x 7" 9 x 17.8cm
Includes fence and scale pipe.

TOMAHAWK POST OFFICE

707-38923 29.00
3-1/2 x 3-1/4" 9 x 8.2cm

YORK'S STORE

707-38924 29.00

BRANCHLINE OIL FACILITY

707-38926 17.00
Many "retired" rail cars lead new lives along the right-of-way, like this tank car converted into a low-cost fuel facility. Kit includes car body, wooden supports and spout.

SMALL FREIGHT HOUSE

707-38925 17.00

SELLEY FINISHING TOUCHES

Easy-to-build kits feature cast metal construction. Structures measure 11/16 x 11/16 x 1" 1.2 x 1.2 x 2.5cm.

OLD TIME CROSSING SHANTY

675-604 13.00

RURAL OUTHOUSE

675-607 6.60
Includes occupant, half-moon door and mail-order catalog.

Division of **Rix Products**

Create a custom business district with these easy-to-build, plastic kits. Each series has a common front wall, which can be painted and detailed for variety. Side walls feature different window and door locations, so models can be used on right or left corners, or in the middle of a block. Small size fits most layouts, and kits can be used in different time periods by adding appropriate signs and other details (sold separately). Parts are molded in appropriate colors.

JOHN'S PLACE

699-6011 8.95
2-3/4 x 5" 7 x 12.8cm
Left-hand corner building.

FURNITURE SHOWROOM

699-6015 11.95
9-1/2 x 4-1/8" 24.2 x 10.5cm
Here's a big building that's right at home in your business district! Typical of large stores, it might be a department store, furrier or perhaps a small factory with a showroom. The finished model includes the large display windows and recessed entry and measures 69 scale feet across the front, by 30 scale feet deep.

ROY'S FIX-IT SHOP

699-6009 8.95
4-3/4 x 2-3/4" 11.9 x 6.9cm

SALLY'S ANTIQUES

699-6010 8.95
4-3/4 x 2-3/4" 11.9 x 6.9cm

KEVIN'S TOY STORE

699-6021 8.95
4-3/4 x 2-3/4" 11.9 x 6.9cm

BONNIE B. BOUTIQUE

699-6022 8.95
4-3/4 x 2-3/4" 11.9 x 6.9cm

TINA'S TART SHOP

699-6000 8.95
4 x 4-1/8" 10 x 10.3cm

BUCK'S BOOK SHOP

699-6024 8.95
4-3/4 x 2-3/4" 11.9 x 6.9cm

FREYTAG'S FURNACE CO.

699-6025 8.95
4-3/4 x 2-3/4" 11.9 x 6.9cm

HAL'S HOBBIES

699-6023 8.95
4-3/4 x 2-3/4" 11.9 x 6.9cm
Right-hand corner building.

MIKE'S MARKET

699-6001 8.95
4-3/4 x 2-3/4" 11.9 x 6.9cm

TONY'S GYM

699-6002 8.95
4-3/4 x 2-3/4" 11.9 x 6.9cm

PARCEL DELIVERY SERVICE

699-6018 8.95
4-1/8 x 4-1/8" 10.5 x 10.5cm

DIME STORE & OFFICE

699-6005 8.95
4 x 4-1/8" 10 x 10.3cm

HARDWARE STORE

699-6006 8.95
4 x 4-1/8" 10 x 10.3cm

OLD INDIAN TOBACCO SHOP

699-6014 8.95
2-3/4 x 5" 7 x 12.8cm

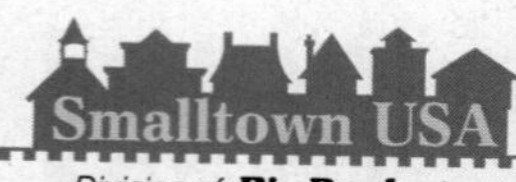

Division of ***Rix Products***

VIVIAN'S FAMILY SHOE STORE

699-6013 8.95
2-3/4 x 5" 7 x 12.8cm

FREIGHT OFFICE

699-6008 8.95
4 x 4-1/8" 10 x 10.3cm

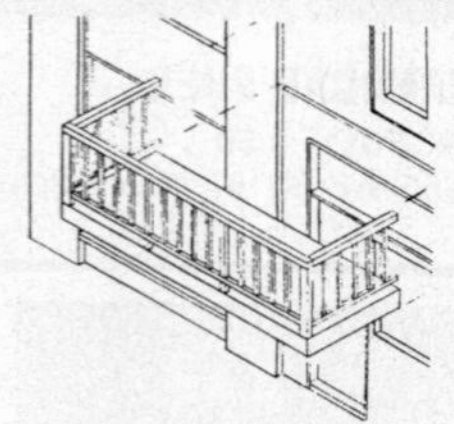

BALCONY KIT

699-6 1.99

DRUG STORE

699-6017 8.95
4-1/8 x 4-1/8" 10.5 x 10.5cm

JESSICA'S SALON

699-6003 8.95
4-3/4 x 2-3/4" 11.9 x 6.9cm

CYCLE REPAIR SHOP

699-6019 8.95
4-1/8 x 4-1/8" 10.5 x 10.5cm

HELEN'S COUNTRY KITCHEN

699-6012 8.95
2-3/4 x 5" 7 x 12.8cm

MADELENE'S DELI

699-6004 7.75
4-3/4 x 2-3/4" 11.9 x 6.9cm

CAB COMPANY

699-6007 8.95
4 x 4-1/8" 10 x 10.3cm

FLORIST'S OFFICE

699-6016 8.95
4 x 4-1/8" 10 x 10.3cm

APPLIANCE MART

699-6020 11.95
5-1/4 x 5" 13.4 x 12.8cm

TALLTOWN BUILDINGS

Make your city skyline more realistic with really tall buildings! They're easy to create from these complete kits, or design your own using the four different modules. Parts are made of plastic.

VICKY'S

699-6027 28.50
You'll find the latest styles in this big five-story store. A prime location for a department store or any commercial venture.

RUSTY'S GRAPHIC ARTS

699-6028 13.50
7-7/8 x 4-13/16" 20 x 12.2cm
Perfect for revitalizing any downtown, Rusty modernized the storefront by adding larger windows and a four-door entry. The kit includes TallTown modules for the brick walls, windows and doors, plus Evergreen stock to build-up the the framing for the new windows.

ROGY'S

699-6030 13.50
9-1/2 x 4-1/8" 23.7 x 10.3cm
Shop for a work of art to decorate your home, or the materials you need to create one at this big double store. A great addition to the business district, the structure features an as-built upper floor with brick walls and older style windows, while the first floor has been modernized. The kit includes injection molded brick walls, along with four TallTown modules and Evergreen strip and sheet styrene. Construction is similar to other kits in the series, but the modernized front needs to be built up from the Evergreen materials.

TALLTOWN MODULES PKG(6) EA 3.00

Use these modules in an endless variety of ways to create custom high-rise buildings for your city scene.

699-7001 #1 Four Doors

699-7002 #2 Four Windows-Equal Panes

699-7003 #3 Two Small End-Two Large Middle Windows

699-7004 #4 Four Large Pane Windows

WALLS

FRONT WALL W/RECESSED ENTRY

699-1 1.50

FRONT WALL W/FLUSH ENTRY

699-2 1.50

FRONT WALL W/CORNER ENTRY

699-3 1.95

SUGAR PINE MODELS

Manufactured by Ye Olde Huff-N-Puff

Craft Train kits feature stripwood, plastic doors, windows and details, plus roofing material (where called for) and complete instructions.

LOGGING ENGINE HOUSE

685-1107 28.00
5-1/2 x 12" 14 x 25.5cm

OIL LOADING FACILITY

685-1105 22.00
2-1/2 x 7" 6.5 x 18cm

SANDHOUSE

685-1114 23.00
1-1/2 x 7" 4 x 18cm

FIREHOUSE (ALPINE HOSE)

685-1103 26.00
3 x 7" 7.5 x 17.8cm
Prototype in Georgetown, Colorado.

BRANCH LINE WATER TANK

685-1112 18.00
2 x 2" 5 x 5cm

SMELTER WORKS

685-1101 17.00
3-3/4 x 4-1/2" 9.5 x 11.5cm

COURT HOUSE

685-1102 21.00
3-3/4 x 4-1/2" 9.5 x 11.5cm

FARM STYLE WATER TANK

685-1111 24.00
2-3/4 x 2-3/4" 7 x 7cm

COVERED AUTO BRIDGE

685-1113 25.00
3 x 9-1/2" 7.5 x 24cm

SAM'S SUPPLY STORE

685-1100 17.00
3-3/4 x 5" 9.5 x 12.7cm
With loading dock.

TWIN TANKS

685-1104 pkg(2) 17.00
2 x 3" 5 x 7.5cm

STATE TOOL & DIE CO.

RAILROAD PRIVY

C&O standard design. Features detailed plastic parts and basic instructions. Can also be used as a small storage shed.

661-500 Single Kit 3.95
661-5003 Set of 3 8.95

PASSENGER SHELTER

661-525 11.95
Assembled structure.

Kits are injection-molded styrene.

400T CONCRETE COALING TOWER

293-7010 135.00
Tower spans two tracks and services a third. Includes separate coal shed with raised track, sand drying house and equipment shed.

COALING TOWER LIFT MECHANISM

293-8008 20.00

HANDCAR SHED

293-7011 9.50
1-5/8 x 2-11/16" 4.1 x 6.8cm

STEEL WATER TANK

293-7012 29.50
5 x 5 x 8-1/2"
12.7 x 12.7 x 21.6cm

OIL TANK

293-7013 15.00

These craft train kits feature precut, color-coded wood, cast window frames, construction board, roofing, aluminum siding and sheet brass where needed, plus illustrated instructions.

ICING PLATFORM
690-3020 39.95
18 x 4" 45.6 x 10.2cm

ICING PLATFORM EXTENSION KIT (ADDS 18")
690-30201 19.95

FREIGHT STATION
690-3030 32.95
6-3/4" x 3-1/4" 16.9 x 8.1cm

YARD OFFICE
690-3040 32.95
4 x 8" 10 x 20cm

LOGGING CAMP
690-3050 32.95
8-1/2 x 11" 21.5 x 28cm

MODERN GRAIN ELEVATOR
690-3060 44.95
13 x 9-1/2" 32.5 x 23.8cm

GRAIN ELEVATOR EXTENSION KIT (ADDS 4 SILOS)
690-30601 19.95
3-3/8 x 4" 8.4 x 10cm

FM AUTOMATIC COALING STATION
690-3080 18.98
2-1/2 x 4" 6.2 x 10cm
Underground storage.

Easy-to-build kits are molded in styrene.

STORAGE TANK KIT
782-50100 pkg(3) **24.95**
Includes mounting bases, ladder and walkway, loading platform, pipelines, pumps and fittings. Less vehicles and figures.

PIPELINES AND FITTINGS
782-62000 6.45
Includes piping, valves, els, tees, unions and pumps.

MILK STOP KIT
782-50200 21.95
6-1/4 x 4-1/2 x 2-1/8"
Features metal roofing, plastic windows doors and milk cans.

LOADING FACILITY
782-50000 21.95
3-3/4 x 5-5/8" 9.6 x 14.2cm
Simulated stud and beam structure. Corrugated metal covering, 5 frame windows and floor. Includes porch, steps and foundation.

YE OLD HUFF-N- PUFF

Wooden Craft Train Kits include Metal and/or plastic details and instructions.

YE OLDE WORK SHOP
792-1001 17.00
3 x 4-1/2" 7.7 x 11.5cm

THE DRAKE OIL WELL
792-1002 30.00
3-1/2 x 5-1/2" 8.9 x 14cm
World's first oil well, near Titusville, Pennsylvania.

CABOOSE WAY STATION
792-1003 21.00

BOX CAR WAY STATION
792-1004 21.00

Information STATION

CIRCUS AND CARNIVAL TRAINS

From the late 1880s to the 1950s, many of America's circuses and carnivals traveled by train. Most used second-hand equipment that had been built for other shows, as circus cars were unique to railroading.

Since railroads charged for the number of cars, not the size, show owners quickly discovered they could carry more on larger cars. Long before high-capacity freight cars appeared, circuses were rolling from town to town on huge 72' long flats, twice the size of the standard 36' car. (Railroads really didn't catch on to the idea until the 1950s when the Pennsy introduced its 75' Truc-Train flat cars for piggyback traffic.)

Before trucks and tractors, teams of horses moved the show from the train to the lot. Once again, the basic 36' car was doubled and horses traveled in 72' long stock cars. On shows that were big enough to carry them, heavier elephant cars were used. These were also 72' long, but had solid wooden sides supported by steel braces and very small vents (elephants are susceptible to respiratory infections).

Fully loaded and moving across your railroad, a complete circus train can be quite a sight! If space is a problem, you could easily convert an older passenger car into an advance car, and have the crew fanning out from the depot, with a crowd of excited residents watching them work.

Kits feature wood construction with plastic parts, hydrocal castings, corrugated or paper shingle roofing and complete instructions. Kits marked EBT are based on structures along the historic East Broad Top Railroad in Pennsylvania.

We have worked closely with this manufacturer to provide accurate delivery information at the time this catalog was published. Items listed in blue ink may not be available at all times. Current delivery information, along with a list of in-stock products for this line, can be found on our Web site at www.walthers.com.

TIMBER TRANSFER CRANE, EBT
771-5 27.45
4 x 6" 10.2 x 15.3cm
Prototype in Mt. Union, Pennsylvania.

LOCO & MACHINE SHOP
771-8 27.95
6 x 8" 15.3 x 20.5cm

SANDING TOWER, EBT
771-1 21.95
2 x 6" 5 x 15.3cm
Prototype in Orbisonia, Pennsylvania.

COLES STATION, EBT
771-2 19.95

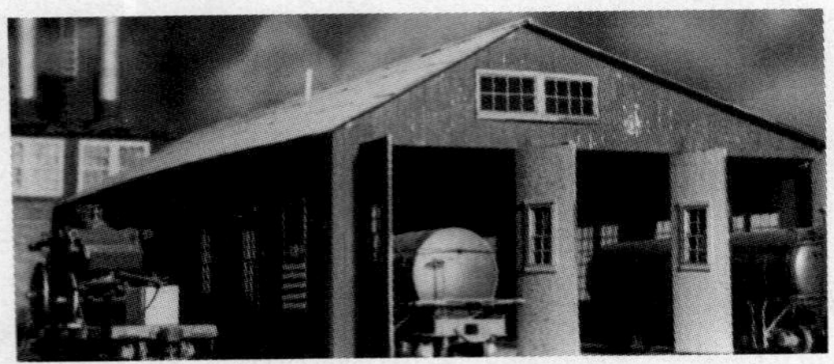

THE CAR SHOP, EBT
771-10 29.95
6 x 10" 15.3 x 25.5cm

FOUNDRY AND PATTERN HOUSE, EBT
771-7 31.90
4 x 14" 10.2 x 32cm
Modeled after the house in the EBT yard in Orbisonia, Pennsylvania.

GEISER MANUFACTURING
771-5007 5.95

ZARFO'S & BURG BUILDING
771-5008 7.95

FOX PIANO BUILDING
771-5009 7.95
4 x 2-3/4" 10.2 x 7cm

ATSAN ICE COMPANY
771-12 32.95
4 x 6" 10.2 x 15.6cm

THREE SPRINGS ORE TIPPLE
771-6 30.75
2 x 8" 5 x 20.5cm
Prototype stood at Three Springs, Pennsylvania.

COALING DOCK, EBT
771-4 32.95
4 x 12" 10.2 x 31cm
Prototype in Orbisonia, Pennsylvania.

THREE SPRINGS STATION, EBT
771-14 27.95

DRYING KILN
771-13 29.99
1-5/8 x 3-7/8" 4.1 x 9.8cm

WOOSTER GAS WAREHOUSE
771-11 31.95
3 x 6" 7.5 x 15.6cm

THE BOILER HOUSE
771-9 29.95
3 x 4" 7.5 x 10.2cm

ENCLOSED WATER TOWER, EBT
771-3 27.45
3 x 4" 7.5 x 10.2cm
Prototype in Saltillo, Pennsylvania.

POSSUM HOLLOW
785-151 24.98
An abandoned caboose has been converted to a home for a rural family. The piles of accumulated junk add to that backwoods atmosphere of the scene.

CABOOSE & SAND FACILITY
785-152 24.98
This is a common sight found around railroad yards. The sand tower supplies the locomotives' needs while the storage shed keeps the caboose well stocked.

OTIS COAL COMPANY
785-153 29.98
Private coal companies like this were found along spur lines throughout the United States. Such facilities served as the links between the long coal trains and the consumer.

TIE AND PLANK MILL
785-154 29.98
Steam powered sawmill...a small industry with lots of possibilities for your layout.

SMILEY'S TOW SERVICE
785-130 24.98

SMOKEHOUSE
785-213 8.49

TOOL SHED
785-216 8.49

PHARMACY
785-221 11.98

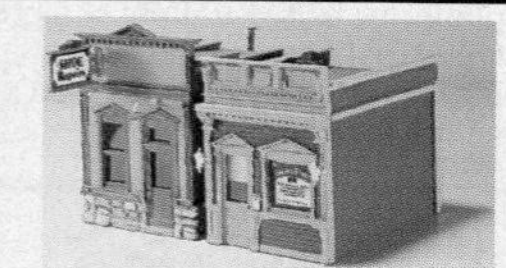

DOCTOR'S OFFICE & SHOE REPAIR
785-224 11.98

ROCKY'S TAVERN
785-238 11.98

BRANCH LINE WATER TOWER
785-241 11.98

AERMOTOR WINDMILL
785-209 6.98

3 OUTHOUSES & MAN
785-214 8.49

ICE HOUSE
785-219 11.98

TICKET OFFICE
785-222 11.98

TRACKSIDE SCALE
785-231 6.98

FLAG DEPOT
785-239 11.98

TUCKER BROTHERS
785-240 11.98

3 FUEL STANDS
785-212 6.98

CHICKEN COOP
785-215 8.49

DANIEL'S OUTFITTERS
785-220 11.98

GAS STATION
785-223 11.98

DIESEL FUEL FACILITY
785-232 6.98

GAZEBO
785-236 8.49

RURAL SAWMILL
785-243 8.49

VOLLMER

BULK MATERIAL CONVEYOR

770-5540 84.99 *NEW*
7-13/64 x 10 x 2-13/64" 18 x 25 x 7cm
Animate your mines or industrial areas with this working conveyor. Includes drive motor and continuous belt, suitable for moving scale coal and other large materials.

HALLE VIADUCT

770-2550 54.99 *NEW*
28-13/16 x 2-13/16 x 9-13/64" 72 x 7 x 23cm
Designed for ease of construction with maximum detail, this modern steel span makes it easy to cross any obstacle along your line. Kit includes support girders and pilings, along with decking and more.

PUMPHOUSE W/LOCO WATER SPOUT

770-5708 33.99 *NEW*
5-1/2 x 1-5/8 x 4-5/8" 13.8 x 11.5 x 4cm
This distinctly different building adds character to any steam-era engine terminal. Prototype houses pumps and machinery, while a wall-mounted water spout serves passing locos.

TAXI STAND W/VEHICLE

770-5150 31.99 *NEW*
7-5/8 x 3-13/64 x 2" 19 x 8 x 5cm
Now you can always find a cab when you need one! Great detail for any modern city, this kit includes a steel and glass passenger shelter, various signs and other details, plus a specially painted Taxi with Vollmer advertising.

BUS STATION/PLATFORMS

770-5148 15.99 *NEW*
Modern detail for metropolitan street scenes. Includes three platforms with a variety of signs, benches and nonworking street lights, plus two modern steel and glass passenger shelters. (Check out the Vehicles and Figures section to create a complete mini-scene for your city!)

SMALL COALING TOWER W/CRANE

770-5718 31.99 *NEW*
6 x 3-5/8 x 4-13/64"
15 x 9 x 10.5cm
Service steam power on branches or shortlines with this super model. Packed with details, the kit includes a positionable jib crane and more.

FELLBACH SIGNAL TOWER

770-5734 35.99 *NEW*
6 x 2-13/64 x 6-13/16"
15 x 7 x 17cm
Handsome three-story structure is perfect for a busy freight yard or passenger terminal. Looks great on steam- or diesel era layouts.

ALTBACH HALF-TIMBER CHURCH

770-3768 59.99 *NEW*
7-13/16 x 5-5/8 x 12"
19.5 x 14 x 30cm
With its distinctive bell/clock tower, this handsome building is ideal for a city scene or a rural area. Realistic parts simulate half-timber and stucco construction, as well as stained glass windows. (Great add-on to your seasonal display or Christmas Village!)

GERA WATER TOWER

770-5707 35.99 *NEW*
4 x 4-13/32 x 10-13/32"
10 x 11 x 26cm
Perfect for a late steam-era engine terminal, large steel tanks like this are a great addition to large industries too! Detailed model includes massive "steel" supports and safety-cage ladders.

VOLLMER

COAL BINS

770-5717 8.99 ***NEW***
4-13/32 x 1-13/32 x 15/16"
11 x 3.5 x 2.3cm
In the steam-era, trackside bins like these could be found at small town lumber yards and grain elevators, many of which sold coal as a sideline. Plastic parts are molded to look like real wood. Add Coal from #770-5223, sold separately, for the final touch of detail.

COAL

770-5223 5.99 ***NEW***
Detail your new Coal Bins (770-5717), Conveyor (770-5540) or Coaling Tower (770-5718, all sold separately). Synthetic material looks like the real thing, but handles easily.

ALPINE LODGE

770-3708 20.99

BUTCHER'S SHOP

770-3674 32.99
4-5/8 x 3-13/16 x 6"
11.5 x 9.5 x 15cm
There's nothing like sinking your teeth into a fresh steak! This neat structure has a ground floor shop, with an elevated stair way. Colorful signs are included.

HALF-TIMBERED HOUSE

770-3673 Gray **19.99**
2 x 3-5/16 x 5-5/16"
5.2 x 8.3 x 13.3cm
Classic construction for the busy city scene.

BOOK STORE

770-3669 29.99
4-3/16 x 3-1/4 x 5-1/2"
10.5 x 8.2 x 13.8cm
You'll have hours of fun shopping for your favorite railroad books in this half-timber building. Lots of add-on details included.

HALF-TIMBERED HOUSE

770-3672 White **19.99**
2 x 3-5/16 x 5-5/16"
5.2 x 8.3 x 13.3cm
A charming blend of old and traditional half-timber and stucco construction, plus modern details such as a TV antenna and chimney are included.

CATHEDRAL

770-3739 99.99
11-3/4 x 5-3/8 x 15-3/4"
30 x 13.5 x 40cm
Built between 1853 and 1855, the prototype of this beautiful cathedral still stands in Germany. Its period architecture is similar to buildings found in many cities throughout the world. For extra realism, full-color stained glass "windows," printed on translucent paper, are included. For a slightly larger and more detailed scene, the Cathedral Steps (770-3738) which measure 16-1/2 x 7-7/8 x 1/2" can be added.

CATHEDRAL STEPS

770-3738 19.99

MORITZBURG STATION

770-3502 99.99 ***NEW***
21-13/64 x 6 x 7-13/64" 53 x 15 x 18cm
This bustling station is perfect for a bigger city along your railroad. The second floor can house company offices, the chief dispatcher or other important officials. Complete with attached station platform, signs and much more.

COVERED BRIDGE

770-2515 26.99
8-13/16 x 3-1/8 x 3-5/8" 22 x 7.8 x 9cm
Some of these old-timers are still standing on less-traveled roads. Plastic parts feature realistic woodgrain detail and color. Perfect for early steam-era layouts.

VOLLMER

HOUSE

770-3670 Tan **19.99**
2 x 3-5/16 x 5-5/16"
5.2 x 8.3 x 13.3cm
This remarkable residence will look great in suburban downtown areas.

HOUSE

770-3671 Yellow **19.99**
2 x 3-5/16 x 5-5/16"
5.2 x 8.3 x 13.3cm
A perfect starter home in the heart of any city.

SWISS DARLIGEN STATION

770-3515 55.99
13-1/2 x 5-1/4"
34.5 x 13.5cm

STORAGE RACKS

770-5748 pkg(3) **16.99**
2-1/4 x 3/4" 6 x 2.1cm

SCHONWIES STATION

770-3525 38.99
9-7/8 x 5-1/8 x 3"
25 x 12.8 x 7.8cm

SCALE HOUSE

770-5721 13.99
1-3/4 x 1-3/8 x 1-3/4"
4.5 x 3.5 x 4.6cm

KOF ENGINE SHED

770-5761 21.99
2-3/4 x 1-5/8" 6.7 x 4cm

OPERATING DIESEL 2-STALL SHED

770-5760 63.99
13 x 5-7/8 x 3-7/8"
33 x 15 x 10cm

RAILWAY WORKSHOP

770-5603 19.99
4-3/8 x 2-1/4 x 2-1/4"
11 x 5.8 x 5.8cm

SINGLE ENGINE SHED

770-5750 37.99
6-1/8 x 4-7/8 x 3-1/2"
15.5 x 12.5 x 9cm

CORRUGATED HUTS

770-5743 pkg(3) **18.99**
2-1/6 x 1-1/16 x 1-5/16"
5.2 x 2.8 x 3.3cm

STATION "REITH"

770-3530 45.99

STATION ROAD VALUE SET

770-3675 124.99
Set includes 1 Each; 3669, 3670, 3671, 3672, 3673 and 3674, perfect for modeling a complete neighborhood on a display layout or module.

FREIGHT SHED W/CRANE & RAMP

770-5701 38.99
11-3/8 x 3-7/8 x 3-1/2"
29 x 10 x 9cm
This busy freight shed will be a good customer for any railroad! A large platform, detailed loading crane and opening doors are all included. A few extra figures and details will bring the finished model to life!

VILLAGE INN

770-3637 49.99
7-13/16 x 5 x 6"
19.5 x 12.5 x 15cm
This delightful kit makes a perfect German restaurant, tourist stop or bread and breakfast. Authentic styling and parts molded in color capture the old-world flavor.

FREIGHT WAREHOUSE

770-3899 38.99
11-1/8 x 4-1/8 x 4-1/8"
28.5 x 10.5 x 10.5cm
Expand your yard or industrial park with this modern structure. Opening freight doors make interior detailing easy! Just add loads and figures for a neat mini-scene on your layout.

WAREHOUSE

770-5604 23.99
6-1/4 x 4 x 2-1/2"
16 x 10 x 6.5cm

ENGINE CLEANING PLANT

770-5747 23.99
4-7/8 x 1-3/16" 12.5 x 3.2cm

COAL BUNKER

770-5719 28.99
5-5/8 x 2-1/2" 13 x 6 X 6.5cm

COVERED PLATFORM

770-3534 25.99
14-5/8 x 1-7/8 x 2-3/4"
37 x 4.8 x 7cm

COVERED PLATFORM

770-3537 22.99
14-5/8 x 1-3/8 x 2-5/8"
37 x 3.4 x 6.7cm

VOLLMER

MODERN COVERED PLATFORM, SMALL

770-3542 27.99
11 x 3-1/8" 28 x 8cm

SERVICE PLATFORM

770-3558 14.99
35-1/4 x 1-1/8 x 1/4"
29 x 10 x 9cm

ALPINE RESTAURANT

770-3706 45.99
6 x 5-7/8 x 4"
17.8 x 15 x 11.5cm

VOLLMER SPECIAL #3

770-5630 61.99
Includes a small trackside building and a specially painted and lettered Marklin box car, with full-color graphics of the Waldbronn Station kit. Great for displays or operation.

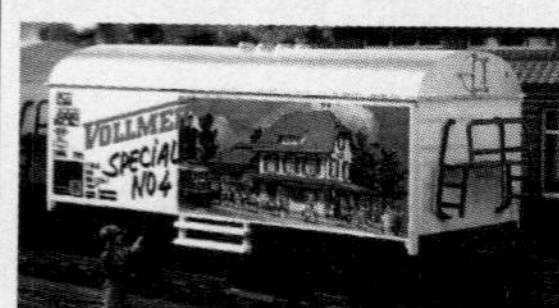

VOLLMER SPECIAL SET #4

770-5631 59.99
Complete your collection with the latest Repair Shed and specially decorated Marklin box car combo

BADEN-BADEN STATION

770-3560 114.99
30-3/4 x 6-1/4 x 7-7/8" 78 x 16 x 20 cm
This beautiful building is typical of large stations built at the turn-of-the century. Its classic design is ideal for American or European theme layouts. The numerous windows invite interior detailing and lighting for spectacular night scenes! Matching platforms (770-3559) are available for modeling the complete station scene.

VOLLMER SPECIAL #1

770-5729 61.99
6-3/8 x 3" 15.5 x 7.5cm

INTERLOCKING YARD TOWER

770-5731 24.99
5-1/8 x 2 x 5-1/8"
13 x 5 x 13cm

COAL DEPOT

770-5615 49.99
7-5/8 x 5-5/8 x 4"
19 x 14 x 10cm
Steam-era homes will welcome this business to the neighborhood! Here, coal was unloaded from hoppers then delivered to customers by wagon or truck. A charming period structure.

TWO-STALL ENGINE HOUSE

770-5753 66.99
12-7/16 x 8-7/16 x 5-1/2"
31 x 21 x 13.8cm
Keep your logging, mining or shortline power ready for its next job. The big stall doors can be built open or closed and many details are included.

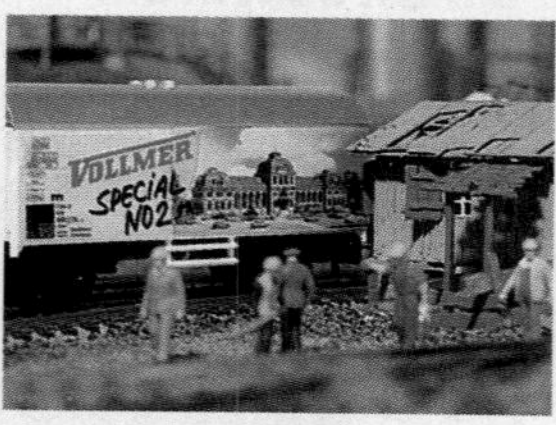

VOLLMER SPECIAL #2

770-5629 61.99
Run-down freight station with specially decorated freight car.

SANDING TOWER

770-5740 33.99
3-1/8 x 2-3/4 x 5-15/16"
8 x 7 x 15.2cm

PLATFORM W/COVER

770-3559 47.99
40-1/2 x 1-7/8 x 2-5/8" 102 x 4.8 x 6.6cm
This ornate platform is based on prototypes at Baden-Baden. Its classic design is perfect for passenger service from the steam-era to modern Amtrak. Printed signs, benches, a newsstand and two non-operating lamps are included. Several can be combined to build a longer platform.

NORDSTADT STATION

770-3561 66.99
21-1/4 x 6-1/4 x 6-1/4" 54 x 16 x 16cm
Serving a suburb or city, this medium-size station is ideal for layouts or modules.

VOLLMER SPECIAL #5

770-5632 59.99 ***NEW***
Includes Tool Shed kit with a specially painted Marklin box car, featuring a full-color view of a Vollmer station.

VOLLMER

CROSSING SHANTY

770-5730 18.99
4-3/8 x 2-3/8 x 3"
11 x 6.1 x 7.5cm

SIGNAL TOWER-DOUBLE TRACK

770-5739 31.99
7-1/2 x 2-3/4 x 5-1/8"
19.2 x 7 x 13cm

KINDERGARTEN

770-3664 48.99
5-5/16 x 4-3/4" 13.5 x 12cm

BERWANG STATION

770-9050 39.99
11 x 6-1/2" 27.3 x 16.5cm

WALTHERS US EXCLUSIVE FOR 2000

"VAMPIRE" VILLA

770-3679 69.99
4-13/16 x 4-13/16 x 5-13/16" 12 x 12 x 14.5cm
Come, spend the night. We dare you! The level of detail on this haunted mansion is downright scary! From the boarded-up windows to the eerie red light that flickers inside, this old house is sure to give you the creeps! And for more frightening fun, a blanket of fog can be generated using Smoke Unit #4114, sold separately.

SIX STALL ROUNDHOUSE

770-5758 159.99
16-1/8 x 35 x 5-1/8" 41 x 89 x 13cm

THREE STALL ROUNDHOUSE

770-5754 99.99
13 x 19-5/8 x 4-7/8" 33 x 50 x 12cm

ROOF SUPPORT FOR #5654

770-5255 6.99
Modifies six stall roundhouse for use with Fleischmann turntable.

EXTENSION PARTS FOR #5754

770-5256 9.99
Modifies roundhouse for use with Marklin turntable. Showcase your motive power in this roundhouse! A must for steam-era layouts, many are still in use. The kit captures the flavor of the prototype, and is small enough to fit any layout. Additional kits can be combined to build a larger structure, even a complete circle! With a 15 degree angle between bays, the round house can be used with various turntables. Locos up to 11-3/8" long can be stored inside.

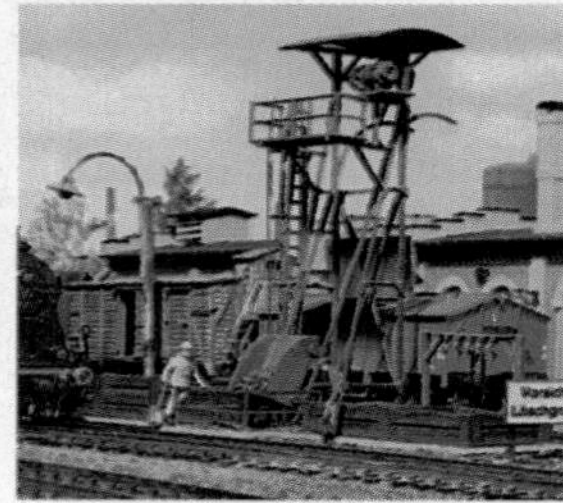

CINDER CONVEYOR

770-5741 27.99
2-9/16 x 1-9/16 x 4-3/16"
6.5 x 4 x 10.6cm

ORNATE WATER TOWER

770-5704 35.99
3-5/8 x 3-5/8" 9 x 9cm

SMOKE GENERATOR FOR #3679

770-4114 35.99

This small engine shed is well suited to shortline operations. Use with steam and diesel locos, or electrics using a catenary section (770-1347) and base frame (770-5253).

2 STALL ENGINE SHED

770-5752 65.99
12 x 7-5/8 x 3-1/2"
30.5 x 19.5 x 9cm

BASE FRAME FOR #5752

770-5253 pkg(2) **6.99**

GARDEN CENTER

770-3644 33.99

SUMMER GARDEN HOUSE

770-3643 21.99

HUNTERS' RAISED HIDE-AWAY

770-3795 13.99
1-3/16 x 1-3/16" 3 x 3cm

VOLLMER

HAYLOFT
770-3794 17.99
2 x 2" 5 x 5cm

BARN
770-3727 35.99
5-1/2 x 3-3/4" 14 x 9.6cm

SMOKEHOUSE
770-3733 16.99
2-3/8 x 2-1/8 x 3"

WINERY FESTIVAL
770-3680 38.99
6-1/4 x 5-1/2" 16 x 14cm
Includes an outdoor serving area with benches, wine press and wooden storage barrel.

STEEL STORAGE DEPOT
770-5616 39.99
12-13/16 x 7 x 4-1/8" 32 x 17.5 x 10.3cm
A perfect addition outside any steel fabrication shop or heavy industry. Includes overhead crane, storage racks and covered work area with realistic steel beams and roof.

FREIGHT STATION
770-5715 53.99
15 x 5-1/8 x 5-3/8" 38 x 13 x 13.5cm
Found in every town and major yards, freight stations served industries without sidings. Vollmer loads, listed in the Scenery section, are perfect for detailing this kit.

RIFLE RANGE
770-3704 61.99
8-3/32 x 8-13/32 x 6-5/8" 20.2 x 21 x 14cm
Set your sites on this handsome structure and you'll have a unique addition to your layout! It's many architectural features make it a natural for a sporting club, golf course or restaurant. And there's a full set of bullseyes and a pit for target practice.

STABLE W/PIGEON LOFT
770-3726 37.99
5-1/2 x 3-1/8" 14 x 8cm

FARMYARD ACCESSORIES
770-3729 18.99
Includes well, pump, rubbish dumps and duck house.

ALPINE HOUSE/FARM
770-3705 51.99
7-1/4 x 5 x 3-1/2"
18.5 x 12.8 x 9.2cm

VINTNER'S LODGE
770-3732 33.99
4-3/4 x 3-1/2 x 5-3/4"
12 x 9 14.5cm

SWITCH TOWER
770-5736 35.99
6 x 3-5/8" 15.2 x 9cm
The prototype for this classic switch tower is still used by the DB, and is located in Wiesbaden, Germany.

FARMHOUSE
770-3730 33.99
4 x 3 x 4-7/8"
10.3 x 7.5 x 12.5cm

HOUSE UNDER CONSTRUCTION
770-3691 42.99
6-7/8 x 5-1/2" 17.5 x 14cm

HOUSE W/BARN
770-3731 33.99
4-7/8 x 2-3/4 x 4-3/4"
12.5 x 7 x 12cm

TANNER'S HOUSE
770-3734 33.99
4-3/8 x 3-3/4"
11 x 8.5 x 12cm

COACH HOUSE
770-3685 31.99
4-1/2 x 4-5/16" 11.4 x 11cm

VOLLMER

HOUSE W/SHOP

770-3723 26.99
6-7/8 x 4-3/8 x 3"
17.5 x 11 x 7.5cm

SCAFFOLDING KIT

770-3690 13.99

LIME WORKS

770-5725 71.99
5-13/16 x 5-13/64 x 12-5/8" 14.5 x 13 x 31.5cm
An essential part of many agricultural, construction and industrial products, lime works mean big business for any railroad. This vertical structure puts a lot of detail in a small space and can easily be "Americanized" as part of a quarry scene.

TIMBERED VILLAGE

770-3735 154.99
Set includes #'s 3730, 3734, 3750 and 3769.

HOUSE W/BAKERY

770-3724 26.99
4-3/4 x 4-3/4 x 3-1/8"
12 x 12 x 8cm
4-3/4 x 3 x 2-1/8"
12 x 7.5 x 5.5cm

GATEKEEPER'S HOUSE

770-3529 47.99
5-1/4 x 3-3/4" 13.2 x 9.5cm

HOUSE W/GARAGE

770-3718 23.99
4-1/2 x 4-3/4 x 3-1/2"
11.5 x 12 x 8.8cm

DURLESBACH STATION

770-3511 57.99
16-3/4 x 5-1/8" 42 x 13cm

RHEINBURG STATION PLATFORM

770-3535 27.99
14-13/16 x 2-5/8 x 2-3/8" 37 x 6.5 x 6cm
Modern style structure protects passengers from any kind of weather. Detailed steel and concrete construction, perfect for modern city scenes. Build a bigger platform with two or more kits, also matches #3536, sold separately.

SEEBURG STATION PLATFORM

770-3536 39.99
38-3/8 x 2-5/8 x 2-3/8" 96 x 6-1/2 x 6cm
Modernize any passenger terminal with this contemporary platform. Perfect for commuter operations or long-distance rail service. Includes one open and one covered platform with plenty of add-on details. Easily combined with additional kits for a longer structure.

DIESEL TANK

770-5530 24.99
7-21/64 x 5-11/16 x 3-13/16"
18.3 x 14.2 x 9.5cm
Dress-up your diesel shops with this fuel storage tank. Looks great by a busy truck terminal, construction company or refinery too! Lots of neat details, including valves, piping, vents, safety cage ladder and more.

ALPINE HOUSE- CHALET STYLE

770-3702 23.99
6-1/8 x 4-3/8 x 3"
15.5 x 11 x 7.5cm

ALPINE CHALET

770-3703 23.99
4-7/8 x 4-3/8 x 3"
12.5 x 11 x 7.5cm

LAKE SHORE HOUSE

770-3711 27.99
7-5/8 x 4-3/4 x 3-3/8"
19.5 x 12 x 8.5cm

VOLLMER

MODERN PARKING STRUCTURE

770-3802 75.99
15 x 7-1/2 x 6-3/4"
38.5 x 19 x 17cm
This modern structure will be easy to "park" on your layout! The kit has the large, realistic appearance of downtown structures, yet it's perfect for modeling a city scene in a small area. To start your scene, the kit includes a Wiking auto, decorated with the Vollmer logo! Just add vehicles, figures and other accessories (which you'll find elsewhere in this Catalog) for a great mini-diorama!

2-STORY HOUSE

770-3700 23.99
7-1/2 x 5-1/2 X 3-1/8"
19 x 14 x 8cm

MOUNTAIN COTTAGE

770-3701 23.99
4-3/4 x 5-3/8 X 3"
12.5 x 13.5 x 7.5cm

MOUNTAIN LODGE

770-3796 30.99
6-1/2 x 3-1/2" 16.5 x 8.5cm

COTTAGE

770-3714 23.99
7-1/2 x 6-1/8 X 3-1/8"
19 x 15.5 x 8cm

COMPLETE FARMSTEAD

770-3737 154.99
Includes one each #3725, 3726, 3727, 3729 and 3733, with walls and gates.
Here's everything you'll need to start farming...in one complete kit! this set includes a farmhouse, Barn, Stable, Accessory Set (well, pump, rubbish dump and duck house), Bake House, plus stone walls and gates. The kits can be arranged in various ways to fit your available space.

VILLAGE INN RATHSKELLER

770-3754 46.99
4-3/4 x 4-3/4 x 5-3/4"
12 x 12 x 14.5cm
HO travelers will enjoy a restful night at this Village Inn. A center of activity in any small town, a few extra details can convert the kit into an "Old World" restaurant for a city scene!

3-DOOR GARAGE

770-3757 16.99
4-3/8 x 2-3/4 x 1-3/4"
11 x 7 x 4.5cm

FORESTER'S HOUSE

770-3792 44.99
5-1/2 x 4-1/2 x 5"
14 x 11.5 x 12.5cm
Nestled in the woods, this handsome kit can serve as a house or hunting lodge.

COUNTRY HOUSE

770-3713 23.99
5-1/8 x 5-1/8 x 2-3/4"
13 x 13 x 7cm

RESTAURANT

770-3781 55.99
6-1/16 x 4-11/16"
15.5 x 12cm

PUBLIC RECORD OFFICE

770-3773 48.99
4-3/8 x 7 x 8"
11 x 10.8 x 20.5cm

STATION RESTAURANT

770-3663 49.99
7-3/4 x 4-3/4" 19.8 x 12cm

VIADUCT

770-2513 36.99
12-1/4 x 2-5/8 x 5-3/4" 30.6 x 6.5 x 14.3cm
This detailed brick viaduct is ideal for a steam- or diesel-era right-of-way. It can be lengthened with #2512 and #2529 (both sold separately) to cross a larger area.

VIADUCT ENLARGEMENT

770-2512 16.99
4 x 2-5/8 x 5-3/4" 10.2 x 6.5 x 14.3cm
Matches the brick construction of #2513, allows for easy expansion of the viaduct, sold separately.

BRIDGE PILING

770-2529 Bridge Piling HO **6.99**
Matches pilings included with kit #2513, for use with kit #2512, sold separately.

VOLLMER

LUIGI'S PIZZERIA
770-3681 46.99
7 x 4-1/2 x 5"
18 x 11.5 x 12.8cm

CITY HOTEL
770-3782 55.99
5-3/8 x 5-1/16" 13.8 x 13cm

CLASSIC STYLE BUILDING W/CAFE
770-3770 48.99
4-3/4 x 4 x 7-3/4"
12 x 10 x 19.6cm

SAWMILL
770-3797 81.99
13-1/8 x 5-1/2" 33 x 14cm

COFFEE SHOP
770-3783 55.99
6-5/8 x 4-11/16" 17 x 12cm

FOOD VENDOR STANDS
770-5144 13.99
2-13/32 x 1-5/8 x 1-13/32"
6 x 4 x 3.5cm
Go where the crowds are with these mobile snack bars. Each is complete with converted camping trailer kit and colorful signs.

CAMPER
770-5147 17.99
2-13/32 x 1-5/8 x 1-13/32"
6 x 4 x 3.5cm
Take the family on a real get-away this year! A great detail for highway scenes behind your favorite car or truck (sold separately) camp grounds or parked by the garage waiting for next year's vacation.

PHOTO SHOP
770-3841 37.99
4 x 3-3/8 x 5-1/2"
10.5 x 8.5 x 14cm

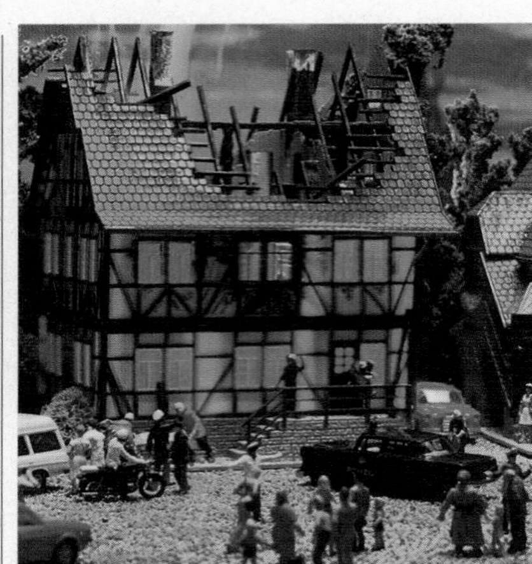

HOUSE ON FIRE
770-3728 45.99
4-3/4 x 3-1/2 x 5-3/4" 12 x 9 x 14.5cm
There's trouble in the neighborhood! This kit can be the beginning of an exciting mini-scene for your layout! The structure is realistically detailed with a burned out roof and exposed trusses. You can build the model with the fire under control, or for extra action, a smoke generator (770-4113) can be installed. Emergency vehicles, figures and other details to complete the scene can be found in the appropriate sections of the catalog.

SMOKE GENERATOR
770-4113 24.99
For #'s 3728 & 3729

4-STORY HOTEL
770-3772 48.99
4-3/8 x 3-3/4 x 8-3/4"
11 x 9.5 x 22cm

CITY COUNCIL OFFICE BUILDING
770-3750 44.99
4-3/4 x 4-1/2 x 5-1/8"
12 x 11.5 x 13cm

FLOWER SHOP
770-3692 48.99
5-3/4 x 5" 14.7 x 12.8cm

CANDY SHOP
770-3683 48.99
5-3/4 x 5 x 4-3/4"
14.7 x 12.8 x 12cm

CASTLE HOTEL
770-3777 67.99
8 x 4-1/2" 20.5 x 12cm

FARM EQUIPMENT REPAIR SHOP
770-3682 45.99
6-3/8 x 4-3/4 x 4-3/4"
15.8 x 12 x 12cm

WAREHOUSE
770-5702 86.99
16-1/8 x 6-1/2" 41x 16.5cm

BICYCLE SHOP
770-3710 43.99
7 x 5-7/8 x 3-1/2"
17.8 x 15 x 8.8cm

PUBLIC RESTROOMS
770-3762 15.99
2 x 2 x 2-3/8"
5.1 x 5.1 x 6cm
7.4 x 5-1/2" 18.5 x 14cm

FOOD STAND
770-5135 13.99

VOLLMER

OLD TIME STORE

770-3749 37.99
4-1/8 x 3-3/8 x 5-1/2"
10.5 x 8.5 x 14cm

MANSION

770-3775 111.99
12-3/8 x 4-1/4 x 8-1/16"
31.5 x 10.8 x 20.5cm
This large structure will add realism to your downtown area. It's perfect for a big city apartment building or townhouse.

BUNGALOW

770-3719 23.99
5-1/8 x 4-3/4 x 2-7/8"
13 x 12 x 7.3cm
Enjoy quiet residential living! All brick construction and a shingle roof make this an ideal starter home. The finished building requires a very small lot, so it's perfect for any neighborhood.

SHANTY

770-5728 18.99
3-1/2 x 2-3/4 x 1-3/4"
9 x 7 x 4.5cm

MODERN OFFICE BUILDING

770-3800 49.99
5-1/2 x 5-1/2 x 7-7/8"
14 x 14 x 20cm

ENGINE SHED

770-9110 29.99
6-1/2 x 5" 16 x 12.5cm

MODERN APARTMENT BUILDING

770-3801 49.99
6 x 4-9/16 x 7-7/8"
15.2 x 11.5 x 20cm

JEWELRY SHOP

770-3840 35.99
3-3/8 x 3-3/8 x 4-7/8"
8.5 x 8.5 x 12.5cm

BOOKSTORE

770-3842 37.99
3-7/8 x 3-3/8 x 5-5/8"
10 x 8.5 x 14.5cm

SUBSTATION OR ANNEX OFFICE

770-5614 16.99
2-3/8 x 2-3/4 x 2-3/4"
6 x 7 x 7cm

ORNAMENTAL FOUNTAIN

770-3758 16.99
2-1/8 x 2-1/8 x 5-3/4"
5.5 x 5.5 x 14.5cm

BURGER KING

770-3632 54.99
7-7/8 x 5-3/4" 20 x 14.8cm

RANCH STYLE HOUSE

770-3712 23.99
5-7/8 x 4-3/8 x 2-1/2" 15. x 11 x 6.5cm

WORKSHOP

770-5612 23.99
5-1/8 x 2-3/4 x 4-3/8"
13 x 7 x 11cm

ST ANDREW'S CHURCH

770-3709 48.99
7-1/4 x 5-1/2" 18.5 x 14cm

LIQUOR STORE

770-3697 55.99
8-1/16 x 5-1/8" 20.5 x 13cm
This building will be the toast of your HO neighborhood. Its ornate design makes it an eye-catching building for any street scene. A handy loading dock makes it easy to load beer and wine barrels.

4-STORY BANK BUILDING

770-3771 48.99
4-1/8 x 3-5/8 x 7-3/4"
10.5 x 9.3 x 19.7cm
This Bank Building adds interest to any downtown scene! Its small size and corner location save valuable layout space. The design lends itself to kit bashing or conversion to match American architectural styles.

CHURCH

770-9210 42.99

See What's Available at

www.walthers.com

VOLLMER

2-STORY FACTORY BUILDING
770-5610 27.99
5-1/8 x 2-3/4 x 5-1/8"
13 x 7 x 13cm

FREIGHT STATION
770-5703 48.99
12 x 6-1/2" 29.8 x 16.5cm

Limited Quantity Available

FARM HOUSE
770-9270 41.99
8-1/8 x 5-1/2" 20.5 x 14cm

EMMA'S GROCERY
770-3688 41.99
6-1/2 x 4-1/8" 16 x 10.5

GRAVEL LOADER
770-5723 86.99
11 x 4-3/8 x 5-7/8"
28 x 11 x 15cm
Electric, operating.

FARM HOUSE
770-3725 59.99
8-1/8 x 6" 20.5 x 15cm

DITZINGEN CHURCH
770-3769 59.99
9-1/2 6-1/8" 23.5 x 15.5cm

DELI/SHOP
770-3678 57.99
5-1/8 x 4-1/2" 13 x 11.5cm

SET OF THREE APARTMENTS
770-3780 109.99
Model a complete city block or housing complex with this set of three structures! The kit includes one each of #3777, 3778 and 3779. The structures can be arranged to fit your available space.

PASSENGER PLATFORM
770-3538 41.99
43-1/8 x 1-7/8 x 2-3/4"
109.5 x 4.8 x 7cm

LARGE COVERED PLATFORM
770-3541 55.99
3-3/8 x 3-13/64" 8.4 x 8cm

OIL LOADING PLATFORM
770-5527 26.99
13-3/8 x 1-7/8 x 3"

STORAGE TANK-TRIPLE
770-5520 22.99
3-3/8 x 2-3/8 x 3"

GAS STORAGE TANK
770-5526 23.99
4-3/4 x 4-3/4 x 4-1/2"

FIRE STATION W/TOWER
770-3752 44.99
4-3/4 x 4-3/4 x 8-5/8"
12 x 12 x 22cm

FIRE STATION DETAIL SET
770-5746 14.99
Details for fire stations or vehicles. Set includes hydrants, hose reels, tools, air bottles, road signs, pylons and more.

POLICE STATION W/JAIL
770-3693 62.99
7-3/4 x 5-1/2" 19.5 x 14cm

PASSENGER STATION NEUFFEN
770-3510 73.99
16-1/8 x 5-3/8 x 5-1/2"
41 x 13.5 x 16.5cm
This branch line station combines a freight house, ticket window and living quarters into one building. Based on an actual German station at Neuffen.

STATION PLATFORM NEUFFEN
770-3539 14.99
17-1/8 x 1-3/8 x 3-1/8"
43.6 x 3.5 x 8cm

VOLLMER

BOUTIQUE

770-3677 48.99
5-1/8 x 5-1/8" 13 x 13cm

Limited Quantity Available

FERRARI DEALER

770-5606 79.99
20 x 14.8cm

SUPERMARKET

770-3660 48.99
16.8 x 14cm

OLD LADIES MILL

770-3628 77.99
14-1/4 x 5-3/4" 35.5 x 14.2cm
Legend has it that if an old lady slips, she'll arrive at the bottom as a young girl! Bring the legend to your layout with this wind mill, based on an actual structure.

WALDBRONN STATION

770-3505 57.99
12-1/2 x 6" 31 x 15cm

CITY HALL

770-3760 83.99
7-1/8 x 4-3/4 x 11-1/4" 18 x 12 x 28.5cm
With its ornate clock tower and solid, stone construction, this handsome public office will be a showplace in any large city.

FIRE STATION

770-3767 69.99
11-7/16 x 4-3/4" 29 x 12cm
Practice makes perfect, for the next alarm just might be the one where you put your life on the line. Much to the delight of some passers-by, the chief has the crew putting on quite a show in front of the station. As one of the most important buildings in any town, this Fire Station is perfect for protecting a small town or suburb. Reflecting the needs of a modern community, the station has five apparatus bays that can hold a variety of equipment, as well as upstairs living quarters. Topped off by the traditional hose tower, the finished model makes a proud addition to your layout. You'll find a well-trained crew ready to go on duty in the Figures section and a complete line up of emergency equipment in Vehicles.

STATION ROAD

770-3650 pkg(4) **115.99**
Build an entire business block from this kit which includes #3645, 3646, 3647 and 3648.

RESTAURANT

770-3645 43.99
6 x 5-13/64 x 5-13/16"
15 x 13 x 14.5cm
Everyone will agree this is the place to go for lunch or dinner. The perfect building for adding a touch of ethnic flavor to any neighborhood.

SHOE SHOP

770-3646 28.99
4-13/64 x 3-1/4 x 5-1/2"
10.5 x 8.2 x 13.8cm
Find shoes for the whole family with a stop here. Detailed from top to bottom, it includes shutters, window boxes and more.

PHOTO SHOP

770-3647 28.99
5 x 3-5/8 x 4-13/16
12.3 x 9 x 12cm
You're sure to smile when you add this building to your business district. It combines a business and home as one building and includes neat "extras" like a satellite dish, vents and chimneys.

PLUMBER'S SHOP

770-3648 28.99
4-13/64 x 3-1/4 x 5-1/2"
10.5 x 8.2 x 13.8cm
Serving residential and commercial accounts, this prosperous plumber lives upstairs in this combined house and shop.

BLACKSMITH

770-3696 43.99
6-1/2 x 5-1/2" 16.5 x 14cm

GAS STATION

770-5744 28.99
3-3/8 x 4 x 1-3/4"
8.5 x 10 x 4.3cm

PUMP ISLANDS ONLY

770-5745 pkg(3) **18.99**

CURVED GIRDER BRIDGE

770-2510 18.99
7-3/8" 13.8cm long
29-7/8" 76cm diameter
This detailed bridge is designed for use on curves. Can be used with Curved Deck Bridges #2507 and #4515.

BABYLAND STORE

770-3661 45.99
12 x 11.5cm
Includes interior details, working lights, a stork and her nest

VOLLMER

BOUTIQUE
770-3694 48.99
7-1/2 x 5-5/16" 19 x 13.5cm

OLD TIME DRUG STORE
770-3747 33.99
3-3/8 x 3-3/8 x 4-7/8"
8.5 x 8.5 x 12.5cm

BUTCHER'S SHOP W/GARAGE
770-3722 26.99
4-5/8 x 3-3/8 x 4"
11.8 x 8.5 x 10.2cm

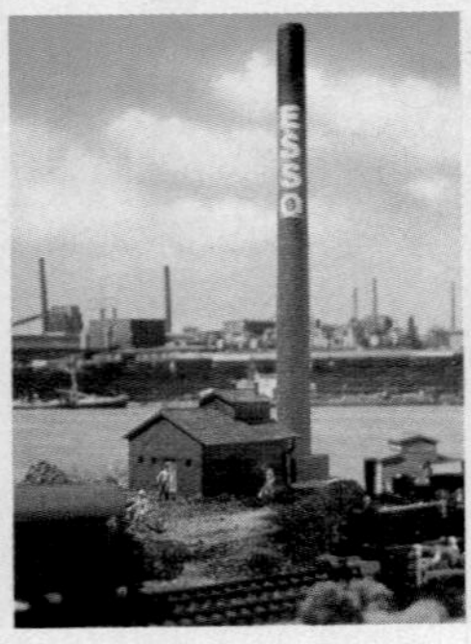

SMOKE STACK ONLY
770-6017 8.99

CAFE
770-3676 48.99
5-1/8 x 4-1/2" 13 x 11.5cm

OIL REFINERY
770-5525 53.99
5-7/8 x 3-7/8 x 9-1/4"
15 x 10 x 23.5cm
This impressive refinery packs lots of detail into a small space. Several can be combined to build a larger complex.

TRAVEL AGENCY
770-3662 42.99
7-13/64 x 4-5/8 x 4-5/8"
16 x 10.5 x 16cm

BIKERS SHOP
770-3666 44.99
6-13/32 x 4-13/64 x 5-5/8"
16 x 10.5 x 16cm

RURAL POLICE HEADQUARTERS
770-3755 67.99
10-5/8 x 5-1/2 x 6-5/8"
27 x 14 x 17cm

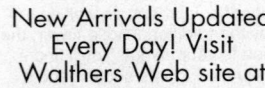

OVERHEAD CRANE
770-5727 23.99
5-5/8 x 2-5/16 x 4-13/16" 14 x 5.8 x 1 2cm
Perfect for loading big loads aboard flats or gondolas. Found at lots of industries. Loaded with details including positionable trolley and more.

OVERHEAD CRANE
770-5624 37.99
10 x 4-3/4 x 6-1/2" 25.5 x 12 x 16.5cm

BREWERY WITH INTERIOR
770-5609 65.99
16-3/8 x 5-1/2" 41.5 x 14cm
Lift your spirits with this Brewery! It's the perfect size for any layout and fits many time periods. Interior details for the boiler house included. The tall smoke stack can be fitted with a smoke generator (#4113) available separately.

PIERS
770-4004 pkg(10) **29.99**
9-1/2" 24cm high
Used to support track ramps. May be cut to shorter lengths.

BASE PLATE
770-4005 pkg(20) **58.99**
Used to support piers.

TOP SECTION
770-4006 pkg(20) **38.99**
Used to secure ramps to piers. Includes 40 mounting screws.

VOLLMER

PIER "DRESSING"
770-4512 pkg(5) **41.99**
Plastic stone for #4004.

UNLOADING RAMP
770-4011 11.99
7 x 3-13/16" 17.5 x 9.5cm

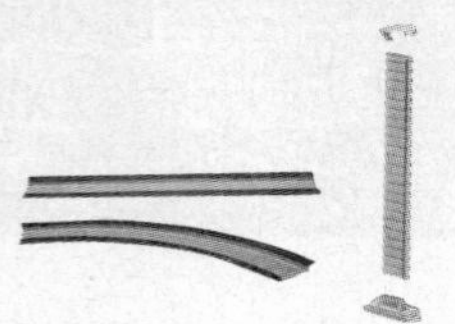

PIER & RAMP STARTER SET
770-4507 71.99
Includes 3 straight track beds #4001, 3 curved track beds #4002, 2 piers #4004, 8 top sections #1200, and bases #4005, and 16 screws.

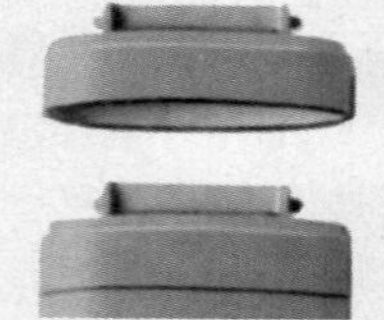

BRIDGE PIER UNITS
770-4016 pkg(20) **27.99**
3/8" 1cm high

BRIDGE PIER
770-2530 9.99
3-1/8 x 1-1/8 x 3"
8 x 3 x 7.7cm

BRIDGE ABUTMENT
770-2531 1 Pair **19.99**
3-5/8 x 1-1/4 x 3-3/4"
9.2 x 3.2 x 9.6cm

STRAIGHT TRACK RAMP
770-4001 pkg(10) **82.99**
14" 35.5cm long

CURVED TRACK RAMP
770-4002 pkg(10) **82.99**
15" Radius
770-4003 pkg(10) **72.99**
18" Radius

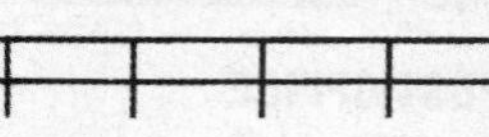

RAILINGS
770-5000 pkg(20) **13.99**
3-1/2" 9cm long

TRUSS BRIDGE
770-2505 25.99
10-5/8 x 3 x 2-1/4"
27 x 7.5 x 5.8cm

FOOT BRIDGE
770-5709 28.99
10 x 8-1/4" 25 x 21cm
HO Scale pedestrians can cross tracks, highways or other obstacles safely on this foot bridge. Standing 5" tall, there's plenty of clearance for most freight and passenger cars. Kit bashers will find lots of ways to build unique variations of the basic model.

STEEL TRUSS BRIDGE-STRAIGHT
770-2511 18.99
7-1/8 x 11 18cm long

MARKET STREET
770-3655 pkg(3) **82.99**
Dress-up your downtown with this complete set of suburban shops featuring kits #3651, 3652 and 3653.

SPORTS SHOP
770-3651 31.99
4-13/64 x 3-1/4 x 5-1/2"
10.5 x 8.2 x 13.8cm
One of the busiest stores on the block, this is THE place to find everything you need for leisure time fun.

GROCERY STORE
770-3652 28.99
5 x 3-5/8 x 4-13/16"
12.3 x 9 x 12cm
Supplying all kinds of foods, beverages and house-hold needs, these little stores can be found on city streets in many of today's cities.

HOUSE
770-3653 28.99
5 x 3-13/64 x 4-13/16"
12.3 x 8 x 12cm
City living at its best! This handsome house blends into the hustle and bustle of Market Street and provides a lovely two story home, or subdivide it and rent it as apartments.

CURVED DECK BRIDGE
770-2507 17.99
Curved bridge deck with two supports. Length: 14-3/4" 37.6cm, Radius: 29-7/8" 76cm

BOX TRUSS BRIDGE
770-2506 37.99
14-1/8 x 3 x 4-3/8"
36 x 7.5 x 11.2cm

CATENARY FOR #2506
770-1351 pkg(2) **10.99**

ARCHED BRIDGE
770-2508 41.99
26 x 6.3 x 9.5cm

ROAD GARAGE
770-3753 35.99
6-3/4 x 4-3/4 x 5-1/2"
17 x 12 x 14cm

MOTOR CROSS
770-3609 89.99
8-7/16 x 7-3/16" 21 x 18cm
Add exciting racing action with this kit. Cycles roll around the course with a hidden motor, which is included.

STONE ARCH BRIDGE - STRAIGHT
770-2509 41.99
14-1/8 x 2 3/8 x 4 1/8"
36 x 6 x 10.5
Whether modern diesel or classic steam, this bridge will fit into any era! Small enough to compliment every layout, the kit draws attention without overwhelming the scene.

HAIRDRESSER SHOP
770-3667 44.99
5-13/64 x 4-13/64 x 6-13/32"
13 x 10.5 x 16cm

ADLER INN W/BEER GARDEN
770-3736 48.99
8-1/4 x 5-1/8" 21 x 13cm

MAINTENANCE DEPOT
770-3756 33.99
5-1/2 x 3-1/8 x 6-5/8"
14 x 8 17cm

VOLLMER

OLD TIME POST OFFICE
770-3748 37.99
4 x 4-3/4 x 7-1/2"
10 x 12 x 19cm

MOUNTAIN VILLAGE
770-9300 96.99
5 building set consisting of railway station and four alpine styled homes.

HAUNTED ROTHENBURG TOWER
770-3900 41.99
3-1/2 x 3-1/2 x 14-1/2"
9 x 9 x 36.5cm
4-3/4 x 5-5/16" 12 x 13.5cm

TOWERGATE
770-3901 45.99
10-3/16 x 2-1/2" 26 x 6.3cm

SAWMILL MOTOR
770-4200 28.99
For #3793m 12V DC

CASTLE WITH GHOST
770-3910 179.99
13-3/4 x 11-3/4" 35 x 30cm

CITY WALLS
770-3903 48.99
13-3/4 x 5-7/8" 35 x 15cm

CAFE/BISTRO
770-3695 48.99
6-3/4 x 5-1/2" 16.8 x 14cm

SAWMILL
770-3793 65.99
8-7/8 x 8-1/8 x 4-1/8"
22.5 x 20.5 x 10.5cm
This attractive model can be used in almost any era! With its attached country home and large water wheel, it will make a great mini-diorama on your layout. For more realism, the wheel can be powered with motor 770-4200.

WINDMILL
770-3630 46.99
Less motor, 19 x 9cm.

POST OFFICE
770-3765 81.99
8-1/4 x 6-1/2" 21 x 16.6cm
Put your stamp of approval on this ornate Post Office! With its classic architecture, it can easily be converted to a school, library or other public building by adding appropriate details and figures.

MODERN FIRE STATION
770-3759 65.99
1-1/4 x 5-7/8" 3.2 x 15cm
Don't be "alarmed", this large firehouse fits any city scene! Three structures (main building, lobby/office and six-story hose tower) are included and can be arranged in a variety of ways. The large glass doors can be opened to display engines parked inside. (See the Vehicles Section for a complete listing of fire fighting vehicles. Engine and figures available separately.)

PLAYGROUND
770-3665 11.99

For Daily Product Updates Point Your Browser to

www.walthers.com

RAILROAD PERSONNEL HOME
770-3786 44.99
5-1/4 x 3-5/8" 13 x 9cm

VOLLMER

HOUSE ENZIAN
770-9253 16.99
5 x 4-1/2" 12.5 x 11cm

FREIGHT PLATFORM
770-5716 35.99
32-13/16 x 2 x 3-16/64"
82 x 4.8 x 16cm

HOUSE AT THE LINE
770-3787 44.99
5-1/4 x 3-5/8" 13 x 9cm

COALING TOWER
770-5720 64.99
7-5/8 x 7-3/16 x 5-5/8"
19 x 18 x 14cm
Refuel your entire steam fleet from this modern facility. Easily adapted to industrial bulk loading of coal, sand, ore and more.

PLATFORM HALL ADD-ON SECTIONS
770-3547 22.99
18-3/8 x 1-15/16 x 3-3/8" 46 x 4.8 x 8.5cm
Open concrete sections and details to build a longer platform scene. Use alone or with #3535, 3536, 3545 or 3546, all sold separately.

STUTTGART SIGNAL TOWER
770-5735 54.99
9-7/16 x 6 x 6-13/16" 26.3 x 15.2 x 17cm
Keep traffic moving through a busy yard or terminal with this elevated tower.

FREIGHT SHED
770-5700 46.99
8-13/16 x 6-5/16 x 4-3/16" 22 x 15.8 x 10.5cm
Ideal for industrial or small town station scenes. Transfer freight from road to rail quickly and easily with this detailed kit along your line.

RAILWAY WORKSHOP KIT
770-5603 19.99
4-1/2 x 2-1/4" 11 x 5.8cm

HOUSE W/VINEYARD
770-5129 25.99

STEAM-ERA STATION PLATFORM HALL
770-3545 39.99
14-3/8 x 5-5/8 x 4-3/16" 37 x 14 x 10.5cm
A smaller version of kit #3546, ideal for stations with less space.

KARLSBAD STEAM-ERA STATION PLATFORM HALL
770-3546 74.99
14-3/8 x 5-5/8 x 4-1/5" 96 x 14 x 10.5cm
Imagine a string of varnished wooden cars, or your favorite heavyweight Pullmans, gliding to a stop beneath this ornate train shed. Detailed plastic parts simulate cast iron filigree of the original. Spans a single track and includes left and right concrete platforms. Perfect for many eras, easily combined with additional kits for a big city station scene.

RESTAURANT
770-3788 54.49
4-5/8 x 4-5/8" 11.5 x 11.5cm

SIGNAL TOWER
770-5738 42.99
6-1/4 x 3" 15.5 x 7.5cm

VOLLMER

INTERLOCKING TOWER

770-5737 18.99
3-1/2 x 2 x 3-3/8"
9 x 5 x 8.5cm

YARD TOWER

770-5733 21.99
3-1/8 x 2-1/4 x 4-3/8"
8 x 5.7 x 11cm

CABINET MAKER'S SHOP

770-3684 39.99
6-5/8 x 4-13/16 x 5-5/16"
16.5 x 12 x 13.3cm
From fine furnishings to new kitchen cabinets, skilled workers will appreciate this handsome shop building. Includes lumber storage area.

FACTORY ON FIRE

770-5601 59.99
13-5/8 x 1-5/8 x 12" 34 x 4 x 30cm
Animate your industrial district with this "burning" building. Includes two red flashing lamps to simulate flames, collapsed wall and burned roof, plus debris. (For more exciting action, a Smoke Generator #770-4114 and fluid #770-4115 are available separately.)

SAVINGS BANK

770-3698 54.99
7-13/16 x 5-5/8 x 5-13/16" 19.5 x 14 x 14.5cm
Dress-up a downtown or suburban scene with this combination building. Ground floor houses a bank, with upstairs apartments or offices.

SINGLE STALL ENGINE SHED

770-5751 49.99
12-13/16 x 10-7/16 x 4-3/4" 32 x 26 x 11.8cm
Shortline, industrial line or tourist road, you name it and this shed is the perfect place to store and service the motive power. Great for steam or diesels.

FARM HOUSE WITH BARN

770-3721 39.99
6-13/16 x 4-13/16 x 4-13/16"
17 x 12 x 12cm
Traditional European design combines house and barn into a single structure.

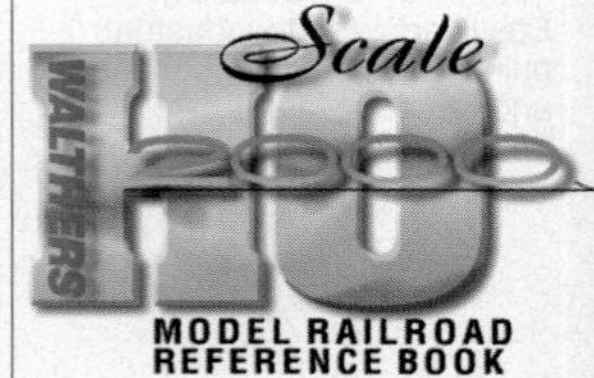

Welcome to The *Magic* of Model Railroading

Models and Photo by Bob Boudreau

Railroading is a business of change as each season begins.

Of course, it only lasts a short time. The railroads pause briefly and begin clearing the line before each storm ends. And while it's pretty, snow brings frozen switches, unsure footing and packed flangeways.

Model railroads are also a place of changes. Many of us start with a simple set and now have vast empires. We run locos and cars from the 1830s to the 1990s. We like buildings of every shape, size and color. All of this variety adds to the fun of our hobby, as you'll see on the pages that follow. Here you'll find a wide range of models, many of which are listed in this book. And as you see how others have transformed them, you'll find new ways of using them on your railroad.

We'd love to see your layout, module or diorama next year, and invite you to send photos for our "Magic of Model Railroading" Photo Contest. Our first place winner receives $250, Second place $100 and Third place $75. All published Honorable Mentions receive $25 and a copy of the catalog. Color slides of any size are preferred, but electronic images can be submitted - please see our Web site at www.walthers.com for full details.

Include a brief description (typed or printed) of the scene, along with any private roadnames, town names and the name of the photographer if different from your own. PLEASE PRINT YOUR NAME AND ADDRESS ON EACH SLIDE and limit submissions to 10 slides. Deadlines will be announced at www.walthers.com and in Walthers publications. Please send entries to:

ATTN: SLIDES FOR CATALOG
C/O Wm. K. Walthers Inc.
PO Box 3039
Milwaukee, WI 53201-3039

Magic

Models and Photo by Jim Hart

"Burning the midnight oil" is the rule, not the exception for railroad employees. In many towns and cities along the line, the night is actually busier than the day! And not just for train crews. During the evening, much of the maintenance and repair that keeps the line running is done. The big city terminals and offices are cleaned at night. Fewer trains allow more time to repair track, bridges, overhead wires and a thousand other items that can't easily be done during the day.

But shop crews will tell you time makes little difference to them.

Eventually, everything from private cars to brand-new diesels needs their attention. It's often a question of when and where something breaks down or its monthly inspection comes due that determines if the day or night will be a busy one.

Of course, somebody, somewhere needs that equipment back in service as soon as possible. So the lights burn 'round the clock here.

And you can't always tell how busy it's been by what's left on the shop floor as the shifts change. Yes, the place is almost empty now, save for one or two troublesome units. But over the last eight hours, a number of engines have been returned to duty. And others are heading here right now as a new day is about to start.

Dawn is breaking over the Old Forge shops in Media, Pennsylvania, where some of Jim Hart's Pennsy motive power rests between runs.

Magic

Models and Photo by Ken Estes

Running slow and running late. Very late. It might not matter with other trains, but the morning intermodal is the hottest on the Lost Creek. Never mind what your watch tells you, when the fog is this thick, you instinctively slow down. Seems drivers have enough trouble seeing you coming on bright, clear days, much less on a morning like this.

"Clear board for the diamond" the conductor suddenly calls out.

Faintly, a green glimmer can be seen ahead.

"Clear board it is" you reply, pulling the whistle lever all the way open - no one will be sleeping late in town this morning!

The pea-soup swirls, then clears just long enough to give you a clear view ahead. You feel the wheels and hear the clatter as the loco rumbles across the diamond. Still off schedule, but at least you're running safely. Early morning finds us trackside on a diorama built by Ken Estes of Lakewood, California. A few simple details and basic structures occupy the crossing, along with a pair of scratchbuilt signals. The working head and class lights on the Athearn GP50 provide a dramatic touch, burning through the rolling fog.

Models and Photo by Fred Lagno

Old timers remember when the chatter of the telegraph key was sweet music. Some learned to "sling lightning" as kids, taught by their fathers or grandfathers who worked for the road. Others remember the excitement of being in the depot and hearing those mysterious dots and dashes flit through the air. A series of clicks and the agent would rise, set the semaphore, then return to type out the message coming across the wires.

In those days, telegraphy was essential, for train orders sent to stations along the line kept things moving safely. In small towns, the telegraph was the only link to a far-away world. Telegrams were only part of it. Locals would drift in to listen in as sporting events or election results were sent live. And the agent who understood the code was looked on as a local hero.

Telephones and centralized traffic control are replacing the Morse Code. Here and there, a few towers are still open, at least until new relays are in place. Colored lights keep today's heavier, faster and longer trains rolling safely.

Passing freights still shake the windows of this tower, but how much longer, no one can say. So amidst the blazing fall colors, we're in time to watch local #2706 take the siding as a long Chessie coal drag snakes by. And if you listen very, very closely, you may hear the sounds of the past.

Magic

Models and Photo by John Bortle

Firing a camelback locomotive is a tough job. Your footing is always in jeopardy on the rocking footplate between the locomotive and tender, and worst of all, you're usually out of touch with the engineer. Any kind of miscommunication and things could get ugly. The day is just beginning as an engineer and fireman have an early morning discussion of the day's schedule prior to departing the NYO&W's Maybrook yard. This class P, 2-8-0 heavy camelback, a very modified Mantua loco, has a long trip ahead of her and her crew wants everything to run smoothly throughout the day. This particular scene was shot out of doors to gain the aspect of early morning light.

Models and Photo by Ken Estes

Witnesses all commented on the same thing; the ear-splitting screech as the cars derailed. Thankfully, no one was hurt, though there is some structural damage to a couple surrounding buildings. The repairs can be easily made, whereas the loss of human life would have been irreversible. The way it stands right now, no one knows how it happened, but rest assured that the inspectors on the scene will figure it out in the end. The accident at Nooks Hill Tower is the first of its kind here and brings out a platoon of rescue and maintenance workers to get the line cleared on Ken Estes' Lost Creek Railroad. A variety of vehicles by Wiking, Roco and Revell help with the clean-up as an Athearn GP50 waits by an old lumber mill crane that has been pressed into service. The structures are by Atlas, scenery by Woodland Scenics and figures by Preiser.

Models and Photo by Pierre Dion

Give 'em a brake! Much like the local Highway Department workers, this maintenance crew has to keep an eye out for traffic passing through. And, just like on the highways, the start of summer is met with a blitz of construction work on the railroads. Protection is provided to the crew and their Custom Finishing and Tichy Train Group equipment by an Alder Models derail. The track workers still must be vigilant, though, and the crew leader pauses in his work to watch CP's #4219 lumber through. In the background a Burro crane goes to work filling up a Proto 2000 gondola with the old broken ties and 40' rails that have been recently discarded.

Magic

Models and Photo by Ralph Schmid

The renovation of historical buildings is never an easy task. The planning, the designing and the actual labor of returning run-down structures to their past glory takes patience, commitment and passion. Once the task is completed, however, all those involved in the project can take real pride in a job well done. Locomotives in this town are playing a vital role in the renovation of the town's historical sites. Here, a locomotive brings a load of tree trunks to the local cottage sawmill. It is here that the wood will be cut into the traditional post-and-beam lumber that is a staple of the community's older facilities. Ralph Schmid uses a narrow gauge locomotive on his layout to accomplish this task.

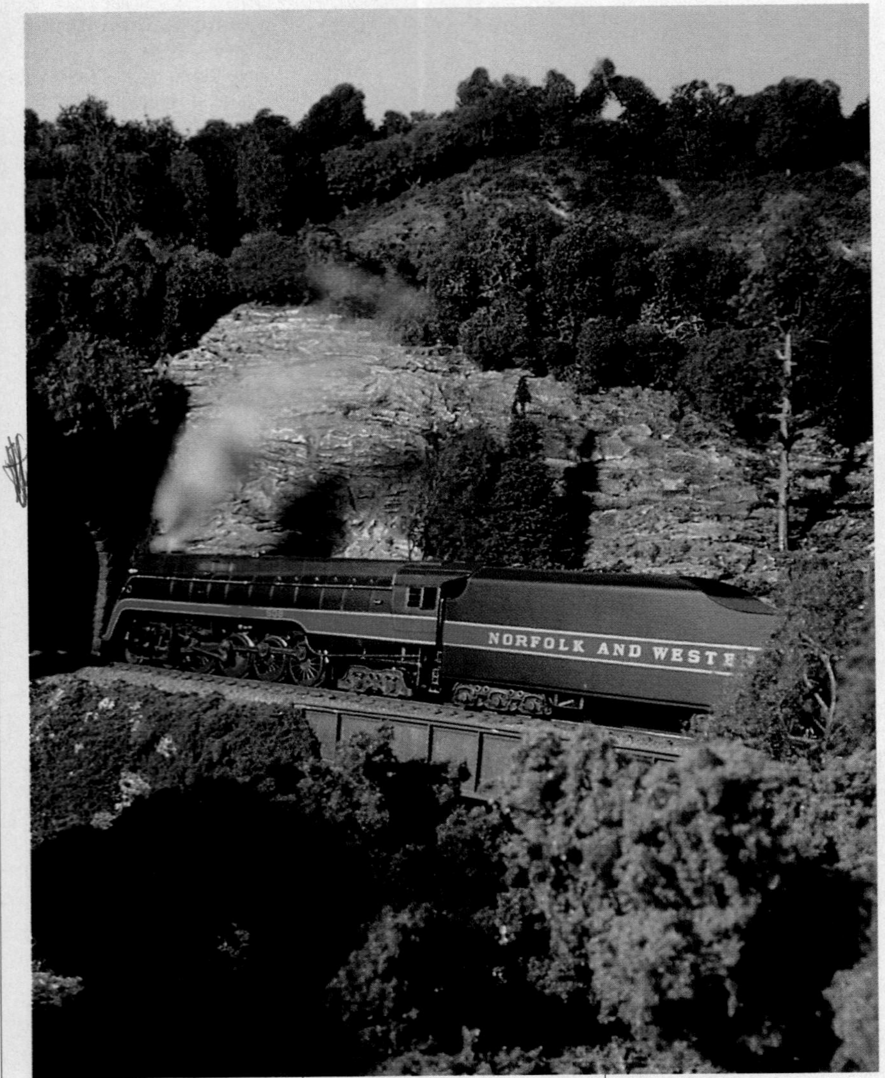

Models and Photo by Gary Hoover

The Appalachian Mountains are America's major mountain system. The mountain range extends approximately 1,600 miles from Quebec, Canada to Alabama. It is said that because of the mountain's rugged natural landscape (including hills, valleys and the eroded remnants of an earlier mountain mass), expansion into the western portions of the United States was rather difficult. However, this layout demonstrates how the locomotive conquered this roadblock to expansion: if you can't get around the mountain, just push your way through it. Gary Hoover of Florissant, Missouri, uses a Bachmann N&W J Class locomotive on this stretch of mountain expanse.

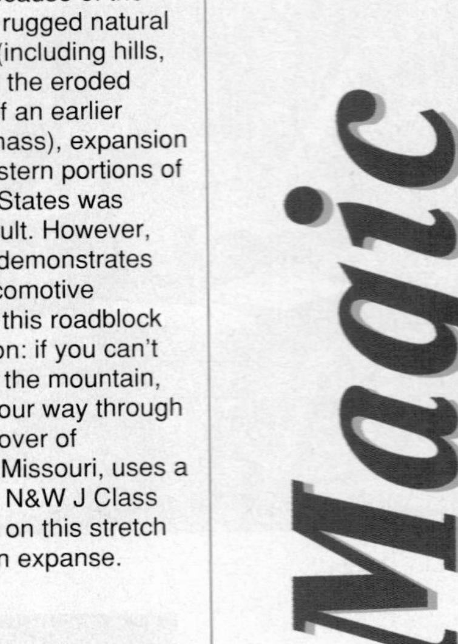

Models and Photo by Philippe Coquet

The engineer of this Athearn UP SD40-2 "Snoot" doesn't need the trailing unit anymore, but boy was he thankful he had it behind him for the trip up the mountain. Now that he is at the peak, things aren't nearly as hard going as they were while trying to get to this point. He doesn't have to push her so hard and he can finally start to make some time. The vegetation and scenery is a bit scarce in this part of the mountains, but soon the train will reach friendlier landscapes. But having just left the West portal, the engineer knows he still has a long ways to go before completing his journey from Elko to Silver City here on Philippe Coquet's freelanced layout.

Models and Photo by Steve Sencaj

The Proto 2000 PRR GP-9 slows a little while rounding a bend as it makes its way under a rural overpass, the first sign that the train and its consist will soon be entering into the busier part of town. As recently as two months ago this train would have worked the siding a mile back at the American Model Builders grain elevator seen in the background, but hard times have fallen upon this sleepy little town and the elevators are now unused. The engineer wonders how much longer they will continue making stops downtown in the so-called "industrial district." The bridge that passes overhead doesn't look sturdy enough to allow any form of traffic to cross it safely, which reaffirms what the engineer already knows about this town. Nonetheless, he trusts his counterparts in the bridge building world and does not fear any incidents.

Models and Photo by Wynn Hammer

Jurassic Layout! No this isn't the Land of the Lost and no that is not a Sleestack. Could it be, however, a relative to the Loch Ness Monster, "Nessie" as some have come to call the creature that many believe to be a plesiosaur? Could a 300 million year old dinosaur still be in existence along the coasts of the Gulf of Mexico? If so, the engineer of this Southern Pacific SW7 is going to have to answer a lot of questions from his superior about his alleged infraction of Rule G (the statute barring railroad personnel from drinking or taking drugs while on duty). Wynn Hammer's photograph bears no real resemblance to the first picture taken of the Loch Ness Monster by Hugh Gray on November 12, 1933, but the substance may be quite the same.

Magic

Magic

Models and Photo by Pierre Dion
Safety is an integral part of the modern railroading experience. It is important that all those aboard any train protect the well-being of everyone aboard the cars, as well as those living in the communities they pass through. Any mistake or oversight could cost lives. The brakeman aboard this RS-23 is prepared to keep a clear path on all unprotected road crossings as the engine makes it way to a nearby paper mill. Pierre Dion used his home region of eastern Quebec to inspire his layout, taken from the period of the late 1980s to the early 1990s.

Models and Photo by Philippe Coquet
Railroad maintenance is not an easy job. In this part of the mountains, you'll find crews working hard to keep passes open and rails in excellent condition so passing locomotives face no hazards in their travels. So when one of this gang's workers takes a break atop the water tank, it's really a well-deserved break after a hard day's work. Philippe Coquet of Paris, France, deserves credit for this layout. Here, an Athearn UP SD40 with 116' nose is used to ride through a mountain railroad. The locomotive features heavy superdetailing and a custom paint job for the snoot.

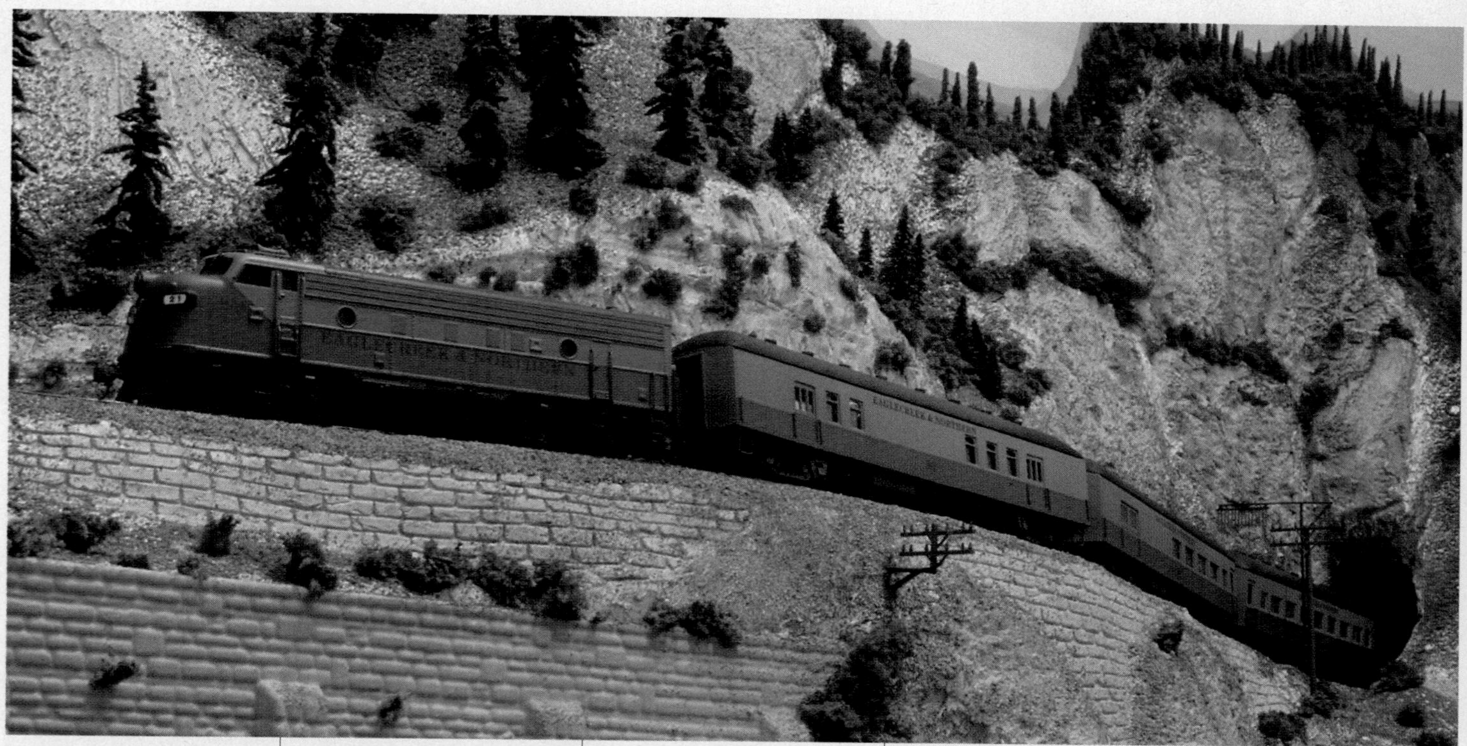

Models and Photo by Flemming Orneholm

Though only fifteen minutes has passed since it left the station, the gentle rocking motion of the daily passenger train, "The Red Arrow" of Flemming Orneholm's freelanced Eaglecreek & Northern, has already lulled some of the passengers to sleep. The Athearn F7 and its consist of Roundhouse Harrimans leave the first tunnel of the trip, laboring slightly as it climbs the 3% incline, and heads west towards Long Neck Creek, the first stop. This crisp, clear day in the fall of 1953 guarantees that passengers will have a great view throughout their journey, making some wonder why anyone would want to travel any other way.

Models and Photo by Alden Armstrong

At this time of the morning, the scenery is so relaxing. Early dawn mist forms below the tracks of a wooden trestle bridge stretching across a mountain range. Autumn reds, golds and oranges burst on the leaves that surround the mountainside. Roaring across the canyon gap along the bridge comes in Red Rock #15 pushing a Missouri Pacific box car. In some settings, the train would seem too out of place due to its size or color. Looking at this picture, however, you can see how the engine becomes a part of the scenery, never upstaging or damaging the view.

Alden A. Armstrong of Grand Junction, Colorado shows how locomotives and scenery work hand-in-hand to create a flawless mountain scene.

Magic

Magic

Models and Photo by Flemming Orneholm

Everyone at the station is bursting with excitement about getting on the approaching train. They've got their tickets purchased, their luggage packed and their destinations in mind. Parents can't wait to show their kids the wonder of traveling on the mighty rails. You can almost feel the anticipation in the air. So when the F7 makes the curve towards the passenger station, you can bet that everyone waiting outside can barely contain their happiness. This train is bringing them one step closer to their dreams. Sweden's Flemming Orneholm uses an Athearn F7, Roundhouse Harriman cars and Preiser figures to detail this scene.

Models and Photo by Alberto Franchi

About four years ago a farmer in this small, unicorporated town decided to try an experiment. In this area there wasn't much of a market for sunflowers, so he created one. Now, several seasons later, the gamble is paying off with a banner crop. As soon as next week he's going to start filling these two grain elevators and with any luck, there won't be enough room. Right now the Canadian National SD40 and its consist are just passing through. But maybe by the time it makes its return run, there will be some business to conduct in this portion of the small, sleepy town. The grain elevators are Northeastern Scale Model kits.

Models and Photo by Martin Pollizotto

Some small towns complain about trains rolling through: the dirt, the noise, the delays of road traffic all contribute to their worries. Some communities, however, find a railroad's presence to be a vital link to their landscape. For this village, the delivery of mixed freight aboard a train being pulled by a Lehigh Valley F3 means a boom to the town's economy. When the businesses get their goods and local residents do their shopping, they'll be sure to thank the railroad for making a path through their city. Credit Martin Pollizotto of East Islip, New York, for this layout scene.

Magic

Models by Michael McChesney and Jim Coon, Photo by Bill McChesney

Whether the locomotive is brand new or a classic still in operation, they always make a welcomed sight coming down the tracks. Here you see two Lehigh Valley locomotives roaring down the tracks. A brand new GE U-23b climbs uphill past an old EMD switcher, hauling behind it a commonwealth flat car. By having both styles working side-by-side on a layout, you can see the enduring legacy of these mighty machines. The newer engine is from Atlas, the older switcher comes from Athearn and Walthers created the flat car. The supply shed behind the locomotives is supplied by Campbell Scale Models.

Models and Photo by Sam Parker

One doesn't appreciate the dramatic size difference between standard and narrow gauge equipment until they are seen next to each other. What the narrow gauge lacks in size and overall cargo space, is made up for by the amount of money saved in the building of smaller cars, locos and the track itself. Sam Parker's layout featuring his Knowlton & Northley Railroad displays the differences between the two gauges nicely, as an HOn30 Car Works 2-6-2 and an HO Bachmann 2-8-0 sit side by side at a freight transfer platform. Transfer platforms like this one existed wherever the two gauges met, as a means to change loads from narrow gauge lines to standard gauge lines and vice versa.

Magic

Models and Photo by Michael and Katherine Connelly

Despite the recent decline in train related accidents, they still occur and two people from the small town of Nanticoke have become another statistic. Medics attend to the passenger of the car while a state policeman and the train crew discuss what exactly happened. Flight for Life is on the way, but until then the driver trapped in the car can only wait. For the engineer, this event goes far beyond an inconvenience. Beside the human lives that have been endangered, he also has to contend with the Bearfence Mountain Railroad standing rule which states that any engineer involved in an accident cannot operate another train until a formal investigation is conducted. This means that the two GP-20s have to stay where they are until another engineer can be sent out to move them, which will effectively shut down this route for quite some time.

Models by Doug Devine, Photo by Bob Boudreau

Traveling through the Canadian winter of the 1950s was no easy task. Heavy snowfall and icy conditions made getting to your appointed destination quite a difficult chore. Thankfully, the Canadian National Railway ran a track to where you needed to go. This passenger train is led by a Fairbanks-Morse "C-Liner" diesel with six-wheel trucks on the rear, common to CN passenger service during this era. Bob Boudreau captures the simple elegance of this winter scene on Doug Devine's layout. Models were kitbashed from former AHM models and sit on modified Athearn PA diesel running gear.

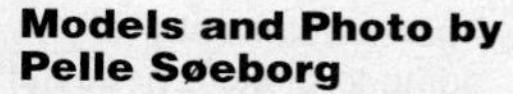

Models and Photo by Pelle Søeborg

"Oh the weather outside is frightful, but aren't the diesel trains delightful"... or something along those lines. The unusual cold day doesn't at all hamper an east bound UP locomotive as it exits Tunnel 1. The tunnel abutment is relatively new, but the smoke from the heavy diesel traffic has already stained the new concrete. The harsh weather of a cold winter in the Tehachapis has also caused the concrete to start to break away. A maintenance crew will have to make a visit out this way as soon as the weather turns a bit warmer to insure that further damage will be avoided in the future winters to come.

Models and Photo by Al Ozell

As the day winds down, the engineer of this double headed PFM Climax and Shay realizes this is going to be the kind of night he lives for. The cloudless sky is going to make a beautiful ride even moreso, and the scenery along this road has made this stretch of track his favorite. Having already travelled up to the highest point of this road, the engineer relaxes a bit for the ride back down. It isn't going to be any easier, but it has always made this man feel better knowing gravity was working with him, rather than against him.

Models and Photo by John Bortle

It's the 1950s and a group of railfans have gathered at Cold Spring, New York, to photo-document a passage of the New York Central's Twentieth Century Limited against the background of the breathtaking Hudson Highlands. The railfans are nearly exploding with anticipation (some things never change, even half a century later) as the rumble of the New York bound consist, pulled by one of the Central's lightning striped PAs, echoes off Storm King Mountain across the Hudson River. The railfans can only hope that this brief moment will bring them the future rewards that they so desire. The photo was taken with a pinhole lens at the actual location and the background is real. The foreground diorama features a modified Athearn PA, Prieser figures and a Praline vehicle.

Models and Photo by Ken Estes

Falling snow can be such a welcoming sight. However, it can also mean a lot of work for anyone who has someplace to go. Trains are no exception. Just because a locomotive packs a lot of power doesn't mean that snow is an insignificant occurrence: moisture and ice can do some serious damage. Here, a set of ATSF F7s head through a tunnel to help a heavy freight climbing the mountain below. Alongside the track, a Lost Creek Railroad Northern prepares to pick up the rotary plow on the siding. Background scenery and snow made of wheat flour gives Ken Estes' layout additional winter detailing.

Magic

Models and Photo by Fred Lagno

He knows the sign says "employees only," but this man wants to get a little closer to the action. The yardmaster gives the passer-by permission to take a look, so why shouldn't he? Imagine his surprise when an Allegheny Central GP9 roars by, fresh from a maintenance stop in a nearby engine facility. What probably seemed to be an inconsequential little detour in this man's day has become a moment he'll never forget. The sound, the sight, the impact of this locomotive will surely leave a lasting impression. Fred Lango of Queenstown, Maryland, sets the stage for a moment in one man's life.

Magic

Models and Photo by Marty Klein

The New Orleans Lake Front Marina, as usual, is bustling with activity. It is a focal point for all types of traffic. A Rivarossi Southern Railroad "Crescent Limited" has completed its run and is heading back into Union Station in New Orleans. Tourists out for a hike have come in off the trails to explore the level boardwalk for a little while to rest their legs. And a young tan-seeking boater tools around the harbor looking for friends or anything interesting that might catch his eye. There is never a dull moment in the Big Easy.

Models and Photo by Lou Sassi

Some layouts show how interesting a railroad or a certain building can look on a layout. Here, Lou Sassi of Charlton, New York, supplies a photograph of his layout that shows the varying scenic elements that a railroad can travel through in one pass. Envy the lucky engineer of this double-headed Boston & Maine freight train traveling across the layout. As the train crosses the river, it will pass through a woody forest region and a small town before it heads into the mountains far in the photograph's background. This train not only will accomplish its mission, but get a great view along the way.

Models by Bob Henry, Photo by Bob Boudreau

Summer: the season of construction. Most people in these parts would swear that the orange cone was the country's, or at least the state's, official form of wildlife. Fortunately, for the townsfolk, this road is not all that heavily traveled. The way it stands now, only the Midland truckers are being inconvenienced as the Public Works Department goes to work on the leaking water main. The workers don't bother to look up as a train passes, they know they have to get done quick. The engineer passing by sighs in relief as he thinks about what a mess it would have been had the water main broke closer to the track, or worse, underneath it. Another near crisis averted.

Models and Photo by Sam Parker

The engineer of this locomotive is headed back to the roundhouse after a long day. Working for a railroad that services passengers and local industry keeps him busy doing many different things. It would be easy to get bored and disinterested in his work. But the beauty of this area's rock formations and tall trees catches his eye. Such scenery makes his job a little less tedious. It also keeps the engineer motivated towards coming into work tomorrow. Sam Parker of Media, Pennsylvania, took this photograph of his HOn30 layout, the Knowlton & Northley Railroad.

Magic

Models and Photo by Ralph Schmid

Around the layout in eighty days! The crew of this hot air balloon is attempting to do what's never been done before; circumvent the world as they know it by balloon. The flight overhead goes mostly unnoticed by the busy town of Neukirch as the populace go about their daily routines. The air balloon crew watches the "ants" below with never-ending amazement, trying to forget about the fact that they have yet to receive clearance as to whether or not they can fly over the next layout. If forced to go around it, their trip would be in jeopardy. Balloon by Faller, structures by Faller and Vollmer and vehicles by Herpa and Wiking.

Models by Mark Verdi and Tom Ludlam, Photo by Shane Deemer

The representatives of the US Army in this area have never really tried to keep what they do a secret. Maybe they don't care, or maybe doing everything out in the open serves a purpose. Only the higher ranking officials know for sure. The only thing that the people in this area are certain of is the fact that something big is about to happen. The factory has been working over-time the last three weeks and during that same time frame, Atlas GP40s like these two have been coming and going like the wind, each heavily laden with military equipment. The locos have been positioning their Roundhouse flat car trains for easy loading onto an endless stream of ships. Is there something going on that the papers have not caught hold of yet? Is there something about to happen that such measures are being taken? Only the future will tell.

Magic

Models and Photo by Jim Hart

It's hard to imagine the coal mining industry without the locomotive playing an inseparable role in its success. Since the earliest days of the industry's development, freight cars took coal from loading stations to its appointed destinations. Many structures were built to accommodate the needs of locomotives parked on tracks below. Jim Hart's layout shows a 2-8-0 from the Western Maryland approaching the West Lima coal dock, preparing to refuel. The engine is a Bachmann locomotive.

Models by Pietro Sedoschi, Photo by Domenico Tromby

Another day, another dollar, or so the well known cliché goes. The saying is definitely not new to the workers in Pietro Sedoschi's scratchbuilt steam engine shed. Everything they need to fix, repair or rebuild steam engines is present. Presses, boring mills, hoists, compressors and hand tools, all showing a bit of wear-and-tear from their constant use, "decorate" the workshop that is home to them at least twelve hours a day. One worker keeps a close eye on the clock as he carries out some repairs on an oil pump, willing it to move faster, but to no avail.

Magic

Models and Photo by Pelle Søeberg

After a long day on the rails, the sunset indicates it's time for the train to come home. A trio of GP60s has been hard at work delivering freight, and is ready to call it a day. Weary from their travels, they make the turn over Bealville Road in Caliente as they head for the engine shed. They'll need the rest; they're being sent out bright and early tomorrow for another round of work. Pelle Søeberg of Denmark used Athearn locomotives and Smokey Valley cabs to maneuver down the tracks of his Tehachapi layout. Detail parts are from Details West and Detail Associates.

Models and Photo by Ken Nelson

This is not the easiest stretch of land to lay track through. The dense rock formations are an obvious deterrent; getting through a wall of granite is never an easy task. There's also the thick forest of trees to think about. Clearing trees out of the way is a lengthy chore. However, human ingenuity can make anything possible. Once the track is laid down and the truss bridge is put in place, the problems of getting the railroad through this area seem nonexistent. The path for this railroad's success looks clear and easy. The Poco Valley Railroad belongs to Ken Nelson from Scotia, New York.

Models and Photo by Erik Kalinski

No matter what kind of a hurry you're in tonight, there's no reason to park your car up on the curb. Of course a patrolling police officer is going to give you a ticket. It might cause some headaches for motorists and pedestrians on this busy street, but the law is the law. This clever street scene comes to life with the use of authentic structures, animated figures, street details and automobiles in vibrant paint schemes. Created by Erik Kalinski from Slovenia, Europe, this picture captures a very specific moment in time and creates a story on its own.

Magic

Models and Photo by Michael and Katherine Connelly

The townspeople of Nanticoke are gathered together to witness a joyous occasion in the town's Methodist church: the wedding of two happy, hopeful people. The residents have donned their fanciest clothes, hitched up the horses to the coaches, and arrived at the chapel for the festivities. Even a man passing by on the street across from the church can't help but stop and take a look. Michael and Katherine Connelly of Raymore, Missouri, use a variety of manufacturers to create this scene — the church is a Lionel kit the figures and coaches come from the Preiser line, and the cemetery behind the church can be credited to Woodland Scenics.

Magic

Models by Ted Grey, Photo by Bob Boudreau

The MicMac Lumber Company Shay locomotive slowly works its way across the highest wood trestle on the railroad's line. The engineer hopes that the falling rock problem has subsided. Between that little threat and his fear of heights, this stretch of the line is by far the most white knuckled of any he has ever worked on. And of course, there are those stories of the hauntings. It has been said by many a trusted fellow engineer that the restless spirits of two men that plunged to their deaths while building this trestle still walk the track occassionally. Supposedly, they are trying to find clues as to what went wrong. It's these three things that make the seven minutes it takes his locomotive to cross this trestle an eternity.

Models by George Micklus, Photo by John Klotz

In the midst of a busy downtown afternoon a New Haven S2 Switcher leaves a caboose on the end of an east bound freight. For most people, living this close to the railroad tracks would drive them insane. The constant noise from the hustle and bustle of the rail yard would be too much to handle on a daily basis. You'd be surprised though, at how easy and fast the inhabitants of this neighborhood have grown accustomed to the never-ending ruckus. It's to the point now where they don't even notice anything is going on. The trains have become no worse than the car and truck traffic; which is no worse than the people talking and yelling out on the street. It all just blends together into one large chorus of city life.

Magic

Models and Photo by Tim Hensch

The yard lights have just come on here at the locomotive shop as the night begins to settle in. This will allow the second shift to work well into the night, both inside the shop and out in the yard. For reasons no one knows, the amount of engines needing repairs has almost doubled. This offers some job security, but at the cost of long hours. A local police officer drives through the yard as a part of his regular beat. The complaints and general sightings of transients has been on the rise of late, so he has been making an effort to drive through this area more often than usual.

Models and Photo by Alden Armstrong

Engineering a locomotive can be hazardous work. That's why those people behind the controls make sure that every caution is exercised. It's not just their own safety that's at stake, though that certainly is a concern: imagine the terror you would feel if you plunged off this trestle bridge into the canyon below. The safety of those who live and work around railroad tracks is also an important concern. That's why you see the engineering crew manning this Shay locomotive looking ahead as it crosses the Chief Ouray mine. This team understands the risks involved, and will take every precaution to guarantee everyone's safety.

Magic

Models and Photo by Fred Lagno

Just another average day at the Silo Yard on the Allegheny Central Railroad. With the recent advent of the logging industry in the area, this brakeman has seen many a load like this one come through of late. He's in constant radio contact with the engineer of switcher #303 as a bulkhead flat car laden with the latest "harvest" is positioned onto track 2. The brakeman begins to laugh gently as the engineer describes his latest idea. He wants to tell the new guy that they now have to unload the bulkhead by hand. But rest assured, they will let the new guy in on the joke before he gets too far.

Models and Photo by Al Ozell

This caboose has seen better days. It's to the point now where the crew has begun to complain, loudly, about the conditions to which they are subjected to while working on the line. They all fear that the next wind storm will be their last if they are caught inside this wheeled albatross. The railroad won't even part with the money to paint the car in a respectable manner. They've been told that this is because the railroad's funds are currently locked up in several expansion projects. It's the engineer's firm belief that you have to walk before you can run, so he does not understand management's position at all. Al Ozell's imported brass model caboose, weathered with Floquil paints, is following a North West Short Line brass log car carrying licorice root logs.

Magic

Models and Photo by Martin Pollizotto

A Lehigh Valley F3 rumbles its way downgrade as it begins its trek out of town, awakening a man who has been waiting for this very moment. You see, he's wanted, and what he did last night isn't going to help the situation any. He needed a place to hole up for the night. He came up with the idea of sleeping by the railroad tracks so he could catch a ride out of town with the first train that passes by. This spot was perfect because traffic of all kinds is around, slowing the train to a nearly hazardless pace. But even as he brushes the dirt from his shoulders, the man doesn't realize he has already made a fatal mistake. He has spent the night sleeping ten feet from a guard tower. Unfortunately for this criminal, the guard recognized him from the early morning news and called the police. The man's life on the run will soon be over, proving once again that crime doesn't pay.

Models by Bill and Christopher McChesney, Photo by Bill McChesney

It has been nearly five years since he retired, but this ex-engineer knew that Mac was still working in a crossing shanty somewhere in this yard. As friendly as he ever was, Mac let him and his son take a little trip down memory lane. The Lehigh Valley S-12 Baldwin Switcher looks mighty lonely parked here at the east end of the Allentown Yard. What's even worse is that the majority of the action here in Allentown often takes place on the west end. Part of him saddens at the thought that #240, the loco that served him so well for so many years, is now only used on rare occasions. The other half is content knowing that "his" train is getting a chance to rest after all its hard years. Either way, he takes solace in the fact that a good man like Mac is watching over her. The loco is by Athearn, the truck is by Alloy Forms and the crossing shanty is a Selley Finishing Touches product.

Magic

Models and Photo by Bill McChesney

As usual, the Allentown diesel service area is rather busy. And, of course, no one is moving nearly as fast as everyone else wants them to. The service area crew is aware of this, but they are already moving as fast as they can. Only so much sand can leave the sanding tower at one time. Whether it helps or not, the waiting engineers seem to be trying to will the sand to move faster. Between you and me, I don't think it's working. The locomotives waiting to receive a load of sand include an Athearn Baldwin S-12 Switcher, an Athearn F7 cab unit, an Athearn SW8 modified from an SW7 and a Walthers SW1.

Models and Photo by Gary Hoover

A three o'clock sun casts shadows down across 2nd Street in the small midwest town of Oak Grove, Illinois. In the background a new Athearn CSX C44-9W slips quietly by, or at least as quiet as a new locomotive can be. It doesn't matter all that much anyway because the residents of Oak Creek have become accustomed to the sight with the factory a scant few miles away. A police car is parked in front of a donut shop, forcing the question "why?" According to the officer, he is there only to finish up his daily paperwork and the shop provides a nice atmosphere in which to do so. But any other air breathing person cannot resist the implicated stereotype that is being presented.

Models and Photo by Philippe Coquet

It's a crisp, clear wintry day here in Gleeson, Nevada. No snow has fallen, but the temperature surely has. Not that there is really anybody around to feel the bite in the air anyway. This copper mine, a Craftsman kit from JV Models, seems to be out of operation and has been that way for quite some time. Years of being battered by the winds and dust of a desert-like climate have taken their toll on this lonely structure. A Shell tank car was left on this siding, for whatever reason, and awaits a diesel to come and take it back to the yard. With any luck, it won't sit by itself as long as the copper mine has. This picture was shot outdoors on a small, 3 x 1' diorama.

Magic

Models and Photo by Pierre Dion

It has been an unusually pleasant and mild spring, allowing this farmer to get into the fields almost two weeks earlier than he has the last three years or so. As he drives his Case in from the fields (there are milking chores to tend to), a train led by #4503 of the Canadian Pacific comes around the bend. This is the third train of the day that has passed through these parts. The farmer doesn't mind in the least bit. His livestock rarely gets spooked at all by the thunderous noise, and besides, these are probably the same trains that transport his crops when he ships them out. He has no problem sharing this little stretch of land with the railroad.

Magic

Models and Photo by Sam Parker

With as much traffic that passes over bridges like this 30' wooden truss bridge on the Knowlton & Northerly Railroad, it is a wonder that they don't need repair more often. The years that these bridges last is a testament to the engineers that designed them and the workers that built them. A Sheepscot Scale barge with a pile driver pauses briefly from its job of adding new pilings to let an HOn30 locomotive pass through. The engineer knows the work being done is more precautionary than necessity, and doesn't fear any adverse occurrences while crossing the small bridge. The buildings in the background and the bridge were scratch built by the modeler.

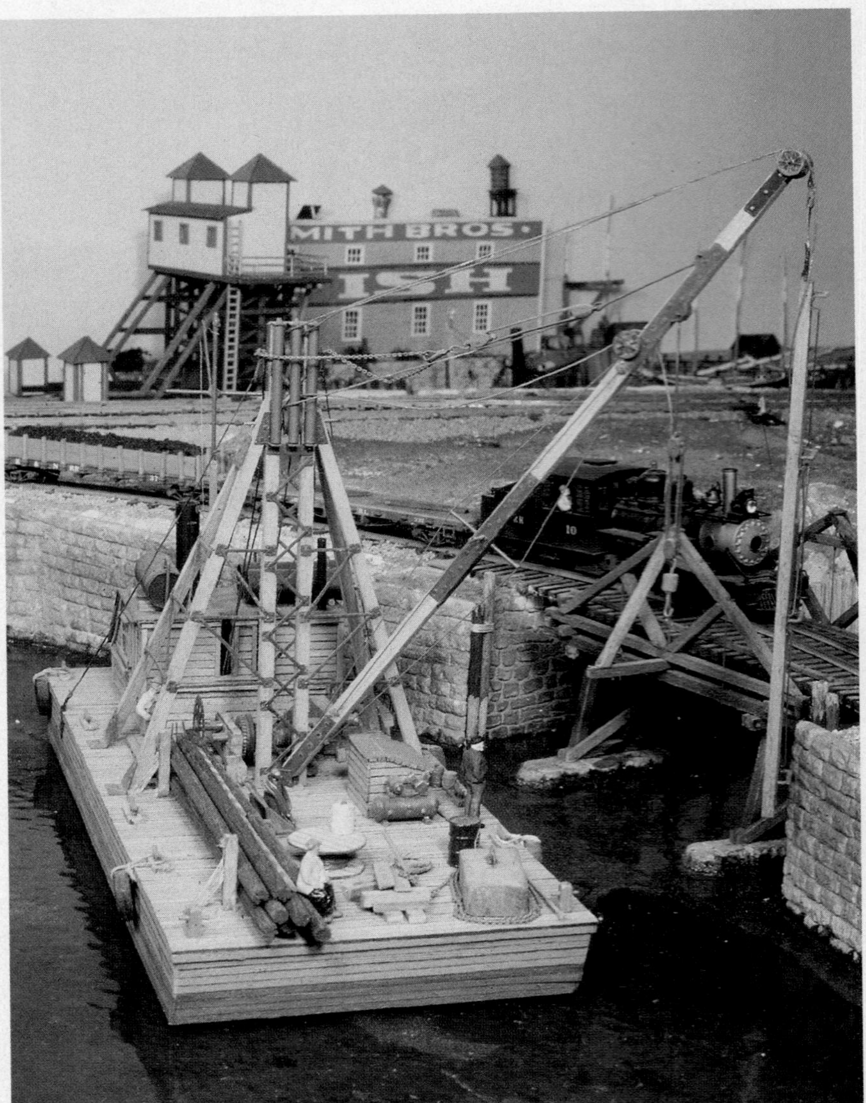

Models and Photo by Ken Estes

It's a beautiful spring day and a chartered Santa Fe excursion consist, complete with a dome car, glides effortlessly between a Lost Creek geep at rest on one side and a Lost Creek caboose on the other. The passengers aboard the speeding train look up in surprise to see objects so close to the track they are traveling on. Those who travel by train often merely raise an eyebrow, the less experienced train travelers spill their drinks, and some people, engrossed in books and what have you, don't notice anything at all. The ever changing scenery is constantly full of surprises. Some happen to be enjoyed more than others. The locomotive and cars are all Athearn products.

Sure, a railroad is equipment. Yellow and maroon, green and gold, yellow and gray. . . all the corporate color schemes are easy clues as to the owner of most locos and cars. But to know the personality of that railroad, you must meet the people who work for it.

Ask around among current employees. Chances are you'll find someone who is the third or fourth generation of their family to work for the same line. You may also be surprised to find how many years he or she has been on the job too.

Or watch a retired railroader's eyes light up as he or she recalls events of long-ago days. Names of old friends come back like smoke from an engine as the years roll away.

Given the size and scope of today's railroading, it's easy to loose sight of the people involved. But without the switchman on the ground or the engineer in the cab, not one wheel would be turning. And for all of the visible jobs like theirs, there are many you never see who are just as important.

Behind the scenes, an army of people keep every railroad in motion. From yard clerk to dispatcher, from section foreman to shop welder, each plays a critical role that defines what his or her railroad is all about.

Next time you see this CN Jordan Spreader, it will be working like brand new. And as you wave to the crew when they pass by, think about the folks in the shops who made it happen. Bob Boudreau takes us out behind the shops for a look at his modified Walthers spreader. The unit features positionable side wings and a smaller front blade. A crew of Preiser figures are getting things ready for tomorrow.

Models and Photo by Bob Boudreau

ATLAS

Unpainted plastic figures

ANIMALS EA 3.25

150-778 Cows & Horses pkg (12)

150-779 Sheep (12 white, 1 black)

PEOPLE

150-793 Assorted Figures pkg(24) **3.25**

BUILDERS IN SCALE

Unpainted HO figures.

RR PERSONNEL EA 2.50

169-5700 Workman
169-5703 Miner Pushing Cart

PEDESTRIANS EA 2.50

169-5701 Male Passenger
169-5702 Leaning Guy
169-5704 40s Fellow

CAMPBELL SCALE MODELS

ANIMALS

Painted Cattle Shown

200-1404 Cattle pkg(12) **11.00**
Unpainted plastic.

Handpainted plastic figures.

RR PERSONNEL PKG(6) EA 7.00

160-42333 Train Crew

160-42334 Work Crew

160-42341 Train Work Crew

PASSENGERS PKG(6) EA 7.00

160-42330 Waiting

160-42342 Sitting

PEDESTRIANS PKG(6) EA 7.00

160-42331 Sitting People

160-42332 Standing People

160-42339 People at Leisure

ANIMALS

160-42201 Cows & Horses pkg(12) **6.00**

MISCELLANEOUS

160-42335 Old West People pkg(6) **7.00**

DYNA-MODEL PRODUCTS COMPANY

Metal cast figures.

DOG ASSORTMENT

Includes Doberman, Shepherd, Spaniel and Dachshund
260-15001 Painted **6.45**
260-1500 Unpainted **3.25**

DOG & FIRE HYDRANTS

260-15131 Painted pkg(6) **6.55**
260-1513 Unpainted pkg(6) **3.25**

DALMATIANS

260-15201 Painted pkg(4) **6.50** *NEW*
260-1520 Unpainted pkg(4) **3.95** *NEW*

CATS

260-15061 Painted pkg(6) **6.45**
250-1506 Unpainted pkg(6) **3.25**

HORSES

260-15071 Painted pkg(3) **8.25**
260-1507 Unpainted pkg(3) **5.45**

SADDLED HORSES W/HITCHING POST

260-15011 Painted pkg(3) **7.25**
260-1501 Unpainted pkg(3) **4.35**

BURROS

260-15161 Painted pkg(4) **8.95**
260-1516 Unpainted pkg(4) **4.35**

PROSPECTOR & PACK BURROS

260-15171 Painted pkg(3) **8.95**
260-1517 Unpainted pkg(3) **5.50**

MULES

260-15151 Painted pkg(3) **8.25**
260-1515 Unpainted pkg(3) **5.45**

MULE TEAM

260-15141 Painted pkg(2) **9.35**
260-1514 Unpainted pkg(2) **6.45**

MILK COWS

260-15101 Painted pkg(5) **9.35**
260-1510 Unpainted pkg(5) **6.45**

STEERS

260-15081 Painted pkg(5) **9.85**
260-1508 Unpainted pkg(5) **6.50**

BEEF COWS

260-15091 Painted pkg(5) **9.35**
260-1509 Unpainted pkg(5) **6.45**

BULL & FOUR CALVES

260-15111 Painted pkg(5) **9.35**
260-1511 Unpainted pkg(5) **6.45**

LONGHORNS

260-15121 Painted pkg(3) **8.25**
260-1512 Unpainted pkg(3) **6.45**

PIGS

260-15041 Painted pkg(4) **6.45**
260-1504 Unpainted pkg(4) **3.25**

SOW & PIGLETS

260-15051 Painted pkg(6) **6.50**
260-1505 Unpainted pkg(6) **3.95**

GOATS

260-15181 Painted pkg(4) **6.50** *NEW*
260-1518 Unpainted pkg(4) **3.95** *NEW*

SHEEP

260-15031 Painted pkg(5) **6.50**
260-1503 Unpainted pkg(5) **3.95**

ROOSTERS & HENS

260-15021 Painted pkg(11) **6.45**
260-1502 Unpainted pkg(11) **3.25**

SKUNKS & TRASHCAN

Each set includes three skunks and one trashcan.

260-15221 Painted **6.50** *NEW*
260-1522 Unpainted **3.95** *NEW*

We have worked closely with this manufacturer to provide accurate delivery information at the time this catalog was published. Items listed in blue ink may not be available at all times. Current delivery information, along with a list of in-stock products for this line, can be found on our Web site at www.walthers.com.

PEDESTRIANS EA 1.99

265-2201 Assorted pkg(7)

FIGURES W/VEHICLES PKG(3) EA 1.99

265-2202 Bicyclists

265-2203 Motorcyclists

MILITARY EA 1.99

265-4500 English Infantry Set #1 pkg(8)

265-4501 Spanish Foreign Legion pkg(7)

265-4502 German Infantry Set #1 pkg(6)

265-4503 Japanese Infantry pkg(7)

2654-4504 German Infantry Set #2 pkg(8)

265-4505 American Infantry pkg(8)

265-4506 English Infantry Set #2 pkg(7)

265-4507 English Infantry Set #3 pkg(6)

265-4508 Swiss Infantry pkg(8)

265-4509 Seated Soldiers pkg(8)

265-4510 Spanish Infantry pkg(8)

265-4511 Russian Infantry pkg(8)

265-4512 US Paratroopers Set #1 pkg(6)

265-4513 US Paratroopers Set #2 pkg(4)

265-4514 Commandos pkg(7)

265-4515 Arab Legion pkg(8)

E-R Models™

NEW SUPPLIER

ANIMALS

262-1010090 Black Bears 10.49 ***NEW***

AMERICAN FIREMEN EA 11.98

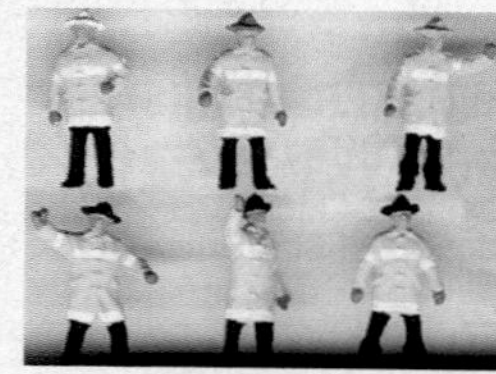

262-100 #1 **11.98** ***NEW***

262-101 #2 **11.98** ***NEW***

POLICE EA 12.98

262-1010059 City Police #1 ***NEW***

262-1010060 Highway Patrol ***NEW***

262-1010061 Sheriff & Deputies ***NEW***

262-1010062 City Police #2 ***NEW***

BOY SCOUTS

262-1010137 **TBA** ***NEW***

by *E-R* Model Importers, Ltd.

PEDESTRIANS EA 2.49

262-110 262-111 262-112

262-110 Woman Wearing Jacket ***NEW***
262-111 Seated Man ***NEW***
262-112 Walking Girl w/Basket ***NEW***

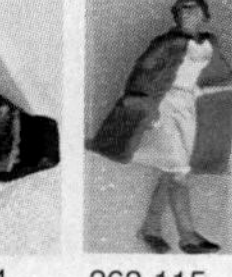

262-113 262-114 262-115

262-113 Seated Girl ***NEW***
262-114 Walking Man w/Suitcase ***NEW***
262-115 Walking Woman w/Coat ***NEW***

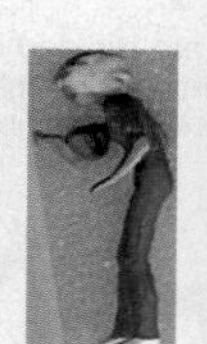
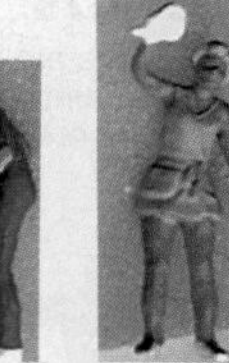

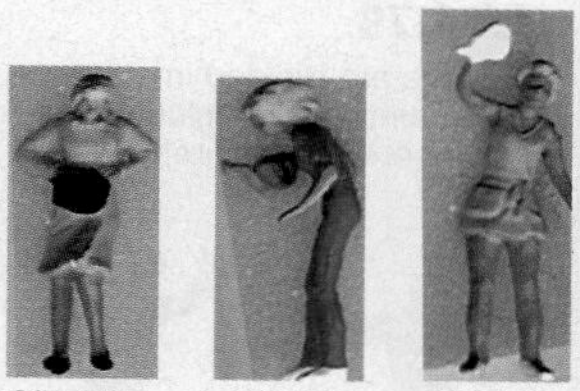

262-116 262-117 262-118

262-116 Woman Searching Purse ***NEW***
262-117 Woman Watering Flowers ***NEW***
262-118 Woman Cleaning Glass ***NEW***

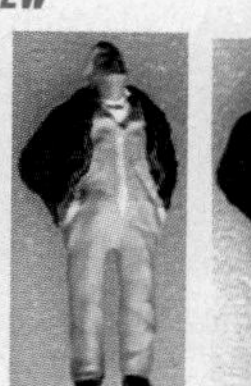

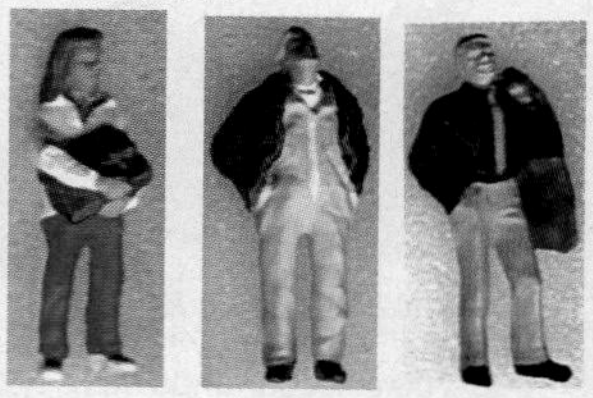

262-119 262-121 262-122

262-119 Girl Carrying Bookbag ***NEW***
262-121 Man w/Hands In Pocket ***NEW***
262-122 Man w/Jacket Over Shoulder ***NEW***

262-123 262-124

262-123 Woman w/Jacket ***NEW***
262-124 Girl w/Jacket In Arm ***NEW***

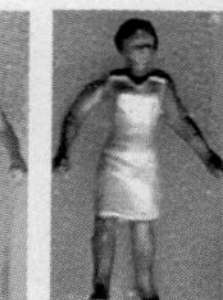

262-125 262-126 262-127

262-125 Fat Man w/Jacket ***NEW***
262-126 Woman w/Handbag ***NEW***
262-127 Walking Woman ***NEW***

PEOPLE WORKING EA 2.49

262-103 262-102

262-103 Chimney Sweep ***NEW***
262-128 Mailman ***NEW***
262-134 Welder ***NEW***
262-139 Chef ***NEW***

SEATED WORKERS

262-102 Worker w/Cap ***NEW***
262-147 Worker w/Hardhat ***NEW***

RAILROAD PERSONNEL

262-129 Engineer **2.49** ***NEW***

RECREATION & SPORTS EA 2.49

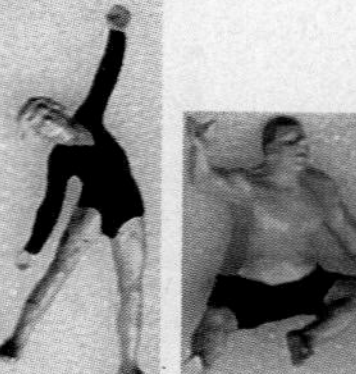
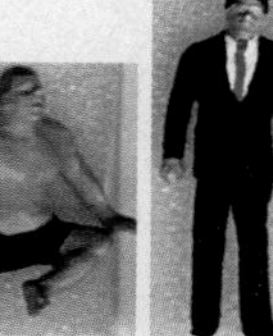

262-106 262-107 262-108

262-106 Female Gymnast ***NEW***
262-107 Fat Man at Beach ***NEW***
262-108 Photographer ***NEW***
262-132 Golfer ***NEW***
262-133 Scuba Diver ***NEW***
262-135 Boy Scout ***NEW***
262-136 Ice Skater ***NEW***
262-138 Bikini Girl ***NEW***

CLOWNS EA 2.49

262-144 1 ***NEW***
262-145 2 ***NEW***
262-146 3 ***NEW***

MISCELLANEOUS EA 2.49

262-104 Nude Girl ***NEW***
262-105 Nude Girl w/Towels ***NEW***
262-108 Politician ***NEW***
262-120 Santa Claus ***NEW***
262-130 Hitchhiker ***NEW***
262-131 Friar ***NEW***
262-140 Woman w/Dog (Puppy Love) ***NEW***
262-141 Man w/Bag (TGIF) ***NEW***
262-142 Businessman ***NEW***
262-143 Bride ***NEW***

kibri

Figures are molded in color and can be converted to different poses.

BACKYARD

405-8100 Backyard Assortment **18.99**
Includes: 2 pools, shed, 2 laundry lines, 2 umbrellas, green house, 4 bikes, fence, 2 sets of tables and more.

CITY CENTER

405-8104 **16.99**
Includes figures, tables w/umbrellas & benches, bikes, fountain & flowers.

PEOPLE ASSORTMENTS EA 12.99

405-8110 Passengers pkg(30)

405-8112 Men pkg(32)

405-8114 Seated Passengers pkg(30)

COW ASSORTMENTS PKG(6) EA 8.99

405-8115 Brown & White

405-8116 Black & White

405-8118 Brown & White

405-8119 Black & White

CONSTRUCTION YARD

405-8313 Construction Assortment **33.99**
Includes: barrels, boxes, dump truck, 4 telephone poles, dumpsters, sheds, fences, walls and more.

LABELLE INDUSTRIES

ENGINEER & FIREMAN EA 4.79

Figures are molded in plastic, fully painted and include one engineer and one fireman per set.

430-7001 Waving & Sitting

430-7002 Slouching & Leaning
430-7004 All four unpainted

International Hobby Corp.

All figures are handpainted plastic.

FIREMEN EA 6.98

348-4260 3 w/Hose, 3 w/Ax

348-4261 6 firemen, 2 extinguishers, stretcher, bullhorn, ax and hose

WORKERS PKG(5) EA 4.98

348-4264 MOW Crew *NEW*
348-4265 Blacksmith Crew *NEW*

MISCELLANEOUS

PKG(6) EA 2.98

348-8852 Winter People

348-8853 Hobo Clowns

PKG(5) EA 4.98

348-4266 The Smith Family *NEW*
348-4267 Passengers *NEW*
348-4268 Travelers *NEW*

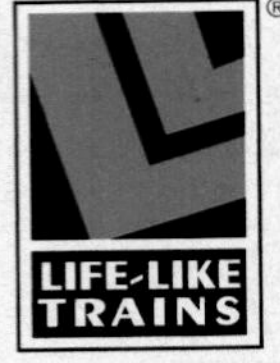

ANIMALS EA 8.75

433-1681 Barnyard Animals pkg(7)
Includes four 3-1/4" fence sections.

433-1682 Hogs pkg(6)

433-1683 Cattle pkg(6)

PEDESTRIANS EA 8.75

433-1682 City People pkg(7)

433-1685 Standing pkg(6)

433-1686 Sitting pkg(6)
Includes 2 park benches.

433-1688 Walking pkg(8)

433-1689 Townspeople pkg(8)

WORKERS PKG(6) EA 8.75

433-1687 Farmers

433-1690 Railroad Workers

Information STATION

Slang Names for Railroaders

Agent - station agent
Air Monkey - air brake repair man
Ashcat - fireman
Bailing Wire Mechanic - a man of little mechanical ability
Ballast Scorcher - an engineer who likes to run fast
Boomer - drifter who went from one railroad job to another
Box Car Tourist - hobo
Brains - conductor, person in charge of the train
Bull - railroad policeman
Car Catcher - rear brakeman
Car Tink - Car inspector (from the days when wheels were checked for cracks by tapping them with a hammer, producing a "tink" sound)
Casey Jones - any engineer, especially one who likes to run fast
Chambermaid - machinist in a roundhouse
Checker - company spy, particularly one checking on loss of materials or a conductor's receipts
Con - conductor
Deadhead - employee riding on a pass; any nonpaying passenger
Dishwashers - engine wipers at roundhouse
Dope Monkey - car inspector
Drummer - yard conductor
Fixed Signal - derisive term for a student brakeman standing on a box car with his lamp out and a cinder in his eye
Flag - assumed name; boomers worked under flag names when their own was blacklisted

FARMERS & ANIMALS

528-11770 Herder w/Sheep, Goats & Dogs **17.99**

528-11740 Milkmaid w/Cows & Calf **17.99**

528-11750 Horses w/Fence pkg(5) **17.99**

528-11430 Farmyard Figures **14.99**

528-11500 Man w/Wheelbarrow & Farm Animals **11.99**

528-11780 Feeding Hut w/Deer **14.99**

528-11801 Cattle & Drover **17.99**

528-11950 Horse-Drawn Wood Cart **20.99**

528-11960 Hay-Making **20.99**

528-11980 Horse-Drawn Hay Wagon **20.99**

528-15710 Farm Animals pkg(6) **8.99**

528-15720 Brown Cows pkg(6) **8.99**

528-15721 Holstein (black & white) Cows pkg(6) **8.99**

528-48250 Chasing Deer **13.99**

RECREATION & SPORTS

528-11270 Windsurfer w/Board **9.99**

528-11410 Hang Glider **11.99**

528-11881 Happy Camper **19.99**
Includes mobile home, printed surfboard and figure.

528-11670 Barbecue Hut **17.99**
Barbecue hut, 3 figures, dog, table, benches and accessories.

528-11690 Scooter Trip-2 Scooters, 3 Figures & 1 Bench **14.99**

528-11720 Riding Horses **17.99**

528-11760 Hunter w/Deer & Dog **17.99**

528-11790 Hunter's Look-Out **14.99**

528-15610 Hunters **8.99**

528-15810 Children Playing pkg(6) **8.99**

528-15830 Winter Sports Figures pkg(6) **8.99**

528-48200 Bathers **13.99**

WORKING PEOPLE

528-11860 Telekom Telephone Repair Person **19.99**
Includes telephone service truck, figure and phone booth.

528-11861 City Worker **19.99**
Includes official truck, 2 traffic signs and figure.

528-11991 Brewery Wagon **31.99**
Includes wagon with beer barrels, 2 horses, driver and helper.

528-15030 Workers pkg(6) **8.99**

528-15910 Early Steam-Era Figures pkg(6) **8.99**

528-15010 Railway Workers **8.99**

528-15020 Construction Workers **8.99**

528-15210 Railway Staff **8.99**

528-11620 Shipping Agents **14.99**

528-11630 Post Office w/Cart & Figures **17.99**

528-11870 Beer Garden **17.99**

528-48240 Farm Workers **13.99**

528-48260 Forest Workers **10.99**

CITY

528-11590 City Park **17.99**
2 figures, phone box, 2 animals and park lamp.

528-15000 Pedestrians pkg(12) **17.99**

528-15440 Seated People pkg(6) **8.99**

528-15450 Heavy-Set Standing People pkg(6) **8.99**

528-15460 Villagers pkg(6) **8.99**

528-15220 Voyagers **8.99**

528-15230 Railway Voyagers **8.99**

528-15410 Passers-by **8.99**

528-15420 Strollers **8.99**

528-15430 Sitting People **8.99**

528-11600 Ice Cream Man & Children **17.99**

528-11501 Wanderer **11.99**

528-11520 Garbage Truck **11.99**

528-11551 City Stop Place **14.99**

528-11810 Vegetable Stand **17.99**

528-11280 Cafe Garden Set w/Figures **11.99**

528-11830 Figure Assortment pkg(6) **20.99**

528-11530 Bus Stop w/Figures **14.99**

528-11540 Town Fountain w/Figures **14.99**

528-11610 Phone Booth w/Figures **17.99**

528-11550 Pedestrian Precinct w/Figures **14.99**

528-11841 Country Market - Market Stand, 2 Figures & 1 Animal **17.99**

MISCELLANEOUS

528-11940 Funeral Scene **20.99**

528-11560 People at Grave Site **17.99**

528-11380 Laundry w/Clothes Line & Figure **11.99**

528-11502 Wood Rest Stop **11.99**

528-11820 At the Station w/Figures **20.99**

528-11660 Figures at Railway Station **17.99**

528-48320 Travelers **17.99**

PLASTRUCT

FAMILY FIGURES

570-93357 Painted pkg(9) **7.95**
570-93353 Unpainted pkg(9) **5.95**

CITY FIGURES

570-93389 Painted pkg(6) **8.95**
570-93333 Unpainted pkg(6) **5.95**

570-93390 Painted pkg(6) **8.95**
570-93340 Unpainted pkg(6) **5.95**

SHEEPSCOT SCALE PRODUCTS

SEAGULLS

668-85006 pkg(38) **10.00**
Sixteen flying, twenty-two perched.

ROCO

IMPORTED FROM AUSTRIA BY WALTHERS

625-40000 Station pkg(24) **4.99**
Undecorated figures.

625-40001 Loco Crew Engineer & Fireman **6.99**

WOODLAND SCENICS

MISCELLANEOUS

785-210 Farmer, Plow, Disc & Horse **6.98**

785-226 Assorted Cats & Dogs w/Man **4.98**

785-227 The Bare Hunter **4.98**

RR PERSONNEL PKG(6) EA 5.98

490-5700 Track Laying Crew

490-5701 Work Crew

490-5704 Train Crew

490-5709 Station Crew
490-5714 Work People

PASSENGERS PKG(6) EA 5.98 (UNLESS NOTED)

490-5702 Station

490-5703 Sitting

490-5706 Sitting

490-5707 Station

490-5708 Standing
490-5725 Sitting w/Bench & Dog **6.50** *NEW*

ANIMALS PKG(6) EA 5.98

490-5726 Assorted Livestock *NEW*

490-5731 Cows & Calves (black & white)
490-5732 Cows & Calves (brown)
490-5734 Deer *NEW*

FURNITURE

490-550 Garage Sale Furniture **7.98**

MILITARY PKG(6) EA 5.98

490-5693 Figures Standing (Olive) *NEW*
490-5694 Figures Sitting (Olive) *NEW*
490-5695 Figures Standing (Desert) *NEW*
490-5696 Figures Sitting (Desert) *NEW*

490-5698 Commando

490-5699 US Combat

PEDESTRIANS PKG(6) EA 5.98 (UNLESS NOTED)

490-5697 Fat People
490-5705 Town People
490-5716 Steam-Era People
490-5717 Street People
490-5718 Young Women w/Children & Strollers
490-5720 Deacon & His Flock **7.50**
490-5721 Commuters
490-5722 Children Playing *NEW*
490-5724 Going To The Train *NEW*
490-5735 Market People *NEW*
490-5736 Tourists **7.50** *NEW*
490-5737 Pastor & Congregants w/Pulpit **7.50** *NEW*

UNPAINTED FIGURES

490-5772 pkg(72) **7.50**

FIRE FIGHTERS

490-9811 Firemen & Accessories **4.98**
Includes six fire fighters, two ladders and ten fire fighting accessories.
490-9810 Firemen w/ Accessories undecorated **1.98**

ACTION PKG(6) EA 5.98

490-5715 Action People
490-5711 Hunters

MINI SCENES

490-5712 Winter 3/4" tall pkg(6) **5.98**

FIGURES & ACCESSORY SET

490-5710 20 Pieces **10.98**
Includes six figures, four benches, three fire hydrants, three mail boxes and three trash cans.

VOLLMER

Bring your models to life with this line of affordably priced people. Each plastic person is molded in a realistic pose and painted in a simplified scheme.

Foreign Travelers 770-2213

PEDESTRIANS PKG(5) EA 8.99 (UNLESS NOTED)

770-2201 People Standing on Station Platform #1

770-2202 Walking Pedestrians

770-2203 Departing Passengers

770-2204 Standing Passengers Set #1

770-2206 Standing Passengers Set #2

770-2207 People Standing on Station Platform

770-2211 Seated Travelers
770-2213 Foreign Travelers pkg(15) **37.99**

770-2214 People Standing on Station Platform #2

770-2221 Hunter w/2 Dogs & 5 Rabbits *NEW*

770-2230 Wedding Party (Bride, Groom, 3 guests) *NEW*

RAILROAD PERSONNEL PKG(5) EA 8.99

770-2208 Switch Crew

770-2209 Track Workers w/Tools-Standing *NEW*

770-2210 Engine Crew

770-2212 Track/Shop Crew

770-2240 Modern Construction/Railroad Workers *NEW*

770-2245 Porters/Red Caps w/Luggage *NEW*

WORKING PEOPLE PKG(5) EA 8.99

770-2205 Farm Hands *NEW*

770-2215 German Fireman Set #1

770-2216 German Fireman Set #2

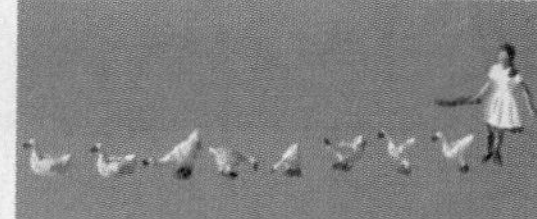
770-2222 Girl w/Flock of 8 Geese *NEW*

770-2223 Shepherd w/Dog & 6 Sheep *NEW*

ANIMALS PKG(4) EA 8.99

770-2217 Horses

770-2218 Cows

770-2219 Cows (3 Brown, 1 Blue "Milka" Advertising Mascot) *NEW*

770-2220 Deer (brown) 1 Stag, 1 Doe & 3 Fawns *NEW*

Bring layout scenes to life with these detailed plastic people. Molded in life-like poses and prepainted, they're ready for all sorts of jobs and leisure activities on your layout.

Geese on Land 447-724

African Rhinos 447-756

Storks w/Two Nests 447-764

Elves w/Deer 447-2303

Fallow Deer 447-2411

Horse Teams 447-2492

Children Playing 447-2197

Singles #1 447-2286

Groups #1 447-2292

Singles #2 447-2295

Groups #2 447-2301

Chubby Singles 447-2399

Chubby Groups 447-2400

First Aid Workers #1 447-982

First Aid Workers #2 447-988

Policemen 447-2246

Traffic Policemen 447-2252

German Fire Fighters-Set #1 447-2371

German Fire Fighters-Set #2 447-2377

American Fire Fighters #1 447-2383

Old-Time People Set #1 447-2156

Old-Time People Set #2 447-2162

ANIMALS EA 8.99

447-724 Geese on Land pkg(12)
447-756 African Rhinos pkg(3) ***NEW***
447-764 Storks w/Two Nests pkg(7)
447-2303 Elves w/Deer pkg(10) ***NEW***
447-2411 Fallow Deer (Small) pkg(12) ***NEW***
447-2492 Horse Teams pkg(4) ***NEW***

CHILDREN

447-2197 Playing pkg(7) **8.99**

PASSENGERS PKG(6) (UNLESS NOTED) EA 8.99

447-2286 Singles #1
447-2292 Groups #1
447-2295 Singles #2
447-2301 Groups #2
447-2399 Chubby Singles pkg(7)
447-2400 Chubby Groups pkg(3)

447-2525 Standing, Waving Partial figures for use in passenger cars, buses, or automobiles with limited interior clearance.

447-2528 Seated #1

EMERGENCY SERVICES PKG(6) EA 8.99

447-982 First Aid Workers #1
447-988 First Aid Workers #2
447-2246 Policemen
447-2252 Traffic Policemen
447-2371 German Fire Fighters-Set #1 (1950s) ***NEW***
447-2377 German Fire Fighters-Set #2 (1950s) ***NEW***
447-2383 American Fire Fighters #1

OLD-TIME PEOPLE PKG(6) EA 8.99

447-2156 Set #1
447-2162 Set #2

Merten M:

LEISURE-TIME PEOPLE PKG(6) (UNLESS NOTED) EA 8.99

447-954 Swimmers-Seated & Laying Down
447-960 Swimmers-Standing in Groups pkg(3)
447-967 Wedding Guests
447-2144 Downhill Skiers-Men *NEW*
447-2150 Downhill Skiers-Women *NEW*
447-2168 Water Skiers *NEW*
447-2174 Musicians on the Beach
447-2209 Organ Grinder & Audience pkg(5)
447-2215 Ice Skaters-Set #1 *NEW*
447-2221 Ice/Figure Skaters *NEW*
447-2227 Ice Skaters-Paired Couples 3 Pair *NEW*
447-2349 Joggers-Men *NEW*
447-2355 Joggers-Women *NEW*
447-2361 Vacationers Reclining in Chaise Lounges *NEW*
447-2398 Happy Drunks
447-2485 Men Running Hurdles (8 Figures; 80 Hurdles) *NEW*
447-2486 Women Running Hurdles (8 Figures; 80 Hurdles) *NEW*
447-2490 Tennis Players (4 Players, 2 Ball Boys, 1 Official) *NEW*
447-2498 Soccer Players pkg(11) *NEW*
447-2499 2 Soccer Goals, 6 Corner Flags, 1 Referee & 2 Linesmen *NEW*
447-2500 Canoeists & Kayakers pkg(4) *NEW*
447-2524 Standing People at Beach Snackbar
447-2526 Nude Swimmers-Standing Females
447-2527 Nude Swimmers-Females Undressing

FIGURE ACCESSORIES EA 8.99

447-2454 Playground Equipment #1
447-2520 Recycling Containers for Glass & Paper

Swimmers-Seated & Laying Down 447-954

Swimmers-Standing in Groups 447-960

Wedding Guests 447-967

Downhill Skiers-Men 447-2144

Downhill Skiers-Women 447-2150

Water Skiers 447-2168

Musicians on the Beach 447-2174

Organ Grinder & Audience 447-2209

Ice Skaters-Set #1 447-2215

Ice/Figure Skaters 447-2221

Ice Skaters-Paired Couples 3 Pair 447-2227

Joggers-Men 447-2349

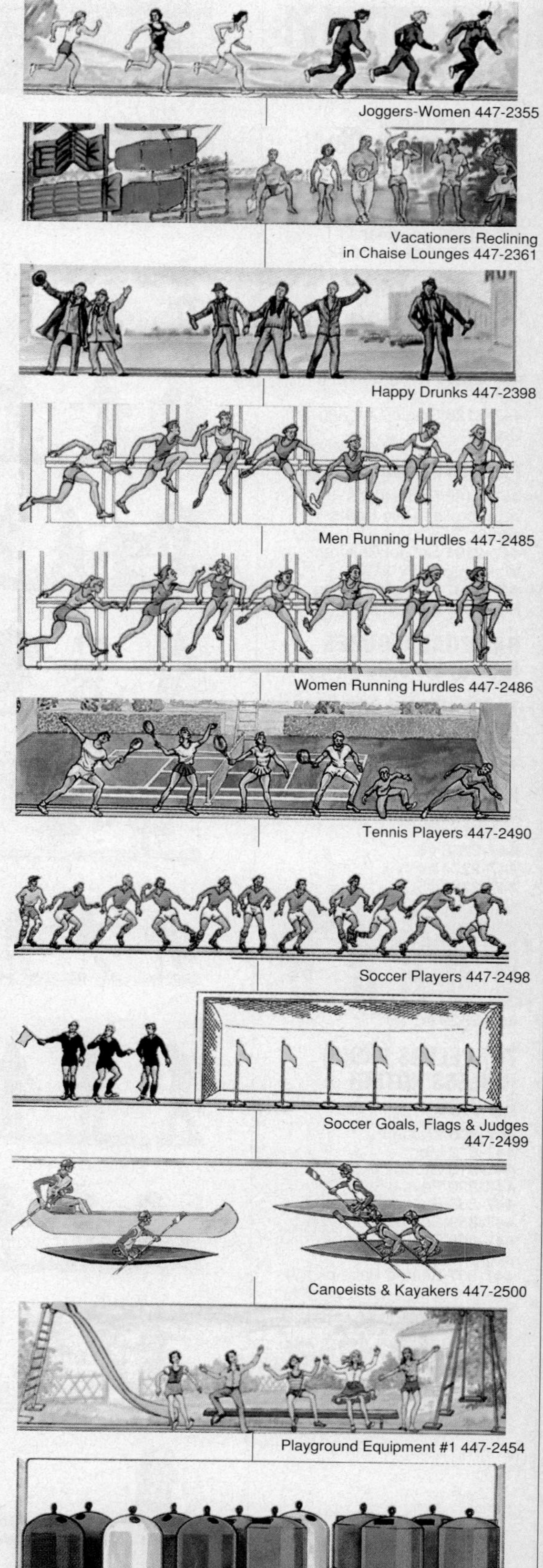

Joggers-Women 447-2355

Vacationers Reclining in Chaise Lounges 447-2361

Happy Drunks 447-2398

Men Running Hurdles 447-2485

Women Running Hurdles 447-2486

Tennis Players 447-2490

Soccer Players 447-2498

Soccer Goals, Flags & Judges 447-2499

Canoeists & Kayakers 447-2500

Playground Equipment #1 447-2454

Reycycling Containers 447-2520

Merten M:

PEDESTRIANS/ PASSERSBY PKG(6) EA 8.99

447-948 Swimmers Set #1 *NEW*
447-2180 Pedestrians #1
447-2502 Passers-By #2

HUNTERS PKG(6) EA 8.99

447-2114 Shooting-Set #2 *NEW*
447-2120 Paired-Carrying Game
447-2126 Single-Carrying Game

PEDESTRIANS EA 8.99

447-2186 Pedestrians w/Umbrellas/Rain Coats pkg(6) *NEW*
447-2191 School Children-Walking pkg(7) *NEW*
447-2397 Beatniks-Young People pkg(6) *NEW*

RAILROAD FIGURES PKG(6) EA 8.99

TRACK REPAIR CREWS

447-876 #2
447-882 #3
447-886 #4 *NEW*

RAILROAD PERSONNEL

447-908 #1
447-914 #2
447-2268 #3
447-2274 #4
447-2280 #5

447-2529 #6

TRAVELERS PKG(6) (UNLESS NOTED) EA 8.99

447-806 Women
447-812 Men
447-818 Groups pkg(2)
447-820 Pairs pkg(3)
447-853 Seated Women
447-859 Seated Men *NEW*
447-865 Seated Groups pkg(2)
447-867 Seated Pairs pkg(3)

447-971 Running Women

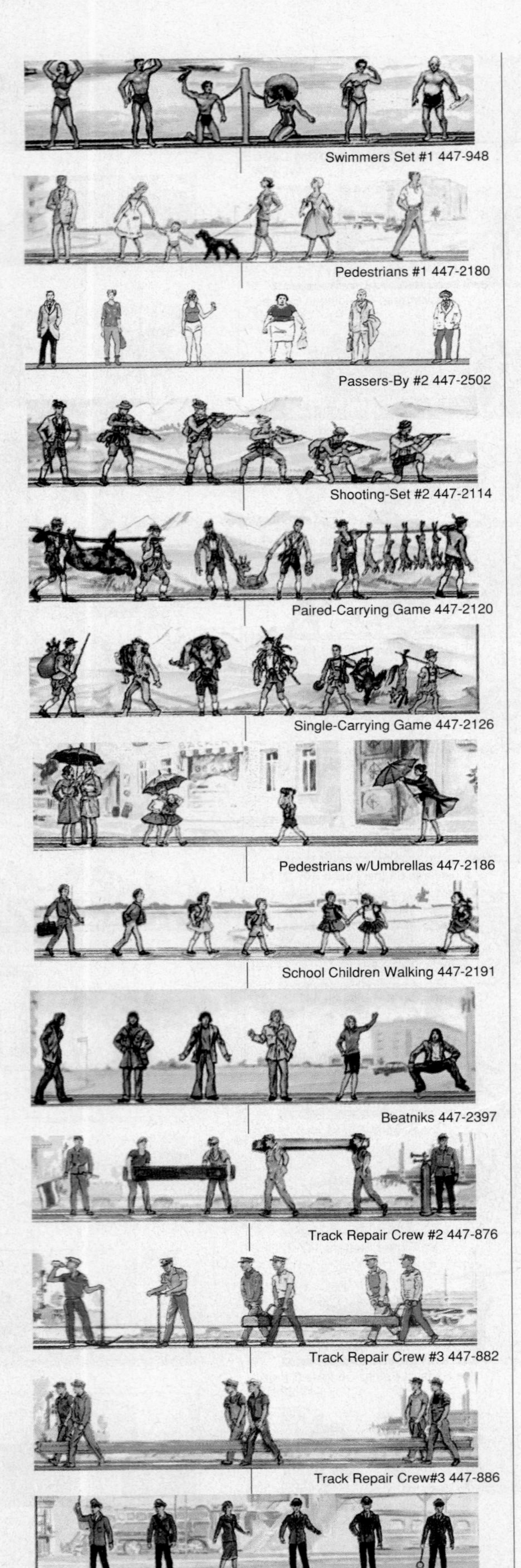

Swimmers Set #1 447-948
Pedestrians #1 447-2180
Passers-By #2 447-2502
Shooting-Set #2 447-2114
Paired-Carrying Game 447-2120
Single-Carrying Game 447-2126
Pedestrians w/Umbrellas 447-2186
School Children Walking 447-2191
Beatniks 447-2397
Track Repair Crew #2 447-876
Track Repair Crew #3 447-882
Track Repair Crew#3 447-886
Railroad Personnel #1 447-908

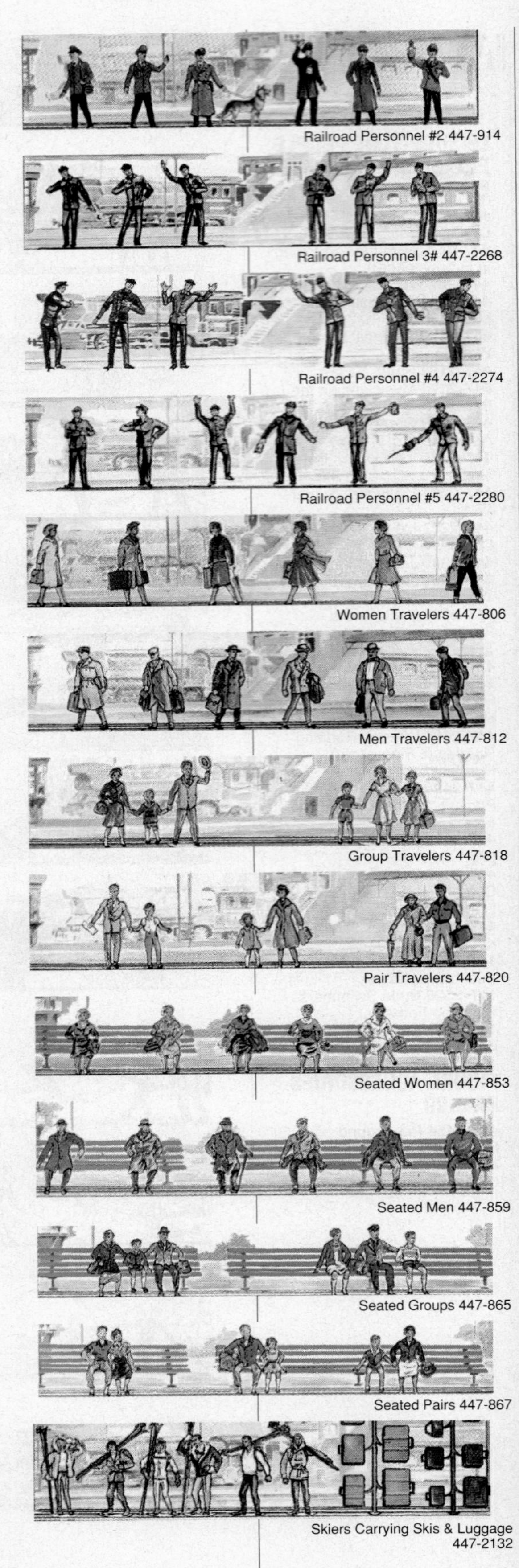

Railroad Personnel #2 447-914
Railroad Personnel 3# 447-2268
Railroad Personnel #4 447-2274
Railroad Personnel #5 447-2280
Women Travelers 447-806
Men Travelers 447-812
Group Travelers 447-818
Pair Travelers 447-820
Seated Women 447-853
Seated Men 447-859
Seated Groups 447-865
Seated Pairs 447-867
Skiers Carrying Skis & Luggage 447-2132

Merten M:

447-2132 Skiers in Winter Clothes Carrying Skis & Luggage *NEW*
447-2515 Seated
447-2516 Walking
447-2517 Seated
447-2519 Seated Passengers *NEW*

447-2523 Foreign Travelers

WORKERS PKG(6) (UNLESS NOTED) EA 8.99

447-800 Street Vendors
447-889 Blacksmiths (4) & Horses (2)
447-891 Foresters & Shepherds pkg(5)
447-896 Farm Workers
447-902 Harvesters
447-920 Harvesters #1
447-926 Harvesters #2
447-2234 Workers Loading #1
447-2240 Workers Loading #2
447-2313 Fruit Stand Vendors & Shoppers w/Bananas *NEW*
447-2319 Women Hanging Laundry pkg(5)
447-2325 Gas Station Workers/Mechanics *NEW*
447-2331 Auto Mechanics
447-2337 Cement Workers
447-2343 Construction Workers
447-2403 Shepherd w/18 Sheep & Dog *NEW*
447-2510 Gardeners
447-2521 People Recycling Glass & Paper *NEW*
Use Recycling Containers from #2520 (sold separately) to model a complete mini-scene.

447-2522 Truck Drivers/Helpers *NEW*

MILITARY

ARMY

447-1009 Mounted Officers w/Horses pkg(3) **8.99** *NEW*

Seated 447-2515

Travelers 447-2516

Seated 447-2517

Seated Passengers 447-2519

Street Vendors 447-800

Blacksmiths & Horses 447-889

Foresters & Shepherds 447-891

Farm Workers 447-896

Harvesters 447-902

Harvesters #1 447-920

Harvesters #2 447-926

Workers Loading #1 447-2234

Workers Loading #2 447-2240

Fruit Stand Vendors & Shoppers w/Bananas 447-2313

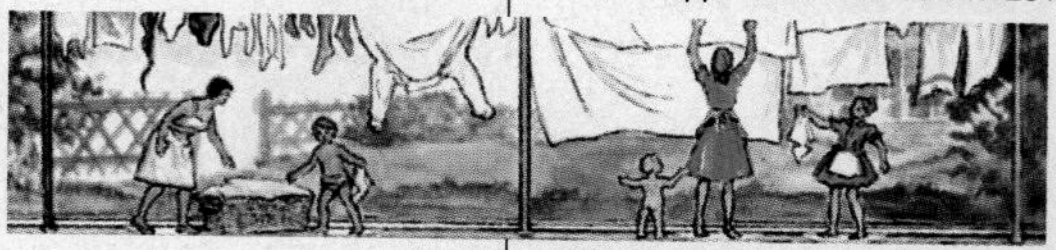

Women Hanging Laundry 447-2319

Gas Station Workers/Mechanics 447-2325

Auto Mechanics 447-2331

Cement Workers 447-2337

Construction Workers 447-2343

Shepherd, Sheep & Dog 447-2403

Gardeners 447-2510

People Recycling 447-2521

Truck Drivers/Helpers 447-2522

Mounted Officers w/Horses 447-1009

Merten M:

ECONOMY FIGURE SETS

EA 5.99

Same detailed plastic figures, but with simplified painting. Great for backgrounds, interiors, or scenes where a large number of figures are needed at a lower cost.

447-5000 Railroad Personnel-Set #2

447-5001 Travelers

447-5002 Seated People Set #1

447-5003 Seated People Set #3

447-5004 Standing People

447-5005 Automobile Drivers

447-5006 People Exercising

447-5007 Skateboarders & Rollerbladers

447-5008 People Dumping Trash

447-5009 Truck Drivers

447-5010 Restaurant Staff

447-5011 Fire Rescue Personnel

447-5012 Fire/Rescue Dive Crew

447-5013 Fire/Rescue Dive Crew in Boat

447-5014 Gardeners-Set #1

447-5015 Gardeners-Set #2

447-5016 Foreign Passers-By

447-5017 Travelers w/Baggage

ANIMALS EA 5.99

447-5018 Horses (brown)

447-5019 Cows (black & white)

CATALOG

447-1997 Merten 1997 Whole Line Catalog **6.99**
Color sketches of figure sets in HO, N, TT, G and O Scales. English, French and German text, 43 pages, softcover.

Unpainted cast brass metal figures, unless noted.

MEN AT WORK EA 2.00

322 324 326

464-322 Art
464-324 Sam
464-326 Chuck

328 300 302

464-328 Dan
464-330 Chris, Kneeling
464-332 Clint, Running Bearded Man
464-300 Tom
464-302 Fred

304 306 320

464-304 Bill
464-306 Ted
464-320 Logan, Kneeling

312 314 316 318

464-312 Valdean
464-314 Arley, Lifting
464-316 Tyrel, Walking
464-318 Joe PA Truck Driver

WORKERS WITH MOVABLE ARMS EA 2.50

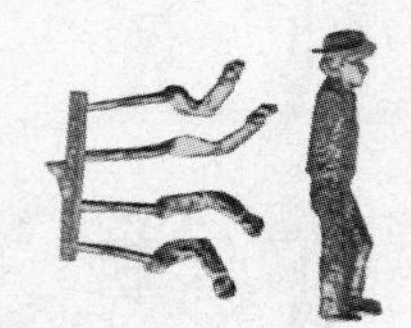
464-308 John

464-310 Jim

ANIMALS

464-618 Rats pkg(5) **2.75**
464-651 Dog pkg(2) **2.50**
464-682 Skunks pkg(2) **1.00**
464-736 Small Birds pkg(4) **1.00** ***NEW***

464-750 Pigeons (White Metal) pkg(6) **1.25**
464-752 Chickens (White Metal) pkg(4) **1.00**

Information STATION

Jesse James

Jesse James was born on September 6, 1847 near the Missouri town of Centerville (now Kearney). In his 34-1/2 years of life he became one of the most famous outlaws in the history of the U.S. Part of his fame was derived from the numerous, and successful, train robberies he participated in as the leader of the James Gang.

The first train robbery that can undoubtedly be traced to Jesse James is the December 12, 1874 heist of the Kansas Pacific Railroad (now Union Pacific). He and his gang achieved this feat by robbing Purdee's general store first, and then made the owner place ties on the track for an impassable obstacle. When the train came to a halt, the James gang liberated it of $30,000 of gold dust, $20,000 in currency, $5,000 in jewelry and all of the passengers' valuables. His next robbery was of the Iron Mountain (now Missouri Pacific) on July 7, 1876 at Rocky Cut, Missouri. He and his gang made away with $16,000. This was followed by the hold-up of a Chicago and Alton express train on October 7, 1879.

In all the years as an outlaw Jesse James never touched the Chicago, Burlington & Quincy train line. It has been said that he stayed away from them because they gave his mother an annual pass for their system as a safety measure.

ORIGINAL Preiser

IMPORTED FROM GERMANY BY WALTHERS
Hand painted, lightweight plastic figures in action poses.

COMPLETE YOUR SCENES WITH THESE CUSTOM FIGURE SETS

Improve dull dioramas and lifeless layout in minutes with custom figure sets from Walthers. Many are exclusives, which feature special groups of figures and custom painting to compliment our structure, passenger car and vehicle kits.

Each figure is molded in a realistic pose and hand-painted to bring out its unique character. Choose from figures for a variety of eras and occupations:

Sales Staff & Customers 590-1010119

Passenger Train Crew 590-10452

Amtrak Train Crew 590-1010054

Pilots, Stewardess & Ground Crew 590-1010055

AUTO DEALERSHIP

590-1010119 Sales Staff & Customers pkg(6) **14.98** ***NEW***
Add action to the sales floor of the Uptown Motors building (933-3077).

PASSENGER TRAIN CREWS

590-10452 Transition-Era Crew pkg(6) **12.99**
Revised with correct figures - a complete crew for any passenger train of the 1940s to the 1960s.

590-1010054 Amtrak Crew pkg(6) **14.98**
Six figures in the current employee uniform, great for station scenes.

Pape rMill Crew 590-1010051

Steel Mill Day Crew 590-1010067

PAPER MILL CREW

590-1010051 Assorted Workers pkg(10) **19.99**
Brings the Superior Paper Mill (933-3060) to life.

"THE WORKS"

Painted especially for use in and around Walthers steel works buildings:

590-1010064 Blast Furnace Crew pkg(6) **13.99**
590-1010065 Electric Furnace Crew pkg(6) **13.99**
590-1010066 Loading Crew pkg(6) **13.99**
590-1010067 Steel Mill Day Crew pkg(10) **19.99**

VINTAGE AIRLINER CREW

590-1010055 Pilots, Stewardess & Ground Crew pkg(6) **14.98**
Super addition to your civilian DC-3 (933-1160 series) display.

MILITARY FIGURES

590-1010056 Standing Pilots & Ground Crew pkg(12) **14.98** ***NEW***
Perfect for detailing any World War Two airfield, these figures look great alongside the C-47 (933-1150) or P-51D (933-1170)

Blast Furnace Crew 590-1010064

Electric Furnace Crew 590-1010065

Loading Crew 590-1010066

POLICE FIGURES

590-10396 US SWAT Team pkg(6) **15.99**
The finishing touch with Walthers Ford Crown Victoria Police Cars (933-1250 series).

590-10397 Mounted Police in Modern Uniform pkg(2) **17.99**
Includes two figures riding detailed horses.

ORIGINAL Preiser

1900S FIGURES

590-12197 Passers-by Wearing Winter Clothes 13.99

590-12193 At the Grocer's 14.99

590-12199 At the Milk Truck 14.99

590-12129 Standing Cyclists 15.99

590-12130 Prussian RR Personnel 13.99

590-12131 Passers-by & Police 13.99

590-12132 Family Walking 13.99

590-12133 Passengers, Men 13.99

590-24608 Group from Spreewald 25.99

590-12134 Bavarian RR Personnel 13.99

590-12135 People Bathing 13.99

590-12136 Passengers, Sitting on Coach 13.99

590-12137 People, Sitting on Platform 13.99

590-12138 Travelers & Passers-by 13.99

590-12139 Passers-by 13.99

590-12196 Wilhelm II Era 13.99

590-12102 Firemen 11.99

590-12187 Seated Firemen 18.99

590-12176 Passers-by 13.99

590-12184 Passers-by Wearing Winter Clothes 13.99

590-12195 People at the Christmas Fair 13.99

590-12198 Postal Officials 14.99

RAILROAD PERSONNEL

590-14017 Track Workers 8.99

590-20261 Circus Workers 15.99

590-20264 Circus Workers w/Driver 15.99

590-10375 Railway Personnel 13.99

590-16348 At the Goods Shed 15.99

590-16500 Tank Crew 7.99
590-17186 Equipment/Vehicle Shop 25.99

590-10236 1989 RR Personnel 11.99

590-14011 Station Personnel 8.99

590-10018 US Personnel & Policeman 11.99

590-10031 Track Workers 11.99

590-10238 Italian RR Workers 13.99

590-14141 Train Personnel DB 1989 8.99

590-10086 French Train Crewmen 11.99

590-10244 Belgian Railway Personnel 15.99

590-10213 Netherlands RR Personnel 15.99

590-10245 Railway Workers 11.99

590-10010 RR Workers 11.99

590-10011 German Railway Personnel 11.99

590-10012 Station Personnel #2 11.99

590-10019 Japanese RR Personnel 11.99

590-14012 German RR Personnel DB 8.99

590-14013 Railway Yard Workers 8.99

590-14014 Steam Engine Crew 8.99

590-14033 Track Workers 8.99

ORIGINAL Preiser

590-14105 Railway Shunters **8.99**

590-10237 1989 Train Personnel **11.99**

590-10087 Swiss Railway Personnel **11.99**

590-12191 Engine-Driver/Stoker **13.99**

590-14403 Track Workers **25.99**

590-10409 Railway Workers pkg(7) **13.99** ***NEW***

590-10410 Railway Workers Great Britain pkg(6) **14.99** ***NEW***

590-10444 Track Workers w/Accessories pkg(6) **16.99** ***NEW***

PASSENGERS

590-10299 Seated **12.99**

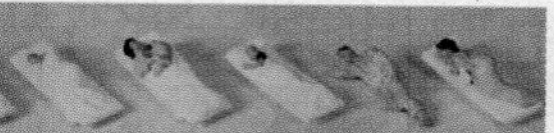
590-10300 Sleeping **13.99**

590-10351 Industrial, Sitting **13.99**

590-10384 Sitting on Bus **12.99**

590-10385 Sitting on Bus **13.99**

590-10406 With Bus Driver pkg(7) **13.99** ***NEW***

590-10386 Sitting on Bus **13.99**

590-10387 Seated Couples **12.99**

590-10388 Dressing **14.99**

590-10391 Passengers Sitting/Eating **12.99**

590-14000 Walking Passengers **8.99**

590-14001 Passers-by **8.99**

590-14002 Standing Passers-by **8.99**

590-14003 Boys & Girls **8.99**

590-14004 Seated Passengers w/Bench **8.99**

590-14005 Youths **8.99**

590-14006 Teenagers **8.99**

590-14007 Children **8.99**

590-10379 Passengers on Platform **13.99**

590-10380 Businessmen **14.99**

590-10381 Businessmen w/Coats **14.99**

590-10382 Passengers w/Steward **13.99**

590-10026 Railfans, Standing **11.99**

590-10027 Seated on Benches **11.99**

590-10028 Arriving **11.99**

590-10029 Departing **11.99**

590-10115 Standing **11.99**

590-10123 Teens Walking **11.99**

590-10124 Senior Citizens **11.99**

590-10281 Travelers w/Luggage **11.99**

590-10020 Passengers **11.99**

590-10114 Waiting **11.99**

590-10103 Seating Diners **11.99**

590-10298 Railway, Seated **11.99**

590-10434 Sitting Travelers pkg(6) **13.99** ***NEW***

590-14020 Passengers **8.99**

590-14028 Arriving **8.99**

590-14029 Travelers Standing **8.99**

590-14104 Passengers **8.99**

590-14123 Teenage Passengers **8.99**

ORIGINAL **Preiser**

590-14400 48 Seated w/Cargo **47.99**

590-14401 24 Standing/ Walking **25.99**

590-10021 21 Seated Persons **10.99**

590-10327 Passengers Hurrying **12.99**

590-14133 Passengers **8.99**

590-14142 Passengers **8.99**

PEOPLE WORKING

590-10100 Emergency Doctors w/Motorcycle pkg(15) **18.99**
590-10212 Office Workshop Personnel **17.99**
590-10220 Construction Workers **18.99**

590-10347 Street Repair Crew w/Accessories pkg(4) **25.99**

590-10445 City Workers w/Accessories pkg(4) **18.99**
NEW

590-10352 Merchant Sailors Ashore pkg(6) **13.99**

590-10353 Ship Crewmen pkg(6) **13.99**

590-10404 2 Swiss Dairymen w/3 Cows pkg(5) **25.99**

590-10405 Street Car Crew w/Pedestrians pkg(7) **15.99**

590-10416 German Federal Railway Personnel pkg(6) **15.99**

590-10418 Track Workers w/Tools pkg(6) **15.99**

590-10419 Policemen w/Warning Vests & Accessories pkg(4) **18.99**

590-10420 Modern Workmen w/Warning Vests pkg(6) **15.99**

590-10421 Film Crew pkg(4) **18.99**

590-10422 Policemen Era III pkg(6) **15.99**

590-10423 Modern Workmen w/Outdoor Gear pkg(6) **15.99**

Construction Workers 590-10220

Office Workshop Personnel 590-10212

Bus-Driver, Passengers 590-14404

Railway Shunters 590-14406

Gardeners Accessories 590-10046

590-14144 Workmen w/Accessories pkg(6) **18.99**

590-14146 Policemen Era III pkg(6) **8.99**

590-14147 Loading Dock Crew pkg(5) **8.99**

590-14148 Figures Standing at Window pkg(6) **8.99**

590-14149 Cleaning Crew pkg(5) **8.99**
590-14406 Railway Shunters **25.99**

590-10350 Industrial/Dock Workers **13.99**

590-10373 Mechanics **11.99**

590-10374 Telephone Workers w/Tent **26.99**

590-10376 Carpenters **17.99**

590-10377 Bakery **18.99**

590-10369 Street Cafe **18.99**

590-10348 Pantomime in cafe **18.99**

590-14009 Truckers **8.99**

590-10014 Different Professions **11.99**

590-10045 Harvest Workers **14.99**
590-10046 Gardeners Accessories **17.99**

590-10037 Crane Operators **11.99**

ORIGINAL **Preiser**

590-10040 Farm Workers #1 **11.99**

590-10044 Farm Workers #2 **12.99**

590-10042 Lumberjacks **11.99**

590-10050 Women Hanging Laundry **11.99**

590-10059 Housewives Working **12.99**

590-10062 TV/Movie Crew **12.99**

590-10089 Photographers **12.99**

590-10016 Delivery Men w/Loads **11.99**

590-10210 Innkeeper/ Waiter/Waitress **14.99**

590-10295 Farm Workers **14.99**

590-14016 Delivery Men w/Loads #2 **8.99**

590-14030 Road Workers **8.99**

590-14040 Farm Workers **8.99**

590-14050 Women Hanging Laundry **8.99**

590-10105 Steeplejacks **11.99**

590-10036 Truck Drivers Standing **11.99**

590-10106 Artists/Models/ Nudes **12.99**

590-10038 Truck Drivers **11.99**

590-10243 Craftsmen **15.99**

590-10248 German Postal Workers **12.99**

590-10048 Cattle Traders **14.99**

590-10294 Stock Workers **18.99**

590-10275 Baker Krause **12.99**

590-10329 Cooks **13.99**

590-10330 Cooks at the Buffet **13.99**

590-10338 Construction Workers **18.99**

590-14127 Standing Truckers **8.99**

590-14128 Crane Personnel **8.99**

590-14129 At the Mill **8.99**

590-14130 Mechanics **8.99**

590-14131 In Front of a Hotel **8.99**

590-10367 At the Restaurant **15.99**

590-10251 Bricklayers/ Accessories **14.99**
590-10328 Tractor Drivers **17.99**

590-10432 German Technical Services 1999 Set #1 pkg(5) **18.99** ***NEW***
590-10433 German Technical Services 1999 Set #2 pkg(5) **18.99** ***NEW***

SPECTATORS

590-10025 Seated **10.99**

590-10301 Spectators #1 **11.99**

590-10302 Spectators #2 **12.99**

590-14025 Seated **8.99**

590-14095 Seated Persons **8.99**

590-10297 Seated Youths **11.99**

590-10346 Night People **17.99**

590-10365 Female Commuters **15.99**

590-10366 Male Commuters **15.99**
590-10368 Tourists, Waiter, Artist **18.99**

590-14143 Spectators **8.99**

VENDORS

590-24695 Market Stall **37.99**

590-24696 Market Stall **37.99**

590-10052 Market Stalls **25.99**

590-10053 Food Vendors/Cart **25.99**

590-10056 Flower Stand/Customers **13.99**

590-10337 Market Stall **14.99**

ORIGINAL Preiser

RECREATION & SPORTS

590-10315 Skaters **12.99**

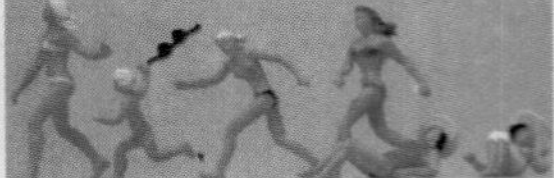

590-10211 Fun at the Beach **11.99**

590-10070 Bathers Standing **10.99**

590-10071 Bathers Reclining **10.99**

590-10078 Tennis Players **12.99**
590-10107 Nude Sunbathers **12.99**

590-10283 Family at Beach **12.99**

590-10424 Sunbathers Eating pkg(6) **14.99** ***NEW***

590-10426 Speedboat Driver & Passengers pkg(6) **13.99** ***NEW***

590-10427 3 Beach Huts w/Figures **25.99** ***NEW***

590-10428 Beachgoers Sitting & Standing pkg(6) **16.99** ***NEW***

590-10429 Sunbathers On Lounges pkg(6) **18.99** ***NEW***

590-10430 Tourists Resting On Folding Chairs pkg(6) **18.99** ***NEW***

590-10431 Sunbathers On Folding Chairs pkg(6) **18.99** ***NEW***

590-10438 Sunbathers & Beach Hut pkg(7) **16.99** ***NEW***
590-10439 Nude Bathers w/2 Lounges pkg(8) **16.99** ***NEW***

590-10290 Wanderers/Hikers **11.99**

590-10316 Skiers **13.99**

See What's Available at

www.walthers.com

Soccer Team 590-10075

Bike Riders w/Bikes 590-10091

Down Hill Skiers 590-10313

590-10072 Family w/Boats **11.99**
590-10075 Soccer Team **18.99**
590-10091 Bike Riders w/Bikes **15.99**

590-10110 Boys & Girls **11.99**

590-10349 Students/Artist in Cafe **18.99**

590-10077 Men Fishing **12.99**

590-10081 3 Cyclists w/Hercules **18.99**

590-10125 3 Mopeds w/Riders **18.99**

590-10126 Motorbikes w/Riders **18.99**

590-10120 Couples Dancing **11.99**

590-10241 Folk Dancers **13.99**

590-24607 Bavarian Group **18.99**
590-10313 Down Hill Skiers **12.99**

590-10314 Figure Skaters **12.99**

590-10240 Bavarian Folk Dancers **13.99**

590-10190 Mountain Climbers **12.99**

590-10113 Hikers **12.99**

590-10441 Hikers At Water Pump pkg(7) **18.99** ***NEW***

590-10442 Hikers Resting pkg(6) **16.99** ***NEW***

590-10443 Hikers At Spring pkg(6) **18.99** ***NEW***

590-10312 Cross Country Skiers **12.99**

590-25100 36 Spectators **47.99**

590-10231 Golfers **13.99**

590-25086 Racing Bicycles **13.99**

ORIGINAL Preiser

590-10128 Motor Bikes & Rider Set **18.99**

590-10249 Divers **14.99**

590-10306 Swimming People **11.99**

590-10307 Children at Pool **11.99**

590-10308 Children/Teens at Pool **11.99**

590-10309 Bathers **11.99**

590-10334 Graffiti Sprayers **13.99**

CYCLE RACERS EA 11.99

590-25000 Team A-Yellow

590-25001 Team B-White

590-25002 Team C-Blue

590-25003 Team D-Red, Yellow

590-25004 Team A-Yellow

590-25005 Team B-White

590-25006 Team C-Blue

590-25007 Team D-Red, Yellow

590-25008 Team F-Blue, Black

590-25009 Team F-Blue, Green

590-10333 Cyclists

590-10336 Cyclists

Travelers 590-14401

Pedestrians 590-14412

PEDESTRIANS

590-10400 Standing Commuters pkg(6) **15.99**

590-10401 Nun w/Small Children pkg(7) **13.99**

590-10402 Nuns w/Luggage pkg(6) **13.99**

590-10403 Standing Travelers w/Luggage, Set #1, Era III pkg(6) **13.99**

590-10407 Modern Swiss Railroad Personnel pkg(7) **15.99**

590-10408 Standing Travelers w/Luggage, Set #2, Era III pkg(6) **13.99**

590-10411 Business Commuters pkg(6) **13.99**

590-10412 Seated Travelers pkg(6) **13.99**

590-10413 Foreign Travelers pkg(6) **13.99**

590-10414 People Waiting for Bus pkg(6) **17.99**

590-10415 Parents & Grandparents w/Children pkg(6) **13.99**

590-10417 Railroad Passengers w/Accessories pkg(6) **15.99**

590-12045 Vintage Passengers 1847 pkg(13) **25.99**

590-12046 Vintage Engine Crew w/Standing Passengers pkg(6) **13.99**
590-14401 Travelers **25.99**

590-14145 Seated Passengers pkg(6) **8.99**
590-14412 Pedestrians pkg(36) **36.99** ***NEW***

590-16800 WWII Civilians Waving pkg(6) **11.99**

590-10378 Passers-by w/Policemen **12.99**

590-10180 Couples Seated **11.99**

590-10181 School Children **11.99**
590-10183 Teens **11.99**

590-10051 Women & Children on Benches **11.99**

590-10090 Drivers & Passengers **11.99**

590-10117 Standing **11.99**

ORIGINAL Preiser

590-10118 Walking 11.99

590-10119 Standing 11.99

590-10096 Seated #2 11.99

590-10097 Seated #3 11.99

590-10258 Girls 11.99

590-10278 Family Picture 11.99

590-10279 Family in City 11.99

590-10280 Alpine Family 11.99

590-10121 Shopping 11.99

590-14125 Passers-by 8.99

590-10284 Family Walking 12.99

590-10116 Walking Passers-by 11.99

590-10095 Seated 11.99

590-10291 Teenagers 11.99

590-10122 Group of Girls 11.99

590-10022 22 Passers-by 11.99

590-10024 Group of Women 11.99

590-10282 Family Sitting 13.99

590-10296 Backpackers 17.99

590-12194 Women & Children 13.99

590-14022 Passers-by 8.99

590-14101 Seated Persons #1 8.99

590-10103 Seated Persons #2 11.99

590-14124 Passers-by 8.99

590-14402 Crowd of 36 37.99

590-10305 Fashion Boutique 25.99

590-10310 Krause Family in Winter 13.99

590-10325 Shopping Promenade 12.99

590-10326 Passers-by Hurrying 12.99

590-10332 People Seated 12.99

590-10335 Arabs 12.99

590-10343 Travelers 12.99

590-10344 School X-ing 13.99

590-14126 Children 8.99

590-14132 Climbing the Stairs 8.99

590-14134 Passers-by 8.99

590-14135 Passers-by 8.99

590-14136 Shopping 8.99

590-14137 Passers-by 8.99

590-14138 Seated Couples 8.99

590-14139 Children 8.99

POLICE & FIREFIGHTERS

590-10435 Republican Guards On Horseback pkg(2) 18.99 *NEW*

590-10389 German Mounted Police In Summer Uniform 17.99

590-10390 German Mounted Police 17.99

590-10392 German Riot Police w/Shields at Side 18.99

590-10393 German Riot Police w/Shields Up 18.99

590-10394 German Mounted Police 1960 15.99

590-10395 German Riot Police w/Shields Down 18.99

590-10396 US SWAT 15.99

ORIGINAL Preiser

590-10397 US Mounted Police **17.99**

590-10398 Italian Mounted Police **18.99**

590-10399 German Mounted Police 1960 **17.99**

590-14008 Policemen **8.99**

590-10214 Firemen **11.99**

590-10101 Emergency Team **10.99**

590-10242 Firemen in Action **12.99**

590-10191 French Police w/Motorcycles **15.99**

590-10064 Traffic Police **12.99**

590-10175 Motorcycle Police **14.99**

590-14200 Firemen #1 **8.99**

590-14201 Firemen #2 **8.99**

590-14202 Firemen #3 **8.99**

590-14203 Firemen #4 **8.99**

590-14204 Firemen #5 **8.99**

590-14205 Firemen #6 **8.99**

590-10370 Policemen, USA **15.99**

590-10371 Policemen, Great Britain **15.99**

590-14206 Firemen #7 **8.99**

590-14207 Firemen Seated **8.99**

590-25107 German Police **13.99**

590-25108 French Police **13.99**

590-10340 German Police **13.99**

590-10341 French Police **13.99**

590-10342 German Firemen **13.99**

SOLDIERS

590-12050 Union Infantry Marching **17.99**

590-12051 Confederate Infantry Marching **17.99**

590-12052 Union Flag Group-1 Each Mounted Officer, Infantry, Flag Bearer, Drummer **18.99**

590-12053 Confederate Flag Group-1 Each Mounted Officer, Infantry, Flag Bearer, Drummer **18.99**

590-12186 Prussian Infantry in Parade Uniform **25.99**

590-16507 Horse Drawn Kitchen Wagon w/Soldier **14.99**

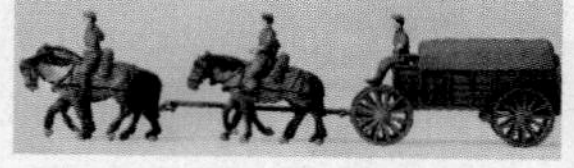
590-16512 Horse Drawn Kitchen Wagon w/Crew **15.99**

590-16513 Horse Drawn 105mm Field Gun w/Cassion & Crew **23.99**

590-16514 105mm Gun w/Crew **19.99**

590-10260 Boy Scouts **12.99**

590-12188 Guards/Officers Marching **25.99**

590-12189 Guards Marching **18.99**

590-24600 Knights/Heralds on Horseback **25.99**

590-24601 Mercenaries **25.99**

WEDDING GROUP

590-10058 Catholic **11.99**
590-10057 Protestant **11.99**

590-14057 Protestant **8.99**

590-14058 Catholic **8.99**

590-10331 Wedding Guests **13.99**

590-10339 Bride/Groom/ Guests **12.99**

590-10436 Formal Guests pkg(6) **13.99** *NEW*

590-10437 Guests On Folding Chairs pkg(6) **18.99** *NEW*

590-10440 Guests At Buffet pkg(6) **16.99** *NEW*

ORIGINAL Preiser

BANDS

590-10206 Tyrolean #1 **15.99**

590-10207 Tyrolean #2 **15.99**

590-10250 Bavarian Band pkg(12) **25.99**

590-24602 pkg(11) **25.99**

MISCELLANEOUS

590-14015 Motorists **8.99**

590-10304 Farmer's Market **18.99**

590-24653 Fair Musicians **18.99**

590-10198 Franciscan Friars **13.99**

590-24604 Figures in National Costumes **17.99**

590-24605 Marksmen **18.99**

590-24606 Figures in Carriage **27.99**

590-25102 Motorcyclist/TV & Press **25.99**

ANIMALS

590-20398 Penguins **10.99**

590-10150 Horses **11.99**

590-10156 Horses **12.99**

590-14150 Horses **8.99**

590-14155 Cows **8.99**

590-14162 Goats & Hogs **8.99**

590-14179 Deer **8.99**

590-14160 Shepherd w/Sheep **8.99**

590-14161 Sheep **8.99**

590-14167 Ducks, Geese, Swans **8.99**

590-10166 Turkey/Peacock **12.99**

590-10151 Donkeys **10.99**

590-10179 Stags & Does **11.99**
590-14411 Sheep pkg(60) **20.99** ***NEW***

590-14165 Cats & Dogs pkg(12) **8.99**

590-20379 Lions **10.99**

590-20383 Camels **14.99**

590-20380 Tigers **10.99**

590-20394 Reindeer **15.99**

590-14178 Reindeer #2 **8.99**

590-20395 Seals **10.99**

590-20392 Kangaroos **10.99**

Horses 590-14407

Cows Black & White 590-14408

Cows Brown & White 590-14409

Sheep 590-14411

Chickens pkg(18) 590-14168

590-20384 Polar Bears **11.99**

590-20386 Brown Bears **11.99**

590-20387 Zebras **11.99**

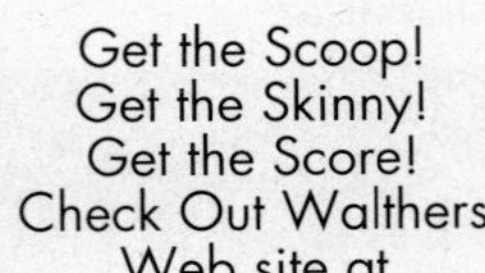

590-20385 Giraffes **11.99**

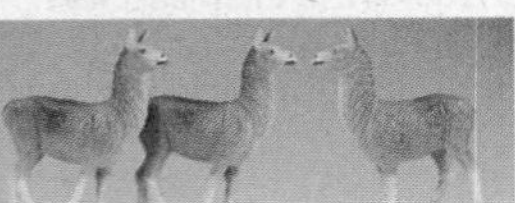
590-20389 Llamas **10.99**

590-20391 Buffalo **14.99**

590-20393 Moose **12.99**
590-14407 Horses **33.99**
590-14408 Cows Black & White **33.99**
590-14409 Cows Brown & White **33.99**
590-14168 Chickens pkg(18) **8.99**

ORIGINAL Preiser

Railroad Personnel & Travelers 590-16325

Passengers & Passers-by 590-16337

Figures & Animals 590-16327

Firemen 590-16339

Federal German Paratroopers 590-16508

Fair/Visitors/Showman 590-16342

Passer-bys/Spectators 590-16343

German Reich Pilots/Crew 590-16503

Sport & Leisure 590-16346

Winter 590-16347

Trades People 590-16326

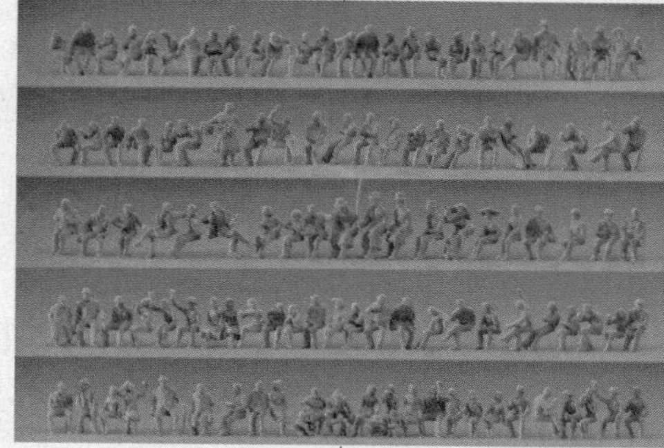
Sitting People 590-16328

Assorted Police 590-16350

Adam & Eve Combination Kits 590-16400

Uniformed People Combination Kit 590-16345

UNPAINTED FIGURE SETS

590-16325 Railroad Personnel & Travelers pkg(120) **24.99**
590-16337 Passengers & Passers-by pkg(120) **24.99**
590-16327 Figures & Animals **24.99**
590-16339 Firemen pkg(60) **12.99**
590-16508 Federal German Paratroopers pkg(30) **6.99**
590-16342 Fair/Visitors/Showman **15.99**
590-16343 Passer-bys/Spectators pkg(130) **24.99**
590-16503 German Reich Pilots/Crew pkg(40) **12.99**
590-16503 German Reich Pilots/Crew pkg(40) **12.99**
590-16346 Sport & Leisure **20.99**
590-16347 Winter **20.99**
590-16326 Trades People pkg(120) **24.99**
590-16328 Sitting People pkg(120) **24.99**
590-16350 Assorted Police pkg(21) **14.99** ***NEW***
590-16400 Adam & Eve Combination Kits pkg(26) **17.99**
590-16345 Uniformed People Combination Kit **12.99**

ORIGINAL Preiser

Armored Infantry 590-16504

Seated Passengers 590-16349

German Infantry WWII 590-16501

Panzer Tank Crew Members WWII 590-16515

German Infantry WWII Walking 590-16519

German SdKfz 251/1 Soldiers WWII 590-16520

Pilots & Ground Crew 590-16502

590-16504 Armored Infantry **6.99**
590-16349 Seated Passengers pkg(36) **9.99**
590-16501 German Infantry WWII pkg(12) **6.99**
590-16515 Panzer Tank Crew Members WWII pkg(20) **7.99**
590-16519 German Infantry WWII Walking pkg(12) **6.99**
590-16520 German SdKfz 251/1 Soldiers WWII pkg(20) **7.99**

590-16521 United States Air Force Standing pkg(12) **6.99**

590-18366 Seated Military Passengers pkg(12) **3.99**
590-16502 Pilots & Ground Crew **12.99**
590-16505 Guards Infantry USSR **6.99**
590-16329 Firemen w/Accessories pkg(42) **11.99**
590-16510 Military #1 pkg(18) **6.99**
590-16506 Federal German Soldiers pkg(50) **8.99**

Firemen w/Accessories 590-16329

Military #1 590-16510

Federal German Soldiers 590-16506

SELLEY Finishing Touches

Unpainted metal.

RR PERSONNEL

675-81 Steam Train Crew pkg(3) **2.00**

675-139 675-231

675-139 Man w/Wheelbarrow **2.00**
675-231 Drivers pkg(3) **2.00**

675-289 Road Gang Working pkg(5) **6.35**

675-294 Brakeman, Crewman pkg(6) **2.25**

675-647 Diesel Train Crew **2.00**
675-701 Handcar Man **1.50**

ANIMALS

675-158 Trough & 6 Pigs **2.75**

675-161 Cows pkg(6) **3.00**

675-162 Bull, Cow & Calf **3.00**

675-163 Horses pkg(6) **3.25**

675-178 Dog & Hydrant **1.80**

675-297 Chickens pkg(12) **2.75**

675-454 Horse & Colt **2.25**

675-456 Elephant **1.75**

675-457 Giraffe **1.75**

675-458 675-520

675-458 Camel **1.75**
675-520 Lion **1.85**

MISCELLANEOUS

675-160 Cowboy & 2 Horses **3.85**

675-662 Hobos & Dogs pkg(5) **2.50**
Includes 4 figures and dog.
675-700 Drunk Leaning On Lamppost **1.50**

675-6571 Prospector w/Burro **3.85**

675-6572 Prospector w/2 Burros **4.75**

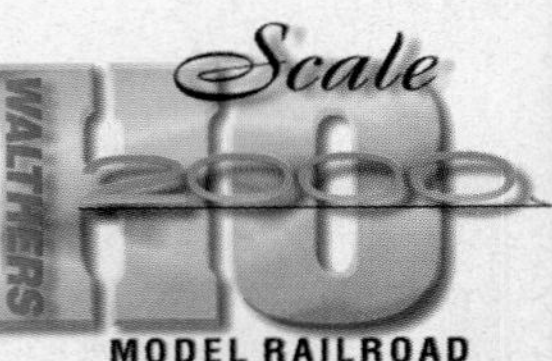

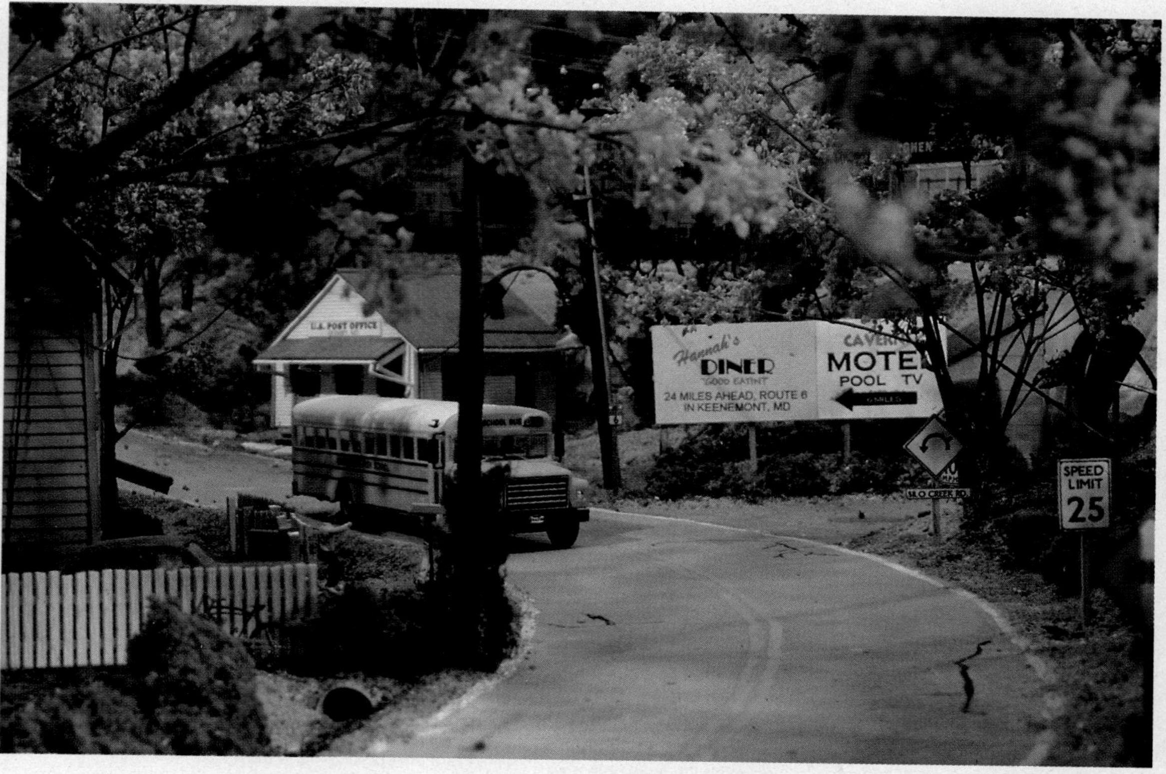

Hard to believe these days, but there was a time when local kids who went to high school rode the train! Most rural schools only taught grades one through eight, so you had to take a train to the nearest big town to attend a real high school. You'll still find students on the morning commuter runs in places like Chicago, Boston or New York, but the bright yellow bus has replaced the passenger car across most of America.

It's back to school time for two local youngsters in tiny Quimby, Maryland. Brakes protest slightly as the driver downshifts on the grade and coasts to a stop. Outside, you can hear the wayfreight working just up the hill at the St. Alban paper mill. Inside the bus, well it's a little too noisy to hear much of anything!

Summer billboards now beckon fall "leaf peakers" in this rural part of Fred Lagno's Allegheny Central Railroad, located in Queenstown, Maryland.

Models and Photo by Fred Lagno

America's DRIVING FORCE

WALTHERS™

Perfect for display, all models are fully assembled and packed in a dust-proof plastic box that provides secure storage and ease of handling. Or, take them out of the package to add a new level of superdetailed realism to the highways along your model railroad. Check out the other new Driving Force accessories in the Structures and Freight Sections of this reference book!

***LICENSED FORD MOTOR CO. REPLICAS**

***FULLY ASSEMBLED HO SCALE**

***DUST-PROOF DISPLAY BOX**

***GREAT LAYOUT DETAIL**

AMERICA'S DRIVING FORCE - MODELING RAILROADS AND THE AUTO INDUSTRY

See the complete listing in the Books-Video-Railroadiana Section of this book!

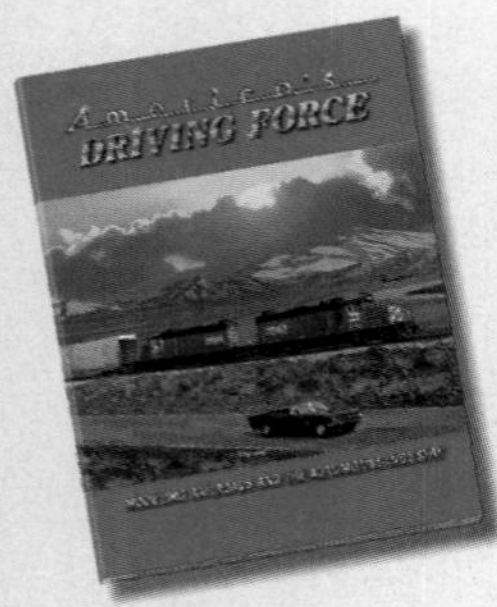

913-104 49.98 *NEW*
Put the pedal to the metal and get your automotive industry modeling in high gear with a copy of America's Driving Force - Modeling Railroads and the Auto Industry. Here at last is a complete look at how autos and trucks are made and the need for railroads at each stage of the operation.

ASSEMBLED AUTOMOBILES

FORD EA 7.98

933-1220 1967 Mustang Fastback *NEW*
It was the most exciting time ever for car fans across America. Faster, sporty, sleek designs, packing high-power engines were the rage on every showroom floor. And leading the pack for 1967 was the Mustang 2-Door Fastback. Facing all-new competition from Camaro, Pontiac and a redesigned Barracuda, the red-hot Mustang got a major restyling. A longer front end nose and deeper side sculpting were added, and the Fastback received a sweeping new roofline that flowed smoothly into the trunk deck. Inside, a new dash layout and an optional swing-away steering wheel were notable features. Under the hood, buyers could select the standard V-6 or one of four optional V-8 powerplants, including the awesome new 390. Depending on which options and engine you selected, you could pay anywhere from $2952 to $2605.

Today, the '67 is as popular as ever among car collectors and Ford fans. And if you can find a real one, expect to pay many times its original sticker price!

But, you can own a detailed replica of this classic, recreated in exacting HO Scale by Walthers.

Licensed by Ford, this miniature marvel captures every line of the real thing. From the sporty grille to the sweeping top, to the signature taillights, it's a fitting tribute to this fantastic car. Clear window glass shows off the interior and rolling wheels with separate tires are standard equipment .

933-1240 1998 Crown Victoria 4-Door Sedan *NEW*
A proud tradition continues with the latest in a long line of Crown Victoria models by Ford. Sleek and stylish, the 1998 model is a favorite with families, but its rugged, powerful performance, ease of handling and bigger size makes it a popular choice with fleet vehicle operators. You'll see them earning a living as taxis, delivery vehicles, unmarked police cars and more.

Daily New Arrival Updates! Visit Walthers Web site at

www.walthers.com

EMERGENCY POLICE VEHICLES

FORD CROWN VICTORIA EA 7.98

Fully assembled and ready to patrol HO Scale highways. Models are painted, and carry the same full-color markings found on the real car. Or, create a custom cruiser for your city, state, county, town or private security firm with the undecorated model. A nonworking lightbar adds the finishing touch to every car.

932-1251 Wisconsin State Patrol *NEW*
932-1252 Illinois State Police *NEW*
932-1253 Iowa State Patrol *NEW*
932-1254 Milwaukee City Police Dept. *NEW*
932-1255 Amtrak Police *NEW*
932-1250 Undecorated *NEW*

Ford logo used by license from Ford Motor Company

ENCLOSED AUTO CARRIERS SINGLE CARS

See the complete listing of these new auto carrying cars in the Freight Section of this book!

89' TRI-LEVEL

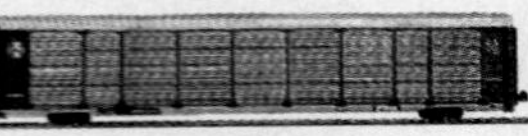

932-4851 ATSF **19.98** *NEW*

THRALL 89' BI-LEVEL KITS

932-4804 GTW (blue with blue panels) **14.98**

LIMITED-RUN CARS

Special paint and lettering schemes make these colorful collectibles that will dress up your distribution facility or auto trains.

932-4812 ATSF **19.98** *NEW*

America's DRIVING FORCE

Ford logo used by license from Ford Motor Company

TRUCKS

FORD

933-1200 LNT 9000 Semi Tractor w/Auto Carrier Semi Trailer **19.98** ***NEW***
You'll see them heading down the highway, maybe taking your new car or truck on it's first long trip! From coast to coast, Auto Carrier Semis move new vehicles from regional centers to dealer's showrooms.

Now, you can slide behind the wheel with an all-new model of these popular transports, recreated in HO Scale. Up front is a handsome, Ford licensed replica of the LNT 9000 semi tractor. The truck cab is equipped with the special rack over the roof so an additional car can be carried. The cab also features a complete interior and window "glass."

Hooked behind is the Auto Carrier Trailer. This superb miniature captures the see-through look of the real thing and is complete right down to the detailed deck where cars are carried.

For more realism, add a load of Ford Crown Victoria Sedans 933-1240, or Expedition sport-utility vehicles 933-1230, both sold separately.

933-1210 1966 F-100 Pickup Truck ***NEW***
Since the first converted Model Ts rolled out of the factory, Ford trucks have earned a reputation for toughness and dependability. Generations of farmers, plumbers, carpenters — anyone who required a go-anywhere, haul-just-about-anything truck found exactly what they needed in the company's pickups.

As the popular F series continued its successful run into 1966, the F-100 sported a redesigned grille that let the world know you were the proud owner of a brand-new model. Designed to be a simple, hard-working hauler, a 240 horsepower, in-line six cylinder engine and three-speed manual transmission were standard.

From the unique grille to the name on the tailgate, this all-new replica is a fitting tribute to this great truck. On the streets of an HO Scale layout, it looks great right out of the box. Or, add some detail parts as a load in the bed, letter it with decals and create a custom hauler for any local business.

933-1230 1998 Expedition SUV ***NEW***
Combining the best of pick-up, luxury car, van and station wagon as one, Sport Utility vehicles have became America's favorite ride! Cruising the freeways or the back woods, they offer drivers a unique freedom and luxury not possible in any other vehicle.

With its stylish appointments inside and out, the Ford Expedition continues to lead the way. Now, you can own a detailed replica of this popular vehicle, produced by Walthers and officially licensed by the Ford Motor Company.

You'll marvel at how the detailed plastic body captures every curve of the real thing, right down to the tiny side mirrors and the unique grille.

Clear window glass shows off the interior details and rolling wheels with separate tires are standard equipment.

DISPLAY YOUR NEW CARS WITH THESE ACCESSORIES

See the complete line of America's Driving Force buildings in the Structures Section.

UPTOWN MOTORS AUTO DEALERSHIP

933-3077 49.98 ***NEW***

AUTO ASSEMBLY PLANT

933-3079 79.98 ***NEW***

933-3077

933-3079

WALTHERS™

AIRCRAFT

DOUGLAS C-47 EA 24.98

Finally, an aircraft kit compatible with Roco Minitanks and Trident military vehicles! Complete your HO Scale military diorama with our new DC-3/C-47.

The DC-3, and its military counterpart the C-47, revolutionized both commercial and military air transport. Sleek DC3s first took to the air in the mid-1930s. Reliable and cheap to operate, they helped to make commercial aviation profitable. With over 10,000 constructed and flown worldwide, the DC-3 was the best-known airliner in the world.

During World War Two, the DC-3 was rebuilt as a cargo carrier for the Army and Navy. Large double-wide cargo/personnel doors were added and the military version was redesignated the C-47.

C-47s were flown by virtually every Allied country. While C-47s were used mainly during W.W. II, some flew in the Korean War and a few even made it into Vietnam.

In the commercial world, versatile DC-3s hauled passengers and freight for most major airlines. They were also used on charters and for special services like survey work and hauling recreational skydivers. Today, over 60 years after the first ones took to the air, many DC-3s, and a few former military C-47s, can still be found in specialized service. In some remote corners of the globe, many still haul passengers.

This display quality HO Scale aircraft kit can be built two ways, as a civilian DC-3 or as a military C-47. Both versions of the kit include correct fuselage sections to make commercial DC-3s with small side-entry doors or military C-47s with double-wide cargo/personnel doors. Models also include separate engines, propellers, wheels and authentic decals.

Best of all, now you can bring together all of your Roco Minitanks, Trident and other HO Scale military vehicles and figures into a single scene featuring the DC-3/C-47. And don't forget, on a model railroad this aircraft flew in both the steam- and diesel-eras!

933-1150 US Army Air Force (W.W.II)
933-1151 US Air Force

DOUGLAS DC-3 EA 24.98

933-1160 North Central
933-1161 Delta
933-1162 Eastern Airlines
933-1163 Pacific Southwest Airlines

933-1164 Ozark
933-1165 North West Airlines
933-1166 Canadian Pacific

AIRLINER CREW

590-1010055 pkg(6) **14.98**
NEW
Dress up your airfield scenes with this set of six authentic figures. Each plastic person is molded in a realistic pose and hand-painted to bring out the fine detailing.

WALTHERS™

P51-D "MUSTANG"

933-1170 pkg(2) **19.98** ***NEW***
"Left waist gunner to crew. . . little friends at four o' clock low!"

To World War Two bomber crews, those were some of the sweetest words ever heard. "Little friends" were escort fighters, protecting the vulnerable bomber formations as they headed to and from the target.

Among the first fighters that could go round-trip with its bigger brothers was the legendary P-51 "Mustang."

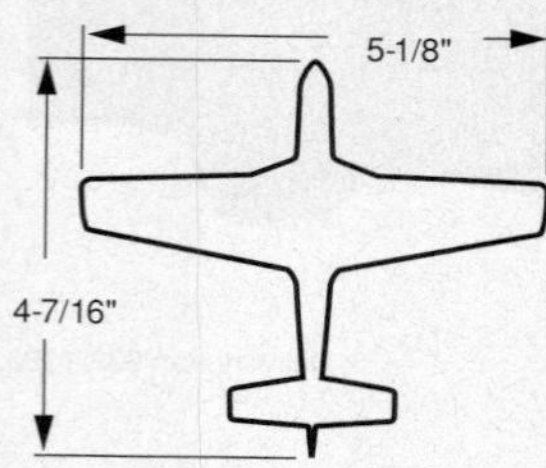

Designed and built for the British in 1940, the P-51 was North American Aviation's first fighter. Its Allison engine proved unsuitable at high-altitudes, but the aircraft was ideal for photo and ground attack missions. By mid 1941, the US Army Air Corps. ordered its first samples.

Lessons learned in combat were quickly incorporated on the production line. In 1942, the Rolls Royce "Merlin" engine was coupled with a new supercharger and a four-blade propeller, dramatically improving performance and range. Designated P51-B/C, the Allies finally had a fighter that could escort bombers to and from the target and take on any opposition.

Later improvements created the P51-D. Its streamlined "bubble" canopy required changes in the fuselage that gave the D a unique appearance. Six .50 caliber, wing-mounted machine guns provided more punch, while stronger pylons allowed bombs or rockets to be carried. Just over 9600 were built and by 1945, most US fighter squadrons flew P51-Ds.

Outdated by jets, Mustangs were quickly transferred to the reserves. Some were briefly recalled to service during the Korean War. And some soldiered on in Latin America and Israel through the late 50s. Others were rebuilt as air racers or preserved as museum pieces, where a few remain in flying condition.

Now, take the controls and add this legendary fighter to your stable of aircraft. All-new tooling captures every line of these sleek planes, from the huge four blade prop to the distinct tail.

Parts for two complete aircraft are included in this first-ever HO Scale kit to get your squadron airborne. And since no fighter of this era is complete without colorful nose art, each kit includes full-color decal markings for four different planes! Based on period photos and research, build your choice of "Betty Lee III", "Louisiana Heat Wave" , "Missouri Armada" or "Scat IV."

Then, park your completed P51s on the flight line with our C-47 (933-1150). Add Roco Minitanks, Trident Miniatures or other HO Scale military vehicles and you'll have the makings of a great diorama. The small size is perfect for wargaming, and makes the finished models much easier to display than larger scale replicas.

625-225

625-444

189-48206

590-1010056

YOUR FLIGHTLINE COMES ALIVE WITH THESE ACCESSORIES

625-225 Dodge 4x4 w/Closed Cab **4.99**
625-444 Willy's Jeep w/Trailer **9.99**
189-48206 US Air Force 1950 Chevrolet Pick-Up **10.99** ***NEW***
590-1010056 US Army Air Force Flight & Ground Figures pkg(12) **14.98** ***NEW***

WALTHERS™

RESIN VEHICLE KITS

Easy-to-build kits feature resin bodies with a high-level of molded-on detail. A basic cab interior is provided and all windows are open, so you can see inside.

AUTOMOBILES

933-4001 Checker Marathon Taxi **8.98**

FARM MACHINERY

933-4016 Modern Farm Tractor **8.98**

933-4008 Grain Truck **12.98**

TRUCKS

933-4012 Logging Truck **19.98**
933-4013 Wood Chip Truck **19.98**
933-1035 Wood Chip Truck Load **2.98**
933-4014 Pulp Wood Truck **19.98**
933-1036 Pulp Wood Truck Load **6.98**

933-4002 Divco Milk Truck **8.98**

933-4003 1941 Pick-Up **8.98**
933-4011 Model R Dump Truck **12.98**

Logging Truck 933-4012

Model R Dump Truck 933-4011

Wood Chip Truck 933-4013

Pulp Wood Truck 933-4014

FARM MACHINERY

933-1047 Combine **32.98** ***NEW***
Grain farmers the world over keep bread on the table with these giant machines. Designed especially for harvesting grains and corn, they're a common sight during the long hours of the harvest season.

Whether working in the fields, parked alongside the machine shed or moving cross country as a flat car load, this detailed kit adds a lot to any rural scene. Plastic parts are molded in color so no painting is needed.

Everything is included, down to the interior details, clear glass and the nonworking strobe light on the roof.

To meet the needs of farmers along your railroad, you can build it with the optional small grain or corn head that comes in every kit. Illustrated instructions and numbered parts, which attach in order, make construction fast and fun.

PLASTIC VEHICLE KITS

CONSTRUCTION EQUIPMENT EA 24.98

Easy-to-build kits feature parts molded in colors.

933-3141 Wheel Loader

933-3142 Terex Heavy Dump Truck

DELIVERY VANS

Kits are available with gold lettering decals, or undecorated for customizing.

933-1591 With Decals **6.98**
933-1590 Undecorated **4.98**

Delivery Van 933-1590

AMERICAN PRECISION

NEW SUPPLIER

TRANSIT BUSES

These licensed replica buses are perfect for the late steam- and early diesel-era. Accurate representation of the buses that transported Americans for four decades. Each model is injection molded, highly detailed and includes complete interiors. Models come fully assembled unless noted.

1949 GMC TDH 4510 EA 15.95

This coach typifies the "old look" city transit buses produced by GMC in various forms from 1949 to 1959. The buses proved to be very popular with city transit operators and were among the most prevalent city buses in use throughout the United States and Canada. They remained in use well into the 1970s.

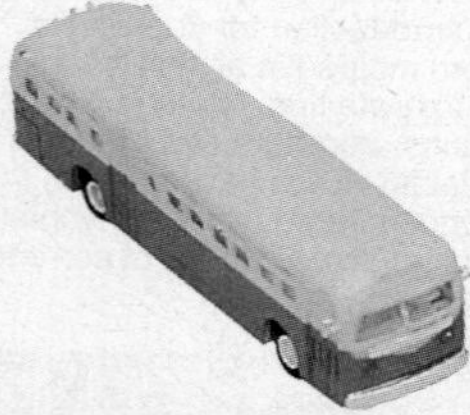

148-390002 Red *NEW*
148-390003 Green *NEW*
148-390004 Orange *NEW*
148-390000 Unassembled Kit **12.95** *NEW*

FLEXIBLE VISICOACH BUS

148-390131 Blue **14.95** *NEW*
This motorcoach was extensively used by intercity and commuter bus operators throughout the United States from the 1940s to the 1970s.

45' Pines Trailer 150-1204

45' Pines Trailer 150-1208

Ford LNT9000 Tractor 150-1224

Ford F-150 Pick-Up Truck 150-1263

45' PINES TRAILER EA 11.95 (UNLESS NOTED)

Each 45' Pines Trailer includes two landing gears-fully extended or retracted, rubber tires and prototypical lettering schemes and numbers.

150-1201 Burlington Motor Carriers **12.95**
150-1202 Chicago Central & Pacific
150-1203 CSX
150-1204 Kankakee, Beaverville & Southern
150-1205 NS
150-1206 Redon
150-1207 Vermont Railway
150-1208 Xtra Intermodal
150-1209 Xtra Lease
150-1200 Undecorated **8.95**

FORD F-150 PICK-UP TRUCKS EA TBA

WITH STANDARD SIDES

150-1241 Black
150-1242 Moonlight Blue
150-1243 Pacific Green
150-1244 Dark Red
150-1245 Tan
150-1246 White
150-1240 Undecorated

WITH FLARED SIDES

150-1261 Black
150-1262 Moonlight Blue
150-1263 Pacific Green
150-1264 Dark Red
150-1265 Tan
150-1266 White
150-1260 Undecorated

FORD LNT9000 TRACTOR EA 7.95 (UNLESS NOTED)

Based on the common prototype of the 1984 Ford LNT 9000 tractor, each features details including seats, steering wheels and rubber tires. This is an officially licensed Ford product.

150-1221 Black
150-1222 Dark Blue
150-1223 Medium Blue
150-1224 Green
150-1225 Orange
150-1226 Red
150-1227 White
150-1228 Yellow
150-1220 Undecorated **5.95**

TRAINS Athearn IN MINIATURE

These easy-to-build kits are based on common styles of semi trucks and trailers, seen throughout the US. Kits are prepainted and lettered (as noted) and require only minor assembly.

AUTOMOBILES

Dealers: MUST Order Dealer Pack of 6.

SEDANS EA 27.00

140-1370 Painted *NEW*
140-1372 Undecorated *NEW*

STATION WAGONS EA 27.00

140-1373 Painted *NEW*
140-1371 Undecorated *NEW*

SEMIS

EA 9.00

Matching tractor and trailer.

140-5481 Bekins
140-5482 Railway Express Agency
140-5483 Safeway
140-5484 Time-DC
140-5485 Lee Way
140-5486 Hertz
140-5487 Chessie
140-5488 BN/NP
140-5489 Penn Central
140-5490 ATSF
140-5491 SP
140-5492 UP
140-5493 CR
140-5480 Undecorated

SEMI TRACTORS

KENWORTH–CONVENTIONAL PKG(6) EA 27.00

DECORATED

140-5666 UP
140-5667 ATSF
140-5668 CR
140-5669 BN
140-5670 Pacific Intermountain Express

140-5671 SP

UNDECORATED

Models are molded in color, but not lettered.

140-5660 Black
140-5661 Yellow
140-5662 Red
140-5663 Blue
140-5664 White
140-5665 Green

WHITE FREIGHTLINER CAB-OVER PKG(6) EA 27.00

140-5501 Bekins
140-5502 Railway Express Agency
140-5503 Safeway
140-5504 Time-DC
140-5505 Lee Way
140-5506 Hertz
140-5507 Chessie
140-5508 BN/NP

140-5509 Penn Central
140-5510 ATSF
140-5511 SP
140-5512 UP
140-5513 CR
140-5500 Undecorated

TRACTOR PARTS

140-55000 Undecorated Tractor Cab **2.00**
140-55001 2-Axle Tractor Frame **1.00**
140-55002 3-Axle Tractor Frame pkg(2) **2.00**
140-55008 Fuel Tank, Tractor pkg(6) **1.50**
140-55009 Battery Box pkg(3) **1.50**
140-55011 Fifth Wheel pkg(3) **1.50**
140-55012 Tires pkg(6) **1.50**
140-55013 Windshield pkg(2) **2.00**
140-55014 Axle pkg(6) **1.20**
140-55015 Accessory Set **1.50**

Capture the look of today's intermodal equipment for railroad or highway with these easy-to-build plastic kits, accessories and decals.

TRAILER KITS

28' PARCEL TRAILER

Drop style "pup" parcel transport trailer. Easy to assemble kit includes undecorated, one-piece plastic body with separate floors, vinyl tires and wheel hubs.

116-50113 **6.25**

116-50512 With Parcel Decal **8.50**

116-50513 With RPS Decal **8.50**

TRAILER DOLLY

116-50114 Parcel **3.50**
Allows two 28' parcel vans to be operated as "doubles."

116-50143 Standard **TBA**

DECORATED 28' WEDGE TRAILER

116-50500 Roadway Express **9.95**
A Walthers Exclusive! Limited-run replica looks great heading down your highways or aboard modern intermodal cars.

28' WEDGE TRAILER

This is an exact replica of the Pines 28' Wedge Trailer. This model has a highly detailed one-piece body, roll-up style rear door, separate floor, landing gear, suspension, separate wheels and rubber tires. This trailer is used by Roadway, ABF, Yellow and others.

UNDECORATED EA 7.95

116-50129 Ribbed
116-50130 Smooth

WITH DECALS EA 9.95

Roadway ribbed trailer decals are longer to fit correctly over ribs.

116-50514, 116-50516

116-50518, 116-50519, 116-50517

116-50514 Smooth w/Yellow Transit Decals (New 1997 Scheme)
116-50516 Smooth w/Yellow Transit (Early) Decals
116-50517 Smooth w/Roadway Express Decals
116-50518 Smooth w/Roadway Decals
116-50519 Ribbed w/Roadway Decals

28' WEDGE TRAILER PARTS

116-50147 Trailer Suspension **3.25**
116-50148 Trailer Floor **2.50**

53' PLATE TRAILER

One of the most distinctive trailers of the rail or road today. Wabash National 53 x 102' Plate Trailers are used by Schneider, National, Werner, Enterprise, XTRA, Heartland Express and others. This easy-to-assemble, highly detailed kit includes one-piece body with separate floor suspension wheels and landing gear.

UNDECORATED EA 9.50

116-50127 All Button
116-50140 No Button
116-50141 Partial Button

PAINTED WHITE W/SILVER RIBS EA 15.95 (UNLESS NOTED)

116-50501 No Decals **13.95**
116-50502 BN Decal (blue, red)
116-50503 BN Decal (blue, black)
116-50504 Alpis Decals

116-50508

116-50510

116-50130

116-50129

116-50532

116-50505 Heartland Decals
116-50506 XTRA Lease w/J.B. Hunt Decals

53' DURAPLATE TRAILER

Wabash National led the market with this 53' plate trailer. Now with the introduction of the uniquely designed and manufactured 53' Duraplate composit wall trailer, Wabash National is in the lead again. A-Line brings this unique trailer to life in HO Scale with exacting detail from manufacturers' blueprints. Available in two sidewall configurations, this highly detailed kit includes unpainted one-piece body with separate suspension wheels, landing gears and separate doors. Available with or without decals.

UNDECORATED TRAILER EA 10.95

116-50520 All Buttons *NEW*
116-50530 No Buttons *NEW*

UNDECORATED TRAILER W/DECALS EA 14.95

Decals include tractor markings.

116-50532 Schneider *NEW*
116-50533 Werner *NEW*
116-50534 Heartland *NEW*
116-50535 JB Hunt *NEW*
116-50536 Swift *NEW*

53' TRAILER ACCESSORIES

116-50132 53' Trailer Floor (Use for Bowser Trailer & Kitbashing) **2.75**
116-50133 Wabash Landing Gear **3.25**
116-50134 Trailer & Container Tie Down Button Covers (etched brass) pkg(48) **2.75**
116-50300 Rib Masking Tape **3.25**
Precut to exact size (.080 x .350') makes detail quick and easy. Just paint trailer silver, tape side ribs, apply finish color and remove for perfect detailing every time.

53' REEFER TRAILER

This distinctive 7-1/2 corrugation side Utility Reefer Trailer is tooled from the original blueprints. Exquisite detail down to the last rivet. New utility land gear, separate rear (swing style) door. Available with or without reefer and fuel tanks. Also available with decals.

UNDECORATED

116-50154 Without Reefer & Tanks **10.95**
116-50507 With Reefer & Tanks **12.95**

WITH DECALS EA 16.95

116-50508 Werner
116-50509 Stevens Transport
116-50510 Market Transport
116-50511 CR England

SWING REEFER DOOR

116-50157 pkg(2) **3.25**

FRUEHAUF 40' "Z" VAN PKG(2) EA 11.50

One of the most widely used trailers in piggyback and road service, prototypes remained in production for years. Kits are molded in aluminum with separate tires, spoked wheel hubs, doorbars and other details. Each includes two undecorated trailers, complete instructions and list of correct decals.

116-50101 Smoothside
Later style, manufactured from 1979 to 1986.

116-50102 Beaded Side
Includes disc and spoked hubs. Manufactured from 1965 to 1978.

5' VAN EXTENSION

An easy conversion kit to model 40' trailers rebuilt into 45' units. This was a common method of extending the life of older trailers from about 1981 to 1984, and many are still in use. Use kit #50101, or complete conversion with trailer and extension, #50116.

116-50115 Extension Kit Only **3.25**
116-50116 40' Van w/Extension **8.95**

TRACTORS EA 10.95

116-50600 Roadway *NEW*
116-50601 Overnight *NEW*

DECAL SETS

A-Line decals are custom designed to be prototypically correct and give excellent detail to all models. These decals are unique to any other decals on the market: they have more detail, different numbers and many decals will do one or more tractors and trailers per package.

SAFETY STRIPES

116-50126 Red & White **2.85**
Improve visibility of any trailer preprinted in the right colors and size.

28' PARCEL DECALS EA 2.85

Decals for one trailer only.

116-50160 Parcel

116-50161 RPS

PARCEL EQUIPMENT EA 4.85

116-50200 28' Trailer, Container, Chassis, Tractor & Dolly
116-50201 40' Drop Trailer, 45' Trailer 48' Martrac Trailer

53' DURAPLATE TRAILER DECALS EA 3.25

Includes tractor marking.

116-50185 Schneider *NEW*
116-50186 Werner *NEW*
116-50187 Heartland *NEW*
116-50188 JB Hunt *NEW*
116-50189 Swift *NEW*

Decal 116-50167

Decal 116-50163

Decal 116-50164

53' REEFER TRAILER DECAL EA 4.85

116-50214 Werner
116-50216 Stevens

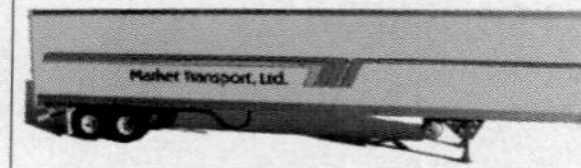

116-50220 Market Tran.
116-50215 CR England

28' WEDGE DECALS

Most contain decals for multiple tractors and trailers. Roadway Express & Carolina decals are longer to fit correctly over ribs.

116-50211 116-50221

116-50212

116-50203

116-50213

116-50203 Roadway's Railway Express **4.85**
116-50211 Yellow **2.85**
116-50212 SAIA-28', 45', 48' & Bobtail **4.85**
116-50213 G.O.D. 28', 48' **4.85**
116-50221 Yellow (new '97) **2.85**

53' PLATE TRAILER DECALS EA 2.85 (UNLESS NOTED)

Most contain decals for tractors and trailers.

116-50163 Schneider
116-50164 Werner
116-50165 XTRA-Lease/J.B. Hunt
116-50166 Burlington (blue, red)
116-50167 Heartland
116-50168 J.B. Hunt **TBA**
116-50184 Alpis **TBA**

FUEL TANKS

LARGE CAPACITY PKG(4) EA 3.80

116-50107 Long
Contains two 150-gallon fuel tanks and two 60" refrigerator fuel tanks.

116-50108 Short
Contains two 120-gallon fuel tanks and two 47" refrigerator fuel tanks.

LARGER, MEDIUM, SMALL CAPACITY PKG(8) EA 3.95

Kits include parts to make small, medium and large tanks.

116-50124 Tractor
116-50125 Reefer Trailer

LANDING GEAR

PKG(2) EA 3.25 (UNLESS NOTED)

Common styles, molded in down position (trailers on flat cars or parked). Includes instructions to modify parts for up position (hitched to tractors). Each includes two sets of gears, with cross support and crank, molded in plastic.

116-50125, 116-50145

116-50112 Trailmobile
116-50133 Wabash
116-50144 Pines
116-50145 Utility
116-50146 Stoughton **TBA**

LARGE TRAILER DETAILS

Ideal for superdetailing Accurail® or McKean 45', Walthers 48' or Bower 53' trailers.

116-50122, 116-50142

116-50122 Sliding Tandem Assembly (leaf spring) **3.60**
116-50142 Air Hose-Trailer **2.50**
Use anywhere hose detail is needed.

MISCELLANEOUS

116-50104 Vinyl Tires **4.50**
Contains 24 tires, use on virtually any model

116-50120 Delrin Vehicle Windshield Wipers pkg(8) **1.95**
116-50123 Record/Document Boxes **2.25**
116-50126 Headache Rack **TBA**
An important detail found on many tractors, especially those pulling flatbeds. Large shield absorbs impact if the load shifts forward because of sudden stops or accidents.

116-50131 Tie-Down Chain (12") **2.95**
A must for holding open loads securely in place on flatbed trailers.

MIRRORS EA 3.15

Finely detailed photo-etched mirrors are easy to install and require no gluing. Very durable, can be used on Herpa, Promotex and most other semi-tractors. Each pack includes four mirrors. Enough for two trucks.

116-50152 Straight
116-50153 Curved

MUD FLAPS PKG(16) EA 2.25

116-50005 Plastic White
116-50117 Vinyl Black
116-50118 Plastic Black

REEFER UNITS EA 3.25 (UNLESS NOTED)

Highly detailed and true-to-prototype, these parts are a neat detail to convert box vans, trailers or containers into refrigerated units. Includes fuel tanks.

THERMO KING

116-50135 Modern
116-50136 Old Style
116-50137 Nose & Underbody

CARRIER

116-50138 Old Style
116-50139 Modern **TBA**

TRAILER FLOORS

116-50132 53' **2.75**
Fits A-Line, Bowser.

116-50159 45' & 48' Universal Trailer Floor & Sliding Tandem
Fits: Frt Range. McKean, Accurail, Walthers and Atlas.

116-50002 53' Universal Floor & Suspension
Great for kitbashing.

REAR TRAILER DOORS PKG(2) EA 3.25

116-50110 Roll-Up 96" Wide
116-50156 Roll-Up 102" Wide
116-50157 Swing Reefer
116-50158 Swing Dry Van

FRONT TRACTOR WHEELS

Authentic replicas of wheels found on modern American trucks. An easy way to make virtually any HO Scale model more realistic.

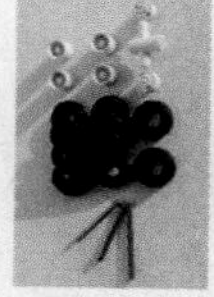

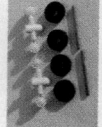

116-50105 116-50106

116-50105 Two-Hole Disc **4.50**
Includes two front and four driving (dual) wheels, 10 tires and axles.

116-50106 Ten-Hole Front Wheels **3.50**
Includes four cast hubs, four tires and axles.

TRAILER DETAIL SETS

116-50103 Up-Grade Kit pkg(2) **4.50**
New tires, hubs and axles for two vans, adaptable to virtually any model.

116-50151 Spoke Wheels & Axles pkg(8) **2.85**
Replacement wheels and axles for American Ltd., Walthers and other intermodal equipment as well as earl trailers.

TRAILER DRESS-UP KITS EA 3.95

116-50119 Spoke Wheels
116-50121 Disk Wheels

TRAILER DETAIL KITS

116-50003 Trailer Upgrade Kit (Disc) **4.50**
116-50103 Spoke Upgrade Kit (Spoke) **4.50**
New tires, wheels and axles for two trailers, adaptable to virtually any model.

116-50004 2-Hole Wheels/Axles **2.85**
116-50006 Atlas 45' Pines Trailer **TBA**

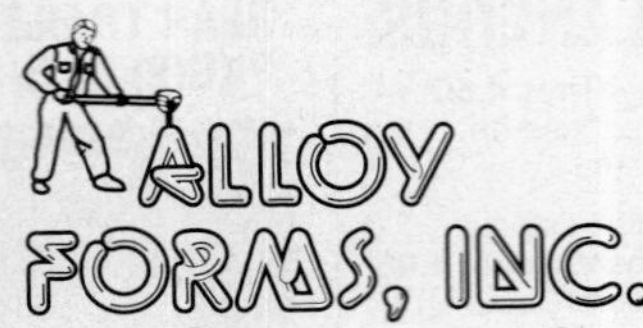

Add detailed cars and trucks to your streets with these metal kits, based on American vehicles. Models consist of unpainted white metal castings. Heavy Truck kits feature numerous metal details, styrene wheels and vinyl tires (unless noted).

AUTOMOBILES & LIGHT TRUCKS

EA 7.49 (UNLESS NOTED)

BUICK

119-2031 1949 Roadmaster

119-2033 1953 Skylark Convertible w/Continental Spare

CADILLAC

119-2024 1955 Fleetwood

119-2032 1959 Eldorado Convertible

CHEVROLET

119-2008 1957 Bel-Air Sports Coupe w/Engine **8.95**

119-2019 1950 4-Door Fastback

119-2020 1955 Bel-Air 2-Door

119-2025 1953 Corvette

119-2029 1955 Nomad Wagon

119-2037 1953 Bel-Air

119-2039 1959 Impala Convertible

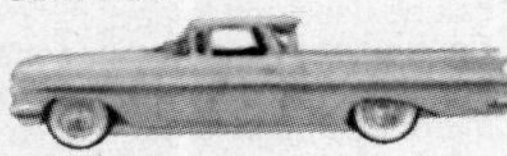

119-2045 1959 El Camino Pickup

DE SOTO

119-2018 1949 4-Door

FORD

119-2021 1956 Pickup **8.95**

119-2022 1956 Thunderbird w/Roof Porthole
119-2038 1955 Thunderbird Without Roof Porthole

119-2030 1948 Convertible w/Engine **8.95**

119-2041 1951 Panel Delivery Truck **8.95**

119-2042 1956 Pickup w/Camper **9.95**
119-2043 1956 Pickup w/Rack & Utility Boxes **9.95**

119-2066 1949 Club Coupe w/Engine **8.95**

HUDSON

119-2023 1949 4-Door

PLYMOUTH

119-2026 1941 Coupe Less Engine
119-2027 1941 Coupe w/Engine **8.95**

MERCURY

119-2028 1949 Two-Door

STUDEBAKER

119-2040 1949 Starline

EMERGENCY VEHICLES

DIAMOND REO/PIERCE EA 24.95

119-7032 CRV-18 Heavy Rescue Unit
119-7036 Suburban Pumper
119-7039 2500 Gallon Tanker

FORD/PIERCE

Models feature Ford truck cabs with Pierce Fire Apparatus bodies.

119-7007 LN Pumper **29.95**
119-7029 LN Suburban Pumper **29.95**
119-7031 LNT CRV-18 Heavy Rescue Unit **24.95**
119-7038 LNT 2500 Gallon Tanker **24.95**

LN9000

119-7061 Pumper **29.95**
119-7069 Suburban Pumper **29.95**
119-7071 CRV-18 Heavy Rescue Vehicle **24.95**
119-7073 2500 Gallon Tanker, Tandem Axle **24.95**

LS/LS9000/LTS

119-7025 LS Pumper **29.95**
119-7030 LS Suburban Pumper **29.95**
119-7037 LTS w/2500 Gallon Tanker **24.95**
119-7068 LS9000 Pumper **29.95**
119-7070 LS9000 Suburban Pumper **29.95**
119-7072 LS9000 2500 Gallon Tanker **24.95**

MACK B42/B61 PUMPER EA 29.95

119-3035 Closed Cab

119-3136 Open Cab

MACK CF

119-7017 2 or 4 Door Pumper **29.95**
119-7040 2500 Gallon Tanker **24.95**
119-7042 "CRV18" Heavy Rescue Unit **31.95**
119-7043 2 or 4 Door Cab Chassis w/Spoke Wheels **22.95**

EQUIPMENT BODIES EA 19.95 (UNLESS NOTED)

119-3086 Generic Fire Pumper Body
Adaptable to various truck kits, complete with ladders, hose reels and other details.

119-7035 Pierce Pumper for Extended Chassis
119-7046 FDNY (New York City) Pumper Body
119-7092 Pierce Pumper
119-7093 Pierce CRV-18 Heavy Rescue Vehicle **9.95**
119-7094 Pierce 2500 Gallon Tanker

FORKLIFT

119-2004 1947 Clark Forklift **4.95**

HEAVY TRUCKS

All kits except #2044 include plastic wheels and vinyl tires.

AUTOCAR

Models feature disc wheels.

119-3100 Tractor **17.95**
119-3101 Dump Truck w/12' Heil Dump Bed **22.95**
119-3102 Three-Axle Concrete Block Truck w/Boom **22.95**
119-3116 "Constructor" Dump Truck w/Curved-Side Body **22.95**
119-3162 "Constructor" Off-Road Tractor **17.95**
Builds single- or dual-axle version, includes disc wheels.

119-7001 Dump Truck-Large Body **24.95**
119-7053 "Constructor" w/Closed Roll Off Trash Compactor Body **22.95**
119-7088 "Constructor" w/Roll-Off Trash Compactor Body & Disc Wheels **22.95**

CHEVROLET

119-2044 1955 2-Ton Stake Truck **9.95**
All metal kit.

DIAMOND REO

Models feature spoked wheels.

119-3109 40' Flatbed **17.95**
119-3114 Tractor **17.95**
119-3115 Van **22.95**
119-3134 14' Dump Body **22.95**
119-3143 11' Low Side Body **22.95**
119-3145 7' Heil Dump Body **22.95**
119-3148 Flatbed **21.95**
119-7033 Dump Truck w/Curved-Side Body **22.95**
119-7049 Short Refrigerated Van **22.95**
119-7050 Fuel Oil Tank Truck **22.95**

FORD

All models feature disc wheels.

LNT

119-3041 Dual Axle Dump Truck w/7' Heil Dump Bed **22.95**
119-3042 Tri-Axle w/12' Heil Dump Body **22.95**
119-3043 Short Refrigerated Van Truck **22.95**
119-3047 Dual Axle Flatbed w/Dual Exhaust, Round Fuel Tanks **21.95**
119-3117 Dump Truck w/Curved-Side Body **22.95**

119-3135 Dual Axle Tractor w/Dual Exhaust, Round Fuel Tanks **17.95**
119-7009 Tractor w/20' Coal/Gravel Dual Axle Trailer **24.95**

ALLOY FORMS, INC.

LTS
119-3151 Dump Truck w/Curved-Side Body **22.95**
119-7020 Dual Axle Tractor w/Dual Exhaust, Round Fuel Tanks **17.95**
119-7021 Dump Truck w/12' Heil Dump Bed **22.95**
119-7022 Dump Truck w/20' Dump Bed **24.95**
119-7023 Boom/Block Truck **22.95**

LN 9000
119-7055 Dual Axle Dump Truck w/7' Heil Dump Body **22.95**
119-7056 Dual Axle Dump Truck w/12' Heil Dump Body **22.95**
119-7057 Short Refrigerated Van Truck **22.95**
119-7059 Dual Axle Heavy Duty Flatbed **21.95**
119-7062 Dual Axle Coal/Gravel Dump Truck **24.95**
119-7075 Dual Axle Tractor w/Dual Exhaust, Round Fuel Tanks **17.95**

LS 9000
119-7063 Dual Axle Tractor w/Round Fuel Tanks **17.95**
119-7064 Dump Truck w/12' Heil Dump Body **22.95**
119-7065 Dual Axle Dump Truck w/20' Dump Body **24.95**

119-7066 Boom/Block Truck **22.95**

GMC ASTRO UNIVERSAL TRACTOR

SLEEPER CABS - DUAL AXLE

119-3012 Single Exhaust, Square Fuel Tanks, Dual Axle **17.95**
Models include sleeper cab, air cleaner and disc wheels.

SHORT CABS
Kits include dual exhaust, round fuel tanks, and spoke wheels.

119-3022 GMC Astro w/16' Van **22.95**

119-3025 Single Axle **17.95**

KENWORTH

1960 "LONG NOSE" CONVENTIONAL
Models feature spoke wheels unless otherwise noted.

119-3112 Dual-Axle Tractor **17.95**

119-3113 Tractor w/20' Dump Body & 20' Dump Trailer **36.95**
Includes fifth wheel dolly and disc wheels
119-7026 Tractor w/30' Tanker Trailer **31.95**
119-7027 Tractor w/30' Highliner Round Nose Van Trailer **31.95**
119-7028 Tractor w/30' Flatbed Stake Trailer **31.95**

MACK

B42/B61 UNIVERSAL TRACTOR
Models feature spoke wheels.

119-3001 Flatbed Truck w/Stakes **21.95**

119-3007 Short Refrigerated Van Truck **22.95**
119-3009 Concrete Block Truck w/Boom **22.95**
119-3018 Ribbed Side Van **22.95**
119-3019 Dump Truck w/Curved-Side Dump Body **22.95**
119-3023 Fuel/Water Tanker **22.95**
119-3027 Box Van w/24' Riveted Smooth Side Body **22.95**

119-3028 Dual Axle Dump Truck w/Heil Dump Bed **22.95**

119-3034 Tri-Axle Dump Truck w/12' Heil Dump Bed **22.95**
119-3138 Tractor Only **17.95**

119-3049 Dual Axle Dump Truck w/12' Heil Dump Bed **22.95**

B71
Models feature disc wheels.
119-3008 Dump Truck w/Curved-Side Body **22.95**

119-3137 Tractor **17.95**
119-3139 Tractor w/Three-Axle Heavy Duty Flatbed **21.95**

DM-800 EA 17.95
119-3011 R-800 Offset Cab Tractor
119-7052 Offset Cab Tractor w/Spoke Wheels

1950 H-60 CABOVER TRACTOR EA 31.95 (UNLESS NOTED)
Models feature spoke wheels unless noted.
119-3014 With 20' Container Trailer
119-3015 With 40' Container Trailer
119-3108 Dual-Axle w/Disc Wheels **17.95**

119-3152 With 30' Highliner Round Nose Trailer
119-3153 With 30' Flatbed Stake Trailer

119-7045 With 30' Tanker Trailer

1930S MACK TRUCKS

BM/BQ
All models feature spoke wheels.
119-3020 Tank Truck **21.95**
119-3031 Single Axle Tractor **17.95**
119-3032 Dual Axle Tractor **17.95**

119-3106 Van **22.95**
119-3107 Stake Truck **21.95**
119-3164 Dump Truck w/Curved Body **22.95**
119-7078 Oil Tanker w/5-Dome Fuel Oil Tank **22.95**
119-7079 Heavy Duty Wrecker **22.95**
119-7081 Single Axle Tractor w/Two Double Bottom Tank Trailers **29.95**
119-7085 Van w/16' Riveted Smooth Side Body **22.95**
119-7086 Dual Axle Oil Tanker w/5-Dome Tank **22.95**

1933 CJ
Models feature spoke wheels.
119-3021 Tank Truck **21.95**
119-3105 Stake Truck **21.95**
119-3104 Van **22.95**
119-3146 Tractor Only **17.95**
119-3147 Oil Truck w/5-Dome Tank Body **22.95**
119-3163 Dump Truck w/Curved Body **22.95** *NEW*
119-7076 City Fuel Oil Truck **22.95**
119-7077 Circus Canvas (Tent) Truck **22.95**

TRAILERS EA 22.95
119-3017 45' Heavy Duty Lowboy Trailer w/Spoke Wheels
119-3029 30' Open Frame Logging Trailer w/Spoke Wheels

119-3110 30' Tri-Axle Dump Trailer w/Spoke Wheels
119-3149 45' Ribbed Sided Van w/Spoke Wheels
119-3154 37' Depressed Center w/Spoke Wheels
119-3181 40' Flatbed Stake **19.95**

119-7003 20' Dump Trailer w/Tongue & Spoked Wheels **19.95**

119-7004 30' Tank Trailer w/Spoke Wheels **22.95**

119-7005 30' Flatbed Trailer w/Stakes **22.95**

119-7006 30' Hi-Liner Van Trailer w/Spoke Wheels **22.95**

119-7010 22' Dump Trailer w/Disc Wheels **22.95**

119-7015 22' Dump Trailer w/Bogie w/Disc Wheels **22.95**

119-7074 UPS Type Over the Road Trailer **22.95**
119-7091 30' Open Frame Trailer pkg(2) **22.95**
119-7095 24' Riveted Side Van w/Spoke Wheels **22.95**

TRAILERS- CONTAINER TRANSPORT
Kits feature spoke wheels.

119-7018 20' **19.95**
119-7019 40' **22.95**

TRUCK BODIES
119-2036 Roll-Off Trash Container Open Top w/End Door **7.95**
119-3024 24' Riveted Smooth Side Van **19.95**
119-3027 24' Riveted Smooth Side Van **19.95**
119-3151 20' Coal/Gravel Dump **19.95**
119-3155 20' Coal/Gravel Dump **19.95** *NEW*
119-3156 1930s Delivery Van **9.95**
119-3157 1930s 20' Canvas Top Van **14.95**
119-3158 1930s Round Tanker **5.95**
119-3159 1930s City Fuel Oil Delivery Tank **9.95**
119-3160 Sloped/Curved Tanker **9.95**
119-3183 Heavy-Duty Flatbed w/Side Stakes **6.95** *NEW*
119-3184 Curved Side Dump **7.95** *NEW*
119-7034 Short Refrigerated Van **9.95**
119-7047 7' Heil Dump **7.95**
119-7048 11' Heil Low Side Dump **7.95**
119-7051 12' Heil Dump **7.95**
119-7054 Trash Compactor **9.95**
119-7080 Heavy Duty Ribbed Side Dump **9.95**
119-7082 5-Dome Fuel Oil Tank **9.95**
119-7084 16' Riveted Smooth Side Van **9.95**
119-7089 1930 Mack Wrecker **9.95**
119-7090 14' Ribbed Side Dump **9.95**
119-7096 Boom/Block Flatbed **9.95**
119-7097 Ribbed Side Van **9.95**
119-7098 Heavy-Duty Flatbed pkg(2) **9.95**
119-7099 Light Duty Flatbed pkg(2) **9.95**

TRUCK LOADS EA 9.95
119-8022 Logs - Stack of 3
119-8050 Banded Lumber pkg(2)
119-8052 Covered Machinery/Lumber pkg(3)
119-8082 Wooden Crates (6 Large, 6 Small) pkg(12)

IMPORTED FROM GERMANY BY WALTHERS

Highways and streets come to life instantly with these detailed models of American and European vehicles. All types of cars, trucks, buses and emergency equipment are offered. Each is fully assembled from plastic parts, with authentic markings where appropriate. Check out the models with working lights for your layout or collection too!

AUTOMOBILES

BENTLEY

189-44411 Convertible Coupe, Top Down **7.99**

BUICK

189-44706 1950 Sedan Limousine **9.99**

CADILLAC

1952 COUPE DEVILLE

189-43408 2-Door Convertible - Top Down **9.99** *NEW*

189-43416 2-Door Hardtop **10.99**

1952 YELLOW CAB

189-43463 **10.99**

1959 EL DORADO TWO-DOOR

189-45110 Pink **9.99**

189-45111 "Just Married" **10.99**

1970 STATION WAGON

189-42903 **9.95**

CHEVROLET

1957 BEL AIR

189-45003 Coupe **10.99**

189-45007 Convertible - Top Down **10.99**

189-45010 2-Door w/Flame Graphics **12.99** *NEW*

1997 S-10 BLAZER SUV

189-46400 Blue **9.99** *NEW*

CAPRICE

189-47601 Classic 1995 **8.99**

189-47616 Beverly Hills Taxi **11.99** *NEW*

1956 CORVETTE

189-45405 Convertible–Top Up **10.99**

CITROEN

AX

189-45602 Two-Door Hardtop w/Sunroof **6.99**

Limited Quantity Available
189-45620 France Telecom **7.99**

189-45619 French Post Office **7.99**

DS 19

189-48000 Plain **10.99**
189-48001 Two-Color **10.99**

189-48004 "Rallye Monte Carlo" (blue) **11.99**

189-48005 Taxi (black) **10.99**

189-48006 "Hydropneumatic" **15.99** *NEW*
Display model based on a prototype created for an ad campaign.

DODGE

MINI-VAN

189-44600 1990 Voyager **10.99** *NEW*

MONACO

189-46603 Four-Door Sedan **8.99**

189-46613 Texas Cab (yellow, blue roof) **10.99**

189-46614 Hodges Dodges "Ramchargers" Drag Car **10.99** *NEW*

FERRARI GTO

189-42601 Red **7.99**

189-42610 "Racing" (blue) **10.99**

189-42611 #86 1962 Race Car (brown) **10.99** *NEW*

FIAT

189-48700 500 F 2-Door 1965 Model **7.99**

FORD

1935 EIFEL CONVERTIBLE

189-41200 Red - Top Up **7.99**

189-41201 White - Top Down **8.99**

CROWN VICTORIA EA 11.99

189-49000 Sedan (red)

189-49004 Chicago Checker Taxi *NEW*

ESCORT

189-45700 Four-Door Hardtop **6.99**

189-45707 Two-Door Convertible-Top Down, Metallic **9.99**

189-45725 Four-Door Hardtop Sport Edition **9.99**

1964 MUSTANG

189-47500 Convertible-Top Down **11.99** *NEW*

189-47501 Convertible-Top Up **11.99** *NEW*

189-47505 Convertible-Top Down, Metallic **11.99**

189-47506 "Crazy Cars" **12.99**

PROBE

189-47400 24V Two-Door Hardtop **9.99**

189-47403 24V-Metallic **10.99**

1956 THUNDERBIRD

189-45210 Convertible-Top Down **10.99**

189-45211 Convertible w/Top-Up **9.99** *NEW*

HORSH

189-41309 853 Convertible (red, black) **10.99**

MG MIDGET TC

189-45907 Convertible **9.99**

MERCEDES-BENZ

170V

189-40507 Convertible-Top Down **9.99**

189-41409 Four-Door Sedan **7.99**

300 SL

189-40800 Coupe **8.99**

1960S 300 LIMOUSINE

189-44801 Kennedy's Berlin Visit w/Figures **23.99**

220 SE

189-40420 Four-Door Hardtop w/Closed Sunroof **8.99**

SSK EA 19.99

189-48302 1928 Two-Seat Roadster-Top Down

189-48303 "Mille Miglia" 1931

189-48304 SSKL-Megamodel **19.99** *NEW*
Includes display box.

A-KLASSE

189-48600 Classic (red) **8.99**
189-48601 Avantgarde w/Open Sunroof (Metallic Blue) **10.99** *NEW*

189-48603 Motorsport (silver, red & black) **14.99**

189-48605 Falk w/Special Map Graphics **15.99** *NEW*

M-KLASSE

189-48500 ML 320 **10.99**

189-48501 Metallic Paint w/Chromed Front End Guard **11.99** *NEW*

189-48507 Off-Road w/Roof Rack & Equipment **13.99** *NEW*

W196 "SILVER ARROW"

189-47000 1955 Race Car-Megamodel **16.99** *NEW*
Includes display box.

MESSERSCHMITT

KABINROLLER KR 200 3-WHEELER

189-48800 1955 Kabinenroller KR 200 Baujahr **7.99**

189-48803 "Castrol" **10.99** *NEW*

MORGAN PLUS 8

189-47104 Metallic **9.99**

189-47107 "Rallye" Race Car **10.99**

189-47109 Brands Hatch 1981 Race Car **11.99** *NEW*

NSU

189-48400 1965 TT Two-Door Hardtop **8.99**

OPEL

RECORD

189-42000 Model C 1966 4-Door Sedan **9.99** *NEW*

1938 OLYMPIA

189-41100 Two-Door **8.99**
189-41110 Convertible - Top Down **7.99**

PONTIAC

189-41700 1973 Trans Am Plain **7.99**

189-41701 Firebird (black, golden eagle) **8.99** *NEW*

RENAULT

189-42500 R5 **6.99**

ROLLS ROYCE

189-44415 Silver Cloud III, Metallic **11.99**

SMART

189-48900 Red & Black **9.99**

VOLKSWAGEN

"BEETLE"

189-42732 1952 Two-Door w/Open Sunroof **6.99**

189-42743 1951 Export Model w/Chrome **8.99**

189-42744 Hippie "Flower Power" **11.99** *NEW*
189-42747 Lufthansa Blue, Yellow **8.99**
189-42748 Light Blue Doors **10.99**

189-42751 German Post **7.99**

189-42761 1953 w/Oval Windows, Whitewall Tires & Chrome **8.99**

189-42762 "1 Million" (gold) **9.99**

189-46705 Convertible, Two-Tone Paint, Top Down **10.99**

189-46706 Convertible-Top Up **9.99**

KARMANN-GHIA 1600

189-45813 1960s Coupe **9.99**

PASSAT

189-48100 1985 Station Wagon **8.99**

189-48108 German Post Office **9.99** *NEW*

VOLVO

189-43906 544 Two-Door Hardtop **9.99**

BIKES & SCOOTERS

189-6013 Two Vespa Scooters, Six Bikes & Two Bike Riders **7.99** *NEW*

BUSES

MERCEDES-BENZ

0-3500 TYPE

189-41039 Roulette **13.99**

189-41044 Dr. Krugmann Travel Center **19.99** *NEW*

LP 809

189-40723 Kreissparkasse **13.99**

189-44350 Belgium **12.99**

SPRINTER

189-47801 Kombi Passenger Van **8.99**

189-47805 "TEC Belgium" **14.99**

189-47813 BVG Omnibus-Technik **12.99**
189-47814 "Europcar" **10.99**

RENAULT

FR1 TYPE

189-45323 Luxemburg "L'aingle de Dalheim" **25.99**

189-45318 Disneyland **19.99**
189-45320 Pays dla Lre **23.99**
189-45321 Terlinden **23.99**

189-45322 FR1 "Euro" (Flag Graphics) **23.99**

R312 TYPE

189-47200 Paris Tour #1 **27.99**

189-47205 Focus Magazine **19.99**
189-47207 Strassburg **23.99**
189-47208 GENF Public Transport **23.99**
189-47209 TEC **27.99**

EMERGENCY EQUIPMENT

FIRE DEPARTMENT SETS

189-49924 Berlin City **46.99**
Includes one each: VW Passat Wagon, Iveco Daily Van and Mecedes LP 809 Equipment Truck with authentic Berin markings, in a special presentation box.

189-49925 New York City **64.99**
Set includes one each: Chevrolet Caprice Chief's Car, American LaFrance Pumper (Engine Co. 73) and an American LaFrance Tractor-Drawn Aerial (Ladder Co. 73), finished in white over red with the City Fire Dept. shield, all in a special presentation box.

189-49927 Chicago City Fire Dept. **74.95** ***NEW***
Finished in the city's traditional black-roof scheme, which originated early in the 20th century when the canvas top of the Chief's new car couldn't be painted red! Set includes one each: Ford Crown Victoria Chief's Car (Battalion Two). American LaFrance Pumper (Engine 3) and an American LaFrance Tractor-Drawn Aerial (Truck 5), all in a special presentation box.

AMERICAN LA FRANCE

OPEN CAB PUMPER

189-46017 White **26.99**

OPEN CAB LADDER TRUCK EA 34.99

189-46013 Green

189-46015 Yellow
189-46016 White

CLOSED CAB LADDER TRUCK EA 34.99

189-46005 Yellow
189-46006 White

OPEN CAB TRACTOR-DRAWN AERIAL EA 34.99

189-46013 Lime Green
189-46015 Yellow
189-46016 White

MIDDLETOWN, PA LIBERTY FIRE CO. #1

Models are painted and lettered in matching blue and white scheme.

189-46020 Closed Cab Pumper **26.99**
189-46021 Closed Cab Tractor-Drawn Aerial Ladder **34.99**

CHEVROLET

BEL AIR

189-45009 1957 2-Door Police Patrol **11.99** ***NEW***

CAPRICE

189-47612 Fire Chief-No Light Bar **10.99**

189-47615 Chicago Police **11.99** ***NEW***

189-47672 Nebraska Safety Patrol **11.99**

189-47674 Michigan State Patrol **11.99**

189-47676 Florida Highway Patrol **13.95**

189-47677 Missouri State Highway Patrol **13.95**

189-47678 Tennessee State Trooper **13.99** ***NEW***

Berlin City Fire Department Set
189-49924

New York City Fire Department Set
189-49925

Chicago City Fire Department Set
189-49927

189-47679 New Jersey State Police **13.99** ***NEW***

189-47680 Nevada Highway Patrol **13.99** ***NEW***

1950 PICK-UP TRUCK

189-48207 Fire District #4 Mini-Pumper **12.99** ***NEW***

CITROEN

JUMPER

189-47353 Slovenian Police Van (blue) **10.99**

189-47354 City of Dortmund Fire Dept. Personnel Van **11.99** ***NEW***

DKW

189-47357 French Police **11.99**

189-40908 German Red Cross-Nürenberg **11.99** ***NEW***

189-40909 Fire Dept. Water System Repair Truck **9.99** ***NEW***

DODGE MONACO

189-46672 Oklahoma State Patrol **11.99**

189-46673 Delaware State Highway Patrol **13.95**

189-46674 Colorado State Highway Courtesy Police **13.95**

Limited Quantity Available
189-46608 Fire Dept. 9.99

FIAT DUCATO

189-43248 Technical Rescue Service (THW) w/2-Axle Trailer 15.99 *NEW*

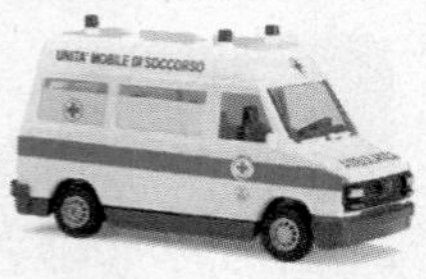

189-43293 Italian Red Cross Ambulance 11.99

189-43297 Red Cross Water Guard Personnel Van 11.99 *NEW*

189-43298 City of Ulm Fire Dept. Personnel Van 11.99 *NEW*

189-47304 Johanniter 12.99

189-47310 Fire–KLAF 11.99

189-47313 Maltese Help Service Ambulance 13.99

189-47314 German Red Cross Ambulance 12.99

189-47317 Post Express 10.99
189-47318 Two Shires Paramedic Ambulance (England) 12.99 *NEW*
189-47321 Stadler Rescue Service Ambulance 12.99 *NEW*
189-47323 Police Personnel Van (German) 9.99 *NEW*

Limited Quantity Available
189-47303 Fire Department 10.99
189-47309 Fire Department
189-43247 Police 9.99
11.99

FORD

Limited Quantity Available
189-43786 Russian Ambulance 10.99
189-43787 DLRG Ambulance (German) 10.99
189-45729 Escort-Hungarian Police 9.99

189-43789 Weimar Fire Dept. Equipment Truck 9.99

TRANSIT VANS

189-42404 THW (orange) 9.99

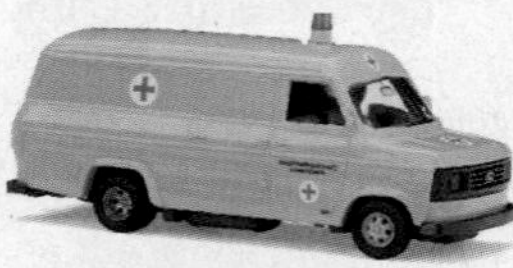

189-42405 Disaster Prevention Ambulance 13.99 *NEW*

189-42406 Fire Dept. Equipment Truck 9.99 *NEW*

Latest New Product News Daily! Visit Walthers Web site at

www.walthers.com

CROWN VICTORIA

189-49003 US Deputy Sheriff 11.99 *NEW*

189-49005 NYPD New York City Patrol Supervisor 11.99 *NEW*

189-49070 Ohio State Police 13.99 *NEW*

189-49071 Utah Highway Patrol 13.99 *NEW*

189-49072 Oregon State Police 13.99 *NEW*

ESCORT EA 9.99 (UNLESS NOTED)

189-45730 Croation Police

189-45731 Indonesian Police 13.99 *NEW*

Limited Quantity Available
189-45726 Fire Dept.
189-45727 Spanish Police
189-45729 Hungarian Police

1931 MODEL AA VAN

189-47706 Police Patro Paddy Wagon 10.99

189-47713 Police Department 11.99 *NEW*

PROBE

189-47407 County Sheriff 10.99 *NEW*

IVECO

DAILY

189-47906 German Red Cross-Karlsruhe 13.99

189-47907 "Pro Medic" Ambulance 18.99

189-47911 Swiss Ambulance 13.99 *NEW*

189-47912 Dutch Fire Dept. Equipment Truck 13.99 *NEW*

189-47971 Swiss Fire Department Flatbed w/Canvas Cover 11.99

189-47972 Fire Dept. Equipment Truck 12.99 *NEW*

Limited Quantity Available
189-47905 Dortmund Fire Dept. Equipment Truck 14.99

MERCEDES-BENZ

507D

189-44309 Police Box Van 8.99

189-44349 Swiss Fire Personnel Bus 11.99

189-44352 Maltese Help Service Mobile Accident Scene Assistance Unit 13.99 *NEW*

189-44353 Vienna, Austria, Fire Dept. Dive Rescue Van 12.99 *NEW*

189-44354 Belgian Civil Defense Telecommunications Van 11.99 *NEW*

200 SE

189-40417 Fire Department 8.99

220

189-40429 Police (green) 8.99

LP 809 EA 14.99

189-40765 Police Horse Transport Truck

189-40772 Hessische Police School

189-40776 THW Mobile Command/Control Unit *NEW*

189-40778 Maltese Help Service Mobile Command/Control Unit 14.99 *NEW*

Limited Quantity Available

189-40774 German Red Cross Mobile Hospital

A-KLASSE

189-48604 Emergency Doctor-Holland 14.99 *NEW*

M-KLASSE

189-48505 Tuscaloosa, Alabama, Sheriff 12.99 *NEW*

189-48506 German Red Cross Emergency Doctor 14.99 *NEW*

SPRINTER

189-47803 Police Prisoner Transport Van 13.99

189-47807 Fire Dept. Personnel Bus 11.99

189-47811 Reinbeck Fire Dept. Mobile Command/ Control Unit 12.99 *NEW*

189-47815 Fire Dept. Rescue Dog Squad 9.99 *NEW*

189-47816 Police Personnel Van 10.99 *NEW*

PEUGEOT

BOXER

189-47381 French Fire Dept. Scuba Divers' Rescue Unit 10.99 *NEW*

189-47377 Fire Department Personnel Bus-Holland 12.99

189-47378 Netherlands Red Cross Ambulance 12.99
189-47379 Holland EMS 13.99

189-47380 Ambulance Belgian Fire 13.99

PLYMOUTH FURY

189-46671 Georgia State Patrol 11.99

See What's Available at

www.walthers.com

RENAULT ESPACE

189-45529 Dutch Police 12.99 *NEW*

Limited Quantity Available

189-45520 Children's Emergency Doctor 8.99
189-45526 Ambulance 9.99
189-45527 Emergency Doctor 10.99

VOLKSWAGEN

PASSAT

189-48103 10.99
189-48106 Technical Help Service (THW) 10.99

189-48107 DB-AG Railroad Police 9.99 *NEW*

189-48105 MHD Emergency Doctor 11.99

MILITARY VEHICLES

BELGIUM

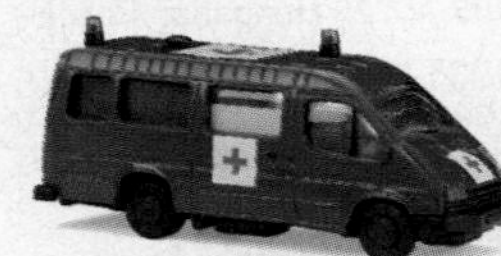

189-43791 Belgian Army Ford Transit Ambulance TBA *NEW*

FRANCE

Limited Quantity Available

189-43287 Peugeot J5 Van 7.99

UNITED STATES

189-48206 US Air Force 1950 Chevrolet Pick-Up 10.99 *NEW*

TRAILERS

189-44903 Tandem for Auto Transport 5.99

Limited Quantity Available

189-44910 Police 8.99
189-44911 Bockmann 9.99

189-44951 Glider w/Trailer 8.99

189-44970 Single Axle 5.99

TRUCKS

FORD

1931 MODEL AA EA 11.99 (UNLESS NOTED)

Based on the one-ton truck chassis, these delivery vehicles were a favorite with many businesses.

189-47704 Kathreiner's

189-47709 Hearse

189-47711 Capital Laundry

189-47712 Berkley Dollar Cleaner Inc. *NEW*
189-47700 Plain 10.99

CITROEN MODEL H

189-41909 Metallic 7.99

IVECO

DAILY

189-47909 Gerber Construction Wide Load Escort 13.99 *NEW*

189-47970 Open Flatbed 9.99 *NEW*

189-47973 Flatbed w/Canvas Cover Street Repair Truck 13.99 *NEW*

MERCEDES-BENZ

LP 809

189-40768 Water Rescue 14.99

189-40769 Flatbed w/Tarpaulin 11.99

189-40780 City Services Ladder Truck 14.99 *NEW*

189-40781 ABX Transport 13.99 *NEW*

TEMPO 3-WHEELER

189-40637 Coal Truck 7.99
189-40638 Becker Coal Delivery 8.99 *NEW*

CHEVROLET

189-48200 Standard **10.99**

189-48208 Circle C Farm Pick-Up w/Stake Body **11.99** *NEW*
Special "peeling" paint job shows gray primer underneath.

VANS

CITROEN

189-47350 Jumper **8.99**

189-47356 French Post Office **9.99**
189-47360 System U Supermarkets (France) **9.99** *NEW*
189-47361 Jumper-Belgian Post Office **10.99** *NEW*

Limited Quantity Available

189-47358 Belgian Post Office **10.99**

C25 EA 10.99

Limited Quantity Available

189-43291 Belgian Post Office "De Post"
189-43292 Belgian Post Office "La Poste"

CHEVROLET

WALTHERS US EXCLUSIVE COLORS!
Add colorful variety to any street scene with these special versions of the Chevy Blazer, available ONLY from Walthers. Turn your Auto Assembly Plant (933-3079), Distribution Facility (933-3076) or Uptown Motors (933-3077) into Chevy facilities with these great models parked nearby. (See the complete listing of America's Driving Force models in the Structures, Vehicles and Freight Sections of this Book.)

189-46492 Red **9.99** *NEW*

189-46493 Black **9.99** *NEW*

1950 PICK-UP

Note: Preproduction Model Shown - Color May Vary Slightly

189-48291 Al's Victory Service Tow Truck **16.98**
Another WALTHERS EXCLUSIVE! This fully assembled Vintage Chevy pick-up sports colorful graphics, airhorns, nonworking amber light, tool box and towing winch. Roadside service is just a phone call away at Al's Victory Service Garage, a Walthers Cornerstone Series® structure found in the Structures section of this Reference Book.

189-48290 "Cornerstone Construction" **9.99**
A WALTHERS EXCLUSIVE! Features special graphics based on the familiar Cornerstone Series® logo. Looks great on any construction site, parked at the new Walton & Sons Lumber Yard or heading down your highways.

DKW

Limited Quantity Available
189-40904 Eichbaum **7.99**

FIAT DUCATO

189-47300 With High Roof **8.99**
189-47305 Kombi **8.99**
189-47319 Swiss EMS Package/Mail Delivery Service **12.99** *NEW*

Limited Quantity Available
189-47302 Busch **7.99**
189-47311 Construction **10.99**
189-47316 SORA ("Vehicles for Mobility & Service) **9.99**

FORD TRANSIT

189-42400 Plain **8.99**

189-43762 RTL "Oldies" Radio **10.99**
189-43790 Märklin w/Model Railroad Graphics **12.99** *NEW*

Limited Quantity Available

189-43779 Wide Load Escort w/Caution Sign **12.99**

IVECO

189-47900 Delivery Van w/Hi Roof **8.99**

DAILY

189-47901 Passenger Van **8.99**

189-47904 "Europcar" **10.99**

Limited Quantity Available
189-47908 THW (blue) **13.99**

MERCEDES-BENZ

189-44348 German Post Office-Modern **9.99**

SPRINTER

189-47800 Van **8.99**

189-47804 "Deutsche Mobilspedition" **13.99**

189-47808 "TNT Express-We Take it Personally" **11.99**

189-47809 "EMS Kurierpost" (German Post Office) **11.99**

189-47810 Bahntrans **11.99**

189-47814 "Europcar" **10.99**
189-47813 Berlin Workers Society (BVG) Engineering **12.99**
189-47814 Europcar **10.99**

189-47817 Belgian Power Company-Electrabel **11.99** *NEW*

Limited Quantity Available

189-41543 170V Postal Service **8.99**
189-44339 Wide Load Escort w/Caution Sign **13.99**

189-47806 "NVS Kurierdienst" **9.99**

PEUGEOT BOXER

Limited Quantity Available
189-47373 Quille **9.99**

RENAULT

189-45500 Van **8.99**

AUTOMOBILES W/WORKING LIGHTS

A bright spot on any highway, day or night. Models feature working head and tail lights, powered by miniature bulbs. Models and electrical equipment are fully assembled, just connect to 14-16V DC or AC power.

189-5641 Ford Escort **15.99**

189-5648 Ford Crown Victoria 4-Door Sedan **16.99** ***NEW***

189-5642 Chevrolet Caprice **16.99**

189-5644 Volkswagen Passat **15.99**

189-5645 A-Klasse **17.99**

189-5646 M-Klasse **19.99**

BUSES W/WORKING LIGHTS

EA 18.99

Put more realism on your roads with these models, featuring working head and tail lights, powered by miniature bulbs. Models and electrical equipment are fully assembled, just connect to 14-16V DC or AC power.

189-5637 Fiat Ducato

189-5639 Mercedes Sprinter

EMERGENCY VEHICLES W/WORKING LIGHTS

These eye-catching models are sure to stop traffic with their working lights! Models come fully assembled with miniature blue or red lamps, flasher circuit and wiring. Simply hook up to 14-16V AC or DC power.

DODGE MONACO

189-5611 US Sheriff **32.95**

FORD

189-5612 State Police (Red Lamps) **27.99** ***NEW***

FIAT DUCATO

189-5601 Ambulance (Blue Lamps) **22.99**

189-5602 Fire Dept. Van (Blue Lamps) **22.90**

AMERICAN LA FRANCE

189-5604 Pumper (Red Lamps) **33.99**

189-5605 Ladder Truck (Red Lamps) **43.99**

IVECO

189-5606 Daily Van-Fire Dept. (Blue Lamps) **23.99**

189-5613 Daily Fire Dept. Truck (Blue Lamps) **24.99** ***NEW***

MERCEDES

189-5607 Sprinter-Police (Blue Lamps) **23.99**

189-5608 MB Fire Truck w/Ladder **31.99**

189-5610 MB LP 308 w/Sand Load **29.99**

189-5615 Sprinter-Police (Blue Lamps) **23.99** ***NEW***

RENAULT ESCAPE

Limited Quantity Available
189-5623 Baby Doctor Ambulance (Blue Lamps) **29.99**

VOLKSWAGEN EA 27.99

189-5603 "Beetle" Set–Police and Fire Dept. (Blue Lamps) pkg(2)

189-5609 Passat Fire & Police Set

189-5614 Passat Wagon Emergency Doctor (Blue Lamps) ***NEW***

TRUCK W/WORKING LIGHTS

189-5643 1950 Chevrolet Pick-Up (Head & Tail Lights) **17.99**

VANS W/WORKING LIGHTS

A bright addition to any scene. Models feature working head and tail lights powered by miniature bulbs. Models and electrical equipment are fully assembled. Connect to 14-16V DC or AC power.

189-5647 Chrysler/Dodge Caravan Mini-Van **16.99** ***NEW***

189-5626 Ford-Wide Load Escort (Yellow Lamps) **25.99**

189-5636 Fiat Ducato **18.99**

189-5638 Mercedes Sprinter **18.99**

VEHICLE ACCESSORIES

CATALOG

189-49993 1999 Busch Vehicles **1.99** *NEW*
A full-color presentation of the entire line of vehicles and accessories. 35 pages, softcover.

DISPLAY BOX

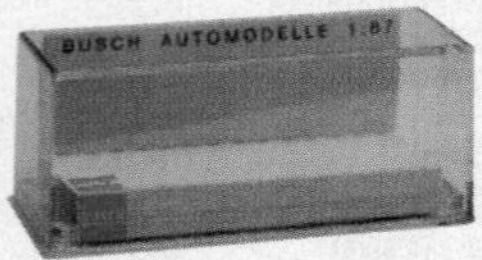

189-49970 Clear Plastic Display Box **1.99**
3 x 1-1/8 x 1-3/8"
7.6 x 3 x 3.4cm
Here's the perfect way to showcase your Busch vehicles! Great protection from dust and curious fingers. Stackable, clear plastic box comes with cardboard base insert.

TIRE & AXLE SET

Sets include three pairs of tires and three axles.

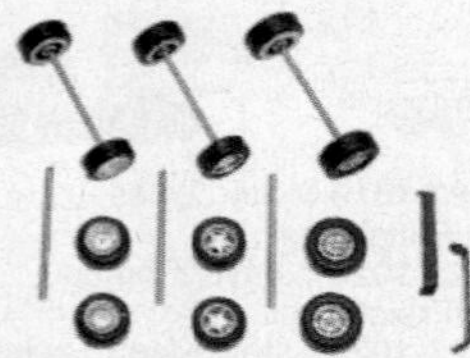

189-49950 Sport (includes 2 spoilers) **3.99**

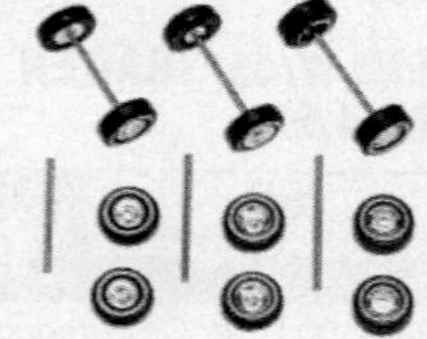

189-49951 6.99

AMERICAN EMERGENCY VEHICLES EA 5.99

Convert HO Scale models into police or fire department vehicles with these accessories. Lights are molded in red or blue plastic and are nonworking.

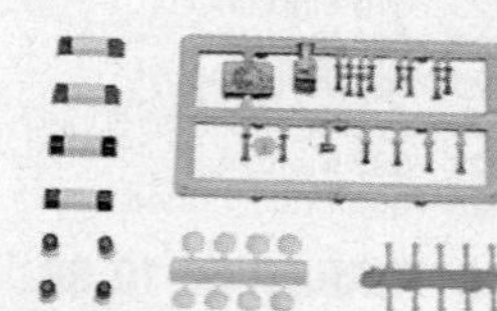

189-49960 Europe

189-49661 Modern American

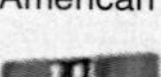

189-49962 1950s-Present *NEW*
Older warning lights, sirens, early light bars and air horns, which can be adapted to vehicles from the 1950s to the present.

189-49963 Modern Vehicles Set #2 *NEW*
Contemporary lightbars and spotlights.

BACHMANN

AUTOMOBILES

160-42206 Automobile Set pkg(6) **6.00**
Preassembled in appropriately colored plastic with painted details.

BRAWA

IMPORTED FROM GERMANY BY WALTHERS

TROLLEY BUSES

Electric trolley buses replaced street cars in many cities and are still used in some areas to provide quiet, non-polluting transportation. Powered models are fully assembled, prepainted in red, blue or yellow, and feature working interior lights and rubber tires. Requires 12-16V AC or DC power supply and #6150 Speed Controller, sold separately. Minimum radius: 8" with poles on inside of curve. Maximum grade: 30%. Minimum Road Dimensions; One-Way Street: Lane width approximately 2" for Standard Bus, 2-1/2" for Articulated or Standard Bus w/Trailer. Two-way street requires about 5" on corners.

186-6100 Standard Bus **127.99**

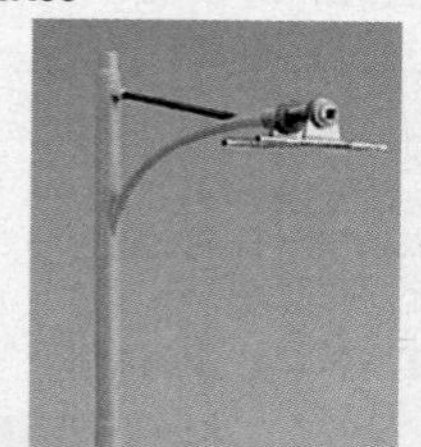

186-6111 Overhead Mast **6.99**
186-6112 Overhead Power Mast **14.99**
186-6115 Overhead Wires pkg(20) **9.99**

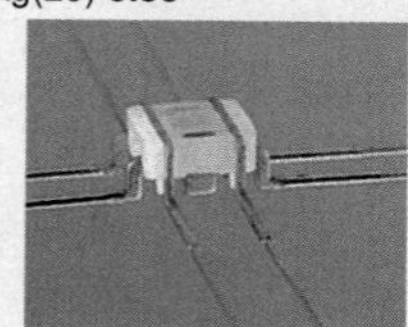

186-6117 Crossing **11.99**

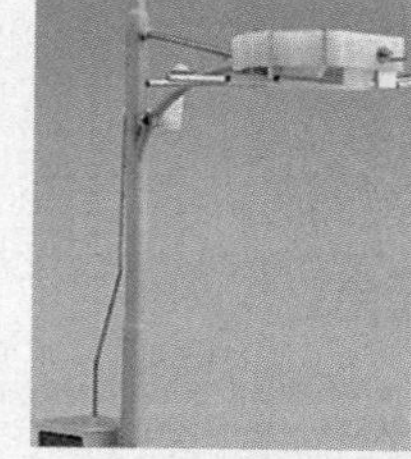

186-6120 Overhead Electric Switch **41.99**
186-6126 Contact Switch Pole **8.99**
186-6127 Insulating Mast **7.99**
186-6133 Rubber Tires pkg(10) **6.99**
Fits 6100 and 6104.

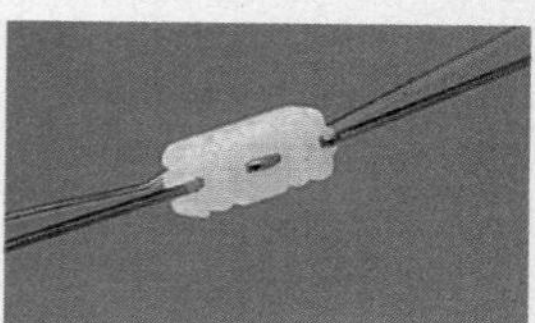

186-6140 Overhead Wire Crossing **9.99**
Use where bus crosses electrified railroad tracks.

186-6143 Wire Connector Sleeves pkg(10) **6.99**
186-6144 Insulating Connector Sleeves **4.99**
186-6148 Overhead Reversing Loop **25.99**

ACCESSORIES

186-60 Trolley Bus Catalog (English/German Text) **17.99**
Information on operations, maintenance and circuits for the Brawa Trolley Bus. Illustrations, color photos, 39 pages, 11 x 8-1/2".

186-6101 Replacement Pantograph **11.99**
Use with 6100 or 6104.

Standard Bus 186-6100

Information STATION

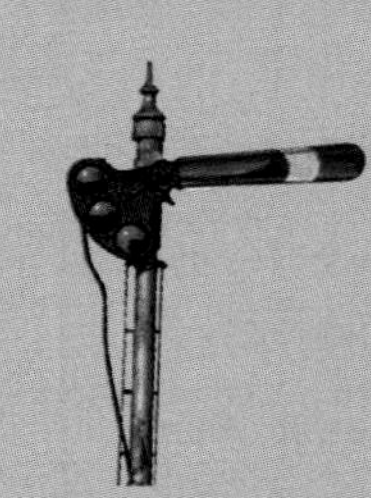

Internet Information

The World Wide Web is a fast, easy and fun way to explore model railroading. Hobbyists with home Internet access are well aware of the many model railroading and hobby related Web sites appearing daily. If you've never explored the Web, ask a friend, coworker, son or daughter to show you how to get started. Many libraries are beginning to offer Internet access for free, and Internet cafes continue to open in many cities.

If you've never visited the Walthers Web site (www.walthers.com), called The Model Railroad Mall®, you're missing out on one of the largest data bases for model railroad products and information available. You'll find pictures, descriptions and listings of more than 75,000 items carried by Walthers, along with new product announcements updated every evening! A search engine used for browsing Walthers on-line catalog makes finding what you're looking for easy. Or, check Walthers warehouse to determine if the item you're looking for is in stock, or when it will be. Then simply place your order through your local hobby shop to receive the items you want.

HO Highways and streets will come to life in minutes with these models. Most are fully assembled, or require only minor assembly of add-on details, such as mirrors, horns etc. Models are prepainted and lettered.

We have worked closely with this manufacturer to provide accurate delivery information at the time this catalog was published. Items listed in blue ink may not be available at all times. Current delivery information, along with a list of in-stock products for this line, can be found on our Web site at www.walthers.com.

AUTOMOBILES

223-220 Audi 100 Avant **2.89**
223-225 Mercedes 300E **2.89**

223-250 Ford Mustang 7.98

MINI-EXACTS EA 6.98 (UNLESS NOTED)

223-4002 Lamborghini **7.98**
223-4003 '69 Mustang **7.98**

223-4004 Ferrari Testerosa **7.98**
223-4005 Ferrari F40 **7.98**
223-4006 1963 Corvette **7.98**
223-4004018 Buick Grand National (black) **5.98**
223-4004019 Buick Grand National (white) **5.98**
223-4004023 Chevy ZR1 Corvette (white) **5.98**
223-4004025 Chevy Stingray Corvette (blue) **5.98**
223-4004029 Chevy 1957 Bel Air (turquoise) **5.98**
223-4004030 Ford Shelby Cobra (red) **5.98**
223-4004031 Ford Shelby Cobra (white) **5.98**
223-4032 Porsche 356 Convertible (silver)
223-4033 Porsche 356 Convertible (green)
223-4034 Porsche 911 Sportster 1966 (yellow)
223-4035 Porsche 911 Sportster 1966 (red)
223-4036 BMW 502 Limo 1950 (ivory)
223-4037 BMW 502 Limo 1950 (black)
223-4038 Beetle 1950s-1960s (blue)
223-4039 Beetle 1950s-1960s (red)
223-4040 Beetle 1950s-1960s (green)

SPORT UTILITY VEHICLE

223-134 Assortment **95.76** pkg(12)

BUSES

EA 10.98

American school buses feature full interior, plastic windows and colorful graphics.

223-1036 County #4

223-1037 Unified #2

223-1038 Helping Hand
223-1043 U.S. Army

223-1044 Camp Woebegon

223-1045 Washington High School

223-1046 Good Shepherd

MISCELLANEOUS TRUCKS

BEVERAGE DELIVERY TRUCKS

LOCAL

223-8601 Chihuahua Beer **13.98**
Navistar truck with roll-up side body.

SEMI

223-8701 Chihuahua Beer **15.98**
Navistar tractor with roll-up side, single axle trailer.

28' VAN TRUCKS EA 13.98

223-1087 Perkins Furniture
223-1088 Amtrak Commissary Truck
223-1090 Pelican Bread

FEED TRUCKS

223-1058 Walenga Staley **13.98**
Includes Walenga dry bulk trailer (prototype works like a covered railroad hopper) and matching Mack tractor.

LOG TRUCK

223-1006 Miller Trucking w/Peterbilt **10.98**
223-10061 Extra Logs for Log Truck pkg(12) **2.98** *NEW*

OLD-TIME TRUCK KITS PKG(2) EA 8.98

1931 FORD

223-17101 Panel Truck
223-17111 Cattle Truck
223-17121 Dump Truck
223-17131 Delivery Truck
223-17141 Stake Truck

1926 MACK "BULLDOG"

223-17001 Coal Truck
223-17011 Stake Truck
223-17021 Van
223-17031 Oil Tanker

STAR GLASS CO. TRUCKS EA 13.98

223-4000100 Dump Truck
223-4002018 Elliptical Tanker for Silica Sand
223-4002019 Kenworth Tractor w/45' Trailer

MOVING VANS

U-HAUL® 26' VAN TRUCKS EA 13.98

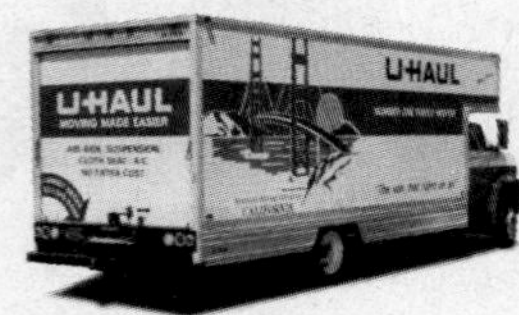

223-7002 California
223-7003 New York
223-7004 Ohio
223-7005 New Mexico
223-7006 Oregon
223-7007 Vermont
223-7008 Alabama
223-7009 Utah
223-7010 Indiana
223-7011 Kentucky
223-7012 Massachusetts
223-7013 Tennessee
223-7014 Wisconsin
223-7015 Oklahoma
223-7016 South Dakota
223-7017 Connecticut
223-7018 Rhode Island
223-7019 Florida
223-7020 Kansas
223-7021 Wyoming
233-7022 Connecticut (Tiger)
223-7023 Montana
223-7000 Undecorated

40' TRAILER EA 10.98

Includes Freightliner

223-1021 Collins 40'

223-1042 Atlas 40'

48' TRAILER

223-1062 Chapparal Van Lines w/Kenworth T-600A **13.98**
223-1071 Huckleberry Farms **14.98**
223-1072 National Van Lines **13.98**
233-1098 Graebel Moving Co. **14.98**

"ELECTRONICS" TRAILER EA 11.98

Includes matching Freightliner tractor.

223-1047 Mayflower
223-1048 Bekins
223-1049 North American

SEMI TRUCKS

SPECIAL EDITION CONTAINER

223-6205 45' Container MR 60th pkg(2) **7.98**

SEMI W/CONTAINER CHASSIS

Sets include decorated Freightliner and three chassis.

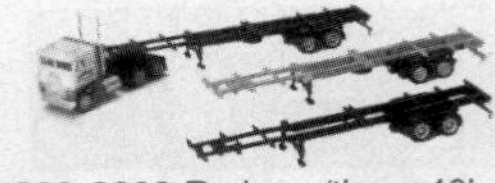

223-8399 Ryder w/three 40' Chassis (No Containers) **9.98**
223-8499 Rail Dispatch w/Three 45' **11.98**
223-8599 Tractor & Container Chassis **11.98**

SEMI W/TRAILER - SPECIAL CHRISTMAS EDITION

223-1994 Christmas 1994 "Santa on Sleigh Graphics" **15.98**
223-1995 Klaus Confectioners 45' Trailer w/Kenworth **14.98**
223-1996 1996 Christmas COE Freightliner w/45' Reefer Trailer **15.98**
223-1997 Christmas 1997 Tractor/Trailer **15.98**
223-4001998 Christmas 1998 Route 66 Collector's Truck **14.98** *NEW*

SEMI W/48' TRAILER EA 13.98 (UNLESS NOTED)

223-1069 Vita Fresh Fruit Juice w/Freightliner
223-1073 Model Railroader 60th Anniversary (white) w/Kenworth **10.38**
223-1076 Covan Tractor Trailer
223-1077 Freight Train Trucking w/Freightliner
223-1078 Modeler Railroader 60th Anniversary (maroon) w/Kenworth
223-1080 Syndicate w/Freightliner
223-1082 Digby w/Kenworth T-600A

SEMI W/40' TRAILER EA 8.98 (UNLESS NOTED)

223-1004 Union 76™ Oil Tanker

223-1008 Brillion w/Freightliner

223-1014 Hi-Way Dispatch w/GMC

223-1019 Melton Lines w/Freightliner
223-1022 Weaver Popcorn w/Freightliner
223-1025 Safety Kleen Tanker **10.98**
223-1028 Chiquita Banana **10.98**

SEMI W/45' TRAILER EA 14.98

223-1100 River City Produce *NEW*
223-1101 Star Market *NEW*
223-1102 Gatto Industrial Platters *NEW*

AMERICAN REDI MIX CONCRETE TRUCK EA 16.98

223-4002023 Material Service (red, yellow)
223-4002024 Tri-County Redi-Mix (blue, yellow)
223-4002025 American Redi-Mix (blue, red w/American Flag)
223-4002026 Palumbo
223-4002027 Granite
223-4002028 Aztec
223-4002029 Kenworth
223-4002030 Undecorated

TRACTORS

FORD AEROMAX EA 8.98

223-651000 With Sleeper
223-652000 No Sleeper

FREIGHTLINER EA 6.98

223-131000 Short Cab-No Sleeper
223-132000 Standard Sleeper Cab
223-133000 Extended Sleeper Cab w/Airfoil

GMC

223-232000 GMC/Chevy Bison Conventional 6.98

MACK EA 8.98

223-511000 Streamlined Conventional w/Sleeper
223-512000 Short Tractor-Less Sleeper

KENWORTH

223-332000 Conventional w/Sleeper **6.98**
223-333000 Conventional w/Aero Sleeper **6.98**
223-334000 Conventional - No Sleeper 6.98
223-335000 Streamline Tractor w/Sleeper **8.98**

223-641000 Streamlined T-600A w/Sleeper **8.98**
223-642000 Streamlined T-600A-No Sleeper **8.98**

PETERBILT

223-432000 Conventional w/Sleeper **6.98**

NAVISTAR

223-751000 Streamlined Tractor **8.98**

TRAILERS

40' PKG(3) EA 10.98 (UNLESS NOTED)

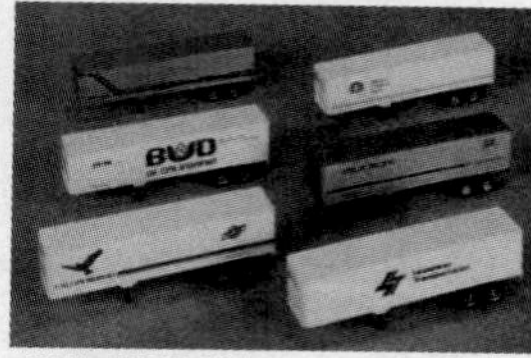

223-8107 UP
223-8108 Budd of California
223-8109 Illinois Central Gulf **9.98**
223-8111 Boston & Maine
223-8114 N&W
223-8115 DRGW

40' OLDIES PKG(2) EA 11.98

223-8139 NP
223-8140 N&W
223-8141 Western Pacific

45' EA 11.98

223-8201 Nitrol
223-8202 Crab Orchard & Egyptian Railway
223-8203 Texas-Mexican Railway
223-8204 Cornucopia Transport
223-8205 CP Rail Intermodal
223-8206 Seaboard System
223-8208 UP w/Flag
223-8209 Lynden Transport w/Alaska Map
223-8210 Illinois Central Gulf
223-8211 BN "Expediter" Logo
223-8213 Co-Op

45' UNDECORATED EA 9.98

223-8200 Rivet Side

223-8250 45' Ribbed Side

48' EA 5.98

223-8502 TransAmerica
223-8503 CP
223-8505 J.B. Hunt
223-8506 Schneider National
223-8507 JB Hunt "Quantum"
223-8508 XTRA Intermodal
223-8500 Undecorated

40' TRAILERS EA 3.98

223-810101 ATSF
223-810301 CR
223-810401 TransAmerica
223-810601 CNW
223-810701 UP
223-810801 Budd of California
223-810901 Illinois Central Gulf
223-811101 Boston & Maine
223-811201 ATSF
223-811401 N&W
223-811501 DRGW
223-812201 IC
223-812401 Strick
223-812601 SOU
223-812701 IC
223-812901 NYC
223-813101 Seaboard Coast Line
223-813201 NP
223-813901 NP
223-814001 N&W
223-814101 Western Pacific
223-814201 B&O
223-814901 Seaboard
223-815501 PRR
223-815601 SSW

45' TRAILERS EA 3.98

223-820101 Nitrol
223-820201 Crab Orchard & Egyptian
223-820301 Texas-Mexican
223-820401 Cornucopia
223-820901 Lynden
223-821001 IC
223-821101 GN
223-821201 Preferred Pool

CONTAINERS

30' BULK TANK CONTAINER W/TRACTOR EA 13.98

223-4002021 UP
223-4002022 Sealand

DYNA MODEL PRODUCTS

CONSTRUCTION EQUIPMENT

COAL CONVEYOR

260-20001 Painted **7.25**
260-2000 Unpainted **5.45**

FORKLIFTS

260-20121 Painted pkg(2) **13.25**
260-2012 Unpainted pkg(2) **7.45**

BAGGAGE TRACTOR W/TWO WAGONS

260-20131 Painted **13.25**
260-2013 Unpainted **5.45**

TRUCKS

1947 FORD

260-20061 Painted **9.35**
260-2006 Unpainted **4.95**

Extendible Chassis Kits 147-7730 and 7740 shown, container sold separately.

EXTENDIBLE CHASSIS KITS

Add detail to any intermodal terminal, highway scene or rail car with these chassis kits. Like the prototype, they'll hold containers from any manufacturer (sold separately), and lock into 40', 45' or 48' positions. Kits include rubber tires. Each comes with a complete set of decals, including mud flap markings, for the companies shown. Choose from individual kits or the money-saving three-packs.

SINGLE CHASSIS EA 7.50

147-7730 Yellow - OOCL & UP
147-7740 Black - APL, Maersk, Matson, Evergreen, Genstar, Flexi-Van

THREE-PACKS EA 17.95

147-7733 Yellow - OOCL & UP
147-7743 Black - APL, Maersk, Matson, Evergreen, Genstar, Flexi-Van

CONTAINER CHASSIS DECALS

147-6230 For Walthers Container Chassis **3.50**
The finishing touch of detail for your Walthers chassis kits (933-3110). Includes the same detailed markings included in American Ltd. Models' own chassis kits.

20' TANK CONTAINER TRAILERS

Replicas of the 40' drop center trailers used to move 20' tank containers, and 20' box containers that are too heavy for a standard chassis. Easy-to-build kits feature rubber tires, photo-etched fenders and custom Micro Scale decals with optional lettering and numbers. Compatible with all 20' tank and box container models.

147-7710 Yellow **9.95**
Includes UP decals, with trailer parts molded in yellow.

147-7720 Blue **9.95**
Used by UP, ASTF and Chemical Leaman, parts are molded in blue.

147-7800 BNSF Tank Container & Chassis Kit **12.95**
Latest markings and 2 optional trailer markings.

147-7810 UP Tank Container & Trailer **12.95**
UP Bulktainer® & yellow trailer.

TRAILER DETAILS

147-7715 Fender & Walkway Kit **2.95**
Tank Container Trailers, set includes four photo-etched stainless steel rear quarter fenders and see-through walkway (prototype provides access to the tank container connections) to detail one trailer.

CAMPBELL SCALE MODELS

BOATS

200-1600 Rowboat w/Oars & Oarlocks **4.98**

IMPORTED FROM SPAIN BY WALTHERS

Vehicles are molded in appropriately colored plastic, with painted details. Markings may vary from what is shown in catalog.

We have worked closely with this manufacturer to provide accurate delivery information at the time this catalog was published. Items listed in blue ink may not be available at all times. Current delivery information, along with a list of in-stock products for this line, can be found on our Web site at www.walthers.com.

AUTOMOBILES

CITROEN EA 1.99

265-2021 2 CV

265-2027 DS 19

265-2048 AMI

265-2076 Break

FIAT EA 1.99

265-2035 1800 Station Wagon

265-2065 Seat 124

265-2108 1500

265-2031 600 Multipla

OPEL EA 1.99

265-2004 1954 Kapitan

265-2039 Rekord

265-2040 Station Wagon

265-2072 Kadett

RENAULT EA 1.99

265-2005 4/4

265-2047 4-L Station Wagon

265-2051 Florida

265-2064 R-8

265-2025 Dauphine

FORD EA 1.99

265-2044 Thunderbird

265-2071 Zephyr

265-2073 Comet

265-2079 Falcon

265-2107 Anglia

265-2085 Consul

JAGUAR 1.99

265-2098 E Coupe

265-2100 Racer

265-2106 Mark Nine

JEEP EA 1.99

265-2026 CJ Type

265-2008 Pickup Truck

265-2078 Wagon

LAND ROVER EA 1.99

265-2033 Land Rover-Open Top

265-2077 Rover 3/L

265-2116 Safari 1.99

MERCEDES BENZ EA 1.99

265-2003 300

265-2010 190SL

265-2049 Racer

265-2011 190SL Coupe

265-2074 220

SEAT EA 1.99

265-2006 Sedan 1400

265-2032 Sedan 1400C

265-2037 Seat 1400 Panel Truck

265-2036 Coupe 600

STUDEBAKER EA 1.99

265-2070 Hawk

265-2075 Avanti

VOLKSWAGEN EA 1.99

265-2001 Beetle

265-2009 Convertible Cabriolet

265-2099 VW Karmann Ghia

265-2080 1500 Coupe

MISCELLANEOUS EA 1.99

265-2002 BMW 501

265-2124 Skoda Coupe

IMPORTED FROM SPAIN BY WALTHERS

265-2109 Borgward Isabella

265-2045 Chevrolet El Camino

265-2105 Alpha Romeo Giuletta Sprint

265-2081 DAF Coupe

265-2082 BMW Coupe

265-2083 SAAB 96

265-2084 Volvo Sport

265-2089 Morris Mini

265-2101 MG 1600

265-2042 De Soto Diplomat

265-2063 Dodge Dart

265-2038 Lincoln Continental

265-2043 Plymouth Suburban

265-2050 Simca Sedan 1000

BOATS

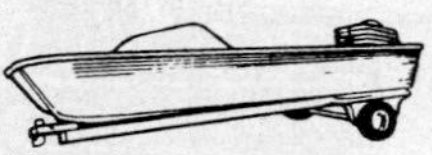
265-2052 Boat & Motor w/Trailer **1.99**

265-2053 Cabin Boat w/Motor & Trailer **1.99**

265-2054 De Soto w/Boat **2.99**

265-2055 Plymouth w/Motor Boat **2.99**

CAMPERS

265-2022 2-Wheel Camping Trailer **1.99**

265-2060 Fiat 1800 w/Trailer **2.99**

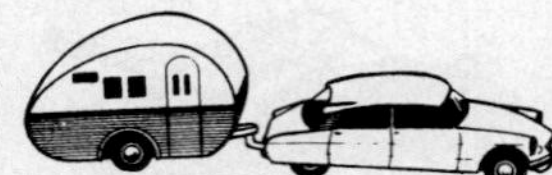
265-2059 Citroen DS-19 w/Trailer **2.99**

265-2061 Volkswagen w/Trailer **2.99**

BUSES

265-2088 Mercedes Microbus **1.99**

265-2102 Pegaso Motor Bus **2.99**

265-2110 Double Decker Alco Bus **2.99**

265-2117 Chausson Motor Bus **2.99**

CONSTRUCTION EQUIPMENT

265-2069 Camion Dump Truck **1.99**

265-2086 4-Wheel Construction Crane **2.99**

265-2087 Dump Truck **2.99**

265-2096 Pegaso Cement Semi-Truck **3.99**

265-2103 Unic Cement Mixer **2.99**

265-2104 Pegaso Cement Mixer **2.99**

265-2112 Caterpillar Earth Mover **2.99**

265-2113 Pala Excavator **2.99**

265-2125 Heavy Duty Berliet Dump Truck **2.99**

EMERGENCY VEHICLES

265-2029 Ford Ambulance **1.99**

265-2019 Fire Truck w/Ladder **2.99**

265-2093 Pegaso Fire Truck **2.99**

265-2097 Pegaso Hook/Ladder Truck **2.99**

FARM MACHINERY

265-2114 Hanamog Farm Tractor **1.99**

MILITARY VEHICLES

WORLD WAR II

TRUCKS-US

265-2056 GMC Truck Flatbed **2.99**

265-2057 GMC Flatbed Truck w/Top **2.99**

265-2058 GMC Tank Truck **2.99**

265-4022 Military Jeep **1.99**

265-4024 GMC 2.5 Ton M-35 **2.99**

265-4025 GMC 2.5 Ton Tank/Truck M35 **2.99**

IMPORTED FROM SPAIN
BY WALTHERS

265-4026 GMC Truck M-35 **2.99**

265-4028 GMC M35 Canvas Covered Truck **2.99**

265-4036 DUKW 6x6 Amphibious "Duck" **3.99**

TANKS-US

265-4012 M4 Sherman **2.99**

ARMORED VEHICLES-US

265-4002 M8 Cochise Armored Car **1.99**

265-4041 M36 **2.99**

TANK-GERMANY EA 2.99

265-4009 Panther

265-4010 Tiger

265-4039 Panzer III

ARMORED VEHICLES-GERMANY

265-4042 KM 8 Ton Anti-Aircraft Half Track **2.99**

ARTILLERY-GERMANY

265-4006 Light Cannon **1.99**

TRUCKS-ENGLAND EA 1.99

265-4023 Military Land Rover

265-4044 Slava Ambulance
265-4045 Large Military Land Rover

TANKS-ENGLAND EA 2.99

265-4004 Centurion

265-4043 Matilda MK II

TANKS-SOVIET UNION

265-4001 T34 Tipo Standard **2.99**

POST-WAR

TRUCKS-US

265-4007 Jeep Truck **1.99**
265-4015 Military Truck **2.99**

265-4016 Military Truck w/Cargo **2.99**

265-4027 GMC M35 Truck w/Rocket **3.99**

TANKS-US EA 2.99

265-4003 M48 General Patton II

265-4008 M47 General Patton

265-4014 M41 Walker Bulldog

ARMORED VEHICLES-US EA 2.99

265-4018 Anti-Aircraft M-42

265-4019 M40

265-4030 T235

265-4031 T245

265-4032 Crane T120

265-4033 T198

265-4034 T113 Troop Transport

TANKS-FRANCE

265-4011 AMX 13 **1.99**

265-4017 Wheeled Tank EBR75 **1.99**

265-4038 AMX **2.99**

TRUCKS-GERMAN

265-4005 Mercedes Unimog **1.99**

265-40051 Unimog w/Light Cannon **2.99**

TANKS-GERMAN

265-4040 Panzer P111 **2.99**

TANKS-SOVIET UNION EA 2.99

265-4013 T54

265-4020 PT76-USSR

265-4029 Stalin

ARMORED VEHICLES-SOVIET UNION

265-4021 BTR50 Personnel Carrier **2.99**

TRUCKS-SPAIN

265-4035 TT90.22 Truck **1.99**

265-4037 Thornycroft Mighty Antar Transport **3.99**
Vehicles are molded in appropriately colored plastic, with painted details. Markings may vary from what is shown in catalog.

TRUCKS

DKW

265-2007 Pickup **1.99**

FORD

265-2013 Flatbed **1.99**

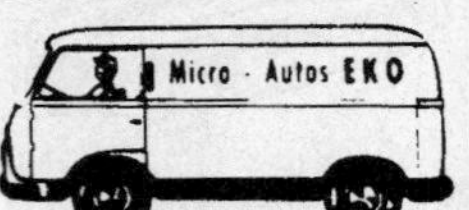

265-2028 Panel Truck **1.99**

265-2020 Gas Oil Tank Truck **2.99**

IMPORTED FROM SPAIN
BY WALTHERS

265-2014 Flatbed w/Canvas Top **2.99**

265-2030 Microbus **1.99**

265-2091 Ford Thames/Flatbed **1.99**

MAGIRUS

265-2015 Flatbed **1.99**

265-2016 Flatbed w/Canvas Top **2.99**

265-2024 Tank Truck **2.99**

PEGASO

265-2092 Delivery Truck **2.99**

265-2066 Cement Delivery **2.99**

265-2094 Tank **2.99**

265-2095 Semi Tank Truck **3.99**

265-2126 Semi w/Van Trailer **3.99**

THAMES EA 2.99

265-2119 Flatbed Truck

265-2120 Soda Delivery Truck

265-2121 Beer Delivery Truck

SAVA EA 2.99

265-2122 Butane Delivery

265-2123 Garbage Truck

SEMI TRUCKS

265-2111 Antar Semi Lo-Boy w/Cargo **2.99**

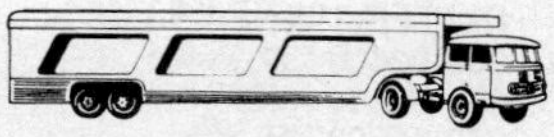

265-2023 Mercedes Car Transport **3.99**

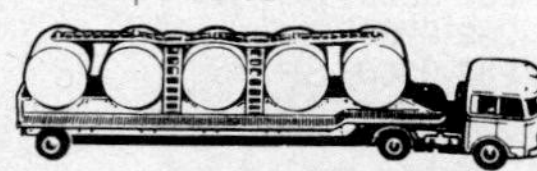

265-2046 Tank Transport **3.99**

265-2068 Double Bottom Truck **3.99**

265-2118 Titan Semi Lo-Boy **4.99**

MISCELLANEOUS

265-2034 Citroen 2CV **1.99**

265-2067 Barreiros Van **2.99**

265-2017 Eko Cola Truck **2.99**

265-2018 Piper Cola Truck **2.99**

265-2090 Panel Truck Furgon **1.99**

For Daily Product Information Click

www.walthers.com

ERTL®

FARM MACHINERY

TRACTORS EA 9.25

264-4214 Modern Case MU7, Maxxum FWA

264-4254 Vintage IH 856

264-5460 Vintage JD 4020

264-5461 Modern JD 8300

COMBINE

264-5468 John Deere 9510 Maximizer Combine **26.99** ***NEW***

TRUCKS

Set the scene along your HO Scale highways with these models of vintage and modern rigs. Each is complete with tractor and trailer.

CONVENTIONAL SEMIS

1948 PETERBILT
With minor changes, this same style of cab was built from 1939 through 1949, making these models ideal for late steam- or early diesel-era layouts.

264-4210 With Flatbed Trailer & 2 International 756 Tractors **40.00**

264-4266 With Vintage Van Trailer **30.00**

264-4517 With Box Trailer **25.00**

264-5458 With Flatbed Trailer & 2 Vintage JD 4020 Tractors **40.00**

KENWORTH® T600B
The T600B provides improved fuel economy and a stylish, modern appearance. The integral sleeper makes this rig a favorite for long-distance runs.

264-4212 With Flatbed Trailer & 2 Maxxum 2wd Tractors **40.00**
264-4518 With Modern Drop-Box Trailer **25.00**
264-5459 With Flatbed Trailer & 2 Modern JD 8300 Tractors **40.00**

Kenworth® T600B w/2 Tractors 264-4212

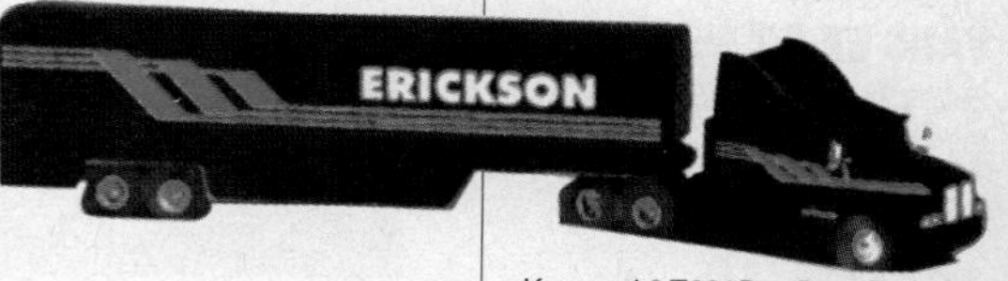

Kenworth® T600B w/Drop Box Trailer 264-4518

Kenworth® T600B w/JD 8300 Tractors 264-5459

E-R Models™

NEW SUPPLIER

AUTOMOBILES

CHEVY

262-93001 Caprice Checker Cab **12.95** *NEW*

BUSES

262-90851 Prisoner Transport **16.95** *NEW*

EMERGENCY VEHICLES

CHEVY

262-90453 Police Van **12.95** *NEW*

262-90501 Yellow Ambulance **14.95** *NEW*

CHEVY BLAZER EA 13.49

262-92608 Highway Patrol 1997 *NEW*
262-92652 New York State Patrol 1997 *NEW*
262-92653 US Border Patrol 1997 *NEW*
262-92681 Fire Chief 1997 *NEW*

JEEP GRAND CHEROKEE EA 13.95

262-90751 Fire Chief *NEW*
262-90752 Airport Police *NEW*

VANS EA 12.95

262-92951 Crime Scene Investigator *NEW*
262-92954 Accident Investigation *NEW*

JEEPS

GRAND CHEROKEE

262-90702 UP **13.95** *NEW*

TRUCKS

CHEVY

RAILROAD PICKUP 1950 EA 12.95

262-92101 NYC *NEW*

262-92102 MOPAC *NEW*

262-92103 SP *NEW*

262-92104 UP *NEW*
262-92105 CNW *NEW*

262-92106 ATSF *NEW*

262-92107 MILW *NEW*
262-92108 NH *NEW*
262-92109 LV *NEW*
262-92110 MKT *NEW*

262-92111 PRR *NEW*

262-92112 D&H *NEW*

262-92113 Railway Express Agency *NEW*

262-92114 Erie *NEW*
262-92115 ROCK *NEW*

BLAZER 1997 EA 13.49

262-92600 CR *NEW*
262-92601 ATSF *NEW*
262-92602 UP *NEW*
262-92603 CSX *NEW*
262-92604 NS *NEW*
262-92605 Amtrak *NEW*
262-92606 SP *NEW*
262-92607 CNW *NEW*

DODGE EA 12.95

262-91012 Dave's Towing *NEW*
262-91013 Tony's Towing *NEW*

FORD

262-92001 AA Railway Express Agency 1931 **13.95** *NEW*

VANS

262-92961 Plumber **12.95** *NEW*
262-92962 Citywide Cable Service **12.95** *NEW*
262-92963 Coroner **12.95** *NEW*
262-92964 Carpet Cleaner **12.95** *NEW*
262-92966 Electrician **12.95** *NEW*
262-92985 Florist **12.95** *NEW*

CHEVY

262-90412 TNT Electric **13.95** *NEW*
262-90413 Water Heater **13.95** *NEW*
262-90417 Port Authority **13.50** *NEW*

CHRYSLER CREW MINIVANS EA 12.95

262-92400 CR *NEW*
262-92401 ATSF *NEW*
262-92402 UP *NEW*
262-92403 CSX *NEW*
262-92404 NS *NEW*
262-92405 Amtrak *NEW*
262-92406 SP *NEW*
262-92407 CNW *NEW*
262-92452 Highway Patrol Commercial Vehicle Enforcement *NEW*

RAILROAD MAINTENANCE EA 12.95

262-92900 CR *NEW*
262-92901 ATSF *NEW*
262-92902 UP *NEW*
262-92903 CSX *NEW*
262-92904 NS *NEW*
262-92905 Amtrak *NEW*
262-92906 SP *NEW*
262-92907 CNW *NEW*

GLOOR CRAFT MODELS

STEP VAN

288-3800 1960s Chevrolet **7.95**
Kit features cast metal construction and is unpainted.

45' TRAILERS

Wood construction with cast metal details. Undecorated.

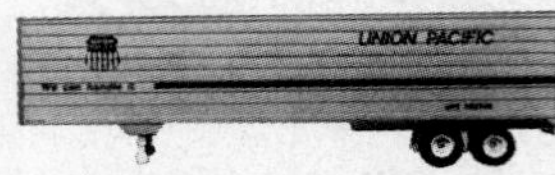

288-3803 Box Van **15.95**

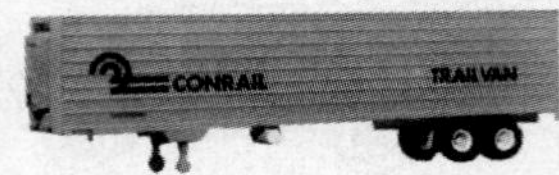

288-3804 Refrigerated **16.95**

MASTER CREATIONS

Brass models, fully assembled.

TRUCKS

464-820 1920 Oldsmobile Truck **24.95**

WAGONS

464-504 Logging Wagon **39.95**

METAL MINIATURES

CONSTRUCTION EQUIPMENT EA 4.00

Unpainted, one-piece cast metal vehicles.

340-32 Clark Fork Lift pkg(2) *NEW*
340-36 Bulldozer

340-44 Caterpillar® Tractor

Information STATION

Standard Time

In the days before Standrad. Time, travel by train could be very difficult.Most communities relied on "sun time," setting clocks when the sun was overhead at noon. Or they depended on a local jeweler or church sexton who set a community clock.As a result, the time in cities just a few miles apart would differ by several minutes. This resulted in nearly one hundred "local" times that railroads were using across the U.S. to set schedules. These were replaced on November 18, 1883 when Standard Time was introduced. This standardization created the four time zones, each one hour apart, whose names are still used today; Eastern, Central, Mountain and Pacific. This idea was sponsored and put into effect by the General Time Convention of Railway Managers. But it took 35 more years until Congress passed the Standard Time Act in March of 1918 that made this the official time for the entire country.

FALLER

IMPORTED FROM GERMANY BY WALTHERS

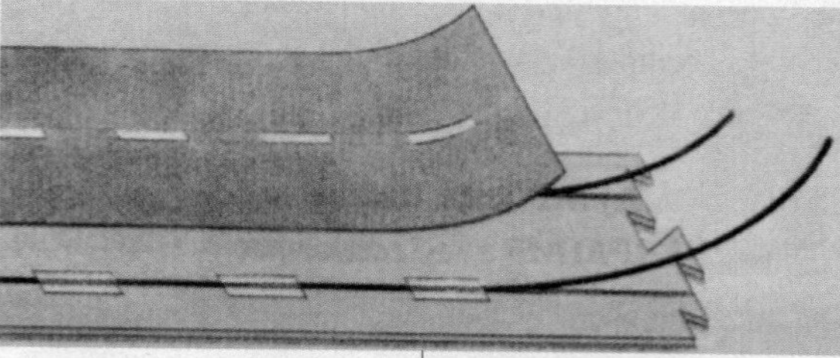

Straight Roadway 272-1650

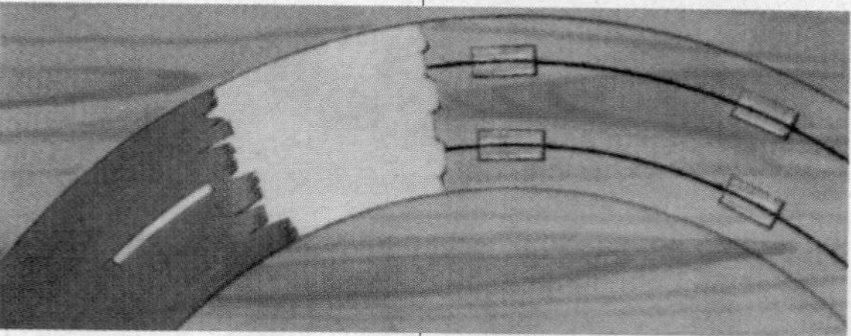

Small Curves Roadway 272-1660

City Tour Car System Starter Set 272-1635

CAR SYSTEM

Add a new dimension of realism to your railroad, as vehicles move along streets and highways under their own power!

CAR SYSTEM STARTER SETS

272-1626 Tour Bus Set **71.99** Includes powered Wiking Bus with 11' (10m) of guide wire, automatic stop switch, roadway filler material, asphalt paint, dry transfer roadway markings, crash barriers and marker posts.

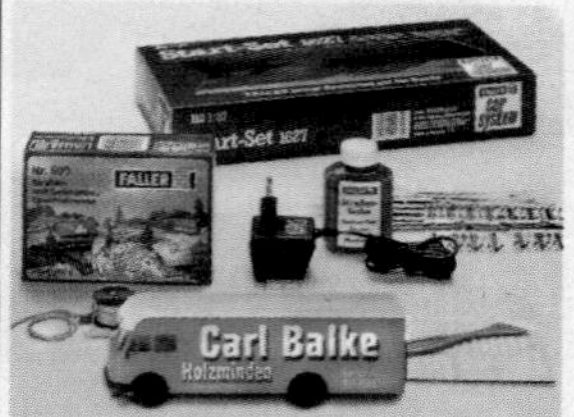

272-1627 Carl Balke House Movers **149.99** Includes powered Brekina moving van with custom graphics, 11' (10m) of guide wire, automatic stopping switch, roadway filler material, asphalt paint, dry transfer roadway markings, crash barriers and marker posts.

272-1629 Garbage Truck **125.99** Make the rounds of your city with this set. Includes MAN Garbage Truck, battery charger, complete oval of roadway and instructions.

272-1630 Südkraft MAN Truck & Trailer **161.99** Includes a powered Herpa truck and two-axle trailer, both decorated for Südkraft International Shippers, plus 11' (10m) of guide wire, automatic stopping switch, roadway filler material, asphalt paint, dry transfer roadway markings, crash barriers and marker posts.

272-1635 City Tour **124.99** *NEW* Includes powered Wiking Bus (Mercedes O 303), eight roadway sections and guide wire.

272-1636 Delivery Truck **74.99** *NEW* Includes powered Herpa Truck (Mercedes SK Box Van), Roadway sections, stop switch and other accessories.

CAR SYSTEM ROADWAY

The Faller Car System roadway offers complete design flexibility, so you can build wide or narrow streets, curves, moderate grades, straights, one-way streets, freeways or virtually any other modern road. Each set includes self-adhesive road surface in realistic colors, diecut cardboard base sections and guide wire. Base pieces interlock like a jigsaw puzzle, so installation is fast and easy. For custom applications, you can cut the various pieces to fit, or just install the guide wire in new or existing streets.

CURVES 2-LANE EA 21.99

272-1660 Small pkg(6) Includes two 90° and four 45° curved sections. Radius is about 8-1/2" 212mm.

272-1665 Large pkg(4) Includes four 45° curved roadway sections, Radius is about 17" 424mm.

STRAIGHT

272-1650 21.99 Includes six straight 2-lane roadway sections, each 12" 30cm long.

CAR SYSTEM ROADWAY ACCESSORIES

272-506 Roadway Paint 7-1/2oz 250ml **7.99** Special formula for use with Car System roadways, dries to a realistic grayish-black.

272-591 Roadway Markings **9.99** Self-adhesive rub-on transfer lines, arrows and more, all in white.

272-592 Crash Barriers **9.99** Includes 32 lane marker posts and 32" 80cm of crash barrier.

272-1670 Guide Wire 33' 9.9m **9.99**

DIVERGING ROUTES

272-1662 Turn-Off Lanes **21.99** Left and right hand diverging routes create more interesting road systems. Includes instructions, requires Switch #1676 or #1677, sold separately.

DIVERGING ROUTE SWITCHES EA 22.99

272-1676 Electro-Mechanical
272-1677 Electrical
Use these switches with #1662 to route vehicles straight ahead or onto a diverging route. Requires 12-16 volts DC or AC power, can be used on right or left.

INTERSECTION

272-1661 22.99 Includes special intersection piece, plus four straight sections. Can be enlarged with 1650,1660, & 1665, sold separately. Measures 5-7/8 x 5-7/8" 15 x 15cm.

BUS STOP

272-1671 129.99 Animate your city streets or rural roads with this conversion. Includes special controls which allow a bus (sold separately) to turn off the main road, come to a stop, then pull back onto the highway.

RAILROAD CROSSING

272-1657 8.99 Specially cut and marked roadway surfaces, plus a track filler piece allow Car System vehicles to cross tracks. Works with most track systems.

STOP SECTION

272-1675 15.99 Brings vehicles to a stop automatically, great for all kinds of special effects. Permanent electro-magnet operates reed switches on all vehicles. Operates on 12-16 volts DC.

TRAFFIC LIGHTS

272-1655 Signals w/Switch pkg(2) **74.99** A great accessory for use with #1661, operates up to four signals through the full sequence of green-yellow-red and brings vehicles to a safe stop in both directions! Includes fully assembled micro-processor to control electronics, operates on 12-16 volts AC or DC.

272-1656 Traffic Lights-Less Switch pkg(2) **39.99** Additional signals for use with #1655.

CAR SYSTEM VEHICLES

Car System vehicles are fully assembled, with a can type motor, and built-in reed switch for use with accessories. Power is supplied by a pair of rechargeable ni-cad batteries. A built-in socket allows batteries to be charged in the vehicle. (Charging time is about seven hours, and vehicles will operate for many hours on a full charge.) Riding on rubber tires, each vehicle actually steers as it moves around corners. The front axle has a fully operational linkage and a strong magnet that follows the hidden guide wire. (Colors and markings of vehicles may vary from what is shown)

POWERED VEHICLES

BUSES

272-1610 Mercedes Small Touring Bus **104.99**

272-1611 Mercedes German Post Office Bus (yellow) **104.99**
272-1612 Mercedes 0 302 **104.99**

FALLER

IMPORTED FROM GERMANY BY WALTHERS

272-1613 Mercedes 0 302 (red) **99.99**
272-1614 City Bus Mercedes O 405 **104.99** ***NEW***

272-1639 Mercedes Sprinter Passenger Van **104.99**
272-1643 Route Service Bus Mercedes O 317K **104.99** ***NEW***
272-1689 Travel Agency Schwenkkraus Tour Bus Setra S315 HDH **104.99** ***NEW***
272-1691 Mercedes 0 405 Dekra **99.99**

272-1692 Setra S 315 HDH **99.99**

272-1694 Mercedes Sprinter **99.99**

EMERGENCY VEHICLES

272-1637 VW Mini-Bus Emergency **104.99**

272-1644 Mercedes G Disaster Control Service **104.99**

272-1693 THW Rescue Truck **109.99**

City Bus Mercedes 272-1614

Route Service Bus Mercedes 272-1643

Travel Agency Schwenkkraus Tour Bus Setra 272-1689

272-1695 Mercedes Sprinter Ambulance **99.99**

Limited Quantity Available

272-1625 Mercedes Unimog Equipment Truck **104.99**

VANS & RVS EA 104.99

272-1624 Mercedes Panel Van
272-1638 Volkswagen Pickup w/Cover "German Post Office"

272-1640 Mercedes Sprinter United German Post Office ***NEW***

TRAILERS

272-1696 Schenker & Faller Car System 4-Wheel Trailers **19.99**

TRUCKS

272-1601 Mercedes Actros Tractor & Trailer **119.99**
272-1602 Mercedes w/Lowenbrau Trailer **119.99**
272-1603 Bussing Moving Van & Trailer Schenker & Co. **119.99**

272-1604 MAN F90 Delivery Truck **114.99**
272-1605 Mercedes SK with Dry Bulk Trailer **119.99**

272-1609 IVECO Truck w/Working Brake Lights **114.99**
272-1619 MAN F2000 w/Dump Trailer **119.99**
272-1621 MAN Diesel Moving Van w/2-Axle Trailer **119.99** ***NEW***

272-1685 MAN & Mercedes SK w/4-Wheel Trailers **199.99**
272-1686 Mercedes Actros 3-Axle Box Van w/2-Axle Trailer **119.99** ***NEW***
272-1687 MAN 2-Axle Box Van w/3-Axle Trailer Alfrede Talke **119.99** ***NEW***

Schenker & Faller Car System 272-1696

Mercedes Actros Tractor & Trailer 272-1601

Mercedes w/ Lowenbrau Trailer 272-1602

Bussing Moving Van & Trailer 272-1603

Mercedes SK w/Dry Bulk Trailer 272-1605

MAN F2000 w/Dump Trailer 272-1619

MAN Diesel Moving Van 272-1621

Mercedes Actros 3-Axle Box Van 272-1686

MAN 2-Axle Box Van 272-1687

IMPORTED FROM GERMANY BY WALTHERS

Limited Quantity Available

272-1606 Mercedes Van & Trailer "Dischinger" **123.99**

272-1608 Mercedes Moving Van w/Trailer **121.49**

272-1617 MAN Moving Van w/Four-Axle Trailer **119.99**

CAR SYSTEM ACCESSORIES

TRUCK-RAIL ROLL-ON/OFF

Add a working intermodal ramp to your Car System equipped layout with this exciting accessory. Trucks actually pull onto flats and drive ahead, coming to a stop on the empty car. At the end of the line, simply switch the motor back on with an electromagnet hidden under the tracks and trucks drive off under their own power! Magnets are designed to fit Marklin or Fleischmann flat cars, (sold separately). Complete ramp requires one each #1680 and 1681.

272-1680 Basic Car Conversion Set **112.99**
Includes one flat car conversion set (two permanent magnets, one for each end of the car), contact wire and two electromagnets. For intermediate size flats such as Marklin 4741, or Fleischmann #5271, sold separately. Designed for use with Ramp #1682, sold separately.

272-1681 Rail Roll-On/Off Add-On Set **59.99** *NEW*
Additional magnets and accessories to convert Intermediate Flats from Marklin (#4741) or Fleischmann (#5271), both sold separately. Includes one car insert with two magnets, contact wire and two electromagnets.

272-1682 Loading Platform Only **15.99**
Installs in minutes, allows trucks to drive directly onto flat cars. For use with Marklin K or M Track (M Track requires transition piece from M to K track) or Fleischmann. Designed for use with Basic Set #1680, sold separately.

VEHICLE BATTERY CHARGER

272-16000 Car System Charger **18.99**
Charges batteries in approximately seven hours. Input: 12 VA 60 Hz 5W Output: 3V DC 200 mA.

UNPOWERED VEHICLES

TRUCKS

272-1025 Mercedes Service Truck **19.49**

Limited Quantity Available

272-1020 MAN F90 w/Self-Loader **15.49**

272-1021 MAN F90 **15.49**

272-1026 Mercedes Service Truck "Break Dancer" **24.99**

TRAILERS

272-1036 3-Axle **17.99**
272-1037 3-Axle w/Stakes **15.49**

272-1038 3-Axle w/Container **18.99**

Limited Quantity Available

272-1032 2-Axle, Long **19.99**

TRAILERS

BARRETT LIVESTOCK TRAILER

Authorized replicas are based on one of the most common designs in use. The easy-to-build plastic kits include photo-etched stainless steel sides, providing the realism of scale thickness and see-through walls. The kits can be used with any HO Scale semi tractor and include decals.

437-4105 Two Hand Hole-Early Style **24.95**

437-4205 Four Hand Hole-Modern Style **24.95**
437-4305 Hog & Sheep, Triple Deck, Three Hand Hole-Early Style **24.95**
437-4405 Hog & Sheep, Triple Deck, Four Hand Hole-Modern Style **24.95**

ASSEMBLED EA 44.95

437-4125 Two Hand Hole-Early Style
437-4225 Four Hand Hole-Modern Style (Assembled)

40' TRAILMOBILE FLATBED TRAILER EA 15.95

Each easy-to-build kit includes a laser-cut wood deck, plus two optional styles of bulkheads. You can also build a straight flatbed with no bulkhead. The kits offer a choice of round dollies or flat feet for the landing gear.

437-5000 Standard (red)
437-5009 Black
437-5010 Construction (yellow)
437-5011 UP (Tuscan Red)
437-5012 BN (green)
437-5013 ATSF (white)
437-5014 US Army (green)
437-5015 Viking Freight (blue)
437-5016 GN (green)
437-5017 Strick Lease (red)
437-5018 JB Hunt *NEW*
437-5019 MOPAC *NEW*
437-5020 ROCK *NEW*
437-5021 D&H *NEW*
437-5022 Schneider National *NEW*
437-5001 Undecorated (gray)

FORD FLATBED LUMBER TRUCK W/20' FLATBED EA 17.95 (UNLESS NOTED)

Kit features a Herpa Ford L9000 assembled truck cab, door decals and a photo-etched grill for protecting the cab's rear window. Door decals are included (with permission from Walthers and Atlas) for the Walthers "Walton & Sons" lumber yard and the Atlas "hillside Lumber" yard to match the graphics in these kits, making them perfect accessories.

437-5200 Black
437-5201 Red
437-5202 Gray
437-5203 Payless Cashways **18.95** *NEW*
Features a special red truck frame.

FORD L9000 W/STAKE BED EA 18.95

437-7001 With Black Bed *NEW*
437-7002 With Blue Bed *NEW*
437-7003 With Red Bed *NEW*
437-7004 With White Bed *NEW*
437-7005 ATSF MOW *NEW*
437-7006 UP MOW *NEW*
437-7007 SP MOW *NEW*
437-7000 With Undecorated Gray Bed *NEW*

STAKE BED (METAL TYPE) EA 9.95

437-7021 Black *NEW*
437-7022 Blue *NEW*
437-7023 Red *NEW*
437-7024 White *NEW*
437-7020 Undecorated Gray *NEW*

20' LUMBER TRUCK BED ONLY EA 9.95

437-5210 Black
437-5211 Red
437-5212 Gray

WILSON GRAIN TRAILER

Constructed of molded aluminum, this grain trailer feature Air Ride suspension and can be built with the tarp open or closed.

437-6000 With Light Blue Tarp **19.95** *NEW*
437-6001 With Black Tarp **19.95** *NEW*
437-6002 With Light Blue Tarp & Prepainted White Panels **21.95** *NEW*
437-6003 With Black Tarp & Prepainted Black Panels **21.95** *NEW*

437-6004 With Dark Blue Tarp **19.95** *NEW*

TRAILER ACCESSORIES

BRAKE DETAIL KITS EA 4.50

437-12200 Black *NEW*
437-12201 Aluminum *NEW*
437-12202 White *NEW*
437-12203 Red *NEW*

TRAILER WHEELS EA 4.50

Each package Includes mud flaps

10-HOLE WHEELS W/TIRES

437-12100 Aluminum *NEW*
437-12101 White *NEW*
437-12102 Chrome *NEW*

WITH TIRES

Includes eight spoked-style wheels, 16 tires and four axles.

437-12001 White
437-12002 Black
437-12003 Silver

WITHOUT TIRES

Contains 16 spoked-style wheels and eight axles.

437-12004 White
437-12005 Black
437-12006 Silver

2-HOLE WHEELS W/TIRES

437-12103 White *NEW*

TIRES ONLY

437-12104 pkg(24) **4.50** *NEW*

TRAILER MUD FLAPS PKG(12) EA 4.50

437-12013 White
437-12014 Black

MARKER & TAIL LIGHT LENSES EA 4.50

Each package features two sets and features 12 tail lights and 48 marker lights.

437-12015 Red
437-12016 Amber
437-12017 Clear
437-12018 Blue
437-12019 Green
437-12020 With Stainless Steel Frame Trim

Set the scene on your highways with these assembled, plastic models based on European and American prototypes. Each is finely detailed with interiors, rolling wheels and "glass." Many are offered in either a standard or a brighter metallic paint scheme. High Tech models feature opening hoods and detailed engines, some also feature metal chassis.

AUTOMOBILE SETS

WKW EXCLUSIVE

326-1 MB/VW Rabbit pkg(2) **9.95**

AMERICAN AUTOMOBILES

BUICK

326-22026 Grand National **8.25**

FORD EA 8.25

326-21975 AC Cobra

326-22019 1969 Mustang

326-22033 1989 Thunderbird

CHEVROLET EA 8.25

326-21982 1957 Bel Air

326-32049 1985 Camaro

CORVETTE

326-21968 1963 Sting Ray

326-21999 Corvette-ZR1

CHRYSLER

GRAND CHEROKEE

326-6187 All-Terrain **7.50**

INDY RACE CARS EA 9.25

326-22170 Type S

326-22187 Type F

PONTIAC

326-22002 Grand Prix **8.25**

EUROPEAN AUTOMOBILES

ALFA ROMEO

326-21876 Racing Version **11.50**

326-22293 1996 White **11.50**

326-22439 155 STW 1997 Racing Version (white) **10.95** *NEW*

For Daily Product Information Click

www.walthers.com

AUDI

326-25201 90 Quattro Coupe **12.50**

326-30922 V8 Metallic Paint **8.95**

A4

326-22477 STW 4-Door Sedan '97 **10.95**

326-22491 Standard **8.75**
326-32490 Metallic **9.50**

CONVERTIBLE

326-21074 Standard **8.50**
326-31073 Metallic Paint **8.95**

COUPE

326-31080 Metallic Paint **8.95**

BMW

AC SCHNITZER

326-22521 Standard **8.95**
326-32520 Metallic **9.50**
326-32568 S5 4-Door Sedan-Metallic Paint **9.50** *NEW*

326-22569 S5 4-Door Sedan **8.75** *NEW*
326-32612 S5 Touring 4-Door Station Wagon-Metallic Paint **9.50** *NEW*

326-22613 S5 Touring 4-Door Station Wagon **8.95** *NEW*

3 SERIES 1998 MODEL

326-22545 Standard **8.75**
326-32544 Metallic **9.50**

528I TOURING

326-22323 Without Roof Rack-Standard **8.95**

326-22347 With Roof Rack-Standard **8.95**
326-32322 Without Roof Rack-Metallic **9.95**
326-32346 With Roof Rack-Metallic **9.95**

1602

326-22309 Standard **8.50**

5 SERIES SEDAN

326-21920 Standard **9.50**
326-31929 Metallic Paint **10.50**

320I

326-188388 Sedan Tucher Brewing (blue w/special graphics) **15.95** *NEW*

325 CONVERTIBLE

326-21388 Standard **8.95**
326-31387 Metallic **9.95**

326-21791 Soft Top **10.50**
326-30892 Sedan-Metallic Paint **9.50**

326-22071 Coupe/Hardtop **10.50**
326-32070 Metallic **11.95**

326-30595 Metallic **7.95**
326-31790 Metallic **11.95**

502

326-22279 4-Door Sedan **9.25**

535I

326-20657 **7.95**
326-30065 Sedan Alpina-Metallic **19.95**

7 SERIES

326-22620 Restyled 1998 4-Door Sedan **8.95** *NEW*
326-32629 Restyled 1998 4-Door Sedan-Metallic Paint **9.95** *NEW*

740I SEDAN

326-31646 Metallic **9.50**

M3

326-22514 Schnitzer-Standard **8.95**
326-32513 Schnitzer-Metallic **9.50**

326-21616 GTR Coupe w/Spoiler **11.50**

M5

326-22644 4-Door Sedan **8.95** *NEW*
326-32643 4-Door Sedan-Metallic Paint **9.95** *NEW*
326-22712 4-Door Sedan w/Trailer & Motorcycle **18.50** *NEW*

Z1 CONVERTIBLE COUPE

326-30748 Metallic Paint **8.95**

Z3

326-21937 Roadster Standard **9.50**

326-22453 Coupe-Standard **8.95**

326-22460 M Coupe-Standard **8.95**

326-22507 Softtop-Standard **9.95**
326-32452 Coupe-Metallic **9.50**
326-32469 M Coupe-Metallic **9.95**
326-32506 Softtop-Metallic **9.95**

CITROEN

2CV SEDAN

326-20817 "Charleston" **6.50**

326-20824 Metallic **5.95**

EVASION MINI VAN

326-21708 Standard **9.50**
326-31707 Metallic **10.95**

FERRARI

All models feature High Tech details.

348 EA 12.50

326-25256 tb (red)

326-25300 ts (red)

TESTAROSSA

326-25454 512 Yellow **12.95**

F-40

326-25102 F40 (Red) **12.50**

F-50 EA 17.95 (UNLESS NOTED)

326-101097 Closed (red) **21.95**

326-25485 Hi-Tech
326-25492 Convertible

GTO

326-32032 1962 Model **8.95**

FIAT

124 SPIDER

326-22354 Standard **8.95**

CINQUECENTO HARDTOP COUPE

326-21142 Standard **6.50**

ULYSSES MINI VAN

326-21715 Standard **9.50**
326-31714 Metallic **10.95**

FORD

GALAXY MINI VAN

326-21821 Standard **9.50**

JAGUAR

326-30205 XJ12 Sedan-Metallic **7.95**
326-32018 E Type **8.95**

HONDA

326-22538 Accord STW 1997 Model (white) **9.95** ***NEW***

LAMBORGHINI COUPE

326-25423 Diablo High Tech (black) **12.95**

MAZDA

323F

326-21739 Standard **8.25**

MX5 CONVERTIBLE COUPE

326-21418 Standard **8.95**
326-31417 Metallic **9.95**

XEDOS 9 SEDAN

326-21500 Standard **8.95**

MERCEDES

CLK

326-22378 Standard **9.50**
326-32377 Metallic **10.50**

326-22583 Convertible Coupe w/Top Up **9.95** ***NEW***
326-32582 Convertible Coupe w/Top Up-Metallic Paint **9.95** ***NEW***

A CLASS

326-22385 Standard **9.50**

326-22415 With Roof Carrier & Surfboard - Standard **13.50**
326-32384 Metallic **10.50**

C CLASS FACELIFT

326-22392 Tour T-Modell-Standard **8.95**

326-22422 Limousine-Standard **8.95**
326-32391 Tour T-Modell-Metallic **9.95**
326-32421 Limousine-Metallic **9.95**

C 180 T

326-22095 Standard **8.95**

326-32094 Metallic **9.95**
326-22255 1996 White **11.50**

C 220 SEDAN

326-31400 Metallic **9.95**

E 280

326-21814 Standard **9.50**
326-31813 Metallic **10.25**

300 SL

326-32025 Gull Wing Coupe **8.95**

E320 CONVERTIBLE COUPE

326-31431 Metallic **9.95**

E320 T STATION WAGON

326-22118 Standard **9.25**
326-32117 Metallic **9.95**

E320 COUPE

326-21456 Standard **8.50**
326-31455 Metallic **9.50**

500 SL COUPE

Metalic with glass roof.

326-25409 High Tech **12.95**
326-25461 High Tech **13.95**

500SL

326-25164 2-Door Hardtop High Tech Series (red) **11.50** ***NEW***

SLK ROADSTER

326-22149 Standard **11.50**
326-32148 Metallic **12.60**

S-CLASS

326-22699 4-Door Sedan **9.95** ***NEW***
326-32698 4-Door Sedan-Metallic Paint **10.50** ***NEW***

V-CLASS

326-32131 Metallic **9.95**

MINI COOPER

FACELIFT

326-22248 Standard **8.75**
326-32247 Metallic **9.50**

326-22330 Folding Top Open, Standard **8.50**
326-32339 Folding Top Open, Metallic **9.50**

SPOKE WHEELS

326-21104 Standard **8.95**
326-31103 Metallic **9.50**

SUNROOF

326-21777 Standard **8.95**
326-32063 Closed Sunroof-Metallic **9.50**

MAYFAIR HARDTOP COUPE

326-31196 Metallic **9.50**

OPEL

CALIBRA

326-21852 Racing Version **11.50**

CORSA GLS COUPE

326-21357 Standard **7.50**
326-42840 German Post Office (New Scheme) **8.95**

CORSA GSI

326-21395 **7.50**
326-31370 4-Door-Metallic **7.50**

"FASTBACK" SEDAN

326-21913 Standard **8.95**

326-31905 Metallic **9.95**

OMEGA

326-31523 GT Sedan-Metallic **9.95**
326-43410 Taxi **12.50**

OMEGA MV6 SEDAN

326-31554 Metallic **9.95**

OMEGA CARAVAN MV6 WAGON

326-21562 Standard **8.95**
326-31561 Metallic **9.95**

TIGRA COMPACT COUPE

326-21746 Standard **8.25**
326-31745 Metallic **8.95**

VECTRA

326-21906 Standard **8.95**
326-31912 Metallic **9.95**

VETRA SEDAN

326-22651 Vectra 1998 STW Sedan w/Spoiler (white) **10.95** *NEW*

VETRA STATION WAGON

326-22156 Standard **9.25**
326-32155 Metallic **9.95**

PEUGEOT

205

326-3069 Turbo (Metallic Paint) **6.50** *NEW*

406

326-22590 Sedan **8.95** *NEW*
326-32599 Sedan-Metallic Paint **9.50** *NEW*
326-22668 STW Street Version **10.50** *NEW*

806 MINI VAN

326-31653 Metallic **10.95**

PORSCHE

356B CABRIOLET

326-22286 Standard **9.25**

996

326-22484 Standard **10.95**

326-22552 Convertible Coupe w/Top Down **9.95** *NEW*
326-32483 Metallic **11.95**
326-32551 Convertible Coupe w/Top Down-Metallic Paint **10.50** *NEW*

911

326-21890 Standard **11.50**
326-32162 Carrera-Metallic **12.50**
326-22163 Carrera **11.50**
326-22231 S-Standard Paint **11.50**

326-22408 1966 Standard **8.95**

326-22606 GT3 2-Door Hardtop w/Spoiler **9.95** *NEW*
326-32674 Carrera 4 Convertible Coupe w/Top Down-Metallic Paint **11.50** *NEW*

326-22675 Carrera 4 Convertible Coupe w/Top Down **10.50** *NEW*

326-22682 Carrera 4 2-Door Hardtop **10.50** *NEW*
326-31899 Metallic **11.50**
326-32087 RS Metallic **12.50**
326-32230 S-Metallic **12.50**
326-32605 GT3 2-Door Hardtop w/Spoiler-Metallic Paint **10.95** *NEW*
326-32681 Carrera 4 2-Door Hardtop-Metallic Paint **11.50** *NEW*
326-37464 Rs Clubsport D.Muller **25.95**

BOXSTER

326-22194 Standard **11.50**
326-32193 Metallic **12.50**

CARRERA S 4

326-21944 Standard **11.50**
326-31943 Metallic **12.50**

TURBO COUPE

326-20602 Standard **7.50**
326-30601 Metallic **7.95**

928

326-45056 Dreams Art Collection-Special Paint **26.95** *NEW*

928 S4 COUPE

326-20718 Standard **7.50**
326-30717 Metallic **7.95**

959 COUPE-HIGH TECH

326-25010 Red **12.50**

RENAULT

LAGUNA SEDAN

326-31622 Metallic **9.50**

R4

326-20190 Sedan **5.95**

TWINGO COMPACT COUPE

326-21517 Top Open **7.50**

SEAT

ALHAMBRA

326-22125 Standard **9.25**
326-32124 Metallic **9.95**

CORDOBA

326-22217 Standard Paint **9.25**
326-32216 Metallic **9.95**

TRABANT

326-44189 601 Station Wagon Altenburg Airport Ground Control **14.50** *NEW*

TRIUMPH

TR 3

326-22316 Standard **8.50**

VOLKSWAGEN

BEETLE '69

326-22361 Standard **8.95**

GOLF

328-43885 Tour Fahrschule **11.95**

CORRADO COUPE

326-20671 Standard **7.50**

GOLF GL CONVERTIBLE COUPE

326-21548 Standard **8.95**
326-31547 Metallic **9.50**

SEDAN
326-31097 Metallic **8.95**

WAGON
326-31639 Metallic **9.50**

GOLF III

326-44172 Station Wagon United German Railways (DB-AG) **10.95** *NEW*

GOLF IV

326-22576 4-Door **8.75** *NEW*
326-32575 4-Door-Metallic Paint **9.50** *NEW*

326-22637 2-Door **8.95** *NEW*
326-32636 2-Door-Metallic Paint **8.95** *NEW*

POLO

326-43953 Station Wagon w/Locksmith Advertising 12.50

COUPE

326-21692 Standard 7.95

SEDAN

326-31752 Metallic 8.50

VENTO GL SEDAN

326-21203 Standard 7.95
326-41928 GL Taxi 8.50

PASSAT

326-22200 Sedan 1996 9.25
326-32209 Sedan 1996-Metallic 9.95
326-22224 Station Wagon 9.25
326-32223 Station Wagon-Metallic 9.95

GL WAGON

326-31660 Metallic 9.95

326-22057 Less Top Carrier 8.95

SHARAN

326-21845 Standard 9.50
326-31844 Metallic 10.95

T4 MINI VAN

326-41379 Zoll 7.50

326-42406 California Coach-Pop-Up Camper 14.50

TRABANT

601S

326-20763 7.50

326-20770 Universal Wagon 7.50

WARTBURG

326-22705 353 1985 4-Door Sedan 10.50 *NEW*

BUSES

326-6100 School Bus 13.95

MAN

326-144957 City Stiftsquelle 28.95

326-145640 City Bus-Undecorated 22.95 *NEW*

MERCEDES

326-43014 100D w/Raised Roof-Frankfurt Airport 13.50

326-43038 207D ADAC Bus/Motorcycle & Trailer 22.95

SETRA

326-140584 S 215 HDH w/"Wild" Graphics 23.95 *NEW*

326-144360 S 215 Articulated Becker Bad Endbach 33.50 *NEW*

326-144940 S315 Schwenkkrauss 28.95

VOLKSWAGEN LT

326-43250 High Roof Bus 9.25

326-43366 LT2 w/Raised Roof Airport Shuttle 15.95 *NEW*
326-43496 With Flat Roof 8.95

CONTAINERS

326-5278 40' Undecorated 3.95
326-75305 Volkswagen-20' pkg(2) 7.95

326-75374 40' Dole Reefer 7.50

326-75381 20' pkg(2) 11.50

EMERGENCY VEHICLES

AUDI

326-43588 V 8 Police 10.50

326-43922 A4 Bavaria Police 11.95

326-44004 Audi A4 Sedan Emergency Doctor 12.95 *NEW*

BMW

323I

326-41164 Police 7.95

325I

326-43205 Touring THW 12.50

502 EA 11.95

326-43724 4-Door Sedan Bavarian Autobahn Police 1950s-60s

326-43779 Fire

520

326-43816 '95 Police 12.50

326-43830 T 1996 Ambulance 13.50

7er

326-44219 Sedan Bamberg Police 11.50 *NEW*

CONTAINERS

326-75596 20' Containers Fire (red) pkg(2) 10.95

326-75633 Fire Dept. Roll-Off Equipment Units pkg(2) 13.50

EMO GROUND SEARCH

326-6220 Bus 14.95 *NEW*
326-6221 Jeep 12.50 *NEW*

FIAT

326-43243 Ulysses ADAC 13.95

FORD GALAXY MINIVAN

326-44059 Ambulance German Red Cross-Mittelhessen 13.30 *NEW*

JEEP

326-43342 Cherokee Fire Chief 14.25
326-43465 Grand Cherokee Medic 14.95

MAN M90

326-41447 LF-16 Pumper 22.95
326-42710 TLF 16 Pumper (Daylight Red) 22.95

326-42833 750L Equipment Truck (Old Timer) 19.95
326-43182 F 2000 Roll-Off Container Truck 25.50

MERCEDES

326-4103 300E Fire Car 6.50
326-41157 207D Fire Rescue 7.95

Limited Quantity Available

326-41263 Gloria LVF 112 Mini Pumper 13.95

326-41423 T2 Equipment Truck **10.95**
326-41867 T2 Ambulance **13.50**
326-42390 207D Ambulance **13.50**

326-42413 TLF 24/48 Pumper **25.50**
326-42475 207D Water Guard Radar **15.95**
326-42529 207D Rescue Service **13.50**
326-42604 Sprinter Van Fire Dept. **14.50**

326-42697 SK 23-12 Aerial Ladder (red) **20.50**
326-42703 SK 23-12 Aerial Ladder (Daylight Red) **22.50**
326-42765 TLF 8/18 Pumper (Daylight Red) **17.95**

326-42772 F8 Pumper **19.75**

326-42826 LF 8/6 Pumper **19.75**

326-42864 German Police E320 Sedan w/Wandel & Goltermann Lightbar **12.50**

For Daily Product Updates Point Your Browser to

www.walthers.com

326-42918 "Police Squad" 300 GE Sport Utility (solid green) **11.50**
326-42925 TLF 24/48 Pumper (Daylight red) **25.50**
326-43076 Fire Dept Truck w/Roll-Off Body **14.25**
326-43083 Sprinter Van Fire Dept.**14.25**
326-43106 309 Berlin Police **14.25**
326-43175 SK w/Cherry Picker **21.65**

326-43229 Sprinter Johann **15.95**

326-43335 Sprinter Hamburg Fire Dept. Equipment Van (Daylight Red) **15.95** ***NEW***
326-43397 T2 Ambulance **15.95**
326-43403 310 D Fire Truck **17.95**
326-43427 E320 Fire Chief **11.95**
326-43441 Truck w/Roll-Off Body **21.95**
326-43519 Vito Paramedic **14.50**

326-43526 L2000 Fire Truck **19.95**

326-43533 Sk Hlf 2000 Fire Truck **24.95**

326-43557 100 Bus, Fire **15.95**

326-43595 300 TE Airport Frankfort **13.500**

326-43618 T2 Rtw Feuerwehr Munchen **15.50**

326-43649 T2 Pick-Up Feuerwehr **15.50**

326-43656 F2000 Roll Off Container, Fire **20.50**

326-43663 C220 Police **11.95**

326-43670 Vito Fire Rescue **15.50**

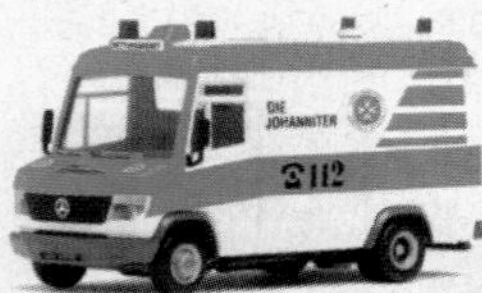

326-43755 T2 Johanniter **15.95**

326-43786 Sprinter Asb Mannheim **15.95**

326-43847 Sprinter w/Motorcycle/Trailer Police **19.95**

326-43854 Sk 1994 Fire Truck (red) **21.50**
326-43892 E 200 Paramedic Passau **14.95**
326-43915 E200 T Service **15.50**
326-43939 T2 Extended Cab **15.50**

326-43946 T2 Ambulance **15.50**

326-43960 T2 Vario/Ziegler TSF-W Sedan Cab-Fire Dept. **17.95** ***NEW***

326-43977 C200 Sedan Wurzburg Fire Dept. **14.95** ***NEW***

326-43984 E200 Station Wagon Ambulance MKT Nuremberg **19.50** ***NEW***

326-44028 T2 Flatbed Pickup w/Sedan Cab & Canvas Cover Fire Dept. **15.95** ***NEW***

326-44042 E200 Station Wagon Ambulance KBH Hannover **19.95** ***NEW***

326-44073 Vito Stuttgart Fire Dept. Incident Command Van **15.95** ***NEW***

326-44097 T2 Flatbed Pickup w/Crew Cab & Canvas Cover THW Detmold **15.95** ***NEW***

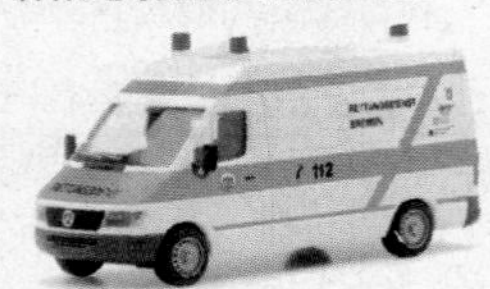

326-44127 Sprinter Van Bremen Fire Dept. Rescue Service Unit **15.95** ***NEW***

326-44134 Sprinter Van Johanniter Ambulance Services-Emergency Pediatrician Nuremberg **14.95** ***NEW***

326-44240 Vito Fire Truck **14.95** ***NEW***

326-144179 SK Dump Truck THW **22.50**
326-144483 Su 240-Fire Nuernberg **28.50**

326-144544 SK 1988 THW **21.50**
326-188345 Mercedes T2 Vario Van Stuttgart Airport Fire Dept. (Daylight Red, white) **14.95** ***NEW***

OPEL

326-42000 Nordrhein Westfalen Police Vectra **10.95**

326-42024 Hansestadt Hamburg Police Omega Sedan **10.95**
326-42291 Police Corsa GLS **9.95**

326-42345 Police Omega Sedan **12.95**

326-42420 Emergency Doctor Omega Station Wagon **12.95**
326-43304 Vectra Police **12.50**
326-43430 Omega Paramedic **13.25**

326-43434 Omega B Station Wagon Aschaffenburg Emergency Doctor **14.50** ***NEW***

326-43564 Omega Police **12.50**

326-44233 Corsa 2-Door Hardtop Dutch Ambulance **11.95** ***NEW***

RENAULT

326-43908 Twingo Police Netherlands **12.95**

326-44035 406 Sedan German Police **11.95** ***NEW***
326-44226 406 Sedan Copenhagen, Denmark, Police (white, black) **11.50** ***NEW***

SCANIA

326-43861 Container Roll-Off Fw Chemieschulz **24.50**

SETRA

326-142854 Police Bus **21,50**

326-145152 S 215 Bus Ulm Fire Brigade (red) **25.95** ***NEW***

TRABANT

326-43694 Universal Station Wagon-Gutersloh Fire Dept. **14.50**

VOLKSWAGEN

326-41362 Police Dept. Station Wagon **9.50**

326-41751 Passat Wagon ADAC **9.75**

326-41850 Police Dept. Golf Sedan **10.95**
326-42093 Passat Emergency ASB **10.95** ***NEW***

326-42321 "Fire Chief" Passat GL Wagon **10.95**
326-42338 Golf Emergency **10.95**

326-42369 Fire Brigade T4 Van **11.95**
326-43991 LT2 Van Ambulance BRK Schwabach **15.95** ***NEW***

326-44158 Beetle German Police **10.95** ***NEW***

326-44165 Beetle German Fire Chief's Car **10.95** ***NEW***

326-44196 Passat Hannover Police Dept. (green, white) **11.50** ***NEW***

326-44202 LT Bus w/Raised Roof THW **14.95** ***NEW***
326-43069 Golf ADAC **14.95**
326-43168 Sharan Emergency **14.95**

326-43373 Sharan w/Trailer & Motor Cycle – Mobile Watch **22.95**
326-43458 Passat Police **12.50**

326-43687 Passat 1997 Police **11.95**

326-43878 Passat Fire (red) **10.50**

Limited Quantity Available

326-41331 Fire Dept. Passat **8.50**

MILITARY VEHICLES

MODERN GERMAN ARMY

326-700436 Opel Vectra Sedan-Staff Car (Bronze Green) **13.50** ***NEW***

326-700443 MB 230 G Military Police Light Truck (tri-color camouflage) **15.95** ***NEW***

326-700450 VW T4 Personnel Van (tri-color camouflage) **16.95** ***NEW***

326-700467 VW T4 Personnel Van-Military Police (Bronze Green) **14.50** ***NEW***

326-740289 MB 5T Single-Axle Canvas Covered Flatbed Truck-Driver Training School **18.50**

LIGHT TRUCKS EUROPEAN

MERCEDES

326-41386 100 Metallic **8.95**

326-41744 100 Flatbed w/Canvas Cover **8.95**

326-42246 T2 Van Unpainted **8.95**

326-42307 100 Camper **13.95**

326-43540 T2 Pick-Up **13.50**

326-43625 Container Pick-Up, Dms Balke **16.95**

326-43632 Sprinter Crewcab, Strassendienst **15.50**

326-44141 T2 Pickup w/Crew Cab & Glass Transport Rack **15.95** ***NEW***

326-145121 Atego 3-Side Dump Truck **15.50** ***NEW***

SPRINTER VAN

326-42536 High Roof Van **9.50**

326-42543 Passenger Van **9.50**

326-42550 Flatbed w/Canvas Cover **9.95**

326-42659 Delivery Van **9.50**

326-42666 Passenger Van w/High Roof **9.50**

326-42680 German Post Office (New Scheme) Van w/High Roof **12.50**

326-42871 Crew-Cab Pickup **9.50**

VOLKSWAGEN

326-41560 Caravelle **8.95**

326-41614 T Van **8.95**

326-41829 T4 Delivery Canvas **9.95**

326-42956 T4 Flatbed Pickup w/Canvas Cover DB (Scheme) **12.50**
326-43311 LT 2 Pick-Up **9.95**

326-43489 LT 2 Crew Cab **9.95**

TAXIS

MERCEDES

326-42284 E 320 **10.95**

326-42642 E220 Sedan **11.50**

326-43571 E 220T **11.50**

326-43809 C200 T **11.50**

VOLKSWAGEN

326-43717 Sharan **11.95**

326-43823 Passat 1996 Sedan **11.50**

326-42437 VW T4 Caravelle **11.95**

MOTORCYCLES

326-50753 BMW RS 1100 Cycle & Trailer **9.95**

TRUCKS–AMERICAN SEMIS

Includes matching tractor and trailer unless noted.

FORD

326-6160 L-9000 w/Elliptical Tanker-Murphy Oil Co. **14.95**
326-6161 L-9000 w/ 27' Doubles-Parcel Service **14.95**
326-6162 Aeromax w/36' Dump Trailer **13.95**
326-6163 L-9000 w/40' Flatbed **13.95**
326-6168 Aeromax Motorcraft **16.95**
326-6177 Anderson Windows **15.95**
326-6203 L 9000, 48' Flatbed w/Wood Load **15.95**
326-6204 Aeromax, 45' Van, Boise Cascade Corrugated Cardboard **15.95**
326-6205 L 9000, Doubles, Ford Motorkraft **14.95**
326-6215 Short Concrete Semi **15.95**
326-6225 Short Tractor w/Double Trailers Hiway 9 **15.95** *NEW*
326-450060 L-9000 w/Elliptical Tank Body (Unpainted) **15.95** *NEW*
326-450100 L-9000 w/Resin Grain Box (red, no lettering) **15.95** *NEW*

GMC GENERAL

326-6053 Overnite–Doubles **13.95**
326-6166 Dump Truck **9.95**
326-6218 Short 40' Reefer Trailer Safeway **14.95**
326-450110 Dump Truck (blue cab) **15.95** *NEW*

INTERNATIONAL (NAVISTAR)

326-6206 26' Straight Truck **9.95**
326-6219 Undecorated (red) **13.95**
326-6223 U-Haul Type Box Van Piano Movers **14.95** *NEW*

BEVERAGE TRUCKS

326-6135 Taylor & Bates w/Trailer **14.95**

326-6136 Taylor & Bates Straight Truck **13.95**

326-6137 Sparkles & Lime w/Trailer **14.95**
326-6138 Sparkles & Lime Straight Truck **13.95**

326-6139 Beverage Trailer Undecorated **10.95**

326-6140 Beverage Straight Truck, Undecorated **9.95**

326-6176 Hazardous Materials Fire Truck **14.95**
Based on a truck in service with the Boston Fire Dept., red with generic imprints to fit any layout, complete with nonworking lightbar.

DELIVERY VANS EA 13.95

326-6149 26' Moving Van
326-6170 Mom's Bakery

FREIGHTLINER

326-6028 Preston–Doubles **13.95**
326-6081 Spector Trailer **14.95**
326-6083 Hennis 40' Trailer **14.95**
326-6123 Weyerhaeuser **13.95**
326-6152 48' Flatbed w/Load **14.95**
326-6216 Medium, Drop-Deck Trailer **14.95**

KENWORTH

326-6198 W-900 C&S Transport w/Skirted Chassis & Airfoil (Bright red) **15.95**
326-6200 T-600 Aero, 45' Van, Boise Cascade Paper Division **15.95**
326-6207 W-900 Logging Truck, Weyerhaeuser **14.50**
326-6208 T-600 Aero Van, Halvor Lines **15.95**
326-6209 T-600 Aero Van, Feed The Children **16.95**

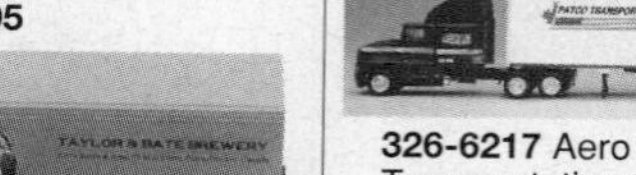
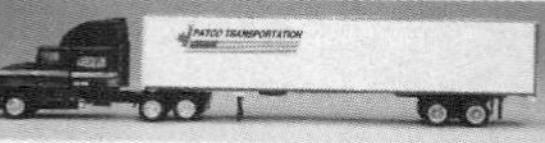

326-6217 Aero Van Patco Transportation **15.95**
326-25230 W-900 w/Sleeper (white) **5.95**
326-25231 W-900 w/Sleeper Painted **6.95**
326-25243 W-900 w/Retooled Chassis (white) **7.95**
326-25244 W-900 w/Retooled Chassis Painted **8.95**
326-6062 Safeway–Triples **16.95**

326-6113 Provost Tank Trailer **16.95**

326-6114 Dump Trailer **14.95**

326-6122 T600 w/45' Trailer **15.95**

326-6127 T600 Weyerhaeuser Flatbed w/Lumber Load **15.95**

326-6141 Reliable Carriers **15.95**
326-6156 T600 w/45' Flatbed **14.95**
326-6171 T600 Interlink 45' Trailer **14.95**
326-6175 T600 Auto Palace 45' Trailer **18.95**
326-6182 T600 Cotton **13.95**
326-6185 T600 Boehmer Box Co. **15.95**
326-6195 W-900 w/48' Flatbed **17.95**
326-6228 W-900 w/Elliptical Tanker Royal America n Shows **12.95** *NEW*
326-6230 T-600 Aerodyne Hill Transport **16.95** *NEW*

Short Concrete Semi 326-6215

Undecorated (red) 326-6219

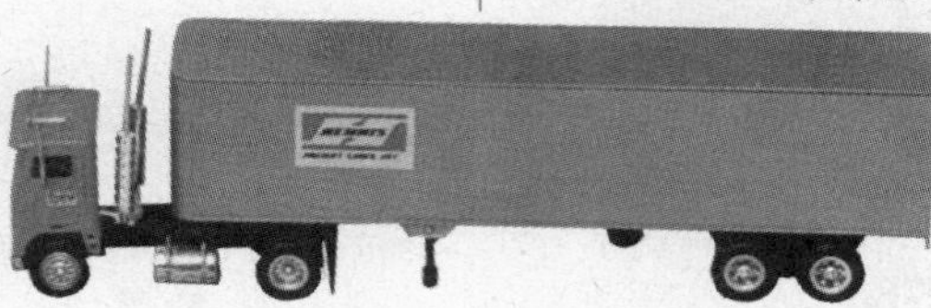

Hennis 40' Trailer 326-6083

Weyerhaeuser 326-6123

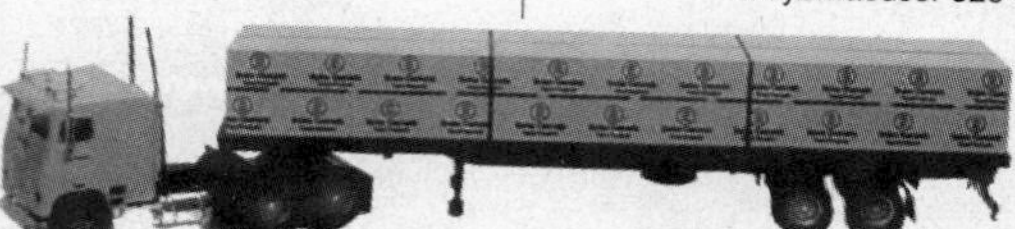

48' Flatbed w/Load 326-6152

326-6231 T-600 8-Compartment Feed Tank Trailer Walinga, Inc. **14.95** ***NEW***
326-25289 T-600 w/Sleeper & Long Flatbed (white) **7.95**
326-25290 T-600 Flatbed w/Sleeper Painted **8.95**
326-144391 W-900 Aero Pkg **16.95**
326-450040 T-600 w/21' Flatbed Body (unpainted cab, no lettering) **15.95** ***NEW***
326-450090 Propane Tanker (maroon truck/yellow tank & wheels) **15.95** ***NEW***

MACK

326-6059 CH 603 Tractor w/Waligna Bulk Feed Trailer Feed Rite **13.95**

326-6071 CH 603 Tractor w/Waligna Bulk Feed Trailer Undcorated **11.95**

326-6124 CH 603 Tractor w/Can Trailer Mowat Express **13.95**

326-6125 CH 603 Tractor w/Slleper & 48' Container Trans X **14.95**

326-6178 CH 603 Tractor w/36' Utilty Trailer & Hiab Crane T-Rex Demolition **15.95**
326-6179 CH 603 Tractor w/45' Trailer Overnite **14.95**
326-6184 CH 603 Tractor Trailer Fleming Foods **15.95**
326-6190 CH 603 Tractor w/45' Trailer Roadway **14.95**
326-6194 CH 603 Tractor w/40' Trailer Eastern Freightways **14.95**
326-6201 CH 613 Tractor w/45' Van Trailer Mega Pizza **15.95**
326-6212 CH 613 Tractor w/48' Chemical Tank Keith Hall & Sons **15.95**

326-6129 Klink Trucking Dump Trailer **13.95**

326-6134 Dairy Product Reefer **14.95**

326-6150 CH Tractor w/Round Tank Trailer **15.95**

326-6151 Short Cab w/40' Trailer **14.95**
326-6224 Short Tractor w/Double Trailers N.Y.C.E. **15.95** ***NEW***
326-6227 CH 613 w/45' Trailer Cool X **14.95** ***NEW***
326-450050 Mack Tank Truck (green cab, silver tank) **15.95** ***NEW***
326-450080 Custom 87 Dump Truck w/Working Tip Mechanism/Rear Tailgate **15.95** ***NEW***

PETERBILT

326-6111 Provisioners **13.95**
326-35232 With New Sleeper, Skirted Chassis **7.95**
326-35233 With New Sleeper, Skirted Chassis, Painted **8.95**
326-6222 Tractor w/New Sleeper & 48' Van Trailer **14.95** ***NEW***
326-6229 Tractor w/New Sleeper Stevens Transport **16.95**

WHITE ROAD COMMANDER

326-6202 Twin-Drive 40' Flatbed w/I-Beams **14.95**

TRACTORS

Kits are fully assembled and include chrome add-ons, such as airhorns, grab irons and mirrors.

UNLETTERED

Cabs are molded in various colors, with no markings.
326-15231 Kenworth W-900 **6.95**
326-15233 Peterbilt **6.95**
326-15235 GMC General **6.95**
326-15264 Mack-No Sleeper **7.95**
326-15290 Kenworth T600 **8.95**
326-15297 International 2-Axle **7.95**
326-15241 Ford L-9000 Short, Painted **7.95**
326-25241 Ford Aeromax w/Sleeper Painted **7.95**
326-15242 Freightliner Single-Axle Medium Cab **6.95**
326-25238 Freightliner Medium Cab **6.95**
326-25239 Freightliner Supercab **6.95**
326-25233 Peterbilt Tractor w//Sleeper **6.95**
326-25264 Mack 613 w/Sleeper **7.95**
326-35231 Kenworth W-900 w/Sleeper **7.95**
326-35290 Kenworth T-600 Aero Sleeper **8.95**
326-25235 GMC General w/Sleeper **6.95**
326-25236 White Road Commander 2-Axle **6.95**
326-25237 White Road Commander 3-Axle **6.95**
326-6226 International/ Navistar U-Haul Type Box Van **9.95** ***NEW***
326-144872 Peterbilt 2-Axle Conventional w/New Sleeper, Chromed Skirts & Airfoil **14.95** ***NEW***
326-450130 Peterbilt w/Modernized Grill & Stacks Painted **9.95** ***NEW***

UNDECORATED

Cabs are white plastic with no markings.
326-15230 Kenworth W-900 **5.95**
326-15232 Peterbilt **5.95**
326-15234 GMC General **5.95**
326-15236 Freightliner 2-Axle **5.95**
326-15237 Freightliner 3-Axle **5.95**
326-15238 Freightliner w/Sleeper **5.95**
326-15239 Freightliner w/Long Sleeper **5.95**
326-15263 Mack-No Sleeper **6.95**
326-15289 Kenworth T600 **7.95**
326-15296 International 2-Axle **6.95**
326-25232 Peterbilt Tractor w/Sleeper **5.95**
326-450000 Ford L 9000 Single-Axle **9.95** ***NEW***
326-450070 International/ Navistar S-Series 2-Axle **9.95** ***NEW***
326-450010 Mack 603 Single-Axle **9.95** ***NEW***
326-450020 Mack 603/613 3-Axle **9.95** ***NEW***
326-450030 Mack 603/613 2-Axle w/Single Idler Axle **9.95** ***NEW***
326-35232 Peterbilt w/New Sleeper & Skirted Chassis **7.95** ***NEW***
326-35233 Peterbilt w/New Sleeper & Skirted Chassis **8.95** ***NEW***
326-450120 Peterbilt Tractor w/Modernized Grill & Stacks **8.95** ***NEW***
326-25263 Mack 613 w/Sleeper **6.95**
326-35230 Kenworth W-900 w/Sleeper **6.95**
326-35289 Kenworth T-600 Aero Sleeper **7.95**
326-25234 GMC General-Short Wheelbase w/Sleeper-White **5.95**
326-15240 Ford L-9000 Short Cab **6.95**
326-25240 Ford Aeromax w/Sleeper **6.95**
326-25242 Freightliner Single-Axle Medium Cab **5.95**

Peterbilt 2-Axel w/New Sleeper 326-144872

Weyand Tractor w/Canvas Trailer 326-145329

EUROPEAN TRUCKS

DAF

326-144452 95 Semi-Fischer Transport **33.95**

326-144643 95 Semi Tanker, Bulkhaul **33.50**

326-144858 95 XF 500 SSC 2-Axle Tractor w/Airfoil, Spoiler & Side Skirts **15.95**

326-144988 95 XF Tractor w/Canvas Side Trailer Monjean **33.95**
326-145329 95 XF 2-Axle Trailer w/Canvas Side Trailer Weyand **33.95** ***NEW***

IVECO

326-143127 Eurotech Tractor Only **15.95**

326-143745 Eurotech Tractor (Undecorated) **14.95**
326-144100 Dump Semi Koegel **19.95**

326-144704 Eurotech Tractor Only w/Air Dam & Spoiler **14.95**

MAN

326-6199 Car Transport w/Jeep **17.95**

326-140560 F90 Double Bottom **22.50**

326-141956 F90 Double Bottom RB **23.95**
326-142205 L2000 Dump Truck **15.50**
326-142984 "Südkraft" F2000 Canvas **27.95**

326-143080 L2000 Car Transporter **16.95**
326-143196 L750 Old-Time Moving Van w/Trailer **22.50**

326-143219 F2000 Single-Axle Tractor **15.50**

326-143479 F90 Tractor Only **14.95**

326-143660 F90 Snowplow **18.50**

326-143691 Dump Truck w/Hiab Crane **16.95**

326-144193 M2000 Tractor/Trailer Spar **31.50**
326-144230 L2000 Multi-Dump **16.95**
326-144407 F2000 Tractor/Trailer Hohlschen **35.50**

326-144599 F2000 Hd Tractor/Trailer Wandt **33.75**

326-144889 F2000 4-Axle Dump **19.50**

326-144902 F2000 3-Axle Dump **18.50**
326-144964 F2000 Semi Grossman **33.95**

326-145282 F2000 2-Axle Restyled Tractor **13.95** ***NEW***
326-145459 F2000 2-Axle Canvas Side Box Van w/2-Axle Canvas Side Trailer Grossman **31.95** ***NEW***

326-145497 F2000 Restyled 2-Axle Flatbed w/Cement Silo Load Maxit **23.95** ***NEW***
326-145572 F2000 2-Axle Evolution Tractor w/Skeleton Log Tractor **26.95** ***NEW***
326-188449 F2000 2-Axle Canvas Side Box Van w/2-Axle Canvas Side Trailer Südkraft **32.95** ***NEW***

MERCEDES

326-41348 Flatbed w/Tarp Roll Off Box **11.50**

326-42277 100 Road Maintenance **15.95**
326-100069 6.0 SL Brabus **19.95**
326-141949 SK 1748 w/Trailer Canvas **24.95**
326-142038 Truck Europcar **21.50**
326-142229 SK Semi Massong **26.95**
326-142519 Tanker Veba-Heizoel **23.95**
326-142663 SK Semi Alfred Talke **25.95**

326-143158 SK Tractor Only **16.95**

326-143356 Logging Truck w/Crane **27.50**

326-143394 Old-Time Moving Van w/Trailer **23.00**

326-143455 SK Tractor Only **14.95**

326-143769 Semi "Rieck" **31.50**
326-143868 SK Garbage Truck Orange **18.50**
326-143929 L 311 Moving Van Carl Balke **31.95**
326-144285 Actros Tanker KTC **33.50**
326-144292 Actros Tractor Only **14.95**
326-144377 Actros Aero Tractor Only **15.95**

326-144582 Actros M Dump Truck **18.50**

326-144605 Sk 1994 Car Carrier, Altmann **22.95**

326-144667 Actros Cement Truck **18.50**

326-144728 Actros w/3-Axle Canvas Side Trailer Fixemer **31.50**

326-144742 Actros Semi Thier **29.95**

326-144780 Actros Auto Carrier Willi Betz **29.95**

326-144803 Actros M Dump Kogel **27.95**

326-144827 814 Cargo Van Schenker **19.50**

Box Van w/Canvas Trailer 326-145459

Tractor w/Log Trailer 326-145572

Box Van w/Canvas Trailer 326-188449

Jumbo Tank Trailer Lehnkering 326-145145

326-144834 814 Auto Carrier w/MB 560 **23.50**

326-144896 Sk 1994 Road Sweeper **15.50**
326-144971 Actros Garbage Alba **20.95**

326-144742 Actros Tractor w/Bulk Container & 3-Axle Trailer "Thier" **29.95** ***NEW***

326-144971 Actros 2-Axle Garbage Truck Alba **20.95**

326-145008 Actros Tractor w/3-Axle Jumbo Tanker (Chromed) Centrans **33.95**

326-145091 Actros 2-Axle Tractor w/3-Axle Canvas Side Trailer Hellmich **31.50** ***NEW***

326-145114 Actros Single-Axle Box Van w/2-Axle Trailer Niemann **33.95** ***NEW***
326-145145 Actros 2-Axle Tractor w/3-Axle Jumbo Tank Trailer Lehnkering **33.95** ***NEW***

326-145237 Actros 2-Axle Tractor w/Refrigerated Trailer Culina Logistik **33.95** ***NEW***

326-145251 Actros S 4-Axle Concrete Mixer **19.50** ***NEW***

326-145268 Actros S 4-Axle Dump Truck **19.50** ***NEW***

326-145336 Actros L 2-Axle Trailer w/3-Axle Glass Transport Trailer Offergeld **31.95** ***NEW***

326-145244 Actros 2-Axle Refrigerated Box Van & 2-Axle Refrigerated Trailer Culina Logistik **33.95** ***NEW***

326-145312 Actros 2-Axle Box Van w/2-Axle Trailer Bi-Fi **34.95** ***NEW***

326-145343 Actros 2-Axle LH Tractor w/5-Axle Lowboy Flatbed Baumann **34.95** ***NEW***

326-145367 Atego 252B 2-Axle 18-Ton Dump Truck **18.50** ***NEW***

326-145374 Actros 2-Axle Stakeside Flatbed w/Crane & 2-Axle Stakeside Flatbed Trailer OBI **32.50** ***NEW***

326-145381 Actros 2-Axle Tractor w/Canvas Side 3-Axle Trailer Offergold **32.50** ***NEW***

326-145398 Actros 2-Axle Tractor w/3-Axle Glass Transport Trailer Rogister **32.50** ***NEW***

326-145404 Actros Single-Axle Tractor w/3-Axle Refrigerated Trailer Marantec **30.95** ***NEW***

326-145411 Actros 2-Axle Trailer w/3-Axle Refrigerated Trailer Offergeld **32.50** ***NEW***

326-145446 Actros 2-Axle Tractor w/3-Axle Canvas Side Trailer Rogister **31.95** ***NEW***

326-145473 Actros L-Tulo 2-Axle Box Van w/2-Axle Trailer Central Trailer Rentco **31.95** ***NEW***

326-145503 Atego Single-Axle Canvas Side Box Van Mercedes Service **18.50** ***NEW***

326-145510 Actros S 2-Axle w/Cherry Picker-Municipal Vehicle (orange) **19.95** ***NEW***

326-145527 Atego Single-Axle Box Van Avis Rent A Car **19.95** ***NEW***

326-145534 Atego 1828 Single-Axle Tractor **14.50** ***NEW***

326-145541 Atego 4140 4-Axle Cement Mixer **18.50** ***NEW***

326-145558 Actros M 2-Axle Tractor w/2-Axle Cement Mixer Trailer **22.95** ***NEW***

326-145589 SK 1994 Model 2-Axle Tractor w/Crane **12.95** ***NEW***

326-188432 Actros LH Single-Axle Tractor w/3-Axle Livestock Trailer Westfleisch **32.95** ***NEW***

326-145619 Actros Single-Axle Tractor w/Bulk Material Tank Trailer Vogt **31.95** ***NEW***

326-188357 Actros Single-Axle Tractor w/Single Axle Low Floor Trailer Schröder **31.95** ***NEW***

326-188418 Actros Single-Axle Tractor w/3-Axle Refrigerated Trailer Frenzel Frozen Foods Limited-Run **34.95** ***NEW***

326-188548 Mercedes Actros L w/Auto Carrier & 6 New Automobile Models 50 Years of Herpa **79.95** ***NEW*** Celebrate the 50th anniversary of Herpa models with this detailed model, featuring special graphics. Includes six brand-new car models for a load.

326-186209 Actros Edition 1997 pkg(3) **37.95**

Limited Quantity Available

326-141727 Schmidbauer **18.25**

RENAULT

326-143493 R390 Tractor Only **14.95**

326-143714 AE 500 Tractor (Undecorated) **14.95**

326-144919 AE 2-Axle Box Van w/2-Axle Trailer Schenker International **33.95**

326-145060 AE 2-Axle Restyled Tractor **13.95**

Refrigerated Box Van w/Trailer 326-145244

Stakeside w/Crane & Flatbed Trailer 326-145374

Marantec Tractor w/Trailer 326-145404

Rogister Tractor w/Trailer 326-145446

Tractor w/Low Floor Livestock Trailer 326-145626

Frozen Foods Tractor w/Trailer 326-188418

Carrier & 6 New Automobile 326-188548

326-145626 AE Restyled Single-Axle Tractor w/3-Axle Low Floor Livestock Trailer MAES **31.95** ***NEW***

326-188456 AE Single-Axle Tractor w/3-Axle Refrigerated Trailer Nosta Transport **32.95** ***NEW***

SCANIA

326-142342 Streamline Aero Tractor Only **15.50**

326-143462 Conventional Tractor Only **14.95**

326-143486 Cab-Over Tractor Only **14.95**

326-143677 Dump Truck **18.50**
326-143899 Conventional 3-Axle Tractor Only **14.95**

326-144087 112 FHK Cement **17.95**

326-144476 Semi-Weyres Transport **31.95**

326-144513 144, Tractor Only **15.95**

326-144520 124 Tractor/ Trailer Ziegelmeier **33.50**

326-144575 124 Bulk Tanker, Spec. Herman **32.95**
326-144742 144 TL w/Sleeper & 3-Axle Jumbo Tank Trailer "Talke" **29.95**

326-144759 144 T L Tanker w/Talke **29.95**

326-144766 144 T L Semi Nor Cargo **33.50**

326-144841 124 Tractor **14.95**

326-144865 124 2-Axle Tractor w/Air Dam & Spoiler **14.95**

326-145046 124 Single-Axle Tractor w/3-Axle Oil Tank Wahr **30.95**
326-145442 Hauber 1996 Conventional 2-Axle Tractor w/3-Axle Dump Trailer Freund **27.95** ***NEW***
326-145480 Hauber 1996 2-Axle Trailer w/3-Axle Low Floor Trailer Sturm **34.95** ***NEW***
326-145565 124 2-Axle Tractor w/3-Axle Dump Trailer **19.95** ***NEW***
326-145596 Hauber 1996 Conventional 2-Axle Tractor w/3-Axle Dump Trailer Monjean **29.95** ***NEW***

326-145602 124 Single-Axle Tractor w/3-Axle Jumbo Tank Trailer (Chromed) Laabs **34.50** ***NEW***

326-188401 144 Topline Single-Axle Tractor w/3-Axle Canvas Side Trailer ASG **31.95** ***NEW***

Tractor w/Dump Trailer 326-145442

Tractor w/Dump Trailer 326-145565

Tractor w/Dump Trailer 326-145596

VOLVO

326-110167 FH16 Globetrotter Tractor Only **25.95**
326-143110 F12 w/Loading Doors **21.95**
326-144018 Steyer NSK Semi **33.50**

326-144810 Fh Semi Scansped **33.50**

326-145183 FH16 Globetrotter XL GL Single-Axle Tractor **13.95** ***NEW***

326-145350 FH Globetrotter XL 2-Axle Trailer w/3-Axle Jumbo Tank Trailer Jongh **34.95** ***NEW***
326-145633 FH XL Single-Axle Tractor w/Jumbo Cargo 2-Axle Trailer Trucking Service Cologne Germany **31.95** ***NEW***

PRIVATE COLLECTION VEHICLES

Models feature chrome rims, wipers, window frames, ornamental fittings and lettering, design stripe, plus chrome embossed or painted rearview mirrors.

AUTOMOBILES

AUDI

326-100502 V-8 EVO **19.95**

326-100939 S2 Coupe **20.95**

BMW

326-100090 735i B11-Metallic **18.50**

BMW M5 Sedan 50 Years of Herpa 326-188562

326-100151 Alpina B10 **19.95**

326-100274 Alpina B 6 **19.95**

326-100977 750i (Calypso Red) **19.95**

326-101011 Alpina B12 **22.95**

326-101080 Alpina, B10 **21.95**

326-100571 325i Convertible w/Optional Hardtop **20.50** ***NEW***

326-101127 Z3 M-Coupé **19.95**

326-101134 3er Sedan 1998 Model **19.95** ***NEW***
326-188562 BMW M5 Sedan 50 Years of Herpa Special Edition **23.95** ***NEW***
One of the most popular BMW autos, reproduced in a special edition to celebrate the 50th anniversary of Herpa models. Finished in Metallic Silver with a blue interior, the model features chrome plated wheel rims and a hot-stamped chrome replica of the ranch exhaust system. The model is attached to a blue plastic base, stamped with anniversary graphics, and protected by a clear plastic cover.

FERRARI TESTAROSSA

326-100038 Red **19.95**
326-100045 White **19.95**
326-100052 F-40 In (red) **21.95** ***NEW***

LAMBORGHINI

326-100380 Lamborghini Diablo VT **21.95**

MAZDA

326-100601 MX5 **19.95**

MERCEDES

326-100014 560 SEC Brabus **18.50**

326-101066 Slk Roadster **21.95**

326-101059 SLK Roadster w/Monobloc IV Wheels (black) **22.95** ***NEW***
326-30064 300 Ce (silver) **19.95** ***NEW***

PORSCHE

326-100106 911 Turbo-Metallic **18.50**

326-100144 928 S4-Metallic **18.50**

326-101073 Boxter **21.95**

326-101110 996 2-Door Hardtop (Green Metallic) **19.95**

326-101141 996 2-Door Convertible w/Top Down (Metallic Silver) **19.95** ***NEW***

326-101158 911 GT3 2-Door Hardtop (Vesuviometallic) **20.95** ***NEW***

TRUCKS

DAF

326-110204 95 500 Supercab **27.50**
326-188425 95 XF SSC Single-Axle Tractor w/3-Axle Trailer D2-CallYa **63.95** ***NEW***
Special multi-color graphics on trailer; limited-run model.

IVECO

326-110020 3-Axle Tractor **25.95** ***NEW***

MERCEDES

Limited Quantity Available
326-110013 Tractor **26.95**

326-110211 Actros LH Tractor w/Side Skirts **25.50** ***NEW***
326-188371 Actros Single-Axle Tractor w/Low Floor 2-Axle Trailer Spartherm **63.95** ***NEW***
Special display truck features different graphics on both sides of trailer.

RENAULT

326-188494 AE Restyled Single-Axle Tractor w/3-Axle Euro Box Trailer Saarland **69.95** ***NEW***
Special multi-color graphics and lettering promoting the Saarland region.

SCANIA

326-110235 144 Tractor **25.95**

326-110242 Conventional Single-Axle Tractor -New Style **23.95** ***NEW***

326-188555 1996 Hauber Single-Axle Conventional w/Euro Box Van 50 Years of Herpa **69.95** ***NEW***
Special edition celebrates 50 years of Herpa scale models. Finished I silver metallic with blue trim with different full-color historic photos reprinted on both sides of the trailer. Model comes attached to a special blue display base with a clear plastic cover, which also carry the special anniversary graphics.

Tractor w/3-Axle Trailer 326-188425

Tractor w/Low Floor Trailer 326-188371

Tractor w/Box Trailer 326-188494

1996 Hauber Single-Axle Conventional w/Euro Box Van 326-188555

TRAILERS

AMERICAN

326-5271 40' Reefer **5.95**
326-5272 40' Dry Van **5.50**
326-5273 27' Trailer **3.95**
326-5274 Converter Dolly **2.00**
326-5275 Elliptical Tank Trailer **7.95**
326-5276 40' Flatbed **6.95**
326-5277 40' Container & Trailer **6.95**
326-5279 40' Trailer & Reefer Container **6.95**
326-5281 36' Dump Trailer **5.95**
326-5280 40' Reefer Container **4.50**
326-5282 Walinga Feed Tank Trailer **6.95**
326-5283 48' Electronics Van **5.95**
326-5285 45' Intermodal Chassis **5.95**
326-5287 Chemical Tank Trailer, Round **7.95**
326-5288 27' Dump Trailer **5.95**
326-5291 48' Container & Trailer **7.95**
326-5292 48' Container **4.95**
326-5294 48' Flatbed **7.95**
326-5300 Dual Axle Trailer Chassis **2.50**
326-5301 Single Axle Trailer Chassis **1.80**
326-5303 40' Container Chassis **3.75**
326-5304 48' Container Chassis **3.95**
326-5312 48' Van **5.95**

326-75398 Electronics-Moving Van **10.95**
326-75503 Two 20' Roll-Off Boxes pkg(2) **10.50**
326-75510 Chrome Tank Trailer **11.95**
326-75527 Chrome Bulk Tank Trailer **11.95**
326-75534 Bulk Tank Trailer-White **10.95**
326-75541 Bulk Tank Trailer-Large **10.95**

326-75589 20' Container Hoyer pkg(2) **11.50**
326-460000 27' 2-Axle Van (Unpainted) **6.95**
326-460010 2-Axle Converter Dolly **4.75** *NEW*
326-460020 45' 3-Axle Van (Unpainted) **9.95** *NEW*
326-460030 45' 2-Axle Van w/Idler (Tag) Axle (Unpainted) **9.95** *NEW*
326-460040 45' Dual Spread Axle Van (Unpainted) **9.95** *NEW*
326-460050 48' 3-Axle Van (Unpainted) **9.95** *NEW*
326-460060 48' 2-Axle w/Idler (Tag) Axle (Unpainted) **9.95** *NEW*
326-460070 48' Dual Spread Axle Van (Unpainted) **9.95** *NEW*
326-460080 40' Single-Axle Van (Unpainted) **9.95** *NEW*
326-460090 21' Flatbed Trailer w/2 Center Axles & Hitch **9.95** *NEW*

EUROPEAN

326-50869 2-Axle Trailer for Car/Light Truck **5.50**

326-75343 Jumbo Box **10.95**

326-75350 Euro-Box **11.50**

326-75404 Euro Canvas **11.50**

326-75411 Curtain Canvas **11.50**

326-75428 Trailer Dry Bulk Chemical **10.95**

326-75435 With 2–20' Containers **10.95**

326-75558 Racing Transport Undecorated **9.95**

326-75565 Canvas Cover w/Working Doors **10.95**

326-75572 Canvas Cover w/Windows **TBA**

326-75602 3-Axle Dump (Unpainted) **10.50** *NEW*

326-75619 3-Axle Round Tank Trailer **13.50** *NEW*

326-75626 2-Axle Dump (Unpainted) **10.50** *NEW*

VANS

MERCEDES

326-42987 Vito **8.95**

326-43199 T2 **10.95**
326-43380 Sprinter **15.95**

326-43793 Vito Sixt **12.95**
326-43328 Vito Passenger Van **9.25** *NEW*

VOLKSWAGEN

326-42109 T4 Caravelle DB **9.50**
326-43144 LT 2 **8.95**
326-43281 LT High Roof **9.25**

VEHICLE ACCESSORIES

CHAIRS

326-51330 Beach Chairs pkg(3) **9.95** *NEW*

DECALS

326-50029 European License Plates **5.25**
326-50074 German Fire Trucks **5.25**
326-50692 German License Plate Set **5.95**

DISPLAY CASES & BOXES

326-29209 Showcase Car/Van (white) **24.95**
326-29216 Truck/Car Collector Box (white) **24.95**
326-29223 Car Collector Box (white) **24.95**
326-29308 Car/Bus Collector Box (brown) **24.95**
326-29315 Truck/Car Collector Box (brown) **24.95**
326-29322 Car Collector Box (brown) **24.95**
326-29339 Showcase Car (white) **12.50**

FIRE TRUCK ACCESSORIES

326-50135 Airhorns, Sirens, Ladders **5.25**
326-50821 Rescue Boat, Hose, Lights, Tools **7.50**

MERCEDES

326-50579 SK Series–Chrome **7.95**

REEFER UNITS EA .50

326-52861 Old Style Thermo King
326-52862 Aerodynamic Carrier
326-52863 Underbelly

SEMI ACCESSORIES

326-50883 Modern Truck Chassis Set **8.95**
326-50791 Trailer Side Protectors **6.50**

STEERING KITS

Includes tie rods, spindles and pins to convert fixed front axles into positionable type for more realism.

326-50517 Construction Equipment **5.50**
326-50333 Trucks **5.25**

TRUCK ACCESSORIES

326-5311 Tractor Chassis **3.95**
326-50227 Truck Tow Bar & Fifth Wheel pkg(3) **5.25**
326-50234 Fuel Tanks & Exhaust **5.95**
326-50364 For DAF **5.25**
326-50371 For MAN **5.25**
326-50449 Truck Loading Crane **5.95**
326-5313 All-Purpose Fifth Wheels pkg(10) **4.95** *NEW*
326-5314 Airfoils (white) pkg(5) **3.95** *NEW*

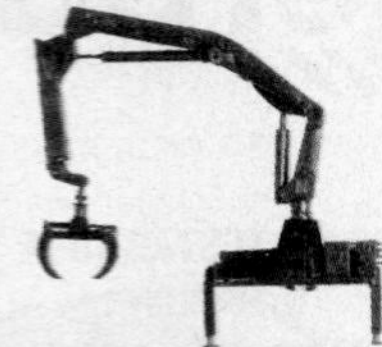

326-51255 Loading Crane w/Wood Grapple **6.95** *NEW*

326-51347 Special Wide Front Tires & Wheels for Trucks **7.50**

TRAILER DETAILS

326-5302 Landing Gear **.50**

TRUCK LOADS

326-5309 Package of Logs **2.95**
326-50470 Gas Cylinders On Pallets **5.50**
326-50555 Cable Drums **5.95**
326-51095 Wood Loads pkg(2) **9.95**

326-75640 Upright Powdered Cement Silos pkg(2) **12.95** *NEW*

WARNING LIGHTS

326-50142 Blue **5.25**
326-50159 Orange **5.25**
326-50425 Hella Warning Light/Siren (blue) **5.25**
326-50494 Light Bars (red, blue & amber) **5.50**
326-50814 Hella Lite-Bar (blue & amber) **5.50**

WHEELS & TIRES

326-5284 Front or Dual Wheels Package **.60**
326-50197 Truck 6-Spoke **5.25**
326-50357 Bus **6.50**
326-50531 Chrome Truck Wheels **6.90**
326-50548 All-Terrain Truck Wheels/Tires **5.95**
326-50852 With Raised White Lettering pkg(5) **7.50**
326-50920 Set of 3 Fifth Wheels **8.25**

Assembled, appropriately colored plastic vehicles, unless noted.

AIRCRAFT

MOTOR PLANES KIT

348-2084 pkg(6) **7.98**

348-2086 2-Motor Planes 4-Gliders Kit pkg(6) **3.98**

1/48 SCALE EA 8.98 (UNLESS NOTED)

P-38 LIGHTNING TWIN ENGINE EA 14.98

348-201031 Black & Silver
348-201032 Silver & Blue

ZERO FIGHTER SINGLE ENGINE
348-202031 Silver
348-202032 White

SPITFIRE SINGLE ENGINE
348-202033 Tan/Brown Camouflage
348-202034 Green/Red Camouflage

ME-109 SINGLE ENGINE
348-202035 Blue
348-202036 Black

P-51 MUSTANG SINGLE ENGINE

348-202037 Silver & Blue
348-202038 Red & White

JETS 1/72 SCALE

F-16 FALCON JET EA 8.98
348-210031 Navy (camouflage)

348-210032 USAF (white)
348-210033 USAF (red, white & blue)

HARRIER JET EA 8.98
348-210034 British (camouflage)
348-210035 Green/Black Camouflage
348-210036 Marines (gray/gray camouflage)

F-14 TOMCAT JET EA 9.98
348-211031 Silver
348-211032 Black
348-211033 White

FA-18 HORNET JET EA 9.98
348-211034 Navy (blue)
348-211035 USAF (silver)
348-211036 Navy (camouflage)

AUTOMOBILES

CLASSIC ASSORTMENTS

348-1720 Cars pkg(6) **7.98**
Diecast metal body with plastic details and underframe.

348-1721 Trucks pkg(6) **9.98**

BUSES
348-11 1940s Style **2.98**

CONSTRUCTION EQUIPMENT
348-140 Front End Loader w/Blade **2.98**
348-150 Front End Loader w/Bucket **2.98**
348-160 Cement Mixer **2.98**
348-226 Road Roller **2.98**

348-4220 Road Grader (yellow) **4.98**

U-Haul Truck

EMERGENCY VEHICLES
348-4200 Pumper (red) **5.98**

FARM MACHINERY
348-3 Harvester **2.98**

TRACTOR/ TRAILERS
348-190 Oil Tanker w/40' Oil Tank **3.98**
348-210 40' **3.98**

TRUCKS

TRUCKS W/CAB OVER ENGINE EA 2.98
348-130 Large Open Bed
348-170 Delivery

LADDER TRUCKS
348-4210 Red **6.98**
348-4212 White **5.49**

LOG TRUCKS W/LOG LOAD EA 11.98
348-14301 Cherry River Boom & Lumber Company *NEW*
348-14302 United States Lumber Company *NEW*
348-14303 Barnhart Lumber Company *NEW*
348-14304 Diamond Lumber Company *NEW*
348-14305 Woodside Lumber Company *NEW*
348-14306 Undecorated *NEW*

SEMI TRUCKS EA 1.98
348-1722 Continental Oil
348-1723 Paradise Bird
348-1724 Westerline Gas
348-1725 Super Star
348-1726 Freeport Cargo
348-1727 Worldrts Cargo
348-1728 Ocean Cargo
348-1729 Top Express

U-HAUL® TRUCKS EA 6.49

348-1130

348-1011 Alabama
348-1014 Arkansas
348-1015 California
348-1111 Hawaii
348-1112 Idaho
348-1113 Iowa
348-1114 Illinois
348-1116 Kansas
348-1117 Kentucky
348-1118 Louisiana
348-1119 Maine
348-1122 Michigan
348-1124 Mississippi
348-1125 Missouri
348-1126 Montana
348-1127 Nebraska
348-1128 Nevada
348-1129 New Hampshire
348-1130 New Jersey
348-1131 New Mexico
348-1134 North Dakota
348-1135 Ohio
348-1136 Oklahoma
348-1137 Oregon
348-1138 Pennsylvania
348-1141 South Dakota
348-1142 Tennessee
348-1143 Texas
348-1144 Utah
348-1145 Vermont
348-1146 Virginia
348-1147 Washington
348-1148 Washington DC
348-1149 West Virginia
348-1150 Wisconsin
348-1151 Wyoming

MISCELLANEOUS EA 2.98 (UNLESS NOTED)
348-12 Tow Truck
348-180 Livestock Transporter
348-200 Flatbed w/Tank Container **3.98**
348-227 Open Truck w/Boom Crane

VANS

348-4222 International Box Van Kit **3.98**

VEHICLE SETS

EA 6.98
348-11101 Rescue
348-11102 Forest Patrol
348-11103 City Maintenance
348-11106 Commercial Trucks

348-11107 City Service Trucks

Information STATION

San Diego Model Railroad Museum

At 24,000 square feet, the non-profit San Diego Model Railroad Museum is the world's largest operating model railroad exhibit. Located in Balboa Park, this one-of-a-kind museum features four scale layouts of enormous size depicting railroads of the southwest. With HO, O and N scale layouts, there's something for everyone including: a toy train gallery with hands-on controls for children, an LGB modular layout and numerous artifacts.

The individual HO layouts are among the largest of their type. The models are constructed and maintained by approximately 300 volunteer club members. The two HO layouts featured at the museum are the San Diego & Arizona Eastern and the Tehachapi Pass. The SD&AE is modeled after the prototype of the same name that connects San Diego with El Cajon and El Centro. The Tehachapi Pass models the Santa Fe line as it runs through the Tehachapi Mountains to near perfection. Included in this layout is a replica of the famous Loop where the engine of a 100-car train spirals up to cross directly over its caboose 90 feet below.

Since it opened in March of 1982, the museum has had over two million visitors.

JORDAN

HIGHWAY MINIATURES

"Highway Miniatures" are detailed replicas of American vehicles from the steam-era. Parts are molded in colors . Kits include step-by-step instructions and are easy to build. However, most include very small parts so some modeling experience is helpful.

1904 Oldsmobile Railroad Inspection Car & Dash Auto 360-228

AUTOMOBILES

ESSEX

360-222 1926 Two-Door Hardtop **4.95**
First popular priced closed car.

FORD

360-241 1914 Model T Touring Car **8.95**

360-226 1920 Model T Sedan **5.95**

360-213 1925 Roadster or Pick-Up **4.95**
Can be built as a Roadster or Pick-Up with top up or down.

360-236 1928 Model A Sedan **6.95**

360-217 1929 Model A Station Wagon **4.95**

360-225 1940 Standard V-8 Sedan **5.95**
Includes optional engine assembly for "hood up" scenes.

OLDSMOBILE

360-228 1904 Railroad Inspection Car & Curved Dash Auto **5.95**
Includes parts for both vehicles.

BUSES

360-229 1934 Ford 21 Passenger Bus **6.95**

EMERGENCY VEHICLES

360-208 1913 Ford Model T Pumper **4.95**
360-220 1923 Mack Aerial Ladder **7.95**

360-221 1927 Ahrens Fox Pumper **6.95**

360-237 1924 American LaFrance Pumper **7.95**

FARM MACHINERY

1920 FORDSON TRACTORS EA 3.95

360-218 Farm–Steel Wheels w/Cleats

360-219 Industrial–Hard Rubber Tires

TRUCKS

FORD

MODEL A

360-240 1928 Pick-Up **6.95**

1929 MODEL AA ONE-TON

360-214 Railway Express Agency **5.95**

360-239 Tank Truck w/ Period Oil/Gas Cans **6.95**

MODEL T EA 4.95 (UNLESS NOTED)

360-207 1911 Delivery Truck **5.95**

360-215 1925 Mail Truck

1923 Mack Aeriel Ladder 360-220

Beer Wagon 360-105

Stage Coach 360-234

360-216 1925 Panel Truck

MODEL TT ONE-TON

360-238 1923 Stake Truck **6.95**

1923 MACK "BULLDOG" TRUCKS EA 6.95

360-209 Stake Truck

360-210 Dump Truck

360-212 Tank Truck

360-227 Mack Hi-Lift Coal Dump Truck

PACKARD

360-231 1922 Stake Truck **6.95**

WAGONS

360-101 Light Delivery **4.95**

360-102 Standard Delivery **4.95**

360-103 Brougham **3.95**

360-104 Buckboard pkg(2) **3.95**

360-301 Baggage w/Bags pkg(2) **3.95**

HORSE-DRAWN WAGONS EA 7.95

360-105 Beer Wagon w/8 Horses
360-234 Stage Coach

EMERGENCY VEHICLES

LADDER TRUCK
490-77675 Red & White Cab **9.98**
Fully assembled, prepainted, diecast metal, patterned after American LaFrance equipment.

TRACTOR/ TRAILERS

TRACTORS 2-PACKS
490-7700 Short Haul without sleeper (white) & long haul w/sleeper (black) **11.98**

SHORT HAUL WITHOUT SLEEPER

WITH BOX TRAILER EA 13.98
490-15000 Trail Rail Service
490-15001 B&O
490-15002 Western Express
490-15003 PFE/UP/ATSF
490-15004 CR
490-15005 SP Pig

WITH TANK TRAILER EA 13.98
490-16000 Water
490-16001 Exxon
490-16002 Union 76
490-16003 Marathon
490-16004 Phillips 66
490-16005 General Cesspool

WITH FLATBED TRAILER
490-19000 Blue **11.98**
490-19001 Red, Black **11.98**
490-19002 D&S w/Wire Cables **13.98**

WITH 2 20' CONTAINERS EA 13.98
490-22000 K-Line Evergreen (white)
490-22001 US Mail-US Army (blue truck)
490-22002 Federal Express-Pennsy
490-22003 ATSF-CP (black truck)

WITH ROUND TANK EA 14.98
490-24000 Compressed Gas *NEW*
490-24001 Medical Waste *NEW*
490-24002 U.S. Army *NEW*
490-24003 Unlettered (silver) *NEW*

LONG HAUL W/SLEEPER

WITH BOX TRAILER EA 12.98
490-17000 Candy Apple Red Baron
490-17001 Black
490-17002 White
490-17003 Coop Shippers
490-17004 Preferred Pool
490-17005 WP Road Rail
490-17006 CP
490-17007 Federal Express

WITH MOVING & RACING TRAILER EA 13.98
490-21000 Black w/Chrome
490-21001 White w/Chrome
490-21002 Racing Dynamics Systems
490-21003 Bekins
490-21004 Dutch Masters

WITH REFRIGERATOR TRAILER EA 13.98
490-23000 Banana
490-23001 Fresh Farms Dairy
490-23002 USDA Meat
490-23003 Union Ice

WITH ROUND TANK EA 14.98
490-25000 Orange Juice *NEW*
490-25001 Milk *NEW*
490-25002 Unlettered (white) *NEW*

KITS

SHORT HAUL
490-26000 With Tank Trailer **11.98** *NEW*
490-29000 With Flat Trailer **10.98** *NEW*
490-32000 With 2 20' Containers **11.98** *NEW*
490-36000 With Container Box Trailer **10.98** *NEW*

LONG HAUL EA 11.98 (UNLESS NOTED)
490-27000 With Box Trailer **10.98** *NEW*
490-31000 With Racing/Moving Trailer *NEW*
490-33000 With Refrigerator Trailer *NEW*

See What's Available at **www.walthers.com**

The following are all unpainted pewter kits of high quality.

FARM EQUIPMENT

284-60001 1950s Red Farm Tractor w/Farmer **12.95** *NEW*

284-60002 1950s Red Manure Spreader **14.95** *NEW*

284-60003 Red 3 Bottom Plow **14.95** *NEW*
284-60004 1960s Green 4020 Farm Tractor w/Farmer **12.95** *NEW*
284-60005 1950s Red Super M-TA w/Front Loader & Farmer **TBA** *NEW*
284-60006 1940s Green 12-A Grain Harvester **TBA** *NEW*
284-60007 1960s Green 4020 Tractor w/237 Corn Picker & Farmer **TBA** *NEW*

284-61001 Bobcat w/Operator Figure **12.95** *NEW*

284-61002 Light Utility Trailer **9.95** *NEW*
284-61003 IT18F Front End Loader w/Operator Figure **TBA** *NEW*
284-61004 1940s D8 8R Tractor w/Logging Arch & Operator Figure **TBA** *NEW*
284-61005 IT18F Log Loader w/Operator Figure **TBA** *NEW*
284-61006 1940s D8 8R Bulldozer w/Operator Figure **TBA** *NEW*
284-61007 V8OE Forklift w/Operator Figure **TBA** *NEW*
284-62001 50 Ton Low Boy Trailer **TBA** *NEW*

AUTOMOBILES

NISSAN 300SX EA 12.00
Detailed replica of the popular twin turbo model has full interior detail and comes prepainted in your choice of five colors. Fully assembled from metal and plastic parts.

381-7150118

381-7150102 Black
381-7150112 Blue
381-7150118 Red
381-7150123 White
381-7150125 Yellow

TOYOTA SUPRA EA 12.98
A perfect addition to modern streets, models are fully assembled with metal chassis, free-rolling wheels, rear spoiler, exhaust pipe and muffler, plus Toyota logo on nose and rear!

381-715021 Red
381-715022 Black
381-715023 White
381-715024 Metallic Silver
381-715025 Metallic Blue

MITSUBISHI FTO EA 12.98
The latest model of Kato sports car, each model is detailed with right-hand steering. Choose from five prepainted colors.

381-7110031 Red
381-7110032 Black
381-7110033 White
381-7110034 Metallic Silver
381-7110035 Blue

LIFE-LIKE®

AMERICAN VEHICLE SETS W/APPLIED PARTS EA 8.75

433-1650 Trucks

433-1657 Cars

MERTEN

HORSE-DRAWN VEHICLES EA 16.99
Set the scene on your steam-era layout, or add an old-fashioned flavor to a modern setting with these wagons. Each comes fully assembled with team and accessories as shown. Additional light and heavy draft horses in harness are available separately to model longer hitches for these and other wagons.

447-2472 European Postal Coach w/Driver, Passenger, Coachman & 2-Horse Team

447-2480 Open Cab w/1 Horse Hitch, Driver & Passengers

447-2496 Lumber Rack Wagon w/Driver, Log Load, Helper & 2-Horse Team

kibri

IMPORTED FROM GERMANY BY WALTHERS

SPECIAL VALUE PRICING SHOWN IN RED

Based on vehicles in service around the world, these easy-to-build kits feature parts molded in realistic colors. All parts are numbered to follow step-by-step, illustrated instructions in each kit. Many also include self-adhesive safety signs, names (German text) and other markings.

SPECIAL BONUS SETS (LIMITED-RUN)

ROAD REPAIR

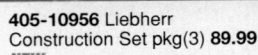

Limited Quantity Available
405-10792 Road Repair Set **63.99**
Make short work of road repairs this season when you have this set of equipment ready. It includes four complete kits; Demag Asphalt Paver, Meiller Road Grader, Hamm Roller and a Mercedes Semi with Dump Trailer.

CONSTRUCTION

Limited Quantity Available
405-10794 Construction Set **75.99**
Get the job done in no time with this set of four vehicles. You'll get an Atlas Tracked Shovel, Schwing Concrete Pumper, Kaelble Wheel Loader and a Scania Semi with Cement Mixer Trailer.

405-10866 Crane Transport Set pkg(7) **159.99**
Celebrates 10 years of Gottwald Crane models from Kibri, includes 10-axle crane, boom transport and five semis with low bed trailers.

405-10868 Salvage/Recovery Cranes Set pkg(4) **73.99**

405-10870 Road-Rail Vehicle Set pkg(4) **79.99**

405-10954 Small Machinery Set pkg(4) **79.99** *NEW*
Great detail for any construction site or shop scene. Includes one each Mobile Crane 405-10490, Front End Loader with Accessories #10340 (yellow), Unimog with Construction Crane #10940 and Backhoe #10692.

405-10956 Liebherr Construction Set pkg(3) **89.99** *NEW*
Heavy machinery for modern building sites. Includes one each #405-10347 Hydraulic Shovel, #10324 Heavy Bulldozer with blade and Ripper and #10202 Builder's Crane.

405-10958 Special Machinery Set pkg(4) **89.99** *NEW*
Get your next big building started right with this set. Includes one each #405-10462, Pile Driver #405-10562, Dragline Crane w/Clamshell and Wrecking Balls, #10550 Drilling Rig on Liebherr Crawler Chassis and Unimog Field Repair Truck #10770.

Transports for Gotwalld "Maxilift" Crane

405-10790

TRANSPORT

405-10790 Transports for Gottwald "Maxilift" Crane **99.99**
This set will make it easy to move the massive Gottwald crane from job to job. It consists of eight Mercedes trucks, all in matching blue, with three six-axle bridge transports, one five-axle low-boy, two Goldhofer platform trailers and two six-axle roller trailers.

TECHNICAL HELP SERVICE (THW)

405-10880 THW Injury Set pkg(4) **49.99**

405-10882 THW Space Clearing Set **39.99** pkg(4)

Limited Quantity Available
405-10732 Support Vehicle Set pkg(6) ~~153.99~~ **89.99**
You're ready for any emergency with this set of six vehicles! Includes: Mercedes Truck w/Flatbed Trailer, Liebherr Shovel, Zettelmeyer Wheel Loader with Accessories, Mercedes Crane, Amphibious "Duck" 6X6 Truck and Emergency Pontoon Bridge.

kibri

IMPORTED FROM GERMANY BY WALTHERS

ASSEMBLED MODELS IN DISPLAY CASE

The perfect choice for the collector or modeler looking for a unique display. Each model features a fully assembled Kibri vehicle in a clear plastic case.

405-15348 Menck M 154 LC Excavator **59.99**
405-15354 DB TLF 5000 H 4XL Fire Engine **44.99**
405-15434 Atlas 2004 LC Excavator **44.99**
405-15512 Kaelble SL26 Wheel Loader **55.99**
405-15618 Terex Quarry Dump Truck **51.99**
405-15638 Liebherr R922 Excavator **79.99**
405-15694 Liebherr R922 Excavator **79.99**
405-15754 Demag AC 665 Telescoping Crane **79.99**

405-15322 Wheel Loader THW **32.99**

405-15324 Liebherr Bulldozer/Excavator **36.99**

405-15394 Demag Road Surfacer **39.99**

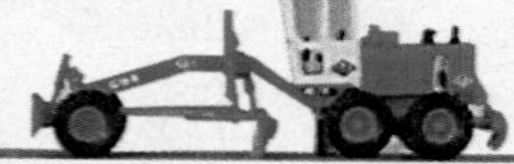

405-15430 O&K Road Grader **32.99**

Modern Push/Pull Tug Boat 405-8520

Container Barge/Lighter 405-8522

Bulk Material Loading Barge 405-8524

405-15454 Off-Road Articulated Dump Truck **32.99**

405-15518 Liebherr 4-Axle LTM 1050 Mobile Crane **39.99**

405-15608 Mercedes Farm Tractor w/Front Hay Cutter & Collection Trailer **39.99**

405-15610 Mercedes Benz Tractor w/Rotating Plow **36.99**

405-15640 Mercedes Benz Unimog w/Loading Crane **29.99**

405-15692 JCB Backhoe **36.99**

DISPLAY CASE

Showcase your favorite Kibri models in these display cases. Molded in clear, with a white top frame and black base, they're an ideal way to keep your models clean and free of dust, and protect them from curious fingers!

405-12060 7-5/8 x 3-1/8 x 4-1/8" 19 x 8 x 10.5cm **12.99**
405-12062 Large-10-3/8 x 2-5/8 x 3-1/8" 26 x 6.5 x 8cm **14.99**
405-12064 Small- 6-3/8 x 6-5/8 x 3-3/8" 16 x 16.5 x 8.5cm **9.99**

BOATS

See the Structures section for additional dockside details and structures from Kibri.

405-8520 Modern Push/Pull Tug Boat **25.99** *NEW*
7-1/4 x 2-1/2 x 3-13/16"
18.2 x 6.2 x 9.5cm
405-8522 Container Barge/Lighter **21.99** *NEW*
11-13/64 x 3-5/8 x 1"
28 x 9 x 2.3cm
405-8524 Bulk Material Loading Barge **21.99** *NEW*
11 x 3-5/8 x 1-1/8"
27.5 x 9 x 2.8cm

CARNIVAL EQUIPMENT

405-11006 Mercedes Industrial Tractor **24.99**
405-10934 Unimog Tractor w/House Trailer **27.99** *NEW*

Unimog Tractor w/Trailer House 405-10934

Mercedes Mixer 405-10928

Limited Quantity Available
405-10504 Showman's House Trailer w/Mercedes Tractor **39.99**

COIL HAULER

405-10578 Scheurle Steel Coil Transporter **42.99**

CONSTRUCTION EQUIPMENT

BACKHOE

405-10692 JCB 4x4 ~~32.99~~ **17.99**

The tractor-mounted backhoe is one of the most versatile pieces of equipment in use today. Found in all types of construction projects, they're also used by railroads, landscapers, cemeteries and others. Model features lots of positionable parts and a detailed cab interior, to duplicate the hard-working prototype.

BULLDOZER

405-10324 Liebherr **33.99**

405-10906 Komatsu Heavy-Duty D575 A-2 **54.99**
World's largest bullldozer.

CEMENT TRUCKS

405-10470 MAN w/Silo & Trailer **19.99**

405-10844 MAN & MB pkg(2) **22.99**

MERCEDES

405-10200 Schwing Concrete Pump (yellow) **36.99**

405-10782 4-Axle Cement Mixer **19.99**
405-10928 Liebherr Articulated Mixer w/Mercedes Actros Cab **23.99** *NEW*

kibri

IMPORTED FROM GERMANY
BY WALTHERS

CRANES

DOCKSIDE

405-8510 Over-Track Crane **54.99**
Plastic baseplate includes craneway and railroad track detail.

DEMAG

405-10754 Telescoping AC 665 Crane **64.99**
This crane can lift up to 250 tons with ease Riding on 16 wheels to spread its weight, it can be operated on the streets.

405-10784 Demag HC 665 w/Super Lift Jib **69.99**

GOTTWALD

405-10388 Telescoping Crane **99.99**

405-10738 LG 1800 "Spacelifter" Heavy Crane
~~149.99~~ **99.99**
An impressive model by itself or alongside a construction project, this big crane is complete with large booms, counterweights, outriggers and many other details.

Demag HC 665 w/Super Lift Jib 405-10784

Telscoping AC 665 Crane 405-10754

Telescopic Mobile Crane 405-10826

LTM 1800 w/Derrick & Pivoted Jib 405-10912

405-10426 Maxilift **118.99**

405-10438 Heavy Girder Frame Crane w/Pivoted Jib **139.99**

405-10788 Gottwald "Maxilift" w/Fly Jib **99.99**

LIEBHERR

405-10912 LTM 1800 w/Derrick & Pivoted Jib **159.99** *NEW*
12 x 7 x 33-5/8"
30 x 17.5 x 84cm

405-10826 LTM 1160/2 Telescopic Mobile Crane **61.99**

405-10962 Telescoping LTM 1160/2 4-Axle **59.99** *NEW*

405-11014 LTF 1030-4 Telescoping Crane **27.99** *NEW*

405-11026 4-Axle Hy-Rail Crane (blue) **33.99** *NEW*

kibri

IMPORTED FROM GERMANY BY WALTHERS

405-10328 Mobile Truck Crane (yellow) **35.99**

405-10390 MAN Truck and Trailer w/20K Construction Crane **43.99**

405-10494 Heavy LTM 1800 w/Pivoted Jib **136.99**
405-10496 Telescopic Crane w/Extended Jib **47.99**
405-10544 Telescopic Crane w/Jib (red) **47.99**
405-10518 4-Axle LTM 1050 **36.99**
405-10672 MAN Tractor w/Builders Crane On Trailer **42.99**

405-10558 4-Axle Hy-Rail Crane **39.99**
405-10560 Heavy LTM 1400 w/Jib **119.99**
405-10760 Liebherr HS 883 HD Litronic w/Clamshell Excavator **66.99**

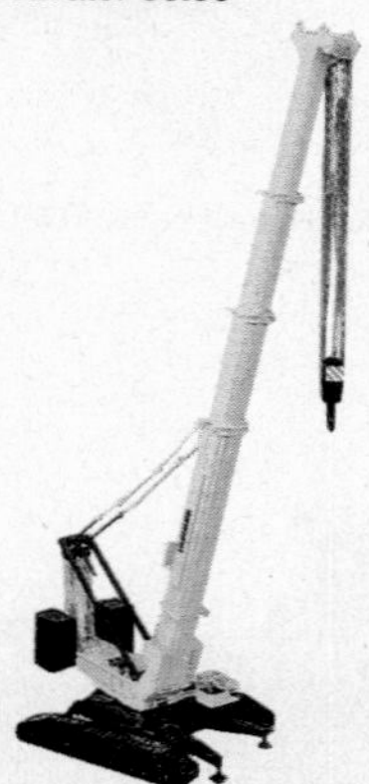

405-10574 LTR 1800 Telescoping Crane **89.99**

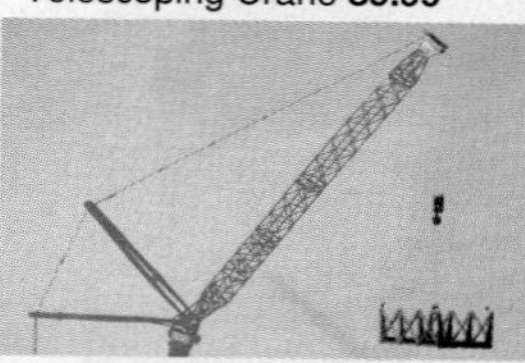

405-10440 Pivoted Jib for Telescoping Cranes **44.99**

405-10612 2-Axle Crane **29.99**

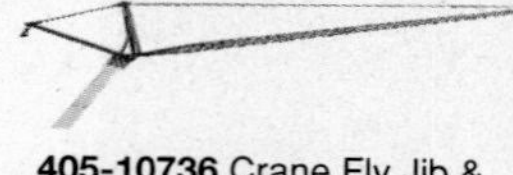

405-10736 Crane Fly Jib & Adapter **33.99**
Give your heavy cranes more lifting capacity with this fly jib. Includes an adapter to fit cranes #10494, 10688 and 10574.

4-Axle LTM 1050 405-10518

MAN Crane on Trailer 405-10672

405-10774 Liebherr LTM 1025 Truck Crane "Breuer" **29.99**
405-10674 4-Axled Telescoping Crane (white) **35.99**

Limited Quantity Available

405-10690 Crane Set pkg(2) **41.99**
Set includes a 4-Axle Truck Crane and a Telescoping Crane with Extending Jib.

405-10734 Telescoping Crane & Equipment Transport pkg(2) **99.99**
This set includes superbly detailed LTM 1400 crane in blue and white, accompanied by a matching MAN tractor pulling a low boy trailer carrying counterweights and other heavy equipment.

MERCEDES-BENZ

405-10634 LTF 1030 3-Axle Crane **36.99**

405-10718 Desert Sand Color w/Air Conditioner **27.99**

MOBILE CRANES EA 16.99

405-10488 Low Cab

405-10490 High Cab

405-10964 Telescoping 3-Axle "Breuer" **31.99** *NEW*

DUMP TRUCKS

DAIMLER-BENZ

405-10352 4-Axle **22.99**

405-10416 High Capacity **23.99**
405-10012 Heavy Duty Semi **19.99**

MERCEDES

405-10700 With Roll On/Off Dump Bed **21.99**

405-10810 Tractor w/2-Axle Dump Trailer **19.99**

405-10812 Low-Side Dump w/3-Axle Dump Trailer **19.99**

405-10814 High-Side Dump w/2-Axle Dump Trailer **19.99**

405-10816 With Meiller Heavy-Duty Dump Body **18.99**

405-10822 Tractor w/2-Axle Dump Trailer **19.99**

405-10930 Actros High Side w/2-Axle Trailer **19.99** *NEW*

MAGIRUS-DEUTZ

405-10914 230D 26 AK 2-Axle **23.99** *NEW*

MAN

405-10212 Double-Bottom **22.99**

405-10650 With Dump Trailer **19.99**

405-10124 With Flatbed Trailer **22.99**

OFF-ROAD TYPES

405-10454 Off-Road **27.99**

405-10618 TEREX (Green) **41.99**

405-10834 MB 4-Axle w/Meiller Dump Body **19.99**

405-10836 4-Axle w/Crane & Dumpster **26.99**

405-10838 MB 3-Axle w/Meiller Dump Body **18.99**

405-10840 Scania 3-Axle w/Meiller Dump Body **18.99**

kibri

IMPORTED FROM GERMANY BY WALTHERS

405-10900 O&K K60 Heavy-Duty Mine Dump Truck **34.99**

405-10904 Komatsu HD 785-3 Heavy-Duty Mine Dump Truck **39.99**

DRILLING RIG

405-10550 Liebherr 974 w/Drilling Equipment **57.99**

FRONT END LOADER

LIEBHERR

405-10146 Tracked **22.99**
405-10638 Heavy-Duty Hydraulic Model R992 **64.99**

FAUN EA 22.99 (UNLESS NOTED)

405-10208 Yellow
405-10294 Red

405-10878 Wheel Loader F1310 (white) **19.99**

405-10944 F 1310 City Street Dept. (orange) **19.99** *NEW*

KAELBLE

405-10512 Heavy-Duty SL30 **44.99**

405-10758 SL26 w/Refuse Loader **42.99**
Great for your recycling center or landfill, comes equipped with large combination grapple and bucket for moving large loads.

KOMATSU

405-10694 Heavy-Duty Model R992 **64.99**

PAVER

405-10394 DEMAG Road Surfacer DF120P **36.99**

ROAD GRADERS EA 29.99

405-10430 Road/Land

405-10902 O&K

See What's Available at

www.walthers.com

Heavy-Duty Hydraulic R992 405-10638

Heavy-Duty Model R992 405-10694

HD Litronic w/Clamshell Excavator 405-10760

Hy-Rail w/Scoop 405-10984

ROLLER

405-10778 Hamm Rubber Tired Compactor **33.99**

405-10280 Hamm Road Roller **21.99**

SHOVELS

ATLAS

405-10434 Tracked **34.99**

405-10894 Model 1064 On Wheels **36.99**
405-10984 Hy-Rail w/Scoop **35.99** *NEW*

LIEBHERR

405-10140 Modern, Wheeled **27.99**

405-10142 Modern, Tracked **27.99**

405-10204 Hy-Rail **28.99**

405-10206 With Grader Blade **28.99**
405-10760 HS 883 HD Litronic w/Clamshell Excavator **66.99**

kibri

IMPORTED FROM GERMANY BY WALTHERS

405-10832 A 922 Tracked Excavator **22.99**

405-10966 HS 883 Heavy-Duty Litronic Cable Excavator w/Accessories **55.99** *NEW*
Includes small and large clamshells, plus small and large wrecking balls.

MENCK

405-10384 With Dragline Bucket **24.99**
405-10562 With Clamshell & Wrecking Balls **47.99**

405-10348 M154 LC Shovel **47.99**

405-10864 Tracked Excavator w/Deep Bucket **45.99** *NEW*

SITE TRAILERS

405-10278 Portable Offices pkg(2) **15.99**

SOIL COMPACTOR

Limited Quantity Available

405-10300 Hamm "Sheepsfoot" Compactor **21.99**

TRUCKS

MERCEDES - UNIMOG EA 29.99 (UNLESS NOTED)

405-10768 Fuel Tank Truck

405-10770 Field Repair Unit

405-10772 Tractor w/Two Site Trailers

405-10884 Road Maintenance w/Plate Compactor

405-10888 Road Maintenance w/Conveyor/Winch

405-10946 Flatbed w/2-Axle Trailer City Street Dept. (orange) *NEW*

405-10948 With Front-Mounted Schmidt Snow Blower City Street Dept. (orange) **31.98** *NEW*

WHEEL LOADER

405-10756 Heavy-Duty **56.99**
A great vehicle wherever loose material needs to be moved, right at home in mine, construction or steel mill service.

EMERGENCY VEHICLES

BOATS

405-8269 Amphibious DUKW "Duck" **16.99**

DAIMLER-BENZ

405-10354 TLF Pumper **29.99**

FORD

405-10332 1950 FK 2500 LF8 Pumper **19.99**

LIEBHERR LTM FIRE DEPT. CRANES

405-10554

405-10330 3-Axle 1050/3 **35.99**
405-10554 4-Axle 1050/4 **38.99**
405-10556 2-Axle 1025 **33.99**

UNIMOG

405-11016 Flatbed w/Loading Crane & 4-Axle Equipment Trailer **23.99** *NEW*

405-10752 Fire Dept. Utility Truck **25.99**
Dispatch this versatile rig to clean-up after a big blaze or hazardous materials situation. Molded in red and black, model is complete with blue lights, siren, loading crane and authentic markings.

SPECIAL SET

405-10796 Fire Dept. Heavy Equipment **69.99**
Everything you need for clean-up after a big blaze in one set. Includes Liebherr LTM 1025 Truck Crane, Mercedes DB-TL Pumper/Light Unit, Dumpster Truck w/Crane and Liebherr 1050/4-Axle Crane, all in red.

TECHNICAL HELP SERVICE (THW) EQUIPMENT

A branch of the German government, this agency is responsible for heavy construction projects, including road and bridge repairs, during war-time or natural disasters. All equipment is painted in a distinctive blue scheme.

LIEBHERR

405-11018 4-Wheel Mobile Crane w/Accessories **27.99** *NEW*

405-11020 Front End Loader on Crawler Chassis **21.99** *NEW*

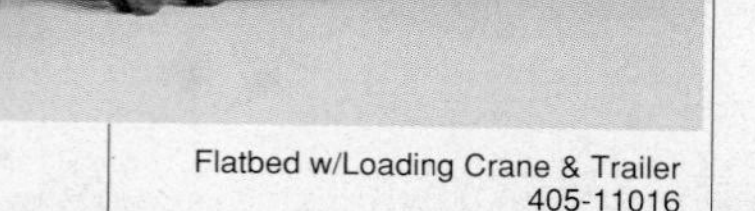

Flatbed w/Loading Crane & Trailer
405-11016

405-10320 Mobile Excavator w/Accessories **27.99**

MAN

405-11022 With 4-Axle Equipment Trailer & Hamm Compactor Roller **43.99** *NEW*

MERCEDES-BENZ

405-10798 Unimog Flatbed w/Meiller Crane **25.99**
405-10800 Dump Truck **19.99**

ZETTELMEYER

405-10322 Wheel Loader w/Accessories **29.99**
Includes optional end loader bucket, backhoe, clamshell, log grapple, air hammer and pile driver

FARM MACHINERY

LEXION 480 CLAAS COMBINES

405-10858 With Grain Head **49.99**

405-10978 With Corn Head & Head Transport Trailer **51.99** *NEW*

kibri

IMPORTED FROM GERMANY
BY WALTHERS

FENDT TRACTORS

405-10762 Vario Favorit 926 Farm Tractor **29.99**

405-10830 With 2 Side-Dump Trailers **32.99**

405-10860 With Mounted Forage Harvester **32.99**

405-10976 Vario Favorit w/CLAAS Round Hay Baler **35.99** *NEW*

405-10982 Favorit 326 w/Earth Rollers **33.99** *NEW*

MERCEDES TRACTORS

405-10484 With Liquid Manure Applicator **29.99**

405-10608 With Front Mower & Hay Rake **38.99**

405-10610 With Reversing Plow **31.99**

405-10646 With Lime Spreader **33.99**

405-10522 With Dump Trailer **19.99**

405-10702 With Tiller and Grain Drill **36.99**

405-10764 4x4 w/Front-Mounted Forage Harvester **36.99**

405-10820 4x4 w/Front-Mounted Bale Lifter, Trailer & Round Hay Bales **31.99**

405-10862 4x4 w/Twin Tires **26.99**

Limited Quantity Available

405-10486 With Feed Trailer **29.99**
405-10350 With Two Wagons **34.99**

FARM IMPLEMENTS EA 19.99

408-10908 Trailer Set pkg(3)
Includes bale throw wagon, dump trailer and liquid manure tank trailer.

408-10910 Tractor Mounted Tool Set pkg(8)
Includes Forage Harvester, Grain Drill, Cultivator, Dump Box, Fork Lift Blades, Loader, Mower/Conditioner and Counterweights.

LIVESTOCK TRUCK

405-10686 Transporter w/Trailer & 12 Cows **35.99**

FLATBED TRACTOR & TRAILER

405-10808 Mercedes Tractor w/3-Axle Flatbed **15.99**

405-10898 Mercedes w/Atlas Crane & 2-Axle Trailer (DB markings) **34.99** *NEW*
405-10936 Unimog Tractor w/Canvas Cover & 4-Axle Flatbed **29.99** *NEW*
405-10986 MAN w/Atlas Load Crane & 5-Axle Trailer **25.99** *NEW*

Limited Quantity Available

405-10312 Scania **25.99**
405-10336 MAN w/Trailer & Forklift **24.99**
405-10850 MB Prefabricated Concrete Loader w/Crane & Trailer **18.99**
405-10856 Scania w/Portable Schwenk Silo on Trailer **18.99**
405-10886 MAN w/2-Axle Trailer **24.99**
405-10890 Tractor w/ 2-Axle Trailer & Fork Lift **32.99**
405-10898 MB Flatbed w/Atlas Loading Crane &Trailer **34.99**

FORK LIFTS

405-10564 Kalmar LMV **23.99**

405-10002 Industrial **7.99**

405-10926 Kaelble SL26 w/Forks **39.99** *NEW*
405-10952 Forklift Bonus Set pkg(4) **62.99** *NEW*
Detail any heavy industrial area with this set of four forklifts. Includes one each #405-10432, 10483, 10002 and 10564

HEAVY-DUTY TRANSPORTS

405-10614 Baumann Mercedes Transport w/Large Tank **69.99**
405-10498 150T VAT and Heavy Hauler w/Rear Control Cabin **69.99**
405-10396 Benz Transporter w/Transformer **49.99**
405-10420 MAN w/Transformer **47.99**
405-10464 4-Axle Mercedes w/Vat and Support **56.99**

Limited Quantity Available

405-10444 Benz Transport w/6-axle Trailer **31.99**
405-10446 Flatbed w/Trailer **39.99**
405-10450 Articulated w/Rungs **16.99**
405-10526 Mercedes Transport w/Pipe Load **21.99**
405-10532 DAF Tractor w/Crane Load **42.99**
405-10534 DAF Transport w/Truck Cabs **33.99**
405-10546 Kalmar Transporter w/Carrier **57.99**
405-10548 Mercedes Heavy Transporter w/Load **47.99**
405-10566 Baumann Mercedes & Special Trailers pkg(5) **114.99**
Specializing in the movement of high, wide, heavy and odd shaped loads, the Baumann fleet is a familiar sight in Europe. Includes Mercedes 3- and 4-Axle heavy tractors, plus a 3-Axle semi tractor, special transporter with transformer load and an additional "bridge" transporter for large construction machinery.

Unimog w/Canvas Cover & Flatbed 405-10936

Load Crane & Trailer 405-10986

Fork Lift Bonus Set pkg(4) 405-10952

kibri

IMPORTED FROM GERMANY BY WALTHERS

405-10568 Baumann MAN & Mercedes w/Trailers pkg(6) **89.99**
Includes two matching tractors and four special equipment trailers, based on heavy moving equipment operated by Baumann.

405-10570 MAN w/Trailer & Boiler **52.99**

Car shown not included

405-10598 Faun Tractor w/Passenger Car Transporter **27.99**

405-10602 Mercedes 850A Tractor w/Trailer **31.99**

405-10740 Mercedes w/Transporter & TEREX Dump Truck **56.99**

405-10670 Electric Steel Furnace in Transit **39.99**

405-10684 Gas Pipe Transporter **35.99**

405-10476 Special Transport w/Transformer Load **89.99**

Car shown not included

405-10502 Kaelble Tractor w/Freight Car Transporter **25.99**

405-10508 Mercedes 4-Axle Tractor & Trailer w/Load **48.99**

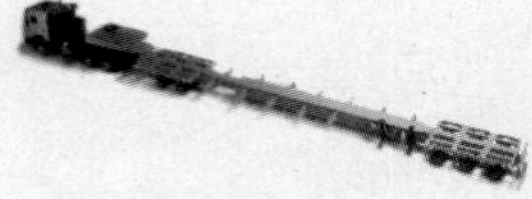

405-10576 Mercedes 3850 Transporter w/Trailer **29.99**

405-10636 Mercedes Transporter for Heavy Load **44.99**

405-10776 Schmidbauer Transport Set **105.99**
Set includes three Mercedes tractors in matching blue, with blue Goldhofer low-boy trailers, plus a Liebherr R 922 Hydraulic Shovel, broken down into chassis, boom cab and bucket for transport.

405-10780 MAN Tractor w/Doll Extendible Flatbed **29.99**

405-10892 MB 4-Axle w/5-Axle Bridge Transporter Trailer **28.99**

INTERMODAL EQUIPMENT

405-10478 Mercedes Semi w/Container **16.99**
Limited Quantity Available

405-10722 Mercedes w/Two 20' Containers **15.99**

402-10876 MB Edelhoff w/Container **18.99** ***NEW***

CONTAINER CRANES

405-10920 Kalmar Telescoping Container Loader **49.99** ***NEW***

Telescoping Container Loader 405-10920

Schmisbauer Transport Set 405-10776

405-10432 Kalmar w/3 20' Containers **29.99**

405-10482 With 40' Containers **29.99**

CONTAINERS

405-10266 20' DB pkg(4) **14.99**

405-10272 Portable Storage Units pkg(2) **9.99**

405-10924 20' Box Type Set pkg(8) **15.99** ***NEW***
Includes four United German Railways (DB-AG) units in current scheme, plus four additional containers in different colors.

405-10922 40' Box Type Set pkg(6) **19.99** ***NEW***
Includes six containers in different colors.
Limited Quantity Available

405-10480 40' pkg(3) **17.99**

INDUSTRIAL TRACTORS

MERCEDES-BENZ

405-10422 Hy-Rail Switcher **27.99**

405-10644 With Trailer & Tank Load **33.99**

405-10706 With Rear Loader **32.99**
Perfect for moving gravel, grain, snow, manure or helping with other chores.

405-10980 With Front Loader & Rear Winches **27.99** ***NEW***

LOWBOY TRACTOR/ TRAILER RIGS

405-10342 MAN Tractor w/Trailer **33.99**

405-10368 Benz w/5-Axle Trailer Platform **25.99**

405-10530 Mercedes Transporter w/Grader **49.99**

405-10708 Baumann Mercedes 4-Axle w/Trailer **32.99**

kibri

IMPORTED FROM GERMANY BY WALTHERS

405-10710 Baumann Mercedes 3-Axle w/Trailer **29.99**
405-10540 Mercedes Transport Trailer w/Crane **27.99**
405-10542 Transport w/Construction Buildings **37.99**

405-10668 Articulated Bulk Carrier **19.99**

405-10896 MB 4-Axle Tractor w/4-Axle Lowboy & 2-Axle Crane **43.99**

405-10596 Faun & Low Loader **36.99**

405-10600 Kaelble Tractor w/Low Loader & Shovel **36.99**

405-10642 Unimog w/4-Axle Trailer & Load **33.99**

405-10712 Mercedes w/Crane Boom in Transit **33.99**

405-10716 MAN w/Well Type Trailer & Pre-Fab Garage **25.99**

405-10938 Unimog w/Loading Crane and 3-Axle Trailer **27.98** ***NEW***

Limited Quantity Available
405-10414 Scania w/Boat Load **59.99**
405-10448 Mercedes w/Articulated Low-Loader **25.99**
405-10536 Mercedes w/Trailer & Off-Road Dump Truck **42.99**
405-10538 Mercedes w/Lowboy & Construction Trailers **39.99**
405-10678 Baumann Site Trailer Transporter **39.99**
405-10680 Scania Dump Truck w/Trailer and Road Roller **44.99**

SEMI TRACTORS

405-10630 MAN Tractor w/Generator **24.99**

405-10660 Mercedes 3-Axle w/Generator **21.99**

405-10662 MAN 3-Axle w/Generator **21.99**

SEMI W/TRAILER

405-10586 MAN Coal Transporter **19.99**

405-10714 Mercedes (Desert Sand Color) w/Air Conditioner & Containers **23.99**

405-10750 Unimog w/Trailer & Lumber Load **33.99**
This short wheelbase 4x4 can negotiate the toughest construction sites! Includes trailer with realistic lumber load.

405-10848 MAN w/Powdered Cement Trailer **16.99**

405-10852 MB Sand Truck/Trailer **16.99**

405-10854 MB Roundnose Tractor w/Lime Spreader **24.99**

405-10916 Mercedes Round Nose Tractor w/Coal Trailer **23.99** ***NEW***

405-10970 Mercedes w/"Kuhn & Nagel" Canvas Side Single Axle Trailer **17.99** ***NEW***

405-10974 Scania w/"Flachglas" 3-Axle Glass Carrier **19.99** ***NEW***

Limited Quantity Available
405-10244 MAN "Kolb-Wellpappe" **11.99**
405-10720 Mercedes w/Covered Trailer "Kibri" **15.99**
405-10724 MAN w/Reefer Trailer "Wiesenhof Ice Cream" **15.99**
405-10726 Mercedes w/Glass Transport Trailer **15.99**

TRACTORS

405-10400 Mercedes 3-Axle **25.99**

405-10424 MAN Heavy Duty **27.99**

405-10458 DAF 95 **27.99**

405-10506 Mercedes 4-Axle **27.99**

405-10510 Mercedes 3-Axle **27.99**

405-10620 Mercedes 4-Axle **22.99**

405-10628 Mercedes 4-Axle w/Generator **24.99**

405-10664 Mercedes-New German Railways 4-Axle **28.99**

TRAILERS

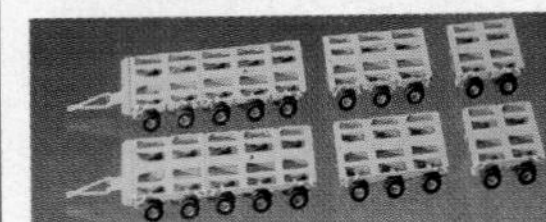

405-10116 Multi-Axle Moving Trailers **24.99**

405-10622 Crane Trailers **27.99**

405-10942 Dump Trailer Assortment pkg(3) **19.99** ***NEW***
Includes 2- and 3-Axle Rear Dump and 2-Axle Side dump types, for use with most trucks and tractors.

TRUCK ACCESSORIES

405-10500 Lettering Set for Trucks (German) **21.99**

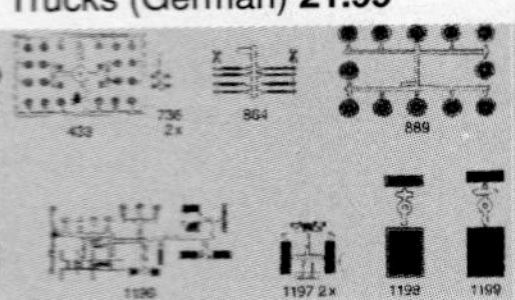

405-10632 Assorted Truck Replacement Parts **27.99**
405-10818 Truck Accessory Set **25.99**
An assortment of add-on details designed to enhance the realism of your Kibri truck fleet. Includes diesel engines, mirrors, air horns and more.

405-11984 Sheet Metal Loads pkg(3) **12.99**

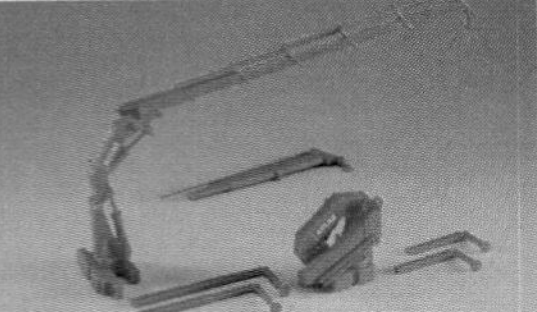

405-10988 Atlas Load Crane & Equipment **13.99** ***NEW***
Features telescoping arm, includes outriggers to convert any truck.

TRUCKS- HEAVY

405-10872 MB Unimog Hy-Rail **24.99**

405-10940 Long Wheelbase Unimog Flatbed w/Canvas Cover & Loading Crane **23.99** ***NEW***

TRUCKS- SPECIAL BODIES

405-10696 MAN w/Crane & Roll On/Off Flat Bed **21.99**

kibri

IMPORTED FROM GERMANY BY WALTHERS

405-10698 Mercedes w/Roll On/Off Scrap Container **21.99**
A great addition to any factory or shop that produces recyclable scrap, such as cardboard, plastic or metals.

405-10748 Short Wheelbase Unimog **25.99**
Designed for use in tight city streets and cramped industrial areas, this go-anywhere, do anything truck is a perfect service vehicle for your fleet.

405-10786 MB Dumpster Loader w/Trailer **29.99**

405-10842 MB 4-Axle w/Roll On/Off Dumpster **22.99**

405-10846 MB w/Trailer & Roll-On/Off Dumpsters **29.99**

405-10874 MB 3-Axle w/Roll On/Off Dumpster (white) **19.99**
405-10932 Mercedes Actros w/Dumpster & 2-Axle Trailer **22.99** *NEW*

BOX VANS W/2-AXLE TRAILERS

405-10802 MAN/"Badisher Wein" **15.99**
405-10804 Mercedes "Sudzucker" **15.99**
405-10968 MAN/"WLZ" **17.99** *NEW*
405-10972 Mercedes "Wiesenhof" Refrigerated Units **17.99** *NEW*

405-10580 Brewery Set **29.99**

DOUBLE-BOTTOM

405-10264 MAN, German Railway **21.99**

Limited Quantity Available
405-10338 MAN "Schenker" **18.99**
405-10260 MAN, German Post Office **19.99**

UTILITY TRUCKS

405-10474 Mercedes w/Crane & Grab **16.99**

405-10640 Unimog w/Loading Crane **25.99**

405-10744 Mercedes w/Cable Trailer **21.99**
Keep the phone lines up and running with this new set. Includes markings for the latest BDP scheme.

405-10746 Long Unimog w/Pole Trailer **29.99**
Just what you need to install new electric or phone service anywhere. Includes long wheelbase Unimog with loading crane and four-axle trailer with pole load.
405-10802 MAN Box Van w/2-Axle Trailer "Badisher Wein" **15.99**
405-10804 Mercedes Box Van w/2-Axle Trailer, Canvas Covers "Südzucker" **15.99**

405-10950 Unimog w/Backhoe & Equipment Trailer **31.99** *NEW*
Set includes Unimog tractor with backhoe and attachments, including jackhammer, timber hooks and clamshell bucket.

WRECKERS

405-10436 Scania Towing & Salvage **25.99**

405-10514 RAU Mercedes 4-Axle Recovery Vehicle **27.99**

LOGGING EQUIPMENT

TRACTORS

405-10824 Kaelble Loader w/Log Grab **39.99**

405-10588 With Logging Trailer **36.99**

MERCEDES-BENZ

405-10590 With Log Loading Crane **33.99**

405-10704 With Crane & Loaded Trailer **32.99**

TRUCKS

405-10828 MB w/Crane & Trailer w/Log Load **29.99**

405-10516 With Crane & Pulpwood Load **27.99**

405-10666 With Articulating Platform & Logs **25.99**

405-10766 MB Unimog w/Log Loading Crane **29.99**
405-10918 Mercedes Round Nose Tractor w/Crane & Skeleton Logging Trailer **23.99** *NEW*

MAN/"WLZ" 405-10968

Box Van w/ Trailer 405-10802

Box Van w/Trailer 405-10804

Mercedes "Wiesenhof" Box Van 405-10972

Dumpster & Trailer 405-10932

Kaelble Loader w/Log Grab 405-10824

Round Nose Tractor w/Crane & Trailer 405-10918

N.J. International

AUTOMOBILES

1964 CORVETTE

525-102 White Metal Kit **7.49**

TRUCKS

DELIVERY TRUCKS

525-103 UPS Type **24.95**
All brass kit.

MACK MB TILT CAB TRACTOR KIT

525-138 White Metal Kit **25.95**

FIRE EQUIPMENT

WHITE METAL KITS

525-130 Mack C Cab & Tillered Ladder Truck **69.95**
525-1301 Mack C Cab Tractor Kit **29.95**
525-1302 Mack Tillered Trailer Kit **45.95**

HY-RAIL TRACTOR

525-4026 Tractor **19.95**
Plastic kit.

NOCH

IMPORTED FROM GERMANY BY WALTHERS
Models are assembled of appropriately colored plastic.

AIRCRAFT

528-11450 Light Mid-Wing Aircraft **11.99**
528-11470 High Performance Glider **11.99**

AUTOMOBILES

AUDI

528-18000 A3 (blue) **8.99**
528-18010 A4 (red) **8.99**
528-18011 A4 Avant (green) **8.99**
528-18020 A6 (black) **9.99**
528-18021 A6 Avant **9.99**
528-18022 A6 Taxi (white) **10.99**
528-18030 TT Coupe **10.99**

FORD EA 8.99

528-18100 Ka (yellow)

528-18110 Fiesta (blue)
528-18120 Puma (red)
528-18130 Mondeo (white)
528-18131 Mondeo Turnier (green)

VOLKSWAGEN

528-18200 Scharan (blue) **8.99**

BOATS

528-10710 Sailboats **7.99**
528-11210 Sailboat w/Fisherman **9.99**
528-11250 Sailboat w/Figure **11.99**
528-11260 Row Boat w/Two People **11.99**
528-11300 Sailboat w/Spinnaker **9.99**

BACKGROUND BOAT KITS

528-35740 Motor Tank **28.99**
528-35750 Pilot Boat **33.99**

EMERGENCY VEHICLES

AUDI EA 9.99 (UNLESS NOTED)

528-18012 A4 Police
528-18023 A6 Fire Dept.
528-18024 A6 Avant Ambulance **12.99**

On-Trak model products

These period trucks and trailers will set the scene on your layout. Each craft train kit features unpainted white metal parts and styrene, wire and wood details.

CONSTRUCTION EQUIPMENT

786-5107 International Concrete Mixer **19.95**
786-5108 Iroquois Steam Road Roller **18.95**

786-5111 Road Repair Set **37.95**
Includes one each #5107 and #5108, plus extra details.

FARM MACHINERY

786-5201 JI Case Steam Tractor **79.95**
Intricately detailed model of 1900s era steam-powered tractor.

TRUCKS

AUTOCAR

786-5105 Stakedbed **14.95**
786-5117 Basic Chassis **13.95**

786-5118 Flatbed **15.95**
786-5126 Kerosene Tank **17.95**
786-5147 Wrecker **16.95**

1947 INTERNATIONAL KB11

786-5040 Flatbed Truck **15.95**
786-5041 Tractor **14.95**
786-5042 Dump Truck **15.95**
786-5044 Tractor w/32' Flatbed Trailer **19.95**
786-5045 Stakebed Truck **16.95**

Prototype Photo

786-5047 Tractor w/28' Van Trailer **20.95**
786-5048 Cab & Chassis–No Body **13.95**

786-5080 Produce Truck **18.85**
786-5084 Square Tank Truck **17.95**

KLEIBER

Built from 1914 to 1937 by the Kleiber Motor Company of San Francisco, California. Flat fenders with cab open.

786-5098 Flatbed Truck **15.70**
786-5099 Flatbed w/Details **17.80**

786-5121 Moving Van **18.45**

OPEN CAB
786-5100 Semi/Tractor **15.70**
786-5101 Semi/Tractor/Trailer **20.95**
786-5103 Dump **16.75**
786-5104 Tank **18.85**
786-5112 Basic Chassis **15.70**
786-5122 Flatbed **16.75**
786-5124 Cement **19.90**
786-5127 Kerosene Tank **19.90**
786-5151 Stakebed **17.80**

CLOSED CAB
786-5114 Delivery Van **18.85**
786-5115 Stakebed **16.75**
786-5122 Flatbed **16.75**
786-5141 Semi Tractor **15.70**
786-5143 Semi Tractor w/Van Trailer **24.10**
786-5148 Basic Chassis **15.70**
786-5149 Tank **18.85**
786-5150 Light Delivery **16.75**
786-5152 Dump **18.85**

GERLINGER LUMBER CARRIER

786-5109 **20.95**

1924 MACK

786-5128 Short Chassis **15.45**
786-5129 Flatbed **16.45**
786-5132 Dump **18.95**
786-5135 Kerosene Tank **18.45**
786-5136 Long Chassis **15.95**
786-5137 Wrecker **18.45**
786-5144 Semi Tractor **15.45**
786-5146 Semi w/Fruehauf Van Tractor **24.45**

786-5403 Railtruck Flatbed **19.75**
786-5413 Log Truck w/Detailed Load **19.95**

TRAILERS
786-5022 40' Flatbed **13.15**
786-5043 32' Single Axle Flatbed **13.15**
786-5110 1920 Freuhauf Semi Van **14.65**

FRUENHAUF PIGGYBACKS
Resin kits with metal wheels.
786-6600 28' **13.95** ***NEW***
786-6610 24' **13.95** ***NEW***
786-6620 32' **15.25** ***NEW***

RZN-MTL© SERIES
One-piece resin cabs on one-piece metal chassis.

FORD C-500 COE

786-6100 Semi Tractor on 96" Wheelbase Basic Chassis **15.95** ***NEW***

TRANSTAR 4200

786-5018 Tractor **16.45**
786-5025 Tractor w/Sleeper **18.65**
786-5029 With Wrecker Body **24.95**

TRANSTAR II EA 16.45

786-5020 Cabover w/Sleeper
86-5021 "Suicide Cab" (No Sleeper)

1926 WHITE
786-5050 Cab & Chassis-No Body, Long Wheelbase **12.95**
786-5051 Flatbed-Long Wheelbase **14.95**
786-5052 Stakebed-Long Wheelbase **16.95**
786-5053 Square Tank-Long Wheelbase **15.95**

786-5055 Log **17.95**
786-5056 Produce **16.75**
786-5066 Semi Tractor Short Wheelbase **12.95**
786-5068 Semi Tractor-Short Wheelbase w/Trailer **20.65**
786-5074 Flatbed-Short Wheelbase **14.95**
786-5075 Cab & Chassis-No Body, Short Wheelbase **12.95**

PIRATE MODELS LTD.

IMPORTED FROM GREAT BRITAIN BY WALTHERS

BUSES

Cast metal, craft train kits are based on popular city and cross-country buses. All models are less seats, interior details and decals.

BLUEBIRD

559-355 1975 School Bus **63.99**

EAGLE EA 69.99

559-3512 05 Interstate

559-3513 05 Combo

559-3514 10 Interstate/ Suburban

FLEXIBLE EA 65.99

559-358 Grumman-Flexible 870
559-3511 Flexible Metro

GMC

559-353 PD4903/4905A Coach **63.99**

559-359 RTS Mark 3 Coach **65.99**

559-3510 RTS Mark 4 **65.99**

559-357 5909/12 Transit **63.99**

MACK

559-354 1930 AB Interstate Coach **63.99**

RENAULT

559-356 IN6C Paris **59.99**

559-3515 1935 TN4H Paris Open Platform **63.99**
559-3517 1935 TN4H Paris Closed Side Entrance **63.99**
559-3516 1935 TN4H Paris Closed Platform **63.99**

559-3518 1934 K63C Paris Open Platform **63.99**
559-3519 1934 K63C Paris Closed Side Entrance **63.99**

TRANSIT EA 63.99

559-351 40' 53SER

559-352 4502/7

Information STATION

Customizing Vehicles

With so many choices in vehicles for your HO Scale layout, you may find that selecting the right automobiles, trucks or farm machinery is a rather daunting task. Once you find the pieces that best suit your needs, you may be tempted to just place them on roads or in parking lots and never give them another thought. However, there are many detailing and customizing options that will give your vehicles a more realistic look on your layout.

Detailing your vehicles through paint gives them a more realistic appearance instead of a one-color mold appearance. The first step is to disassemble as much of the vehicle as you can. With the wheels usually painted black, you can add silver paint to make the hubcaps stand out. You can also add the same silver paint to parts like door handles and grills. Adding red and silver paint to headlights and taillights is also a strong customizing feature.

Besides paint, there are other vehicle accessories you can look into using to detail your vehicles. Try adding license plate decals to give various cars an authentic feel. You can also place figures in a few of the vehicles. Some manufacturers do produce seated figures to place in cars, though a little plastic surgery (i.e., cutting figures off at the waist) can produce the same effect.

AUTOMOBILES

PKG(5) EA 10.95

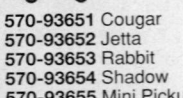

570-93651 Cougar
570-93652 Jetta
570-93653 Rabbit
570-93654 Shadow
570-93655 Mini Pickup
570-93656 VW Bug

570-93657 Thunderbird
570-93658 Toronado
570-93659 Falcon
570-93660 Stationwagon
570-93661 Mustang
570-93662 Karmen Ghia

BICYCLES

570-93416 Bicycles pkg(3) **9.95**

BUSES

PKG(2) EA 9.50

570-93481 City Transit Bus
570-93491 Old School Bus
570-93496 Trolley Bus

PLEASURE BOATS

570-93541 Pleasure Boat Set pkg(4) **4.95**

IMPORTED FROM GERMANY BY WALTHERS
Assembled, precolored plastic European autos, trucks and buses. Markings and colors may vary from what is shown in catalog.

Limited Quantity Available On All Items

AUTOMOBILES

CITROEN AX

583-5607 Rally **7.99**

583-5609 EDF/GDF **6.99**

EMERGENCY VEHICLES

FORD TRANSIT

583-3723 Rescue Doctor/ Ambulance w/High Roof **8.99**

583-3744 Ambulance w/High Roof **7.99**

FIAT

583-3229 Ducato Rescue Van w/Dayglow Orange Stripes **7.99**

MERCEDES-BENZ

583-4045 1320 GW-Chemie (Chemicals) **13.99**

507D

583-4321 Rescue Van w/Ladder, Trailer & Boat **14.99**

TRUCKS

MERCEDES-BENZ

1320 W/TRAILER

583-3504 Pasin Papir **14.99**

583-3507 Edeka **17.99**

LP 809

583-3804 Highway Dept. w/Sand Load **10.99**

SCANIA SEMI W/TRAILER EA 17.99

583-1815 Mayflower Moving Co.

583-1816 Navajo

VANS

FORD

583-3758 Duisberger **6.99**

MERCEDES-BENZ

507D

583-4337 Metallic **8.99**

583-4373 Reiterequippe **12.99**

583-4374 Glass Transporter **8.99**

PEUGEOT J5

583-3243 "Kurierdienst" w/Trailer **11.99**

RENAULT

583-5503 Taxi **7.99**

VEHICLE SETS

583-30 Set 3-Europe pkg(6) **29.99**
Collector's set includes: Citroen H Metallic, Ferrari GTO, Volvo 544 Sedan, Rolls Royce Sedan, Renault Espace Sedan and a Citroen AX Sedan.

SELLEY Finishing Touches

Kits are easy-to-build and feature cast metal construction.

FARM MACHINERY

FORKLIFT

675-146 Forklift Truck **1.75**

HY-RAIL INSPECTION CAR

675-642 Crazy Inspection Car **5.50**

IMPLEMENTS

675-157 Wagon **3.85**

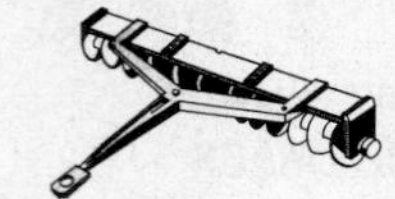

675-228 Tractor-Drawn Harrow **2.00**

PLATFORM TRACTOR

675-147 Platform Mule **1.75**

TRACTORS EA 2.75

675-226 #2

675-227 #1

MILITARY EQUIPMENT

TANK

675-288 Sherman Tank **5.25**

Sheepscot Scale Products

Bring a new level of detail to your layout with these craft train kits. Models feature brass photo-etched parts and castings, plus strip wood and complete instructions. Trailers and truck bodies are plaster castings with separate wheels.

Contractor's Barge #1 668-1110

100' Barge w/100-Ton Crane 668-1231

400-Ton Coal Barge 668-1221

80' Ferry 668-1311

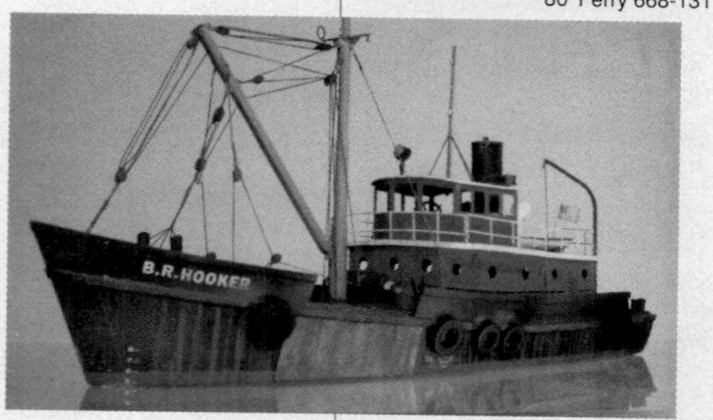

80' Workboat 668-1312

BOATS

668-1191 Yard Tug "Snapper" **55.00**
Model measures just 55 scale feet long. A plaster former is included to simplify construction of the hull, and the deckhouse is made of brass.

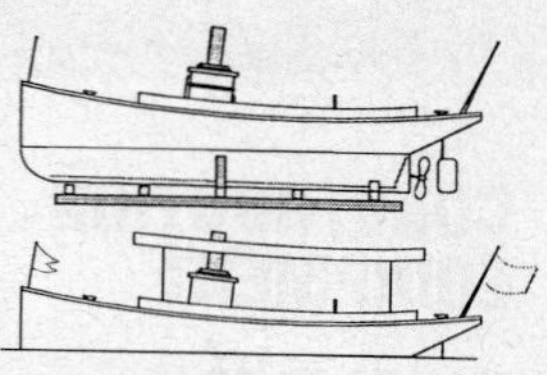

668-1245 Steam Launch **26.00**
Small steam-powered launches like this could be found on many lakes and rivers. Metal kit can be built for display on land with a full hull, or as a waterline model (no lower hull) for an action scene. Made of cast metal and complete with flag and top.

668-1311 80' Ferry **105.00**
668-1312 80' Workboat **130.00**
Model can be used as a Coast Guard buoy tender, a coastal or harbor contractor's workboat or an island packet. Measuring 11 x 4", the work boat features a solid plaster hull former with sheer, flare and deck camber built in, cast-metal lifeboat and vents, brass tubing on the mast and boom, and photo-etched parts such as the brass deckhouse and pilothouse.

668-1325 Tug Boat 85' (12") NYC Steam #16 **TBA** *NEW*

668-1360 60' Fishing Dragger Boat **TBA** *NEW*

BARGES

668-1110 Contractor's Barge #1 **95.00**
Packs loads of realism into just 4 x 10". Rigs of this type can often be found making repairs on railroad bridges, trestles, and piers. Model is complete with derrick and deck details.

668-1221 400-Ton Coal Barge **25.00**
Adaptable to all types of bulk freight, this model is based on barges built for the Army during WWII for general cargo

668-1231 100' Barge w/100-Ton Crane **205.00**
This intricate model features a 100-ton capacity crane on a 100' barge. Crane features a photo-etched boom, with tab and slot construction for ease of assembly. Lots of metal castings and complete instructions round out the model.

CONSTRUCTION EQUIPMENT

668-95021 Truck Crane, Bucyrus Erie 15-B w/75' Boom **30.00** *NEW*
Truck not included.

LINK-BELT SPEEDERS EA TBA

668-95221 LS-98 Crawler w/100 + 30' Boom, Clamshell, Magnet *NEW*
668-95222 HC-108 Truck Crane w/100 + 30' Boom, 8 x 4 Carrier *NEW*
668-95223 LS-98 Short Crawler w/Backhoe Attachment *NEW*
668-95224 UC-108 8 x 4 "Wagon Crane" w/100 + 30' Boom *NEW*

TRAILERS

These vintage trailers look great on steam-era highways, and you may still see them serving other purposes today. Based on equipment used from the 1930s to the 1950s, each is cast in plaster and is easily painted and installed on your favorite chassis, sold separately.

DUMP TRAILERS

668-95010 With Load pkg(2) **15.00**
668-95028 16-Yard **10.00** *NEW*

ROUND NOSE VAN TRAILERS

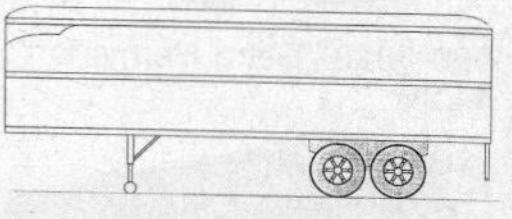

668-95011 32' Dual Axle, pkg(2) **15.00**

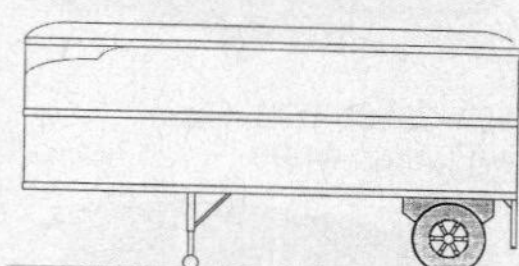

668-95012 24' Single Axle, pkg(2) **18.00**

MOVING VAN TRAILERS

668-95013 28' pkg(2) **15.00**

FLATBED TRAILERS

668-95030 18' Covered w/Stakes, 1930s Era **7.00** *NEW*

TANK TRAILERS

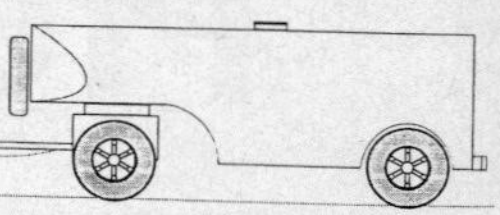

668-95014 20' 1930s pkg(3) **18.00**

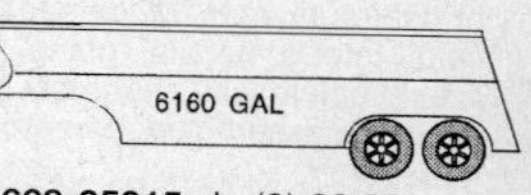

668-95015 pkg(3) **28.00**
Available in three sizes: 4300, 6160 and 6700 gallons.

BRASS TRAILERS

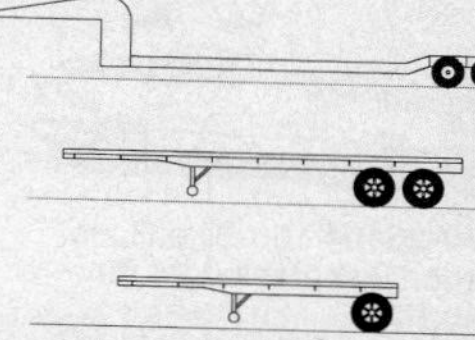

668-95008 Gooseneck & Flats pkg(3) **35.00**
Includes parts for a gooseneck low bed machinery trailer, plus 25' and 35' high profile flatbed trailers.

TRUCKS

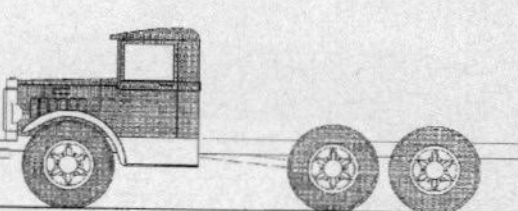

668-95101 Mack 1938 BX Cab & Chassis **TBA**
Cast-metal frame, wheels and cab details (some cab details are photo-etched brass). Details include headlights on brass brackets, rear-view mirrors, windshield wipers and steering wheel.

668-95104 Sterling Late 1940s Heavy-Duty 6 x 4 **24.00** *NEW*
Heavy-duty truck features 24" rubber, cab and chassis.

TRUCK BODIES EA 4.00 (UNLESS NOTED)

VAN BODIES

668-95016 15' Deep Wheel Well & Partial Wheel Well **16.00**
668-95019 Moving w/Over Cab Extension *NEW*
668-95023 15' w/Shallow Wheel Wells *NEW*
668-95024 15' w/Deep Wheel Wells *NEW*

DUMP TRUCK BODIES

With loads.

668-95009 20-Yard pkg(6) **15.00**
668-95025 18-Yard *NEW*
668-95026 6-Yard *NEW*
668-95027 12-Yard *NEW*

ORIGINAL Preiser

IMPORTED FROM GERMANY BY WALTHERS

These easy to build, hi ghly detailed vehicles are ideal for collecting or use on layouts. Models feature realistic plastic parts molded in color, interior details, "glass", mirrors, wheels and much more. All are complete with assembly instructions. Some models are also available assembled, as noted.

AUTOMOBILES

AUDI

590-25104 100 Bike Race Escort-Assembled **24.99**

590-25106 200 Bike Race Escort-Assembled **24.99**

590-38024 80 Avant **11.99**

590-38025 A8 **12.99**

590-38030 A4 **9.99**

590-38031 Convertible w/2 Figures **10.99**

590-38037 Convertible **9.99**

FIAT TIPO

590-25103 Bike Race Escort-Assembled **23.99**

590-38028 With Sunroof **9.99**

OPEL ASTRA EA 24.99

590-25105 Bike Race Escort-Assembled
590-33229 Station Wagon-Assembled

SUZUKI

590-33228 410 Sport Utility w/Jacobs "Swing" Trailer **23.99**

BUSES

590-33221 Uhrebian **39.99**
590-33233 Kassbohrer w/Figures **44.99**

590-33234 Setra-Hermsdorf **44.99**

590-33235 B. B. Risen w/Figures **44.99**

590-33236 Will Markgrafler **44.99**

Car Pulling Boat w/2 Figures 590-33242

"Paddy Wagon" US Police 590-33240

CONSTRUCTION EQUIPMENT

MAN EA 23.99

590-31300 Municipal Three-Way Dump Truck

590-37019 3-Way Dump Truck

MERCEDES

590-35014 LA 1924 Dump Truck **23.99**

590-38003 1722L Cab w/Meiller Dumpster-Assembled **24.99**

590-38014 Multi-Purpose Vehicle **24.99**

Limited Quantity Available

590-1162 LA1924 3-Way Dump Truck w/Crane **14.99**
590-1208 LA1513 Cab w/Meiller Dumpster **15.99**
590-1228 LAK 1113 3-Way Dump Truck **15.49**

BOATS

590-17304 Speed Boats pkg(2) **19.99**
590-33242 Car Pulling Boat w/2 Figures **29.99** *NEW*

EMERGENCY VEHICLES

AUDI

590-37025 Model 100 - Police w/2 Figures **11.99**

AIRPORT CRASH TRUCKS

FAUN FLF80/200

590-31167 Kit **19.99**
590-31165 Hamburg Airport GTLF18 **23.99**

590-35008 Assembled **31.99**

MERCEDES

590-31163 FTLF8000 Berlin Airport **23.99**

590-31294 1113 Berlin Airport **23.99**

590-35009 DLK23-12 Ladder Berlin Airport-Assembled **32.99**

590-35027 LF 8 408 D Equipment Van **16.99**

590-35028 L 613 Medical Van **16.99**

CHEVROLET EA 27.99

Specially painted and lettered Trident models, each includes two figures and accessories.

590-33237 Suburban, German

590-33239 Suburban, German
590-33240 "Paddy Wagon," US Police

CRANE

590-31100 Fire Dept. Telescoping Crane (Red) **31.99**

FORD

TRANSIT

590-33226 German Police w/3 Figures **27.99**

590-35020 Fire Brigade **13.99**

ESCORT

590-35024 Fire Chief Station Wagon w/2 Figures **11.99**

Preiser

HORSE-DRAWN FIRE EQUIPMENT EA 26.99 (UNLESS NOTED)

Models are fully assembled, based on German prototypes, but similar to equipment used in other countries.

590-30425 Hand Pumper

590-30426 Water Wagon

590-30427 "Flying Squad" Personnel Wagon

590-30428 Steam Pumper **33.99**

590-30429 Coal Tender

HORSE-DRAWN FIRE MUSEUM SETS

590-30405 Hand Pump, Water Tank & Personnel Wagon pkg(3) **31.99**

590-30406 Steam Pumper & Coal Tender pkg(2) **19.99**

MERCEDES

590-31116 Meiller Multi-Purpose Truck w/4 Bodies **25.99**
Includes office, tall dumpster, low-side flatbed and equipment bodies.

Fire Engines 590-31209

Technical Rescue Service 590-31211

Sedan Cab W/Turntable Ladder 590-31268

590-31128 F-16-2 Compartment Pumper **20.99**

590-31144 AF/36 Hose Carrier **18.99**
590-31172 TLF 48/50-5 Tank Pumper **31.99**

590-31178 TLF 24/50 Tank Pumper **22.99**
590-31180 LA 1924 w/Simon Snorkel **29.99**
590-31182 1017 Rescue Unit w/Crane **25.99**
590-31207 Fire Dept. Dump Truck **23.99**
590-31209 Fire Engines (4 Different) **39.99**
590-31211 Mercedes 508 Technical Rescue Service Set pkg(4) **39.99**
This set includes two crew-cab equipment trucks and two personnel van kits. One pair is molded in orange the other in the traditional blue.
590-31222 LA1519 w/Fire Dept. Dumpster **24.99**
590-31230 LF16 Squad Tender **23.99**

590-31246 LAF1113 Hose Carrier **23.99**

590-31248 TLF16 Tank Pumper **23.99**

590-31252 RW1 Rescue Unit **23.99**
590-31268 LF1113 Sedan Cab w/DLK 23-12 Turntable Ladder **32.99**

590-31270 LF1313 w/DLK 23-12 Turntable Ladder **32.99**

590-31280 LF16TS Squad Tender/Pumper **24.99**

590-31284 TroLF 750 Dry Powder Unit **23.99**

590-31286 TLF 16/28-5 Tank Pumper **23.99**
590-35000 F-16-2 Compartment Pumper Kit Assembled (Red) **23.99**

590-35001 TLF16 Pumper-Assembled **23.99**

590-35002 TroTLF16 Dry Powder Unit-Assembled **23.99**

590-35003 DLK 23-12 Ladder-Assembled **32.99**
590-35004 Clean-up Unit w/Meiler Dumpster-Assembled **23.99**

590-35011 O 309 Command Van-Assembled **14.99**

590-35013 Sedan Cab Pumper **24.99**

590-35015 Equipment Truck w/Crewcab & Covered Bed **17.99**

590-35018 GW Breath Care **15.99**

590-35019 Truck-Mounted Light Plant **20.99**

590-35021 LF8 Pumper **16.99**

590-35022 LF16 Pumper - Frankfurt Fire Dept. **25.99**

590-35023 Roll-On/Off Truck w/Tank Container **25.99**

590-35025 Emergency Unit - Berlin Fire Dept. **15.99**

590-35026 Mercedes 408 D Fire Dept. Squad Truck **16.99**
590-37004 LA911 Police, Green-Assembled **23.99**
590-37020 L508D Police Bus **15.99**

Limited Quantity Available
590-1234 LA911 Red Cross **15.49**
590-1236 LA911 Police **15.99**

590-1258 1922AK Export Pumper **15.99**
590-31210 Fire Dept. Dumpster Truck 1632 **24.99**

MAGIRUS

590-31134 DLK23 Ladder (red) **31.99**
590-31202 F200D Water Tanker **23.99**
590-31203 Turntable Ladder **32.99**
590-31204 F200D Rescue Squad **23.99**

590-31215 150D 3-Way Fire Dept. Dump Truck w/Compressor **23.99**
590-31218 150D 10FA Pumper **20.99**

590-31219 F150 D 10 **23.99**
NEW

ORIGINAL **Preiser**

590-31224 Magirus F150D **22.99**
590-31242 125A Foam Sprayer **20.99**
590-31259 Hose Truck SW 2000 **23.99** *NEW*

590-31260 F200D 16A Water Container ZB6 **23.99**

590-31261 TroTLF16 w/Sedan Cab **23.99**

590-31263 LF 16 Sedan Cab Pumper on Mercur 150 A Chassis **23.99**

590-31272 M125A LF 16TS **23.99**

590-31265 F 150 D 10 w/Extension Ladder **37.99**

590-31276 M125A Hose SW2000 **23.99**

590-31292 200 D16 Articulated Elevated Platform **31.99**
590-31308 Fire Dept. Tools & Gear Truck **23.99**

590-35012 DLK 23-12 Ladder **33.99**

590-35016 F200 Pollution Control Equipment Truck **23.99**
590-35029 AW Hannover Fire Truck **24.99** *NEW*

Limited Quantity Available

590-1186 150D/TLF16 Pumper **15.49**

590-1198 ZLF3000 Foam Sprayer **15.99**

590-1206 1500 Street Sander **15.99**

590-1216 F125A Pumper **15.49**
590-31200 F125A Driver Training **15.99**

590-31274 M125A Pumper, TLF16 **24.49**

590-31278 M126D 10A Tanker **24.49**

MAN

590-31201 Flatbed w/Crane **23.99**

590-31296 HA LF Water/Dry Powder **25.99**

590-31298 HA LF Pumper **25.99**
590-31302 1 Tender HA LF **25.99**
590-35005 HA LF Pumper-Assembled **23.99**
590-35006 Tender HA LF-Assembled **24.99**

590-35007 Tool & Gear Carrier-Assembled **23.99**

Limited Quantity Available
590-1169 LA 911A Emergency Service **16.99**
Same as 31168, less interior equipment.

ZIEGLER

590-31112 Firefighting Trailer **8.99**

590-31254 Hose Trailer **11.99**

590-35010 2B/2C w/Hose Trailer **12.99**

EMERGENCY VEHICLE ACCESSORIES

590-31000 Fire Dept. Dry Transfers **9.99**

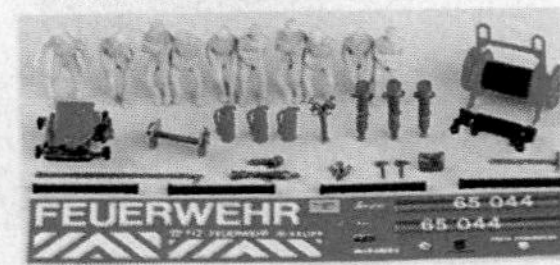

590-31010 Seated Firemen, Hose Reels, Nozzles Lettering **12.99**

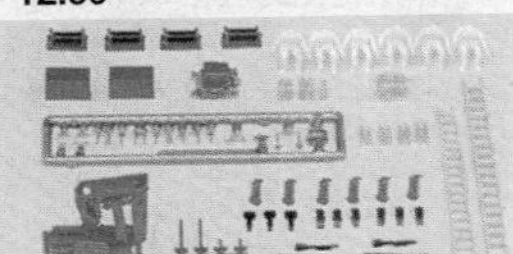

590-31013 Fire Truck Details w/Loading Crane **11.99**

AW Hannover Fire Truck 590-35029

Hose Truck SW 2000 590-31259

590-31114 Foam Sprayer & Water Cannon Trailers pkg(2) **8.99**

590-31148 Kuli Portable Lighting Plants pkg(2) **12.99**

590-31152 CO2 & Pressure Suction Container For #1116 **18.99**
590-31213 Loading Platform **12.99**

TECHNICAL HELP SERVICE (THW)

Models feature parts molded in blue

MERCEDES EA 23.99 (UNLESS NOTED)

590-31168 911A Fire Truck w/Interior
590-37000 911A Fire Truck Assembled-Less Interior

590-37001 LA1113B Assembled
590-37002 LA113 Assembled blue

590-37007 L 407D Medical Van Assembled **22.99**
590-37023 508D Box Van **14.99**

Limited Quantity Available
590-31226 LAK 1113 **20.99**
590-31238 LA113 Rescue **20.99**

MAGIRUS

590-31306 Tool & Gear Truck **23.99**

590-31307 Generator Truck **24.99**

RESCUE EQUIPMENT

Limited Quantity Available
590-31193 Light Plant, Rubber Raft & Generator pkg(3) **17.49**

See What's Available at

www.walthers.com

ORIGINAL **Preiser**

FARM EQUIPMENT

HORSE-DRAWN

590-30431 Farmer w/Horse-Drawn Plow **27.99**

IMPLEMENTS

590-17918 Manure Spreader, Trailer & Plow **17.99**

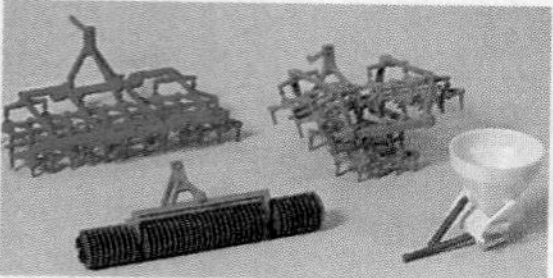

590-17919 Drag Disc, Harrow & Manure Spreader **15.99**

MITSUBISHI

590-33238 Pajero w/Livestock Trailer, 4 Figures & Reluctant Cow **27.99**

TRACTORS

590-17927 Tractor Special Implement **16.99** ***NEW***

DEUTZ

590-17913 Tractor w/Mower-Assembled **11.99**

590-17914 Tractor w/Wagon-Assembled **15.99**
590-17920 Tractors pkg(2) **18.99**

DEUTZ D6206 TRACTOR KITS

590-17922 With Shovel & Fork **20.99**
Can be built with or without roll-over protective structure.

590-17923 With Enclosed Cab & Snow Plow **17.99**

590-17924 With Enclosed Cab, Shovel & Fork **17.99**

HANOMAG R55

590-17915 Farm Tractor-Assembled **12.99**

590-17916 Forestry Model (gray) w/Winch-Assembled **12.99**

590-21000 Closed Cab (red) Assembled **13.99**

590-24679 Set of 2 (white) **19.99**
Includes parts to build two complete tractors, one with roll-over protective structure, the other with fully enclosed cab.

LANZ

590-17921 Farm Tractor-Assembled **13.99**

590-17925 D2416 with Sickle Bar Mower **13.99**

590-17926 D2416 Farm Tractor **17.99** ***NEW***

TRAILERS

590-17917 Single Axle Dump & Tank Trailers pkg(2) **13.99**

HORSE-DRAWN WAGONS

590-24609 Beer Wagon w/Driver, 4-Horse Hitch, Load & Sign **37.99**
590-30430 Royal Bavarian Assembled **26.99**

590-30450 Closed White Marriage Coach w/4 Figures Assembled **26.99**

590-30451 Open White Marriage Coach w/4 Figures Assembled **26.99**

590-30452 Closed Taxi w/3 Figures Assembled **26.99**

590-30454 1900 German Coach w/Figures **26.99**

590-30457 Furniture Wagon w/Two Horses Assembled **26.99**

590-30462 1890s Beer Wagon **26.99**

Beer Wagon 590-24609

Flatbed Wagon 590-30434

Liquid Manure 590-30435

Hay Rack 590-30436

Lowenbrau Beer Wagon 590-30437

Spatenbrau Beer Wagon 590-30438

590-30434 Flatbed Wagon w/Driver, Horses & Cargo **26.99**
590-30435 Liquid Manure Wagon w/Driver, Team & Wooden Tank **26.99**
590-30436 Hay Rack w/Horses, Driver & Helper **24.99**
590-30437 Beer Wagon w/Horses Lowenbrau **52.99** ***NEW***
590-30438 Beer Wagon w/Horses Spatenbrau **52.99** ***NEW***

590-30465 Log Wagon w/Driver & Load **26.99**

590-30468 Ore Wagon w/Driver & Horses Assembled **19.99**

590-30470 Cargo Wagon w/Horses Assembled **23.99**

590-30472 Hay Wagon w/Driver & Load Assembled **23.99**

590-30474 Manure Wagon w/Driver Load & Ox **23.99**

590-30477 Hay Wagon w/Driver & Load **26.99**

ORIGINAL Preiser

MILITARY VEHICLES

GERMAN ARMY W.W.II

SDKFZ 251/SERIES HALF-TRACK

590-16516 Personnel Carrier w/Machine Gun **11.99**

590-16517 Field Radio Unit **12.99**

590-16518 Engineering Unit **12.99**

590-16522 251/2 w/Mortar **12.99**

590-16523 251/9 w/Cannon **12.99**

HORSE-DRAWN EQUIPMENT

590-16507 Field Kitchen w/Crew Kit **14.99**
Includes hand-painted two-horse hitch and driver.

590-16512 Supply Wagon w/Crew Kit **15.99**
Includes hand-painted four-horse hitch, two outriders and driver.

ARTILLERY

590-16513 105mm Gun Kit w/Caisson, Crew & 6-Horse Hitch **23.99**
An impressive kit suitable for display or war gaming. Includes six-horse hitch with harness, three outriders, one mounted rider, four-man crew riding on caisson and 105mm gun.

590-16514 105mm Gun w/Crew **19.99**
Includes gun and hand-painted 8-man crew.

MODERN GERMAN ARMY

FORD

Limited Quantity Available

590-37022 Transit Van **13.99**

Fleld Kitchen 590-16507

SUpply Wagon 590-16512

10mm Gun Kit 590-16513

105mm Gun Kit 590-16514

MERCEDES

590-37010 3-Way Dump Truck - German Federal Army **20.99**

590-37011 Ambulance-Assembled **23.99**

590-37015 Hanomag R55 Tractor NATO-Assembled **13.99**

590-37017 L508 Border Guard Van **14.99**

590-37027 German Border Guard Mercedes Heavy Tractor **23.99**

Limited Quantity Available
590-1232 LA911 German Border Guard Truck **15.99**

590-31264 LA911/42 w/Fuel Tank for Helicopters **24.49**
590-31266 911/42 Driving School Truck **20.49**
590-37005 LA911/42 Border Guard Truck-Assembled **23.49**

590-37009 L508 Van-Assembled **13.99**

TRAILERS

590-31310 4-Axle Flatbed-German Post Office **24.99**

VANS

FORD TRANSIT EA 27.99

590-33227 Kerschbaum Carpenters w/Figures-Assembled
590-33230 Krause's Bakery w/Figures-Assembled
590-33231 Delivery Service w/3 Figures-Assembled

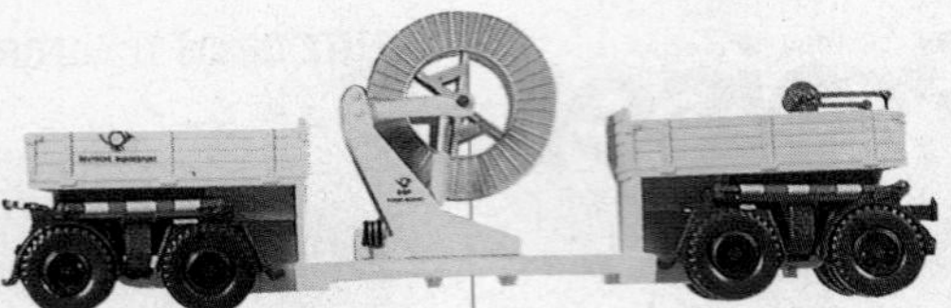

4-Axle Flatbed 590-31310

Kerschbaum Carpenters 590-33227

Krause's Bakery 590-33230

Delivery Service 590-33231

TRUCKS

DAIMLER

590-38038 1-1/2 Ton Truck Circa 1896 **22.99**

MERCEDES

590-33215 508D w/Plumbers **29.99**

590-33216 508D w/Compressor & Figures **29.99**

590-33241 Mercedes Moving Van w/Lift Gate, Figure & 2 Carts **23.99**

590-37018 508 Road Maintenance Truck **15.99**

590-38004 Cattle Carrier-Assembled **23.99**

590-38005 "Schulteis Beer" Brewery Truck **26.99**

590-38007 German Federal Postal Service Van Assembled **14.99**
590-38036 508D Transporter (dark gray) **12.99**

ORIGINAL Preiser

590-38039 408 D Tow Truck **22.99**

Limited Quantity Available

590-38006 1625 S/32 Refrigerator Assembled **29.49**
590-38008 KG Assembled **29.49**
590-38010 Cattle Carrier **24.49**

TRACTORS

590-31309 Mercedes 1362 German Post Office **22.99**

Limited Quantity Available

590-1120 Heavy Tractor LAK 2624/36 **10.99**

MITSUBISHI L300

590-33209 Flower Shop w/5 Figures-Assembled **25.99**
590-38033 "L. Kerschbaum" **11.99**

TRUCK ACCESSORIES

590-17202 Waste Container/Dustbin **12.99**

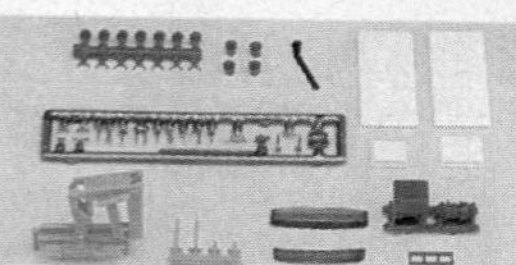

590-31014 Truck Accessories **11.99**

590-31214 Dumpster Container pkg(4) **12.99**

RAIL POWER PRODUCTS

TRAILERS

40' DROP TRAILER

60-800 With Decals **7.00**

28' INTERMODAL PARCEL TRAILER W/DECALS

60-801 Container w/Chassis **7.00**
60-802 Container Only **3.75**

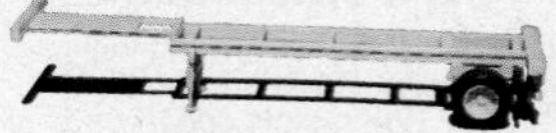

60-803 Chassis Only **3.75**
60-804 Extra UPS Decals **1.50**

28' WEDGE TRAILER EA 7.00

Fill up empty loading docks, intermodal freght yards, trailer-less cabs or flat cars with these highly detailed 28' trailers.

RIBBED

60-805 ABF
60-806 CF
60-807 NWT
60-808 Roadway

60-809 Overnite

60-810 Carolina
60-811 CF
60-812 Transcon
60-813 Preston
60-814 Leeway

SMOOTH SIDE

60-820 Roadway
60-821 Overnite
60-822 Yellow

60-823 Carolina
60-824 Roadway
60-825 Viking
60-826 Preston

60-827 Yellow (new logo)

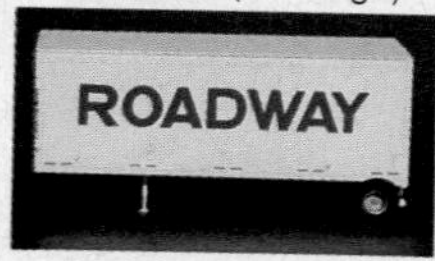

60-828 Roadway (new logo)

48' RIBBED WEDGE TRAILER EA 8.00

60-850 Roadway
60-851 Preston
60-852 N.W. Trans
60-853 C.F. Freight
60-854 Carolina
60-855 Overnight
60-856 Leeway
60-857 Transcon
60-858 Yellow Freight

SEMI TRUCK DETAILS

DOLLY

60-900 Converter Dolly **3.75**

AIRDAM

60-902 Cabover Airdam **2.50**

MIRRORS

60-903 Tractor Side (2 Pairs) **1.25**

TIRES

60-904 Spare Tire Mounted on 2-Hole Disc Wheel pkg(3) **1.25**

WHEELS EA 1.50

60-901 Tractor Fifth Wheel pkg(3)
60-905 5 Hole Rims w/Tires (4 Rims, 8 Tires) ***NEW***

SS LTD
SCALE STRUCTURES LIMITED

CONSTRUCTION EQUIPMENT

650-9120 Ford Inspection Car **25.95**

650-9121 Wood Mine Car **9.95**

650-9122 Electric Mine Loco **12.95**

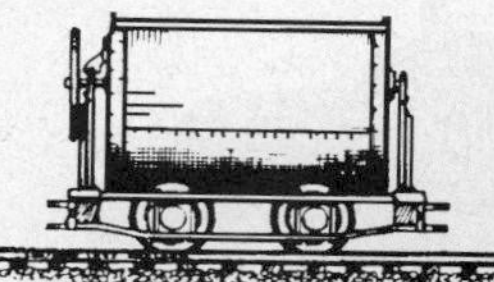

650-9123 Side Dump Mining Car **9.95**

650-9124 Jensen Oil Pump **25.95**

650-9125 Jennings Lumber Co. Log Skidder **32.95**

For Daily Product Information Click

www.walthers.com

650-9126 V&T Jib Crane **31.95**

EMERGENCY VEHICLES

650-9119 Gould 1890 Fire Engine **19.95**

FARM MACHINERY

650-9139 Drag Disc **5.95**

650-9140 Harrow (Drag Rack) **5.95**

650-9141 Foot Treadle Grinding Wheel **4.95**
650-9142 Plow **5.95**

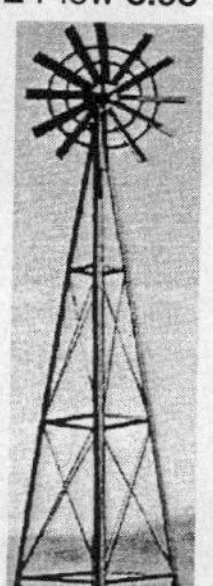

650-9143 Windmill **12.95**

Detail trackside scenes across your layout with this line of easy-to-build kits. Parts are cast in resin, which is assembled, painted and sanded like styrene. Most kits can be built with positionable parts and rolling wheels. The bodies of most models are hollow castings and interiors are included.

EMERGENCY VEHICLES

Seagrave Fire Apparatus Trademark(s) Used Under License from FWD Corporation

ANNIVERSARY CAB FIRE ENGINES

Serving departments large and small, these fire engines were built from 1951 through 1970.

PUMPERS EA 18.99

627-401 Open Cab
627-402 Canopy Cab
627-403 Sedan Cab

LADDER TRUCKS EA 37.99

Models are complete with three-section, photo-etched nickel silver ladder.

627-404 Open Cab
627-405 Closed Cab

Open Cab 627-401

Canopy Cab 627-402

Sedan Cab 627-403

Modern Log Skidder 627-201

Six-Wheel Pulp Forwarders 627-202

Four-Weel Pulp Forwarders 627-209

LOGGING EQUIPMENT

627-201 Modern Log Skidder **20.99**
Parts are molded in yellow.

PULP FORWARDERS

Choose from large or small versions. Parts are molded in color with hollow cab.

627-202 Six-Wheel **22.99**
627-209 Four-Wheel **20.99**

LOGGING DETAILS PKG(3) EA 3.49

Detailed resin castings are ready to paint.

627-208 Chain Saws w/Photo-Etched Saw Bar
627-207 Portable Generators

TRUCKS

627-301 1956 Cab-Over Semi Tractor **8.99**
The model is molded in color and features a hollow cab.

Complete Model 627-503

BOATS

GREAT LAKES ORE CARRIER S.S. EDMUND FITZGERALD

This full-size, HO Scale replica builds into an impressive model. The modular design allows you to build various lengths to fit your available space. Kits include detailed resin castings, with photo-etched detail, and a flat bottom to simulate a vessel in the water.

627-501 Waterline Bow and Stern **449.99**
This kit includes the bow (front) and stern (rear), with two 12" long center sections. (1) kit #501 plus (3) #502 are needed to make full ship as shown below. 522 Scale Feet.

627-502 Waterline 72' Center Section Only **59.99**
Matching Center Section is 12" long and can be used to increase the length of the basic kit #501, sold separately.

627-503 S.S. Edmund Fitzgerald Complete Model w/Full Hull **649.99**
This kit includes all parts needed to build a full-length replica of the vessel. This version features the full hull, suitable for use as a display model. Measures 729 scale feet long, Approximately 8-1/2'.

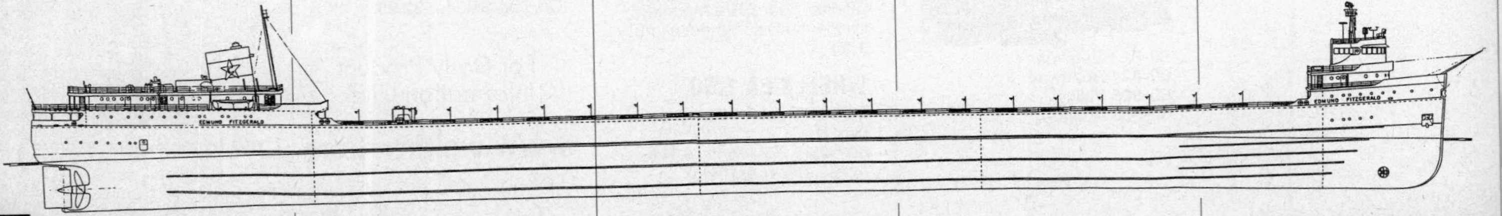

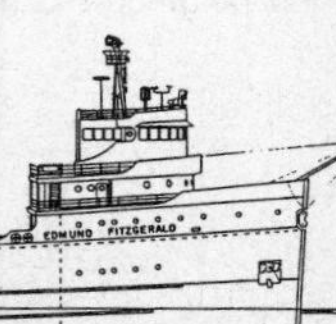

IMPORTED FROM AUSTRIA BY WALTHERS
Ready-to-run, pre-colored vehicles.

AUTOMOBILES

VOLKSWAGEN PKG(3) EA 7.99

625-1440 1500 2-Door

625-1441 1600 TL 2-Door

BUSES

625-1451 Ford FK 1000 2-Tone **9.99**

625-1604 Saurer Travel Agency "Chiemgau-Reisen" **16.99**

CONSTRUCTION VEHICLES

"MOONLIGHT BUILDERS" SERIES

Vehicles in this series are painted and lettered for "Schwarz" Moonlight Builders.

625-1490 Volkswagen T4 Crew Cab Flatbed w/Canvas Cover **9.99**

625-1493 Unimog U 1700 Flatbed w/Crane, Canvas Cover & Equipment Trailer **26.99** *NEW*

625-1513 GMC 2-1/2 Ton Flatbed w/Fuel Tanks **12.99**

625-1671 Mercedes SK 94 3-Axle Dump Truck **31.99** *NEW*

625-1672 Unimog & Crane **39.99**

Limited Quantity Available
625-1543 3-Axle Dump w/Trailer, Magirus **22.99**

DELIVERY TRUCKS

625-1453 Ford FK 1000 Panel Van **9.99** *NEW*

625-1454 Bakery Panel Van Ford FK 1000 **9.99** *NEW*

625-1486 Sun Farmer's Market VW T4 Flatbed w/Cover **8.99** *NEW*

625-1663 Brenta Heating Oil Delivery VW T3 Pick-Up **11.99** *NEW*

625-1679 Schuon Forwarding Unimog w/Terminal/Airport Trailers **29.99** *NEW*

625-1631 GMC 6x6 Flatbed Truck "Herkules Bier" **11.99**

625-1634 Mercedes L5000 w/DB "House-to-House" Container **19.99** *NEW*

Limited Quantity Available
625-1584 Renault **13.99**
625-1594 Mercedes 1838 **29.99**
625-1596 Steyr 91 **28.99**

EMERGENCY VEHICLES

AMBULANCES

625-1438 VW Baby Doctor w/High Roof **10.99**

625-1452 Johanniter Ford FK 1000 (white) **11.99** *NEW*

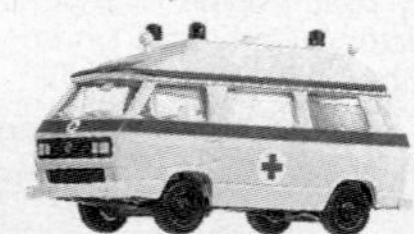

625-1460 VW T3 w/Raised Roof (white, red) **11.99** *NEW*

625-1478 VW-T4 Marktschellenberg Mountain Rescue Service Van **7.99**

625-1480 Emergency Baby Doctor VW T4 **11.99** *NEW*

Limited Quantity Available
625-1377 Ambulance **8.99**

HELICOPTERS

625-2200 Bo 105 German Emergency Air Patrol **11.99**

625-2201 BO105 Air Rescue **10.99**

625-2210 Eurocopter EC 135 **TBA** *NEW*

SERVICE TRUCKS

625-1362 VW Double Cab, Fire Dept. **8.99**

625-1413 Unimog S404 **7.99**

625-1449 Dodge Fire Dept. Field Workshop Truck **9.99**
625-1445 VW T3 Bus DB Railway Fire Department **9.99**
625-1467 VW T3 "Civil Defense" **9.99**

625-1472 VW T4 Bus "ADAC" **8.99**

625-1488 Freidrichshafen Fire Dept. VW T4 Crew Cab Flatbed w/Tarp **9.99** *NEW*

625-1489 Disaster Prevention VW T4 Crew Cab Flatbed w/Tarp **9.99** *NEW*

625-1495 Fire Dept. Unimog U1300 Crew Cab Flatbed **13.99** *NEW*

625-1499 Unimog U1300 Aircraft Tractor w/Helicopter Flatbed "Ambulance Air Service" **14.99**

625-1683 Celle Fire Dept. MAN 630 L2A Squad Truck **10.99** *NEW*

625-1728 Fire Dept. Mercedes Wolf SUV **10.99** *NEW*

625-1729 Windeck Fire Dept. Land Rover **10.99** *NEW*

625-2050 Salzburg Fire Dept. VW T4 Vans pkg(2) **21.99** *NEW*
Includes one each personnel van and sedan cab pick-up with canvas covered bed, both in red and white.

Limited Quantity Available
625-1367 VW Synchro Fire Fighting Van **10.99**
625-1370 VW Type 2 Command Car **8.99**
625-1399 Mercedes 1017 "ASB" **13.99**
625-1463 VW-T3 Fire Brigade Personnel Van **9.99**
625-1464 VW-T3 "ASB" Crew Cab Pick-Up **9.99**
625-1473 VW T4 Bus "Fire Brigade" **8.99**

LADDER TRUCKS

625-1346 Magirus DLK 23-12 **24.99**

Limited Quantity Available
625-1349 Magirus 23-12 **19.99**
625-1371 DLK 23-12 w/Renault Cab **19.99**
625-1397 Mercedes DL **22.99**

POLICE VEHICLES

625-1394 VW Minibus Type 2 German Railroad Police **8.99**

625-1416 VW Type 2 Van German Police Traffic Accident Command **11.99**

625-1483 German Highway Patrol VW T4 Personnel Van **11.99** *NEW*

625-1497 Unimog U1700 German Police Crew Cab w/Rescue/Removal Equipment **21.99**

625-1658 Unimog U1300 Flatbed (green) **11.99** *NEW*

625-1659 MAN 630 L2A Squad Truck (green) **10.99** *NEW*

625-2411 VW-T4 Zürich Police **9.99**
625-2466 VW-T3 Set Gendarmerie & Police **22.99**

625-2413 Swiss Canton Police Van Set pkg(2) **22.99** *NEW*
Includes one each VW T3 and T4 personnel vans in white and orange with full color markings.

625-2466 French VW T3 Personnel Van Set pkg(2) **22.99** *NEW*
Includes one "Gendarmie" in white with red lettering and one "Police" van in white with blue lettering.

RED CROSS

625-1439 MB German Red Cross **14.99**

625-1727 Pinzgauer 4x4 Truck (white, red) **9.99** *NEW*

Limited Quantity Available
625-1301 Munga **5.99**
625-1339 MAN 5T w/Trailer **8.99**
625-1360 VW Crew Cab Pickup w/Canvas Cover **11.99**

TECHNICAL HELP SERVICE - THW

625-1431 Mercedes 1017 w/4-Axle Trailer **20.99**

625-1448 Unimog U1300L-Camouflage Scheme **17.99**

625-1461 VW T3 Van w/Crew Cab & Special Body(blue) **11.99** *NEW*

625-1462 VW T3 Crew Cap Pick-Up & T4 Personnel Van **21.99**
625-1498 Unimog w/Clean-Up/Removal Equipment **24.99**

625-1629 MAN N4520/N4620 7t 6x6 Flatbed Truck **9.99**

625-1636 Volvo FH12 Semi Tractor & Canvas Covered Flatbed (blue) **26.99** *NEW*

625-1646 MAN 452 Heavy Truck (camouflage) **23.99** *NEW*

625-1730 VW T3 Personnel Van, Boat & Trailer (blue) **16.99** *NEW*

625-1731 VW T3 Crew Cab Pick-Up (white, UN/THW markings) **9.99** *NEW*

625-1732 Unimog U1300L Flatbed w/Canvas Cover (blue) **8.99** *NEW*

Limited Quantity Available
625-1378 Man 630 L2A **11.99**

PUMPERS

625-1395 Magirus LF-16-TS **19.99**
625-1398 Opel Blitz TLF15 **14.99**

625-1450 Ford FK 1000 Fire Brigade Van **11.99**

625-1457 Flachau Ford FK 1250 Van Mini-Pumper **11.99** *NEW*

625-1458 St. Gilgen Ford FK 1250 Van Mini-Pumper **11.99** *NEW*

625-1680 Steyr 586 TLF 1500 w/Fender Mounted Headlights **17.99**

625-1681 Mercedes LF 8 Oelsa Volunteer Fire Brigade **13.99**
625-1699 Unimog Two-Axle U2450 Fire Engine **19.99**

625-1684 Oshkosh Airport/Industrial Fire Engine Set pkg(2) **49.99** *NEW*
Includes two complete rigs based on the 8x8 HEMTT military truck. One is painted blue and white, the other high visibility yellow and red. Perfect for protecting airports or refineries, chemical plants and other large industries.

625-1685 Itzehoe Fire Dept. Mercedes LF 25 **17.99** *NEW*

625-1686 Lenggries Fire Dept. Magirus TLF 16 **17.99** *NEW*

625-1687 Munich Fire Dept. VW T4 Personnel Van & Magirus LF 16 TS Set **28.99** *NEW*

625-1688 United German Railways DB-AG Fire Dept. Magirus LF 16 **17.99** *NEW*

Limited Quantity Available
625-1342 Steyr 680 TLF **15.99**
625-1351 Mercedes LF8 **10.99**
625-1357 Magirus Deutz TroTLF16 Sedan Cab **19.99**
625-1375 Mercedes LF8 w/Trailer & Portable Pump **16.99**
625-1682 Magirus LF 16 TS **17.99**

INTERMODAL

625-1805 Container Gantry Crane w/Lettering **39.99**

Prototype Photo

625-1916 Road Railer 3-Axle Curtain Side Trailer "BTZ" **29.99**

Ready-to-run, pre-colored vehicles.

625-1924 Road Railer Basic Set w/Pirelli & Royal Greenland Containers **59.99**

625-1925 Road Railer Supplement w/Canvas Cover Jagermeister **29.99**

625-1926 Danish State Railways Unimog Hy-Rail Tractor (Nonpowered, yellow) **19.99** ***NEW***

Piggyback Flat w/Load 625-1901

Well Flat w/Tractor & Trailer 625-1917

Road Railer Basic Set 625-1918

Road Railer DB Trailer Train 625-1903

Road Railer Platform & Trailer 625-1914

Styer 860 Bottle Flatbed & Trailer 625-2051

SEMI TRUCKS

625-1649 Magerius w/Airfield Tank Trailer "DAF" **24.99**
625-1901 Piggyback Flat w/Load **69.99**
625-1903 Road Railer DB Trailer Train **59.99**
625-1914 Road Railer Platform & "Danzas" Trailer **29.99**
625-1917 Well Flat w/Frigo Tractor & Trailer **59.99**
625-1918 Road Railer Basic Set (3 platforms, 2 Trailers) **59.99**
625-2051 Union Brewery (Brau AG) Styer 860 Bottle Flatbed & Trailer **26.99** ***NEW***

Limited Quantity Available

625-1430 Volvo FL10 **15.99**
625-1514 Tractor Trailer Steyr 91 **14.99**
625-1520 Semi, Ischler Saltz (salt) Steyr 91 **15.99**
625-1557 Steyr 91 Gondrand 3-Axle **16.99**
625-1570 Volvo FL10 "Kuhne & Nagel" **25.99**
625-1571 Mercedes 1838 "Kieserling" **29.99**
625-1572 1838 Tractor w/3-Axle Trailer "Fahrschule Hinterlechner" **29.99**
625-1576 Mercedes 1838 Schenker **24.99**
625-1577 Mercedes 1838 **28.99**
625-1579 Mercedes 1838 **29.99**
625-1582 "Bahlsen" Truck & Trailer **34.99**
625-1586 Volvo FH 12 Pewag **29.99**
625-1589 Volvo FL10 "Maxilaterale" **27.99**
625-1613 BMW 1850 w/Refrigerator Trailer **29.99**
625-1618 Volvo FH12 Globetrotter w/Refrigerated Trailer "Transdanubia" **28.99**
625-1661 Volvo FL 10 w/Curtains Side **26.99**
625-1902 Piggyback Flat w/Truck & Trailer **79.99**

MAINTENANCE/ UTILITY VEHICLES

625-1465 VW-T3 Van w/DR Reichsbahn Logo **7.99**

625-1479 VW-T4 Personnel Van TWS Gas Service **7.99**
625-1491 VW T4 Crew Cab Flatbed w/Canvas Cover "Community Service" **9.99**
625-1492 VW T4 Crew Cab United German Railways DB-AG **9.99**

625-1494 Unimog Crew Cab-Telekom **14.99**

625-1496 Unimog w/Front End Loader (orange) **12.99** ***NEW***

625-1657 Mercedes Benz 1017 Community Services **10.99**

625-1647 MAN Off-Road Truck Pro-Log Rally Support **13.99**

625-1923 Unimog U1650L Hy-Rail Overhead Line Truck **32.99**

Limited Quantity Available

625-1436 VW Type 2 **11.99**

RECREATIONAL VEHICLES

625-1709 Land Rover w/Horse Trailer **17.99**

625-1724 Mercedes Benz Convertible Sport Utility **8.99**

625-1725 Hummer-Civilian Sport Utility **9.99**

VOLKSWAGEN VANS

625-1469 T3 German Post Office **8.99**

625-1470 T4 Van "Junghenrich Service" **11.99**
625-1476 T4 "Jungheinrich" **8.99**

625-1477 T4 NDR North German TV/Radio **8.99**

625-1481 United German Railways DB-AG T4 Passenger Van **7.99** ***NEW***

625-1484 Miele Automated Washer T4 **7.99** ***NEW***

625-1662 Armored Car **7.99** ***NEW***

625-2477 DSB Cargo Van (red, white) **7.99** ***NEW***

Limited Quantity Available

625-1415 Minibus w/Antenna Mast **10.99**
625-1428 Type II **8.99**
625-1433 Telekom **9.99**
625-1468 T3 Feldschlosschen Diet Pills **11.99**
625-1475 T4 DHL Worldwide Express **8.99**
625-1554 German Federal Mail **9.99**
625-1555 Type II Double Cab German Railways **6.99**
625-1566 Three Unit Set - Heitkamp pkg(3) **21.99**
625-1660 Van "Winkler & Berner" **8.99**

TRUCK ACCESSORIES

625-1747 Whelen 9000 Emergency Vehicle Light Bar (Blue) **4.99**
625-1753 Spotlights **4.99**
One each clear, black and chrome, for spotlights, auxiliary road lamps, fog lights etc.

625-1758 Emergency Lights (Blue) **4.99**
625-1760 Fire Engine Accessories **4.99**
For models 1300, 1303, 1304, 1311 & others.

625-1761 Fire Engine Accessories **4.99**
For models 1304, 1311 & others.

625-1762 Fire Engine Accessories **4.99**
Includes hoses, portable foam generator, roll-up doors, etc.

625-1772 Steering Set **4.99**
For Steyr 91 or Steyr 660, includes parts to change other vehicles.

625-1775 Snowplow Kit pkg(2) **5.99**
Type "Kalmbach," attachment plates for 2 trucks are supplied.

625-1777 Salt Spreader **5.99**

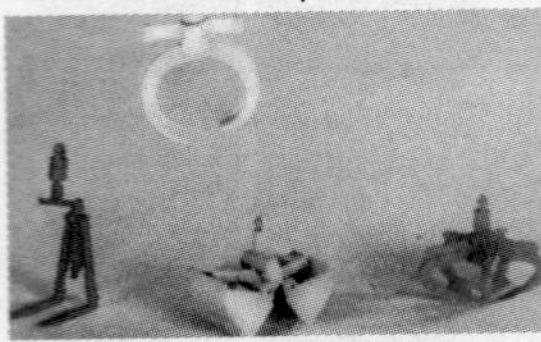

625-1778 Crane Attachments pkg(4) **5.99**
625-1781 Michelin Figures pkg(10) **4.99**
625-1783 Beverage Crates pkg(18) **4.99**
625-1796 Siren/Light (Blue) for Emergency Vehicles **4.99**
625-1807 20' Container Set pkg(3) **14.99**
Includes 1 Each Canada Maritime, Cronos and Grimaldi Group.

625-1808 40' Container Set pkg(3) **16.99**
Includes 1 Each Consent Leasing, Norasia and Maersk.

625-1809 20' Reefer Container Set pkg(3) **15.99**
Includes 1 Each Hasseroder, Bohmisches and Mauritius Pilsener.

Limited Quantity Available

625-1754 Construction Hitches & Towbars **4.99**
625-1755 Roof Spoilers pkg(3) **4.99**
625-1792 Steering Set Accessory for #625-1366 **4.99**
625-1806 Interchangeable Flatbed Covers pkg(3) **14.99**
Includes 1 Each TGF Transfrracht, Zufall and Bahntrans.

TRUCK DECALS & DRY TRANSFERS

All sets are decals unless noted.

625-1787 50s Vehicles **4.99**

Limited Quantity Available

625-1765 Fire Dept. Lettering Dry Transfer **8.49**
625-1768 Day Glow Red **4.99**
625-1773 Trucks/Trailers #1 **3.99**
625-1774 Trucks/Trailers #2 **3.99**
625-1784 Trucks (Self-Adhesive) **4.99**
625-1785 Vehicle I.D. (Self-Adhesive) **4.99**

CATALOG

625-81298 1998-2000 Miniature Model **2.00**

Roco MINITANKS

IMPORTED FROM AUSTRIA BY WALTHERS
Ready-to-run, pre-colored vehicles.

MILITARY VEHICLES

AUSTRIA

625-320 Pinzgauer 710 M 4x4 Troop Carrier w/Canvas Cover **6.99**

625-551 Steyr 680M3 w/Flatbed **10.99**
625-559 Steyr 680 M3 **9.99**

625-564 Puch G/KP Staff Car-Short Wheelbase w/Removable Top **7.99**
625-589 Steyr Puch G **7.99**

625-611 5-Ton Truck w/Yale Building Crane **9.99**
625-628 Steyr 680 M w/Crane **9.99**

Limited Quantity Available

625-380 Steyr 586 TLF 2000 **12.99**

FRANCE

625-410 VW Bus Military Police **11.99**

625-565 Peugeot P4 VLTT Staff Car-Short Wheelbase w/Removable Top **7.99**

625-590 Peugeot P4 Without Top **7.99**

Limited Quantity Available

625-586 Peugeot P4 Gendarmerie **8.99**

FEDERAL GERMAN FRONTIER GUARD

625-399 VW 1600 TL Staff Car NATO Green **2.99**

625-446 4-Wheel, 4-Ton Trailer **9.99**
625-546 VW Type 2 **8.99**

Prototype Photo

625-578 Unimog w/Clean-Up/Removal Equipment **19.99**

625-581 VW 1600 TL Staff Car Black-Green **2.99**

625-631 VW T4 Personnel Bus (Mint Green) **8.99**

625-817 VW Type 2 **7.99**

GERMAN ARMY - WORLD WAR II

AIRCRAFT

625-459 Junkers JU 52 G2 **13.99**

BATTLE TANKS

625-102 Panther V **4.99**

625-105 Grille, w/88mm Anti-Aircraft Gun **5.99**

625-107 Panzer IZ-F2 & H-K **5.99**
Optional parts.

625-111 Anti-Aircraft **5.99**
Optional quad 20mm or 3.7 cm guns

625-171 Panzer VI Hunting Tiger **5.99**

625-174 Panzer III Short Gun **4.99**
Optional long and short 75mm guns included.

625-176 Assault Gun II **5.99**
Optional 105 or 75mm guns.

Roco Minitanks

625-700 VI Tiger Version E **8.99**
625-702 "Tiger" Pz.Kpfw. VI w/Markings for Tunisian Campaign **11.99** *NEW*

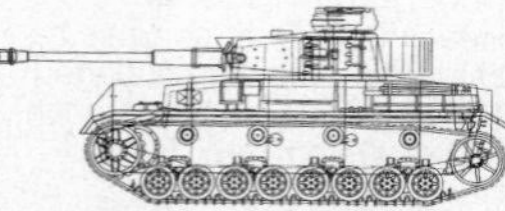

625-705 Medium Pz.Kpfw IV-H Series **TBA** *NEW*

625-701 Tank Recovery Vehicle on Tiger Chassis **8.99**

625-888 PzKpfw VI Tiger **26.99**
Finished in special camouflage scheme, includes display box.

TRUCKS

625-228 Half Track w/Anti-Aircraft Gun **5.99**
Optional quad 20mm or 3.7 cm guns.

625-235 VW Kubelwagen Type 82 **5.99**

625-236 VW Schwimmwagen Amphibious Type 166 **5.99**

625-338 Opel Tank Fire Extinguisher TL F15 **11.99**

625-370 Opel Blitz w/Canvas **6.99**

625-418 Mercedes DL Ladder Truck **17.99**

RAILROAD EQUIPMENT

625-836 Class R 10 Flat Car w/Half Track **LIMITED-RUN** **32.99**

625-839 Flat Car w/Two VW Kubelwagens **39.99** *NEW*

GERMAN ARMY - POST 1945

AIRCRAFT

625-860 Eurocopter EC 635 Prototype **TBA** *NEW*

BATTLE TANKS

625-256 Leopard 1 A2 Tank w/105mm Gun **7.99**

625-270 Gepard Anti-Aircraft **8.99**

625-275 Leopard 1A4 **7.99**
625-599 Leopard 2A5 KWS II **8.99**

625-329 Leopard 2, Battle **8.99**
625-391 Leopard 1A1A1 **8.99**
625-819 Kpz Leopard 2 **22.99**

ARMORED VEHICLES

625-212 HS30 Rocket Carrier **4.99**

625-219 M48 Armored Bridge Carrier **7.99**

625-222 M2 Alligator Bridge **9.99**

625-257 Tank Recovery **7.99**

625-284 LANCE Missile Transport & Loading Vehicle **7.99**

"Tiger" Pz.Kpfw. VI Battle Tank 625-702

625-347 M113 A1G **7.99**

625-416 M109 A3 **8.99**

Prototype Photo

625-426 M113 Artillery Fire Control Vehicle Mortar **8.99**

625-427 Armored Bridge Erector **16.99**
625-440 M113 Artillery Fire Control Vehicle Gun **8.99**
625-448 Hummel **10.99**

625-453 Luchs Spatch Pz2 **9.99**

625-475 Marder 1 A2 **6.99**

625-476 Roland II Anti-Aircraft Gun on Marder Chassis **12.99**
625-506 TPz 1 Fuchs **11.99**
625-507 Fuchs ABC Armed Radiation Vehicle **10.99**

625-544 German SMART Fox Chemical Unit **13.99**

Prototype Photo

625-566 Marder 1A3 **7.99**

625-592 M113 A1G ABRA Artillery Observation Radar Unit **7.99**
625-594 M113 A1G KrKw Ambulance **9.99**

625-616 M113 A1G IFAB Artillery Observation Unit **8.99**
625-710 Wiesel w/TOW **7.99**

Roco MINITANKS

625-711 Wiesel (Weasel) Personnel Carrier w/Cannon **7.99** ***NEW***

625-720 PZ Jaguar 2 w/TOW **9.99**

625-730 Self-Propelled Howitzer PzH 2000 w/Extra Armor **TBA** ***NEW***
625-822 TPz 1 Fuchs w/Camouflage Paint **19.99**

TRUCKS

625-240 LKW Unimog S **5.99**
625-242 Unimog S404, Radio **5.99**

625-246 Jupiter MD 7 + 6 x 6, Closed **5.99**

625-281 Munga 4x4 **5.99**

625-327 VW Iltis **5.99**
625-414 VW Type 2, Flatbed Truck **5.99**
625-436 Airfield Fuel Tanker/Semi **18.99**
625-445 4-Wheel, 4-Ton Trailer **9.99**
625-449 MAN N4530 **10.99**
625-451 Daimler Benz 1017A **10.99**
625-452 Unimog U 1300L w/Trailer **10.99**
625-470 MAN N4510 **9.99**

625-472 Unimog U1300L Communications Truck **8.99**
625-502 Mercedes 1017A Fuel Truck **12.99**

625-504 LARS Multiple Rocket Launcher 110 SF2 **13.99**
625-505 MAN 4520/N **8.99**
625-508 Unimog U 1300L DB Ambulance **11.99**

625-541 VW T4 Personnel Van **7.99**
625-543 MAN w/Transport Trailer 4540 **19.99**
625-554 MAN N 45/40/4640 **10.99**

Prototype Photo

625-557 US M1025 Hummer w/Weapons **12.99**

625-568 M200 A1 Generator **4.99**
625-569 MAN 10t N4540 w/Crane **11.99**
625-580 VW T4 Van **7.99**
625-587 Mercedes Benz 230G "Wolf" **7.99**

625-591 Unimog U1300 Helicopter Tractor & Flatbed **12.99**
625-593 Unimog U1300 TLF 8/18 **11.99**
625-810 VW Fire Brigade **19.99**
625-556 MB 230/290 Wolf Off-Road Vehicle-Closed Top **7.99**

625-619 MB Wolf Off-Road Vehicle-Open Top w/Machine Gun **6.99**

625-620 Unimog U 24050 6x6 **8.99**

625-625 VW T4 EK P/P Flatbed **6.99**

625-626 VW T4 DK P/P Crew Cab **6.99**
625-630 "Elefant" Heavy-Duty Tank Transporter **19.99**

625-650 Roland LVB Field Radar Tracking/Control Unit (medium green) **18.99** ***NEW***

625-654 Unimog U 1250 Sedan Cab Flat Bed (Olive Green) **14.99** ***NEW***

625-655 Ford FK 1000 Ambulance (medium green, red & white markings) **11.99** ***NEW***

625-656 Unimog U 1300L Range Control Officer (tan) **9.99** ***NEW***

625-657 VW T3 Sedan Cab w/Special Body **8.99** ***NEW***

625-658 VW T3 Sedan Cab w/Fire Equipment Body **9.99** ***NEW***

625-660 Ford FK 1000 Personnel Van (medium green) **8.99** ***NEW***
625-661 Ford FK 1000 Van (medium green) **8.99** ***NEW***

625-834 Magirus Airfield Semi Tanker-Camouflage **41.99**

625-837 Unimog Aircraft Tractor w/BO 105 Helicopter & Trailer **34.99** ***NEW***
Special set features truck and helicopter in camouflage paint.

625-842 VW T4 Sedan Cab Flatbed Pick-Ups pkg(2) **29.99** ***NEW***
Includes one each in blue and camouflage.

RAILROAD TRANSPORT

625-820 Flat Cars w/Bridge Layer **79.99**
Includes two cars; one Samms class flat carrying an armored "Biber" bridge layer and the second carrying pontoon bridge sections. Vehicle and bridges are finished in camouflage.

625-826 Flat Car w/MLRS/MARS **59.99**
Heavy-Duty Samms class flat car comes with camouflaged MLRS/MARS multiple launch rocket system vehicle.

625-835 Samms Flat Car w/Camouflaged Leopard Tank in Display Case **59.99**
Fully assembled display models.

Limited Quantity Available
625-420 Magirus 168M11FL w/Tanks **12.99**
625-454 Magirus/Iveco 1681Fl **10.99**
625-595 Marder 1A3 Driver's School **6.99**

625-825 Unimog Hy Rail w/Loaded Flat **89.99**
Neat touch for any base or embarkation area. Includes unpowered Unimog hy-rail tractor in green, plus a class Kbs flat carrying a Unimog truck and ambulance, both in camouflage.

GREAT BRITAIN

ARMORED VEHICLES-W.W.II

625-237 Saladin Recon **5.99**

TANKS- POST 1945

625-200 Chieftain **6.99**

TRUCKS - POST 1945
625-408 VW Van "Royal Military Police" **11.99**
625-612 VW T3 Royal Air Force Police **9.99**

RAILROAD TRANSPORT

625-829 Parlor Car-British Army **64.99**

IFOR

BATTLE TANKS
625-604 M992 Howitzer & M109A2 Ammunition Transporter **16.99**
Finished in International Forces colors and graphics

SOVIET UNION

ARMORED VEHICLES POST-1945

625-250 SCUD-A Missile Carrier **7.99**
625-1260 Armored Personnel Carrier BRDM-2 **6.99**

625-1261 Armored Personnel Carrier BRDM-2 w/Rocket Launcher **6.99**

TANKS-WORLD WAR II

625-1200 T35-1933 Version **6.99**

625-1201 T35 TU-1933 Version **5.99**

625-1202 T35-1938 Version **5.99**

625-1203 T28-1935 Version **5.99**

625-1204 T-28 TU-1935 Version **5.99**

625-1205 T28-1938 Version w/Conical Turrets **5.99**

625-1206 T-26 1931 **6.99**

625-1207 T-26 1933 **6.99**

625-1208 T-26 1933 TU Combat **6.99**
625-1209 T-26 1937 **6.99**

625-1211 BT-2 1931 **6.99**
625-1212 BT-2 1933 **6.99**

625-1213 BT-5 1934 **6.99**

625-1214 BT-7 1936 **6.99**
625-1222 T34/76-1941 Version **6.99**
625-1225 T34/85-1944 Version **6.99**
625-1240 SU-85 Assault Gun-1944 Version **6.99**
625-1241 SU-100 Assault Gun-1945 Version **6.99**
625-1242 SU-152 Assault Gun **6.99**
625-1250 KW-1 Heavy Duty-1940 Version **6.99**
625-1251 KW-2 Heavy Duty-1940 Version **6.99**

TRUCKS ZIS-5 WORLD WAR II EA 5.99

625-1270 P/P Canvas Covered Flatbed

625-1271 Wooden Box Body

UNITED NATIONS UN

625-634 MAN 454 Cargo Truck w/2 Weisel APCs w/TOW Weapons (white, black) **34.99** *NEW*

625-635 Unimog TLF 1000 Fire Engine (green, white) **10.99** *NEW*

UNITED STATES

WORLD WAR II - U.S. & ALLIES

ARMORED VEHICLES

625-104 M40 155mm Gun Carriage **5.99**
625-178 M4 Artillery Tractor **5.99**
625-205 Tank Destroyer **4.99**
Includes parts for M10 or M36.

ARTILLERY

625-183 Light Howitzer M2A1 105mm **5.99**

TANKS

625-202 MH A3 Sherman **4.99**

TRAILERS

625-151 Trailer w/2 Assault Boats **4.99**

TRUCKS

625-179 M26 Tank Transporter **9.99**

625-225 4 x 4 Dodge, Closed **4.99**

625-278 M21 MMC w/.50 Caliber Machine Gun **5.99**

625-279 M16 Anti-Aircraft (Quad .50 Machine Gun Mount) **6.99**

625-280 M3 Half-Track Personnel Carrier w/Canvas Cover **5.99**

625-444 Willy's Jeep **9.99**

625-583 GMC CCKW Mobile Shop **11.99**

625-605 GMC 6x6 w/Breakdown Equipment **11.99**

625-606 Chevrolet 2-1/2 Ton Truck **11.99**

625-627 GMC 6X6 w/Hard Top Cab & Quad .50 Anti-Aircraft Gun **11.99**

625-632 Willy's Jeep Military Police (white) **8.99**

625-645 Willys Jeep-Military Police (Olive Green) **8.99** *NEW*

Roco MINITANKS

625-646 GMC Cargo/Personnel Truck w/Canvas Bed Cover (Olive Green, white star & lettering) **14.99** ***NEW***
625-840 M26 "Draggin' Wagon" Heavy Tank Recovery Tractor & Trailer w/Sherman Tank **39.99** ***NEW***
Authentic model of the World War Two tractor and trailer, complete with a special Sherman tank load. Models come fully assembled in a special clear display box.

GMC Cargo/Personnal Truck 625-646

M26 "Draggin' Wagon" Heavy Tank Recovery Tractor & Trailor 625-840

POST-WAR U.S. ARMY

AIRCRAFT

625-248 Bell UH-1D Helicopter **8.99**

625-318 Bell AH1G Cobra Helicopter **8.99**

ARMORED PERSONNEL CARRIER

625-346 M113 **7.99**

625-348 Command Post M577 A1 **8.99**

625-349 Command Vehicle w/Tent **8.99**

625-351 M113 A1G w/20mm Mortar **7.99**

625-406 M901/M981 **10.99**

625-469 M113 A3 ACAV **9.99**

625-494 M3 Bradley CFV-Sand Color **12.99**
625-512 M2 A2/M3 A2 Bradley IFV **12.99**

625-552 US M923 w/3 Tanks **12.99**
625-828 M113 in MERDC Camouflage **22.99**

ARMORED VEHICLES

625-232 M88 Recovery Vehicle **6.99**

625-283 Missile Carrier M667 **7.99**

625-289 M548 **7.99**

625-290 Anti-Aircraft Missile Launcher M730 **8.99**
625-355 M132 Flame Thrower **9.99**
625-376 Mine Launcher on M548 **10.99**
625-492 Tank Recovery Unit M578 **8.99**

625-555 M270 MLRS/MARS **11.99**
625-572 M106 Mortar Carrier **7.99**
625-584 M992 Artillery Ammo Support Vehicle **9.99**

625-600 M9 ACE Armored Recovery Vehicle **12.99**

ARTILLERY

625-187 Medium Howitzer M1/M114 115mm **6.99**

BATTLE TANKS

625-182 M103 120mm **5.99**

625-220 M48 A1 Patton II w/90mm Gun **5.99**

625-221 M47 General Patton **5.99**

625-254 M551 Sheridan **5.99**

625-419 M1E1 Abrams **9.99**

625-821 US M1A2 Abrams w/Camouflage Paint **27.99**

625-181 M60/M60A1 w/105mm Gun **5.99**

SELF-PROPELLED GUNS

625-208 M42 Anti-Aircraft Gun **4.99**

625-388 M107 SF Gun Carriage **6.99**
Optional parts for 203mm Gun

625-514 M109 A2 **8.99**

RAILROAD EQUIPMENT

625-830 Heavy Duty Flat Car Rlmmp USTC w/2 M-113 APCs **44.99**

625-838 Limited-Run US Transportation Corps. Railway Diner Era III (green, yellow, silver-gray roof) **49.99** ***NEW***

Limited Quantity Available
625-827 Stake Flat Car w/Camouflaged 7 Ton MAN Truck **54.99**

Roco Minitanks

TRUCKS

625-282 AM General M151 MUTT A2 **5.99**

625-359 Dodge M880 w/Radio Cabin **7.99**

625-389 M561 Gama Goat **7.99**
Includes canvas cover and radio cabin.

625-413 VW Type 2 **5.99**

625-417 M939 **11.99**

625-428 Hummer Cargo/ Troop Carrier **7.99**

625-477 HEMTT M977 Cargo **19.99**

625-478 Hummer w/TOW Missile Carrier **10.99**

625-479 M1038 Open Hummer **7.99**

625-482 Ford MUTT w/Trailer M151 A2 **8.99**

625-483 M34 w/Water Tank Trailer **13.99**

625-484 M35 A2 2.5-Ton w/Flatbed **10.99**

625-487 M1038 Hummer w/Radio Cabin **9.99**

625-488 HEMTT w/Fuel Supply Equipment **21.99**

625-489 M1038 Hummer **9.99**

625-493 M934 Van w/M200 **19.99**

625-516 M923 w/M105 **17.99**

625-526 M923 **15.99**

625-535 M1039 Hummer Desert Storm **9.99**

625-538 5-Ton Dump Truck pkg(2) **11.99**
Builds either a M929 without winch of the M930 w/winch. Includes canvas cover

625-539 M93A1 5-Ton Wrecker **13.99**

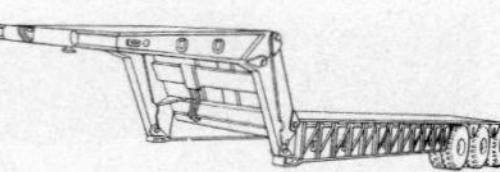

625-540 M931 5-Ton Truck w/40 Ton Low Bed Trailer **22.99**

625-545 M1038 Hummer & M101Trailer **11.99**

625-547 M997 Hummer Ambulance **11.99**

625-548 HEMTT M978 Tanker **19.99**

625-570 US M923 w/3 Fuel Tanks **16.99**

625-571 M35A2 Truck w/Ammo Boxes **12.99**

625-577 Military Police Set pkg(3) **28.99**
Includes three Volkswagen trucks (Traffic Section, Accident Investigation and a personnel van) with all lettering in English.

Prototype Photo

625-579 M109A3 Mobile Shop **12.99**

625-582 Hummer w/Shelter & Telephone Cable Splicer Trailer **12.99**

625-597 VW T3 Fire Department pkg(2) **19.99**
Includes Van and crew-cab pickup w/canvas cover, both in special Army Fire Dept. graphics.

625-601 M931+M969A1 5-Ton Tractor w/5000 Gallon Trailer **19.99**

625-602 M931 5-Ton Tractor-Single Width Tires **10.99**

625-603 M929 5-Ton Dump Truck-Single Width Tires **11.99**

625-618 Ford MUTT M151 A2 w/TOW **8.99**

625-629 US Fire Department VW Pick-Up & Van (red) **19.99**

625-640 Dodge Field Maintenance Unit w/Rubber Tires **8.99**

625-641 M923/M925 5-Tonner w/Special Body **11.99**

625-643 M 35A2 Cargo Truck w/Wrecker Hoist (Olive Green) **10.99** *NEW*

625-659 VW T3 Sedan Cab w/Special Body **7.99** *NEW*

625-814 VW Type 2 Military Police pkg(2) **20.99**

625-815 M998 HMMWV Hummer Personnel **19.99**

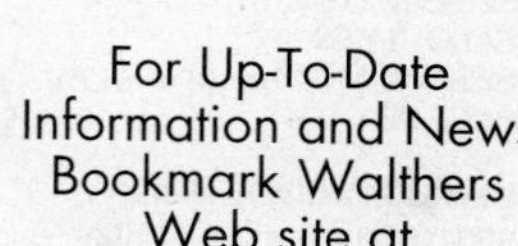

For Up-To-Date Information and News Bookmark Walthers Web site at

www.walthers.com

MILITARY ACCESSORIES

TRAILERS

625-287 M10 Munitions Trailer **3.99**

625-328 1-1/2 Ton 1 Axle Trailer pkg(2) **5.99**

625-462 M101A/M1050A2 Trailer Set **5.99**

625-474 Water Tank Trailers pkg(2) **6.99**

625-573 US M332 Ammo-Trailer **3.99**

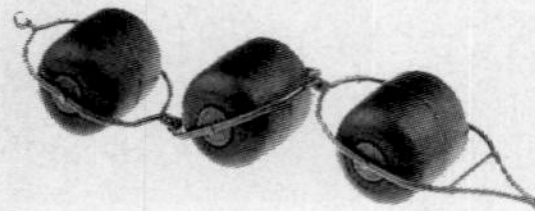

625-617 Portable Fuel Bladders **6.99**

FIGURES EA 3.99

625-117 Combat Group pkg(12)

625-154 American Infantry pkg(16)

625-263 WWII German Soldiers pkg(15)
625-265 Russian Soldiers pkg(10)

625-272 Infantry Assault Group pkg(18)

625-298 Soldiers, Sitting pkg(16)

625-299 Soldiers, Sitting pkg(18)

625-300 Command Group pkg(8)

625-302 Infantry Soldiers pkg(16)

625-309 Tank Commanders & Divers pkg(14)

625-463 Tank Commanders

DECALS

A/UN

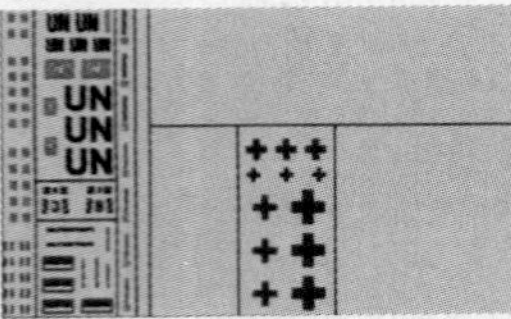

625-335 Assortment #4 **4.99**

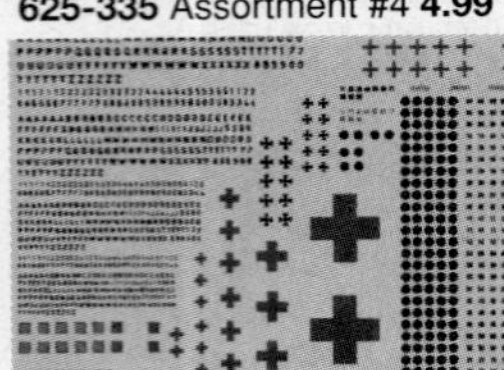

625-371 Tactical Signs **4.99**
625-373 Decal Set 6 **4.99**
For tank trucks, danger and flammable contents.

625-560 US Army Decals, Set A **10.99**
625-561 US Army Decals, Set B **11.99**
625-562 US Army Decals, Set C **11.99**
625-500 MT Plus Accessory Set **5.99**

Limited Quantity Available
625-1050 German Frontier Guard **4.99**

PAINT EA 2.99

625-360 Leather Brown
625-368 Tar Black
625-375 Paint - Forest Green
625-403 Paint NATO Green pkg(3)

DETAIL PARTS

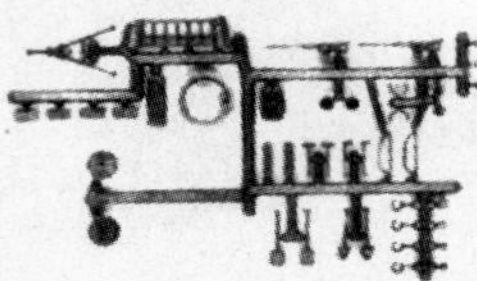

625-277 Accessory Set **3.99**
Includes rifles, shovels, axes, tripod, and more.

625-317 Barbed Wire Rolls **4.99**

625-319 Ammo Boxes **5.99**
625-354 Weapons Set - US/German **4.99**
625-362 Machine Guns **4.99**

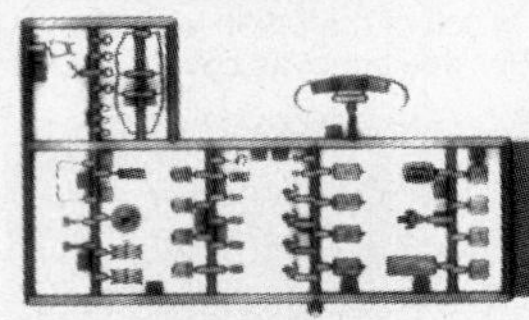

625-364 Accessories for M60 A1 **3.99**

625-365 Radio Boxes pkg(2) **3.99**

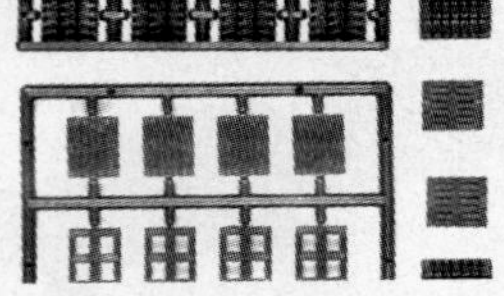

625-422 Gas Cans w/Pallets **4.99**
625-442 Machine Gun Set **4.99**
625-464 Flashing Lights **3.99**
625-496 Rubber Tires for US Trucks **5.99**
625-497 Antenna (Aerial) Wire, Oxidized Black **3.99**
625-500 MT Plus Accessory Set **5.99**

625-542 Sandbags,Less Howitzer **4.99**

625-549 German Wheel Sets pkg(36) **5.99**
Includes 9 Sand, 9 Standard, 9 Rims with and 9 Rims without Nut-Protection

625-550 Artillery Set **4.99**
625-576 Maintenance Accessory Set **4.99**

625-585 Containers 3 x 10' **5.99**
625-596 Radio Antennas-German Federal Army **4.99**

625-608 Federal German Army Number Plates **4.99**
625-609 German Border Guard Number Plates **4.99**
625-1051 Accessory Set **4.99**

625-1052 External Stowage Bins for M113 Armored Personnel Carriers (sold separately) pkg(40) **4.99** ***NEW***

Limited Quantity Available
625-400 Window Set **3.99**
Mirrors, towing hooks, pintles, lamps, Friend/Foe recognition equipment and more.

625-441 Steering Set for #417 **3.49**

NISSEN HUTS

Wherever US forces went during W.W.II, these pre-fab metal buildings weren't far behind. Easy to transport and assemble, they were used to construct just about any kind of building. The models feature the correct 1/2 round, corrugated profile and come in a Basic or Extended version

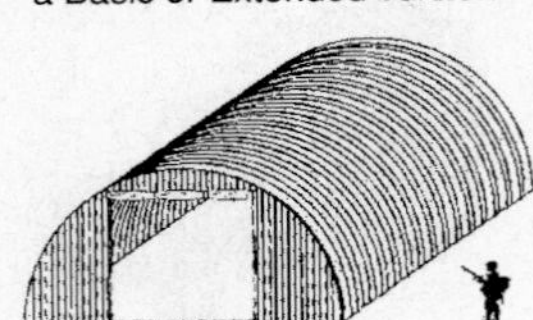

625-614 Basic **8.99**

625-615 Extended **9.99**

MILITARY CATALOGS

625-1001 Catalog of Vehicle Types **23.99**
625-1002 Catalog of Vehicle Types 1st Edition German **14.99**
625-1003 Catalog of Vehicle Types 2nd Extension-German **14.99**
625-81898 1998 Mini-Tank **3.99**

TENTS & STRUCTURES

625-218 Assorted Tents & Cargo **3.99**

625-255 10-Man Tent **3.99**

625-292 2-Stall Garage **12.99**

DISPLAY CASE EA 6.99

625-898 Clear Plastic Case 6" 15cm
Perfect way to display your favorite Minitanks. Protects models from dust and discourages others from handling easily damaged miniatures.

625-899 8-1/2" 21cm

Easy-to-build white metal kits include detailed parts and assembly instructions.

CONSTRUCTION EQUIPMENT EA 6.99

652-3502 Cement Mixer

652-3515 Fork Lift Truck
These gasoline powered fork lifts are found outside all types of industries. Includes several pallets.

CONVEYOR

652-3508 2-Wheel Belt Conveyor **8.95**

SEQUOIA SCALE MODELS

VELOCIPEDES

135-13 HOn3 **8.95**
Prototype was hand-powered track inspection vehicle. Kit features cast-metal construction.

NEW SUPPLIER

Ideal for dioramas, war games and collecting, this line of HO Scale military equipment includes Soviet and German vehicles from various eras. Kits are unpainted plastic.

MILITARY EQUIPMENT

GERMAN - W.W.II

BATTLE TANKS - PZ.KFW.38(T) EA 13.99
This light tank originated in Czechoslovakia in the early 1930s. After German authorities took over production in 1939, the improved model was called panzerkampfwagen 38(t), indicating the country of origin, tscheche, or Czechoslovakia in German. Equipped with a 37mm gun and two 7.92mm machine guns, the 38(t) saw service in Poland, France, Yugoslavia, Greece and Russia during 1940-41, comprising as much as 25% of the German tank force at the time. Although quickly replaced by heavier tanks, the chassis was later adapted to self-propelled guns, anti-tank weapons, artillery tractors and other specialized armored vehicles.

737-87001 Model G ***NEW***
A later production variant, 500 were constructed, making it the most common version.

737-87002 Model C ***NEW***
Identical to the earlier B model, but with the recuperator on top of the gun. A total of 110 were built.

PZ.KFW.38(T) Model C Tank
737-87002

Tatra 13 6 x 6 Truck
737-111086

SOVIET UNION & WARSAW PACT-POST WAR

TRUCKS

737-87011 ZiL-157 Cargo Truck w/Stake Body **12.99** ***NEW***

737-87012 ZiL-157 Radio Truck **12.99** ***NEW***

737-87013 KaMAZ-4310 Cargo/Personnel Truck **12.99** ***NEW***

737-87016 KaMAZ-4310 w/Engine Driven Generator Unit **13.99** ***NEW***

737-87017 ZiL-131 Cargo/Personnel Truck **13.99** ***NEW***

737-87018 ZiL-131 Radio Truck **13.99** ***NEW***
737-111086 German Democratic Republic (DDR)Tatra 813 6x6 **14.99** ***NEW***

Information STATION

Scenery Books

Real railroads were built through the existing scenery. But if they had had a choice, they might have made things a lot easier! For modelers, scenery construction is a fast and easy part of creating a complete layout. You don't have to be an artist, and you can work at your own pace over areas large or small. There's a huge range of materials available to recreate everything from snow-capped mountains, to lush forests to barren deserts.

To help you understand what materials are available and how they can be used, here are just a few of the innovative and interesting books and videos you can select:

Kalmbach has several books dedicated to improving the scenery on a layout. *HO Railroad from Set to Scenery* (400-12144) offers advice for beginners, including plenty of hands-on scenery construction tips. *303 Tips For Detailing Model Railroad Scenery and Structures* (400-12153) offers practical and effective advice for improving the realism of the buildings and scenery on your model railroad. *The Pennsy Middle Division in HO Scale* (400-12170) shows how to use many of today's scenery materials to capture the look of a real railroad.

trident

IMPORTED FROM AUSTRIA BY WALTHERS

Modernize your layout with these civilian vehicles, based on American prototypes, and military equipment from the US and other countries. All 90000 series models are assembled plastic with clear "glass" and full interiors. The 80000 series models are craft train kits, featuring detailed metal castings.

BUSES & VANS

CHEVROLET

729-90071 "Air Shuttle Service" **12.99**

729-90076 Safe Line School Bus **13.99**

729-90116 Chevy Suburban School Bus **12.99**

SPORT VAN EA 11.99

729-900411 White
729-900412 Red
729-900413 Blue
729-900414 Green

CARGO VAN EA 11.99 (UNLESS NOTED)

729-900461 White
729-900462 Red
729-900463 Blue
729-900464 Yellow
729-900465 Green

729-90073 "City Wide Water" **12.99**

729-90074 "TNT" **12.99**

729-90075 "Rockway" **13.99**

729-90102 DHL Worldwide Express Delivery **12.99**

729-90103 FedEx **13.99**

729-90114 Opel Racing Team **13.99**

729-90123 U Drive Truck Rentals **13.99**

CONSTRUCTION EQUIPMENT

729-90055 MAN F8 16.192 FAK Dump Truck **14.99**

729-90093 CCC Tri-Axle Dump Truck **TBA**

729-90094 Heavy-Duty Forklift **15.99**

EMERGENCY VEHICLES

Plastic models are fully assembled and feature colorful graphics.

AMBULANCES

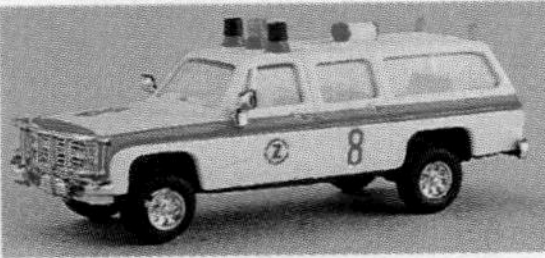

729-90060 Airport **12.99**

729-90061 Rescue **13.99**
729-90063 Advanced Life Support Rescue Vehicle **13.99**

729-90065 Paramedic Ambulance **14.99**

729-90077 Ambulance w/Chevy Van Cab **17.98**

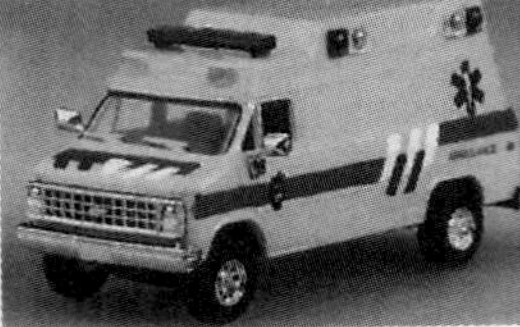

729-90098 Chevy Ambulance (yellow) **14.99**

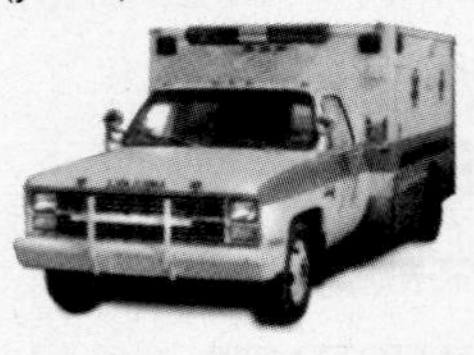

729-90024 Ambulance **12.99**
729-90100 Metropolitan Ambulance **14.99**

729-900631 Advanced Life Support Unit **13.99**
729-90018 Fire Dept. Command Vehicle **9.99**

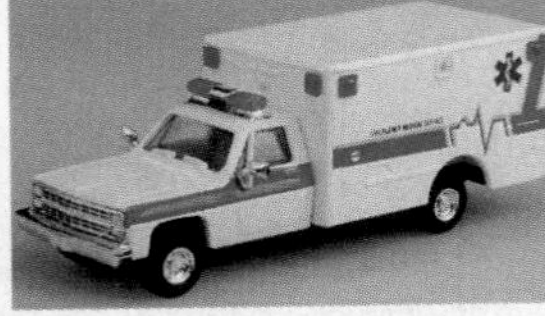

729-90105 Emergency Medical Service **13.99**

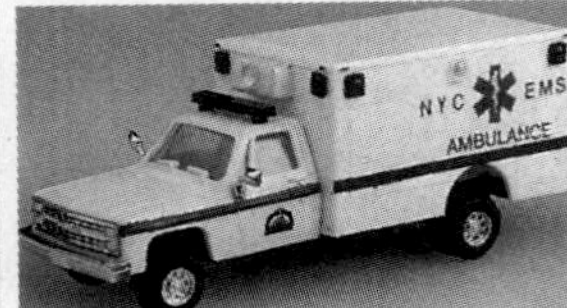

729-90107 NYC EMS **13.99**

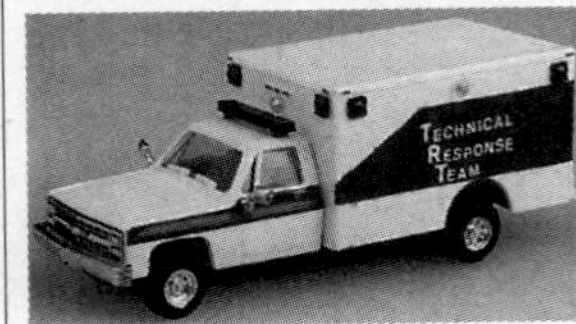

729-90119 Technical Response Team **13.99**

729-90130 Mercy Paramedic **13.99**

Limited Quantity Available
729-90049 Chevy Van Fire/Rescue **14.99**

FIRE ENGINES EA 13.99

"SCAT" MINI-PUMPER

729-90062 Red
729-900621 White
729-900622 Lime Green

RESCUE PUMPERS

729-901171 White
729-901172 Red
729-901173 Lime Green

FIRE DEPT. CHEVROLET SUBURBAN

729-90057 "Subi" Fire Command **13.99**

729-90064 York City (FDNY) Fire Chief **13.99**
729-900541 Emergency Medical Services EMS **13.99**

729-900581 "Florian 13" Airport Fire Command **12.99**

POLICE VEHICLES

729-90042 Sheriff Dive Rescue Team-Chevy Blazer **12.99**

trident

729-90082 Police "Paddy Wagon"-Chevy Pickup Cab **13.99**
729-90118 Texas State Police **13.99**

729-90120 Personnel Van **12.99**

729-90131 Dutch Traffic Police **14.99**

NEW YORK CITY POLICE EA 12.99 (UNLESS NOTED)

729-90096 Chevy Personnel Van

729-90097 Chevy Cargo Van

729-90106 Parks Police

729-90108 Patrol Unit **13.99**

TECHNICAL HELP SERVICE -THW

729-90070 MAN F8 Dump Truck w/Crane (Blue) **15.99**

MILITARY VEHICLES

AUSTRIA

729-80170 Steyr Armored Personnel Carrier **29.99**
729-80171 Steyr KSPz Armored Personnel Carrier **29.99**
729-80172 Steyr-Puch 500D Mini Staff Car **12.99**
729-90045 Steyr 12MIB 5t Truck, Plastic **TBA**

CANADA

Assembled plastic.

729-90011 LAV-AT Anti Tank Version **11.99**
729-90012 LAV-M 81mm Mortar Carrier **9.99**

729-90013 LAV-C2 Command Control Vehicle **9.99**

729-90027 LAV-R Armored Recovery **11.99**

ENGLAND

729-80167 Bedford MK 4 Ton Cargo Truck w/Canvas Cover **29.99**

729-80168 Land-Rover 109 APC **27.99**

729-80173 Land Rover 101FC Truck **26.99**

729-90025 M119 Light Gun, Plastic **7.99**

729-90029 M105 Light Gun, Plastic **7.99**

FRANCE

729-80161 AMX-10P APC w/20mm Gun **29.99**

729-80162 Thomson-CSF "Crotale 4000" **37.99**
729-80163 Thomson-CSF "Crotale Radar" **36.99**

729-80164 Panhard Armed Reconnaissance Vehicle **TBA**
729-80177 AMX 10 VOA Armored Observation Carrier **TBA**

GERMANY

729-80158 Rheinmetall Anti-Aircraft Gun MK20 RH 202 **19.99**
729-80160 Volkswagen LT 45D/E Utility Truck **26.99**

GERMAN ARMY W.W.II

SDKFZ SERIES HALF-TRACKS EA 11.99 (UNLESS NOTED)

729-90090 251/1 Armored Infantry Carrier

729-90091 251/2 Armored Mortar Carrier
729-90092 251/9 Self-Propelled Gun

729-90124 2 Kettenkraftrad Motorcycle **TBA**

729-90127 251/7 Armored Engineer Carrier **12.99**

729-90128 251/6 Armored Flame-Thrower **TBA**

729-90129 251/21 Self-Propelled Anti-Aircraft Gun **TBA**

JAPAN

729-80150 Type 89 Armored Personnel Carrier **29.99**

SOVIET UNION AIRBORNE ASSAULT WEAPONS EA 25.99

729-80033 ASU-85 w/85mm Gun

729-80133 BMD-2 Airborne Combat Vehicle

ANTI-AIRCRAFT & ARTILLERY

729-80052 ZSU-23-4 Gun w/Quad 23mm Guns **29.99**
729-80065 BMP-SON Artillery Radar Vehicle **27.99**

729-80093 SA-13 TELAR 1 "Strela 10" Anti-Aircraft System **31.99**
729-80174 LANCE Missile System Vehicle **TBA**

ARMORED PERSONNEL CARRIERS

729-80031 MT-LBW Troop Transporter/Artillery Tractor **25.99**

729-80037 BTR 60PB Armored **29.99**
729-80039 BRM-1 Reconnaissance Vehicle w/75mm Gun **25.99**

trident

729-80040 BMP-1 Armored w/73mm Gun **25.99**
729-80041 BRDM2 Reconnaissance Vehicle **26.99**
729-80049 BTR-70 Armored **29.99**

729-80050 BMP-2 w/30mm Gun **29.99**
729-80064 BTR-60PA Armored **29.99**

729-80121 BTR-80 Armored **29.99**

729-80132 BRDM-26 Armored Command Vehicle **26.99**
729-80155 "Anona" Assault Gun 120mm **27.99**
729-80156 BMD-2 Combat **29.99**
729-80157 BMP-3 **29.99**

BATTLE TANKS & SELF-PROPELLED GUNS

729-80020 T-72 w/125mm Gun **27.99**

729-80025 T-64 w/125mm Gun **29.99**

729-80043 T-72 w/125mm Gun **29.99**
729-80094 T-72 M1 w/125mm Gun **29.99**

729-80034 "Akatsiya" 152mm Howitzer **31.99**

729-80038 "Gvozdika" 125mm Howitzer **27.99**

729-80131 T-80 ERA w/125mm Gun & Reactive Armor **31.99**

MILITARY TRUCKS & VANS

729-80137 ZIL-131, 3, 5 Ton Cargo w/Canvas Top **29.99**

729-80165 Russian UAZ-452 Personnel Van **23.99**

729-80166 KRAZ-255B Heavy Truck **TBA**

729-80175 ZIL-157 Truck Tractor **29.99**

MISSILE WEAPONS

729-80028 BRDM-2/PUR-64 Tank Destroyer **27.99**

729-80042 BRDM-2/AT5 "Spandrel" Tank Destroyer **27.99**

729-80075 BM-21 "Grad" Truck w/URAL-375 122mm Rocket Launcher **31.99**

SWITZERLAND

729-80146 Anti-Aircraft Missile System **29.99**

729-80159 Fire Control Trailer **31.99**

729-80169 MOWAG "Piranha" PzJg 90 Anti-Tank Vehicle **TBA**
729-80176 MOWAG "Piranha" Armored Personnel Carrier **31.99**

UNITED NATIONS-INTERNATIONAL FORCES

MAN/OAF F8 5-TON TRUCK EA 13.99

729-900191 IFOR (Olive Green, white)

Limited Quantity Available
729-900192 UN (white, blue & white logo)

UNITED STATES

AIR FORCE

M1031 UTILITY TRUCK EA 9.99

729-90017 Maintenance
729-900171 Red
729-900172 Blue
729-900173 Yellow

FIRE CHIEF TRUCK

729-90110 Fire Chief 1 **11.99**

729-90111 Fire Chief **12.99**
729-901111 Assistant Fire Chief **12.99**

US ARMY

HAWK MISSILE SYSTEM MIM-23B USA

729-80081 M78 Launcher w/3 Surface-To-Air missiles **25.99**
729-80082 M501 Loader **19.99**

729-80083 M390C Transporter w/3 Surface-To-Air Missiles **24.99**

729-80084 AN/MPQ-51 Range Only Radar **25.99**

729-80085 AN/MPQ-55 Acquisition Radar **25.99**

729-80086 AN/MPQ-46 Target Illuminator Radar **26.99**

729-80087 AN/MPQ-35 Target Acquisition Radar **31.99**

729-80088 AN/MSQ-110 Information Coordination Center **25.99**
729-80089 AN/MSM-43 Missile Test Shop **12.99**

729-80090 AN/TSW-11 Battery Control Center **19.99**

trident

729-80091 HF45D Generator **9.99**

US ARMY-TRUCKS

729-80141 M988 "Hummer" One-Ton Multi-Purpose **19.99**

729-80144 M715 Cargo **19.99**

729-90003 M1009 Utility Blazer Body, Plastic **9.99**

729-90004 M1008 Troop Carrier Pickup w/Side Rails, Plastic **9.99**

729-90005 M1008 Troop Carrier w/Canvas Cover, Plastic **9.99**
729-90006 M1028 Radio Truck Pickup Body, Plastic **9.99**

729-90007 M1010 Ambulance Pick-Up Cab, Plastic **9.99**

729-90021 Ambulance, Plastic **11.99**

729-90047 LMTV Cargo 2.5 Ton, Plastic **13.99**

729-90048 MTV, 5 Ton, Plastic **14.99**

729-90066 Personnel Van, Plastic **11.99**

729-90083 Cargo Van, Plastic **12.99**

729-90084 Heavy Duty Forklift, Plastic **15.99**

729-90085 M1082 LMTV Single-Axle Trailer **TBA**

729-90086 M1087 LMTV 2.5-Ton Cargo Truck w/Canvas Cover **15.99**

729-90087 M1083 MTV 5-Ton Cargo Truck w/Canvas Cover **15.99**

729-90088 M9088 5-Ton Truck Tractor **TBA**

729-90089 M917 20-Ton Tri-Axle Dump Truck **TBA**

Limited Quantity Available
729-90030 M1008 Troop Carrier (Sand Color) Plastic **9.99**
729-90034 Shelter Carrier (Sand Color) Plastic **9.99**

M1031 MAINTENANCE TRUCK

729-90020 Corps of Engineers **9.99**
729-90052 Maintenance Vehicle **11.99**

729-90126 Multi-Use Shelter **TBA**

729-90125 M1079 2-1/2 Ton Truck w/Shelter **TBA**

Limited Quantity Available
729-90032 M1009 Utility (Sand Color) Plastic **8.99**

US 2-1/2 TON TRUCKS

729-80106 CCKW 353 w/ "Le-Roi" Air Compressor **31.99**

729-80111 CCKW 352 Utility w/Canvas Top **26.99**
729-80112 CCKW 352 Wrecker **26.99**

US SEMI TRACTOR

Assembled plastic.

729-90028 M915 w/M872 Tri-Axle Flatbed **22.99**

729-90043 M915 w/Refrigerator Container & Chassis **22.99**

729-90081 M915A1 w/MILVAN 20' Reefer Container **22.99**

729-90051 M915A1, 14 Ton Tractor **14.99**

729-90053 Wrecker **14.99**

M920

729-90080 M920 Tri-Axle Heavy Tractor **TBA**

729-90109 M915A1 Tractor w/M969A1 5000-Gallon Trailer **22.99**

SEMI TRAILERS

729-90068 M872 Tri-Axle Flatbed **15.99**

729-90069 M872A3 Tri-Axle Flatbed w/Sides **19.99**

729-90079 20' Container & Chassis - MILVAN **15.99**

US NAVY

729-90112 Personnel Van **11.99**

MARINE CORPS EA 9.99 (UNLESS NOTED)

729-90010 LAV-25 w/25mm Cannon

729-90026 LAV-L Logistics
729-90036 LAV Anti-Tank (Sand Color) **11.99**
729-90037 LAV Mortar/Carrier (Sand Color)
729-90038 Command/Control (Sand Color)
729-90039 LAV Logistics Vehicle (Sand Color)
729-90040 LAV Recovery (Sand Color) **11.99**

729-90067 LAV-AD Air Defense Carrier **TBA**

trident

TRUCKS

CHEVROLET

FULL SIZE BLAZER EA 9.99

729-90001 Blue w/White Rear Roof
729-900011 Red
729-900012 Blue

4X4 PICKUP EA 9.99

729-90002 White
729-900021 Red

FLEETSIDE LONG BOX PICKUP EA 9.99

729-900081 Red
729-900082 Gray

NINE PASSENGER SUBURBAN

729-900141 Red **9.99**
729-900142 White **9.99**
729-900591 Two-Tone Red **11.99**

OFF-ROAD RACING TRUCK

729-90050 Rally 4x4 Truck **TBA**

STEP SIDE 4X4 PICKUP EA 9.99 (UNLESS NOTED)

729-90015 Black

729-90115 Stripe Graphics **12.99**
729-900151 Red
729-900152 White

TOW TRUCK EA TBA

729-900721 White
729-900722 Red
729-900723 Blue
729-900724 Yellow

FORD

F-350 PICK-UP CREW CAB EA TBA

This model depicts the popular crew cab, with double doors and rear seat. Trucks like this are common wherever work crews need transportation, and are especially popular with railroads, construction companies and others.

729-900781 White
729-900782 Red
729-900783 Blue
729-900784 Yellow

STANDARD PICK-UP EA TBA

729-900951 White
729-900952 Red
729-900953 Blue
729-900954 Yellow

1-TON DELIVERY TRUCKS

729-90113 Furniture & More **12.99**

729-90121 U Drive Truck Rentals **13.99**

729-90122 U Drive Truck Rentals **13.99**

729-90104 Federal Express **13.99**
729-901011 Unlettered-White **11.99**
729-901012 Unlettered-Blue **11.99**
729-901013 Unlettered-Gray **11.99**

VEHICLE ACCESSORIES

729-96003 Emergency Vehicle Warning Lights (blue & clear) **4.99**
729-96011 Towing Device **4.99**

VEHICLE CATALOG

729-97000 1997-98 Catalog **8.99**
A great reference for collectors and model builders. Includes 34 pages of color and black and white photos of prototypes, models and accessories.

Easy-to-assemble kits are unpainted, soft metal castings and include complete instructions.

TRUCKS

1914 DIAMOND T

785-217 Service Truck **7.98**
Dry transfers included.

785-218 Grain Truck **7.98**

785-242 Tank Truck **8.98**
Dry transfers included.

785-244 Tractor & Trailer **8.98**

FEDERAL

785-247 Dump Truck **8.98**

CONSTRUCTION EQUIPMENT

785-233 Bulldozer-Tractor w/Blade **7.98**

785-234 Motor Grader **7.98**

785-235 Track Type Loader Traxcavator **7.98**

785-237 Back Hoe-Insley Model "K" **10.98**

785-246 Hyster Logging Cruiser **10.98**

FARM MACHINERY

Tractors are based on the very popular John Deere Model A, in original (unstyled on steel wheels) and later styled (streamlined hood and rubber tires) types.

785-207 Styled Tractor w/Disc (1938-1946) **6.49**

785-208 Styled Tractor w/Planter (1938-1946) **6.49**

785-211 Original Unstyled (1928-1938) pkg(2) **6.49**

MOTORCYCLES

785-228 Motorcycle Set **4.49**
Includes two motorcycles, one side car and one rider.

TRUCKS-N-STUFF

SEMIS

Models are fully assembled and include tractor and trailer in colorful, prototype schemes.

FORD

AEROMAX W/SLEEPER EA 19.99

734-202 Swift Transportation (New Scheme) 28' Doubles
734-203 Swift Transportation (Old Scheme) 28' Doubles

AEROMAX EA 17.99

734-512 Gilbert Feeds w/Bulk Trailer (red)

734-516 Nutrena Feeds w/Bulk Trailer (white, green, silver)

FREIGHTLINER

734-502 Cherokee Freight w/45' Trailer (yellow, brown, silver) **17.49**

734-508 Redfearn w/45' Trailer (black & gold Tractor) **17.49**

734-510 Lodi Truck Service w/48' Container (60th Anniversary Scheme) **19.67**
734-522 COE Poppy State Express w/45' Reefer Trailer **17.99** *NEW*

734-537 BNSF 3-Axle w/53' Trailer **18.99** *NEW*

734-1051 Conti Trucking w/48' Flatbed & Cable Rolls **20.99**
734-1056 H&S Trucking 48' Flatbed w/Tin Plate Steel Load **20.99**
734-1057 Gigli Hay & Grain 48' Flatbed w/Small Hay Bales **20.99**

SHORT WHEELBASE (2-AXLE) CABOVER

734-205 Wallace Transport w/Modern Hi-Cube 28' 6" Vans **19.99**
734-206 Westside Transport Inc. w/Hi-Cube 28' 6" Vans **19.99**
734-209 Viking Freight System w/Hi-Cube Doubles **20.99**
734-520 Northern w/45' Reefer Van **17.99**

734-1007 Cherokee Freight Lines Double Flatbeds w/Grape Tanks **21.99**
734-1008 A&A Trucking Double Flatbeds w/Tomato Tubs **20.99**
734-1009 Nepote Ranches Double Flatbeds w/Loaded Grape Tanks **21.99**
734-1010 Panella Trucking Double Flatbeds w/Case Goods **20.99**
734-1011 Tiger Lines Double Flatbeds w/Loaded Grape Tanks **21.99**
734-1013 Nepote Ranches Double Flatbeds w/Painted Sack Load **21.99**
734-1018 Ed Rocha Double Flatbeds w/Hay Loads **20.99**
734-1019 Ed Rocha Double Flatbeds w/Grape Tanks **21.99**
734-1021 Wallace Transport Double Flatbeds w/Tomato Tubs **20.99**

734-1022 Wallace Transport Double Flatbeds w/Case Goods **20.99**
734-1023 BJJ Trucking Double Flatbeds w/Loaded Grape Tanks **21.99**
734-1024 BJJ Trucking Double Flatbeds w/Tomato Tubs **20.99**
734-1027 Joe Coehlo Trucking Double Flatbeds w/Tomato Tubs **20.99**

734-1028 Joe Coehlo Trucking Double Flatbeds w/Sugar Beet Load **20.99**
734-1029 Westside Transport Double Flatbeds w/Tomato Tubs **20.99**
734-1033 Gigli Hay Double Flatbeds w/Hay Loads **20.99**
734-1048 Bernie Gorman Trucking Double Flatbeds w/Tomato Tubs **20.99**
734-1049 Broadway Trucking Double Flatbeds w/Tomato Tubs **20.99**
734-1050 Wallace Transport Double Flatbeds w/Cotton Bales **20.99**
734-1052 WTI Double Flatbeds & Cotton Bales **20.99**
734-1053 Gigli Hay & Grain Double Flatbeds w/Sacks **20.99**
734-1055 A&A Trucking Double Flatbeds w/Garlic Boxes **20.99**
734-1061 COE Dairy Feed w/Double Hi-Cube Vans **20.99** *NEW*

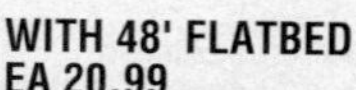

WITH 48' FLATBED EA 20.99

734-1059 COE BJJ Trucking 3-Axle w/Sacked Load *NEW*

734-1079 COE BJJ Trucking 3-Axle w/Lumber Load *NEW*
734-1083 Rocha Trucking 3-Axle w/Orange Boxes *NEW*
734-1089 Gannon Trucking 3-Axle w/Tarped Load *NEW*

734-1095 COE Valley Material Transport w/Lumber Load *NEW*
734-1096 COE Valley Material Transport w/Tarped Load *NEW*

WITH DOUBLE FLATBEDS EA 20.99 (UNLESS NOTED)

734-1060 COE Dairy Feed Transport 2-Axle w/Sack Load *NEW*
734-1062 COE Panella Trucking 2-Axle w/Grain Hoppers w/Extension *NEW*

734-1081 COE Wallace Transport 2-Axle w/Grain Hoppers *NEW*
734-1090 Rausser Bros. w/Hay Load *NEW*

Freightliner w/48' Flatbed 734-1083

Freightliner w/48' Flatbed 734-1089

Freightliner w/Double Flatbed 734-1090

Kenworth T600 734-529

734-1092 JSG Trucking w/Tarped Load *NEW*

734-2003 Gannon Trucking w/28' 6" Double Flats w/Case Goods **25.99** *NEW*

KENWORTH

CONVENTIONAL

734-511 Van de Pol w/Tank Trailer (green, silver) **17.49**

T600

734-500 Farley Trucking w/45' Van **17.99**

734-501 Tiger Lines w/45' Van **17.99**

734-503 Associated Feed w/Bulk Trailer **17.49**

734-506 Panella Trucking w/Trailer (red & white) **17.49**

734-514 RETSI Refrigerated Services w/45' Reefer (turquoise & white) **17.99**
734-515 H&S Trucking w/45' Trailer (blue & white) **17.99**
734-517 Zacky Farms w/45' Trailer **17.99**
734-523 Panella Trucking w/40' Reefer Van Safeway **17.99** *NEW*
734-524 Swift Transportation w/53' Dry Van **18.99** *NEW*
734-529 Tiger Lines w/53' Reefer Safeway **18.99** *NEW*

TRUCKS-N-STUFF

SLEEPER W/53' TRAILER EA 18.99

734-531 HTC *NEW*

734-533 Farley Transportation *NEW*

734-534 Tiger Lines *NEW*
734-540 RETSI *NEW*

AEROSLEEPER W/TRAILER

734-204 Tiger Lines w/28' 6" Modern Hi-Cube Doubles **19.99**

734-207 Metro Freight Systems w/Hi-Cube Doubles **19.99**
734-208 Viking Freight System w/Hi-Cube Doubles **20.99**
734-210 Interstate Dist. Co. w/Hi-Cube Doubles **20.99**

734-518 CH Dredge w/45' Van **17.99**

734-519 Panella Motorsports Transport Race Truck **19.99**

734-521 Duraflame w/45' Trailer **17.99**

734-539 RETSI w/53' Van **18.99** *NEW*
734-541 Zacky Farms w/53' Reefer Van **18.99** *NEW*
734-544 Duraflame w/53' Van **18.99** *NEW*

FLAT TOP SLEEPER EA 20.99

734-1025 Joe Coehlo Trucking Double Flatbeds w/Hay Loads
734-1026 Joe Coehlo Trucking Double Flatbeds w/Case Goods

734-1046 Swift Transport 48' Spread Axle Flatbed w/Tarped Machinery
734-1047 Swift Transport w/48' Flatbed & Tall Tarped Load
734-1065 Roy E. Lay w/Tarped Load *NEW*

WITH 48' SPREAD AXLE FLATBED TRAILER EA 20.99

734-1035 Joe Coehlo w/Tarped Load
734-1038 John Perez w/Tarped Machinery

WITH DOUBLE FLATBEDS EA 20.99

734-1040 John Perez w/Tomato Tubs
734-1041 John Perez w/Grain Hoppers

734-1042 John Perez w/Tarped Feed Load

734-1043 Valley Farms w/Tomato Tubs
734-1044 Valley Farms w/Grain Hoppers
734-1045 Valley Farms w/Sugar Beet Boxes
734-1066 Roy E. Lay Double Flatbeds w/Sack Load *NEW*
734-1070 Bernie Gorman w/Loaded Grain Hopper *NEW*
734-1076 Button Transport Double Flatbeds w/Sugar Beet Load *NEW*
734-1077 Button Transport w/48' Flatbeds w/Coil Steel Tarped *NEW*

MACK

734-504 Associate Feed w/Bulk Trailer (blue & white) **17.49**

734-505 Lodi Nut w/45' Trailer **17.99**

734-509 BJJ w/Tank Trailer (silver & black) **17.98**
734-542 Lodi Nut Sleeper w/53' Trailer **18.99** *NEW*
734-1072 Royal Trucking w/Sleeper & 48' Flat w/Tarped Load **20.99** *NEW*

CONVENTIONAL

734-1014 Panella Trucking Double Flatbeds w/Painted Grain Hoppers **19.99**
734-1015 Panella Trucking Double Flatbeds w/Tin Plate Steel Load **20.99**
734-1016 Ed Rocha Trucking Double Flatbeds w/Case Goods Load **20.99**
734-1017 Ed Rocha Trucking Double Flatbeds w/Tomato Tubs **20.99**

734-1034 Frank Alegre Trucking w/Aluminum Bottom Dump Doubles **19.99**

SHORT WHEELBASE TRACTOR EA 20.99

734-1036 Panella Trucking 48' Flatbed w/Case Goods

734-1037 Frank Alegre 48' Flatbed w/Tarped Load
734-1039 Ed Rocha 48' Flatbed w/Tarped Steel Coils
734-1063 Panella Trucking w/Loaded Bottom Dumps *NEW*
734-1071 Royal Trucking w/Loaded Bottom Dumps *NEW*

PETERBILT

734-535 Paul E Vaz w/New Chassis w/Tanker **18.99** *NEW*

Kenworth Sleeper w/53' Trailer 734-531

Peterbilt Conventional 734-536

Peterbilt Conventional w/Loaded Double Trailers 734-1080

734-2005 Fairchild Conversion 3-Axle w/Multi Deck Cowboy w/Loader **25.99** *NEW*

734-2008 Teresi Trucking w/Multi Deck Lowboy w/Loader **25.99** *NEW*

CONVENTIONAL EA 18.99

734-532 Nepote Ranchers w/New Chassis & 53' Trailer *NEW*
734-536 Boycite Petroleum w/Gas Tanker *NEW*

734-538 Cargill Salt w/53' Van Trailer *NEW*

CONVENTIONAL W/LOADED DOUBLE TRAILERS EA 20.99 (UNLESS NOTED)

734-1012 Mike Lowrie Flatbeds w/Grain Hoppers-Painted **19.99**
734-1020 TVT Trucking Flatbeds w/Tomato Tubs

734-1030 Westside Transport Double Flatbeds w/Tarped Load

734-1031 Westside Transport Double Flatbeds w/Garlic Boxes

734-1032 Granite Construction w/Painted Double Bottom Dumps **19.99**
734-1054 Mike Lowrie Double Flatbeds w/Garlic Boxes

734-1058 WTI Double Flatbeds w/Small Hay Bales
734-1067 Sagara Trucking Flatbeds w/Sack Load *NEW*
734-1069 Sagara Trucking Flatbeds w/Tomato Tubs *NEW*
734-1074 Button Transport Flatbeds w/Tomato Tubs *NEW*

734-1078 Sagara Trucking w/Double Grain Hoppers *NEW*
734-1080 Ryder Logistics Flatbeds w/Case Goods *NEW*

TRUCKS-N-STUFF

734-1084 Paul Vaz w/Set of Double Bottom Dumps *NEW*

734-1085 Paul Vaz Flatbeds w/Grape Tanks *NEW*

734-1088 Silva Trucking Flatbeds w/Tarped Load *NEW*

734-1091 JSG Trucking w/Double Grain Hoppers *NEW*
734-1094 Mr. Trucker 2-Axle w/Double Bottom Dumps Loaded *NEW*
734-1097 Doug Winn w/Double Bottom Dumps *NEW*

734-2000 T&T Trucking w/Double Bulk Air Tanks *NEW*

734-2001 Conti Materials w/Double Bulk Air Tanks **25.99** *NEW*

734-2006 Santa Clara Transfer 2-Axle w/Double Air Tanks **25.99** *NEW*

WITH 48' FLATBED EA 20.99

734-1064 Mike Lowrie SWB w/Loaded *NEW*
734-1068 Sagara Trucking w/Tarped Load *NEW*
734-1073 American Forest Products w/Lumber Plywood Load *NEW*
734-1075 Button Transport w/Sacked Rice Load *NEW*

734-1082 Panella Trucking w/New Chassis & Sleeper w/Tarped Load *NEW*

734-1086 Paul Vaz w/New Chassis & Sleeper w/Lumber Load *NEW*

734-1087 Teresi Trucking w/Sheet Steel Load *NEW*

734-1093 Clark Trucking w/Sheet Steel Load *NEW*

WITH TRUCK & TRAILER TRANSFER EA 25.99

734-2002 Cowti Materials Transport (Custom) *NEW*
734-2004 Fairchild (Custom) *NEW*
734-2009 Mr. Trucker (Custom) *NEW*

734-2011 Valley Material Transport *NEW*
734-2012 D.H. Winn (Custom) *NEW*

SLEEPERS

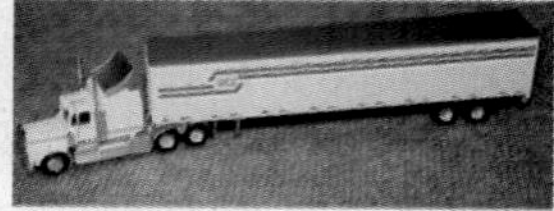
734-530 Paul Vaz w/New Chassis & 53' Van Trailer **18.99** *NEW*

734-2007 With Multi Deck Lowboy w/Load **25.99** *NEW*

734-2010 Mr Trucker w/Cowboy w/Tarped Load **25.99** *NEW*

SEMI TRACTORS

KENWORTH T600 W/SLEEPER EA 9.99

734-708 Swift Transport - New Scheme
734-733 Metro Freight System *NEW*
734-734 Interstate Distribution *NEW*
734-735 Viking Freight System *NEW*
734-738 Victory Express *NEW*

FORD AEROMAX W/SLEEPER EA 9.99

734-709 Swift Transport-Old Scheme
734-737 Knight Transportation w/Sleeper *NEW*

FREIGHTLINER

734-736 COE Viking Freight System **9.99** *NEW*

SEMI KITS

Easy-to-build, plastic models include prepainted and lettered tractor and painted trailers.

FLATBED DOUBLES EA 20.99

Kits include cast plaster load as noted.

734-1001 Panella Trucking - Freightliner w/Tomato Tubs
734-1002 Tiger Lines - Freightliner w/Tomato Tubs
734-1003 H&S - Freightliner w/Tomato Tubs

734-1004 Farley - Freightliner w/Hay Bales

734-1005 Farley - Freightliner w/Sack Load

734-1006 Mike Lowrie - Peterbilt Conventional w/Tomato Tubs

28' HI-CUBE

734-200 Conti Trucking - Freightliner (white) **19.99**

734-201 H&S Trucking **18.99**

TRAILERS

734-740 53' Trailer BNSF **9.99** *NEW*

BOTTOM DUMP

734-101 Dirt Trailer-Doubles **9.99**

W/LOAD EA 14.99

734-714 Low Tarped Load
734-715 Tall Tarped Load
734-716 Tarped Machinery
734-717 Tarped Steel Coils

28' HI-CUBE

734-109 Intermodal Smoothside (white) **5.39**

53' REEFER VAN W/REEFER UNIT

734-118 Undecorated **7.99**

53' DRY VANS EA 9.99 (UNLESS NOTED)

734-726 Swift Transportation *NEW*
734-727 Metro Freight System *NEW*
734-728 Knight Transportation *NEW*
734-729 Victory Express *NEW*
734-119 Undecorated **6.49**

SPREAD AXLE FLATBED

734-111 Complete Kit **9.99**

28' HI-CUBE VAN EA 7.39

734-706 Swift Transport-New Scheme
734-707 Swift Transport-Old Scheme
734-730 Metro Freight System *NEW*
734-731 Interstate Distribution *NEW*
734-732 Viking Freight System *NEW*

24' FLATBED-DOUBLES EA 14.99 (UNLESS NOTED)

PAINTED W/LOAD

Easy-to-build kits include prepainted flatbed doubles and cast plaster loads as noted.

734-700 With Tomato Tubs

734-701 With Hay Load

734-702 With Sack Load

734-703 With Cases

734-704 With Grain Hoppers **12.99**
734-705 Assorted Colors w/Grape Tanks
734-710 With Tin Plate Steel Load
734-711 With Tarped Load

734-712 With Garlic Boxes
734-713 With Sugar Beet Boxes
734-718 With Cotton Bales

UNPAINTED

734-105 Flatbed **8.99**

734-106 Grain Hoppers **9.99**

TRUCK ACCESSORIES

734-110 Trailer Sub Frames w/Flaps pkg(2) **1.99**
734-102 2-Hole White Wheels w/Tires pkg(12) **2.99**
734-104 Trailer Dollies-Complete **2.49**
734-107 Landing Gear w/Flat Pads pkg(10) **3.99**
734-108 Fenders w/Flaps pkg(2) **1.29**

IMPORTED FROM GERMANY BY WALTHERS
Detailing modern streets is easy with this large selection of vehicles. Autos from Austin to Volkswagen, classic autos and trucks, vans, emergency, construction and recreation vehicles. Each item is preassembled in appropriately colored plastic. (Markings and colors may vary from photos.)

AUTOMOBILES

AUSTIN HEALEY EA 11.99

3000

781-81605 Convertible Top Down (red)

781-81601 Green

AUDI

781-12401 A6 (black) **10.99**

781-82602 Font **7.99**

BMW

781-829 Convertible **9.99**

ISETTA EA 10.99

781-80801 Blue
781-80802 Red

3ER EA 8.99

781-19403 Convertible Top Down (violet)

781-19902 Touring Station Wagon (red)

520I

781-19301 **6.99**

750I

781-19201 **5.99**

BORGWARD ISABELLA

781-82301 Red **5.99**

CHEVROLET

781-81902 Corvette **11.99**

CITROEN

781-80701 ID 19 **11.99**
781-82202 15-Six (green) **5.99**

781-80703 ID 19 (brown) **12.99** *NEW*

2CV

781-80901 **8.99**
781-80902 Open **8.99**

FERRARI 348TS

781-18901 Red **8.99**

FORD

781-29940 Galaxy **10.99**

781-81101 17 M **11.99**

TAURUS

781-82001 **5.99**

Limited Quantity Available
781-79906 12M w/Case **18.99**

HORCH

Different Color Shown
781-82502 1937 Sedan (blue) **5.99**

JAGUAR

ROADSTER

781-80101 Sport (black) **5.99**
781-81701 E Type (black) **11.99**

MAZDA MX-5 CONVERTIBLE

781-18804 With Top Down **8.99**

MERCEDES

781-14702 E230 Mercedes Benz (black) **9.99**

781-83501 1936 540K (brown) **8.99**

C240

781-14440 Silver **11.99**

MB 320 SE

781-14302 Blue **7.99**

V230

781-28802 Box Van (black) **10.99**

220S
781-82401 **11.99**

230GE SPORT UTILITY
781-26602 Blue **9.99**

300B

781-836 Black **7.99**

300 SL

781-83302 Coupe **12.99**

781-83404 Roadster (black) **10.99**

320E SEDAN

Limited Quantity Available
781-15803 Blue **8.99**

500 SL
781-14102 Gray/Green **7.99**
781-14202 Convertible (black) **8.99**

MITSUBISHI

PAJERO

781-6601 Black w/Horse Trailer **12.99**

781-26302 Maroon **8.99**

PORSCHE

CARRERRA 4
781-16402 Yellow **7.99**

ROLLS ROYCE

Different Color Shown
781-83802 1951 Silver Wrath (brown) **7.99**

TRIUMPH

TR4 EA 10.99
781-81501 Blue

781-81503 Convertible w/Top Down (Dark Green)

VOLKSWAGEN

BEETLE

781-831 Post Office **5.99**

781-80202 Convertible w/Top Down (orange) **5.99**

781-81002 Green **10.99** *NEW*

GOLF
781-46 Cabriolet **7.99**

781-5104 4 Door **8.99**
781-5201 GTI **7.99**

781-5302 Convertible (red) **10.99**

781-5402 Variant (black) **8.99**

781-5701 A IV (Dark Green) **10.99**

WIKING

POLO
781-3603 4-Door Sedan (Cosmic Green) **10.99** *NEW*
781-4903 Deutsche Post Yellow **8.99**

VENTO
781-5502 Black **3.99**

Limited Quantity Available
781-5501 Maroon **7.99**

VOLVO

Different Color Shown

781-26403 850 (black) **9.99**

BUSES

781-70502 Hinged "MUG" **21.99**

781-87303 D38 Berliner Double Decker **15.99**

MERCEDES

Limited Quantity Available
781-87301 1939 Double Decker **15.99**

CONSTRUCTION EQUIPMENT

781-663 Forklift **5.99**

781-65701 Street Cleaner **10.99**

781-66401 Still R 70-16 Forklift **6.99**

GROVE
781-63202 "Thomen" Hydraulic Crane 6-Axle **40.99**

"Thomen" Hydraulic Crane 781-63202

MAN

781-67303 Dump Truck (brown) **10.99**

781-68902 F90 w/Asphalt Boiler **20.99**

UNIMOG

781-64602 With Snowplow **13.99**

WIMO BAU
Special green-and-red scheme for Wimo Builders.

781-50503 With Loader "Wimo-Bau" **26.99**

781-64701 Unimog w/Loading Crane **15.99**

781-65002 Road Roller **8.99**
781-66001 O&K Shovel **12.99**

781-67502 MAN Dump Truck w/Crane **13.99**
781-67602 MAN Dump Truck **15.99**

Limited Quantity Available
781-65001 Road Roller Wimo-Bau **8.99**
781-67302 MAN Dump Truck **8.99**

EMERGENCY VEHICLES

FORD

781-10407 Galaxy Police **15.99**

781-86401 17 M Police **12.99**

IVECO
781-61101 LF 16 Pumper **17.99**
781-61901 Euro DLK23-12 Ladder Truck **23.99**

MAGIRUS

Limited Quantity Available
781-693 Equipment Truck **10.99**

MERCEDES
781-70 230 TE Ambulance **8.99**

781-605 Fire Dept. Van **10.99**

781-616 Pumper **11.99**

781-6602 Dutch Police G320 w/Horse Trailer **20.99**
781-10402 C 200 Police **12.99**
781-10601 MB G350 Police (green) **8.99**
781-60101 MB 570D Fire Dept. **10.99**
781-61801 DLK 23-12 French Fire **17.99**

Limited Quantity Available
781-103 230TE Autobahn Police **10.99**
781-278 Ambulance **8.99**
781-609 VRW Command Car **8.99**
781-628 1617 Fire Truck **9.99**
781-60801 Fire Dept. Sprinter Van **12.99**

OPEL

781-862 1939 Ladder Truck **7.99**

781-863 LF8 Blitz 1939 Fire Truck **8.99**

781-10408 Senator - Police Canton Zurich, Switzerland **16.99**

PORSCHE

781-10405 Automobile Police **11.99**

UNIMOG

781-622 TLF 8/18 Fire Water Truck **10.99**

VOLKSWAGEN
781-7102 Emergency Doctor **13.99**

781-10901 Automobile Police VW Caravan **12.99**

781-86101 Beetle Fire Brigade **10.99**

Limited Quantity Available
781-78 ADAC **11.99**

CARAVELLE
781-320 Ambulance **8.99**

GOLF

781-4904 A III Post Office **11.99**

PASSAT

Limited Quantity Available
781-10404 Automobile Police **12.99**

VOLVO

781-10406 850 Swedish Police **15.99**

FARM MACHINERY

TRACTORS

CLAAS

781-38301 Front Mount Hay Cutter for Tractor **7.99**

DEUTZ

781-386 Enclosed Cab (green) **6.99**

781-88101 1950s/60s (Styled, No Cab, green) **11.99**

FENDT EA 17.99

781-37901 Favorit 926
781-38001 "Xylon" Mid-Mounted Engine

781-38002 Xylon w/Platform

LANZ-1938 BULLDOG

781-88001 Blue **5.99**

WAGONS

781-879 Open **5.99**

781-38701 Claas Dump **13.99**

KRONE EA 7.99

781-38801 Trailer Agricultural w/Low Platform (green)

781-38840 Trailer High (green)

TECHNICAL HELP SERVICE (THW)

MERCEDES

Limited Quantity Available
781-695 Covered Van **8.49**

TRUCKS

781-840 1939 Opel Blitz **10.99**
781-876 Trailer 2-Axle **8.99**

781-63302 Euro Wiking OAMTC Wrecker (yellow) **16.99**
781-85802 Van w/Tri-Axle Trailer "German Federal Railways" **20.99**

BUSSING 8000 OLD-TIMERS

781-88302 8000 Tanker **12.99**
781-85803 Wandt w/Trailer (green w/white covers) **25.99**
NEW

Limited Quantity Available
781-468 330 w/Trailer **15.99**
781-478 Van w/2 Trailers **17.49**
781-886 Kraft Ketchup Double-Bottom **19.99**
781-85802 Van w/Tri-Axle Trailer "German Federal Railways" **20.99**

DAF

Limited Quantity Available
781-467 Double-Bottom **17.99**

GOLI 3-WHEELER

781-84104 Automobile **10.99**

Limited Quantity Available
781-84103 Stark **8.99**

HANOMAG

Limited Quantity Available
781-850 ST100 w/Two Trailers **19.99**

IVECO

781-43902 Euro Cargo Truck "DB" **16.99**
781-55204 Euro Van–Swiss Post Office **15.99**
781-55205 Euro Cargo Truck Post **20.99**

Limited Quantity Available
781-439 Delivery Euro Cargo **15.99**
781-474 Double-Bottom Van **17.99**
781-516 Euro Star **23.99**

MAGIRUS S750

781-85503 S7500 w/Trailer (blue w/white covers) **21.99**
NEW

MAN

Limited Quantity Available
781-459 Double-Bottom Van **15.99**
781-511 Covered Flatbed **13.99**
781-541 Covered Flatbed **15.99**
781-551 Double-Bottom Post Office **19.99**
781-570 F90 w/Trailer **19.99**
781-643 Recycling Container **9.99**

Wandt w/Trailer (green w/white covers)
781-85803

S7500 w/Trailer (blue w/white covers)
781-85503

781-859 L6600 Delivery **11.99**
781-860 L6600 Post Office **12.99**
781-44102 Racing BP **29.99**
781-44103 Racing Dehnhardt **29.99**
781-44104 Racing DEA **35.99**

781-57402 Truck & Trailer DB **27.99**

MERCEDES

781-571 Double-Bottom Trailer **26.99**

781-575 2244 Silo Transporter **20.99**
781-56101 Box Van w/Trailer Alpiners **29.99**

781-57105 MB-SK Hydrotherm w/Trailer **37.99**

781-78003 Tractor/Trailer Shell **25.99**

781-63902 MB Garbage **13.99**
781-63903 MB Garbage "Paris" **20.99**

PETERBILT

781-63101 American Wrecker **15.99**

Limited Quantity Available
781-456 2632 Double-Bottom Covered Flatbed **13.99**
781-457 2632 Double-Bottom **17.99**
781-573 Double-Bottom **27.99**

RENAULT

781-52702 With 40' Trailer-Puma **20.99**

SCANIA

781-51801 Semi-Covered Flatbed **29.99**

781-52801 Refrigerated Semi **28.99**

Limited Quantity Available
781-51004 Semi w/Tri-Axle Canvas Side Trailer **29.99**
781-87001 Early Model 411-Open Cab **9.99**

UNIMOG

Limited Quantity Available
781-405 With Tar Kettle Trailer **11.99**

VOLKSWAGEN

781-26801 "Gypsy" Motor Home Camper **15.99**

781-29803 Delivery **11.99**

VOLVO FL10

Limited Quantity Available
781-519 Semi **16.99**
781-548 Moving Van **17.99**
781-787 With Gas Cylinders **13.99**

VANS

MERCEDES

781-28101 Sprinter MB **8.99**
781-28301 Sprinter Box (blue) **9.99**

VOLKSWAGEN

781-9201 Caravan Detleffs 530 **11.99**
781-29601 Combi (black) **8.99**
781-29903 Sharan Knirps **10.99**

VEHICLE ACCESSORIES

781-10 Truck Accessories **6.99**
Assorted details include windshields, bumpers, mirrors and more.

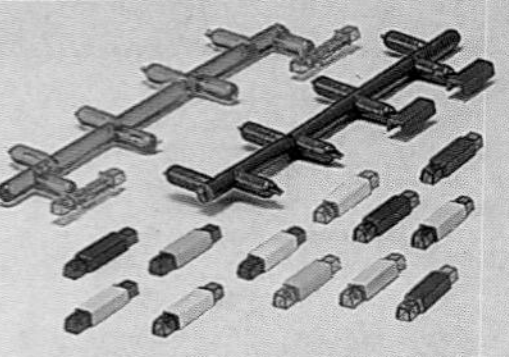

781-11 Emergency Lights **5.99**

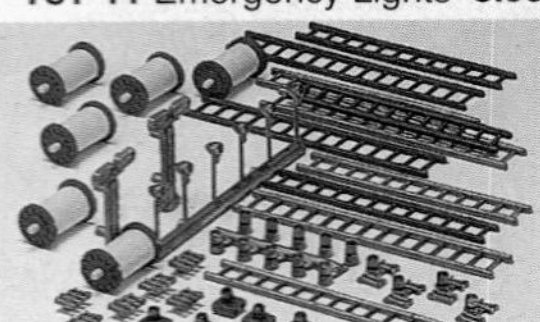

781-12 Firefighting Accessories **9.99**

781-13 Assorted Wheels **7.99**

781-14 Wheels & Axles **9.99**

Easy-to-build, plastic kits. All Photos show prototype aircraft or vehicle.

AIRCRAFT

CORBEN

782-52500 Super-Ace **6.45**

PITCAIRN AUTOGIRO

782-52600 Less Decals **6.45**
782-52601 With Decals **8.95**
This unique design combined the features of an airplane with an unpowered rotary wing in an early attempt to increase vertical lift.

STEARMANN

782-52700 PT-17 Trainer **7.65**
The classic "pilot maker" served as a primary trainer for both Army and Navy flyers during W.W.II and many were purchased by civilians after the war.

AUTOMOBILES

Add authentic American vehicles to your layout with these easy-to-build kits. All parts are molded in clear plastic, so the one-piece body has flush windows. Just mask and paint, add the one-piece frame with seats, glue on the wheels and you're ready for the road.

CHEVROLET EA 5.45

782-54100 1957 Bel Air Two-Door Hardtop
No other car symbolizes the fabulous 50s quite like this. As popular now as they were when new, this model looks great in period or modern street scenes.

782-54130 1995 Caprice Four-Door
These big sedans were among the last Caprice models and were often used as police cars and taxis.

782-54500 1932 Cabriolet
Build as a Convertible or Hardtop.

782-54700 1955 Nomad Wagon
A great car for the family or surfers heading for the beach.

CORD

782-56100 1937 Convertible **5.45**
A legend when new, a true classic today! This super-charged beauty could easily hit 110 mph! It boasted the first disappearing headlamps, hidden fuel filler, full wheel covers and license plate light.

DODGE

782-55500 1977 Four-Door Sedan **5.45**
Matches 1971-1978 models, which had only minor styling changes. Very popular with police departments and other fleet vehicle operators.

FORD EA 5.45

782-53100 1939 Deluxe Sedan
Restyled for 1939, this model featured integral headlamps and an all-new grill.

782-53110 1957 Fairlane 500 Two-Door
Head out to the suburbs in style behind the wheel of this late 50s favorite!

782-53120 1957 Thunderbird
One of the best-loved Fords of all time, these models still turn heads today.

782-53200 1956 Crown Victoria
Always popular, this version came packed with features, including a plastic sunroof!

Less figure

782-53500 1940 Coupe

782-53600 1935 Four-Door Sedan

782-53800 Taurus

MERCURY

782-53700 1949 Two-Door Hardtop **5.45**
The "Jimmy Dean" Merc remains a favorite with collectors and street rodders!

PONTIAC

782-56200 1964 GTO **5.45**
Considered the first of the great 60s muscle cars, the GTO could outrun a Ferrari and sold new for just $3800!

TRUCKS

CHEVROLET EA 5.45

782-54110 1950 Pick-Up
Perfect for the busy contractor, farmer or as a restored truck on today's streets.

782-54120 1950 Stake Truck
Remove the bed from your old pick-up, add a flatbed, some side stakes and you have a rig that can carry any kind of load.

782-54600 1932 Pick-Up

782-54800 El Camino
The styling and interior of a car, and the versatile hauling capacity of a truck made the El Camino a favorite with city and country residents.

782-54900 1995 Blazer
One of the most popular sport utilities, equally at home on the freeway or off-roading.

FORD EA 5.45

782-53130 1955 Panel Truck
Making local deliveries will be a snap with this handsome truck. The father of today's vans, panels were used by all kinds of businesses.

782-53300 1953 F-100 Pick-Up
This 50th Anniversary model featured lots of innovations. Tailgate is a separate piece so it can be built open or closed. Box is also separate, ideal for kitbashing!

782-53400 1953 Stake Bed

782-53900 1992 Explorer Four-Door

YE OLDE HUFF-N-PUFF

FARM EQUIPMENT

792-1025 Tractor & Disc **9.00**

HORSE-DRAWN WAGON

792-1026 Amish Buggy w/Horse & Ma & Pa Figures **15.00**

The Wheel Works

A DIVISION OF
MICRO ENGINEERING

Kits feature white metal parts.

AUTOMOBILES

1932 FORD EA 9.95

778-96105 Roadster (Top Down)

778-96106 Roadster (Top Up)

778-96121 Victoria Sedan

778-96122 Coupe

778-96130 Station Wagon

FARM MACHINERY

TRACTORS

778-96115 Ford **7.30**

TRUCKS

778-96157 Terminal **12.35**

HY-RAIL EA 12.35

778-96111 HOn3
778-96113 HO

1934 FORD

778-96101 Pick-Up **9.95**

778-96102 Panel Truck **10.45**
Includes decals.

778-96103 Stake Body Truck **13.60**
Includes decals.

778-96108 Cab & Chassis **9.95**

778-96109 Small Stake Truck **9.95**
Features plastic stake bed.

778-96112 Log Truck **16.75**
Includes logs.

778-96114 REA Panel Truck **14.65**
Includes decals.

778-96117 Service Truck **12.35**

778-96127 Flatbed Truck **10.45**

778-96128 Flatbed w/Tractor **16.75**

778-96129 Dump Truck **10.95**

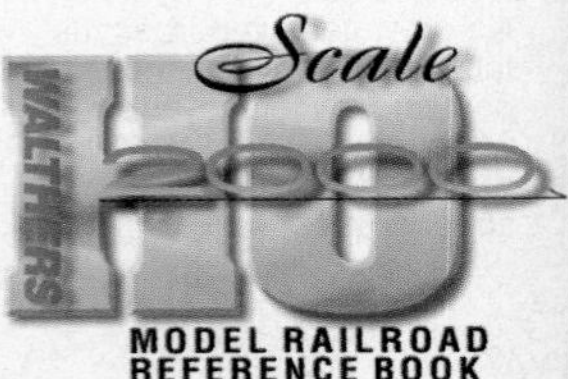

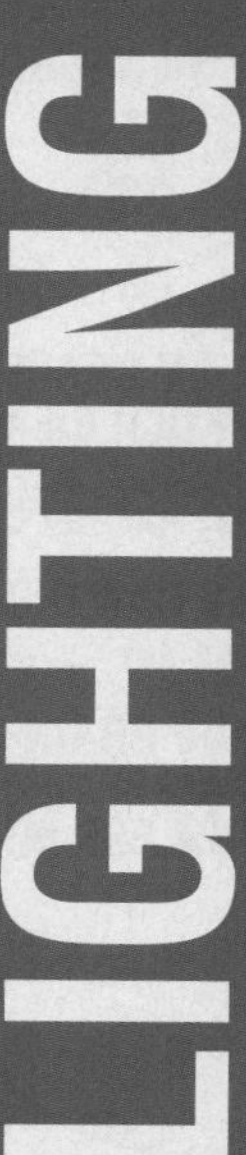

Burning the midnight oil" is the rule, not the exception for railroad employees. In many towns and cities along the line, the night is actually busier than the day! And not just for train crews. During the evening, much of the maintenance and repair that keeps the line running is done. The big city terminals and offices are cleaned at night. Fewer trains allow more time to repair track, bridges, overhead wires and a thousand other items that can't easily be done during the day.

But shop crews will tell you time makes little difference to them. Eventually, everything from private car to brand-new diesel needs their attention. It's often a question of when and where something breaks down or its monthly inspection comes due that determines if the day or night will be a busy one.

Of course, somebody, somewhere needs that equipment back in service as soon as possible. So the lights burn 'round the clock here.

And you can't always tell how busy it's been by what's left on the shop floor as the shifts change. Yes, the place is almost empty now, save for one or two troublesome units. But over the last eight hours, a number of engines have been returned to duty. And others are heading here right now as a new day is about to start.

Dawn is breaking over the Old Forge shops in Media, Pennsylvania, where some of Jim Hart's Pennsy motive power rests between runs.

Models and Photo by Jim Hart

WALTHERS

BULBS

16V MINI-BULB PKG(3) EA 4.98

For longer bulb life, our 16V bulbs can be operated from a 12V power supply.

942-3491 Amber
942-3493 Clear
942-3495 Green
942-3496 Red

1.5V MICRO BULB

942-433 Clear **5.98**

1.5V GRAIN-O-RICE PKG(3) EA 4.98

942-435 Clear
942-436 12V Clear

6V GRAIN-O-WHEAT

942-441 Clear pkg(2) **2.98**

16V GRAIN-O-WHEAT PKG(3) EA 4.98 (UNLESS NOTED)

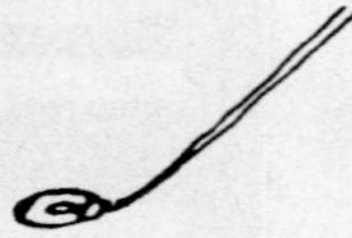

942-3451 Amber
942-3453 Clear
942-3455 Green
942-3456 Red
942-13453 Clear pkg(50) **59.98**

16V SUB-MINIATURE BULB

942-365 Clear pkg(3) **6.98**

FLUORETTES PKG(3) EA 6.98

942-352 16V White
942-353 8V White

SOCKETS

FLUORETTE

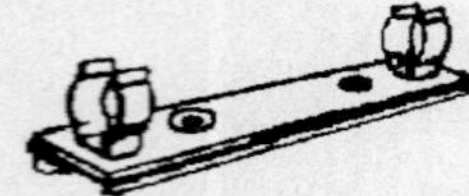

942-362 Panel w/Clips pkg(3) **4.98**

SOCKETS

942-350 pkg(6) **4.98**

HOOK-UP WIRE

942-414 6', 4 Colors **2.49**

LIGHTING KITS

Easily installed, these insulated sockets can be connected directly to a metal, plastic or wood roof. Frosted tubular bulbs fit snugly out of the way of interior details and give uniform, diffuse lighting over a large area. Wired as directed, bulbs give realistic illumination and last for hundreds and hundreds of hours. Kit contains bulbs and sockets.

933-717 Standard 2-Bulb Kit **6.98**
Two 942-352 16V bulbs included.
933-718 4-Bulb **12.98**
933-963 1-Bulb (No Instructions) **3.98**

ATLAS

LAYOUT WIRE EA 5.45

20 gauge standard copper, 50' spool.

151-315 Black
151-316 Red
151-317 Green
151-318 Yellow
151-319 Blue

ATHEARN

MOTORS

140-84047 5/8" Arm With 3/4" Flywheel **14.50**
140-84048 1/2" Arm w/Flywheel **14.50**
140-84049 5/8" Arm With 5/8" Flywheel **14.50**
140-84060 C44-9W Hi Performance **16.50**
140-84067 C44-9W Hi Performance w/Flywheel **19.25**

NARROW CAN MOTORS EA 9.75

140-84030 Small
140-84040 Large

ASSEMBLY CLIP

140-84017 Jet 400 pkg(4) **2.00**
140-84025 Bottom Jet 400 pkg(3) **1.50**

MOTOR MOUNT PADS

140-84020 Jet 400 pkg(12) **3.00**
140-84021 Jet 600 pkg(6) **1.50**
140-84022 Spg 400 **1.50**
140-84024 Dpg 600 **1.50**

MISCELLANEOUS

140-84014 Brush Spring Jet 400 pkg(36) **3.60**
140-84019 Thrust Washer 1/8" I.D. pkg(6) **1.20**
140-90037 Motor Brushes pkg(24) **7.20**
140-90043 Motor Bearing Oilite pkg(6) **1.80**
140-90107 Spline Hollow 7/16" pkg(6) **1.80**
140-90108 Ball Coupling Jet 400/600 pkg(6) **1.80**

BACHMANN

ELECTRICAL ACCESSORIES

WATER PUMP ELECTRIC, MINI

160-42219 12.00

INTERIOR LIGHTING KIT W/WIRE

160-42240 pkg(2) **6.00**

POWER PACKS

160-44207 28.00
160-44209 G Scale **33.00**
NEW

BL HOBBY PRODUCTS

ELECTRICAL ACCESSORIES

DIODES

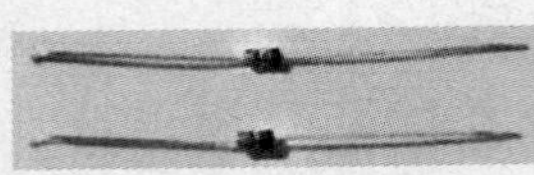

183-261 pkg(5) **2.50**

LEDS PKG(4) EA 3.75

Small

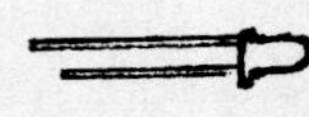

Regular

183-250 Small (red), 3/32" Lens
183-251 Small (green), 3/32" Lens
183-252 Small (yellow), 3/32" Lens
183-253 Regular T-1 (red)
183-254 Regular T-1 (green)
183-255 Regular T-1 (yellow)

RESISTORS

183-260 Drop 560 ohms pkg(5) **2.00**
183-262 Sensing pkg(10) **4.00**
4700 ohm surface-mount resistors are used across wheels of cars to sensitize the cars for operating auto block control. Instructions included.

FIBER OPTICS

FIBERS

183-700 Fiber Optic Assortment **4.95**
5' each, 10, 20 and 30mm fiber.

183-701 100', 10mm Fiber **7.25**
183-702 30', 20mm Fiber **6.00**
183-703 15', 30mm Fiber **6.25**
183-704 15', 40mm Fiber **6.75**

FIBER W/LIGHT SOURCE EA 6.25

Includes two each of 20mm and 30mm optic fiber.

183-711 Clear
183-712 Green
183-713 Red
183-714 Yellow
183-715 Multiple Light Source **11.95**
A light source to be used with multiple strands of fiber optic. Many strands of different sizes can use this common source. Operates on 6 watt, 110V bulb. Full instructions are included.

LIGHT KITS

STARS IN YOUR SKY

Places lighted stars in your backdrop sky. Includes various sizes of fiber optic, light source and full instructions.

183-532 HO Scale **44.00**
183-530 Z Scale **37.00**
183-531 N Scale **39.00**

MOON IN YOUR SKY

183-535 12.00
Place a moon in sky backdrop. Light source, materials and instructions included.

AUTO

183-720 7.75
With 1 red and 1 clear bulb, 3' each of 20 and 30mm fiber optic material.

FLASHER

183-721 7.75
With 2 red bulbs.

INTERNATIONAL HOBBY CORP.

LIGHTING KITS

For passenger cars. 12 in each package.

348-4245 4-Wheel **13.98**
348-4246 6-Wheel **16.98**

25' WIRE MULTI-STRAND

348-4411 1.49

GEARHEAD MOTOR

348-5188 39.98

BLINKING BEACON LIGHTS

Blinking unit with LED.

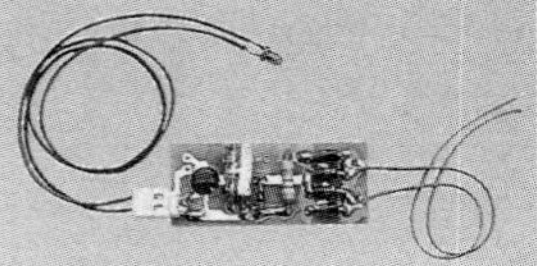

348-5200 Red
348-5201 Yellow

DELUXE MOTORIZING KIT

348-5190 For Circus Rides **7.98**

Figure 1

Figure 2

Figure 3

Figure 4

Figure 5

Figure 6

Accurate Lighting has developed four styles of lighting systems. They all provide the same effect but derive their power from different sources. Make sure that you select the effect and power source that best meets your needs.

PRO LINE SERIES

Accurate Lighting's Pro Line Series Lighting Systems are designed to offer the most realistic directional lighting available. Installed in series with the locomotive's motor, the lights operate at full intensity before the unit moves. All locomotives operated in multi-units must have a lighting system installed. The lighting systems include all the necessary bulbs/lenses and hardware to complete installation.

SWITCHERS

144-10101 Forward/Reverse Lighting For Athearn SW7 Cow, SW7 Calf & S12 Switcher **27.95**
See Figure 8.

144-12121 Forward/Reverse Lighting For Athearn SW7 Cow, SW7 Calf & S12 Switcher w/Ditch Lights **29.95**
NEW
See Figure 17.

144-10202 Forward/Reverse Lighting For Athearn SW1000 & SW1500 Switchers (except SP version) **27.95**
See Figure 1.

144-10404 Redesigned Forward/Reverse Lighting For Athearn SP Version of SW1500 Switcher **29.95**
Use this unit if you want ditch lights for all SW1500 and SW1000 Switchers.
See Figure 5.

DIESEL LOCOMOTIVES

FORWARD/REVERSE LIGHTING

144-101014 For Model Die Casting ALCO RS-3 **28.95**
Redesigned. See Figure 16.

144-10212 With Constant Cab Light **29.95**
For Athearn GP-9, GP38-2, GP40-2, GP50, GP60, SD9, SD40-2, SD40T-2 (except SP and SSW version).
See Figures 2 and 18.

144-12212 With Constant Cab Light **31.95**
For Athearn F45, FP45, GP35, RDC, SD40T-2 (SP and SSW versions only), SD45, SDP40, U28B, U28C, U30B, U30C, U33B, U33C and DD40.
See Figures 3 and 18.

14414204 Ditch Lights & Operating Red Marker Lights **32.95**
For Athearn AMD103 P40/P42 Locomotives. See Figures 6 and 9.

Figure 7

144-14212 With Constant Cab Light **32.95**
Includes six forward lights, one constant cab light and two reverse lights. Works on all Athearn locos that require extra lights for ditch, truck and step lights. See Figures 7 and 18.

144-14222 With Ditch & Number Board Lights **32.95**
For Athearn GE C44-9W and AC4400. See Figures 3 and 18.

144-40202 Directional Constant Lighting **26.95**
For Walthers Trainline® Series ALCO FA-1/FB-1, GE DASH 8-40B and EMD F40PH.
See Figures 12 and 14.

144-50101 Directional Lighting For GE C449W **27.95**
Replaces amber LEDs with clear bulbs to light defuser bar. See Figures 3 and 18.

144-50212 Directional Lighting For Kato GP35 **31.95**
See Figures 3 and 18.

CONSTANT LIGHTING MODULE

144-30010 **24.95**
Matches current draw for non-lighted powered units.

figure 8

FORWARD LIGHTING ONLY

144-20210 Constant Lighting w/Directional Cab Light **27.95**
For Athearn locos operated in multi-units. GP9, GP38-2, GP40-2, GP50, GP60, SD9, SD40T-2 (except SP and SSW version). See Figure 2.

144-22210 With Directional Cab Light **29.95**
For Athearn locos operated in multi-units. F45, FP45, GP35, RDC, SD40T-2 (SP and SSW versions), SD45, SDP40, U28B, U28C, U30B, U30C, U33B, U33C and DD40.
See Figure 3.

144-24210 Constant Lighting w/Directional Cab Light For Locos in Multi-Units **32.95**
All Athearn locos needing extra lights for ditch lights, step lights, truck lights, etc. Includes six forward lights and one directional cab light.
See Figure 7.

144-24220 With Nose & Ditch Lights & 2 Number Board Lights **32.95**
For Athearn GE C44-9W and AC4400. See Figure 3.

Figure 9

FORWARD/REVERSE DIRECTIONAL LIGHTING W/ROOF BEACON

144-102125 With Amber Strobe Flasher **39.95**
For Athearn GP9, GP38-2, GP40-2, GP50, GP60, SD9, SD40-2, SD40T-2 (except SP and SSW versions). Unit includes roof mounted beacon detail. See Figure 20.

144-122125 With Amber Strobe Flasher **39.95**
For Athearn F45, FP45, GP35, RDC, SD40T-2 (SP and SSW versions only), SD45, SDP40, U28B, U28C, U30B, U30C, U33B and U33C. Unit includes roof mounted beacon detail.
See Figure 20.

FORWARD ONLY DIRECTIONAL LIGHTING W/ROOF BEACON

144-202105 With Amber Strobe Flasher **39.95**
For Athearn GP9, GP38-2, GP40-2, GP50, GP60, SD9, SD40-2 and SD40T-2 (except SP and SSW versions). Unit includes roof mounted beacon detail. See Figure 20.

144-222105 With Amber Strobe Flasher **39.95**
For Athearn F45, FP45, GP35, RDC, SD40T-2 (SP and SSW versions only), SD45, SDP40, U28B, U28C, U30B, U30C, U33B and U33C. Unit includes roof mounted beacon detail.
See Figure 20.

ATHEARN F7A/B

144-22000 Forward Only Constant Lighting **29.95**
For Athearn F7A and F7B powered units. See Figure 4.

Figure 10

144-220005 Forward Only Directional Lighting w/Amber Strobe Flasher **39.95**
For Athearn F7A, includes Western Cullen style beacon detail. See Figure 10.

STEAM LOCOS

Figure 11

144-40011 Forward Only Lighting w/Single 1.5V Bulb **19.95**
See Figure 11.

144-40012 Forward Only Lighting w/Two 1.5V Bulbs **19.95**
See Figure 11.

144-40021 Constant Lighting w/Single 1.5V Bulb **19.95**
See Figure 11.

144-40022 Constant Lighting w/Two 1.5V Bulbs **19.95**
See Figure 11.

CATALOG

144-1 Catalog **Free**

"WE'VE DONE THE HARD WORK FOR YOU"

Figure 12

FORWARD/REVERSE LIGHTING FOR OVERLAND MODEL DRIVES

144-102126 29.95
For Overland Model drives requiring two roof lights, one constant cab light and two backup lights. See Figures 2 and 12.

144-122126 31.95
For Overland Model drives requiring two roof lights, ditch or nose lights, one constant cab light and two backup lights. See Figures 3 and 18.

144-142126 33.95
For Overland Model drives requiring two roof lights, two ditch lights, two nose lights, one constant cab light and two backup lights. See Figures 7 and 18.

BATTERY POWERED STROBE FLASHERS

.90 x .55 x .32" battery pack and flasher unit, on/off switch, dot style LED-suited for diesel roof flashers, emergency vehicle warning lights and structure warning lights. See Figure 10.

144-62001 Red **9.98**
144-62002 Amber **9.98**
144-62003 Yellow **9.98**
144-62009 Replacement Batteries pkg(6) **1.79**

"Modelers TIP"
Where to start? Install a 144-10212 Lighting Unit into an Athearn Locomotive just out of the box. Amaze yourself and your friends with the lighting effects.

ELECTRICAL PICKUPS

144-31000 Direct Wiring Kit **3.49**
For two Athearn, Roundhouse and Lifelike locos. Replaces the comutator strip and assures electrical conductivity between trucks and motor.

144-1001 Side Frame Electrical Pickup pkg(8) **5.95**
For six axle Athearn locos. Pickup power at the truck, great for DCC. Includes parts for two locos.

144-1004 Side Frame Electrical Pickups pkg(8) **5.95**
For four axle Athearn locos. Pick up power at the truck, great for DCC. Parts for two locos.

DIGITAL COMMAND CONTROL LIGHTING

The lighting systems are designed to be easily incorporated with all DCC manufacturers modules. The lighting systems include the bulbs and lens retainer to provide the very best lighting systems for the DCC operator.

FOR DIGITRAX DH 84/DH 140 DECODERS

144-70212 2 Each of Forward Roof & Backup Lights **28.95**
Plugs into decoder. Each set of lights runs off a separate function. See Figures 18 and 19.

144-72212 2 Each of Forward Roof, Nose/Ditch & Backup Lights **29.95**
Plugs into decoder. Each set of lights runs off a separate function. See Figures 13 and 18.

144-74212 2 Each of Forward Roof, Nose, Ditch & Backup Lights **31.95**
Plugs into decoder. Each set of lights runs off a separate function. See Figures 7 and 18.

ALL OTHER DECODERS

These lighting units are placed in line with the decoder and provide the lighting effects as described.

144-80212 2 Each of Forward Roof & Backup Lights **28.95**
Each set of lights runs off a separate function. See Figures 18 and 19.

144-82212 2 Each of Forward Roof, Nose/Ditch & Backup Lights **29.95**
Each set of lights runs off a separate function. See Figures 18 and 19.

144-84212 2 Each of Forward Roof, Nose, Ditch & Backup Lights **31.95**
Each set of lights runs off a separate function. See Figures 18 and 19.

Figure 13

GENESIS SERIES

Accurate Lighting's Genesis Series Lighting Systems are designed to offer the modeler a system that operates with other locomotives that do not have lighting systems. Installed in parallel with the loco's motor, the lights operate from the track power. It takes up to 2.5V before the lighting system comes on and the units will have started to move. The lighting units contain all the necessary bulbs/lens retainers and hardware to complete installation. The locos listed are Athearn, but can be installed in any manufacturer's unit with similar shells.

144-60101 Forward/Reverse Lighting **29.95** *NEW*
For Athearn SW7 Cow, SW7 Calf and S12 Switcher. See Figure 8.

144-60202 Forward/Reverse Lighting **29.95** *NEW*
For Athearn SW1000 and SW1500 Switchers (except SP version). See Figures 1 and 8.

144-60404 Forward/Reverse Lighting w/Constant Cab Light **29.95** *NEW*
For Athearn SP version of SW1500 Switcher. Use this unit if you want ditch lights for all SW1500 and SW1000 Switchers. See Figures 5 and 17.

Figure 14

144-60212 Forward/Reverse Lighting w/Constant Cab Light **31.95** *NEW*
For Athearn GP9, GP38-2, GP40-2, GP50, GP60, SD9, SD40-2, SD40T-2 (except SP and SSW version) locos. See Figures 2 and 14.

144-62212 Forward/Reverse Lighting w/Constant Cab Light **33.95** *NEW*
For Athearn F45, FP45, GP35, RDC, SD40T-2 (SP and SSW versions only), SD45, SDP40, U28B, U28C, U30B, U30C, U33B, U33C, and DD40. See Figures 15 and 18.

144-64204 Forward/Reverse Lighting, Ditch Lights & Operating Red Marker Lights **32.95** *NEW*
For Athearn AMD103 P40/P42 locos. See Figures 6 and 9.

144-64222 Forward/Reverse Lighting w/Ditch & Number Board Lights **32.95** *NEW*
For Athearn GE C44-9W and AC4400. See Figures 3 and 18.

144-64212 Forward/Reverse Lighting w/Constant Cab Light **34.95** *NEW*
Six forward lights, one constant cab light and two reverse lights. Works on all Athearn locos that require extra lights for ditch, truck and step lights. See Figures 7 and 18.

FORWARD LIGHTING ONLY

144-60210 Constant Lighting w/Directional Cab Light **28.95** *NEW*
For Athearn locos operated in multi-units. GP9, GP38-2, GP40-2, GP50, GP60, SD9, SD40T-2 (except SP and SSW versions). See Figure 2.

144-62210 Constant Lighting w/Directional Cab Light **30.95** *NEW*
For Athearn locos operated in multi-units. F45, FP45, GP35, RDC, SD40T-2 (SP and SSW versions), SD45, SDP40, U28B, U28C, U30B, U30C, U33B, U33C and DD40. See Figure 3.

144-64210 Constant Lighting w/Directional Cab Light **32.95** *NEW*
For locos operated in multi-units. All Athearn locos needing extra lights for ditch lights, truck lights, step lights, etc. Six forward lights and one directional light. See Figure 7.

"WE'VE DONE THE HARD WORK FOR YOU"

Figure 15

Figure 16

Figure 17

Figure 18

Figure 19

Figure 20

TECHNICAL QUESTIONS E-MAIL US AT ACCLIGHTIN@AOL.COM

Figure 1

CABOOSE LIGHTING SYSTEM

Comes with plastic details to make a round or square light receptacle.

Figure 2

STREAMLINE PASSENGER LIGHTING SYSTEM

Mount lights in the shell's casting to provide EOT effect.

Figure 3

END OF THE TRAIN DEVICE

Mounted on Kadee #5 Coupler with 1.5V flashing bulb installed in casting.

Figure 4

SIDE MOUNTED END OF TRAIN DEVICE

Mounted on Kadee #5 Coupler with flashing LED. Prototype shown.

BATTERY POWERED

CABOOSE FLASHING EOT EA 16.95

See Figure 1.

144-61005 Amber
144-61006 Red

STREAMLINE PASSENGER RED WARNING LIGHT

See Figure 2.

144-61003 Constant **12.95**
144-61004 Flashing **16.95**

END OF TRAIN DEVICES

TOP MOUNTED EA 21.95
See Figure 3.

144-61001 Amber
144-61002 Red

SIDE MOUNTED
144-610 Red **24.95**
See Figure 4.

TRACK POWERED DC & DCC

Wheels and pickups not included with lighting units.

CABOOSE FLASHING EOT EA 18.95

With interior lights.
See Figure 1.

144-715 Amber
144-716 Red

CABOOSE CONSTANT EOT EA 16.95

With interior lights.
See Figure 1.

144-717 Amber
144-718 Red

STREAMLINE PASSENGER RED WARNING LIGHT EA 16.95

See Figure 2.

144-7110 Flashing
144-7111 Constant

END OF TRAIN DEVICES

TOP MOUNTED EA 23.95
See Figure 3.

144-711 Amber
144-712 Red

SIDE MOUNTED
144-710 Red **26.95** *NEW*
See Figure 4.

PICKUPS
144-1005 For 1 Caboose or Freight Car **5.95**

LATCHING REED SWITCH

144-62014 On/Off **6.95**

TWO PIN CONNECTORS

Both male and female connectors have 8" ribbon wire to extend your power source between units. Rated at 1 Amp.

144-10 Miniature, Black Wire pkg(2) **6.95**
144-11 Miniature, White Wire pkg(2) **6.95** *NEW*
144-12 Micro Miniature, Black Wire pkg(2) **7.95**
144-13 Micro Miniature, White Wire pkg(2) **7.95** *NEW*

DITCH LIGHTS

EMD TOP MOUNTED

Includes 1.5V focused bulbs and 8" leads. Unpainted.

144-28 With Resistor **6.95**
144-281 Without Resistor **6.49**

EMD END MOUNTED

144-29 With Resistor **6.95**
144-291 Without Resistor **6.49**

DROPPING RESISTORS PKG(6) EA 1.49

For 1.5V bulbs when used with DCC systems and other projects. 1/4 Watt.

144-20

144-20 150 Ohm
144-21 560 Ohm
144-22 240 Ohm
144-23 180 Ohm
144-24 300 Ohm
144-25 360 Ohm
144-26 430 Ohm
144-27 470 Ohm

DIODES

144-505 1 Amp 50PIV **1.49**

MAGNETS

144-62015 Activates Reed Switch #62014 **1.95**
1-3/4 x 3/16".

144-6215 Magnetic Tape w/Self Adhesive Backing **2.95**
Ideal for placing under chassis of loco to trip momentary reed switches.

BULBS

Replacement bulbs for Accurate Lighting systems and other special projects. If a lens retainer is enclosed, it fills the gap between the bulb and the slightly larger openings found on some Athearn locos.

144-71 Focused 1.5V **2.98**
With dropping resistor and lens retainer.

144-72 Focused 1.5V 1 Pair **4.50**
With dropping resistor and lens retainer.

144-74 Focused 1.5V 2 Pair **8.98**
With dropping resistor and lens retainer.

144-503 14V Ballast Bulb **1.98**
144-62016 Focused 1.5V **2.19**
With lens retainer.

144-62017 Focused Single Filament Bulb 1.0V **2.19**
For Athearn F7 and Life-Like Proto 2000™ GP30.

144-62018 Bi-Pin High Intensity Bulb 2.0V **4.19**
Ideally suited for Athearn S12 and SW7.

144-62019 Axial Bulb 1.5V **2.98**
With two 1" leads. 15mA draw, .032 x .115".

144-62023 Clear Micro Bulb 1.5V **2.19**
With 1" leads. 15mA draw, .054 x .10".

144-62024 Red Micro Bulb 1.5V **2.19**
With 1" leads. 15mA draw, .054 x .10".

144-62025 For RS3 1.5V **2.19**
With 10" leads. 15mA draw.

144-62026 Focused Bulb For Number Board 1.5V **2.19**
With 8" leads. 15mA draw.

DOT STYLE LEDS EA 2.49

144-150 Red
144-151 Amber

BI-COLOR LED

144-155 Green/Red **4.49**
144-156 Ultra Bright Green/Red **4.98**

BATTERY HOLDERS

Single battery holders with double sided tape on the bottom for easy installation.

144-130 AA Plastic Holder **2.49**
With 6" red and black leads. 2.25 x .64 x .57".

144-131 AA Metal Holder **2.49**
Ideally suited to solder on components for electronic projects. 2.03 x .64 x .65".

144-132 AAA Metal Holder **2.98**
Ideally suited to solder on components for electronic projects. 2.03 x .45 x .42".

144-133 N Plastic Holder **2.49**
With 6" red and black leads. 1.37 x .51 x .49".

144-135 C Plastic Holder **2.49**
With 6" red and black leads. 2.44 x 1.18 x .49".

144-137 9V Battery Snap Connector **1.49**
With 6" red and black leads. 1.08 x .60 x .22".

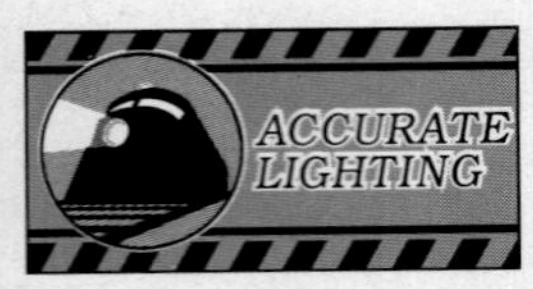

BATTERY HOOKUP KITS EA 9.98

Include battery holder, latching reed switch and magnet. Build a circuit you can turn on/off with a magnet. Ideal for heavyweights, lanterns, drumheads, caboose warning lights, etc. Soldering required.

144-1302 AA Kit
144-1312 Metal AA Kit
144-1322 Metal AAA Kit
144-1332 N Kit
144-1352 C Kit
144-1372 9V Kit

HOOKUP WIRE

18 GAUGE MULTI-STRANDED WIRE PKG(50') EA 8.98

Ideal as a bus line from power pack to blocks.

144-181 White
144-182 Black
144-183 Red
144-184 Green

24 GAUGE MULTI-STRANDED WIRE PKG(25') EA 5.98

Ideal as jumpers from bus line to track sections.

144-241 White
144-242 Black
144-243 Red
144-244 Green

30 GAUGE MULTI-STRANDED WIRE PKG(25') EA 5.98 (UNLESS NOTED)

Ideal as motor hookup wire.

144-301 White
144-302 Black
144-303 Red
144-304 Green
144-3001 White Ribbon Wire, 2 Strands pkg(20') **4.98**

32 GAUGE MULTI-STRANDED WIRE PKG(25') EA 5.98

Ideal for those wiring projects that require a very fine, flexible wire.

144-321 White
144-322 Black
144-323 Red
144-324 Green

40 GAUGE WIRE

144-401 Lacquer Coated pkg(20') **4.98** *NEW*
Thread-like lacquer coated wire for those low voltage projects that require almost invisible wire.

HEAT SHRINK TUBING

144-120 3.99
Shrinks to half its diameter when heated with high voltage hair dryer or professional heat gun. Used to insulate electrical connections. Total of 3' of black tubing in three sizes: 3/64, 1/16 and 3/32".

JUMPER CABLE SET

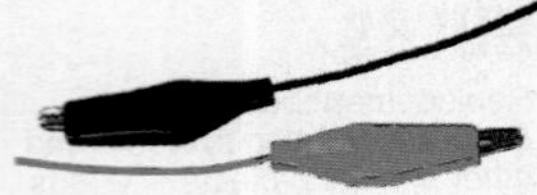

144-115 pkg(2) **2.99**
Features alligator clip on each end with 14" leads. Each cable is a different color.

SPRING CLIPS

144-3 Quick Connect/Disconnect Fahnestock Clips pkg(10) **4.99**
Ideal for power pack connections and other projects.

LIGHTING MODULES

Operate off the AC or DC side of a secondary power pack. The 1.5V bulb can be used to light switch stands, building lights, street lights and more.

144-501 14V Ballast Bulb w/Diodes & Hookup Wire **3.98**
Will power 1.5V bulb(s) from power pack. Requires soldering.

144-502 Constant Intensity Light Source Unit **5.98**
Comes assembled with one 1.5V bulb.

CAMPFIRE SIMULATION UNITS

144-90010 Flame Magic I **12.98**
Driven by FM stereo radio.

144-90011 Flame Magic II **21.98**
Computer programmed to simulate campfire effect. Operates off AC side of power pack.

VEHICLE LIGHTS

144-60 Head Lights & Tail Lights **19.98** *NEW*
The 1.5V bulbs are powered from the AC or DC side of a secondary power pack. Each vehicle will have to be customized to accept the lights. See Figure 2.

NAVIGATION LIGHTS FOR DC-3

The 1.5V bulbs are powered from the AC or DC side of a secondary power pack. Must be installed prior to final assembly.

Figure 1

144-1100 For Walthers Douglas DC-3 **15.98** *NEW*
See Figure 1.

144-1200 With Roof Beacon For Walthers Douglas DC-3 **19.98** *NEW*
See Figure 1.

BOWSER AEROTRAIN

144-1002 Forward Only Constant Lighting **28.95** *NEW*
Includes end of train lighting.

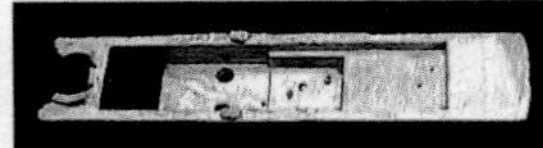

144-1003 Power Frame for Aerotrain **24.95**
With the frame you can add an Athearn Switcher front power truck, motor and drive shaft to make this loco come alive.

ATHEARN HUSTLER

144-50 Gear Set **21.95**
Easy to install. Replaces rubber band drive.

144-130900 Replacement Can Motor & Ernst #2 Gear Set **32.95**
For Athearn Hustler.

Figure 2

LOCOMOTION

REPLACEMENT CAN MOTORS

Can motors can be used to upgrade existing steam and diesel locos. The can motors have mounts that snap into the original motor's frame (some units may require modifications). The can motors for the Athearn locos include presoldered clips, so no soldering is required. All motors include flywheels unless noted and are wired in the same direction as the motor it is to replace.

144-130000 For Bowser K-4, L-1, M-1, M-1a & Northern 4-8-2 **47.97**
See Style 2.

144-130100 For Mantua 0-4-0/0-6-0 Tank, 0-6-0 Big 6, 0-4-0 Pony & Prairie. **42.95**
See Style 3.

144-130115 For Bowser A-3 Dockside & A-5 Shifter **42.95**
See Style 3.

144-130125 For Mantua 0-4-0 Camel & 0-4-0 Goat **42.95**
See Style 3.

144-130200 For Life-Like GP18 & Roundhouse RS-3 **42.95**
See Style 6.

144-130250 For Bowser K-11 & USRA Light Pacific **47.95**
See Style 2.

144-130275 For Bowser USRA Mikado 2-8-2 **47.95**
See Style 2.

144-130300 For Stewart RS-3 **42.95**
See Style 6.

144-130400 For Bowser H-9 & E6 **47.95**
See Style 4.

144-130450 For Bowser T1 4-4-4 Twin Motors **89.95** *NEW*
Not shown.

144-130500 For Mantua 4-6-2 Pacific & 4-6-4 Hudson **47.95**
See Style 1.

144-130550 For Mantua 2-8-2 Mikado & 2-8-2 Camel **47.95**
See Style 1.

144-130600 For Bowser Old Style I-1 Decapod 2-10-0, PRRN-2 & USRA 2-10-2 **47.95** *NEW*
See Style 2.

144-130700 For New Style I-1 Decapod 2-10-0 **47.95**
See Style 2.

144-130800 For Bowser H10-44, Front Range GP7, GP9 & GP30. **42.95**
See Style 8.

144-130850 For Athearn Hustler **29.95**
See Style 7.

144-180000 Without Mount & Flywheels **32.95**
Ideal for Atlas FP, GP38 and SD35; Walthers H-10-44 and other repowering projects.
See Style 5.

144-180100 For Life-Like C-628 **42.95**

144-180150 For Stewart AS16/616 **42.95**
See Style 6.

144-180200 For Athearn Cab & Road Diesels **42.95**
See Style 8.

144-180250 For Athearn SD40-2, SD40T-2 & GE9-44CW **42.95**
See Style 8.

Style 1

Style 2

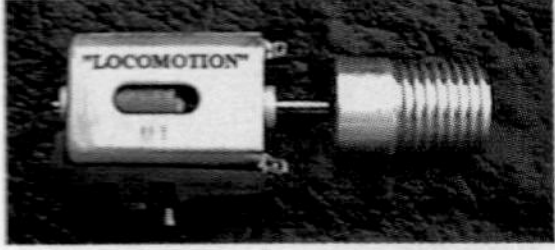

Style 3

Style 4

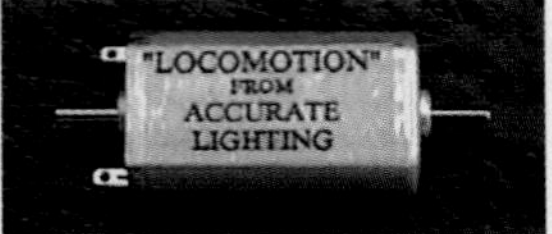

Style 5

Style 6

Style 7

Style 8

CONTROLLERS

LIGHTED SWITCH CONTROLLERS

Will operate all switches and switch motors, including Lionel, Atlas and others. Light remains on after corresponding button is pressed. Instructions, red and green light bulbs, mounting screws and self-stick number sheet are included.

Each #498 and #444 is complete with red and green bulbs, contact plate, number sheet, mounting screws and easy-to-follow instructions.

Each #894 and #888 is equipped with electro-mechanical switching circuitry controls and switches red and green light automatically. No need for contact plates or relays; unit is completely self contained. Bulbs use the AC current from the power supply.

SURFACE MOUNT

105-444 Standard **8.95**
105-888 Electro-Mechanical **14.95**

INSERT MOUNT

105-498 7.95
105-894 13.95
105-4994 GE Bulb 12-18V (red) pkg(2) **.70**
105-4995 GE Bulb 12-18V (blue) pkg(2) **.70**

PANELS

FRAME-MOUNTED

With polished aluminum mounting frame.

105-401 Operates 1 Switches **4.65**
105-402 Operates 2 Switches **6.35**
105-403 Operates 3 Switches **7.95**
105-404 Operates 4 Switches **9.65**
105-405 Operates 5 Switches **10.65**
105-406 Operates 6 Switches **12.45**
105-407 Operates 7 Switches **13.95**
105-408 Operates 8 Switches **15.95**

105-916 Operates 16 Switches **29.95**

TERMINAL

105-416 Less Switch **7.95**

105-516 With Switch **9.65**

FLUSH-MOUNTED

EXCLUSIVE FEATURE: All Acme switch controllers are equipped with crimp or solder terminals.

105-301 Operates 1 Switches **3.95**
105-302 Operates 2 Switches **5.25**
105-303 Operates 3 Switches **6.75**
105-304 Operates 4 Switches **8.45**
105-305 Operates 5 Switches **9.65**
105-306 Operates 6 Switches **11.25**
105-307 Operates 7 Switches **12.85**
105-308 Operates 8 Switches **14.45**

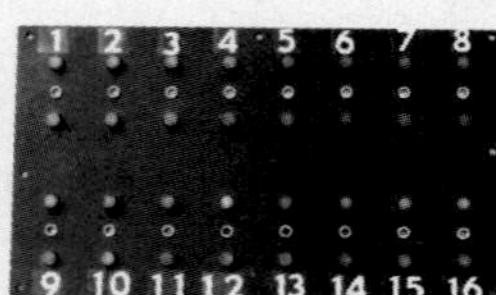

105-816 Operates 16 Switches **26.55**

PUSH-BUTTON UNIT

105-439 Double **2.50**
Can be installed in any position. Dealers MUST order multiples of 12.

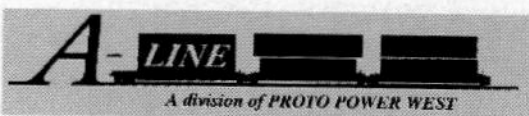

MOTORS

FLAT CAN MOTORS EA 26.95

Five-pole with skewed armature and 2.0 mm shaft.

116-40321 18 x 33mm, DS
116-40322 18 x 24mm, DS

MOTOR MOUNT TAPE

116-12020 pkg(8) **1.65**
Two-sided foam tape.

ELECTRICAL HOOK-UP KIT

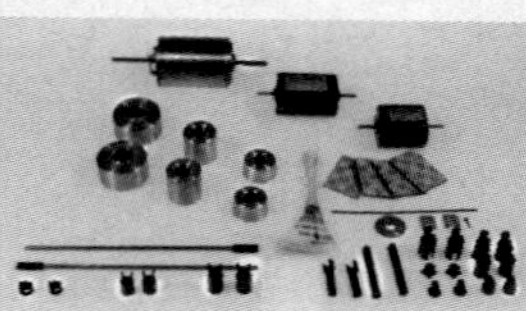

116-12040 3.25
For upgrading electrical connections on stock Athearn Locos. Also for installing can motors in Athearn and other locos. Will complete two locos.

HOOK-UP WIRE

116-12041 pkg(2') **1.65**
Very fine, white, flexible multi-stranded wire for all repowering jobs.

REPOWERING PARTS

116-12052 Long Spline Shafts pkg(6) **2.00**
Longer than standard Athearn shafts, can be cut to any length.

LOCOMOTIVE REPOWERING KITS EA 33.95

For use with Athearn diesels. Kits include can motor, brass flywheels, wiring hardware and instructions.

116-70321 Basic 4 & 6 Axle Diesels
Motor measures 18 x 33mm.

116-80321 Diesel Switchers
18 x 33mm motor, tapered #20021 flywheels.

116-90321 Short Wheel Base Diesel/Steam Loco
18 x 24mm motor, fits Athearn GP38, GP40 & GP50; also can be used for steam locomotive repowering.

FLYWHEELS EA 6.85 (UNLESS NOTED)

Precision machined from brass stock, flywheels are drilled and reamed for slip fit on drive shaft. Each pack includes two flywheels, with Athearn couplings installed and complete instructions. Dimensions shown are outside diameter, length and shaft size. Possible applications are listed with each item.

116-20004 1 x 1/2 x 3.0" pkg(2)
Micro or Holland can motor fits Athearn F7, PA, F&FP45, Cary F&E, Train Miniature FA, Bachmann F9, Model Power/AHM E and most units with wide hoods.

116-20006 21/32 x 11/16 x 2.0" pkg(2)
Flat can motor fits narrow hood units; Atlas, Athearn/GSB SD40-2, SD40T-2, Mantua GP20, Bachmann GP30, DD40X, BQ23-7, AHM RS2, SD40. Fits on stock motored Atlas units. Also fits narrow hood brass imports and plastic diesels.

116-20013 11/16 x 3/8" x 2.4mm *NEW*
Can motor in Athearn S12, SW1500 and most short wheelbase locomotives.

116-20021 11/16 x 3/8" x 2.0" pkg(2) **7.85**
Flat can motor fits Athearn S12, SW1500 and most narrow hood units with short wheelbase, AHM, ALCO 1000. Can also be used for steam locomotive repowering.

FLYWHEEL CEMENT

116-20010 2.65

UNIVERSAL COUPLING ASSORTMENT

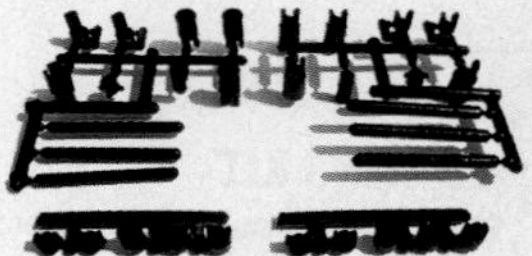

116-12030 6.50
21-piece kit includes assorted male and female universal joints and various length spines, all cast in Delrin®.

UNIVERSAL COUPLING KIT

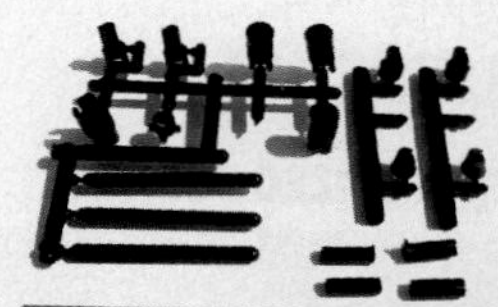

116-12031 6.50
8-piece kit includes two 105mm steel shafts with plastic splines and universal joint components (enough parts to retrofit one brass or plastic locomotive).

MOTOR MOUNT CRADLE WEIGHTS EA 4.75

Unique system for adding weight and mounting motor. Custom shaped lead weight is designed to fit many popular units. Easy to install: puts weight where you want it in the base of chassis; motor is fixed to cradle with silicon or double stick tape.

ATHEARN
116-12400 SD40-2, SD40T-2, C44-9W
116-12403 GP35, GP30, GP20
116-12404 F7 *NEW*
116-12405 GP38, GP40, GP50, GP60, AMD-103
116-12407 SD45, UC, E-UNIT F45, FP45 *NEW*
116-12808 Train Miniature FA **TBA** *NEW*

RPP
116-12401 GP60, GP60B, GP60M
116-12402 SD60, SD45-2, SD90 MAC
116-12406 C40-8W, C44-9W

DIMI TRAINS

LIGHTING KIT
236-8000 Athearn Passenger Car **TBA**

FALLER

IMPORTED FROM GERMANY BY WALTHERS

LIGHTING

MOTORIZED BLINKER

272-631 39.99
Pulses are used for rhythmic switching, blinkers or church bells.

STRUCTURE LIGHT

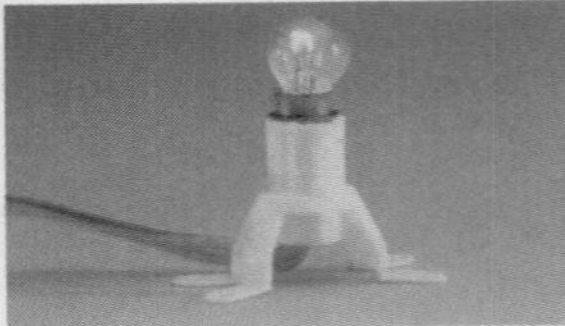

272-670 1.99
Set comes with lighting socket, bulb, cables and plugs.

WELDING FLASH MODULE

272-640 37.99
16V AC, generates a bluish-white flickering light.

12-16V GRAIN OF WHEAT BULB EA 3.99

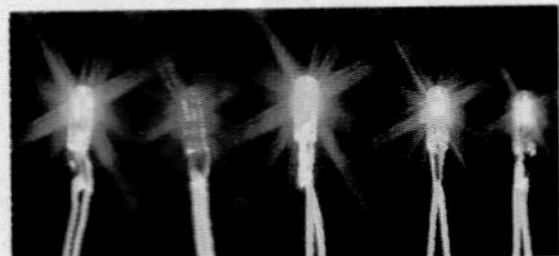

272-671 Clear
272-672 Red
272-673 Yellow
272-674 Green
272-676 Blue

MICRO BULBS

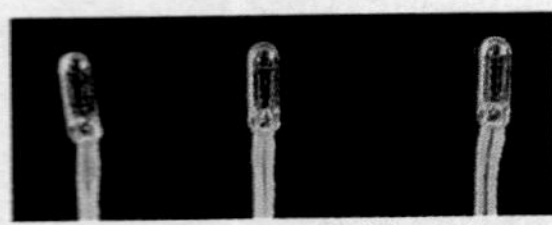

272-677 White, 12-16V AC 35mA w/Wire Leads **5.99** ***NEW***

LIGHT CONDUCTOR FILAMENT

Limited Quantity Available
272-634 17.99
For #633. 10m of flexible light filament.

LIGHTING CONTROL

272-680 16 VAC 8 Output **26.99**
This lighting control has a wide variety of uses, and allows you to switch lights on and off in individual rooms in structures on your layout. Ready for operation from 16v AC, it can power eight outputs to which either 10 grain of wheat bulbs (671-676) per output or three lighting bases (670) can be connected.

ELECTRICAL ACCESSORIES

SYNCHRONOUS MOTORS

272-628 Extra Power **26.99**
Provides 35% more power than #629 for a variety of applications. Speed of 4/15 RPM, with reversible rotation. 12-16V AC, 60mA.

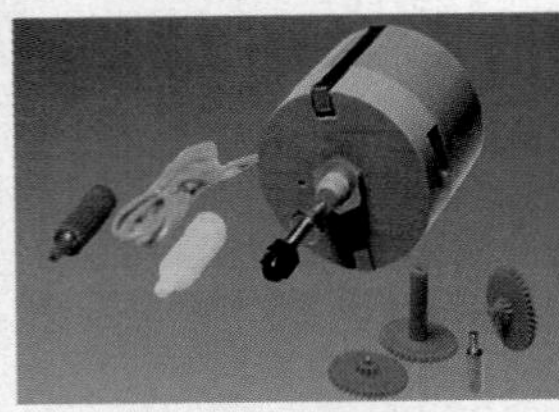

272-629 22.99
Speed of 4/15 RPM. Revolves clockwise or counter-clockwise. 16V AC.

MULTI-FUNCTION SWITCH UNIT

272-632 39.99
Electro-mechanical for switching functions, one connection for permanent contact. Ready for operation with 12-16V AC.

ELECTRIC FIRE SIREN

272-637 39.99
Ready to use for 12-16V DC or AC. Loudspeaker included.

PLUG STRIP

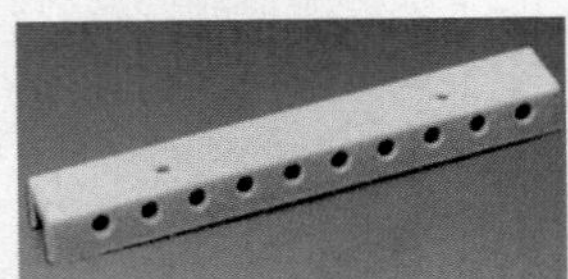

272-686 3.99
Features 10 pairs of sockets.

Labelle industries

We have worked closely with this manufacturer to provide accurate delivery information at the time this catalog was published. Items listed in blue ink may not be available at all times. Current delivery information, along with a list of in-stock products for this line, can be found on our Web site at www.walthers.com.

LIGHTING

1.2 V ANGEL HAIR BULBS
430-6663 Clear pkg(2) **1.98**

16V "ROUND" BULBS PKG(2) EA 1.69

430-6441 Clear
430-6443 Green
430-6444 Yellow
430-6445 Frosted (street lamps)

LOCOMOTIVE HEADLIGHT BULBS
430-2431 Small ea **1.99**
430-2432 Large **1.69**

"PEPPER BULBS" PKG(3) EA 1.69

430-6411 Clear 3V

WIRE

HOOK-UP WIRE, MULTI-STRAND-33'
430-6001 23 Gauge Single Conductor Black, Red, Green **2.99**
430-6002 23 Gauge Two Conductor Brown, Yellow **3.99**
430-6003 23 Gauge Three Conductor Red, Green, Yellow **4.99**
430-6004 23 Gauge Four Conductor **4.99**

Information STATION

Outdoor Wiring

Wiring for outdoor operation presents unique challenges and opportunities. Because most transformers and rectifiers are designed to be used indoors rather than outdoors, you need to be sure of your equipment's capabilities. Not all products are made to be used out in the elements.

The wiring will have to be able to stand up to the rigors of Mother Nature. Insulated 14 gauge household wiring cables will suffice. The wires themselves can lay on top of the ground without problems, however, aesthetically speaking, it is better to bury them to hide their presence. This can be easily done by digging a small trench to place the wires in.

Another way of doing this is to place the wiring in plastic or metal tubing and then bury the tubing. This presents a safeguard against accidental cutting of the wires by someone digging in the wrong place. It also makes it a little easier to retrieve and replace specific wires in the ground.

Due to the forces of nature, oxidation becomes a problem for every outdoor modeler. When it occurs, an insulating coat forms on the rails which weakens the flow of electricity, possibly even stopping it altogether. The oxidation occurs most frequently around rail joints.

IMPORTED FROM GERMANY BY WALTHERS
Brawa offers a comprehensive line of electrical accessories, lighting equipment and wire suitable for use with all model railroad systems.

ELECTRICAL ACCESSORIES

ELECTRONIC SPEED CONTROLLER

186-6150 79.99
Variable speed throttle for Brawa cableways, trolleybuses and DC railroad systems. Unit operates from AC contacts on transformer (24V maximum). Can power AC or DC accessories. Built-in short circuit protection with red LED indicator.

RELAYS

Relays 2760 or 2761 feature matching color-coded wiring for Brawa signals and accessories. Units may be operated manually, or automatically with reed switches.

186-2760 Double 10-20V AC **47.99**

186-2761 Triple 10-24V AC **62.99**

ADJUSTABLE RESISTOR

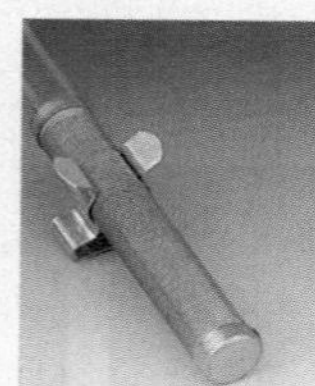

186-6154 18.99
Adjustable output clip.
Reduces train speed for slow-running train blocks. 0-100 ohms; 1/4 x 2".

BRIDGE RECTIFIER

186-2185 10.99
3/4 x 1/2 x 1/4". 10-16V, 1A

DISTRIBUTOR

Several distributors can be connected to supply more accessories.

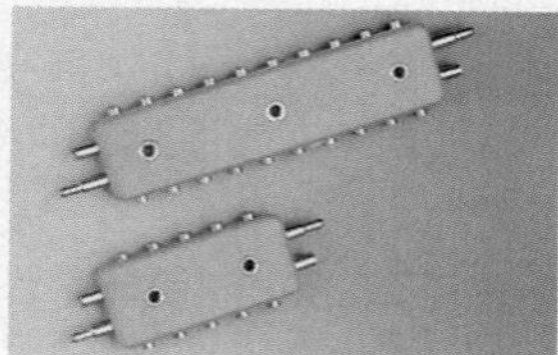

186-2591 5-Way, 2-Pole **4.99**
186-2592 10-Way, 2-Pole **6.99**

SCREW TERMINAL STRIP

186-3094 2.99
12 Way; 4" Long

WIRE HOLDER

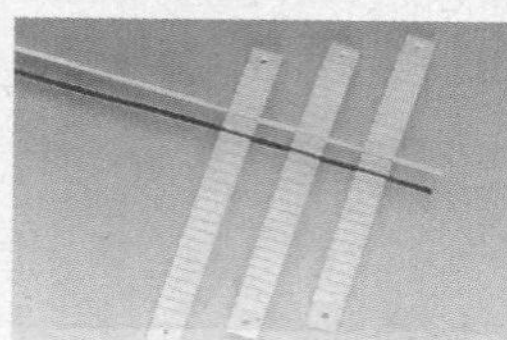

186-3910 pkg(10) **5.99**
Holds up to 25 wires or leads securely.

PUSH-BUTTON

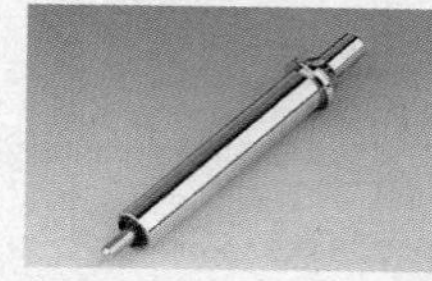

186-3500 Panel, Nickel-Plated **6.99**
Multi-purpose on/off switch, with retaining clip. 1/4 x 1-1/2".

186-3573 Push-Button 3/4" pkg(4) **6.99**

MOMENTARY CONTACT PUSH-BUTTON EA 6.99

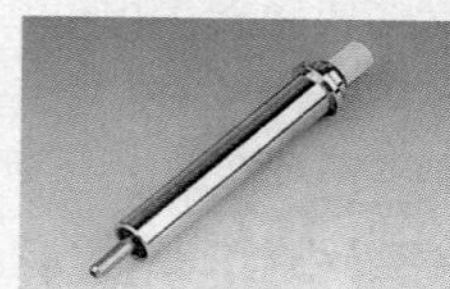

186-3501 Yellow pkg(2)
186-3502 Red
186-3503 Green
186-3505 Blue pkg(2)
186-3508 Black pkg(2)
186-3509 White pkg(2)

ILLUMINATED PUSH-BUTTON EA 8.99

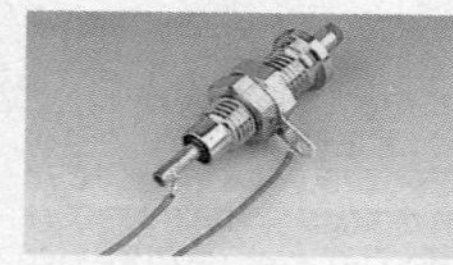

186-3511 Yellow
186-3512 Red
186-3513 Green
186-3519 White

NON-ILLUMINATED PUSH-BUTTON EA 4.99

1/4" Diameter.

186-3471 Yellow
186-3472 Red
186-3473 Green
186-3475 Blue
186-3478 Black
186-3479 White

SPST PANEL PUSH-BUTTON SWITCH W/NUT

186-3524 pkg(2) **5.99**
Base approx. 1 x 1/2"; threaded neck length is approx. 1/2".

SIGNAL SWITCHES

For manual operation of signals. 1A/25V.

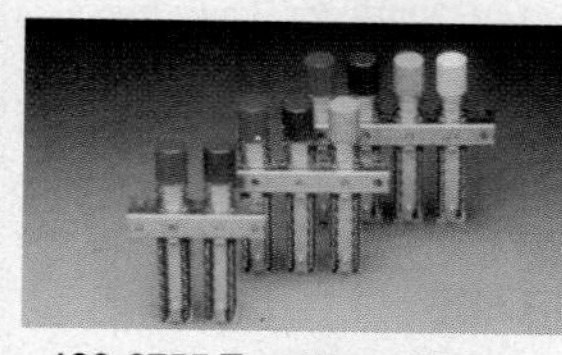

186-2755 Two-Way **18.99**
Red-Green; 1-1/2".

186-2756 Three-Way **19.99**
Red-Green-Yellow; 2".

186-2757 Four-Way **26.99**
Red-Green-Yellow-white; 2-1/2".

TOGGLE-SWITCH - ON/OFF

220 V/2A.

186-3520 Single-Pole **6.99**
186-3574 Tumbler Toggle Switch 3/4" pkg(4) **6.99**

MAGNETIC REED SWITCH

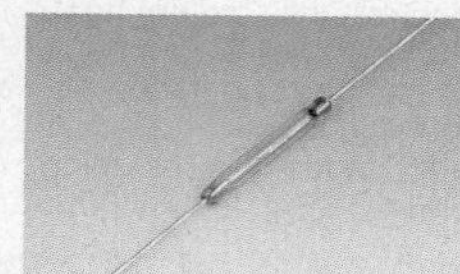

186-3530 Inert Gas-Filled Tube Contact **2.99**
Contact load is 0.5A capacity, 3/4 x .1".

MAGNETS

186-3543 Bar Magnet **2.99**
For use with 3530; 1/4 x 1/2" (6 x 12 x 4mm).

PLUG & SOCKET

FOR MARKLIN

186-3070 4.99
8 crosshole plugs, 8 sleeves.

30 PIECE SET

186-3071 8.99
15 plugs, 15 sockets in 5 colors.

SOCKET 2-POLE

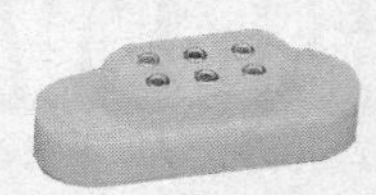

186-3570 pkg(5) **4.99**

PLUG 2-POLE

186-3571 pkg(5) **4.99**
1/3" centers

BATTERY CAP SOCKET 6-POLE

186-3572 1.99

ROUND PLUGS PKG(10) EA 2.99

With crossover hole.

186-3051 Yellow
186-3052 Red
186-3053 Green
186-3054 Brown
186-3055 Blue
186-3056 Orange
186-3057 Gray
186-3058 Black
186-3059 White

PANEL SOCKETS PKG(10) EA 11.99

For use on control panels.

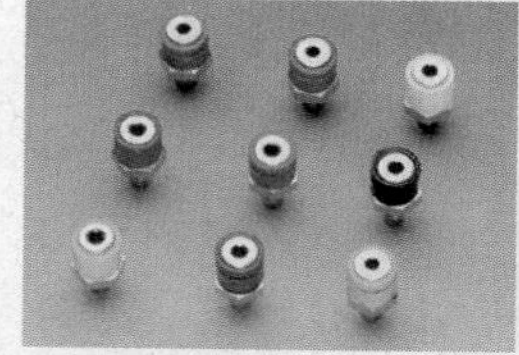

186-3081 Yellow
186-3082 Red
186-3083 Green
186-3084 Brown
186-3085 Blue
186-3086 Orange
186-3087 Gray
186-3088 Black
186-3089 White

ROUND SOCKET PKG(10) EA 2.99

186-3041 Yellow
186-3042 Red
186-3043 Green
186-3044 Brown
186-3045 Blue
186-3046 Orange
186-3047 Gray
186-3048 Black
186-3049 White

LIGHTING

TALL STRUCTURE LIGHTS

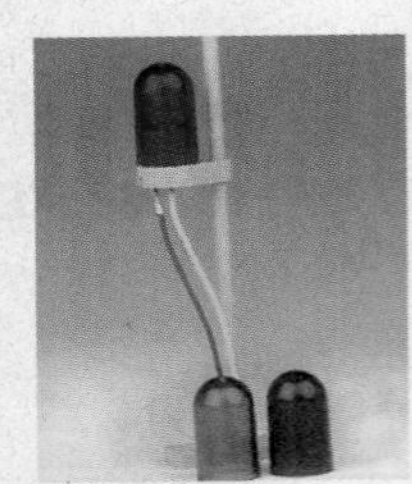

186-3405 3.99
Adjustable for all size structures. Can be mounted in buildings, or under benchwork. Bayonet fitting helps prevent bulb from working loose. Includes colored bulb cover for unusual lighting effects. 16V.

MINI PIN TERMINAL STRIP

186-3091 6.99
20 contacts, can be separated at any point; for use as pin and tubular socket. Spacing 1", 2.54mm, for all systems.

LED PANEL LIGHT EA 6.99

Each LED features a built-in ballast resistor. Each 1/4" diameter, installed depth 1". 14-16V.

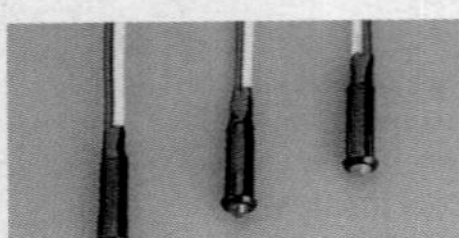

186-3481 Yellow
186-3482 Red
186-3483 Green

SCREW PANEL LIGHT PKG(2) EA 8.99

Size E5.5 for use on control panel. Current draw 50mA at 14-16V

Limited Quantity Available

186-3441 Yellow
186-3442 Red
186-3449 White

INDICATOR BULB COVER PKG(2)EA 6.49

Limited Quantity Available

186-3455 Blue
For use only with 3304 spherical bulbs.

MINIATURE BULB PKG(2) EA 7.99 (UNLESS NOTED)

14V, 30mA; for Brawa metal signals.

186-3259 Clear **6.99**
186-3260 Yellow
186-3261 Red
186-3262 Green

LEDS

Connect only through 1000 Ohm resistor.

186-3295 Yellow, 2mm pkg(2) **2.99**
186-3296 Red, 2mm pkg(2) **2.99**
186-3297 Red, 1mm pkg(2) **5.99**
186-3298 Red, 3mm pkg(2) **2.99**
Miniature type for #4806. Approximate size 1/4" x 5/32".

186-3339 For Marklin Loco pkg(4) **5.99**
186-3913 1000 Ohm Resistor pkg(10) **2.99**

Limited Quantity Available

186-3360 Yellow pkg(2) **5.49**
186-3361 Red pkg(2) **5.49**
186-3362 Green pkg(2) **5.49**

PUSH IN PANEL LIGHTS EA 8.99

For control panels and other installations where small diameter indicator lamps are needed. Units feature heat-resistant black plastic body with colored cap, nickel plated mounting ring, long life bulb and 6" leads. Fits mounting hole of 3/16". 12-14V. 60mA.

186-3461 Amber
186-3462 Red
186-3463 Green
186-3465 Blue
186-3469 White

SPECIAL BULBS PKG(2) EA 4.99

With 2 electrodes. Replacement bulb for Brawa HO and N plastic signals made before 1981. 16V, 30mA.

Limited Quantity Available

186-3257 Green
186-3258 Yellow

LILIPUT BULB

186-3263 24V, Clear pkg(2) **9.99**

16V, 35MA PKG(2) EA 4.99

186-3271 Clear
186-3272 Red
186-3273 Green
186-3274 Yellow

GRAIN-O-WHEAT BULB

16V, 30mA, unless otherwise noted.

186-3254 Clear pkg(2) **2.99**
2 exposed electrodes, 16V, 35mA.
186-3286 Short, Green pkg(2) **7.99**
186-3287 2-Wire, Clear **4.99**
186-3288 Clear for 5760, 14V, 40mA **3.99**
186-3291 Clear for Z Lights, 10V, 30mA pkg(2) **3.99**
186-3293 Clear, 1 Black Wire ea **3.99**
186-3290 Spare Bulb for Z Lights pkg(2) **6.99**
2 exposed electrodes, clear, 10V, 30mA.
186-3292 Miniature Bulb **3.99**
2 electrodes for 7942;1.5V 15mA; connect only through resistor.
186-3267 Micro Bulb, Clear, 3V pkg(2) **3.99**
186-3268 Mini Bulb, Clear, 3V **4.99**

MISCELLANEOUS BULBS

186-3264 Screw-In Bulb for #4621 & 4591 pkg(2) **6.99**
186-3289 For Z Spotlight, 6V pkg(2) **3.99**
186-3279 Valve Base 16V Clear pkg(2) **5.99**
186-3337 Flat Top 19V Red pkg(4) **7.99**
186-3338 Replacement Bulb For Marklin #60008 pkg(4) **7.99**
186-3344 14V Fleischmann Bulb pkg(4) **5.99**
186-3345 14V Trix Bulb pkg(4) **5.99**
186-3348 Mini Bayonet Bulb, 14V **2.99**

FESTOON BULB

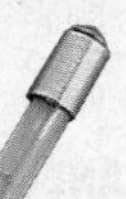

186-3250 Frosted 16V 30mA pkg(2) **6.99**
186-3276 Candle Bulb, Amber pkg(4) **6.99**
Fits socket size E5.5, 19V 65mA
186-3277 Candle Bulb, Clear pkg(4) **6.99**
Fits socket size E5.5, 19V 65mA

186-3278 Reflector Bulb, Clear pkg(2) **8.99**
80mA, 1 watt, approx. total length 3/4", 16V

19V TUBULAR BULB

186-3282 32mm pkg(2) **4.99**
186-3283 42mm pkg(2) **6.99**

PUSH-IN BULB

186-3340 Clear pkg(4) **4.99**
For Marklin, 19V, 50mA.
186-3341 Red pkg(4) **5.99**
For Marklin, 19V, 50mA.
186-3342 Green pkg(4) **5.99**
For Marklin, 19V, 50mA.

186-3343 Clear pkg(4) **5.99**
Marklin, new pattern w/locating lugs;19V, 50mA.

186-3344 Clear pkg(4) **5.99**
For Fleischmann, 14V 50mA.

186-3345 Clear pkg(4) **5.99**
For Trix, 14V 50mA.

186-3251 Clear pkg(2) **6.99**
3 x 2.55, 16V, 30mA.

THREAD SPHERICAL BULB

Fits E5.5 size sockets.

186-3300 1.5V Clear, 100mA, 5mm pkg(4) **5.99**
186-3301 3.5V Clear, 200mA, 5mm pkg(4) **5.99**
186-3302 6V Clear, 100mA, 5mm pkg(4) **5.99**
186-3303 14V Clear, 50mA, 5mm pkg(4) **5.99**
186-3304 19V Clear, 60mA, 5mm pkg(4) **4.99**
186-3307 19V Clear, 50mA, 5mm pkg(4) **4.99**
186-3310 19V Red, 50mA, 5mm pkg(4) **4.99**
186-3311 19V Yellow, 50mA, 5mm pkg(4) **4.99**
186-3275 19V, 50mA Clear pkg(4) **4.99**
186-3316 3.5V Clear, 200mA 8mm pkg(4) **4.99**
186-3318 14V Clear, 50mA 8mm pkg(4) **5.99**
186-3319 19V Clear, 50mA 8mm pkg(4) **4.99**
186-3322 19V Green, 50mA 8mm pkg(4) **5.99**
186-3325 1.5V Clear, 100mA 8mm pkg(4) **5.99**

FITS E10 SIZE SOCKETS

186-3330 3.5V Clear, 200mA pkg(4) **4.99**
186-3331 19V Clear, 100mA pkg(4) **6.99**
186-3332 3.5V Red, 200mA pkg(4) **5.99**
186-3333 19V Red, 100mA pkg(4) **7.99**
186-3334 3.5V Green, 200mA pkg(4) **5.99**
186-3335 3.5V Green, 100mA pkg(4) **7.99**

BULB ACCESSORIES

186-3400 Building Light **1.99**
Plastic, with brass socket (male) and 16" brown and yellow leads 16V; 2 (female) plastic plugs for simple hook up.

186-3422 Screw Metal Base w/2 Connectors Size E5.5 pkg(10) **7.99**

186-3423 Recessed Base w/Bracket Size E5.5 pkg(10) **12.99**
186-3424 E5 Screw Base, Raised pkg(10) **11.99**
186-3433 E10 Screw Base, Raised pkg(10) **10.99**

WIRE

SOLID STRAND

Solid Strand copper wire with PVC insulation. Max load 6A; length, 11 yards per coil, approx. diameter, .048.

BRAWA

33' ROLL EA 1.50
Dealers MUST order Multiples of 10.

186-3100 Purple
186-3101 Yellow
186-3102 Red
186-3103 Green
186-3104 Brown
186-3105 Blue
186-3107 Gray
186-3108 Black
186-3109 White

Limited Quantity Available

186-3197 Brown pkg(33') **7.49**

80' ROLL EA 4.99
186-3201 Yellow
186-3202 Red
186-3203 Green
186-3204 Brown
186-3205 Blue
186-3207 Gray
186-3208 Black
186-3209 White

328' ROLL EA 15.99
186-3110 Purple
186-3111 Yellow
186-3112 Red
186-3113 Green
186-3114 Brown
186-3115 Blue
186-3117 Gray
186-3118 Black
186-3119 White

FINE STRAND
Fine stranded copper wire, approx. .036" diameter. Maximum load 2.5A.

33' ROLL EA 1.50
186-3160 Purple
186-3161 Yellow
186-3162 Red
186-3163 Green
186-3164 Brown
186-3165 Blue
186-3168 Black

133' ROLL EA 17.99
186-3222 Red
186-3228 Black

SINGLE CONDUCTOR EXTRA-FLEXIBLE WIRE

186-3240 #18 pkg(33') **4.99**

Limited Quantity Available

186-3246 #15 pkg(10') **6.49**

MULTI-CONDUCTOR FLAT CABLE HOOK-UP WIRE
#24 solid copper wires in assorted colors, maximum load, 6A per wire.

186-3170 Brown/Yellow pkg(16') **1.99**
186-3171 Brown/Yellow pkg(164') **18.99**
186-3172 Blue/Yellow/Blue pkg(16') **3.99**
For use with Marklin.
186-3173 Blue/Yellow/Blue pkg(164') **32.99**
For use with Marklin.
186-3174 Yellow/Red/Blue pkg(16') **3.99**
For use with Marklin.
286-3175 Yellow/Red/Blue pkg(164') **32.99**
For use with Marklin.
186-3176 Gray/Violet/Blue pkg(16') **3.99**
For use with Arnold.
186-3177 Gray/Violet/Blue pkg(164') **32.99**
For use with Arnold.
186-3182 Blue/Yellow/Red/Green pkg(16') **4.99**
186-3184 Five Conductor pkg(16') **5.99**
186-3186 Blue/Brown/Yellow/Red/Green/Black pkg(16') **7.99**
186-3188 Yellow/Brown/Red/Green/Blue/Gray/Black/White pkg(16') **9.99**
186-3189 Same as 3188 pkg(164') **99.99**
186-3139 #24 2 Conductor, pkg(164") White **15.99**
186-3230 #18 2 Conductor, Orange, White pkg(65") **21.99**
186-3235 #18 3 Conductor, pkg(65') **32.99**
Yellow/White/Green.

Limited Quantity Available

186-3193 #24 10 Conductor, pkg(164") White **123.99**

#24 2 CONDUCTOR PKG (16') EA 1.49
Dealers MUST order Multiples of 10.

186-3122 Red
186-3123 Green
186-3128 Black
186-3129 White

WIRE ACCESSORIES

186-3091 29\0 Pin Miniature Connector **6.99**
186-3914 Terminal Strip, 30 Position **8.99**
186-3913 Resistor 1000 ohm pkg(10) **2.99**

186-3915 Soldering Plates 10 Terminal **8.99**
186-3916 Soldering Plates 20 Terminal **14.99**

Limited Quantity Available

186-3211 Stand for Spooled Wire **28.99**

BUSCH

IMPORTED FROM GERMANY BY WALTHERS

Add electronic animation to your layout with these accessories. Each unit comes fully assembled, with bulbs and/or LEDs. Small component size is adaptable to most any HO scale building or vehicle.

LIGHT & SOUND

189-5751 Crossing Blinkers w/Bell Sound **73.99**

189-5755 Building Site w/Sound **124.99**

189-5750 Blue Blinker Set w/Sound **69.99**
Light & sound control unit w/speaker & 2 bulbs.

189-49965 Vehicle Accessory Warning Set **6.99**
189-5938 Blinking Blue Siren with 2 LEDs **23.99**

BLINKER SETS

FLASHING LIGHTBAR
189-5922 Blue Lamps **19.99**
NEW
Complete flasher circuit and modern HO Scale lightbar converts your favorite models, sold seperately, into emergency vehicles.

TWO ALTERNATING
189-5935 With Blinker Control Blue **15.99**

189-5918 Yellow **18.99**
189-5919 Red **18.99**

FOUR ALTERNATING
189-5929 Yellow Warning Blinker **21.99**

AUTO LIGHTS

189-5927 Headlights & Tail Lights **17.99**

TIMERS

189-5961 With Infra Red Unit **32.99**
189-5963 Without Infra Red Unit **24.99**

CABLE LAMP WITH 250 MM OF CABLE
189-4290 Clear 16V/30mA **4.99**
189-4291 Red 5V/60mA **5.99**
189-4292 Amber 5V/60mA **5.99**
189-4293 Blue 5V/60mA **5.99**
189-4294 Turquoise 5V/60mA **5.99**

CONDUCTIVE PAINT
189-5900 Silver **10.99**
With the stroke of a brush you have a painted line which will conduct electricity on plastic, wood, glass, etc. It can be painted over and still carry current.

SCENES

189-5408 Summer Night Party Set **23.99**
Everything you need for any backyard event. Complete with working string of colored lights (12 LEDs), two support poles, four benches and two tables.

189-5409 Christmas Tree w/7 LEDs **22.99**
Holiday magic all year 'round. Fully assembled, snow-covered tree has seven yellow LEDs for a festive touch in any scene. Great accessory for Christmas villages too!

189-5450 American Construction Zone Blinkers **29.99**
Keep highway crews safe with this set of working construction flashers. Includes four stanchions, two of which are equipped with yellow LEDs and a flasher control unit.

189-5631 Complete Speed Trap Set **33.99**

189-5400 Luminous Advertising **22.99**
Includes 8 LEDs and extra letters (dry decals). Perfect for advertising restaurants, clubs and more.

189-5405 Flexible Light Band **24.99**
Features a string of 12 yellow LEDs. A nice addition to campsites, restaurants or as Christmas lights.

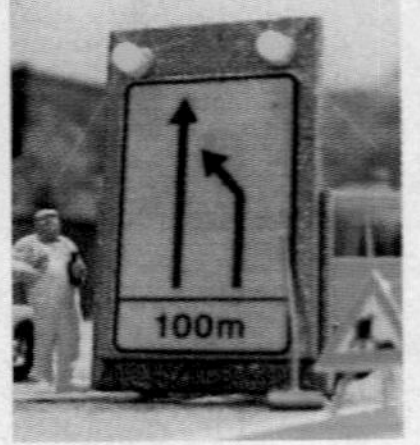

189-5930 Blinking Trailer with Control Unit **23.99**
Warn motorists of upcoming construction zones with this blinking trailer.

189-5937 Construction Zone Blinkers 7 Stantion (4 blink) and Control Unit **27.99**
When it's time to repair city streets and sewers, keep motorists alert with these construction zone blinkers.

189-5940 Radar Trap Set **31.99**
Keep traffic under control with this modern accessory along a busy highway. Set includes an unmarked Peugeot police van with white flashing unit, photographic unit with red flashing light, simulated calculator and accumulator. Electronic control unit is fully assembled and flashes both lights every five seconds.

189-5921 Flames **25.99**

189-5920 Advertising Signs **59.99**

189-5928 Christmas Tree & Lights **22.99**

189-5931 Electronic Welder **22.99**

STRUCTURE LIGHTS

189-4280 Building Lights pkg(2) **2.99**
Fully assembled sockets with wire leads and replaceable bulbs. Ideal for interior lighting in most structures.

FOGGY MOUNTAIN

The Millennium Series of locomotive lighting units and accessories are manufactured using the latest state-of-the-art solid state integrated circuits and technology and are rated at 1.25 Amps for 12V. They may be used in any scale as long as the motor has a continuous current draw of less than the indicated rating. Plated brass pin connectors and holders are included, where required, as are complete installation instructions.

CONSTANT LIGHTING

280-2000 Constant Non-Directional Lighting **5.75**
Lights are on in both directions. Use with one or two 1.5V lamps up to 90MA each. Includes Pin Connectors. Dimensions: .40 x .5625 x .125".

280-2001 Constant Directional Lighting w/o Bulbs **6.75**
Lights operate in direction of travel. May be used with up to four additional 1.5V lamps up to 90MA each. Includes Pin Connectors. Dimensions: .50 x .5625 x .094".

280-2002 Constant Directional Lighting w/Bulbs **9.50**
Lights operate in direction of travel. Up to four additional 1.5V lamps may be added in each direction if ditch lights are needed. Includes Pin Connectors. Dimensions: .50 x .5625 x .094".

PIN CONNECTORS

All are sub-miniature plated brass.

280-2010 Set of 2 **1.50**
280-2011 Set of 3 **2.00**
280-2012 Set of 4 **2.60**
280-2013 Set of 10 **6.00**
280-2014 Set of 32 **17.75**

JAY-BEE

INTERIOR LIGHTING & END OF TRAIN FLASHER KIT

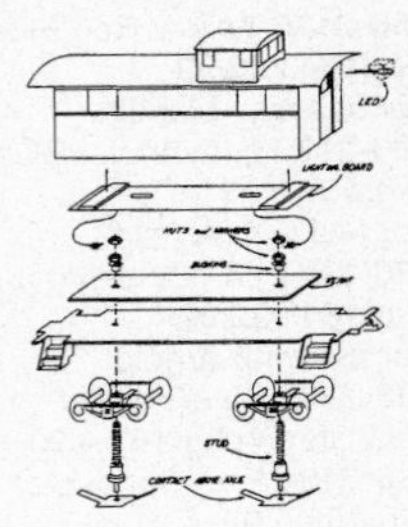

369-157 Athearn Cabooses **20.50**
This HO Scale lighting unit is designed for the three styles of Athearn cabooses and includes brass wheelsets, contacts, mounting studs, prewired circuit board and red LED. The easy-to-install kit is track powered with no wiring or soldering required. Lighting is constant, with full brightness attained at only 3.5/4 track volts. LED has a flashing rate of 70 per minute.

ELECTRICAL PICKUP

369-1533 Athearn Freight Truck **6.75**
This easy-to-assemble HO Scale kit includes parts to modify the Athearn freight truck for electrical pickup from track. Metal wheelsets included.

KIBRI

IMPORTED FROM GERMANY BY WALTHERS

SINGLE BULBS W/SOCKET

405-5840

405-5839 Bulb Assortment pkg(5) **9.99**
405-5840 Single Bulb **3.99**

Information STATION

Workbench/Layout Lighting

One of the more significant tools used throughout the model building process is proper lighting. Workbenches and layouts should be set up so that at least two light sources project onto them. This will allow the modeler to work without having to be in the shadows of his/her own hands.

It is also a good idea to have identical lighting for the workbench and layout areas. This guarantees that all colors, weathering effects, etc. will look the same on the workbench as when applied to the layout.

The type of lighting is purely a matter of personal preference. Incandescent bulbs give off a softer light than fluorescent bulbs and can be easily wired to dimmers for evening/night effects. But they also give off quite a bit of heat and use more electricity to equal the light output of fluorescent bulbs. The choice is yours.

We have worked closely with this manufacturer to provide accurate delivery information at the time this catalog was published. Items listed in blue ink may not be available at all times. Current delivery information, along with a list of in-stock products for this line, can be found on our Web site at www.walthers.com.

LIGHTING SYSTEMS

Circuitron products are constructed on printed circuit boards and designed to mount by snapping into a section of Circuitron's PCMT (Printed Circuit Mounting Track). Solid State integrated circuit technology. Connections to any Circuitron printed circuit board can be made using .110" female solderless connectors or by soldering the leads directly to the terminals on the board. Complete instructions are included. One year limited warranty.

FL1 STROBE FLASHERS EA 13.95

Bright flash, small package, battery operation. Long battery life; 6 months continuous operation from one AA alkaline cell. Will operate off hearing aid or watch cell. 1/2 x 3/4" high. HO 1.5 Volts, O 3.0 Volts , N 1.5 Volts.

800-1001 HO, Orange LED
800-1002 HO, Red LED
800-1003 HO, Yellow LED
800-1011 O, Orange LED
800-1012 O, Red LED
800-1013 O, Yellow LED
800-1021 N, Orange LED
800-1022 N, Red LED
800-1023 N, Yellow LED

FLW WHITE STROBES

Bright white flash from small incandescent lamp (included). Battery or track power adapter powered. Same size as FL-1.

800-1031 Bright 1.4mm Lamp, 1.5 Volt **13.95**
800-1032 Very Bright 1.7mm Lamp, 3.0 Volt **14.95**
800-1033 Extra Bright 2.4mm Lamp, 3.0 Volt **14.95**

CF-1 CABOOSE FLASHER EA 13.95

Single rear facing bulb slowly flashes on and off. Includes CF-1 circuit board, subminiature LED and battery clip. A 9V battery provides about 100 hours of flashing.

800-1200 Red
800-1201 Yellow

ML-2 MARS LIGHT

800-1502 16.95
Alternately flashes two 1.7mm diameter, high intensity, lens-end lamps (included) at a prototypical speed. Lamps may be mounted in dual headlight housings or side-by-side in larger headlight openings. Requires 2.4-3.0 volt DC input which can be provided by batteries, 800-2002 TP-2 or 800-2003 TP-3 Track Power Adapters.

FLA AMTRAK-STYLE STROBE FLASHER

800-1100 14.95
Duplicates the action of twin Xenon strobes found on many Amtrak locos. Designed for mounting inside HO Scale dummy locos, uses 9V transistor type battery to provide approximately 100 hours of flashing. Twin white lamps flash brightly about once a second.

800-9341 Replacement Lamp 0.1" dia pkg(2) **5.95**

ML-1 MARS LIGHT

800-1500 16.95
Realistic simulation of the gyrating beacon seen on many locos. Utilizing a special design, high intensity lens end dual-filament, the ML-1 can be used in most HO locos. Uses 2.4-3.0 volt DC from batteries, 800-2002 TP-2 or the 800-2003 TP-3 Track Power Adapters, sold separately.

800-9340 Replacement Dual Filament Lamp, 3V **2.95**

DITCH LIGHTS

Alternately flashes two 1.7mm diameter, high intensity, lens-end lamps (included) at a slow rate to simulate ditch lights. With the addition of a DPST or DPDT switch, the DL-1 circuit can be bypassed so the lights stay on. Requires 2.4-3.0 volt DC input from batteries, TP-2 800-2002 or TP-3 800-2003 Track Power Adapters, sold separately.

800-1400 DL-1 Oscillating Ditch Lights **16.95**
800-9123 Subminī Slide Switch, DPDT pkg(2) **2.95**
800-742402 Replacement Lamp Set for DL-1 pkg(2) **4.95**

EOT/FRED FLASHERS EA 12.95

Scale size housing, easily mounted on any freight car. High-intensity LED slowly flashes a bright light rearward. Requires 3V input, easily obtained from two small batteries; the TP-1 Track Power Adapter, 800-2001, can be used if the car is equipped with track power pickups.

800-1302 Red
800-1303 Yellow

EMERGENCY FLASHER EA 14.95

A low-cost circuit that alternately flashes two LEDs at a constant rate. Available with either .080" or .120" LEDs in red or yellow. Animate emergency vehicles, signs, barricades, towers, etc. Simple to install. Powered by a 9V battery, or by using a PS-3.

800-3002 .120" Red
800-3003 .120" Yellow
800-3022 .080" Red
800-3023 .080" Yellow

BASIC FLASHERS

Simple, inexpensive circuits for flashing LEDs or lamps (sold separately).

800-1601 Fixed Rate LED Flasher **6.95**
800-1602 Fixed Rate Lamp (<250 ma.) Flasher **10.95**
800-1603 Adjustable Rate and Duty Cycle Flasher for Lamp or LED (<250 ma.) **12.95**

DIODES

800-9350 3 Amp pkg(2) **1.50**
800-9351 1 Amp pkg(6) **1.50**
800-9352 6 Amp pkg(2) **2.95**
800-935012 3 Amp pkg(12) **6.95**
800-935212 6 Amp pkg(12) **12.95**

OPTO-SENSORS

.185" diameter. For use with all CIRCUITRON Detection Circuits.

800-9201 Single **3.95**
800-9202 Set of 2 **7.50**
800-9206 Set of 6 **19.95**

TL-1 TRAFFIC LIGHT CONTROLLER

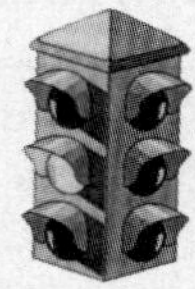

800-5820 29.95
Timing circuitry for standard traffic light. Outputs drive LED or lamp signals (not included). If LEDs are used, they must be common anode design. All four times are adjustable. Requires 10-18V AC or DC input. Red, yellow and green outputs provided for each direction (6 total) and each can drive a 250mA maximum load. Adaptable for all scales.

PL-8, PL-12 PROGRESSIVE LAMP CIRCUITS

Create unique signs. Sequence for both circuits is the same, only the maximum number of letters (and lamps) is different. Can also light fewer letters. Lights each lamp in succession with all previous lamps remaining on until all lamps are lit. The speed is adjustable. All lamps remain on, then go out. Finally, all lamps come on, then go out. Time on /off is adjustable. The sequence automatically repeats. The PL-8 and PL-12 include 8 and 12 lamps respectively (12-18 volt, 3mm dia.) but other lamps may be substituted for specific application. Construction of the actual sign will depend upon application and is left to the modeler. The PL-8 and PL-12 require a 12 volt AC or DC supply for proper operation. Adaptable for HO and larger scales.

800-5808 PL-8 **44.95**
800-5812 PL-12 **54.95**

CL-1, CL-2 CHASE LIGHTS, 10-STEP EA 39.95

10 step sequence with one lamp lit at a time. Ideal for "moving" sign and marquee applications. CL-1 includes 10 micro-lamps (1.4mm dia.), perfect for the edge of signs. CL-2 includes 10 high-output 2.4mm lamps for direct viewing in larger scales or with 10 mil fiber optics. Both circuits provide adjustable step speed and operate off 10-18V AC or DC. An additional flasher output is provided to backlight a sign or marquee, and flashes at 1/10 the step speed. Fiber optics and sign material not included.

800-5831 CL-1 w/Micro Lamps
800-5832 CL-2 w/2.4mm Lamps

SQ-8 SEQUENCING STROBE

800-5838 39.95
Provides a rapid sequencing of 8 high intensity white strobe lights (included). When the lamps are aligned, the effect is one of a light sweep from one end to the other. This type of lighting effect is commonly used near airports on the approaches, but can also be very effective on signs and other applications. Both the sweep speed and the delay between the sweeps are independently adjustable. Requires a 10-18 volt AC or DC input. For use with HO and larger scales.

AW-1, AW-2 ARC WELDER CIRCUITS EA 18.95

Circuits utilize two lamps, one yellow and one blue, along with a circuit that provides a random flickering effect of the lamps. The result is a very convincing representation of an arc welder in operation.

AW-1 includes micro-bulbs and is designed for direct viewing in all scales. A small wisp of cotton placed over the lamps will serve to diffuse the light and produce a very realistic smoke effect.

AW-2 includes larger lamps and is designed to illuminate a window from within a structure. If the window is frosted to represent years of grime, the flickering effect is very realistic. The AW-1 and AW-2 require a 10-18 volt AC or DC input for proper operation. Adaptable for all scales.

800-5841 AW-1
800-5842 AW-2

REPLACEMENT LAMP SET PKG(2) EA 4.95

800-9342 AW-1
800-9343 AW-2

FIRELITES™ FLICKERING FLAME CIRCUITS

800-5851 FF-1 **17.95**
800-5852 FF-2 **18.95**
800-5853 FF-3 **19.95**
These circuits produce a realistic, random flash that can be used for campfires, barrel fires or inside structures. FF-1 includes a single 1.4mm amber lamp, ideal for direct viewing. FF-2 includes both amber and red bulbs which flicker and flash independently, ideal for large fires viewed directly, hidden inside a barrel or when illuminating crumpled cellophane. The FF-3 is a high power unit with larger (2.4mm) amber and red lamps which can be used for backlighting effects inside structures. The FF-3 will handle up to 20 total lamps for use in multiple locations or to simulate a very large fire. All units require 10-18V AC or DC input.

REPLACEMENT LAMP SETS

800-9344 Amber & Yellow (1 Each) for FF-2 **4.95**
800-9345 Amber & Yellow (1 Each) for FF-3 **4.95**
800-7416302 Amber for FF-1 pkg(2) **4.95**
800-9341306 Amber pkg(6) **11.95**
800-9341706 Red pkg(6) **11.95**

LIGHTING ACCESSORIES

TRACK POWER ADAPTERS

TP-1

800-2001 10.95
Miniature voltage regulator can power any CIRCUITRON LED-type Strobe Flasher or EOT flasher from track power. Can be used as a constant lighting unit in unpowered rolling stock. 35 mA output will power 2-3 Strobes or EOT Flashers, LEDs with a 47 ohm resistor, one #7418 or two #7414 Mitey Lites™ wired in series. Bi-Directional, output will be present whether train is moving forward or backward. Can be used with DC, AC or Carrier Control systems. 0.3 x 0.3 x 0.8".

RELATIVE INTENSITY OF MITEY LITES:

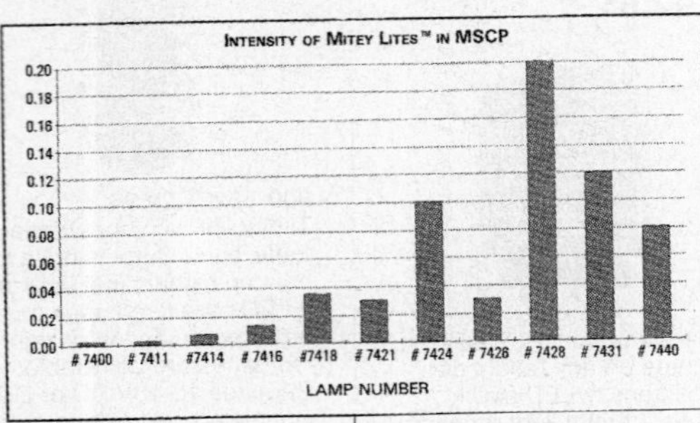

TP-2

800-2002 10.95
Will power the ML-1 Mars Light and Strobe Flashers and also has outputs that will provide directional constant lighting. Fits most HO locos, can be used with motors drawing up to 1 amp.

TP-3

800-2003 14.95
Adjustable output (1.5 or 3.0V DC). Ideal for constant lighting source in unpowered rolling stock. No ballast lamps or motors required. Will power Mars flasher in models driven by low current can motors. Works with all forms of track power. Max current output is 1/2 amp.

PS-3 POWER SUPPLY

800-5304 10.95
Designed to power the EF-1 Emergency Flasher in situations where battery operation is undesirable. Accepts AC or DC input of 10 to 18 volts and converts it to 9V DC.

ADJUSTABLE CONVERTER AND REGULATOR

800-5305 PS-2A **26.95**
A self-contained AC to DC converter with an adjustable voltage regulated output. The output voltage can be adjusted anywhere between 1.25 and 12.00 volts DC. Maximum continuous current output of the PS-2A is in excess of one amp. Ideal for powering any low current DC accessories including 1.5V micro-lamps. The AC or unfiltered DC input should be about 5-6V higher than the desired regulated output voltage to allow maximum current output. The input voltage may be as high as 22V, but this may result in reduced current available at the output, particularly at lower voltage settings.

BATTERY HOLDERS

For use with HO and O Scale Strobe Flashers.

800-9611 AA, 1 cell, 1.5V **2.50**
800-9612 AA, 2 cell, 3V **3.00**
800-9613 AAA, 1 cell, 1.5V **2.50**
800-9614 AAA, 2 cell, 3V **3.00**
800-9615 N, 1 cell, 1.5V **2.50**
800-9616 N, 2 cell, 3V **3.00**

HIDDEN ACCESSORY SWITCH

A completely hidden switch for controlling Strobe Flashers, marker lights or other rolling stock electrical accessories. Reed switch kits are turned on and off simply by bringing an external magnet up to the outside of the locomotive or car body. No external projections detract from the appearance of the model. Kits contain a subminiature reed switch and a tiny bias magnet.

800-9101 RS-1 Reed Switch Kit **4.95**
Requires adjustment before mounting.

800-9102 RS-2 Reed Switch Kit **6.95**
Requires no adjustment.

800-9100 External Magnet for Actuating Reed Switches **1.50**
800-9103 Sub-Miniature Slide Switches SPDT pkg(2) **2.95**

MINIATURE SWITCHES

Sub-Miniature Toggle Switches for panel mounting. 6 amp rating. Solder lug terminals. Chrome handle. 1/4" panel hole.

800-911002 SPDT On-On pkg(2) **5.50**
800-911006 SPDT On-On pkg(6) **14.95**
800-911102 SPDT On-Off-On pkg(2) **6.50**
800-911106 SPDT On-Off-On pkg(6) **17.95**
800-911202 SPDT On-Off-On Momentary pkg(2) **6.95**
800-911206 SPDT On-Off-On Momentary pkg(6) **18.95**
800-912002 DPDT On-On pkg(2) **6.50**
800-912006 DPDT On-On pkg(6) **17.95**
800-912102 DPDT On-Off-On pkg(2) **6.95**
800-912106 DPDT On-Off-On pkg(6) **18.95**
800-912202 DPDT On-Off-On Momentary pkg(2) **7.50**
800-912206 DPDT On-Off-On Momentary pkg(6) **19.95**
800-9128 Red Plastic Sleeve for Handle pkg(6) **2.50**
800-9129 Black Plastic Sleeve for Handle pkg(6) **2.50**

SOLDERLESS CONNECTORS EA 2.95

Female .110" Solderless Connectors for all Circuitron printed circuit boards.

800-9602 Non-Insulated pkg(8)
800-9603 Insulated pkg(6)

HEAT SHRINK TUBING EA 2.95

Use to insulate and protect wire connections quickly and easily. Shrinks to half the listed diameter when heated with a match, soldering iron or heat gun.

800-8700 Assortment ***NEW***
Includes 6" 15cm of each diameter from 3/64 to 3/16".
800-8703 3/64" 1.191mm Diameter - 36" 0.9m Long ***NEW***
800-8704 1/16" 1.588mm Diameter - 36" 0.9m Long ***NEW***
800-8706 3/32" 2.381mm Diameter - 36" 0.9m Long ***NEW***
800-8708 1/8" 3.175mm Diameter - 30" 75cm Long ***NEW***
800-8712 3/16" 4.763mm Diameter - 30" 75cm Long ***NEW***

ULTRAFINE HOOK-UP WIRE

Ultrafine stranded wire measures just 0.015" 0.397mm outside diameter. Vinyl insulation is easily stripped. Ideal for wiring locomotive lights, signals, signs and other small models. Each pack includes 10' 2.9m.

800-8610 Black ***NEW***
800-8612 Red ***NEW***
800-8619 White ***NEW***

LAMPS

7400 SUB-MICRO

0.75mm diameter axial lead. 1.5 V, 18 mA w/1" bare wire leads. Use for marker lights, number boards, step lights, etc.

800-740002 pkg(2) **3.95**
800-740006 pkg(6) **9.95**
800-740012 pkg(12) **16.95**
800-940012 Dropping Resistor For 12V pkg(10) **1.95**
800-940016 Dropping Resistor For 16V pkg(10) **1.95**

7411 STANDARD OUTPUT

1.40mm diameter lens end, w/8" black stranded wires. 1.5V, 13mA.

800-741102 pkg(2) **3.50**
800-741106 pkg(6) **7.75**
800-741112 pkg(12) **12.95**
800-741125 pkg(25) **24.95**
800-941112 Dropping Resistor For 12V pkg(10) **1.95**
800-941116 Dropping Resistor For 16V pkg(10) **1.95**

7414 MEDIUM OUTPUT
1.40mm diameter lens end w/8" black wire leads. 1.5V, 30mA. Ideal for headlights, mars lights, ditch lights, etc. to minimize total current draw.

800-741402 pkg(2) **4.95**
800-741406 pkg(6) **11.95**
800-741412 pkg(12) **16.95**
800-941612 Dropping Resistor For 12V pkg(6) **1.95**

7416 HIGH OUTPUT
1.40mm diameter lens end, w/8" black wire leads. 1.5V, 60mA. Very bright! Use for headlights, etc.

800-741602 pkg(2) **4.95**
800-741606 pkg(6) **11.95**
800-741612 pkg(12) **16.95**
800-941612 Dropping Resistor For 12V pkg(6) **1.95**
800-941616 Dropping Resistor For 16V pkg(6) **1.95**

COLORED LAMPS
Same specifications as #7416 lamps. Use same dropping resistors as #7416. Ideal for warning lights, signals, signs and more.

SET OF 2 EA 4.95
800-7416202 Red
800-7416302 Amber
800-7416402 Green
800-7416502 Blue

SET OF 6 EA 11.95
800-7416206 Red
800-7416306 Amber
800-7416406 Green
800-7416506 Blue

7418 VERY HIGH OUTPUT
1.40mm diameter lens end, w/8" black wire leads. 3.0V, 26mA. Ideal for headlight, mars light, etc.

800-741802 pkg(2) **4.95**
800-741806 pkg(6) **11.95**
800-741812 pkg(12) **16.95**
800-941812 Dropping Resistor For 12V pkg(6) **1.95**
800-941816 Dropping Resistor For 16V pkg(6) **1.95**

7421 VERY HIGH OUTPUT
1.70mm diameter lens end, with 8" black wire leads. 1.5V, 75mA. Extremely bright! Ideal for headlights, mars lights, or ditch lights.

800-742102 pkg(2) **4.95**
800-742106 pkg(6) **11.95**
800-942112 Dropping Resistor For 12V pkg(4) **1.95**
800-942116 Dropping Resistor For 16V pkg(4) **1.95**
2.4mm diameter lens end, with 8" black wire leads. 3V 120mA. Our brightest lamp!

7426 VERY HIGH OUTPUT
2.4mm diameter lens end, with 8" black wire leads. 1.5V, 90mA. Extremely bright! Use for headlights, etc.

800-742602 pkg(2) **4.95**
800-742606 pkg(6) **11.95**
800-942612 Dropping Resistor For 12V pkg(4) **1.95**
800-942616 Dropping Resistor For 16V pkg (4) **1.95**

7424 EXTRA HIGH OUTPUT
1.70mm diameter lens end with 8" black wire leads. 3.0V, 105mA. Extremely bright! Ideal for headlights, mars lights or ditch lights.

800-742402 pkg(2) **4.95**
800-742406 pkg(6) **11.95**
800-942412 Dropping Resistor For 12V pkg(4) **1.95**
800-942416 Dropping Resistor For 16V pkg(4) **1.95**

7431 VERY HIGH OUTPUT
2.4mm diameter lens end, with 8" black wire leads. 12-14V, 50mA. Ideal for headlights in locomotives not equipped with constant lighting and for structure lighting.

800-743102 pkg(2) **4.95**
800-743106 pkg(6) **11.95**

7428 MAXIMUM OUTPUT
2.4mm diameter lens end with 8" black wire leads. 3.0V, 120mA. Extremely bright! Ideal for headlights, mars lights or ditch lights, etc.

800-742802 pkg(2) **4.95**
800-742806 pkg(6) **11.95**
800-942812 Dropping Resistor For 12V pkg(4) **1.95**
800-942816 Dropping Resistor For 16V pkg(4) **1.95**

7440 GENERAL PURPOSE
Long life miniature lamp. 3.0mm diameter lens end, w/8" wire leads. 14-16V, 30mA. Use for equipment and structure lighting.

800-744006 pkg(6) **3.95**
800-744012 pkg(12) **5.95**
800-744025 pkg(25) **10.95**

LEDS

.125" DIA PKG (2) EA 2.95
Super-bright, diffused lens, ideal for strobe flashers, signs, signals and more.

800-9301 Orange
800-9302 Red
800-9303 Yellow
800-9304 Green
800-9306 Red/Green, Bi-Color

.200" DIA PKG (2) EA 2.95
800-9311 Orange
800-9312 Red
800-9313 Yellow
800-9314 Green
800-9316 Red/Green, Bi-Color

.75" DIA PKG (2) EA 2.95
800-9321 Orange
800-9322 Red
800-9323 Yellow
800-9324 Green

FIBER OPTICS
PMMA plastic fibers with a special fluoro-polymer coating. Light entering the end is transmitted along the length by internal reflection and exits the far end with very little loss in intensity. Use for signals, signs and special effects.

800-8020 0.020" dia 30' **5.25**
800-8030 0.030" dia 20' **5.25**
800-8040 0.040" dia 15' **6.25**
800-8060 0.060" dia 10' **6.25**

MANUAL & PROJECT BOOK
800-7833 2.95
Fiber optics instructions and complete plans to build a moving light theater marquee using Circuitron fiber optics and chase light circuits.

CIRCUITRON CATALOG & APPLICATION BOOK

800-9999 Fifty-two pages **5.00**

Grandt Line

DELRIN SPROCKETS
Material is Dupont Delrin 500 (acetal resin). All fit 1/8" shaft, except #300-70153, which fits 3/16" shaft. Dimension indicates outside diameter.

300-70082 8 Teeth, .371" **1.60**
300-70092 9 Teeth, .409" **1.60**
300-70102 10 Teeth, .456" **1.60**
300-70122 12 Teeth, .535" **1.60**
300-70152 15 Teeth, .650" **1.85**
300-70153 15 Teeth, 3/16" Shaft, .65" **3.15**
300-70162 16 Teeth, .69" **1.85**
300-70182 18 Teeth, .789" **2.05**
300-70202 20 Teeth, .848" **2.05**

GEARS
300-7007 1/8" Outside Diameter pkg(2) **1.85**
10 teeth, V bevel

300-7030 2:1 Ratio **5.75**
Cross-Box, .078" coupling, 3/32" axle material, less wheels.

300-7036 2:1 Ratio **5.50**
Cross-Box, .078" bore U-Joints, 3/32" axle material, less wheels.

300-7034 1:1 Bevel pkg(2) **4.40**
In Line, 15 teeth, 3mm bore, 48DP, Delrin.

300-7035 1:1 Bevel pkg(2) **4.40**
Same as 7034 with 3/32" bore.

300-7037 1:1 Ratio **6.30**
In Line, mounting bracket .089", coupling each 3/32". Will clear wheels as small as .32 diameter, 24" gauge.

300-7040 1:1 Skew Bevel pkg(2) **5.40**
1/8" Offset w/Cross-Box, .078" bore and axle material.

300-7077 1:1 Skew Bevel pkg(2) **4.40**
.078" Bore, .125" Offset-Delrin.

300-7078 2:1 Skew Bevel pkg(2) **4.40**
.062" & .125" Bore, .100" Offset-Delrin.

MOTOR

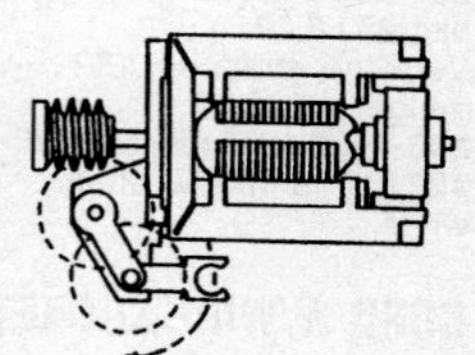

300-7094 Mabuchi Motor **25.95**
Gearing for 80:1 or 160:1 reduction. (80:1 configuration shown above.)

UNIVERSAL JOINTS

300-7009 .093" Set, pkg(2) **2.05**

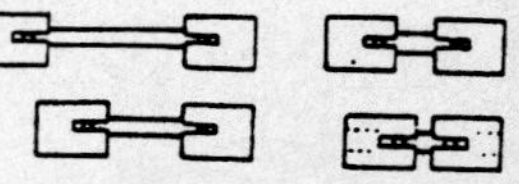

300-7011 .079" Set, .600" to 1.00" pkg(4) **2.40**

300-7004 Bores 3mm & 3/32" pkg(2) **2.05**

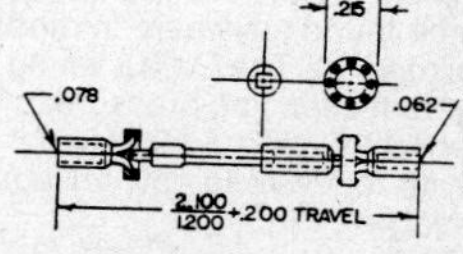

300-7039 Climax Set, Delrin **4.40**

300-7010 .078" 2mm, Delrin pkg(2) **2.05**
300-7013 Bore w/U-Joint **7.30**
300-7012 Bore w/Cross-Box **4.75**

MISCELLANEOUS

300-7005 Electrical Pick-Up Shoe for Loco Drivers **5.20**

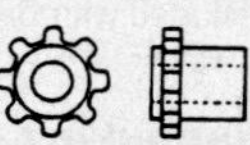

300-7006 Delrin Chain & 8-Tooth Sprocket **8.25**

300-7008 Flexible Delrin Shaft Coupling pkg(2) **3.10**
3/32" and .078" bores.
300-7033 Cross-Box for #300-7077 Gears **1.60**

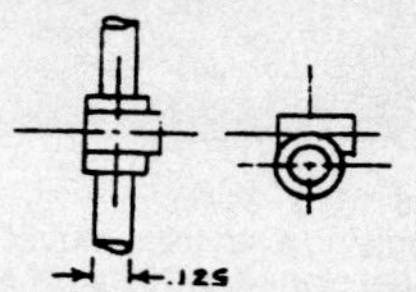

300-7079 Delrin Climax Cross-Boxes pkg(4) **4.40**

300-7083 Brass Bevel Pinion, 12-Tooth, 48DP **5.95**

300-70001 Delrin 6" Chain **6.25**

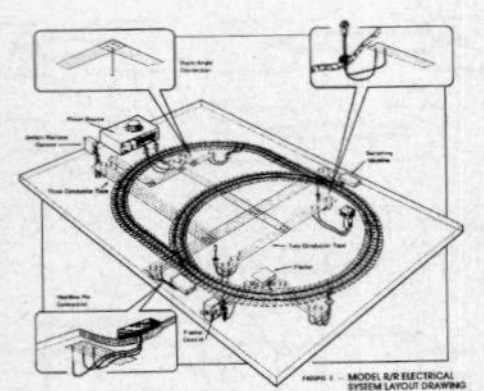

The Cir-Kit "concept" of electrical interconnection provides one of the most flexible means of circuit wiring to be found anywhere in model railroading. The Cir-Kit wiring system uses flat, pressure-sensitive, adhesive-backed Mylar tapewire for low-voltage wiring.

The system includes sockets and adapters for joining the tapewire to conventional wiring systems, tools and complete instructions for installation.

WIRING

INSTALLATION INSTRUCTION BOOKLET

206-1039 1.95
Illustrated 22-page instruction booklet outlining all steps necessary for installing Cir-Kit Concepts electrical components. Explains how to use brads, make solderless connections, interconnect conventional and tapewiring systems, and how to test circuits. Included with Basic Wiring Kit (#206-1040).

BASIC WIRING KIT I

206-1040 31.95
Contains everything required to get started. A 15' roll of two-conductor tape, a 10' roll of three-conductor tape, 60 1/8" brass brads, 36 headless pins, 22 wire sockets, 5 two-conductor 4" cords with sockets, map tack, pilot hole punch, instruction book, GOW bulb and test probe for trouble shooting.

BASIC WIRING KIT II

206-105 26.45
Includes transformer lead-in wire, junction splice, pilot hole punch and needles, 15' tapewire, test probe and 1/8" brass brads.

TAPEWIRE

Tapewire is an adhesive-backed Mylar tape containing electrical conductors. The tape is .005" thick by 5/8" wide and can be painted. It can be run under grass mats or behind wallpaper. Tapewire can be used throughout the layout, but is most useful where "invisible" wiring is desired. Connections are pinned together (with brads) and do not require soldering.

206-1001 2 Conductor (15') **7.95**
206-1017 2 Conductor (50') **23.95**
206-10291 3 Conductor (50') **27.95**
206-10292 3 Conductor (10') **6.98**

MINIATURE WIRE

For connections where flat tape is not practical.

206-203 2 Conductor Hookup pkg(25') **3.39**
Very fine, stranded, #32 gauge.
206-2032 1 Conductor **1.98**
#32 gauge with 50' shank, white.

CORD W/WIRE SOCKET

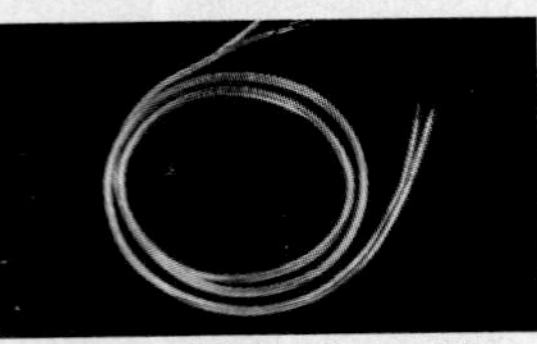

206-10282 2 Conductor **.99**

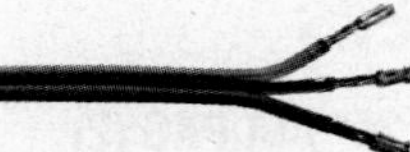

206-10283 3 Conductor **1.19**
A four-inch length of conductor cord with pin sockets on one end. For connecting tape to conventional wiring systems.

TRANSFORMER LEAD-IN

206-1008 4.75
For connecting transformer to tapewire system. Plug on one end mates with Junction Splice (#206-1007). Opposite (spade lug) ends of 6' lead connect to transformer terminals.

ADAPTER CORD

206-10281 18" Long **1.98**
Plug on one end accepts tape conductors. Opposite (stripped) ends may be connected to screw terminals, track or conventional wiring.

12V PLUG-IN TRANSFORMER

206-10090 22.95
Provides AC power for lights. Not for running trains. Will handle up to 23 16V bulbs. 10-watt rating. Built-in circuit breaker.

DIMMER

206-802 Dimmer Extension Cord **24.95**
With this all-electric variable controller, any lamp up to 300 watts may be dimmed or the speed regulated for a small power tool up to 2.5 amps.

WIRE SOCKETS

One end is crimped onto conventional wire. The other end may be plugged into headless pins and pinned to tapewire systems.

206-1032 pkg(22) **3.98**
206-10321 pkg(60) **8.98**

JUNCTION SPLICE

206-1007 3.19
For connecting tapewire system to transformer lead-in. Use with #206-1008.

IN-LINE FUSE HOLDER

206-1026 1.75
Fuse holder and wire sockets for in-line connection. Fuse not included.

LIGHTING

DROPPING RESISTOR

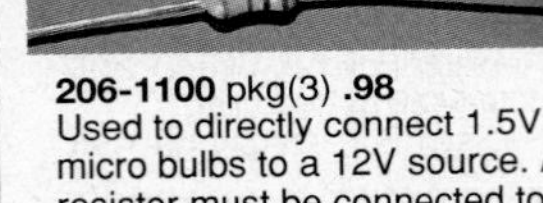

206-1100 pkg(3) **.98**
Used to directly connect 1.5V micro bulbs to a 12V source. A resistor must be connected to each bulb.

BULB SOCKET

206-10108 With 8" Black Wires **1.49**

GRAIN-OF-WHEAT BULBS

Bulb consumes between 50 and 60mA at 12V. Outside diameter approximately 1/8".

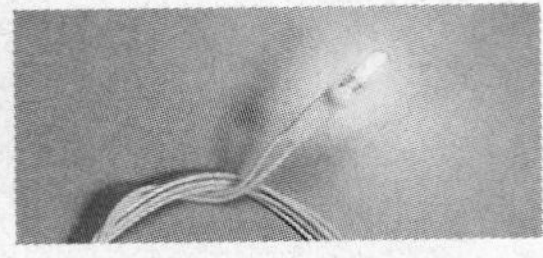

206-10101 12V w/1/8" Black Wire **1.25**
206-10102 16V w/8" Black Wire **1.25**
206-101011 12V w/Wire Leads **1.25**
206-101018 3V w/8" White Wire **1.25**
206-101021 12V w/12" Brown Wire **1.30**
206-101022 12V w/18" Brown Wire **1.35**
206-1010182 3V w/8" Black Wire **1.49**
206-10101822 3V w/8" Black Wire pkg(100) **126.65**

SCREW BASE BULB

206-10107 12V **1.49**

GRAIN-OF-RICE BULBS EA 1.49 (UNLESS NOTED)

206-10106 12V Clear w/Black Wire
206-101020 12V w/12" Brown Wire **1.59**
206-101023 12V w/8" Brown Wire
206-101062 12V Clear w/White Wire
206-101063 16V Clear w/Black Wire

MICRO BULBS 1.5V EA 1.59 (UNLESS NOTED)

206-101013 With Black Wire
206-101014 With White Wire
206-101015 With Wire Terminals
206-1010130 With Black Wire pkg(100) **135.15**

SWIVEL SPOTLIGHT

206-101010 3.25
Miniature swivel spotlight features top-mounted 360° rotation and 180° side-to-side movement. Large size bulb is a highly focused lens for light concentration and will burn for 5000+ hours. Bulb snaps in and works on a 12V system. 7/8" long, 3/8" diameter.

GLOWING EMBERS

206-865 11.95
Works with any 12V system and requires no separate transformer. The orange-colored bulb is a replaceable screw-base type with a MH658 plug attached to the small gauge along with a 24" long power cord.

ACCESSORIES

PILOT HOLE PUNCH

For making small holes for brass brads. Eliminates the risk of making holes that are too large.

206-10141 3.98
206-10143 Pilot Hole Punch Needles pkg(2) **1.29**

BRASS BRADS & HEADLESS PINS

Used for connecting tapewire and conventional wiring systems. No soldering is required.

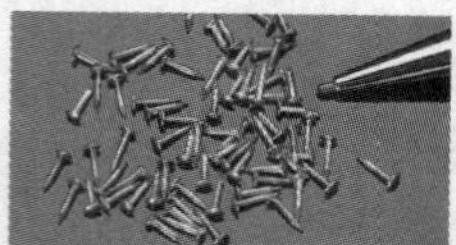

206-1021 1/8" Brass Brads pkg(300) **7.45**
206-10211 1/8" Brass Brads pkg(60) **1.98**
206-1031 Headless Pins pkg(36) **1.89**
206-10223 Brass Pins #18 pkg(50) **1.59**
206-1045 Wood Screws #0 pkg(20) **1.79**

SWITCHES

SPDT, for turning lights and accessories on and off. Only 1/4 x 7/16" in size. For tape or conventional wiring systems. Instructions included. Pound-in construction.

206-1011 Miniature Slide **4.98**
206-10481 Small Slide **1.98**

206-1048 In-Line **2.29**

EYELETS

206-1023 Hollow, Small pkg(20) **.98**
206-10231 Hollow, Small pkg(110) **4.98**

TERMINAL BLOCKS

206-1049 2-Pole **3.75**
206-10491 4-Pole **4.10**
206-10492 6-Pole **4.39**

See What's Available at

www.walthers.com

KATO

MOTORS

381-31500 HM 5 w/Double Shaft **19.98**

WITH DUAL FLYWHEEL AND SADDLE

381-956010 For Kato Hood Units **30.00**
381-956020 For Kato Switcher **35.00**

LIFE LIKE

BULBS EA 3.75

433-1203 Lamp Bulb pkg(3) For use with Old Time Lamp Post #433-1201.

433-1204

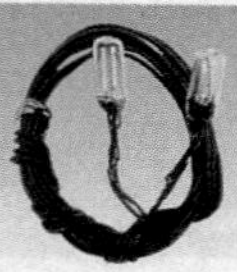

433-1210

433-1204 With Wired Socket pkg(2)
433-1210 Grain Of Wheat pkg(2)
For use with Light Pole #433-1206 and Gas Light #433-1505.

HOOK-UP WIRE

433-1431 2-Strand, Brown pkg(10) **3.75**

HOUSE LIGHTING KIT

433-1200 With Base **3.75**

CIRCUITS

LIGHT SENSITIVE CIRCUIT

464-1200 19.95
Unit controls three 1.5mv bulbs. Circuit includes a photo-cell which activates the 3 lights at 3 different times when room lights are dimmed. The 3 lights also turn off at 3 different times when light in room is increased. The unit's light sensitivity is adjustable. The unit accepts 7.5 to 12 volts in either AC or DC for power input.

LIGHT SENSITIVE CIRCUIT II

464-1210 21.95
Unit controls six 1.5mv bulbs. Circuit includes a photo-cell which activates the 6 lights at 3 different times when room lights are dimmed. The 3 lights also turn off at 3 different times when light in room is increased. The unit's light sensitivity is adjustable. The unit accepts 7.5 to 12 volts in either AC or DC for power input.

BULBS

MINIATURE LIGHT BULB

464-1250 1.25
1.5mm in size, designed for long life. Accepts only 1.5 volts for power (more volts will destroy bulb).

MODELTRONICS

MOTORS

510-3002 Reversing HO/N 1.0 Amp **11.95**
510-3003 Reversing HO/O 3.0 Amp **15.95**
510-3004 Non-Reversing HO/N 1.0 Amp **7.95**
510-3005 Non-Reversing HO/O 3.0 Amp **13.95**
510-3006 Non-Reversing HO/O 2.0 Amp **11.95**

WIRE

All purpose, color coded, flexible pre-tinned wire.

490-5201 1 Conductor Red pkg(400') **22.00**
490-5202 2 Conductor Red, Black pkg(200') **24.00**
490-5203 3 Conductor Red, White, Black pkg(100') **22.00**
490-5204 4 Conductor Red, White, Yellow, Black pkg(100') **24.00**
490-2401 1 Conductor Green, Red, Brown, Blue, Gray & Black pkg(35') **1.89**
490-2402 2 Conductor Red, Black pkg(17.5') **1.89**
490-2403 3 Conductor Blue, White, Black pkg(11.5') **1.89**
490-2404 4 Conductor Green, Red, White, Black pkg(8.5') **1.89**
490-2301 1 Conductor cd **1.99**
490-2302 2 Conductor cd **1.99**
490-2303 3 Conductor cd **1.99**
490-2304 4 Conductor cd **1.99**
490-2310 18 Gauge Wire 1 Conductor pkg(25') **2.98**
490-2311 18 Gauge Wire 2 Conductor pkg(12.5') **2.98**
490-2299 2 Spools #1 Conductor Wire, Extra Fine-2 Colors pkg(50') **1.99**

BULBS

14V GRAIN-O-SAND PKG(3) EA 4.50

490-146 Clear, 1.2mm
490-147 Red, 1.2mm
490-148 Green, 1.2mm
490-149 Amber, 1.2mm

GRAIN-O-RICE

1.5V PKG(3) EA 3.98

490-152 Clear, 2.2mm
490-153 Red, 2.2mm
490-154 Green, 2.2mm
490-155 Amber, 2.2mm

3V

490-345 Clear, 150mA pkg(3) **3.49**

14V PKG(3) EA 3.98

490-252 Clear, 2.2mm
490-253 Red, 2.2mm
490-254 Green, 2.2mm
490-255 Amber, 2.2mm

GRAIN-O-WHEAT

1.5V

490-344 Pointed, 150mA pkg(3) **3.49**

3V PKG(3) EA 2.49

490-391 Clear, 3.2mm
490-392 Red, 3.2mm
490-393 Green, 3.2mm
490-394 Amber, 3.2mm

14V PKG(3) EA 2.49

490-381 Clear, 3.2mm
490-382 Red, 3.2mm
490-383 Green, 3.2mm
490-384 Amber, 3.2mm

14V GAS PEA LAMPS PKG(2) EA 2.98

490-395 Clear, 6mm
490-396 White, 6mm

HEADLIGHTS PKG(3) EA 3.49

490-340 16V 70mA Wired Flat Head
490-341 14V 70mA Flat Head Screw
490-342 14V Oval Screw
490-343 14V Oval Bayonet

BAYONET BASE 6V

490-51960 #51 Clear pkg(2) **2.98**

BAYONET BASE 14V

490-398 Pointed, N Scale w/14V G-O-W Bulbs pkg(3) **3.49**
490-53961 #53 Clear pkg(2) **2.98**
490-53962 #53 Red pkg(2) **2.98**
490-257961 BB pkg(2) **2.98**
490-257962 #257 Red pkg(2) **3.49**
490-363961 #363 Clear pkg(2) **3.49**

BAYONET BASE 18V

490-144596 #1445 Clear pkg(2) **2.98**

BUILDING LIGHTS

490-491 Socket Stand & Bulb pkg(2) **2.89**
490-492 12V w/Screw Base pkg(6) **4.98**
490-9898 Fire Lighting **4.98**
490-10096 With Screw Base pkg(2) **2.98**

LAMP POST BULBS

490-10095 pkg(2) **2.98**

SCREW BASE 14V PKG(2) EA 2.98

490-144996 #1449 Clear
490-144997 #1449 Red
490-144998 #1449 Green
490-258961 #258 Clear
490-430961 #430 Clear
490-432961 #432 Clear
490-432962 #432 Red
490-432963 #432 Green
490-461961 #461 Clear

SCREW BASE 18V

490-144796 #1447 Clear pkg(2) **2.98**

1.5V SUB MINI

490-145 Clear, 12.5mA pkg(3) **4.50**
Angels Hair 1.2mm.

3V BRITE

490-397 Clear, GOW pkg(3) **3.49**

14V BLINKER PKG(2) EA 2.98

Blinks after 20 second warm-up.

490-10097 Clear, 250mA
490-10098 Red, 250mA
490-10099 Amber, 250mA

LIGHTING KITS

SUPER MICROLAMPS EA 2.49 (UNLESS NOTED)

These tiny light bulbs are perfect for use with signals, headlights or wherever space is limited. Bulbs are designed for use with 1.5V DC (15mA) and measure 1.4mm. Long life design.

296-100 Clear
296-101 Red
296-102 Green
296-103 Amber
296-104 Flame
296-10001 Clear pkg(25) **39.95**

LAMP W/PAINTED SHADE

296-105 3.95
Typical outdoor/security lamp, found on all types of buildings. Includes 1.5V bulb and painted metal shade with instructions. HO and larger.

LITEPAC™

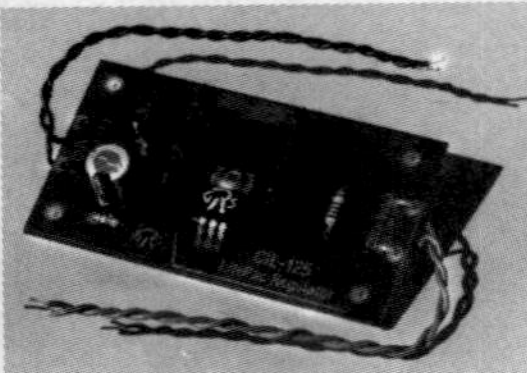

296-125 1.5V **34.95**
Powers up to 50 or more micro15mA bulbs on a layout, diorama or module using any 4-20V AC or DC power source. Unlike AC transformer devices, the Litepac provides fully regulated and filtered DC voltage which can extend lamp life up to 30%. The "Lamp Saver" circuit helps prevent harmful AC over-volt conditions from destroying delicate 1.5V microlamps. Litepac comes fully assembled with built-in overload protection, instructions and mounting hardware.

LITEPAC™ STARTER SET

296-135 49.95
Includes 12 #100 light bulbs.

LED POWER CONVERTER

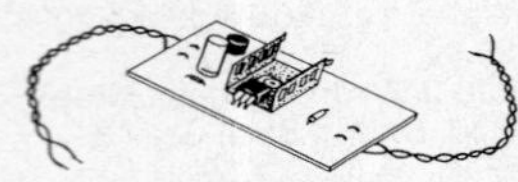

296-140 34.95
Converter can power up to fifty 20mA, 2.1 to 3.0V LEDs. Automatic safety feature shuts down the unit in event of overload, overheating or short. Ballast resistors are not required. Input: 6-20V AC/DC (variable or steady); output: 2.4V DC (regulated) 1.0 amp. max.

HEAVY DUTY SUPER MICROLAMPS

Bulbs are designed for use with 1.8V DC (60mA) and measure 1.3mm in diameter.

296-200 Clear **5.95**
296-201 Red **5.95**
296-202 Green **5.95**
296-205 Flamemaker™ Lamp Kit **4.39**
296-301 Frosted Globe **4.49**
6.0mm in diameter.

STREET LIGHTS

296-302 Street Light Kit **7.98**
Typical street light includes 4" diameter post adjustable to 12' high (HO Scale Feet), 1.5V DC Frosted Globe lamp (6mm), and instructions. Can be used with N & S Scales.

296-303 Old Time Gas Street Light HO & Up **7.98**

HEAVY DUTY FLOURETTE LAMPS

Can be used to light building interiors or passenger car interiors. 12-16V AC/DC.

296-400 Frosted **1.89**
296-401 Frosted pkg(6) **9.95**
296-402 Lamp Holder **1.89**
296-403 Lamp Holder pkg(6) **9.95**

ULTIMATE MICROLAMP™

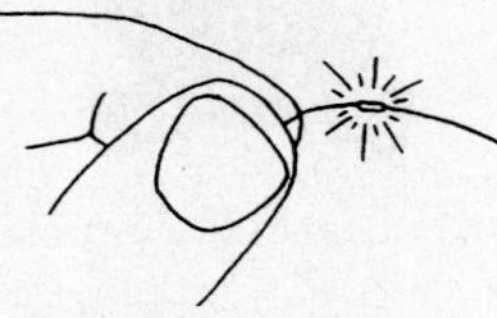

296-500 3.95
Can be used with the CLM series Loco Liting modules for working head, ditch, marker or numberboard lights on locos, plus marker lights for cabooses and passenger equipment. Also used for military, aircraft and vehicle models. Requires 1.5V power source, draws a low 15mA of current. Using the CIL-125 LitePac™, (#269-125) 50 to 75 of these bulbs can be used on a layout. Includes one assembled axial-design bulb with 1" wire leads, (bulbs are pre-tested before packaging) insulation material and instructions.

HIGH INTENSITY 3V SUPER MICROLAMPS EA 3.95

Replacement Lamps for #296-1013 & #296-1014.

296-501 Blue
296-502 Rose
296-503 Flame
296-504 Clear

CLM LOCOLITE™

Fully assembled constant lighting modules ready for installation. HO and larger.

296-900 Single Headlamp **11.95**

296-901 Two Headlamps **14.95**
Auto-reverse on one lamp.
296-902 Two Headlamps **14.95**
Auto-reverse on both lamps.

296-908 Replacement Lamp **2.49**
For #s 900, 901, and 902. 1.4V DC 1.3mm dia 10mA.

SINGLE HEADLAMP

296-903 Heavy Duty Single Headlamp **13.95** ***NEW***
Less Lamp, 2A. For S, O and G scale.

2-PIN MICRO CONNECTOR™

Gold plated, assembled.

296-906 With 5" 30ga Color-Coded Leads (1 set) **4.95**
296-907 Less Leads (2 sets) **5.95**

MICRO FLAMEMAKER™

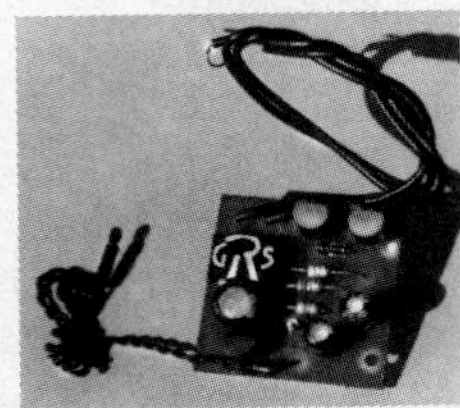

296-1000 27.50
Unit simulates the flickering light produced by a small bonfire or campfire. 6-20V AC/DC. Used with all scales. 1 x 1 x 3/8".

MICROFLASHER™ SLOW

296-1001 27.50
For model signs, billboards, beacons, etc. Includes two clear heavy-duty microbulbs. 12-20V.

MICROFLASHER™ FAST

296-1002 27.50
For model signs, billboards, emergency vehicles, planes, boats, etc. Flashes two clear heavy-duty microlamps which are included. 12-20V.

MICROSTROBE™

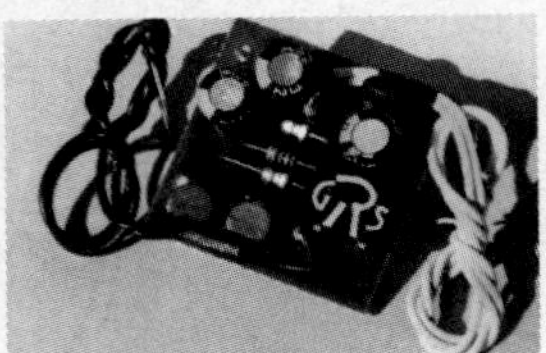

296-1003 27.50
Pure white strobe effect achieved through two strobe blue microlamps, included. For use on model signs, trains, planes, boats, etc. 6-20V.

SUPER FLAMEMAKER™

Unit simulates larger fires such as a working blast furnace or a burning structure. Can be used in any scale. 16-20V AC. Circuit board 1 x 1 x 5/8" high. Lamp assembly 3/16" diameter, 7/8" long.

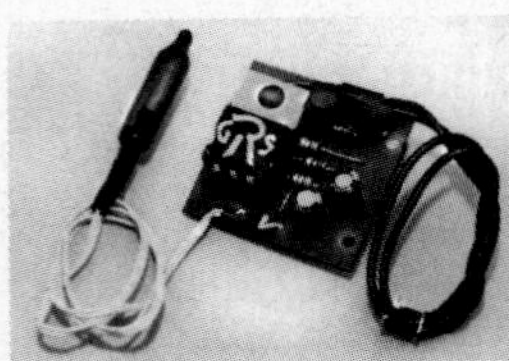

296-1004 27.50
296-300 Lamp Replacement For #1004 **4.39**

VEHICLE LIGHTING KITS

Kits come complete with assembled electronics, 1.5V Heavy Duty Super Microlamps, hardware and instructions. 6-18V AC/DC.

1005

1008

1011

1012

296-1005 Rotating Beacon (red) **27.50**
296-1008 Dual Litebar (red/blue) **36.95**
296-1011 Rotating Beacon (yellow) **27.50**
296-1012 Basic Vehicle Lighting Kit **17.95**

ULTIMATE ARC WELDER

296-1013 39.95
Adjustable action and brightness to model the color and sporadic action of an actual arc welder. Great in railroad shops like Allied Rail Rebuilders. Includes assembled driver, blue- and rose-colored lamps (can be viewed directly or indirectly) and mounting Velcro for driver. 12-20V AC/DC required.

WIRE

MICRO-WIRE

296-5006 32 Gauge, 2 Strand, Insulated **3.95**

LIGHT WORKS USA

By Miller Engineering

NEW SUPPLIER

ELECTROLUMINESCENT SIGN KITS

Each sign is made of special plastic that's only .008" thick for a near scale appearance. The sign is coated on one side with phosphor, which glows when current is applied. This produces a soft, neon-like light that's bright enough to be seen under regular room lights, but generates no heat. Each kit comes with an assembled 3V power supply, which requires two AAA batteries, not included. Complete instructions cover all of the steps needed for installation and operation.

VERTICAL

Left and right version may be mounted together to create a sign that lights on both sides.

BENTENS BAR & GRILL

502-12011 Medium, Left 14.95 *NEW*
502-12012 Medium, Right 14.95 *NEW*
502-12021 Small, Left 13.95 *NEW*
502-12022 Small, Right 13.95 *NEW*

CAFE

502-13011 Large, Left 16.95 *NEW*
502-13012 Large, Right 16.95 *NEW*
502-13021 Medium, Left 14.95 *NEW*
502-13022 Medium, Right 14.95 *NEW*

HOTEL

502-14011 Large, Left 16.95 *NEW*
502-14012 Large, Right 16.95 *NEW*
502-14021 Medium, Left 14.95 *NEW*
502-14022 Medium, Right 14.95 *NEW*

MOTEL

502-15011 Large, Left 16.95 *NEW*
502-15012 Large, Right 16.95 *NEW*
502-15021 Medium, Left 14.95 *NEW*
502-15022 Medium, Right 14.95 *NEW*

PIZZA - (SQUARE) EA 14.95

502-16011 Medium, Left *NEW*
502-16012 Medium, Right *NEW*

STAR DRUG EA 14.95

502-31021 Medium, Left *NEW*
502-31022 Medium, Right *NEW*

MID STATE BANK EA 14.95

502-14111 Medium, Left *NEW*
502-14112 Medium, Right *NEW*

AAA LOGO

502-33011 Large, Left 14.95 *NEW*
502-33012 Large, Right 14.95 *NEW*
502-33021 Medium, Left 13.95 *NEW*
502-33022 Medium, Right 13.95 *NEW*

BARBER SHOP

502-34011 Large, Left 14.95 *NEW*
502-34012 Large, Right 14.95 *NEW*
502-34021 Medium, Left 13.95 *NEW*
502-34022 Medium, Right 13.95 *NEW*

ROOMS

502-35011 Large, Left 16.95 *NEW*
502-35012 Large, Right 16.95 *NEW*
502-35021 Medium, Left 15.95 *NEW*
502-35022 Medium, Right 15.95 *NEW*

OPEN

502-36011 Large, Left 15.95 *NEW*

502-36012 Large, Right 15.95 *NEW*
502-36021 Medium, Left 14.95 *NEW*
502-36022 Medium, Right 14.95 *NEW*

PAWN SHOP

502-37011 Large, Left 15.95 *NEW*
502-37012 Large, Right 15.95 *NEW*
502-37021 Medium, Left 14.95 *NEW*
502-37022 Medium, Right 14.95 *NEW*

PIZZA (ROUND)

502-38011 Large, Left 15.95 *NEW*
502-38012 Large, Right 15.95 *NEW*
502-38021 Medium, Left 14.95 *NEW*
502-38022 Medium, Right 14.95 *NEW*

REXALL

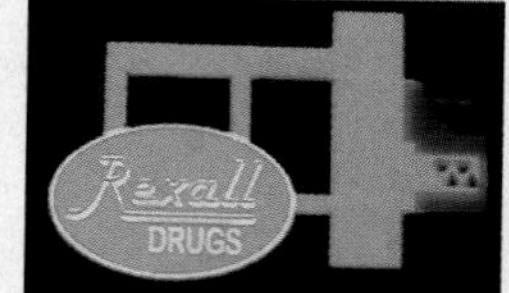

502-39011 Large, Left 14.95 *NEW*
502-39012 Large, Right 14.95 *NEW*
502-39021 Medium, Left 13.95 *NEW*
502-39022 Medium, Right 13.95 *NEW*

MERCANTILE

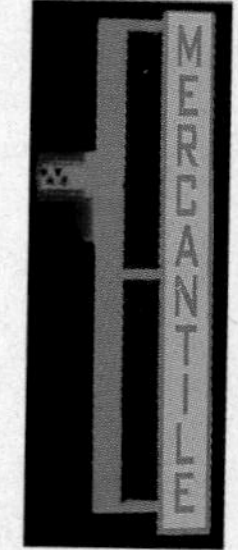

502-40011 Large, Left 15.95 *NEW*
502-40012 Large, Right 15.95 *NEW*
502-40021 Medium, Left 14.95 *NEW*
502-40022 Medium, Right 14.95 *NEW*

THEATER

502-41011 Large, Left 16.95 *NEW*
502-41012 Large, Right 16.95 *NEW*
502-41021 Medium, Left 15.95 *NEW*
502-41022 Medium, Right 15.95 *NEW*

BIJOU

502-42011 Large, Left 15.95 *NEW*
502-42012 Large, Right 15.95 *NEW*
502-42021 Medium, Left 14.95 *NEW*
502-42022 Medium, Right 14.95 *NEW*

HORIZONTAL

Horizontal signs are designed to mount on a roof or wall.

CAFE

502-1701 Large 14.95 *NEW*
502-1702 Medium 13.95 *NEW*

GILMOR HOTEL

502-1801 Large 17.95 *NEW*
502-1802 Medium 14.95 *NEW*

DINER

502-1901 Large 17.95 *NEW*
502-1902 Medium 13.95 *NEW*

LIGHT WORKS USA

HOTEL

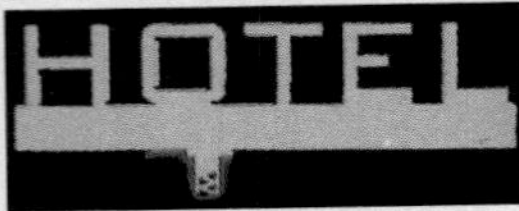

502-2101 Large **14.25** *NEW*
502-2102 Medium **13.95** *NEW*

MOTEL

502-2201 Large **14.25** *NEW*
502-2202 Medium **13.95** *NEW*

TRIANGLE HOTEL

502-2401 Large **17.95** *NEW*
502-2402 Medium **14.95** *NEW*

PARKWAY DINER

502-2801 Large **19.95** *NEW*
502-2802 Medium **15.95** *NEW*

HOTEL BELMONT

502-2901 Large **17.95** *NEW*
502-2902 Medium **14.95** *NEW*

CLOCK

Left and right are the same.

502-3201 Large **13.95** *NEW*
502-3202 Medium **12.95** *NEW*

"N"-WAY PRODUCTS

LIGHTING

FLASHING DIESEL BEACONS EA 8.95

Prototype flashing warning beacon lights sit atop modern diesels and emit a colored flash from a LED. Require drilling and soldering.

535-551 Orange, Track Operated
535-552 Red, Track Operated

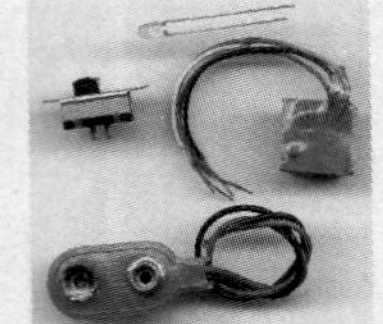

535-555 Orange, Battery Powered
535-556 Red, Battery Powered

FLASHING STROBES EA 14.95

Flashing strobe unit produces a pure white flash from small light bulb. Instructions included.

535-553 Track Operated

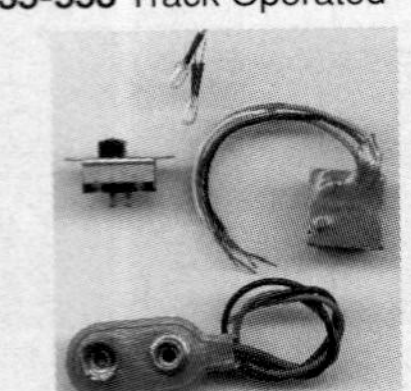

535-557 9V Battery Powered

EMERGENCY FLASHING LIGHT KITS

Can be attached to all plastic HO cars, fire engines and fire trucks to transform them into police, fire and highway emergency vehicles. The flasher will operate 3 sets of emergency lights. Requires two 9V batteries or the N-Way Power Supply Kit. Vehicle not included.

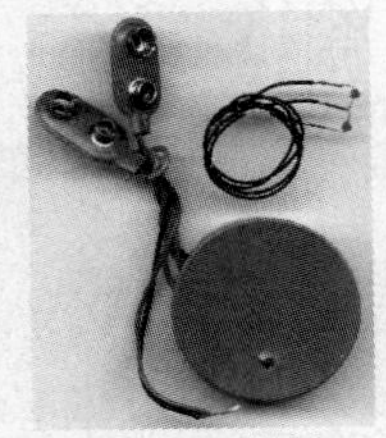

535-651 Orange Lights w/Flasher **10.95**
535-652 Red Lights w/Flasher **10.95**
535-655 Orange Lights Only **5.95**
535-656 Red Lights Only **5.95**

LIGHTING & ELECTRICAL

BRASS ENCASED 12V PKG(2) EA 3.99

525-9006 Clear
525-9007 Red
525-9008 Green
525-9009 Amber

PANEL INDICATOR 12V EA 3.99

525-9026 White
525-9027 Red
525-9028 Green
525-9029 Yellow

SMALL CLEAR BULBS

SUPER MICRO 1.4MM

525-9145 1.5V pkg(3) **15.99**

MICRO 1.8MM EA 3.99

525-9182 12V
525-9185 1.5V

SUBMIN 2.5MM EA 3.29

525-9252 12V
525-9255 1.5V

GRAIN OF RICE 2.5MM, 12V PKG(2) EA 3.99

525-9256 Clear
525-9257 Red
525-9258 Green
525-9259 Amber

GRAIN OF WHEAT 3.2MM

1.5V PKG(2) EA 3.99

525-9306 Clear
525-9307 Red
525-9308 Green
525-9309 Amber

3V PKG(2) EA 3.99

525-9316 Clear
525-9317 Red
525-9318 Green
525-9319 Amber

12V PKG(2) EA 3.29

525-9326 Clear
525-9327 Red
525-9328 Green
525-9329 Amber

LED PANEL LIGHTS 12V EA 3.99

525-9057 Red
525-9058 Green

LIGHTING KIT

525-8801 **1.99**
Use for lighting structures. Kit includes bulb socket, mounting base, bulb, wire and screws.

PANEL METERS

525-8360 DC Volt Meter, 20-0-20 **16.99**
525-8361 DC Amp Meter, 5-0-5 **14.99**
525-8362 DC Amp Meter, 0-2 **14.99**
525-8363 DC Volt Meter, 0-16 **16.99**

MINIATURE SWITCHES

525-8528 Momentary Switch (SPDT) 3 Pole-Bat Type Lever On-Off-On **4.99**
525-8529 Momentary Switch (DPDT) 6 Pole-Bat Type Lever On-On **5.99**
525-8540 2-Pole (SPST) Chrome Lever w/Blue Dot On End On-Off **3.99**
525-8541 2-Pole (SPST) w/Red Dot On End On-Off **3.99**
525-8586 6-Pole (DPDT) Chrome Lever w/Blue Dot On-Off-On **4.99**
525-8587 6-Pole (DPDT) Chrome Lever w/Red Dot On-Off-On **4.99**

SPOOLED WIRE

1 CONDUCTOR 50' EA 2.99

525-8420 Red
525-8421 Green
525-8427 Brown
525-8428 Yellow

2 CONDUCTOR 35'

525-8422 **4.99**

4 CONDUCTOR 20'

525-8423 **5.29**

ELECTRICAL CONNECTORS PKG(10) EA 3.29

525-8450 Male Red
525-8451 Male Green
525-8452 Male Orange
525-8453 Male White
525-8454 Male Black
525-8455 Male Blue
525-8456 Male Gray
525-8457 Male Brown
525-8458 Male Yellow
525-8460 Female Red
525-8461 Female Green
525-8462 Female Orange
525-8463 Female White
525-8464 Female Black
525-8465 Female Blue
525-8466 Female Gray
525-8467 Female Brown
525-8468 Female Yellow

UTAH PACIFIC

CONSTANT LIGHTING KITS

Reversing headlight and back-up light. Constant light for numberboards, cab lights, etc. Kit includes diodes and polarity board. Less light bulbs.

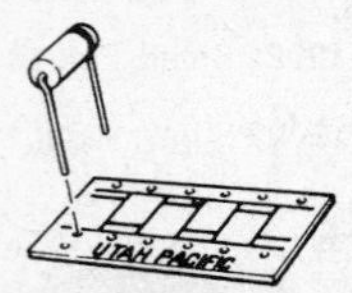

755-96 Locomotive **5.95**

755-66 Non-Directional **4.00**

VOLLMER

IMPORTED FROM GERMANY BY WALTHERS

LIGHTING ACCESSORIES

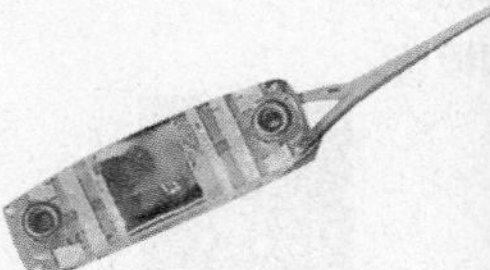

770-6550 Lighting Strip 2-Socket **8.99**

FLASHING BARRICADE KITS

652-1501 7.95
Includes prepainted orange and white barricade assembly, wire, 1 x 1" circuit board and yellow LED. Makes one operating and five dummy units.

652-1505 19.95
Includes circuit and materials to construct 5 operational Flashing Barricades. Each barricade will flash independently, but in a specific sequence. Use of two or more FBK-5 kits to construct a complete construction scene will result in a seemingly random flash sequence among all the barricades.

FLASHING HIGHWAY SIGN KIT

652-1520 14.95
Includes materials and circuit to construct one operational diamond shaped highway warning sign with dual alternating yellow flashing lamps. The sign can be assembled in a number of ways to duplicate most prototype situations. Pre-printed yellow and black signboards in a large variety of styles are included. The FS-1 requires a 9 volt DC power source or the CIRCUITRON PS-3 may be used to power the FS-1 directly from a power pack.

STOP SIGNS

Post mounted, scale sized sign kit includes pre-assembled electronic flasher circuit. 9 volt DC operation. May be battery powered, or Circuitron PS-3 to power from power-pack. Circuit can flash up to 3 additional signs.

652-1525 With Red Light & Flashing Circuit Kit **14.95**
652-1526 With Red Light Flashing Circuit Pre-assembled **22.95**
652-1528 With Red LED-No Flasher Kit **6.95**
652-1529 With Red LED-Pre-assembled **12.95**

PLASTRUCT

FIBRE OPTICS

Can be used for lighting building interiors and exteriors, street lights, signs and much more. Clear Acrylic and Styrene lamination provides high quality illumination.

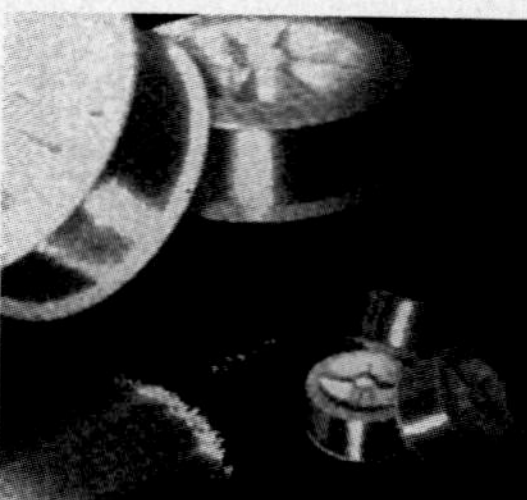

570-92501 .010" O.D. x 12' pkg(10) **5.50**
570-92502 .020" O.D. x 12' pkg(5) **6.50**
570-92503 .030" O.D. x 12' pkg(4) **7.50**
570-92504 .040" O.D. x 12' pkg(2) **8.50**
570-92505 .060" O.D. x 12' **12.50**
570-92551 Jacketed Multi-Strand .010" x 6' **20.00**

SCALE SHOPS

Make your models more realistic with this assortment of miniature electronic supplies!

We have worked closely with this manufacturer to provide accurate delivery information at the time this catalog was published. Items listed in blue ink may not be available at all times. Current delivery information, along with a list of in-stock products for this line, can be found on our Web site at www.walthers.com.

LIGHTING

SUPER CONSTANT LIGHTING UNITS

Add NI-CAD battery powered lights to cars or locos with these lighting units. These units charge a battery which provides power for the bulb.

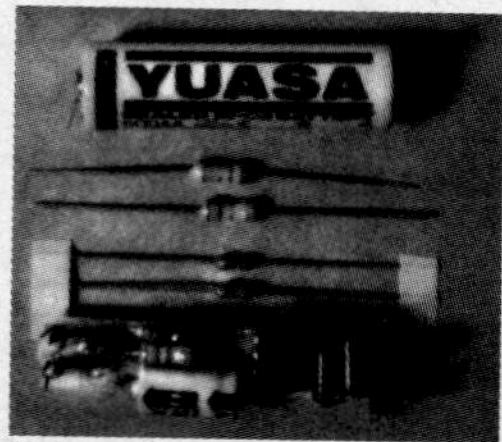

649-7060 LM317T 3.49
649-7061 With LM317T Assembled 15.98
649-7065 Kit **6.98**
649-7066 Assembled **25.95**
649-7076 #7075, Less Battery Assembled 23.95

CROSSING FLASHER

649-7010 Kit 3.98
649-7011 Assembled 13.98
649-7013 Magnets for Engines #7012, 4048 3.98

CONTROL UNITS

Requires #7028 or #7029.

MARS LIGHT

649-7030 Kit 6.98
649-7031 Assembled 17.98

STROBE/F.R.E.D

649-7040 Kit 4.98
649-7041 Assembled **15.98**
649-7042 Unit 1.5V Bulb Assembled 15.98

WIRE

649-4242 24 AWG **6.98**
649-4243 Flexible 24AWE (red) pkg(10') **6.98**
649-4245 6' Five Conductor Flexible Cable 8.98

CONNECTORS

Miniature-size multi-pin connectors feature gold-plated contacts for reliable operation.

MINIATURE

649-3020 2-Pin **1.49**
649-3030 3-Pin **1.98**
649-3040 4-Pin **2.98**
649-3200 20-Pin **13.98**

SUB-MINIATURE

649-3420 2-Pin **1.98**
649-3430 3-Pin **2.98**
649-3440 4-Pin **3.98**
649-3442 20-Pin **18.98**

CONNECTOR CLIP REPLACEMENT KIT

649-6015 pkg(6) **1.98**
For Athearn engines, 1 set.

649-6025 Reverse Loop Control Kit **7.98**

DIODES

50 PIV EA .98

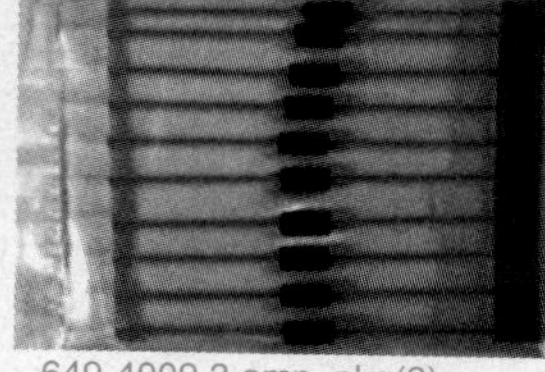

649-4009 3 amp, pkg(3)
649-4010 1 amp, pkg(10)

CONSTANT/DIRECTIONAL LIGHTING DIODES KIT

649-7051 1.98
Rear light on and headlight dims in reverse.

LEDS EA .98

.085" DIAMETER x.115" HIGH
649-5030 Red
649-5031 Green

Limited Quantity Available
649-5032 Yellow

R-Y-G
649-5049 5mm Diameter
649-5110 Right Angle each

3MM DIAMETER PKG(2)
649-5080 Red
649-5090 Green
649-5100 Yellow
649-5105 Orange

5MM DIAMETER PKG(2)
649-5106 Red
649-5107 Green
649-5108 Yellow
649-5109 Orange

T1 3MM LED
649-5040 Blue pkg(12) **3.49**

MOUNTING CLIPS PKG(10) EA 1.98

649-5132 T1-3/4 LEDs

BULBS

MICRO MINI BULB WITHOUT INSULATORS

649-5021 1.5V, .052" dia pkg(2) **1.39**

SWITCHES

MINIATURE TOGGLE

649-4049 SPST 2.19
649-4050 SPDT **2.79**

SPDT SLIDES EA .98

649-4052 Miniature
649-4053 Sub-Miniature

SUBMINIATURE TOGGLES EA 2.98

649-4060 DPDT/CO
649-4070 DPDT

HEAT SHRINK TUBING

PKG(12") BLACK

649-4501 3/64" dia **1.39**
649-4502 1/16" dia **1.49**
649-4503 1/8" dia **1.69**
649-4504 3/16" dia **1.89**
649-4505 3/32" dia **1.59**
649-4600 Assortment **2.98**
4" of each listed above.

PKG(12") RED

649-4601 3/64" dia **1.39**
649-4602 1/16" dia **1.49**
649-4603 1/8" dia **1.69**
649-4604 3/16" dia **1.89**
649-4605 3/32" dia **1.59**
649-4700 Assortment **2.98**
4" of each listed above.

MISCELLANEOUS

POWER REGULATOR

649-7028 Assembled 14.98
649-7029 Kit 3.98

MARS/PYLE/BEACON SLOW

649-7032 Kit 7.98
649-7033 Assembled 18.98

PHOSPHOR BRONZE SHEET

649-8003 1-5/8 x 6 x .003" **3.98**
649-8008 1-5/8 x 6 x .088" **5.98**

NorthWest Short Line

12 VOLT CAN TYPE MOTORS

These high precision heavy duty motors, with skewed 5 pole armatures, are suitable for all scales from O to N. They have a high efficiency (low battery drain) with high torque/speed characteristics, plus silence and maintenance free operation. Fully enclosed cylindrical type. Mounting screws (packed with motor) must not be inserted more than 2mm into motor case. Uses long life ceramic & ferrite magnets.

Note: All dimensions on the chart are in millimeters.

*203279 Can Motor has double shafts to serve as a replacement in Tenshado or AHM regeared locos. This motor is designed to perform 70% faster than a standard 20 x 32 motor.

12 VOLT DC FLAT CAN MOTORS

Flat sides permit more power in narrow spaces.

53-183349 Single Shaft 18 x 23 x 33mm **31.95**
53-183359 Double Shaft 18 x 23 x 33mm **33.95**
53-183519 Double Shaft 18 x 23 x 36mm **31.95**
53-183679 Double 15mm Shaft 18 x 23 x 36mm **31.95** ***NEW***

BRUSH CAP EA 5.50

53-100209 20mm diameter
For can motors only.

OPEN FRAME MOTOR

53-101539 Open Frame Motor **20.95**
Has a double shaft.

MOTOR MOUNT

53-1996 1.00
Sticky plastic for temporary or permanent attachment.

12 VOLT DC FLAT CAN MOTORS

Number	Price	Width	Length	Shaft Dia.	Shaft Length	RPM	Amps
122539	32.95	12	25	1.5	15	17,800	0.04
123039	32.95	12	30	1.5	15	15,000	0.04
142039	29.95	14	20	1.5	15	28,000	0.24
142539	30.95	14	25	1.5	15	17,000	0.05
162059	24.95	16	20	2	15	16,800	0.14
163049	26.95	16	29.5	2	25	14,900	0.10
163059	26.95	16	29.5	2	15	14,900	0.10
202739	28.95	20	26.5	2.4	15	9,100	0.10
203229	30.95	20	31.5	2.4	25	9,800	0.10
203239	30.95	20	31.5	2.4	15	9,800	0.10
203279	25.95	20	31.5	2.4	15	16,500	
222439	22.95	22	24	2.4	15	17,000	0.16
223139	25.95	22	31	2.4	15	11,000	0.11
223619	25.95	22	36	2.4	15	9,800	0.075
224039	26.95	22	40	2.4	15	9,500	0.075
282419	23.95	28	24	2.4	15	9,800	0.13
283019	25.95	28	30	2.4	15	8,200	0.09
283519	26.95	28	35	2.4	15	7,000	0.1
284019	27.95	28	40	2.4	15	8,300	0.01

SHAFT/AXLE STOCK EA 1.00

Precision ground steel rod for shafts, axles and worm shafts. Each package includes one 6" length.

53-20154 O.D 1.5mm
53-20204 O.D 2.0mm
53-20244 O.D 2.4mm
Often used in place of 3/32" in import models.

53-20254 O.D. 2.5mm
53-20304 O.D. 3.0mm
Used in place of 1/8" in import models and axles.

53-20624 O.D 1/16"
53-20934 O.D 3/32"
Common as motor shaft size.

53-21254 O.D. 1/8"
Loco axles, some motor shafts in US models.

EA 1.50

53-20404 O.D 4.0mm
53-20504 O.D 5.0mm
53-20584 O.D 5.8mm
53-20604 O.D 6.0mm
53-21564 O.D 5/32"
53-21874 O.D 3/16"
53-22504 O.D 1/4"

UNIVERSAL DRIVELINE COUPLER SETS EA 2.95

Ball type universal driveline coupling for use as double universal or as two single joints. Sets with the same ball sizes may be combined to couple different shaft sizes. Easy to install press-fit or cup can be drilled and tapped for set screw. Made of celcon acetal engineering plastic. 2.4mm fits 3/32".

53-4956 Universal Shaft 5/32-1/8"
53-4966 Universal Shaft 5/32-3"
53-4976 Universal Shaft 5/32, 2.4mm

REWHEEL KIT

53-1106 F/AHM E8 **12.95**

72' DP STEEL WORMS

.1875 O.D worms match gears listed above.

53-100006 3/32" Bore **4.00**
53-104006 1.5mm Bore **4.49**
53-105006 2mm Bore **4.50**

Universal Driveline Couplers

No.	Primary Cups Shaft	Add'l Cups	Horned Ball Shaft	Ball Dia.	Price
4806	1/8"	None	2.4mm	3/16"	1.95
4816	2.4mm	None	2.4mm	3/16"	1.95
4826	2.0mm	1.5, 2.4mm	2.0mm	1/8"	2.95
4836	1.5mm	2.0, 2.4mm	1.5mm	3/32"	2.95
4846	2.4mm	2.4mm	2.0mm	1/8"	2.95
4856	1.2mm	1.5, 2.0mm	1.5mm	3/32"	2.95
4866	3.0mm	None	2.4mm	3/16"	1.95
4876	1.5mm	1.5mm	1.5mm	3/32"	2.95
4886	2.4mm	2.0mm			2.95
4896	2.0mm	2.0mm			2.95
4906	2.4mm				2.95
4916	2.0mm	2.4mm			2.95

NorthWest Short Line

FLANGED BEARINGS

BRASS PKG(8) EA 2.95
53-3546 3/32 x 1/8"
53-3556 9/64 x 5/32" for WSM K-37

BRONZE PKG(2) EA 1.50
53-3566 2.0mm x 1/8"
53-3576 1.5mm x 4.0mm
53-3586 2.4mm x 3.9mm
53-3596 2.0mm x 3.9mm
53-3606 1.5mm x 3.9mm
53-3616 1/8 x 3/16"
53-3636 1.5mm x 2.5mm

PILLOW BLOCK

53-3706 2.4 Hole **2.50**

GEARBOXES

Idler and standard gearboxes and a "high-rise" double idler to allow horizontal motor installation in the boiler. Power is transferred to driven axle via quiet, slow speed worm gears.

53-1366 28:1 Double Idler, 3.0mm axle **19.95**
53-1396 28:1 Idler, 3.0mm axle **17.95**
53-1406 28:1, 3.0mm axle **15.95**
53-1416 28:1, Doubler Idler, 1/8" axle **19.95**
53-1426 28:1, Doubler Idler, 1/8" axle **17.95**
53-1436 28:1, 1/8" axle **15.95**
53-1466 28:1, Idler, 2.4mm axle **17.95**
53-1476 28:1, 2.4mm axle **15.95**
53-1506 36:1 Idler, 3.0mm axle **17.95**
53-1516 36:1, 3.0mm axle **15.95**
53-1536 36:1 Idler, 1/8" axle **17.95**
53-1546 36:1, 1/8" axle **15.95**
53-1736 50-1 Compound for HOn3, 1.5mm Shaft; 3.0mm Axle **31.95** ***NEW***
53-2116 14:1, 2.4/3.0mm axle **12.95**
53-2216 Transfer Gearbox **15.95**
53-2236 Transfer Gearbox, 1:89, 2.4mm axle **14.95**
53-2246 Transfer Case, 1:1 2.4mm axle **19.95**
53-2406 28:1 Idler, 3.0mm axle **18.95**
53-2416 28:1,3.0mm axle **15.95**
53-2426 28:1 Idler, 1/8" axle **18.95**
53-2436 28:1, 1/8" axle **15.95**
53-2446 28:1 Idler, 4.0mm axle (5/32") **18.95**
53-2456 28:1, 4.0mm axle (5/32") **15.95**

72' DP GEARS EACH 4.00

All bores are light press fit. All gears are machine cut, not injection molded.

BRASS 3.0MM BORE(.118")

Number of Teeth	Spur Gear	Worm Gear	Reverse Worm Gear	O.D.
15	177156	117156	147156	0.24
20	177206	117206	147206	0.306
24	177246	177246	147246	0.361
30	177306	117306	147306	0.444
36	177366	147366	147366	0.527
40	177406	117406	147406	0.583

DELRIN 3.0MM BORE(.118")

Number of Teeth	Spur Gear	Worm Gear	Reverse Worm Gear	O.D.
15	187156	127156	157156	0.24
20	187206	127206	157206	0.306
24	187246	127246	157246	0.361
30	187306	127306	157306	0.444
36	187366	127366	157366	0.527
40	187406	127406	157406	0.583

BRASS 3/32" BORE(.0937")

Number of Teeth	Spur Gear	Worm Gear	Reverse Worm Gear	O.D.
10	170106	110106	140106	0.178
15	170156	110156	140156	0.24
20	170206	110206	140206	0.306
24	170246	110246	140246	0.361
30	170306	110306	140306	0.444
36	170366	110366	140366	0.527
40	170406	110406	140406	0.583

DELRIN 33/2" BORE(.0937")

Number of Teeth	Spur Gear	Worm Gear	Reverse Worm Gear	O.D.
15	180156	120156	150156	0.24
20	180206	120206	150206	0.306
24	180246	120246	150246	0.361
30	180306	120306	150306	0.444
36	180366	120366	150366	0.527
40	180406	120406	150406	0.583

KMT BRASS TOWER GEARS

Will also fit Tenshodo diesels and some others.

EA 4.00
53-776096 9T
53-776106 10T
53-776246 24T
53-776096 26T
53-776136 13T
53-776146 14T
53-776156 15T
53-776176 17T
53-776186 18T
53-776196 19T
53-776216 21T

PKG(6) 16.20
53-776116 11T
53-776126 12T
53-776166 16T
53-776206 20T
53-776226 22T
53-776236 23T

KMT TOWER GEAR SERVICE

53-1056 59.95

THRUST WASHERS

For miscellaneous fine tuning application. All slip fit dimensions listed.

Number	I.D.	O.D.	Thickness	Metal	Pkg	Price
1004	3/32"	3/16"	.005"	bronze	10	0.90
11004	3/32"	3/16"	.005"	bronze	100	4.50
11034	3/32"	3/16"	.010"	bronze	100	4.50
1034	3/32"	3/16"	.010"	bronze	10	0.90
1064	1/8"	3/16"	.010"	bronze	10	0.90
11064	1/8"	3/16"	.010"	bronze	100	4.50
1084	2.0mm	3.0mm	.010"	bronze	10	0.90
11084	2.0mm	3.0mm	.010"	bronze	100	4.50
1104	1/16"	3.0mm	.010"	bronze	10	0.90
11104	1/16"	3.0mm	.010"	bronze	100	4.50
1124	.064"	.120"	.020"	nylon	10	0.90
11124	.060"	.120"	.020"	nylon	100	5.50
1144	3/32"	1/4"	.016"	bronze	10	0.90
11144	3/32"	1/4"	.016"	bronze	100	4.50
1164	4"	4"	7"	bronze	50	4.50
11164	4"	4"	7"	bronze	50	4.50
1174	5"	8"	.010"	bronze	50	4.50
1184	6"	6"	.010"	bronze	50	4.50
1194	2"	2"	4.2"	bronze	50	4.50

NorthWest Short Line

GEAR ALIGNER EA 6.95

A gear truing tool designed to check and minimize gear wobbling which can occur when installing gears on axles and shafts. Can sometimes straighten wobbling gear.

53-324 For 2.4mm (3/32") Axles and Shafts
53-334 For 3.0mm Axles and Shafts
53-384 For 1/8" Axles and Shafts

GEARBOX INPUT SHAFT CONVERSION EA 5.00

53-1446 2.0mm Right Hand
53-1456 1.5mm Right Hand
Converts wormshaft bore size (double idler and non-idler types only).

53-1646 2.0mm Left Hand
53-1656 1.5mm Left Hand
Converts worm shaft bore size for idler styles 1396, 1426, 1506, 1536 and 1466 (idler style only)

HI-LOW GEARBOXES

For quiet HO Mallets and articulated locomotives. Features a quiet direct line drive system, molded of celcon acetal plastic with bronze worm shaft bearings, steel worm and machined brass gears. Eliminates noisy tower spur gears.

53-1486 28:1, 3mm Axle **29.95**
53-1496 28:1, 1/8" Axle **29.95**
53-1586 36:1, 3mm Axle **31.95**
53-1596 36:1, 1/8" Axle **31.95**
53-2486 28:1, 1/8" Axle .04 Module **29.95**

GEAR & RE-GEAR SETS

KMT DIESEL RE-GEAR KIT

53-1006 4-Axle **18.95**
53-1016 6-Axle **24.95**

SPEED REDUCTION GEAR

53-1206 Benson Shay **12.95**
53-1216 PC Shay **12.95**
53-3126 42% Reduction, AHM 0-8-0 **8.95**
Vertical motor shaft type only.

53-3136 AHM 4-8-4 **8.95**
53-3076 AHM Hudson, Pacific **9.95**

PFM SHAY

53-1236 (7T) 2mm Bore **15.50**
53-1246 (12T) 2.6mm Bore **15.00**
53-1266 (7T) 2.4mm Bore **15.00**
53-1276 (7T) 2.4mm Bore **14.00**

MINI GEARBOXES 50-1 RATIO EA 25.95 (UNLESS NOTED)

53-1706 2.4 x 1.5mm
53-1716 2.0 x 1.5mm
53-1726 1.5 x 1.5mm
53-1736 3.0 x 1.5mm **31.95**

MDC LOCOS

53-1806 72:1 for Small Motor, 2.0mm Shaft **16.95**
53-1816 45:1 for Small Motor, 2.0mm Shaft **16.95**
53-1826 72:1 for Large Motor, 3/32" Shaft **16.95**
53-1836 45:1 for Large Motor, 3/32" Shaft **16.95**
53-1886 Gear Upgrade Kit - Bull Gear **10.95**

HON3 MDC

53-1846 14.95
Uses existing motor.

53-1856 44.95
Includes 1225 can motor.

53-3056 26T Idler Gear Westside Models **5.50**

PARTIAL RE-GEAR KIT FOR MDC

53-1866 2-Truck Shay **19.95**
53-1876 3-Truck Shay **24.95**

AHM

53-3086 Mikado **8.95**
53-3096 0-4-0 & 0-6-0T **8.95**
53-3106 USRA 0-6-0 **9.95**
53-3016 2-8-4 **7.95**
And larger, except 4-8-4.

SAMHONGSA

53-3226 E-B 22T pkg(2) **9.95**
53-3236 SD38-2 22T pkg(2) **9.95**
53-3246 22T pkg(2) **8.95**
53-3256 21T pkg(2) **9.95**
53-3266 25T pkg(2) **9.95**
53-3276 36T pkg(2) **8.95**
53-3296 10T pkg(4) **12.95**

KEYSTONE/SAMHONGSA SHAY

53-3386 pkg(2) **8.95**

FOR WSM

53-3346 E-Unit **19.95**

REPLACEMENT GEAR PKG(2)

53-3396 For Keystone/ Samhongsa Shay (27T) **8.95**
53-3336 21T Alco, SHS **8.95**
53-3356 15T Alco, SHS **9.95**
53-3206 Mantua **8.95**

IDLER WORM GEAR

53-3366 Keystone/Samhongsa GP7, 28T pkg(2) **9.95**
53-3376 Samhongsa H15-44/GP7, 23T pkg(2) **8.95**

SPUR GEAR FOR SAMHONGSA PKG(2) EA 9.95

53-3416 SD38-2, 14T
53-3426 SD38-2, 15T
53-3436 RSD-15/DL-600B, 15T
53-3446 20T
53-3456 RSD-15/DL600B, 21T
53-3476 RS-3/RS-32, 21T

SPUR GEAR FOR ORIENTAL

53-3466 F3, 20T pkg(2) **9.95**

REVERSE WORM GEAR PKG(2) 8.95

(By Special Order Only)

53-3486 For Hallmark Whitcomb, 25T
53-3496 Hi-angle for Samhansa Diesels, 15T

ARMATURE EA 8.95

Double-shaft Sagami 5-pole armature upgrades the Rivarossi 154 x 20mm 3 pole motor used in N Scale articulated locos and Atlas 4-6-2.

53-100869 For #101539 Motor
53-100889 For #101519 Motor

ATHEARN RE-POWER KITS

Athearn diesel re-motor kit with Sagami motor and NWSL flywheel allows slower, smoother speed, more power with loco amp draw (run more locos at a time) and no need to re-gear. Plugs directly to Athearn universals.

53-1614 All But Narrow Hood **34.95**
53-1624 Large **34.95**
53-1634 SD40-2 **36.95**
Includes two precision turned brass flywheels and shafts bushed to fit the existing Athearn couplings.

53-1654 Switcher **36.95**
Includes #1833 motor, NWSL flywheel & universal couplings.

ATLAS RE-POWER KITS

53-1664 FP7 **34.95**

POWER SYSTEM PLANNING KIT

53-26 3.00
Consists of translucent sheets of motor, gearbox and drive unit outlines printed at actual size. Sheets can be overlaid on scale drawings of the model to determine fit, position and location of components.

KEYSTONE DRIVE KITS

Kit will convert the dummy Keystone Shay to a powered version; all four axles.

53-12086 HO (fits KLW 105) **69.95**
53-12096 HOn3 (fits KLW 153) **69.95**

SAGAMI MOTOR INFORMATION BOOKLET

53-9 .50

RIBBONRAIL

PILOT LIGHTS

Compact panel mounting. Features all-brass housing, colored lens and simple wiring. Requires 5/16" 7.9cm mounting hole and will fit panels up to 3/8" 9.5cm thick.

14V W/GRAIN-OF-WHEAT BULB EA 2.20

Includes rubber retainer and clear grain-of-wheat bulb. Operates on 12-16V DC.

170-141 Red Lens
170-142 Amber Lens
170-143 Green Lens
170-144 Blue Lens
170-145 White Lens

14V W/AUTOMOTIVE BULB EA 2.40

Includes spring retainer and clear automotive type bulb. One wire grounded, brass, operates on 12-16V DC.

170-151 Red Lens
170-152 Amber Lens
170-153 Green Lens
170-154 Blue Lens
170-155 White Lens

PILOT LIGHT HOUSING EA 1.60

Includes rubber retainer, bulbs sold separately.

170-161 Red Lens
170-162 Amber Lens
170-163 Green Lens
170-164 Blue Lens
170-165 White Lens

MINIATURE SWITCHES

Functions as a single pole switch or as a momentary contact pushbutton. Both are avilable in press mount (simply drill hole and tap switch in place) for panels over 3/16" thick or in screw mount (with ring and nut retainer) for thinner panels.

MIDGET TYPE

7/16" 11.1cm diameter

170-1 Press Mount **1.25**
170-2 Screw Mount **2.75**

MINI TYPE

1/4" 6.3cm diameter.

170-3 Press Mount **1.00**
170-4 Screw Mount w/Set Screws **2.50**
Includes 4/40 set screws and allen wrench.

FLYWHEELS

Dimensions from left to right are: Outside Diameter, Length and Hole & Shaft bore.

DUALS

170-52 11/16" - 5/8"- 3/32" **6.00**
170-53 11/16" -5/8" - 1/8" **6.00**
170-54 3/4" - 19/32" 1/8" **6.00**
170-56 15/16" - 3/8" - 1/8" **7.00**
170-57 1" - 3/8" x 1/8" **7.00**
170-58 1" - 5/8" - 2mm **7.00**
170-59 1" - 5/8" - 3/32" **8.00**
170-60 1" - 5/8" - 1/8" **8.00**

SINGLES

170-61 11/16" - 5/8"- 3/32" **3.25**
170-62 11/16" -5/8" - 1/8" **3.25**
170-63 3/4" - .600" 1/8" **3.25**
170-64 15/16" - 3/8" - 1/8" **3.75**
170-65 1" - 3/8" x 1/8" **3.75**
170-66 1" - 5/8" - 2mm **4.25**
170-67 1" - 5/8" - 3/32" **4.25**
170-68 1" - 5/8" - 1/8" **4.25**

STATE TOOL & DIE CO.

WIRE TIES - REUSABLE

661-26512 4-1/2" pkg(30) **4.50**

661-26519 3-1/2" pkg(30) **3.50**

IMPORTED FROM AUSTRIA
BY WALTHERS

MOTORS

CAN

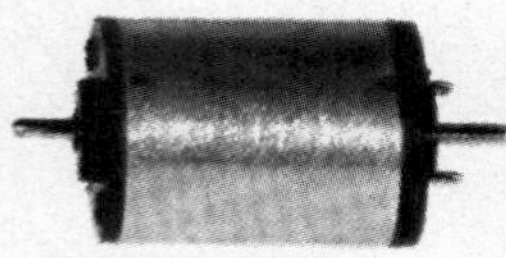

625-85029 39.99
Five-pole, 14V DC, Single-End Shaft Flat

OPEN FRAME EA 18.99 (UNLESS NOTED)

17,000 RPM, 85mA, 21 x 14mm.

625-85020 Double-End Shaft
625-85033 Double Shaft 33 x 20mm
625-85035 Single Shaft 33 x 20mm **39.99**
625-85018 17,000 RPM, 100mA Double End Shaft 17 x 14mm

SWITCHES

Each switch unit contains four single push-buttons or switches. The switch unit intended for turnout control has an additional position indication return, which is a true return indication and does not require additional cabling. Manual operation at the turnout will produce a correct red or green indication.

625-10520 w/Return Indication **28.99**
625-10521 2-Position w/o Return Indication **19.99**
625-10522 Push-button **16.99**
625-10524 2-Position w/ Center Off Switch **19.99**

LEVER SWITCHES EA 4.49

For signals, alternating power feed to track sections.

Limited Quantity Available
625-10503 On-Off Switch (blue)
625-10504 2-Way (yellow)

SWITCH CONTROL 2/3-WAY

625-10526 28.99
Two-position switch with return indication for single slips and symmetrical 3-way turnouts. These two turnout designs require, if properly controlled, the exclusion of one of the four possible turnout positions. The switch 10526 offers a definite control of the three permissible turnout settings.

POWER PACKS

TRANSFORMER 40VA

625-10718 94.99

CONTROL UNIT 15V

625-10719 69.99

CIRCUIT CONTROL UNIT

Limited Quantity Available
625-10700 84.99
To be used with universal transformers-continuous voltage regulation & polarity reverse with "O" position.

ACCESSORIES

PLUG CONNECTORS

Limited Quantity Available
625-10601 pkg(6) **2.49**

BULBS

Limited Quantity Available
625-10026 12V Bayonet, Short **2.49**

RELAYS

625-10019 Universal Relay **18.99**

1-CONDUCTOR WIRE PKG(6) EA 19.99

10 meter roll.

625-10630 Black
625-10631 Brown
625-10632 Red
625-10633 Orange
625-10634 Yellow
625-10635 Green
625-10636 Blue
625-10637 Violet
625-10638 Green

TIMEWELL
PRECISION FLYWHEELS

FLYWHEELS

These Precision Flywheels may be used as Athearn replacement parts or on other motors. OD=outside diameter, L=length, SD=shaft diameter.

712-101 2.50
For: Alco, Balboa, Trains, 2.25 Hallmark, Westside Imports, Athearn Hi-Fi (old). OD: 3/4", L: 3/8", SD: 3/32".

712-102 2.50
For: Suydam, Custom Brass Electrics. OD: 11/16", L: 3/8", SD: 3/32".

712-115 2.00
For: NWSL Can Motors. OD: 1/2", L: 3/16", SD: 1.5mm.

712-120 2.50
For: NWSL Can Motors. OD: 5/8", L: 5/16", SD: 2.0mm.

712-124 2.50
For: NWSL Can Motors. OD: 3/4", L: 5/16", SD: 2.4mm.

712-130 3.25
For: NWSL Can Motors. OD: 7/8", L: 3/8", SD: 2.4mm.

712-135 3.75
For: NWSL Can Motors. OD: 1", L: 3/8", SD: 2.4mm.

712-1031 3.00
For: Athearn U28, U30, U33, PA1. OD: 5/8", L: 5/8", SD: 1/8".

712-1032 3.00
For: Athearn F7, GP9, SD9, RDC, GP30, FP35, and BART. OD: 3/4", L: 1/2", SD: 1/8".

712-1033 2.50
For: Athearn S12, SW1500. OD: 3/4", L: 5/16", SD: 1/8".

712-1034 3.00
For: Athearn, F45, FP45, SDP40, SD45. OD: 3/4", L: 3/4", SD: 1/8".

TRAIN TRONICS

SWITCHES

REED SWITCH & MAGNET

723-406 6.95
Provides momentary switch that is activated by magnets placed on bottom of train. Use to operate various track detection systems, controls and signals.

PUSH-BUTTON

723-407 6.95
SPST - normally open, momentary, mounts in 5/16" hole. Kit contains 4 switches.

LIGHTING

CONSTANT LIGHT KITS

Installed in any HO or N Scale engine, the headlight remains "on" even when engine is stopped. 102 contains 2 bulbs: may be used for cab light & 1 headlight or dual headlight engines.

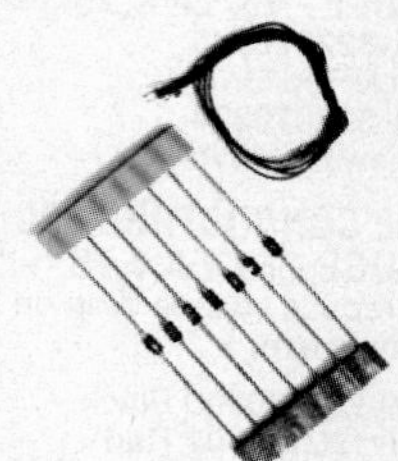

723-101 One Bulb **4.25**
723-102 Two Bulb **4.50**

REVERSING CONSTANT LIGHT KIT

723-103 Two Bulb **4.95**
Rear light operates when reversing. Front headlight stays on without dimming as on the real railroads. Rear light will go out when loco again moves forward.

REPLACEMENT BULBS

723-104 1.5V For #101,102,103 **3.95**
723-108 12V-.080 Amps .2 Diameter 6" Leads pkg(3) **3.40**
723-107 12V GOW Red pkg(3) **3.95**
723-109 12V-.27 Amps Bulbs Flasher Type, Min Bayonet Base pkg(2) **4.40**
723-110 12V-.2 Amps Bulbs Min. Bayonet Base, Clear pkg(3) **3.30**

LIGHT EMITTING DIODES

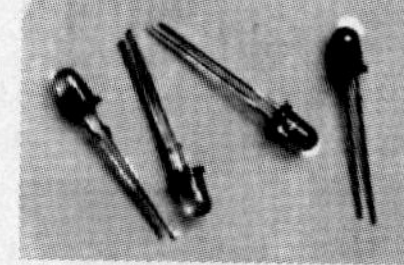

No heat, low current drain, low voltage, .120 diameters.

PKG(4) EA 3.50
723-402 Red
723-403 Green
723-404 Yellow

FIBER OPTICS

Fiber optics can be used in dwarfs, street lights, airplane marker lights and railroad block signals to name a few applications. 401 optics can be used with Train Tronics Chase Light Kit #201 to make larger illuminated or animated signs. EA pkg(25').

723-401 .020" Diameter **8.95**
723-413 .030" Diameter **8.95**
723-414 .040" Diameter **12.95**

TAURUS PRODUCTS/ TROUT CREEK ENG.

POWER PICK-UP

707-2001 Track Slider Power Pick-Up System pkg(4) **3.00**

TOMAR INDUSTRIES

CONTACT WIPERS

81-825 5.95
Package contains enough materials to make approximately eight wipers. Includes circuit board material, phophor bronze, screws and hook-up wire.

Western Rail Products

LIGHTING KITS EA 10.95

757-101 End of Train Flasher w/Batteries
Flashing red LED, electronic circuit, on/off switch and batteries included.

757-103 Diesel Engine Strobe Flasher w/Batteries
Kit includes flashing yellow strobe LED, electronic control circuit, switch and batteries.

757-105 Caboose Flashing, Warning Lights
Kit comes completely wired and ready for installation.

SWITCHES

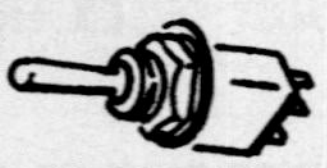

757-401 SPDT pkg(2) **4.95**
Single-pole double-throw miniature toggle switch. On-Off-On positions. Rated 6 amps of 125V.

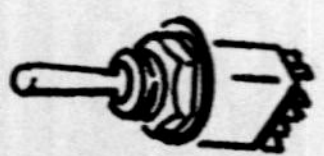

757-402 DPDT pkg(2) **5.95**
Double-pole double-throw miniature toggle switch. On-Off-On positions. Rated 6 amps of 125V.

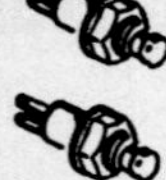

757-403 Switch Push Button pkg(2) **1.95**
Miniature push button switches. Momentary-on push buttons.

BATTERIES

757-902 pkg(2) **1.95**
Small "watch type" batteries are replacements for original batteries sold with EOT flasher (#101) Diesel Engine Strobe Light (#103) and the Caboose Flasher (#105).

WIRE WORKS

WIRE

A wide range of electrical wire easily adaptable to any sort of miniature electronics. Features stranded for flexibility, tinned for soldering ease, large selection for color coding, application guide on each package, and realistic quantities.

ONE CONDUCTOR - #22 GAUGE - 50' EA 3.00

851-122070500 Black
851-122070501 Brown
851-122070502 Red
851-122070503 Orange
851-122070504 Yellow
851-122070505 Green
851-122070506 Blue
851-122070509 White

ONE CONDUCTOR - #22 GAUGE - 90' EA 4.75

851-122070900 Black
851-122070902 Red
851-122070905 Green
851-122070909 White

TWO CONDUCTOR - #22 GAUGE - 30' EA 4.75

851-222070300 Black/Red
851-222070304 Yellow/Blue
851-222070305 Green/Brown

THREE CONDUCTOR - #22 GAUGE - 23' EA 4.75

851-322070230 Black/Red/Green
851-322070234 Yellow/Blue/White

ONE CONDUCTOR - #20 GAUGE - 70' EA 4.75

To reduce voltage drop on HO layouts over 8".

851-120100700 Black
851-120100702 Red
851-120100704 Yellow
851-120100705 Green
851-120100706 Blue
851-120100709 White

TWO CONDUCTOR - #20 GAUGE - 25'

851-220100250 Black/Red **4.75**

HEAT SHRINK TUBING EA 2.00

Add extra protection around splices, exposed wires and connectors with heat shrinkable tubing. Simply slide over wire and heat with match, soldering iron or heat gun.

851-21062 1/16" shrinks to 1/32"
851-21093 3/32" shrinks to 3/64"
851-21125 1/8" shrinks to 1/16"
851-21187 3/16" shrinks to 3/32"
851-21250 1/4" shrinks to 1/8"

Yesterday, December 7, 1941....

By late afternoon of this dreadful Sunday, the nation's railroads are fighting back. Extra crews are called. By evening, the first troop trains are moving. Empty freight cars are readied for on-line customers. Trains are moving as fast as the dispatchers will allow. Southern Pacific is among the busiest - and most vulnerable - of the nation's railroads on this somber day.

Monday, December 7, 1942. Everything from staples to Sherman tanks hurries across SP rails this morning. Armed guards watch every junction, bridge, and yard - anywhere there's even a hint of potential trouble. With its connections to ship yards, oil refineries, piers and docks, aircraft plants and army and navy bases, the threat of an air attack is likely. So real is the threat that engines working the coast have their headlights shrouded to meet black-out regulations. Signals and switch lamps are shrouded too.

Even the "Daylight," SP's finest passenger train, is not immune. The mighty class GS-4 "Northerns" that pull these trains trade their colorful civilian scheme for drab black "fatigues." Much of the streamlined boiler casing is removed, making it easier to lubricate critical parts and shorten station shops.

And very likely, the engine wipers, hostlers and helpers out here on the "dawn patrol" are women.

Morning comes slowly through the fog, but the workload will not wait. Turning to meet the next assignment, GS-4 #4430 will soon join a parade of engines on the ready tracks, as a busy work day begins on Alden Armstrong's layout in Grand Junction, Colorado.

Models and Photo by Alden Armstrong

A "TRAINATORIAL"

Announcing the NEW Radio Controlled On-Board System from Aristo-Craft

Brought to You by "TATE"

The Aristo Train Engineer

Just in time for the new millennium, Aristo-Craft is introducing its state-of-the-art Radio Controlled On-Board System (#614-55000). Ease the handling of multiple train operation with the innovative, patented technology of Aristo-Craft.

This new system offers:

- **Easy Programming for Prototypical Operation**
- **Maximum Performance from Cutting Edge Digital Technology**
- **The Ultimate In Realistic Speed Control**
- **Clear Indication of Loco Direction and Speed**
- **Control Over Sound Volume**
- **And Much More!**

"Look Ma, No Wires!"

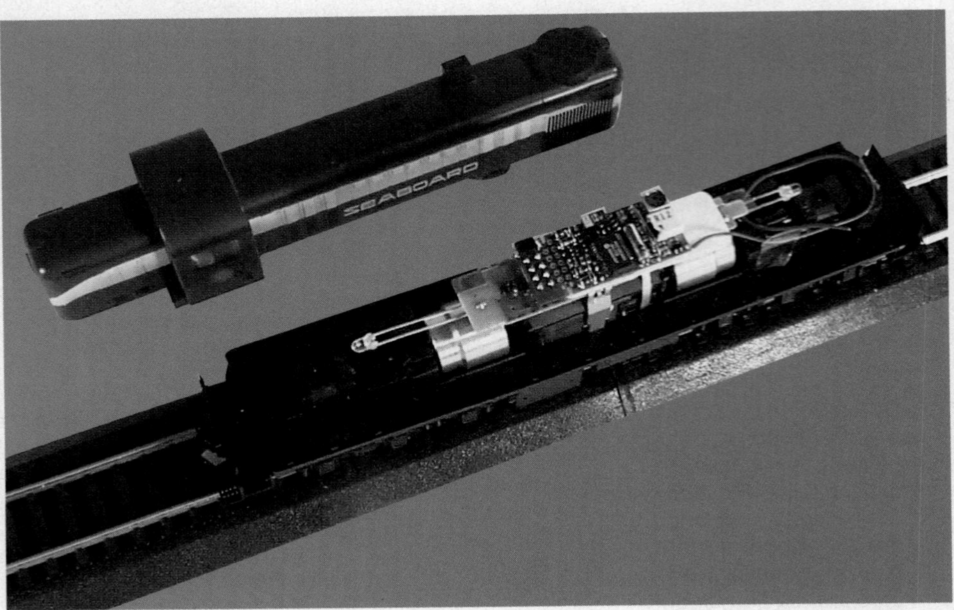

614-55001 Receiver
Locomotive Not Included

614-55003
75 MHz Transmitter
Only Preproduction sample shown, some details will vary.

614-55000 Combo Pack
TBA New
Start operations with this handy set which includes both the #55003 Transmitter and #55001 Receiver.

614-55001 Receiver Only
TBA New
Combination speed control and radio control receiver, easily installed in most motive power, uses the same socket as a DCC decoder.

614-55003 75 MHz Transmitter Only **TBA**
New
Extra hand-held unit allows each engineer to have his or her own wireless throttle controlling up to 10 frequencies. Great for operating sessions, club shows and other busy times. *NOTE: Output of 75 megahertz is suitable only for use in the United States and Canada.

Here's How Easy it is to Set Up

Simply plug the combination speed control and radio controlled receiver into your locomotive's DCC port, set your frequency, step back and control the action with the Aristo-Craft Hand Held Transmitter.

Together these two items form an impressive system that gives you the ability to operate up to ten locomotives independently of each other, either on the same track or on multiple tracks.

With Aristo-Craft's patented Seeker™ technology, changing frequencies is a breeze! No longer do you need to change crystals in order to set frequencies. All you need to do is place the Hand Held Transmitter within one foot of the locomotive and press the "code set" button on the transmitter. That's it! With the push of a button, you have just linked your loco to your transmitter. Nothing else needs to be done! Your trains will remember the last command given and will follow that command on "cruise control" until they are told to do otherwise. Up to ten different frequencies can be used at the same time.

Best of all, this new system is wireless! You can now enjoy the independence of a 100′ (33m) transmitter range and never have to worry about wires getting in the way. Finally, you can enjoy the best of DCC command with the liberating freedom of wireless technology.

AMPS

614-5450 4 Amp Deluxe **179.95**
Features include: high temperature protection, over current protection, built-in LED current display, power indicator light, binding post for easy connection, strong flame retardent plastic case and double insulation.

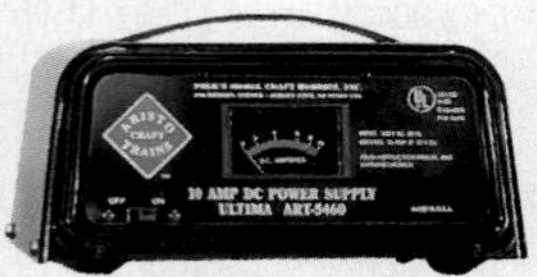

614-5460 Ultima 10 Amp Linear **149.95**
614-5461 Ultima 10 Amp Power Supply w/10 Channel Controller **219.95** *NEW*

THE TRAIN ENGINEER

Revolutionize your model railroad with this wireless walkaround throttle system. You'll be able to run trains and accessories from up to 300' away - with your current power pack and wiring!

The Original Train Engineer (614-5470) includes a special receiver which operates with your current power pack. Simply connect the receiver into the existing wiring between the pack and the track. No modifications to locos or cars are needed!

Now you're ready to run a train with the hand-held transmitter, which controls speed and direction by broadcasting a multi-directional, low-power FM signal (27 megahertz) to the receiver. Built-in Pulse-Code-Modulation (PCM) eliminates outside signal interference.

For more fun and easy remote control operations, add the Remote Accessory Unit (614-5474, sold separately) to run trackside turnouts, signals and lights with your Transmitter. Connect additional units to run up to 50 different accessories!

For club or show layouts, or just running trains with another person, additional receivers (614-5471) and Transmitters (614-5473) are available separately.

614-5470 Original Train Engineer Walkaround Control 2 Piece Set **189.95**
Includes Receiver and Hand-Held Transmitter.

614-5471 Original Train Engineer Additional Receiver Only **134.95**

614-5473 Original Train Engineer Transmitter (27 Megahertz) **99.95**

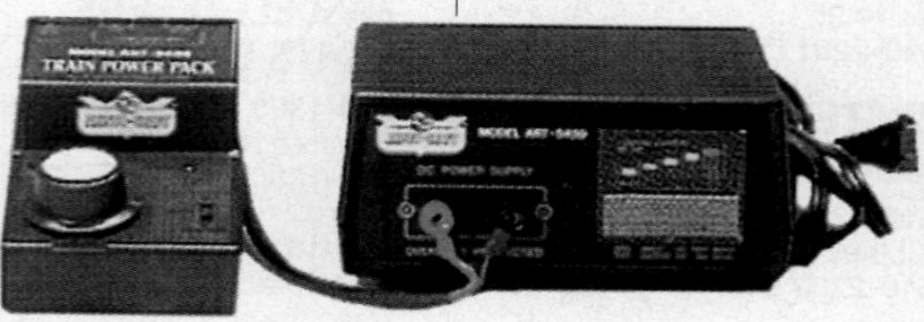

4 Amp Deluxe 610-5450

Train Engineer Walkaround Control Two-Piece Set 614-5470

614-5474 Original Train Engineer Remote Accessory Controller **69.95**
Operates up to five lights, turnouts or accessories; additional units can be combined to control up to 50 accessories.

614-5475 Original Train Engineer Accessory Receiver **79.95**
Designed for remote control of turnouts only. Operates up to five turnouts; additional units can be combined to control up to 50 turnouts.

614-5480 Basic DC/Train Engineer 2 Amp w/100' Range **99.95**
Simplified version of Train Engineer. A wireless radio control system for all DC electric trains. Includes one transmitter and one receiver.

614-5491 FM Radio Crystals-27 Megahertz 1 Pair **19.95**

614-5499 Cooling Fan for Receiver **14.95**
Increases airflow to keep interior components of Receiver (#614-5471; also included with #5470, both sold separately) cooler.

POWER PACKS

614-5400 1.8 Amp w/Pulse Width Control **59.95**
Perfect for those just starting out in the hobby. Features include: 1.8 amp and directional control, auto electronic circuit protection, power and over current indicator lights, constant voltage pulse width speed control and automatic electronic momentum circuit smooth operation.

614-5492 On Board RX and Transmitter **249.95**

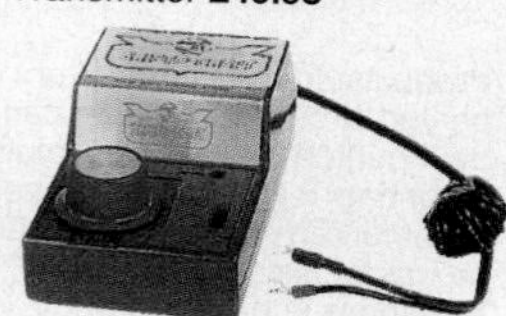

614-5401 Control Pack Adaptor For 10 Amp **79.95**
Convert your present power pack into a Pulse Width Control power pack. Features include: directional control with amp, auto electronic circuit protection, power and over current indicator lights, constant voltage pulse width speed control and automatic electronic momentum circuit for smooth operation.

614-5451 3.5 Amp DC Power Supply **114.95**

WALTHERS

TRAINLINE® POWER PACK

931-2000 Starter Set Power Pack **24.98**
Ideal for powering your first layout as well as displays and test tracks. UL-listed unit delivers full forward and reverse speed control, with center-off. Simple two-wire hook up to track DC terminals. Includes AC terminals to power lights and other accessories, sold separately. Suitable for most HO Scale trains.

A.J. FRICKO COMPANY

Electrical accessories for HO & larger scales.

CONVERTO

274-805 24.95
Solid-state electronic device converts AC universal motor. Direction is then controlled by polarity in rail, not by the traditional E unit. (For Marklin, Lionel, American Flyer or any AC transformer.)

ATLAS

POWER PACK

150-310 Atlas Custom-Power® 1700 Power Pack **34.95**
Features Include: a transistor that protects circuitry and a thermal fuse power for overload protection, circuit breaker protection, an overload indicator lamp, separate power and reversing switches and no pulse power to damage precision motors. Output: 14V DC, 17V AC, 1.2 Amps at no load. Listed by Underwriter Laboratories.

BACHMANN

SMOKE FLUID

160-99993 2-1/4oz **3.00**

ATHEARN

ATHEARN TRAINPAK™

140-9997 Power Pack **29.50**
NEW
The Athearn Trainpak is the perfect choice for you to start building your model railroad empire. Can be used with HO or N Scale layouts. Includes overload warning light, power indicator, speed control dial and direction control switch. 16V, 7VA.

FALLER

IMPORTED FROM GERMANY BY WALTHERS

ELECTRICAL BELL

272-638 **34.99**
Church bell sound.

BUSCH

IMPORTED FROM GERMANY BY WALTHERS

SOUND SYSTEMS

RAILWAY STATION

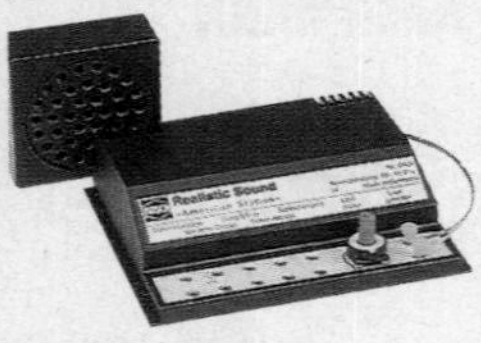

189-5768 American Railway Station **99.99**
Realistic sounds, stored on a chip, create the atmosphere of a busy railway station. Sounds include Western bell, steam whistle, crossing bell, station voice announcement and "Tickets, please" voice announcement. Includes separate speaker; operates on 10-16V AC or DC.

CITY SOUNDS EA 99.99

189-5764 Street Traffic
189-5765 Church Bells

Products are constructed on printed circuit boards that can be mounted on Printed Circuit Mounting Track. Connections to Circuitron circuit boards can be made using .110" female solderless connectors or by soldering leads to terminals on the board. Solid-state integrated circuit technology. Complete instructions. One year limited warranty.

SOUND SYSTEMS

DIESEL HORN

800-5701 DH-1 Diesel Horn **28.95**
Electronic multi-chime horn with speaker and push button. With external switches, unit can produce three different single frequency or dual chime tones or a three chime tone. Requires 10-18V AC or DC input.

800-9150 Speaker 2-1/4" (8 ohm) **4.95**
800-9610 Push Button **1.50**

STEAM SOUND

Easily installed in HO Scale models. Circuitry has individually controlled accurate "chuff" sound with constant background hiss. Self-contained SS-1 is powered by 9V battery for use with any form of track power. Includes 1 x 1 x 1/2" circuit board, 9V battery holder, subminiature slide switch, 1" diameter speaker, volume control resistors, chuff contact wire, insulating material and complete instructions.

800-4000 SS-1 Steam Sound Kit **39.95**
800-9104 Spring Pickup Wire pkg(4) **2.00**
Four 3" lengths, 28 gauge (.0126") beryllium copper spring wire.
800-9105 Sound System Synchronizing Insulation **3.00**
800-9151 Speaker **9.95**
23mm (7/8") diameter, 3/8" thick high-output transducer.

MODELTRONICS

510-6200 Locomotive Shown Not Included

SOUND SYSTEMS & ACCESSORIES

DIESEL SOUND

510-6200 MKII Diesel Sound System **74.95**
From a gentle idle to a throaty growl, add the sound of your favorite prime mover to your miniature motive power. While idling, the internal machinery clatter can be heard. As the engine begins moving and working harder, the diesel engine sound grows louder. When slowing down, the sound drops. There's also an adjustable turbocharger, which you can set to match your favorite engines. Idle sound starts at about 1.5 to 3.0 volts. Ready to install, select the speaker (sold separately) that best fits your model from the list below. Custom integrated circuit also provides constant brightness lighting system, less bulbs. Unit is easy to install and comes with complete instructions. Small size (3/4 x 2-3/16 x 5/8") is ideal for use inside powered or dummy units.

STEAM SOUND

510-2000 Micro-Sound II Steam **74.95**
Give your steamers all the sound and power of the real thing with these easy-to-install units. Operates with any throttle system and since they're self-contained, each engine generates its own level of sound. Exhaust cutoff and drift control are built in and regulated by the engine power, so a hard working engine sounds louder. Output is fully synchronized with the drive wheels using special slip-on cams, so wheels and valve gear do not have to be removed for installation. Can be installed in most locos, tenders or head-end cars. Select the speaker (sold separately) that best fits your model from the list below. Can also be enhanced with Air Pumps #1930 or 1940 (sold separately) to match the era of your loco for more realistic sound.

AIR PUMP SOUNDS EA 39.95

As your train eases to a stop, the sounds of the air compressor pumping up the train line can be heard. These circuits add a new dimension to your steam fleet by matching the sound of earlier Single Phase or later Cross Compound pumps. Modules can be combined for bigger engines equipped with two compressors.

510-1930 Cross Compound Air Compressor (Later Steam)
510-1940 Single Phase Air Compressor (Early Steam)

SOUND CAR KITS

An economical way to add sound to your entire fleet. Start with a Sound System #2000 or 6200, a speaker and accessories (sold separately). Then, install System B (#2200) or System C (#2202) in a headend car such as an RPO or a freight car. Parts are also included to convert one loco. Additional locos can be fitted with Engine Kits #2201 or 2203. Connect to the equipped car and the loco comes to life with sound.

SYSTEM B - LOCO MOUNTED SPEAKER

510-2200 Complete Car/Loco Kit **14.95**
510-2201 Loco Only **11.75**

SYSTEM C - CAR MOUNTED SPEAKER

510-2202 Complete Car/Loco Kit **9.95**
510-2203 Loco Only **7.95**

SPEAKERS ONLY EA 11.95

510-1511 Round 1"
510-1513 Round 1-1/4"
510-1515 Round 1-1/2"
510-1523 Oval 1.85 x 2.85"

SOUND SYSTEM PARTS & ACCESSORIES

Designed especially for use with Diesel or Steam Sound systems, sold separately.

CONSTANT BRIGHTNESS LIGHT KITS

510-3002 Reversing **11.95**
Maximum 1.0 Amp, suitable for HO and N Scale.

510-3003 Reversing **15.95**
Maximum 3.0 amps, suitable for HO & O Scale.

510-3004 Forward Only **7.95**
Maximum 1.0 Amp, suitable for HO and N Scale.

510-3005 Forward Only **13.95**
Maximum 3.0 amps, suitable for HO & O Scale.

510-3006 Forward Only **11.95**
Maximum 2.0 amps, suitable for HO & O Scale.

510-6001 Constant Light/Speed Reducer **11.95**
Will slow locos not equipped with Modeltronics sound system and provides constant lighting. Suitable for all scales.

SUB-MINI CONNECTOR-GOLD PLATED

510-1339 One Pin **8.95**
510-1340 Two Pin 1/16x1/8" **10.95**
510-1341 Three Pin **11.95**
510-1342 Four Pin **12.95**
510-1343 Six Pin **13.95**

FLEXIBLE WIRE EA 1.75

Each pack includes 10'.

510-3020 28 Ga. Black
510-3022 30 Ga. Black
510-3024 30 Ga. Red
510-3026 30 Ga. Blue
510-3028 30 Ga. Yellow

BATTERY HOLDERS EA 2.95

510-1350 Small
510-1351 Large

MISCELLANEOUS PARTS EA 2.95

510-1300 Articulated Engine Synchro Kit
510-1330 Power Filter (Adds Echo)
510-1370 Small On/Off Switch
510-3010 Heat Shrink Tube Assortment includes 3/64, 3/8, 1/16 and two 4" lengths.
510-3015 Solder Kit **4.95**

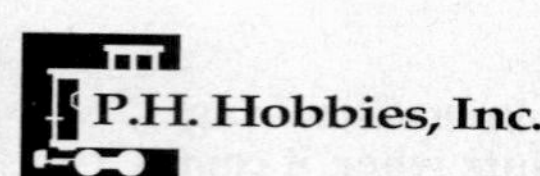

POWER SUPPLIES

PS3 POWER PACK

567-3 PS3 3-Amp Throttle **99.95**
The PS3 has a 16-gauge aluminum case with a flat black finish. Fully filtered 3 amp pure DC power supply, with power indicator light.

PS6 & PS10 SERIES POWER PACKS

PS6 and PS10 Series Power Supplies have a 16-gauge aluminum case with a baked gunmetal gray metallic finish upper case, and a black lower case. Fan-cooled and can be used with all DC trains in all gauges and scales.

PS6

567-6 PS6–6 Amp **238.00**

567-67 PS6G–6 Amp w/Volt & Ammeter **285.00**

PS10

567-10 PS10–10 Amp **264.00**

567-107 PS10G–10 Amp w/Volt & Ammeter **310.00**

REVERSING UNIT

567-1 62.00
A reversing shuttle circuit for point-to-point (station-to-station) operation with timer delay.

LIFE-LIKE®

SMOKE FLUID

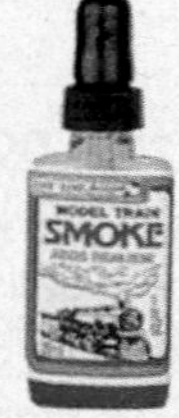

433-1417 1oz **5.75**
Can be used in any smoke generator designed for petroleum-based smoke fluid.

SCALE SHOPS

VOLTROLLERS

Voltrollers are offered in two different versions. The hand-held throttle is primarily designed for Can motors, while the cabinet/panel models are intended for all motors. Most units are available assembled or in kit form. All units are DC less momentum, pulse or brake. Power is controlled by a rotational knob for speed, and a slide switch for direction. All Voltrollers have a 6' cable. Throttle dimensions are 3-5/16 x 2-1/8 x 1-3/8".

1.5 AMP

649-1315 Walk-Around Throttle Kit **39.98**
649-1316 Walk-Around Throttle, Assembled **69.98**
649-1317 Cabinet Throttle Kit **29.98**
649-1318 Cabinet Throttle, Assembled **59.98**
649-1319 Panel Throttle Kit **19.98**

3 AMP

649-1335 Walk-Around Throttle Kit **49.98**
649-1336 Walk-Around Throttle, Assembled **79.98**
649-1337 Cabinet Throttle Kit **39.98**
649-1338 Cabinet Throttle, Assembled **69.98**
649-1339 Panel Throttle Kit **29.98**

5 AMP

649-1355 Walk-Around Throttle Kit **69.98**
649-1356 Walk-Around Throttle, Assembled **99.98**
649-1357 Cabinet Throttle Kit **54.98**
649-1358 Cabinet Throttle, Assembled **84.98**
649-1359 Panel Throttle Kit **39.98**

ACCESSORIES

649-3500 Velcro Hook & Loop, 1 x 2" **1.29**
Adhesive back for throttle mount.

649-3501 Velcro Hook, 1 x 4" **1.29**
Adhesive back for extra throttle mounts.

649-4093 Din Plug & Socket **6.98**
649-4094 Din Socket **1.98**
649-4245 Cable, 6' Five Conductor **8.98**

SOUND SYSTEMS

SPEAKER

649-4090 1" Round **5.98**
8 ohm, .2 watts; for on-board sound systems.

MODEL POWER

SMOKE FLUID

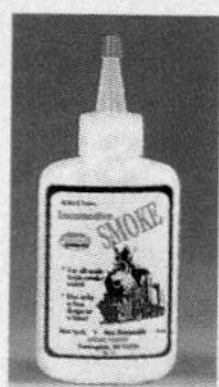

490-12 4oz **4.98**
For any scale of trains. Use only a few drops at a time. Non-toxic and non-flammable

N-WAY PRODUCTS

POWER SUPPLY KIT

535-425 14.95
This kit will eliminate the two 9V batteries necessary to power the N-Way Flashing Crossing Signals & Boulevard Crossing Signals. One Power Supply Kit will power 4 sets of signals. This kit will also power the N-Way Train Detection Kit. Requires 110V input for operation.

Information STATION

Magnetic Levitation

We all know about the steam- and the diesel-era, but there might be a brand-new era coming to prototype railroads in the near future. The latest innovation is magnetic levitation, which is defined as the support and often propulsion of objects or vehicles by magnetic fields.

In operation, the field "supports" the train, lifting it up and away from a guideway which replaces the traditional right-of-way. Since there's no contact with any surface, friction is all but eliminated.

Engineers feel magnetic levitation is an ideal possibility for travel at high speeds of 275-300mph/435-475 kph.

Right now, a typical maglev train resembles a railroad or monorail car and travels along a guideway. Lifting force comes from numerous electromagnets in the train as well as the guideway.

"I got my MRC DCC Command 2000 set up in about 10 minutes by just hooking up four wires."

"Now I can run up to ten decoder-equipped locomotives at one time, independently, with no additional wiring!"

My name is Paul Podlaski. I'm a model railroader who hates wiring, soldering and fancy electronics. In fact, I'm a real klutz when it comes to programming anything—even my VCR.

I've got to tell you, I got my MRC DCC Command 2000 set up in about 10 minutes by just hooking up four wires—two wires to the power station and two to the track.

Programming my UP FA1 took about three minutes and once that was done I had a train running almost instantly. I got a second locomotive, a BN GP9M, programmed and running in no time and within a few minutes I had two trains running independently on the same mainline!

As soon as I equip the rest of my locomotives with decoders, I'll be able to control up to 10 trains on the same line with no major rewiring and no headaches. In the meantime, I can still run nondecoder-equipped locomotives without any problems. It's great!

I'm in the process of expanding my layout. I want to run more trains without having to add additional wiring. Besides having simple installation, once you switch over to Command 2000 DCC, you can add complex track work to your layout without rotary switches or block toggles. If I hadn't already had block wiring, adding Command 2000 would have been even easier because I wouldn't have needed blocks or toggles. Four wires would have done the job! I just wish I had started off this way instead of waiting until I needed to expand.

You also get features that are a pain to add with conventional wiring. Command 2000 lets you program the acceleration rate and the starting voltage of your locomotives. You can also add constant and directional lighting. And, when your train is in the siding for a meet, you can even turn off the lights just like on the real railroads!

Thank you, MRC, for Command 2000.

Sincerely,

Paul Podlaski

Paul Podlaski

Here's how MRC Command 2000 DCC works:

MRC uses advanced microprocessor technology. Command 2000 increases the realism, control and satisfaction of model railroading like no other introduction in the past 50 years.

The DCC unit feeds a constant voltage to the track along with a digital control signal addressed to a decoder installed in your locomotive. Each decoder is designed to read only those signals that have been addressed to it specifically, allowing for independent control of locomotives on the same line.

The MRC Command 2000 System also offers accessories like a handheld memory walkaround throttle, additional decoders available in single and three packs, a DCC Auto Reverse unit to control reverse loops and Power Station 8 which boosts your output to 8 amps so you can run bigger locomotives. If you need to control more than 10 trains, the Bus System allows you to link more than one Command 2000 console so you can run 20 trains or more.

Command 2000 comes in three versions:

Command 2000 only

Command 2000 with a decoder-equipped loco

Command 2000 with a 65 -watt power supply and a decoder-equipped loco

Model Rectifier Corporation (MRC) is the largest supplier of train controllers in North America. Most MRC power packs are backed by a 5-year limited warranty, and most include the following basic features: UL listed; on-off switch; overload indicator light; circuit breaker protected; directional control (reverse switch); and AC terminals for accessories. Manufacturer's Rating: 1 amp will handle one average HO or two average N Scale trains. Fixed 12 volt DC expansion terminals (where noted) allow you to add another speed and direction control as long as the capacity of the pack is not exceeded.

DIGITAL COMMAND CONTROL

500-90

COMMAND 2000

Affordable, easy-to-use Digital Command Control! Control up to ten different engines at once—one standard and nine decoder-equipped locos. Easy to use, with simple controls for adjusting starting voltage, acceleration and deceleration.

500-2000 Console w/Decoder Equipped Locomotive **244.98**
500-90 Console Only **169.98**
500-110 Console w/Power Supply & Loco **269.98**

500-501 DCC Power Station 8 **289.98**
You can boost your DCC Command 2000 (sold separately) up to eight powerful amperes with an easy hookup to run more trains or engines with bigger motors. Includes power supply and has adjustable output voltage capability. Simple hookup.

HO DECODERS

500-305 14 Step No Plug **19.98** ***NEW***
500-310 Single **26.98**
500-340 3-Pack **74.98**

Comes with connector for easy installation in locos equipped with DCC plug; can be wired in to those that do not. Fits in most HO Scale locos, measures 32.5 x 16.5 x 7.5mm.

WALKAROUND 2000

500-300 Handheld Throttle w/Memory **37.98**
Control up to four decoder-equipped locomotives with the Command 2000. Features two independent throttles, plus direction and light controls. Memory function keeps the locomotive running even after you unplug the controller. Comes with a standard 15' four-conductor telephone cable.

DCC ACCESSORY POWER SUPPLY

500-510 39.98
AC power unit supplies up to 50VA of power. Use with Command 2000 for peak performance, can be used as a stand-alone power supply for accessories.

500-511 Turn Power Box **39.98** ***NEW***
AC accessory pack. 12 & 18V.

DCC AUTO REVERSE

500-520 39.98
Automatically controls reverse loop circuits. No manual switching required; eliminates conventional block and switch systems.

BUS SYSTEM

500-600 19.98 ***NEW***
Links two or more Command 2000 units together; one bus unit and two Consoles will run up to 20 trains. Requires a Power Booster.

CAB CONTROL 55

500-70 32.98 ***NEW***
A remote cab control that's a convenient and inexpensive way to add an extra train on a separate track. Hooks up to any AC power supply.

POWER PACKS

TECH II SERIES

The TECH II Series introduces Proportional Tracking Control (PTC) to MRC's durable, feature-rich line of power packs. PTC provides instant response from locomotives throughout the entire speed range and automatically adjusts pulse characteristics to match the locomotive's motor. The result is tighter, surer command of your trains. Tech II units will operate HO, HOn3, TT and N Scale trains; #2400 and #2500 will also operate S, O, On3 and G Scale trains.

500-1400 Railpower 1400 **44.98**
Superior speed control at a sensible price. Features on/off switch, Throttlemaster knob, automatic circuit protector and much more. Enough muscle to run three average HO trains or six average N Scale trains.

500-1440 Tru-Sound 1440 w/Speaker **61.98**
Bring your layout to life with the sounds of real railroading! This versatile power pack boasts all the great features of the Railpower 1400—including PTC and enough power to run three HO trains—and also adds digital steam whistle and diesel horn sounds. Sounds are activated by a push button; a 4" speaker and 12' of cable are included. Can be used for both HO and N Scale layouts.

500-1500 Locomotion 1500 w/Momentum Control **60.98**
Combines advanced PTC with precise momentum circuitry and realistic braking—advance the throttle and the 1500 slowly, realistically brings your locomotive up to speed. Also features double insulation for safety, Power monitor light, spring-loaded brake switch and much more. Power for running three average HO trains.

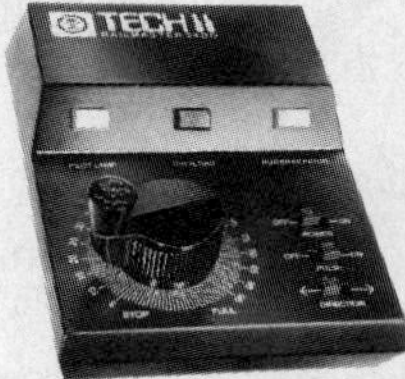

500-2400 Railmaster 2400 **60.98**
If you want more power—enough to run five average HO trains—the Railmaster 2400 is the right pack for you. Loaded with features to keep you in control of your railroad, including PTC, pulse injection on-off switch, overload indicator light, pilot light, power monitor light, automatic circuit protector and much more.

PART NUMBER	DESCRIPTION	EXTENDED RANGE SPEED CONTROL	OVERLOAD LIGHT INDICATOR	DIRECTION CONTROL	REVERSE LOOP	ON-OFF SWITCH	AUTOMATIC PULSE OR PULSE SWITCH POWER	AMMETER AND VOLTMETER	TOTAL AMPERAGE	POWER FOR AVERAGE TRAINS	FIXED 12V FOR DC EXPANSION
500-1300	RAILPOWER 1300	•		•		•			0.6	3	
500-1370	RAILPOWER 1370	•	•	•		•	•		1.5	4-5	
500-1400	RAILPOWER 1400	•	•	•		•	•		1.1	2-3	
500-1440	TRU-SOUND 1440	•	•	•		•	•		1.1	2-3	
500-1500	LOCOMOTION 1500	•	•	•		•	•		1	2-4	•
500-2400	RAILMASTER 2400	•	•	•		•	•		1.45	4-5	•
500-2500	LOCOMOTION 2500	•	•	•		•	•		1.34	4-6	•
500-2800	DUALPOWER 2800	2	•	2		•	•		1.2	2-3	
500-3000	THROTTLE CONTROL 3000	3	•	•	•		•		N/A	N/A	
500-7000	SOUND & POWER 7000		•	•		•			2.5	4-6	
500-9500	POWER COMMAND 9500		•	•		•		•	2.5	4-6	•

500-2500 Locomotion 2500 w/Momentum Control **75.98**
The top of the Tech II line, the Locomotion 2500 is packed with power and all the features you need for realistic train operation, including PTC, precise momentum circuitry and braking control. The speed control is so exact, you'll believe you're handling a prototype locomotive. Offers enough output to run five average HO trains.

500-2800 Dualpower 2800 **77.98**
Double your operations! The Dualpower 2800 is a PTC-equipped dualpack with independent controls, allowing you to operate two different locomotives—even with common rail circuits. Features two Throttlemaster control knobs, two direction switches and two power monitors. The durable housing is double insulated for safety.

Limited Quantity Available
500-3000 Throttle Control 3000 **49.98**
Not a power source but a full-featured cab control complete with automatic pulse, spring-loaded brake switch and all the features you find in Tech II power packs. The perfect controller for that remote switching operation on your layout. Accepts up to 2.5 amps of power. Requires a power controller to operate.

TECH 3 POWER COMMAND

Here is the power pack for the serious modeler! Get maximum control: Ammeter and voltmeter let you monitor loco operation and identify problems before damage occurs. Achieve maximum realism: Advanced Proportional Tracking Control, momentum circuitry, plus braking and acceleration control make you feel like you're running a real locomotive. Available with 30VA of power, pack can run HO, N, G and other DC trains. Covered by a limited five-year warranty, comes with Throttle Master control knob, 300° of control, thermostat protection, AC terminals for accessories and much more.

500-9500 Power Command (30VA) **99.98**

STANDARD POWER PACKS

Maximum realism at an economical price. Check out the features on these durable power packs: extended range control throttle, master on-off switch, mainline direction switch and much more.

500-1300 Railpower 1300 **30.98**
For use with HO, N and Z scale trains. Total output 7VA on solid state circuitry, designed to deliver superior slow-speed acceleration for increased realism. Features a mainline direction switch, 300° speed control, circuit protection to guard against overload and more.

500-1370 Railpower 1370 **39.98**
Power for up to 5 average HO trains! Solid state circuitry delivers 18VA output and superior slow-speed acceleration. Mainline direction switch, on-off switch, red LED pilot light, 300° speed control and circuit protection.

500-6200 Trainpower 6200 **112.98**
Maximum power for G Scale , but also runs HO. Unit provides 60VA output power, plus 0-18.5 volts DC track voltage. Includes AC output for accessories, mode switch to select HO & N Scale or Large Scale, 300° throttle control and power monitor lamp. Delivers 3.6 amps of power to trains.

TECH 4 TRAIN CONTROLS

Delivers precise, ultra-slow speed control for realistic operation. Adjustable voltage and momentum. Turbo boost circuitry. Programmable momentum simulates the drag of a heavy train or a light engine movement. Programmable voltage maximizes performance. Open the throttle, and an impulse circuit delivers a burst of power at the right moment for smooth, jerk-free starts. Set top-end voltage for exact speed control at every position on the throttle. Best of all, you get the same peak performance from every engine. Optional Walk-Around Throttle (#500-251, sold separately) with modular plug lets you work at trackside or enjoy the company of another operator.

500-250 Tech 4250 **99.98**
17VA.

500-251 Walkaround Throttle System **32.98**
You can have full mobility with this unit, giving you memory, direction, brake, stop, LED light and 300° throttle plus a 15' wired cable all at the touch of a button.

500-350 Tech 4350 **109.98**
30VA w/built-in memory.

WALKAROUND CONTROL

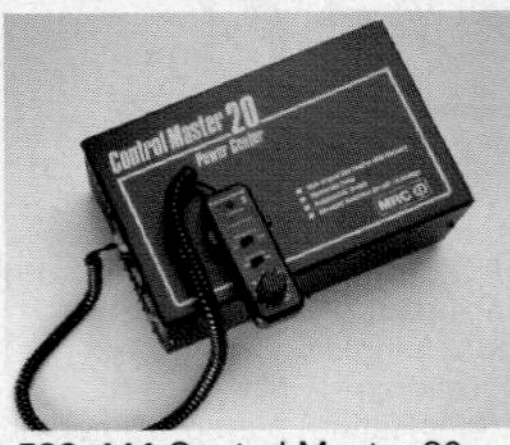

500-444 Control Master 20 **184.98**
Power to run trains with the convenience of a walkaround cab. Hand-held control with memory function—unplug the control and your train keeps moving. HO/N Scale. Terminals for ammeter and voltmeter hookup, filtered and regulated DC output, momentum circuitry, nudge switch control and a mode switch. 5.0 amps plus reserve power.

ACCESSORIES

500-800 On-Board Speaker System **29.98**
500-810 Fixed 3" Speaker & Wire **8.98**
500-820 Speaker Wire, 12' **2.98**
500-2025 Circuit Breaker Loco GD1 **3.00**
500-2026 Circuit Breaker Pike GD2 **3.00**
500-2030 Throttlemaster Knob **2.25**
500-2040 Terminal Strip-Plain **5.98**
500-2041 Terminal Strip-Wired **6.98**
500-4441 Walkaround for CM20 **29.98**
500-1 MRC Information Flyer **No Charge**

SOUND SYSTEMS

500-210 SoundMaster 210 **209.98**
Broadcast any of 12 sounds from a moving train, then with the flick of a switch, direct one of 10 sounds from a fixed speaker. Generates 12 digital sounds: steam locomotive whistle, conductor's "All-aboard", rail clacking, crossing gate bell, circus calliope, diesel horn, steam whistle, engine bell, traveling diesel horn, steam air release, diesel rumble and steam chuff. A built-in tape jack lets you hear your own recorded music or sounds. Installs easily in standard rolling stock. Slide controls adjust both fixed and on-board sound. Includes 1" speaker, 3" speaker and receiver for on-board sound.

500-8000 Sound Generator 8000 **75.98**
Make your models sound like the real thing. With the flick of a switch you can go from the rumble and horn of a diesel to the chuff and whistle of a steamer. Easy-to-use controls let you synchronize the sound to the speed of your loco and adjust the volume to the size of your layout. Easy to hook up; includes one 4" fixed-location speaker and 12' of wire.

SOUNDMASTER ACCESSORIES

500-830 Speaker Enclosure **35.98**
An additional speaker for maximum listening pleasure and sound quality.

500-840 Stock Car w/Assembled Receiver **39.98**
Athearn model.

500-7000 Sound n' Power 7000 **179.98**
Back by popular demand, the Sound n' Power 7000 provides realistic sound, high power and control in one unit. The steam and diesel locomotive sound system, including steam whistle and diesel horn, provides a new dimension to your model railroading pleasure, plus all the high power demanded by sophisticated railroaders. 60VA.

SWITCHES

500-2001 SPST Slide **1.98**
500-2003 DPDT Slide **2.98**
500-2011 SPST E1 Toggle Switch **3.49**
500-2014 SPDT CENTER-OFF Toggle Switch **3.49**
500-2015 DPDT E5 Switch **3.98**
500-2016 DPDT 3W CENTER-OFF SW Wired Switch **5.98**
500-2017 SPDT E7 CENTER-OFF Momentary Switch **4.98**

SOUND SYSTEMS

DIESEL HORN

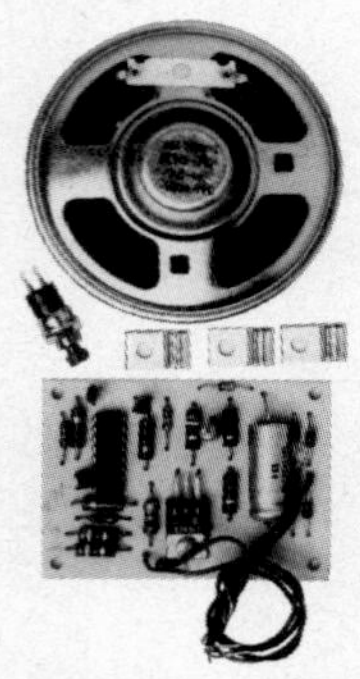

723-301 3-Toned Diesel Horn Kit **27.95**
Tones of 311, 370 and 420 cycles are duplicated simultaneously. Solid state circuitry throughout can be connected to 6 to 16 volt AC/DC (not included). Kit includes pushbutton speaker mounting clips and 3" speaker. To expand system add 723-415 speakers at various points around your layout.

STEAM WHISTLE W/DIESEL HORN

723-305 89.95
Provides both 3-toned steam whistle and 3-chimed diesel horn. For authenticity steam whistle provides background steam hiss; use slide control on steam for varying pitch and volume of whistle. Kit contains solid state prebuilt and tested circuit, pushbutton, slide control, speaker and mounting clips.

SPEAKER

723-415 5.95
Can be used in conjuction with Train Tronics #301 3-Toned Diesel Horn or #305 Steam Whistle to add diesel horn or steam whistle sound to other areas of your layout. 8 ohm, 3" in diameter.

SWITCH POWER

SWITCH MACHINE POWER UNIT

Capable of operating up to 20 turnouts simultaneously, with "positive snap-action." Features instantaneous recycling with LED ready indicator. Current limiting to prevent coil burnout. Operates any type of dual coil switch machine.

723-603 Switchman Capacitive Discharge Unit **39.95**

723-1801 AC Converter for Zero-1 **7.95**
(By Special Order Only)

723-1804 Conductive Paint for Zero-1 **2.50**
(By Special Order Only)

723-1805 Power Booster for Zero-1 **99.95**
(By Special Order Only)

SPECTRUM

(Division of Bachmann)

POWER PACKS

160-44281 Magnum .9 Amp **41.00**
The perfect beginner's power pack. Features include precision throttle control, master on-off switch, direction control, AC output for accessories and shockproof casing. Covered by a lifetime warranty.

160-44207 HO & N **28.00**

SEUTHE®

IMPORTED FROM GERMANY BY WALTHERS

A quality line of smoke/steam generators for various foreign and domestic locomotives. Generators for structures and ships are also available.

SMOKE & STEAM

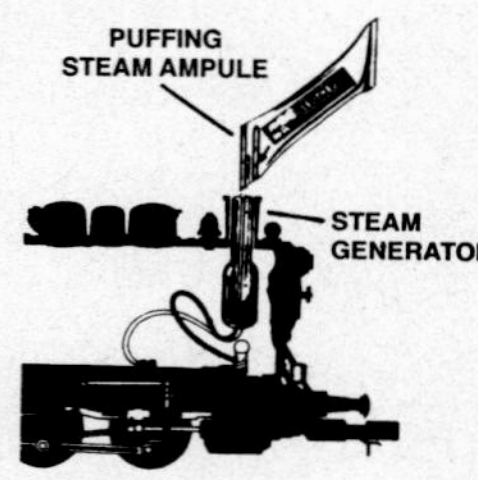

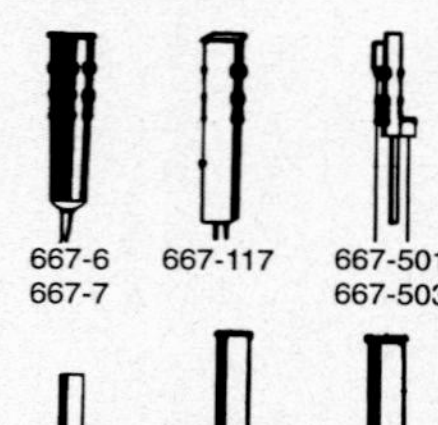

STEAM GENERATORS

667-6 Operating Voltage 14V **19.99**
For model structures and factory chimneys as well as all O Gauge locomotives.

667-7 Operating Voltage 16V **19.99**
For model structures and factory chimneys as well as all O Gauge locomotives. Especially for Marklin 5700.

667-8 Operating Voltage 16V, Metal **19.99**
For all types of locomotives with metal bodies.

667-9 Operating Voltage 14V **19.99**
For Fleischmann 4170, 4175, 4177 and 4178; also, Marklin-Hamo DC (8335).

667-10 Maximum 16V AC/DC **19.99**
For Marklin 3046, 3047, 3048, 3084, 3085 and 3102 locomotives as well as Fleischmann and Liliput locomotives.

667-11 Maximum 16V AC/DC **19.99**
Same as #10 except for Marklin digital.

667-12 Operating Voltage 16V **19.99**
Same as #100 except for Marklin digital.

667-20 Maximum 16V AC/DC **19.99**
For Marklin 3083, 3091 and 3093 also Hamo 8391, 8392 and 8393.

667-21 Maximum 16V AC/DC **19.99**
Universal type for all locomotives with metal bodies and extremely slim chimneys.

667-22 Maximum 16V AC/DC **19.99**
Universal type for all locomotives with plastic bodies and extremely slim chimneys.

667-23 Maximum 16V AC/DC **19.99**
Same as #22 except for Marklin digital.

667-24 Maximum 16V AC/DC **19.99**
Same as #20 except for Marklin digital.

667-99 Operating Voltage 14V **19.99**
For all types of locomotives with plastic bodies.

667-100 Operating Voltage 16V **19.99**
For all types of locomotives with plastic bodies.

CONSTANT GENERATORS

The generator creates realistic puffing smoke while locomotive is stationary or in motion. The #50 Electronic Smoke Unit is used with #51 and #52 smoke generators, regulating the current flow to allow the operation of these two generators.

667-50 Electronic Control (SDE #50) **23.99**
667-51 Small Stack Smoke Generator **19.99**
667-52 Large Stack Smoke Generator **19.99**

SMOKE GENERATORS

667-5 Smoke Generator, Ships **19.99**
Smoke generator for ships and similar models, 6V.

667-117 Smoke Chimney 16V **10.99**
Smoke generator for house or building.

SUPER SMOKE UNITS

667-500 Ship Models/Large Chimneys **28.99**
667-501 12V w/Smoke Fluid **25.99**
667-503 16V w/Smoke Fluid **25.99**

ACCESSORIES

667-101 Loco Smoke 4cc pkg(3) **3.99**
For use with Arnold and Marklin locomotives.

667-103 Steam Distillate 4cc pkg(3) **3.49**
Three tubes, three different scents: neutral, pine and locomotive.

667-105 Neutral Steam Distillate, 50ml **7.99**
667-106 Neutral Steam Distillate, 250ml **15.99**
667-200 Steam Pipes pkg(6) **5.99**
For use with 667-10 Steam Generator.
667-400 Neutral Scent 4cc pkg(3) **2.99**
667-401 Locomotive Smoke 4cc pkg(3) **2.99**
667-402 Pine Scent 4cc pkg(3) **2.99**
667-404 Continuous Smoke pkg(3) **2.99**
For use with chimney.

VOLLMER

IMPORTED FROM GERMANY BY WALTHERS

SMOKE UNIT

770-4114 Smoke Generator **35.99**
Features a large tank for smoke-making. Includes enough fluid for 70 minutes of smoke.

770-4115 Smoke Fluid Refill, 50ml **8.99**

Scale
WALTHERS
HO
2000
MODEL RAILROAD
REFERENCE BOOK

ADHESIVES

Running slow and running late. Very late. It might not matter with other trains, but the morning intermodal is the hottest on the Lost Creek. Never mind what your watch tells you: when the fog is this thick, you instinctively slow down. Seems drivers have enough trouble seeing you coming on bright, clear days, much less on a morning like this.

"Clear board for the diamond," the conductor suddenly calls out.

Faintly, a green glimmer can be seen ahead.

"Clear board it is," you reply, pulling the whistle lever all the way open - no one will be sleeping late in town this morning!

The pea-soup swirls, then clears just long enough to give you a clear view ahead. You feel the wheels and hear the clatter as the loco rumbles across the diamond. Still off schedule, but at least you're running safely.

Early morning finds us trackside on a diorama built by Ken Estes of Lakewood, California. A few simple details and basic structures occupy the crossing, along with a pair of scratchbuilt signals. The working head and class lights on the Athearn GP50 provide a dramatic touch, burning through the rolling fog.

Models and Photo by Ken Estes

WALTHERS™

Goo® 904-299

ADHESIVES

GOO®

904-299 1-1/8oz **2.98**

- **ALL PURPOSE ADHESIVE** GOO is the permanent rubber base adhesive that grips most anything. It never lets go.
- **FAST-SETTING JOINTS** Easy contact action opens new possibilities for fast-setting joints with any material.

Walthers GOO is the perfect adhesive for building or repairing jobs on your layout and around the house!

The easy contact action of GOO produces fast-setting joints with any material. GOO works with all types of metals (including steel, brass, aluminum, copper and others) plus items like wood, plastic, cardboard, china, leather, vinyl, ceramics, paper, concrete and many more, on any smooth or porous surface.

GOO is a permanent rubber base adhesive that's shockproof, waterproof and crackproof–it's as flexible as rubber. Joints won't crack when flexed back and forth, won't break loose when the temperature changes and won't weaken when wet or damp. It sticks forever!

Dealers: MUST order in multiples of 6.

MIKRO TIP

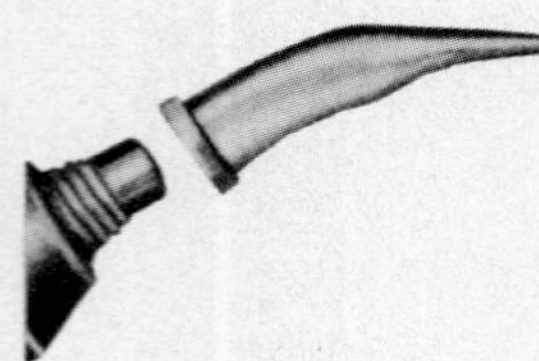

904-302 pkg(10) **2.98**

FOR PRECISION GLUING FITS MOST ANY GLUE TUBE

- Easily added to GOO Adhesive Tube
- Helps eliminate waste and mess
- Allows more precise application of glue
- Mounts on 3/16" diameter glue nozzle

CLEANERS

BRIGHT BOY ABRASIVE TRACK CLEANER

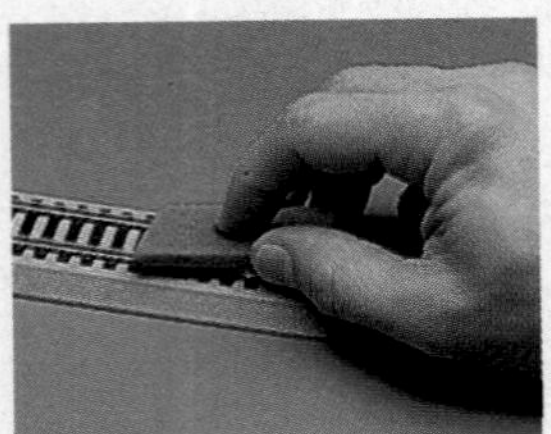

949-521 **4.98**
Improve the conductivity of your tracks by keeping them clean with easy-to-use Bright Boy!

AMBROID®

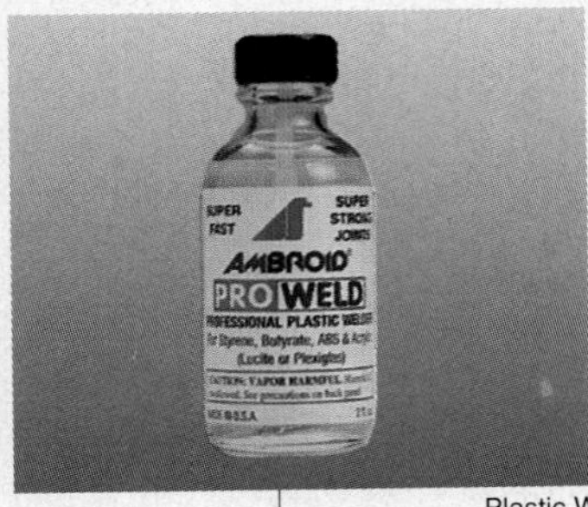

Plastic Welder 130-110

ADHESIVES

LIQUID CEMENT

Waterproof cement for use on wood, leather, canvas, metal, most fabrics and glass.

130-101 Regular Cement 1.8oz Tube **2.29**

130-102 Regular Cement 3.2oz Tube **3.59**

Dealers: MUST order Dealer Pack of 12.

130-1511 Regular Cement 1oz Tube **1.99**

FAS'N-ALL ADHESIVE/SEALANT

130-157 1oz **2.29**
Rubber-based general purpose adhesive and sealant. Cured material remains flexible, waterproof and shock absorbent.

STYRENE PLASTIC CEMENT

130-1521 5/8oz Tube **1.79**
Improved, fast-drying, more aggressive formula. Dries clear. Resistant to running.

CLEAR VINYL CEMENT

130-1611 5/8oz Tube **1.89**
Crystal-clear cement for joining or mending rigid or flexible vinyl. Made for joining vinyl figure models. Waterproof.

TAC-N-PLACE ADHESIVE

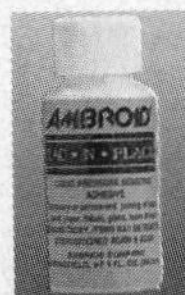

130-158 1oz **1.99**
Nontoxic, brush-on, pressure-sensitive adhesive. For temporary or permanent joining of plastic, wood, paper, fabric, glass, foam and metal. Remains tacky.

PLASTIC WELDER

130-110 Pro Weld 2oz **2.89**
A clear, super fast plastic fusing adhesive. Bonds styrene, butyrate, ABS and acrylic.

RESIN GLUE

130-126 Se•Cur•It 4oz **2.29**
Great for porous materials. Sandable resin glue will not stain and is nonflammable.

EZ MASK

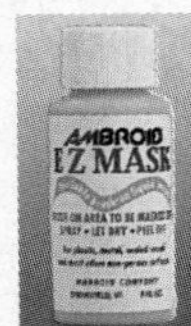

130-154 1oz Bottle **1.99**
Eliminate the use of messy tape with this brush-on, peel-off, water soluble masking liquid.

Information STATION

Working Safely with Adhesives

Adhesives and their fumes have chemical components that can cause irritation to skin, nose, eyes and mouth. It's important that you work safely and follow directions when working with these materials.

Start by reading the directions for the safe handling, use and disposal of the material. Here are three more things you can do when using adhesive products to protect yourself:

1. Work in an area that has plenty of ventilation so fumes do not build up.
2. Take frequent breaks to reduce long-term exposure to fumes.
3. Stop what you are working on immediately if you begin to feel dizzy. Get some fresh air to clear your head and check the room ventilation - you may need to use an exhaust fan or open several windows.

Cyanoacrylate adhesives, better known as CAs or "super glues," can bond instantly to skin in a matter of seconds. Protect yourself by using gloves and covering any exposed skin. If you do get bonded to something, DO NOT PRY THE ITEM LOOSE. Use a commercial debonder (nail polish remover or acetone will work in a pinch but will destroy most plastics) to help free you from the object.

See a doctor immediately if you get any in your eyes or other sensitive area.

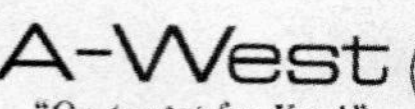

"On target for You!"

TURBO OIL

Non-petroleum product for plastics or metal. Bottle is fitted with a plastic dropper applicator tip and overcap.

158-3 1oz **2.59**
158-14 4oz w/Needle Tip **5.29**

STAINLESS NEEDLEPOINT APPLICATOR BOTTLES

Precision application of solvent, flux, paint, oil, glue, ink, cement, contact cleaner, fuel, and ceramic decor. Length 1" or 4" snaps into bottle neck. Includes 1oz bottle, cap and cleaning wire. od = outer diameter; id = inner diameter

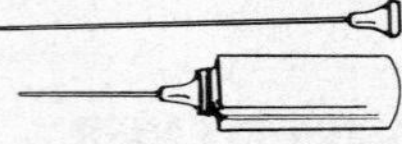

1" NEEDLE EA 2.59 (UNLESS NOTED)

158-16 Blue .016od .008id flow 1
158-20 Yellow .020od .010id flow 2
158-25 Red .025od .013id flow 3
158-35 White .035od .023id flow 8
158-50 Black .050od .033id flow 17
158-65 Clear .065od .047id flow 35
158-73 Set #1 **5.99**
Includes tips for kit #'s 16, 25, 50 and 1 Bottle.
158-76 Set #2 **10.99**
Includes tips for kit #'s 16, 20, 25, 35, 50, 65 and 1 Bottle.

4" NEEDLE EA 3.69

158-164 Blue .016od .008id flow 1
158-204 Yellow .020od .010id flow 2
158-254 Red .025od .013id flow 3
158-354 White .035od .023id flow 8
158-504 Black .050od .033id flow 17
158-654 Clear .065od .047id flow 35

G-GUN

Makes applying grease, glue, putty, or latex/plaster molding material to delicate or hard-to-reach places easy.

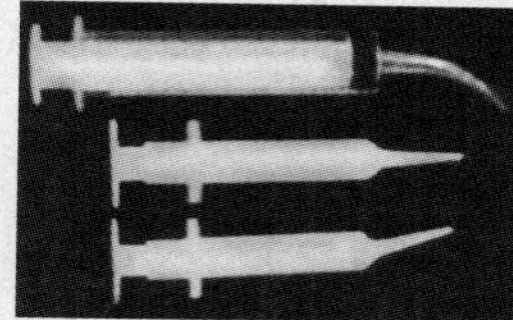

158-900 1/2oz **1.98**
158-901 Jr G-Gun pkg(2) **1.98**
158-902 Jr. G-Gun & Dropper **1.29**

A.J. FRICKO COMPANY

TRACK & MOTOR CLEANER

274-8 Cleano 30ml **34.95**
Universal track and motor cleaner for layouts and locomotives. Just one drop per rail per 4 x 8' area remains effective for 1 year. Cleano will protect against rust even in the dampest basements.

A-LINE

TRACK CLEANING PAD KIT

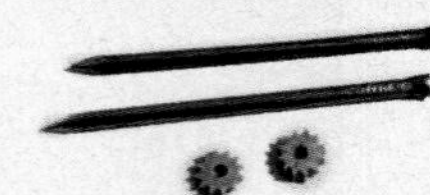

116-10003 3.65
Easily converts most 40' box cars into track cleaning cars. Soft-abrasive pad wipes away built-up grime without scratching rail.

FLYWHEEL CEMENT

116-20010 .02oz **2.65**

SMOKE FLUID & TRACK CLEANER

614-29601 3.50
For improved conductivity and engine performance, keep your track and wheels clean with Aristo-Craft Track Cleaner. It also doubles as smoke fluid, for the cleanest smoke around without the buildup.

LUBRICANTS EA 3.50

Lubricants inhibit rust as well as prevent friction, heat and wear.

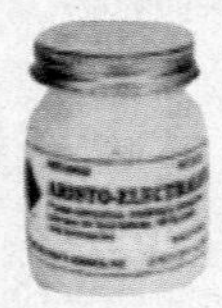

614-29602 Lubricant-Conductive
Add extra conductivity and smooth operation to locomotives by adding to axle bearings and bushings.

614-29603 Aristo-Lube Oil 1.125oz
614-29604 Aristo-Grease 1oz

CARL GOLDBERG MODELS, Inc.

INSTANT ADHESIVES (CYANOACRYLATES)

Normal shelf life is approximately 12 months, which can be extended by refrigeration.

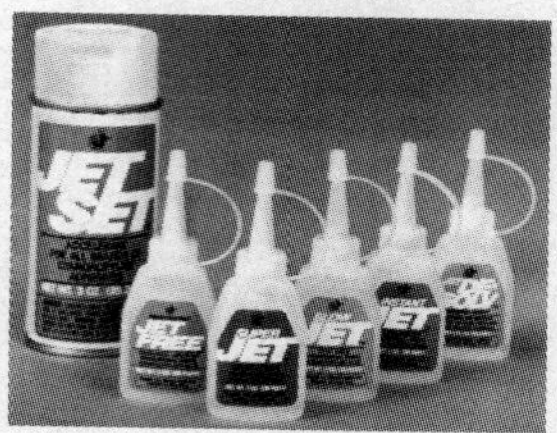

INSTANT JET

Jet instant glue flows like water through 1/4" to 1/2" of a tightly-fitted joint. May be used to bond balsa, hardwood, plywood, many plastics, rubber, glass, ceramics, metal, leather and some fabrics. Apply sparingly and hold parts firmly together for about 15 seconds. Nontoxic.

289-762 1/2oz **3.99**
289-763 1oz **6.49**

SUPER JET

Super Jet may be used to bond balsa, hardwood, celluloid, polyester and epoxy fiberglass, epoxy castings, metals, rubber, ceramics, leather, naugahyde, most plastics and some fabrics. It has gap-filling qualities and sets up in 15-20 seconds.

289-767 1/2oz **3.99**
289-768 1oz **6.49**

SLOW JET

Slow-drying thick formula is excellent for gap filling and delicate, critical fit applications. Dries in 1-2 minutes.

289-772 1/2oz **3.99**
289-773 1oz **6.49**
289-774 2oz **11.99**

JET SET PUMP

Acclerator for all brands of cyanoacrylate adhesives for fast setting and strong glue joints. Can also be used to make instant bonds and fill large and small gaps. Material is freon-free with a very mild odor.

289-777 2oz **5.99**
289-778 Pump Refill 8oz **9.99**

JET DESOLV

289-781 1oz **3.99**
Will dissolve Instant Jet, Super Jet, Slow Jet and other brands of CA glue. Excellent for clean-up.

JET PAC CAP & TIPS

289-789 3.99
Includes cap, five sizes of tips and 12" of pipette tubing. Fits Goldberg adhesive bottles.

EPOXY PLUS

289-790 2oz **9.99**
Eight-minute set-up epoxy is non-sagging, sandable, carvable and paintable. Is 25% lighter than other epoxies.

JET EPOXY

289-791 6 min **11.99**
289-792 20 min **9.99**

MODEL MATE FILLER

289-795 5.49
Filler material for wood, fiberglass or Styrofoam. Putty is nonshrinking, odorless and nontoxic. Easily sanded. Compatible with all types of paints and finishes, can be colored using water colors or latex pigments.

BACHMANN

LUBRICATION

160-99986 Conductive Contact Lube **7.00**

GREASE

160-99987 7.00

OIL EA 7.00

160-99988 Heavy Gear
160-99989 Light Gear

FLOQUIL-POLLY S COLOR CORP.

POLLY SCALE PLASTIC CEMENT

270-505408 Liquid Cement 1/2oz (15ml) **1.99**
Features applicator brush on cover.

BUSCH

ADHESIVE KLEBER

189-7597 10g **10.99**
For plastic, metal, rubber, wood, ceramic, leather.

ADHESIVE HAFTKLEBER

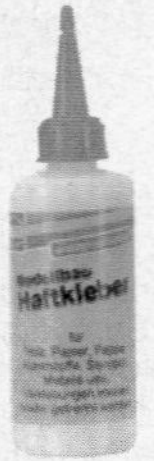

189-7598 100g **7.99**
For wood, paper, cardboard, plastic, styrofoam, metal. Ideal for slippery gravel and much more. Drys quickly and transparent.

CREATIONS UNLIMITED

TOUCH-N-FLOW

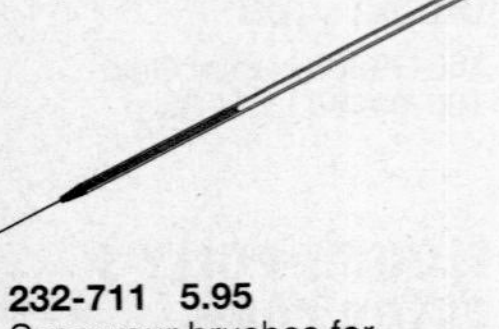

232-711 **5.95**
Save your brushes for painting! Touch-N-Flow applies liquid plastic cements with pinpoint accuracy. Use with Tenax-7R, Ambroid Proweld and CA Activators. Eliminates accidental spillage and evaporation because bottles remain closed and off workbench.

APPLICATOR BOTTLES EA 5.50

One-drop applicators for precise use of thin liquids

232-6003 With 2 Tubes
232-6051 With "Flex" Tube

FALLER

IMPORTED FROM GERMANY BY WALTHERS

PLASTIC CEMENT

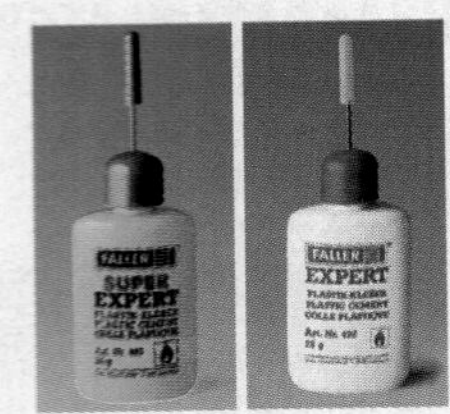

272-490 272-492

272-490 Super EXPERT Cement **4.44**
Bonds quickly and durably, with special hollow needle and protective cap. Dealers MUST order multiples of 24.

272-492 EXPERT Liquid **4.14**
Liquid cement in a plastic bottle with needle applicator for very fine work. Nontoxic, Nonflammable, 25ml. Dealers MUST order multiples of 24.

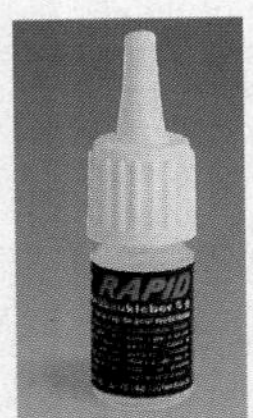

272-491 EXPERT Rapid Cement **5.37**
Split-second modeling cement. Dealers MUST order multiples of 12.

LUBRICANT

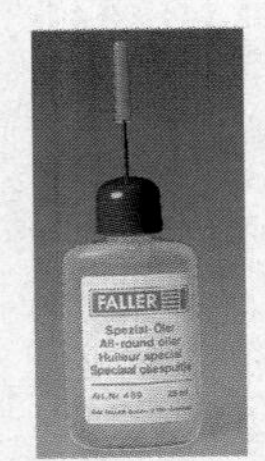

272-489 Special Oiler **6.99**
All-around oiler for small motors and gears. Resin and acid free. 25g.

INTERNATIONAL HOBBY CORP.

TRACK CLEANING PADS

348-4398 pkg(6) **3.98**
Replacement pads for IHC Track Cleaning Car.

Hob-E-Lube

by Woodland Scenics

NEW PREMIUM OILS

HOB-E-LUBE

Premium oils from Woodland Scenics are specially formulated for specific uses. All paint and plastic compatible.

785-661 Ultra-Lite Oil **6.98**
Contains proven anti-wear additives. Use on HO or smaller scales of model trains, precision instruments or where a light oil is needed.

785-662 Lite Oil **6.98**
Multi-viscosity additives for trouble free operation, even at extreme temperatures. Great for home and workshop applications.

785-663 Medium Oil **6.98**
Prevents metal contact and surface scuffing. Specially formulated for use on R/C cars, airplanes, boats and HO Scale and larger model trains.

785-664 Gear Lube **6.98**
A true gear lubricant, where tough, lasting gear oil is needed.

OILS & GREASE

Complete line of oils, greases and dry lubricants for model railroad equipment of any scale. All seven are paint and plastic compatible.

785-650 Workbench Assortment **19.98**
Get all seven in one pack and save yourself over five dollars!

785-651 Dry Graphite **3.79**
With molybdenum. Does not attract dust and dirt.

785-652 Dry White Lube w/Teflon **3.79**
White, non-staining lube doesn't conduct electricity. Use on electrical switches, N & Z worm and gears.

785-653 Ultra Lite Oil **3.79**
Use with close tolerance precision parts.

785-654 Lite Oil **3.79**
General purpose hobby lube, rust preventing.

785-655 Gear Lube **3.79**
Tough, long-lasting lube with high adhesion to prevent dripping.

785-656 Moly Grease **3.79**
With molybdenum, covers entire surface and maintains high viscosity. Ideal for parts exposed to water.

785-657 White Grease w/Teflon **3.79**
Non-staining lube with corrosion protection and water proof lubrication. Good for use outside.

ADHESIVES

HOB-E-TAC

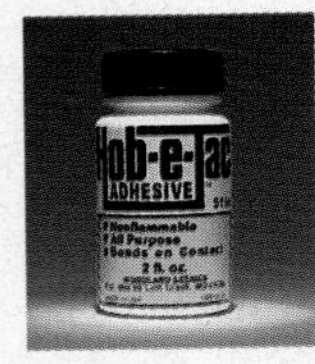

785-195 Hob-e-Tac 2oz **4.79**
All purpose, nonflammable, aggressive high tack adhesive. For making trees and for attaching Clump-Foliage, Field Grass and Foliage Clusters. Can also be used as a contact adhesive.

GLUE

FOAM TACK GLUE

785-1444 Foam Tack Glue 12oz **9.98**
This specially formulated glue is high tack and effective on most materials. Use as a contact cement whenever bonding two large surfaces.

LOW TEMP FOAM GLUE

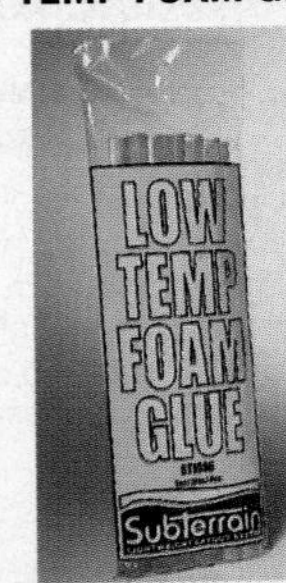

785-1446 pkg(10) **3.98**
Low Temp Glue Sticks melt at a temperature that will not damage foam. Use with Glue Gun #785-1445, sold separately.

KADEE®

LUBRICANT

380-231 Greas-Em Tube **1.95**
A fine dry lubricant ideal for couplers, bearing surfaces and many other model railroad applications.

KIBRI

IMPORTED FROM GERMANY BY WALTHERS

PLASTIC CEMENT

Liquid cement with brush.

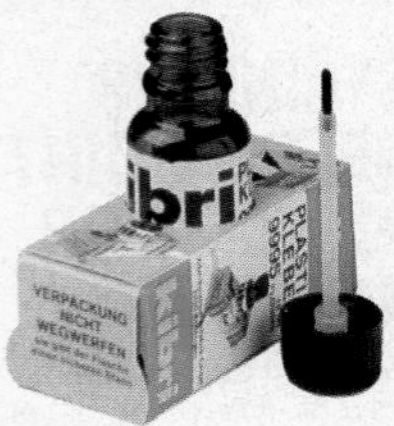

405-9995 .45oz (15ccm) **2.99**
405-9996 3.4oz (100ccm) **6.99**

LIFE-LIKE®

TRACK CLEANER

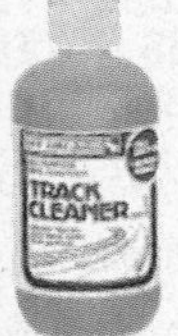

433-1415 8oz **4.75**

433-1440 Track Brite **4.00**

MAINTENANCE KIT

433-8629 **13.25**
Includes Grease Gun, Oil Gun, Track Cleaner, Track Brite and Trouble Shooter Circuit Tester.

Labelle Lubricants inhibit rust when applied to metal parts, as well as preventing friction, heat and wear.

LUBRICANTS

EA 3.99

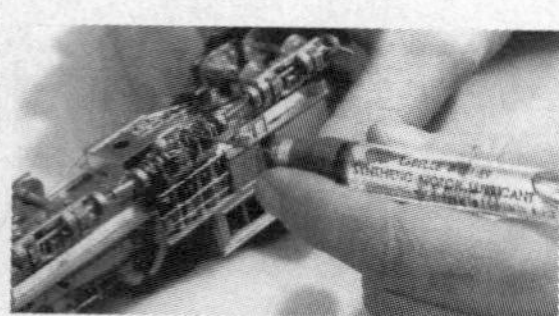

430-101 Synthetic Multi-Purpose Oil 1/2oz
Very light oil for motors, bearings, etc. Natural penetrating action will usually free a "frozen" motor, will damage paints and some plastics.

430-102 Plastic Compatible Gear Lubricant 1/2oz
A true gear oil. Should NOT be used on bushings, bearings, etc. Can be used on plastic.

430-104 Synthetic Multi-Purpose Oil 1/2oz
Medium weight, non-gumming, long lasting. For small power tools, major appliances, etc. Will damage paints and some plastics.

430-106 Plastic Compatible Grease w/Teflon™ 1/2oz
Compatible with other lubricants and can be applied over them if necessary. Non-staining, non-toxic.

430-107 Plastic Compatible Motor Oil 1/2oz
Medium weight lubricant for large scale models with high torque motors.

430-108 Plastic Compatible Motor Oil 1/2oz
Light weight lubricant for small locomotives with low and medium torque motors, precision instruments, sewing machines, etc. Will not harm plastics, painted surfaces. Non-staining.

430-111 Racing Oil 1/2oz
For road race cars. A clean, white, dry, non-staining powdered lubricant. Will not harm plastics or paints. Use dry or add to oils or greases to make them "slipperier".

430-134 Micro-Fine Powdered Teflon™

430-1001 HO Oiler Starter Assortment **12.49**
Medium weight.

MASCOT® PRECISION TOOLS

INSTANT ADHESIVE

230-752 3 Gram Tube (.10 fl oz) Gel **2.99**
High performance, extended range adhesive that bonds metal, plastic, rubber, ceramics and glass in seconds. Bonds colorless, eliminating the "white frosting" effect of other adhesives. No-drip formula fills gaps and is ideal for use on vertical surfaces.

FLITZ METAL POLISH

230-975 10 Gram Tube (.35 fl oz) **4.25**
Cleans, polishes and protects! Acid free, nontoxic, nonabrasive paste rubs on and wipes off. For use on gold, silver brass, platinum, chrome, copper and marble. Concentrated so a little goes a long way.

MICRO ENGINEERING CO.

PLIOBOND® ADHESIVE

For gluing Delrin track or hand-laid rail to ties.

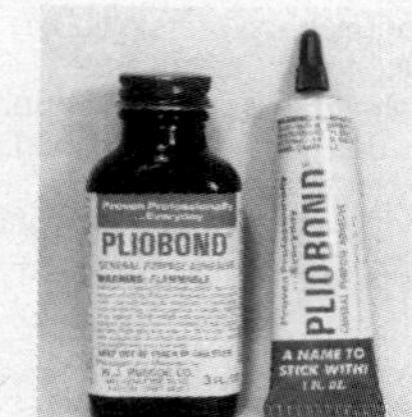

255-49101 With Brush Top 3oz **6.25**

255-49102 With Fine Tip Tube 1oz **4.15**

MICROSCALE INDUSTRIES INC®

LIQUID CEMENT

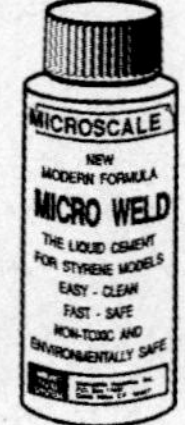

460-109 Micro Weld--Plastic 1oz bottle **2.00**
Colorless liquid plastic-fusing adhesive. (Dissolves a thin layer of each surface to be joined and forms a welded joint.)

460-116 Micro Metal Foil Adhesive 1oz **2.00**
Bonds aluminum foil to models.

MICRO MASK

460-110 1oz bottle **2.00**
Liquid masking that can be brushed on plastic, wood, metal and over paints, etc. After painting is completed, the mask can be peeled off leaving a good delineation.

MODEL POWER

ADHESIVE

490-15 Vunder Glue **3.25**

TRACK CLEANER

490-14 4oz **4.98**

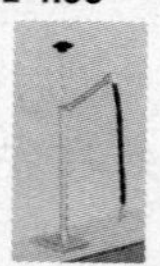

490-250 Cleaning Block **2.49**
Blue ceramic stone.

ADHESIVES

RAIL ZIP

547-452 1oz **4.49**
Liquid track cleaner and corrosion inhibitor. Penetrates existing corrosion layers and restores electrical conductivity to the track. Also retards future corrosion. Nontoxic, contains no solvents, acids, alkalies or alcohols—safe for all metals and plastics.

ZAP-A-GAP/CA + FILLING ADHESIVE

Bonds woods, veneers, cork, vinyl, fabrics, rubber, leather, plastics, metals, stone and porcelain. Also works on oily, fuel-soaked surfaces or prestained miniature pieces.

547-425 4oz **20.99**
547-429 2oz **11.99**
547-431 1oz **6.59**
547-433 1/2oz **3.99**
547-435 1/4oz **2.99**

FLEX ZAP

547-454 20g **7.99**
For use on fiberglass, carbon fiber and plywood. 10-15 second set time

ZAP GEL

A form of thick CA, Zap Gel has the same great formula and is ideal for areas that will be under high stress or load-bearing parts. Concentrated formula will not run, even when applied on vertical surfaces. Perfect for dozens of hobby and household projects.

547-26 20g **6.99** ***NEW***
547-27 3g **1.49** ***NEW***

ZAP/CA SUPER THIN INSTANT ADHESIVE

Very thin, penetrating, instant curing cyanoacrylate adhesive. Parts are held tightly together and a drop of ZAP/CA is applied to the joint and cures in 1-5 seconds. Bonds close fitting balsa, cloth, all woods, veneers, plastics, metals, rubber, oily surfaces, etc.

547-426 4oz **20.99**
547-428 2oz **11.99**
547-430 1oz **6.59**
547-432 1/2oz **3.99**
547-434 1/4oz **2.99**

ZAP-O-CA+ ODORLESS

547-458 20g **9.99**
Bonds balsawood, plywood and fiberglass to Styrofoam without any primers. Bonds Styrofoam to Styrofoam without melting the foam pieces.

PLASTI-ZAP CA++ INSTANT PLASTIC GLUE

547-442 1/3oz **3.49**
For assembly of plastic parts or kits. Will not attack painted surfaces, tacking cures in 10-20 seconds, full cure in 1-3 minutes. Can be removed with debonder or accelerated with ZIP-KICKER. Nonflammable, non-sniffable.

CANOPY GLUE

547-56 Bottle **3.59**
Works on balsa, plywood, plastics, film coverings, fiberglass and any primed or painted surfaces and dries clear.

Z-ENDS DISPENSING TIPS & TUBES

547-441 Z-Ends pkg(10) **3.59**
Extra nozzle extension reaches into tight spots and has a molded ring for storage on bottle neck. 10 Z-Ends tips plus 10 teflon micro dropper tubes included.

ZIP-KICKER GLUE ACCELERATOR

"ZIP-KICKER" accelerator for super glues forces immediate cure for all cyanoacrylates. Use of this accelerator also expands gap filling ability, permits structural fillet forming and solves tough-to-bond combinations of materials.

547-438 2oz **5.99**
547-453 8oz Refill **9.99**

SLO-ZAP CA—SLOW CURE ADHESIVE

547-443 1oz **6.89**
High viscosity, slow cure adhesive has a 30-40 second positioning time and cures in 1-2 minutes. The high viscosity formula permits use on poorly fitting surfaces, large bond areas and is a surface sealing agent for cloth and porous surfaces. Bonds oily surfaces.

POLY-ZAP

547-422 1/2oz **5.49**
Glues and repairs Lexan®. Glues space age plastics and nylon. Doesn't fog parts if glue is applied to film. Repairs EZ kits, too.

Z-7 DEBONDER DEBONDING AGENT

547-439 1oz **3.99**
Waterbased material softens and removes cured cyanoacrylates, paint and hobby decals. Also removes ball point pen inks, permanent marker inks, typist correction fluid, nail polish and scuff marks from painted surfaces. Safe for most plastics.

RIBBONRAIL

TRACK CLEANING BLOCK

Manual cleaning block for rail and wheels consists of an abrasive stone block (1 x 3 x 1/4").

170-11 Less Handle **4.00**
170-12 With Handle **5.25**

NOCH

IMPORTED FROM GERMANY BY WALTHERS

TRACK CLEANING BLOCK

528-50140 7.99
Removes built-up dirt and grime from your tracks.

PECO

IMPORTED FROM GREAT BRITAIN BY WALTHERS

LUBRICANT

552-640 Electro Lube Cleaner & Oil **6.99**
Use to lube motors, gears, commutators and bearings. Pen-type applicator for reaching small parts. Safe for most plastics.

SCALE SCENICS

DIVISION OF CIRCUITRON

SOLDER

652-1502 pkg(10') **2.95**
Ultra-fine rosin core solder (.014" diameter), is electronics grade (60% tin, 40% lead). Ideal for soldering miniature circuits, detailing for brass models or to simulate scale size hose or piping.

PLASTRUCT

PLASTIC SOLVENT CEMENT

570-2 Plastic Weld 2oz Bottle **3.25**
A colorless, liquid, plastic-fusing adhesive. Dissolves a thin layer of each surface to form a welded joint as strong as the surrounding area. Bonds styrene, ABS, butyrate and acrylics.

570-3 Bondene 2oz Bottle **3.25**
A colorless, liquid, plastic-fusing adhesive. Dissolves a thin layer of each surface to form a welded joint as strong as the surrounding area. Bonds styrene to styrene, ABS to ABS and most other alike plastic combinations.

570-4 Weldene 2oz Bottle **3.95**
A nontoxic, colorless, liquid, plastic-fusing adhesive. Instantly tacky, cures in hours. Provides a permanent bond. Environmentally friendly. Bonds styrene to styrene only.

Information STATION

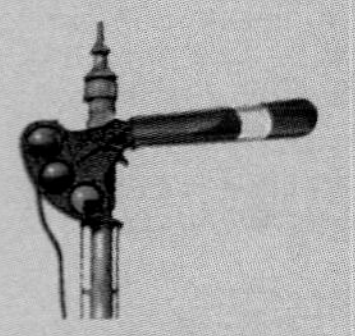

John Henry

John Henry (aka Jawn Henry) was a "steel drivin' man." He worked at building railroad cuts and tunnels throughout the south. Like all steel driving men, he used a ten-pound hammer to drive steel drill bits into solid rock. These holes were then filled with nitroglycerin or black powder in order for the railroad companies to blast through the mountains.

Shortly after the Civil War a steam-powered drilling machine arrived on the scene. All six feet four inches of John Henry didn't like the sight of it one bit and openly displayed his contempt. Thus, a man vs. machine contest was born. It was because of this contest that John Henry became a legend.

The wager was a hundred dollars, and of course, Henry's pride and prestige. A crowd of people gathered and a time limit was set.

According to legend, Henry wielded two twenty-pound hammers, one in each hand, and drove two holes seven feet deep. The steam-powered machine drilled one hole nine feet deep. Man had won and the legend was born.

It's been said that Henry died immediately after that contest. Also, that he lived into the night and died in his sleep. It has even been said that he didn't die at all that day; rather he lived for years after working for the railroads.

Regardless of what happened or how it happened, the truth remains that John Henry defied the odds, bested the machine, and became part of railroad history.

Satellite City
"HOT STUFF"

ADHESIVES

HOT STUFF™
Cyanoacrylate, colorless liquid instant adhesive that bonds wood, glass, metal, leather, fabric, rubber and most plastics in 5-10 seconds. Nontoxic.

639-54 2oz **9.95**
639-58 4oz **18.95**
639-501 1/2oz **3.60**
639-502 1/4oz **2.50**
639-504 1oz **5.75**

SUPER T™
Gap-filling clear cyanoacrylate glue with a cure rate of 10-25 seconds, allowing time to position parts after glue is applied. Besides having the speed and strength of HOT STUFF, SUPER T's thick density makes it especially suitable for joining parts that don't fit perfectly.

639-499 4oz **18.95**
639-505 1oz **5.75**
639-506 1/2oz **3.60**
639-507 1/4oz **2.50**
639-508 2oz **9.95**

SPECIAL T™
Thick, clear, cyanoacrylate glue with a consistency five times that of SUPER T. Thick consistency allows up to 50 seconds positioning time (most materials bond 30 to 50 seconds).

639-514 4oz **20.95**
639-515 2oz **10.95**
639-516 1oz **6.50**

UFO™ INSTANT GLUE

THIN
Penetrating, odorless and no curing fumes. Instant clear glue for the cyano-sensitive modeler. Will not attack white foam, allows full joint coverage of all bonds.

639-519 1oz **11.95**
639-520 2oz **20.95**

THICK
Odorless and no curing fumes. Ultra Gap Filling clear instant glue. Set time of 50-60 seconds. Use for assembly work.

639-521 1oz **11.95**
639-522 2oz **20.95**

NCF™ ACCELERATOR
An extremely fast-acting accelerator for all instant glues. Parts may be sprayed up to 8 minutes in advance of bonding. May melt some expanded foam products. Non-Freon, dries instantly.

639-2 Pump Spray 2oz **6.95**
639-5 Pump Spray 4.9oz **11.95**
639-18 Refill 18oz **39.95**

MILD FORMULA
For use with HOT STUFF, UFO, Odorless THIN, SUPER T, SPECIAL T and UFO Odorless THICK. Works in four ways: easier, faster, stronger and able to bond some unusual materials. May melt some expanded foam products.

639-213 Pump Spray 2oz **5.95**
639-5131 Pump Spray 4.9oz **9.95**
639-1813 Refill 18oz **35.95**

SPRAY 'N CURE
Free of all chlorinated and fluorinated solvents. Works just like HOT SHOT accelerator. Has a 2-minute on-part life after area is completely dry. Allow 50 to 60 seconds (at room temperature) for complete drying before bonding.

639-510 Pump Spray 2oz **5.25**
639-5016 Refill 16oz **28.95**

REPLACEMENT ACCESSORIES
639-100 Spray Pumps pkg(2) **1.95**
For accelerators.

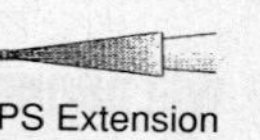

639-101 Pro-TIPS Extension Applicators pkg(12) **1.95** *NEW*
Fits all Hot Stuff spout sizes.
639-500 18" Tube Teflon pkg(10) **5.00**

For #s 501 and 504.

639-509 12" Tube Super T pkg(10) **5.00**
For #s 406, 505 and 508.
Dealers: MUST order pack of 10.

639-511

639-600

639-511 Small Hot Tips pkg(2) **1.25**
No clog, for #s 501 and 506.

639-600 Large Hot Tips pkg(2) **1.95**
639-700 Hot Tips–UFO pkg(2) **1.95**
No clog spouts.

DEBONDER SOLVENT

639-512 Ultra Super Solvent 2oz **5.98**
Nitroparaffin based for cyanoacrylate/super glues.

SQUADRON PRODUCTS

PLASTIC PUTTY

SQUADRON FILLER PUTTY EA 2.98
Make sure your models look their best before painting with these filler putties.
A long-time favorite with aviation, military, figure and automobile modelers, Squadron Green and White Filler Putty is ideal for railroad models too.

Designed to quickly and easily fill gaps between plastic or metal parts, or repair surface scratches and nicks, the putty is fine grained (especially nice for small scale models) and quick drying. Just apply, allow to dry for 30 minutes, then sand to final shape.

Each tube includes 2.3oz of putty, enough for several projects. Two different colors are offered to provide a suitable contrast on your models. This makes it easier to sand just the areas that need to be filled without removing surrounding detail. Choose from white (which is somewhat finer) for lighter-colored kits, or green for darker-colored kits.

680-9055 Green (for Dark Color Plastics)
680-9065 White (for Light Color Plastics)

ROCO

IMPORTED FROM AUSTRIA BY WALTHERS

OILER
625-10906 **11.99**
Prevents friction, heat and wear.

RUBBER TRACK CLEANER

625-10002 **9.99**
For cleaning and removing dirt & oil deposits from your tracks.

GREASE FOR LOCO GEARS

625-10905 8g **7.99**

STEWART PRODUCTS

TRACK CLEANER

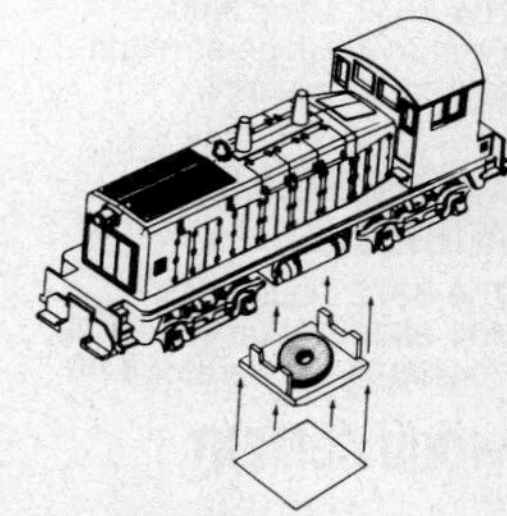

683-501 **9.95**
The track cleaner slips over the fuel tank of the Athearn SW-7 and rubs rails by gravity. Each cleaner includes 10 self-abrasive sanding pads for easy replacement.

REPLACEMENT PADS
683-502 pkg(30) **7.95**

TRU-SCALE MODELS

RAIL CLEANER
730-1425 **4.00**
Abrasive track cleaner, curved for easy use on hard to reach track.

ADHESIVES

Fast drying, non-yellowing cements.

PLASTIC CEMENT

704-3501 Tube 5/8oz **1.00**
Dealers: MUST order Dealer Pack of 48.

704-3502 Liquid–Bottle 1oz **1.98**
For clean, transparent plastic-to-plastic joints.
Dealers: MUST order Dealer Pack of 12.

704-3507 Liquid Cement w/Precision Applicator **3.49**
Dealers: MUST order Dealer Pack of 6.

704-3515 Clear Parts Cement 3oz **3.49**

NON-TOXIC PLASTIC CEMENT

704-3521 Tube 5/8oz **1.00**
For use by children.
Dealers: MUST order Dealer Pack of 48.

CEMENT PEN

704-3532 1/3oz **3.00**
Fast-drying, high-strength cement for plastic.

MODEL MASTER ADHESIVES

704-8872 Liquid **4.49**
704-8874 Instant Glue **4.98**
704-8875 Accelerator **4.98**

WOOD CEMENT

EXTRA-FAST DRYING

Hot fuel proof.

704-3503 5/8oz **1.29**
Dealers: MUST order Dealer Pack of 24.

704-3504 1-3/4oz **2.29**
Dealers: MUST order Dealer Pack of 12.

FAST DRYING

704-3505 5/8oz **1.29**
Dealers: MUST order Dealer Pack of 24.

704-3506 1-3/4oz **2.29**
Dealers: MUST order Dealer Pack of 12.

GLUING TIPS

704-8805 pkg(5) **1.49**
Fits most tubes of glue for precise glue application.
Dealers: MUST order Dealer Pack of 12

DECAL SETTING SOLUTION

704-8804 1/4oz Bottle **1.10**

PLASTIC PUTTY

704-3511 5/8oz **1.49**
Can be used to fill, sculpture or redesign a surface.
Dealers: MUST order Dealer Pack of 24.

SOLDER

- Indium-based solder
- Melts at 275° F (150° lower than lead-tin solders—with a much higher wetting ability)
- Specific Gravity is 8.6
- Bonding holding strength is 4,000 lbs. PSI

Will never tarnish; contains no silver or bismuth and will solder to platinum, gold, silver and numerous alloys. Solid state components can be soldered without using a heat sink. Repairs to printed circuit boards are simple as the low melting point will not damage the board. Use with any flux, rosin, chloride or acid.

118-1 20 Sticks **10.85**
118-2 60 Sticks **31.50** *NEW*

FLUX

Works on most metals and alloys and may be used with any soft solder. Water soluble and will wash off after drying. If a possibility of corrosion exists, may be neutralized by a solution of bicarbonate of soda.

118-3 1/2oz **2.85**
118-4 2oz **4.65** *NEW*
118-5 8oz **14.55** *NEW*
118-6 16oz **23.35** *NEW*

ANTI-FLUX

Fast drying liquid inhibitor. Apply over area where solder is not wanted. Solder immediately after applying. Water soluble, may be washed or brushed off and used with any soft solder.

118-7 1/2oz **2.85**
118-8 2oz **4.65** *NEW*
118-9 8oz **14.55** *NEW*
118-10 16oz **23.35** *NEW*

WELDBOND

WELDBOND

All-around wood glue, ballast cement, sealer, hardener, weather-proofer and more. Dries clear. Porous and non-porous applications. Safe to use. For ballast cement, mix one part Weldbond with two parts water.

A Weldbond application book is available at no charge. Please send a self-addressed stamped envelope to Walthers.

797-125 4oz **3.39**
797-185 8oz **4.95**
797-795 1/2gal **22.20**
797-1395 1gal **37.00**

YE OLDE HUFF-N-PUFF

FLUX

792-2015 1oz Bottle **3.00**
Non-corrosive soft solder liquid flux.

TENAX-7R

The Space Age Plastic Welder.

SPACE AGE CONSTRUCTION KIT

731-8 **16.99** *NEW*
This new kit includes one bottle of Tenax-7R, one "Touch-N-Flow" liquid applicator, one "Easi-Fill" applicator filling bottle, one 25 unit packet of "Microbrushes" and instructions.

PLASTIC WELDER

731-7 **2.50**
Tenax-7R causes plastic to become its own bonding agent. Works on styrene, butyrate, ABS and acrylic plastics. Apply Tenax-7R with a fine hair bristled brush or a Touch-N-Flow applicator (232-711). Nonflammable, non-sniffable, non-sticky and leaves no residue. Tenax-7R bonds in seconds and dries in minutes.

Dealers: MUST Order Dealer Pack of 12.

VOLLMER

IMPORTED FROM GERMANY BY WALTHERS

CLEAR PLASTIC CEMENT

For use on plastic kits. Delayed drying time allows gluing of larger surface areas. Non-toxic, nonflammable.

770-6016 Supercement 25ml **4.99**

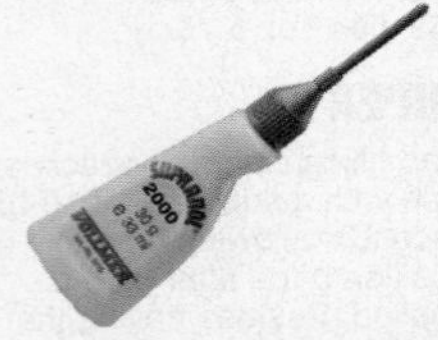

770-6115 Supranol 33ml **5.99**

PAINT

On the endless prairies of western Canada, they are often the only signs of civilization. A pair of steel rails, shiny or dark with rust, and an aging grain elevator.

They stand in colorful contrast to the changing seasons. Stark and bright against the green fields of spring. Muted and somber against the gray-white days of winter.

In between, the long days and nights are broken by the passing trains. Today's bright schemes and bold lettering are a far cry from the days when the line was new. The brown box cars and black steamers of yesterday are only memories now.

Watch the action on a typical day and you'll see a rainbow of schemes. Bright orange and black diesels streak past, and the occasional run-through units stand out even more. Brightly painted and lettered containers from around the world can be seen on the many intermodal trains. Once a day, you can watch a VIA passenger train fly by. And in the fall, the sidings glow with brightly painted covered hoppers.

As the tallest point for miles, the elevator is a natural landmark for railfans who wander out this far. Alberto Franchi offers a dramatic bird's eye view of the action from high atop his scratchbuilt elevators. Northeastern lumber and Grandt Line windows were used in construction, and the building was finished with Testors colors and Letra-Set dry transfers. The brass import diesels were done with Accu-Colors and weathered with various Floquil shades.

Models and Photo by Alberto Franchi

WALTHERS™

DECAL SETTING SOLUTION

904-470 Solvaset 2oz 60ml **2.98**
Dealers: MUST Order Multiples of 6

Make decals snuggle down on any surface. Softens decal film so it stretches over surface details like rivets, seams and hinges. Eliminates air bubbles, white spots and draping without hiding detail.

MASKING LIQUID

904-106 Magic Masker 20cc **2.98**
Dealers: MUST Order Multiples of 12

An easy way to mask off small areas or odd shaped parts where tape won't work. Just brush it on and allow to dry. Then spray your color, let dry and peel off. Works on plastic, wood, metal, paint, doped surfaces, chrome and silver.

SMP INDUSTRIES Accu-paint

Capture the color of railroading in the eastern U.S. with these All-Purpose paints. Most are matched to actual samples of prototype paint. Finely ground, lead-free pigments cover smoothly without hiding details. Brush or spray directly on wood, metals or plastics without the need for a barrier coat. Dries to a hard, glossy finish in minutes.

We have worked closely with this manufacturer to provide accurate delivery information at the time this catalog was published. Items listed in blue ink may not be available at all times. Current delivery information, along with a list of in-stock products for this line, can be found on our Web site at www.walthers.com.

RAILROAD COLORS 1 OZ (30ML) EA 3.50

102-1 Stencil White
102-2 Stencil Black
102-3 Boston & Maine Blue
102-4 Bangor & Aroostook Blue
102-5 D&H Blue
102-6 Grand Trunk Western Blue
102-7 CR Blue
102-8 Vermilion
102-9 Cornell Red
102-10 Chinese Red
102-11 CP Rail Action Red
102-12 Oxide Brown
102-15 Warm Orange
102-16 NH Red-Orange
102-17 CN Orange
102-18 CN Red-Orange
102-19 CN Yellow
102-20 Medium Yellow
102-21 MEC Harvest Yellow
102-22 Imitation Gold
102-24 EL Yellow
102-25 Hunters Green
102-26 MEC Pine Green
102-27 401 Green
102-30 CN Green
102-31 Brunswick Green
102-32 Jade Green
102-33 RDG Green
102-34 EL Maroon
102-35 Passenger Maroon
102-36 Engine Maroon
102-38 CP Tuscan Red
102-39 Alkyd Brown
102-40 Aluminum
102-41 Rich Gold
102-42 CN Lettering Gray
102-43 CP Gray
102-45 NYC Light Gray
102-46 NYC Dark Gray
102-48 EL Gray
102-51 CP Rail Action Green
102-52 CP Rail Action Yellow
102-53 Deep Red
102-54 Rich Oxide Brown
102-55 Erie Green
102-56 Gray-Green
102-59 Iron Oxide
102-61 VIA Blue
102-62 Weathered Black
102-63 ATSF War Bonnet Blue
102-64 ATSF War Bonnet Yellow
102-65 SP Lark Dark Gray
102-67 UP/MILW Armour Yellow
102-68 UP/MILW Harbor Mist Gray
102-69 ATSF War Bonnet Red
102-70 BN Green
102-71 IC Gulf Orange
102-72 DRGW Yellow
102-74 Chessie Blue
102-75 Southern Green
102-76 Guilford Gray
102-78 NP Dark Green
102-79 NP Light Green
102-80 CSX Blue
102-81 CSX Gray

PRIMER

102-98 Metal-Plastic 1oz (30ml) **3.50**
Special primer-sealer for use on plastics or metals when spraying Accu-Paint colors. Provides an ideal surface to prevent chipping, peeling or lifting. Can be sprayed without thinning.

THINNER

Specially formulated for thinning All-Purpose series colors, will not attack most modeling plastics. Can also be used to clean spray equipment or brushes.

102-100 Bottle 1oz (30ml) **3.50**
102-10016 Pint Can 16oz (480ml) **14.95**

FINISHES 1OZ (30ML) EA 3.50

Crystal-clear finishes with varying amounts of flattening agents, for shiny, semi-gloss or flat finish.

102-101 Satin Finish
102-102 Semi-Gloss Finish
102-103 Gloss Finish
102-104 Weathering Finish
Weather models in a single step! Special satin finish has a transparent grime color to dirty and dull models with less work.

DECAL SETTING SOLUTION

102-500 Accu-Set 1oz (30ml) **3.39**

GB ENGINEERING

WORK HOLDER

298-600 Painting Handle **5.95**
Hold models securely and keep your hands clean while you paint. Works well with all types of models. "V"-shaped aluminum handle has foam pads on ends to prevent damage. Spring-loaded legs are adjusted with screw and nut to provide constant holding force. Secure grip lets you safely turn model to any position while airbrushing or spray painting.

BUILDERS IN SCALE

WEATHERING

169-106 Silverwood Stain 4oz **6.98**
Give new wood an aged, weather-beaten look in minutes. Premixed and packaged, Silverwood is perfect for use on wooden kits, scratchbuilding projects and produces an especially nice effect on shingled roofs. Material is alcohol based. Includes applicator.

CHALKS

169-107 Weathering Chalk Set **14.98**
Add lots of neat weathering effects to your models with this set of eight chalks. Includes Terra Cotta, Red-Brown, Brown, Rust, Black, Light Gray, Medium Gray and Dark Gray chalks, plus an applicator brush.

CUSTOM HOBBYIST, INC.®

PAINT STRIPPER

CHAMELEON™ STRIPPER

Safely remove paint from plastic or metal in minutes. Chameleon stripper is noncaustic, water soluble and biochemically degradable so it won't hurt the environment. Safe for most hobby plastics, works in about 15 minutes. Can be reused.

359-1000

359-1 Pint **11.99**
359-2 Quart **17.99**
359-1000 8oz **6.99**

CHAMELEON™ GEL

Same formula as regular Chameleon stripper, but in a thicker gel coat that clings to models. Great for removing stubborn paint. Choose from three convenient sizes.

359-10 8oz **6.99**
359-11 16oz **9.99**
359-12 32oz **14.99**

FALLER

PAINT MARKER PENS

272-690 Modeler's Color Pens pkg(6) **25.99**
Ideal for painting any kind of models. Water-based paints are opaque, economic and quick drying. Set includes red, yellow, orange, lavender, blue and green.

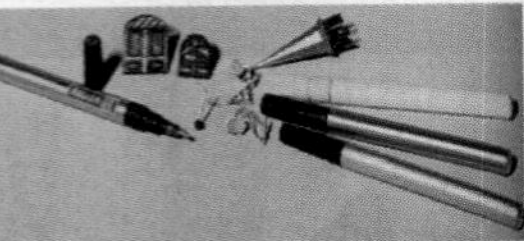

272-691 Metallic Paint Pens pkg(4) **22.99**
A fast and easy way to simulate a variety of natural metal finishes on your models. Includes white for base coat, plus gold, silver and copper. Colors are durable, permanent and quick drying.

GYROS

RED SABLE PAINT BRUSHES

SETS PKG(3) EA 6.65

Brush sets can be used with water or oil paint, enamels, varnish, lacquer, etc.

321-1900 3/0, 00 & 0
321-1910 #1, #3 & #5
321-1920 10/0, 5/0 & 4/0

WATER COLOR BRUSHES

Short handles, each pack includes six brushes of the same size.

321-5270 #0 **26.29**
321-5271 #1 **28.59**
321-5272 #2 **32.29**
321-5273 #3 **37.89**
321-52720 #00 **25.75**
321-52730 #000 **25.75**
321-52740 #0000 **25.75**

Airbrushes, parts and accessories, ideal for finishing all types of models, home, craft and art projects or professional painting and illustration. Brushes are equipped with spray head assembly and needle to produce one of three adjustable spray patterns:

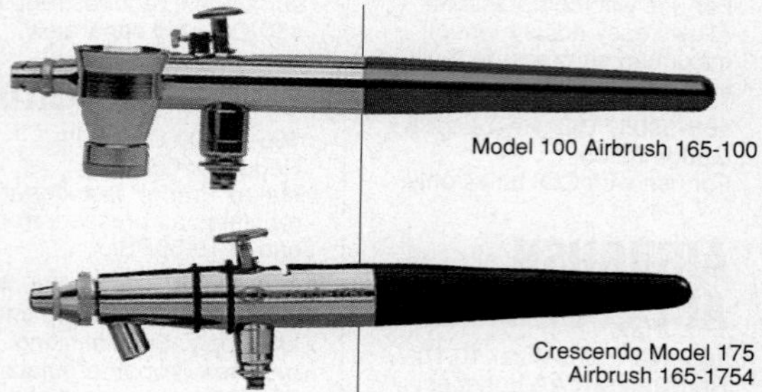

Model 100 Airbrush 165-100

Crescendo Model 175 Airbrush 165-1754

CAUTION: For your safety, the use of a properly vented spray booth and a respirator which is paint mist and vapor compatible, is strongly recommended when painting with an airbrush.

AIRBRUSHES

MODEL 100 AIRBRUSH

Dual action, internal mix for fine detail work, each features: color cup or cavity, counter-balanced handle, self-lubricating Teflon® needle bearing, and head seal, plus a non-slip, one-piece trigger that can be used in either hand.

165-100 Fine **94.00**
Model 100 Airbrush with Fine needle and head, 1/16oz (2cc) color cup, protective cap, spare needle, wrench for head, hanger, instruction book and storage case.

165-101 Medium **94.00**
Same as #100, with Medium needle and head.

165-102 Gravity Feed - Fine **106.00**
Same as #100, but with gravity feed airbrush with color cup which holds 1/16oz. (2cc).

MODEL 100 LG GRAVITY FEED AIRBRUSH BASIC SETS EA 106.00

For use with thinned artist acrylics and vinyls, and lighter viscosity materials.

Model 100 LG series airbrush with permanent top-mounted color cup and fitted cover (holds 1/3oz (10.5cc) of color), hanger, extra needle, protective cap, wrench and padded case.

165-1005 Fine
165-1006 Medium
165-1007 Heavy

MODEL 100SG AIRBRUSH

165-1008 Extra Fine **94.00**
Includes Model 100 gravity feed airbrush with built in fluid cavity. Designed to spray precise amounts.

MODEL 150 AIRBRUSH

Identical to model 100, but use jars or a removable color cup to hold paint.

BASIC SETS EA 101.00

Model 150 airbrush, attachable 3/4oz (22cc) and 2oz (60cc) paint jars with covers for big jobs, or force-fit color cup for smaller work, case, hanger, wrench, protective cap, self-lubricating Teflon® needle bearing, head seal and siphon tube, plus non-slip, one-piece trigger.

165-150 Fine
165-153 Heavy

DELUXE SETS

165-152 Fine **135.00**
Fine head assembly and needle, 8' (2.45m) braided air hose, 1/4" pipe thread adapter (for use with compressor or CO^2 tank), wrench for head, hanger, instruction booklet and wooden case.

165-1507 Fine & Heavy **124.00**
Same as 165-152, but with Fine and Heavy head assemblies and needles, plus cardboard storage box.

CRESCENDO MODEL 175 AIRBRUSH

Bottom-feed, dual action, internal mix design.

AIRBRUSH ONLY EA 87.00

165-1754 Fine
165-1755 Medium
165-1756 Heavy

BASIC SETS EA 106.00

Includes Model 175 airbrush, 1/4oz (7cc) metal color cup, 3/4oz (22cc) jar with adapter, 2oz (60cc) jar, spare needle, instruction book, protective cap, hanger and plastic case.

165-1751 Fine
165-1752 Medium
165-1753 Large

DELUXE SET

165-1757 Crescendo Set **125.00**
Crescendo 175 Airbrush with all three tips (Fine, Medium and Heavy), spray regulators and needles, 8 ft (2.45m) braided air hose, 3/4oz (22cc) jar with adapter, two 2oz (60cc) paint jars, one 1/4oz metal paint cup, hanger, protective cap and instruction book.

MODEL 200 AIRBRUSH

Single action delivers a pre-set amount of fluid

BASIC SETS EA 66.00

Model 200 airbrush, attachable 3/4oz (22cc) jar and 2oz (60cc) jar with cover, protective cap and wrench.

165-2001 Medium
165-2002 Large

DELUXE SETS

165-2003 Fine **81.00**
6' (1.83m) vinyl hose, propel regulator, attachable 3/4oz jar, spare 3/4oz jar with cover and can of Propel®.

165-2004 Medium w/Compressor **280.00**
Model 180 portable diaphragm compressor, 10' (3.05m) braided airhose, 1/4" pipe thread fitting (adapts brush to compressor or CO^2 tank), attachable and spare 3/4oz jar, one 2oz jar with cover and protective cap.

165-2005 Medium Only **78.00**
Includes: 6' (1.83m) vinyl airhose, Propel® regulator, attachable and spare 3/4oz jars, one 2oz jar with cover and protective cap.

GRAVITY FEED BASIC SETS EA 65.00 (UNLESS NOTED)

Identical to Model 200, but with permanently attached 1/16oz (2cc) color cup, ideal for smaller jobs. All sets include protective cap, wrench for head and storage case.

165-2009 Fine
165-20010 Medium
165-20011 Fine w/Built-in Cavity **60.00**
Built-in color cavity holds enough color for small jobs.

MODEL 250 AIRBRUSH

Single action, external mix, bottom feed design. Spray pattern adjusts from 3/4" (18.9mm) to 2" (50.8mm).

BASIC SETS

Model 250 airbrush with 3/4oz (22cc) jars and cover, 6' (1.83m) vinyl air hose and Propel® regulator.

165-2501 Boxed Set **23.00**

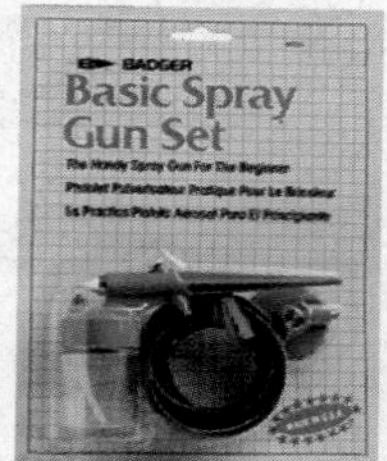

165-2502 Carded Set **20.00**
165-2503 With Propel® **30.00**
Same as #2501, but includes a can of Propel®

165-2504 Large Capacity Set **31.00**
Same as #2503, with larger Model 250 Airbrush and attached 4oz (120cc) jar.

165-2507 Basic Spray Gun Hobby Set **45.00**
Includes Model 250 airbrush with attached and spare 3/4oz (22cc) jars and cover, 6' (1.83m) vinyl air hose and Propel® regulator, three hobby colors, mixing pipette, how-to book and instructions.

MODEL 350 AIRBRUSH

Single action, external mix, bottom feed design. Makes a larger dot spray pattern.

BASIC SETS EA 48.00

Include: Model 350 airbrush, 2oz (60cc) jar with cover, attachable 3/4oz (22cc) jar, wrench for head and instruction booklet, plus storage box.

165-3501 Fine
165-3504 Medium
165-3505 Heavy

BASIC SETS W/ACCESSORIES

165-3502 Medium **54.00**
6' (1.83m) vinyl air hose and Propel® regulator.

165-3503 Medium **62.00**
6' vinyl air hose, 1/4oz (7cc) self-standing color cup, can of Propel® and regulator.

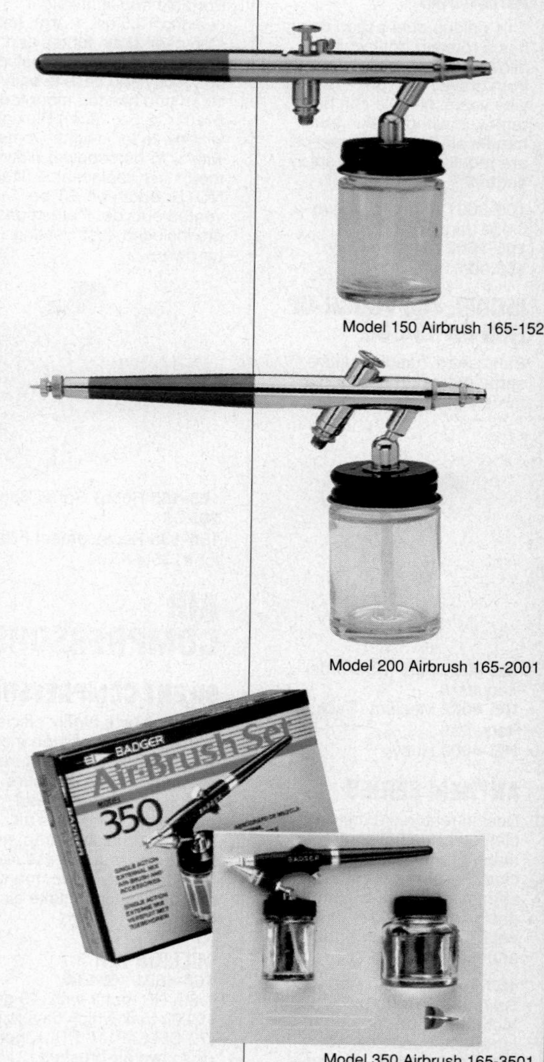

Model 150 Airbrush 165-152

Model 200 Airbrush 165-2001

Model 350 Airbrush 165-3501

DELUXE SETS

165-3506 Complete Craft Set **88.00**
Model 350 medium tip w/attachable 3/4oz (22cc) jar, 6' (1.83m) vinyl air hose, Propel® can and regulator, 3/4oz jar w/cover, 3 reusable Mylar stencils, 2 sheets BriteWhite airbrush paper, 5 Air-Tex textile colors, one 1oz Air Tex cleaner, hanger, and how-to booklet.

165-35004 Model 350 Airbrush Set **84.00**
Includes 3 tips (Fine, Medium and Heavy) & needles, attached 3/4oz (22cc) jar, 2oz (60cc) jar with cover, plus 8' (2.45m) braided air hose and 1/4" pipe thread fitting (converts airbrush for use with compressor or CO2 tank).

MODEL 360 UNIVERSAL AIRBRUSH

This unique dual-action design has a rotating front which allows a quick conversion from from gravity to syphon feed or vise versa. Needle can be removed without taking the handle off. No additional tips are required to change spray patterns.

165-3601 Airbrush w/Two 3/4oz Jars **160.00**
165-3602 Airbrush Only **153.00**

MODEL 400 TOUCH-UP GUN EA 134.00

Fan control needle adjusts spray pattern from round to fan-shape.

165-4001 Fine (Backorder Required)
165-4002 Medium (Backorder Required)
165-4003 Heavy

ANTHEM SERIES

Design features a thinner diameter needle; spray material without having to change spray heads. Body is a streamlined, light-weight design that provides exacting balance for easy operation and maximum user comfort.

165-1551 Anthem Airbrush Starter Set **107.00**
Includes 1/4oz cup, 3/4oz jar/adapter and 2oz jar.
165-1552 Anthem Airbrush Only **87.00**

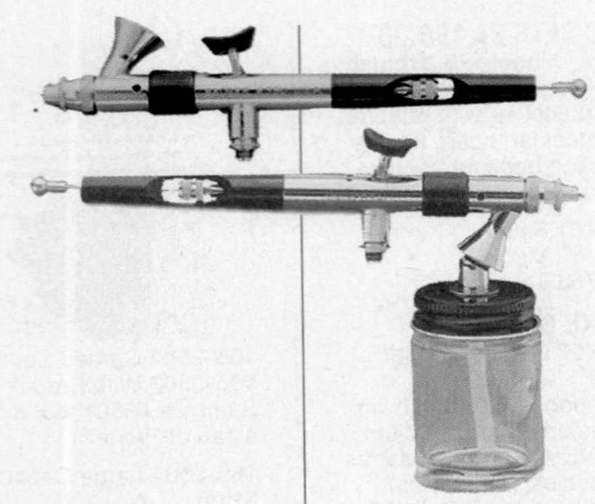

Model 360 Universal Airbrush
165-3601

165-1557 Anthem Airbrush Complete Set **119.00**
Includes brush, hose, 3 jars w/adapter, color cup, hanger and display box.

SPRAY BOOTH

Portable and lightweight (weighs 10.5lbs, 4.7kg), helps stop overspray, fumes and odors. Lightweight, translucent polypropylene case is easy to clean and has top mounted 5 x 8" (12.5 x 20cm) Plexiglas window to let in light. Comes with 1/25 horsepower blower motor with replaceable filter. NOTE: Booth MUST be vented outside. Instructions are included, less venting hardware.

165-135 Hobby Spray Booth **263.55**
165-136 Replacement Filter for #135 **4.55**

AIR COMPRESSORS

SILENT COMPRESSORS

Powered by a highly efficient, oil reciprocating piston motor, silent compressors feature automatic on/off pressure switch, thermal overload protection, adjustable air regulator, moisture trap, gauge for line pressure, pressure release safety valve, manual on/off valve and intake air filter.

MILLION-AIR

165-4801 634.00
1/6th HP motor with .45 gallon (1.70l) tank which develops .70 CFM at 116 PSI. Operates up to two air-brushes.

BILLION-AIR

165-4802 754.00
1/4 HP motor with 1.06 gallon (4.08l) tank which develops .90 CFM at 116 PSI. Operates up to three airbrushes.

TRILLION-AIR

165-4803 889.00
1/2 HP piston motor with 1.06 gallon (4.08l) tank which develops 1.75 CFM at 116 PSI. Operates up to five airbrushes.

CYCLONE I AIR COMPRESSORS

Oil-less, diaphragm type compressor has internal bleed, allowing use with any airbrush. Develops .80 CFM at 25 PSI. 1/12 horsepower motor, maximum air pressure: 40 pounds.
Measures 8-1/4 x 4-3/4 x 7" (20.6 x 11.8 x 17.5 cm).

165-1801 Standard **212.00**
165-18011 Automatic Shut-Off **273.00**
Same as #1801 but shuts off automatically when you release airbrush trigger.

WHIRLWIND II COMPRESSOR

165-802 160.00
Portable, very lightweight (5lbs, 4.53kg) and quiet. Oil-less, diaphragm type compressor has internal bleed, allowing use with any airbrush. Develops .40 CFM at 20 PSI. 1/20 horsepower motor, maximum air pressure: 35 pounds. Measures 8 x 4-1/2 x 5" (20 x 11.2 x 12.5 cm)

COMPRESSOR ACCESSORIES

165-50023 1/4" Pipe Thread Fitting Adapter **3.45**
Adapts airhose to compressor or CO^2 tank.

165-50051 Moisture Trap **42.00**
Air filter and water trap for air compressors.

165-50054 Air Regulator Filter & Gauge Set **60.65**
For use with compressors. Allows easy adjustment of maximum air pressure, built-in filter traps moisture.

165-50057 CO^2 Regulator & Gauge **82.55**
For use with CO^2 tanks only.

AIRBRUSH ACCESSORIES

165-121 Paint Mixer **10.10**
Requires two AA batteries, sold separately.

OIL & LUBRICANT

165-122 REGDAB™ Airbrush Lubricant 1oz (30cc) **4.30**
Maintains smooth trigger action and eliminates needle friction caused by dried paint.

165-50052 Replacement Oil 24oz (.75l) **10.30**
Special lightweight oil for use in all Silent compressors.

AIRBRUSH HOLDERS

165-125 Model 125 **27.30**
Heavy-duty unit holds two airbrushes; rotates, swivels and clamps on any surface up to 2" thick.

165-50021 Airbrush Hanger **3.25**
Metal holder included with sets.

PAINT FILTER

165-502016 Paint Filter **5.45**
For all airbrushes using jars or bottles. Micro screen mesh filter passes only particles which will flow through the airbrush.

COLOR CUPS EA 7.05 (UNLESS NOTED)

165-50048 1/8oz (3.5cc)
Self-standing, for Model 100 side feed airbrushes. Screw-off bottom for easy cleaning.

165-500482 1/4oz (7cc)
Self-standing, fits 150 and 200 only.

165-500483 1/4oz (7cc)
Self-standing, fits 350 only.

165-50047 1/6oz (2cc) **6.95**

CLEANING REAMERS

165-50060 Cleaning Reamer for Heads 100-200 **4.35**
165-50061 3-Cornered for Models 100 & 200 **5.45**

JARS & COVERS

165-500052 3/4oz (22cc) **1.25**
For models 200, 250, 350 and 150

165-500053 2oz (60cc)
For Models 200, 250, 350 & 150 **1.70**

BADGER PROPEL®

165-50002 11oz (33ml) **8.15**
165-50202 17oz (51ml) **10.65**
Works with all types of airbrushes, requires regulator #50200, sold separately.

PROPEL® REGULATOR

165-50200 Complete Regulator **6.90**
Makes Propel® last longer, regulates air pressure from can at 10-50PSI.

165-50029 Tire Adapter **4.55**
Convert any spare tire into an air supply. Special fitting modifies Propel® regulator #50200 (sold separately) to fit standard valve stem.

165-50117 Stem w/O-Ring **3.55**
165-50118 O-Ring Only **1.10**
165-50119 Washer **1.10**

AIR HOSE

165-502011 Braided w/Connections **15.75**
10' (3.05m) of heavy duty hose for use with compressors. Swivel connections at both ends.

VINYL AIRHOSE

165-50001 Six Foot **5.90**
165-500011 Ten Foot **8.55**
Flexible, lightweight, sturdy hose. With connectors at each end. Not recommended for use with compressors.

10' RE-COIL™ HOSE EA 17.70

165-504011 For Badger
165-504012 For Binks
Stretches to a maximum of 10' (3.05m). Recoil feature.

IN-LINE MOISTURE FILTER

165-502025 With Hose **28.00**
Complete assembly with 10' (3.05m) braided air hose.

165-502014 Filter Only **16.00**
For use with #502025 Air Hose only.

RESPIRATOR

165-1901 Double Cartridge Type **76.45**
Protects against paint mists and vapors.

165-1902 Replacement Cartridge for #1901 **16.05**
165-1903 Replacement Pre-Filter for #1901 **8.05**

FOTO-FRISKET FILM

165-600 pkg(10) **13.15**
Low tack, easy lift-off masking film.

AIR ABRASIVE GUN

Removes rust or paint from metal, and roughs the surface for improved paint adhesion.
NOTE: Use of wrap-around safety goggles and a dust mask or respirator is recommended. Not for use by children.

165-2603 Starter Set **42.00**
Set includes: gun w/attached 4oz (120cc) jar, 8' (240cm) hose and 12oz (336kg) net weight of aluminum oxide, face mask, Propel® and regulator.

165-2601 Gun Only **30.00**

HOW-TO BOOKS

165-500 Hobby & Craft Guide to Airbrushing **6.85**
Includes instructions on preparation for painting, mixing paint, cleaning and maintenance. Softcover, 32 pages, over 130 full color illustrations, 8-1/2 x 11".

165-505 Step by Step Modelers Guide to Airbrushing **10.10**
Painting models, figures and dioramas. Includes techniques from shadowing to mixing paint. Softcover, over 180 color photos, 32 pages, 8-1/2 x 11" .

CATALOG

165-96 Badger 1996 Catalog **1.00**

MODELFLEX™ PAINT

Specially formulated for models, goes on super thin (.25 to .50 thousands) to color without hiding fine details. Non-toxic and with no foul odor, Modelflex cleans up with water and can be sprayed or brushed.

MODELFLEX SETS EA 22.00

165-1701 Railroad Rolling Stock
One each: Engine Black, Reefer White, Reefer Gray, Reefer Yellow, Reefer Orange, Dark Tuscan Red, Light Tuscan Red.

165-1702 Weathering & Railroad Off-Line
One each: Weathered Black, Antique White, Primer Gray, Concrete Gray, Sand, Signal Red, Light Green.

165-1703 Railroad Private Colors
One each: Caboose Red, Rail Box Yellow, Mopac Blue, Pullman Green, Super Gloss Black, Maroon, Tuscan Red, Santa Fe Silver.

165-1704 Military Colors
One each: Forest Green, Olive Drab, European Dark Green, Armor Sand, Field Drab, Medium Green, Camouflage Gray.

165-1705 Gloss Auto Colors Set
One each: Black, White, Red, Blue, Brown, Yellow, Green.

INDIVIDUAL PAINTS 1OZ (30CC) EA 3.25

165-1601 Engine Black
165-1602 Reefer White
165-1603 Grimy Black
166-1604 Reefer Gray
165-1605 Weathered Black
165-1606 Antique White
165-1607 Signal Red
165-1608 Caboose Red
165-1609 Reefer Orange
165-1610 Reefer Yellow
165-1611 Concrete Gray
165-1612 Primer Gray
165-1613 Dark Tuscan Oxide Red
165-1614 Light Tuscan Oxide Red
165-1615 Maroon Tuscan Oxide Red
165-1616 Brunswick Green
165-1617 Pullman Green
165-1618 Soo Line Maroon
165-1619 Soo Line Dulux Gold
165-1620 Super Gloss Black
165-1621 PRR Green
165-1622 PRR Maroon
165-1623 CNW Dark Green
165-1624 UP Armor Yellow
165-1625 UP Harbor Mist Gray
165-1626 BN Green
165-1627 NYC Gray Dark 1
165-1628 NYC Gray Light 1
165-1629 Conrail Blue
165-1630 Sand
165-1631 ATSF Red
165-1632 ATSF Silver
165-1633 ATSF Yellow
165-1634 ATSF Blue
165-1635 SP Lark Light Gray
165-1636 SP Daylight Red
165-1637 SP Scarlet Red
165-1638 SP Daylight Orange
165-1639 SP Letter Gray
165-1640 SP Lark Dark Gray
165-1641 SP Armor Yellow
165-1642 MILW Orange
165-1643 MILW Maroon
165-1644 MILW Gray
165-1645 MILW Brown
165-1646 SOU Sylvan Green
165-1647 Light Green
165-1648 Weyerhaeuser Yellow Green
165-1649 CSX Blue
165-1650 Insignia Yellow
165-1651 EL Gray
165-1652 ELYellow
165-1653 EL Maroon
165-1654 Rail Box Yellow
165-1655 CNW Old Yellow
165-1656 CNW Zeto Yellow
165-1657 Soo Line Red
165-1658 Amtrak Red
165-1659 Amtrak Blue
165-1660 B&M Blue
165-1661 DRGW Orange
165-1662 DRGW Gold
165-1663 GN Big Sky Blue
165-1664 GN Orange
165-1665 GN Green
165-1666 Grand Trunk Western Blue
165-1667 C&O Royal Blue
165-1668 C&O Yellow
165-1669 B&O Enchantment Blue
165-1670 CSX Gray
165-1671 WC Maroon
165-1672 WC Cream
165-1673 IC Orange
165-1674 IC Cream
165-1675 Gulf, Mobile & Ohio Red
165-1676 D&H Blue
165-1677 NP Light Green
165-1678 NP Yellow
165-1679 Rock Island Blue
165-1680 Katy Green
165-1681 Katy Yellow
165-1682 L&N Blue
165-1683 L&N Gray
165-1684 L&N Yellow
165-1685 RDG Green
165-1686 MP Blue
165-1687 Missabe Road Maroon
165-1688 Missabe Road Yellow
165-1689 WP Orange
165-1690 Penn Central Green
165-16151 BNSF Green
165-16152 BNSF Orange
165-16153 CB&Q Chinese Red
165-16154 CB&Q Gray
165-16155 Wabash Blue
165-16156 Wabash Gray
165-16157 Frisco Orange
165-16158 CP Action Yellow
165-16159 CP Action Red
165-16160 CP Tuscan Red
165-16161 CP Yellow
165-16162 CP Gray
165-16163 CN Red #11
165-16164 CN Green #11
165-16165 CN Orange #10
165-16166 CN Yellow #11
165-16167 CN Gray #11
165-16168 Trailer Train Yellow
165-16169 MP Eagle Blue
165-16170 MP Eagle Roof Gray
165-16171 MP Eagle Gray
165-16172 Rust
165-16173 Mud
165-16174 Earth
165-16175 Rail Brown
165-16176 Roof Brown
165-16177 NH Hunter Green *NEW*
165-16178 NH Warm Orange *NEW*
165-16179 NH Imitation Silver *NEW*
165-16180 NH Pullman Green *NEW*
165-16181 NH Imitation Gold *NEW*
165-16182 NH Red-Orange *NEW*
165-16183 NH Socony Red *NEW*
165-16184 LV Cornell Red *NEW*
165-16185 SAL Pullman Green *NEW*
165-16186 AC Imitation Aluminum *NEW*
165-16187 CNW Red *NEW*
165-16188 D&H Gray *NEW*
165-16189 B&M Maroon *NEW*
165-16190 B&O Dulux Gold *NEW*
165-16191 Pullman Harbor Mist Gray *NEW*
165-16192 Western Pacific Green *NEW*
165-16193 CB&Q Imitation Aluminum *NEW*
165-16194 CB&Q Red *NEW*
165-16195 BNSF Silver *NEW*
165-16196 BNSF Yellow *NEW*
165-16197 SP/ATSF Overland Light Gray *NEW*
165-16198 SP/ATSF Overland Dark Gray *NEW*
165-16199 Rock Maroon *NEW*
165-16200 Rock Red *NEW*
165-16201 Rock Aluminum White *NEW*
165-16202 John Deere Yellow *NEW*
165-16203 John Deere Green *NEW*
165-16204 Light Flesh *NEW*
165-16205 Medium Flesh *NEW*
165-16206 Dark Flesh *NEW*

MILITARY COLORS

165-1691 Bomber Green
165-1692 SAC Bomber Green
165-1693 Bomber Blue
165-1694 Field Drab
165-1695 Green Drab
165-1696 Olive Drab
165-1697 Camouflage Gray
165-1698 Camouflage Brown
165-1699 Flat Gull Gray
165-16100 Euro Dark Green
165-16101 Medium Field Green
165-16102 Forest Green
165-16103 Armor Sand
165-16104 Dark Green
165-16105 Medium Green

GLOSS COLORS

165-16106 Black
165-16107 White
165-16108 Red
165-16109 Orange
165-16110 Blue
165-16111 Green
165-16112 Yellow
165-16113 Brown
165-16114 Silver
165-16115 Midnight Blue
165-16116 Deep Red
165-16117 Bright Orange
165-16118 Sunset Yellow

FLAT COLORS

165-16119 Flat Black
165-16120 Flat White

CLEAR FINISH

165-16601 Flat
165-16602 Satin
165-16603 Gloss

EXTENDER

165-16600 Extender

MARINE PAINTS & RACKS 1OZ BOTTLES EA 3.25

165-16401 Anti-Fouling Red Oxide *NEW*
165-16402 Navy Red *NEW*
165-16403 Coast Guard Red *NEW*
165-16404 Coast Guard Orange *NEW*
165-16405 Deck Tan *NEW*
165-16406 Navy Brown *NEW*
165-16407 Quartermaster Brown *NEW*
165-16408 Navy Buff *NEW*
165-16409 Panama Buff *NEW*
165-16410 Navy White *NEW*
165-16411 Deck Green *NEW*
165-16412 Hull Black *NEW*
165-16413 Wrought Iron Balck *NEW*
165-16414 Bulwarks Red *NEW*
165-16415 Caprail Green *NEW*
165-16416 Midship Blue *NEW*
165-16417 White *NEW*
165-16418 Slate Gray *NEW*
165-16419 Umber *NEW*
165-16420 Yellow Ochre *NEW*
165-16421 Hull Cream *NEW*
165-16422 Windjammer White *NEW*
165-16423 Windjammer Yellow *NEW*
165-16424 Windjammer Red *NEW*
165-16425 Windjammer Green *NEW*
165-16426 Windjammer Blue *NEW*
165-16427 Salmon Buff *NEW*
165-16428 Orange Ochre *NEW*
165-16429 Shipyard Rust *NEW*
165-16430 Shipyard Grimy Gray *NEW*
165-16431 Deck Red *NEW*
165-16432 Dark Deck Gray *NEW*
165-16433 Tug Light Blue *NEW*
165-16434 Tug Medium Blue *NEW*
165-16435 Tug Deep Blue *NEW*
165-16436 Tug Light Green *NEW*
165-16437 Tug Olive Green *NEW*
165-16438 Tug Orange *NEW*
165-16439 Tug Yellow *NEW*
165-16440 Tug Light Gray *NEW*
165-16441 Army Corps Enginner Buff *NEW*
165-16442 Golden Yellow *NEW*
165-16443 Bright Silver *NEW*
165-16444 #5 Standard Navy Gray *NEW*
165-16445 #20 Standard Deck Gray *NEW*
165-16446 5-L Light Gray (Early 1941) *NEW*
165-16447 5-0 Ocean Gray (Early 1941) *NEW*
165-16448 5-D Dark Gray (Early 1941) *NEW*
165-16449 5-H Haze Gray (Late 1941) *NEW*
165-16450 5-0 Ocean Gray (Late 1941) *NEW*
165-16451 5-S Sea Blue A (Late 1941) *NEW*
165-16452 5-N Navy Blue (Late 1941) *NEW*
165-16453 Deck Blue 20B (Late 1941) *NEW*
165-16454 #82 Black (1943) *NEW*
165-16455 5-P Pale Gray (1943) *NEW*
165-16456 5-L Light Gray (1946) *NEW*
165-16457 Dull Coat *NEW*
165-16458 Matte Coat *NEW*
165-16459 Gloss Coat *NEW*
165-16460 Retarder *NEW*

CLEANER

165-16606 16oz **9.00**

FLOQUIL®

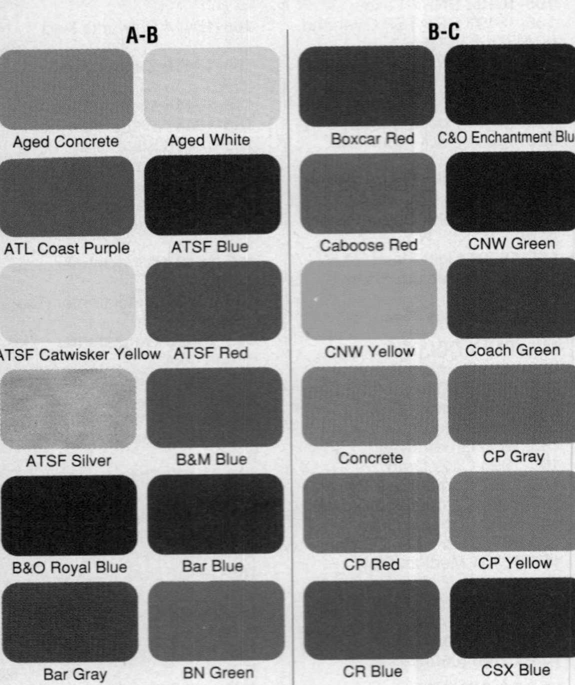

C-D

CSX Gray, CSX Tan, CSX Yellow, D&H Avon Blue, D&H Gray, Dark Green, Depot Buff, Depot Olive, Dirt, DRGW Building Brown, DRGW Building Cream, DRGW Freight Car Red, DRGW Orange, DRGW Yellow

D-G

DTI Cherry Red, Dust, E/L Gray, E/L Maroon, E/L Yellow, Earth, Engine Black, Flat Aluminum, GN Big Sky Blue, GN Empire Green, GN Glacier Green, GN Orange, Grimy Black, GTW Blue

Due to the printing process, the colors above are only representative of the actual colors.

Made especially for painting miniatures, Floquil colors cover without hiding detail. Floquil is solvent based, while Polly Scale™ colors are water-reducible acrylics. Dealers: Ask about merchandising display racks.

RAILROAD COLORS

270-110001 Thinner-Brush Cleaner **2.49**
Only chemical compatible solvent for Floquil colors, can be used for thinning, mixing and cleaning equipment.

270-110002 Retarder **2.49**
Slows drying time of solvent-based colors, for airbrushing and covering large areas.

270-110003 Hi-Gloss **2.49**
Light amber colored coating for indoor use. Heat, water and alcohol resistant. Dries in about four hours with an extremely high-gloss finish.

270-110004 Crystal Cote **2.49**
Water clear, quick-drying gloss and fixative. Use indoors or out, does not yellow. Durable, resists abrasion and most common chemicals except alcohol.

270-110005 Glaze **2.49**
Amber colored, semi-gloss coating. Use indoors or out. Dries in about 15-20 minutes and resists water, alcohol and most common chemicals. Can be used for priming, or mix with solvent-based colors for an eggshell finish.

RAILROAD COLORS 1OZ (30ML) EA 2.49

270-110006 Dust
270-110007 Rail Brown
270-110009 Primer
270-110010 Engine Black
270-110011 Reefer White
270-110012 Reefer Gray
270-110013 Grimy Black
270-110014 Railroad Tie Brown
270-110015 Flat Finish
270-110016 Aged Concrete
270-110017 Weathered Black
270-110020 Caboose Red
270-110023 Flesh Tone Base
270-110025 Tuscan Red
270-110030 Reefer Orange
270-110031 Reefer Yellow
270-110033 Railbox Yellow
270-110034 Brunswick Green
270-110035 BN Green
270-110040 Dark Green
270-110041 Light Green
270-110044 Depot Olive
270-110045 Pullman Green
270-110048 Coach Green
270-110050 Dark Blue
270-110051 Light Blue
270-110056 GN Big Sky Blue
270-110058 CR Blue
270-110065 Signal Red
270-110070 Roof Brown
270-110073 Rust
270-110074 Box Car Red
270-110081 Earth
270-110082 Concrete
270-110083 Mud
270-110084 Foundation
270-110085 Antique White
270-110086 Grime
270-110087 Depot Buff
270-110088 D&H Caboose Red
270-110100 Old Silver (metallic)
270-110101 Bright Silver (metallic)
270-110103 Bright Gold (metallic)
270-110104 Brass (metallic)
270-110105 Copper (metallic)
270-110108 Gun Metal (metallic)
270-110119 Graphite (metallic)
270-110130 SP Lettering Grey
270-110131 SP Lark Light Grey
270-110132 SP Lark Dark Grey
270-110133 SP Armour Yellow
270-110134 SP Daylight Orange
270-110135 SP Daylight Red
270-110136 SP Scarlet
270-110144 Platinum Mist (metallic)
270-110166 UP Armour Yellow
270-110167 UP Harbor Mist Gray
270-110168 UP Light Orange
270-110174 SOU Green
270-110175 SOU Freight Car Brown
270-110176 ATSF Red
270-110177 ATSF Blue
270-110178 ATSF Yellow
270-110179 ATSF Mineral Brown
270-110183 RDG Green
270-110184 Tuscan Red #2
270-110186 Railroad Oxide Red
270-110250 CN Orange #11
270-110252 CN Grey #17
270-110254 CN Yellow #12
270-110256 CN Green #12
270-110260 CNW Yellow
270-110262 CNW Green
270-110280 WC Gold
270-110282 WC Maroon
270-110310 TTX Yellow
270-110320 MKT Green
270-110330 NYC Jade Green
270-110350 CSX Gray
270-110352 CSX Blue
270-110354 CSX Black
270-110356 CSX Yellow
270-110450 SOO Red
270-110601 Zinc Chromate Primer

THINNER-BRUSH CLEANER

Only chemically compatible solvent for Floquil colors. Use for thinning, mixing, correcting, cleaning brushes, air brushes and solvent-resistant surfaces.

270-120001 Bottle - 2oz (60ml) **2.50**
270-140001 Can - 8oz (240ml) **5.75**
270-150001 Pint (0.24l) **6.75**
270-160001 Quart (0.95l) **9.50**
270-151611 Airbrush Thinner 16oz (0.24l) **6.95**

RAILROAD AEROSOLS 5OZ (150ML) EA 5.50

Same colors, but in spray cans for covering large areas, or quick paint jobs.

270-130004 Crystal Cote
270-130007 Rail Brown
270-130009 Primer
270-130010 Engine Black
270-130011 Reefer White
270-130012 Reefer Gray
270-130013 Grimy Black
270-130015 Flat Finish
270-130016 Instant Weathering
270-130020 Caboose Red
270-130025 Tuscan Red
270-130030 Reefer Orange
270-130031 Reefer Yellow
270-130040 Dark Green
270-130045 Pullman Green
270-130048 Coach Green
270-130050 Dark Blue
270-130070 Roof Brown
270-130074 Box Car Red
270-130081 Earth
270-130082 Concrete
270-130101 Bright Silver (metallic)
270-130601 Zinc Chromate Primer

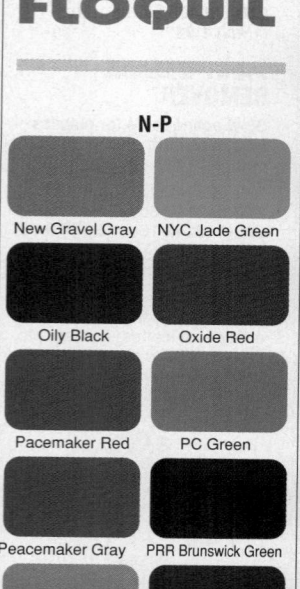

FLOQUIL®

N-P

New Gravel Gray
NYC Jade Green
Oily Black
Oxide Red
Pacemaker Red
PC Green
Peacemaker Gray
PRR Brunswick Green
PRR Buff
PRR Maroon

P-R

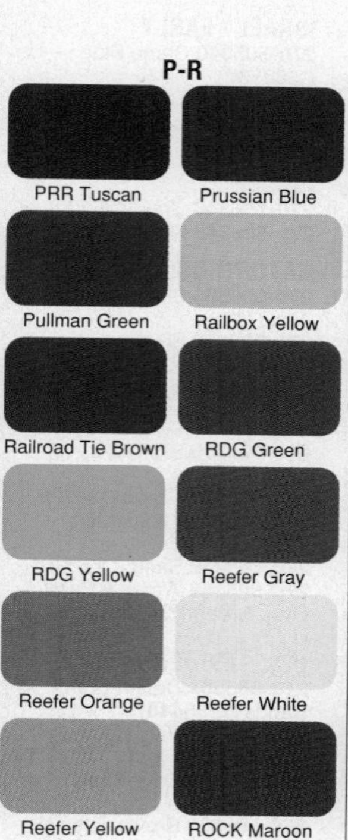

S

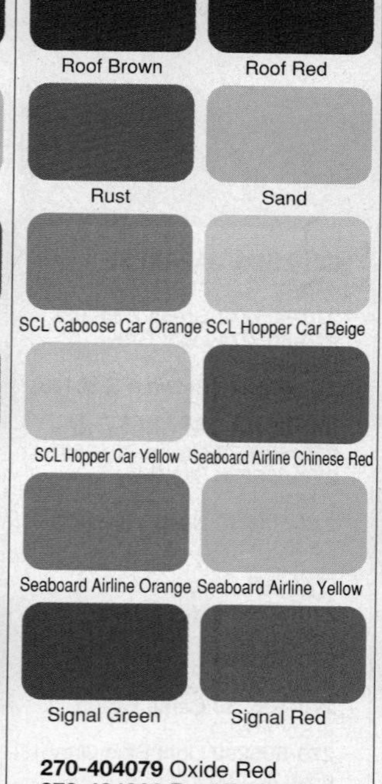

S

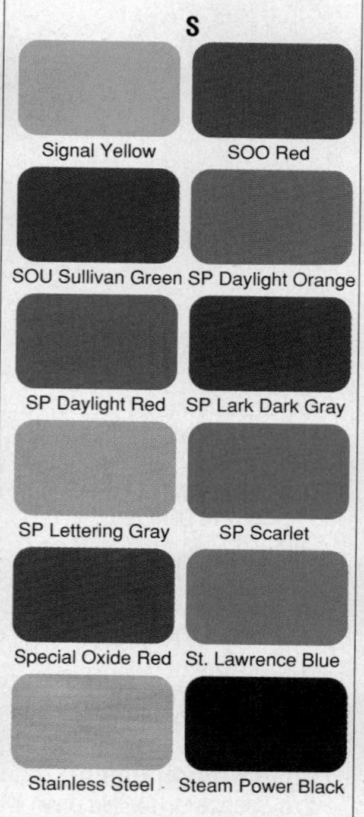

T-Z

AEROSOL FIGURE PRIMER 5OZ EA 5.50

Permanent, high-adherence primers resist chipping. Made especially for metal figures and miniatures, works well on most models. Fine pigments cover completely without filling in or hiding fine details. Can be used as a base under water-or solvent-based paints. Available in four colors to highlight detail and simplify application of finish coats.

270-330022 Figure Flat
270-330009 Light Gray
270-330010 Base Black
270-330021 Base White

POLLY SCALE™

A comprehensive line of user-friendly acrylics, Polly Scale colors are water-reducible, odor-free and environmentally safe. A wide selection of railroad and military colors are available, excellent for plastics, metals and brass. Fine ground pigments cover without hiding surface details and the formula is self leveling. Easily brushed, drybrushed and airbrushed. Can be sprayed at low pressure. Use plain water for clean-up or thinning. All colors are intermixable with older Polly S paints.

PAINT SETS PKG(8) EA 8.49

Sets include a brush and organizing tray.

270-490001 Railroad Colors Set
1 Each: Reefer White, Reefer Yellow, Dark Green, Box Car Red, Reefer Gray, Caboose Red, Roof Brown and Engine Black.

270-490002 Railroad Weathering Colors Set
1 Each: Aged White, Dirt, Aged Concrete, Railroad Tie Brown, Grimy Black, Mud, Rust and New Gravel Gray.

270-590001 Aircraft Interior Colors Set
1 Each: Zinc Chromate, Interior Green, Dull Dark Green, Bronze Green, Instrument Black, Dark Olive Drab, Medium Green and Neutral Gray

270-590002 Air & Armor Weathering Colors Set
1 Each: Burnt Aluminum, Flat Aluminum, Rust, Earth, Oxidized Aluminum, Scale Black, Dirt and Concrete.

RAILROAD COLORS - 1/2OZ (15ML) EA 1.99

270-404046 Atlantic Coast Line Purple
270-404049 Maine Central Harvest Gold
270-404052 Maine Central Pine Green
270-404055 Toronto, Hamilton & Buffalo Cream
270-404058 CP Yellow
270-404061 CP Red
270-404064 PRR Buff
270-404067 TTX Yellow
270-404070 Depot Olive
270-404073 MOW Grey
270-404076 Coach Green
270-404079 Oxide Red
270-404082 Roof Red
270-404085 Signal Yellow
270-404088 Signal Green
270-404091 Signal Red
270-404094 Utility Orange
270-404097 Prussian Blue

RAILROAD COLORS - 1OZ (30ML) EA 2.49

270-414110 Steam Power Black
270-414113 Reefer White
270-414116 Reefer Grey
270-414119 Reefer Orange
270-414122 Reefer Yellow
270-414125 Railbox Yellow
270-414128 Caboose Red
270-414131 Aged White
270-414134 Undercoat Light Gray
270-414137 Grimy Black
270-414140 Tarnished Black
270-414143 ATSF Silver
270-414146 ATSF Catwhisker Yellow
270-414149 ATSF Red
270-414150 ATSF Blue
270-414152 MILW Orange
270-414155 MILW Maroon
270-414158 MILW Gray
270-414161 PRR Maroon
270-414164 PRR Brunswick Green
270-414167 PRR Tuscan
270-414170 UP Armor Yellow
270-414173 UP Dark Gray
270-414176 UP Harbor Gray
270-414179 SP Letter Gray
270-414182 SP Lark Dark Gray
270-414183 SP Scarlet
270-414185 SP Daylight Orange
270-414186 SP Daylight Red
270-414188 CNW Green
270-414191 CNW Yellow
270-414194 D&H Avon Blue
270-414197 D&H Gray
270-414200 WC Maroon
270-414203 GN Big Sky Blue
270-414206 CR Blue
270-414209 BN Green
270-414212 SOO Red
270-414215 CSX Yellow
270-414218 CSX Grey
270-414221 CSX Blue
270-414222 CSX Tan
270-414224 GN Orange
270-414227 GN Empire Green
270-414228 GN Glacier Green
270-414230 Bangor & Aroostook Blue
270-414233 Bangor & Aroostook Gray
270-414236 EL Yellow
270-414239 EL Grey
270-414242 EL Maroon
270-414245 B&M Blue
270-414248 ROCK Maroon
270-414251 CP Grey
270-414254 DRGW Orange
270-414255 DRGW Cream
270-414256 DRGW Brown
270-414257 DRGW Yellow
270-414258 DRGW Freight Red
270-414260 C&O Enchantment Blue
270-414263 Pacemaker Red
270-414266 Pacemaker Grey
270-414269 B&O Royal Blue
270-414272 Dark Green
270-414275 Roof Brown
270-414278 Depot Buff
270-414281 Box Car Red
270-414284 Pullman Green
270-414287 Vermont Green
270-414290 Engine Black
270-414293 Zinc Chromate Primer
270-414296 Stainless Steel
270-414299 Flat Aluminum
270-414302 Sand
270-414305 Dust
270-414308 Dirt
270-414311 Earth
270-414314 Mud
270-414317 Concrete
270-414320 Aged Concrete
270-414323 Rust
270-414326 Oily Black
270-414329 Railroad Tie Brown
270-414332 New Gravel Grey
270-414350 Mineral Red
270-414352 Light Freight Oxide Red
270-414354 Special Oxide Red
270-414356 GTW Morency Orange
270-414358 GTW Blue
270-414360 LV Cornell Red
270-414362 Detroit, Toledo & Ironton Cherry Red
270-414364 St. Lawrence Blue
270-414366 Weyerhauser Green
270-414368 Penn Central Green
270-414370 NYC Jade Green
270-414372 Guilford Gray
270-414374 SOU Sylvan Green
270-414376 RDG Green
270-414378 RDG Yellow
270-414380 L&N Gray
270-414382 Seaboard Air Line Chinese Red
270-414384 Seaboard Air Line Yellow
270-414386 Seaboard Air Line Orange
270-414388 Seaboard Coast Line Hopper Car Beige
270-414390 Seaboard Coast Line Hopper Car Yellow
270-414392 Seaboard Coast Line Caboose Orange

POLLY SCALE AIR/ARMOR COLORS 1/2OZ (15ML) EA 1.99

Recreate equipment from World War I to the present. Matched to Army/Navy (AN), Federal Standard 595 (FS) and German WWII (RLM orders) as noted. Colors marked * indicate an approximate match to the Federal Standard color listed.

270-505011 White (RLM 21 *37886)
270-505014 Scale Black (RLM 66 *36081)
270-505017 Yellow (RLM 04 *33538)

FLOQUIL®

270-505020 Red (RLM 23 FS 31302)
270-505023 Dark Blue (RLM 24 *25053)
270-505026 Green (RLM 25 *34108)
270-505029 Doped Linen (*33727)
270-505032 Brown Drab PC-10 (FS 34098)
270-505035 German Mauve (FS 37144)
270-505038 FR/FOK Dark Green (FS 34096)
270-505041 FR Chestnut Brown (FS 20140)
270-505044 FR Beige (FS 33546)
270-505051 Light Blue (RLM 65 *35352)
270-505055 Black Green (RLM 70 *34050)
270-505056 Dark Green (RLM 71 *34083)
270-505059 Dark Gray (RLM 74 *36081)
270-505060 Gray Violet (RLM 75 *36152)
270-505061 Light Gray (RLM 76 *36473)
270-505070 Brown Violet (RLM 81 *34079)
270-505071 Dark Green (RLM 82 *34083)
270-505072 Light Green (RLM 83 *34138)
270-505075 Gray (RLM 02 *16165)
270-505080 US Olive Drab (A/N613 *33070)
270-505082 US Medium Green (A/N612 *34092)
270-505084 US Sand (A/N616 *30279)
270-505086 US Neutral Gray (A/N603 *36118)
270-505088 USN Blue Gray (*35189)
270-505090 USN Light Gray (A/N602 *36440)
270-505092 USN Sea Blue (A/N607 *35045)
270-505094 USN Intermediate Blue (A/N608 *35164)
270-505096 US Interior Green (A/N611 *34089)
270-505098 US Olive Drab (*34088)
270-505110 Panzer Dark Gray (*36152)
270-505111 Panzer Dark Yellow (*33440)
270-505112 Panzer Red Brown (*30111)
270-505113 Panzer Olive Green (*34092)

POLLY SCALE MODEL & HOBBY COLORS 1/2OZ (15ML) EA 1.99

Matched to Federal Standard 595 (FS) and German WWII (RLM orders) as noted. Colors marked * indicate an approximate match to the Federal Standard color listed.

270-505200 Rust (FS 30215)
270-505202 Dust (FS 37778)
270-505204 Grimy Black (FS 36081)
270-505205 Dirty White
270-505206 Mud (FS 33440)

270-505208 Dirt (FS 30095)
270-505210 Old Concrete (FS 30318)
270-505212 Flesh (*32648)
270-505214 Night Black (22) (FS 37038)

U.S. ARMY AIR CORPS
270-505216 Blue (23) (*15102)
270-505218 Olive Drab (22) (FS 10118)
270-505220 Orange Yellow (4) (FS 13432)

U.S. ARMY
270-505222 Khaki (*30219)
270-505224 Olive Drab (FS 34087)

SOVIET UNION (USSR)
270-505226 Underside Blue (FS 15200)
270-505228 Light Earth Brown (FS 33434)
270-505230 Topside Green (FS 34201)
270-505232 Dark Topside Gray (FS 36176)
270-505234 Light Topside Gray (FS 36270)

FRANCE
270-505236 Dark Blue Gray (FS 35164)
270-505238 Khaki (FS 34127)
270-505240 Earth Brown (*30140)
270-505242 Light Blue Gray (FS 36238)

ROYAL AUSTRALIAN AIR FORCE
270-505244 Earth Brown (FS 30099)
270-505246 Foliage Green (FS 34092)
270-505248 Sky Blue (FS 35550)

ROYAL AIR FORCE - BRITAIN
270-505250 Dark Green (*34079)
270-505252 Dark Earth (*30118)
270-505254 Sky (Type "S" *34504)
270-505256 Ocean Grey (*35237)
270-505258 Sea Grey Med (FS 36293)
270-505260 Middlestone (*30266)
270-505262 Azure Blue (*35231)
270-505264 Extra Dark Sea Grey (*36118)
270-505266 Dark Slate Grey (*34096)
270-505268 P.R.U. Blue (*35189)
270-505270 Interior Grey Green (*34226)

IMPERIAL JAPANESE ARMY
270-505272 Green (*34098)
270-505274 Light Grey (*36628)
270-505276 Brown (FS 30108)

IMPERIAL JAPANESE NAVY
270-505278 Green (*34058)
270-505280 Sky Gray (*36495)
270-505282 Deep Yellow (*33538)

ITALIAN
270-505284 Hazel Tan (*30219)
270-505286 Camo Brown 2 (FSb 10076)
270-505288 Camo Green (FSb 34227)
270-505290 Light Blue Grey 1 (FSb 36307)
270-505292 Camo Yellow 2 (FSb 33481)
270-505294 Camo Yellow 3 (FSb 33434)
270-505296 Dark Olive Green 2 (FSb 34052)

GERMANY
270-505298 Uniform Gray (*34158)
270-505300 Dark Brown (RLM 61 - *30040)
270-505302 Green (RLM 62 *34128)
270-505304 Light Gray (RLM 63 - *36375)
270-505306 Light Blue (RLM 64 - *25414)
270-505308 Dark Olive Green (RLM 67 - *34151)
270-505310 Light Olive Green (RLM 68 - *34258)
270-505312 Light Tan (RLM 69 - *33695)
270-505314 72 Green (RLM 72 - *36081)
270-505316 73 Green (RLM 73 - *34064)
270-505318 78 Light Blue (RLM 78 - *35414)
270-505320 Sand Yellow (RLM 79 - *30215)
270-505322 Olive Green (RLM 80 *34083)
270-505324 Sky Green (RLM 84 - *34554)

U.S. NAVY
270-505326 Pale Blue Gray 5P (*36440)
270-505328 Light Gray 5L (*36373)
270-505330 Haze Gray 5H (*36251)
270-505332 Ocean Gray 50 (*36173)
270-505334 Navy Blue 5N (*36081)
270-505336 Deck Tan (FS 1735)
270-505338 Weathered Deck Blue 20-B (*36076)

ISRAEL - EARLY
270-505340 Camo Blue (*35053)
270-505342 Tan (*31433)
270-505344 Light Gray (*37722)

ISRAEL
270-505346 Gray (*36300)
270-505348 Khaki (*30277)

NATO TRICOLOR
270-505350 Black (FS 37038)
270-505352 Brown (FS 30051)
270-505354 Green (FS 34094)

SOVIET
270-505356 Brown #2 (*32473)
270-505358 Green (*34226)
270-505360 Khaki #2 (*34088)
270-505362 Sand (*33798)
270-505368 Warsaw Pact Gray Green (*34258)

U.S. - MODERN
270-505364 Desert Storm Sand (FS 33446)
270-505366 Earth Red (FS 30117)
270-505370 Olive Drab (FS 34087)
270-505372 Brown Special (FS 30140)
270-505374 Dark Ghost Gray (FS 36320)
270-505376 Light Ghost Gray (FS 36375)
270-505378 Dark Gull Gray (FS 36231)
270-505380 Light Gull Gray (FS 36440)
270-505382 Gunship Gray (FS 36118)
270-505384 Neutral Gray (FS 36270)
270-505386 Tan Special (FS 10400)
270-505388 Tac Dark Green (FS 34079)
270-505390 Tac Mid-Green (FS 34102)
270-505392 USTAC Tan
270-505394 Tac Light Gray (FS 36622)
270-505396 Light Blue (FS 35622)

POLLY SCALE™ ACCESSORIES

CLEAR FINISHES EA 1.79
270-404100 Gloss
270-404103 Satin
270-404106 Flat

DECAL SETTING SOLUTION EA 1.79
270-505401 Polly Sol
A stronger solution, makes decals snuggle down in problem areas where surface detail is more pronounced.

270-505403 Polly Set
Softens decal film to hug surface details. Works fast.

PLASTIC CEMENT
270-505408 Liquid 1/2oz (15ml) **1.99**

PAINT & DECAL REMOVER
Slow acting, safe for plastics. Removes both paint and decals.

270-522142 2oz (60ml) **2.95**
270-542143 8oz (240ml) **6.95**
270-542144 16oz (0.47l) **9.95**

PLASTIC PREP
A pre-painting cleaner for use on plastics. Removes mold release, silicones, grease, etc. Leaves plastic clean, static-free and dust-free.

270-546007 8oz (240ml) **4.95**
270-556007 16oz (0.47l) **6.95**

AIRBRUSH THINNER
Made for airbrush application of colors. For smoother mixing, better flow and faster drying.

270-546008 8oz (240ml) **4.95**
270-556008 16oz (0.47l) **6.95**

MIXING BOTTLES
Empty glass bottle with seals and lids. Ideal for mixing and storing custom colors or thinned paints for airbrushing.

270-190231 1/2oz (15ml) pkg(6) **3.60**

270-190232 1oz (30ml) pkg(6) **3.90**

FLOQUIL

BRUSHES

Manufactured and designed especially for the demands of hobby painting, all brushes are hand-made from the finest materials. Natural hairs or synthetic fibers are set in seamless nickel ferrules. Brushes come in five basic styles:

Brights: Flat brushes with chisel-sharp edges for controlled application of color, can be used to leave a clean, sharp edge to the coating.

Flats: Same as Brights, but with longer hairs (also called shaders), hold more coating and allow quick, controlled application of coating over a large area.

One-Stroke: Large, wide, full-bodied, square-tipped brush for laying on a large, smooth application of coating in a single stroke. (Lacquering brushes have a similar shape.)

Rounds: Full-bodied brushes tapered to a needle tip, which offer excellent control for detail applications of colors.

Scroller: Made for script lettering and ultra-fine detail work, stocks are semi-flat with rounded edges forming a saber-like point.

RED SABLE

All-natural tail hair from the Kolinsky Sable, used in the best brushes. Prized for its ability to hold a needle point, found in detail and specific-use brushes.

FLAT
270-622001 #1 **4.00**
270-622002 #2 **4.50**
270-622003 #3 **5.00**
270-622004 #4 **6.00**

ROUND EA 4.00 (UNLESS NOTED)
270-677000 #0
270-677001 #1
270-677002 #2
270-677010 10/0 "Super Spotter" **6.00**
270-677030 3/0
270-677050 5/0

WHITE BRISTLE

A natural hair obtained from hogs, with a natural split on each end that holds color in heavy amounts until applied to the surface. Brushes are well suited to applying base coatings or covering large areas.

FLAT
270-633001 #1 **3.50**
270-633002 #2 **3.50**
270-633003 #3 **4.00**
270-633004 #4 **4.50**

FLOQUIL SUPREMES

270-699000 #0 **5.50**
270-699001 #1 **6.00**
270-699002 #2 **6.50**
270-699003 #3 **9.00**
270-699030 3/0 **5.00**
270-699050 5/0 **4.50**

ULTIMATE DETAILING BRUSHES EA 8.95

A top-quality brush made with pure Red Sable hairs, and packed in a reusable screw-top storage case.

270-655001 #1 Round
270-655002 #2 Scroller
270-655003 #3 Flat

OX HAIR FLAT-SINGLE STROKE

A natural hair which is soft and flexible, but holds large amount of color. Brush characteristics fall between bristle and soft hair type.

270-666012 1/2" **6.00**
270-666014 1/4" **4.00**
270-666038 3/8" **5.00**

CAMEL HAIR

A blend of natural hairs obtained from various animals. Brushes are versatile and can be used with all types of colors.

WATER COLOR ROUND
Dealer MUST order multiples of 12.

270-644003 #3 **2.50**
270-644004 #4 **2.50**
270-644005 #5 **3.00**
270-644007 #7 **4.00**

LACQUER FLAT
270-651701 1" **7.00**
270-651712 1/2" **4.00**
270-651714 1/4" **3.00**
270-651734 3/4" **5.50**

SILVER FOX

Brushes feature synthetic fibers, designed to provide excellent performance and longer life, with performance qualities like red sable.

ROUND
270-688200 #0 **4.00**
270-688201 #1 **4.50**
270-688202 #2 **5.50**
270-688203 #3 **6.00**
270-688230 #3/0 **4.00**

BRIGHT
270-688001 #1 **4.50**
270-688002 #2 **4.50**
270-688003 #3 **5.00**
270-688004 #4 **5.00**

FLAT - SINGLE STROKE
270-688112 1/2" **8.00**
270-688114 1/4" **5.00**
270-688138 3/8" **6.50**

PRECISION LINER
270-688350 5/0 **4.00**
Long, flexible tip for striping, detail painting and script lettering.

New Arrivals Updated Every Day! Visit Walthers Web site at

www.walthers.com

BRUSH SETS

270-606000 Starter Set **12.99**
Includes five assorted brushes.
270-669006 Dust Flogger pkg(3) **11.99**
Remove dust, not details, from your favorite models! Set includes a Stiff Duster for crevices, a Scrubber for hard, tough dust and a Dust Flogger for final soft dusting.

POLLY SCALE™ BRUSHES

Made especially for use with acrylics.

GOLDEN FOX
Synthetic fiber.

DETAIL ROUNDS
270-768000 #0 **4.00**
270-768001 #1 **4.00**
270-768010 10/0 **5.00**
270-768020 20/0 **5.00**
270-768030 3/0 **4.00**
270-768050 5/0 **4.00**

FLATS
270-768102 #2 **4.00**
270-768104 #4 **4.50**

WHITE BRISTLE
270-768212 1/2" **2.49**

CAMEL HAIR-ONE STROKE EA 1.95

270-768314 1/4"
270-768338 3/8"

CAMEL HAIR-WATER COLOR EA 1.49

270-768501 #1
270-768502 #2
270-768503 #3

RECOMMENDED AIR PRESSURES AND THINNING RATIOS FOR AIRBRUSHING

All measurements are approximate. Thinning ratio and pressure needed may vary, depending upon the type of finish required or brand of compressor.

ALWAYS TEST FIRST!

Floquil solvent-based Model Railroad.

Thinning Ratio: 75% color, 5% glaze, 20% Thinner-Brush Cleaner. Approximate Pressure: 12-20 lbs.

CLEAR COATINGS
Crystal-Cote Thinning Ratio: Usually none required, if needed use Airbrush Thinner. Approximate Pressure: 12-20 lbs.

POLLY SCALE COLORS
Thinning Ratio: 10-15% distilled water. Approximate Pressure: 15-20 lbs.

IMPORTANT: For best results, it's imperative that your airbrush be cleaned thoroughly when you are done spraying to keep paint from drying inside and clogging the spray tip. This should be done immediately, especially when using acrylics, which set up faster than enamels and lacquers.

MARINE COLORS

Match paint and coatings used on vessels from the 18th century to the present. Perfect for ship and boat models in any scale. Solvent base colors are compatible with plastic, fiberglass, woods, metals and Lexan. Colors followed by A/N match Army/Navy standards from 1943; FS indicates Federal Standard color, matched to (TT-C-595, 1950) FS 595.

Limited Quantity Available on All Items

FLOQUIL MARINE 1 OZ (30ML) EA 2.49

270-818590 Pale Blue Gray 5P
270-818592 Light Gray 5L
270-818594 Haze Gray 5H
270-818596 Ocean Gray 5-0
270-818598 Navy Blue 5N
270-818600 Weather Deck Blue 20B

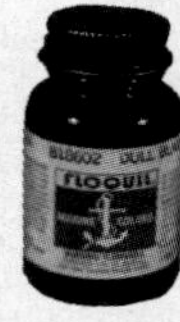

270-818602 Dull Black 13
270-818605 Haze Green 5HG
270-818606 Ocean Green 5-OG
270-818608 Navy Green 5NG
270-818610 Black Boottopping (A/N514)
270-818612 Red Boottopping (FS 1705)
270-818614 Anti-Fouling Red (FS 1020)
270-818616 Deck Green (A/N503)
270-818618 Deck Tan (FS 1735)
270-818620 Quartermaster Brown (FS 1005)
270-818622 Navy Brown #41 (A/N510)
270-818624 Navy Buff #22 (FS 1750)
270-818626 Panama Buff (A/N507)
270-818628 Navy Red #40 (FS 1110)
270-818632 Coast Guard Red (A/N509)
270-818634 Coast Guard Orange (A/N508)
270-818636 Marine Corps Green (FS 1415)
270-818638 8638 Sea Blue (A/N623)
270-818640 Navy Blue (A/N502)
270-818642 Maritime Blue (A/N501)
270-818644 Navy Light Blue #43 (FS 1525)
270-818646 Navy Dark Gray #21 (A/N513)
270-818648 Navy Medium Gray (FS 1615)
270-818650 Navy Light Gray (FS 1650)
270-818652 Battleship Gray (FS 1640)
270-818654 Bright Silver
270-818656 Iron Black
270-818658 New Manila Stain
270-818660 Weathered Manila Stain
270-818662 Light Stockholm Tar
270-818664 Dark Stockholm Tar
270-818666 Teak
270-818668 Mahogany
270-818670 Bright Oil

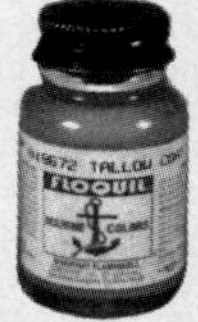

270-818672 Tallow Coat
270-818674 Pine Tar Oil
270-818676 Tar
270-818678 Salmon Buff
270-818680 Yellow Ochre
270-818682 Orange Ochre
270-818684 Umber
270-818686 Slate Gray
270-818688 Midship Blue
270-818690 Caprail Green
270-818692 Bulwarks Red
270-818694 Hull Cream
270-818696 Verdigris
270-818698 Bulwark White
270-818700 Deck Gray
270-818702 Gallery Yellow
270-818704 Deckhouse Blue (Matches USN Thayer Blue)
270-818706 Pearl
270-818708 Stone

MARINE COLOR SET

270-898500 **24.43**
Includes: Hull Black, Bulwark White, Caprail Green, Quarter Gallery Yellow, Deck Gray, Deckhouse Blue, 2oz (120ml) bottle of thinner and #3 Floquil brush in plastic case.

THINNER-BRUSH CLEANER

270-826607 Brush Cleaner 2oz (60ml) **2.50**
270-848601 Airbrush Thinner 8oz (240ml) **5.75**

COLOR CARDS EA 3.00

270-890689 Modern Marine Card
Actual color chips from 22 Modern Marine colors, plus airbrushing information.

270-890789 Classic Marine Card.
Complete set of 21 actual color chips for 18th - and 19th - century vessels.

REFLECTANCE REDUCER

Use as a finish coat over Marine and other colors to reduce reflectivity. Initial coat will take the gloss from 90° to about 10° reflectance. With additional coats, finish can be varied from flat to semi-gloss to satin. As a final top-coat, this material serves as a protective coating and aides in waterproofing.

270-828613 2oz (60ml) **2.95**
270-848602 8oz (240ml) **8.95**

BINKS

AIRBRUSHES

Designed to meet the painting needs of modelers, illustrators, artists and others, creating custom models is easy with this complete line of airbrushes and accessories.

CAUTION: For your safety, the use of a properly vented spray booth and a respirator which is paint mist and vapor compatible is strongly recommended when painting with an airbrush.

WREN AIRBRUSH

An all-purpose airbrush, great for hobby and craft projects, but versatile enough for bigger jobs. Single action, external mix design uses a siphon feed. Spray pattern can be adjusted from 1/16" 15cm to 1-1/2" 3.75cm. Three body sizes and nozzle openings are available to suit the types of material you are working with:

A: Small, for fine lines. Use with inks, stains, dyes, etc. Also fits B&C style bodies.

B: Medium opening, use with thinned lacquers and enamels. Also Fits C style body.

C: Largest opening, use with any material that does not require fine control. Also fits B style body.

WREN AIRBRUSH ONLY EA 82.50

177-10001 Small - A
177-10002 Medium - B
177-10021 Large - C
B and C models have same air orifice and can be interchanged.

SET #1 EA 93.00

Includes 1/2oz (15ml) color bottle assembly, packed in a durable styrene storage case.

177-10003 Small - A
177-10004 Medium - B
177-10022 Large - C

SET #2 EA 120.00

Includes 1/4, 1/2 & 2-1/2oz (7.5, 15 & 75ml) color bottle assemblies and #60 air hose with connections, packed in a durable styrene storage case.

177-10005 Small - A
177-10006 Medium - B
177-10023 Large - C

SET #5

Limited Quantity Available

177-10011 Small - A **146.00**
All items in Set #4, and two #70 Wren-Paks.

SPRAY GUN

Color Cup sold separately

177-115 163.00
Designed for larger jobs, produces fine finishes. Ideal for touch-up, shading and spotting. Features one-piece drop-forged aluminum body, brass fluid passage insert, curved overhead trigger to fit index finger, self-centering brass air nozzle, with adjustable spray pattern. Can be used with 8oz 2.4dl Color Cup #177-81540, sold separately below.

COLOR CUP

177-81540 8oz 24dl **34.50**
Designed for use with spray gun #177-115, sold separately.

ACCESSORIES

AIR COMPRESSOR

177-342035 220.00
Electric motor delivers 1/15 HP, permits continuous running without overheating. Delivers 30PSI with A brushes, 28PSI with B and C brushes. Weight 9lbs 4.05kg, 110V, 60C.

177-5984 Foot Switch for #342025 **55.50**
Turns compressor on/off without having to plug and unplug cord. Capacity to 7 amp, 125/250 VAC. With 6' 1.8m cord.

WREN-PAK PROPELLANT

Limited Quantity Available

177-5975 Case pkg(12) **81.00**
Harmless Freon propellant for use with Wren Airbrush. Supplies power for spraying liquid material. Sufficient to airbrush the contents of a 2-1/2oz 75ml color bottle. (PAK life depends on material viscosity.)

WREN-PAK VALVE

177-5962 Valve Body **8.10**
177-5963 Needle Stem **3.95**
177-5964 Propellant Valve Seat pkg(2) **2.45**

AIR HOSE

Standard vinyl or braided air hose with connection for Wren airbrush and 1/4" connector for compressor. All are 1/8" 3.1cm interior diameter.

VINYL

177-5960 6' 1.8m **7.80**
177-5994 10' 3m **9.20**
177-5995 12' 3.6m **9.70**
177-5996 15' 4.5m **10.50**

HEAVY DUTY BRAIDED

177-5961 6' 1.8m **10.50**
177-5997 10' 3m **14.25**
177-5998 12' 3.6m **15.75**
177-5999 15' 4.5m **18.25**

BLOW GUN & ACCESSORIES

177-152 Blow Gun **17.75**
For cleaning, dusting or releasing castings from molds.

177-715003 Braided Hose Assembly **12.00**
1/4" .6cm interior diameter x 5' 150cm, for connecting #152 Blow Gun to #86836 Extractor or Compressor. Includes #72312 connectors.

177-72312 Connector **3.95**
1/4" .6cm for use with #715003.

177-83576 DM Nipple for Blow Gun **2.14**
To connect #715003 Hose to #152 Blow Gun.

CAP ASSEMBLY

177-5927 For 1/4oz 7.5ml Bottle **8.30**
177-5928 For 1/2oz 15ml Bottle **8.80**
177-5929 For 2.5oz 75ml Bottle **9.40**

SIPHON BOTTLE ASSEMBLY

With friction connection.

177-5930 Glass 1/4oz 7.5ml **10.75**
177-5931 Glass 1/2oz 15ml **11.00**

Limited Quantity Available
177-5981 Plastic 2oz 60ml **19.75**

BOTTLE & CAP ASSEMBLY

With seal tight cover.

177-5934 Glass 1/2oz 15ml **3.45**
177-5978 Plastic 2oz 60ml **4.55**

CAPS ONLY PKG(2)

177-5957 Fits 1/4oz 7.5ml Jar **1.10**
177-5958 Fits 1/2oz 15ml Jar **1.10**
177-5959 Fits 2.5oz 75ml Jar **1.10**
177-5940 Siphon Tube **3.25**
177-5950 Nut for Hose-Airbrush pkg(3) **1.41**
177-5951 Tailpiece for Hose-Airbrush pkg(3) **2.00**
177-5952 Tailpiece for Hose-Compressor **1.95**
177-5953 Ferrule for Hose-Tailpiece **.95**
177-202673 Hanger Screw pkg(20) **2.00**

AIRBRUSH TOOLS

177-59100 Airbrush Repair Kit **137.00**
Ideal for hobby shops, includes a complete assortment of the most commonly replaced parts from the Wren airbrush. Also includes all-purpose tool to completely disassemble and reassemble the airbrush.

177-59102 User Repair Kit **10.25**
Contains spare parts and special tool for complete disassembly and reassembly of airbrushes.

177-5983 Airbrush Wrench **1.10**

RAVEN PARTS

177-593 Trigger Button **4.50**
177-5137 Handle Only **2.35**
177-5920 Air Valve Housing **6.30**
177-59131 Handle Only, Plastic **3.45**
177-59151 Cup Assembly 1/16oz **28.00**
177-59164 Color Cup-Assembly 1/8oz **38.50**
177-59165 Cup Sub-Assembly 1/8oz **32.50**
177-59184 Adapter **6.90**
177-59209 Fine Needle pkg(6) **46.50**
177-59238 Trigger Assembly **22.50**

Limited Quantity Available
177-59137 Needle Chuck Nut **2.90**
177-59141 Air Valve Spring pkg(10) **5.00**
177-59145 Air Cap **3.00**
177-59153 Cup Sub-Assembly 1/8oz **20.00**
177-59156 Protective Cap **4.90**
177-59160 Hanger **2.50**
177-59169 Lower Case Insert **2.40**
177-59170 Spring Retainer **2.80**
177-59181 Spare Parts Kit **10.25**
177-59226 Body Assembly for Raven II - Shell Only **64.00**
177-59229 Air Valve **2.20**
177-59233 Needle Adjustment **1.60**
177-59234 Adjustment Knob **4.55**
177-59235 Lock Knob **1.00**
177-59244 Trigger Cam **.95**

RAVEN II BODIES ONLY EA 54.00

177-591 10001 A
177-592 10002 B
177-595 10021 C

FLUID CONTROL ASSEMBLIES ONLY EA 31.50

177-599 For #10001
177-5910 For #10002
177-59101 For #10021

USER REPAIR KIT #1

177-59206 20.50
Includes two each of #59146, 59144, 59134, 59140 and one of 59175.

FEDERAL EQUIPMENT CO.

The perfect spray equipment for small jobs, including model building, art work and crafts. Handles all common hobby materials. Brushes are durable and easy to clean.

CAUTION: For your safety, the use of a properly vented spray booth and a respirator which is paint mist and vapor compatible, is strongly recommended when painting with an airbrush.

AIRBRUSHES

787-2 Quickchange Airbrush (medium) & Mini-Sandblast Gun **60.00** ***NEW***

787-812 Compact Hobby Gun **19.00**
External mix, siphon feed with adjustable nozzle. Includes 1oz (30ml) jar & 8' (2.4m) air hose with 1/4" fitting.

787-831 Quickchange Intermediate Airbrush **32.00** ***NEW***
787-832 Airbrush Quickchange **32.00**
Easy snap-in, snap-out jar makes changing colors and cleaning easier than ever. Uses fine and heavy jar/nozzle assemblies to handle a wide range of materials. Wide base for stability on any horizontal surface. Wide-mouth jars are easy to clean.

787-835 Complete Set **56.00**
Includes fine, medium and heavy quick change jar assemblies, plus 8' (2.4m) air hose with 1/4" fitting.
787-850 Dual Action Airbrush **70.00** ***NEW***
Fine with 1oz jar and hose.
787-855 Dual Action Airbrush Set **96.00** ***NEW***
Includes fine, medium and heavy tips, a 1oz jar, cup and hose.

787-1832 Medium Nozzle **32.00**
Quick change jar and nozzle assembly with medium spray opening, allows easy cleanup and color changes. Wide base allows unit to stand on any horizontal surface.

AIRBRUSH & COMPRESSOR SETS

787-211 Hobby Spray Set **169.00**
Includes #201 Compressor, Hobby Gun #812, 8' (2.4m) air hose and extra 1oz (30ml) and 2oz (60ml) jars with covers.

787-414 Spray & Inflating Outfit **195.00**
An all-purpose set with lots of uses around the house. Includes 410 compressor, 112 Spray Gun, 812 Hobby Gun, Viscosity Meter, 15' (4.5m) air hose and inflater fitting kit with tire chuck.

787-430 Complete Airbrush Kit **184.00**
Includes 1/10 HP compressor with bleeder valve and on/off switch, external mix airbrush with adjustable air flow and 8' (2.4m) air hose.

AIR COMPRESSORS

787-201 Piston **142.00**
1/12 horsepower oil-less piston compressor, delivers up to 40 PSI. Operates on 115 volt, 60 cycle. Includes bleeder valve. Weight 6-1/2lbs (2.92kg)

787-410 Diaphragm **162.00**
1/10 horsepower oil-less diaphragm air compressor, delivers up to 45 PSI. Operates on 115 volts, 60 cycle. Includes bleeder valve. Weight 12lbs (5.4kg)

787-1000 MC-1000 Compressor **150.00**
A lightweight compressor for household and hobby chores. Delivers 0.6 CFM at 20lbs. (Output can be adjusted to 0.8 CFM, maximum output is 45 lbs) Perfect for all types of airbrushing, including models, clothing and more. Provides enough power to inflate toys and operate mini sandblast guns and touch-up painting equipment.

ACCESSORIES

AIRBRUSH ACCESSORIES

787-15 Airbrush Propellant (15oz) **8.00**
787-90 Propellant Adapter for Airbrush Hose **9.00** ***NEW***
787-820 Miniature Pressure Regulator w/Gauge **27.00** ***NEW***
60 PSI, 1/4" fitting.

787-802

787-822

787-802 1/4" Bleeder Valve **10.00**
1/4" thread, 1/4" fittings.

787-822 Regulator w/Gauge **30.00**
Provides constant, uniform pressure from 0-140 PSI.

AIR FILTER KITS

787-220 Miniature Air Filter - Moisture Trap **27.00** ***NEW***
1/4" fitting.

787-240 Air Filter - Moisture Trap **29.00** ***NEW***
1/4" fitting.

787-704 Air Filter - Pressure Regulator Kit **53.00** ***NEW***
787-722 Miniature Air Filter - Pressure Regulator Kit **52.00** ***NEW***

AIR HOSE

Includes standard 1/4" fittings.

787-818 8' (2.4m) **9.00**
787-910 10' **17.00** ***NEW***
787-920 20' **22.00** ***NEW***

Limited Quantity Available
787-415 15' (4.5m) **13.95**

ALUMINUM OXIDE SANDBLAST GRIT

787-35 3/4 Pound **6.00** ***NEW***
787-355 5 Pound **24.00** ***NEW***

JAR & NOZZLE ASSEMBLIES EA 15.00

787-31 Light
787-32 Medium
787-33 Heavy

PAINT JARS

787-1520 1oz (30ml) pkg(3) **6.00**
787-1521 2oz (60ml) pkg(3) **7.00**
787-1522 4.5oz (135ml) pkg(3) **10.00**

MINI-SANDBLAST GUN

Cleans curved surfaces or hard-to-reach areas, can also etch designs on glass or wood. Unit includes 4oz (120ml) jar, 8' (2.4m) air hose, 12oz (360ml) of 220 grit aluminum oxide and a face mask. Use with a 1/10th horsepower or higher compressor (sold separately).

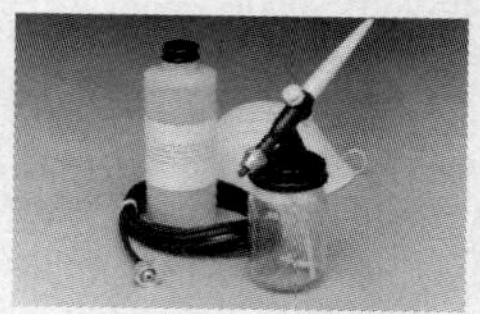

787-342 Mini-Sandblast Gun Only **35.00**
787-452 Mini-Sandblaster w/#410 Compressor **179.00**
787-805 Mini-Sandblast Booth **45.00**
For use with #342 or #452.

MICROSCALE®

LIQUID DECAL FILM 1OZ (30ML) EA 2.00

460-117 Micro Liquid Decal Film
To make your own decals, brush super film on a flat clean surface, allow to dry and draw or paint on your image. When brushed over an old decal, film seals and provides a new surface.

MASKING LIQUID 1OZ (30ML) EA 2.00

460-110 Micro Mask
Just brush on and allow to dry. Can be cut with hobby knife to create special effects. For use with solvent based paints. (Micro Mask is water soluble.)

DECAL SETTING SOLUTION 1OZ (30ML) EA 2.00

These setting solutions soften decal film, allowing it to stretch over details for the most realistic appearance. Prevents air bubbles and results in an invisible carrier film, reducing silvering. Formulated especially for MicroScale decals, can be used with most other brands.

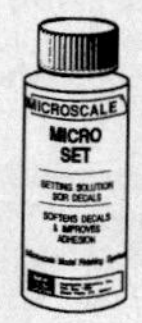

460-104

460-105

460-104 Micro Set
Brush over area where decal is to be applied. Special wetting agents cut oils in new paint and strengthens adhesive on decal.

460-105 Micro Sol
A stronger formula, for use on larger details or stubborn areas. Just brush on, actually makes decal part of the paint.

CLEAR FINISH EA 2.00

These water clear, nonyellowing, acrylic resins adhere strongly to paint and plastics and hide decal film. Can be applied with a brush, or airbrushed (40lbs pressure recommended). Clean-up with water.

460-103 Micro Coat Flat
Dead-flat finish for a dirty, weathered or camouflaged look.

460-106 Micro Coat Satin
Semi-gloss, for a less shiny or slightly dirty look.

460-108 Micro Coat Gloss
Provides a smooth surface for decaling and produces a high-gloss, "wet look" when dry.

ADHESIVES 1OZ (30ML) EA 2.00

460-109 Micro Weld Plastic Cement
Formulated for styrene, produces strong joints without crazing or warping thin parts. Nontoxic and environmentally friendly, mild flammability.

460-114 Micro Krystal Kleer
Perfect for attaching clear parts. Dries clear, or tint with food coloring. Can be used to model window "glass" by applying a thin layer to window openings. Cleans up with water, waterproof when dry.

460-115 Micro Liquitape
Holds parts securely, but allows you to remove and replace them over and over. Also for attaching patterns. Cleans up with water.

460-116 Micro Metal Foil Adhesive
Works with household aluminum foil, copper, stainless steel and other metallic foils.

Paasche Airbrush Co.

A complete line of airbrushes and accessories, suitable for all types of model painting, crafts and other hobbies as well as fine art illustration.

CAUTION: For your safety, the use of a properly vented spray booth and a respirator which is paint mist and vapor compatible, is strongly recommended when painting with an airbrush.

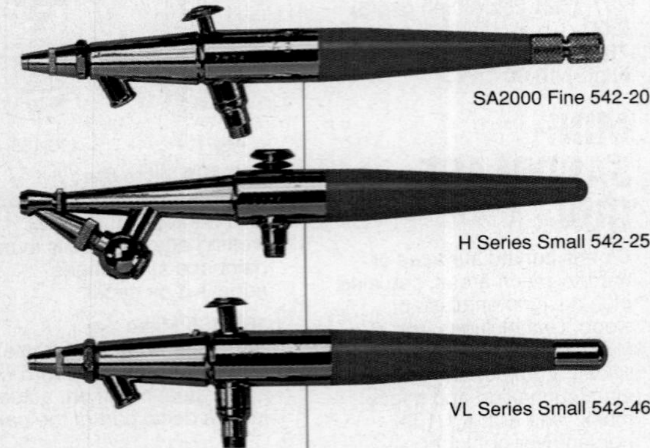

SA2000 Fine 542-20

H Series Small 542-25

VL Series Small 542-46

AIRBRUSHES

F SERIES

542-50 F#1 **38.00**
This inexpensive airbrush is the perfect choice for simple hobby work, students learning how to airbrush or touch-up work. Easy to master single action, external mix siphon-feed design is perfect for beginners. Spray pattern adjusts from 1/32 to 3/4" and is suitable for use with light fluids. Optional color cups and bottles are also available separately.

H SERIES

AIRBRUSHES EA 44.00 (UNLESS NOTED)
This popular single action, siphon-feed, external mix airbrush is highly recommended for beginners. Sturdy and flexible, it can be adapted to practically any hobby use. Available in three sizes of spray patterns; each brush can be converted to another size with Aircaps and Color Adjusting Part, sold separately. Suitable for left or right hand users. Optional color cups and bottles are also available separately.

542-25 Small 1/32-1"
542-26 Medium 1/32-1-1/4"
542-27 Large 1/16-1-1/2"

542-2001 2000H Hobby Kit **55.00**
Includes single action, internal mix airbrush plus two 1/2oz bottle assemblies, air hose with coupling, airbrush hanger, adjusting wrench, Allen wrench and "22 Airbrush Lessons" book.

542-3 Travel Set **77.00**
Includes large spray pattern, single action airbrush, two 8oz (240ml) cans of Propellant, bottle assembly, color cup, air hose, tank valve, "22 Airbrush Lessons" book and parts list.

VJR EA 85.00

These gravity-feed, internal mix, dual-action brushes provide super control for weathering, camouflage, tinting and shading. Built-in color cup makes color changes fast and easy and makes this brush ideal for left or right handed users. Spray heads handle the viscosity shown.

542-42 Light Fluids
542-43 Medium Fluids

VLS

542-53 Swivel Set **118.00**
Identical to #52, but with a screw-on swivel airbrush connector.

AIRBRUSH CARD SET EA 43.00

Sets include one airbrush, wrench, air regulator valve, 6' hose assembly and color jar with cap.

542-32 H Series ***NEW***
542-49 F Series ***NEW***
542-51 VL Series ***NEW***

VL SERIES

AIRBRUSHES EA 94.00
Maximum versatility for virtually any hobby or craft painting project. Double-action, internal mix, siphon-fed brush can spray fine lines or cover broad areas. Available in three sizes of spray patterns; each brush can be converted to another size with Aircaps and Color Adjusting Part, sold separately. Optional color cups and bottles are also available separately.

542-46 Small 1/32-1"
542-47 Medium 1/32-1-1/4"
542-48 Large 1/32-1-1/2"

SETS

542-11 Travel Set **108.00**
Large spray airbrush, two 8oz (240ml) cans of Propellant, bottle assembly, color cup, air hose, tank valve, instructions and parts list.

542-2002 Hobby Kit **90.00**
Small spray pattern airbrush, two 1/2oz bottle assemblies, air hose with coupling, airbrush hanger, adjusting wrench, Allen wrench and instructions are all included.

SA2000 EA 64.00

Easy to use and operate, these single action, internal mix, siphon fed airbrushes are adaptable to all types of modeling, art and craft projects and can be used with all types of hobby paints.

542-20 Fine 1/64-1"
542-21 Medium 1/32-1-1/4"
542-22 Heavy 1/16-1-1/2"

VSR

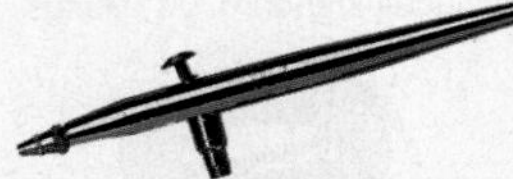

542-55 VSR90#1 Set **98.00**
This gravity-feed, internal mix, dual-action brush allows quick color changes using three different size cups, which are included. Cups attach to the top of the brush and swivel to left or right for a clear view of your work, or to fit either hand. Extra needle, aircap and tip are also included for use with heavier materials or broader coverage.

VL Set 542-52

H Set 542-31

Millennium 542-100

VL SET

542-52 Model VL Small Pattern **110.00**
Includes Small spray pattern airbrush, plus spray assemblies and needles for Medium and Large (VL5) applications, 1/4oz (7cc) color cup, 3oz (90ml) and 1oz (30ml) bottle assemblies, 1oz (30ml) plain bottle and cap, hanger, wrench, air hose with couplings, head protector, instructions and parts list.

H SET

542-31 Model H Small Pattern **77.00**
Includes small spray pattern, single action airbrush, 1/4oz (7cc) color cup, 3oz (90ml) and 1oz (30ml) bottle assemblies, 1oz (30ml) bottle and cap, color adjusting parts, hanger, wrenches, air hose with couplings, aircaps, "22 Airbrush Lessons" instruction booklet and parts list.

MILLENNIUM

542-100 Complete Set **86.00**
This double-action, internal-mix, siphon-feed brush features a thin barrel grip that allows for easy pullback of the needle mechanism to clear clogs. A rounded trigger button offers greater comfort and better control. Set includes Medium Airbrush (1/32-1-1/4" spray pattern), 1/4oz color cup, 1/2oz bottle, 6' air hose, wrench, hangar, storage case and instructions.

SA SET

542-2003 Hobby Kit **72.00**
Set includes two 1/2oz bottle assemblies, air hose with coupling, airbrush hanger, wrenches, and instructions.

Paasche Airbrush Co.

MINI SANDBLAST GUN

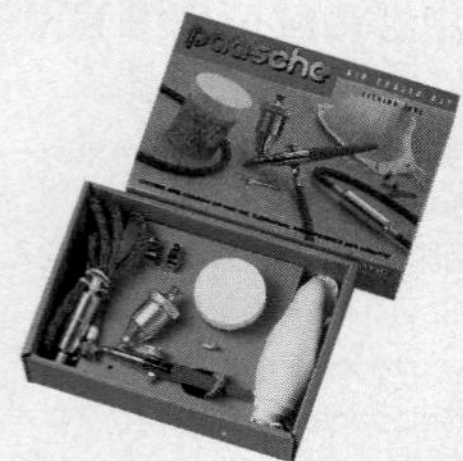

542-19 Air Eraser Set **88.00**
Etch glass or remove paint and rust. Set includes air eraser, fast cutting compound, air hose with moisture trap wrench, hanger and five disposable respirators.

FAST CUT COMPOUND

542-1905 5lb **17.15**
542-1906 6oz **3.75**

AIRBRUSH PROPELLANT

Portable, disposable cans of airbrush propellant. Use when a compressor or electricity is not available. Provides air pressure for varying amount of time, depending on brush and type of work. Propellant has no CFCs which harm the ozone layer. To control the air volume between the can and the brush, use the Pressure Tank Valve, sold separately.

542-6236 Large 11oz (330ml) **9.90**
542-6238 Small 8.5oz (255ml) **7.55**
542-1456 Pressure Tank Valve **6.20**
Use with #6236 or #6238. Controls air volume from tank to airbrush. All-brass construction.

PAINTING SUPPLIES

REGULATOR

542-75 In-Line **54.10**
Low pressure unit has a 60 PSI gauge and moisture drain. Easy adjustment of pressure and provides clean, dry air.

AIR HOSE

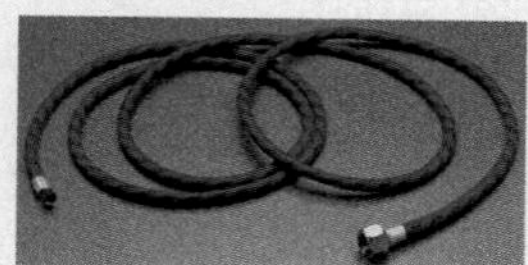

542-2118 Braided w/Couplings **9.60**
1/8" (3.175mm) diameter, 8' (2.4m) long.

MOISTURE TRAP

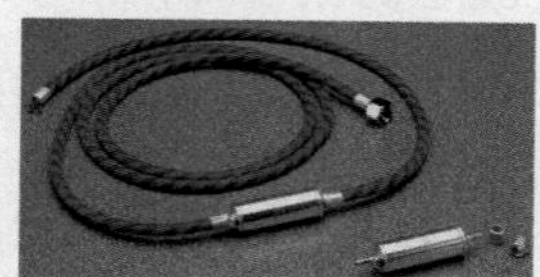

542-6171 **13.95**
Fits 1/8"(3.175mm) air hose to remove moisture from air.

SPRAY BOOTHS

542-10000 **279.00**
Paint safely by venting paint and fumes. Filter removes larger particles, but will not remove hazardous materials, so exhaust should be vented outside. Compact in size: 24" wide x 18" high (60 x 45cm) and easy to assemble. Provides 80 to 100 LFM air movement. Complete with motor.

SPRAY BOOTH FILTERS

542-10001 Polyester **1.55**
542-10002 Charcoal **5.20**

REPLACEMENT PARTS & ACCESSORIES

H SERIES AIRBRUSHES

COLOR ADJUSTING PARTS EA 10.65

542-5381 For H#1 Small
542-5429 For H#3 Medium
542-5433 For H#5 Large

TIPS EA 4.80

542-5621 For H#1 Small
542-5623 For H#3 Medium
542-5625 For H#5 Large

NEEDLES EA 7.00

542-5631 #1 Fine
542-5633 #3 Medium
542-5635 #5 Heavy

AIRCAPS EA 3.50

542-5516 For H#1
542-5518 For H#3
542-5519 For H#5

MISCELLANEOUS

542-5387 1/4oz (7cc) Metal Color Cup **5.37**
542-1455 "O" Ring **.80**

VL/SA SERIES AIRBRUSHES

MULTIHEAD ASSEMBLIES EA 16.60

542-9575 For VL#1 Small
542-9576 For VL#3 Medium
542-9577 For VL#5 Large

AIRTIPS EA 3.45

542-9553 For VL#1 Small
542-9554 For VL#3 Medium
542-9555 For VL#5 Large

AIRCAPS EA 4.15

542-9561 For VL#1 Small
542-9563 For VL#3 Medium
542-9565 For VL#5 Large
542-174 Finger Lever Assembly **7.00**

REPLACEMENT NEEDLES EA 3.45 (UNLESS NOTED)

542-9552 Reamer **5.70**
542-9578 For VL#1 Small
542-9581 For VL#3 Medium
542-9583 For VL#5 Large

SA 2000 NEEDLES EA 4.70

(All other replacement parts for SA2000 are the same as the VL series.)

542-2631 #1 Fine
542-2633 #3 Medium
542-2635 #5 Heavy

COLOR BOTTLE ASSEMBLIES

542-9511 1oz (30ml) **4.65**
542-9549 3oz (90ml) **4.85**

COLOR CUP

542-9515 1/4oz (7cc) **5.35**

UNIVERSAL PARTS

Parts fit all Paasche airbrushes.

COLOR BOTTLE ASSEMBLIES

542-5383 1oz (30ml) **4.65**
542-5430 3oz (90ml) **4.85**

BOTTLES

542-5388 3oz (90ml **1.00**
542-5435 1oz (30ml) **.80**

PLAIN COVERS EA .40

Less gaskets.

542-190 For 3oz Bottle
542-191 For 1oz Bottle

GASKETS EA .45

542-3107 For 3oz Cup
542-5007 For 1oz Cup

INSTRUCTION BOOK

542-99999 22 Airbrush Lessons for Beginners **1.50**
Teaches the basics of airbrush control along with the proper use of masks, stencils and frisket paper. Easy to follow with illustrated lessons. Included with brushes and sets.

HEAVY-DUTY SPRAYERS

MODEL 62 EA 50.00

Great for jobs requiring more than an airbrush, but are small enough that an airgun is too much. Complete with 3oz jar.

542-6213 Light Fluids
542-6223 Medium Fluids

MANUAL SPRAY GUNS

Finish, decorate and coat with this unique design for results unobtainable with other spray systems.

Adjusts from 3" fan to round pattern; available in small (0), medium (00), or large (000) pattern. NOTE: Siphon Jar must be ordered separately.

AUF EA 112.00

542-110 AUF-0
542-111 AUF-00
542-112 AUF-000

AUTF EA 121.00

542-115 AUTF-0
542-116 AUTF-00
542-117 AUTF-000

SIPHON JAR ASSEMBLY

542-4300 3oz **10.95**
Use with AUF or AUTF spray guns, sold separately.

L SERIES

SPRAYER EA 45.00

Ideal for hobbyists who need to cover large areas, or spray heavy paints and varnishes.

Available in four tip sizes for light to heavy fluids. **NOTE**: Quart Cups are sold separately - sizes for the Sprayer and Cup MUST BE IDENTICAL.

542-121 Light L#1
542-122 Medium L#2
542-123 Heavy L#3
542-124 Very Heavy L#4

1 QUART CUPS EA 41.45

542-1211 LSC #1
542-1212 LSC #2
542-1213 LSC #3
542-1214 LSC #4

COMPRESSOR

542-62 1/4 Horsepower **245.00**
Small, quiet unit with oil-less diaphragm, designed for home, office or studio use. Delivers up to 35 pounds of pressure and can be used with any airbrush. Equipped with three-wire cord and On/Off switch. Delivers .5CFM at 20 PSI. Weighs approximately 24 pounds.

542-63 1/10 Horsepower **171.00**
An economical unit with oil-less diaphragm, suitable for use with properly thinned fluids. Delivers up to 30 pounds of air and can be used with any airbrush. Equipped with three-wire cord. Delivers .5 CFM at 20 PSI. Weighs approximately 12 pounds.

542-64 1/4 Horsepower Silentaire **799.00**
Heavy-duty model can handle three brushes at once. Quiet operation makes it ideal for home or office. Includes output pressure regulator with gauge. Delivers up to 114 P.S.I., output 1.08 C.F.M
Specifications: 1 CFM 100 PSI, 115V, 60 Cycle, weighs approximately 42 pounds.

Compressor 542-63

K-TOOL PRODUCTS

PAINT FILTER

211-1 Airbrush Paint Filter **4.95**
Keep your airbrush operating at peak performance with this special filter. Fine stainless steel mesh will pass only particles that should normally flow through airbrush. Larger particles are trapped before they can enter and cause clogs. Fits all airbrushes that use bottles; slides easily on and off siphon tube for easy clean-up.

ROBART

PAINT SHAKER

Keep your hobby paints mixed and ready to use. Great for mixing thinner and paint when airbrushing or blending custom colors. Eliminates messy stirring sticks and paint spills. Paint is shaken at 5,000 cycles/minute. Adjustable rubber strap holds all 1/4, 1/3, 1/2, 5/8 and 1 ounce bottles. Assembled and ready for use.

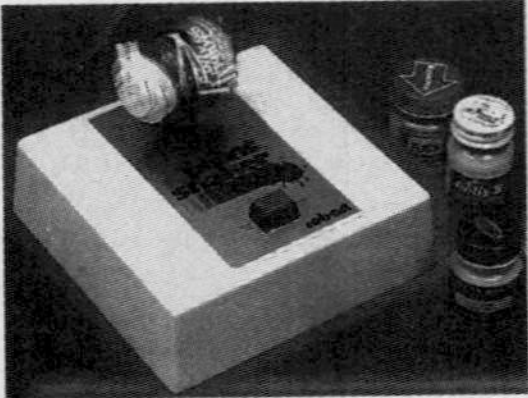

547-410 Battery Powered **24.95**
Use anywhere electricity is not available. Requires 4 D batteries, sold separately.

547-411 Electrically Powered **34.95**
Complete with transformer, plugs into any U.S. standard outlet (110V AC).

547-415 Replacement Straps pkg(5) **5.45**
Adjustable replacement straps for either shaker.

SCALECOAT

Create authentic models of your favorite equipment with this complete line of colors. Designed especially for use on metal without the need for a primer coat. Premixed for brushing, all colors can be thinned (3 parts paint to one part thinner is recommended) for airbrushing. All colors, except 640-1, 2 and 3 dry to a high gloss finish, so no clear coat is required for decaling. Can be applied to plastics with a base coat of Shieldcoat, or use Scalecoat II colors which are plastic compatible. When ordering, ask for the free technical sheet, #640-100.

SCALECOAT I RAILROAD COLORS 2OZ (60 ML)

LOCOMOTIVE COLORS EA 3.25

640-1 Locomotive Black (Low Gloss Finish)
640-2 Oxide Red (Low Gloss Finish)
640-3 Graphite & Oil (Low Gloss Finish)
640-5 Smoke Box Gray
640-6 Brunswick Green

STANDARD COLORS EA 3.25

640-8 D&H Yellow
640-9 D&H Blue
640-10 Black
640-11 White
640-12 Tuscan Red
640-13 Box Car Red
640-14 Caboose Red
640-15 Reefer Yellow
640-16 Reefer Orange
640-17 Pullman Green
640-18 Coach Olive
640-19 SOU Green
640-20 MOW Gray
640-21 Roof Brown
640-22 UP Yellow
640-23 Silver
640-24 ATSF Blue
640-25 GN Green
640-26 ATSF Red
640-27 IC Orange
640-28 SP Dark Gray
640-29 SP Scarlet
640-30 SP Daylight Orange
640-31 SP Daylight Red
640-32 UP Harbor Mist Gray
640-33 UP Dark Gray
640-35 CNW Yellow
640-36 CNW Green
640-37 B&O Royal Blue
640-38 BN Green
640-40 DRGW New Orange
640-41 EL Gray
640-42 EL Maroon
640-43 EL Yellow
640-45 GN Empire Builder Green
640-46 GN Empire Builder Orange
640-47 Aluminum
640-60 NP Light Green
640-61 NP Dark Green
640-62 LV Cornell Red
640-63 D&H Gray
640-65 NYC Light Gray
640-66 NYC Dark Gray
640-69 CP Tuscan Red
640-75 CR Blue
640-76 CB&Q Chinese Red
640-77 RDG Green
640-78 BNSF Orange
640-79 BNSF Green
640-80 BNSF White
640-81 PRR Freight Car Red
640-82 N&W Red
640-83 MILW Orange
640-84 UP Hopper Car Gray
640-85 New UP Yellow ***NEW***
640-86 NH Hunter Green ***NEW***
640-87 Box Car Red #2 ***NEW***
640-88 Box Car Red #3 ***NEW***
640-89 CP Rail Bright Red ***NEW***
640-90 NH Orange ***NEW***
640-91 C&O Blue ***NEW***

SCALECOAT THINNER

640-48 Can 8oz .24L **4.25**
640-49 Can 1qt .95L **7.95**
640-50 Bottle 2oz 60mL **2.65**

STRIPPERS

640-56 Paint Remover 16oz .47L **8.95**
Safe for use on most plastics, can be re-used. Big bottle handles lots of jobs.

640-59 Metal Stripper 32oz .48L Can **10.95**
Formulated to remove paint from metal (great for brass models) and reusable.

COATINGS

SHIELDCOAT

640-55 2oz (60ml) **3.25**
Scalecoat colors can be applied to plastics treated with a base coat of Shieldcoat. Helps insure uniform coverage of paint and prevents crazing. Must be thinned with Scalecoat thinner for spraying.

GLAZE 2 OZ 60ML EA 3.25

Protect paint and hide decal film. Gloss and Flat can be mixed to create a desired satin finish. (Thin 3-4 parts thinner to 1 part finish.)

640-51 Flat
640-52 Gloss
Semi-gloss finish, with less shine than actual paint finish.

SANDING SEALER

Seals wood surfaces for application of Scalecoat colors.

640-53 Wood Sealer 2oz 60mL **3.25**

640-57 Thinner 2oz 60mL **2.65**
Special formula, for use only with #53 Sanding Sealer.

SCALECOAT II RAILROAD COLORS 2OZ 60ML

EA 3.25

Matching colors formulated especially for use on plastics. Drying time can be increased by adding Quick-Dry.

640-2001 Locomotive Black
640-2002 Oxide Red
640-2003 Graphite & Oil
640-2006 PRR Brunswick Green
640-2010 Black
640-2011 White
640-2012 Tuscan Red
640-2013 Box Car Red
640-2014 Caboose Red
640-2015 Reefer Yellow
640-2016 Reefer Orange
640-2017 Pullman Green
640-2019 SOU Green
640-2020 MOW Gray
640-2021 Roof Brown
640-2022 UP Yellow
640-2023 Silver
640-2024 ATSF Blue
640-2025 GN Green
640-2026 ATSF Red
640-2032 UP Harbor Mist Gray
640-2037 B&O Royal Blue
640-2038 BN Green
640-2047 Aluminum
640-2075 CR Blue
640-2076 CB&Q Chinese Red
640-2077 RDG Green
640-2078 BNSF Orange
640-2079 BNSF Green
640-2080 BNSF White
640-2081 PRR Freight Car Red
640-2082 N&W Red
640-2083 MILW Orange
640-2084 UP Hopper Car Gray
640-2085 New UP Yellow ***NEW***
640-2086 NH Hunter Green ***NEW***
640-2087 Box Car Red #2 ***NEW***
640-2088 Box Car Red #3 ***NEW***
640-2089 CP Rail Bright Red ***NEW***
640-2090 NH Orange ***NEW***
640-2091 C&O Blue ***NEW***

SCALECOAT II THINNER

640-2048 Can 8oz .24L **4.25**
640-2049 Can 1qt .97L **7.95**
640-2050 Bottle 2oz 60mL **2.65**

QUICK DRY

640-54 Quick-Dry 2oz 60mL **3.25**
Speeds drying time of Scalecoat colors on plastic and wood, which can't be oven baked. Drying time varies with amount added to paint.

Information STATION

GRAFFITI ALONG YOUR RAILROAD

Trying to think of that extra added touch of realism that will complete your latest car? Graffiti may be the answer you're looking for. Unfortunately, graffiti is a part of all railroads in this day and age, but what better way to add that bit of reality to your layout?

There are basically two types of graffiti found on trains. One is the hand written chalk messages generally from yard conductors in order to speed up local switching. The other type is the "advertising" of local vandals or taggers.

One method of creating model graffiti is to draw a design or some words on tissue paper. Then, coat the back of the tissue with pastel color desired. Next, tape the design into place. Finally, trace over the design to transfer the image (this process works like carbon paper). After the graffiti has been applied spray it with a flat finish to seal it.

Another method involves fine or ultra-fine tipped markers and blank decal paper. First draw the design/words on the film. Next, seal the film with a very thin application of gloss coat finish. Let it set for 10-15 minutes and then add more coats as desired. Finally, use the film like a regular decal.

A third way of creating graffiti is to use a technical drafting pen and apply the design/words directly to the car. The advantage of this method is the colorfast and quick drying ink that is used with these pens.

A complete line of colors for railroad, automobile and military modelers. Enamel, acrylic and lacquer formulas are available to meet your painting needs.

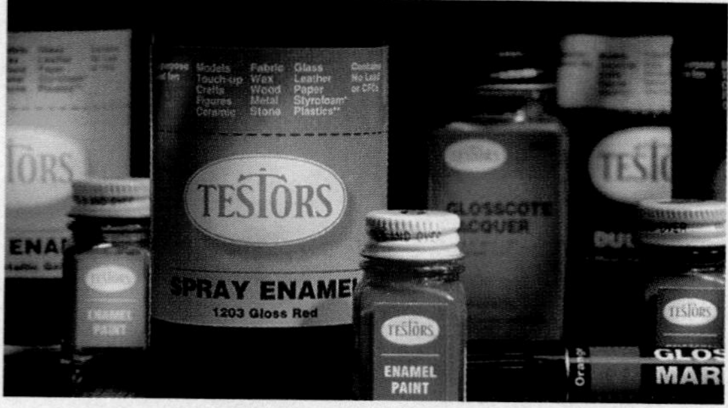

PLA ENAMELS

BOTTLES - 1/4OZ (7.5ML) EA 1.10

All-purpose paints are fast drying, easy to apply and can be used on many different surfaces. Colors are carefully controlled from batch to batch so that each bottle exactly matches the corresponding spray. Use on styrene, ABS plastic, wood, metal, leather, glass, wax and other materials. Colors dry fast to a hard gloss finish (unless noted).

Dealers MUST order multiples of 12.

704-1103 Red
704-1104 Dark Red
704-1108 Light Blue
704-1110 Medium Blue
704-1111 Dark Blue
704-1112 Pale Yellow
704-1114 Yellow
704-1116 Cream
704-1124 Green
704-1127 Orange
704-1133 Light Brown
704-1134 Purple
704-1138 Gray
704-1140 Brown
704-1141 Wood
704-1144 Gold
704-1145 White Gloss
704-1146 Silver
704-1147 Black Gloss
704-1149 Flat Black
704-1150 Flat Red
704-1151 Copper
704-1152 Metallic Red

BRUSH-ON METAL FLAKE

704-1529 Ruby Red
704-1530 Jade Green
704-1531 Burgundy Purple
704-1539 Sapphire Blue
704-1542 Lime Gold

FLUORESCENT COLORS

704-1173 Orange
704-1174 Green
704-1175 Red
704-1176 Blue
704-1177 Yellow
704-1178 Pink

MILITARY FLAT COLORS

704-1162 Sky Blue
704-1163 Battle Gray
704-1164 Olive Drab Green
704-1165 Army Olive
704-1166 Military Brown
704-1167 Desert Tan
704-1168 White
704-1169 Yellow
704-1170 Light Tan
704-1171 Beret Green
704-1172 Sea Blue
704-1180 Steel
704-1181 Aluminum
704-1182 Brass
704-1183 Rubber
704-1184 Zinc Chromate
704-1185 Rust

PLA SPRAY ENAMELS

3OZ (90ML) EA 3.00

Matching colors for bottled colors in a handy spray can. Dries to hard gloss finish unless noted.

Dealers MUST order multiples of 3.

704-1203 Red
704-1204 Dark Red
704-1208 Light Blue
704-1210 Bright Blue
704-1211 Dark Blue
704-1214 Yellow
704-1224 Green
704-1226 Aircraft Gray
704-1231 Bright Red
704-1233 Flat Light Gray
704-1234 Purple
704-1237 Primer
704-1238 Gray
704-1240 Brown
704-1241 Wood
704-1244 Gold
704-1245 White Gloss
704-1246 Silver
704-1247 Black Gloss
704-1249 Flat Black
704-1250 Flat Red
704-1251 Copper
704-1257 Transparent Blue
704-1258 Flat White
704-1261 Glosscote *NEW*
704-1265 Flat Olive Drab *NEW*

SPRAY CUSTOM COLORS

704-1601 Candy Emerald Green
704-1605 Candy Apple Red
704-1607 Candy Hot Rod Red
704-1617 Candy Grape
704-1628 Competition Orange

SPRAY METAL FLAKE

704-1629 Ruby Red
704-1630 Jade Green
704-1631 Burgundy Purple
704-1639 Sapphire Blue
704-1642 Lime Gold

CHROME SPRAY

704-1290 Chrome Silver

AUTOMOTIVE ENAMELS

704-1273 Orange
704-1274 Green
704-1275 Red
704-1277 Yellow
704-1278 Pink
704-1801 Cherry Red
704-1804 Blue Pearl Metallic
704-1813 Black Pearl
704-1814 High Gloss Clear

STOCK CAR COLORS

1/2OZ EA 1.99

704-52740 Instrument Panel Matte Black *NEW*
704-52741 Suspension Gloss Black *NEW*
704-52742 Fire Extinguisher Red *NEW*
704-52743 Engine Silver *NEW*
704-52744 Drive Shaft Flat White *NEW*
704-52745 Steel *NEW*
704-52746 Aluminum *NEW*
704-52747 Chassis Gloss Gray *NEW*
704-52748 Distributer Intermediate Blue *NEW*
704-52749 Semigloss Black *NEW*

TEAM LICENSED COLORS 3OZ EA 3.60

704-52940 #3 RCR Racing Black *NEW*
704-52941 #4 Kodak Film Racing Yellow *NEW*
704-52942 #5 Kelloggs Racing Yellow *NEW*
704-52943 #5 Kelloggs Racing Red *NEW*
704-52944 #6 Valvoline Racing Dark Blue *NEW*
704-52945 #6 Valvoline Racing White *NEW*
704-52946 #8 Circuit City Racing Black *NEW*
704-52947 #8 Circuit City Racing Red *NEW*
704-52949 #16 Primestar Racing Red *NEW*
704-52951 #31 RCR Racing Blue *NEW*
704-52952 #31 RCR Racing Yellow *NEW*
704-52953 #36 Skittles Racing Blue *NEW*
704-52954 #36 Skittles Racing Red *NEW*
704-52955 #43 Petty Racing Blue *NEW*
704-52957 #75 Remington Racing Metallic Green *NEW*
704-52958 #88 Ford Credit Racing Red *NEW*
704-52959 #88 Ford Quality Care Racing Blue *NEW*
704-52960 #94 McDonald's Racing Red *NEW*
704-52961 #97 John Deere Racing Light Green *NEW*
704-52962 #97 John Deere Racing Dark Green *NEW*
704-52963 #97 John Deere Racing Yellow *NEW*
704-52964 #99 Excide Batteries Racing Pink Magenta *NEW*
704-52965 #9 Excide Batteries Racing Black
704-52966 Flat White Primer *NEW*
704-52967 Flat Gray Primer *NEW*
704-52968 Satin Black *NEW*
704-52969 Clear Gloss *NEW*
704-52970 #43 Petty Racing Red *NEW*
704-52971 Roll Cage Grey *NEW*
704-52972 #16 Primestar Yellow *NEW*
704-52973 #75 Remington Racing Yellow *NEW*
704-52974 #75 Remington Racing Orange *NEW*
704-52975 #44 Hot Wheels Metallic Racing Blue *NEW*
704-52976 #24 Dupont Racing Blue *NEW*
704-52977 #24 Dupont Racing Red *NEW*

MODEL MASTER

FS ENAMELS 1/2OZ (15ML) BOTTLES EA 1.99

FS Series colors match Federal Standard number indicated. Bottled paints are specially formulated for airbrushing, with popular colors also offered in spray cans. Dealers MUST order in multiples of 6.

704-1705

704-1701 Military Brown (FS 30117)
704-1702 Field Drab (FS 30118)
704-1704 Armor Sand (FS 30277)
704-1705 Insignia Red (FS 31136)
704-1706 Sand (FS 33531)
704-1707 Chrome Yellow (FS 13538)
704-1708 Insignia Red (FS 33538)
704-1709 Radome Tan (FS 33613)
704-1710 Dark Green (FS 34079)
704-1711 Olive Drab (FS 34087)
704-1712 Field Green (FS 34097)
704-1713 Medium Green (FS 34102)
704-1714 Forest Green 34127)
704-1715 Interior Green (FS 34151)
704-1716 Pale Green (FS 34227)
704-1717 Dark Sea Blue (FS 15042)
704-1718 Flat Sea Blue (FS 35042)
704-1719 Insignia Blue (FS 35044)
704-1720 Intermediate Blue (FS 35164)
704-1721 Medium Gray (FS 35237)
704-1722 Duck Egg Blue (FS 35622)
704-1723 Gunship Gray (FS 36118)
704-1725 Neutral Gray (FS 36270)
704-1726 Light Sea Gray (FS 36307)
704-1728 Light Ghost Gray (FS 36375)
704-1729 Gloss Gull Gray (FS 16440)
704-1730 Flat Gull Gray (FS 36440)
704-1731 Aircraft Gray (FS 16473)
704-1732 Light Gray (FS 36495)
704-1733 Camouflage Gray (FS 36622)
704-1734 Green Zinc Chromate
704-1735 Wood
704-1736 Leather
704-1740 Dark Gull Gray (FS 36231)
704-1741 Dark Ghost Gray (FS 36320)
704-1742 Dark Tan (FS 30219)
704-1744 Gold
704-1745 Insignia White (FS 17875)
704-1747 Gloss Black (FS 17038)
704-1749 Flat Black (FS 37038)
704-1764 Euro Dark Green (FS 34092)
704-1768 Flat White (FS 37875)
704-1772 Blue Angel Blue (FS 15050)
704-1775 Florescent Red (FS 28915)
704-1780 Steel
704-1781 Aluminum
704-1782 Brass
704-1785 Rust
704-1786 Medium Field Green (FS 34095)
704-1787 Green Drab (FS 34086)
704-1788 Euro 1 Gray (FS 36081)
704-1790 Chrome Silver (FS 17178)
704-1791 Navy Gloss Gray (FS 16081)
704-1792 SAC Bomber Tan (FS 34201)
704-1793 SAC Bomber Green (FS 34159)
704-1794 Navy Aggressor Gray (FS 36251)
704-1795 Gunmetal
704-1796 Jet Exhaust
704-2021 Tan (FS 20400)
704-2022 International Orange (FS 12197 - Gloss)
704-2023 Blue Angels Yellow (FS 13655 - Gloss)
704-2024 US Army Helo Drab (FS 34031)

704-2025 Marine Corps Green (FS 34052)
704-2026 Dark Drab (B-52 FS 24091- Semi-Gloss)
704-2027 Dark Green (B-52 FS 34096)
704-2028 Willow Green (FS 14187 - Gloss)
704-2029 Green (FS 34258)
704-2030 True Blue (FS 15102 - Gloss)
704-2031 Blue (FS 35109)
704-2032 Bright Blue (FS 35183)
704-2033 Blue (FS 35414)
704-2034 Engine Gray (FS 36076)
704-2035 Air Mobility Command Gray (FS 36173)
704-2036 Dark Gray (F-15 FS 36176)
704-2037 Flint Gray (FS 36314)
704-2038 Light Gray (FS 36492)
704-2039 Canadian Voodoo Gray (FS 16515)
704-2040 Aircraft Interior Black (FS 37031)
704-2041 Fluorescent Red-Orange (FS 28913-Semi Gloss)

FIGURE COLORS
Special flat colors for skin tones and uniforms.

704-2001 Skin Tone-Light Base
704-2002 Skin Tone-Dark Base
704-2003 Skin Tone-Warm Tint
704-2004 Skin Tone-Shadow Tint
704-2005 Burnt Umber
704-2006 Raw Umber
704-2007 Burnt Sienna
704-2008 Raw Sienna
704-2009 British Crimson
704-2010 Piping Pink
704-2011 Cadmium Yellow Light
704-2012 Cobalt Blue
704-2013 Napolenoic Violet
704-2014 German Uniform Feldgrau
704-2015 Flat Clear Lacquer *NEW*
704-2016 Semi-Gloss Clear Lacquer *NEW*
704-2017 Gloss Clear Lacquer *NEW*
704-2018 Thinner *NEW*

DECAL SOLUTIONS EA 1.99
704-2145 Solvent *NEW*
704-2146 Setting *NEW*

WORLD WAR II UNITED STATES & ROYAL AIR FORCE
704-2048 RAF Azure Blue (ANA 609)
704-2049 RAF Sky Type "S" (ANA 610)
704-2050 Olive Drab (ANA 613)
704-2051 Faded Olive Drab
704-2052 RAF Middlestone (ANA 615)
704-2053 Sand (ANA 616)
704-2054 Dark Earth (ANA 617)
704-2055 Navy Blue Grey
704-2056 RAF Dark Slate Grey
704-2057 RAF Ocean Grey
704-2058 RAF Medium Sea Grey
704-2059 RAF Dark Sea Grey
704-2060 RAF Dark Green
704-2061 RAF P.R.U. Blue
704-2062 RAF Interior Green
704-2063 RAF Trainer Yellow

WORLD WAR I GERMAN LUFTWAFFE
These semi-gloss colors match the RLM specifications for camouflage colors used on German Aircraft during World War One.

704-2071 Grun (RLM 02)
704-2072 Gelb (RLM 04)
704-2073 Rot (RLM 23)
704-2074 Dunkelblau (RLM 24)
704-2075 Dunkelbraun (RLM 61)
704-2076 Grun (RLM 62)
704-2077 Licthgrau (RLM 63)
704-2078 Hellblau (RLM 65)
704-2079 Schwarzgrau (RLM 66)
704-2080 Schwarzgrun (RLM 70)
704-2081 Dunkelgrun (RLM 71)
704-2082 Grun (RLM 72)
704-2083 Grun (RLM 73)
704-2084 Graugrun (RLM 74)
704-2085 Grauviolett (RLM 75)
704-2086 Licthblau (RLM 76)
704-2087 Hellblau (RLM 78)
704-2088 Sandgelb (RLM 79)
704-2089 Olivgrun (RLM 80)
704-2090 Braunviolett (RLM 81)
704-2091 Dunkelgrun (RLM 82)
704-2092 Licthgrun (RLM 83)

WORLD WAR II GERMAN PANZER COLORS
704-2094 Schwarzgrau (1939-43 RAL 7021)
704-2095 Panzer Dunkelgelb
704-2096 Schokololaden-braun (1943 RAL 8017)
704-2097 Panzer Olivgrun 1943
704-2098 Afrika Khakibraun 1941 (RAL 7008)
704-2099 Afrika Grunbraun 1941 (RAL 8000)
704-2100 Signalbraun (RAL 8002)
704-2101 Anthracitgrau (RAL 7016)
704-2102 Afrika Braun 1942 (RAL 8020)
704-2103 Afrika Dunkelgrau 1942 (RAL 7027)
704-2104 Panzer Interior Buff-Semi-Gloss

WORLD WAR II FRENCH COLORS
704-2105 Dark Blue Gray
704-2106 Khaki
704-2107 Chestnut
704-2108 Earth Brown
704-2109 Light Blue Green

WORLD WAR II ITALIAN COLORS
704-2110 Italian Sand
704-2111 Italian Dark Brown
704-2112 Italian Olive Green
704-2113 Italian Blue Gray

WORLD WAR II JAPANESE COLORS
704-2114 Imperial Japanese Army Green
704-2115 Imperial Japanese Army Light Gray
704-2116 Imperial Japanese Navy Green
704-2117 Imperial Japanese Navy Gray
704-2118 Deep Yellow
704-2119 Interior Metallic Blue

WORLD WAR II RUSSIAN COLORS
704-2120 Topside Gray
704-2121 Underside Gray
704-2122 Topside Green
704-2123 Underside Blue
704-2124 Earth Brown
704-2125 Earth Gray
704-2126 Topside Blue
704-2127 Marker Red
704-2128 Marker Yellow
704-2129 Russian Armor Green

MODERN RUSSIAN COLORS
All colors have a semi-gloss finish.

704-2130 Flanker Pale Blue
704-2131 Flanker Medium Blue
704-2132 Flanker Blue/Gray
704-2133 Fulcrum Gray
704-2134 Fulcrum Gray/Green
704-2135 Interior Blue/Green

MODERN ARMOR (GULF WAR) COLORS
704-2136 US Army/Marines Gulf Armor Sand
704-2137 British Gulf Armor Light Stone
704-2138 Israeli Armor Sand/Gray

TINT WHITES
704-2142 Flat White (FS 37295)
704-2143 Semi-Gloss White (RLM 21)
704-2144 Gloss White (FS 17295)

AUTOMOTIVE ENAMELS
704-2705 Burgundy Red Metallic
704-2709 Light Ivory
704-2710 Sand Beige
704-2711 Anthracite Gray Metallic
704-2712 Graphite Metallic
704-2713 Black Metallic
704-2714 German Silver Metallic
704-2715 French Blue
704-2716 British Green Metallic
704-2717 Bright Yellow
704-2718 Guards Red
704-2719 Italian Red
704-2720 Classic White
704-2721 Classic Black
704-2723 Turn Signal Amber
704-2724 Stop Light Red
704-2725 Header Flat White
704-2726 Ford Engine Light Blue
704-2727 Ford/GM Engine Blue
704-2728 Pontiac Engine Blue
704-2729 Oldsmobile Engine Blue
704-2730 Chrysler Engine Blue
704-2731 Chevy Engine Red
704-2732 Chrysler Engine Red
704-2733 Ford Engine Red
704-2734 Silver Chrome Trim
704-2735 Black Chrome Trim
704-2736 Clear Top Coat
704-2737 Gray Primer

SPRAY ENAMELS 3OZ (90ML) EA 3.30
Dealers MUST order multiples of 3.

704-1910 Dark Green (FS 34079)
704-1911 Olive Drab (FS 34087)
704-1913 Medium Green (FS 34102)
704-1917 Dark Sea Blue (FS 15042)
704-1920 Intermediate Blue (FS 35164)
704-1923 Gunship Gray (FS 36118)
704-1926 Light Sea Gray (FS 37307)
704-1929 Gloss Gull Gray (FS 16440)
704-1930 Flat Gull Gray (FS 36440)
704-1933 Camouflage Gray (FS 36622)
704-1942 Dark Tan (FS 30219)
704-1947 Gloss Black (FS 17038)
704-1949 Flat Black (FS 37038)
704-1950 Panzer Gray (FS 36076)
704-1954 Light Earth (FS 30140)
704-1955 Afrika Mustard (FS 30266)
704-1972 Blue Angel Blue (FS 15050)
704-1988 Euro 1 Gray (FS 36081)
704-1992 SAC Bomber Tan (FS 34201)
704-1993 SAC Bomber Green (FS 34159)
04-1994 Navy Aggressor Gray (FS 36251)

AUTOMOTIVE COLORS
704-2901 Silver Blue Metallic
704-2902 Arctic Blue Metallic
704-2905 Burgundy Red Metallic
704-2909 Light Ivory
704-2910 Sand Beige
704-2913 Black Metallic
704-2914 German Silver Metallic
704-2915 French Blue
704-2916 British Green Metallic
704-2917 Bright Yellow
704-2918 Guards Red
704-2919 Italian Red
704-2920 Classic White
704-2921 Classic Black
704-2922 Champagne Gold Metallic
704-2936 Clear Top Coat
704-2937 Gray Primer
704-2938 Racing Orange
704-2939 Racing Red
704-2940 Racing Blue
704-2942 1950s Aqua
704-2943 Bright White
704-2944 Gloss Pearl Clear Coat
704-2945 Turquoise Metallic
704-2947 Deep Pearl Purple
704-2948 White Primer
704-2949 Transparent Black Window Tint

CLEAR FINISH - ENAMEL
704-1959 Satin
704-1960 Flat
704-1961 Gloss

THINNER - ENAMEL
Dealers MUST order multiples of 12.

704-1148 1/4oz (7.5ml) Bottle **1.10**
704-1156 1-3/4oz (52.5ml) Bottle **1.98**

PAINT MARKERS EA 3.00
Perfect for painting small parts, doing touch-up and more. Colors match PLA Enamels and sprays. Fast drying, with double chisel tip for fine lines or bold strokes. 1/3oz.

Dealers MUST order multiples of 6.

704-2503 Gloss Red
704-2508 Gloss Light Blue
704-2511 Gloss Dark Blue
704-2414 Gloss Yellow
704-2524 Gloss Green
704-2527 Gloss Orange
704-2538 Gloss Gray
704-2540 Gloss Brown
704-2545 Gloss White
704-2547 Gloss Black
704-2544 Metallic Gold
704-2546 Metallic Silver
704-2549 Flat Black
704-2575 Fluorescent Red

MODEL MASTER METALIZER LACQUER
Recreate virtually any natural metal finish on plastic models using these special lacquer colors. Designed for airbrush application only, colors are premixed in Buffing (which can be polished to various degrees of sheen) or Nonbuffing types.

BUFFING 1/2OZ (15ML) BOTTLE EA 1.99
Dealers MUST order multiples of 6.

704-1401 Aluminum Plate
704-1402 Stainless Steel
704-1403 Magnesium
704-1404 Titanium
704-1405 Gunmetal
704-1406 Exhaust
704-1412 Dark Anodonic Gray
704-1415 Burnt Metal

BUFFING SPRAY 3OZ (90ML) EA 3.30
Same great colors in easy to use spray cans.

Dealers MUST order multiples of 3.

704-1451 Aluminum Plate
704-1452 Stainless Steel
704-1453 Magnesium
704-1454 Titanium
704-1455 Gunmetal
704-1459 Metalizer Sealer

NONBUFFING 1/2OZ (7.5ML) BOTTLE EA 1.99
Dealers MUST order multiples of 6.

704-1417 Brass
704-1418 Aluminum
704-1420 Steel
704-1423 Gunmetal
704-1424 Burnt Iron

METALIZER THINNER & SEALER EA 1.89

Special formulas for use with Metallizer colors. 1-3/4oz (52.5ml) bottle.

Dealers MUST order multiples of 12.

704-1409 Sealer
704-1419 Thinner

PAINT SETS

704-9120 Auto Detail **8.49**
Get a new model builder revved up for his or her first project with this set. Complete with six 1/4oz bottles of paint, a 1/4oz bottle of thinner, a paint brush, cement pen for clean and easy application of model glue and a handy storage tray.

704-9121 Aircraft **8.49**
Make ready on the flight deck with this starter set! Comes with six 1/4oz bottles of paint, a 1/4oz bottle of thinner, a paint brush, cement pen to make gluing easier and a storage tray.

704-9131 Military Flats **7.99**
Black, blue, gray, green, brown, tan, white and blue.
704-9146 Promotional Paint Set **7.29**
704-507 Hobby/Craft Flat Color **8.99** *NEW*

704-9116 Standard Finishing - Model Building **7.99** *NEW*
704-9137 Promotional Stock Car Detail Set **9.00** *NEW*

ACRYLIC SPRAY SETS

Sets include five 1/4oz nontoxic colors, 1/2oz primer, propellant and spray cap.

704-9215 Model Car **14.00** *NEW*

704-9216 Military Aircraft **14.00** *NEW*
704-9135 Model Car Refill Set **9.99** *NEW*
704-9136 Model Aircraft Refill Set **9.99** *NEW*

ACRYLIC POT SETS

Each includes a paint brush and mixing tray.

HOBBY CRAFT

704-9184 12 Colors **4.19** *NEW*

704-9186 18 Colors **5.39** *NEW*

MODEL CAR

704-9185 12 Colors **4.19** *NEW*

704-9187 18 Colors **5.39** *NEW*

SUPPLIES KIT

704-9111 Model Building Supplies Kit **6.99**
Drop cloth, three brushes, hobby knife, five gluing tips and five sanding films.

FINISHING CENTER

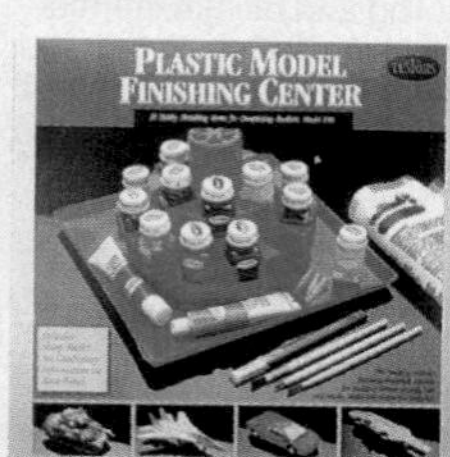

704-9172 Lazy Susan Finishing Center **23.98**
Revolving carousel with 9 gloss and flat enamels, thinner, plastic cement, putty, three paint brushes, knife, gluing tips and drop cloth.

PLASTIC MODEL FINISHING KITS EA 17.99

11 bottles of enamel, 1 bottle thinner, 1 tube plastic cement, putty, broad tip brush, fine tip brush, 1/4" (.6cm) brush, hobby knife, drop cloth, three gluing tips, five sanding films and plastic tray.

704-9160 Flat
704-9161 Gloss
704-9115 Enamel Set - Small **6.99**
Red, yellow, blue, silver, white and black, plus brush.

CLEANERS, THINNERS & COATINGS

AIRBRUSH THINNER

MODEL MASTER FS ENAMELS

704-1789 1-3/4oz (52.5ml) Bottle **2.49**
Dealers MUST order multiples of 12.

704-1799 8oz (0.12l) pkg(6) Can **5.49**
Dealers MUST order multiples of 6.

MODEL MASTER & TESTORS ENAMELS

704-8824 8oz (.12l) Can **5.49**
704-8825 1-3/4oz (52.5ml) Bottle **2.49**

CLEAR FINISH

DULLCOTE

A protective, transparent lacquer that dries dead flat without altering the color.

704-1160 1-3/4oz (52.5ml) **1.98**
Dealers: MUST order Dealer Pack of 12.

704-1260 Spray 3oz (90ml) **3.00**
Dealers MUST order multiples of 3.

GLOSSCOTE

Clear lacquer dries to a transparent, high gloss protective finish that does not alter the color.

704-1161 Bottle 1-3/4oz (52.5ml) **1.98**
Dealers MUST order multiples of 12.

704-1261 Spray 3oz (90ml) **3.00**
Dealers MUST order multiples of 3.

LACQUER BRUSH CLEANER

Dealers MUST order multiples of 6

704-1159 1oz (30ml) Bottle **1.79**
Use with Clear and Dull Coat.

DECAL SETTING SOLUTION

Softens decal film to conform to surface details.

704-8804 1/4oz (7.5ml) **1.10**
Dealers: MUST order Dealer pack of 12.

704-1737 1/2oz (15ml) **1.99**
Dealers: MUST order Dealer pack of 6

PAINT BRUSHES

Applying colors, highlighting fine details, washes, weathering, drybrushing and many other painting jobs are easy with this complete selection of brushes. Choose from natural and synthetic hairs in various shapes and sizes.

ROUND EA 3.75 (UNLESS NOTED)

704-8731 #3 *NEW*
704-8732 #0 *NEW*
704-8733 #2 **4.00** *NEW*

FLAT

704-8734 5/16" **5.00** *NEW*

MODEL MASTER

These top quality brushes help insure professional results. All Model Master brushes are made with solid birch handles and seamless nickel-plated ferrules.

Dealers MUST order multiples of 12.

SABLE

704-8841 #2 Red Sable Round **4.50**
For fine detail work and pinpoint washes.

704-8842 #3/0 Red Sable Round **4.00**
For precise, small scale work.

704-8861 1/2" Black Sable Flat **5.00**
For broad color applications and washes

CAMEL

704-8851 3/8" Camel Hair Flat **4.50**
Soft, fine bristles designed for high gloss finishes.

SYNTHETIC

704-8831 #2 Round **4.25**
Fine tip and good body, for painting small assemblies.

704-8832 #0 Round **4.00**
Durable bristles and fine point are ideal for applying liquid cement.

704-8833 1/4" Chisel **5.50**
Use for blending, such as secondary camouflage patterns.

SHED PROOF SYNTHETIC

Unique brushes feature nylon bristles stapled in the tip to keep them from falling out. Dealers MUST order multiples of 12.

INDIVIDUAL BRUSHES

704-8701 Broad Tip **.79**

704-8702 Fine Tip **.79**

704-8705 1/4" Tip **1.19**

SETS

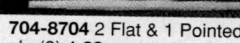

704-8703 1 Flat Tip & 1 Pointed pkg(2) **1.10**

704-8704 2 Flat & 1 Pointed pkg(3) **1.39**

704-8706 Flat, Pointed, and 1-1/4" Tips pkg(3) **1.59**

AIRBRUSHES

CAUTION:
For your safety, the use of a properly vented spray booth and a respirator which is paint mist and vapor compatible, is strongly recommended when painting with an airbrush.

TESTORS AIRBRUSH SETS

Use standard paint bottles to supply color and speed color changes. Spray width is adjusted by turning nozzle, volume can be changed by raising or lowering bottle.

704-8821 Airbrush Set **29.95**
With organizing tray, single-action external mix airbrush, mixing pipette, propellant control assembly, three 1/2oz (15ml) jars, 6' (1.8m) flexible hose and instruction manual. Also includes 9oz (270ml) ozone safe propellant.

704-9174 Airbrushing Set for Models **59.95** *NEW*
Set combines a double-action, internal-mix Aztek Airbush with Testor nontoxic acrylic paints. Includes storage carousel for paints.

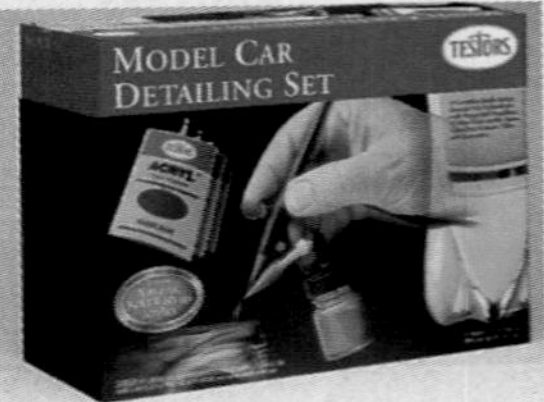

704-9176 Model Car Detailing Set **49.95** *NEW*
Set includes Aztek 1270 airbrush with three nozzles, propellant, 12 gloss acrylic paints in flexible pouches, paint mizing tray, detailing paint brush, compressor adapter, paint stencil, pouch storage rack and instructional video.

AZTEC AIRBRUSHES

Easy to use and maintain. Available in both single- and dual-action, as well as internal or external mix. Bodies are acetal resin, which is impervious to solvents, lightweight and nearly unbreakable.

EXTERNAL MIX

Fully assembled, single-action, with 6' air hose.

MODEL A220
704-2203 Set **19.95**
704-2206 Set w/6oz Can Ozone Safe Propellant **27.95**
Includes airbrush, two 1/2 ounce (15cc) bottles, 28mm quick change cap, compressor adapter and instructions.

MODEL A270
704-2705 Set **29.95**
704-2706 Set w/6 oz Can Ozone Safe Propellant **34.95**
Includes airbrush, 28 and 33mm bottle/cap assemblies, compressor adapter, instruction book and video.

MODEL A320
704-3205 Set **49.95**
704-3208 Set w/6 oz Can Ozone Safe Propellant **59.95**
Includes airbrush, general detail nozzle (.53mm), 28 and 33mm siphon caps and bottles, compressor adapter, instruction book and video.

INTERNAL MIX

Superb control, with interchangeable nozzles. Paint travels through the nozzle, not the body, so only the nozzles need to be cleaned. Gravity feed color cup can be positioned for right or left hand. Dual-action brushes are fully assembled and include air hose.

MODEL A430
704-4305 Set w/Plastic Storage Case **79.95**
704-4308 Set w/Wooden Storage Case **99.95**
Includes airbrush with 10' hose, general detail, medium coverage and large coverage nozzles, 7.5cc gravity feed color cup, 28 and 33mm siphon bottle and cap, instruction manual and video, plus storage case.

MODEL A470
704-4702 Set w/Plastic Storage Case **99.95**
704-4709 Set w/Wooden Storage Case **149.99**
Includes airbrush with 15' air hose, fine, medium and large nozzles, 2.5, 3 and 7.5cc gravity feed color cups, 28 and 33mm siphon bottles and caps, aircan hose adapter, instruction manual and video, plus storage case.

AIRBRUSH ACCESSORIES

AIR HOSE 10'

704-9311 Straight **14.95**
704-9312 Coiled **18.95**

ADAPTER

704-9313 Air Can Hose Adapter **8.95**

SIPHON CAPS & BOTTLES EA 5.95

704-9314 33mm
704-9319 28mm *NEW*
704-9326 Bottles 1/2oz pkg(2) *NEW*

704-9327 Bottles 2/3oz *NEW*

AZTEK NOZZLES EA 9.95 (UNLESS NOTED)

704-9304 Fineline (.30mm)
704-9305 General Coverage (.40mm)
704-9306 High Flow (.50mm)
704-9342 General (.53mm)
704-9343 Medium (.70mm)
704-9344 Large (1.02mm)
704-9302 Nozzle Set 4 Assorted **40.00** *NEW*

ACRYLIC PAINT NOZZLES EA 9.95

704-9340 .40mm
704-9341 .50mm

CLEANING STATION

704-9315 Airbrush Cleaning Station **29.95**
704-9316 Replacement Filters for #9315 **7.95**
Convenient, environmentally sound way to clean your airbrush. Simply insert in the adjustable neck and spray. Solvent passes through the nozzle, then through a filter and is trapped in the jar.

COLOR CUPS

704-9347 3.0cc **3.25**
704-9348 7.5cc **3.25**
704-9349 12.0cc **4.00**
704-9308 1.0cc Side Feed **3.25** *NEW*
704-9309 2.5cc Side Cup **3.25** *NEW*
704-9310 8.0cc Side Cup **4.00** *NEW*
704-9303 Color Cup Set **9.95** *NEW*
704-9346 12cc Top Feed **4.00** *NEW*
One each of 9308, 9309 and 9310.

MODEL MASTER

PIPETTES

704-50642 pkg(6) **2.98**
Transfer color or thinner for mixing custom colors. Plastic, easy to clean and reusable.

MASKING

704-50622 Modeling Tape **5.49**
1/2"x 20' (1.25cm x 6m)

For sharp separations between colors. Light adhesive will not lift paint under normal use.

704-50641 Parafilm M Masking Film **7.95**
2 x 25" (5 x 62.5cm)

Create custom masking, stencils, camouflage patterns and more. Light adhesive will not lift paint under normal usage.

PROPELLANT

704-8822 15oz (450ml) **10.00**
Ozone safe air supply with fittings. For any airbrush designed to accept propellant cans.

CLEANERS

704-65160 4oz **2.99** *NEW*
704-65162 32oz **9.95** *NEW*

HOBBY TOOLS

704-50628 Sprue Cutters **13.50**

AIR COMPRESSORS

Rugged and reliable, available in two sizes, ideal for hobby and craft work. NOTE: All Compressors are available by special order only.

AZTEK

704-50201 AC 100 **199.00**
NEW
Boasting maximum power and a compact design, this compressor is perfect for most airbrushing. Features 1/8 horsepower, 1.58 CFM, 35 psi maximum pressure, an oil-less diaphragm, 1/4 NPS air hose fitting and an on/off switch. 110V .08 amps.

704-50202 AC 200 **300.00**
Delivers up to 25lbs of air. Built-in moisture trap and pressure gauge. Rubber feet minimize vibration and noise With oil-less operation, fan cooling and built-in thermal protection switch. 2 year guarantee and 10,000 hour service life.

704-50203 AC 400 **350.00**
Delivers up to 30lbs of air. Heavy-duty, diaphragm-type with 1/12 horsepower motor and features of the AC 200.

705-50206 AC 600 **499.00**
NEW
This superior compressor is quiet, compact and powerful enough to run two airbrushes at the smae time. The fan-cooled unit is piston operated, weighs 12lbs and has a tank capacity of 1/3 gallons. Features 50 psi maximum pressuere, pressure relief valve, automatic thermal protector, pressure regulator and gauge, air-pressure auto-shutoff switch, a pressure holding tank with a water drain valve. 115 V 2.2amps.

705-50205 AC 500 **349.00**
NEW
A quiet and powerful unit that is distinguished by a pressure-holding tank with an automatic pressure switch, allowing the unit to maintain contant pressure while reducing pulsing. Features 1/8 horsepower, 1.58 CFM, 32 psi maximum pressure, an air pressue auto-shutoff switch, air pressure gauge and a pressure holding tank with a water drain valve. 110V .08 amps; weight: 16-1/2lbs; tank capacity: one gallon.

COMPRESSOR ACCESSORIES

REGULATOR & MOISTURE TRAP

704-50680 **66.65**
Built-in regulator to increase or decrease pressure. Moisture trap dries air. Fully assembled, fits most compressors.

PRESSURE GAUGE

704-50681 **22.25**
Large, easy to read black and white markings. Fully assembled, fits most compressors.

SPRAY BOOTH

704-50210 **449.95**
20W x 15D x 14H"
(50 x 37.5 x 35cm)
Powered fan collects overspray in three-stage filter system and vents vapors. Clear window area lets in plenty of light; mounting brackets provided for additional lighting (sold separately).

TAMIYA COLOR

Capture the color of the prototype with this line of water-soluble acrylics. Suitable for brushing or airbrushing, colors can be used on resins, styrofoam, wood, glass, metal and all common modeling plastics.

ACRYLIC BOTTLES 3/4OZ (23ML) EA 2.40

GLOSS FINISH

865-81001 Black
865-81002 White
865-81003 Royal Blue
865-81004 Blue
865-81005 Green
865-81006 Orange
865-81007 Red
865-81008 Lemon Yellow
865-81009 Brown
865-81010 Gun Metal
865-81011 Chrome Sliver
865-81012 Gold Leaf
865-81013 Metallic Blue
865-81014 Sky Blue
865-81015 Light Green
865-81016 Purple
865-81017 Pink
865-81028 Park Green

FLAT

865-81301 Black
865-81302 White
865-81303 Yellow
865-81304 Yellow Green
865-81305 Green
865-81306 Copper
865-81307 Red
865-81308 Blue
865-81309 Hull Red
865-81310 Brown
865-81311 Japanese Navy Green
865-81312 Japanese Navy Gray
865-81313 Japanese Army Green
865-81314 Japanese Army Gray
865-81315 Flesh
865-81316 Aluminum
865-81317 Sea Blue
865-81318 Medium Blue
865-81319 Sky Gray
865-81320 Medium Gray
865-81321 Sky
865-81322 RLM Gray
865-81323 Light Blue
865-81324 Dark Gray
865-81325 Light Sea Gray
865-81326 Deep Green
865-81327 Black Green
865-81349 Khaki
865-81350 Field Blue
865-81351 Khaki Drab
865-81352 Earth
865-81353 Neutral Gray
865-81354 Dark Sea Gray
865-81355 Deck Tan
865-81356 Metallic Gray
865-81357 Buff
865-81358 Olive Green
865-81359 Desert Yellow
865-81360 Dark Yellow
865-81361 Dark Green
865-81362 Olive Drab
865-81363 German Gray
865-81364 Red Brown
865-81365 Field Gray
865-81366 Light Gray

CLEAR COLORS 3/4OZ (23ML) BOTTLES EA 2.40

Special clear tints can be used to create stained glass, turn signals, brake lamps, tinted automobile glass, warning lamps and more. Dries with a clear gloss finish.

865-81019 Smoke
865-81023 Clear Blue
865-81024 Clear Yellow
865-81025 Clear Green
865-81026 Clear Orange

CLEAR FINISH 3/4OZ (23ML) BOTTLES EA 2.40

865-81021 Flat Base
Mix with glossy paints to reduce their shine as needed. For semi-gloss add about 15% flat base; for dead flat, add about 30% flat base.

865-81022 Clear

SEMI-GLOSS ACRYLIC

865-81018 Black **2.40**
3/4oz (23ml) bottle.

ACRYLIC THINNER

865-81020 Small (.69oz 23ml) **2.40**
865-81030 Medium (1.2oz 40ml) **2.70**
865-81040 Large (7-1/2oz 250ml) **6.50**

PAINT MARKERS

ENAMEL EA 3.20

Enamel paint markers are used as you would use a marking pen. Use on plastic, wood, metal and glass, and can be applied over acrylics and lacquers. Tip is 5/32 x 3/64" (4mm x 1mm).

865-89001 Black
865-89002 White
865-89003 Royal Blue
865-89005 Green
865-89006 Orange
865-89007 Red
865-89008 Lemon Yellow
865-89011 Chrome Silver
865-89012 Gold Leaf
865-89301 Flat Black
865-89315 Flat Flesh
865-89356 Metallic Gray

POLYCARBONATE EA 4.00

Formulated for use on polycarbonate plastics (used in RC car bodies) and works well on some engineering plastics used for handrails on locos and cars.

865-88001 White
865-88002 Red
865-88003 Light Blue
865-88004 Blue
865-88005 Black
865-88006 Yellow
865-88007 Orange
865-88008 Light Green
865-88010 Purple
865-88011 Pink
865-88012 Silver

PAINT BRUSHES

Featuring a variety of sizes and hair types, these brushes are made especially for painting models.

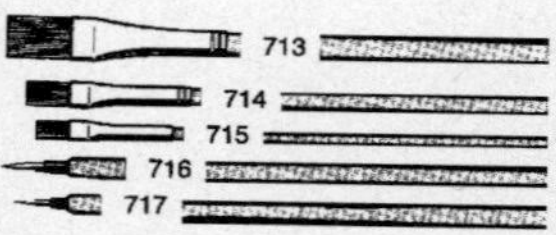

HORSE HAIR

865-713 #5 Flat **2.40**
865-714 #3 Flat **1.75**
865-715 #0 Flat **1.65**
865-716 Medium Pointed **2.40**
865-717 Small Pointed **2.40**

WEASEL HAIR

865-718 Medium Pointed **6.10**
865-719 Small Pointed **5.50**

AIRBRUSH

865-74501 Spray Works Airbrush System **145.00**
A small, portable air compressor and airbrush in one unit. Electric motor provides smooth steady pressure (15CFM) for an even spray. Airbrush can be adjusted to spray thin lines or wide areas. Power can be supplied by 7.2V Ni-Cad battery pack or a suitable AC adapter, both sold separately.

PAINT

Designed for Woodland Scenics Mini Scenes, details and structures, these paints can be used to finish any hobby project.

EARTH COLOR KIT

785-1215 14.98
A simple system for staining rocks, terrain, and plaster castings such as portals. Beginners get quality results. The Earth Color Kits include instructions, applicator, palette, and eight 1oz bottles each of Earth Color Liquid Pigment (White, Black, Concrete, Stone Gray, Slate Gray, Raw Umber, Burnt Umber, Yellow Ocher).

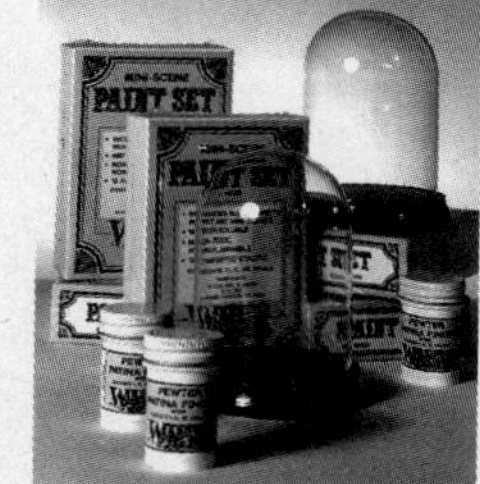

785-125 Paint Set pkg(12) **4.49**
Includes 12 water-based, non-toxic colors, each 1-1/2oz (44ml): Red, Yellow, Blue, White, Gray, Black, Earth, Clay, Terra Cotta, Sand, Beige and Golden Rod.

785-126 Pewter Patina Finish 7/8oz (30ml) **1.98**
Gives any metal the look of fine pewter castings. Great for figures or special effects. Dealers MUST order multiples of 5.

TOP COAT EA 3.98

785-1453 Asphalt 4oz
785-1454 Concrete 4oz

Scale
WALTHERS
HO
2000
MODEL RAILROAD REFERENCE BOOK

TOOLS

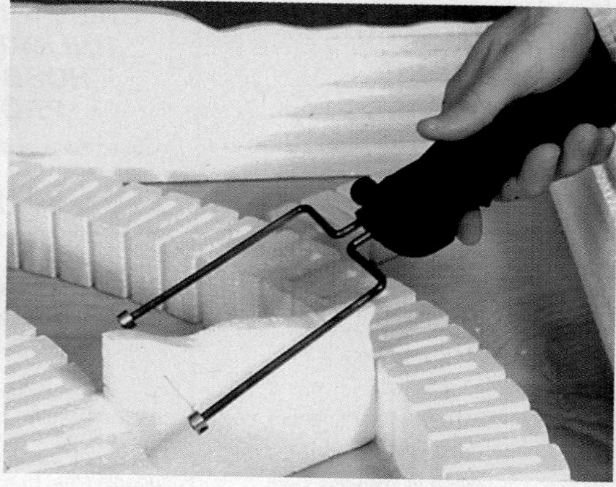

In the early days, building a railroad was tough, back-breaking work. Tunnels, bridges, cuts, fills, grading... all of it had to be done by hand with simple tools. Late in the 19th Century steam was harnessed to run the heavier machinery. In the 20th Century, gasoline and diesel powered equipment took over.

Building a model railroad has also gotten easier as the tools have gotten better. Early on, basic carpentry tools and single-edge razor blades were often the only things available. But in the 1940s, bigger companies began making smaller tools for war production and many found their way into hardware stores and hobby shops. And as the hobby grew in the 50s, a number of jewelry tool-makers, medical and dental instrument makers and art supply companies discovered the hobby market. Specialized pliers, tiny screwdrivers, magnifiers, hammers, tweezers, clamps and vises, hobby knives and blades, soldering equipment, fine-toothed saws and miniaturized power tools were readily available.

We still use many of these tools of course, and today, you'll find an incredible variety of specialized items to make every job easier and faster.

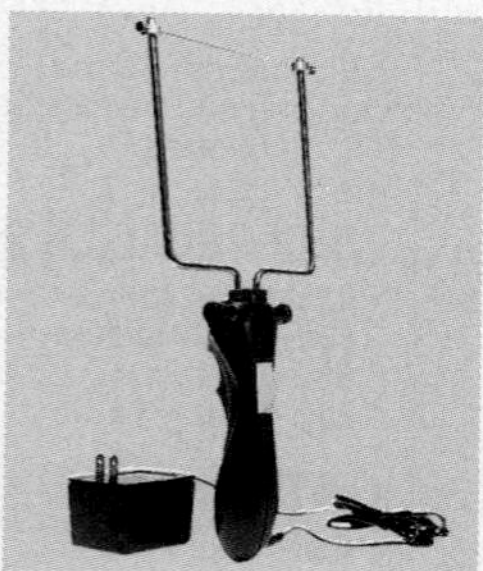

Some of the most recent innovations have been developed to build complete layouts and scenery from lightweight foam. Perfect for beginners who lack space or woodworking skills, these new materials and tools make it easy to build a layout anywhere. Best of all, they eliminate the noise and dust associated with other methods.

Using an inexpensive Hot Wire Foam Cutter, a Low Temperature Glue Gun and Nontoxic Foam products, everyone from novice to experienced modeler can easily build a layout of any size or design.

The Hot Wire Foam Cutter is great for cutting and shaping nontoxic foam. It produces clean, smooth edges wherever it's used, and there's no dusty mess to clean up afterwards. Using the Cutter is easy. Just plug it into the nearest outlet and you're ready to go. In addition to cutting and shaping scenery, you can carve elaborate patterns for craft projects, or use a straightedge to make precision cuts.

Since foam products have low melting points, a Low Temperature Glue Gun is the best way to join pieces. Other glue guns generate too much heat and can actually damage foam sections. Since it works at a cooler temperature, this unit is also ideal for all sorts of household projects and repairs that require a strong, quick-drying adhesive.

Pictured in action above are the Woodland Scenics Hot Wire Foam Cutter and Low Temperature Glue Gun, along with various nontoxic products from their SubTerrain Lightweight Layout System. (See the complete listing in the Scenery Section of this Book.)

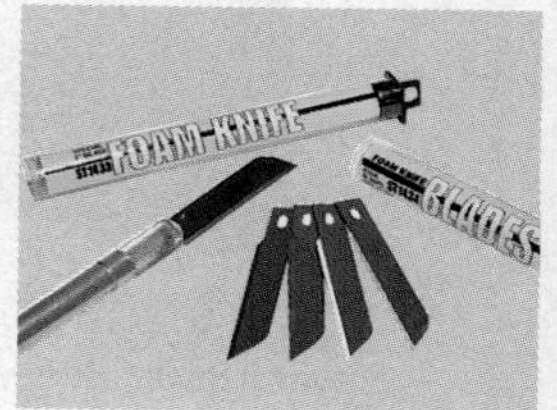

Check out these items, along with a complete selection of other time-saving, innovative tools on the following pages.

Layouts and Photos by Woodland Scenics

ACCURATE LIGHTING

WIRE STRIPPERS

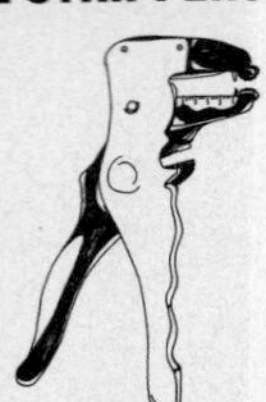

144-100 14.95
Avoid faulty connections. Strip wires more easily and precisely with Accurate Lighting Wire Strippers.

PIN VISE DRILL BIT HOLDERS EA 19.95

Drill bit holder for screwdrivers, including electric/cordless drills.

144-604 Holds #40-60
144-608 Holds #60-80

CIR-KIT CONCEPTS

MINI DRILL

206-201 6.95
High speed and hand operated; will drill small accurate holes in all types of material. 4-1/2" long, 3-to-1 ratio and accepts number size bits 61 through 80. Hollow handle stores your extra bits.

HAMMER

206-1041 Brass Head Hammer **9.95**
Designed to pound brass brads. 5-1/2" long with a solid brass head and serrated steel handle.

FORCEPS

206-10461 5" Locking **7.98**
Grips and holds 1/8" brads. Surgical stainless steel, serrated teeth.

A.J. FRICKO COMPANY

PINHOLE LENS FOR 35MM SLR CAMERA* EA 189.95

Focusing pinhole lens with colens to overcome fuzziness.

*Must have a camera with removable lens. Pinhole lens fits onto a camera body.

Lens features:

- 0.018 diameter aperture
- 105 f/stop
- etched in stainless steel
- a much sharper image
- a brighter viewing screen
- a shorter exposure time
- depth of field from 1" to infinity

274-842 Canon
Manual focus camera body.
274-843 Konika
274-844 Minolta
Manual focus camera body.
274-845 Nikon
Either manual or auto focus camera body.

274-846 Olympus
274-847 Pentax K
Bayonet mount, also works for Ricoh.
274-848 Pentax S
Universal screw mount for all screw mount body types.
274-849 Yashica/Contax
274-851 Minolta Maxxum
274-852 Canon EOS

DRS

MINI VACUUM ATTACHMENT KIT

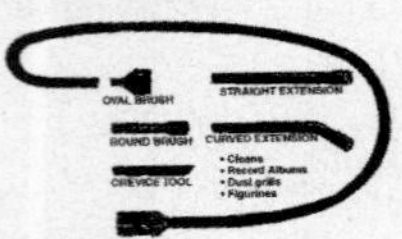

312-1 18.95
Great for cleaning in hard-to-reach places. Attach the adapter to the hose end of your vacuum cleaner. Includes an oval brush, round brush, crevice tool, straight extension, curved extension and an adapter.

CREATIONS UNLIMITED HOBBY PRODUCTS

FLEX-I-FILE™

Tough flexible tapes, for wet or dry sanding, on lightweight, high strength, anodized aluminum frames. Unlike needle files, FLEX-I-FILE automatically follows compound curves, contour changes and fillets without leaving scratches or flat-spots.

- Removes flash from plastic or metal castings
- Smoothes and polishes rough surfaces and seams
- Follows irregular or flowing contours
- Provides a delicate touch for hairline accuracy

STARTER SET

232-700 7.95
An inexpensive introduction to "Flex-I-File" uses and capabilities. Includes frame and two each fine, medium and coarse tapes.

COMBO SET

232-123 15.50
Includes frame with 8 each fine, medium and coarse tapes, plus one bonus tape on frame.

3-IN-1 SET

232-301 22.50
Includes 3 frames plus 7 each fine, medium and coarse tapes.

TOOL-TENDER PLUS

232-401 34.95
Four complete sets with room for five. Five-place tool stand in a clear plastic storage case.

TOOL TENDER ONLY

232-400 15.95

REPLACEMENT TAPES PKG(6) EA 2.50

232-150 Coarse
232-280 Medium
232-320 Fine
232-600 X-Fine

SCRIBES

SCRIBE-N-CUT

232-6087 Folding Knife **4.95**
Large blade is ideal for cutting big sheets of styrene, vacuum-formed models and more. Blade folds into handle for safe storage.

NEEDLE POINT SCRIBER

Engrave new details, scribe seams or restore recessed lines on plastic models. Can also be used to make delicate cuts to remove molded-on detail with minimum surface damage. Top unscrews for safe needle storage.

232-6114 Ultra-Fine Scriber w/2 Needle Points **4.95**
232-6115 Replacement Needles for #6114 pkg(3) **2.50**

FLEX-PAD

Flexible sanders with new angled end. Available in handy 1/2 x 6" sizes.

INDIVIDUAL EA 2.10

232-1500 Coarse
232-2800 Medium
232-3200 Fine
232-6000 X-Fine

INTRO SET

232-525 11.50
One each of above, plus triple-grit polisher.

FLEX SET

232-550 15.50
Includes Flex-I-File with an assortment of tapes and Flex-Pads.

POLISHER

232-3210 Triple Grit **3.10**
Three-in-one polisher/finisher. Black area removes blemishes and scratches, white area smoothes and removes paint, gray buffs to restore high gloss finish.

Information STATION

A Basic Tool Set

What kinds of tools do you need for model railroading? Basic carpentry tools are great for projects such as benchwork construction, but for the small sizes of hobby parts, you'll need a few specialized tools. Your selection may vary depending on what you're building, but this list includes some of the most basic items.

There are several brands of hobby knives available with interchangeable blades. These come in a variety of sizes for cutting various types of materials such as plastic, wood and paper. You can also find carving blades for use in various soft woods.

Saws come in a variety of sizes with both fixed and interchangeable blades. These are ideal for cutting various thickness of plastics, woods and metals, as well as some other items such as rail. The most common type are "Razor Saws" which look like an old-fashioned straight razor, and can handle most cutting chores.

Tweezers come in many different kinds of blade styles and are a great way to handle small parts during assembly and installation. A needlepoint is ideal for most fine detail work. Cross-locking types, where the blades remain closed, are great for holding small parts while painting or completing subassemblies.

DREMEL®

MULTIPRO®

MULTIPRO SUPER KIT

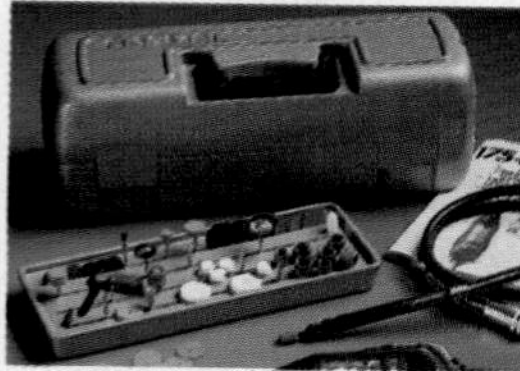

250-3956 152.70
MultiPro tool with a flex-shaft for precision, hands free operation, a new customized storage case, 72 assorted accessories and a 175+ Uses Book. Allows you to cut, grind, carve, rout, sharpen, drill, polish, sand and more.

VARIABLE SPEED MULTIPRO KIT

250-3955 131.90
Features everything necessary to grind, sharpen, drill, polish sand and more, including: variable speed MultiPro tool, storage case, 72 assorted accessories and a 175+ Uses Book.

2-SPEED MULTI-PURPOSE KIT

250-2850 97.90
Ideal for multiple applications on a variety of materials. Includes two speed MultiPro tool, quick change collet nut, storage case, wrench, 30 assorted accessories and a 175+ Uses Book.

SINGLE SPEED MULTIPRO

250-275 62.20
Ideal for sanding, carving and drilling. Features a single speed MultiPro tool, quick change collet nut, wrench, 5 assorted accessories and a 175+ Uses Book.

CORDLESS MULTIPRO

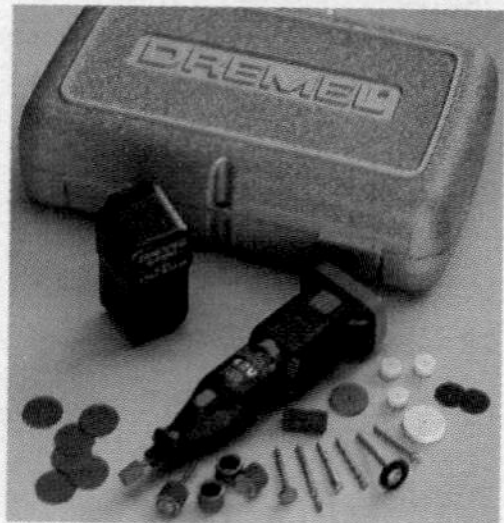

250-7700 76.80
Includes 7.2V two speed cordless MultiPro, quick change collet nut, storage case, 3 hour charger, 25 assorted accessories and a 175+ Uses Book.

MINIMITE

Cordless rotary tool with 5 accessories.

250-750 MiniMite **51.60**
250-755 MiniMite Removable Battery Pack **22.30**
250-756 MiniMite Battery Charger **11.40**

MULTIPRO ACCESSORIES

DRILL PRESS STAND

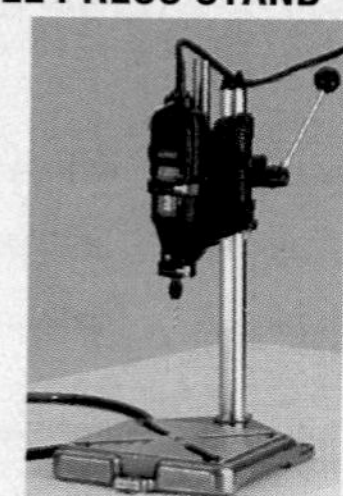

250-212 58.70
For models #275, 285 and 395. MultiPro not included.

ROUTER/SHAPER TABLE

250-231 44.30
Converts Moto-Tool into bench mounted wood shaper. Pilot bit routing and sanding. Use with #245, 250, 270, 275, 280, 285, 2750 and Freewheeler Model 850.

ROUTER ATTACHMENT

250-330 36.50
Router Attachment Featuring New Double-Handle Design

VERSATIP PLUS

1550 VERSA-TIP PLUS

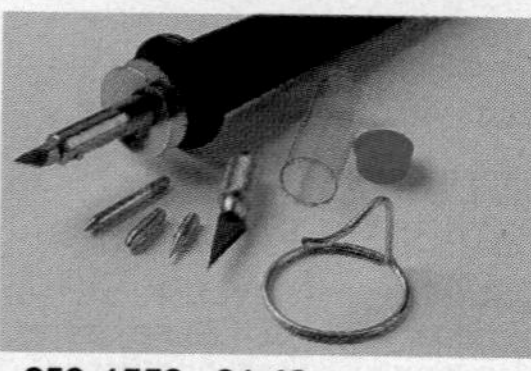

250-1550 31.40
Multi-purpose tool for woodburning, soldering, hot knife cutting, etc. Features a powerful 30 watt, high efficiency, bronze core heating element that delivers up to 1,050°F of tip temperature, double insulated, UL and CSA listed.

250-470 Soldering Tip **3.60**
250-472 Grading Tip **3.60**
250-473 Script Tip **3.60**

MULTIPRO AND FLEX-SHAFT ACCESSORIES

WRENCH

250-90962 Open End Wrench **1.40**

250-2222 Flex-Shaft Tool Stand **29.10**
Suspends Flex-Shaft Tool above workbench. Adjustable height from 12-42".

FOOT OPERATED SPEED CONTROL

250-221 68.10
Variable speed control to power HD Flex tool. Speed from 0-20,000 RPM.

MULTIPRO CHUCK

250-4486 Keyless, Knurled, 3-Jaw Chuck **12.25**
For quick bit changes. Not for use with cordless or Flex-Shaft tools.

ADAPTER SLEEVE

250-55091 3.90
For MultiPro tools 275, 285 and 395.

LAMP

250-1304 3 Diopter Magnifier Lamp **34.90**
4" diameter lens. 3 diopter lens enlarges the viewed area clearly and allows hands free to work. Constructed of metal and nylon; black enamel finish. 39" long flexible arm rotates 360°. Includes mounting bracket. (Black only).

BIT SETS

20 PIECE CUTTING/CARVING SET

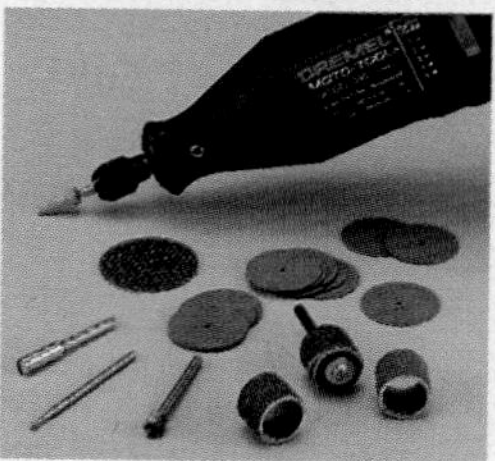

250-605 11.50

16 PIECE CLEANING/POLISHING SET
250-624 16.85

30 PIECE CUTTING/CARVING SET
250-625 16.85

44 PIECE SANDING/GRINDING SET
250-626 16.85

50 PIECE GENERAL PURPOSE SET
250-627 16.85

10 PIECE CLEANING/ POLISHING SET
250-604 11.50

34 PIECE ACCESSORY SET
250-90349 55.35

6 PIECE ENGRAVING CUTTER SET
250-300 13.15

HIGH SPEED CUTTER SETS
250-326 6 Pieces **26.45**
Includes #s 115, 125, 134, 144, 192 and 196.

REPAIR KIT

250-90800 Moto-Tool Repair Kit **8.65**
For series 2 or newer, #s 270, 280, 370 and 380. Includes 1 pair of No. 90827 brushes, 2 No. 990813 brush caps, 1 each collets 480, 481, 482 and 483.

HIGH SPEED STEEL CUTTERS W/ 1/8" STEEL SHANKS EA 5.85

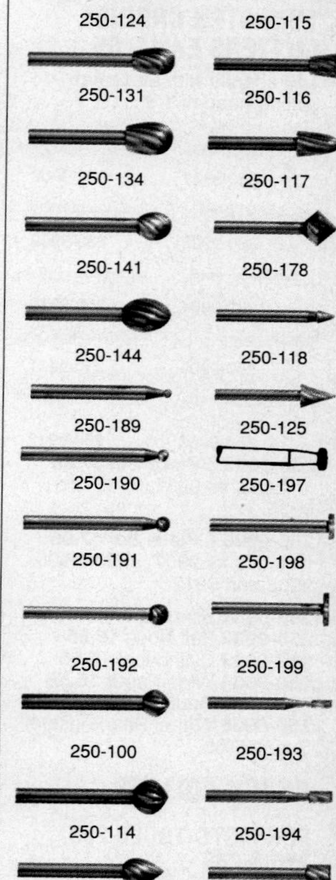

SMALL ENGRAVING CUTTERS EACH 2.95

Quality cutters for detail engraving, carving, routing in wood, fiberglass, plastic and soft metals. Not for use with hardened materials. 3/32" shanks only.

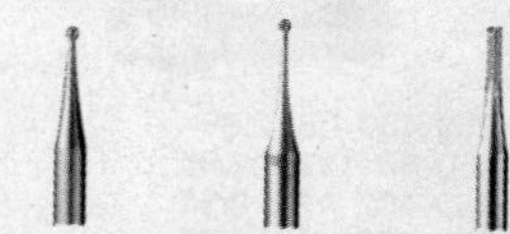

250-105 Small
250-106 Medium
250-107 Large
250-108 Small
250-109 Medium
250-110 Large
250-111 Small
250-112 Medium
250-113 Large

DREMEL®

TUNGSTEN CARBIDE CUTTERS EA 11.05

1/8" shanks with maximum cutting head of 1/8".

250-9901 250-9902

250-9903 250-9909

250-9904 250-9910

250-9905 250-9911

250-9906 250-9912

250-9923 3 Piece Set **37.85**
Includes #s 9931, 9933 and 9935.

250-9925 5 Piece Set **47.05**
Includes #s 9907, 9903, 9905, 9908 and 9912.

250-9931 Slim Taper **15.55**
250-9932 Ball Nose **15.55**
250-9933 Cylindrical **15.55**
250-9934 Wide Taper **15.55**
250-9935 Round **15.55**
250-9936 Wheel Shape (Rotor Saw) **15.55**

CHUCK COLLETS

FOR MOTO-TOOLS 260, 270 & 280

250-434 1/8" **3.00**
250-435 3/32" **7.60**
250-436 1/16" **7.60**
250-437 1/32" **7.60**

FOR MOTO-TOOLS SERIES 2 OR LATER.

250-480 1/8" **2.95**
250-481 3/32" **2.95**
250-482 1/16" **2.95**
250-483 1/32" **2.95**

MOTOR BRUSHES PKG(2) EA 4.15

250-90828 Carbon Brush
250-90826 For #260 Moto-Tool
250-90827 For #270, 280, 370, 380 & 395
250-90825 For #245, 250, 246, 275 & 2750
250-90929 For #275, 285 & 395

ALUMINUM OXIDE ABRASIVE WHEEL EA 6.45

250-500 1" Dia Medium Grit
250-501 1" Dia Fine Grit

CUT OFF WHEELS

250-409 .025" Thick, 15/16" Dia. pkg(36) **5.90**
250-420 Heavy Duty .40" Thick 15/16" Dia. pkg(20) **6.35**
250-426 Super Duty pkg(5) **8.50**
Fiberglass (1-1/4" dia.) long lasting. Larger diameter for cutting thicker materials.

250-540 1-1/4 x 1/16" **4.40**
Cut-off, groove and trim metals, woods and ceramics. Use with Mandrel 402.

GRINDING WHEEL

250-541 7/8 x 1/8" **2.95**
Use for deburring, removing rust and general purpose grinding. Use with Mandrel 402.

SPIRAL CUTTING GUIDE KIT

250-565 22.20
Make your Dremel MultiPro™ Tool even more versatile! Allows controlled cuts with maximum visibility. Easy depth adjustment. Includes: 2 drywall cutting bits and 1 spiral cutting bit.

250-560 Drywall Cutting Bit **3.30**
Gives fast, clean cuts in drywall.

250-561 Spiral Cutting Bit **4.40**
Cuts through all types of wood and wood composites.

250-562 Tile Cutting Bit **13.30**
Cuts ceramic wall tile, cement board and plaster.

SANDING DISCS PKG(36) EA 3.30

250-411 Coarse
250-412 Medium
250-413 Fine

DRUM SANDERS

1/2" DIAMETER DRUM SANDER & BANDS

250-407 Drum Sander **4.00**
250-408 Coarse Grit pkg(6) **2.95**
250-432 Fine Grit pkg(6) **2.95**

1/4" DRUM SANDER & BANDS

250-430 Drum 1/4" w/Coarse Band **4.00**
250-431 Sander Bands 1/4" Coarse pkg(6) **2.95**

3/8" DRUM SANDER & BANDS

250-439 3/8" Drum Sander **4.00**
250-440 3/8" Sander Bands-Coarse pkg(6) **2.95**

BRASS BRUSHES EA 3.90

Brass brushes are non-sparking and softer than steel, so they will not scratch softer metals. Use on gold, copper, brass and other precious metals.

250-535 Wheel Shape
250-536 Cup Shape
250-537 End Shape

STAINLESS STEEL BRUSHES EA 3.90

Stainless steel brushes do not cause "after-rust" when used on stainless steel or other corrosive-resistant materials. Use on pewter, aluminum, stainless steel and other metals.

250-530 Wheel Shape

250-531 Cup Shape

250-532 End Shape

BRUSHES EA 2.95

Not to be used over 15,000 rpm.

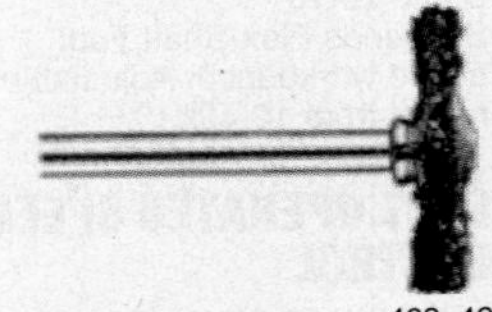

403, 428

250-403 Bristle

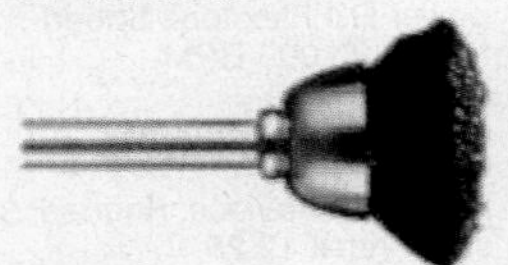

404, 442

250-404 Bristle

405, 443

250-405 Bristle
250-428 Wire
250-442 Wire
250-443 Wire

MANDRELS

250-401 Screw Mandrel **2.95**
Used with polishing accessories, 1/8" shank.

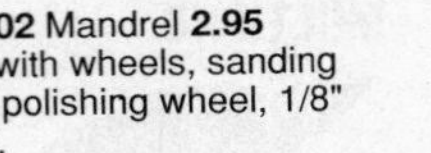

250-402 Mandrel **2.95**
Used with wheels, sanding discs, polishing wheel, 1/8" shank.

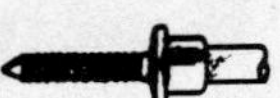

250-424 Screw Mandrel for #427 **2.95**
Used with 427 polishing wheel, 1/8" shank.

250-460 Polishing Point and Mandrel **5.20**

STEEL ROUTER BITS

250-615 Piloted Corner Rounding Bit **10.25**

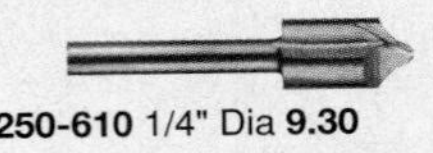

250-610 1/4" Dia **9.30**

250-632 1/4" Dia **8.65**

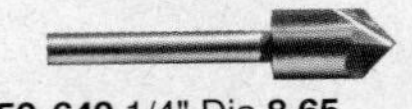

250-640 1/4" Dia **8.65**
(By Special Order Only)

250-650 1/8" Dia **8.65**

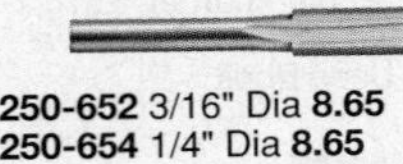

250-652 3/16" Dia **8.65**
250-654 1/4" Dia **8.65**

250-612 3/32" Dia **10.25**

250-613 3/16" Dia **10.25**

250-614 1/8" Dia **10.25**
250-602 High Speed Router Bit Set **47.90**

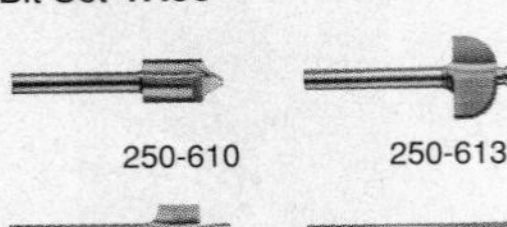

250-610 250-613

250-614 250-650

Use with router attachment #229. Includes router bits. #610, #614, #615, #650 and #654.

MOUNTED EMERY WHEEL POINTS EA 2.95

250-941 250-945 250-952

250-953 250-954 250-932

250-971 250-992 250-997

250-921 250-903 250-911

PLAIN SHAPED WHEEL POINTS EA 2.95

1/8" shanks, dimensions in inches.

250-8153 3/16 x 3/8
250-8181 5/8 x 1/8
250-8215 1 x 1/8
250-8193 5/8 x 3/8
250-8175 3/16 x 3/8

DIAMOND WHEEL POINTS EA 12.00

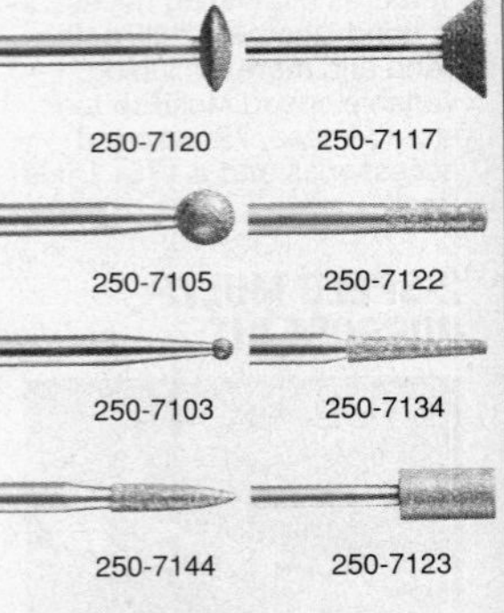

250-7120 250-7117

250-7105 250-7122

250-7103 250-7134

250-7144 250-7123

4 PIECE SET

250-9927 32.90
Includes #7103, 7122, 7134 and 7144.

DREMEL

POLISHING WHEELS EA 3.00

250-423 Cloth Polishing Wheel
1" dia use 402 mandrel.

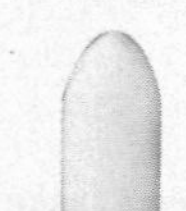

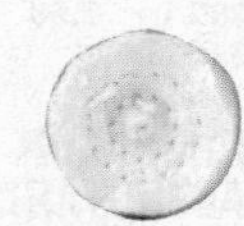

250-422 250-414

250-422 Felt Polishing Tip 3/8" diameter use 401 mandrel.

250-414 1/2" Dia Felt Polishing Wheel
Use 402 mandrel.

250-429 1" Dia Felt Polishing Wheel
Use mandrel #402, 1/2" diameter.

250-425 Emery Impregnated
Use with #402 mandrel, 7/8" diameter.

250-421 Polishing Compound

POLISHING POINTS

EMERY IMPREGNATED

Use with #424 mandrel.

250-427 2.95

POLISHING RUBBER CYLINDER

250-461 2.95

SILICON GRINDING POINTS EACH 2.95

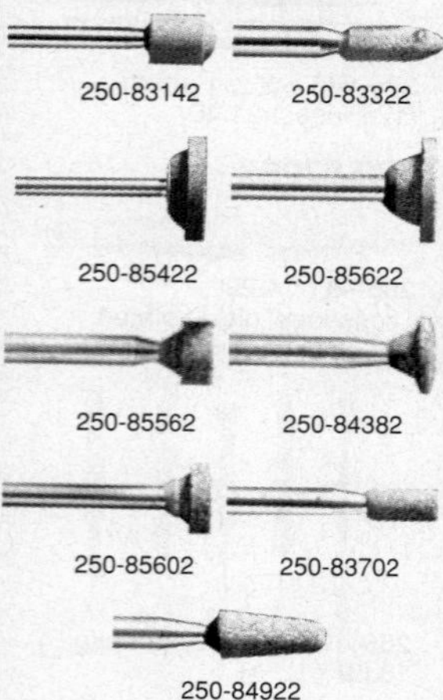

DONEGAN OPTICAL COMPANY

OPTIVISOR EA 34.95

The Optivisor is a precision-made binocular magnifier that is worn on the head leaving both hands free. Can be instantly tilted downward when needed and upward when not in use. Can be worn over regular prescription or safety glasses. Comes with dial, adjustable, conforming headband, high impact visor, genuine leather padded comfort band and optical glass lenses mounted in an interchangeable frame. Six lens powers available, plus an attachable auxiliary OptiLOUPE lens for additional magnification.

240-402 1-1/2x, 20" Focal Length
240-403 1-3/4x, 14" Focal Length
240-404 2x, 10" Focal Length
240-405 2-1/2x, 8" Focal Length
240-407 2-3/4x, 6" Focal Length
240-410 3-1/2x, 4" Focal Length
For extremely fine work.

ACCESSORIES FOR OPTIVISOR

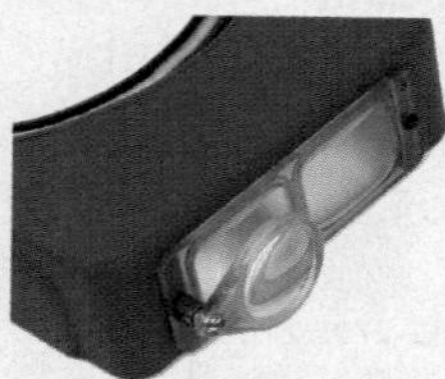

240-300 OptiLOUPE **5.95**
Adds 2-1/2x to all other lenses.

OPTIVISOR LENS PLATE EA 18.95

240-2 Lens Plate 2
240-3 Lens Plate 3
240-4 Lens Plate 4
240-5 Lens Plate 5
240-7 Lens Plate 7
240-10 Lens Plate 10

CLIP-ON BINOCULAR MAGNIFIER EA 24.95

Hands free magnification for detailed tasks. Lightweight frame can be used with frame included, or easily clipped onto most eyeglass frames. Pivots up when magnification is not needed. Relieves eye strain and increases accuracy.

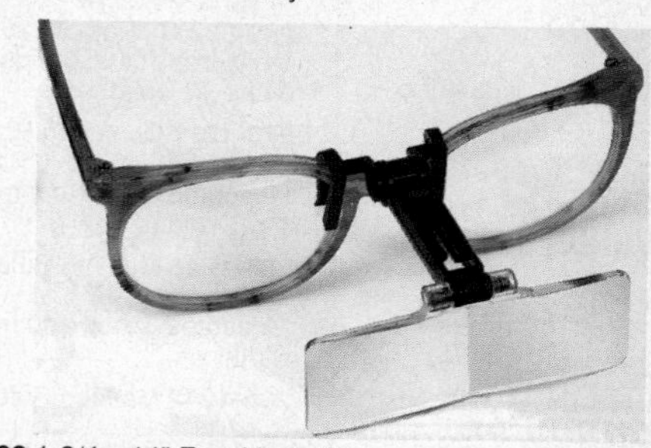

240-503 1-3/4x, 14" Focal Length
240-504 2x, 10" Focal Length
240-505 2-1/2x, 8" Focal Length
240-507 2-3/4x, 6" Focal Length

POCKET MAGNIFIERS

240-703 3x **5.95**
240-704 4x **5.95**
240-705 5x **5.95**

240-903 Single Fold 3x **5.95**
240-904 Single Fold 4x **5.95**
240-905 Single Fold 5x **5.95**

240-937 Double Fold 3/4/7x **6.95**
240-949 Double Fold 4/5/9x **6.95**

240-700416 Assortment pkg(10) **52.50**

FLEX ARM MAGNIFIERS W/OPTICAL GLASS LENS

240-1013 5" Round w/Clamp **82.50**

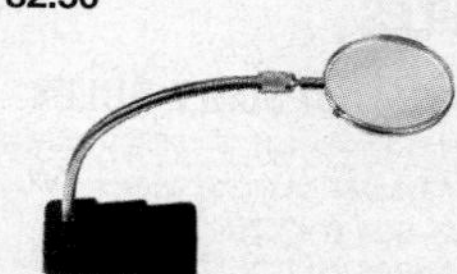

240-1014 5" Round w/Base **82.50**
240-1043 4" Round w/Clamp **70.80**
240-1044 4" Round w/Base **70.80**

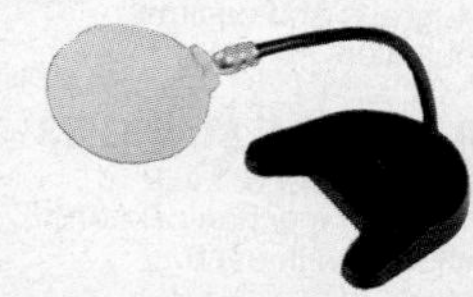

240-204 Flex-a-Mag **25.95**
Features optical grade acrylic material which has been selected for its hard surface qualities as well as its refractive index. Weighted Case.

ERNST MANUFACTURING

HOBBY TRAYS

259-158 Regular 11 x 16" **3.95**
Features a variety of compartment sizes for unlimited storage versatility. 1-1/2" deep.

259-159 Deluxe 10-1/2 x 10-1/2" **5.95**
Features 3" long compartments. 1-1/2" deep.

FALLER

IMPORTED FROM GERMANY BY WALTHERS

MODELER KNIFE

272-687 With 3 blades **11.99**

ABRASIVE FILES

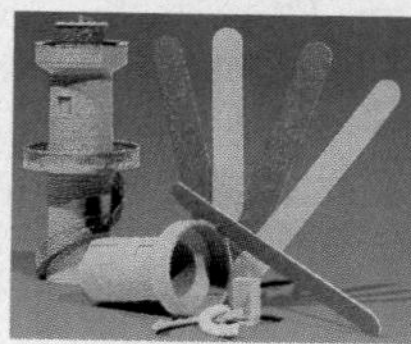

272-689 pkg(5) **6.99**

STRIPPING KNIFE

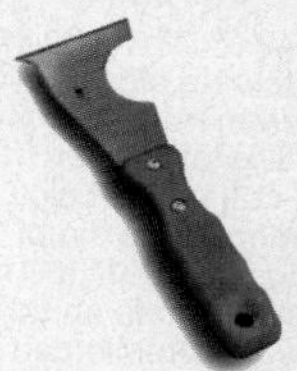

272-694 11.99
Special shape allows you to get into nooks and crannies, between rails and other locations where conventional putty knives won't work as well. Can also be used to carve rock formations and scenic features.

TROWEL

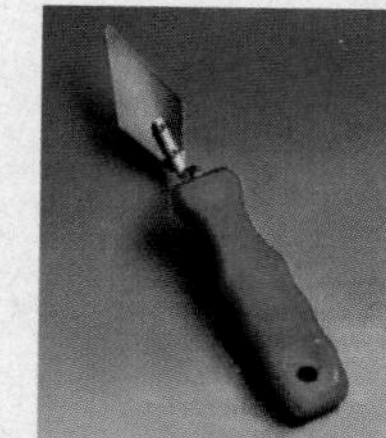

272-695 9.99
For use in close quarters along any layout or diorama. Perfect for applying and smoothing plaster, roadway fillers and more, as well as carving rock formations.

SANDING SPONGES

272-696 pkg(2) **6.99**
Use on wood, plastic, metal and more. One is covered with fine and medium grit, the other with medium and coarse. Easily washed and used over and over.

Measuring, marking and assembly tools for hobbyists, industry or specialty trades.

CALIPERS

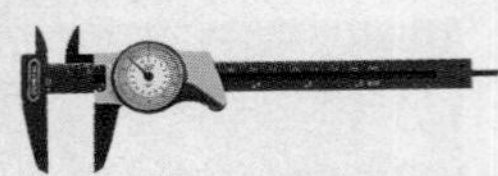

285-142 6" Dial Caliper **29.49**
Dial caliper 0 to 6" by .01 reading.

285-143 6" Digital **82.49**
Get accurate digital measurements every time with the 6" Digital Caliper! This Swiss-crafted precision instrument gives direct readings of 0.001" (0.1mm). Features include an adjustable 0, fiberglass reinforced super polyamid, friction thumb roller and 4-way measurement (outside, inside, depth and step).

285-144 Metric Version of #142 **29.00**
Capacity of 0 to 150mm by .01mm.

285-1405 Dial Caliper O Gauge **33.19**
Same as #285-1404 except O Gauge.

285-1401 HO **33.19**
Equipped with "HO" dial, one turn equals 3 "HO" feet. "HO" scale is at bottom with corresponding "O" gauge feet at top of beam for cross reference. Inside, outside, step and depth measurements. Comes with table of relationship for scale conversion into English and metric. Made of heavy duty, lightweight, fiberglass reinforced plastic.

PRECISION SCREWDRIVERS

285-704

285-701 #00 Cross **3.85**
285-702 #0 Cross **3.45**
285-703 #1 Cross **3.85**
285-704 5/64 **3.98**
285-705 3/32 **3.10**
285-706 1/8 **3.49**
285-707 9/64 **3.98**
285-708 5/32 **3.49**
285-700 5-Piece Set **15.45**
Includes Precision Screwdrivers #701, #702, #703, #705 and #706.

RULES

RAILROAD SCALE RULES

285-651 6" **3.75**
Includes HO, N, Z, O and S Scales. Stainless steel.

285-1251 12" **6.35**
12" flex model railroad rule. 1" wide with HO, S, O, N, MM, 64, grads and decimal equivalent.

ULTRA RULE STAINLESS STEEL RULES

Precision mechanical pencil included with each.

6" FLEXIBLE

285-30 Protractor **26.65** ***NEW***
Measures degrees, 1/2 degrees and 32nds. 3-7/8" width.

285-641 Marking Rule **7.65** ***NEW***
Measures 32nds and mm. 7/8" width.

285-642 Marking Rule **7.65** ***NEW***
Measures 32nds and 10ths. 7/8" width.

285-831 "T" Rule **17.65** ***NEW***
Measures 16ths, 32nds and 64ths. 2" width.

285-1250 UltraBend Ruler **24.50**
16 and 32 with end grads.

12" FLEXIBLE

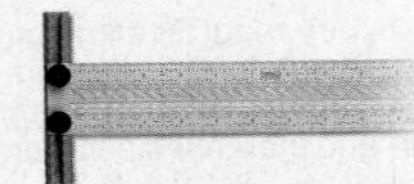

285-832 "T" Rule **27.25** ***NEW***
Measures 16ths, 32nds and 64ths. 2" width.

285-1211 Centering Rule **19.39** ***NEW***
Measures 32nds and mm. 1-5/8" width.

285-1241 Marking Rule **11.65** ***NEW***
Measures 32nds and mm. 7/8" width.

285-1242 Marking Rule **11.65** ***NEW***
Measures 32nds and 10ths. 7/8" width.

MULTI USE RULE & GAUGE

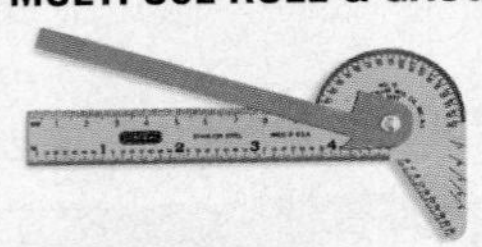

285-16 9.25
Steel 4" rule has etched graduations in 64th and millimeters, plus performs these five functions: drill point gauge checks 59° angle drill points, bevel protractor for measuring angles, center finder locates center of shafts and circles, circle divider for dividing circles into sectors and tap and drill table for National form of thread.

285-1203 12" Flexible Rule **5.65**
12" flex rule 15/32" wide with mm, .5mm, 32, 64 grads.

DRILL GAGES

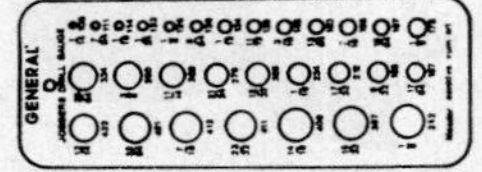

285-13 #61-80 **12.59** ***NEW***
285-15 #1-60 **11.15** ***NEW***
285-24 Hobby 1/16 to 1/2" in 64ths **4.89** ***NEW***

LEVELS

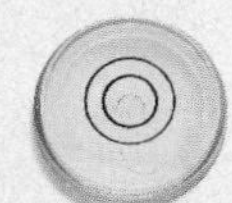

285-847 Bull's Eye **3.65**
1-3/8" diameter

285-839 9" Magnetic Torpedo **17.79**

PUNCHES

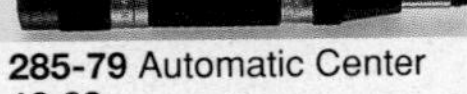

285-79 Automatic Center **19.60**
Precise means of punching center holes for drilling. Adjustable light to heavy stroke, single-handed operation. 5 x 1/2" body with replaceable point.

285-7924 Solid Point **2.95**

VISES

PIN VISES

285-90 Pin Vise **10.49**
Nickel-plated body is hollow to permit use of long rods, 3-3/4" long with 5/16" body. Two double-ended collets, capacity .0 to .125, .0 to 3.2mm.

285-93 Heavy Duty Adjustable Pin Vise **10.59**
Holds small drills, wires, files, etc. Three jaw hardened steel keyless chuck, sturdy plastic handle. 6-7/8" overall length, 1" diameter. Capacity .040 to .250, 1mm to 6.4mm.

285-92 Swivel Head Pin Vise **7.95**
Exceptional for delicate work. Single collet made of hardened tool steel. Large free-wheeling swivel head. 4" overall, 5/16" diameter body.

VACUUM VISE

285-1850 63.19
Multi-angle swivel vacuum vise holds firmly in any position. Portable, attaches instantly with quick lever action and features a universal ball joint with positive lock. "V"-grooved steel jaws (3" wide, 2-5/8" capacity) and slide-on-soft jaws for fragile work

MECHANICS STEEL SQUARE

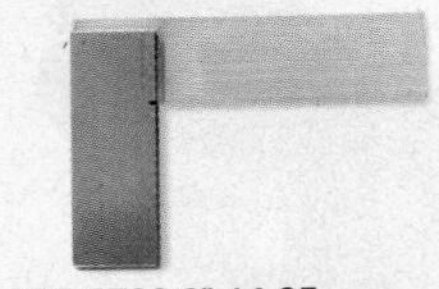

285-2702 2" **14.35**

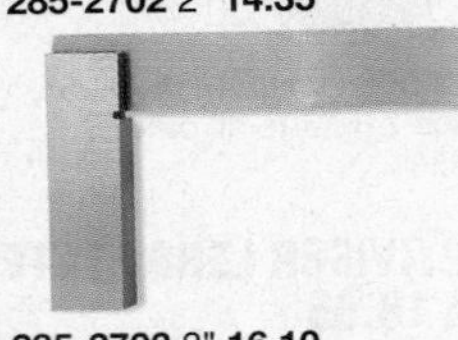

285-2703 3" **16.10**

285-2704 4" **17.29**

PICK-UP

285-388 Mini Mechanical **4.49**
Four-prong steel jaws retrieve small objects up to 1/2" (14mm). Tapered point for hard-to-reach work areas.

POCKET SCRIBER

285-81 3.98
3/8" body.

PRECISION ADJUSTABLE TRAMMEL

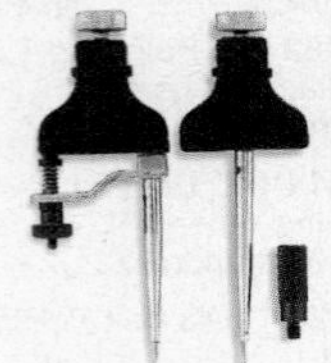

285-520 25.99
Diecast body with hardened and ground 3" needlepoint legs will draw circles and measure sizable distances with the accuracy of a divider. Points are removable and accurately set with fine adjusting screw. Clamp opening for beam is 3/8 x 3/4".

NEEDLE FILE SET

285-475 Swiss Pattern (12 Pieces) **21.40**

TWEEZERS

285-411 4.29
Cross-lock, nickel-plated, self-closing point.

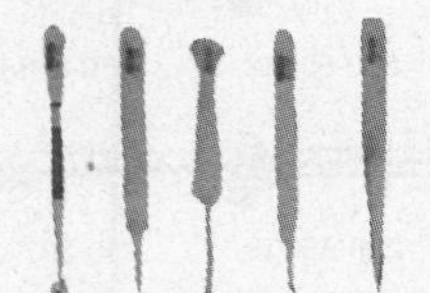

285-422 Tweezer Set pkg(5) **18.59**

POWER MAGNET

285-3704 15.55
4oz magnet with 20# pull.

DRILL BITS

CARBON PKG(2)

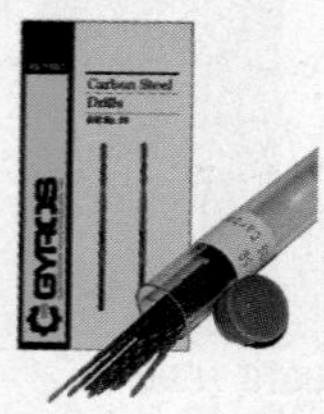

321-4510250

321-4510242 #42 2.60 *NEW*
321-4510243 #43 2.60 *NEW*
321-4510244 #44 2.60 *NEW*
321-4510245 #45 2.60 *NEW*
321-4510246 #46 2.60 *NEW*
321-4510247 #47 2.60 *NEW*
321-4510248 #48 2.60 *NEW*
321-4510249 #49 2.60 *NEW*
321-4510250 #50 2.60 *NEW*
321-4510251 #51 2.60 *NEW*
321-4510252 #52 2.60 *NEW*
321-4510253 #53 2.60 *NEW*
321-4510254 #54 2.60 *NEW*
321-4510255 #55 2.60 *NEW*
321-4510256 #56 2.60 *NEW*
321-4510257 #57 2.60 *NEW*
321-4510258 #58 2.75 *NEW*
321-4510259 #59 2.75 *NEW*
321-4510260 #60 2.75 *NEW*
321-4510261 #61 2.75 *NEW*
321-4510262 #62 2.75 *NEW*
321-4510263 #63 2.75 *NEW*
321-4510264 #64 2.75 *NEW*
321-4510265 #65 2.75 *NEW*
321-4510266 #66 2.75 *NEW*
321-4510267 #67 2.75 *NEW*
321-4510268 #68 2.75 *NEW*
321-4510269 #69 2.75 *NEW*
321-4510270 #70 2.75 *NEW*
321-4510271 #71 2.75 *NEW*
321-4510272 #72 2.75 *NEW*
321-4510273 #73 2.75 *NEW*
321-4510274 #74 2.75 *NEW*
321-4510275 #75 2.75 *NEW*
321-4510276 #76 2.75 *NEW*
321-4510277 #77 2.75 *NEW*
321-4510278 #78 2.75 *NEW*
321-4510279 #79 2.75 *NEW*
321-4510280 #80 3.85 *NEW*

HIGH-SPEED STEEL PKG(2)

321-4520242 #42 2.95 *NEW*
321-4520243 #43 2.95 *NEW*
321-4520244 #44 2.95 *NEW*
321-4520245 #45 2.95 *NEW*
321-4520246 #46 2.95 *NEW*
321-4520247 #47 2.95 *NEW*
321-4520248 #48 2.95 *NEW*
321-4520249 #49 2.95 *NEW*
321-4520250 #50 2.95 *NEW*
321-4520251 #51 2.95 *NEW*
321-4520252 #52 2.95 *NEW*
321-4520253 #53 2.95 *NEW*
321-4520254 #54 2.95 *NEW*
321-4520255 #55 2.95 *NEW*
321-4520256 #56 2.95 *NEW*
321-4520257 #57 2.95 *NEW*
321-4520258 #58 3.15 *NEW*
321-4520259 #59 3.15 *NEW*
321-4520260 #60 3.15 *NEW*
321-4520261 #61 3.15 *NEW*
321-4520262 #62 3.15 *NEW*
321-4520263 #63 3.15 *NEW*
321-4520264 #64 3.15 *NEW*
321-4520265 #65 3.15 *NEW*
321-4520266 #66 3.15 *NEW*
321-4520267 #67 3.15 *NEW*
321-4520268 #68 3.15 *NEW*
321-4520269 #69 3.15 *NEW*
321-4520270 #70 3.15 *NEW*
321-4520271 #71 3.15 *NEW*
321-4520272 #72 3.15 *NEW*
321-4520273 #73 3.15 *NEW*
321-4520274 #74 3.70 *NEW*
321-4520275 #75 3.70 *NEW*
321-4520276 #76 3.70 *NEW*
321-4520277 #77 3.70 *NEW*
321-4520277 #78 3.70 *NEW*
321-4520279 #79 3.70 *NEW*
321-4520280 #80 4.39 *NEW*

DRILL SETS

Each set includes #61-80 drill bits.

CARBON

321-4512010 Plastic Storage Dome **41.69** *NEW*
321-4512020 Metal Storage Box **37.50** *NEW*

HIGH-SPEED STEEL

321-4522010 Plastic Storage Dome **43.35** *NEW*
321-4522020 Metal Storage Box **39.19** *NEW*

TUNGSTEN STEEL TAPS

321-1700 00-90 **7.69**
321-1701 0-80 **5.79**
321-1702 1-72 **5.25**
321-1703 2-56 **4.49**
321-1704 3-48 **4.49**
321-1705 4-40 **4.25**
321-1706 5-40 **4.25**
321-1707 6-32 **4.25**
321-1708 8-32 **3.75**

TAP SETS EA 23.50

321-1712 One each: #2-56, 3-48, 4-40, 6-32 & 8-32.
321-1714 One each: #00-90, 0-80, 1-72 & 2-56.

ADJUSTABLE SPLIT DIES 13/16" DIA

321-1720 00-90 **17.69**
321-1721 0-80 **16.49**
321-1722 1-72 **16.49**
321-1723 2-56 **12.25**
321-1724 3-48 **12.25**
321-1725 4-40 **12.25**
321-1726 5-40 **12.25**
321-1727 6-32 **12.25**

321-1728 9.58

TAP WRENCH

321-1710 #0-1/4" **15.49**

TAP & DIE SET

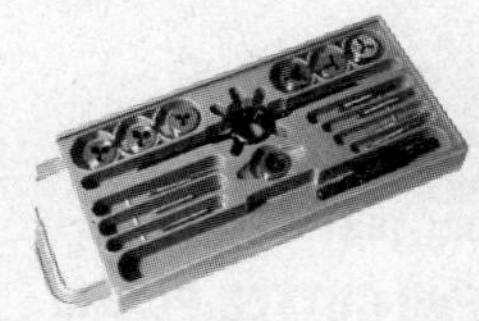

321-1716 13/16 Dia **136.69**
16-piece set includes die holder, tap wrench, seven taps and seven dies, numbers; 00-90, 0-80, 1-72, 2-56, 3-48, 4-40 and 6-32, and a 10 x 6-3/4" molded storage case.

RATCHET DRILL/VISE

321-1837 15.25
Tool can be used as pin vise or as hand drill by pushing the quick return center piece along the twisted bar. Uses drills 61-80.

SWIVEL HEAD PIN VISE

321-1818 8.15
Holds drills, taps, reamers, etc, from 0 to 1/8" diameter. Steel, 4" long.

RAZOR SAWS

Cuts wood, plastic and brass without dulling. 9-1/4" overall with hardwood handle and brass back. Cuts 3/4" deep, with 60 teeth per inch. Blade is 5-1/4" long and .008" thin.

321-8316008 Model Makers Razor Saw **21.25**
321-8416008 Replacement Blade for #8316008 **10.75**

RIP SAW BLADES

With fine teeth set for smooth, controlled, split free cutting of all soft and hard woods. Ideal for plastics. Non-binding.

321-8132018 Thin, Fine 2" x .018" w/140 Teeth **13.25**
321-8232208 Same as 321-92413 w/Mandrel **16.25**
321-8132009 Extra Thin, 2" x .009" w/140 teeth **13.89**
321-8232009 Same as 321-92414 w/Mandrel **16.89**
321-8232000 3-Piece Combo Set **25.85**
Includes #321-92413, 321-92414 and mandrel.

SAW BLADES

Circular, tempered carbon steel blades with 1/8" hole. Use with mandrel #2, #321-83983. Dimension indicates diameter.

321-8120715 Coarse, 3/4", 36 Teeth **11.35**
321-8110715 Fine, 3/4", 60 Teeth **11.35**
321-8110815 Fine, 7/8", 80 Teeth **11.79**
321-8120815 Coarse, 7/8", 40 Teeth **11.79**
321-8111015 Fine, 1", 68 Teeth **12.29**
321-8121015 Coarse, 1", 34 Teeth **12.29**
321-8111215 Fine, 1-1/4", 80 Teeth **13.59**
321-8111515 Fine, 1-1/2", 100 Teeth **15.35**
321-8112015 Fine, 2", 140 Teeth **21.00**
321-8211000 1 Each of Thick & Thin pkg(2) **17.69**
321-8130821 Coarse 7/8" **7.45**
321-8111225 1-1/4" **7.45**
321-8230821 7/8" w/Mandrel pkg(2) **15.69**
321-8211225 1-1/4", w/Mandrel **10.65**
321-8131222 Coarse, 1-1/4" **10.49**
321-8231222 Coarse, 1-1/4" w/Mandrel **13.25**
321-8220515 Saw Mounted Medium 1/2" **10.98**
321-8220715 Coarse, 3/4" w/Mandrel **14.00**
321-8210715 Fine, 3/4" w/Mandrel **14.00**
321-8210815 Fine, 7/8" w/Mandrel **14.59**
321-8220815 Coarse, 7/8" Mandrel **14.59**
321-8211015 Fine, 1" w/Mandrel **15.00**
321-8221015 Coarse, 1" w/Mandrel **15.00**
321-8211215 Fine, 1-1/4" w/Mandrel **16.35**
321-8211515 Fine, 1-1/2" w/Mandrel **18.00**
321-8212015 Fine, 2" w/Mandrel **23.98**
321-8120515 Medium, 1/2" **8.15**

CIRCULAR STEEL SAWS

For wood, plastic and soft metal. Includes two washers.

321-8110805 .005" **6.00**
321-8210805 .005" w/Mandrel **8.29**

For Daily Product Information Click
www.walthers.com

FIBER DISKS

Cuts and grinds many materials, and resists breakage.

93102 and 93104 can be used on glass, plastic, stone, ceramic, wood, aluminum, copper, brass and other low tensile strength materials. 1/16" hole use mandrel #4 (321-84025).

321-93102 1" Dia x 1/32", Hard pkg(2) **3.35**
321-93104 1-1/2" Dia x 1/32", Hard pkg(2) **3.75**

Heavy Duty—93106 and 93108 are ideal on steel, steel alloys, hard bronze and other high tensile strength materials.

321-93106 1-1/2" Dia x 1/32", Hard pkg(2) **3.75**
1/16" hole, use with Mandrel #4 (#321-84025).
321-93108 2" Dia x 1/32", Hard pkg(2) **4.85**
1/8" hole, use with Mandrel #2 (#321-83985).
321-93109 2-1/2" Hard **3.39**

LOW TENSILE

321-1132100 1 x 1/32 x 1/16" Hole **1.95** *NEW*
321-1132102 1 x 1/32 x 1/16" Hole pkg(2) **3.35** *NEW*
321-1132153 1-1/2 x 1/32 x 1/16" Hole **2.00** *NEW*
321-1132154 1-1/2 x 1/32 x 1/16" Hole pkg(2) **3.75** *NEW*

HIGH TENSILE

321-1132155 1-1/2 x 1/32 x 1/16" Hole **2.00** *NEW*
321-1132156 1-1/2 x 1/32 x 1/16" Hole pkg(2) **3.75** *NEW*
321-1132207 2 x 1/32 x 1/8" Hole **2.45** *NEW*
321-1132208 2 x 1/32 x 1/8" Hole pkg(2) **4.85** *NEW*
321-1132250 2-1/2 x 1/32 x 1/4" Hole pkg(2) **6.50** *NEW*
321-1132259 2-1/2 x 1/32 x 1/4" Hole **3.40** *NEW*

1/8" CHUCKS

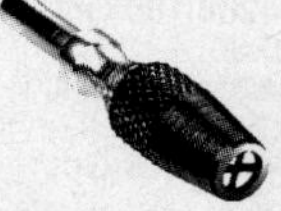

321-4501801 Mini Adaptor **6.15**
Collet capacity 0" to .390" (drill no. 61). Used in hand or electric drills for fast accurate centering of 61-80 drill bits.

321-4501819 Adaptor **14.00** *NEW*
For use with drills #42-80. The all-purpose chuck has two collets with a range of .0-.094". Features a cross-drilled hole for easily tightening larger drills.

MANDRELS

Mandrels for saws and fiber cut-off discs.

321-839851 Saw Mandrel Small Dia **2.79**

1/8" SHANK

321-83986 2.75
321-84027 #4 **3.45**
321-840252 1/4" Screw **3.45**

321-8018100 1/4" Body **2.75**
NEW **321-8018101** 3/16" Body **2.75**
NEW **321-8018102** 1/8" Body **2.75**
NEW **321-8018104** 1/8" Body Pointed Screw Top **2.75** *NEW*
321-8018105 5/16" Body **3.45**
NEW

3/32" EA 2.75

321-8033200 1/4" Body *NEW*
321-8033201 3/32" Body Pointed Screw Top *NEW*
321-8033202 3/32" Body *NEW*

FLAP WHEEL

For use on metal and wood. Polishes, sands, deburs, blends seams, removes old finish, rust and scale. 1/2 x 3/8" with 1/8" shank.

321-94207 80 Grit, Medium **8.65**
321-94208 180 Grit, Fine **8.65**
321-94209 360 Grit, Very Fine **8.65**
321-94200 80 Grit, 1-1/4" x 3/8" **8.65**
321-94201 180 Grit, 1-1/4" x 1/4" **8.25**
321-94202 180 Grit, 1-1/4" x 3/8" **8.65**
321-94203 180 Grit, 1-1/2" x 3/8" **10.30**
321-94204 360 Grit, 1-1/4" x 1/4" **8.25**
321-94205 360 Grit, 1-1/4" x 3/8" **8.65**
321-94206 360 Grit, 1-1/2" x 3/8" **10.30**

MOUNTED WIRE WHEEL

321-84285 2.75

NEEDLE FILE SETS

DELICATE

With round handles 4" files for delicate filing. #2 cut, with plastic folding wallet

321-1402 6-Piece **9.39**

321-1403 12-Piece **20.15**

ECONOMY

321-1406 5-1/2", 6-Piece **6.80**
One each #3 cut: Flat pointed, rat tail, equalizing, square, half round and triangular.

LONG

321-1407 7", 5-Piece **12.65**
One each #0 cut: Triangular, square, 1/2 round, round and flat.

METAL AND WOOD

For all metals and wood. With plastic folding wallet #2 cut unless noted.

321-1400 5-1/2", 6-Piece **12.00**
321-1401 5-1/2", 12-Piece **20.80**
321-1404 4", 4-Piece - Extra Fine **7.50**
One each: equal, round, 1/2 round, 3 square.

5-1/2" FILES EA 1.20

Dealers MUST order multiples of 12.

321-1460 1/2" Round
321-1461 Knife
321-1462 Round
321-1463 Square
321-1464 Triangle
321-1465 Equaling

321-1466 Flat

RASP SET

NEEDLE

321-1405 15.49
Coarse cut for plaster, wood plastic and stone. Includes square, equal, 1/2 round, 3 square, round and flat 5-1/2", with plastic wallet.

CURVED

321-1485 6-Piece **29.89**

HOBBY HAND BRUSHES EA 3.49

Fine wire brush cleans files, saws and drill bits. Removes rust, tarnish, dirt. 3/8", wire bristles, .005"; 8" overall. Smooth wood handle.

321-1822 Stainless
321-1824 Brass

END CUTTER PLIERS

321-1307 6.25

MINI-VISE

321-1827 8.69
Clamp-on tiny diecast steel vise fits 3/4" table top. 7/8" opening.

RIFFLER SETS

Double-ended riffler files for wood, metal, plastic and stone. 6" long. Each tool has two shaped ends.

321-1486 12-Piece Set Medium Cut **40.95**

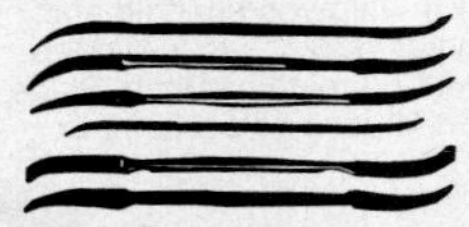

321-1488 6-Piece Set **25.75**
321-1489 Mini 3-Piece Set **16.20**
321-1490 Mini 4-Piece Set **21.50**

MINI-PICK 5 PIECE ASSORTMENT

321-1840 24.19
Stainless tiny picks, probes, scrapers, hooks. 6" long.

MINI-WATCHMAKERS PLIERS SET

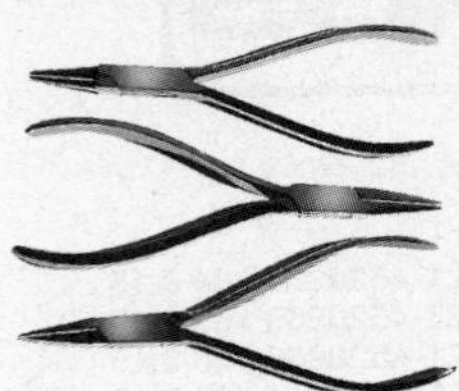

321-1333 21.35
Smooth jaw, box joint, 4-1/2" set includes flat, round and chain.

TINY TINSNIP

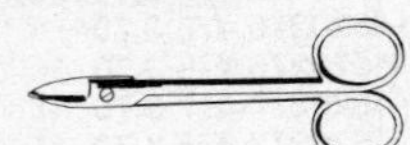

321-1830 6.50
4-1/4", one serrated jaw.

TWEEZERS EA 6.00

Swiss-style watchmakers tweezers. Nonmagnetic, stainless steel, fine point 4-5/8" long.

321-1741 Straight

321-1742 Curved

HEMOSTATS EA 7.75

Use to grip, pull or clamp. Ideal for soldering, wire work and other modeling needs. 5-1/2" long.

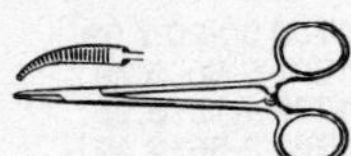

321-1820 Curved

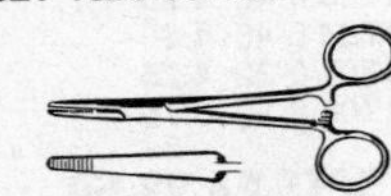

321-1821 Straight

DRILL SET

321-1285 37.00
20 high-speed drills sizes 61-80. Includes storage box with plastic dome.

INTERNATIONAL HOBBY CORP.

SCALE CONVERTER

348-5070 1.98
For O, S, HO, N and Z

KIBRI

IMPORTED FROM GERMANY BY WALTHERS

CUTTING & WORK BOARD

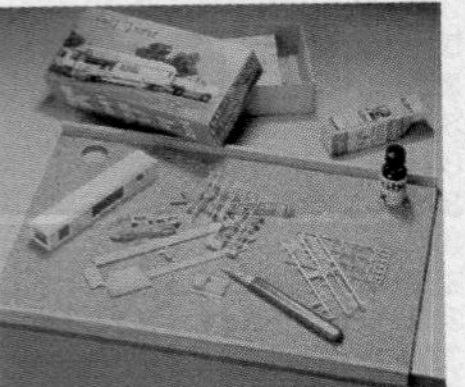

405-5092 15.99
Fiberboard surface with built-up wood edges and a 2" wood slant. Screws for permanent mounting included.
15-3/4 x 10 x 12"
40 x 26.5cm.

KADEE®

LOCO-DRIVER CLEANER

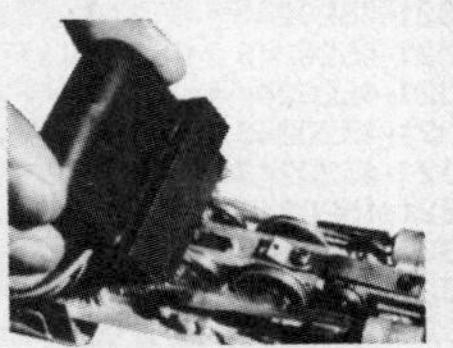

380-843 Speedi Driver Cleaner Brush **9.95**
No special wiring needed to operate. Cleans corrosion from loco drivers or wheel treads, or diesel wheels to improve electrical conductivity.

ENGINEERING

Soldering tools, various tool sets and accessory items for model builders.

SOLDERING GUN

370-1210 Electric Soldering Gun **15.95**
With tip, 110V, 100 watts.

SOLDERING IRON

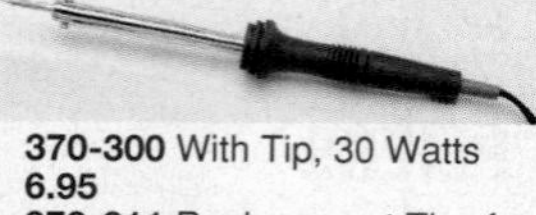

370-300 With Tip, 30 Watts **6.95**
370-311 Replacement Tips for #300 **1.95**

370-910 Heavy Duty w/Tip, 60 Watts **7.95**
370-911 Replacement Tips for #910 **2.00**

370-212 Soldering Iron Pencil **5.95**
12v, 30 watt capacity. Features 6' cord, lightweight construction, clips onto car battery for outdoor use.

WIRE BENDERS

370-322 Mighty **19.95**
Bends 1/4" music wire and square or rectangular shaped metal. You can produce your own clamps, brackets, landing gear, hangers and more.

370-323 Mini **9.95**
Bends music wire or brass wire diameters of 1/8" and smaller as well as square and rectangular shaped metal.

COIL WINDER

370-324 21.95
For winding wire up to 1/4" in diameter.

SAW

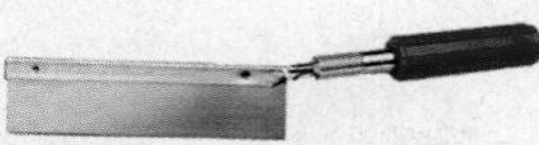

370-295 Precision Metal Saw **6.95**
Designed for cutting tubing and small metal shapes of brass and copper. 52 teeth per inch for fine cutting.

HEMOSTATS

370-805 Straight **5.95**

PLIERS EA 4.95

Vinyl grip handles with finger guards.

370-810 Long Nose
370-811 Wire Cutter
370-812 Round Nose

SANDPAPER PKG (9 SHEETS) EA 1.29

Dealer: MUST order 24 packs.

370-475 Assortment
370-476 Wet/Dry

Contains 3 each: 180 coarse grit, 240 med. grit, 280 fine grit.

TAPS EA 2.95 (UNLESS NOTED)

370-435 0-80
370-436 1-72
370-437 2-56
370-438 3-48
370-439 4-40
370-434 Tap Handle **4.95**

ADJUSTABLE THREADING DIES EA 5.95 (UNLESS NOTED)

High speed, steel, 13/16" diameter dies, with unified threads.

370-415 0-80
370-416 1-72
370-417 2-56
370-418 3-58
370-419 4-40
370-420 Die Handle **9.95**
Carbon steel, positive lock die stock handle.

NEEDLE FILE SET

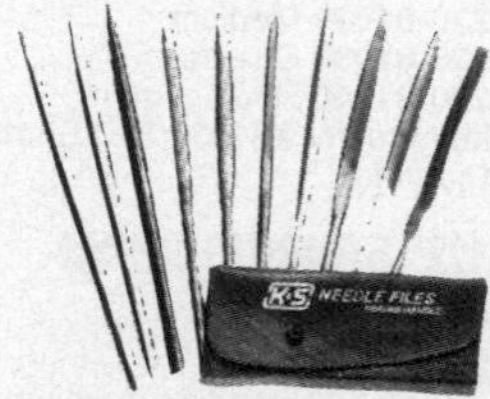

370-430 6" pkg(10) **8.95**

TUBING CUTTER

370-296 3.95

TUBING BENDER KIT

370-321 2.75
Bend tubing in the following sizes: 1/16", 3/32", 1/8", 5/32" and 3/16" OD.

FLEX-I-GRIT EA 1.65

1 sheet each: 23 micron, silicon carbon, light gray, 23 micron aluminum oxide, tan, 8 micron silicon carbide, dark gray. 0.5 micron chromium oxide, green, 1.5 micron cerium oxide, burnt orange (Micron = 1 millionth of a meter). Five 4 x 5-1/2" sheets per pack.

Dealer: MUST order dealer pack of 36 (all one number).

370-4001 "A" Regular, Assorted Grits
For general purpose hobby sanding, 1 sheet each: SIL 150 coarse grit, GAR 280 medium grit, SIL 320 fine grit, AL 400 extra-fine grit, AL 600 ultra-fine grit.

370-4002 "B" Micro-Fine, Assorted
For exceedingly high finishes.

FLEX-I-GRIT SANDING SHEETS PKG(5) EA 1.65

- Sand any surface: wood, plastic, metal, paint.
- Fit to any shape, won't crack, peel or clog
- Flex to clean

Use over and over, wet or dry. Reusable abrasive coated polyester. Silicon carbide.

Dealers: MUST Order dealer pack of 36.

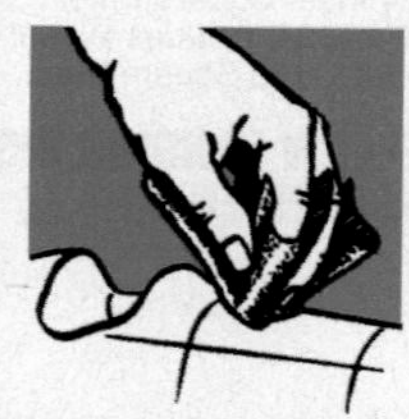

370-4011 150 Coarse
370-4031 320 Fine

PRECISION MICROMETER

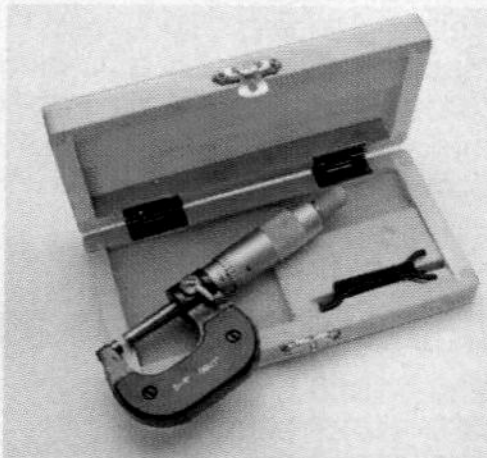

370-800 29.95
High quality design, ratchet thimble, positive locking clamp, enamel finish, accuracy to .0001. Comes complete with an adjustment tool and wooden storage case.

K-TOOL PRODUCTS

MITER BOX

Cuts any angle from 0° to 60°, in 5° increments, right or left (plus 22-1/2°, half of 45°).

- Cutting depth 1/4" with razor blade (more with saw blade).
- Cuts all woods, plastics and thin wall metal tubing.
- Handle accepts "Zona" saw or single-edged razor blades. (One of each included).
- Adjustable slide-stop for cutting many same-length pieces.
- 7-1/2 x 7-1/2" cutting surface.
- Lexan base with non-skid rubber feet.
- Designed for either right- or left hand operation.

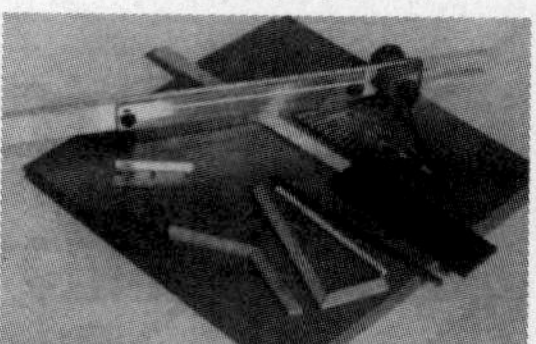

211-2 29.95
211-21 Extra Handle for #2 **8.50**

GRADE GAUGE

211-150 13.95
A must for anyone building or modifying a model railroad layout to quickly and accurately determine any track grade. Easy to use: attach to any standard 24" or 48" carpenter's level. Set gauge to desired incline percent. Lay on roadbed. Raise roadbed until bubble balances. Secure roadbed using standard construction practices.

Information STATION

Soldering

The word "soldering" is mentioned and the room goes quiet, no one speaks. There seems to be a mystery about this integral part of model railroading, a Taboo of sorts that most model railroaders tend to stay away from unless absolutely unavoidable.

It is, however, not as mysterious or difficult as one might think. With the correct tools: soldering gun or pencil, rosin core solder, tin/lead solder and flux, one can achieve wonders.

The correct sized iron is important. The smaller ones generally run about 25 or 40 watts, which for the most part is sufficient for the majority of model railroading jobs. The higher the wattage, the more heat is produced through the iron. Having the correct amount of heat is vital to a good soldering job. Too little or too much will lead to problems.

Be sure to tin the solder iron to prevent oxidation, which in turn would restrict the transfer of heat from the iron to the piece being worked on. This is done by cleaning the tip of the iron until it is shiny with fine sandpaper or a file. Then heat the iron and touch solder to it until it is covered. Finally, with a cotton cloth wipe the tip clean. You are now ready to begin.

MASCOT PRECISION TOOLS

Mascot tools are quality engineered to give top performance and satisfaction.

MOTORIZED HANDPIECE ACCESSORIES

SANDER SET

230-980 39.00
Rotary Tool Accessory Kit (18 pieces) 1/8" and 1/32" shanks. Fits all electric portable rotary tools.

ADAPTER CHUCK

230-982 7.75
The 3/32" shaft fits all portable electric rotary tools. Holds miniature drills from #80 (.014") to #43 (.089").

MOUNTED METAL BRUSHES WITH 3/32" SHANKS EA 2.99

230-81000 Crimped Steel Cup Brush 9/16"

230-81001 Crimped Brass Cup Brush 9/16"

230-81002 Straight Steel End Brush 3/16"

230-81003 Crimped Steel End Brush 1/4"
230-81004 Crimped Brass End Brush 3/16"

MOUNTED NATURAL HAIR BRUSHES WITH 3/32" SHANKS EA 2.50

230-81006 Wheel Brush Stiff 3/4"

230-81007 Wheel Brush Medium 3/4"

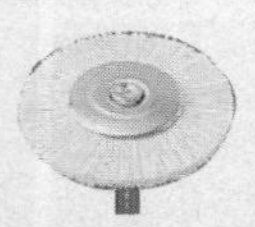

230-81008 Wheel Brush Soft 3/4"

230-81009 End Brush Soft 1/4"

230-81010 End Brush Stiff 1/4"

230-81011 Cup Brush Soft 1/2"

230-81012 Cup Brush Stiff 5/8"

BUR & WHEEL STAND

230-81049 For 3/32" Shank Burs **5.99**
Holds all your shaft tools upright and ready for quick access.

MINIATURE HIGH SPEED STEEL BURS EA 2.99

Made of the finest quality high speed steel and finished to exacting standards, these Swiss burs have a head diameter of 2.7mm (less than 7/64") and are perfect for precise detail work. Shank size 3/32".

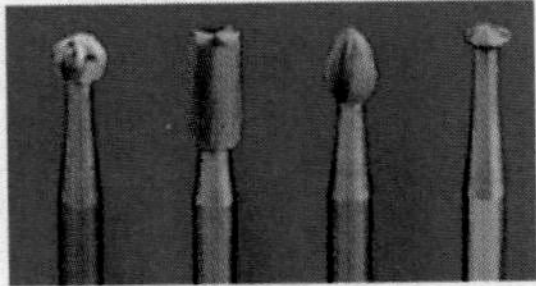

81013 81019 81016 81020

81018 81014 81017 81015

230-81013 Ball
230-81014 Wheel
230-81015 Cone
230-81016 Bud
230-81017 Cone Square Plain
230-81018 Cup
230-81019 Cylinder Square Plain
230-81020 Hart

SWISS HIGH SPEED STEEL BUR SET EA 7.99

230-81022 Includes Ball, Cone & Cone Square Plain
230-81023 Includes Ball, Bud & Cylinder Square Plain
230-81024 Includes Wheel, Hart & Cone Square Plain

YELLOW SANDING DISK ASSORTMENT

230-81025 Assorted w/Mandrel (3/32" Shank) pkg(30) **7.99**
Yellow Sanding Disks are made of high quality aluminum oxide bonded to flexible paper, making hard-to-reach places accessible.

YELLOW SANDING DISKS PKG(50) EA 4.99

230-81026 Fine
230-81027 Medium
230-81028 Coarse

SANDING DISK MANDREL

230-81029 Press On/Flip Off Mandrel With 3/32" Shank **4.99**

CUT OFF DISKS

230-81030 7/8" pkg(50) **9.99**
These high speed resin-bonded aluminum oxide disks offer fast, cool and smooth cutting on all metal.

1/4" SANDING DRUM ASSORTMENT

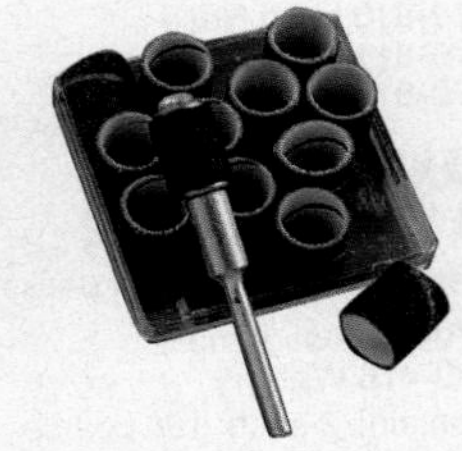

230-81031 5.99
Includes 4 each fine, medium, coarse with 1/8" mandrel.

1/4" SANDING DRUMS PKG(12) EA 3.99

230-81032 Fine
230-81033 Medium
230-81034 Coarse
230-81035 Replacement Mandrel for #81031 1/8" Shaft Diameter

3/8" SANDING DRUM ASSORTMENT

230-81036 5.99
Includes 4 each fine, medium, coarse with 1/8" mandrel.

3/8" SANDING DRUMS PKG(12) EA 3.99

230-81037 Fine
230-81039 Medium
230-81039 Coarse
230-81040 Replacement Mandrel for #81036 3/8" Shaft Diameter

1/2" SANDING DRUM ASSORTMENT

230-81041 6.50
Includes 4 each fine, medium, coarse with 1/8" mandrel.

1/2" SANDING DRUMS PKG(12) EA 3.99

230-81042 Fine
230-81043 Medium
230-81044 Coarse
230-81045 Replacement Mandrel for #81041 1/2" Shaft Diameter

HEATLESS WHEEL KIT

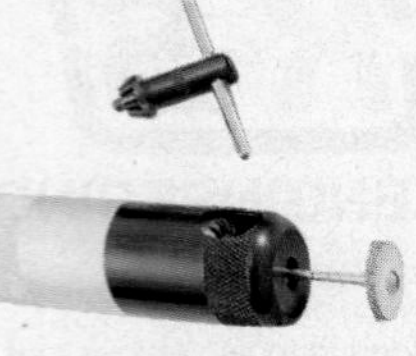

230-81046 6 Assorted w/Mandrel **6.99**
These outstanding hard, square-edged wheels are used for deburring and finishing. The real benefit to the hobbyist is the loose, coarse construction which makes the grinding process cool and suitable for plastic finishing.

HEATLESS WHEELS PKG(10) EA 7.99

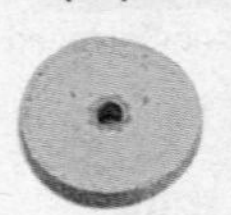
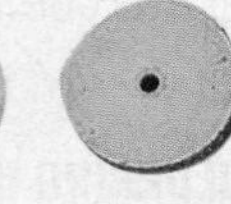

230-81047 230-81048

230-81047 1/2 x 3/32"
230-81048 5/8 x 3/32"

PLIERS

JOINT PLIERS EA 11.99

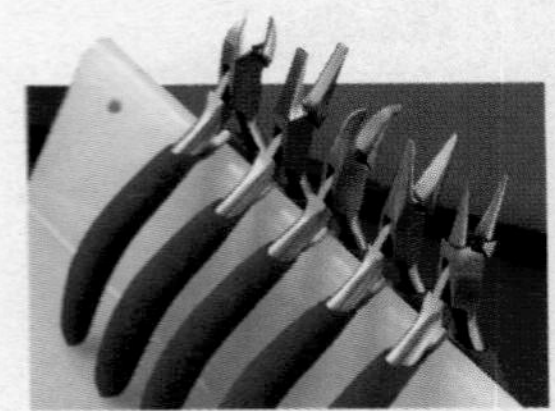

230-480 Flat Nose
230-481 Chain Nose
230-483 Diagonal Cutters
230-485 Bent Nose
230-488 Round Nose

LONG RANGER PLIERS EA 10.99

These unique pliers have an entire long body that gets the user closer to the work than regular pliers. The hinged joint of the plier jaws is closer to the working end of the tool, giving the maximum possible holding power. Each has matte finish with closed cell handle covers and leaf spring return.

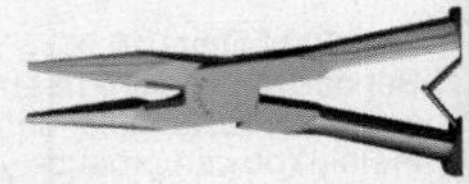

230-495 Lineman's w/Cutter
230-496 Diagonal Cutters

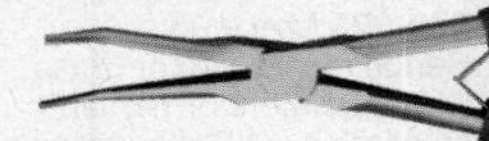

230-497 Bent Nose
230-498 Serrated Jawed Needle Nose

MASCOT PRECISION TOOLS

SPRUE & FINE WIRE CUTTING PLIERS

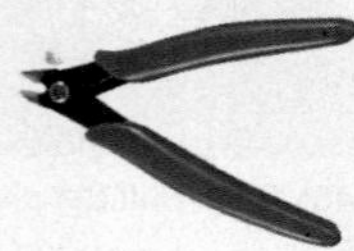

230-450 10.75
Features hardened, slim-line, razor sharp jaws, cushion grips and is perfect for cutting sprue cleanly. Can also cut wire up to .40" 1mm.

MINIATURE ELECTRONIC PLIERS EA 7.99

Features double leaf spring return for extra smooth and quiet, nonbinding opening and closure.

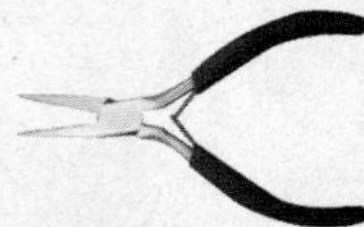

230-380 Flat Nose
230-383 Diagonal
230-384 End Nippers

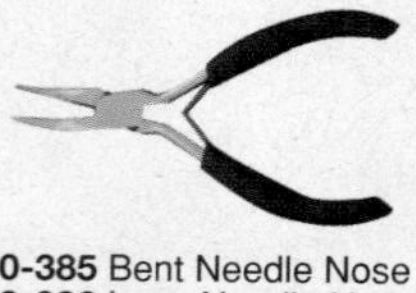

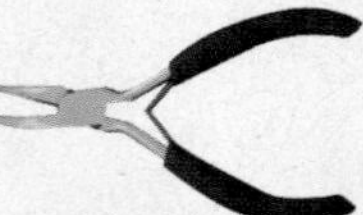

230-385 Bent Needle Nose
230-386 Long Needle Nose
230-387 Needle Nose

PREMIER PLIERS

230-400 Flat Nose **22.99**
230-402 Needle Nose **24.99**
230-403 Wire Cut **29.99**

MINIATURE PLIERS EA 4.99

Each pliers offers a brushed satin finish, spring action return with a solid feel.

230-370 Flat Nose
230-371 Needle Nose

230-373 Diagonal

230-374 End Nippers

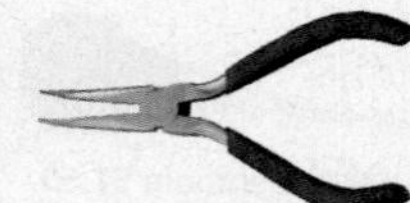

230-375 Bent Needle Nose
230-376 Long Nose

TWEEZERS

230-531 Decal Tweezers 4-1/2" **6.99**
Nickel plated steel tweezers with thin, smooth spade points, angled to allow perfect placement of decals.

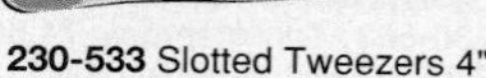

230-532 Utility Solder Tweezer 4" **5.50**

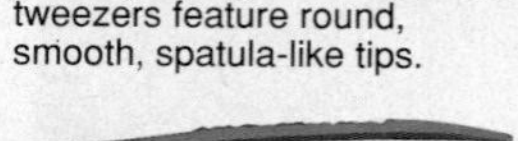

230-533 Slotted Tweezers 4" **6.99**

230-534 Soft Tipped Decal Tweezer 5" **3.99**
Ultra-lightweight flexible plastic tweezers feature round, smooth, spatula-like tips.

230-515 Glass Filled Tweezer Non-Conductive/ Anti-Magnetic **1.99**

230-530 Magnifying Tweezers **7.99**

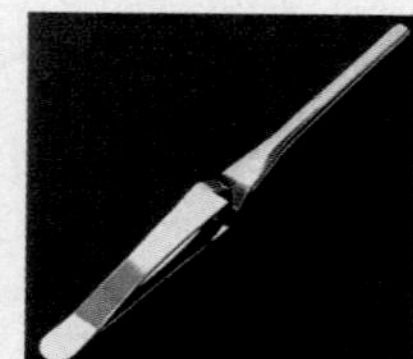

230-500 Cross-Locking 6-3/8" **4.99**
Tips serrated for sure grip. 1-12 lb tension. Fits #200.

230-501 Fine-Pointed 4-1/4" **12.75**
Sharp tips and light tension for fine work. Nickel-plated steel. Magnetic.

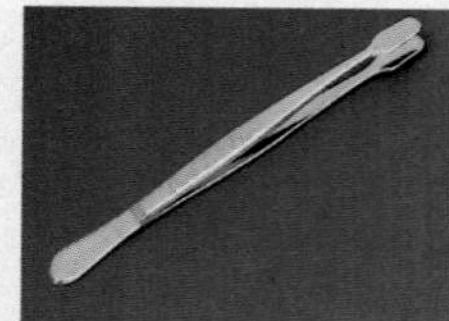

230-503 Stamp 4-1/2" **3.50**
Smooth, wafer thin points. Nickel-plated steel.

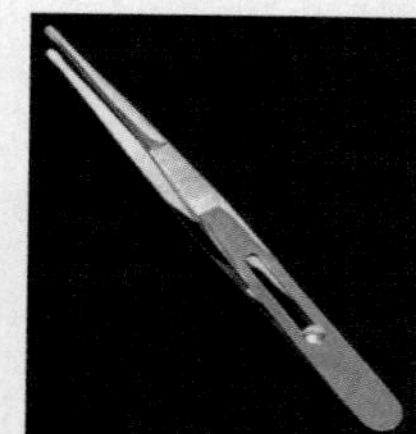

230-504 Slide Lock 5-7/8" **7.75**
Thin serrated tips for firm grip, thin flat back permits holding tweezer vise. Chrome plated.

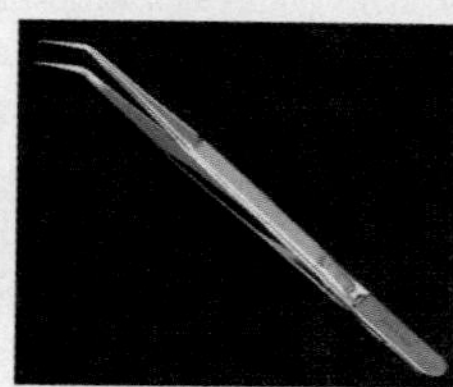

230-505 Curved 6" **6.25**
Nickel-plated steel with slender tips, serrated for positive grip.

230-506 Sharp Pointed 4-3/4" **5.50**

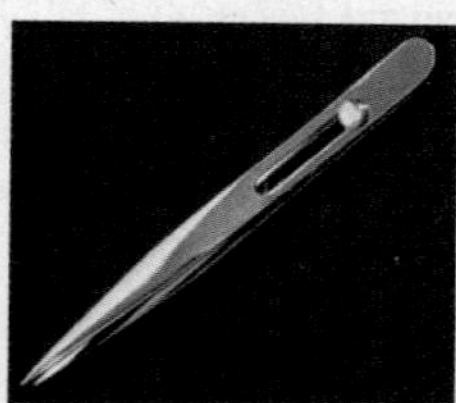

230-507 Slide Lock 4-3/4" **5.50**

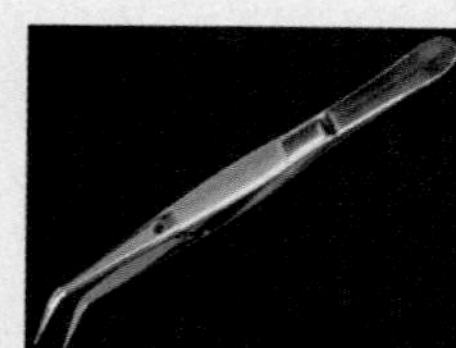

230-508 Curved 4-1/2" **5.50**
230-509 Cross Lock 4-1/2" **5.50**

230-510 Curved 6-7/8" **5.50**
230-511 Straight 7" **4.99**

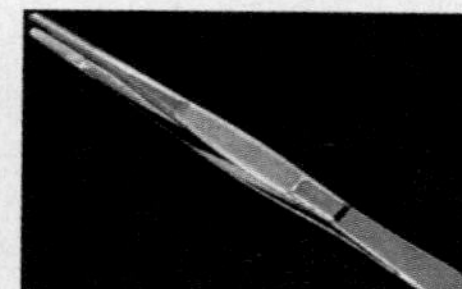

230-512 Round Point 6" **4.99**

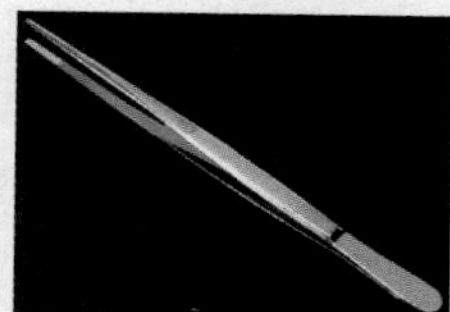

230-520 Retrieving 8" **7.95**

ALL PURPOSE TWEEZER SET

230-521 21.00
4-3/4" stamp, 4-1/2" sharp pointed, 6" retrieving, 6" curved, 6-1/2" curved and 6-1/2" self-closing.

KNIVES

SCALPEL W/BLADES

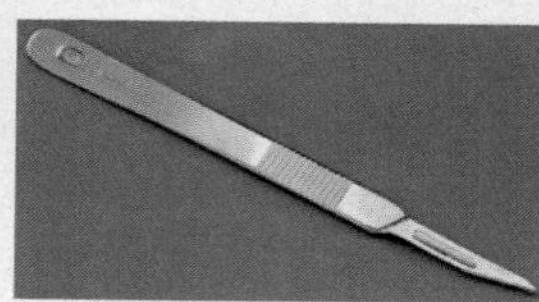

230-30 4.99
True medical-surgical instrument with slim line stainless steel scalpel handle. Includes 2 German engineered scalpel blades.

230-3011 Replacement Blades pkg(5) **3.25**

UTILITY KNIVES

MINI UTILITY KNIFE

230-110 3.79

#1 LIGHTWEIGHT W/BLADE

230-1 2.40
230-111 With 3 Blades **4.80**

#2 MED WEIGHT W/BLADES

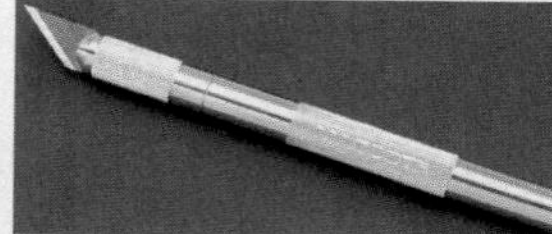

230-2 3.60

#5 HEAVY DUTY W/BLADE

230-5 4.15

KNIFE SETS

PRECISION KNIFE SET

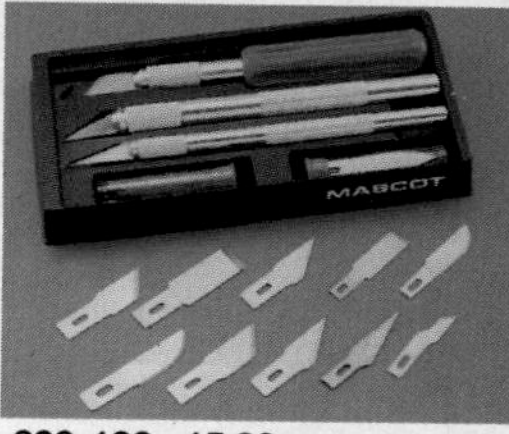

230-182 15.00
Includes a lightweight, medium weight and heavy duty knife plus a plastic storage tray.

DELUXE KNIFE SET

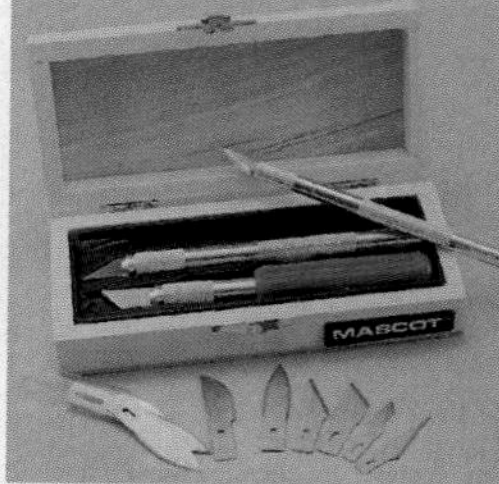

230-865 18.75
Same knives as #182 plus 10 assorted blades and wooden storage box.

DELUXE HOBBY-CRAFT MODELERS KNIFE & TOOL SET

230-866 39.90
Contains 1 each lightweight, medium weight, heavy-duty knife, hobby awl, mitre box, razor saw, sander, screwdriver and 20 assorted blades.

KNIFE BLADES W/SAFE VIAL

BLADES FOR #230-1 KNIFE HANDLE

230-11 #11 pkg(5) **1.99**

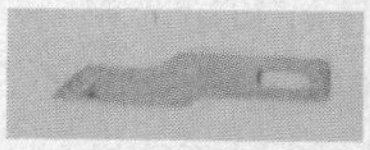

230-16 #16 pkg(5) **1.85**

MASCOT PRECISION TOOLS

BLADES FOR #230-2, 230-5, 230-9 KNIFE HANDLES

230-19 #19 pkg(5) **2.29**

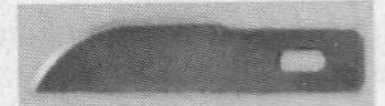

230-22 #22 pkg(5) **3.29**

230-23 #23 pkg(5) **5.29**

230-24 #24 pkg(5) **2.19**

BLADES FOR #230-110 KNIFE HANDLES

230-1101 Mini Knife Blades pkg(5) **2.60**

SAWS

RAZOR SAW BLADE

230-102 1-1/4" **4.10**
Fits #2 and #5 handles.

POCKET HACKSAW

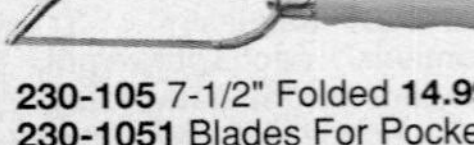

230-105 7-1/2" Folded **14.99**
230-1051 Blades For Pocket Hacksaw pkg(3) **2.70**

HOBBY SAW W/BLADES

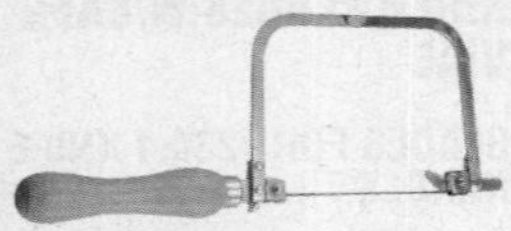

230-99 9.99
Holds blades securely. Offers rigidity for accurate cut. Includes 12 Swiss-made jeweler's saw blades.

JEWELER'S SAWS

Includes 12 blades.
230-100 2" Throat **19.99**

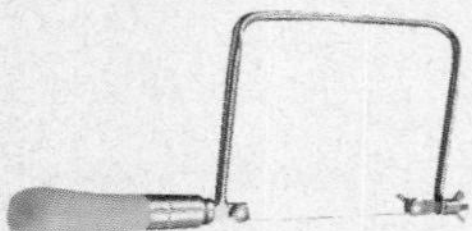

230-103 4" Throat **22.99**

JEWELER'S SAW BLADES

230-1001 pkg(24) **6.50**
12 coarse #8, 12 medium #4.
230-1004 pkg(24) **5.50**
12 fine #1, 12 extra fine #2/0.
230-1005 pkg(24) **5.70**
12 super fine #4/0, 12 ultra fine #8/0.

JEWELER'S SAW BLADES, BULK PACKS PKG(144) EA 25.92

230-120 Blade #3
230-121 Blade #2
230-122 Blade #1
230-123 Blade #0
230-124 Blade #2/0
230-125 Blade #4/0

BLADES #4 FLAT

230-492041 4.00

SPIRAL SAW BLADES

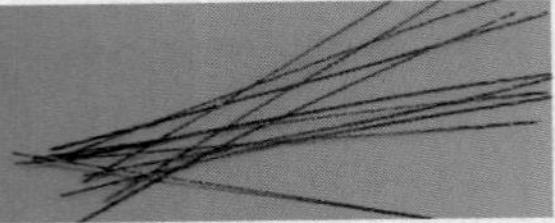

230-1003 pkg(24) **7.00**
Contains 12 medium and 12 coarse blades, fitting all jeweler's saw frames.

MITRE BOXES

MINI MITRE BOX

230-208 3.99
A must for on-the-go club members.

PORTABLE BENCH DOUBLE MITRE BOX

230-209 4.99

ALUMINUM MITRE BOX

230-206 7.99
Just 5-1/2 x 2". Uses 1-1/4" blade, has two 45° slots and one 90° slot.

FILES

UTILITY FILE SET

230-780 6pcs **16.95**

SWISS SINGLE CUT SET

230-777 3pcs **11.00**
Includes 3 shapes, three-square, round and half-round. 5-1/2" long.

SWISS SINGLE CUT SET

230-778 6pcs **21.50**
Includes round, half-round, square, flat, three-square and equaling. 5-1/2" long.

INDIVIDUAL FILES EA 3.90

230-770 Flat
230-771 Half round
230-772 Round
230-773 Square
230-774 Equaling
230-775 Three-Square

REAMERS

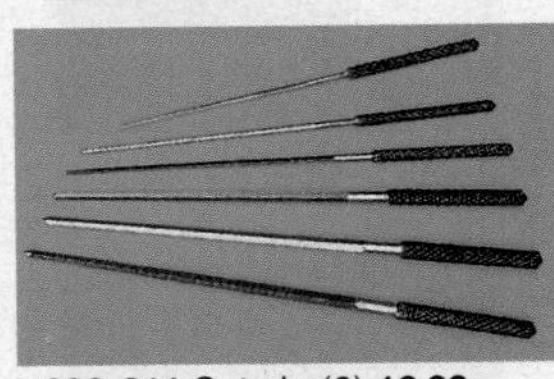

230-311 Set pkg(6) **16.99**

DOUBLE END SCRIBER

230-300 7" **9.99**

WOODWORKING TOOLS

WOODWORKING TOOL SET-STANDARD

Each set has five basic shapes and you have a choice of palm-grip mushroom-shape handles (862) or the conventional straight handle styling (861). Both sets include one each of the following: a bent square chisel (5/16"), straight skew chisel (5/16"), straight small gouge (5/32"), bent large gouge (5/16") and a "V" parting tool (5/32").

230-861 Mushroom **57.50**
230-862 Straight **65.95**

WOODWORKING TOOL SET-MINIATURE

Both sets include one each of the following: a bent square chisel (7/32"), straight skew chisel (1/4"), straight small gouge (3/32"), bent large gouge (7/32") and a "V" parting tool (3/32").

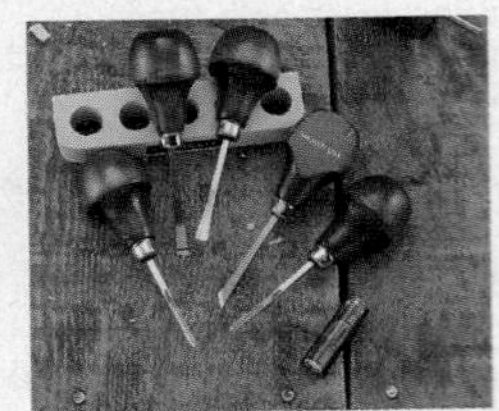

230-863 Mini Mushroom **71.50**
230-864 Mini Straight **64.95**

WOODCARVING KNIFE SET

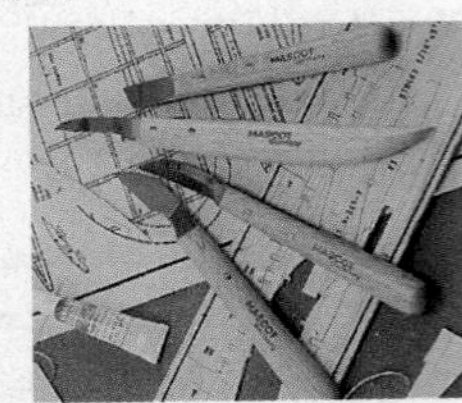

230-860 4 Pieces **61.00**
Finely balanced knives with alloy blades and wooden handles. Designed for carving, incising, shaving, splicing and notching.

WOOD RASP SET

230-779 29.99
Equaling, flat, half-round, round and three-square. Overall 5-1/2" in length.

BURNISHERS EA 7.99

230-295 Straight Blade

230-296 Curved Blade

SCRAPER

230-297 9.99

JEWELER'S TOOLS

MODEL MAKING

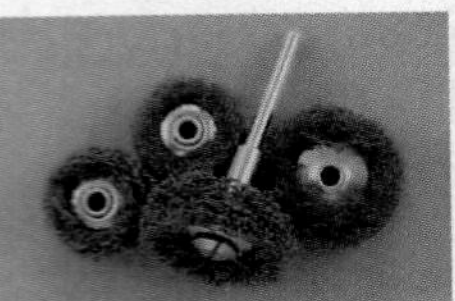

230-461 Satin Buff Set pkg(5) **11.99**

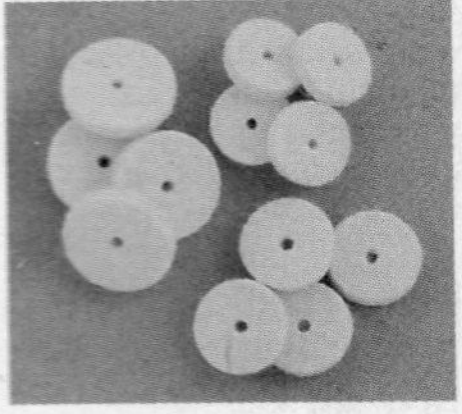

230-462 Felt Wheel Set pkg(12) **6.99**

230-463 Chamois Buff Set pkg(6) **9.99**

230-464 Muslin Buff Set pkg(4) **6.99**

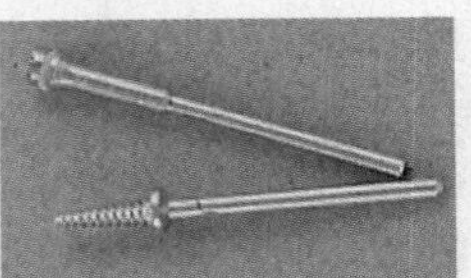

230-465 Mandrel Set - 3/32" **3.99**

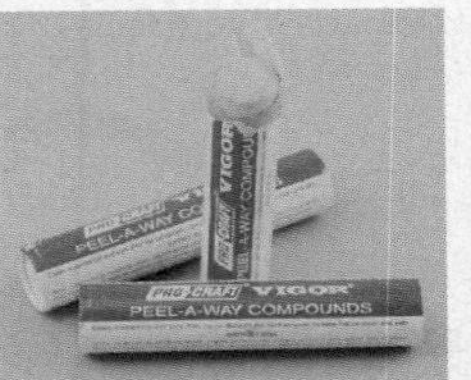

230-469 Rouge Set (red, tripoli & yellow) **12.99**
230-470 Jeweler's Wax Set **15.99**
230-475 Wax Carver/Spatula Set pkg(3) **9.99**

MASCOT
PRECISION TOOLS

DRILLS

230-840 Mini Hand Drill **9.25**

230-841 Spiral Drill **16.99**

PRECISION DRILL SET

230-177 28.75
#61-80 set (20pc) carbon drills with plastic case.

CARBON TWIST DRILLS

Carbon twist drills are only available in packages of 12.

PKG(12)
EA 9.00
230-50 #50
230-51 #51
230-52 #52
230-53 #53
230-54 #54
230-55 #55
230-56 #56
230-57 #57
230-58 #58
230-59 #59
230-60 #60

PKG(12)
EA 12.00
230-68 #68
230-69 #69
230-70 #70
230-71 #71
230-72 #72
230-73 #73
230-74 #74
230-75 #75
230-76 #76
230-77 #77
230-78 #78

PKG(12)
EA 10.98
230-61 #61
230-62 #62
230-63 #63
230-64 #64
230-65 #65
230-66 #66
230-67 #67

PKG(12)
EA 12.75
230-79 #79
230-80 #80

HIGH SPEED STEEL TWIST DRILLS

Only available in packages of 12.

230-643 #43 **9.95**
230-648 #48 **9.95**
230-650 #50 **9.95**
230-656 #56 **10.55**
230-660 #60 **11.24**
230-665 #65 **11.50**
230-667 #67 **11.50**
230-668 #68 **11.50**
230-670 #70 **12.08**
230-672 #72 **13.30**
230-674 #74 **13.67**
230-675 #75 **13.67**
230-676 #76 **13.67**
230-678 #78 **14.31**
230-680 #80 **16.80**

CARBON TWIST DRILL ASSORTMENTS

230-86 6 Carbon Twist Drills **5.99**
Assortment of the top six drill sizes preferred by hobbyists and craftsmen, 50, 56, 60, 65, 70 and 76.

12 CARBON TWISTS DRILLS

230-178 10.50
Includes one dozen assorted drills from #50 to 80.

PIN VISES

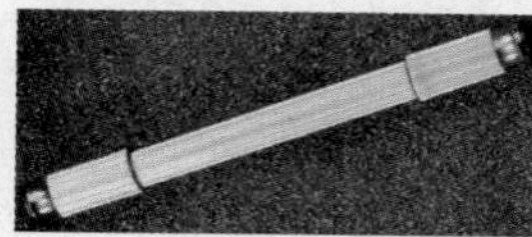

230-810 Double End **6.99**

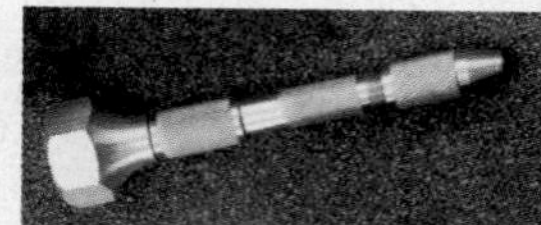

230-811 Swivel Head **7.39**
230-815 Slide Lock **8.29**

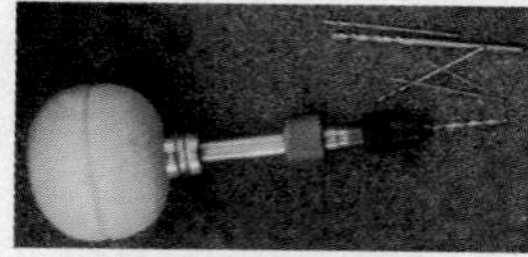

230-812 Wood Head Pin Vise Drill Set **18.75**
230-822 Pin Vise & Drill Set **12.90**

CLAMPS

MINI CLAMPS PKG(2)

Made of rigid, high impact, nylon filled plastic, these clamps are lightweight and virtually indestructible.

230-213 1" **4.99**
230-214 2" **5.99**

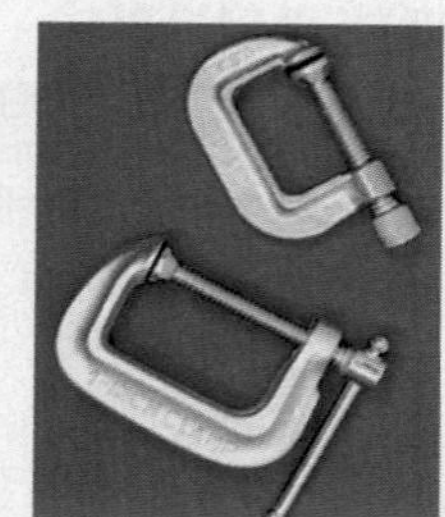

230-210 8.25
Includes 1" and 3/4".

C-CLAMP

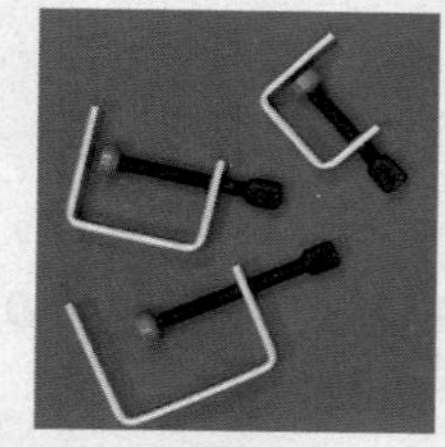

230-212 pkg(3) **6.50**

NON-MAR WEDGE CLAMP

230-202 11.99
Leather-lined jaws grip securely without marring. Resin body.

FILE BLOCK AND CLAMP

230-150 7.50

THE THIRD HAND

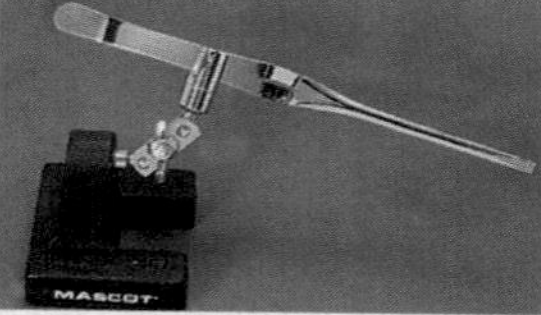

230-200 13.95
Tweezer mounted work positioner.

TWIN GRIP POSITIONER

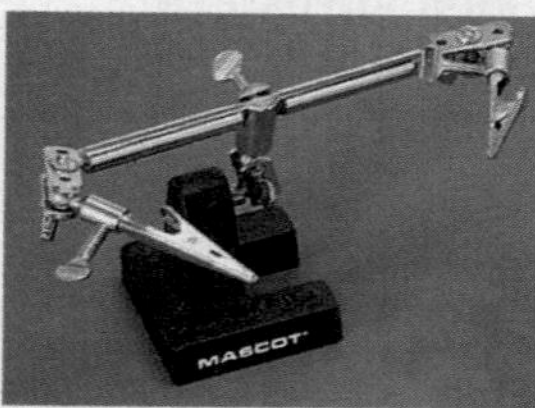

230-201 18.99

TWIN GRIP W/MAGNIFIER

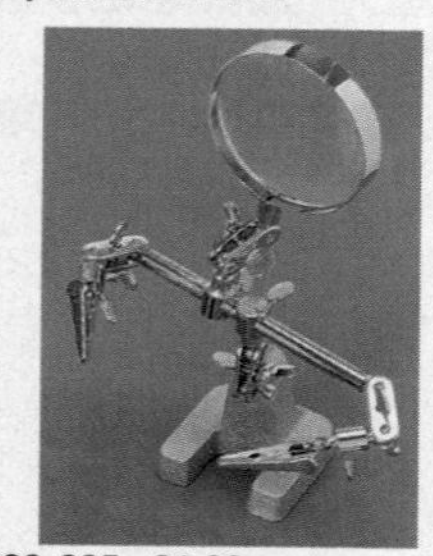

230-205 21.00

WOOD HANDLE HANDVISE

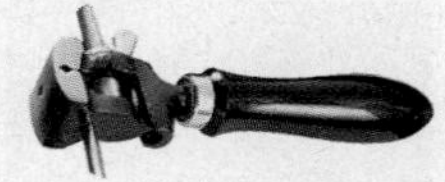

230-199 11.99

MAGNIFIERS

230-904 Dual Focus Magnifier **4.99**

230-899 Spectacle Loupe (2x) **4.99**
Loupe fits securely to right or left lens. Flips out of way for convenience. Scratch proof plastic coated clip. Lightweight.

230-903 With Case (4x & 5x) **12.99**

230-909 Bench Magnifier (3x) **22.99**

230-900 Eyepiece (2.5x) **7.50**

230-901 Pocket (10x) **10.99**

230-999 Lighted Head Band Magnifier **39.99**
230-910 Binocular (3x) **18.50**

Daily New Product Announcements! Visit Walthers Web site at

www.walthers.com

MALLETS & HAMMERS

230-600 Mascot Multi Hammer w/6 Heads **12.99**

230-601 Swiss Style Watchmakers Hammer **7.99**
Double-faced head is only 2-1/4" long with flat and chisel faces. Forged head mounted on a hardwood handle. Overall length 8".

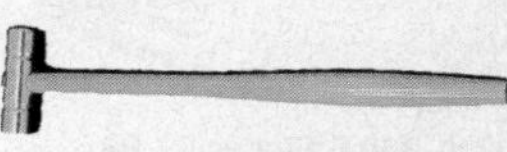

230-602 Brass Mallet **9.99**
Overall length is 9" with 2" head.

230-603 Mallet w/Interchangable Face **17.50**
Includes brass, fiber and nylon faces. Overall length is 9" with 2" head. Comes with wrench for changing faces.

HAMMER/ SCREWDRIVERS SET

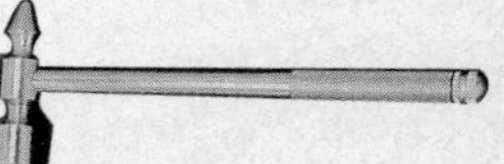

230-604 5 Pieces **15.95**

SCREWDRIVERS

PRECISION SCREWDRIVER SET

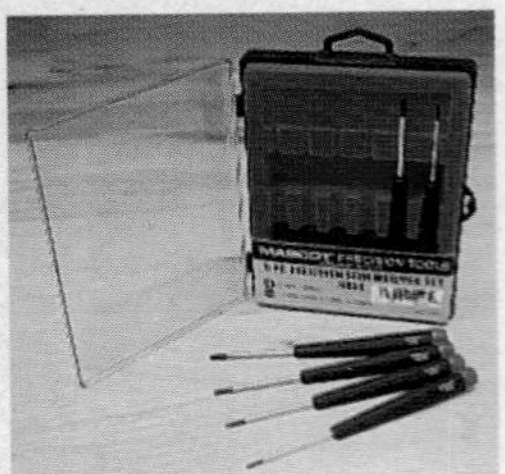

230-850 6 Pieces **17.99**
This one-of-a-kind set features non-rolling handles with contoured swivel heads, shafts made of molybdenum steel (hardened and chrome plated for strength and torque) and precision ground tips for sure fit and absolute control. Includes 4 slotted heads (1.5 x 50 mm, 2 x 50 mm, 3 x 50mm) and 2 Phillips head sizes (00 x 50mm, 0 x 50mm) and a handy hard-plastic carrying case.

PRECISION SCREWDRIVER SET

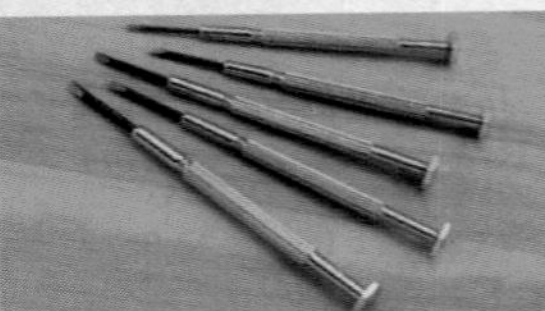

230-855 5 Pieces **12.50**
Nickel plated, with swivel heads. 3" to 3-5/8" length, sizes .048" to .085". Blades permanently fixed in handles.

METRIC SCREWDRIVER SET W/2 PHILLIPS

230-853 6 Pieces **4.99**

REVERSIBLE BLADE SCREWDRIVERS

230-800 Flat Head **6.50**
Blade has 1/16" and 3/32" ends with swivel head.

230-806 Phillips **7.50**
Blade has size #0 and #1 Phillips ends.

POCKET EYEGLASS SCREWDRIVER

230-804 2.10

SCREWDRIVER SHARPENER

230-847 9.99
Spring action device holds screwdriver firmly in place while rolled over sharpening stone (stone not included).

MISCELLANEOUS

TITANIUM SOLDER PICK

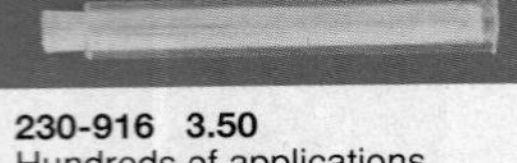

230-917 6.30
Use to move solder to and from desired spot.

STEEL SCRATCH BRUSH

230-916 3.50
Hundreds of applications. Features straight steel wire tightly packed in vinyl sleeve that can be peeled away as brush wears.

INSPECTION MIRRORS

1" diameter, stainless steel mirrors mounted in 8" long handle.

230-905 Plain Mirror **7.45**
230-906 Magnifying Mirror **8.35**

PRONG HOLDERS

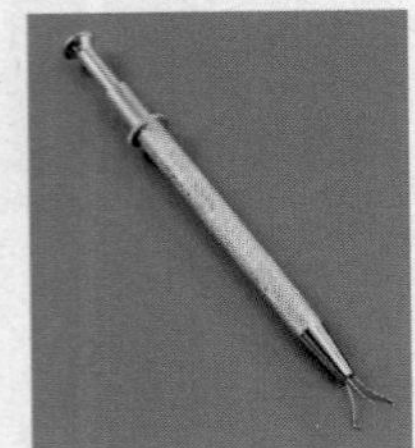

230-203 3 Prongs **5.99**

230-204 4 Prongs **6.50**

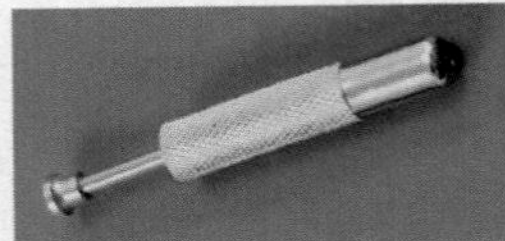

230-2031 Mini 3 Prong **5.99**

MINIATURE OPEN END WRENCH SET

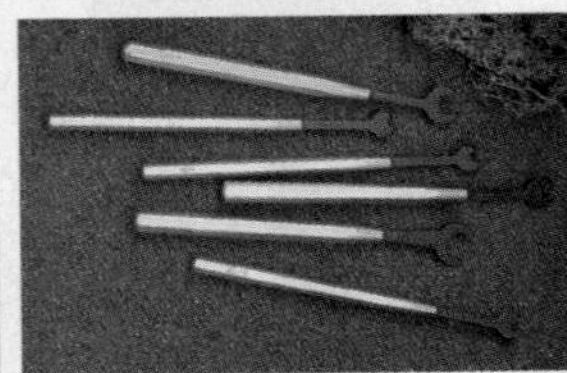

230-856 16.75
Sizes include 3/32", 1/8", 5/32", 3/16", 1/4" and 5/16".

MICRO CLEANER SET

230-700 5.99
Assortment of five micro cleaning wire brushes in sizes: .09", .12", .15", .18" and .30". Includes a separate handle that will accommodate all but the largest brush. Packed in a reusable plastic vial.

DENTAL PROBES

230-303 Set(3) **7.20**

MINI-AUTOMATIC PUNCH

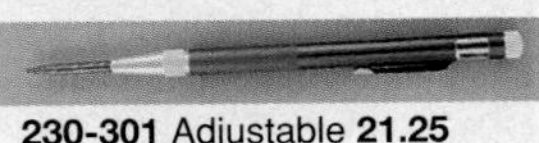

230-301 Adjustable **21.25**

POCKET LEVEL

230-805 2.08

ELECTRICIAN SCISSORS

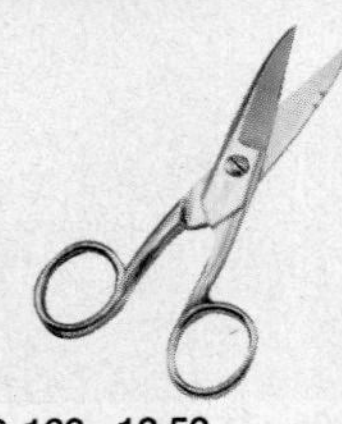

230-163 12.50
Double plate, chrome over nickel with notches for stripping wire. 5" long.

METRIC NUT DRIVER SET

230-858 5.80
Sizes 3.0mm, 3.5mm, 4.0mm, 4.5mm and 5.0mm.

HEMOSTATS EA 7.90

230-340 Straight Blade

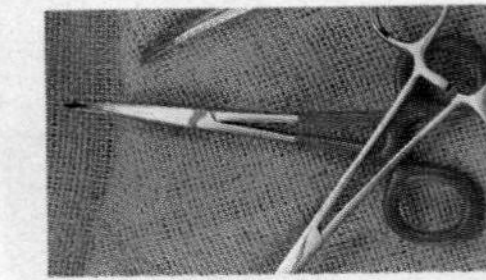

230-341 Curved Blade

BLOWER

230-915 6.99

GEAR PULLERS

230-220 Stationary **11.50**
230-221 Adjustable **19.99**

RULERS

6" METRIC/ENGLISH RULER

230-710 2.69

12" MODEL RR SCALE

230-711 8.99
Scale conversions for HO, O and S gauges.

TRACK CLEANERS

230-971 Tunnel Tablet Track Cleaner **13.95**

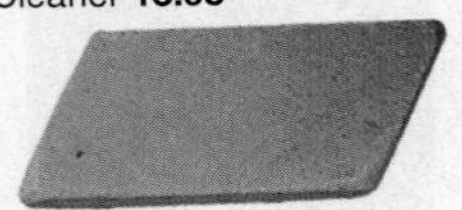

230-970 Track & Tool Cleaning Tablet **6.00**

MASCOT HOBBY TOOL CATALOG

230-997 N/C

Power Tools For Hobby Projects

As modelbuilding has become a more sophisticated hobby, tool makers have created a variety of power tools for the experienced builder.

The most common is probably the hand-held motor tool. With a high speed fixed or variable RPM motor and interchangeable bits, these units can perform all kinds of jobs. Typical applications include cutting, grinding and polishing metals, as well as sanding, carving and routing wood. Wire brushes and various types of polishing equipment are also offered. These units are ideal for use with softer metals and virtually any kind of wood. The variable speed models are better suited to use with plastics, as more control is needed to prevent softening and distorting the material.

Power sanders are offered by some manufacturers. These can be adapted to the finer grades of abrasives used with hobby materials and work much like their larger versions.

For electrical work or soldering of various metals, there are many kinds of soldering pencils, soldering guns and butane torches.

For advanced metal and wood work, you'll find smaller size lathes available. These will do everything the full-size models can, but are sized for more practical use around the home workshop.

microflame

TORCHES & ACCESSORIES

Microflame features "Micronox," a laboratory tested and proven gas used as a fuel oxidizer. It has a longer operating and shelf life than oxygen, extends the operating life of butane and produces a neutralizing flame.

MINIATURE TORCH SETS

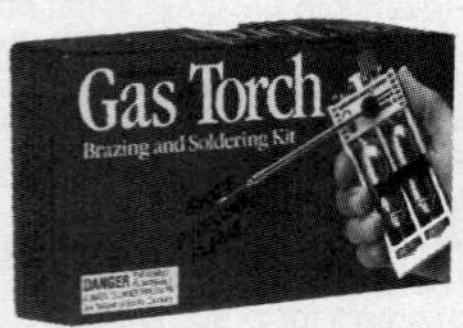

450-1000 Hobby **39.99**
Torch set solders and brazes and has a 5000°F pinpoint flame. Contains torch, flame tips, gaskets, 1 butane and 2 Micronox cylinders, brazing rod and flux. Also included is a 1/2" thick fireproof board and a working surface on which the Microflame torch can be used safely.

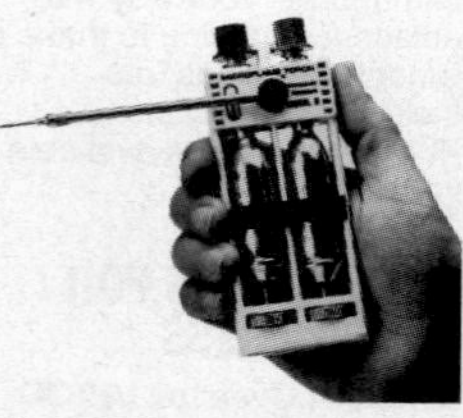

450-1201 Economy **24.99**
Contains torch, flame tip, one Micronox, butane cylinder and instructions.

450-4200 Standard **34.99**
Contains torch, two flame tips, gaskets, one butane and two Micronox cylinders, three brazing rods and flux tube.

450-4400 Deluxe Hardware-Gas Set **59.95**
Injection molded carrying case with form-fitted recessed compartments. Contains torch, 2 flame tips, 1 butane tip, 6 Micronox and 3 butane cylinders, spark lighter, 6 brazing rods and tube of flux.

BRAZING RODS & FLUX

450-3000 Brazing Rods pkg(4) **18.99**
Gold colored 45% silver alloy with flux core.

450-3102 Aluminum Brazing Rods pkg(6) **2.00**

450-3104 Aluminum Flux Jar 1.5oz **2.49**

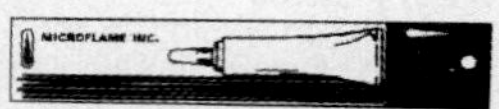

450-3111 Brazing Rods & Flux pkg(6) **6.75**
40% silver alloy rods and brazing rod flux.

REPLACEMENT CYLINDERS

MICRONOX™

450-1001 pkg(2) **3.25**
Fits all miniature torches.

450-1002 Butane pkg(2) **4.99**
Fits all miniature torches.

450-4300 Cylinder Kit **10.75**
Contains 4 Micronox and 2 butane cylinders.

450-8100 Supercharger Refill **3.99**
2-hour replacement butane cylinder for Super Cub torch.

ACCESSORIES

450-7400 Orifice Cup pkg(3) **2.75**
450-10031 Threaded Flame Tips pkg(2) **2.75**

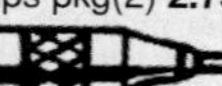

450-1003 Slotted Flame Tips pkg(3) **2.75**
16-gauge tips to fit all torches.

450-10040 Cylinder Gaskets pkg(4) **1.25**
Fits all torches manufactured prior to April 1977.

450-1004 Cylinder Gaskets pkg(4) **1.25**
Fits all Model B dual cylinder miniature torches.

450-10060 Micronox Piercing Knob **3.49**
Fits all Dual cylinder torches manufactured prior to April 1977.

450-1006 Micronox Piercing Knob **3.49**
Fits all Model B Dual Cylinder Miniature Torches manufactured after 1977.

450-10070 Butane Piercing Knob **3.49**
Fits dual cylinder torches manufactured prior to April 1977.

450-1007 Butane Piercing Knob **3.49**
Fits all Model B dual cylinder Miniature torches manufactured after 1977.

450-1008 Spark Lighter **2.25**

450-1009 Slotted Butane Tip **7.50**
Attaches to any torch to permit use of butane gas only.

450-10091 Threaded Butane Tip **7.50**

450-1005 Threaded Rotary Assembly **4.49**

450-8700 Super Cub Torch Head **10.50**

BUTANE TORCH SETS

450-9510 Dragon Torch Head Only **22.00**

450-8000 Super Cub **12.95**
Delivers more than 2 hours of burning time at controlled high temperature flame (2000°F, 1080°C). Contains threaded torch head and 25 gram butane cylinder.

N.J. INTERNATIONAL

TOOLS

525-6604 Part Picker **3.99**

NMRA

STANDARDS GAUGE EA 10.00

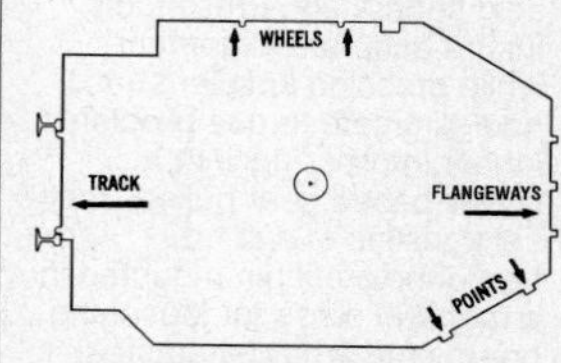

Designed and developed by the NMRA (National Model Railroad Association) Engineering Committee, this pocket-sized gauge enables you to check all important dimensions on your track and rolling stock as follows:

- Gauge of track and turnouts
- Flangeway depth and "check gauge"
- Clearance
- Height of loading platform and coupler

If cars do not run correctly, this gauge will pinpoint the trouble for you. Complete instructions come with each gauge.

098-1 HO Standard Gauge
098-2 HOn3 Standard Gauge
098-5 O Standard Gauge
098-6 On3/00 Standard Gauge
098-7 Sn3 Standard Gauge
098-8 N Standard Gauge

NOCH

IMPORTED FROM GERMANY BY WALTHERS

SCALE RULER

528-71400 HO, N & Z **8.99**

RIBBONRAIL

WORK CRADLES

Hold your favorite models safely and securely while detail painting, decaling, or making repairs. Made of Alclad aluminum, easy-to-assemble holder is adjustable and padded to protect the finish of your work.

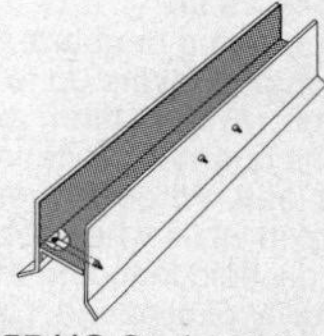

170-55 HO Scale **12.95**
170-1055 N Scale **7.50**

ROCO

IMPORTED FROM AUSTRIA BY WALTHERS

CRANKPIN WRENCH

625-10903 **7.99**
Box spanner socket wrench for removal of crankpins on locomotives with coupling rods.

STATE TOOL & DIE CO.

GLUE & PAINT DISHES

661-800 pkg(6) **2.00** *NEW*

NorthWest Short Line

THE QUARTERER

53-444 29.95
For quartering or quarter checking of drivers up to 1" O.D. on 1/8" or 3.0mm axles. Permits quartering either right or left lead. Wheel is pressed onto axle while wheelset is still securely held in tool to avoid possibility of slippage. Can be used to compare quartering of existing drivers. Includes operating instructions and 2 index pins (crank pin substitutes). Requires .100" space on each side of gear to fit driver into tool.

THE PULLER

53-454 7.95
A rigid, precision tool for removing wheels, drivers and gears from axles and shafts. Made for HO Scale modeling, but handles larger and smaller scales. Capacity: axles 1/16" to 1/8"; drivers, wheels and gears up to 1-5/8" O.D. Maximum press depth 1". Puller comes complete with 2 press screws, V-plate, Allen wrench and operation suggestions. Allen wrench not usually needed, finger pressure being adequate in most cases.

PRESS SCREWS

Optional for #454 with thumb screw head (will not accept Allen wrench).

53-45314 1/16" Tip **1.95**
53-45324 3/32" Tip **1.95**
53-45334 Cone Tip **1.75**
53-45344 Flat Tip **1.50**

V-PLATE

53-45074 V-Plate for Puller **.75**

THE PULLER II

53-554 8.95 *NEW*
With greater depth, this Puller is ideal for O, S and #1 Scale models. It can remove gears from a shaft with a distance of 1-5/8" 4cm from the face of the gear to the shaft end. Wheels up to 1-1/4" 3.1cm (Scale 55" in O; 33" in #1) can be pressed from their axles. Great for repairs or rebuilding in smaller scales and repowering slot or RC cars too.

PROFESSIONAL PRESS TOOL SETS

Use with the Puller (#53-454) and the Puller II (53-554), both sold separately. Press tools insure accurate alignment while pressing smaller shafts and eliminate torque problems inherit in pressing with a screw-based gear puller. Each set consists of a short, hardened steel pin mounted in a mandrel press for loosening gears, and a hardened steel pin fitted in a mandrel press to "break" the shaft free of the gear. The mandrel includes a "stabilizer" bar to reduce rotational force when pressing, for consistent alignment and less chance of damage. The tools can also help in the accurate assembly of short, small shafts with gears and wheels.

53-45394 Complete Set pkg(4) **29.95** *NEW*
Includes one each 53-45404, 45424, 45444 and 45464.

INDIVIDUAL PRESS TOOLS EA 9.95

53-45404 1mm *NEW*
53-45414 1.6mm *NEW*
53-45424 1.2mm *NEW*
53-45434 3/16" 2.4mm *NEW*
53-45444 1.5mm *NEW*
53-45464 2.4mm *NEW*

THE BENDER

53-484 36.95
Press bending brake to bend brass or other light sheet metals up to 90° (depends on how far you tighten press screws) up to 3" bend length, up to .020" half hard brass capacity. Depth guide permits duplication of bend placement on stock being bent. Includes reversible die operation suggestions and alternate urethane die material.

REPLACEMENT PRESS SCREW

53-48164 pkg(2) **2.00**
1-1/2" head, 1/4" diameter and 20 threads per inch for #484.

SANDING STICKS EA 2.95

53-25019 120 grit (red)
53-25029 240 grit (blue)
53-25039 320 grit (green)
53-25049 400 grit (yellow)
53-25059 600 grit (black)

REPLACEMENT BELTS FOR SANDING STICKS EA .79

53-28069 For #25019
53-28079 For #25029
53-28089 For #25039
53-28099 For #25049
53-28109 For #25059

URETHANE DIE MATERIAL

Permits bends without marking material, for #484

53-48154 pkg(3) **2.00**

THE DUPLICUTTER

53-524 22.95
Designed for working with sheet styrene (scribing, squaring and cutting to size) but can also be used with wood modeling and cutting locomotive window glass to size. Accepts standard size styrene sheets 6-1/2". Comes complete with a set of 4 scales O, HO, S and N.

THE RIVETER+

53-514 49.95
Rivet tables can be easily attached to Sensipress+ (not included.) Comes with .015 (1-1/2" HO) rivet embossing punch and die. Tool enables "accurate rivet spacing". Advancing knob is calibrated in .001" increments.

OPTIONAL EMBOSSING PUNCHES & DIES FOR #514

PUNCHES

53-51004 Universal **3.00**
53-51104 .010" **4.00**
53-51154 .015" **4.00**
53-51204 .020" **3.00**
53-51304 .030" **3.00**
53-51404 .040" **3.00**
53-51504 .050" **3.00**

DIES

53-51164 .015" **4.00**
53-51214 .020" **3.00**
53-51314 .030" **3.00**
53-51414 .040" **3.00**
53-51514 .050" **3.00**

RIVET EMBOSSING PUNCH/DIE SET FOR RIVETER+

53-51014 29.95
Includes one each to the following sizes of punches and dies: .010", .020", .030", .040" and .050" and a universal punch.

THE ALIGNER GEAR ALIGNMENT TOOL EA 6.95

Installing a gear squarely (without wobble) on a shaft or axle is tedious and sometimes unsuccessful. This tool will "square-up" and salvage most problem gears in place.

53-324 For 2.4mm or 3/32" Axle
53-334 For 3mm Axle
53-384 For 1/8" Axle

THE TRUE-SANDER

53-574 29.95
Combination holding jig and sanding block for finishing and squaring off stripwood and strip styrene. Jig can be adjusted to hold anything from thinnest stripwood up to an HO body shell (angle adjustment to 90°). Makes perfect fits easier.

THE CHOPPER

53-494 21.95
Heavy duty strip wood length cutter. Also can do mitre cuts (guides for 30, 45 and 60° included). Adjustable stop piece permits setting any cut length up to 3-1/4" for exactly duplicate cut pieces–for car decking ties, trestle building, etc. Four blades and operating suggestions included. No special blades needed, uses single edge razor blades. Also cuts styrene and other model making plastics. Safety top keeps handle from slipping or raising dangerously high.

53-49154 Extra Blades pkg(8) **1.00**

CHOPPER III

53-594 Chopper III **29.95**
Heavy duty wide base version of the Chopper allows easier handling of long pieces of material. Chopper III provides for installation of up to 3 handles, permitting multiple set-ups. Includes one handle only, additional handles are available (see #49144 below). The 18" wide base is a sturdier work area and the safety top keeps handle from slipping or raising dangerously high.

53-49144 Extra Handle **9.95**

DRILL & TAP SETS

53-30505 1/6-60W each **18.75**
53-30605 1.0mm x 0.25 each **12.75**
53-30625 1.2mm x 0.25 each **12.50**
53-30645 1.4mm x 0.3 each **11.75**
53-30675 1.7mm x 0.35 each **11.25**
53-30705 2.0mm x 0.4 each **11.00**
53-30765 2.6mm x 0.45 each **10.25**
53-30805 3.0mm x 0.5 each **10.25**

THE SENSIPRESS + ARBOR PUNCH PRESS

53-504 79.95
Use the press for assembling parts, wheels, etc. and as a gear puller to disassemble. Small enough to give a sensitive touch and also sturdy enough to supply up to 250 pounds of pressure. Reversible 3/8" ram is flat on one end and bored 3/16" on the other so you can interchange various tools. Ram set screw retains the tool. 3/32" tip for gear and wheel pulling is included. Gibbed and adjustable overarm for precision alignment.

ARBOR PRESS PUNCH ADAPTER FOR #504

53-50014 2.95
Punches up to 1/8" holes easily in brass and styrene, larger holes may exceed tool capacity depending on material and thickness. You can "nibble" your way with adjacent punching to make car window openings, etc. Includes ram adapter. Punches and dies available separately.

ACCESSORIES FOR ARBOR PRESS

53-50504 Oversize 1/2" OD Tool **1.50**
53-50514 Blank Flat End Tool **.75**
53-50524 1/16" Diameter Tip **1.50**
53-50534 3/32" Diameter Tip **1.50**
53-50544 Cone End, Concave **1.00**
53-50564 Bored 2.0mm Tool **1.00**
53-50574 Bored 3/32" Tool **1.00**
53-50584 Bored 1/8" Tool **1.00**
53-50594 Interchange Tool Set **8.75**
Set of all the above except 50534.

53-50604 "V" Plate **3.00**

ROUND HOLE PUNCHES & DIES FOR #504 EA 4.95

PUNCHES

53-50104 1/16"
53-50124 5/64"
53-50144 3/32"
53-50164 1/8"

DIES

53-50114 1/16"
53-50134 5/64"
53-50154 3/32"
53-50174 1/8"

PANAVISE®

WORK HOLDERS

PanaVise work holder tool systems are very versatile. All movements are controlled by one variable-pressure knob, making it possible to move the work to any desired position.

550-324 Work Center **76.99**
Standard Base, tray base mount, circuit board holder and solder station. (Solder and soldering iron not included).

550-301 Standard PanaVise **42.99**
Standard height base and vertical jaw vise head with nylon jaws.

550-381 Vacuum Base PanaVise **54.99**
Vacuum base and vertical jaw vise head with nylon jaws included.

550-396 Wide-Opening Head PanaVise **45.99**
Standard height base and wide opening jaw vise head #366 with Neoprene jaw pads.

550-201 PV Jr. Work Vise **21.95**

550-203 PV Jr. Vise Head **20.91**

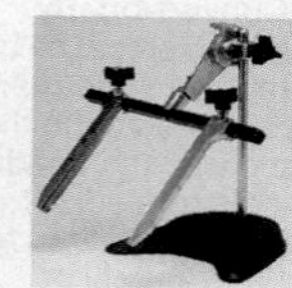

550-333 Circuit Board Holder **64.99**
Spring loaded circuit board holder features 8-position rotating adjustment, indexing at 45° increments and 6 lock positions. Extra arms can be added for multiple board holding. Includes two pre-drilled and tapped flanges.

550-350 Multi-Purpose Work Center **74.99**
Wide opening head, standard base and tray base mount with 6 trays for small parts and tools.

HEADS

550-376 Extra Wide Opening **41.99**
Self-centering double action jaws (opens to 9") and reversible jaw pads. Fits #300 Series bases. Base not included.

550-303 Original Vise Head **23.99**
Nylon jaws. Fits #300 Series bases.

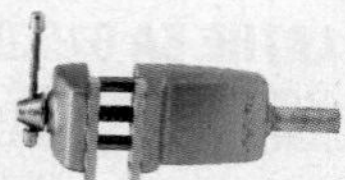

550-304 Low Profile Vise Head **30.99**
Steel jaws. Fits #300 Series bases.

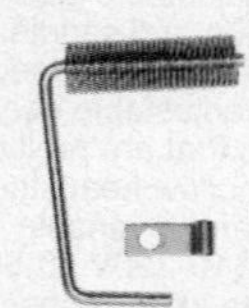

550-358 Universal Holder **21.33**

550-366 Wide Opening Head **30.99**
Wide opening head features Neoprene jaw pads. Fits all #300 Series bases.

550-315 Circuit Board Holder **29.99**
Complete with 14" cross-bar. Fits all #300 Series bases. Ideal for holding boxcars for lettering.

550-316 Extra Arms 1 Pair **17.99**
For #315 circuit board holder.

550-317 Support Unit for #315 **10.49**

550-318 14" Cross Bar **5.29**
For #315 circuit board holder (lengths to 30" on special order).

550-371 Solder Station **10.99**
Solder and iron holder attach to #312 and all bases (except #380), to bench, wall, or free standing. Includes two sponges and mounting screws.

BASES

550-300 Standard Height (Original) **19.99**

550-305 Low Profile **19.99**

550-380 Vacuum PanaVise Base **31.99**

550-400 Heavy Duty PanaVise Base **37.99**

PANAPRESS

550-502 Precision Panapress **109.99**
Although it weighs less than 6 pounds and stands only 7" high, this hand arbor press exerts pressure up to a quarter-ton. Ideal for pressing bearings, sleeves or collars, forming and assembling small parts, punching, riveting, broaching, staking and dozens of other operations.

Arbor and table-plate die-cast of high strength Zamak III. Operating mechanism of hardened and ground steel. Ram is reversible.

ACCESSORIES

REPLACEMENT JAWS

550-343 Nylon Jaws w/Screws 1 Pair **2.49**
For #303 and #304 heads.

550-344 Grooved Nylon Jaws w/Screws 1 Pair **3.49**
With horizontal groove, for #303 and #304 heads.

550-346 Deluxe Neoprene Jaw Pads for #366 1 Pair. **2.99**

550-352 Teflon Jaws w/Screws each. **11.49**
For #303 and #304.

550-353 Plated Steel Jaws w/Screws 1 Pair. **5.99**
For #303 and #304.

550-354 Brass Jaws w/Screws 1 Pair **7.49**
For #303 and #304.

CROSSBARS

For 315, 324 and 333.

550-31822 22" **6.89**
550-31830 30" **8.49**

FIXTURING HEADS

550-337 Fixturing Head Face Plate **16.99**
Fits all #300 Series bases.

550-437 Heavy Duty Face Plate **19.99**
For #400 Series heavy duty base.

MOUNTINGS

550-308 Mounting Plate, Weighted **27.99**
Complete with mounting holes and mounting screws, for #300 and #305 bases.

550-310 Surface Plate **91.99**
Blanchard ground, with mounting holes for #300 and #305 bases with mounting screws.

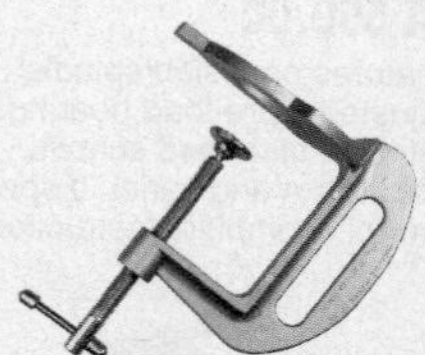

550-311 Bench Clamp **38.99**
Complete with mounting screws, for #300 and #305 bases.

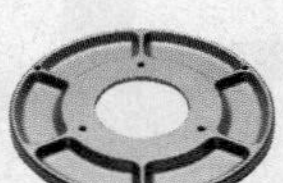

550-312 Tray Base Mount **19.99**
Includes mounting screws, for #300 and #305 bases.

MISCELLANEOUS

550-319 Circuit Board Replacement Knobs pkg(4) **3.99**

SHERLINE

Milling Machine can be used for milling, drilling, fly-cutting and boring. Use lathe for turning wood, plastic or metal. Sherline machines have inch-feed threads.

MILLS & ATTACHMENTS

Technical Specifications listed for both 5000 and 5100:

Max Clearance Table Spindle: 8", 203mm; Throat: 2.25", 50mm; Travel "X" Axis: 9", 228mm; Travel "Y" Axis: 3", 76mm; Travel "Z" Axis: 6.5", 165mm; Hole through Spindle: .405", 10mm; Spindle Nose Thread: 3/4 x 16 TPI; Spindle Taper: #1 Morse; Handwheel Graduations: .001", .01mm; Electronically Controlled Spindle Speed: 70-2800 rpm; Overall Width: 14.75", 375mm; Overall Depth: 11.75", 298mm; Overall Height: 20.75", 527mm; Table Size: 2.75 x 13", 70 x 330mm; Hold Down Provisions: 2 "T" Slots; Shipping Weight: 33lbs, 15kgs

VERTICAL MILL TABLE EA 100.00

This accessory is used on the lathe to accomplish some light milling tasks. Table mounts on the cross slide, allowing stock to be moved in three axis. Cutters are held in headstock.

677-1184 Metric
677-1185 English (Inches)

VERTICAL MILL EA 550.00

Features precision spindle adjustable pre-load bearings, anti-backlash feed screws, table locks and variable speed control. Complete instructions.

677-5000 Englis Version
677-5100 Metric Version

DELUXE MILL PACKAGE EA 650.00

677-5400
For deluxe Packages: Vertical Mill (5000) with 12" Base, 5" travel Y axis, drill chuck (3072) and mill spacer (1297) and laser engraved scales; comes with 2 adjustable 2" handwheels and 1/2.5 adjustable hand wheel.

677-5410 Metric Version

8-DIRECTION VERTICAL MILLING MACHINE EA 875.00 (UNLESS NOTED)

Includes 14" 35cm base.

677-2000 English ***NEW***
677-2010 Metric ***NEW***
677-2000418 8-Way Mill w/Digital Readout Installed **1,150.00** ***NEW***

DIGITAL READOUT EA 350.00

3-axis rpm indicator gauge for mills.

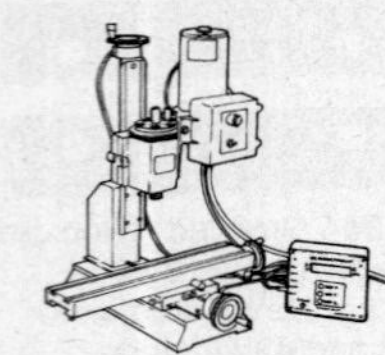

677-8100 English ***NEW***
677-8160 Metric ***NEW***

XY/XYZ BASE

The Vertical Mill can be purchased without the headstock and motor/speed control. This allows lathe owners to swap their headstock and motor/speed control from the lathe to the mill in approximately 30 seconds.

677-5200 XY Base **230.00**
677-5201 XYZ Base **315.00**

SPECIAL MILL PACKAGE EA 610.00

5000 Mill with two, 2" resettable handwheels and one 2-1/2" resettable handwheel with ball thrust bearings.

677-5500
677-5510 Metric Version

RIGHT ANGLE ATTACHMENT

677-3701 55.00
For use with #3700. Mounts the rotary table in the vertical position. Has a locking mechanism that is positive and does not move the table as it is locked. Black oxide base.

4" ROTARY TABLE

677-3700 Rotary Table **250.00**
Designed to work with the Model 5000 and 5100 Sherline Milling Machines. Can be used on any mill whenever the 4-inch size would be an advantage. 2" high and 4" (100mm) in diameter. Features solid bar stock steel and weighs 7 pounds. Hardened worm gear case. Engraved with a laser, giving sharp and precise lines every 5°, numbered every 15°. These lines are calibrated with the 72-tooth worm gear which is driven by the handwheel. The handwheel is divided into 50 parts, making each line on the handwheel 1/10°. This allows a circle to be divided into 3600 increments without interpolation. It takes 72 revolutions of the handwheel to rotate the table one revolution. Includes two holddown clamps and "T" nut fasteners. Plus an adapter that allows the Sherline 3-4 jaw chucks to be mounted directly to the Rotary Table and 6 page instruction manual.

OPTIONAL TAILSTOCK

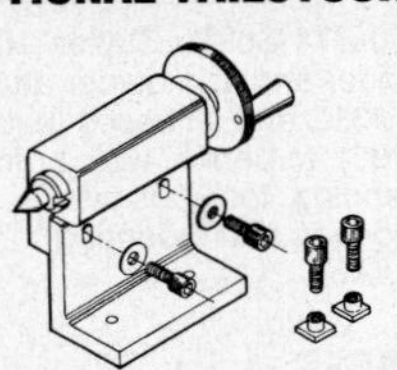

677-3702 For 4" Rotary Table (#3700) **55.00**
With the table mounted vertically, an optional tailstock can be mounted to the mill table. It is used to support and stabilize the other end of long work held in a chuck or otherwise attached to the rotary table.

INDEXING ATTACHMENT

677-3200 165.00
A unique design that provides a very economical means of accurately rotating a part so that things such as the flats on a nut or the teeth on a gear can be added.

HORIZONTAL MILLING CONVERSION

677-6100 120.00
Increase the size of work that can be machined with the addition of the Horizontal Milling Conversion. By allowing the vertical column to be mounted in various positions in relation to the table, and with the headstock and spindle rotated 90° into the horizontal position, a tremendous variety of machining possibilities are opened up. Plus, the mill can remain mounted to the conversion base and still operate in its conventional vertical mode as well.

COVERS

677-3015 Toggle Switch Dust Cover **5.00** ***NEW***
677-4150 Lathe Cover **10.00**
677-5150 Vinyl Mill Cover **12.00**

SLITTING SAW ACCESSORIES

677-3065 Holder **35.00**
677-7302 #40 (.020") Blade **11.25**
677-7303 #57 (.032") Blade **12.30**

LATHES & ATTACHMENTS

Technical Specifications for both 4000 and 4100: Swing Over Bed: 3.5", 90mm; Swing Over Carriage: 1.88", 48mm; Distance Between Centers: 8", 200mm; Hole Through Spindle: 0.405", 10mm; Spindle Nose Thread: 3/4" x 16 TPI; Spindle Nose Taper: #1 Morse; Travel of Cross Slide: 4.25", 110mm; Travel of Tailstock Spindle: 1.5", 38mm; Taper of Tailstock Spindle: #0 Morse; Headstock Swivel: 360°; Protractor Graduations: 0° to 45° by 5°; Handwheel Dial Graduations: 0.001", .01mm; Electronically Controlled Spindle Speed Range: 70-2800 rpm; Length Overall: 23", 584mm; Width Overall: 10.25", 260mm; Height Overall: 8", 203mm; Shipping Weight: 24lbs.

24" LATHE EA 675.00

677-44001 24" Bed ***NEW***
677-44101 Metric ***NEW***

3" LATHE MACHINE BASE

Features fully dovetailed slides, adjustable gibs on cross-slide and saddle, protected lead and feed screws, adjustable headstock bearings that are prelubricated for life, hollow headstock spindle and a variable speed motor. (110-220V 50-60Hz) Complete instructions.

677-4000 Englis Version **460.00**
677-4100 Metric Version **460.00**
677-40001 #4000 w/Accessories **550.00** ***NEW***

SPECIAL LATHE PACKAGE EA 510.00

4000 with two 2" resettable handwheels.

677-4500 English Version
677-4530 Metric Version

SPECIAL LATHE PACKAGE EA 595.00

Lathe 4500 and Chucks #1041 and #1072.

677-45001 English Version
677-45301 Metric Version

VERTICAL MILLING COLUMN EA 130.00

Attachment features solid aluminum base, dovetailed steel vertical column and adjustable saddle. Various functions possible include grooving, keyway cutting and flycutting.

677-3050 English Version
677-3053 Metric Version
677-4150 Lathe Cover **10.00**

MULTI-DIRECTION VERTICAL MILLING COLUMN EA 350.00

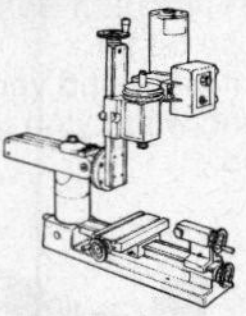

677-3580 English ***NEW***
677-3585 Metric ***NEW***

QUICK-CHANGE TOOLPOST & ACCESSORIES

677-2250 Toolpost & 3 Interchangeable Tool Holders **250.00** ***NEW***
677-2255 Toolholder for 3/8" Inserted Carbide Tips **85.00** ***NEW***
Fits #2250, sold separately.

DIGITAL READOUT EA 300.00

3-axis rpm indicator gauge for lathes.

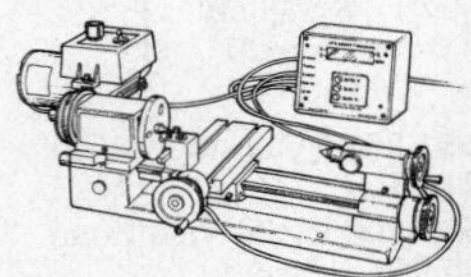

677-8200 English ***NEW***
677-8260 Metric ***NEW***

SHERLINE

ACCESSORIES

ADJUSTABLE LIVE CENTER

677-1201 **55.00**
Allows you to position the center. The center is attached to one plate, while the shaft is part of another. Two slightly over-size holes in one side allow adjustment screws to be loosened, the center located and then locked down where you want it.

TAILSTOCK CHUCK HOLDER

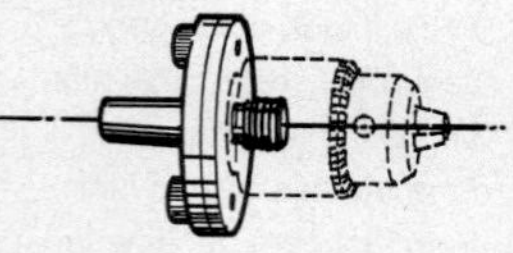

677-1202 **40.00**
Holds a tailstock chuck in alignment. Allows perfect centering for the chuck.

TAILSTOCK CUSTOM TOOL HOLDER

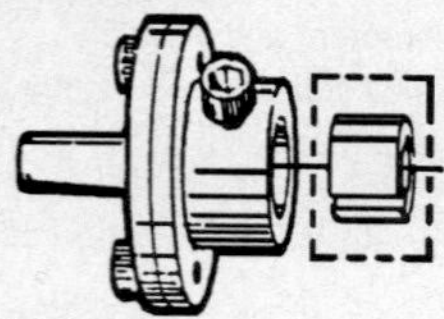

677-1203 **40.00**
By making your own custom split collet with a 5/8" outside diameter, this part can hold virtually any tool you wish to adapt to it.

WOOD TOOL REST SET

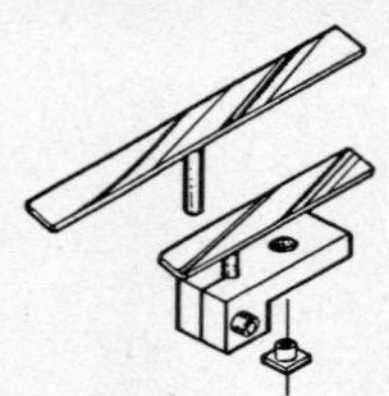

677-3038 **50.00**

OVERSIZE HANDWHEEL

677-3400 **15.00**
Allows the machinist to reset the handwheel to "zero" (or any desired setting) at any time during a machining operation.

RESETTABLE HANDWHEELS

677-3420 2" Adjustable, English **35.00**
677-3430 2" Adjustable, Metric **35.00**
677-3440 2-1/2" Adjustable, English **40.00**
677-3450 2-1/2" Adjustable, Metric **40.00**

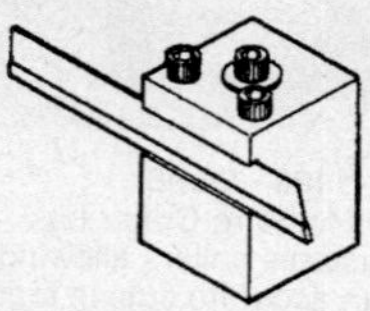

677-3018 Rear Mount Cutoff Tool Holder and Tool **45.00** *NEW*
677-8700 Self-Contained CNC Rotary Table Indexer **TBA** *NEW*
Includes 4" rotary table with installed stepper motor, microprocesser unit with numeric keypad and 115 VAC power source. This item is a stand alone unit but can be connected to an existing CNC control to function as a fourth radial axis in that system.

LATHE ACCESSORIES

677-1010 "Zero Jacobs Taper" 5/32" Drill Chuck & Key w/#1 Morse Arbor (Headstock) **60.00** *NEW*
677-1015 "Zero Jacobs Taper" 5/32" Chuck & Key w/#0 Morse Arbor (Tailstock) **55.00** *NEW*
677-1041 3-Jaw Self-Centering Chuck **90.00**
677-1044 4-Jaw Chuck **90.00**
677-1160 Collet Set (1/8 - 5/16") pkg(5) **80.00**
677-1072 Tailstock Chuck & Key **45.00**
677-1074 Steady Rest **40.00**
677-1161 WW Collet Adapter & Draw Bar **35.00**
677-1191 Live Center **35.00**

677-1220 Tailstock Spindle Extender **30.00**
677-1270 Compound Slide **100.00**
677-1290 Steady Rest Riser **30.00**
677-1291 Spacer Block Kit **65.00**

677-2049 Spindle Handwheel **40.00** *NEW*
677-2083 1" (25.4mm) WW Collet Blank **25.00**
677-2085 WW Collet "T" Stock Adapter **50.00**
677-2086 8mm Collet "T" Stock Adapter **50.00**
677-2110 W.R. Smith "T" Rest **175.00**
677-2200 Radius Cutting Attachment **115.00**
677-2295 Quick Change Carbide Insert Holder **85.00** *NEW*
677-3001 Power Feed for Lathe **80.00**
677-3002 Cut-Off-Tool & Holder **45.00**
677-3003 Two Position Tool Post **15.00**
677-3005 1/4" sq. High Speed Tool Blank **3.00**
677-3006 Carbide Tool Set **18.00**
677-3007 High Speed Tool Set **25.00**
677-3012 Hold Down Set **20.00**
677-3020 Allen "T" Driver **6.00**
For cap screws used on machines.
677-3021 Center Drill Set **15.00**
677-3100 Screw Cutting Attachment **110.00**
677-4360 Chip Guard **14.00**
677-7600 Insert Holder Tool Post **20.00**
677-7610 55° Negative Rake Insert Holder **60.00**

MILL ACCESSORIES

677-1187 Chuck to Tee Slot Adapter **5.00**

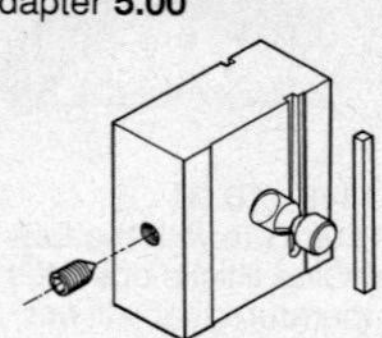

677-1297 Mill Headstock Riser **40.00**
677-3061 Boring Tool for #3054 **15.00**
677-3052 Fly Cutter **35.00**
Adjustable 3" and 5" rests are placed near the work and the cutting tool is rested on and moved across their surface to cut wood.

677-3054 Boring Head **60.00**
677-3055 Morse # 1 Tool Blank **15.00**
677-3056 T Nut 10/32" pkg(10) **7.50**
677-3057 Rocker Tool Post **30.00**
677-3058 4-Jaw Hold Down Set **5.00**
677-3060 Milling Collets **40.00**
677-3061 Boring Tool (1-5/16") **15.00**
677-3072 Drill Chuck & Draw Bar **40.00**
677-3079 End Mill Holder 3/8" **30.00**
677-3063 Boring Tool for #3054 **15.00**
677-3080 End Mill Set **30.00**
677-3551 Milling Vise **65.00**

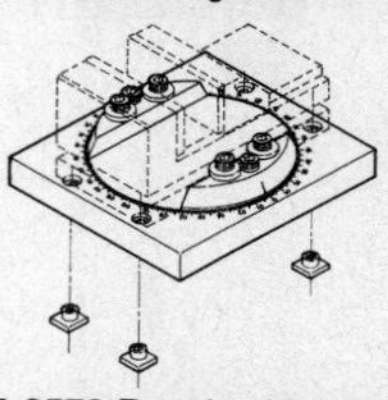

677-3570 Rotating Vise Base **90.00** *NEW*
677-3575 Rotating Vise Base w/Mill Vise Included (#3551) **145.00** *NEW*

MILL CUTTER ARBORS EA 50.00

Designed to hold 7/8 or 1" I.D. cutters for milling or gearcutting. These steel arbors are for use in the Sherline headstock spindle and are available in short (3/4") or long (1-3/4") sizes.

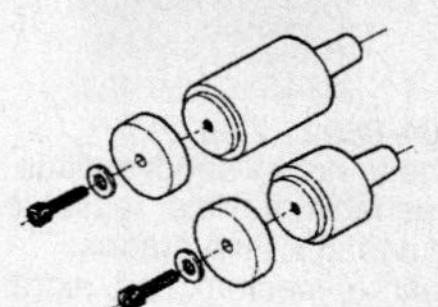

677-3230 7/8" Diameter Short *NEW*
677-3231 7/8" Diameter Long *NEW*
677-3235 1" Diameter Short *NEW*
677-3236 1" Diameter Long *NEW*
677-3575 Rotating Vise Base w/Mill Vise Included (#3551) **145.00** *NEW*

MISCELLANEOUS

677-4004 Drive Belt **7.50**
677-5300 Home Machinist's Handbook **20.00**
677-5325 Sherline Catalog **2.00**
677-5327 Complete Instruction Manual **10.00**

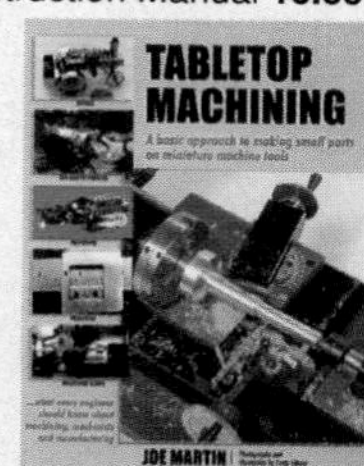

677-5301 Book-Tabletop Machining **40.00** *NEW*

ROBART

RIGHT ANGLE DRIVE

Smooth ball bearing action allows you to drill, grind, polish and more, in places that are tight or around corners. Easy to attach and uses the same collet system as the Moto-Tool.

547-421 **38.45**
For use with Moto-Tool #s 395, 285, 275 series and #800 freewheel.

547-4200 **38.45**
For use with older model Moto-Tools.

CARBIDE CUTTERS EA 7.95

Tungsten carbide cutters on 1/8" steel shanks for all woods, fiberglass and plastics.

CONE CUTTER
547-4602 Fine Grit

1/4" BALL CUTTER
547-4621 Coarse Grit
547-4622 Fine Grit

3/8" BALL CUTTER
547-4611 Coarse Grit

1/4" ROD CUTTER
547-4631 Coarse Grit

DISC CUTTER
547-4651 Coarse Grit

HOBBY KNIVES

Specially designed for building plastic kits. Blade can be resharpened.

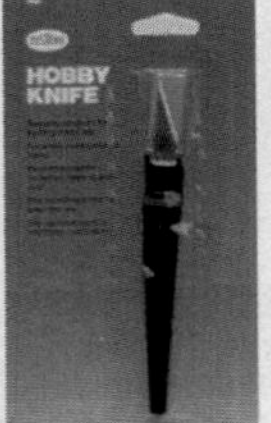
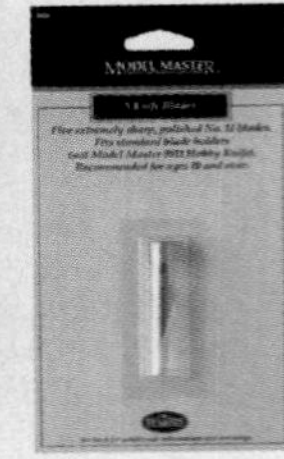

704-8801 704-8816

704-8801 Hobby Knife **1.49**
Dealers MUST Order Packs of 12

704-8816 Knife Blades pkg(5) **2.79**

DECAL APPLICATOR SYSTEM

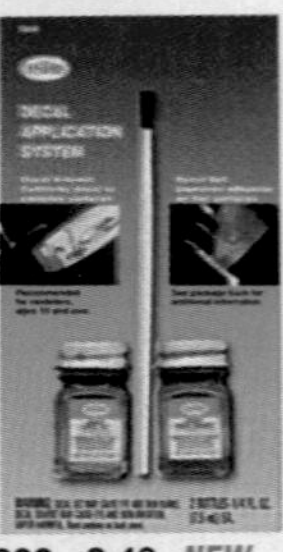

704-8809 2.49 ***NEW***
System helps decals conform to difficult shapes through improved adhesion. System includes two bottles of decal solution and one brush.

DROP CLOTH

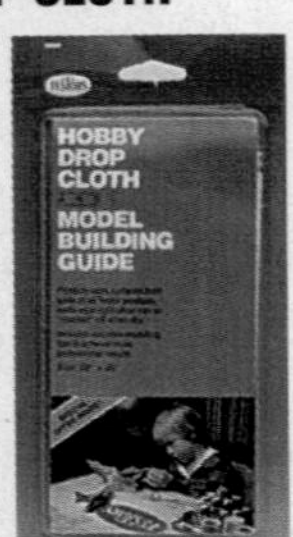

704-8803 2.98 ***NEW***
24 x 36" sheet is impervious to most solvents.

NEEDLE FILE SET

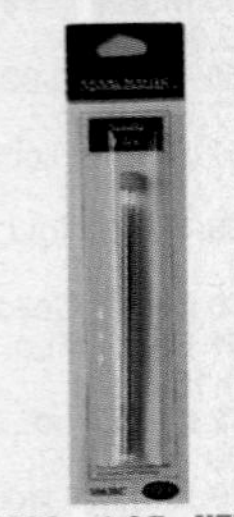

704-50630 4.95 ***NEW***

PIN VISE

704-50629 12.95 ***NEW***
With six drill bits.

SANDPAPER

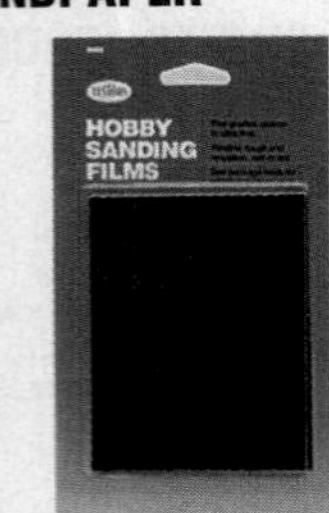

704-8802 2.49 ***NEW***
These hobby sanding films are washable, flexible, reusable and tough. Five grades: coarse, medium, fine, extra-fine and ultra-fine.

SPRUE CUTTERS

704-50628 13.50 ***NEW***

TWEEZERS

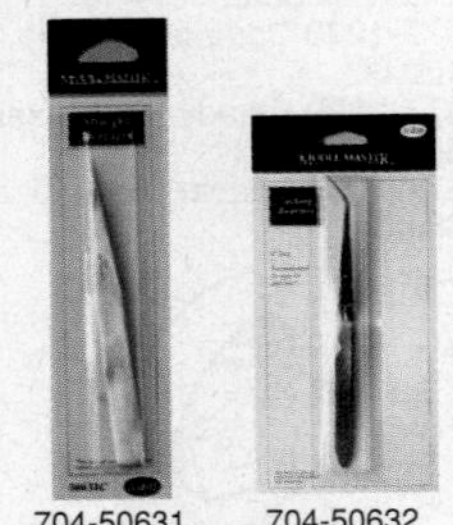

704-50631 704-50632

704-50631 Straight **3.95** ***NEW***
704-50632 Lock **4.95** ***NEW***

DIES EA 29.98

785-877 00-90
785-878 0-80
785-879 1-72
785-880 2-56

WRENCHES EA 4.49

785-885 00-90
785-886 0-80
785-887 1-72
785-888 2-56

TAPS EA 3.29

785-895 00-90
785-896 0-80
785-897 1-72
785-898 2-56

LOW TEMP FOAM GLUE GUN

785-1445 16.98
The Glue Gun with the Low Temp Glue Sticks operates at a temperature that will not damage foam.

785-1446 pkg(10) **3.98**
10" Glue Sticks.

FOAM KNIFE

785-1433 5.98

FOAM KNIFE BLADES

785-1434 pkg(4) **4.98**
The Foam Knife comes with a 2" replaceable blade that is ideal for cutting thick pieces of foam.

HOT WIRE FOAM CUTTER

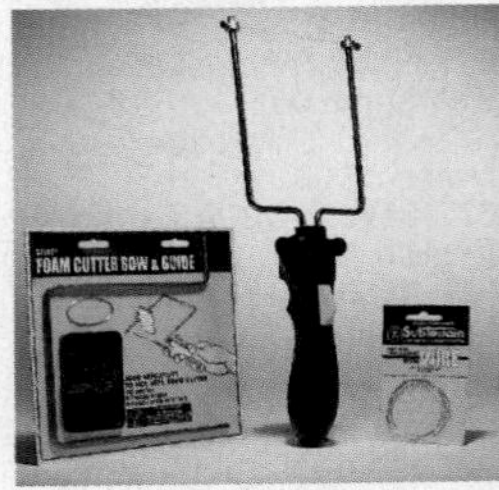

785-1435 29.98
The Hot Wire Cutter has adjustable collars allowing for clean accurate cuts in foam. Attach the guide for more precise cutting. The Bow attachment adds versatility to the Hot Wire Cutter. Woodland Scenics recommends using only on SubTerrain white foam which emits no toxic fumes. Use only special nichrome replacement wire.

HOT WIRE REPLACEMENT WIRE

785-1436 4' **1.98**

FOAM CUTTER BOW & GUIDE

785-1437 7.49

TAMIYA

DECAL SCISSORS

865-74031 21.50
Coated with a special material to resist sticking to adhesives when cutting decals and stickers. Sharp, fine blades allow for delicate work.

Information STATION

Pensions

Nowadays, there is nothing new or exciting about a pension plan. Many present day companies have instituted such a policy. At the beginning of the Twentieth Century, however, these plans were few and far between. In fact, the first railroad in the United States to have a formal pension plan for all level of employees was the PRR; it took effect on January 1, 1900. This plan applied to all employees from the age of 70, which from that date became the mandatory retiring age.

The Federal Railroad Retirement Act (USA) came into effect thirty-seven years later on July 1, 1937. This act replaced voluntary retirement and disability benefits on about 80 of the major railroads.

X-ACTO®

Designed for artists, craftsmen/women and hobbyists. X-ACTO began producing precision knives and tools in 1935. Included are cutting tools and accessories, drills, tweezers, pliers, files, woodcarving sets and other craft tools that are ideal for miniature work.

KNIVES

X-2000™ PRECISION KNIVES EA 5.50

This safer stylish knife offers anti-roll design, no-slip grip, center barrel blade release for fast and easy blade changing, greater stability, snap-on safety cap and four colors.

790-3721 Teal
790-3722 Cranberry
790-3723 Blue
790-3724 Black

HOBBY KNIVES

790-3021 #1 Knife w/Safety Grip **3.55**
Includes #11 blade and tri-angular safety grip to prevent rolling.

790-3295 X-Calibre Retractable Knife **12.75**
Executive design with metal pocket clip. Balanced, lightweight; perfect for most light duty cutting.

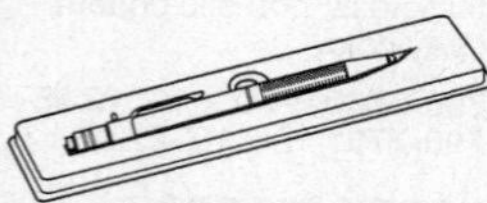

790-5095 X-Calibre RT Set **15.50**
Stainless steel blade retracts with push button pocket clip.

790-3685 Cut-All® Knife **2.75**
Assorted colors with safety cap.

790-3209 9RX Knife **9.95**

790-3201 #1 Light Duty Knife **2.65**
790-3601 #1 Knife w/Safety Cap **3.15**

790-3202 #2 Medium Duty Knife **3.75**
790-3602 #2 Knife w/Safety Cap **4.65**

790-3203 #3 Pen-Knife **5.40**

790-5204 #4 Stencil Knife w/#204 Blades **5.75**

790-3205 #5 Heavy Duty Knife **4.95**

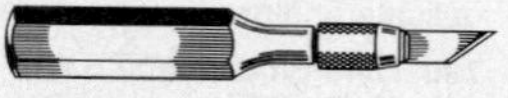

790-3206 #6 Heavy Duty Knife **8.15**

790-3241 Craft Swivel Knife **7.65**
The perfect precision tool for all light-duty cutting.

790-3261 Woodcarving Knife **8.60**

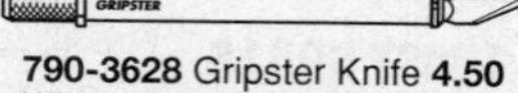

790-3628 Gripster Knife **4.50**
With safety cap, assorted colors.

UTILITY KNIVES & ACCESSORIES

790-3008 #8R Utility Knife **1.65**
Compact with lightweight plastic handle, adjustable cutting depth and retractable, reversible blade.

790-3208 #8R Retractable Utility Knife **1.95**
Cycolac handle w/2 blades.

790-3272 Plastic Retractable Utility Knife **5.60**
790-3274 Metal Retractable Utility Knife **7.75**
790-7747 Board Cutter **15.50**
Contoured shape and soft grip allow perfect 90° cuts through mat board and foam board up to 1/2" thick, and cuts precise 45° bevel with special adapter.

SAWS

790-7043 Jeweler's Saw w/Blade **29.95**
790-7044 Coping Saw **6.85**
Comes with one standard saw blade. Adjustable grips.

RAZOR SAW SETS

790-75310 Razor Saw & Knife Set **15.95**
#5 Handle, 234, 235 and 236 blades, #15 keyhole saw blade and 5 knife blades.

790-75300 #5 Handle Set **8.50**
Includes #234 and #235 blades.

790-75350 Extra-Fine Set **7.50**
790-75380 6-1/2" Set **8.50**
Includes #5 knife with #240 blades.

MITRE BOXES

790-75320 Mitre Box Set Carded **15.95**
Contains aluminum mitre box #7533, #236 razor saw blade and #5 handle. For use with #236 blade only.

790-75330 Mitre Box Only, Carded **8.50**
Extruded aluminum, 6" long, 3/4 x 1-3/4" capacity. Grooves on base to hold wood, etc. from 1/16 to 1/4".

790-75370 SurGrip Mitre Box Set **29.75**
790-75360 SurGrip Mitre Box Only, Carded **21.95**

TOOL SETS

KNIFE SETS

790-5211 Knife Set #51 **4.50**
#1 knife with 5 assorted blades.

790-5212 Knife Set #52 **6.40**
#2 knife with 5 assorted blades.

790-5262 Double Knife Set #62 **11.50**
#1 and #2 knives with 10 assorted blades.

799-5281 Triple Knife Set **15.50**
#1, #2 and #5 knives plus 10 assorted blades in plastic case.

790-5282 Carded Knife Chest #82 **21.50**
#1, #2 and #5 knives plus 10 assorted blades.

790-5083 Deluxe Knife Set **30.50**
#1, #2 and #6 knives plus 14 assorted blades.

790-5028 Carded Do-It-Yourself Set **22.95**
#2 and woodcarving knives, plus 8 assorted blades.

CARVING TOOL SETS

790-5175 Carving Chest **31.95**
Deluxe woodcarver set. #5 handle with 5 assorted blades, two 3" blades, 6 gouges and 4 routers.

790-5177 Woodcarving Set Basic **16.95**
#5 handle with 6 gouge-blades, 4 regular blades, two 3-inch blades.

790-5179 Carving Tool Set **33.75**
Six hardwood handled chisels.

790-5224 Standard Woodcarving Set **22.50**
For narrow cuts, deep cross cuts, leveling, whittling, general carving, initial shaping and outlining in wood. Includes #5 Knife with blades 19, 15, 18, 22, 24, 26 and A, B, C, D, E and F gouges.

KNIFE AND TOOL SETS

790-5076 Basic Craft Tool Set **31.95**
790-5087 Deluxe Craft Tool Set **67.50**
Complete assortment of knives, blades and tools including coping saw, block plane, sander, jeweler's screwdriver, spoke shave, balsa stripper pin vise, 3 drill bits, 4 gouges, 2 routers and 9 assorted blades.

790-5086 "The Crafter" Tool Set **48.95**
#1, #2 and #5 knives and assortment of blades, gouger, routers, plus plane, sander, spoke shave and balsa stripper in a wood chest.

BLADES

KNIFE BLADES

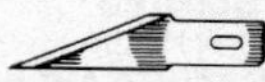

790-2 #2 Blade **2.20**
Sharp angle precision cutting of medium to heavyweight materials. Fits knife handle #s 2, 2 SGK, 5, 6 and wood-carving handle.

790-202 Carded pkg(5) **2.20**
790-402 Carded Safety Dispenser pkg(15) **6.05**

790-208 Carded **2.30**

790-9 #9RX Blade pkg(5) **6.75**
For light duty stencil and frisket cutting. Also used as a lifter. Fits knife handle #9XR.

790-209 Carded pkg(5) **6.75**

790-10 #10 Blade pkg(5) **3.30**
For general cutting, light carving and slicing. Fits handles 1, 1SGK, Super No. 1 X-Press, Gripster, Cut All and #3 Pen.

790-210 Carded pkg(5) **3.30**

790-610 Bulk Pack pkg(100) **55.00**

790-11 #11 Blade **2.10**
Sharp angle for delicate, precision cutting, trimming and stripping. Fits knife handle #s 1, 1SGK, Super No. 1 X-Press, Gripster, Cut All and #3 Pen.

790-211 Carded pkg(5) **2.10**
790-411 Carded Safety Dispenser pkg(15) **5.15**
790-611 Bulk Pack pkg(100) **27.00**
790-291 Broad Tip #11 pkg(5) **2.30**
Modified blade provides a stronger, more flexible point.

790-212 Carded pkg(5) **7.95**
For delicate paper cutting, stenciling and carving. Fits knife handles 1, 1SGK, Super No. 1 X-Press, Gripster, Cut All and #3 Pen.

790-213 #13 Blade pkg(5) **3.30**
For precision cutting of plastics, balsa and thin metals. Fits knife handles 1, 1SGK, Super No. 1 X-Press, Gripster, Cut All and #3 Pen.

790-215 #15 Keyhole Saw Blade pkg(5) **6.50**
For small interior cuts. Fits knife handles 2, 5, 6 and woodcarving handle.

790-16 #16 Blade pkg(5) **2.10**
For stenciling, etching and scoring and printed circuit boards. Fits knife handles 1, 1SGK, Super No. 1 X-Press, Gripster, Cut All and #3 Pen.

790-216 Carded pkg(5) **2.10**
790-616 Bulk Pack(100) **27.00**

790-17 #17 Blade pkg(5) **2.10**
For precision wood chiseling with 1/4" chisel. Fits knife handles 1, Super No. 1 X-Press, Gripster and Cut All.

790-217 Carded pkg(5) **2.10**

790-18 #18 Blade pkg(5) **2.30**
For deep cross and smooth chiseling of wood with 1/2" surface. Fits handle #2.

790-218 Carded pkg(5) **2.30**

X-ACTO

790-19 #19 Blade pkg(5) **2.30**
For light chiseling, shaping, deburring and trimming. Fits handles 2 and 2 SGK.

790-219 Carded pkg(5) **2.30**

790-22 #22 Blade pkg(5) **4.05**
For long, heavy-pressure, woodworking, whittling, carving and trimming in confined spaces. Fits handles 2 and 2 SGK.

790-222 Carded pkg(5) **4.05**

790-23 #23 Blade pkg(5) **8.25**
For corner cuts, stripping and trimming in confined spaces. Fits handle #s 2 and 2 SGK.

790-223 Carded pkg(5) **8.25**

790-24 #24 Blade pkg(5) **2.10**
For close corner cuts on templates and mats, deburring, stripping and gasket cutting. Fits handle #s 2 and 2 SGK.

790-224 Carded pkg(5) **2.10**

790-225 Carded pkg(5) **7.40**
For heavy-pressure cutting, whittling, carving and trimming. Fits handles 2 and 2 SGK.

790-226 #26 pkg(5) **4.60**
Blade 2-5/16" cutting edge for general purpose whittling and trimming. Fits handle #2.

790-227 #27 pkg(5) **5.75**
Blade for general purpose cutting of lightweight and medium woods. 3" length allows deeper cuts. Fits handle #2.

790-28 #28 pkg(5) **11.25**
For whittling, leather and linoleum. Fits handles 2 and 2 SGK.

790-228 Carded pkg(5) **11.25**

790-245 Craft Swivel Knife Blade pkg(2) **2.85**
Designed to rotate 360° for easy cutting of curves and circles in lightweight materials.

790-292 Heavy Duty Utility pkg(5) **2.70**
For #3272 and 3274. For cutting mats, carpeting, wallboard, wallpaper, tile, plastic and wood.

790-295 X-Calibre RT Knife Blade pkg(5) **6.80**
For fine cutting, trimming paperwork and stenciling. Stainless steel resists corrosion, won't rust.

STAINLESS STEEL BLADES

790-221 Carded pkg(5) **2.30**
790-421 Carded Safety Dispenser pkg(15) **6.80**
790-621 Bulk pkg(100) **36.50**

BLADE ASSORTMENT #1

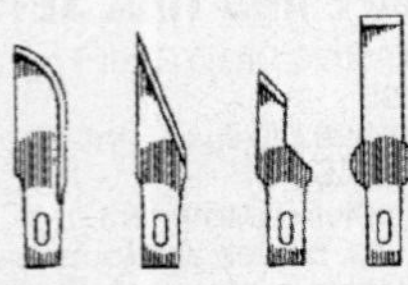

790-231 Carded pkg(5) **2.20**
Includes two #11 and one each of #s 10, 16 and 17.

BLADE ASSORTMENT #2

790-232 Carded pkg(5) **3.05**
Includes blades 18, 19, 22 and two 24s.

SAW BLADES

#234 RAZOR SAW BLADE

790-234 Fine Saw Blade **3.05**
For delicate sawing, cutting circuit boards, model construction and shaping balsa wood. Cutting edge 4-1/2" long, 3/4" deep.

#235 RAZOR SAW BLADE

790-235 Medium Saw Blade **2.95**
For delicate sawing, cutting circuit boards, model construction and shaping balsa wood, cutting fiberglass, plastic, narrow gauge tubing, metals and railroad tracks. Cutting edge 4-1/2" long, 1" deep.

#236 RAZOR SAW BLADE

790-236 Course Saw Blade **3.35**
For coarse sawing of wood, plastic, fiberglass, metals and moldings. Cutting edge 5-1/2" long, 1-1/4" deep.

790-239 Extra Fine Saw Blade **3.35**
For delicate sawing work in confined space, cutting circuit boards, model construction, shaping balsa wood, cutting fiberglass, plastic, metals and railroad tracks. Cutting edge 5-1/2" long, 1-1/4" deep.

#240 RAZOR SAW BLADE

790-240 Heavy Duty Saw Blade **7.65**
For heavy duty sawing of railroad track, moldings, narrow gauge tubing, metals, plastic and fiberglass. Cutting edge 6-1/2" long, 2-1/16" deep.

COPING SAW BLADE

790-734 pkg(5) **6.40**

JEWELER'S SAW BLADES PKG(12) EA 6.40

For #7043 saw.

790-746 #6/0 Extra Fine Cut
790-752 #2/0 Fine Cut
790-753 #3 Medium Cut

SINGLE EDGE RAZOR BLADES

790-270 pkg(5) **2.00**
790-670 pkg(100) **14.50**

CARVING BLADES EA 3.50

790-103 Convex pkg(2)
For carving cylindrical shapes, rug cutting and linoleum cutting.

790-104 Concave, 3/4" Radius pkg(2)
For general carving.

790-105 Concave, 1-3/8" Radius
Initial shaping and carving.

PRECISION TOOLS

GOUGES

790-134 Gouge Assortment pkg(5) **10.15**
Contains 3/16" chisel, 3/32" U gouge, 3/16" V gouge, 3/8" V gouge and 3/8" U gouge. Fit knife handles #5 and #6.

790-151 A-Chisel Gouge 3/16" **3.50**

ROUTERS

790-135 Routers Assortment pkg(4) **10.15**
Fit knife handles #5 and #6. For carving out grooves, hollows and recesses.

FILE SETS

790-73580 File Set **9.95**
Includes 3 files and handle.

790-73610 Needle File Set w/Handle Carded **18.95**

NEEDLE FILES PKG(12) EA 25.60

790-6367 Half Round
790-6368 Knife
790-6369 Round
790-6371 3-Square
790-6372 Equaling
790-6375 Flat
790-6376 Marking Half Round

SANDERS

790-7042 Block Sander 2 x 5" **4.10**

SANDING ACCESSORIES

790-7036 Sanding Belt Assortment **6.15**

BLOCK PLANE

3-3/4" long single bevel steel blade. Molded body for delicate and accurate planing.

790-7040 Block Plane **6.65**
790-29 Refill Blades pkg(2) **2.30**

HAND DRILL PIN VISE

790-73220 Double-Ended Hand Drill Pin Vise **5.25**
Contains chucks that will accept #49-#80 bits.

DRILL CHUCK ADAPTER

790-73210 Precision Chuck Set **9.75**
3 collets with interchangeable handle for sizes 45-80 drills.

TWIST DRILLS

790-6409 Drills 55-80 Assorted (12) **13.75**
790-6410 Drills 45-60 Assorted (12) **13.75**
790-6411 Drills 1/16-3/16" Assorted (9) **13.75**
790-6412 Drill Stand Set **29.95**
With 20 drills 61-80, stand and cover.

TWEEZERS

790-73350 5" Fine Point **11.75**
790-73360 Soldering Tweezer 4-1/2" **4.25**
Medium sharp points.

790-73370 Pointed Tweezer 6-1/2" **4.50**
Self-closing.

790-73380 Soldering Tweezer 6-12" **4.95**
Self-closing, blunt serrated points.

790-73430 Angular Tweezer **4.65**
Fine serrated points.

PLIERS

Plastic cushion grip handles, lap joint construction.

790-75040 Long Nose, Side Cutting **9.25**
790-75050 Diagonal Cutting **9.25**
790-75060 Flat Nose, 4-1/2" **9.25**
790-75070 Snipe Nose, 4-1/2" **9.25**
790-75100 Extra Long **13.75**
790-75110 Bent Nose **10.25**

VISE

790-73700 Mini Vacu-Vise **9.50**

HAMMER SET

790-7050 Hammer Set **15.95**
Includes 6 interchangeable heads.

SOLDERING IRON

790-73780 Soldering Iron 110V **15.95**
With tip and hot knife blade.

SOLDERING AIDS

790-7456 Cross-Action Clamp Heat Sink pkg(3) **3.25**
Six tools with carrying case.

X-TRA HANDS

Double alligator spring clamps and double ball joints hold work firmly.

790-75130 Single **12.50**
790-75140 Double **13.50**
790-75170 With 2x Magnifier **15.95**

CLAMPS

790-7003 Small Clamp, Plastic pkg(2) **3.75**
3-1/4" long with 1" throat.
790-7004 Large Clamp, Plastic pkg(2) **7.25**
7-1/4" long with 2-1/16" throat.
790-7446 "C" Clamp Set pkg(4) **10.25**
790-7450 Mini "C" Clamp Assortment pkg(3) **7.25**

SCREWDRIVERS

790-7068 Jeweler's pkg(5) **9.95**

SELF-HEALING MAT

One-inch grid pattern, 3mm thickness, non-slip bottom. Gray color.

790-7760 8-1/2 x 12" **12.95**
790-7761 12 x 18" **22.95**

HOBBY RULERS

RULER PREPACK

Contains six of each of the following: 18" with metric and inch; 12" with HO and O Scales, metric and inch; 12" with 1/24", 1/32", 1/72" scales, metric and inch; 3 x 4" Square, 3" Triangle, 6" with HO and O Scales, metric and inch; 6" with 1/24", 1/32", 1/72" scales, metric and inch on back

790-7725 3" Triangle, Inches Only **7.75**
790-7726 3 x 4" Square, Inches Only **7.75**

MISCELLANEOUS

790-7100 Pinpoint Oiler **3.85**
790-73800 Part Picker **7.50**

SHEARS

These high-precision shears have a special ultra-tapered shape that provides a simple way to quickly and cleanly cut in hard-to-reach areas. Perfect for cutting sprue and wire.

791-90001 Premium Quality Shear - Oval Head **19.99**

791-90005 Premium Quality Shear - Tapered Head **19.99**

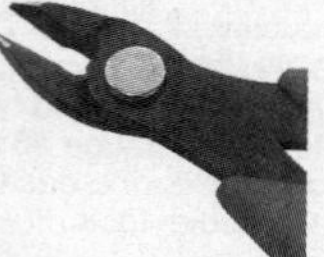

791-90026 Crafter's Shear **12.99**

791-90028 Track Cutter **12.99**

791-90033 Hard Wire & Cable Cutter **15.99**

791-90036 Ultraflush Cutting Shear **10.49**

791-90039 High Precision Shear **10.49**

791-90043 Angled High Precision Shear **17.49**

791-90046 Photo Etch Shear **15.99**

SCISSORS

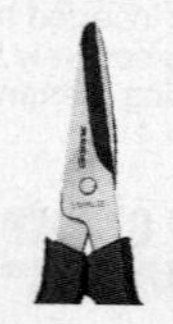

791-90118 Modeler's **18.99**
This handy stainless-steel scissors easily cuts mylar, fabric, styrene, soft aluminum or brass sheet stock.

791-90128 High Durability **21.99** ***NEW***
These user-friendly scissors are designed to cut through tough Kevlar fibers, but can be used to trim photo-etched parts. Feature high carbon steel blades, ultra-durable plasma spray coating and serrations on one edge.

PLIERS

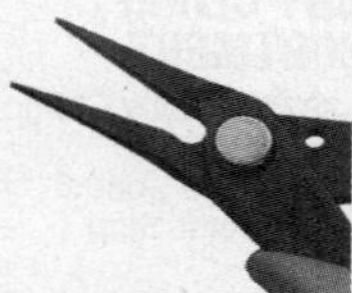

791-90065 Tweezernose, Smooth **17.99**
791-90066 Tweezernose, Serrated **17.99**

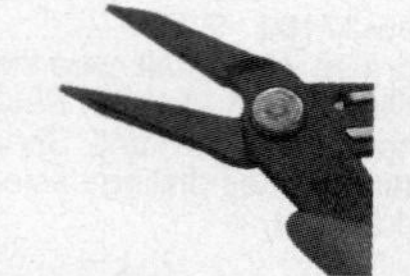

791-90075 Longnose, Smooth **10.99**

791-90122 Round Nose **14.99**

791-90123 Combination Tip **14.99**

791-90124 Split Ring **12.99**

791-90125 Micro Former **16.99**

STAINLESS STEEL TWEEZERS

High-quality Swiss-manufactured electronic-grade tweezers manufactured from anti-magnetic, anti-acid stainless steel.

791-90105 Precise, Straight Tips **21.99**

791-90107 Tapered, Extra Fine Tips **21.99**

791-90108 Precise, Thin, Curved Tips **21.99** ***NEW***

791-90109 Rounded, Straight Tips **21.99**

791-90113 Precise, Very Strong **21.99**

TOOL KITS

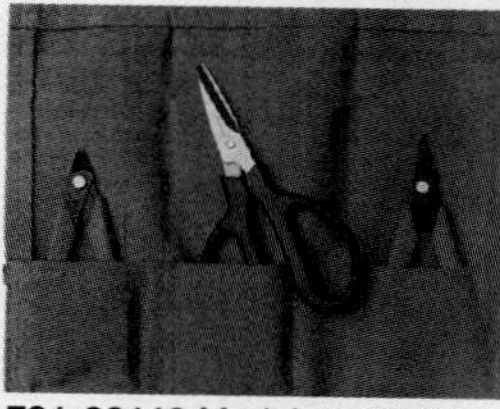

791-90119 Modeler's **47.00**
Includes #90039 High Precision Shear, #90065 Tweezernose™ pliers and #90118 Modeler's Scissors in a durable tri-fold pouch.

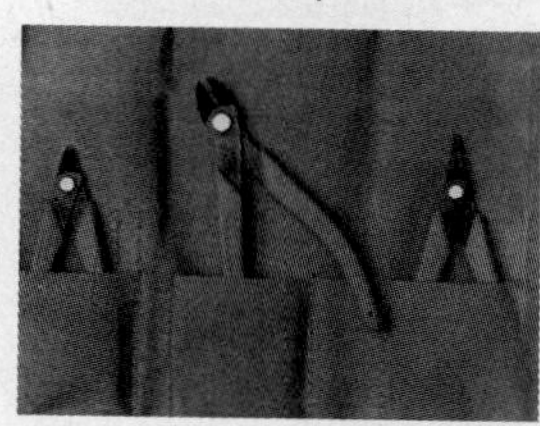

791-90120 Railroader's **47.00**
Features the #90028 Xuron Track Cutter, #90039 High Precision Shear and #90066 Serrated Tweezernose™ pliers in a tri-fold fabric pouch.

DISPENSING BOTTLES

EA 4.49

Polyethylene bottles with stainless steel dispensing tubes for controlled dispensing of a wide variety of liquids, including solvents. 2oz.

791-90115 0.010" ID Needle
791-90116 0.020" ID Needle
791-90117 0.040" ID Needle
791-90114 2oz Dispensing Bottle Nozzle Spout **1.99**

Information STATION

HO Scale

The HO Scale has only grown in popularity since its introduction more than 50 years ago. Today it has the honor of being the most popular size in the model railroading community with well over 100,000 modelers choosing it as their scale of choice. But exactly what is HO Scale?

The term "HO" refers to two different things, the first being scale. In this scale, everything is 1/87th the size as it is in real life, making the model of an 87 foot prototype freight car only one foot long.

"HO" refers to the track gauge as well. Track gauge is the distance between the two inside edges of the rails. In the real world, on a standard railroad, this distance is 4' 8-1/2", which translates to 16.5 mm in the modeling world.

This scale was originated in England and was derived from halving the popular O Scale sizes, giving us the "Half-O" Scale. This was soon shortened to just plain "HO."

4 IN 1 SAW SET

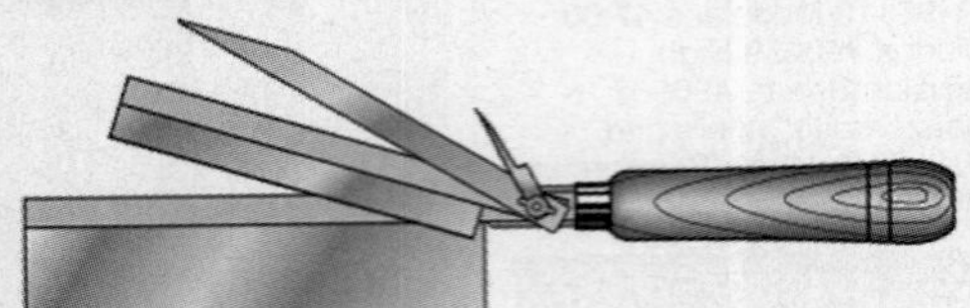

795-35140 7.95
Versatile set for all kinds of cutting. Includes four interchangeable blades that attach with a wing nut and screw.

4 IN 1

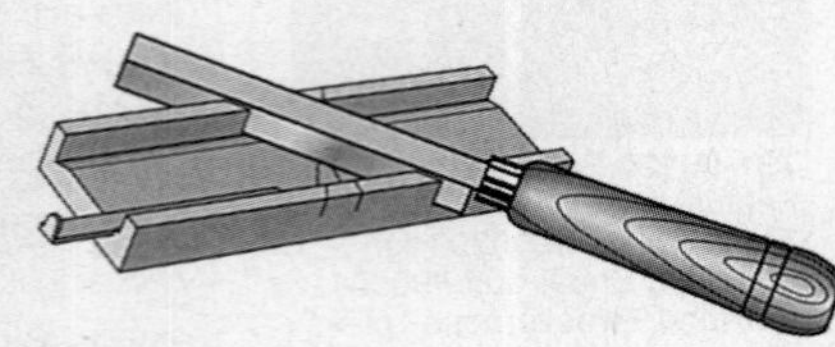

REPLACEMENT BLADES

795-36406 Keyhole Saw Blade (Pull Style) pkg(3) **1.80**
795-36408 Keyhole Saw Blade (Push Style) pkg(3) **1.80**
795-36458 Saber Saw Blade **1.00**
795-36050 Razor Saw Blade, 13/32" Cutting Depth **1.00**
795-36555 Razor Saw Blade, 1-3/16" Cutting Depth **1.50**

MINI MITER BOX W/SAW

795-251 7.50
Combination saw and miter box (w/#200 saw).

795-250 3.95
Designed to fit all razor-type saws. Adjustable stop and beveled channel.

THIN SLOT MITER W/THIN GAUGE SAW

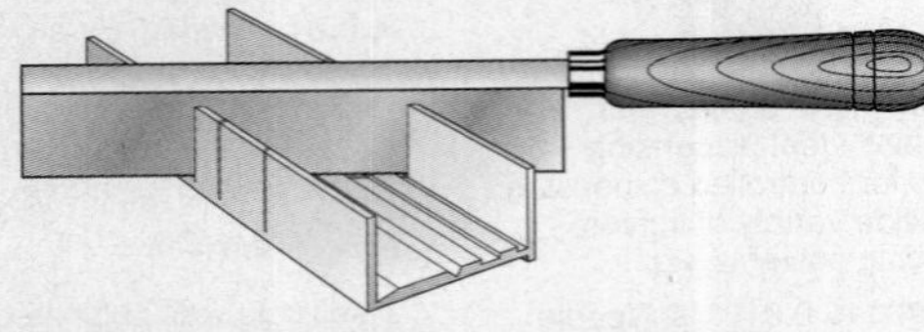

795-35241 Set Includes 4 Extra Blades **15.95** *NEW*
Aluminum miter box with unique narrow slots to maintain accurate cuts. Cuts material up to 2" wide and 7/8" thick at 90, 45, and 30 angles. Comes with 42 tpi razor saw.

795-240 Thin Slot - .140" Miter Box Only **10.95**
795-245 Medium Slot - .025" Miter Box Only **10.95**

RETRACTABLE KNIFE SET

795-39850 4.95
Knife with #11 blade in handle and five additional #11 blades.

SOFT GRIP KNIFE

795-39910 With Fine Point Blade **3.95**
Put an end to blisters with the Soft Grip Knife. The soft grip handle provides extra comfort and control, and features an anti-roll design. Perfect for cutting wood, paper, plastic film, balsa wood, vinyl, foamboard and rubber.

795-39920 Set Includes 4 Extra Blades **5.95**

ULTRA THIN SAWS EA 3.95

The thinnest razor saws available with ultra thin .008" thick blades. #150 is ideal for super fine cuts in wood and plastic without splitting or ragged edges. #200 offers longer wear in metal cutting applications. Both have shorter cutting depths plus steel backs for greater blade stability.

795-150 42 TPI
795-200 32 TPI
795-35050 52 TPI

24 TPI WOODCRAFT SAW

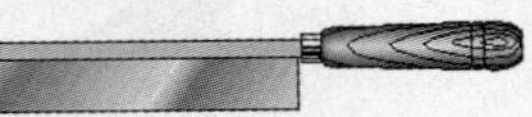

795-300 4.95
.015" thick blade, 6-1/2" long, 7/8" cutting depth.

32 & 42 TPI UNIVERSAL SAWS

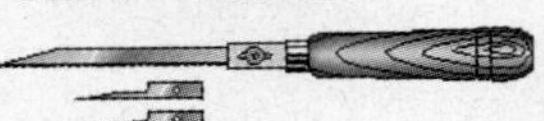

795-500 5.50
A good all-purpose saw. .022" thick blade, 6-1/2" long, 1-3/16" cutting depth.

795-35550 Extra Fine Cuts **5.50**
A good all-purpose saw for model and miniature making and smooth precision cuts in balsa and other wood, plastic, copper or brass.

SABER SAW SET

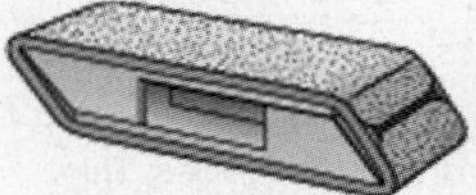

795-450 5.95
.022" thick blade, 4-1/2" long, 3/8" wide. Ideal for large inside cuts and for cutting through thick material. Set also includes #36408 "push" and the #36406 "pull" miniature keyhole saber blades.

MINI SANDING BLOCK

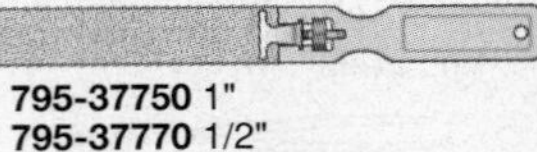

795-37730 pkg(5) **3.95**

1" & 1/2" SANDING STICKS EA 8.95

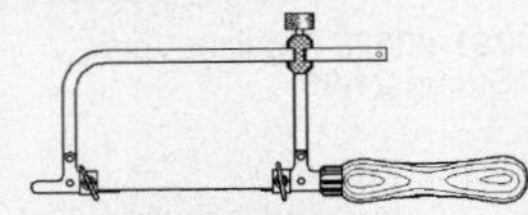

795-37750 1"
795-37770 1/2"

JEWELER'S SAW

795-35750 Adjustable Jeweler's Saw **12.95**

JEWELER'S SAW BLADES EA 2.50

795-36475 .019 x .0095" x 61 TPI
795-36476 .020 x .010" x 56 TPI
795-36480 .028 x .013" x 43 TPI

JUNIOR HACK SAW

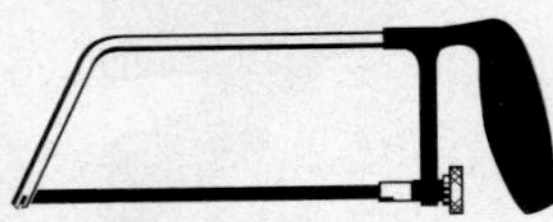

795-650 7.95
Has a well balanced and sturdy, solid, metal frame with comfortable handle grip. Several different blades can be easily inserted and tightened securely in this frame using the tensioning screw.

HOBBY CLAMPS BERNA ASSEMBLERS®

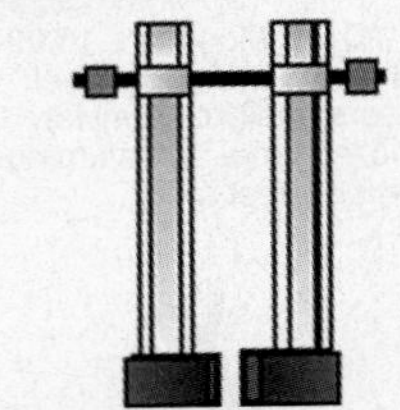

795-38710 4.95
Assembled, 3" beam with 3" jaws.

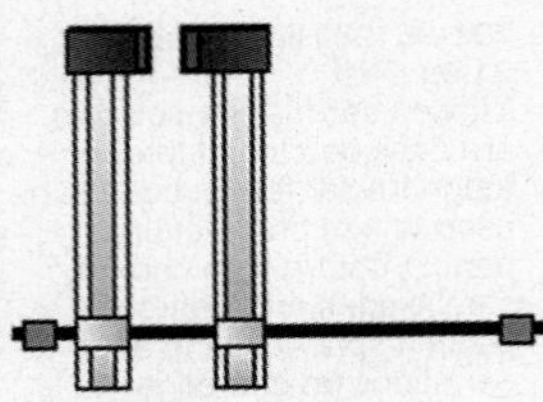

795-38720 5.95
8" beam with 3" jaws.

HOBBY CLAMP ASSORTMENT

795-38725 Hobby Clamp Assortment **16.95**
Includes two 8", one 3" clamps and Connector Strip.

SPIRAL HAND DRILL W/SPRING

795-37160 9.95
For use with small, wire sized drills from #80 to #70. Push ring down to turn drill. Spring return makes drilling easier and faster.

3" TRIANGLE

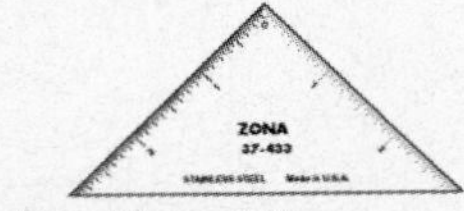

795-37433 6.95

SWIVEL HEAD PIN VISE

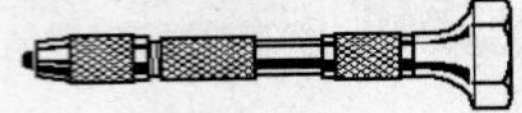

795-37140 6.95
Comes with two double-ended collets in the handle with 0 to .125" range. Holds any small tool with round shank: drills, burs, reamers, taps, needles, scribers, etc.

TOOL HOLDER W/TWO CHUCKS

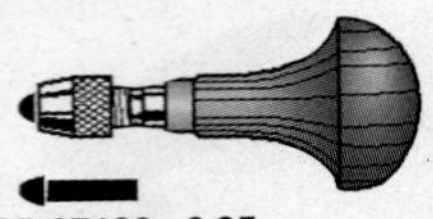

795-37130 6.95
Includes two collets with capacity range of 0 to .118" diameter. Ideal for use with small tools including: chisels, files, reamers, beading tools, burs and gravers.

HANGING DRILL SET

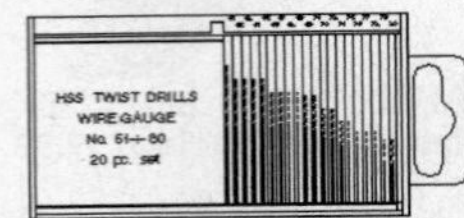

795-37150 20 Pieces **25.95**
Contains high speed twist drills in wire gauge #61 through #80, one each. For use in above tools.

TWEEZER SET

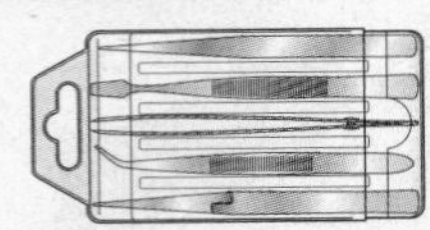

795-37540 21.95 *NEW*
A selection of five quality tweezers for handling small objects. Includes one each of fine point, flat blade, slide lock, curved point and cross locking tweezers.

L-SQUARE 3" X 4"

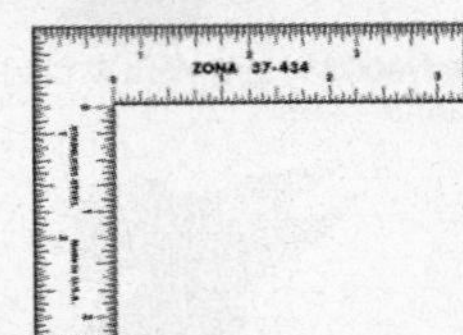

795-37434 6.95

SCRATCH BUILDING

It seems the amount of stuff you have always expands to fill the available space. And if you think your attic, basement or garage is bad, consider the average railroad shop!

Now it's one thing if the company likes one brand of locomotives - you can maintain a pretty basic inventory of parts. But like most shortlines, the Fundy Northern fixes a wide range of older motive power and just doesn't have the money to throw much away.

So it all has to be kept somewhere, usually in a vacant spot along the roundhouse walls. But there comes a day when there simply is no more space. You toss what you can, sell some of it for scrap and start filling out the requisition forms to get a proper storage building built.

After meeting with everyone from accountant to insurance agent, the shop foreman of the Fundy Northern has successfully convinced them of the need for a new supply building. (We hear he just took them on tour through the storage areas, making sure to pass close to those oily engine parts and dirty shelves. His overalls were fine, but those three-piece suits. . . .)

Work started the next day and has progressed nicely. The bridges and building crew have plenty to do before it's finished, but it should be a long time until this building is too small to hold everything!

Bob Boudreau's modular layout is the setting for this Campbell kit shown under construction. Along with all of the interior braces, trusses and wood components, board lumber, home-made ladder and sawhorses can be seen. The roundhouse was scratchbuilt, and a converted low-nose Athearn GP9 can be seen idling nearby.

Models and Photo by Bob Boudreau

WALTHERS™

Walthers provides a complete range of miniature hardware for hobby projects. Wood, machine and nylon screws, plus hex nuts and washers in assorted sizes are available for your special needs. Look for the Walthers Miniature Screw display at your Dealer. (Machine and wood screws may be brass or brass plated.) Fine detail work is easier with the right tools. Walthers offers miniature drill bits from size 43 to 80, pin vises, the Screw Sticker and more.

SIZE INFORMATION

SIZE	00-90	0-80	1-72	2-56
Screw Body Diameter	.047	.060	.073	.086
Clearance Drill Number	.55	52	48	43
Tap Drill Number	.61	55	53	50
Hex Head Across Flat	.078	.097	.109	.123
Height	.042	.042	.055	.064
Round Head Diameter	.089	.108	.136	.164
Height	.041	.047	.055	.065
Flat Head Diameter	.089	.108	.136	.164
Height	.024	.035	.043	.051

HARDWARE

ROUND HEAD BRASS MACHINE SCREWS PKG EA 2.79

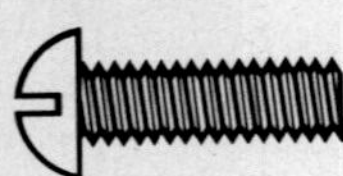

00-90
947-1002 3/16 x.047" pkg(12)
947-1003 1/4 x .047" pkg(12)
947-1005 3/8 x .047" pkg(12)
947-1006 1/2 x .047" pkg(10)

0-80
947-1012 3/16 x .060" pkg(16)
947-1013 1/4 x .060" pkg(16)
947-1015 3/8 x .060" pkg(12)
947-1016 1/2 x .060" pkg(10)

1-72
947-1022 3/16 x .073" pkg(16)
947-1023 1/4 x .073" pkg(16)
947-1025 3/8 x .073" pkg(12)
947-1026 1/2 x .073" pkg(10)

2-56
947-1032 3/16 x .086" pkg(16)
947-1033 1/4 x .086" pkg(16)
947-1035 3/8 x .086" pkg(12)
947-1036 1/2 x .086" pkg(10)

HEX HEAD BRASS MACHINE SCREWS PKG EA 2.79

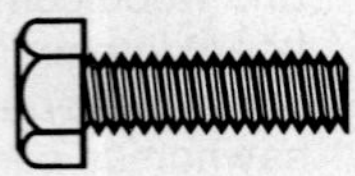

00-90
947-1122 3/16 x.047" pkg(12)
947-1123 1/4 x .047" pkg(12)
947-1125 3/8 x .047" pkg(12)
947-1126 1/2 x .047" pkg(10)

0-80
947-1132 3/16 x .060" pkg(12)
947-1133 1/4 x .060" pkg(12)
947-1135 3/8 x .060" pkg(12)
947-1136 1/2 x .060" pkg(10)

1-72
947-1142 3/16 x .073" pkg(12)
947-1143 1/4 x .073" pkg(12)
947-1145 3/8 x .073" pkg(12)
947-1146 1/2 x .073" pkg(10)

2-56
947-1152 3/16 x .086" pkg(12)
947-1153 1/4 x .086" pkg(12)
947-1155 3/8 x .086" pkg(12)
947-1156 1/2 x .086" pkg(10)

ROUND HEAD NYLON MACHINE SCREWS PKG EA 2.79

947-1163 1-72 1/4 x .073" pkg(12)
947-1177 2-56 5/8 x .086" pkg(12)
947-1188 4-40 3/4 x .112" pkg(12)

SELF TAPPING STEEL SHEET METAL SCREWS PKG EA 2.79

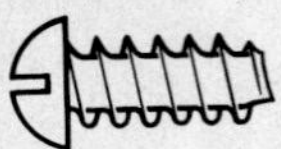

#2 PKG(24)
947-1189 3/16 x .088"
947-1190 1/4 x .088"
947-1191 1/2 x .088"

FLAT HEAD BRASS MACHINE SCREWS PKG EA 2.79

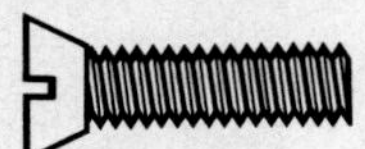

00-90
947-1042 3/16 x .047" pkg(12)
947-1043 1/4 x .047" pkg(12)
947-1045 3/8 x .047" pkg(12)
947-1046 1/2 x .047" pkg(10)

0-80
947-1052 3/16 x.060" pkg(16)
947-1053 1/4 x .060" pkg(16)
947-1055 3/8 x .060" pkg(12)
947-10561/2 x .060" pkg(10)

1-72
947-1062 3/16 x.073" pkg(16)
947-1063 1/4 x .073" pkg(16)
947-1065 3/8 x .073" pkg(12)
947-1066 1/2 x .073" pkg(10)

2-56
947-1072 3/16 x.086" pkg(16)
947-1073 1/4 x .086" pkg(16)
947-1075 3/8 x .086" pkg(12)
947-1076 1/2 x .086" pkg(10)

WOOD SCREWS-BRASS OR BRASS PLATED PKG EA 2.79

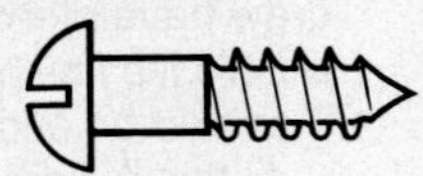

#0 PKG(24)
947-1195 3/8 x.060"

#1 PKG(24)
947-1196 3/8" x .073"
947-1197 1/2 x .073"

#2 PKG(24)
947-1198 #2 3/8 x .086"
947-1199#2 1/2 x .086"

HEX NUTS PKG EA 2.79

BRASS PKG(12)
947-1250 00-90 (.040 x 5/64")
947-1251 0-80 (.050 x 5/32")
947-1252 1-72 (.062 x 7/64")
947-1253 2-56 (.072 x 1/8")

NYLON PKG(12)
947-1255 2-56 (.075 x 3/16")
947-1256 4-40 (.100 x 1/4")

WASHERS

BRASS PKG(16) EA 2.79
947-1270 #00
(O.D=105" I.D=060" .020" Thick)
947-1271 #0
(O.D=125" I.D=068" .020" Thick)
947-1272 #1
(O.D=156" I.D=084" .025" Thick)
947-1273 #2
(O.D=188 I.D=094" .025" Thick)

TOOLS

DRILL BITS PKG(2) EA 1.98

947-43 .089
947-48 .076
947-50 .070
947-52 .064
947-53 .060
947-55 .052
947-56 .047
947-57 .043
947-58 .042
947-60 .040

DRILL BITS PKG(2) EA 2.29

947-61 .039
947-62 .038
947-63 .037
947-64. 036
947-65 .035
947-66 .033
947-67 .032
947-68 .031
947-69 .0292
947-70 .028
947-71 .026
947-72 .025
947-73 .024
947-74 .0225
947-75 .021
947-76 .020
947-77 .018
947-78 .016
947-79 .0145
947-80 .0135

DRILL SET & ACCESSORIES

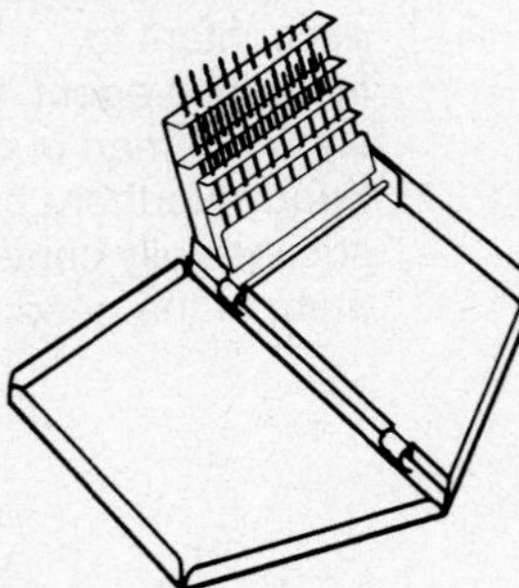

949-659 Set of 20 Bits w/Case **18.98**
Set of 20 hard-to-find #61-80 drill bits, conveniently organized in a metal case.

949-660 Drill Case Only **4.98**
A neat and safe way to store drill bits between projects.

WRENCHES EA 3.98

Will fit Brass Hex Nuts & Hex Head screws.
947-1321 #00
947-1322 #0
947-1323 #1
947-1324 #2

949-662 Wrench Set pkg(4) **14.98**
Includes one each #1321-1324.

WORK HOLDER

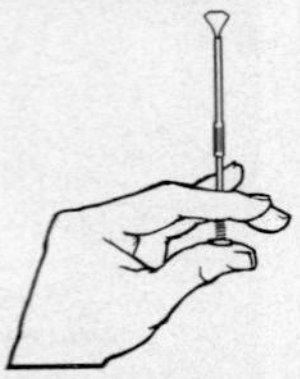

949-519 Screw Sticker **5.98**
Get a firm grip on tiny screws, parts and more. One-handed operation makes the miniature fingers an extension of your own.

PIN-VISE

949-664 Double Ended **7.98**
Includes two single end collets. Holds bits from #42 to #70.

TAP & DIE HOLDER

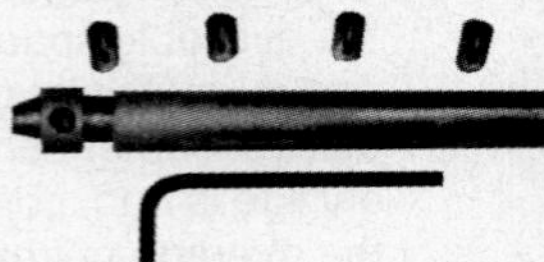

949-663 Tap Holder **14.98**
Holds taps and dies securely while cutting threads. Includes storage case, holder, Allen wrench and collets for 00-90, 0-80, 1-72 and 2-56 taps.

TAPS EA 2.79

947-1301 00-90
947-1302 0-80
947-1303 1-72
947-1304 2-56

POURABLE METAL

TEMP-LOW

949-525 3oz (84g) **4.98**
An easy way to add weight to any model, Temp-Low™ melts in hot water (158° to 190° F). It's ideal for brass locos, as you just melt and pour in without fear of unsoldering detail. You can also make custom castings in cardboard, rubber or plaster molds. And it makes a great filler to support tubing while bending.

WALTHERS™

ADHESIVE

FIX IT FOREVER WITH GOO®!

•ALL PURPOSE ADHESIVE
GOO is the permanent rubber base adhesive that grips most anything. It never lets go.

•FAST SETTING JOINTS
Easy contact action opens new possibilities for fast-setting joints with any material.

GOO is the perfect adhesive for building or repairing jobs on your layout and around the house!

The easy contact action of GOO produces fast-setting joints with any material. GOO works with all types of metals (including steel, brass, aluminum, copper and others.) plus items like wood, plastic, cardboard, china, leather, vinyl, ceramics, paper, concrete and many more, on any smooth or porous surface.

GOO is a permanent rubber base adhesive that's shockproof, waterproof and crack proof–it's as flexible as rubber. Joints won't crack when flexed back and forth, won't break loose when the temperature changes and won't weaken when wet or damp. It sticks forever! **Dealers MUST order multiples of 6**

904-299 GOO® Adhesive, Large Tube 1-1/8 oz **2.98**

PAINTING ACCESSORIES

MASKING LIQUID

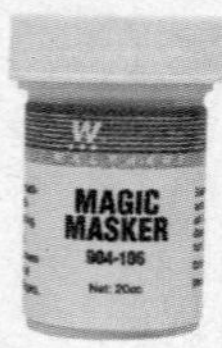

904-106 Magic Masker (20cc) **2.98**
Get professional results when you mask your models the easy way! Magic Masker makes quick work of covering odd shaped or small areas, such as windows, without the time and trouble of cutting and fitting tape. Brush it on the area to be masked off and allow to dry. Then spray your color, let dry and peel off Magic Masker. Works on plastic, wood, metal, paint, chrome and silver. **Dealers MUST order multiples of 12.**

DECAL SETTING SOLUTION

904-470 Solvaset 2oz **2.98**
Solvaset softens the decal film so it snuggles down on the surface, over rivets and other details without hiding them. Also eliminates air bubbles, white spots and draping. **Dealers MUST order multiples of 6.**

Daily New Arrival Updates! Visit Walthers Web site at

www.walthers.com

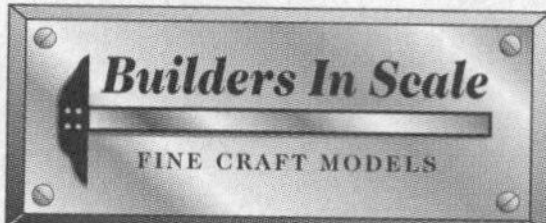

SHINGLES

VICTORIAN-PAPER EA 4.59

Natural wood color, laser-cut on self-adhesive material. Each package covers approximately 14 square inches.

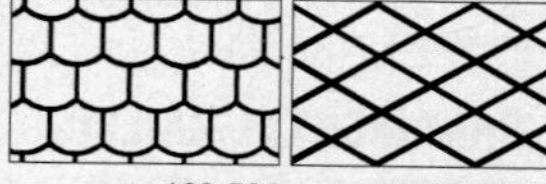

169-504 169-505

169-504 Curved, "Fishscale"
169-505 Diamond

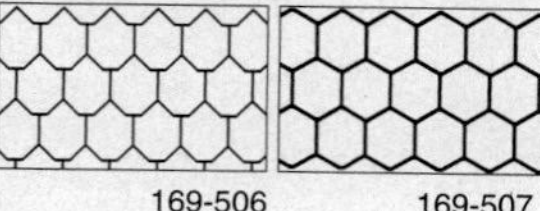

169-506 169-507

169-506 Octagonal
169-507 Hexagonal

TRUEWOOD™ EA 8.98

169-508 ShakeShingles
Laser-cut from real wood and self-adhesive for easy installation. Each package covers over 15 square inches, depending on the amount of reveal.

SLATE EA 4.98

Laser-cut, self-adhesive, authentically textured and colored slate shingles. Each package covers over 12 square inches. These easy-to-install shingles add dimension and realism to a structure's roof.

169-509 Quarry Gray
169-510 Slate Green
169-511 Shale Black

SHAKE

169-513 **5.98**
Self-adhesive strips.

METAL SIDING PKG(6) EA 3.98 (UNLESS NOTED)

Ribbed seam, 7-1/2" long. Dimension indicates scale width.

169-500 4'
169-501 8'
169-502 12'
169-512 12' (Copper) **4.98**

TAR PAPER EA 3.49

This prototypically thin material has two sides — the weathered color on one side, black on the other — which can be used to model composition tar papers. Each package has over 55 square inches (#169-264 has over 75 square inches).

169-260 Faded Gray/Black
169-261 Red/Black
169-262 Worn Green/Black
169-263 Dusty Blue/Black
169-264 Assorted 4 Colors **4.59**

ALPINE DIVISION SCALE MODELS

TIN SIDING SHEETS

.010" CORRUGATED
700-100 4 x 12" pkg(6) **7.50**
700-101 2 x 12" pkg(6) **5.00**

.010" PLAIN
700-102 4 x 12" pkg(6) **5.50**

90° ANGLE
700-104 1/8 x 12" pkg(6) **3.75**

ALUMINUM PAPER

700-1001 Corrugated, 4 x 11-1/2" pkg(6) **3.65**

Information STATION

Vocabulary

Air Monkey - air brake repair man

Alley - clear track in railroad yard

Ashcat - locomotive fireman

Bailing Wire Mechanic - a man of little mechanical ability

Ball of Fire - a fast run

Band Wagon - pay car from which wages are handed out to railroad employees

Bend the Iron - change the position of a switch, also called bend the rust or bend the rail

Big Hole - emergency application of air brake valve, causing a quick stop

Big Hook - wrecking crane

Bird Cage - brakeman or switchman's lantern

Black Diamonds - company coal

Black Snake - solid train of loaded coal cars

Blow Smoke - brag

Board - fixed signal regulating railroad traffic

Bootlegger - train that runs over more than one railroad

Boomer - drifter who went from one railroad job to another

Boxcar Tourist - hobo

Bull - railroad policeman

Calliope - steam locomotive

Can - tank car

Car Catcher - rear brakeman

Carry a White Feather - show a plume of steam over the safety valves of the engine

Casey Jones - any locomotive engineer, especially a fast one

Catwalk - plank walk on top of boxcars

Chambermaid - machinist in roundhouse

IMPORTED FROM GERMANY
BY WALTHERS

PLASTIC SHEETS EA 4.99

Ideal for all kinds of scratchbuilding projects, each pack includes two sheets measuring 4 x 6". Thickness varies from 1/32 to .039.

186-2800 186-2801

186-2800 Wood Flooring (Dark Brown)
186-2801 Wood Flooring (Natural Finish)

186-2805 186-2806

186-2805 Cobblestones
186-2806 Historic Cobblestones (Gray)

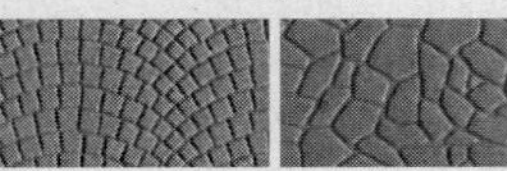

186-2810 186-2815

186-2810 Curved Cobblestones
186-2815 Random Stone Paving

186-2825 186-2826

186-2825 Masonry Slabs (Sandstone)
186-2826 Masonry Slabs (Brick Red)

186-2830 186-2835

186-2830 Sidewalk Paving
186-2835 Ribbed Metal Sheet (Silver)
186-2836 Ribbed Metal Sheet (Black)

186-2840 186-2845

186-2840 Window Glazing
186-2845 Artificial Paving Stone

186-2855 186-2856

186-2855 Corrugated Metal Sheet (Gray)
186-2856 Corrugated Sheet (Translucent)

186-2867 Wall Tiles (Brick Red)

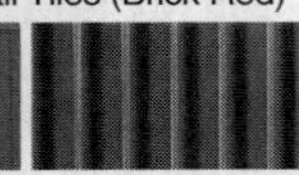

186-2827 186-2850

186-2827 Brick Wall Sheet
186-2850 Sheet Piling

TUBING/RODS

Brass tube and angles are 12" long, unless noted; dimensions shown are external diameter x wall thickness in millimeters. Dealers MUST order multiples of 10.

Limited Quantity Available on All Items

RECTANGULAR TUBE

186-3732 2.0 x 4.0 x 0.30 **2.90**

U-SECTION

186-3738 2.0 x 2.0 x 2.0 x 0.30 **2.05**
186-3740 3.0 x 3.0 x 3.0 x 0.30 **2.25**
186-3742 4.0 x 4.0 x 4.0 x 0.30 **2.40**

T-SECTION

186-3774 4.0 x 4.0 x 0.50 **5.75**
186-3776 2.5 x 2.5 x 0.40 **3.29**

SQUARE TUBE

186-3716 1.5 x 1.5 x 0.30 **2.45**
186-3718 2.0 x 2.0 x 0.30 **2.35**
186-3720 3.0 x 3.0 x 0.30 **2.90**
186-3722 4.0 x 4.0 x 0.30 **2.90**

HEXAGON TUBE

186-3750 3.0 x 0.30 **2.45**
186-3752 4.0 x 0.30 **2.60**

ANGLE

186-3763 3.0 x 3.0 x 0.50 **3.30**
186-3764 4.0 x 4.0 x 0.50 **5.45**
186-3766 2.5 x 2.5 x 0.40 **3.20**
186-3767 3.5 x 3.5 x 0.30 **3.85**

H-SECTION

186-3781 2.5 x 1.5 x 0.50 **3.65**
186-3782 3.0 x 2.0 x 0.50 **3.80**

FALLER

SIDEWALK TILES

272-597 9.99
Two large sidewalk tiles that can be divided into 8 footway tiles, 4 footway sheets. 16 separate edging strips are included.

ORNAMENTAL RAILING

272-598 9.99
3" 72cm long decorative railing for bridges, fences, etc.

Hob-Bits

by Woodland Scenics

Hob-Bits® are made of brass and are available in four small sizes.

FILLISTER HEAD SCREWS

00-90 PKG(5) EA 1.49
785-821 1/8 x .046"
785-822 1/4 x .046"
785-823 3/8 x .046"
785-824 1/2 x .046"

0-80 PKG(5) EA 1.49
785-825 1/8 x .058"
785-826 1/4 x .058"
785-827 3/8 x .058"
785-828 1/2 x .058"

0-72 PKG(5) EA 1.49
785-829 1/8 x .072"
785-830 1/4 x .072"
785-831 3/8 x .072"
785-832 1/2 x .072"

2-56 PKG(5) EA 1.49
785-833 1/8 x .085"
785-834 1/4 x .085"
785-835 3/8 x .085"
785-836 1/2 x .085"

FLAT HEAD SCREWS

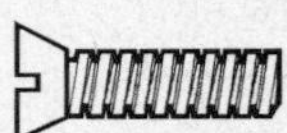

00-90 PKG(5) EA 1.49
785-841 1/8 x .046"
785-842 1/4 x .046"
785-843 3/8 x .046"
785-844 1/2 x .046"

0-80 PKG(5) EA 1.49
785-845 1/8 x .058"
785-846 1/4 x .058"
785-847 3/8 x .058"
785-848 1/2 x .058"

1-72 PKG(5) EA 1.49
785-849 1/8 x .072"
785-850 1/4 x .072"
785-851 3/8 x .072"
785-852 1/2 x .072"

2-56 PKG(5) EA 1.49
785-853 1/8 x .085"
785-854 1/4 x .085"
785-855 3/8 x .085"
785-856 1/2 x .085"

HEX HEAD SCREWS

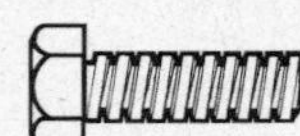

00-90 PKG(5) EA 1.49
785-861 1/8 x .046"
785-862 1/4 x .046"
785-863 3/8 x .046"
785-864 1/2 x .046"

0-80 PKG(5) EA 1.49
785-865 1/8 x .058"
785-866 1/4 x .058"
785-867 3/8 x .058"
785-868 1/2 x .058"

1-72 PKG(5) EA 1.49
785-869 1/8 x .072"
785-870 1/4 x .072"
785-871 3/8 x .072"
785-872 1/2 x .072"

2-56 PKG(5) EA 1.49
785-873 1/8 x .085"
785-874 1/4 x .085"
785-875 3/8 x .085"
785-876 1/2 x .085"

ROUND HEAD SCREWS

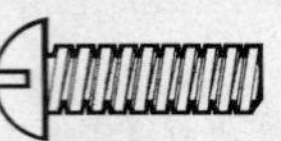

00-90 PKG(5) EA 1.49
785-801 1/8 x .046"
785-802 1/4 x .046"
785-803 3/8 x .046"
785-804 1/2 x .046"

0-80 PKG(5) EA 1.49
785-805 1/8 x .058"
785-806 1/4 x .058"
785-807 3/8 x .058"
785-808 1/2 x .058"

1-72 PKG(5) EA 1.49
785-809 1/8 x .072"
785-810 1/4 x .072"
785-811 3/8 x .072"
785-812 1/2 x .072"

2-56 PKG(5) EA 1.49
785-813 1/8 x .085"
785-814 1/4 x .085"
785-815 1/2 x .085"
785-816 1/2 x .085"

HEX NUTS

PKG(5) EA 1.49
785-881 00-90
785-882 0-80
785-883 1-72
785-884 2-56

WASHERS

PKG(5) EA 1.49
785-891 00-90
785-892 0-80
785-893 1-72
785-894 2-56

DIES EA 29.98

785-877 00-90
785-878 0-80
785-879 1-72
785-880 2-56

WRENCHES EA 4.49

785-885 00-90
785-886 0-80
785-887 1-72
785-888 2-56

TAPS EA 3.29

785-895 00-90
785-896 0-80
785-897 1-72
785-898 2-56

evergreen scale models

Styrene is one of the most common modeling plastics. It can be used to simulate concrete, metal or wooden surfaces and is easily cut and sanded to virtually any shape. When cutting sheets, simply score with a sharp knife, then "break" on the scored line. Small strips and very thin sheets can be cut through. Parts can be joined with plastic solvents, while epoxies and CA adhesives can be used to join painted parts or other materials. Before brush painting with Floquil, Scalecoat or other lacquers, a primer coat of Floquil Barrier or Scalecoat Shieldcoat should be applied to prevent the paint from "attacking" the plastic.

SIDING

Duplicate many common types of building siding with these opaque white sheets. Each is pre-scribed to match different widths of lumber.

V-GROOVE

Used on freight and passenger cars, railroad, commercial and residential buildings. Many 19th- and early 20th-century structures had panels of v-groove siding applied in horizontal, vertical and diagonal patterns, or in combination with clapboard and novelty siding for decorative effects. * Part dimension indicates spacing.

6 x 12" SHEET EA 3.29

.020" THICK

269-2025 .025"
269-2030 .030"
269-2040 .040"
269-2050 .050"
269-2060 .060"
269-2080 .080"
269-2100 .100"
269-2125 .125"

.040" THICK

269-4030 .030"
269-4040 .040"
269-4050 .050"
269-4060 .060"
269-4080 .080"
269-4100 .100"
269-4125 .125"
269-4188 .188"
269-4250 .250"

12 x 24 SHEETS EA 11.60

.020" THICK SHEET

269-12025 .025"
269-12030 .030"
269-12040 .040"
269-12050 .050"
269-12060 .060"
269-12080 .080"
269-12100 .100"
269-12125 .125"

.040" THICK SHEET

269-14030 .030"
269-14040 .040"
269-14050 .050"
269-14060 .060"
269-14080 .080"
269-14100 .100"
269-14125 .125"
269-14188 .188"
269-14250 .250"

NOVELTY

Many buildings of the mid 19th to early 20th century used novelty siding, also known as shiplap or drop siding. It consisted of overlapping boards, with a rabbet in the bottom of each board, overlapping in the round cove on the top of the board below. * Part dimension indicates spacing.

6 x 12 x.040" SHEET EA 3.29

269-4062 .060"
5-1/4 HO Scale inches, 9-1/2 N Scale inches.

269-4083 .083"
7-1/4 HO Scale inches.

269-4109 .109"
9-1/4 HO Scale inches.

269-4150 .150"

BOARD & BATTEN

* Part dimension indicates spacing.

6 x 12 x .040" SHEET EA 3.29

269-4542 .075
269-4543 .100
269-4544 .125

12 x 24 x .040" SHEET EA 11.60

269-14542 .075
269-14543 .100
269-14544 .125

CLAPBOARD

One of the most common sidings (often called lap siding) is a prominent feature of many wooden railroad buildings as well as city, town and farm structures of all kinds. * Part dimension indicates spacing.

6 x 12 x .040" SHEET EA 3.29

269-4031 .030"
269-4041 .040"
269-4051 .050"
269-4061 .060"
269-4081 .080"
269-4101 .100"

12 x 24 x .040" SHEET EA 11.60

269-14031 .030"
269-14041 .040"
269-14051 .050"
269-14061 .060"
269-14081 .080"
269-14101 .100"

CORRUGATED METAL

* Part dimension indicates spacing.

6 x 12 x .040" SHEETS EA 3.29

269-4525 .030"
269-4526 .040"
269-4527 .060"
269-4528 .080"
269-4529 .100"
269-4530 .125"

12 x 24 x .040" SHEETS EA 11.60

269-14525 .030"
269-14526 .040"
269-14527 .060"
269-14528 .080"
269-14529 .100"
269-14530 .125"

PASSENGER CAR

Each 6 x 12" sheet has grooves running the entire length to eliminate splicing.

269-3025 .030" **3.29**
Grooved with 2-1/4" scale spacing, thickness matches Grandt Line molded windows and doors.

FREIGHT CAR EA 3.29

269-2020 .020" N
269-2037 .020" HO
269-4037 .040" HO

STRIPS

DIMENSIONAL EA 1.79

14" long, opaque white strips.

.010" THICK PKG(10)

269-100 .020"
269-101 .030"
269-102 .040"
269-103 .060"
269-104 .080"
269-105 .100"
269-106 .125"
269-107 .156"
269-108 .188"
269-109 .250"

.015" THICK PKG(10)

269-110 .020"
269-111 .030"
269-112 .040"
269-113 .060"
269-114 .080"
269-115 .100"
269-116 .125"
269-117 .156"
269-118 .188"
269-119 .250"

.020" THICK PKG(10)

269-120 .020"
269-121 .030"
269-122 .040"
269-123 .060"
269-124 .080"
269-125 .100"
269-126 .125"
269-127 .156"
269-128 .188"
269-129 .250"

.030" THICK PKG(10)

269-131 .030"
269-132 .040"
269-133 .060"
269-134 .080"
269-135 .100"
269-136 .125"
269-137 .156"
269-138 .188"
269-139 .250"

.040" THICK PKG(10)

269-142 .040"
269-143 .060"
269-144 .080"
269-145 .100"
269-146 .125"
269-147 .156"
269-148 .188"
269-149 .250"

.060" THICK

269-153 .060" pkg(10)
269-154 .080" pkg(10)
269-155 .100" pkg(10)
269-156 .125" pkg(10)
269-157 .156" pkg(9)
269-158 .188" pkg(9)
269-159 .250" pkg(8)

.080" THICK

269-164 .080" pkg(9)
269-165 .100" pkg(8)
269-166 .125" pkg(8)
269-167 .156" pkg(8)
269-168 .188" pkg(8)
269-169 .250" pkg(7)

.100" THICK

269-175 .100" pkg(8)
269-176 .125" pkg(7)
269-177 .156" pkg(7)
269-178 .188" pkg(7)
269-179 .250" pkg(6)

.125" THICK

269-186 .125" pkg(6)
269-187 .156" pkg(6)
269-188 .188" pkg(6)
269-189 .250" pkg(5)

SQUARE EA 1.79

269-196 3/16 x 3/16" pkg(4)
269-199 1/4 x 1/4" pkg(3)

HO SCALE PKG(10) EA 1.79

Dimensions shown are HO Scale inches. Strips are 14" long, opaque white and packed in resealable poly bags.

269-8102 1 x 2"
269-8103 1 x 3"
269-8104 1 x 4"
269-8106 1 x 6"
269-8108 1 x 8"
269-8110 1 x 10"
269-8112 1 x 12"
269-8202 2 x 2"
269-8203 2 x 3"
269-8204 2 x 4"
269-8206 2 x 6"
269-8208 2 x 8"
269-8210 2 x 10"
269-8212 2 x 12"
269-8404 4 x 4"
269-8406 4 x 6"
269-8408 4 x 8"
269-8410 4 x 10"
269-8412 4 x 12"
269-8606 6 x 6"
269-8608 6 x 8"
269-8610 6 x 10"
269-8612 6 x 12"

STRUCTURAL SHAPES

14" actual length, molded in opaque white styrene.

STYRENE SHAPE ASSORTMENTS PKG(48) EA 85.00

269-46 Update for Floor Rack
269-47 Update for Counter Displays
Two packages each of 24 new sizes.

ANGLES EA 1.79

269-291 .060" pkg(4)
269-292 .080" pkg(4)
269-293 .100" pkg(4)
269-294 .125" pkg(4)
269-295 .156" pkg(3)
269-296 .188" pkg(3)
269-297 .250" pkg(3)

CHANNELS EA 1.79

269-261 .060" pkg(4)
269-262 .080" pkg(4)
269-263 .100" pkg(4)
269-264 .125" pkg(4)
269-265 .156" pkg(4)
269-266 .188" pkg(3)
269-267 .250" pkg(3)
269-268 .312" pkg(3)

H-COLUMNS EA 1.79

269-281 .060" pkg(4)
269-282 .080" pkg(4)
269-283 .100" pkg(4)
269-284 .125" pkg(3)
269-285 .156" pkg(3)
269-286 .188" pkg(3)
269-287 .250" pkg(2)

I-BEAMS EA 1.79

269-271 .060" pkg(4)
269-272 .080" pkg(4)
269-273 .100" pkg(4)
269-274 .125" pkg(4)
269-275 .156" pkg(3)
269-276 .188" pkg(3)
269-277 .250" pkg(3)
269-278 .312" pkg(2)
269-279 .375" pkg(2)

ROD & TUBING

Each piece 14" actual length, molded in white styrene.

269-217 Rod & Tube Assortment pkg(7) **1.79**

ROUND EA 1.79

269-210 .030" pkg(10)
269-211 .040" pkg(10)
269-212 .080" pkg(6)
269-213 .100" pkg(5)
269-214 1/8" pkg(4)
269-218 .020" pkg(10)
269-219 .025" pkg(10)
269-220 .035" pkg(10)
269-221 .047" pkg(10)
269-222 .062" pkg(8)

Evergreen Scale Models

ROUND TUBING EA 1.79

269-223 .093" pkg(6)
269-224 1/8" pkg(5)
269-225 5/32" pkg(4)
269-226 3/16" pkg(4)
269-227 7/32" pkg(4)
269-228 1/4" pkg(3)
269-229 9/32" pkg(3)
269-230 5/16" pkg(3)
269-231 11/32" pkg(3)
269-232 3/8" pkg(2)
269-234 7/16" pkg(2)
269-236 1/2" pkg(2)

HALF ROUND EA 1.79

269-240 .040" pkg(6)
269-241 .060" pkg(5)
269-242 .080" pkg(4)
269-243 .100" pkg(3)
269-244 1/8" pkg(3)

QUARTER ROUNDS EA 1.79

269-246 .030" pkg(5)
269-247 .040" pkg(5)
269-248 .060" pkg(4)
269-249 .080" pkg(3)
269-250 .100" pkg(3)

SQUARE TUBING EA 1.79

269-252 .125" pkg(3)
269-253 .187" pkg(3)
269-254 .250" pkg(3)
269-255 .312" pkg(2)
269-256 .375" pkg(2)

RECTANGULAR TUBING EA 1.79

269-257 .125 x .250" pkg(3)
269-258 .187 x .312" pkg(2)
269-259 .250 x .375" pkg(2)

STYRENE SHEETS

Part dimension indicates thickness.

WHITE 6 x 12" EA 1.99

269-9008 Assortment
Includes one each .010, .020 and .040"

269-9009 .005" pkg(3)
269-9010 .010" pkg(4)
269-9015 .015" pkg(3)
269-9020 .020" pkg(3)
269-9030 .030" pkg(2)
269-9040 .040" pkg(2)
269-9060 .060"
269-9080 .080"

11 x 14" EA 14.40

269-9210 .010" pkg(15)
269-9215 .015" pkg(12)
269-9220 .020" pkg(12)
269-9230 .030" pkg(8)
269-9240 .040" pkg(6)
269-9260 .060" pkg(4)
269-9280 .080" pkg(3)

12 x 24"

INDIVIDUAL SHEETS

269-19010 .010" **1.44**
269-19015 .015" **1.80**
269-19020 .020" **1.80**
269-19030 .030" **2.70**
269-19040 .040" **3.60**
269-19060 .060" **5.40**
269-19080 .080" **7.20**
269-19100 .100" **9.00**
269-19125 .125" **10.00**

MULTI-PACKS EA 21.60 (UNLESS NOTED)
Dealers MUST order in these quantities.

269-19010 .010" pkg(15)
269-19015 .015" pkg(12)
269-19020 .020" pkg(12)
269-19030 .030" pkg(8)
269-19040 .040" pkg(6)
269-19060 .060" pkg(4)
269-19080 .080" pkg(3)
269-19100 .100" pkg(2) **18.00**
269-19125 .125" pkg(2) **20.00**

SHEET ASSORTMENT

269-9002 Odds & Ends **4.69**
A scratchbuilder's delight–a full half pound (8oz) of sheet plastic in various thicknesses and lengths.

CLEAR EA 1.99

6 x 12"
269-9005 .005" pkg(3)
269-9006 .010" pkg(3)
269-9007 .015" pkg(2)

TILES

Scribed in squares to represent flooring. Opaque white sheets are .040" thick.

6 x 12" EA 3.29

269-4501 1/16" square
269-4502 1/12" square
269-4503 1/8" square
269-4504 1/6" square
269-4505 1/4" square
269-4506 1/3" square
269-4507 1/2" square

12 x 24" EA 11.60

269-14501 1/16" square
269-14502 1/12" square
269-14503 1/8" square
269-14504 1/6" square
269-14505 1/4" square
269-14506 1/3" square
269-14507 1/2" square

SIDEWALKS

Opaque white sheets are .040" thick, scribed in squares, just paint and cut to model sidewalks.

6 x 12" SHEET EA 3.29

269-4514 1/8" square
269-4515 3/16" square
269-4516 1/4" square
269-4517 3/8" square
269-4518 1/2" square

12 x 24" SHEET EA 11.60

269-14514 1/8" square
269-14515 3/16" square
269-14516 1/4" square
269-14517 3/8" square
269-14518 1/2" square

LADDER KITS

269-201 HO Scale (1/810) **1.79**
Features slotted stringers, makes 24" of ladder.

STANDING SEAM ROOFING

6 x 12" SHEET EA 4.69

With seam strips, measures .040" thick.

269-4521 3/16" square
269-4522 1/4" square
269-4523 3/8" square
269-4524 1/2" square

HANDBOOK

269-12 Styrene Handbook **1.00**

BUILDING MATERIAL

Embossed sheets are made of Vinylite plastic which is easily bent, scored and cut. The material is rigid enough to stand alone, but develops greater strength when glued to wood or cardstock backing. Dealers must order in multiples of six.

BRICK & BLOCK

340-1011 White (3-1/2 x 20") **2.50**
340-1013 White (8-1/4 x 20") **5.00**
340-1012 Red (3-1/2 x 20") **2.50**
340-1014 Red (8-1/4 x 20") **5.00**
340-1411 1" Scale Brick (5 1/4 x 20") **3.50**
340-1413 1" Scale Brick (8 1/4 x 20") **5.00**
340-2121 1/2" Scale Brick (8 x 20") **5.00**

340-1050 Cement Block (3-1/2 x 18") **2.50**

ROOFING

3-1/2 X 18" EA 2.50 (UNLESS NOTED)

340-1030

340-1040

340-1030 Asphalt Roofing
340-1040 Shake Roofing
340-2123 1/2" Scale Roof (8 x 18") **5.00**

STONE

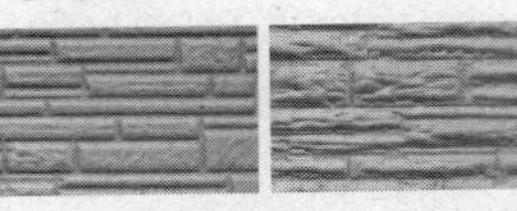
340-1020 340-1070

340-1020 Stone (3-1/2 x 18") **2.50**
340-1070 Lannon Stone (3-1/2 x 18") **2.50**

340-1220

340-2127

340-1220 Field Stone (3-1/2 x 18") **2.50**
340-2127 Pebblestone (5-1/8 x 14") **3.50**
340-142 1/2" Cut Stone (8 1/2 x 20") **5.00**

GRANDT LINE

PLASTIC RODS PKG(12) EA 4.75

8" long, flexible. Dimension indicates diameter.

300-3901 .010"
300-3902 .020"
300-3903 .030"
300-3904 .040"
300-3905 .050"

For Daily Product Information Click

www.walthers.com

KADEE®

STAINLESS STEEL HARDWARE

0-80 PKG(12) EA 2.45

380-1640 Nuts
380-1641 Washers

ROUND HEAD SCREWS
380-1643 1/8"
380-1646 1/4"
380-1648 3/8"
380-1649 1/2"

1-72 PKG(12) EA 2.45

380-1680 Nuts
380-1681 Washers

ROUND HEAD SCREWS
380-1683 1/8"
380-1686 1/4"
380-1688 3/8"
380-1689 1/2"

2-56 PKG(12) EA 2.45

380-1700 Nuts
380-1701 Washers

ROUND HEAD SCREWS
380-1703 1/8"
380-1706 1/4"
380-1708 3/8"
380-1709 1/2"
380-1710 5/8"
380-1711 3/4"

A complete selection of stripwood and scale lumber, cut to match common construction sizes

SCALE LUMBER

Dimensions are in HO Scale inches, (1 x 2", etc.) with actual length of 12 or 24" as noted.

1" EA 2.50

12" ACTUAL LENGTH
385-200 x 2" pkg(11)
385-201 x 3" pkg(11)
385-202 x 4" pkg(10)
385-203 x 6" pkg(10)
385-204 x 8" pkg(9)
385-205 x 10" pkg(8)
385-206 x 12" pkg(7)
385-207 x 14" pkg(7)
385-208 x 16" pkg(6)
385-209 x 18" pkg(6)
385-210 x 20" pkg(6)
385-212 x 24" pkg(6)

24" ACTUAL LENGTH
385-300 x 2" pkg(6)
385-301 x 3" pkg(6)
385-302 x 4" pkg(5)
385-303 x 6" pkg(5)
385-304 x 8" pkg(5)
385-305 x 10" pkg(4)
385-306 x 12" pkg(4)
385-307 x 14" pkg(4)
385-308 x 16" pkg(3)
385-309 x 18" pkg(3)
385-310 x 20" pkg(3)
385-311 x 22" pkg(3)
385-312 x 24" pkg(3)

2" EA 2.50

12" ACTUAL LENGTH
385-213 x 2" pkg(14)
385-214 x 3" pkg(14)
385-215 x 4" pkg(14)
385-216 x 6" pkg(14)
385-217 x 8" pkg(11)
385-218 x 10" pkg(11)
385-219 x 12" pkg(10)
385-220 x 14" pkg(10)
385-221 x 16" pkg(10)
385-222 x 18" pkg(10)
385-223 x 20" pkg(10)
385-224 x 22" pkg(8)
385-225 x 24" pkg(8)

24" ACTUAL LENGTH
385-313 x 2" pkg(7)
385-314 x 3" pkg(7)
385-315 x 4" pkg(7)
385-316 x 6" pkg(7)
385-317 x 8" pkg(6)
385-318 x 10" pkg(6)
385-319 x 12" pkg(6)
385-320 x 14" pkg(5)
385-321 x 16" pkg(5)
385-322 x 18" pkg(5)
385-323 x 20" pkg(5)
385-324 x 22" pkg(5)
385-325 x 24" pkg(5)

3" EA 2.50

12" ACTUAL LENGTH
385-226 x 3" pkg(14)
385-227 x 4" pkg(14)
385-228 x 6" pkg(12)
385-229 x 8" pkg(12)
385-230 x 9" pkg(11)
385-231 x 12" pkg(10)
385-233 x 10" pkg(11)
385-234 x 14" pkg(12)
385-235 x 16" pkg(12)
385-236 x 18" pkg(12)
385-237 x 20" pkg(12)

24" ACTUAL LENGTH
385-326 x 3" pkg(7)
385-328 x 6" pkg(6)
385-329 x 8" pkg(6)
385-330 x 9" pkg(6)
385-331 x 12" pkg(6)
385-333 x 10" pkg(6)
385-334 x 14" pkg(6)
385-335 x 16" pkg(6)
385-336 x 18" pkg(6)
385-337 x 20" pkg(6)

4" EA 2.50

12" ACTUAL LENGTH
385-238 x 4" pkg(14)
385-239 x 6" pkg(12)
385-240 x 8" pkg(11)
385-241 x 10" pkg(11)
385-242 x 12" pkg(10)
385-243 x 14" pkg(10)
385-244 x 16" pkg(8)
385-245 x 18" pkg(8)
385-246 x 20" pkg(8)
385-247 x 22" pkg(8)
385-248 x 24" pkg(6)

24" ACTUAL LENGTH
385-338 x 4" pkg(7)
385-339 x 6" pkg(6)
385-340 x 8" pkg(6)
385-341 x 10" pkg(6)
385-342 x 12" pkg(5)
385-343 x 14" pkg(5)
385-344 x 16" pkg(4)
385-345 x 18" pkg(4)
385-346 x 20" pkg(4)
385-347 x 22" pkg(4)
385-348 x 24" pkg(3)

6" EA 2.50

12" ACTUAL LENGTH
385-249 x 6" pkg(12)
385-250 x 8" pkg(11)
385-251 x 10" pkg(10)
385-252 x 12" pkg(9)
385-253 x 14" pkg(9)
385-254 x 16" pkg(9)
385-255 x 18" pkg(8)
385-256 x 20" pkg(8)
385-257 x 22" pkg(6)
385-258 x 24" pkg(6)

24" ACTUAL LENGTH
385-349 x 6" pkg(6)
385-350 x 8" pkg(6)
385-351 x 10" pkg(5)
385-352 x 12" pkg(5)
385-353 x 14" pkg(5)
385-354 x 16" pkg(5)
385-355 x 18" pkg(4)
385-356 x 20" pkg(4)
385-357 x 22" pkg(3)
385-358 x 24" pkg(3)

8" EA 2.50

12" ACTUAL LENGTH
385-259 x 8" pkg(10)
385-260 x 10" pkg(10)
385-261 x 12" pkg(9)
385-262 x 14" pkg(8)
385-263 x 16" pkg(8)
385-264 x 18" pkg(6)
385-265 x 20" pkg(6)
385-266 x 22" pkg(6)
385-267 x 24" pkg(6)

24" ACTUAL LENGTH
385-359 x 8" pkg(5)
385-360 x 10" pkg(5)
385-361 x 12" pkg(5)
385-362 x 14" pkg(4)
385-363 x 16" pkg(4)
385-364 x 18" pkg(3)
385-365 x 20" pkg(3)
385-366 x 22" pkg(3)
385-367 x 24" pkg(3)

10" EA 2.50

12" ACTUAL LENGTH
385-268 x 10" pkg(9)
385-269 x 12" pkg(8)
385-270 x 14" pkg(8)
385-271 x 16" pkg(8)
385-272 x 18" pkg(6)
385-273 x 20" pkg(6)
385-274 x 22" pkg(6)
385-275 x 24" pkg(6)

24" ACTUAL LENGTH
385-368 x 10" pkg(5)
385-369 x 12" pkg(4)
385-370 x 14" pkg(4)
385-371 x 16" pkg(4)
385-372 x 18" pkg(3)
385-373 x 20" pkg(3)
385-374 x 22" pkg(3)
385-375 x 24" pkg(3)

12" EA 2.50

12" ACTUAL LENGTH
385-276 x 12" pkg(8)
385-277 x 14" pkg(6)
385-278 x 16" pkg(6)
385-279 x 18" pkg(6)
385-280 x 20" pkg(6)
385-281 x 22" pkg(6)
385-282 x 24" pkg(6)

24" ACTUAL LENGTH
385-376 x 12" pkg(4)
385-377 x 14" pkg(4)
385-378 x 16" pkg(3)
385-379 x 18" pkg(3)
385-380 x 20" pkg(3)
385-381 x 22" pkg(3)

STRIPWOOD

Dimensions shown are actual size.

12" ACTUAL LENGTH EA 2.50

385-101 1/32 x 1/32" pkg(14)
385-102 1/32 x 1/16" pkg(14)
385-103 1/32 x 3/32" pkg(12)
385-104 1/32 x 1/8" pkg(12)
385-105 1/32 x 5/32" pkg(10)
385-106 1/32 x 3/16" pkg(10)
385-107 1/32 x 1/4" pkg(10)
385-108 1/32 x 5/16" pkg(8)
385-109 1/32 x 3/8" pkg(8)
385-110 1/32 x 7/16" pkg(6)
385-111 1/32 x 1/2" pkg(6)
385-112 1/32 x 3/4" pkg(6)
385-113 1/32 x 1" pkg(4)
385-115 1/16 x 1/16" pkg(12)
385-116 1/16 x 3/32" pkg(12)
385-117 1/16 x 1/8" pkg(10)
385-118 1/16 x 5/32" pkg(10)
385-119 1/16 x 3/16" pkg(10)
385-120 1/16 x 1/4" pkg(8)
385-121 1/16 x 5/16" pkg(8)
385-122 1/16 x 3/8" pkg(6)
385-123 1/16 x 7/16" pkg(6)
385-124 1/16 x 1/2" pkg(6)
385-125 1/16 x 3/4" pkg(4)
385-126 1/16 x 1" pkg(4)
385-128 3/32 x 3/32" pkg(10)
385-129 3/32 x 1/8" pkg(10)
385-130 3/32 x 5/32" pkg(10)
385-131 3/32 x 3/16" pkg(8)
385-132 3/32 x 1/4" pkg(8)
385-133 3/32 x 5/16" pkg(6)
385-134 3/32 x 3/8" pkg(6)
385-135 3/32 x 7/16" pkg(6)
385-136 3/32 x 1/2" pkg(4)
385-137 3/32 x 3/4" pkg(4)
385-138 3/32 x 1" pkg(2)
385-140 1/8 x 1/8" pkg(10)
385-141 1/8 x 5/32" pkg(8)
385-142 1/8 x 3/16" pkg(8)
385-143 1/8 x 1/4" pkg(6)
385-144 1/8 x 5/16" pkg(6)
385-145 1/8 x 3/8" pkg(6)
385-146 1/8 x 7/16" pkg(4)
385-147 1/8 x 1/2" pkg(4)
385-148 1/8 x 3/4" pkg(4)
385-149 1/8 x 1" pkg(2)
385-151 5/32 x 5/32" pkg(8)
385-152 5/32 x 3/16" pkg(6)
385-153 5/32 x 1/4" pkg(6)
385-154 5/32 x 5/16" pkg(6)
385-155 5/32 x 3/8" pkg(4)
385-156 5/32 x 7/16" pkg(4)
385-157 5/32 x 1/2" pkg(4)
385-158 5/32 x 3/4" pkg(4)
385-159 5/32 x 1" pkg(2)
385-161 3/16 x 3/16" pkg(6)
385-162 3/16 x 1/4" pkg(6)
385-163 3/16 x 5/16" pkg(4)
385-164 3/16 x 3/8" pkg(4)
385-165 3/16 x 7/16" pkg(4)
385-166 3/16 x 1/2" pkg(4)
385-167 3/16 x 3/4" pkg(2)
385-168 3/16 x 1" pkg(2)
385-170 1/4 x 1/4" pkg(6)
385-171 1/4 x 5/16" pkg(4)
385-172 1/4 x 3/8" pkg(4)
385-173 1/4 x 7/16" pkg(4)
385-174 1/4 x 1/2" pkg(2)
385-175 1/4 x 3/4" pkg(2)
385-176 1/4 x 1" pkg(2)
385-178 5/16 x 5/16" pkg(4)
385-179 5/16 x 3/8" pkg(4)
385-180 5/16 x 7/16" pkg(2)
385-181 5/16 x 1/2" pkg(2)
385-182 5/16 x 3/4" pkg(2)
385-183 5/16 x 1" pkg(2)
385-185 3/8 x 3/8" pkg(2)
385-186 3/8 x 7/16" pkg(2)
385-187 3/8 x 1/2" pkg(2)
385-188 3/8 x 3/4" pkg(2)
385-189 3/8 x 1" pkg(2)
385-191 7/16 x 7/16" pkg(4)
385-192 7/16 x 1/2" pkg(4)
385-193 7/16 x 3/4" pkg(4)
385-194 7/16 x 1" pkg(4)
385-196 1/2 x 1/2" pkg(4)
385-197 1/2 x 3/4" pkg(4)
385-198 1/2 x 1" pkg(4)

24" ACTUAL LENGTH EA 2.50

385-901 .012 x 1/32" pkg(5)
385-902 .012 x.040" pkg(6)
385-903 .012 x 3/64" pkg(6)
385-904 .012 x 1/16" pkg(6)
385-905 .012 x 3/32" pkg(5)
385-906 .012 x 3/32" pkg(5)
385-907 .012 x 1/8" pkg(5)
385-908 .012 x 5/32" pkg(5)
385-909 .012 x 3/16" pkg(5)
385-910 .012 x 7/32" pkg(5)
385-911 .012 x 1/4" pkg(4)
385-921 .020 x 1/32" pkg(7)
385-922 .020 x .040" pkg(7)
385-923 .020 x 3/64" pkg(7)
385-924 .020 x 1/16" pkg(7)
385-925 .020 x 5/64" pkg(6)
385-926 .020 x 3/32" pkg(6)
385-927 .020 x 1/8" pkg(6)
385-928 .020 x 5/32" pkg(5)
385-929 .020 x 3/16" pkg(5)
385-930 .020 x 7/32" pkg(5)
385-931 .020 x 1/4" pkg(4)
385-941 .040 x 1/32" pkg(8)
385-942 .040 x .040" pkg(8)
385-943 .040 x 3/64" pkg(8)
385-944 .040 x 1/16" pkg(6)
385-945 .040 x 5/64" pkg(6)
385-946 .040 x 3/32" pkg(6)
385-947 .040 x 1/8" pkg(5)
385-948 .040 x 5/32" pkg(5)
385-949 .040 x 3/16" pkg(5)
385-950 .040 x 7/32" pkg(5)
385-951 .040 x 1/4" pkg(4)
385-971 3/64 x 1/32" pkg(6)
385-972 3/64 x 3/64" pkg(6)
385-973 3/64 x 1/16" pkg(6)
385-974 3/64 x 5/64" pkg(6)
385-975 3/64 x 3/32" pkg(6)
385-976 3/64 x 1/8" pkg(5)
385-977 3/64 x 5/32" pkg(5)
385-978 3/64 x 3/16" pkg(5)
385-979 3/64 x 1/4" pkg(4)
385-981 5/64 x 1/32" pkg(6)
385-983 5/64 x 1/16" pkg(6)
385-984 5/64 x 5/64" pkg(6)
385-985 5/64 x 3/32" pkg(6)
385-986 5/64 x 1/8" pkg(5)
385-987 5/64 x 5/32" pkg(4)
385-988 5/64 x 3/16" pkg(4)
385-989 5/64 x 1/4" pkg(4)
385-990 5/64 x 5/16" pkg(4)
385-991 5/64 x 1/2" pkg(4)
385-992 .400 x 3/64" pkg(4)
385-994 .400 x 5/64" pkg(4)
385-996 .400 x 1/8" pkg(3)
385-997 .400 x 5/32" pkg(3)
385-998 .400 x 3/16" pkg(3)
385-999 .400 x 1/4" pkg(1)

STRUCTURAL ACCESSORIES

40' FENCE PKG(2) EA 3.50

385-608 3 Rail
385-610 4 Rail

10' GATE EA 2.50

385-609 3 Rail
385-611 4 Rail

WOODEN LADDERS

385-600 26' HO Scale Length pkg(2) **2.75**

FUZZ

EA 2.50

Fuzz is a prepackaged, multi-scale wood material for use in scratchbuilding and railroad scenery.

385-620 Extra Fine 7.5oz (210g)
385-621 Fine 6.5oz (182g)
385-622 Medium 4oz (112g)
385-623 Coarse 1.5oz (42g)
385-624 Extra Coarse 4.5oz (182g)

Precut strips and shapes in metal and plastic can be used Precut strips and shapes in metal and plastic can be used for a variety of custom building applications in any scale. All items are available as single pieces (first price shown) or in multi-packs (second price). NOTE: Tubing size indicates outside diameter. Dealer Displays available, call for information. Dealers MUST order dealer packs.

TUBES & TUBING

ASSORTED TUBING

370-707 Sizes & Shapes **5.95**
A large assortment of brass, copper and aluminum tubing and shapes.

370-320 Tube Assortment–Small Pieces **1.95**

ALUMINUM

ROUND

12"

370-100 1/16" **.35** pkg(15) **5.25**
370-101 3/32" **.40** pkg(12) **4.80**
370-102 1/8" **.40** pkg(12) **4.80**
370-103 5/32" **.45** pkg(12) **5.40**
370-104 3/16" **.50** pkg(12) **6.00**
370-105 7/32" **.55** pkg(10) **5.50**
370-106 1/4" **.60** pkg(10) **6.00**
370-107 9/32" **.65** pkg(8) **5.20**

36"

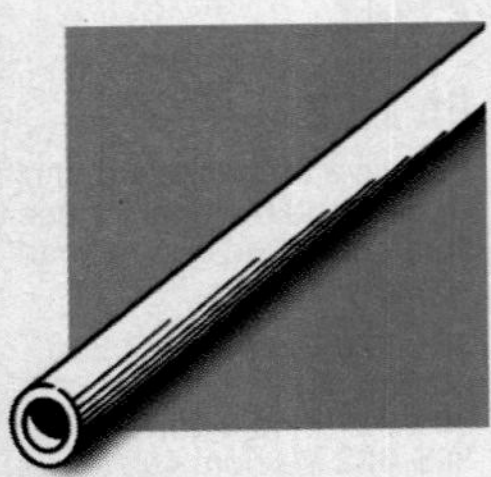

370-1108 3/32" **1.20** pkg(8) **9.60**
370-1109 1/8" **1.20** pkg(8) **9.60**
370-1110 5/32" **1.35** pkg(6) **8.10**
370-1111 3/16" **1.50** pkg(6) **9.00**
370-1112 7/32" **1.65** pkg(6) **9.90**
370-1113 1/4" **1.80** pkg(5) **9.00**
370-1114 9/32" **1.95** pkg(5) **9.75**
370-1115 5/16" **2.25** pkg(4) **9.00**

.035" WALL THICKNESS

370-3030 3/16" **1.70** pkg(6) **10.20**
370-3031 1/4" **1.80** pkg(4) **7.20**
370-3032 5/16" **2.00** pkg(4) **8.00**
370-3033 3/8" **2.10** pkg(3) **6.30**
370-3034 7/16" **2.50** pkg(3) **7.50**
370-3035 1/2" **2.75** pkg(2) **5.50**

.049" WALL THICKNESS

370-3060 3/16" **1.80** pkg(5) **9.00**
370-3061 1/4" **2.00** pkg(4) **8.00**
370-3062 5/16" **2.20** pkg(4) **8.80**
370-3063 3/8" **2.50** pkg(3) **7.50**

12" SQUARE

370-3010 3/32 x 3/32" **1.00** pkg(7) **7.00**
370-3011 1/8 x 1/8" **1.10** pkg(6) **6.60**
370-3012 5/32 x 5/32" **1.20** pkg(6) **7.20**
370-3013 3/16 x 3/16" **1.30** pkg(5) **6.50**
370-3014 7/32 x 7/32" **1.40** pkg(5) **7.00**
370-3015 1/4 x 1/4" **1.80** pkg(5) **9.00**

35" STREAMLINE

370-1100 1/4" **2.75** pkg(5) **13.75**
370-1101 5/16" **3.00** pkg(5) **15.00**
370-1102 3/8" **3.25** pkg(4) **13.00**
370-1103 1/2" **3.75** pkg(4) **15.00**
370-1104 5/8" **5.00** pkg(3) **15.00**
370-1105 3/4" **5.50** pkg(2) **11.00**

ROUND COPPER 12"

370-117 1/16" **.50** pkg(20) **10.00**
370-118 3/32" **.60** pkg(15) **9.00**
370-119 5/32" **.65** pkg(12) **7.80**
370-120 1/8" **.65** pkg(12) **7.80**

BRASS

12" SQUARE

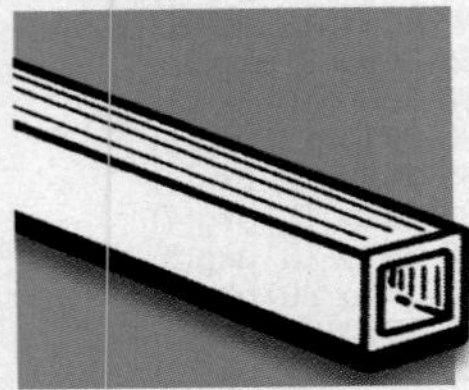

370-149 1/16" **.90** pkg(12) **10.80**
370-150 3/32" **1.00** pkg(12) **12.00**
370-151 1/8" **1.05** pkg(12) **12.60**
370-152 5/32" **1.20** pkg(10) **12.00**
370-153 3/16" **1.40** pkg(6) **8.40**
370-154 7/32" **1.50** pkg(6) **9.00**
370-155 1/4" **1.70** pkg(6) **10.20**

12" RECTANGLE

370-262 3/32 x 3/16" **1.70** pkg(4) **6.80**
370-264 1/8 x 1/4" **1.90** pkg(4) **7.60**
370-266 5/32 x 5/16" **2.10** pkg(4) **8.40**
370-268 3/16 x 3/8" **2.30** pkg(4) **9.20**

12" HEXAGON

370-271 3/32" **.65** pkg(8) **5.20**
370-272 1/8" **.75** pkg(7) **5.25**
370-273 5/32" **.85** pkg(6) **5.10**
370-274 3/16" **.95** pkg(5) **4.75**

12" STREAMLINE

370-122 Small **1.25** pkg(4) **5.00**

ROUND

12"

370-125 1/16" **.50** pkg(20) **10.00**
370-126 3/32" **.60** pkg(15) **9.00**
370-127 1/8" **.65** pkg(15) **9.75**
370-128 5/32" **.65** pkg(12) **7.80**
370-129 3/16" **.75** pkg(12) **9.00**
370-130 7/32" **.80** pkg(10) **8.00**
370-131 1/4" **.90** pkg(8) **7.20**
370-132 9/32" **1.00** pkg(8) **8.00**
370-133 5/16" **1.10** pkg(6) **6.60**
370-134 11/32" **1.20** pkg(6) **7.20**
370-135 3/8" **1.30** pkg(6) **7.80**
370-136 13/32" **1.50** pkg(4) **6.00**
370-137 7/16" **1.60** pkg(4) **6.40**
370-138 15/32" **1.65** pkg(4) **6.60**
370-139 1/2" **1.75** pkg(4) **7.00**
370-140 17/32" **2.00** pkg(3) **6.00**
370-141 9/16" **2.10** pkg(3) **6.30**
370-142 19/32" **2.30** pkg(2) **4.60**
370-143 5/8" **2.45** pkg(2) **4.90**
370-144 21/32" **2.60** pkg(2) **5.20**

36"

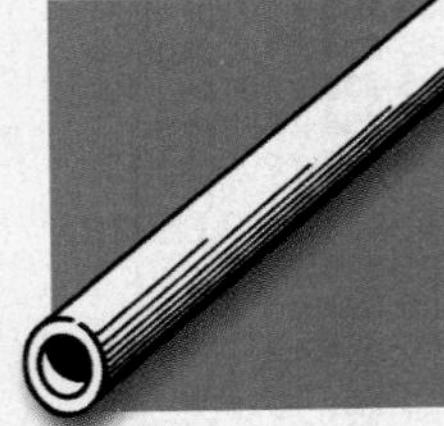

370-1143 1/16" **1.50** pkg(10) **15.00**
370-1144 3/32" **1.80** pkg(8) **14.40**
370-1145 1/8" **1.95** pkg(8) **15.60**
370-1146 5/32" **1.95** pkg(6) **11.70**
370-1147 3/16" **2.25** pkg(6) **13.50**
370-1148 7/32" **2.40** pkg(6) **14.40**
370-1149 1/4" **2.70** pkg(5) **13.50**
370-1150 9/32" **3.00** pkg(5) **15.00**
370-1151 5/16" **3.30** pkg(4) **13.20**
370-1152 11/32" **3.60** pkg(4) **14.40**
370-1153 3/8" **3.90** pkg(3) **11.70**

RODS 12"

SOLID ALUMINUM

370-3040 1/32" **.30** pkg(20) **6.00**
370-3041 1/16" **.36** pkg(20) **7.20**
370-3042 3/32" **.40** pkg(15) **6.00**
370-3043 1/8" **.70** pkg(10) **7.00**
370-3044 3/16" **.90** pkg(8) **7.20**
370-3045 1/4" **1.40** pkg(6) **8.40**
370-3046 5/16" **1.80** pkg(4) **7.20**
370-3047 3/8" **2.20** pkg(4) **8.80**
370-3048 1/2" **2.90** pkg(3) **8.70**

BRASS

370-159 .020" **.20** pkg(50) **10.00**
370-160 1/32" **.20** pkg(50) **10.00**
370-161 3/64" **.25** pkg(34) **8.50**
370-162 1/16" **.35** pkg(20) **7.00**
370-163 3/32" **.50** pkg(16) **8.00**
370-164 1/8" **.70** pkg(10) **7.00**
370-165 5/32" **.95** pkg(8) **7.60**
370-166 3/16" **1.05** pkg(5) **5.25**
370-167 .114" **.60** pkg(10) **6.00**
370-168 .081" **.55** pkg(10) **5.50**
370-169 .072" **.45** pkg(16) **7.20**

MUSIC WIRE 36"

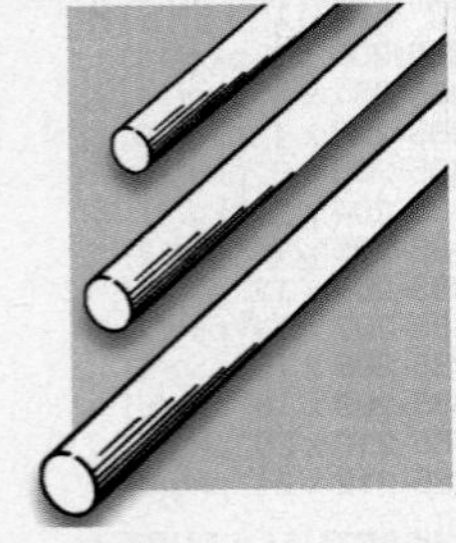

370-497 .039" **.25** pkg(25) **6.25**
370-498 .015" **.20** pkg(50) **10.00**
370-499 .020" **.15** pkg(42) **6.30**
370-500 .025" **.15** pkg(34) **5.10**
370-501 .032" (1/32") **.20** pkg(34) **6.80**
370-502 .047" **.25** pkg(34) **8.50**
370-503 .055" **.30** pkg(32) **9.60**
370-504 .062" (1/16) **.30** pkg(25) **7.50**
370-505 .078" **.40** pkg(20) **8.00**
370-506 3/32" **.55** pkg(13) **7.15**
370-507 1/8" **.80** pkg(9) **7.20**
370-508 5/32" **1.15** pkg(7) **8.05**
370-509 3/16" **1.65** pkg(4) **6.60**
370-510 7/32" **2.25** pkg(4) **9.00**
370-511 1/4" **2.80** pkg(3) **8.40**

SHEETS

STRIP & SHEET ASSORTMENT

370-727 5.95
Brass, copper and aluminum strips and sheets in a variety of thicknesses, widths and lengths.

CLEAR PLASTIC

9 x 12", flexible and clear as glass. Vacuum formable.

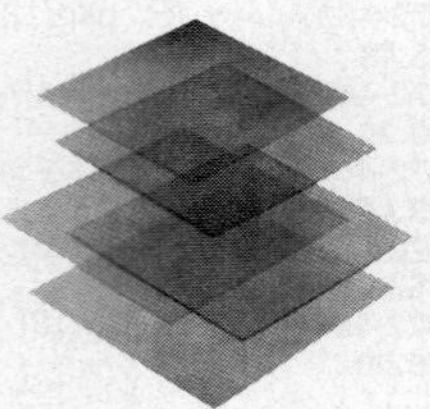

370-1301 .010" **2.29** pkg(10) **22.90**
370-1304 .015" **2.59** pkg(10) **25.90**
370-1306 .030" **2.59** pkg(10) **25.90**

ALUMINUM

Each piece measures 6 x 12", dimension shown is thickness.

370-3070 .064" **5.50** pkg(2) **11.00**
370-3071 .090" **7.50** pkg(2) **15.00**
370-3072 .125" **9.50** pkg(2) **19.00**

METAL

4 X 10"

370-250

370-255

370-250 .005" Brass **1.60** pkg(6) **9.60**
370-251 .010" Brass **1.60** pkg(6) **9.60**
370-252 .015" Brass **2.10** pkg(6) **12.60**
370-253 .032" Brass **3.80** pkg(3) **11.40**
370-254 .008" Tin **1.10** pkg(6) **6.60**
370-255 .016" Aluminum **1.20** pkg(6) **7.20**
370-256 .032" Aluminum **1.60** pkg(6) **9.60**
370-257 .064" Aluminum **2.35** pkg(6) **14.10**
370-258 Assorted Brass **3.10** pkg(6) **18.60**
370-259 .025" Copper **4.10** pkg(3) **12.30**

12 X 30" EA 11.00 (UNLESS NOTED)

370-6005 .002" Brass
370-6010 .005" Soft Brass
370-6015 .002" Copper
370-6020 .005" Soft Copper
370-6025 .005" Aluminum **6.00**
370-6030 .002" Stainless Steel

BRASS PARTS

CHANNELS

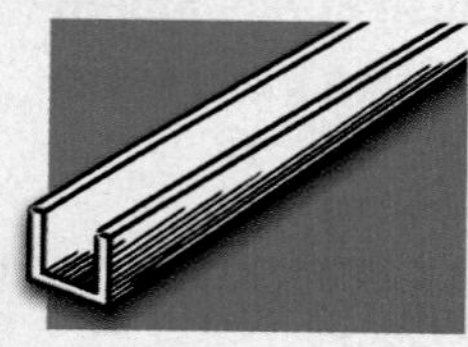

370-181 1/8" **.85** pkg(10) **8.50**
370-182 5/32" **.95** pkg(8) **7.60**
370-183 3/16" **.80** pkg(7) **5.60**
370-184 7/32" **.80** pkg(6) **4.80**
370-185 1/4" **.85** pkg(5) **4.25**

ANGLES

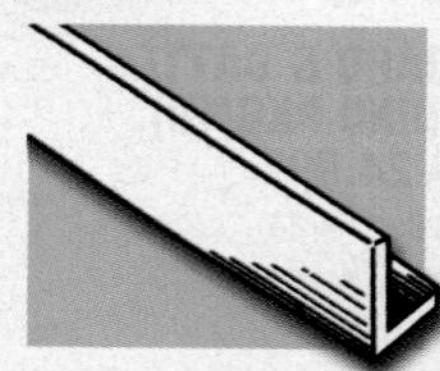

370-171 1/8 x 1/8" **.70** pkg(10) **7.00**
370-172 5/32 x 5/32" **.80** pkg(10) **8.00**
370-173 3/16 x 3/16" **.70** pkg(8) **5.60**
370-174 7/32 x 7/32" **.75** pkg(7) **5.25**
370-175 1/4 x 1/4" **.75** pkg(6) **4.50**

SOFT BRASS FUEL LINE

370-121 1/8" **.80** pkg(10) **8.00**

STRIPS

370-230 .016 x 1/4" **.45** pkg(20) **9.00**
370-231 .016 x 1/2" **.50** pkg(15) **7.50**
370-232 .016 x 1" **.70** pkg(10) **7.00**
370-233 .016 x 3/4 **.60** pkg(10) **6.00**
370-234 .016 x 2" **1.25** pkg(5) **6.25**
370-235 .025 x 1/4" **.55** pkg(15) **8.25**
370-236 .025 x 1/2" **.60** pkg(10) **6.00**
370-237 .025 x 1" **1.00** pkg(6) **6.00**
370-238 .025 x 3/4" **.85** pkg(6) **5.10**
370-239 .025 x 2" **1.90** pkg(3) **5.70**
370-240 .032 x 1/4" **.60** pkg(15) **9.00**
370-241 .032 x 1/2" **.65** pkg(10) **6.50**
370-242 .032 x 1" **1.10** pkg(5) **5.50**
370-243 .032 x 3/4" **.90** pkg(6) **5.40**
370-244 .032 x 2" **2.10** pkg(3) **6.30**
370-245 .064 x 1/4" **.85** pkg(8) **6.80**
370-246 .064 x 1/2" **1.30** pkg(4) **5.20**
370-247 .064 x 3/4" **1.75** pkg(3) **5.25**
370-248 .064 x 1" **2.25** pkg(2) **4.50**
370-249 .064 x 2" **3.65** pkg(3) **10.95**

JL INNOVATIVE DESIGN

STUCCO

361-222 Peel & Stick Sheets pkg(4) **4.99**
An easy way to create stucco walls, each sheet measures 2 x 5-1/2". Package covers 44 square inches.

JV MODELS

PAPER BUILDING MATERIAL

345-8401 Brick pkg(3) **3.98**
Red brick wall or foundation material. 4-1/2 x 7-1/2" sheets.

MASTER CREATIONS

SHINGLES EA 3.50

Laser-cut shingles are peel and stick for easy installation.

464-1000 Random Cedar

464-1002 Fish Scale

464-1004 Octagonal

464-1006 Diamond

464-1008 Saw Tooth

SCREEN WIRE

464-1100 Scale Screen Wire **4.50**
Ultra-fine wire screen, 270 mesh per square inch, made from .0016" diameter wire. Package includes 12 square inches of screening.

SCALE HOSE

464-1105 Hose **1.50**
A fine rubber hose that acts and feels like the real thing. Includes 12" (30cm) per package, can also be used in S Scale.

MAGNET WIRE

464-1110 1.50
Fine diameter (.0055"), varnish insulated, solderable, current carrying magnetic wire. Perfect for exposed wiring with a scale conduit appearance. Can be painted with water base colors. Package includes 3' (0.9m).

Information STATION

Modeling Plastics

Plastics have become the most important and widely used materials for both manufactured and scratchbuilt models. Each type has unique characteristics that make it more suitable for certain applications. Virtually all can be used together, though this may require different types of adhesives to produce a good, strong bond. Some of the most commonly used plastics include:

STYRENE (hi-impact polystyrene) - Lightweight, strong and easily worked, styrene is the most common hobby plastic. Pellets are used in injection molding and make up the balance of parts in most assembled models. For scratchbuilding, you'll find styrene in a wide variety of shapes and sheets. Most are easily cut with a sharp hobby knife. However, some thicker sizes may require a fine saw. Styrene can also be scribed to simulate wood or steel construction, so it's perfect for virtually any kind of model. However, it's easily damaged by most solvents, so use only compatible paints and glues.

ABS (Acrylonitrile-butadiene-styrene) - A chemically engineered polymer that combines the best of acrylics, butyrates and styrene into one, resulting in a material that is extremely versatile.

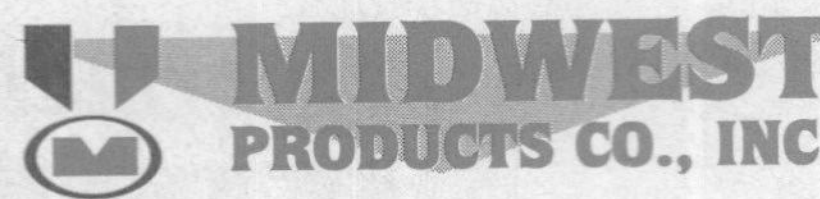

Create unique models for your layout with this selection of precut wood strips, shapes, dowels and more.

BALSA

STRIPS

All items are 36" long.

472-6022 1/16 x 1/16" pkg(60) 12.60
472-6024 1/16 x 1/8" pkg(57) 14.82
472-6025 1/16 x 3/16" pkg(36) 12.96
472-6026 1/16 x 1/4" pkg(30) 12.60
472-6029 1/16 x 1/2" pkg(24) 14.40
472-6033 3/32 x 3/32" pkg(48) 12.48
472-6035 3/32 x 3/16" pkg(36) 12.96
472-6038 3/32 x 3/8" pkg(20) 12.40
472-6044 1/8 x 1/8" pkg(36) 12.96
472-6045 1/8 x 3/16" pkg(36) 15.12
472-6046 1/8 x 1/4" pkg(30) 15.60
472-6048 1/8 x 3/8" pkg(20) 13.60
472-6049 1/8 x 1/2" pkg(15) 12.45
472-6055 3/16 x 3/16" pkg(25) 11.75
472-6056 3/16 x 1/4" pkg(20) 11.40
472-6058 3/8 x 3/16" pkg(15) 12.45
472-6059 3/16 x 1/2" pkg(12) 12.96
472-6066 1/4 x 1/4" pkg(20) 13.60
472-6068 1/4 x 3/8" pkg(15) 13.20
472-6069 1/4 x 1/2" pkg(12) 14.16
472-6088 3/8 x 3/8" pkg(12) 14.16
472-6089 3/8 x 1/2" pkg(10) 16.50
472-6099 1/2 x 1/2" pkg(9) 17.19

SHEETS

472-6102 1/16 x 1" pkg(20) 22.60
472-6103 3/32 x 1" pkg(20) 24.80
472-6104 1/8 x 1" pkg(20) **26.80**
472-6105 3/16 x 1" pkg(10) 17.00
472-6106 1/4 x 1" pkg(10) **20.10**
472-6108 3/8 x 1" pkg(10) **25.80**
472-6109 1/2 x 1" pkg(10) **27.80**
472-6201 1/32 x 2" pkg(20) 25.80
472-6202 1/16 x 2" pkg(20) 26.80
472-6203 3/32 x 2" pkg(20) 29.80
472-6204 1/8 x 2" pkg(20) **33.00**
472-6205 3/16 x 2" pkg(10) 19.60
472-6206 1/4 x 2" pkg(10) **23.70**
472-6208 3/8 x 2" pkg(5) **15.95**
472-6209 1/2 x 2" pkg(5) **20.35**
472-6301 1/32 x 3" pkg(20) 28.80
472-6302 1/16 x 3" pkg(20) 28.80
472-6303 3/32 x 3" pkg(20) 35.00
472-6304 1/8 x 3" pkg(20) **39.20**
472-6305 3/16 x 3" pkg(10) 25.20
472-6306 1/4 x 3" pkg(10) **30.40**
472-6308 3/8 x 3" pkg(5) **23.20**
472-6309 1/2 x 3" pkg(5) **28.35**
472-6401 1/32 x 4" pkg(20) 44.40
472-6402 1/16 x 4" pkg(20) 44.40
472-6403 3/32 x 4" pkg(15) 38.70
472-6404 1/8 x 4" pkg(15) **42.45**
472-6405 3/16 x 4" pkg(10) 35.50
472-6406 1/4 x 4" pkg(10) **42.70**
472-6408 3/8 x 4" pkg(5) **29.60**
472-6409 1/2 x 4" pkg(5) **35.80**
472-6601 1/32 x 6" pkg(10) 35.50
472-6602 1/16 x 6" pkg(10) 36.10
472-6603 3/32 x 6" pkg(10) 40.70
472-6604 1/8 x 6" pkg(10) **50.00**
472-6605 3/16 x 6" pkg(5) **27.05**
472-6606 1/4 x 6" pkg(5) **31.65**
472-6608 3/8 x 6" pkg(5) **41.70**

BASSWOOD

SHEETS

All items are 24" long.

472-4102 1/16 x 1" pkg(15) 16.20
472-4103 3/32 x 1" pkg(15) 17.70
472-4104 1/8 x 1" pkg(15) **20.10**
472-4105 3/16 x 1" pkg(10) 16.50
472-4106 1/4 x 1" pkg(10) **19.10**
472-4301 1/32 x 3" pkg(15) 19.35
472-4302 1/16 x 3" pkg(15) 20.85
472-4303 3/32 x 3" pkg(15) 24.00
472-4304 1/8 x 3" pkg(15) **27.75**
472-4305 3/16 x 3" pkg(10) 21.10
472-4306 1/4 x 3" pkg(10) **24.20**
472-4308 3/8 x 3" pkg(5) **17.00**
472-4309 1/2 x 3" pkg(5) **27.05**
472-4401 1/32 x 4" pkg(15) 32.40
472-4402 1/16 x 4" pkg(15) 33.15
472-4403 3/32 x 4" pkg(15) 34.80
472-4404 1/8 x 4" pkg(15) **39.45**
472-4405 3/16 x 4" pkg(10) 30.40
472-4406 1/4 x 4" pkg(10) **37.10**
472-4110 1/32 x 2" pkg(15) 16.95
472-4111 1/16 x 2" pkg(15) 18.60
472-4112 3/32 x 2" pkg(15) 20.10
472-4113 1/8 x 2" pkg(15) **23.25**
472-4114 3/16 x 2" pkg(10) 17.00
472-4115 1/4 x 2" pkg(10) **20.10**
472-4116 3/8 x 2" pkg(5) **14.15**
472-4117 1/2 x 2" pkg(5) **20.10**
472-4125 1/16 x 6" pkg(10) 55.60
472-4126 3/32 x 6" pkg(10) 58.20
472-4127 1/8 x 6" pkg(10) **65.90**
472-4128 3/16 x 6" pkg(5) **35.55**
472-4129 1/4 x 6" pkg(5) **45.05**

STRIPS

All items are 24" long.

472-4022 1/16 x 1/16" pkg(60) 11.40
472-4024 1/16 x 1/8" pkg(48) 12.00
472-4026 1/16 x 1/4" pkg(42) 15.96
472-4029 1/16 x 1/12" pkg(24) 15.36
472-4033 3/32 x 3/32" pkg(60) 14.40
472-4044 1/8 x 1/8" pkg(48) 12.48
472-4045 1/8 x 3/16" pkg(36) 12.96
472-4046 1/8 x 1/4" pkg(30) 13.20
472-4049 1/8 x 1/2" pkg(15) 12.75
472-4050 5/32 x 5/32" pkg(36) 12.96
472-4055 3/16 x 3/16" pkg(36) 14.40
472-4058 3/16 x 3/8" pkg(20) 14.20
472-4059 3/16 x 1/2" pkg(15) 14.10
472-4066 1/4 x 1/4" pkg(20) 13.20
472-4068 1/4 x 3/8" pkg(16) 12.96
472-4069 1/4 x 1/2" pkg(12) 13.56
472-4077 5/16 x 5/16" pkg(18) 14.58
472-4088 3/8 x 3/8" pkg(15) 16.20
472-4099 1/2 x 1/2" pkg(10) 17.50

ARCHITECTURAL SCALE LUMBER

All items are 11" long.

PKG(17) EA 1.95
472-8000 .0208 x .0208"
472-8001 .0208 x .0312"
472-8002 .0208 x .0416"

PKG(15) EA 1.95
472-8003 .0208 x .625"
472-8004 .0208 x .0833"
472-8005 .0208 x .1041"
472-8006 .0208 x .1251"
472-8016 .0416 x .0416"
472-8017 .0416 x .0625"
472-8018 .0416 x .0833"
472-8019 .0416 x .1041"
472-8020 .0415 x.125"

FLOORING/SIDING

3 x 24". Measurement indicates spaced groove.

PKG(15) EA 28.65

472-4440 1/4"
472-4441 3/8"
472-4442 1/2"
472-4443 Random Groove

PKG(10) EA 19.90
472-4434 1/16 x 1/32"
472-4435 3/32 x 1/32"
472-4436 1/8 x 1/32"
472-4437 1/16 x 1/16"
472-4438 3/32 x 1/16"
472-4439 1/8 x 1/16"

CLAPBOARD SIDING

1/16 X 3 X 24" PKG(10) EA 24.90
472-4448 1/16"
472-4449 3/32"

3 X 24" PKG(10) EA 24.70 (UNLESS NOTED)

472-4450 1/8" **22.70**
472-4451 1/4"
472-4452 3/8"
472-4453 1/2"

BOARD & BATTEN SIDING PKG(10) EA 24.90

1/16 x 3 x 24".

472-4444 1/16"
472-4445 3/32"

MINIATURE MOLDINGS

472-3100 Base Board pkg(7) 10.43
472-3103 Door Trim, Interior pkg(7) **8.26**
472-3104 Door & Window Casing pkg(6) **8.64**
472-3106 Window Trim, Interior pkg(10) **11.50**
472-3109 1/4" Chair Rail pkg(10) **8.80**
472-3110 3/16" Chair Rail pkg(25) **14.25**
472-3114 3/32" Quarter Round pkg(25) **13.00**
472-3116 2/8" Quarter Round pkg(25) **14.25**
472-3124 3/16" Cove pkg(20) 14.60
472-3125 /14" Cove pkg(15) 14.10

SHINGLES

472-4500 Tapered Cedar 144 Square Inches pkg(12) **4.95**
472-4505 Basswood 200 Square Inches pkg(12) **4.75**

CORNER ANGLES

Angles measure 24" long.

472-4463 3/8 x 3/8" pkg(10) 23.20
472-4464 1/2 x 1/2" pkg(10) 25.80

DOWELS

Measurement indicates diameter.

12" LONG

472-7903 1/16" **1.20**

HARDWOOD 36" LONG

472-7904 1/8" pkg(45) **11.25**
472-7905 3/16" pkg(36) **14.40**
472-7906 1/4" pkg(30) **15.00**
472-7907 5/16" pkg(25) **15.00**
472-7908 3/8" pkg(20) **15.00**
472-7909 1/2" pkg(12) **13.80**

HARDWOODS

All hardwoods are 24" long.

WALNUT

472-4601 1/16 x 1/16" pkg(30) 10.80
472-4618 1/8 x 1/8" pkg(25) 13.00
472-4620 1/8 x 1/4" pkg(15) 14.10
472-4637 1/4 x 1/4" pkg(12) 15.48
472-4670 1/32 x 3" pkg(15) 40.20
472-4671 1/16 x 3" pkg(15) 42.45
472-4673 1/8 x 3" pkg(15) 55.65
472-4675 1/4 x 3" pkg(10) 55.60

MAHOGANY

472-4701 1/16 x 1/16" pkg(45) 13.95
472-4718 1/8 x 1/8" pkg(25) 13.00
472-4720 1/8 x 1/4" pkg(20) 15.60
472-4737 1/4 x 1/4" pkg(18) 18.54
472-4770 1/32 x 3" pkg(15) 38.70
472-4771 1/16 x 3" pkg(15) 40.20
472-4773 1/8 x 3" pkg(15) 49.50
472-4775 1/4 x 3" pkg(10) 49.40

CHERRY

472-4801 1/16 x 1/16" pkg(30) 9.30
472-4818 1/8 x 1/8" pkg(25) 13.00
472-4820 1/8 x 1/4" pkg(15) 11.70
472-4837 1/4 x 1/4" pkg(12) 12.36
472-4870 1/32 x 3" pkg(15) 38.70
472-4871 1/16 x 3" pkg(15) 40.20
472-4873 1/8 x 3" pkg(15) 49.50
472-4875 1/4 x 3" pkg(10) 49.40

NorthWest Short Line

SCREWS

NICKEL-PLATED METRIC SCREWS EA .95

FLAT HEAD
53-11535 1.4 x .3 x 3mm pkg(8)
53-11545 1.4 x .3 x 4mm pkg(8)
53-11565 1.4 x .3 x 6mm pkg(8)
53-11995 1.7 x .35 x 16mm pkg(8)
53-12255 2 x .4 x 5mm pkg(10)
53-12755 2.6 x .45 x 5mm pkg(10)
53-12295 2 x 18 x .4mm pkg(6)

PAN HEAD
53-11035 1 x .25 x 3mm pkg(6)
53-11075 1.0 x .25 x 7mm pkg(6)
53-11235 1.2 x .25 x 3mm pkg(6)
53-11245 1.2 x .25 x 4mm pkg(6)
53-11255 1.2 x .25 x 5mm pkg(6)
53-11435 1.4 x .3 x 3mm pkg(8)
53-11445 1.4 x 3 x 4mm pkg(8)
53-11465 1.4 x 3 x 6mm pkg(8)
53-11505 1.4 x 3 x 10mm pkg(8)
53-11725 1.7 x .35 x 1.8mm pkg(8)
53-11755 1.7 x .35 x 5mm pkg(8)
53-11885 1.7 x .35 x 18mm pkg(8)
53-12035 2 x 4 x 3mm pkg(10)
53-12045 2 x 4 x 4mm pkg(10)
53-12055 2 x 4 x 5mm pkg(10)
53-12065 2 x 4 x 6mm pkg(10)
53-12085 2 x 4 x 8mm pkg(10)
53-12105 2 x 4 x 10mm pkg(8)
53-12125 2 x 4 x 12mm pkg(8)
53-12635 2.6 x .45 x 3mm pkg(10)
53-12655 2.6 x .45 x 5mm pkg(10)
53-12665 2.6 x .45 x 6mm pkg(10)
53-12685 2.6 x .45 x 8mm pkg(10)
53-12705 2.6 x .45 x 10mm pkg(10)
53-12755 2.6 x .45 x 5mm pkg(10)
53-13055 3 x 5 x 5mm pkg(10)
53-13105 3 x 10 x 5mm pkg(10)

SET SCREW PKG(6)
53-16725 1.7 x .35 Steel
53-16835 2 x 4mm

PLASTIC INSULATING PAN HEAD SCREWS PKG(4) EA .95

53-51435 1.4 x 3mm
53-51745 1.4 x 4mm x .35

NYLON SCREWS

FILLISTER HEAD PKG(10)
53-41745 0-80 x 1/8" **.95**
53-41765 0-80 x 1/2" **1.25**

FLAT HEAD
53-42245 0-80 x 9/32" pkg(10) **.95**
53-42455 2-56 x 3/8" pkg(10) **1.00**

PAN HEAD
53-41255 0-80 x 3/8" pkg(8) **.95**
53-41365 1-72 x 1/2" pkg(10) **.95**
53-41475 2-56 x 1/2" pkg(10) **1.00**

BLACK-PLATED PAN HEAD SCREWS EA .95

PAN HEAD
53-211425 1.4 x 2 x .3mm pkg(8)
53-211435 1.4 x 3 x .3mm pkg(8)
53-211455 1.4 x 5 x .3mm pkg(8)
53-211465 1.4 x 6 x .3mm pkg(8)
53-211485 1.4 x 8 x .3mm pkg(8)
53-212065 2 x 6 x .4mm pkg(8)
53-212085 2 x 8 x .4mm pkg(8)
53-216415 1.4 x 1.5mm pkg(6)

STEEL SCREWS

53-18065 2 x 6mm pkg(8) **.95**

HEX NUTS

EA .95

53-10105 1 x .25mm pkg(6)
53-10125 1.2 x .25mm pkg(6)
53-10145 1.4 x .3mm pkg(8)
53-10175 1.7 x .35mm pkg(8)
53-10205 2 x .4mm pkg(10)
53-10265 2.6 x .45mm pkg(10)
53-10305 3 x .5mm pkg(10)

BUILDING MATERIAL

CAP TILES

541-1008 For Concrete Sheets **1.50**

CONCRETE BLOCK WALLS EA 1.99

Molded in gray plastic, use to create warehouses, gas stations, garages and other concrete structures. Measurement in HO scale feet.

541-1004 14-1/2 x 28' pkg(4)
541-1005 14-1/2 x 18-1/2' pkg(4)
541-1006 14-1/2 x 9-1/4' pkg(8)

PREFAB STEEL WAREHOUSE WALLS

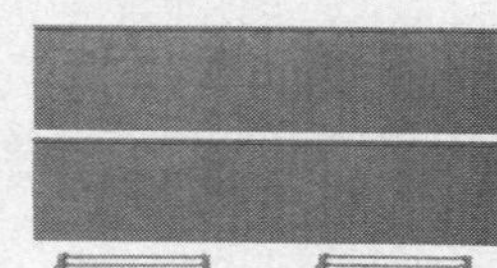

541-1011 Two Wall Panels & Downspouts (18 x 80' scale feet) **3.50**

541-1012 Peaked End Panels pkg(2) **3.00**

541-1013 Two Roof Panels & Supports (15 x 80' scale feet) **3.50**

SHINGLES

541-1007 Panels (7-3/16 x 2-1/32") pkg(2) **2.25**
541-1015 Roof (5 x 8") **2.95**

SIDING

541-1014 Board & Batten (5 x 8') **2.95**

SCALE SCENICS

DIVISION OF CIRCUITRON

MICRO-MESH

Lightweight, non-woven, raised diamond pattern mesh. Measures just .005" thick; 3 x 6" 7.5 x 15cm.

shown actual size

652-3500 Aluminum **3.95**
652-3501 Brass **4.50**
May be soldered.

GEARS

652-2001 Gear Assortment **3.95**

FLAT WIRE

652-1504 Nickel Silver **2.50**
Used for simulating strapping. Measures .010 x .030". Package contains 5' (150cm) of wire.

SUPERIOR HOBBY PRODUCTS

SCALE LUMBER

Rough sawn basswood lumber. Dimensions shown are HO scale inches.

Limited Quantity Available
697-729 8 x 8" pkg(10) **1.79**
Each piece is one actual foot long.

TAURUS PRODUCTS/ TROUT CREEK ENG.

EMBOSSED BUILDING PAPERS EA 4.00

707-21000 Wallpaper Assortment (Red, Yellow, Blue) pkg(8)
707-21001 Small Brick/Block Pattern (White) pkg(3)
707-21002 Large Brick/Block Pattern (White) pkg(3)
707-21003 Fieldstone (white) pkg(3)

WILLIAMS BROS.

ALUMINUM SHEETS PKG(2) EA 3.25

Real stamped aluminum, with a variety of layout and diorama uses. Each pack includes 72 square inches of material.

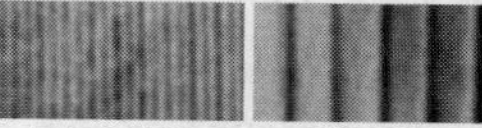

782-60000 782-60100

782-60000 Corrugated Aluminum
782-60100 Crimped Aluminum

782-60200 Square Tile

All items are prepackaged and available only in the quantities shown.

SCALE LUMBER

11" LONG EA 2.00

Large dimension is height, small dimension is thickness. Decimals are actual size.

1 SCALE INCH
(Actual size .012")

521-3001 x 2 (x .024) pkg(15)
521-3002 x 3 (x .036) pkg(15)
521-3003 x 4 (x .048) pkg(15)
521-3004 x 6 (x .072) pkg(13)
521-3005 x 8 (x .096) pkg(13)
521-3006 x 10 (x .120) pkg(13)

2 SCALE INCHES
(Actual size .024")

521-3010 x 2 (x .024) pkg(15)
521-3011 x 3 (x .036) pkg(15)
521-3012 x 4 (x .048) pkg(15)
521-3013 x 6 (x .072) pkg(13)
521-3014 x 8 (x .096) pkg(13)
521-3015 x 10 (x .120) pkg(13)
521-3016 x 12 (x .144) pkg(11)

3 SCALE INCHES
(Actual size .036")

521-3020 x 3 (x .036) pkg(15)
521-3021 x 4 (x .048) pkg(15)
521-3022 x 6 (x .072) pkg(13)
521-3023 x 8 (x .096) pkg(13)
521-3024 x 10 (x .120) pkg(13)
521-3025 x 12 (x .144) pkg(11)

4 SCALE INCHES
(Actual size .048")

521-3030 x 4 (x .048) pkg(13)
521-3031 x 6 (x .072) pkg(13)
521-3032 x 8 (x .096) pkg(13)
521-3033 x 10 (x .120) pkg(13)
521-3034 x 12 (x .144) pkg(13)

6 SCALE INCHES
(Actual size .072")

521-3040 x 6 (x .072) pkg(13)
521-3041 x 8 (x .096) pkg(11)
521-3042 x 10 (x .120) pkg(11)
521-3043 x 12 (x .144) pkg(11)

8 SCALE INCHES
(Actual size .096")

521-3050 x 8 (x .096) pkg(11)
521-3051 x 10 (x .120) pkg(11)
521-3052 x 12 (x .144) pkg(11)

10 SCALE INCHES
(Actual size .120")

521-3060 x 10 (x .120) pkg(11)
521-3061 x 12 (x .144) pkg(9)

12 SCALE INCHES
(Actual size .144")

521-3070 x 12 (x .144) pkg(9)

STRIPWOOD

Each piece is 24" 60cm long. Large dimension indicates thickness, small dimension indicates width.

1/32"

521-70120 x 1/32" pkg(10) **2.00**
521-70122 x 3/64" pkg(10) **2.00**
521-70123 x 1/16" pkg(10) **2.00**
521-70124 x 5/64" pkg(10) **2.40**
521-70125 x 3/32" pkg(10) **2.40**
521-70126 x 1/8" pkg(10) **2.40**
521-70127 x 5/32" pkg(10) **2.70**
521-70128 x 3/16" pkg(10) **2.70**
521-70130 x 1/4" pkg(10) **3.20**
521-70131 x 5/16" pkg(10) **3.50**
521-70132 x 3/8" pkg(10) **4.90**
521-70134 x 1/2" pkg(10) **5.50**
521-70135 x 3/4" pkg(10) **5.55**
521-70136 x 1" pkg(5) **3.30**
521-70137 x 2" pkg(5) **5.85**
521-70138 x 3" pkg(2) **3.45**
521-70139 x 4" pkg(2) **4.40**

3/64"

521-70161 x 3/64" pkg(10) **2.70**
521-70162 x 1/16" pkg(10) **2.70**
521-70163 x 5/64" pkg(10) **2.70**
521-70164 x 3/32" pkg(10) **2.70**
521-70165 x 1/8" pkg(10) **2.70**
521-70166 x 5/32" pkg(10) **3.20**
521-70167 x 3/16" pkg(10) **3.20**
521-70169 x 1/4" pkg(10) **4.00**
521-70170 x 5/16" pkg(10) **4.40**
521-70171 x 3/8" pkg(10) **4.90**
521-70173 x 1/2" pkg(10) **5.50**
521-70174 x 3/4" pkg(10) **5.50**
521-70175 x 1" pkg(5) **3.60**
521-70176 x 2" pkg(5) **7.45**
521-70177 x 3" pkg(2) **3.95**
521-70178 x 4" pkg(2) **5.02**

1/16"

521-70180 x 1/16" pkg(10) **2.70**
521-70181 x 5/64" pkg(10) **2.70**
521-70182 x 3/32" pkg(10) **2.70**
521-70183 x 1/8" pkg(10) **3.20**
521-70184 x 5/32" pkg(10) **3.20**
521-70185 x 3/16" pkg(10) **3.50**
521-70187 x 1/4" pkg(10) **4.40**
521-70188 x 5/16" pkg(10) **4.40**
521-70189 x 3/8" pkg(10) **5.55**
521-70191 x 1/2" pkg(10) **6.25**
521-70192 x 3/4" pkg(10) **7.35**
521-70193 x 1" pkg(5) **4.55**
521-70194 x 2" pkg(5) **7.50**
521-70195 x 3" pkg(2) **3.95**
521-70196 x 4" pkg(2) **5.02**

5/64"

521-70198 x 5/64" **2.70**
521-70199 x 3/32" pkg(10) **3.20**
521-70200 x 1/8" pkg(10) **3.20**
521-70201 x 5/32" pkg(10) **3.20**
521-70202 x 3/16" pkg(10) **3.50**
521-70204 x 1/4" pkg(10) **4.40**
521-70205 x 5/16" pkg(10) **4.95**
521-70206 x 3/8" pkg(10) **6.25**
521-70208 x 1/2" pkg(10) **6.25**
521-70209 x 3/4" pkg(10) **7.45**
521-70210 x 1" pkg(5) **4.60**
521-70211 x 2" pkg(5) **7.80**
521-70212 x 3" pkg(2) **4.23**
521-70213 x 4" pkg(2) **5.78**

3/32"

521-70215 x 3/32" pkg(10) **3.20**
521-70216 x 1/8" pkg(10) **3.20**
521-70217 x 5/32" pkg(10) **3.20**
521-70218 x 3/16" pkg(10) **3.50**
521-70220 x 1/4" pkg(10) **4.40**
521-70221 x 5/16" pkg(10) **4.95**
521-70222 x 3/8" pkg(10) **6.25**
521-70224 x 1/2" pkg(10) **6.85**
521-70225 x 3/4" pkg(10) **7.45**
521-70226 x 1" pkg(5) **4.50**
521-70227 x 2" pkg(5) **7.70**
521-70228 x 3" pkg(2) **4.25**
521-70229 x 4" pkg(1) **3.19**

1/8"

521-70231 x 1/8" pkg(10) **3.20**
521-70232 x 5/32" pkg(10) **4.00**
521-70233 x 3/16 pkg(10) **4.20**
521-70235 x 1/4" pkg(10) **4.90**
521-70236 x 5/16" pkg(10) **4.95**
521-70237 x 3/8" pkg(10) **6.25**
521-70239 x 1/2" pkg(10) **8.05**
521-70240 x 3/4" pkg(10) **9.45**
521-70241 x 1" pkg(5) **5.25**
521-70242 x 2" pkg(5) **8.50**
521-70243 x 3" pkg(2) **4.59**
521-70244 x 4" pkg(1) **3.51**

5/32"

521-70246 x 5/32" pkg(5) **2.20**
521-70247 x 3/16" pkg(5) **2.30**
521-70249 x 1/4" pkg(5) **2.65**
521-70250 x 5/16" pkg(5) **3.25**
521-70251 x 3/8" pkg(5) **3.35**
521-70253 x 1/2" pkg(5) **4.25**
521-70254 x 3/4" pkg(5) **5.00**
521-70255 x 1" pkg(2) **2.33**
521-70256 x 2" pkg(2) **4.09**
521-70257 x 3" pkg(2) **4.78**
521-70258 x 4" pkg(1) **3.51**

3/16"

521-70260 x 3/16" pkg(5) **2.65**
521-70262 x 1/4" pkg(5) **2.95**
521-70263 x 5/16" pkg(5) **3.35**
521-70264 x 3/8" pkg(5) **4.20**
521-70266 x 1/2" pkg(5) **4.60**
521-70267 x 3/4" pkg(5) **5.20**
521-70268 x 1" pkg(2) **2.47**
521-70269 x 2" pkg(2) **4.09**
521-70270 x 3" pkg(2) **5.16**
521-70271 x 4" pkg(1) **3.82**

1/4"

521-70285 x 1/4" pkg(5) **3.35**
521-70286 x 5/16" pkg(5) **3.35**
521-70287 x 3/8" pkg(5) **4.50**
521-70289 x 1/2" pkg(5) **5.15**
521-70290 x 3/4" pkg(5) **5.60**
521-70291 x 1" pkg(2) **2.94**
521-70292 x 2" pkg(2) **4.59**
521-70293 x 3" pkg(2) **5.78**
521-70294 x 4" pkg(1) **4.40**

5/16"

521-70296 x 5/16" pkg(5) **4.60**
521-70297 x 3/8" pkg(5) **5.15**
521-70299 x 1/2" pkg(5) **5.50**
521-70300 x 3/4" pkg(5) **6.05**
521-70301 x 1" pkg(2) **2.94**
521-70302 x 2" pkg(2) **4.97**
521-70303 x 3" pkg(2) **6.68**

3/8"

521-70306 x 3/8" pkg(5) **5.25**
521-70308 x 1/2" pkg(5) **5.60**
521-70309 x 3/4" pkg(5) **6.10**
521-70310 x 1" pkg(2) **2.94**
521-70311 x 2" pkg(2) **4.97**
521-70312 x 3" pkg(2) **6.68**

1/2"

521-70323 x 1/2" pkg(2) **2.47**
521-70324 x 3/4" pkg(2) **2.65**
521-70325 x 1" pkg(2) **3.19**
521-70326 x 2" pkg(2) **5.66**
521-70327 x 3" pkg(2) **7.54**

3/4"

521-70330 x 3/4" pkg(2) **3.09**
521-70331 x 1" pkg(2) **3.31**
521-70332 x 2" pkg(1) **3.08**
521-70333 x 3" pkg(1) **4.45**

BULK PACKS-50 PIECES

Each piece is 24" 60cm long.

521-120 1/32 x 1/32" **8.00**
521-123 1/32 x 1/16" **8.00**
521-125 1/32 x 3/32" **10.00**
521-126 1/32 x 1/8" **10.00**
521-161 3/64 x 3/64" **11.50**
521-180 1/16 x 1/16" **11.50**
521-183 1/16 x 1/8" **14.00**
521-231 1/8 x 1/8" **14.00**

SCRIBED SHEATHING

PKG(2) EA 5.90

First dimension indicates scribe spacing, second is thickness. Each item is 24" long.

521-70350 .025 x 1/32"
521-70351 1/32 x 1/32"
521-70353 3/64 x 1/32"
521-70354 1/16 x 1/32"
521-70355 3/32 x 1/32"
521-70356 1/8 x 1/32"
521-70357 3/16 x 1/32"
521-70358 1/4 x 1/32"
521-70359 3/8 x 1/32"
521-70360 1/2 x 1/32"
521-70361 Random x 1/32"
521-70362 .025 x 1/16"
521-70363 1/32 x 1/16"
521-70365 3/64 x 1/16"
521-70366 1/16 x 1/16"
521-70367 3/32 x 1/16"
521-70368 1/8 x 1/16"
521-70369 3/16 x 1/16"
521-70370 1/4 x 1/16"
521-70371 3/8 x 1/16"
521-70372 1/2 x 1/16"
521-70373 Random x 1/16"

SIDING

CLAPBOARD PKG(2) EA 5.90

Dimension indicates lap spacing. Each item is 24" long.

521-70375 1/32"
521-70377 3/64"
521-70378 1/16"
521-70379 3/32"
521-70380 1/8"
521-70381 3/16"
521-70382 1/4"
521-70383 3/8"
521-70384 1/2"

BOARD & BATTEN PKG(2) EA 5.90

Dimension indicates cap spacing.

521-70402 1/16"
521-70403 3/32"
521-70404 1/8"
521-70405 3/16"
521-70406 1/4"
521-70407 3/8"
521-70408 1/2"
521-70409 3/4"

IMPRINTED CONCRETE PKG(2) EA 5.90

521-70415 1/16"
521-70417 1/8"
521-70418 3/16"

CORRUGATED PKG(2) EA 5.90

Dimension indicates corrugation spacing.

521-70424 .40"
521-70426 1/16"
521-70436 3/32"
521-70437 1/8"

STEEL PKG(2) EA 5.90

521-70347 HO Steel Siding
521-70349 O Steel Siding

LOG

521-6030 Log Scribed pkg(2) 4.25

ROOFING

SELF-ADHESIVE SHINGLES PKG(2) EA 3.45

Put a new roof on any HO Scale structure with these easy-to-use shingles. Each comes preprinted and die-cut on self-adhesive paper. Eliminates the mess and bother of glue, just peel and stick in place on your models. Easily painted to simulate a variety of roofing materials. Each includes two matching sheets.

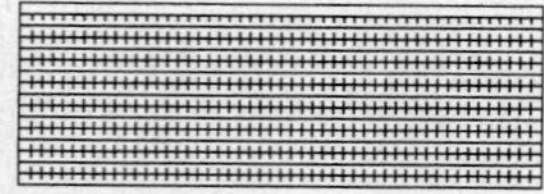

521-80701 Slate

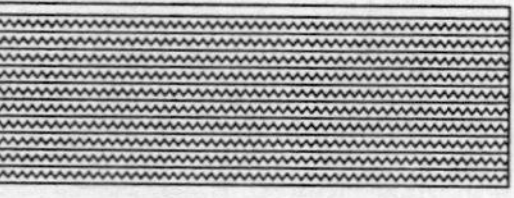

521-80703 Diamond

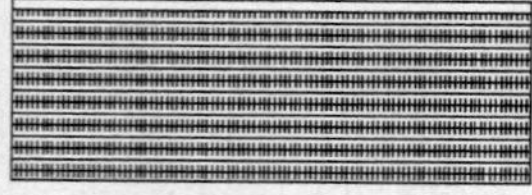

521-80704 Random

521-80706 Roll Roofing

STRUCTURAL SHAPES

All items are 22" 55cm long unless noted.

ANGLES

11" MULTI-PACKS EA 3.40

521-5001 1/32" pkg(8)
521-5002 1/16" pkg(7)
521-5003 3/32" pkg(7)
521-5004 1/8" pkg(6)

22" MULTI-PACKS

521-70499 1/32" pkg(5) 3.90
521-70500 3/64" pkg(5) 3.90
521-70501 1/16" pkg(5) 4.15
521-70502 5/64" pkg(5) 4.15
521-70503 3/32" pkg(5) 4.15
521-70504 1/8" pkg(5) 4.65
521-70505 5/32" pkg(5) 5.15
521-70506 3/16" pkg(5) 5.15
521-70507 1/4" pkg(5) 5.40
521-70508 5/16" pkg(2) 2.70
521-70509 3/8" pkg(2) 3.60
521-70527 1/2" pkg(2) 4.30

CHANNELS

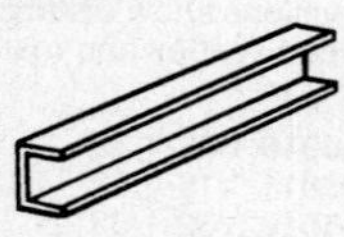

11" MULTI-PACKS EA 3.40

521-5012 1/16" pkg(7)
521-5013 3/32" pkg(7)
521-5014 1/8" pkg(6)

22" MULTI-PACKS

521-70540 1/16" pkg(5) 4.15
521-70541 5/64" pkg(5) 4.15
521-70542 3/32" pkg(5) 4.15
521-70543 1/8" pkg(5) 4.65
521-70544 5/32" pkg(5) 5.15
521-70545 3/16" pkg(5) 5.15
521-70546 1/4" pkg(5) 5.40
521-70547 5/16" pkg(2) 2.70
521-70548 3/8" pkg(2) 3.60
521-70549 1/2" pkg(2) 4.30

H COLUMN

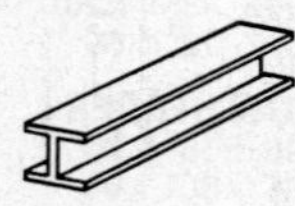

11" MULTI-PACKS EA 3.40

521-5018 1/16" pkg(7)
521-5019 3/32" pkg(7)
521-5020 1/8" pkg(6)

22" MULTI-PACKS

521-70550 1/16" pkg(5) 4.15
521-70551 5/64" pkg(5) 4.15
521-70552 3/32" pkg(5) 4.15
521-70553 1/8" pkg(5) 4.65
521-70554 5/32" pkg(5) 5.15
521-70555 3/16" pkg(5) 5.15
521-70556 1/4" pkg(5) 5.40
521-70557 5/16" pkg(2) 2.70
521-70558 3/8" pkg(2) 3.60
521-70559 1/2" pkg(2) 4.30

I BEAMS

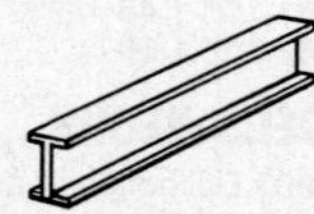

11" MULTI-PACKS EA 3.40

521-5015 1/16" pkg(7)
521-5016 3/32" pkg(7)
521-5017 1/8" pkg(6)

22" MULTI-PACKS

521-70560 1/16" pkg(5) 4.15
521-70561 5/64" pkg(5) 4.15
521-70562 3/32" pkg(5) 4.15
521-70563 1/8" pkg(5) 4.65
521-70564 5/32" pkg(5) 5.15
521-70565 3/16" pkg(5) 5.15
521-70566 1/4" pkg(5) 5.40
521-70567 5/16" pkg(2) 2.70
521-70568 3/8" pkg(2) 3.60
521-70569 1/2" pkg(2) 4.30

TEES

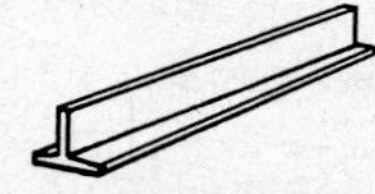

521-70510 3/64" pkg(5) 3.90
521-70511 1/16" pkg(5) 4.15
521-70512 5/64" pkg(5) 4.15
521-70513 3/32" pkg(5) 4.15
521-70514 1/8" pkg(5) 4.65
521-70515 5/32" pkg(5) 5.15
521-70516 3/16" pkg(5) 5.15
521-70517 1/4" pkg(5) 5.40
521-70518 5/16" pkg(2) 2.70
521-70519 3/8" pkg(2) 3.60
521-70525 1/32" pkg(5) 3.90

ZEES

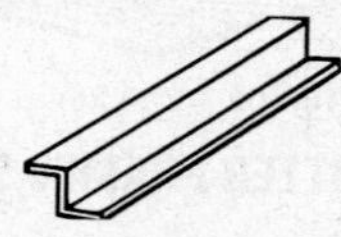

11" MULTI-PACKS EA 3.40

521-5009 3/64" pkg(8)
521-5010 1/16" pkg(7)
521-5011 3/32" pkg(7)

22" MULTI-PACKS

521-70520 3/64" pkg(5) 3.90
521-70521 1/16" pkg(5) 4.15
521-70523 3/32" pkg(5) 4.15

MOULDINGS

All items are 24" 60cm long unless noted.

CORNER POSTS

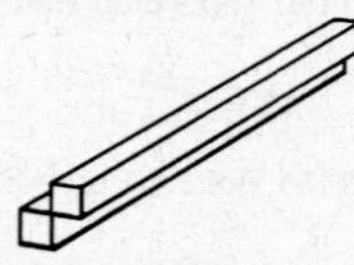

521-593 1/8" .85
521-595 3/16" .95

COVE

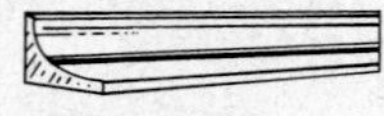

521-91 1/16" .75
521-92 5/64" .75
521-93 3/12" .75
521-94 1/8" .90
521-95 5/32" .95
521-96 3/16" .95
521-98 1/4" 1.05

DOUBLE BEAD

521-871 1/8" .90
521-872 3/32" .75
521-873 5/64" .75
521-874 1/16" .75
521-875 3/64" .70

HALF ROUND

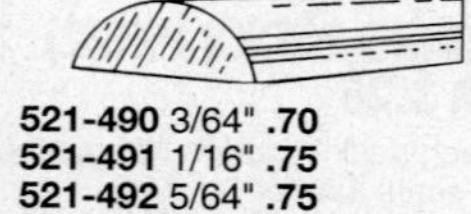

521-490 3/64" .70
521-491 1/16" .75
521-492 5/64" .75
521-493 3/32" .75
521-494 1/8" .90
521-495 5/32" .95
521-496 3/16" .95
521-498 1/4" 1.05

QUARTER ROUND

521-570 3/64" .70
521-571 1/16" .75
521-572 5/64" .75
521-573 3/32" .75
521-574 1/8" .90

ROUND

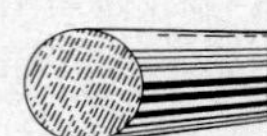

521-485 3/64" .70
521-486 1/16" .75
521-487 5/64" .75
521-488 3/32" .75
521-489 1/8" .90

WINDOW SASH

521-880 3/16" .95
521-881 5/32" .95
521-882 1/8" .90
521-883 1/4" 1.05
521-842 Threshold .45

DOLLHOUSE MINIATURES 1" SCALE (1/12)

All items are 24" 60cm long unless noted.

BASEBOARD

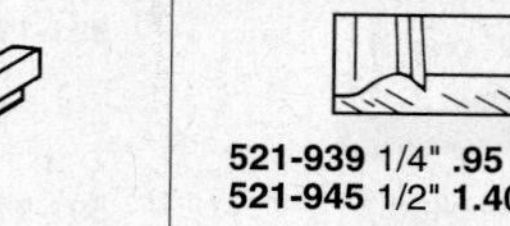

521-939 1/4" .95
521-945 1/2" 1.40

521-946 1/2" 1.40

521-947 1/2" 1.40

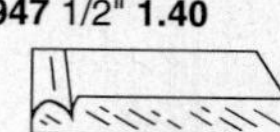

521-949 1/2" 1.40

CHAIR RAIL

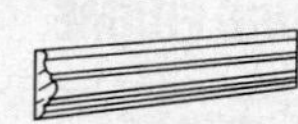

521-951 3/16" .90
521-952 1/4" .95

521-957 1/4" .95

CHANNEL, DOLLHOUSE

521-1066 1/4 x 22" 1.00
521-1067 3/8 x 22" 1.30

BEADED CLAPBOARD EA 2.65

521-387 3-7/16", 3/8" Spacing
521-389 3-7/16", 1/2" Spacing

CORNER BLOCK EA 2.45

521-954 5/64 x 9/16 x 22"
521-955 5/64 x 9/16 x 22"

CORNER TRIM

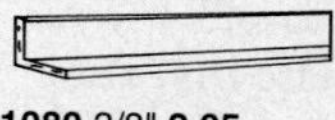

521-1080 3/8" 2.05
521-1081 1/2" 2.20

521-4018 3/8" pkg(3) 4.35
521-4019 1/2" pkg(2) 4.35

CORNICE

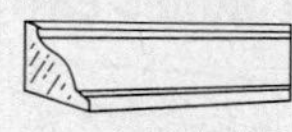

521-948 5/16" 1.05
521-950 1/2" 1.40

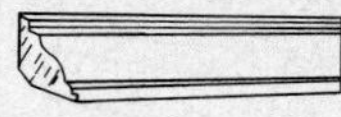

521-967 3/8" .90

CROWN CORNICE EA 4.35

521-4012

521-4013

521-4012 5/16" pkg(4)
521-4013 1/2" pkg(3)

DOOR CASING

521-941 1/2" 1.40

521-942 1/2" 1.40

521-943 3/8" 1.25

521-944 3/8" 1.25

DOOR/WINDOW CASING

521-929 1/4" .95
521-930 1/2" 1.40

521-931 1/4" .95
521-933 3/8" 1.25

521-940 1/2" 1.40

DOOR FRAMES

521-1030 7/16" **1.60**

521-1031 7/16" **1.60**
521-1032 5/8" **1.75**
521-1033 5/8" **1.75**
521-1034 3/4" **1.90**
521-1035 3/4" **1.90**

DOOR JAMBS EA 1.40

521-961 1/2"

521-966 1/2"

DOOR PANEL TRIM EA 1.05

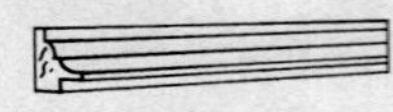

521-1075 Back Band

521-1076 Cap

521-1077 Cap

DOOR PANELS

Raised on both sides.

521-1050 521-1051

521-1050 3 Panel 2-3/16 x 3" **1.25**
521-1051 3 High, 3 Wide 2 x 3" **1.25**

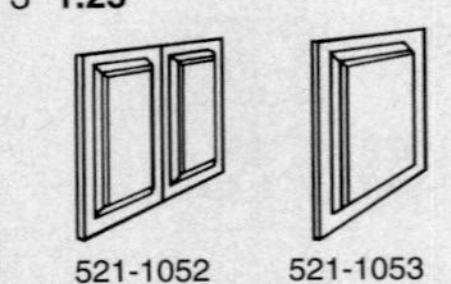

521-1052 521-1053

521-1052 3 High 2-3/16 x 3" **1.25**
521-1053 Single 2-3/16 x 2-3/16" pkg(3) **3.00**

GUTTER

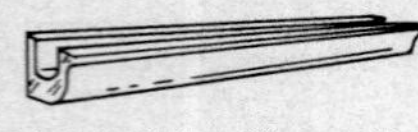

521-956 3/8" **1.60**

HANDRAIL

521-959 1/2" **1.75**

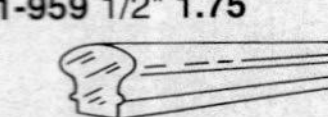

521-960 1/4" **1.10**

MOULDING PACKS

Each package decorates two or more typical dollhouse rooms.

BASEBOARD EA 4.35

521-4010 1/2" pkg(3)

521-4011 1/2" pkg(3)

CHAIR RAIL

521-4014 1/4" pkg(5) **4.35**

CASING DOOR/WINDOW EA 4.35

521-4015 1/2" pkg(3)

521-4016 1/4" pkg(5)

521-4017 3/8" pkg(4)

PANEL, WAINSCOT

521-1073 1 Panel x 2-3/16" **1.00**

PICTURE FRAME

521-901 3/32" **.75**
521-902 1/8" **.90**
521-904 3/16" **.95**
521-905 1/4" **1.05**

521-907 1/8" **.90**
521-909 3/16" **.95**
521-910 1/4" **1.05**

521-914 3/16" **.95**
521-915 1/4" **1.05**

521-917 1/8" **.90**
521-919 3/16" **.95**

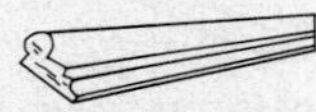

521-922 5/32" **.95**

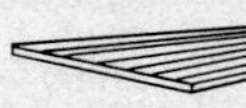

521-923 3/16" **.95**

RANDOM FLOORING

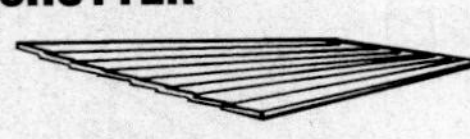

521-440 1/16 x 3-1/2" Sheet **2.65**

SHUTTER

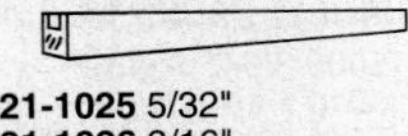

521-1060 3-1/2" **4.25**

SHUTTER FRAMES EA .95

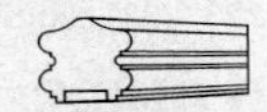

521-1025 5/32"
521-1026 3/16"

STAIR & PORCH RAILING

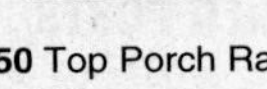

521-1140 Fancy Hand Rail **1.50**

521-1150 Top Porch Rail **1.40**

521-1151 Bottom Porch Rail **.95**

STAIR PARTS

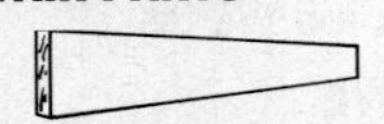

521-344 Riser 37/64 x 1/16 x 24" **.75**

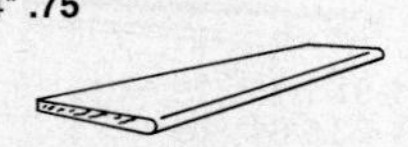

521-345 Tread 27/32 x 1/16 x 24" **.95**

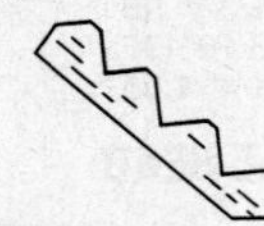

521-897 Stair Stringer 3/4 x 14" **1.25**
521-896 Stair Stringer 3/4 x 22" **1.60**

THRESHOLD

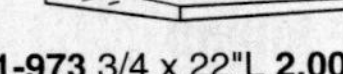

521-973 3/4 x 22"L **2.00**

SIDING PACKS PKG(2) EA 3.25

Each pack includes two pieces of scale lumber 3 x 11".

BOARD AND BATTEN

521-6006 3/32"
521-6007 1/8"
521-6008 3/16"

CLAPBOARD

521-6001 1/16"
521-6002 3/32"
521-6003 1/8"

CORRUGATED

521-6020 1/16"
521-6021 3/32"
521-6022 1/8"

SCRIBED

Dimensions show distance between scribes and material thickness.

521-6010 1/32-1/32"
521-6011 1/16-1/32"
521-6012 3/32-1/32"
521-6013 1/8-1/32"
521-6015 1/16-1/16"
521-6016 3/32-1/16"
521-6017 1/8-1/16"

WINDOW SASH RECESS

521-885 5/32" **.85**

WINDOW SECTIONS

WINDOW CASING OUTSIDE

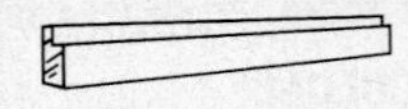

521-1005 .335" **1.20**
521-1007 1/2" **1.60**

WINDOW HEADER

521-995 .335" **1.20**
521-996 .460" **1.60**
521-997 1/2" **1.60**

WINDOW JAMB

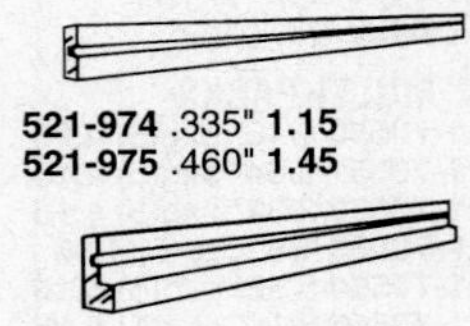

521-974 .335" **1.15**
521-975 .460" **1.45**

521-976 1/2" **1.45**

WINDOW SILL

521-981 1/2" **1.45**
521-982 5/8" **1.60**

MISCELLANEOUS

521-1003 Dollhouse of a Dollhouse **13.75**

Information STATION

Interstate Commerce Commissioin

On February 4, 1887, President Grover Cleveland signed an Act of Congress that created the Interstate Commerce Commission (ICC). As the first U.S. regulatory agency, it was created in response to malpractices in the railroad industry. At the time it allowed the government to regulate rates, services, abandonments of services and force the laws regarding railroads, trucking, pipelines, inland water carriers and freight forwarders engaged in interstate commerce. In later years it expanded to bus lines and express agencies.

At the time of its inception, the ICC regulated 100% of railroad traffic. In 1967 all the safety functions were transferred to the Department of Transportation. The deregulation of the late 1970s and 80s further reduced the ICC's role. Finally, in 1996 the Interstate Commerce Commission was abolished, ending over a century of service to the United States and its people.

ABS PLASTIC

Stronger than styrene, ABS is ideal for all types of model building, especially architectural models, or items subject to frequent handling. For easy identification, Plastruct ABS products are molded in gray.

ABS SHEET

Each sheet measures 7 x 12", thickness shown.

570-91001 .010" pkg(5) **3.25**
570-91002 .020" pkg(5) **4.25**
570-91003 .030" pkg(4) **4.25**
570-91004 .040" pkg(3) **4.50**
570-91005 .060" pkg(2) **4.00**
570-91006 .080" pkg(2) **5.25**
570-91007 .100" pkg(2) **6.50**
570-91008 .125" pkg(2) **8.00**

ABS STRIP STOCK

Each piece measures 1-1/4 x 24", thickness shown.

570-90361 Concrete .020" pkg(5) **5.25**
570-90362 Concrete .030" pkg(4) **4.75**
570-90365 Steel .020" pkg(5) **5.25**
570-90366 Steel .030" pkg(4) **4.75**

ABS ROD

Each solid piece is 15" long, outside height and width shown.

570-90351 1/8" pkg(5) **4.25**
570-90352 1/8 x 1/4" pkg(5) **4.75**

ABS RECTANGULAR & SQUARE TUBING

Each piece is 15" long, height and width shown.

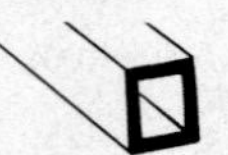

570-90221 1/4 x 3/16" pkg(6) **4.75**
570-90222 5/16 x 1/4" pkg(5) **4.50**
570-90223 3/8 x 1/4" pkg(5) **5.25**

570-90201 1/8" pkg(7) **4.75**
570-90202 3/16" pkg(6) **5.00**
570-90203 1/4" pkg(5) **4.75**
570-90204 5/16" pkg(4) **4.50**
570-90205 3/8" pkg(4) **5.00**

BUTYRATE ROUND TUBING

Each piece is 15" long, outside diameter shown.

570-90101 3/64" Wire pkg(15) **5.00**
570-90102 1/16" Wire pkg(12) **4.75**

570-90103 3/32" pkg(10) **4.25**
570-90104 1/8" pkg(10) **4.75**
570-90105 3/16" pkg(9) **5.25**
570-90106 1/4" pkg(7) **5.00**
570-90107 5/16" pkg(6) **5.25**
570-90108 3/8" pkg(5) **5.25**

INSERT WIRE FOR BUTYRATE ROUND TUBING

Brass wire for 3/32" or 1/8" Butyrate tube, adds stiffness and allows bending to almost any configuration.

570-90121 For 3/32" Tube .045" Outside Diameter. pkg(10) **3.75**

570-90122 For 1/8" Tube .058" Outside Diameter. pkg(10) **4.25**

BUTYRATE HALF-ROUND PROFILE

Each piece is 15" long, outside diameter shown.

570-90171 3/16" pkg(4) **4.25**
570-90172 1/4" pkg(4) **4.50**
570-90173 5/16" pkg(4) **4.75**

ABS STRUCTURAL SHAPES

ABS ANGLES

Height and length shown.

570-90001 3/64 x 10" pkg(10) **4.25**
570-90002 1/16 x 10" pkg(10) **4.75**
570-90003 3/32 x 15" pkg(8) **4.50**
570-90004 1/8 x 15" pkg(7) **4.75**
570-90005 3/16 x 24" pkg(5) **4.75**
570-90006 1/4 x 24" pkg(4) **4.50**
570-90007 5/16 x 24" pkg(4) **5.25**
570-90008 3/8 x 24" pkg(3) **4.75**

ABS I BEAMS

Height and length shown.

570-90021 1/16 x 10" pkg(10) **4.75**
570-90022 3/32 x 10" pkg(8) **4.25**
570-90023 1/8 x 15" pkg(7) **4.75**
570-90024 3/16 x 24" pkg(5) **4.75**
570-90025 1/4 x 24" pkg(4) **4.50**
570-90026 5/16 x 24" pkg(4) **5.00**
570-90027 3/8 x 15" pkg(5) **4.75**
570-90028 7/16 x 15" pkg(4) **4.25**
570-90029 1/2 x 15" pkg(4) **4.75**
570-90030 9/16 x 15" pkg(4) **5.25**
570-90031 5/8 x 15" pkg(3) **4.75**

ABS CHANNELS

Height and length shown.

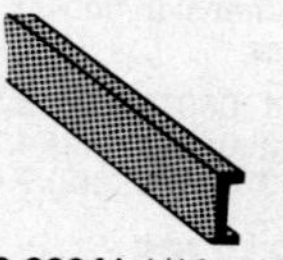

570-90041 1/16 x 10" pkg(10) **4.75**
570-90042 3/32 x 10" pkg(8) **4.75**
570-90043 1/8 x 15" pkg(7) **4.75**
570-90044 3/16 x 15" pkg(5) **4.00**
570-90045 1/4 x 24" pkg(4) **4.25**
570-90046 5/16 x 24" pkg(4) **5.00**

ABS H COLUMNS

Height and length shown.

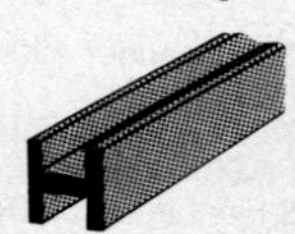

570-90061 1/16 x 10" pkg(8) **5.00**
570-90062 3/32 x 15" pkg(6) **4.25**
570-90063 1/8 x 15" pkg(5) **4.00**
570-90064 3/16 x 24" pkg(4) **4.75**
570-90065 1/4 x 15" pkg(5) **4.25**
570-90066 5/16 x 15" pkg(5) **4.75**
570-90067 3/8 x 15" pkg(4) **4.25**

ABS TEES

Height and length shown.

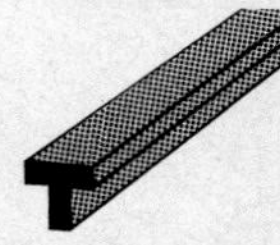

570-90081 3/64 x 10" pkg(10) **4.75**
570-90082 1/16 x 10" pkg(8) **4.25**
570-90083 3/32 x 15" pkg(8) **5.00**
570-90084 1/8 x 15" pkg(7) **5.00**
570-90085 3/16 x 24" pkg(5) **5.25**
570-90086 1/4 x 24" pkg(4) **4.75**

ABS LADDER

570-90421 N Scale 3" Long pkg(2) **1.75**
570-90422 HO Scale 5" Long pkg(2) **2.00**
570-90423 O Scale 15" Long pkg(2) **4.25**

ABS LADDER W/SAFETY CAGE

570-90431 HO Scale 5" Long **3.25**
570-90432 O Scale 12" Long **5.50**

ABS HANDRAILS

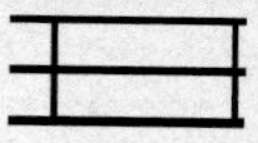

570-90471 N Scale 3-5/8" Long pkg(2) **1.75**
570-90472 HO Scale 6" Long pkg(2) **2.00**
570-90473 O Scale 24" Long **3.50**

ABS STAIRS

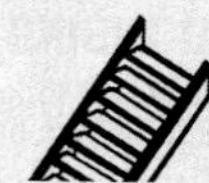

570-90441 N Scale 3" Long pkg(2) **2.50**
570-90442 HO Scale 5" Long pkg(2) **3.00**
570-90443 O Scale 12" Long **3.75**

ABS STAIR RAILS

570-90481 N Scale 3-5/8" Long pkg(2) **1.75**
570-90482 HO Scale 6" Long pkg(2) **2.00**
570-90483 O Scale 24" Long **3.50**

ABS OPEN WEB TRUSS

Warren Style 2.

570-90401 1/8 x 6" pkg(2) **3.25**
570-90402 3/16 x 6" pkg(2) **3.75**
570-90403 1/4 x 6" pkg(2) **4.25**
570-90404 3/8 x 6" pkg(2) **4.75**
570-90405 1/2 x 12" pkg(2) **5.25**
570-90406 5/8 x 12" pkg(2) **5.75**
570-90407 3/4 x 12" pkg(2) **6.50**
570-90408 1 x 12" pkg(2) **7.00**

ABS OPEN WEB TRUSS

Warren Style 1.

570-90411 1/8 x 3" pkg(2) **4.75**
570-90412 13/64 x 3" pkg(2) **5.00**
570-90413 9/32 x 5" pkg(2) **5.50**
570-90414 13/32 x 7" pkg(2) **5.75**
570-90415 1/2 x 9" pkg(2) **6.25**
570-90416 5/8 x 11" **3.50**
570-90417 3/4 x 11" **3.75**
570-90418 1 x 11" **4.00**

ACRYLIC PLASTICS

Rigid plastic is ideal for thicker objects, such as rods, sheets and special shapes. Plastruct Acrylic products are crystal clear unless noted.

ACRYLIC BALLS

Outside diameter shown.

570-92001 1/8" pkg(10) **1.75**
570-92002 5/32" pkg(10) **1.75**
570-92003 3/16" pkg(10) **1.75**
570-92004 1/4" pkg(10) **2.25**
570-92005 9/32" pkg(10) **2.75**
570-92006 5/16" pkg(10) **2.75**
570-92007 3/8" pkg(10) **3.25**
570-92008 7/16" pkg(10) **3.75**
570-92009 1/2" pkg(10) **3.75**
570-92010 5/8" pkg(10) **4.75**
570-92011 3/4" pkg(5) **4.75**
570-92012 7/8" pkg(3) **4.00**
570-92013 1" pkg(2) **3.50**
570-92014 1-1/4" **3.25**

ACRYLIC CUBES

Perfectly square, use for modern buildings, sculpture or craft projects. Length, width and height shown.

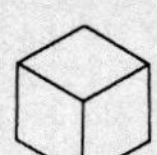

570-92021 1/4" pkg(10) **3.25**
570-92022 3/8" pkg(10) **3.75**
570-92023 1/2" pkg(10) **4.75**
570-92024 5/8" pkg(5) **2.75**
570-92025 3/4" pkg(5) **4.00**
570-92026 1" pkg(3) **4.00**
570-92027 1-1/4" **3.50**

ACRYLIC DOMES

One piece, easy way to model ends of oil, water, gas or food storage tanks. Outside diameter shown.

ELLIPTICAL

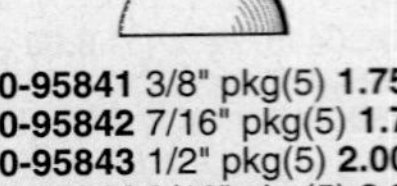

570-95741 3/8" pkg(5) **1.75**
570-95742 7/16" pkg(5) **1.75**
570-95743 1/2" pkg(5) **2.00**
570-95744 9/16" pkg(5) **2.00**
570-95745 5/8" pkg(5) **2.25**
570-95746 3/4" pkg(5) **2.50**
570-95747 7/8" pkg(5) **2.75**
570-95748 1" pkg(5) **3.00**
570-95749 1-1/8" pkg(5) **3.25**
570-95750 1-1/4" pkg(5) **3.75**
570-95751 1-1/2" pkg(5) **5.00**
570-95755 2" pkg(2) **4.20**
570-95759 3" pkg(2) **6.60**
570-95763 4" **5.00**
570-95767 5" **6.30**
570-95771 6" **7.60**

HEMISPHERICAL

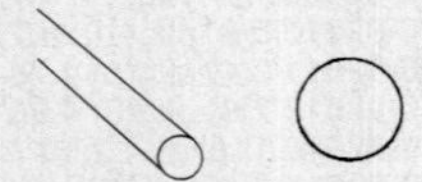

570-95841 3/8" pkg(5) **1.75**
570-95842 7/16" pkg(5) **1.75**
570-95843 1/2" pkg(5) **2.00**
570-95844 9/16" pkg(5) **2.25**
570-95845 5/8" pkg(5) **2.50**
570-95846 3/4" pkg(5) **2.75**
570-95847 7/8" pkg(5) **3.00**
570-95848 1" pkg(5) **3.25**
570-95849 1-1/8" pkg(5) **3.50**
570-95850 1-1/4" pkg(5) **4.25**
570-95851 1-1 /2" pkg(5) **6.50**
570-95855 2" pkg(2) **4.70**
570-95859 3" pkg(2) **7.60**
570-95863 4" **5.40**
570-95867 5" **7.00**
570-95871 6" **9.00**

ACRYLIC ROD

All pieces are 17-1/2" long unless noted.

SOLID ROUND

Simulate bracing, wiring, cabling, piping, conduit or use anywhere round stock is needed. Outside diameter shown.

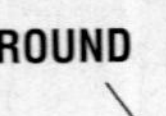

570-90291 1/16 x 8-1/2" Long pkg(40) **5.50**
570-90292 1/8 x 8-1/2" Long pkg(30) **5.50**
570-92031 1/16" pkg(20) **5.50**
570-92032 1/8" pkg(10) **3.75**
570-92033 3/16" pkg(5) **2.75**
570-92034 1/4" pkg(5) **3.25**
570-92035 5/16" pkg(5) **4.75**
570-92036 3/8" pkg(3) **4.25**
570-92037 7/16" pkg(2) **3.50**
570-92038 1/2" pkg(2) **4.50**
570-92039 9/16" **3.00**
570-92040 5/8" **4.00**
570-92041 3/4" **5.00**

HALF-ROUND

Extruded in crystal clear acrylic. Outside diameter shown.

570-92051 1/2" pkg(3) **4.00**
570-92052 5/8" pkg(2) **3.75**
570-92053 3/4" **3.00**
570-92054 1" **4.50**

SQUARE

Perfect square, ideal for glass columns and special affects. Width and height shown.

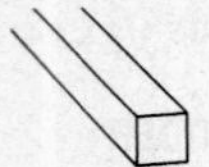

570-92061 1/8" pkg(10) **4.75**
570-92062 3/16" pkg(5) **4.25**
570-92063 1/4" pkg(3) **3.25**
570-92064 3/8" pkg(2) **3.25**
570-92065 1/2" **3.00**
570-92066 5/8" **5.25**
570-92067 3/4" **7.00**

RECTANGULAR

Extruded in crystal clear acrylic. Width and height shown.

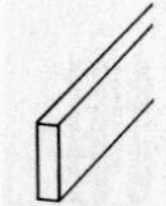

570-92071 5/8 x 1/8" pkg(3) **3.25**
570-92072 3/4 x 3/16" pkg(2) **3.50**
570-92074 1 x 1/4" **3.25**

SPIRAL

Outside diameter shown.

570-92091 3/8" pkg(2) **3.75**
570-92092 1/2" **2.75**
570-92093 5/8" **3.75**
570-92094 3/4" **5.50**
570-92095 1" **8.50**

ACRYLIC TUBING

All pieces are 15" long. Outside dimensions shown.

ROUND

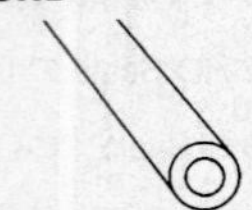

570-90131 3/32" pkg(10) **4.25**
570-90132 1/8" pkg(10) **4.75**
570-90133 3/16" pkg(7) **4.00**
570-90134 1/4" pkg(5) **3.50**

SQUARE

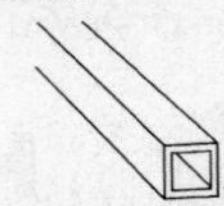

570-90241 1/8" pkg(5) **4.25**
570-90242 3/16" pkg(5) **4.75**
570-90243 1/4" pkg(4) **4.25**

CLEAR SHEET

BUTYRATE & ACRYLIC

These plastics are tougher than styrene and resist splitting and shattering when cut. Each sheet measures 7 x 12", dimension shown is thickness.

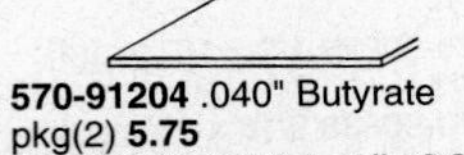

570-91204 .040" Butyrate pkg(2) **5.75**
570-91206 .060" Acrylic **6.00**

COPOLYESTER

Tougher than styrene, resists splitting and shattering when cut. Each sheet measures 7 x 12", dimension shown is thickness.

570-91251 .030" pkg(3) **5.50**
570-91252 .040" pkg(2) **4.75**
570-91253 .060" pkg(2) **7.00**

LADDER CLIPS

Use to secure ladders (sold separately) against structures or towers. Simply trim the stem length to adjust mounting clearance from the surface. Use pipe clip flanges or drill 3/32" hole for mounting. Parts are injection molded in clear acrylic plastic.

570-95435 Fits Ladder #90423 (O) pkg(5) **2.00** ***NEW***
570-95437 Fits Ladder #90425 (G) pkg(5) **2.50** ***NEW***
570-95438 Fits Ladder #90426 (1/16) pkg(5) **2.75** ***NEW***

FLUORESCENT ACRYLIC ROD

Gathers light from the sides and emits it from the ends. Molded in color, can be used for all types of special effects, such as signals, switch lamps, neon signs, auto and truck lamps etc. Each piece is 10" long, outside diameter shown.

BLUE

570-90251 1/16" pkg(10) **3.75**
570-90252 3/32" pkg(8) **4.25**
570-90253 1/8" pkg(7) **4.75**
570-90254 5/32" pkg(5) **4.50**

GREEN

570-90261 1/16" pkg(10) **3.75**
570-90262 3/32" pkg(8) **4.25**
570-90263 1/8" pkg(7) **4.75**
570-90264 5/32 pkg(5) **4.50**

RED

570-90271 1/16" pkg(10) **3.75**
570-90272 3/32" pkg(8) **4.25**
570-90273 1/8" pkg(7) **4.75**
570-90274 5/32" pkg(5) **4.50**

YELLOW

570-90281 1/16" pkg(10) **3.75**
570-90282 3/32" pkg(8) **4.25**
570-90283 1/8" pkg(7) **4.75**
570-90284 5/32" pkg(5) **4.50**

FLUORESCENT ACRYLIC SHEET PKG(2) 4.25

Acrylic sheet matches fluorescent rods and can be used for special lighting, such as neon signs. Light is gathered across the surface and emitted at the edges; images etched on the surface will also glow. Sheets are 12 x 7 x .010".

570-91301 Blue
570-91302 Green
570-91303 Red
570-91304 Yellow

CEMENT

BONDENE SOLVENT CEMENT

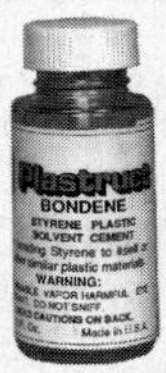

570-3 Bondene 2oz Bottle **3.25**
A colorless, liquid, plastic-fusing adhesive. Dissolves a thin layer of each surface to form a welded joint as strong as the surrounding area. Bonds Styrene to Styrene, ABS to ABS and most other alike plastic combinations. Dealers MUST order in multiples of 12.

PLASTIC WELD SOLVENT CEMENT

570-2 Plastic Weld 2oz Bottle **3.25**
This colorless, liquid, plastic-fusing adhesive bonds Styrene, ABS, Butyrate, and Acrylics. Dissolves a thin layer of each surface to form a welded joint as strong as the surrounding area. Dealers MUST order multiples of 12.

WELDENE SOLVENT CEMENT

570-4 Weldene 2oz Bottle **3.95**
A non-toxic, colorless, liquid, plastic-fusing adhesive for bonding Styrene to Styrene ONLY. Instantly tacky, cures in hours. Provides a permanent bond. Environmentally friendly. Dealers MUST order multiples of 12.

STYRENE PLASTIC

The most common modeling plastic, available in sheets, strips and special shapes, as well as vacuum-formed parts. For ease of identification, Plastruct styrene products are molded in white, unless noted. Easily cut, drilled, sanded or scored & snapped. Bonds with most Styrene cements. Accepts most acrylic paints; a primer coat is recommended. Dealers MUST order in multiples as shown.

STRIPS, RODS & SHEETS

STYRENE STRIPS

Each piece is 10" long, unless noted. Width and height shown.

570-90710 .010 x .020" pkg(10) **1.75**
570-90711 .010 x .030" pkg(10) **1.75**
570-90712 .010 x .040" pkg(10) **1.75**
570-90713 .010 x .060" pkg(10) **1.75**
570-90714 .010 x .080" pkg(10) **1.75**
570-90715 .010 x .100" pkg(10) **1.75**
570-90716 .010 x .125" pkg(10) **1.75**
570-90717 .010 x .156" pkg(10) **1.75**
570-90718 .010 x .187" pkg(10) **1.75**
570-90719 .010 x .250" pkg(10) **1.75**
570-90721 .020 x .030" pkg(10) **1.75**
570-90722 .020 x .040" pkg(10) **1.75**
570-90723 .020 x .060" pkg(10) **1.75**
570-90724 .020 x .080" pkg(10) **1.75**
570-90725 .020 x .100" pkg(10) **1.75**
570-90726 .020 x .125" pkg(10) **1.75**

Plastruct

570-90727 .020 x .156" pkg(10) **1.75**
570-90728 .020 x .187" pkg(10) **1.75**
570-90729 .020 x .250" pkg(10) **1.75**
570-90732 .030 x .040" pkg(10) **1.75**
570-90733 .030 x .060" pkg(10) **1.75**
570-90734 .030 x .080" pkg(10) **1.75**
570-90735 .030 x .100" pkg(10) **1.75**
570-90736 .030 x .125" pkg(10) **1.75**
570-90737 .030 x .156" pkg(10) **1.75**
570-90738 .030 x .187" pkg(10) **1.75**
570-90739 .030 x .250" pkg(10) **1.75**
570-90743 .040 x .060" pkg(10) **1.75**
570-90744 .040 x .080" pkg(10) **1.75**
570-90745 .040 x .100" pkg(10) **1.75**
570-90746 .040 x .125" pkg(10) **1.75**
570-90747 .040 x .156" pkg(10) **1.75**
570-90748 .040 x .187" pkg(10) **1.75**
570-90749 .040 x .250" pkg(10) **1.75**
570-90754 .060 x .080" pkg(10) **1.75**
570-90755 .060 x .100" pkg(10) **1.75**
570-90756 .060 x .125" pkg(10) **1.75**
570-90757 .060 x .156" pkg(10) **1.75**
570-90758 .060 x .187" pkg(10) **1.75**
570-90759 .060 x .250" pkg(10) **1.75**
570-90765 .080 x .100" pkg(10) **2.25**
570-90766 .080 x .125" pkg(10) **2.25**
570-90767 .080 x .156" pkg(10) **2.25**
570-90768 .080 x .187" pkg(10) **2.25**
570-90769 .080 x .250" pkg(10) **2.25**
570-90776 .100 x .125" pkg(10) **2.25**
570-90777 .100 x .156" pkg(10) **2.25**
570-90778 .100 x .187" pkg(10) **2.25**
570-90779 .100 x .250" pkg(10) **2.25**
570-90787 .125 x .156" pkg(10) **2.50**
570-90788 .125 x .187" pkg(10) **2.50**
570-90789 .125 x .250" pkg(10) **2.50**
570-90798 .156 x .187" pkg(5) **1.25**
570-90799 .156 x .250" pkg(5) **1.25**
570-90809 .187 x .250" pkg(5) **1.75**
570-90641 .020 x 1-1/4 x 24" pkg(5) **3.75**
570-90642 .030 x 1-1/4 x 24" pkg(5) **4.25**

STYRENE ROUND ROD
Each piece is 10" long, outside diameter shown.

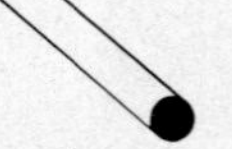

570-90850 .010" pkg(10) **1.75**
570-90851 .020" pkg(10) **1.75**
570-90852 .025" pkg(10) **1.75**
570-90853 .030" pkg(10) **1.75**
570-90854 .035" pkg(10) **1.75**
570-90855 .040" pkg(10) **2.25**
570-90856 .045" pkg(10) **2.25**
570-90857 .050" pkg(10) **2.25**
570-90858 .060" pkg(10) **2.25**
570-90859 .080" pkg(5) **1.25**
570-90860 .100" pkg(5) **1.50**
570-90861 .125" pkg(5) **1.50**
570-90862 .156" pkg(5) **1.75**
570-90863 .187" pkg(5) **2.00**
570-90864 .250" pkg(5) **2.25**
570-90849 .015" pkg(10) **1.75** *NEW*

HALF-ROUND ROD
Each piece is 10" long, outside diameter shown.

570-90879 .030" pkg(10) **1.75**
570-90880 .040" pkg(10) **2.25**
570-90881 .060" pkg(10) **2.25**
570-90882 .080" pkg(10) **2.50**
570-90883 .100" pkg(10) **2.50**
570-90884 .125" pkg(5) **1.50**
570-90885 .156" pkg(5) **1.75**
570-90886 .187" pkg(5) **2.00**
570-90887 .250" pkg(5) **2.25**

STYRENE SQUARE ROD
Each piece is 10" long, height and width shown.

570-90709 .010" pkg(10) **1.75**
570-90720 .020" pkg(10) **1.75**
570-90730 .030" pkg(10) **1.75**
570-90740 .040" pkg(10) **1.75**
570-90750 .060" pkg(10) **1.75**
570-90760 .080" pkg(10) **2.25**
570-90770 .100" pkg(10) **2.25**
570-90780 .125" pkg(10) **2.75**
570-90790 .160" pkg(5) **1.25**
570-90800 .190" pkg(5) **1.75**
570-90810 .250" pkg(5) **2.25**

STYRENE QUARTER-ROUND ROD
Each piece is 10" long, height and width shown.

570-90891 .030" pkg(10) **1.75**
570-90892 .040" pkg(10) **2.25**
570-90893 .060" pkg(10) **2.25**
570-90894 .080" pkg(10) **2.50**
570-90895 .100" pkg(5) **1.50**
570-90896 .125" pkg(5) **1.50**

STYRENE TRIANGULAR ROD
Each piece is 10" long, height and width shown.

570-90841 .030" pkg(10) **1.75**
570-90842 .040" pkg(10) **2.25**
570-90843 .060" pkg(10) **2.25**
570-90844 .080" pkg(10) **2.50**
570-90845 .100" pkg(5) **1.50**
570-90846 .125" pkg(5) **1.50**

HEXAGONAL ROD
570-90871 .020" pkg(10) **1.75** *NEW*
570-90872 .030" pkg(10) **1.75** *NEW*
570-90873 .040" pkg(10) **2.25** *NEW*
570-90874 .060" pkg(10) **2.25** *NEW*
570-90875 .080" pkg(10) **2.50** *NEW*
570-90876 .100" pkg(5) **1.50** *NEW*
570-90877 .125" pkg(5) **1.50** *NEW*

CLEAR STYRENE SHEET
570-91201 .010" pkg(3) **4.50**
Each sheet measures 7 x 12", dimension shown is thickness.

WHITE STYRENE SHEET
Each sheet measures 7 x 12", dimension shown is thickness.

570-91101 .010" pkg(8) **3.75**
570-91102 .020" pkg(7) **4.25**
570-91103 .030" pkg(5) **4.00**
570-91104 .040" pkg(4) **4.25**
570-91105 .060" pkg(3) **4.75**
570-91106 .080" pkg(2) **4.25**
570-91107 .100" pkg(2) **5.50**
570-91108 .125" pkg(2) **7.00**

COLORED STYRENE SHEET
Each sheet measures 7 x 12", dimension shown is thickness.

570-91151 .020" Red pkg(2) **4.75**
570-91161 .020" Beige pkg(2) **4.75**
570-91171 .020" Gray pkg(2) **4.75**

STYRENE TUBING

STYRENE ROUND TUBING
Each piece is 15" long, outside diameter shown.

570-90603 3/32" pkg(15) **4.25**
570-90604 1/8" pkg(10) **3.25**
570-90605 3/16" pkg(8) **3.00**
570-90606 1/4" pkg(7) **3.25**
570-90607 5/16" pkg(6) **3.50**
570-90608 3/8" pkg(5) **3.25**

STYRENE SQUARE TUBING
Each piece is 15" long, height and width shown.

570-90621 1/8" pkg(7) **3.25**
570-90622 3/16" pkg(6) **3.25**
570-90623 1/4" pkg(5) **2.75**
570-90624 5/16" pkg(5) **3.25**
570-90625 3/8" pkg(4) **3.00**

STYRENE RECTANGULAR TUBING
Each piece is 15" long, height and width shown.

570-90631 1/4 x 3/16" pkg(5) **2.75**
570-90632 5/16 x 1/4" pkg(5) **3.25**
570-90633 3/8 x 1/4" pkg(4) **3.00**

STYRENE STRUCTURAL SHAPES

ANGLES
Height and length shown.

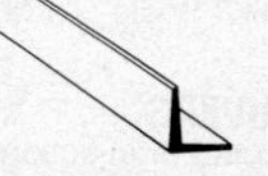

570-90501 3/64 x 10" pkg(10) **3.25**
570-90502 1/16 x 10" pkg(10) **3.75**
570-90503 3/32 x 15" pkg(8) **3.75**
570-90504 1/8 x 15" pkg(7) **3.50**
570-90505 3/16 x 24" pkg(5) **3.50**
570-90506 1/4 x 24" pkg(5) **3.75**
570-90507 5/16 x 24" pkg(4) **3.75**
570-90508 3/8 x 24" pkg(4) **4.25**

I BEAMS
Height and length shown.

570-90511 1/16 x 10" pkg(10) **3.25**
570-90512 3/32 x 10" pkg(10) **3.75**
570-90513 1/8 x 15" pkg(8) **3.75**
570-90514 5/32 x 15" pkg(6) **3.50**
570-90515 3/16 x 24" pkg(5) **3.50**
570-90516 1/4 x 24" pkg(5) **4.00**
570-90517 5/16 x 24" pkg(4) **3.75**
570-90518 3/8 x 15" pkg(5) **3.00**
570-90519 7/16 x 15" pkg(5) **3.50**
570-90520 1/2 x 15" pkg(4) **3.50**
570-90521 9/16 x 15" pkg(3) **2.75**
570-90522 5/8 x 15" pkg(3) 3.25

CHANNELS
Height and length shown.

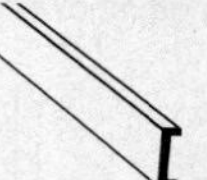
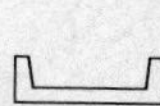

570-90531 1/16 x 10" pkg(10) **3.25**
570-90532 3/32 x 10" pkg(10) **3.75**
570-90533 1/8 x 15" pkg(8) **3.75**
570-90534 5/32 x 15" pkg(6) **3.50**
570-90535 3/16 x 15" pkg(5) **3.25**
570-90536 1/4 x 24" pkg(5) **4.00**
570-90537 5/16 x 24" pkg(4) **3.75**

DEEP CHANNELS
Height and length shown.

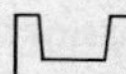

570-90581 1/16 x 10" pkg(10) **3.25**
570-90582 3/32 x 10" pkg(10) **3.75**
570-90583 1/8 x 15" pkg(8) **3.75**
570-90584 3/16 x 15" pkg(5) **3.00**
570-90585 1/4 x 24" pkg(5) **4.00**

COLUMNS
Height and length shown.

570-90541 1/16 x 10" pkg(10) **3.25**
570-90542 3/32 x 15" pkg(10) **4.00**
570-90543 1/8 x 15" pkg(8) **3.75**
570-90544 5/32 x 15" pkg(6) **3.50**
570-90545 3/16 x 24" pkg(5) **3.75**
570-90546 1/4 x 15" pkg(5) **2.75**
570-90547 5/16 x 15" pkg(5) **3.50**
570-90548 3/8 x 15" pkg(4) **3.50**

TEES
Height and length shown.

570-90561 3/64 x 10" pkg(10) **3.25**
570-90562 1/16 x 10" pkg(10) **3.75**
570-90563 3/32 x 15" pkg(8) **3.75**
570-90564 1/8 x 15" pkg(7) **3.75**
570-90565 3/16 x 24" pkg(5) **3.50**
570-90566 1/4 x 24" pkg(5) **4.00**

ZEES
Height and length shown.

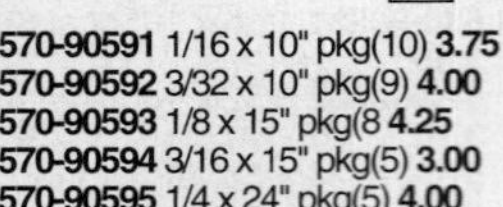

570-90591 1/16 x 10" pkg(10) **3.75**
570-90592 3/32 x 10" pkg(9) **4.00**
570-90593 1/8 x 15" pkg(8 **4.25**
570-90594 3/16 x 15" pkg(5) **3.00**
570-90595 1/4 x 24" pkg(5) **4.00**

BALCONY RAILINGS
Molded in brown.

570-90901 N Scale 6-1/2" Long pkg(2) **5.00**
570-90902 HO Scale 6-1/2" Long pkg(2) **5.25**
570-90903 O Scale 6-1/2" Long pkg(2) **5.75**

LADDERS

570-90671 N Scale 3" Long pkg(2) **1.50**
570-90672 HO Scale 5" Long pkg(2) **1.75**

HANDRAILS

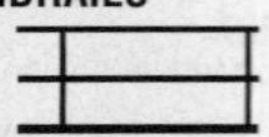

570-90681 N Scale 3-5/8" Long pkg(2) **1.50**
570-90682 HO Scale 6" Long pkg(2) **1.75**

STAIRS

570-90661 N Scale 3-5/8" Long pkg(2) **1.50**
570-90662 HO Scale 5" Long pkg(2) **2.00**

OPEN WEB TRUSSES
WARREN STYLE 2

570-90651 1/8 x 6" pkg(2) **2.50**
570-90652 3/16 x 6" pkg(2) **3.00**
570-90653 1/4 x 6" pkg(2) **3.25**
570-90654 3/8 x 6" pkg(2) **3.75**
570-90655 1/2 x 12" pkg(2) **4.25**
570-90656 5/8 x 12" pkg(2) **5.00**
570-90657 3/4 x 12" pkg(2) **5.75**
570-90658 1 x 12" pkg(2) **6.25**

PRATT STYLE

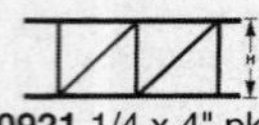

570-90921 1/4 x 4" pkg(2) **3.75**
570-90922 5/16 x 4" pkg(2) **3.75**
570-90923 7/16 x 7" pkg(2) **4.00**
570-90924 43/64 x 7" pkg(2) **4.50**
570-90925 27/32 x 8" pkg(2) **4.75**
570-90926 1-1/4 x 7" pkg(2) **5.50**
570-90927 1-5/8 x 8" pkg(2) **6.25**

CELLFORM STYLE

570-90931 1/8 x 4" pkg(2) **3.75**
570-90932 7/32 x 4" pkg(2) **4.00**
570-90933 5/16 x 4" pkg(2) **4.25**
570-90934 13/32 x 4" pkg(2) **4.50**

STAIR RAILS

570-90691 N Scale 3-5/8" Long pkg(2) **1.50**
570-90692 HO Scale 6" Long pkg(2) **1.75**

STEPS/LOUVERS
Vacuum-formed or injection molded, dimensions shown indicate width and length.

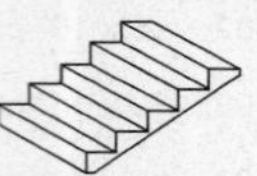

570-90951 N Scale 34° 3-7/8 x 2-1/8" **3.50**
570-90956 N Scale 17° 3-7/8 x 2-1/8" **2.25** ***NEW***
570-90952 HO Scale 34° 3-7/8 x 2-1/8" **4.25**
570-90957 HO Scale 17° 3-7/8 x 2-1/8" **2.45** ***NEW***
570-90953 O Scale 34° 7 x 12" **6.00** ***NEW***

PATTERNED SHEETS

Vacuum formed from .020 styrene. Scales shown indicate relative size, most items can be used for larger or smaller models. Sheets measure 12 x 7" unless noted, dimension shown is the size of an individual object in the pattern. See Landscaping section for additional patterns.

BRICK

570-91611 .145" (HO) pkg(2) **8.25**
570-91608 .062" (N) pkg(2) **8.25**
570-91609 .100 (TT) pkg(2) **8.25**
570-91613 .187" (O) pkg(2) **8.25**
570-91616 .375" (G) 24 x 7" **8.95**
570-91601 .730" (1/12) 24 x 7" **8.95**

BRICK RELIEF
For use around doors and windows, includes two sets of arches, sills and corners. Use with 570-91601. Sheet measures 24 x 7".

570-91603 .720" (1/12) **13.95**

ROUGH BRICK

570-91605 .150" (HO) pkg(2) **8.25**
570-91606 .200" (O) pkg(2) **8.25**
570-91604 .400" (G) pkg(2) **8.25**
570-91616 .400" (G) 24 x 7" **8.95**
570-91607 .800" (1/12) 24 x 7" **8.95**

CONCRETE BLOCK

570-91620 .175" (HO) pkg(2) **8.25**
570-91621 .325" (O) pkg(2) **8.25**
570-91624 .650" (G) pkg(2) **8.25**
570-91618 .650" (G) 24 x 7" **8.95**
570-91622 1.30" (1/12) 24 x 7" **8.95**

FLOORING PKG(2) EA 8.25 (UNLESS NOTED)

PLANKING

570-91531 .078" (HO)
570-91530 .039" (N)
570-91532 .120" (O)
570-91533 .210" (G)
570-91766 .210" (G) Single 24 x 7" 60 x 17.5cm Sheet **8.95**

SQUARE TILES
WHITE

570-91539 .125" (All)
570-91540 .050" (All)
570-91541 .055" (All)
570-91542 .180" (All)
570-91543 .075" (All)
570-91544 .235" (All)
570-91545 .485" (All)
570-91546 .960" (All)

RED
570-91749 .125" (All) ***NEW***
570-91750 .050" (All)
570-91751 .055" (All)
570-91752 .180" (All)
570-91753 .075" (All)
570-91754 .235" (All)
570-91755 .485" (All)
570-91756 .960" (All)

CLEAR
570-91739 .125" (All)
570-91740 .050" (All)
570-91741 .055" (All)
570-91742 .180" (All)
570-91743 .075" (All)
570-91744 .235" (All)
570-91745 .485" (All)
570-91746 .960" (All)

ROOFING EA 8.25 (UNLESS NOTED)

ASPHALT SHINGLE

570-91630 .125" (HO) pkg(2)
570-91631 .250" (O) pkg(2)
570-91633 .475" (G) pkg(2)
570-91642 .475" (G) 24 x 7" **8.95**
570-91636 .980" (1/12) 24 x 7" **8.95**

RIBBED METAL PKG(2)

570-91511 .093" (HO)
570-91512 .200" (O)
570-91513 .287" (G)

SCALLOPED TILE

570-91650 .125" (HO) pkg(2)
570-91651 .250" (O) pkg(2)
570-91654 .375" (G) pkg(2)
570-91643 .375" (G) 24 x 7" **8.95**
570-91653 .785" (1/12) 24 x 7" **8.95**

SPANISH TILE

570-91638 .087" (HO) pkg(2)
570-91640 .048" (N) pkg(2)
570-91637 .125" (O) pkg(2)
570-91632 .250" (G) pkg(2)
570-91619 .250" (G) 24 x 7" **8.95**
570-91639 .500" (1/12) 24 x 7" **8.95**

WOOD SHAKE SHINGLE

570-91656 .125" (HO) pkg(2)
570-91655 .250" (O) pkg(2)
570-91659 .375" (G) pkg(2)
570-91644 .375" (G) 24 x 7" **8.95**
570-91658 .750" (1/12) 24 x 7" **8.95**

RIDGED CLAY TILE PKG(2)

570-91665 .110" (HO)
570-91666 .220" (O)

SIDING PKG(2) EA 8.25 (UNLESS NOTED)

CLAPBOARD SIDING

570-91550 .062" (All)
570-91551 .125" (All)
570-91552 .187" (All)
570-91554 .250" (All) 11 x 7"
570-91558 .250" (All) 22 x 7" **8.95**
570-91556 .312" (All) 11 x 7"
570-91767 . 375" (All) 24 x 7" **8.95** ***NEW***
570-91769 .312" (All) 22 x 7" **8.95**

CORRUGATED SIDING

570-91509 .050" (HO)
570-91510 .030" (N)
570-91519 .080" (O)
570-91520 .125" (1/32) 11 x 7"
570-91521 .187" (G) 11 x 7"
570-91522 .250" (1/16) 11 x 7"

STONE PKG(2) EA 8.25 (UNLESS NOTED)

DRESSED STONE / BLOCK

570-91590 .212" (HO)
570-91587 .375" (O)
570-91592 .875" (G)
570-91774 24 x 7 x 1-3/4" **8.95** ***NEW***

INTERLOCKING PAVING

570-91670 .082" (HO)
570-91671 .150" (O)
570-91672 .350" (G)
570-91645 .350" (G) 24 x 7" **8.95**
570-91673 .650" (1/12) 24 x 7" **8.95**

RANDOM/FIELD STONE

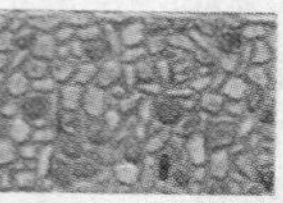

570-91581 .170" (HO)
570-91580 .240" (HO)

RANDOM COURSED STONE

570-91561 .312" (HO)
570-91562 .100" (N)
570-91560 .450" (O)

FIELD STONE

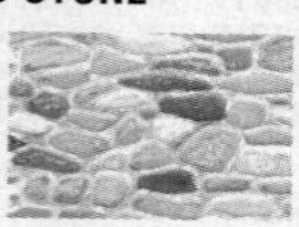

570-91563 .250" (HO)
570-91565 .325" (O)
570-91564 .575" (G)
570-91583 .750" (1/12) 24 x 7" **8.95**

ROUND FIELD STONE

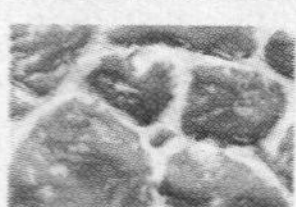

570-91591 .810" (1/12)

RANDOM POLISHED

570-91582 .225" (HO)
570-91584 .125" (N)
570-91588 .312" (O)
570-91589 .375" (G)
570-91615 .375" (G) 24 x 7" **8.95**
570-91586 1" (1/12) 24 x 7" **8.95**

PATIO STONE

570-91593 .750" (G)

STONE WALL

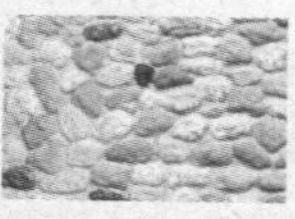

570-91559 .310" (All)

ROCK EMBANKMENT

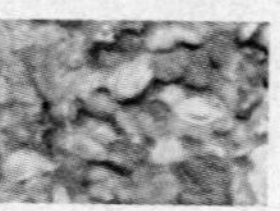

570-91570 .125" (HO)
570-91571 .225" (O)

SAFETY TREAD

CHECKER PLATE

570-91680 .125" (HO) Clear pkg(2) **8.25**

TREAD PLATE PKG(2) EA 5.75 (UNLESS NOTED)

570-91681 .100" (HO) pkg(2) **8.25**
570-91701 .035" (Z) 3-7/8 x 2-1/4"
570-91702 .055" (N) 3-7/8 x 2-1/4"
570-91703 .200" (O) 3-7/8 x 2-1/4"
570-91704 .280" (G) 3-7/8 x 2-1/4"

DOUBLE DIAMOND PLATE PKG(2) EA 9.50

570-91682 .150" (G)
570-91683 .187" (1/16)

SINGLE DIAMOND PLATE PKG(2) EA 9.50

570-91687 .030" (HO)
570-91684 .050" (O)
570-91685 .083" (G)
570-91686 .125" (1/16)

RUBBER TREAD PKG(2) EA 5.75

570-91711 .070 (O)3-7/8 x 2-1/4"
570-91712 .140 (G)3-7/8 x 2-1/4"

STUCCO WALL PKG(2) EA 8.25

570-91572 Smooth (All)
570-91573 Coarse (All)

TUBE FITTINGS & ACCESSORIES

Use with Butyrate tubing to model industrial and commercial pipe lines, race car roll cages, exhaust systems, custom chassis or plumbing in doll houses. Parts are molded in Butyrate (white or gray) or ABS plastics as noted. Parts are designed to allow temporary press-fit, however final assembly must be cemented.

COLUMN BASE MOUNTS

These ABS parts simplify mounting vertical columns for all kinds of construction.

570-95411 Fits 570-90063 pkg(5) **2.25**
570-95412 Fits 570-90064 pkg(5) **2.50**
570-95413 Fits 570-90065 pkg(5) **2.75**
570-95414 Fits 570-90066 pkg(5) **3.00**
570-95415 Fits 570-90067 & 7/16" pkg(5) **3.25**
570-95416 Fits 1/2 & 9/16" pkg(5) **3.50**
570-95417 Fits 5/8 & 3/4" pkg(5) **3.75**

COLUMN BLOCKS

ABS Column Blocks are a quick and effective way to mount vertical square tubing on your model base. Great for concrete pads, lamp bases and similar supports.

570-95401 Fits 570-90205 pkg(5) **2.00**
570-95402 Fits 7/16" pkg(5) **2.25**
570-95403 Fits 1/2" pkg(5) **2.50**
570-95404 Fits 9/16" pkg(5) **2.75**
570-95405 Fits 5/8" pkg(5) **3.00**
570-95406 Fits 3/4" pkg(5) **3.25**

COUPLINGS

Clear Butyrate plastic.

570-95081 Fits 570-90101 pkg(5) **1.50**
570-95082 Fits 570-90102 pkg(5) **1.50**
570-95083 Fits 570-90103 pkg(5) **1.75**
570-95084 Fits 570-90104 pkg(5) **1.75**
570-95087 Fits 570-90105 pkg(5) **2.00**
570-95088 Fits 570-90106 pkg(5) **2.00**
570-95089 Fits 570-90107 pkg(5) **2.25**
570-95090 Fits 570-90108 pkg(5) **2.25**

ELBOWS

White Butyrate plastic

90° ELBOWS

570-95001 Fits 570-90103 pkg(5) **1.75**
570-95002 Fits 570-90104 pkg(5) **2.00**
570-95003 Fits 570-90105 pkg(5) **2.00**
570-95004 Fits 570-90106 pkg(5) **2.25**
570-95005 Fits 570-90107 pkg(5) **2.25**
570-95006 Fits 570-90108 pkg(5) **2.50**

90° FEMALE ELBOWS

570-95041 Fits 570-90103 pkg(5) **1.75**
570-95042 Fits 570-90104 pkg(5) **2.00**
570-95043 Fits 570-90105 pkg(5) **2.00**
570-95044 Fits 570-90106 pkg(5) **2.25**
570-95045 Fits 570-90107 pkg(5) **2.25**
570-95046 Fits 570-90108 pkg(5) **2.50**

45° ELBOWS

570-95021 Fits 570-90103 pkg(5) **1.75**
570-95022 Fits 570-90104 pkg(5) **2.00**
570-95023 Fits 570-90105 pkg(5) **2.00**
570-95024 Fits 570-90106 pkg(5) **2.25**
570-95025 Fits 570-90107 pkg(5) **2.25**
570-95026 Fits 570-90108 pkg(5) **2.50**

45° FEMALE ELBOWS

570-95061 Fits 570-90103 pkg(5) **1.75**
570-95062 Fits 570-90104 pkg(5) **2.00**
570-95063 Fits 570-90105 pkg(5) **2.00**
570-95064 Fits 570-90106 pkg(5) **2.25**
570-95065 Fits 570-90107 pkg(5) **2.25**
570-95066 Fits 570-90108 pkg(5) **2.50**

FIVE DIAMETER BENDS

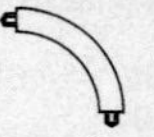

570-95101 Fits 570-90105 pkg(5) **2.50**
570-95102 Fits 570-90106 pkg(5) **2.75**
570-95103 Fits 570-90107 pkg(5) **3.00**
570-95104 Fits 570-90108 pkg(5) **3.25**

THREE DIAMETER BENDS

570-95111 Fits 570-90105 pkg(5) **2.50**
570-95112 Fits 570-90106 pkg(5) **2.75**
570-95113 Fits 570-90107 pkg(5) **3.00**
570-95114 Fits 570-90108 pkg(5) **3.25**

FLANGES

White Butyrate plastic.

570-95171 Fits 570-90101 pkg(5) **1.75**
570-95172 Fits 570-90102 pkg(5) **1.75**
570-95173 Fits 570-90103 pkg(5) **1.75**
570-95174 Fits 570-90104 pkg(5) **2.00**
570-95175 Fits 570-90105 pkg(5) **2.00**
570-95176 Fits 570-90106 pkg(5) **2.25**
570-95177 Fits 570-90107 pkg(5) **2.25**
570-95178 Fits 570-90108 pkg(5) **2.50**

LIGHT SHADES

Molded in Green ABS plastic, with open center for mounting.

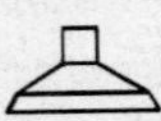

570-95901 5/16" O.D. pkg(5) **2.00**
570-95902 7/16" O.D. pkg(5) **2.25**
570-95903 5/8" O.D. pkg(5) **2.50**
570-95904 15/16" O.D. pkg(5) **2.75**

MANWAYS

Use to model access hatches or clean-outs in tanks. Molded in Gray ABS plastic.

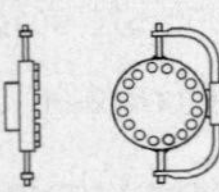

570-95641 13/16" O.D. pkg(3) **2.25**
570-95642 1-1/16" O.D. pkg(3) **3.00**
570-95643 1-1/2" O.D. pkg(3) **3.75**

MOTORS

These nonoperating details simulate the large electrical motors found at all types of industries. Easily modified for special applications. Molded in Green ABS plastic.

570-95911 3/8" pkg(3) **2.25**
570-95912 1/2" pkg(3) **2.55**
570-95913 5/8" pkg(3) **2.85**
570-95914 3/4" pkg(3) **3.15**

MOTOR AND PUMP SETS

A neat detail for any industrial or commercial application where a motor-driven pump would be found. Each set includes a nonoperating motor, pump and base plate. The motor and pump can easily be modified to simulate special applications such as turbines, blowers and more. Molded in Gray and Green ABS, except 570-95921, which is metal.

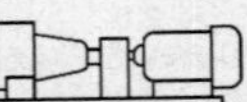

570-95921 9/16 x 3/16 x 1/4" pkg(5) **5.00**
570-95922 1-1/16 x 1/4 x 1/2" **2.75**
570-95923 1-9/16 x 3/8 x 5/8" **3.00**
570-95924 1-5/8 x 1/2 x 5/8" **3.25**
570-95929 2-7/32 x 5/8 x 3/4" **4.25** ***NEW***

NOZZLES

Gray ABS plastic.

570-95601 Fits 570-90101 pkg(5) **1.75**
570-95602 Fits 570-90102 pkg(5) **1.75**
570-95603 Fits 570-90103 pkg(5) **2.00**
570-95604 Fits 570-90104 pkg(5) **2.00**
570-95605 Fits 570-90105 pkg 5) **2.25**
570-95606 Fits 570-90106 pkg 5) **2.25**
570-95607 Fits 570-90107 pkg(5) **2.50**
570-95608 Fits 570-90108 pkg(5) **2.50**

REDUCERS

White Butyrate plastic.

CONCENTRIC

570-95132 Reduces 90104 to 90103 pkg(5) **2.00**
570-95133 Reduces 90105 to 90103 pkg(5) **2.25**
570-95134 Reduces 90106 to 90104 pkg(5) **2.25**
570-95135 Reduces 90106 to 90105 pkg(5) **2.50**
570-95136 Reduces 90107 to 90105 pkg(5) **2.50**
570-95137 Reduces 90107 to 90106 pkg(5) **2.75**
570-95139 Reduces 90108 to 90107 pkg(5) **3.00**

ECCENTRIC

570-95161 Reduces 90105 to 90103 pkg(5) **2.00**
570-95162 Reduces 90606 to 90604 pkg(5) **2.25**
570-95163 Reduces 90607 to 90605 pkg(5) **2.50**
570-95164 Reduces 90608 to 90606 pkg(5) **2.75**

RINGS

Use to model tank flanges or heat exchanger rings. Molded in Gray ABS plastic.

570-95621 Fits 3/8" pkg(5) **1.75**
570-95622 Fits 7/16" pkg(5) **2.00**
570-95623 Fits 1/2" pkg(5) **2.25**
570-95624 Fits 9/16" pkg(5) **2.50**
570-95625 Fits 5/8" pkg(5) **2.75**
570-95626 Fits 3/4" pkg(5) **3.00**
570-95627 Fits 7/8" pkg(5) **3.25**
570-95628 Fits 1" pkg(5) **3.50**
570-95629 Fits 1-1/8" pkg(5) **3.75**
570-95630 Fits 1-1/4" pkg(5) **4.00**

SADDLES

Use to support horizontal tanks or platforms. Molded in Gray ABS plastic.

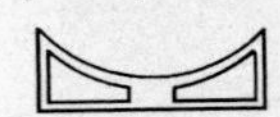

570-95661 Fits 570-90106 pkg(5) **1.50**
570-95662 Fits 570-90107 pkg(5) **1.75**
570-95663 Fits 570-90108 pkg(5) **1.75**
570-95664 Fits 7/16" pkg(5) **2.00**
570-95665 Fits 1/2" pkg(5) **2.00**
570-95666 Fits 9/16" pkg(5) **2.25**
570-95667 Fits 5/8" pkg(5) **2.25**
570-95668 Fits 3/4" pkg(5) **2.50**

TEES

White Butyrate plastic.

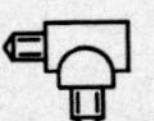

570-95201 Fits 570-90103 pkg(5) **1.75**
570-95202 Fits 570-90104 pkg(5) **2.00**
570-95203 Fits 570-90105 pkg(5) **2.00**
570-95204 Fits 570-90106 pkg(5) **2.25**
570-95205 Fits 570-90107 pkg(5) **2.25**
570-95206 Fits 570-90108 pkg(5) **2.50**

SNAP-ON TEES

White Butyrate plastic.

570-95241 Fits 570-90101 pkg(5) **1.50**
570-95242 Fits 570-90102 pkg(5) **1.50**
570-95243 Fits 570-90103 pkg(5) **1.75**
570-95244 Fits 570-90104 pkg(5) **1.75**
570-95245 Fits 570-90105 pkg(5) **2.00**
570-95246 Fits 570-90106 pkg(5) **2.00**
570-95247 Fits 570-90107 pkg(5) **2.25**
570-95248 Fits 570-90108 pkg(5) **2.25**

STUB-IN TEES

White Butyrate plastic.

570-95221 Fits 570-90105 pkg(5) **2.00**
570-95222 Fits 570-90106 pkg(5) **2.00**
570-95223 Fits 570-90107 pkg(5) **2.25**
570-95224 Fits 570-90108 pkg(5) **2.25**

TUBE CAPS

White Butyrate plastic.

570-95301 Fits 570-90103 pkg(5) **1.75**
570-95302 Fits 570-90104 pkg(5) **2.00**
570-95303 Fits 570-90105 pkg(5) **2.00**
570-95304 Fits 570-90106 pkg(5) **2.25**
570-95305 Fits 570-90107 pkg(5) **2.25**
570-95306 Fits 570-90108 pkg(5) **2.50**

VALVES

Gray Butyrate plastic.

ANGLE VALVES

570-95532 Fits 570-90102 pkg(5) **2.00**
570-95533 Fits 570-90103 pkg(5) **2.25**
570-95534 Fits 570-90104 pkg(5) **2.25**
570-95535 Fits 570-90105 pkg(5) **2.50**
570-95536 Fits 570-90106 pkg(5) **2.50**

CONTROL VALVES

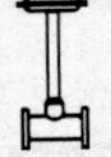

570-95521 Fits 570-90101 pkg(5) **2.00**
570-95522 Fits 570-90102 pkg(5) **2.00**
570-95523 Fits 570-90103 pkg(5) **2.25**
570-95524 Fits 570-90104 pkg(5) **2.25**
570-95525 Fits 570-90105 pkg(5) **2.50**
570-95526 Fits 570-90106 pkg(5) **2.50**

GATE VALVES

570-95501 Fits 570-90101 pkg(5) **2.00**
570-95502 Fits 570-90102 pkg(5) **2.00**
570-95503 Fits 570-90103 pkg(5) **2.25**
570-95504 Fits 570-90104 pkg(5) **2.25**
570-95505 Fits 570-90105 pkg(5) **2.50**
570-95506 Fits 570-90106 pkg(5) **2.50**
570-95507 Fits 570-90107 pkg(5) **2.75**
570-95508 Fits 570-90108 pkg(5) **3.00**

PLUG VALVES

570-95551 Fits 570-90102 pkg(5) **2.00**
570-95552 Fits 570-90103 pkg(5) **2.25**
570-95553 Fits 570-90104 pkg(5) **2.25**
570-95554 Fits 570-90105 pkg(5) **2.50**
570-95555 Fits 570-90106 pkg(5) **2.50**

SUPPORT CLIPS

Gray Butyrate plastic.

570-95561 Fits 570-90101 pkg(5) **1.50**
570-95562 Fits 570-90102 pkg(5) **1.50**
570-95563 Fits 570-90103 pkg(5) **1.75**
570-95564 Fits 570-90104 pkg(5) **1.75**
570-95565 Fits 570-90105 pkg(5) **2.00**
570-95566 Fits 570-90106 pkg(5) **2.00**
570-95567 Fits 570-90107 pkg(5) **2.25**
570-95568 Fits 570-90108 pkg(5) **2.25**

SKYLIGHTS

Clear Copolyester plastic.

PYRAMID

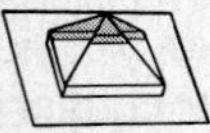

570-93001 1/4" pkg(2) **4.20**
570-93002 3/8" pkg(2) **4.40**
570-93003 1/2" pkg(2) **4.60**
570-93004 5/8" pkg(2) **4.90**

DOME

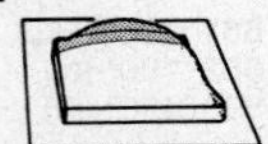

570-93011 1/4" pkg(2) **4.20**
570-93012 3/8" pkg(2) **4.40**
570-93013 1/2" pkg(2) **4.60**
570-93014 3/4" pkg(2) **5.00**

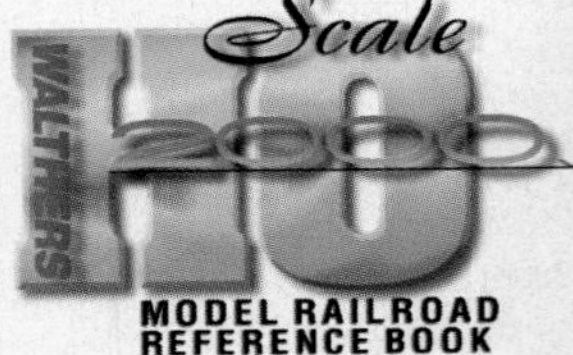

PARTS

What does it take to keep the railroad running? Most people would answer it's the trains themselves. After all, without cars and locos, you have no railroad.

Others would say it's the miles of track. Gleaming steel rails, thousands of ties, knife-edge ballast, glowing signals - these are the things that make railroads run and separate them from the other forms of transportation.

Some might point to the big corporate office building, massive steel bridges, huge shops and roundhouses, small-town depots, or the tiny trackside sheds for the maintenance crews.

There are those who would point out the many employees, from college kids hired for summer track projects, to the president of the line. Each and every person who works the road makes a difference.

In truth, it is all of these things and many more that keep the road running. But much of what is required takes place behind the scenes, out of the public eye. Among the places usually off-limits are the shops, where workers rebuild and repair everything from air horns to complete engines. But thanks to the talents of Pietro Sedoschi, of Udine, Italy, we're getting an insider's view of the work. This interior shot shows only a small portion of his beautiful steam-era workshop. Everything you would need in the real world has been included; tiny hand tools, safety signs, welding equipment, workbenches, calendar, large lathes, a first aid kit and yes, even a sink for washing up - complete with faucets! Working lights provide dramatic effects and help show the action as one of the many figures sets up a boring mill. The structure is part of a display layout Pietro scratchbuilt, which measures 64 x 28" and includes literally hundreds of tiny details.

Models by Pietro Sedoschi
Photo by Domenico "Nic" Tromby

Parts are metal castings.

We have worked closely with this manufacturer to provide accurate delivery information at the time this catalog was published. Items listed in blue ink may not be available at all times. Current delivery information, along with a list of in-stock products for this line, can be found on our Web site at www.walthers.com.

CABOOSE AWNING PKG(4) EA .65

120-2201 24" Wide
120-2202 30" Wide

CHIMNEYS PKG(2) EA .75

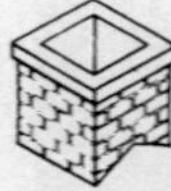

120-2701 120-2705 120-2706

120-2701 Fancy
120-2705 Brick
120-2706 Stone

COACH SEATS EA .95

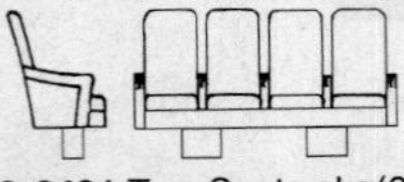

120-3401 Two Seats pkg(6)
120-3402 Three Seats pkg(4)
120-3403 Four Seats pkg(4)

CORBELS

120-1401 120-1403

120-1401 pkg(12) .95
120-1403 pkg(4) 1.25

DOORS

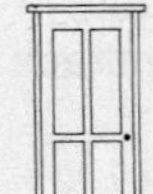

120-2403 120-2404 120-2405

120-2403 With 4-Pane Window pkg(3) **1.75**
120-2404 With Transom pkg(4) **1.50**
120-2405 4-Panel pkg(4) **1.50**

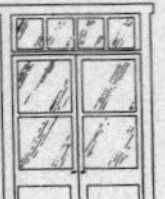
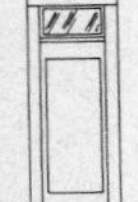

120-2406 120-2407 120-2408

120-2406 Double pkg(2) 1.75
120-2407 Solid Panel pkg(4) 1.50
120-2408 3-Panel pkg(4) **1.50**

120-2409 120-2410 120-2411

120-2409 With 2 Windows pkg(4) 1.50
120-2410 4-Panel pkg(4) **1.50**
120-2411 With 4 Windows pkg(4) 1.50

FREIGHT DOORS

120-1602 120-2401 120-2402

120-1602 Ghost Town **.49**
120-2401 With Transom .65
120-2402 Plain .65

GEARS PKG(2) EA .75 (UNLESS NOTED)

120-414 120-415 120-416

120-414 Large (9/16")
120-415 Small (7/16")
120-416 Pinion (9/16")

GINGERBREAD

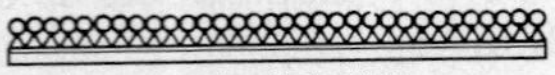

120-1101 pkg(10) **1.75**

120-1102 pkg(10) 1.50

120-1103 pkg(10) **1.50**

120-1104 pkg(10) 1.75

120-1105 pkg(10) **1.50**

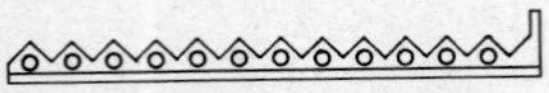

120-1106 Ridge Trim pkg(10) 1.40

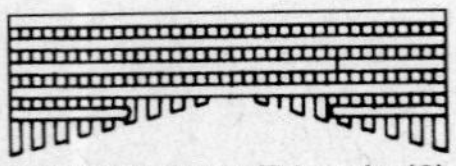

120-2900 Lattice Trim pkg(6) **1.50**

HATCHES

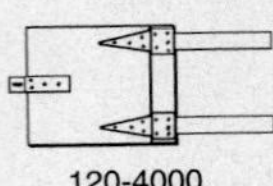

120-4000 120-4002

120-4000 Ice, Narrow Gauge pkg(4) **.65**
120-4002 Small pkg(4) **1.50**

LAMPS

120-1800 Outside Kerosene Lamp pkg(6) 1.50

LOCOMOTIVE DETAILS

120-1301 Engineer's & Fireman's Seats (1 each) 1.25

120-2203 Diesel Sunshade Awnings pkg(2) **.59**

MINE EQUIPMENT

120-2801 Latrine Car (2' Gauge) **2.50**

120-2821 Kanawha Mine Car (HOn3) **4.25**
120-9804 18" Gauge Mine Track Kick Switch pkg(2) 1.40

PLUG DOORS PKG(2) EA 1.25

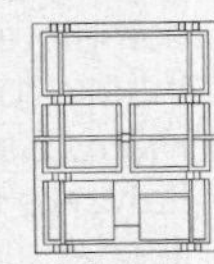

120-301 Hi Cube

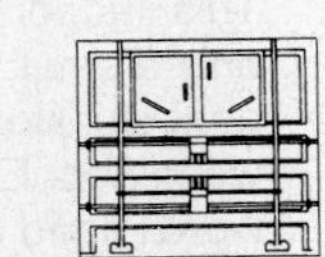

120-302 Youngstown
120-303 60' Auto Door

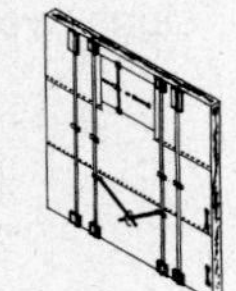

120-304 Superior

PORCH SUPPORTS PKG(6) EA 1.50

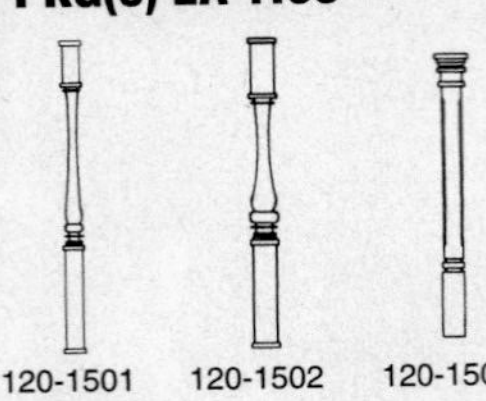

120-1501 120-1502 120-1503

120-1501 Long
120-1502 Short
120-1503 Square

PULLEYS PKG(4) EA .75

120-424 Large 1/4" Diameter
120-425 Small 3/16" Diameter

RAILINGS & GATES

120-1601 Ghost Town pkg(6) **1.00**

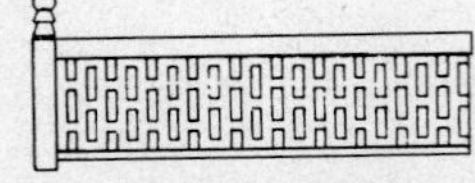

120-2301 Porch Railings pkg(6) 1.50

120-2302 Porch Railings pkg(6) 1.50

120-3000 Fence Gate pkg(4) **1.40**

ROLLING STOCK DETAILS

120-3801 4-Rung Ladders pkg(4) .75

ROOF BRACES

120-1402 120-2001 120-2002

120-1402 Support pkg(12) **.65**
120-2001 Large pkg(12) **1.50**
120-2002 Small pkg(12) 1.50

SMOKE JACKS PKG(4) EA .75

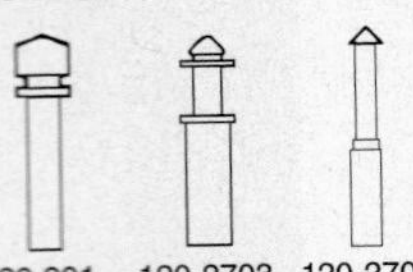

120-901 120-2703 120-2704

120-901 Caboose
120-2703 Short
120-2704 Tall

STAIRS & STEPS

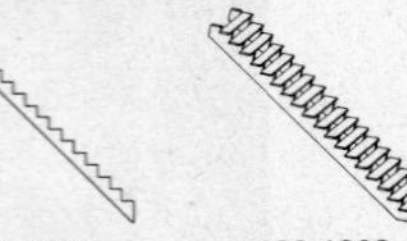

120-1201 120-1202

120-1201 Stair Riser pkg(6) **1.40**
120-1202 Open Stair Section 1/2 x 2-7/8" 1.10

120-1203 120-1204

120-1203 Short Stair Section 7/16 x 1-3/4" **.50**
120-1204 Medium Stair Section **.85**

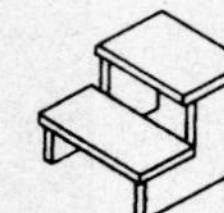

120-1205 120-1207

120-1205 Long Stair Section 7/16 x 4-1/4" 1.50
120-1207 Short Step pkg(2) .60

TOOLS

120-2603 Lathe/Tool Makers **2.00**

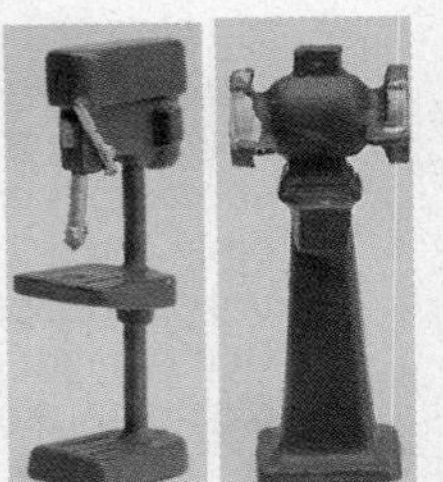

120-2604 120-2605

120-2604 Modern Drill Press - Floor Model **.75**
120-2605 Pedestal Tool Grinder **.50**

120-2606 Bridgeport Vertical Milling Machine **2.00**

TRACKSIDE DETAILS

Make your right-of-way look as good as the rest of your models with these cast-metal details. Smaller items are single pieces, ready for painting and installation. Larger models have a minimum of parts for easy assembly. Additional information and pictures appeared in "Add Right-of-Way Signal Detail" in the June 1975 issue of Model Railroader.

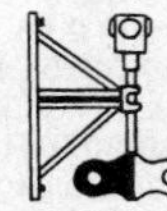

120-1001 120-1002

120-1001 Train Order Board **1.50**
120-1002 Train Order Board **1.50**
Nonoperating, prototypes were mounted on stations.

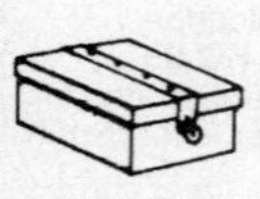
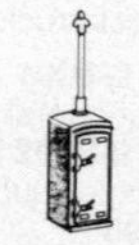

120-3101 120-3102

120-3101 Ground Relay Box pkg(2) **.60**
120-3102 Instrument Case **1.25**
Houses circuit relays for smaller installations. Mast provides connections from underground signal cables to line wire paralleling the track.

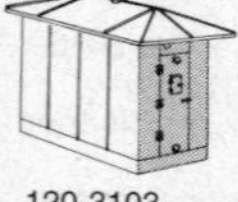
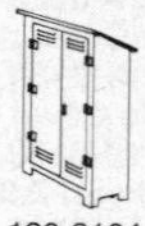

120-3103 120-3104

120-3103 Signal Relay Equipment House **1.75**
For housing banks of relays and other electrical equipment at large and important signal installations.

120-3104 Relay Enclosure **1.00**
House relays and electrical equipment for smaller installations such as single pairs of signals or crossing flashers.

120-3105 120-3107

120-3105 Battery Box, Double pkg(2) **1.10**
Used to enclose primary or back-up batteries. Also used as a relay housing where batteries are the primary power.

120-3107 Electrical Switch Motor pkg(6) **1.50**
Powers mainline turnouts at passing sidings and crossovers, enabling them to be thrown remotely by tower operator or dispatchers.

120-3108 Circuit Controller pkg(10) **1.50**
Provides position indication for interlocking hand-thrown turnouts with signal system.

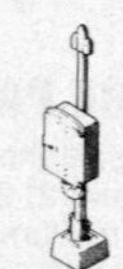

120-3109 Cable Junction Box pkg(3) **1.50**
Provides a terminal point between overhead and underground lines to signals. It may also house a telephone or a signal relay.

120-3110 Vault Cover pkg(4) **.95**
Used to cover underground concrete vaults at all signal locations.

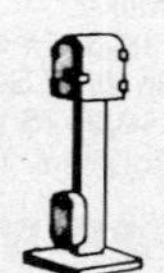

120-3111 120-3112

120-3111 Remote Signal Indicator pkg(3) **1.50**
A low-level, dual block signal indicator used to guide track crews and switchmen. Repeats distant signal aspect. Sometimes used to indicate position of remote turnout.

120-3112 Electrical Lock pkg(3) **1.50**
Secures hand-thrown turnouts on a signaled mainline. Lock may be released only by tower personnel or dispatcher.

120-3113 Equipment Base pkg(6) **1.40**

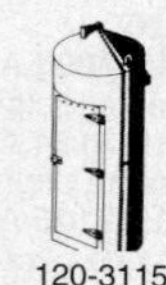

120-3114 120-3115

120-3114 Wooden Telephone Shelter **1.75**
Provides shelter and communications for road and track crews at unmanned junctions, spurs and crossings. Cast interior includes phone and junction box.

120-3115 Concrete Telephone Shelter **1.50**
Modern, smaller unit used like #3114.

VENTS PKG(4) EA .75

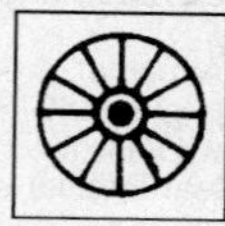

120-701 120-1701

120-701 Exhaust Fans
120-1701 Passenger Car

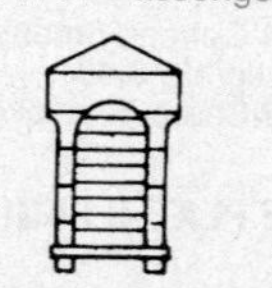

120-1900 Louvered

WINDOWS

120-2101 Ticket **1.50**

120-2504 120-2505

120-2504 pkg(4) **1.50**
120-2505 pkg(4) **1.50**

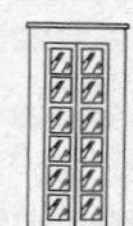

120-2506 120-2507

120-2506 pkg(4) **1.50**
120-2507 French pkg(4) **1.75**

120-2508 120-2509

120-2508 Large pkg(2) **1.75**
120-2509 pkg(2) **1.75**

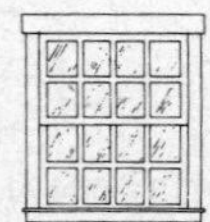

120-2510 120-2511

120-2510 pkg(4) **1.60**
120-2511 pkg(4) **1.60**

120-2512 120-2513

120-2512 Twelve-Pane pkg(4) **1.75**
120-2513 Transom pkg(4) **1.50**

120-2514 120-2515

120-2514 Four-Pane pkg(4) **1.50**
120-2515 Single pkg(4) **1.50**

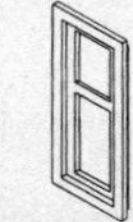

120-2516 120-2517

120-2516 Single Interlock pkg(4) **1.50**
120-2517 Double for Interlock Tower pkg(4) **1.50**

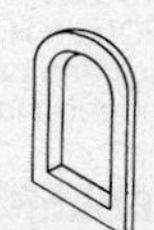

120-2518 120-2520

120-2518 Curio Shop pkg(2) **1.75**
120-2520 Small Arched pkg(4) **1.50**

120-2521 120-2522

120-2521 Large, Arched pkg(4) **1.50**
120-2522 Two-Pane pkg(4) **1.50**

MISCELLANEOUS

120-408 120-409

120-408 Valve pkg(5) **1.50**
120-409 Elbow pkg(5) **1.50**
120-410 Fire Extinguisher pkg(5) **1.50**

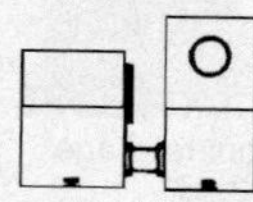
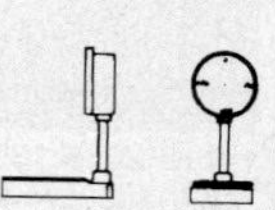

120-801 120-3201

120-801 Electrical Boxes pkg(4) **.65**
120-3201 Scale 200# Capacity pkg(4) **1.25**
120-1603 Tombstones, Assorted pkg(12) **1.50**

120-3301 120-3901

120-3301 Manhole Covers pkg(10) **1.50**
120-3901 Water Tank Spout **.75**

AM MODELS

Parts are molded in brown plastic (unless noted).

DOORS & WINDOWS

129-201 Doors & Windows **1.50**
Includes four doors and twelve windows.

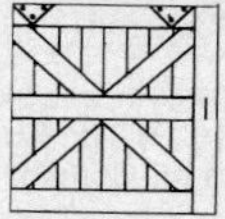

129-203 Freight Doors pkg(4) **1.50**
Molded in white plastic.

PALLETS & SKIDS

129-50112 pkg(12) **1.50**
129-50136 pkg(36) **3.50**

BRASS CAR SIDES

CAR ENDS

173-200 Streamlined **3.95**
One-piece castings match ends used by Pullman Standard or American Car & Foundry on lightweight, flat-top cars. Made of American pewter metal, castings can be used with any Brass Car Sides conversion and are included with Basic Body kit (173-101), listed in the Passenger Car section.

BAGGAGE-MAIL DOORS PKG(2) EA 3.75

One-piece, photo-etched brass.

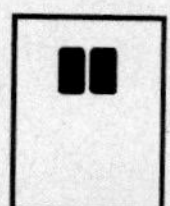

173-300 173-301

173-300 3' Two-Window
173-301 5' Three-Window

DETAIL PARTS

AIR CONDITIONERS

119-2007 Window pkg(7) **2.39**
119-2016 20-Ton Roof Mounted Air Conditioner **3.49**

CHAIN

119-1000 24" Copper (36 links per inch) **2.95**

55 GALLON DRUMS PKG(7) EA 2.95 (UNLESSS NOTED)

119-2002 Used & Abused

119-2003 New Condition
119-2011 Barrel Rack Set **4.95**

FENCE

119-2013 Corrugated Iron Fence w/Gates **12.95**
Kit includes 200 scale feet of fence material.

JUNK YARD DETAILS

119-2046 Junk Autos pkg(5) **7.95**
Five different disabled car bodies to create an auto wrecking yard, or smash and stack to use as flat car or truck loads.

119-2036 24' Roll-Off Body Kit **7.95**

119-2010 Portable "A" Frame w/Chain Hoist Kit **4.95**
Includes brass parts and copper chain.

LADDERS

119-2014 6-ft. Wooden Stepladder pkg(2) **2.39**

MISCELLANEOUS

119-2005 4 x 8' Scale Raised Diamond Plate Sheets pkg(7) **2.95**

119-2015 18" Squirrel Cage Exhaust Blower **3.49**

119-2006 1000 lb. Hydraulic Pallet Jack pkg(2) **2.39**
119-2012 Work Table Set (3 pieces) **4.95**

119-2017 Wooden Reels pkg(3) **3.49**
119-2034 Roof Top Water Tower **5.95**
119-2048 Skipper's Dog House pkg(2) **2.39**

VEHICLE DETAILS

AUTO PARTS

119-2047 Assorted Auto Parts **5.95**
119-2051 Brass Airplane Hood Ornament pkg(6) **3.49**
119-2052 Window Glass for Chevy Coupe (Clear Plastic) pkg(2) **2.39**
119-2053 White Walls for Autos (Self-Adhesive Paper) pkg(6) **3.49**
119-2054 Generic Steering Wheels pkg(12) **3.49**
119-3133 Spare Tires pkg(4) **2.95**

LICENSE PLATES PKG(12) EA 3.49

119-2050 1950
119-2055 1955
119-2056 1956
119-2057 1957
119-2058 1948
119-2059 1959
119-2060 1941
119-2061 1951
119-2062 1949
119-2063 1953

TRUCK PARTS

BATTERY BOXES PKG(4) 2.95

119-3083 With Air Tank
119-3084 With Small Tank

BOGIES EA 3.95

119-3122 With Offset Springs & Tires
119-3123 With Centered Springs & Tires

BUMPERS EA 2.95

119-3161 Front, Off-Road (2 Types) for Ford Trucks 2 Pair
119-3167 Rear Drop Step for Trailers/Flatbeds pkg(2)
119-3169 Front For GMC Astro 2 Pair
119-3171 Heavy-Duty Front (2 Types) for Diamond Reo/Autocar 2 Pair

CAB DETAILS

119-3004 Air Deflector pkg(3) **2.95**
119-3065 Mack Bulldog Radiator Caps (Brass) pkg(6) **2.95**
119-3069 1/4 Tractor Fenders pkg(2) **1.95**
Mount in front of dual wheels.
119-3074 Air Dam for Cab Roof pkg(3) **2.95**
119-3081 Sun Visors Mack B42/61/71 pkg(3) **1.95**

CAB SEATS PKG(2) EA 1.95

119-3058 Standard
119-3059 Modern Hi-Back Type
119-3071 Truck Seat Bench Type

DECALS

119-3053 Decals for Mack & GMC pkg(2) **2.95**

EXHAUST PIPES & ACCESSORIES

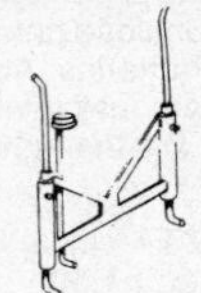

119-3057 Dual w/Air Cleaner for Athearn Freightliner **1.95**
119-3054 Dual for Mack B-42/61/71 pkg(2) **2.95**
119-3056 Dual for Ulrich Kenworth **2.95**
119-3063 Dual w/"Snorkel" Air Cleaner for GMC **1.95**
119-3046 Dual for Mack H-60 **1.95**
119-3062 Single Pipe/Air Cleaner pkg(2) **1.95**
119-3180 Stacks (3 Types) for Autocar, Diamond Reo, Ford pkg(6) **2.95**

FIRE TRUCK PARTS

119-3052 Spotlights w/Brackets pkg(2) **2.95**
119-3087 Fire Pumper Detail Set **6.95**
Includes two hose reels with stand, two cluster hose connections and two extinguishers.
119-3099 Update Detail Parts/Fire Trucks **2.95**
119-3172 Rectangular Light Bars pkg(6) **2.95**
119-3173 Detail Kit **6.95**
Includes 3 and 5" hose fittings, hose guides and water cannon. Enough parts for two trucks.
119-3174 Ladders (Large & Small) 2 Sets **2.95**
119-3175 Hoses-Single, Double & Triple 2 Sets **2.95**

FIFTH WHEEL DOLLY

119-3078 Tandem Axle **7.95**
119-3079 Single Axle pkg(2) **6.95**
119-3182 Dual Axle pkg(2) **6.95** *NEW*

GAS & AIR TANKS

119-3050 GMC Astro Rectangular w/Recessed Steps pkg(2) **2.95**
119-3051 GMC Astro Cylindrical pkg(2) **2.95**
119-3067 Mack B-42/61 w/Step pkg(2) **1.95**
119-3082 Ford "L" Round w/Steps pkg(2) **1.95**
119-3085 Air Tank w/Mounting Bracket pkg(4) **2.95**
119-3090 Autocar Rectangular **2.95**
119-3124 Air Tank-Long Frame pkg(4) **2.95**
119-3125 Air Tank-Short Frame pkg(4) **2.95**
119-3126 Air Tank Less Mounts pkg(4) **2.95**
119-3128 Air Tank-Short, Fat Frame pkg(4) **2.95**
119-3131 Air Tanks-Rear Mount pkg(3) **2.95**

LIGHTS EA 2.95

119-3093 Torpedo Running Lights pkg(2)
119-3094 Headlight - Autocar Style pkg(4)
119-3095 Tail Lights/Tractors
119-3096 Tail Lights/Trailers pkg(2)

MIRRORS PKG(2) EA 1.95

119-3055 Mack DM 800-Etched Brass
119-3060 GMC (Plastic)
119-3066 Mirrors - Etched Brass (Mack B & Ford LNT/LTS)
119-3098 Mirrors - Etched Brass (Autocar)

REFRIGERATION UNIT

119-3080 Trailer Refrigerator Units pkg(2) **2.95**

TRUCK ACCESSORIES

119-2035 Engine Kits pkg(3) **5.95**
119-3010 Sleeper Box **2.95**
119-3037 Bed Stakes (Plastic) **2.95**
119-3038 Wheel Bogies **2.95**
119-3064 Athearn Tractor Detail Kit **2.95**
119-3068 Mud Flaps pkg(4) **1.95**
119-3070 Fender for Dual Axles Set **2.95**
119-3073 Handle-Brass pkg(6) **2.95**
119-3075 Lumber Headache Rack pkg(2) **2.95**
119-3076 Radiator Guards for Tractors pkg(3) **1.95**
119-3077 Jack Stands for Trailers - Wheel Type pkg(3) **1.95**
119-3088 Tri-Axle Conversion Kit **6.95**
119-3089 Loading Boom & Cradle **4.95**
Converts flatbed to concrete block truck.

119-3091 Air Cleaner-Horizontal pkg(4) **2.95**
119-3092 Power Steering Oil Cooler/Lubrifiner Filter pkg(4) **2.95**
119-3097 Air Horns pkg(6) **1.95**
119-3118 5th Wheel Plate & Base pkg(2) **1.95** *NEW*
119-3120 Hose & Cable Rack pkg(4) **2.95**
119-3121 Standard Differential & Drive Shaft pkg(3) **2.95**
119-3127 Air Horns-Short Single pkg(6) **2.95**
119-3129 Spare Tire Holder w/Cover pkg(3) **2.95**
119-3130 Spare Tire Holder-No Cover pkg(3) **2.95**
119-3132 Mack Air Cleaner pkg(4) **2.95**
119-3165 Generic Steering Wheels pkg(6) **2.95**
119-3166 Heavy-Duty Winch for Flatbeds pkg(2) **2.95**
119-3167 Spare Tire & Holder (No Cover) 1930s Trucks pkg(3) **2.95**
Plastic and rubber parts.

119-3168 Spare Tire Holder & Cover **2.95** *NEW*
119-3170 Arched Front & Rear Springs w/Differential 2 Sets **2.95**

119-3176 Detail Kit for B Series Macks **6.95**
Includes air horns, air cleaner, Bulldogs, battery box, exhausts and gas tanks.

119-3177 Head & Tail Lights for 1930s Trucks (2 Types) 2 Sets **2.95**
119-3178 Pistons for Dump Body/Trailer 2 Sets **2.95**
Includes two each, small medium and large sizes.
119-3179 Flat Rear Springs w/Differential For Dump or Flatbed Trailers pkg(2) **2.95**

TRUCK TIRES PKG(10) EA 2.95

119-3061 Large
119-3072 Small

ULRICH UPGRADE KITS

Sets include mirrors, wheel rims, tires and axles. Metal, plastic and brass parts.

119-3005 Kenworth Tractors **6.95**
119-3006 All Trailers **6.95**

MACK TRACTORS

119-3002 Single-Axle **5.95**
119-3003 Dual-Axle **6.95**

WHEEL SETS EA 2.95

Includes wheels, axles, tires and hubs.

119-3119 Duals pkg(4)
119-3039 Budd Disc
119-3040 6 Spoke
119-3045 Low Boy

BH MODELS

Limited Quantity Available On All Items.

24' DIAMETER TANK ROOFS

Plastic parts are molded in black or silver. Matches parts from former BH Models or RIX Products tank kits. Great for scratchbuilding.

FLAT

159-5 Silver **2.50**

15° PEAKED EA 3.00

159-2 Black
159-6 Silver

30° PEAKED EA 3.00

159-3 Black
159-7 Silver

ACCURAIL®

Molded plastic parts can be adapted to all types of kits or scratchbuilt models.

DOORS PKG(4) EA 1.49

PLUG/YOUNGSTOWN

112-110 10' Plug & Youngstown

112-111 8' Youngstown

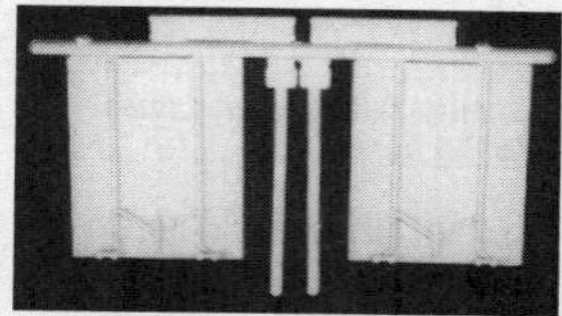

112-115 8' Plug

PS-1

112-112 8'

112-116 6'

SUPERIOR PANEL

112-113 6' Doors

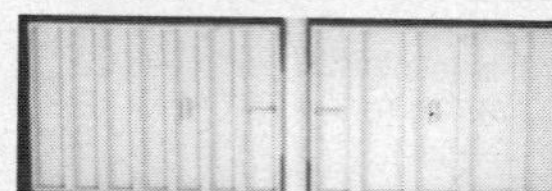

112-114 7' Doors

DUMMY COUPLERS

112-109 For Unit Train pkg(12) **2.49**

GRADE CROSSING MAT

112-117 Modern Rubber Mat pkg(6) **1.99**

BOX CAR PARTS EA 1.98

112-107 Steel Roof

112-108 Body Detail Set

HATCH & OUTLET SET

112-118 ACF Hopper **1.49**

UNDERFRAMES EA 2.98

112-105 40' Fishbelly

112-106 40' Steel

ALPINE DIVISION
Scale Models

Suitable for detailing structures and other models.

CABOOSE INTERIOR

700-421 6.50 ***NEW***

CRATES & BARRELS

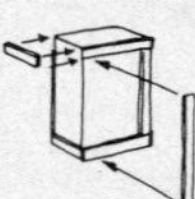

700-512

700-513

700-512 Wood Platform Crates Kit **2.50**
700-513 Barrels pkg(6) **1.10**

FREIGHT CAR LOAD

700-431 Flat Car Crate Load **3.95**
2 large and 1 small machinery crates.

DOORS

700-109 Sheet Metal pkg(6) **1.95**

ICE BLOCKS

700-569 300 Pound Blocks pkg(12) **2.50**

PACIFIC ELECTRIC DECALS

700-121 15/16" pkg(4) **3.98**
NEW
700-122 1-7/8" pkg(2) **3.98**
NEW

PACIFIC ELECTRIC PILOTS

700-185 Standard Wood **3.95**

STRUCTURAL DETAILS

700-106 5 Tread Steps (Wood) pkg(6) **2.75**
700-120 Station Shed Support **7.75**

WINDOWS EA. 1.25

Windows printed on acetate sheets.

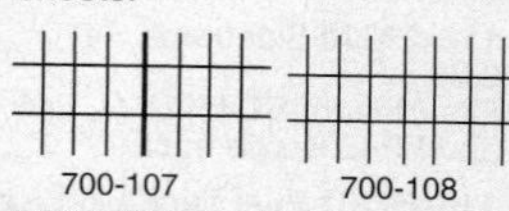

700-107 Industrial
700-108 Skylights

700-118 House

VENTS EA 3.45

700-113

700-114

700-113 Cast "A" pkg(12)
700-114 Cast Roof pkg(6)

NEOPRENE "O" RING DRIVE BELT PKG(6) EA 5.25

700-180 9/16"
700-1179 1/2"
700-1180 7/16"

MISCELLANEOUS

700-110 Wood Louver Strip 5/8 x 4" pkg(6) **3.45**
700-173 Motor Pulley Twin Groove pkg(3) **4.50**
700-177 Dynamotor/ Compressor (brass) each **1.50**
700-1186 Cast Brass Foot Boards for Box Motors pkg(4) **4.00**

Information STATION

ATTACHING NEW PARTS

If you're new at adding superdetails, it's a lot easier than you think. Most parts are made of metal (brass or various soft alloys) or injection molded styrene plastic.

When existing details have to be removed, carve them away with a hobby knife with a brand-new blade. Put some heavy tape (electrical tape works well) around the edges to protect other details and the body before starting. Finish up by sanding the surface.

Many parts are made with runners which can be mounted in a hole drilled into the model using small (#60 - 80) drill bits. A hand-held pin vise is a must for this work. Once the fit is to your liking, position the part. Apply a drop of glue from the inside to the runner. Use an instant glue (CA) when joining dissimilar materials like metal and plastic.

You can also add your own runners to small parts. Simply drill a small hole in a hidden spot and install a short piece of brass wire. Mount and glue like any other part.

Some larger parts may be glued directly to the body. Remove unwanted details first, then test fit. Look for high or low spots and fix them before final gluing.

DETAIL PARTS

AEI TAGS

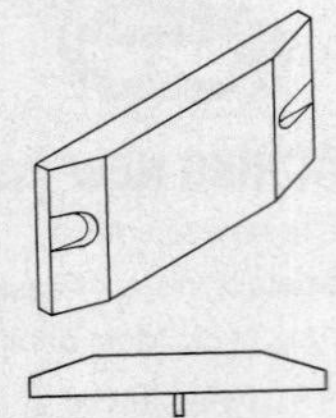

116-29460 1.95
Now appearing on locos and cars, Automatic Equipment Identification (AEI) tags are part of a computerized system that keeps track of prototype equipment. Prototypically correct, tags feature small mounting pins for easy installation on painted models without damaging the finish.

WINDSHIELD WIPERS

Molded in nonbreakable Delrin.

116-29200 Long & Short pkg(8) **3.15**
116-29201 Short Only pkg(8) **2.15**

BRASS DIESEL STEPS EA 3.50 (UNLESS NOTED)

Give your diesel fleet a new level of detail with these photo-etched steps, which provide scale thickness and see-through realism. Can be installed directly on your model, or used to replace molded steps. Available for many popular models.

FOR ATHEARN SHELLS

116-29236 SD40-2
116-29237 GP60, 50, 40, 38
116-29249 C44-9W
116-29252 UB/UC
116-29255 SW7 ***NEW***
116-29256 F45/FP45 ***NEW***

FOR RAILPOWER SHELLS

116-29230 SD45
116-29231 SD60
116-29232 840CW
116-29233 B23-7
116-29234 SD60M
116-29235 GP35
116-29244 GP60B, M
116-29245 GP35
116-29246 C32-8/840B
116-29247 SD45-2
116-29248 944CW
116-29250 SD40/38
116-29257 SD90 MAC **4.95**

FOR ASSORTED SHELLS

116-29253 Atlas C30-7
116-29239 FR GP7/9

KATO SHELLS

116-29238 SD40
116-29258 SD45
116-29259 GP35
116-29260 C44-9W

CHAIN

116-29216 40 Links Per Inch **2.95**
Includes 12" of brass chain.

E UNIT PARTS

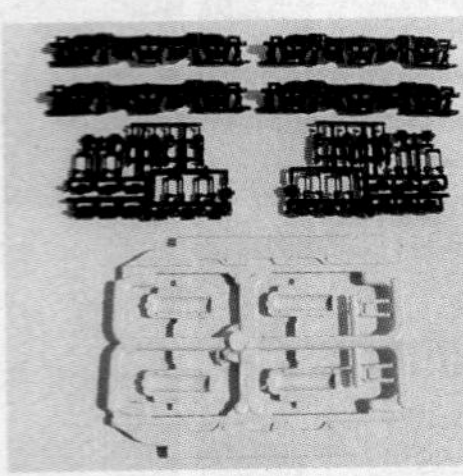

116-29300 Sideframe Set **8.35**
Fits Athearn SD45, U, C, F45 and FP45 3-axle truck.

116-29301 Fuel Tank Skirt/Air Tank Set **3.25**

FREIGHT CAR PARTS

116-29400 Tank Car Ends pkg(6) **3.50**
Includes two each GATX, ACF and Trinity "soft edge" types, fits MDC 50' car.

GRAB IRONS

116-29100 pkg(50) **3.50**
Fine scale, formed brass wire is unplated for better paint adhesion. Use on locos and cars.

SCALE LABEL SET

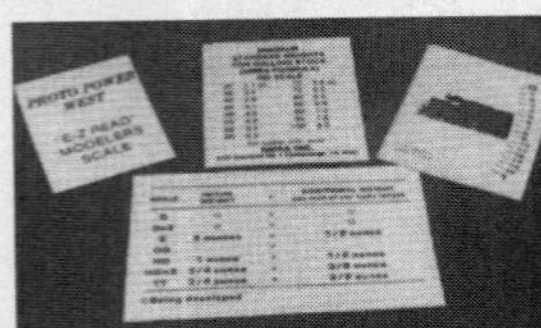

116-13111 2.65
Improve the performance of your freight car fleet by making sure every car meets NMRA weight standards. Self-adhesive label converts a 16oz postal scale (sold separately) to an E-Z read modeler's weighting scale. Use with A-Line "weigh-it yourself" lead weights.

STIRRUPS PKG(25) EA 3.50

116-29000 116-29001 116-29002

116-29000 Style "A"
116-29001 Style "B"
116-29002 Style "C"

SUN SHADES SET EA 2.75

Replace fragile plastic shades with durable brass etchings. Great for models which are handled often. Shades are adjustable and include mounting instructions.

116-29210 116-29211 116-29212

116-29210 Hood Unit Diesels pkg(6)
116-29211 E&F Unit pkg(6)
116-29212 Comfort Cab pkg(4)

WEIGHTS

Motor Mount Cradle Weights for locos are listed in the Lighting-Electrical-Motors section.

ATHEARN 85' FLAT CAR

116-13202 Flat Car w/End Weights **11.75**
Improve the looks and operation of Athearn 85' Flat Cars with this custom weight set. Parts fit center sill and ends, lowering the car to a more prototypical height. Lower center of gravity and additional weight improve tracking, so the car can be operated easily without a load. Can be used on cushioned or noncushioned cars and adds more realistic detail to the end of the car. Includes complete Athearn kit, end weight castings and instructions.

WEIGHT SETS EA 5.95

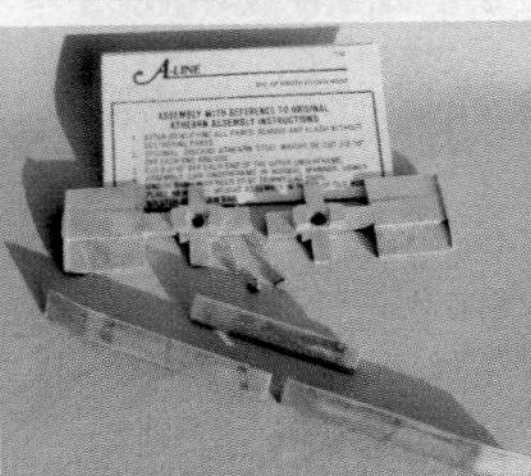

116-13200 85' Flat Car End Weight Kit
116-13201 Center Sill Kit
Fits Athearn 85' and Custom Rail 89' flat cars, plus Walthers Auto Rack.

FLAT WEIGHTS EA 4.50

An easy way to add extra weight to locos and cars. Lead is precut, with double-sided backing tape for easy installation. Thickness dimension includes tape.

116-13000 1/2 x 1/2 x 3/16" 12.7 x 12.7 x 4.7mm 3oz 84g pkg(2)
116-13001 1/2 x 3/4 x 5/32" 12.7 x 19 x 3.9mm 3oz 84g pkg(2)
116-13002 1/2 x 3/4 x 1/4" 12.7 x 19 x 6.3mm 6oz 168g

MOLDABLE LEAD

116-13010 1oz (28g) **2.95**
Add extra weight in small or odd-shaped areas. Lead putty contains over 90% lead, yet is easily shaped with fingers. Nonhardening, can be glued with most adhesives.

POURABLE LEAD

116-13015 6oz (168g) **3.75**
An easy way to add weight in tight spaces, tiny lead balls are .080 or about 5/64" diameter. Easily poured into any area and set with diluted white glue.

Custom Railway Supply

Photo-etched and chemically milled parts are a unique way to detail equipment and structures. Made from brass sheet, each is soft enough to be trimmed with a modeler's knife for proper shape and fit. They are easily painted for added detail. Illustrations are not to scale.

Limited Quantity Available On All Items.

BACKHEADS EA 6.85

Add realistic cab detail to modern or old-time steam locos. Kits are cast metal.

212-1053 Belpaire Firebox

212-1057 1895 Era for MDC Locos
Fits locos with backhead approximately 3/4" wide.

POSTAGE STAMP SERIES EA 1.75

Small details made from chemically milled brass, designed to assemble with only minor cutting, filing and bending. Prime and paint for the finishing touch.

212-1060 Bicycle & Park Bench

212-1062 Tool Set

BANISTERS EA 3.95

212-1074 Elevated Walkway
212-1076 Walkway

STAIRWAYS EA 5.75

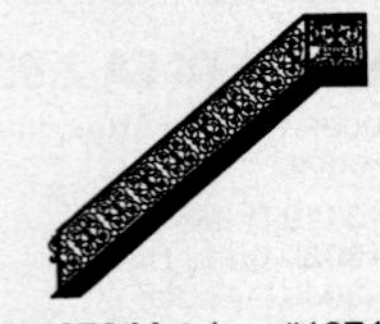

212-1072 Matches #1074

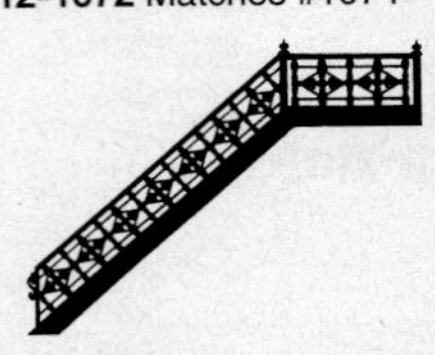

212-1075 Matches #1076

Add the finishing touch of realism to your models with this selection of white metal, wood, plastic and brass (as noted) parts.

FREIGHT CAR DETAILS

CAR FLOORS

Laser-cut flooring adds a level of realistic detail to open cars.

152-233 Walthers 54' GSC Flat Car w/Bolt Holes **7.95**
152-234 Walthers 54' GSC Flat Car Without Bolt Holes **3.25**
152-320 Athearn 40' Flat Cars **4.95**
152-321 Athearn 50' Flat Cars **4.95**
152-322 Proto 2000™ Gondolas **4.95**
152-323 Athearn Gondolas **4.95**
152-324 MDC Gondolas **4.95**
152-325 MDC 60' Flat Cars pkg(2) **5.95** *NEW*
152-326 Red Caboose 42' Flat Cars pkg(2) **5.95** *NEW*
152-328 InterMountain Flat Cars **5.95** *NEW*
152-329 Proto 2000 53' Flat Cars **5.95** *NEW*

ROOFWALKS EA 4.95

152-293 Athearn Box Car
152-294 InterMountain Box Car
152-296 Athearn 50' Box Car
152-297 Walthers 50' Automobile Box Car
152-299 Proto 2000 50' Box Cars

TACK BOARDS

152-298 For Freight Cars **2.95**

CABOOSE PARTS

152-226 Axle Generator pkg(2) **5.95**
152-227 Modernization Kit Athearn Santa Fe Caboose **11.95**

LOCOMOTIVE DETAILS

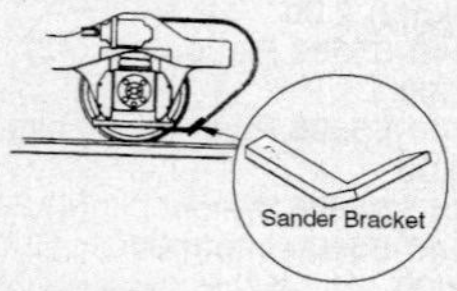

152-208 EMD Sander Brackets pkg(8) **1.75**

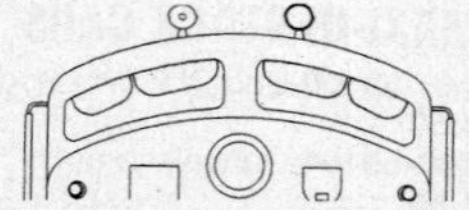

152-222 Cab Unit Sun Shades pkg(4) **1.85**

STEAM GENERATORS

152-223 Roof Vent pkg(2) **1.95**

F AND E UNIT NOSE DOORS PKG(2) EA 1.95

152-219 Less Headlight
152-220 With Headlight

GULF, MOBILE & OHIO F-UNIT PARTS

152-206 Poling Pockets pkg(4) **1.75**
152-207 Pilot Steps pkg(4) **1.75**
152-213 Roof Mounted Cooling Coil pkg(2) **1.95**

WINDOW SETS

Easy to install flush-mounted window "glass" for your favorite locos and rolling stock. Clear plastic parts are laser-cut for precise fit and premasked on front and back for easy painting.

WALTHERS EA 4.95

152-259 SW1
152-263 Dash 8-40B

ATHEARN EA 4.95 (UNLESS NOTED)

152-228 Scale F-Units **5.95**
Correct-size windshields, engine requires modification.

152-229 Semi-Scale F-Units
Larger windshields fit standard Athearn opening.

152-230 Modern GP & SD Locos **3.95**
152-231 SW7 **3.95**
152-232 SW1000/1500 **3.95**
152-235 GP7/9 **3.95**
152-236 Wide Vision Caboose **5.95**
152-237 U-Boats
152-238 Dash 9-44CW
152-251 F45
152-253 FP45
152-276 SD9
152-277 Trainmaster SP
152-278 Trainmaster Standard
152-290 PA-1
152-291 PB-1
152-292 S-12
152-2289 B Units (2 sets) **3.95**
152-2381 Dash-9 for Low Number Board Cab
152-2382 Dash-9 for Gull Wing Cab

BOWSER PENNSYLVANIA CABOOSES

152-255 N-5 Cars **4.95**
152-256 N-5C Cars **5.95**

LIFE-LIKE/PROTO 2000 EA 4.95

152-248 Proto 2000 E7A
152-249 Proto 2000 E7B
152-250 F40 PH
152-254 Proto 2000 E8/9
152-300 Proto 2000 PA *NEW*

RAIL POWER PRODUCTS EA 4.95 (UNLESS NOTED)

152-240 SD45 **3.95**
152-241 SD60 **3.95**
152-242 CF7 w/Topeka Cab
152-243 Dash 8-40C w/Santa Fe Cab
152-244 SD60M
152-245 GP35 **3.95**
152-246 CF7 w/Round Cab
152-247 SD7/9 **3.95**
152-252 Dash 8-40B
152-257 SD90 MAC
152-264 SD38/40
152-265 SD60M 3 Piece Windshield
152-266 GP60
152-267 GP60M
152-268 SD45-2
152-269 B23-7
152-274 C30-7
152-275 C32-8
152-2390 Dash 8-40CW9-44CW

MANTUA

152-262 GP20 **3.95**

IHC/RIVAROSSI PASSENGER CARS EA 8.50

152-270 Streamlined Coach
152-271 Dome Car

TRAINSTATION PRODUCTS EA 6.95

152-258 Window Set for High Level Passenger Cars
152-295 Coach/Dorm
152-305 Diner *NEW*

MISCELLANEOUS

152-106 Stationary Boiler Kit **28.95**

152-107 Stationary Steam Engine Kit **32.95**
152-205 Wheelstops pkg(2) **1.95**
152-224 Steam Driven Water Pump pkg(2) **3.00**

152-401 Winches pkg(2) **6.60**
152-402 Hooks pkg(8) **2.95**
152-404 Fire Hydrants pkg(8) **2.75**
152-407 Bolt Wheels pkg(8) **2.75**
152-411 Pillow Blocks pkg(16) **2.75**
152-413 Gas Engine **5.95**

STRUCTURE PARTS

CHIMNEYS EA 2.50

152-279 Smoke Jacks
152-280 Santa Fe - Rio Grande Style pkg(3)
152-281 Single Farber Style pkg(3)
152-282 Double Farber Style pkg(2)

SHINGLES

152-283 Santa Fe Style **20.95**
152-284 Hex Shaped **11.95**
152-285 Tabbed **13.50**
152-286 Rolled Roofing **7.95**

SCREEN DOORS & WINDOWS EA 4.95

152-310 Atlantic Coast Line Depot
152-311 Post Office
152-312 Dill's Market

LOADING DOCK SET

152-327 pkg(2) **11.95**
One Each "L" Shaped & Straight

COLUMBIA VALLEY MODELS

White metal castings.

GAS PUMP

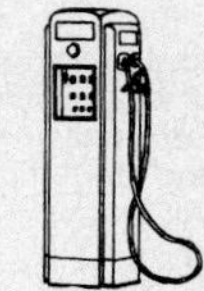

216-187 1940-50s Era pkg(2) **3.95**
Cast metal pumps include nozzles, hoses and "This Sale" signs.

VICTORIAN STRUCTURE DETAILS

216-387 Gable Trim pkg(3) **2.50**
216-487 Gingerbread Trim 3" Strips pkg(4) **3.25**

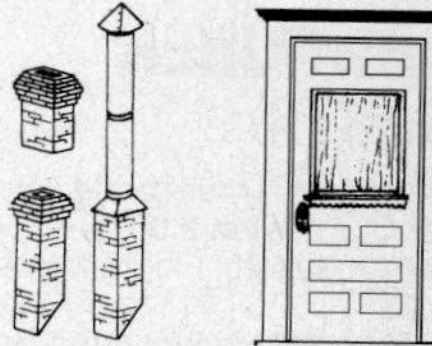

216-587 Chimneys pkg(3) **1.75**
216-687 Front Door pkg(3) **2.50**

CENTRAL VALLEY

UNDERFRAME KIT

210-1000 Steel pkg(3) **5.49**
Detailed black plastic parts upgrade most 40' freight car kits, or use as a starting point for scratchbuilt models.

BRAKE SHOE END BEAM

210-1124 Brake & Beam Details **2.79**
Includes parts to detail one pair of Central Valley 4-wheel passenger car trucks, sold separately. Adaptable to 6-wheel trucks and other brands. Parts are injection-molded, black styrene.

Ideal for customizing, scratchbuilding or repairs, parts are plastic except for weights, loco underframes, light bulbs, screws, etc. Parts are available only for current production models. Items not listed in this catalog are temporarily out of stock.

AIRPLANE PARTS

140-13760 Body **2.50**
140-13761 Upper Body **1.50**
140-13762 Lower Body **1.50**
140-13763 Landing Gear & Prop pkg(2) **1.00**
140-13765 Wing pkg(2) **1.00**
140-13766 Skid **1.00**

BOAT PARTS

140-13750 Body **2.50**
140-13751 Hull **1.00**
140-13752 Cockpit Insert **1.00**
140-13753 Deck **1.00**
140-13754 Window **1.00**
140-13757 Skid - Fore & Aft **1.00**

CONTAINER PARTS

140-20300 Undecorated Body 20' Corrugated **2.00**
140-20301 20' Floor pkg(2) **2.00**
140-20400 Undecorated Body 20' Smoothside **2.00**
140-20500 Undecorated Body 20' Beveled **2.00**
140-20600 Undecorated Body 20' Ribbed Side **2.00**
140-57000 Undecorated Body 48' **4.00**
140-57001 48' Floor pkg(2) **2.00**
140-57400 Undecorated Body 40' **3.00**
140-57401 48' Floor pkg(2) **2.00**

SEMI TRAILER PARTS

140-14253 Wheel Assembly 25' Van pkg(2) **1.50**
140-14259 25' Chassis **2.00**
140-51510 Undecorated 40' Trailer Body **3.00**
140-56000 Undecorated 45' Trailer Body **3.50**
140-56005 45' Trailer Hardware **2.00**

KENWORTH TRUCK

140-56600 Body **2.00**
140-56613 Windshield pkg(2) **2.00**
140-56615 Parts Group **1.50**

FREIGHT CAR PARTS

140-90600 Brake Wheels for Freight Cars pkg(6) **2.00**

40' BOX CAR

140-12000 Undecorated Body **3.00**
140-12022 Steel Door pkg(6) **1.50**
140-12023 Door Guide pkg(12) **1.50**
140-12024 Floor Simulated Wood pkg(2) **1.50**
140-12025 Modern Roofwalk pkg(3) **1.50**
140-12027 Floor 40' Hi-Cube pkg(2) **1.50**
140-12029 Door Guide 40' Hi-Cube pkg(12) **1.50**
140-12026 Underframe pkg(2) **1.50**
140-12028 Hi-Cube Door pkg(6) **1.50**
140-19500 Undecorated Body-Hi-Cube **3.00**
140-19600 Undecorated Body-Smoothside Hi-Cube **3.00**
140-52300 Undecorated Body-Wood **3.00**

50' BOX CAR

140-13098 Sliding Door pkg(6) **1.50**
140-13107 Floor-Plug Door pkg(2) **1.50**
140-13109 Floor-Sliding Door pkg(2) **1.50**
140-13113 Door Guide-Sliding pkg(12) **1.50**
140-55200 Shell Outside Braced pkg(4) **3.50**
140-55201 Door-Outside Braced pkg(4) **2.00**

50' DOUBLE DOOR BOX CAR

140-13099 Doors-Small pkg(6) **1.50**
140-13102 Doors pkg(4) **1.00**
140-13103 Door Guide pkg(12) **1.50**
140-13104 Floor pkg(2) **1.50**
140-13105 Roofwalk pkg(2) **1.50**
140-13106 Underframe pkg(2) **1.50**

50' RAILBOX CAR

140-50700 Undecorated Body-Double Door **3.00**
140-50701 Double Doors pkg(4) **1.50**
140-50702 Double Door Guides pkg(4) **1.50**
140-50703 Large Double Doors pkg(4) **1.50**
140-50704 Small Double Doors pkg(4) **1.50**

UNDECORATED BOX CAR BODIES

140-13290 Smoothside Plug Door **3.00**
140-13360 Plug Door **3.00**
140-50500 Side Box **3.00**

86' HIGH-CUBE BOX CAR EA 1.50

140-90717 Steel Weight
140-19741 Floor
140-19742 Underframe
140-19743 Drawbar pkg(4)

86' HI-CUBE BOX CAR BODIES EA 6.00

140-19740 Undecorated 4-Door
140-19850 Undecorated 8-Door

STOCK CAR

140-17740 Undecorated Body **3.00**
140-17752 Door pkg(6) **1.50**
140-17753 Floor pkg(2) **1.50**
140-17754 Roofwalk pkg(2) **1.50**
140-17755 Underframe pkg(4) **1.50**

HEAVY-DUTY FLAT CAR

140-13002 Floor **1.50**
140-13003 Brake Wheel pkg(6) **1.50**
140-13004 Brake Wheel Staff pkg(6) **1.50**
140-13005 Span Bolster pkg(2) **1.50**
140-13006 Coupler Cover pkg(6) **1.50**
140-13009 Underframe **1.50**
140-13040 Undecorated Body **3.00**
140-90706 Large Weight pkg(2) **1.50**
140-90707 Small Weight pkg(2) **1.50**

40' FLAT CAR

140-13490 Undecorated Body **3.00**
140-13502 Upper Underframe pkg(2) **1.50**
140-13503 Lower Underframe pkg(2) **1.50**
140-13504 Stakes pkg(12) **1.50**

50' FLAT CAR

140-13990 Undecorated Body **3.00**
140-14002 Upper Underframe pkg(2) **1.50**
140-14003 Lower Underframe pkg(2) **1.50**
140-14257 Dual Trailer Mount pkg(2) **1.50**

PULPWOOD FLAT CAR

140-14490 Undecorated Body **3.00**

HUSKY STACK CARS

140-59000 Body **5.00**
140-59001 Catwalks pkg(4) **1.50**
140-59002 Walkway Step pkg(4) **1.50**
140-59003 Bolster pkg(4) **1.50**
140-59004 Ladder pkg(4) **1.50**
140-59005 Tri-Valve pkg(4) **1.50**
140-59006 Frame pkg(4) **1.50**
140-59007 Brake Wheel pkg(4) **1.50**
140-59008 Weight pkg(3) **1.50**
140-59009 Drawbar pkg(6) **6.00**

IMPACK CARS

140-55500 End Body **3.00**
140-55501 End Underframe pkg(2) **2.00**
140-55502 Platform pkg(2) **2.00**
140-55505 Parts Group pkg(2) **2.00**
140-55506 Weight pkg(4) **2.00**
140-55600 Intermediate Body **3.00**
140-55601 Underframe pkg(2) **2.00**

MAXI-III STACK CARS

140-59100 End Platform Body **4.50**
140-59101 Catwalk pkg(4) **1.50**
140-59102 Bolster-Male pkg(4) **1.50**
140-59103 Bolster-Female pkg(4) **1.50**
140-59104 Small DD pkg(4) **1.50**
140-59105 Intermediate Valve pkg(4) **1.50**
140-59108 Intermediate Weight pkg(4) **1.50**
140-59109 Span Bolster pkg(4) **1.50**
140-59500 Intermediate Body pkg(4) **4.50**

85' PIGGYBACK FLAT EA 1.50 (UNLESS NOTED)

140-20000 Piggyback Flat Floor **3.50**
140-20011 Upper Underframe
140-20012 Lower Underframe
140-20013 Body Bolster pkg(4)
140-20021 Steel Weight
140-20022 Coupler Draw Bar pkg(4)
140-20025 Trailer Hitch Set
140-20026 Container Shoe Set
140-20150 All-Purpose Flat Floor **3.50**

TANK CAR

140-14990 Undecorated Body 3-Dome Tank **3.00**

62' TANK CAR

140-15200 Undecorated Body **3.00**
140-15231 Bottom Sheet pkg(2) **2.00**
140-15232 Underframe pkg(2) **1.50**
140-15233 Center Sill pkg(2) **1.50**
140-15234 Ladder pkg(6) **1.50**
140-15235 Platform Rail pkg(6) **1.80**
140-15236 Handrail pkg(6) **1.80**
140-15237 Platform pkg(3) **1.50**
140-90716 Weight pkg(2) **1.50**

40' TANK CAR

140-15502 Bottom Sheet pkg(3) **1.50**
140-15503 Underframe pkg(3) **1.50**
140-15504 Center Sill pkg(3) **1.50**
140-15505 Brake Gear Box pkg(6) **1.50**
140-15506 Placard Holder pkg(12) **1.50**
140-15507 Ladder pkg(6) **1.80**
140-15508 Handrail pkg(6) **1.80**
140-15511 Manway Cover pkg(6) **1.50**

40' CHEMICAL TANK CAR

140-15490 Undecorated Body **3.00**
140-15512 Platform pkg(3) **1.50**
140-15513 Platform Rail pkg(6) **1.80**
140-15514 Manway Cover pkg(6) **1.50**
140-15700 Body Shell 1-Dome, Undecorated **3.00**
140-90705 Steel Weight pkg(2) **1.50**

PICKLE CARS

140-14749 Top & Ends **2.50**
140-14752 Floor pkg(2) **1.50**
140-14753 Underframe pkg(3) **1.50**
140-14754 Center Support pkg(3) **1.50**
140-14755 Roofwalk pkg(3) **1.50**
140-14758 Truss Rod pkg(12) **1.50**
140-14759 Side, Undecorated pkg(2) **2.50**

REFRIGERATOR CARS

140-16002 Ice Hatch/Latch Set pkg(2) **1.80**

40' REEFERS

140-15990 Undecorated Body-40' Steel Reefer **3.00**
140-16005 Roofwalk pkg(3) **1.50**
140-16006 Underframe pkg(2) **1.50**
140-52000 Undecorated Body-40' Wood Reefer **3.00**

50' EXPRESS REEFERS

140-53300 Undecorated Body **3.50**
140-53301 50' Express Floor pkg(2) **2.00**
140-53302 Underframe **2.00**
140-53303 Roofwalk pkg(2) **1.50**
140-53304 Ice Hatch **2.00**
140-53306 Steel Weight pkg(2) **2.00**
140-53308 Trucks pkg(2) **2.00**

50' REEFER UNDECORATED BODIES EA 3.00

140-16240 Single Sheathed
140-16310 Outside Braced

57' MECHANICAL REEFER

140-54601 Floor pkg(2) **2.00**
140-54603 Steel Weight pkg(2) **2.00**
140-13108 Fuel Tank - Plug Door Box/57' Reefer pkg(6) **1.50**
140-54600 Undecorated Body **3.50**
140-54602 Underframe pkg(2) **2.00**

GONDOLA

140-16470 Undecorated Body-50' Gondola **3.00**
140-16755 Frozen Food Locker pkg(3) **1.80**
140-16756 50' Roof pkg(4) **1.60**
140-16758 50' Roof & Roofwalk **1.50**

QUAD HOPPERS

140-17490 Undecorated Body **3.00**
140-17502 Brake Gear pkg(4) **1.50**
140-17503 Doors pkg(4) **2.00**
140-17504 Underframe pkg(4) **1.50**

CENTERFLOW HOPPER

140-19000 Undecorated Body **3.50**
140-19052 Roofwalk pkg(2) **1.50**
140-19053 Long Hatch Set **1.50**
140-19055 Individual Hatch pkg(8) **1.50**
140-19056 Latch Bar pkg(4) **1.50**
140-19057 Steel Weight pkg(2) **2.00**
140-19058 Underframe pkg(2) **2.00**
140-90597 Brake Wheel pkg(6) **2.00**

54' COVERED HOPPER

140-53000 Undecorated Body **3.00**
140-53001 Underframe **1.00**
140-53002 A End Wall pkg (3) **1.50**
140-53003 B End Wall pkg (3) **1.50**
140-53004 Roofwalk pkg(2) **1.50**
140-53005 Hatch pkg(2) **1.20**
140-53006 Outlet pkg(3) **1.80**
140-53007 Brake Wheel pkg(6) **1.80**
140-53008 Brake Set **1.00**
140-53009 Round Signboards pkg(3) **1.50**
140-53011 Square Signboards pkg(3) **1.50**
140-53012 Rectangular Signboards pkg(3) **1.50**

34' HOPPER

140-54001 Underframe pkg(2) **2.00**
140-90701 Steel Weight pkg(4) **1.50**

34' UNDECORATED BODIES EA 3.00

140-54000 Offset
140-54200 Composite
140-54070 Offset-Flat Top
140-54400 Ribbed w/Peak Ends
140-54470 Ribbed Side w/Flat Ends

200 TON CRANE

140-16990 Cab, Undecorated **3.00**
140-17002 Chassis **3.00**
140-17004 Right Support pkg(2) **1.50**
140-17005 Right & Left Floor pkg(2) **1.50**
140-17014 Friction Spring pkg(3) **1.50**
140-17024 Crane Coupler Cover Plate pkg(4) **1.50**
140-17006 Right Floor pkg(2) **1.50**
140-17007 Boom **1.50**
140-17008 Boom Arm pkg(2) **1.50**
140-17009 Cover Hatch pkg(2) **1.50**
140-17013 Windlass pkg(3) **1.50**
140-17015 Large Sheave pkg(3) **1.50**
140-17016 Small Sheave pkg(3) **1.50**
140-17017 Large Hooks pkg(3) **1.50**
140-17018 Small Hooks pkg(3) **1.50**
140-17019 Snatch Block pkg(3) **1.50**
140-17022 Snatch Block Plate pkg(4) **1.50**
140-17023 Coupler Box w/Cover pkg(4) **1.50**
140-17025 Crank pkg(4) **1.50**
140-90704 Steel Weight pkg(2) **.80**
140-99205 Sheave Pin for Cranes pkg(12) **1.50**

ROTARY SNOW PLOW

140-11940 Undecorated Body **3.50**
140-11961 Long Roofwalk pkg(6) **1.80**
140-11962 Short Roofwalk pkg(6) **1.80**
140-11963 Smokebox Door pkg(6) **1.00**
140-11964 Deflector pkg(6) **1.80**
140-11965 Rotor w/Shaft pkg(2) **1.80**
140-11966 Rotor Housing Subframe **2.25**
140-11967 SubFrame **1.50**
140-11968 Rotor Shaft pkg(6) **1.80**
140-11969 Thrust Washer pkg(12) **1.50**
140-11971 Retainer pkg(12) **1.80**
140-11972 Underframe **1.50**
140-11973 Flanger pkg(3) **1.65**
140-11975 Coupler Box pkg(6) **1.50**
140-11976 Rotor & Shaft **1.50**

CABOOSE

140-12490 Undecorated Body **3.50**
140-12503 Regular Floor pkg(2) **1.50**
140-12504 Regular Ladder pkg(4) **2.00**
140-12505 Roofwalk Long Regular pkg(3) **1.50**
140-12506 Regular Short Roofwalk pkg(3) **1.50**
140-12507 Railing pkg(6) **1.80**
140-12508 Accessory Set **1.50**
140-12509 Regular Underframe pkg(2) **.55**
140-12512 Cupola pkg(2) **1.50**

WORK CABOOSE

140-12740 Undecorated Body **3.50**
140-12756 Long Roofwalk pkg(3) **1.50**
140-12757 Short Roofwalk pkg(3) **1.20**
140-12758 Boom Support pkg(3) **1.50**
140-12759 Smoke Jack pkg(6) **1.50**
140-12911 Floor **1.50**
140-12914 Tool Box (Right & Left) pkg(3) **1.50**

BAY WINDOW CABOOSE

140-12850 Shell-Undecorated **3.50**
140-12851 Floor pkg(2) **1.50**
140-12852 Underframe pkg(2) **1.50**
140-12853 Steel Weight pkg(2) **1.50**
140-12854 Roofwalk pkg(2) **1.50**
140-12855 Smoke Jack pkg(6) **1.50**

WIDE VISION CABOOSE

140-53600 Undecorated Body **3.50**
140-53601 Cupola, Undecorated pkg(2) **1.40**
140-53602 Short Roofwalk pkg(3) **1.00**
140-53603 Long Roofwalk pkg(3) **1.50**
140-53604 Floor pkg(2) **1.50**
140-53605 Underframe pkg(2) **1.50**
140-53606 Air Brake Set pkg(2) **1.50**
140-53607 Steel Weight pkg(2) **1.50**

LOCOMOTIVE DETAILS & ACCESSORIES

C44-9W

140-10428 Short Stanchion pkg(36) **3.50**
140-10429 Long Stanchion pkg(6) **1.00**
140-49401 Handrail Set **5.50**
140-49410 Cab Window pkg(2) **2.00**
140-49411 Lens Sets pkg(2) **2.00**
140-49415 Air Conditioner pkg(2) **2.00**
140-49416 Radiator Grilles pkg(2) **2.00**
140-49417 Accessory Set **2.00**
140-49418 Tank Set-Black **3.00**
140-49419 Tank Set-Silver **3.00**
140-49430 Frame-Black **15.00**
140-49431 Frame-Silver **15.00**
140-49432 Frame-UP Gray **15.00**
140-49433 Frame-SP Gray **15.00**
140-49434 Powered Mechanism **54.50**
140-49435 Dummy Mechanism **26.50**
140-49440 Front Power Truck-Black **7.00**
140-49441 Front Power Truck-Silver **7.00**
140-49450 Rear Power Truck-Black **7.00**
140-49451 Rear Power Truck-Silver **7.00**
140-49460 Front Dummy Truck-Black **6.00**
140-49461 Front Dummy Truck-Silver **6.00**
140-49470 Rear Dummy Truck-Black **6.00**
140-49471 Rear Dummy Truck-Silver **6.00**
140-49478 Sideframe Set-Black **3.00**
140-49479 Sideframe Set-Silver **3.00**
140-49492 Brake Set-Black pkg(2) **2.00**
140-49493 Brake Set-Silver pkg(2) **2.00**
140-49500 Undecorated Body-High Number Boards & Cab **14.75**
140-49501 Undecorated Cab w/High Number Boards **5.00**
140-49503 Cab-Hi Number Board **5.00**
140-49800 Undecorated Body-Low Number Boards & Cab **14.75**
140-49801 Undecorated Cab w/Low Number Boards **5.00**
140-49810 Undecorated Body w/Gull Wing Cab **14.75**
140-49811 Undecorated Cab w/Gull Wings **5.00**
140-49880 Phase 2 Body/Gullwing Cab **16.75**

HUSTLER

140-29900 Undecorated Body **5.00**
140-29901 Motor Connector Clip pkg(2) **1.50**
140-29905 Idler Pulley w/Bracket pkg(6) **1.50**
140-29907 Hustler Idler Pulley Bracket pkg(6) **1.50**
140-29912 Master Shaft Pulley pkg(6) **.90**
140-29913 Underframe Left Hand **1.50**
140-29914 Underframe Right Hand **1.50**
140-29915 Insulating Plates pkg(4) **1.50**
140-29916 Insulated Washer pkg(12) **1.50**

GP9

140-10511 Undecorated Cab pkg(2) **1.50**
140-10522 Radiator pkg(6) **1.50**
140-10523 Right Hand Step Guard pkg(6) **1.50**
140-10524 Left Hand Step Guard pkg(6) **1.50**
140-10533 Headlight Lens pkg(6) **1.80**
140-10536 Air Tank pkg(6) **1.80**
140-11529 Handrail Set **4.00**
140-30510 Undecorated Body **6.25**
140-33051 Dummy Mechanism **15.00**
140-33151 Powered Mechanism **27.50**
140-42004 Underframe **5.50**
140-90604 Horns pkg(6) **1.50**

GP50/GP38-2

140-45900 Undecorated Body GP50-Phase II **7.75**
140-46017 Step Guard Right Hand **1.50**
140-46018 Step Guard Left Hand **1.50**
140-46026 Connector Clip pkg(2) **1.50**
140-46027 Handrail Set **4.00**
140-46029 Underframe GP38-2 **7.50**
140-46031 Window & Lens Set **2.00**
140-46037 Truck Accessory Set **2.00**
140-46038 Dynamic Brake Hatch GP38-2 **2.00**
140-46039 Nondynamic Hatch GP38-2 **2.00**
140-46040 GP38-2 Weights pkg(2) **2.00**
140-46042 Powered Mechanism GP38-2 **32.50**
140-46052 Dummy Mechanism GP38-2 **15.75**
140-46500 Undecorated Body-w/Dynamics GP38-2 **7.75**
140-46620 Undecorated Body-Nondynamic GP38-2 **7.75**
140-46638 Dynamic Brake Housing, GP50 pkg(2) **2.00**
140-46727 Handrail Set - GP50 **4.00**
140-46729 Underframe GP50 **7.50**
140-46740 GP50 Weights pkg(2) **2.00**
140-46760 Undecorated Body-GP50 w/Dynamics **7.75**
140-46770 Undecorated Body-Nondynamic GP50 **7.75**

GP40-2

140-46742 Powered Mechanism-GP40-2, 50 & 60 **34.50**
140-46752 Dummy Mechanism-GP40-2, 50 & 60 **16.25**
140-47200 Undecorated Body-w/Dynamics **8.00**
140-47201 Dynamic Brake Hatch **2.00**
140-47202 Nondynamic Brake Hatch pkg(2) **2.00**
140-47210 Undecorated Body-Nondynamic **8.00**

F7

140-30230 Shell F7A w/2 Headlights-Undecorated **5.75**
140-30240 Shell F7B Undecorated **5.75**
140-30390 Shell F7A w/1 Headlight-Undecorated **5.75**
140-42005 Black Underframe **5.50**
140-60209 Long Truck Clip pkg(3) **1.50**
140-60210 Short Truck Clip pkg(3) **1.50**
140-90604 Horns pkg(6) **1.50**
140-90709 Weight **1.50**
140-90710 Super Gear Weights **4.00**

RAIL DIESEL CAR

140-11713 Underframe **4.50**
140-11714 Coupler Box pkg(6) **1.50**
140-11715 Coupler Box Cover pkg(12) **2.00**
140-11716 Centering Spring pkg(12) **1.50**
140-11717 Drive Shaft pkg(6) **1.50**
140-11718 Drive Shaft Coupling pkg(12) **1.50**
140-11720 Motor Connector Clip pkg(6) **1.00**
140-11726 RDC1 Window Set **1.50**
140-11727 RDC3 Window Set **1.50**
140-20700 Undecorated Body-RDC-1 **6.00**
140-20750 Undecorated Body-RDC-3 **6.00**

AC4400

140-43401 Handrail Set **6.00**
140-43410 Accessory Sprue **3.00**
140-43412 R Sand Fill Housing pkg(2) **2.00**
140-43413 Auxiliary Cabinet **2.00**
140-43414 Cantilever & Strut Set pkg(2) **2.00**
140-43700 Body-2 Dynamic High Board Cab **16.75**
140-43701 Cab High Boards **6.00**
140-43710 Body-3 Dynamic Low Board Cab **16.75**
140-43711 Cab Low Boards **6.00**
140-43900 2 Dynamic Low Board Cab **16.75**
140-43910 GE Demo Version (Gullwing Cab, 3 Dynamic, Phase I Rear Grills) **16.75**

PA1 A & B UNITS

140-33210 Undecorated Body-PA-1 **8.75**
140-33218 Window Set PA1 & PB1 **1.50**
140-33221 Underframe **5.00**
140-33226 Front Power Truck-PA1 **6.50**
140-33227 Rear Power Truck-PA/PB1 **6.50**
140-33228 Front Gear Cover Boxes for PA1 pkg(3) **1.50**
140-33232 Motor Connector Clip pkg(2) **1.50**
140-33235 Numberboard Set PA1 **1.50**
140-33301 Powered PA1 Mechanism **40.50**
140-33302 Powered PB1 Mechanism **40.50**
140-33321 Dummy PA1 Mechanism **19.25**
140-33322 Dummy PB1 Mechanism **19.25**
140-33410 PA Sideframe Set **4.00**
140-33411 PA1 Light Bracket pkg(3) **1.50**
140-33412 PA1 Bulb Shroud pkg(3) **1.50**
140-33413 PA1 Light Wiper Clip pkg(3) **1.50**
140-33610 Shell PB1 Undecorated **8.75**

U-BOATS (U28B, U28C, U33B & U33C)

140-34001 Loco Cab pkg(2) **2.00**
140-34005 Brake Wheels pkg(6) **1.80**
140-34006 Air Horn Cluster U33B/C pkg(6) **1.80**
140-34007 Bell pkg(6) **1.80**
140-34014 GE-B Underframe **5.00**
140-34015 Air Tank pkg(3) **1.50**
140-34019 U28B/U30B Handrail Sets **4.00**
140-34026 Motor Connector Clip GE-B pkg(2) **1.50**
140-34027 Motor Drive Assembly pkg(12) **16.20**
140-34028 Sideframe GE-B **4.00**
140-34050 Powered B Mechanism **28.50**
140-34060 Dummy B Mechanism **13.25**
140-34070 Powered C Mechanism **29.50**
140-34080 Dummy C Mechanism **14.25**
140-34100 Shell U28B Undecorated **6.50**
140-34206 C Underframe **5.00**
140-34212 Front Power Truck-C Units **6.50**
140-34214 Front Dummy Truck-C Units **3.50**
140-34217 C Spline 1" pkg(6) **1.80**
140-34218 Sideframe C Plastic **4.00**
140-34228 Window Set pkg(2) **1.75**
140-34229 U28C/U30C Handrail Sets **4.50**
140-34300 Undecorated Body-U28C **6.50**
140-34500 Undecorated Body-U30B **6.50**
140-34700 Undecorated Body-U30C **6.50**
140-34900 Undecorated Body-U33B, **6.50**
140-35100 Undecorated Body-U33C **6.50**
140-40002 Windshield pkg(4) **1.50**

F45 & FP45

140-36050 F45 Powered Mechanism **29.50**
140-36051 F45 Underframe **5.00**
140-36060 F45 Dummy Mechanism **13.75**
140-36070 FP45 Powered Mechanism **29.50**
140-36071 FP45 Underframe **5.00**
140-36080 FP45 Dummy Mechanism **13.50**
140-36100 Undecorated Body-F45 **6.75**
140-36101 Number Board F45 & FP45 pkg(2) **2.00**
140-36106 Window Set **1.50**
140-36111 Handrail Set **4.00**
140-36113 Motor Connector Clip FP45 pkg(2) **1.50**
140-36114 Light Bracket 8-Axle Loco pkg(4) **1.50**
140-36115 Gear Box Clip Top 6-Axle pkg(4) **1.50**
140-36116 Gear Box Clip Bottom 6-Axle pkg(4) **1.50**
140-36300 Undecorated Body-FP45 **6.75**
140-40067 Brake Cylinders-All 45s **2.00**

BALDWIN S-12

140-37200 Undecorated Body Shell **6.25**
140-37201 Cab, Undecorated pkg(2) **2.00**
140-37209 Window & Lens Set **1.50**
140-37211 Handrail Set **4.00**

SD9

140-38001 Cab, Undecorated pkg(2) **2.00**
140-38005 Window/Numberboard **1.50**
140-38010 Step Guard Set **1.50**
140-38011 Air Tank pkg(3) **5.00**
140-38017 Handrail Set **4.50**
140-38018 Underframe **5.00**
140-38023 Powered Mechanism **27.50**
140-38024 Dummy Mechanism **13.75**
140-38025 Sideframe Set **4.00**
140-38200 Undecorated Body **6.75**

DD40

140-40042 Handrail Set **6.00**
140-40043 Dual Motor Connector Clip pkg(2) **1.80**
140-40045 Drive Shaft Assembly **1.50**
140-40046 Radiator pkg(6) **2.00**
140-40047 Step Guards-Right pkg(6) **1.80**
140-40048 Step Guards-Left pkg(4) **1.80**
140-40049 Spline 8" Long pkg(12) **3.60**
140-40050 Light Bracket pkg(4) **1.20**
140-42000 Worm Drive Assembly **1.30**
140-42007 Worm Housing Half 1 PA/DD pkg(4) **2.00**
140-42008 Worm Housing Half S PA/DD pkg(4) **2.00**
140-42021 Gear Box Cover pkg(2) **1.50**
140-42032 Truck Front Dummy DD40 **5.00**
140-42033 Underframe **11.00**
140-42600 Undecorated Body **10.00**
140-44240 Powered Mechanism-Single Motor **34.50**
140-44260 Dummy Mechanism **18.50**
140-44280 Powered Mechanism-Dual Motor **43.50**

SW1000/1500

140-39001 Standard SW1500 Cab **2.50**
140-39002 SP Version SW1500 Cab **2.50**
140-39003 Numberboard SP Version pkg(4) **1.50**
140-39004 SW1500 Step Guard pkg(4) **1.50**
140-39008 Window & Lens Set **2.50**
140-39015 Handrail Set **4.00**
140-39016 SW1500 Underframe **5.50**
140-39020 Sideframe Set **3.00**
140-39024 SW1500 Dummy Front Truck **4.50**
140-39200 Undecorated Body-SW1500 **7.75**
140-39201 SW1500 Powered Mechanism **34.75**
140-39202 SW1000 Powered Mechanism **34.75**
140-39203 SW1500 Dummy Mechanism **15.75**
140-39204 SW1000 Dummy Mechanism **15.75**
140-39210 Undecorated Body-SW1500-Southern Pacific **7.75**
140-39500 Undecorated Body-SW1000 **7.75**

SW7 COW AND CALF

140-40510 Undecorated Body-SW7 Cow **6.50**
140-40760 Undecorated Body-SW7 Calf **6.50**
140-41001 Hood Shell-Calf Undecorated pkg(2) **2.00**
140-41002 Cab, Undecorated pkg(2) **2.00**
140-41007 Bell pkg(6) **1.50**
140-41015 Horn pkg(6) **1.50**
140-41018 Underframe SW7/S12 **4.25**
140-41021 Sideframe SW7/1000 **2.50**
140-41023 Rear Power Truck **5.00**
140-41024 Front Power Truck **5.00**
140-41029 Handrail Set Cow or Calf **4.00**
140-41033 Motor Connector Clip SW/S12 pkg(2) **1.50**
140-41035 Gear Box Clip - Bottom SW/S12 pkg(6) **1.80**
140-41036 Light Bracket SW/S12 pkg(4) **1.60**
140-41039 Light Assembly Switcher **2.00**
140-41045 Window & Lens Set **2.50**
140-44001 Powered Mechanism-SW7 & S12 **27.50**
140-44051 Dummy Mechanism-SW7 & S12 **12.75**

FAIRBANKS-MORSE H24-66 TRAINMASTER

140-10426 Handrail Stanchions - Long pkg(36) **3.50**
140-43001 Powered Mechanism **29.50**
140-43015 Underframe **5.00**
140-43021 Gear Box Clip Bottom pkg(4) **2.00**
140-43022 Gear Box Clip Top pkg(4) **2.00**
140-43051 Dummy Mechanism **15.75**
140-43101 Handrail Set **4.25**
140-43107 Headlight Lens & Marker Boards pkg(2) **1.50**
140-43108 Airtanks pkg(2) **1.50**
140-43109 Window pkg(2) **1.50**
140-43200 Undecorated Body **6.75**
140-43201 Cab, Undecorated pkg(2) **.80**
140-43210 Undecorated Body-SP Type **6.75**
140-43211 Cab, Undecorated SP Type pkg(2) **1.50**

GP35, SDP40, SD45

140-40001 Horn pkg(6) **1.50**
140-40002 Lens Numberboard pkg(4) **1.50**
140-40003 Cab Window pkg(4) **1.50**
140-40004 Headlight Lens pkg(6) **1.50**
140-40005 Back-Up Light Lens pkg(4) **1.50**
140-40006 Radiator SD45 pkg(4) **1.50**
140-40007 Cab Roof pkg(4) **1.60**
140-40008 Right Hand Step Guards Pkg(6) **1.50**
140-40009 Left Hand Step Guards Pkg(6) **1.80**
140-40017 Underframe SD40/45 **5.00**
140-40066 Sideframe Set, All 45s **4.00**
140-40067 Brake Cylinder, All 45s pkg(8) **2.00**
140-41200 Undecorated Body-SDP40 **6.75**
140-41800 SD45 Shell-Undecorated **6.75**
140-42003 Underframe, GP35 **5.50**
140-42019 GP35 Handrail Set **4.00**
140-42200 Undecorated Body-GP35 **6.25**
140-44100 Powered Mechanism-SD45 **35.50**
140-44120 Dummy Mechanism-SD45 **17.75**
140-44200 Powered Mechanism-GP35 **27.50**
140-44220 Dummy Mechanism-GP35 **13.75**

SD40-2/SD40T-2

140-40035 SDP40 & SD45 Handrail Set **4.50**
140-45015 Light Bracket SD40-2 pkg(6) **1.20**
140-45016 Motor Connector Clip SD40-2 pkg(2) **1.50**
140-45018 Step Guard Left-Hand SD40-2 pkg(4) **1.50**
140-44029 SD40-2 Handrail Set **4.50**
140-44042 Powered Mechanism-SD40-2 **37.50**
140-44052 Dummy Mechanism-SD40-2 **17.75**
140-44106 Window Set **2.00**
140-44500 Undecorated Body-Dynamic SD40-2 **8.75**
140-44590 Undecorated Body-Nondynamic SD40-2 **8.75**
140-45017 Step Guard-Right-SD40-2 pkg(4) **1.50**
140-45019 Underframe **7.50**
140-45036 Sideframe Set **4.00**
140-45037 Brake Cylinder & Shock Set **2.00**
140-45038 SD40-2 Dynamic Brake Hatch pkg(2) **2.00**
140-45039 SD40-2 Nondynamic Brake Hatch pkg(2) **2.00**
140-45042 Powered Mechanism-SD40T-2 **37.50**
140-45052 Dummy Mechanism-SD40T-2 **17.75**
140-45106 SD40T-2 Window Set-Long **2.00**
140-45500 SD40-2 Undecorated Body-Long Nose **8.75**
140-45529 SD40T-2 Underframe **7.50**
140-45540 SD40-2 Undecorated Body-Standard **8.75**
140-45580 SD40-2 Long Handrail Set **4.50**
140-45590 SD40-2 Short Handrail Set
140-95009 Light Bracket Assembly **5.00**

GP60

140-10427 Handrail Stanchions pkg(36) **3.50**
140-47638 Dynamic Brake Hatch **1.50**
140-47700 Undecorated Body w/Brake Lever **8.50**
140-47710 Undecorated Body w/Brake Wheel **8.50**
140-47727 Handrail Set **4.00**

HEADLIGHTS & LIGHTING

140-90200 4-Wheel Passenger Car Lighting **2.00**
140-90201 6-Wheel Passenger Car Lighting **2.00**
140-90360 Headlight Bulb pkg(2) **2.00**
140-90378 Light Kit Conductor Strip pkg(6) **1.80**
140-90587 Light Bracket, F7 & GP pkg(6) **1.80**
140-95010 Bracket Receptacle Loco pkg(3) **1.50**
140-95011 Bulb Retainer Clip Loco pkg(3) **1.50**
140-95013 Light Bracket Assembly Switch **2.50**
140-95014 Light Bracket Assembly 4-Wheel, Low Nose **2.50**
140-95015 Light Bracket Assembly 6-Wheel, Low Nose **2.50**

HANDRAIL STANCHIONS PKG(36) 3.50

140-10424 Short
140-10425 Long

LOCO POWER TRAIN PARTS

FLYWHEELS & BUSHINGS

140-95004 5/16" Bushing Only pkg(4) **2.00**
140-95005 Flywheel 5/16 x 3/4" pkg(2) **4.75**
140-95007 Flywheel for GP50/38-2 pkg(2) **4.75**
140-95008 Brass, 3/4" long, .670 Diameter pkg(2) **4.75**

COUPLINGS

140-40020 Worm & Shaft Assembly pkg(12) **9.00**
140-40022 1/4" Worm pkg(12) **3.60**
140-40051 1/8" Worm, DD40 pkg(12) **3.60**
140-41017 Universal Slotted, S12 pkg(6) **1.80**
140-90105 Female w/Keyway pkg(12) **3.60**
140-90103 5/16" Female pkg(6) **1.80**
140-90102 3/32" Female pkg(6) **1.80**

WORM ASSEMBLY

140-40054 GP9 & GP35 pkg(12) **16.20**
140-41032 S12 & SW1500 pkg(6) **8.10**
140-41037 F7 pkg(6) **8.10**
140-41031 Worm Housing SW/S12 pkg(4) **1.80**
140-41034 Worm Coupling SW1500/S12 pkg(6) **1.80**

THRUST WASHERS

140-84019 1/8" Inside Diameter pkg(6) **1.20**
140-99201 3/32" pkg(12) **2.40**

GEARS, GEAR PLATE & BOX COVER

140-40030 23-Tooth pkg(4) **1.50**
140-40031 45-Tooth pkg(4) **1.80**
140-40055 Bottom Cog F7/GP pkg(6) **1.80**
140-40056 Top Box, Clip F7/GP pkg(6) **1.80**
140-41020 16-Tooth, SW & S12 pkg(6) **1.80**
140-60023 Loco Axle Gear 12-Tooth pkg(6) **1.80**
140-60024 Drive Gear-SD40-2 pkg(6) **1.50**

SPLINES

140-34025 3/4" Long, GE-B pkg(12) **3.60**
140-40015 1-1/4" Long FP45 pkg(12) **3.60**
140-90109 1-1/8" pkg(12) **3.60**
140-90099 5/8" Long Coupling pkg(6) **1.80**
140-90106 1/2" Long Coupling pkg(12) **3.60**

BEARINGS & HOUSINGS

140-40021 Round Worm-PA/DD pkg(12) **3.60**
140-40052 Square Worm-DD40 pkg(12) **3.60**
140-40053 DD40 Housing pkg(12) **4.80**
140-45035 Plastic Wheel Bearing for Locos pkg(4) **2.00**
140-46639 Nondynamic GP50 Housing pkg(2) **2.00**

MISCELLANEOUS

140-40019 40" Drive Wheel pkg(12) **13.80**
140-40057 Oilite Sideframe Bearing pkg(12) **3.60**
140-90101 HI-FI Drive Rubber Band pkg(24) **2.40**
140-95012 Loco Wiper Clip pkg(3) **1.50**
140-99203 Armature Washer pkg(12) **2.40**
140-99206 Sheave Pins-Medium pkg(12) **1.50**
140-99207 Sheave Pins-Short pkg(12) **1.50**

PASSENGER CAR PARTS

STREAMLINED CARS

140-17800 Undecorated Body-Baggage **4.50**
140-17802 Baggage Floor **2.00**
140-17803 Baggage Window Set pkg(2) **2.00**
140-17900 Undecorated Body-Diner **4.50**
140-17903 Diner Window Set pkg(2) **2.00**
140-18000 Undecorated Body-RPO **4.50**
140-18002 RPO Floor **2.00**
140-18003 RPO Window Set **2.00**
140-18100 Coach **4.50**
140-18102 Coach Floor pkg(2) **2.00**
140-18103 Coach Window Set **2.00**
140-18200 Undecorated Body-Vista-Dome **4.50**
140-18202 Vista-Dome/Diner Floor pkg(2) **2.00**
140-18203 Lower Vista-Dome Windows **2.00**
140-18204 Vista-Dome Window pkg(4) **1.50**
140-18300 Undecorated Body-Observation **4.50**
140-18302 Observation Floor **2.00**
140-18303 Observation Window Set **2.00**
140-90598 Streamline Brake Wheels pkg(6) **2.00**

STANDARD (HEAVYWEIGHT) CARS

140-18400 Undecorated Body-RPO **4.50**
140-18402 RPO Floor **2.00**
140-18403 RPO Windows **1.50**
140-18404 Side Door Window Set for RPO **1.50**
140-18500 Undecorated Body-Monitor Roof Coach **4.50**
140-18502 Coach/Pullman Floor **2.00**
140-18503 Coach Window Set **2.00**
140-18540 Undecorated Body-Clerestory Roof Coach **4.50**
140-18600 Undecorated Body-Pullman **4.50**
140-18603 Pullman Window Set **2.00**
140-18700 Undecorated Body-Observation **4.50**
140-18702 Observation Floor **2.00**
140-18703 Observation Window Set **2.00**
140-18704 Observation Rear Wall pkg(2) **2.00**
140-18708 Observation Rear Window pkg(2) **2.00**
140-18709 Railing Standard Observation pkg(2) **2.00**
140-18800 Undecorated Body-Baggage **4.50**
140-18802 Baggage/Diner Floor **2.00**
140-18900 Undecorated Body-Diner **4.50**
140-18903 Diner Window Set **1.60**
140-90376 Offset Steel Weight pkg(2) **1.50**
140-90377 Flat Steel Weight pkg(2) **1.80**
140-90599 Standard Brake Wheels pkg(6) **2.00**

COMPLETE PART SETS

Includes complete bag of parts, as included with kit shown.
140-75001 Hi-Cube Grain Box Car **4.00**
140-75002 40/50' Box & Reefer **4.00**
140-75003 Cupola Caboose **4.00**
140-75004 Work Caboose **4.00**
140-75006 Bay Window Caboose **4.00**
140-75007 Heavy Duty Flat - B **4.00**
140-75008 Heavy Duty Flat - A **3.00**
140-75009 Rotary Snowplow **4.00**
140-75010 Pulpwood Flat **4.00**
140-75011 40' Flat w/Stakes **4.00**
140-75012 50' Flat w/Stakes **4.00**
140-75013 50' Flat w/Van **4.00**
140-75014 Pickle Car w/Tanks **4.00**
140-75015 Chemical Tank **4.00**
140-75016 62' Tank Car **4.00**
140-75017 40' Tank Car **4.00**
140-75018 Pickle Car w/Sides **4.00**
140-75019 200 Ton Crane **5.00**
140-75020 Derrick Car **4.00**
140-75021 Quad Hopper **4.00**
140-75022 Streamlined Passenger Car **5.00**
140-75023 Standard Passenger Car **5.00**
140-75024 Standard Baggage Car **5.00**
140-75025 Observation Car **5.00**
140-75026 Centerflow Hopper **4.00**
140-75027 86' Hi-Cube Box Car **4.00**
140-75028 85' Flat Cars **4.00**
140-75029 Two 40' Vans **4.00**
140-75030 #2 Van Reefer **4.00**
140-75031 54' Covered Hopper **4.00**
140-75032 Express Reefer **4.00**
140-75033 34' Hopper **4.00**
140-75035 Freightliner Tractor **4.00**
140-75036 Wide Vision Caboose **4.00**
140-75037 Railbox **4.00**
140-75038 57' Mechanical Reefer **4.00**
140-75041 Impack Ends **5.00**
140-75042 Impack Intermediates **5.00**
140-75043 45' Trailers **4.00**
140-75044 Husky Trucks & Weights **4.00**
140-75045 Husky-Undecorated **5.00**
140-75046 Husky-Yellow **5.00**
140-75047 Husky-Red **5.00**
140-75048 Husky Drawbar **9.00**
140-75049 Maxi-Undecorated **5.00**
140-75050 Maxi-Yellow **5.00**
140-75051 Maxi-Red **5.00**
140-75052 Maxi-Blue **5.00**
140-75053 Maxi-Green **5.00**
140-75054 Maxi Trucks & Weights **7.50**
140-75058 Husky Drawbar **7.50**
140-75101 SW7 Cow **6.00**
140-75102 SW7 Calf **6.00**
140-75103 DD40 **6.00**
140-75104 SD7 **6.00**
140-75105 GP35 **6.00**
140-75106 SDP40 **6.00**
140-75107 SD45 **6.00**
140-75108 FP45 **6.00**
140-75109 S12 **6.00**
140-75110 PA1 **6.00**
140-75111 U Boats-B **6.00**
140-75112 U Boats-C **6.00**
140-75113 SD9 **6.00**
140-75114 Trainmaster **6.00**
140-75115 SD40-2 **6.00**
140-75116 F7 **6.00**
140-75117 SD40T-2 Short **6.00**
140-75118 SD40T-2 Long **6.00**
140-75119 GP38-2 **6.00**
140-75120 GP50 **6.00**
140-75121 SW1500 **6.00**
140-75122 SW1000 **6.00**
140-75123 SW1500-SP **6.00**
140-75124 Hustler **5.00**
140-75125 RDC1 & 3 **5.00**
140-75126 GP60-50 Phase II **6.00**
140-75127 GP60 Demo **6.00**
140-75128 C44-9W **6.00**

MISCELLANEOUS

140-42012 Blomberg B Truck Detail Set **2.00**
140-44501 Cab, SD40-2, GP50 & GP38-2 pkg(2) **2.00**

AUTO LOADER

140-14075 Undecorated Body **3.00**

STEEL WEIGHTS PKG(2) EA 1.50

140-90700 40' Freight Car
140-90702 Regular Caboose
140-90703 50' Freight Car

KIT BOXES

Empty boxes are ideal for storing models.
140-76300 7-1/2" **1.00**
140-76301 10-1/2" **1.25**
140-76302 12-1/2" **1.50**
140-76303 Maxi III **2.00**

2/56 MACHINE SCREWS PKG(24) 1.75

Machine screws available in the following lengths:
140-99000 1/8"
140-99001 3/16"
140-99002 1/4"
140-99003 5/16"
140-99004 3/8"
140-99005 7/16"
140-99006 1/2"
140-99007 1/4" Flat Head
140-99008 3/16" Sheet Metal
140-99009 5/16" Sheet Metal

SD70/SD75

141-63801 Body **24.98** ***NEW***
Includes long hood, SD75 cabinet, step guard, battery box, blower housing, left and right side grills, exhaust stack, dynamic cover, etched dynamic grill, brakewheel housing, "Q" fan covers and fans (3) and sand filler.

141-63820 Tank Set **4.98** ***NEW***
Includes left and right fuel tanks and two air tanks.

141-63824 Snow Plow Set **3.98** ***NEW***
Comes with high and low plow.

141-63825 Ditch Lights w/Bulbs **4.98** ***NEW***
Left and right.

141-63826 Etched Dynamic Grill **2.98** ***NEW***
141-63827 Dynamic Set **7.98** ***NEW***
Features etched dynamic grill, dynamic housing, exhaust stack and left and right side grills.

141-63830 Mechanism **79.98** ***NEW***
This powered mechanism includes fuel and air tanks, brake details, circuit board and wire locks.

141-63833 Power Truck (black) **19.98** ***NEW***
Includes brake details.

141-63835 Drive Axle Assembly pkg(6) **19.98** ***NEW***
141-63836 Idler Gear pkg(6) **3.98** ***NEW***
141-63854 Grab Iron Set **4.98** ***NEW***

HANDRAIL SETS EA 6.98

141-63852 Molded Black ***NEW***
141-63853 Molded Silver ***NEW***

UNDERFRAME EA 19.98

141-63831 Black ***NEW***
141-63832 Silver ***NEW***

SD70

141-63834 Drive Line **9.98** ***NEW***
Includes 2 each of SD70 worm housing, dog bone shaft, female coupling, worm assembly, Teflon® washer and square bearing.

141-63837 Axle Gear pkg(6) **3.98** ***NEW***

"Q" FANS

141-63850 Molded Black pkg(4) **6.98**
141-63851 Molded Silver pkg(4) **6.98**

SD70M/SD75M

141-63810 Window Set **4.98** ***NEW***
Includes cab windows and front door window.

141-63811 Cab Doors **3.98** ***NEW***
Includes right and left doors with hinges.

141-63812 Cab Interior **3.98** ***NEW***

WALKWAY SETS EA 8.98

141-63815 SD70M ***NEW***
Features SD70M walkway, front anticlimber and rear anticlimber.

141-63816 SD75M ***NEW***
Features SD75M walkway, front anticlimber and rear anticlimber.

SD70I/SD75I CAB

141-63802 Canadian **9.98** ***NEW***
Features cab without louvers, back wall, left and right front doors, number board less lights, left and right window inserts, cab windows, cab interior and nose door window.

SD75I CAB

141-63803 BNSF **9.98** ***NEW***
Includes cab with louvers, back wall, left and right front doors, number board less lights, left and right window inserts, cab windows, cab interior and nose door window.

MISCELLANEOUS

141-63838 Genesis Wire Locks pkg(32) **3.98** ***NEW***
141-63840 Genesis Circuit Board **9.98** ***NEW***
141-63841 Genesis Motor Assembly **39.98** ***NEW***
Includes motor, two flywheels and motor mounts.

141-63842 Genesis Motor Only **29.98** ***NEW***
141-63843 Genesis Light Bulbs pkg(4) **3.98** ***NEW***
141-63844 Genesis Teflon® Washer pkg(12) ***NEW***
141-63845 Genesis Coupler Covers pkg(6) **3.98** ***NEW***
141-63846 #1 Self Tapping Screws pkg(12) **1.98** ***NEW***
141-63487 #0 Self Tapping Screws pkg(12) **1.98** ***NEW***

A. W. Enterprises, Inc.

STEAM LOCO DETAIL PARTS

Turn plain models into detailed miniatures with these unpainted brass investment castings.

AIR BRAKE PARTS

157-4 157-10 157-11

157-4 Distributor Valve **1.50**
157-10 Westinghouse Cross Compound Compressor **3.00**
157-11 Air Pump Strainer **1.50**

BELL

157-18 Air Ringer Type **2.00**

DRIVER CENTERS FOR 57" DRIVERS PKG(2) EA 1.75

157-2 157-3

157-2 Medium Counterweight
157-3 Heavy Counterweight

ENGINE PARTS

157-1 157-5

157-1 72' Smokebox Front **2.95**
157-5 Engine Frame for 0-8-0 or 2-8-0 (Left & Right) **15.00**

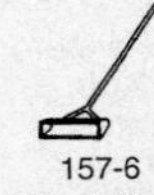

157-6 157-8

157-6 Blow Down Muffler pkg(2) **1.50**
157-8 SP Style Smoke Stack **2.25**

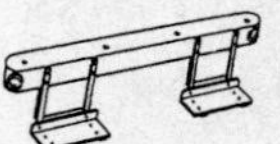

157-9 157-16

157-9 Switcher Pilot **3.50**
157-16 Power Reverse **3.25**

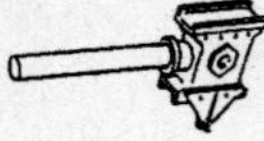

157-17 157-19

157-17 Cab Lubricator **2.00**
157-19 Alligator Crossheads 1 Pair **2.25**

157-22 157-25

157-22 Fire Door Early Oil Type **2.25**
157-25 Generator **2.50**

157-26 157-27

157-26 Fire Extinguisher pkg(2) **2.00**
157-27 Pilot Steps pkg(2) **2.00**

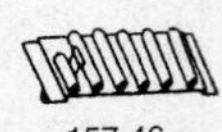

157-45 157-46

157-45 Boiler Back Head for SP 0-8-0, 2-8-0 **2.75** ***NEW***
157-46 Tool Rack **1.25** ***NEW***

157-47 157-48

157-47 Shelf On Backhead **1.25** ***NEW***
157-48 Stoker **2.75** ***NEW***

157-49 157-50

157-49 Grate Shaker Triple - Manual pkg(2) **2.25** ***NEW***
157-50 Butterfly Firedoor & Step **2.75** ***NEW***

157-51 157-52

157-51 Brake Valve **3.00** ***NEW***
157-52 Lift Rings pkg(6) **1.75** ***NEW***

FREIGHT CAR PARTS

157-28 157-53

157-28 Air Hose pkg(10) **3.00** ***NEW***
157-53 Ratchet & Pawl pkg(2) **1.25** ***NEW***

HATCHES

157-12 157-20

157-12 Oil Bunker **.75**
157-20 Tall Water Tank **2.50**

HEADLIGHTS-SP STYLE

157-7 157-23

157-7 With Bracket **2.25**
157-23 No Bracket **2.00**

LOCOMOTIVE BRAKE SHOES & HANGERS 1 PAIR EA 1.25

157-35 157-36

157-35 Short ***NEW***
157-36 Long ***NEW***

OIL DIPSTICKS EA .75

157-13 157-14

157-13 Long
157-14 Short

PASSENGER CAR DETAILS

157-29 157-30

157-29 Brake Cylinder w/Levers **2.75** ***NEW***
157-30 Universal Valve **1.50** ***NEW***

157-31 157-32

157-31 Belt Generator **2.25** ***NEW***
157-32 Axle Generator Three-Piece Set **4.75** ***NEW***

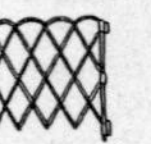

157-33 157-34

157-33 Safety Tail Gate pkg(2) **3.25** ***NEW***
157-34 Air Compressor (Air Conditioning) **3.75** ***NEW***

TANK STAYS PKG(4) EA 1.75

157-43 157-44

157-43 Water ***NEW***
157-44 Oil ***NEW***

TENDER PARTS

157-21 157-37

157-21 Rerail Frogs pkg(2) **2.00**
157-37 Front Pilot Beam w/Poling Pockets **2.25** ***NEW***

157-38 157-39 157-40

157-38 Water Gauge Tricocks **1.75** ***NEW***
157-39 Brake Cylinder w/Brackets **2.25** ***NEW***
157-40 Water Leg Valves pkg(2) **2.00** ***NEW***

157-41 157-42

157-41 Pipe Detail SP **1.75** ***NEW***
157-42 Water Hose & Coupling pkg(2) **2.00** ***NEW***

TOOL BOXES

157-15 157-24

157-15 Underbody Mount **2.25**
157-24 Long **2.00**

Metal details for layout scenes.

STREET DETAILS

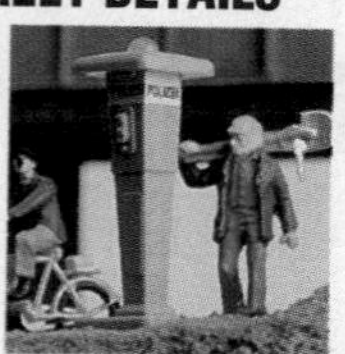

186-5440 Police Emergency Phone **9.99**
Green, approx. 1" 25.4cm tall, illuminated.

186-5441

186-5444

186-5445

186-5441 Illuminated Phone Booth **13.99**
186-5444 Booth-Pay Phone **14.99**
186-5445 Freestanding Pay Phone (yellow) **11.99**
186-5446 Freestanding - Tall Pay Phone **11.99**

TRACKSIDE DETAILS

186-2652 Distance Posts pkg(10) **5.99**
Prototypes are spaced 100 meters apart.

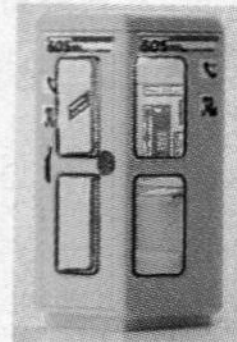

186-5442 Phone Shanty **13.99**

186-2653 Switch Heater **12.99**
Includes two propane tanks, 3-3/4" 9.3cm wide.

186-2654 Lineside Phone Box **6.99**
1 x 3/4" 2.5 x 1.8cm.

Limited Quantity Available
186-673 Brass Bumper Post pkg(2) **33.99**

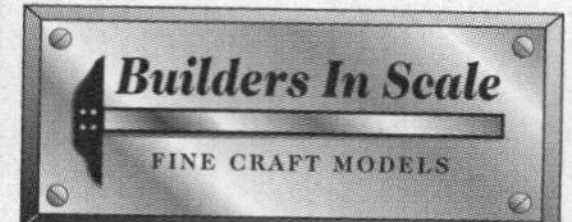

CHAIN

Each package includes 18" of brass chain.

DETAIL - 40 LINKS PER INCH

169-250 Black **2.98**
169-251 Brass **2.59**

HEAVY DUTY - 15 LINKS PER INCH

169-254 Black **2.98**
169-255 Brass **2.59**

ORNATE - 12 LINKS PER INCH

169-256 Black **2.98**
169-257 Brass **2.59**

WINDOW TREATMENTS

169-503 Venetian Blind Set pkg(10) **3.49**
Laser-cut paper, great detail for home or office interiors. Includes ten different sizes, can be modeled with slats open or closed. Includes instructions.

169-253 Lace Curtains **5.98**
Make any empty window look like home! Laser-cut lace curtains add detail and dimension to otherwise plain windows. Eight pairs of curtains in several sizes.

LOBSTER TRAPS

169-591 pkg(8) **9.98**
Perfect detail for dockside scenes or boats. Parts are made of finely detailed, photo-etched brass. Includes eight traps and assorted lobsters.

MINE HOIST

169-609 Mine Hoist w/Ore Skip **14.49**
Includes 17 white metal parts and wooden base.

DETAIL CASTING SETS EA 5.98

Turn plain models into superdetailed scenes with these parts. Each includes at least 10 related metal castings, which you just paint and install.

169-5500 Backyard Details
Add realism to residential areas with the dog house, bird bath, swing set and other items in this assortment.

169-5501 Alley Details
Great details for the back of any building, set includes an electric meter, trash cans, drums, crates and other items

169-5502 Warehouse Details
Put life in any loading dock with these tanks, pallets, crates, drums and more.

169-5503 Depot Details
Your depot becomes a busy place with the luggage cart, suitcases, trunks, platform steps and more in this set.

169-5504 Nautical Detail Set
The waterfront is buzzing with detail when you add boat cleats, life ring, buoys, anchors, oars and more from this set.

169-5505 Office Detail Set
It's another day at the office when you add items included in this set, such as a desk, filing cabinets, chairs, a clock, phones and other office essentials.

169-5506 Mine Junk Detail Set
Looking for gold? With mine buckets and cars, dynamite crates, bull wheels, and other equipment, this set is the genuine item.

169-5507 Workshop Detail Set
Hard work pays off when you show off the welding set, sawhorse, tool crib, anvil, workbench and other workshop materials included in this set.

PLYWOOD SHEETS

231-1010 1/2 x 1" pkg(12) **1.95**
Real wood cut to a scale 4 x 8' sheet, great for lumber yards, freight car or pickup bed loads, boarded-up windows or scale models of layouts!

12" DIAMETER ROOF VENT

231-241 1.95

18" DIAMETER ROOF VENTS EA 1.95

White metal castings.

231-240

231-242

231-240 Round pkg(5)
231-242 Stacked Cones pkg(4)

18" DIAMETER WIND VANE VENTS PKG(3) EA 1.95

White metal castings.

231-243

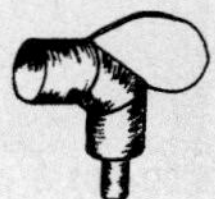
231-244

231-243 Mouth Down Wind
231-244 Mouth Up Wind

SLAT VENT KITS EA 8.95

These larger slatted vents can be used on engine sheds, industrial buildings or any structure that needs realistic roof detail.

231-17 Small
9/16 x 1-1/8" (1.4 x 2.8cm)
Makes up to five vents.

231-18 Medium
3/4 x 1-1/2" (1.9 x 3.8cm)
Makes up to four vents.

231-19 Large
1 x 2" (2.5 x 5cm) Makes up to three vents.

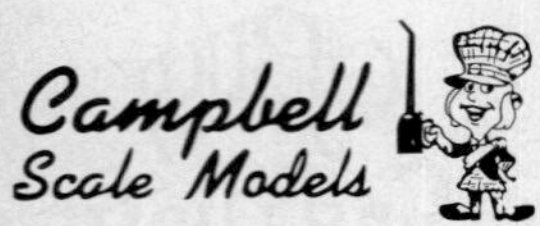

Use these parts to detail modern, Old West or Victorian-era buildings. Windows, doors and trim are molded in white plastic unless noted.

BARRELS

Made from turned hardwood, with raised trim and bands.

200-249 Red pkg(12) **5.00**
200-250 Plain pkg(12) **4.50**

CHAIN

200-256 Black **4.35**
12" length, 36 links per inch.
Dealers: Must order in multiples of 6.

CORRUGATED ALUMINUM EA 5.75

Easy way to model corrugated walls or roofing. Width is shown in HO Scale feet, each sheet is 7-1/2" long by .002" thick. Dimension listed is scale width.

200-801 8' pkg(9)
200-802 10' pkg(7)
200-803 12' pkg(6)
200-804 4' pkg(10)
200-805 6' pkg(9)

DOORS EA 3.00

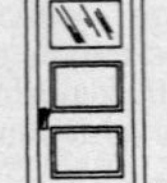

200-912 200-913 200-914

200-912 pkg(3)
200-913 pkg(3)
200-914 pkg(2)

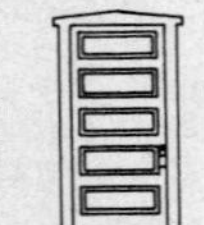
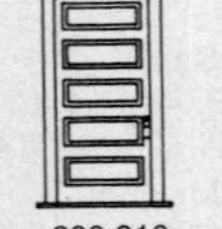

200-915 200-916 200-917

200-915 pkg(3)
200-916 pkg(3)
200-917 pkg(2)

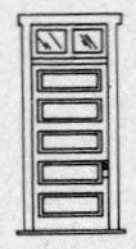
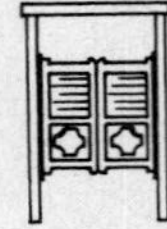

200-918 200-919

200-918 pkg(2)
200-919 pkg(2)
200-941 Victorian Door/Vent pkg(2)

OIL DRUMS PKG (12) EA 5.00 (UNLESS NOTED)

200-251 Plain **4.50**
200-252 Silver
200-253 Black
200-254 Red

PROFILE SHINGLES

200-800 100' Roll **8.00**
Modeling realistic shingled roofs is easy with Profile Shingles. Made of paper with a natural wood color, one edge is notched to resemble individual shingles, while the other is solid. The back is coated with water-soluble glue. Simply cut to length, moisten and apply in overlapping strips. Enough material to cover approximately 9 x 12".

SKYLIGHTS EA 3.00

200-909 200-910

200-909 pkg(2)
200-910 Corrugated pkg(4)

STRUCTURAL DETAILS EA 3.00

200-920 200-927

200-920 Bell & Bracket
200-927 Cyclone Vent pkg(3)

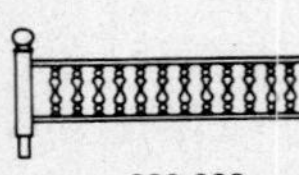

200-921 200-922

200-921 Corbels pkg(28)
200-922 Porch Railing pkg(4)

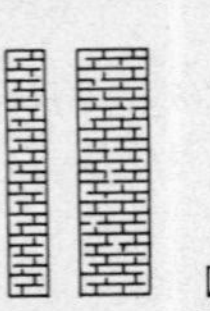
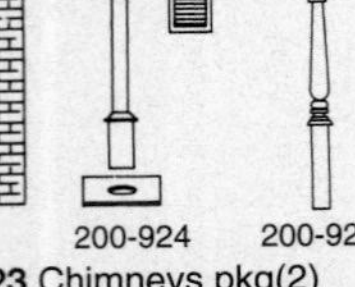

200-923 200-924 200-926

200-923 Chimneys pkg(2)
200-924 Two Smoke Jacks & Four Attic Vents
200-926 Turned Post pkg(5)

200-932 Spool Trim pkg(4)

200-933 Step Stringer pkg(4)

WINDOWS EA 3.00

200-900 200-901 200-902

200-900 pkg(4)
200-901 pkg(5)
200-902 pkg(5)

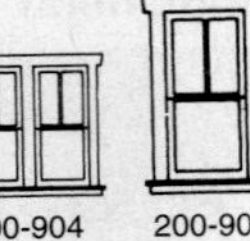

200-903 200-904 200-905

200-903 pkg(6)
200-904 pkg(3)
200-905 pkg(4)

200-906 200-907 200-908

200-906 pkg(4)
200-907 pkg(4)
200-908 pkg(3)

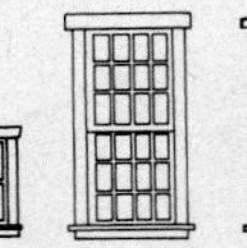

200-911 200-929 200-937

200-911 pkg(3)
200-929 pkg(2)
200-937 pkg(3)

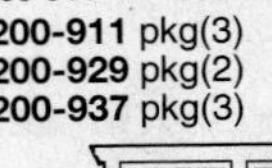

200-936 pkg(3)
200-939 Large Victorian pkg(3)
200-940 Small Victorian pkg(3)

MISCELLANEOUS

200-255 200-925 200-938

200-255 Brass Light Shades pkg(6) **4.50**
Dealers: Must order in multiples of 6.

200-925 Nuts & Bolts pkg(60) **3.00**
One-piece plastic, molded in gunmetal gray, but easily painted to match your project.

200-938 Air Cooler Evaporator pkg(2) **3.00**

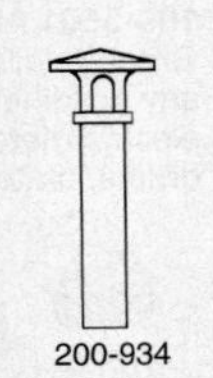

200-931 200-934

200-931 Flagpole & 48 Star Flag **3.25**
Plastic pole, printed paper flag and basic assembly instructions.

200-934 Smoke Stack pkg(2) **3.00**
Molded in black plastic.

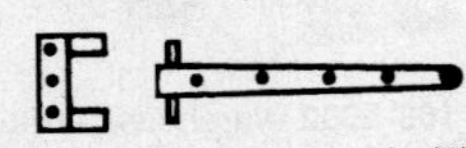

200-935 Hinges, Large pkg(8) **3.00**
Molded in black plastic.

200-930 Park Benches pkg(4) **3.50**
Plastic sides with wooden slats.

200-1606 Stone Bridge w/Highway Accessories **6.50**
Easy-to-build plastic kit is great for rural scenes.

We have worked closely with this manufacturer to provide accurate delivery information at the time this catalog was published. Items listed in blue ink may not be available at all times. Current delivery information, along with a list of in-stock products for this line, can be found on our Web site at www.walthers.com.
All parts are made of cast metal.

FINIAL PKG(6) EA 1.50

Typically installed atop signal posts, can be used for other applications.

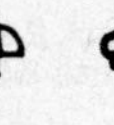

1361 1362 1363 1364

215-1361 Pointed
215-1362 Round
215-1363 Teardrop
215-1364 Dome

GAS STATION DETAILS

215-100 215-101

215-100 Early "Clockface" Gas Pump pkg(2) **2.25**
215-101 Oil Bunker pkg(4) **1.95**

TRACKSIDE DETAILS

215-113 215-125

215-113 Battery Box pkg(6) **1.95**
215-125 Electric Car Puller **2.25**

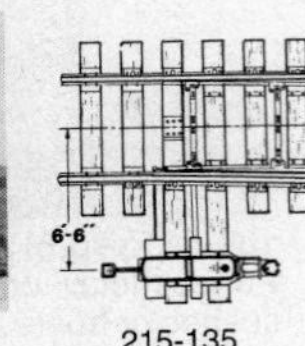

215-120 215-135

215-120 Oil Column **2.25**
215-135 Switch Motor pkg(2) **2.75**

MOONSHINE STILL

215-180 Moonshine Still **3.25**
Complete kit looks great hidden in a rural area.

PASSENGER CAR DETAILS

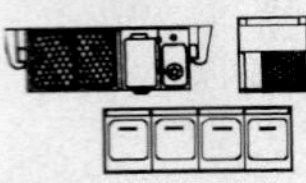

215-200 Waukesha Air Conditioner **2.00**
Kit models a common style of passenger car air conditioners and includes ice engine, sub cooler and bottled gas box.

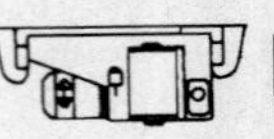

215-205 215-211

215-205 Engine Generator **2.25**
215-211 Pullman Cover pkg(4) **1.75**

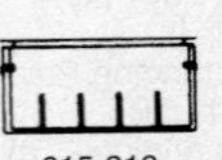
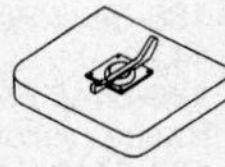

215-213 215-220

215-213 Cover Only pkg(4) **1.75**
215-220 Water Fill Hatch 2 Pair **1.50**
215-221 Waste Drain Pipe pkg(6) **1.50**

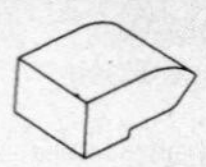

215-250 215-255

215-250 Utility, Round Roof pkg(12) **2.25**
For heavyweight passenger cars.

215-255 Streamlined Car Roof Vent pkg(8) **1.75**

STAIRS

215-155 45° Stairway pkg(2) **1.50**

VENTS PKG(3) EA 1.95

215-150 215-151

215-150 Roof
215-151 Large Cyclone

CMA Creative Model Associates

Make your models look their best with these plastic parts.

CRATES

363-1020 pkg(8) **4.95** *NEW*

COAL BINS

363-1024 pkg(3) **5.95** *NEW*

GRAB IRONS

363-1018 Bracket Type pkg(48) **4.95**
Injection molded in gray styrene.

ICE BLOCKS

363-1012 For Reefers pkg(64) **4.95**

LADDERS

363-1010 For Freight Car pkg(16) **4.95**

MILK CANS

363-1006 pkg(45) **4.95**

OUTDOOR LIGHTS

363-1017 Lamps w/Brackets pkg(24) **4.95**
Great detail for industrial or railroad buildings. Nonworking lamps feature one-piece shade with bulb detail and separate building mounting bracket.

PALLETS

363-1003 **4.95**
Dress-up any loading dock.

PHOSPHOR BRONZE WIRE EA 2.50

Make handrails, grab irons, plumbing and more. Harder than brass and easier to work, each piece is 8" long and perfectly straight. Packed in a rigid plastic tube for protection and storage.

363-1100 .008" pkg(10)
363-1101 .010" pkg(12)
363-1102 .015" pkg(12)
363-1103 .020" pkg(12)
363-1104 .025" pkg(12)
363-1105 .032" pkg(12)

ROOFWALKS

363-1016 40' Steel pkg(3) **5.95**
Make any 40' box car, stock car or reefer more realistic with these parts. One-piece roofwalk and separate corner walkways have a very thin cross section, and see-through tread.

SACKS

363-1019 Burlap Sacks pkg(64) **4.95**
Nearly every industry used to receive and ship raw materials in bags, and many still do! Great detail for loading docks, freight car or truck loads and more.

DEPOTS BY JOHN

DETAILED REPLICAS IN SCALE

AIR CONDITIONER

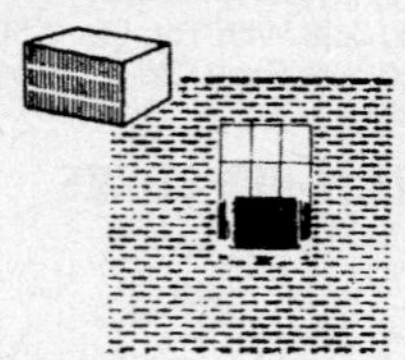

87-109 Window Air Conditioner Kit pkg(2) **3.50**
Easy-to-build kit with pre-cut wood block, metal grill and foil covering.

CHIMNEYS

87-124 36' Tall w/Caps **2.95**

87-125 18" Square w/Caps **2.49**

87-126 Victorian **2.49**

COMMUNICATION BOXES

87-121 Telephone & Waybill Boxes pkg(6) **1.95**
Commonly installed on stations, interlocking towers and shanties to house company phones and store waybills for transfers. Also seen mounted on posts at trackside.

CORBELS EA 2.49

87-111 Long w/Channel

87-112 Curved Design

DOORS

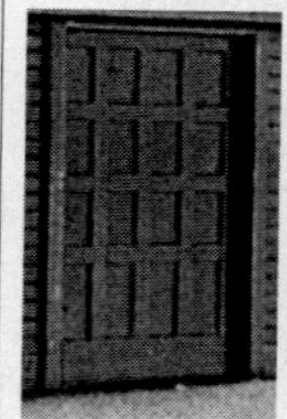

87-133

87-134

87-133 16-Panel Freight Door CNW pkg(2) **2.49**
87-134 2-Lite Door w/2-Lite Transom pkg(2) **1.95**

EAVE BRACKETS PKG(8) EA 1.95

87-123

87-127

87-128

87-123 Curved, Center Brace
87-127 Right Angle
87-128 Acute Angle

STEPS

87-129 Concrete Steps pkg(2) **2.49**
87-135 Brass Roof Vents **1.95** *NEW*

CRESCENT STATION

WHITEWALLS

513-601 Whitewalls for Tires pkg(24) **3.00**
Die-cut, self-adhesive stickers to model wide whitewalls popular in the 40s and 50S.

Parts are metal castings unless noted.

CABOOSE PARTS

254-16 254-24

254-16 Windows, Doors & Steps **8.95**
254-24 Steps pkg(8) **2.95**

CHAIN

254-121 Brass (12") **2.50**

CHIMNEYS

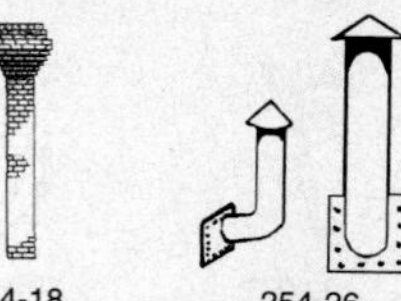

254-18 254-26

254-18 Victorian Chimney **1.95**
254-26 Smoke Jack pkg(3) **2.25**

COAL BUCKETS

254-76 With Handle pkg(2) **3.25**
Used at small coaling facilities, can be used as small buckets in O Scale.

HEADLIGHT

254-45 Rio Grande, Early Box Type pkg(2) **2.25**

INTERIOR DETAILS

254-108 Stove **1.95**
254-122 Box of Bottles pkg(4) **2.50**
254-123 Cafe Chairs pkg(8) **1.95**
Used in Columbine Cafe #254-118.

MINIATURE TOOLS EA 1.95 (UNLESS NOTED)

254-104 Ladder, Plastic pkg(2) **2.25**
254-106 Rerailer Shoes pkg(4)
254-107 Large Tool Boxes pkg(2)
254-109 Lanterns pkg(4)
254-110 Shovels pkg(4)
254-111 Brooms pkg(4)

PLASTIC DOORS PKG(4) EA 1.95

254-62

254-63

254-62 With Transom
254-63 Four Panel

PLASTIC WINDOWS DOUBLE-HUNG EA 1.95

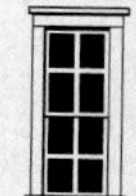

254-60

254-61

254-60 Tall pkg(4)
254-61 Double pkg(2)

SCREWS

254-127 Wood Truck (1/4") pkg(12) **1.95**

WATER TANK

254-124 Round Roof-Top **5.95**

WOODEN BARRELS

254-15 Large pkg(4) **2.25**
254-23 Small pkg(10) **2.50**

MISCELLANEOUS

254-34 Bridge Shoes pkg(4) **1.95**

254-25

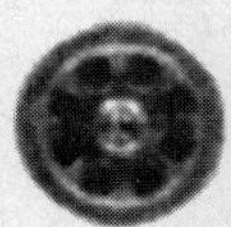

254-128

254-25 Rural Mailbox pkg(5) **1.95**
254-128 Speeder Wheels pkg(4) **1.95**

254-93

254-94

254-93 Auto Tires pkg(12) **4.95**
254-94 Assorted Gears pkg(8) **4.50**

From the golden age of steam to the latest diesels, modeling your favorite equipment is easy with these brass and plastic parts.

STEAM DETAILS

AIR BRAKES

190-284 Westinghouse "AB" Brass Set **8.00**
Twelve-piece set can be adapted to many freight cars. Includes reservoir, control valve, dust collector, bell cranks, Ajax housing and wheel, plus other details.

190-313 "ABD" Plastic pkg(2) **3.50**
Three-piece, for modern freight cars.

WESTINGHOUSE "KC" SETS - COMPLETE

190-291 Brass **6.75**
Standard for steam-era cars. Includes underbody and end details, brake staff and chart of wire sizes to model piping.

TENDER BRAKE SET

190-306 Westinghouse "U" Set **8.00**
Standard equipment on most tenders built from 1920-1950.

LOCOMOTIVE AIR BRAKES

190-272 Double Kit **3.35**

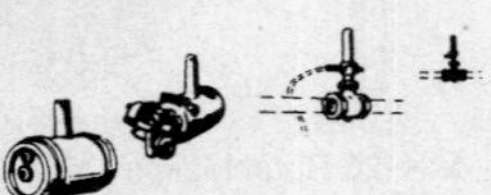

190-273 Single Phase **3.35**
Three-piece set, use with engines equipped with single phase air pump.

STEAM LOCO CAB BRAKE STANDS EA 3.80

190-366 Single Valve, Older or Smaller Engines
190-367 Standard Era-All Engines (2 Valve)
190-368 Modern Medium and Large Engines

AIR CONDITIONING RECEPTACLE

190-355 Air Conditioning Receptacle pkg(2) **3.10**

AIR HOSES

190-276 Freight Car & Caboose, Plastic pkg(20) **2.95**
Standard design, enough for 10 cars.

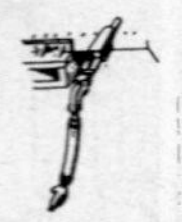
190-277

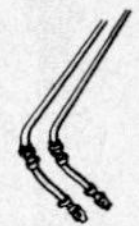
190-319

190-277 Standard Type-Brass pkg(4) **2.55**
Use on locomotives, tenders and cars.

190-319 Steam Freight Locos pkg(2) **2.10**
A single hose was installed on the pilot of most freight service engines. Includes parts for two locos.

PASSENGER AIR, SIGNAL, STEAM LINES

190-274

190-275

190-320

190-274 Loco & Tender-Brass **4.90**
Set of five hoses and brackets for equipping a single engine and tender.

190-275 Passenger Car & Express Reefer-Plastic pkg(2) **4.20**
Includes twelve hoses and brackets, enough for two cars

190-320 Bracketed Air & Signal Lines pkg(2) **2.10**
Air and signal lines in a mounting bracket, as installed on the pilot of dual service and passenger locos. Parts for two engines.

AIR PUMPS

190-240 190-334 190-2002

190-240 Westinghouse Cross Compound **3.80**

190-334 Side Mounting **5.90**
Dual pumps mounted side by side, with full piping. Used on right side of most locos. This is a different configuration than smokebox mounted pumps (#190-349).

190-2002 Double Pump Set **8.25**
Includes two air pumps, plus distributing valve and equalizing reservoir.

CROSS COMPOUND-PIPED EA 5.20

Pumps include basic air piping, which can be bent for custom installations, or expanded with wire and fittings, sold separately.

190-346 190-347 190-349

190-346 With Remote Strainer
190-347 Standard Strainer
190-349 Front Mounting
Used on front of smoke boxes, most locos had two.

SINGLE PHASE W/BRACKET EA 4.50

Older style with single cylinder, used on early steam locos.

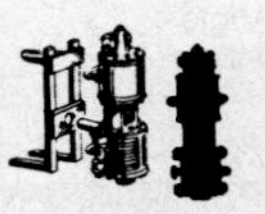
190-256

190-257

190-256 9-1/2"
190-257 11"

ALTERNATOR

190-365 Passenger Car **2.65**
Prototype converts DC to AC for car lighting systems.

ASH PANS

190-248 190-249 190-479

190-248 Drop-Door Type pkg(2) **3.80**
Typically used on engines with small fire boxes built between 1900 and late 1930s.

190-249 Commonwealth Cast Type pkg(2) **4.95**
Used on larger, modern engines but also applied to older types. Castings can be cut to fit any length fire box.

190-479 Pennsylvania Type pkg(2) **3.75**

BACKHEAD DETAILS

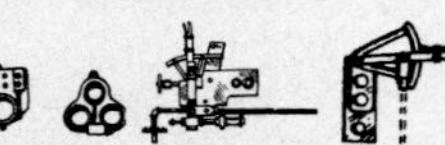
190-372 190-373 190-374

190-372 Gauges, Engineer's & Fireman's Side **3.50**

190-373 Reverse Quadrant for Power Reverse **4.20**
190-374 Small Quadrant pkg(2) **3.40**
Use for injectors, small power reverse, etc.

BATTERY RECEPTACLES

190-354 Battery Receptacles pkg(2) **3.10**

BELLS

190-281 190-285

190-299

190-281 Standard Rope Pull **3.35**
190-285 Air Ringer **3.35**
190-299 Angle Bracket Boiler Front Mounting **3.95**

190-317

190-328

190-329

190-317 Modern Steam Loco **3.35**
190-328 With Top Bar **3.50**
190-329 Rigid Old Ball Top **2.65**

BLOW-OFF COCKS

190-308 Blow-Off Cocks (2) & Inspection Plugs (6) **3.80**

BRAKE CYLINDERS

190-219

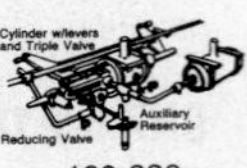

190-220

190-219 Engines pkg(2) **3.75**
190-220 Westinghouse "PC" High Speed System (3 pieces) **6.40**
Used on older engine tenders and passenger cars. Includes cylinder with levers and triple valve, reducing valve and auxiliary reservoir.

190-221 Tender **3.00**

BRAKE SHOES EA. 10.50

Each set includes insulated bushing.

190-444 Fits 57 to 64"
190-445 Fits 64 to 80"
190-446 Fits Bowser M1, M1A, Northern & USRA Mountain
190-447 Fits Bowser G-5

BRAKE WHEELS

190-289

190-351

190-289 Brass, 6-Spoke pkg(6) **3.80**
190-351 Plastic Set(6) **4.20**

CAB DETAILS

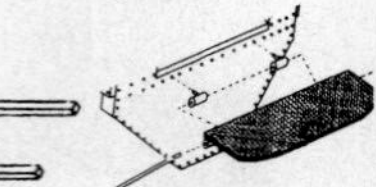
190-381 190-385

190-381 Roof Hatch **2.50**
190-385 Deck Plate w/Hinges **4.75**

CAB WALKWAYS PKG(2) EA 2.80

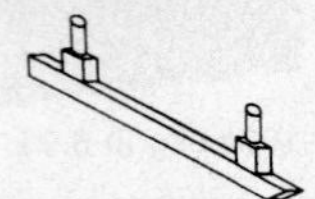

190-379 25/32" (19.8mm)
190-380 1-1/16" (26.9mm)

COAL PUSHER

190-255 Standard **4.50**

DAMPER

190-269 Damper Control **2.10**
Used on all sizes of steamers, from 0-6-0s to Shays to articulateds.

DETAIL KITS

190-2001 Modern Pennsy Freight Engines **10.50**
Modernize Bowser engines with this kit and #236 Smoke Box front. Includes modern headlight, Pyle dual generator, bracket for generator, modern Pennsy marker lights, Keystone number plate and chin platform.

DOMES

AUXILIARY

Each includes dome base, valves and whistle.

190-227

190-228

190-227 Exposed Set **4.40**
190-228 Exposed w/Fittings **3.80**

1860-70 VINTAGE DOMES EA 8.25
Each includes sand and steam domes.

190-338 190-342

190-338 Round Steam Tapered Sand Domes
190-342 Fluted Sand, Tapered Steam Domes

ECCENTRIC CRANK

190-384 pkg(2) **4.75**

ELESCO FEEDWATER HEATER

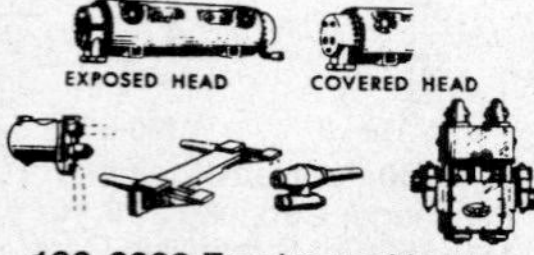

190-2003 Feedwater Heater Kit (8 Pieces) **10.50**
Build with exposed or covered head, castings for both are included.

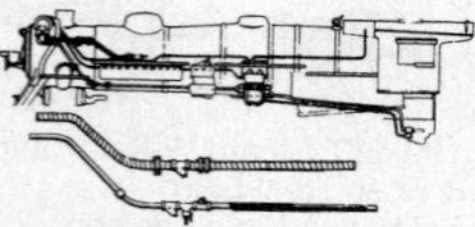

190-343 Feedwater Pipe Set **5.20**
Includes one each hot and cold water pipes. Smaller pipe carries cold water from pump to heater. Wrapped pipe carries heated water to left side or top feed injector. Bend pipes carefully to fit your application.

GENERATORS EA 2.65

190-211 190-212

190-211 Turbo
190-212 Sunbeam

190-213 190-214

190-213 Loco Light
190-214 Buda Ross

190-215 190-234

190-215 Pyle-GE
190-234 Pyle, Dual Voltage

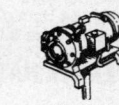

190-335 190-362

190-335 With Muffler
190-348 Passenger Car
190-362 Large, Dual Voltage

SPICER SHAFT DRIVEN TYPES
190-352 Type GL, 20kw **6.00**
190-353 Type GL, 25kw **6.00**
190-357 Type G, 35kw **6.40**

HEADLIGHTS

190-204 190-206 190-207

190-204 Lima Arc **2.65**
190-206 Standard, w/Wing Board & Visor **2.65**
190-207 Plain **2.65**

190-208 190-263 190-282

190-208 Northern Pacific Style **2.65**
190-263 Mars Light - Twin Type **2.95**
Used on steam and diesels, includes bracket for mounting on steam loco smokebox.
190-282 GN Style **2.65**
190-304 Switcher **3.50**
Used at front and rear on small locos and as back-up light on bigger tenders.

190-305 Large Baldwin Oil Lamp (1890s) **4.00**

PENNSYLVANIA STYLES

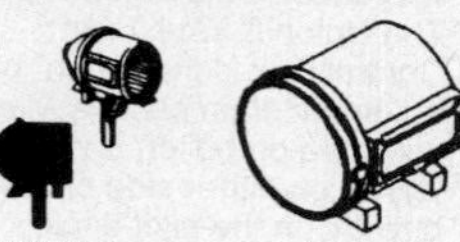
190-235 190-477

190-235 Modern **2.65**
190-477 Flat Back **2.65**

PYLE EA 2.65

190-201 190-205 190-230

190-201 With Visor
190-205 With Wing Board
190-230 Twin Sealed Beam

PYLE - FLAT SIDED EA 2.65

190-327 190-331

190-327 Standard
190-331 With Visor

SUNBEAM EA 2.65

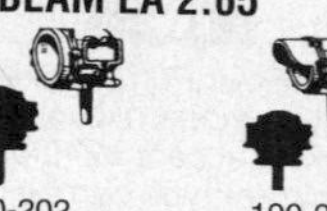
190-202 190-229

190-202 Standard
190-229 With Visor

SANTA FE STYLES

190-203 190-209 190-210

190-203 Large, Old **2.65**
190-209 With Bracket **2.95**
190-210 Standard **2.65**

HEADLIGHT BRACKETS

190-241 190-246 190-478

190-241 Standard w/Numberboard **2.65**
190-246 High Mounting w/Grab Irons **3.80**
Fits all Cal-Scale headlights.
190-478 Pennsy Type **2.10**
Use with headlights #235 or 477, sold separately.

CENTER-MOUNTING EA 2.65

190-258 190-279

190-258 UP
190-279 CNW

HEATERS

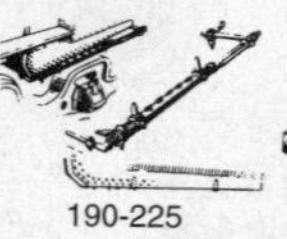

190-225 190-270

190-225 Locomotive Oil Heater **3.80**
190-270 Worthington Type SA Feedwater Heater (3 Pieces) **8.25**

INJECTORS

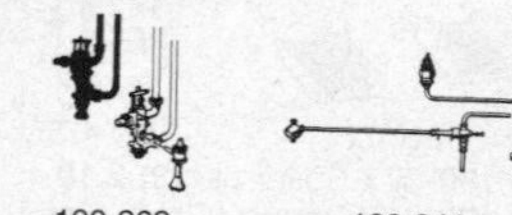
190-262 190-341

190-262 Non-Lifting Nathan Type "4000" **2.95**
190-341 Check Valve & Injector (3 Pieces) **6.20**

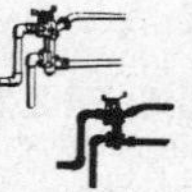
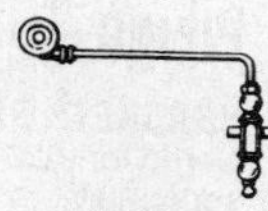
190-264 190-337

190-264 Non-Lifting Sellers Type **2.95**
190-337 Check Valve & Injector Set **5.80**
Check valves and pumps mount on each side of boiler, injector on the left side only.
190-288 Lifting, Large Monitor pkg(2) **5.90**

MARKERS EA. 2.65

FOR CABOOSE

190-325 190-463

190-325 Caboose, less jewels pkg(2)
190-463 Pennsylvania Style pkg(2)

190-464 190-465

190-464 PRR, PC & CR pkg(2)
190-465 CR pkg(2)

FOR LOCOMOTIVES

190-280 190-312 190-375

190-280 Modern pkg(2)
190-312 "Standard Era" including USRA pkg(2)
190-375 A&W Style pkg(2)
Used on some early engines, passenger cars and cabooses.

FOR PASSENGER CARS

190-490 PRR Type 2 Pair

MISCELLANEOUS

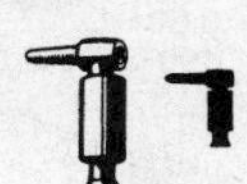
190-226 190-239

190-226 Locomotive Radiator **2.95**
190-239 Over-Fire Jet Set pkg(16) **7.20**
Used on the prototype to create better combustion in the fire box.

190-271 Mechanical Lubricators w/Brackets pkg(4) **5.70**

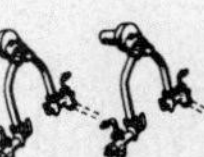

190-286 190-326

190-286 Sanders pkg(2) **3.45**
190-326 Wood Burning Stack w/Spark Arrestor Screen **8.25**

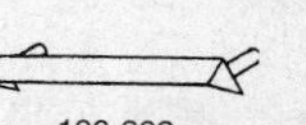
190-382 190-383

190-382 Window Shade pkg(2) **2.80**
190-383 Three-Way Junction Box pkg(2) **2.50**

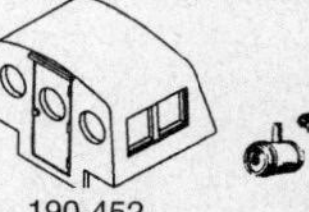
190-452 190-2004

190-452 PRR Modern "Dog House" **8.20**
Installed on tender deck of some larger PRR steam locos, housed a seat for the head brakeman.

190-493 PRR Tender Water Scoop Controls (3 Piece Set) **2.65**
190-2004 Water Scoop Kit **8.25**
Installed on some tenders to allow taking water without stopping. Complete with scoop, control and other details.

MUFFLERS

190-222 190-223

190-222 Exhaust w/Valve **3.00**
190-223 Exhaust, Wilson **2.65**

NUMBER BOARDS

190-260 190-389

190-260 4 Character pkg(2) **3.30**
190-389 Oval pkg(2) **2.40**

NUMBER PLATES

190-238 PRR pkg(3) **2.10**

190-244 190-245

190-244 B&O Capitol Dome pkg(2) **2.10**
190-245 Plain pkg(3) **2.10**

PILOTS

190-261 190-387

190-261 Commonwealth Drop Coupler **7.20**
Used on 4-8-4s, Big Boys and Challengers
190-387 PRR **6.75**

190-298 190-388

190-298 General Steel Castings w/Coupler **7.20**
190-388 PRR-Slatted w/Stops **6.75**

190-296 190-336

190-296 Commonwealth w/Swing Coupler pkg(5 Pieces) **7.20**
190-336 Wood, 5'6", CP **7.20**

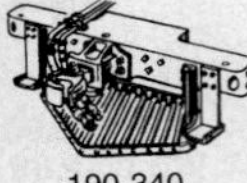

190-340 190-344

190-340 Wood, 4'6", UP **7.20**
190-344 Commonwealth Cast Late Version w/couplers **7.20**

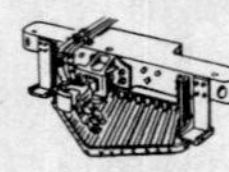
190-315 190-318

190-315 Standard Boiler Tube **7.20**
190-318 Boiler Tube w/Coupler, Hoses, Sheet Metal Guard **7.20**

PIPING

BRACKETS PKG(6) EA 2.20

Cored for .020 wire, sold separately.

190-480 190-481 190-482

190-480 Four Hole
190-481 Three Hole
190-482 Two Hole

CLAMPS

190-483 Clamp for .020 Wire pkg(10) **2.45**

UNIONS EA 3.50

190-484 190-485

190-484 Hexagonal pkg(8)
Includes six medium and two large unions.
190-485 Square & Round pkg(16)
Includes eight square and eight round unions; four each large and small sizes.

POWER REVERSE

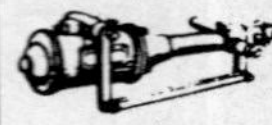
190-217 190-218

190-217 Type "T" **3.85**
190-218 Type "P" **3.10**

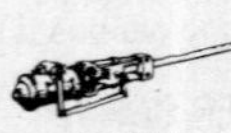

190-216 190-303

190-216 Type "C" **3.85**
190-303 Early 1900s **3.80**

190-297 190-330

190-297 Articulated Locos **3.80**
190-330 Ragonnet B **3.80**

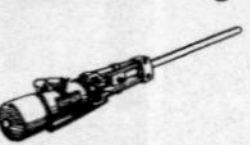

190-237 190-332

190-237 Pennsylvania-Modern **3.80**
190-332 Ragonnet B1 **3.80**

190-360 190-363

190-360 Standard Reverse Gear (Rear) **3.80**
Typically used on small engines.
190-363 Large Reverse Gear Rear Facing **3.80**

SHIELDS

Available separately or in kits containing pump mounting brackets, radiator casting and equalizing reservoir.

190-259 Air Pump Shield **5.90**
Used on modern locomotives. Brackets accept #240 pumps, any similar type can be used. Pipes can be fabricated with standard brass handrail wire, prototype pipes are 2" outside diameter.

LARGE 7'-9"

190-266 Shield Only **4.90**
190-2005 Kit **8.25**
Used on UP Challengers, Big Boys and other large, modern locomotives.

SMALL 7'-3"

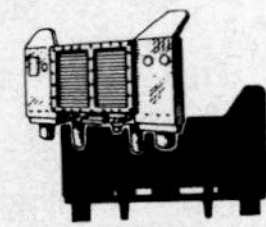

190-267 Shield Only **4.90**
190-2006 Kit **8.25**
Used on conventional sized locomotives.

SMOKE BOX FRONTS

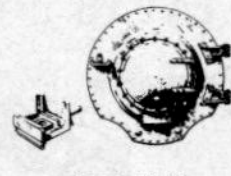
190-243 190-278

190-243 USRA Type, 81" Diameter w/Number Plate **4.70**
190-278 CNW w/Bracket **4.40**

190-236 190-242

190-236 PRR Modern 7'-6" w/Number Plate **4.50**
Used on K-5s and M-1s.
190-242 Harriman Type 86" Diameter w/Number Plate **4.70**

STEPS

190-377 190-475

190-377 Boiler pkg(2) **2.10**
190-475 Pennsy Cabin Car (Caboose) pkg(4) **4.20**

STOKER ENGINES

190-224 190-254

190-224 Standard Two Cylinder **4.85**
190-254 Single Cylinder Duplex Type **3.35**

TENDER HATCHES

190-231 190-232 190-233

190-231 Large **4.40**
190-232 Rectangular Base **3.35**
190-233 Rounded Base **3.35**

TOOL BOX

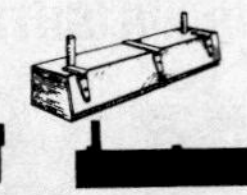
190-295 190-364

190-295 Loco Tool Box **3.10**
190-364 Tool Box, Tender **4.20**
Underslung between trucks.

THROTTLES

190-268 Front End w/Rods & Guides **3.35**

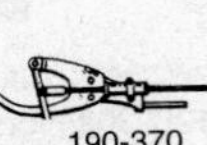
190-369 190-370

190-369 Horizontal-Early Engines **3.10**
190-370 Front End, Medium & Large #1 **3.80**

190-371 190-376

190-371 Front End, Medium & Large #2 **3.80**
190-376 Dome, Mounts on Side of Steam Dome **2.65**

TRAIN CONTROL

190-252 190-390

190-252 Train Control Box w/Bracket, Union 3-speed **5.60**
The Union 3-Way Train Control Box is the "brain" of automatic train control. May be mounted on boiler, under or on walks, on either side of or directly on the pilot deck.
190-390 Trailing Truck Bearing Plates pkg(2) **2.65**

VALVES

190-247 Pop-Valves, Large set (6 Pieces) **2.10**

CHECK VALVES

190-251 Nathan Double Top Feed **2.65**

190-253 With Stop Valve pkg(2) **2.95**

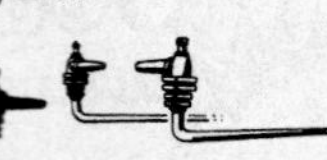

190-265 Vertical pkg(2) **2.95**

STARTER VALVES

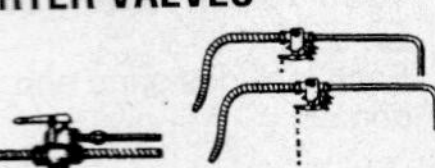
190-293 190-294

190-293 Large (Left Hand) **3.35**
190-294 Small (Right & Left Hand) pkg(2) **3.80**

GLOBE VALVES

190-314 190-361

190-314 Valves & Drain Cocks pkg(13) **4.90**
190-361 2 & 3" Valves pkg(4) **3.80**

VAPOR TRAPS

190-350 190-358

190-350 For Heavyweight Passenger Cars pkg(2) **3.10**
190-358 For Streamline Cars pkg(2) **3.80**

WATER PUMP

190-287 190-333

190-287 Steam Water Pump & Hose Reel **5.90**
Fairbanks-Morse design, mounted on some work cars and locos, as well as tank cars. Includes bracket, valve and hose reel.
190-333 Low Water Alarm **3.50**

WHISTLES & ACCESSORIES

190-250 190-307

190-250 Large Modern Type **2.10**
Mounted on boiler or on smoke box by stack.
190-307 Saturated Steam w/Pipe **3.80**

190-339 190-378

190-339 Assorted Whistles pkg(3) **4.10**
190-378 Whistle Shield **2.40**

DIESEL DETAILS

ANTENNA SUPPORTS

Accurate models of the induction phone (an early form of radio) antennas and brackets used on Pennsylvania cabooses and locos.

DIESEL SETS EA 9.95 (UNLESS NOTED)

Correct brackets for specific diesels. Brass parts, plus complete instructions with photos. Installs with simple hand tools and your favorite adhesive. (Use .020 wire to complete, sold separately.)

190-401 RS-3
190-402 F-Unit
190-403 Alco PA
190-404 FM Trainmaster
190-405 Baldwin S-12
190-406 GP30
190-407 RS-1
190-408 GP7/9
190-409 Baldwin Sharks
190-410 U-25B
190-411 RS-11
190-412 E-Unit **10.50**
190-438 FP7 **10.50**
190-459 FA **9.50**
190-466 RS12 **10.50**

CABOOSES

190-455 N5 Stand & Receiver-Brass **11.25**
190-474 Brackets & Receiver-Plastic **4.20**
Includes basic installation and assembly instructions, less wire.

RECEIVERS EA 2.10

190-457

190-458

190-457 GP7/9
190-458 FM Trainmaster

190-391

190-392

190-391 Transmitter - Loco & Caboose pkg(2) **3.40**
190-392 Antenna Stand Only pkg(2) **3.80**

AIR HORNS-NATHAN

Illustrations are approximately twice actual size.

190-316 5-Chime **3.10**
190-400 3-Chime w/Mounting Brackets **4.50**

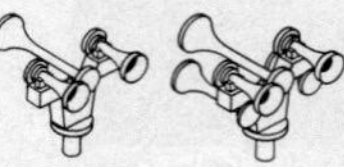
190-420 190-421 190-422

190-420 3-Chime P3 **5.20**
190-421 5-Chime P5 **7.20**
190-422 KS-1 pkg(2) **2.65**

190-423 190-424 190-425

190-423 KS-2 pkg(2) **2.65**
190-424 2-Chime K2 **5.20**
190-425 3-Chime K3 **5.20**
190-426 4-Chime K4 **5.20**

190-427

190-428

190-429

190-427 5-Chime K5 **7.20**
190-428 3-Chime M3 **6.20**
190-429 5-Chime M5 **7.20**

COUPLER LIFT BAR

190-476 Lift Bar w/Stanchions pkg(2) **3.95**
Typical of lift bars used on many diesels, includes two bars and six stanchions, for both ends of the unit

MU STANDS PKG(2) EA 2.70

190-393

190-394

190-393 With Nonworking Light & Battery Connector
190-394 With Battery Connector

BELLS

190-322

190-430 190-435

190-322 Hood Unit - Bracketed **2.85**
190-430 Underframe Mounted pkg(2) **3.10**
190-435 Road Switcher Style w/Bracket EL **3.75**

FUEL SYSTEM

190-431

190-432

190-431 Fillers pkg(3) **2.65**
Includes three different styles of filler pipes.
190-432 Filters pkg(2) **4.00**

HEADLIGHTS

190-417 Mars Light for F3A **2.10**

PYLE NATIONAL PKG(2) EA 2.70

190-395

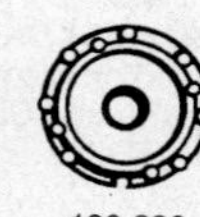
190-396

190-395 Dual Sealed Beam
190-396 Single Beam

GE 44 TONNER PKG(2) EA 2.65

190-413

190-414

190-413 Modern
190-414 Visor

SPARK ARRESTOR PKG(2) EA 2.95

190-439

190-440

190-439 Half-Round Top
190-440 Flat Top

NUMBERBOARDS

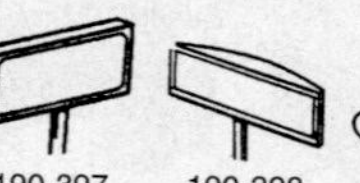
190-397 190-398 190-416

190-397 3-Character pkg(2) **2.95**
190-398 5-Character pkg(2) **3.25**
190-416 Early F Unit w/Marker pkg(2) **2.65**
190-443 PRR E&F Unit pkg(2) **2.65**

PILOTS - F UNITS

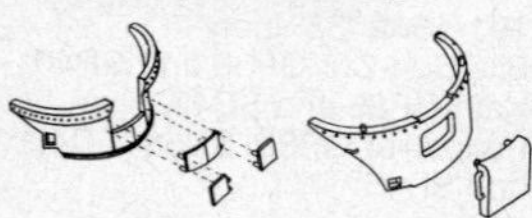
190-441 190-442

190-441 Doors Only **2.65**
Model in open or closed position, use with virtually any F unit.
190-442 Passenger Pilot w/Coupler Cover **11.25**
Complete assembly for Athearn F & Cary E units.

STEPS

190-399

190-434

190-399 Step pkg(2) **2.40**
190-434 Stanchion Style - End Platform EL **6.20**

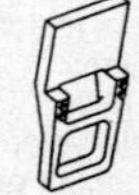
190-448

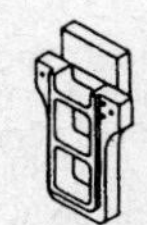
190-449

190-448 E, F & BL2 pkg(6) **3.75**
190-449 For FP45 & F45 (4 large & 1 small) pkg(5) **3.75**
190-450 For PA, PBs & FAs pkg(4) **3.75**

ALCO FA PARTS

190-460

190-461

190-460 Water Cooled Turbo Exhaust Stack **2.10**
190-461 Dynamic Brake-Plastic **2.10**
190-462 Dynamic Brake-Brass **5.40**

MISCELLANEOUS DETAILS

190-415

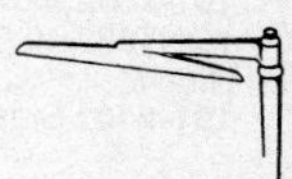
190-419

190-415 Nose Lift Rings EMD F&E pkg(2) **2.10**
190-419 Windshield Wipers pkg(4) **3.75**

190-418

190-436

190-418 Ladder for Baldwin Shark **3.10**
190-436 Dynamic Brake Access Panel **2.10**

190-433

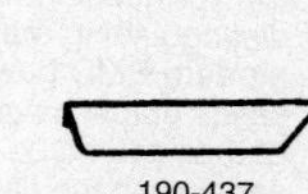
190-437

190-433 RS Marker Lights EL pkg(4) **4.20**
190-437 Sunshade w/Mounting Lugs **4.20**

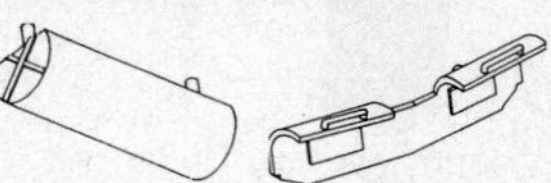
190-451 190-456

190-451 Water Tank FP/7 **6.20**
190-456 Modern Pilot Plow **6.25**

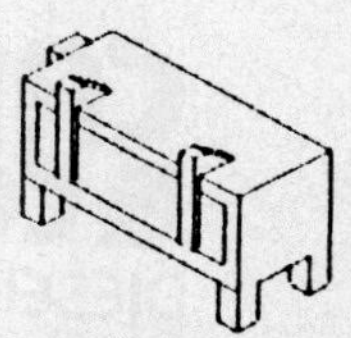

190-488 Receiver Box for PRR RS Locos **2.65**

190-489 Slack Adjuster for PRR RS Locos 2 Pair **2.65**

CAR PARTS

PASSENGER DETAILS

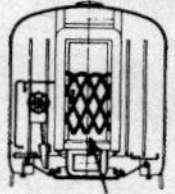
190-309

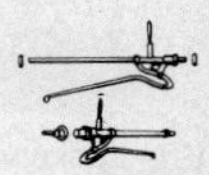
190-345

190-309 Tailgate-Brass pkg(2) **3.80**
190-321 End Railing Set Wood Cars **9.25**
190-345 Mail Catcher for Railway Post Office pkg(2) **4.80**

STEPS

190-356

190-386

190-356 Passenger Car - Standard Era pkg(4) **7.20**
190-386 Passenger/Baggage Car pkg(4) **6.50**

BRAKE SETS

190-359 Westinghouse HSC (6 Pieces) **7.20**
Used on streamline cars.

FREIGHT DETAILS

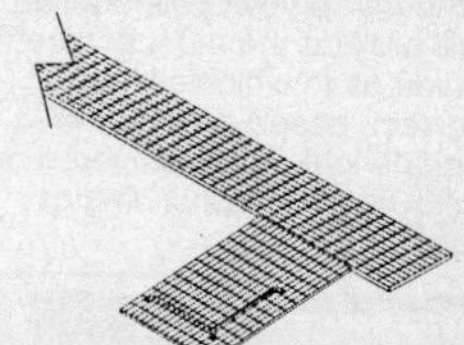

190-491 Styrene Roofwalks (2 35' Walks & 4 Laterals) **4.65**
Just .020" thick with see-through surface, matches later steel type used on many cars. Molded in styrene with .046" mouting posts. Walks can be spliced to model a walk up to 70' long.

190-494 Brake Levers - Plastic 4 Pair **TBA** ***NEW***

CANNON & COMPANY DIESEL COMPONENTS

Make your motive power look like the real thing with these injection molded parts. Each is carefully engineered to match major structural components of second and third generation EMD locomotives. Parts are molded in light gray styrene. Easily added to most plastic locos and a great starting point for scratchbuilt or kitbashing projects. Most include basic instructions for assembly and installation.

Erie Lackawanna SDP45 #3637, featured in the March and April 1999 RMC, was kitbashed using a Kato mechanism, Rail Power Products shell and Cannon & Company components. This unique prototype may be built using the following parts:

191-1001 Hood Doors
191-1002 Hood Doors
191-1003 Hood Doors
191-1004 Hood Doors
191-1005 Hood Doors
191-1006 Hood Doors
191-1007 Hood Doors
191-1008 Generator/Alternator Access Door
191-1103 81" Low Short Hood Kit
191-1152 40 Series Hood End
191-1201 Cab Sub Base Kit
191-1304 Inertial Filter Screens
191-1353 Inertial Filter Hatch
191-1404 Radiator Grilles
191-1502 40 Series Cab Kit
191-1505 Laser-Cut Cab Windows
191-1551 Cab Sunshades
191-1602 Blower Housing
191-1952 40 Series Turbo Hatch
191-2101 Small Anticlimber

ANTICLIMBERS EA 2.95

Change or upgrade the look of any EMD, from the first GP35s to the latest SD90. Description is the most common usage, but most could be found on other engines as well. The time frame you are modeling will provide the most accurate guide as to which style is correct, based on how the engine looked as-delivered or following later rebuilding or repairs.

191-2101

191-2102

191-2101 Small pkg(4)
Includes two different styles.

191-2102 Full Width pkg(2)
Used on early SD units.

191-2103

191-2104

191-2103 Standard Dash 2 Type pkg(2)

191-2104 Tunnel Motor Style pkg(2)
Used on SD40T-2 and SD45T-2 Rear, includes two styles.

191-2105

191-2106

191-2105 50 Series, Late Dash 2 and GP15-1 pkg(2)

191-2106 SD60, SD60M & SD50 pkg(2)
Used on front and rear.

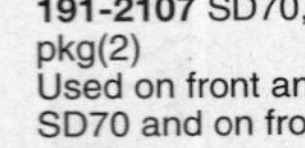
191-2107 191-2108

191-2107 SD70, Late GP60 pkg(2)
Used on front and rear of SD70 and on front of GP60.

191-2108 SD80/90 Front & Rear w/Ditch Lights pkg(2)
Includes one set of forward ditch lights.

EMD BLOWER HOUSINGS PKG(2) 3.50

Blower housings are a distinguishing feature of modern EMD power. The four styles below have every detail of their prototype and include separate base flanges and thin mounting edges.

191-1601

191-1602

191-1601 Angled
Used on some GP/SD40-2s, GP/SD50s, all GP/SD60s and the SD70MAC.

191-1602 35 & 40
Used on all GP/SD35s, most GP/SD38s, GP/50, GP40s and SD45s.

191-1603

191-1604

191-1603 Late-40
Used on 1971 built GP/50 GP/SD38, GP/SD40s and SD45s.

191-1604 Dash 2
Used on the majority of Dash 2 GPs and SDs, plus all early GP/SD50s.

THINWALL EMD CAB KITS & ACCESSORIES

Designed to fit EMD locomotive models from various manufacturers. Cab kits feature "thinwall" construction for a highly realistic appearance. Doors and windows (with flush fitting "glass," included in all kits) are separate and can be modeled open or closed. Hood Unit Cabs (#1501 and 1502) include two styles of fronts, separate doors and handles, side windows, sunshade brackets and numberboards. In addition to various separate and optional details, Switcher Cabs (#1503 and 1504) also include a detailed interior floor and electrical cabinet. Kits includes complete assembly instructions.

HOOD UNITS EA 5.95

191-1501

191-1502

191-1501 Dash 2, 50/60/70 Series
Fits Athearn SD40-2, SD40T-2, GP38-2, GP40-2, GP50 and GP60. Also fits Railpower SD45-2, GP60 and SD60. Includes optional front wall with "L" shaped window used by some roads.

191-1502 "35" Line
Fits Con-Cor GP38 and GP40, Kato GP35 and SD40, plus Railpower GP35, SD38, SD40 and SD45.

SWITCHER CABS EA 8.50

191-1503

191-1504

191-1503 Early Switcher
Arched window style used on SW1s through SW7s built from 1939 to 1950. Fits Athearn SW7, Kato NW2 and Walthers SW1.

191-1504 Late Switcher
Squared window style used on SW7-SW1200s built from 1950-1966. Fits Athearn SW7, Life-Like SW9/SW1200.

WINDOW SETS

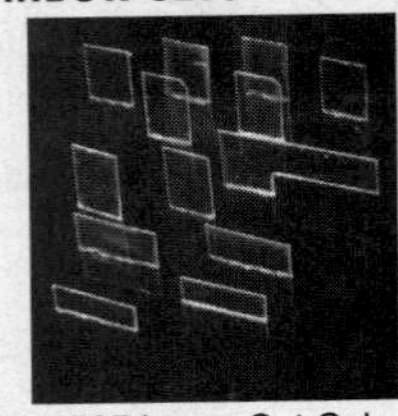

191-1505 Laser-Cut Cab Windows **2.95**
Precision laser-cut window sets for #1501 and 1502 cab kits. Window material is exceptionally clear and virtually scratch proof. One side is masked, the other paper protected.

EMD CAB DETAILS

191-1551 Sunshades pkg(8) **2.95**
Traditional styled sunshades with reinforcing bracket and razor-sharp edges. Exact fit for brackets in Cannon cab kits and carefully molded to be flexible.

191-1552 Padlocks & Wiper Motors pkg(17) **2.50**
External barrel padlocks in three styles for security on modern units, along with two versions of wiper motors to detail open cab doors.

EMD SHORT HOOD KITS & ACCESSORIES EA 6.95

Five different conversion kits to replicate the variety of short hoods used by EMD from 1963 to the present. Each kit includes at least 40 parts to cover the many differences in brake gear, class lights, vents and other appliances.

191-1101

191-1103

191-1101 High Nose
Used by Southern, N&W and NS on most units from the GP/SD35 through the GP50. Includes clear numberboard material.

191-1103 81"
Introduced in 1963, used on all hood units, from early 35 line through early Dash 2s.

191-1104

191-1105

191-1104 88"
Introduced in 1977, this is the standard nose for all post-1977 Dash 2s through the GP60s and SD70s.

191-1105 116"
The first of the "snoots," used on early SP SD40T-2 "tunnel motors" and UP SD40-2s

191-1106 123"
The final version of the "snoot," used on ATSF and Kansas City Southern SD40-2s, plus SP and SSW SD40T-2s.

SHORT HOOD ACCESSORIES

191-1102

191-1107

191-1102 EMD Low Nose Toilet Hatch pkg(4) **1.95**
A post-1981 addition to most 88" low noses (use with #1104) used on both GP and SD units.

191-1107 88" Optional Left Side pkg(2) **2.95**
Recessed brake wheel side for post-1990 units with 88" nose, use with #1104 (sold separately).

EMD LONG HOOD ENDS PKG(2) EA 3.50

Four different components essential to upgrade any scale width EMD long hood to an exact prototype match. Kit #1151 has the headlight molded in place. Kits 1152-1154 have three styles of separate housings and a separate headlight, allowing easy conversions and painting.

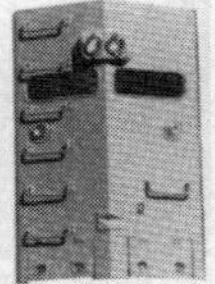
191-1151

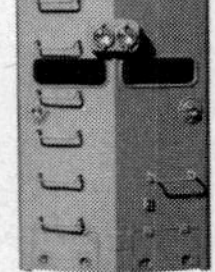
191-1152

191-1151 35 Series
Correct hood end for GP/SD28s and 35s.

191-1152 40 Series
Standard hood end for GP/SD38s, 39s and 40s

CANNON & COMPANY DIESEL COMPONENTS

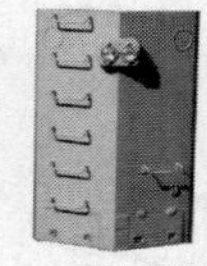
191-1153 191-1154

191-1153 Dash 2
Fully equipped hood end with numberboards and class lights, for Dash 2s, plus 50, 60 and 70 Series.

191-1154 Blank Dash 2
Blank hood end for later Dash 2, 50, 60 and 70 Series locos.

EMD HOOD UNIT DOORS

Four sizes of engine compartment doors, three sizes of radiator compartment doors, along with both styles of generator/alternator access doors and plates permit the construction or modification of most of the recent EMD long hood door arrangements.

ENGINE COMPARTMENT DOORS PKG(8) EA 1.95

18 x 78"

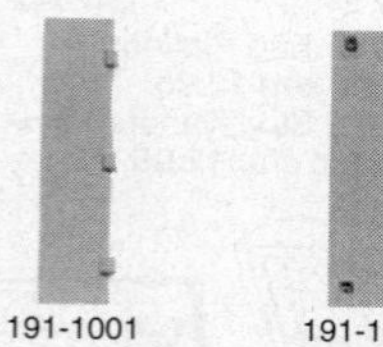
191-1001 191-1002

191-1001 Plain
191-1002 Latched
22 x 78"

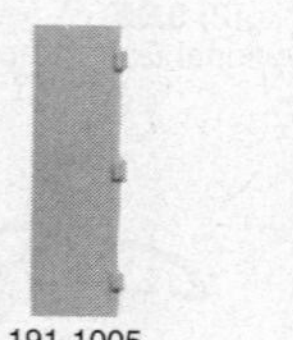

191-1005 191-1006

191-1005 Plain
191-1006 Latched

RADIATOR COMPARTMENT DOORS PKG(8) EA 1.95

22 x 65"

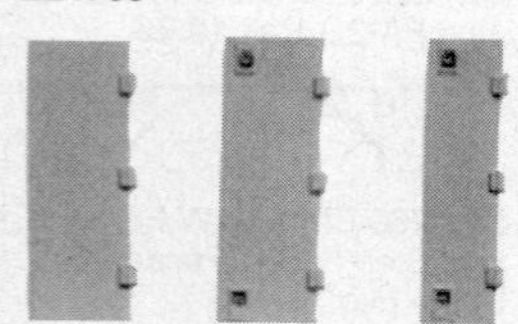
191-1003 191-1004 191-1007

191-1003 Plain
191-1004 Latched
191-1007 16 x 17 x 65"
Includes both Plain and Latched types.

GENERATOR/ALTERNATOR ACCESS PKG(4) EA 1.95

Includes access doors and plates.

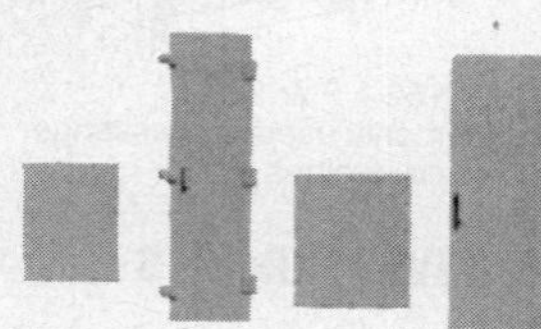
191-1008 191-1009

191-1008 35/40 Series
191-1009 Dash 2, 50/60/70 Series

AIR FILTER HATCH

191-1901 AAF Angled Paper Filter **2.95**
Correct for post-1976 GP38-2s and SD38-2s.

EMD CAB SUB BASE & OPTIONAL DOORS

Kits replace the entire structure under the cab and nose. Includes enough parts to build two different sub bases, including all prototype variations for the period covered. Photos show only a few of the possible door arrangements. Optional doors are shown installed on appropriate sub bases.

191-1201 All 35 Line & 40 Series Units 2 Pair **6.95**

191-1202 All Dash 2 & 50/60 Series Units 1 Pair **6.95**

191-1203 SP "Split" Equipment Doors pkg(6) **2.95**

191-1204 CR "Split" Battery Box Doors, Chessie "Mailslot" Battery Box Doors pkg(8) **2.95**

INERTIAL FILTER SCREENS

These screens all feature correct depth and contour as well as hex head bolts on the extra-thin mounting flange. For ease of use they are all surface mount components.

191-1301 Late Dash 2 GPs pkg(4) **1.95**
Correct for late GP38-2s, GP39-2s, GP40-2s and SD38-2s.

191-1302 35 Line, GP pkg(4) **2.95**
Correct for GP35 and SD35 and some SD39s.

191-1303 pkg(4) **2.50**
Correct for GP38, GP39, GP40 and some SD39s. Also used on early GP38-2, GP39-2, GP40-2, GP15-1 and SD38-2s.

191-1304 pkg(4) **2.50**
Correct for SD38, SD40, SD45 and early SD40-2 and SD45-2.

191-1305 Post 1984 EMD SD40-2 pkg(4) **2.50**
Correct for post 1984 SD40-2s. May be modified for SD50 and SD60.

191-1306 Inertial Filter Screens **2.50**
Set includes long and short for GP49, GP50, GP59 and GP60.

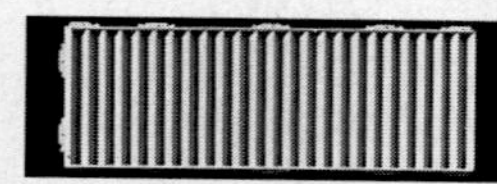

191-1307 SD50 to SD90 pkg(4) **2.50** ***NEW***
Used on SD50, SD60, SD60M, SD70, SD75, SD80 and SD90.

RADIATOR GRILLES & SCREENS

The early radiator grilles feature all of the visible layers of detail right back to the shutters. The later style screens accurately represent the depth and rounded corrugations of the prototype. Both feature hex bolt detail on ultra-thin mounting flanges.

191-1401 Radiator Screens Pkg(4) **2.50**
Used on late GP38-2, GP39-2 and SD45-2.

191-1402 35 Line Radiator Grilles pkg(4) **3.50**
Used on all 35 Line units: GP28, GP35, SD28 and SD35.

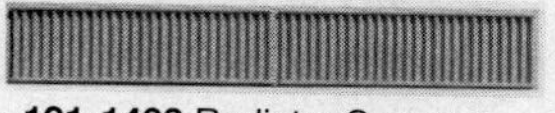

191-1403 Radiator Screens pkg(4) **3.50**
Used on late GP40-2s and SD40-2s.

191-1404 Radiator Grilles pkg(4) **3.95**
Correct for all GP40s and SD40s, also early GP40-2s and SD40-2s.

191-1405 Radiator Grilles pkg(4) **3.95**
Precise wire mesh grilles for GP/SD38/39 and Phase 1 GP39-2, plus early GP38-2.

191-1406 GP50/60 Radiator Screens pkg(2) **3.95** ***NEW***
Used on GP49, GP50, GP59 and all versions of GP60.

191-1407 SD50-75 Radiator Screens pkg(2) **3.95** ***NEW***
Used on SD50, SD60, SD60M, SD70 and SD75.

191-1408 SD80/90 Radiator Screens pkg(2) **3.95** ***NEW***
Used on SD80 and SD90.

INERTIAL FILTER HATCHES PKG(2) EA 2.95

One of the more prominent features on the roof, inertial filter hatches or "dust bins" can be found atop second and third generation EMD hood units. Each kit features deeply molded, ultra-fine exhaust grilles, hex-head mounting bolts, precise dimensional accuracy and a raised mounting surface that "floats" the hatch just off the top of the long hood.

191-1351 191-1352

191-1351 Early 35 Line Units
191-1352 GP/SD38

191-1353 191-1354

191-1353 Late 35 Line Units
Used on GP/SD39, GP/SD40, SD45 and SD38-2, SD40-2, SD45-2.

191-1354 GP38-2, GP15-1, GP15T

191-1355 191-1356

191-1355 GP40-2 and Phase I GP39-2
191-1356 Phase II GP39-2
191-1357 GP49 and GP50
191-1358 GP59, GP60, GP60B, GP60M
191-1359 SD50, SD60M
191-1360 SD70, SD70M

PILOT LIFT TABS

191-2051 EMD 40 Series Through SD90 pkg(24) **2.50**

TURBO HATCHES PKG(2) EA 3.95

One of the most visible and interesting features on the roof of second generation diesels. Correct exhaust assemblies for any turbocharged unit from the first GP/SD35s to the last Dash 2s before silencers were mandated. Components feature see-through stacks with .080" bars, plus correct angles and dimensions.

191-1951 GP/SD35
191-1952 40 Series & Dash 2

CAST BRAKEWHEELS

191-1108 22" pkg(6) **3.95** ***NEW***
Used on almost all EMD units and all GEs up to the Dash 7.

STEP GUARD

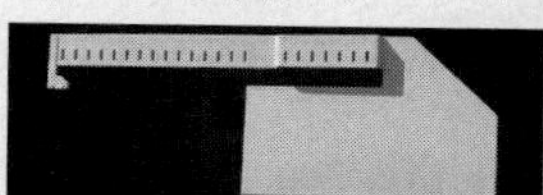

191-1605 For SD80 and SD90 **2.95** ***NEW***

Custom Finishing

Add a new dimension to your models with this line of brass and pewter detail parts for locos and passenger cars. Each is finely detailed and ready for installation. Most items include basic mounting instructions and can be attached using ACC or solder.

AIR FILTERS

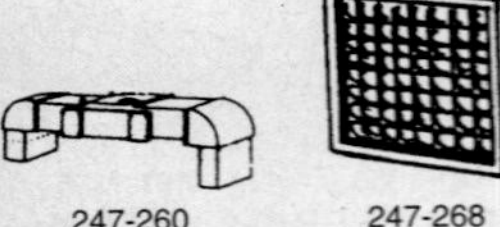

247-260 247-268

247-260 Air Filtration Unit/HORST **8.95**
Fits Atlas GP-7 locos.

247-268 Car Body Filters pkg(12) **12.95**

AIRTANKS

247-235 12" Roof Top Mount pkg(2) **6.59**

247-290 Extended Range Fuel Tank Air Reservoirs pkg(4) **4.95**

ANTENNAS

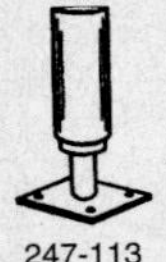

247-113 247-201

247-113 Firecracker pkg(2) **4.95**
247-181 NYC Observation/ Lounge Antenna Stanchions (42 Pieces) **26.95**
247-201 Sinclair pkg(2) **3.95**

ATS/CAB SIGNAL DETAILS

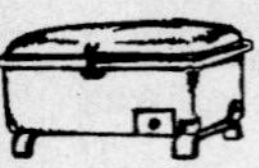

247-101 247-116

247-101 CTC for NYC/B&O **4.95**
247-116 Cab Type for NYC **5.95**
Commonly used on passenger service RS-3s.

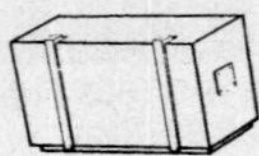

247-125 247-149

247-125 Cab Type Box w/Exciter **8.95**
Used on New Haven RS-3s, can be adapted to other Haven engines.

247-149 Modern Cab Type **4.95**
247-153 Pennsylvania Type **4.95**

247-202 Pick-Up & Connector pkg(3) **6.95**

247-208 Motor **4.95**

247-229 Pickup Shoe **4.59**
For mounting on truck side frames.

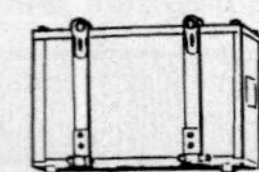

247-297 Two Strap ATS Cabinet **2.95**
Used by Conrail and others.

BATTERY BOXES

247-172 **2.95**
247-304 50" Single Door **7.59**

BELLS EA 4.95

HIGH-HOOD MOUNT

247-109 247-110

247-109 Boston & Maine Type
247-110 MEC 1

247-111 MEC Type 2

247-137 247-138

247-137 Side Mount
247-138 Dual Lever

247-139 247-140

247-139 Boiler Side Mount
247-140 Old Time NH

247-230 247-231

247-230 Hood Mount
247-231 Cab Mount

247-246 247-250

247-246 Hood
247-250 EMD SW

247-281 Side Mount

BRAKE DETAILS

247-147 Hand Brake Chain Guide pkg(6) **5.95**

247-198 247-278

247-198 12x10 Brake Cylinder w/Lever pkg(4) **12.95**
247-278 EMD Cast Iron Brake Wheel **3.95**
247-308 Brake Equalization Valve **2.59**

247-303 Pullman Brake Bracket pkg(6) **3.59**
Used on all types of baggage and passenger cars built by Pullman.

BRAKE SYSTEM SETS

247-307 UC **5.59**
247-312 PC Dual Cylinder **5.95**

BRAKE STANDS EA 4.95

247-279 247-280

247-279 EMD Loco w/Wheel
247-280 Peacock

COOLING COILS

247-152 1 Pair **3.95**
Commonly used on passenger service engines.

CONVERSION KITS

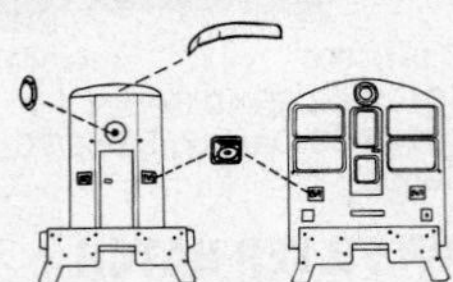

247-264 Fairbanks-Morse H12-44 Conversion **11.95**
Convert your Walthers H10-44 into an early H12-44 with this set. Includes cast brass nose piece to match roof contour, replacement front headlight (accepts 1.5V mini-bulb and MV lens #159, both sold separately) and sloped sand filler hatches for nose and rear of cab. Illustrated instruction sheet.

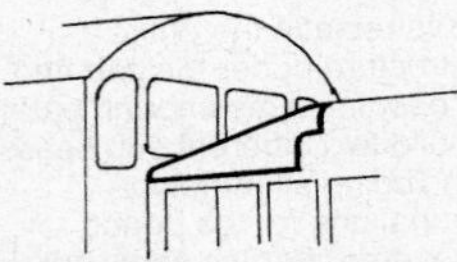

247-285 SW-1 Loco Hood Conversion **3.95**
One-piece metal casting, converts Walthers SW-1 into a later production engine with a smooth taper from hood to cab.

247-316 Retrofit Kit for Pressure Unloading Tank Car **12.95**

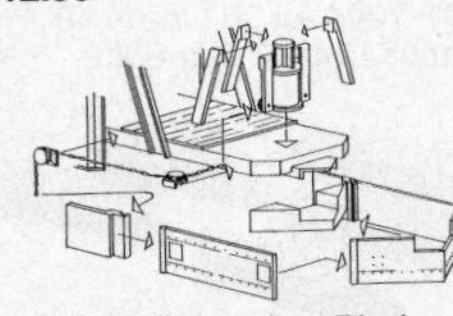

247-317 Snowplow Blade Conversion for Jordan Spreader **7.95**

COUPLER PARTS

247-313 Truck & Coupler Adapters for Con-Cor 73' Passenger Cars 1 Pair **3.59**

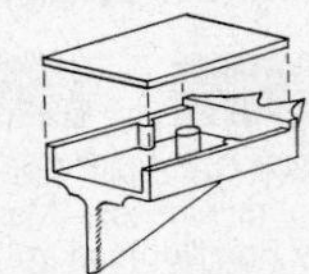

247-311 Front Coupler Pocket For Walthers Russell Plow **2.59**

DIESEL DETAILS

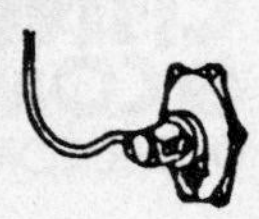

247-195 247-196

247-195 Wheel Slip Modulator pkg(4) **4.95**
247-196 Speed Recorder pkg(4) **4.95**

247-203 247-205

247-203 Number Boards CV, GT, CP pkg(2) **5.95**
247-205 RS-2/3 Curved Grab Irons pkg(10) **3.59**
247-212 Lighting Box Alco RS-3 **5.95**

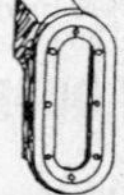

247-226 247-228

247-226 Fuel Tank Sight Glass pkg(2) **4.59**
247-228 EMD Speed Recorder Drive Unit **3.95**

247-241 247-242

247-241 End Platform (6 piece set) **12.95**
247-242 Side Handrail (14 piece set) **12.95**

247-239 247-245

247-239 Extended Vision Side Windows pkg(2) **9.95**
247-245 Optional Equipment Box **6.59**

247-248 247-249

247-248 End Platform Lift Rings (4 pieces) **5.95**
247-249 Icicle Breakers E&F Units (3 piece set) **12.95**
247-262 Fuel Tank Skirts for Alco FA-2 1 Pair **12.95**

247-263 EMD/MLW FB Unit End Step Skirts (Passenger Units) pkg(4) **7.95**
247-306 RS-1 Locomotive Bumper 1 Pair **2.59**

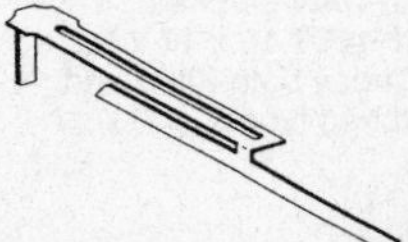

247-314 Photo-Etched Brass Windshield Wipers Dual Arm Articulated Type 2 Pair **3.95**

Custom Finishing

DITCH LIGHTS

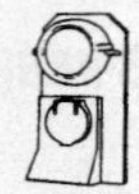
247-126

247-293

247-126 Deck Mounted pkg(2) **4.95**
Applied to modern diesels, left and right lights with MU stand.

247-293 Modern Deck Mounted pkg(2) **4.95**

247-236

247-237

247-236 Bracket Mounted pkg(2) **4.59**
247-237 Built-on Type pkg(2) **3.95**

247-238

247-251

247-238 Built-on Type for E&F Units pkg(2) **3.95**
One-piece castings for Left & Right mounting on round nose.
247-251 Platform End Mount pkg(2) **5.59**
Cored to accept micro-bulbs, sold separately.

247-294 Modern Deck Mount w/MU **3.59**
247-315 Deck Mounted Ditch Lights 1 Pair **2.59**

ELECTRICAL

247-145

247-148

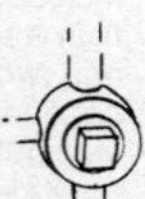
247-154

247-145 Round Junction pkg(8) **4.95**
247-148 Rectangular Electrical Box pkg(6) **4.95**
247-154 Small Junction pkg(6) **3.95**

247-105 NH pkg(2) **4.95**
247-119 Short Insulators pkg(6) **5.958**

247-163 Air Conditioning Receptacle pkg(2) **4.95**
247-164 Amplidyne Inverter **6.95**

END STEPS

247-276

247-277

247-276 Three Straight Up GP38-2s
247-277 Three Up SD40s
247-267 Four Straight Up GP/SD Units

FREIGHT CAR DETAILS

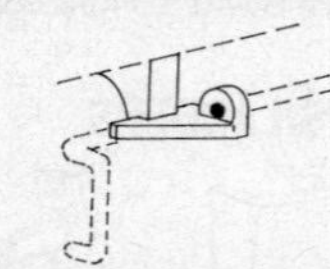

247-326 Modern Freight Car Cut Lever Brackets pkg(12) **TBA** ***NEW***

WINE HOPPER LATCHES

247-273 Twin Hopper pkg(4) **5.59**
247-274 Triple Hopper pkg(6) **6.59**
247-275 Quad Hopper pkg(8) **6.59**

HEADLIGHTS/LIGHTING

247-102

247-106

247-102 12" Pyle National **4.95**
Steel wrapped headlight, used by NYC and B&A. Can be illuminated with modification. Accepts MV Products lens #136.

247-106 EMD Back-Up Light **4.95**
Applied to many E units, cored for 1.5V bulb (.055 diameter). Accepts MV Products lens #29.

247-123

247-124

247-123 Golden Glow-NH **4.95**
Can be illuminated with modification. Accepts MV Products lens #166. Used on many types of New Haven steam locos.

247-124 Bracket for #123 **4.95**
Use for mounting Golden Glow headlight on smokebox door.

247-210 Single Beam Headlight for Bachmann BL2 **4.95**

PYLE DUAL BEAM EA 3.95

One of the most common modern headlights, available in three styles to match your favorite prototype. Lights are cored to accept micro-bulbs, sold separately.

247-253

247-254

247-253 Vertical Mounting w/Visors
247-254 Horizontal Mounting w/Visors

247-255

247-256

247-255 Standard, No Visors
247-256 Pyle Twin Mars Light (CB&Q Style) **4.95**

247-112

247-114

247-112 Ground Light w/Bracket pkg(2) **4.95**
247-114 Early Marker Light pkg(2) **4.95**
Single lens, accepts jewels .042" in diameter.

247179-

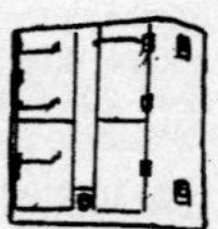
247-213

247-179 Bracket pkg(8) **4.95**
247-213 GP7 Light Equipment Box pkg(2) **14.95**

HORNS

247-120 pkg(2) **4.95**

247-197

247-215

247-197 Shrouded Type - CB&Q **4.95**
247-215 EMD Single Chime pkg(2) **5.95**

LESLIE STYLE HORNS

Used on many diesels.

247-219

247-220

247-219 RS-25 Single Chime **4.95**
247-220 RSM-25-2R Double Chime **4.95**

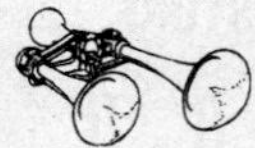
247-221

247-222

247-221 RSL-3L Three Chime **5.95**
247-222 RS-3L Three Chime **5.95**

247-223

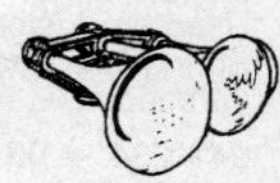
247-224

247-223 RSU-3L Three Chime **5.95**
247-224 RSU-3C Three Chime **5.95**

247-225 RS-5T Five Chime **7.95**

JEWELS

Sized to fit most steam and diesel marker lights, 1mm size is just under four HO Scale inches.

247-127 Clear
247-128 Amber
247-129 Red
247-130 Green

LINESIDE DETAILS

247-171

247-194

247-171 Buda Wheel Stops pkg(2) **6.95**
247-194 Durable Bumper Model D **7.95**

247-173

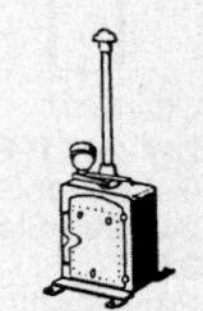
247-174

247-173 Pole Mounted Relay **6.95**
247-174 Large Relay Box **7.95**

247-175

247-192

247-175 Remote Block Signal Indicator **5.95**
247-192 Flanger Sign pkg(2) **6.95**

247-193 Lineside Electrical Relay Cabinet **8.95**
247-176 Switch **4.95**
247-283 Switch Heater w/Propane Tank **4.59**
A great detail for any right-of-way winter or summer! Based on actual installation, complete kit includes propane tank, simulated burner details and basic instructions.

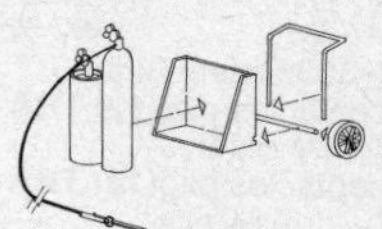

247-327 Industrial-Size Acetylene Cutting Torch w/Cart Pewter & Brass Wire Kit **TBA** ***NEW***

LUBRICATION CABINETS EA 2.89

Prototypes are applied on some diesels to automatically lubricate wheel flanges when units pass through curves. Includes manifold and cabinet.

247-296 Single Handle Door
247-295 Two-Handled Door

MU'S

247-257 247-258

247-257 3-Hose **7.95**
247-258 Diesel **7.95**
With bracket; 2 left, 2 right.
247-298 Standard 6.5" MU Head pkg(12) **4.95**

PASSENGER CAR DETAILS

247-161 Diaphragm Buffer Springs pkg(2) **5.95**

247-291 Pullman Detail Set (33 pieces) **12.95**
Includes details commonly found on cars serving the eastern US.

247-292 Supplemental Detail Set (14 pieces) **9.95**
247-302 Standard 40" Stirrup Step **3.59**

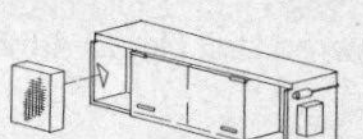

247-321 Safety A/C Fresh Air Intake & Exhaust Vents, Clestory Mount Type Set **TBA** ***NEW***

Custom Finishing

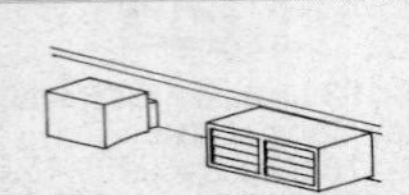

247-322 Pullman Smoothside Underbody Detail Set **TBA** *NEW*

247-323 247-324

247-323 Safety Battery Receptacles pkg(12) **TBA** *NEW*
247-324 Safety AC Receptacles pkg(12) **TBA** *NEW*

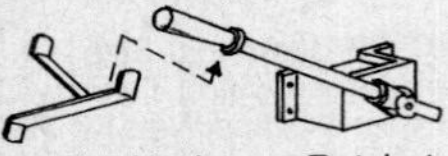

247-325 Lindstrom Ratchet Brake Lever 1 Pair **TBA** *NEW*

PILOTS

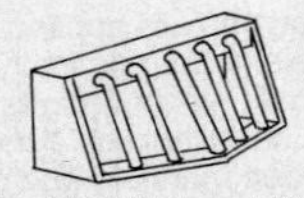

247-319 ALCO Diesel Pilot Insert 1 Pair **TBA** *NEW*

PLOWS

247-243 Pilot w/Hoses **6.59**
Fits Atlas GP7 locos.

QUEEN POSTS PKG(8) EA 4.95

Ideal for use with turnbuckles #165 and 166.

247-184 Flush Type
247-168 6"
247-169 8"

REFRIGERATION DETAILS

247-286 247-287

247-286 Freight Car Retrofit Unit (white metal) **4.59**
247-287 Modern Trailer Diesel Unit **4.95**

247-288 247-289

247-288 Medium Duty pkg(2) **4.59**
247-289 Older Style Gas Powered Unit pkg(2) **4.59**

SPARK ARRESTORS

247-131 247-234

247-131 Large, Round Style pkg(2) **4.95**
Used on Boston & Maine and Springfield Terminal GP7 and GP9 locos.

247-234 4.95

SPRINGS

247-252 Return pkg(2) **2.95**
.062" diameter, .050" eye diameter, .655" eye centers.

STACKS (INTAKE/EXHAUST)

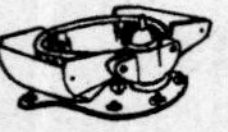

247-150 Working Clamshell Stack **9.95**

247-122 247-151

247-122 Turbo Stack **4.95**
Simulate engines with original aircooler or rebuilt with turbochargers.

247-151 Steam Generator Stack **4.95**

247-206 247-211

247-206 Steam Generator Intake pkg(2) **4.95**
247-211 R-S11 Steam Generator Stack Set **4.95**

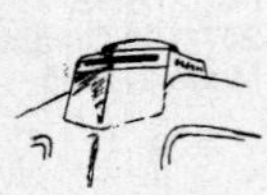

247-207 247-209

247-207 R-S1/R-S3 Steam Generator Stack pkg(2) **2.95**
247-209 Steam Generator Stack **3.95**
Parts for the Proto 2000 BL2 from Life-Like.

247-214 247-247

247-214 EMD Steam Generator pkg(2) **4.95**
247-247 Extended Height Exhaust Stack GP, SD pair **4.95**

247-269 247-284

247-269 Extended Height Turbo Cooled Exhaust Stack **4.95**
247-284 EMD Early Switcher Exhaust Stack/Short pkg(2) **4.95**
With bracket; 2 left, 2 right.

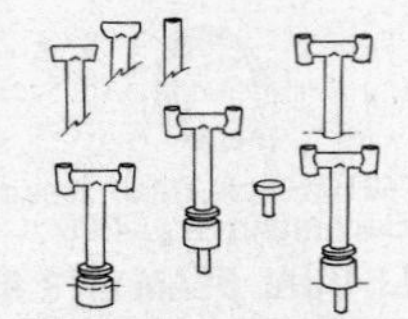

247-320 2 Caboose Stacks & 3 Vents **TBA** *NEW*

STEAM LOCO DETAILS

247-136 Pipe Hangers pkg(2) **3.95**
Cored .040", generally used on the injector pipe to check valves.

247-142 247-143

247-142 Dome Fittings pkg(8) **4.95**
Accepts up to .028" wire for discharge pipes.

247-135 247-170

247-135 Air Strainer **3.95**
247-170 Cab Seats-Left & Right pkg(2) **6.95**
Cored for use with .018" wire

247-178 247-204

247-178 Oval Dome Covers pkg(4) **4.95**
247-204 Flag Stanchion w/Saddle pkg(4) **4.95**

VALVES

247-143 pkg(16) **5.95**
Can be used with #142.

247-144 With Pipe **5.95**

247-141 247-160

247-141 Boiler Strap Stays pkg(9) **4.95**
247-160 Drain Cock pkg(6) **3.95**

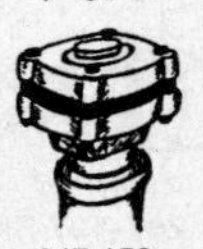

247-158 247-159

247-158 Check Valves Left & Right pkg(2) **4.95**
247-159 Relief pkg(2) **3.95**
247-167 Long Stem Globe pkg(4) **8.95**

WESTINGHOUSE

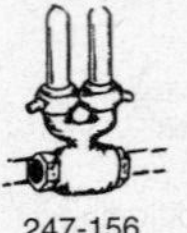

247-156 247-157

247-156 AD
247-157 SD

SNOWSHIELDS EA 12.95

Each kit is a two-piece set.

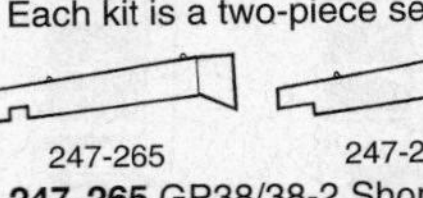

247-265 247-266

247-265 GP38/38-2 Short Notch
247-266 GP38/38-2 Long Notch

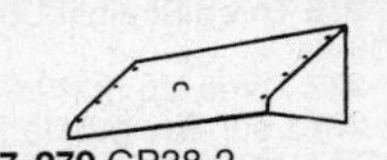

247-270 GP38-2
247-271 SD40/SD40-2 Short Notch
247-272 SD40/SD40-2 Long Notch

STEPS/LADDERS

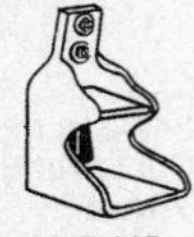

247-108 247-115

247-108 Walkway pkg(2) **5.49**
247-115 Pilot pkg(2) **5.95**

247-155 Loco pkg(2) **5.95**
247-299 18" Stirrup Set pkg(8) **3.95**

PENNSY TENDER EA 11.95

247-182 247-183

247-182 Short
247-183 Long

TENDER DETAILS

247-121 Coal Rake **3.29**

247-133 247-134

247-133 Stoker Feed (Alco) **4.95**
247-134 Coal Pusher, Alco **5.95**
Mounts under main deck, simulates connection for automatic stoker.

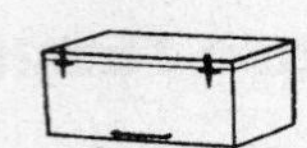

247-162 Tool Box **3.95**
Can also be used on cabooses, tenders or maintenance equipment.

TRUCK DETAILS PKG(4) EA 7.95

247-199 Slack Adjuster

247-200 Bolster Anchor

TRUCKS

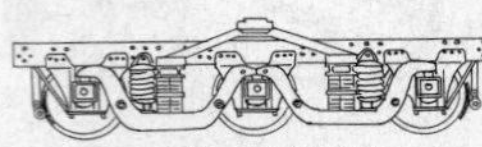

247-305 6-Wheel **28.95**

TRUCK WHEELS 1 PAIR EA 21.95

247-309 Friction Bearings
247-310 Roller Bearings

TURNBUCKLES

247-165 Short for Freight Cars pkg(4) **4.95**

247-166 Long for Passenger Cars pkg(4) **3.98**

VENTS/VENTING

247-117 247-118

247-117 Globe pkg(2) **4.95**
Used for passenger car washrooms; angled base.

247-118 Pintsch Roof pkg(10) **5.95**
Includes eight short vents with flat bases for roof mounting and two long vents with angled bases for mounting over vestibules. Used on early cars equipped with gas lights and frequently left in place after electric lighting was installed.

247-146 Garland pkg(8) **7.95**

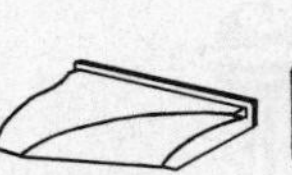

247-300 247-301

247-300 Ward Type for Heavyweight Cars pkg(12) **4.59**
247-301 Garland A-1 Type pkg(12) **4.95**
Clerestory style used on baggage and passenger cars.

Custom Finishing

WHISTLES PKG(2) EA 4.95

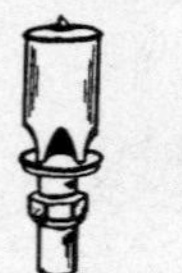

247-103 247-104 247-107

247-103 Electric-NH
247-104 NYC/Boston & Albany
247-107 Electric-NYC/GN

WINTERIZATION HATCHES

247-240 247-259

247-240 High Type F-Units **5.59**
247-259 Split, CP Style (Fits Life-Like FA-2) **12.95**

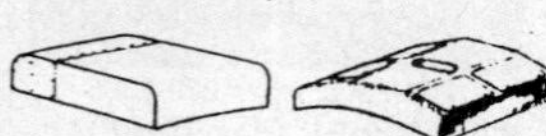
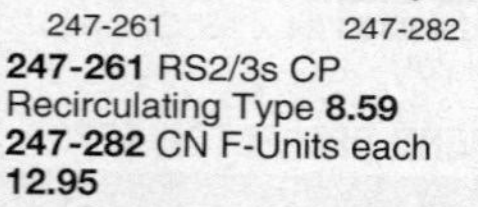

247-261 247-282

247-261 RS2/3s CP Recirculating Type **8.59**
247-282 CN F-Units each **12.95**

EKO

BARRELS, BOXES & SACKS

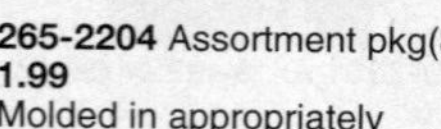

265-2204 Assortment pkg(8) **1.99**
Molded in appropriately colored plastic.

FALLER

TABLES AND CHAIRS

272-579 Tables and Chairs. **6.99**
An assortment with four tables and 24 chairs. Ideal for pubs and outdoor restaurants.

DYNA-MODEL PRODUCTS COMPANY

Cast metal, unpainted parts.

DOORS PKG(2) EA 2.45

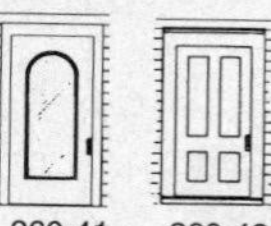

260-41 260-42 260-43

260-41 Arched Window
260-42 4-Panel
260-43 Double 4-Panel

260-44 260-45

260-44 Half Window
260-45 Full Window

WINDOWS

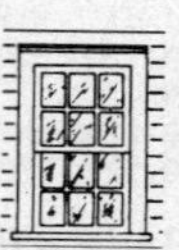

260-81 260-82

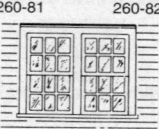

260-83

260-81 Double Pane pkg(6) **3.00**
260-82 6-Pane pkg(6) **3.00**
260-83 Double 6-Pane pkg(2) **2.45**

260-84 260-85

260-84 4-Pane pkg(6) **3.00**
260-85 Attic/Tower pkg(6) **2.45**

SHINGLES

260-61 Shake Shingle **3.50**
9 x 9" formed plastic sheet.

EAVE BRACKETS

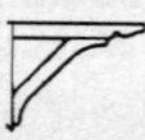

260-71 Bracket pkg(6) **2.45**

UTILITY POLE DETAILS

260-2025 Pole Detail Kit **5.95**
Includes 10 cast metal crossarms with six insulators, crossarm braces, 10 side mount telephone line insulators and a transformer.

ROOF FOR COVERED GONDOLA

117-9116 52' 6" Mid-Height **8.00**
Fits Walthers, E&C Shops, Roundhouse, Life-Like and Con-Cor cars.

BRAKE EQUIPMENT EA 4.00

117-9109 Handbrake Assortment
117-9110 Brake Assortment

CABOOSE DETAIL SET

117-9111 Superdetails for Athearn & MDC Cars **10.00**
Fits center cupola models.

CABOOSE PARTS EA 4.00

117-9106 Grab Irons
117-9107 Detail Parts

CABOOSE WINDOW SETS EA 3.00

117-9108 Bowser N5c
117-9113 Bowser N5

COVERED HOPPER PARTS

117-9100 M&K Ballast Doors **3.00**
117-9105 Detail Set **4.00**

COVERED HOPPER ROOFS EA 5.00

117-9112 MDC 70 Ton PS-2
117-9114 ACF CH-29

FLOATS & FITTINGS

117-9118 Marine Car Float & GMA Barge Fittings **10.00** *NEW*
Includes 1 each of #s 9119, 9120, 1921 and 9122.

117-9119 Marine Car Bitts **3.00** *NEW*
117-9120 Kleets & Chocks **3.00** *NEW*
117-9121 Barge Hatches & Bollards **3.00** *NEW*
117-9122 Car Float Toggles **3.00** *NEW*

PASSENGER CAR DETAILS EA 3.00

117-9101 Pennsylvania Ice Air Conditioner
117-9102 Car Roof Vents
117-9115 Car Stirrup **5.00**

PASSENGER CAR UNDERBODY DETAILS EA 5.00

117-9103 Pennsylvania/ Pullman
117-9104 New Haven

WOOD PANEL BAGGAGE DOORS EA 5.00

For B-60 Baggage Car Kit (#1010), sold seperately.

117-9123 PRR *NEW*
117-9124 N&W *NEW*

INTERNATIONAL HOBBY CORP.

DETAIL ASSORTMENTS

348-4408 Rooftop & Street Accessories **1.49**
Fire hydrant, skylight, clothes line with hanging wash, pedestal base, step railings, chaise lounge, park bench and more.

FLAGS

348-4410 US & All 50 States pkg(66) **2.98**
Full-color paper flags, plus three white and three gray plastic poles with bases.

KWIK KITS EA 3.98

These easy-to-build plastic details assemble in minutes and add realism to any scene. Parts are molded in silver. Kits include basic instructions.

348-4552 Rural Assortment pkg(9)
Fuel oil tank, two TV antennas, satellite dish, two trash cans and three rural mail boxes.

348-4553 City Assortment pkg(17)
Large mail storage box, city letter mail box, two trash cans, six parking meters, two fire hydrants, two window air conditioners, phone booth and two TV antennas.

Information STATION

JUNK

What about it? How about the fact that it is probably one of the most common elements present in our world today. Though this is true, it is often overlooked by model railroaders when planning their layouts, which is odd because it is found everywhere. Backyards, construction sites, around garages, some front yards and of course, junk yards, are all places where junk can be found. It may not be the item of choice, but what better way to add novelty and realism to a layout?

It is fairly easy to model junk. There are no uniformed plans for it, in fact, the more sloppier and random the better. Everything and anything can be used for junk. The best way to find materials is by looking through your scrap materials. All the extra wheels, wood strips, ties, kit parts, etc., are perfect for creating believable junk. Or, for those who lack imagination or time, commercial junk castings are also available. Realism can be further achieved with good coloring. Generally, weathering colors work the best.

Turn any model into a detailed replica with this line of injection molded plastic, brass and cast metal parts. Many items include basic assembly and installation instructions.

DIESEL DETAILS

AIR HORNS

NATHAN PKG(2) EA 1.75

229-1601 229-1602

229-1601 3-Chime M3
229-1602 5-Chime M5

229-1603 P3/P5

HANCOCK

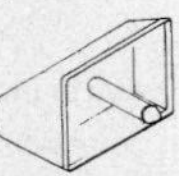

229-1604 Air Chime **1.75** ***NEW***
Soft metal.

ALCO PKG(2) EA 1.50

Soft metal.

229-1605 229-1606

229-1605 FA/PA ***NEW***
229-1606 RS ***NEW***

LESLIE

229-1608 Tyfon A200 pkg(4) **2.00**

AIR FANS

229-2003 Dynamic Brake 48" Flat Top pkg(4) **2.75**

COOLING FANS PKG(4) EA 2.75

229-2001 229-2004

229-2001 34" Flat Top
229-2004 48" Flat Top

COOLING FANS EA TBA

Q TYPE

229-2005 48" ***NEW***
229-2006 48" pkg(3) ***NEW***
229-2007 52" ***NEW***
229-2008 52" pkg(3) ***NEW***

AIR FILTERS

Cast metal.

229-2706 Horst Paducah **3.25**
229-2707 Horst Paper **3.85**
Large weather hoods.

229-2708 Paper, AMT Type **3.50**
Low profile dynacell.

AIR GRILLES

EMD-EARLY

Etched stainless steel.

229-2701 229-2704

229-2701 "Farr" F&E Units pkg(2) **8.00**
229-2704 F7A pkg(2) **5.50**

229-2705 229-2711

229-2705 F7B pkg(2) **5.50**
229-2711 "Chicken Wire" - Early F Units pkg(2) **8.50**
229-2727 Proto 2000 SW9/1200 **5.00**

EMD-LATE

229-2012 48" Flat Top Grille pkg(2) **3.00**
Photo-etched metal.

ALCO

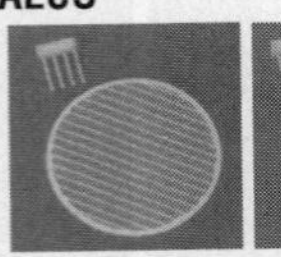

229-2702 229-2703

229-2702 64" Diameter pkg(2) **3.00**
229-2703 57" Diameter pkg(2) **3.00**
Sets include photo-etched round grill and plastic bolts.

229-2716 Century Series Brake Grid pkg(2) **1.25**

229-2730 Grille Set C628, Stewart **TBA**

EMC FT, STEWART EA TBA

229-2728 Fan & Dynamic Brake Grilles
229-2729 Side Air Intake Grilles ***NEW***

FAIRBANKS-MORSE

229-2712 Exhaust, Vent & Intake pkg(4) **2.50**

GE EA 6.00

229-2717 Dash 8-40C
229-2718 Dash 8-40B
229-2722 C32-8

C44-9 EA 7.50

229-2723 For Railpower
229-2724 For Athearn

AIR RESERVOIRS

229-3201 229-3202

229-3201 Single 15" Diameter Top or Side Mount pkg(2) **2.25**
229-3202 Double 12" Diameter Top Mount pkg(2) **2.25**

229-3203 15" GP35-40 Side Mount pkg(4) **2.25**

EMD PKG(2) EA 1.50 (UNLESS NOTED)

Soft metal.

229-3204 SW1200 ***NEW***
229-3205 SW1200/GP38/GP40 ***NEW***

229-3206 GP20 ***NEW***

229-3207 GP30 ***NEW***

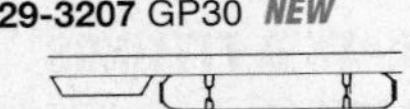

229-3208 GP35/DD35/DD35A ***NEW***

229-3209 GP38-2/GP40-2/SD40/SD45T-2 ***NEW***

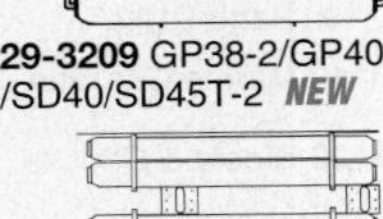

229-3210 GP7/GP9 Roof Mount pkg(4) **2.10** ***NEW***

AIR VENTS

229-1901 229-1902

229-1901 Round pkg(12) **1.00**
Mounted on cab roof or low nose.

229-1902 Flat - Roof or Side Mount pkg(8) **1.00**

229-1903 229-1904

229-1903 Flat - Roof Mount pkg(4) **1.50**
229-1904 Dynamic Brake pkg(2) **1.50**
Mounted on roof of hood units.

229-1905 EMD Body Louvers **3.95**

AIR HOSES

229-1508 MU pkg(16) **2.50**
229-6206 Freight Car pkg(6) **1.50**

BELLS PKG(2) EA 1.25 (UNLESS NOTED)

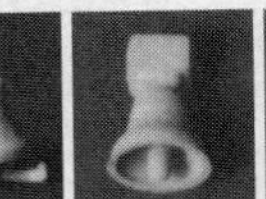
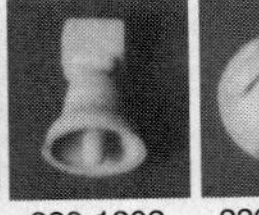

229-1201 229-1202 229-1204

229-1201 EMD Cab Mount **1.50**
229-1202 Underframe Mount
229-1204 Western

BRAKE CYLINDERS

229-2801 Diesel Trucks pkg(8) **2.00**

BRAKE GEAR SETS

229-6238 229-6401

229-6238 Hand Brake & Valve pkg(2) **1.50**
229-6247 ABDXL Brake Set **TBA**
229-6401 Equipco pkg(2) **1.25**

229-6402 229-6403

229-6402 Miner pkg(2) **1.25**
229-6403 Ukeco pkg(2) **1.25**

CABS-NORTH AMERICAN SAFETY DESIGN EA 9.95 (UNLESS NOTED)

229-3604 Canadian Type **10.95**
229-3601 EMD Type
229-3602 Phase I
229-3603 Phase 2

CAB DETAILS

AIR CONDITIONERS EA 1.50

229-2308 229-2309

229-2308 "Prime"
229-2309 "Vapor"

AIR DEFLECTORS "PRIME" TYPE PKG(4) 1.25

Molded in clear plastic, with raised frame, which can be painted for added realism.

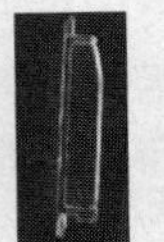

229-2310 229-2311 229-2312

229-2310 Deflector/Mirror-UP Type
229-2311 Angled
229-2312 Straight

ARMRESTS EA 1.25

229-2302 229-2303

229-2302 24" Plain pkg(8)
229-2303 24 x 36" Stepped pkg(4)

WIND DEFLECTOR SET

229-2304 pkg(3) **2.50**
Includes three styles of scale thickness deflectors, made of photo-etched brass. Eyebolts are included so deflectors can be open or closed.

WINDOWS

229-2301 All Weather pkg(2) **3.00**
Double type for GP, SD units.

229-3306 EMD pkg(4) **1.25**
229-2551 Clear Plastic Window Material pkg(5) **1.00**
229-3307 Window Plugs pkg(4) **1.25**
Fits Athearn GE locos, fills in small oval windows on side of cab.

CHAIN

229-2210 Safety Chain (black) 12" Long-40 Links Per Inch **2.25**

CLASSIFICATION LIGHTS

229-1017

229-1018

229-1017 Early EMD pkg(6) **1.25**
Used on GP7, GP9, GP18, GP20 and SD24.

229-1018 With Access Door - SD7 pkg(4) **1.50**
Converts Athearn SD9 to SD7.

229-1019

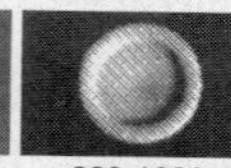
229-1020

229-1019 Late EMD pkg(8) **1.25**
Used from GP30 on, can be illuminated from inside.

229-1020 Blank Knock-Out pkg(8) **1.25**
Used On EMD Dash 2s.

COUPLER LIFT BARS

Parts match equipment on front and rear of most hood units. Bars are preformed wire and fit plastic (or brass) brackets.

AAR TYPE 1

229-2211 Bar & Brackets pkg(2) **2.50**
229-2212 Bar Only pkg(10) **5.50**
229-2226 F/E Cab Units **TBA**

EMD MODERN, TYPE 2 EA TBA

229-2227 pkg(2) ***NEW***
229-2228 pkg(10) ***NEW***

GE MODERN EA TBA

229-2229 Inside Loop pkg(2) ***NEW***
229-2230 Inside Loop pkg(10) ***NEW***
229-2231 Outside Loop pkg(2) ***NEW***
229-2232 Outside Loop pkg(10) ***NEW***

BRACKETS ONLY

229-2213 Plastic pkg(4) **3.00**
229-102213 Brass pkg(8) **2.75**

FREIGHT CAR

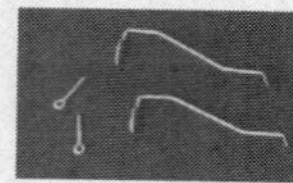

229-6215 Standard Type pkg(10) **2.50**
Formed wire cut lever and eyebolt for mounting on end of car.

229-6240 Modern pkg(6) **2.25**

PASSENGER CAR

229-6642 Modern Cars pkg(4) **2.50**.

MISCELLANEOUS

229-2204 Bar w/Bracket pkg(2) **2.00**
229-2205 Bar Only pkg(10) **2.75**

COVERED HOPPER PARTS

229-6212

229-6218

229-6212 Square Hatch pkg(8) **2.75**
229-6218 Round Hatch pkg(8) **2.00**

229-6229 Discharge Gate pkg(4) **2.00**
229-6429 Roping/Lift Tab for ACF Cars pkg(8) **1.50**

DECAL SETS

WP BOX CAR EA 3.50

229-9001 Modern 15" (white)
229-9002 Early 1950s (silver)
229-9003 Late 1950s (yellow)
229-9004 40' "Western Way"(yellow)
229-9005 50' "Western Way"(yellow)
229-9006 Script "Western Way" (yellow)
229-9007 Cushion Protection (yellow)

DIESEL TRUCK JOURNAL PKG(8) EA 2.25

229-2805

229-2804 Hyatt Roller Bearing
229-2805 EMD Blomberg Square Type
229-2806 EMD Blomberg Slope Style

DOOR OPENER

229-6216 Hennesy pkg(2) **2.00**

DREADNAUGHT END PKG(4) EA 1.75

40S & 50S AAR BOX CAR

229-6235 4/5 Type
229-6236 5/5 Type

DROP STEPS

EMD PKG(2) EA 1.50

229-1401

229-1402

229-1401 EMD Early GP, SD, SW
229-1402 Late GP, SD

229-1404 Dash 2 Series

GENERAL ELECTRIC

229-1403 U Series pkg(2) **1.50**

ALCO EA 3.00 (UNLESS NOTED)

229-1405

229-1406

229-1405 Short-RS/RSDs pkg(2)
229-1406 Long-Century pkg(2)
229-1408 Long-RSD pkg(2)
229-1409 C628/C630 ***NEW***

FAIRBANKS-MORSE

229-1407 Trainmaster **3.00**

CABOOSE

229-6502 With End Platform pkg(2) **2.50**

DYNAMIC BRAKE BOX

229-3402 GE C36-7 **4.95**
229-3403 GE B30-7A1B **4.95**
229-3404 Dynamic Brake & Steam Generator **2.95**

DYNAMIC BRAKE HOUSING

229-2015 EMD SW **2.15** ***NEW***
Soft metal.

END DETAILS

229-6430 Walkover w/Handrail Set **1.75.**
229-6431 Endframe Ladders-ACF Centerflow Hopper pkg(2) **3.50**

EXHAUST SILENCERS EA 1.85

Soft metal.

EMD MP15AC/DC

229-2406 High Stacks ***NEW***

229-2407 Low Stacks ***NEW***

EXHAUST STACKS

EMD

229-2401

229-2402

229-2401 F3, F7, F9, BL2 pkg(2) **1.25**
229-2402 Non-Turbo pkg(2) **1.25**

229-2403 GP20/SD24 pkg(2) **1.50**
229-2404 GP60/SD60/SD70 pkg(2) **2.00**

229-2405 Repowered **1.85** ***NEW***
Soft metal.

FLASHERS PKG(2) EA 1.50

Nonoperating units feature base and appropriately colored globe.

229-2901

229-2902

229-2903

229-2901 Western Cullen
229-2902 Stratolite
229-2903 Xenon Strobe

FOOTBOARDS PKG(2) EA 4.50

229-2208

229-2209

229-2208 Metal
229-2209 Wood

FREIGHT CAR PARTS

229-6211

229-6213

229-6211 Brake Platform pkg(4) **2.75**
229-6213 Handles, Hatches & Tack Boards (14 Pieces) **2.25**
229-6214 Roping Ring Flat, Gondola or Hopper, Wire Formed pkg(12) **1.50** ***NEW***
229-6247 Modern Brake Set 1980s w/ABDW Valve 1 Set **4.75** ***NEW***

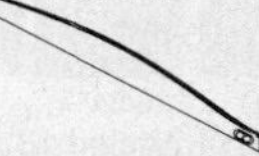

229-6512 Caboose Roof Ends pkg (2) **1.50** ***NEW***
229-6219 Dome for Athearn 40' Cars **3.50**

229-6224

229-6237

229-6224 Box Car Roof Plug pkg(8) **1.50**
229-6227 AB Brake Set **3.25**
229-6237 Tank Car Placards pkg(8) **1.25**
229-6246 AEI Data Tag "Amtech" pkg(10) **1.25**

WINDOWS PKG(4) EA 1.60 (UNLESS NOTED)

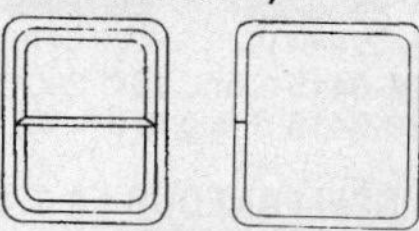

229-6505 2-Pane ***NEW***
229-6506 Large ***NEW***

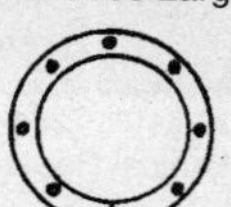

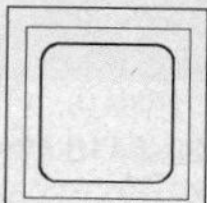

229-6507 Round ***NEW***
229-6508 Square, NE Style ***NEW***

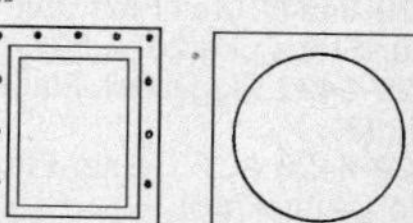

229-6509 Rectangle, NE Style ***NEW***
229-6510 Round, NE Style pkg(8) **1.85** ***NEW***

ALCO EA 1.50

Soft metal.

229-2408 RS-2/RS-3 ***NEW***
229-2409 RS-2/RS-3 w/Extension ***NEW***

FREIGHT CAR STIRRUPS

OFFSET BOTTOM MOUNT PKG(8) EA 1.65

229-6411 229-6412 229-6413

229-6411 Angled 18 x 12-1/2"
229-6412 Stepped 17 x 14"
229-6413 Double 18-1/2 x 12"

STRAIGHT BOTTOM MOUNT PKG(8) EA 1.65

229-6414 229-6417

229-6414 16 x 11-1/2"
229-6417 8-1/2 x 13"

SIDE MOUNT PKG(8) EA 1.65

229-6415 229-6416

229-6415 Slant, 13-1/2 x 13"
229-6416 Straight, 9 x 12"

MISCELLANEOUS EA 1.75 (UNLESS NOTED)

  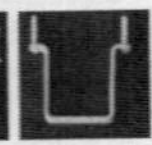
229-6418 229-6419 229-6420

229-6418 Mechanical Reefer pkg(7)
229-6419 Gunderson Type pkg(8)
229-6420 Thrall Type pkg(8)
229-6421 Thrall Five Unit Well Car Steps pkg(20) **3.50**
229-6422 Piggyback Flat Car pkg(8)
229-6428 ACF Center Flow Hoppers pkg(8)

FUEL TANK PARTS

229-3101 229-3102

229-3101 EMD Flush-Mount Fuel Gauge pkg(6) **1.00**
229-3102 Fitting Set pkg(8) **1.00**
Includes filler necks, plus sight gauge and flush mount gauge.

GONDOLA PARTS

229-6221 229-6222 229-6223

229-6221 Dreadnaught Ends pkg(2) **1.75**
229-6222 Riveted Ends pkg(2) **1.75**
229-6223 Drop Doors pkg(8) **2.50**
229-6225 GS Steel Plate pkg(8) **2.50**
229-6226 GS-Drop Chain, Open/Closed "Enterprise" pkg(32) **4.50**

GRAB IRONS

Scale size, made of formed wire and precut (unless noted).

DROP TYPE

229-2201 229-2202

229-2201 With Nut/Bolt/ Washer Castings pkg(18) **2.25**
229-2202 Grab Irons Only pkg(24) **2.50**

ALCO CURVED EA TBA

229-2233 C628/C630 *NEW*
229-2234 RS/RSD/RSC *NEW*

STRAIGHT TYPE PKG(12) EA 2.00

229-2224 11"
229-2225 14"
229-6605 36"

229-6210 With Nut/Bolt/ Washer Castings

PASSENGER CAR PKG(12) EA 1.75

 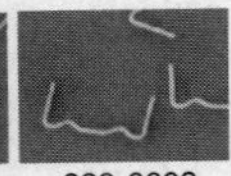
229-6601 229-6603

229-6601 Vestibule
229-6602 Roof
229-6603 Roof Ladder

CABOOSE PKG(12) EA 2.25

229-6503 229-6504

229-6503 Curved - Ends & Sides
229-6504 "L" Shaped - Ends

FREIGHT CARS PKG(12) EA 2.00 (UNLESS NOTED)

229-6205 229-6209

229-6205 Running Board Corner **2.25**
229-6209 Bracket Type, 22" pkg(8)
Molded in Delrin® plastic.
229-6217 18" Curved for Tank Car
229-6423 22" Straight
229-6424 22" Drop-Piggyback
229-6425 22" Drop
229-6426 19-1/2" Straight
229-6427 19-1/2" Drop

LOCOMOTIVES

229-2215 28" Ladder Grabs for E & F Units **2.00**

229-2219 Walkway Guard (EMD 60 Series) **1.00**

PILOT

229-2216 Curved, Anti-Climber pkg(12) **2.00**
229-2220 Pilot Grab Bar - SW/GP, 8'4" pkg(6) **1.25**

FAN PKG(3) EA 1.50

Mounted on roof of hood units in front of the last radiator fan.

229-2217 Circular, GP30-GP/SD60
229-2218 Angular Dash 2

ROOF

229-2221 Cab Roof Grab Bar pkg(6) **1.25**

HEADLIGHTS

OSCILLATING PYLE

229-1001 Plastic pkg(2) **1.00**
229-101001 Brass **1.35**

OSCILLATING MARS

229-1005 229-1008

229-1005 Plastic pkg(2) **1.00**
229-101005 Brass **1.35**
229-1008 Dual Plastic pkg(2) **1.00**
229-101008 Dual Brass **1.50**

OSCILLATING DUAL PYLE GYRALIGHT

229-1002 229-1009

229-1002 Plastic pkg(2) **1.00**
229-1009 Recessed pkg(2) **1.00**
229-101002 Brass **1.35**

DUAL PYLE

229-1003 229-1004

229-1003 EMD-Late Plastic pkg(2) **1.00**
229-101003 EMD-Late Brass **1.35**
229-1004 Early Plastic pkg(2) **1.00**
229-101004 Early Brass **1.35**
229-101023 Brass w/Horizontal Shield **1.35** *NEW*
229-101024 Brass w/Vertical Shield **1.35** *NEW*

PYLE - LARGE "MOUNTAIN" TYPE FOR WP, CN, CP

229-1010 Plastic pkg(2) **1.25**
229-101010 Brass **1.50**

PYLE - DUAL W/VISORS PKG(2) 1.00

229-1023 Horizontal
229-1024 Vertical

PYLE CONVERSION PLATE

229-1012 For 14-1/2" Headlight pkg(2) **1.00**
Modifies older single beam units into dual sealed beam lights, used on many first generation units.

EMD SWITCHERS

229-1011 229-1015

229-1011 Dual Pyle w/Numberboards & Sealed Beams **3.00**
229-1015 Original (Large, Single Beam) NW/SW Series pkg(2) **1.50**

DUAL MARS PKG(2) EA 1.00

229-1006 229-1007

229-1006 Standard
229-1007 Oscillating Dual Recessed

LIGHT HOUSING

229-1016 For SP Baldwin **3.95**

REAR LIGHT BRACKET

229-1021 SP Late GP/SDs pkg(2) **1.25**

BACK UP LIGHT

229-1014 Canadian Type pkg(2) **1.00**

DITCH LIGHTS

229-1013 Canadian Type pkg(2) **1.00**

229-1022 With Stand pkg(4) **1.25**
229-1026 MU Stand-SP High Type **1.25**
229-1029 BN Style Strobe Flashers pkg(2) **1.25**

229-6511 Caboose pkg(4) **1.55** *NEW*

SOUTHERN PACIFIC TYPES PKG(2)

229-1025 High Type w/MU Stand **1.25**
229-1027 Low Type **1.00**

LADDERS

229-2207 229-6207

LOCOMOTIVE

229-2207 SD 7/9 Kit **3.50**

FREIGHT CAR

229-6208 Short (Modern) pkg(8) **2.00**
229-6207 Long pkg(10) **2.85**
dders Amtrak MHC **2.95**

LADDER SETS EA 2.25

229-6241 8-Rung
229-6242 7-Rung

LENSES PKG(12) EA 1.25

CLEAR CLASSIFICATION LIGHTS

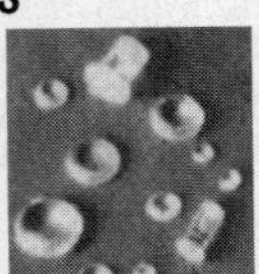

229-1708 4-1/2" (.052") Diameter
229-1709 7" (.080") Diameter

HEADLIGHT LENSES

229-1710 12" (.138") Diameter
229-1711 14-1/2" (.167") Diameter

LIFT RINGS

  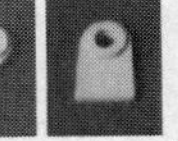
229-1104 229-1102 229-1103

229-1104 Tabs - Roof and Side Hood Mount pkg(16) **1.50**
229-1102 EMD F&E Unit Nose pkg(6) **1.25**
229-1103 Flat - Mounts on Pilot Beam pkg(8) **1.25**

229-1105 229-1106 229-1107

229-1105 Switcher Side Mount pkg(4) **1.50**
229-1106 Alco FA/PA Century Type pkg(12) **1.25**
229-1107 Alco S/RS Type pkg(12) **1.25**
229-1108 GE w/Hinges pkg(12) **1.50**

EYE BOLTS

229-2206 Formed Wire pkg(24) **3.00**
229-2222 Long Shank pkg(24) **3.00**
229-1101 Plastic pkg(36) **1.50**
229-101101 Brass pkg(24) **2.25**

MINIATURE TOOLS

229-7101 229-7202

229-7101 Hand Tool Set, Photo-etched, 35 pieces **3.25**
229-7102 Screw Jack pkg(2) **1.35**

229-7103 229-7104

229-7103 Rerail Frog pkg(2) **1.35**
229-7104 Oil Can pkg(2) **1.35**

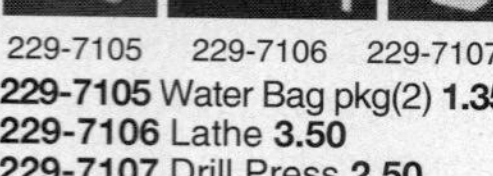

229-7105 229-7106 229-7107

229-7105 Water Bag pkg(2) **1.35**
229-7106 Lathe **3.50**
229-7107 Drill Press **2.50**

MISCELLANEOUS

229-2307 SD7-35 Circular Access Cover pkg(6) **1.00**
229-2313 Battery Compartment Door & Handbrake SD60M **4.95**
229-2809 Truck Air Line EMD Blomberg "B" pkg(4) **1.50**

MU STANDS PKG(2) EA 1.25

EARLY GP

229-1501 229-1502

229-1501 Low
229-1502 High

INTERMEDIATE GP/SD

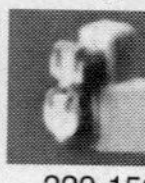

229-1503 229-1504

229-1503 Single
229-1504 Double

LATE GP/SD

229-1505 229-1506

229-1505 Single
229-1506 Double

MU RECEPTACLES

229-1507 Receptacles & Blank Covers pkg(30) **1.25**
Three different types of receptacles and two styles of covers.

229-101507 Brass pkg(30) **2.25**
229-1509 Receptacles **1.25**
229-1510 Head-End Power Receptacle Set **1.25**

NUMBERBOARDS

ALCO PKG(4) EA 3.00

Plastic boards and brackets, with photo-etched brass fronts for large or five-digit style numberboards.

229-2602 229-2603

229-2602 Curved Back
229-2603 Angled Back

MISCELLANEOUS

1 2 3 4 5 6 7 8 9 0 X -
1 2 3 4 5 6 7 8 9 0 X -

229-2601 Stencils (Photoetched Brass) **2.50**

229-2604 Numberboard & Headlight WP/UP GP35/40 **3.50**
229-4501 GE U33C (Fits Atlas Series 1) **4.00**
229-4502 EMD GP35 (Fits Kato Series 1) **4.00**

NUT/BOLT/WASHER CASTINGS EA 2.00

Simulates 3/4" bolt with 2" washer.

229-2203 Plastic pkg(48)
229-102203 Brass pkg(18)

PILOTS

229-2214 Passenger for Cab Unit **5.95**
229-2223 For Bowser FM H16-44 **3.25**

RADIATORS

EMD SWITCHERS PKG(2) EA 3.50

Kits include photo-etched screen and plastic frame to model large radiators on the front of EMD switchers. Includes instructions.

229-2709 SW Units
229-2710 NW Units

FAIRBANKS-MORSE

229-2713 Photo-Etched Fan Screen **2.75**

EMD SD45 GRILLS PKG(2) EA 1.25

229-2714 Late Type
229-2715 Early Type

MISCELLANEOUS GRILLS

229-2719 SD50-2 Radiators & Air Intake Grills pkg(2) **4.95**
229-2720 40" Series pkg(4) **3.95**
GP/SD 40 and some GP/SD40-2 units.

RADIO ANTENNAS

229-1801 229-1802 229-1803

CAN TYPE

Used by ATSF and UP.

229-1801 Plastic pkg(6) **1.00**
229-101801 Brass pkg(3) **1.35**

WHIP TYPE

Used by ATSF and UP.

229-1802 Plastic pkg(3) **1.00**
229-101802 Brass pkg(3) **1.35**

SINCLAIR

229-1803 Plastic pkg(4) **1.50**
229-101803 Brass pkg(4) **2.50**
229-1806 Small **TBA**

MOTOROLA FIRECRACKER

229-1805 pkg(6) **1.25**
229-101805 Brass pkg(3) **2.00** *NEW*

MISCELLANEOUS

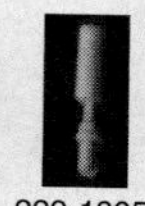

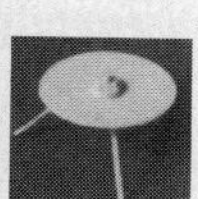

229-1804 229-1805 229-6501

229-1804 Wagon Wheel pkg(3) **3.25**
Photo-etched brass with plastic antenna casting.

229-6501 Caboose Dish Type pkg(3) **2.50**

RUNNING BOARDS (FREIGHT CARS)

Includes pre-formed corner grab irons.

WOOD EA 3.75

229-6201 229-6202

229-6201 40' Cars
229-6202 50' Cars

METAL EA 6.50

Photo-etched metal.

229-6203 229-6204

229-6203 40' Cars
229-6204 50' Cars

SAND FILLERS PKG(3) EA TBA

MODERN

229-3005 EMD *NEW*
229-3006 GE *NEW*

ALCO C628/C630

229-3007 Early *NEW*
229-3008 Late *NEW*

SAND HATCHES

EMD LOCOS

229-3001 229-3002

229-3001 Late-GP35 pkg(6) **1.25**
229-3002 Early-GP7/9 pkg(4) **1.00**

EMD CAB UNITS PKG(4) EA 1.00

229-3003 229-3004

229-3003 Early
229-3004 Late

SHOCK ABSORBER/ SNUBBER PKG(4) EA 1.75

229-2803

229-2802 EMD Style
229-2803 GE Style

SHORT NOSE CONVERSIONS EA 6.95

229-3605 CP Rail 102"
229-3606 UP 115" "Snoot"
229-3607 KCS 123" "Snoot"

SIGNAL BOXES PKG(2) EA 1.50

229-2305 229-2306

229-2305 3 Strap-Early
229-2306 2 Strap-Late

SPARK ARRESTORS

MILW TYPES PKG(2) EA 2.50

Cast metal.

229-2105 229-2106

229-2105 SW Switchers
229-2106 F Units

EMD EA 1.85

Soft metal.

229-2107 229-2108

229-2107 SW, CN/CP High *NEW*
229-2108 GP, CN/CP Low *NEW*

MISCELLANEOUS

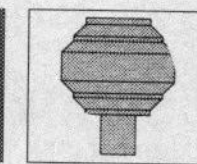

229-2101 229-2104 229-2102

229-2103 229-4001

229-2101 Super Flared Switcher Type pkg(2) **1.25**
229-2104 ATSF Type Cast Metal pkg(2) **1.85**
229-2102 Round Type pkg(2) **1.25**
229-2103 Round Wire Screen Type pkg(2) **1.85**
Used on EMD Switchers, cast metal.

229-4001 Steam Locos **2.00**
229-102102 Round, Brass pkg(2) **2.35**

SPEED RECORDERS PKG(4) EA 1.75

229-2807 Flange Type
229-2808 GE Type

SUNSHADES

PLASTIC

229-1301

229-1302

229-1301 GP/SD Units pkg(6) **1.50**
229-1302 F&E Units pkg(4) **1.25**

229-1303

229-1303 EMD Wide Cabs pkg(4) **1.50**

BRASS

229-101301 GP/SD Units pkg(2) **2.25**
229-101302 F&E Units pkg(4) **1.75**

SUPERIOR PANEL DOORS PKG(2) EA 2.85

229-6306

229-6301 6 x 8'3", 5-Panel
229-6302 6 x 8'3", 6-Panel
229-6306 8 x 9', 7-Panel
229-6311 10' x 9'3", 6-Panel

STEAM GENERATOR STACK

229-2410 Alco RS-2/RS-3 pkg(2) **1.60** *NEW*
Soft metal.

WINDOW SETS EA 1.75 (UNLESS NOTED)

Individual clear plastic windows replace solid window casting in hood units.

229-3301 Athearn SW
229-3302 Athearn S-12
229-3303 Athearn F7A
229-3304 Athearn F7B **1.00**
229-3305 Atlas FP7

WINDSHIELD WIPERS

229-2314 Offset Blade, Single & Double Arm pkg(8) **2.50** *NEW*
229-2315 Inline Blade, Single & Double Arm **TBA** *NEW*
229-2316 Dual Single Arm **TBA** *NEW*
229-2317 Dual Double Arm **TBA** *NEW*
229-2318 Amtrak Single Long Arm **TBA** *NEW*

WINTERIZATION HATCHES

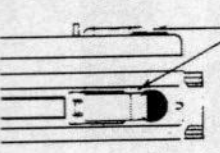

229-2011 Alco RS2/RS3 **1.90** *NEW*
Soft metal.

229-2013

229-2014

229-2013 GP9 & GP18 **2.00**
229-2014 GP/SD60 **2.00**

STRUCTURE DETAILS

229-7201

229-7202

229-7201 Baggage Door 48" **1.50**
229-7202 Footing Piers, Concrete pkg(24) **1.50**

PASSENGER CAR DETAILS

229-6604 Roof Vent-Harriman Type pkg(12) **1.75**
229-6609 Head-End Power Receptacle Set **1.25**

PASSENGER CAR STEPS EA 1.75

229-6606 Superliner pkg(8)
229-6607 Material Handling Car pkg(6)
229-6608 Stirrup for Baggage Car pkg(6)

DETAIL KITS

FREIGHT CARS EA 10.50 (UNLESS NOTED)

229-501 C&BT Shops 40' Steel Box Car **10.50**
Use with single or double door cars.
229-503 Walthers 10,000 Gallon Tank Cars **10.50**
229-504 Proto 2000 Series **5.50**
229-505 Proto 2000 PS 4470 Covered Hopper *NEW*
229-550 Caboose American Model Builders **7.50**

LOCOMOTIVES

229-701 Stewart F3A, F7A, F9A Units **7.50**
229-702 Stewart F3B, F7B, F9B Units **7.00**
229-704 Highliner EMD FB Units **7.00**
229-707 Basic 1980 Era Diesel Detail Kit **8.50**
229-708 GE U33C Detail Kit - Atlas **8.50**
229-709 Stewart EMC, EMD FT-A **5.00** *NEW*
229-710 EMC (EMD) FT-B Stewart **5.00**
229-711 Athearn GE P32, P40, P42, ADM103 **17.50** *NEW*
229-712 Stewart Alco C628, C630 **TBA** *NEW*
229-713 Railpower EMD SD90MAC **TBA** *NEW*
229-3608 Alco "Hammerhead" Conversion **7.95**
229-3609 Alco RS-2 Conversion **8.95**

PASSENGER CARS

229-901 Superliner Con-Cor **10.50**
229-902 Mail/Material Handling Car Con-Cor **8.50**
229-903 Horizon Car - Walthers **9.50** *NEW*
229-904 Budd Hi-Level - Train Station Products **9.50** *NEW*

HARDWARE

WIRE EA 2.50

FLAT BRASS PKG(6)

229-2530 .015 x .060
229-2522 .015 x .018
229-2524 .015 x .030
229-2526 .015 x .024
229-2528 .015 x .042

ROUND BRASS

Ideal for modeling all types of pipe, railings etc., brass wire is easily bent to fit your applications. Size is outside diameter in HO Scale inches, followed by actual dimensions.

Number	Size	Outside Diameter	Wire Size	Pkg
229-2501	1/4"	0.5400"	.006"	5
229-2502	3/8"	0.6750"	.008"	5
229-2503	1/2"	0.8400"	.010"	10
229-2504	3/4"	1.2150"	.012"	10
229-2505	1"	1.6600"	.015"	10
229-2506	1-1/4"	1.9900"	.019"	10
229-2507	1-1/2"	2.3750"	.022"	10
229-2508	2"	2.8750"	.028"	10
229-2509	2-1/2"	3.5000"	.033"	10
229-2510	3"	4.0000"	.040"	6
229-2511	3-1/2"	4.0000"	.046"	6
229-2512	4"	4.5000"	.052"	6

STAINLESS STEEL

Measurement indicates diameter.

229-3503 .010" pkg(5) *NEW*
229-3504 .012" pkg(10) *NEW*
229-3505 .015" pkg(10) *NEW*
229-3506 .019" pkg(10) *NEW*

HARDWARE (continued)

STEEL PANHEAD SCREWS PKG(6) EA .85

2/56

229-2552 1/8"
229-2553 3/16"
229-2554 1/4"
229-2555 1/2"
229-2556 3/8"

1/72

229-2561 1/8"
229-2562 3/16"
229-2563 1/4"
229-2564 3/8"

STEEL HEX NUTS PKG(6) EA .85

229-2557 2/56
229-2565 1/72

STEEL WASHERS PKG(12) EA .85

229-2558 2/56
229-2566 1/72

Information STATION

PAINTING NEW PARTS

Installing new parts on factory-painted models often creates a new challenge - matching the paint.

Although common colors are used, which are mixed to the same pigment formula, no two batches are actually identical. While the new paint is the same color, it probably does not look right.

To see how closely your touch-up paint matches, brush a small amount on a scrap of cardboard or plastic. When dry, place the model and the paint chip together on your layout. Examine the paint under the normal lighting conditions of your layout room, and decide if it's too light or dark.

Make up a color swatch card on some scrap material by mixing one drop of your base color with black (if too light) or white (if too dark) paint in varying amounts, starting with one drop and working up. Record the formula as you apply the drop of paint to the card. When dry, compare the final samples under the layout lighting to see which is the closest match.

Remember, real equipment is often repaired and overhauled and the paint doesn't match. You can also "camouflage" new parts with some weathering to make them blend in.

Detail parts are metal castings.

AUTO PARTS EA 2.25

261-625 261-649 261-653

261-625 Tires pkg(5)
261-649 Truck Wheels pkg(6)

261-652 Car/Truck Springs pkg(6)
261-653 Radiator pkg(4)

261-654 Rear End pkg(4)

261-655 Muffler pkg(3)

261-656 261-657

261-656 Transmission pkg(3)
261-657 Engine Block pkg(3)

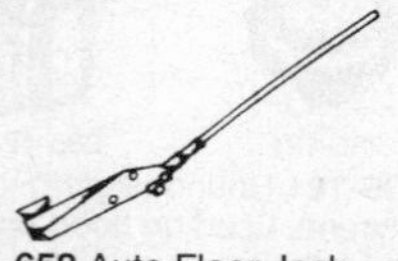

261-658 Auto Floor Jack pkg(3)

BOILER KIT

261-505 6.95
American Hoist & Derrick prototype can be used for all types of small steam-powered machinery.

BOXES & CRATES EA 2.25

261-644 261-645 261-662

261-644 Assorted Boxes
261-645 Empty Crates pkg(6)
261-662 Box of Produce pkg(5)

BUCK SAWS

261-614 Hand Powered **3.75**

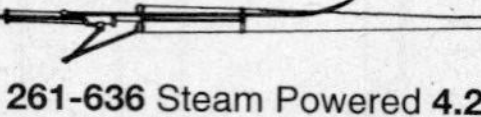

261-636 Steam Powered **4.25**

CANS & DRUMS EA 2.25

261-609 261-613 261-659

261-609 Lube Cans Set pkg(12)
261-613 2-1/2 Gallon Gas Can pkg(4)
261-659 Milk Can pkg(6)

261-618 261-623 261-661

261-618 25-Gallon Drum pkg(5)
261-623 Oil Can w/Handle pkg(4)
261-661 Garbage Can pkg(4)

GAS STATION EQUIPMENT

261-651 261-601

261-651 Oil High Boy pkg(2) **2.25**
261-601 Gravity-Feed Gas Pump **2.75**

HOIST

261-506 AH&D Two-Spool Hoist **23.95**

INTERIOR DETAILS EA 2.25 (UNLESS NOTED)

261-626 261-637 261-638

261-626 Work Bench **2.50**
261-637 Toilet pkg(2)
261-638 Sink & Towel Dispenser

261-639 261-640

261-639 Wall Telephone pkg(3)
261-640 Radio pkg(3)

261-641 261-642

261-641 Chair pkg(2)
261-642 Stove & Pipe

261-646 2-Drawer File Cabinet pkg(3)

261-647 261-648

261-647 Desk Top & File Cabinet Set **2.50**
261-648 Pool Table & Cue Rack Set **3.50**

261-660 Lamp Shade pkg(6)

LOGGING TOOLS

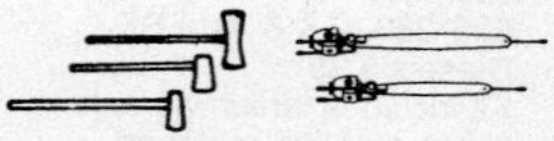

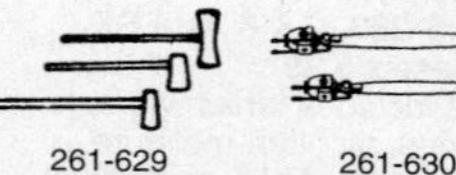

261-629 261-630

261-629 Assorted Axes & Mauls pkg(2) **2.25**
261-630 Chain Saws **5.50**
261-501 Woodsman Set **13.95**

MINIATURE TOOLS EA 2.25 (UNLESS NOTED)

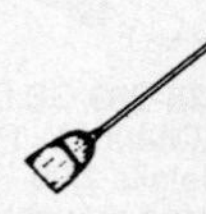

261-602 261-603

261-602 Push Broom pkg(4)
261-603 Straight Broom pkg(4)

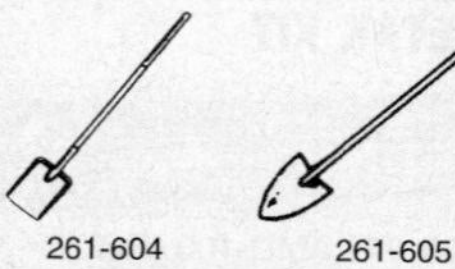

261-604 261-605

261-604 Shovel pkg(4)
261-605 Spade pkg(4)
261-607 Canteen pkg(5)
261-608 Railroad Car Jack pkg(4)
261-610 Kerosene Lanterns pkg(5)

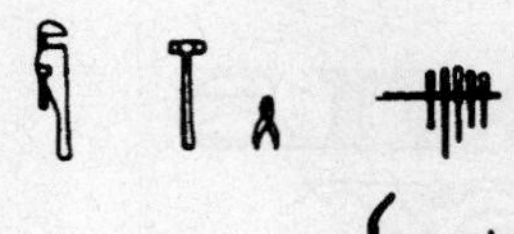

261-612 Tool Set **2.75**
261-615 Vise pkg(3)
261-616 Grinder pkg(3)

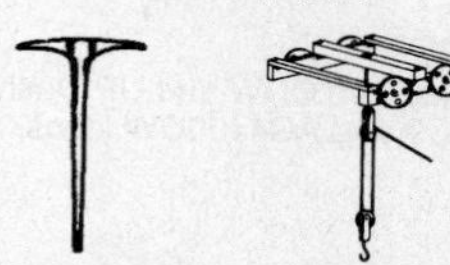

261-621 261-634

261-621 Picks pkg(6)
261-631 Motor Drive
261-634 Overhead Rolling Block & Tackle **3.00**
261-650 Fire Extinguisher pkg(5)

PEAVEYS PKG(4) EA 2.25

261-627 Long

261-628 Short

POWER METER

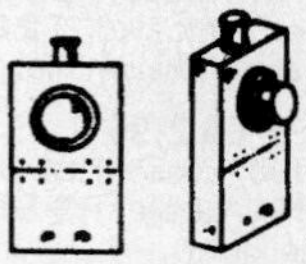

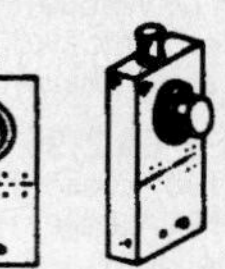

261-606 Power Head/Box **2.25**

ROLLER BEARINGS PKG(4) EA 2.25

261-632 Small
261-633 Large

SMOKE JACKS EA 2.25

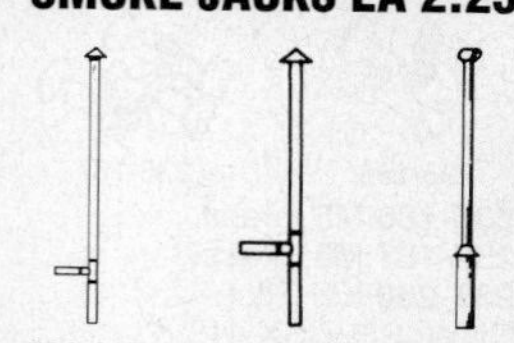

261-617 261-619 261-643

261-617 Tall-Wall Mount pkg(2)
261-619 Short-Wall Mount pkg(2)
261-643 Short-Roof Mount pkg(3)

STATIONARY ENGINE

261-510 Stationary Cat Engine **12.95**

WELDING TANKS PKG(5) EA 2.25

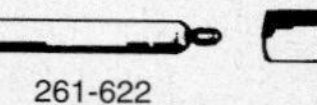

261-622 261-624

261-622 Oxygen Bottle
261-624 Acetylene Bottle

kibri

IMPORTED FROM GERMANY BY WALTHERS

Special Value Price Shown In Red
Plastic parts molded in colors.

OIL DRUMS

405-9386 Assorted Oil Drums pkg(24) **9.99**

405-9458 Shipping Container Pallets & Oil Drums
~~19.99~~ **9.99**

WIRE CABLE DRUMS

405-9921 Wire Cable Drums pkg(2) **10.99**

TRANSFORMER

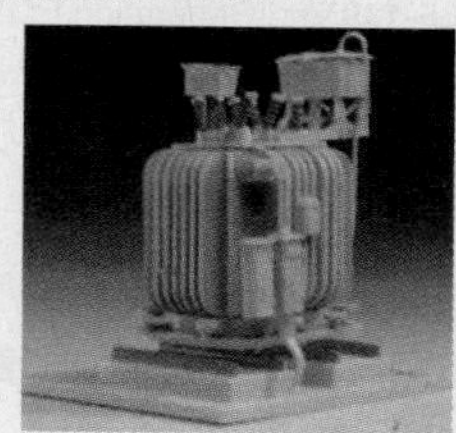

405-9922 High Volume Transformer **13.99**

These diesel detail parts are white metal castings or styrene parts. Illustrations are not to scale.

DIESEL DETAIL PARTS

AIR CONDITIONERS

235-158 235-159

235-158 Vapor Type **1.00**
Mounted atop cab of 2nd generation hood units. Styrene.
235-159 Prime Type **1.25**
Roof mount with adapter for GE hood unit. Styrene.

235-260 Dayton/Phoenix Type **2.00**
For GE Dash 9, white metal.

AIR FILTERS

EARLY TYPES EA 1.00

235-139 235-154

235-139 2nd Generation EMD & GE Units pkg(2)
235-154 1st & Early 2nd Generation Hood Units

PRIME TYPE EA. 1.25

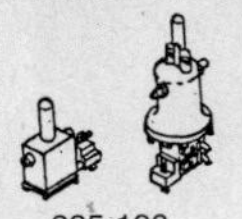
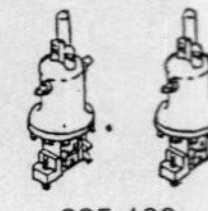

235-198 235-199

235-198 Prime Type 1
235-199 Prime Type 2
Used on second generation EMD hood units.

SALEM TYPE

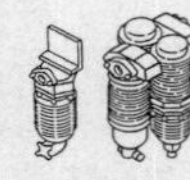

235-225 235-226

235-225 Small pkg(2) **1.50**
235-226 Set pkg(2) **1.75**

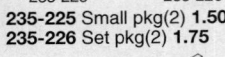

235-237 Air Dryer Filter w/Pipes & Mounts **4.75**.

GE TYPE

Used on CNW and UP Dash 8, 9 and AC4400CW locos.

235-248 Filter Set w/Mount & Pipes **2.25**.

AIR HORNS

235-131 235-173 235-174

235-131 Hancock Type 4700 pkg(2) **1.00**
Used by PC, MILW, L&N, Seaboard Coast Line and others, also used on industrial switchers.
235-173 Flat Type Single Chime pkg(2) **2.95**
For 1st generation diesels, brass.
235-174 Wabco Type E, Single Chime pkg(2) **2.95**
For 1st generation diesels.

LESLIE EA 2.95

235-190 "Leslie" RSL-3L-R
235-191 "Leslie" RS-ST-RF, 5 Chime Horn

NATHAN EA 2.95

235-175 P3, Three Chime
For all types of 1st and 2nd generation units, brass.

235-186 235-187

235-186 M3, brass.
235-187 M5, brass.
235-250 K5HR24
CNW, SP, CSX, NS & Canadian roads, brass.
235-251 K5 Low Profile w/Reverse #3 & 4 Bells
CSX, DRGW, NS & others, brass.
235-252 K5 Low Profile w/All Bells Forward Amtrak, CSX, NS, Metro, brass.
235-253 K3 w/Reverse #4 Bell
ATSF, BNSF, CN, CP, SP & others, brass.
235-254 K3 w/All Bells Forward CP, CN & others, brass.

AIR HOSE PKG(2) EA 1.25

235-267 Locomotive Type w/Bracket

235-268 Locomotive Type w/Extension & Angle Cock

AIR TANKS

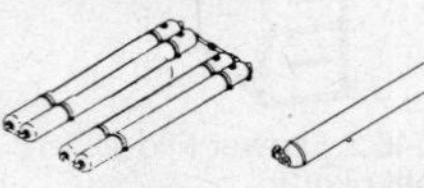

235-146 235-204

235-146 Geeps-Roof Mount **2.50**
Used on EMD GP7 through GP20s and CNW GP35s.
235-204 EMD Hood Units-Underframe **1.95**

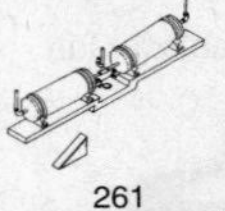

261 263

235-261 Bottom-Mount for Post 1995 GE Dash 9 AC4400CW **5.25**
Kit includes tanks w/brackets, cast metal.
235-263 4- & 6-Axle GE Diesels **5.25**
Kit includes tanks w/brackets, pipes, air filter, moisture ejector and bell, cast metal.

AIR TANK DETAILS

235-242 Pipes & Moisture Ejectors-Set **1.95.**

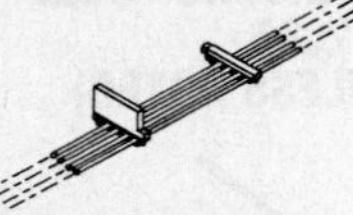

235-259 GE Dash 8, 9 & AC4400CW Pipe & Bracket Details **2.95**
Used on right side underframe, white metal & brass.

AMTRAK LOCO SUPER DETAIL KIT

235-271 AMD-103 (P-40, P-42) **22.95** ***NEW***
Kit includes sander brackets, underframe bell, screen guard, toilet drain, K5LA horn, HEP cables, air dryers with mounts, battery box brackets, Sinclair radio antenna and many pipe assortments. Parts are white metal and brass.

ANTENNAS

235-157 235-214

235-157 "Firecracker" Type pkg(5) **1.95**
Brass, used on all types of locos and cabooses.
235-214 Sinclair w/Ground Plain **1.50**
Used by SP, ATSF and others.

ANTENNA MOUNTING STANDS PKG(2) 1.75

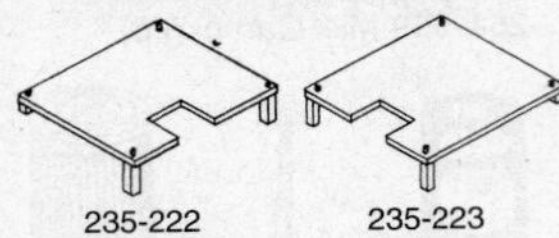

235-222 235-223

235-222 Style 1
235-223 Style 2

ANTICLIMBERS

235-189 EMD SD Locos **1.25**
Styrene.

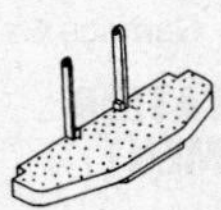

235-262 GE C30-7 Front w/2 Middle Stanchions **1.95**
White metal.

AUTOMATIC TRAIN CONTROL

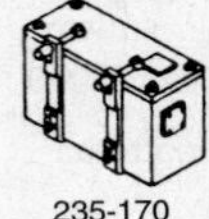

235-170 235-184

235-170 Control Box **1.50**
For hood units of PRR (later PC, CR) ATSF, UP and others.
235-184 Automatic Train Stop **1.25**
Used by Santa Fe, Amtrak.

BELLS EA 1.25 (UNLESS NOTED)

235-127 235-128

235-127 Frame Mount pkg(2)
For all types of units.
235-128 Fabricated Type pkg(2)
Standard equipment for EMD switchers, post 1952.

235-129 235-134

235-129 Hood-Side Mount pkg(2)
GE and other hood units.
235-134 Roof Mount pkg(2)
GE hood units.

235-135 235-151

235-135 Front Mount pkg(2) **1.50**
N&W and SOU hood units
235-151 Curved Base-Fabricated Type pkg(2)
For Alco-built switchers.

235-152 235-176

235-152 Gong Type pkg(2) **1.00**
For nose of CNW and Detroit, Toledo & Ironton units, also installed on Bangor and Aroostook, BN and MP power.
235-176 Hood-Side Mount pkg(2)

235-238 End of Fuel Tank Mount pkg(2)

BEARING CAP

235-244 Axle Bearing Caps pkg(4) **1.25.**

BRAKE VENT VALVE

235-245 Brake Vent Regulator Valve pkg(2) **1.25.**

CAB & BODY VENTS EA 1.00

235-121 235-122

235-121 Round pkg(12)
Styrene, used on hood units and cabooses.
235-122 Square pkg(12)
Used on cabs of 2nd generation EMD and GE units.

VENT & ELECTRICAL CABINET SETS EA 1.00

235-107 235-161

235-107 Late 2nd Generation
235-161 EMD Dash-2
Cast metal, includes vent for top of hood and electrical cabinet filter.

DETAILS WEST

COOLING FANS

STYRENE PARTS

235-142 235-143

235-142 36" Cap-Top pkg(4)
Used for radiator and/or dynamic brake on F7/9, GP20, GP30, GP35, SD7/9, SD18, SD24, SD35, F8/9 **1.50**

235-143 48" Cap-Top pkg(2) **1.00**
Dynamic brake for F7, F9, GP7/9, E8/9.

235-144 235-145

235-144 48" Pan-Top pkg(3) **1.25**
Radiator and/or dynamic brake for late GP9, GP18, GP20, GP30, GP35, SD9, SD18, SD24.

235-145 48" Flared-Top pkg(4) **1.25**
Radiator for EMD GP20.

COUPLER KNUCKLE BRACKETS

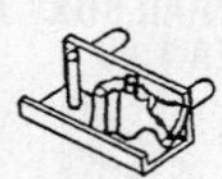
235-196 235-210

235-196 Spare Knuckle/ Bracket pkg(2) **1.00**
235-210 Knuckle Holder GP50/60 **1.75**
Many roads install these brackets on locos, so crews have spare knuckles handy for occasional repairs.

DIESEL PARTS

235-118 235-119

235-118 Steam Generator Set (3 pieces) **1.50**
235-119 Rerail Frog Set **1.50**
Includes two "butterfly" rerailers, right and left hanging brackets and basic instructions.

235-172 235-188 235-189

235-172 Loco and Cab Step Lights pkg(8) **1.25**
For virtually all diesels and many road's cabooses.
235-188 Diesel Sun Visor, Styrene pkg(4) **1.00**

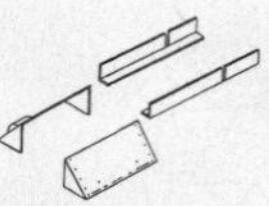
235-194 235-195

235-194 Awning/Smoke Deflector **1.50**
235-195 Coupler Buffer Plate pkg(2) **1.50**
Fills empty space below couplers on most plastic hood units, includes installation instructions.

TRACTION MOTOR CABLE SETS

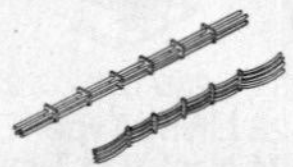

235-224 Traction Motor Cable Set **1.95**

235-239 Traction Motor Cable Set **3.25.**

END-OF-TRAIN DEVICE

235-227 End-of-Train Device w/Red Bulb **1.95**
One-piece metal casting, simulates devices used to protect modern freight trains.

FUEL FILLERS PKG(4) EA 1.00

235-149 235-166 235-167

235-149 GE Hood Units
235-166 EMD Road Units
235-167 EMD Switcher Type

235-258 GE Dash 8, 9 & AC4400CW Fillers & Gauges **2.95**

FUEL TANK MOUNTS

235-111 Breather Pipe **1.00**
For SD7/9, 18, 24 and 26.

FUEL TANK BRACKETS

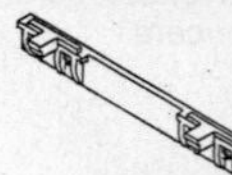

235-197 235-240

235-197 End Bracket pkg(2) **1.50**
235-240 GE Style Brackets pkg(4) **1.75.**

FUEL SHUT-OFF

235-247 Emergency Fuel Shut-Off Box pkg(2) **1.25.**

F UNIT PARTS EA 5.50

For Athearn, Stewart and other F units.

235-208 235-209

235-208 A Unit
Includes front step, walkway platform, coupler draft gear, draft gear detail and rear door.
235-209 B Unit
Includes door, coupler draft gear and backup light for each end.

GE DETAIL SETS

Complete sets of parts to detail your Dash 9-44CW or AC4400CW to match specific prototypes.
235-230 SP, CSX, NS and CP **15.95.**
235-231 CNW, UP **13.95.**
235-232 Santa Fe **14.95.**

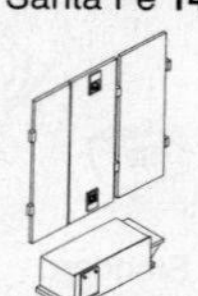

235-269 Brass Etched Access Doors & Capacitor Starter Box **3.95** *NEW*
White metal and bronze. For post 1995 GE AC4400CW.

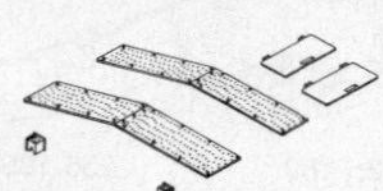

235-270 Bronze Etched Walkway Detail Set **5.95** *NEW*
White metal and bronze. For GE Dash 9-44CW or AC4400CW. Includes rear radiator walkway plates, walkway access hatches and lifting lugs

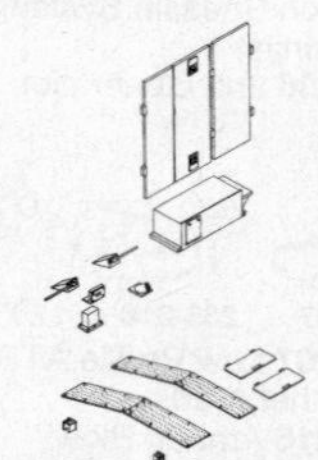

235-272 Locomotive Detail Set **12.50** *NEW*
White metal, brass and bronze. Set includes brass access doors, capasitor starter box, etched bronze walkway plates, lifting lugs and fuel filler.

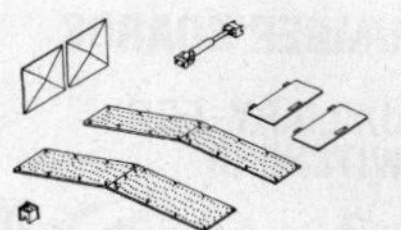

235-273 Bronze Etched Detail Kit **8.50** *NEW*
White metal and bronze. Set includes radiator plates, access hatches, lifting lugs, 4 "x" panels and anti-hunting dampers for BNSF and NS GE Dash 9-44CWs.

HANDBRAKES

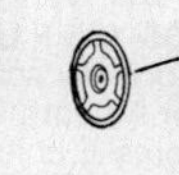

235-179 235-132 235-177

235-179 EMD/GE Wheel Only pkg(2) **1.00**
235-132 Ratchet Handbrake **1.00**
Standard on most EMD and other hood units.
235-177 Locomotive Type - Wheel w/Gear Box **1.50**
235-246 Handbrake Chain Pulley Beam pkg(2) **1.50.**

235-1016 Handbrake and Pulley Mount **1.50**

SP BARREL TYPE HEADLIGHTS EA 1.25

235-108 235-109

235-108 Bolted Face
235-109 Hinged Face
For first generation GP and SD units.

PYLE HEADLIGHTS

TWIN SEALED BEAM PKG(2) EA 1.00

235-114 235-117

235-114 Early
235-117 Late

GYRALIGHT PKG(2) EA 1.00

235-115 235-116 235-148

235-115 Single
235-116 Twin - Early
235-148 Twin - Flush Mount

MARS LIGHTS PKG(2) EA 1.00

235-112 235-113

235-112 Signal
235-113 Twin Signal

NOSE MOUNTED LIGHTS EA 1.00

235-137 235-138

235-137 Mars
235-138 Pyle
Integral with nose, used on some EMD 2nd generation hood units, one-piece casting with mounting instructions, locos require modification.

235-133 235-162

235-133 Barrel Type pkg(2) **2.00**
For GP7/9s of WP and CN.
235-162 E&F Unit Back-Up Light, pkg(2) **1.00**
Single sealed beam.

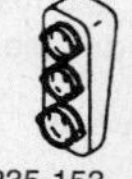

235-153 235-200

235-153 Oscitrol pkg(2) **1.00**
For Amtrak E units and ICG rebuilt hood units.
235-200 Nose Headlight/Warning Light **1.25**
Used by SP and some other roads, mounted on low nose.

DITCH LIGHTS

235-228 235-229

235-228 EMD Style (Pilot Top Mount) **2.95**
235-229 GE Style w/Bulbs (Pilot End Mount) **2.95**
Working accessory, includes lamp housings and micro-bulbs.

235-243 With Platforms & Bulbs **3.50.**

HEADLIGHT SETS - SOUTHERN PACIFIC

To make diesels more visible, SP applied additional warning lights to virtually all types of diesels. Sets are complete with mounting brackets, lights and basic instructions.

MARS LIGHTS, PRE-1958 HOOD UNITS

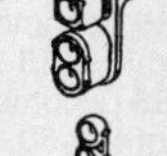

235-100 235-101

235-100 Single End (6 pieces) **2.25**
235-101 Double End (8 pieces) **2.75**

MARS LIGHTS, SD7/9

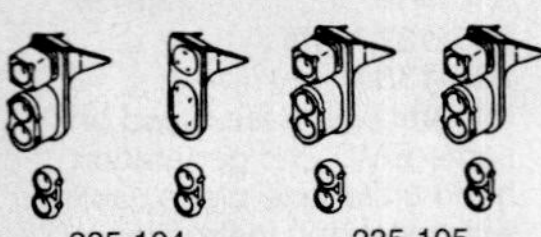
235-104 235-105

235-104 Single End (6 pieces) **2.25**
235-105 Double End (8 pieces) **2.75**

PYLE LIGHTS, POST 1958 HOOD UNITS

235-102 235-103

235-102 Single End (6 pieces) **2.25**
235-103 Double End (8 pieces) **2.75**

SP REBUILD

235-178 Modern-Rear **1.50**
Use with #235-200 (sold separately) for most 2nd generation SP power.

MU CABLES EA 1.95 (UNLESS NOTED)

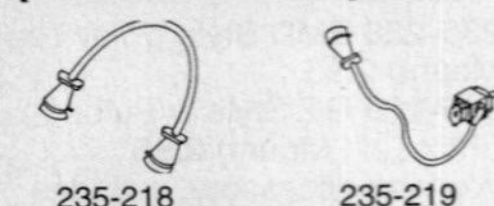
235-218 235-219

235-218 Double Plugs pkg(4)
235-219 Receptacle, Plug pkg(2)

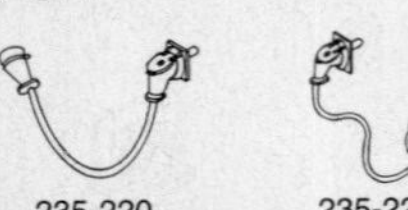
235-220 235-221

235-220 Receptacle w/Two Plugs pkg(2)
235-221 Dummy Receptacle pkg(2)
235-236 Double-Ended Receptacle & Two Receptacle pkg(2)

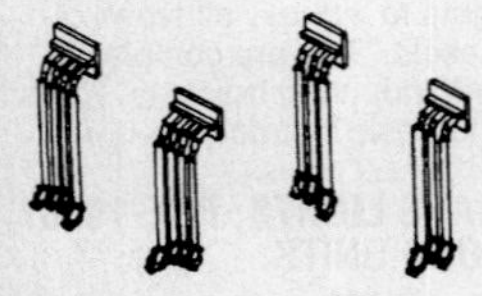
265 266

235-265 Locomotive 4 Cluster Set pkg(4) **3.75**
235-266 Locomotive 3 Cluster Set pkg(4) **3.50**
235-452 With Two Types of Stands **2.95**

NUMBER BOARDS

AUXILIARY- FOR SWITCHERS

235-136 235-156

235-136 EMD pkg(2) **1.00**
235-156 Alco pkg(2) **1.25**

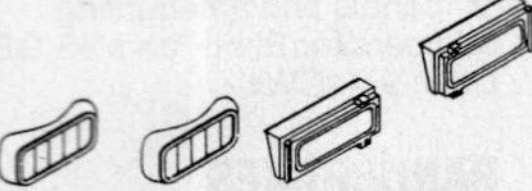
235-165 235-249

235-165 F Unit pkg(2) **1.00**
Correctly scaled and designed for Athearn F7A, also used on some E units.
235-249 GE Dash 7/8/9, AC4400CW pkg(2) **1.35**

PILOTS

235-130 235-141

235-130 Low Profile Snowplow **1.75**
Replaces footboards on 2nd generation EMD and GE hood units.
235-141 Passenger GP9 **2.50**
Used on SP units.

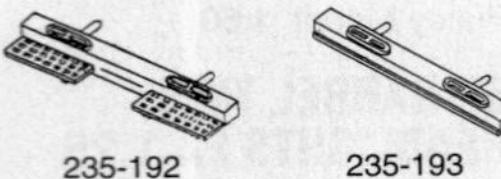
235-192 235-193

235-192 Beam w/Footboards pkg(2) **1.50**
235-193 Beam Only pkg(2) **1.25**

ROTARY BEACONS

White metal base with styrene lens.

235-106 235-126

235-106 Roof Mount **1.00**
235-126 "Western-Cullen" **1.00**
Type D-312 used by UP, BN, ATSF and others.

SAND FILLER HATCHES PKG(4) EA 1.25

235-201 235-202 235-203

235-201 EMD GP7 through GP20
235-202 Alco
235-203 GE
235-241 GE Dash 8, 9 & AC Series-Set **1.75**.
Rear housing and filler hatches for newer GE power.

SNOW PLOWS EA 1.75 (UNLESS NOTED)

Metal castings duplicate various styles of pilot plows installed on many diesels.

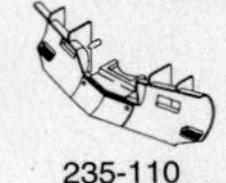

235-110 235-120

235-110 With Footboards
For 2nd generation hood units of SP, UP and WP.
235-120 Early Hood Units
1st and some 2nd generation hood units of Spokane, Portland & Seattle (BN), IC, SP, CN including Alco Centuries.

235-140 235-150

235-140 Western Style
Used on 2nd generation hood units of SP, UP, and WP.
235-150 Weed Cutter
For hood units of ATSF, Conrail and others

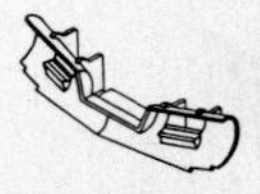

235-155 235-160

235-155 Standard
Most common type, used by ATSF, BN, CNW and WP.
235-160 F & E Unit Type **2.25**
Used by Amtrak, GN (BN), SP and WP.

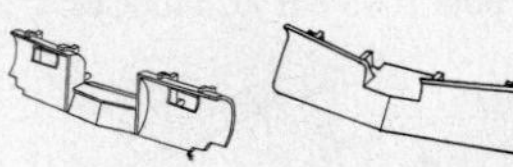
235-180 235-185

235-180 Flat
235-185 Low Profile, NP

235-205 235-206

235-205 Convex
Used on Chessie System EMD hood units.
235-206 2nd Generation Hood Units

235-207 235-216 235-217

235-207 Low Profile ATSF and other roads.
235-216 Amtrak Plow
235-217 EMD Passenger Hood Unit Plow

235-233 235-234 235-235

235-233 SP, CP Type
235-234 CNW & UP Type
235-235 Santa Fe Type
235-255 Open MU Doors - ATSF & BN
235-256 CSX, NS
235-257 Canadian Roads - BCR & CN

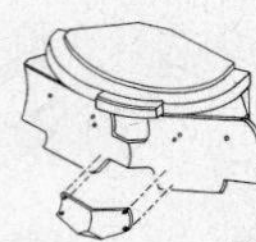

235-264 Alco PA Pilot (SP) **2.50**

SPARK ARRESTORS PKG(2) EA 1.50

"SUPER"

Used on nonturbocharged units

235-123 235-124 235-125

235-123 Lifting Type
235-124 Nonlifting Type
For EMD units of DRGW, MP, CNW, GM&O and SOO.
235-125 Harco Centrifugal Type pkg(2)
For nonturbocharged EMDs from UP, BN, BAR and ARR.

WINTERIZATION HATCHES

Used on locos of roads operating in colder areas. Hatches redirect radiator heat back into the hood to keep electrical equipment warm and dry. Styrene parts.

EARLY EMD EA 1.00

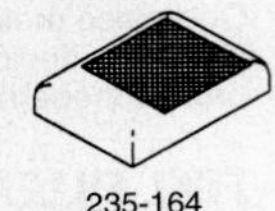
235-163 235-164

235-163 F Units
Used on both A and B units
235-164 GP/SD Units
For EMD GP7/9, GP20 and SD7/9.

48" - LATER EMD EA 1.50

235-211 235-212 235-213

235-211 GP50
235-212 SD45, F45, GP18
235-213 Square - SD45, F45

FREIGHT CAR DETAILS

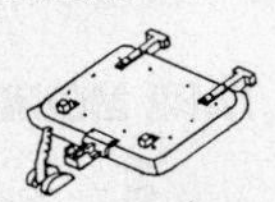

235-1003 Equipco Reefer Hatch pkg(4) Styrene **2.00**

BRAKE GEAR SETS EA 1.85

Complete exterior and underbody details for box cars, adaptable to other cars. Styrene.

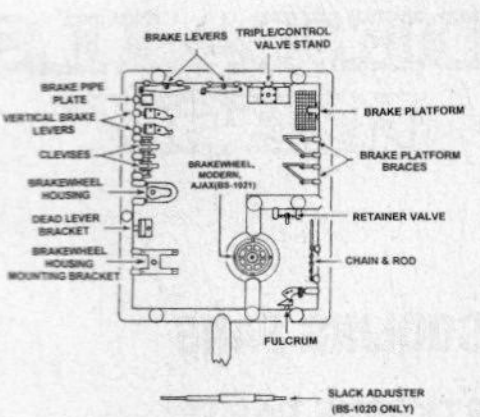

235-1020 Modern 1960-Present
Includes slack adjuster and vertical "Hook & Eye" lever detail.

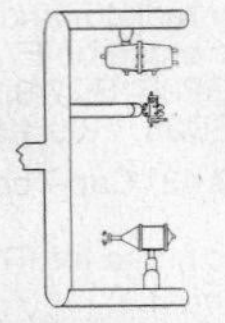

235-1021 Early 1940-1975
Includes Ajax brakewheel.

CUSHION COUPLER POCKETS EA 2.50

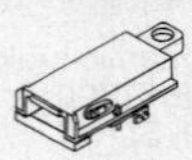
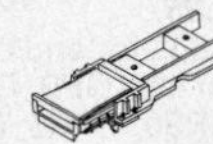
235-1009 235-1010

235-1009 Caboose & Freight Cars pkg (2)
235-1010 Most 60' Cars

DOORS

"RAILBOX" TYPES PKG(2) EA 1.00

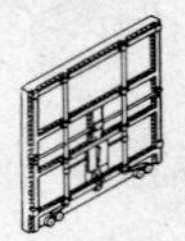

235-147 235-168

235-147 10' Plug
235-168 10' Sliding
For Athearn "Railbox" car, can be installed on other 50' to 60' cars.

8' DOORS

235-181 235-1002

235-181 With Guides & Tack Boards pkg(2) **1.75**
235-1002 Panel Door pkg(2) **2.00**

DREADNAUGHT ENDS PKG(2) EA 2.00

4-4 style, one-piece styrene parts replace ends on many freight cars.

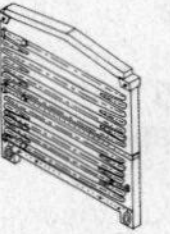
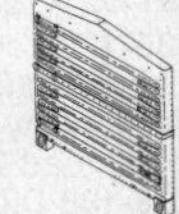
235-1000 235-1001

235-1000 Square Corners
Used on cars built 1930-1940.

235-1001 Round Corners
Used on cars built 1940-1950.

DETAILS WEST

HITCHES EA 3.45 (UNLESS NOTED)

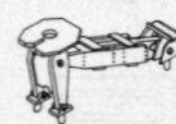
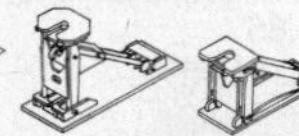

235-1004 235-1007 235-1008

235-1004 Piggyback Hitch **6.95**

235-1007 Pullman-Standard Rigid

235-1008 ACF Model 6-2 Cushioned Fixed Hitch

235-1011 235-1012 235-1013

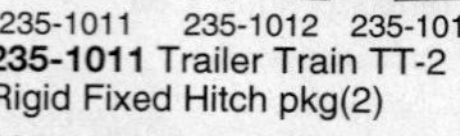

235-1011 Trailer Train TT-2 Rigid Fixed Hitch pkg(2)

235-1012 Pullman-Standard Cushioned Fixed Hitch pkg(2)

235-1013 ACF Model 5 Rigid-Wrench Operated Retractable Hitch pkg(2)

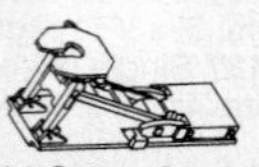

235-1014 Spine Car Hitch pkg(5) **7.95**

INTERMODAL DETAILS

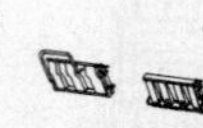

235-1015 235-1017

235-1015 Flat Car Restraint Curbs **5.95**
Includes container end fixed restraint curbs and fold down restraint curbs, fits 60' and 89' Flat cars.

235-1017 Bridge Plates for Piggyback Flats pkg(2) **1.75**

LADDERS

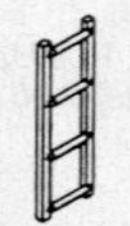

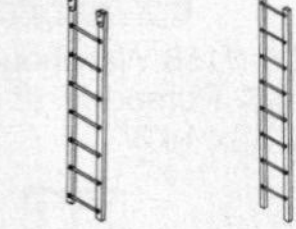

235-169 235-1006 235-1005

235-169 4-Rung Ladder pkg(8) **1.00**
Standard on new and rebuilt freight cars, styrene.

235-1006 7-Rung Ladder w/Brackets pkg(4) **1.25**

235-1005 8-Rung ladder pkg(4) **1.25**

LOG BUNKS

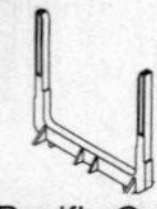

235-171 Pacific Car & Foundry Type pkg(4) **2.50**
Converts 40' and 50' flat cars into log carriers, used by BN, MILW and UP.

UNDERFRAMES EA 1.75 (UNLESS NOTED)

Styrene parts can be used with many freight car kits, include under-car cushioning details.

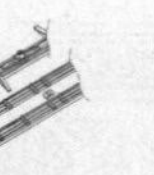
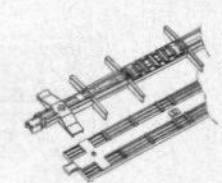

235-182 235-183

235-182 50' Hydra-Cushion
235-183 50' Evans
235-182 50' Hydra-Cushion w/Brake Set **2.25**
235-183 50' "Evans 20" Cushion w/Brake Set **2.25**

DETAIL KIT

235-1018 Spine Car Detail Kit **15.95**

CABOOSE PARTS

235-1019 Smoke Stack, Vent and Antenna Set **2.95**

TRACKSIDE DETAILS

BATTERY VAULTS

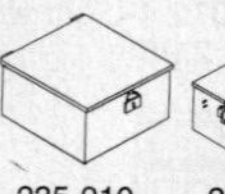

235-909 235-910 235-911

235-909 Small pkg(2) **1.25**
235-910 Medium pkg(2) **1.50**
235-911 Large pkg(2) **1.75**
Prototypes house storage batteries to power trackside signals, crossing protection and other electrical gear.

ELECTRIC RELAY CABINETS

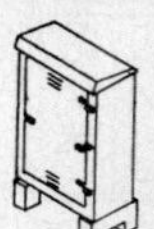
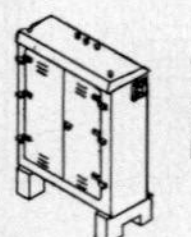
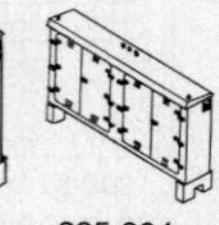

235-901 235-902 235-904

235-901 1 Door **1.75**
235-902 2 Door **1.85**
235-904 4 Door **1.95**
Prototypes house controls for crossing gates, flashers, signals, etc.

INSTRUMENT SHEDS

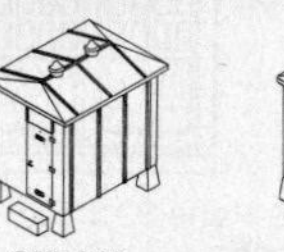
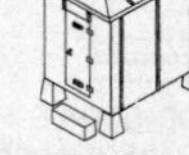
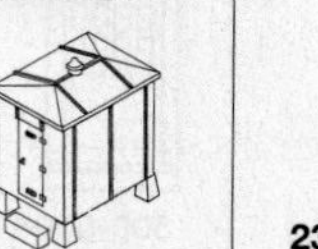

235-907 235-908

235-907 6 x 8' **3.95**
235-908 5 x 7' **2.95**

DETECTORS

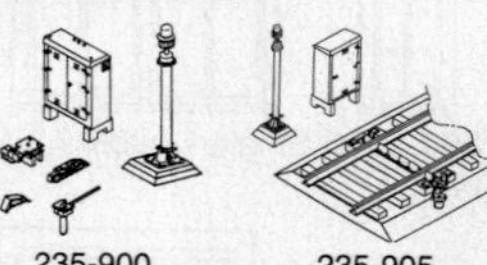

235-900 235-905

235-900 Hot Box **7.95**
235-905 Dragging Equipment **4.95**
To prevent derailments, the prototypes of this equipment monitor passing trains for overheated wheel bearings (#900) or anything dragging beneath a car (#905). Nonworking kits include castings to build a typical installation and instructions.

LUBRICATOR

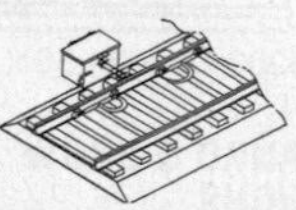

235-906 Flange Lubricator Set **2.95**
Installed on curves to reduce wheel and flange wear, prototype automatically applies grease to passing wheel flanges before car or loco enters a curve.

RAIL DETAILS

TURNOUT RAIL BRACES EA 2.95

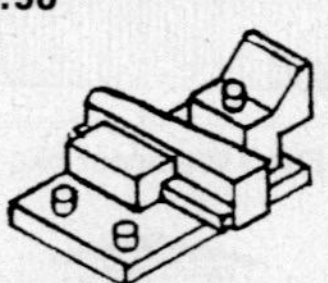

235-919 Adjustable pkg(12) ***NEW***

235-920 Rigid pkg(12) ***NEW***

RAIL BARS EA 2.75

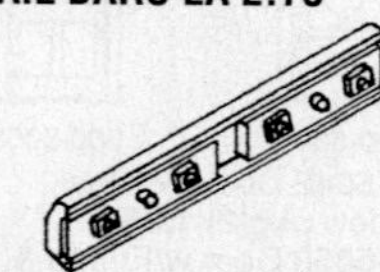

235-921 3 Bolt Fish Plate, Code 83, 70 pkg(12) ***NEW***

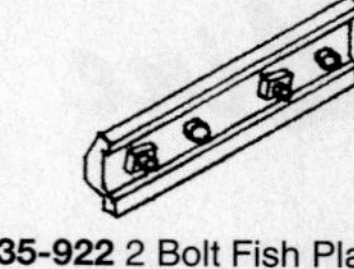

235-922 2 Bolt Fish Plate, Code 70 pkg(12) ***NEW***

SWITCH CONTROLS

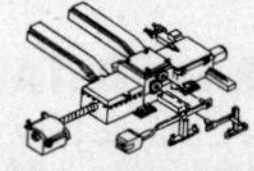

235-903 Motor & Tie Mount **1.50**
Simulates electric motors used on prototype turnouts controlled by a dispatcher.

SWITCH STANDS

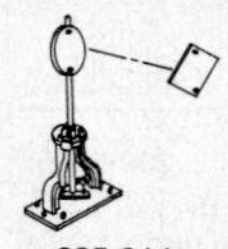

235-914 235-915

235-914 Style 1 pkg(2) **2.95**
235-915 Style 2 pkg(2) **2.95**

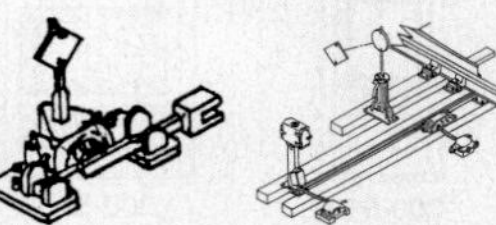

235-916 235-917

235-916 Ground Throw Switch 2 Sets **2.75**
235-917 With Interlock **3.75**

JACK & STANDS

235-450 Air Jack & Car Stands pkg(2) **2.25**
Used in shops to lift and support freight cars being repaired.

MEN WORKING SIGN/BLUE FLAG

235-451 Men At Work Sign **1.95**
Collapsible sign with bracket, mounts between tracks, includes decal sign. Prototype protects repair or inspection crews working on equipment.

PHONE BOX

235-912 Telephone Box w/Wood Post **1.50**

CROSSING FLASHER

235-913 Crossing Signal w/LEDs **19.95**
Includes crossbuck, pole, base and LEDs.

MISCELLANEOUS

HY-RAIL WHEELS

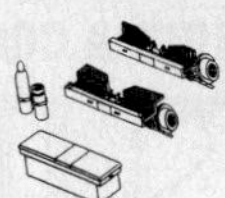

235-918 For Trident Vehicles Set **6.95**
Converts Chevy Pickup, Suburban or Blazer to railroad inspection/repair vehicle. Includes front and rear hy-rail wheels, toolbox and welding tanks.

KEIL-LINE MODELS

We have worked closely with this manufacturer to provide accurate delivery information at the time this catalog was published. Items listed in blue ink may not be available at all times. Current delivery information, along with a list of in-stock products for this line, can be found on our Web site at www.walthers.com.

HOPPER WEIGHTS PKG(2) EA 4.49

Improve car operation without hiding detail. Cast weights are designed for hidden installations. Bring light cars up to NMRA recommended weight for improved performance. No glue needed.

382-8707 Walthers Twin Hopper
382-8708 Athearn 2-Bay Hopper

AIR CONDITIONER UNIT

382-87962 For Passenger Car pkg(2) **5.99** ***NEW***

Grandt Line

Parts for HO and HOn3 equipment are highly detailed, made of injection molded styrene plastic unless noted.

STRUCTURAL DETAILS

BRACKETS & CORBELS

300-5074 Double-S Corbels 38" pkg(12) **2.05**

300-5151

300-5178

300-5151 14 x 17-1/2" Bracket pkg(20) **1.85**
300-5178 Porch Bracket pkg(24) **1.85**

300-5171

300-5172

300-5171 Victorian Corbels pkg(28) **2.05**
300-5172 Eave Bracket & Louvered Vent pkg(4) **2.05**

BUILDING DETAILS EA 2.05

300-5218

300-5219

300-5218 Corrugated Metal Roofing (2 sheets)
300-5219 Date Plaques/Numbers (2 sets)

CATALOG

300-9991 Grandt Line Catalog **4.25**

CHIMNEY & VENTS

300-5084

300-5107

300-5084 Engine House Stack Set pkg(3) **2.90**
Includes two 18" and one 9" stacks.
300-5107 Louvered Victorian Attic Vents pkg(4) **2.05**

CORNICE

300-5076 300-5020

300-5076 6 x 6 x 20" pkg(120) **3.40**
300-5020 "Wells Fargo" Office-Brick Set pkg(4) **2.05**

CRANK PIN DETAIL

300-5082 Plastic pkg(10) **1.85**
300-86082 Brass **5.65**

DEPOT DETAILS

RIO GRANDE SOUTHERN - "OPHIR"

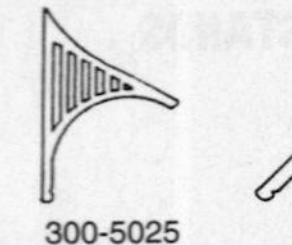

300-5025

300-5026

300-5025 Eaves pkg(6) **2.05**
300-5026 Gables pkg(4) **2.05**

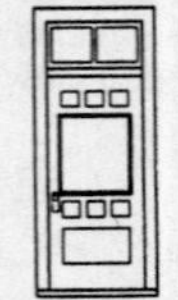

300-5197

300-5198

300-5197 36 x 84" Doors pkg(4) **2.05**
300-5198 Freight Doors pkg(3) **2.65**

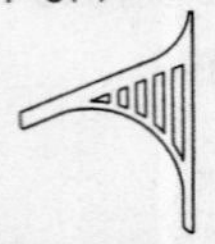

300-5200

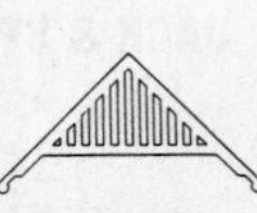

300-5201

300-5200 Eave Trim pkg(4) **1.85**
300-5201 Gable Trim pkg(4) **1.85**

300-5202 300-5027

300-5202 Roof Cresting Trim **2.95**
300-5027 Station Roof (7 Pieces) **3.10**

300-5263 Residence Door w/Arched Window Set **1.85**

RGS DEPOT WINDOWS EA 2.05

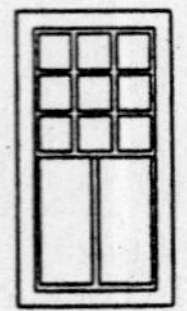

300-5193

300-5195

300-5193 36 x 76" pkg(8)
300-5195 4-Pane 36 x 82" pkg(4)

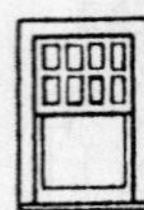

300-5194 9-Pane 32 x 53", 58 x 53" each

300-5196 Single/Double pkg(4)

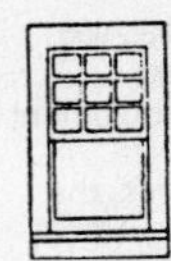

300-5199 10-Pane, 24 x 44", 51.5 x 51"

300-5203 Double, 36 x 82" pkg(4)

DURANGO & DRGW STATIONS

300-5013

300-5014

300-5013 Doors pkg(2) **1.85**
300-5014 Windows 36 x 87" pkg(8) **3.15**

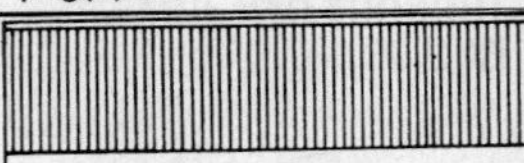

300-5015 Wainscot pkg(5) **2.35**

300-5016 Windows 36 x 44" pkg(8) **2.05**

300-5042

300-5058

300-5042 Doors w/Oval Window pkg(2) **1.85**
300-5058 Door w/Frame & Transom pkg(3) **2.05**

300-5057 Chimney pkg(3) **2.05**

300-5080 Baggage Room Door pkg(3) **2.05**

DOOR GRAB BOX

300-5243 15.25

DOORS

300-5021

300-5022

300-5021 Five Panel w/Frame pkg(3) **1.85**
300-5022 "Assay Office" Double, 5'9" pkg(2) **1.85**

300-5028

300-5072

300-5028 30" w/Window & Separate Frame pkg(3) **1.85**
300-5072 4-Light w/Transom pkg(4) **2.05**

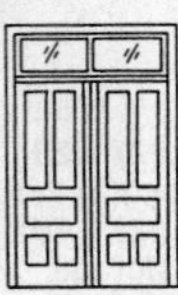

300-5073

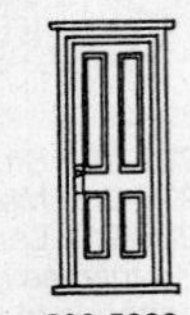

300-5088

300-5073 Double pkg(2) **1.85**
300-5088 Station 4-Panel, 2'6" x 7'6" pkg(3) **2.05**

300-5102

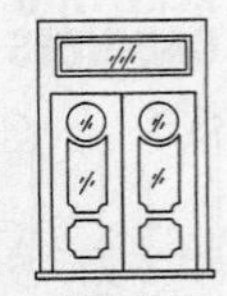

300-5109

300-5102 Engine House w/Hinges pkg(4) **2.95**
300-5109 Double w/Transom Round & Rectangular Panes pkg(3) **2.05**

300-5115 Victorian Store Front **1.85**

300-5131 2-Panel w/Frame (Tongue & Groove) pkg(3) **1.85**

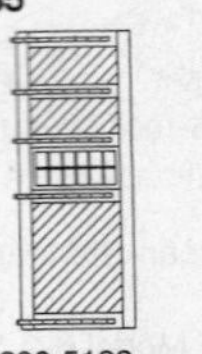

300-5133

300-5134

300-5133 Roundhouse w/Windows & Doors **2.65**
Fits 14'6" x 19' opening.
300-5134 36" w/Window and Transom pkg(3) **1.85**

300-5136

300-5137

300-5136 Double w/Iron Shutters, 5' x 9'7" pkg(2) **2.05**
300-5137 Single w/Iron Shutters, 4'2" x 9'7" pkg(2) **2.05**

300-5139

300-5149

300-5139 Factory Front w/Transom pkg(2) **1.85**
For masonry buildings, measures a scale 39 x 92"
300-5149 Double w/Transom & 2 Side Lights pkg(2) **1.85**

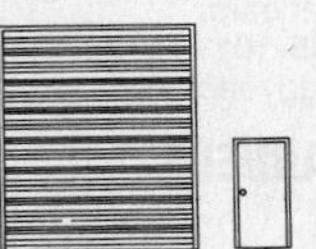

300-5158 Warehouse, Roll-Up & 36" Personnel (2 sets) **2.05**
12'6" x 14'3"

300-5163 33" w/Window & Transom pkg(3) **2.05**

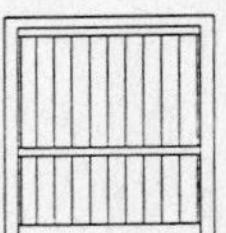

300-5267

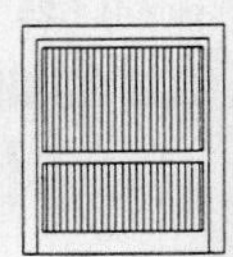

300-5268

300-5267 Warehouse .9 x 1.05" pkg(2) **2.05** ***NEW***
300-5268 Warehouse .8 x 1" pkg(2) **2.05** ***NEW***

Grandt Line

FENCE

300-5119 Victorian Picket Fence Set **2.05**

HINGES

300-5168 Reefer Door Hinge pkg(48) **2.05**

300-5095 Assortment (2 sets) **1.85**
300-86095 Assortment (Brass) **5.65**

LATTICE WORK

300-5064 Band Stand Lattice Work pkg(8) **2.90**
Can be adapted to Campbell Bandstand.

LOUVERED SHUTTERS PKG(16) EA 2.05

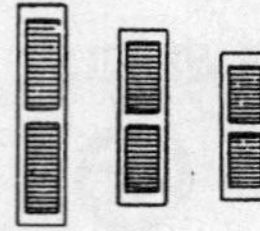

300-5173 18 x 56"
300-5174 18 x 68"
300-5175 18 x 87"

NUT-BOLT-WASHER

Illustrations enlarged to show detail.

7/8" NUT, 3-3/16" STEEL WASHERS

300-5101 Plastic pkg(175) **2.05**
300-86105 Brass pkg(35) **5.65**

2-1/2" NUT ON RECTANGULAR WASHERS

300-5113 Plastic pkg(100) **2.05**
300-86113 Brass pkg(20) **5.65**

2-1/2" NUT, 6-1/2" CAST IRON WASHERS

300-5123 Plastic pkg(100) **2.05**
300-86123 Brass pkg(20) **5.65**

2-1/2" HEX NUT-BOLT, NO WASHER

300-5135 Plastic pkg(100) **2.05**
300-86135 Brass pkg(20) **5.65**

300-5156 2-1/2" Cored, .020" pkg(80) **2.05**

1" SQUARE

300-5045 Plastic pkg(175) **2.05**
300-86045 Brass pkg(35) **5.65**

1-3/4" SQUARE NUT, BOLT, WASHER

300-5046 Plastic pkg(175) **2.05**
300-86046 Brass pkg(35) **5.65**

1-1/4" NUT, 3" MALLEABLE IRON WASHER

300-5066 Plastic pkg(175) **2.05**
300-86066 Brass pkg(20) **5.65**

2-1/2" NUT, 5" MALLEABLE IRON WASHER

300-5093 Plastic pkg(100) **2.05**
300-86093 Brass pkg(20) **5.65**

2-1/2" NUT, CARTER BROTHERS ELLIPTICAL WASHER

300-5094 Plastic pkg(100) **2.05**
300-86094 Brass pkg(20) **5.65**

2-1/2" NUT, 6" SQUARE WASHER

300-5096 Plastic pkg(100) **2.05**
300-86096 Brass pkg(20) **5.65**

2-1/4" NUT-BOLT, 4-1/2" FLAT STEEL WASHER

300-5098 Plastic pkg(100) **2.05**
300-86098 Brass pkg(35) **5.65**

3" NUT, 4-1/2" FLAT STEEL WASHER

300-5099 Plastic pkg(100) **2.05**
300-86099 Brass pkg(35) **5.65**

1-3/4" NUT-BOLT, 2-1/2" STEEL WASHERS

300-5100 Plastic pkg(175) **2.05**
300-86100 Brass pkg(35) **5.65**

STAR

300-5270 pkg(100) **2.05** *NEW*

PORCH RAILINGS EA 2.05 (UNLESS NOTED)

300-5017 300-5019

300-5017 "Wells Fargo" Balcony pkg(3)
300-5019 "Gay Nineties" pkg(4)

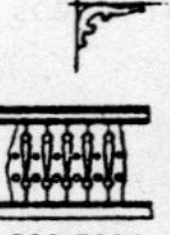

300-5034 300-5035

300-5034 Ornamental w/Roof Bracket (4 Pieces)
300-5035 Turned Spindle pkg(3)

300-5065 "Masonic Hall" Balcony, Brackets (2 Pieces) **2.35**

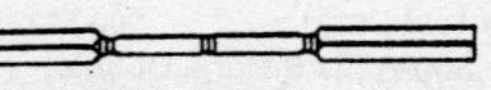

300-5079 Porch Pillar Turned Wood Type pkg(8)

300-5083 35" High, 1" Bars on 6" Centers pkg(6) **2.90** (Approximately 100 scale feet)

ROOFS EA 3.95

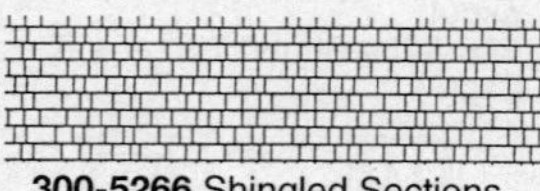

300-5266 Shingled Sections pkg(8) *NEW*
Two sections 3.58 x 1.65", one section 2.4 x 1.475", one section 1.3 x 1.5".

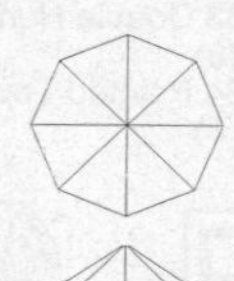

300-5269 Octagonal Bandstand *NEW*

SHEAVES

MINEHEAD FRAME - 60" DIAMETER

300-5091 Plastic (2 sets) **1.85**
300-86091 Brass **5.65**
With pillow blocks.

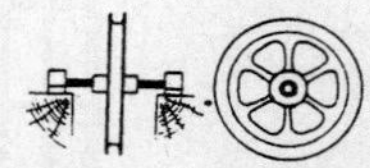

300-5122 43" Diameter Cable Sheave w/Bearings pkg(2) **1.85**

SHINGLES

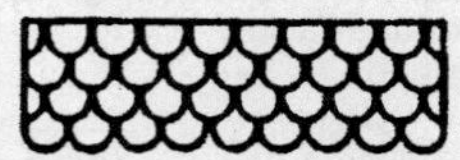

300-5216 Scalloped pkg(2) **2.05**

STAIRCASES

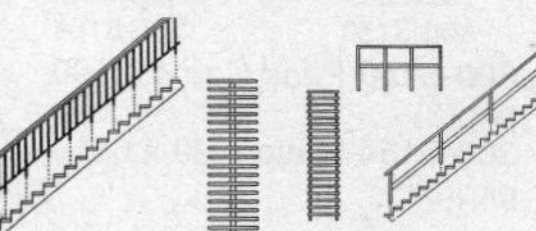

300-5176 300-5177

300-5176 Modern Cast Iron **2.05**
300-5177 Open Wood **2.65**

STATION DETAILS

300-5089 Rotary Order Board **2.05**
Used by many Colorado narrow gauge lines.

300-5062 Lamp Reflectors & Bulbs pkg(18) **2.05**
Nonworking, molded in clear plastic. Simulates outdoor lighting used on all types of railroad, commercial and industrial buildings.

STOVES EA 1.85

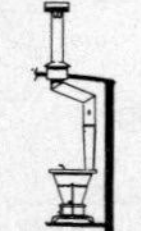
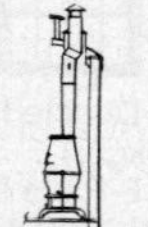

300-5007 300-5008 300-5023

300-5007 DRGW Caboose Car w/Stack
300-5008 DRGW Passenger Car w/Stack
300-5023 Stovepipe w/Elbow Bonnet, Thimble

TRIM

300-5018 Spool for Upper Porch (4 Pieces) **2.05**
300-5075 Corbel Double S 26" **2.05**

300-5152 Entrance pkg(8) **1.85**
300-5162 Queen Anne Trim **2.05**

300-5211 Architectural Details-Dentils pkg(3) **1.85**

300-5227 300-5228

300-5227 Gable pkg(4) **1.85**
300-5228 Newel Post pkg(8) **1.85**

300-5229 Spool Bracket pkg(8) **1.85**

300-5246 Widow's Walk Iron Railing (4 Pieces) **3.05**

300-5258 Gable Trim Assortment pkg(2) **2.05**

TRIM GRAB BOX

300-5244 17.50
Assorted trim pieces, ideal for scratchbuilding, kitbashing or superdetailing.

WATER TANK PARTS

300-5038 Hoop Fasteners pkg(99) **3.40**

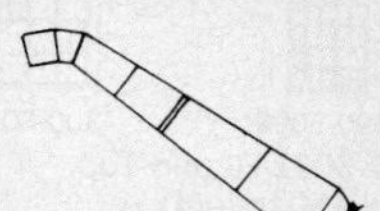

300-5054 Spout Set **2.05**

WINDOWS EA 2.05 (UNLESS NOTED)

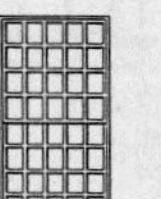
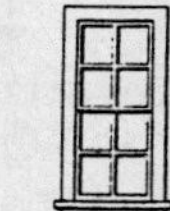

300-5009 300-5010 300-5029

300-5009 Double Hung 36 x 56" pkg(8)
300-5010 Roundhouse, 60 x 120" pkg(6)
300-5029 27 x 64" Double Hung pkg(8)

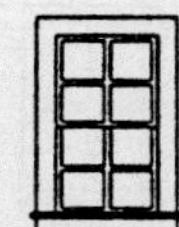

300-5011 300-5030

300-5011 30" Silverton Station Attic pkg(4)
300-5030 Double Hung 27 x 48" pkg(8)

Grandt Line

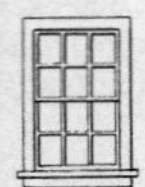

300-5031 300-5032

300-5031 Double Hung 36 x 64" pkg(8)
300-5032 Double Hung 36 x 52" pkg(8)

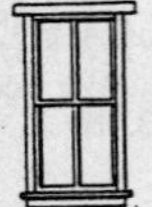

300-5060 300-5081

300-5060 Station 30 x 69" pkg(8)
300-5081 Horizontal Sliding 52 x 33" pkg(8)

300-5087 300-5077

300-5087 Gothic Church 48 x 90" pkg(4)
300-5077 Double-Hung Masonry 72 x 102" pkg(4)

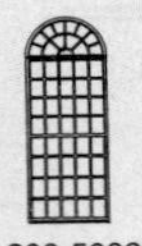
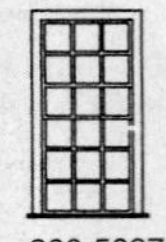
300-5092 300-5097

300-5092 Round Top, 60 x 150" pkg(4)
300-5097 Engine House 18-Pane, 42 x 91" pkg(8)

300-5112 Attic, Rectangular 6-Light pkg(8)

300-5116 Victorian, 4 Single, 2 Double (2 sets)

300-5117 300-5126

300-5117 Double Hung 36 x 64", 4-Pane pkg(8)
300-5126 Gothic Church and Residence pkg(4)

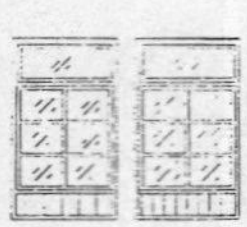
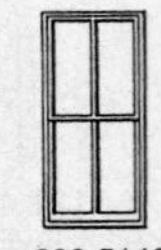
300-5138 300-5140

300-5138 Store Window, 65 x 115" pkg(4)
300-5140 Double Hung 4-Pane Factory 42 x 91" pkg(4)

300-5150 300-5154

300-5150 Peak Cap 41 x 90" pkg(8)
300-5154 Mason, 30 x 65" pkg(8)

300-5157 Window & Door Set 115 x 97" (2 sets) **2.05**

300-5160 300-5161

300-5160 Queen Anne pkg(3)
300-5161 Queen Anne Single pkg(3)

300-5165 Storefront Set **2.65**

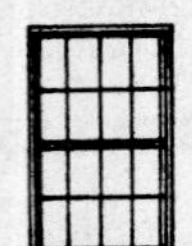

300-5179 Double Hung, 42 x 72" pkg(6)
300-5204 6-Pane Double Hung, Triple 100 x 92" pkg(3)

300-5205 4-Pane Double Hung, Double 65 x 92" pkg(3)

300-5206 Diamond Patterned pkg(2) **1.85**

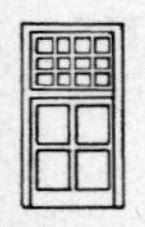
300-5208 300-5209

300-5208 Double Hung 85 x 48"
300-5209 Double Hung 34 x 67"

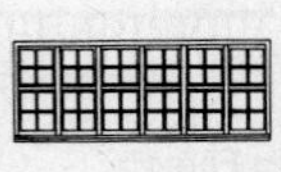

300-5210 300-5220

300-5210 48-Pane Double Hung 186 x 70" pkg(2)
300-5220 Double Pointed, 33 x 88" pkg(8)

300-5212 300-5215

300-5212 Double Round-Top
300-5215 Double 4-Pane 30 x 62"

300-5221 300-5222

300-5221 8-Pane Double, 63 x 69" pkg(4)
300-5222 16-Pane Double, 59 x 64" pkg(4)

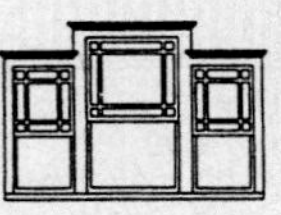
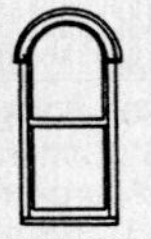
300-5223 300-5230

300-5223 Dormer/Gable pkg(4)
300-5230 Round Top, 2' x 6' pkg(8)

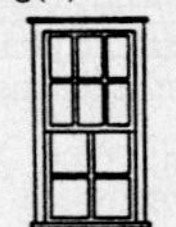

300-5233 300-5234

300-5233 Double Hung, 32 x 70" pkg(8)
300-5234 Pointed Top 30 x 86" pkg(8)

300-5239 300-5240

300-5239 Single Sash 28 x 26" pkg(4)
300-5240 Round, Masonry 65" Diameter pkg(2) **1.85**

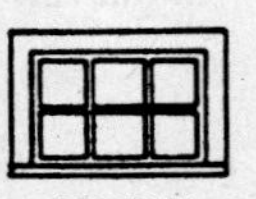
300-5060 300-5242

300-5241 Shed or Attic pkg(8)
300-5242 Horizontal pkg(8)

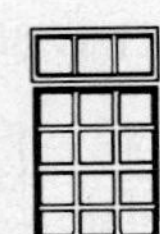

300-5245 Window/Transom Set pkg(4)

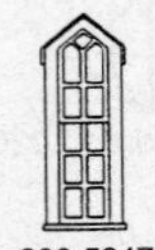

300-5247 300-5248

300-5247 Double Hung 11-Pane pkg(8)
300-5248 Attic Peaked Single Pane pkg(8)

300-5251 300-5252

300-5251 Horizontal pkg(8) **2.05**
300-5252 Double pkg(8)

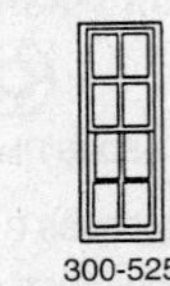
300-5254 300-5255

300-5254 Gothic pkg(8)
300-5255 8-Pane Double-Hung pkg(8)

300-5249 300-5256

300-5249 Victorian Attic pkg(8)
300-5256 20-Pane Arched pkg(8)

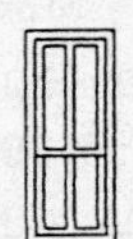

300-5250 Double-Hung 4-Pane pkg(8)
300-5261 Windows 4 Pane pkg(8)

300-5262 Half Round 13-Pane pkg(6)

300-5259 Peaked Top Window/Door Set pkg(2)

300-5264 300-5265

300-5264 4-Pane Single, 8-Pane Double pkg(2)
300-5265 4-Pane pkg(8)

WINDOW GRAB BOX

300-5192 Grab Box **17.80**
An assortment of windows for kitbashing, scratchbuilding, etc.

FREIGHT CAR DETAILS

BRAKE GEAR SETS

WESTINGHOUSE NARROW GAUGE TYPE K

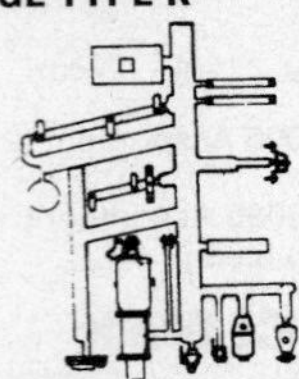

300-5040 Plastic **1.60**
300-86040 Brass **9.40**
300-5224 Colorado & Southern NY Type **1.60**
Used on C&S cars with truss rod underframes, also used on F&CC box cars.

300-5232 Westinghouse AB **3.40**
Complete set with reservoirs, valve, rods, bell levers, chain and more.

BRAKE WHEELS

300-5225 C&S Brake Wheel pkg(4) **2.05**

15" LOVSTED

300-5067 Plastic pkg(4) **2.05**
300-86067 Brass pkg(2) **11.55**

DRGW 16" SPOKE

300-5037 Plastic pkg(4) **2.05**
300-86037 Brass pkg(2) **11.55**

BRAKE RODS

300-5184 With Clevis pkg(6) **2.05**
300-5189 With Chain pkg(2) **1.85**

REEFER DOOR LATCH KITS EA 2.05

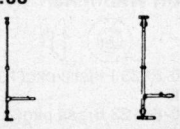

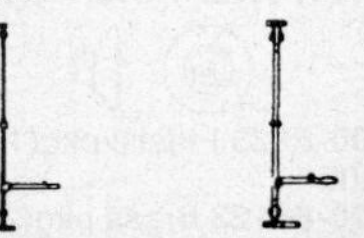
300-5166 300-5167

300-5166 Narrow Gauge pkg(4)
300-5167 Standard Gauge pkg(2)

Grandt Line

CABOOSE DETAILS

RIO GRANDE/RIO GRANDE SOUTHERN

Short Rio Grande/Rio Grande Southern caboose end detail, bolsters & needlebeams.

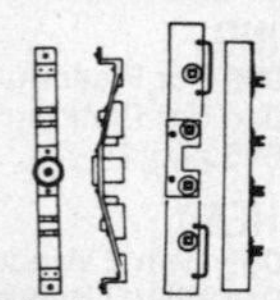

300-5090 Plastic **2.05**
300-86090 Brass pkg(2) **11.55**

COLORADO & SOUTHERN

300-5236 Pedestals & Journal Box Lids pkg(4) **2.40**

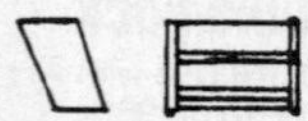

300-5237 Steps **1.60**

300-5238 Ladders pkg(2) **2.65**

FLAT CAR DETAILS

Includes bolster, end beam, striker plate & coupler used on DRGW 6000 series narrow gauge flat cars.

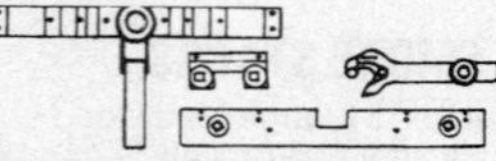

300-5183 Plastic-2 Complete Sets **1.85**
300-86183 Brass **5.65**

FREIGHT CAR DOORS

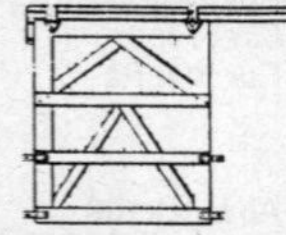

300-5170 Narrow Gauge Stock Car pkg(2) **1.85**
300-5207 Standard Box Car w/Camel Hardware pkg(2) **2.05**

GONDOLA PARTS

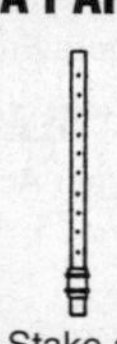

300-5108 Stake and Stake Pockets for 12" Boards pkg(40) **2.65**

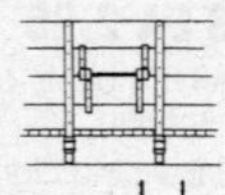

300-5118 Hinge Set for Side Dump Gondola (2 sets) **1.85**

300-5125 Standard Gauge Bolster pkg(4) **1.85**
Based on modified cast steel bolsters on high-side gondolas.

300-5128

300-5190

300-5128 Needlebeam & Subassembly for High Side Gondola pkg(4) **2.05**
300-5190 DRGW Stirrups pkg(20) **2.05**

300-86103 Brass Pillow Blocks pkg(12) **5.65**
Used on drop bottom door release bar.

GRAB IRONS

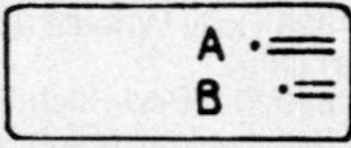

300-5191 Grab Iron Bending Fixture **1.60**
Make scale 17 and 20" straight grab irons for your equipment in minutes with this handy tool. Just insert a length of .008" wire (sold separately), bend with gentle finger pressure and trim.

HARDWARE KITS

Sets include the steel parts found on the prototypes.

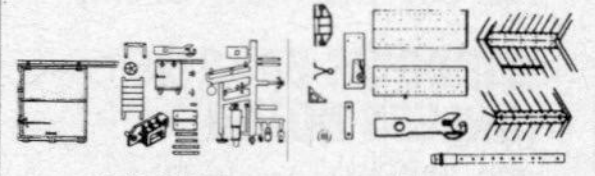

300-5001 300-5002

300-5001 DRGW Box Car **3.95**
300-5002 DRGW High Side Gondola **3.40**

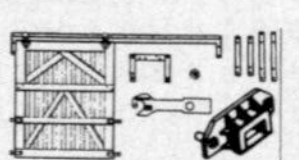

300-5004 DRGW Stock Car **3.40**
300-5103 Russell Log Car **1.85**

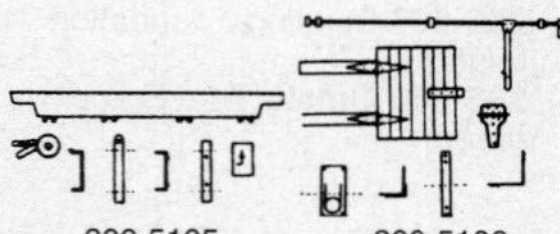

300-5105 300-5106

300-5105 Westside Lumber Co. Flat Car **1.85**
300-5106 Standard Gauge Reefer **3.15**

LOG BUNKS

300-5104 Pacific Car & Foundry Type pkg(2) **1.85**

NARROW GAUGE FREIGHT CAR DETAILS

300-5056 300-5068

300-5056 DRGW Box Car End Roof Walks pkg(4) **2.05**
300-5068 UTLX Tank Car Ends, 77" pkg(2) **1.85**

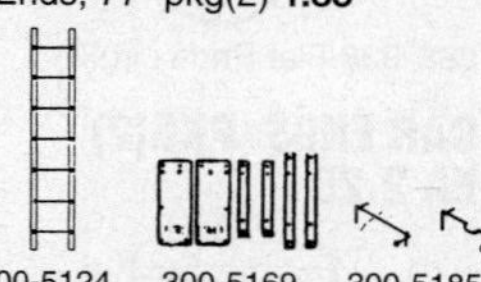

300-5124 300-5169 300-5185

300-5124 Ladders pkg(20) **1.85**
300-5169 Box Car Corner Plates pkg(4) **2.05**
300-5185 Uncoupling Levers pkg(2) **2.05**

QUEENPOSTS

6" W/BEAM HON3

300-5180 Plastic pkg(4) **2.05**
300-86180 Brass **5.65**

6" PLAIN

300-5050 Plastic pkg(24) **2.05**
300-86050 Brass pkg(6) **5.65**

3" W/BEAM

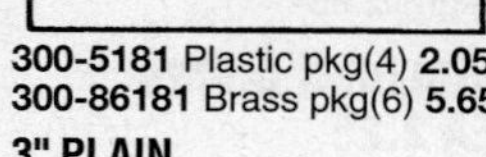

300-5181 Plastic pkg(4) **2.05**
300-86181 Brass pkg(6) **5.65**

3" PLAIN

300-5052 Plastic pkg(24) **2.05**
300-86052 Brass pkg(6) **5.65**

5" QUEENPOST ONLY

300-5051 Plastic pkg(24) **2.05**
300-86051 Brass pkg(6) **5.65**

10" QUEENPOST ONLY

300-5053 Plastic pkg(24) **2.05**
300-86053 Brass pkg(6) **5.65**

REEFER DETAILS

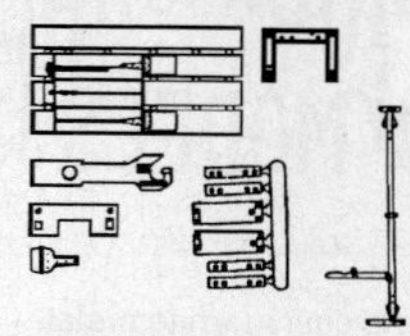

300-5005 DRGW Hardware Kit **3.40**

STAKE POCKETS

SINGLE U-BOLT

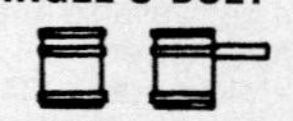

300-5012 Plastic pkg(24) **2.05**
300-86012 Brass pkg(12) **10.75**

DRGW DOUBLE U-BOLT

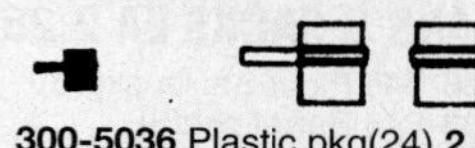

300-5036 Plastic pkg(24) **2.05**
300-86036 Brass pkg(12) **12.60**

STIRRUP STEPS

Used on box cars, flat cars, stock cars and high-side gondolas.

300-5129 Red Delrin pkg(24) **2.05**

300-5130 Black Delrin pkg(24) **2.05**
300-86129 Brass pkg(4) **5.95**

TURNBUCKLES

DRGW prototypes are full-scale and cored for .015 wire.

300-5039 Plastic pkg(24) **2.05**
300-86039 Brass pkg(16) **11.55**

PASSENGER CAR PARTS

CAR WINDOWS

300-5059 Outfit (Work) Car pkg(8) **2.05**

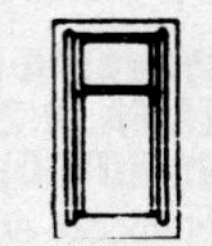

300-5069 Narrow for DRGW Coach pkg(30) **2.60**

DRGW DOORS PKG(4) EA 2.05

300-5063 Caboose

300-5071 Combine Baggage

COACH END

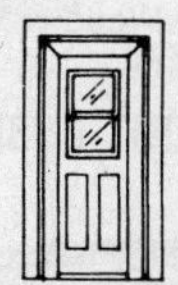

300-5070 Straight Top

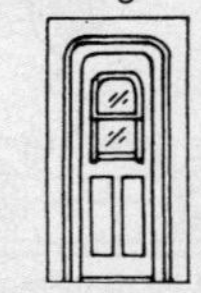

300-5078 Arch Top

ROOF DETAIL

Vents, smokejacks and more.

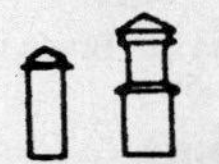

300-5043 Plastic **2.05**
300-86043 Brass **5.65**

MISCELLANEOUS

BAGGAGE WAGON KIT

300-5033 Plastic **2.35**
300-86033 Brass **20.25**
Common four-wheel type used at stations large and small.

CRIBBING

300-5260 Cribbing Sections 1 x 4" pkg(6) **5.25**

DRIVER CENTERS

Unmachined brass, for DRGW narrow gauge locos from Baldwin.

300-86101 36" C-16 pkg(8) **31.50**
300-86102 46" T-12 pkg(6) **26.25**

Grandt Line

DRUMS & BARRELS

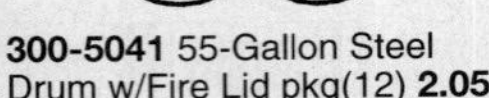

300-5041 55-Gallon Steel Drum w/Fire Lid pkg(12) **2.05**

300-5217 Wooden Barrels pkg(12) **2.40**

FAIRMONT PUSH CAR KITS

300-5164 HO **2.05**

300-5024 HOn3-Plastic **2.05**
300-86024 HOn3-Brass **12.60**

300-86104 16" Brass Wheels pkg(4) **11.55**

LIFT RINGS

300-5085 Plastic Assortment pkg(108) **2.05**
300-86085 Brass **5.65**

WAGON WHEELS

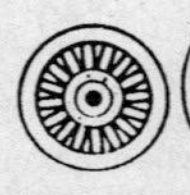

300-5143 Circus Wagon **2.40** Includes 36" front and 48" diameter rear wheels, adaptable to other types of heavy wagons.

Gloor Craft Models

Parts cast in white metal.

We have worked closely with this manufacturer to provide accurate delivery information at the time this catalog was published. Items listed in blue ink may not be available at all times. Current delivery information, along with a list of in-stock products for this line, can be found on our Web site at www.walthers.com.

BARRELS, CRATES, CANS & SACKS EA 2.25

288-845 Flour Sacks pkg(6)
288-846 Barrel pkg(3)
288-847 Crate pkg(3)
288-848 55 Gallon Drum pkg(3)
288-851 Cream Cans pkg(3)

BRAKE GEAR EA 2.25

288-826 5 Piece Brake Set
288-813 Brake Wheel Platform pkg(6)
288-822 Brake Wheel Platform pkg(6)
288-844 Ratchet Brake Arm pkg(4)
288-862 Brake Wheel pkg(4)
288-888 Brake Wheel w/Pin pkg(4)
288-890 Ajax Holder pkg(4)
288-896 "K" Brake Cylinder, Large pkg(4)

CAR DETAILS EA 2.25 (UNLESS NOTED)

288-820 Freight Car Steps pkg(2)
288-859 Coupler Pocket, Flared pkg(4)
288-861 Grab Irons pkg(12) **3.25**
288-863 Caboose Steps, AAR Style pkg(4) **3.25**
288-884 Freight Car Steps pkg(2)
288-897 Poling Pocket pkg(12)
288-898 "Z" Braces pkg(8)

PENNSYLVANIA CAR DETAILS EA. 2.25 (UNLESS NOTED)

288-824 Caboose Antenna **3.25**
288-869 Caboose Steps pkg(4) **3.25**
288-870 Smokejack pkg(2)
288-886 Caboose Doors pkg(2)
288-887 Caboose Window pkg(4)
288-893 ND Type Steps **3.25**
288-894 ND Wheel Housing pkg(4)
288-895 ND Brake Shoe with Arm pkg(8)

FLAT CAR PARTS EA 2.25

288-885 Stake Pocket pkg(12)
288-889 End Sill pkg(2)

TANK CAR PARTS EA 2.25

288-834

288-835

288-834 Manway Covers pkg(3)
288-835 Vents pkg(4)
288-836 Unloading Valves pkg(4)
288-837 Placard pkg(12)

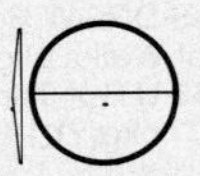

288-838 Flat Ends pkg(2)

CAR ENDS PKG(2) EA 2.25

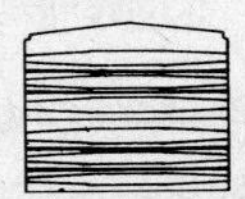

288-832 Express
288-812 Freight
288-831 Hi Cube

CHIMNEY & VENTS EA 2.25

288-865 Roof Vent
288-872 Chimney, Short pkg(2)

FREIGHT CAR PLUG DOORS EA 2.25

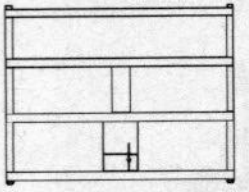

288-830

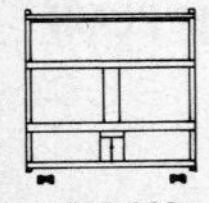

288-833

288-830 10' w/Opener Wheels pkg(2)
288-833 10 x 12' pkg(2)
288-892 Plug Door w/Handles pkg(2) **2.95**

BUILDING DOORS EA 2.25

288-858 Freight, Single pkg(2)
288-866 Entrance pkg(4)
288-879 6-Panel, Tall pkg(3)

DOWN SPOUTS EA 2.25

288-868 Down Spout pkg(4)
288-881 Short pkg(6)

HATCHES & COVERS EA 2.25

288-825 Long Coupler Pockets w/Covers pkg(2)

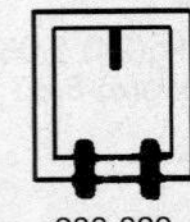

288-839

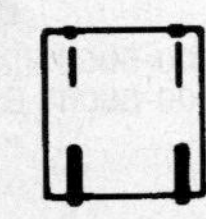

288-840

288-839 Reefer Hatches pkg(4)
288-840 Covered Hopper Hatch pkg(4)

LIGHTS EA 2.25

Nonworking models of various types of lighting.

288-849 Building Light, Antique pkg(4)
288-871 Marker Light pkg(4)
288-882 Vapor Lights pkg(4)
288-883 Building Lights, Small, Modern pkg(6)

STEPS & STAIRS EA 2.25

288-811 Stair Riser, 9-Step pkg(6)
288-855 Riser pkg(15)

MINIATURE TOOLS EA 2.25

288-852 Shovel pkg(3)
288-853 Broom pkg(6)
288-854 Fire Extinguisher pkg(3)

TRAILER DETAILS EA 2.25 (UNLESS NOTED)

288-827

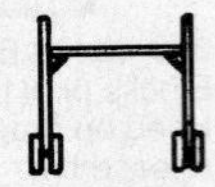

288-828

288-827 Dual Wheels pkg(4) **4.35**
288-828 Dolly Wheels (Landing Gear) pkg(2)
288-819 Flat Bed Hitch Set
288-842 Trailer Bumper pkg(4)
288-843 Suspension pkg(2)

WALKWAYS EA 2.25

288-829 End Walks pkg(6)
288-821 Corner End Walk pkg(4)
288-860 Roof Walk Set (3 Pieces)
288-891 End Walk Platform

WINDOWS EA. 2.25 (UNLESS NOTED)

288-856 4-Pane pkg(4)
288-857 12-Pane pkg(4)
288-864 Bay Window Set **4.35**
288-873 2-Pane, Large pkg(3)
288-874 5-Pane, Narrow pkg(4)
288-875 6-Pane, Large pkg(3)
288-876 1-Pane, Large pkg(4)
288-877 6-Pane, Long pkg(3)
288-878 5-Pane, Long pkg(3)

MISCELLANEOUS EA 2.25

288-823 Wire Coil pkg(6)
288-841 Flat Car Ramp pkg(6)
288-867 Building Foundation pkg(2)
288-880 Ornate Trim Brace pkg(6)

All parts are molded plastic unless noted.

DOORS EA .89

LOADING
411-1008 For Platform
411-1014 For Platform pkg(2)
411-1025 pkg(2)

OVERHEAD
411-1009 With 2 Windows
411-1011 With 2 Windows
411-1012 Overhead/Tailgate Doors
411-1015 Hinge Style

ENTRYWAYS W/2 WINDOWS EA .89

411-1006 Main
411-1016 Store Front

LOADING DOCK

411-1018 Use with #411-1008 & #411-1014 **.98**

MAIL BOXES

411-129 Four Each 1930s & 1960s Styles pkg(8) **2.95**
411-1021 Early 1900s Style pkg(4) **.89**
411-1022 1960s Style pkg(4) **.89**

ROOF DETAILS EA .89

411-1023 Asphalt Roof Section
411-1024 Coping for Top of Building

SIDEWALK

411-1019 With Corner **.89**

SMOKE STACKS

411-131 Large Metal for Factory pkg(4) **3.45**
411-1020 pkg(2) **.89**

TWO-STORY FRAMES EA .89

411-1002 For Windows
411-1003 First Floor
411-1004 For Inserts

WALL

411-1010 All Brick **.89**

WINDOWS

411-130 40-Pane for Factory pkg(6) **2.95**
411-1005 With Brick **.89**
411-1007 Office Windows w/Brick **.89**
411-1017 Store Front **.89**

WINDOW "GLASS"

411-1900 Clear Acetate **.89**

HI-TECH DETAILS
FOR THE DISCRIMINATING MODELER

Carefully engineered for prototype accuracy and ease of construction, each thinwall kit is designed for use on locos with scale width hoods. Each cab features separate windows and doors of the correct size, which can be positioned open or closed. Separate door handles are provided for extra realism. The roof contour matches the real thing.

GE DIESEL CABS EA 6.95 (UNLESS NOTED)

PRE 1972

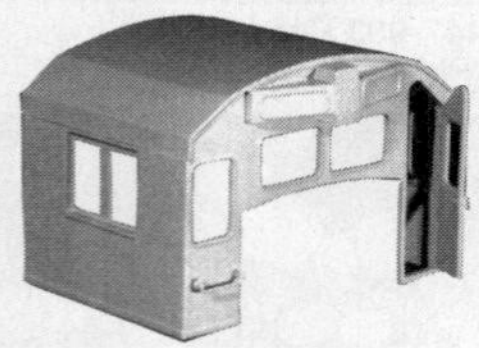

331-5000 2 Window
331-5001 4 Window
331-5002 4 Window w/Small Windows Plated Over

POST 1972
331-5003 2 Window

331-5004 4 Window
331-5005 4 Window w/Small Windows Plated Over

HIGH HOOD
331-5006 2 Window Cab
331-5007 4 Window Cab

331-5008 4 Window Cab w/Small Windows

U-25 SERIES

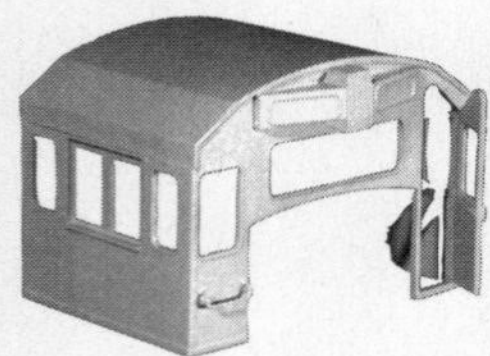

331-5010 Single-Pane Front Window

SP CAB KIT

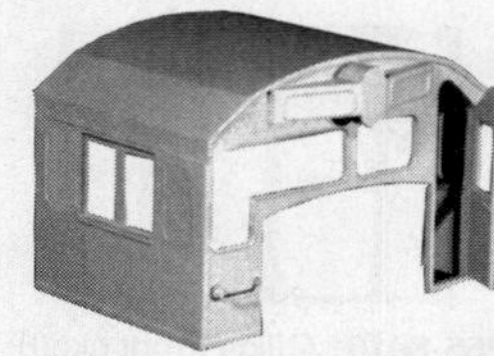

331-5009 "L" Window **7.50**

WIDE CAB
331-6011 Nose Door **2.95** *NEW*

B UNIT CONVERSION KITS

331-5011 For Proto 2000 GP9 Diesels UP/PRR **6.95**
331-5013 EMD GP30B UP (Cabless GP30 Unit) **19.95** *NEW*

GE HIGH NOSE KIT
331-5012 2.95 *NEW*

GE EXHAUST STACK EA 2.95

331-6000 U-Boats Thru Dash-7
331-6001 Dash-7 Thru Dash-8
331-6002 Dash-8 Thru Dash-9

UNIVERSAL ANTENNA DOME EA 2.95

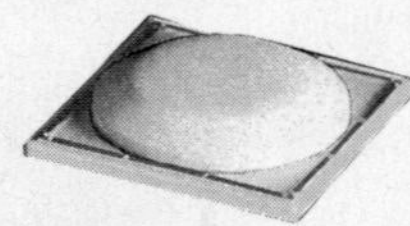

331-6003 Round

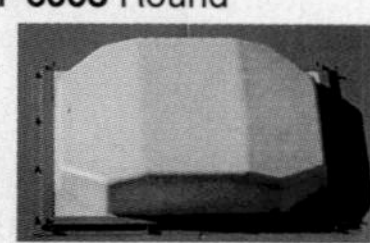

331-6007 Octagon

GE ANTICLIMBER
331-6004 C-30-7 **2.95**

INTAKE GRILLES EA 2.95
331-6005 C-30-7 Rear
331-6006 C-36-7 Dynamic

WASTE FLUID CONTAINMENT TANK EMD EA 2.95
331-6008 Square
331-6009 Angled Corners
331-6010 UP Style

WEIGHTS EA 2.95
85-4001041 Cylindrical Covered Hopper pkg(8)
85-4003041 4750 Cubic Foot 3-Bay Hopper pkg(6)

40' PS-1 BOX CAR PARTS EA 4.95
85-4040001 8' PS Door (Box Car Red)
85-4040002 6' Youngstown Door (Box Car Red)
85-4040051 8' PS Door (gray)
85-4040052 6' Youngstown Door (gray)
85-4040006 PS Roof (Box Car Red)
85-4040016 Underframe
85-4040018 Underbody Details

40' OR 50' PS-1 BOX CAR PARTS EA 4.95
85-4040009 Body Details (Box Car Red)
85-4040013 PS Ends (Box Car Red)
85-4040059 Body Details (gray)
85-4040063 PS Ends (gray)

50' PS-1 BOX CAR PARTS EA 4.95
85-4060001 8' PS Door (Box Car Red) DD
85-4060002 8' Youngstown Door (Box Car Red) DD
85-4060003 8' Plug Door (Box Car Red)
85-4060006 PS Roof (Box Car Red)
85-4060051 8' PS Door (gray) DD
85-4060052 8' Youngstown Door (gray) DD
85-4060053 8' Plug Door (Gray)
85-4090001 9' PS Door (Box Car Red)
85-4090016 Underframe
85-4090018 Underbody Details
85-4090051 9' PS Door (gray)

1937 AAR BOX CAR PARTS EA 4.95
85-4070001 Youngstown Door (Box Car Red)
85-4070006 Murphy Brown (Box Car Red)
85-4070009 Body Details (Box Car Red)
85-4070013 Dreadnaught Ends (Box Car Red)
85-4070016 Underframe
85-4070018 Underbody Details
85-4070051 Youngstown Door (gray)
85-4070059 Body Details (gray)
85-4070063 Dreadnaught Ends (gray)

MODIFIED AAR BOX CAR PARTS EA 4.95
85-4080013 Dreadnaught Ends (Box Car Red)
85-4080063 Dreadnaught Ends (gray)

R-40-23 REEFER CAR PARTS EA 4.95
85-4050006 Murphy Roof (Box Car Red)
85-4050009 Roof & End Details (Box Car Red)
85-4050010 Side Details (black)
85-4050013 Dreadnaught Ends (Box Car Red)
85-4050056 Murphy Roof (black)

KADEE®

ACETAL SCREWS

380-256 Roundhead 1/2" Insulating Screws pkg(12) **1.65**
Insulated phillips head screws. Uses include mounting couplers, draft gear boxes and trucks. Can be easily trimmed to appropriate length.

FREIGHT CAR DETAILS EA 1.35

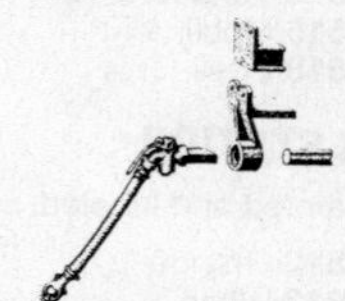

380-438 Air Hose & Angle Cock w/Mounting Bracket pkg(20)

380-439 Nut-Bolt-Washer Detail pkg(36)

PS-1 40' BOX CAR LADDERS 1 SET EA 2.75
Complete sets of end and side ladders as used on PS-1 box cars. Adaptable to most post-war box cars and reefers. Molded in color shown.

380-2101 Oxide Red *NEW*
380-2102 Box Car Red *NEW*
380-2103 Black *NEW*

BRAKE WHEELS

METAL

380-440 18" Metal pkg(6) **1.35**

PLASTIC PKG(8) EA 2.40

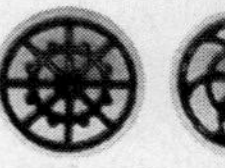
380-2040

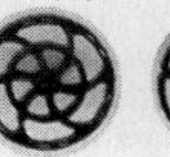
380-2041

380-2042

380-2043

380-2044

AJAX
380-2020 Box Car Red *NEW*
380-2030 Red Oxide *NEW*
380-2040 Black *NEW*

EQUIPCO
380-2021 Box Car Red *NEW*
380-2031 Red Oxide *NEW*
380-2041 Black *NEW*

MINER
380-2022 Box Car Red *NEW*
380-2032 Red Oxide *NEW*
380-2042 Black *NEW*

UNIVERSAL
380-2023 Box Car Red *NEW*
380-2033 Red Oxide *NEW*
380-2043 Black *NEW*

CHAMPION
380-2024 Box Car Red *NEW*
380-2034 Red Oxide *NEW*
380-2044 Black *NEW*

JL INNOVATIVE DESIGN

ASSORTED CRATES PKG(4) EA 3.79

A variety of food product crates with colorful labels, including: Irish Beauty, Smoky Jim's Sweet Potatoes, Washington Apples, Jo Jo Melons, Greenspot, American Maid Pears, Red Crown and Big Chief Tomatoes.

LARGE

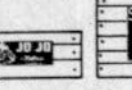

361-323 Assorted-Brown
361-423 Assorted-Gray
361-523 Assorted-Green

SMALL

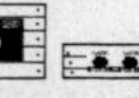

361-324 Assorted-Brown
361-424 Assorted-Gray
361-524 Assorted-Green

AUTO PARTS CRATES PKG(4) EA 3.98

361-823 Brown ***NEW***
361-824 Gray ***NEW***
361-825 Green ***NEW***

BARRELS PKG(5) EA 3.98

Prepainted barrels with product labels. Great detail for railroad shop, gas stations and bulk oil dealers, refineries, farms and almost any industry.

GAS STATION

Labels from Blau, Deep Rock, Texaco, Pennzoil, Veedol, Sunoco and Sinclair.

361-312 Green
361-313 Red

INDUSTRIAL

Labels from FMC, Dow, Monsanto, RP, J&L Steel, Glidden, BPS and IC.

361-412 Silver
361-413 Yellow

FEED & SEED FERTILIZER

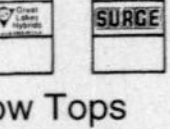

361-512 Blue w/Yellow Tops

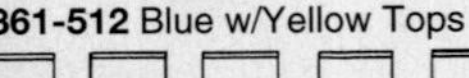

361-513 Black

FOOD & FLOUR LABELS

361-712 Custom Barrels Wood (brown) Includes labels from Karo, Gold Medal, Pasier Pickles, Swan Flour and Fleischmanns Yeast.

CUSTOM FENCING

361-305 Assorted Custom 6" Boardfence **3.79**

GAS PUMPS

Prepainted and decorated with the logo of the company shown.

CUSTOM PKG(2) EA 5.49 (UNLESS NOTED)

361-619 Gulf **6.49** ***NEW***

361-814

361-817

361-814 Texaco
361-815 Mobil
361-816 Sinclair
361-817 Phillips 66

DELUXE CUSTOM PKG(2) EA 6.49

361-514 Texaco ***NEW***
361-515 Mobil ***NEW***
361-518 Shell ***NEW***

DELUXE CUSTOM PKG(2) EA 6.49

361-514 Texaco ***NEW***
361-515 Mobil ***NEW***
361-518 Shell ***NEW***

GAS STATION

Prepainted and labeled.

361-812 Orange
361-813 White

ICE BLOCKS

361-205 pkg(25) **2.50**

LADDERS

CUSTOM 6" PKG(2) EA 1.98

361-552 Metal (silver)
361-553 Wood (brown

CUSTOM LADDERS EA 1.79

361-554 8' Step (brown)
361-555 10' Lean-To Ladders (unfinished) pkg(4)

OIL HIGHBOYS PKG(2) EA 3.98

Prepainted and decorated with the logo of the company shown.

361-914 Texaco

361-915 Mobil
361-916 Sinclair
361-917 Phillips 66
361-918 Shell ***NEW***
361-919 Gulf ***NEW***

OIL RACKS

361-826 Mixed Brands pkg(3) **4.49** ***NEW***

SODA CASES

361-827 Mixed Brands pkg(3) **4.49** ***NEW***

TIRE DISPLAYS

361-314 Closed-Unfinished **2.50**
361-315 Open-Unfinished **2.50**

361-316 Painted & Labeled pkg(3) **4.49**

Detailed, injection-molded styrene plastic, unless noted.

BRIDGE PARTS

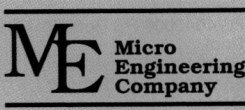

255-80166 50' Plate Girder pkg(4) **3.95**
255-80167 30' Plate Girder pkg(4) **3.50**

255-80174 Barrel Platform w/Barrel **2.75**

255-80034 Bridge Shoes-White Metal pkg(4) **2.45**

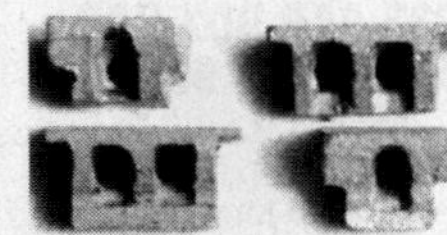

255-80035 Assorted Bridge Shoes-White Metal pkg(16) **6.85**

DOORS EA 2.25

255-80161 Office Front pkg(8)
255-80162 Warehouse Personnel pkg(4)
255-80062 Transom pkg(4)
255-80063 Four Panel pkg(4)
255-80065 Baggage pkg(3)
255-80160 Warehouse Overhead pkg(3)
255-80165 Store Front pkg(4)

WINDOWS EA 2.25

255-80060

255-80061

255-80060 30 x 81" pkg(8)
255-80061 Double 66 x 104" pkg(2)

255-80064 255-80067 255-80068

255-80064 28 x 64" pkg(8)
255-80067 25 x 50" pkg(8)
255-80068 28 x 64" pkg(8)

BUILDING DETAILS

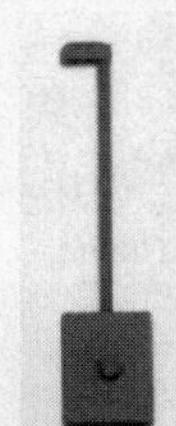

255-80164 Electric Meter Box & Mast pkg(2) **2.25**
255-80163 Gutters & Downspouts pkg(6) **2.25**
255-80066 Board Walks pkg(2) **2.25**

255-80105 Pallets pkg(12) **2.25**
255-80173 Ore Gate **2.50**

MERTEN

DETAIL PARTS EA 8.99

Plastic parts are molded in realistic colors and ready to install.

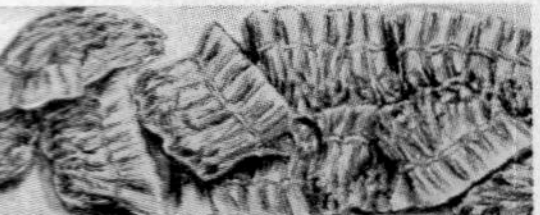

447-932 Grain Stacks-Wheat Sheaves pkg(12) ***NEW***

447-933 Railroad Ties (Plastic) pkg(150) ***NEW***

447-2369 Wooden Barrels-7 Sizes pkg(70) ***NEW***

447-2370 Wooden Boxes-6 Sizes pkg(90) ***NEW***

447-2418 Split-Rail Fence 44-1/2" 113cm ***NEW***

DIESEL DETAILS

Undecorated, plastic parts unless noted.

AIR HORNS EA 1.25

3-CHIME
381-950011 Black
381-950012 Gray
381-950013 Silver
381-950014 Blue
381-950015 Red
381-950016 Yellow

1-CHIME PKG(2)
381-950020 Maroon *NEW*
381-950021 Black *NEW*
381-950022 Gray *NEW*
381-950024 Blue *NEW*

AIR TANKS RS/RSC-2 EA 2.00

381-954061 Black *NEW*
381-954062 Gray *NEW*

BODY SHELLS EA 35.00

GE DASH 9
381-951050 Low Numberboards, 6-Step Wide
381-951060 Low Numberboards, 6-Step Narrow
381-951070 High Numberboards, 5-Step Wide
381 951080 High Numberboards, 6-Step Narrow
381-951085 High Numberboards 6-Step Wide

DASH 9 GULLWING CABS
381-951090 5-Step
381-951095 6-Step Wide

GP35
381-951040 Phase 1B

RS/RSC-2 UNDECORATED
381-951110 Water Cooled *NEW*
381-951120 Air Cooled *NEW*

BRASS BELLS EA 1.75

381-963010 For Hood Units
381-963030 Medium
381-963031 Frame Mount

BRAKE SET FOR DASH 9 TRUCKS EA 2.50

381-964021 Black
381-964022 Gray
381-964023 Silver

BRAKE WHEELS EA 1.00

DASH 9
381-965031 Black
381-965032 Gray
381-965033 Silver
381-965036 Yellow
381-965039 Orange

SD45
381-965041 Black
381-965042 Gray
381-965044 Blue
381-965046 Yellow

RS/RSC-2 PKG(2)
381-967051 Black *NEW*
381-967052 Gray *NEW*
381-967054 Blue *NEW*
381-967055 Red *NEW*
381-967059 Orange *NEW*

CAB DETAILS EA 1.00

381-965010 Cab Sunshade-Undecorated
381-965020 Numberboards/ Inserts for Dash 9 pkg(2)

CIRCUIT BOARD PARTS

381-966010 Power Clips pkg(6) 1.00
381-966012 Power Buss pkg(2) 1.00 *NEW*

COUPLER PARTS

381-953010 Coupler & Pin Set-Hood Units 2.00

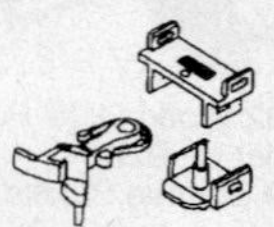

381-953020 Coupler, Pocket & Foot Board-Switchers 1.25
381-953030 Coupler & Screw for Hood Unit 2.00
381-900100 Screw Frame Mount Coupler pkg(6) 1.00 *NEW*

CYLINDER & SWING HANGER FOR GP EA 1.00

381-964011 Black
381-964012 Gray
381-964013 Silver

DRIVE GEARS

381-960010 Hood Units 4.00
381-960020 Switchers 2.50

EXHAUST STACKS EA 1.00

381-965050 GE Dash 9
381-965080 NW2 Switcher
381-965081 RS/RSC-2 *NEW*

FRAMES EA 30.00

381-955040 Dash 9
381-955042 RS/RSC-2 Black *NEW*

FUEL TANKS EA 2.00

SD40

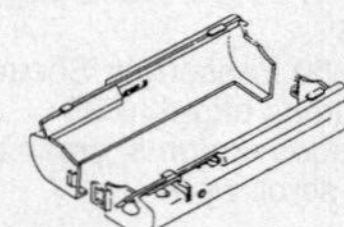

381-954011 Black
381-954012 Gray

GP35
381-954021 Black
381-954022 Gray

NW2-PHASE 1
381-954031 Black

NW2-PHASE 2
381-954041 Black
381-954042 Gray

DASH 9
381-954051 Black
381-954052 Gray
381-954053 Silver

GLASS SET EA 5.50

381-951500 SD45
381-951510 Dash 9
381-951520 RS-21 RSC-2 *NEW*

HANDRAILS

SD40
381-952011 Black 3.00

GP35 EA 3.00
381-952021 Black
381-952022 Gray

NW2 EA 3.00
381-952031 Black
381-952032 Gray

DASH 9
381-952041 Black 3.00

SD45 EA 3.00
381-952051 Black
381-952052 Gray

RS/RSC-2 PKG(2) EA 6.00
381-952061 Black *NEW*
381-952062 Gray *NEW*

HEADLIGHT ASSEMBLY EA 10.00 (UNLESS NOTED)

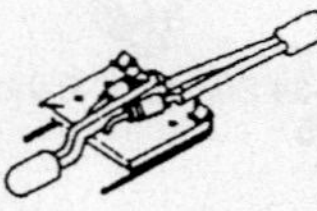

381-903010 Switchers - Front 6.00
381-958010 Hood Units
381-958020 Switchers - Rear

HEADLIGHT HOUSING

381-965045 Dash 9 1.00

HOOD UNITS

381-961500 Worm set pkg(2) 5.00 *NEW*

IDLER GEARS

381-961020 Switchers 2.50

381-962010 Geared Wheel Set 5.00

FOR HOOD UNITS PKG(5) EA 4.00

381-961010 15T
381-961030 17T *NEW*
381-961040 22T *NEW*

LIGHT CIRCUIT BOARD & ANALOG PLUG EA 12.50

381-958031 For SD40/45
381-958032 For Dash 9
381-958033 For RS/RSC-2 *NEW*

MOTORS & PARTS

381-31500 HM - 5 Motor 19.98
381-956010 Motor w/Dual Flywheels for Hood Units 30.00
381-956020 Motor w/Dual Flywheels for Switchers 35.00
381-957010 Motor Brushes 2.00
381-956030 Motor for RS Units 30.00 *NEW*
381-966011 Motor Shoe Retainer 1.00 *NEW*

NUMBERBOARDS

381-965021 RS/RSC-2 (black) pkg(4) 1.00 *NEW*

ROOF HATCHES

GP35 EA 1.00
381-965060 Dynamic Brake-Undecorated
381-965070 Nondynamic-Undecorated

SD45
381-965061 Dynamic Fan Hatch 1.50

SCREWS

381-900110 Flat Head 2 x 8mm pkg(6) 1.00 *NEW*

SWITCHER HORN/BELL BRACKET EA 2.50

381-963021 Black
381-963022 Gray
381-963024 Blue

TRUCK ASSEMBLIES

SD UNITS EA 25.00
381-959011 Black
381-959013 Silver

GP UNITS EA 20.00
381-959021 Black
381-959022 Gray
381-959023 Silver

SWITCHERS EA 20.00
381-959031 Black
381-959032 Gray
381-959033 Silver

DASH 9 EA 25.00
381-959041 Black
381-959042 Gray
381-959043 Silver

SD45 EA 23.00
381-959051 Black
381-959052 Gray
381-959053 Silver

REV. DASH 9 EA 25.00
381-959061 Black
381-959063 Silver

RS-2 ROLLER BEARING EA 23.00
381-959071 Black *NEW*
381-959072 Gray *NEW*

RS-2 FRICTION BEARING EA 23.00
381-959081 Black *NEW*
381-959083 Silver *NEW*

RSC-2 FRICTION BEARING EA 23.00
381-959091 Black *NEW*
381-959093 Silver *NEW*

UNIVERSALS

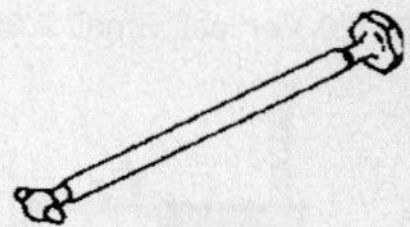

381-967010 Dash 9 2.00
381-967011 SD40/SD45 2.00
381-967012 RS/RSC-2 pkg(2) 2.00 *NEW*

WEIGHT SETS EA 12.00

381-966020 Add-on for GP35/SD40
Includes weight, bracket and screws.
381-966021 For RS/RSC-2 12.00 *NEW*

FREIGHT DETAILS

COVERED HOPPER PARTS EA 3.00 (UNLESS NOTED)

381-850000 33" Wheel Set pkg(8) 9.60
381-850010 Roofwalks Undecorated pkg(6)
381-850011 Hatches Undecorated pkg(6)
381-850012 Brake Pieces Undecorated pkg(6)
381-850013 Doors Undecorated pkg(6)

Keystone Locomotive Works

Parts are metal pressure castings; kits include brass rod and wire as required. Illustrations are NOT to scale.

BOILERS

395-20 Vertical, Small **2.25**

395-101 Horizontal, Portable **15.95**

CAST RAFTERS

395-43 13-1/2' pkg(6) **2.45**
395-44 25' pkg(6) **3.25**
395-45 48-1/2' pkg(6) **4.25**

JUNK

395-2 Engine House **3.95**
Includes stacks, domes, sideframes, drivers, rods, loco fittings and lots of other odds and ends.

395-12 Set of 8 Drivers and Axles **5.95**
Includes eight 64" spoked steam engine drivers.

395-15 Diesel Engine House **5.95**
Approximately 35 pieces of assorted "scrapped" diesel parts from EMD, Alco and GE including: sideframes, roof fans, spark arrestors, stacks, traction motors, loco brake cylinders, wheels, brake shoes and nose assembly.

395-14 Logging **3.95**
Includes 70- and 90-Ton Shay sideframes, Shay sandbox, domes and cab front, headlight, backhead, tender filler hatch, geared Shay drivers and tires, log bunks, compressors and cylinders.

FREIGHT CAR DETAILS

395-4 Small Brake Cylinder w/Clevis **1.25**
395-5 Log Buggy Shoo-Fly pkg(2) **1.25**

395-6 Riveted Flat Car Stakes pkg(12) **1.95**

PULPWOOD CAR CONVERSION KITS EA 2.95

Add-on details simulate equipment used on freight cars handling pulpwood.
395-52 Flat Car Rack Bulkhead End
395-53 Gondola, Low End, Solid Bulkhead
395-54 Gondola, Tall, Open End Bulkhead

TACONITE CAR SIDE EXTENSIONS

395-59 DM&IR Taconite Extensions **TBA**
Applied to ore cars rebuilt to carry taconite pellets.

LOCO DETAILS

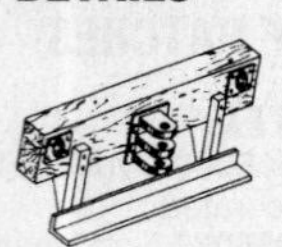

395-10 Shay Engine Pilot **1.25**

395-8

395-11

395-8 Single Stage Air Compressor **1.25**
395-11 Diesel Spark Arrestor **1.25**
Used by Canadian National and Grand Trunk.

395-21

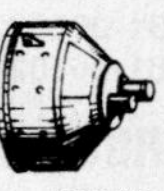

395-22

395-21 Traction Motor pkg(2) **3.25**
395-22 2500 HP Generator **3.25**
395-23 Old Time Headlight **1.25**
395-29 Shay Steam Cylinders w/U-joints **9.95**
395-49 GE44-Tonner Delrin U-Joint Retrofit **3.00**
Replaces rubber tubing on early models.
395-51 Air Tank (Approximately 2 x 6') **1.25**
395-58 Pilot Filler for Athearn SD9 pkg(2) **1.95**
Fills in opening below coupler pocket.

ENGINES

395-31 Donkey Engine C&D **12.95**
395-32 Boiler w/Small Mill Engine **11.95**

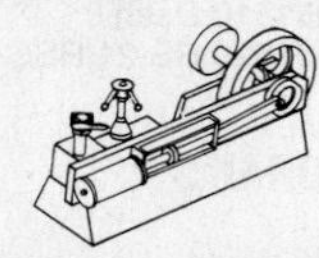

395-1106 Large Horizontal Engine Only **14.95**

MINIATURE TOOLS

395-1 Logging Tool Set **3.95**
Includes two peaveys, two pikes, one saw and two axes.

OUTHOUSE

395-42 **2.25**

SAWMILL DETAILS

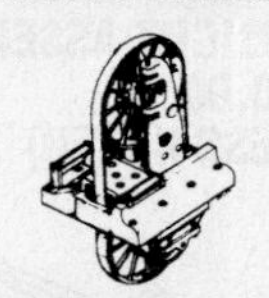

395-34 Sumner 6' Band Saw **12.95**

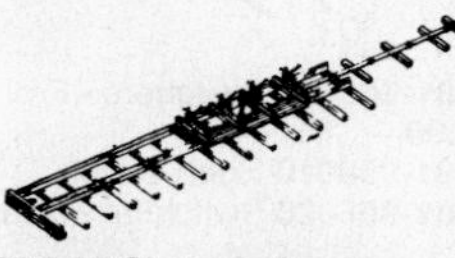

395-35 Shotgun Carriage w/Ways & Track **10.95**

395-36 Edger Kit **10.95**

395-37 Live Rolls **10.95**

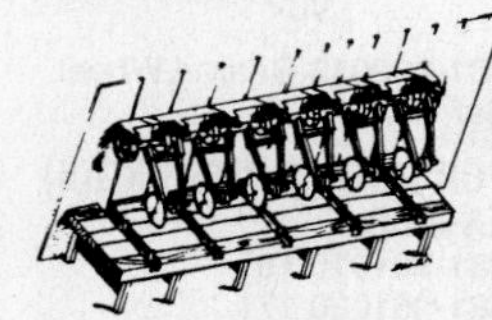

395-38 Cut-off Saw **10.95**
Used to cut lumber to length.

395-39 Logging Mill Transfer Table **10.95**

395-40 Log Deck & Jack Slip **21.95**
395-41 Grinder pkg(2) **1.95**

395-48 Lumber Carts 2' Gauge pkg(2) **2.45**

395-102 Working Jill Poke Unloader Kit **9.95**
395-19 Cheese Blocks pkg(4) **1.25**

SHAY LOCO DOMES EA 1.25

395-26 Steam
395-27 Sand

STEAM LOCO STACKS

395-3

395-7

395-3 Lima Diamond **2.95**
Replaces PFM B-2 & B-3 stack.
395-7 Congdon Type **1.25**

395-25

395-24

395-25 Shotgun **1.25**
395-24 Small Diamond **1.25**

STRUCTURE DETAILS

395-17 Corrugated Metal Roll, 5' x 1-1/4" **2.95**
395-33 Blacksmith Forge & Anvil **3.25**
395-46 Concrete Pier, 1/8 x 1/8" pkg(15) **2.45**
395-47 Angle Brace pkg(24) **2.45**
395-50 Passenger Shelter Columns pkg(6) **6.95**
Includes uprights, cross arms, and scroll work.

TRACKSIDE DETAILS

395-18 Switch Stand pkg(2) **3.95**

WINDSHIELD WIPER EA 1.98

395-3401 Metal pkg(4)
Generic style for diesels.

395-3405 Plastic
For 2nd Generation diesels.

WINTERIZATION HATCHES EA 1.45

Cast metal, fits 48" fans.
395-55 SD18 & Others, Rounded Corners.
395-56 Long-2nd Generation Diesels, Square Corners.
395-57 Short-For GP38-2 & Others, Square Corners.

NORTHWEST SHORTLINE

BALDWIN DETAILS

53-4625 Cylinder Saddle, HOn3 **.50**
Slide valve saddle used on 4-4-0 and 2-6-0 locos circa 1880-1910. Brass plated casting.

LOCO DRIVER SPRINGS

4mm long springs w/2mm diameters.

53-14004 Wimpy pkg(8) **1.95**
53-14014 Light pkg(8) **1.95**
53-14024 Medium pkg(8) **1.95**
53-14104 Wimpy pkg(100) **9.95**
53-14114 Light pkg(100) **9.95**
53-14124 Medium pkg(100) **9.95**

UPGRADE KIT

53-106 Upgrade for SW-1 **3.95**

N.J. INTERNATIONAL

DETAIL PARTS

525-312 Aldon Car Puller **1.99**
525-321 LCL Cement Container **1.79**
525-326 Union Switch Indicator **1.79**
525-407 Brass Chain 18" **1.99**
525-410 Air Horn pkg(2) **.99**
525-6175 Sacks - Freight pkg(12) **3.29**
525-6180 Tables, Stools, Benches **3.29**

Add a touch of realism to any scene with these detailed brass castings (unless noted).

AUTO PARTS

464-758 Automobile Transmission **1.50**
464-706 Rear Axle **1.25**

PIERCE-ARROW TRUCK PARTS

464-695 Front Axle **5.95**
464-697 Rear Axle **7.95**
464-705 Exhaust Manifold **1.25**
464-715 Gas Tank **1.50**
464-716 Front Wheel/Tire pkg(2) **2.00**
464-717 Steering Column **1.25**
464-718 Rear Wheel/Tire **1.50**
464-739 Hood **1.50**
464-754 Intake Manifold **1.25**
464-755 Radiator **1.95**
464-756 Engine **3.95**
439-763 Water Manifold **1.00**
464-771 Seat **3.95**
464-775 Floor Assembly **3.95**
464-778 Main Frame **12.95**
464-779 Running Lamp Set **1.95**
464-782 Shift Assembly **1.25**
464-783 Battery Box **1.95**
464-785 Hand Crank **1.00**
464-787 Drive Shaft **1.00**

BUILDING DETAILS

464-665 Watt Moreland Finial **1.00**
464-740 Lightning Rod pkg(6) **1.00**
464-744 Flag Pole **1.25**
Building mount style.
464-745 Spiral Lightning Rod w/Glass Ball **1.25**

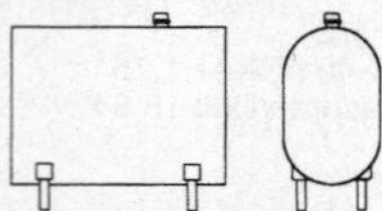

464-765 Fuel Oil Tank w/Valve **4.95**

BUILDING INTERIOR DETAILS

464-675 J.L. Mott Water Closet **4.50**
464-710 File Cabinet pkg(2) **2.00**
464-719 Pot Belly Stove (brass & white metal) **1.75**
464-924 Victorian Wallpaper **1.95**

CANS & DRUMS

464-720

464-757

464-720 Jug pkg(6) **1.00**
464-757 Milk Cans pkg(2) **1.75**
464-730 Five Gallon Cans pkg(6) **1.00**

464-760 55 Gallon Drum pkg(4) **1.25**

WOODEN BARRELS PKG(2) EA 2.95

Brass castings.
464-612 Large
464-614 Small

DEPOT BAGGAGE CART

464-654 Hand Truck **6.95**
Southern Railway prototype with working wheels and fine details.

DISHES

464-605 Tin Plates pkg(5) **2.75**
464-607 Frying Pan pkg(5) **2.75**
464-620 Bottles (4 types) pkg(8) **2.95**
464-630 Coffee Cups pkg(6) **2.50**
464-684 Coffee Pot pkg(2) **1.75**
464-797 Water Bottle pkg(6) **1.00**

DOORS & WINDOWS

Laser-cut details; #784 includes clear window "glass."

464-780 Freight Door **1.50**
464-784 Skylight Window **2.50**

ENGINE HOUSE DETAILS

464-776 Engine House Detail Set **24.95**
Over 65 brass and white metal castings, including many tools, a figure and exterior details. Great for any shop scene, includes three full-color photos showing how details were used in other kits.

ENGINE & PUMP

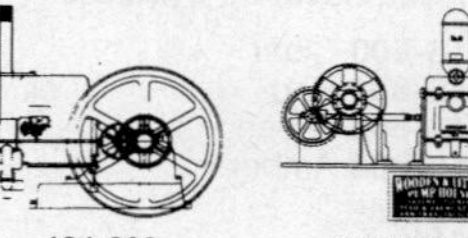
464-699 464-700

464-699 8-Horse Stover Engine **9.95**
464-700 1876 Challenger Pump **6.95**

FREIGHT CAR DETAILS

464-616 Brake Wheels-Clear Creek Style pkg(4) **2.00**
464-621 C&S/RGS Reefer Hinge pkg(4) **1.50**
464-629 Box Car Door Guides-Colorado & Southern pkg(2) **1.00**
464-633 Box Car Bolsters-Colorado & Southern pkg(2) **1.00**
464-635 Log Car Bolsters pkg(2) **1.00**
464-662 Stake Pockets-CCM pkg(6) **2.25**
464-670 Lift Rings-CCM pkg(10) **1.50**
464-734 Tiffany Reefer Hinges **2.75**
464-738 Clear Creek Freight Car Hardware **5.95**
464-794 1893 Rio Grande Reefer Vents pkg(2) **1.00**

GAS PUMPS

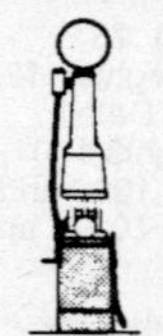
464-762

464-764

464-762 Filter Style **2.75**
464-764 Glass Style **3.50**

464-774 Detail Set **19.95**
Complete with three-color decals, two oil bunkers with crank arms, two filler pipe stands and vapor vents for simulated underground storage tanks, air compressor, inner tube test tank, concrete lube pad, pump island, vehicle lift, two gas pumps and more.

464-772 Gas Pump Island Set **8.95**
Includes urethane island, two pumps, oil bottles, water can and decals.

464-788 Fry Model 117 "Mae West" Gas Pump **3.95**

GAS STATION DETAILS

464-711 Hydraulic Auto Hoist **4.50**
464-712 Gas Tank Filter Vent Pipe **1.25**

HANDLES & HINGES

464-746

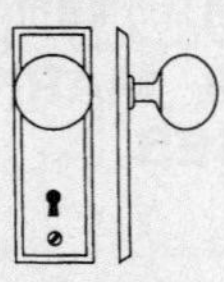
464-747

464-746 Door Handle Set **1.50**
464-747 Door Knob & Plate pkg(2) **1.50**
464-641 Photo-Etched Hinges pkg(6) **2.45**
464-652 Drawer Pull pkg(2) **1.25**
464-737 Door Latch Assembly **1.50** *NEW*

MINE DETAILS

464-792 Chute Assembly **5.00**
464-796 Head Gear **2.00**

MINIATURE TOOLS

464-690

464-790

464-690 Solder Pots pkg(2) **2.00**
464-790 Pick Ax **1.25**
464-714 Hand Lantern pkg(2) **2.50**
464-601 Hand Oil Can pkg(5) **2.75**
464-602 Lunch Box pkg(2) **1.50**
464-604 Bucking Saw **TBA**
464-606 Falling Saw **TBA**
464-608 Logger's Lube Cans pkg(2) **2.00**
464-609 Wire Spool pkg(2) **1.25**
464-610 Broadax pkg(2) **1.75**
464-611 Saw Anvil pkg(2) **1.00**
464-613 Pliers pkg(5) **2.75**
464-619 Small Tongs pkg(5) **2.75**
464-622 Shovel pkg(2) **2.50**
464-623 Anvil pkg(2) **2.50**
464-625 Large Tongs pkg(4) **2.25**
464-626 Straw Broom pkg(2) **1.50**
464-631 Short Screwdriver pkg(5) **2.75**
464-632 Fire Extinguisher pkg(2) **1.75**
464-636 Peavy pkg(2) **1.70**
464-637 Grease Gun pkg(5) **2.75**
464-638 Falling Ax pkg(2) **1.75**
464-639 Tool Set **2.00**
Mallet, crowbar, gouge and file.
464-640 Metal Buckets (hollow cast) pkg(2) **2.00**
464-642 Wooden Buckets (hollow cast) pkg(2) **2.00**
464-643 Coal Scoop pkg(5) **2.75**
464-645 Pickaroon (Logging Tool) pkg(2) **1.75**
464-647 Square Mallet pkg(5) **2.75**
464-653 Paint Cans pkg(5) **2.75**
464-656 "Glass" Insulators pkg(5) **2.75**
464-658 Knife Switch pkg(5) **2.75**
464-663 "Candlestick" Phone pkg(2) **2.00**
464-664 Hand Drill pkg(5) **2.75**
464-667 Crow Bar pkg(5) **2.75**
464-668 Wood Gouge pkg(5) **2.75**
464-672 Chisel pkg(5) **2.75**
464-678 Sledge Hammer pkg(5) **2.75**
464-680 Blow Torch pkg(2) **1.75**
464-686 Wood Mallet pkg(5) **2.75**
464-692 Saw Mallet pkg(5) **2.75**
464-694 File pkg(5) **2.75**
464-696 Screw Drivers pkg(5) **2.75**
464-703 Oil Funnel pkg(2) **1.75**
464-707 Lube Valve **1.25**
464-708 Drill Press **2.75**
464-709 Air Line Tee **1.25**
464-722 Oil Can pkg(2) **1.75**
464-724 Hi-Boy Oil Container **2.25**
464-726 Air Compressor **2.50**
464-728 Tube Test Tank w/Tire pkg(2) **1.75**
464-731 Vice pkg(2) **1.75**
464-741 Junk Box pkg(3) **1.00**
464-742 Junk Barrel **1.00**
464-770 Tool Box **1.75**
464-786 Oil Can Tall pkg(2) **2.00**
464-789 Tool Set pkg(4) **2.00**
464-791 Spade pkg(2) **2.00**
464-793 Broom pkg(2) **1.25**
464-799 Leaning Sacks pkg(4) **1.00**

MISCELLANEOUS

464-598 Out House pkg(2) **2.25**
464-599 Tomb Stone Set pkg(13) **1.50**
464-628 Wooden Tub pkg(2) **3.50**
464-649 Control Lever pkg(2) **2.00**
464-655 Large Band Wheel **3.00**
464-659 Head Block **1.50**
464-660 Pallet **1.25**
464-661 Bearing Supports **1.50**
464-666 Set Works **1.50**
464-743 Hog Set **17.95**
Brass body, drive housing and pipe.
464-751 Angle Insulator **1.00**

PIPES PKG (2) EA 1.50

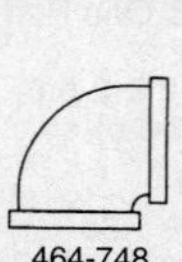
464-748

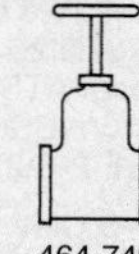
464-749

464-748 Elbow
464-749 Valve

ROOF VENTS

464-624 Short Vent pkg(4) **1.25**
464-634 Factory Roof Vent **1.45**

SMOKEJACKS PKG(2) EA 1.00

464-759 Bent
464-761 "T" - Top
464-781 Cone Top
464-798 Common

STREET DETAILS

464-732 Lamp Post **1.00**

STUMPS

464-650 Stump Set pkg(9) **5.95**
Set of nine pewter castings with realistic detail.

VEGETABLES PKG(6) EA 1.25

464-701 Water Melons
464-702 Pumpkins
464-704 Gourds

M.V. PRODUCTS
HEADLIGHT & MARKER LENSES

HEADLIGHT & MARKER LENSES

Add realistic headlights to your favorite models with this unique lens system. Each comes fully assembled, with an ultra-thin, parabolic metal mirror mounted behind a solid lens made of a hybrid polymer. This design picks up and reflects all available light for a highly realistic appearance. The lens is heat-resistant, and may be illuminated with small bulbs for more realism. Adaptable to any scale, many lenses are also available precolored red, green, amber or blue. These can be used as model railroad signals, or to detail vehicles, aircraft and other models in larger scales.

Lighting the Lens – Make a starter hole with a sharp tool (such as an awl) in the center of the metal backing. Use a drill size proportional to the lens and drill approximately halfway through. During power-on operation, the lamp makes the whole lens glow, with a bright center that looks like a scale bulb.

HO Scale sizes are shown for individual lenses, along with actual diameter in inches and drill number needed for mounting.

ENGINE SETS

Designed for brass steam engines, most include lenses for headlight(s) and/or tender back-up lamp. Some include a red lamp for emergency stop signals.

516-1 One Clear & One Red pkg(2) **1.75**
PFM ATSF 4-6-4, 4-8-4, 2-10-4.

516-2 Clear 18" pkg(2) **1.85**
PFM ATSF #1337 4-6-2, B2 & B3 Shays with balloon stacks, Michigan 3 cylinder Shay, Custom Brass NP A & A1 4-8-4.

516-3 Clear pkg(2) **1.75**
Balboa/Hallmark ATSF 9000 series 0-6-0.

516-4 Two Clear & One Red pkg(3) **2.25**
Sunset ATSF 0-8-0 & 2-8-0, Custom Brass/Balboa/Key ATSF 2-6-2.

516-5 Clear pkg(2) **1.85**
Hallmark ATSF 2-8-0 #2507.

516-6 Clear pkg(2) **1.30**
Tenshodo GN M2, N3, R2, P2 and Q1, Westside NYC J1e 4-6-4, PFM MoPac 4-8-4.

516-7 Clear pkg(2) **1.30**
Tenshodo GN, S1, S2 and O8. Van Hobbies CN N-5d 2-8-0, CP T-1a, and H.1a.b 4-6-4.

516-8 Clear pkg(3) **2.70**
Westside/Balboa/Max Gray SP GS4.

516-9 Two Clear & One Red pkg(3) **2.70**
PFM CNW 4-6-2 E2a. Westside/Max Gray UP FEF2 & FEF3.

516-10 Clear pkg(2) **1.75**
PFM SOU F1 & PS4, WP 4-8-2.

516-12 Clear pkg(2) **1.75**
Athearn Alco PA.

516-13 Clear pkg(2) **1.85**
PFM Pacific Coast Shay & NP S4 4-6-0. NWSL E2a 4-6-2.

516-14 Clear pkg(2) **1.85**
PFM Frisco 2-10-0, Westside SP B1. Alco Models SP C15 2-8-0.

516-15 Clear pkg(2) **1.75**
PFM Western Pacific 2-8-2, DRGW L131, C&O K4, UP FEF1, MILW F6a.

516-16 Clear pkg(2) **1.30**
PFM DRGW & Western Pacific 4-6-0, MoPac 4-6-2 & 4-8-4. Westside NYC J3a, J3b & J1e. Van Hobbies CN #6060.

INDIVIDUAL LENSES

4-1/2" PKG(4) EA 2.00 (UNLESS NOTED)
Measures .052", Drill #55. Class lights for most EMD hood units and GE U-Boats. Fits Detail Associates headlights 1017, 1018, 1019 and 1020. Drop-in mount for marker light castings from Cal-Scale, Precision Scale and most HO brass steam engines.

516-300 Clear
516-301 Red
516-302 Green
516-303 Amber
516-304 Blue
516-500 One Red, One Green & One Amber set(3) **1.50**

5-1/2" PKG(4) EA 1.50 (UNLESS NOTED)
Measures .063", Drill #52. Class lights for Athearn, AHM and most brass U-Boats, headlights for Athearn RDC and various Alco Models. Also fits Cal-Scale, Precision Scale and most brass steam loco marker light castings.

516-22 Clear
516-220 Red
516-221 Green
516-222 Amber
516-223 Blue
516-501 One Red, One Green & One Amber set(3) **1.00**

6-1/8" PKG(4) EA 1.50
Measures .070", Drill #50.

516-600 Clear
516-601 Red
516-602 Green
516-603 Amber

6-1/2"
Measures .073", Drill #49.

516-18 Six Clear & One Red pkg(7) **2.55**
Athearn U-Boats, Details West headlight 102 and 1012.

516-26 Clear pkg(4) **1.50**
Details West headlight 117 and 138, Detail Associates headlight 1003.

516-103 Eight Clear & Two Red pkg(10) **3.75**
Details West headlight 103.

6-3/4"
Measures .078", #47 Drill.

516-19 Six Clear & One Red pkg(7) **2.55**
Athearn EMDs, Atlas GP40, AHM U25C, Gem SDP40F, AHM, Model Power, Trains and PMI EMD FP45. Details West headlights 100 and 104.

516-23 Four Clear & One Red pkg(5) **1.85**
Athearn F45, FP45, SD9. Alco Models Century Series, SD40, GP40, C643. Details West headlights 101 and 105 - use two sets.

516-24 Red pkg(2) **.75**
Details West headlights 112, 113, 115 and 116. Detail Associates headlights 1001, 1002, 1005, 1007, 1008 and 1009. Utah Pacific 70, 71 and 84.

516-25 Clear pkg(4) **1.50**
Athearn SD9. Details West headlights 113, 114, 116 and 137. Detail Associates headlights 1002-1004, 1006-1009 and 1011.

7"
Measures .082", #45 Drill.

516-28 One Clear, One Red pkg(2) **.75**
Cal-Scale #263 Mars light, PFM Burlington 05 with Mars light.

516-280 Clear pkg(4) **1.50**
Sealed beam headlights for EMD hood units, GE U-Boat & electrics - all manufacturers.

516-281 Red pkg(4) **1.50**

7-1/2" PKG(4) EA 1.50 (UNLESS NOTED)
Measures .086", #44 Drill.

516-20 Clear
516-27 Clear - Tender pkg(2) **.75**
516-200 Red
516-201 Green
516-202 Amber
516-203 Blue
516-502 One Red, One Green & One Amber set(3) **1.00**

8-1/2" PKG(2) EA 1.00
Measures .096", #44 Drill.

516-409 Clear
516-410 Red
516-411 Green
516-412 Amber

9" PKG(2) EA 1.00
Measures .101", #38 Drill.

516-29 Clear
Headlights for SS Ltd. old trucks and 1/43 Scale (measures 4.46") vehicles.

516-30 Red
516-31 Amber
516-32 Blue

9-1/2" PKG(2) EA 1.50
Measures .110", Drill #35.

516-109 Clear
516-110 Red

10" EA .85
Measures .116", Drill #32.

516-116 Clear
516-117 Red

10-3/4"
Measures .118"

516-118 Red, Clear & Black **.85**
NEW

11"
Measures .128", Drill #30.

516-17 Clear pkg(2) **1.65**
Athearn SW7 Cow, Alco/ Westside GE 44-ton Diesel.

1/35 & 1/43 VEHICLE LIGHTS EA .85

11" lamps in HO Scale. Use for head/tail lights on larger models; measures 4.46" in 1/35 Scale, 5.7" in 1/43 Scale.

516-128 Clear
516-129 Red
516-130 Amber
516-131 Blue
516-132 Black (For infra-red lamps.)
516-800 One Red, One Green & One Amber set(3) **2.25**
Approximately 11" in HO, measures .125", drill 1/8". 1/32 Scale aircraft recognition lights.

12"
Measures .136", Drill #29.

516-136 Clear
516-137 Red
516-138 Amber
516-139 Blue

ATHEARN BALDWIN S12

516-21 Clear pkg(2) **1.65**

13" EA .85
Measures .149", Drill #25.

516-149 Clear
516-150 Red

14"
Measures .159", Drill #21.

516-159 Clear **.75**
516-160 Red **.85**

14-1/2" EA .95
Measures .166", Drill #19. Use for vehicle lights in 1/35 Scale (measures 5.7") or 1/43 (measures 7").

516-166 Clear
516-167 Red
516-168 Amber
516-169 Blue

15" EA .85
Measures .173", Drill #17.

516-173 Clear
516-174 Red

15-1/2" EA .85
Measures .180", Drill #15.

516-180 Clear
516-181 Red
516-182 Amber
516-183 Blue

16"
516-185 Clear **.85**
Measures .185", Drill #13.

17"
516-193 Clear **.85**
Measures .193", Drill #10.

17-1/2" EA .95
Measures .199", Drill #8. Use with 7" lamps on 1/35 scale vehicles.

516-197 Amber
516-198 Red
516-199 Clear

ATHEARN F7A

Scale 17-1/2" fits nose and front door headlights. Some roads equipped one lamp with a red emergency stop signal, which can be modeled with #111.

SET(2) EA 1.85
516-11 Clear
516-111 One Clear & One Red

18"
516-204 Clear **.95**
Measures .204", Drill #6.

18-1/2" EA .95
Measures .209", Drill #4. Ideal for marker lights (measures 4-1/2") in G Scale.

516-209 Clear
516-210 Red
516-211 Green
516-212 Amber

19" EA .95
Measures .221", Drill #2. Use for 7" lamps in 1/32 Scale.

516-216 Red
516-217 Amber
516-218 Clear

20" EA .95
Measures .228", Drill #1. Use for 5.7" lamps in 1/24-1/25 Scale vehicles.

516-228 Clear
516-229 Red
516-230 Amber
516-231 Blue

21-1/2"
516-401 Clear **1.75**
Measures/Drill 15/64".

22"
516-248 Clear **1.00**
Measures .248", Drill 1/4".

23"
516-402 Clear **1.75**
Measures/Drill 17/64".

24-1/2" EA 1.75
Measures/Drill 9/32". Use for 7" lamps on 1/24 - 1/25 Scale vehicles.

516-403 Clear
516-414 Red
516-415 Amber

26"
516-404 Clear **1.75**
Measures/Drill 19/64".

CATALOG

516-1001 Catalog & Usage List **FREE**
A comprehensive list of all MV lenses, with sizes and applications for various models.

METAL MINIATURES

Parts are lead alloy castings. Illustrations are not to scale.

WEIGHTS EA 4.00

340-175 Freight Car Weights pkg(8)
340-176 Athearn PA1
340-177 Athearn SW7
340-178 Athearn GE U28B or U28C

DIESEL SNOW PLOWS EA 3.00

340-50

340-53

340-50 GP/SD Series Locos
Fits Athearn locos, adaptable to Tyco and PFM.

340-53 No Mounting Brackets
Adaptable to various diesels.

340-51

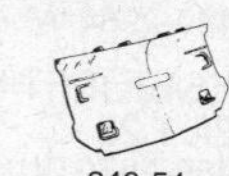
340-54

340-51 F Unit
Larger style applied to some F-units. Fits Athearn F7A, adaptable to others.

340-54 Medium
Used for clearing yards and sidings. Fits Athearn SW, GP & SD models.

340-52 SP & Others
Slightly different from #50, used by several major roads.

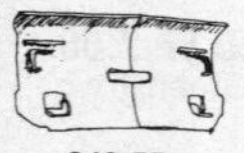
340-55

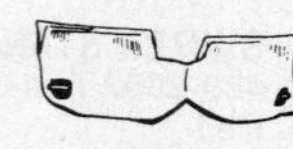
340-65

340-55 Square Nose
For Athearn PA and Walthers FA diesels with square front.

340-65 Southern Pacific F Units
Used for many years on Fs.

1960s-1970s DIESELS

Used on many EMD GP and SD, and GE U28-U33 units. Fits Athearn, Life-Like and Bachmann as well as Alco and imported brass locos.

340-56

340-57

340-56 Notched Corner
340-57 Small Coupler Opening

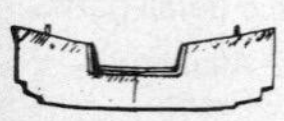
340-58

340-61

340-58 No Cable Opening
340-61 EJ&E, LIRR "Weedcutter" Style

340-59

340-60

340-59 Large Coupler Opening
340-60 CNW Type

340-62 340-64

340-62 Chessie System/CSX Type
340-64 GE U-Boat Type

PASSENGER CAR PARTS

340-75 Air Conditioning Unit **3.00**
Pullman type, 1931, adaptable to most heavyweight cars.

TRACKSIDE DETAIL

340-100 Track Siding Bumper Post **4.00**
Bolted tie crib and earth works, for all types of shortline or industrial trackage.

340-33 Portable Generator **4.00**

FORK LIFT

340-32 Clark Fork Lift Trucks pkg(2) **4.00**

CAR LOADS EA 4.00

One-piece casting loads ideal for open cars.
340-34 Covered Machinery
340-35 Crated Machinery

NOCH

IMPORTED FROM GERMANY BY WALTHERS

Made of appropriately colored plastic with molded and painted details.

PARK BENCHES

528-11200 pkg(10) **11.99**

WASTE CONTAINERS

528-11490 **11.99**

WATERING TROUGH

528-10880 **6.99**

WIRE FASTENERS

528-60160 pkg(10) **7.99**

ON-TRAK model products

All items are cast in a lead-tin-antimony alloy.

DETAIL PARTS

786-55 Spread-Lift Bar (for crane) pkg(2) **2.00**
786-110 20" Hook w/Pulley pkg(2) **1.50**
786-200 Hayes Track Bumper pkg(2) **2.75**
786-219 Depot Roof Support pkg(12) **2.75**
786-370 Stove Pipe pkg(6) **1.95**
786-377 Pulley Set pkg(36) **5.20**
786-427 Highway Pylons pkg(12) **1.95**
786-434 Eave Set (for SOO Depot) pkg(20) **3.35**
786-462 Industrial Stack pkg(4) **1.75**
786-511 Tall Stack (SOO) pkg(3) **3.20**
786-534 Bolster 8' x 9" pkg(8) **3.50**
786-588 End Railing pkg(4) **3.50**
786-595 Screw Jack Large pkg(6) **2.25**
786-598 Screw Jack Small pkg(6) **1.75**
786-602 Old Milk Can pkg(8) **2.45**
786-621 Spare Tire pkg(4) **2.00**
786-623 Truck Dual pkg(8) **2.75**
786-625 Front Tire pkg(4) **2.20**
786-645 Garbage Cans pkg(6) **2.10**
786-646 5-Gallon Grease Cans pkg(12) **2.25**
786-679 Power Axle w/Divider pkg(2) **1.75**
786-680 Power Axle w/Divider pkg(2) **1.50**
786-700 Jib Crane Kit **5.25**
786-702 Abandoned Model T in Swamp - Mini Diorama **7.95** *NEW*
786-725 Riveted Bolster w/Screws pkg(4) **2.45**
786-746 1940s Truck Rear Axle pkg(2) **1.50**
786-805 Tool Box 10 x 22" pkg(4) **1.75**
786-817 Pulley w/Frame pkg(4) **2.45**
786-821 Mack Truck Hood pkg(2) **3.25**
786-875 Wood Spoked Rims w/Tires pkg(4) **2.25**
786-879 Crane Boom pkg(2) **2.75**
786-883 Pulleys w/Bracket pkg(12) **2.50**
786-886 Exhaust Pipe w/Muffler pkg(3) **1.75**

786-946 Raccoon Raiding Barrel pkg(2) **2.50** *NEW*
786-947 Battered Wooden Kegs pkg(4) **2.49**
786-948 Grain Sacks (4 Single, 4 Double) **2.70**
786-998 Gas Station Air Compressor **1.65**

786-749 Cab Assembly 7 Piece Set **4.75**

POLA

IMPORTED FROM GERMANY BY WALTHERS

INTERIOR DETAILS

578-460 **11.99**

ROCO

IMPORTED FROM AUSTRIA BY WALTHERS

PANTOGRAPHS EA 10.99

Working metal pantographs.

625-85225 Austrian Type II With "Wanisch" mount.

625-85233 DBB Type SBS #54 For AC (Black)
625-85234 DB Type SBS #67 (Red)
Same as #85216, but with wider wiper to fit 3-rail AC systems.

WHEEL BLOCKS

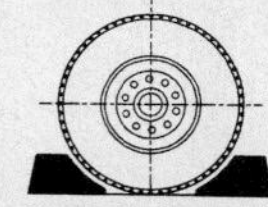

625-40005 Plastic Wheel Blocks for Trucks pkg(12) **4.99**

WIPERS EA 3.99

625-40002 Replacement AC Wiper (2.2" 56mm)
Fits 14111, 14120, 14126, 14138, 14145, 14148 and 14191.

625-40003 Replacement AC Wiper (1.6" 42mm)
Fits 14178 and 14183.

SMALLTOWN U.S.A.

Molded plastic detail parts.

DOORS PKG(2) EA 1.50

699-4

699-5

699-4 Overhead, 10 x 12'
699-5 Hinged Freight, 10 x 9'

"ScRRatch Stuff" EA 2.69

Includes easy-to-build mini kits and ready-to-use accessories that range from baggage carts to track tool sets. Made from fine Britannia castings and/or laser cut wood components.

482-6001 Baggage Cart Mini Kit

482-6002 Wood Barrels w/Pallets

482-6003 Window Kit - Double Hung, 4-Pane

482-6004 Window Coolers pkg(2)

482-6005 Cast Metal Double Doors pkg(2)

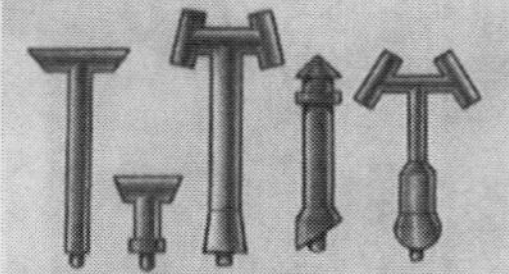

482-6006 Cast Metal Smokestacks pkg(5)

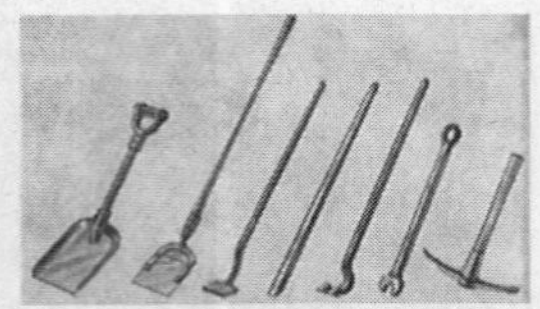

482-6007 Track Tool Set pkg(7)

482-6010 Dory

482-6008 Concrete Telephone Booth

482-6011 Hand Cart Mini Kit

482-6012 Block & Tackle

ASSORTMENT

482-6000 Detail Assortment pkg(48) **129.12**
Includes four each of the 12 ScRRatch Stuff products shown above.

RAIL POWER PRODUCTS

Plastic parts are designed to fit Rail Power diesel locomotive shells, but can be adapted to other models.

AIR CONDITIONERS

60-103 GE **1.00**
60-111 GE Dash 8 **1.00**
60-127 GE Dash 8-40CW Deck Mount **1.50**
60-141 GE Dash 9-44CW **1.50**

AIR TANKS EA 1.00 (UNLESS NOTED)

60-118 Dash 8-40B
60-126 Dash 8-40CW pkg(2)
60-135 SD7/9
60-153 SD90MAC **2.00**

ANTI-CLIMBER

60-144 GE C32-8 **1.00**

BLOWER

60-108 EMD SD60 Blower Housing pkg(2) **1.00**

BRAKE HATCHES EA 2.00

GP35

60-120 Dynamic w/Fan
60-121 Nondynamic

SD7/9

60-133 Dynamic w/Fan
60-134 Nondynamic

SD40

60-147 Dynamic w/Fan
60-148 Nondynamic

SD38

60-149 Dynamic w/Fan
60-150 Nondynamic

GP60/GP60M

60-158 Dynamic w/Fan

BRAKE WHEEL

60-107 Locomotive Type pkg(6) **1.00**

CABS EA 8.00

60-122 Dash 8-40CW
60-129 Dash 8-40CW-ATSF
60-130 SD60
60-137 SD60M
60-138 GP60M
60-152 SD90MAC "I" Cab
60-156 GP60B Cab & Dynamic Brake Without Fan
60-157 GP60 Cab w/Number Board

CHASSIS EA 12.00

Diecast metal parts designed to fit Rail Power body shells, listed in the Locomotives Section.

60-115 Dash 8-40B
60-119 CF7
60-123 Dash 8-40CW
60-128 SD60, SD60M
60-131 SD7/9
60-136 SD45-2
60-139 GP60M/B, GP40X
60-140 Dash 9-44CW
60-146 SD38, 40 & 45
60-151 SD90MAC

DOORS

60-110 EMD Hood Unit Cab Doors pkg(3) **1.00**

DRIVE SHAFT

60-145 1-1/2" for Athearn Drive pkg(4) **1.50**

EXHAUST STACKS EA .50 (UNLESS NOTED)

60-101 Dash 8 Early
60-102 Dash 7/8 Large
60-105 EMD Silencer **1.00**
60-112 GE Bathtub Silencer
60-125 8-40CW&B
60-142 9-44CW

FANS EA 1.25

60-104 EMD "Q" Fan Set pkg(3)
60-155 SD38 36" Dynamic Brake Fans

FUEL TANK

60-132 SD7/9 Half **1.50**

IMPAC BRACES

60-124 Container Braces for Athearn Impac pkg(4) **2.50**

"NOSE" KIT

60-106 EMD 116" Snoot **4.00**

NUMBER BOARDS

60-109 C32-8 pkg(4) **.50**
60-116 CF7 Light/Number **1.00**

RADIATORS

60-154 SD90MAC Radiator Section w/Fans **3.75**

ROOF SECTION

60-159 GP60B Engine Compartment Roof Section **1.25**
60-160 SD90MAC-H Engine Roof w/Exhaust **5.00** *NEW*

SIDEFRAMES

60-114 FB-2 pkg(4) **7.00**
60-143 GE Dash 9-44CW Hi-Adhesion Truck pkg(4) **7.00**
60-161 GP40X HTB **8.50** *NEW*

CAR PARTS EA 2.50

480-2990 AB Brake Set pkg(3)
480-2992 Box Car Doors 6' 2 Pair

HANDRAIL PKG(12) EA 2.50

480-2977 Locomotive Posts
480-2978 Caboose (Curved, Angled & Platform)

HOPPER ENDS EA 2.50

480-2991 Oval 3 Pair
480-2993 Peaked 3 Pair

JEWELS

MARKER PKG(12) EA 1.25

480-2961 Red
480-2962 Green
480-2963 Amber
480-2964 White

HEADLIGHT PKG(2) EA 1.25

480-2970 3/16" Diameter
480-2971 5/32" Diameter

MARKER LAMPS

CABOOSE PKG(2) EA 2.50

480-2950 Three Green, One Red
480-2951 Three Amber, One Red

LOCO

480-2954 Two Green, Two White pkg(2) **2.50**

SWITCH STAND EA 2.50

480-2952 Two Green, Two Red
480-2953 Two Amber, Two Red

ASSORTMENTS

Includes 2 lamps and assorted jewels.

480-2955 Assortment **2.95**
480-2956 Classification Lamp **1.75**

SCREWS

480-2959 Screw Assortment pkg(36) **1.50**

TRACK GAUGE

480-2975 HO Track Gauge **1.50**

VALVE GEAR KITS EA 10.00

Brass and plastic detail parts.

480-2840 4-4-2 Atlantic
480-2841 2-6-2 Prairie

PLANO

Made of photo-etched metal for near scale thickness, and see-through surfaces on grilles, platforms and walkways.

DETAIL PARTS

AIR GRILLES

565-181 Farr Grille-Rock Island U25B pkg(2) **2.75**
Fits Stewart loco.

ACF ATHERN HOPPERS WALKWAY RISERS EA 2.00

565-118 Same Size
565-119 Two Sizes

BRACKETS EA 2.25 (UNLESS NOTED)

565-182 Rotary Beacon Light Bracket-Cab Corner pkg(3)
565-183 Rotary Beacon Light Bracket-Cab Center Low pkg(4)
565-184 Small Antenna Bracket-Cab Center pkg(3)
565-200 Box Car Roofwalk Brass pkg(6) **3.75** *NEW*

BRAKE PLATFORM PKG(2) EA 1.25 (UNLESS NOTED)

For early box cars.
565-130 Open Round
565-131 Slotted
565-132 Diamond
565-13112 Apex Slotted Pattern pkg(12) **5.75** *NEW*

BRASS LIFT RINGS

565-120 pkg(60) **2.25** *NEW*

COUPLER PLATFORMS

PARTIAL CAR WIDTH EA 1.95

565-127 Round
565-128 Slotted
565-129 Open Diamond

FULL CAR WIDTH EA 2.75

565-133 Round
565-134 Slotted Pattern
565-135 Diamond US Gypsum

CONVERSION

565-1284 Apex slotted pattern pkg(4) **6.00** *NEW*

CONTAINER CAR DETAILS

565-136 Brake Rod Support for A-Line Gunderson Container pkg(4) **1.00**
565-137 End Load Guides, Set(20) **1.75**
565-138 Locator Boxes, Set(10) **2.75**
565-139 Lift Rings w/Gussets (40-45' Wells) Set(20) **2.00**
565-140 Freight Car Lift Rings pkg(24) **1.00**
565-171 A-Line Husky Stack Replacement Detail Parts **3.00**

FAN HATCHES EA 3.50 (UNLESS NOTED)

565-180 SD45 **4.00** *NEW*
565-185 SD40-2
565-186 GP35
565-187 GP38
565-188 GP38-2

REPLACEMENT THRALL STANCHIONS

565-321 WKW pkg(8) **3.00** *NEW*

SLOTTED MATERIAL EA 10.50

Large, photo-etched sheets feature a slotted pattern. Each measures 1.8 x 8.5".
565-201 Stainless
565-202 Brass

MORTON ROUND PATTERN EA 10.50

565-203 Stainless Steel
565-204 Brass

STEP GUARDS

565-189 EMD Blower Housing-Angled Slots pkg(4) **1.00**
Photo-etched brass, fits many EMD hood units.

TRUCK AND TRAILER DETAILS

CROSS OVER PLATFORMS/STEPS PKG(3) EA 2.25 (UNLESS NOTED)

565-366 Round Pattern
565-367 Slotted Pattern
565-368 Diamond Pattern
565-369 Diamond Tread Plate
565-370 12' Frame Steps
565-371 18' Frame Steps **2.50**

FENDERS

565-372 Chrome Quarter Finders pkg(2) **2.25**

MUDFLAPS

Fits Herpa and Promotex trucks, adaptable to others.
565-352 Chrome Tipped Flaps pkg(2) **2.25**

PLACARD FRAMES

565-310 Tank Cars **1.75**
565-311 Truck/Trailer-Flush Mount **1.50**

RACKS FOR TRIDENT CHEVY PICKUPS

565-378 Pipe Rack, 8' Box **3.25**
565-379 Louvered Headache Rack **2.00**

RADIATOR GRILLES PKG(2) EA 2.25

Etched stainless, fits Herpa and Promotex tractors.

FORD

565-353 Aeromax

INTERNATIONAL

565-356 IHC Tractors

MACK

565-350 With MACK lettering
565-351 Plain (UPS style) with NO lettering

RUNNING BOARDS FOR TRIDENT CHEVYS

565-381 Pickup **2.50**
565-382 Blazer **2.50**
565-383 Suburban **3.00**
565-384 Van **3.00**

TAILGATE

565-380 Louvered w/5th Wheel Cutout for Trident Chevy Pickup **2.00**

TRUCK MIRROR SETS EA 2.00 (UNLESS NOTED)

565-354 Ford Aeromax Set #1
565-355 Ford Aeromax Set #2
565-357 International Set #1
565-374 International Set #2
565-358 Mack CH13 Set #1
565-373 Mack CH13 Set #2
565-359 "Lollipop" Style pkg(8)
565-360 Front Corner Bumper Post pkg(8)
565-361 Front Finder Set #1
565-362 Front Finder Set #2
565-363 Front Finder Set #3
565-364 Front Finder Set #4
565-365 Front Finder Set #5
565-375 KW T600 Set for Herpa **2.25**
565-376 UPS/Mack Truck Mirrors/Details for Herpa **3.24**
565-377 UPS Box Delivery Van Mirror/Detail Set for Walthers & N.J. International

DRILL TEMPLATES

565-174 Athearn Husky Stack Maxi III **5.00**
565-175 A-Line Husky Stack **4.50**
565-176 A-Line Thrall Long & Short Ends, Standard 40' & 45' APL **6.50**
565-177 A-Line Thrall 45' TTX Short End **2.75**
565-178 A-Line Thrall Electric Long & Short Ends **7.50**
565-179 A-Line 40' Gunderson Car **2.50**

FRAME KITS

Designed for A-Line Thrall cars.

40' DOUBLE STACK CARS

565-161 End Units (Two 40' "End" Wells) pkg(2) **8.75**
565-162 Mid Units (Two 40' "Mid" Wells) pkg(2) **8.25**
565-163 Five Unit Set (Five 40' Wells) pkg(5) **17.95**

45'

565-164 APL Mid-Units pkg(2) **8.95**
Two 45' middle wells.
565-165 APL Five-Unit Set pkg(5) **18.95**
Two 40' ends, three 45' middles.
565-166 APL Mid-Units pkg(2) **8.95**
Two 45' middle wells.
565-167 TTX Five-Unit Set pkg(5) **18.95**
Two 40' ends, three 45' middles.

GUNDERSON

565-168 40' Gunderson, Five-Unit pkg(5) **4.50**
Five wells.

THRALL-ELECTRIC VERSIONS

565-169 End Units pkg(2) **9.75**
Two 40' "end" wells.
565-170 Five Units pkg(5) **19.25**
Five 40' wells.

PASSENGER CAR PARTS

BLINDS

565-300 Venetian Blinds 3 Sizes, Stainless Steel **8.50**

WALKWAYS

Photo-etched metal for scale thickness and see-through tread in round, slotted, and diamond patterns, as used on prototype cars.

WALTHERS

50' AIRSLIDE COVERED HOPPERS

565-95 Single-Bay Apex, Slotted **3.75**
565-98 Double-Bay Apex, Slotted **4.50**
565-99 Double-Bay Morton, Round **4.50**

FRONT RUNNER PLATFORMS

565-126 2 Sets **3.00** *NEW*

AUTO RACKS

565-325 Side Panels **TBA**

CEMENT HOPPERS

565-86 2-Bay **5.75**

PULLMAN-STANDARD PS2CD COVERED HOPPERS EA 8.50

565-87 Morton, Round
565-88 Apex, Slotted

PRESSURE DIFFERENTIAL (PD) COVERED HOPPERS

565-114 Morton, Round **7.25**

COIL CARS, FULL-LENGTH EA 5.50

565-121 Morton, Round
565-123 Apex, Slotted

COIL CARS, ENDS ONLY EA 3.75

565-122 Morton, Round
565-124 Apex, Slotted

FUNNEL-FLOW TANK CARS

565-301 Platform Walkway **5.25**

65' LPG/ANHYDROUS AMMONIA TANK CARS

565-302 Center Handrail **7.75**
565-303 Outside Handrail **6.75**
565-304 Inside Handrail **6.75**

SPINE CARS

565-158 Walkways **2.25**

20' TANK CONTAINER

565-316 Walkways **2.00**

48' THRALL WELL CARS

565-153 Stand-Alone Single, Round **4.25**
565-154 Five Car Set **8.75**

48' THRALL DOUBLE STACK CONTAINER CAR

565-1533 3 Sets **7.50** *NEW*

HUSKY STACK

565-125 General Purpose Husky Stack Walkway **5.25**

A-LINE

THRALL DOUBLE STACK

565-141 40' End Units Only **2.75**
Two ends.
565-142 40' Mid Units Only **2.75**
Two middles.
565-143 40' Five Unit Set **5.75**
Two ends, three middles.
565-144 45' APL Style Mid Unit **3.00**
Two 45' middles.
565-145 APL Style Five Unit Set **5.95**
Two 45' ends, three 40' middles.
565-146 45' TTX Style Mid Unit **3.00**
Two 45' middles.
565-147 45' TTX Style Five Unit Set **5.95**
Two 40' ends, three 45' middles.

DOUBLE STACK

565-148 40' Gunderson Five Unit Set **1.75**
Walkways with lift rings.

THRALL ELECTRIC VERSIONS

565-149 End Unit **2.75**
Two 40' end wells.
565-150 Five Unit **5.75**
Five 40' wells.

HUSKY STACK

565-151 Walkway & Detail Parts **7.75**

AMERICAN LIMITED

20' TANK CONTAINERS

565-315 Bulktainer **2.25**
565-317 20' Tank **2.00**
565-318 UP Style w/Placards **3.50**

ATHEARN

PULLMAN-STANDARD PS-3 COVERED HOPPERS EA 8.50

565-84 Morton, Round
565-85 Apex, Slotted

PLANO

4-BAY ACF COVERED HOPPERS EA 9.25
565-110 Morton, Round
565-111 Apex, Slotted

HUSKY STACK
565-155 Walkways & Detail Parts **7.75**
565-156 Maxi III Walkways 5-Unit **13.50**
565-157 Brass Details-Maxi III 5-Unit **10.25**

IMPAC CARS
565-152 Walkway Set-Round **2.00**

ATLAS

565-96 ACF Cylindrical Hopper Walkway with Risers **9.50**
535-307 33,000 Gallon Tank Car **6.25** *NEW*

BOWSER

565-91 ACF 70-Ton 2-Bay Walkway Kit **3.50** *NEW*
Also works with Kato.
565-320 Roadrailer Coupler Mate Detail Set **4.25**

CENTRALIA CAR SHOPS

565-451 UP CA-3 Caboose **4.75**
Includes steps, end platforms, and walkways.

CON-COR

565-92 PS2 3-Bay Covered Hopper Apex, Slotted **4.50**

DETAIL ASSOCIATES

ACF TWO-BAY COVERED HOPPER EA 7.25
565-76 Morton
565-77 Apex
565-78 US Gypsum

INTERMOUNTAIN

PULLMAN STANDARD COVERED HOPPERS-MORTON, ROUND EA 9.00
565-82 Trinity Style
565-83 PS4750

CYLINDRICAL HOPPERS EA 8.25
565-97 Canadian Hopper-Morton
565-100 Canadian Grain Cars

R-40-23 REEFERS - PFE EA 2.25
565-196 Morton, Round
565-197 Apex, Slotted
565-198 US Gypsum, Diamond
565-199 Transco, Diamond

SANTA FE REEFERS EA 4.50
565-205 Morton, Round
565-206 Apex, Slotted
565-207 Transco, Diamond

MCKEAN

ACF CENTERFLOW COVERED HOPPERS
Apex pattern for Front Range cars.
565-102 2-Bay **7.50** *NEW*
565-105 3-Bay **8.25** *NEW*

FRONT RUNNER EA 2.25
Each includes two sets of walkways.
565-159 Round
565-160 Diamond

MODEL DIE CASTING

FMC COVERED HOPPERS EA 9.25
565-80 Morton, Round
565-81 Apex, Slotted

TANK CAR PLATFORM
565-305 Modern Car **5.25**

RED CABOOSE
565-306 10,000 Gallon Type 103W Tank Car Platforms **4.25**

PS-2 TWO BAY COVERED HOPPERS
565-89 Apex Slotted **3.50**
565-90 US Gypsum Diamond **3.50**
565-893 Apex pkg(3) **8.00** *NEW*

BOX CAR WALKWAYS
Fits virtually any 40 or 50' box car models.

40' EA 4.00 (UNLESS NOTED)
565-190 Round
565-191 Slotted
565-192 Diamond
565-1916 Apex Slotted Pattern pkg(6) **18.25** *NEW*

50' EA 4.50 (UNLESS NOTED)
565-193 Morton, Round
565-194 APEX, Slotted
565-195 US Gypsum

HUSKY STACK CARS 2 + 2 WALKWAYS W/BRASS DETAILS EA 9.25
565-172 Early Style with Side Patterns
565-173 Late Style without Side Platforms

OUTDOOR FURNITURE

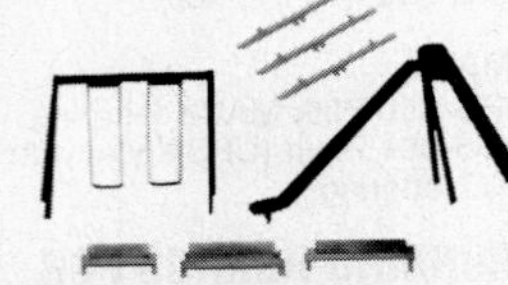

570-94702 Playground Set **9.95**

570-94705 Basketball Set pkg(2) **2.95**

570-94708 Diving Board **2.75**

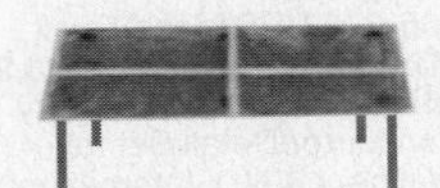

570-94712 Ping Pong Table **3.25**
570-94752 Umbrella Tables pkg(3) **4.50**

570-94762 Patio Chair Set pkg(3) **5.50**

570-94772 Park Bench Set pkg(5) **2.75**

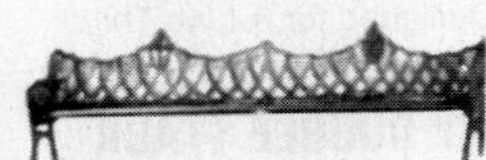

570-94767 1800s Park Bench pkg(2) **5.50**

GAS PUMPS

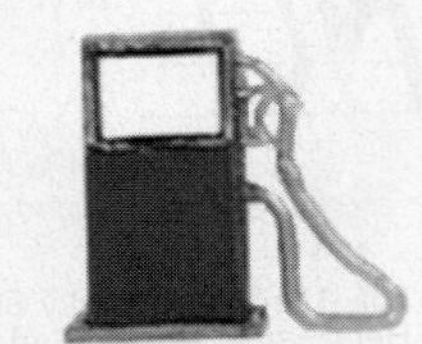

570-94872 1960s Style pkg(3) **3.95**

FOUNTAINS

570-94733 1" Square **5.25**
570-94732 1-1/2" Square **6.25**
570-94735 1" Hexagon **5.25**

SWIMMING POOL

570-94710 4-5/8 x 4" **5.95**

GEORGIAN COLUMN

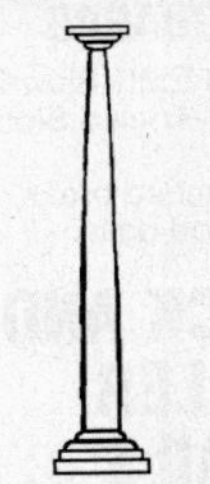

570-90993 1-31/32" **4.95**

LATTICES/TRELLIS

570-90911 2-1/8 x 15/16" **4.00**

570-90912 1-1/4 x 4" pkg(2) **5.00**

570-90913 4-1/8 x 2" pkg(2) **5.00**
570-90914 2 -7/16 x 4" pkg(2) **5.00**
570-90915 1-7/16 x 1-7/8" **4.00**
570-90916 5-7/8 x 2-7/8 x 1/8" **7.00**
570-90917 2-7/8 x 5-7/8" **7.00**

Information STATION

Casey Jones, America's Most Famous Engineer

John Luther Jones was a real person, born in southeast Missouri on March 14, 1864. His family later moved to Caycee, Kentucky. This was the origin of his nickname "Casey," which distinguished him from other John Joneses working on the Illinois Central. By age 26, Jones was engineer of the "Cannonball Express" between Memphis, Tennessee, and Canton, Mississippi.

On April 30, 1900, Casey made his mark in history. Around 4:00 a.m., the "Cannonball" neared tiny Vaughan, Mississippi, where passing tracks allowed trains to meet.

Running late and hurtling through the foggy darkness at 50mph, Jones had no idea one of two freights stopped up ahead was too long for the siding. Its crew planned a "saw by," a slow speed switching trick that permitted the shorter mail train to pass the rear, then the front of the freight. The rear brakeman had gone back 3,000 feet behind his train and placed warning signals on the track. Out of the darkness, the "Cannonball" suddenly roared past, never acknowledging his warnings nor slowing. A hundred feet from the stopped freight train, Casey realized a crash was inevitable. He told his fireman to jump, but he stayed on trying to stop the train.

When they pulled his body from the wreck, they found one hand on the whistle cord and the other on the airbrake lever. Wallace Stevens, an engine wiper on the IC, wrote a poem about Casey's last run, which eventually became the "Ballad of Casey Jones."

Division of Rix Products

Parts are molded in plastic.

STRUCTURAL DETAILS

DOORS

541-1100 Roll-Up Freight pkg(2) **1.50**

541-1101 30 Panel Wood pkg(2) **1.50**

541-1102 541-1103 541-1104

541-1102 Solid pkg(3) **1.50**
541-1103 Door w/Large Window pkg(3) **1.50**
541-1104 Door w/3-Panel Window pkg(3) **1.50**

541-1105 Window/Door Combo pkg(2) **1.50**

541-1106 Store Front & Window **1.50**

541-1110 Two Car Garage, 16 x 7' pkg(2) **1.50**

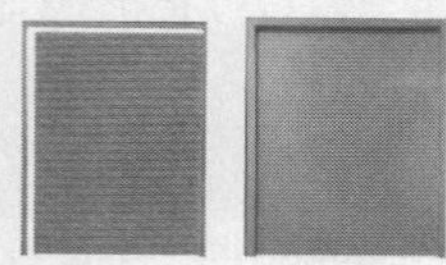

541-1108 541-1109

541-1108 Engine House Door/Frame pkg(2) **1.75**
541-1109 Roll-Up Loading, 9-1/2 x 12' pkg(2) **1.50**

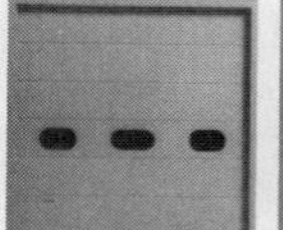

541-1107 541-1111

541-1107 12 x 12' Freight pkg(2) **1.50**
541-1111 Double Personnel pkg(2) **1.50**
541-1112 Fire Station Door w/Separate Frame (Open) pkg(2) **1.50**

541-1113

541-1115

541-1113 Roll-Up Freight Door, 9-1/2 x 10' pkg(2) **1.50**
541-1115 Window & Center Door Combo pkg(2) **1.50**
541-1200 Personnel Doors pkg(6) **2.25**
541-1201 Windows Assorted pkg(6) **2.25**
541-1202 Freight Doors Assorted pkg(6) **3.00**

541-1203 Doors & Windows Assorted pkg(6) **3.00**

WINDOWS EA 1.50

541-2100 541-2102

541-2100 1-Story pkg(3)
541-2102 Two-Story (Metal Buildings) pkg(2)

541-2101 Vertical Pane Slide Window pkg(3)

541-2103 541-2104

541-2103 Four-Pane pkg(3)
541-2104 Eight-Pane pkg(2)

DOWNSPOUTS

541-1116 Large Overhang pkg(4) **1.25**

541-3101 Small Overhang pkg(6) **1.50**

GUARDRAIL

Kits include plastic molded parts and illustrated instructions.

541-3 Guard **1.15**
541-12 Highway Guardrail pkg(3) **2.50**
541-13 Highway Guardrail pkg(6) **4.00**

MACHINE SHOP DOORS/WINDOWS

541-3000 Doors & Windows pkg(8) **2.50**
541-3002 Windows pkg(4) **1.50**

PARKING BARRIER

541-1016 Concrete pkg(12) **1.50**

STAIR PARTS EA 1.50

514-1010 541-1114

541-1010 Concrete Staircase pkg(3)
541-1114 Staircase Handrails pkg(2)

VENTILATORS

541-1009 541-3102

541-1009 Louvered pkg(3) **1.50**
541-3102 Roof Ridge pkg(4) **1.99**

BUILDING DETAIL SET

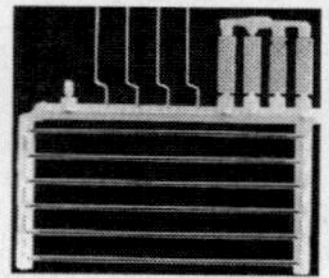

541-3001 Gutters, Downspouts, Chimney & Electric Meter **2.50**

CAR DETAILS

PANEL HOPPER CONVERSION

"Blisters" were applied on the side panels of some older cars to increase carrying capacity. Complete set fits Athearn 34' ribbed side hoppers.

541-4000 1.99

PASSENGER CAR SEATS PKG(36) EA 3.99

For lightweight and streamlined cars.

541-4100 Brown
541-4101 Gray
541-4102 Red
541-4103 Blue
541-4104 Green

DOME CAR WINDOW

541-1 Dome Insert **3.00**
See-through green plastic dome fits Oriental Limited "California Zephyr" car, or any brass model of a Budd prototype dome car.

GLAZING PKG(4) EA 1.50

Each measures 1 x 3" 2.5 x 7.5cm
541-1002 Green Tint
541-1003 Smoke Tint

RED CABOOSE

FREIGHT CAR PARTS

FLAT CARS

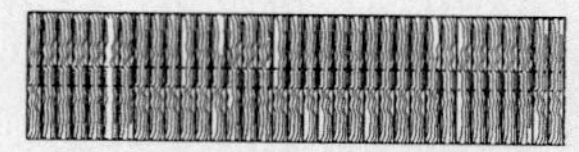

629-220001 42' Laser-Cut Wood Flat Car Deck **3.95** *NEW*
With peel and stick backing.

629-220012 Flat Car Detail Kit **2.75**

TANK CARS

629-300002 Frame **2.75**
629-300006 Detail Sprue **1.85**
629-300008 Frame Grab Irons **1.85**
629-300009 Body Grab Irons **1.85**
629-300011 Car Handrail - Metal **1.85**

REEFERS

629-400001 R-30-9/12 Reefer Laser-Cut Wood Roofwalk **2.95** *NEW*
629-400009 Roof & Roofwalk (Box Car Red) **2.75**
629-400010 K Brakes & Air Hoses **1.85**
629-400011 Wood Ice Hatch/Platform **2.75**
629-400012 Reefer Detail Kit **3.50**
629-400019 R-30-12-9 Reefer Underframe (black) **2.75**
629-400020 Frame Crossmembers **1.85**

BOX CAR

629-800001 40' Roof Walkway **2.75**
629-800005 6' Doors (2 Youngstown, 2 Superior) **2.00**
629-800002 Frame **2.50**
629-800003 Underbody/Brake Sprue **2.50**
629-800004 Ladder/Detail Sprue **2.00**
629-800006 Grab Irons **1.85**
629-800007 AAR Laser-Cut Wood Roofwalk **2.95** *NEW*

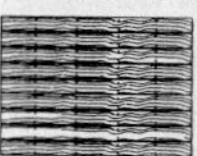

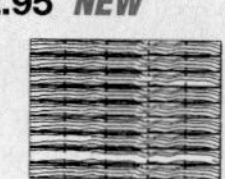

629-800008 10' Wooden Laser-Cut Interior & Roofwalk **9.95** *NEW*
With peel and stick backing.

629-800009 10' 6" Wooden Laser-Cut Interior **6.95** *NEW*
With peel and stick backing.

629-800010 10' Double Door Wooden Laser-Cut Interior & Roofwalk **9.95** *NEW*
With peel and stick backing.

629-800011 10' 6" Double Door Wooden Laser-Cut Interior & Roofwalk **6.95** *NEW*
With peel and stick backing.

MATHER CARS

629-100001 K-Brake Detail **2.75**
629-100002 Underframe **2.95**
629-100003 Ladder/Grab/End Details **2.75**
629-100004 Wooden Laser-Cut Hatches **2.50**
629-100005 Underbody Details **1.85**
629-100006 Roof & Roofwalk **2.75**
629-100007 Mather Laser-Cut Wood Roofwalk **2.95** *NEW*

X-29

629-700001 Underframe **4.00**
629-700002 Door/Detail **5.00**
629-700003 Roof & Roofwalk **2.75**

629-700006 X-29/ARA Box Car Laser-Cut Wood Roofwalk **2.95** *NEW*
629-700007 X-29/ARA Laser-Cut Box Car Interior & Wood Roofwalk **9.95** *NEW*
With peel and stick backing.

ORIGINAL **Preiser**

IMPORTED FROM GERMANY BY WALTHERS

MISCELLANEOUS DETAILS

590-16509 Parachute Kit Less Figures pkg(4) **4.99**

590-17005 Luggage Assortment pkg(90) **11.99**

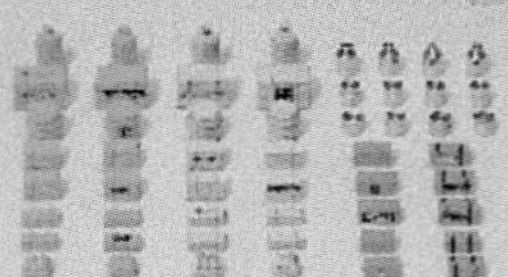
590-17100 Cargo Kit pkg(54) **11.99**

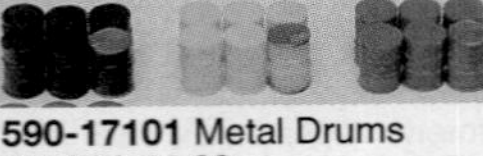
590-17101 Metal Drums pkg(30) **11.99**

590-17102 Sacks pkg(60) **11.99**

590-17103 Handcarts (Assorted) pkg(8) **11.99**

590-17104 Pallets pkg(60) **11.99**

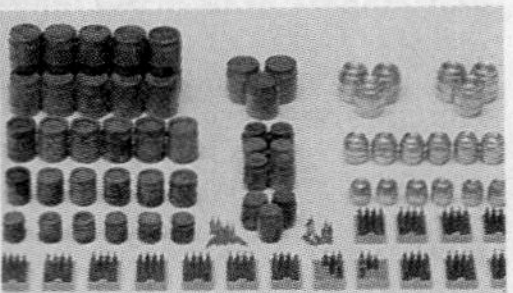
590-17105 Beer Barrels & Crates w/Bottles **11.99**

590-17107 Fork Lifts, Wheelbarrows pkg(26) **24.99**

590-17110 Lattice Box, Pallets, Crates pkg(38) **32.99**
590-17111 Cargo Accessories **31.99**

590-17112 Postal Carts **18.99**

590-17113 Plastic Boxes Kit **11.99**

590-17175 Accessories for Track Workers **17.99**
590-17177 Concrete Mixer, Tool Kit **18.99**

590-17178 Traffic Control Accessory Kit **11.99**

590-17184 Office Equipment **29.99**

590-17185 Workshop Equipment **25.99**

590-17200 Park Benches (unpainted) pkg(24) **11.99**

590-17219 Banquet Tables & Chairs pkg(12) **11.99** ***NEW***
590-17220 Tableware & Food for Tables **14.99** ***NEW***
590-17308 Beach Chairs, Lounges & Huts pkg(18) **16.99** ***NEW***

590-17201 8 Tables & 48 Chairs w/Umbrella **11.99**

590-17209 Garden Umbrellas Multi-Colored pkg(5) **11.99**

590-17325 Soccer Goals **6.99**

590-17500 Market Stalls & Sunshades **16.99**

590-17501 Fruit & Vegetable Boxes **16.99**

590-17502 Baskets Fruit/Vegetables **14.99**
590-18225 Flag Assortment **10.99**
590-18325 Concrete Slabs Kit **11.99**
590-18326 Airfield Lights **18.99**
590-18337 Barbed Wire/Stakes Kit **11.99**
590-21025 Waste Containers **17.99**

590-24705 Dance Floor Less Figures **18.99**
590-25175 Barriers Kit **11.99**

590-17114 Cable Roll and Transport Box **11.99**

590-17179 Telephone Construction Set **19.99**

MILITARY

590-18338 Military Guard Tower **23.99**

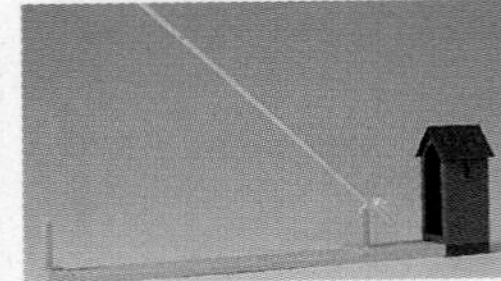
590-18339 Military Sentry Gate Post **6.99**

590-18350 Wooden Supply Crates **3.99**

590-18351 Steel Drums **3.99**

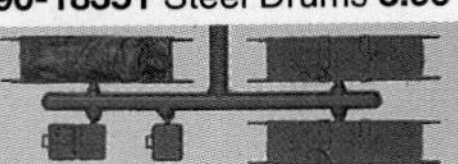
590-18352 Stretchers (Assorted) **3.99**

590-18353 Pallet Jack & Pallets **3.99**

590-18354 Powered Hand Truck **3.99**

590-18355 Drill Press & Lathe **3.99**

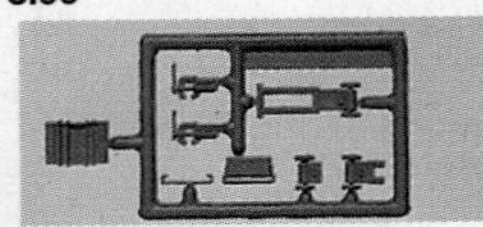
590-18356 Hand Tools (Assorted) **3.99**

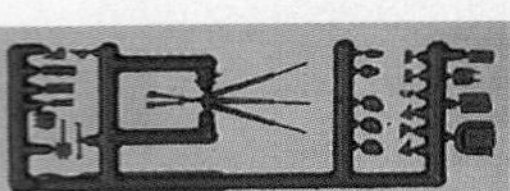
590-18357 Weapon & Gear Set #1 WWII (Assorted) **3.99**

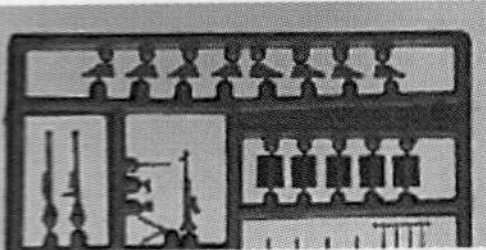
590-18358 Weapon & Gear Set #2 WWII (Assorted) **3.99**

590-18359 Folding Lawn Chairs **3.99**

590-18360 Air Compressor on Wheels **6.99**

590-18361 Steel Storage Chests **3.99**

590-18362 Military Motorcycle **6.99**

590-18363 Steel Storage Baskets **3.99**

590-18364 Generators **3.99**

590-18365 Weapons & Gear Set #3, Modern **3.99**

590-18367 Rafts w/Oars & Life Jackets **3.99**

PRECISION SCALE CO

Super Detailing Parts, Kits and Supplies in Brass and Plastic.

Within the pages of these three catalogs, a modeler will find everything needed to outfit a freight car, passenger car or locomotive the way it should be done. Easy to use, each catalog is organized alphabetically by the more common terms used by modelers. Full of valuable information like critical dimensions and correct scale sizes, these catalogs give readers exactly what they need. Some items have even been enlarged to show more and better detail.

Throughout these fully illustrated catalogs you will find many "Super Detailing Kits" which will enable you to detail existing wood, plastic and brass models. Each catalog includes a complete listing of Precision Scale detail parts for its respective category.

H0 & H0n3
CATALOG OF DETAILING PARTS
FOR
PASSENGER & FREIGHT CARS
Catalog No. 2
PRECISION SCALE CO

HO/HOn3 585-9739

585-9739 HO/HOn3 Passenger/Freight Car **8.00**
Softcover, 8-1/2 x 11" format, 124 pages.

AIR CONDITIONING SYSTEMS

585-31003

585-33212

585-31003 Passenger Car Air Conditioner Compressor (Frigidare) pkg(2) **4.00**
585-33212 Pullman Car Reservoir **2.00**
585-33214 Pullman Car Mechanical Speed Control **3.00**
585-33215 Pullman HW Car Rock Guard for Compressor w/Screen **2.50**
585-33233 Pullman Car Mechanical Standby Switch Box **1.75**

CHAIN & CHAIN HOOKS

585-3304 Inboard Chain Hooks pkg(6) **2.50**
585-3305 Outboard Chain Hooks pkg(6) **2.50**
585-32042 Inboard Chain Hooks, Plastic pkg(10) **2.00**
585-32043 Outboard Chain Hooks, Plastic pkg(10) **2.00**

HON3 FREIGHT CAR KITS

These craft train kits consist of unpainted brass, plastic and wood parts.

585-614 34' Stock Car DRGW **21.95**
585-684 Tank Car UTLX **21.95**
585-10608 30' Wood Reefer DRGW **23.75**
585-10640 40' Wood Reefer DRGW **22.50**

UNDERFRAMES

585-31032 HOn3 Box Car, Brass **9.75**
585-31567 HOn3 Box Car, Plastic **2.50**
585-31569 HOn3 Caboose C&S 4-Wheel w/Pedestals & 26" Wheels, 9' Wheelbase **9.00**

PRECISION SCALE CO INC
HO AND HOn3
STEAM LOCOMOTIVE CATALOG
OF DETAILING PARTS
IN
BRASS & PLASTIC
CATALOG NO.1

HO/HOn3 585-9740

585-9740 HO/HOn3 Steam Locomotive **16.00**
Softcover, 8-1/2 x 11" format, over 200 pages.

BOOSTER ENGINES

585-3297 Franklin Type for Tender **4.00**
585-3299 Franklin Type w/Steam Joint, Kit **6.25**
585-3447 Steam Piping for SP GS-Series pkg(2) **2.75**

585-3296 Franklin Type Plumbing Connections pkg(2) **2.75**

AIR PUMPS

585-3092

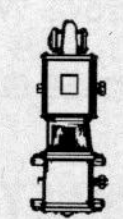
585-3188

585-3092 8-1/2" Wabco Cross Compound **3.25**
585-3188 9-1/2" Single Phase Westinghouse **2.50**

HO SCALE
DIESEL LOCOMOTIVE
DETAILING PARTS
Brass & Plastic
Catalog No. 2
PRECISION SCALE CO INC
FINEST QUALITY

HO/HOn3 585-9742

585-9742 HO/HOn3 Diesel Locomotive **5.00**
Softcover, 8-1/2 x 11" format, 54 pages.

AIR HORNS

585-39044 Alco pkg(2) **2.25**
585-39083 Alco pkg(2) **2.50**
585-39084 3-Chime w/Ring Mount, Plastic **2.75**
585-39085 3-Chime w/Bracket, Plastic **2.75**

AIR HOSES

585-3150 With Angle Cock & Glad Hand pkg(6) **2.75**
585-3152 With Angle Cock, Less Glad Hand pkg(6) **2.75**
585-3307 HOn3 Short w/Angle Cock & Glad Hand pkg(4) **2.75**
585-3281 Dual w/Bracket for Pilot **2.00**

WIRE

585-4867 Straight Brass pkg(6) **2.50**
.008" O.D., 12" long.
585-4877 Half Round Brass pkg(12) **2.75**
.056 x .031" O.D., 12" long.

PIPE

585-4842 Machined Lagged Pipe pkg(3) **2.75**
.019" O.D., 6" long.
585-4845 Cast Lagged Pipe w/Union pkg(3) **3.25**
.022" O.D., 1-1/2" long.

SPRINGS

585-44 Journal Undersize pkg(4) **3.00**
585-381 Driver Small pkg(12) **2.75**
585-382 Driver Large pkg(12) **2.75**
585-8054 Journal Oversize pkg(16) **1.50**

GEAR BOXES & ACCESSORIES

585-31214 HOn3 C-16 Gear Cover **1.50**
585-48283 Worm, Short 13:1 Steel 3.50
585-48324 13:1 Nylon Gear 2.00

TRACK

A new concept in flex track that allows long wheelbase locos to negotiate sharper curves. All rail is nickel silver, scale 9' ties and 36" track length.

585-4925 Straight Flex, Code 100 pkg(6) **23.75**
585-4926 Curved Flex Elevated, Code 100 pkg(6) **23.75**
585-4927 Straight Flex, Code 83 pkg(6) **22.75**
585-4928 Curved Flex Elevated, Code 83 pkg(6) **23.75**
585-4929 Straight Flex, Code 70 pkg(6) **22.75**
585-4930 Curved Flex Elevated, Code 70 pkg(6) **23.75**
585-4931 Straight Flex Code 83 HO/HOn3 pkg(6) **27.00**
585-4932 Curved Flex Main Line Code 83 pkg(6) **23.75**

SEATS

585-39091

585-39092

585-39091 Engineer Cab Seat **2.25**
585-39092 Diesel Cab Seat, Auxiliary **2.25**
585-3413 Cab Seat, Modified pkg(2) **2.25**

650-9999 HO #9 Catalog Add more realism to your layout with the complete line of structures, cast metal parts and details from SS Ltd. The complete selection is illustrated in this catalog, and all items are available from Walthers by special order

CAST METAL DETAILS

All castings are unpainted white metal.

BRACKETS

650-2019 650-2021

650-2019 Double pkg(6) **2.99**
650-2021 Finial Small pkg(12) **2.39**

650-2022 Porch "Fan" pkg(6) **2.59**

650-2023 650-2024

650-2023 Eave Small pkg(10) **2.59**
650-2024 Eave Medium pkg(10) **2.89**

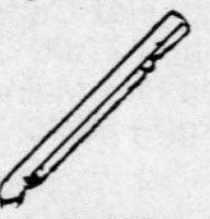

650-2025 650-2026

650-2025 Eave Large pkg(10) **3.19**
650-2026 Porch pkg(3) **2.39**

650-2027 650-2060

650-2027 Sign pkg(3) **2.39**
650-2060 Eave Ornate pkg(6) **2.99**

650-2107 Roof Overhang Eave pkg(6) **2.99**
650-2172 Eave Support pkg(10) **3.19**
650-2285 Eave-Large pkg(10) **3.19**
650-2286 Eave-Small pkg(10) **2.89**
650-2289 Ornate Eave-Large pkg(10) **2.59**
650-2290 Ornate Eave-Small pkg(10) **2.49**
650-2527 Eave pkg(3) **2.39**
650-2548 Wooden Eave pkg(3) **2.39**
650-2556 Gable End pkg(4) **2.39**

CHIMNEYS

650-2005 650-2006

650-2005 Tenement Chimney Porch Roof 3 Vent **2.59**
650-2006 Tenement Chimney Floor Roof 3 Vent **2.59**

650-2007 650-2008

650-2007 Tenement Chimney Porch Roof 4 Vent **2.89**
650-2008 Tenement Chimney Flat Roof 4 Vent **2.89**

650-2032 650-2033

650-2032 Emporium Chimney **2.59**
650-2033 Tall Brick Chimney pkg(2) **2.59**
650-2166 Short Smokejack-Pitched pkg(4) **2.49**
650-2167 Tall Smokejack-Pitched pkg(4) **2.49**

650-2178 Stackable Brick Chimney pkg(2) **2.19**
650-2284 Short Brick Chimney pkg(2) **1.99**

650-2329 Two-Vent Brick Chimney **2.49**
650-2358 Short Chimney pkg(2) **2.19**
650-2428 Chimney 7' w/Tapered Flue **2.49**
650-2441 Smokejack w/Taper-Straight pkg(2) **2.59**
650-2443 Smokejack w/Taper "T" pkg(2) **2.59**
650-2452 Cone Top Smokejack w/Taper pkg(2) **2.59**
650-2487 Tenement Chimney pkg(2) **1.99**
650-2499 Brick Chimney Flat pkg(2) **1.99**
650-2503 Brick Chimney Stone pkg(2) **1.99**
650-2505 Tall Chimney Stone Cap pkg(2) **2.59**
650-2506 Brick Chimney Brick Cap pkg(2) **1.99**
650-2515 Tenement Chimney 2 Vent **2.49**
650-2517 Tall Brick Chimney pkg(2) **2.59**
650-2518 Short Brick Chimney pkg(2) **1.99**
650-2519 Round Smokestack pkg(2) **2.59**
650-2532 T-Style Smokejack **2.89**
650-2536 Tall Round Smokejack **2.59**
650-2542 Brick Chimney Stone pkg(2) **1.99**
650-2544 Large Stone Chimney pkg(4) **2.59**
650-2546 Short Brick Chimney Concrete pkg(2) **1.99**
650-2550 Short Chimney w/Flue pkg(2) **1.99**
650-2551 Tall Chimney w/Flue pkg(2) **2.59**
650-2553 Brick Chimney w/Taper pkg(2) **1.99**

CITY STREET DETAILS

650-2011 650-2012

650-2011 City Tree Planters w/Post Small pkg(2) **2.89**
650-2012 City Tree Planters w/Post Large pkg(2) **2.89**

650-2036 650-2037

650-2036 Industrial Lamp Large pkg(10) **2.19**
650-2037 Industrial Lamp Small pkg(10) **1.99**

650-2039 650-2040

650-2039 Porch Lamp pkg(2) **2.19**
650-2040 Back Door Lamp pkg(2) **2.19**
650-2058 City Canopy pkg(2) **2.39**
650-2318 Electric Street Lamp-Single Light (Nonworking) **2.89**

650-2319 Gas Street Lamp-Single Light (Nonworking) **2.89**
650-2320 Park Bench pkg(2) **2.49**
650-2333 Manhole Cover pkg(6) **1.99**
650-2334 Sewer Grating pkg(3) **1.99**
650-2335 Police Call Box-Wall Mount pkg(3) **1.99**

650-2336 Fire Call Box on Post pkg(3) **2.19**
650-2337 Water Hydrant pkg(4) **2.59**
650-2345 Electric Street Lamp-Double Light (Nonworking) **3.99**

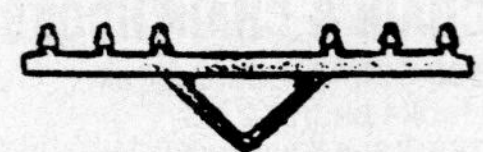

650-2393 Telephone Pole Crossarms pkg(12) **2.49**
650-2427 Drinking Fountain pkg(3) **1.99**
650-2486 Street Lamp J Top **3.39**
650-2491 Fire Plug No. 2 pkg(4) **1.99**
650-2493 Cast Iron Bench **2.49**
650-2516 Barber Pole pkg(2) **2.49**
650-2525 Two Arm Utility Pole pkg(2) **3.59**
650-2534 Four Arm Utility Pole pkg(2) **4.39**
650-2549 Metal Lamp pkg(10) **2.19**

CRATES

650-2151 650-2152

650-2151 24 x 18 x 24" pkg(4) **2.59**
650-2152 42 x 30 x 18" pkg(4) **2.59**

650-2153 650-2154

650-2153 36 x 30 x 36" pkg(3) **2.59**
650-2154 30 x 36 x 66" pkg(3) **2.59**

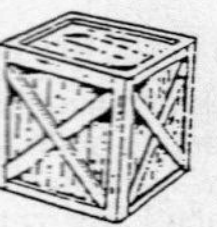

650-2155 650-2156

650-2155 54 x 54 x 54" pkg(3) **2.99**
650-2156 Stacked 2-High Empty pkg(4) **1.99**

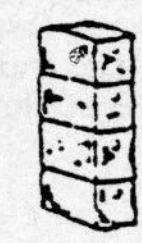

650-2157 650-2158

650-2157 Stacked 3-High Empty pkg(4) **2.19**
650-2158 Stacked 4-High Empty pkg(4) **2.39**

650-2159 650-21560

650-2159 Stacked 2-High Filled pkg(4) **1.99**
650-2160 Stacked 3-High Filled pkg(4) **2.19**
650-2161 Stacked 4-High Filled pkg(4) **2.39**
650-2278 Stack of Filled-5 High pkg(4) **2.49**
650-2279 Single-Filled pkg(4) **1.99**
650-2280 Single-Empty pkg(4) **1.99**
650-2310 Stack of Crates-Empty (5 High) pkg(4) **2.49**
650-2385 Filled (3)-Flat pkg(4) **2.19**
650-2386 Empty (3)-Flat pkg(4) **2.19**

DEPOT DETAILS

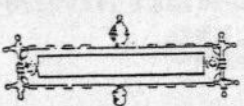

650-2096 Station Signboard pkg(2) **3.79**

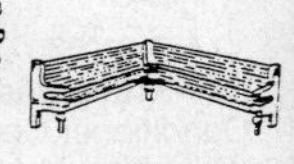

650-2148 650-2149

650-2148 Station Bench (Interior/Exterior) Straight pkg(2) **3.19**
650-2149 Station Bench (Interior/Exterior) Corner In pkg(2) **3.19**

650-2150 Station Bench (Interior/Exterior) Corner Out pkg(2) **3.19**

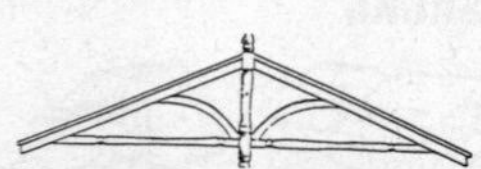

650-2176 Passenger Station Platform Truss pkg(2) **3.99**
650-2182 Telegraph Sounder pkg(3) **2.19**
650-2275 Train Order Signal pkg(2) **1.99**

650-2276

650-2281

650-2276 Passenger Assist Steps pkg(4) **2.39**
650-2281 Two Wheel Dolly pkg(2) **2.89**

650-2282 Cast Iron Bench w/Wood Slates pkg(2) **2.49**
650-2283 Baggage Barrow **3.99**
650-2369 Train Order Signal **7.95**
650-2370 Station Platform Lamps pkg(3) **4.95**
650-2387 Ornate Sign Panel pkg(2) **3.29**
650-2390 Bay Ticket Window **3.19**
650-2501 Large Wooden Pallets pkg(6) **3.39**
650-2540 Telegraph Pole pkg(2) **3.59**

DOORS

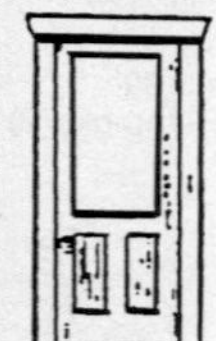
650-2061

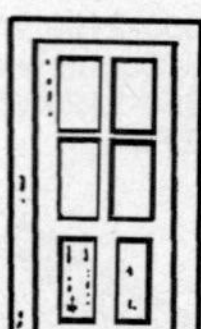
650-2062

650-2061 2-Panel 1-Lite pkg(2) **2.19**
650-2062 2-Panel, 4-Lite Steel Frame pkg(2) **2.19**
650-2085 Door Hinges pkg(12) **2.19**

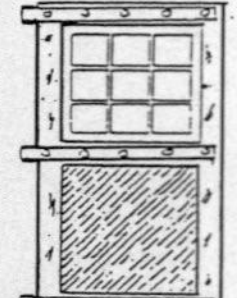
650-2111

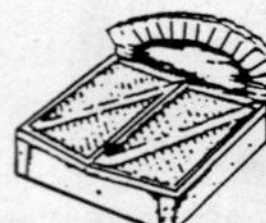
650-2139

650-2111 English House Door w/Hinge pkg(2) **3.59**
650-2139 Cellar Door, Brick, Set **2.89**
650-2165 Commercial-Recessed **2.89**

650-2199 650-2256

650-2199 Narrow 4-Panel 6-Lite pkg(2) **2.19**
650-2256 Virginia City pkg(2) **2.59**
650-2200 Narrow 2-Panel 1 Lite pkg(2) **2.19**
650-2258 Colonial Arch pkg(2) **2.59**
650-2260 4-Panel w/Transom pkg(2) **2.59**
650-2262 Colonial Ornate pkg(2) **2.59**
650-2264 2-Panel, 4-Lite pkg(2) **2.19**
650-2265 Saloon pkg(2) **2.39**
650-2268 6-Panel pkg(2) **2.19**
650-2269 4-Panel pkg(2) **2.19**
650-2327 Ornate to Match #2326 pkg(2) **2.59**
650-2351 Curved Arch Door pkg(2) **2.59**
650-2360 Store Front **2.49**
650-2363 Freight w/Transom **2.49**
650-2364 Steel w/9-Lite Window pkg(2) **2.19**

650-2365 Freight Without Transom pkg(2) **2.49**
650-2366 Steel Fire pkg(2) **2.59**
650-2367 Wood Frame, 1-Lite, 2-Panel pkg(2) **2.19**
650-2368 Victorian 2-Lite pkg(2) **2.59**
650-2435 Wood Brace, Factory **2.49**
650-2444 4-Panel, 3-Lite Transom pkg(2) **2.19**
650-2446 Double 6-Lite pkg(2) **2.59**
650-2482 2-Lite Door w/Transom pkg(2) **2.19**
650-2524 Two Panel Wood Door pkg(2) **2.19**

DRUMS

650-2328 55-Gallon Oil pkg(6) **2.39**

650-2349 Stack 55-Gallon Drums **2.49**
650-2417 15-Gallon pkg(8) **2.39**
650-2418 30-Gallon pkg(7) **2.39**
650-2419 #2 55-Gallon pkg(6) **2.39**
650-2449 55-Gallon w/Trash pkg(5) **2.39**

650-2462 Open/Used 55-Gallon pkg(6) **2.90**
650-2463 Open/New 55-Gallon pkg(6) **2.90**
650-2488 55-Gallon Oil No. 3 pkg(6) **2.39**
650-2514 55-Gallon Oil No. 4 pkg(6) **2.39**

FENCES

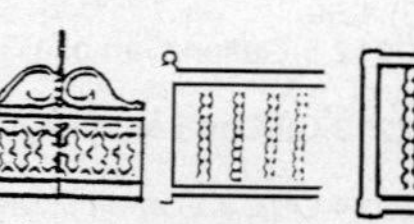
650-2030 650-2042

650-2043

650-2030 Ornate Gate pkg(3) **2.19**
650-2042 Ornate Section pkg(3) **1.99**
650-2043 Gate for #2042 pkg(2) **1.99**

650-4126 Corrugated Iron w/Gates Scale 200' (Plastic) Kit **9.95**
650-4127 Corrugated Iron Fence w/Gates Scale 200' (Metal) Kit **12.95**

650-4128 Chain Link w/Gates Scale 200' (Brass) Kit **19.95**
650-2497 Crossing Gate Kit-2 Gates **5.99**

FREIGHT CAR LOADS EA 9.95

Resin castings.

650-8050 Banded Lumber pkg(4)
650-8051 Covered Machine pkg(3)

GAS STATION DETAILS

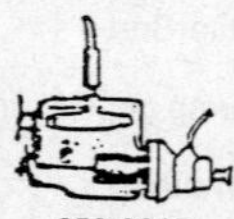
650-2015

650-2016

650-2015 Engine Block 4 Cycle w/Exhaust & Transmission **2.19**
650-2016 Engine Block 4 Cycle w/Exhaust, Transmission & Mounts **2.19**
650-2067 Gas Station Hoist Platform **2.49**

650-2068 650-2098 650-2174

650-2068 Ornate 1929 Gas Pump **3.59**
650-2098 Electric Motor Large pkg(2) **2.39**
650-2174 Oil Can Rack pkg(2) **1.99**
650-2175 Oil Highboy (Bulk Oil) pkg(3) **2.99**
650-2308 Tires pkg(10) **2.19**
650-2321 1929 Gas Pump **3.59**
650-2381 Small Electric Motor pkg(4) **2.19**
650-2394 Gas Pump Island **1.99**
650-2401 1930s Gas Pump **3.59**
650-2402 Round Gas Can pkg(4) **2.19**

650-2407

650-2409

650-2407 Auto Tires #2 pkg(10) **2.19**
650-2408 Auto Tires #3 pkg(10) **2.19**
650-2409 Auto Tires #4 pkg(10) **2.19**

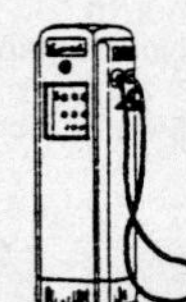

650-2453 1950s Electric Gas Pump pkg(2) **2.19**
650-2454 Junk Barrel w/Trash Pile pkg(3) **2.39**
650-2476 Auto Engines Kit pkg(3) **5.95**
650-2496 Auto Tire Stand pkg(2) **1.99**
650-2520 Gas Station Hoist Kit **2.19**
650-2521 Auto Tire Pump w/Stand pkg(4) **2.19**
650-8028 Auto Junk Piles **14.95**

INTERIOR DETAIL SETS

Complete sets of parts.

650-7200 Commercial Office Interior **41.95**
650-7201 Grocery Store Interior **47.95**
650-7202 Passenger Depot, Exterior/Interior **34.95**
650-7203 General Store, Exterior/Interior **49.95**
650-7204 Roundhouse Interior **49.95**
650-7207 Pool Hall **47.95**
650-7208 Barber Shop **39.95**

650-7209 Farm Machinery **37.95**
650-7212 Service Station **24.95**
650-7217 Living Room w/Walls **14.95**
650-7218 Country Kitchen w/Walls **19.95**
650-7219 Master Bedroom w/Walls **11.95**
650-7220 Guest Bedroom w/Walls **11.95**
650-7221 Dining Room w/Walls **11.95**
650-7222 Study w/Walls **18.95**
650-7223 Family Room w/Walls **18.95**
650-7224 Full Bath w/Walls **11.95**

650-7225 Doll's Dollhouse w/Furniture **44.95**

650-7226 Machine Shop **42.95**
650-7227 Street Details **11.95**
650-7228 San Francisco Office Building Millwork (For Kit #1113) **14.95**

650-7229 The Store Interior (For Kit #1118) **84.95**

LOCO DETAILS

650-2189 Gauge Cluster pkg(2) **1.99**

650-2222

650-2223

650-2222 Loco Cab Seat pkg(2) **2.49**
650-2223 Johnson Bar pkg(2) **2.49**

SCALE STRUCTURES LIMITED

650-2224 Coal Rake pkg(3) **2.19**
650-4138 Ornate Observation Car Rail #1 (Standard Gauge) pkg(2) **9.95**
650-4139 Ornate Observation Car Rail #2 (Narrow Gauge) pkg(2) **9.95**

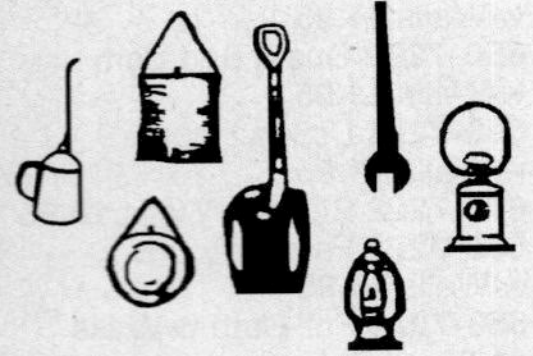

650-7230 Loco Detail Set #1 **5.95**
650-7231 Loco Detail Set #2 **5.95**

LOGS & STUMPS

All except #650-2539 are resin castings.

650-2539 Tree Stump Small & Large pkg(2) **3.59**

650-8007 Small Stumps **9.95**
650-8008 Large Stumps **9.95**

650-8020 Large Floating Logs pkg(9) **4.95**
650-8021 Small Floating Logs pkg(18) **9.95**

MASTER TOUCH DETAILS

650-7233 Industrial Roof-Top Set **19.95**

650-7234 Commerical Roof-Top Set **19.95**

650-7235 For Bachmann Sears Home **24.95**
Set of interior furnishings and additional exterior details, designed especially for the "Sears Catalog House" kit.

MINIATURE TOOLS

650-2048

650-2049

650-2048 Dynamite Plunger pkg(3) **2.19**
650-2049 Dynamite Keg pkg(4) **2.19**

650-2089

650-2090

650-2101

650-2089 Steel Ladder pkg(4) **2.39**
650-2090 Fire Extinguisher No. 2 pkg(6) **2.59**
650-2101 Nuts/Bolts/Washers-15° pkg(12) **2.19**
650-2102 Nuts/Bolts/Washers-30° pkg(12) **2.19**
650-2115 Manure Fork pkg(3) **2.19**

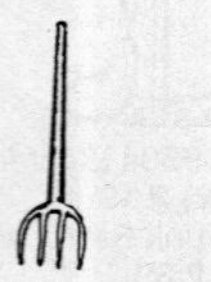
650-2116

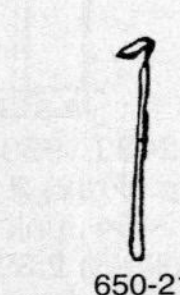
650-2117

650-2116 Pitch Fork pkg(3) **2.19**
650-2117 Hoe pkg(3) **2.19**
650-2118 Post Hole Digger pkg(3) **2.39**

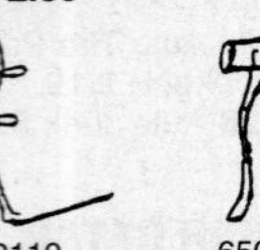
650-2119 650-2123

650-2119 Scythe w/Blade pkg(3) **2.39**
650-2123 Hand Axe pkg(3) **1.99**

650-2146

650-2147

650-2146 Fire Axe pkg(3) **1.99**
650-2147 Anvil pkg(2) **1.99**
650-2168 Small Winch pkg(2) **3.59**

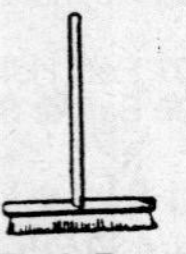

650-2201 Push Broom pkg(3) **2.19**
650-2202 Tamp Bar pkg(3) **2.19**
650-2203 Spike Maul pkg(3) **2.19**
650-2204 Pry Bar pkg(3) **2.19**
650-2205 Spud Wrench pkg(4) **1.99**
650-2206 Monkey Wrench pkg(3) **2.19**
650-2207 Screw Jack pkg(3) **2.89**
650-2208 Track Jack pkg(3) **2.89**
650-2209 Vice-Jaws Closed pkg(2) **2.39**
650-2210 Bench Grinder pkg(3) **2.19**
650-2211 C-Clamp-Large pkg(3) **1.99**
650-2212 5-Gallon Can pkg(3) **1.99**
650-2213 Oil Can-Large pkg(4) **1.99**
650-2214 Oil Can-Small pkg(4) **1.99**

650-2215 Pail w/Handle Up pkg(3) **2.19**
650-2216 Pail w/Handle Down pkg(3) **2.19**
650-2217 Canteen pkg(3) **2.19**
650-2218 Water Bag pkg(3) **1.99**
650-2219 Water Keg pkg(2) **2.39**
650-2220 Tin Dipper pkg(6) **2.39**
650-2221 Grease Pot pkg(3) **1.99**
650-2233 Scoop pkg(6) **2.39**

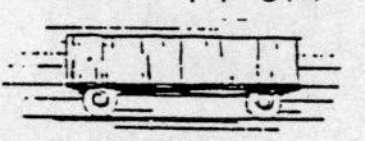

650-2234 Push Cart pkg(2) **2.59**
650-2238 Scoop Shovel pkg(3) **2.19**
650-2239 Long Handle Shovel pkg(3) **2.19**
650-2240 Spade Shovel pkg(3) **2.19**
650-2298 Lanterns pkg(6) **2.59**
650-2299 Acetylene Bottle w/Valve pkg(3) **2.19**
650-2300 Oxygen Bottle w/Valve pkg(3) **2.19**
650-2301 Tiny Tools-Set A **2.89**
650-2302 Tiny Tools-Set B **2.89**
650-2303 Tool Box pkg(3) **2.19**
650-2304 Lug Wrench pkg(4) **2.19**
650-2305 Oil Bottle-Small pkg(12) **2.19**
650-2306 Tire Pump pkg(4) **2.19**
650-2307 Air Compressor **2.19**

650-2311 Welding Cart **2.49**
650-2312 Welding Hose & Nozzle **1.99**
650-2313 Straight Broom pkg(3) **1.99**
650-2322 Work Cart **3.19**
650-2324 Fire Extinguisher #1 pkg(6) **2.59**
650-2379 Cross Cut Saw & Ax pkg(2) **2.19**
650-2391 Arc Welder Kit **2.89**
650-2410 Air Compressor, Large **2.39**
650-2412 Small Welding Cart & Tanks pkg(6) **1.99**
650-2415 Acetylene Tanks #2 pkg(4) **1.99**
650-2416 Oxygen Tanks #2 pkg(4) **1.99**

650-2468 Portable "A" Frame Hoist **4.95**

650-2470 Work Tables (3 types) **4.95**

650-2471 6' Wooden Stepladder pkg(2) **2.35**
650-2504 Wooden Ladder pkg(4) **2.39**
650-2507 Long Spade Shovel pkg(3) **2.19**
650-2508 Long Scoop Shovel pkg(3) **2.19**
650-2509 Straight Broom No. 2 pkg(3) **2.19**
650-2535 Step Stool pkg(4) **2.39**
650-7211 Blacksmith's Tools & Equipment **8.95**

RAILS & POSTS

650-2028 650-2029

650-2028 Ornate Rail w/Post Small pkg(3) **2.19**
650-2029 Ornate Rail w/Post Large pkg(3) **2.39**

650-2133 Post w/Carved Top 11' pkg(4) **2.49**

650-2134 Post w/Carved Top 10' pkg(4) **2.49**

650-2135 Post w/Carved Top and Bottom pkg(4) **2.49**

650-2136 Fluted Post 1/2 Round 13'6" pkg(4) **2.49**

650-2137 Fluted Post Round 13'6" pkg(4) **2.89**

650-2138 Fluted Post Square 12' pkg(4) **2.59**
650-2291 Balcony Railing pkg(2) **1.99**
650-2292 Railing w/Post pkg(3) **2.39**
650-2295 Post-Small pkg(4) **2.59**
650-2296 Post-Large pkg(4) **2.89**
650-2343 Stoop Railing pkg(2) **1.99**
650-2459 Round Post w/Taper for Roof pkg(3) **2.39**
650-2481 Post w/Finial Top pkg(4) **2.59**
650-2483 Post w/Double Corbal pkg(4) **2.59**
650-2484 Post w/Flatback **2.59**

SACKS

650-2031

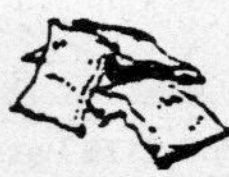
650-2126

650-2031 Stack of 6 pkg(3) **1.99**
650-2126 Pile of 4 pkg(3) **1.99**

650-2127

650-2128

650-2127 Stack of 18 **1.99**
650-2128 3 Leaning pkg(3) **1.99**
650-2229 Grain pkg(6) **2.59**
650-2230 Flour pkg(6) **2.59**
650-2231 Open Feed pkg(6) **2.59**
650-2232-Leaning pkg(6) **2.59**
650-2338 Stack of Three pkg(3) **1.99**
650-2350 Stack of 36 **3.29**

TRACKSIDE DETAILS

650-2052 650-2053 650-2054

650-2052 Switch Stand Harp (Dummy) **2.59**
650-2053 Switch Stand w/Cast Base (Dummy) **2.59**
650-2054 Switch Stand w/Frame Base (Dummy) **2.59**

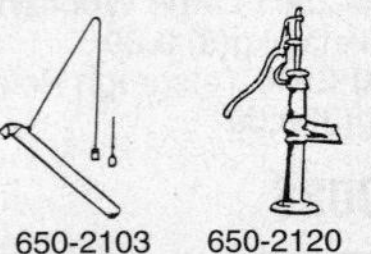
650-2103 650-2120

650-2103 Water Tank Spout w/Counterweights **3.99**
650-2120 Water Pump pkg(2) **2.89**

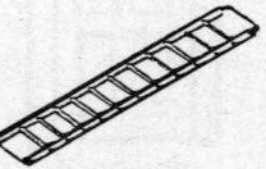
650-2124

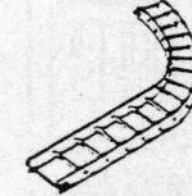
650-2125

650-2124 Freight Roller Straight Section pkg(3) **2.59**
650-2125 Freight Roller 90° Curve Section pkg(2) **2.39**

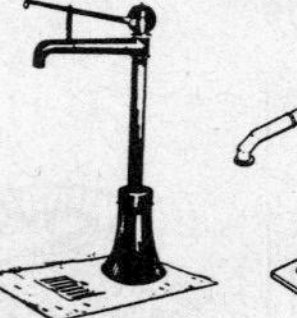
650-2375 650-2434

650-2375 Water Column **5.95**

SCALE STRUCTURES LIMITED

650-2426 Water Tank Spout Kit **3.99**
650-2434 DRGW Water Column **4.95**
650-2460 Water Tank Spout w/Counterweights #2 **2.89**

VENTS

650-2047 650-2108

650-2047 Tank pkg(5) **1.99**
650-2084 Foundation pkg(10) **2.19**
650-2108 Roof w/Fin pkg(2) **3.59**
650-2330 Roof Vent pkg(3) **2.39**
650-2382 Turbine Vent-Flat Roof **2.89**
650-2383 Turbine Vent-Slope Roof pkg(2) **2.89**
650-2423 Globe 24" pkg(4) **2.39**
650-2450 Mushroom Roof pkg(6) **2.19**
650-2489 Large Flat Roof pkg(3) **2.39**
650-2498 Round Industrial Roof pkg(3) **2.39**
650-2500 Round Roof pkg(3) **2.19**
650-2502 Large Round Roof **2.19**
650-2512 Roof & Wind Vane pkg(2) **2.19**
650-2529 Roof for Peak pkg(2) **1.99**
650-2543 24" Globe Roof pkg(3) **2.49**
650-2554 Roof Pitch Roof pkg(2) **2.59**

WINDOWS

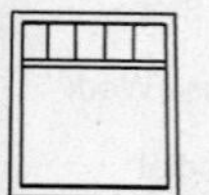

650-2063 650-2064 650-2069

650-2063 Emporium Front pkg(2) **2.59**
650-2064 Emporium Side pkg(3) **2.59**
650-2069 Brick Cellar 2-Lite pkg(4) **2.59**

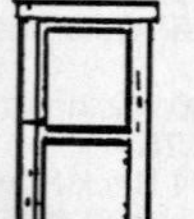
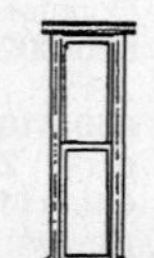
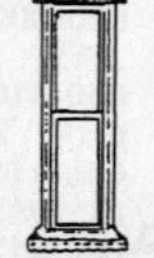
650-2070 650-2071 650-2072

650-2070 Elliptical pkg(4) **2.19**
650-2071 Double Hung pkg(3) **2.39**
650-2072 Ornate Narrow 2-Lite pkg(3) **2.49**

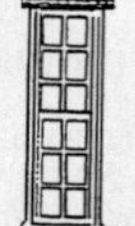

650-2073 650-2074 650-2075

650-2073 Tall Narrow 12-Lite pkg(3) **2.59**
650-2074 Double - Double Hung 4-Lite pkg(2) **2.39**
650-2075 Ornate Double Hung 2-Lite pkg(3) **2.59**

650-2076 650-2077 650-2078

650-2076 Short Double Hung pkg(3) **2.39**
650-2077 Steel Sash 9-Lite Double pkg(2) **2.39**
650-2078 Steel Sash 9-Lite pkg(3) **2.39**

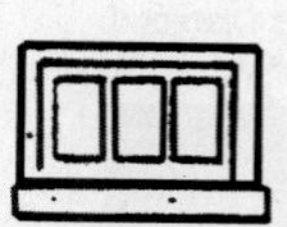
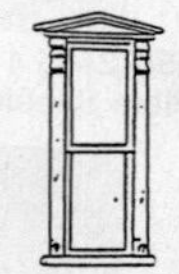
650-2079 650-2080

650-2079 Steel Sash 3-Lite Basement pkg(5) **2.59**
650-2080 Tall Virginia City 2-Lite pkg(3) **2.59**

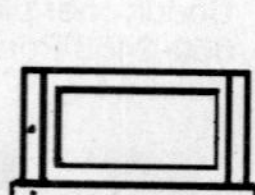
650-2081 650-2082

650-2081 Double-Double Hung 2-Lite Ornate pkg(2) **2.49**
650-2082 Steel Sash 1-Lite Basement pkg(5) **2.59**
650-2083 Steel Sash 18-Lite pkg(3) **2.59**

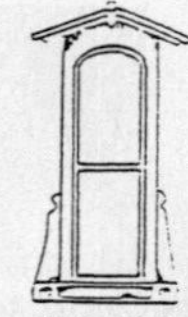
650-2094 650-2095

650-2094 Double Dormer 2-Lite pkg(2) **2.89**
650-2095 Tall Ornate 2-Lite pkg(3) **2.89**

650-2129 650-2130

650-2129 Factory 9-Lite Without Frame pkg(3) **2.89**
650-2130 Factory 9-Lite w/Frame pkg(3) **2.99**

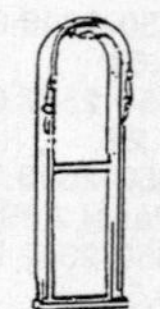
650-2140 650-2141

650-2140 Mansard 2-Lite Small pkg(3) **2.19**
650-2141 Mansard 2-Lite Tall pkg(3) **3.29**

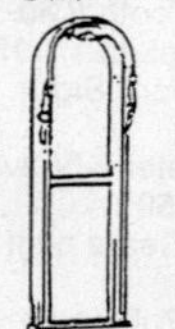
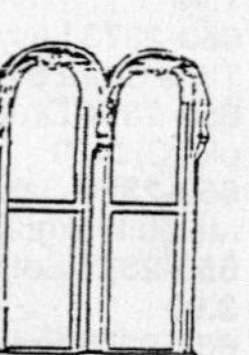
650-2142 650-213

650-2142 Victorian Round Top 2-Lite Tall pkg(2) **3.29**
650-2143 Victorian Double Top 2-Lite Tall pkg(3) **2.59**

650-2179 650-2263

650-2179 Ornate Bay **2.89**
650-2257 Virginia City pkg(3) **2.59**
650-2259 Colonial Arch pkg(3) **2.59**

650-2261 650-2356

650-2261 Double Hung 3-Lite pkg(3) **2.39**
650-2263 Colonial Ornate pkg(3) **2.59**
650-2266 Double, Double Hung 3-Lite pkg(2) **2.39**
650-2267 Tall 4-Lite pkg(3) **2.49**
650-2270 Tall 8-Lite Victorian pkg(3) **2.89**
650-2271 Double 5-Lite Victorian pkg(3) **2.89**
650-2272 Round Gable pkg(3) **2.19**
650-2325 Tall City Double Hung 8-Lite pkg(3) **2.59**
650-2326 Ornate Double Double Hung 3-Lite pkg(2) **2.39**
650-2352 Curved Arch Double 2-Lite **2.49**
650-2353 Curved Arch Tall 3-Lite pkg(3) **3.29**
650-2354 Curved Arch Short 3-Lite pkg(3) **2.89**
650-2355 Cast Concrete 2-Lite-Single pkg(3) **3.19**
650-2356 Cast Concrete 2-Lite-Double **2.49**
650-2357 Cast Concrete 2-Lite-Triple **2.89**
650-2361 Store Front 1-Lite **2.99**
650-2362 Store Foyer 1-Lite **2.99**
650-2437 Double Hung 4-Pane pkg(6) **2.19**
650-2442 Double-Hung 8-Pane pkg(2) **2.59**
650-2523 Wood 2-Lite pkg(3) **2.39**
650-2526 Wood 2-Lite pkg(3) **2.39**
650-2532 Two-Story Bay **3.79**

MISCELLANEOUS

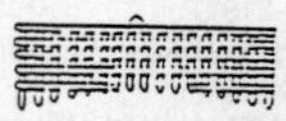

650-2010 Porch Lattice Curved pkg(4) **2.59**

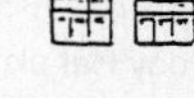
650-2013 650-2014

650-2013 Box Style Roof Trim pkg(4) **2.49**
650-2014 Ridge Trim, DRGW Style pkg(4) **2.59**

650-2017 650-2018

650-2017 Barrel w/Top (separate) pkg(4) **2.39**
650-2018 Small Power Head w/Meter pkg(3) **1.99**

650-2020 650-2035

650-2020 Porch Header Ornate pkg(4) **2.59**
650-2034 City Apartment Mailbox Cluster pkg(4) **2.19**
650-2035 McClellan Saddle pkg(2) **2.19**

650-2038 650-2041

650-2038 Spitoon Number 4 pkg(4) **2.19**
650-2041 Stair Stringer 6 Riser pkg(8) **1.99**

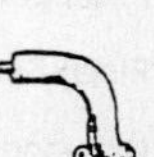

650-2044 650-2045 650-2046

650-2044 8" Pipe w/Flange, Straight pkg(4) **1.99**
650-2045 8" Pipe w/Flange, 90° pkg(3) **1.99**
650-2046 8" Gate Valve w/Wheel pkg(2) **2.19**
650-2056 Spanish Tile Ridge Trim pkg(4) **2.59**
650-2065 Smokejack Pitch Roof w/Cap pkg(4) **2.59**

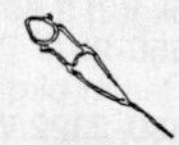
650-2050 650-2051

650-2050 Bed Roll pkg(3) **1.99**
650-2051 Bridle pkg(3) **2.89**

650-2055 650-2057

650-2055 Spanish Tile Roof Peak pkg(5) **2.19**
650-2057 Octagon Gusset Plate pkg(12) **1.99**

650-2059 650-2066

650-2059 Ornate Building Cap No. 1 **3.29**
650-2066 Tall 2 Vent Jack pkg(4) **2.89**

650-2091 Front Stoop, Round pkg(2) **2.59**

650-2092 650-2093

650-2092 Wood Window Casement Detail pkg(2) **2.19**
650-2093 Wall Cap Strip Narrow pkg(4) **2.89**

650-2099 650-2100

650-2099 Concrete Pier Single pkg(6) **2.89**
650-2100 Concrete Pier Double pkg(6) **3.29**

650-2104 650-2105 650-2106

650-2104 Strap Turnbuckles pkg(10) **2.39**
650-2105 Valve, 3-Way pkg(3) **1.99**
650-2106 Old-Time Passenger Car Water Cooler pkg(3) **2.39**

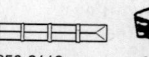

650-2112 650-2113

650-2112 Wall Capstrip Wide pkg(4) **2.99**
650-2113 Shingle Bolt pkg(10) **2.59**

650-2114 Cyclone w/Support Bracket **3.99**
650-2121 Horse Collar pkg(3) **2.39**
650-2122 Water Tub **2.49**

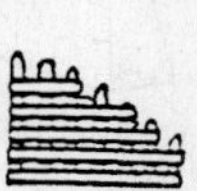
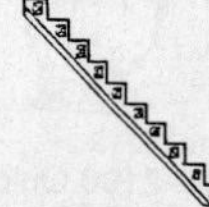
650-2144 650-2145

650-2144 Ornate Stair Stringer 14-Riser pkg(4) **2.59**
650-2145 Corner Lattice pkg(6) **2.59**
650-2162 Reed Basket pkg(3) **1.99**

SCALE STRUCTURES LIMITED

650-2163 Lug Box pkg(3) **1.99**
650-2164 Bushel Basket pkg(3) **1.99**
650-2169 Curved Eave Trim pkg(4) **2.59**
650-2170 Ornate Half-Round Column pkg(4) **2.49**
650-2171 Electric Main Switch-Small pkg(3) **1.99**

650-2173 Ornate Storefront Cornice **3.79**
650-2177 Drawer Cluster **1.99**
650-2180 Store Corner Trim pkg(4) **2.49**
650-2181 Ornate Cornice #3 pkg(2) **2.89**
650-2183 Pillow Blocks pkg(8) **2.39**
650-2184 Small Gears pkg(6) **1.99**
650-2185 Large Gears & Sheave pkg(3) **1.99**
650-2186 24" Gauge-18" Diameter Wheels & Axles pkg(6) **2.49**
650-2187 24" Gauge-24" Diameter Wheels & Axles pkg(6) **2.49**
650-2188 Valve Cluster pkg(3) **2.19**

650-2189

650-2190

650-2189 Gauge Cluster pkg(2) **1.99**
650-2190 6" Pipe Expansion Union pkg(3) **1.99**
650-2191 Tee Section 8" pkg(3) **2.19**

650-2192 650-2195

650-2192 Electric Insulators pkg(12) **2.19**
650-2193 Pipe w/Gas Line Valve pkg(3) **1.99**
650-2194 Pipe Section w/Inlet Valve pkg(3) **1.99**
650-2195 Check Valve pkg(3) **1.99**

650-2196

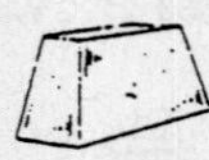
650-2197

650-2196 Quick Close Valve pkg(3) **2.89**
650-2197 Concrete Pier Triple pkg(4) **2.89**

650-2198

650-2237

650-2198 Bridge Girder Section pkg(2) **3.99**
650-2237 Wagon Wheel-Large pkg(4) **2.59**
650-2225 Western Saddle pkg(2) **2.49**
650-2226 Pack Rack pkg(2) **1.99**
650-2227 Colt .45 w/Holster pkg(3) **2.19**
650-2228 Rifle pkg(3) **2.19**
650-2234 Push Cart pkg(2) **2.59**
650-2235 Scale-Large pkg(2) **2.49**
650-2236 Cowboy Hat pkg(6) **2.49**
650-2241 Desk #1 **2.49**
650-2242 Desk Top for #2241 **2.19**
650-2243 Swivel Chair Without Arms pkg(2) **2.19**
650-2244 Steel Safe-Large pkg(2) **2.19**
650-2245 Wall Phone pkg(3) **2.19**
650-2246 Extension Phone pkg(3) **2.19**
650-2247 Candlestick Phone pkg(3) **2.19**
650-2248 Typewriter pkg(2) **2.19**
650-2249 Books pkg(4) **2.19**
650-2250 Desk Lamp #1 pkg(2) **2.19**
650-2251 Pot Belly Stove #1 pkg(2) **2.89**
650-2252 Coal Hod pkg(3) **2.19**
650-2253 Coal Scoop pkg(3) **1.99**
650-2254 Cuspidor #1 pkg(4) **2.19**
650-2255 Wall Clock w/Print Sheet **1.99**
650-2273 Round Gable Vent pkg(3) **2.19**
650-2274 Trunk pkg(2) **1.99**
650-2277 Milk Can pkg(6) **2.19**
650-2287 Finial-Large pkg(8) **1.99**
650-2288 Finial-Small pkg(8) **1.99**
650-2293 Diamond Roof Trim pkg(4) **2.59**
650-2294 Low Relief Roof Trim pkg(4) **2.49**
650-2297 Lamps (7 Kinds) pkg(7) **2.89**
650-2309 Wagon Wheels-Small pkg(4) **2.39**
650-2314 Trash Can pkg(3) **2.39**
650-2315 Water Cooler w/Faucet pkg(3) **2.19**
650-2316 Pot Belly Stove #2 pkg(2) **2.49**
650-2317 Passenger Car Heater pkg(2) **2.39**
650-2322 Work Cart **3.19**
650-2323 Ice Wagon **3.19**
650-2331 Industrial Power Head-Large pkg(3) **1.99**
650-2332 Industrial Power Head-Small pkg(3) **1.99**
650-2339 Pot Belly Stove #3 pkg(2) **2.39**
650-2340 Flower Pot pkg(12) **1.99**
650-2341 Lattice, Style #1 pkg(4) **2.59**
650-2342 Stoop w/Worn Mat **2.49**
650-2344 Skylight-Small pkg(2) **2.59**
650-2346 Ornate Cornice #4 **3.59**
650-2347 Ornate Cornice #5 **3.29**
650-2348 Ornate Gable End Panel **2.89**
650-2359 Exterior Staircase **3.59**
650-2371 Large Boot (Old-Time Store Sign) pkg(2) **1.99**
650-2372 Large Dentures (Old-Time Store Sign) pkg(2) **1.99**
650-2373 Large Tooth (Old-Time Store Sign) pkg(2) **1.99**
650-2374 Drug Store Sign pkg(2) **3.29**
650-2376 Gas Meter w/Valve-Medium pkg(2) **2.59**
650-2377 Set of Gears pkg(12) **3.99**
650-2378 Set of Pulleys #1 pkg(4) **2.49**
650-2380 Single Water Faucet pkg(10) **2.59**
650-2384 Coal Bin pkg(2) **1.99**
650-2388 Factory Whistle pkg(4) **2.19**
650-2389 Set of Pulleys #2 **2.49**
650-2395 Extra Large Ball Finial pkg(4) **2.19**
650-2396 Residential Power Head pkg(6) **2.39**
650-2397 Residential Gas Regulator pkg(6) **2.39**
650-2398 Pulley Trolley & Hook pkg(3) **2.59**
650-2399 Wall-Mounted Fire Plug pkg(6) **2.19**
650-2400 Power Control Panel pkg(4) **2.19**
650-2403 Garbage Can 30-Gallon pkg(3) **2.39**
650-2404 Open Top Coke Machine pkg(2) **2.59**
650-2405 Upright Coke Machine pkg(2) **2.59**
650-2406 Cream Cans pkg(6) **1.99**
650-2411 Fuel Oil Tank 200-Gallon **3.95**
650-2413 Exterior Plumbing-4 Pieces, 2 Types **1.99**
650-2414 Electrical Meter Box pkg(6) **1.99**
650-2420 Oil Bunker #2 pkg(3) **2.59**
650-2421 Open Garbage Can 30-Gallon pkg(3) **2.39**
650-2422 Coke Button Sign pkg(4) **1.29**
650-2424 Oil Can Rack #2 pkg(2) **1.99**
650-2425 Hand Water Pump #2 pkg(3) **2.19**
650-2429 Open Garbage Can 20-Gallon pkg(4) **2.39**
650-2430 Garbage Can 20-Gallon pkg(4) **2.39**
650-2431 Portable Scale pkg(2) **2.49**
650-2432 Ornate Cornice #6 **3.59**
650-2433 Ball Finial Large **2.39**
650-2436 Gate Hinges, Large pkg(8) **2.39**
650-2438 Tall Ornate Flat Iron Post pkg(4) **2.59**
650-2439 Ornate Square Post pkg(4) **2.59**
650-2440 Hydraulic Pump Jack pkg(3) **2.39**
650-2445 Ornate Ceiling Panels pkg(2) **2.89**
650-2447 Concrete Pier - Rectangular pkg(2) **2.39**
650-2448 Concrete Pier w/Tank Saddle pkg(2) **2.39**
650-2451 Extra Small Ball Finial pkg(8) **2.19**
650-2455 Wood Pallets (3 ea Small & Large) pkg(6) **2.85**
650-2456 Shaded Lamp w/Wire Loop pkg(5) **2.39**
650-2457 Large Pack for Horse pkg(6) **2.59**
650-2458 Small Pack for Mule pkg(3) **2.39**
650-2461 Rubbish Bin **2.35**

650-2464 Clark Forklift (1947 Model) **4.95**

650-2465 4 x 8' Diamond Plate Sheets pkg(3) **2.90**

650-2466 Hydraulic Pallet Jack pkg(2) **2.35**
650-2467 Window Air Conditioner pkg(7) **2.35**
650-2468 Portable "A" Frame Hoist **4.95**

650-2469 Wood Barrel Racks w/6 Barrels **4.95**
650-2470 Work Tables (3 types) **4.95**
650-2471 6' Wooden Stepladder pkg(2) **2.35**

650-2472 Squirrel Cage Exhaust Blower **3.45**

650-2473 20-Ton Roof Air Conditioner **3.45**

650-2474 Wooden Reels (Small, Medium, Large) pkg(9) **3.45**

650-2475 Roof Water Tower **5.95**

650-2477 Roll Off Trash Body Kit **6.95**

650-2478 Skipper's Dog House pkg(2) **2.35**

650-2479 Safety Cones pkg(7) **2.35**
650-2480 Pot Belly Stove No. 4 pkg(2) **2.89**
650-2485 Drain Scuppers **1.99**
650-2490 Roof Top Cyclone No. 2 **3.29**
650-2492 Corner Mailbox No. 2 pkg(3) **2.19**
650-2494 Small Ornate Eagle **2.19**
650-2495 Bell w/Bracket pkg(3) **2.59**
650-2510 Building Corner Stone pkg(2) **2.19**
650-2511 Wooden Ramp pkg(3) **2.19**
650-2513 Swivel Chair w/Arms pkg(2) **2.19**
650-2522 Deck Braces pkg(4) **2.99**
650-2528 Steel Stantions pkg(6) **2.49**
650-2530 Platform Roof Support pkg(3) **3.79**
650-2531 Pot Belly Stove w/Pipe pkg(2) **2.89**
650-2537 Gable End Trim pkg(4) **2.49**
650-2538 Wooden Steps pkg(4) **2.49**
650-2541 Warehouse Work Station pkg(2) **2.49**
650-2545 Ornate Metal Column pkg(4) **2.89**
650-2547 Industrial Electric Insulator pkg(8) **2.49**
650-2552 Long Wooden Stairs pkg(3) **2.89**
650-2555 Small Wood Beer Keg pkg(4) **2.19**
650-2557 Short Wooden Counter pkg(2) **2.49**
650-3026 Walter the Welder **.89**
650-4100 Facing Brick-Brown pkg(3) **2.75**
650-4111 Brick Row Lock (Brown) pkg(3) **2.75**
650-4124 Rubble Stone-Brown pkg(3) **2.75**
650-4125 Facing Stone-Brown pkg(3) **2.75**
650-5161 Cash Register & Paper Roll **2.89**
650-7232 Fire Hose Stand Kit **7.95**

Easy-to-build white metal kits (unless noted) include detailed parts and assembly instructions.

ELECTRIC MOTORS

652-3512 Industrial Electric Motors **4.95**

FENCE HARDWARE

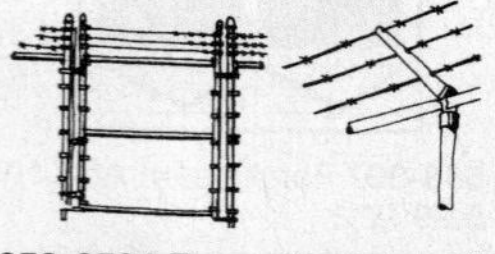

652-3504 Fence Hardware Kit **6.95**
Great detail around any factory, business, parking lot, locomotive on display in the city park, or anywhere you need a realistic security fence. Includes cast metal posts, gate, latch and flat wire. Posts are 12 scale feet tall, can be cut. (Also makes a nice smaller fence in O or S Scale). For the finishing touch, add Micro-Mesh fence material (sold separately) and barbed wire.

FLAT WIRE

Measures .010 x .030", can be used to model load restraint banding.

652-1504 Nickel Silver (5') **2.50**

GEARS

Use for scratch-building machinery or as junk. May include heavy machinery parts.

652-2001 Gear Assortment **3.95**

LP TANK

652-3505 LP Gas Tank pkg(2) **3.95**
Industrial sized propane tanks are common throughout rural areas. Includes styrene parts for two tanks.

MICRO-MESH

Micro-expanded metal can be used for all types of air intakes, chainlink fence, walkways and more. Includes a single 3 x 6" (7.5 x 15cm) sheet in aluminum or brass.

652-3500 Aluminum **3.95**
652-3501 Brass **4.50**

PALLETS

652-5002 Wooden Pallet pkg(12) **1.95**
4' square, molded in brown styrene.

SCALE WORKS MODELS

Cast metal details.

BLOCK & PULLEY

644-9206 pkg(2) **3.19**

CHIMNEYS/DOORS

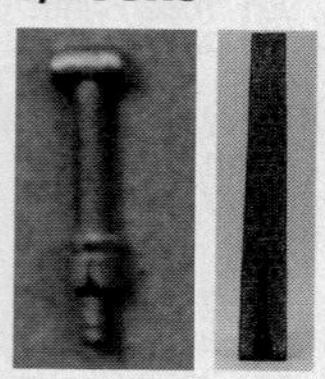

644-9203 644-9205 644-9211

644-9203 "Z" Frame, Wood pkg(2) **1.89**
644-9205 "T" Smoke Jack 4" High pkg(2) **1.49**
644-9207 Small pkg(2) **.69**
644-9211 7-1/4' Square at Base **6.95**

WINDOWS

644-9201 644-9202

644-9201 Mill-36 Pane Side by Side 6 x 7' pkg(3) **2.89**
644-9202 Mill-Horizontal 18 Pane 6 x 3-1/2' pkg(3) **2.65**

644-9204 Shed-4 Pane 2-1/2' sq. pkg(4) **2.89**

Selley Finishing Touches

Details are unpainted metal castings.

BOAT

675-673 Rowboat **1.75**

BRAKE PARTS EA 1.50

675-50 Brake Cylinder
675-265 Freight Car Brake Wheels

CANS, CASES, BUCKETS, BARRELS & DRUMS EA 2.50 (UNLESS NOTED)

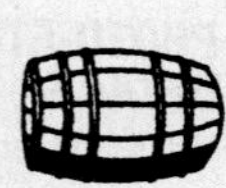

675-151 675-152

675-151 Oil Drums pkg(12)
675-152 Flour Barrels pkg(12)

675-153 675-154

675-153 Packing Cases pkg(12)
675-154 Milk Cans pkg(12)

675-298 675-299

675-298 Buckets pkg(3) **1.75**
675-299 Beer Kegs pkg(12)

CARTS, TRAILERS & TRUCKS

675-144 675-145

675-144 4-Wheel Baggage Truck **3.00**
675-145 2-Wheel Baggage Truck **2.00**

675-143 675-148

675-143 Baggage Cart **3.00**
675-148 Industrial Trailer pkg(2) **1.75**

675-142 675-149

675-142 Hand Truck **1.75**
675-149 Stake Trailer **2.00**

FEEDWATER HEATER

675-379 Elesco Type w/Bracket **1.50**

FIRE HOSE

675-595 Fire Hose on Rack **1.50**

GAS PUMPS W/MAN EA 2.75

675-175 Shell
675-176 ESSO
675-177 Texaco

INTERIORS

675-166 675-646

675-166 Pump & Tub **1.75**
675-646 Stove, Hod & Shovel **2.00**

675-419 Country Store Set **6.60**
Includes figures, scale, pot belly stove, pail & shovel, dolly, two chairs, barrel, hatchet and assorted cases.

LUGGAGE

675-150 pkg(12) **3.00**

675-656 Trunks (Assortment) pkg(6) **2.50**

MAILBOXES EA 2.00 (UNLESS NOTED)

675-173 Letter Boxes pkg(4)
675-174 Package Mail Boxes pkg(3)
675-235 Rural Mail Boxes pkg(4)
675-641 Mail Crane **2.55**

MINIATURE TOOLS

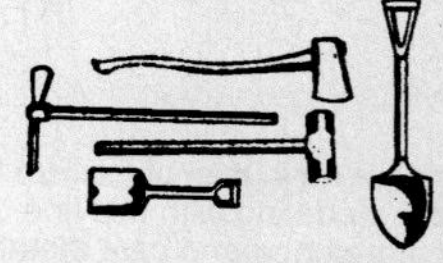

675-140 Tools (Set of 5) **2.00**
675-141 Scales pkg(2) **1.75**

675-290 675-605

675-290 Mower & Roller **2.00**
675-605 Step Ladder **2.00**

675-659 675-1391

675-659 Compressor Kit **2.75**
675-1391 Wheelbarrows pkg(2) **1.75**

MOW CAR KITS

675-283 Hand Car **5.00**
675-608 Go Devil **10.00**

PASSENGER CAR WEIGHTS EA 2.25

Flat, cast metal weights for improved rolling performance.

675-703 1/2oz Athearn pkg(4)
675-704 1/2oz pkg(4)
675-705 3/4oz pkg(3)
675-706 1-1/4oz pkg(2)
675-707 1oz pkg(2)

STREET DETAILS

675-230 Barricade **2.25**
675-113 Parking Meters pkg(12) **2.25**
675-172 Fire Alarm Boxes pkg(4) **2.00**
675-180 Fire Hydrants pkg(12) **2.50**
675-184 Trash Boxes pkg(2) **1.75**

TRANSFORMERS

675-257 675-510

675-257 Large **5.45**
675-510 Giant **6.60**

675-637 Line Pole Type pkg(6) **2.55**

VENDING MACHINES

675-679 pkg(3) **2.75**
Includes ice, soft drink and newspaper machines.

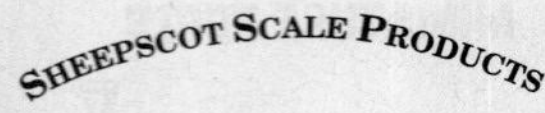

Bring a new level of realism to your modeling with this line of photo-etched and cast metal details.

CAST METAL DETAILS

MISCELLANEOUS EA 10.00

668-85001 #1
Pile of melons, 6 pumpkins, pile of pumpkins, 8 blue hubbard squash, stack of feed sacks, pile of watermelons and five 40-quart milk cans.

668-85502 #2
Three piles of grain sacks, four large potato sacks, pile of cement bags, group of milk cans, three groups of potato sacks and two groups of apple baskets.

668-85003 #3
Two groups of half-bushel baskets, group of milk cans, group of bushel boxes, two groups of bushel baskets, two groups of apple boxes, two groups of bushel boxes and a stack of bushel boxes.

668-85004 #4
Seven sea gulls, three half-bushel feed tubs, pile of small grain sacks, six vegetable boxes, stacks of bushel baskets and two groups of large potato sacks.

TRUCK PARTS

668-85005 Truck Tires-11.00-20 pkg(10) **5.00**
Includes spoke wheels for two front and four rear duals. Suitable for highway trucks from late 1930s to the present.

668-85007 Truck Tires 9.00-24 pkg(10) **5.00**
Includes spoke wheels for two front and four rear duals. Replaces hard rubber tires/wheels on Mack AC Bulldog, or other 1930s vintage trucks.

668-85008 Truck Tires 12.00-24 pkg(10) **6.00**
Includes spoke wheels for two front and four rear duals. For heavy duty on/off road trucks from the 1930s to the 1960s, fits Alloy Forms Autocar and Mack DM800.

668-85009 Truck Tires 10.00-15 pkg(10) **5.00**
Includes spoke wheels, makes eight sets of rear duals. Use for 18 ton "tag-along" (2 axle) or 50-ton low bed trailer, from the late 1930s to the present. Also good for idler (nondriven) axles on tri-axle dump trucks and cement mixers.

668-85010 Truck Tires 10.00-20 pkg(10) **5.00**
Includes six-hole disc (Budd) wheels for two front and four rear duals. For medium duty trucks from the 1930s to the present.

668-85011 Truck Detail Parts **6.00**
Five pair of west coast mirrors, four pair of 8 x 12" mirrors, three pair of older, round mirrors, four pair of mud flaps, four rear body sills with taillights, rear body sill with bumper, spare tire carrier and pintle hook and eye.

FIREWOOD EA 10.00

Great scenic detail alongside buildings, can be used to hide imperfections in the building foundation.

668-85013 Piles
Five log piles of 12 logs, each 30" long, four 8' long logs about 15" diameter and one log pile of six logs about 4' long.

668-85014 #2
One log pile of 11, each 8' long, six 8' long logs about 15" diameter, one log pile of random lengths and two log piles of six, 4' long logs.

GRANITE EA 10.00

Plaster casting.

668-85016 Blocks pkg(18)
Includes 18 blocks of quarried granite, weighing from five to 36 tons. Great for loads on trucks, flat cars, gondolas, barges, or use to build retaining walls or other scenic detail.

668-85017 Walls
1-1/2 x 18". Made of granite blocks up to 8' long and 16" high, total wall height 109" in HO Scale. Makes a wall with a total length of 18 actual inches with an inside and outside corner.

PHOTO-ETCHED DETAILS

Unassembled brass.

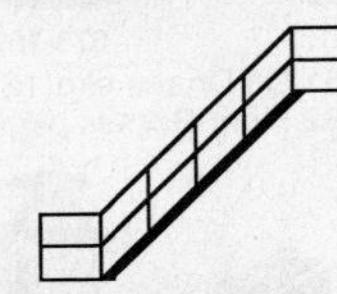

668-75001 Fire Escape - 5 Flights **10.00**
Great detail for any building, includes parts for five flights of stairs, with landings and railings. Additional kits can be combined for taller buildings.

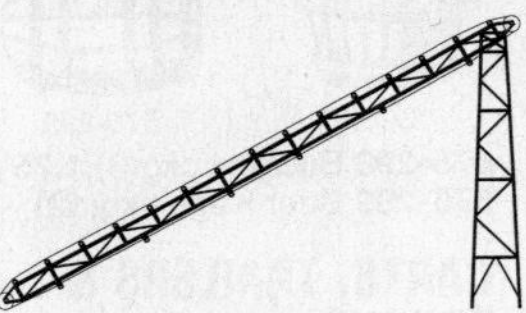

668-75002 Conveyor 60' **10.00**
Lattice work measures 60 scale feet, includes 15 top and six return rollers.

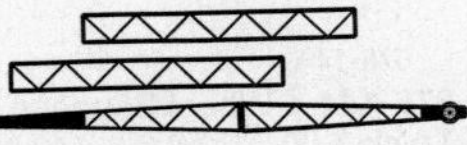

668-75004 Crane Boom **10.00**
35' long, with two 20' inserts, can be used to build a 75' boom.

668-75012 100-Ton Crane Boom **20.00**
100' long, includes 60' basic boom and two 20' inserts.

STEWART HOBBIES

All parts are plastic except where noted.

LOCOMOTIVE DETAILS

RS-3 BODY SHELLS EA 11.00

Undecorated shells include handrails.

691-1075 PH-1B
691-2075 PH-2A
691-3075 PH-3

RS-3 UNDERBODY

691-1076 Frame, Metal **3.00**
691-1077 Fuel Tank **2.00**

AS-16/AS-616

691-4049 Windows/Lens Set **3.00**
691-4075 Undecorated Body, Cab & Deck **9.00**
691-4076 Handrail Set **3.00**
691-4077 Coupler Liftbars pkg(2) **1.00**
691-4078 Air Tanks pkg(2) **1.00**
691-4079 Bell **1.00**
691-4080 Horn **1.00**
691-4081 Frame, Metal **5.00**
691-4082 Weight Set **5.00**

U25B

691-7049 Windows/Lens Set **3.00**
691-7075 Phase I Body **17.00**
691-7076 Handrail Set, 8 Pieces **4.00**
691-7077 Horn, 3-Chime **1.00**
691-7078 Screen Set, 6 Pieces **6.00**
691-7079 Ladder **1.00**
691-7080 Brakewheel **1.00**
691-7081 Airtanks pkg(2) **2.00**
691-7082 Frame **5.00**
691-7475 Phase IV/U28B Body **17.00**
691-7476 Phase III Body **17.00**
691-7477 Weight Set pkg(6) **5.00**

RS12

691-4575 Body Shell **9.00**
691-4576 Handrail Set **3.00**
691-4577 Weight Set **5.00**

S&S HOBBY

PHOTO-ETCHED DIESEL GRILLE KITS

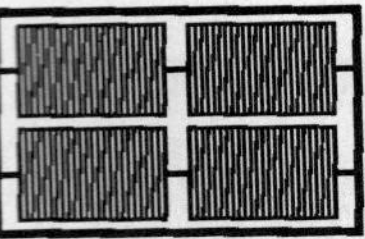

643-306 For Athearn SD40T-2 **4.99** ***NEW***

643-307 For Athearn AMD103 **5.99** ***NEW***

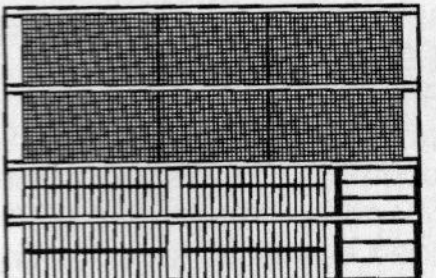

643-308 For Walthers F40PH **6.99** ***NEW***

STATE TOOL & DIE CO.

CABOOSE CONVERSION KIT

661-900 C&O Caboose Conversion Kit **4.25**
This set of plastic parts matches the steps and sun visors installed on C&O cabooses. They can also be used to create a custom model for your road. Designed for the PROTO 2000 Center Cupola car, the parts can be adapted to other models. (Parts shown on model, sold separately.)

KLING LADLE KIT

661-760 6.95

All items are cast in white metal unless noted.

CANS, DRUMS & KEGS EA 2.25 (UNLESS NOTED)

135-1011 135-2024

135-1011 Milk Cans pkg(8)
135-2024 Oil Cans pkg(5)
135-1014 Nail Kegs pkg(10)
135-2057 55-Gallon Drums pkg(6) **2.50**
135-2068 Garbage Cans pkg(4)
135-2072 Assorted Containers, Small pkg(9)

CHIMNEYS & SMOKE JACKS EA 2.25

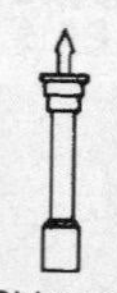

135-1007 Chimney
135-2070 Brick Chimney, Small pkg(2)
135-2073 Smoke Jack pkg(2)

CITY DETAILS

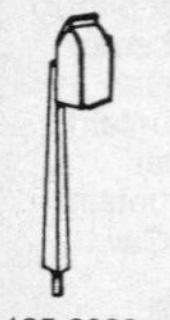
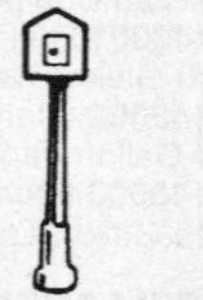

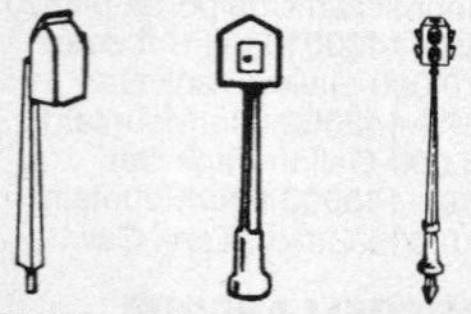

135-2022 135-2023 135-2029

135-2022 Mail Box pkg(2) **2.25**
135-2023 Fire Alarm Box pkg(2) **2.25**
135-2029 Traffic Light (2-Light w/Jewels) **2.50**

CORBEL & SUPPORTS EA 2.25

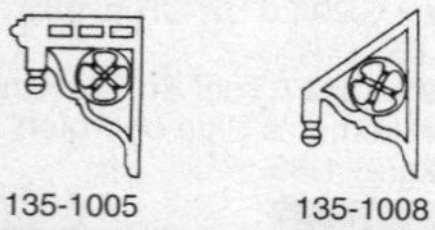

135-1005 135-1008

135-1005 Corbel pkg(2)
135-1008 Corbel Angle pkg(2)

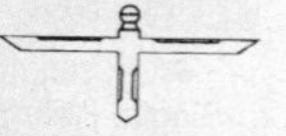

135-1010 135-1024

135-1010 Eave Support pkg(3)
135-1024 Corbel pkg(6)
135-1025 Corbel pkg(8)
135-1026 Eave Supports pkg(2)

CRATES PKG(3) EA 2.25

135-2066 Small
135-2067 Large

DOORS PKG(2) EA 2.25

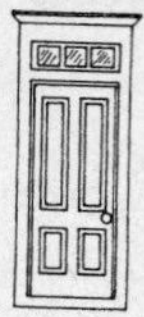

135-1004 135-1015 135-1017

135-1004 With Three-Pane Transom
135-1015 Victorian
135-1017 With Single-Pane Transom

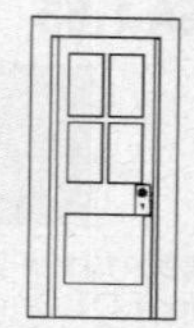

135-1019 135-1020

135-1019 Double
135-1020 Single

FENCE

135-2028 Prefab Fences **4.50**

GEAR

135-2062 Large Spoke pkg(3) **1.95**

HANDCART

135-14 pkg(2) **4.95**

HOIST

135-4002 Repair Hoist (Wood Kit) **6.95**

LAMPS EA 2.25

Nonworking models.

135-1002 Station Lamp w/Fount pkg(2)
135-2058 Lamp Shades pkg(12)

LOCOMOTIVE DETAILS

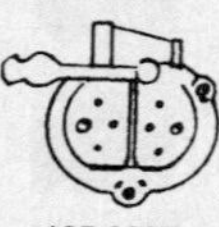

135-2036 135-2037

135-2036 Cab Seats pkg(4) **2.25**
135-2037 Fire Door pkg(2) **2.25**

135-3011 Backhead Set pkg(9 Pieces) **4.95**
Cast metal details.

LOGGING WAGON

135-4004 Logging Wagon Kit **9.95**

135-4006 Log Drag pkg(2) **9.50**

MARKER JEWELS PKG(12) EA 1.95

Extra small.
135-5002 Red
135-5003 Amber
135-5004 Green
135-5005 Clear

POSTS PKG(3) EA 2.25

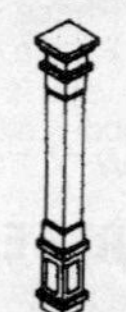

135-1023 Ornate
135-1028 Porch, Corner
135-1029 Porch, Middle

POTBELLY STOVE

135-2061 With Stack pkg(2) **2.25**

RAILING W/POST PKG(2) EA 2.25

135-1021 Western

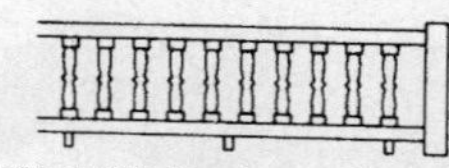

135-1022 Porch

ROOF TRIM

135-1006 Victorian w/Finial pkg(5) **2.50**

STAIRCASE

135-2056 pkg(6) **2.75**

TRACKSIDE DETAILS

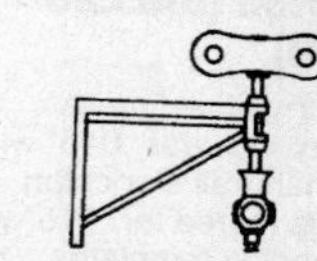

135-1001 DRG Order Board Signal **2.25**
135-2001 Bumper pkg(2) **3.25**

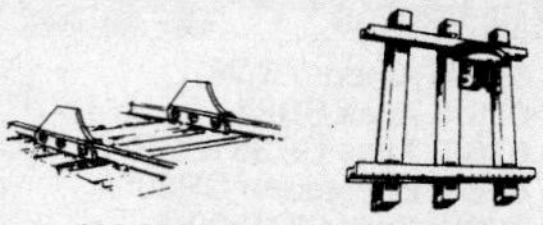

135-2005 135-2006

135-2005 Wheel Stops pkg(4) **2.95**
135-2006 Hinged Derail pkg(2) **2.25**

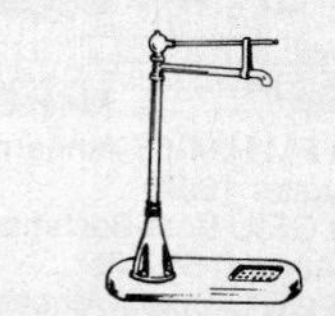

135-2009 Water Column **4.25**

135-2011 Rail Greaser & 3 Drums Set **4.50**

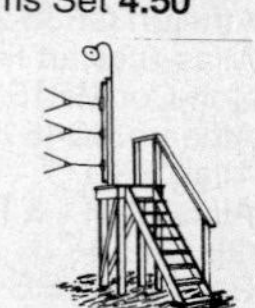

135-2012 Train Order Rack **5.50**

135-2016 135-2017

135-2016 Large Relay Box **2.50**
135-2017 Small Relay Box pkg(2) **2.25**

135-2019 Telephone Box pkg(2) **2.25**
135-2021 HOn3 Wheel Stops pkg(6) **2.75**

135-2026 Cattle Guard Set (5 Pieces) **2.75**

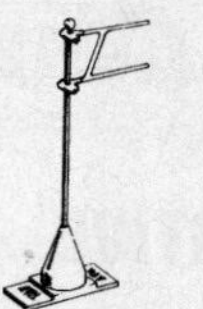

135-2031 135-2034

135-2031 Metal Mail Crane **2.25**
135-2034 Relay Cast pkg(2) **2.25**

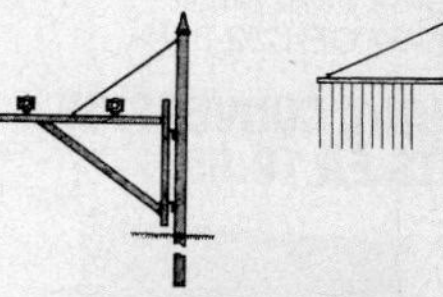

135-4001 135-4003

135-4001 Branchline Crossing Gate (wood/metal) **3.95**
135-4003 Telltale Kit Wood pkg(2) **3.95**

WHEELS EA 2.25

135-1012 Sheffield, 18" pkg(4)
135-1013 Sheffield, 15" pkg(4)
135-2038 Wagon, Small pkg(2)
135-2039 Wagon, Large pkg(2)

WINDOWS EA 2.25 (UNLESS NOTED)

135-1003 135-1009

135-1003 8-Pane pkg(3)
135-1009 Bay Window **2.50**

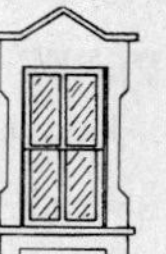
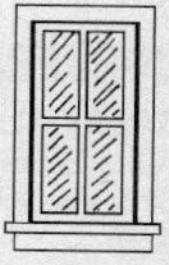

135-1016 135-1018

135-1016 Victorian pkg(3)
135-1018 pkg(3)
135-1027 Four-Pane pkg(3)

LOCOMOTIVE DETAILS

ANTICLIMBERS & END SILLS EA 2.95

676-66 EMD Large
676-67 GP50
676-69 EMD Small
676-97 GE C32-8

B UNIT CONVERSION KITS EA 19.95

676-1 GP/SD9B
Includes 2 sides and 1 top casting, complete handrail set (.015" wire).

676-2 Atlas SD24B
Kit features all metal parts, plus handrails and stanchions.

676-43 Front Range GP9B

B UNIT ACCESSORIES

676-72 GE High Short Hood/Dash 7 **6.95**

676-73 GE Utility Cabs/B30-73 **6.95**
Shown with #676-72.

676-98 EMD Battery Box Doors pkg(8) **2.95**

BRAKE PARTS

676-131 Brake Cylinder for Diesel Trucks pkg(16) **3.95**

CONVERSION PARTS

676-94 Alco S-1/3 Hood fits Atlas S2 **6.95**
676-46 GP7/9 to Switcher **4.95**
Mountings to convert to AAR switcher trucks.

DIESEL 2-AXLE TRUCKS

676-251 2 Axle Dummy Trucks with Brass Wheels pkg(2) **8.95**
Fits GP, F, B U-Boats or Dash 8 B locos (not intended for switcher). Compatible with Train Station or Athearn sideframes. Blackened brass wheels. Some assembly required.

END BRACKETS

For Alco road switchers.
676-109 Late pkg(4) **7.95**
676-111 Early Road & All Yard Switchers pkg(2) **4.95**

HANDRAIL KITS EA 15.95 (UNLESS NOTED)

Make any diesel more realistic. Includes .015" wire, brass handrail stanchion castings (cored for .015" wire) and bending templates.

676-4 Athearn SD9
676-3 Atlas SD24
676-5 Atlas GP38 & GP40
676-6 Bachmann GP30
676-8 Cary SW1500
676-9 AHM SD40
676-10 Atlas SD35
676-11 AHM GP18/Tyco GP20
676-12 Bachmann GP40

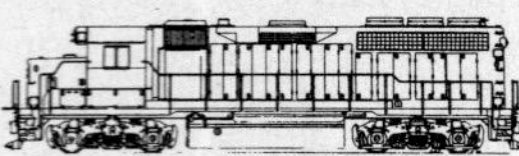

676-13 FM H24-66 Athearn Trainmaster **16.95**
676-14 GE U Boat-Bachmann U36B, Athearn B Units
676-15 GE U Boats-Athearn C Units
676-16 Bachmann BQ23-7
676-17 Cary S-2/4 and AHM S-4
676-18 AHM Alco Road Switcher
676-19 T&D SD40-2, SD40-2T & Athearn SD40-2
676-20 Athearn GP50
676-21 Railpower SD50, SD60
676-23 Cary & Athearn SW1500/SW1000.
676-30 Athearn GP38-2/40-2
676-31 Atlas-Stewart RS-3
676-41 Con-Cor MP15
676-42 Athearn SD45 & SDP40
676-44 Atlas RS-1
676-45 Atlas RS-11 & RSD-12
676-47 GE C32-8
676-68 Rail Power GE Dash 8-40B
676-82 Atlas GP7 **16.95**
676-86 Bachmann Dash 8-40C
676-87 Railpower CF7
676-200 Dash 8-40CW **16.95**
676-210 Rail Power SD60M **16.95**
676-211 GP60M
676-212 GP60B
676-213 GP60
676-214 GP35
676-215 GE Dash 8-40BW
676-216 GE AC4400 CW **16.95**
676-252 SD90MAC **16.95**

HANDRAIL STANCHIONS

BRASS

Castings cored for .015" wire, sold separately.

676-100 EMD 1st Generation **12.95**
GP/SD7 and Early GP9

676-101 Old GP/SD9 pkg(28) **11.95**
Fits GP9, GP18 and GP20; SD9, SD18 and SD24.

676-103 Modern GP pkg(28) **11.95**
Also fits SD second generation diesels.

676-104 Modern SD pkg(37) **11.95**
676-105 EMD GP30 pkg(28) **11.95**
676-106 FM Trainmaster pkg(30) **12.95**
676-107 Alco Yard Switchers pkg(16) **7.95**
676-108 Alco Road Switchers -Old pkg(22) **7.95**
676-110 GE U Boats pkg(30) **11.95**
676-113 GE C32-8 pkg(36) **11.95**
676-115 GE Dash 8-40B pkg(32) **11.95**
676-117 Alco RS-11 & RSD-12 **5.95**
676-118 GE Dash 8/9 CW **12.95**
676-132 Alco RS-1 **11.95**
676-135 SD60 pkg(59) **12.95**
676-190 SD90M **12.95**

PLASTIC EA 5.95

676-205 EMD 2nd Generation pkg(28)
676-206 GP9, GP18, GP20, GP50, GP18, GP20, GP24
676-207 GP30

HANDRAIL TEES

676-102 Plastic Handrail Tees pkg(8) **3.95**

GP15-1 PARTS

BODY SHELLS EA 19.95

Unpainted kits detailed to match specific prototypes. Models are less cabs, but will accept Cannon & Co. or Athearn Dash 2 cab, sold separately. Includes assembly instructions.

676-48 MP Phase Two
676-49 MP Phase One
676-50 CR
676-51 Frisco
676-52 CNW

DECK PARTS EA 2.95

676-65 Side Sills
676-70 Steps

HANDRAIL KITS EA 15.95

Wire and brass stanchions to fit specific GP15-1 body shells.
676-53 MP Phase I/CNW
676-54 MP Phase II/Frisco
676-55 CR

HOOD TOPS

676-71 Front & Rear pkg(2) **2.95**

UNDERBODY

Body Shell Sold Separately

676-56 Frame **10.95**
One-piece metal casting, fits all versions of GP15-1 body shell.

676-62 Fuel Tank **4.95**
Plastic, use with #56.

SHORT NOSES EA 6.95

Fits EMD GP and SD units.
676-58 80"
676-59 86"

Turn a plain model into a detailed replica with this line of metal castings.

LOCOMOTIVE DETAILS

ANTENNAS PKG(6) EA 1.85

695-13124 UHF Sinclair Style for EOT Device *NEW*
695-13125 ATCS Tear Drop Style UP *NEW*

DITCH LIGHTS

695-13100 GE Dash 8/9 pkg(4) **1.85**

HEADLIGHTS

695-13101

695-13102

695-13101 Light Cluster UP & BN SD7/9 pkg(4) **3.50**
695-13102 GE Nose Light U30/33/36 B & C **1.85**

695-13103

695-13106

695-13103 GE Nose/Cab Gyralight-SP **1.95**
695-13106 Dual Pyle-Early (All Roads) **1.85**
695-13104 GE Nose Light Bracket w/Cover Plate **1.85**
695-13105 GE Nose Light - BN/D&H **1.85**

695-13107

695-13109

695-13107 Dual Pyle-Late (All Roads) **1.85**
695-13109 Gyralight for Nose-NP GEs **1.85**
695-13108 Gyralight NP/SP/SLSF **2.00**

695-13110

695-13116

695-13110 GP9 Cluster Bracket w/Cover Plates Dual Pyle-Early **1.95**
695-13116 GP9 Cluster Bracket w/Cover Plates Dual Pyle-Late **1.95**
695-13111 GP9 Cluster Assembly (4 Pieces) **3.95**
695-13112 SP Cluster Light Bracket w/Dual Pyle **2.00**
695-13113 SP Cluster Bracket-GP/SD 35/40 **3.25**
695-13114 SP Nose Light Cluster-Assembled **2.50**
695-13115 GP9 Cluster Bracket-Pyle (4 Pieces) **3.95**
695-13117 Dual Pyle Oscillator w/Shields pkg(2) **1.85**
695-13118 SP Light Cluster 1-H113, H-114, H-117 pkg(3) **3.75**
695-13119 SP Nose Cluster Bracket w/Dual Beam/Cover Plate **1.85**
695-13120 SP Nose Cluster Bracket w/Dual Beam-Round **1.85**

MASHIMA MOTOR MOUNTS EA 4.95

695-141000 Long 24mm 1"
695-141001 Short 13mm 1/2"

WEIGHTS EA 4.95

695-143000 E&C Shops Johnstown Coalporter pkg(2)
695-143001 Red Caboose 10,000-Gallon Tank Car
695-143002 InterMountain 8,000-Gallon Tank Car
695-143003 InterMountain 10,000-Gallon Tank Car

MISCELLANEOUS

695-13121 Bell w/Bracket for Hood Unit GPs pkg(3) **1.95**

695-13126

695-13127

695-13126 Central Air Filter Box GP9/20 SP/CR pkg(2) **1.85** *NEW*
695-13127 Tool Box SP Units Brakeman's Side on Porch pkg(2) **1.85** *NEW*

695-13200

695-13300

695-13200 Horn-Single, Rear for E & F B Units pkg(4) **1.85**
695-13300 Speed Recorder-Cone Type **1.85**

CAST METAL DETAILS EA 2.95

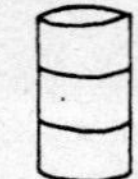

683-809 55-Gallon Oil Drum pkg(10)

683-820 Open Barrels pkg(10)

683-808 Flood Lights (Non-operating) pkg(3)

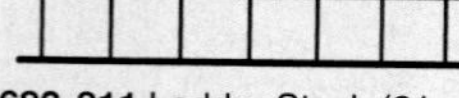

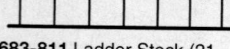

683-811 Ladder Stock (21 rungs) pkg(3)

683-815 Crane Magnet & Hook (2 Sets)

683-804 Fire Extinguishers pkg(10)

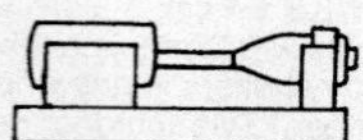

683-802 Fuel & Water Pump pkg(4)

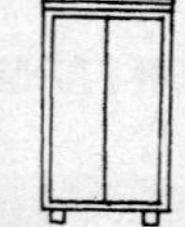

683-800 Signal Relay pkg(3)

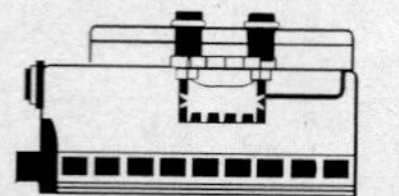

683-821 Diesel Engine *NEW*

Cast metal details.

CHIMNEY & SMOKE JACK EA 2.00

707-20008 707-20003

707-20008 Smokejack pkg(4)
707-20003 Brick Chimney pkg(2)

EAVE SUPPORTS

707-20004 Eave Supports pkg(4) **2.00**

LADDERS

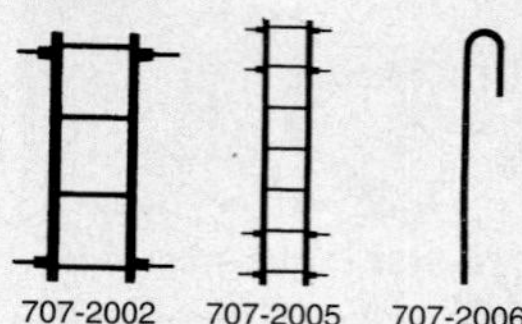

707-2002 707-2005 707-2006

707-2002 Caboose pkg(2) **5.00**
707-2005 Freight Car, Long pkg(4) **4.00**
.010" thick. Includes instructions to adapt to cars using 5, 6 or 7 rung ladders.

707-2006 Freight Car, Short pkg(8) **4.00**
.010" thick.

LIFT RINGS EA 3.00

Measures .010" thick.

707-2007 Tiny pkg(48)
707-2008 Large pkg(36)

PORCH POSTS EA 3.00

707-20010 Tall *NEW*
707-20011 Short *NEW*

ROOFING

707-20001 Ornamental Iron Roof **4.00**
.010" thick, 84 HO Scale feet long.

STOVE PIPE

707-20009 Elbow Stove Pipe pkg(3) **2.00**

STAIRCASE

707-20002 Ornamental Iron Staircase **6.00**
0.10" thick. Includes stripwood for stairs and scribed wood porch.

TRIM & RAILING

707-20006 Gable Small pkg(2) **2.00**
707-20007 Gable Large pkg(2) **2.00**

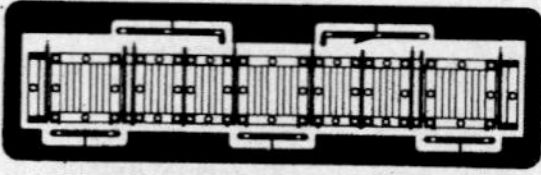

707-2004 Platform Railings for Observation Cars Kit **3.00**
Includes brake stanchion and handle.

707-20005 Gingerbread **6.00**

TROLLEY FENDER

707-2003 Eclipse Kit pkg(2) **9.00**

TICHY TRAIN GROUP

Precision injection-molded impact-grade styrene parts.

BRACKETS

293-8011 pkg(8) **1.50**

BRAKE PARTS

293-3003 Brake Wheel, Bracket & Staff pkg(4) **1.50**
For 1895-1920 era flats and gondolas. Cored for .018 and .020 wire.

293-3005 KC West Brake **2.50**
293-3013 AB Brake Set **2.50**
293-3034 Split K Brake System **2.50**

CAR ENDS EA 2.50

BOX CAR

293-3058 7/8 1 Pair *NEW*

USRA REBUILT CARS

293-3031 With Top Rib
293-3032 Less Top Rib

YOUNGSTOWN PRESSED STEEL PKG(2)

For USRA 40-ton freight cars. End has separate order board and facia strip.

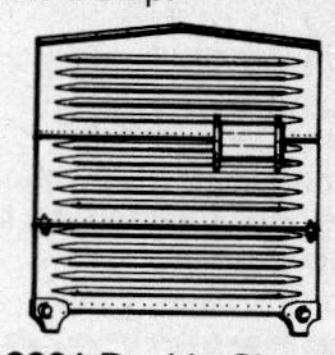

293-3001 Double-Sheathed Cars
293-3020 Single-Sheathed Cars

COAL DOCK DETAILS

293-8003 Coal Chute **3.00**
293-8004 Coal Shed **9.50**
293-8005 Hoist House & Sand House **9.50**

DOORS

293-3017 6' Wood w/Tracks pkg(2) **2.50**
293-3018 6' Steel w/Tracks pkg(2) **2.50**
293-3055 Steel Youngstown 6 x 9' **3.00**
293-8009 Wooden Structure pkg(3) **1.50**
293-8015 Double Steel pkg(3) **1.50** *NEW*

EYEBOLTS

293-3037 pkg(80) **3.00**

GRAB IRONS EA 3.00

Preformed wire.
293-3015 18" Drop pkg(100)
293-3021 18" Straight pkg(100)
293-3028 Roof Corner pkg(100)
293-3053 24" Straight pkg(50)
293-3054 Curved Caboose pkg(25)
293-3057 24" Drop pkg(50) *NEW*

JIB CRANE

293-8007 5.95

LADDERS

293-3033 Freight Car (Assorted) **2.50**
293-8002 Safety Cage Ladder/Staircase **3.00**

PIPE RAILINGS

293-8013 pkg(4) **1.50**

PLATFORMS

293-3023 Reefer Wood Ice pkg(4) **2.50**
293-8001 Open Grate **3.00**

RETAINING WALLS

293-8012 pkg(3) **1.50**

ROOFWALK

293-3029 40' Wood **2.00**

STAKE POCKETS

293-3006 pkg(32) **1.50**

STIRRUP STEPS PKG(10) EA 1.50

293-3038 293-3039 293-3040

293-3038 Straight Side Mount
293-3039 Straight Bottom Mount
293-3040 Short Straight Bottom Mount

293-3041 293-3042 293-3043

293-3041 Slant Side Mount
293-3042 Angled Offset Bottom Mount
293-3043 Double Offset Bottom Mount

293-3044 293-3045

293-3044 Stepped Offset Bottom Mount
293-3045 Straight Double Step Side Mount Bottom

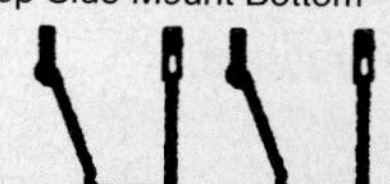

293-3046 293-3047

293-3046 Angled Side/Bottom Mount
293-3047 Angled Offset Side Mount

TANK CAR PARTS

293-3007 Detail Set **4.95**
293-3011 Frame **3.75**

TRUCK BEARINGS

293-3059 Nylon pkg(48) **3.00** *NEW*

TWEEZERS

293-5000 Plastic pkg(4) **2.00** *NEW*

UNDERFRAMES EA 3.75

293-3019 USRA Single-Sheathed Freight Car
293-3030 R-40 PFE Reefer

WATER COLUMN

293-8006 4.95

WINDOWS EA 1.50

293-8010 Six Lite pkg(6)
293-8014 Double Hung pkg(3) *NEW*

All products made in the USA.

DIESEL DETAILS

DYNAMIC BRAKE HATCH

732-88 EMD Late GPs **8.95**
For EMD GP60 Phase II, fits Athearn GP50/60.

GRILLES

732-138 GP9 **2.95**
Designed to backdate the Proto2000 GP18 to a GP9. Can be adapted to other engines where a see-through GP9 grille is desired.

EMD FANS W/ROTATING BLADES

48" ORIGINAL

732-139 Single **2.95**
732-140 Set of Three **7.95**
For GP50, GP60 and GP60M dynamic brakes. Also used on F45, FP45, SDP40F, SD40-2, SD40T-2 and other GP and SD units.

48" Q FANS

732-143 Set of Three **7.95**
For later GP and SD units.

52"

732-141 Single **2.95**
For SD50, SD60, SD60M, SD70 and other units.

DAMPERS

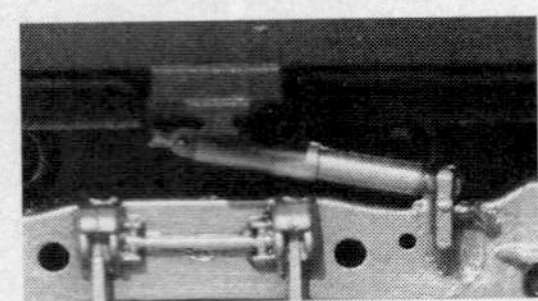

732-144 EMD Anti-Hunting Dampers pkg(4) **2.95**
For late GP or rebuilt Blomberg 2-axle (4-wheel) trucks. Includes enough parts for two engines.

PASSENGER CAR PARTS

DOOR GATES

732-408 Passenger Car End pkg(4) **2.95**
Fits Con-Cor, AHM, Rivarossi, Walthers, Athearn, brass and other passenger cars. Two basic styles of gates are included.

STEP COVERS

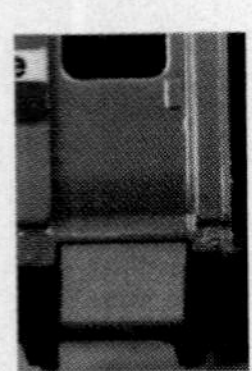

732-430 pkg(4) **2.95**
Fits Walthers Amtrak Horizon Cars. Can be used on other passenger cars where a smooth step cover is needed.

EXHAUST PIPES

732-431 pkg(4) **2.95**
Fits Train Station Products/ Detail Associates Budd "El Capitan" Hi-Level passenger cars.

WHEEL RECORDERS

732-432 Decelostats pkg(8) **2.95**
Fits journal covers of Train Station Products/Detail Associates Outside Swing Hanger Passenger Car Trucks. Used by UP, ATSF and others.

WINDOW INSERTS

732-433 Superliner II Sleeping Car **2.95**
Converts Con-Cor Superliner Sleeper windows to Superliner II Sleeper or Transition Sleeper configuration. Includes enough parts for four Superliner II cars, or one Transition Car

ROOF VENTS

732-435 Rectangular Wire Screen pkg(12) **2.95**
Commonly used on most modern Budd passenger cars. Enough parts for two or three cars, depending on number of prototype vents.

STIRRUP STEPS

732-436 pkg(12) **2.95**
Same parts as used on Train Station High-Level cars. Same style is used on prototype Budd and other cars. Enough parts to convert three to six cars.

TRUCK MOUNTING POSTS

732-439 pkg(4) **3.95** *NEW*
Fits Train Station Products, Rivarossi, Con-Cor and other trucks to the floor/frame of a car. Enough parts for two cars.

UNDERFRAME/FLOOR

732-800 85' **5.95**
Same parts used in Train Station Products/Detail Associates High-Level Car kits. Suitable for scratchbuilding

BODY SHELLS EA 10.95 (UNLESS NOTED)

Undecorated shells for Budd Hi-Level cars.

732-801 Step-Up Coach
732-802 Coach
732-803 Diner
732-804 Hi-Level Lounge **TBA**

WHITEGROUND MODEL WORKS

ICE BLOCKS

771-5006 pkg(12) **2.00**
Clear plastic.

VOLLMER

IMPORTED FROM GERMANY BY WALTHERS

ACCESSORIES

Detailed plastic parts.

770-3761 Town Square Items pkg(28) **17.99**
Set of 28 parts including 2 cobblestone sheets (6-3/8 x 9-5/8" 16 x 24cm), trash bins, parking meters, police and fire alarm boxes and more.

770-5021 Structural Shapes **9.99**

770-5131 Postal Accessories **9.99**

770-5132 Garden Furniture w/Accessories **12.99**

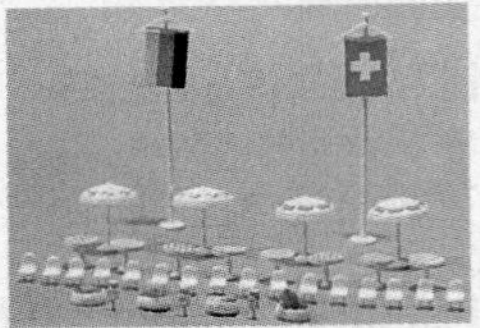

770-5142 Round Tables & Chairs **10.99**

770-5143 Rectangular Tables & Chairs **10.99**

770-5241 Brick Piles & Pipe **6.99**
1/2 x 1/4 x 1/4"
11.5 x 7 x 7 mm.

770-5242 Wooden Cases pkg(10) **6.99**

770-5742 Bicycle Stands pkg(3) **16.99**

770-5705 Loading Gauge & Water Spout **13.99**
Column: 2-1/2 x 1 x 3"
6.2 x 2.5 x 7.5 cm.
Gauge: 2-3/4 x 13/32 x 2-1/2"
7 x 1 x 6.5 cm.

770-6524 Water Column Only **7.99**
2-1/2 x 1 x 2-3/4"
6 x 2.4 x 7.2 cm

PARTY TENTS

770-5130 **7.99**
1-13/32 x 1-13/32 x 1-5/8"
3.5 x 3.5 x 4 cm
Guests will appreciate these handy shelters in any kind of weather. Great outdoor detail for wedding scenes, restaurants, carnival or fair midways, backyards and more.

OUTDOOR FARMER'S MARKET

770-5141 **20.99**
A great detail for the busy downtown, this set is complete with snackbar trailers, tables, umbrellas, tents and other details.

Parts are lost wax brass castings unless noted.

AIR HORN

755-60 Five Chime for GE U-Boats, etc. **2.00**

ANTENNA MASTS

755-91 Brass pkg(25) **5.00**
755-92 Plastic pkg(25) **2.50**

ARM RESTS PKG(2) EA 2.00

755-79

755-80

755-79 Two Brackets
755-80 Three Brackets

BELLS

755-81

755-98

755-81 Diesel pkg(2) **1.50**
755-98 Brass w/Bracket pkg(2) **2.25**

BRAKE PARTS

755-68 Brake Wheel **2.00**

755-82 Brake Cylinder Assembly **1.50**

CABOOSE STACKS EA 2.00

755-73 27" Tall
755-74 54" Tall

DYNAMIC BRAKE KIT

755-78 **5.00**

EXHAUST STACK

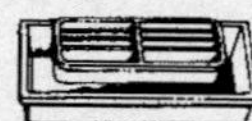

755-69 GE Type **2.50**

GRAB IRONS

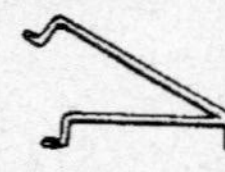

755-55 Corner, Brass pkg(2) **1.95**

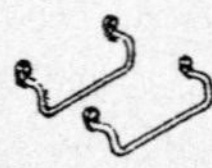

755-54 Drop, Brass pkg(12) **5.95**

HANDRAIL STANCHIONS

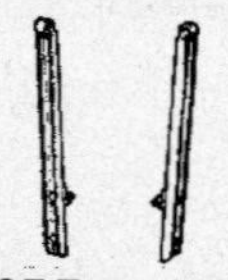

755-87 GE Type pkg(32) **8.95**
Cast in Beryllium copper.

HAPCO SPARK ARRESTORS

755-75

755-76

755-75 Stack Only **2.00**
755-76 Two Stacks & Two Bases **5.00**

LIFT RINGS

755-62 GE Type pkg(10) **2.00**

MARKER LIGHTS

755-63 Adlake Caboose Marker pkg(2) **4.00**

MIRRORS

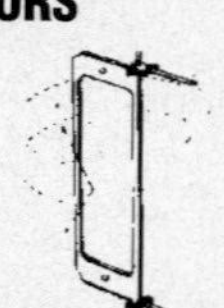

755-77 Cab Mirror w/Brackets pkg(2) **2.00**

PYLE GYRALITES

755-70

755-71

755-70 Single **1.50**
755-71 Single w/Bracket **1.75**

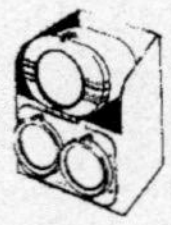

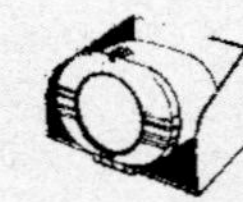
755-84 755-85

755-84 Single w/Headlight - Nose Mount **2.00**
755-85 Single - Nose Mount **1.50**

SNOW PLOW

755-99 Pilot Plow **4.95**

SNOW SHIELD

755-83 pkg(2) **5.00**
Used on UP and Amtrak E units.

SPEED RECORDERS

755-61

755-65

755-61 Early GE pkg(2) **1.50**
Early GE axle generator loco overspeed control.

755-65 Axle Wheel Slip pkg(5) **2.00**
Chicago Pneumatic, axle-mounted speed recorder drive unit.

SUN VISORS

755-93 Diesel Cab Visors pkg(4) **2.00**
Photo-etched in .005" brass.

TANK CAR DETAILS

755-53 Dome & Vent **2.00**

TRACTION MOTOR

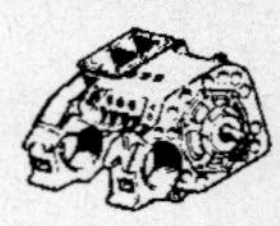

755-67 GE 752 Style **3.00**
Early traction motor, less gear case.

VENTS

755-72 Roof Vents **1.50**
For cabooses, passenger cars, structures, etc.

WINDSHIELD WIPERS

For diesel and electric locos.

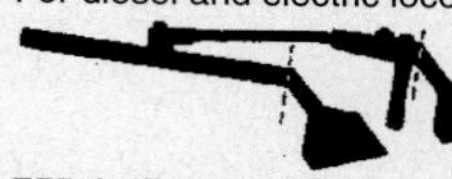

755-94 Beryllium Copper pkg(4) **2.50**

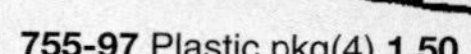

755-97 Plastic pkg(4) **1.50**

Ye Olde Huff-N-Puff

BARRELS

792-2000 Wooden Barrels pkg(12) **2.00**

BOILER

792-1027 Horizontal Stationary Boiler **13.00**
Fine detail, includes many metal castings.

BRASS CHAIN EA 2.00

Each chain is 10" in length.

792-2001 Extra-Fine - 36 links per inch
792-2002 Fine - 27 links per inch
792-2003 Heavy - 20 links per inch

BRASS STRIPS & BARS EA 2.00

792-2008 Strip .005 x 3/32" (6')
792-2009 Strip .005 x 1/8" (6')
792-2016 Bar 3/32 x 3/32 x 12" pkg(2)
792-2021 Brass Strip .005 x 1/4 x 24"

LADDERS

792-2020 Brass Ladder Stock .005 x 1/4 x 24" **2.00**

RIVET STRIP EA 2.00

792-2013 3/32" wide (3')
792-2014 1/8" wide (3')

SMOKE JACK

792-2005 Brass for Caboose pkg(2) **2.00**

TRUSS ROD

792-2004 Nylon Truss Rod Line (black) (20') **2.00**

WASHERS PKG(48) EA 2.00

792-2010 Fibre (1/16 x 5/16", 5/32" hole diameter)
792-2011 Flat Steel (3/32 x 7/16", 5/32" hole diameter)

WINDOWS PKG(5) EA 2.00

792-2006 Cast nylon frames 13/32 x 1/2"
792-2007 Plastic frames 7/32 x 1/2"

SUPER DETAILING PARTS

BOOKS & VIDEO

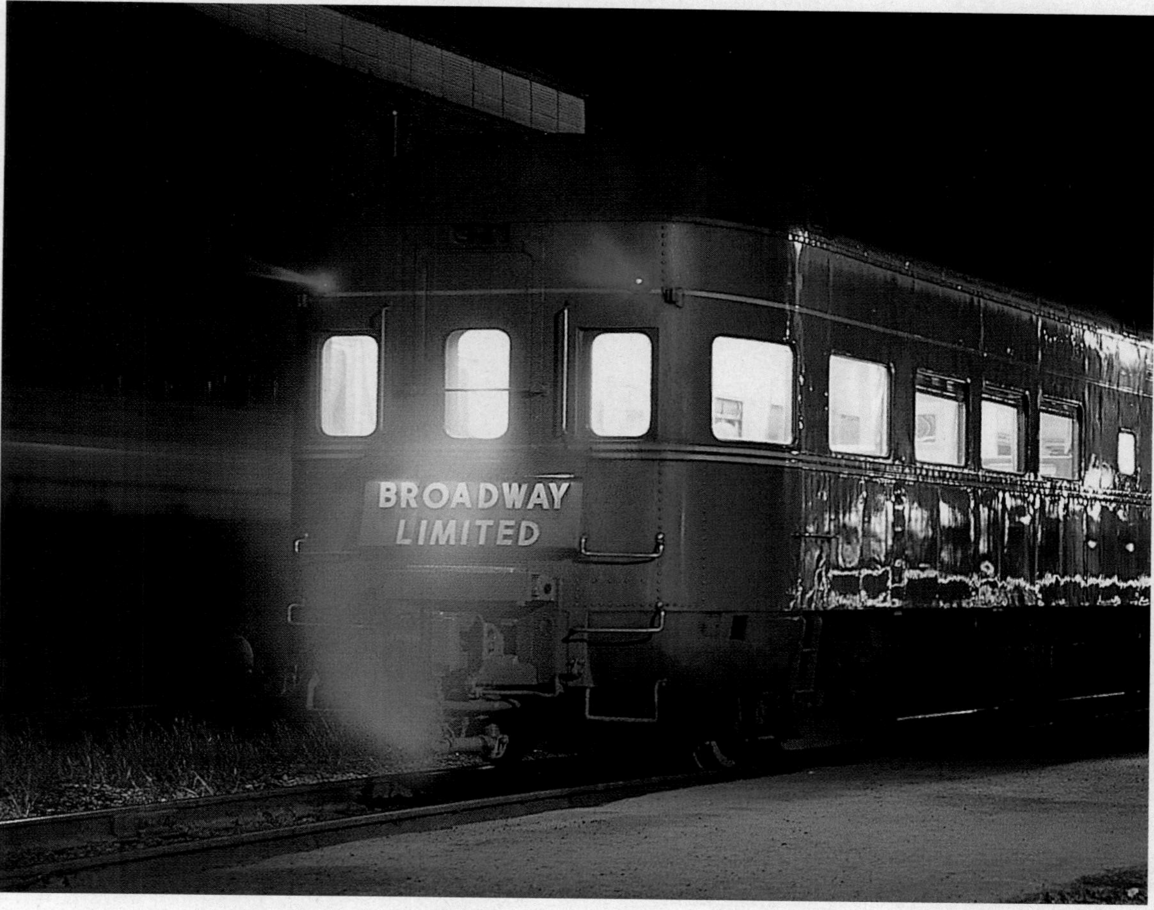

Tickets in hand, you make your way sleepily out onto the platform. A fine October breeze, cool and bracing as fresh apple cider, blows through as the doors open. Lights gleam invitingly from the platform. A Porter appears to carry your bags and make sure you get to the proper track.

Just ahead, the great "Broadway Limited" waits patiently in the darkness. Walking past the observation "Mountain View," you glance up and find the car deserted. Not surprising given the lateness of the hour. But it begins to nag at you. There really aren't many people on board after all. A Trainmen sees you aboard safely and directs you to your berth and some much needed sleep.

October 1966: the westbound Broadway Limited at Altoona Pennsylvania. The hour is late, literally and figuratively. In little more than a year, the all-Pullman Broadway, the most luxurious train in America, will be terminated.

The trains may be gone, but you can still travel back to those wonderful days in videos and books. Here, you can discover new ideas and methods to model the great trains of yesterday or today. And if you're fascinated by freight operations, the glory of passenger travel or the romance of railroading, exciting reading and viewing opportunities are waiting on the pages ahead.

You'll also find lots of new titles, including Pennsy Streamliners: The Blue Ribbon Fleet, by well-known passenger train expert Joe Welsh. In this, the most in-depth treatment of the Pennsy story available, Welsh covers every detail a railfan could want. From passenger car rosters to interviews with former employees, Pennsy Streamliners presents a complete history of the famous line's rise, dominance, and decline in the high-class luxury rail-service industry. Packed with historical accounts from the 1930s to 1960s, the 160-page Pennsy Streamliners includes rare color photos and passenger fleet exterior photos in color, as well as more than 100 black-and-white photos. Item #400-1077 is now available from Kalmbach Publishing Co.

Photo by Robert Malinoski

WALTHERS™

AMERICA'S DRIVING FORCE - MODELING RAILROADS AND THE AUTO INDUSTRY

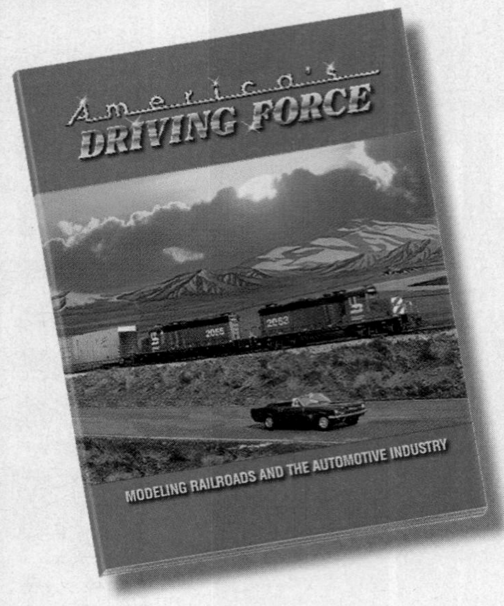

913-104 49.98 *NEW*
Put the pedal to the metal and get your automotive industry modeling in high gear with a copy of *America's Driving Force - Modeling Railroads and the Auto Industry*. Here at last is a complete look at how autos and trucks are made and the need for railroads at each stage of the operation.

Separate chapters examine the fascinating history and growth of the auto industry, manufacturing operations from raw materials to final delivery and the ever-changing and vital role of railroads and their specialized equipment.

A great addition to your modeling or prototype reference library, a large 8-1/2 x 11" format showcases the many model and prototype photos found in this one-of-a-kind, 120-page, hardcover book.

Next, we'll show you how to model this amazing industry. Fascinating articles provide ideas for modeling vehicles, auto rack cars, loading and unloading facilities, assembly plants, supporting parts plants and more. And, you'll discover lots of new operations possibilities, from simply adding auto industry bridge traffic, to using an auto plant and its many support industries as the central theme of your layout.

RAILROADING ALONG THE WATERFRONT

913-103 49.98
Wherever rails and water meet, in big city harbors, lake ports, river landings or coastal towns, you'll find some of the most interesting operations. This exciting and unique hardcover, 120-page book is a gold-mine of ideas, prototype photos and information that make it easy to model virtually any kind of rail/marine operations on your layout.

The modeling chapter provides over 30 pages of practical "how-to-do-it" advice. Great ideas for modeling water, building a barge, adding carfloat operations and a chart of industries and the freight cars that serve them are just a few of the articles you'll find here, along with more color photos. And, there's a glossary to explain many of the technical terms and colorful slang used in the text and along the docks.

Separate chapters cover the unique flavor of each region of the US, while large photos (most in full-color) showcase equipment in operation.

TRAINS TRACKS & TALL TIMBER

913-102 49.98
This hardcover, 120-plus page book takes you into the woods, through the sawmills and the paper mills, alongside the machinery and on board the trains that serve America's wood products industry. You'll experience history first hand, from the rough-and-tumble life of an early logging camp, to the mechanized operations of the present day.

Modelers will find two full chapters, over 40 pages in all, of practical tips and ideas for modeling a logging operation in any scale. Dozens of photos, track plans, and drawings explain the workings of the mills and their relationship to the railroads and support operations. Then, put your new skills to work on one of 12 different modeling projects, covering everything from making trees and logs to realistic operations.

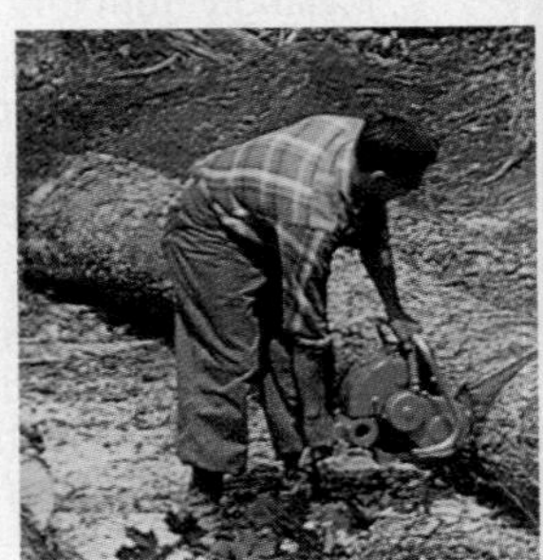

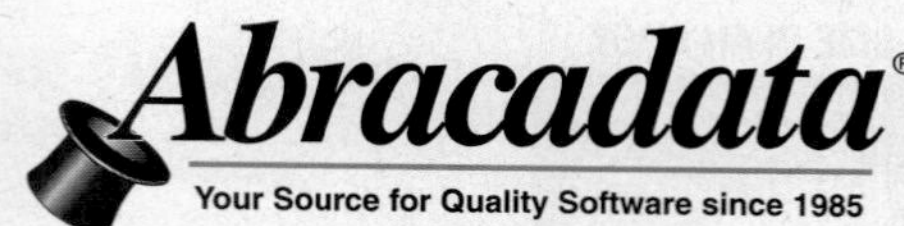

Abracadata®
Your Source for Quality Software since 1985

TRAIN-TEASERS

SOFTWARE

TRAIN-TEASERS
EA 19.99

Slider Puzzles 124-21730

Jigsaw Puzzles 124-21530

ConcenTRAINtion 124-21830

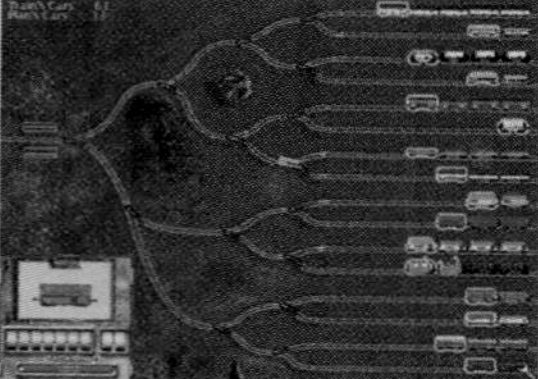

Hump Yard 124-21630

Train Jumpers 124-21930

The all-new Train Teaser series will "deliver" pleasure to all. Kids from 4 to 84 will have hours of fun working through these "old time" favorites. These easy-to-learn games combine original train theme pictures with the classic puzzles that everyone enjoys.

"The Hump Yard" is a tetris type game where the different cars must be sorted onto the correct track while controlling the switches and retarder. You control game speed, retarder pressure and type of game. Choose the "Frantic Yardmaster," the "Consist" or a "Combination" of both.

With the next four games in the series, "Jigsaw Puzzles", "Train Jumpers", "Slider Puzzles" and "ConcenTRAINtion," you can control different game play aspects. For example, you control the number and size of pieces, the rotation, the playing speed, background color, card back design and more. All these features, spread throughout five games, make puzzle solving as challenging as you like. At the end of each game you are rewarded with competition scoring and beautiful original train photographs taken by fellow train enthusiasts.

Windows 95/98/NT, Pentium 60 or higher, 16MB RAM (32 recommended), 50 MB HD, CD-ROM, SVGA monitor, 16-Bit graphics card or higher.

124-21530 Jigsaw Puzzles *NEW*
124-21630 Hump Yard *NEW*
124-21730 Slider Puzzles *NEW*
124-21830 ConcenTRAINtion *NEW*
124-21930 Train Jumpers *NEW*

3D RAILROAD CONCEPT AND DESIGN

124-21230

124-21230 View I

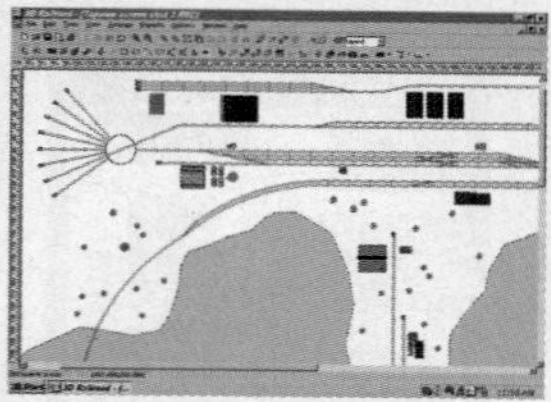

124-21230 View II

As you draw 2D layouts in any scale, this innovative program creates a materials list automatically. Choose from a variety of track pieces or create your own. Control elevation, grade, roadbed, ties and rail attributes with ease. You can view your layout in spectacular 3D graphics. Easily place actual manufacturer objects from the many libraries and then enter your layout and move through it in a colorful, textured, virtual 3D world.

With the version 2.0 for Windows you can also enjoy these added features. The "Terrain Tool" allows you to create custom terrain by drawing the shape and size you want, then simply lifting the grid to the shape you desire. The terrain then conforms to the track and buildings you place. The "Track Wizard" is just that. Enter the appropriate dimensions and the "Wizard" will create the perfect track piece.

124-21230 Windows **99.99**
Windows 95/98/NT, Pentium 166 or higher, 32MB RAM, 30 to 50MB HD, CD-ROM, 256 color monitor or better (16-bit or higher is recommended).

124-21240 Macintosh **99.99**
Power Mac, System 7.5 or higher, 24MB RAM, 15 to 80MB HD, CD-ROM, 256 color monitor or better.

3D RAILROAD MASTER

124-21330

124-21330 View I

124-21330 View II

The "3D Railroad Master" simulator puts you in the engineer's seat of your very own model railroad. Use actual cab controls to adjust speed, apply braking, give crossing warnings, control train direction and track switching. Each layout comes with its own pick-up and delivery schedule that you must adhere to if you want to succeed. Simultaneously control up to four trains per layout, but watch out for the animated pedestrians, livestock and vehicles. Accidents could cause the loss of time, money and even lives!

124-21330 Windows **59.99**
NEW
Windows `95, Pentium 166 or higher, 32MB RAM, 40 to 105MB HD, CD-ROM, SVGA 256 color monitor or better, mouse.

TRIPLE TRAIN PAK

Triple Train Pak

2D Railroad Architect

Train Engineer Deluxe

Trains The Screen Saver

Screen Saver's modules keep your desktop moving right along. Next comes Train Engineer Deluxe which allows you to run the game on a custom layout you build yourself. Finally, 2D Railroad Architect contains all the tools needed to create a precision layout available in our full 3D program without all the glitz.

124-20930 Windows **69.99**
NEW
486/DX2/66, Windows '95, 16MB RAM, 256 color monitor or better, 2X CD-ROM or faster.

TRAIN PAK MAC

124-20940 Macintosh **29.99**
A favorite product for those who don't own newer Macintoshes. Contains the original "Train Engineer" plus the first program created to "Design Your Own Railroad." With these, you can create top view layouts in any scale, or become the engineer to play the game. Are you planning on a new Mac later? We offer an upgrade path. System 6.0.7 or higher, 4MB RAM, 6MB hard drive.

SOFTWARE

RIGHT TRACK

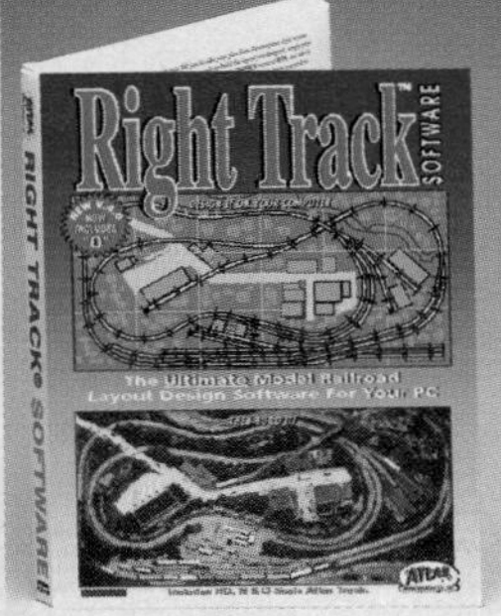

150-370 Version 4.0 **34.95**
Users can draw in the size and shape of their layout table; place and connect track; add elevations, helices, parallel tracks, transition curves, roadbed and more.

Features new Atlas O libraries; updated graphical user interface; the ability to create crossovers and ladders and to search and replace elements; gradients can now be calculated; several undo steps (adjustable); color can be added to elements according to layer, number or height; easier zoom function; autosave function and more.

System requirements: PC with Windows 95, 98 or NT; Pentium I, 66Mhz; 16MB RAM; 10MB free disk space.

ATLAS CD-ROM LIBRARY

150-371 19.95
The Atlas CD-ROM Library includes the entire contents of Atlas' 6 HO and N Scale layout instruction books, plus the Parts Catalog, Wiring Book and product catalog. Access every one of Atlas' 54 layout plans, locomotive diagrams and any other piece of information Atlas has printed. Requires a PC with system 486SX or better, Windows 3.1 or '95, 4MB RAM, 5MB free disk space and a mouse.

BOOKS

SEVEN STEP-BY-STEP HO RAILROADS

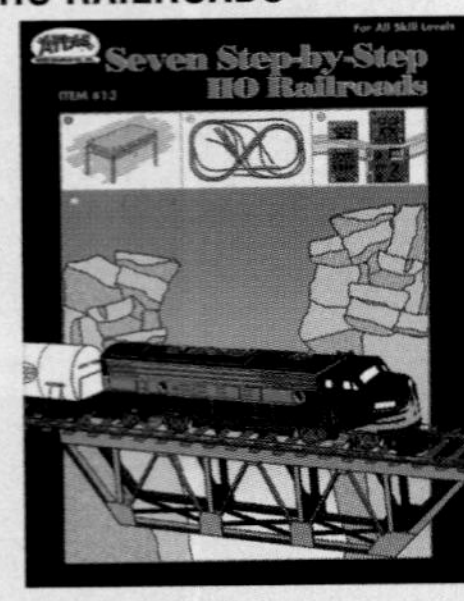

150-13 4.95
This book will show you, step-by-step, how to build the layout of your choice. Includes tips on benchwork, track laying, wiring and scenery. All skill levels.

HO LAYOUTS FOR EVERY SPACE

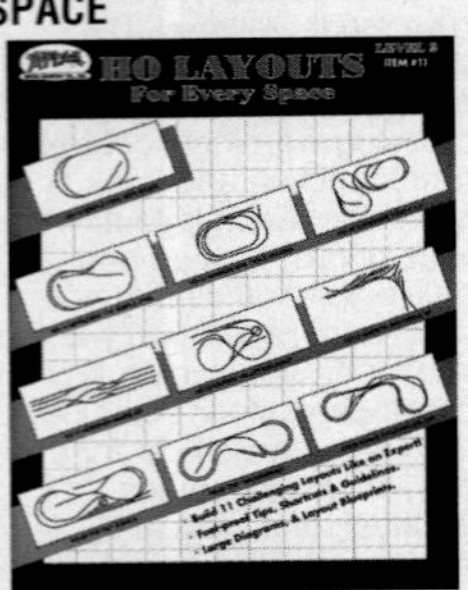

150-11 4.95
Contains 11 challenging layouts for unusual spaces, both large and small. Each plan is accompanied by complete instructions on benchwork, tracklaying, wiring, scenery and more. Intermediate to advanced skill levels.

ROLLING THUNDER-A PORTRAIT OF NORTH AMERICAN RAILROADING

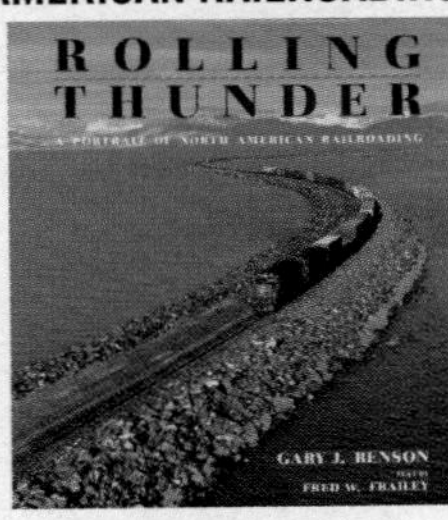

150-16 19.95
Breathtaking, 192-page, full-color journey contains 164 photos capturing the breadth and drama of trains in the 1990s. More than 40 railroads depicted in on-location photos by noted railroad photographer Gary Benson. Text by Fred Frailey.

THE COMPLETE ATLAS WIRING BOOK

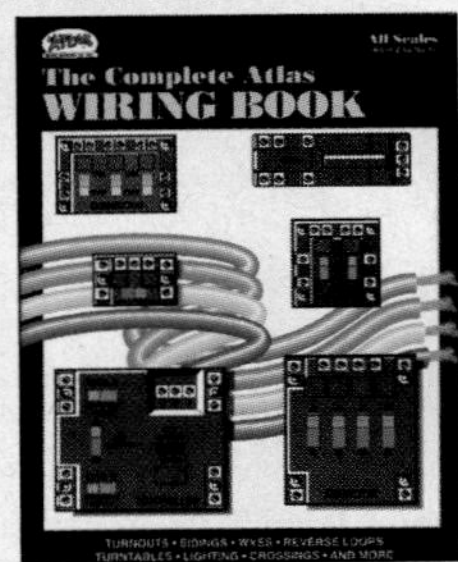

150-12 4.95
Learn how to install and use Atlas' quality components on any layout. Starts beginners with the basics of wiring, and takes advanced modelers through some complex wiring situations. Complemented by more than 100 diagrams and complete glossary. For all scales and skill levels.

BEGINNER'S GUIDE TO HO MODEL RAILROADING

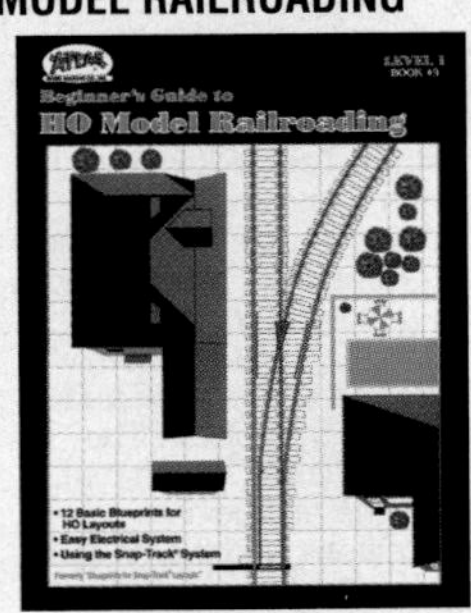

150-9 3.95
Perfect for the novice, this book contains twelve layouts built with either Atlas code 100 or code 83 track. Now includes code 83 track products required listings (in addition to code 100 listings); large, clear layout diagrams; and complete construction and wiring instructions. Written in modern, simple language.

KING-SIZE PLAN BOOK

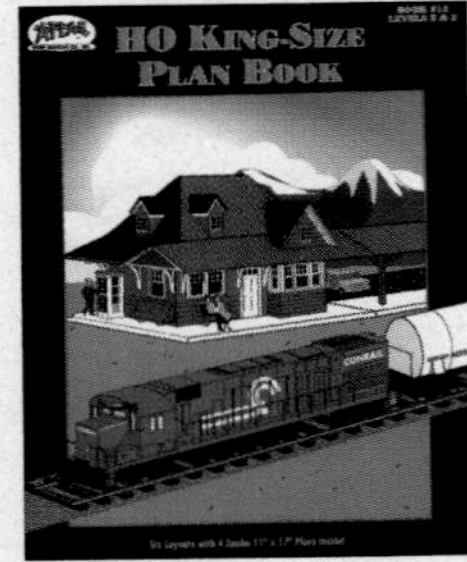

150-14 6.95
Contains six layout plans that are large and relatively complex. Four out of the six plans fold out to 11 x 17", and each plan is in a 2" to the foot scale format. Includes complete building instructions, including detailed diagrams for a few cookie-cutter layout plans. Intermediate to advanced skill levels.

ATLAS PARTS CATALOG

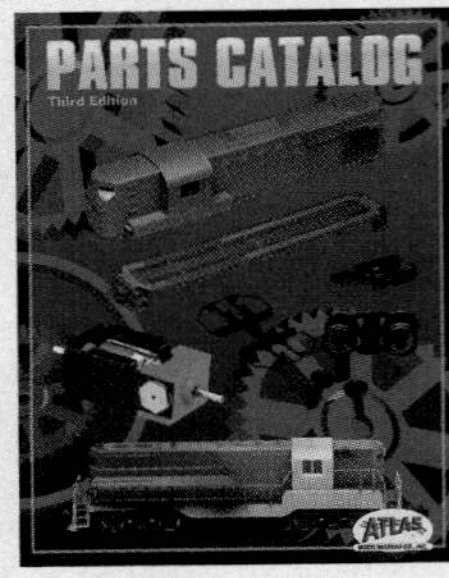

150-3 5.00
Contains exploded diagrams of Atlas locomotives with part numbers labeled for easy identification. Complete list of available parts and prices for all locomotives, freight cars and miscellaneous products. Some assembly, repair and maintenance information included.

PRINTS

ALL-AMERICAN LOCOMOTIVES EA 6.95

Full-color, 24 x 36".

150-352 Midwest Terminal
150-353 Union Pacific Fast Freight
159-354 Santa Fe "War Bonnet"
150-355 Mainline Action

Get Daily Info, Photos and News at

www.walthers.com

BACHMANN

BOOKS

E-Z TRACK MANUAL

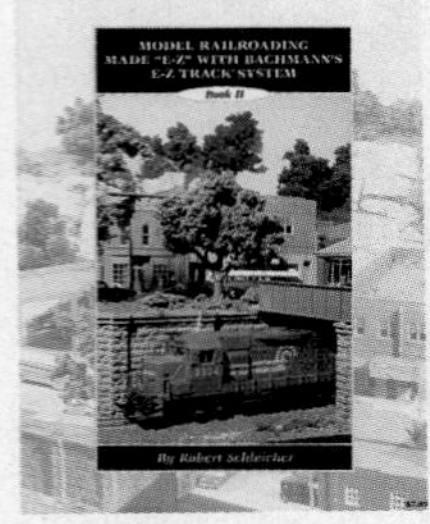

160-99978 #2 **7.95** ***NEW***

MODEL RAILROADING MADE E-Z

160-99979 #1 **4.00**

CATALOGS

1999 SPECTRUM CATALOG

160-99981 5.00 ***NEW***
See what Spectrum has to offer in this full-color, 52-page catalog.

1999 BACHMANN CATALOG

160-99998 6.00 ***NEW***
Full-color catalog displays Bachmann's current line of products. 92 pages.

BOOKS

AIR BRUSHING

HOBBY & CRAFT GUIDE TO AIR-BRUSHING

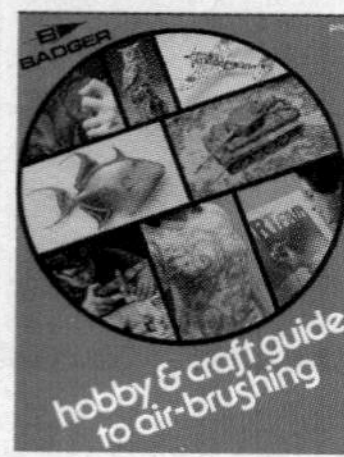

165-500 6.85
Preparation for painting, mixing paint, cleaning and maintenance. 32 pages, 8-1/2 x 11".

STEP BY STEP MODELERS GUIDE TO AIR-BRUSHING

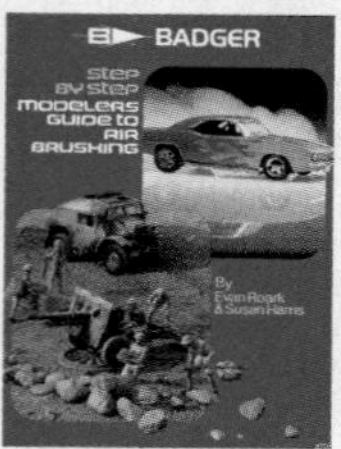

165-505 10.10
Covers painting models, figures and dioramas. Techniques from shadowing to properly mixing paint. 32 pages, 8-1/2 x 11".

ANYONE CAN AIR BRUSH

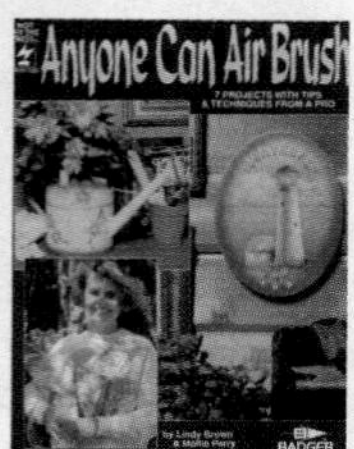

165-502020 7.60
Basic tips and techniques for handling, cleaning and working with your airbrush. Softcover, 24 pages.

INTRODUCTION TO AIRBRUSHES, ACCESSORIES & AIRBRUSHING MEDIUMS
165-222001 24.95

THE FUNDAMENTALS OF AIRBRUSH TECHNIQUE: BASIC EXERCISES
165-222002 Volume I **24.95**

INTERMEDIATE AIRBRUSH TECHNIQUE: WORKING IN COLOR
165-222003 Volume II **24.95**

BL HOBBY PRODUCTS

FLASHER LAPEL PIN

183-580 19.95
Pin is a plastic HO Scale operating railroad crossing flasher that uses a 9V battery. Includes 10" wires and printed circuit board, less battery.

BRAWA

1999-2000 CATALOG

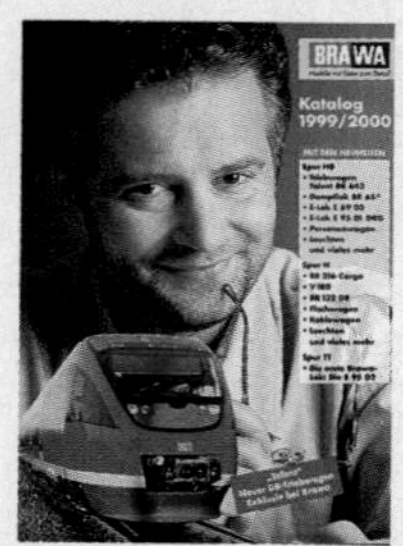

186-98 12.49
147 pages of full-color photos of locos, scenery, signals and all other items. German text.

BUSCH

2000 CATALOGS

Discover the entire exciting line of Busch models with these new catalogs. Full-color photos of the entire selection of scenery, electronic accessories, signals, vehicles and much more.

189-9890 2000 Catalog (German Text) w/CD-ROM (English, German & French Text) **8.99** ***NEW***
189-9892 Printed Catalog Only (English/French Text) **5.99** ***NEW***

C M SHOPS, INC.

MUGS

Full-color, baked enamel ceramic mugs. Dishwasher safe.

RAILROAD HERALDS EA 5.95

12-9095

12-9001 EL
12-9002 CNJ
12-9003 D&H
12-9004 Lehigh & Hudson River
12-9005 B&O
12-9006 Family Line
12-9007 BN
12-9008 Illinos Central Gulf
12-9009 Lehigh & New England
12-9010 CNW (Employee Owned)
12-9011 PRR (Keystone)
12-9012 PC
12-9013 RDG
12-9014 Erie
12-9015 DL&W
12-9016 ATSF
12-9017 DRGW
12-9018 Chessie
12-9019 NH (Script)
12-9020 CNW
12-9021 The Rock
12-9022 NYC
12-9023 LV
12-9024 SOU
12-9025 UP
12-9026 Erie Western
12-9027 CB&Q
12-9028 WP
12-9029 MILW
12-9030 GN
12-9031 WM
12-9032 Seaboard Air Line
12-9033 Providence & Worchester
12-9034 Richmond, Fredericksburg &Potomac
12-9035 MOPAC
12-9036 Boston &Maine
12-9037 SP
12-9038 New York Susquehanna & Western
12-9039 Frisco
12-9040 NP
12-9041 PENN-RDG Seashore Lines
12-9042 New York, Ontario & Western
12-9043 Kansas City Southern
12-9044 Ann Arbor
12-9045 MKT
12-9046 C&O
12-9047 Maine Central
12-9048 Detroit, Toledo & Ironton
12-9049 CR
12-9050 N&W
12-9051 SOO
12-9052 Rock Island
12-9053 Green Bay & Western
12-9054 Rutland
12-9055 Raritan River
12-9056 Wabash
12-9057 Vermont Railway
12-9058 Gulf Mobile &Ohio
12-9059 Illinois Central
12-9060 Long Island-Dash Dan
12-9061 Bangor & Aroostook
12-9062 Duluth, Missabe & Iron Range
12-9063 NKP
12-9064 L&N
12-9065 SOO-Modern
12-9066 CN-Maple Leaf
12-9067 SSW-Blue Streak
12-9068 Clinchfield
12-9069 NH (McGinnis)
12-9070 Pittsburgh & Lake Erie
12-9072 Florida East Coast
12-9073 New York Susquehanna & Western - Susie Q
12-9074 Chicago Great Western
12-9075 Clinchfield
12-9076 Spokane, Portland & Seattle
12-9077 Minneapolis, Northfield & Southern
12-9078 Atlantic Coast Line
12-9079 CV-Old
12-9080 Grand Trunk Western
12-9081 CP-Old
12-9082 Delaware Otsego
12-9083 Seaboard
12-9085 Morristown & Erie
12-9086 Chicago & Illinois Midland
12-9087 Texas & Pacific
12-9089 Appalachicola Northern
12-9090 Central of Georgia
12-9091 Seaboard Coast Line
12-9092 MON
12-9093 Bessemer & Lake Erie
12-9094 Amtrak
12-9095 Colorado Midland
12-9096 NS
12-9097 Alaska
12-9098 Virginian
12-9099 Texas-Mexican-Railway
12-9100 NJ Transit
12-9101 Mexican National Railways
12-9102 CNW System
12-9103 C&O Kitten
12-9104 Boston & Maine (McGinnis)
12-9105 CP Rail
12-9106 Erie Centennial
12-9107 GN (Big Sky Blue)
12-9108 Minneapolis & St. Louis
12-9109 Montana Rail Link
12-9110 WC
12-9111 UP "Overland"
12-9112 Trona
12-9113 Toronto, Hamilton & Buffalo
12-9114 Reading Anthracite
12-9115 British Columbia
12-9116 Belt Railway of Chicago
12-9117 Bangor & Aroostook (shield)
12-9118 Monongahela
12-9119 Connecticut Central
12-9120 Ashley, Drew & Northern
12-9121 BNSF
12-9122 Chicago & Eastern Illinois
12-9123 Housatonic
12-9124 Detroit, Toledo & Ironton - Compass Herald

F UNITS EA 5.95

12-8012

12-8015

12-8001 Ontario &Western
12-8002 LV
12-8003 GN
12-8004 DRGW
12-8005 CNW
12-8006 Gulf Mobile & Ohio
12-8007 SP
12-8008 L&N
12-8009 CN
12-8010 EL
12-8011 ATSF
12-8012 NYC
12-8013 PRR
12-8014 Wabash
12-8015 UP
12-8016 PRR
12-8017 Southern
12-8018 ATSF
12-8019 Erie
12-8020 Clinchfield
12-8021 Burlington Route
12-8022 NP
12-8023 Frisco
12-8024 WP
12-8025 CP
12-8026 B&O

ANNIVERSARY EA 5.95

12-9084 MR 50th
12-9088 NMRA 50th

CAMPBELL SCALE MODELS

CLOTH PATCH

200-1 1.25
The Campbell Scotsman on a cloth patch, stitched as shown here (red, black and white). For your vest, hat or bib-overalls. Actual size is 2 x 3-1/4" oval.

Beautifully cast belt buckles showing exquisite detail. Fits belts up to 1-3/4" wide.

204-1050

204-1172

204-1440

204-14745 204-15045

204-15205 204-16005

204-38

204-14675

BELT BUCKLES

ANTIQUE PEWTER FINISH EA 9.95

For color add the number 5 to the end of the part number. Color increases price to $11.95.

204-1045 Durango Highline
204-1050 C&O #614 Montage
204-1088 Broadway Limited
204-1089 Western Pacific F7
204-1172 ATSF "Super Chief"
204-1440 The American 4-4-0
204-1467 Durango Station
204-1474 Southern Pacific
204-1502 New York Central E9
204-1504 UP Overland Route
204-1511 California Zephyr
204-1513 Rio Grande Zephyr
204-1520 The Southern "Serves the South" *NEW*
204-1522 B&O
204-1534 Seaboard Air Line Railroad *NEW*
204-1535 Central of Georgia
204-1537 The Galloping Goose
204-1564 Mountain Pass

204-10885

204-38985

204-1591 Lineman
204-1608 SP Diesel Freight (Pewter only)
204-1691 Warbonnet
204-3898 Santa Fe
204-16005 Lineman

EPOXY COLOR EA 11.95 (UNLESS NOTED)

204-38 The Golden Spike 125 Years **19.95**
204-10885 Broadway Limited
204-14675 Durango Station
204-14745 Southern Pacific
204-15045 UP Overland Route
204-15205 The Southern "Serves the South"
204-15205 The Southern "Serves the South"(Color only)
204-15225 B&O
204-15345 Seaboard Air Line Railroad
204-15345 Seaboard Air Line Railroad (Color only)
204-38985 Santa Fe (Color only)

KEY RINGS EA 5.95

204-1324 Railroad Crossing
204-1329 SP Diesel Freight
204-13245 Railroad Crossing w/Epoxy Color

CRESCENT STATION

NOTE CARDS PKG(6) EA 2.95

Six cards of the same design with envelops and blank interiors for personal messages. A great way to share your hobby with friends and family!

513-505 Santa arrives at Ives Station

513-506 Great Northern S-2 in Snow
513-507 Manchester

CUSTOM RAILWAY SUPPLY

LENAHAN'S LOCOMOTIVE LEXICONS EA 9.95

Limited Quantity Available

212-1003 Volume 1
HO Scale steam and electric loco production from 1920 to 1970. Information on early brass industry plus origins of steam loco wheel arrangements and names. Over 350 photos, softcover, 96 pages, 8-1/2 x 11".

212-1004 Volume 2
Provides a listing of all logging steamers, diesel and miscellaneous steam produced until 1970. Information on collecting HO and a look at early power drives. Photos.

DESIGN PRESERVATION

STRUCTURE CATALOG

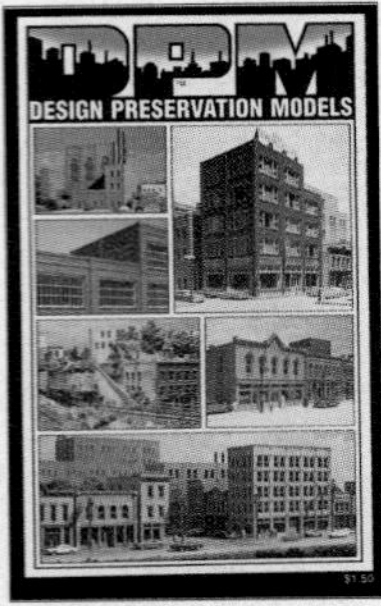

243-13 1.50
A complete listing of all HO (plus N and O Scale) kits, shown in full-color

DPA-LTA ENTERPRISES

OFFICIAL LOCOMOTIVE ROSTERS & NEWS

The most vital resource any railfan can own! Rosters cover all major systems, plus rental fleets and 750 shortlines, 20 pages color.

237-1 1994/1995 **19.95**
237-2 1996 **19.95**
237-3 1997 **19.95**

237-5 1999 **26.95**
4 x 6-3/4". 60 pages of color photos.
237-6 2000 **26.95** *NEW*
The most vital resource any railfan can own! Features every major rail system and shortlines (almost 750), all new locomotives ordered for 2000-2001 delivery, all short-term rental units on major lines, all major locomotive museums and all railroads in North America from Alaska to Mexico in alphabetical order with complete current locomotives. 20 pages of color builders' photographs.

DOVER PUBLICATIONS

BOOKS

HISTORICAL RAILROAD

THE RAILROAD STATION

241-28627 14.95
Chronicles the evolution of the architecture of the railroad station from the 1830s to the 1950s. Examines the station as a structure for which there was no precedent. Studies the station's role in the opening of the frontier. 155 halftones, 76 line illustrations. 320 pages, 6-1/2 x 9-1/4".

A HISTORY OF THE AMERICAN LOCOMOTIVE: 1830-1880

241-23818 24.95
The American locomotive; design and history from 1830-1880. Scale drawings, plans, photos, illustrations, 528 pages, 8-3/8 x 8".

EARLY AMERICAN LOCOMOTIVES

241-22772 10.95
Historical (1804-1874), main-line (post-1870), special and foreign locomotive engravings from the late 19th century. 200 pages, 11-3/8 x 8-1/4".

ANTIQUE LOCOMOTIVES COLORING BOOK

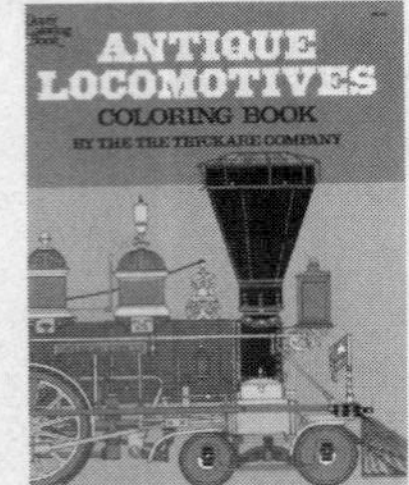

241-23293 2.95
Coloring book of famous locomotives. 48 pages, 8-1/4 x 11".

THE LONG ISLAND RAILROAD IN EARLY PHOTOGRAPHS

241-26301 13.95
Details the upheaval that followed as railroad service ended the isolation on Long Island. Over 220 rare photographs, softcover, 152 pages, 8-7/8 x 11-3/4".

POSTCARDS

241-25320 Old Trolley pkg(24) **4.95**
Full-color, ready-to-mail reproductions of early 1900s cards.

Carstens
PUBLICATIONS, INC.

BOOKS

An assortment of railroad publications from plan books to electrical handbooks. Books are softcover unless noted.

RAILROADS

NC&STL DIXIE LINE
205-87 Hardcover **26.95**
Enjoy this look at the Nashville, Chattanooga & St. Louis Railway. Many pictures of the road's steam and diesel operations compliment an informative history. 98 pages.

CONNECTICUT COMPANY STREETCARS
205-82 21.95
Depicts operations in Hartford, New Haven, Norwich, New London, Derby, Waterbury, Bridgeport and more. Over 150 photos and illustrations.

CONNECTICUT COMPANY
205-84 Hardcover **25.95**

EXTRA SOUTH
205-53 21.95
Nostalgic look at southern steam railroading. Reprint of 1964 edition with expanded text and photos. 144 pages, 8-1/2 x 11".

SUSQUEHANNA: NYS&W

205-80 15.95
New York, Susquehanna & Western from Erie Steam and railcars through RS-1s to GP18s. 98 pages, 11 x 8-1/2".

BALTIMORE & OHIO HERITAGE: 1945-1955
205-52 7.95
From 2-8-8-4s and 2-10-2s to 4-4-2s on the old Buffalo & Susquehanna. 48 pages, 11 x 8-1/2".

SLIM GAUGE CARS
205-72 19.95
This plan book includes virtually every popular type of narrow-gauge freight car. Many photos in full color.

UPRR: THE OVERLAND ROUTE
205-60 12.95
Big power and long trains of this great American carrier in the last great days of steam. 11 x 8".

THE FINAL YEARS: NYO&W RY
205-61 15.95
Photo coverage of the final 20 years of steam and diesel operation. 100 pages, 11 x 8".

CUMBERLAND & PENNSYLVANIA
205-63 9.95
Western Maryland acquired the famous old C&P. photos of steam power and unusual gas-electrics operating in the Alleghenies. 11 x 8".

GRAND TRUNK HERITAGE
205-66 13.95
Covers Grand Trunk steam in Maine, New Hampshire and Quebec. 64 pages.

LEHIGH & NEW ENGLAND
205-81 13.95
Covers the road's turbulent history as a bridge road and major coal hauler. Photos, 80 pages.

RAILS BEYOND THE RUTLAND

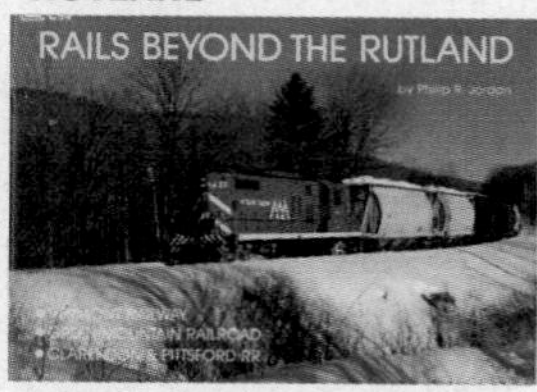

205-54 12.95
Contemporary operations of the Vermont Railway, Green Mountain Railroad and Clarendon & Pittsford. Pictures of rail action in Vermont's green mountains and a remembrance of Rutland steam power.

COLORADO MEMORIES OF THE NARROW GAUGE CIRCLE
205-59 15.95
Photographs of the narrow gauge circle in Colorado from 1935 to 1960. 130 pages, 11 x 8".

THE RAILROAD THAT CAME OUT AT NIGHT
205-65 12.95
Covers railroading in and around Boston as it was from the time South Station was built through the present.

LACKAWANNA HERITAGE 1947-1952
205-69 8.95
Covers the DL&W's final transition years before merger with Erie. 8 x 11".

MODELING

TRACTION PLANBOOK (2ND EDITION)
205-16 9.95
Enlarged and revised. Packed with specially drawn traction plans. Photos, 98 pages, 8 x 11".

THE V&O STORY
205-47 19.95
Examines the philosophy, concepts and history behind W. Allen McClelland's mythical Virginia & Ohio super layout. Photos (some color), 100 pages, 8-1/2 x 11".

TRACKWORK HANDBOOK FOR MODEL RAILROADS

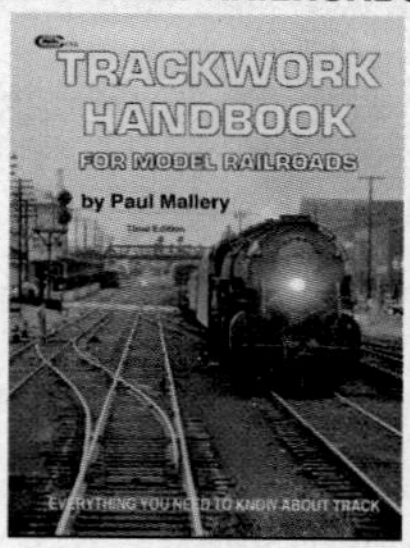

205-90 13.95
Covers a wide range of trackwork subjects including tablework, roadbed and subroadbed, track types and track laying, switches and crossings, track wiring basics, wheels and couplers, switch stands and machines, and trackwork scenery.

OPERATION HANDBOOK FOR MODEL RAILROADERS
205-74 12.95
Provides in-depth information of methods and procedures of prototype railroads for transporting freight and passengers and on means successfully used to duplicate prototype activities on model railroads.

BRIDGE & TRESTLE HANDBOOK
205-79 18.95
Includes information about railroad bridges, from elementary bridge engineering to building the bridge that's right for your layout. Fourth edition, photos, 156 pages.

COMPLETE LAYOUT PLANS (3RD EDITION)
205-73 7.95
A track book for beginners and others who prefer sectional track whether in N, HO, TT, S or O. Nearly 150 designs, 186-piece track-planning kit, 36 pages, 8 x 11".

TRACK DESIGN (3RD EDITION)

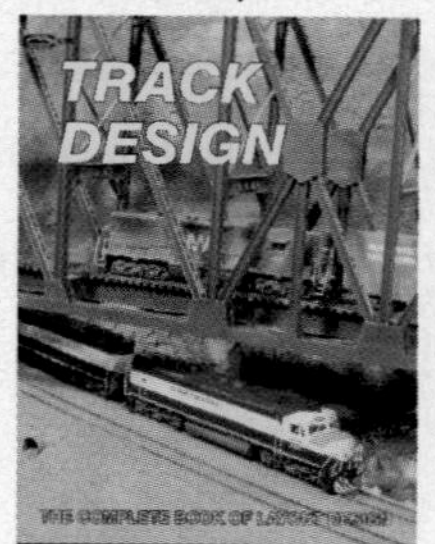

205-88 11.95
Everything you always wanted to know about designing large and small model railroads is back!

DESIGN HANDBOOK FOR MODEL RAILROADERS
205-71 8.95
Paul Mallery explains how to design large and small model railroads. 66 pages, 8-1/4 x 11".

ELECTRICAL HANDBOOK FOR MODEL RAILROADS VOLUME 2, 4TH EDITION

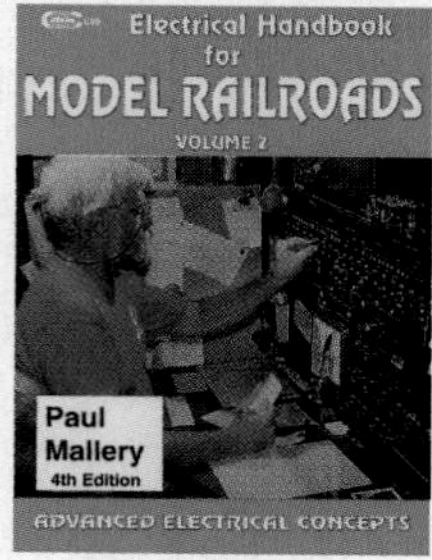

205-89 14.95
Paul Mallery tackles hundreds of electrical concepts and shows you how it's done.

MISCELLANEOUS

THE LIFE AND TIMES OF A LOCOMOTIVE ENGINEER

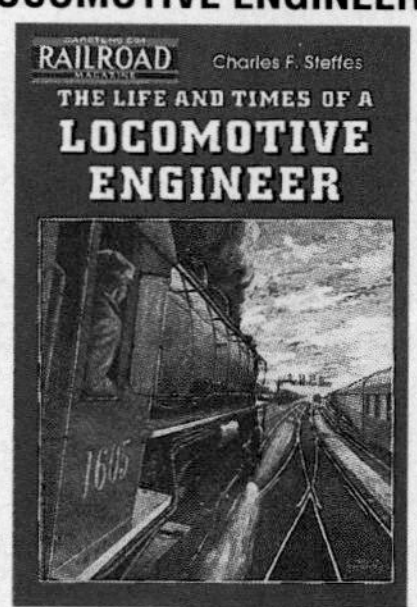

205-94 19.95 *NEW*
Charles F. Steffes gives a first-person account of his nearly 40 years as an employee of the SP Railroad. 312 pages.

LIONEL STANDARD GAUGE ERA
205-13 4.00
Locos and car type made by Lionel in Standard Gauge 1906-1941. 34 pages, 8-1/2 x 11".

TOY TRAINS OF YESTERYEAR
205-67 5.00
Collection of articles reprinted from "Toy Trains Magazine," 52 pages, 8-1/4 x 11".

BASSETT-LOWKE CENTENNIAL BOOK
205-1004 12.00
Photos and information on Britain's famed Bassett-Lowke Works. Numbered limited edition, hardcover (with case), 136 pages, 11 x 8".

TALKING TO THE WORLD FROM PAN AM'S CLIPPERS
205-91 21.95 *NEW*
Join Flight Radio Officer Francis Allan Chapman as he describes his worldwide flying adventures aboard Pan American Airways Clippers from 1939 to 1949. 128 pages.

VIDEOS

MODELING ALP WAYFREIGHT OPERATIONS
205-3001 19.95
Ride along as Whitney Towers operates his well-known HO Scale layout. 30 minutes.

FALLER

SCENIC MODELING MADE EASY

272-840 10.99
English text, covers tools, materials and techniques. Over 120 color illustrations, softcover, 35 pages, 8-1/4 x 11-1/2".

1999-2000 CATALOG
272-879 7.99 *NEW*
Latest edition, with nearly 300 pages of full-color photos. Complete listing of structures, auto system cars and accessories, scenery materials, lighting and more, all in one handy reference. English text.

CHARLES S. GREGG PUBLISHER

BOOKS

TRAIN SHED CYCLOPEDIAS

The Train Shed reprints contain the plans and photos from the various "cyclopedias" referred to in the listings. Excellent sources for reference on all types of cars and locomotives.

SIGNALS & SIGNAL SYMBOLS

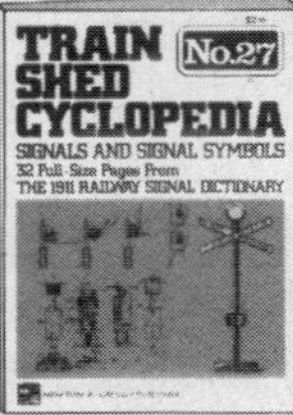

310-857 TS 27 **2.50**

INDEX TO TRAIN SHEDS 1 THRU 42
310-874 **2.95**

BRIDGES & TRESTLES FROM VARIOUS RAILWAY ENGINEERING & MAINTENANCE CYCLOPEDIAS FROM 1921
310-889 TS 54 **4.50**

HEAVY TRACTION 1922-1941
310-844 TS 15 **4.95**

PASSENGER CARS FROM THE 1943 CAR BUILDERS' CYCLOPEDIA
310-851 TS 21 **4.50**

DIESEL & GAS ELECTRIC LOCOMOTIVES
310-849 TS 20, 80 pages **5.95**
1925-1938, with full-color photos.

STEAM LOCOMOTIVES FROM THE 1938 LOCOMOTIVE
310-853 Part 2, TS 23, 80 pages. **4.50**

ELECTRIC MOTOR CARS 1888-1928
310-855 TS 25 **4.55**

RAILWAY SERVICE CARS 1928-1943
310-856 TS 26 **4.95**

CARS, SCALES & GATES FROM THE 1909 BUDA CATALOG
310-859 TS 28 **5.50**
160 full-size pages reprinted as 80 pages from the original edition.

FREIGHT CARS, 1892 BY WILLIAM VOSS
310-860 TS 29 **5.50**

RAIL MOTOR CARS 1919-1928
310-861 TS 30 **4.50**

LOCOMOTIVES, TENDERS & TRUCKS FROM THE 1927 LOCOMOTIVE CYCLOPEDIA EA 5.50
80 pages.
310-862 Part 1, TS 31
310-863 Part 2, TS 32

BUILDINGS & STRUCTURES OF AMERICAN RAILROADS, 1893 EA 4.95 (UNLESS NOTED)

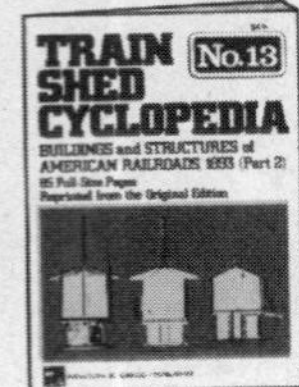

310-848 Part 3, TS 19, 80 pages **4.50**
310-854 Part 4, TS 24
310-864 Part 5, TS 33
310-869 Part 6, TS 38

INDUSTRIAL & FOREIGN LOCOS 1930
310-868 TS 37 **4.95**

VOSS PASSENGER CARS 1892
310-870 **5.50**

LOCOMOTIVE CABS & FITTINGS FROM THE 1927 LOCOMOTIVE CYCLOPEDIA EA 3.00
40 pages.
310-871 Part 1, TS 40
310-872 Part 2, TS 41

DIESEL & OIL ELECTRICS FROM WESTINGHOUSE (1930) & INGERSOLL-RAND (1936)
310-875 TS 43 **4.50**

LOCOS FROM BALDWIN LOGGING LOCO CATALOG 1913 & LOCOMOTIVE STOKER CATALOG 1919
310-876 TS 44 **4.50**

FLATS, GONDOLAS & HOPPERS FROM THE 1931 CAR BUILDERS' CYCLOPEDIA EA 4.50
64 pages.
310-878 Part 1, TS 46
310-880 Part 2, TS 48

LOCOS OF THE 40S & 50S FROM THE 1941 LOCO CYCLOPEDIA & RAILWAY MECHANICAL ENGINEER EA 4.50 (UNLESS NOTED)
Steam locomotives. 64 pages.
310-877 Part 1, TS 45
310-879 Part 2, TS 47
310-881 Part 3, TS 49
310-882 Part 4, TS 50
310-883 Part 5, TS 51
310-891 Part 6, TS 56
Diesel locomotives. 64 pages.
310-893 Part 7, TS 58
310-895 Part 8, TS 60
310-899 Part 9, TS 64
310-901 Part 10, TS 66
310-915 Part 11, TS 80 **4.95**

THE 1925 CAR BUILDERS' CYCLOPEDIA EA 4.50
64 pages.
310-896 Part 1, TS 61
310-897 Part 2, TS 62
310-898 Part 3, TS 63
310-900 Part 4, TS 65
310-902 Part 5, TS 67
310-903 Part 6, TS 68

GONDOLAS & HOPPERS
310-905 Part 2, TS 70 **4.50**

HOPPERS, TANKS CONTAINERS & CABOOSES
310-906 Part 3, TS 71 **4.50**

CAR BUILDERS' CYCLOPEDIA (1943) BOX, STOCK & FLAT CARS
310-846 Part 1, TS 17 **3.95**

CABOOSES-FREIGHT CAR CONSTRUCTION DETAILS
310-910 Part 4, TS 75 **4.50**

FREIGHT CAR CONSTRUCTION, UNDERFRAMES & BRAKES
310-912 Part 5, TS 77 **4.50**

SAFETY APPLIANCES & TRUCKS
310-916 Part 6, TS 81 **4.95**

FREIGHT CARS, INDUSTRIAL & EXPORT CARS
310-918 Part 7, TS 83 **4.95**

MOTOR CARS & PASSENGER CONSTRUCTION
310-921 Part 8, TS 86, 64 pages **4.95**

PASSENGER CONSTRUCTION & INTERIOR FITTINGS
310-923 Part 9, TS 88 **4.95**

FREIGHT & PASSENGER CARS, SHOPS & TERMINALS OF THE 1940S & 1950S EA 4.95 (UNLESS NOTED)
64 pages.
310-908 Part 1, TS 73 **4.50**
310-914 Part 2, TS 79
310-920 Part 3, TS 85
310-925 Part 4, TS 90

FROM THE 1919 LOCO CYCLOPEDIA EA 4.95
310-917 Boilers, Part 3, TS 82
310-919 Smoke Boxes & Stokers, Part 4, TS 84
310-922 Frames, Cylinders & Gears, Part 5, TS 87
310-924 Pistons & Trucks, Part 6, TS 89

DICTIONARIES

LOCOMOTIVES SELECTED FROM THE 1916 LOCOMOTIVE DICTIONARY
310-847 TS 18 **4.95**

FREIGHT CARS FROM THE 1919 CAR BUILDERS' DICTIONARY EA 5.50
80 pages.
310-866 Part 1, TS 35
310-867 Part 2, TS 36

PASSENGER CARS FROM THE 1919 CAR BUILDERS' DICTIONARY
310-873 TS 42 **3.00**

STEAM LOCOMOTIVES FROM THE 1919 LOCOMOTIVE DICTIONARY & ENCYCLOPEDIA EA 4.50
64 pages.
310-884 Part 1, TS 52
310-885 Part 2, TS 53

FREIGHT & PASSENGER CARS FROM THE 1898 CAR BUILDERS' DICTIONARY EA 4.50
64 pages.
310-890 Part 1, TS 55
310-892 Part 2, TS 57
310-894 Part 3, TS 59

LOCOMOTIVE DICTIONARY 1912 EA 4.50
64 pages.
310-904 Locomotive Photos, Part 1, TS 69
310-907 Locomotive Drawings & Boilers, Part 2, TS 72
310-909 Smoke Boxes, Stokers, Valve Gears/Trucks, Part 3, TS 74
310-911 Cow Catchers, Cabs/ Fittings & Tenders, Part 4, TS 76
310-913 Electric Locomotives & Motor Cars, Part 5, TS 78

FINE SCALE MINIATURES

THE FABULOUS FRANKLIN & SOUTH MANCHESTER RAILROAD

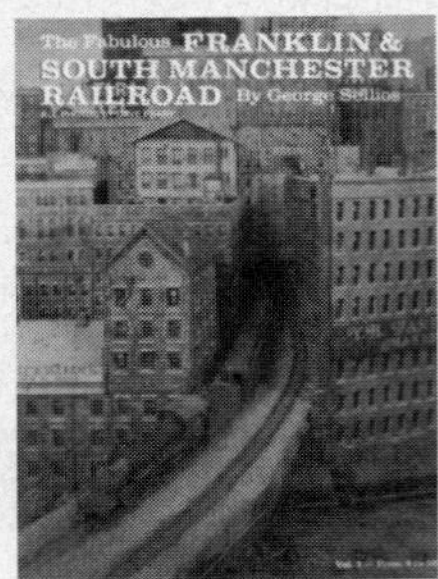

275-1 Volume 1 **19.95**
A visual treat, from the towering 20-story buildings, down to the tiniest details, such as weeds growing in sidewalk cracks. Softcover, 82 color photos, 80 pages, 8-1/2 x 11".

Information STATION

GARDENING BOOKS SIMPLIFY SCENERY

The tracks are done, the trains are running. Now it's time to add scenery to your outdoor empire. Unlike your basement layout, a garden railroad is a living environment that presents lots of new challenges. A good gardening book can help you at each step of the way, from initial planning to final planting.

When creating realistic garden railroads, scenery is every bit as significant as for inside set-ups. The challenge of outdoor scenery is not necessarily making it look realistic, but making it look right.

Now you may know a 4-8-4 from an SD40-2, but how much do you know about gardening? If you don't already have a green thumb, or have never considered the special challenges of gardening for a layout, a book will come in handy in a hurry.

You'll want to know what kinds of plants work well along a layout, but you'll also need to know if they do well in sun or shade, how much water and fertilizer they need, how to recognize insects or diseases and how tall or wide they are when fully mature.

Understanding your local weather and climate conditions are also important factors. This defines the average dates from the last to the first frost each year (growing season), average high and low temperatures, average annual rainfall and similar factors. This will help you make the right choices.

Knowing what type of ground cover grows well with little light, or what type of plants can last through a long winter and which ones can make it without harm through a 100° summer can save a lot of time and money.

It's also important to understand how much maintenance the garden portion of the layout requires. Do you want to, or do you have the time to give the care and attention that some plants need? How much time do you want to spend gardening compared to model railroading?

Country Trains

Let the world know you're a railfan with this collection of signs and scenes that add humor and interest to any office, den or train room. Items are printed in full color except as noted.

WALL SIGNS EA 2.49 (UNLESS NOTED)

Printed in prototypical colors on heavy cardboard. 12 x 12" unless otherwise noted.

203-914 203-916 203-922

203-914
203-916
203-922 (24 x 24")

203-918 203-923 203-932

203-918 (23 x 23")
203-923
203-932

203-910 203-915 203-927

203-910
203-915 (12 x 18")
203-927 (12 x 18")

203-917 750 Tracks (6 x 12")

203-900 203-919

203-900 Don't Touch Dem Trains
203-919 Stop, Look & Listen (6 x 12")
203-872 My Job
203-873 To Restroom
203-874 Temporary Parking Reserved for Model Railroader (12 x 18")
203-875 To the Trains
203-920 Model RR Only
203-921 Private RR Crossing
203-924 Train Buff X-ing
203-925 Watch Your Step
203-966 Passenger Car Rules
203-967 Quiet Loco Zone
203-969 No Smoking Unless .98 (4 x 12")

203-928 You Want to Be A Model Railroader? **.98** (6 x 12")

ROADNAME SIGNS EA 2.49

All signs are heavy cardboard.

203-885 203-896 203-899

203-885 Sandy River
203-896 Canadian National Maple Leaf (12 x 12")
203-899 MILW (12-1/2 x 8-1/2")

203-956 203-975

203-956 Erie (12 x 12")
203-975 ATSF (11-3/4 x 11-3/4")
203-877 D&H (10 x 12")
203-878 SSW (11 x 11")
203-884 LV
203-888 CNW
203-892 Seaboard Airline
203-893 Burlington Route (10 x 11")
203-894 IC (7 x 11")
203-895 CP
203-897 Rock Island (11-1/4 x 8")
203-901 Boston & Maine
203-902 Atlantic Coast Line
203-903 Seaboard System
203-904 Pacific Electric (12 x 12")
203-906 Virginian
203-907 Texas & Pacific
203-908 N&W
203-909 MEC
203-911 Bangor Aroostook
203-913 Georgia Railroad
203-926 Railway Express Agency
203-929 NKP
203-930 MKT (10 x 11")
203-931 WM
203-940 CR
203-941 Chessie System
203-942 Central of Georgia (8 X 12")
203-943 CNJ (12 x 12")
203-944 C&O (12 x 12")
203-945 Clinchfield (7 x 12")
203-946 CSX (9 x 12")
203-947 Frisco (6 x 12")
203-948 Gulf, Mobile & Ohio (6 x 12")
203-949 Kansas City Southern (12 x 12")
203-950 Long Island "Dashing Dan" (12 x 12")
203-951 MON (12 x 12")
203-952 NYNH&H (6 x 12")
203-953 NYC Oval
203-954 NYC Lines (5 x 12")
203-955 NH (8 x 12")
203-957 NS "Horse" (8 x 12")
203-958 RDG (9-1/2 x 11")
203-959 Lackawanna Railroad (9 x 12")
203-960 PC (5 x 12")
203-961 B&O (12 x 12")
203-963 Wabash (12 x 12")
203-964 Virginia & Truckee (12 x 12")
203-965 L&N
203-970 MP Lines (18 x 12")
203-971 NP (10 x 11")
203-972 SOO
203-973 WP (12-1/8 x 12-1/8")
203-974 Amtrak (12-1/2 x 7")
203-976 GN (11-3/4 x 11-3/4")
203-978 SP (12-1/8 x 12-1/8")
203-979 SP Daylight (12 x 6")
203-981 PRR (12-1/8 x 12-1/8")
203-982 Rio Grande Southern
203-983 Belfast & Moosehead Lake (12 x 12")
203-984 CR Quality (4-1/2 x 12")
203-985 Florida East Coast Palms (12 x 12")
203-986 Seaboard Coast Line (12 x 12")
203-988 DRGW (9 x 12")
203-991 BN (12 x 8-3/4")
203-992 UP (12 x 12")
203-996 SOU
203-998 SCL/L&N

LICENSE PLATE FRAMES EA 2.95

White plastic with silkscreened blue lettering.

203-100 Get Jolly Ride A Trolley
203-104 My Other Car Is A Pullman

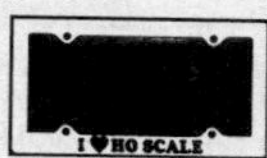

203-109 I Love HO Scale
203-111 I (Love) Model Railroading
203-112 I (Love) Trains
203-114 Please Pray For My Husband He Is A Model Railroader
203-115 So The Car Smokes A Little, So Do Locomotives

BUMPER STICKERS EA .89

Silkscreen printed, red and black. 10 x 2"

203-17 I Love N Scale
203-18 I Love HO Scale
203-19 I Love O Scale
203-20 I Love Model Railroading
203-21 I Love Trains
203-22 I Love Locomotives
203-23 My Other Car is a Pullman (2 x 10")
203-24 My Wife Says If I Buy One More Train She'll Leave Me. Gee, I'll Miss Her. (4 x 8")
203-25 Pray For Me, My Husband Chases Trains. (2 x 10")
203-26 I Love Live Steam (2 x 10")
203-27 I Love S Scale (2 x 10")
203-28 I'd Rather Be On A Train (2 x 10")
203-29 No Smoking Unless You Are a Locomotive (2 x 10")
203-30 Pray for Me, My Wife Likes Trains (2 x 10")
203-31 Watch Your Step
203-34 Happiness Is Being A Train Buff (2 x 12")
203-36 Pass With Caution, I'm A Model Railroader (2 x 12").
203-37 Honk If You're A Model Railroader (2 x 10")
203-38 SB Throttle - Caution
203-39 Railroaders Love To Couple Up (2 x 12").
203-40 So the Car Smokes A Little, So Do Locomotives
203-41 Steam Locomotives Have A Tender Behind
203-42 Get a Jolly Ride A Trolley
203-43 Caution Light At End Of Tunnel May Be A Train

LOGOS EA 1.98

8 x 8" decal stickers.

203-301 Atlantic Coast Line
203-302 Bangor & Aroostook
203-303 Boston and Maine
203-304 BN
203-306 Chessie
203-307 CNW
203-308 CR
203-309 DRGW
203-311 Erie
203-312 IC
203-313 LV
203-315 MKT
203-316 MP Lines
203-317 MoPac
203-318 N&W
203-319 PC
203-320 RDG
203-321 SOU
203-322 Texas & Pacific
203-323 Virginian
203-340 GN
203-341 ATSF
203-342 SP
203-343 UP
203-344 WP
203-345 Amtrak
203-347 PRR
203-348 B&O
203-349 MILW
203-350 Seaboard Air Line
203-351 D&H
203-357 Lackawanna Railroad
203-359 Long Island RR
203-360 MEC
203-361 NH
203-362 NYNH&H
203-363 NKP
203-364 NP
203-365 NS
203-366 NYC
203-368 REA
203-369 Rock Island
203-370 "Rock"
203-371 Sandy River
203-372 Sierra Railroad
203-373 Seaboard Coast Line

DRUMHEADS EA 4.95 (UNLESS NOTED)

Printed on translucent (11 x 11") flexible plastic.

203-2401 203-2419

203-2401 WP
203-2419 PRR "Broadway Limited"
203-2400 California Zephyr
203-2404 ATSF "Super Chief"
203-2408 SP "Overland Limited" **2.95**
203-2410 NP "North Coast Limited"
203-2412 ATSF "El Capitan"
203-2413 ATSF "KC Chief"
203-2414 ATSF "Texas Chief"
203-2417 UP "Overland" (1920)
203-2425 GN
203-2427 MILW "Olympian Hiawatha"
203-2434 NYC "20th Century"
203-2436 ATSF "San Diegan" **2.95**
203-2437 NJC "Blue Comet"
203-2438 DRGW "Mainline"
203-2440 MKT "The Texas Special"
203-2441 DRGW "Royal George"
203-2442 UP "Challenger"

International Hobby Corp.

BOOKS

All books hardcover.

RAILROAD

STEAM LOCOMOTIVE 3-D POP-UP BOOK

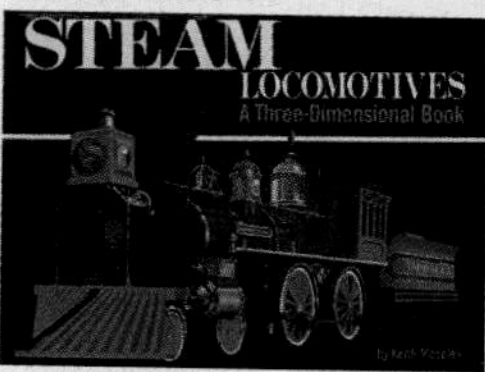

348-51795 3.98
A pop-up guide to the history and use of steam engines. Seven intricate dimensional spreads show famous steam locomotives, and the accompanying text is full of facts.

STATIONS

348-52100 3.98
The fictional journey we each take along the tracks of memory, where time and place intersect the lost world of home.

IRON HORSE-HOW THE RAILROADS CHANGED AMERICA

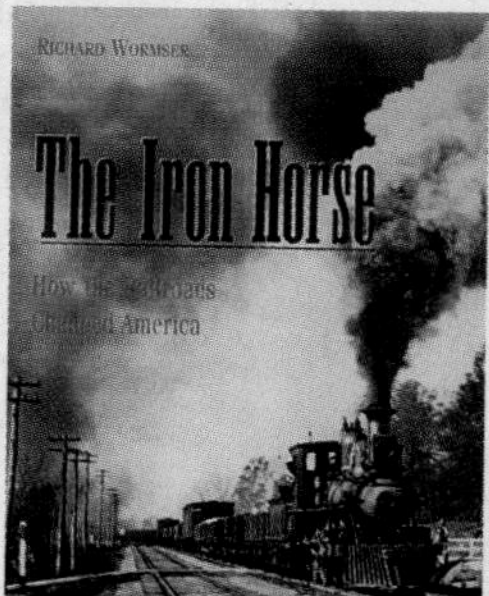

348-78221 3.98
Great for train enthusiasts and history buffs. Includes inventors and immigrants who toiled to lay track, corrupt "robber barons," infamous bandits and hijackers, wrecks, disasters and more.

RAILROAD MAGNETS

EA 2.98

Authentic graphics and durable construction. Sized approximately 2 x 2", 2 x 3" and 2-1/4" round.

234-1 234-2

234-1 Lionel Trains
234-2 American Flyer Trains

234-3 234-4

234-3 Amtrak
234-4 Atlantic Coast Line

234-6 234-7

234-6 B&O
234-7 BN

234-8 234-9

234-8 Burlington Route
234-9 C&O

234-10 234-11

234-10 Chessie System
234-11 CNW

234-12 234-13

234-12 Cotton Belt
234-13 Durango Silverton

234-16 234-17

234-16 Frisco
234-17 GN

234-18 234-19

234-18 IC
234-19 L&N

234-20 234-21

234-20 MKT
234-21 Maine Central

234-22 234-23

234-22 MILW
234-23 MON

234-24 234-25

234-24 Mopac Eagle
234-25 N&W

234-26 234-27

234-26 NYC
234-27 NH

234-28 234-29

234-28 NKP
234-29 NP

234-31 234-32

234-31 PRR
234-32 RDG

234-33 234-34

234-33 DRGW
234-34 ROCK

234-36 234-37

234-36 ATSF Chief
234-37 Seaboard Railroad

Info, Images, Inspiration! Get It All at

www.walthers.com

234-38 234-39

234-38 SOO
234-39 SP

234-41 234-42

234-41 UP
234-42 Virginia & Truckee

234-43 234-44

234-43 Wabash
234-44 Western Pacific

234-45 234-46

234-45 White Pass & Yukon Route
234-46 Railway Express Agency

234-47 234-48

234-47 Wells Fargo & Co. Express
234-48 Railroad Crossing

234-53 234-54

234-53 McCormick-Deering
234-54 Minneapolis Moline

234-55 234-56

234-55 Allis Chalmers
234-56 J. I. Case

234-57 234-58

234-57 New Idea
234-58 Waterloo Boy

234-61 234-62

234-61 Farmall
234-62 John Deere

234-63 Massey-Harris
234-5 B&M
234-14 Erie
234-15 Florida East Coast
234-35 ATSF
234-40 Southern
234-49 Finks Overalls
234-50 AT&T
234-51 I Love Trains
234-52 Public Telephone
234-59 Oliver
234-60 Ferguson System
234-64 WC *NEW*

RAILROAD SIGNS

EA 15.99

Colorful, authentic graphics on porcelain/enamel base. Sized 8 x 8", 8 x 12" and 9" round. Graphics identical to magnets shown at left.

234-101 NYC Pay Toilet 3-1/2 x 12"
234-102 ATSF "The Chief"
234-103 BN
234-104 Railway Express Agency
234-105 Wells Fargo & Co. Express
234-106 Maine Central
234-108 Boston & Maine
234-109 Finck's Overalls
234-110 Telephone
234-200 ATSF
234-201 WP
234-202 NKP
234-203 Erie
234-204 UP Overland
234-205 Chessie 12 x 8"
234-206 MILW
234-207 SP
234-208 GN RY
234-209 NP
234-210 ROCK 12 x 8"
234-211 Seaboard Railroad
234-212 CNW
234-213 IC
234-214 PRR
234-215 MKT
234-216 Atlantic Coast Line
234-217 Burlington Route
234-218 Lionel Trains
234-219 American Flyer
234-220 B&O
234-222 Southern
234-223 Amtrak
234-224 Mopac Eagle
234-225 MON
234-226 N&W
234-228 NYC
234-229 Wabash
234-230 RDG
234-231 SOO
234-232 Railroad Crossing
234-233 White Pass
234-234 L&N
234-235 Frisco
234-236 Durango & Silverton
234-237 NH
234-238 Florida East Coast
234-239 NS
234-240 CR
234-241 CNJ
234-242 "To the Trains"
234-243 Kansas City Southern
234-244 D&H
234-245 San Francisco Cable Car Crossing
234-246 WC *NEW*

KATO

CATALOGS

JAPANESE PROTOTYPE CATALOG

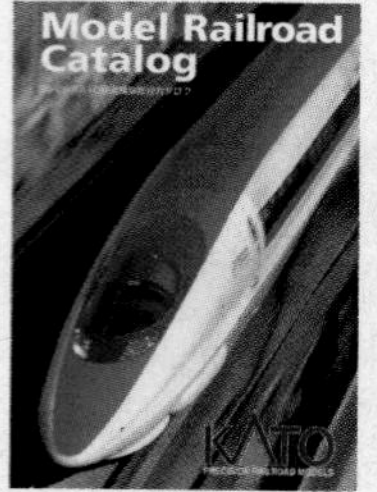

381-25000 18.00
Color photos of all Kato Japanese products. Over 200 pages, Japanese text.

INTERNATIONAL MODEL RAILROAD CATALOG

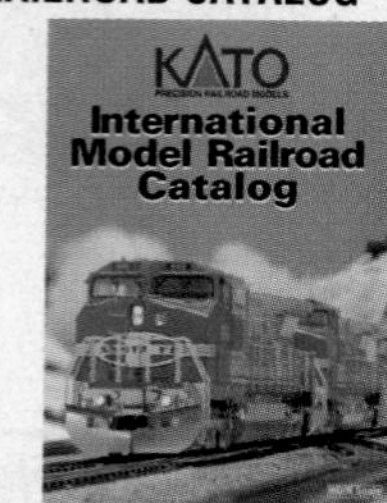

381-25100 9.98
68-pages, English and German text. Full-color photographs of every North American model produced by Kato. Selected foreign models also included.

KIBRI

CATALOG

405-99900 1999-2000 Edition
6.99 *NEW*
A full-color guide to the complete line of Kibri structures and vehicles in HO Scale, plus scenery and N Scale items too!

GIL REID

RAILROAD PRINTS

THE GREAT TRAINS OF AMERICA SERIES

Four color process. Each print has 19 x 13" image printed on 22 x 16" stock with clear border on all sides. Newer prints have a title printed in bottom margin. Interurban prints smaller size.

CNW TEN-WHEELER TRADITION

70-27 11.50
R1 1385 and SD45s at Butler, Wisconsin.

MILW-ROARING THROUGH RONDOUT

70-8 11.50
Hiawatha sweeps north at 100 mph.

PRR-PENNSY'S FINEST

70-11 11.50
K4 5425 is smoking it up (fireman's side).

SP-GRAY PLUS ORANGE AND RED

70-12 11.50
Lark headed by Daylight 4-8-4.

NKP-BERKSHIRE AT MIDNIGHT

70-14 11.50
S-2 765s crew ready for a fast run.

TEXAS & PACIFIC-THE SNUFF DIPPER
70-16 11.50
2-10-2 tries lignite fuel experiment.

NYC-CENTURIES PASS AT NIGHT

70-13 11.50
J3a passes Valley series observation car.

NEW YORK CENTRAL & HUDSON RIVER 999

70-28 11.50
The day before 112.5 mph and the Empire State Express.

MILW-HAPPY HIAWATHA HOLIDAY

70-31 11.50
Engine 1 leaves Milwaukee in 1935.

THE COMPETITORS

70-32 11.50
A Milwaukee Road Twin Cities time freight speeds under the CNW bridge. CNW hotshot 488 Class H3002 goes over it.

ERIE-NO. 1, OF COURSE

70-17 11.50
Loco 2942 heads west with the Erie Limited.

NYC'S GREAT HUDSON
70-1014 Signed **16.00**
The J-1d, NYC's Hudson 5298, is ready, waiting for the next call for mainline service.

ALMOST HOME
70-1 11.50
Late night arrival. Train lurches through switches.

NYC/PRR RACE OF THE CENTURY
70-2 11.50
Competitors roar east out of Englewood, Illinois.

CUT-QUEEN CITY QUIETUDE
70-3 11.50
Five locos at Cincinnati engine terminal

PRR-NO. 65 THE AMERICAN
70-4 11.50
Stays on time despite driving snow.

MILW-NO. 5, DAY EXPRESS
70-5 11.50
Double-header slams through Brookfield.

WABASH, IC, CHICAGO & ALTON
70-6 11.50
Those Night Trains at St. Louis Union Station.

UP FLAGSHIP-NO. 27
70-7 11.50
The Overland Limited fights night snowstorm.

CNW-CLASS D ON THE RUN
70-9 11.50
81" drivered 4-4-2 takes a curve.

SEABOARD AIR LINE - A NAME LIKE A COCKTAIL
70-10 11.50
The Orange Blossom Special at speed.

PRR-PENNSY PERFECTION
70-18 11.50
GG1 4895 passes MP54 owl car 569.

IC-6.6 MILES FROM DESTINY
70-19 11.50
It's Casey Jones on No. 1 tonight!

PRR-STILL ON THE PAYROLL 1935
70-30 11.50
K2s roll out of Richmond, Ind.

NEW YORK CENTRAL & HUDSON RIVER THE DAY BEFORE 112.5 MPH
70-280 35.00
Numbered print signed by artist.

EMPERORS OF THE ROAD SERIES

4-color lithograph on heavy paper. Each print has a 22 x 15-1/4" image printed on 25 x 19" stock, with clear border on all sides. Title is printed in bottom margin. Separate insert gives history and details.

NYC-HEADQUARTERS IS WATCHING
70-24 19.95
Road foreman joins 3005s crew.

PRR-HAND OFF AT HARRISBURG
70-26 19.95
Two K4s take over Broadway Limited.

INTERURBANS

Prints are four color process. 8-3/4 x 11-1/4" image printed on 12 x 15" stock.

70-22 70-20

CHICAGO NORTH SHORE & MILWAUKEE 763 WITH DINER PASSES 757
70-20 11.50

CHICAGO, SOUTH SHORE & SOUTH BEND IN CHICAGO JUICE VS. STEAM
70-21 11.50

CINCINNATI & LAKE ERIE RED DEVIL FAST AS A PLANE
70-22 11.50

YAKIMA VALLEY NILES CAR 100
70-23 11.50

MISCELLANEOUS

RAILROAD GHOSTS

70-1015 Signed **27.50**
SOO #2700 crosses Milwaukee Road tracks at Duplainville, Wisconsin. Photo; 18-7/8 x 13-15/16" image on Kodak Professional paper, 20 x 16" overall.

ACTION AT DUPLAINVILLE

70-34 16.00
17-1/2 x 11-1/2" image on 22 x 16" heavy stock.

THE CANNONBALL - MILWAUKEE ROAD

70-1016 Signed **27.50**
Westbound Cannonball at the Brookfield, Wisconsin, station in the 1960s. This is a color photo of a 19 x 13-1/4" image on 20 x 16" Kodak Professional paper.

PENNSYLVANIA STANDARD

70-1019 Color Print **50.00**
NEW
Train number 29, the New York to Chicago Broadway Limited, roars past the M1a 6750 at the Rockville Bridge.

OMAHA UNION STATION

70-1017 Signed **38.00**
Symbolizes trains and locomotives operating in and out of Omaha Station during the changeover from steam to diesel power. A representation of trains one might see within a 24 hour time period. The color print has a 23 x 8" image on 24 x 10" Kodak Professional paper.

NYC 79 MPH

70-1018 Signed **42.00**
The 5405 was one of the last Hudson locomotives built for the New York Central. Color photo of a 28 x 5-3/16" image on 30 x 8" Kodak Professional paper.

PRR T1 5536: 120 MPH PLUS?
70-35 Signed **16.00**
23 x 9" image on 25 x 12" heavy stock.

THE C.A. REISS COAL CO. 1880-1980
70-290 29.95
Special edition of 500 prints commemorates the 100th anniversary of the Reiss Coal Company in 1980. 22 x 12-3/4" image printed on 26 x 17" stock.

KROMER CAP CO.

RAILROAD CAP

407-775 Adjustable Cap **7.75**
Blue-and-white striped cotton cap. Fully washable. Pleated one-piece top.

Golden West Books

BOOKS

Nearly every phase of American railroading is represented: steam, locos, diesels, logging and mining roads, interurbans and histories of the Santa Fe and the railroad caboose. All books are hardcover unless otherwise noted.

RAILROAD BOOKS

THE RAILROAD CABOOSE
290-14 15.00
The 100-year history of the railroad caboose. Illustrated, 237 pages, 6 x 9".

MOUNT LOWE: RAILWAY IN THE CLOUDS
290-51 51.95
Chronicles the building of the great cable incline on a 62% grade, plus construction of the narrow gauge to Alpine Tavern. Illustrated, 284 pages, 8-1/2 x 11".

AMERICAN NARROW GAUGE

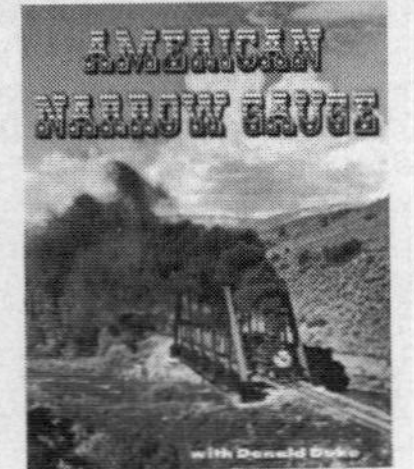

290-59 20.00
An account of narrow-gauge lines in operation after WWII. Follows the DRGW, East Broad Top, East Tennessee & Western North Carolina and more. More than 400 illustrations, maps, bibliography and index.

TEHACHAPI!
290-67 54.95 *NEW*

TRACTION CLASSICS: VOLUME 2
290-71 20.00
Features streamline high-speed cars, private cars, sleeping cars and parlor-observation cars. 258 pages, 8-1/2 x 11".

THE SOUTHERN PACIFIC OF MEXICO
290-76 39.95
An in-depth look at operations in Mexico. Over 330 illustrations. Nine maps and all-time roster. 168 pages, 8-1/2 x 11".

THE TIME OF THE TROLLEY
290-78 42.95
A revised and updated version of the classic by William D. Middleton. 700 pages, over 700 illustrations, 8-1/2 x 11".

BAJA CALIFORNIA RAILWAYS
290-79 15.00
A study of railroads south of the California border. Features an all-time roster of steam and diesel locomotives, maps and more than 225 illustrations. 350 pages, 6-1/2 x 8-1/2".

SUPER CHIEF: STAR'S TRAIN

290-83 17.00
On-the-spot narrative of the train's story. Illustrated, 256 pages, 8-1/2 x 11".

BEAUMONT HILL: SOUTHERN PACIFIC'S SOUTHERN CALIFORNIA GATEWAY
290-86 48.95
1870s to the heavy double-stack trains of today. 265 illustrations, 8 maps and 12 color plates. 174 pages, 8-1/2 x 11".

PIGGYBACK AND CONTAINERS: A HISTORY OF RAIL INTERMODAL ON AMERICA'S STEEL HIGHWAY
290-87 47.95
A complete history of American intermodel operation and equipment. Features the container phenomenon with its double-stack trains; also discusses the loading and unloading process. 205 illustrations, 192 pages, 8-1/2 x 11".

THE GREAT YELLOW FLEET
290-90 45.95
Complete story of the refrigerator car from its origin to mechanical refrigerator cars and piggyback refrigerator trailers. Illustrations, specifications, 165 pages, 8-1/2 x 11".

DRGW NARROW GAUGE: THEN & NOW
290-93 14.95
All-color book contains 56 illustrations featuring Denver & Rio Grande narrow gauge from 1956 to current date. Illustrations, 48 pages, 11 x 8-1/2".

SANTE FE RR GATEWAY: VOLUME 2
290-956 59.95
Passenger and freight services, steam and diesel motive-power, stations and terminals, branch lines, Fred Harvey system, signals and communications.

THE BEAUTY OF RAILROAD BRIDGES

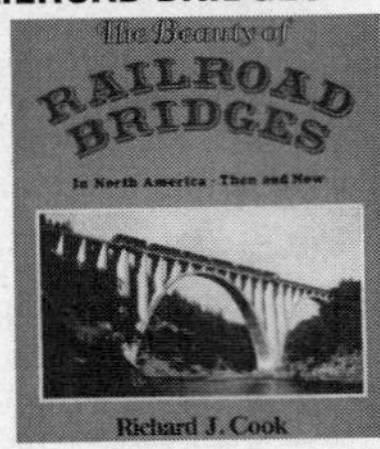

290-952 44.95

BLUE RIDGE TROLLEY
290-953 39.95
Hagerstown & Frederick story of the development, operation and quaint trolley cars. 8-1/2 x 11".

SANTE FE RR GATEWAY: VOLUME 1

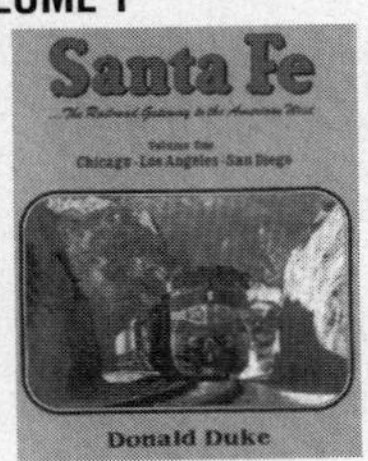

290-955 59.95
Ventures into Mexico, developments in California, electrification possibilities, ATSF bus system, air-rail transportation, ATSF Skyways and mergers including pending BN merger. 455 illustrations, 288 pages, 8-1/2 x 11".

DINNER IS SERVED: FINE DINING ABOARD THE SOUTHERN PACIFIC
290-957 39.95
Everything about great trains and the meals they served. More than 115 illustrations and 36 recipes.

EAST BROAD TOP
290-958 49.95
An account of the EBT as a coal hauler from the mines to Mount Union. 360 illustrations, maps, profile and rosters.

DONNER PASS
290-959 57.95
Experience the grade that is Donner Pass.

RAILROAD FREEWAY
290-960 18.95
Covers entire operating procedures for commuter systems in Los Angeles, Orange, Riverside, San Bernardino, San Diego and Ventura. Gives directions to major sites using the Metrolink line. 222 pages, 45 color maps, 8-1/2 x 11".

INCLINE RAILWAYS OF LOS ANGELES & SOUTHERN CALIFORNIA
290-961 39.95 *NEW*
Learn how a dozen incline railways travel the peaks, hills and valleys of Los Angeles and Southern California. Over 300 illustrations, 250 pages, 5 x 8".

hobby helpers

RAILROAD CAPS

EA 7.95

Lightweight cloth cap and brim with nylon mesh back. One size fits all; adjustable plastic band.

99-701 MILW
99-702 Milwaukee (Hiawatha)
99-703 SOO (Modern)
99-704 SOO (Old)
99-705 MILW/SOO
99-706 NYC
99-707 CNW
99-708 NP
99-709 GN

99-710 ROCK (Old)
99-711 Chessie
99-712 ATSF
99-713 Frisco
99-714 NKP
99-715 Burlington Route
99-716 PRR (Keystone)
99-717 B&O (Capital)

I'M AN ALCO-haulic

99-719 I'm an Alco-haulic

This Budd's for You!

99-720 This Budd's For You!

99-721 Not Pulling a Full Train

I ♥ TRAINS

99-722 I Love Trains
99-723 I Love O Gauge
99-724 I Love HO Gauge
99-725 I'm an N-Thusiast
99-726 I'm a Model Railroad Widow
99-727 N&W
99-728 Cotton Belt
99-729 BN
99-730 UP
99-731 SP (Modern)
99-732 SP

99-733 Amtrak
99-734 SOU
99-735 DRGW
99-736 Spokane, Portland & Seattle Railway
99-737 IC Gulf
99-738 CN
99-739 CB&Q Zephyr
99-740 Chicago Belt Railway
99-741 Chicago, Milwaukee & St. Paul
99-742 Kansas City Southern
99-744 North Shore

99-745 The Headlights On, But No One's In The Cab

99-746 Derailed
99-747 In Training

NARROWMINDED
&
PROUD OF IT!

99-748 Narrowminded & Proud of It

OFFICIAL
MODEL RAILROAD
NITPICKER

99-749 Official Model Railroad Nitpicker
99-750 Dies with Most Trains Wins
99-752 Ferroequinologist at Large

99-753 99-755

99-753 Caution! Railfan at Large!
99-755 Caution! Railfan with Camera
99-754 Model RRing is Contagious—Catch It!

99-756 99-757

99-756 Construction—Enter at Own Risk!
99-757 No One's On Board!
99-758 Stops at All Hobby Shops
99-759 Still Plays with Trains
99-760 Gulf, Mobile & Ohio
99-761 WM
99-762 Chicago, Missouri & Western
99-763 L&N (Old)
99-764 MKT (Old)
99-765 WC

GREEN FROG PRODUCTIONS

VHS VIDEO TAPES

EARLY DIESELS VOLUME 6
302-53145 19.95
Footage from ATSF, UP, DRGW, MILW, NYC, Gulf, Mobile & Ohio, SOO, B&O, EL, PRR, NKP and ROCK. 60 minutes.

THE ROADRAILERS
302-53146 14.95
First introduced by C&O as far back as 1955, this unique method of freight operation still exists today. 30 min.

NORFOLK SOUTHERN-ATLANTA TO CHATTANOOGA

302-53124 19.95
Norfolk Southern's Georgia Division from Atlanta to Chattanooga. 60 minutes with Digital Stereo Hi-Fi sound.

THREE DECADES OF EXCURSIONS
302-53134 24.95
See and hear number 4501 as she pulls three decades of steam excursions. Color, with Stereo Hi-Fi sound and a running time of 90 minutes.

CSX VOLUME 6

302-53135 Pittsburgh to Willard, Ohio **29.95**
Follow over 200 miles of track through beautiful fall scenery. 60 minutes. Stereo Digital Audio.

CSX-7 JACKSONVILLE TO PLANT CITY, FLORIDA
302-53139 Volume VII **29.95**

CSX VOLUME 9
302-53162 Willard to Deshler, Ohio **29.95** *NEW*
You'll see the addition of a new main, an expansion addition to the yard at Willard and contractors installing new track and new signaling systems. Visit a hobo stew party, meet locals of Deshler and learn about the important history of this town to the B&O. 60 minutes

CSX VOLUME 10
302-53169 Augusta to Spartanburg **29.95** *NEW*
Travel along CSX's hilly regions between August, GA, and Spartanburg, SC. Includes heavy freight action with helpers at the rear, a cab ride in a new wide cab AC engine, visits to the yards on both ends of the line and more. 60 minutes.

CONRAIL PITTSBURGH TO CRESTLINE

302-53133 19.95
Go through over 20 locations, including Conway Yard, where over 4000 cars a day are classified. Digital Stereo sound, 60 minutes.

CONRAIL'S BIG-4
302-53154 29.95 *NEW*
Visit places such as Terre Haute, Greencastle and Avon, Indiana, as well as Effingham and East St. Louis, Illinois and more. Highlights include IC, UP, BN, NS and CSX. 60 minutes.

Got a Mouse? Click Walthers Web Site at

www.walthers.com

TRAIN MOUNTAIN MUSEUM

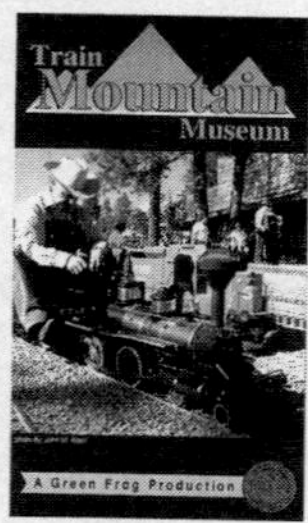

302-53136 14.95
Located in Southern Oregon near Chiloquin, Train Mountain has over 200 acres of operation, including storage and maintenance facilities that would make a real railroad pale by comparison. 45 minutes. Stereo Hi-Fi sound.

RAILFANNING THE SANTA FE
302-53125 19.95
Build scenes that are realistic and photogenic, as Gary Hoover takes you through the intricacies of building a prototype scene for photography. 60 minutes, Stereo Hi-FI sound.

CONRAIL MIDDLE DIVISION
302-53126 19.95
From Altoona to Harrisburg, visit the "longest stone arch bridge in the world" at Rockville, Pa, the famous Horseshoe Curve, and more. Stereo Digital sound. 60 minutes.

THE RIO GRANDE SOUTHERN/DENVER & RIO GRANDE WESTERN

302-53127 19.95
Visit the Black Canyon at Gunnison, now under a lake, as well as Lizard Head Pass, Durango, Cerro Summit and many more. Stereo Hi-Fi sound, 60 minutes.

THE PENN CENTRAL
302-53128 Volume I, 1969-1970 **49.95**
Volume one, 1968-1970. Scenes before the PRR and NYC merger around Valparaiso, Indiana, and Wayne, Michigan. Post merger scenes include Detroit and St. Louis. Tape two: later operations in Michigan, Ohio, Windsor, Canada, and Buffalo, New York. Two tapes, color, narration, Stereo Hi-Fi sound and 180 minute running time.

LOGGING RAILROADS/MODELING THE PROTOTYPE
302-53130 19.95
A look at the logging industry. The operations of several logging railroads are examined. Shows how the trees were cut and loaded, then unloaded at the saw mill. 60 minutes. Stereo Hi-Fi sound.

STEAM GIANTS ACROSS AMERICA

302-53131 19.95
Witness the exciting action of massive articulated steam locomotives. Featuring Stereo Hi-Fi sound. 60 minutes.

UNION PACIFIC SUPER RAILROAD

302-53115 24.95
Lots of action, multiple train meets and more from western Illinois to Cheyenne, Wyoming. 60 minutes.

302-53129 Volume II **24.95**
Cheyenne to Ogden. Visit the mines in the Powder River Basin, follow the UP to Sherman Hill, by way of the Hermosa tunnels, and much more! Stereo Hi-Fi sound and 90 minute running time.

302-53132 Volume III **19.95**
Butte to Pocatello.

302-53137 Volume IV **24.95**
The Oregon Short Line.

302-53140 Volume V **19.95**
The Lagrande Subdivision.

THE BEST OF UNION PACIFIC SUPER RAILROAD
302-53170 19.95 *NEW*
The best of five volumes of UP action. Includes mountain railroading, helper service, fast freights, a cab ride, coal fields, yard action and more. 60 minutes.

PASSENGER TRAINS OF THE 60s
Passenger Trains of Birmingham.
302-53141 Volume I **14.95**
302-53142 Volume II **14.95**
302-53143 Volume III **19.95**

TRACTION N' TROLLEYS

302-53149 19.95 *NEW*
Great film from the 30s, 40s and some from the 50s and 60s. Shows how it used to be when traction and trolleys were an integral part of our economy. 60 minutes.

THE CIRCUS AND THE RAILROAD

302-53150 19.95 *NEW*
In the "good ole' days" most circuses traveled by railroad. You'll get to see how it was done first hand as you view how equipment and animals were loaded and unloaded, a circus parade and Wisconsin's Circus World Museum. 30 minutes.

MAINLINE RAILROAD

PREVIEWS
Selections of current videos. 75 minutes.

302-1 Volume I **14.95**

Short, selected scenes not found on Volume I (such as IC, GP9s, Rails to Steel City, Illinois Hot Spots and NASA Railroad). 40 minutes.
302-2 Volume II **14.95**
302-3 Volume III **19.95**
302-4 Volumes I, II, III **39.95**

35 YEARS OF CASS SCENIC RAILROAD
302-53120 24.95

THE ENTIRE FLORIDA EAST COAST
302-53121 19.95

RAILS NEW ORLEANS
302-53123 19.95

THE SIERRA RAILROAD
302-53066 14.95
Hollywood's most photographed railroad. Digital Stereo sound Running time: 40 minutes.

CLASSIC STEAM OF THE 20s THROUGH THE 40s
302-53114 19.95
B&W, 60 minutes.

GREEN FROG PRODUCTIONS

TWILIGHT OF STEAM
302-53106 19.95
A fantastic collection of steam from the 1960s and 70s. 60 minutes.

STEAM SHORTLINES OF THE SOUTH
302-53109 14.95
A fantastic tape of 15 different steam operated railroads in the South, shot in the 1950s and 60s.

STEAM IN THE 50s
Three volumes cover steam's final years. Volume I: MoPac, NP, Pennsy, IC, B&O and more; 60 minutes. Volume II: UP, DM&IR, CNW and more; 35 minutes. Volume III: NP, Klickitat Lumber, N&W and more; 60 min.

302-53006 Volume I **19.95**
302-53061 Volume II **14.95**
302-53092 Volume III **19.95**

THE NEW GEORGIA RAILROAD
302-53002 14.95
Operations of former Florida East Coast 4-6-2 #750. An E8 in New Georgia Railroad colors is also highlighted. Color, 28 minutes with stereo sound.

RAILS BUFFALO
302-53040 19.95
Video action of modern day Buffalo, New York. 60 minutes.

RAILS CHICAGO
302-53011 19.95
Switching and mainline running in the "Windy City". Running time: 56 minutes. Revised.

RAILS CHICAGO 1995
302-53112 19.95
Spectacular action at Hammond, Indiana; Blue Island; Joliet; Elmhurst; Franklin Park; Homewood and more .

RAILS CANADA
302-53012 14.95
Modern operations of CN and CP. 25 minutes.

WESTERN MARYLAND—END OF AN ERA
302-53010 19.95
Original color films chronicling the final years of the Western Maryland. 70 minutes.

MICHIGAN FAST FREIGHT
302-53009 19.95
Railroad action in Michigan's lower peninsula, circa 1967. 54 minutes.

DETROIT, TOLEDO & IRONTON
Volume I: Traces the development from the 1920s through 1983. Volume II: The last years of Detroit, Toledo & Ironton operations, to integration and merger with the Grand Trunk Western.

302-53013 Volume I **19.95**
302-53014 Volume II **14.95**

THE ILLINOIS CENTRAL
302-53024 39.95
Two tape set chronicles 37 years of the IC, from steam to diesel. Color with stereo sound, over two hours.

CANADIAN STEAM
302-53018 14.95
CN 4-4-0 and CP 4-8-4.

RAILS IN TRANSITION
Volume I: SLSF, PRR, N&W, Gulf, Mobile & Ohio and more. 60 minutes. Volume II: CNW, South Shore, Katy, MILW, ATSF, C&O, B&O and CB&Q. 40 minutes.

302-53016 Volume I **19.95**
302-53039 Volume II **14.95**

RAILS TO STEEL CITY
302-53022 19.95
Activity around the Pittsburgh area. Color, 60 minutes.

THE GP9s
302-53023 14.95
Sights and sounds of EMD's General Purpose diesels. Color with stereo sound, 70 minutes.

ILLINOIS HOTSPOTS
302-53025 19.95
Color, 60 minutes.

SOUTH SHORE LINE
302-53118 39.95
A look at the South Shore in 1975-78. 60 minutes.

THE BEST OF PASSENGER TRAINS
302-53110 The West Volume III **19.95**
Great photography, action and color. 60 minutes.

NASA RAILROAD
302-53026 14.95
An in-depth look at a truly different railroad that moves rocket motors, rocket fuel and a wide range of items with a fleet of special cars. Color, 60 minutes.

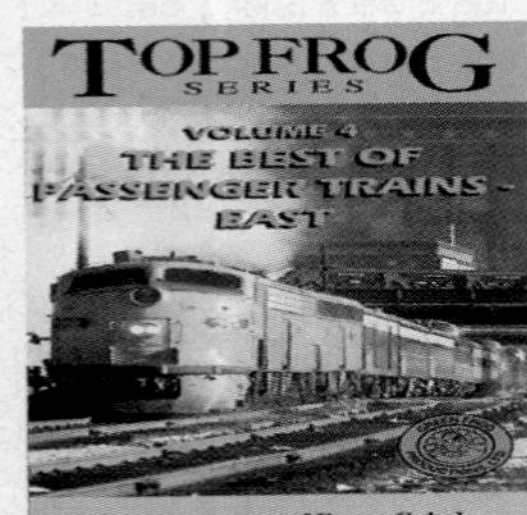

302-53138 Volume IV-East **19.95**
1950s to 1970s passenger train action from NYC, PRR, EL, MON, MP, CB&Q, Gulf, Mobile & Ohio, B&O, IC, C&O, MILW, PC and Grand Trunk. 60 minutes.

TOP FROG VOLUME 6
302-53155 DRGW 50s & 60s **14.95**
Covers the DRGW action of the 50s and 60s on the now abandoned line between Durango and Chama. 30 minutes.

TOP FROG VOLUME 7
302-53156 The CB&Q **19.95**
50s, 60s and 70s equipment and trains are featured in this 45 minute video. Highlights include passenger, freight and many first generation diesels of CB&Q.

CONRAIL - THE WEST SLOPE
302-53119 19.95
Tremendous action between Gallitzin, PA and Johnstown, PA. 60 minutes.

THE ST. LOUIS SOJOURN
302-53113 19.95
Visit St. Louis Station and other locations in and around St. Louis. 60 minutes.

SUWANEE STEAM SPECIAL
302-53028 14.95
Features #1218 in the Florida sun. 60 minutes.

THE EAST BROAD TOP
302-53031 24.95
Includes coverage from the early 1950s through the 1970s. 120 minutes.

THE MONONGAHELA RAILROAD
302-53032 19.95
Filmed in Pennsylvania and Virginia hills. 60 minutes.

ROCK ISLAND RAILROAD
302-53033 19.95
Follow the history of the Rock Island with photography captured from 1958 to 1970. Color.

WESTERN MARYLAND SCENIC RAILROAD
302-53038 14.95

NEW YORK CENTRAL ODYSSEY
302-53036 49.95
Two-tape set features action of first-generation diesels. 150 minutes.

RAILFAIR 1991
302-57000 14.95
Follow the UP Challenger and Northern as they double-head through the spectacular mountain scenery to Sacramento. 60 minutes.

Latest New Product News Daily! Visit Walthers Web site at

www.walthers.com

NARROW GAUGE STEAM

DRGW AND THE BUMBLEBEE—#268

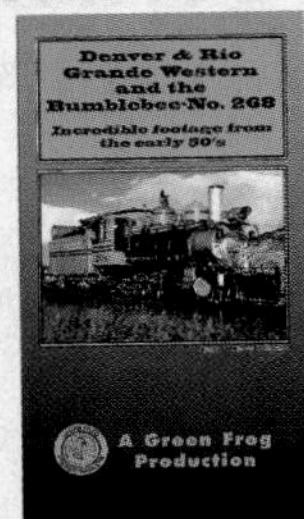

302-53144 19.95
Incredible 1950s narrow gauge action shot around Gunnison, Alamosa, the Farmington branch, the Monarch branch and between Durango and Chama. 45 minutes.

C&T IN '73
302-53017 14.95
Features the Cumbres & Toltec during the fall of 1973. Color, 36 minutes with stereo sound.

COLORADO - STEAM MECCA
302-53084 19.95
Coverage of all Colorado major steam railroads. Digital stereo sound.

WORKTRAIN TO SILVERTON
302-53005 14.95
Ride along with a work train of drop bottom gondolas on their way to Silverton. 23 minutes.

SWITCHIN' ALONG THE RIO GRANDE
302-53008 14.95
Switching and servicing operations at various stops.

THE CHAMA TURN
302-53003 19.95
Action and operations over Cumbres. 60 minutes.

COLORADO NARROW GAUGE PASSENGER CHASE
302-53020 19.95
Filmed in 1965, features the last passenger run the Rocky Mountain Railroad Club took of the Rio Grande narrow gauge. Color, 45 minutes.

ROTARY ON THE RIO GRANDE NARROW GAUGE
302-53021 19.95
Follow the Cumbres & Toltec in 1975 and 1976 as it opened its line using the former Rio Grande rotary snow plow OM. Color, 70 minutes.

BEST OF NARROW GAUGE
302-53035 19.95
Rio Grande narrow-gauge action assembled from previously released footage by Emery Gulash. All material has been re-edited, including all-new narration. 62 minutes.

TWILIGHT OF THE RIO GRANDE
302-53004 14.95
40 minutes.

IN SEARCH OF NARROW GAUGE MIKADOS
302-53054 24.95
Color, 70 minutes.

VINTAGE STANDARD GAUGE

GHOST TRAIN FROM THE PAST

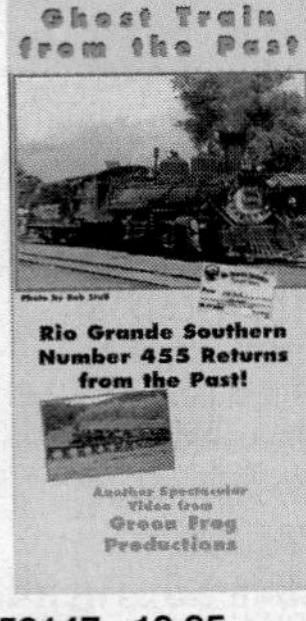

302-53147 19.95
Follow the Rio Grand Southern in 1997 on its journey through such locations as Lower Gallagher, Keystone Hill, Bridge 45A and Brown/Meadow Creek. Plus, discussions with train crews, old-timers who road the real RGS, and noted author Mallory Hope Ferrell. 60 minutes.

ATLANTA RAILROADS-THEIR HISTORY AND THEIR STORY
302-53087 19.95
A documentary covering the history from the very first train to today's operations. 60 minutes.

SANTA FE ODYSSEY
Each is an action-packed two-tape set. Volume I: Steam and diesels in switching, freight and passenger service. Color, 150 minutes. Volume II: Santa Fe revitalizes its diesel fleet in the 1970s. 120 minutes. Volume III: Santa Fe from the 1950s to the present. 105 minutes.

302-53019 Volume I **49.95**
302-53029 Volume II **49.95**
302-53037 Volume III **49.95**

ERIE LACKAWANNA
302-53063 49.95
Begins in early 1962 after the merger of the Erie and Delaware, Lackawanna & Western and continues to the formation of Conrail in 1976. Full color, stereo. 2 hours 10 minutes. Two tape set.

GREEN FROG PRODUCTIONS

THE BOSTON & MAINE

302-53158 19.95 ***NEW***
Follow the Boston & Maine's wrenching change from steam to diesel power. Includes rare scenes of P4 Pacific #3713 in snow melter service. 42 minutes.

STEAM ON NORTHERN PACIFIC

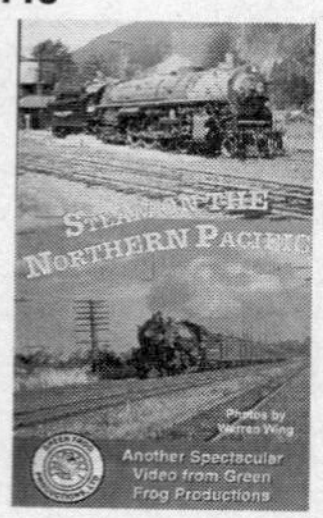

302-53163 29.95 ***NEW***
Follow the NP through the 40s and witness train wrecks, snow scenes, lots of loco action and more. Mostly color, 60 minutes.

NEW YORK CENTRAL ODYSSEY
302-53069 Volume II **49.95**
Summer 1963. Transition to the Cigar Band Herald, action on Toledo Division and merger into Penn Central. 2 hours 40 minutes. 2 tape set.

TOP FROG—BEST OF STEAM
302-53074 19.95
Steam scenes from the 50s along with fan trip runs in the 60s and 70s. 1 hour.

THE CALIFORNIA ZEPHYR
302-53027 19.95
Filmed in 1965 aboard and trackside the California Zephyr. 60 minutes.

PENNSYLVANIA RAILROAD
302-53043 19.95
From 1952 until the merger with the NYC, covers the end of steam and classic First Generation diesels.

WABASH RAILROAD
302-53044 19.95
From 1954 until the merger with the N&W. First Generation diesels and plenty of passenger trains. 60 minutes.

CHICAGO ODYSSEY
Action in and around Chicago in the 1950s and 1960s. 2-1/2 hours.
302-53047 Volume I **49.95**
302-53079 Volume II **49.95**

RIO GRANDE ODYSSEY
302-53049 49.95
From the early 60s until the 80s, see First Generation Geeps, narrow gauge steam and great freight and passenger train action. 2-1/2 hours.

THE NICKEL PLATE

302-53048 19.95
Steam and 1st Generation diesels in the 50s and 60s as well as the Akron, Canton & Youngstown. 45 minutes.

TRAVELIN' TRAINS
302-53050 14.95
About hobos in the depression era, accompanied by blues music. 30 minutes.

PACIFIC NORTHWEST KALEIDOSCOPE
302-53102 19.95
Full color, 16 mm footage in the 1930s through early 1970s. Lots of Milwaukee Road action. 60 minutes.

MODERN DAY RAILROADING

CSX ATLANTA TO CHATTANOOGA
302-53068 Volume I **29.95**
Fast paced action meets, branch line operations and yard activity. 60 minutes.

CSX CHATTANOOGA TO NASHVILLE
302-53085 Volume II **29.95**
Spectacular scenery including Cowan tunnel, Cumberland Mountain and Nickajack Lake. 60 minutes.

CSX NASHVILLE TO LOUISVILLE
302-53097 Volume III **29.95**
See two ex-L&N branch lines, CF-7s and the Kentucky Railroad Museum. Civil War history, fast paced CSX action, including Radner Yard. 60 minutes.

CSX LOUISVILLE TO CINCINNATI
302-53108 Volume IV **29.95**
Travel the line from yard to yard and see fantastic bridges, tunnels and fast paced action. 60 minutes.

THE WAY WEST
302-53073 Volume I **19.95**
Modern action from the Mississippi to the Feather River Canyon. Stereo sound, running time: 60 minutes.

CSX EVANSVILLE TO CHICAGO

302-53117 29.95
This one covers fast paced action at the Ohio River bridge, night action at Evansville yard; Vincennes, Indiana; Terra Haute and more.

THE BEST OF CSX
302-53157 19.95 ***NEW***
The best of over eight volumes of CSX material, giving the viewer tremendous action, cab rides, yard visits shop action and much more. 60 minutes.

AMTRAK'S CALIFORNIA ZEPHYR: DISCOVERING THE GREAT AMERICAN WEST
302-53070 19.95
Chicago to the West coast, aboard and off train. Visit with crews, stop at the Golden Spike Monument, and visit the California State Railroad Museum. 48 minutes.

MAINTENANCE OF WAY YESTERDAY & TODAY
302-53090 19.95
Hear from the experts how railroads manage this impressive operation and see how it's done. 45 minutes.

AMTRAK'S CALIFORNIA ZEPHYR
Behind the scenes with Amtrak's crews, along with cab scenes and aerials. Tour of the California Rail Museums, scenic photography with natural sound; no narration. Brief descriptions of each scene appear on screen. Your trip will cover the Zephyr route from Chicago to the West Coast.
302-53076 14.95
302-53083 Volume II **19.95**

RAILROADING THROUGH THE WINTER OF '93
302-53065 19.95
Great coverage of the blizzard of 1993 in the Northeast corner of the U.S. and in Southeast Canada. You'll see CN, CP, Amtrak, CSX, Grand Trunk, VIA Rail, Go Transit at Aldershot, Burlington West, Niagara Falls, Fort Erie, Copetown, Dundas and Bayview Junction. 60 minutes.

MARION HOT SPOTS
302-53045 19.95
The train watching capitol of Ohio. More than 30 scheduled trains a day on CSX and NS. 60 minutes.

MAGNOLIA CUT-OFF OF THE CSX
302-53056 19.95
Sweeping curves, tunnels, trestles and fall foliage serve as a back drop for GP40s, GP50s and rare U30-Cs. 60 minutes. Color.

STEEL RAILS-THE SPECIAL TRAIN
302-53104 14.95
Run-bys and aerial shots. 30 minutes.

EMPIRE BUILDER

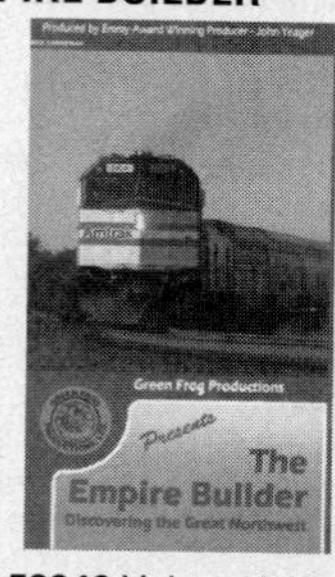

302-53046 Volume I **19.95**
302-53052 Volume II **14.95**
Volume I is a documentary about the Amtrak train from Chicago. Includes interviews with crew members. Volume II is a railfan-oriented tape, with aerial shots, in-cab scenes, run-bys and train action.

THE TOLEDO, PEORIA & WESTERN
302-53055 19.95

THE GOLDEN HORSESHOE FOREIGN POWER INVADES CANADA
302-53089 19.95
Action abounds from Niagara Falls to east of Toronto. 60 minutes.

STEEL RAILS-PRIVATE VARNISH
302-53103 19.95
Action inside and out of the best private cars in North America. 60 minutes.

FROM COAL TO KILOWATTS – THE COAL TRAINS OF DETROIT EDISON
302-53077 24.95
The most comprehensive coal train tape ever produced. From the mines to dumping at the power plant. 90 minutes.

GODERICH & EXETER
302-53093 14.95
Venture into Canada to see this shortline in winter and summer. Great action with chop-nosed GP9s, cab rides and deep, cold snow! 60 minutes.

UNION PACIFIC ODYSSEY
Volume I: History of the UP. 120 minutes. Volume II: More First Generation diesels, "City" trains, new Second Generation diesels, more turbines, Centennials and DD 35s. 120 minutes, Color.
302-53034 Volume I **49.95**
302-53059 Volume II **49.95**

TRAINS, TRAINS, TRAINS! FOR KIDS 2 TO 92
302-53107 14.95
K.C. Frog takes you on a tour of old and new trains, talks about steam and diesel engines and how they work, and takes you on a cab ride through the mountains.

K-27 1995 FREIGHT TRAIN

302-53152 19.95 ***NEW***
Follow the Rio Grande K-27 through the mountains and prairies of the Rockies. 60 minutes.

K-27 1997 RIO GRANDE MOW TRAIN

302-53153 19.95 ***NEW***
Witness the only time this K-27 train, with its authentic MOW cars and caboose, appears in this configuration as it goes from Chama to Antonito and back. 60 minutes.

VIDEO MAGAZINE

RAILROAD VIDEO MAGAZINE
302-53075 19.95
Broadcast quality footage of the fascinating world of railroading. Tour short lines in Canada and Florida, the CSX Queensgate Hump Yard, see steam fan trips from the 1960s and tour the Allegheny Railroad, once part of the mighty Pennsy system. Running time: 65 minutes.

MODEL AND TOY TRAINS

APPALACHIAN COAL-MODELING THE PROTOTYPE
302-53078 19.95
Visits to two layouts and comparisons to the prototype. 60 minutes.

THE RIO GRANDE SOUTHERN - MODELING THE PROTOTYPE
302-53091 19.95
On3 layout. Learn about the RGS and how you can model it, buildings, scenery, etc. 60 minutes.

PAINTING IN BACKDROPS
302-53122 19.95

BUILDING A MODEL RAILROAD - THE APPLE VALLEY BRANCH
302-70000 109.95
Ten tapes that cover everything from design to operation of the Apple Valley Branch. A quick and easy way to get them all at a great price! Each tape is 30 minutes in length.

THE APPLE VALLEY BRANCH
302-70001 14.95
Provides an introduction to the entire project. Describes design, construction and operational possibilities.

BENCHWORK 1
302-70002 14.95
Shows step-by-step how to assemble the legs, L-girder and lower level benchwork construction.

BENCHWORK 2
302-70003 14.95
Continues with the cutting of roadbed and construction of the upper level and techniques for attaching the two halves.

LAYING TRACK
302-70004 14.95
Covers track-laying techniques for smooth operation. Laying roadbed, placing turnouts, cutting and fitting flex track, installing bridges and more.

WIRING FOR COMMAND CONTROL
302-70005 14.95
Shows the easy wiring and simple use of command control.

BUILDING STRUCTURES
302-70006 14.95
Covers a variety of techniques including preparing pieces before assembly, painting, scratch building, decaling, dry transfers, mortar and bricks and weathering.

ROLLING STOCK
302-70007 14.95
Building different types of freight cars and how to air brush and letter them. Also, weathering and the installation of couplers.

SCENERY
302-70008 14.95
Make your layout come alive. Tips on color, foliage, adding water, building roads and installing tunnel portals.

ADDING REALISM
302-70009 14.95
Provides ideas to make a scene stand out and look like people inhabit your model world. 30 minutes.

OPERATING
302-70010 14.95
Shows operating possibilities and traffic movement around the layout and discusses how real railroads would do it. 30 minutes.

COMPACT DISCS

Test your sound system and your ears with these digitally recorded, edited and mastered CDs. Sit back and enjoy a listening experience that makes you feel like you are on location.

K-27 #463

302-60000 14.95 *NEW*

SHAY SOUNDS

302-60001 14.95 *NEW*

SOUNDS OF THE JOINT LINE

302-60002 14.95 *NEW*
Listen to the sounds of diesels working their way up steep grades along the front range of the Rockies. 56 minutes.

THUNDERING NARROW GAUGE
302-60003 14.95 *NEW*
Features the sounds of almost all the locos on the roster for both the Cumbres & Toltec and the Durango & Silverton. 45 minutes.

REMEMBERING STEAM-CAB RIDE
302-60004 14.95 *NEW*
A 45 minute trip in the cab of a 2-8-0 on the five mile long line of the Tennessee Valley Railroad Museum. Includes all the sounds one would expect to hear from a inside a cab such as injector, coal shoveling, bell, brakes, side rod clank and more!

AUDIO TAPES

High quality Dolby cassette tapes of railroad sounds, digitally mastered and dubbed in real time for outstanding reproduction.

SOUNDS OF STEEL MILLS
302-55020 10.95
You'll hear it all, including the wail of sirens and switcher bells, the hiss of escaping steam and air, the rumbling of machinery and overhead cranes and more. Cassette tape.

REMEMBERING STEAM
302-55018 Volume III Cab Ride **10.95**
You'll hear exhaust sounds, whistle, injector, coal shoveling, bell, brakes, side rod clank, etc. Cassette tape, 45 minutes.

STEAM & DIESEL SOUNDS OF THE 1950S
302-54000 8.95
Nickel Plate Berkshires, Alco PA's, F3's and more. 20 minutes.

THUNDERING NARROW GAUGE
302-54005 10.95
Outstanding action recordings of Colorado narrow gauge. 38 minutes.

SOUNDS OF THE NEW GEORGIA RAILROAD
302-54006 8.95
Hear a former Florida East Coast 4-6-2 in action. 20 minutes.

DIESELS '87
302-54108 11.95
The contemporary sounds of modern railroading, including a GP50, rebuilt GP7s and more. 43 minutes.

STEAM AND DIESEL SOUNDS OF THE 1980s
302-54110 11.95
A wide range of active and restored locos in service across America, including an Alco RS-1, 0-6-0, 4-84 GP7 and more. 47 minutes.

DIESELS 1986
Two volumes of diesels still operating in the late 80s. Each tape has a playing time of 20 minutes.

302-54003 Volume I **8.95**
302-54004 Volume II **8.95**

SOUNDS OF THE EAST BROAD TOP
302-54113 10.95
Steam power of the Pennsylvania narrow gauge line captured in stereo during 1988. 36 minutes.

THE GP9s
302-54112 12.95
Original sounds of EMD's General Purpose diesel that changed the face of railroading forever. 56 minutes.

STEAM SOLILOQUY
302-54114 12.95
Features 4-6-2s, 2-8-0s, 2-8-2s and more. 60 minutes.

FIRST GENERATION DIESELS
302-54115 11.95
Features GP7s, GP9s, RS-1s, F3s, Fs, PAs and E8s. Many locos are in tandem, some are as single units. 44 minutes.

SOUNDS OF THE SILVERTON
302-54116 12.95

SOUNDS OF JOINT LINE
302-54118 12.95

SOUNDS OF THE 1218
302-54119 12.95
Captures the most powerful operating steam loco on a ferry trip and in service as an excursion train in Florida. 60 minutes.

REMEMBER STEAM—TRACKSIDE
302-55016 9.95

REMEMBER STEAM—TRAIN RIDE
302-55017 9.95

THE K-27 UNDER STEAM

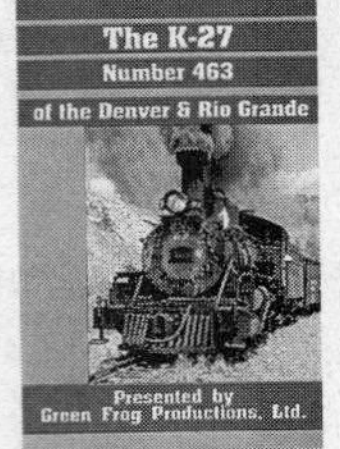

302-54120 9.95 *NEW*
Sit back and enjoy the way a real narrow gauge sounded... and felt. 66 minutes.

BACKGROUND SERIES

Basic railroad background sounds designed to be played in the background of a layout with birds (daytime) and crickets (nighttime). Each tape is 60 minutes.

COUNTRY EA 10.95
302-55000 Daytime Steam
302-55001 Daytime Diesel Contemporary
302-55002 Daytime Diesel 1st Generation
302-55003 Nighttime Steam
302-55004 Nighttime 1st Generation Diesel
302-55005 Nighttime Diesel Contemporary

CITY EA 10.95
302-55006 Daytime Diesel 1st Generation
302-55007 Daytime Diesel Contemporary
302-55008 Daytime Steam
302-55009 Nighttime Diesel 1st Generation
302-55010 Nighttime Diesel Contemporary
302-55011 Nighttime Steam

BAR ROOM/STATION ANNOUNCEMENTS
302-55014 10.95

HARBOR SOUNDS
302-55015 10.95

NARROW GAUGE EA 10.95
302-55012 Daytime Steam
302-55013 Nighttime Steam

LIFE-LIKE®

BOOKS

BASICS FOR BEGINNERS 12TH EDITION

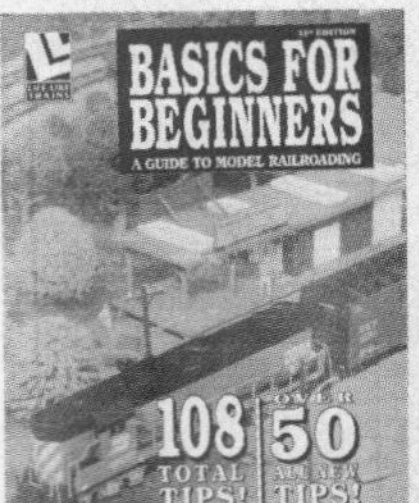

433-8003 1.00
Useful tips on detailing, building and landscaping your layout.

HEIMBURGER HOUSE PUBLISHING

Heimburger House books cover a wide range of illustrated model and prototype railroad titles. Most books feature color covers and glossy enamel paper stock for the text. All books are softcover unless noted.

BOOKS

PROTOTYPE RAIL

TWO FEET TO THE QUARRIES
30-92 32.00 *NEW*
Learn this history of the Monson Railroad, the last operating two-foot-gauge railroad in North America. Features nearly 200 photographs.

TRAINS OF CUBA
30-920698468 16.95 *NEW*
Find out how steam, diesel and electric trains are an essential part of business and transportation in Cuba. 96 pages, 8-1/2 x 5-1/2".

NARROW GAUGE RAILWAY SCENES
30-920698417 24.95 *NEW*
Author Adolf Hungry Wolf details the history and stories of most every notable narrow gauge operation of the last 50 years. 224 pages, 11 x 8-1/2".

WHERE RAILS MEET THE SEA: AMERICA'S CONNECTION BETWEEN SHIPS & TRAINS
30-1567995977 22.98 *NEW*
The connection between the shipping industry and the development of the steam engine is explained in this 176-page book. Features over 200 photographs and illustrations.
8-11/16 x 11-5/8".

VANCOUVER ISLAND RAILROADS
30-1550390775 36.95 *NEW*
This section of Canada has a rich history of railroading, involving its mining and logging operations. Learn more about it in these 186 pages, featuring over 250 B&W photos and maps.
8-1/2 x 11".

V&S: THE VICTORIA AND SIDNEY RAILWAY 1892-1919
30-969251114 26.95 *NEW*
This award-winning book examines the growth of the V&S Railway since its debut in the late 1800s. 236 pages, 8-1/2 x 11", over 250 photos and maps.

STEAMWHEELERS AND STEAM TUGS
30-1550390899 42.95 *NEW*
The book's subtitle explains it best: "An illustrated history of the Canadian Pacific Railway's British Columbia lake and river service." 288 pages, 8-1/2 x 11", full of maps, photos and illustrations.

LOGGING BY RAIL: THE BRITISH COLUMBIA STORY
30-1550390651 42.95 *NEW*
An award-winning examination of British Columbia railroad logging from the late 1880s to the last steam and dieselized lines. Over 500 photos, 326 pages, 8-1/2 x 11".

STEAM ON THE KETTLE VALLEY: A RAILWAY HERITAGE RECOMMENDED
30-1550390635 19.95 *NEW*
Learn how the Kettle Railway persevered over extreme weather conditions and difficult topography to become an important rail line in British Columbia. 120 pages, 9 x 8", over 175 photos.

THE SKYLINE LIMITED: THE KASLO & SLOCAN RAILWAY
30-1550390406 52.95 *NEW*
From the 1890s through the early 1900s, this Great Northern narrow gauge railroad ran through British Columbia's Slocan mountains. 296 pages, 8-1/2 x 11". Over 300 illustrations.

IN SEARCH OF THE NARROW GAUGE
30-1550390694 19.95 *NEW*
Author Bob Whetham goes to 17 different countries to locate different narrow gauge railroads. Over 120 photographs and illustrations chronicle his journey. 108 pages, 8-1/2 x 7".

WORKING STEAM: VINTAGE LOCOMOTIVES TODAY
30-1567997767 19.98 *NEW*
Details the over 300 working steam locomotives in Canada and the United States. Hardcover, 120 pages, 11-1/4 x 11-14".

NORTH SHORE/SOUTH SHORE
30-93 41.95 *NEW*
The history of these interurban stalwarts is detailed in 200 striking color photographs. Over 140 pages.

UNITED STATES RAILROAD MAP
30-89 7.95
47 x 29", all color.

CHICAGO'S RAILROADS AND PARMALEE'S TRANSFER COMPANY: A CENTURY OF TRAVEL

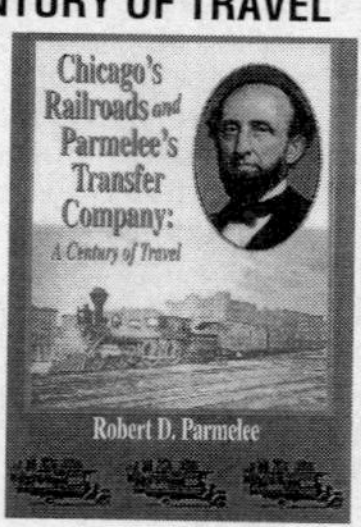

30-91 19.95
Documents the development and growth of Chicago railroads and their relationship with the Parmalee Transfer Company. Over 150 illustrations, 8.5 x 11".

NEVADA COUNTY NARROW GAUGE

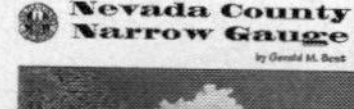

30-911581464 39.95
Written by Gerald Best, recounts the story of the railroad that served the quartz gold mines of Northern California. 8-1/2 x 11", 224 pages.

TIE HACKERS TO TIMBER HARVESTERS/THE HISTORY OF LOGGING IN THE BC INTERIOR

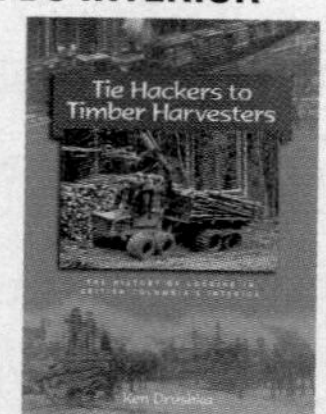

30-1550171895 45.95
Author Ken Drushka delves into the interior forest industry, a vital element of British Columbia's economy. 240 pages.

GILPIN GOLD TRAM

30-29 36.95
Review the history of Colorado's only two-foot gauge railroad, used to haul ore from Central City to Blackhawk. Hardcover, 120 B&W photographs, 120 pages.

THE SEARCH FOR STEAM

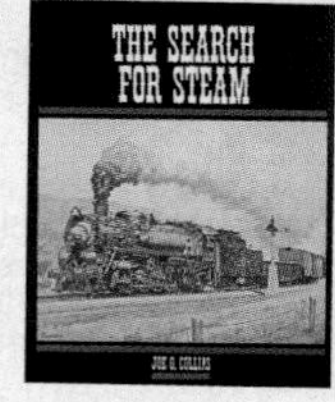

30-37 45.95
This mammoth collection of over 420 photographs honors the course and contributions of steam railroading, an era which drew to a close by the late 1950s. Hardcover, 360 pages.

AMERICA'S RAIL PICTORIAL

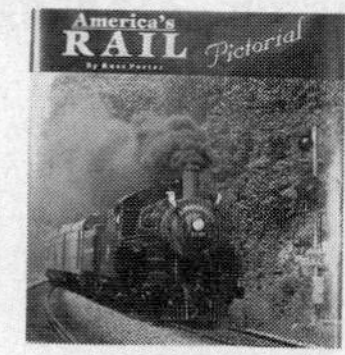

30-88 44.95
Loaded with all-color photographs, readers can survey the development of the American railroad from the 1950s through the 1970s. Hardcover, 152 pages, 10 x 11".

THE MAINE TWO-FOOTERS

30-911581472 44.95
Written by Linwood Moody.

FIDDLETOWN & COPPEROPOLIS
30-12 14.95
The hilarious history of the narrow gauge railroads. 144 pages, one cartoon per page.

THE MAN WHO LIVES IN PARADISE
30-22 24.95
Autobiography of A. C. Gilbert, best known for the American Flyer train sets and Erector Sets.

HOLLYWOOD TRAINS

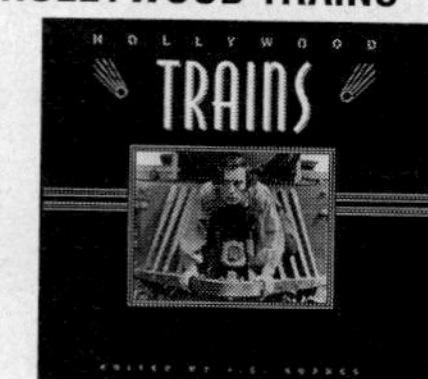

30-41 12.95
Documents the many films that featured railroads Stunning B&W photos by Hollywood's premier lensmen. 240 pages, 8-1/2 x 11".

MONON ROUTE

30-58 49.95
Covers the Monon's history. Includes 463 photographs, maps, drawings and illustrations. Hardcover, 323 pages.

GREAT AMERICAN RAILROAD STATIONS

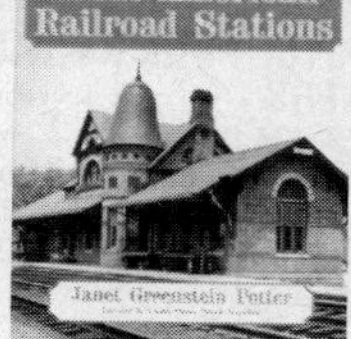

30-59 29.95
Discover the biographical profiles of more than 700 stations across the United States. More than 500 archival photographs and drawings. 570 pages.

SAN FRANCISCO CABLE CARS

30-60 19.95
History of San Francisco's cable car and the characters that built, ran and protected them. Many large B&W pictures. 144 pages.

RAILROAD TIMETABLES, TRAVEL BROCHURES & POSTERS: HISTORY & GUIDE FOR COLLECTORS
30-61 44.95
The only book focused exclusively on American railroad paper ephemera of the 19th and 20th century.

LANTERNS THAT LIT OUR WORLD EA 14.95
Comprehensive guides to identify, date and restore old railroad, marine, fire, carriage, farm and other lanterns.

30-62 Book One
30-63 Book Two

CLASSIC NORTH AMERICAN STEAM
30-66 19.95
Steam locomotives are back in action. Beautiful photos. 10-1/2 x 14-1/4".

HEIMBURGER HOUSE PUBLISHING

KINSEY PHOTOGRAPHER: THE LOCOMOTIVE PORTRAITS
30-73 19.98
Stunning portraits of the steam locos used by the logging industry in northwest Washington during the first half of the twentieth century.

WORKING IN THE WOODS
30-78 44.95
A hardbound history of logging in British Columbia. Large B&W photos, 8-1/2 x 11".

WHISTLE PUNKS & WIDOW MAKERS
30-79 24.95
Robert Swanson tells about the legendary heroes of the golden age of logging in British Columbia.

TRANSIT IN BRITISH COLUMBIA: THE FIRST 100 YEARS.
30-80 44.95
Tells the story of the first 100 years of public transit in Canada west of the Rockies.

BRITISH COLUMBIA RAILWAY

30-83 79.95
466 spectacular color photographs of the British Columbia Railway from the 1950s to the 1990s.

TRAIN COUNTRY

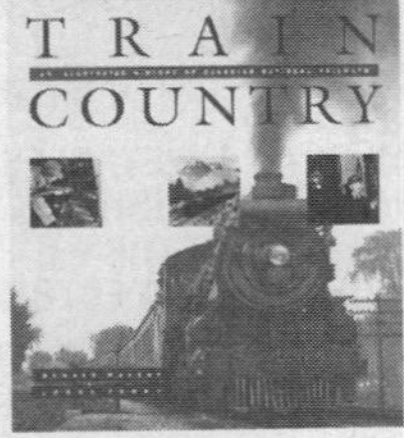

30-47 24.95
Covers the Canadian National Railway with photographs of early and late steam, gas electrics, freight and passenger trains, diesels, structures, stations, bridges, troop trains, 1920 ski trains and streamlined Northern-type locomotives. 11 x 10".

WABASH
30-9 41.95
History of the Wabash, as well as a dozen of its predecessor lines. Photos, roster, maps, timetables. Hardcover, 320 pages, 8-1/2 x 11".

GLOVER STEAM LOCOMOTIVES: THE SOUTH'S LAST STEAM BUILDER
30-55 38.95
The story of Glover Locomotive Works of Marietta, Georgia, and the 200 small locomotives they manufactured between 1902 and the 1930s. Hardcover, 128 pages, 10 x 10".

THE AMERICAN STREAMLINER (PREWAR)
30-56 44.95
A color tribute to the streamliners that graced the American rails between 1933 and WWII. Hardcover, 172 pages, 200 color and B&W photos, 10 x 10".

ALONG THE EAST BROAD TOP

30-15 41.95
Detailed history of the Pennsylvania shortline, including station and car drawings. 350 photos, 8 color, hardcover, 248 pages, 8-1/2 x 11".

LOGGING RAILROADS OF SOUTH CAROLINA
30-18 42.95
Details hundreds of lumber railroads and shortlines that dotted South Carolina during the logging heyday. 175 B&W photos, 82 maps, hardcover, 8-1/2 x 11".

TRAINS OF AMERICA
30-19 44.95
Full color photo essay of American railroads, from late steam to early diesel. Photos arranged alphabetically by railroad name, and includes shortlines, class I and regional lines. Hardcover, 206 pages, 11 x 10".

THE LAST OF STEAM
30-38 41.95
The waning years of steam railroading throughout the United States. Hardcover, 272 pages, 300 photos (279 large engine pictures), 8-1/2 x 11".

ILLINOIS CENTRAL: MAIN LINE OF MID-AMERICA

30-46 42.95
Bursting with beautiful color photos of steam, diesels, passenger equipment, scenes from online towns and more. 128 pages, hardcover, 10 x 11".

NORFOLK AND WESTERN COAL CAR EQUIPMENT
30-28 5.95
Covers the N&W coal hauling routes, rolling stock and motive power procedures during the mid-1940s. Summary of equipment, along with specific car examples that give general arrangement drawings, specifications, car series number and a photograph of each car. 24 pages.

WABASH STANDARD PLANS & REFERENCE
30-30 22.95
Map of line; 55 standard plans such as trestles, markers, signs, milepost markings, spring switches, bulletin boards, crossings, telltales, telephone boxes, freight house skids, weights of rail and tie renewal references. 150 pages, 11 x 8-1/2".

COLORFUL EAST BROAD TOP
30-31 24.95
The East's last original narrow gauge railroad in glorious color during the 1950s. Features the major points of Railroading/Mining interest in Pennsylvania. Includes steam locos, freight and passenger cars, action trains, Orbisonia shops, timber transfer, mixed freights and more. Includes unpublished color photos, map and text. 88 pages, 11 x 8-1/2".

LEHIGH VALLEY RAILROAD
30-33 44.95
A comprehensive history of the line's founding, expansion, prosperity, decline and dissolution. 655 photographs, maps and drawings, 372 pages, 8-1/2 x 11".

CHICAGO & NORTH WESTERN MILWAUKEE ROAD PICTORIAL

30-36 29.95
Features nearly 120 photos from both the CNW and the Milwaukee Road. Artist Russ Porter includes 10 of his beautiful CNW and Milwaukee oil paintings as part of the illustrative material. Photographs depict both late steam and early diesel trains in Wisconsin and Illinois. 76 pages, 11 x 8-1/2".

RIO GRANDE STEAM LOCOMOTIVES: STANDARD GAUGE
30-42 41.95
Traces the development of Rio Grande's steam locomotives from the early days to the last days of steam. Hardcover, laminated, 140 photos, 26 folio drawings, maps, timetables and rosters from 1891 to 1956, 9 x 12".

UINTAH RAILWAY: THE GILSONITE ROUTE

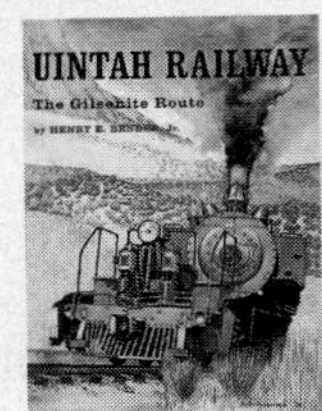

30-43 39.95
A complete and colorful account of one of the last narrow-gauge lines built in the Rockies. Includes an addendum and errata, 240 pages, 290 photos, maps, notes, and rosters, 8-1/2 x 11".

JOHN NORWOOD

RIO GRANDE NARROW GAUGE BY JOHN NORWOOD

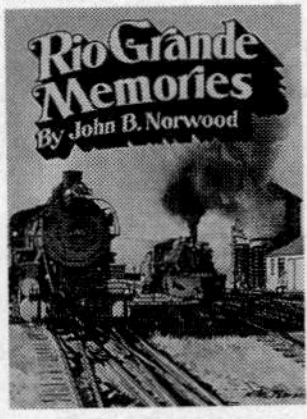

30-7 44.95
Features operations of the Rio Grande narrow gauge lines in southern Colorado and northern New Mexico. 275 illustrations, 8 color, hardcover, 312 pages.

RIO GRANDE NARROW GAUGE RECOLLECTIONS
30-14 41.95
John Norwood's personal account of 40 years service with the Rio Grande narrow gauge. A look at the daily operations, equipment and people. Over 250 photos (some color), maps, timetables and a glossary. Hardcover, 272 pages, 8-1/2 x 11".

RIO GRANDE MEMORIES BY JOHN NORWOOD
30-25 41.95
Hundreds of B&W photos and an 8-page color photo section. Index, hardcover, 192 pages, 8-1/2 x 11".

JOHN NORWOOD'S RAILROADS

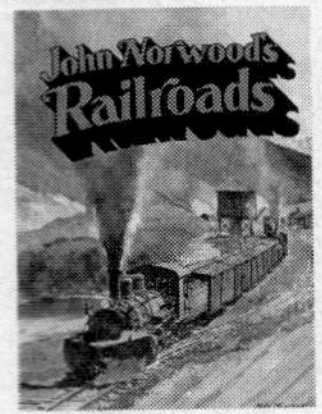

30-39 44.95
John Norwood recounts his experiences and the historical background of numerous standard and narrow gauge lines in the US. Hardcover, 8-1/2 x 11".

MODELING

S GAUGE LOCOMOTIVES & CARS
30-3 3.50
Techniques of model railroad rolling stock and loco construction. Emphasis on S Scale, but information is appropriate for all other scales. 40 pages, 8-1/2 x 11".

AMERICAN FLYER INSTRUCTION BOOK
30-16 4.95
Originally published in 1952 by A.C. Gilbert Co., includes instructions and suggestions on operating S Gauge, 2-rail trains and track tips. 14 track plans, layouts, 64 pages, 5-1/4 x 8-1/2".

SOUVENIR EDITION OF S GAUGIAN
30-27 4.50
Magazine highlighting all the American Flyer S gauge trains made by Lionel from 1979-1989. Includes a detailed, handy reference list of items made. Color photos, 68 pages.

A.C. GILBERT'S FAMOUS AMERICAN FLYER TRAINS

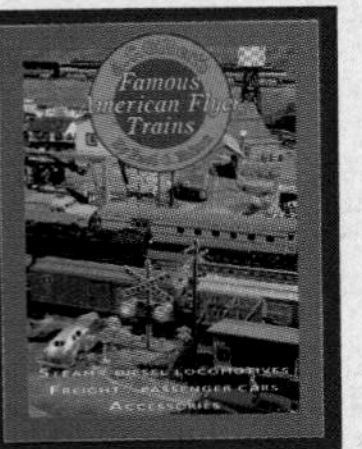

30-911581480 41.95 ***NEW***
Explore the product history of the A.C. Gilbert Company from 1946 to 1966. Hardcover, 200 pages, 8-1/2 x 11".

HEIMBURGER HOUSE PUBLISHING

PHOTOGRAPHY

KINSEY PHOTOGRAPHY
30-72 29.98
A magnificent collection of 206 classic photos of the Pacific Northwest taken in the first half of the century by renowned photographers Darius and Tabitha Kinsey. 10-1/4 x 13-1/4".

GHOST TOWNS OF COLORADO
30-896584186 19.95 ***NEW***
Philip Varney and John Drew visit 90 towns and sites that make up the spirit that was once the Wild West. 160 pages, 8-1/2 x 11", over 165 photographs.

NICHOLAS MORANT'S CANADA
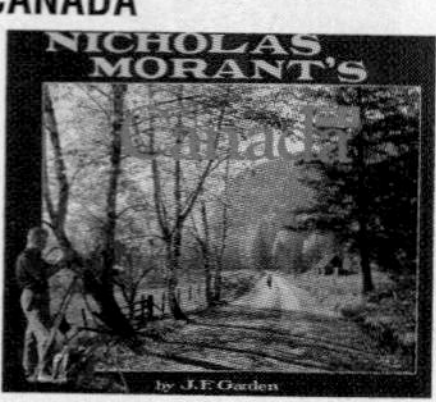

30-969162162 59.95 ***NEW***
Learn about the life and adventures of Nicholas Morant, premier photographer for the Canadian Pacific Railway. 276 pages, 11 x 10-1/4".

VEHICLES

THE FIRE ENGINE
30-831732660 19.95 ***NEW***
Chronicles the development of the fire engine, from its inception to its design as a sophisticated, modern vehicle. Features over 140 color photographs.

TRACKS IN THE FOREST
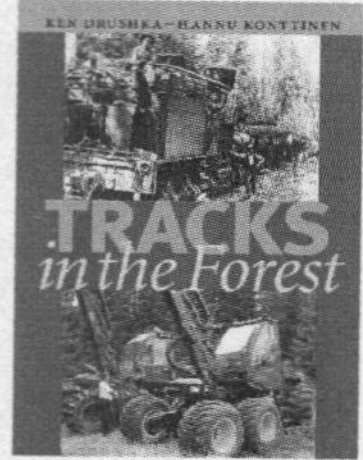

30-9529086164 39.95 ***NEW***
Analyzes the development, design and evolution of mechanized logging equipment. Hardcover, 254 pages.

H&M PRODUCTIONS

BOOKS
Softcover 11 x 8-1/2" format, except as noted.

THE SUBWAY
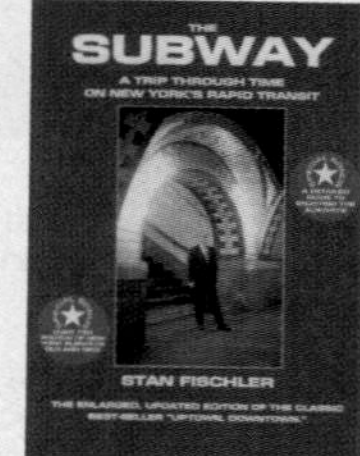

91-401 29.95
This enlarged, updated edition of "Uptown, Downtown" features more than 150 photos of the New York subway and includes a detailed guide.

BY THE EL

Limited Quantity Available
91-1000 38.95
New York at mid-century. Hardcover book has 124 pages with over 100 color photos to take you back.

NEW YORK CITY MAP BONANZA BARGAIN
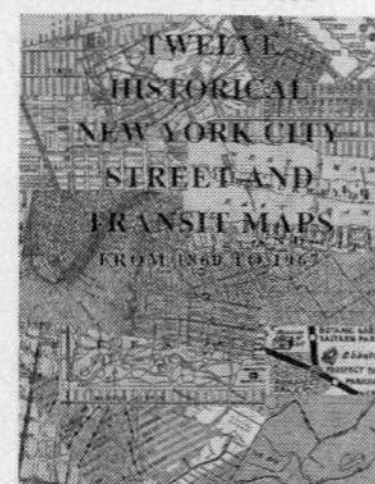

Limited Quantity Available
91-1100 29.95
A book of 12 historical New York City street and transit maps from 1860 to 1967. Suitable for framing (some as large as 13 x 19").

JERSEY CITY WESTBOUND
91-1 29.95
Photographic study of Jersey Central Passenger Operations.

FOUR GREAT DIVISIONS
91-50 36.95
Covers the New York Central's Hudson division. Erie Lackawanna's New York and Scranton divisions and the Northern Pacific Burlington Northern Rocky Mountain Division.

TWILITE OF THE MONONGAHELA
91-201 32.95
Full color story of the railway in its last year.

CONFESSIONS OF A TROLLEY DODGER FROM BROOKLYN
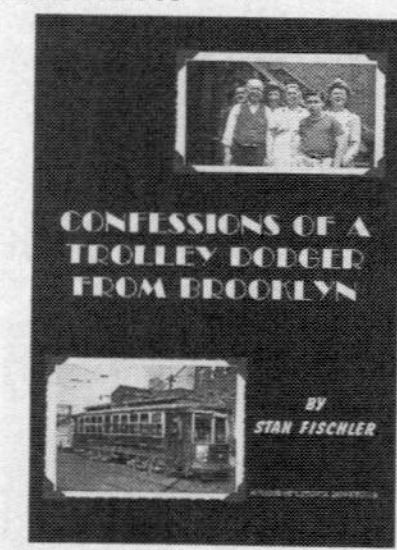

91-202 24.95

CABINS, CRUMMIES & HACKS
91-103 Volume IV **29.95**
Covers the cabooses of the Southwest and Mexico. Full color.

91-105 Volume V: Northern North America **33.95**
Full color, 80 pages, hardcover.

GOTHAM TURNSTILES

91-400 33.95
Rapid transit of New York 1958-1968.

CLASSIC FREIGHT CARS: THE SERIES

91-304 Volume V **24.95**
Covers Northeast railroad work equipment.

91-307 Volume VII **24.95**
More 40' boxcars.

91-308 Volume VIII **26.95**
50' boxcars.

91-309 Volume IX: Insulated Boxcars and Mechanical Reefers **26.95**

91-310 Volume X: North American Work Trains **26.95**

91-311 Volume XI: High Capacity Covered Hoppers **27.95** ***NEW***

Limited Quantity Available
91-305 Volume VI **24.95**
Loaded flats and gondolas.

CLASSIC LOCOMOTIVES - THE SERIES
91-501 Volume I - Alco Switchers S-1 to S-7 **32.95**
More than 210 color photos of Alco switchers. Horizontal format, 80 pages, softcover.

91-502 Volume II - EMD SD45s **32.95**
Over 160 color photos. Horizontal format, 80 pages, softcover.

91-503 Volume III - EMD GP30s **32.95**
Over 140 color photos. 80 pages.

91-504 Volume IV RS3 **39.95**

Information STATION

MODEL TRAIN MUSEUMS
Layout ideas can come from anywhere. Books, videos, conventions — all these are great venues of inspiration for the model train hobbyist. But to get the best look at the history and innovations of this hobby, why not check out a museum? A number of model train museums, dedicated to the preservation and enjoyment of classic model trains, are currently in operation.
Strasburg, Pennsylvania is home to the National Toy Train Museum. Boasting an impressive collection of floor toys, electric trains and train-related accessories in five different scales, the museum displays items originating from the mid-19th century to contemporary models. The museum also is home to a movie theater, gift shop and extensive library of books, catalogs and magazines related to toy trains.
The San Diego Model Railroad Museum is home to the largest operating model railroad exhibit. Located in California's Balboa Park, the unique SDMRM displays four different layouts dedicated to railroads of the Southwest: an O-Scale Cabrillo & Southwestern ; HO Scale depictions of the San Diego & Arizona Eastern and the Tehachapi Pass; and a Pacific Desert Lines exhibit in N Scale. There's also a toy train gallery to keep the kids — and the kid inside every collector — thoroughly entertained.
Another museum you might be interested in visiting is the South Florida Railway Museum, located in Deerfield Beach, Florida. The museum prides itself on being more than just a place to look at collectible trains. Instead, the museum devotes its energy to "preserve the history of railroads in southern Florida, and educate the public about the importance of railroads in the region past and present."

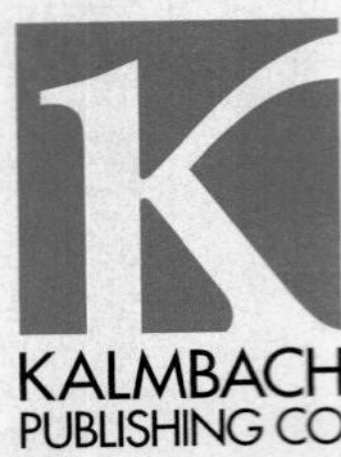

MODEL RAILROADING & SCALE MODELING

MODELING TANKS & MILITARY VEHICLES

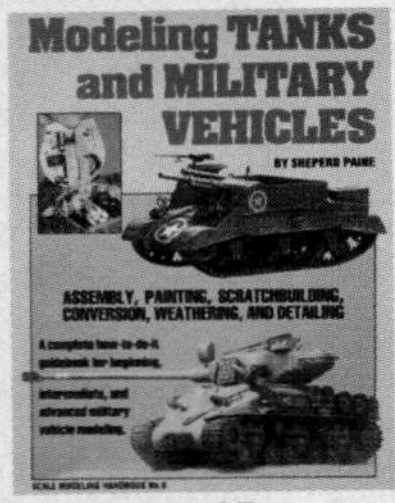

400-12058 14.95
Assembly, painting, scratchbuilding, weathering and detailing for building realistic armor models. 76 pages, 260 photos, 8-1/4 x 11-1/4".

MODEL RAILROADER'S GUIDE TO INTERMODAL EQUIPMENT & OPERATIONS

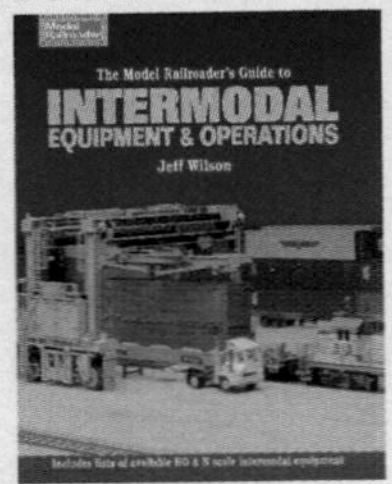

400-12190 15.95
This must-have book uses detailed photographs and illustrations to explain this dynamic part of railroading. Plus tips, techniques and instructions for modeling intermodal transportation on your layout. 80 pages, 140 color and 40 B&W photos, 8-1/4 x 10-3/4".

A REALISTIC HO LAYOUT FOR BEGINNERS

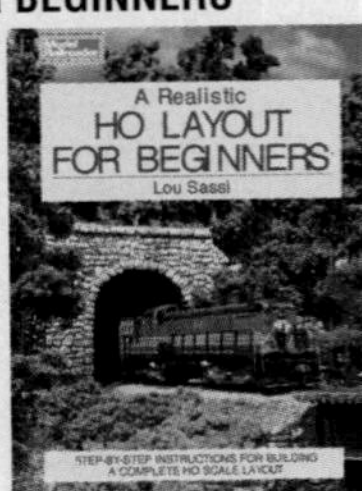

400-12141 16.95
Shows how to build a realistic HO layout with all the details. 96 pages, 120 B&W and 60 color photos, 8-1/4 x 10-7/8".

BASIC MODEL RAILROADING: GETTING STARTED IN THE HOBBY

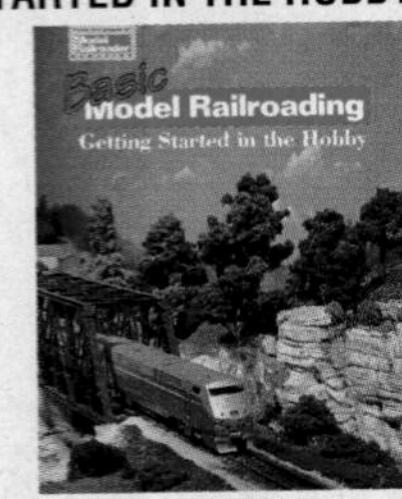

400-12197 14.95
Packed with simple tips and techniques, detailed photos, diagrams and drawings. Basics of tracklaying, wiring, maintaining locomotives, scenery, painting, weathering and more. 80 pages, 150 color photos, 8-1/4 x 10-3/4".

DETAILING SCALE MODEL AIRCRAFT

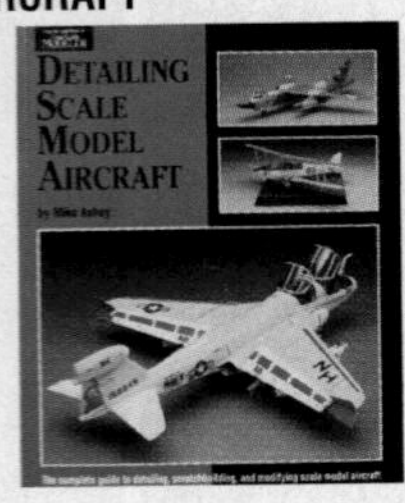

400-12137 16.95
Teaches how to create accurate and realistic scale aircraft from scratchbuilding to painting. Includes simple techniques for interior and exterior details, removing seams, applying decals and weathering. 104 pages, 249 photos, 8-1/4 x 10-3/4".

MODEL AIRCRAFT TIPS & TECHNIQUES: AN ILLUSTRATED GUIDE

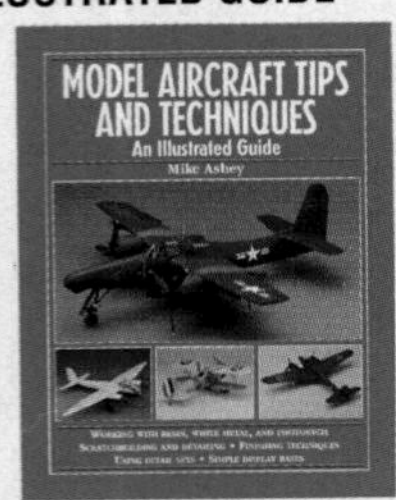

400-12165 16.95
Shows how to detail cockpits, guns, wheel wells and more. 112 pages, 400 B&W and 24 color photos, 8-1/4 x 10-3/4".

TRACK PLANNING FOR REALISTIC OPERATIONS

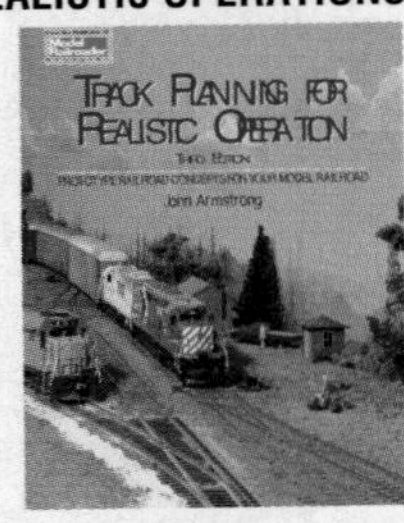

400-12148 3rd Edition **18.95**
Must-have for track planning and design tips and techniques. 144 pages, 45 B&W and 120 illustrations, 8-1/4 x 10-3/4".

BUILDING AND DISPLAYING SCALE MODEL AIRCRAFT WITH PAUL BOYER

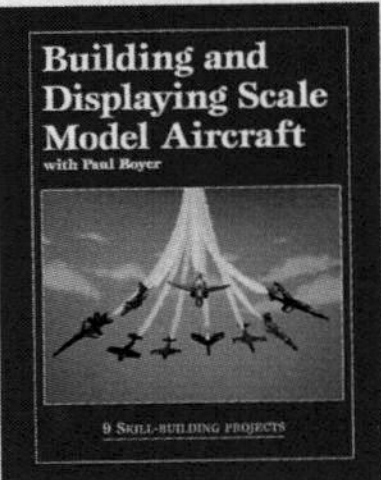

400-12151 12.95
Teaches basic aircraft modeling preparation and assembly techniques. Includes suggestions for painting and decaling with special attention to creative displays and mounting tips for finished projects. 88 pages, 110 B&W and 50 color photos, 8-1/4 x 10-3/4".

BUILDING & DETAILING SCALE MODEL SHIPS

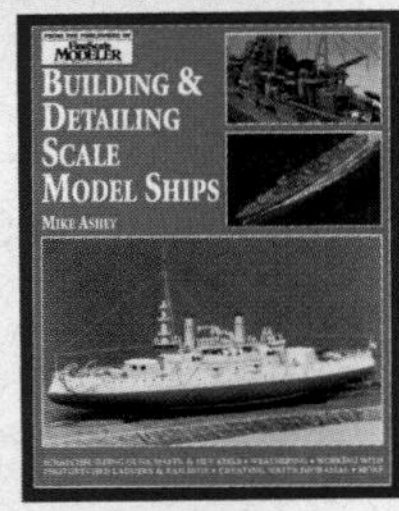

400-12152 18.95
Provides hundreds of simple techniques for building, detailing, scratchbuilding and modifying scale model ships. Hundreds of close-up photos and tips on scratchbuilding detailed parts, seam removal, weathering and more. 112 pages, 240 B&W and 32 color photos, 8-1/4 x 10-3/4".

BUILDING & DETAILING SCALE MODEL PICKUP TRUCKS

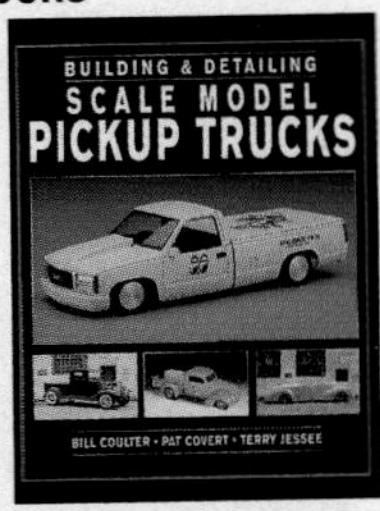

400-12164 14.95
Teaches how to assemble, combine and customize truck kits. Teaches painting, finishing and weathering techniques for street rods, customized trucks and more. 88 pages, 180 B&W and 84 color photos, 8-1/4 x 10-3/4".

BUILDING & DETAILING SCALE MODEL TRUCKS & EMERGENCY VEHICLES

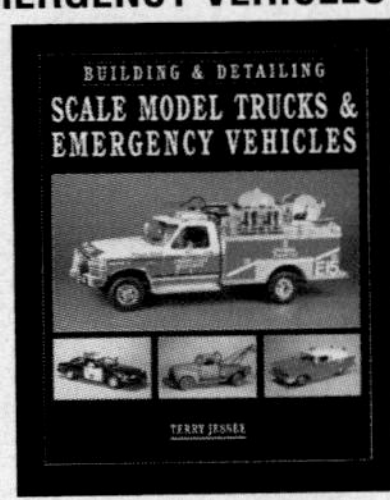

400-12188 16.95 ***NEW***
Provides detailed instruction on modeling ambulances, tow trucks, police cruisers and more. Includes step-by-step assembly instructions for vehicle build-ups and kitbashing. Softcover, 96 pages, 180 B&W and 48 color photos, 8-1/4 x 10-3/4".

BUILDING AND DETAILING SCALE MODEL STOCK CARS

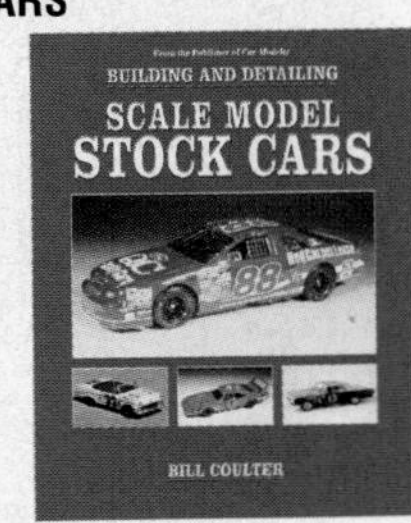

400-12172 17.95
Shows how to create replicas of NASCAR winners, with step-by-step instructions for building and detailing over a dozen cars. 112 pages, 220 B&W and 64 color photos, 8-1/4 x 10-3/4".

MODEL RAILROADING IN SMALL SPACES

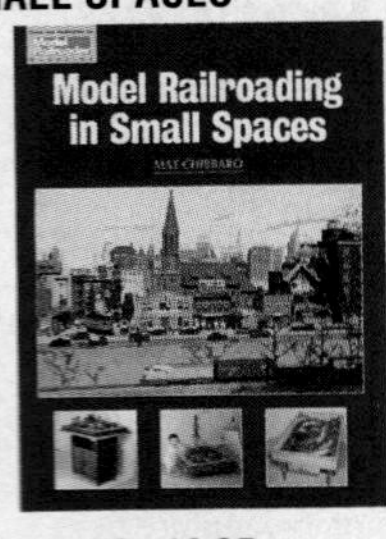

400-12176 16.95
How to build an impressive layout in nearly any space. Step-by-step instructions for building layouts in closets, drawers, on tables and more. 96 pages, 80 B&W and 30 color photos, 40 illustrations, 8-1/4 x 10-3/4".

BUILDING AND DETAILING SCALE MODEL MUSCLE CARS

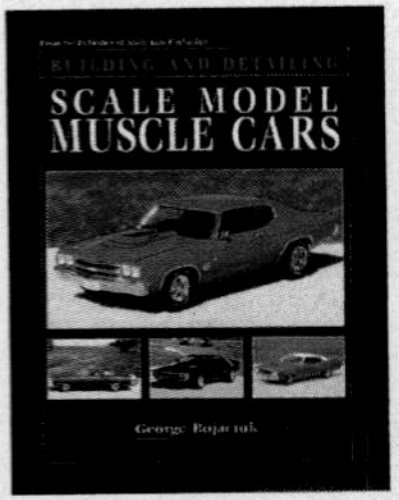

400-12180 15.95
Easy-to-follow directions for building and detailing over a dozen cars. 88 pages, 189 B&W and 48 color photos, 8-1/4 x 10-3/4".

CUSTOM CAR MODELING

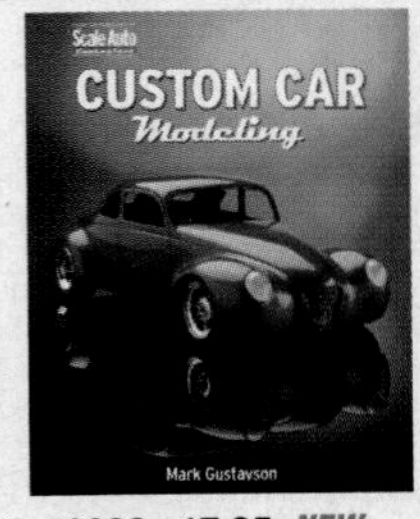

400-12202 17.95 ***NEW***
Learn how to customize any ordinary model kit to build the car of your dreams. Step-by-step instructions as well as tips and techniques are included. Softcover, 96 pages, 190 B&W and 32 color photos, 8-1/4 x 10-3/4".

BASICS OF SCALE AUTOMOTIVE MODELING: GETTING STARTED IN THE HOBBY

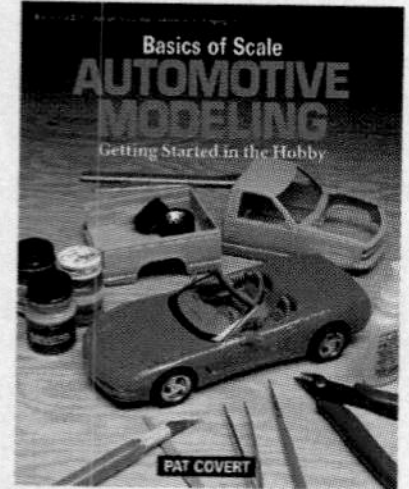

400-12192 15.95 ***NEW***
Covers the basics of assembling, gluing, decaling, masking and painting. Softcover, 88 pages, 139 B&W and 40 color photos, 8-1/4 x 10-3/4".

BUILDING THE P-40 WARHAWK

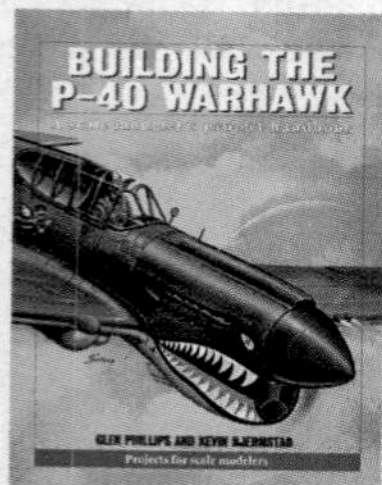

400-12181 15.95
Directions and techniques for building 11 variations of this famous warplane using existing kits. Includes walkaround detail photos of actual P-40s. 88 pages, 180 B&W and 24 color photos, 25+ illustrations, 8-1/4 x 10-3/4".

BUILDING THE MESSERSCHMITT BF-109

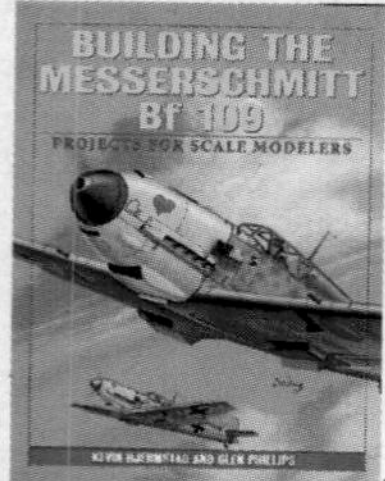

400-12185 16.95 ***NEW***
Includes a detailed colors and markings section for accurate modeling, step-by-step projects for all skill levels and walkaround photography of an actual Bf-109. Softcover, 88 pages, 180 B&W and 26 color photos, 8-1/4 x 10-3/4".

TODAY IS THE FIRST DAY OF THE REST OF YOUR LAYOUT

400-12193 9.95
A humorous look at model railroading. 80 pages, 78 illustrations, 5 1/4 x 8".

THIS IS NOT THE HONEYMOON I ANTICIPATED

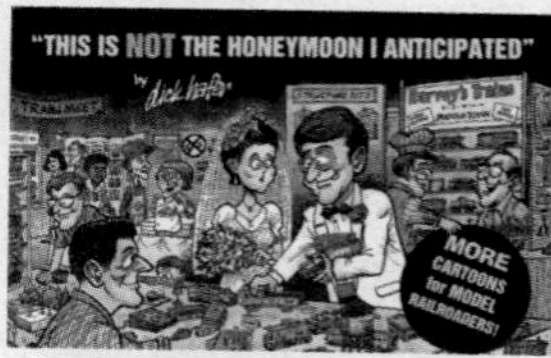

400-12183 8.95
Find a multitude of new barbs and jabs aimed at the stereotypical model railroader in its pages. 80 pages with 76 cartoons, 8 x 5-1/4".

SCALE MODEL DETAILING PROJECTS YOU CAN DO FROM FINESCALE MODELER

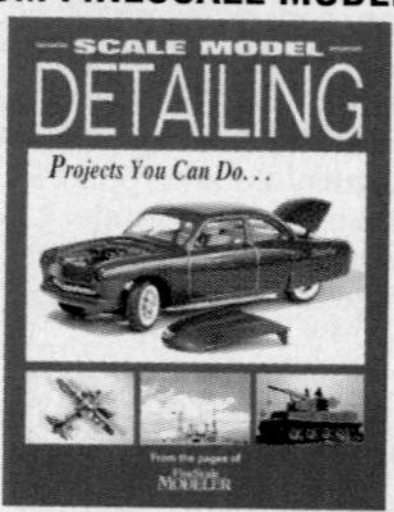

400-12139 14.95
Learn step-by-step how to convert scale figures, weather aircraft, model a rusty 1949 Mercury and more! 104 pages, 8-1/4 x 10-3/4".

BUILDING BETTER SCALE MODEL CARS & TRUCKS: DETAILING TIPS & TECHNIQUES

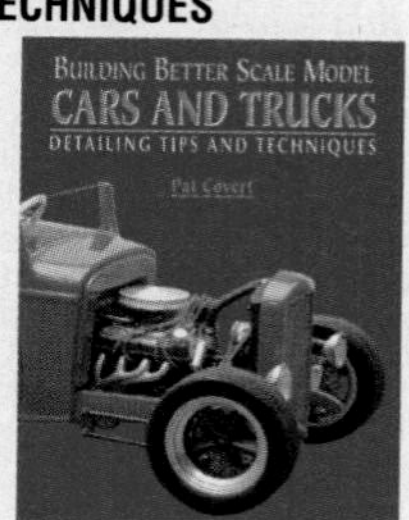

400-12174 14.95 ***NEW***
Includes easy-to-follow photographs and text as well as tips that appeal to all levels of modelers and apply to any car project. Softcover, 88 pages, 145 B&W and 39 color photos, 8-1/4 x 10-3/4".

ARMOR CONVERSION AND DETAILING PROJECTS FROM FINESCALE MODELER

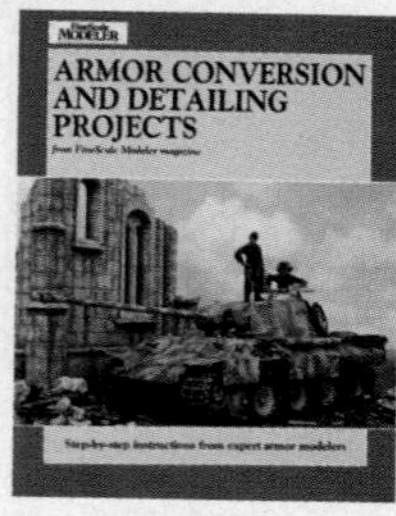

400-12166 15.95
Shows how to convert commercial kits into dramatically detailed armored and tactical vehicles. 104 pages, 160 B&W and 44 color photos, 8-1/4 x 10-3/4".

FREIGHT CAR PROJECTS AND IDEAS

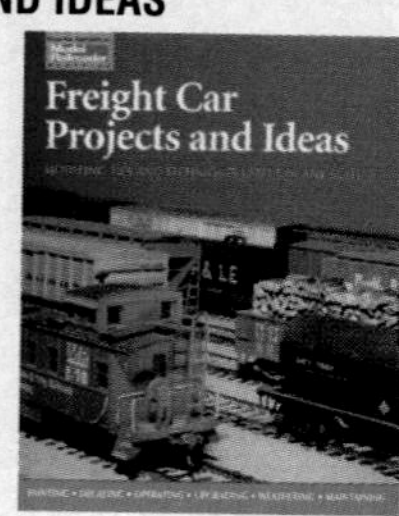

400-12171 16.95
Techniques that can improve the realism of any freight car. 80 pages, 120 B&W and 75 color photos, 45 illustrations, 8-1/4 x 10-3/4".

HOW TO DETAIL DIESEL LOCOMOTIVES

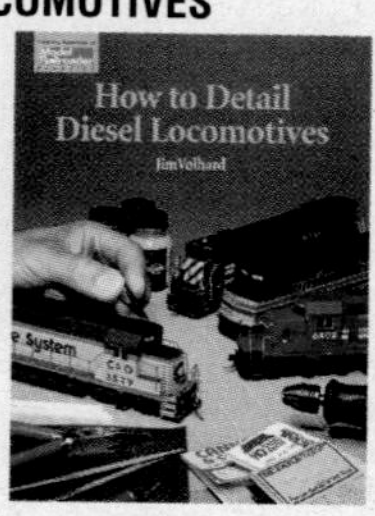

400-12186 16.95
Learn the basic skills needed for successful detailing. 96 pages, 150 B&W and 25 color photos, 35 illustrations, 8-1/4 x 10-3/4".

PAINTING AND WEATHERING RAILROAD MODELS

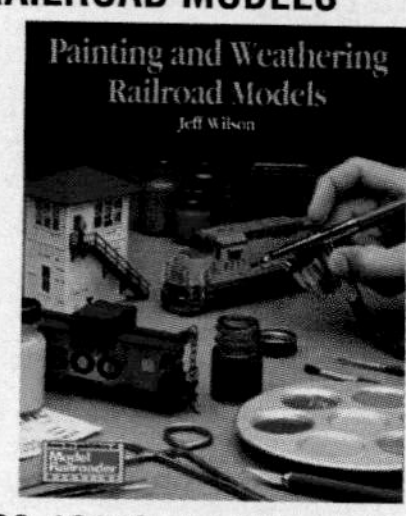

400-12142 14.95
Introduces the basic materials, tools and techniques, then walks through specific projects from start to finish. 80 pages, 100 B&W and 50 color photos, 8-1/4 x 10-3/4".

HO RAILROAD FROM SET TO SCENERY

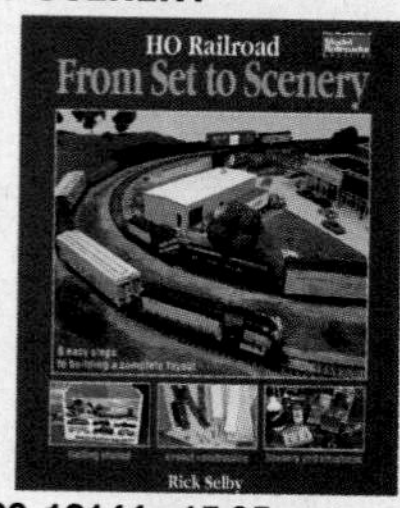

400-12144 15.95
Helpful hints on selecting a starter train set and progresses to benchwork construction, track laying, wiring, building scenery and future expansion of layout. 96 pages, 100 B&W and 60 color photos, 8-1/4 x 10-3/4".

KITBASHING HO MODEL RR STRUCTURES

400-12154 2nd Edition **11.95**
Art Curren shows how to use plastic kits to create unique customized buildings. 88 pages, 110 B&W and 18 color photos, 75 diagrams, 8-1/4 x 10-3/4".

303 TIPS FOR DETAILING MODEL RAILROAD SCENERY AND STRUCTURES

400-12153 16.95
Effective hints for improving the realism of the buildings and scenery on your model railroad. 96 pages 170 photos, 8-1/4 x 10-3/4".

DIESEL DETAILING PROJECTS FROM MODEL RAILROADER

400-12161 14.95
Each project includes a list of required parts and materials. 96 pages, 150 B&W and 50 color photos, 8-1/4 x 10-3/4".

SOMETIMES YOU GOTTA COMPROMISE

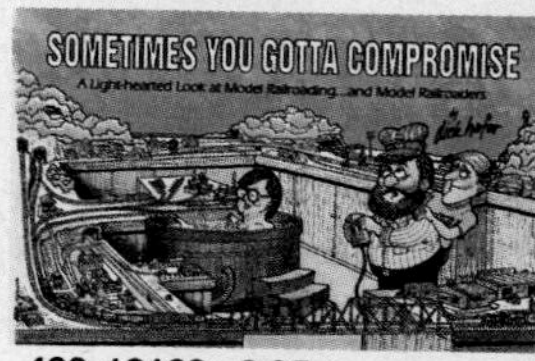

400-12163 8.95
Laugh along at the lighter side of model railroading and don't be surprised if you recognize yourself or a friend. 80 pages, 8 x 5-1/5".

HO LINESIDE INDUSTRIES YOU CAN BUILD

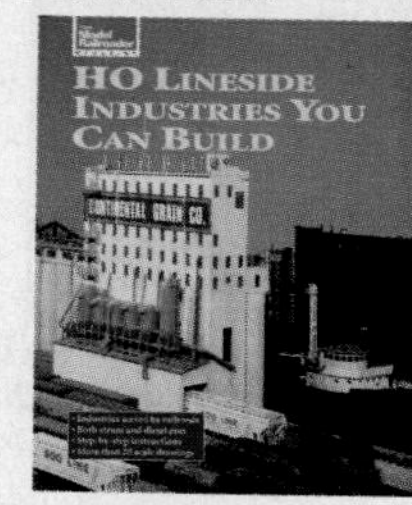

400-12168 14.95
The photos, step-by-step instructions and accurate drawings and plans provide ideas that can be modified or built as illustrated. 120 pages, 200 B&W and 35 color photos, 8-1/4 x 10-3/4".

THE PENNSY MIDDLE DIVISION IN HO SCALE

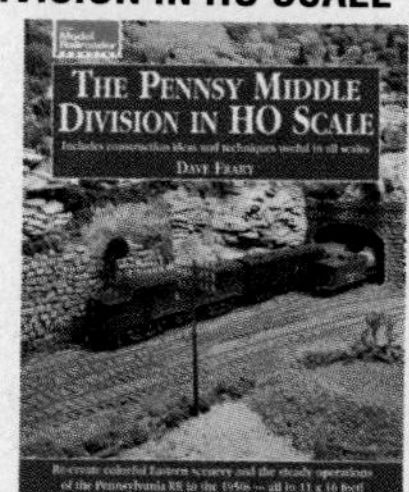

400-12170 11.95
Construction of a 11 x 16' replica of the Pennsylvania's Middle Division. Includes track planning, benchwork construction, wiring, trackwork and scenery techniques. 64 pages, 30 B&W and 90 color photos, 8-1/4 x 10-3/4".

THE PRACTICAL GUIDE TO HO MODEL RAILROADING

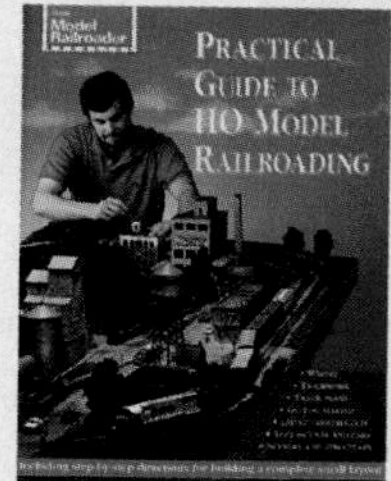

400-12075 10.95
Step-by-step practical guide to HO Scale model railroading. Answers modelers questions about subjects from track planning, to wiring, to scenery construction. 88 pages, 8-1/4 x 11- 1/4".

SMALL RAILROADS YOU CAN BUILD

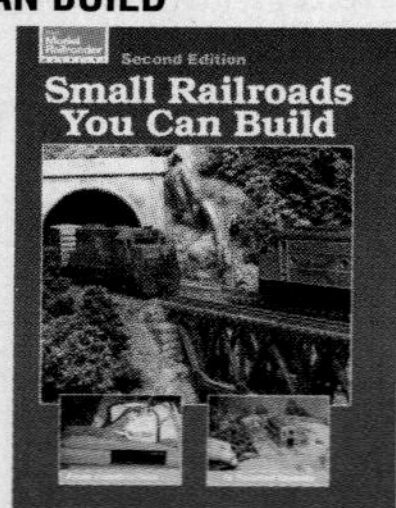

400-12146 2nd Edition **10.95**
Revised and expanded with new N, HO and O Scale layouts to build in a small room. Each project includes step-by-step instructions applicable to all scales. 64 pages, 100 B&W and 50 color photos, 8-1/4 x 10-1/4".

HOW TO BUILD DIORAMAS

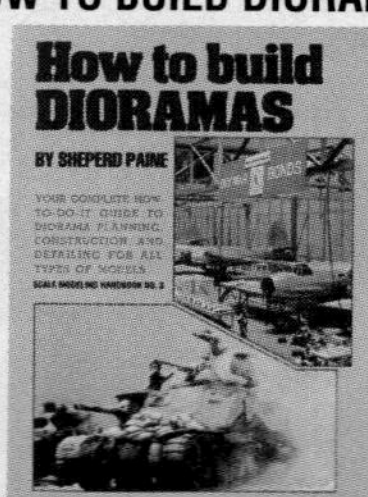

400-12047 16.95
Sheperd Paine shows how to design and build dioramas from the ground up. He explains weathering, covers figures and shadow box construction and even details model photography. 104 pages, 8-1/4 x 11".

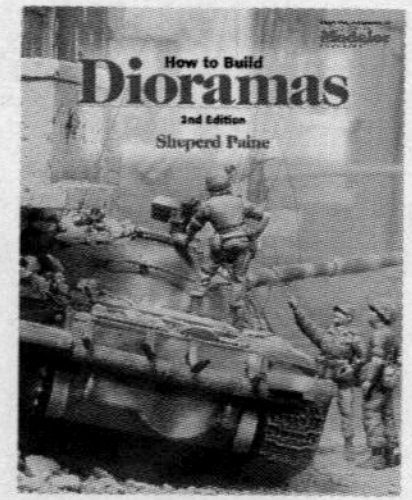

400-12136 2nd Edition **24.95**
NEW
With this newly updated book, making realistic dioramas has never been easier. Includes new projects and photos, along with tips on weathering, painting, detailing and more. Softcover, 144 pages, 290+ photos, 41 illustrations, 8-1/4 x 10-3/4".

HOW TO BUILD MODEL RAILROAD BENCHWORK

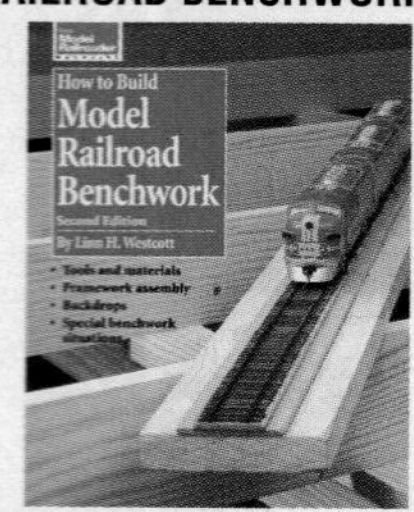

400-12175 2nd Edition **12.95**
New tools, materials and techniques that make benchwork construction easy. 80 pages, 115 B&W photos and 120 illustrations.

SCENERY TIPS & TECHNIQUES

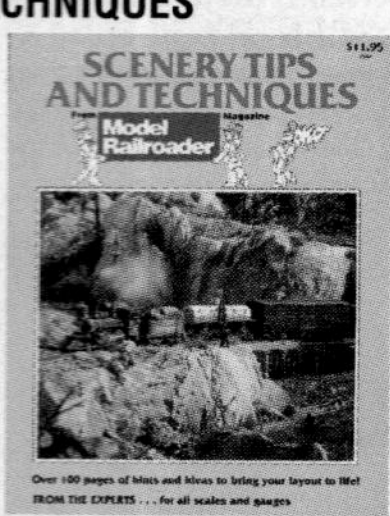

400-12084 15.95
A collection of scenery articles from Model Railroader magazine. Covers all scales, new ideas and new materials. 116 pages, 8-1/4 x 10-3/4".

A TREASURY OF MODEL RR PHOTOS

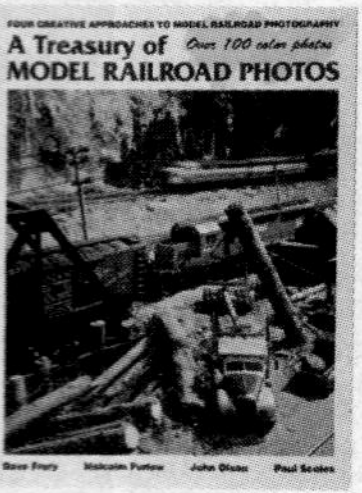

400-12095 16.95
Four respected model railroad photographers chronicle their work with over 100 examples of their craft. 104 pages, over 100 color photos, 8-1/4 x 11-1/4".

HOW TO BUILD REALISTIC MODEL RAILROAD SCENERY

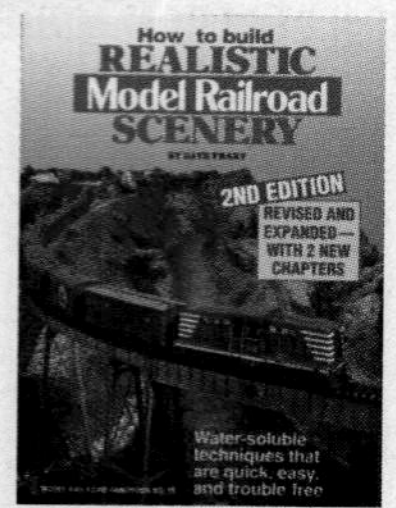

400-12100 2nd Edition **18.95**
A "cookbook" approach to creating workable scenery. 132 pages, B&W and color photos, 8-1/2 x 11-1/4".

MODEL RAILROAD BRIDGES AND TRESTLES

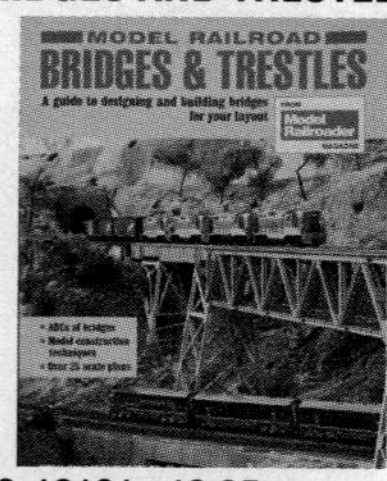

400-12101 19.95
Includes 12 construction plans, prototype photos and over 20 sets of scale drawings. 152 pages, 8-1/2 x 11".

HO RAILROAD FROM START TO FINISH

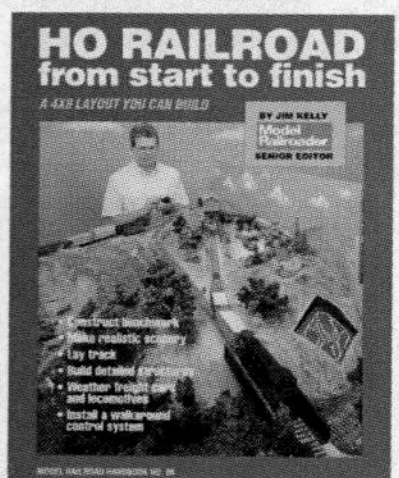

400-12121 14.95
Beginner's book on the construction of the HO Scale Cripple Creek Central. Covers everything from benchwork to rolling stock, avoids power tools and messy materials. 100 photos, 8-1/4 x 10 x 3/4".

HOW TO PAINT REALISTIC MILITARY FIGURES

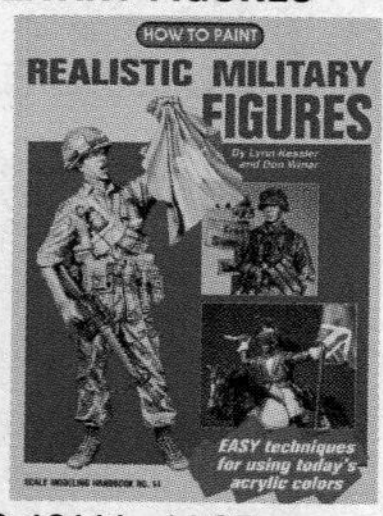

400-12111 14.95
Easy techniques for using todays acrylic colors. Advice on choosing the proper tools, light and shadow effects for displaying figures and creating simple dioramas. 84 pages, 116 color photos, 8-1/4 x 11-1/4".

222 TIPS FOR BUILDING MODEL RAILROAD STRUCTURES

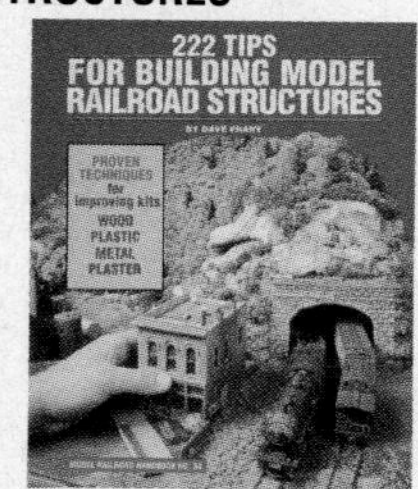

400-12115 11.95
Answers to hundreds of questions. 8-1/2 x 11".

EASY MODEL RAILROAD WIRING

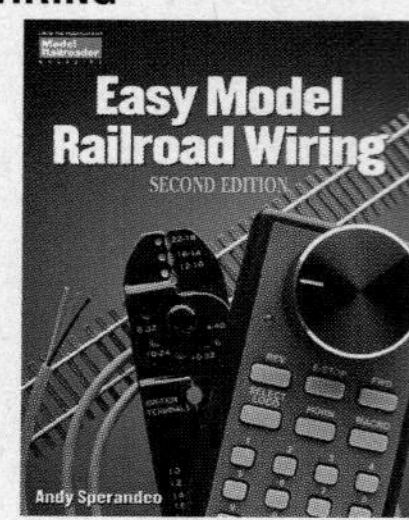

400-12207 2nd Edition **19.95**
NEW
Provides easy and reliable layout wiring techniques that every level of modeler needs to know. Each chapter includes photos, illustrations and detailed schematics. Softcover, 128 pages, 80 B&W photos, 160 illustrations, 8-1/4 x 10-3/4".

MAINTAINING & REPAIRING YOUR SCALE MODEL TRAINS

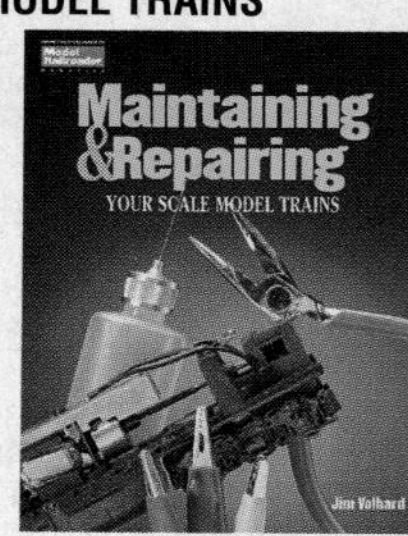

400-12210 15.95 ***NEW***
With simple, instructional information, this book covers the basic techniques needed to maintain and repair DC-powered scale model locos, rolling stock and layouts. 80 pages, 150 B&W photos, 8-1/4 x 10-3/4".

48 TOP-NOTCH TRACK PLANS FROM MODEL RAILROADER

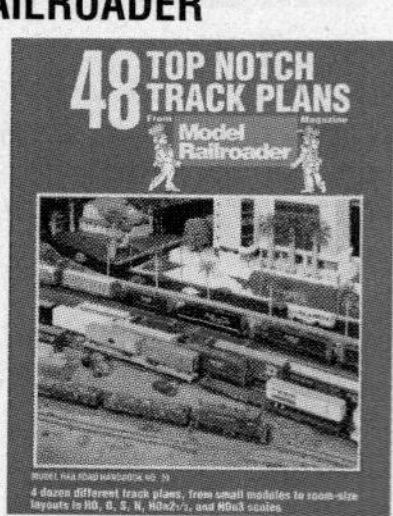

400-12132 16.95
You'll find a layout to fit any space limit or scale preference including HO (HOn2-1/2 and HOn3), O, S, N and Z scales. 120 pages, 220 B&W and 100 color photos, 8-1/4 x 10-3/4".

See What's Available at

www.walthers.com

6 HO RAILROADS YOU CAN BUILD FROM MODEL RAILROADER

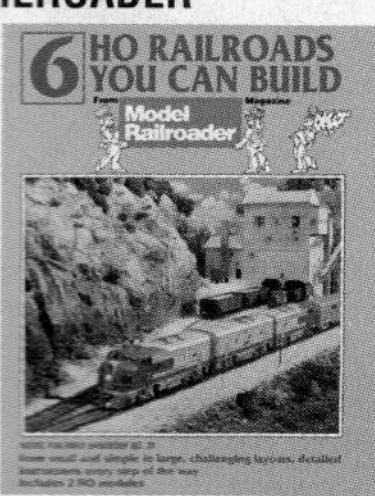

400-12131 18.95
Six HO layout plans ranging from beginning through more complicated and challenging projects. Detailed instructions cover everything. 144 pages, 200 color photos, 8-1/4 x 10-3/4".

HO TRACKSIDE STRUCTURES YOU CAN BUILD

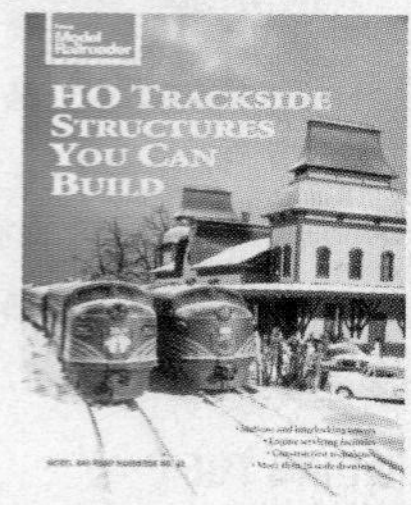

400-12143 14.95
A variety of railroad structures and construction techniques. Techniques cover both wood and styrene construction, and drawings of additional structures are included. 120 pages, 145 B&W and 15 color photos, 150 illustrations, 8-1/4 x 10-3/4".

20 CUSTOM DESIGNED TRACK PLANS

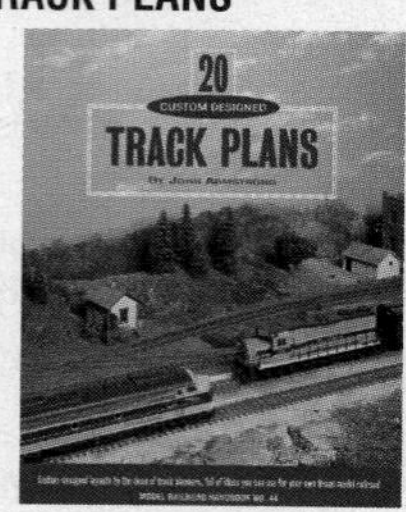

400-12133 15.95
Each plan begins with the size of railroad desired, era, operating priorities etc. Then a track plan is created. 96 pages, 50 B&W photos, 40 illustrations, 8-1/2 x 10-3/4".

RAILROADS & REFERENCE

TWILIGHT OF THE GREAT TRAINS

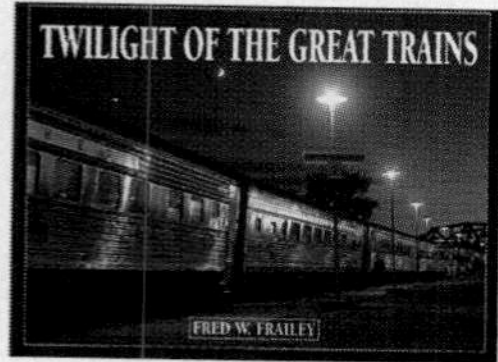

400-1066 49.95
Reveals the never-before-told story of how and why passenger service declined in the years after World War II. Traces the fall of the pre-Amtrak passenger train and how eleven rail systems fought off the inevitable. 200 pages, 150 B&W and 64 color photos, 11 x 8-1/2".

BURLINGTON NORTHERN ACROSS THE HEARTLAND

400-1087 18.95
Dramatic action photos feature the classy stainless steel Zephyr passenger train as well as steam and diesel-powered trains. 128 pages, 120 B&W photos, 11 x 8-1/2".

NEW HAVEN RAILROAD ALONG THE SHORELINE

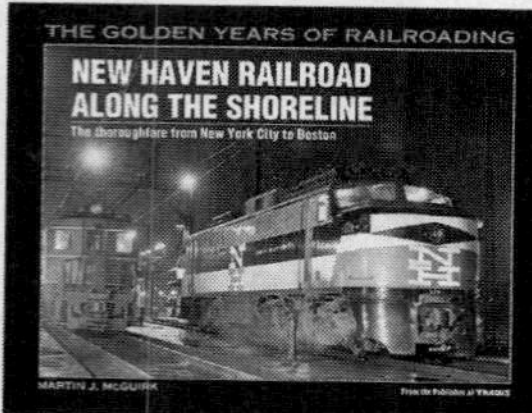

400-1088 18.95
Timeless photos capture the steam, diesel and electric locomotives and the eclectic paint schemes of the 1940s and 50s, as well as historic landmarks in New York City and Boston. 128 pages, 120 B&W photos, 11 x 8-1/2".

THE HISTORICAL GUIDE TO NORTH AMERICAN RAILROADS

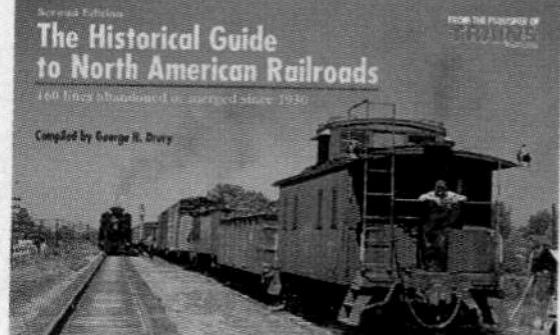

400-1092 2nd Edition **28.95**
NEW
If a line has merged, closed or been abandoned, it is listed here. This book contains a comprehensive listing of all the important railroad mergers since 1930. Softcover, 480 pages, 249 B&W photos, 128 illustrations, 8-1/4 x 5-1/2".

CONTEMPORARY DIESEL SPOTTER'S GUIDE

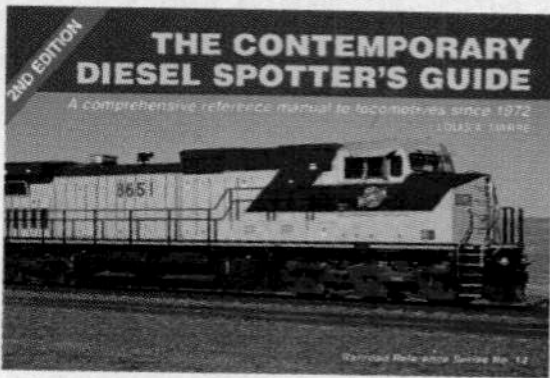

400-1068 2nd Edition **21.95**
Photos and descriptions of locomotives built for service in North America since 1972. 352 pages, 500 B&W photos and 5 illustrations, 8-1/4 x 5-1/2".

F UNITS: THE DIESELS THAT DID IT

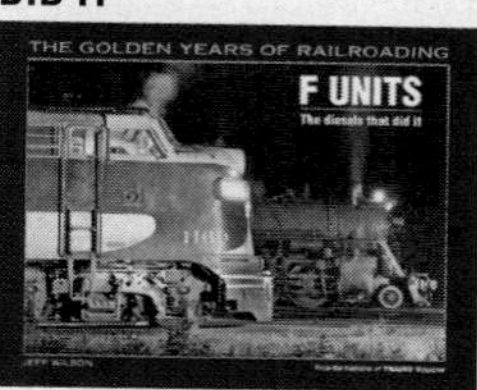

400-1098 19.95 *NEW*
Experience the diesel locomotive that ran steam locos out of operation with this book full of vintage photos and action shots of FTs, F3s, F7s, F9s and more. Features production histories and some prototype illustrations. Softcover, 128 pages, 120 B&W photos, 11 x 8-1/2".

WISCONSIN CENTRAL: RAILROAD SUCCESS STORY

400-1069 49.95
Analyzes the Wisconsin Central and what makes it the most successful regional railroad. Hardcover, 160 pages, 106 color photos, 3 maps, 11 x 8-7/16".

SOUTHERN PACIFIC IN THE BAY AREA: THE SAN FRANCISCO-SACRAMENTO-STOCKTON TRIANGLE

400-1070 18.95
Southern Pacific from the golden years just before WWII to the mid-1950s. 128 pages, 120 B&W photos, 11 x 8-1/2".

DOMELINERS: YESTERDAY'S TRAINS OF TOMORROW

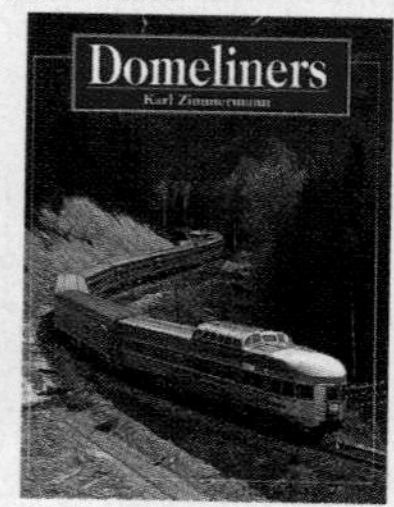

400-1076 49.95
Traces the history of dome cars from their earliest construction to the end of their era. Hardcover, 128 pages, 60 B&W and 60 color photos.

PENNSY STREAMLINERS: THE BLUE RIBBON FLEET

400-1077 48.95 *NEW*
An in-depth look at the history of the Pennsy passenger fleet with documentation from the Pennsy archives. Covers the rise, dominance and decline of the famous line's luxury rail service. Hardcover, 160 pages, 104 B&W and 36 color photos, 11 x 8-3/4".

HEART OF THE PENNSYLVANIA RAILROAD

Limited Quantity Available
400-1071 18.95
Nostalgic look at the Pennsylvania from just prior to WWII through the mid-1950s. 128 pages 120 B&W photos, 11 x 8-1/2".

AMERICAN SHORTLINE RAILWAY GUIDE

400-1073 5th Edition **24.95**
A ready reference for nearly 600 shortline and regional railroads in the United States and Canada. 320 pages, 100 B&W photos, 8-1/4 x 5-1/2".

PULLMAN PAINT AND LETTERING NOTEBOOK

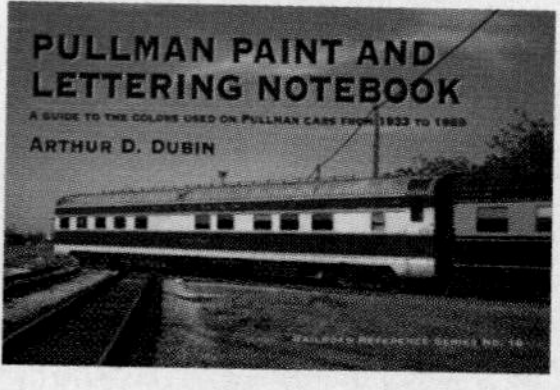

400-1075 24.95
Provides details on the paint schemes of the Pullman Company passenger cars of the 1930s and 40s. 160 pages, 40 B&W photos, 250 illustrations, 40 paint samples, 8-1/4 x 5-1/2".

MILWAUKEE ROAD IN ITS HOMETOWN

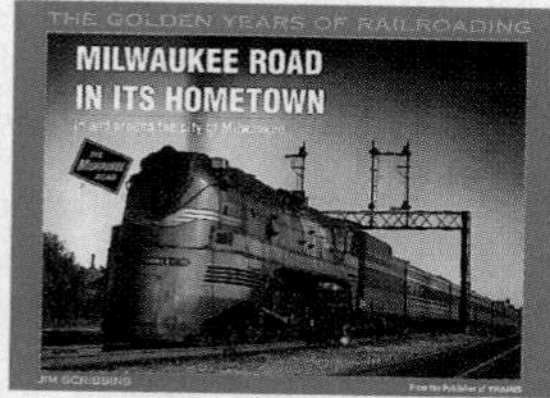

400-1080 18.95
A guided tour from 1945 to 1955. 128 pages, 120 B&W photos, 11 x 8-1/2".

CONFESSIONS OF A TRAIN-WATCHER FOUR DECADES OF RAILROAD WRITING

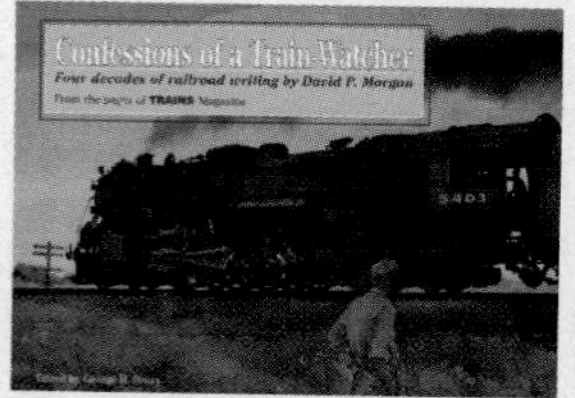

400-1081 39.95
David P. Morgan, longtime editor of Trains magazine, takes the reader back to the 50s, 60s and 70s, detailing locomotives, passenger trains, train travel and more. 160 pages, 85 B&W photos, 11 x 8-7/16".

NORFOLK AND WESTERN IN THE APPALACHIANS

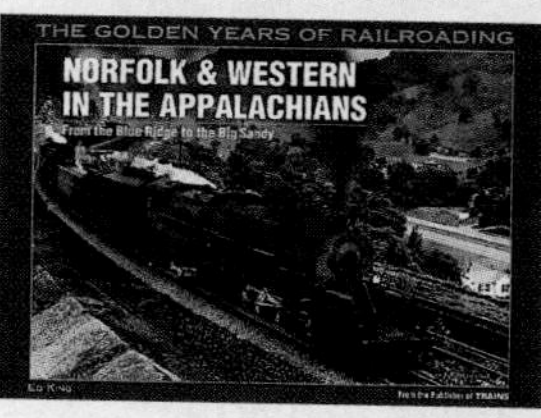

400-1083 18.95
A look back at the last major railroad to use steam locomotives. 128 pages, 120 B&W photos, 11 x 8-1/2".

MODEL RAILROADER CYCLOPEDIA VOL 1: STEAM LOCOMOTIVES

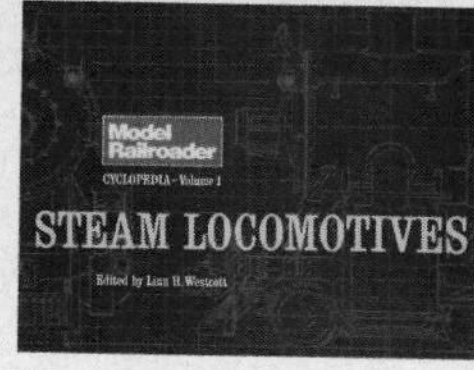

400-1001 49.95
Tells what all the piping, springs and pumps are for. 272 pages, 127 HO Scale drawings, 700 photos, 14 x 11".

MODEL RAILROADER CYCLOPEDIA VOL 2: DIESEL LOCOMOTIVES

400-1033 34.95
Large-format pages of HO Scale plans and photos of diesel locos are included, also a primer on diesel operation and components. 160 pages, photos, illustrations, 14 x 11".

THE ART OF RAILROAD PHOTOGRAPHY: TECHNIQUES FOR TAKING DRAMATIC TRACKSIDE PICTURES

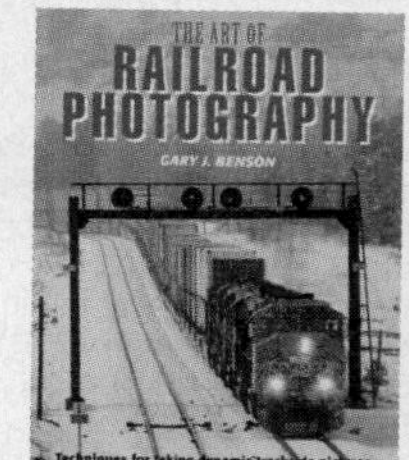

400-1055 39.95
Color pictorial filled with grand and unconventional photography, plus tested techniques for improving your own shots. Hardcover, 152 pages, 130+ color photos, 8-1/4 x 11-1/4".

GUIDE TO NORTH AMERICAN STEAM LOCOMOTIVES

400-1051 27.95
The development of steam locomotives on all North American railroads since 1900. 400 pages, 400 + B&W photos, 8-1/4 x 5-1/2".

DIESEL LOCOMOTIVES: THE FIRST 50 YEARS

400-1054 27.95
How did the diesel evolve? How did that design evolve? What about the designs that didn't? How do you distinguish one from another? Find out as the history of the diesel is traced. 480 pages, 500 photos, 8-1/4 x 5-1/2".

MANHATTAN GATEWAY

Limited Quantity Available
400-1057 44.95
The history of Pennsylvania Station from the first proposals in the late 1800s to the glory years in the 1920s, to demolition of the building in the 1960s. 160 pages, 150 B&W and 16 color photos, 8-1/2 x 11".

THE NICKEL PLATE STORY

400-1059 74.95
The entire story of this historic line is told from its early days through its final mainline steam run in 1958 and merger with N&W in 1964. Hardcover, 484 pages, 600 B&W photos, 15 illustrations, 8-1/2 x 11".

SANTA FE IN THE MOUNTAINS

400-1060 18.95
Santa Fe over the Tehachapi Mountains, Raton Pass and Cajon Pass. 128 pages, 120 photos, 11 x 8-1/2".

BURLINGTON NORTHERN DIESEL LOCOMOTIVES: 3 DECADES OF BN POWER

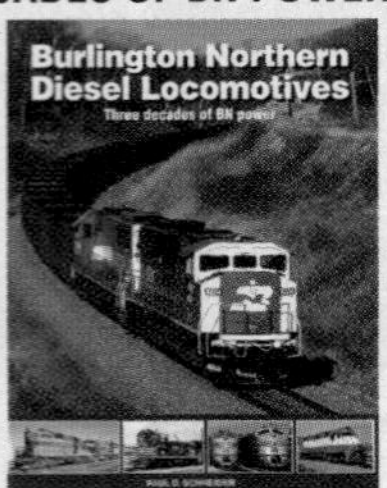

400-1053 54.95
Former BN employee traces the motive power history of Burlington Northern. Hardcover, 160 pages, 175 color photos, 8-1/4 x 11-1/4".

UP ACROSS SHERMAN HILL: BIG BOYS, CHALLENGERS & STREAMLINERS

400-1091 19.95 ***NEW***
Sherman Hill, Wyoming, provides the perfect backdrop for the hardworking Big Boys and Challengers. Included are a route map of the railway, vintage photos and prototype details. Softcover, 128 pages, 120 B&W photos, 11 x 8-1/2".

SOUTHERN PACIFIC'S BLUE STREAK MERCHANDISE

400-1048 39.95
Author Fred Frailey reveals how the train survived six decades from its beginnings during the Great Depression. Hardcover, 168 pages, 8-1/2 x 11-1/2".

COMPENDIUM OF RAILROAD RADIO FREQUENCIES

400-1101 15th Edition **18.95**
NEW
This is the ultimate source for listening to railroad communications. Includes frequencies for the U.S. and six other countries. Softcover, 208 pages, 10 maps, 8-1/2 x 5-1/2".

GUIDE TO TOURIST RAILROAD & MUSEUMS

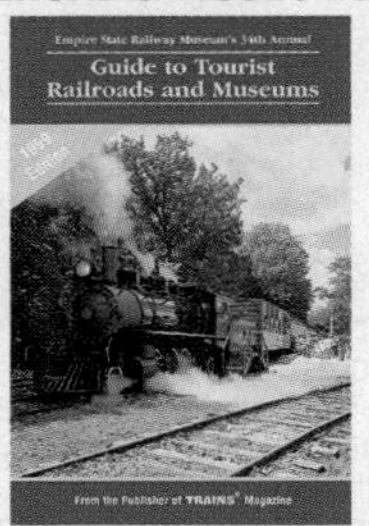

400-1099 34th Edition **15.95**
NEW
This updated version of the popular best seller once again has all the information you need to plan a railroading trip across the country. Includes coupons for savings on entrance fees and tickets and 73 new listings. Softcover, 512 pages, 400 B&W photos, 5-1/2 x 8-1/2".

VIDEOS

AIRBRUSHING WITH ACRYLIC PAINTS

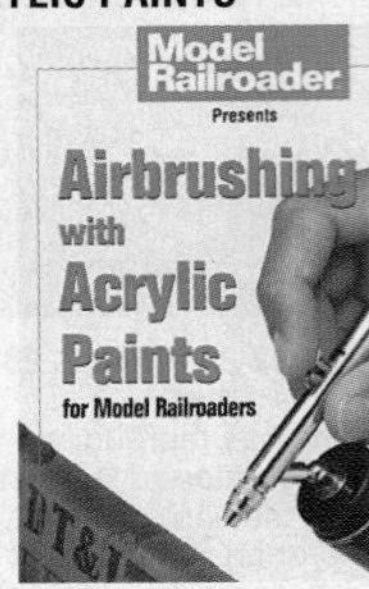

400-15007 29.95
Teaches painting techniques to create one-of-a-kind pieces for your layout.

MODEL RAILROAD SCENERY MADE EASY

400-15049 29.95
Watch as the staff of Model Railroader reveals the mysteries of building layout scenery. Learn everything from carving rocks, to mixing paints, pouring water and planting trees. 60 minutes.

MODEL RAILROADER PRESENTS UNION PACIFIC'S DONNER PASS

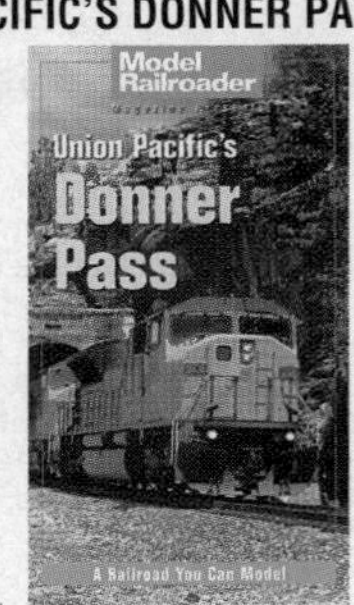

400-15038 29.95
Includes everything you need to recreate Donner Pass on your layout including tracks, tunnels, bridges, maps and more. 60 minutes.

Hot New Products Announced Daily! Visit Walthers Web site at

www.walthers.com

RAILS AROUND THE BAY AREA

400-15034 29.95
Check out the hot spots of the beautiful Bay Area.

CAJON PASS, CALIFORNIA

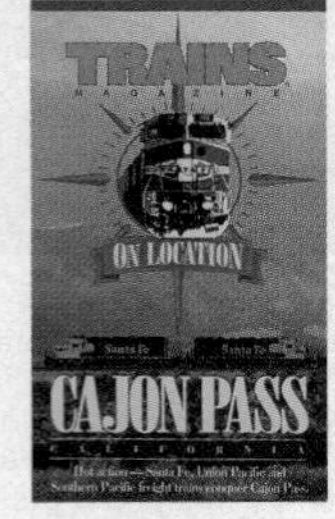

400-15025 29.95
Experience the drama. 60 minutes.

HORSESHOE CURVE: CONRAIL'S MOUNTAIN RAILROAD

400-15026 29.95
Visit Conrail's main line through the mountains of Pennsylvania. 60 minutes.

BURLINGTON NORTHERN'S CHICAGO RACETRACK

400-15027 29.95
One of the Midwest's busiest, fastest railroads—Burlington Northern's Chicago-Aurora main line. 60 minutes.

CASCADE CROSSING: SOUTHERN PACIFIC IN OREGON

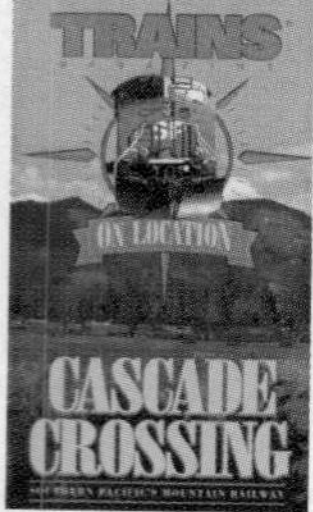

400-15029 29.95
The story of Southern Pacific's mountainous main line in the Cascade range of western Oregon. 60 minutes.

CONRAIL'S CHICAGO GATEWAY

400-15030 29.95
Tour Conrail's busy main line across Northwestern Indiana and through its "gateway" to Chicago. 60 minutes.

AMTRAK'S NORTHEAST CORRIDOR

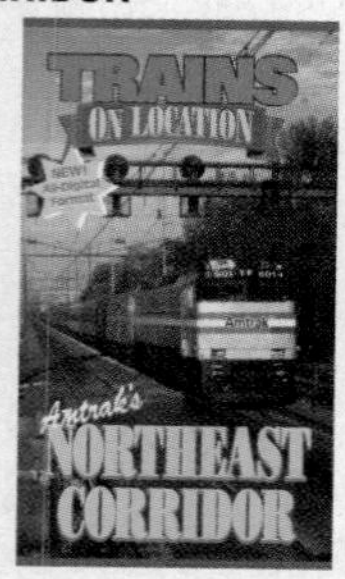

400-15031 29.95
Ride with Amtrak witnessing high-speed trains behind AEM-7 and E60 electrics, as well as the 30th Street Station in Philadelphia. 60 minutes.

TEHACHAPI!

400-15032 29.95
The most celebrated train-watching location in the West—Southern Pacific's crossing of the Tehachapi Mountains in Southern California. 60 minutes.

HEART OF THE WISCONSIN CENTRAL

400-15033 29.95
Experience the excitement of America's premier regional railroad. 60 minutes.

SAND PATCH IN THE ALLEGHANY MOUNTAINS

400-15035 29.95
Travel the CSX main line between Cumberland, Maryland, and the summit of the Alleghenies at Sand Patch, Pennsylvania.

CONRAIL IN NEW ENGLAND

400-15043 29.95 ***NEW***
Enjoy one last look at the "big blue railroad's" most scenic main lines as you visit some of New England's most popular train watching spots.

STEVENS PASS: BNSF CONQUERS THE CASCADES

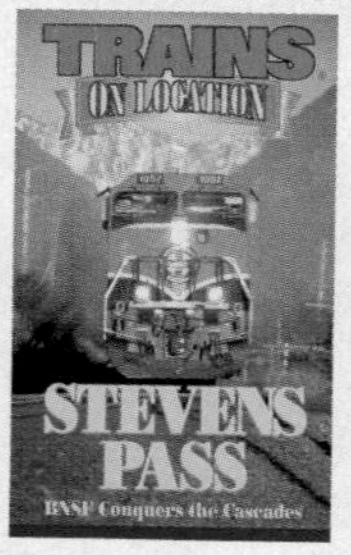

400-15036 29.95
Discover why this is one of the premier train-watching spots in America!

TODAY'S EMD DIESELS

400-15037 19.95
The best of EMD locomotives from the files of Trains On Location video series.

FEATHER RIVER: UNION PACIFIC'S CANYON CROSSING

400-15039 29.95
Journey through the canyon to horseshoe curve at James, the Honeymoon Tunnels, Williams Loop and Keddie Wye. 60 minutes.

MOJAVE MAINLINE

400-15040 29.95
See exotic desert scenery as the BNSF Needles Sub covers 168 miles of double-track main line from Needles to Barstow, California. 60 minutes.

CANADIAN CROSSROADS

400-15041 29.95
Some of Canada's most exciting railroading comes alive on Canadian Crossing. 60 minutes.

POWDER RIVER SHOWDOWN

400-15042 29.95
Witness the thundering parade of countless BNSF and UP coal trains serving rich eastern Wyoming coal mines. 60 minutes.

COLORADO'S JOINT LINE

400-15044 29.95 ***NEW***
Visit 119 miles of railroad jointly operated by BNSF and UP. Enjoy the history, operations and rolling stock of this amazing line. Color, 60 minutes.

APPALACHIAN CONQUEST: CSX'S CORBIN LINE

400-15028 29.95
CSX's Corbin Division main line in Kentucky and Tennessee. 60 minutes.

CALENDARS

MODEL RAILROADER 2000 CALENDAR

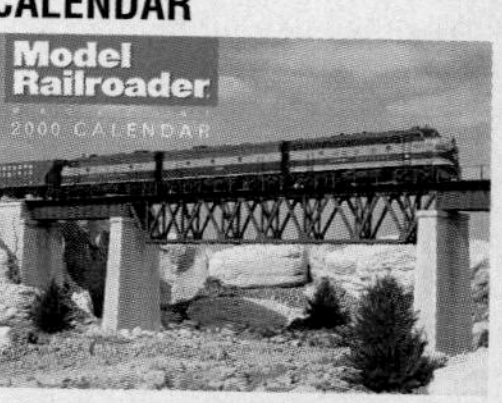

400-68110 12.95 ***NEW***
Captures the amazing lifelike scenes of model railroading in full-color. Detailed information is provided with each photo.

CLASSIC TOY TRAINS 2000 CALENDAR

400-68112 12.95 ***NEW***
Detailed information accompanies every photo of the action packed layouts from Lionel, American Flyer, Marx Hi-Rail and more.

TRAINS 2000 CALENDAR

400-68113 12.95 ***NEW***
Spectacular trains and breathtaking scenery show today's railroads hard at work. Detailed descriptions accompany each of the twelve photos.

TRAINS CLASSIC 2000 CALENDAR: GOLDEN YEARS OF RAILROADING

400-68115 12.95 ***NEW***
Each month features a classic black and white photo that brings back the Golden Years of Railroading.

krause publications

Read about your favorite kinds of model railroading in this line of affordable softcover books.

THE HO MODEL RAILROADING HANDBOOK 3RD EDITION

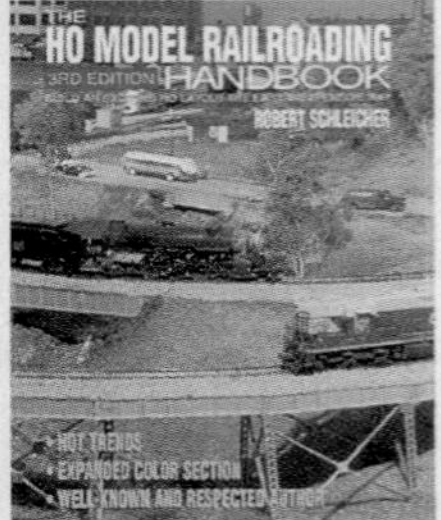

213-8346 19.95
Learn to build layouts with up-to-the minute techniques and products. Presented in an easy to use style with ideas for modelers of all skill levels. Third edition, 8-1/2 x11", 224 pages.

STANDARD GUIDE TO ATHEARN MODEL TRAINS

213-6317 24.95
Features more than 4,000 models and a handy checklist to track your collection. Designed for use by novices and professional collectors. 8-1/2 x 11", 288 pages.

COLLECTING TOY TRAINS-IDENTIFICATION & VALUE GUIDE

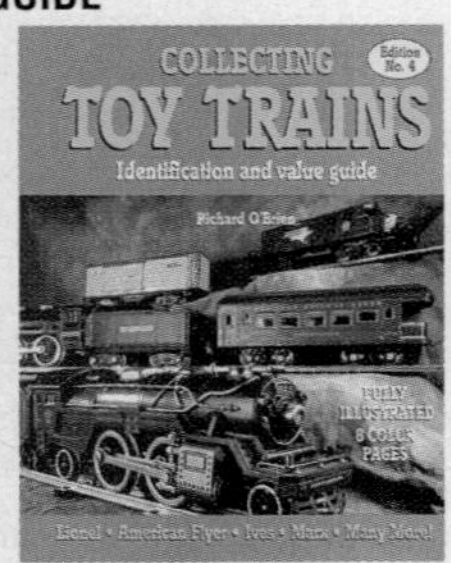

213-1203 24.95
Examines the history of notable American toy train makers, including Ives, American Flyer, Lionel and more. Selected examples of current collector's market prices too. 1200 black and white photos plus 37 color photos, 8-1/2 x 11", 432 pages.

LARGE SCALE MODEL RAILROADING HANDBOOK

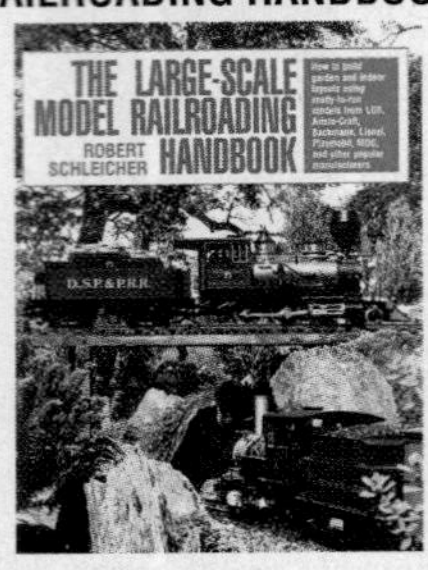

213-8229 18.95
Learn how to build, design and operate a large scale layout indoors or out. Also includes tips for maintaining and upgrading locos. 8-1/4 x 10-7/8", 224 pages.

THE BROWN BOOK OF BRASS LOCOMOTIVES-THIRD EDITION

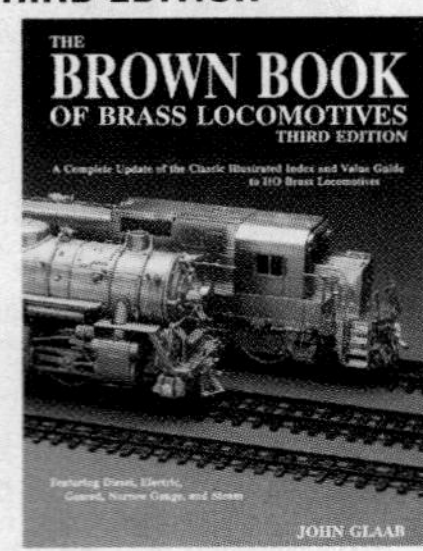

213-8395 24.95
Market prices for all types of brass locos in an updated third edition. Engines are listed by class, manufacturer and importer. Information on production run size, original selling price and many illustrations help you buy or sell models. 8-1/4 x 10-7/8", 288 pages.

COLLECTOR'S GUIDE TO AMERICAN TOY TRAINS

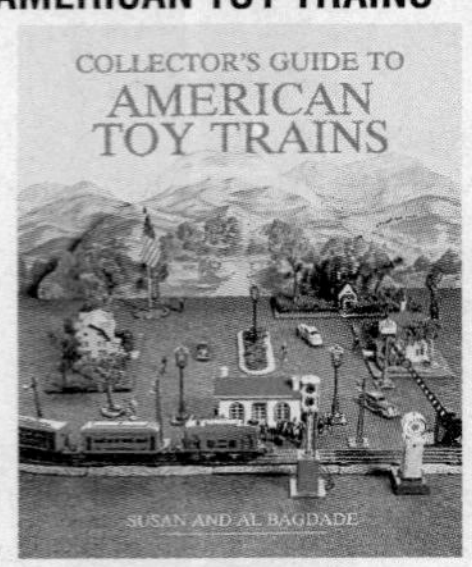

213-1204 19.95
Accurate identification and latest market prices for Lionel, Marx, American Flyer, Ives, Buddy L and other popular lines. Top collectors provide price information for models. New photos and many first-time listings have been added. 7-1/2 x 9", 244 pages with 4 color pages!

SCENERY FOR MODEL RAILROADS, DIORAMAS AND MINIATURES

213-8503 22.95 ***NEW***
Details the easiest and most effective methods for creating scenery. Techniques are explained with easy-to-follow directions. Includes reference cards providing recipes for colors, an expanded color section and directions for all-season scenery. 8-1/2 x 11", 120 B&W photos, 16 page color section,160 pages.

L & H
RAILSONICS
EST. 1978

RAILROAD RECORDINGS

L&H Railsonics cassettes and CDs are stereo recordings. Opened cassettes and CDs will be replaced if defective, but cannot be returned for credit or refund.

DIESEL SUPER POWER

138-4017 Cassette **9.98**
SW1500, GP20, GP30, GP35, SD40-2, SDP40F, SD45 SDP45, SD45T-2, F45, DD35 A & B, DD40AX, U23B, U25B, DL-640 and DL-721. Features recordings at Donner and Cajon Pass.

HIGH COUNTRY STEAM

138-4058 Cassette **9.98**
Cumbres & Toltec passenger trains, caught in a thunderstorm, steam rotary OM and the days of common carrier freight operation. Recordings made on DRGW Narrow Gauge in the 1960s and 1970s.

DIESEL TRACKS-BIG ENGINES AND HEAVY RAIL

138-4096 Cassette **9.98**
UP Williams Loop, BN SD60s in the Columbia River Gorge, two NS freights on Old Fort Mtn., Santa Fe freights roaring across the desert at 70mph and grinding up Tehachapi, Horsehoe Curve, Amtrak Zephyr at Blue Canyon and more.

A DECADE OF STEAM VOL 1

138-4067 Cassette **9.98**
UP 3985 4-6-6-4, SOU 2716 2-8-4, SP 4449 4-8-4, SOU 610 2-10-4, Chessie 614 4-8-4, UP 8444 4-8-4, RDG 2102 4-8-4, Sierra 28-2-8-0, Sierra 34 2-8-2, SOU 2839 4-6-4.

STEAM TRACKS VOL 3 "GIANTS MEET"

The engines that attended Railfair '91, the '91 and '92 Conventions and the '90 Yakima steam meet. Hear the big engines working hard and running fast.

138-4111 Cassette **9.98**
138-6111 CD **12.98**

THE SOUND OF STEAM (NOSTALGIA SERIES)

138-7002 Cassette **11.98**
PRR K-4 Pacifics, RDG T-1s, CN 4-8-4s, CP 4-4-0 and 4-6-0 DM&IR 2-8-8-4s and much more.

MODELERS SOUNDS, STEAM

138-3001 Cassette **9.98**
Steam engine sounds with long sequences of stack talk and whistling. Especially for railroad background sounds.

FIRST GENERATION DIESELS VOL 1

138-4010 Cassette **9.98**
Features early EMD, Alco and Baldwin power.

FIRST GENERATION DIESELS VOL 2

138-4055 Cassette **9.98**
EMD: F3, F7, F9, FL9, GP7; Alco: PA1, RS1, RS2, RS3; FM: H10-44, H12-44; Baldwin: S12, RS12.

DAYLIGHT 4449 SOUNDS RECORDING OF THE WORLD'S FAIR DAYLIGHT

138-4078 Cassette **9.98**

STEAM TRACKS VOL 1

138-4085 Cassette **9.98**
Locomotives include Norfolk & Southern 2-6-6-4 1218, SP 4-8-4 4449, NKP 2-8-4 765 plus engines from the Pennsy, RDG and Sierra.

STEAM TRACKS VOL 2

CN 6060, CP (BCR) 2860 and 3716 "Alberta Bound," NKP 587, NS 611 and 1218, UP 8444, Grand Canyon Railway, SP 4449 on Cantara Loop, East Broad Top.

138-4095 Cassette **9.98**
138-6095 CD **12.98**

STEAM'S SUNSET

138-7000 Cassette **9.98**
Sounds of steam on the Canadian Prairies and Duluth, Missabe & Iron Range Yellowstones, 1958-59.

Mayfair Games

GAMES

Silverton 487-469

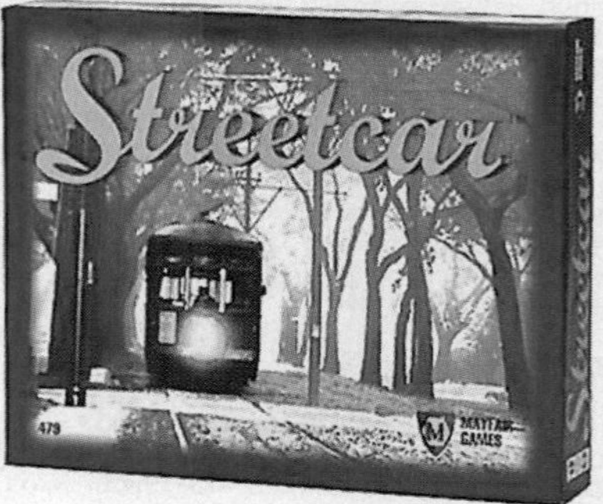

Streetcar™ 487-479

SILVERTON
487-469 45.00
Railroad through Colorado, Utah and New Mexico during the gold and silver rushes of the late 1800s. Acquire various freight loads and discover the best routes to succeed. Ages 10 to adult, up to six players.

STREETCAR™
487-479 30.00
Be the first to complete your route and race your trolley across New Orleans.

UNCLE HAPPY'S TRAIN

487-466 14.95
Simplified version of Empire Builder. For 2-6 players, ages 6 to adult.

FREIGHT TRAIN
487-484 20.00
Get points by building trains from the engine up.

EMPIRE BUILDER

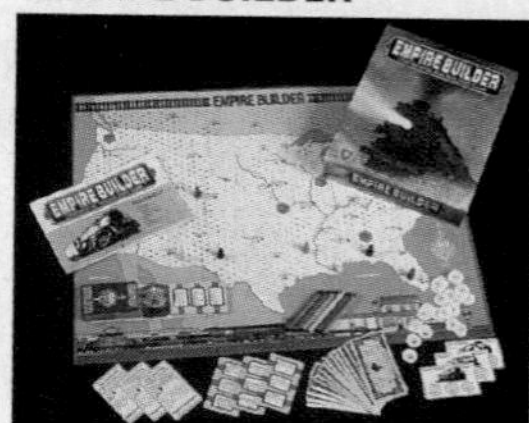

487-450 35.00
Operate a rail empire in an effort to accumulate the most money. For 2 to 6 players, ages 12 to adult.

1870™

487-471 45.00
Takes players to the trans-Mississippi Valley. For 3 to 7 players, ages 16 and up.

EMPIRE BUILDER MINIATURES
487-1040 5.95
Includes four locos: the Big Boy, the J, the GP30 and the Consolidation. Each is designed for use with Empire Builder and related games and/or as collectibles.

1835™
487-550 60.00
Railway building and share speculation set in Germany. Players that become directors of companies manipulate their railroads, making their companies stronger and themselves rich. For 3 to 7 players, ages 16 to adult.

INDIA RAILS

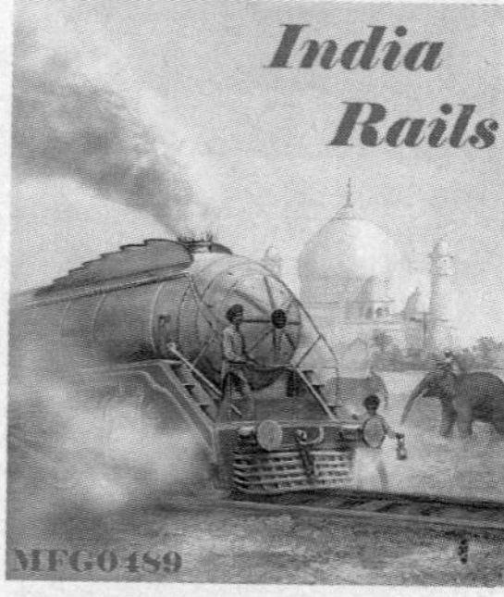

487-489 35.00
Features the exotic lands of India and exotic cargoes like gypsum, indigo, jute and rugs. The latest Empire Builder® System game in boxed format, complete with pilgrims.

EURORAILS

487-457 35.00
Eurorails allows players to amass fortune and power. For 2 to 6 players, ages 12 to adult.

DAMPFROSS

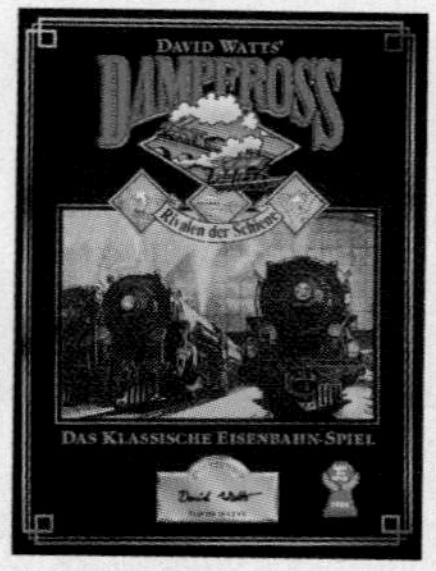

487-556 50.00
A game of building rail lines and racing trains. Includes English and German rules, 3 to 6 players, ages 10 and up.

1856™

487-472 45.00
Explores the growth of railroads in southern Ontario. Engage in corporate raiding, stock manipulation and insider trading. For 3 to 7 players, ages 16 and up.

IRON DRAGON

487-467 30.00
Fantasy and reality meet in this exciting game. The Iron Dragons cross a make-believe world, delivering treasures to those in need. Magical items make every game a new adventure through the unknown.

EXPRESS

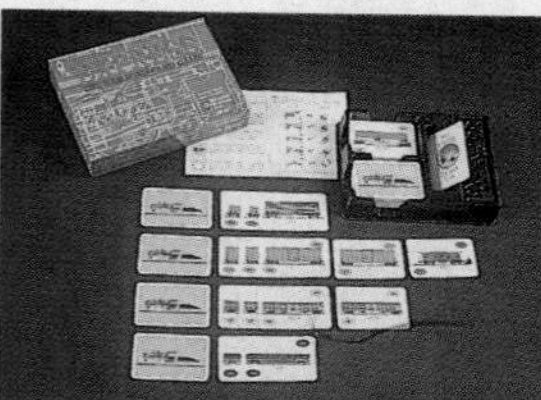

487-458 15.00
A unique card game as easy to learn as rummy. Players start with a one-car train and build on to maximize points and bonuses. For 2 to 6 players, ages 8 to adult.

BRITISH RAILS/NIPPON RAILS/AUSTRALIAN RAILS EA 25.00
Travel the world in this exciting series of games from the Empire Builder® system.

487-1450 Nippon Rails
Railbuilding on the islands of Japan.
487-1452 British Rails
Explore railroading in the United Kingdom.
487-1453 Australia Rails
Takes the railroad fan "Down Under" to Australia.

MOUNTAINS IN MINUTES

WALL SIGN/PLAQUE

473-840 Beware of the Trains
9.98
Made of high-density foam, 14 x 10".

NMRA

CABOOSE COUNTRY!

98-12 9.95
Includes portraits of the caboose from early "bobber" types to current "state of the art" cabooses.

FREIGHT TERMINALS & TRAINS
98-14 44.95 *NEW*
Provides detailed information on freight train operations and the design and operation of the facilities that serve them.

1953 OFFICIAL RAILWAY EQUIPMENT REGISTER
98-15 54.95 *NEW*
Lists nearly all the cars used on North American railroads including car numbers and dimensions - inside and out - for cars of all kinds.

NOCH

CATALOG

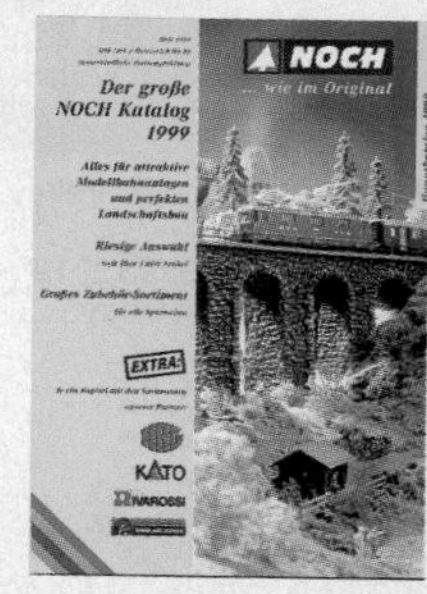

528-71990 6.99 *NEW*
Full-color photos of the entire line of scenery products and supplies for HO, N&Z and G Scales. 162 pages, German text.

ART PRINTS

Duo-tone color process prints, (printed in brown and black) representing both narrow and standard gauge and the 4-4-0 to the 2-8-8-4 locomotives. Printed on 15 x 20" six point cover stock.

Included with each print is a description of each loco, a short informative statement on its wheel arrangement and its disposition.

SIGNATURE SERIES EA 19.95 (UNLESS NOTED)

413-2 Wildcat RR "2" 2-6-2 **15.95**

413-700 The Wabash Cannonball

413-198603 WSL Shay "9" Tuolomne

413-198609 Sumpter Valley, Baker
413-199004 RDG G3 "219"
413-199005 West Point

MIGHTY MALLET SIGNATURE SERIES (13 X 16") EA 19.95

413-1981 GN "1981" 2-6-8-0

413-2601 Erie L-1 Class Mallet
413-4294 Cab Forward

STREAMLINER SIGNATURE SERIES EA 19.95

413-1380 Southern "1380"

413-2102 LV "2102"

413-5304 B&O "5304"

MOUNTAIN CLASS SIGNATURE SERIES

413-179 WP "179" FEC 414, MT44 **19.95**

CALIFORNIA CLASSICS EA 19.95

413-9205 SP "2412" at Milbrae
413-9206 Napa Valley Line "60"

FULL-COLOR PRINT

413-47300 The Winter San Juan Express - Limited Edition **65.00**
A dramatic full-color rendering. 22 x 30", numbered, signed and dated.

413-9039 Up "9039" On Archer Hill **30.00**
This special "unpublished" print by Mike Kotowski is available signed and numbered of a run of 500. 18 x 14-1/4".

413-2479 SP "2479" **40.00**
18 x 22" print of engine No. 2479 at San Jose, California, in the 1930s. Image size 17 x 24". Limited edition of 300 prints; signed and numbered by the artist.

SIGNED PRINTS EA 19.95

413-7 "Skookum" Deep River 2-4-4-2
413-100 MILW "100"
413-118 RDG "118"
413-200 Out of the Moffat Tunnel
413-208 WP, M-80 Class Mallets
413-652 SP "652"
413-800 Virginian 800 Class Mallet
413-808 UP "808" Kansas
413-836 UP "836"
413-1026 Frisco "1026"
413-1218 Class "A" Number 1218
413-1399 ATSF Passenger Mallet
413-1400 NYH&H "1400"
413-1460 Saluda Mountain "1460"
413-1522 Frisco "1522" at Fork Valley
413-1601 Allegheny Barrels Toward Sunlight
413-1607 DRGW "1607" M-75 Heavyweight
413-1801 Dixie Flyers
413-2102 LV "2102"
413-2523 GN "2523" Fast Tracking
413-2584 The First High Stepping GN
413-2860 UP "2860" (13 x 16")
413-2906 UP "2906"
413-2925 All the Way w/ATSF
413-3000 An Ageless High Stepper, SP
413-3001 NYC Mohawk "3001"
413-3003 The Northern Racers
413-3460 The Tallest High Stepper, ATSF
413-3703 DRGW
413-3705 DRGW "J705" Challenger
413-3768 PRR "3768"
413-4001 CNW "4001"
413-4015 UP Big Boy
413-4117 Hercules "4117" B&M
413-4352 San Joaquin SP "4352"
413-5011 SP "5011"
413-5200 The Hudson
413-5302 B&O
413-5304 Royal, Blue—and Fast, B&O
413-5450 NYC J3A "5450"
413-5594 F3 Class "5994" B&O
413-6755 PRR "6755"
413-7002 Pony Express "7002" UP
413-8000 The Race of the Iron Thouroughbreds
413-8444 The Last of the High
413-9201 Pacific Coast "105" at Santa Maria
413-9202 ATSF "3450" at Fresno
413-9203 SP "2921" at Capitola Trestle
413-9204 SP "2479" at San Jose
413-9207 SP "4100" at Niles Tower
413-9208 SP "4402" at Salinas
413-9209 Modesto & Empire Traction "100"
413-9210 WP "94" & SP "3025" at Altamont Pass
413-9211 Stockton Terminal & Eastern "1"
413-9212 ATSF "3940" at Pinole
413-9213 Spokane, Portland & Seattle "700"
413-9214 Sierra Railroad "3" & "34"
413-9215 Cotton Belt "819"
413-9216 NKP "765" vs Pere Marquette "1225"
413-9217 Nevada Northern "40"
413-9218 SP "2472"
413-9219 Cumbres & Toltec "488"
413-9220 Atlantic & West Point "290"
413-9221 ATSF "3731"
413-9222 N&W "611"
413-9223 UP "3985"
413-9224 Blue Mountain & RDG "2102"
413-44492 A Reprieve from the Past
413-60603 Bullet Nose Betty "6060"
413-198601 White Pass & Yukon Dead Horse Gulch
413-198602 Pacific Coast Ry "106"
413-198604 Lake Tahoe's Railroad
413-198605 The Suntan Route
413-198606 Rio Grande Southern at Trout Lake
413-198607 Uintah Ry, Morro Castle
413-198608 Morenci Southern
413-198610 DRGW at Chama
413-198611 SP Narrow Gauge from Keeler
413-198612 Nevada County Narrow Gauge Bear River Bridge
413-199001 NYC's Niagra "5500"
413-199002 NKP
413-199003 SP Espees
413-199006 ATSF
413-199007 N&W's Last Y-66 "2200"
413-199008 NP's Last Challenger "5149"
413-199009 C&O "1309"
413-199010 Rutlands
413-199011 PRR
413-199012 Big Boy

SIGNED PRINTS EA 15.95

413-4 Clover Valley "4" 2-6-6-2T
413-29 Virginia & Truckee "29" 2-8-0
413-94 WP "94" 4-6-0
413-488 DRGW "488" 2-8-2
413-610 Texas & Pacific "610" 2-10-4
413-765 NKP "765" 2-8-4
413-2839 Southern "Royal Hudson" "2839" 4-6-4
413-3025 SP "3025"
413-3811 SP "3811"
413-6060 CN "6060"

BOOKS

LIONEL INSPIRATION

484-998 49.95

ALCO OFFICIAL COLOR

484-1008 49.95 ***NEW***
Find out what your favorite ALCO looked like when it was brand new! Includes 128 pages of company photos from the early 1950s to the very end.

FAIRBANKS MORSE IN COLOR
484-978 49.95

PULLMAN-STANDARD COLOR GUIDE TO FREIGHT EQUIPMENT
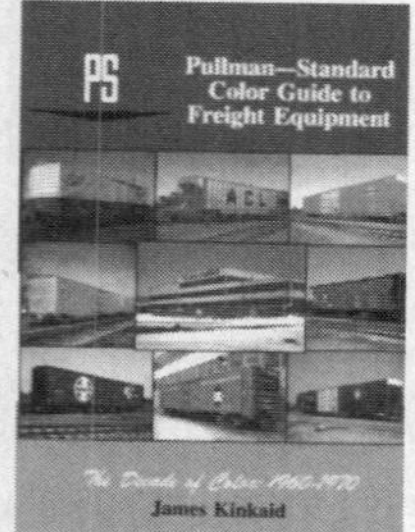

484-955 49.95

NEW YORK CENTRAL LIGHTNING STRIPES
484-67 Volume I **45.00**
Over 200 color photos of steam, diesel and electric locos from the Midwest to Canada. 128 pages.

484-165 Volume II **49.95**
End-to-end tour of the NYC between 1946 and 1968, with special focus on diesel and electric power.

NEW YORK CENTRAL TRACKSIDE WITH EUGENE VAN DUSEN

484-950 49.95
This all-color book features classic 1940s and 50s trackside photos of NYC's Hudsons, Mohawks and Niagaras.

NEW YORK CENTRAL COLOR PHOTOGRAPHY OF ED NOWAK
484-92 Volume I **45.00**
Ed Nowak details his work during 1943-1968 shooting steam and diesel.

484-73 Volume II **49.95**
Takes you behind the lens of NYC's official photographer as he visits New York City, the Hudson River Valley, Buffalo, Chicago and other hot spots during the 1940s, 50s and 60s.128 pages.

484-246 Volume III **49.95**
The concluding book of this series include the GCT, the West Shore, Hudson Division, NE STATES, De Witt, Collinwood and more.

NYC COLOR GUIDE TO FREIGHT AND PASSENGER EQUIPMENT
484-228 49.95
Over 300 color photographs taken from the postwar years into the 1960s with commentary.

NEW YORK CENTRAL STEAM IN COLOR
484-227 49.95
NYC steam is captured in this all-color portfolio of vintage views.

READING COMPANY
484-1002 Volume I **49.95**
Take a ride on the Reading in over 230 color shots of diesels and electrics in operation.

READING STEAM IN COLOR
484-983 49.95
Over 200 color photographs of steam during 1946-1956.

RDG COLOR GUIDE TO FREIGHT AND PASSENGER EQUIPMENT
484-226 49.95
More than 300 color photographs from the postwar period, through the sixties right up to Conrail.

DELAWARE & HUDSON IN COLOR
484-106 Volume I **45.00**
Covers 1946 to 1968 in 185 color photos including 47 rare steam shots. 128 pages.

484-270 Volume II **49.95**
Join us for a trip over the D&H in the between lightning stripes and Guilford. Hardcover, 128 pages.

D&H COLOR GUIDE
484-992 49.95
Over 300 vintage views of the rolling stock of this important bridge line.

LEHIGH VALLEY IN COLOR

484-1014 Volume III **49.95**
NEW
A 128 page hardcover book containing 222 color photos of the many paint schemes of the LV as well as the different diesels during the years of 1952 -1976. An emphasis is placed on the immediate years before CR.

LEHIGH VALLEY IN COLOR
Some 222 pages of color photos, showing units in action from 1952 through 1976.
484-59 Volume I **45.00**
484-33 Volume II **45.00**

CNJ/LV COLOR GUIDE FREIGHT/ PASSENGER
484-954 49.95

JERSEY CENTRAL LINES IN COLOR
484-9 Volume I **45.00**
Mid 1960s. Approximately 200 photos, 128 pages.

484-19 Volume II **49.95**
Camelbacks, Mikados and tangerine & blue Baldwin babyfaces and F3s. Special emphasis is also given to the Pennsylvania Division. 128 pages.

SP&S COLOR GUIDE TO FREIGHT AND PASSENGER EQUIPMENT
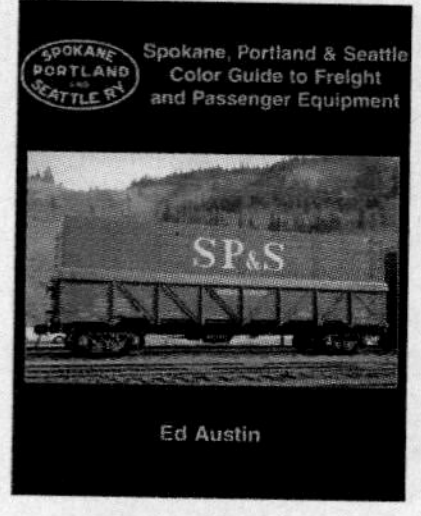

484-945 49.95
The colorful rolling stock of the Pacific Northwest's own railroad is examined through more than 300 color photos.

NORTHERN PACIFIC COLOR GUIDE TO FREIGHT AND PASSENGER CARS
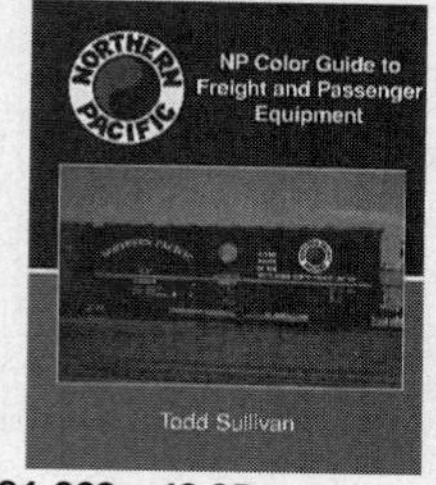

484-963 49.95

GN STEAM & ELECTRIC IN COLOR
484-1016 54.95 ***NEW***

GN COLOR GUIDE FREIGHT/PASSENGER EQUIPMENT

484-952 49.95

CB&Q COLOR GUIDE FREIGHT/ PASSENGER EQUIPMENT
484-953 49.95

CHICAGO BURLINGTON & QUINCY IN COLOR

484-229 Volume I **49.95**
484-959 Volume II **49.95**

ERIE LACKAWANNA COLOR GUIDE TO FREIGHT AND PASSENGER CARS
484-964 49.95

ERIE LACKAWANNA IN COLOR
484-5 Volume I: The West End **45.00**
Take a trip from Chicago to Meadville, PA.

484-122 Volume II: NY State **45.00**
Mainlines and branches are thoroughly documented in color.

484-211 Volume III: The East End **49.95**
The East End highlights the former DL&W mainline Bloomsburg Branch and myriad New Jersey branches. Hardcover, 128 pages

484-994 Volume IV: The Early Years **49.95**
The pre-SD45 black and yellow era replete with lots of cab units and diesel oddities. Hardcover, all color.

ERIE RAILROAD IN COLOR
484-17 45.00
Starts at the ferry slips of Jersey City and proceeds west to Chicago. Photographed in full color between World War II and 1960. 128 pages.

ERIE RAILROAD TRACKSIDE W/ROBERT F. COLLINS
484-1000 49.95
Third book on the Erie showcases the photos of Bob Collins and provides over 225 vintage color views of steam and diesel power in action.

LACKAWANNA RAILROAD TRACKSIDE
484-1017 54.95 ***NEW***

LACKAWANNA RAILROAD IN COLOR
484-83 45.00
Approximately 200 color photos, 128 pages.

SEABOARD AIR LINE COLOR GUIDE TO FREIGHT AND PASSENGER EQUIPMENT
484-1004 49.95
More than 300 color photos of this road which disappeared in 1967.

N&W IN COLOR

484-988 Volume I **49.95**
Focuses on steam and early diesels that rostered the pre-expanded N&W.

SOUTHERN RAILWAY IN COLOR
484-1013 Volume II **49.95**
NEW
A 128 page hardcover book containing over 240 vintage pictures of the SOU.

SOUTHERN COLOR GUIDE TO FREIGHT AND PASSENGER CARS
484-977 49.95

IC IN COLOR
484-975 49.95
Early 1950s right up to the 1972 ICG merger. Half of the book is steam, while still covering black Geeps, handsome E-units and the later orange and white 2nd generation diesels. 128 page, hardcover.

FRISCO IN COLOR
484-961 49.95

PENN CENTRAL COLOR GUIDE TO FREIGHT AND PASSENGER EQUIPMENT

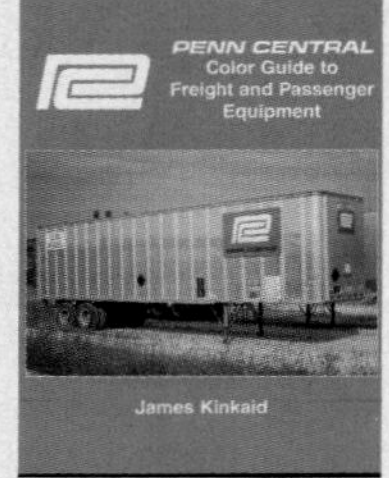

484-948 49.95
The Penn Central had a fascinating eclectic collection of rolling stock, which looks great when new and freshly painted.

PRR TROLLEYS IN COLOR
484-995 Volume I **49.95**
Covers the state's smaller companies in Scranton, Wilkes-Barre, Allentown, Reading, Altoona, Hershey and Lancaster.

484-1001 Volume II The Philadelphia Region **49.95**
An all-color look at trolleys of the Keystone state, featuring the Philadelphia region. This second volume covers the PTC, Red Arrow, P&W and Fairmount Park systems.

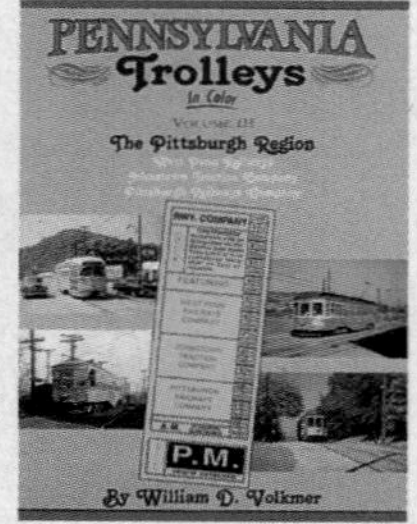

484-1022 Volume III: The Pittsburgh Region **54.95** ***NEW***
The West Penn, Pittsburgh Railways and Johnstown Traction are all covered in the last installment of this series. Includes more than 250 nostalgic color scenes. Hardcover, 128 pages.

PRR: HUDSON TO HORSESHOE
484-231 49.95

PENNSYLVANNIA-READING SEASHORE IN COLOR
484-976 49.95
Covers PRR, RDG and PRSL steam/diesel action in New Jersey.

PRR COLOR GUIDE TO FREIGHT AND PASSENGER EQUIPMENT
484-76 Volume I **45.00**
Everything from baggage cars to business cars, cabins to coaches, wagontops to wire cars are portrayed. 325 color photos, 128 pages.

484-968 Volume II **49.95**
Features early photography of Paul Winters around Columbus, Ohio.

PENNSY STANDARD RAILROAD OF THE WORLD
484-1018 Volume 1 **54.95**
NEW

PENNSY ELECTRIC YEARS
484-7 45.00
Pennsy electric locomotives. 190 full color photos, 128 pages.

PENNSY DIESEL YEARS
484-32 Volume II **45.00**
The diverse diesels of the mighty PRR: such oddities as the rubber-tired diesels, steam-diesel tandems, the unique RS3 "hammerhead," and the rare LS25 Lima transfer unit. Approximately 200 color photos.

484-75 Volume III **45.00**
Travel aboard a Centipede-drawn excursion that starts out at Harrisburg and ends in Detroit! 128 page full color.

484-91 Volume IV **45.00**
A photographic tour of each region, before and after the 1955 realignment. Hundreds of photos, 128 pages.

484-157 Volume V **49.95**
484-967 Volume VI **49.95**
Take trips on the South Wind and Broadway Ltd. in this final installment of the series.

PENNSY STEAM YEARS
Pennsy steam from the forties and fifties. Color, 128 pages.
484-84 Volume I **45.00**
484-996 Volume II **49.95**

UP COLOR GUIDE TO FREIGHT AND PASSENGER EQUIPMENT

484-986 Volume II **49.95**
Since the early 1950s, Lou Schmitz has been shooting color slides of freight, passenger and nonrevenue equipment.

UP STEAM IN COLOR
484-957 49.95

UP TRACKSIDE

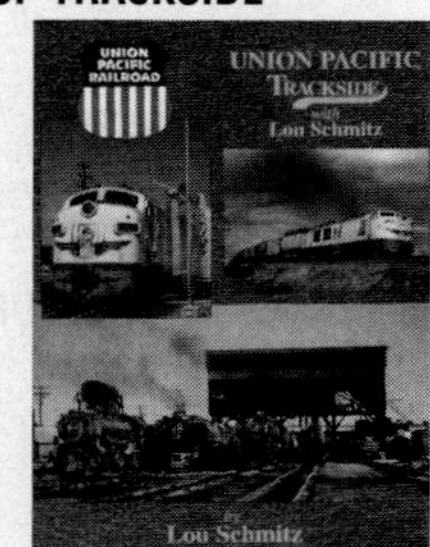

484-1006 49.95 ***NEW***
Shows the steam to diesel transition on the Eastern District of the UP. Over 260 pictures of everything from 4-8-8-4s to F3s to Centennials.

UNION PACIFIC OFFICIAL PHOTOGRAPHY
484-254 Volume I **49.95**
Straight from the UP archives comes the road's 1940s-50s steam and early diesel color photography reproduced to 1990s standards. Hardcover.

UP COLOR GUIDE TO FREIGHT & PASSENGER EQUIPMENT
484-262 Volume I **49.95**
250 of the UP's official 4x5 color transparencies and descriptions of new or rebuilt passenger and freight equipment. Hardcover, 128 pages.

THE NYO&W IN COLOR
484-990 49.95
Magnificent collection of color photos dating back to 1941. Rare views of steam, diesels and rolling stock. 128 page hardcover book.

B&O COLOR GUIDE TO FREIGHT AND PASSENGER CARS

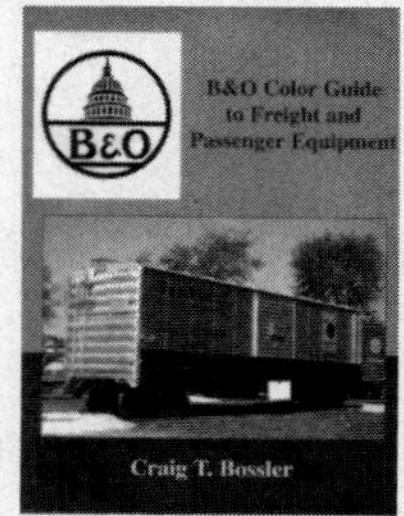

484-969 49.95

BALTIMORE & OHIO TRACKSIDE WITH WILLIS MCCALEB
484-1005 49.95
B&O steam in all its glory, captured in the Midwest by noted rail photographer Willis McCaleb in this 128-page all-color book. Includes every type of B&O steam working in the Midwest during the fifties.

C&O COLOR GUIDE TO FREIGHT AND PASSENGER EQUIPMENT

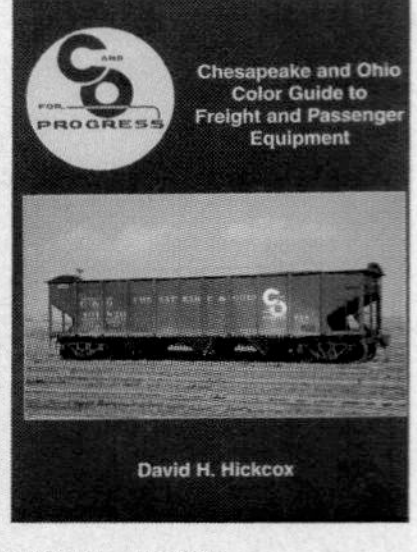

484-944 49.95
C&O rostered some very attractive passenger and general merchandise equipment. Contains over 300 (Pre-Chessie) color photos.

TRACKSIDE IN THE ALBANY, NY GATEWAY 1949-74

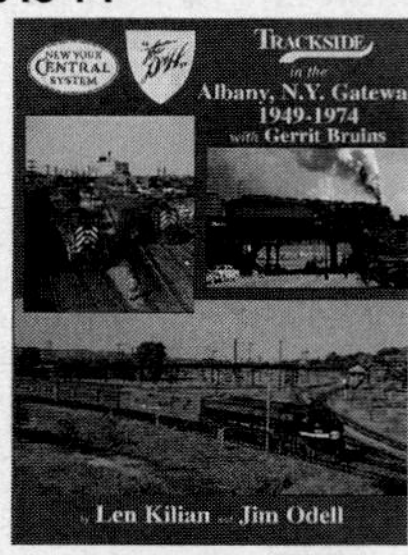

484-1012 49.95 ***NEW***
See the Albany-Rensselaer-Troy area of New York during some of the most exciting times to be trackside.

TRACKSIDE/EAST OF THE HUDSON: 1941-1953 WITH BILL MCCHESNEY

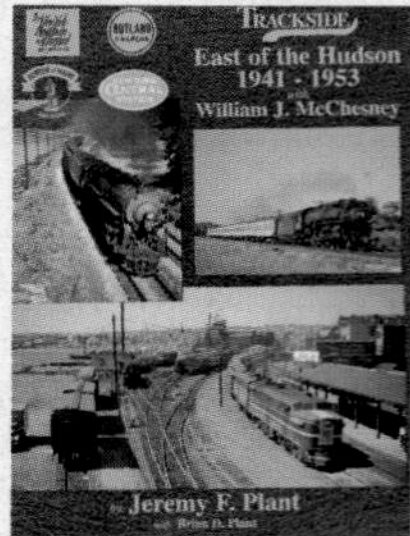

484-949 49.95
Bill McChesney's color coverage of eastern railroading began immediately before WWII. These early color efforts of rare subjects like NH steam are treasures for the railfan community .

BOSTON & MAINE IN COLOR
484-991 49.95
Over 240 color photos of steam and diesel across the system from the forties to Guilford.

MEC IN COLOR

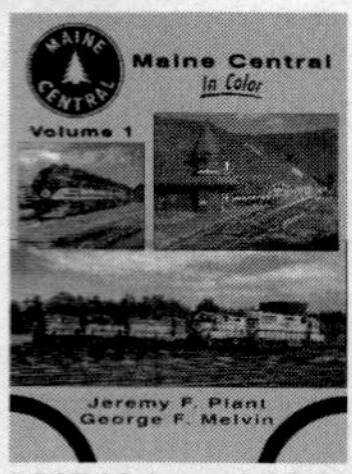

484-1007 Volume I **49.95**
NEW
From the 1950s to Guilford, the authors provide a detailed tour of the MEC. Includes over 240 color pictures.

WESTERN MARYLAND IN COLOR
484-956 Volume I **49.95**
484-966 Volume II **49.95**

NH COLOR GUIDE TO FREIGHT & PASSENGER EQUIPMENT

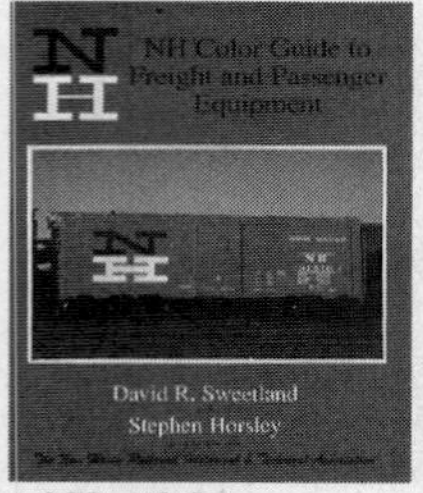

484-960 49.95

NH TRACKSIDE

484-1010 49.95 ***NEW***
Explore what the NH was like in the 1950s and 60s. Photos range from the heavy-duty electrified zone to bucolic branches to four unit FAs on Maybrook merchandise trains.

NORTHERN NEW ENGLAND COLOR GUIDE TO FREIGHT & PASSENGER EQUIPMENT
484-233 49.95

For Up-To-Date Information and News Bookmark Walthers Web site at

www.walthers.com

CANADIAN PACIFIC COLOR GUIDE TO FREIGHT AND PASSENGER EQUIPMENT

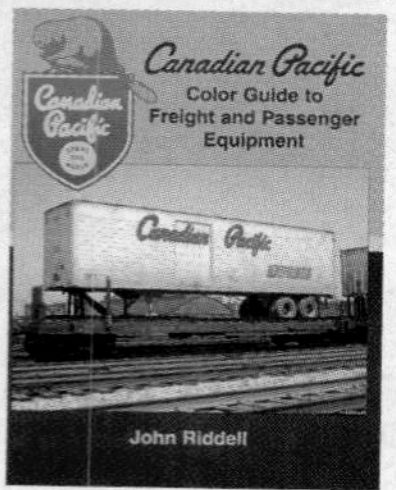

484-947 49.95
A comprehensive look at rolling stock during the 1950s, 60s and 70s. 128-pages, hardcover.

CGW COLOR GUIDE TO FREIGHT & PASSENGER EQUIPMENT

484-1009 49.95 ***NEW***
Various rolling stock of the "Corn Belt" are displayed through color photos and expert commentary.

CHICAGO GREAT WESTERN IN COLOR

484-987 49.95
Tour the "X" shaped system from Chicago westward and see diesels in action as far back as the early 1950s.

MINNEAPOLIS & ST. LOUIS

484-984 49.95
The Minneapolis & St. Louis route is followed and explained in 240 wonderful color photos.

SOO LINE IN COLOR

484-993 49.95
A 128 page book containing over 240 vintage views during the years when steam and early diesels roamed the system.

CNW OFFICIAL COLOR PHOTOGRAPHY

484-1020 54.95 ***NEW***
Straight from CNW's archives comes over 200 classic views from the 1940s and 50s. Includes photos of new equipment, special events, day-to-day operations and more. Hardcover, 128 pages, full-color.

NICKEL PLATE ROAD COLOR PHOTOGRAPHY

484-965 Volume I **49.95**
484-980 Volume II **49.95**
484-989 Volume III **49.95**

CNW IN COLOR, 1941 - 1953

484-997 Volume I **49.95**

ILLINOIS TERMINAL IN COLOR

484-1003 Volume I **49.95**
All-color look at the Illinois Terminal through the personal photos of noted traction authority Gordon Lloyd. Covers operations from 1952 through the N&W takeover.

ROCK ISLAND IN COLOR

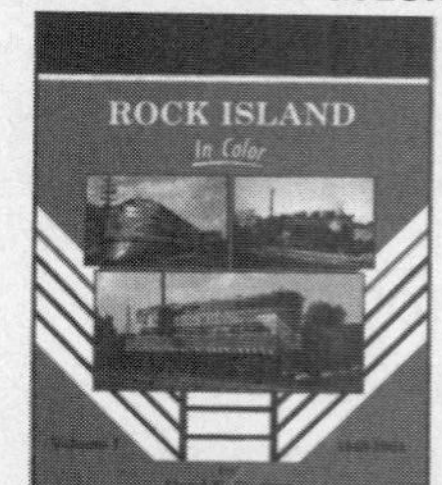

484-234 Volume I: 1948-1964 **49.95**
484-951 Volume II 1965-1980 **49.95**
484-981 Guide to Frieght & Passenger Equipment. **49.95**

INSULL CHICAGO INTERURBANS IN COLOR

484-979 49.95

WABASH IN COLOR

484-41 45.00
Over 180 color photos, 128 pages.

MISSOURI-KANSAS-TEXAS IN COLOR

484-225 49.95
Take a color tour of the famous "Katy" System. Hardcover.

MILW COLOR GUIDE TO FREIGHT & PASSENGER EQUIPMENT

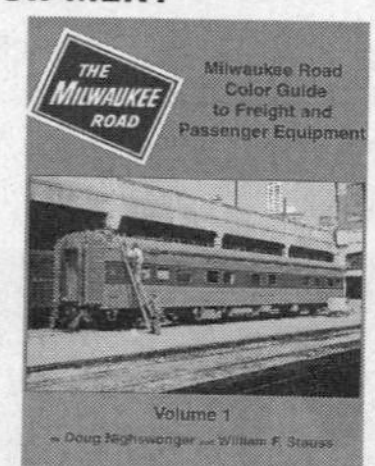

484-974 Volume I **49.95** ***NEW***
Covers the passenger fleet in maroon, orange and yellow schemes. Also contains cabooses and non-revenue equipment.

MILWAUKEE ROAD IN COLOR

484-962 Volume I: The East End **49.95**
484-970 Volume II: The Milwaukee Area **49.95**
484-971 Volume III: Wisconsin & Michigan **49.95**

UNDER MILWAUKEE WIRES

484-985 49.95
Beautiful Kodachromes of Bi-polars and maroon and orange "Little Joes" magnificently reproduced in this 128 page hardcover.

SP COLOR GUIDE TO FREIGHT AND PASSENGER EQUIPMENT

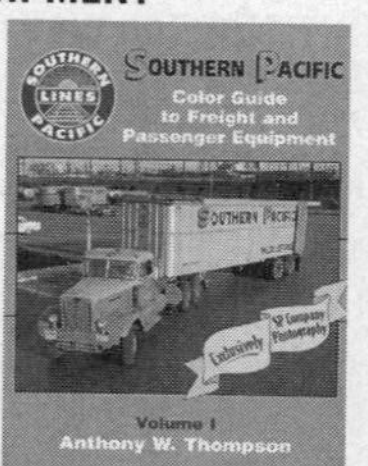

484-1015 Volume I **49.95** ***NEW***
Contains pictures taken by the company's marketing, purchasing and PR departments mainly during the 50s and 60s. Not a comprehensive look at the road's roster, but offers plenty for the rubbertire enthusiast.

SOUTHERN PACIFIC IN COLOR

484-238 49.95
Details the glory years after WWII to the early 1960s. The last of steam with pioneering diesels. 128 pages.

PACIFIC ELECTRIC IN COLOR

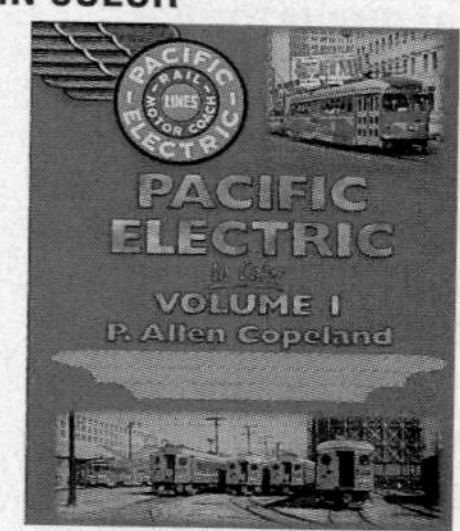

484-999 49.95
This electrified railroad blanketed the Los Angeles area. The "Big Red Cars," Southern Pacific influence, vintage street scenes are all to be found in this book.

RIO GRANDE COLOR GUIDE TO FREIGHT AND PASSENGER CARS

484-982 Volume I **49.95**

RIO GRANDE IN COLOR

484-114 Volume I Colorado **45.00**
The Mainline through the Rockies, from the late steam, early diesel period. 200 color photos, 128 pages.

RIO GRANDE IN COLOR

484-946 Volume II: Utah **49.95**
Tour the DRGW from Grand Junction to SP Interchange at Ogden through more than 230 vintage color photographs.

RIO GRANDE TRACKSIDE

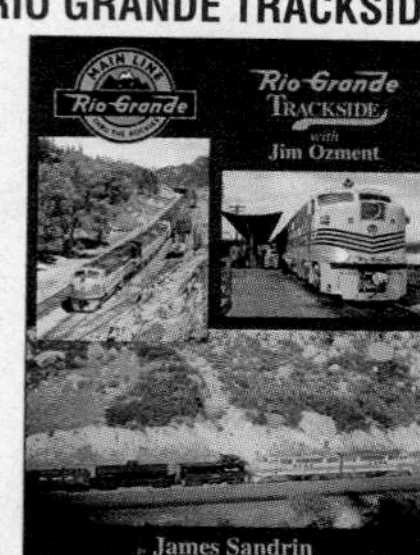

484-1019 54.95 ***NEW***

SANTA FE COLOR GUIDE TO FREIGHT & PASSENGER EQUIPMENT

484-958 49.95

SANTE FE ALL THE WAY

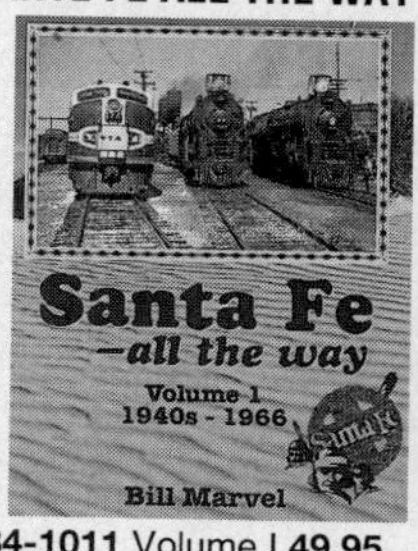

484-1011 Volume I **49.95**
NEW
A look back at the ATSF during its steam and 1st generation heyday. Includes over 240 classic photographs from the 1940s, 50s and 60s.

SANTA FE TRACKSIDE

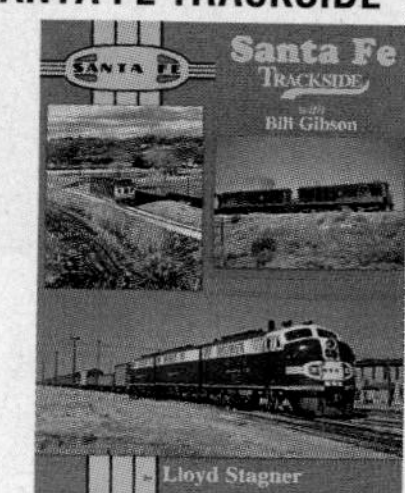

484-1021 54.95 ***NEW***
Tenth in the series, this book tours the Santa Fe of the 1950s and 60s in the area south of Kansas City. See everything from FTs to six-wheeled road switchers. Hardcover, 128 pages, full-color.

SANTA FE 1940-1971 IN COLOR

484-30 Volume I: Chicago-K.C **49.95**
First in a four volume series. Shows Santa Fe steam at its best and at least one of every diesel class that the road had during this period.

484-130 Volume II: KC-Albuquerque **49.95**
See rare DL-109s in K.C. and then spend a day in 1946 as everything from 2-10-2s to FTs pass by.

484-224 Volume III: Albuquerque - L.A. **49.95**
Visit Tehachapi and Cajon in the days when big steam worked side-by-side with the first generation of diesels.

484-232 Volume IV: Texas - El Capitan **49.95**

BESSEMER & LAKE ERIE IN COLOR

484-230 49.95

A GOLDEN DECADE OF TRAINS: THE 1950S IN COLOR

484-608 45.00
Rail photographer Robert R. Malinoski displays color work from his journeys across the nation during the 1950s. 128 pages.

Motorbooks International

This listing does not contain the only products sold by Motorbooks International. We have hundreds of of other titles on a variety of topics available from Walthers. Check it out!

503-1 Motorbooks International Catalog **N/C** *NEW*

RAILROAD HISTORY

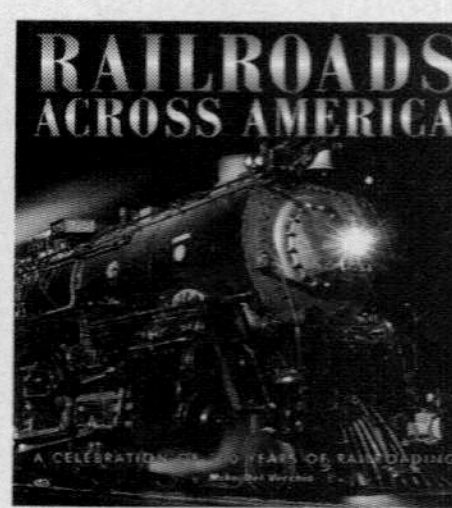

RAILROADS ACROSS AMERICA/150 YEARS OF THE IRON ROAD
503-760306427 24.95

CHESSIE THE RAILROAD KITTEN
503-96220031 11.95

CNW RAILWAY
503-188225676 29.95

AMERICAN TRAIN DEPOTS & ROUNDHOUSES
503-76030038 29.95

CLASSIC AMERICAN RAILROADS

503-760302391 29.95

THE AMERICAN RAILROAD

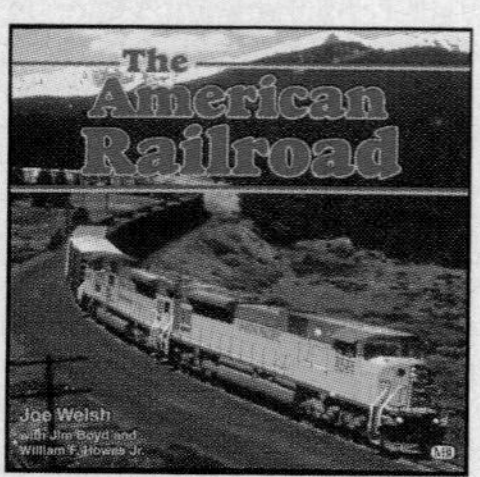

503-760305129 29.95 *NEW*

A CENTURY OF RAILWAYS
503-860935353 75.00

C&O IN THE COAL FIELDS
503-939487241 22.95

PENNSYLVANIA RAILROAD COLOR HISTORY
503-760303797 21.95

SANTA FE RAILROAD COLOR HISTORY
503-760303800 21.95

SOUTHERN PACIFIC RAILROAD

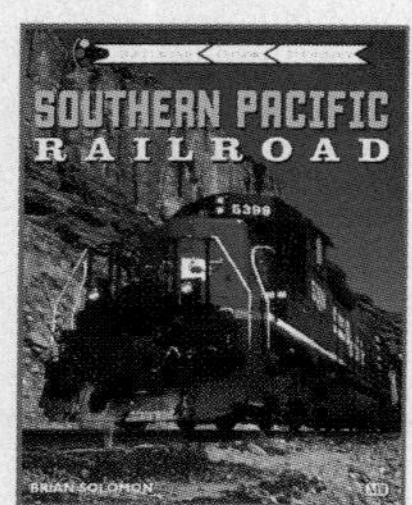

503-760306141 21.95 *NEW*

COLORADO & SOUTHERN
503-944119034 13.95

LAKE MICHIGAN'S RAILROAD FERRIES
503-944119115 24.95

ILLINOIS CENTRAL MONDAY MORNIN' RAILS
503-944119131 49.95

NEW YORK, ONTARIO & WESTERN IN THE DIESEL AGE
503-944119158 29.95

THE CHESSIE ERA
503-962200328 14.95

THE VIRGINIAN ERA
503-962200395 14.95

GN RAILWAY 1945-70
503-1882256565 29.95

AMERICA'S FIGHTING RAILROADS W.W.II PICTORIAL
503-1575100010 12.95

RAILWAY DISASTERS OF THE WORLD
503-1852603232 32.95

MILWAUKEE ROAD 1850-1960
503-1882256611 29.95

CHICAGO, MILWAUKEE & ST. PAUL RAILWAY
503-1882256670 29.95

SOO LINE 1975-1982
503-1882256689 29.95

TRAINS OF THE TWIN PORTS PHOTO ARCHIVE

503-1583880038 29.95 *NEW*

WISCONSIN CENTRAL LIMITED
503-1882256751 29.95

WISCONSIN CENTRAL RAILWAY 1871-1909
503-1882256786 29.95

WEST VIRGINIA LOGGING RAILROADS
503-1883089034 19.95

APPALACHIAN COAL MINES & RAILROADS
503-1883089085 15.95

L&N THE OLD RELIABLE
503-1883089190 29.95

NEW YORK CENTRAL RAILROAD

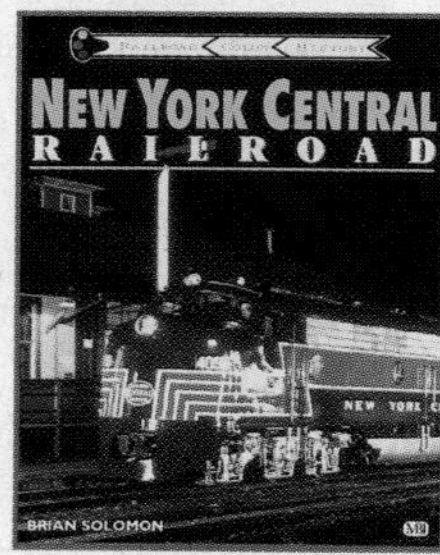

503-760306133 21.95 *NEW*

SEABOARD AIR LINE RAILWAY

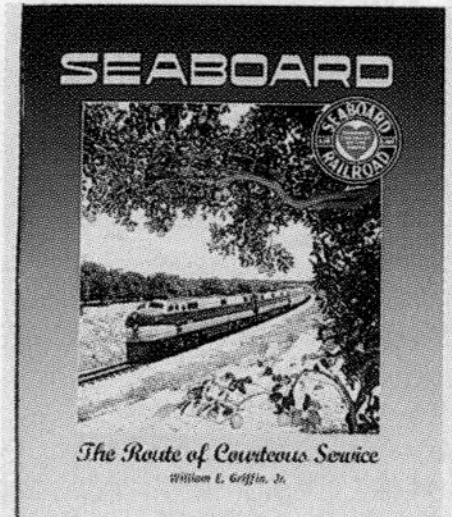

503-1883089441 29.95 *NEW*
Hardcover, 8-12 x 11" format, 224 pages, 250 B&W photos, 16 pages of color.

NICKEL PLATE PUBLICITY PHOTOS 1943-52
503-1883089220 Volume I 25.95
503-1883089387 Volume II 25.95

SOUTHERN RAILWAY SPENCER SHOPS
503-1883089239 22.95

BERKSHIRE NKP

503-1883089395 26.95 *NEW*

LACKAWANNA-SUPER-POWER RAILROAD OF THE NORTHEAST
503-1883089328 26.95

WEST VIRGINIA MANN CREEK RAILROAD
503-1883089379 29.95

GHOST TRAIN!

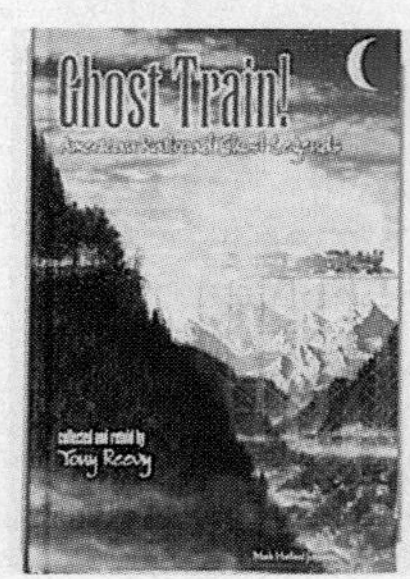

503-1883089417 14.95 *NEW*

BRITISH MAIN LINE SERVICES IN THE AGE OF STEAM 1900-1968
503-860935361 46.95

CHICAGO NORTHWESTERN MILWAUKEE ROAD PICTORIAL
503-911581308 29.95

CLASSIC TRAINS
503-752211609 24.95

DRGW
503-1883089484 28.95 *NEW*

GREAT NORTHERN RAILWAY
503-1882256794 29.95

THE GENERAL & THE TEXAS

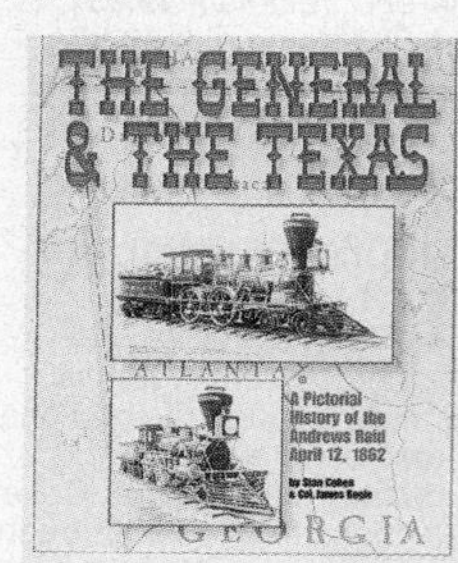

503-1575100606 17.95 *NEW*

NEW YORK CENTRAL SYSTEM
503-188308946 28.95 *NEW*

RAILWAYS IN CAMERA
503-750910607 29.98

FREIGHT

CABOOSE

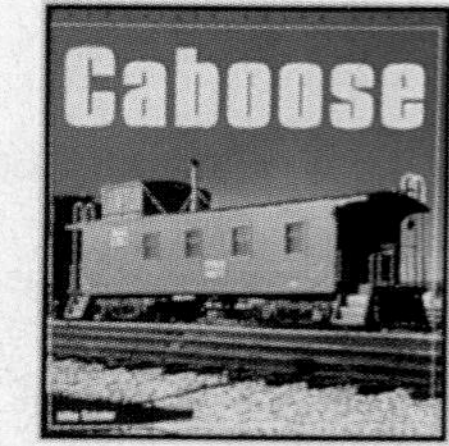

503-760303762 13.95

B&O CABOOSES
503-1883089115 Volume I 26.95

N&W COAL CARS
503-1883089360 29.95

FREIGHT TRAIN CARS

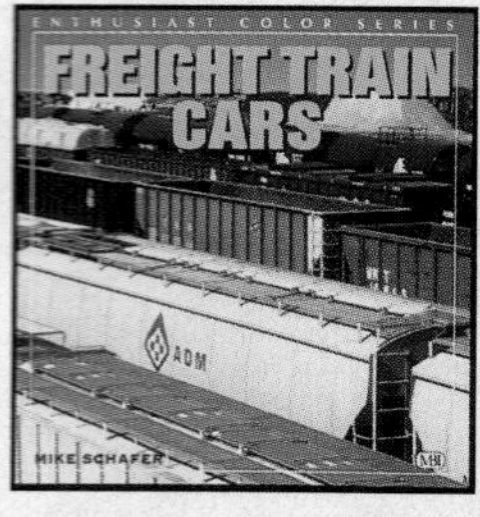

503-760306125 13.95 *NEW*

PASSENGER TRAINS & TRAVEL

BY STREAMLINER FROM FLORIDA TO NEW YORK
503-944119114 39.95

B&O PASSENGER SERVICE 1945-1971
503-188308900 24.95

NYC TRAINS OF THE FUTURE
503-188308928 26.95

VENICE-SIMPLON ORIENT EXPRESS
503-760302669 29.95

CLASSIC AMERICAN STREAMLINERS
503-760303770 29.95

STREAMLINER MEMORIES

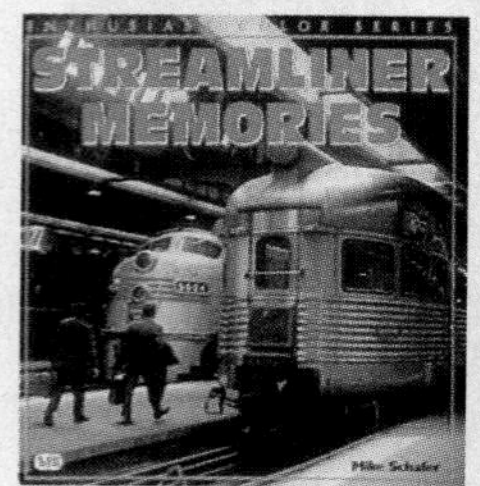

503-760306192 13.95 *NEW*

C&O STREAMLINERS
503-939487217 29.95

CHICAGO'S COMMUTER RAILROADS
503-944119093 24.95

IC STREAMLINERS
503-1883089107 19.95

NYC MERCURY
503-962200344 14.95

NYC GREAT STEEL FLEET IN COLOR
503-1883089182 22.95

B&O PASSENGER SERVICE 1945-71-VOLUME II
503-1883089212 26.95

NYC LIGHTWEIGHT PASSENGER CARS
503-1883089255 28.95

20TH CENTURY LIMITED
503-1883089263 19.95

Motorbooks International

NEW HAVEN RAILROAD STREAMLINE ERA
503-1883089336 33.95

ATLANTIC COAST LINE PASSENGER SERVICE
503-188308945 26.95 NEW

LOCOMOTIVES

STEAM THROUGH FIVE CONTINENTS
503-750906278 19.95

L&N DIESEL LOCOS
503-188308931 26.95

MODERN DIESEL LOCOMOTIVES
503-760301999 13.95

AMERICAN STEAM LOCOMOTIVES

503-760303363 29.95

KATY: DIESELS TO THE GULF
503-944119050 39.95

N&W: DIESEL'S LAST CONQUEST
503-962200360 14.95

N&W RAILROAD-MAGNIFICENT MALLETS
503-1883089018 14.95

VIRGINIAN RAILWAY LOCOMOTIVES
503-1883089050 15.95

B&O E UNIT PASSENGER LOCOS
503-1883089069 15.95

NYC EARLY DIESEL LOCOS
503-1883089166 29.95

CLASSIC DIESELS OF THE SOUTH
503-1883089204 26.95

WM DIESEL LOCOMOTIVES
503-1883089247 4.95

VINTAGE DIESEL LOCOMOTIVES

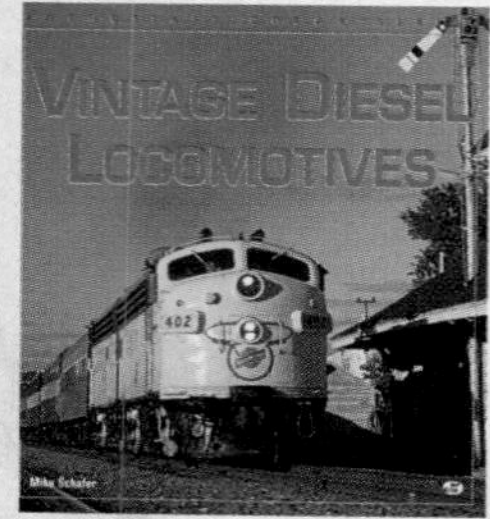

503-760305072 13.95

NARROW GAUGE STEAM LOCOMOTIVES

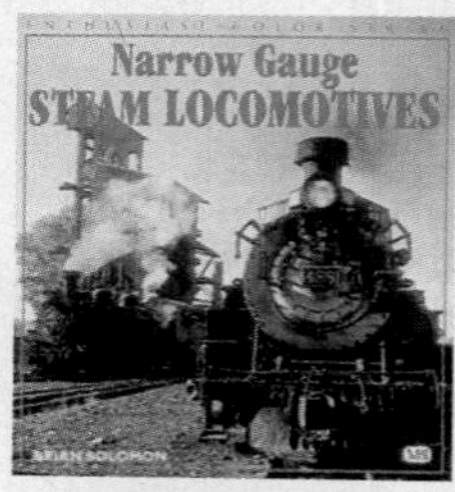

503-760305439 13.95 NEW

WESTERN PACIFIC LOCOMOTIVES
503-1883089344 24.95

NICKEL PLATE DIESEL LOCOS
503-1883089352 26.95

HOW TO PREPARE, FIRE & DRIVE A STEAM LOCO
503-860935396 34.95

LOCOMOTION
503-563367407 26.95

CHESSIE SYSTEM DIESEL LOCOMOTIVES
503-1883089425 36.95 NEW

MODEL RAILROADING

DIESEL MODELER'S GUIDE EA 14.95
503-965536505 Volume I
503-96553653 Volume II

THE AMERICAN TOY TRAIN

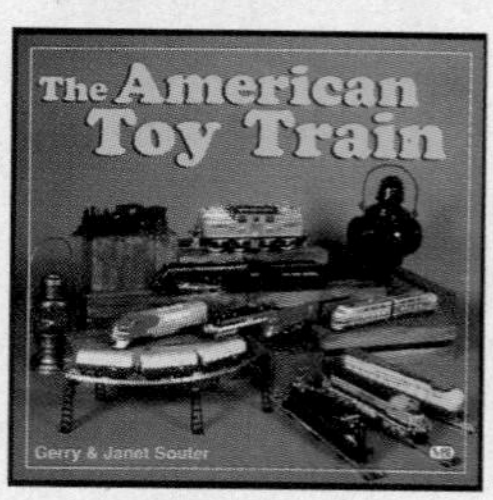

503-760306206 29.95 NEW

INTERMODAL MODELER'S GUIDE EA 14.95
503-965536513 Volume I
503-965536521 Volume II

AMERICAN HISTORY

GOING, GOING, GONE-VANISHING AMERICANA
503-811819191 19.95

AMERICAN SERVICE STATIONS 1943-53
503-1882256271 29.95

THE AMERICAN CAR DEALERSHIP

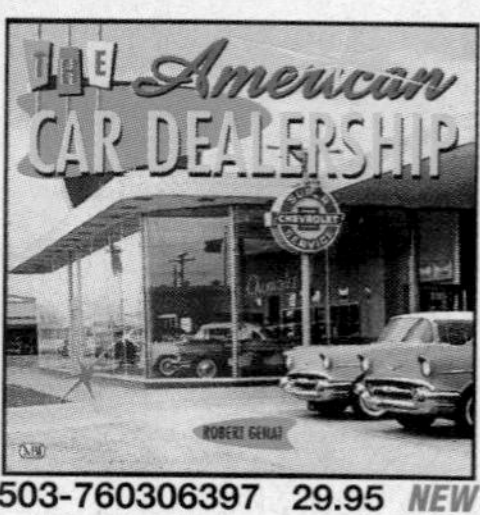

503-760306397 29.95 NEW

THE AMERICAN GAS STATION
503-760306494 19.95 NEW

THE AMERICAN DRIVE-IN
503-879389192 29.95 NEW

THE AMERICAN STATE FAIR
503-760306567 29.95 NEW

THE AMERICAN DINER

503-760301107 29.95 NEW

CRUISIN'
503-760301484 29.95 NEW

ROUTE 66 REMEMBERED
503-76030114 29.95 NEW

PHILLIPS 66 GAS STATIONS 1945-54
503-1882256425 29.95

COCA-COLA: HISTORY IN PHOTOS
503-1882256468 29.95

COCA-COLA: ITS VEHICLES
503-1882256476 29.95

BUSES

AMERICAN BUSES
503-760304327 24.95

CONSTRUCTION EQUIPMENT

SUPER-DUTY EARTHMOVERS
503-760306451 21.95 NEW

GIANT EARTHMOVERS: III
503-76030369 19.95

GIANT EARTHMOVING EQUIPMENT
503-760300321 14.98

ROAD CONSTRUCTION
503-760300402 12.95

CATERPILLAR
503-1882256700 24.95

ERIE SHOVELS

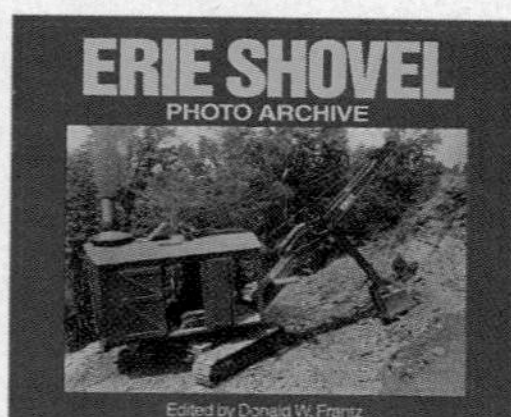

503-1882256697 32.95

FARM HISTORY & MACHINERY

ALLIS-CHALMERS
503-760301085 Allis-Chalmers Tractors 13.95
503-879388285 The Allis-Chalmers Story 34.95
503-929355547 Allis-Chalmers Farm Equipment 39.95

INSIDE JOHN DEERE: A FACTORY HISTORY

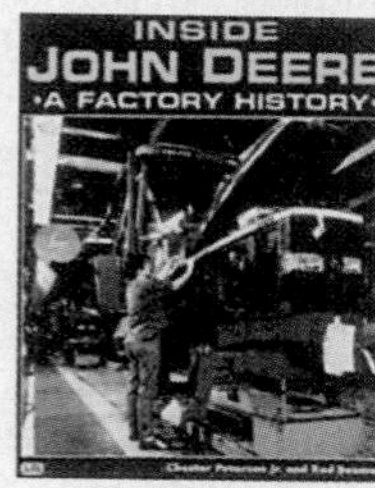

503-760304416 24.95 NEW

THE AMERICAN BARN
503-760301093 29.95

CLASSIC FARM TRACTORS
503-760302464 15.98

THE AMERICAN FAMILY FARM
503-760302847 29.95

THE AMERICAN FARM TRACTOR
503-879385324 29.95

TRUCKS

THE AMERICAN PICKUP TRUCK
503-760304734 29.95 NEW

AMERICAN BEER TRUCKS
503-760304408 21.95 NEW

NEW CAR CARRIERS 1910-1998
503-1882256980 19.95 NEW

DELIVERY TRUCKS
503-760306265 21.95 NEW

LOGGING TRUCKS, TRACTORS & CRAWLERS
503-760302332 19.95

EUCLID AND TEREX EARTH MOVING EQUIPMENT

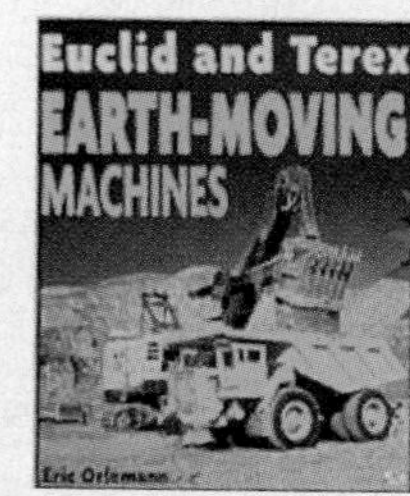

503-760302936 24.95

BIG RIGS IN ACTION
503-760303452 13.95

Daily New Arrival Updates! Visit Walthers Web site at

www.walthers.com

GAS & OIL TRUCKS
503-76030212 21.95

WORLD'S GREATEST WORKING TRUCKS
503-96496456 19.95

PICTORIAL HISTORY OF AMERICAN TRUCKS
503-1870979567 19.95

CLASSIC AMERICAN HEAVY TRUCKS
503-1901432084 24.95

BEVERAGE TRUCKS 1910-75
503-1882256603 29.95

EMERGENCY VEHICLES

PUMPERS WORKHORSE FIRE ENGINES
503-760306729 21.95 NEW

VOLUNTEER & RURAL FIRE APPARATUS PHOTO GALLERY

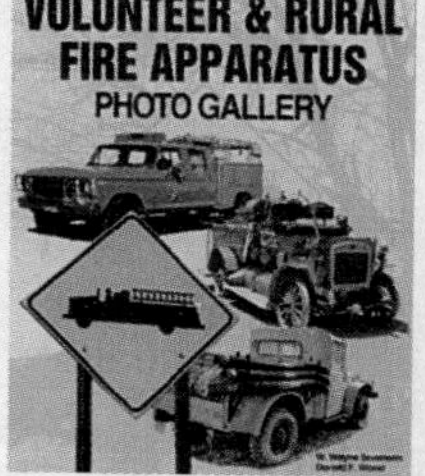

503-1583880054 24.95 NEW

ENCYCLOPEDIA OF AMERICAN POLICE CARS
503-760304491 44.95 NEW

FIRE CHIEF CARS 1900-97
503-1882256875 19.95

FIRE TRUCKS IN ACTION
503-879389273 13.95

THE AMERICAN FIRE STATION
503-760305277 29.95

Limited Quantity Available

ILLUSTRATED HISTORY OF BRITISH RAILWAY WORKSHOPS
503-860935035 39.95

. . . AND GONE FOREVER
503-860935264 (British Steam) 29.98

TROLLEYCARS, STREETCARS, TRAMS
503-879389729 19.95

TAKING THE TRAIN-BRITISH RAILWAYS
503-1852604093 14.98

ALL ABOARD!
503-1550541889 19.95

MORE GREAT RAILWAY JOURNEYS
503-563387173 29.95

THE PRESIDENT TRAVELS BY TRAIN
503-1883089174 39.95

THE AMERICAN FIRE ENGINE
503-879387505 29.95

BOOKS

CLASSIC POWER SERIES

NO. 5 PRR Q CLASS

525-7205 23.95

NO.9 THE JETS NH EP-5 ELECTRICS
525-7209 29.95

PLAN & PHOTO SERIES

Drawings, photos and statistical data.

NO. 1A CABOOSES OF THE NH&NYC RAILROADS
525-7501 14.95

ELECTRIC LOCOMOTIVE PLAN BOOK VOLUME 1
525-7504 24.95

NO. 3 CABOOSES OF THE NARROW GAUGE & LOGGING RAILROADS
525-7505 14.95

OTHER BOOKS

BROOKLYN TROLLEYS
525-7604 29.95
A unique book detailing Brooklyn's transportation heritage. 120 pages, 230 photos, diagrams and system map.

3-AXLE STREET CARS-ROBINSON TO RATHGEBER
525-7614 Vol. I **29.95**
History and development of 3-Axle Street Cars.

NEW YORK RAILWAYS-THE GREEN LINE
525-7615 19.95
New York's last street railway system. 64 pages, 115 photos, rosters and maps.

CROSS CONTINENT ELECTRICS

525-7616 24.95
Development, testing and learning the operation of GN/PRR electric Locos. 64 pages, B&W and color photos.

3-AXLE STREET CARS-ROBINSON TO RATHGEBER
525-7617 Vol. II **31.95**
Building, operation and development of 3-axle street cars worldwide.

SECOND AVE ELEVATED IN MANHATTAN
525-7618 29.95
South Ferry to 129 St. History, drawings and photos. 64 pages, 140 photos, rosters and maps.

THIRD AVE. RAILWAY SYSTEM IN MANHATTAN
525-7619 27.95
History, system operation, routes, street and system maps. 64 pages, B&W and color photos.

BRT TROLLEY LINES IN QUEENS
525-7620 29.95
Complete history from horse cars to Peter Witt. 88 pages, photos, diagrams, rosters and maps.

HEDLEY-DOYLE STEPLESS STREETCAR
525-7622 22.95
80 pages, 100 photos, 40 equipment drawings, full fleet coverage worldwide.

OSO PUBLISHING CO.

NEW
SUPPLIER

BOOKS

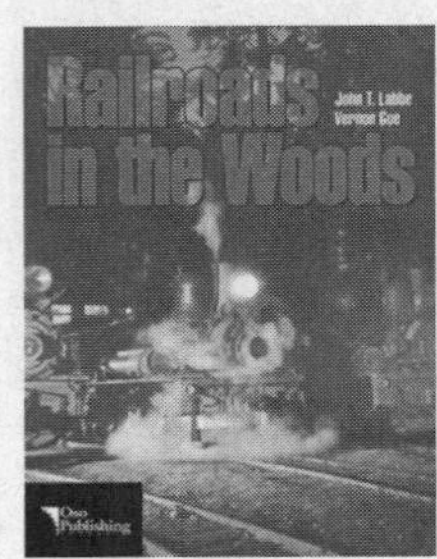

537-52107 Railroads in the Woods **39.95**

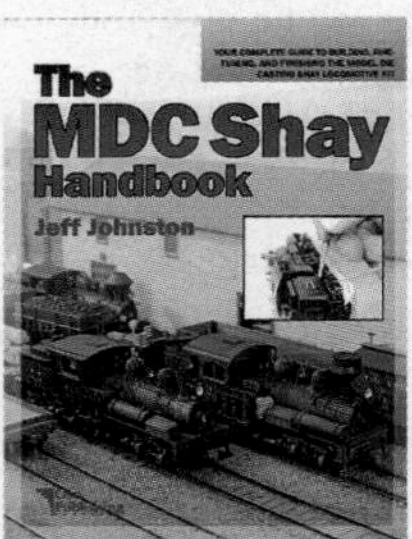

537-52115 The MDC Shay Handbook **17.95**

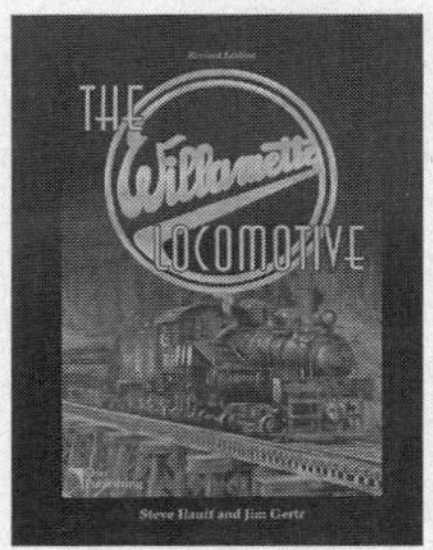

537-52131 The Wilamette Locomotive **39.95**

NATIVE GROUND MUSIC

SINGING RAILS "RAILROADIN' SONGS, JOKES, AND STORIES"

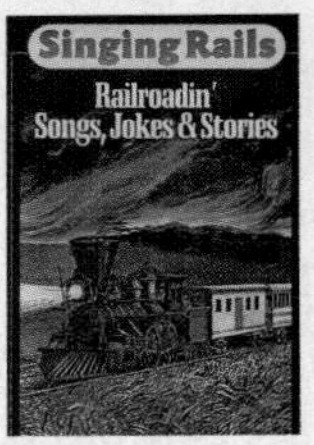

518-206260 5.95
Packed full of railroad facts, superstitions, songs and tall tales, you'll find this book hard to put down. Softcover, 68 pages, 8-1/2 x 5-1/2".

NORTHWEST SHORT LINE

LOGGING TO THE SALT CHUCK-SIMPSON TIMBER-

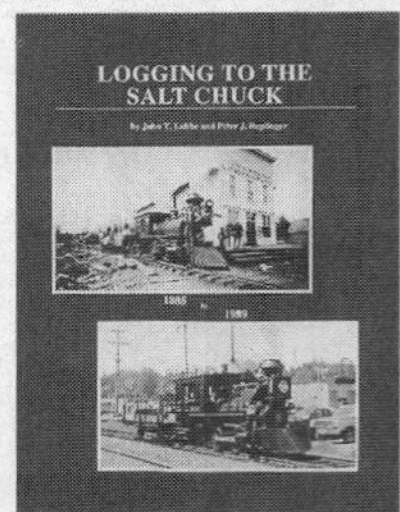

53-5069 Hardcover **45.95**

NWSL FULL LINE CATALOG
53-1 7.00

NORTHERN PACIFIC RAILWAY
53-5109 49.95

LOGGING IN SKAGIT CO.
53-5089 59.95

THE PACIFIC NORTHWEST RAILROADS OF MCGEE & NIXON
53-5099 59.95

Information STATION

IS MY OLD TRAIN SET WORTH MONEY?

If you've been modeling for any length of time, you've probably been asked that question. While there is a lot of demand for antiques and collectibles, many factors determine if toy trains are really valuable. There are many guide books and histories available that will help you identify toy trains, as well as determine the current market prices. Typically, collectors look at the following:
Condition: Probably the most important factor. The most desirable items were never played with nor removed from their original box. These are referred to as mint-in-box (MIB) or new-in-box (NIB). Since this is rare, such items command the best prices. While beauty is in the eye of the beholder, condition is usually judged on a sliding scale ranging from MIB down to poor and prices vary accordingly.
Packaging: The overall condition of the package will substantially impact value. Boxes were often torn when first opened, treated roughly over time, soiled and damaged during handling or storage, or simply thrown away. An excellent original box can double the value of a used toy. Packaging can also be judged from excellent to poor.
Age: To be considered an antique, an item must be 100 years old or more. Since toys were once a luxury item made in small numbers, older items are more desirable. The age of the toy will also determine what it is made of, such as metal or plastic.
Scarcity: If fewer items were made, they are much more likely to be collectable. Items like one-off prototype models built for engineering studies, or factory errors with the wrong color or lettering are good examples. Some items produced only for specific sets and not sold separately qualify as well. Sets produced with unique colors and packaging, often for a regional customer such as a large department store, may fit into this group.

Quadrant Press, Inc.

BOOKS

All books feature B&W photos and are softcover unless noted.

RAILROADS

CZ-THE STORY OF THE CALIFORNIA ZEPHYR
69-429 19.95
Includes car diagrams, roster, menus and timetables. More than 125 photos, 104 pages. By Karl Zimmermann.

BALTIMORE'S LIGHT RAIL
69-55 15.95
Baltimore's most remarkable transit renaissance. Provides a detailed look at the system's unique heritage and its creative reconstruction. 149 photographs, maps and drawings, 96 pages.

SANTA FE STREAMLINERS
69-41 17.95
Comprehensive survey of ATSF's famed streamliners, beginning with the inaugural of the "Super Chief" in the 30s up to Amtrak's "Southwest Limited".

TOURING PITTSBURGH BY TROLLEY
69-5 14.95
A pictorial review of the extensive network of trolley lines operated by Pittsburgh Railways in the 1950s and 1960s. By Harold A. Smith.

OCEAN LINERS OF THE WORLD
69-43 11.50
Covers transatlantic ships and principal liner routes around the globe since WWII. 125 photos, 96 pages

ERIE LACKAWANNA EAST
69-12 9.95
Covers operations from the 1960 merger through 1975. 146 photos. 80 pages.

BUILDING THE INDEPENDENT SUBWAY
69-50 15.95
Focusing on New York City's 15-year struggle to build its own subway system. The book includes information on construction, the 207th Street shops and subway rolling stock. More than 120 photos, 80 pages.

TWILIGHT ON THE NARROW GAUGE
69-14 8.50
Reissued story of the DRGW of the 1950s. Photos, 64 pages, 11 x 8-1/2".

THE REMARKABLE GG-1

69-16 12.95
The famous Pennsy electrics from #4800 to the rededication of #4935 in May 1977. 110 photos, 72 pages, 11 x 8-1/2".

LIGHT RAIL TRANSIT ON THE WEST COAST

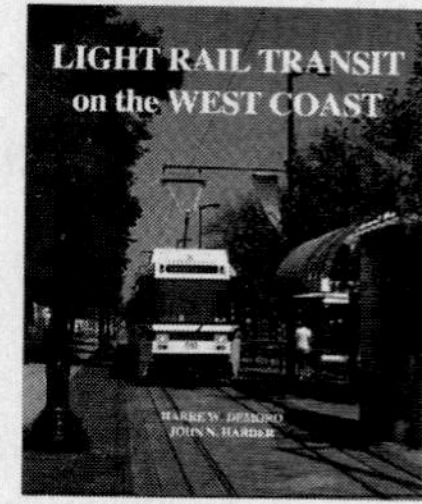

69-49 13.95
How, why and where the trolley car is returning to the West Coast in the form of light rail transit. 96 pages, 125 photos.

AMERICA'S WORKHORSE LOCOMOTIVE: THE 2-8-2
69-54 14.95
Contains a photo-history of the 2-8-2 from 1884 to 1949. 160 photos, 80 pages, 8-1/2 x 11".

RAILS TO SAN FRANCISCO BAY
69-51 15.95
A look at the years from 1900 to 1955 when the SP, WP, ATSF and several electric lines operated rail-maritime service in the San Francisco Bay area. 120 photos, 96 pages, 8-1/2 x 11".

NEW YORK TRANSIT MEMORIES

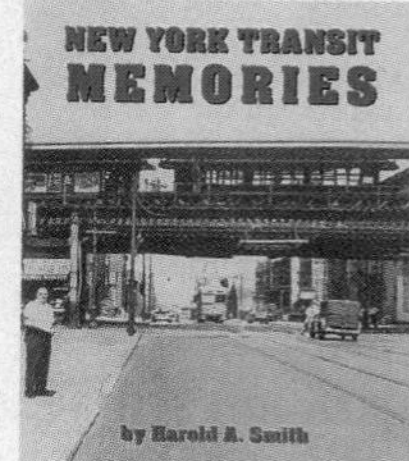

69-52 16.95
Covers the various forms of transit used in the five boroughs of New York City from the 1930s to the 1960s. Over 170 photos, 88 pages.

ERIE MEMORIES
69-93 39.95
Reviews each division with background material, its own map and gradient profile. Hardcover, 219 photos, 160 pages.

COMMUTER TRAINS TO GRAND CENTRAL TERMINAL
69-45 7.95
150 years of commuter train operation north and northeast of New York City. 100 photos, 64 pages.

RAILROAD AVENUE ENTERPRISES

All books are softcover.

CONRAIL'S SD40 & SD40-2

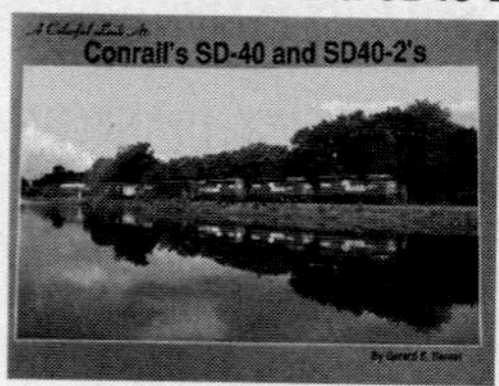

615-17 19.95
Complete roster and mechanical specifications. 66 color photos.

PHILADELPHIA TRANSPORTATION COMPANY RAILS

615-18 21.95
More than 200 pictures and illustrations capture the city's streetcars, subway-el, workcars, transfers, tokens and more.

THE HARD COAL CARRIERS
615-14 Vol 1 First Generation Geeps **19.95**
Covers the CNJ, Lackawanna, Erie, EL, LV and RDG with complete roster information and detail data. 11 color and 119 B&W photos, 80 pages.

615-16 Vol 2 Camelback Twilight **19.95**

PENNSY K-4'S REMEMBERED
615-15 6.95

CHANGE AT OZONE PARK
615-13 18.95

RAILROAD STATIONS OF NEW ENGLAND
615-5 Volume 1 **7.95**
190 photos, 72 pages, 8-1/2 x 11".

LEHIGH VALLEY PASSENGER CARS
615-6 13.95

26 MILES TO JERSEY CITY
615-7 8.95

THE MORRISTOWN & ERIE RAILWAY
615-9 8.95

THE HANDSOMEST TRAINS IN THE WORLD
615-10 15.95

A COLORFUL LOOK AT THE CHICAGO & NORTH WESTERN

615-19 19.95
Looks at the line from the mid 60s to the UP merger. Includes 80 color photos showcasing a wide range of diesels across the system. 48 pages, full-color.

ANTHRACITE COUNTRY COLOR

615-20 19.95
Pennsylvania's central coal region during the 1950s. Includes 64 photos from the RDG, CNJ, Pennsy and LV operating in Schuylkill and Carbon County. Lots of steam and early diesels from a by-gone era. 48 pages, full-color.

DIAMONDBUGS
615-21 14.95 ***NEW***
Over 80 black and white photos illustrate the evolution of the gas-electrics on the Erie. Also included are diagrams and charts giving a comprehensive look as these cars. 64 pages.

COLORFUL MEMORIES OF READING'S SHAMOKIN DIVISION
615-22 TBA ***NEW***
Covers the Reading Co. during the steam to diesel transition era with 48 pages of full color.

R·ROBB LTD.

NARROW GAUGE PICTORIALS
Colorado narrow gauge equipment, from various roads, is featured in these softcover books. Each has a horizontal format and more than 100 B&W photos.

THE MUDHENS

622-795 28.00

PASSENGER CARS OF THE DRGW
622-2 Vol II **23.50**
191 pages, 11 x 8-1/2".

GONDOLAS, BOX CARS & FLAT CARS OF THE DRGW
622-3 Vol III **33.00**

DRGW REFRIGERATOR, STOCK AND TANK CARS
622-4 Vol IV **25.00**

DRGW CABOOSES
622-5 Vol V **24.00**

WORK EQUIPMENT OF THE DRGW
622-7 Vol VII **28.50**
224 pages, 11 x 8-1/2".

COLORADO & SOUTHERN ROLLING STOCK
622-8 Vol VIII **35.00**

RGS RICO TO DURANGO

622-9 Vol IX **22.00**
160 pages.

LOCOMOTIVES OF THE DRGW
622-11 Volume XI **33.00**
Includes roster, folios and photographs of all modern narrow gauge steam locomotives.

THE GRAND MOUNTAINS
622-101 35.00
1st in a series of DRGW steam motive power volumes. Features 4-8-2 Mountain class M-67, M-69, M-75 and M-78 locomotives.

Limited Quantity Available

PINO GRANDE BY R.S. POLKINGHORN
622-201 29.00
Softbound reprint of Howell North publication.

BOOKS

SAN DIEGO TROLLEY
341-114 25.95

AMERICA'S FIRST TRANS-CONTINENTAL RAILWAY
341-922 9.95

DONE HONEST & TRUE: RICHARD STEINHEIMER'S 1/2 CENTURY OF RAIL PHOTOGRAPHY
561-9849 29.95 *NEW*

FROM THE CAB; STORIES OF A RAILROAD ENGINEER
561-9850 14.95 *NEW*

CONRAIL: MOTIVE POWER REVIEW
561-9853 Volume I 29.95

CROOKEDEST RAILROAD IN THE WORLD
561-9910 24.95 *NEW*

FEATHER RIVER CANYON
561-96000 49.95

WALT DISNEY'S RAILROAD STORY
561-97000 59.95

CROSSROADS OF THE WEST-A PHOTOGRAPHIC LOOK AT 50 YEARS OF RAILROADING IN UTAH
561-98000 49.95 *NEW*

VIDEOS

From contemporary operations to the classic trains of yesteryear, you'll find a wide range of railroad action in these top-quality railroad videos. Each is in full-color with sound (unless noted).

DAYLIGHT TO THE FAIR
561-11 39.95

THE ALASKA RAILROAD
561-21 39.95

BRITISH COLUMBIA RAILWAY
561-31 39.95

DENVER & RIO GRANDE WESTERN
561-91 39.95

CUMBRES & TOLTEC'S SCENIC FREIGHT TRAIN
561-103 29.95

TODAY'S CHICAGO RAILROADS
561-106 39.95

EASTERN KENTUCKY COAL LINES
561-109 39.95

SOUTHERN PACIFIC'S SHASTA DIVISION
561-193 39.95

CUMBRES & TOLTEC'S ROTARY SNOW PLOW
561-194 24.95

WISCONSIN CENTRAL
561-197 39.95

BEST OF 1987
561-201 29.95

RAILROADS OF MEXICO EA 39.95
561-202 Northern Mexico Rails
561-203 Central Mexico Rails

CANFOR'S ENGLEWOOD RAILWAY
561-205 24.95

LTV MINING RAILROAD
561-207 39.95

WESTERN MARYLAND SCENIC RR
561-208 19.95

SANTA FE 3751—RETURN TO STEAM
561-209 29.95

CHATTANOOGA STEAM REUNION
561-210 24.95

MISSOURI-KANSAS-TEXAS THE KATY
561-211 39.95

LOGGING RAILROADS OF THE SIERRAS
561-212 24.95

ACROSS MARIAS PASS
561-214 39.95

ACROSS DONNER SUMMIT
561-215 39.95

LAST OF THE GIANTS
561-216 Volume I 19.95
561-252 Volume II 39.95
561-256 Vol III 39.95

UNION PACIFIC'S FEATHER RIVER ROUTE
561-217 39.95

POWDER RIVER BASIN COAL TRAINS
561-219 39.95

MEXICO'S PACIFICO RAILROAD
561-220 39.95

ARKANSAS & MISSOURI
561-221 39.95

SAN DIEGO MODEL RAILROAD MUSEUM
561-224 19.95

A GREAT RAILROAD AT WORK, NEW YORK, NEW HAVEN & HARTFORD
561-226 19.98

ALONG THE HUDSON DIVISION
561-227 39.95

PACIFIC ELECTRIC—TWILIGHT YEARS
561-229 29.95

LOS ANGELES TRANSIT—THE FINAL YEARS
561-230 29.95

THE GREEN BAY ROUTE
561-233 39.95

SOUTHERN PACIFIC 2472
561-235 29.95

AMTRAK NORTHEAST CORRIDOR SERIES
561-236 NY to Philadelphia 39.95
561-238 Cab Ride D.C. to Philadelphia 29.95
561-9237 NY-Philadelphia/ Philadelphia-D.C Set pkg(2) 69.95

CLINCHFIELD CHALLENGE
561-240 29.95

THIS IS MY RAILROAD - DIESEL
561-241 29.95

TODAY'S MAINE RAILROADS
561-242 39.95

UP FEATHER RIVER ROTARY
561-244 29.95

TODAY'S NORTHWESTERN PACIFIC
561-245 39.95

STEAM ACROSS AMERICA
561-247 Volume I 39.95

AMTRAK'S X2000 DEMONSTRATION
561-249 19.95

GREAT AMERICAN TRAIN RIDES EA 14.95
561-250 Volume I
561-9532 Volume III

UNION PACIFIC'S 40TH ANNIVERSARY STEAM EXCURSION
561-253 29.95

CHICAGO STEAM CELEBRATION
561-254 29.95

EASTERN QUEBEC'S ORE LINES
561-257 Volume I 29.95
561-9311 Volumes I & II 49.95

CANADIAN DOUBLEHEADER STEAM
561-261 29.95

WINTER ALONG THE UPPER MISSISSIPPI
561-263 39.95

NEW YORK CENTRAL: AN INSIDER'S VIEW
561-266 39.95

SANTA FE SUPER CHIEF
561-361 14.95

MICHIGAN ORE LINES
561-441 19.95

HORSESHOE CURVE
561-481 39.95

SAND PATCH GRADE
561-521 39.95

TODAY'S ST. LOUIS RAILROADS
561-531 39.95

SNOW ON THE RUN
561-551 19.95

SIERRA PACIFIC LINES
561-631 39.95

THE COPPER CANYON—CHIHUAHUA PACIFICO RAILROAD
561-641 39.95

KANSAS CITY SOUTHERN
561-651 39.95

CASS SCENIC RAILROAD
561-671 29.95

MONTANA RAIL LINK
561-681 39.95

UNION PACIFIC 3985 CHALLENGER
561-691 29.95

BURLINGTON NORTHERN E-UNITS
561-701 39.95

CHESAPEAKE & OHIO 2765
561-941 29.95

CSX SOUTHERN WEST VIRGINIA COAL
561-942 39.95

TEHACHAPI
561-943 29.95

ATSF NEW MEXICO MAINLINE EA 39.95
561-948 Volume I

SP DAYLIGHT 4449
561-1101 19.95

UNION PACIFIC 3985
561-1103 19.95

SANTA FE SALUTE
561-9413 29.95

AMTRAK'S AUTO TRAIN
561-9417 39.95

GREAT NORTHERN RAILWAY SERIES EA 29.95
561-9514 Volume I
561-9515 Volume II
561-9516 Volume III

CONRAIL HOT SPOTS EAST
561-9517 39.95

INTO THE ALLEGHENY RANGE
561-9519 Volume II 19.95
561-9520 Volume III 39.95

TRAIN WRECKS, CRASHES, DISASTERS
561-9521 29.95

TRAGEDY AT CAJON PASS
561-9522 29.95

HISTORIC SPOTS: SOUTHERN CALIFORNIA IN THE 1950s
561-9523 39.95

THE FRASER CANYON ROUTE
561-9526 19.95

THROUGH THE RATHOLE-CAB RIDE
561-9527 19.95

THE RATHOLE
561-9528 39.95

HISTORIC HOT SPOTS: SANTA FE'S PASADENA SUBDIVISION
561-9529 39.95

DURANGO & SILVERTON NARROW GAUGE RAILROAD
561-9530 19.95

ORANGE EMPIRE MUSEUM
561-9531 19.95

DOUBLESTACKS OVER TEHACHAPI
561-9534 19.95

TODAY STEAM ACROSS AMERICA
561-9535 19.95

STEAMTOWN GRAND OPENING
561-9536 29.95

SANTA FE THE DIESEL LOCOMOTIVE
561-9537 Vol.I 19.95

THE JOINT LINE
561-9538 29.95

U-BOAT SURVIVORS
561-9539 39.95

THE STORMY
561-9541 39.95

THE CALIFORNIA NORTHERN
561-9542 39.95

BN'S CRAWFORD HILL
561-9543 29.95

THE MILWAUKEE ROAD SERIES
561-9544 Volume I 19.95
561-9616 Three-Volume Set 49.95

SWISS RAIL JOURNEYS SET, VOLUME II
561-9617 99.95

THE GLACIER EXPRESS REVISITED
561-9619 39.95

AMTRAK ACROSS AMERICA
561-9620 19.95

DAYLIGHT 4449'S OREGON JOURNEY
561-9621 29.95

SP'S CENTRAL CALIFORNIA MAINLINE
561-9622 29.95

SP'S GEEPS AND CADILLACS
561-9623 29.95

SOUTHERN PACIFIC 3-TAPE SET
561-9624 59.95

EARLY BALDWIN DIESELS ON THE SP
561-9625 19.95

OPERATION FAST FREIGHT
561-9626 19.95

COUNTDOWN TO MERGER
561-9627 29.95

ACROSS THE HEARTLAND
561-9628 29.95

ALONG THE POCAHONTAS DISTRICT
561-9629 39.95

CALIFORNIA ZEPHYR
561-9630 19.95

CONRAIL HOTSPOTS WEST
561-9631 39.95

CHRISTMAS TRAINS
561-9632 19.95

FEATHER RIVER CANYON E-9S
561-9633 19.95

TOUR OF THE M-10000
561-9712 29.95

TODAY'S IC EA 29.95
561-9713 Volume I: North
561-9714 Volume II: South

EUREKA & PALISADE
561-9715 19.95

TOWER 55
561-9716 19.95

CUBA STEAM
561-9717 19.95

INTO ALLEGHENY RANGE, VOLUME IV
561-9718 39.95

MT. RAINIER SCENIC'S
561-9719 19.95

TRACKS AHEAD EA 19.95
561-9720 Volume I
561-9721 Volume II
561-9722 Volume III
561-9727 Volume IV

SUNRISE/SUNSET: A DAY AT GIBBON JUNCTION
561-9723 19.95

SANTA FE VINTAGE DIESELS
561-9724 19.95

DAYLIGHT TO VANCOUVER
561-9725 14.95

THE GENERAL
561-9726 19.95

UP MARYSVILLE SUBDIVISIONS EA 29.95
561-9728 Volume 1
561-9729 Volume 2

WHEELS A'ROLLING
561-9730 19.95

BURLINGTON NORTHERN'S FUNNEL
561-9731 19.95

A STEAM DRIVEN MAN

561-9732 19.95

CLASSIC CHICAGO RAILROADING
561-9733 19.95

STEAM OVER TENNESSEE PASS
561-9734 29.95

EAST BROAD TOP
561-9735 29.95

STEAM TO SQUAMISH
561-9736 19.95

BC RAIL CAB RIDE - FROM SEA TO SKY
561-9737 29.95

BIG BOYS ON TV

561-9738 29.95

TRIBUTE TO TENNESSEE PASS
561-9739 29.95

SUPER TRAINS
561-9740 19.95

WORKIN' ON THE COAST STARLIGHT

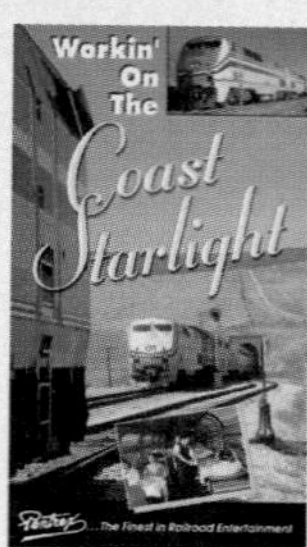

561-9812 19.95

THOSE INCREDIBLE ALCOS EA 29.95

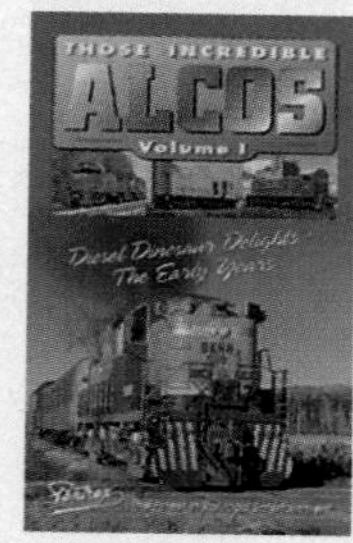

561-9815 Volume I: Diesel Dinosaur Delights
561-9817 Volume II: Notch-Nosed Wonders *NEW*
561-9818 Volume III: Sleek Century Behemoths *NEW*

GRAND CANYON RAILWAY
561-9816 29.95 *NEW*

TRAINS UNLIMITED BOX SET
561-9820 4 Tapes **39.95** *NEW*
These pieces from The History Channel document a variety of railroad operations. Episodes include "Steam Trains", "Atchison, Topeka & Santa Fe", "Built For Speed" and "Grand Central." Includes bonus episode "When Giants Roamed: The Golden Age Of Steam."

BRITISH RAIL JOURNEYS III

561-9821 29.95 *NEW*
The four-tape set explores the beauty of the British Isles. Includes: The Severn Valley & the Cotswold, Bridgnorth to Oxford; The North East, Middelborough to Pickering; South Wales & The Borders, Shrewsbury to Pembroke; and Southwest Scotland, Largs to Stranraer.

DECADES OF STEAM

561-9822 29.95 *NEW*
Learn how steam locomotives helped to define the golden years of Great Britian's railroading (1920s through the 1960s) in this four-tape set.

HISTORY OF BRITISH TRAINS

561-9823 29.95 *NEW*
Trace the development of railroads in Great Britian. Four-tape set includes: Volume I: The Cradle of Railways, Volume II: The Industrail Heartland, Volume III: Commuters & Holidays and Volume IV: Valleys & Mountains.

RAIL AWAY EA 29.95

561-9824 Set 1 *NEW*
Five hours of world travel. Volume I: Orient Express, India and Sri Lanka; Volume II: Portugal, Spain and Greece; Volume III: Finalnd, Scotland, Denmark & Sweden; Volume IV: Cumba, Tunisia, Eastern & Oriental.

561-9825 Set 2 *NEW*
International travel at its most glamorous! Volume I: Australia and Peru; Volume II: Holland, Switzerland and Norway; Volume III: Ireland, Canada, Scotland and England; Volume IV: Romania, South Africa and Hungary.

SWISS RAIL JOURNEYS III

561-9826 29.95 *NEW*
Tour Switzerland aboard vintage locomotives in this box set of videos. Tapes include: The Bernia Express, The Engadine Line and The Gruyere Railway.

WORLD STEAM JOURNEYS EA 29.95

561-9827 Volume I *NEW*
Includes four tapes: Patagonia Express, Relics of the Raj, Rails to Arabia and African Steam.

561-9828 Volume II *NEW*
Four tapes: Steam to the Gobi Desert, Wheels of Fire, Return to the Blue Ridge, Narrow Gauges of Eastern Europe and The Last Stronghold of Steam in Europe.

ALL ABOARD SERIES EA 19.95 (UNLESS NOTED)

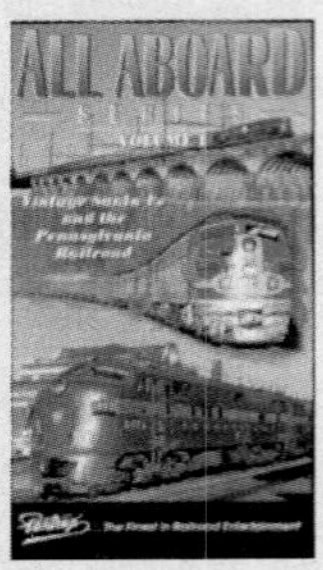

561-9829 Volume I: Vintage Santa Fe & The Pennsylvania Railroad **4.95** *NEW*

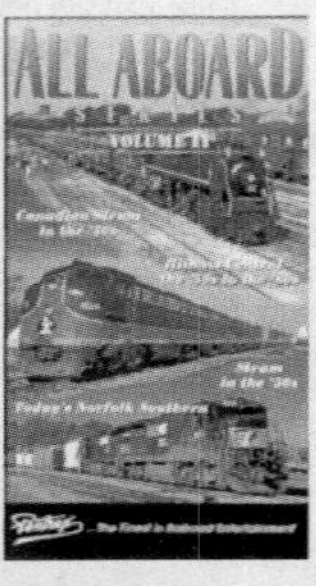

561-9830 Volume II: Canadian Steam, Illinois Central 50s-80s *NEW*

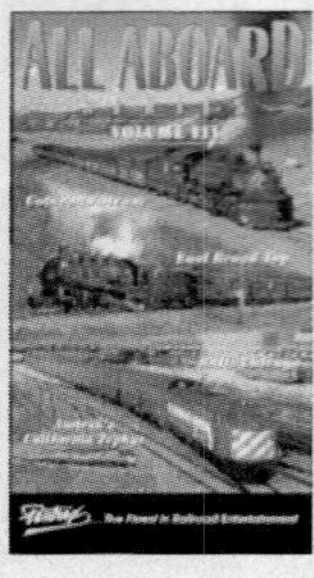

561-9819 Volume III: Col. Steam, EBT, Rails Chicago, Amtrak's CZ *NEW*

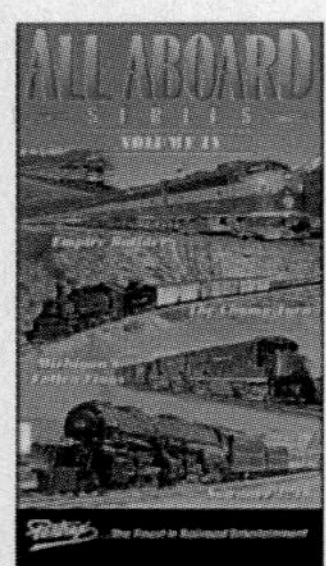

561-9831 Volume IV: Empire Builder, The Chama Turn, Suwanee *NEW*

561-9832 Volume V:1965 San Juan Passenger Special *NEW*

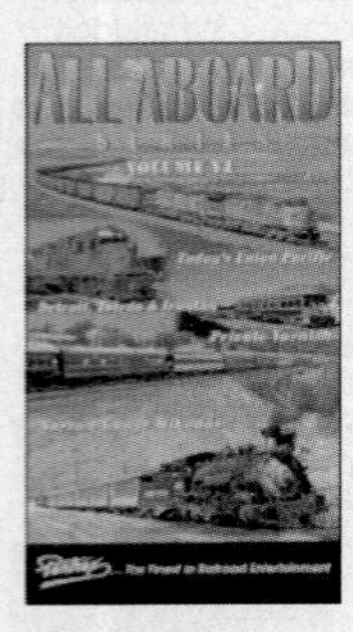

561-9833 Volume VI: Today's Union Pacific *NEW*

561-9834 Volume VII: Volume VII: FEC, Rockets & Rails, Early Diesels of St. Louis *NEW*

HOT RAILS THROUGH THE TWIN CITES

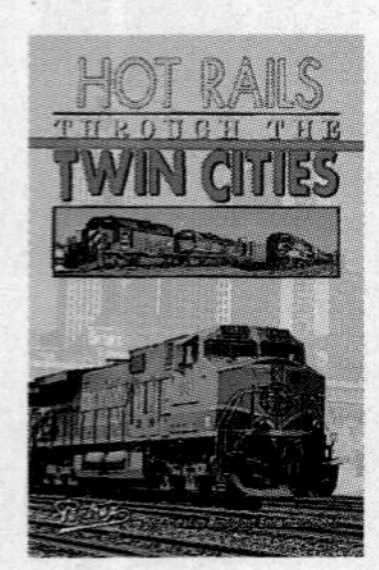

561-9835 29.95 *NEW*
Travel through Minneapolis/St. Paul, home to eight different railroads as well as Amtrak passenger trains

GRAND ISLAND

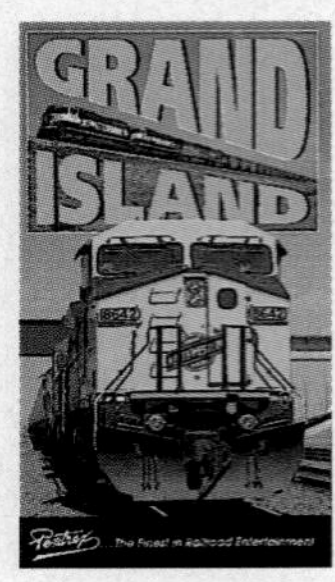

561-9836 19.95 *NEW*
Watch Burlington Northern and Union Pacific travel through Nebraska to their point of intersection: Grand Island.

COASTER

561-9837 19.95 *NEW*
Enjoy the Pacific Ocean aboard commuter servce stretching from San Diego to Oceanside, California.

PITTSBURGH LINE BLUES "FAREWELL TO CONRAIL"

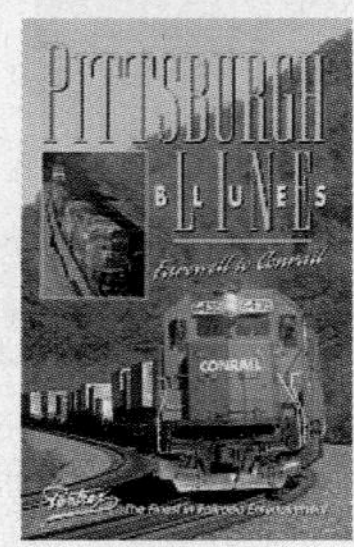

561-9838 19.95 *NEW*
Watch "Big Blue" pull freight as it ventures through the Allegheny Mountains.

STEAM 1998

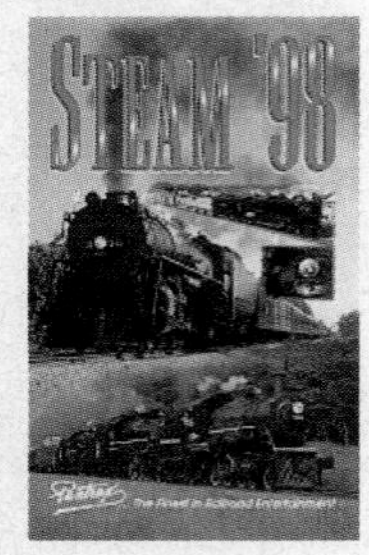

561-9839 19.95 *NEW*
Watch steam locomotives from Union Pacific and Milwaukee Road travel the country during the summer of 1998.

UNION PACIFIC'S MIGHTY TURBINES

561-9840 19.95 *NEW*
Learn how Union Pacific became the first railroad to place a fleet of gas turbine-electric locomotives into use, and how these engines differ from diesel-electric units.

OZARK COUNTRY CAB RIDE: "BNSF IN MISSOURI - THE CUBA SUB"

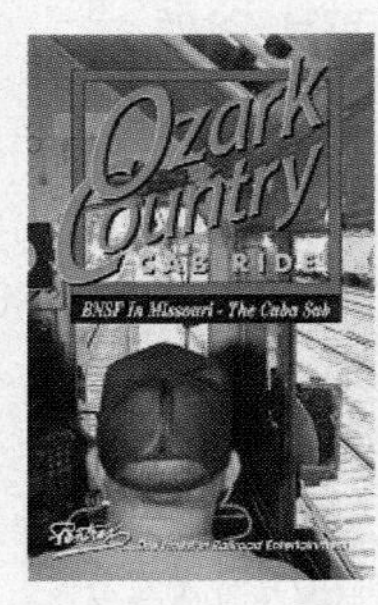

561-9841 19.95 *NEW*
Ride the hilly and curvy territory between St. Louis and Springfield aboard an intermodal train.

PENTREX PREVIEWS

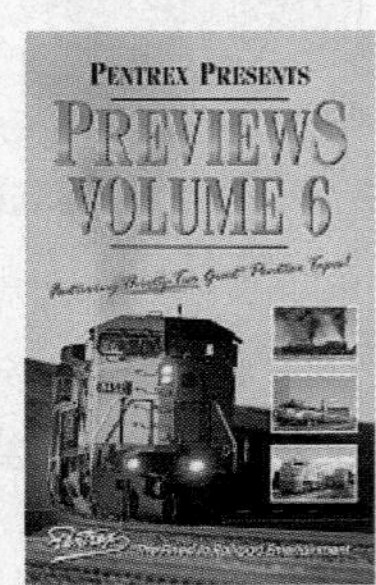

561-9842 Volume VI **19.95** *NEW*
Sample 32 of Pentrex's latest videos in this 90-minute adventure.

THE BEST OF THE MIDWEST

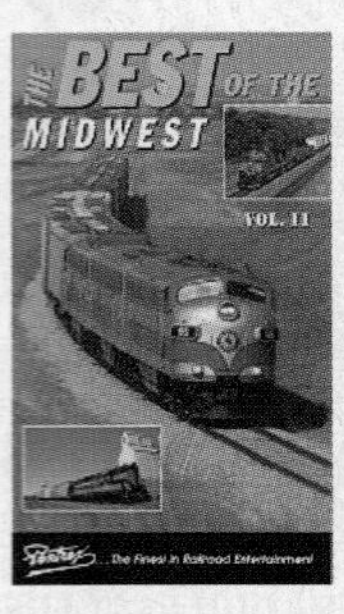

561-9843 Volume II **19.95** *NEW*
Visit Missouri, Nebraska, Iowa, South Dakota and Minnesota to learn the value of regional railroads to the Midwest.

TRAINS ON THE HIGH PLAINS

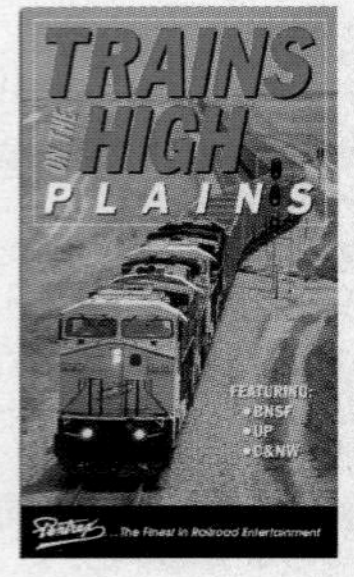

561-9844 19.95 *NEW*
Learn how coal travels from Wyoming's Powder River Basin to power plants.

RIDING THE RAILS
561-9845 19.95 *NEW*

TRACKS AHEAD EA 19.95
561-9846 Volume V *NEW*
561-9847 Volume VI *NEW*

CALIFORNIA ELECTRIC TRILOGY

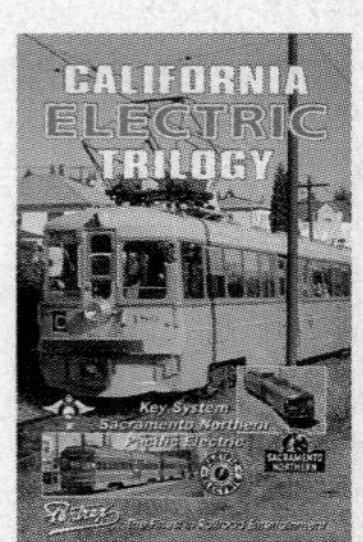

561-9848 29.95 *NEW*
See how three electric railroads maneuvered through California during the 1950s and 1960s

THE STANDARD RAILROAD OF THE WORLD: PRR
561-9851 39.95

MONON: SHE'S A HOOSIER LINE
561-9852 39.95

RUNAWAY TRAINS
561-70349 19.95 *NEW*

ROCO

IMPORTED FROM AUSTRIA BY WALTHERS

BERLIN CITY RAILWAY
625-84000 22.99
History of the Berlin City Railway. 120 pages, 100 illustrations, German text.

GLASKATEN
625-84001 22.99
History of the Glaskaten locomotives and Bavarian coach models. German text.

40 YEARS OF DB
625-84002 22.99
German text.

ROCO LINE TRACK PLAN SHEET
625-81455 9.99

ROCO LINE TRACK SYSTEM
Limited Quantity Available
625-81457 1.00

SINGLE SHOT GALLERY

All books are softcover and 8-1/2 x 11".

SHAY INSTRUCTION SHEETS #2
671-8000 9.00
Reprint of 11 Class B Shay service bulletins, first issued by Lima in July of 1923. 32 pages.

THE LIMA SHAY CATALOG (1925)

671-9502 9.00
Reproduced Shay photos and documentation. 32 pages.

INSTRUCTIONS FOR THE CARE OF THE SHAY LOCOMOTIVE
671-9507 9.00
Period photographs and isometric drawings highlight this 32-page book.

Sandia Software

CADRAIL

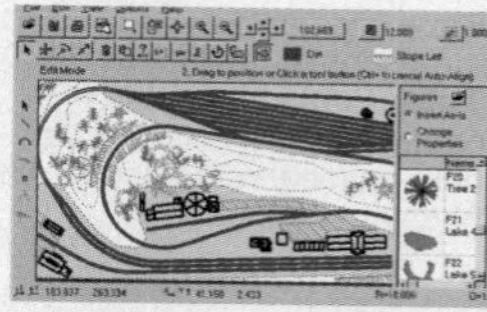

645-3 Version 7 for MS Windows 95 **99.95**
The premier Computer Assisted Design (CAD) program for model railroaders. Works in any scale and includes hundreds of powerful, easy-to-use CAD tools that allow you to plan, profile and 3D view. Provides hundreds of drawings including: buildings, bridges, rolling stock, scenery, sample layouts, symbols and track libraries. Requires: VGA, Mouse, CD ROM.

645-10 Cadrail Junior **49.95**
NEW
Based on Cadrail's CAD shell, Cadrail Junior comes with easy to learn drag and drop tools. This is a system for railroad design for those who don't want a complete CAD program. Includes its own library of track layouts or allows you to make your own. Features automatic track section alignment, ability to draw any size or scale, unlimited user defined styles and layers, ability to work with elevations, grades and coordinates, library of sample plans that includes numerous brand names and complete computerized help and examples. Requires MS Windows 95 or 98, VGA, mouse and CD ROM.

S & S HOBBY

MY TRAIN COLORING BOOK

643-700 4.49
Fun for kids of all ages. Twenty pages of the many faces of North America's Railroads.

SUPERIOR HOME VIDEO

VIDEOS

RAILROAD VIDEOS

CHOO CHOO TRAINS: CLOSE UP AND VERY PERSONAL
662-4 14.95 ***NEW***
See trains from steam locos to modern wonders. 30 minutes.

STEVENS PASS
662-6 29.95 ***NEW***
Ride through Washington's Stevens Pass. 60 minutes.

HISTORY OF AMERICAN RAILROADS
662-18 24.95 ***NEW***
A historical study of railroad development. 80 minutes.

GHOST TRAIN
662-19 29.95
Visit the Virginia & Truckee and the Old West. 73 minutes.

STEAMING UP THE NEW RIVER GORGE
662-28 39.95
Ride through the wilds of the New River Gorge. 90 minutes.

GIANTS ON THE RAILS
662-29 19.95
Ride some of America's steam locomotives. 60 minutes.

THE ALPHABET TRAIN
662-100 8.98 ***NEW***
Exposure kids to railroading with this one-hour video.

RETURN OF THE GALLOPING GOOSE
662-1008 24.95 ***NEW***
60 minutes.

CUMBRES & TOLTEC SCENIC RAILWAY
662-1009 24.95 ***NEW***
70 minutes.

CHASED BY A STEAM TRAIN EA 29.95
Travel the Rocky Mountains on a passenger (Volume I) or freight (Volume 2) train. Each video runs 90 minutes.

662-101 Volume 1 ***NEW***
662-102 Volume 2 ***NEW***

FIRST TRAIN TO TOLTEC
662-313 29.95 ***NEW***
Cumbres & Toltec railroad tours Rockies. 60 minutes.

ROCKY MOUNTAIN SNOWPLOW
662-323 29.95 ***NEW***
Trains clear snow from the Cumbres & Toltec Scenic Railroad. 90 minutes.

DURANGO TO SILVERTON
662-1004 14.95 ***NEW***
A train heads from Durango to Silverton. 25 minutes.

FREIGHT TRAINS - ACROSS THE AMERICAN WEST
662-1005 14.95 ***NEW***
Engines push through to Salt Lake City. 25 minutes.

TENNESSEE PASS AND THE ROYAL GORGE ROUTE
662-603 29.95 ***NEW***
Travel through a stretch of the Colorado Rockies. 90 minutes.

THUNDER ON THE RAILS
662-4785 9.95
Covers Virginia & Truckee and Nevada Northern. 30 minutes.

HAWAII'S SUGAR CANE TRAIN
662-732 14.95 ***NEW***
Locomotive tours Hawaiian island. 40 minutes.

THE SPIRIT OF MOUNTAIN RAILROADING
662-1001 19.95 ***NEW***
100 years of Durango & Silverton railroad. 60 minutes.

EUREKA'S INCREDIBLE JOURNEY
662-1002 19.95 ***NEW***
Owner and crew discuss their experiences. 60 minutes.

THE 8:30 TO SILVERTON
662-1003 19.95 ***NEW***
Travel from Durango to Silverton. 60 minutes.

THE WINTER HOLIDAY TRAINS
662-1006 14.95 ***NEW***
Travel through wintery San Juan Mountains. 25 minutes.

LOTS & LOTS OF TRAINS EA 14.95
Each video runs approximately 30 minutes.

662-7201 Volume 1 ***NEW***
662-7202 Volume 2 ***NEW***

TITANS OF THE TRACKS
662-7700 14.95

BRANSON SCENIC RAILWAY
662-61238 14.95 ***NEW***
Branson, Missouri, comes to life in this 30-minute tour.

ALL ABOARD: THE LEGEND OF THE RAILS
662-80893 19.95 ***NEW***
Explore passenger car development. 60 minutes.

CANADA THE TRAIN JOURNEY
662-653015 24.95
60 minutes.

DAYLIGHT EXPRESS
662-378262 39.95
103 minutes.

ALL ABOARD THE POTOMAC EAGLE
662-99 19.95 ***NEW***
Travel West Virginia on a diesel Train. 60 minutes.

PIKE'S PEAK BY RAIL
662-26 19.95 ***NEW***
Discover America's famous mountain. 39 minutes.

THE GEORGETOWN LOOP RAILROAD
662-34 19.95 ***NEW***
Travel through the Colorado Mountains. 30 minutes.

ALL ABOARD FOR EUREKA
662-38 19.95 ***NEW***
Explore Ozarks. 30 minutes.

THE SUGAR CANE TRAIN
662-47 19.95 ***NEW***
Learn about Maui's last working railroad. 30 minutes.

SCENIC RAILWAY OF THE WORLD
662-49 19.95 ***NEW***
Tour of the White Pass & Yukon Route. 30 minutes.

STEAM CLOUDS
662-138 39.95 ***NEW***
Travel through the Columbia River Gorge. 90 minutes.

THE ALASKA RAILROAD
662-107 19.95 ***NEW***
Explore America's 49th state. 35 minutes.

PIKE'S PEAK ROUTE
662-66 19.95 ***NEW***
Travel from Colorado Springs to Grand Junction. 55 minutes.

KLONDIKE GOLD RUSH DOUBLE FEATURE
662-53 19.95 ***NEW***
Learn about mining for gold, 60 minutes.

THE GOLD RUSH RAILROAD
662-55 19.95 ***NEW***
Railroad development during the Gold Rush. 50 minutes.

AN ENGINEER'S POINT OF VIEW
662-57 19.95 ***NEW***
Drive upfront with an engineer. 57 minutes.

DISCOVERING CANADA BY RAIL EA 19.95
Each video runs 70 minutes.

662-1101 West Coast Explorations ***NEW***
662-1102 Gold Country ***NEW***
662-1103 Inside British Columbia ***NEW***
662-1104 Rugged Northern Beauty ***NEW***
662-1105 East To West Panorama ***NEW***
662-1106 Along The Waterways ***NEW***
662-1107 Historical Adventures ***NEW***
662-1108 French Canadian Journeys ***NEW***
662-1109 Four Tape Set 1101-1104 **49.95** ***NEW***
662-1110 Four Tape Set 1105-1108 **49.95** ***NEW***

FAREWELL TO STEAM - NORTHERN PACIFIC
662-103 19.95 ***NEW***
30 minutes.

RAYONIER - LAST STEAM LOGGER
662-104 19.95 ***NEW***
30 minutes.

STEWART PRODUCTS

RECORD BOOKS

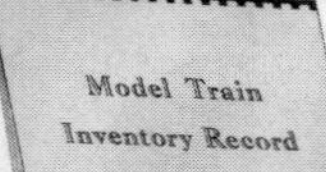

683-509 Model Train Inventory **7.95**

Limited Quantity Available

683-508 Trainwatcher's Scratchpad **5.95**

TESTORS

CD-ROM

HOW TO BUILD MODEL AIRPLANES

704-1 24.95 ***NEW***
Get started in model building with answers to the most-asked questions in the hobby.

VOLLMER

IMPORTED FROM GERMANY BY WALTHERS

98-99 CATALOG

770-9998 6.99
Separate sections for G, HO, N & Z Scale, with measurements for all buildings. Full-color. 8-1/4 x 11-3/4".

Virnex Industries, Inc.

DECALS

Full color railroad herald decals, 2-1/2" to 3" in size.

RAILROAD EA 1.50 EXCEPT AS NOTED

762-106

762-101 DRGW
762-102 GN
762-103 Indiana Harbor Belt
762-104 N&W
762-105 South Shore
762-106 CP
762-107 CB&Q
762-108 MP
762-109 Gulf, Mobile & Ohio
762-110 NYC
762-111 Frisco
762-112 CNW
762-113 PRR
762-114 MILW
762-115 Chessie
762-116 Elgin, Joliet & Eastern
762-117 Illinois Central Gulf
762-118 North Shore
762-119 UP
762-120 NKP
762-121 EL
762-122 Rock Island
762-123 L&N
762-124 Belt Railway of Chicago
762-125 Central Vermont
762-100 Assortment pkg(25) **35.50**
One each of #101-125.

Amtrak

762-155

762-161

762-171

Western Pacific

762-173

762-151 BN
762-152 Grand Trunk
762-153 CR
762-154 CN
762-155 Amtrak
762-156 ATSF
762-157 CP
762-158 The Rock
762-159 Florida East Coast
762-160 GN (Blue)
762-161 Kansas City Southern
762-162 MKT
762-163 Monon
762-164 New York, Ontario & Western
762-165 PC
762-166 Seaboard Coast Line
762-167 SOU
762-168 SP
762-169 Vermont Railway
762-170 Wabash
762-171 NP
762-172 Family Lines
762-173 WP
762-174 Atlantic Coast Line
762-175 SOO
762-150 Assortment pkg(25) **35.50**
One each of #151-175.
762-201 B&O
762-202 C&O
762-203 CNJ
762-204 Chicago & Eastern Illinois
762-205 Chicago Great Western
762-206 SSW
762-207 Detroit, Toledo & Ironton
762-208 Green Bay & Western
762-209 Green Mountain
762-210 MEC
762-211 NS
762-212 RDG
762-213 MP Buzz Saw
762-214 Chicago & Illinois Midland
762-215 WC

MISCELLANEOUS

762-131 "I am a Railfan" **1.50**
762-132 "Pray for Me—My husband collects trains" **1.50**

HOT PAD

"PRAY FOR ME—MY HUSBAND COLLECTS TRAINS"

762-432 2.50
6 x 6" White with red lettering.

BOOKS

MAKING THE SCENE

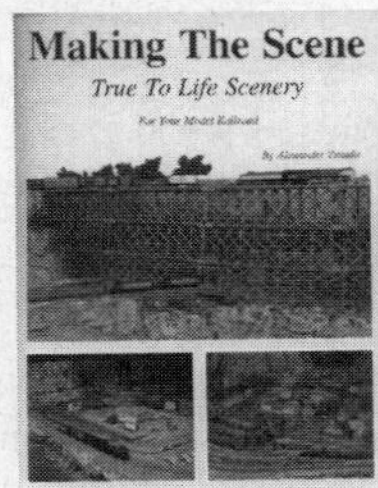

762-801 9.95
Includes chapters on track and trackwork, roadbed and ballasting, creating rivers and lakes, rockwork and more. Softcover, 74 pages.

WEEKEND CHIEF PUBLISHING

Weekend Chief publishes and distributes a wide range of prototype railroading books, with a special focus on operations in the eastern United States. Each book is loaded with photos, making them an ideal reference for the modeler or historian.

BOOKS

RAILROAD BOOKS

HOWARD FOGG AND THE DIESEL IMAGE

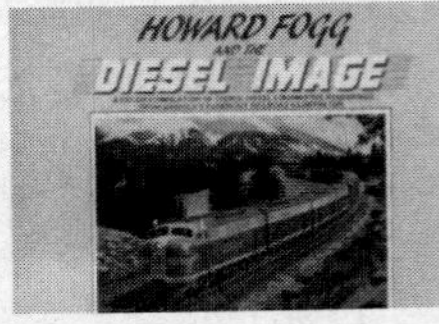

779-1 39.95
Showcase of diesel loco prints by noted rail artist Howard Fogg. Full-page prints with caption information. Full-color, hardcover, 175 pages, indexed by railroad, 12 x 9".

RAILWAY PROTOTYPE CYCLOPEDIA

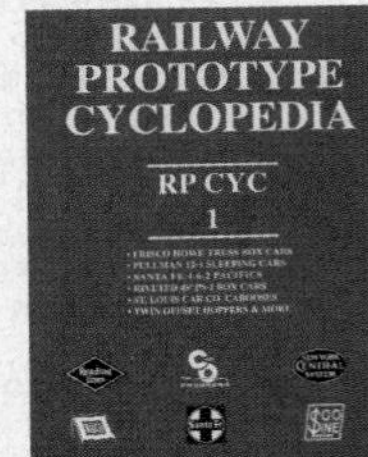

779-2 20.95
Softcover, 96 pages

MAINLINE STEAM REVIVAL
779-4 39.95

PENNSY POWER
779-14 50.00 ***NEW***

NEW YORK CENTRAL'S EARLY POWER 1831-1916

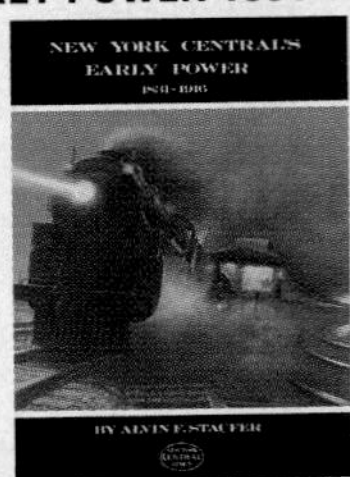

779-17 50.00 ***NEW***
Learn more about the many smaller railroads that make up the New York Central System. Over 800 photographs and drawings, 352 pages.

B&O POWER
779-18 50.00 ***NEW***

NEW HAVEN POWER
779-19 80.00 ***NEW***

NEW YORK CENTRAL LATER POWER
779-20 70.00 ***NEW***

THOROUGHBREDS
779-21 65.00 ***NEW***

BROOKLYN'S WATERFRONT RAILWAYS
779-109 24.95
Brooklyn steam, diesel and electrics in color and black & white. Maps and brochures. Softcover, 64 pages.

DIESEL DEMONSTRATORS

779-110 TBA

DIESELS TO PARK AVENUE: THE FL-9 STORY

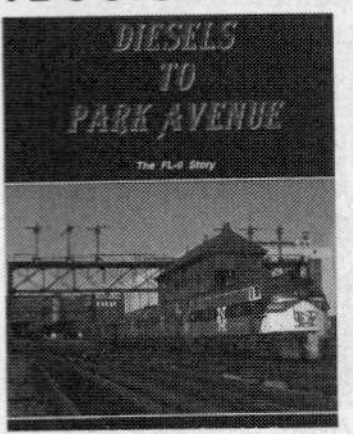

779-111 44.00

THE LATE GREAT PENNSYLVANIA STATION

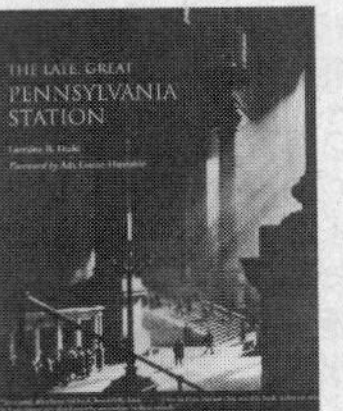

779-112 16.95

VICTORIAN RR STATION
779-1004 39.95

RAILROAD ATLASES EA 23.95 (UNLESS NOTED)

799-10

779-5 North Eastern USA **24.95**
779-6 Arizona - New Mexico
779-7 Colorado - Utah
779-8 California - Nevada
779-9 Great Lakes - East
779-10 Great Lakes - West
779-11 Piedmont Area
779-12 Washington - Oregon

RAILROAD BOOKS

Expand your railroad library with this series of prototype books. Each volume has an 8-1/2 x 11" format and is packed with photos that will provide endless ideas for modeling projects.

NS

NORFOLK SOUTHERN LOCOMOTIVE DIRECTORY 1998-1999

95-71 14.95 *NEW*
Get the most up-to-date listing of NS power, including the recent addition of Conrail locomotives. 112 pages, 100 photos.

NORFOLK SOUTHERN 1982-1994

95-1200 28.95

PRR SERIES

Pennsy experimented with diesels like no other railroad, creating an incredibly diverse roster with examples from every major US builder. This softcover series examines specific models and provides a comprehensive collection of photos.

VOLUME I: ALCO RS SERIES

95-61 14.95
A must-have for Alco fans, 60 pages of pictures.

VOLUME II: BALDWIN SWITCHERS & ROAD SWITCHERS

95-62 16.95
Some of the rarest and most unusual American diesels, presented in 80 pages of photos.

VOLUME III: EMD SECOND GENERATION ROAD SWITCHERS

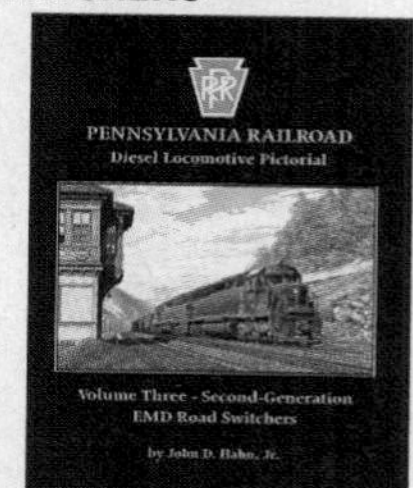

95-63 16.95
Starts in 1963 with the purchase of GP30s and ends with the last pre-merger six-axle SD45s. 80 pages with over 150 photos.

VOLUME IV: BALDWIN CAB & TRANSFER UNITS

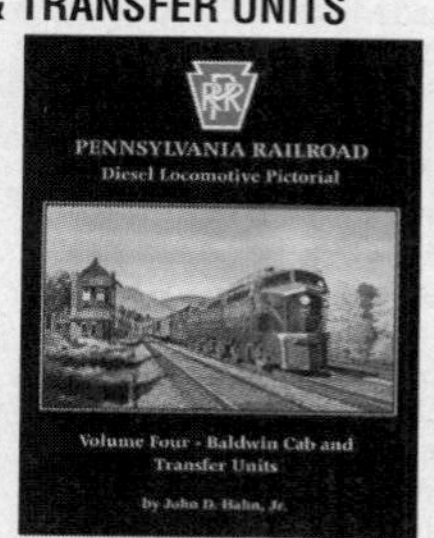

95-69 16.95
Any diesel fan will treasure this collection, featuring over 125 B&W photographs. 72 pages.

CROSSROADS OF COMMERCE: THE PENNSYLVANIA RAILROAD CALENDAR ART OF GRIF TELLER

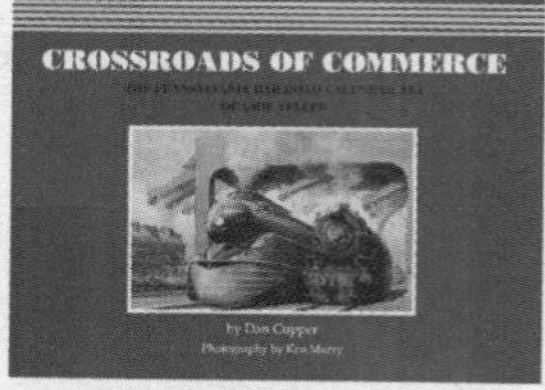

95-74 49.95 *NEW*
This 184-page award-winning book showcases the calendar paintings used as advertising by the Pennsylvania Railroad. Also features a biography of the man responsible for these impressive works of art. 184 pages featuring over 200 photos (150 in color).

FAIRBANKS-MORSE

C-LINERS F-M'S CONSOLIDATION LINE OF LOCOMOTIVES

95-64 22.95
Fairbanks-Morse and Canadian Locomotive Co. enter the 1950s fighting for a share of the cab unit market. In-depth look at both four- and six-axle versions, along with the P-12-42. Softcover with 80 pages and over 250 photos.

TRAIN MASTER-THE MOST USEFUL LOCOMOTIVE EVER BUILT

95-250 29.95
Hauling everything from commuters to coal, the H24-66 proved the versatility of high-horsepower, six-axle engines. Complete look at the history and heritage of this milestone in diesel design. Softcover, 112 pages (24 in color) and 250+ B&W images.

N&W SECOND GENERATION DIESELS

95-500 48.00

UP

SWITCHERS & SLUGS

95-65 24.95
Expanded coverage of EMC/EMD models featured in Diesel Era magazine, plus sections on Alco, Baldwin, FM, GE and non-revenue industrial models. Softcover, 116 pages (24 in color) with over 275 B&W photos.

UNION PACIFIC LOCOMOTIVE DIRECTORY 1999

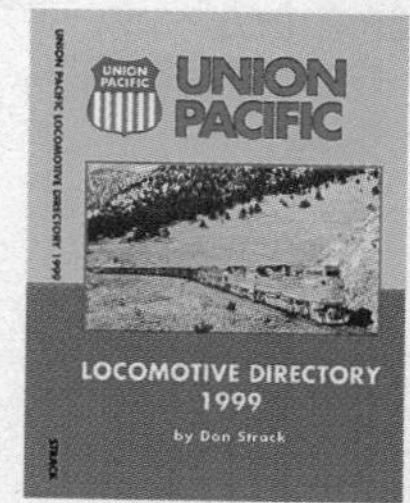

95-72 19.95 *NEW*

UNION PACIFIC'S SHERMAN HILL IN THE DIESEL ERA

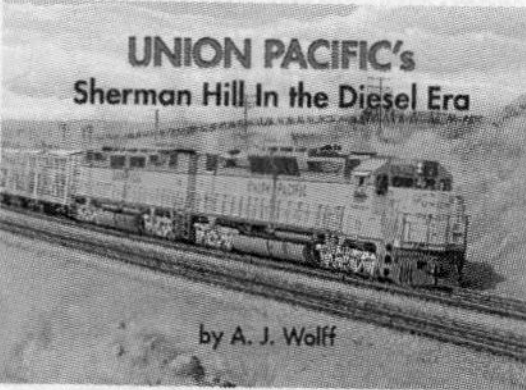

95-75 48.00 *NEW*
Written by A.J. Wolff.

CONRAIL

THE FINAL YEARS

95-66 48.00
Here's a last look at the motive power, from 1992 through 1997, with a special section on the SD80MAC. Hardcover, 200 pages with over 500 color and B&W photos. Great companion to #95-100, which covers 1986-1991, sold separately.

MOTIVE POWER REVIEW 1986-1991

95-100 48.00
A motive power photo essay, with a detailed roster of new acquisitions and still-in-service classics like GP30s and E8s. Hardcover, 252 pages with 870 photos. Great companion to #95-66, which covers 1992-1997, sold separately.

MISCELLANEOUS

DIESELS OF THE SOUTHERN RAILWAY 1939-1982

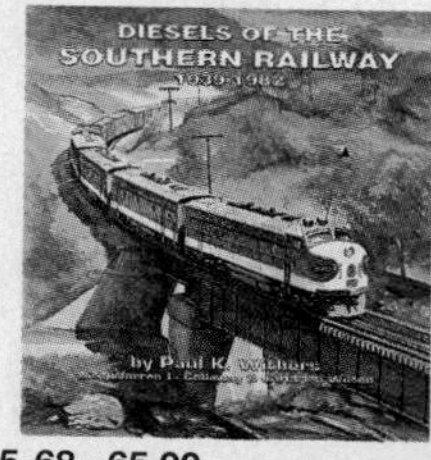

95-68 65.00
Coverage from the first FTs to the last GEs. Hardcover, 384 pages with more than 1,000 photos. Complete roster lists modifications, retirements, dispositions and specifications for Southern and all subsidiaries.

EMD'S SD60 SERIES-STEPPINGSTONE TO THE 21ST CENTURY

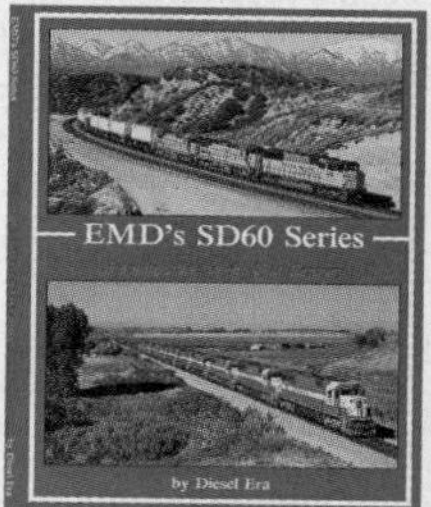

95-60 29.95
A look at the loco that paved the way for today's EMDs. Plenty of roster and detail views for modeling projects, along with action shots. Softcover, 164 pages with 12 HO Scale drawings and over 250 B&W photos.

THE GP20 AND SD24 EMD'S TURBOCHARGED DUO

95-70 29.95 *NEW*
See how the addition of a turbocharger revolutionized these locomotives--and the industry itself. 112 pages, over 200 color and B&W photos.

KANSAS CITY SOUTHERN IN THE DERAMUS ERA

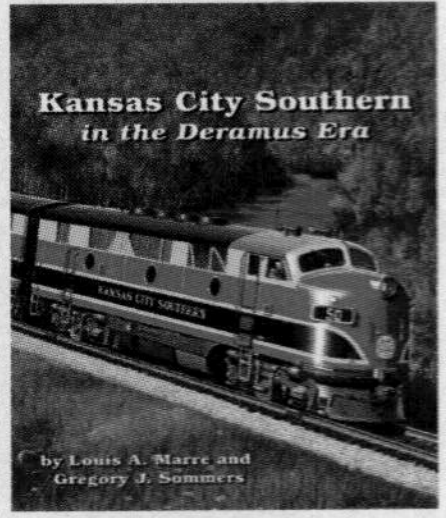

95-73 48.00 ***NEW***
Study how one family's multigenerational control of Kansas City Southern shaped the line's motive power and train operation. Hardcover, 224 pages featuring maps, rosters and over 500 photos.

ATLANTIC COAST LINE-THE DIESEL YEARS
95-800 49.95
Covers all models from 1939 through the 1967 merger with the Seaboard. Hardcover, 196 pages, 443 photos.

DIESELS OF THE CNW

95-900 59.95
A look at internal combustion units from 1926 to the final units delivered before the 1995 UP merger. Includes locos from merged lines like Chicago Great Western, and used engines purchased for rebuilding programs. Hardcover, 320 pages (32 in full-color) and 400+ photos.

HORSESHOE HERITAGE
95-950 9.95 ***NEW***
The official booklet of the Horseshoe Curve National Historical Landmark. 60 pages, 117 color and B&W photos.

THE REVOLUTIONARY FT-EMC'S ASSAULT ON MAIN LINE FREIGHT OPERATIONS

95-1000 24.95
Here's the story of the diesel that dethroned steam as king of the rails, and laid the groundwork for the future of railroading. Softcover second edition with 132 pages, 250+ color and B&W photos.

GE'S DASH 8 SERIES: THE DIESEL ERA'S THIRD GENERATION

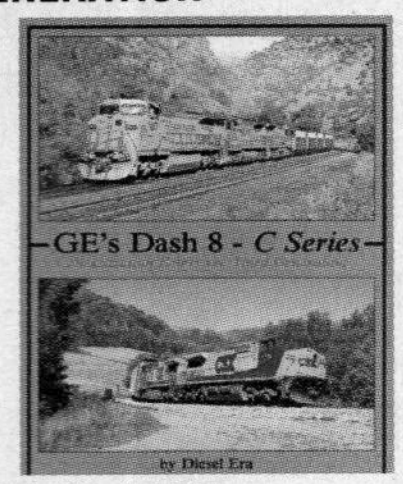

95-1100 24.95
Unveiled in 1987, many consider this the engine that introduced the latest generation of diesels to railroading. Covers all six-axle Dash 8 owners in the US and Canada with roster, detail and in-action shots. Softcover, 120 pages 250+ color and B&W photos.

WHISTLES UNLIMITED

WOOD TRAIN WHISTLES

753-10 Regular **4.95**
753-20 Junior **4.50**
753-30 Mini **4.00**

New Arrivals Updated Every Day! Visit Walthers Web site at

www.walthers.com

COLORADO'S COLORFUL JOINT LINE

798-32 39.95
See BN, DRGW and ATSF trains make a spectacular run along the Rockies. 60 min.

THE FIFTIES EXPRESS
798-23 39.95
The newest diesels, electrics and steam in action. 52 min.

ALLEGHENY RAILS
798-24 Volume I **39.95**
B&O steam comes to life on this tape compiled from original 8mm films. 55 min.
798-25 Volume II **39.95**
WM trains of the mid 1950s return to the mainline. 52 min.

THE MILWAUKEE'S MIGHTY ELECTRICS
798-28 39.95
See the "Joes" in action over Pipestone Pass and "Box Cabs" crossing the Columbia River in the 1960s.

SANTA FE'S NEW MEXICO MAIN
798-39 39.95
The desolate beauty of Santa Fe's New Mexico mainline. 60 min.

SILVER RAILS GOLDEN MEMORIES
798-26 39.95
A tribute to the 50th anniversary of the Rocky Mountain Railroad Club.

ASSAULT ON SNOW
798-27 39.95
Man and machine battle the elements as Wyoming & Colorado F units buck drifts, and a UP rotary works west of Laramie. 52 min.

KINDIG'S DIESELS
798-29 Part 1 **29.95**
Color movies of diesel power from 1971 and 1972.

AMERICA ON RAILS
Series begins in the 1930s showing a cross section of America's railroads with an emphasis on interurbans and passenger trains.

798-30 Section 1 **29.95**
798-36 Section 2 **29.95**
798-37 Section 3 **29.95**

TEHACHAPI-PARTS 1 & 2
Part 1 covers the Santa Fe, Part 2 features Southern Pacific.

798-20 Part 1 **39.95**
798-21 Part 2 **39.95**

THE RIO GRANDE TODAY
798-22 39.95
Profiles operations on the Rio Grande. 2 hrs.

EXCURSION TO THE THIRTIES
798-3 39.95
Reproduced from original films made from 1937 to 1941. A rare look at pre-war narrow gauge operations on the C&S, DRGW and RGS. 52 min.

THE LAST STEAMERS OF THE C&S
798-19 39.95
Original footage from 1958-60 shows 2-10-2, 2-8-2, 2-8-0, rotary snow plow and more. 52 minutes.

A FORTIES MEMORY
798-10 24.95
Postwar railroading including ATSF, DRGW, SP, RGS and others. 24 min.

CHALLENGER '82
798-2 39.95
A study of UP 3985 from delivery in 1943 to restoration and fantrip service in 1982.

SANTA FE'S RATON ROUTE
798-42 39.95
Modern Santa Fe power against a panorama of the Old West filmed between 1989 and 1991. 112 min.

UP "CHALLENGER" 3985
798-1 39.95
Covers the testing and operation of the famous 4-6-6-4 in 1981.

RIO GRANDE NARROW GAUGE IN THE 50S
798-4 39.96
Follow K-36 and K-27 Mikados in freight and passenger service through Colorado in 1950.

STEAM OVER SHERMAN
798-11 39.95
Steam's last days on the UP. 54 min.

DIESELS ON THE UP
798-13 39.95
A look at contemporary operations from Cheyenne to Dale Junction. 60 min.

UNION PACIFIC'S LAST STEAM GIANTS
798-38 24.95
It's summer, 1958, at Cheyenne, and UP's 4-8-8-4s are being readied for their last months of service. 24 min.

NARROW GAUGE VIDEO VIGNETTE
798-5 24.95
Large and small DRGW narrow gauge locos are featured. 55 min.

DIESELS WEST
798-8 39.95
High-horsepower diesels in action along the UP and DRGW. 55 min.

LEGEND OF THE RIO GRANDE ZEPHYR
798-9 39.95
The last privately owned and operated streamliner on its final run April 24, 1983.

DRGW NARROW GAUGE FREIGHT TRAINS
798-6 29.95
From films made in 1967, this tape follows freights behind K-37s 493 and 497. 60 min.

HEAVY FREIGHT AND UNION PACIFIC 3985

798-40 39.95
UP 3985 pulls a freight train between Cheyenne and North Platte in August 1990. 60 min.

RAILS ACROSS THE SUMMIT
798-12 19.95
Cumbres and Toltec Scenic Railway Mikado 483 heads for Cumbres Summit. 28 minutes, color and sound.

DIESELS ON THE UP—THE SEQUEL
798-14 39.95
SD40s, U30Cs and DDA40Xs do battle with a Wyoming blizzard.

RIO GRANDE OF THE ROCKIES
798-15 39.95
Colorado mainline and narrow gauge DRGW operations in the 1950s. 59 min.

DOUBLE HEADER '83
798-16 19.95
In October 1983, Peter-Built Locomotive Works sponsored a two-engine freight over the Cumbres & Toltec Scenic Railroad, rolling back time to the 1940s. 28 min.

RAILS ALONG THE ROCKIES

798-31 39.95
BN, Rio Grande and Santa Fe trains on Colorado's Joint Line. 60 min.

DRGW NARROW GAUGE STOCK TRAIN AND COLOR KARAVAN

798-7 29.95
Filmed in October 1966.

SNOWTRAIN: RIO GRANDE'S SKI SPECIAL

798-17 29.95
Filmed in 1984. 28 min.

THE SUGAR CANE TRAIN

798-18 19.95
Ride behind steam on the Lahaina, Kaanipall & Pacific.

SANTA FE SELIGMAN SUB

798-33 39.95
A variety of trains thunder over the Arizona Divide. 60 min.

BLUE RIDGE STEAM

798-35 39.95
Action along the Blue Ridge Summit, the Christianburg grade and the Shenandoah Line in the late 1950s. 82 min.

UNION PACIFIC SUPER CABS & STEAM

798-41 39.95
Wide cab SD60Ms and GE Dash 8-40CWs take the lead on Sherman Hill.

A SALUTE TO SOLDIER SUMMIT

798-34 39.95
All trains on the DRGW's Utah Division have a common goal—to reach Soldier Summit.

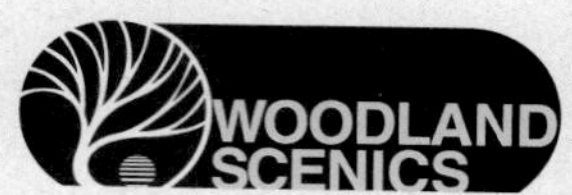

SUBTERRAIN SYSTEM

HOW TO VIDEO
785-1401 24.98
Approx. 60 minutes. A step-by-step video that shows you how to build a model railroad layout with the revolutionary SubTerrain Layout System.

HOW TO MANUAL
785-1402 4.98
An illustrated how-to manual that teaches you how to create the ideal base for scenery and landscaping from start to finish.

THE SCENERY MANUAL

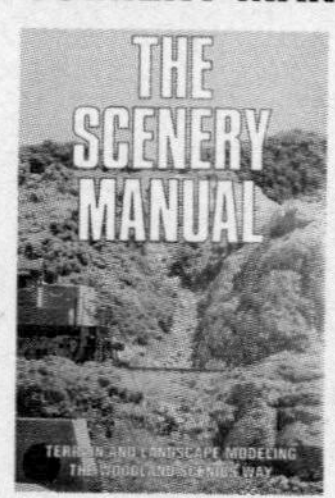

785-1207 9.98
An illustrated start-to-finish guide to terrain construction and landscaping. It is full of basics for beginners and secrets of skilled scenery modelers.

VIDEO

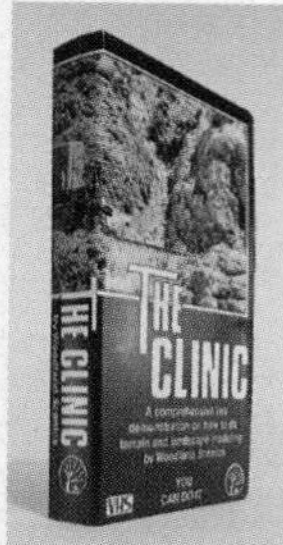

THE CLINIC
785-990 24.98
Learn by watching the professionals demonstrate landscaping and terrain modeling techniques. In this video, you'll see just how easy it is. 1 hour and 15 min. length.

JOIN THE NATIONAL MODEL RAILROAD ASSOCIATION

You may know that the NMRA developed interchange standards for model railroad products. Maybe you've been to a club open house, or heard about regional and national conventions. But there are many other benefits for members.

Whether you invest in a brass loco, a bag of detail parts or a complete kit, you expect to get your money's worth of fun and relaxation from your purchase. A one-year membership is just $32.00, far less than most craft train kits, a brass model or a hardcover book. And the return on your investment, in the form of new friends, knowledge and modeling skills, is priceless.

In today's fast-changing world, the NMRA can help you keep up with your favorite hobby. The monthly "Bulletin" provides the latest news, along with how-to articles and much more. An annual periodical index (published in The Bulletin) makes it easy to locate prototype and model information for your latest project. The Kalmbach Memorial Library, located near the National Headquarters in Chattanooga, Tennessee, houses thousands of articles, books and other reference materials on model and prototype railroading. And, the NMRA is also publishing prototype reference books, in addition to the Data Sheets covering recommended practices.

Whether on a local, regional or national level, you'll be able to meet fellow modelers.

We think you'll agree that it makes good sense to belong to an organization that's doing so much for so many people—and doing it all for fun! Use the application blank below (or make a photocopy) and join today.

Phil Walthers

MEMBERSHIP APPLICATION

NMRA, INC. • 4121 CROMWELL RD. • CHATTANOOGA, TN 37421
Telephone (423) 892-2846 • Fax (423) 899-4869

❑ **Regular**, One Year $32.00
❑ **Regular**, Two Year $64.00
❑ **Sustaining**, One Year $64.00
❑ **Youth**, One Year .... $21.00 (Under 20 Years)
❑ **Affiliate**, One Year . . .(No Bulletin $16.00
❑ **Family Member**, One Year .... $6.00 (Available to Spouse or Minor Child of Member)
❑ **Life Membership**, Apply to Headquarters Office with date of birth for a quotation.

I enclose . . . ❑ Check ❑ Money Order ❑ Charge

Occupation ____________ Date of Birth ____________
Scale & Gauge ____________ NMRA # (renewals only) ____________
Special Interests (include prototype) ____________
(U.S. FUNDS ONLY) ❑ NEW ❑ RENEWAL
Name ____________
Street ____________
City ____________
State & Zip ____________
Telephone ____________

Annual Dues of $32.00 includes $15.00 for subscription to the NMRA BULLETIN

Charge to:
❑ American Express
❑ VISA ❑ Master Card ❑ Discover
Expiration Date ____________
CARD NUMBER ____________

JW/Revised 3/95

Recommended by **WALTHERS** Signature ____________

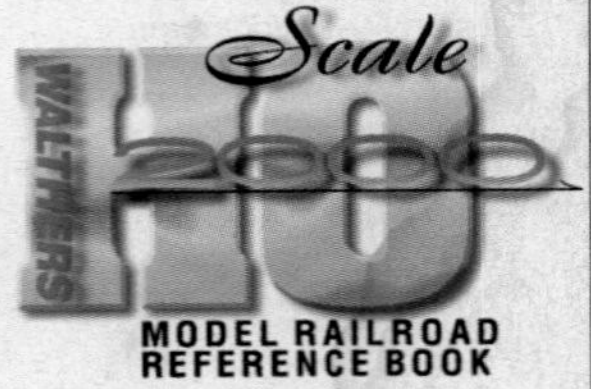
Scale
WALTHERS
HO
2000
MODEL RAILROAD
REFERENCE BOOK